The grass withers,
the flower fades;
but the word of
our God will
stand for ever.

—Isaiah 40:8

Presented

TO ______________________________

BY ______________________________

OCCASION ______________________________

DATE ______________________________

SCEPTER

DAILY BIBLE

REVISED STANDARD VERSION

CATHOLIC EDITION

Scepter

Scepter Daily Bible

Published by Scepter Publishers Inc.
info@scepterpublishers.org
www.scepterpublishers.org
800-322-8773
New York

Nihil Obstat
Thomas Hanlon, S.T.L., L.S.S., PH.L.

Imprimatur
†Gordon Joseph
Archbishop of Saint Andrews and Edinburgh
Feast of Epiphany 1966

Interior design, typesetting, and cartography by Adept Concept Solutions, Urbana, IL.

ISBN: 9781594173554 - Black faux leather
ISBN: 9781594173561 - Burgundy faux leather
ISBN: 9781594173547 - Black bonded leather

FOREWORD

Despite the decline of religious practice, the appetite of English people for new versions of Scripture is, paradoxically, greater than ever. Educated people are still expected to have some acquaintance with the Bible even though religious convictions are no longer demanded. One does not need to be either a Christian or a scholar to recognize the Bible as great literature. With the growth of literacy, greater numbers are able to enjoy the Bible's unique appeal. No other religious writing however exalted can compete with the inspired text.

We welcome a Catholic edition of the Revised Standard Version, not only because it will lead more of your people to read the Bible, but also because of its ecumenical value. May all who read it grow in the knowledge and love of God's own word.

✠ JOHN CARDINAL HEENAN
Archbishop of Westminster
December 1965

The Editors of this edition, Dom Bernard Orchard, O.S.B. and the Reverend R.C. Filler, D.D.D., L.S.S., wish to express appreciation for permission to use, with authorized changes, the Revised Standard Version of the Bible, copyrighted, 1946, 1952, and 1957.

THE NAMES AND THE ORDER OF THE BOOKS OF

THE OLD TESTAMENT

Alternate names used for the books of the Bible are in parentheses.

THE NAMES AND THE ORDER OF THE BOOKS OF

THE NEW TESTAMENT

Alternate names used for the books of the Bible are in parentheses.

INTRODUCTION

This version of the Revised Standard Version of the Bible has been prepared for the use of Catholics by a committee of the Catholic Biblical Association of Great Britain. It is published with ecclesiastical approval and by agreement with the Standard Bible Committee and the Division of Christian Education of the National Council of the Churches of Christ in the United States of America.

The Revised Standard Version itself needs no lengthy introduction, being already well known and widely read. It is, as its Preface states, "an authorized revision of the American Standard Version, published in 1901, which was a revision of the King James Version, published in 1611." In Britain, the King James Version is more commonly called the Authorized Version. It occupies a unique place in English Biblical and indeed literary tradition. The Standard Bible of 1901 was the work of an American committee revising it in the light of modern textual criticism. In 1937 it was decided to make a revision of the Standard Version which should "embody the best results of modern scholarship as to the meaning of the Scriptures, and express this meaning in English diction which is designed for use in public and private worship and preserves those qualities which have given to the King James Version a supreme place in English literature." The New Testament in this new version was published in 1946 and the whole Bible in 1952.

The remarkable success which attended the new revision on its appearance seems to be ample justification of the revisers' aims and it has been acclaimed on all sides as a translation which combines accuracy and clarity of meaning with beauty of language and traditional diction.

For four hundred years, following upon the great upheaval of the Reformation, Catholics and Protestants have gone their separate ways and suspected each other's translations of the Bible of having been in some way manipulated in the interests of doctrinal presuppositions. It must be admitted that these suspicions were not always without foundation. At the present time, however, the sciences of textual criticism and philology, not to mention others, have made such great advances that the Bible text used by translators is substantially the same for all—Protestants and Catholics alike.

Today, and indeed since the appearance in 1943 of the Encyclical Letter Divino Afflante Spiritu, encouraging Biblical studies, Catholics like every one else go back to the original languages and base their translations on the same critical principles.

With the improvement in interdenominational relations and the advance of Biblical knowledge, the possibility of producing a Bible common to all Christians was mooted as far back as 1953. It was felt that, if such a thing could be achieved, it would be of incalculable benefit in wiping away remaining misconceptions and prejudices and in fostering still further good relations between the Churches. The Word of God would then not only be our common heritage and unifying link but be recognized as such, and those engaged in theological discussion could appeal to the same authoritative text. A decisive step toward this objective could be made by editing the Revised Standard Version for Catholic use.

A small committee of members of the Catholic Biblical Association was formed and permission obtained to examine this translation and suggest any changes that might be required to make it acceptable to Catholics. The Standard Bible Committee of the U.S.A. was then approached and they gave warm welcome to the proposal. Here was a wonderful opportunity to make a real step forward in the field of ecumenical relations. However, ideas of this kind take time to penetrate all levels and many difficulties and delays ensued. But a change of mind has taken place and what seemed to many in 1953 to be a novel idea of doubtful value or even of no value at all is now generally recognized to be a legitimate and desirable goal.

In the present edition the aim has not been to improve the translation as such. No doubt there are many places where a different rendering might have been chosen on critical grounds. This has been avoided. But there are other places where, the critical evidence being evenly balanced, considerations of Catholic tradition have favored a particular rendering or the inclusion of a passage omitted by the RSV translators.

In the Old Testament it has not been thought necessary to make any changes in the text. There is, however, the very important difference in the number of books. Catholic Bibles include seven extra books and parts of two others. These are known to Catholics as "deuterocanonical" and are regarded as an integral part of the Canon of the Old Testament. They are here printed in the order in which they appear in the Latin Vulgate, with the exception of the extra parts of the Book of Esther. But not regarding them as canonical he put them together at the end of the Hebrew text regardless of their historical or logical sequence. In this edition of the RSV they have been restored to their proper place in the narrative. These books and parts of books are regarded by Protestants as apocryphal.

This question of the "Apocrypha" is the one big problem left and needs to be carefully considered when discussing the possibility of a common Bible. The books known as the Apocrypha are: 1 and 2 Esdras (3 and 4 Esdras), Tobit, Judith, Wisdom, Sirach (Ecclesiasticus), Baruch with the Letter of Jeremiah, 1 and 2 Maccabees, Additions to Daniel

ABBREVIATIONS

In the notes to the books of the Old Testament, the following abbreviations are: Ms for manuscript; Mss for manuscripts. Heb denotes the Hebrew of the consonantal Masoretic Text of the Old Testament; and MT denotes the Hebrew of the pointed Masoretic Text of the Old Testament. The ancient versions of the Old Testament are indicated by:

Gk	Septuagint, Greek Version of Old Testament
Lat	Latin Version of Tobit, Judith, and 2 Maccabees
Sam	Samaritan Hebrew text of Old Testament
Syr	Syriac Version of Old Testament
Tg	Targum
Vg	Vulgate, Latin Version of Old Testament

Cn indicates a correction made where the text has suffered in transmission and the versions provide no satisfactory restoration but the Committee agrees with the judgment of competent scholars as to the most probable reconstruction of the original text.

References to quoted and parallel passages are given following the notes on pages where these are relevant. The abbreviations on the following page are used for the books of the Bible.

ABBREVIATIONS OF THE BOOKS OF

THE OLD TESTAMENT

Gen	Genesis	Tob	Tobit	Dan	Daniel
Ex	Exodus	Jud	Judith	Hos	Hosea
Lev	Leviticus	Esther	Esther	Joel	Joel
Num	Numbers	Job	Job	Amos	Amos
Deut	Deuteronomy	Ps	Psalms	Obad	Obadiah
Josh	Joshua	Prov	Proverbs	Jon	Jonah
Judg	Judges	Eccles	Ecclesiastes	Mic	Micah
Ruth	Ruth	Song	Song of Solomon	Nahum	Nahum
1 Sam	1 Samuel	Wis	Wisdom	Hab	Habakkuk
2 Sam	2 Samuel	Sir	Sirach	Zeph	Zephaniah
1 Kings	1 Kings	Is	Isaiah	Hag	Haggai
2 Kings	2 Kings	Jer	Jeremiah	Zech	Zechariah
1 Chron	1 Chronicles	Lam	Lamentations	Mal	Malachi
2 Chron	2 Chronicles	Bar	Baruch	1 Mac	1 Maccabees
Ezra	Ezra	Ezek	Ezekiel	2 Mac	2 Maccabees
Neh	Nehemiah				

ABBREVIATIONS OF THE BOOKS OF

THE NEW TESTAMENT

Mt	Matthew	Eph	Ephesians	Philem	Philemon
Mk	Mark	Phil	Philippians	Heb	Hebrews
Lk	Luke	Col	Colossians	Jas	James
Jn	John	1 Thess	1 Thessalonians	1 Pet	1 Peter
Acts	Acts of the Apostles	2 Thess	2 Thessalonians	2 Pet	2 Peter
Rom	Romans	1 Tim	1 Timothy	1 Jn	1 John
1 Cor	1 Corinthians	2 Tim	2 Timothy	2 Jn	2 John
2 Cor	2 Corinthians	Tit	Titus	3 Jn	3 John
Gal	Galatians			Jude	Jude
				Rev	Revelation (Apocalypse)

SCEPTER

DAILY BIBLE

REVISED STANDARD VERSION

CATHOLIC EDITION

OLD TESTAMENT

THE FIRST BOOK OF MOSES COMMONLY CALLED

GENESIS

SIX DAYS OF CREATION AND THE SABBATH

1 *In the beginning God created[a] the
heavens and the earth. 2The earth
was without form and void, and dark-
ness was upon the face of the deep;
and the Spirit[b] of God was moving
over the face of the waters.

3 And God said, "Let there be
light"; and there was light. 4And God
saw that the light was good; and God
separated the light from the darkness.
5God called the light Day, and the
darkness he called Night. And there
was evening and there was morning,
one day.

6 And God said, "Let there be a
firmament in the midst of the waters,
and let it separate the waters from the
waters." 7And God made the firma-
ment and separated the waters which
were under the firmament from the
waters which were above the firma-
ment. And it was so. 8And God called
the firmament Heaven. And there was
evening and there was morning, a sec-
ond day.

9 And God said, "Let the waters
under the heavens be gathered togeth-
er into one place, and let the dry land
appear." And it was so. 10God called
the dry land Earth, and the waters
that were gathered together he called
Seas. And God saw that it was good.
11And God said, "Let the earth put
forth vegetation, plants yielding seed,
and fruit trees bearing fruit in which
is their seed, each according to its
kind, upon the earth." And it was so.
12The earth brought forth vegetation,
plants yielding seed according to their
own kinds, and trees bearing fruit in
which is their seed, each according
to its kind. And God saw that it was
good. 13And there was evening and
there was morning, a third day.

14 And God said, "Let there be
lights in the firmament of the heav-
ens to separate the day from the night;
and let them be for signs and for sea-
sons and for days and years, 15and let
them be lights in the firmament of the
heavens to give light upon the earth."
And it was so. 16And God made the
two great lights, the greater light to
rule the day, and the lesser light to
rule the night; he made the stars also.
17And God set them in the firmament
of the heavens to give light upon the
earth, 18to rule over the day and over
the night, and to separate the light
from the darkness. And God saw that
it was good. 19And there was evening
and there was morning, a fourth day.

20 And God said, "Let the waters
bring forth swarms of living crea-
tures, and let birds fly above the earth
across the firmament of the heavens."
21So God created the great sea mon-
sters and every living creature that
moves, with which the waters swarm,
according to their kinds, and every
winged bird according to its kind.
And God saw that it was good. 22And
God blessed them, saying, "Be fruit-
ful and multiply and fill the waters in
the seas, and let birds multiply on the
earth." 23And there was evening and
there was morning, a fifth day.

24 And God said, "Let the earth
bring forth living creatures accord-
ing to their kinds: cattle and creep-
ing things and beasts of the earth
according to their kinds." And it was
so. 25And God made the beasts of the
earth according to their kinds and the
cattle according to their kinds, and ev-
erything that creeps upon the ground
according to its kind. And God saw
that it was good.

26 Then God said, "Let us make
man in our image, after our likeness;
and let them have dominion over the

[a] Or *When God began to create*
[b] Or *wind*

fish of the sea, and over the birds of
the air, and over the cattle, and over
all the earth, and over every creeping
thing that creeps upon the earth." 27 So
God created man in his own image, in
the image of God he created him; male
and female he created them. 28 And
God blessed them, and God said to
them, "Be fruitful and multiply, and
fill the earth and subdue it; and have
dominion over the fish of the sea and
over the birds of the air and over ev-
ery living thing that moves upon the
earth." 29 And God said, "Behold, I
have given you every plant yielding
seed which is upon the face of all the
earth, and every tree with seed in its
fruit; you shall have them for food.
30 And to every beast of the earth, and
to every bird of the air, and to every-
thing that creeps on the earth, every-
thing that has the breath of life, I have
given every green plant for food." And
it was so. 31 And God saw everything
that he had made, and behold, it was
very good. And there was evening and
there was morning, a sixth day.

2 Thus the heavens and the earth
were finished, and all the host of
them. 2 And on the seventh day God
finished his work which he had done,
and he rested on the seventh day from
all his work which he had done. 3 So
God blessed the seventh day and hal-
lowed it, because on it God rested
from all his work which he had done
in creation.

4 These are the generations of the
heavens and the earth when they were
created.

ANOTHER ACCOUNT OF THE CREATION

*In the day that the LORD God
made the earth and the heavens,
5 when no plant of the field was yet
in the earth and no herb of the field
had yet sprung up—for the LORD God
had not caused it to rain upon the
earth, and there was no man to till
the ground; 6 but a mist[a] went up from
the earth and watered the whole face
of the ground 7 then the LORD God
formed man of dust from the ground,
and breathed into his nostrils the
breath of life; and man became a liv-
ing being. 8 And the LORD God plant-
ed a garden in Eden, in the east; and
there he put the man whom he had
formed. 9 And out of the ground the
LORD God made to grow every tree
that is pleasant to the sight and good
for food, the tree of life also in the
midst of the garden, and the tree of
the knowledge of good and evil.

10 A river flowed out of Eden to
water the garden, and there it divid-
ed and became four rivers. 11 The name
of the first is Pishon; it is the one
which flows around the whole land
of Hav′ilah, where there is gold; 12 and
the gold of that land is good; bdellium
and onyx stone are there. 13 The name
of the second river is Gihon; it is the
one which flows around the whole
land of Cush. 14 And the name of the
third river is Tigris, which flows east
of Assyria. And the fourth river is the
Euphra′tes.

15 The LORD God took the man
and put him in the garden of Eden to
till it and keep it. 16 And the LORD God
commanded the man, saying, "You
may freely eat of every tree of the gar-
den; 17 but of the tree of the knowledge
of good and evil you shall not eat, for
in the day that you eat of it you shall
die."

18 Then the LORD God said, "It
is not good that the man should be
alone; I will make him a helper fit
for him." 19 So out of the ground the
LORD God formed every beast of the
field and every bird of the air, and
brought them to the man to see what
he would call them; and whatever the
man called every living creature, that
was its name. 20 The man gave names
to all cattle, and to the birds of the air,
and to every beast of the field; but for
the man there was not found a helper
fit for him. 21 So the LORD God caused

[a] Or *flood*

a deep sleep to fall upon the man, and
while he slept took one of his ribs and
closed up its place with flesh; 22and
the rib which the LORD God had taken
from the man he made into a woman
and brought her to the man. 23Then
the man said,

"This at last is bone of my
bones
and flesh of my flesh;
she shall be called Woman,[b]
because she was taken out of
Man."[c]

24 Therefore a man leaves his father and his mother and cleaves to
his wife, and they become one flesh.
25And the man and his wife were both
naked, and were not ashamed.

THE FIRST SIN AND ITS PUNISHMENT

3 Now the serpent was more subtle
than any other wild creature that
the LORD God had made. He said to
the woman, "Did God say, 'You shall
not eat of any tree of the garden'?"
2And the woman said to the serpent,
"We may eat of the fruit of the trees of
the garden; 3but God said, 'You shall
not eat of the fruit of the tree which
is in the midst of the garden, neither
shall you touch it, lest you die.'" 4But
the serpent said to the woman, "You
will not die. 5For God knows that
when you eat of it your eyes will be
opened, and you will be like God,
knowing good and evil." 6So when the
woman saw that the tree was good for
food, and that it was a delight to the
eyes, and that the tree was to be desired to make one wise, she took of its
fruit and ate; and she also gave some
to her husband, and he ate. 7Then the
eyes of both were opened, and they
knew that they were naked; and they
sewed fig leaves together and made
themselves aprons.

8 And they heard the sound of
the LORD God walking in the garden
in the cool of the day, and the man
and his wife hid themselves from the
presence of the LORD God among the
trees of the garden. 9But the LORD
God called to the man, and said to
him, "Where are you?" 10And he said,
"I heard the sound of thee in the garden, and I was afraid, because I was
naked; and I hid myself." 11He said,
"Who told you that you were naked?
Have you eaten of the tree of which
I commanded you not to eat?" 12The
man said, "The woman whom thou
gavest to be with me, she gave me
fruit of the tree, and I ate." 13Then the
LORD God said to the woman, "What
is this that you have done?" The woman said, "The serpent beguiled me,
and I ate." 14The LORD God said to the
serpent,

"Because you have done this,
cursed are you above all
cattle,
and above all wild animals;
upon your belly you shall go,
and dust you shall eat
all the days of your life.
15I will put enmity between you
and the woman,
and between your seed and
her seed;
he shall bruise your head,*
and you shall bruise his
heel."

16To the woman he said,

"I will greatly multiply your
pain in childbearing;
in pain you shall bring forth
children,
yet your desire shall be for your
husband,
and he shall rule over you."

17And to Adam he said,

"Because you have listened to
the voice of your wife,
and have eaten of the tree
of which I commanded you,
'You shall not eat of it,'
cursed is the ground because
of you;
in toil you shall eat of it all
the days of your life;

[b]Heb *ishshah*
[c]Heb *ish*

18 thorns and thistles it shall bring
forth to you;
and you shall eat the plants
of the field.
19 In the sweat of your face
you shall eat bread
till you return to the ground,
for out of it you were taken;
you are dust,
and to dust you shall
return."

20 The man called his wife's name
Eve,[a] because she was the mother of
all living. 21 And the LORD God made
for Adam and for his wife garments of
skins, and clothed them.
22 Then the LORD God said,
"Behold, the man has become like
one of us, knowing good and evil; and
now, lest he put forth his hand and
take also of the tree of life, and eat,
and live for ever" 23 therefore the LORD
God sent him forth from the garden
of Eden, to till the ground from which
he was taken. 24 He drove out the man;
and at the east of the garden of Eden
he placed the cherubim, and a flam-
ing sword which turned every way, to
guard the way to the tree of life.

CAIN MURDERS ABEL

4 *Now Adam knew Eve his wife, and
she conceived and bore Cain, say-
ing, "I have gotten[b] a man with the
help of the LORD." 2 And again, she
bore his brother Abel. Now Abel was
a keeper of sheep, and Cain a tiller
of the ground. 3 In the course of time
Cain brought to the LORD an offering
of the fruit of the ground, 4 and Abel
brought of the firstlings of his flock
and of their fat portions. And the
LORD had regard for Abel and his of-
fering, 5 but for Cain and his offering
he had no regard. So Cain was very
angry, and his countenance fell. 6 The
LORD said to Cain, "Why are you an-
gry, and why has your countenance
fallen? 7 If you do well, will you not be
accepted? And if you do not do well,
sin is couching at the door; its desire
is for you, but you must master it."
8 Cain said to Abel his broth-
er, "Let us go out to the field."[c] And
when they were in the field, Cain rose
up against his brother Abel, and killed
him. 9 Then the LORD said to Cain,
"Where is Abel your brother?" He
said, "I do not know; am I my brother's
keeper?" 10 And the LORD said, "What
have you done? The voice of your
brother's blood is crying to me from
the ground. 11 And now you are cursed
from the ground, which has opened its
mouth to receive your brother's blood
from your hand. 12 When you till the
ground, it shall no longer yield to you
its strength; you shall be a fugitive
and a wanderer on the earth." 13 Cain
said to the LORD, "My punishment is
greater than I can bear. 14 Behold, thou
hast driven me this day away from the
ground; and from thy face I shall be
hidden; and I shall be a fugitive and
a wanderer on the earth, and whoev-
er finds me will slay me." 15 Then the
LORD said to him, "Not so![d] If any one
slays Cain, vengeance shall be taken
on him sevenfold." And the LORD put
a mark on Cain, lest any who came
upon him should kill him. 16 Then Cain
went away from the presence of the
LORD, and dwelt in the land of Nod,[e]
east of Eden.

BEGINNINGS OF CIVILIZATION

17 Cain knew his wife, and she con-
ceived and bore Enoch; and he built a
city, and called the name of the city
after the name of his son, Enoch. 18 To
Enoch was born Irad; and Irad was the
father of Mehu´ja-el, and Mehu´ja-
el the father of Methu´sha-el, and
Methu´sha-el the father of Lamech.
19 And Lamech took two wives; the
name of the one was Adah, and the

[a] The name in Hebrew resembles the word for *living*
[b] Heb *qanah,* get
[c] Sam Gk Syr Compare Vg: Heb lacks *Let us go out to the field*
[d] Gk Syr Vg: Heb *Therefore*
[e] That is *Wandering*

name of the other Zillah. 20Adah bore
Jabal; he was the father of those who
dwell in tents and have cattle. 21His
brother's name was Jubal; he was the
father of all those who play the lyre
and pipe. 22Zillah bore Tubal-cain; he
was the forger of all instruments of
bronze and iron. The sister of Tubal-
cain was Na´amah.

23 Lamech said to his wives:
"Adah and Zillah, hear my
voice;
you wives of Lamech, heark-
en to what I say:
I have slain a man for wound-
ing me,
a young man for striking me.
24If Cain is avenged sevenfold,
truly Lamech
seventy-sevenfold."

25 And Adam knew his wife again,
and she bore a son and called his name
Seth, for she said, "God has appointed
for me another child instead of Abel,
for Cain slew him." 26To Seth* also a
son was born, and he called his name
Enosh. At that time men began to call
upon the name of the LORD.

ADAM'S DESCENDANTS TO NOAH AND HIS SONS

5 This is the book of the generations*
of Adam. When God created man,
he made him in the likeness of God.
2Male and female he created them,
and he blessed them and named them
Man when they were created. 3When
Adam had lived a hundred and thirty
years, he became the father of a son
in his own likeness, after his image,
and named him Seth. 4The days of
Adam after he became the father of
Seth were eight hundred years; and he
had other sons and daughters. 5Thus
all the days that Adam lived were nine
hundred and thirty years; and he died.

6 When Seth had lived a hundred
and five years, he became the father
of Enosh. 7Seth lived after the birth
of Enosh eight hundred and seven
years, and had other sons and daugh-
ters. 8Thus all the days of Seth were
nine hundred and twelve years; and
he died.

9 When Enosh had lived ninety
years, he became the father of Kenan.
10Enosh lived after the birth of Kenan
eight hundred and fifteen years, and
had other sons and daughters. 11Thus
all the days of Enosh were nine hun-
dred and five years; and he died.

12 When Kenan had lived sev-
enty years, he became the father of
Mahal´alel. 13Kenan lived after the
birth of Mahal´alel eight hundred
and forty years, and had other sons
and daughters. 14Thus all the days of
Kenan were nine hundred and ten
years; and he died.

15 When Mahal´alel had lived six-
ty-five years, he became the father
of Jared. 16Mahal´alel lived after the
birth of Jared eight hundred and thirty
years, and had other sons and daugh-
ters. 17Thus all the days of Mahal´alel
were eight hundred and ninety-five
years; and he died.

18 When Jared had lived a hundred
and sixty-two years he became the fa-
ther of Enoch. 19Jared lived after the
birth of Enoch eight hundred years,
and had other sons and daughters.
20Thus all the days of Jared were nine
hundred and sixty-two years; and he
died.

21 When Enoch had lived six-
ty-five years, he became the father
of Methu´selah. 22Enoch walked with
God after the birth of Methu´selah
three hundred years, and had other
sons and daughters. 23Thus all the
days of Enoch were three hundred
and sixty-five years. 24Enoch walked
with God; and he was not, for God
took him.

25 When Methu´selah had lived
a hundred and eighty-seven years,
he became the father of Lamech.
26Methu´selah lived after the birth of
Lamech seven hundred and eighty-
two years, and had other sons and
daughters. 27Thus all the days of
Methu´selah were nine hundred and
sixty-nine years; and he died.

28 When Lamech had lived a hun-
dred and eighty-two years, he became
the father of a son, 29and called his
name Noah, saying, "Out of the ground
which the LORD has cursed this one
shall bring us relief from our work and
from the toil of our hands." 30Lamech
lived after the birth of Noah five hun-
dred and ninety-five years, and had
other sons and daughters. 31Thus all
the days of Lamech were seven hun-
dred and seventy-seven years; and he
died.

32 After Noah was five hundred
years old, Noah became the father of
Shem, Ham, and Japheth.

THE WICKEDNESS OF MANKIND

6 When men began to multiply on the
face of the ground, and daughters
were born to them, 2the sons of God*
saw that the daughters of men were
fair; and they took to wife such of
them as they chose. 3Then the LORD
said, "My spirit shall not abide in man
for ever, for he is flesh, but his days
shall be a hundred and twenty years."
4The Nephilim were on the earth in
those days, and also afterward, when
the sons of God came in to the daugh-
ters of men, and they bore children
to them. These were the mighty men
that were of old, the men of renown.

5 The LORD saw that the wicked-
ness of man was great in the earth,
and that every imagination of the
thoughts of his heart was only evil
continually. 6And the LORD was sorry
that he had made man on the earth,
and it grieved him to his heart. 7So
the LORD said, "I will blot out man
whom I have created from the face of
the ground, man and beast and creep-
ing things and birds of the air, for I
am sorry that I have made them." 8But
Noah found favor in the eyes of the
LORD.

NOAH PLEASES GOD

9 These are the generations of
Noah. Noah was a righteous man,
blameless in his generation; Noah
walked with God. 10And Noah had
three sons, Shem, Ham, and Japheth.

11*Now the earth was corrupt in
God's sight, and the earth was filled
with violence. 12And God saw the
earth, and behold, it was corrupt;
for all flesh had corrupted their way
upon the earth. 13And God said to
Noah, "I have determined to make
an end of all flesh; for the earth is
filled with violence through them;
behold, I will destroy them with
the earth. 14Make yourself an ark
of gopher wood; make rooms in the
ark, and cover it inside and out with
pitch. 15This is how you are to make
it: the length of the ark three hun-
dred cubits, its breadth fifty cubits,
and its height thirty cubits. 16Make a
roof[a] for the ark, and finish it to a cu-
bit above; and set the door of the ark
in its side; make it with lower, sec-
ond, and third decks. 17For behold, I
will bring a flood of waters upon the
earth, to destroy all flesh in which is
the breath of life from under heaven;
everything that is on the earth shall
die. 18But I will establish my covenant
with you; and you shall come into the
ark, you, your sons, your wife, and
your sons' wives with you. 19And of
every living thing of all flesh, you
shall bring two of every sort into
the ark, to keep them alive with you;
they shall be male and female. 20Of
the birds according to their kinds,
and of the animals according to their
kinds, of every creeping thing of the
ground according to its kind, two of
every sort shall come in to you, to
keep them alive. 21Also take with you
every sort of food that is eaten, and
store it up; and it shall serve as food
for you and for them." 22Noah did
this; he did all that God commanded
him.

THE GREAT FLOOD

7 Then the LORD said to Noah,
"Go into the ark, you and all your

[a]Or *window*

household, for I have seen that you are righteous before me in this generation. 2 Take with you seven pairs of all clean animals, the male and his mate; and a pair of the animals that are not clean, the male and his mate; 3 and seven pairs of the birds of the air also, male and female, to keep their kind alive upon the face of all the earth. 4 For in seven days I will send rain upon the earth forty days and forty nights; and every living thing that I have made I will blot out from the face of the ground." 5 And Noah did all that the LORD had commanded him.

6 Noah was six hundred years old when the flood of waters came upon the earth. 7 And Noah and his sons and his wife and his sons' wives with him went into the ark, to escape the waters of the flood. 8 Of clean animals, and of animals that are not clean, and of birds, and of everything that creeps on the ground, 9 two and two, male and female, went into the ark with Noah, as God had commanded Noah. 10 And after seven days the waters of the flood came upon the earth.

11 In the six hundredth year of Noah's life, in the second month, on the seventeenth day of the month, on that day all the fountains of the great deep burst forth, and the windows of the heavens were opened. 12 And rain fell upon the earth forty days and forty nights. 13 On the very same day Noah and his sons, Shem and Ham and Japheth, and Noah's wife and the three wives of his sons with them entered the ark, 14 they and every beast according to its kind, and all the cattle according to their kinds, and every creeping thing that creeps on the earth according to its kind, and every bird according to its kind, every bird of every sort. 15 They went into the ark with Noah, two and two of all flesh in which there was the breath of life. 16 And they that entered, male and female of all flesh, went in as God had commanded him; and the LORD shut him in.

17 The flood continued forty days upon the earth; and the waters increased, and bore up the ark, and it rose high above the earth. 18 The waters prevailed and increased greatly upon the earth; and the ark floated on the face of the waters. 19 And the waters prevailed so mightily upon the earth that all the high mountains under the whole heaven were covered; 20 the waters prevailed above the mountains, covering them fifteen cubits deep. 21 And all flesh died that moved upon the earth, birds, cattle, beasts, all swarming creatures that swarm upon the earth, and every man; 22 everything on the dry land in whose nostrils was the breath of life died. 23 He blotted out every living thing that was upon the face of the ground, man and animals and creeping things and birds of the air; they were blotted out from the earth. Only Noah was left, and those that were with him in the ark. 24 And the waters prevailed upon the earth a hundred and fifty days.

THE FLOOD SUBSIDES

8 But God remembered Noah and all the beasts and all the cattle that were with him in the ark. And God made a wind blow over the earth, and the waters subsided; 2 the fountains of the deep and the windows of the heavens were closed, the rain from the heavens was restrained, 3 and the waters receded from the earth continually. At the end of a hundred and fifty days the waters had abated; 4 and in the seventh month, on the seventeenth day of the month, the ark came to rest upon the mountains of Ar´arat. 5 And the waters continued to abate until the tenth month; in the tenth month, on the first day of the month, the tops of the mountains were seen.

6 At the end of forty days Noah opened the window of the ark which he had made, 7 and sent forth a raven; and it went to and fro until the waters were dried up from the earth. 8 Then he sent forth a dove from him, to see if

the waters had subsided from the face
of the ground; 9but the dove found no
place to set her foot, and she returned
to him to the ark, for the waters were
still on the face of the whole earth.
So he put forth his hand and took
her and brought her into the ark with
him. 10He waited another seven days,
and again he sent forth the dove out
of the ark; 11and the dove came back
to him in the evening, and lo, in her
mouth a freshly plucked olive leaf; so
Noah knew that the waters had sub-
sided from the earth. 12Then he waited
another seven days, and sent forth the
dove; and she did not return to him
any more.

13 In the six hundred and first
year, in the first month, the first day
of the month, the waters were dried
from off the earth; and Noah removed
the covering of the ark, and looked,
and behold, the face of the ground
was dry. 14In the second month, on
the twenty-seventh day of the month,
the earth was dry. 15Then God said to
Noah, 16"Go forth from the ark, you
and your wife, and your sons and your
sons' wives with you. 17Bring forth
with you every living thing that is
with you of all flesh—birds and an-
imals and every creeping thing that
creeps on the earth—that they may
breed abundantly on the earth, and be
fruitful and multiply upon the earth."
18So Noah went forth, and his sons
and his wife and his sons' wives with
him. 19And every beast, every creeping
thing, and every bird, everything that
moves upon the earth, went forth by
families out of the ark.

GOD'S PROMISE TO NOAH

20 Then Noah built an altar to the
LORD, and took of every clean animal
and of every clean bird, and offered
burnt offerings on the altar. 21And
when the LORD smelled the pleas-
ing odor, the LORD said in his heart,
"I will never again curse the ground
because of man, for the imagination
of man's heart is evil from his youth;
neither will I ever again destroy every
living creature as I have done. 22While
the earth remains, seedtime and har-
vest, cold and heat, summer and win-
ter, day and night, shall not cease."

THE COVENANT WITH NOAH

9 And God blessed Noah and his sons,
and said to them, "Be fruitful and
multiply, and fill the earth. 2The fear of
you and the dread of you shall be upon
every beast of the earth, and upon ev-
ery bird of the air, upon everything that
creeps on the ground and all the fish
of the sea; into your hand they are de-
livered. 3Every moving thing that lives
shall be food for you; and as I gave you
the green plants, I give you everything.
4Only you shall not eat flesh with its
life, that is, its blood. 5For your life-
blood I will surely require a reckoning;
of every beast I will require it and of
man; of every man's brother I will re-
quire the life of man. 6Whoever sheds
the blood of man, by man shall his
blood be shed; for God made man in his
own image. 7And you, be fruitful and
multiply, bring forth abundantly on the
earth and multiply in it."

8 Then God said to Noah and to his
sons with him, 9"Behold, I establish
my covenant with you and your de-
scendants after you, 10and with every
living creature that is with you, the
birds, the cattle, and every beast of
the earth with you, as many as came
out of the ark.[a] 11I establish my cove-
nant with you, that never again shall
all flesh be cut off by the waters of a
flood, and never again shall there be a
flood to destroy the earth." 12And God
said, "This is the sign of the covenant
which I make between me and you
and every living creature that is with
you, for all future generations: 13I set
my bow in the cloud, and it shall be a
sign of the covenant between me and
the earth. 14When I bring clouds over
the earth and the bow is seen in the
clouds, 15I will remember my covenant

[a] Gk: Heb repeats *every beast of the earth*

which is between me and you and ev-
ery living creature of all flesh; and
the waters shall never again become a
flood to destroy all flesh. 16When the
bow is in the clouds, I will look upon
it and remember the everlasting cov-
enant between God and every living
creature of all flesh that is upon the
earth." 17God said to Noah, "This is
the sign of the covenant which I have
established between me and all flesh
that is upon the earth."

NOAH AND HIS SONS

18 The sons of Noah who went
forth from the ark were Shem, Ham,
and Japheth. Ham was the father of
Canaan. 19These three were the sons
of Noah; and from these the whole
earth was peopled.

20Noah was the first tiller of the
soil. He planted a vineyard; 21and he
drank of the wine, and became drunk,
and lay uncovered in his tent. 22And
Ham, the father of Canaan, saw the
nakedness of his father, and told his
two brothers outside. 23Then Shem
and Japheth took a garment, laid it
upon both their shoulders, and walked
backward and covered the nakedness
of their father; their faces were turned
away, and they did not see their father's
nakedness. 24When Noah awoke from
his wine and knew what his youngest
son had done to him, 25he said,

"Cursed be Canaan;
a slave of slaves shall he be
to his brothers."

26He also said,

"Blessed by the LORD my God
be Shem;[b]
and let Canaan be his slave.
27God enlarge Japheth,
and let him dwell in the
tents of Shem;
and let Canaan be his slave."

28 After the flood Noah lived three
hundred and fifty years. 29All the days
of Noah were nine hundred and fifty
years; and he died.

NATIONS DESCENDED FROM NOAH

10 These are the generations* of the
sons of Noah, Shem, Ham, and
Japheth; sons were born to them after
the flood.

2 The sons of Japheth: Gomer,
Magog, Madai, Javan, Tubal, Me-
shech, and Tiras. 3The sons of Gomer:
Ash´kenaz, Riphath, and Togar´mah.
4The sons of Javan: Eli´shah, Tarshish,
Kittim, and Do´danim. 5From these
the coastland peoples spread. These
are the sons of Japheth[c] in their lands,
each with his own language, by their
families, in their nations.

6 The sons of Ham: Cush, Egypt,
Put, and Canaan. 7The sons of Cush:
Seba, Hav´ilah, Sabtah, Ra´amah, and
Sab´teca. The sons of Ra´amah: Sheba
and Dedan. 8Cush became the father
of Nimrod; he was the first on earth
to be a mighty man. 9He was a mighty
hunter before the LORD; therefore
it is said, "Like Nimrod a mighty
hunter before the LORD." 10The be-
ginning of his kingdom was Babel,
Erech, and Accad, all of them in the
land of Shinar. 11From that land he
went into Assyria, and built Nin´eveh,
Reho´both-Ir, Calah, and 12Resen be-
tween Nin´eveh and Calah; that is the
great city. 13Egypt became the father
of Ludim, An´amim, Leha´bim, Naph-
tu´him, 14Pathru´sim, Caslu´him
(whence came the Philistines), and
Caph´torim.

15 Canaan became the father
of Sidon his first-born, and Heth,
16and the Jeb´usites, the Amorites,
the Gir´gashites, 17the Hivites, the
Arkites, the Sinites, 18the Ar´vadites,
the Zem´arites, and the Ha´mathites.
Afterward the families of the
Canaanites spread abroad. 19And the
territory of the Canaanites extended
from Sidon, in the direction of Gerar,
as far as Gaza, and in the direction
of Sodom, Gomor´rah, Admah, and
Zeboi´im, as far as Lasha. 20These are
the sons of Ham, by their families,

[b] Or *Blessed be the* LORD, *the God of Shem*
[c] Compare verses 20, 31. Heb lacks *These are the sons of Japheth*

their languages, their lands, and their
nations.

21To Shem also, the father of all
the children of Eber, the elder broth-
er of Japheth, children were born.
22The sons of Shem: Elam, Asshur,
Arpach´shad, Lud, and Aram. 23The
sons of Aram: Uz, Hul, Gether, and
Mash. 24Arpach´shad became the fa-
ther of Shelah; and Shelah became the
father of Eber. 25To Eber were born
two sons: the name of the one was
Peleg,[a] for in his days the earth was
divided, and his brother's name was
Joktan. 26Joktan became the father of
Almo´dad, Sheleph, Hazarma´veth,
Jerah, 27Hador´am, Uzal, Diklah,
28Obal, Abim´a-el, Sheba, 29Ophir,
Hav´ilah, and Jobab; all these were
the sons of Joktan. 30The territory
in which they lived extended from
Mesha in the direction of Sephar to
the hill country of the east. 31These
are the sons of Shem, by their fami-
lies, their languages, their lands, and
their nations.

32 These are the families of the
sons of Noah, according to their ge-
nealogies, in their nations; and from
these the nations spread abroad on
the earth after the flood.

THE TOWER OF BABEL

11 *Now the whole earth had one
language and few words. 2And
as men migrated from the east, they
found a plain in the land of Shinar and
settled there. 3And they said to one
another, "Come, let us make bricks,
and burn them thoroughly." And they
had brick for stone, and bitumen for
mortar. 4Then they said, "Come, let
us build ourselves a city, and a tower
with its top in the heavens, and let us
make a name for ourselves, lest we be
scattered abroad upon the face of the
whole earth." 5And the LORD came
down to see the city and the tow-
er, which the sons of men had built.
6And the LORD said, "Behold, they
are one people, and they have all one
language; and this is only the begin-
ning of what they will do; and noth-
ing that they propose to do will now
be impossible for them. 7Come, let us
go down, and there confuse their lan-
guage, that they may not understand
one another's speech." 8So the LORD
scattered them abroad from there over
the face of all the earth, and they left
off building the city. 9Therefore its
name was called Babel, because there
the LORD confused[b] the language of
all the earth; and from there the LORD
scattered them abroad over the face of
all the earth.

DESCENDANTS OF SHEM

10 These are the descendants of
Shem. When Shem was a hundred
years old, he became the father of
Arpach´shad two years after the
flood; 11and Shem lived after the birth
of Arpach´shad five hundred years,
and had other sons and daughters.

12 When Arpach´shad had lived
thirty-five years, he became the father
of Shelah; 13and Arpach´shad lived af-
ter the birth of Shelah four hundred
and three years, and had other sons
and daughters.

14 When Shelah had lived thirty
years, he became the father of Eber;
15and Shelah lived after the birth of
Eber four hundred and three years,
and had other sons and daughters.

16 When Eber had lived thirty-four
years, he became the father of Peleg;
17and Eber lived after the birth of
Peleg four hundred and thirty years,
and had other sons and daughters.

18 When Peleg had lived thirty
years, he became the father of Re´u;
19and Peleg lived after the birth of
Re´u two hundred and nine years, and
had other sons and daughters.

20 When Re´u had lived thir-
ty-two years, he became the father
of Serug; 21and Re´u lived after the
birth of Serug two hundred and

[a] That is Division
[b] Compare Heb *balal,* confuse

border of the wilderness; 7then they
turned back and came to En-mish´pat
(that is, Kadesh), and subdued all
the country of the Amal´ekites,
and also the Amorites who dwelt in
Haz´azon-ta´mar. 8Then the king of
Sodom, the king of Gomor´rah, the
king of Admah, the king of Zeboi´im,
and the king of Bela (that is, Zo´ar)
went out, and they joined battle in
the Valley of Siddim 9with Ched-or-
lao´mer king of Elam, Tidal king of
Goi´im, Am´raphel king of Shinar,
and Ar´ioch king of Ella´sar, four
kings against five. 10Now the Valley of
Siddim was full of bitumen pits; and
as the kings of Sodom and Gomor´rah
fled, some fell into them, and the rest
fled to the mountain. 11So the ene-
my took all the goods of Sodom and
Gomor´rah, and all their provisions,
and went their way; 12they also took
Lot, the son of Abram's brother, who
dwelt in Sodom, and his goods, and
departed.

13 Then one who had escaped
came, and told Abram the Hebrew,
who was living by the oaks[b] of Mamre
the Amorite, brother of Eshcol and
of Aner; these were allies of Abram.
14When Abram heard that his kinsman
had been taken captive, he led forth
his trained men, born in his house,
three hundred and eighteen of them,
and went in pursuit as far as Dan.
15And he divided his forces against
them by night, he and his servants,
and routed them and pursued them to
Hobah, north of Damascus. 16Then he
brought back all the goods, and also
brought back his kinsman Lot with his
goods, and the women and the people.

ABRAM BLESSED BY MELCHIZEDEK

17 After his return from the defeat
of Ched-or-lao´mer and the kings who
were with him, the king of Sodom
went out to meet him at the Valley
of Shaveh (that is, the King's Valley).
18And Melchiz´edek* king of Salem
brought out bread and wine; he was
priest of God Most High. 19And he
blessed him and said,

"Blessed be Abram by God
Most High,
maker of heaven and earth;
20and blessed be God Most High,
who has delivered your
enemies into your
hand!"

21And the king of Sodom said to
Abram, "Give me the persons, but
take the goods for yourself." 22But
Abram said to the king of Sodom, "I
have sworn to the LORD God Most
High, maker of heaven and earth,
23that I would not take a thread or
a sandal-thong or anything that is
yours, lest you should say, 'I have
made Abram rich.' 24I will take noth-
ing but what the young men have eat-
en, and the share of the men who went
with me; let Aner, Eshcol, and Mamre
take their share."

GOD'S COVENANT WITH ABRAM

15 After these things the word of the
LORD came to Abram in a vision,
"Fear not, Abram, I am your shield;
your reward shall be very great."*
2But Abram said, "O Lord GOD, what
wilt thou give me, for I continue
childless, and the heir of my house is
Elie´zer of Damascus?" 3And Abram
said, "Behold, thou hast given me
no offspring; and a slave born in my
house will be my heir." 4And behold,
the word of the LORD came to him,
"This man shall not be your heir; your
own son shall be your heir." 5And he
brought him outside and said, "Look
toward heaven, and number the stars,
if you are able to number them."
Then he said to him, "So shall your
descendants be." 6And he believed the
LORD; and he reckoned it to him as
righteousness.

7 And he said to him, "I am the
LORD who brought you from Ur of
the Chalde´ans, to give you this land
to possess." 8But he said, "O Lord
GOD, how am I to know that I shall

[b]Or *terebinths*

possess it?" 9He said to him, "Bring
me a heifer three years old, a she-goat
three years old, a ram three years old,
a turtledove, and a young pigeon."
10And he brought him all these, cut
them in two, and laid each half over
against the other; but he did not cut
the birds in two. 11And when birds of
prey came down upon the carcasses,
Abram drove them away.

12 As the sun was going down, a
deep sleep fell on Abram; and lo, a
dread and great darkness fell upon
him. 13Then the LORD said to Abram,
"Know of a surety that your descen-
dants will be sojourners in a land
that is not theirs, and will be slaves
there, and they will be oppressed for
four hundred years; 14but I will bring
judgment on the nation which they
serve, and afterward they shall come
out with great possessions. 15As for
yourself, you shall go to your fathers
in peace; you shall be buried in a good
old age. 16And they shall come back
here in the fourth generation; for the
iniquity of the Amorites is not yet
complete."

17 When the sun had gone down
and it was dark, behold, a smoking
fire pot and a flaming torch passed
between these pieces. 18On that day
the LORD made a covenant with
Abram, saying, "To your descen-
dants I give this land, from the river
of Egypt to the great river, the river
Euphra´tes, 19the land of the Ken´ites,
the Ken´izzites, the Kad´monites, 20the
Hittites, the Per´izzites, the Reph´aim,
21the Amorites, the Canaanites, the
Gir´gashites and the Jeb´usites."

THE BIRTH OF ISHMAEL

16 Now Sar´ai, Abram's wife, bore
him no children. She had an
Egyptian maid whose name was
Hagar; 2and Sar´ai *said* to Abram,
"Behold now, the LORD has prevent-
ed me from bearing children; go in to
my maid; it may be that I shall obtain
children by her." And Abram hear-
kened to the voice of Sar´ai. 3So, af-
ter Abram had dwelt ten years in the
land of Canaan, Sar´ai, Abram's wife,
took Hagar the Egyptian, her maid,
and gave her to Abram her husband
as a wife. 4And he went in to Hagar,
and she conceived;* and when she saw
that she had conceived, she looked
with contempt on her mistress. 5And
Sar´ai said to Abram, "May the wrong
done to me be on you! I gave my maid
to your embrace, and when she saw
that she had conceived, she looked
on me with contempt. May the LORD
judge between you and me!" 6But
Abram said to Sar´ai, "Behold, your
maid is in your power; do to her as
you please." Then Sar´ai dealt harshly
with her, and she fled from her.

7 The angel of the LORD found her
by a spring of water in the wilderness,
the spring on the way to Shur. 8And
he said, "Hagar, maid of Sar´ai, where
have you come from and where are
you going?" She said, "I am fleeing
from my mistress Sar´ai." 9The an-
gel of the LORD said to her, "Return
to your mistress, and submit to her."
10The angel of the LORD also said to
her, "I will so greatly multiply your
descendants that they cannot be num-
bered for multitude." 11And the angel
of the LORD said to her, "Behold, you
are with child, and shall bear a son;
you shall call his name Ish´mael;[a] be-
cause the LORD has given heed to your
affliction. 12He shall be a wild ass of a
man, his hand against every man and
every man's hand against him; and he
shall dwell over against all his kins-
men." 13So she called the name of the
LORD who spoke to her, "Thou art a
God of seeing"; for she said, "Have I
really seen God and remained alive
after seeing him?"[b] 14 Therefore the
well was called Beer-la´hai-roi;[c] it lies
between Kadesh and Bered. 15And
Hagar bore Abram a son; and Abram
called the name of his son, whom

[a] That is *God hears*
[b] Cn: Heb *have I even here seen after him who sees me?*
[c] That is *the well of one who sees and lives*

Hagar bore, Ish´mael. 16 Abram was
eighty-six years old when Hagar bore
Ish´mael to Abram.

THE SIGN OF THE COVENANT

17 When Abram was ninety-nine
years old the LORD appeared to
Abram, and said to him, "I am God
Almighty;[d] walk before me, and be
blameless. 2 And I will make my cov-
enant between me and you, and will
multiply you exceedingly." 3 Then
Abram fell on his face; and God said
to him, 4 "Behold, my covenant is with
you, and you shall be the father of a
multitude of nations. 5 No longer shall
your name be Abram,[e] but your name
shall be Abraham;[f] for I have made
you the father of a multitude of na-
tions. 6 I will make you exceedingly
fruitful; and I will make nations of
you, and kings shall come forth from
you. 7 And I will establish my covenant
between me and you and your de-
scendants after you throughout their
generations for an everlasting cov-
enant, to be God to you and to your
descendants after you. 8 And I will give
to you, and to your descendants after
you, the land of your sojournings, all
the land of Canaan, for an everlasting
possession; and I will be their God."

9 And God said to Abraham, "As
for you, you shall keep my covenant,
you and your descendants after you
throughout their generations. 10 This
is my covenant, which you shall keep,
between me and you and your descen-
dants after you: Every male among
you shall be circumcised. 11 You shall
be circumcised in the flesh of your
foreskins, and it shall be a sign of the
covenant between me and you. 12 He
that is eight days old among you shall
be circumcised; every male through-
out your generations, whether born in
your house, or bought with your mon-
ey from any foreigner who is not of
your offspring, 13 both he that is born
in your house and he that is bought
with your money, shall be circum-
cised. So shall my covenant be in your
flesh an everlasting covenant. 14 Any
uncircumcised male who is not cir-
cumcised in the flesh of his foreskin
shall be cut off from his people; he has
broken my covenant."

15 And God said to Abraham, "As
for Sar´ai your wife, you shall not call
her name Sar´ai, but Sarah shall be
her name. 16 I will bless her, and more-
over I will give you a son by her; I will
bless her, and she shall be a mother
of nations; kings of peoples shall come
from her." 17 Then Abraham fell on his
face and laughed, and said to himself,
"Shall a child be born to a man who
is a hundred years old? Shall Sarah,
who is ninety years old, bear a child?"
18 And Abraham said to God, "O that
Ish´mael might live in thy sight!"
19 God said, "No, but Sarah your wife
shall bear you a son, and you shall
call his name Isaac.[g] I will establish
my covenant with him as an everlas-
ing covenant for his descendants after
him. 20 As for Ish´mael, I have heard
you; behold, I will bless him and make
him fruitful and multiply him exceed-
ingly; he shall be the father of twelve
princes, and I will make him a great
nation. 21 But I will establish my cov-
enant with Isaac, whom Sarah shall
bear to you at this season next year."

22 When he had finished talking
with him, God went up from Abraham.
23 Then Abraham took Ish´mael his son
and all the slaves born in his house or
bought with his money, every male
among the men of Abraham's house,
and he circumcised the flesh of their
foreskins that very day, as God had
said to him. 24 Abraham was nine-
ty-nine years old when he was cir-
cumcised in the flesh of his foreskin.
25 And Ish´mael his son was thirteen
years old when he was circumcised in
the flesh of his foreskin. 26 That very

[d] Heb *El Shaddai*
[e] That is *exalted father*
[f] Here taken to mean *father of a multitude*
[g] That is *he laughs*

day Abraham and his son Ish´mael
were circumcised; 27and all the men
of his house, those born in the house
and those bought with money from a
foreigner, were circumcised with him.

A SON PROMISED TO ABRAHAM AND SARAH

18 And the LORD appeared to him by
the oaks[a] of Mamre, as he sat at
the door of his tent in the heat of the
day. 2He lifted up his eyes and looked,
and behold, three men stood in front
of him. When he saw them, he ran
from the tent door to meet them, and
bowed himself to the earth, 3and said,
"My lord, if I have found favor in your
sight, do not pass by your servant.
4Let a little water be brought, and
wash your feet, and rest yourselves
under the tree, 5while I fetch a morsel
of bread, that you may refresh your-
selves, and after that you may pass
on—since you have come to your ser-
vant." So they said, "Do as you have
said." 6And Abraham hastened into
the tent to Sarah, and said, "Make
ready quickly three measures[b] of fine
meal, knead it, and make cakes." 7And
Abraham ran to the herd, and took a
calf, tender and good, and gave it to
the servant, who hastened to prepare
it. 8Then he took curds, and milk, and
the calf which he had prepared, and
set it before them; and he stood by
them under the tree while they ate.

9 They said to him, "Where is
Sarah your wife?" And he said, "She
is in the tent." 10The LORD said, "I
will surely return to you in the spring,
and Sarah your wife shall have a son."
And Sarah was listening at the tent
door behind him. 11Now Abraham and
Sarah were old, advanced in age; it
had ceased to be with Sarah after the
manner of women. 12So Sarah laughed
to herself, saying, "After I have grown
old, and my husband is old, shall I
have pleasure?" 13The LORD said to
Abraham, "Why did Sarah laugh, and
say, 'Shall I indeed bear a child, now
that I am old?' 14Is anything too hard[c]
for the LORD? At the appointed time I
will return to you, in the spring, and
Sarah shall have a son." 15But Sarah
denied, saying, "I did not laugh"; for
she was afraid. He said, "No, but you
did laugh."

JUDGMENT PRONOUNCED ON SODOM

16 Then the men set out from
there, and they looked toward Sodom;
and Abraham went with them to set
them on their way. 17The LORD said,
"Shall I hide from Abraham what I am
about to do, 18seeing that Abraham
shall become a great and mighty na-
tion, and all the nations of the earth
shall bless themselves by him?[d] 19No,
for I have chosen[e] him, that he may
charge his children and his house-
hold after him to keep the way of the
LORD by doing righteousness and jus-
tice; so that the LORD may bring to
Abraham what he has promised him."
20Then the LORD said, "Because the
outcry against Sodom and Gomor´rah
is great and their sin is very grave, 21I
will go down to see whether they have
done altogether according to the out-
cry which has come to me; and if not,
I will know."

22 So the men turned from there,
and went toward Sodom; but Abraham
still stood before the LORD. 23Then
Abraham drew near, and said, "Wilt
thou indeed destroy the righteous
with the wicked? 24Suppose there are
fifty righteous within the city; wilt
thou then destroy the place and not
spare it for the fifty righteous who are
in it? 25Far be it from thee to do such
a thing, to slay the righteous with the
wicked, so that the righteous fare as
the wicked! Far be that from thee!
Shall not the Judge of all the earth do
right?" 26And the LORD said, "If I find

[a] Or *terebinths*
[b] Heb *seahs*
[c] Or *wonderful*
[d] Or *in him all the nations of the earth shall be blessed*
[e] Heb *known*

at Sodom fifty righteous in the city,
I will spare the whole place for their
sake." 27 Abraham answered, "Behold,
I have taken upon myself to speak
to the Lord, I who am but dust and
ashes. 28 Suppose five of the fifty righ-
teous are lacking? Wilt thou destroy
the whole city for lack of five?" And
he said, "I will not destroy it if I find
forty-five there." 29 Again he spoke
to him, and said, "Suppose forty are
found there." He answered, "For the
sake of forty I will not do it." 30 Then
he said, "Oh let not the Lord be angry,
and I will speak. Suppose thirty are
found there." He answered, "I will not
do it, if I find thirty there." 31 He said,
"Behold, I have taken upon myself to
speak to the Lord. Suppose twenty are
found there." He answered, "For the
sake of twenty I will not destroy it."
32 Then he said, "Oh let not the Lord be
angry, and I will speak again but this
once. Suppose ten are found there."
He answered, "For the sake of ten I
will not destroy it." 33 And the LORD
went his way, when he had finished
speaking to Abraham; and Abraham
returned to his place.

THE DEPRAVITY OF SODOM

19 *The two angels came to Sodom
in the evening; and Lot was sit-
ting in the gate of Sodom. When Lot
saw them, he rose to meet them,
and bowed himself with his face to
the earth, 2 and said, "My lords, turn
aside, I pray you, to your servant's
house and spend the night, and wash
your feet; then you may rise up early
and go on your way." They said, "No;
we will spend the night in the street."
3 But he urged them strongly; so they
turned aside to him and entered his
house; and he made them a feast, and
baked unleavened bread, and they ate.
4 But before they lay down, the men
of the city, the men of Sodom, both
young and old, all the people to the
last man, surrounded the house; 5 and
they called to Lot, "Where are the
men who came to you tonight? Bring
them out to us, that we may know
them." 6 Lot went out of the door to
the men, shut the door after him, 7 and
said, "I beg you, my brothers, do not
act so wickedly. 8 Behold, I have two
daughters who have not known man;
let me bring them out to you, and do
to them as you please; only do nothing
to these men, for they have come un-
der the shelter of my roof." 9 But they
said, "Stand back!" And they said,
"This fellow came to sojourn, and he
would play the judge! Now we will
deal worse with you than with them."
Then they pressed hard against the
man Lot, and drew near to break the
door. 10 But the men put forth their
hands and brought Lot into the house
to them, and shut the door. 11 And they
struck with blindness the men who
were at the door of the house, both
small and great, so that they wearied
themselves groping for the door.

SODOM AND GOMORRAH DESTROYED

12 Then the men said to Lot, "Have
you any one else here? Sons-in-law,
sons, daughters, or any one you have
in the city, bring them out of the
place; 13 for we are about to destroy
this place, because the outcry against
its people has become great before the
LORD, and the LORD has sent us to
destroy it." 14 So Lot went out and said
to his sons-in-law, who were to mar-
ry his daughters, "Up, get out of this
place; for the LORD is about to destroy
the city." But he seemed to his sons-
in-law to be jesting.

15 When morning dawned, the an-
gels urged Lot, saying, "Arise, take your
wife and your two daughters who are
here, lest you be consumed in the pun-
ishment of the city." 16 But he lingered;
so the men seized him and his wife
and his two daughters by the hand, the
LORD being merciful to him, and they
brought him forth and set him outside
the city. 17 And when they had brought
them forth, they[f] said, "Flee for your

[f] Gk Syr Vg: Heb *he*

life; do not look back or stop anywhere
in the valley; flee to the hills, lest you
be consumed." 18And Lot said to them,
"Oh, no, my lords; 19behold, your ser-
vant has found favor in your sight, and
you have shown me great kindness in
saving my life; but I cannot flee to the
hills, lest the disaster overtake me,
and I die. 20Behold, yonder city is near
enough to flee to, and it is a little one.
Let me escape there—is it not a little
one?—and my life will be saved!" 21He
said to him, "Behold, I grant you this
favor also, that I will not overthrow the
city of which you have spoken. 22Make
haste, escape there; for I can do noth-
ing till you arrive there." Therefore
the name of the city was called Zo′ar.[a]
23The sun had risen on the earth when
Lot came to Zo′ar.

24 Then the LORD rained on Sodom
and Gomor′rah brimstone and fire
from the LORD out of heaven; 25and
he overthrew those cities, and all the
valley, and all the inhabitants of the
cities, and what grew on the ground.
26But Lot's wife behind him looked
back, and she became a pillar of salt.
27And Abraham went early in the
morning to the place where he had
stood before the LORD; 28and he looked
down toward Sodom and Gomor′rah
and toward all the land of the valley,
and beheld, and lo, smoke of the land
went up like the smoke of a furnace.

29 So it was that, when God de-
stroyed the cities of the valley, God
remembered Abraham, and sent Lot
out of the midst of the overthrow,
when he overthrew the cities in which
Lot dwelt.

THE SHAMEFUL ORIGIN OF MOAB AND AMMON

30 Now Lot went up out of Zo′ar,
and dwelt in the hills with his two
daughters, for he was afraid to dwell
in Zo′ar; so he dwelt in a cave with
his two daughters. 31And the first-born
said to the younger, "Our father is
old, and there is not a man on earth to
come in to us after the manner of all
the earth. 32Come, let us make our fa-
ther drink wine, and we will lie with
him, that we may preserve offspring
through our father." 33So they made
their father drink wine that night; and
the first-born went in, and lay with
her father; he did not know when she
lay down or when she arose. 34And on
the next day, the first-born said to the
younger, "Behold, I lay last night with
my father; let us make him drink wine
tonight also; then you go in and lie with
him, that we may preserve offspring
through our father." 35So they made
their father drink wine that night also;
and the younger arose, and lay with
him; and he did not know when she lay
down or when she arose. 36Thus both
the daughters of Lot were with child by
their father. 37The first-born bore a son,
and called his name Moab; he is the fa-
ther of the Moabites to this day. 38The
younger also bore a son, and called his
name Ben-ammi; he is the father of the
Ammonites to this day.

ABRAHAM AND SARAH AT GERAR

20 From there Abraham journeyed
toward the territory of the Negeb,
and dwelt between Kadesh and Shur;
and he sojourned in Gerar. 2And
Abraham said of Sarah his wife, "She
is my sister." And Abim′elech king of
Gerar sent and took Sarah. 3But God
came to Abim′elech in a dream by
night, and said to him, "Behold, you
are a dead man, because of the wom-
an whom you have taken; for she is
a man's wife." 4Now Abim′elech had
not approached her; so he said, "Lord,
wilt thou slay an innocent people?
5Did he not himself say to me, 'She is
my sister'? And she herself said, 'He
is my brother.' In the integrity of my
heart and the innocence of my hands
I have done this." 6Then God said to
him in the dream, "Yes, I know that
you have done this in the integrity of
your heart, and it was I who kept you
from sinning against me; therefore I

[a] That is *Little*

did not let you touch her. 7Now then
restore the man's wife; for he is a
prophet, and he will pray for you, and
you shall live. But if you do not restore
her, know that you shall surely die,
you, and all that are yours."
8 So Abim'elech rose early in the
morning, and called all his servants,
and told them all these things; and
the men were very much afraid. 9Then
Abim'elech called Abraham, and said
to him, "What have you done to us?
And how have I sinned against you,
that you have brought on me and my
kingdom a great sin? You have done to
me things that ought not to be done."
10And Abim'elech said to Abraham,
"What were you thinking of, that you
did this thing?" 11Abraham said, "I did
it because I thought, There is no fear
of God at all in this place, and they will
kill me because of my wife. 12Besides
she is indeed my sister, the daughter
of my father but not the daughter of
my mother; and she became my wife.
13And when God caused me to wan-
der from my father's house, I said to
her, 'This is the kindness you must do
me: at every place to which we come,
say of me, He is my brother.'" 14Then
Abim'elech took sheep and oxen, and
male and female slaves, and gave them
to Abraham, and restored Sarah his
wife to him. 15And Abim'elech said,
"Behold, my land is before you; dwell
where it pleases you." 16To Sarah he
said, "Behold, I have given your broth-
er a thousand pieces of silver; it is
your vindication in the eyes of all who
are with you; and before every one you
are righted." 17Then Abraham prayed
to God; and God healed Abim'elech,
and also healed his wife and female
slaves so that they bore children. 18For
the LORD had closed all the wombs of
the house of Abim'elech because of
Sarah, Abraham's wife.

THE BIRTH OF ISAAC

21 The LORD visited Sarah as he had
said, and the LORD did to Sarah
as he had promised. 2And Sarah con-
ceived, and bore Abraham a son in his
old age at the time of which God had
spoken to him. 3Abraham called the
name of his son who was born to him,
whom Sarah bore him, Isaac. 4And
Abraham circumcised his son Isaac
when he was eight days old, as God
had commanded him. 5Abraham was a
hundred years old when his son Isaac
was born to him. 6And Sarah said,
"God has made laughter for me; every
one who hears will laugh over me."
7And she said, "Who would have said
to Abraham that Sarah would suckle
children? Yet I have borne him a son
in his old age."

HAGAR AND ISHMAEL SENT AWAY

8 And the child grew, and was
weaned; and Abraham made a great
feast on the day that Isaac was
weaned. 9But Sarah saw the son of
Hagar the Egyptian, whom she had
borne to Abraham, playing with her
son Isaac.[b] 10So she said to Abraham,
"Cast out this slave woman with her
son; for the son of this slave woman
shall not be heir with my son Isaac."
11And the thing was very displeasing
to Abraham on account of his son.
12But God said to Abraham, "Be not
displeased because of the lad and be-
cause of your slave woman; whatever
Sarah says to you, do as she tells you,
for through Isaac shall your descen-
dants be named. 13And I will make a
nation of the son of the slave woman
also, because he is your offspring."
14So Abraham rose early in the morn-
ing, and took bread and a skin of wa-
ter, and gave it to Hagar, putting it on
her shoulder, along with the child,
and sent her away. And she departed,
and wandered in the wilderness of
Beer-sheba.
15 When the water in the skin was
gone, she cast the child under one of
the bushes. 16Then she went, and sat
down over against him a good way off,
about the distance of a bowshot; for

[b]Gk Vg: Heb lacks *with her son Isaac*

she said, "Let me not look upon the
death of the child." And as she sat
over against him, the child lifted up
his voice[a] and wept. 17 And God heard
the voice of the lad; and the angel of
God called to Hagar from heaven,
and said to her, "What troubles you,
Hagar? Fear not; for God has heard the
voice of the lad where he is. 18 Arise,
lift up the lad, and hold him fast with
your hand; for I will make him a great
nation." 19 Then God opened her eyes,
and she saw a well of water; and she
went, and filled the skin with water,
and gave the lad a drink. 20 And God
was with the lad, and he grew up; he
lived in the wilderness, and became
an expert with the bow. 21 He lived
in the wilderness of Paran; and his
mother took a wife for him from the
land of Egypt.

ABRAHAM AND ABIMELECH MAKE A COVENANT

22 At that time Abim´elech and
Phicol the commander of his army
said to Abraham, "God is with you in
all that you do; 23 now therefore swear
to me here by God that you will not
deal falsely with me or with my off-
spring or with my posterity, but as I
have dealt loyally with you, you will
deal with me and with the land where
you have sojourned." 24 And Abraham
said, "I will swear."

25 When Abraham complained
to Abim´elech about a well of wa-
ter which Abim´elech's servants had
seized, 26 Abim´elech said, "I do not
know who has done this thing; you
did not tell me, and I have not heard
of it until today." 27 So Abraham took
sheep and oxen and gave them to
Abim´elech, and the two men made
a covenant. 28 Abraham set seven
ewe lambs of the flock apart. 29 And
Abim´elech said to Abraham, "What
is the meaning of these seven ewe
lambs which you have set apart?" 30 He
said, "These seven ewe lambs you will
take from my hand, that you may be a
witness for me that I dug this well."
31 Therefore that place was called Beer-
sheba;[b] because there both of them
swore an oath. 32 So they made a cov-
enant at Beer-sheba. Then Abim´elech
and Phicol the commander of his army
rose up and returned to the land of the
Philistines. 33 Abraham planted a tam-
arisk tree in Beer-sheba, and called
there on the name of the LORD, the
Everlasting God. 34 And Abraham so-
journed many days in the land of the
Philistines.

THE COMMAND TO SACRIFICE ISAAC

22 After these things God test-
ed Abraham, and said to him,
"Abraham!" And he said, "Here am
I." 2 He said, "Take your son, your only
son Isaac, whom you love, and go to
the land of Mori´ah, and offer him
there as a burnt offering upon one
of the mountains of which I shall tell
you." 3 So Abraham rose early in the
morning, saddled his ass, and took
two of his young men with him, and
his son Isaac; and he cut the wood for
the burnt offering, and arose and went
to the place of which God had told
him. 4 On the third day Abraham lift-
ed up his eyes and saw the place afar
off. 5 Then Abraham said to his young
men, "Stay here with the ass; I and the
lad will go yonder and worship, and
come again to you." 6 And Abraham
took the wood of the burnt offering,
and laid it on Isaac his son;* and he
took in his hand the fire and the knife.
So they went both of them together.
7 And Isaac said to his father Abraham,
"My father!" And he said, "Here am
I, my son." He said, "Behold, the fire
and the wood; but where is the lamb
for a burnt offering?" 8 Abraham said,
"God will provide himself the lamb
for a burnt offering, my son." So they
went both of them together.

9 When they came to the place of
which God had told him, Abraham

[a] Gk: Heb *she lifted up her voice*
[b] That is *Well of seven* or *Well of the oath*

built an altar there, and laid the wood
in order, and bound Isaac his son, and
laid him on the altar, upon the wood.
10Then Abraham put forth his hand,
and took the knife to slay his son.
11But the angel of the LORD called to
him from heaven, and said, "Abraham,
Abraham!" And he said, "Here am I."
12He said, "Do not lay your hand on
the lad or do anything to him; for now
I know that you fear God, seeing you
have not withheld your son, your only
son, from me." 13And Abraham lifted
up his eyes and looked, and behold,
behind him was a ram, caught in a
thicket by his horns; and Abraham
went and took the ram, and offered it
up as a burnt offering instead of his
son. 14So Abraham called the name of
that place The LORD will provide;[c] as
it is said to this day, "On the mount of
the LORD it shall be provided."[d]

15 And the angel of the LORD called
to Abraham a second time from heav-
en, 16and said, "By myself I have sworn,
says the LORD, because you have done
this, and have not withheld your son,
your only son, 17I will indeed bless you,
and I will multiply your descendants
as the stars of heaven and as the sand
which is on the seashore. And your
descendants shall possess the gate
of their enemies, 18and by your de-
scendants shall all the nations of the
earth bless themselves, because you
have obeyed my voice." 19So Abraham
returned to his young men, and they
arose and went together to Beer-sheba;
and Abraham dwelt at Beer-sheba.*

THE CHILDREN OF NAHOR

20 Now after these things it was
told Abraham, "Behold, Milcah also
has borne children to your brother
Nahor: 21Uz the first-born, Buz his
brother, Kemu´el the father of Aram,
22Chesed, Hazo, Pildash, Jidlaph, and
Bethu´el." 23Bethu´el became the fa-
ther of Rebekah. These eight Milcah
bore to Nahor, Abraham's brother.
24Moreover, his concubine, whose
name was Reumah, bore Tebah, Ga-
ham, Tahash, and Ma´acah.

SARAH'S DEATH AND BURIAL

23 Sarah lived a hundred and
twenty-seven years; these were
the years of the life of Sarah. 2And
Sarah died at Kir´iath-ar´ba (that is,
Hebron) in the land of Canaan; and
Abraham went in to mourn for Sarah
and to weep for her. 3And Abraham
rose up from before his dead, and
said to the Hittites, 4"I am a strang-
er and a sojourner among you; give
me property among you for a burying
place, that I may bury my dead out
of my sight." 5The Hittites answered
Abraham, 6"Hear us, my lord; you are
a mighty prince among us. Bury your
dead in the choicest of our sepulchres;
none of us will withhold from you his
sepulchre, or hinder you from bury-
ing your dead." 7Abraham rose and
bowed to the Hittites, the people of
the land. 8And he said to them, "If
you are willing that I should bury my
dead out of my sight, hear me, and en-
treat for me Ephron the son of Zohar,
9that he may give me the cave of
Mach-pe´lah, which he owns; it is at
the end of his field. For the full price
let him give it to me in your presence
as a possession for a burying place."
10Now Ephron was sitting among the
Hittites; and Ephron the Hittite an-
swered Abraham in the hearing of the
Hittites, of all who went in at the gate
of his city, 11"No, my lord, hear me; I
give you the field, and I give you the
cave that is in it; in the presence of the
sons of my people I give it to you; bury
your dead." 12Then Abraham bowed
down before the people of the land.
13And he said to Ephron in the hear-
ing of the people of the land, "But if
you will, hear me; I will give the price
of the field; accept it from me, that I
may bury my dead there." 14Ephron
answered Abraham, 15"My lord, listen

[c] Or *see*
[d] Or *he will be seen*

to me; a piece of land worth four hun-
dred shekels of silver, what is that be-
tween you and me? Bury your dead."
16 Abraham agreed with Ephron; and
Abraham weighed out for Ephron the
silver which he had named in the hear-
ing of the Hittites, four hundred shek-
els of silver, according to the weights
current among the merchants.

17 So the field of Ephron in Mach-
pe´lah, which was to the east of
Mamre, the field with the cave which
was in it and all the trees that were in
the field, throughout its whole area,
was made over 18 to Abraham as a pos-
session in the presence of the Hittites,
before all who went in at the gate of
his city. 19 After this, Abraham buried
Sarah his wife in the cave of the field
of Mach-pe´lah east of Mamre (that is,
Hebron) in the land of Canaan. 20 The
field and the cave that is in it were
made over to Abraham as a possession
for a burying place by the Hittites.

THE MARRIAGE OF ISAAC AND REBEKAH

24 Now Abraham was old, well ad-
vanced in years; and the LORD
had blessed Abraham in all things.
2 And Abraham said to his servant, the
oldest of his house, who had charge of
all that he had, "Put your hand under
my thigh, 3 and I will make you swear
by the LORD, the God of heaven and
of the earth, that you will not take a
wife for my son from the daughters
of the Canaanites, among whom I
dwell, 4 but will go to my country and
to my kindred, and take a wife for my
son Isaac." 5 The servant said to him,
"Perhaps the woman may not be will-
ing to follow me to this land; must I
then take your son back to the land
from which you came?" 6 Abraham
said to him, "See to it that you do not
take my son back there. 7 The LORD,
the God of heaven, who took me from
my father's house and from the land
of my birth, and who spoke to me and
swore to me, 'To your descendants I
will give this land,' he will send his
angel before you, and you shall take a
wife for my son from there. 8 But if the
woman is not willing to follow you,
then you will be free from this oath of
mine; only you must not take my son
back there." 9 So the servant put his
hand under the thigh of Abraham his
master, and swore to him concerning
this matter.

10 Then the servant took ten of his
master's camels and departed, tak-
ing all sorts of choice gifts from his
master; and he arose, and went to
Mesopota´mia, to the city of Nahor.
11 And he made the camels kneel down
outside the city by the well of water
at the time of evening, the time when
women go out to draw water. 12 And
he said, "O LORD, God of my master
Abraham, grant me success today, I
pray thee, and show steadfast love to
my master Abraham. 13 Behold, I am
standing by the spring of water, and
the daughters of the men of the city
are coming out to draw water. 14 Let
the maiden to whom I shall say, 'Pray
let down your jar that I may drink,'
and who shall say, 'Drink, and I will
water your camels'—let her be the one
whom thou hast appointed for thy ser-
vant Isaac. By this I shall know that
thou hast shown steadfast love to my
master."

15 Before he had done speaking,
behold, Rebekah, who was born to
Bethu´el the son of Milcah, the wife of
Nahor, Abraham's brother, came out
with her water jar upon her shoulder.
16 The maiden was very fair to look
upon, a virgin, whom no man had
known. She went down to the spring,
and filled her jar, and came up. 17 Then
the servant ran to meet her, and said,
"Pray give me a little water to drink
from your jar." 18 She said, "Drink, my
lord"; and she quickly let down her jar
upon her hand, and gave him a drink.
19 When she had finished giving him a
drink, she said, "I will draw for your
camels also, until they have done
drinking." 20 So she quickly emptied
her jar into the trough and ran again
to the well to draw, and she drew for

all his camels. 21The man gazed at her
in silence to learn whether the LORD
had prospered his journey or not.

22 When the camels had done
drinking, the man took a gold ring
weighing a half shekel, and two brace-
lets for her arms weighing ten gold
shekels, 23and said, "Tell me whose
daughter you are. Is there room in
your father's house for us to lodge in?"
24She said to him, "I am the daughter
of Bethu´el the son of Milcah, whom
she bore to Nahor." 25She added,
"We have both straw and proven-
der enough, and room to lodge in."
26The man bowed his head and wor-
shiped the LORD, 27and said, "Blessed
be the LORD, the God of my master
Abraham, who has not forsaken his
steadfast love and his faithfulness to-
ward my master. As for me, the LORD
has led me in the way to the house of
my master's kinsmen."

28 Then the maiden ran and told
her mother's household about these
things. 29Rebekah had a brother whose
name was Laban; and Laban ran out
to the man, to the spring. 30When he
saw the ring, and the bracelets on his
sister's arms, and when he heard the
words of Rebekah his sister, "Thus the
man spoke to me," he went to the man;
and behold, he was standing by the
camels at the spring. 31He said, "Come
in, O blessed of the LORD; why do you
stand outside? For I have prepared
the house and a place for the camels."
32So the man came into the house; and
Laban ungirded the camels, and gave
him straw and provender for the cam-
els, and water to wash his feet and the
feet of the men who were with him.
33Then food was set before him to eat;
but he said, "I will not eat until I have
told my errand." He said, "Speak on."

34 So he said, "I am Abraham's ser-
vant. 35The LORD has greatly blessed
my master, and he has become great;
he has given him flocks and herds, sil-
ver and gold, menservants and maid-
servants, camels and asses. 36And
Sarah my master's wife bore a son to
my master when she was old; and to
him he has given all that he has. 37My
master made me swear, saying, 'You
shall not take a wife for my son from
the daughters of the Canaanites, in
whose land I dwell; 38but you shall go
to my father's house and to my kin-
dred, and take a wife for my son.' 39I
said to my master, 'Perhaps the wom-
an will not follow me.' 40But he said to
me, 'The LORD, before whom I walk,
will send his angel with you and pros-
per your way; and you shall take a
wife for my son from my kindred and
from my father's house; 41then you
will be free from my oath, when you
come to my kindred; and if they will
not give her to you, you will be free
from my oath.'

42 "I came today to the spring,
and said, 'O LORD, the God of my
master Abraham, if now thou wilt
prosper the way which I go, 43behold,
I am standing by the spring of water;
let the young woman who comes out
to draw, to whom I shall say, "Pray
give me a little water from your jar
to drink," 44and who will say to me,
"Drink, and I will draw for your cam-
els also," let her be the woman whom
the LORD has appointed for my mas-
ter's son.'

45 "Before I had done speaking in
my heart, behold, Rebekah came out
with her water jar on her shoulder;
and she went down to the spring, and
drew. I said to her, 'Pray let me drink.'
46She quickly let down her jar from
her shoulder, and said, 'Drink, and
I will give your camels drink also.'
So I drank, and she gave the camels
drink also. 47Then I asked her, 'Whose
daughter are you?' She said, 'The
daughter of Bethu´el, Nahor's son,
whom Milcah bore to him.' So I put
the ring on her nose, and the bracelets
on her arms. 48Then I bowed my head
and worshiped the LORD, and bless-
ed the LORD, the God of my master
Abraham, who had led me by the right
way to take the daughter of my mas-
ter's kinsman for his son. 49Now then,

if you will deal loyally and truly with
my master, tell me; and if not, tell me;
that I may turn to the right hand or
to the left."

50 Then Laban and Bethu´el an-
swered, "The thing comes from the
LORD; we cannot speak to you bad
or good. 51 Behold, Rebekah is before
you, take her and go, and let her be
the wife of your master's son, as the
LORD has spoken."

52 When Abraham's servant heard
their words, he bowed himself to the
earth before the LORD. 53 And the ser-
vant brought forth jewelry of silver
and of gold, and raiment, and gave
them to Rebekah; he also gave to her
brother and to her mother costly or-
naments. 54 And he and the men who
were with him ate and drank, and
they spent the night there. When they
arose in the morning, he said, "Send
me back to my master." 55 Her brother
and her mother said, "Let the maiden
remain with us a while, at least ten
days; after that she may go." 56 But he
said to them, "Do not delay me, since
the LORD has prospered my way; let
me go that I may go to my master."
57 They said, "We will call the maid-
en, and ask her." 58 And they called
Rebekah, and said to her, "Will you
go with this man?" She said, "I will
go." 59 So they sent away Rebekah their
sister and her nurse, and Abraham's
servant and his men. 60 And they bless-
ed Rebekah, and said to her, "Our sis-
ter, be the mother of thousands of ten
thousands; and may your descendants
possess the gate of those who hate
them!" 61 Then Rebekah and her maids
arose, and rode upon the camels and
followed the man; thus the servant
took Rebekah, and went his way.

62 Now Isaac had come from[a] Beer-
la´hai-roi, and was dwelling in the
Negeb. 63 *And Isaac went* out to medi-
tate in the field in the evening; and he
lifted up his eyes and looked, and be-
hold, there were camels coming. 64 And
Rebekah lifted up her eyes, and when
she saw Isaac, she alighted from the
camel, 65 and said to the servant, "Who
is the man yonder, walking in the field
to meet us?" The servant said, "It is
my master." So she took her veil and
covered herself. 66 And the servant told
Isaac all the things that he had done.
67 Then Isaac brought her into the tent,[b]
and took Rebekah, and she became his
wife; and he loved her. So Isaac was
comforted after his mother's death.

ABRAHAM MARRIES KETURAH

25 Abraham took another wife, whose
name was Ketu´rah. 2 She bore him
Zimran, Jokshan, Medan, Mid´ian,
Ishbak, and Shuah. 3 Jokshan was the
father of Sheba and Dedan. The sons of
Dedan were Asshu´rim, Letu´shim, and
Le-um´mim. 4 The sons of Mid´ian were
Ephah, Epher, Hanoch, Abi´da, and
Elda´ah. All these were the children of
Ketu´rah. 5 Abraham gave all he had to
Isaac. 6 But to the sons of his concu-
bines Abraham gave gifts, and while
he was still living he sent them away
from his son Isaac, eastward to the
east country.

THE DEATH OF ABRAHAM

7 These are the days of the years of
Abraham's life, a hundred and seven-
ty-five years. 8 Abraham breathed his
last and died in a good old age, an old
man and full of years, and was gath-
ered to his people. 9 Isaac and Ish´mael
his sons buried him in the cave of
Mach-pe´lah, in the field of Ephron
the son of Zohar the Hittite, east of
Mamre, 10 the field which Abraham
purchased from the Hittites. There
Abraham was buried, with Sarah his
wife. 11 After the death of Abraham
God blessed Isaac his son. And Isaac
dwelt at Beer-la´hai-roi.

ISHMAEL'S DESCENDANTS

12 These are the descendants
of Ish´mael, Abraham's son, whom

[a] Syr Tg: Heb *from coming to*
[b] Heb adds *Sarah his mother*

Hagar the Egyptian, Sarah's maid,
bore to Abraham. 13These are the
names of the sons of Ish´mael, named
in the order of their birth: Neba´ioth,
the first-born of Ish´mael; and Kedar,
Adbeel, Mibsam, 14Mishma, Dumah,
Massa, 15Hadad, Tema, Jetur, Naphish,
and Ked´emah. 16These are the sons of
Ish´mael and these are their names,
by their villages and by their encamp-
ments, twelve princes according to
their tribes. 17(These are the years of
the life of Ish´mael, a hundred and
thirty-seven years; he breathed his
last and died, and was gathered to his
kindred.) 18They dwelt from Hav´ilah
to Shur, which is opposite Egypt in the
direction of Assyria; he settled[c] over
against all his people.

THE BIRTH AND YOUTH OF ESAU AND JACOB

19*These are the descendants of
Isaac, Abraham's son: Abraham was
the father of Isaac, 20and Isaac was
forty years old when he took to wife
Rebekah, the daughter of Bethu´el the
Arame´an of Paddan-aram, the sister
of Laban the Arame´an. 21And Isaac
prayed to the LORD for his wife, be-
cause she was barren; and the LORD
granted his prayer, and Rebekah his
wife conceived. 22The children strug-
gled together within her; and she said,
"If it is thus, why do I live?"[d] So she
went to inquire of the LORD. 23And the
LORD said to her,

> "Two nations are in your
> womb,
> and two peoples, born of
> you, shall be divided;
> the one shall be stronger than
> the other,
> the elder shall serve the
> younger."

24When her days to be delivered
were fulfilled, behold, there were
twins in her womb. 25The first came
forth red, all his body like a hairy
mantle; so they called his name Esau.
26Afterward his brother came forth,
and his hand had taken hold of Esau's
heel; so his name was called Jacob.[e]
Isaac was sixty years old when she
bore them.

27 When the boys grew up, Esau
was a skilful hunter, a man of the field,
while Jacob was a quiet man, dwelling
in tents. 28Isaac loved Esau, because
he ate of his game; but Rebekah loved
Jacob.

ESAU SELLS HIS BIRTHRIGHT

29 Once when Jacob was boiling
pottage, Esau came in from the field,
and he was famished. 30And Esau
said to Jacob, "Let me eat some of
that red pottage, for I am famished!"
(Therefore his name was called
Edom.[f]) 31Jacob said, "First sell me
your birthright." 32Esau said, "I am
about to die; of what use is a birth-
right to me?" 33Jacob said, "Swear to
me first."[g] So he swore to him, and
sold his birthright to Jacob. 34Then
Jacob gave Esau bread and pottage of
lentils, and he ate and drank, and rose
and went his way. Thus Esau despised
his birthright.

ISAAC AND ABIMELECH

26 Now there was a famine in the
land, besides the former famine
that was in the days of Abraham. And
Isaac went to Gerar, to Abim´elech
king of the Philistines. 2And the LORD
appeared to him, and said, "Do not
go down to Egypt; dwell in the land
of which I shall tell you. 3Sojourn
in this land, and I will be with you,
and will bless you; for to you and to
your descendants I will give all these
lands, and I will fulfil the oath which
I swore to Abraham your father. 4I
will multiply your descendants as the
stars of heaven, and will give to your
descendants all these lands; and by

[c] Heb *fell*
[d] Syr: Heb obscure
[e] That is *He takes by the heel* or *He supplants*
[f] That is *Red*
[g] Heb *today*

your descendants all the nations of
the earth shall bless themselves: [5]be-
cause Abraham obeyed my voice and
kept my charge, my commandments,
my statutes, and my laws."

6 So Isaac dwelt in Gerar. [7]When
the men of the place asked him
about his wife, he said, "She is my
sister"; for he feared to say, "My
wife," thinking, "lest the men of the
place should kill me for the sake of
Rebekah"; because she was fair to
look upon. [8]When he had been there
a long time, Abim′elech king of the
Philistines looked out of a window
and saw Isaac fondling Rebekah his
wife. [9]So Abim′elech called Isaac, and
said, "Behold, she is your wife; how
then could you say, 'She is my sis-
ter'?" Isaac said to him, "Because I
thought, 'Lest I die because of her.'"
[10]Abim′elech said, "What is this you
have done to us? One of the people
might easily have lain with your wife,
and you would have brought guilt
upon us." [11]So Abim′elech warned all
the people, saying, "Whoever touches
this man or his wife shall be put to
death."

12 And Isaac sowed in that land,
and reaped in the same year a hun-
dredfold. The LORD blessed him,
[13]and the man became rich, and
gained more and more until he be-
came very wealthy. [14]He had posses-
sions of flocks and herds, and a great
household, so that the Philistines en-
vied him. [15](Now the Philistines had
stopped and filled with earth all the
wells which his father's servants had
dug in the days of Abraham his fa-
ther.) [16]And Abim′elech said to Isaac,
"Go away from us; for you are much
mightier than we."

17 So Isaac departed from there,
and encamped in the valley of Gerar
and dwelt there. [18]And Isaac dug
again the wells of water which had
been dug in the days of Abraham his
father; for the Philistines had stopped
them after the death of Abraham;
and he gave them the names which
his father had given them. [19]But when
Isaac's servants dug in the valley
and found there a well of springing
water, [20]the herdsmen of Gerar quar-
reled with Isaac's herdsmen, saying,
"The water is ours." So he called
the name of the well Esek,[a] because
they contended with him. [21]Then they
dug another well, and they quarreled
over that also; so he called its name
Sitnah.[b] [22]And he moved from there
and dug another well, and over that
they did not quarrel; so he called its
name Reho′both,[c] saying, "For now
the LORD has made room for us, and
we shall be fruitful in the land."

23 From there he went up to Beer-
sheba. [24]And the LORD appeared to
him the same night and said, "I am
the God of Abraham your father; fear
not, for I am with you and will bless
you and multiply your descendants for
my servant Abraham's sake." [25]So he
built an altar there and called upon
the name of the LORD, and pitched his
tent there. And there Isaac's servants
dug a well.

26 Then Abim′elech went to him
from Gerar with Ahuz′zath his advis-
er and Phicol the commander of his
army. [27]Isaac said to them, "Why have
you come to me, seeing that you hate
me and have sent me away from you?"
[28]They said, "We see plainly that the
LORD is with you; so we say, let there
be an oath between you and us, and
let us make a covenant with you,
[29]that you will do us no harm, just
as we have not touched you and have
done to you nothing but good and
have sent you away in peace. You are
now the blessed of the LORD." [30]So
he made them a feast, and they ate
and drank. [31]In the morning they rose
early and took oath with one anoth-
er; and Isaac set them on their way,
and they departed from him in peace.
[32]That same day Isaac's servants came

[a]That is *Contention*
[b]That is *Enmity*
[c]That is *Broad places* or *Room*

and told him about the well which
they had dug, and said to him, "We
have found water." 33He called it
Shibah; therefore the name of the city
is Beer-sheba to this day.

ESAU'S HITTITE WIVES

34 When Esau was forty years old,
he took to wife Judith the daughter
of Be-e´ri the Hittite, and Bas´emath
the daughter of Elon the Hittite; 35and
they made life bitter for Isaac and
Rebekah.

ISAAC BLESSES JACOB

27 When Isaac was old and his eyes
were dim so that he could not see,
he called Esau his older son, and said
to him, "My son"; and he answered,
"Here I am." 2He said, "Behold, I
am old; I do not know the day of my
death. 3Now then, take your weapons,
your quiver and your bow, and go out
to the field, and hunt game for me,
4and prepare for me savory food, such
as I love, and bring it to me that I may
eat; that I may bless you before I die."
5 Now Rebekah was listening
when Isaac spoke to his son Esau. So
when Esau went to the field to hunt
for game and bring it, 6Rebekah said
to her son Jacob, "I heard your father
speak to your brother Esau, 7'Bring
me game, and prepare for me savory
food, that I may eat it, and bless you
before the LORD before I die.' 8Now
therefore, my son, obey my word as I
command you. 9Go to the flock, and
fetch me two good kids, that I may
prepare from them savory food for
your father, such as he loves; 10and
you shall bring it to your father to eat,
so that he may bless you before he
dies." 11But Jacob said to Rebekah his
mother, "Behold, my brother Esau is
a hairy man, and I am a smooth man.
12Perhaps my father will feel me, and
I shall seem to be mocking him, and
bring a curse upon myself and not a
blessing." 13His mother said to him,
"Upon me be your curse, my son; only
obey my word, and go, fetch them to
me." 14So he went and took them and
brought them to his mother; and his
mother prepared savory food, such
as his father loved. 15Then Rebekah
took the best garments of Esau her
older son, which were with her in
the house, and put them on Jacob her
younger son; 16and the skins of the
kids she put upon his hands and upon
the smooth part of his neck; 17and she
gave the savory food and the bread,
which she had prepared, into the hand
of her son Jacob.
18 So he went in to his father, and
said, "My father"; and he said, "Here
I am; who are you, my son?" 19Jacob
said to his father, "I am Esau your
first-born. I have done as you told me;
now sit up and eat of my game, that
you may bless me." 20But Isaac said
to his son, "How is it that you have
found it so quickly, my son?" He an-
swered, "Because the LORD your God
granted me success." 21Then Isaac said
to Jacob, "Come near, that I may feel
you, my son, to know whether you
are really my son Esau or not." 22So
Jacob went near to Isaac his father,
who felt him and said, "The voice is
Jacob's voice, but the hands are the
hands of Esau." 23And he did not rec-
ognize him, because his hands were
hairy like his brother Esau's hands;
so he blessed him. 24He said, "Are you
really my son Esau?" He answered, "I
am." 25Then he said, "Bring it to me,
that I may eat of my son's game and
bless you." So he brought it to him,
and he ate; and he brought him wine,
and he drank. 26Then his father Isaac
said to him, "Come near and kiss me,
my son." 27So he came near and kissed
him; and he smelled the smell of his
garments, and blessed him, and said,

"See, the smell of my son
is as the smell of a field
which the LORD has
blessed!
28May God give you of the dew of
heaven,
and of the fatness of the
earth,

and plenty of grain and
wine.
29 Let peoples serve you,
and nations bow down to
you.
Be lord over your brothers,
and may your mother's sons
bow down to you.
Cursed be every one who curs-
es you,
and blessed be every one
who blesses you!"

ESAU'S LOST BLESSING

30 As soon as Isaac had finished
blessing Jacob, when Jacob had scarce-
ly gone out from the presence of Isaac
his father, Esau his brother came in
from his hunting. 31 He also prepared
savory food, and brought it to his fa-
ther. And he said to his father, "Let my
father arise, and eat of his son's game,
that you may bless me." 32 His father
Isaac said to him, "Who are you?" He
answered, "I am your son, your first-
born, Esau." 33 Then Isaac trembled
violently, and said, "Who was it then
that hunted game and brought it to
me, and I ate it all[a] before you came,
and I have blessed him?—yes, and he
shall be blessed." 34 When Esau heard
the words of his father, he cried out
with an exceedingly great and bitter
cry, and said to his father, "Bless me,
even me also, O my father!" 35 But he
said, "Your brother came with guile,
and he has taken away your blessing."
36 Esau said, "Is he not rightly named
Jacob? For he has supplanted me these
two times. He took away my birth-
right; and behold, now he has tak-
en away my blessing." Then he said,
"Have you not reserved a blessing for
me?" 37 Isaac answered Esau, "Behold,
I have made him your lord, and all his
brothers I have given to him for ser-
vants, and with grain and wine I have
sustained him. What then can I do for
you, my son?" 38 Esau said to his fa-
ther, "Have you but one blessing, my
father? Bless me, even me also, O my
father." And Esau lifted up his voice
and wept.
39 Then Isaac his father answered
him:
"Behold, away from[b] the fat-
ness of the earth shall
your dwelling be,
and away from[c] the dew of
heaven on high.
40 By your sword you shall live,
and you shall serve your
brother;
but when you break loose
you shall break his yoke
from your neck."

JACOB ESCAPES ESAU'S FURY

41 Now Esau hated Jacob because
of the blessing with which his father
had blessed him, and Esau said to
himself, "The days of mourning for
my father are approaching; then I
will kill my brother Jacob." 42 But the
words of Esau her older son were told
to Rebekah; so she sent and called
Jacob her younger son, and said to
him, "Behold, your brother Esau com-
forts himself by planning to kill you.
43 Now therefore, my son, obey my
voice; arise, flee to Laban my brother
in Haran, 44 and stay with him a while,
until your brother's fury turns away;
45 until your brother's anger turns
away, and he forgets what you have
done to him; then I will send, and
fetch you from there. Why should I be
bereft of you both in one day?"
46 Then Rebekah said to Isaac, "I
am weary of my life because of the
Hittite women. If Jacob marries one of
the Hittite women such as these, one
of the women of the land, what good
will my life be to me?"

28 Then Isaac called Jacob and bless-
ed him, and charged him, "You
shall not marry one of the Canaanite
women. 2 Arise, go to Paddan-aram to
the house of Bethu'el your mother's

[a] Cn: Heb *of all*
[b] Or *of*
[c] Or *of*

father; and take as wife from there
one of the daughters of Laban your
mother's brother. 3God Almighty[d]
bless you and make you fruitful and
multiply you, that you may become
a company of peoples. 4May he give
the blessing of Abraham to you and
to your descendants with you, that
you may take possession of the land
of your sojournings which God gave
to Abraham!" 5Thus Isaac sent Jacob
away; and he went to Paddan-aram
to Laban, the son of Bethu'el the
Arame'an, the brother of Rebekah,
Jacob's and Esau's mother.

ESAU MARRIES ISHMAEL'S DAUGHTER

6 Now Esau saw that Isaac had
blessed Jacob and sent him away to
Paddan-aram to take a wife from there,
and that as he blessed him he charged
him, "You shall not marry one of the
Canaanite women," 7and that Jacob
had obeyed his father and his mother
and gone to Paddan-aram. 8So when
Esau saw that the Canaanite women
did not please Isaac his father, 9Esau
went to Ish'mael and took to wife, be-
sides the wives he had, Ma'halath the
daughter of Ish'mael Abraham's son,
the sister of Neba'ioth.

JACOB'S DREAM AT BETHEL

10 Jacob left Beer-sheba, and went
toward Haran. 11And he came to a
certain place, and stayed there that
night, because the sun had set. Taking
one of the stones of the place, he put
it under his head and lay down in
that place to sleep. 12And he dreamed
that there was a ladder set up on
the earth, and the top of it reached
to heaven; and behold, the angels of
God were ascending and descending
on it! 13And behold, the LORD stood
above it[e] and said, "I am the LORD,
the God of Abraham your father and
the God of Isaac; the land on which
you lie I will give to you and to your
descendants; 14and your descendants
shall be like the dust of the earth, and
you shall spread abroad to the west
and to the east and to the north and
to the south; and by you and your de-
scendants shall all the families of the
earth bless themselves.[f] 15 Behold, I
am with you and will keep you wher-
ever you go, and will bring you back to
this land; for I will not leave you until
I have done that of which I have spo-
ken to you." 16Then Jacob awoke from
his sleep and said, "Surely the LORD
is in this place; and I did not know it."
17And he was afraid, and said, "How
awesome is this place! This is none
other than the house of God, and this
is the gate of heaven."

18 So Jacob rose early in the morn-
ing, and he took the stone which he
had put under his head and set it up
for a pillar and poured oil on the top
of it. 19He called the name of that place
Bethel;[g] but the name of the city was
Luz at the first. 20Then Jacob made a
vow, saying, "If God will be with me,
and will keep me in this way that I
go, and will give me bread to eat and
clothing to wear, 21so that I come
again to my father's house in peace,
then the LORD shall be my God, 22and
this stone, which I have set up for a
pillar, shall be God's house; and of
all that thou givest me I will give the
tenth to thee."*

JACOB MEETS RACHEL

29 Then Jacob went on his jour-
ney, and came to the land of the
people of the east. 2As he looked, he
saw a well in the field, and lo, three
flocks of sheep lying beside it; for out
of that well the flocks were watered.
The stone on the well's mouth was
large, 3and when all the flocks were
gathered there, the shepherds would
roll the stone from the mouth of the
well, and water the sheep, and put the
stone back in its place upon the mouth

[d]Heb *El Shaddai*
[e]Or *beside him*
[f]Or *be blessed*
[g]That is *The house of God*

of the well.

4 Jacob said to them, "My brothers, where do you come from?" They said, "We are from Haran." 5 He said to them, "Do you know Laban the son of Nahor?" They said, "We know him." 6 He said to them, "Is it well with him?" They said, "It is well; and see, Rachel his daughter is coming with the sheep!" 7 He said, "Behold, it is still high day, it is not time for the animals to be gathered together; water the sheep, and go, pasture them." 8 But they said, "We cannot until all the flocks are gathered together, and the stone is rolled from the mouth of the well; then we water the sheep."

9 While he was still speaking with them, Rachel came with her father's sheep; for she kept them. 10 Now when Jacob saw Rachel the daughter of Laban his mother's brother, and the sheep of Laban his mother's brother, Jacob went up and rolled the stone from the well's mouth, and watered the flock of Laban his mother's brother. 11 Then Jacob kissed Rachel, and wept aloud. 12 And Jacob told Rachel that he was her father's kinsman, and that he was Rebekah's son; and she ran and told her father.

13 When Laban heard the tidings of Jacob his sister's son, he ran to meet him, and embraced him and kissed him, and brought him to his house. Jacob told Laban all these things, 14 and Laban said to him, "Surely you are my bone and my flesh!" And he stayed with him a month.

JACOB MARRIES LABAN'S DAUGHTERS

15 Then Laban said to Jacob, "Because you are my kinsman, should you therefore serve me for nothing? Tell me, what shall your wages be?" 16 Now Laban had two daughters; the name of the older was Leah, and the name of the younger was Rachel. 17 Leah's eyes were weak, but Rachel was beautiful and lovely. 18 Jacob loved Rachel; and he said, "I will serve you seven years for your younger daughter Rachel." 19 Laban said, "It is better that I give her to you than that I should give her to any other man; stay with me." 20 So Jacob served seven years for Rachel, and they seemed to him but a few days because of the love he had for her.

21 Then Jacob said to Laban, "Give me my wife that I may go in to her, for my time is completed." 22 So Laban gathered together all the men of the place, and made a feast. 23 But in the evening he took his daughter Leah and brought her to Jacob; and he went in to her. 24 (Laban gave his maid Zilpah to his daughter Leah to be her maid.) 25 And in the morning, behold, it was Leah; and Jacob said to Laban, "What is this you have done to me? Did I not serve with you for Rachel? Why then have you deceived me?" 26 Laban said, "It is not so done in our country, to give the younger before the first-born. 27 Complete the week of this one, and we will give you the other also in return for serving me another seven years." 28 Jacob did so, and completed her week; then Laban gave him his daughter Rachel to wife. 29 (Laban gave his maid Bilhah to his daughter Rachel to be her maid.) 30 So Jacob went in to Rachel also, and he loved Rachel more than Leah, and served Laban for another seven years.

31 When the LORD saw that Leah was hated, he opened her womb; but Rachel was barren. 32 And Leah conceived and bore a son, and she called his name Reuben;[a] for she said, "Because the LORD has looked upon my affliction; surely now my husband will love me." 33 She conceived again and bore a son, and said, "Because the LORD has heard[b] that I am hated, he has given me this son also"; and she called his name Simeon. 34 Again she conceived and bore a son, and said, "Now this time my husband will be

[a] That is *See, a son*
[b] Heb *shama*

joined[c] to me, because I have borne
him three sons"; therefore his name
was called Levi. 35And she conceived
again and bore a son, and said, "This
time I will praise[d] the LORD"; there-
fore she called his name Judah; then
she ceased bearing.

30 When Rachel saw that she bore
Jacob no children, she envied her
sister; and she said to Jacob, "Give me
children, or I shall die!" 2Jacob's anger
was kindled against Rachel, and he
said, "Am I in the place of God, who
has withheld from you the fruit of the
womb?" 3Then she said, "Here is my
maid Bilhah; go in to her, that she may
bear upon my knees, and even I may
have children through her." 4So she
gave him her maid Bilhah as a wife;
and Jacob went in to her. 5And Bilhah
conceived and bore Jacob a son. 6Then
Rachel said, "God has judged me, and
has also heard my voice and given me
a son"; therefore she called his name
Dan. 7Rachel's maid Bilhah conceived
again and bore Jacob a second son.
8Then Rachel said, "With mighty
wrestlings I have wrestled[e] with my
sister, and have prevailed"; so she
called his name Naph´tali.

9 When Leah saw that she had
ceased bearing children, she took her
maid Zilpah and gave her to Jacob as a
wife. 10Then Leah's maid Zilpah bore
Jacob a son. 11And Leah said, "Good
fortune!" so she called his name Gad.[f]
12Leah's maid Zilpah bore Jacob a sec-
ond son. 13And Leah said, "Happy am
I! For the women will call me happy";
so she called his name Asher.[g]

14 In the days of wheat harvest
Reuben went and found mandrakes
in the field, and brought them to his
mother Leah. Then Rachel said to
Leah, "Give me, I pray, some of your
son's mandrakes." 15But she said to
her, "Is it a small matter that you have
taken away my husband? Would you
take away my son's mandrakes also?"
Rachel said, "Then he may lie with you
tonight for your son's mandrakes."
16When Jacob came from the field in
the evening, Leah went out to meet
him, and said, "You must come in to
me; for I have hired you with my son's
mandrakes." So he lay with her that
night. 17And God hearkened to Leah,
and she conceived and bore Jacob a
fifth son. 18Leah said, "God has given
me my hire[h] because I gave my maid to
my husband"; so she called his name
Is´sachar. 19And Leah conceived again,
and she bore Jacob a sixth son. 20Then
Leah said, "God has endowed me
with a good dowry; now my husband
will honor[i] me, because I have borne
him six sons"; so she called his name
Zeb´ulun. 21Afterwards she bore a
daughter, and called her name Dinah.
22Then God remembered Rachel, and
God hearkened to her and opened her
womb. 23She conceived and bore a son,
and said, "God has taken away my
reproach"; 24and she called his name
Joseph,[j] saying, "May the LORD add to
me another son!"

JACOB PROSPERS AT LABAN'S EXPENSE

25 When Rachel had borne Joseph,
Jacob said to Laban, "Send me away,
that I may go to my own home and
country. 26Give me my wives and my
children for whom I have served you,
and let me go; for you know the ser-
vice which I have given you." 27But
Laban said to him, "If you will allow
me to say so, I have learned by divina-
tion that the LORD has blessed me be-
cause of you; 28name your wages, and I
will give it." 29Jacob said to him, "You
yourself know how I have served you,

[c] Heb *lawah*
[d] Heb *hodah*
[e] Heb *niphtal*
[f] That is *Fortune*
[g] That is *Happy*
[h] Heb *sakar*
[i] Heb *zabal*
[j] That is *He adds*

and how your cattle have fared with
me. 30For you had little before I came,
and it has increased abundantly; and
the LORD has blessed you wherever I
turned. But now when shall I provide
for my own household also?" 31He
said, "What shall I give you?" Jacob
said, "You shall not give me anything;
if you will do this for me, I will again
feed your flock and keep it: 32let me
pass through all your flock today,
removing from it every speckled and
spotted sheep and every black lamb,
and the spotted and speckled among
the goats; and such shall be my wag-
es. 33So my honesty will answer for me
later, when you come to look into my
wages with you. Every one that is not
speckled and spotted among the goats
and black among the lambs, if found
with me, shall be counted stolen."
34Laban said, "Good! Let it be as you
have said." 35But that day Laban re-
moved the he-goats that were striped
and spotted, and all the she-goats
that were speckled and spotted, every
one that had white on it, and every
lamb that was black, and put them in
charge of his sons; 36and he set a dis-
tance of three days' journey between
himself and Jacob; and Jacob fed the
rest of Laban's flock.

37 Then Jacob took fresh rods of
poplar and almond and plane, and
peeled white streaks in them, expos-
ing the white of the rods. 38He set the
rods which he had peeled in front of
the flocks in the runnels, that is, the
watering troughs, where the flocks
came to drink. And since they bred
when they came to drink, 39the flocks
bred in front of the rods and so the
flocks brought forth striped, speck-
led, and spotted. 40And Jacob separat-
ed the lambs, and set the faces of the
flocks toward the striped and all the
black in the flock of Laban; and he put
his own droves apart, and did not put
them with Laban's flock. 41Whenever
the stronger of the flock were breed-
ing Jacob laid the rods in the runnels
before the eyes of the flock, that they
might breed among the rods, 42but
for the feebler of the flock he did not
lay them there; so the feebler were
Laban's, and the stronger Jacob's.
43Thus the man grew exceedingly rich,
and had large flocks, maidservants
and menservants, and camels and
asses.

JACOB FLEES WITH FAMILY AND FLOCKS

31 Now Jacob heard that the sons
of Laban were saying, "Jacob has
taken all that was our father's; and
from what was our father's he has
gained all this wealth." 2And Jacob
saw that Laban did not regard him
with favor as before. 3Then the LORD
said to Jacob, "Return to the land of
your fathers and to your kindred, and
I will be with you." 4So Jacob sent
and called Rachel and Leah into the
field where his flock was, 5and said to
them, "I see that your father does not
regard me with favor as he did before.
But the God of my father has been
with me. 6You know that I have served
your father with all my strength;
7yet your father has cheated me and
changed my wages ten times, but God
did not permit him to harm me. 8If he
said, 'The spotted shall be your wag-
es,' then all the flock bore spotted;
and if he said, 'The striped shall be
your wages,' then all the flock bore
striped. 9Thus God has taken away the
cattle of your father, and given them
to me. 10In the mating season of the
flock I lifted up my eyes, and saw in a
dream that the he-goats which leaped
upon the flock were striped, spotted,
and mottled. 11Then the angel of God
said to me in the dream, 'Jacob,' and I
said, 'Here I am!' 12And he said, 'Lift
up your eyes and see, all the goats that
leap upon the flock are striped, spot-
ted, and mottled; for I have seen all
that Laban is doing to you. 13I am the
God of Bethel, where you anointed
a pillar and made a vow to me. Now
arise, go forth from this land, and re-
turn to the land of your birth.'" 14Then
Rachel and Leah answered him, "Is

there any portion or inheritance left
to us in our father's house? 15 Are we
not regarded by him as foreigners? For
he has sold us, and he has been using
up the money given for us. 16 All the
property which God has taken away
from our father belongs to us and to
our children; now then, whatever God
has said to you, do."

17 So Jacob arose, and set his sons
and his wives on camels; 18 and he
drove away all his cattle, all his live-
stock which he had gained, the cattle
in his possession which he had ac-
quired in Paddan-aram, to go to the
land of Canaan to his father Isaac.
19 Laban had gone to shear his sheep,
and Rachel stole her father's house-
hold gods. 20 And Jacob outwitted
Laban the Arame´an, in that he did
not tell him that he intended to flee.
21 He fled with all that he had, and
arose and crossed the Euphra´tes, and
set his face toward the hill country of
Gilead.

LABAN OVERTAKES JACOB

22 When it was told Laban on the
third day that Jacob had fled, 23 he
took his kinsmen with him and pur-
sued him for seven days and followed
close after him into the hill country
of Gilead. 24 But God came to Laban
the Arame´an in a dream by night,
and said to him, "Take heed that you
say not a word to Jacob, either good
or bad."

25 And Laban overtook Jacob. Now
Jacob had pitched his tent in the hill
country, and Laban with his kins-
men encamped in the hill country
of Gilead. 26 And Laban said to Jacob,
"What have you done, that you have
cheated me, and carried away my
daughters like captives of the sword?
27 Why did you flee secretly, and cheat
me, and did not tell me, so that I
might have sent you away with mirth
and songs, with tambourine and lyre?
28 And why did you not permit me to
kiss my sons and my daughters fare-
well? Now you have done foolishly.
29 It is in my power to do you harm;
but the God of your father spoke to
me last night, saying, 'Take heed that
you speak to Jacob neither good nor
bad.' 30 And now you have gone away
because you longed greatly for your
father's house, but why did you steal
my gods?" 31 Jacob answered Laban,
"Because I was afraid, for I thought
that you would take your daughters
from me by force. 32 Any one with
whom you find your gods shall not
live. In the presence of our kinsmen
point out what I have that is yours,
and take it." Now Jacob did not know
that Rachel had stolen them.

33 So Laban went into Jacob's
tent, and into Leah's tent, and into
the tent of the two maidservants,
but he did not find them. And he
went out of Leah's tent, and entered
Rachel's. 34 Now Rachel had taken
the household gods and put them
in the camel's saddle, and sat upon
them. Laban felt all about the tent,
but did not find them. 35 And she said
to her father, "Let not my lord be
angry that I cannot rise before you,
for the way of women is upon me."
So he searched, but did not find the
household gods.

36 Then Jacob became angry, and
upbraided Laban; Jacob said to Laban,
"What is my offense? What is my
sin, that you have hotly pursued me?
37 Although you have felt through all
my goods, what have you found of
all your household goods? Set it here
before my kinsmen and your kins-
men, that they may decide between
us two. 38 These twenty years I have
been with you; your ewes and your
she-goats have not miscarried, and
I have not eaten the rams of your
flocks. 39 That which was torn by wild
beasts I did not bring to you; I bore
the loss of it myself; of my hand you
required it, whether stolen by day or
stolen by night. 40 Thus I was; by day
the heat consumed me, and the cold
by night, and my sleep fled from my
eyes. 41 These twenty years I have been

in your house; I served you fourteen
years for your two daughters, and six
years for your flock, and you have
changed my wages ten times. 42 If the
God of my father, the God of Abraham
and the Fear of Isaac, had not been on
my side, surely now you would have
sent me away empty-handed. God
saw my affliction and the labor of my
hands, and rebuked you last night."

LABAN AND JACOB MAKE A COVENANT

43 Then Laban answered and said
to Jacob, "The daughters are my
daughters, the children are my chil-
dren, the flocks are my flocks, and
all that you see is mine. But what can
I do this day to these my daughters,
or to their children whom they have
borne? 44 Come now, let us make a
covenant, you and I; and let it be a
witness between you and me." 45 So
Jacob took a stone, and set it up as
a pillar. 46 And Jacob said to his kins-
men, "Gather stones," and they took
stones, and made a heap; and they
ate there by the heap. 47 Laban called
it Je´gar-sahadu´tha:[a] but Jacob
called it Galeed.[b] 48 Laban said, "This
heap is a witness between you and
me today." Therefore he named it
Galeed, 49 and the pillar[c] Mizpah,[d] for
he said, "The LORD watch between
you and me, when we are absent one
from the other. 50 If you ill-treat my
daughters, or if you take wives be-
sides my daughters, although no man
is with us, remember, God is witness
between you and me."

51 Then Laban said to Jacob, "See
this heap and the pillar, which I have
set between you and me. 52 This heap is
a witness, and the pillar is a witness,
that I will not pass over this heap to
you, and you will not pass over this
heap and this pillar to me, for harm.
53 The God of Abraham and the God of
Nahor, the God of their father, judge
between us." So Jacob swore by the
Fear of his father Isaac, 54 and Jacob of-
fered a sacrifice on the mountain and
called his kinsmen to eat bread; and
they ate bread and tarried all night on
the mountain.

55[e] Early in the morning Laban
arose, and kissed his grandchildren
and his daughters and blessed them;
then he departed and returned home.

32 Jacob went on his way and the an-
gels of God met him; 2 and when
Jacob saw them he said, "This is God's
army!" So he called the name of that
place Mahana´im.[f]

JACOB SENDS PRESENTS TO APPEASE ESAU

3 And Jacob sent messengers be-
fore him to Esau his brother in the
land of Se´ir, the country of Edom,
4 instructing them, "Thus you shall
say to my lord Esau: Thus says your
servant Jacob, 'I have sojourned with
Laban, and stayed until now; 5 and I
have oxen, asses, flocks, menservants,
and maidservants; and I have sent to
tell my lord, in order that I may find
favor in your sight.'"

6 And the messengers returned
to Jacob, saying, "We came to your
brother Esau, and he is coming to
meet you and four hundred men with
him." 7 Then Jacob was greatly afraid
and distressed; and he divided the
people that were with him, and the
flocks and herds and camels, into two
companies, 8 thinking, "If Esau comes
to the one company and destroys it,
then the company which is left will
escape."

9 And Jacob said, "O God of my fa-
ther Abraham and God of my father
Isaac, O LORD who didst say to me,
'Return to your country and to your
kindred, and I will do you good;

[a] In Aramaic *The heap of witness*
[b] In Hebrew *The heap of witness*
[c] Compare Sam: Heb lacks *the pillar*
[d] That is *Watchpost*
[e] Ch 32.1 in Heb
[f] Here taken to mean *Two armies*

am not worthy of the least of all the
steadfast love and all the faithfulness
which thou hast shown to thy servant,
for with only my staff I crossed this
Jordan; and now I have become two
companies. 11Deliver me, I pray thee,
from the hand of my brother, from
the hand of Esau, for I fear him, lest
he come and slay us all, the mothers
with the children. 12But thou didst
say, 'I will do you good, and make
your descendants as the sand of the
sea, which cannot be numbered for
multitude.'"

13 So he lodged there that night,
and took from what he had with him
a present for his brother Esau, 14two
hundred she-goats and twenty he-
goats, two hundred ewes and twenty
rams, 15thirty milch camels and their
colts, forty cows and ten bulls, twen-
ty she-asses and ten he-asses. 16These
he delivered into the hand of his ser-
vants, every drove by itself, and said to
his servants, "Pass on before me, and
put a space between drove and drove."
17He instructed the foremost, "When
Esau my brother meets you, and asks
you, 'To whom do you belong? Where
are you going? And whose are these
before you?' 18then you shall say,
'They belong to your servant Jacob;
they are a present sent to my lord
Esau; and moreover he is behind us.'"
19He likewise instructed the second
and the third and all who followed the
droves, "You shall say the same thing
to Esau when you meet him, 20and
you shall say, 'Moreover your servant
Jacob is behind us.'" For he thought,
"I may appease him with the present
that goes before me, and afterwards
I shall see his face; perhaps he will
accept me." 21So the present passed
on before him; and he himself lodged
that night in the camp.

JACOB WRESTLES AT PENIEL

22 The same night he arose and
took his two wives, his two maids,
and his eleven children, and crossed
the ford of the Jabbok. 23He took them
and sent them across the stream,
and likewise everything that he had.
24And Jacob was left alone; and a man
wrestled with him until the breaking
of the day. 25When the man saw that
he did not prevail against Jacob, he
touched the hollow of his thigh; and
Jacob's thigh was put out of joint as
he wrestled with him. 26Then he said,
"Let me go, for the day is breaking."
But Jacob said, "I will not let you go,
unless you bless me." 27And he said
to him, "What is your name?" And
he said, "Jacob." 28Then he said,
"Your name shall no more be called
Jacob, but Israel,[g] for you have striv-
en with God and with men, and
have prevailed." 29Then Jacob asked
him, "Tell me, I pray, your name."
But he said, "Why is it that you
ask my name?" And there he bless-
ed him. 30So Jacob called the name
of the place Peni´el,[h] saying, "For I
have seen God face to face, and yet
my life is preserved." 31The sun rose
upon him as he passed Penu´el, limp-
ing because of his thigh. 32Therefore
to this day the Israelites do not eat
the sinew of the hip which is upon
the hollow of the thigh, because he
touched the hollow of Jacob's thigh
on the sinew of the hip.*

JACOB AND ESAU MEET

33 And Jacob lifted up his eyes
and looked, and behold, Esau
was coming, and four hundred men
with him. So he divided the children
among Leah and Rachel and the two
maids. 2And he put the maids with
their children in front, then Leah with
her children, and Rachel and Joseph
last of all. 3He himself went on before
them, bowing himself to the ground
seven times, until he came near to his
brother.

4 But Esau ran to meet him, and
embraced him, and fell on his neck

[g]That is *He who strives with God* or *God strives*
[h]That is *The face of God*

and kissed him, and they wept. 5And
when Esau raised his eyes and saw
the women and children, he said,
"Who are these with you?" Jacob
said, "The children whom God has
graciously given your servant." 6Then
the maids drew near, they and their
children, and bowed down; 7Leah
likewise and her children drew near
and bowed down; and last Joseph
and Rachel drew near, and they
bowed down. 8Esau said, "What do
you mean by all this company which
I met?" Jacob answered, "To find
favor in the sight of my lord." 9But
Esau said, "I have enough, my broth-
er; keep what you have for yourself."
10Jacob said, "No, I pray you, if I have
found favor in your sight, then accept
my present from my hand; for truly
to see your face is like seeing the
face of God, with such favor have you
received me. 11Accept, I pray you, my
gift that is brought to you, because
God has dealt graciously with me,
and because I have enough." Thus he
urged him, and he took it.

12 Then Esau said, "Let us jour-
ney on our way, and I will go before
you." 13But Jacob said to him, "My lord
knows that the children are frail, and
that the flocks and herds giving suck
are a care to me; and if they are over-
driven for one day, all the flocks will
die. 14Let my lord pass on before his
servant, and I will lead on slowly, ac-
cording to the pace of the cattle which
are before me and according to the
pace of the children, until I come to
my lord in Se´ir."

15 So Esau said, "Let me leave
with you some of the men who are
with me." But he said, "What need is
there? Let me find favor in the sight of
my lord." 16So Esau returned that day
on his way to Se´ir. 17But Jacob jour-
neyed to Succoth,[a] and built himself
a house, and made booths for his cat-
tle; therefore the name of the place is
called Succoth.

JACOB REACHES SHECHEM

18 And Jacob came safely to the
city of Shechem, which is in the land
of Canaan, on his way from Paddan-
aram; and he camped before the
city. 19And from the sons of Hamor,
Shechem's father, he bought for a
hundred pieces of money[b] the piece of
land on which he had pitched his tent.
20There he erected an altar and called
it El-El´ohe-Israel.[c]

THE RAPE OF DINAH

34 Now Dinah the daughter of Leah,
whom she had borne to Jacob,
went out to visit the women of the
land; 2and when Shechem the son of
Hamor the Hivite, the prince of the
land, saw her, he seized her and lay
with her and humbled her. 3And his
soul was drawn to Dinah the daugh-
ter of Jacob; he loved the maiden and
spoke tenderly to her. 4So Shechem
spoke to his father Hamor, saying,
"Get me this maiden for my wife."
5Now Jacob heard that he had defiled
his daughter Dinah; but his sons were
with his cattle in the field, so Jacob
held his peace until they came. 6And
Hamor the father of Shechem went
out to Jacob to speak with him. 7The
sons of Jacob came in from the field
when they heard of it; and the men
were indignant and very angry, be-
cause he had wrought folly in Israel by
lying with Jacob's daughter, for such a
thing ought not to be done.

8 But Hamor spoke with them,
saying, "The soul of my son Shechem
longs for your daughter; I pray you,
give her to him in marriage. 9Make
marriages with us; give your daugh-
ters to us, and take our daughters
for yourselves. 10You shall dwell with
us; and the land shall be open to you;
dwell and trade in it, and get property
in it." 11Shechem also said to her fa-
ther and to her brothers, "Let me find
favor in your eyes, and whatever you
say to me I will give. 12Ask of me ever

[a] That is *Booths*
[b] Heb *a hundred qesitah*
[c] That is *God, the God of Israel*

so much as marriage present and gift,
and I will give according as you say to
me; only give me the maiden to be my
wife."

13 The sons of Jacob answered
Shechem and his father Hamor de-
ceitfully, because he had defiled their
sister Dinah. 14They said to them, "We
cannot do this thing, to give our sister
to one who is uncircumcised, for that
would be a disgrace to us. 15Only on
this condition will we consent to you:
that you will become as we are and ev-
ery male of you be circumcised. 16Then
we will give our daughters to you, and
we will take your daughters to our-
selves, and we will dwell with you and
become one people. 17But if you will
not listen to us and be circumcised,
then we will take our daughter, and
we will be gone."

18 Their words pleased Hamor
and Hamor's son Shechem. 19And
the young man did not delay to do
the thing, because he had delight in
Jacob's daughter. Now he was the
most honored of all his family. 20So
Hamor and his son Shechem came to
the gate of their city and spoke to the
men of their city, saying, 21"These men
are friendly with us; let them dwell in
the land and trade in it, for behold,
the land is large enough for them; let
us take their daughters in marriage,
and let us give them our daughters.
22Only on this condition will the men
agree to dwell with us, to become one
people: that every male among us be
circumcised as they are circumcised.
23Will not their cattle, their proper-
ty and all their beasts be ours? Only
let us agree with them, and they will
dwell with us." 24And all who went
out of the gate of his city hearkened
to Hamor and his son Shechem; and
every male was circumcised, all who
went out of the gate of his city.

DINAH'S BROTHERS AVENGE THEIR SISTER

25 On the third day, when they
were sore, two of the sons of Jacob,
Simeon and Levi, Dinah's brothers,
took their swords and came upon
the city unawares, and killed all the
males. 26They slew Hamor and his son
Shechem with the sword, and took
Dinah out of Shechem's house, and
went away. 27And the sons of Jacob
came upon the slain, and plundered
the city, because their sister had been
defiled; 28they took their flocks and
their herds, their asses, and whatever
was in the city and in the field; 29all
their wealth, all their little ones and
their wives, all that was in the hous-
es, they captured and made their prey.
30Then Jacob said to Simeon and Levi,
"You have brought trouble on me by
making me odious to the inhabitants
of the land, the Canaanites and the
Per´izzites; my numbers are few, and
if they gather themselves against me
and attack me, I shall be destroyed,
both I and my household." 31But they
said, "Should he treat our sister as a
harlot?"

JACOB RETURNS TO BETHEL

35 God said to Jacob, "Arise, go up
to Bethel, and dwell there; and
make there an altar to the God who
appeared to you when you fled from
your brother Esau." 2So Jacob said to
his household and to all who were
with him, "Put away the foreign gods
that are among you, and purify your-
selves, and change your garments;
3then let us arise and go up to Bethel,
that I may make there an altar to the
God who answered me in the day of
my distress and has been with me
wherever I have gone." 4So they gave
to Jacob all the foreign gods that they
had, and the rings that were in their
ears; and Jacob hid them under the
oak which was near Shechem.

5 And as they journeyed, a terror
from God fell upon the cities that were
round about them, so that they did not
pursue the sons of Jacob. 6And Jacob
came to Luz (that is, Bethel), which is
in the land of Canaan, he and all the
people who were with him, 7and there
he built an altar, and called the place

El-bethel,[a] because there God had re-
vealed himself to him when he fled from
his brother. 8And Deb´orah, Rebekah's
nurse, died, and she was buried under
an oak below Bethel; so the name of it
was called Al´lon-bacuth.[b]

9 God appeared to Jacob again,
when he came from Paddan-aram, and
blessed him. 10And God said to him,
"Your name is Jacob; no longer shall
your name be called Jacob, but Israel
shall be your name." So his name was
called Israel. 11And God said to him,
"I am God Almighty:[c] be fruitful and
multiply; a nation and a company of
nations shall come from you, and kings
shall spring from you. 12The land which
I gave to Abraham and Isaac I will give
to you, and I will give the land to your
descendants after you." 13Then God
went up from him in the place where
he had spoken with him. 14And Jacob
set up a pillar in the place where he
had spoken with him, a pillar of stone;
and he poured out a drink offering
on it, and poured oil on it. 15So Jacob
called the name of the place where God
had spoken with him, Bethel.

THE BIRTH OF BENJAMIN AND THE DEATH OF RACHEL

16 Then they journeyed from
Bethel; and when they were still some
distance from Ephrath, Rachel tra-
vailed, and she had hard labor. 17And
when she was in her hard labor, the
midwife said to her, "Fear not; for
now you will have another son."
18And as her soul was departing (for
she died), she called his name Ben-
o´ni;[d] but his father called his name
Benjamin.[e] 19So Rachel died, and she
was buried on the way to Ephrath
(that is, Bethlehem), 20and Jacob set
up a pillar upon her grave; it is the
pillar of Rachel's tomb, which is there
to this day. 21Israel journeyed on, and
pitched his tent beyond the tower of
Eder.

22 While Israel dwelt in that land
Reuben went and lay with Bilhah his
father's concubine; and Israel heard
of it.

Now the sons of Jacob were twelve.
23The sons of Leah: Reuben (Jacob's
first-born), Simeon, Levi, Judah, Is´-
sachar, and Zeb´ulun. 24The sons of
Rachel: Joseph and Benjamin. 25The
sons of Bilhah, Rachel's maid: Dan
and Naph´tali. 26The sons of Zilpah,
Leah's maid: Gad and Asher. These
were the sons of Jacob who were born
to him in Paddan-aram.

THE DEATH OF ISAAC

27 And Jacob came to his father
Isaac at Mamre, or Kir´iath-ar´ba
(that is, Hebron), where Abraham and
Isaac had sojourned. 28Now the days
of Isaac were a hundred and eighty
years. 29And Isaac breathed his last;
and he died and was gathered to his
people, old and full of days; and his
sons Esau and Jacob buried him.

ESAU'S DESCENDANTS

36 These are the descendants of
Esau (that is, Edom). 2Esau took
his wives from the Canaanites: Adah
the daughter of Elon the Hittite,
Oholiba´mah the daughter of Anah
the son[f] of Zib´eon the Hivite, 3and
Bas´emath, Ish´mael's daughter, the
sister of Neba´ioth. 4And Adah bore
to Esau, Eliphaz; Bas´emath bore
Reu´el; 5and Oholiba´mah bore Je´ush,
Jalam, and Korah. These are the sons
of Esau who were born to him in the
land of Canaan.

6 Then Esau took his wives, his
sons, his daughters, and all the mem-
bers of his household, his cattle, all
his beasts, and all his property which
he had acquired in the land of Canaan;

[a]That is *God of Bethel*
[b]That is *Oak of weeping*
[c]Heb *El Shaddai*
[d]That is *Son of my sorrow*
[e]That is *Son of the right hand* or *Son of the South*
[f]Sam Gk Syr: Heb *daughter*

and he went into a land away from his brother Jacob. 7For their possessions were too great for them to dwell together; the land of their sojournings could not support them because of their cattle. 8So Esau dwelt in the hill country of Se´ir; Esau is Edom.

9 These are the descendants of Esau the father of the E´domites in the hill country of Se´ir. 10These are the names of Esau's sons: El´iphaz the son of Adah the wife of Esau, Reu´el the son of Bas´emath the wife of Esau. 11The sons of El´iphaz were Teman, Omar, Zepho, Gatam, and Kenaz. 12(Timna was a concubine of El´iphaz, Esau's son; she bore Am´alek to El´iphaz.) These are the sons of Adah, Esau's wife. 13These are the sons of Reu´el: Nahath, Zerah, Shammah, and Mizzah. These are the sons of Bas´emath, Esau's wife. 14These are the sons of Oholiba´mah the daughter of Anah the son[g] of Zib´eon, Esau's wife: she bore to Esau Je´ush, Jalam, and Korah.

CLANS AND KINGS OF EDOM

15 These are the chiefs of the sons of Esau. The sons of El´iphaz the first-born of Esau: the chiefs Teman, Omar, Zepho, Kenaz, 16Korah, Gatam, and Am´alek; these are the chiefs of El´iphaz in the land of Edom; they are the sons of Adah. 17These are the sons of Reu´el, Esau's son: the chiefs Nahath, Zerah, Shammah, and Mizzah; these are the chiefs of Reu´el in the land of Edom; they are the sons of Bas´emath, Esau's wife. 18*These are the* sons of Oholiba´mah, Esau's wife: the chiefs Je´ush, Jalam, and Korah; these are the chiefs born of Oholiba´mah the daughter of Anah, Esau's wife. 19These are the sons of Esau (that is, Edom), and these are their chiefs.

20 These are the sons of Se´ir the Horite, the inhabitants of the land: Lotan, Shobal, Zib´eon, Anah, 21Dishon, Ezer, and Dishan; these are the chiefs of the Horites, the sons of Se´ir in the land of Edom. 22The sons of Lotan were Hori and Heman; and Lotan's sister was Timna. 23These are the sons of Shobal: Alvan, Man´ahath, Ebal, Shepho, and Onam. 24These are the sons of Zib´eon: A´iah and Anah; he is the Anah who found the hot springs in the wilderness, as he pastured the asses of Zib´eon his father. 25These are the children of Anah: Dishon and Oholiba´mah the daughter of Anah. 26These are the sons of Dishon: Hemdan, Eshban, Ithran, and Cheran. 27These are the sons of Ezer: Bilhan, Za´avan, and Akan. 28These are the sons of Dishan: Uz and Aran. 29These are the chiefs of the Horites: the chiefs Lotan, Shobal, Zib´eon, Anah, 30Dishon, Ezer, and Dishan; these are the chiefs of the Horites, according to their clans in the land of Se´ir.

31 These are the kings who reigned in the land of Edom, before any king reigned over the Israelites. 32Bela the son of Be´or reigned in Edom, the name of his city being Din´habah. 33Bela died, and Jobab the son of Zerah of Bozrah reigned in his stead. 34Jobab died, and Husham of the land of the Te´manites reigned in his stead. 35Husham died, and Hadad the son of Bedad, who defeated Mid´ian in the country of Moab, reigned in his stead, the name of his city being Avith. 36Hadad died, and Samlah of Masre´kah reigned in his stead. 37Samlah died, and Shaul of Reho´both on the Euphra´tes reigned in his stead. 38Shaul died, and Ba´al-ha´nan the son of Achbor reigned in his stead. 39Ba´al-ha´nan the son of Achbor died, and Hadar reigned in his stead, the name of his city being Pau; his wife's name was Mehet´abel, the daughter of Matred, daughter of Me´zahab.

40 These are the names of the chiefs of Esau, according to their families and their dwelling places, by their names: the chiefs Timna, Alvah,

[g]Gk Syr: Heb *daughter*

Jetheth, 41Oholiba´mah, Elah, Pinon, 42Kenaz, Teman, Mibzar, 43Mag´diel, and Iram; these are the chiefs of Edom (that is, Esau, the father of Edom), according to their dwelling places in the land of their possession.

JOSEPH DREAMS OF GREATNESS

37 Jacob dwelt in the land of his father's sojournings, in the land of Canaan. 2This is the history of the family of Jacob.

*Joseph, being seventeen years old, was shepherding the flock with his brothers; he was a lad with the sons of Bilhah and Zilpah, his father's wives; and Joseph brought an ill report of them to their father. 3Now Israel loved Joseph more than any other of his children, because he was the son of his old age; and he made him a long robe with sleeves. 4But when his brothers saw that their father loved him more than all his brothers, they hated him, and could not speak peaceably to him.

5 Now Joseph had a dream, and when he told it to his brothers they only hated him the more. 6He said to them, "Hear this dream which I have dreamed: 7behold, we were binding sheaves in the field, and lo, my sheaf arose and stood upright; and behold, your sheaves gathered round it, and bowed down to my sheaf." 8His brothers said to him, "Are you indeed to reign over us? Or are you indeed to have dominion over us?" So they hated him yet more for his dreams and for his words. 9Then he dreamed another dream, and told it to his brothers, and said, "Behold, I have dreamed another dream; and behold, the sun, the moon, and eleven stars were bowing down to me." 10But when he told it to his father and to his brothers, his father rebuked him, and said to him, "What is this dream that you have dreamed? Shall I and your mother and your brothers indeed come to bow ourselves to the ground before you?" 11And his brothers were jealous of him, but his father kept the saying in mind.

JOSEPH IS SOLD BY HIS BROTHERS

12 Now his brothers went to pasture their father's flock near Shechem. 13And Israel said to Joseph, "Are not your brothers pasturing the flock at Shechem? Come, I will send you to them." And he said to him, "Here I am." 14So he said to him, "Go now, see if it is well with your brothers, and with the flock; and bring me word again." So he sent him from the valley of Hebron, and he came to Shechem. 15And a man found him wandering in the fields; and the man asked him, "What are you seeking?" 16"I am seeking my brothers," he said, "tell me, I pray you, where they are pasturing the flock." 17And the man said, "They have gone away, for I heard them say, 'Let us go to Dothan.'" So Joseph went after his brothers, and found them at Dothan. 18They saw him afar off, and before he came near to them they conspired against him to kill him. 19They said to one another, "Here comes this dreamer. 20Come now, let us kill him and throw him into one of the pits; then we shall say that a wild beast has devoured him, and we shall see what will become of his dreams." 21But when Reuben heard it, he delivered him out of their hands, saying, "Let us not take his life." 22And Reuben said to them, "Shed no blood; cast him into this pit here in the wilderness, but lay no hand upon him"—that he might rescue him out of their hand, to restore him to his father. 23So when Joseph came to his brothers, they stripped him of his robe, the long robe with sleeves that he wore; 24and they took him and cast him into a pit. The pit was empty, there was no water in it.

25 Then they sat down to eat; and looking up they saw a caravan of Ish´maelites coming from Gilead, with their camels bearing gum, balm, and myrrh, on their way to carry it down to Egypt. 26Then Judah said to his brothers, "What profit is it if we slay our brother and conceal his

blood? [27]Come, let us sell him to the
Ish´maelites, and let not our hand be
upon him, for he is our brother, our
own flesh." And his brothers heeded
him. [28]Then Mid´ianite traders passed
by; and they drew Joseph up and lift-
ed him out of the pit, and sold him to
the Ish´maelites for twenty shekels of
silver; and they took Joseph to Egypt.

29 When Reuben returned to the
pit and saw that Joseph was not in the
pit, he rent his clothes [30]and returned
to his brothers, and said, "The lad is
gone; and I, where shall I go?" [31]Then
they took Joseph's robe, and killed
a goat, and dipped the robe in the
blood; [32]and they sent the long robe
with sleeves and brought it to their
father, and said, "This we have found;
see now whether it is your son's robe
or not." [33]And he recognized it, and
said, "It is my son's robe; a wild beast
has devoured him; Joseph is without
doubt torn to pieces." [34]Then Jacob
rent his garments, and put sackcloth
upon his loins, and mourned for his
son many days. [35]All his sons and all
his daughters rose up to comfort him;
but he refused to be comforted, and
said, "No, I shall go down to Shol
to my son, mourning." Thus hisfa-
ther wept for him. [36]Meanwhile he
Mid´ianites had sold him in Egypto
Pot´i-phar, an officer of Pharaoh,he
captain of the guard.

JUDAH AND TAMAR

38 It happened at that time at
Judah went down from is
brothers, and turned in to a cerin
Adul´lamite, whose name was Hh.
[2]There Judah saw the daughter a
certain Canaanite whose name is
Shua; he married her and went to
her, [3]and she conceived and boa
son, and he called his name Er. [4]An
she conceived and bore a son, ance
called his name Onan. [5]Yet agaire
bore a son, and she called his re
Shelah. She[a] was in Chezib where
bore him. [6]And Judah took a wifr
Er his first-born, and her name was
Tamar. [7]But Er, Judah's first-born,
was wicked in the sight of the LORD;
and the LORD slew him. [8]Then Judah
said to Onan, "Go in to your brother's
wife, and perform the duty of a broth-
er-in-law to her, and raise up offspring
for your brother." [9]But Onan knew
that the offspring would not be his; so
when he went in to his brother's wife
he spilled the semen on the ground,
lest he should give offspring to his
brother. [10]And what he did was dis-
pleasing in the sight of the LORD, and
he slew him also. [11]Then Judah said to
Tamar his daughter-in-law, "Remain
a widow in your father's house, till
Shelah my son grows up"—for he
feared that he would die, like his
brothers. So Tamar went and dwelt in
her father's house.

12 In course of time the wife of
Judah, Shua's daughter, died; and
when Judah was comforted, he went
up to Timnah to his sheepshearers, he
and his friend Hirah the Adullamite.
[13]And when Tamar was told, "Your
father-in-law is going up to Timnah
to shear his sheep," [14]she put off her
widow's garments, and put on a veil,
wrapping herself up, and sat at the en-
trance to Enaim, which is on the road
to Timnah; for she saw that Shelah was
grown up, and she had not been giv-
en to him in marriage. [15]When Judah
saw her, he thought her to be a har-
lot, for she had covered her face. [16]He
went over to her at the road side, and
said, "Come, let me come in to you,"
for he did not know that she was his
daughter-in-law. She said, "What will
you give me, that you may come in to
me?" [17]He answered, "I will send you
a kid from the flock." And she said,
"Will you give me a pledge, till you
send it?" [18]He said, "What pledge shall
I give you?" She replied, "Your signet
and your cord, and your staff that is
in your hand." So he gave them to her,
and went in to her, and she conceived
by him. [19]Then she arose and went

[a]Gk: Heb *He*

away, and taking off her veil she put
on the garments of her widowhood.
20 When Judah sent the kid by his
friend the Adullamite, to receive the
pledge from the woman's hand, he
could not find her. 21And he asked the
men of the place, "Where is the harlot[a]
who was at Enaim by the wayside?"
And they said, "No harlot[b] has been
here." 22So he returned to Judah, and
said, "I have not found her; and also
the men of the place said, 'No harlot[c]
has been here.'" 23And Judah replied,
"Let her keep the things as her own,
lest we be laughed at; you see, I sent
this kid, and you could not find her."
24 About three months later Judah
was told, "Tamar your daughter-in-
law has played the harlot; and more-
over she is with child by harlotry."
And Judah said, "Bring her out, and
let her be burned." 25As she was be-
ing brought out, she sent word to her
father-in-law, "By the man to whom
these belong, I am with child." And
she said, "Mark, I pray you, whose
these are, the signet and the cord and
the staff." 26Then Judah acknowledged
them and said, "She is more righteous
than I, inasmuch as I did not give her
to my son Shelah." And he did not lie
with her again.
27 When the time of her delivery
came, there were twins in her womb.
28And when she was in labor, one put
out a hand; and the midwife took and
bound on his hand a scarlet thread,
saying, "This came out first." 29But
as he drew back his hand, behold, his
brother came out; and she said, "What
a breach you have made for yourself!"
Therefore his name was called Perez.[d]
30Afterward his brother came out with
the scarlet thread upon his hand; and
his name was called Zerah.

JOSEPH AND POTIPHAR'S WIFE

39 Now Joseph was taken down to
Egypt, and Pot´i-phar, an officer
of Pharaoh, the captain of the guard,
an Egyptian, bought him from the
Ish´maelites who had brought him
down there. 2The LORD was with
Joseph, and he became a successful
man; and he was in the house of his
master the Egyptian, 3and his master
saw that the LORD was with him, and
that the LORD caused all that he did
to prosper in his hands. 4So Joseph
found favor in his sight and attended
him, and he made him overseer of his
house and put him in charge of all that
he had. 5From the time that he made
him overseer in his house and over
all that he had the LORD blessed the
Egyptian's house for Joseph's sake;
the blessing of the LORD was upon all
that he had, in house and field. 6So he
left all that he had in Joseph's charge;
and having him he had no concern for
anything but the food which he ate.
Now Joseph was handsome and
good-looking. 7And after a time his
master's wife cast her eyes upon
Joseph, and said, "Lie with me." 8But
he refused and said to his master's
wife, "Lo, having me my master has no
concern about anything in the house,
and he has put everything that he has
in my hand; 9he is not greater in this
house than I am; nor has he kept back
anything from me except yourself,
because you are his wife; how then
can I do this great wickedness, and
sin against God?" 10And although she
spoke to Joseph day after day, he would
not listen to her, to lie with her or to be
with her. 11But one day, when he went
into the house to do his work and none
of the men of the house was there in
the house, 12she caught him by his gar-
ment, saying, "Lie with me." But he
left his garment in her hand, and fled
and got out of the house. 13And when
she saw that he had left his garment
in her hand, and had fled out of the
house, 14she called to the men of her
household and said to them, "See, he

[a]Or *cult prostitute*
[b]Or *cult prostitute*
[c]Or *cult prostitute*
[d]That is *A breach*

has brought among us a Hebrew to in-
sult us; he came in to me to lie with
me, and I cried out with a loud voice;
15 and when he heard that I lifted up
my voice and cried, he left his garment
with me, and fled and got out of the
house." 16 Then she laid up his garment
by her until his master came home,
17 and she told him the same story, say-
ing, "The Hebrew servant, whom you
have brought among us, came in to me
to insult me; 18 but as soon as I lifted up
my voice and cried, he left his garment
with me, and fled out of the house."

19 When his master heard the
words which his wife spoke to him,
"This is the way your servant treat-
ed me," his anger was kindled. 20 And
Joseph's master took him and put
him into the prison, the place where
the king's prisoners were confined,
and he was there in prison. 21 But the
LORD was with Joseph and showed
him steadfast love, and gave him fa-
vor in the sight of the keeper of the
prison. 22 And the keeper of the pris-
on committed to Joseph's care all the
prisoners who were in the prison; and
whatever was done there, he was the
doer of it; 23 the keeper of the prison
paid no heed to anything that was in
Joseph's care, because the LORD was
with him; and whatever he did, the
LORD made it prosper.

THE DREAMS OF TWO PRISONERS

40 Some time after this, the but-
ler of the king of Egypt and his
baker offended their lord the king of
Egypt. 2 And Pharaoh was angry with
his two officers, the chief butler and
the chief baker, 3 and he put them in
custody in the house of the captain
of the guard, in the prison where
Joseph was confined. 4 The captain of
the guard charged Joseph with them,
and he waited on them; and they con-
tinued for some time in custody. 5 And
one night they both dreamed—the
butler and the baker of the king of
Egypt, who were confined in the pris-
on—each his own dream, and each
dream with its own meaning. 6 When
Joseph came to them in the morning
and saw them, they were troubled. 7 So
he asked Pharaoh's officers who were
with him in custody in his master's
house, "Why are your faces downcast
today?" 8 They said to him, "We have
had dreams, and there is no one to
interpret them." And Joseph said to
them, "Do not interpretations belong
to God? Tell them to me, I pray you."

9 So the chief butler told his dream
to Joseph, and said to him, "In my
dream there was a vine before me,
10 and on the vine there were three
branches; as soon as it budded, its
blossoms shot forth, and the clusters
ripened into grapes. 11 Pharaoh's cup
was in my hand; and I took the grapes
and pressed them into Pharaoh's
cup, and placed the cup in Pharaoh's
hand." 12 Then Joseph said to him,
"This is its interpretation: the three
branches are three days; 13 within
three days Pharaoh will lift up your
head and restore you to your office;
and you shall place Pharaoh's cup in
his hand as formerly, when you were
his butler. 14 But remember me, when it
is well with you, and do me the kind-
ness, I pray you, to make mention of
me to Pharaoh, and so get me out of
this house. 15 For I was indeed stolen
out of the land of the Hebrews; and
here also I have done nothing that
they should put me into the dungeon."

16 When the chief baker saw that
the interpretation was favorable, he
said to Joseph, "I also had a dream:
there were three cake baskets on my
head, 17 and in the uppermost basket
there were all sorts of baked food for
Pharaoh, but the birds were eating it
out of the basket on my head." 18 And
Joseph answered, "This is its inter-
pretation: the three baskets are three
days; 19 within three days Pharaoh will
lift up your head—from you!—and
hang you on a tree; and the birds will
eat the flesh from you."

20 On the third day, which was
Pharaoh's birthday, he made a feast

for all his servants, and lifted up the
head of the chief butler and the head
of the chief baker among his servants.
21He restored the chief butler to his
butlership, and he placed the cup in
Pharaoh's hand; 22but he hanged the
chief baker, as Joseph had interpreted
to them. 23Yet the chief butler did not
remember Joseph, but forgot him.

JOSEPH INTERPRETS PHARAOH'S DREAM

41 After two whole years, Pharaoh
dreamed that he was standing by
the Nile, 2and behold, there came up
out of the Nile seven cows sleek and
fat, and they fed in the reed grass.
3And behold, seven other cows, gaunt
and thin, came up out of the Nile after
them, and stood by the other cows on
the bank of the Nile. 4And the gaunt
and thin cows ate up the seven sleek
and fat cows. And Pharaoh awoke.
5And he fell asleep and dreamed a sec-
ond time; and behold, seven ears of
grain, plump and good, were growing
on one stalk. 6And behold, after them
sprouted seven ears, thin and blight-
ed by the east wind. 7And the thin
ears swallowed up the seven plump
and full ears. And Pharaoh awoke,
and behold, it was a dream. 8So in the
morning his spirit was troubled; and
he sent and called for all the magi-
cians of Egypt and all its wise men;
and Pharaoh told them his dream, but
there was none who could interpret it[a]
to Pharaoh.

9 Then the chief butler said to
Pharaoh, "I remember my faults to-
day. 10When Pharaoh was angry with
his servants, and put me and the chief
baker in custody in the house of the
captain of the guard, 11we dreamed on
the same night, he and I, each having
a dream with its own meaning. 12A
young Hebrew was there with us, a
servant of the captain of the guard;
and when we told him, he interpreted
our dreams to us, giving an interpre-
tation to each man according to his
dream. 13And as he interpreted to us,
so it came to pass; I was restored to
my office, and the baker was hanged."

14 Then Pharaoh sent and called
Joseph, and they brought him hast-
ily out of the dungeon; and when he
had shaved himself and changed his
clothes, he came in before Pharaoh.
15And Pharaoh said to Joseph, "I have
had a dream, and there is no one who
can interpret it; and I have heard
it said of you that when you hear a
dream you can interpret it." 16Joseph
answered Pharaoh, "It is not in me;
God will give Pharaoh a favorable an-
swer." 17Then Pharaoh said to Joseph,
"Behold, in my dream I was standing
on the banks of the Nile; 18and seven
cows, fat and sleek, came up out of the
Nile and fed in the reed grass; 19and
seven other cows came up after them,
poor and very gaunt and thin, such
as I had never seen in all the land of
Egypt. 20And the thin and gaunt cows
ate up the first seven fat cows, 21but
when they had eaten them no one
would have known that they had eat-
en them, for they were still as gaunt
as at the beginning. Then I awoke.
22I also saw in my dream seven ears
growing on one stalk, full and good;
23and seven ears, withered, thin, and
blighted by the east wind, sprouted
after them, 24and the thin ears swal-
lowed up the seven good ears. And I
told it to the magicians, but there was
no one who could explain it to me."

25 Then Joseph said to Pharaoh,
"The dream of Pharaoh is one; God has
revealed to Pharaoh what he is about
to do. 26The seven good cows are seven
years, and the seven good ears are sev-
en years; the dream is one. 27The seven
lean and gaunt cows that came up after
them are seven years, and the seven
empty ears blighted by the east wind
are also seven years of famine. 28It is
as I told Pharaoh, God has shown to
Pharaoh what he is about to do. 29There
will come seven years of great plenty
throughout all the land of Egypt, 30but
after them there will arise seven years

[a]Gk: Heb *them*

of famine, and all the plenty will be for-
gotten in the land of Egypt; the famine
will consume the land, 31 and the plenty
will be unknown in the land by reason
of that famine which will follow, for it
will be very grievous. 32 And the dou-
bling of Pharaoh's dream means that
the thing is fixed by God, and God will
shortly bring it to pass. 33 Now there-
fore let Pharaoh select a man discreet
and wise, and set him over the land of
Egypt. 34 Let Pharaoh proceed to ap-
point overseers over the land, and take
the fifth part of the produce of the
land of Egypt during the seven plente-
ous years. 35 And let them gather all the
food of these good years that are com-
ing, and lay up grain under the authori-
ty of Pharaoh for food in the cities, and
let them keep it. 36 That food shall be a
reserve for the land against the seven
years of famine which are to befall the
land of Egypt, so that the land may not
perish through the famine."

JOSEPH'S RISE TO POWER

37 This proposal seemed good to
Pharaoh and to all his servants. 38 And
Pharaoh said to his servants, "Can we
find such a man as this, in whom is
the Spirit of God?" 39 So Pharaoh said
to Joseph, "Since God has shown you
all this, there is none so discreet and
wise as you are; 40 you shall be over my
house, and all my people shall order
themselves as you command; only as
regards the throne will I be great-
er than you." 41 And Pharaoh said to
Joseph, "Behold, I have set you over
all the land of Egypt." 42 Then Pharaoh
took his signet ring from his hand and
put it on Joseph's hand, and arrayed
him in garments of fine linen, and put
a gold chain about his neck; 43 and he
made him to ride in his second char-
iot; and they cried before him, "Bow
the knee!"[b] Thus he set him over all
the land of Egypt. 44 Moreover Pharaoh
said to Joseph, "I am Pharaoh, and
without your consent no man shall
lift up hand or foot in all the land of
Egypt." 45 And Pharaoh called Joseph's
name Zaph´enath-pane´ah; and he
gave him in marriage As´enath, the
daughter of Poti´phera priest of On.
So Joseph went out over the land of
Egypt.

46 Joseph was thirty years old when
he entered the service of Pharaoh
king of Egypt. And Joseph went out
from the presence of Pharaoh, and
went through all the land of Egypt.
47 During the seven plenteous years the
earth brought forth abundantly, 48 and
he gathered up all the food of the sev-
en years when there was plenty[c] in the
land of Egypt, and stored up food in
the cities; he stored up in every city
the food from the fields around it.
49 And Joseph stored up grain in great
abundance, like the sand of the sea,
until he ceased to measure it, for it
could not be measured.

50 Before the year of famine came,
Joseph had two sons, whom As´enath,
the daughter of Poti´phera priest of
On, bore to him. 51 Joseph called the
name of the first-born Manas´seh,[d]
"For," he said, "God has made me
forget all my hardship and all my fa-
ther's house." 52 The name of the sec-
ond he called E´phraim,[e] "For God
has made me fruitful in the land of my
affliction."

53 The seven years of plenty that
prevailed in the land of Egypt came
to an end; 54 and the seven years of
famine began to come, as Joseph had
said. There was famine in all lands;
but in all the land of Egypt there was
bread. 55 When all the land of Egypt
was famished, the people cried to
Pharaoh for bread; and Pharaoh said
to all the Egyptians, "Go to Joseph;
what he says to you, do." 56 So when
the famine had spread over all the

[b] *Abrek,* probably an Egyptian word similar in sound to the Hebrew word meaning *to kneel*
[c] Sam Gk: Heb *which were*
[d] That is *Making to forget*
[e] From a Hebrew word meaning *to be fruitful*

land, Joseph opened all the storehous-
es,[a] and sold to the Egyptians, for
the famine was severe in the land of
Egypt. 57 Moreover, all the earth came
to Egypt to Joseph to buy grain, be-
cause the famine was severe over all
the earth.

JOSEPH'S BROTHERS GO TO EGYPT

42 When Jacob learned that there
was grain in Egypt, he said to his
sons, "Why do you look at one an-
other?" 2 And he said, "Behold, I have
heard that there is grain in Egypt; go
down and buy grain for us there, that
we may live, and not die." 3 So ten of
Joseph's brothers went down to buy
grain in Egypt. 4 But Jacob did not
send Benjamin, Joseph's brother, with
his brothers, for he feared that harm
might befall him. 5 Thus the sons of
Israel came to buy among the others
who came, for the famine was in the
land of Canaan.

6 Now Joseph was governor over
the land; he it was who sold to all
the people of the land. And Joseph's
brothers came, and bowed them-
selves before him with their faces to
the ground. 7 Joseph saw his brothers,
and knew them, but he treated them
like strangers and spoke roughly to
them. "Where do you come from?"
he said. They said, "From the land of
Canaan, to buy food." 8 Thus Joseph
knew his brothers, but they did not
know him. 9 And Joseph remembered
the dreams which he had dreamed of
them; and he said to them, "You are
spies, you have come to see the weak-
ness of the land." 10 They said to him,
"No, my lord, but to buy food have
your servants come. 11 We are all sons
of one man, we are honest men, your
servants are not spies." 12 He said to
them, "No, it is the weakness of the
land that you have come to see." 13 And
they said, "We, your servants, are
twelve brothers, the sons of one man
in the land of Canaan; and behold, the
youngest is this day with our father,
and one is no more." 14 But Joseph said
to them, "It is as I said to you, you are
spies. 15 By this you shall be tested: by
the life of Pharaoh, you shall not go
from this place unless your youngest
brother comes here. 16 Send one of you,
and let him bring your brother, while
you remain in prison, that your words
may be tested, whether there is truth
in you; or else, by the life of Pharaoh,
surely you are spies." 17 And he put
them all together in prison for three
days.

18 On the third day Joseph said to
them, "Do this and you will live, for I
fear God: 19 if you are honest men, let
one of your brothers remain confined
in your prison, and let the rest go and
carry grain for the famine of your
households, 20 and bring your young-
est brother to me; so your words will
be verified, and you shall not die."
And they did so. 21 Then they said to
one another, "In truth we are guilty
concerning our brother, in that we
saw the distress of his soul, when he
besought us and we would not listen;
therefore is this distress come upon
us." 22 And Reuben answered them,
"Did I not tell you not to sin against
the lad? But you would not listen.
So now there comes a reckoning for
his blood." 23 They did not know that
Joseph understood them, for there
was an interpreter between them.
24 Then he turned away from them and
wept; and he returned to them and
spoke to them. And he took Simeon
from them and bound him before
their eyes. 25 And Joseph gave orders to
fill their bags with grain, and to re-
place every man's money in his sack,
and to give them provisions for the
journey. This was done for them.

JOSEPH'S BROTHERS RETURN TO CANAAN

26 Then they loaded their asses
with their grain, and departed. 27 And
as one of them opened his sack to
give his ass provender at the lodging
place, he saw his money in the mouth

[a] Gk Vg Compare Syr: Heb *all that was in them*

of his sack; 28and he said to his broth-
ers, "My money has been put back;
here it is in the mouth of my sack!"
At this their hearts failed them, and
they turned trembling to one anoth-
er, saying, "What is this that God has
done to us?"

29 When they came to Jacob their
father in the land of Canaan, they told
him all that had befallen them, saying,
30"The man, the lord of the land, spoke
roughly to us, and took us to be spies of
the land. 31But we said to him, 'We are
honest men, we are not spies; 32we are
twelve brothers, sons of our father; one
is no more, and the youngest is this day
with our father in the land of Canaan.'
33Then the man, the lord of the land,
said to us, 'By this I shall know that
you are honest men: leave one of your
brothers with me, and take grain for
the famine of your households, and go
your way. 34Bring your youngest broth-
er to me; then I shall know that you are
not spies but honest men, and I will de-
liver to you your brother, and you shall
trade in the land.'"

35 As they emptied their sacks, be-
hold, every man's bundle of money was
in his sack; and when they and their fa-
ther saw their bundles of money, they
were dismayed. 36And Jacob their father
said to them, "You have bereaved me
of my children: Joseph is no more, and
Simeon is no more, and now you would
take Benjamin; all this has come upon
me." 37Then Reuben said to his father,
"Slay my two sons if I do not bring him
back to you; put him in my hands, and
I will bring him back to you." 38But he
said, "My son shall not go down with
you, for his brother is dead, and he
only is left. If harm should befall him
on the journey that you are to make,
you would bring down my gray hairs
with sorrow to Sheol."

THE BROTHERS COME AGAIN, BRINGING BENJAMIN

43 Now the famine was severe in the
land. 2And when they had eaten
the grain which they had brought from
Egypt, their father said to them, "Go
again, buy us a little food." 3But Judah
said to him, "The man solemnly warned
us, saying, 'You shall not see my face,
unless your brother is with you.' 4If you
will send our brother with us, we will
go down and buy you food; 5but if you
will not send him, we will not go down,
for the man said to us, 'You shall not
see my face, unless your brother is with
you.'" 6Israel said, "Why did you treat
me so ill as to tell the man that you had
another brother?" 7They replied, "The
man questioned us carefully about
ourselves and our kindred, saying, 'Is
your father still alive? Have you anoth-
er brother?' What we told him was in
answer to these questions; could we in
any way know that he would say, 'Bring
your brother down'?" 8And Judah said
to Israel his father, "Send the lad with
me, and we will arise and go, that we
may live and not die, both we and you
and also our little ones. 9I will be surety
for him; of my hand you shall require
him. If I do not bring him back to you
and set him before you, then let me
bear the blame for ever; 10for if we had
not delayed, we would now have re-
turned twice."

11 Then their father Israel said to
them, "If it must be so, then do this:
take some of the choice fruits of the
land in your bags, and carry down to the
man a present, a little balm and a lit-
tle honey, gum, myrrh, pistachio nuts,
and almonds. 12Take double the money
with you; carry back with you the mon-
ey that was returned in the mouth of
your sacks; perhaps it was an oversight.
13Take also your brother, and arise, go
again to the man; 14may God Almighty[b]
grant you mercy before the man, that
he may send back your other brother
and Benjamin. If I am bereaved of my
children, I am bereaved." 15So the men
took the present, and they took double
the money with them, and Benjamin;
and they arose and went down to
Egypt, and stood before Joseph.

[b]Heb *El Shaddai*

16 When Joseph saw Benjamin
with them, he said to the steward of
his house, "Bring the men into the
house, and slaughter an animal and
make ready, for the men are to dine
with me at noon." 17The man did as
Joseph bade him, and brought the
men to Joseph's house. 18And the
men were afraid because they were
brought to Joseph's house, and they
said, "It is because of the money,
which was replaced in our sacks the
first time, that we are brought in, so
that he may seek occasion against us
and fall upon us, to make slaves of us
and seize our asses." 19So they went
up to the steward of Joseph's house,
and spoke with him at the door of the
house, 20and said, "Oh, my lord, we
came down the first time to buy food;
21and when we came to the lodging
place we opened our sacks, and there
was every man's money in the mouth
of his sack, our money in full weight;
so we have brought it again with us,
22and we have brought other money
down in our hand to buy food. We do
not know who put our money in our
sacks." 23He replied, "Rest assured, do
not be afraid; your God and the God
of your father must have put treasure
in your sacks for you; I received your
money." Then he brought Simeon out
to them. 24And when the man had
brought the men into Joseph's house,
and given them water, and they had
washed their feet, and when he had
given their asses provender, 25they
made ready the present for Joseph's
coming at noon, for they heard that
they should eat bread there.

26 When Joseph came home, they
brought into the house to him the
present which they had with them,
and bowed down to him to the ground.
27And he inquired about their welfare,
and said, "Is your father well, the old
man of whom you spoke? Is he still
alive?" 28They said, "Your servant our
father is well, he is still alive." And
they bowed their heads and made
obeisance. 29And he lifted up his eyes,
and saw his brother Benjamin, his
mother's son, and said, "Is this your
youngest brother, of whom you spoke
to me? God be gracious to you, my
son!" 30Then Joseph made haste, for his
heart yearned for his brother, and he
sought a place to weep. And he entered
his chamber and wept there. 31Then
he washed his face and came out;
and controlling himself he said, "Let
food be served." 32They served him
by himself, and them by themselves,
and the Egyptians who ate with him
by themselves, because the Egyptians
might not eat bread with the Hebrews,
for that is an abomination to the
Egyptians. 33And they sat before him,
the first-born according to his birth-
right and the youngest according to
his youth; and the men looked at one
another in amazement. 34Portions were
taken to them from Joseph's table, but
Benjamin's portion was five times as
much as any of theirs. So they drank
and were merry with him.

JOSEPH DETAINS BENJAMIN

44 Then he commanded the steward
of his house, "Fill the men's sacks
with food, as much as they can car-
ry, and put each man's money in the
mouth of his sack, 2and put my cup,
the silver cup, in the mouth of the
sack of the youngest, with his money
for the grain." And he did as Joseph
told him. 3As soon as the morning was
light, the men were sent away with
their asses. 4When they had gone but
a short distance from the city, Joseph
said to his steward, "Up, follow af-
ter the men; and when you overtake
them, say to them, 'Why have you re-
turned evil for good? Why have you
stolen my silver cup?[a] 5Is it not from
this that my lord drinks, and by this
that he divines? You have done wrong
in so doing.'"

6 When he overtook them, he
spoke to them these words. 7They said
to him, "Why does my lord speak such

[a]Gk Compare Vg: Heb lacks *Why have you stolen my silver cup?*

words as these? Far be it from your
servants that they should do such a
thing! 8Behold, the money which we
found in the mouth of our sacks, we
brought back to you from the land of
Canaan; how then should we steal
silver or gold from your lord's house?
9With whomever of your servants it be
found, let him die, and we also will
be my lord's slaves." 10He said, "Let
it be as you say: he with whom it is
found shall be my slave, and the rest
of you shall be blameless." 11Then ev-
ery man quickly lowered his sack to
the ground, and every man opened
his sack. 12And he searched, begin-
ning with the eldest and ending with
the youngest; and the cup was found
in Benjamin's sack. 13Then they rent
their clothes, and every man loaded
his ass, and they returned to the city.

14 When Judah and his brothers
came to Joseph's house, he was still
there; and they fell before him to the
ground. 15Joseph said to them, "What
deed is this that you have done? Do
you not know that such a man as I
can indeed divine?" 16And Judah said,
"What shall we say to my lord? What
shall we speak? Or how can we clear
ourselves? God has found out the guilt
of your servants; behold, we are my
lord's slaves, both we and he also in
whose hand the cup has been found."
17But he said, "Far be it from me that I
should do so! Only the man in whose
hand the cup was found shall be my
slave; but as for you, go up in peace to
your father."

JUDAH PLEADS FOR BENJAMIN'S RELEASE

18 Then Judah went up to him and
said, "O my lord, let your servant, I
pray you, speak a word in my lord's
ears, and let not your anger burn
against your servant; for you are like
Pharaoh himself. 19My lord asked his
servants, saying, 'Have you a father, or
a brother?' 20And we said to my lord,
'We have a father, an old man, and a
young brother, the child of his old age;
and his brother is dead, and he alone
is left of his mother's children; and his
father loves him.' 21Then you said to
your servants, 'Bring him down to me,
that I may set my eyes upon him.' 22We
said to my lord, 'The lad cannot leave
his father, for if he should leave his fa-
ther, his father would die.' 23Then you
said to your servants, 'Unless your
youngest brother comes down with
you, you shall see my face no more.'
24When we went back to your servant
my father we told him the words of
my lord. 25And when our father said,
'Go again, buy us a little food,' 26we
said, 'We cannot go down. If our
youngest brother goes with us, then
we will go down; for we cannot see
the man's face unless our youngest
brother is with us.' 27Then your ser-
vant my father said to us, 'You know
that my wife bore me two sons; 28one
left me, and I said, Surely he has been
torn to pieces; and I have never seen
him since. 29If you take this one also
from me, and harm befalls him, you
will bring down my gray hairs in sor-
row to Sheol.' 30Now therefore, when
I come to your servant my father, and
the lad is not with us, then, as his life
is bound up in the lad's life, 31when
he sees that the lad is not with us, he
will die; and your servants will bring
down the gray hairs of your servant
our father with sorrow to Sheol. 32For
your servant became surety for the lad
to my father, saying, 'If I do not bring
him back to you, then I shall bear the
blame in the sight of my father all my
life.' 33Now therefore, let your servant,
I pray you, remain instead of the lad
as a slave to my lord; and let the lad
go back with his brothers. 34For how
can I go back to my father if the lad is
not with me? I fear to see the evil that
would come upon my father."

JOSEPH REVEALS HIMSELF TO HIS BROTHERS

45 Then Joseph could not control
himself before all those who
stood by him; and he cried, "Make
every one go out from me." So no

one stayed with him when Joseph
made himself known to his broth-
ers. 2And he wept aloud, so that the
Egyptians heard it, and the household
of Pharaoh heard it. 3And Joseph said
to his brothers, "I am Joseph; is my
father still alive?" But his brothers
could not answer him, for they were
dismayed at his presence.

4 So Joseph said to his brothers,
"Come near to me, I pray you." And
they came near. And he said, "I am
your brother, Joseph, whom you sold
into Egypt. 5And now do not be dis-
tressed, or angry with yourselves, be-
cause you sold me here; for God sent
me before you to preserve life. 6For the
famine has been in the land these two
years; and there are yet five years in
which there will be neither plowing
nor harvest. 7And God sent me before
you to preserve for you a remnant on
earth, and to keep alive for you many
survivors. 8So it was not you who sent
me here, but God; and he has made me
a father to Pharaoh, and lord of all his
house and ruler over all the land of
Egypt. 9Make haste and go up to my
father and say to him, 'Thus says your
son Joseph, God has made me lord of
all Egypt; come down to me, do not
tarry; 10you shall dwell in the land of
Goshen, and you shall be near me, you
and your children and your children's
children, and your flocks, your herds,
and all that you have; 11and there I
will provide for you, for there are yet
five years of famine to come; lest you
and your household, and all that you
have, come to poverty.' 12And now your
eyes see, and the eyes of my brother
Benjamin see, that it is my mouth that
speaks to you. 13You must tell my fa-
ther of all my splendor in Egypt, and of
all that you have seen. Make haste and
bring my father down here." 14Then he
fell upon his brother Benjamin's neck
and wept; and Benjamin wept upon his
neck. 15And he kissed all his brothers
and wept upon them; and after that
his brothers talked with him.

16 When the report was heard in
Pharaoh's house, "Joseph's brothers
have come," it pleased Pharaoh and
his servants well. 17And Pharaoh said
to Joseph, "Say to your brothers, 'Do
this: load your beasts and go back to
the land of Canaan; 18and take your
father and your households, and come
to me, and I will give you the best of
the land of Egypt, and you shall eat
the fat of the land.' 19Command them[a]
also, 'Do this: take wagons from the
land of Egypt for your little ones and
for your wives, and bring your father,
and come. 20Give no thought to your
goods, for the best of all the land of
Egypt is yours.'"

21 The sons of Israel did so; and
Joseph gave them wagons, according
to the command of Pharaoh, and gave
them provisions for the journey. 22To
each and all of them he gave festal
garments; but to Benjamin he gave
three hundred shekels of silver and
five festal garments. 23To his father he
sent as follows: ten asses loaded with
the good things of Egypt, and ten
she-asses loaded with grain, bread,
and provision for his father on the
journey. 24Then he sent his brothers
away, and as they departed, he said
to them, "Do not quarrel on the way."
25So they went up out of Egypt, and
came to the land of Canaan to their
father Jacob. 26And they told him,
"Joseph is still alive, and he is ruler
over all the land of Egypt." And his
heart fainted, for he did not believe
them. 27But when they told him all the
words of Joseph, which he had said to
them, and when he saw the wagons
which Joseph had sent to carry him,
the spirit of their father Jacob revived;
28and Israel said, "It is enough; Joseph
my son is still alive; I will go and see
him before I die."

JACOB BRINGS HIS WHOLE FAMILY TO EGYPT

46 So Israel took his journey with
all that he had, and came to

[a]Compare Gk Vg: Heb *you are commanded*

Beer-sheba, and offered sacrifices
to the God of his father Isaac. 2And
God spoke to Israel in visions of the
night, and said, "Jacob, Jacob." And
he said, "Here am I." 3Then he said,
"I am God, the God of your father;
do not be afraid to go down to Egypt;
for I will there make of you a great
nation. 4I will go down with you to
Egypt, and I will also bring you up
again; and Joseph's hand shall close
your eyes." 5Then Jacob set out from
Beer-sheba; and the sons of Israel
carried Jacob their father, their little
ones, and their wives, in the wagons
which Pharaoh had sent to carry him.
6They also took their cattle and their
goods, which they had gained in the
land of Canaan, and came into Egypt,
Jacob and all his offspring with him,
7his sons, and his sons' sons with him,
his daughters, and his sons' daughters;
all his offspring he brought with him
into Egypt.

8 Now these are the names of the
descendants of Israel, who came into
Egypt, Jacob and his sons. Reuben,
Jacob's first-born, 9and the sons of
Reuben: Hanoch, Pallu, Hezron,
and Carmi. 10The sons of Simeon:
Jem´uel, Jamin, Ohad, Jachin, Zohar,
and Sha´ul, the son of a Canaanitish
woman. 11The sons of Levi: Gershon,
Kohath, and Merar´i. 12The sons of
Judah: Er, Onan, Shelah, Perez, and
Zerah (but Er and Onan died in the
land of Canaan); and the sons of
Perez were Hezron and Hamul. 13The
sons of Is´sachar: Tola, Puvah, Iob,
and Shimron. 14The sons of Zeb´ulun:
Sered, Elon, and Jah´leel 15(these are
the sons of Leah, whom she bore to
Jacob in Paddan-aram, together with
his daughter Dinah; altogether his
sons and his daughters numbered thir-
ty-three). 16The sons of Gad: Ziph´ion,
Haggi, Shuni, Ezbon, Eri, Aro´di, and
Are´li. 17The sons of Asher: Imnah,
Ishvah, Ishvi, Beri´ah, with Serah
their sister. And the sons of Beri´ah:
Heber and Mal´chi´el 18(these are the
sons of Zilpah, whom Laban gave to
Leah his daughter; and these she bore
to Jacob—sixteen persons). 19The sons
of Rachel, Jacob's wife: Joseph and
Benjamin. 20And to Joseph in the land
of Egypt were born Manas´seh and
E´phraim, whom As´enath, the daugh-
ter of Poti´phera the priest of On, bore
to him. 21And the sons of Benjamin:
Bela, Becher, Ashbel, Gera, Na´aman,
Ehi, Rosh, Muppim, Huppim, and Ard

22(these are the sons of Rachel,
who were born to Jacob—fourteen
persons in all). 23The sons of Dan:
Hushim. 24The sons of Naph´tali:
Jahzeel, Guni, Jezer, and Shillem
25(these are the sons of Bilhah, whom
Laban gave to Rachel his daughter,
and these she bore to Jacob—seven
persons in all). 26All the persons be-
longing to Jacob who came into Egypt,
who were his own offspring, not in-
cluding Jacob's sons' wives, were six-
ty-six persons in all; 27and the sons
of Joseph, who were born to him in
Egypt, were two; all the persons of the
house of Jacob, that came into Egypt,
were seventy.

JACOB SETTLES IN GOSHEN

28 He sent Judah before him to
Joseph, to appear[b] before him in
Goshen; and they came into the land
of Goshen. 29Then Joseph made ready
his chariot and went up to meet Israel
his father in Goshen; and he present-
ed himself to him, and fell on his
neck, and wept on his neck a good
while. 30Israel said to Joseph, "Now
let me die, since I have seen your face
and know that you are still alive."
31Joseph said to his brothers and to his
father's household, "I will go up and
tell Pharaoh, and will say to him, 'My
brothers and my father's household,
who were in the land of Canaan, have
come to me; 32and the men are shep-
herds, for they have been keepers of
cattle; and they have brought their
flocks, and their herds, and all that
they have.' 33When Pharaoh calls you,

[b] Sam Syr Compare Gk Vg: Heb *to show the way*

and says, 'What is your occupation?'
34you shall say, 'Your servants have
been keepers of cattle from our youth
even until now, both we and our fa-
thers,' in order that you may dwell in
the land of Goshen; for every shepherd
is an abomination to the Egyptians."

47 So Joseph went in and told
Pharaoh, "My father and my
brothers, with their flocks and herds
and all that they possess, have come
from the land of Canaan; they are
now in the land of Goshen." 2And
from among his brothers he took five
men and presented them to Pharaoh.
3Pharaoh said to his brothers, "What
is your occupation?" And they said
to Pharaoh, "Your servants are shep-
herds, as our fathers were." 4They said
to Pharaoh, "We have come to sojourn
in the land; for there is no pasture for
your servants' flocks, for the famine
is severe in the land of Canaan; and
now, we pray you, let your servants
dwell in the land of Goshen." 5Then
Pharaoh said to Joseph, "Your father
and your brothers have come to you.
6The land of Egypt is before you; settle
your father and your brothers in the
best of the land; let them dwell in the
land of Goshen; and if you know any
able men among them, put them in
charge of my cattle."

7 Then Joseph brought in Jacob his
father, and set him before Pharaoh,
and Jacob blessed Pharaoh. 8And
Pharaoh said to Jacob, "How many
are the days of the years of your life?"
9And Jacob said to Pharaoh, "The
days of the years of my sojourning are
a hundred and thirty years; few and
evil have been the days of the years of
my life, and they have not attained to
the days of the years of the life of my
fathers in the days of their sojourn-
ing." 10And Jacob blessed Pharaoh,
and went out from the presence of
Pharaoh. 11Then Joseph settled his fa-
ther and his brothers, and gave them
a possession in the land of Egypt, in
the best of the land, in the land of
Ram´eses, as Pharaoh had command-
ed. 12And Joseph provided his father,
his brothers, and all his father's
household with food, according to the
number of their dependents.

THE FAMINE IN EGYPT

13 Now there was no food in all
the land; for the famine was very se-
vere, so that the land of Egypt and the
land of Canaan languished by reason
of the famine. 14And Joseph gathered
up all the money that was found in
the land of Egypt and in the land of
Canaan, for the grain which they
bought; and Joseph brought the mon-
ey into Pharaoh's house. 15And when
the money was all spent in the land
of Egypt and in the land of Canaan,
all the Egyptians came to Joseph, and
said, "Give us food; why should we
die before your eyes? For our money is
gone." 16And Joseph answered, "Give
your cattle, and I will give you food
in exchange for your cattle, if your
money is gone." 17So they brought
their cattle to Joseph; and Joseph gave
them food in exchange for the horses,
the flocks, the herds, and the asses:
and he supplied them with food in
exchange for all their cattle that year.
18And when that year was ended, they
came to him the following year, and
said to him, "We will not hide from my
lord that our money is all spent; and
the herds of cattle are my lord's; there
is nothing left in the sight of my lord
but our bodies and our lands. 19Why
should we die before your eyes, both
we and our land? Buy us and our land
for food, and we with our land will be
slaves to Pharaoh; and give us seed,
that we may live, and not die, and that
the land may not be desolate."

20 So Joseph bought all the land
of Egypt for Pharaoh; for all the
Egyptians sold their fields, because
the famine was severe upon them.
The land became Pharaoh's; 21and
as for the people, he made slaves of

them[a] from one end of Egypt to the
other. 22 Only the land of the priests he
did not buy; for the priests had a fixed
allowance from Pharaoh, and lived
on the allowance which Pharaoh gave
them; therefore they did not sell their
land. 23 Then Joseph said to the people,
"Behold, I have this day bought you
and your land for Pharaoh. Now here
is seed for you, and you shall sow the
land. 24 And at the harvests you shall
give a fifth to Pharaoh, and four fifths
shall be your own, as seed for the field
and as food for yourselves and your
households, and as food for your lit-
tle ones." 25 And they said, "You have
saved our lives; may it please my lord,
we will be slaves to Pharaoh." 26 So
Joseph made it a statute concerning
the land of Egypt, and it stands to
this day, that Pharaoh should have the
fifth; the land of the priests alone did
not become Pharaoh's.

THE LAST DAYS OF JACOB

27 Thus Israel dwelt in the land of
Egypt, in the land of Goshen; and they
gained possessions in it, and were
fruitful and multiplied exceedingly.
28 And Jacob lived in the land of Egypt
seventeen years; so the days of Jacob,
the years of his life, were a hundred
and forty-seven years.

29 And when the time drew near
that Israel must die, he called his son
Joseph and said to him, "If now I have
found favor in your sight, put your
hand under my thigh, and promise to
deal loyally and truly with me. Do not
bury me in Egypt, 30 but let me lie with
my fathers; carry me out of Egypt and
bury me in their burying place." He
answered, "I will do as you have said."
31 And he said, "Swear to me"; and he
swore to him. Then Israel bowed him-
self upon the head of his bed.

JACOB BLESSES JOSEPH'S SONS

48 After this Joseph was told,
"Behold, your father is ill"; so
he took with him his two sons,
Manas´seh and E´phraim. 2 And it was
told to Jacob, "Your son Joseph has
come to you"; then Israel summoned
his strength, and sat up in bed. 3 And
Jacob said to Joseph, "God Almighty[b]
appeared to me at Luz in the land of
Canaan and blessed me, 4 and said to
me, 'Behold, I will make you fruitful,
and multiply you, and I will make of
you a company of peoples, and will
give this land to your descendants
after you for an everlasting posses-
sion.' 5 And now your two sons, who
were born to you in the land of Egypt
before I came to you in Egypt, are
mine; E´phraim and Manas´seh shall
be mine, as Reuben and Simeon are.
6 And the offspring born to you after
them shall be yours; they shall be
called by the name of their brothers
in their inheritance. 7 For when I came
from Paddan, Rachel to my sorrow
died in the land of Canaan on the way,
when there was still some distance
to go to Ephrath; and I buried her
there on the way to Ephrath (that is,
Bethlehem)."

8 When Israel saw Joseph's sons,
he said, "Who are these?" 9 Joseph
said to his father, "They are my sons,
whom God has given me here." And
he said, "Bring them to me, I pray you,
that I may bless them." 10 Now the eyes
of Israel were dim with age, so that
he could not see. So Joseph brought
them near him; and he kissed them
and embraced them. 11 And Israel said
to Joseph, "I had not thought to see
your face; and lo, God has let me see
your children also." 12 Then Joseph re-
moved them from his knees, and he
bowed himself with his face to the
earth. 13 And Joseph took them both,
E´phraim in his right hand toward
Israel's left hand, and Manas´seh in
his left hand toward Israel's right
hand, and brought them near him.
14 And Israel stretched out his right
hand and laid it upon the head of

[a] Sam Gk Compare Vg: Heb *he removed them to the cities*
[b] Heb *El Shaddai*

E´phraim, who was the younger, and his left hand upon the head of Manas´seh, crossing his hands, for Manas´seh was the first-born.
15And he blessed Joseph, and said,

"The God before whom my
fathers Abraham and
Isaac walked,
the God who has led me all my
life long to this day,
16the angel who has redeemed
me from all evil, bless the
lads;
and in them let my name be
perpetuated, and the
name of my fathers
Abraham and Isaac;
and let them grow into a multi-
tude in the midst of the
earth."

17 When Joseph saw that his father laid his right hand upon the head of E´phraim, it displeased him; and he took his father's hand, to remove it from E´phraim's head to Manas´seh's
head. 18And Joseph said to his father, "Not so, my father; for this one is the first-born; put your right hand upon
his head." 19But his father refused, and said, "I know, my son, I know; he also shall become a people, and he also shall be great; nevertheless his younger brother shall be greater than he, and his descendants shall become
a multitude of nations." 20So he blessed them that day, saying,

"By you Israel will pronounce
blessings, saying,
'God make you as E´phraim
and as Manas´seh'";

21Then Israel said to Joseph, "Behold, I am about to die, but God will be with you, and will bring you again to the land of your fathers.
22Moreover I have given to you rather than to your brothers one mountain *slope*[a] *which I took from the hand* of the Amorites with my sword and with my bow."

JACOB'S LAST WORDS TO HIS SONS

49 *Then Jacob called his sons, and said, "Gather yourselves together, that I may tell you what shall befall you in days to come.

2Assemble and hear, O sons of
Jacob,
and hearken to Israel your
father.
3Reuben, you are my first-born,
my might, and the first
fruits of my strength,
pre-eminent in pride and
pre-eminent in
power.
4Unstable as water, you shall not
have pre-eminence
because you went up to your
father's bed;
then you defiled it—you[b]
went up to my couch!
5Simeon and Levi are brothers;
weapons of violence are
their swords.
6O my soul, come not into their
council;
O my spirit,[c] be not joined
to their company;
for in their anger they slay
men,
and in their wantonness
they hamstring oxen.
7Cursed be their anger, for it is
fierce;
and their wrath, for it is
cruel!
I will divide them in Jacob
and scatter them in Israel.
8Judah, your brothers shall praise
you;
your hand shall be on
the neck of your
enemies;
your father's sons shall bow
down before you.
9Judah is a lion's whelp;
from the prey, my son, you
have gone up.
He stooped down, he couched
as a lion,

[a]Heb *shekem,* shoulder
[b]Gk Syr Tg: Heb *he*
[c]Or *glory*

and as a lioness; who dares
rouse him up?
10The scepter shall not depart
from Judah,
nor the ruler's staff from
between his feet,
until he comes to whom it
belongs;[d]
and to him shall be the obedience of the peoples.
11Binding his foal to the vine
and his ass's colt to the
choice vine,
he washes his garments in wine
and his vesture in the blood
of grapes;
12his eyes shall be red with wine,
and his teeth white with
milk.
13Zeb´ulun shall dwell at the shore
of the sea;
he shall become a haven for
ships,
and his border shall be at
Sidon.
14Is´sachar is a strong ass,
crouching between the
sheepfolds;
15he saw that a resting place was
good,
and that the land was
pleasant;
so he bowed his shoulder to
bear,
and became a slave at forced
labor.
16Dan shall judge his people
as one of the tribes of Israel.
17Dan shall be a serpent in the
way,
a viper by the path,
that bites the horse's heels
so that his rider falls
backward.
18I wait for thy salvation, O LORD.
19Raiders[e] shall raid Gad,
but he shall raid at their
heels.
20Asher's food shall be rich,
and he shall yield royal
dainties.
21Naph´tali is a hind let loose,
that bears comely fawns.[f]
22Joseph is a fruitful bough,
a fruitful bough by a spring;
his branches run over the
wall.
23The archers fiercely attacked
him,
shot at him, and harassed
him sorely;
24yet his bow remained unmoved,
his arms[g] were made agile
by the hands of the Mighty One
of Jacob
(by the name of the
Shepherd, the Rock
of Israel),
25by the God of your father who
will help you,
by God Almighty[h] who will
bless you
with blessings of heaven
above,
blessings of the deep that
couches beneath,
blessings of the breasts and
of the womb.
26The blessings of your father
are mighty beyond the blessings of the eternal
mountains,[i]
the bounties of the everlasting hills;
may they be on the head of
Joseph,
and on the brow of him who
was separate from his
brothers.
27Benjamin is a ravenous wolf,
in the morning devouring
the prey,
and at even dividing the
spoil."

[d] Syr Compare Tg: Heb *until Shiloh comes* or *until he comes to Shiloh*
[e] Heb *gedud,* a raiding troop
[f] Or *who gives beautiful words*
[g] Heb *the arms of his hands*
[h] Heb *El Shaddai*
[i] Compare Gk: Heb *of my progenitors to*

JACOB'S DEATH AND BURIAL

28 All these are the twelve tribes of Israel; and this is what their father said to them as he blessed them, blessing each with the blessing suitable to him. 29 Then he charged them, and said to them, "I am to be gathered to my people; bury me with my fathers in the cave that is in the field of Ephron the Hittite, 30 in the cave that is in the field at Mach-pe´lah, to the east of Mamre, in the land of Canaan, which Abraham bought with the field from Ephron the Hittite to possess as a burying place. 31 There they buried Abraham and Sarah his wife; there they buried Isaac and Rebekah his wife; and there I buried Leah— 32 the field and the cave that is in it were purchased from the Hittites." 33 When Jacob finished charging his sons, he drew up his feet into the bed, and breathed his last, and was gathered to his people.

50 Then Joseph fell on his father's face, and wept over him, and kissed him. 2 And Joseph commanded his servants the physicians to embalm his father. So the physicians embalmed Israel; 3 forty days were required for it, for so many are required for embalming. And the Egyptians wept for him seventy days.

4 And when the days of weeping for him were past, Joseph spoke to the household of Pharaoh, saying, "If now I have found favor in your eyes, speak, I pray you, in the ears of Pharaoh, saying, 5 My father made me swear, saying, 'I am about to die: in my tomb which I hewed out for myself in the land of Canaan, there shall you bury me.' Now therefore let me go up, I pray you, and bury my father; then I will return." 6 And Pharaoh answered, "Go up, and bury your father, as he made you swear." 7 So Joseph went up to bury his father; and with him went up all the servants of Pharaoh, the elders of his household, and all the elders of the land of Egypt, 8 as well as all the household of Joseph, his brothers, and his father's household; only their children, their flocks, and their herds were left in the land of Goshen. 9 And there went up with him both chariots and horsemen; it was a very great company. 10 When they came to the threshing floor of Atad, which is beyond the Jordan, they lamented there with a very great and sorrowful lamentation; and he made a mourning for his father seven days. 11 When the inhabitants of the land, the Canaanites, saw the mourning on the threshing floor of Atad, they said, "This is a grievous mourning to the Egyptians." Therefore the place was named A´bel-mizraim;[a] it is beyond the Jordan. 12 Thus his sons did for him as he had commanded them; 13 for his sons carried him to the land of Canaan, and buried him in the cave of the field at Mach-pe´lah, to the east of Mamre, which Abraham bought with the field from Ephron the Hittite, to possess as a burying place. 14 After he had buried his father, Joseph returned to Egypt with his brothers and all who had gone up with him to bury his father.

JOSEPH FORGIVES HIS BROTHERS

15 When Joseph's brothers saw that their father was dead, they said, "It may be that Joseph will hate us and pay us back for all the evil which we did to him." 16 So they sent a message to Joseph, saying, "Your father gave this command before he died, 17 'Say to Joseph, Forgive, I pray you, the transgression of your brothers and their sin, because they did evil to you.' And now, we pray you, forgive the transgression of the servants of the God of your father." Joseph wept when they spoke to him. 18 His brothers also came and fell down before him, and said, "Behold, we are your servants." 19 But Joseph said to them, "Fear not, for am I in the place of God? 20 As for you, you meant evil against me; but God meant it for good, to bring it about that many

[a]That is *meadow* (or *mourning*) *of Egypt*

people should be kept alive, as they are
today. 21So do not fear; I will provide
for you and your little ones." Thus he
reassured them and comforted them.

JOSEPH'S LAST DAYS AND DEATH

22 So Joseph dwelt in Egypt, he
and his father's house; and Joseph
lived a hundred and ten years. 23And
Joseph saw E´phraim's children of
the third generation; the children
also of Machir the son of Manas´seh
were born upon Joseph's knees. 24And
Joseph said to his brothers, "I am
about to die; but God will visit you,
and bring you up out of this land to
the land which he swore to Abraham,
to Isaac, and to Jacob." 25Then Joseph
took an oath of the sons of Israel, say-
ing, "God will visit you, and you shall
carry up my bones from here." 26So
Joseph died, being a hundred and ten
years old; and they embalmed him,
and he was put in a coffin in Egypt.

THE SECOND BOOK OF MOSES COMMONLY CALLED

EXODUS

1 These are the names of the sons of
Israel who came to Egypt with Jacob,
each with his household: 2Reuben,
Simeon, Levi, and Judah, 3Is´sachar,
Zeb´ulun, and Benjamin, 4Dan and
Naph´tali, Gad and Asher. 5All the
offspring of Jacob were seventy per-
sons; Joseph was already in Egypt.
6Then Joseph died, and all his broth-
ers, and all that generation. 7But the
descendants of Israel were fruitful
and increased greatly; they multiplied
and grew exceedingly strong; so that
the land was filled with them.

THE ISRAELITES ARE OPPRESSED

8 Now there arose a new king over
Egypt, who did not know Joseph.
9And he said to his people, "Behold,
the people of Israel are too many and
too mighty for us. 10Come, let us deal
shrewdly with them, lest they mul-
tiply, and, if war befall us, they join
our enemies and fight against us and
escape from the land." 11Therefore
they set taskmasters over them to
afflict them with heavy burdens; and
they built for Pharaoh store-cities,
Pithom and Raam´ses. 12But the more
they were oppressed, the more they
multiplied and the more they spread
abroad. And the Egyptians were in
dread of the people of Israel. 13So
they made the people of Israel serve
with rigor, 14and made their lives bit-
ter with hard service, in mortar and
brick, and in all kinds of work in the
field; in all their work they made them
serve with rigor.

15 Then the king of Egypt said to
the Hebrew midwives, one of whom
was named Shiph´rah and the other
Pu´ah, 16"When you serve as midwife
to the Hebrew women, and see them
upon the birthstool, if it is a son, you
shall kill him; but if it is a daughter,
she shall live." 17But the midwives
feared God, and did not do as the king
of Egypt commanded them, but let
the male children live. 18So the king of
Egypt called the midwives, and said
to them, "Why have you done this,
and let the male children live?" 19The
midwives said to Pharaoh, "Because
the Hebrew women are not like the
Egyptian women; for they are vig-
orous and are delivered before the
midwife comes to them." 20So God
dealt well with the midwives; and
the people multiplied and grew very
strong. 21And because the midwives
feared God he gave them families.
22Then Pharaoh commanded all his
people, "Every son that is born to the
Hebrews[a] you shall cast into the Nile,
but you shall let every daughter live."

BIRTH AND YOUTH OF MOSES

2 Now a man from the house of Levi
went and took to wife a daughter
of Levi. 2The woman conceived and
bore a son; and when she saw that
he was a goodly child, she hid him
three months. 3And when she could
hide him no longer she took for him
a basket made of bulrushes, and
daubed it with bitumen and pitch; and
she put the child in it and placed it
among the reeds at the river's brink.
4And his sister stood at a distance,
to know what would be done to him.
5Now the daughter of Pharaoh came
down to bathe at the river, and her
maidens walked beside the river; she
saw the basket among the reeds and
sent her maid to fetch it. 6When she
opened it she saw the child; and lo,
the babe was crying. She took pity
on him and said, "This is one of the
Hebrews' children." 7Then his sister
said to Pharaoh's daughter, "Shall I go
and call you a nurse from the Hebrew
women to nurse the child for you?"
8And Pharaoh's daughter said to her,

[a] Sam Gk Tg: Heb lacks *to the Hebrews*

"Go." So the girl went and called the
child's mother. 9And Pharaoh's daugh-
ter said to her, "Take this child away,
and nurse him for me, and I will give
you your wages." So the woman took
the child and nursed him. 10And the
child grew, and she brought him to
Pharaoh's daughter, and he became
her son; and she named him Moses,[b]
for she said, "Because I drew him out[c]
of the water."

MOSES FLEES TO MIDIAN

11 One day, when Moses had grown
up, he went out to his people and
looked on their burdens; and he saw
an Egyptian beating a Hebrew, one of
his people. 12He looked this way and
that, and seeing no one he killed the
Egyptian and hid him in the sand.
13When he went out the next day, be-
hold, two Hebrews were struggling
together; and he said to the man that
did the wrong, "Why do you strike
your fellow?" 14He answered, "Who
made you a prince and a judge over
us? Do you mean to kill me as you
killed the Egyptian?" Then Moses was
afraid, and thought, "Surely the thing
is known." 15When Pharaoh heard of
it, he sought to kill Moses.

But Moses fled from Pharaoh, and
stayed in the land of Mid´ian; and he
sat down by a well. 16Now the priest
of Mid´ian had seven daughters; and
they came and drew water, and filled
the troughs to water their father's
flock. 17The shepherds came and drove
them away; but Moses stood up and
helped them, and watered their flock.
18*When they came* to their father
Reu´el, he said, "How is it that you
have come so soon today?" 19They said,
"An Egyptian delivered us out of the
hand of the shepherds, and even drew
water for us and watered the flock."
20He said to his daughters, "And where
is he? Why have you left the man? Call
him, that he may eat bread." 21And
Moses was content to dwell with the
man, and he gave Moses his daugher
Zippo´rah. 22She bore a son, and he
called his name Gershom; for he said,
"I have been a sojourner[d] in a foreign
land."

23 In the course of those many days
the king of Egypt died. And the people
of Israel groaned under their bond-
age, and cried out for help, and their
cry under bondage came up to God.
24And God heard their groaning, and
God remembered his covenant with
Abraham, with Isaac, and with Jacob.
25And God saw the people of Israel,
and God knew their condition.

MOSES AT THE BURNING BUSH

3 Now Moses was keeping the flock of
his father-in-law, Jethro, the priest
of Mid´ian; and he led his flock to the
west side of the wilderness, and came
to Horeb, the mountain of God. 2And
the angel of the LORD appeared to
him in a flame of fire out of the midst
of a bush; and he looked, and lo, the
bush was burning, yet it was not con-
sumed. 3And Moses said, "I will turn
aside and see this great sight, why the
bush is not burnt." 4When the LORD
saw that he turned aside to see, God
called to him out of the bush, "Moses,
Moses!" And he said, "Here am I."
5Then he said, "Do not come near;
put off your shoes from your feet, for
the place on which you are standing
is holy ground." 6And he said, "I am
the God of your father, the God of
Abraham, the God of Isaac, and the
God of Jacob." And Moses hid his face,
for he was afraid to look at God.

7 Then the LORD said, "I have
seen the affliction of my people who
are in Egypt, and have heard their cry
because of their taskmasters; I know
their sufferings, 8and I have come
down to deliver them out of the hand
of the Egyptians, and to bring them up
out of that land to a good and broad
land, a land flowing with milk and
honey, to the place of the Canaanites,

[b] Heb *Mosheh*
[c] Heb *mashah*
[d] Heb *ger*

the Hittites, the Amorites, the
Per´izzites, the Hivites, and the
Jeb´usites. 9And now, behold, the cry
of the people of Israel has come to me,
and I have seen the oppression with
which the Egyptians oppress them.
10Come, I will send you to Pharaoh
that you may bring forth my people,
the sons of Israel, out of Egypt." 11But
Moses said to God, "Who am I that I
should go to Pharaoh, and bring the
sons of Israel out of Egypt?" 12He said,
"But I will be with you; and this shall
be the sign for you, that I have sent
you: when you have brought forth the
people out of Egypt, you shall serve
God upon this mountain."

THE DIVINE NAME REVEALED

13 Then Moses said to God, "If I
come to the people of Israel and say
to them, 'The God of your fathers
has sent me to you,' and they ask me,
'What is his name?' what shall I say
to them?" 14God said to Moses, "I AM
WHO I AM."[a]* And he said, "Say this
to the people of Israel, 'I AM has sent
me to you.'" 15God also said to Moses,
"Say this to the people of Israel, 'The
LORD,[b] the God of your fathers, the
God of Abraham, the God of Isaac,
and the God of Jacob, has sent me to
you': this is my name for ever, and
thus I am to be remembered through-
out all generations. 16Go and gather
the elders of Israel together, and say
to them, 'The LORD, the God of your
fathers, the God of Abraham, of Isaac,
and of Jacob, has appeared to me, say-
ing, "I have observed you and what
has been done to you in Egypt; 17and
I promise that I will bring you up out
of the affliction of Egypt, to the land
of the Canaanites, the Hittites, the
Amorites, the Per´izzites, the Hivites,
and the Jeb´usites, a land flowing with
milk and honey."' 18And they will
hearken to your voice; and you and the
elders of Israel shall go to the king of
Egypt and say to him, 'The LORD, the
God of the Hebrews, has met with us;
and now, we pray you, let us go a three
days' journey into the wilderness,
that we may sacrifice to the LORD our
God.' 19I know that the king of Egypt
will not let you go unless compelled
by a mighty hand.[c] 20So I will stretch
out my hand and smite Egypt with all
the wonders which I will do in it; af-
ter that he will let you go. 21And I will
give this people favor in the sight of
the Egyptians; and when you go, you
shall not go empty, 22but each woman
shall ask of her neighbor, and of her
who sojourns in her house, jewelry of
silver and of gold, and clothing, and
you shall put them on your sons and
on your daughters; thus you shall de-
spoil the Egyptians."

MOSES' MIRACULOUS POWER

4 Then Moses answered, "But behold,
they will not believe me or listen
to my voice, for they will say, 'The
LORD did not appear to you.'" 2The
LORD said to him, "What is that in
your hand?" He said, "A rod." 3And he
said, "Cast it on the ground." So he
cast it on the ground, and it became a
serpent; and Moses fled from it. 4But
the LORD said to Moses, "Put out your
hand, and take it by the tail"—so he
put out his hand and caught it, and it
became a rod in his hand 5"that they
may believe that the LORD, the God
of their fathers, the God of Abraham,
the God of Isaac, and the God of
Jacob, has appeared to you." 6Again,
the LORD said to him, "Put your hand
into your bosom." And he put his hand
into his bosom; and when he took it
out, behold, his hand was leprous, as
white as snow. 7Then God said, "Put
your hand back into your bosom." So
he put his hand back into his bosom;
and when he took it out, behold, it
was restored like the rest of his flesh.
8"If they will not believe you," God

[a] Or *I AM WHAT I AM* or *I WILL BE WHAT I WILL BE*
[b] The word *LORD* when spelled with capital letters, stands for the divine name, *YHWH*, which is here connected with the verb *hayah*, to be
[c] Gk Vg: Heb *no, not by a mighty hand*

said, "or heed the first sign, they may
believe the latter sign. 9 If they will not
believe even these two signs or heed
your voice, you shall take some water
from the Nile and pour it upon the dry
ground; and the water which you shall
take from the Nile will become blood
upon the dry ground."

10 But Moses said to the LORD,
"Oh, my Lord, I am not eloquent, ei-
ther heretofore or since thou hast
spoken to thy servant; but I am slow
of speech and of tongue." 11 Then the
LORD said to him, "Who has made
man's mouth? Who makes him dumb,
or deaf, or seeing, or blind? Is it not
I, the LORD? 12 Now therefore go, and
I will be with your mouth and teach
you what you shall speak." 13 But he
said, "Oh, my Lord, send, I pray, some
other person." 14 Then the anger of
the LORD was kindled against Moses
and he said, "Is there not Aaron,
your brother, the Levite? I know that
he can speak well; and behold, he is
coming out to meet you, and when he
sees you he will be glad in his heart.
15 And you shall speak to him and put
the words in his mouth; and I will be
with your mouth and with his mouth,
and will teach you what you shall do.
16 He shall speak for you to the people;
and he shall be a mouth for you, and
you shall be to him as God. 17 And you
shall take in your hand this rod, with
which you shall do the signs."

MOSES RETURNS TO EGYPT

18 Moses went back to Jethro his
father-in-law and said to him, "Let
me go back, I pray, to my kinsmen in
Egypt and see whether they are still
alive." And Jethro said to Moses, "Go
in peace." 19 And the LORD said to
Moses in Mid′ian, "Go back to Egypt;
for all the men who were seeking
your life are dead." 20 So Moses took
his wife and his sons and set them on
an ass, and went back to the land of
Egypt; and in his hand Moses took the
rod of God.

21 And the LORD said to Moses,
"When you go back to Egypt, see that
you do before Pharaoh all the miracles
which I have put in your power; but I
will harden his heart, so that he will
not let the people go. 22 And you shall
say to Pharaoh, 'Thus says the LORD,
Israel is my first-born son, 23 and I say
to you, "Let my son go that he may
serve me"; if you refuse to let him
go, behold, I will slay your first-born
son.'"

24 At a lodging place on the way
the LORD met him and sought to kill
him. 25 Then Zippo′rah took a flint and
cut off her son's foreskin, and touched
Moses' feet with it, and said, "Surely
you are a bridegroom of blood to me!"
26 So he let him alone. Then it was that
she said, "You are a bridegroom of
blood," because of the circumcision.

27 The LORD said to Aaron, "Go
into the wilderness to meet Moses." So
he went, and met him at the mountain
of God and kissed him. 28 And Moses
told Aaron all the words of the LORD
with which he had sent him, and all
the signs which he had charged him to
do. 29 Then Moses and Aaron went and
gathered together all the elders of the
people of Israel. 30 And Aaron spoke all
the words which the LORD had spo-
ken to Moses, and did the signs in the
sight of the people. 31 And the people
believed; and when they heard that
the LORD had visited the people of
Israel and that he had seen their af-
fliction, they bowed their heads and
worshiped.

BRICKS WITHOUT STRAW

5 Afterward Moses and Aaron went
to Pharaoh and said, "Thus says the
LORD, the God of Israel, 'Let my peo-
ple go, that they may hold a feast to
me in the wilderness.'" 2 But Pharaoh
said, "Who is the LORD, that I should
heed his voice and let Israel go? I do
not know the LORD, and moreover I
will not let Israel go." 3 Then they said,
"The God of the Hebrews has met
with us; let us go, we pray, a three
days' journey into the wilderness, and

sacrifice to the LORD our God, lest he
fall upon us with pestilence or with
the sword." 4 But the king of Egypt
said to them, "Moses and Aaron, why
do you take the people away from
their work? Get to your burdens."
5 And Pharaoh said, "Behold, the peo-
ple of the land are now many and you
make them rest from their burdens!"
6 The same day Pharaoh commanded
the taskmasters of the people and
their foremen, 7 "You shall no longer
give the people straw to make bricks,
as heretofore; let them go and gather
straw for themselves. 8 But the number
of bricks which they made heretofore
you shall lay upon them, you shall by
no means lessen it; for they are idle;
therefore they cry, 'Let us go and of-
fer sacrifice to our God.' 9 Let heavier
work be laid upon the men that they
may labor at it and pay no regard to
lying words."

10 So the taskmasters and the fore-
men of the people went out and said
to the people, "Thus says Pharaoh,
'I will not give you straw. 11 Go your-
selves, get your straw wherever you
can find it; but your work will not be
lessened in the least.'" 12 So the people
were scattered abroad throughout all
the land of Egypt, to gather stubble for
straw. 13 The taskmasters were urgent,
saying, "Complete your work, your
daily task, as when there was straw."
14 And the foremen of the people of
Israel, whom Pharaoh's taskmasters
had set over them, were beaten, and
were asked, "Why have you not done
all your task of making bricks today,
as hitherto?"

15 Then the foremen of the people
of Israel came and cried to Pharaoh,
"Why do you deal thus with your
servants? 16 No straw is given to your
servants, yet they say to us, 'Make
bricks!' And behold, your servants are
beaten; but the fault is in your own
people." 17 But he said, "You are idle,
you are idle; therefore you say, 'Let
us go and sacrifice to the LORD.' 18 Go
now, and work; for no straw shall be
given you, yet you shall deliver the
same number of bricks." 19 The fore-
men of the people of Israel saw that
they were in evil plight, when they
said, "You shall by no means lessen
your daily number of bricks." 20 They
met Moses and Aaron, who were
waiting for them, as they came forth
from Pharaoh; 21 and they said to them,
"The LORD look upon you and judge,
because you have made us offensive in
the sight of Pharaoh and his servants,
and have put a sword in their hand to
kill us."

ISRAEL'S DELIVERANCE ASSURED

22 Then Moses turned again to the
LORD and said, "O LORD, why hast
thou done evil to this people? Why
didst thou ever send me? 23 For since
I came to Pharaoh to speak in thy
name, he has done evil to this people,
and thou hast not delivered thy people
at all."

6 But the LORD said to Moses, "Now
you shall see what I will do to
Pharaoh; for with a strong hand he
will send them out, yea, with a strong
hand he will drive them out of his
land."

2 And God said to Moses, "I am
the LORD. 3 I appeared to Abraham, to
Isaac, and to Jacob, as God Almighty,[a]
but by my name the LORD I did not
make myself known to them. 4 I also
established my covenant with them,
to give them the land of Canaan, the
land in which they dwelt as sojourn-
ers. 5 Moreover I have heard the groan-
ing of the people of Israel whom the
Egyptians hold in bondage and I have
remembered my covenant. 6 Say there-
fore to the people of Israel, 'I am the
LORD, and I will bring you out from
under the burdens of the Egyptians,
and I will deliver you from their bond-
age, and I will redeem you with an
outstretched arm and with great acts
of judgment, 7 and I will take you for

[a] Heb *El Shaddai*

my people, and I will be your God; and you shall know that I am the LORD your God, who has brought you out from under the burdens of the Egyptians. 8And I will bring you into the land which I swore to give to Abraham, to Isaac, and to Jacob; I will give it to you for a possession. I am the LORD.'" 9Moses spoke thus to the people of Israel; but they did not listen to Moses, because of their broken spirit and their cruel bondage.

10 And the LORD said to Moses, 11"Go in, tell Pharaoh king of Egypt to let the people of Israel go out of his land." 12But Moses said to the LORD, "Behold, the people of Israel have not listened to me; how then shall Pharaoh listen to me, who am a man of uncircumcised lips?" 13But the LORD spoke to Moses and Aaron, and gave them a charge to the people of Israel and to Pharaoh king of Egypt to bring the people of Israel out of the land of Egypt.

THE GENEALOGY OF MOSES AND AARON

14 These are the heads of their fathers' houses: the sons of Reuben, the first-born of Israel: Hanoch, Pallu, Hezron, and Carmi; these are the families of Reuben. 15The sons of Simeon: Jemu'el, Jamin, Ohad, Jachin, Zohar, and Shaul, the son of a Canaanite woman; these are the families of Simeon. 16These are the names of the sons of Levi according to their generations: Gershon, Kohath, and Merar'i, the years of the life of Levi being a hundred and thirty-seven years. 17The *sons of Gershon: Libni* and Shim'e-i, by their families. 18The sons of Kohath: Amram, Izhar, Hebron, and Uz'ziel, the years of the life of Kohath being a hundred and thirty-three years. 19The sons of Merar'i: Mahli and Mushi. These are the families of the Levites according to their generations. 20Amram took to wife Joch'ebed his father's sister and she bore him Aaron and Moses, the years of the life of Amram being one hundred and thirty-seven years. 21The sons of Izhar: Korah, Nepheg, and Zichri. 22And the sons of Uz'ziel: Mi'shael, Elza'phan, and Sithri. 23Aaron took to wife Eli'sheba, the daughter of Ammin'adab and the sister of Nahshon; and she bore him Nadab, Abi'hu, Elea'zar, and Ith'amar. 24The sons of Korah: Assir, Elka'nah, and Abi'asaph; these are the families of the Ko'rahites. 25Elea'zar, Aaron's son, took to wife one of the daughters of Pu'ti-el; and she bore him Phin'ehas. These are the heads of the fathers' houses of the Levites by their families.

26 These are the Aaron and Moses to whom the LORD said: "Bring out the people of Israel from the land of Egypt by their hosts." 27It was they who spoke to Pharaoh king of Egypt about bringing out the people of Israel from Egypt, this Moses and this Aaron.

MOSES AND AARON OBEY GOD'S COMMANDS

28 On the day when the LORD spoke to Moses in the land of Egypt, 29the LORD said to Moses, "I am the LORD; tell Pharaoh king of Egypt all that I say to you." 30But Moses said to the LORD, "Behold, I am of uncircumcised lips; how then shall Pharaoh listen to me?"

7 And the LORD said to Moses, "See, I make you as God to Pharaoh; and Aaron your brother shall be your prophet. 2You shall speak all that I command you; and Aaron your brother shall tell Pharaoh to let the people of Israel go out of his land. 3But I will harden Pharaoh's heart, and though I multiply my signs and wonders in the land of Egypt, 4Pharaoh will not listen to you; then I will lay my hand upon Egypt and bring forth my hosts, my people the sons of Israel, out of the land of Egypt by great acts of judgment. 5And the Egyptians shall know that I am the LORD, when I stretch forth my hand upon Egypt and bring out the people of Israel from among them." 6 And Moses and Aaron did so; they did as the LORD commanded them. 7 Now Moses was eighty years old, and Aaron eighty-three years old, when they spoke to Pharaoh.

AARON'S MIRACULOUS ROD

8 And the LORD said to Moses and Aaron, 9 "When Pharaoh says to you, 'Prove yourselves by working a miracle,' then you shall say to Aaron, 'Take your rod and cast it down before Pharaoh, that it may become a serpent.'" 10 So Moses and Aaron went to Pharaoh and did as the LORD commanded; Aaron cast down his rod before Pharaoh and his servants, and it became a serpent. 11 Then Pharaoh summoned the wise men and the sorcerers; and they also, the magicians of Egypt, did the same by their secret arts. 12 For every man cast down his rod, and they became serpents. But Aaron's rod swallowed up their rods. 13 Still Pharaoh's heart was hardened, and he would not listen to them; as the LORD had said.

THE FIRST PLAGUE: WATER TURNED TO BLOOD

14 *Then the LORD said to Moses, "Pharaoh's heart is hardened, he refuses to let the people go. 15 Go to Pharaoh in the morning, as he is going out to the water; wait for him by the river's brink, and take in your hand the rod which was turned into a serpent. 16 And you shall say to him, 'The LORD, the God of the Hebrews, sent me to you, saying, "Let my people go, that they may serve me in the wilderness; and behold, you have not yet obeyed." 17 Thus says the LORD, "By this you shall know that I am the LORD: behold, I will strike the water that is in the Nile with the rod that is in my hand, and it shall be turned to blood, 18 and the fish in the Nile shall die, and the Nile shall become foul, and the Egyptians will loathe to drink water from the Nile."'" 19 And the LORD said to Moses, "Say to Aaron, 'Take your rod and stretch out your hand over the waters of Egypt, over their rivers, their canals, and their ponds, and all their pools of water, that they may become blood; and there shall be blood throughout all the land of Egypt, both in vessels of wood and in vessels of stone.'"

20 Moses and Aaron did as the LORD commanded; in the sight of Pharaoh and in the sight of his servants, he lifted up the rod and struck the water that was in the Nile, and all the water that was in the Nile turned to blood. 21 And the fish in the Nile died; and the Nile became foul, so that the Egyptians could not drink water from the Nile; and there was blood throughout all the land of Egypt. 22 But the magicians of Egypt did the same by their secret arts; so Pharaoh's heart remained hardened, and he would not listen to them; as the LORD had said. 23 Pharaoh turned and went into his house, and he did not lay even this to heart. 24 And all the Egyptians dug round about the Nile for water to drink, for they could not drink the water of the Nile.

THE SECOND PLAGUE: FROGS

25 Seven days passed after the LORD had struck the Nile.

8[a] Then the LORD said to Moses, "Go in to Pharaoh and say to him, 'Thus says the LORD, "Let my people go, that they may serve me. 2 But if you refuse to let them go, behold, I will plague all your country with frogs; 3 the Nile shall swarm with frogs which shall come up into your house, and into your bedchamber and on your bed, and into the houses of your servants and of your people,[b] and into your ovens and your

[a] Ch 7.26 in Heb
[b] Gk: Heb *upon your people*

kneading bowls; 4the frogs shall come
up on you and on your people and on
all your servants.'"" 5[c] And the LORD
said to Moses, "Say to Aaron, 'Stretch
out your hand with your rod over
the rivers, over the canals, and over
the pools, and cause frogs to come
upon the land of Egypt!'" 6So Aaron
stretched out his hand over the waters
of Egypt; and the frogs came up and
covered the land of Egypt. 7But the
magicians did the same by their secret
arts, and brought frogs upon the land
of Egypt.

8 Then Pharaoh called Moses and
Aaron, and said, "Entreat the LORD to
take away the frogs from me and from
my people; and I will let the people
go to sacrifice to the LORD." 9Moses
said to Pharaoh, "Be pleased to com-
mand me when I am to entreat, for
you and for your servants and for your
people, that the frogs be destroyed
from you and your houses and be
left only in the Nile." 10And he said,
"Tomorrow." Moses said, "Be it as you
say, that you may know that there is
no one like the LORD our God. 11The
frogs shall depart from you and your
houses and your servants and your
people; they shall be left only in the
Nile." 12So Moses and Aaron went out
from Pharaoh; and Moses cried to the
LORD concerning the frogs, as he had
agreed with Pharaoh.[d] 13And the LORD
did according to the word of Moses;
the frogs died out of the houses and
courtyards and out of the fields.
14And they gathered them together in
heaps, and the land stank. 15But when
Pharaoh saw that there was a respite,
he hardened his heart, and would not
listen to them; as the LORD had said.

THE THIRD PLAGUE: GNATS

16 Then the LORD said to Moses,
"Say to Aaron, 'Stretch out your rod
and strike the dust of the earth, that
it may become gnats throughout all
the land of Egypt.'" 17And they did
so; Aaron stretched out his hand with
his rod, and struck the dust of the
earth, and there came gnats on man
and beast; all the dust of the earth be-
came gnats throughout all the land of
Egypt. 18The magicians tried by their
secret arts to bring forth gnats, but
they could not. So there were gnats on
man and beast. 19And the magicians
said to Pharaoh, "This is the finger of
God." But Pharaoh's heart was hard-
ened, and he would not listen to them;
as the LORD had said.

THE FOURTH PLAGUE: FLIES

20 Then the LORD said to Moses,
"Rise up early in the morning and
wait for Pharaoh, as he goes out to
the water, and say to him, 'Thus says
the LORD, "Let my people go, that
they may serve me. 21Else, if you will
not let my people go, behold, I will
send swarms of flies on you and your
servants and your people, and into
your houses; and the houses of the
Egyptians shall be filled with swarms
of flies, and also the ground on which
they stand. 22But on that day I will set
apart the land of Goshen, where my
people dwell, so that no swarms of
flies shall be there; that you may know
that I am the LORD in the midst of
the earth. 23Thus I will put a division[e]
between my people and your people.
By tomorrow shall this sign be."'"
24And the LORD did so; there came
great swarms of flies into the house of
Pharaoh and into his servants' houses,
and in all the land of Egypt the land
was ruined by reason of the flies.

25 Then Pharaoh called Moses and
Aaron, and said, "Go, sacrifice to your
God within the land." 26But Moses
said, "It would not be right to do so;
for we shall sacrifice to the LORD
our God offerings abominable to the
Egyptians. If we sacrifice offerings
abominable to the Egyptians before
their eyes, will they not stone us? 27We
must go three days' journey into the

[c] Ch 8.1 in Heb
[d] Or *which he had brought upon Pharaoh*
[e] Gk Vg: Heb *set redemption*

wilderness and sacrifice to the LORD
our God as he will command us."
28So Pharaoh said, "I will let you go,
to sacrifice to the LORD your God in
the wilderness; only you shall not go
very far away. Make entreaty for me."
29Then Moses said, "Behold, I am go-
ing out from you and I will pray to the
LORD that the swarms of flies may de-
part from Pharaoh, from his servants,
and from his people, tomorrow; only
let not Pharaoh deal falsely again by
not letting the people go to sacrifice
to the LORD." 30So Moses went out
from Pharaoh and prayed to the LORD.
31And the LORD did as Moses asked,
and removed the swarms of flies from
Pharaoh, from his servants, and from
his people; not one remained. 32But
Pharaoh hardened his heart this time
also, and did not let the people go.

THE FIFTH PLAGUE: LIVESTOCK DISEASED

9 Then the LORD said to Moses,
"Go in to Pharaoh, and say to him,
'Thus says the LORD, the God of the
Hebrews, "Let my people go, that they
may serve me. 2For if you refuse to let
them go and still hold them, 3behold,
the hand of the LORD will fall with a
very severe plague upon your cattle
which are in the field, the horses, the
asses, the camels, the herds, and the
flocks. 4But the LORD will make a dis-
tinction between the cattle of Israel
and the cattle of Egypt, so that noth-
ing shall die of all that belongs to the
people of Israel."'" 5And the LORD set
a time, saying, "Tomorrow the LORD
will do this thing in the land." 6And
on the morrow the LORD did this
thing; all the cattle of the Egyptians
died, but of the cattle of the people
of Israel not one died. 7And Pharaoh
sent, and behold, not one of the cat-
tle of the Israelites was dead. But the
heart of Pharaoh was hardened, and
he did not let the people go.

THE SIXTH PLAGUE: BOILS

8 And the LORD said to Moses and
Aaron, "Take handfuls of ashes from
the kiln, and let Moses throw them to-
ward heaven in the sight of Pharaoh.
9And it shall become fine dust over
all the land of Egypt, and become
boils breaking out in sores on man
and beast throughout all the land of
Egypt." 10So they took ashes from the
kiln, and stood before Pharaoh, and
Moses threw them toward heaven,
and it became boils breaking out in
sores on man and beast. 11And the ma-
gicians could not stand before Moses
because of the boils, for the boils were
upon the magicians and upon all the
Egyptians. 12But the LORD hardened
the heart of Pharaoh, and he did not
listen to them; as the LORD had spo-
ken to Moses.

THE SEVENTH PLAGUE: THUNDER AND HAIL

13 Then the LORD said to Moses,
"Rise up early in the morning and
stand before Pharaoh, and say to him,
'Thus says the LORD, the God of the
Hebrews, "Let my people go, that they
may serve me. 14For this time I will
send all my plagues upon your heart,
and upon your servants and your peo-
ple, that you may know that there is
none like me in all the earth. 15For by
now I could have put forth my hand
and struck you and your people with
pestilence, and you would have been
cut off from the earth; 16but for this
purpose have I let you live, to show
you my power, so that my name may
be declared throughout all the earth.
17You are still exalting yourself against
my people, and will not let them go.
18Behold, tomorrow about this time I
will cause very heavy hail to fall, such
as never has been in Egypt from the
day it was founded until now. 19Now
therefore send, get your cattle and
all that you have in the field into safe
shelter; for the hail shall come down
upon every man and beast that is in
the field and is not brought home, and
they shall die."'" 20Then he who feared
the word of the LORD among the ser-
vants of Pharaoh made his slaves and
his cattle flee into the houses; 21but he

who did not regard the word of the
LORD left his slaves and his cattle in
the field.
22 And the LORD said to Moses,
"Stretch forth your hand toward heav-
en, that there may be hail in all the
land of Egypt, upon man and beast
and every plant of the field, through-
out the land of Egypt." 23 Then Moses
stretched forth his rod toward heaven;
and the LORD sent thunder and hail,
and fire ran down to the earth. And
the LORD rained hail upon the land
of Egypt; 24 there was hail, and fire
flashing continually in the midst of
the hail, very heavy hail, such as had
never been in all the land of Egypt
since it became a nation. 25 The hail
struck down everything that was in
the field throughout all the land of
Egypt, both man and beast; and the
hail struck down every plant of the
field, and shattered every tree of the
field. 26 Only in the land of Goshen,
where the people of Israel were, there
was no hail.
27 Then Pharaoh sent, and called
Moses and Aaron, and said to them,
"I have sinned this time; the LORD is
in the right, and I and my people are
in the wrong. 28 Entreat the LORD; for
there has been enough of this thun-
der and hail; I will let you go, and you
shall stay no longer." 29 Moses said to
him, "As soon as I have gone out of
the city, I will stretch out my hands
to the LORD; the thunder will cease,
and there will be no more hail, that
you may know that the earth is the
LORD's. 30 But as for you and your
servants, I know that you do not yet
fear the LORD God." 31 (The flax and
the barley were ruined, for the barley
was in the ear and the flax was in bud.
32 But the wheat and the spelt were not
ruined, for they are late in coming up.)
33 So Moses went out of the city from
Pharaoh, and stretched out his hands
to the LORD; and the thunder and the
hail ceased, and the rain no longer
poured upon the earth. 34 But when
Pharaoh saw that the rain and the hail
and the thunder had ceased, he sinned
yet again, and hardened his heart, he
and his servants. 35 So the heart of
Pharaoh was hardened, and he did not
let the people of Israel go; as the LORD
had spoken through Moses.

THE EIGHTH PLAGUE: LOCUSTS

10 Then the LORD said to Moses, "Go
in to Pharaoh; for I have hardened
his heart and the heart of his ser-
vants, that I may show these signs of
mine among them, 2 and that you may
tell in the hearing of your son and of
your son's son how I have made sport
of the Egyptians and what signs I have
done among them; that you may know
that I am the LORD."
3 So Moses and Aaron went in to
Pharaoh, and said to him, "Thus says
the LORD, the God of the Hebrews,
'How long will you refuse to humble
yourself before me? Let my people go,
that they may serve me. 4 For if you
refuse to let my people go, behold, to-
morrow I will bring locusts into your
country, 5 and they shall cover the face
of the land, so that no one can see the
land; and they shall eat what is left to
you after the hail, and they shall eat
every tree of yours which grows in the
field, 6 and they shall fill your houses,
and the houses of all your servants
and of all the Egyptians; as neither
your fathers nor your grandfathers
have seen, from the day they came on
earth to this day.'" Then he turned
and went out from Pharaoh.
7 And Pharaoh's servants said to
him, "How long shall this man be a
snare to us? Let the men go, that they
may serve the LORD their God; do
you not yet understand that Egypt is
ruined?" 8 So Moses and Aaron were
brought back to Pharaoh; and he said
to them, "Go, serve the LORD your
God; but who are to go?" 9 And Moses
said, "We will go with our young and
our old; we will go with our sons
and daughters and with our flocks
and herds, for we must hold a feast
to the LORD." 10 And he said to them,

"The Lord be with you, if ever I let
you and your little ones go! Look, you
have some evil purpose in mind.[a] 11No!
Go, the men among you, and serve
the Lord, for that is what you de-
sire." And they were driven out from
Pharaoh's presence.

12 Then the Lord said to Moses,
"Stretch out your hand over the land
of Egypt for the locusts, that they may
come upon the land of Egypt, and eat
every plant in the land, all that the
hail has left." 13So Moses stretched
forth his rod over the land of Egypt,
and the Lord brought an east wind
upon the land all that day and all that
night; and when it was morning the
east wind had brought the locusts.
14And the locusts came up over all
the land of Egypt, and settled on the
whole country of Egypt, such a dense
swarm of locusts as had never been
before, nor ever shall be again. 15For
they covered the face of the whole
land, so that the land was darkened,
and they ate all the plants in the land
and all the fruit of the trees which
the hail had left; not a green thing
remained, neither tree nor plant of
the field, through all the land of
Egypt. 16Then Pharaoh called Moses
and Aaron in haste, and said, "I have
sinned against the Lord your God,
and against you. 17Now therefore, for-
give my sin, I pray you, only this once,
and entreat the Lord your God only
to remove this death from me." 18So he
went out from Pharaoh, and entreat-
ed the Lord. 19And the Lord turned
a very strong west wind, which lifted
the locusts and drove them into the
Red Sea; not a single locust was left
in all the country of Egypt. 20But the
Lord hardened Pharaoh's heart, and
he did not let the children of Israel go.

THE NINTH PLAGUE: DARKNESS

21 Then the Lord said to Moses,
"Stretch out your hand toward heaven
that there may be darkness over the
land of Egypt, a darkness to be felt."
22So Moses stretched out his hand
toward heaven, and there was thick
darkness in all the land of Egypt three
days; 23they did not see one another,
nor did any rise from his place for
three days; but all the people of Israel
had light where they dwelt. 24Then
Pharaoh called Moses, and said, "Go,
serve the Lord; your children also
may go with you; only let your flocks
and your herds remain behind." 25But
Moses said, "You must also let us
have sacrifices and burnt offerings,
that we may sacrifice to the Lord our
God. 26Our cattle also must go with us;
not a hoof shall be left behind, for we
must take of them to serve the Lord
our God, and we do not know with
what we must serve the Lord until
we arrive there." 27But the Lord hard-
ened Pharaoh's heart, and he would
not let them go. 28Then Pharaoh said
to him, "Get away from me; take heed
to yourself; never see my face again;
for in the day you see my face you
shall die." 29Moses said, "As you say! I
will not see your face again."

WARNING OF THE FINAL PLAGUE

11 The Lord said to Moses, "Yet
one plague more I will bring upon
Pharaoh and upon Egypt; afterwards
he will let you go hence; when he lets
you go, he will drive you away com-
pletely. 2Speak now in the hearing of
the people, that they ask, every man
of his neighbor and every woman of
her neighbor, jewelry of silver and of
gold." 3And the Lord gave the people
favor in the sight of the Egyptians.
Moreover, the man Moses was very
great in the land of Egypt, in the sight
of Pharaoh's servants and in the sight
of the people.

4 And Moses said, "Thus says the
Lord: About midnight I will go forth
in the midst of Egypt; 5and all the
first-born in the land of Egypt shall
die, from the first-born of Pharaoh
who sits upon his throne, even to the
first-born of the maidservant who is

[a]Heb *before your face*

behind the mill; and all the first-born
of the cattle. 6And there shall be a
great cry throughout all the land of
Egypt, such as there has never been,
nor ever shall be again. 7But against
any of the people of Israel, either man
or beast, not a dog shall growl; that
you may know that the LORD makes a
distinction between the Egyptians and
Israel. 8And all these your servants
shall come down to me, and bow down
to me, saying, 'Get you out, and all the
people who follow you.' And after that
I will go out." And he went out from
Pharaoh in hot anger. 9Then the LORD
said to Moses, "Pharaoh will not listen
to you; that my wonders may be multi-
plied in the land of Egypt."

10 Moses and Aaron did all these
wonders before Pharaoh; and the
LORD hardened Pharaoh's heart, and
he did not let the people of Israel go
out of his land.

THE FIRST PASSOVER INSTITUTED

12 *The LORD said to Moses and
Aaron in the land of Egypt, 2"This
month shall be for you the beginning
of months; it shall be the first month
of the year for you. 3Tell all the con-
gregation of Israel that on the tenth
day of this month they shall take ev-
ery man a lamb according to their fa-
thers' houses, a lamb for a household;
4and if the household is too small for
a lamb, then a man and his neighbor
next to his house shall take according
to the number of persons; according
to what each can eat you shall make
your count for the lamb. 5Your lamb
shall be without blemish, a male a
year old; you shall take it from the
sheep or from the goats; 6and you
shall keep it until the fourteenth day
of this month, when the whole assem-
bly of the congregation of Israel shall
kill their lambs in the evening.[b] 7Then
they shall take some of the blood, and
put it on the two doorposts and the
lintel of the houses in which they eat
them. 8They shall eat the flesh that
night, roasted; with unleavened bread
and bitter herbs they shall eat it. 9Do
not eat any of it raw or boiled with wa-
ter, but roasted, its head with its legs
and its inner parts. 10And you shall let
none of it remain until the morning,
anything that remains until the morn-
ing you shall burn. 11In this manner
you shall eat it: your loins girded, your
sandals on your feet, and your staff
in your hand; and you shall eat it in
haste. It is the LORD's passover. 12For
I will pass through the land of Egypt
that night, and I will smite all the
first-born in the land of Egypt, both
man and beast; and on all the gods of
Egypt I will execute judgments: I am
the LORD. 13The blood shall be a sign
for you, upon the houses where you
are; and when I see the blood, I will
pass over you, and no plague shall fall
upon you to destroy you, when I smite
the land of Egypt.

14 "This day shall be for you a me-
morial day, and you shall keep it as a
feast to the LORD; throughout your
generations you shall observe it as
an ordinance for ever. 15Seven days
you shall eat unleavened bread; on
the first day you shall put away leav-
en out of your houses, for if any one
eats what is leavened, from the first
day until the seventh day, that per-
son shall be cut off from Israel. 16On
the first day you shall hold a holy
assembly, and on the seventh day a
holy assembly; no work shall be done
on those days; but what every one
must eat, that only may be prepared
by you. 17And you shall observe the
feast of unleavened bread, for on this
very day I brought your hosts out of
the land of Egypt: therefore you shall
observe this day, throughout your
generations, as an ordinance for ever.
18In the first month, on the fourteenth
day of the month at evening, you shall
eat unleavened bread, and so until the
twenty-first day of the month at eve-
ning. 19For seven days no leaven shall
be found in your houses; for if any

[b]Heb *between the two evenings*

one eats what is leavened, that person
shall be cut off from the congregation
of Israel, whether he is a sojourner
or a native of the land. 20You shall eat
nothing leavened; in all your dwell-
ings you shall eat unleavened bread."

21 Then Moses called all the elders
of Israel, and said to them, "Select
lambs for yourselves according to your
families, and kill the passover lamb.
22Take a bunch of hyssop and dip it in
the blood which is in the basin, and
touch the lintel and the two doorposts
with the blood which is in the basin;
and none of you shall go out of the
door of his house until the morning.
23For the LORD will pass through to
slay the Egyptians; and when he sees
the blood on the lintel and on the two
doorposts, the LORD will pass over
the door, and will not allow the de-
stroyer to enter your houses to slay
you. 24You shall observe this rite as an
ordinance for you and for your sons
for ever. 25And when you come to the
land which the LORD will give you, as
he has promised, you shall keep this
service. 26And when your children say
to you, 'What do you mean by this ser-
vice?' 27you shall say, 'It is the sacrifice
of the LORD'S passover, for he passed
over the houses of the people of Israel
in Egypt, when he slew the Egyptians
but spared our houses.'" And the peo-
ple bowed their heads and worshiped.

28 Then the people of Israel went
and did so; as the LORD had com-
manded Moses and Aaron, so they did.

THE TENTH PLAGUE: DEATH OF THE FIRSTBORN

29 At midnight the LORD smote
all the first-born in the land of Egypt,
from the first-born of Pharaoh who sat
on his throne to the first-born of the
captive who was in the dungeon, and
all the first-born of the cattle. 30And
Pharaoh rose up in the night, he, and
all his servants, and all the Egyptians;
and there was a great cry in Egypt, for
there was not a house where one was
not dead. 31And he summoned Moses
and Aaron by night, and said, "Rise
up, go forth from among my people,
both you and the people of Israel; and
go, serve the LORD, as you have said.
32Take your flocks and your herds, as
you have said, and be gone; and bless
me also!"

THE EXODUS: FROM RAMESES TO SUCCOTH

33 And the Egyptians were urgent
with the people, to send them out of
the land in haste; for they said, "We
are all dead men." 34So the people took
their dough before it was leavened,
their kneading bowls being bound up
in their mantles on their shoulders.
35The people of Israel had also done as
Moses told them, for they had asked
of the Egyptians jewelry of silver and
of gold, and clothing; 36and the LORD
had given the people favor in the sight
of the Egyptians, so that they let them
have what they asked. Thus they de-
spoiled the Egyptians.

37 And the people of Israel jour-
neyed from Ram′eses to Succoth,
about six hundred thousand men on
foot, besides women and children. 38A
mixed multitude also went up with
them, and very many cattle, both
flocks and herds. 39And they baked
unleavened cakes of the dough which
they had brought out of Egypt, for it
was not leavened, because they were
thrust out of Egypt and could not
tarry, neither had they prepared for
themselves any provisions.

40 The time that the people of Israel
dwelt in Egypt was four hundred and
thirty years. 41And at the end of four
hundred and thirty years, on that very
day, all the hosts of the LORD went
out from the land of Egypt. 42It was
a night of watching by the LORD, to
bring them out of the land of Egypt; so
this same night is a night of watching
kept to the LORD by all the people of
Israel throughout their generations.

DIRECTIONS FOR THE PASSOVER

43 And the LORD said to Moses
and Aaron, "This is the ordinance of

the passover: no foreigner shall eat
of it; 44but every slave that is bought
for money may eat of it after you have
circumcised him. 45No sojourner or
hired servant may eat of it. 46In one
house shall it be eaten; you shall not
carry forth any of the flesh outside the
house; and you shall not break a bone
of it. 47All the congregation of Israel
shall keep it. 48And when a strang-
er shall sojourn with you and would
keep the passover to the LORD, let all
his males be circumcised, then he may
come near and keep it; he shall be as
a native of the land. But no uncircum-
cised person shall eat of it. 49There
shall be one law for the native and
for the stranger who sojourns among
you."

50 Thus did all the people of Israel;
as the LORD commanded Moses and
Aaron, so they did. 51And on that very
day the LORD brought the people of
Israel out of the land of Egypt by their
hosts.

13 The LORD said to Moses, 2"Con-
secrate to me all the first-born;
whatever is the first to open the womb
among the people of Israel, both of
man and of beast, is mine."

THE FESTIVAL OF UNLEAVENED BREAD

3 And Moses said to the peo-
ple, "Remember this day, in which
you came out from Egypt, out of the
house of bondage, for by strength
of hand the LORD brought you out
from this place; no leavened bread
shall be eaten. 4This day you are to
go forth, in the month of Abib. 5*And*
when the LORD brings you into the
land of the Canaanites, the Hittites,
the Amorites, the Hivites, and the
Jeb´usites, which he swore to your fa-
thers to give you, a land flowing with
milk and honey, you shall keep this
service in this month. 6Seven days you
shall eat unleavened bread, and on
the seventh day there shall be a feast
to the LORD. 7Unleavened bread shall
be eaten for seven days; no leavened
bread shall be seen with you, and no
leaven shall be seen with you in all
your territory. 8And you shall tell your
son on that day, 'It is because of what
the LORD did for me when I came out
of Egypt.' 9And it shall be to you as a
sign on your hand and as a memorial
between your eyes, that the law of the
LORD may be in your mouth; for with
a strong hand the LORD has brought
you out of Egypt. 10You shall therefore
keep this ordinance at its appointed
time from year to year.

THE CONSECRATION OF THE FIRSTBORN

11 "And when the LORD brings
you into the land of the Canaanites,
as he swore to you and your fathers,
and shall give it to you, 12you shall
set apart to the LORD all that first
opens the womb. All the firstlings of
your cattle that are males shall be the
LORD's. 13Every firstling of an ass you
shall redeem with a lamb, or if you
will not redeem it you shall break its
neck. Every first-born of man among
your sons you shall redeem. 14And
when in time to come your son asks
you, 'What does this mean?' you shall
say to him, 'By strength of hand the
LORD brought us out of Egypt, from
the house of bondage. 15For when
Pharaoh stubbornly refused to let us
go, the LORD slew all the first-born in
the land of Egypt, both the first-born
of man and the first-born of cattle.
Therefore I sacrifice to the LORD all
the males that first open the womb;
but all the first-born of my sons I re-
deem.' 16It shall be as a mark on your
hand or frontlets between your eyes;
for by a strong hand the LORD brought
us out of Egypt."

THE PILLARS OF CLOUD AND FIRE

17 When Pharaoh let the people go,
God did not lead them by way of the
land of the Philistines, although that
was near; for God said, "Lest the peo-
ple repent when they see war, and re-
turn to Egypt." 18But God led the peo-
ple round by the way of the wilderness

toward the Red Sea. And the people of
Israel went up out of the land of Egypt
equipped for battle. 19And Moses took
the bones of Joseph with him; for
Joseph had solemnly sworn the people
of Israel, saying, "God will visit you;
then you must carry my bones with
you from here." 20And they moved
on from Succoth, and encamped at
Etham, on the edge of the wilderness.
21And the LORD went before them by
day in a pillar of cloud to lead them
along the way, and by night in a pil-
lar of fire to give them light, that they
might travel by day and by night; 22the
pillar of cloud by day and the pillar of
fire by night did not depart from be-
fore the people.

Crossing the Red Sea

14 Then the LORD said to Moses,
2"Tell the people of Israel to turn
back and encamp in front of Pi-ha-
hi´roth, between Migdol and the sea,
in front of Ba´al-zephon; you shall
encamp over against it, by the sea.
3For Pharaoh will say of the people
of Israel, 'They are entangled in the
land; the wilderness has shut them
in.' 4And I will harden Pharaoh's
heart, and he will pursue them and I
will get glory over Pharaoh and all his
host; and the Egyptians shall know
that I am the LORD." And they did so.

5 When the king of Egypt was told
that the people had fled, the mind
of Pharaoh and his servants was
changed toward the people, and they
said, "What is this we have done, that
we have let Israel go from serving us?"
6So he made ready his chariot and took
his army with him, 7and took six hun-
dred picked chariots and all the other
chariots of Egypt with officers over all
of them. 8And the LORD hardened the
heart of Pharaoh king of Egypt and he
pursued *the people of Israel* as they
went forth defiantly. 9The Egyptians
pursued them, all Pharaoh's horses
and chariots and his horsemen and his
army, and overtook them encamped at
the sea, by Pi-ha-hi´roth, in front of
Ba´al-zephon.

10 When Pharaoh drew near, the
people of Israel lifted up their eyes,
and behold, the Egyptians were
marching after them; and they were
in great fear. And the people of Israel
cried out to the LORD; 11and they said
to Moses, "Is it because there are no
graves in Egypt that you have tak-
en us away to die in the wilderness?
What have you done to us, in bring-
ing us out of Egypt? 12Is not this what
we said to you in Egypt, 'Let us alone
and let us serve the Egyptians'? For
it would have been better for us to
serve the Egyptians than to die in
the wilderness." 13And Moses said to
the people, "Fear not, stand firm, and
see the salvation of the LORD, which
he will work for you today; for the
Egyptians whom you see today, you
shall never see again. 14The LORD will
fight for you, and you have only to be
still." 15The LORD said to Moses, "Why
do you cry to me? Tell the people of
Israel to go forward. 16Lift up your rod,
and stretch out your hand over the sea
and divide it, that the people of Israel
may go on dry ground through the
sea. 17And I will harden the hearts of
the Egyptians so that they shall go in
after them, and I will get glory over
Pharaoh and all his host, his chariots,
and his horsemen. 18And the Egyptians
shall know that I am the LORD, when
I have gotten glory over Pharaoh, his
chariots, and his horsemen."

19 Then the angel of God who
went before the host of Israel moved
and went behind them; and the pil-
lar of cloud moved from before them
and stood behind them, 20coming be-
tween the host of Egypt and the host
of Israel. And there was the cloud and
the darkness; and the night passed[a]
without one coming near the other all
night.

21 Then Moses stretched out his
hand over the sea; and the LORD drove
the sea back by a strong east wind all

[a] Gk: Heb *and it lit up the night*

night, and made the sea dry land, and
the waters were divided. 22And the
people of Israel went into the midst of
the sea on dry ground, the waters be-
ing a wall to them on their right hand
and on their left. 23The Egyptians pur-
sued, and went in after them into the
midst of the sea, all Pharaoh's horses,
his chariots, and his horsemen. 24And
in the morning watch the LORD in the
pillar of fire and of cloud looked down
upon the host of the Egyptians, and
discomfited the host of the Egyptians,
25clogging[b] their chariot wheels so that
they drove heavily; and the Egyptians
said, "Let us flee from before Israel;
for the LORD fights for them against
the Egyptians."

THE PURSUERS DROWNED

26 Then the LORD said to Moses,
"Stretch out your hand over the sea,
that the water may come back upon
the Egyptians, upon their chari-
ots, and upon their horsemen." 27So
Moses stretched forth his hand over
the sea, and the sea returned to
its wonted flow when the morning
appeared; and the Egyptians fled
into it, and the LORD routed[c] the
Egyptians in the midst of the sea.
28The waters returned and covered
the chariots and the horsemen and
all the host[d] of Pharaoh that had
followed them into the sea; not so
much as one of them remained. 29But
the people of Israel walked on dry
ground through the sea, the waters
being a wall to them on their right
hand and on their left.

30 Thus the LORD saved Israel that
day from the hand of the Egyptians;
and Israel saw the Egyptians dead
upon the seashore. 31And Israel saw
the great work which the LORD did
against the Egyptians, and the peo-
ple feared the LORD; and they be-
lieved in the LORD and in his servant
Moses.

[b]Or *binding*. Sam Gk Syr: Heb *removing*
[c]Heb *shook off*
[d]Gk Syr: Heb *to all the host*
[e]Or *its chariot*

THE SONG OF MOSES

15 Then Moses and the people of
Israel sang this song to the LORD,
saying,

"I will sing to the LORD, for
he has triumphed
gloriously;
the horse and his rider[e] he
has thrown into the
sea.
2The LORD is my strength and my
song,
and he has become my
salvation;
this is my God, and I will
praise him,
my father's God, and I will
exalt him.
3The LORD is a man of war;
the LORD is his name.
4"Pharaoh's chariots and his host
he cast into the sea;
and his picked officers are
sunk in the Red Sea.
5The floods cover them;
they went down into the
depths like a stone.
6Thy right hand, O LORD, glorious
in power,
thy right hand, O LORD,
shatters the enemy.
7In the greatness of thy majesty
thou overthrowest thy
adversaries;
thou sendest forth thy fury,
it consumes them like
stubble.
8At the blast of thy nostrils the
waters piled up,
the floods stood up in a
heap;
the deeps congealed in the
heart of the sea.
9The enemy said, 'I will pursue, I
will overtake,
I will divide the spoil, my
desire shall have its
fill of them.
I will draw my sword, my

hand shall destroy
them.'
10Thou didst blow with thy wind,
the sea covered them;
they sank as lead in the
mighty waters.
11"Who is like thee, O LORD,
among the gods?
Who is like thee, majestic in
holiness,
terrible in glorious deeds,
doing wonders?
12Thou didst stretch out thy right
hand,
the earth swallowed them.
13"Thou hast led in thy steadfast
love the people whom thou
hast redeemed,
thou hast guided them by
thy strength to thy
holy abode.
14The peoples have heard, they
tremble;
pangs have seized on the in-
habitants of Philistia.
15Now are the chiefs of Edom
dismayed;
the leaders of Moab, trem-
bling seizes them;
all the inhabitants of Canaan
have melted away.
16Terror and dread fall upon them;
because of the greatness of
thy arm, they are as
still as a stone,
till thy people, O LORD,
pass by,
till the people pass by whom
thou hast purchased.
17Thou wilt bring them in, and
plant them on thy own
mountain,
the place, O LORD, which
thou hast made for
thy abode,
the sanctuary, O LORD,
which thy hands have
established
18The LORD will reign for ever and
ever."

THE SONG OF MIRIAM

19 For when the horses of Pharaoh
with his chariots and his horsemen
went into the sea, the LORD brought
back the waters of the sea upon them;
but the people of Israel walked on dry
ground in the midst of the sea. 20Then
Miriam, the prophetess, the sister of
Aaron, took a timbrel in her hand; and
all the women went out after her with
timbrels and dancing. 21And Miriam
sang to them:

"Sing to the LORD, for he has
triumphed gloriously;
the horse and his rider he has
thrown into the sea."

BITTER WATER MADE SWEET

22 Then Moses led Israel onward
from the Red Sea, and they went into
the wilderness of Shur; they went
three days in the wilderness and found
no water. 23When they came to Marah,
they could not drink the water of
Marah because it was bitter; therefore
it was named Marah.[a] 24And the peo-
ple murmured against Moses, saying,
"What shall we drink?" 25And he cried
to the LORD; and the LORD showed
him a tree, and he threw it into the
water, and the water became sweet.

There the LORD[b] made for them a
statute and an ordinance and there he
proved them, 26saying, "If you will dili-
gently hearken to the voice of the LORD
your God, and do that which is right
in his eyes, and give heed to his com-
mandments and keep all his statutes, I
will put none of the diseases upon you
which I put upon the Egyptians; for I
am the LORD, your healer."

27 Then they came to Elim, where
there were twelve springs of water
and seventy palm trees; and they en-
camped there by the water.

BREAD FROM HEAVEN

16They set out from Elim, and all
the congregation of the people of
Israel came to the wilderness of Sin,

[a]That is *Bitterness*
[b]Heb *he*

which is between Elim and Sinai, on
the fifteenth day of the second month
after they had departed from the land
of Egypt. 2And the whole congrega-
tion of the people of Israel murmured
against Moses and Aaron in the wil-
derness, 3and said to them, "Would
that we had died by the hand of the
LORD in the land of Egypt, when we
sat by the fleshpots and ate bread to
the full; for you have brought us out
into this wilderness to kill this whole
assembly with hunger."

4 Then the LORD said to Moses,
"Behold, I will rain bread from heav-
en for you; and the people shall go
out and gather a day's portion every
day, that I may prove them, whether
they will walk in my law or not. 5On
the sixth day, when they prepare what
they bring in, it will be twice as much
as they gather daily." 6So Moses and
Aaron said to all the people of Israel,
"At evening you shall know that it was
the LORD who brought you out of the
land of Egypt, 7and in the morning you
shall see the glory of the LORD, be-
cause he has heard your murmurings
against the LORD. For what are we,
that you murmur against us?" 8And
Moses said, "When the LORD gives
you in the evening flesh to eat and in
the morning bread to the full, because
the LORD has heard your murmurings
which you murmur against him—
what are we? Your murmurings are
not against us but against the LORD."

9 And Moses said to Aaron, "Say to
the whole congregation of the people
of Israel, 'Come near before the LORD,
for he has heard your murmurings.'"
10And as Aaron spoke to the whole
congregation of the people of Israel,
they looked toward the wilderness,
and behold, the glory of the LORD ap-
peared in the cloud. 11And the LORD
said to Moses, 12"I have heard the mur-
murings of the people of Israel; say to
them, 'At twilight you shall eat flesh,
and in the morning you shall be filled
with bread; then you shall know that I
am the LORD your God.'"

13 In the evening quails came up
and covered the camp; and in the
morning dew lay round about the
camp. 14And when the dew had gone
up, there was on the face of the wil-
derness a fine, flake-like thing, fine
as hoarfrost on the ground.* 15When
the people of Israel saw it, they said
to one another, "What is it?"[c] For
they did not know what it was. And
Moses said to them, "It is the bread
which the LORD has given you to eat.
16This is what the LORD has com-
manded: 'Gather of it, every man of
you, as much as he can eat; you shall
take an omer apiece, according to the
number of the persons whom each of
you has in his tent.'" 17And the peo-
ple of Israel did so; they gathered,
some more, some less. 18But when
they measured it with an omer, he
that gathered much had nothing
over, and he that gathered little had
no lack; each gathered according to
what he could eat. 19And Moses said
to them, "Let no man leave any of it
till the morning." 20But they did not
listen to Moses; some left part of it
till the morning, and it bred worms
and became foul; and Moses was an-
gry with them. 21Morning by morning
they gathered it, each as much as he
could eat; but when the sun grew hot,
it melted.

22 On the sixth day they gathered
twice as much bread, two omers
apiece; and when all the leaders of the
congregation came and told Moses,
23he said to them, "This is what the
LORD has commanded: 'Tomorrow is
a day of solemn rest, a holy sabbath
to the LORD; bake what you will bake
and boil what you will boil, and all
that is left over lay by to be kept till
the morning.'" 24So they laid it by till
the morning, as Moses bade them; and
it did not become foul, and there were
no worms in it. 25Moses said, "Eat it
today, for today is a sabbath to the
LORD; today you will not find it in

[c]Or *"It is manna."* Heb *man hu*

the field. 26 Six days you shall gather it; but on the seventh day, which is a sabbath, there will be none." 27 On the seventh day some of the people went out to gather, and they found none. 28 And the LORD said to Moses, "How long do you refuse to keep my commandments and my laws? 29 See! The LORD has given you the sabbath, therefore on the sixth day he gives you bread for two days; remain every man of you in his place, let no man go out of his place on the seventh day." 30 So the people rested on the seventh day.

31 Now the house of Israel called its name manna; it was like coriander seed, white, and the taste of it was like wafers made with honey. 32 And Moses said, "This is what the LORD has commanded: 'Let an omer of it be kept throughout your generations, that they may see the bread with which I fed you in the wilderness, when I brought you out of the land of Egypt.'" 33 And Moses said to Aaron, "Take a jar, and put an omer of manna in it, and place it before the LORD, to be kept throughout your generations." 34 As the LORD commanded Moses, so Aaron placed it before the testimony, to be kept. 35 And the people of Israel ate the manna forty years, till they came to a habitable land; they ate the manna, till they came to the border of the land of Canaan. 36 (An omer is the tenth part of an ephah.)

WATER FROM THE ROCK

17 All the congregation of the people of Israel moved on from the wilderness of Sin by stages, according to the commandment of the LORD, and camped at Reph´idim; but there was no water for the people to drink. 2 Therefore the people found fault with Moses, and said, "Give us water to drink." And Moses said to them, "Why do you find fault with me? Why do you put the LORD to the proof?" 3 But the people thirsted there for water, and the people murmured against Moses, and said, "Why did you bring us up out of Egypt, to kill us and our children and our cattle with thirst?" 4 So Moses cried to the LORD, "What shall I do with this people? They are almost ready to stone me." 5 And the LORD said to Moses, "Pass on before the people, taking with you some of the elders of Israel; and take in your hand the rod with which you struck the Nile, and go. 6 Behold, I will stand before you there on the rock at Horeb; and you shall strike the rock, and water shall come out of it, that the people may drink." And Moses did so, in the sight of the elders of Israel. 7 And he called the name of the place Massah[a] and Mer´ibah,[b] because of the faultfinding of the children of Israel, and because they put the LORD to the proof by saying, "Is the LORD among us or not?"

AMALEK ATTACKS ISRAEL AND IS DEFEATED

8 Then came Am´alek and fought with Israel at Reph´idim. 9 And Moses said to Joshua, "Choose for us men, and go out, fight with Am´alek; tomorrow I will stand on the top of the hill with the rod of God in my hand." 10 So Joshua did as Moses told him, and fought with Am´alek; and Moses, Aaron, and Hur went up to the top of the hill. 11 Whenever Moses held up his hand, Israel prevailed; and whenever he lowered his hand, Am´alek prevailed. 12 But Moses' hands grew weary; so they took a stone and put it under him, and he sat upon it, and Aaron and Hur held up his hands, one on one side, and the other on the other side; so his hands were steady until the going down of the sun. 13 And Joshua mowed down Am´alek and his people with the edge of the sword.

14 And the LORD said to Moses, "Write this as a memorial in a book and recite it in the ears of Joshua,

[a] That is *Proof*
[b] That is *Contention*

that I will utterly blot out the remem-
brance of Am′alek from under heav-
en." 15And Moses built an altar and
called the name of it, The LORD is my
banner, 16saying, "A hand upon the
banner of the LORD![c] The LORD will
have war with Am′alek from genera-
tion to generation."

JETHRO'S ADVICE

18 Jethro, the priest of Mid′ian,
Moses' father-in-law, heard of all
that God had done for Moses and for
Israel his people, how the LORD had
brought Israel out of Egypt. 2Now
Jethro, Moses' father-in-law, had
taken Zippo′rah, Moses' wife, after
he had sent her away, 3and her two
sons, of whom the name of the one
was Gershom (for he said, "I have
been a sojourner[d] in a foreign land"),
4and the name of the other, Elie′zer[e]
(for he said, "The God of my father
was my help, and delivered me from
the sword of Pharaoh"). 5And Jethro,
Moses' father-in-law, came with his
sons and his wife to Moses in the wil-
derness where he was encamped at
the mountain of God. 6And when one
told Moses, "Lo,[f] your father-in-law
Jethro is coming to you with your wife
and her two sons with her," 7Moses
went out to meet his father-in-law,
and did obeisance and kissed him;
and they asked each other of their
welfare, and went into the tent. 8Then
Moses told his father-in-law all that
the LORD had done to Pharaoh and to
the Egyptians for Israel's sake, all the
hardship that had come upon them in
the way, and how the LORD had deliv-
ered them. 9And Jethro rejoiced for all
the good which the LORD had done to
Israel, in that he had delivered them
out of the hand of the Egyptians.
10 And Jethro said, "Blessed be
the LORD, who has delivered you out
of the hand of the Egyptians and out
of the hand of Pharaoh. 11Now I know
that the LORD is greater than all gods,
because he delivered the people from
under the hand of the Egyptians,[g]
when they dealt arrogantly with
them." 12And Jethro, Moses' father-in-
law, offered[h] a burnt offering and sac-
rifices to God; and Aaron came with
all the elders of Israel to eat bread
with Moses' father-in-law before God.
13 On the morrow Moses sat to
judge the people, and the people
stood about Moses from morning till
evening. 14When Moses' father-in-law
saw all that he was doing for the peo-
ple, he said, "What is this that you are
doing for the people? Why do you sit
alone, and all the people stand about
you from morning till evening?"
15And Moses said to his father-in-law,
"Because the people come to me to
inquire of God; 16when they have a
dispute, they come to me and I decide
between a man and his neighbor, and
I make them know the statutes of God
and his decisions." 17Moses' father-in-
law said to him, "What you are doing
is not good. 18You and the people with
you will wear yourselves out, for the
thing is too heavy for you; you are not
able to perform it alone. 19Listen now
to my voice; I will give you counsel,
and God be with you! You shall repre-
sent the people before God, and bring
their cases to God; 20and you shall
teach them the statutes and the deci-
sions, and make them know the way in
which they must walk and what they
must do. 21Moreover choose able men
from all the people, such as fear God,
men who are trustworthy and who
hate a bribe; and place such men over
the people as rulers of thousands, of
hundreds, of fifties, and of tens. 22And
let them judge the people at all times;
every great matter they shall bring to

[c] Cn: Heb obscure
[d] Heb *ger*
[e] Heb *Eli,* my God, *ezer,* help
[f] Sam Gk Syr: Heb *I*
[g] Transposing the last clause of v. 10 to v. 11
[h] Syr Tg Vg: Heb *took*

you, but any small matter they shall decide themselves; so it will be easier for you, and they will bear the burden with you. 23If you do this, and God so commands you, then you will be able to endure, and all this people also will go to their place in peace."

24 So Moses gave heed to the voice of his father-in-law and did all that he had said. 25Moses chose able men out of all Israel, and made them heads over the people, rulers of thousands, of hundreds, of fifties, and of tens. 26And they judged the people at all times; hard cases they brought to Moses, but any small matter they decided themselves. 27Then Moses let his father-in-law depart, and he went his way to his own country.

THE ISRAELITES REACH MOUNT SINAI

19 On the third new moon after the people of Israel had gone forth out of the land of Egypt, on that day they came into the wilderness of Sinai. 2And when they set out from Reph´idim and came into the wilderness of Sinai, they encamped in the wilderness; and there Israel encamped before the mountain. 3And Moses went up to God, and the LORD called to him out of the mountain, saying, "Thus you shall say to the house of Jacob, and tell the people of Israel:* 4You have seen what I did to the Egyptians, and how I bore you on eagles' wings and brought you to myself. 5Now therefore, if you will obey my voice and keep my covenant, you shall be my own possession among all peoples; for all the earth is mine, 6and you shall be to me a kingdom of priests and a holy nation. These are the words which you shall speak to the children of Israel."

7 So Moses came and called the elders of the people, and set before them all these words which the LORD had commanded him. 8And all the people answered together and said, "All that the LORD has spoken we will do." And Moses reported the words of the people to the LORD. 9And the LORD said to Moses, "Lo, I am coming to you in a thick cloud, that the people may hear when I speak with you, and may also believe you for ever."

THE PEOPLE CONSECRATED

9 Then Moses told the words of the people to the LORD. 10And the LORD said to Moses, "Go to the people and consecrate them today and tomorrow, and let them wash their garments, 11and be ready by the third day; for on the third day the LORD will come down upon Mount Sinai in the sight of all the people. 12And you shall set bounds for the people round about, saying, 'Take heed that you do not go up into the mountain or touch the border of it; whoever touches the mountain shall be put to death; 13no hand shall touch him, but he shall be stoned or shot; whether beast or man, he shall not live.' When the trumpet sounds a long blast, they shall come up to the mountain." 14So Moses went down from the mountain to the people, and consecrated the people; and they washed their garments. 15And he said to the people, "Be ready by the third day; do not go near a woman."

16 On the morning of the third day there were thunders and lightnings, and a thick cloud upon the mountain, and a very loud trumpet blast, so that all the people who were in the camp trembled. 17Then Moses brought the people out of the camp to meet God; and they took their stand at the foot of the mountain. 18And Mount Sinai was wrapped in smoke, because the LORD descended upon it in fire; and the smoke of it went up like the smoke of a kiln, and the whole mountain quaked greatly. 19And as the sound of the trumpet grew louder and louder, Moses spoke, and God answered him in thunder. 20And the LORD came down uponMount Sinai, to the top of the mountain; and the LORD called Moses to the top of the mountain, and Moses went up. 21And the LORD

said to Moses, "Go down and warn
the people, lest they break through to
the LORD to gaze and many of them
perish. 22 And also let the priests who
come near to theLORD consecrate
themselves, lest the LORD break out
upon them." 23 And Moses said to
the LORD, "The people cannot come
up to Mount Sinai; for thou thyself
didst charge us, saying, 'Set bounds
about the mountain, and consecrate
it.'" 24 And the LORD said to him, "Go
down, and come up bringing Aaron
with you; but do not let the priests
and the people break through to come
up to the LORD, lest he break out
against them." 25 So Moses went down
to the people and told them.

THE TEN COMMANDMENTS

20 And God spoke all these words,
saying,*
2 "I am the LORD your God, who
brought you out of the land of Egypt,
out of the house of bondage.
3 "You shall have no other gods be-
fore[a] me.
4 "You shall not make for yourself
a graven image, or any likeness of any-
thing that is in heaven above, or that
is in the earth beneath, or that is in
the water under the earth; 5 you shall
not bow down to them or serve them;
for I the LORD your God am a jealous
God, visiting the iniquity of the fa-
thers upon the children to the third
and the fourth generation of those
who hate me, 6 but showing steadfast
love to thousands of those who love
me and keep my commandments.
7 "You shall not take the name of
the LORD your God in vain; for the
LORD will not hold him guiltless who
takes his name in vain.
8 "Remember the sabbath day, to
keep it holy. 9 Six days you shall labor,
and do all your work; 10 but the seventh
day is a sabbath to the LORD your God;
in it you shall not do any work, you, or
your son, or your daughter, your man-
servant, or your maidservant, or your
cattle, or the sojourner who is within
your gates; 11 for in six days the LORD
made heaven and earth, the sea, and
all that is in them, and rested the sev-
enth day; therefore the LORD blessed
the sabbath day and hallowed it.
12 "Honor your father and your
mother, that your days may be long
in the land which the LORD your God
gives you.
13 "You shall not kill.
14 "You shall not commit adultery.
15 "You shall not steal.
16 "You shall not bear false witness
against your neighbor.
17 "You shall not covet your neigh-
bor's house; you shall not covet your
neighbor's wife, or his manservant, or
his maidservant, or his ox, or his ass,
or anything that is your neighbor's."
18 Now when all the people per-
ceived the thunderings and the light-
nings and the sound of the trum-
pet and the mountain smoking, the
people were afraid and trembled;
and they stood afar off, 19 and said to
Moses, "You speak to us, and we will
hear; but let not God speak to us, lest
we die." 20 And Moses said to the peo-
ple, "Do not fear; for God has come
to prove you, and that the fear of him
may be before your eyes, that you may
not sin."

THE LAW CONCERNING THE ALTAR

21 And the people stood afar off,
while Moses drew near to the thick
darkness where God was. 22 And the
LORD said to Moses, "Thus you shall
say to the people of Israel: 'You have
seen for yourselves that I have talked
with you from heaven. 23 You shall not
make gods of silver to be with me, nor
shall you make for yourselves gods
of gold. 24 An altar of earth you shall
make for me and sacrifice on it your
burnt offerings and your peace offer-
ings, your sheep and your oxen; in ev-
ery place where I cause my name to
be remembered I will come to you and
bless you. 25 And if you make me an

[a]Or *besides*

altar of stone, you shall not build it of
hewn stones; for if you wield your tool
upon it you profane it. 26And you shall
not go up by steps to my altar, that
your nakedness be not exposed on it.'

THE LAW CONCERNING SLAVES

21 "Now these are the ordinances
which you shall set before them.
2When you buy a Hebrew slave, he
shall serve six years, and in the sev-
enth he shall go out free, for nothing.
3If he comes in single, he shall go out
single; if he comes in married, then
his wife shall go out with him. 4If his
master gives him a wife and she bears
him sons or daughters, the wife and
her children shall be her master's and
he shall go out alone. 5But if the slave
plainly says, 'I love my master, my
wife, and my children; I will not go
out free,' 6then his master shall bring
him to God, and he shall bring him
to the door or the doorpost; and his
master shall bore his ear through with
an awl; and he shall serve him for life.
7 "When a man sells his daughter
as a slave, she shall not go out as the
male slaves do. 8If she does not please
her master, who has designated her[a]
for himself, then he shall let her be re-
deemed; he shall have no right to sell
her to a foreign people, since he has
dealt faithlessly with her. 9If he des-
ignates her for his son, he shall deal
with her as with a daughter. 10If he
takes another wife to himself, he shall
not diminish her food, her clothing, or
her marital rights. 11And if he does not
do these three things for her, she shall
go out for nothing, without payment
of money.

THE LAW CONCERNING VIOLENCE

12 "Whoever strikes a man so that
he dies shall be put to death. 13But
if he did not lie in wait for him, but
God let him fall into his hand, then I
will appoint for you a place to which
he may flee. 14But if a man willfully
attacks another to kill him treacher-
ously, you shall take him from my al-
tar, that he may die.
15 "Whoever strikes his father or
his mother shall be put to death.
16 "Whoever steals a man, whether
he sells him or is found in possession
of him, shall be put to death.
17 "Whoever curses his father or
his mother shall be put to death.
18 "When men quarrel and one
strikes the other with a stone or with
his fist and the man does not die but
keeps his bed, 19then if the man rises
again and walks abroad with his staff,
he that struck him shall be clear; only
he shall pay for the loss of his time,
and shall have him thoroughly healed.
20 "When a man strikes his slave,
male or female, with a rod and the
slave dies under his hand, he shall be
punished. 21But if the slave survives a
day or two, he is not to be punished;
for the slave is his money.
22 "When men strive together, and
hurt a woman with child, so that there
is a miscarriage, and yet no harm fol-
lows, the one who hurt her shall[b] be
fined, according as the woman's hus-
band shall lay upon him; and he shall
pay as the judges determine. 23If any
harm follows, then you shall give life
for life, 24eye for eye, tooth for tooth,
hand for hand, foot for foot, 25burn
for burn, wound for wound, stripe for
stripe.
26 "When a man strikes the eye
of his slave, male or female, and de-
stroys it, he shall let the slave go free
for the eye's sake. 27If he knocks out
the tooth of his slave, male or female,
he shall let the slave go free for the
tooth's sake.

LAWS CONCERNING PROPERTY

28 "When an ox gores a man or
a woman to death, the ox shall be
stoned, and its flesh shall not be eaten;
but the owner of the ox shall be clear.
29But if the ox has been accustomed

[a] Another reading is *so that he has not designated her*
[b] Heb *he shall*

to gore in the past, and its owner has
been warned but has not kept it in, and
it kills a man or a woman, the ox shall
be stoned, and its owner also shall be
put to death. 30If a ransom is laid on
him, then he shall give for the redemp-
tion of his life whatever is laid upon
him. 31If it gores a man's son or daugh-
ter, he shall be dealt with according to
this same rule. 32If the ox gores a slave,
male or female, the owner shall give
to their master thirty shekels of silver,
and the ox shall be stoned.

33 "When a man leaves a pit open,
or when a man digs a pit and does not
cover it, and an ox or an ass falls into
it, 34the owner of the pit shall make it
good; he shall give money to its own-
er, and the dead beast shall be his.

35 "When one man's ox hurts an-
other's, so that it dies, then they shall
sell the live ox and divide the price of
it; and the dead beast also they shall
divide. 36Or if it is known that the ox
has been accustomed to gore in the
past, and its owner has not kept it in,
he shall pay ox for ox, and the dead
beast shall be his.

LAWS OF RESTITUTION

22[c] "If a man steals an ox or a sheep,
and kills it or sells it, he shall pay
five oxen for an ox, and four sheep for a
sheep.[d] He shall make restitution; if he
has nothing, then he shall be sold for his
theft. 4If the stolen beast is found alive
in his possession, whether it is an ox or
an ass or a sheep, he shall pay double.

2[e] "If a thief is found breaking in,
and is struck so that he dies, there
shall be no bloodguilt for him; 3but
if the sun has risen upon him, there
shall be bloodguilt for him.

5 "When a man causes a field or
vineyard to be grazed over, or lets his
beast loose and it feeds in another
man's field, he shall make restitution
from the best in his own field and in
his own vineyard.

6 "When fire breaks out and catch-
es in thorns so that the stacked grain
or the standing grain or the field is
consumed, he that kindled the fire
shall make full restitution.

7 "If a man delivers to his neigh-
bor money or goods to keep, and it is
stolen out of the man's house, then, if
the thief is found, he shall pay double.
8If the thief is not found, the owner
of the house shall come near to God,
to show whether or not he has put his
hand to his neighbor's goods.

9 "For every breach of trust, wheth-
er it is for ox, for ass, for sheep, for
clothing, or for any kind of lost thing,
of which one says, 'This is it,' the case
of both parties shall come before God;
he whom God shall condemn shall pay
double to his neighbor.

10 "If a man delivers to his neigh-
bor an ass or an ox or a sheep or any
beast to keep, and it dies or is hurt or
is driven away, without any one see-
ing it, 11an oath by the LORD shall be
between them both to see whether he
has not put his hand to his neighbor's
property; and the owner shall accept
the oath, and he shall not make res-
titution. 12But if it is stolen from him,
he shall make restitution to its owner.
13If it is torn by beasts, let him bring it
as evidence; he shall not make restitu-
tion for what has been torn.

14 "If a man borrows anything of
his neighbor, and it is hurt or dies, the
owner not being with it, he shall make
full restitution. 15If the owner was
with it, he shall not make restitution;
if it was hired, it came for its hire.[f]

SOCIAL AND RELIGIOUS LAWS

16 "If a man seduces a virgin who
is not betrothed, and lies with her,
he shall give the marriage present for
her, and make her his wife. 17If her fa-
ther utterly refuses to give her to him,

[c] Ch 21.37 in Heb
[d] Restoring the second half of verse 3 and the whole of verse 4 to their place immediately following verse 1
[e] Ch 22.1 in Heb
[f] Or *it is reckoned in* (Heb *comes into*) *its hire*

he shall pay money equivalent to the
marriage present for virgins.
18 "You shall not permit a sorcer-
ess to live.
19 "Whoever lies with a beast shall
be put to death.
20 "Whoever sacrifices to any god,
save to the LORD only, shall be utterly
destroyed.
21 "You shall not wrong a stranger
or oppress him, for you were strangers
in the land of Egypt. 22 You shall not
afflict any widow or orphan. 23 If you
do afflict them, and they cry out to
me, I will surely hear their cry; 24 and
my wrath will burn, and I will kill you
with the sword, and your wives shall
become widows and your children
fatherless.
25 "If you lend money to any of my
people with you who is poor, you shall
not be to him as a creditor, and you
shall not exact interest from him. 26 If
ever you take your neighbor's garment
in pledge, you shall restore it to him
before the sun goes down; 27 for that is
his only covering, it is his mantle for
his body; in what else shall he sleep?
And if he cries to me, I will hear, for I
am compassionate.
28 "You shall not revile God, nor
curse a ruler of your people.
29 "You shall not delay to offer
from the fulness of your harvest and
from the outflow of your presses.
"The first-born of your sons you shall
give to me. 30 You shall do likewise
with your oxen and with your sheep:
seven days it shall be with its dam; on
the eighth day you shall give it to me.
31 "You shall be men consecrated
to me; therefore you shall not eat any
flesh that is torn by beasts in the field;
you shall cast it to the dogs.

JUSTICE FOR ALL

23 "You shall not utter a false re-
port. You shall not join hands
with a wicked man, to be a malicious
witness. 2 You shall not follow a mul-
titude to do evil; nor shall you bear
witness in a suit, turning aside after
a multitude, so as to pervert justice;
3 nor shall you be partial to a poor man
in his suit.
4 "If you meet your enemy's ox or
his ass going astray, you shall bring
it back to him. 5 If you see the ass of
one who hates you lying under its
burden, you shall refrain from leaving
him with it, you shall help him to lift
it up.[a]
6 "You shall not pervert the justice
due to your poor in his suit. 7 Keep far
from a false charge, and do not slay
the innocent and righteous, for I will
not acquit the wicked. 8 And you shall
take no bribe, for a bribe blinds the
officials, and subverts the cause of
those who are in the right.
9 "You shall not oppress a strang-
er; you know the heart of a stranger,
for you were strangers in the land of
Egypt.

SABBATICAL YEAR AND SABBATH

10 "For six years you shall sow your
land and gather in its yield; 11 but the
seventh year you shall let it rest and
lie fallow, that the poor of your people
may eat; and what they leave the wild
beasts may eat. You shall do likewise
with your vineyard, and with your ol-
ive orchard.
12 "Six days you shall do your work,
but on the seventh day you shall rest;
that your ox and your ass may have
rest, and the son of your bondmaid,
and the alien, may be refreshed. 13 Take
heed to all that I have said to you; and
make no mention of the names of oth-
er gods, nor let such be heard out of
your mouth.

THE ANNUAL FESTIVALS

14 "Three times in the year you
shall keep a feast to me. 15 You shall
keep the feast of unleavened bread, as
I commanded you, you shall eat un-
leavened bread for seven days at the
appointed time in the month of Abib,
for in it you came out of Egypt. None

[a] Gk: Heb obscure

shall appear before me empty-handed. 16 You shall keep the feast of harvest, of the first fruits of your labor, of what you sow in the field. You shall keep the feast of ingathering at the end of the year, when you gather in from the field the fruit of your labor. 17 Three times in the year shall all your males appear before the Lord GOD.

18 "You shall not offer the blood of my sacrifice with leavened bread, or let the fat of my feast remain until the morning.

19 "The first of the first fruits of your ground you shall bring into the house of the LORD your God. "You shall not boil a kid in its mother's milk.

THE CONQUEST OF CANAAN PROMISED

20 "Behold, I send an angel before you, to guard you on the way and to bring you to the place which I have prepared. 21 Give heed to him and hearken to his voice, do not rebel against him, for he will not pardon your transgression; for my name is in him.

22 "But if you hearken attentively to his voice and do all that I say, then I will be an enemy to your enemies and an adversary to your adversaries.

23 "When my angel goes before you, and brings you in to the Amorites, and the Hittites, and the Per´izzites, and the Canaanites, the Hivites, and the Jeb´usites, and I blot them out, 24 you shall not bow down to their gods, nor serve them, nor do according to their works, but you shall utterly overthrow *them and break their pillars in* pieces. 25 You shall serve the LORD your God, and I[b] will bless your bread and your water; and I will take sickness away from the midst of you. 26 None shall cast her young or be barren in your land; I will fulfil the number of your days. 27 I will send my terror before you, and will throw into confusion all the people against whom you shall come, and I will make all your enemies turn their backs to you. 28 And I will send hornets before you, which shall drive out Hivite, Canaanite, and Hittite from before you. 29 I will not drive them out from before you in one year, lest the land become desolate and the wild beasts multiply against you. 30 Little by little I will drive them out from before you, until you are increased and possess the land. 31 And I will set your bounds from the Red Sea to the sea of the Philistines, and from the wilderness to the Euphra´tes; for I will deliver the inhabitants of the land into your hand, and you shall drive them out before you. 32 You shall make no covenant with them or with their gods. 33 They shall not dwell in your land, lest they make you sin against me; for if you serve their gods, it will surely be a snare to you."

THE BLOOD OF THE COVENANT

24 And he said to Moses, "Come up to the LORD, you and Aaron, Nadab, and Abi´hu, and seventy of the elders of Israel, and worship afar off. 2 Moses alone shall come near to the LORD; but the others shall not come near, and the people shall not come up with him."

3 Moses came and told the people all the words of the LORD and all the ordinances; and all the people answered with one voice, and said, "All the words which the LORD has spoken we will do." 4 And Moses wrote all the words of the LORD. And he rose early in the morning, and built an altar at the foot of the mountain, and twelve pillars, according to the twelve tribes of Israel. 5 And he sent young men of the people of Israel, who offered burnt offerings and sacrificed peace offerings of oxen to the LORD. 6 And Moses took half of the blood and put it in basins, and half of the blood he threw against the altar. 7 Then he took the book of the covenant, and read it in the hearing of the people; and they said, "All that the LORD has spoken

[b] Gk Vg: Heb *he*

we will do, and we will be obedient."
8 And Moses took the blood and threw
it upon the people, and said, "Behold
the blood of the covenant which the
LORD has made with you in accor-
dance with all these words."

ON THE MOUNTAIN WITH GOD

9 Then Moses and Aaron, Nadab,
and Abi´hu, and seventy of the elders
of Israel went up, 10 and they saw the
God of Israel; and there was under his
feet as it were a pavement of sapphire
stone, like the very heaven for clear-
ness. 11 And he did not lay his hand on
the chief men of the people of Israel;
they beheld God, and ate and drank.

12 The LORD said to Moses, "Come
up to me on the mountain, and wait
there; and I will give you the tables of
stone, with the law and the command-
ment, which I have written for their
instruction." 13 So Moses rose with
his servant Joshua, and Moses went
up into the mountain of God. 14 And
he said to the elders, "Tarry here for
us, until we come to you again; and,
behold, Aaron and Hur are with you;
whoever has a cause, let him go to
them."

15 Then Moses went up on the
mountain, and the cloud covered the
mountain. 16 The glory of the LORD
settled on Mount Sinai, and the
cloud covered it six days; and on the
seventh day he called to Moses out
of the midst of the cloud. 17 Now the
appearance of the glory of the LORD
was like a devouring fire on the top of
the mountain in the sight of the peo-
ple of Israel. 18 And Moses entered the
cloud, and went up on the mountain.
And Moses was on the mountain forty
days and forty nights.

OFFERINGS FOR THE TABERNACLE

25 The LORD said to Moses, 2 "Speak
to the people of Israel, that they
take for me an offering; from every
man whose heart makes him willing
you shall receive the offering for me.
3 And this is the offering which you
shall receive from them: gold, silver,
and bronze, 4 blue and purple and scar-
let stuff and fine twined linen, goats'
hair, 5 tanned rams' skins, goatskins,
acacia wood, 6 oil for the lamps, spic-
es for the anointing oil and for the
fragrant incense, 7 onyx stones, and
stones for setting, for the ephod and
for the breastpiece. 8 And let them
make me a sanctuary, that I may dwell
in their midst. 9 According to all that
I show you concerning the pattern of
the tabernacle, and of all its furniture,
so you shall make it.

THE ARK OF THE COVENANT

10 "They shall make an ark of
acacia wood; two cubits and a half
shall be its length, a cubit and a half
its breadth, and a cubit and a half
its height. 11 And you shall overlay it
with pure gold, within and without
shall you overlay it, and you shall
make upon it a molding of gold round
about. 12 And you shall cast four rings
of gold for it and put them on its four
feet, two rings on the one side of it,
and two rings on the other side of it.
13 You shall make poles of acacia wood,
and overlay them with gold. 14 And you
shall put the poles into the rings on
the sides of the ark, to carry the ark
by them. 15 The poles shall remain in
the rings of the ark; they shall not be
taken from it. 16 And you shall put into
the ark the testimony which I shall
give you. 17 Then you shall make a mer-
cy seat[a] of pure gold; two cubits and
a half shall be its length, and a cubit
and a half its breadth. 18 And you shall
make two cherubim of gold; of ham-
mered work shall you make them, on
the two ends of the mercy seat. 19 Make
one cherub on the one end, and one
cherub on the other end; of one piece
with the mercy seat shall you make
the cherubim on its two ends. 20 The
cherubim shall spread out their wings
above, overshadowing the mercy seat
with their wings, their faces one to

[a] Or *cover*

another; toward the mercy seat shall
the faces of the cherubim be. 21And
you shall put the mercy seat on the
top of the ark; and in the ark you
shall put the testimony that I shall
give you. 22There I will meet with you,
and from above the mercy seat, from
between the two cherubim that are
upon the ark of the testimony, I will
speak with you of all that I will give
you in commandment for the people
of Israel.

THE TABLE FOR THE BREAD OF THE PRESENCE

23 "And you shall make a table of
acacia wood; two cubits shall be its
length, a cubit its breadth, and a cu-
bit and a half its height. 24You shall
overlay it with pure gold, and make a
molding of gold around it. 25And you
shall make around it a frame a hand-
breadth wide, and a molding of gold
around the frame. 26And you shall
make for it four rings of gold, and
fasten the rings to the four corners at
its four legs. 27Close to the frame the
rings shall lie, as holders for the poles
to carry the table. 28You shall make
the poles of acacia wood, and overlay
them with gold, and the table shall
be carried with these. 29And you shall
make its plates and dishes for incense,
and its flagons and bowls with which
to pour libations; of pure gold you
shall make them. 30And you shall set
the bread of the Presence on the table
before me always.

THE LAMPSTAND

31 "And you shall make a lamp-
stand of pure gold. The base and the
shaft of the lampstand shall be made
of hammered work; its cups, its cap-
itals, and its flowers shall be of one
piece with it; 32and there shall be six
branches going out of its sides, three
branches of the lampstand out of one
side of it and three branches of the
lampstand out of the other side of
it; 33three cups made like almonds,
each with capital and flower, on one
branch, and three cups made like al-
monds, each with capital and flower,
on the other branch—so for the six
branches going out of the lampstand;
34and on the lampstand itself four
cups made like almonds, with their
capitals and flowers, 35and a capital
of one piece with it under each pair
of the six branches going out from
the lampstand. 36Their capitals and
their branches shall be of one piece
with it, the whole of it one piece of
hammered work of pure gold. 37And
you shall make the seven lamps for it;
and the lamps shall be set up so as to
give light upon the space in front of it.
38Its snuffers and their trays shall be
of pure gold. 39Of a talent of pure gold
shall it be made, with all these uten-
sils. 40And see that you make them
after the pattern for them, which is
being shown you on the mountain.

THE TABERNACLE

26 "Moreover you shall make the
tabernacle with ten curtains of
fine twined linen and blue and pur-
ple and scarlet stuff; with cherubim
skilfully worked shall you make them.
2The length of each curtain shall be
twenty-eight cubits, and the breadth
of each curtain four cubits; all the
curtains shall have one measure.
3Five curtains shall be coupled to one
another; and the other five curtains
shall be coupled to one another. 4And
you shall make loops of blue on the
edge of the outmost curtain in the
first set; and likewise you shall make
loops on the edge of the outmost cur-
tain in the second set. 5Fifty loops you
shall make on the one curtain, and fif-
ty loops you shall make on the edge of
the curtain that is in the second set;
the loops shall be opposite one anoth-
er. 6And you shall make fifty clasps of
gold, and couple the curtains one to
the other with the clasps, that the tab-
ernacle may be one whole.

7 "You shall also make curtains
of goats' hair for a tent over the

tabernacle; eleven curtains shall you
make. 8The length of each curtain
shall be thirty cubits, and the breadth
of each curtain four cubits; the eleven
curtains shall have the same measure.
9And you shall couple five curtains by
themselves, and six curtains by them-
selves, and the sixth curtain you shall
double over at the front of the tent.
10And you shall make fifty loops on
the edge of the curtain that is outmost
in one set, and fifty loops on the edge
of the curtain which is outmost in the
second set.

11 "And you shall make fifty clasps
of bronze, and put the clasps into the
loops, and couple the tent together
that it may be one whole. 12And the
part that remains of the curtains
of the tent, the half curtain that re-
mains, shall hang over the back of the
tabernacle. 13And the cubit on the one
side, and the cubit on the other side,
of what remains in the length of the
curtains of the tent shall hang over
the sides of the tabernacle, on this
side and that side, to cover it. 14And
you shall make for the tent a covering
of tanned rams' skins and goatskins.

THE FRAMEWORK

15 "And you shall make upright
frames for the tabernacle of acacia
wood. 16Ten cubits shall be the length
of a frame, and a cubit and a half the
breadth of each frame. 17There shall
be two tenons in each frame, for fit-
ting together; so shall you do for all
the frames of the tabernacle. 18You
shall make the frames for the taber-
nacle: twenty frames for the south
side; 19and forty bases of silver you
shall make under the twenty frames,
two bases under one frame for its two
tenons, and two bases under another
frame for its two tenons; 20and for the
second side of the tabernacle, on the
north side twenty frames, 21and their
forty bases of silver, two bases under
one frame, and two bases under an-
other frame; 22and for the rear of the
tabernacle westward you shall make
six frames. 23And you shall make two
frames for corners of the tabernacle
in the rear; 24they shall be separate
beneath, but joined at the top, at the
first ring; thus shall it be with both of
them; they shall form the two corners.
25And there shall be eight frames, with
their bases of silver, sixteen bases;
two bases under one frame, and two
bases under another frame.

26 "And you shall make bars of aca-
cia wood, five for the frames of the
one side of the tabernacle, 27and five
bars for the frames of the other side
of the tabernacle, and five bars for
the frames of the side of the taberna-
cle at the rear westward. 28The mid-
dle bar, halfway up the frames, shall
pass through from end to end. 29You
shall overlay the frames with gold,
and shall make their rings of gold for
holders for the bars; and you shall
overlay the bars with gold. 30And you
shall erect the tabernacle according to
the plan for it which has been shown
you on the mountain.

THE CURTAIN

31 "And you shall make a veil of
blue and purple and scarlet stuff and
fine twined linen; in skilled work
shall it be made, with cherubim; 32and
you shall hang it upon four pillars of
acacia overlaid with gold, with hooks
of gold, upon four bases of silver.
33And you shall hang the veil from the
clasps, and bring the ark of the testi-
mony in thither within the veil; and
the veil shall separate for you the holy
place from the most holy. 34You shall
put the mercy seat upon the ark of
the testimony in the most holy place.
35And you shall set the table outside
the veil, and the lampstand on the
south side of the tabernacle opposite
the table; and you shall put the table
on the north side.

36 "And you shall make a screen for
the door of the tent, of blue and pur-
ple and scarlet stuff and fine twined
linen, embroidered with needlework.
37And you shall make for the screen

five pillars of acacia, and overlay them
with gold; their hooks shall be of gold,
and you shall cast five bases of bronze
for them.

THE ALTAR OF BURNT OFFERING

27 "You shall make the altar of aca-
cia wood, five cubits long and five
cubits broad; the altar shall be square,
and its height shall be three cubits.
2And you shall make horns for it on its
four corners; its horns shall be of one
piece with it, and you shall overlay
it with bronze. 3You shall make pots
for it to receive its ashes, and shovels
and basins and forks and firepans; all
its utensils you shall make of bronze.
4You shall also make for it a grating, a
network of bronze; and upon the net
you shall make four bronze rings at
its four corners. 5And you shall set it
under the ledge of the altar so that the
net shall extend halfway down the al-
tar. 6And you shall make poles for the
altar, poles of acacia wood, and over-
lay them with bronze; 7and the poles
shall be put through the rings, so that
the poles shall be upon the two sides
of the altar, when it is carried. 8You
shall make it hollow, with boards; as
it has been shown you on the moun-
tain, so shall it be made.

THE COURT AND ITS HANGINGS

9 "You shall make the court of
the tabernacle. On the south side
the court shall have hangings of fine
twined linen a hundred cubits long for
one side; 10their pillars shall be twen-
ty and their bases twenty, of bronze,
but the hooks of the pillars and their
fillets shall be of silver. 11And likewise
for its length on the north side there
shall be hangings a hundred cubits
long, their pillars twenty and their
bases twenty, of bronze, but the hooks
of the pillars and their fillets shall be
of silver. 12And for the breadth of the
court on the west side there shall be
hangings for fifty cubits, with ten
pillars and ten bases. 13The breadth
of the court on the front to the east
shall be fifty cubits. 14The hangings
for the one side of the gate shall be
fifteen cubits, with three pillars and
three bases. 15On the other side the
hangings shall be fifteen cubits, with
three pillars and three bases. 16For
the gate of the court there shall be
a screen twenty cubits long, of blue
and purple and scarlet stuff and fine
twined linen, embroidered with nee-
dlework; it shall have four pillars and
with them four bases. 17All the pillars
around the court shall be filleted with
silver; their hooks shall be of silver,
and their bases of bronze. 18The length
of the court shall be a hundred cubits,
the breadth fifty, and the height five
cubits, with hangings of fine twined
linen and bases of bronze. 19All the
utensils of the tabernacle for every
use, and all its pegs and all the pegs of
the court, shall be of bronze.

THE OIL FOR THE LAMP

20 "And you shall command the
people of Israel that they bring to you
pure beaten olive oil for the light, that
a lamp may be set up to burn contin-
ually. 21In the tent of meeting, outside
the veil which is before the testimony,
Aaron and his sons shall tend it from
evening to morning before the LORD.
It shall be a statute for ever to be ob-
served throughout their generations
by the people of Israel.

VESTMENTS FOR THE PRIESTHOOD

28 "Then bring near to you Aaron
your brother, and his sons with
him, from among the people of Israel,
to serve me as priests—Aaron and
Aaron's sons, Nadab and Abi´hu,
Elea´zar and Ith´amar. 2And you shall
make holy garments for Aaron your
brother, for glory and for beauty. 3And
you shall speak to all who have abili-
ty, whom I have endowed with an able
mind, that they make Aaron's gar-
ments to consecrate him for my priest-
hood. 4These are the garments which
they shall make: a breastpiece, an
ephod, a robe, a coat of checker work,

a turban, and a girdle; they shall make holy garments for Aaron your brother and his sons to serve me as priests.

THE EPHOD

5 "They shall receive gold, blue and purple and scarlet stuff, and fine twined linen. 6And they shall make the ephod of gold, of blue and purple and scarlet stuff, and of fine twined linen, skilfully worked. 7It shall have two shoulder-pieces attached to its two edges, that it may be joined together. 8And the skilfully woven band upon it, to gird it on, shall be of the same workmanship and materials, of gold, blue and purple and scarlet stuff, and fine twined linen. 9And you shall take two onyx stones, and engrave on them the names of the sons of Israel, 10six of their names on the one stone, and the names of the remaining six on the other stone, in the order of their birth. 11As a jeweler engraves signets, so shall you engrave the two stones with the names of the sons of Israel; you shall enclose them in settings of gold filigree. 12And you shall set the two stones upon the shoulder-pieces of the ephod, as stones of remembrance for the sons of Israel; and Aaron shall bear their names before the LORD upon his two shoulders for remembrance. 13And you shall make settings of gold filigree, 14and two chains of pure gold, twisted like cords; and you shall attach the corded chains to the settings.

THE BREASTPLATE

15 "And you shall make a breastpiece of judgment, in skilled work; like the work of the ephod you shall make it; of gold, blue and purple and scarlet stuff, and fine twined linen shall you make it. 16It shall be square and double, a span its length and a span its breadth. 17And you shall set in it four rows of stones. A row of sardius, topaz, and carbuncle shall be the first row; 18and the second row an emerald, a sapphire, and a diamond; 19and the third row a jacinth, an agate, and an amethyst; 20and the fourth row a beryl, an onyx, and a jasper; they shall be set in gold filigree. 21There shall be twelve stones with their names according to the names of the sons of Israel; they shall be like signets, each engraved with its name, for the twelve tribes. 22And you shall make for the breastpiece twisted chains like cords, of pure gold; 23and you shall make for the breastpiece two rings of gold, and put the two rings on the two edges of the breastpiece. 24And you shall put the two cords of gold in the two rings at the edges of the breastpiece; 25the two ends of the two cords you shall attach to the two settings of filigree, and so attach it in front to the shoulder-pieces of the ephod. 26And you shall make two rings of gold, and put them at the two ends of the breastpiece, on its inside edge next to the ephod. 27And you shall make two rings of gold, and attach them in front to the lower part of the two shoulder-pieces of the ephod, at its joining above the skilfully woven band of the ephod. 28And they shall bind the breastpiece by its rings to the rings of the ephod with a lace of blue, that it may lie upon the skilfully woven band of the ephod, and that the breastpiece shall not come loose from the ephod. 29So Aaron shall bear the names of the sons of Israel in the breastpiece of judgment upon his heart, when he goes into the holy place, to bring them to continual remembrance before the LORD. 30And in the breastpiece of judgment you shall put the Urim and the Thummim, and they shall be upon Aaron's heart, when he goes in before the LORD; thus Aaron shall bear the judgment of the people of Israel upon his heart before the LORD continually.

OTHER PRIESTLY VESTMENTS

31 "And you shall make the robe of the ephod all of blue. 32It shall have in it an opening for the head, with a

woven binding around the opening,
like the opening in a garment,[a] that
it may not be torn. [33]On its skirts
you shall make pomegranates of blue
and purple and scarlet stuff, around
its skirts, with bells of gold between
them, [34]a golden bell and a pomegran-
ate, a golden bell and a pomegranate,
round about on the skirts of the robe.
[35]And it shall be upon Aaron when
he ministers, and its sound shall be
heard when he goes into the holy
place before the LORD, and when he
comes out, lest he die.

36 "And you shall make a plate of
pure gold, and engrave on it, like the
engraving of a signet, 'Holy to the
LORD.' [37]And you shall fasten it on
the turban by a lace of blue; it shall
be on the front of the turban. [38]It shall
be upon Aaron's forehead, and Aaron
shall take upon himself any guilt in-
curred in the holy offering which the
people of Israel hallow as their holy
gifts; it shall always be upon his fore-
head, that they may be accepted be-
fore the LORD.

39 "And you shall weave the coat
in checker work of fine linen, and you
shall make a turban of fine linen, and
you shall make a girdle embroidered
with needlework.

40 "And for Aaron's sons you shall
make coats and girdles and caps; you
shall make them for glory and beauty.
[41]And you shall put them upon Aaron
your brother, and upon his sons with
him, and shall anoint them and ordain
them and consecrate them, that they
may serve me as priests. [42]And you
shall make for them linen breeches to
cover their naked flesh; from the loins
to the thighs they shall reach; [43]and
they shall be upon Aaron and upon
his sons, when they go into the tent of
meeting, or when they come near the
altar to minister in the holy place; lest
they bring guilt upon themselves and
die. This shall be a perpetual statute for
him and for his descendants after him.

[a]The Hebrew word is of uncertain meaning
[b]Gk: Heb *girdles, Aaron and his sons*
[c]Heb *all*

THE ORDINATION OF THE PRIESTS

29 "Now this is what you shall do
to them to consecrate them, that
they may serve me as priests. Take
one young bull and two rams with-
out blemish, [2]and unleavened bread,
unleavened cakes mixed with oil, and
unleavened wafers spread with oil.
You shall make them of fine wheat
flour. [3]And you shall put them in one
basket and bring them in the basket,
and bring the bull and the two rams.
[4]You shall bring Aaron and his sons to
the door of the tent of meeting, and
wash them with water. [5]And you shall
take the garments, and put on Aaron
the coat and the robe of the ephod,
and the ephod, and the breastpiece,
and gird him with the skilfully woven
band of the ephod; [6]and you shall set
the turban on his head, and put the
holy crown upon the turban. [7]And you
shall take the anointing oil, and pour
it on his head and anoint him. [8]Then
you shall bring his sons, and put coats
on them, [9]and you shall gird them
with girdles[b] and bind caps on them;
and the priesthood shall be theirs by
a perpetual statute. Thus you shall or-
dain Aaron and his sons.

10 "Then you shall bring the bull
before the tent of meeting. Aaron and
his sons shall lay their hands upon the
head of the bull, [11]and you shall kill
the bull before the LORD, at the door
of the tent of meeting, [12]and shall take
part of the blood of the bull and put it
upon the horns of the altar with your
finger, and the rest of[c] the blood you
shall pour out at the base of the altar.
[13]And you shall take all the fat that
covers the entrails, and the appendage
of the liver, and the two kidneys with
the fat that is on them, and burn them
upon the altar. [14]But the flesh of the
bull, and its skin, and its dung, you
shall burn with fire outside the camp;
it is a sin offering.

15 "Then you shall take one of the
rams, and Aaron and his sons shall lay

their hands upon the head of the ram, 16 and you shall slaughter the ram, and shall take its blood and throw it against the altar round about. 17 Then you shall cut the ram into pieces, and wash its entrails and its legs, and put them with its pieces and its head, 18 and burn the whole ram upon the altar; it is a burnt offering to the LORD; it is a pleasing odor, an offering by fire to the LORD.

19 "You shall take the other ram; and Aaron and his sons shall lay their hands upon the head of the ram, 20 and you shall kill the ram, and take part of its blood and put it upon the tip of the right ear of Aaron and upon the tips of the right ears of his sons, and upon the thumbs of their right hands, and upon the great toes of their right feet, and throw the rest of the blood against the altar round about. 21 Then you shall take part of the blood that is on the altar, and of the anointing oil, and sprinkle it upon Aaron and his garments, and upon his sons and his sons' garments with him; and he and his garments shall be holy, and his sons and his sons' garments with him.

22 "You shall also take the fat of the ram, and the fat tail, and the fat that covers the entrails, and the appendage of the liver, and the two kidneys with the fat that is on them, and the right thigh (for it is a ram of ordination), 23 and one loaf of bread, and one cake of bread with oil, and one wafer, out of the basket of unleavened bread that is before the LORD; 24 and you shall put all these in the hands of Aaron and in the hands of his sons, and wave them for a wave offering before the LORD. 25 Then you shall take them from their hands, and burn them on the altar in addition to the burnt offering, as a pleasing odor before the LORD; it is an offering by fire to the LORD.

26 "And you shall take the breast of the ram of Aaron's ordination and wave if for a wave offering before the LORD; and it shall be your portion. 27 And you shall consecrate the breast of the wave offering, and the thigh of the priests' portion, which is waved, and which is offered from the ram of ordination, since it is for Aaron and for his sons. 28 It shall be for Aaron and his sons as a perpetual due from the people of Israel, for it is the priests' portion to be offered by the people of Israel from their peace offerings; it is their offering to the LORD.

29 "The holy garments of Aaron shall be for his sons after him, to be anointed in them and ordained in them. 30 The son who is priest in his place shall wear them seven days, when he comes into the tent of meeting to minister in the holy place.

31 "You shall take the ram of ordination, and boil its flesh in a holy place; 32 and Aaron and his sons shall eat the flesh of the ram and the bread that is in the basket, at the door of the tent of meeting. 33 They shall eat those things with which atonement was made, to ordain and consecrate them, but an outsider shall not eat of them, because they are holy. 34 And if any of the flesh for the ordination, or of the bread, remain until the morning, then you shall burn the remainder with fire; it shall not be eaten, because it is holy.

35 "Thu you shall do to Aaron
and to his ons, according to all that
I have comanded you; through sev-
en days sill you ordain them, 36 and
every day ou shall offer a bull as a sin
offering f atonement. Also you shall
offer a si offering for the altar, when
you mak atonement for it, and shall
anoint it consecrate it. 37 Seven days
you sha make atonement for the al-
tar, and nsecrate it, and the altar
shall be ost holy; whatever touches
the alta hall become holy.

HE DAILY OFFERINGS

38 "w this is what you shall of-
fer up the altar: two lambs a year
old da day continually. 39 One lamb
you s offer in the morning, and
the o lamb you shall offer in the

evening; 40and with the first lamb a
tenth measure of fine flour mingled
with a fourth of a hin of beaten oil,
and a fourth of a hin of wine for a li-
bation. 41And the other lamb you shall
offer in the evening, and shall offer
with it a cereal offering and its liba-
tion, as in the morning, for a pleasing
odor, an offering by fire to the LORD.
42It shall be a continual burnt offering
throughout your generations at the
door of the tent of meeting before the
LORD, where I will meet with you, to
speak there to you. 43There I will meet
with the people of Israel, and it shall
be sanctified by my glory; 44I will con-
secrate the tent of meeting and the
altar; Aaron also and his sons I will
consecrate, to serve me as priest.
45And I will dwell among the people
of Israel, and will be their God. 46And
they shall know that I am the LORD
their God, who brought them forth
out of the land of Egypt that I might
dwell among them; I am the LORD
their God.

THE ALTAR OF INCENSE

30 "You shall make an altar to burn
incense upon; of acacia wood
shall you make it. 2A cubit shall be its
length, and a cubit its breadth; it shall
be square, and two cubits shall be its
height; its horns shall be of one piece
with it. 3And you shall overlay it with
pure gold, its top and its sides round
about and its horns; and you shall
make for it a molding of gold round
about. 4And two golden rings shall
you make for it; under its molding
*on two opp*osite sides of it shall you
make them, and they shall be holders
for poles with which to carry it. 5You
shall make the poles of acacia wood,
and overlay them with gold. 6And you
shall put it before the veil that is by
the ark of the testimony, before the
mercy seat that is over the testimo-
ny, where I will meet with you. 7And
Aaron shall burn fragrant incense
on it; every morning when he dress-
es the lamps he shall burn it, 8and
when Aaron sets up the lamps in the
evening, he shall burn it, a perpetual
incense before the LORD throughout
your generations. 9You shall offer no
unholy incense thereon, nor burnt
offering, nor cereal offering; and
you shall pour no libation thereon.
10Aaron shall make atonement upon
its horns once a year; with the blood
of the sin offering of atonement he
shall make atonement for it once in
the year throughout your generations;
it is most holy to the LORD."

THE HALF SHEKEL FOR THE SANCTUARY

11 The LORD said to Moses,
12"When you take the census of the
people of Israel, then each shall give a
ransom for himself to the LORD when
you number them, that there be no
plague among them when you number
them. 13Each who is numbered in the
census shall give this: half a shekel
according to the shekel of the sanctu-
ary (the shekel is twenty gerahs), half
a shekel as an offering to the LORD.
14Every one who is numbered in the
census, from twenty years old and up-
ward, shall give the LORD's offering.
15The rich shall not give more, and
the poor shall not give less, than the
half shekel, when you give the LORD's
offering to make atonement for your-
selves. 16And you shall take the atone-
ment money from the people of Israel,
and shall appoint it for the service of
the tent of meeting; that it may bring
the people of Israel to remembrance
before the LORD, so as to make atone-
ment for yourselves."

THE BRONZE BASIN

17 The LORD said to Moses, 18"You
shall also make a laver of bronze, with
its base of bronze, for washing. And
you shall put it between the tent of
meeting and the altar, and you shall
put water in it, 19with which Aaron
and his sons shall wash their hands
and their feet. 20When they go into the
tent of meeting, or when they come
near the altar to minister, to burn an

offering by fire to the LORD, they shall
wash with water, lest they die. 21They
shall wash their hands and their
feet, lest they die: it shall be a statute for ever to them, even to him and
to his descendants throughout their
generations."

THE ANOINTING OIL AND INCENSE

22 Moreover, the LORD said to
Moses, 23"Take the finest spices: of
liquid myrrh five hundred shekels,
and of sweet-smelling cinnamon half
as much, that is, two hundred and fifty, and of aromatic cane two hundred
and fifty, 24and of cassia five hundred,
according to the shekel of the sanctuary, and of olive oil a hin; 25and you
shall make of these a sacred anointing oil blended as by the perfumer;
a holy anointing oil it shall be. 26And
you shall anoint with it the tent of
meeting and the ark of the testimony, 27and the table and all its utensils,
and the lampstand and its utensils,
and the altar of incense, 28and the altar of burnt offering with all its utensils and the laver and its base; 29you
shall consecrate them, that they may
be most holy; whatever touches them
will become holy. 30And you shall
anoint Aaron and his sons, and consecrate them, that they may serve me
as priests. 31And you shall say to the
people of Israel, 'This shall be my holy
anointing oil throughout your generations. 32It shall not be poured upon the
bodies of ordinary men, and you shall
make no other like it in composition;
it is holy, and it shall be holy to you.
33Whoever compounds any like it or
whoever puts any of it on an outsider
shall be cut off from his people.'"

34 And the LORD said to Moses,
"Take sweet spices, stacte, and onycha, and galbanum, sweet spices with
pure frankincense (of each shall there
be an equal part), 35and make an incense blended as by the perfumer, seasoned with salt, pure and holy; 36and
you shall beat some of it very small,
and put part of it before the testimony
in the tent of meeting where I shall
meet with you; it shall be for you
most holy. 37And the incense which
you shall make according to its composition, you shall not make for yourselves; it shall be for you holy to the
LORD. 38Whoever makes any like it to
use as perfume shall be cut off from
his people."

BEZALEL AND OHOLIAB

31 The LORD said to Moses, 2"See, I
have called by name Bez´alel the
son of Uri, son of Hur, of the tribe of
Judah: 3and I have filled him with the
Spirit of God, with ability and intelligence, with knowledge and all craftsmanship, 4to devise artistic designs,
to work in gold, silver, and bronze,
5in cutting stones for setting, and in
carving wood, for work in every craft.
6And behold, I have appointed with
him Oho´liab, the son of Ahis´amach,
of the tribe of Dan; and I have given
to all able men ability, that they may
make all that I have commanded you:
7the tent of meeting, and the ark of the
testimony, and the mercy seat that is
thereon, and all the furnishings of
the tent, 8the table and its utensils,
and the pure lampstand with all its
utensils, and the altar of incense, 9and
the altar of burnt offering with all its
utensils, and the laver and its base,
10and the finely worked garments, the
holy garments for Aaron the priest
and the garments of his sons, for their
service as priest, 11and the anointing
oil and the fragrant incense for the
holy place. According to all that I have
commanded you they shall do."

THE SABBATH LAW

12 And the LORD said to Moses,
13"Say to the people of Israel, 'You
shall keep my sabbaths, for this is a
sign between me and you throughout
your generations, that you may know
that I, the LORD, sanctify you. 14You
shall keep the sabbath, because it is
holy for you; every one who profanes
it shall be put to death; whoever does

any work on it, that soul shall be cut off from among his people. 15 Six days shall work be done, but the seventh day is a sabbath of solemn rest, holy to the LORD; whoever does any work on the sabbath day shall be put to death. 16 Therefore the people of Israel shall keep the sabbath, observing the sabbath throughout their generations, as a perpetual covenant. 17 It is a sign for ever between me and the people of Israel that in six days the LORD made heaven and earth, and on the seventh day he rested, and was refreshed.'"

THE TWO TABLETS OF THE COVENANT

18 And he gave to Moses, when he had made an end of speaking with him upon Mount Sinai, the two tables of the testimony, tables of stone, written with the finger of God.

THE GOLDEN CALF

32 When the people saw that Moses delayed to come down from the mountain, the people gathered themselves together to Aaron, and said to him, "Up, make us gods, who shall go before us; as for this Moses, the man who brought us up out of the land of Egypt, we do not know what has become of him." 2 And Aaron said to them, "Take off the rings of gold which are in the ears of your wives, your sons, and your daughters, and bring them to me." 3 So all the people took off the rings of gold which were in their ears, and brought them to Aaron. 4 And he received the gold at their hand, and fashioned it with a *graving tool, and* made a molten calf; and they said, "These are your gods, O Israel, who brought you up out of the land of Egypt!" 5 When Aaron saw this, he built an altar before it; and Aaron made proclamation and said, "Tomorrow shall be a feast to the LORD." 6 And they rose up early on the morrow, and offered burnt offerings and brought peace offerings; and the people sat down to eat and drink, and rose up to play.

7 And the LORD said to Moses, "Go down; for your people, whom you brought up out of the land of Egypt, have corrupted themselves; 8 they have turned aside quickly out of the way which I commanded them; they have made for themselves a molten calf, and have worshiped it and sacrificed to it, and said, 'These are your gods, O Israel, who brought you up out of the land of Egypt!'" 9 And the LORD said to Moses, "I have seen this people, and behold, it is a stiff-necked people; 10 now therefore let me alone, that my wrath may burn hot against them and I may consume them; but of you I will make a great nation."

11 But Moses besought the LORD his God, and said, "O LORD, why does thy wrath burn hot against thy people, whom thou hast brought forth out of the land of Egypt with great power and with a mighty hand? 12 Why should the Egyptians say, 'With evil intent did he bring them forth, to slay them in the mountains, and to consume them from the face of the earth'? Turn from thy fierce wrath, and repent of this evil against thy people. 13 Remember Abraham, Isaac, and Israel, thy servants, to whom thou didst swear by thine own self, and didst say to them, 'I will multiply your descendants as the stars of heaven, and all this land that I have promised I will give to your descendants, and they shall inherit it for ever.'" 14 And the LORD repented of the evil which he thought to do to his people.

15 And Moses turned, and went down from the mountain with the two tables of the testimony in his hands, tables that were written on both sides; on the one side and on the other were they written. 16 And the tables were the work of God, and the writing was the writing of God, graven upon the tables. 17 When Joshua heard the noise of the people as they shouted, he said to Moses, "There is a noise of war in the camp." 18 But he said, "It is not the sound of shouting for victory,

or the sound of the cry of defeat, but
the sound of singing that I hear."
19 And as soon as he came near the
camp and saw the calf and the danc-
ing, Moses' anger burned hot, and he
threw the tables out of his hands and
broke them at the foot of the moun-
tain. 20 And he took the calf which they
had made, and burnt it with fire, and
ground it to powder, and scattered it
upon the water, and made the people
of Israel drink it.

21 And Moses said to Aaron, "What
did this people do to you that you have
brought a great sin upon them?" 22 And
Aaron said, "Let not the anger of my
lord burn hot; you know the people,
that they are set on evil. 23 For they
said to me, 'Make us gods, who shall
go before us; as for this Moses, the
man who brought us up out of the
land of Egypt, we do not know what
has become of him.' 24 And I said to
them, 'Let any who have gold take it
off!'; so they gave it to me, and I threw
it into the fire, and there came out
this calf."

25 And when Moses saw that the
people had broken loose (for Aaron
had let them break loose, to their
shame among their enemies), 26 then
Moses stood in the gate of the camp,
and said, "Who is on the LORD's side?
Come to me." And all the sons of Levi
gathered themselves together to him.
27 And he said to them, "Thus says the
LORD GOD of Israel, 'Put every man
his sword on his side, and go to and
fro from gate to gate throughout the
camp, and slay every man his broth-
er, and every man his companion,
and every man his neighbor.'" 28 And
the sons of Levi did according to the
word of Moses; and there fell of the
people that day about three thousand
men. 29 And Moses said, "Today you
have ordained yourselves[a] for the
service of the LORD, each one at the
cost of his son and of his brother,
that he may bestow a blessing upon
you this day."

30 On the morrow Moses said to
the people, "You have sinned a great
sin. And now I will go up to the LORD;
perhaps I can make atonement for
your sin." 31 So Moses returned to the
LORD and said, "Alas, this people have
sinned a great sin; they have made for
themselves gods of gold. 32 But now,
if thou wilt forgive their sin—and if
not, blot me, I pray thee, out of thy
book which thou hast written." 33 But
the LORD said to Moses, "Whoever
has sinned against me, him will I blot
out of my book. 34 But now go, lead the
people to the place of which I have
spoken to you; behold, my angel shall
go before you. Nevertheless, in the
day when I visit, I will visit their sin
upon them."

35 And the LORD sent a plague
upon the people, because they made
the calf which Aaron made.

THE COMMAND TO LEAVE SINAI

33 The LORD said to Moses, "De-
part, go up hence, you and the
people whom you have brought up
out of the land of Egypt, to the land
of which I swore to Abraham, Isaac,
and Jacob, saying, 'To your descen-
dants I will give it.' 2 And I will send
an angel before you, and I will drive
out the Canaanites, the Amorites, the
Hittites, the Per´izzites, the Hivites,
and the Jeb´usites. 3 Go up to a land
flowing with milk and honey; but I
will not go up among you, lest I con-
sume you in the way, for you are a
stiff-necked people."

4 When the people heard these evil
tidings, they mourned; and no man
put on his ornaments. 5 For the LORD
had said to Moses, "Say to the people
of Israel, 'You are a stiff-necked peo-
ple; if for a single moment I should go
up among you, I would consume you.
So now put off your ornaments from
you, that I may know what to do with
you.'" 6 Therefore the people of Israel
stripped themselves of their orna-
ments, from Mount Horeb onward.

[a] Gk Vg See Tg: Heb *ordain yourselves*

THE TENT OUTSIDE THE CAMP

7 Now Moses used to take the tent
and pitch it outside the camp, far off
from the camp; and he called it the
tent of meeting. And every one who
sought the LORD would go out to the
tent of meeting, which was outside
the camp. 8 Whenever Moses went out
to the tent, all the people rose up, and
every man stood at his tent door, and
looked after Moses, until he had gone
into the tent. 9 When Moses entered
the tent, the pillar of cloud would
descend and stand at the door of the
tent, and the LORD would speak with
Moses. 10 And when all the people saw
the pillar of cloud standing at the door
of the tent, all the people would rise
up and worship, every man at his tent
door. 11 Thus the LORD used to speak to
Moses face to face, as a man speaks to
his friend. When Moses turned again
into the camp, his servant Joshua the
son of Nun, a young man, did not de-
part from the tent.

MOSES' INTERCESSION

12 Moses said to the LORD, "See,
thou sayest to me, 'Bring up this peo-
ple'; but thou hast not let me know
whom thou wilt send with me. Yet
thou hast said, 'I know you by name,
and you have also found favor in my
sight.' 13 Now therefore, I pray thee, if I
have found favor in thy sight, show me
now thy ways, that I may know thee
and find favor in thy sight. Consider
too that this nation is thy people."
14 And he said, "My presence will go
with you, and I will give you rest."
15 And he said to him, "If thy presence
will not go with me, do not carry us up
from here. 16 For how shall it be known
that I have found favor in thy sight, I
and thy people? Is it not in thy going
with us, so that we are distinct, I and
thy people, from all other people that
are upon the face of the earth?"

17 And the LORD said to Moses,
"This very thing that you have spoken
I will do; for you have found favor in
my sight, and I know you by name."
18 Moses said, "I pray thee, show me
thy glory." 19 And he said, "I will make
all my goodness pass before you, and
will proclaim before you my name
'The LORD'; and I will be gracious
to whom I will be gracious, and will
show mercy on whom I will show mer-
cy. 20 But," he said, "you cannot see my
face; for man shall not see me and
live." 21 And the LORD said, "Behold,
there is a place by me where you shall
stand upon the rock; 22 and while my
glory passes by I will put you in a cleft
of the rock, and I will cover you with
my hand until I have passed by; 23 then
I will take away my hand, and you
shall see my back; but my face shall
not be seen."

MOSES MAKES NEW TABLETS

34 The LORD said to Moses, "Cut
two tables of stone like the first;
and I will write upon the tables the
words that were on the first tables,
which you broke. 2 Be ready in the
morning, and come up in the morning
to Mount Sinai, and present yourself
there to me on the top of the moun-
tain. 3 No man shall come up with
you, and let no man be seen through-
out all the mountain; let no flocks or
herds feed before that mountain." 4 So
Moses cut two tables of stone like the
first; and he rose early in the morn-
ing and went up on Mount Sinai, as
the LORD had commanded him, and
took in his hand two tables of stone.
5 And the LORD descended in the cloud
and stood with him there, and pro-
claimed the name of the LORD. 6 The
LORD passed before him, and pro-
claimed, "*The LORD, the LORD*, a God
merciful and gracious, slow to anger,
and abounding in steadfast love and
faithfulness, 7 keeping steadfast love
for thousands, forgiving iniquity and
transgression and sin, but who will
by no means clear the guilty, visiting
the iniquity of the fathers upon the
children and the children's children,
to the third and the fourth genera-
tion." 8 And Moses made haste to bow

his head toward the earth, and wor-
shiped. 9And he said, "If now I have
found favor in thy sight, O Lord, let
the Lord, I pray thee, go in the midst
of us, although it is a stiff-necked peo-
ple; and pardon our iniquity and our
sin, and take us for thy inheritance."

THE COVENANT RENEWED

10 And he said, "Behold, I make
a covenant. Before all your people
I will do marvels, such as have not
been wrought in all the earth or in
any nation; and all the people among
whom you are shall see the work of
the LORD; for it is a terrible thing that
I will do with you.

11 "Observe what I command you
this day. Behold, I will drive out before
you the Amorites, the Canaanites, the
Hittites, the Per´izzites, the Hivites,
and the Jeb´usites. 12Take heed to
yourself, lest you make a covenant
with the inhabitants of the land
whither you go, lest it become a snare
in the midst of you. 13You shall tear
down their altars, and break their
pillars, and cut down their Ashe´rim
14(for you shall worship no other god,
for the LORD, whose name is Jealous,
is a jealous God), 15lest you make a
covenant with the inhabitants of the
land, and when they play the harlot
after their gods and sacrifice to their
gods and one invites you, you eat of
his sacrifice, 16and you take of their
daughters for your sons, and their
daughters play the harlot after their
gods and make your sons play the har-
lot after their gods.

17 "Your shall make for yourself no
molten gods.

18 "The feast of unleavened bread
you shall keep. Seven days you shall
eat unleavened bread, as I command-
ed you, at the time appointed in the
month Abib; for in the month Abib you
came out from Egypt. 19All that opens
the womb is mine, all your male[a] cat-
tle, the firstlings of cow and sheep.
20The firstling of an ass you shall re-
deem with a lamb, or if you will not
redeem it you shall break its neck. All
the first-born of your sons you shall
redeem. And none shall appear before
me empty.

21 "Six days you shall work, but
on the seventh day you shall rest; in
plowing time and in harvest you shall
rest. 22And you shall observe the feast
of weeks, the first fruits of wheat
harvest, and the feast of ingathering
at the year's end. 23Three times in the
year shall all your males appear before
the LORD God, the God of Israel. 24For
I will cast out nations before you, and
enlarge your borders; neither shall
any man desire your land, when you
go up to appear before the LORD your
God three times in the year.

25 "You shall not offer the blood of
my sacrifice with leaven; neither shall
the sacrifice of the feast of the pass-
over be left until the morning. 26The
first of the first fruits of your ground
you shall bring to the house of the
LORD your God. You shall not boil a
kid in its mother's milk."

27 And the LORD said to Moses,
"Write these words; in accordance
with these words I have made a cove-
nant with you and with Israel." 28And
he was there with the LORD forty days
and forty nights; he neither ate bread
nor drank water. And he wrote upon
the tables the words of the covenant,
the ten commandments.[b]

THE SHINING FACE OF MOSES

29 When Moses came down from
Mount Sinai, with the two tables of
the testimony in his hand as he came
down from the mountain, Moses did
not know that the skin of his face
shone because he had been talking
with God. 30And when Aaron and all
the people of Israel saw Moses, be-
hold, the skin of his face shone, and
they were afraid to come near him.
31But Moses called to them; and Aaron

[a] Gk Theodotion Vg Tg: Heb uncertain
[b] Heb *words*

and all the leaders of the congregation
returned to him, and Moses talked
with them. 32And afterward all the
people of Israel came near, and he
gave them in commandment all that
the LORD had spoken with him in
Mount Sinai. 33And when Moses had
finished speaking with them, he put a
veil on his face; 34but whenever Moses
went in before the LORD to speak with
him, he took the veil off, until he came
out; and when he came out, and told
the people of Israel what he was com-
manded, 35the people of Israel saw the
face of Moses, that the skin of Moses'
face shone; and Moses would put the
veil upon his face again, until he went
in to speak with him.

SABBATH REGULATIONS

35 Moses assembled all the congre-
gation of the people of Israel, and
said to them, "These are the things
which the LORD has commanded you
to do. 2Six days shall work be done,
but on the seventh day you shall have
a holy sabbath of solemn rest to the
LORD; whoever does any work on it
shall be put to death; 3you shall kindle
no fire in all your habitations on the
sabbath day."

PREPARATIONS FOR MAKING THE TABERNACLE

4 Moses said to all the congrega-
tion of the people of Israel, "This is
the thing which the LORD has com-
manded. 5Take from among you an
offering to the LORD; whoever is of
a generous heart, let him bring the
LORD's offering: gold, silver, and
bronze; 6blue and purple and scarlet
stuff and fine twined linen; goats'
hair, 7tanned rams' skins, and goat-
skins; acacia wood, 8oil for the light,
spices for the anointing oil and for
the fragrant incense, 9and onyx stones
and stones for setting, for the ephod
and for the breastpiece.

10 "And let every able man among
you come and make all that the LORD
has commanded: the tabernacle, 11its
tent and its covering, its hooks and its
frames, its bars, its pillars, and its bas-
es; 12the ark with its poles, the mercy
seat, and the veil of the screen; 13the
table with its poles and all its utensils,
and the bread of the Presence; 14the
lampstand also for the light, with its
utensils and its lamps, and the oil for
the light; 15and the altar of incense,
with its poles, and the anointing oil
and the fragrant incense, and the
screen for the door, at the door of
the tabernacle; 16the altar of burnt
offering, with its grating of bronze,
its poles, and all its utensils, the la-
ver and its base; 17the hangings of the
court, its pillars and its bases, and the
screen for the gate of the court; 18the
pegs of the tabernacle and the pegs of
the court, and their cords; 19the finely
wrought garments for ministering in
the holy place, the holy garments for
Aaron the priest, and the garments of
his sons, for their service as priests."

OFFERINGS FOR THE TABERNACLE

20 Then all the congregation of the
people of Israel departed from the pres-
ence of Moses. 21And they came, every
one whose heart stirred him, and ev-
ery one whose spirit moved him, and
brought the LORD's offering to be used
for the tent of meeting, and for all its
service, and for the holy garments. 22So
they came, both men and women; all
who were of a willing heart brought
brooches and earrings and signet rings
and armlets, all sorts of gold objects,
every man dedicating an offering of
gold to the LORD. 23And every man
with whom was found blue or purple or
scarlet stuff or fine linen or goats' hair
or tanned rams' skins or goatskins,
brought them. 24Every one who could
make an offering of silver or bronze
brought it as the LORD's offering; and
every man with whom was found acacia
wood of any use in the work, brought it.
25And all women who had ability spun
with their hands, and brought what
they had spun in blue and purple and

scarlet stuff and fine twined linen; 26all
the women whose hearts were moved
with ability spun the goats' hair. 27And
the leaders brought onyx stones and
stones to be set, for the ephod and for
the breastpiece, 28and spices and oil for
the light, and for the anointing oil, and
for the fragrant incense. 29All the men
and women, the people of Israel, whose
heart moved them to bring anything
for the work which the LORD had com-
manded by Moses to be done, brought
it as their freewill offering to the LORD.

BEZALEL AND OHOLIAB

30 And Moses said to the people of
Israel, "See, the LORD has called by
name Bez′alel the son of Uri, son of
Hur, of the tribe of Judah; 31and he has
filled him with the Spirit of God, with
ability, with intelligence, with knowl-
edge, and with all craftsmanship, 32to
devise artistic designs, to work in
gold and silver and bronze, 33in cut-
ting stones for setting, and in carving
wood, for work in every skilled craft.
34And he has inspired him to teach,
both him and Oho′liab the son of
Ahis′amach of the tribe of Dan. 35He
has filled them with ability to do every
sort of work done by a craftsman or by
a designer or by an embroiderer in blue
and purple and scarlet stuff and fine
twined linen, or by a weaver—by any
sort of workman or skilled designer.

36 Bez′alel and Oho′liab and every
able man in whom the LORD has
put ability and intelligence to know
how to do any work in the construc-
tion of the sanctuary shall work in
accordance with all that the LORD has
commanded."

2 And Moses called Bez′alel and
Oho′liab and every able man in whose
mind the LORD had put ability, ev-
ery one whose heart stirred him up
to come to do the work; 3and they
received from Moses all the freewill
offering which the people of Israel
had brought for doing the work on the
sanctuary. They still kept bringing
him freewill offerings every morning,
4so that all the able men who were do-
ing every sort of task on the sanctuary
came, each from the task that he was
doing, 5and said to Moses, "The peo-
ple bring much more than enough for
doing the work which the LORD has
commanded us to do." 6So Moses gave
command, and word was proclaimed
throughout the camp, "Let neither
man nor woman do anything more for
the offering for the sanctuary." So the
people were restrained from bringing;
7for the stuff they had was sufficient
to do all the work, and more.

CONSTRUCTION OF THE TABERNACLE

8 And all the able men among the
workmen made the tabernacle with
ten curtains; they were made of fine
twined linen and blue and purple and
scarlet stuff, with cherubim skilfully
worked. 9The length of each curtain
was twenty-eight cubits, and the
breadth of each curtain four cubits; all
the curtains had the same measure.

10 And he coupled five curtains to
one another, and the other five cur-
tains he coupled to one another. 11And
he made loops of blue on the edge of
the outmost curtain of the first set;
likewise he made them on the edge
of the outmost curtain of the second
set; 12he made fifty loops on the one
curtain, and he made fifty loops on
the edge of the curtain that was in
the second set; the loops were oppo-
site one another. 13And he made fifty
clasps of gold, and coupled the cur-
tains one to the other with clasps; so
the tabernacle was one whole.

14 He also made curtains of goats'
hair for a tent over the tabernacle; he
made eleven curtains. 15The length of
each curtain was thirty cubits, and the
breadth of each curtain four cubits; the
eleven curtains had the same measure.
16He coupled five curtains by them-
selves, and six curtains by themselves.
17And he made fifty loops on the edge
of the outmost curtain of the one set,
and fifty loops on the edge of the other

connecting curtain. 18And he made fif-
ty clasps of bronze to couple the tent
together that it might be one whole.
19And he made for the tent a covering
of tanned rams' skins and goatskins.

20 Then he made the upright
frames for the tabernacle of acacia
wood. 21Ten cubits was the length of
a frame, and a cubit and a half the
breadth of each frame. 22Each frame
had two tenons, for fitting together;
he did this for all the frames of the
tabernacle. 23The frames for the tab-
ernacle he made thus: twenty frames
for the south side; 24and he made for-
ty bases of silver under the twenty
frames, two bases under one frame
for its two tenons, and two bases un-
der another frame for its two tenons.
25And for the second side of the tab-
ernacle, on the north side, he made
twenty frames 26and their forty bases
of silver, two bases under one frame
and two bases under another frame.
27And for the rear of the tabernacle
westward he made six frames. 28And
he made two frames for corners of
the tabernacle in the rear. 29And they
were separate beneath, but joined at
the top, at the first ring; he made two
of them thus, for the two corners.
30There were eight frames with their
bases of silver: sixteen bases, under
every frame two bases.

31 And he made bars of acacia
wood, five for the frames of the one
side of the tabernacle, 32and five bars
for the frames of the other side of
the tabernacle, and five bars for the
frames of the tabernacle at the rear
westward. 33And he made the middle
bar to pass through from end to end
halfway up the frames. 34And he over-
laid the frames with gold, and made
their rings of gold for holders for the
bars, and overlaid the bars with gold.

35 And he made the veil of blue
and purple and scarlet stuff and fine
twined linen; with cherubim skilful-
ly worked he made it. 36And for it he
made four pillars of acacia, and over-
laid them with gold; their hooks were
of gold, and he cast for them four bas-
es of silver. 37He also made a screen for
the door of the tent, of blue and pur-
ple and scarlet stuff and fine twined
linen, embroidered with needlework;
38and its five pillars with their hooks.
He overlaid their capitals, and their
fillets were of gold, but their five bas-
es were of bronze.

MAKING THE ARK OF THE COVENANT

37 Bez'alel made the ark of acacia
wood; two cubits and a half was its
length, a cubit and a half its breadth,
and a cubit and a half its height. 2And
he overlaid it with pure gold within
and without, and made a molding of
gold around it. 3And he cast for it four
rings of gold for its four corners, two
rings on its one side and two rings
on its other side. 4And he made poles
of acacia wood, and overlaid them
with gold, 5and put the poles into the
rings on the sides of the ark, to carry
the ark. 6And he made a mercy seat of
pure gold; two cubits and a half was
its length, and a cubit and a half its
breadth. 7And he made two cherubim
of hammered gold; on the two ends
of the mercy seat he made them, 8one
cherub on the one end, and one cherub
on the other end; of one piece with the
mercy seat he made the cherubim on
its two ends. 9The cherubim spread out
their wings above, overshadowing the
mercy seat with their wings, with their
faces one to another; toward the mercy
seat were the faces of the cherubim.

MAKING THE TABLE FOR THE BREAD OF THE PRESENCE

10 He also made the table of acacia
wood; two cubits was its length, a cu-
bit its breadth, and a cubit and a half
its height; 11and he overlaid it with
pure gold, and made a molding of gold
around it. 12And he made around it a
frame a handbreadth wide, and made
a molding of gold around the frame.
13He cast for it four rings of gold, and
fastened the rings to the four corners

at its four legs. 14Close to the frame
were the rings, as holders for the
poles to carry the table. 15He made
the poles of acacia wood to carry the
table, and overlaid them with gold.
16And he made the vessels of pure gold
which were to be upon the table, its
plates and dishes for incense, and its
bowls and flagons with which to pour
libations.

MAKING THE LAMPSTAND

17 He also made the lampstand of
pure gold. The base and the shaft of
the lampstand were made of ham-
mered work; its cups, its capitals, and
its flowers were of one piece with it.
18And there were six branches going
out of its sides, three branches of the
lampstand out of one side of it and
three branches of the lampstand out
of the other side of it; 19three cups
made like almonds, each with cap-
ital and flower, on one branch, and
three cups made like almonds, each
with capital and flower, on the oth-
er branch—so for the six branches
going out of the lampstand. 20And on
the lampstand itself were four cups
made like almonds, with their capi-
tals and flowers, 21and a capital of one
piece with it under each pair of the six
branches going out of it. 22Their cap-
itals and their branches were of one
piece with it; the whole of it was one
piece of hammered work of pure gold.
23And he made its seven lamps and
its snuffers and its trays of pure gold.
24He made it and all its utensils of a
talent of pure gold.

MAKING THE ALTAR OF INCENSE

25 He made the altar of incense of
acacia wood; its length was a cubit,
and its breadth was a cubit; it was
square, and two cubits was its height;
its horns were of one piece with it.
26He overlaid it with pure gold, its
top, and its sides round about, and its
horns; and he made a molding of gold
round about it, 27and made two rings
of gold on it under its molding, on two
opposite sides of it, as holders for the
poles with which to carry it. 28And he
made the poles of acacia wood, and
overlaid them with gold.

MAKING THE ANOINTING OIL AND THE INCENSE

29 He made the holy anointing oil
also, and the pure fragrant incense,
blended as by the perfumer.

MAKING THE ALTAR OF BURNT OFFERING

38 He made the altar of burnt of-
fering also of acacia wood; five
cubits was its length, and five cubits
its breadth; it was square, and three
cubits was its height. 2He made horns
for it on its four corners; its horns
were of one piece with it, and he over-
laid it with bronze. 3And he made all
the utensils of the altar, the pots, the
shovels, the basins, the forks, and the
firepans; all its utensils he made of
bronze. 4And he made for the altar a
grating, a network of bronze, under
its ledge, extending halfway down.
5He cast four rings on the four cor-
ners of the bronze grating as holders
for the poles; 6he made the poles of
acacia wood, and overlaid them with
bronze. 7And he put the poles through
the rings on the sides of the altar, to
carry it with them; he made it hollow,
with boards.

8 And he made the laver of bronze
and its base of bronze, from the mir-
rors of the ministering women who
ministered at the door of the tent of
meeting.

MAKING THE COURT OF THE TABERNACLE

9 And he made the court; for the
south side the hangings of the court
were of fine twined linen, a hundred
cubits; 10their pillars were twenty and
their bases twenty, of bronze, but the
hooks of the pillars and their fillets
were of silver. 11And for the north side
a hundred cubits, their pillars twenty,
their bases twenty, of bronze, but the
hooks of the pillars and their fillets

were of silver. 12And for the west side
were hangings of fifty cubits, their
pillars ten, and their sockets ten; the
hooks of the pillars and their fillets
were of silver. 13And for the front to
the east, fifty cubits. 14The hangings
for one side of the gate were fifteen
cubits, with three pillars and three
bases. 15And so for the other side; on
this hand and that hand by the gate
of the court were hangings of fifteen
cubits, with three pillars and three
bases. 16All the hangings round about
the court were of fine twined linen.
17And the bases for the pillars were
of bronze, but the hooks of the pil-
lars and their fillets were of silver;
the overlaying of their capitals was
also of silver, and all the pillars of the
court were filleted with silver. 18And
the screen for the gate of the court
was embroidered with needlework
in blue and purple and scarlet stuff
and fine twined linen; it was twenty
cubits long and five cubits high in its
breadth, corresponding to the hang-
ings of the court. 19And their pillars
were four; their four bases were of
bronze, their hooks of silver, and the
overlaying of their capitals and their
fillets of silver. 20And all the pegs for
the tabernacle and for the court round
about were of bronze.

MATERIALS OF THE TABERNACLE

21 This is the sum of the thingsor
the tabernacle, the tabernacle ofıe
testimony, as they were counteat
the commandment of Moses, forıe
work of the Levites under the dı-
tion of Ith´amar the son of Aarone
priest. 22Bez´alel the son of Uri, sof
Hur, of the tribe of Judah, madıl
that the LORD commanded Mo;
23and with him was Oho´liab thei
of Ahis´amach, of the tribe of Da
craftsman and designer and emb-
derer in blue and purple and sct
stuff and fine twined linen.

24 All the gold that was usec
the work, in all the construc
of the sanctuary, the gold from
offering, was twenty-nine talents and
seven hundred and thirty shekels, by
the shekel of the sanctuary. 25And the
silver from those of the congregation
who were numbered was a hundred
talents and a thousand seven hundred
and seventy-five shekels, by the shek-
el of the sanctuary: 26a beka a head
(that is, half a shekel, by the shekel of
the sanctuary), for every one who was
numbered in the census, from twenty
years old and upward, for six hundred
and three thousand, five hundred and
fifty men. 27The hundred talents of sil-
ver were for casting the bases of the
sanctuary, and the bases of the veil;
a hundred bases for the hundred tal-
ents, a talent for a base. 28And of the
thousand seven hundred and sev-
enty-five shekels he made hooks for
the pillars, and overlaid their capi-
tals and made fillets for them. 29And
the bronze that was contributed was
seventy talents, and two thousand
and four hundred shekels; 30with it
he made the bases for the door of the
tent of meeting, the bronze altar and
the bronze grating for it and all the
utensils of the altar, 31the bases round
about the court, and the bases of the
gate of the court, all the pegs of the
tabernacle, and all the pegs round
about the court.

MAKING THE VESTMENTS FOR THE PRIESTHOOD

39And of the blue and purple and
scarlet stuff they made finely
wrought garments, for ministering
in the holy place; they made the holy
garments for Aaron; as the LORD had
commanded Moses.

2 And he made the ephod of gold,
blue and purple and scarlet stuff, and
fine twined linen. 3And gold leaf was
hammered out and cut into threads to
work into the blue and purple and the
scarlet stuff, and into the fine twined
linen, in skilled design. 4They made
for the ephod shoulder-pieces, joined
to it at its two edges. 5And the skilful-
ly woven band upon it, to gird it on,

was of the same materials and work-
manship, of gold, blue and purple and
scarlet stuff, and fine twined linen; as
the LORD had commanded Moses.

6 The onyx stones were prepared,
enclosed in settings of gold filigree
and engraved like the engravings of a
signet, according to the names of the
sons of Israel. 7And he set them on the
shoulder-pieces of the ephod, to be
stones of remembrance for the sons of
Israel; as the LORD had commanded
Moses.

8 He made the breastpiece, in
skilled work, like the work of the
ephod, of gold, blue and purple and
scarlet stuff, and fine twined linen. 9It
was square; the breastpiece was made
double, a span its length and a span
its breadth when doubled. 10And they
set in it four rows of stones. A row of
sardius, topaz, and carbuncle was the
first row; 11and the second row, an em-
erald, a sapphire, and a diamond; 12and
the third row, a jacinth, an agate, and
an amethyst; 13and the fourth row, a
beryl, an onyx, and a jasper; they were
enclosed in settings of gold filigree.
14There were twelve stones with their
names according to the names of the
sons of Israel; they were like signets,
each engraved with its name, for the
twelve tribes. 15And they made on the
breastpiece twisted chains like cords,
of pure gold; 16and they made two
settings of gold filigree and two gold
rings, and put the two rings on the two
edges of the breastpiece; 17and they
put the two cords of gold in the two
rings at the edges of the breastpiece.
18Two ends of the two cords they had
attached to the two settings of filigree;
thus they attached it in front to the
shoulder-pieces of the ephod. 19Then
they made two rings of gold, and put
them at the two ends of the breast-
piece, on its inside edge next to the
ephod. 20And they made two rings of
gold, and attached them in front to the
lower part of the two shoulder-pieces
of the ephod, at its joining above the
skilfully woven band of the ephod.
21And they bound the breastpiece by
its rings to the rings of the ephod with
a lace of blue, so that it should lie upon
the skilfully woven band of the ephod,
and that the breastpiece should not
come loose from the ephod; as the
LORD had commanded Moses.

22 He also made the robe of the
ephod woven all of blue; 23and the
opening of the robe in it was like
the opening in a garment, with a
binding around the opening, that it
might not be torn. 24On the skirts of
the robe they made pomegranates of
blue and purple and scarlet stuff and
fine twined linen. 25They also made
bells of pure gold, and put the bells
between the pomegranates upon the
skirts of the robe round about, be-
tween the pomegranates; 26a bell and a
pomegranate, a bell and a pomegran-
ate round about upon the skirts of the
robe for ministering; as the LORD had
commanded Moses.

27They also made the coats, woven
of fine linen, for Aaron and his sons,
28and the turban of fine linen, and
the caps of fine linen, and the linen
breeches of fine twined linen, 29and
the girdle of fine twined linen and
of blue and purple and scarlet stuff,
embroidered with needlework; as the
LORD had commanded Moses.

30 And they made the plate of the
ho crown of pure gold, and wrote
upo it an inscription, like the engrav-
ingof a signet, "Holy to the LORD."
31Al they tied to it a lace of blue, to
fasn it on the turban above; as the
Lo had commanded Moses.

THE WORK COMPLETED

Thus all the work of the taber-
naof the tent of meeting was fin-
ish and the people of Israel had
doaccording to all that the LORD
hammanded Moses; so had they
do33And they brought the taberna-
cleMoses, the tent and all its uten-
sils hooks, its frames, its bars, its
pil and its bases; 34the covering of
tai rams' skins and goatskins, and

the veil of the screen; 35the ark of the
testimony with its poles and the mer-
cy seat; 36the table with all its utensils,
and the bread of the Presence; 37the
lampstand of pure gold and its lamps
with the lamps set and all its utensils,
and the oil for the light; 38the golden
altar, the anointing oil and the fra-
grant incense, and the screen for the
door of the tent; 39the bronze altar,
and its grating of bronze, its poles,
and all its utensils; the laver and its
base; 40the hangings of the court, its
pillars, and its bases, and the screen
for the gate of the court, its cords,
and its pegs; and all the utensils for
the service of the tabernacle, for the
tent of meeting; 41the finely worked
garments for ministering in the holy
place, the holy garments for Aaron the
priest, and the garments of his sons to
serve as priests. 42According to all that
the LORD had commanded Moses, so
the people of Israel had done all the
work. 43And Moses saw all the work,
and behold, they had done it; as the
LORD had commanded, so had they
done it. And Moses blessed them.

THE TABERNACLE ERECTED AND ITS EQUIPMENT INSTALLED

40 The LORD said to Moses, 2"On
the first day of the first month
you shall erect the tabernacle of the
tent of meeting. 3And you shall put in
it the ark of the testimony, and you
shall screen the ark with the veil.
4And you shall bring in the table, and
set its arrangements in order; and you
shall bring in the lampstand, and set
up its lamps. 5And you shall put the
golden altar for incense before the
ark of the testimony, and set up the
screen for the door of the tabernacle.
6You shall set the altar of burnt offer-
ing before the door of the tabernacle
of the tent of meeting, 7and place the
laver between the tent of meeting and
the altar, and put water in it. 8And you
shall set up the court round about,
and hang up the screen for the gate
of the court. 9Then you shall take the
anointing oil, and anoint the taberna-
cle and all that is in it, and consecrate
it and all its furniture; and it shall
become holy. 10You shall also anoint
the altar of burnt offering and all its
utensils, and consecrate the altar; and
the altar shall be most holy. 11You shall
also anoint the laver and its base, and
consecrate it. 12Then you shall bring
Aaron and his sons to the door of the
tent of meeting, and shall wash them
with water, 13and put upon Aaron the
holy garments, and you shall anoint
him and consecrate him, that he may
serve me as priest. 14You shall bring
his sons also and put coats on them,
15and anoint them, as you anointed
their father, that they may serve me
as priests: and their anointing shall
admit them to a perpetual priesthood
throughout their generations."

16 Thus did Moses; according to all
that the LORD commanded him, so he
did. 17And in the first month in the sec-
ond year, on the first day of the month,
the tabernacle was erected. 18Moses
erected the tabernacle; he laid its bas-
es, and set up its frames, and put in its
poles, and raised up its pillars; 19and
he spread the tent over the tabernacle,
and put the covering of the tent over it,
as the LORD had commanded Moses.
20And he took the testimony and put
it into the ark, and put the poles on
the ark, and set the mercy seat above
on the ark; 21and he brought the ark
into the tabernacle, and set up the veil
of the screen, and screened the ark of
the testimony; as the LORD had com-
manded Moses. 22And he put the table
in the tent of meeting, on the north
side of the tabernacle, outside the veil,
23and set the bread in order on it before
the LORD; as the LORD had command-
ed Moses. 24And he put the lampstand
in the tent of meeting, opposite the
table on the south side of the taberna-
cle, 25and set up the lamps before the
LORD; as the LORD had commanded
Moses. 26And he put the golden altar
in the tent of meeting before the veil,
27and burnt fragrant incense upon it;

as the LORD had commanded Moses.
28And he put in place the screen for
the door of the tabernacle. 29And he
set the altar of burnt offering at the
door of the tabernacle of the tent of
meeting, and offered upon it the burnt
offering and the cereal offering; as the
LORD had commanded Moses. 30And
he set the laver between the tent of
meeting and the altar, and put water
in it for washing, 31with which Moses
and Aaron and his sons washed their
hands and their feet; 32when they went
into the tent of meeting, and when they
approached the altar, they washed; as
the LORD commanded Moses. 33And he
erected the court round the tabernacle
and the altar, and set up the screen of
the gate of the court. So Moses fin-
ished the work.

THE CLOUD AND THE GLORY

34Then the cloud* covered the tent
of meeting, and the glory of the LORD
filled the tabernacle.

35And Moses was not able to en-
ter the tent of meeting, because the
cloud abode upon it, and the glory
of the LORD filled the tabernacle.
36Throughout all their journeys, when-
ever the cloud was taken up from over
the tabernacle, the people of Israel
would go onward;

37but if the cloud was not taken up,
then they did not go onward till the
day that it was taken up.

38For throughout all their journeys
the cloud of the LORD was upon the
tabernacle by day, and fire was in it
by night, in the sight of all the house
of Israel.

THE THIRD BOOK OF MOSES COMMONLY CALLED

LEVITICUS

THE BURNT OFFERING

1 The LORD called Moses, and spoke
to him from the tent of meeting,
saying, 2 "Speak to the people of Israel,
and say to them, When any man of
you brings an offering to the LORD,
you shall bring your offering of cattle
from the herd or from the flock.

3 "If his offering is a burnt offering
from the herd, he shall offer a male
without blemish; he shall offer it at
the door of the tent of meeting, that
he may be accepted before the LORD;
4 he shall lay his hand upon the head
of the burnt offering, and it shall be
accepted for him to make atonement
for him. 5 Then he shall kill the bull
before the LORD; and Aaron's sons the
priests shall present the blood, and
throw the blood round about against
the altar that is at the door of the
tent of meeting. 6 And he shall flay the
burnt offering and cut it into pieces;
7 and the sons of Aaron the priest shall
put fire on the altar, and lay wood
in order upon the fire; 8 and Aaron's
sons the priests shall lay the pieces,
the head, and the fat, in order upon
the wood that is on the fire upon the
altar; 9 but its entrails and its legs he
shall wash with water. And the priest
shall burn the whole on the altar, as
a burnt offering, an offering by fire, a
pleasing odor to the LORD.

10 "If his gift for a burnt offering
is from the flock, from the sheep or
goats, he shall offer a male without
blemish; 11 and he shall kill it on the
north side of the altar before the
LORD, and Aaron's sons the priests
shall throw its blood against the altar
round about. 12 And he shall cut it into
pieces, with its head and its fat, and
the priest shall lay them in order upon
the wood that is on the fire upon the
altar; 13 but the entrails and the legs he
shall wash with water. And the priest
shall offer the whole, and burn it on
the altar; it is a burnt offering, an of-
fering by fire, a pleasing odor to the
LORD.

14 "If his offering to the LORD is a
burnt offering of birds, then he shall
bring his offering of turtledoves or of
young pigeons. 15 And the priest shall
bring it to the altar and wring off its
head, and burn it on the altar; and its
blood shall be drained out on the side
of the altar; 16 and he shall take away
its crop with the feathers, and cast it
beside the altar on the east side, in the
place for ashes; 17 he shall tear it by its
wings, but shall not divide it asunder.
And the priest shall burn it on the al-
tar, upon the wood that is on the fire;
it is a burnt offering, an offering by
fire, a pleasing odor to the LORD.

GRAIN OFFERINGS

2 "When any one brings a cereal of-
fering as an offering to the LORD,
his offering shall be of fine flour; he
shall pour oil upon it, and put frank-
incense on it, 2 and bring it to Aaron's
sons the priests. And he shall take
from it a handful of the fine flour and
oil, with all of its frankincense; and
the priest shall burn this as its memo-
rial portion upon the altar, an offering
by fire, a pleasing odor to the LORD.
3 And what is left of the cereal offering
shall be for Aaron and his sons; it is a
most holy part of the offerings by fire
to the LORD.

4 "When you bring a cereal offer-
ing baked in the oven as an offering, it
shall be unleavened cakes of fine flour
mixed with oil, or unleavened wafers
spread with oil. 5 And if your offering
is a cereal offering baked on a griddle,
it shall be of fine flour unleavened,
mixed with oil; 6 you shall break it in
pieces, and pour oil on it; it is a ce-
real offering. 7 And if your offering is

a cereal offering cooked in a pan, it
shall be made of fine flour with oil.
8And you shall bring the cereal offer-
ing that is made of these things to the
LORD; and when it is presented to the
priest, he shall bring it to the altar.
9And the priest shall take from the
cereal offering its memorial portion
and burn this on the altar, an offering
by fire, a pleasing odor to the LORD.
10And what is left of the cereal offer-
ing shall be for Aaron and his sons; it
is a most holy part of the offerings by
fire to the LORD.

11 "No cereal offering which you
bring to the LORD shall be made with
leaven; for you shall burn no leaven
nor any honey as an offering by fire
to the LORD. 12As an offering of first
fruits you may bring them to the
LORD, but they shall not be offered
on the altar for a pleasing odor. 13You
shall season all your cereal offerings
with salt; you shall not let the salt of
the covenant with your God be lack-
ing from your cereal offering; with all
your offerings you shall offer salt.

14 "If you offer a cereal offering of
first fruits to the LORD, you shall of-
fer for the cereal offering of your first
fruits crushed new grain from fresh
ears, parched with fire. 15And you
shall put oil upon it, and lay frankin-
cense on it; it is a cereal offering. 16And
the priest shall burn as its memorial
portion part of the crushed grain and
of the oil with all of its frankincense;
it is an offering by fire to the LORD.

OFFERINGS OF WELL-BEING

3 "If a man's offering is a sacrifice of
peace offering, if he offers an ani-
mal from the herd, male or female,
he shall offer it without blemish be-
fore the LORD. 2And he shall lay his
hand upon the head of his offering
and kill it at the door of the tent of
meeting; and Aaron's sons the priests
shall throw the blood against the altar
round about. 3And from the sacrifice
of the peace offering, as an offering
by fire to the LORD, he shall offer the
fat covering the entrails and all the fat
that is on the entrails, 4and the two
kidneys with the fat that is on them
at the loins, and the appendage of the
liver which he shall take away with
the kidneys. 5Then Aaron's sons shall
burn it on the altar upon the burnt of-
fering, which is upon the wood on the
fire; it is an offering by fire, a pleasing
odor to the LORD.

6 "If his offering for a sacrifice of
peace offering to the LORD is an an-
imal from the flock, male or female,
he shall offer it without blemish. 7If he
offers a lamb for his offering, then he
shall offer it before the LORD, 8laying
his hand upon the head of his offering
and killing it before the tent of meet-
ing; and Aaron's sons shall throw its
blood against the altar round about.
9Then from the sacrifice of the peace
offering as an offering by fire to the
LORD he shall offer its fat, the fat tail
entire, taking it away close by the
backbone, and the fat that covers the
entrails, and all the fat that is on the
entrails, 10and the two kidneys with
the fat that is on them at the loins,
and the appendage of the liver which
he shall take away with the kidneys.
11And the priest shall burn it on the al-
tar as foodoffered by fire to the LORD.

12 "If his offering is a goat, then he
shall offer it before the LORD, 13and
lay his hand upon its head, and kill
it before the tent of meeting; and the
sons of Aaron shall throw its blood
against the altar round about. 14Then
he shall offer from it, as his offering
for an offering by fire to the LORD, the
fat covering the entrails, and all the fat
that is on the entrails, 15and the two
kidneys with the fat that is on them
at the loins, and the appendage of the
liver which he shall take away with the
kidneys. 16And the priest shall burn
them on the altar as food offered by
fire for a pleasing odor. All fat is the
LORD's. 17It shall be a perpetual stat-
ute throughout your generations, in
all your dwelling places, that you eat
neither fat nor blood."

SIN OFFERINGS

4 And the LORD said to Moses, 2"Say
to the people of Israel, If any one
sins unwittingly in any of the things
which the LORD has commanded not
to be done, and does any one of them,
3if it is the anointed priest who sins,
thus bringing guilt on the people,
then let him offer for the sin which he
has committed a young bull without
blemish to the LORD for a sin offer-
ing. 4He shall bring the bull to the
door of the tent of meeting before the
LORD, and lay his hand on the head of
the bull, and kill the bull before the
LORD. 5And the anointed priest shall
take some of the blood of the bull and
bring it to the tent of meeting; 6and
the priest shall dip his finger in the
blood and sprinkle part of the blood
seven times before the LORD in front
of the veil of the sanctuary. 7And the
priest shall put some of the blood on
the horns of the altar of fragrant in-
cense before the LORD which is in the
tent of meeting, and the rest of the
blood of the bull he shall pour out at
the base of the altar of burnt offer-
ing which is at the door of the tent of
meeting. 8And all the fat of the bull
of the sin offering he shall take from
it, the fat that covers the entrails and
all the fat that is on the entrails, 9and
the two kidneys with the fat that is on
them at the loins, and the appendage
of the liver which he shall take away
with the kidneys 10(just as these are
taken from the ox of the sacrifice of
the peace offerings), and the priest
shall burn them upon the altar of
burnt offering. 11But the skin of the
bull and all its flesh, with its head, its
legs, its entrails, and its dung, 12the
whole bull he shall carry forth outside
the camp to a clean place, where the
ashes are poured out, and shall burn it
on a fire of wood; where the ashes are
poured out it shall be burned.

13 "If the whole congregation of
Israel commits a sin unwittingly and
the thing is hidden from the eyes of
the assembly, and they do any one
of the things which the LORD has
commanded not to be done and are
guilty; 14when the the sin which they
have committed becomes known, the
assembly shall offer a young bull for
a sin offering and bring it before the
tent of meeting; 15and the elders of
the congregation shall lay their hands
upon the head of the bull before the
LORD, and the bull shall be killed be-
fore the LORD. 16Then the anointed
priest shall bring some of the blood
of the bull to the tent of meeting,
17and the priest shall dip his finger in
the blood and sprinkle it seven times
before the LORD in front of the veil.
18And he shall put some of the blood
on the horns of the altar which is in
the tent of meeting before the LORD;
and the rest of the blood he shall pour
out at the base of the altar of burnt of-
fering which is at the door of the tent
of meeting. 19And all its fat he shall
take from it and burn upon the altar.
20Thus shall he do with the bull; as he
did with the bull of the sin offering,
so shall he do with this; and the priest
shall make atonement for them, and
they shall be forgiven. 21And he shall
carry forth the bull outside the camp,
and burn it as he burned the first bull;
it is the sin offering for the assembly.

22 "When a ruler sins, doing un-
wittingly any one of all the things
which the LORD his God has com-
manded not to be done, and is guilty,
23if the sin which he has committed is
made known to him, he shall bring
as his offering a goat, a male without
blemish, 24and shall lay his hand upon
the head of the goat, and kill it in the
place where they kill the burnt offer-
ing before the LORD; it is a sin offer-
ing. 25Then the priest shall take some
of the blood of the sin offering with
his finger and put it on the horns of
the altar of burnt offering, and pour
out the rest of its blood at the base
of the altar of burnt offering. 26And
all its fat he shall burn on the altar,
like the fat of the sacrifice of peace
offerings; so the priest shall make

atonement for him for his sin, and he
shall be forgiven.

27 "If any one of the common peo-
ple sins unwittingly in doing any one
of the things which the LORD has
commanded not to be done, and is
guilty, 28when the sin which he has
committed is made known to him he
shall bring for his offering a goat, a
female without blemish, for his sin
which he has committed. 29And he
shall lay his hand on the head of the
sin offering, and kill the sin offering
in the place of burnt offering. 30And
the priest shall take some of its blood
with his finger and put it on the horns
of the altar of burnt offering, and pour
out the rest of its blood at the base of
the altar. 31And all its fat he shall re-
move, as the fat is removed from the
peace offerings, and the priest shall
burn it upon the altar for a pleasing
odor to the LORD; and the priest shall
make atonement for him, and he shall
be forgiven.

32 "If he brings a lamb as his offer-
ing for a sin offering, he shall bring a
female without blemish, 33and lay his
hand upon the head of the sin offering,
and kill it for a sin offering in the place
where they kill the burnt offering.
34Then the priest shall take some of
the blood of the sin offering with his
finger and put it on the horns of the
altar of burnt offering, and pour out
the rest of its blood at the base of the
altar. 35And all its fat he shall remove
as the fat of the lamb is removed from
the sacrifice of peace offerings, and
the priest shall burn it on the altar,
upon the offerings by fire to the LORD;
and the priest shall make atonement
for him for the sin which he has com-
mitted, and he shall be forgiven.

5 "If any one sins in that he hears
a public adjuration to testify and
though he is a witness, whether he
has seen or come to know the matter,
yet does not speak, he shall bear his
iniquity. 2Or if any one touches an un-
clean thing, whether the carcass of an
unclean beast or a carcass of unclean
cattle or a carcass of unclean swarm-
ing things, and it is hidden from him,
and he has become unclean, he shall
be guilty. 3Or if he touches human
uncleanness, of whatever sort the un-
cleanness may be with which one be-
comes unclean, and it is hidden from
him, when he comes to know it he
shall be guilty. 4Or if any one utters
with his lips a rash oath to do evil or to
do good, any sort of rash oath that men
swear, and it is hidden from him, when
he comes to know it he shall in any of
these be guilty. 5When a man is guilty
in any of these, he shall confess the sin
he has committed, 6and he shall bring
his guilt offering to the LORD for the
sin which he has committed, a female
from the flock, a lamb or a goat, for a
sin offering; and the priest shall make
atonement for him for his sin.

7 "But if he cannot afford a lamb,
then he shall bring, as his guilt offer-
ing to the LORD for the sin which he
has committed, two turtledoves or
two young pigeons, one for a sin of-
fering and the other for a burnt offer-
ing. 8He shall bring them to the priest,
who shall offer first the one for the sin
offering; he shall wring its head from
its neck, but shall not sever it, 9and
he shall sprinkle some of the blood
of the sin offering on the side of the
altar, while the rest of the blood shall
be drained out at the base of the al-
tar; it is a sin offering. 10Then he shall
offer the second for a burnt offering
according to the ordinance; and the
priest shall make atonement for him
for the sin which he has committed,
and he shall be forgiven.

11 "But if he cannot afford two tur-
tledoves or two young pigeons, then
he shall bring, as his offering for the
sin which he has committed, a tenth
of an ephah of fine flour for a sin of-
fering; he shall put no oil upon it, and
shall put no frankincense on it, for it
is a sin offering. 12And he shall bring it
to the priest, and the priest shall take
a handful of it as its memorial portion

and burn this on the altar, upon the
offerings by fire to the LORD; it is a sin
offering. 13Thus the priest shall make
atonement for him for the sin which
he has committed in any one of these
things, and he shall be forgiven. And
the remainder shall be for the priest,
as in the cereal offering."

OFFERINGS WITH RESTITUTION

14 The LORD said to Moses, 15"If
any one commits a breach of faith and
sins unwittingly in any of the holy
things of the LORD, he shall bring, as
his guilt offering to the LORD, a ram
without blemish out of the flock, val-
ued by you in shekels of silver, accord-
ing to the shekel of the sanctuary; it is
a guilt offering. 16He shall also make
restitution for what he has done amiss
in the holy thing, and shall add a fifth
to it and give it to the priest; and the
priest shall make atonement for him
with the ram of the guilt offering, and
he shall be forgiven.

17 "If any one sins, doing any of the
things which the LORD has command-
ed not to be done, though he does not
know it, yet he is guilty and shall bear
his iniquity. 18He shall bring to the
priest a ram without blemish out of
the flock, valued by you at the price
for a guilt offering, and the priest shall
make atonement for him for the error
which he committed unwittingly, and
he shall be forgiven. 19It is a guilt of-
fering; he is guilty before the LORD."

6[a] The LORD said to Moses, 2"If any
one sins and commits a breach of
faith against the LORD by deceiving
his neighbor in a matter of deposit
or security, or through robbery, or if
he has oppressed his neighbor 3or has
found what was lost and lied about
it, swearing falsely—in any of all the
things which men do and sin there-
in, 4when one has sinned and become
guilty, he shall restore what he took by
robbery, or what he got by oppression,
or the deposit which was committed
to him, or the lost thing which he
found, 5or anything about which he
has sworn falsely; he shall restore it
in full, and shall add a fifth to it, and
give it to him to whom it belongs, on
the day of his guilt offering. 6And he
shall bring to the priest his guilt offer-
ing to the LORD, a ram without blem-
ish out of the flock, valued by you at
the price for a guilt offering; 7and the
priest shall make atonement for him
before the LORD, and he shall be for-
given for any of the things which one
may do and thereby become guilty."

INSTRUCTIONS CONCERNING SACRIFICES

8[b] The LORD said to Moses,
9"Command Aaron and his sons, say-
ing, This is the law of the burnt of-
fering. The burnt offering shall be on
the hearth upon the altar all night
until the morning, and the fire of
the altar shall be kept burning on it.
10And the priest shall put on his linen
garment, and put his linen breeches
upon his body, and he shall take up
the ashes to which the fire has con-
sumed the burnt offering on the altar,
and put them beside the altar. 11Then
he shall put off his garments, and put
on other garments, and carry forth
the ashes outside the camp to a clean
place. 12The fire on the altar shall be
kept burning on it, it shall not go out;
the priest shall burn wood on it every
morning, and he shall lay the burnt of-
fering in order upon it, and shall burn
on it the fat of the peace offerings.
13Fire shall be kept burning upon the
altar continually; it shall not go out.

14 "And this is the law of the ce-
real offering. The sons of Aaron shall
offer it before the LORD, in front of
the altar. 15And one shall take from it
a handful of the fine flour of the ce-
real offering with its oil and all the
frankincense which is on the cereal
offering, and burn this as its memo-
rial portion on the altar, a pleasing

[a]Ch 5.20 in Heb
[b]Ch 6.1 in Heb

odor to the LORD. 16And the rest of it
Aaron and his sons shall eat; it shall
be eaten unleavened in a holy place; in
the court of the tent of meeting they
shall eat it. 17It shall not be baked with
leaven. I have given it as their portion
of my offerings by fire; it is a thing
most holy, like the sin offering and
the guilt offering. 18Every male among
the children of Aaron may eat of it, as
decreed for ever throughout your gen-
erations, from the LORD's offerings by
fire; whoever touches them shall be-
come holy."

19 The LORD said to Moses, 20"This
is the offering which Aaron and his
sons shall offer to the LORD on the
day when he is anointed: a tenth of an
ephah of fine flour as a regular cere-
al offering, half of it in the morning
and half in the evening. 21It shall be
made with oil on a griddle; you shall
bring it well mixed, in baked[a] pieces
like a cereal offering, and offer it for
a pleasing odor to the LORD. 22The
priest from among Aaron's sons, who
is anointed to succeed him, shall offer
it to the LORD as decreed for ever; the
whole of it shall be burned. 23Every ce-
real offering of a priest shall be wholly
burned; it shall not be eaten."

24 The LORD said to Moses, 25"Say
to Aaron and his sons, This is the law
of the sin offering. In the place where
the burnt offering is killed shall the
sin offering be killed before the LORD;
it is most holy. 26The priest who offers
it for sin shall eat it; in a holy place
it shall be eaten, in the court of the
tent of meeting. 27Whatever[b] touches
its flesh shall be holy; and when any
of its blood is sprinkled on a garment,
you shall wash that on which it was
sprinkled in a holy place. 28And the
earthen vessel in which it is boiled
shall be broken; but if it is boiled in
a bronze vessel, that shall be scoured,
and rinsed in water. 29Every male
among the priests may eat of it; it is
most holy. 30But no sin offering shall
be eaten from which any blood is
brought into the tent of meeting to
make atonement in the holy place; it
shall be burned with fire.

7 "This is the law of the guilt offer-
ing. It is most holy; 2in the place
where they kill the burnt offering
they shall kill the guilt offering, and
its blood shall be thrown on the altar
round about. 3And all its fat shall be
offered, the fat tail, the fat that covers
the entrails, 4the two kidneys with the
fat that is on them at the loins, and
the appendage of the liver which he
shall take away with the kidneys; 5the
priest shall burn them on the altar as
an offering by fire to the LORD; it is a
guilt offering. 6Every male among the
priests may eat of it; it shall be eaten
in a holy place; it is most holy. 7The
guilt offering is like the sin offering,
there is one law for them; the priest
who makes atonement with it shall
have it. 8And the priest who offers any
man's burnt offering shall have for
himself the skin of the burnt offering
which he has offered. 9And every cere-
al offering baked in the oven and all
that is prepared on a pan or a griddle
shall belong to the priest who offers
it. 10And every cereal offering, mixed
with oil or dry, shall be for all the sons
of Aaron, one as well as another.

FURTHER INSTRUCTIONS

11 "And this is the law of the sacri-
fice of peace offerings which one may
offer to the LORD. 12If he offers it for a
thanksgiving, then he shall offer with
the thank offering unleavened cakes
mixed with oil, unleavened wafers
spread with oil, and cakes of fine flour
well mixed with oil. 13With the sacri-
fice of his peace offerings for thanks-
giving he shall bring his offering with
cakes of leavened bread. 14And of such
he shall offer one cake from each of-
fering, as an offering to the LORD; it
shall belong to the priest who throws

[a]Meaning of Heb is uncertain
[b]Or *Whoever*

the blood of the peace offerings. 15And the flesh of the sacrifice of his peace offerings for thanksgiving shall be eaten on the day of his offering; he shall not leave any of it until the morning. 16But if the sacrifice of his offering is a votive offering or a freewill offering, it shall be eaten on the day that he offers his sacrifice, and on the morrow what remains of it shall be eaten, 17but what remains of the flesh of the sacrifice on the third day shall be burned with fire. 18If any of the flesh of the sacrifice of his peace offering is eaten on the third day, he who offers it shall not be accepted, neither shall it be credited to him; it shall be an abomination, and he who eats of it shall bear his iniquity.

19 "Flesh that touches any unclean thing shall not be eaten; it shall be burned with fire. All who are clean may eat flesh, 20but the person who eats of the flesh of the sacrifice of the LORD's peace offerings while an uncleanness is on him, that person shall be cut off from his people. 21And if any one touches an unclean thing, whether the uncleanness of man or an unclean beast or any unclean abomination, and then eats of the flesh of the sacrifice of the LORD's peace offerings, that person shall be cut off from his people."

22 The LORD said to Moses, 23"Say to the people of Israel, You shall eat no fat, of ox, or sheep, or goat. 24The fat of an animal that dies of itself, and the fat of one that is torn by beasts, may be put to any other use, but on no account shall you eat it. 25For every person who eats of the fat of an animal of which an offering by fire is made to the LORD shall be cut off from his people. 26Moreover you shall eat no blood whatever, whether of fowl or of animal, in any of your dwellings. 27Whoever eats any blood, that person shall be cut off from his people."

28 The LORD said to Moses, 29"Say to the people of Israel, He that offers the sacrifice of his peace offerings to the LORD shall bring his offering to the LORD; from the sacrifice of his peace offerings 30he shall bring with his own hands the offerings by fire to the LORD; he shall bring the fat with the breast, that the breast may be waved as a wave offering before the LORD. 31The priest shall burn the fat on the altar, but the breast shall be for Aaron and his sons. 32And the right thigh you shall give to the priest as an offering from the sacrifice of your peace offerings; 33he among the sons of Aaron who offers the blood of the peace offerings and the fat shall have the right thigh for a portion. 34For the breast that is waved and the thigh that is offered I have taken from the people of Israel, out of the sacrifices of their peace offerings, and have given them to Aaron the priest and to his sons, as a perpetual due from the people of Israel. 35This is the portion of Aaron and of his sons from the offerings made by fire to the LORD, consecrated to them on the day they were presented to serve as priests of the LORD; 36the LORD commanded this to be given them by the people of Israel, on the day that they were anointed; it is a perpetual due throughout their generations."

37 This is the law of the burnt offering, of the cereal offering, of the sin offering, of the guilt offering, of the consecration, and of the peace offerings, 38which the LORD commanded Moses on Mount Sinai, on the day that he commanded the people of Israel to bring their offerings to the LORD, in the wilderness of Sinai.

THE RITES OF ORDINATION

8 The LORD said to the Moses, 2"Take Aaron and his sons with him, and the garments, and the anointing oil, and the bull of the sin offering, and the two rams, and the basket of unleavened bread; 3and assemble all the congregation at the door of the tent of meeting." 4And Moses did as the LORD commanded him; and the

congregation was assembled at the
door of the tent of meeting.
5 And Moses said to the congre-
gation, "This is the thing which the
LORD has commanded to be done."
[6]And Moses brought Aaron and his
sons, and washed them with water.
[7]And he put on him the coat, and gird-
ed him with the girdle, and clothed
him with the robe, and put the ephod
upon him, and girded him with the
skilfully woven band of the ephod,
binding it to him therewith. [8]And he
placed the breastpiece on him, and in
the breastpiece he put the Urim and
the Thummim. [9]And he set the tur-
ban upon his head, and on the turban,
in front, he set the golden plate, the
holy crown, as the LORD commanded
Moses.
10 Then Moses took the anointing
oil, and anointed the tabernacle and
all that was in it, and consecrated
them. [11]And he sprinkled some of it
on the altar seven times, and anointed
the altar and all its utensils, and the
laver and its base, to consecrate them.
[12]And he poured some of the anoint-
ing oil on Aaron's head, and anointed
him, to consecrate him. [13]And Moses
brought Aaron's sons, and clothed
them with coats, and girded them
with girdles, and bound caps on them,
as the LORD commanded Moses.
14 Then he brought the bull of the
sin offering; and Aaron and his sons
laid their hands upon the head of the
bull of the sin offering. [15]And Moses
killed it, and took the blood, and with
his finger put it on the horns of the
altar round about, and purified the
altar, and poured out the blood at the
base of the altar, and consecrated it,
to make atonement for it. [16]And he
took all the fat that was on the en-
trails, and the appendage of the liver,
and the two kidneys with their fat,
and Moses burned them on the altar.
[17]But the bull, and its skin, and its
flesh, and its dung, he burned with
fire outside the camp, as the LORD
commanded Moses.
18 Then he presented the ram of
the burnt offering; and Aaron and his
sons laid their hands on the head of
the ram. [19]And Moses killed it, and
threw the blood upon the altar round
about. [20]And when the ram was cut
into pieces, Moses burned the head
and the pieces and the fat. [21]And when
the entrails and the legs were washed
with water, Moses burned the whole
ram on the altar, as a burnt offering,
a pleasing odor, an offering by fire to
the LORD, as the LORD commanded
Moses.
22 Then he presented the other
ram, the ram of ordination; and Aaron
and his sons laid their hands on the
head of the ram. [23]And Moses killed
it, and took some of its blood and put
it on the tip of Aaron's right ear and
on the thumb of his right hand and on
the great toe of his right foot. [24]And
Aaron's sons were brought, and Moses
put some of the blood on the tips of
their right ears and on the thumbs
of their right hands and on the great
toes of their right feet; and Moses
threw the blood upon the altar round
about. [25]Then he took the fat, and the
fat tail, and all the fat that was on the
entrails, and the appendage of the liv-
er, and the two kidneys with their fat,
and the right thigh; [26]and out of the
basket of unleavened bread which was
before the LORD he took one unleav-
ened cake, and one cake of bread with
oil, and one wafer, and placed them on
the fat and on the right thigh; [27]and
he put all these in the hands of Aaron
and in the hands of his sons, and
waved them as a wave offering before
the LORD. [28]Then Moses took them
from their hands, and burned them on
the altar with the burnt offering, as an
ordination offering, a pleasing odor,
an offering by fire to the LORD. [29]And
Moses took the breast, and waved it
for a wave offering before the LORD;
it was Moses' portion of the ram of
ordination, as the LORD commanded
Moses.
30 Then Moses took some of the

anointing oil and of the blood which
was on the altar, and sprinkled it
upon Aaron and his garments, and
also upon his sons and his sons' gar-
ments; so he consecrated Aaron and
his garments, and his sons and his
sons' garments with him.

31 And Moses said to Aaron and
his sons, "Boil the flesh at the door
of the tent of meeting, and there eat it
and the bread that is in the basket of
ordination offerings, as I commanded,
saying, 'Aaron and his sons shall eat
it'; 32 and what remains of the flesh
and the bread you shall burn with fire.
33 And you shall not go out from the
door of the tent of meeting for seven
days, until the days of your ordination
are completed, for it will take seven
days to ordain you. 34 As has been done
today, the LORD has commanded to be
done to make atonement for you. 35 At
the door of the tent of meeting you
shall remain day and night for seven
days, performing what the LORD has
charged, lest you die; for so I am com-
manded." 36 And Aaron and his sons
did all the things which the LORD
commanded by Moses.

AARON'S PRIESTHOOD INAUGURATED

9 On the eighth day Moses called
Aaron and his sons and the elders
of Israel; 2 and he said to Aaron, "Take
a bull calf for a sin offering, and a ram
for a burnt offering, both without
blemish, and offer them before the
LORD. 3 And say to the people of Israel,
'Take a male goat for a sin offering,
and a calf and a lamb, both a year old
without blemish, for a burnt offering,
4 and an ox and a ram for peace offer-
ings, to sacrifice before the LORD, and
a cereal offering mixed with oil;
today the LORD will appear to you
5 And they brought what Moses co
manded before the tent of meeti
and all the congregation drew n
and stood before the LORD. 6 A
Moses said, "This is the thing wh
the LORD commanded you to do; a
the glory of the LORD will appear
you." 7 Then Moses said to Aaron,
"Draw near to the altar, and offer your
sin offering and your burnt offering,
and make atonement for yourself and
for the people; and bring the offering
of the people, and make atonement for
them; as the LORD has commanded."

8 So Aaron drew near to the altar,
and killed the calf of the sin offering,
which was for himself. 9 And the sons
of Aaron presented the blood to him,
and he dipped his finger in the blood
and put it on the horns of the altar,
and poured out the blood at the base
of the altar; 10 but the fat and the kid-
neys and the appendage of the liver
from the sin offering he burned upon
the altar, as the LORD commanded
Moses. 11 The flesh and the skin he
burned with fire outside the camp.

12 And he killed the burnt offer-
ing; and Aaron's sons delivered to
him the blood, and he threw it on the
altar round about. 13 And they deliv-
ered the burnt offering to him, piece
by piece, and the head; and he burned
them upon the altar. 14 And he washed
the entrails and the legs, and burned
them with the burnt offering on the
altar.

15 Then he presented the people's
offering, and took the goat of the sin
offering which was for the people, and
killed it, and offered it for sin, like
the first sin offering. 16 And he pre-
sented the burnt offering, and offered
it according to the ordinance. 17 And
he presented the cereal offering, and
filled his hand from it, and burned it
upon the altar, besides the burnt of-
fering of the morning.

18 He killed the ox also and the
ram, the sacrifice of peace offerings
for the people; and Aaron's sons de-
livered to him the blood, which he
threw upon the altar round about,
19 and the fat of the ox and of the ram,
the fat tail, and that which covers
the entrails, and the kidneys, and
the appendage of the liver; 20 and they
put the fat upon the breasts, and he
burned the fat upon the altar, 21 but

the breasts and the right thigh Aaron
waved for a wave offering before the
LORD; as Moses commanded.
22 Then Aaron lifted up his hands
toward the people and blessed them;
and he came down from offering the
sin offering and the burnt offering and
the peace offerings. 23And Moses and
Aaron went into the tent of meeting;
and when they came out they blessed
the people, and the glory of the LORD
appeared to all the people. 24And fire
came forth from before the LORD and
consumed the burnt offering and the
fat upon the altar; and when all the
people saw it, they shouted, and fell
on their faces.

NADAB AND ABIHU

10 Now Nadab and Abi′hu, the sons
of Aaron, each took his censer,
and put fire in it, and laid incense on
it, and offered unholy fire before the
LORD, such as he had not commanded
them. 2And fire came forth from the
presence of the LORD and devoured
them, and they died before the LORD.
3Then Moses said to Aaron, "This is
what the LORD has said, 'I will show
myself holy among those who are near
me, and before all the people I will be
glorified.'" And Aaron held his peace.
4 And Moses called Mish′a-el and
Elza′phan, the sons of Uz′ziel the un-
cle of Aaron, and said to them, "Draw
near, carry your brethren from before
the sanctuary out of the camp." 5So
they drew near, and carried them in
their coats out of the camp, as Moses
had said. 6And Moses said to Aaron
and to Elea′zar and Ith′amar, his sons,
"Do not let the hair of your heads hang
loose, and do not rend your clothes,
lest you die, and lest wrath come upon
all the congregation; but your breth-
ren, the whole house of Israel, may be-
wail the burning which the LORD has
kindled. 7And do not go out from the
door of the tent of meeting, lest you
die; for the anointing oil of the LORD
is upon you." And they did according
to the word of Moses.

8 And the LORD spoke to Aaron,
saying, 9"Drink no wine nor strong
drink, you nor your sons with you,
when you go into the tent of meeting,
lest you die; it shall be a statute for
ever throughout your generations.
10You are to distinguish between the
holy and the common, and between
the unclean and the clean; 11and you
are to teach the people of Israel all the
statutes which the LORD has spoken
to them by Moses."
12 And Moses said to Aaron and to
Elea′zar and Ith′amar, his sons who
were left, "Take the cereal offering
that remains of the offerings by fire
to the LORD, and eat it unleavened be-
side the altar, for it is most holy; 13you
shall eat it in a holy place, because it
is your due and your sons' due, from
the offerings by fire to the LORD; for
so I am commanded. 14But the breast
that is waved and the thigh that is of-
fered you shall eat in any clean place,
you and your sons and your daughters
with you; for they are given as your
due and your sons' due, from the sac-
rifices of the peace offerings of the
people of Israel. 15The thigh that is of-
fered and the breast that is waved they
shall bring with the offerings by fire
of the fat, to wave for a wave offering
before the LORD, and it shall be yours,
and your sons' with you, as a due for
ever; as the LORD has commanded."
16 Now Moses diligently inquired
about the goat of the sin offering, and
behold, it was burned! And he was
angry with Elea′zar and Ith′amar, the
sons of Aaron who were left, saying,
17"Why have you not eaten the sin of-
fering in the place of the sanctuary,
since it is a thing most holy and has
been given to you that you may bear
the iniquity of the congregation, to
make atonement for them before the
LORD? 18Behold, its blood was not
brought into the inner part of the
sanctuary. You certainly ought to have
eaten it in the sanctuary, as I com-
manded." 19And Aaron said to Moses,
"Behold, today they have offered their

sin offering and their burnt offering before the LORD; and yet such things as these have befallen me! If I had eaten the sin offering today, would it have been acceptable in the sight of the LORD?" 20 And when Moses heard that, he was content.

CLEAN AND UNCLEAN FOODS

11 *And the LORD said to Moses and Aaron, 2 "Say to the people of Israel, These are the living things which you may eat among all the beasts that are on the earth. 3 Whatever parts the hoof and is cloven-footed and chews the cud, among the animals, you may eat. 4 Nevertheless among those that chew the cud or part the hoof, you shall not eat these: The camel, because it chews the cud but does not part the hoof, is unclean to you. 5 And the rock badger, because it chews the cud but does not part the hoof, is unclean to you. 6 And the hare, because it chews the cud but does not part the hoof, is unclean to you. 7 And the swine, because it parts the hoof and is cloven-footed but does not chew the cud, is unclean to you. 8 Of their flesh you shall not eat, and their carcasses you shall not touch; they are unclean to you.

9 "These you may eat, of all that are in the waters. Everything in the waters that has fins and scales, whether in the seas or in the rivers, you may eat. 10 But anything in the seas or the rivers that has not fins and scales, of the swarming creatures in the waters and of the living creatures that are in the waters, is an abomination to you. 11 They shall remain an abomination to you; of their flesh you shall not eat, and their carcasses you shall have in abomination. 12 Everything in the waters that has not fins and scales is an abomination to you.

13 "And these you shall have in abomination among the birds, they shall not be eaten, they are an abomination: the eagle, the vulture, the osprey, 14 the kite, the falcon according to its kind, 15 every raven according to its kind, 16 the ostrich, the nighthawk, the sea gull, the hawk according to its kind, 17 the owl, the cormorant, the ibis, 18 the water hen, the pelican, the carrion vulture, 19 the stork, the heron according to its kind, the hoopoe, and the bat.

20 "All winged insects that go upon all fours are an abomination to you. 21 Yet among the winged insects that go on all fours you may eat those which have legs above their feet, with which to leap on the earth. 22 Of them you may eat: the locust according to its kind, the bald locust according to its kind, the cricket according to its kind, and the grasshopper according to its kind. 23 But all other winged insects which have four feet are an abomination to you.

UNCLEAN ANIMALS

24 "And by these you shall become unclean; whoever touches their carcass shall be unclean until the evening, 25 and whoever carries any part of their carcass shall wash his clothes and be unclean until the evening. 26 Every animal which parts the hoof but is not cloven-footed or does not chew the cud is unclean to you; every one who touches them shall be unclean. 27 And all that go on their paws, among the animals that go on all fours, are unclean to you; whoever touches their carcass shall be unclean until the evening, 28 and he who carries their carcass shall wash his clothes and be unclean until the evening; they are unclean to you.

29 "And these are unclean to you among the swarming things that swarm upon the earth: the weasel, the mouse, the great lizard according to its kind, 30 the gecko, the land crocodile, the lizard, the sand lizard, and the chameleon. 31 These are unclean to you among all that swarm; whoever touches them when they are dead shall be unclean until the evening. 32 And anything upon which any of them falls when they are dead shall be unclean, whether it is an article of

wood or a garment or a skin or a sack,
any vessel that is used for any pur-
pose; it must be put into water, and
it shall be unclean until the evening;
then it shall be clean. 33 And if any of
them falls into any earthen vessel, all
that is in it shall be unclean, and you
shall break it. 34 Any food in it which
may be eaten, upon which water may
come, shall be unclean; and all drink
which may be drunk from every such
vessel shall be unclean. 35 And every-
thing upon which any part of their
carcass falls shall be unclean; wheth-
er oven or stove, it shall be broken in
pieces; they are unclean, and shall
be unclean to you. 36 Nevertheless a
spring or a cistern holding water shall
be clean; but whatever touches their
carcass shall be unclean. 37 And if any
part of their carcass falls upon any
seed for sowing that is to be sown,
it is clean; 38 but if water is put on the
seed and any part of their carcass falls
on it, it is unclean to you.

39 "And if any animal of which
you may eat dies, he who touches its
carcass shall be unclean until the eve-
ning, 40 and he who eats of its carcass
shall wash his clothes and be unclean
until the evening; he also who carries
the carcass shall wash his clothes and
be unclean until the evening.

41 "Every swarming thing that
swarms upon the earth is an abomina-
tion; it shall not be eaten. 42 Whatever
goes on its belly, and whatever goes on
all fours, or whatever has many feet,
all the swarming things that swarm
upon the earth, you shall not eat; for
they are an abomination. 43 You shall
not make yourselves abominable with
any swarming thing that swarms; and
you shall not defile yourselves with
them, lest you become unclean. 44 For
I am the LORD your God; consecrate
yourselves therefore, and be holy, for
I am holy. You shall not defile your-
selves with any swarming thing that
crawls upon the earth. 45 For I am the
LORD who brought you up out of the
land of Egypt, to be your God; you
shall therefore be holy, for I am holy."

46 This is the law pertaining to
beast and bird and every living crea-
ture that moves through the waters
and every creature that swarms upon
the earth, 47 to make a distinction be-
tween the unclean and the clean and
between the living creature that may
be eaten and the living creature that
may not be eaten.

PURIFICATION OF WOMEN AFTER CHILDBIRTH

12 The LORD said to Moses, 2 "Say
to the people of Israel, If a wom-
an conceives, and bears a male child,
then she shall be unclean seven days;
as at the time of her menstruation, she
shall be unclean. 3 And on the eighth
day the flesh of his foreskin shall be
circumcised. 4 Then she shall contin-
ue for thirty-three days in the blood
of her purifying; she shall not touch
any hallowed thing, nor come into the
sanctuary, until the days of her purify-
ing are completed. 5 But if she bears a
female child, then she shall be unclean
two weeks, as in her menstruation;
and she shall continue in the blood of
her purifying for sixty-six days.

6 "And when the days of her puri-
fying are completed, whether for a son
or for a daughter, she shall bring to the
priest at the door of the tent of meeting
a lamb a year old for a burnt offering,
and a young pigeon or a turtledove for a
sin offering, 7 and he shall offer it before
the LORD, and make atonement for her;
then she shall be clean from the flow of
her blood. This is the law for her who
bears a child, either male or female.
8 And if she cannot afford a lamb, then
she shall take two turtledoves or two
young pigeons, one for a burnt offering
and the other for a sin offering; and the
priest shall make atonement for her,
and she shall be clean."

LEPROSY, VARIETIES AND SYMPTOMS

13 The LORD said to Moses and
Aaron, 2 "When a man has on the

skin of his body a swelling or an erup-
tion or a spot, and it turns into a lep-
rous disease on the skin of his body,
then he shall be brought to Aaron the
priest or to one of his sons the priests,
3and the priest shall examine the dis-
eased spot on the skin of his body;
and if the hair in the diseased spot has
turned white and the disease appears
to be deeper than the skin of his body,
it is a leprous disease; when the priest
has examined him he shall pronounce
him unclean. 4But if the spot is white
in the skin of his body, and appears
no deeper than the skin, and the hair
in it has not turned white, the priest
shall shut up the diseased person for
seven days; 5and the priest shall ex-
amine him on the seventh day, and
if in his eyes the disease is checked
and the disease has not spread in the
skin, then the priest shall shut him up
seven days more; 6and the priest shall
examine him again on the seventh
day, and if the diseased spot is dim
and the disease has not spread in the
skin, then the priest shall pronounce
him clean; it is only an eruption; and
he shall wash his clothes, and be
clean. 7But if the eruption spreads in
the skin, after he has shown himself
to the priest for his cleansing, he shall
appear again before the priest; 8and
the priest shall make an examination,
and if the eruption has spread in the
skin, then the priest shall pronounce
him unclean; it is leprosy.

9 "When a man is afflicted wit
leprosy, he shall be brought to th
priest; 10and the priest shall make a
examination, and if there is a whit
swelling in the skin, which has turne
the hair white, and there is quick ra
flesh in the swelling, 11it is a chron
leprosy in the skin of his body, and th
priest shall pronounce him unclea
he shall not shut him up, for he is u
clean. 12And if the leprosy breaks o
in the skin, so that the leprosy cove
all the skin of the diseased pers
from head to foot, so far as the prie
can see, 13then the priest shall ma
an examination, and if the leprosy
has covered all his body, he shall pro-
nounce him clean of the disease; it has
all turned white, and he is clean. 14But
when raw flesh appears on him, he
shall be unclean. 15And the priest shall
examine the raw flesh, and pronounce
him unclean; raw flesh is unclean,
for it is leprosy. 16But if the raw flesh
turns again and is changed to white,
then he shall come to the priest, 17and
the priest shall examine him, and if
the disease has turned white, then the
priest shall pronounce the diseased
person clean; he is clean.

18 "And when there is in the skin of
one's body a boil that has healed, 19and
in the place of the boil there comes
a white swelling or a reddish-white
spot, then it shall be shown to the
priest; 20and the priest shall make an
examination, and if it appears deeper
than the skin and its hair has turned
white, then the priest shall pronounce
him unclean; it is the disease of lepro-
sy, it has broken out in the boil. 21But
if the priest examines it, and the hair
on it is not white and it is not deep-
er than the skin, but is dim, then the
priest shall shut him up seven days;
22and if it spreads in the skin, then the
priest shall pronounce him unclean; it
is diseased. 23But if the spot remains
in one place and does not spread, it
is the scar of the boil; and the priest
shall pronounce him clean.

24 "Or, when the body has a burn
on its skin and the raw flesh of the
burn becomes a spot, reddish-white
or white, 25the priest shall examine it,
and if the hair in the spot has turned
white and it appears deeper than the
skin, then it is leprosy; it has broken
out in the burn, and the priest shall
pronounce him unclean; it is a lep-
rous disease. 26But if the priest ex-
amines it, and the hair in the spot is
not white and it is no deeper than the
skin, but is dim, the priest shall shut
him up seven days, 27and the priest
shall examine him the seventh day;
if it is spreading in the skin, then the

priest shall pronounce him unclean; it
is a leprous disease. 28But if the spot
remains in one place and does not
spread in the skin, but is dim, it is a
swelling from the burn, and the priest
shall pronounce him clean; for it is the
scar of the burn.

29 "When a man or woman has a
disease on the head or the beard, 30the
priest shall examine the disease; and
if it appears deeper than the skin,
and the hair in it is yellow and thin,
then the priest shall pronounce him
unclean; it is an itch, a leprosy of the
head or the beard. 31And if the priest
examines the itching disease, and it
appears no deeper than the skin and
there is no black hair in it, then the
priest shall shut up the person with
the itching disease for seven days,
32and on the seventh day the priest
shall examine the disease; and if the
itch has not spread, and there is in it
no yellow hair, and the itch appears
to be no deeper than the skin, 33then
he shall shave himself, but the itch he
shall not shave; and the priest shall
shut up the person with the itching
disease for seven days more; 34and
on the seventh day the priest shall
examine the itch, and if the itch has
not spread in the skin and it appears
to be no deeper than the skin, then
the priest shall pronounce him clean;
and he shall wash his clothes, and be
clean. 35But if the itch spreads in the
skin after his cleansing, 36then the
priest shall examine him, and if the
itch has spread in the skin, the priest
need not seek for the yellow hair; he is
unclean. 37But if in his eyes the itch is
checked, and black hair has grown in
it, the itch is healed, he is clean; and
the priest shall pronounce him clean.

38 "When a man or a woman has
spots on the skin of the body, white
spots, 39the priest shall make an ex-
amination, and if the spots on the
skin of the body are of a dull white,
it is tetter that has broken out in the
skin; he is clean.

40 "If a man's hair has fallen from
his head, he is bald but he is clean.
41And if a man's hair has fallen from
his forehead and temples, he has bald-
ness of the forehead but he is clean.
42But if there is on the bald head or
the bald forehead a reddish-white dis-
eased spot, it is leprosy breaking out
on his bald head or his bald forehead.
43Then the priest shall examine him,
and if the diseased swelling is red-
dish-white on his bald head or on his
bald forehead, like the appearance of
leprosy in the skin of the body, 44he
is a leprous man, he is unclean; the
priest must pronounce him unclean;
his disease is on his head.

45 "The leper who has the dis-
ease shall wear torn clothes and let
the hair of his head hang loose, and
he shall cover his upper lip and cry,
'Unclean, unclean.' 46He shall remain
unclean as long as he has the disease;
he is unclean; he shall dwell alone in a
habitation outside the camp.

47 "When there is a leprous disease
in a garment, whether a woolen or a
linen garment, 48in warp or woof of
linen or wool, or in a skin or in any-
thing made of skin, 49if the disease
shows greenish or reddish in the gar-
ment, whether in warp or woof or in
skin or in anything made of skin, it is
a leprous disease and shall be shown
to the priest. 50And the priest shall
examine the disease, and shut up
hat which has the disease for seven
lays; 51then he shall examine the dis-
ase on the seventh day. If the disease
as spread in the garment, in warp or
oof, or in the skin, whatever be the
e of the skin, the disease is a ma-
nant leprosy; it is unclean. 52And
shall burn the garment, whether
eased in warp or woof, woolen or
en, or anything of skin, for it is a
lignant leprosy; it shall be burned
he fire.

53 "And if the priest examines,
the disease has not spread in the
nent in warp or woof or in any-
g of skin, 54then the priest shall
mand that they wash the thing in

which is the disease, and he shall shut
it up seven days more; 55and the priest
shall examine the diseased thing af-
ter it has been washed. And if the
diseased spot has not changed color,
though the disease has not spread,
it is unclean; you shall burn it in the
fire, whether the leprous spot is on
the back or on the front.

56 "But if the priest examines, and
the disease is dim after it is washed,
he shall tear the spot out of the gar-
ment or the skin or the warp or woof;
57then if it appears again in the gar-
ment, in warp or woof, or in anything
of skin, it is spreading; you shall burn
with fire that in which is the disease.
58But the garment, warp or woof, or
anything of skin from which the dis-
ease departs when you have washed it,
shall then be washed a second time,
and be clean."

59 This is the law for a leprous dis-
ease in a garment of wool or linen, ei-
ther in warp or woof, or in anything
of skin, to decide whether it is clean
or unclean.

PURIFICATION OF LEPERS AND LEPROUS HOUSES

14 The LORD said to Moses, 2"This
shall be the law of the leper for
the day of his cleansing. He shall be
brought to the priest; 3and the priest
shall go out of the camp, and the priest
shall make an examination. Then, if
the leprous disease is healed in the
leper, 4the priest shall command them
to take for him who is to be cleansed
two living clean birds and cedarwood
and scarlet stuff and hyssop; 5and the
priest shall command them to kill one
of the birds in an earthen vessel over
running water. 6He shall take the liv-
ing bird with the cedarwood and the
scarlet stuff and the hyssop, and dip
them and the living bird in the blood
of the bird that was killed over the
running water; 7and he shall sprinkle
it seven times upon him who is to be
cleansed of leprosy; then he shall pro-
nounce him clean, and shall let the
living bird go into the open field. 8And
he who is to be cleansed shall wash
his clothes, and shave off all his hair,
and bathe himself in water, and he
shall be clean; and after that he shall
come into the camp, but shall dwell
outside his tent seven days. 9And on
the seventh day he shall shave all his
hair off his head; he shall shave off his
beard and his eyebrows, all his hair.
Then he shall wash his clothes, and
bathe his body in water, and he shall
be clean.

10 "And on the eighth day he shall
take two male lambs without blemish,
and one ewe lamb a year old without
blemish, and a cereal offering of three
tenths of an ephah of fine flour mixed
with oil, and one log of oil. 11And the
priest who cleanses him shall set
the man who is to be cleansed and
these things before the LORD, at the
door of the tent of meeting. 12And
the priest shall take one of the male
lambs, and offer it for a guilt offering,
along with the log of oil, and wave
them for a wave offering before the
LORD; 13and he shall kill the lamb in
the place where they kill the sin of-
fering and the burnt offering, in the
holy place; for the guilt offering, like
the sin offering, belongs to the priest;
it is most holy. 14The priest shall take
some of the blood of the guilt offer-
ing, and the priest shall put it on the
tip of the right ear of him who is to
be cleansed, and on the thumb of his
right hand, and on the great toe of his
right foot. 15Then the priest shall take
some of the log of oil, and pour it into
the palm of his own left hand, 16and
dip his right finger in the oil that is
in his left hand, and sprinkle some oil
with his finger seven times before the
LORD. 17And some of the oil that re-
mains in his hand the priest shall put
on the tip of the right ear of him who
is to be cleansed, and on the thumb of
his right hand, and on the great toe of
his right foot, upon the blood of the
guilt offering; 18and the rest of the oil
that is in the priest's hand he shall

put on the head of him who is to be cleansed. Then the priest shall make atonement for him before the LORD. 19 The priest shall offer the sin offering, to make atonement for him who is to be cleansed from his uncleanness. And afterward he shall kill the burnt offering; 20 and the priest shall offer the burnt offering and the cereal offering on the altar. Thus the priest shall make atonement for him, and he shall be clean.

21 "But if he is poor and cannot afford so much, then he shall take one male lamb for a guilt offering to be waved, to make atonement for him, and a tenth of an ephah of fine flour mixed with oil for a cereal offering, and a log of oil; 22 also two turtledoves or two young pigeons, such as he can afford; the one shall be a sin offering and the other a burnt offering. 23 And on the eighth day he shall bring them for his cleansing to the priest, to the door of the tent of meeting, before the LORD; 24 and the priest shall take the lamb of the guilt offering, and the log of oil, and the priest shall wave them for a wave offering before the LORD. 25 And he shall kill the lamb of the guilt offering; and the priest shall take some of the blood of the guilt offering, and put it on the tip of the right ear of him who is to be cleansed, and on the thumb of his right hand, and on the great toe of his right foot. 26 And the priest shall pour some of the oil into the palm of his own left hand; 27 and shall sprinkle with his right finger some of the oil that is in his left hand seven times before the LORD; 28 and the priest shall put some of the oil that is in his hand on the tip of the right ear of him who is to be cleansed, and on the thumb of his right hand, and on the great toe of his right foot, in the place where the blood of the guilt offering was put; 29 and the rest of the oil that is in the priest's hand he shall put on the head of him who is to be cleansed, to make atonement for him before the LORD. 30 And he shall offer, of the turtledoves or young pigeons such as he can afford, 31 one[a] for a sin offering and the other for a burnt offering, along with a cereal offering; and the priest shall make atonement before the LORD for him who is being cleansed. 32 This is the law for him in whom is a leprous disease, who cannot afford the offerings for his cleansing."

33 The LORD said to Moses and Aaron, 34 "When you come into the land of Canaan, which I give you for a possession, and I put a leprous disease in a house in the land of your possession, 35 then he who owns the house shall come and tell the priest, 'There seems to me to be some sort of disease in my house.' 36 Then the priest shall command that they empty the house before the priest goes to examine the disease, lest all that is in the house be declared unclean; and afterward the priest shall go in to see the house. 37 And he shall examine the disease; and if the disease is in the walls of the house with greenish or reddish spots, and if it appears to be deeper than the surface, 38 then the priest shall go out of the house to the door of the house, and shut up the house seven days. 39 And the priest shall come again on the seventh day, and look; and if the disease has spread in the walls of the house, 40 then the priest shall command that they take out the stones in which is the disease and throw them into an unclean place outside the city; 41 and he shall cause the inside of the house to be scraped round about, and the plaster that they scrape off they shall pour into an unclean place outside the city; 42 then they shall take other stones and put them in the place of those stones, and he shall take other plaster and plaster the house.

43 "If the disease breaks out again in the house, after he has taken out the stones and scraped the house and plastered it, 44 then the priest shall go and look; and if the disease has spread

[a] Gk Syr: Heb *afford, 31 such as he can afford, one*

in the house, it is a malignant leprosy
in the house; it is unclean. 45And he
shall break down the house, its stones
and timber and all the plaster of the
house; and he shall carry them forth
out of the city to an unclean place.
46Moreover he who enters the house
while it is shut up shall be unclean un-
til the evening; 47and he who lies down
in the house shall wash his clothes;
and he who eats in the house shall
wash his clothes.

48 "But if the priest comes and
makes an examination, and the dis-
ease has not spread in the house af-
ter the house was plastered, then
the priest shall pronounce the house
clean, for the disease is healed. 49And
for the cleansing of the house he shall
take two small birds, with cedar-
wood and scarlet stuff and hyssop,
50and shall kill one of the birds in an
earthen vessel over running water,
51and shall take the cedarwood and
the hyssop and the scarlet stuff, along
with the living bird, and dip them in
the blood of the bird that was killed
and in the running water, and sprin-
kle the house seven times. 52Thus he
shall cleanse the house with the blood
of the bird, and with the running wa-
ter, and with the living bird, and with
the cedarwood and hyssop and scarlet
stuff; 53and he shall let the living bird
go out of the city into the open field;
so he shall make atonement for the
house, and it shall be clean."

54 This is the law for any leprous
disease: for an itch, 55for leprosy in
a garment or in a house, 56and for a
swelling or an eruption or a spot, 57to
show when it is unclean and when it is
clean. This is the lw for leprosy.

CONCERNING BOLY DISCHARGES

15 The LORD sa to Moses and
Aaron, 2"Say the people of
Israel, When any m has a discharge
from his body, hiischarge is un-
clean. 3And this is e law of his un-
cleanness for a dharge: whether
his body runs withs discharge, or
his body is stopped from discharge, it
is uncleanness in him. 4Every bed on
which he who has the discharge lies
shall be unclean; and everything on
which he sits shall be unclean. 5And
any one who touches his bed shall
wash his clothes, and bathe himself in
water, and be unclean until the eve-
ning. 6And whoever sits on anything
on which he who has the discharge
has sat shall wash his clothes, and
bathe himself in water, and be un-
clean until the evening. 7And whoev-
er touches the body of him who has
the discharge shall wash his clothes,
and bathe himself in water, and be un-
clean until the evening. 8And if he who
has the discharge spits on one who is
clean, then he shall wash his clothes,
and bathe himself in water, and be un-
clean until the evening. 9And any sad-
dle on which he who has the discharge
rides shall be unclean. 10And whoever
touches anything that was under him
shall be unclean until the evening;
and he who carries such a thing shall
wash his clothes, and bathe himself
in water, and be unclean until the
evening. 11Any one whom he that has
the discharge touches without having
rinsed his hands in water shall wash
his clothes, and bathe himself in wa-
ter, and be unclean until the evening.
12And the earthen vessel which he
who has the discharge touches shall
be broken; and every vessel of wood
shall be rinsed in water.

13 "And when he who has a dis-
charge is cleansed of his discharge,
then he shall count for himself seven
days for his cleansing, and wash his
clothes; and he shall bathe his body
in running water, and shall be clean.
14And on the eighth day he shall take
two turtledoves or two young pigeons,
and come before the LORD to the door
of the tent of meeting, and give them
to the priest; 15and the priest shall
offer them, one for a sin offering and
the other for a burnt offering; and the
priest shall make atonement for him
before the LORD for his discharge.

16 "And if a man has an emission of
semen, he shall bathe his whole body
in water, and be unclean until the eve-
ning. 17And every garment and every
skin on which the semen comes shall
be washed with water, and be unclean
until the evening. 18If a man lies with
a woman and has an emission of se-
men, both of them shall bathe them-
selves in water, and be unclean until
the evening.

19 "When a woman has a discharge
of blood which is her regular dis-
charge from her body, she shall be in
her impurity for seven days, and who-
ever touches her shall be unclean un-
til the evening. 20And everything upon
which she lies during her impurity
shall be unclean; everything also upon
which she sits shall be unclean. 21And
whoever touches her bed shall wash
his clothes, and bathe himself in wa-
ter, and be unclean until the evening.
22And whoever touches anything upon
which she sits shall wash his clothes,
and bathe himself in water, and be
unclean until the evening; 23whether
it is the bed or anything upon which
she sits, when he touches it he shall
be unclean until the evening. 24And if
any man lies with her, and her impuri-
ty is on him, he shall be unclean seven
days; and every bed on which he lies
shall be unclean.

25 "If a woman has a discharge of
blood for many days, not at the time of
her impurity, or if she has a discharge
beyond the time of her impurity, all
the days of the discharge she shall
continue in uncleanness; as in the
days of her impurity, she shall be un-
clean. 26Every bed on which she lies,
all the days of her discharge, shall
be to her as the bed of her impurity;
and everything on which she sits shall
be unclean, as in the uncleanness of
her impurity. 27And whoever touches
these things shall be unclean, and
shall wash his clothes, and bathe him-
self in water, and be unclean until
the evening. 28But if she is cleansed
of her discharge, she shall count for
herself seven days, and after that she
shall be clean. 29And on the eighth day
she shall take two turtledoves or two
young pigeons, and bring them to the
priest, to the door of the tent of meet-
ing. 30And the priest shall offer one for
a sin offering and the other for a burnt
offering; and the priest shall make
atonement for her before the LORD for
her unclean discharge.

31 "Thus you shall keep the people
of Israel separate from their unclean-
ness, lest they die in their unclean-
ness by defiling my tabernacle that is
in their midst."

32 This is the law for him who has
a discharge and for him who has an
emission of semen, becoming unclean
thereby; 33also for her who is sick with
her impurity; that is, for any one, male
or female, who has a discharge, and
for the man who lies with a woman
who is unclean.

THE DAY OF ATONEMENT

16 The LORD spoke to Moses, af-
ter the death of the two sons of
Aaron, when they drew near before
the LORD and died; 2and the LORD
said to Moses, "Tell Aaron your broth-
er not to come at all times into the
holy place within the veil, before the
mercy seat which is upon the ark, lest
he die; for I will appear in the cloud
upon the mercy seat. 3But thus shall
Aaron come into the holy place: with
a young bull for a sin offering and a
ram for a burnt offering. 4He shall put
on the holy linen coat, and shall have
the linen breeches on his body, be
girded with the linen girdle, and wear
the linen turban; these are the holy
garments. He shal bathe his body in
water, and then pu them on. 5And he
shall take from t e congregation of
the people of Israe wo male goats for
a sin offering, andne ram for a burnt
offering.

6 "And Aaron all offer the bull
as a sin offering f himself, and shall
make atonemen r himself and for
his house. 7Then shall take the two

goats, and set them before the LORD at the door of the tent of meeting; 8and Aaron shall cast lots upon the two goats, one lot for the LORD and the other lot for Aza′zel. 9And Aaron shall present the goat on which the lot fell for the LORD, and offer it as a sin offering; 10but the goat on which the lot fell for Aza′zel shall be presented alive before the LORD to make atonement over it, that it may be sent away into the wilderness to Aza′zel.

11 "Aaron shall present the bull as a sin offering for himself, and shall make atonement for himself and for his house; he shall kill the bull as a sin offering for himself. 12And he shall take a censer full of coals of fire from the altar before the LORD, and two handfuls of sweet incense beaten small; and he shall bring it within the veil 13and put the incense on the fire before the LORD, that the cloud of the incense may cover the mercy seat which is upon the testimony, lest he die; 14and he shall take some of the blood of the bull, and sprinkle it with his finger on the front of the mercy seat, and before the mercy seat he shall sprinkle the blood with his finger seven times.

15 "Then he shall kill the goat of the sin offering which is for the people, and bring its blood within the veil, and do with its blood as he did with the blood of the bull, sprinkling it upon the mercy seat and before the mercy seat; 16thus he shall make atonement for the holy place, because of the uncleannesses of the people of Israel, and because of their transgressions, all their sins; and so he shall do for the tent of meeting, which abides with them in the midst of their uncleannesses. 17There shall be no man in the tent of meeting when he enters to make atonement in the holy place until he comes out and has made atonement for himself and for his house and for all the assembly of Israel. 18Then he shall go out to the altar which is before the LORD and make atonement for it, and shall take some of the blood of the bull and of the blood of the goat, and put it on the horns of the altar round about. 19And he shall sprinkle some of the blood upon it with his finger seven times, and cleanse it and hallow it from the uncleannesses of the people of Israel.

20 "And when he has made an end of atoning for the holy place and the tent of meeting and the altar, he shall present the live goat; 21and Aaron shall lay both his hands upon the head of the live goat, and confess over him all the iniquities of the people of Israel, and all their transgressions, all their sins; and he shall put them upon the head of the goat, and send him away into the wilderness by the hand of a man who is in readiness. 22The goat shall bear all their iniquities upon him to a solitary land; and he shall let the goat go in the wilderness.

23 "Then Aaron shall come into the tent of meeting, and shall put off the linen garments which he put on when he went into the holy place, and shall leave them there; 24and he shall bathe his body in water in a holy place, and put on his garments, and come forth, and offer his burnt offering and the burnt offering of the people, and make atonement for himself and for the people. 25And the fat of the sin offering he shall burn upon the altar. 26And he who lets the goat go to Aza′zel shall wash his clothes and bathe his body in water, and afterward he may come into the camp. 27And the bull for the sin offering and the goat for the sin offering, whose blood was brought in to make atonement in the holy place, shall be carried forth outside the camp; their skin and their flesh and their dung shall be burned with fire. 28And he who burns them shall wash his clothes and bathe his body in water, and afterward he may come into the camp.

29 "And it shall be a statute to you for ever that in the seventh month, on the tenth day of the month, you shall

afflict yourselves, and shall do no
work, either the native or the strang-
er who sojourns among you; 30 for on
this day shall atonement be made for
you, to cleanse you; from all your sins
you shall be clean before the LORD.
31 It is a sabbath of solemn rest to you,
and you shall afflict yourselves; it is
a statute for ever. 32 And the priest
who is anointed and consecrated as
priest in his father's place shall make
atonement, wearing the holy linen
garments; 33 he shall make atonement
for the sanctuary, and he shall make
atonement for the tent of meeting
and for the altar, and he shall make
atonement for the priests and for all
the people of the assembly. 34 And this
shall be an everlasting statute for you,
that atonement may be made for the
people of Israel once in the year be-
cause of all their sins." And Moses did
as the LORD commanded him.

THE SLAUGHTERING OF ANIMALS

17 *And the LORD said to Moses,
2 "Say to Aaron and his sons, and
to all the people of Israel, This is the
thing which the LORD has command-
ed. 3 If any man of the house of Israel
kills an ox or a lamb or a goat in the
camp, or kills it outside the camp,
4 and does not bring it to the door of
the tent of meeting, to offer it as a gift
to the LORD before the tabernacle of
the LORD, bloodguilt shall be imputed
to that man; he has shed blood; and
that man shall be cut off from among
his people. 5 This is to the end that the
people of Israel may bring their sacri-
fices which they slay in the open field,
that they may bring them to the LORD,
to the priest at the door of the tent of
meeting, and slay them as sacrifices
of peace offerings to the LORD; 6 and
the priest shall sprinkle the blood on
the altar of the LORD at the door of
the tent of meeting, and burn the fat
for a pleasing odor to the LORD. 7 So
they shall no more slay their sacrifices
for satyrs, after whom they play the
harlot. This shall be a statute for ever
to them throughout their generations.
8 "And you shall say to them, Any
man of the house of Israel, or of the
strangers that sojourn among them,
who offers a burnt offering or sacri-
fice, 9 and does not bring it to the door
of the tent of meeting, to sacrifice it
to the LORD; that man shall be cut off
from his people.

EATING BLOOD PROHIBITED

10 "If any man of the house of
Israel or of the strangers that sojourn
among them eats any blood, I will
set my face against that person who
eats blood, and will cut him off from
among his people. 11 For the life of the
flesh is in the blood; and I have given it
for you upon the altar to make atone-
ment for your souls; for it is the blood
that makes atonement, by reason of
the life. 12 Therefore I have said to the
people of Israel, No person among
you shall eat blood, neither shall any
stranger who sojourns among you eat
blood. 13 Any man also of the people of
Israel, or of the strangers that sojourn
among them, who takes in hunting
any beast or bird that may be eaten
shall pour out its blood and cover it
with dust.
14 "For the life of every creature is
the blood of it;[a] therefore I have said
to the people of Israel, You shall not
eat the blood of any creature, for the
life of every creature is its blood; who-
ever eats it shall be cut off. 15 And ev-
ery person that eats what dies of itself
or what is torn by beasts, whether he
is a native or a sojourner, shall wash
his clothes, and bathe himself in wa-
ter, and be unclean until the evening;
then he shall be clean. 16 But if he does
not wash them or bathe his flesh, he
shall bear his iniquity."

SEXUAL RELATIONS

18 And the LORD said to Moses,
2 "Say to the people of Israel, I am
the LORD your God. 3 You shall not

[a] Gk Syr Compare Vg: Heb *for the life of all flesh, its blood is in its life*

do as they do in the land of Egypt,
where you dwelt, and you shall not do
as they do in the land of Canaan, to
which I am bringing you. You shall not
walk in their statutes. 4You shall do
my ordinances and keep my statutes
and walk in them. I am the LORD your
God. 5You shall therefore keep my
statutes and my ordinances, by doing
which a man shall live: I am the LORD.
6 "None of you shall approach
any one near of kin to him to uncov-
er nakedness. I am the LORD. 7You
shall not uncover the nakedness of
your father, which is the nakedness
of your mother; she is your mother,
you shall not uncover her nakedness.
8You shall not uncover the nakedness
of your father's wife; it is your father's
nakedness. 9You shall not uncover the
nakedness of your sister, the daugh-
ter of your father or the daughter of
your mother, whether born at home or
born abroad. 10You shall not uncover
the nakedness of your son's daughter
or of your daughter's daughter, for
their nakedness is your own naked-
ness. 11You shall not uncover the na-
kedness of your father's wife's daugh-
ter, begotten by your father, since she
is your sister. 12You shall not uncover
the nakedness of your father's sister;
she is your father's near kinswoman.
13You shall not uncover the nakedness
of your mother's sister, for she is your
mother's near kinswoman. 14You shall
not uncover the nakedness of your fa-
ther's brother, that is, you shall not
approach his wife; she is your aunt.
15You shall not uncover the nakedness
of your daughter-in-law; she is your
son's wife, you shall not uncover her
nakedness. 16You shall not uncover
the nakedness of your brother's wife;
she is your brother's nakedness. 17You
shall not uncover the nakedness of a
woman and of her daughter, and you
shall not take her son's daughter or
her daughter's daughter to uncover
her nakedness; they are your[b] near
kinswomen; it is wickedness. 18And
you shall not take a woman as a rival
wife to her sister, uncovering her na-
kedness while her sister is yet alive.
19 "You shall not approach a wom-
an to uncover her nakedness while
she is in her menstrual uncleanness.
20And you shall not lie carnally with
your neighbor's wife, and defile your-
self with her. 21You shall not give any
of your children to devote them by fire
to Molech, and so profane the name of
your God: I am the LORD. 22You shall
not lie with a male as with a woman; it
is an abomination. 23And you shall not
lie with any beast and defile yourself
with it, neither shall any woman give
herself to a beast to lie with it: it is
perversion.
24 "Do not defile yourselves by
any of these things, for by all these
the nations I am casting out before
you defiled themselves; 25and the land
became defiled, so that I punished its
iniquity, and the land vomited out its
inhabitants. 26But you shall keep my
statutes and my ordinances and do
none of these abominations, either
the native or the stranger who so-
journs among you 27(for all of these
abominations the men of the land
did, who were before you, so that the
land became defiled); 28lest the land
vomit you out, when you defile it, as
it vomited out the nation that was be-
fore you. 29For whoever shall do any of
these abominations, the persons that
do them shall be cut off from among
their people. 30So keep my charge nev-
er to practice any of these abominable
customs which were practiced before
you, and never to defile yourselves by
them: I am the LORD your God."

RITUAL AND MORAL HOLINESS

19 And the LORD said to Moses, 2"Say
to all the congregation of the peo-
ple of Israel, You shall be holy; for I the
LORD your God am holy. 3Every one of
you shall revere his mother and his fa-
ther, and you shall keep my sabbaths:
I am the LORD your God. 4Do not turn

[b] Gk: Heb lacks *your*

to idols or make for yourselves molten
gods: I am the LORD your God.

5 "When you offer a sacrifice of
peace offerings to the LORD, you shall
offer it so that you may be accepted.
6It shall be eaten the same day you of-
fer it, or on the morrow; and anything
left over until the third day shall be
burned with fire. 7If it is eaten at all
on the third day, it is an abomination;
it will not be accepted, 8and every one
who eats it shall bear his iniquity, be-
cause he has profaned a holy thing of
the LORD; and that person shall be cut
off from his people.

9 "When you reap the harvest of
your land, you shall not reap your
field to its very border, neither shall
you gather the gleanings after your
harvest. 10And you shall not strip your
vineyard bare, neither shall you gath-
er the fallen grapes of your vineyard;
you shall leave them for the poor and
for the sojourner: I am the LORD your
God.

11 "You shall not steal, nor deal
falsely, nor lie to one another. 12And
you shall not swear by my name false-
ly, and so profane the name of your
God: I am the LORD.

13 "You shall not oppress your
neighbor or rob him. The wages of a
hired servant shall not remain with
you all night until the morning. 14You
shall not curse the deaf or put a stum-
bling block before the blind, but you
shall fear your God: I am the LORD.

15 "You shall do no injustice in
judgment; you shall not be partial to
the poor or defer to the great, but in
righteousness shall you judge your
neighbor. 16You shall not go up and
down as a slanderer among your peo-
ple, and you shall not stand forth
against the life[a] of your neighbor: I
am the LORD.

17 "You shall not hate your broth-
er in your heart, but you shall reason
with your neighbor, lest you bear sin
because of him. 18You shall not take
vengeance or bear any grudge against
the sons of your own people, but you
shall love your neighbor as yourself: I
am the LORD.

19 "You shall keep my statutes. You
shall not let your cattle breed with a
different kind; you shall not sow your
field with two kinds of seed; nor shall
there come upon you a garment of
cloth made of two kinds of stuff.

20 "If a man lies carnally with a
woman who is a slave, betrothed to
another man and not yet ransomed or
given her freedom, an inquiry shall be
held. They shall not be put to death,
because she was not free; 21but he
shall bring a guilt offering for himself
to the LORD, to the door of the tent
of meeting, a ram for a guilt offering.
22And the priest shall make atonement
for him with the ram of the guilt offer-
ing before the LORD for his sin which
he has committed; and the sin which
he has committed shall be forgiven
him.

23 "When you come into the land
and plant all kinds of trees for food,
then you shall count their fruit as for-
bidden;[b] three years it shall be forbid-
den to you, it must not be eaten. 24And
in the fourth year all their fruit shall
be holy, an offering of praise to the
LORD. 25But in the fifth year you may
eat of their fruit, that they may yield
more richly for you: I am the LORD
your God.

26 "You shall not eat any flesh with
the blood in it. You shall not practice
augury or witchcraft. 27You shall not
round off the hair on you temples or
mar the edges of your beard. 28You
shall not make any cuttings in your
flesh on account of the dead or tattoo
any marks upon you: I am the LORD.

29 "Do not profane your daughter
by making her a harlot, lest the land
fall into harlotry and the land become
full of wickedness. 30You shall keep
my sabbaths and reverence my sanc-
tuary: I am the LORD.

[a]Heb *blood*
[b]Heb *their uncircumcision*

31 "Do not turn to mediums or
wizards; do not seek them out, to be
defiled by them: I am the LORD your
God.
32 "You shall rise up before the
hoary head, and honor the face of an
old man, and you shall fear your God:
I am the LORD.
33 "When a stranger sojourns with
you in your land, you shall not do him
wrong. 34The stranger who sojourns
with you shall be to you as the native
among you, and you shall love him
as yourself; for you were strangers in
the land of Egypt: I am the LORD your
God.
35 "You shall do no wrong in judg-
ment, in measures of length or weight
or quantity. 36You shall have just bal-
ances, just weights, a just ephah, and
a just hin: I am the LORD your God,
who brought you out of the land of
Egypt. 37And you shall observe all my
statutes and all my ordinances, and do
them: I am the LORD."

PENALTIES FOR VIOLATIONS OF HOLINESS

20 The LORD said to Moses, 2"Say to
the people of Israel, Any man of
the people of Israel, or of the strang-
ers that sojourn in Israel, who gives
any of his children to Molech shall be
put to death; the people of the land
shall stone him with stones. 3I myself
will set my face against that man, and
will cut him off from among his peo-
ple, because he has given one of his
children to Molech, defiling my sanc-
tuary and profaning my holy name.
4And if the people of the land do at all
hide their eyes from that man, when
he gives one of his children to Molech,
and do not put him to death, 5then I
will set my face against that man and
against his family, and will cut them
off from among their people, him and
all who follow him in playing the har-
lot after Molech.
6 "If a person turns to mediums
and wizards, playing the harlot after
them, I will set my face against that
person, and will cut him off from
among his people. 7Consecrate your-
selves therefore, and be holy; for I am
the LORD your God. 8Keep my stat-
utes, and do them; I am the LORD who
sanctify you. 9For every one who curs-
es his father or his mother shall be put
to death; he has cursed his father or
his mother, his blood is upon him.
10 "If a man commits adultery
with the wife of[c] his neighbor, both
the adulterer and the adulteress shall
be put to death. 11The man who lies
with his father's wife has uncovered
his father's nakedness; both of them
shall be put to death, their blood is
upon them. 12If a man lies with his
daughter-in-law, both of them shall
be put to death; they have commit-
ted incest, their blood is upon them.
13If a man lies with a male as with a
woman, both of them have committed
an abomination; they shall be put to
death, their blood is upon them. 14If a
man takes a wife and her mother also,
it is wickedness; they shall be burned
with fire, both he and they, that there
may be no wickedness among you. 15If
a man lies with a beast, he shall be put
to death; and you shall kill the beast.
16If a woman approaches any beast and
lies with it, you shall kill the woman
and the beast; they shall be put to
death, their blood is upon them.
17 "If a man takes his sister, a
daughter of his father or a daughter of
his mother, and sees her nakedness,
and she sees his nakedness, it is a
shameful thing, and they shall be cut
off in the sight of the children of their
people; he has uncovered his sister's
nakedness, he shall bear his iniquity.
18If a man lies with a woman having
her sickness, and uncovers her naked-
ness, he has made naked her fountain,
and she has uncovered the fountain of
her blood; both of them shall be cut
off from among their people. 19You
shall not uncover the nakedness of
your mother's sister or of your father's
sister, for that is to make naked one's

[c] Heb repeats *if a man commits adultery with the wife of*

near kin; they shall bear their iniqui-
ty. 20 If a man lies with his uncle's wife,
he has uncovered his uncle's naked-
ness; they shall bear their sin, they
shall die childless. 21 If a man takes his
brother's wife, it is impurity; he has
uncovered his brother's nakedness,
they shall be childless.

22 "You shall therefore keep all my
statutes and all my ordinances, and
do them; that the land where I am
bringing you to dwell may not vomit
you out. 23 And you shall not walk in
the customs of the nation which I am
casting out before you; for they did all
these things, and therefore I abhorred
them. 24 But I have said to you, 'You
shall inherit their land, and I will give
it to you to possess, a land flowing
with milk and honey.' I am the LORD
your God, who have separated you
from the peoples. 25 You shall therefore
make a distinction between the clean
beast and the unclean, and between
the unclean bird and the clean; you
shall not make yourselves abomina-
ble by beast or by bird or by anything
with which the ground teems, which
I have set apart for you to hold un-
clean. 26 You shall be holy to me; for I
the LORD am holy, and have separated
you from the peoples, that you should
be mine.

27 "A man or a woman who is a me-
dium or a wizard shall be put to death;
they shall be stoned with stones, their
blood shall be upon them."

THE HOLINESS OF PRIESTS

21 And the LORD said to Moses,
"Speak to the priests, the sons
of Aaron, and say to them that none
of them shall defile himself for the
dead among his people, 2 except for his
nearest of kin, his mother, his father,
his son, his daughter, his brother, 3 or
his virgin sister (who is near to him
because she has had no husband; for
her he may defile himself). 4 He shall
not defile himself as a husband among
his people and so profane himself.
5 They shall not make tonsures upon
their heads, nor shave off the edges
of their beards, nor make any cuttings
in their flesh. 6 They shall be holy to
their God, and not profane the name
of their God; for they offer the offer-
ings by fire to the LORD, the bread
of their God; therefore they shall be
holy. 7 They shall not marry a harlot
or a woman who has been defiled;
neither shall they marry a woman
divorced from her husband; for the
priest is holy to his God. 8 You shall
consecrate him, for he offers the bread
of your God; he shall be holy to you;
for I the LORD, who sanctify you, am
holy. 9 And the daughter of any priest,
if she profanes herself by playing the
harlot, profanes her father; she shall
be burned with fire.

10 "The priest who is chief among
his brethren, upon whose head the
anointing oil is poured, and who has
been consecrated to wear the gar-
ments, shall not let the hair of his
head hang loose, nor rend his clothes;
11 he shall not go in to any dead body,
nor defile himself, even for his father
or for his mother; 12 neither shall he go
out of the sanctuary, nor profane the
sanctuary of his God; for the conse-
cration of the anointing oil of his God
is upon him: I am the LORD. 13 And he
shall take a wife in her virginity. 14 A
widow, or one divorced, or a woman
who has been defiled, or a harlot,
these he shall not marry; but he shall
take to wife a virgin of his own peo-
ple, 15 that he may not profane his chil-
dren among his people; for I am the
LORD who sanctify him."

16 And the LORD said to Moses,
17 "Say to Aaron, None of your descen-
dants throughout their generations
who has a blemish may approach to
offer the bread of his God. 18 For no one
who has a blemish shall draw near, a
man blind or lame, or one who has a
mutilated face or a limb too long, 19 or
a man who has an injured foot or an
injured hand, 20 or a hunchback, or a
dwarf, or a man with a defect in his
sight or an itching disease or scabs

or crushed testicles; 21no man of the
descendants of Aaron the priest who
has a blemish shall come near to of-
fer the LORD's offerings by fire; since
he has a blemish, he shall not come
near to offer the bread of his God. 22He
may eat the bread of his God, both of
the most holy and of the holy things,
23but he shall not come near the veil or
approach the altar, because he has a
blemish, that he may not profane my
sanctuaries; for I am the LORD who
sanctify them." 24So Moses spoke to
Aaron and to his sons and to all the
people of Israel.

THE USE OF HOLY OFFERINGS

22 And the LORD said to Moses,
2"Tell Aaron and his sons to keep
away from the holy things of the peo-
ple of Israel, which they dedicate to
me, so that they may not profane my
holy name: I am the LORD. 3Say to
them, 'If any one of all your descen-
dants throughout your generations
approaches the holy things, which
the people of Israel dedicate to the
LORD, while he has an uncleanness,
that person shall be cut off from my
presence: I am the LORD. 4None of the
line of Aaron who is a leper or suffers
a discharge may eat of the holy things
until he is clean. Whoever touch-
es anything that is unclean through
contact with the dead or a man who
has had an emission of semen, 5and
whoever touches a creeping thing by
which he may be made unclean or a
man from whom he may take unclean-
ness, whatever his uncleanness may
be 6the person who touches any such
shall be unclean until the evening and
shall not eat of the holy things un-
less he has bathed his body in water.
7When the sun is down he shall be
clean; and afterward he may eat of the
holy things, because such are his food.
8That which dies of itself or is torn by
beasts he shall not eat, defiling him-
self by it: I am the LORD. 9They shall
therefore keep my charge, lest they
bear sin for it and die thereby when
they profane it: I am the LORD who
sanctify them.
10 "An outsider shall not eat of a
holy thing. A sojourner of the priest's
or a hired servant shall not eat of a
holy thing; 11but if a priest buys a slave
as his property for money, the slave
may eat of it; and those that are born
in his house may eat of his food. 12If a
priest's daughter is married to an out-
sider she shall not eat of the offering
of the holy things. 13But if a priest's
daughter is a widow or divorced, and
has no child, and returns to her fa-
ther's house, as in her youth, she may
eat of her father's food; yet no outsid-
er shall eat of it. 14And if a man eats of
a holy thing unwittingly, he shall add
the fifth of its value to it, and give the
holy thing to the priest. 15The priests
shall not profane the holy things of
the people of Israel, which they offer
to the LORD, 16and so cause them to
bear iniquity and guilt, by eating their
holy things: for I am the LORD who
sanctify them."

ACCEPTABLE OFFERINGS

17 And the LORD said to Moses,
18"Say to Aaron and his sons and all
the people of Israel, When any one of
the house of Israel or of the sojourn-
ers in Israel presents his offering,
whether in payment of a vow or as a
freewill offering which is offered to
the LORD as a burnt offering, 19to be
accepted you shall offer a male with-
out blemish, of the bulls or the sheep
or the goats. 20You shall not offer any-
thing that has a blemish, for it will not
be acceptable for you. 21And when any
one offers a sacrifice of peace offer-
ings to the LORD, to fulfil a vow or as
a freewill offering, from the herd or
from the flock, to be accepted it must
be perfect; there shall be no blemish
in it. 22Animals blind or disabled or
mutilated or having a discharge or an
itch or scabs, you shall not offer to the
LORD or make of them an offering by
fire upon the altar to the LORD. 23A
bull or a lamb which has a part too

long or too short you may present for
a freewill offering; but for a votive
offering it cannot be accepted. 24Any
animal which has its testicles bruised
or crushed or torn or cut, you shall not
offer to the LORD or sacrifice within
your land; 25neither shall you offer as
the bread of your God any such ani-
mals gotten from a foreigner. Since
there is a blemish in them, because of
their mutilation, they will not be ac-
cepted for you."

26 And the LORD said to Moses,
27"When a bull or sheep or goat is
born, it shall remain seven days with
its mother; and from the eighth day on
it shall be acceptable as an offering by
fire to the LORD. 28And whether the
mother is a cow or a ewe, you shall not
kill both her and her young in one day.
29And when you sacrifice a sacrifice of
thanksgiving to the LORD, you shall
sacrifice it so that you may be accept-
ed. 30It shall be eaten on the same day,
you shall leave none of it until morn-
ing: I am the LORD.

31 "So you shall keep my com-
mandments and do them: I am the
LORD. 32And you shall not profane
my holy name, but I will be hallowed
among the people of Israel; I am the
LORD who sanctify you, 33who brought
you out of the land of Egypt to be your
God: I am the LORD."

THE SABBATH AND APPOINTED FESTIVALS

23 The LORD said to Moses, 2"Say to
the people of Israel, The appoint-
ed feasts of the LORD which you shall
proclaim as holy convocations, my
appointed feasts, are these. 3Six days
shall work be done; but on the seventh
day is a sabbath of solemn rest, a holy
convocation; you shall do no work; it
is a sabbath to the LORD in all your
dwellings.

PASSOVER AND UNLEAVENED BREAD

4 "These are the appointed feasts
of the LORD, the holy convocations,
which you shall proclaim at the time
appointed for them. 5In the first
month, on the fourteenth day of the
month in the evening,[a] is the LORD'S
passover. 6And on the fifteenth day
of the same month is the feast of un-
leavened bread to the LORD; seven
days you shall eat unleavened bread.
7On the first day you shall have a holy
convocation; you shall do no laborious
work. 8But you shall present an offer-
ing by fire to the LORD seven days; on
the seventh day is a holy convocation;
you shall do no laborious work."

THE OFFERING OF FIRST FRUITS

9 And the LORD said to Moses,
10"Say to the people of Israel, When
you come into the land which I give
you and reap its harvest, you shall
bring the sheaf of the first fruits of
your harvest to the priest; 11and he
shall wave the sheaf before the LORD,
that you may find acceptance; on the
morrow after the sabbath the priest
shall wave it. 12And on the day when
you wave the sheaf, you shall offer a
male lamb a year old without blem-
ish as a burnt offering to the LORD.
13And the cereal offering with it shall
be two tenths of an ephah of fine flour
mixed with oil, to be offered by fire
to the LORD, a pleasing odor; and the
drink offering with it shall be of wine,
a fourth of a hin. 14And you shall eat
neither bread nor grain parched or
fresh until this same day, until you
have brought the offering of your God:
it is a statute for ever throughout your
generations in all your dwellings.

THE FESTIVAL OF WEEKS

15 "And you shall count from the
morrow after the sabbath, from the
day that you brought the sheaf of the
wave offering; seven full weeks shall
they be, counting fifty days to the
morrow after the seventh sabbath;
then you shall present a cereal offer-
ing of new grain to the LORD. 17You
shall bring from your dwellings two
loaves of bread to be waved, made of

[a] Heb *between the two evenings*

two tenths of an ephah; they shall be
of fine flour, they shall be baked with
leaven, as first fruits to the LORD.
18And you shall present with the
bread seven lambs a year old without
blemish, and one young bull, and two
rams; they shall be a burnt offering to
the LORD, with their cereal offering
and their drink offerings, an offering
by fire, a pleasing odor to the LORD.
19And you shall offer one male goat for
a sin offering, and two male lambs a
year old as a sacrifice of peace offer-
ings. 20And the priest shall wave them
with the bread of the first fruits as a
wave offering before the LORD, with
the two lambs; they shall be holy to
the LORD for the priest. 21And you
shall make proclamation on the same
day; you shall hold a holy convocation;
you shall do no laborious work: it is a
statute for ever in all your dwellings
throughout your generations.
22 "And when you reap the harvest
of your land, you shall not reap your
field to its very border, nor shall you
gather the gleanings after your har-
vest; you shall leave them for the poor
and for the stranger: I am the LORD
your God."

THE FESTIVAL OF TRUMPETS

23 And the LORD said to Moses,
24"Say to the people of Israel, In the
seventh month, on the first day of the
month, you shall observe a day of sol-
emn rest, a memorial proclaimed with
blast of trumpets, a holy convocation.
25You shall do no laborious work; and
you shall present an offering by fire to
the LORD."

THE DAY OF ATONEMENT

26 And the LORD said to Moses,
27"On the tenth day of this seventh
month is the day of atonement; it
shall be for you a time of holy con-
vocation, and you shall afflict your-
selves and present an offering by fire
to the LORD. 28And you shall do no
work on this same day; for it is a day
of atonement, to make atonement for
you before the LORD your God. 29For
whoever is not afflicted on this same
day shall be cut off from his people.
30And whoever does any work on this
same day, that person I will destroy
from among his people. 31You shall
do no work: it is a statute for ever
throughout your generations in all
your dwellings. 32It shall be to you a
sabbath of solemn rest, and you shall
afflict yourselves; on the ninth day of
the month beginning at evening, from
evening to evening shall you keep
your sabbath."

THE FESTIVAL OF BOOTHS

33 And the LORD said to Moses,
34"Say to the people of Israel, On the
fifteenth day of this seventh month
and for seven days is the feast of
booths[b] to the LORD. 35On the first day
shall be a holy convocation; you shall
do no laborious work. 36Seven days
you shall present offerings by fire to
the LORD; on the eighth day you shall
hold a holy convocation and present
an offering by fire to the LORD; it is
a solemn assembly; you shall do no la-
borious work.
37 "These are the appointed feasts
of the LORD, which you shall proclaim
as times of holy convocation, for pre-
senting to the LORD offerings by fire,
burnt offerings and cereal offerings,
sacrifices and drink offerings, each on
its proper day; 38besides the sabbaths
of the LORD, and besides your gifts,
and besides all your votive offerings,
and besides all your freewill offerings,
which you give to the LORD.
39 "On the fifteenth day of the
seventh month, when you have gath-
ered in the produce of the land, you
shall keep the feast of the LORD sev-
en days; on the first day shall be a
solemn rest, and on the eighth day
shall be a solemn rest. 40And you
shall take on the first day the fruit
of goodly trees, branches of palm
trees, and boughs of leafy trees, and

[b]Or *tabernacles*

willows of the brook; and you shall
rejoice before the LORD your God
seven days. 41You shall keep it as a
feast to the LORD seven days in the
year; it is a statute for ever through-
out your generations; you shall keep
it in the seventh month. 42You shall
dwell in booths for seven days; all
that are native in Israel shall dwell
in booths, 43that your generations
may know that I made the people of
Israel dwell in booths when I brought
them out of the land of Egypt: I am
the LORD your God."

44 Thus Moses declared to the peo-
ple of Israel the appointed feasts of
the LORD.

THE LAMP

24 The LORD said to Moses, 2"Com-
mand the people of Israel to bring
you pure oil from beaten olives for the
lamp, that a light may be kept burn-
ing continually. 3Outside the veil of
the testimony, in the tent of meeting,
Aaron shall keep it in order from eve-
ning to morning before the LORD con-
tinually; it shall be a statute for ever
throughout your generations. 4He
shall keep the lamps in order upon
the lampstand of pure gold before the
LORD continually.

THE BREAD FOR THE TABERNACLE

5 "And you shall take fine flour,
and bake twelve cakes of it; two
tenths of an ephah shall be in each
cake. 6And you shall set them in two
rows, six in a row, upon the table of
pure gold. 7And you shall put pure
frankincense with each row, that it
may go with the bread as a memori-
al portion to be offered by fire to the
LORD. 8Every sabbath day Aaron shall
set it in order before the LORD contin-
ually on behalf of the people of Israel
as a covenant for ever. 9And it shall be
for Aaron and his sons, and they shall
eat it in a holy place, since it is for him
a most holy portion out of the offer-
ings by fire to the LORD, a perpetual
due."

BLASPHEMY AND ITS PUNISHMENT

10 Now an Israelite woman's son,
whose father was an Egyptian, went
out among the people of Israel; and
the Israelite woman's son and a man
of Israel quarreled in the camp, 11and
the Israelite woman's son blasphemed
the Name, and cursed. And they
brought him to Moses. His mother's
name was Shelo´mith, the daughter of
Dibri, of the tribe of Dan. 12And they
put him in custody, till the will of the
LORD should be declared to them.

13 And the LORD said to Moses,
14"Bring out of the camp him who
cursed; and let all who heard him lay
their hands upon his head, and let all
the congregation stone him. 15And
say to the people of Israel, Whoever
curses his God shall bear his sin.
16He who blasphemes the name of
the LORD shall be put to death; all
the congregation shall stone him;
the sojourner as well as the native,
when he blasphemes the Name, shall
be put to death. 17He who kills a man
shall be put to death. 18He who kills a
beast shall make it good, life for life.
19When a man causes a disfigurement
in his neighbor, as he has done it shall
be done to him, 20fracture for fracture,
eye for eye, tooth for tooth; as he has
disfigured a man, he shall be disfig-
ured. 21He who kills a beast shall make
it good; and he who kills a man shall
be put to death. 22You shall have one
law for the sojourner and for the na-
tive; for I am the LORD your God." 23So
Moses spoke to the people of Israel;
and they brought him who had cursed
out of the camp, and stoned him with
stones. Thus the people of Israel did
as the LORD commanded Moses.

THE SABBATICAL YEAR

25 The LORD said to Moses on
Mount Sinai, 2"Say to the people
of Israel, When you come into the land
which I give you, the land shall keep a
sabbath to the LORD. 3Six years you
shall sow your field, and six years you
shall prune your vineyard, and gather

in its fruits; 4but in the seventh year there shall be a sabbath of solemn rest for the land, a sabbath to the LORD; you shall not sow your field or prune your vineyard. 5What grows of itself in your harvest you shall not reap, and the grapes of your undressed vine you shall not gather; it shall be a year of solemn rest for the land. 6The sabbath of the land shall provide food for you, for yourself and for your male and female slaves and for your hired servant and the sojourner who lives with you; 7for your cattle also and for the beasts that are in your land all its yield shall be for food.

THE YEAR OF JUBILEE

8 "And you shall count seven weeks[a] of years, seven times seven years, so that the time of the seven weeks of years shall be to you forty-nine years. 9Then you shall send abroad the loud trumpet on the tenth day of the seventh month; on the day of atonement you shall send abroad the trumpet throughout all your land. 10And you shall hallow the fiftieth year, and proclaim liberty throughout the land to all its inhabitants; it shall be a jubilee for you, when each of you shall return to his property and each of you shall return to his family. 11A jubilee shall that fiftieth year be to you; in it you shall neither sow, nor reap what grows of itself, nor gather the grapes from the undressed vines. 12For it is a jubilee; it shall be holy to you; you shall eat what it yields out of the field.

13 "In this year of jubilee each of you shall return to his property. 14And if you sell to your neighbor or buy from your neighbor, you shall not wrong one another. 15According to the number of years after the jubilee, you shall buy from your neighbor, and according to the number of years for crops he shall sell to you. 16If the years are many you shall increase the price, and if the years are few you shall diminish the price, for it is the number of the crops that he is selling to you. 17You shall not wrong one another, but you shall fear your God; for I am the LORD your God.

18 "Therefore you shall do my statutes, and keep my ordinances and perform them; so you will dwell in the land securely. 19The land will yield its fruit, and you will eat your fill, and dwell in it securely. 20And if you say, 'What shall we eat in the seventh year, if we may not sow or gather in our crop?' 21I will command my blessing upon you in the sixth year, so that it will bring forth fruit for three years. 22When you sow in the eighth year, you will be eating old produce; until the ninth year, when its produce comes in, you shall eat the old. 23The land shall not be sold in perpetuity, for the land is mine; for you are strangers and sojourners with me. 24And in all the country you possess, you shall grant a redemption of the land.

25 "If your brother becomes poor, and sells part of his property, then his next of kin shall come and redeem what his brother has sold. 26If a man has no one to redeem it, and then himself becomes prosperous and finds sufficient means to redeem it, 27let him reckon the years since he sold it and pay back the overpayment to the man to whom he sold it; and he shall return to his property. 28But if he has not sufficient means to get it back for himself, then what he sold shall remain in the hand of him who bought it until the year of jubilee; in the jubilee it shall be released, and he shall return to his property.

29 "If a man sells a dwelling house in a walled city, he may redeem it within a whole year after its sale; for a full year he shall have the right of redemption. 30If it is not redeemed within a full year, then the house that is in the walled city shall be made sure in perpetuity to him who bought it, throughout his generations; it shall

[a]Or *sabbaths*

not be released in the jubilee. 31But the
houses of the villages which have no
wall around them shall be reckoned
with the fields of the country; they
may be redeemed, and they shall be
released in the jubilee. 32Nevertheless
the cities of the Levites, the houses
in the cities of their possession, the
Levites may redeem at any time. 33And
if one of the Levites does not exer-
cise[a] his right of redemption, then
the house that was sold in a city of
their possession shall be released in
the jubilee; for the houses in the cit-
ies of the Levites are their possession
among the people of Israel. 34But the
fields of common land belonging to
their cities may not be sold; for that is
their perpetual possession.

35 "And if your brother becomes
poor, and cannot maintain himself
with you, you shall maintain him; as
a stranger and a sojourner he shall
live with you. 36Take no interest from
him or increase, but fear your God;
that your brother may live beside you.
37You shall not lend him your money
at interest, nor give him your food for
profit. 38I am the LORD your God, who
brought you forth out of the land of
Egypt to give you the land of Canaan,
and to be your God.

39 "And if your brother becomes
poor beside you, and sells himself to
you, you shall not make him serve
as a slave: 40he shall be with you as a
hired servant and as a sojourner. He
shall serve with you until the year of
the jubilee; 41then he shall go out from
you, he and his children with him, and
go back to his own family, and return
to the possession of his fathers. 42For
they are my servants, whom I brought
forth out of the land of Egypt; they
shall not be sold as slaves. 43You shall
not rule over him with harshness,
but shall fear your God. 44As for your
male and female slaves whom you may
have: you may buy male and female
slaves from among the nations that
are round about you. 45You may also
buy from among the strangers who
sojourn with you and their families
that are with you, who have been born
in your land; and they may be your
property. 46You may bequeath them
to your sons after you, to inherit as
a possession for ever; you may make
slaves of them, but over your brethren
the people of Israel you shall not rule,
one over another, with harshness.

47 "If a stranger or sojourner with
you becomes rich, and your brother
beside him becomes poor and sells
himself to the stranger or sojourn-
er with you, or to a member of the
stranger's family, 48then after he is
sold he may be redeemed; one of his
brothers may redeem him, 49or his un-
cle, or his cousin may redeem him, or
a near kinsman belonging to his family
may redeem him; or if he grows rich he
may redeem himself. 50He shall reck-
on with him who bought him from
the year when he sold himself to him
until the year of jubilee, and the price
of his release shall be according to
the number of years; the time he was
with his owner shall be rated as the
time of a hired servant. 51If there are
still many years, according to them he
shall refund out of the price paid for
him the price for his redemption. 52If
there remain but a few years until the
year of jubilee, he shall make a reckon-
ing with him; according to the years of
service due from him he shall refund
the money for his redemption. 53As a
servant hired year by year shall he be
with him; he shall not rule with harsh-
ness over him in your sight. 54And if he
is not redeemed by these means, then
he shall be released in the year of jubi-
lee, he and his children with him. 55For
to me the people of Israel are servants,
they are my servants whom I brought
forth out of the land of Egypt: I am the
LORD your God.

REWARDS FOR OBEDIENCE

26 "You shall make for yourselves no
idols and erect no graven image or

[a]Compare Vg: Heb *exercises*

pillar, and you shall not set up a fig-
ured stone in your land, to bow down
to them; for I am the LORD your God.
2You shall keep my sabbaths and rev-
erence my sanctuary: I am the LORD.

3 "If you walk in my statutes and
observe my commandments and do
them, 4then I will give you your rains
in their season, and the land shall
yield its increase, and the trees of
the field shall yield their fruit. 5And
your threshing shall last to the time
of vintage, and the vintage shall last
to the time for sowing; and you shall
eat your bread to the full, and dwell
in your land securely. 6And I will
give peace in the land, and you shall
lie down, and none shall make you
afraid; and I will remove evil beasts
from the land, and the sword shall not
go through your land. 7And you shall
chase your enemies, and they shall fall
before you by the sword. 8Five of you
shall chase a hundred, and a hundred
of you shall chase ten thousand; and
your enemies shall fall before you by
the sword. 9And I will have regard for
you and make you fruitful and multi-
ply you, and will confirm my covenant
with you. 10And you shall eat old store
long kept, and you shall clear out the
old to make way for the new. 11And I
will make my abode among you, and
my soul shall not abhor you. 12And I
will walk among you, and will be your
God, and you shall be my people. 13I
am the LORD your God, who brought
you forth out of the land of Egypt,
that you should not be their slaves;
and I have broken the bars of your
yoke and made you walk erect.

PENALTIES FOR DISOBEDIENCE

14 "But if you will not hearken to
me, and will not do all these command-
ments, 15if you spurn my statutes, and
if your soul abhors my ordinances, so
that you will not do all my command-
ments, but break my covenant, 16I will
do this to you: I will appoint over you
sudden terror, consumption and fever
that waste the eyes and cause life to
pine away. And you shall sow your
seed in vain, for your enemies shall
eat it; 17I will set my face against you,
and you shall be smitten before your
enemies; those who hate you shall
rule over you, and you shall flee when
none pursues you. 18And if in spite of
this you will not hearken to me, then
I will chastise you again sevenfold for
your sins, 19and I will break the pride
of your power, and I will make your
heavens like iron and your earth like
brass; 20and your strength shall be
spent in vain, for your land shall not
yield its increase, and the trees of the
land shall not yield their fruit.

21 "Then if you walk contrary to
me, and will not hearken to me, I will
bring more plagues upon you, seven-
fold as many as your sins. 22And I will
let loose the wild beasts among you,
which shall rob you of your children,
and destroy your cattle, and make you
few in number, so that your ways shall
become desolate.

23 "And if by this discipline you are
not turned to me, but walk contrary to
me, 24then I also will walk contrary to
you, and I myself will smite you sev-
enfold for your sins. 25And I will bring
a sword upon you, that shall execute
vengeance for the covenant; and if you
gather within your cities I will send
pestilence among you, and you shall
be delivered into the hand of the ene-
my. 26When I break your staff of bread,
ten women shall bake your bread in
one oven, and shall deliver your bread
again by weight; and you shall eat,
and not be satisfied.

27 "And if in spite of this you will
not hearken to me, but walk contrary
to me, 28then I will walk contrary to
you in fury, and chastise you myself
sevenfold for your sins. 29You shall eat
the flesh of your sons, and you shall
eat the flesh of your daughters. 30And
I will destroy your high places, and
cut down your incense altars, and cast
your dead bodies upon the dead bodies
of your idols; and my soul will abhor
you. 31And I will lay your cities waste,

and will make your sanctuaries desolate, and I will not smell your pleasing odors. 32 And I will devastate the land, so that your enemies who settle in it shall be astonished at it. 33 And I will scatter you among the nations, and I will unsheathe the sword after you; and your land shall be a desolation, and your cities shall be a waste.

34 "Then the land shall enjoy[a] its sabbaths as long as it lies desolate, while you are in your enemies' land; then the land shall rest, and enjoy[a] its sabbaths. 35 As long as it lies desolate it shall have rest, the rest which it had not in your sabbaths when you dwelt upon it. 36 And as for those of you that are left, I will send faintness into their hearts in the lands of their enemies; the sound of a driven leaf shall put them to flight, and they shall flee as one flees from the sword, and they shall fall when none pursues. 37 They shall stumble over one another, as if to escape a sword, though none pursues; and you shall have no power to stand before your enemies. 38 And you shall perish among the nations, and the land of your enemies shall eat you up. 39 And those of you that are left shall pine away in your enemies' lands because of their iniquity; and also because of the iniquities of their fathers they shall pine away like them.

40 "But if they confess their iniquity and the iniquity of their fathers in their treachery which they committed against me, and also in walking contrary to me, 41 so that I walked contrary to them and brought them into the land of their enemies; if then their uncircumcised heart is humbled and they make amends for their iniquity; 42 then I will remember my covenant with Jacob, and I will remember my covenant with Isaac and my covenant *with Abraham, and I will* remember the land. 43 But the land shall be left by them, and enjoy[a] its sabbaths while it lies desolate without them; and they shall make amends for their iniquity, because they spurned my ordinances, and their soul abhorred my statutes. 44 Yet for all that, when they are in the land of their enemies, I will not spurn them, neither will I abhor them so as to destroy them utterly and break my covenant with them; for I am the LORD their God; 45 but I will for their sake remember the covenant with their forefathers, whom I brought forth out of the land of Egypt in the sight of the nations, that I might be their God: I am the LORD."

46 These are the statutes and ordinances and laws which the LORD made between him and the people of Israel on Mount Sinai by Moses.

VOTIVE OFFERINGS

27 The LORD said to Moses, 2 "Say to the people of Israel, When a man makes a special vow of persons to the LORD at your valuation, 3 then your valuation of a male from twenty years old up to sixty years old shall be fifty shekels of silver, according to the shekel of the sanctuary. 4 If the person is a female, your valuation shall be thirty shekels. 5 If the person is from five years old up to twenty years old, your valuation shall be for a male twenty shekels, and for a female ten shekels. 6 If the person is from a month old up to five years old, your valuation shall be for a male five shekels of silver, and for a female your valuation shall be three shekels of silver. 7 And if the person is sixty years old and upward, then your valuation for a male shall be fifteen shekels, and for a female ten shekels. 8 And if a man is too poor to pay your valuation, then he shall bring the person before the priest, and the priest shall value him; according to the ability of him who vowed the priest shall value him.

9 "If it is an animal such as men offer as an offering to the LORD, all of such that any man gives to the LORD is holy. 10 He shall not substitute anything for it or exchange it, a good

[a] Or *pay for*

for a bad, or a bad for a good; and if he makes any exchange of beast for beast, then both it and that for which it is exchanged shall be holy. 11And if it is an unclean animal such as is not offered as an offering to the LORD, then the man shall bring the animal before the priest, 12and the priest shall value it as either good or bad; as you, the priest, value it, so it shall be. 13But if he wishes to redeem it, he shall add a fifth to the valuation.

14 "When a man dedicates his house to be holy to the LORD, the priest shall value it as either good or bad; as the priest values it, so it shall stand. 15And if he who dedicates it wishes to redeem his house, he shall add a fifth of the valuation in money to it, and it shall be his.

16 "If a man dedicates to the LORD part of the land which is his by inheritance, then your valuation shall be according to the seed for it; a sowing of a homer of barley shall be valued at fifty shekels of silver. 17If he dedicates his field from the year of jubilee, it shall stand at your full valuation; 18but if he dedicates his field after the jubilee, then the priest shall compute the money-value for it according to the years that remain until the year of jubilee, and a deduction shall be made from your valuation. 19And if he who dedicates the field wishes to redeem it, then he shall add a fifth of the valuation in money to it, and it shall remain his. 20But if he does not wish to redeem the field, or if he has sold the field to another man, it shall not be redeemed any more; 21but the field, when it is released in the jubilee, shall be holy to the LORD, as a field that has been devoted; the priest shall be in possesion of it. 22If he dedicates to the LORD a field which he has bought, which is not a part of his possession by inheritance, 23then the priest shall compute the valuation for it up to the year of jubilee, and the man shall give the amount of the valuation on that day as a holy thing to the LORD. 24In the year of jubilee the field shall return to him from whom it was bought, to whom the land belongs as a possession by inheritance. 25Every valuation shall be according to the shekel of the sanctuary: twenty gerahs shall make a shekel.

26 "But a firstling of animals, which as a firstling belongs to the LORD, no man may dedicate; whether ox or sheep, it is the LORD's. 27And if it is an unclean animal, then he shall buy it back at your valuation, and add a fifth to it; or, if it is not redeemed, it shall be sold at your valuation.

28 "But no devoted thing that a man devotes to the LORD, of anything that he has, whether of a man or beast, or of his inherited field, shall be sold or redeemed; every devoted thing is most holy to the LORD. 29No one devoted, who is to be utterly destroyed from among men, shall be ransomed; he shall be put to death.

30 "All the tithe of the land, whether of the seed of the land or of the fruit of the trees, is the LORD's; it is holy to the LORD. 31If a man wishes to redeem any of his tithe, he shall add a fifth to it. 32And all the tithe of herds and flocks, every tenth animal of all that pass under the herdsman's staff, shall be holy to the LORD. 33A man shall not inquire whether it is good or bad, neither shall he exchange it; and if he exchanges it, then both it and that for which it is exchanged shall be holy; it shall not be redeemed."

34 These are the commandments which the LORD commanded Moses for the people of Israel on Mount Sinai.

THE FOURTH BOOK OF MOSES COMMONLY CALLED

NUMBERS

THE FIRST CENSUS OF ISRAEL

1 The LORD spoke to Moses in the
wilderness of Sinai, in the tent of
meeting, on the first day of the sec-
ond month, in the second year af-
ter they had come out of the land of
Egypt, saying, 2"Take a census of all
the congregation of the people of
Israel, by families, by fathers' houses,
according to the number of names, ev-
ery male, head by head; 3from twen-
ty years old and upward, all in Israel
who are able to go forth to war, you
and Aaron shall number them, com-
pany by company. 4And there shall
be with you a man from each tribe,
each man being the head of the house
of his fathers. 5And these are the
names of the men who shall attend
you. From Reuben, Eli´zur the son of
Shed´eur; 6from Simeon, Shelu´mi-el
the son of Zurishad´dai; 7from Judah,
Nahshon the son of Ammin´adab;
8from Is´sachar, Nethan´el the son of
Zu´ar; 9from Zeb´ulun, Eli´ab the son
of Helon; 10from the sons of Joseph,
from E´phraim, Elish´ama the son
of Ammi´hud, and from Manas´seh,
Gama´liel the son of Pedah´zur;
11from Benjamin, Abi´dan the son of
Gideo´ni; 12from Dan, Ahi-e´zer the
son of Ammishad´dai; 13from Asher,
Pa´giel the son of Ochran; 14from Gad,
Eli´asaph the son of Deu´el; 15from
Naph´tali, Ahi´ra the son of Enan."
16These were the ones chosen from
the congregation, the leaders of their
ancestral tribes, the heads of the clans
of Israel.

17 Moses and Aaron took these
men who have been named, 18and on
the first day of the second month, they
assembled the whole congregation to-
gether, who registered themselves by
families, by fathers' houses, according
to the number of names from twenty
years old and upward, head by head,
19as the LORD commanded Moses. So
he numbered them in the wilderness
of Sinai.

20 The people of Reuben, Israel's
first-born, their generations, by their
families, by their fathers' houses, ac-
cording to the number of names, head
by head, every male from twenty years
old and upward, all who were able to
go forth to war: 21the number of the
tribe of Reuben was forty-six thou-
sand five hundred.

22 Of the people of Simeon, their
generations, by their families, by
their fathers' houses, those of them
that were numbered, according to the
number of names, head by head, ev-
ery male from twenty years old and
upward, all who were able to go forth
to war: 23the number of the tribe of
Simeon was fifty-nine thousand three
hundred.

24 Of the people of Gad, their gen-
erations, by their families, by their
fathers' houses, according to the num-
ber of the names, from twenty years
old and upward, all who were able to
go forth to war: 25the number of the
tribe of Gad was forty-five thousand
six hundred and fifty.

26 Of the people of Judah, their
generations, by their families, by
their fathers' houses, according to the
number of names, from twenty years
old and upward, every man able to go
forth to war: 27the number of the tribe
of Judah was seventy-four thousand
six hundred.

28 Of the people of Is´sachar, their
generations, by their families, by their
fathers' houses, according to the num-
ber of names, from twenty years old
and upward, every man able to go
forth to war: 29the number of the tribe
of Is´sachar was fifty-four thousand
four hundred.

30 Of the people of Zeb´ulun, their
generations, by their families, by their

fathers' houses, according to the num-
ber of names, from twenty years old
and upward, every man able to go
forth to war: 31 the number of the tribe
of Zeb´ulun was fifty-seven thousand
four hundred.

32 Of the people of Joseph, name-
ly, of the people of E´phraim, their
generations, by their families, by
their fathers' houses, according to the
number of names, from twenty years
old and upward, every man able to go
forth to war: 33 the number of the tribe
of E´phraim was forty thousand five
hundred.

34 Of the people of Manas´seh,
their generations, by their families, by
their fathers' houses, according to the
number of names, from twenty years
old and upward, every man able to go
forth to war: 35 the number of the tribe
of Manas´seh was thirty-two thou-
sand two hundred.

36 Of the people of Benjamin, their
generations, by their families, by their
fathers' houses, according to the num-
ber of names, from twenty years old
and upward, every man able to go
forth to war: 37 the number of the tribe
of Benjamin was thirty-five thousand
four hundred.

38 Of the people of Dan, their gen-
erations, by their families, by their
fathers' houses, according to the
number of names, from twenty years
old and upward, every man able to go
forth to war: 39 the number of the tribe
of Dan was sixty-two thousand seven
hundred.

40 Of the people of Asher, their
generations, by their families, by
their fathers' houses, according to the
number of names, from twenty years
old and upward, every man able to go
forth to war: 41 the number of the tribe
of Asher was forty-one thousand five
hundred.

42 Of the people of Naph´tali, their
generations, by their families, by their
fathers' houses, according to the num-
ber of names, from twenty years old
and upward, every man able to go
forth to war: 43 the number of the tribe
of Naph´tali was fifty-three thousand
four hundred.

44 These are those who were
numbered, whom Moses and Aaron
numbered with the help of the lead-
ers of Israel, twelve men, each rep-
resenting his fathers' house. 45 So the
whole number of the people of Israel,
by their fathers' houses, from twen-
ty years old and upward, every man
able to go forth to war in Israel 46 their
whole number was six hundred and
three thousand five hundred and fifty.

47 But the Levites were not num-
bered by their ancestral tribe along
with them. 48 For the LORD said to
Moses, 49 "Only the tribe of Levi you
shall not number, and you shall not
take a census of them among the peo-
ple of Israel; 50 but appoint the Levites
over the tabernacle of the testimo-
ny, and over all its furnishings, and
over all that belongs to it; they are to
carry the tabernacle and all its fur-
nishings, and they shall tend it, and
shall encamp around the tabernacle.
51 When the tabernacle is to set out,
the Levites shall take it down; and
when the tabernacle is to be pitched,
the Levites shall set it up. And if any
one else comes near, he shall be put
to death. 52 The people of Israel shall
pitch their tents by their companies,
every man by his own camp and every
man by his own standard; 53 but the
Levites shall encamp around the tab-
ernacle of the testimony, that there
may be no wrath upon the congrega-
tion of the people of Israel; and the
Levites shall keep charge of the taber-
nacle of the testimony." 54 Thus did the
people of Israel; they did according to
all that the LORD commanded Moses.

THE ORDER OF ENCAMPMENT AND MARCHING

2 The LORD said to Moses and Aaron,
2 "The people of Israel shall en-
camp each by his own standard, with
the ensigns of their fathers' houses;
they shall encamp facing the tent of

meeting on every side. 3 Those to en-
camp on the east side toward the sun-
rise shall be of the standard of the
camp of Judah by their companies, the
leader of the people of Judah being
Nahshon the son of Ammin´adab, 4 his
host as numbered being seventy-four
thousand six hundred. 5 Those to en-
camp next to him shall be the tribe of
Is´sachar, the leader of the people of
Is´sachar being Nethan´el the son of
Zu´ar, 6 his host as numbered being fif-
ty-four thousand four hundred. 7 Then
the tribe of Zeb´ulun, the leader of
the people of Zeb´ulun being Eli´ab
the son of Helon, 8 his host as num-
bered being fifty-seven thousand four
hundred. 9 The whole number of the
camp of Judah, by their companies,
is a hundred and eighty-six thousand
four hundred. They shall set out first
on the march.

10 "On the south side shall be the
standard of the camp of Reuben by
their companies, the leader of the peo-
ple of Reuben being Eli´zur the son
of Shed´eur, 11 his host as numbered
being forty-six thousand five hun-
dred. 12 And those to encamp next to
him shall be the tribe of Simeon, the
leader of the people of Simeon being
Shelu´mi-el the son of Zurishad´dai,
13 his host as numbered being fif-
ty-nine thousand three hundred.
14 Then the tribe of Gad, the leader of
the people of Gad being Eli´asaph the
son of Reu´el, 15 his host as numbered
being forty-five thousand six hundred
and fifty. 16 The whole number of the
camp of Reuben, by their companies,
is a hundred and fifty-one thousand
four hundred and fifty. They shall set
out second.

17 "Then the tent of meeting shall
set out, with the camp of the Levites
in the midst of the camps; as they en-
camp, so *shall* they set out, each in
position, standard by standard.

18 "On the west side shall be the
standard of the camp of E´phraim by
their companies, the leader of the
people of E´phraim being Elish´ama
the son of Ammi´hud, 19 his host as
numbered being forty thousand five
hundred. 20 And next to him shall
be the tribe of Manas´seh, the lead-
er of the people of Manas´seh being
Gama´liel the son of Pedah´zur, 21 his
host as numbered being thirty-two
thousand two hundred. 22 Then the
tribe of Benjamin, the leader of the
people of Benjamin being Abi´dan
the son of Gideo´ni, 23 his host as num-
bered being thirty-five thousand four
hundred. 24 The whole number of the
camp of E´phraim, by their compa-
nies, is a hundred and eight thousand
one hundred. They shall set out third
on the march.

25 "On the north side shall be
the standard of the camp of Dan by
their companies, the leader of the
people of Dan being Ahi-e´zer the
son of Ammishad´dai, 26 his host as
numbered being sixty-two thou-
sand seven hundred. 27 And those
to encamp next to him shall be the
tribe of Asher, the leader of the peo-
ple of Asher being Pa´giel the son
of Ochran, 28 his host as numbered
being forty-one thousand five hun-
dred. 29 Then the tribe of Naph´tali,
the leader of the people of Naph´tali
being Ahi´ra the son of Enan, 30 his
host as numbered being fifty-three
thousand four hundred. 31 The whole
number of the camp of Dan is a hun-
dred and fifty-seven thousand six
hundred. They shall set out last,
standard by standard."

32 These are the people of Israel
as numbered by their fathers' houses;
all in the camps who were numbered
by their companies were six hundred
and three thousand five hundred and
fifty. 33 But the Levites were not num-
bered among the people of Israel, as
the LORD commanded Moses.

34 Thus did the people of Israel.
According to all that the LORD com-
manded Moses, so they encamped by
their standards, and so they set out,
every one in his family, according to
his fathers' house.

THE SONS OF AARON

3These are the generations of Aaron
and Moses at the time when the
LORD spoke with Moses on Mount
Sinai. 2These are the names of the sons
of Aaron: Nadab the first-born, and
Abi´hu, Elea´zar, and Ith´amar; 3these
are the names of the sons of Aaron, the
anointed priests, whom he ordained
to minister in the priest's office. 4But
Nadab and Abi´hu died before the
LORD when they offered unholy fire
before the LORD in the wilderness of
Sinai; and they had no children. So
Elea´zar and Ith´amar served as priests
in the lifetime of Aaron their father.

THE DUTIES OF THE LEVITES

5 And the LORD said to Moses,
6"Bring the tribe of Levi near, and set
them before Aaron the priest, that
they may minister to him. 7They shall
perform duties for him and for the
whole congregation before the tent of
meeting, as they minister at the tab-
ernacle; 8they shall have charge of all
the furnishings of the tent of meeting,
and attend to the duties for the people
of Israel as they minister at the taber-
nacle. 9And you shall give the Levites
to Aaron and his sons; they are wholly
given to him from among the people of
Israel. 10And you shall appoint Aaron
and his sons, and they hall attend to
their priesthood; but i any one else
comes near, he shall beut to death."

11 And the LORD sid to Moses,
12"Behold, I have taken tl Levites from
among the people of Isel instead of
every first-born that ops the womb
among the people of Isra The Levites
shall be mine, 13for all e first-born
are mine; on the day thaslew all the
first-born in the land of lpt, I conse-
crated for my own all thrst-born in
Israel, both of man and beast; they
shall be mine: I am the Lb."

A CENSUS OF THE LIES

14 And the LORD saic Moses in
the wilderness of Sinar"Number
the sons of Levi, by fathers' houses
and by families; every male from a
month old and upward you shall num-
ber." 16So Moses numbered them ac-
cording to the word of the LORD, as he
was commanded. 17And these were the
sons of Levi by their names: Gershon
and Kohath and Merar´i. 18And these
are the names of the sons of Gershon
by their families: Libni and Shim´e-i.
19And the sons of Kohath by their
families: Amram, Izhar, Hebron, and
Uz´ziel. 20And the sons of Merar´i
by their families: Mahli and Mushi.
These are the families of the Levites,
by their fathers' houses.

21 Of Gershon were the family
of the Libnites and the family of the
Shim´e-ites; these were the families of
the Gershonites. 22Their number ac-
cording to the number of all the males
from a month old and upward was[a]
seven thousand five hundred. 23The
families of the Gershonites were to
encamp behind the tabernacle on the
west, 24with Eli´asaph, the son of La´el
as head of the fathers' house of the
Gershonites. 25And the charge of the
sons of Gershon in the tent of meeting
was to be the tabernacle, the tent with
its covering, the screen for the door of
the tent of meeting, 26the hangings of
the court, the screen for the door of
the court which is around the taber-
nacle and the altar, and its cords; all
the service pertaining to these.

27 Of Kohath were the family of
the Amramites, and the family of
the Izhar´ites, and the family of the
He´bronites, and the family of the
Uz´zielites; these are the families
of the Ko´hathites. 28According to
the number of all the males, from a
month old and upward, there were
eight thousand six hundred, attending
to the duties of the sanctuary. 29The
families of the sons of Kohath were to
encamp on the south side of the tab-
ernacle, 30with Eli-za´phan the son of
Uz´ziel as head of the fathers' house of
the families of the Ko´hathites. 31And

[a]Heb *their number was*

their charge was to be the ark, the ta-
ble, the lampstand, the altars, the ves-
sels of the sanctuary with which the
priests minister, and the screen; all
the service pertaining to these. 32And
Elea´zar the son of Aaron the priest
was to be chief over the leaders of the
Levites, and to have oversight of those
who had charge of the sanctuary.

33 Of Merar´i were the family of
the Mahlites and the family of the
Mushites: these are the families of
Merar´i. 34Their number according to
the number of all the males from a
month old and upward was six thou-
sand two hundred. 35And the head of
the fathers' house of the families of
Merar´i was Zu´riel the son of Abiha´il;
they were to encamp on the north side
of the tabernacle. 36And the appointed
charge of the sons of Merar´i was to be
the frames of the tabernacle, the bars,
the pillars, the bases, and all their ac-
cessories; all the service pertaining
to these; 37also the pillars of the court
round about, with their bases and pegs
and cords.

38 And those to encamp before the
tabernacle on the east, before the tent
of meeting toward the sunrise, were
Moses and Aaron and his sons, having
charge of the rites within the sanctu-
ary, whatever had to be done for the
people of Israel; and any one else who
came near was to be put to death. 39All
who were numbered of the Levites,
whom Moses and Aaron numbered
at the commandment of the LORD, by
families, all the males from a month
old and upward, were twenty-two
thousand.

THE REDEMPTION OF THE FIRSTBORN

40 And the LORD said to Moses,
"Number all the first-born males of
the people of Israel, from a month
old and upward, taking their number
by names. 41And you shall take the
Levites for me—I am the LORD—in-
stead of all the first-born among the
people of Israel, and the cattle of the
Levites instead of all the firstlings
among the cattle of the people of
Israel." 42So Moses numbered all the
first-born among the people of Israel,
as the LORD commanded him. 43And
all the first-born males, according to
the number of names, from a month
old and upward as numbered were
twenty-two thousand two hundred
and seventy-three.

44 And the LORD said to Moses,
45"Take the Levites instead of all the
first-born among the people of Israel,
and the cattle of the Levites instead
of their cattle; and the Levites shall
be mine: I am the LORD. 46And for
the redemption of the two hundred
and seventy-three of the first-born of
the people of Israel, over and above
the number of the male Levites, 47you
shall take five shekels apiece; reck-
oning by the shekel of the sanctuary,
the shekel of twenty gerahs, you shall
take them, 48and give the money by
which the excess number of them is
redeemed to Aaron and his sons." 49So
Moses took the redemption money
from those who were over and above
those redeemed by the Levites; 50from
the first-born of the people of Israel
he took the money, one thousand
three hundred and sixty-five shekels,
reckoned by the shekel of the sanctu-
ary; 51and Moses gave the redemption
money to Aaron and his sons, accord-
ing to the word of the LORD, as the
LORD commaded Moses.

IE KOHATHITES

4 The LORDaid to Moses and Aaron,
2"Take acensus of the sons of
Kohath fro among the sons of Levi,
by their fiilies and their fathers'
houses, 3fn thirty years old up to
fifty yearld, all who can enter the
service, to the work in the tent of
meeting. his is the service of the
sons of Kath in the tent of meeting:
the mostly things. 5When the camp
is to set, Aaron and his sons shall
go in atake down the veil of the
screen, cover the ark of the testi-
mony v it; 6then they shall put on

it a covering of goatskin, and spread over that a cloth all of blue, and shall put in its poles. 7 And over the table of the bread of the Presence they shall spread a cloth of blue, and put upon it the plates, the dishes for incense, the bowls, and the flagons for the drink offering; the continual bread also shall be on it; 8 then they shall spread over them a cloth of scarlet, and cover the same with a covering of goatskin, and shall put in its poles. 9 And they shall take a cloth of blue, and cover the lampstand for the light, with its lamps, its snuffers, its trays, and all the vessels for oil with which it is supplied: 10 and they shall put it with all its utensils in a covering of goatskin and put it upon the carrying frame. 11 And over the golden altar they shall spread a cloth of blue, and cover it with a covering of goatskin, and shall put in its poles; 12 and they shall take all the vessels of the service which are used in the sanctuary, and put them in a cloth of blue, and cover them with a covering of goatskin, and put them on the carrying frame. 13 And they shall take away the ashes from the altar, and spread a purple cloth over it; 14 and they shall put on it all the utensils of the altar, which are used for the service there, the firepans, the forks, the shovels, and the basins, all the utensils of the altar; and they shall spread upon it a covering of goatskin, and shall put in its poles. 15 And when Aaron and his sons have finished covering the sanctuary and all the furnishings of the sanctuary, as the camp sets out, after that the sons of Kohath shall come to carry these, but they must not touch the holy things, lest they die. These are the things of the tent of meeting which the sons of Kohath are to carry.

16 "And Elea´zar the son of Aaron the priest shall have charge of the oil for the light, the fragrant incense, the continual cereal offering, and the anointing oil, with the oversight of all the tabernacle and all that is in it, of the sanctuary and its vessels."

17 The LORD said to Moses and Aaron, 18 "Let not the tribe of the families of the Ko´hathites be destroyed from among the Levites; 19 but deal thus with them, that they may live and not die when they come near to the most holy things: Aaron and his sons shall go in and appoint them each to his task and to his burden, 20 but they shall not go in to look upon the holy things even for a moment, lest they die."

THE GERSHONITES AND MERARITES

21 The LORD said to Moses, 22 "Take a census of the sons of Gershon also, by their families and their fathers' houses; 23 from thirty years old up to fifty years old, you shall number them, all who can enter for service, to do the work in the tent of meeting. 24 This is the service of the families of the Gershonites, in serving and bearing burdens: 25 they shall carry the curtains of the tabernacle, and the tent of meeting with its covering, and the covering of goatskin that is on top of it, and the screen for the door of the tent of meeting, 26 and the hangings of the court, and the screen for the entrance of the gate of the court which is around the tabernacle and the altar, and their cords, and all the equipment for their service; and they shall do all that needs to be done with regard to them. 27 All the service of the sons of the Gershonites shall be at the command of Aaron and his sons, in all that they are to carry, and in all that they have to do; and you shall assign to their charge all that they are to carry. 28 This is the service of the families of the sons of the Gershonites in the tent of meeting, and their work is to be under the oversight of Ith´amar the son of Aaron the priest.

29 "As for the sons of Merar´i, you shall number them by their families and their fathers' houses; 30 from thirty years old up to fifty years old, you shall number them, every one that can

enter the service, to do the work of
the tent of meeting. 31And this is what
they are charged to carry, as the whole
of their service in the tent of meeting:
the frames of the tabernacle, with
its bars, pillars, and bases, 32and the
pillars of the court round about with
their bases, pegs, and cords, with all
their equipment and all their acces-
sories; and you shall assign by name
the objects which they are required to
carry. 33This is the service of the fam-
ilies of the sons of Merar′i, the whole
of their service in the tent of meeting,
under the hand of Ith′amar the son of
Aaron the priest."

CENSUS OF THE LEVITES

34 And Moses and Aaron and the
leaders of the congregation numbered
the sons of the Ko′hathites, by their
families and their fathers' houses,
35from thirty years old up to fifty
years old, every one that could enter
the service, for work in the tent of
meeting; 36and their number by fami-
lies was two thousand seven hundred
and fifty. 37This was the number of the
families of the Ko′hathites, all who
served in the tent of meeting, whom
Moses and Aaron numbered according
to the commandment of the Lord by
Moses.

38 The number of the sons of
Gershon, by their families and their
fathers' houses, 39from thirty years old
up to fifty years old, every one that
could enter the service for work in the
tent of meeting 40their number by their
families and their fathers' houses was
two thousand six hundred and thirty.
41This was the number of the families
of the sons of Gershon, all who served
in the tent of meeting, whom Moses
and Aaron numbered according to the
commandment of the Lord.

42 The number of the families of
the sons of Merar′i, by their families
and their fathers' houses, 43from thir-
ty years old up to fifty years old, ev-
ery one that could enter the service,
for work in the tent of meeting 44their
number by families was three thou-
sand two hundred. 45These are those
who were numbered of the families
of the sons of Merar′i, whom Moses
and Aaron numbered according to the
commandment of the Lord by Moses.

46 All those who were numbered of
the Levites, whom Moses and Aaron
and the leaders of Israel numbered,
by their families and their fathers'
houses, 47from thirty years old up to
fifty years old, every one that could
enter to do the work of service and the
work of bearing burdens in the tent of
meeting, 48those who were numbered
of them were eight thousand five hun-
dred and eighty. 49According to the
commandment of the Lord through
Moses they were appointed, each to
his task of serving or carrying; thus
they were numbered by him, as the
Lord commanded Moses.

UNCLEAN PERSONS

5 The Lord said to Moses, 2"Com-
mand the people of Israel that they
put out of the camp every leper, and
every one having a discharge, and
every one that is unclean through
contact with the dead; 3you shall put
out both male and female, putting
them outside the camp, that they may
not defile their camp, in the midst of
which I dwell." 4And the people of
Israel did so, and drove them outside
the camp; as the Lord said to Moses,
so the people of Israel did.

CONFESSION AND RESTITUTION

5 And the Lord said to Moses,
6"Say to the people of Israel, When
a man or woman commits any of the
sins that men commit by breaking
faith with the Lord and that person is
guilty, 7he shall confess his sin which
he has committed; and he shall make
full restitution for his wrong, adding
a fifth to it, and giving it to him to
whom he did the wrong. 8But if the
man has no kinsman to whom resti-
tution may be made for the wrong, the
restitution for wrong shall go to the

LORD for the priest, in addition to the
ram of atonement with which atone-
ment is made for him. 9 And every of-
fering, all the holy things of the peo-
ple of Israel, which they bring to the
priest, shall be his; 10 and every man's
holy things shall be his; whatever any
man gives to the priest shall be his."

CONCERNING AN UNFAITHFUL WIFE

11 And the LORD said to Moses,
12 "Say to the people of Israel, If any
man's wife goes astray and acts un-
faithfully against him, 13 if a man lies
with her carnally, and it is hidden
from the eyes of her husband, and
she is undetected though she has de-
filed herself, and there is no witness
against her, since she was not taken in
the act; 14 and if the spirit of jealousy
comes upon him, and he is jealous of
his wife who has defiled herself; or if
the spirit of jealousy comes upon him,
and he is jealous of his wife, though
she has not defiled herself; 15 then the
man shall bring his wife to the priest,
and bring the offering required of her,
a tenth of an ephah of barley meal; he
shall pour no oil upon it and put no
frankincense on it, for it is a cereal
offering of jealousy, a cereal offering
of remembrance, bringing iniquity to
remembrance.

16 "And the priest shall bring her
near, and set her before the LORD
17 and the priest shall take holy water
in an earthen vessel, and take some
of the dust that is on the floor of the
tabernacle and put it into the water.
18 And the priest shall set the woman
before the LORD and unbind the hair
of the woman's head, and place in her
hands the cereal offering of remem-
brance, which is the cereal offering of
jealousy. And in his hand the priest
shall have the water of bitterness that
brings the curse. 19 Then the priest
shall make her take an oath, saying, 'If
no man has lain with you, and if you
have not turned aside to uncleanness,
while you were under your husband's
authority, be free from this water of
bitterness that brings the curse. 20 But
if you have gone astray, though you
are under your husband's authority,
and if you have defiled yourself, and
some man other than your husband
has lain with you, 21 then' (let the
priest make the woman take the oath
of the curse, and say to the woman)
'the LORD make you an execration
and an oath among your people, when
the LORD makes your thigh fall away
and your body swell; 22 may this water
that brings the curse pass into your
bowels and make your body swell and
your thigh fall away.' And the woman
shall say, 'Amen, Amen.'

23 "Then the priest shall write
these curses in a book, and wash
them off into the water of bitterness;
24 and he shall make the woman drink
the water of bitterness that brings the
curse, and the water that brings the
curse shall enter into her and cause
bitter pain. 25 And the priest shall take
the cereal offering of jealousy out of
the woman's hand, and shall wave the
cereal offering before the LORD and
bring it to the altar; 26 and the priest
shall take a handful of the cereal of-
fering, as its memorial portion, and
burn it upon the altar, and afterward
shall make the woman drink the wa-
ter. 27 And when he has made her drink
the water, then, if she has defiled her-
self and has acted unfaithfully against
her husband, the water that brings the
curse shall enter into her and cause
bitter pain, and her body shall swell,
and her thigh shall fall away, and the
woman shall become an execration
among her people. 28 But if the woman
has not defiled herself and is clean,
then she shall be free and shall con-
ceive children.

29 "This is the law in cases of jeal-
ousy, when a wife, though under her
husband's authority, goes astray and
defiles herself, 30 or when the spirit of
jealousy comes upon a man and he is
jealous of his wife; then he shall set
the woman before the LORD and the
priest shall execute upon her all this

law. 31The man shall be free from in-
iquity, but the woman shall bear her
iniquity."

THE NAZIRITES

6And the LORD said to Moses, 2"Say
to the people of Israel, When either
a man or a woman makes a special
vow, the vow of a Nazirite,[a] to sepa-
rate himself to the LORD 3he shall sep-
arate himself from wine and strong
drink; he shall drink no vinegar made
from wine or strong drink, and shall
not drink any juice of grapes or eat
grapes, fresh or dried. 4All the days
of his separation[b] he shall eat nothing
that is produced by the grapevine, not
even the seeds or the skins.

5 "All the days of his vow of sep-
aration no razor shall come upon his
head; until the time is completed for
which he separates himself to the
LORD he shall be holy; he shall let the
locks of hair of his head grow long.

6 "All the days that he separates
himself to the LORD he shall not go
near a dead body. 7Neither for his fa-
ther nor for his mother, nor for brother
or sister, if they die, shall he make him-
self unclean; because his separation to
God is upon his head. 8All the days of
his separation he is holy to the LORD

9 "And if any man dies very sud-
denly beside him, and he defiles his
consecrated head, then he shall shave
his head on the day of his cleansing;
on the seventh day he shall shave it.
10On the eighth day he shall bring two
turtledoves or two young pigeons to
the priest to the door of the tent of
meeting, 11and the priest shall offer
one for a sin offering and the other
for a burnt offering, and make atone-
ment for him, because he sinned
by reason of the dead body. And he
shall consecrate his head that same
day, 12and separate himself to the
LORD for the days of his separation,
and bring a male lamb a year old for
a guilt offering; but the former time
shall be void, because his separation
was defiled.

13 "And this is the law for the
Nazirite, when the time of his sepa-
ration has been completed: he shall
be brought to the door of the tent of
meeting, 14and he shall offer his gift
to the LORD one male lamb a year old
without blemish for a burnt offering,
and one ewe lamb a year old without
blemish as a sin offering, and one ram
without blemish as a peace offering,
15and a basket of unleavened bread,
cakes of fine flour mixed with oil,
and unleavened wafers spread with
oil, and their cereal offering and their
drink offerings. 16And the priest shall
present them before the LORD and
offer his sin offering and his burnt
offering, 17and he shall offer the ram
as a sacrifice of peace offering to the
LORD with the basket of unleavened
bread; the priest shall offer also its
cereal offering and its drink offering.
18And the Nazirite shall shave his con-
secrated head at the door of the tent of
meeting, and shall take the hair from
his consecrated head and put it on the
fire which is under the sacrifice of the
peace offering. 19And the priest shall
take the shoulder of the ram, when
it is boiled, and one unleavened cake
out of the basket, and one unleavened
wafer, and shall put them upon the
hands of the Nazirite, after he has
shaven the hair of his consecration,
20and the priest shall wave them for
a wave offering before the LORD they
are a holy portion for the priest, to-
gether with the breast that is waved
and the thigh that is offered; and after
that the Nazirite may drink wine.

21 "This is the law for the Nazirite
who takes a vow. His offering to the
LORD shall be according to his vow
as a Nazirite, apart from what else
he can afford; in accordance with the
vow which he takes, so shall he do ac-
cording to the law for his separation
as a Nazirite."

[a]That is *one separated* or *one consecrated*
[b]Or *Naziriteship*

THE PRIESTLY BENEDICTION

22 The LORD said to Moses, 23"Say
to Aaron and his sons, Thus you shall
bless the people of Israel: you shall
say to them, 24

The LORD bless you and keep you:
25The LORD make his face to shine
upon you, and be gracious
to you:
26The LORD lift up his counte-
nance upon you, and give
you peace.

27 "So shall they put my name
upon the people of Israel, and I will
bless them."

OFFERINGS OF THE LEADERS

7 On the day when Moses had fin-
ished setting up the tabernacle, and
had anointed and consecrated it with
all its furnishings, and had anointed
and consecrated the altar with all its
utensils, 2the leaders of Israel, heads
of their fathers' houses, the leaders of
the tribes, who were over those who
were numbered, 3offered and brought
their offerings before the LORD six
covered wagons and twelve oxen, a
wagon for every two of the leaders,
and for each one an ox; they offered
them before the tabernacle. 4Then the
LORD said to Moses, 5"Accept these
from them, that they may be used in
doing the service of the tent of meet-
ing, and give them to the Levites, to
each man according to his service."
6So Moses took the wagons and the
oxen, and gave them to the Levites.
7Two wagons and four oxen he gave
to the sons of Gershon, according to
their service; 8and four wagons and
eight oxen he gave to the sons of
Merar'i, according to their service,
under the direction of Ith'amar the
son of Aaron the priest. 9But to the
sons of Kohath he gave none, because
they were charged with the care of
the holy things which had to be car-
ried on the shoulder. 10And the leaders
offered offerings for the dedication of
the altar on the day it was anointed;
and the leaders offered their offering
before the altar. 11And the LORD said
to Moses, "They shall offer their of-
ferings, one leader each day, for the
dedication of the altar."

12 He who offered his offering
the first day was Nahshon the son of
Ammin'adab, of the tribe of Judah;
13and his offering was one silver plate
whose weight was a hundred and thir-
ty shekels, one silver basin of seventy
shekels, according to the shekel of the
sanctuary, both of them full of fine
flour mixed with oil for a cereal offer-
ing; 14one golden dish of ten shekels,
full of incense; 15one young bull, one
ram, one male lamb a year old, for a
burnt offering; 16one male goat for a
sin offering; 17and for the sacrifice of
peace offerings, two oxen, five rams,
five male goats, and five male lambs
a year old. This was the offering of
Nahshon the son of Ammin'adab.

18 On the second day Nethan'el the
son of Zu'ar, the leader of Is'sachar,
made an offering; 19he offered for
his offering one silver plate, whose
weight was a hundred and thirty
shekels, one silver basin of seventy
shekels, according to the shekel of the
sanctuary, both of them full of fine
flour mixed with oil for a cereal offer-
ing; 20one golden dish of ten shekels,
full of incense; 21one young bull, one
ram, one male lamb a year old, for a
burnt offering; 22one male goat for a
sin offering; 23and for the sacrifice of
peace offerings, two oxen, five rams,
five male goats, and five male lambs
a year old. This was the offering of
Nethan'el the son of Zu'ar.

24 On the third day Eli'ab the son
of Helon, the leader of the men of
Zeb'ulun: 25his offering was one silver
plate, whose weight was a hundred
and thirty shekels, one silver basin
of seventy shekels, according to the
shekel of the sanctuary, both of them
full of fine flour mixed with oil for
a cereal offering; 26one golden dish
of ten shekels, full of incense; 27one
young bull, one ram, one male lamb
a year old, for a burnt offering; 28one

male goat for a sin offering; 29 and for
the sacrifice of peace offerings, two
oxen, five rams, five male goats, and
five male lambs a year old. This was
the offering of Eli´ab the son of Helon.

30 On the fourth day Eli´zur the
son of Shed´eur, the leader of the men
of Reuben: 31 his offering was one sil-
ver plate whose weight was a hundred
and thirty shekels, one silver basin
of seventy shekels, according to the
shekel of the sanctuary, both of them
full of fine flour mixed with oil for
a cereal offering; 32 one golden dish
of ten shekels, full of incense; 33 one
young bull, one ram, one male lamb
a year old, for a burnt offering; 34 one
male goat for a sin offering; 35 and for
the sacrifice of peace offerings, two
oxen, five rams, five male goats, and
five male lambs a year old. This was
the offering of Eli´zur the son of
Shed´eur.

36 On the fifth day Shelu´mi-el
the son of Zurishad´dai, the leader of
the men of Simeon: 37 his offering was
one silver plate, whose weight was a
hundred and thirty shekels, one silver
basin of seventy shekels, according to
the shekel of the sanctuary, both of
them full of fine flour mixed with oil
for a cereal offering; 38 one golden dish
of ten shekels, full of incense; 39 one
young bull, one ram, one male lamb
a year old, for a burnt offering; 40 one
male goat for a sin offering; 41 and for
the sacrifice of peace offerings, two
oxen, five rams, five male goats, and
five male lambs a year old. This was
the offering of Shelu´mi-el the son of
Zurishad´dai.

42 On the sixth day Eli´asaph the
son of Deu´el, the leader of the men
of Gad: 43 his offering was one silver
plate, whose weight was a hundred
and thirty shekels, one silver basin
of seventy shekels, according to the
shekel of the sanctuary, both of them
full of fine flour mixed with oil for
a cereal offering; 44 one golden dish
of ten shekels, full of incense; 45 one
young bull, one ram, one male lamb
a year old, for a burnt offering; 46 one
male goat for a sin offering; 47 and for
the sacrifice of peace offerings, two
oxen, five rams, five male goats, and
five male lambs a year old. This was
the offering of Eli´asaph the son of
Deu´el.

48 On the seventh day Elish´ama
the son of Ammi´hud, the leader of
the men of E´phraim: 49 his offering
was one silver plate, whose weight
was a hundred and thirty shekels, one
silver basin of seventy shekels, ac-
cording to the shekel of the sanctuary,
both of them full of fine flour mixed
with oil for a cereal offering; 50 one
golden dish of ten shekels, full of in-
cense; 51 one young bull, one ram, one
male lamb a year old, for a burnt offer-
ing; 52 one male goat for a sin offering;
53 and for the sacrifice of peace offer-
ings, two oxen, five rams, five male
goats, and five male lambs a year old.
This was the offering of Elish´ama the
son of Ammi´hud.

54 On the eighth day Gama´liel the
son of Pedah´zur, the leader of the
men of Manas´seh: 55 his offering was
one silver plate, whose weight was a
hundred and thirty shekels, one silver
basin of seventy shekels, according to
the shekel of the sanctuary, both of
them full of fine flour mixed with oil
for a cereal offering; 56 one golden dish
of ten shekels, full of incense; 57 one
young bull, one ram, one male lamb
a year old, for a burnt offering; 58 one
male goat for a sin offering; 59 and for
the sacrifice of peace offerings, two
oxen, five rams, five male goats, and
five male lambs a year old. This was
the offering of Gama´liel the son of
Pedah´zur.

60 On the ninth day Abi´dan the
son of Gideo´ni, the leader of the
men of Benjamin: 61 his offering was
one silver plate, whose weight was a
hundred and thirty shekels, one silver
basin of seventy shekels, according to
the shekel of the sanctuary, both of
them full of fine flour mixed with oil
for a cereal offering; 62 one golden dish

of ten shekels, full of incense; 63 one
young bull, one ram, one male lamb
a year old, for a burnt offering; 64 one
male goat for a sin offering; 65 and for
the sacrifice of peace offerings, two
oxen, five rams, five male goats, and
five male lambs a year old. This was
the offering of Abi′dan the son of
Gideo′ni.

66 On the tenth day Ahi-e′zer the
son of Ammishad′dai, the leader of
the men of Dan: 67 his offering was
one silver plate, whose weight was a
hundred and thirty shekels, one silver
basin of seventy shekels, according to
the shekel of the sanctuary, both of
them full of fine flour mixed with oil
for a cereal offering; 68 one golden dish
of ten shekels, full of incense; 69 one
young bull, one ram, one male lamb
a year old, for a burnt offering; 70 one
male goat for a sin offering; 71 and for
the sacrifice of peace offerings, two
oxen, five rams, five male goats, and
five male lambs a year old. This was
the offering of Ahi-e′zer the son of
Ammishad′dai.

72 On the eleventh day Pa′giel the
son of Ochran, the leader of the men
of Asher: 73 his offering wa one silver
plate, whose weight was ı hundred
and thirty shekels, one sver basin
of seventy shekels, accorꞑg to the
shekel of the sanctuary, bh of them
full of fine flour mixed vth oil for
a cereal offering; 74 one gden dish
of ten shekels, full of incse; 75 one
young bull, one ram, oneıale lamb
a year old, for a burnt offing; 76 one
male goat for a sin offeg; 77 and
for the sacrifice of peacofferings,
two oxen, five rams, five ıle goats,
and five male lambs a yeold. This
was the offering of Pa′giee son of
Ochran.

78 On the twelfth dayhi′ra the
son of Enan, the leader oe men of
Naph′tali: 79 his offering wne silver
plate, whose weight washundred
and thirty shekels, one er basin
of seventy shekels, accorg to the
shekel of the sanctuary, b of them
full of fine flour mixed with oil for
a cereal offering; 80 one golden dish
of ten shekels, full of incense; 81 one
young bull, one ram, one male lamb
a year old, for a burnt offering; 82 one
male goat for a sin offering; 83 and for
the sacrifice of peace offerings, two
oxen, five rams, five male goats, and
five male lambs a year old. This was
the offering of Ahi′ra the son of Enan.

84 This was the dedication offering
for the altar, on the day when it was
anointed, from the leaders of Israel:
twelve silver plates, twelve silver
basins, twelve golden dishes, 85 each
silver plate weighing a hundred and
thirty shekels and each basin seventy,
all the silver of the vessels two thou-
sand four hundred shekels according
to the shekel of the sanctuary, 86 the
twelve golden dishes, full of incense,
weighing ten shekels apiece according
to the shekel of the sanctuary, all the
gold of the dishes being a hundred and
twenty shekels; 87 all the cattle for the
burnt offering twelve bulls, twelve
rams, twelve male lambs a year old,
with their cereal offering; and twelve
male goats for a sin offering; 88 and all
the cattle for the sacrifice of peace
offerings twenty-four bulls, the rams
sixty, the male goats sixty, the male
lambs a year old sixty. This was the
dedication offering for the altar, after
it was anointed.

89 And when Moses went into the
tent of meeting to speak with the
Lord he heard the voice speaking to
him from above the mercy seat that
was upon the ark of the testimony,
from between the two cherubim; and
it spoke to him.

THE SEVEN LAMPS

8 Now the Lord said to Moses, 2 "Say
to Aaron, When you set up the
lamps, the seven lamps shall give
light in front of the lampstand." 3 And
Aaron did so; he set up its lamps to
give light in front of the lampstand,
as the Lord commanded Moses.
4 And this was the workmanship of

the lampstand, hammered work of
gold; from its base to its flowers, it
was hammered work; according to the
pattern which the LORD had shown
Moses, so he made the lampstand.

CONSECRATION AND SERVICE OF THE LEVITES

5 And the LORD said to Moses,
6"Take the Levites from among the
people of Israel, and cleanse them.
7And thus you shall do to them, to
cleanse them: sprinkle the water of
expiation upon them, and let them go
with a razor over all their body, and
wash their clothes and cleanse them-
selves. 8Then let them take a young
bull and its cereal offering of fine
flour mixed with oil, and you shall
take another young bull for a sin offer-
ing. 9And you shall present the Levites
before the tent of meeting, and assem-
ble the whole congregation of the peo-
ple of Israel. 10When you present the
Levites before the LORD the people of
Israel shall lay their hands upon the
Levites, 11and Aaron shall offer the
Levites before the LORD as a wave of-
fering from the people of Israel, that it
may be theirs to do the service of the
LORD12Then the Levites shall lay their
hands upon the heads of the bulls; and
you shall offer the one for a sin offer-
ing and the other for a burnt offering
to the LORD to make atonement for
the Levites. 13And you shall cause the
Levites to attend Aaron and his sons,
and shall offer them as a wave offer-
ing to the LORD

14 "Thus you shall separate the
Levites from among the people of
Israel, and the Levites shall be mine.
15And after that the Levites shall go
in to do service at the tent of meet-
ing, when you have cleansed them
and offered them as a wave offering.
16For they are wholly given to me from
among the people of Israel; instead of
all that open the womb, the first-born
of all the people of Israel, I have tak-
en them for myself. 17For all the first-
born among the people of Israel are
mine, both of man and of beast; on the
day that I slew all the first-born in the
land of Egypt I consecrated them for
myself, 18and I have taken the Levites
instead of all the first-born among
the people of Israel. 19And I have giv-
en the Levites as a gift to Aaron and
his sons from among the people of
Israel, to do the service for the people
of Israel at the tent of meeting, and
to make atonement for the people of
Israel, that there may be no plague
among the people of Israel in case the
people of Israel should come near the
sanctuary."

20 Thus did Moses and Aaron and
all the congregation of the people of
Israel to the Levites; according to all
that the LORD commanded Moses
concerning the Levites, the people of
Israel did to them. 21And the Levites
purified themselves from sin, and
washed their clothes; and Aaron of-
fered them as a wave offering before
the LORD and Aaron made atonement
for them to cleanse them. 22And after
that the Levites went in to do their
service in the tent of meeting in at-
tendance upon Aaron and his sons;
as the LORD had commanded Moses
concerning the Levites, so they did to
them.

23 And the LORD said to Moses,
24"This is what pertains to the Levites:
from twenty-five years old and up-
ward they shall go in to perform the
work in the service of the tent of
meeting; 25and from the age of fifty
years they shall withdraw from the
work of the service and serve no more,
26but minister to their brethren in the
tent of meeting, to keep the charge,
and they shall do no service. Thus
shall you do to the Levites in assign-
ing their duties."

THE PASSOVER AT SINAI

9 And the LORD spoke to Moses
in the wilderness of Sinai, in the
first month of the second year af-
ter they had come out of the land
of Egypt, saying, 2"Let the people

of Israel keep the passover at its appointed time. 3On the fourteenth day of this month, in the evening, you shall keep it at its appointed time; according to all its statutes and all its ordinances you shall keep it." 4So Moses told the people of Israel that they should keep the passover. 5And they kept the passover in the first month, on the fourteenth day of the month, in the evening, in the wilderness of Sinai; according to all that the LORD commanded Moses, so the people of Israel did. 6And there were certain men who were unclean through touching the dead body of a man, so that they could not keep the passover on that day; and they came before Moses and Aaron on that day; 7and those men said to him, "We are unclean through touching the dead body of a man; why are we kept from offering the LORD's offering at its appointed time among the people of Israel?" 8And Moses said to them, "Wait, that I may hear what the LORD will command concerning you."

9 The LORD said to Moses, 10"Say to the people of Israel, If any man of you or of your descendants is unclean through touching a dead body, or is afar off on a journey, he shall still keep the passover to the LORD. 11In the second month on the fourteenth day in the evening they shall keep it; they shall eat it with unleavened bread and bitter herbs. 12They shall leave none of it until the morning, nor break a bone of it; according to all *the statute for the passover* they shall keep it. 13But the man who is clean and is not on a journey, yet refrains from keeping the passover, that person shall be cut off from his people, because he did not offer the LORD's offering at its appointed time; that man shall bear his sin. 14And if a stranger sojourns among you, and will keep the passover to the LORD according to the statute of the passover and according to its ordinance, so shall he do; you shall have one statute, both for the sojourner and for the native."

THE CLOUD AND THE FIRE

15 On the day that the tabernacle was set up, the cloud covered the tabernacle, the tent of the testimony; and at evening it was over the tabernacle like the appearance of fire until morning. 16So it was continually; the cloud covered it by day[a] and the appearance of fire by night. 17And whenever the cloud was taken up from over the tent, after that the people of Israel set out; and in the place where the cloud settled down, there the people of Israel encamped. 18At the command of the LORD the people of Israel set out, and at the command of the LORD they encamped; as long as the cloud rested over the tabernacle, they remained in camp. 19Even when the cloud continued over the tabernacle many days, the people of Israel kept the charge of the LORD and did not set out. 20Sometimes the cloud was a few days over the tabernacle, and according to the command of the LORD they remained in camp; then according to the command of the LORD they set out. 21And sometimes the cloud remained from evening until morning; and when the cloud was taken up in the morning, they set out, or if it continued for a day and a night, when the cloud was taken up they set out. 22Whether it was two days, or a month, or a longer time, that the cloud continued over the tabernacle, abiding there, the people of Israel remained in camp and did not set out; but when it was taken up they set out. 23At the command of the LORD they encamped, and at the command of the LORD they set out; they kept the charge of the LORD at the command of the LORD by Moses.

THE SILVER TRUMPETS

10 The LORD said to Moses, 2"Make two silver trumpets; of hammered work you shall make them; and you

[a]Gk Syr Vg: Heb lacks *by day*

shall use them for summoning the
congregation, and for breaking camp.
3And when both are blown, all the
congregation shall gather themselves
to you at the entrance of the tent of
meeting. 4But if they blow only one,
then the leaders, the heads of the
tribes of Israel, shall gather them-
selves to you. 5When you blow an
alarm, the camps that are on the east
side shall set out. 6And when you blow
an alarm the second time, the camps
that are on the south side shall set
out. An alarm is to be blown whenever
they are to set out. 7But when the as-
sembly is to be gathered together, you
shall blow, but you shall not sound an
alarm. 8And the sons of Aaron, the
priests, shall blow the trumpets. The
trumpets shall be to you for a perpet-
ual statute throughout your gener-
ations. 9And when you go to war in
your land against the adversary who
oppresses you, then you shall sound
an alarm with the trumpets, that you
may be remembered before the LORD
your God, and you shall be saved from
your enemies. 10On the day of your
gladness also, and at your appointed
feasts, and at the beginnings of your
months, you shall blow the trumpets
over your burnt offerings and over
the sacrifices of your peace offerings;
they shall serve you for remembrance
before your God: I am the LORD your
God."

DEPARTURE FROM SINAI

11 In the second year, in the sec-
ond month, on the twentieth day of
the month, the cloud was taken up
from over the tabernacle of the tes-
timony, 12and the people of Israel set
out by stages from the wilderness of
Sinai; and the cloud settled down in
the wilderness of Paran. 13They set
out for the first time at the command
of the LORD by Moses. 14The standard
of the camp of the men of Judah set
out first by their companies; and over
their host was Nahshon the son of
Ammin'adab. 15And over the host of
the tribe of the men of Is'sachar was
Nethan'el the son of Zu'ar. 16And over
the host of the tribe of the men of
Zeb'ulun was Eli'ab the son of Helon.

17 And when the tabernacle was
taken down, the sons of Gershon and
the sons of Merar'i, who carried the
tabernacle, set out. 18And the stan-
dard of the camp of Reuben set out by
their companies; and over their host
was Eli'zur the son of Shed'eur. 19And
over the host of the tribe of the men
of Simeon was Shelu'mi-el the son
of Zurishad'dai. 20And over the host
of the tribe of the men of Gad was
Eli'asaph the son of Deu'el.

21 Then the Ko'hathites set out,
carrying the holy things, and the tab-
ernacle was set up before their arriv-
al. 22And the standard of the camp
of the men of E'phraim set out by
their companies; and over their host
was Elish'ama the son of Ammi'hud.
23And over the host of the tribe of the
men of Manas'seh was Gama'liel the
son of Pedah'zur. 24And over the host
of the tribe of the men of Benjamin
was Abi'dan the son of Gideo'ni.

25 Then the standard of the camp
of the men of Dan, acting as the rear
guard of all the camps, set out by their
companies; and over their host was
Ahi-e'zer the son of Ammishad'dai.
26And over the host of the tribe of the
men of Asher was Pa'giel the son of
Ochran. 27And over the host of the
tribe of the men of Naph'tali was
Ahi'ra the son of Enan. 28This was the
order of march of the people of Israel
according to their hosts, when they
set out.

29 And Moses said to Hobab the
son of Reu'el the Mid'ianite, Moses'
father-in-law, "We are setting out for
the place of which the LORD said, 'I
will give it to you'; come with us, and
we will do you good; for the LORD
has promised good to Israel." 30But
he said to him, "I will not go; I will
depart to my own land and to my kin-
dred." 31And he said, "Do not leave us,
I pray you, for you know how we are

to encamp in the wilderness, and you
will serve as eyes for us. 32 And if you
go with us, whatever good the LORD
will do to us, the same will we do to
you."

33 So they set out from the mount
of the LORD three days' journey; and
the ark of the covenant of the LORD
went before them three days' journey,
to seek out a resting place for them.
34 And the cloud of the LORD was over
them by day, whenever they set out
from the camp.

35 And whenever the ark set out,
Moses said, "Arise, O LORD and let
thy enemies be scattered; and let them
that hate thee flee before thee." 36 And
when it rested, he said, "Return, O
LORD to the ten thousand thousands
of Israel."

COMPLAINING IN THE DESERT

11 And the people complained in the
hearing of the LORD about their
misfortunes; and when the LORD
heard it, his anger was kindled, and
the fire of the LORD burned among
them, and consumed some outlying
parts of the camp. 2 Then the people
cried to Moses; and Moses prayed
to the LORD and the fire abated. 3 So
the name of that place was called
Tab´erah,[a] because the fire of the
LORD burned among them.

4 Now the rabble that was among
them had a strong craving; and the
people of Israel also wept again, and
said, "O that we had meat to eat! 5 We
remember the fish we ate in Egypt for
nothing, the cucumbers, the melons,
the leeks, the onions, and the garlic;
6 but now our strength is dried up, and
there is nothing at all but this manna
to look at."

7 Now the manna was like corian-
der seed, and its appearance like that
of bdellium. 8 The people went about
and gathered it, and ground it in mills
or beat it in mortars, and boiled it in
pots, and made cakes of it; and the
taste of it was like the taste of cakes
baked with oil. 9 When the dew fell
upon the camp in the night, the man-
na fell with it.

10 Moses heard the people weeping
throughout their families, every man
at the door of his tent; and the anger
of the LORD blazed hotly, and Moses
was displeased. 11 Moses said to the
LORD, "Why hast thou dealt ill with
thy servant? And why have I not found
favor in thy sight, that thou dost lay
the burden of all this people upon me?
12 Did I conceive all this people? Did I
bring them forth, that thou shouldst
say to me, 'Carry them in your bosom,
as a nurse carries the sucking child,'
to the land which thou didst swear
to give their fathers? 13 Where am I to
get meat to give to all this people? For
they weep before me and say, 'Give us
meat, that we may eat.' 14 I am not able
to carry all this people alone, the bur-
den is too heavy for me. 15 If thou wilt
deal thus with me, kill me at once, if I
find favor in thy sight, that I may not
see my wretchedness."

THE SEVENTY ELDERS

16 And the LORD said to Moses,
"Gather for me seventy men of the
elders of Israel, whom you know to
be the elders of the people and of-
ficers over them; and bring them
to the tent of meeting, and let them
take their stand there with you. 17 And
I will come down and talk with you
there; and I will take some of the spir-
it which is upon you and put it upon
them; and they shall bear the burden
of the people with you, that you may
not bear it yourself alone. 18 And say
to the people, 'Consecrate yourselves
for tomorrow, and you shall eat meat;
for you have wept in the hearing of
the LORD saying, "Who will give us
meat to eat? For it was well with us in
Egypt." Therefore the LORD will give
you meat, and you shall eat. 19 You shall
not eat one day, or two days, or five
days, or ten days, or twenty days, 20 but
a whole month, until it comes out at

[a] That is *Burning*

your nostrils and becomes loathsome to you, because you have rejected the LORD who is among you, and have wept before him, saying, "Why did we come forth out of Egypt?"'" 21But Moses said, "The people among whom I am number six hundred thousand on foot; and thou hast said, 'I will give them meat, that they may eat a whole month!' 22Shall flocks and herds be slaughtered for them, to suffice them? Or shall all the fish of the sea be gathered together for them, to suffice them?" 23And the LORD said to Moses, "Is the LORD's hand shortened? Now you shall see whether my word will come true for you or not."

24 So Moses went out and told the people the words of the LORD and he gathered seventy men of the elders of the people, and placed them round about the tent. 25Then the LORD came down in the cloud and spoke to him, and took some of the spirit that was upon him and put it upon the seventy elders; and when the spirit rested upon them, they prophesied. But they did so no more.

26 Now two men remained in the camp, one named Eldad, and the other named Medad, and the spirit rested upon them; they were among those registered, but they had not gone out to the tent, and so they prophesied in the camp. 27And a young man ran and told Moses, "Eldad and Medad are prophesying in the camp." 28And Joshua the son of Nun, the minister of Moses, one of his chosen men, said, "My lord Moses, forbid them." 29But Moses said to him, "Are you jealous for my sake? Would that all the LORD's people were prophets, that the LORD would put his spirit upon them!" 30And Moses and the elders of Israel returned to the camp.*

THE QUAILS

31 And there went forth a wind from the LORD and it brought quails from the sea, and let them fall beside the camp, about a day's journey on this side and a day's journey on the other side, round about the camp, and about two cubits above the face of the earth. 32And the people rose all that day, and all night, and all the next day, and gathered the quails; he who gathered least gathered ten homers; and they spread them out for themselves all around the camp. 33While the meat was yet between their teeth, before it was consumed, the anger of the LORD was kindled against the people, and the LORD smote the people with a very great plague. 34Therefore the name of that place was called Kib'roth-hatta'avah,[a] because there they buried the people who had the craving. 35From Kib'roth-hatta'avah the people journeyed to Haze'roth; and they remained at Haze'roth.

AARON AND MIRIAM JEALOUS OF MOSES

12 Miriam and Aaron spoke against Moses because of the Cushite woman whom he had married, for he had married a Cushite woman; 2and they said, "Has the LORD indeed spoken only through Moses? Has he not spoken through us also?" And the LORD heard it. 3Now the man Moses was very meek, more than all men that were on the face of the earth. 4And suddenly the LORD said to Moses and to Aaron and Miriam, "Come out, you three, to the tent of meeting." And the three of them came out. 5And the LORD came down in a pillar of cloud, and stood at the door of the tent, and called Aaron and Miriam; and they both came forward. 6And he said, "Hear my words: If there is a prophet among you, I the LORD make myself known to him in a vision, I speak with him in a dream. 7Not so with my servant Moses; he is entrusted with all my house. 8With him I speak mouth to mouth, clearly, and not in dark speech; and he beholds the form of the LORD. Why then were you not afraid to speak against

[a]That is *Graves of craving*

my servant Moses?"
9 And the anger of the LORD was
kindled against them, and he depart-
ed; 10and when the cloud removed
from over the tent, behold, Miriam
was leprous, as white as snow. And
Aaron turned towards Miriam, and
behold, she was leprous. 11And Aaron
said to Moses, "Oh, my lord, do not[b]
punish us because we have done fool-
ishly and have sinned. 12Let her not be
as one dead, of whom the flesh is half
consumed when he comes out of his
mother's womb." 13And Moses cried to
the LORD"Heal her, O God, I beseech
thee." 14But the LORD said to Moses,
"If her father had but spit in her face,
should she not be shamed seven days?
Let her be shut up outside the camp
seven days, and after that she may be
brought in again." 15So Miriam was
shut up outside the camp seven days;
and the people did not set out on the
march till Miriam was brought in
again. 16After that the people set out
from Haze´roth, and encamped in the
wilderness of Paran.

SPIES SENT INTO CANAAN

13 The LORD said to Moses, 2"Send
men to spy out the land of Canaan,
which I give to the people of Israel;
from each tribe of their fathers shall
you send a man, every one a leader
among them." 3So Moses sent them
from the wilderness of Paran, accord-
ing to the command of the LORD all
of them men who were heads of the
people of Israel. 4And these were their
names: From the tribe of Reuben,
Sham´mu-a the son of Zaccur; 5from
the tribe of Simeon, Shaphat the son
of Hori; 6from the tribe of Judah,
Caleb the son of Jephun´neh; 7from
the tribe of Is´sachar, Igal the son of
Joseph; 8from the tribe of E´phraim,
Hoshe´a the son of Nun; 9from the
tribe of Benjamin, Palti the son of
Raphu; 10from the tribe of Zeb´ulun,
Gad´diel the son of Sodi; 11from the
tribe of Joseph (that is from the tribe
of Manas´seh), Gaddi the son of Susi;
12from the tribe of Dan, Am´miel the
son of Gemal´li; 13from the tribe of
Asher, Sethur the son of Michael;
14from the tribe of Naph´tali, Nahbi
the son of Vophsi; 15from the tribe of
Gad, Geu´el the son of Machi. 16These
were the names of the men whom
Moses sent to spy out the land. And
Moses called Hoshe´a the son of Nun
Joshua.
17 Moses sent them to spy out the
land of Canaan, and said to them, "Go
up into the Negeb yonder, and go up
into the hill country, 18and see what
the land is, and whether the people
who dwell in it are strong or weak,
whether they are few or many, 19and
whether the land that they dwell in
is good or bad, and whether the cit-
ies that they dwell in are camps or
strongholds, 20and whether the land
is rich or poor, and whether there is
wood in it or not. Be of good cour-
age, and bring some of the fruit of the
land." Now the time was the season of
the first ripe grapes.
21 So they went up and spied out
the land from the wilderness of Zin to
Rehob, near the entrance of Hamath.
22They went up into the Negeb,
and came to Hebron; and Ahi´man,
Sheshai, and Talmai, the descen-
dants of Anak, were there. (Hebron
was built seven years before Zo´an in
Egypt.) 23And they came to the Valley
of Eshcol, and cut down from there a
branch with a single cluster of grapes,
and they carried it on a pole between
two of them; they brought also some
pomegranates and figs. 24That place
was called the Valley of Eshcol,[c] be-
cause of the cluster which the men of
Israel cut down from there.

THE REPORT OF THE SPIES

25 At the end of forty days they re-
turned from spying out the land. 26And
they came to Moses and Aaron and to

[b]Heb *lay not sin upon us*
[c]That is *Cluster*

all the congregation of the people of
Israel in the wilderness of Paran, at
Kadesh; they brought back word to
them and to all the congregation, and
showed them the fruit of the land.
27And they told him, "We came to the
land to which you sent us; it flows
with milk and honey, and this is its
fruit. 28Yet the people who dwell in the
land are strong, and the cities are for-
tified and very large; and besides, we
saw the descendants of Anak there.
29The Amal´ekites dwell in the land of
the Negeb; the Hittites, the Jeb´usites,
and the Amorites dwell in the hill
country; and the Canaanites dwell by
the sea, and along the Jordan."

30 But Caleb quieted the people
before Moses, and said, "Let us go up
at once, and occupy it; for we are well
able to overcome it." 31Then the men
who had gone up with him said, "We
are not able to go up against the peo-
ple; for they are stronger than we." 32So
they brought to the people of Israel an
evil report of the land which they had
spied out, saying, "The land, through
which we have gone to spy it out, is a
land that devours its inhabitants; and
all the people that we saw in it are
men of great stature. 33And there we
saw the Nephilim (the sons of Anak,
who come from the Nephilim); and
we seemed to ourselves like grasshop-
pers, and so we seemed to them."

THE PEOPLE REBEL

14 Then all the congregation raised a
loud cry; and the people wept that
night. 2And all the people of Israel
murmured against Moses and Aaron;
the whole congregation said to them,
"Would that we had died in the land
of Egypt! Or would that we had died
in this wilderness! 3Why does the
LORD bring us into this land, to fall
by the sword? Our wives and our little
ones will become a prey; would it not
be better for us to go back to Egypt?"

4 And they said to one another,
"Let us choose a captain, and go back
to Egypt." 5Then Moses and Aaron fell
on their faces before all the assembly
of the congregation of the people of
Israel. 6And Joshua the son of Nun
and Caleb the son of Jephun´neh, who
were among those who had spied out
the land, rent their clothes, 7and said
to all the congregation of the people
of Israel, "The land, which we passed
through to spy it out, is an exceeding-
ly good land. 8If the LORD delights in
us, he will bring us into this land and
give it to us, a land which flows with
milk and honey. 9Only, do not rebel
against the LORD and do not fear the
people of the land, for they are bread
for us; their protection is removed
from them, and the LORD is with us;
do not fear them." 10But all the congre-
gation said to stone them with stones.

Then the glory of the LORD ap-
peared at the tent of meeting to all the
people of Israel. 11And the LORD said
to Moses, "How long will this people
despise me? And how long will they
not believe in me, in spite of all the
signs which I have wrought among
them? 12I will strike them with the
pestilence and disinherit them, and I
will make of you a nation greater and
mightier than they."

MOSES INTERCEDES FOR THE PEOPLE

13 But Moses said to the LORD
"Then the Egyptians will hear of it,
for thou didst bring up this people
in thy might from among them, 14and
they will tell the inhabitants of this
land. They have heard that thou, O
LORD art in the midst of this people;
for thou, O LORD art seen face to face,
and thy cloud stands over them and
thou goest before them, in a pillar
of cloud by day and in a pillar of fire
by night. 15Now if thou dost kill this
people as one man, then the nations
who have heard thy fame will say,
16'Because the LORD was not able to
bring this people into the land which
he swore to give to them, therefore
he has slain them in the wilderness.'
17And now, I pray thee, let the pow-
er of the LORD be great as thou has

promised, saying, 18'The LORD is slow
to anger, and abounding in steadfast
love, forgiving iniquity and transgres-
sion, but he will by no means clear the
guilty, visiting the iniquity of fathers
upon children, upon the third and
upon the fourth generation.' 19Pardon
the iniquity of this people, I pray
thee, according to the greatness of thy
steadfast love, and according as thou
hast forgiven this people, from Egypt
even until now."

20 Then the LORD said, "I have
pardoned, according to your word;
21but truly, as I live, and as all the
earth shall be filled with the glory of
the LORD, 22none of the men who have
seen my glory and my signs which I
wrought in Egypt and in the wilder-
ness, and yet have put me to the proof
these ten times and have not hear-
kened to my voice, 23shall see the land
which I swore to give to their fathers;
and none of those who despised me
shall see it. 24But my servant Caleb,
because he has a different spirit and
has followed me fully, I will bring
into the land into which he went,
and his descendants shall possess it.
25Now, since the Amal´ekites and the
Canaanites dwell in the valleys, turn
tomorrow and set out for the wilder-
ness by the way to the Red Sea."

AN ATTEMPTED INVASION IS REPULSED

26 And the LORD said to Moses
and to Aaron, 27"How long shall this
wicked congregation murmur against
me? I have heard the murmurings
of the people of Israel, which they
murmur against me. 28Say to them,
'As I live, says the LORD what you
have said in my hearing I will do to
you: 29your dead bodies shall fall in
this wilderness; and of all your num-
ber, numbered from twenty years old
and upward, who have murmured
against me, 30not one shall come into
the land where I swore that I would
make you dwell, except Caleb the son
of Jephun´neh and Joshua the son of
Nun. 31But your little ones, who you
said would become a prey, I will bring
in, and they shall know the land
which you have despised. 32But as for
you, your dead bodies shall fall in
this wilderness. 33And your children
shall be shepherds in the wilderness
forty years, and shall suffer for your
faithlessness, until the last of your
dead bodies lies in the wilderness.
34According to the number of the days
in which you spied out the land, forty
days, for every day a year, you shall
bear your iniquity, forty years, and
you shall know my displeasure.' 35I,
the LORD have spoken; surely this will
I do to all this wicked congregation
that are gathered together against me:
in this wilderness they shall come to
a full end, and there they shall die."

36 And the men whom Moses sent
to spy out the land, and who returned
and made all the congregation to mur-
mur against him by bringing up an
evil report against the land, 37the men
who brought up an evil report of the
land, died by plague before the LORD.
38But Joshua the son of Nun and Caleb
the son of Jephun´neh remained alive,
of those men who went to spy out the
land.

39 And Moses told these words to
all the people of Israel, and the peo-
ple mourned greatly. 40And they rose
early in the morning, and went up to
the heights of the hill country, saying,
"See, we are here, we will go up to
the place which the LORD has prom-
ised; for we have sinned." 41But Moses
said, "Why now are you transgressing
the command of the LORD for that
will not succeed? 42Do not go up lest
you be struck down before your ene-
mies, for the LORD is not among you.
43For there the Amal´ekites and the
Canaanites are before you, and you
shall fall by the sword; because you
have turned back from following the
LORD the LORD will not be with you."
44But they presumed to go up to the
heights of the hill country, although
neither the ark of the covenant of
the LORD nor Moses, departed out

of the camp. 45 Then the Amal'ekites
and the Canaanites who dwelt in that
hill country came down, and defeat-
ed them and pursued them, even to
Hormah.

VARIOUS OFFERINGS

15 The LORD said to Moses, 2 "Say
to the people of Israel, When you
come into the land you are to inhabit,
which I give you, 3 and you offer to the
LORD from the herd or from the flock
an offering by fire or a burnt offering
or a sacrifice, to fulfil a vow or as a
freewill offering or at your appointed
feasts, to make a pleasing odor to the
LORD, 4 then he who brings his offer-
ing shall offer to the LORD a cereal
offering of a tenth of an ephah of fine
flour, mixed with a fourth of a hin of
oil; 5 and wine for the drink offering,
a fourth of a hin, you shall prepare
with the burnt offering, or for the
sacrifice, for each lamb. 6 Or for a ram,
you shall prepare for a cereal offering
two tenths of an ephah of fine flour
mixed with a third of a hin of oil; 7 and
for the drink offering you shall offer a
third of a hin of wine, a pleasing odor
to the LORD. 8 And when you prepare
a bull for a burnt offering, or for a
sacrifice, to fulfil a vow, or for peace
offerings to the LORD, 9 then one shall
offer with the bull a cereal offering of
three tenths of an ephah of fine flour,
mixed with half a hin of oil, 10 and you
shall offer for the drink offering half
a hin of wine, as an offering by fire, a
pleasing odor to the LORD

11 "Thus it shall be done for each
bull or ram, or for each of the male
lambs or the kids. 12 According to the
number that you prepare, so shall you
do with every one according to their
number. 13 All who are native shall do
these things in this way, in offering an
offering by fire, a pleasing odor to the
LORD. 14 And if a stranger is sojourn-
ing with you, or any one is among you
throughout your generations, and he
wishes to offer an offering by fire, a
pleasing odor to the LORD he shall do
as you do. 15 For the assembly, there
shall be one statute for you and for
the stranger who sojourns with you,
a perpetual statute throughout your
generations; as you are, so shall the
sojourner be before the LORD. 16 One
law and one ordinance shall be for
you and for the stranger who sojourns
with you."

17 The LORD said to Moses, 18 "Say
to the people of Israel, When you
come into the land to which I bring
you 19 and when you eat of the food of
the land, you shall present an offer-
ing to the LORD. 20 Of the first of your
coarse meal you shall present a cake
as an offering; as an offering from the
threshing floor, so shall you present
it. 21 Of the first of your coarse meal
you shall give to the LORD an offering
throughout your generations.

22 "But if you err, and do not ob-
serve all these commandments which
the LORD has spoken to Moses, 23 all
that the LORD has commanded you
by Moses, from the day that the LORD
gave commandment, and onward
throughout your generations, 24 then
if it was done unwittingly without the
knowledge of the congregation, all the
congregation shall offer one young
bull for a burnt offering, a pleasing
odor to the LORD with its cereal of-
fering and its drink offering, accord-
ing to the ordinance, and one male
goat for a sin offering. 25 And the priest
shall make atonement for all the con-
gregation of the people of Israel, and
they shall be forgiven; because it was
an error, and they have brought their
offering, an offering by fire to the
LORD and their sin offering before
the LORD for their error. 26 And all the
congregation of the people of Israel
shall be forgiven, and the stranger
who sojourns among them, because
the whole population was involved in
the error.

27 "If one person sins unwitting-
ly, he shall offer a female goat a year
old for a sin offering. 28 And the priest
shall make atonement before the

Lord for the person who commits an
error, when he sins unwittingly, to
make atonement for him; and he shall
be forgiven. 29You shall have one law
for him who does anything unwitting-
ly, for him who is native among the
people of Israel, and for the stranger
who sojourns among them. 30But the
person who does anything with a
high hand, whether he is native or a
sojourner, reviles the Lord and that
person shall be cut off from among
his people. 31Because he has despised
the word of the Lord and has broken
his commandment, that person shall
be utterly cut off; his iniquity shall be
upon him."

PENALTY FOR VIOLATING THE SABBATH

32 While the people of Israel were
in the wilderness, they found a man
gathering sticks on the sabbath day.
33And those who found him gather-
ing sticks brought him to Moses and
Aaron, and to all the congregation.
34They put him in custody, because it
had not been made plain what should
be done to him. 35And the Lord said
to Moses, "The man shall be put to
death; all the congregation shall stone
him with stones outside the camp."
36And all the congregation brought
him outside the camp, and stoned
him to death with stones, as the Lord
commanded Moses.

FRINGES ON GARMENTS

37 The Lord said to Moses,
38"Speak to the people of Israel, and
bid them to make tassels on the cor-
ners of their garments throughout
their generations, and to put upon the
tassel of each corner a cord of blue;
39and it shall be to you a tassel to look
upon and remember all the command-
ments of the Lord to do them, not to
follow after your own heart and your
own eyes, which you are inclined to go
after wantonly. 40So you shall remem-
ber and do all my commandments,
and be holy to your God. 41I am the
Lord your God, who brought you out
of the land of Egypt, to be your God: I
am the Lord your God."

REVOLT OF KORAH, DATHAN, AND ABIRAM

16 Now Korah the son of Izhar, son of
Kohath, son of Levi, and Dathan
and Abi´ram the sons of Eli´ab, and
On the son of Peleth, sons of Reuben,
2took men; and they rose up before
Moses, with a number of the people
of Israel, two hundred and fifty lead-
ers of the congregation, chosen from
the assembly, well-known men; 3and
they assembled themselves togeth-
er against Moses and against Aaron,
and said to them, "You have gone too
far! For all the congregation are holy,
every one of them, and the Lord is
among them; why then do you exalt
yourselves above the assembly of the
Lord?" 4When Moses heard it, he fell
on his face; 5and he said to Korah and
all his company, "In the morning the
Lord will show who is his, and who is
holy, and will cause him to come near
to him; him whom he will choose he
will cause to come near to him. 6Do
this: take censers, Korah and all his
company; 7put fire in them and put in-
cense upon them before the Lord to-
morrow, and the man whom the Lord
chooses shall be the holy one. You
have gone too far, sons of Levi!" 8And
Moses said to Korah, "Hear now, you
sons of Levi: 9is it too small a thing
for you that the God of Israel has sep-
arated you from the congregation of
Israel, to bring you near to himself,
to do service in the tabernacle of the
Lord and to stand before the congre-
gation to minister to them; 10and that
he has brought you near him, and all
your brethren the sons of Levi with
you? And would you seek the priest-
hood also? 11Therefore it is against the
Lord that you and all your company
have gathered together; what is Aaron
that you murmur against him?"

12 And Moses sent to call Dathan
and Abi´ram the sons of Eli´ab; and
they said, "We will not come up. 13Is it
a small thing that you have brought us

up out of a land flowing with milk and
honey, to kill us in the wilderness,
that you must also make yourself a
prince over us? 14Moreover you have
not brought us into a land flowing
with milk and honey, nor given us in-
heritance of fields and vineyards. Will
you put out the eyes of these men? We
will not come up."

15 And Moses was very angry, and
said to the LORD"Do not respect their
offering. I have not taken one ass from
them, and I have not harmed one of
them." 16And Moses said to Korah,
"Be present, you and all your com-
pany, before the LORD you and they,
and Aaron, tomorrow; 17and let every
one of you take his censer, and put
incense upon it, and every one of you
bring before the LORD his censer, two
hundred and fifty censers; you also,
and Aaron, each his censer." 18So ev-
ery man took his censer, and they put
fire in them and laid incense upon
them, and they stood at the entrance
of the tent of meeting with Moses and
Aaron. 19Then Korah assembled all
the congregation against them at the
entrance of the tent of meeting. And
the glory of the LORD appeared to all
the congregation.

20 And the LORD said to Moses
and to Aaron, 21"Separate yourselves
from among this congregation, that
I may consume them in a moment."
22And they fell on their faces, and said,
"O God, the God of the spirits of all
flesh, shall one man sin, and wilt thou
be angry with all the congregation?"
23And the LORD said to Moses, 24"Say
to the congregation, Get away from
about the dwelling of Korah, Dathan,
and Abi´ram."

25 Then Moses rose and went to
Dathan and Abi´ram; and the elders
of Israel followed him. 26And he said
to the congregation, "Depart, I pray
you, from the tents of these wicked
men, and touch nothing of theirs,
lest you be swept away with all their
sins." 27So they got away from about
the dwelling of Korah, Dathan, and
Abi´ram; and Dathan and Abi´ram
came out and stood at the door of
their tents, together with their wives,
their sons, and their little ones. 28And
Moses said, "Hereby you shall know
that the LORD has sent me to do all
these works, and that it has not been
of my own accord. 29If these men die
the common death of all men, or if
they are visited by the fate of all men,
then the LORD has not sent me. 30But
if the LORD creates something new,
and the ground opens its mouth, and
swallows them up, with all that be-
longs to them, and they go down alive
into Sheol, then you shall know that
these men have despised the LORD."

31 And as he finished speaking all
these words, the ground under them
split asunder; 32and the earth opened
its mouth and swallowed them up,
with their households and all the men
that belonged to Korah and all their
goods. 33So they and all that belonged
to them went down alive into Sheol;
and the earth closed over them, and
they perished from the midst of the
assembly. 34And all Israel that were
round about them fled at their cry; for
they said, "Lest the earth swallow us
up!" 35And fire came forth from the
LORD and consumed the two hundred
and fifty men offering the incense.

36[a] Then the LORD said to Moses,
37"Tell Elea´zar the son of Aaron the
priest to take up the censers out of
the blaze; then scatter the fire far and
wide. For they are holy, 38the censers
of these men who have sinned at the
cost of their lives; so let them be made
into hammered plates as a covering
for the altar, for they offered them be-
fore the LORD therefore they are holy.
Thus they shall be a sign to the peo-
ple of Israel." 39So Elea´zar the priest
took the bronze censers, which those
who were burned had offered; and
they were hammered out as a covering
for the altar, 40to be a reminder to the
people of Israel, so that no one who

[a]Ch 17.1 in Heb

is not a priest, who is not of the de-
cendants of Aaron, should draw near
to burn incense before the LORD lest
he become as Korah and as his com-
pany—as the LORD said to Elea´zar
through Moses.

41 But on the morrow all the con-
gregation of the people of Israel mur-
mured against Moses and against
Aaron, saying, "You have killed the
people of the LORD" 42And when the
congregation had assembled against
Moses and against Aaron, they turned
toward the tent of meeting; and be-
hold, the cloud covered it, and the glo-
ry of the LORD appeared. 43And Moses
and Aaron came to the front of the
tent of meeting, 44and the LORD said
to Moses, 45"Get away from the midst
of this congregation, that I may con-
sume them in a moment." And they
fell on their faces. 46And Moses said
to Aaron, "Take your censer, and put
fire therein from off the altar, and lay
incense on it, and carry it quickly to
the congregation, and make atone-
ment for them; for wrath has gone
forth from the LORD the plague has
begun." 47So Aaron took it as Moses
said, and ran into the midst of the as-
sembly; and behold, the plague had al-
ready begun among the people; and he
put on the incense, and made atone-
ment for the people. 48And he stood
between the dead and the living; and
the plague was stopped. 49Now those
who died by the plague were four-
teen thousand seven hundred, besides
those who died in the affair of Korah
50And Aaron returned to Moses at th
entrance of the tent of meeting, whe
the plague was stopped.

THE BUDDING OF AARON'S ROD

17[b] The LORD said to Moses, 2"Spk
to the people of Israel, and et
from them rods, one for each fathrs'
house, from all their leaders accorng
to their fathers' houses, twelve ds.
Write each man's name upon hisod,
3and write Aaron's name upon throd
of Levi. For there shall be one rod for
the head of each fathers' house. 4Then
you shall deposit them in the tent of
meeting before the testimony, where
I meet with you. 5And the rod of the
man whom I choose shall sprout;
thus I will make to cease from me the
murmurings of the people of Israel,
which they murmur against you."
6Moses spoke to the people of Israel;
and all their leaders gave him rods,
one for each leader, according to their
fathers' houses, twelve rods; and the
rod of Aaron was among their rods.
7And Moses deposited the rods before
the LORD in the tent of the testimony.

8 And on the morrow Moses went
into the tent of the testimony; and be-
hold, the rod of Aaron for the house
of Levi had sprouted and put forth
buds, and produced blossoms, and
it bore ripe almonds. 9Then Moses
brought out all the rods from before
the LORD to all the people of Israel;
and they looked, and each man took
his rod. 10And the LORD said to Moses,
"Put back the rod of Aaron before the
testimony, to be kept as a sign for the
rebels, that you may make an end of
their murmurings against me, lest
they die." 11Thus did Moses; as the
LORD commanded him, so he did.

12 And the people of Israel said to
Moses, "Behold, we perish, we are un-
done, we are all undone. 13Every one
who comes near, who comes near to
the tabernacle of the LORD shall die.
Are we all to perish?"

RESPONSIBILITY OF PRIESTS AND LEVITES

18 So the LORD said to Aaron, "You
and your sons and your fathers'
house with you shall bear iniquity
in connection with the sanctuary;
and you and your sons with you shall
bear iniquity in connection with your
priesthood. 2And with you bring your
brethren also, the tribe of Levi, the
tribe of your father, that they may join
you, and minister to you while you
and your sons with you are before the

[b]Ch 17.16 in Heb

tent of the testimony. 3They shall at-
tend you and attend to all duties of the
tent; but shall not come near to the
vessels of the sanctuary or to the al-
tar, lest they, and you, die. 4They shall
join you, and attend to the tent of
meeting, for all the service of the tent;
and no one else shall come near you.
5And you shall attend to the duties of
the sanctuary and the duties of the al-
tar, that there be wrath no more upon
the people of Israel. 6And behold, I
have taken your brethren the Levites
from among the people of Israel; they
are a gift to you, given to the LORD to
do the service of the tent of meeting.
7And you and your sons with you shall
attend to your priesthood for all that
concerns the altar and that is within
the veil; and you shall serve. I give
your priesthood as a gift,[a] and any
one else who comes near shall be put
to death."

THE PRIESTS' PORTION

8 Then the LORD said to Aaron,
"And behold, I have given you what-
ever is kept of the offerings made to
me, all the consecrated things of the
people of Israel; I have given them to
you as a portion, and to your sons as
a perpetual due. 9This shall be yours
of the most holy things, reserved from
the fire; every offering of theirs, every
cereal offering of theirs and every sin
offering of theirs and every guilt of-
fering of theirs, which they render to
me, shall be most holy to you and to
your sons. 10In a most holy place shall
you eat of it; every male may eat of it;
it is holy to you. 11This also is yours,
the offering of their gift, all the wave
offerings of the people of Israel; I have
given them to you, and to your sons
and daughters with you, as a perpetu-
al due; every one who is clean in your
house may eat of it. 12All the best of the
oil, and all the best of the wine and of
the grain, the first fruits of what they
give to the LORD, I give to you. 13The
first ripe fruits of all that is in their
land, which they bring to the LORD,
shall be yours; every one who is clean
in your house may eat of it. 14Every
devoted thing in Israel shall be yours.
15Everything that opens the womb of
all flesh, whether man or beast, which
they offer to the LORD, shall be yours;
nevertheless the first-born of man you
shall redeem, and the firstling of un-
clean beasts you shall redeem. 16And
their redemption price (at a month
old you shall redeem them) you shall
fix at five shekels in silver, according
to the shekel of the sanctuary, which
is twenty gerahs. 17But the firstling
of a cow, or the firstling of a sheep,
or the firstling of a goat, you shall
not redeem; they are holy. You shall
sprinkle their blood upon the altar,
and shall burn their fat as an offering
by fire, a pleasing odor to the LORD;
18but their flesh shall be yours, as the
breast that is waved and as the right
thigh are yours. 19All the holy offer-
ings which the people of Israel pres-
ent to the LORD I give to you, and to
your sons and daughters with you, as
a perpetual due; it is a covenant of salt
for ever before the LORD for you and
for your offspring with you." 20And
the LORD said to Aaron, "You shall
have no inheritance in their land, nei-
ther shall you have any portion among
them; I am your portion and your in-
heritance among the people of Israel.

21 "To the Levites I have given ev-
ery tithe in Israel for an inheritance,
n return for their service which they
erve, their service in the tent of
meeting. 22And henceforth the people
of Israel shall not come near the tent
o meeting, lest they bear sin and die.
23ut the Levites shall do the service
of he tent of meeting, and they shall
ber their iniquity; it shall be a per-
pe al statute throughout your gener-
atis; and among the people of Israel
the shall have no inheritance. 24For
the the of the people of Israel, which
they present as an offering to the
LOR I have given to the Levites for

[a]Heb *service of gift*

an inheritance; therefore I have said of them that they shall have no inheritance among the people of Israel."

25 And the LORD said to Moses, 26"Moreover you shall say to the Levites, 'When you take from the people of Israel the tithe which I have given you from them for your inheritance, then you shall present an offering from it to the LORD, a tithe of the tithe. 27And your offering shall be reckoned to you as though it were the grain of the threshing floor, and as the fulness of the wine press. 28So shall you also present an offering to the LORD from all your tithes, which you receive from the people of Israel; and from it you shall give the LORD's offering to Aaron the priest. 29Out of all the gifts to you, you shall present every offering due to the LORD, from all the best of them, giving the hallowed part from them.' 30Therefore you shall say to them, 'When you have offered from it the best of it, then the rest shall be reckoned to the Levites as produce of the threshing floor, and as produce of the wine press; 31and you may eat it in any place, you and your households; for it is your reward in return for your service in the tent of meeting. 32And you shall bear no sin by reason of it, when you have offered the best of it. And you shall not profane the holy things of the people of Israel, lest you die.'"

CEREMONY OF THE RED HEIFER

19 Now the LORD said to Moses and to Aaron, 2"This is the statute of the *law which the LORD has* commanded: Tell the people of Israel to bring you a red heifer without defect, in which there is no blemish, and upon which a yoke has never come. 3And you shall give her to Elea´zar the priest, and she shall be taken outside the camp and slaughtered before him; 4and Elea´zar the priest shall take some of her blood with his finger, and sprinkle some of her blood toward the front of the tent of meeting seven times. 5And the heifer shall be burned in his sight; her skin, her flesh, and her blood, with all her dung, shall be burned; 6and the priest shall take cedarwood and hyssop and scarlet stuff, and cast them into the midst of the burning of the heifer. 7Then the priest shall wash his clothes and bathe his body in water, and afterwards he shall come into the camp; and the priest shall be unclean until evening. 8He who burns the heifer shall wash his clothes in water and bathe his body in water, and shall be unclean until evening. 9And a man who is clean shall gather up the ashes of the heifer, and deposit them outside the camp in a clean place; and they shall be kept for the congregation of the people of Israel for the water for impurity, for the removal of sin. 10And he who gathers the ashes of the heifer shall wash his clothes, and be unclean until evening. And this shall be to the people of Israel, and to the stranger who sojourns among them, a perpetual statute.

11 "He who touches the dead body of any person shall be unclean seven days; 12he shall cleanse himself with the water on the third day and on the seventh day, and so be clean; but if he does not cleanse himself on the third day and on the seventh day, he will not become clean. 13Whoever touches a dead person, the body of any man who has died, and does not cleanse himself, defiles the tabernacle of the LORD, and that person shall be cut off from Israel; because the water for impurity was not thrown upon him, he shall be unclean; his uncleanness is still on him.

14 "This is the law when a man dies in a tent: every one who comes into the tent, and every one who is in the tent, shall be unclean seven days. 15And every open vessel, which has no cover fastened upon it, is unclean. 16Whoever in the open field touches one who is slain with a sword, or a dead body, or a bone of a man, or a grave, shall be unclean seven days.

17 For the unclean they shall take some
ashes of the burnt sin offering, and
running water shall be added in a ves-
sel; 18 then a clean person shall take
hyssop, and dip it in the water, and
sprinkle it upon the tent, and upon all
the furnishings, and upon the persons
who were there, and upon him who
touched the bone, or the slain, or the
dead, or the grave; 19 and the clean per-
son shall sprinkle upon the unclean
on the third day and on the seventh
day; thus on the seventh day he shall
cleanse him, and he shall wash his
clothes and bathe himself in water,
and at evening he shall be clean.

20 "But the man who is unclean
and does not cleanse himself, that
person shall be cut off from the midst
of the assembly, since he has defiled
the sanctuary of the LORD; because
the water for impurity has not been
thrown upon him, he is unclean. 21 And
it shall be a perpetual statute for them.
He who sprinkles the water for impu-
rity shall wash his clothes; and he who
touches the water for impurity shall be
unclean until evening. 22 And whatever
the unclean person touches shall be
unclean; and any one who touches it
shall be unclean until evening."

THE WATERS OF MERIBAH

20 And the people of Israel, the
whole congregation, came into
the wilderness of Zin in the first
month, and the people stayed in
Kadesh; and Miriam died there, and
was buried there.

2 Now there was no water for the
congregation; and they assembled
themselves together against Moses and
against Aaron. 3 And the people con-
tended with Moses, and said, "Would
that we had died when our brethren
died before the LORD! 4 Why have you
brought the assembly of the LORD
into this wilderness, that we should
die here, both we and our cattle? 5 And
why have you made us come up out of
Egypt, to bring us to this evil place? It
is no place for grain, or figs, or vines,
or pomegranates; and there is no wa-
ter to drink." 6 Then Moses and Aaron
went from the presence of the assem-
bly to the door of the tent of meeting,
and fell on their faces. And the glory of
the LORD appeared to them, 7 and the
LORD said to Moses, 8 "Take the rod,
and assemble the congregation, you
and Aaron your brother, and tell the
rock before their eyes to yield its wa-
ter; so you shall bring water out of the
rock for them; so you shall give drink
to the congregation and their cattle."
9 And Moses took the rod from before
the LORD, as he commanded him.

10 And Moses and Aaron gathered
the assembly together before the rock,
and he said to them, "Hear now, you
rebels; shall we bring forth water for
you out of this rock?" 11 And Moses
lifted up his hand and struck the rock
with his rod twice; and water came
forth abundantly, and the congre-
gation drank, and their cattle. 12 And
the LORD said to Moses and Aaron,
"Because you did not believe in me, to
sanctify me in the eyes of the people
of Israel, therefore you shall not bring
this assembly into the land which I
have given them." 13 These are the wa-
ters of Mer′ibah,[a] where the people of
Israel contended with the LORD, and
he showed himself holy among them.

PASSAGE THROUGH EDOM REFUSED

14 Moses sent messengers from
Kadesh to the king of Edom, "Thus
says your brother Israel: You know
all the adversity that has befallen us:
15 how our fathers went down to Egypt,
and we dwelt in Egypt a long time; and
the Egyptians dealt harshly with us
and our fathers; 16 and when we cried
to the LORD, he heard our voice, and
sent an angel and brought us forth out
of Egypt; and here we are in Kadesh,
a city on the edge of your territory.
17 Now let us pass through your land.
We will not pass through field or vine-
yard, neither will we drink water from

[a] That is *Contention*

a well; we will go along the King's
Highway, we will not turn aside to
the right hand or to the left, until we
have passed through your territory."
18But Edom said to him, "You shall
not pass through, lest I come out
with the sword against you." 19And
the people of Israel said to him, "We
will go up by the highway; and if we
drink of your water, I and my cattle,
then I will pay for it; let me only pass
through on foot, nothing more." 20But
he said, "You shall not pass through."
And Edom came out against them
with many men, and with a strong
force. 21Thus Edom refused to give
Israel passage through his territory;
so Israel turned away from him.

THE DEATH OF AARON

22 And they journeyed from Ka-
desh, and the people of Israel, the
whole congregation, came to Mount
Hor. 23And the LORD said to Moses
and Aaron at Mount Hor, on the bor-
der of the land of Edom, 24"Aaron shall
be gathered to his people; for he shall
not enter the land which I have given
to the people of Israel, because you
rebelled against my command at the
waters of Mer'ibah. 25Take Aaron and
Elea'zar his son, and b ng them up to
Mount Hor; 26and stri Aaron of his
garments, and put then pon Elea'zar
his son; and Aaron sh be gathered
to his people, and sh die there."
27Moses did as the LOR ommanded;
and they went up Mou Hor in the
sight of all the congre ion. 28And
Moses stripped Aaron of garments,
and put them upon Ele r his son;
and Aaron died there on top of the
mountain. Then Moses Elea'zar
came down from the mo in. 29And
when all the congregat saw that
Aaron was dead, all the h of Israel
wept for Aaron thirty day

THE BRONZE SERP

21 When the Canaanite, king of
Arad, who dwelt in Negeb,
heard that Israel was coming by the
way of Atharim, he fought against
Israel, and took some of them captive.
2And Israel vowed a vow to the LORD,
and said, "If thou wilt indeed give this
people into my hand, then I will utter-
ly destroy their cities." 3And the LORD
hearkened to the voice of Israel, and
gave over the Canaanites; and they ut-
terly destroyed them and their cities;
so the name of the place was called
Hormah.[b]

4 From Mount Hor they set out by
the way to the Red Sea, to go around
the land of Edom; and the people be-
came impatient on the way. 5And the
people spoke against God and against
Moses, "Why have you brought us up
out of Egypt to die in the wilderness?
For there is no food and no water, and
we loathe this worthless food." 6Then
the LORD sent fiery serpents among
the people, and they bit the people,
so that many people of Israel died.
7And the people came to Moses, and
said, "We have sinned, for we have
spoken against the LORD and against
you; pray to the LORD, that he take
away the serpents from us." So Moses
prayed for the people. 8And the LORD
said to Moses, "Make a fiery serpent,
and set it on a pole; and every one who
is bitten, when he sees it, shall live."
9So Moses made a bronze serpent, and
set it on a pole; and if a serpent bit
any man, he would look at the bronze
serpent and live.*

THE JOURNEY TO MOAB

10 And the people of Israel set out,
and encamped in Oboth. 11And they
set out from Oboth, and encamped at
I'ye-ab'arim, in the wilderness which
is opposite Moab, toward the sunrise.
12From there they set out, and en-
camped in the Valley of Zered. 13From
there they set out, and encamped on
the other side of the Arnon, which is
in the wilderness that extends from
the boundary of the Amorites; for
the Arnon is the boundary of Moab,

[b] Heb *Destruction*

between Moab and the Amorites.
14Wherefore it is said in the Book of
the Wars of the LORD,

"Waheb in Suphah,
and the valleys of the Arnon,
15and the slope of the valleys
that extends to the seat of Ar,
and leans to the border of
Moab."

16 And from there they continued
to Beer;[a] that is the well of which the
LORD said to Moses, "Gather the peo-
ple together, and I will give them wa-
ter." 17Then Israel sang this song:

"Spring up, O well!—Sing to
it!—
18the well which the princes dug,
which the nobles of the people
delved,
with the scepter and with their
staves."

19and from Mat´tanah to Naha´liel,
and from Naha´liel to Bamoth, 20and
from Bamoth to the valley lying in the
region of Moab by the top of Pisgah
which looks down upon the desert.[b]

KING SIHON DEFEATED

21 Then Israel sent messengers
to Sihon king of the Amorites, say-
ing, 22"Let me pass through your
land; we will not turn aside into
field or vineyard; we will not drink
the water of a well; we will go by
the King's Highway, until we have
passed through your territory." 23But
Sihon would not allow Israel to pass
through his territory. He gathered
all his men together, and went out
against Israel to the wilderness, and
came to Jahaz, and fought against
Israel. 24And Israel slew him with the
edge of the sword, and took posses-
sion of his land from the Arnon to the
Jabbok, as far as to the Ammonites;
for Jazer was the boundary of the
Ammonites.[c] 25And Israel took all
these cities, and Israel settled in
all the cities of the Amorites, in
Heshbon, and in all its villages. 26For
Heshbon was the city of Sihon the
king of the Amorites, who had fought
against the former king of Moab and
taken all his land out of his hand, as
far as the Arnon. 27Therefore the bal-
lad singers say,

"Come to Heshbon, let it be
built,
let the city of Sihon be
established.
28For fire went forth from
Heshbon,
flame from the city of Sihon.
It devoured Ar of Moab,
the lords of the heights of
the Arnon.
29Woe to you, O Moab!
You are undone, O people of
Chemosh!
He has made his sons fugitives,
and his daughters captives,
to an Amorite king, Sihon.
30So their posterity perished from
Heshbon,[d] as far as Dibon,
and we laid waste until fire
spread to Med´eba."[e]

KING OG DEFEATED

31 Thus Israel dwelt in the land of
the Amorites. 32And Moses sent to spy
out Jazer; an they took its villages,
and disposs sed the Amorites that
were there. 33Then they turned and
went up by e way to Bashan; and Og
the king o Bashan came out against
them, he d all his people, to bat-
tle at Ed i. 34But the LORD said to
Moses, " not fear him; for I have
given hi nto your hand, and all his
people, his land; and you shall do
to him ou did to Sihon king of the
Amorit who dwelt at Heshbon."
35So th ew him, and his sons, and
all his le, until there was not one
surviv ft to him; and they pos-
sessed land.

[a]That is *Well*
[b]Or *Jeshimon*
[c]Gk: Heb *the boundary of the Ammonites was strong*
[d]Gk: Heb *we have shot at them. Heshbon has perished*
[e]Compare Sam and Gk: Heb *we have laid waste to Noph ch to Medeba*

BALAK SUMMONS BALAAM TO CURSE ISRAEL

22 Then the people of Israel set out, and encamped in the plains of Moab beyond the Jordan at Jericho. 2And Balak the son of Zippor saw all that Israel had done to the Amorites. 3And Moab was in great dread of the people, because they were many; Moab was overcome with fear of the people of Israel. 4And Moab said to the elders of Mid′ian, "This horde will now lick up all that is round about us, as the ox licks up the grass of the field." So Balak the son of Zippor, who was king of Moab at that time, 5sent messengers to Balaam the son of Be′or at Pethor, which is near the River, in the land of Amaw to call him, saying, "Behold, a people has come out of Egypt; they cover the face of the earth, and they are dwelling opposite me. 6Come now, curse this people for me, since they are too mighty for me; perhaps I shall be able to defeat them and drive them from the land; for I know that he whom you bless is blessed, and he whom you curse is cursed."

7 So the elders of Moab and the elders of Mid′ian departed with the fees for divination in their hand; and they came to Balaam, and gave him Balak's message. 8And he said to them, "Lodge here this night, and I will bring back word to you, as the LORD speaks to me"; so the princes of Moab stayed with Balaam. 9And God came to Balaam and said, "Who are these men with you?" 10And Balaam said to God, "Balak the son of Zippor, king of Moab, has sent to me, saying, 11'Behold, a people has come out of Egypt, and it covers the face of the earth; now come, curse them for me; perhaps I shall be able to fight against them and drive them out.'" 12God said to Balaam, "You shall not go with them; you shall not curse the people, for they are blessed." 13So Balaam rose in the morning, and said to the princes of Balak, "Go to your own land; for the LORD has refused to let me go with you." 14So the princes of Moab rose and went to Balak, and said, "Balaam refuses to come with us."

15 Once again Balak sent princes, more in number and more honorable than they. 16And they came to Balaam and said to him, "Thus says Balak the son of Zippor: 'Let nothing hinder you from coming to me; 17for I will surely do you great honor, and whatever you say to me I will do; come, curse this people for me.'" 18But Balaam answered and said to the servants of Balak, "Though Balak were to give me his house full of silver and gold, I could not go beyond the command of the LORD my God, to do less or more. 19Pray, now, tarry here this night also, that I may know what more the LORD will say to me." 20And God came to Balaam at night and said to him, "If the men have come to call you, rise, go with them; but only what I bid you, that shall you do."

BALAAM, THE DONKEY, AND THE ANGEL

21 So Balaam rose in the morning, and saddled his ass, and went with the princes of Moab. 22But God's anger was kindled because he went; and the angel of the LORD took his stand in the way as his adversary. Now he was riding on the ass, and his two servants were with him. 23And the ass saw the angel of the LORD standing in the road, with a drawn sword in his hand; and the ass turned aside out of the road, and went into the field; and Balaam struck the ass, to turn her into the road. 24Then the angel of the LORD stood in a narrow path between the vineyards, with a wall on either side. 25And when the ass saw the angel of the LORD, she pushed against the wall, and pressed Balaam's foot against the wall; so he struck her again. 26Then the angel of the LORD went ahead, and stood in a narrow place, where there was no way to turn either to the right or to the left. 27When the ass saw the angel of the

LORD, she lay down under Balaam;
and Balaam's anger was kindled, and
he struck the ass with his staff. 28Then
the LORD opened the mouth of the ass,
and she said to Balaam, "What have I
done to you, that you have struck me
these three times?" 29And Balaam said
to the ass, "Because you have made
sport of me. I wish I had a sword in
my hand, for then I would kill you."
30And the ass said to Balaam, "Am I
not your ass, upon which you have rid-
den all your life long to this day? Was
I ever accustomed to do so to you?"
And he said, "No."

31 Then the LORD opened the eyes
of Balaam, and he saw the angel of
the LORD standing in the way, with
his drawn sword in his hand; and
he bowed his head, and fell on his
face. 32And the angel of the LORD
said to him, "Why have you struck
your ass these three times? Behold,
I have come forth to withstand you,
because your way is perverse before
me; 33and the ass saw me, and turned
aside before me these three times. If
she had not turned aside from me,
surely just now I would have slain
you and let her live." 34Then Balaam
said to the angel of the LORD, "I have
sinned, for I did not know that thou
didst stand in the road against me.
Now therefore, if it is evil in thy
sight, I will go back again." 35And the
angel of the LORD said to Balaam,
"Go with the men; but only the
word which I bid you, that shall you
speak." So Balaam went on with the
princes of Balak.*

36 When Balak heard that Balaam
had come, he went out to meet him
at the city of Moab, on the boundary
formed by the Arnon, at the extremity
of the boundary. 37And Balak said to
Balaam, "Did I not send to you to call
you? Why did you not come to me?
Am I not able to honor you?" 38Balaam
said to Balak, "Lo, I have come to you!
Have I now any power at all to speak
anything? The word that God puts in
my mouth, that must I speak." 39Then
Balaam went with Balak, and they
came to Kir´iath-hu´zoth. 40And Balak
sacrificed oxen and sheep, and sent to
Balaam and to the princes who were
with him.

BALAAM'S FIRST ORACLE

41 And on the morrow Balak
took Balaam and brought him up to
Bamothba´al; and from there he saw
the nearest of the people.

23 And Balaam said to Balak, "Build
for me here seven altars, and
provide for me here seven bulls and
seven rams." 2Balak did as Balaam
had said; and Balak and Balaam of-
fered on each altar a bull and a ram.
3And Balaam said to Balak, "Stand
beside your burnt offering, and I
will go; perhaps the LORD will come
to meet me; and whatever he shows
me I will tell you." And he went to a
bare height. 4And God met Balaam;
and Balaam said to him, "I have pre-
pared the seven altars, and I have
offered upon each altar a bull and a
ram." 5And the LORD put a word in
Balaam's mouth, and said, "Return
to Balak, and thus you shall speak."
6And he returned to him, and lo, he
and all the princes of Moab were
standing beside his burnt offering.
7And Balaam took up his discourse,
and said,

"From Aram Balak has brought
me,
the king of Moab from the
eastern mountains:
'Come, curse Jacob for me,
and come, denounce Israel!'
8How can I curse whom God has
not cursed?
How can I denounce whom
the LORD has not
denounced?
9For from the top of the moun-
tains I see him,
from the hills I behold him;
lo, a people dwelling alone,
and not reckoning itself
among the nations!
10Who can count the dust of Jacob,

or number the fourth part[a]
of Israel?
Let me die the death of the
righteous,
and let my end be like his!"

11 And Balak said to Balaam,
"What have you done to me? I took
you to curse my enemies, and be-
hold, you have done nothing but bless
them." 12And he answered, "Must I
not take heed to speak what the LORD
puts in my mouth?"

BALAAM'S SECOND ORACLE

13 And Balak said to him, "Come
with me to another place, from which
you may see them; you shall see only
the nearest of them, and shall not
see them all; then curse them for me
from there." 14And he took him to the
field of Zophim, to the top of Pisgah,
and built seven altars, and offered a
bull and a ram on each altar. 15Balaam
said to Balak, "Stand here beside
your burnt offering, while I meet the
LORD yonder." 16And the LORD met
Balaam, and put a word in his mouth,
and said, "Return to Balak, and thus
shall you speak." 17And he came to
him, and lo, he was standing beside
his burnt offering, and the princes
of Moab with him. And Balak said to
him, "What has the LORD spoken?"
18And Balaam took up his discourse,
and said,

"Rise, Balak, and hear;
hearken to me, O son of
Zippor:
19God is not man, that he should
lie,
or a son of man, that he
should repent.
Has he said, and will he not
do it?
Or has he spoken, and will
he not fulfil it?
20Behold, I received a command
to bless:
he has blessed and I cannot
revoke.
21He has not beheld misfortune
in Jacob;
nor has he seen trouble in
Israel.
The LORD their God is with
them,
and the shout of a king is
among them.
22God brings them out of Egypt;
they have as it were the
horns of the wild ox.
23For there is no enchantment
against Jacob,
no divination against Israel;
now it shall be said of Jacob
and Israel,
'What has God wrought!'
24Behold, a people! As a lioness it
rises up
and as a lion it lifts itself;
it does not lie down till it
devours the prey,
and drinks the blood of the
slain."

25 And Balak said to Balaam,
"Neither curse them at all, nor bless
them at all." 26But Balaam answered
Balak, "Did I not tell you, 'All that
the LORD says, that I must do'?" 27And
Balak said to Balaam, "Come now, I
will take you to another place; per-
haps it will please God that you may
curse them for me from there." 28So
Balak took Balaam to the top of Pe´or,
that overlooks the desert.[b]

29And Balaam said to Balak, "Build
for me here seven altars, and provide
for me here seven bulls and seven
rams." 30And Balak did as Balaam had
said, and offered a bull and a ram on
each altar.

BALAAM'S THIRD ORACLE

24 When Balaam saw that it pleased
the LORD to bless Israel, he did
not go, as at other times, to look for
omens, but set his face toward the
wilderness. 2And Balaam lifted up his
eyes, and saw Israel encamping tribe
by tribe. And the Spirit of God came

[a] Or *dust clouds*
[b] Or *Jeshimon*

upon him, 3and he took up his dis-
course, and said,

"The oracle of Balaam the son
of Be´or,
the oracle of the man whose
eye is opened,[a]
4the oracle of him who hears the
words of God,
who sees the vision of the
Almighty,
falling down, but having his
eyes uncovered:
5How fair are your tents, O Jacob,
your encampments, O
Israel!
6Like valleys that stretch afar,
like gardens beside a river,
like aloes that the LORD has
planted,
like cedar trees beside the
waters.
7Water shall flow from his
buckets,
and his seed shall be in
many waters,
his king shall be higher than
Agag,
and his kingdom shall be
exalted.
8God brings him out of Egypt;
he has as it were the horns
of the wild ox,
he shall eat up the nations his
adversaries,
and shall break their bones
in pieces,
and pierce them through
with his arrows.
9He couched, he lay down like a
lion,
and like a lioness; who will
rouse him up?
Blessed be every one who
blesses you,
and cursed be every one who
curses you."

BALAAM'S FOURTH ORACLE

10 And Balak's anger was kindled
against Balaam, and he struck his
hands together; and Balak said to
Balaam, "I called you to curse my en-
emies, and behold, you have blessed
them these three times. 11Therefore
now flee to your place; I said, 'I will
certainly honor you,' but the LORD
has held you back from honor." 12And
Balaam said to Balak, "Did I not tell
your messengers whom you sent to
me, 13'If Balak should give me his
house full of silver and gold, I would
not be able to go beyond the word of
the LORD to do either good or bad of
my own will; what the LORD speaks,
that will I speak'? 14And now, behold,
I am going to my people; come, I will
let you know what this people will
do to your people in the latter days."
15And he took up his discourse, and
said,

"The oracle of Balaam the son
of Be´or,
the oracle of the man whose
eye is opened,[b]
16the oracle of him who hears the
words of God,
and knows the knowledge of
the Most High,
who sees the vision of the
Almighty,
falling down, but having his
eyes uncovered:
17I see him, but not now;
I behold him, but not nigh:
a star shall come forth out of
Jaob,
and a cepter shall rise out
of Israel;
it shall cush the forehead[c] of
Mab,
and beak down all the sons
of Sheth.
18Edom shl be dispossessed,
Se´irlso, his enemies, shall
be dispossessed,
whilsrael does valiantly.
19By Jacobhall dominion be
excised,
ande survivors of cities be
destroyed!"

[a]Or *closed* or *perfect*
[b]Or *closed* or *perfect*
[c]Heb *corners* (of the head)

20 Then he looked on Am′alek, and
took up his discourse, and said,

"Am′alek was the first of the
nations,
but in the end he shall come to
destruction."

21 And he looked on the Kenite,
and took up his discourse, and said,

"Enduring is your dwelling
place,
and your nest is set in the
rock;
22nevertheless Kain shall be
wasted.
How long shall Asshur take
you away captive?"

23 And he took up his discourse,
and said,

"Alas, who shall live when God
does this?
24But ships shall come from
Kittim
and shall afflict Asshur and
Eber;
and he also shall come to
destruction."

25 Then Balaam rose, and went
back to his place; and Balak also went
his way.

WORSHIP OF BAAL OF PEOR

25 While Israel dwelt in Shittim the
people began to play the harlot
with the daughters of Moab. 2These
invited the people to the sacrifices
of their gods, and the people ate, and
bowed down to their gods. 3So Israel
yoked himself to Ba′al of Pe′or. And
the anger of the LORD was kindled
against Israel; 4and the LORD said to
Moses, "Take all the chiefs of the peo-
ple, and hang them in the sun before
the LORD that the fierce anger of the
LORD may turn away from Israel."
5And Moses said to the judges of
Israel, "Every one of you slay his men
who have yoked themselves to Ba′al of
Pe′or."

6 And behold, one of the people of
Israel came and brought a Mid′ianite
woman to his family, in the sight of
Moses and in the sight of the whole
congregation of the people of Israel,
while they were weeping at the
door of the tent of meeting. 7When
Phin′ehas the son of Elea′zar, son of
Aaron the priest, saw it, he rose and
left the congregation, and took a spear
in his hand 8and went after the man of
Israel into the inner room, and pierced
both of them, the man of Israel and
the woman, through her body. Thus
the plague was stayed from the peo-
ple of Israel. 9Nevertheless those that
died by the plague were twenty-four
thousand.

10 And the LORD said to Moses,
11"Phin′ehas the son of Elea′zar, son
of Aaron the priest, has turned back
my wrath from the people of Israel,
in that he was jealous with my jeal-
ousy among them, so that I did not
consume the people of Israel in my
jealousy. 12Therefore say, 'Behold, I
give to him my covenant of peace;
13and it shall be to him, and to his de-
scendants after him, the covenant of a
perpetual priesthood, because he was
jealous for his God, and made atone-
ment for the people of Israel.'"

14 The name of the slain man
of Israel, who was slain with the
Mid′ianite woman, was Zimri the son
of Salu, head of a fathers' house be-
longing to the Simeonites. 15And the
name of the Mid′ianite woman who
was slain was Cozbi the daughter of
Zur, who was the head of the people
of a fathers' house in Mid′ian.

16 And the LORD said to Moses,
17"Harass the Mid′ianites, and smite
them; 18for they have harassed you
with their wiles, with which they be-
guiled you in the matter of Pe′or, and
in the matter of Cozbi, the daughter
of the prince of Mid′ian, their sister,
who was slain on the day of the plague
on account of Pe′or."

A CENSUS OF THE NEW GENERATION

26 After the plague the LORD said
to Moses and to Elea′zar the son
of Aaron, the priest, 2"Take a census
of all the congregation of the people

of Israel, from twenty years old and
upward, by their fathers' houses, all
in Israel who are able to go forth to
war." 3And Moses and Elea´zar the
priest spoke with them in the plains
of Moab by the Jordan at Jericho, say-
ing, 4"Take a census of the people,[a]
from twenty years old and upward,"
as the LORD commanded Moses. The
people of Israel, who came forth out of
the land of Egypt, were:

5 Reuben, the first-born of Israel;
the sons of Reuben: of Hanoch,
the family of the Ha´nochites; of
Pallu, the family of the Pal´luites;
6of Hezron, the family of the
Hez´ronites; of Carmi, the family of
the Carmites. 7These are the families
of the Reubenites; and their num-
ber was forty-three thousand seven
hundred and thirty. 8And the sons
of Pallu: Eli´ab. 9The sons of Eli´ab:
Nem´uel, Dathan, and Abi´ram.
These are the Dathan and Abi´ram,
chosen from the congregation, who
contended against Moses and Aaron
in the company of Korah, when they
contended against the LORD, 10and
the earth opened its mouth and swal-
lowed them up together with Korah,
when that company died, when the
fire devoured two hundred and fif-
ty men; and they became a warning.
11Notwithstanding, the sons of Korah
did not die.

12 The sons of Simeon according to
their families: of Nem´uel, the family
of the Nem´uelites; of Jamin, the fami-
ly of the Ja´minites; of Jachin, the fam-
ily of the Ja´chinites; 13of Zerah, the
family of the Zer´ahites; of Shaul, the
family of the Sha´ulites. 14These are
the families of the Simeonites, twen-
ty-two thousand two hundred.

15 The sons of Gad according to
their families: of Zephon, the family
of the Ze´phonites; of Haggi, the fami-
ly of the Haggites; of Shuni, the family
of the Shunites; 16of Ozni, the family
of the Oznites; of Eri, the family of
the Erites; 17of Ar´od, the family of
the Ar´odites; of Are´li, the family of
the Are´lites. 18These are the families
of the sons of Gad according to their
number, forty thousand five hundred.

19 The sons of Judah were Er
and Onan; and Er and Onan died in
the land of Canaan. 20And the sons
of Judah according to their families
were: of Shelah, the family of the
Shela´nites; of Perez, the family of
the Per´ezites; of Zerah, the family
of the Zer´ahites. 21And the sons of
Perez were: of Hezron, the family of
the Hez´ronites; of Hamul, the fami-
ly of the Hamu´lites. 22These are the
families of Judah according to their
number, seventy-six thousand five
hundred.

23 The sons of Is´sachar according
to their families: of Tola, the family
of the To´laites; of Puvah, the family
of the Punites; 24of Jashub, the fami-
ly of the Jash´ubites; of Shimron, the
family of the Shim´ronites. 25These
are the families of Is´sachar according
to their number, sixty-four thousand
three hundred.

26 The sons of Zeb´ulun, according
to their families: of Sered, the family
of the Ser´edites; of Elon, the family
of the E´lonites; of Jah´leel, the fam-
ily of the Jah´leelites. 27These are the
families of the Zeb´ulunites according
to their number, sixty thousand five
hundred.

28 The sons of Joseph accord-
ing to their families: Manas´seh and
E´phraim. 29The sons of Manas´seh: of
Machir, the family of the Ma´chirites;
and Machir was the father of Gil-
ead; of Gilead, the family of the
Gil´eadites. 30These are the sons of
Gilead: of Ie´zer, the family of the
Ie´zerites; of Helek, the family of the
He´lekites; 31and of As´riel, the fami-
ly of the As´rielites; and of Shechem,
the family of the She´chemites;
32and of Shemi´da, the family of the
Shemi´daites; and of Hepher, the
family of the He´pherites. 33Now
Zeloph´ehad the son of Hepher had

[a] Supplying *take a census of the people* Compare verse 2

no sons, but daughters: and the names
of the daughters of Zeloph´ehad were
Mahlah, Noah, Hoglah, Milcah, and
Tirzah. 34These are the families of
Manas´seh; and their number was fif-
ty-two thousand seven hundred.

35 These are the sons of
E´phraim according to their fami-
lies: of Shu´thelah, the family of the
Shu´thelahites; of Becher, the family
of the Bech´erites; of Tahan, the fam-
ily of the Ta´hanites. 36And these are
the sons of Shu´thelah: of Eran, the
family of the E´ranites. 37These are
the families of the sons of E´phraim
according to their number, thirty-two
thousand five hundred. These are
the sons of Joseph according to their
families.

38 The sons of Benjamin according
to their families: of Bela, the family
of the Be´la-ites; of Ashbel, the fam-
ily of the Ash´belites; of Ahi´ram,
the family of the Ahi´ramites; 39of
Shephu´pham, the family of the
Shu´phamites; of Hupham, the fam-
ily of the Hu´phamites. 40And the
sons of Bela were Ard and Na´aman:
of Ard, the family of the Ard´ites; of
Na´aman, the family of the Na´amites.
41These are the sons of Benjamin ac-
cording to their families; and their
number was forty-five thousand six
hundred.

42 These are the sons of Dan ac-
cording to their families: of Shuham,
the family of the Shu´hamites. These
are the families of Dan according to
their families. 43All the families of the
Shu´hamites, according to their num-
ber, were sixty-four thousand four
hundred.

44 The sons of Asher according to
their families: of Imnah, the family of
the Imnites; of Ishvi, the family of the
Ishvites; of Beri´ah, the family of the
Beri´ites. 45Of the sons of Beri´ah: of
Heber, the family of the Heberites; of
Mal´chi-el, the family of Mal´chi-
elites. 46And the name of the daugh-
ter of Asher was Serah. These are
the families of the sons of Asher
according to their number, fifty-three
thousand four hundred.

48 The sons of Naph´tali according
to their families: of Jahzeel, the family
of the Jah´zeelites; of Guni, the family
of the Gunites; 49of Jezer, the family of
the Je´zerites; of Shillem, the family of
the Shil´lemites. 50These are the fam-
ilies of Naph´tali according to their
families; and their number was for-
ty-five thousand four hundred.

51 This was the number of the
people of Israel, six hundred and one
thousand seven hundred and thirty.

52 The LORD said to Moses: 53"To
these the land shall be divided for
inheritance according to the number
of names. 54To a large tribe you shall
give a large inheritance, and to a small
tribe you shall give a small inheri-
tance; every tribe shall be given its
inheritance according to its numbers.
55But the land shall be divided by lot;
according to the names of the tribes of
their fathers they shall inherit. 56Their
inheritance shall be divided accord-
ing to lot between the larger and the
smaller."

57 These are the Levites as
numbered according to their fam-
ilies: of Gershon, the family of the
Gershonites; of Kohath, the family
of the Ko´hathites; of Merar´i, the
family of the Merar´ites. 58These
are the families of Levi: the fam-
ily of the Libnites, the family of
the He´bronites, the family of the
Mahlites, the family of the Mushites,
the family of the Kor´ahites. And
Kohath was the father of Amram.
59The name of Amram's wife was
Joch´ebed the daughter of Levi, who
was born to Levi in Egypt; and she
bore to Amram Aaron and Moses and
Miriam their sister. 60And to Aaron
were born Nadab, Abi´hu, Elea´zar
and Ith´amar. 61But Nadab and Abi´hu
died when they offered unholy fire be-
fore the LORD. 62And those numbered
of them were twenty-three thousand,
every male from a month old and up-
ward; for they were not numbered

among the people of Israel, because there was no inheritance given to them among the people of Israel.

63 These were those numbered by Moses and Elea´zar the priest, who numbered the people of Israel in the plains of Moab by the Jordan at Jericho. 64But among these there was not a man of those numbered by Moses and Aaron the priest, who had numbered the people of Israel in the wilderness of Sinai. 65For the LORD had said of them, "They shall die in the wilderness." There was not left a man of them, except Caleb the son of Jephun´neh and Joshua the son of Nun.

THE DAUGHTERS OF ZELOPHEHAD

27 Then drew near the daughters of Zeloph´ehad the son of Hepher, son of Gilead, son of Machir, son of Manas´seh, from the families of Manas´seh the son of Joseph. The names of his daughters were: Mahlah, Noah, Hoglah, Milcah, and Tirzah. 2And they stood before Moses, and before Elea´zar the priest, and before the leaders and all the congregation, at the door of the tent of meeting, saying, 3"Our father died in the wilderness; he was not among the company of those who gathered themselves together against the LORD in the company of Korah, but died for his own sin; and he had no sons. 4Why should the name of our father be taken away from his family, because he had no son? Give to us a possession among our father's brethren."

5 Moses brought their case before the LORD. 6And the LORD said to Moses, 7"The daughters of Zeloph´ehad are right; you shall give them possession of an inheritance among their father's brethren and cause *the inheritance of* their father to pass to them. 8And you shall say to the people of Israel, 'If a man dies, and has no son, then you shall cause his inheritance to pass to his daughter. 9And if he has no daughter, then you shall give his inheritance to his brothers. 10And if he has no brothers, then you shall give his inheritance to his father's brothers. 11And if his father has no brothers, then you shall give his inheritance to his kinsman that is next to him of his family, and he shall possess it. And it shall be to the people of Israel a statute and ordinance, as the LORD commanded Moses.'"

JOSHUA APPOINTED MOSES' SUCCESSOR

12 The LORD said to Moses, "Go up into this mountain of Ab´arim, and see the land which I have given to the people of Israel. 13And when you have seen it, you also shall be gathered to your people, as your brother Aaron was gathered, 14because you rebelled against my word in the wilderness of Zin during the strife of the congregation, to sanctify me at the waters before their eyes." (These are the waters of Mer´ibah of Kadesh in the wilderness of Zin.) 15Moses said to the LORD, 16"Let the LORD the God of the spirits of all flesh, appoint a man over the congregation, 17who shall go out before them and come in before them, who shall lead them out and bring them in; that the congregation of the LORD may not be as sheep which have no shepherd." 18And the LORD said to Moses, "Take Joshua the son of Nun, a man in whom is the spirit, and lay your hand upon him; 19cause him to stand before Elea´zar the priest and all the congregation, and you shall commissin him in their sight. 20You shall inv t *him* with some of your authorityhat all the congregation of the peopof Israel may obey. 21And he shall sta before Elea´zar the priest, who shanquire for him by the judgment ofe Urim before the LORD at his worney shall go out, and at his word thshall come in, both he and all the ple of Israel with him, the whole cregation." 22And Moses did as the D commanded him; he took Joshua caused him to stand before Elr the priest and the whole

congregation, 23 and he laid his hands
upon him, and commissioned him as
the LORD directed through Moses.

DAILY OFFERINGS

28 The LORD said to Moses, 2 "Com-
mand the people of Israel, and
say to them, 'My offering, my food
for my offerings by fire, my pleasing
odor, you shall take heed to offer to
me in its due season.' 3 And you shall
say to them, This is the offering by
fire which you shall offer to the LORD
two male lambs a year old without
blemish, day by day, as a continual of-
fering. 4 The one lamb you shall offer
in the morning, and the other lamb
you shall offer in the evening; 5 also a
tenth of an ephah of fine flour for a
cereal offering, mixed with a fourth of
a hin of beaten oil. 6 It is a continual
burnt offering, which was ordained
at Mount Sinai for a pleasing odor, an
offering by fire to the LORD. 7 Its drink
offering shall be a fourth of a hin for
each lamb; in the holy place you shall
pour out a drink offering of strong
drink to the LORD. 8 The other lamb
you shall offer in the evening; like the
cereal offering of the morning, and
like its drink offering, you shall of-
fer it as an offering by fire, a pleasing
odor to the LORD

SABBATH OFFERINGS

9 "On the sabbath day two male
lambs a year old without blemish, and
two tenths of an ephah of fine flour
for a cereal offering, mixed with oil,
and its drink offering: 10 this is the
burnt offering of every sabbath, be-
sides the continual burnt offering and
its drink offering.

MONTHLY OFFERINGS

11 "At the beginnings of your
months you shall offer a burnt of-
fering to the LORD two young bulls,
one ram, seven male lambs a year old
without blemish; 12 also three tenths
of an ephah of fine flour for a cereal
offering, mixed with oil, for each bull;
and two tenths of fine flour for a cere-
al offering, mixed with oil, for the one
ram; 13 and a tenth of fine flour mixed
with oil as a cereal offering for every
lamb; for a burnt offering of pleasing
odor, an offering by fire to the LORD.
14 Their drink offerings shall be half a
hin of wine for a bull, a third of a hin
for a ram, and a fourth of a hin for a
lamb; this is the burnt offering of each
month throughout the months of the
year. 15 Also one male goat for a sin of-
fering to the LORD it shall be offered
besides the continual burnt offering
and its drink offering.

OFFERINGS AT PASSOVER

16 "On the fourteenth day of the
first month is the LORD's passover.
17 And on the fifteenth day of this
month is a feast; seven days shall un-
leavened bread be eaten. 18 On the first
day there shall be a holy convocation:
you shall do no laborious work, 19 but
offer an offering by fire, a burnt of-
fering to the LORD two young bulls,
one ram, and seven male lambs a year
old; see that they are without blem-
ish; 20 also their cereal offering of fine
flour mixed with oil; three tenths of
an ephah shall you offer for a bull, and
two tenths for a ram; 21 a tenth shall
you offer for each of the seven lambs;
22 also one male goat for a sin offering,
to make atonement for you. 23 You shall
offer these besides the burnt offering
of the morning, which is for a contin-
ual burnt offering. 24 In the same way
you shall offer daily, for seven days, the
food of an offering by fire, a pleasing
odor to the LORD it shall be offered be-
sides the continual burnt offering and
its drink offering. 25 And on the seventh
day you shall have a holy convocation;
you shall do no laborious work.

OFFERINGS AT THE FESTIVAL OF WEEKS

26 "On the day of the first fruits,
when you offer a cereal offering of
new grain to the LORD at your feast
of weeks, you shall have a holy con-
vocation; you shall do no laborious

work, 27 but offer a burnt offering, a
pleasing odor to the LORD two young
bulls, one ram, seven male lambs a
year old; 28 also their cereal offering of
fine flour mixed with oil, three tenths
of an ephah for each bull, two tenths
for one ram, 29 a tenth for each of the
seven lambs; 30 with one male goat, to
make atonement for you. 31 Besides the
continual burnt offering and its cere-
al offering, you shall offer them and
their drink offering. See that they are
without blemish.

OFFERINGS AT THE FESTIVAL OF TRUMPETS

29 “On the first day of the seventh
month you shall have a holy
convocation; you shall do no labori-
ous work. It is a day for you to blow
the trumpets, 2 and you shall offer a
burnt offering, a pleasing odor to the
LORD one young bull, one ram, seven
male lambs a year old without blem-
ish; 3 also their cereal offering of fine
flour mixed with oil, three tenths of
an ephah for the bull, two tenths for
the ram, 4 and one tenth for each of
the seven lambs; 5 with one male goat
for a sin offering, to make atonement
for you; 6 besides the burnt offering of
the new moon, and its cereal offering,
and the continual burnt offering and
its cereal offering, and their drink of-
fering, according to the ordinance for
them, a pleasing odor, an offering by
fire to the LORD

OFFERINGS ON THE DAY OF ATONEMENT

7 “On the tenth day of this seventh
month you shall have a holy convoca-
tion, and afflict yourselves; you shall
do no work, 8 but you shall offer a
burnt offering to the LORD a pleasing
odor: one young bull, one ram, seven
male lambs a year old; they shall be to
you without blemish; 9 and their cereal
offering of fine flour mixed with oil,
three tenths of an ephah for the bull,
two tenths for the one ram, 10 a tenth
for each of the seven lambs: 11 also one
male goat for a sin offering, besides
the sin offering of atonement, and the
continual burnt offering and its cereal
offering, and their drink offerings.

OFFERINGS AT THE FESTIVAL OF BOOTHS

12 “On the fifteenth day of the
seventh month you shall have a holy
convocation; you shall do no laborious
work, and you shall keep a feast to the
LORD seven days; 13 and you shall offer
a burnt offering, an offering by fire,
a pleasing odor to the LORD thirteen
young bulls, two rams, fourteen male
lambs a year old; they shall be without
blemish; 14 and their cereal offering of
fine flour mixed with oil, three tenths
of an ephah for each of the thirteen
bulls, two tenths for each of the two
rams, 15 and a tenth for each of the
fourteen lambs; 16 also one male goat
for a sin offering, besides the contin-
ual burnt offering, its cereal offering
and its drink offering.

17 “On the second day twelve young
bulls, two rams, fourteen male lambs
a year old without blemish, 18 with the
cereal offering and the drink offerings
for the bulls, for the rams, and for the
lambs, by number, according to the or-
dinance; 19 also one male goat for a sin
offering, besides the continual burnt
offering and its cereal offering, and
their drink offerings.

20 “On the third day eleven bulls,
two rams, fourteen male lambs a year
old without blemish, 21 with the cereal
offering and the drink offerings for
the bulls, for the rams, and for the
lambs, by number, according to the or-
dinance; 22 also one male goat for a sin
offering, besides the continual burnt
offering and its cereal offering and its
drink offering.

23 “On the fourth day ten bulls,
two rams, fourteen male lambs a year
old without blemish, 24 with the cereal
offering and the drink offerings for
the bulls, for the rams, and for the
lambs, by number, according to the
ordinance; 25 also one male goat for
a sin offering, besides the continual
burnt offering, its cereal offering and
its drink offering.

26 "On the fifth day nine bulls, two
rams, fourteen male lambs a year old
without blemish, 27 with the cereal of-
fering and the drink offerings for the
bulls, for the rams, and for the lambs,
by number, according to the ordi-
nance; 28 also one male goat for a sin
offering; besides the continual burnt
offering and its cereal offering and its
drink offering.

29 "On the sixth day eight bulls,
two rams, fourteen male lambs a year
old without blemish, 30 with the cereal
offering and the drink offerings for
the bulls, for the rams, and for the
lambs, by number, according to the
ordinance; 31 also one male goat for
a sin offering; besides the continual
burnt offering, its cereal offering, and
its drink offerings.

32 "On the seventh day seven bulls,
two rams, fourteen male lambs a year
old without blemish, 33 with the cereal
offering and the drink offerings for
the bulls, for the rams, and for the
lambs, by number, according to the
ordinance; 34 also one male goat for
a sin offering; besides the continual
burnt offering, its cereal offering, and
its drink offering.

35 "On the eighth day you shall
have a solemn assembly: you shall
do no laborious work, 36 but you shall
offer a burnt offering, an offering
by fire, a pleasing odor to the LORD
one bull, one ram, seven male lambs
a year old without blemish, 37 and the
cereal offering and the drink offerings
for the bull, for the ram, and for the
lambs, by number, accoding to the or-
dinance; 38 also one mal goat for a sin
offering; besides the cntinual burnt
offering and its cereal ćering and its
drink offering.

39 "These you shaloffer to the
LORD at your appoind feasts, in
addition to your votivefferings and
your freewill offerings,r your burnt
offerings, and for you:ereal offer-
ings, and for your drinkferings, and
for your peace offerings

40[a] And Moses told the people of
Israel everything just as the LORD had
commanded Moses.

VOWS MADE BY WOMEN

30 Moses said to the heads of the
tribes of the people of Israel,
"This is what the LORD has com-
manded. 2 When a man vows a vow to
the LORD or swears an oath to bind
himself by a pledge, he shall not break
his word; he shall do according to all
that proceeds out of his mouth. 3 Or
when a woman vows a vow to the
LORD and binds herself by a pledge,
while within her father's house, in
her youth, 4 and her father hears of her
vow and of her pledge by which she
has bound herself, and says nothing
to her; then all her vows shall stand,
and every pledge by which she has
bound herself shall stand. 5 But if
her father expresses disapproval to
her on the day that he hears of it, no
vow of hers, no pledge by which she
has bound herself, shall stand; and
the LORD will forgive her, because
her father opposed her. 6 And if she is
married to a husband, while under her
vows or any thoughtless utterance of
her lips by which she has bound her-
self, 7 and her husband hears of it, and
says nothing to her on the day that he
hears; then her vows shall stand, and
her pledges by which she has bound
herself shall stand. 8 But if, on the day
that her husband comes to hear of
it, he expresses disapproval, then he
shall make void her vow which was on
her, and the thoughtless utterance of
her lips, by which she bound herself,
and the LORD will forgive her. 9 But
any vow of a widow or of a divorced
woman, anything by which she has
bound herself, shall stand against her.
10 And if she vowed in her husband's
house, or bound herself by a pledge
with an oath, 11 and her husband heard
of it, and said nothing to her, and did
not oppose her; then all her vows shall
stand, and every pledge by which she

[a] Ch 30.1 in Heb

bound herself shall stand. 12But if her
husband makes them null and void
on the day that he hears them, then
whatever proceeds out of her lips con-
cerning her vows, or concerning her
pledge of herself, shall not stand: her
husband has made them void, and the
LORD will forgive her. 13Any vow and
any binding oath to afflict herself, her
husband may establish, or her hus-
band may make void. 14But if her hus-
band says nothing to her from day to
day, then he establishes all her vows,
or all her pledges, that are upon her;
he has established them, because he
said nothing to her on the day that he
heard of them. 15But if he makes them
null and void after he has heard of
them, then he shall bear her iniquity."

16 These are the statutes which the
LORD commanded Moses, as between
a man and his wife, and between a
father and his daughter, while in her
youth, within her father's house.

WAR AGAINST MIDIAN

31 The LORD said to Moses, 2"Avenge
the people of Israel on the
Mid'ianites; afterward you shall be
gathered to your people." 3And Moses
said to the people, "Arm men from
among you for the war, that they may
go against Mid'ian, to execute the
LORD's vengeance on Mid'ian. 4You
shall send a thousand from each of
the tribes of Israel to the war." 5So
there were provided, out of the thou-
sands of Israel, a thousand from each
tribe, twelve thousand armed for war.
6And Moses sent them to the war, a
thousand from each tribe, together
with Phin'ehas the son of Elea'zar the
priest, with the vessels of the sanc-
tuary and the trumpets for the alarm
in his hand. 7They warred against
Mid'ian, as the LORD commanded
Moses, and slew every male. 8They
slew the kings of Mid'ian with the rest
of their slain, Evi, Rekem, Zur, Hur,
and Reba, the five kings of Mid'ian;
and they also slew Balaam the son of
Be'or with the sword. 9And the people
of Israel took captive the women of
Mid'ian and their little ones; and they
took as booty all their cattle, their
flocks, and all their goods. 10All their
cities in the places where they dwelt,
and all their encampments, they
burned with fire, 11and took all the
spoil and all the booty, both of man
and of beast. 12Then they brought the
captives and the booty and the spoil
to Moses, and to Elea'zar the priest,
and to the congregation of the people
of Israel, at the camp on the plains of
Moab by the Jordan at Jericho.

RETURN FROM THE WAR

13 Moses, and Elea'zar the priest,
and all the leaders of the congregation,
went forth to meet them outside the
camp. 14And Moses was angry with
the officers of the army, the com-
manders of thousands and the com-
manders of hundreds, who had come
from service in the war. 15Moses said
to them, "Have you let all the women
live? 16Behold, these caused the people
of Israel, by the counsel of Balaam, to
act treacherously against the LORD in
the matter of Pe'or, and so the plague
came among the congregation of the
LORD. 17Now therefore, kill every male
among the little ones, and kill every
woman who has known man by lying
with him. 18But all the young girls
who have not known man by lying
with him, keep alive for yourselves.
19Encamp outside the camp seven days;
whoever of you has killed any person,
and whoever has touched any slain,
purify yourselves and your captives on
the third day and on the seventh day.
20You shall purify every garment, every
article of skin, all work of goats' hair,
and every article of wood."

21 And Elea'zar the priest said to
the men of war who had gone to battle:
"This is the statute of the law which
the LORD has commanded Moses:
22only the gold, the silver, the bronze,
the iron, the tin, and the lead, 23every-
thing that can stand the fire, you shall
pass through the fire, and it shall be

clean. Nevertheless it shall also be pu-
rified with the water of impurity; and
whatever cannot stand the fire, you
shall pass through the water. 24You
must wash your clothes on the seventh
day, and you shall be clean; and after-
ward you shall come into the camp."

DISPOSITION OF CAPTIVES AND BOOTY

25 The LORD said to Moses, 26"Take
the count of the booty that was tak-
en, both of man and of beast, you and
Elea´zar the priest and the heads of
the fathers' houses of the congrega-
tion; 27and divide the booty into two
parts, between the warriors who went
out to battle and all the congregation.
28And levy for the LORD a tribute
from the men of war who went out
to battle, one out of five hundred, of
the persons and of the oxen and of
the asses and of the flocks; 29take it
from their half, and give it to Elea´zar
the priest as an offering to the LORD.
30And from the people of Israel's half
you shall take one drawn out of every
fifty, of the persons, of the oxen, of
the asses, and of the flocks, of all the
cattle, and give them to the Levites
who have charge of the tabernacle of
the LORD." 31And Moses and Elea´zar
the priest did as the LORD command-
ed Moses.

32 Now the booty remaining of the
spoil that the men of war took was:
six hundred and seventy-five thou-
sand sheep, 33seventy-two thousand
cattle, 34sixty-one thousand asses,
35and thirty-two thousand persons in
all, women who had not known man
by lying with him. 36And the half, the
portion of those who had gone out to
war, was in number three hundred
and thirty-seven thousand five hun-
dred sheep, 37and the LORD's tribute
of sheep was six hundred and seven-
ty-five. 38The cattle were thirty-six
thousand, of which the LORD's trib-
ute was seventy-two. 39The asses
were thirty thousand five hundred,
of which the LORD's tribute was six-
ty-one. 40The persons were sixteen
thousand, of which the LORD's tribute
was thirty-two persons. 41And Moses
gave the tribute, which was the offer-
ing for the LORD to Elea´zar the priest,
as the LORD commanded Moses.

42 From the people of Israel's half,
which Moses separated from that of
the men who had gone to war—43now
the congregation's half was three
hundred and thirty-seven thousand
five hundred sheep, 44thirty-six thou-
sand cattle, 45and thirty thousand five
hundred asses, 46and sixteen thou-
sand persons—47from the people of
Israel's half Moses took one of every
fifty, both of persons and of beasts,
and gave them to the Levites who had
charge of the tabernacle of the LORD
as the LORD commanded Moses.

48 Then the officers who were over
the thousands of the army, the cap-
tains of thousands and the captains of
hundreds, came near to Moses, 49and
said to Moses, "Your servants have
counted the men of war who are un-
der our command, and there is not a
man missing from us. 50And we have
brought the LORD's offering, what
each man found, articles of gold, arm-
lets and bracelets, signet rings, ear-
rings, and beads, to make atonement
for ourselves before the LORD." 51And
Moses and Elea´zar the priest received
from them the gold, all wrought arti-
cles. 52And all the gold of the offering
that they offered to the LORD from
the commanders of thousands and
the commanders of hundreds, was
sixteen thousand seven hundred and
fifty shekels. 53(The men of war had
taken booty, every man for himself.)
54*And Moses and Elea´zar* the priest
received the gold from the command-
ers of thousands and of hundreds, and
brought it into the tent of meeting, as
a memorial for the people of Israel be-
fore the LORD

CONQUEST AND DIVISION OF TRANSJORDAN

32 Now the sons of Reuben and the
sons of Gad had a very great mul-
titude of cattle; and they saw the land

of Jazer and the land of Gilead, and
behold, the place was a place for cat-
tle. 2So the sons of Gad and the sons
of Reuben came and said to Moses and
to Elea´zar the priest and to the lead-
ers of the congregation, 3"At´aroth,
Dibon, Jazer, Nimrah, Heshbon,
Elea´leh, Sebam, Nebo, and Be´on,
4the land which the LORD smote be-
fore the congregation of Israel, is a
land for cattle; and your servants
have cattle." 5And they said, "If we
have found favor in your sight, let this
land be given to your servants for a
possession; do not take us across the
Jordan."

6 But Moses said to the sons of
Gad and to the sons of Reuben, "Shall
your brethren go to the war while
you sit here? 7Why will you discour-
age the heart of the people of Israel
from going over into the land which
the LORD has given them? 8Thus did
your fathers, when I sent them from
Ka´desh-bar´nea to see the land. 9For
when they went up to the Valley of
Eshcol, and saw the land, they dis-
couraged the heart of the people of
Israel from going into the land which
the LORD had given them. 10And the
LORD's anger was kindled on that
day, and he swore, saying, 11'Surely
none of the men who came up out of
Egypt, from twenty years old and up-
ward, shall see the land which I swore
to give to Abraham, to Isaac, and to
Jacob, because they have not wholly
followed me; 12none except Caleb the
son of Jephun´neh the Ken´izzite and
Joshua the son of Nun, for they have
wholly followed the LORD.' 13And the
LORD's anger was kindled against
Israel, and he made them wander in
the wilderness forty years, until all
the generation that had done evil in
the sight of the LORD was consumed.
14And behold, you have risen in your
fathers' stead, a brood of sinful men,
to increase still more the fierce an-
ger of the LORD against Israel! 15For
if you turn away from following him,
he will again abandon them in the
wilderness; and you will destroy all
this people."

16 Then they came near to him, and
said, "We will build sheepfolds here
for our flocks, and cities for our little
ones, 17but we will take up arms, ready
to go before the people of Israel, until
we have brought them to their place;
and our little ones shall live in the for-
tified cities because of the inhabitants
of the land. 18We will not return to our
homes until the people of Israel have
inherited each his inheritance. 19For
we will not inherit with them on the
other side of the Jordan and beyond;
because our inheritance has come to
us on this side of the Jordan to the
east." 20So Moses said to them, "If you
will do this, if you will take up arms to
go before the LORD for the war, 21and
every armed man of you will pass over
the Jordan before the LORD until he
has driven out his enemies from be-
fore him 22and the land is subdued
before the LORD then after that you
shall return and be free of obligation
to the LORD and to Israel; and this
land shall be your possession before
the LORD. 23But if you will not do so,
behold, you have sinned against the
LORD and be sure your sin will find
you out. 24Build cities for your little
ones, and folds for your sheep; and do
what you have promised." 25And the
sons of Gad and the sons of Reuben
said to Moses, "Your servants will
do as my lord commands. 26Our little
ones, our wives, our flocks, and all our
cattle, shall remain there in the cities
of Gilead; 27but your servants will pass
over, every man who is armed for war,
before the LORD to battle, as my lord
orders."

28 So Moses gave command con-
cerning them to Elea´zar the priest,
and to Joshua the son of Nun, and to
the heads of the fathers' houses of the
tribes of the people of Israel. 29And
Moses said to them, "If the sons of
Gad and the sons of Reuben, every
man who is armed to battle before
the LORD will pass with you over the

Jordan and the land shall be subdued
before you, then you shall give them
the land of Gilead for a possession;
30 but if they will not pass over with you
armed, they shall have possessions
among you in the land of Canaan."
31 And the sons of Gad and the sons of
Reuben answered, "As the LORD has
said to your servants, so we will do.
32 We will pass over armed before the
LORD into the land of Canaan, and the
possession of our inheritance shall re-
main with us beyond the Jordan."

33 And Moses gave to them, to the
sons of Gad and to the sons of Reuben
and to the half-tribe of Manas´seh the
son of Joseph, the kingdom of Sihon
king of the Amorites and the kingdom
of Og king of Bashan, the land and its
cities with their territories, the cities
of the land throughout the country.
34 And the sons of Gad built Dibon,
At´aroth, Aro´er, 35 At´roth-sho´phan,
Jazer, Jog´behah, 36 Beth-nim´rah and
Beth-har´an, fortified cities, and folds
for sheep. 37 And the sons of Reuben
built Heshbon, Elea´leh, Kiriatha´im,
38 Nebo, and Ba´al-me´on (their names
to be changed), and Sibmah; and they
gave other names to the cities which
they built. 39 And the sons of Machir
the son of Manas´seh went to Gilead
and took it, and dispossessed the
Amorites who were in it. 40 And Moses
gave Gilead to Machir the son of
Manas´seh, and he settled in it. 41 And
Ja´ir the son of Manas´seh went and
took their villages, and called them
Hav´voth-ja´ir.[a] 42 And Nobah went
and took Kenath and its villages, and
called it Nobah, after his own name.

THE STAGES OF ISRAEL'S JOURNEY FROM EGYPT

33 These are the stages of the peo-
ple of Israel, when they went
forth out of the land of Egypt by their
hosts under the leadership of Moses
and Aaron. 2 Moses wrote down their
starting places, stage by stage, by
command of the LORD and these are
their stages according to their starting
places. 3 They set out from Ram´eses in
the first month, on the fifteenth day
of the first month; on the day after
the passover the people of Israel went
out triumphantly in the sight of all the
Egyptians, 4 while the Egyptians were
burying all their first-born, whom the
LORD had struck down among them;
upon their gods also the LORD execut-
ed judgments.

5 So the people of Israel set out
from Ram´eses, and encamped at
Succoth. 6 And they set out from
Succoth, and encamped at Etham,
which is on the edge of the wilder-
ness. 7 And they set out from Etham,
and turned back to Pi-hahi´roth,
which is east of Ba´al-ze´phon; and
they encamped before Migdol. 8 And
they set out from before Hahi´roth,
and passed through the midst of the
sea into the wilderness, and they
went a three days' journey in the wil-
derness of Etham, and encamped at
Marah. 9 And they set out from Marah,
and came to Elim; at Elim there were
twelve springs of water and seventy
palm trees, and they encamped there.
10 And they set out from Elim, and en-
camped by the Red Sea. 11 And they set
out from the Red Sea, and encamped
in the wilderness of Sin. 12 And they
set out from the wilderness of Sin,
and encamped at Dophkah. 13 And they
set out from Dophkah, and encamp-
ed at Alush. 14 And they set out from
Alush, and encamped at Reph´idim,
where there was no water for the peo-
ple to drink. 15 And they set out from
Reph´idim, and encamped in the wil-
derness of Sinai. 16 And they set out
from the wilderness of Sinai, and en-
camped at Kib´roth-hatta´avah. 17 And
they set out from Kib´roth-hatta´avah,
and encamped at Haze´roth. 18 And
they set out from Haze´roth, and en-
camped at Rithmah. 19 And they set
out from Rithmah, and encamped at
Rim´mon-per´ez. 20 And they set out
from Rim´mon-per´ez, and encamped

[a] That is *the villages of Jair*

at Libnah. 21And they set out from
Libnah, and encamped at Rissah.
22And they set out from Rissah, and
encamped at Kehela´thah. 23And they
set out from Kehela´thah, and en-
camped at Mount Shepher. 24And they
set out from Mount Shepher, and en-
camped at Hara´dah. 25And they set
out from Hara´dah, and encamped at
Makhe´loth. 26And they set out from
Makhe´loth, and encamped at Tahath.
27And they set out from Tahath, and
encamped at Terah. 28And they set out
from Terah, and encamped at Mithkah.
29And they set out from Mithkah, and
encamped at Hashmo´nah. 30And they
set out from Hashmo´nah, and en-
camped at Mose´roth. 31And they set
out from Mose´roth, and encamped
at Bene-ja´akan. 32And they set out
from Bene-ja´akan, and encamped at
Hor-haggid´gad. 33And they set out
from Hor-haggid´gad, and encamp-
ed at Jot´bathah. 34And they set out
from Jot´bathah, and encamped at
Abro´nah. 35And they set out from
Abro´nah, and encamped at E´zion-
ge´ber. 36And they set out from
E´zion-ge´ber, and encamped in the
wilderness of Zin (that is, Kadesh).
37And they set out from Kadesh, and
encamped at Mount Hor, on the edge
of the land of Edom.

38 And Aaron the priest went up
Mount Hor at the command of the
LORD and died there, in the forti-
eth year after the people of Israel
had come out of the land of Egypt,
on the first day of the fifth month.
39And Aaron was a hundred and twen-
ty-three years old when he died on
Mount Hor.

40 And the Canaanite, the king of
Arad, who dwelt in the Negeb in the
land of Canaan, heard of the coming
of the people of Israel.

41 And they set out from Mount
Hor, and encamped at Zalmo´nah.
42And they set out from Zalmo´nah,
and encamped at Punon. 43And they
set out from Punon, and encamped
at Oboth. 44And they set out from
Oboth, and encamped at I´ye-ab´arim,
in the territory of Moab. 45And they
set out from I´yim, and encamped at
Dibon-gad. 46And they set out from
Dibon-gad, and encamped at Al´mon-
diblatha´im. 47And they set out from
Al´mon-diblatha´im, and encamped
in the mountains of Ab´arim, before
Nebo. 48And they set out from the
mountains of Ab´arim, and encamped
in the plains of Moab by the Jordan
at Jericho; 49they encamped by the
Jordan from Beth-jesh´imoth as far
as Abel-shittim in the plains of Moab.

DIRECTIONS FOR THE CONQUEST OF CANAAN

50 And the LORD said to Moses in
the plains of Moab by the Jordan at
Jericho, 51"Say to the people of Israel,
When you pass over the Jordan into
the land of Canaan, 52then you shall
drive out all the inhabitants of the
land from before you, and destroy all
their figured stones, and destroy all
their molten images, and demolish
all their high places; 53and you shall
take possession of the land and settle
in it, for I have given the land to you
to possess it. 54You shall inherit the
land by lot according to your families;
to a large tribe you shall give a large
inheritance, and to a small tribe you
shall give a small inheritance; wherev-
er the lot falls to any man, that shall
be his; according to the tribes of your
fathers you shall inherit. 55But if you
do not drive out the inhabitants of the
land from before you, then those of
them whom you let remain shall be as
pricks in your eyes and thorns in your
sides, and they shall trouble you in
the land where you dwell. 56And I will
do to you as I thought to do to them."

THE BOUNDARIES OF THE LAND

34 The LORD said to Moses, 2"Com-
mand the people of Israel, and say
to them, When you enter the land of
Canaan (this is the land that shall fall
to you for an inheritance, the land of

Canaan in its full extent), 3your south
side shall be from the wilderness of
Zin along the side of Edom, and your
southern boundary shall be from the
end of the Salt Sea on the east; 4and
your boundary shall turn south of
the ascent of Akrab´bim, and cross
to Zin, and its end shall be south of
Ka´desh-bar´nea; then it shall go on
to Ha´zar-ad´dar, and pass along to
Azmon; 5and the boundary shall turn
from Azmon to the Brook of Egypt,
and its termination shall be at the sea.

6 "For the western boundary, you
shall have the Great Sea and its[a] coast;
this shall be your western boundary.

7 "This shall be your northern
boundary: from the Great Sea you
shall mark out your line to Mount
Hor; 8from Mount Hor you shall mark
it out to the entrance of Hamath, and
the end of the boundary shall be at
Zedad; 9then the boundary shall ex-
tend to Ziphron, and its end shall
be at Hazar-enan; this shall be your
northern boundary.

10 "You shall mark out your east-
ern boundary from Hazar-enan to
Shepham; 11and the boundary shall
go down from Shepham to Riblah on
the east side of A´in; and the bound-
ary shall go down, and reach to the
shoulder of the sea of Chin´nereth on
the east; 12and the boundary shall go
down to the Jordan, and its end shall
be at the Salt Sea. This shall be your
land with its boundaries all round."

13 Moses commanded the people
of Israel, saying, "This is the land
which you shall inherit by lot, which
the LORD has commanded to give to
the nine tribes and to the half-tribe;
14for the tribe of the sons of Reuben
by fathers' houses and the tribe of the
sons of Gad by their fathers' houses
have received their inheritance, and
also the half-tribe of Manas´seh; 15the
two tribes and the half-tribe have re-
ceived their inheritance beyond the
Jordan at Jericho eastward, toward
the sunrise."

TRIBAL LEADERS

16 The LORD said to Moses,
17"These are the names of the men
who shall divide the land to you for
inheritance: Elea´zar the priest and
Joshua the son of Nun. 18You shall
take one leader of every tribe, to di-
vide the land for inheritance. 19These
are the names of the men: Of the tribe
of Judah, Caleb the son of Jephun´neh.
20Of the tribe of the sons of Simeon,
Shem´uel the son of Ammi´hud. 21Of
the tribe of Benjamin, Eli´dad the
son of Chislon. 22Of the tribe of the
sons of Dan a leader, Bukki the son
of Jogli. 23Of the sons of Joseph: of the
tribe of the sons of Manas´seh a lead-
er, Han´niel the son of Ephod. 24And
of the tribe of the sons of E´phraim a
leader, Kem´uel the son of Shiphtan.
25Of the tribe of the sons of Zeb´ulun
a leader, Eli-za´phan the son of
Parnach. 26Of the tribe of the sons of
Is´sachar a leader, Pal´tiel the son of
Azzan. 27And of the tribe of the sons
of Asher a leader, Ahi´hud the son of
Shelo´mi. 28Of the tribe of the sons of
Naph´tali a leader, Pedah´el the son
of Ammi´hud. 29These are the men
whom the LORD commanded to divide
the inheritance for the people of Israel
in the land of Canaan."

CITIES FOR THE LEVITES

35 The LORD said to Moses in the
plains of Moab by the Jordan at
Jericho, 2"Command the people of
Israel, that they give to the Levites,
from the inheritance of their posses-
sion, cities to dwell in; and you shall
give to the Levites pasture lands
round about the cities. 3The cities
shall be theirs to dwell in, and their
pasture lands shall be for their cat-
tle and for their livestock and for all
their beasts. 4The pasture lands of
the cities, which you shall give to the
Levites, shall reach from the wall of
the city outward a thousand cubits
all round. 5And you shall measure,
outside the city, for the east side two

[a] Syr: Heb lacks *its*

thousand cubits, and for the south side two thousand cubits, and for the west side two thousand cubits, and for the north side two thousand cubits, the city being in the middle; this shall belong to them as pasture land for their cities. [6]The cities which you give to the Levites shall be the six cities of refuge, where you shall permit the manslayer to flee, and in addition to them you shall give forty-two cities. [7]All the cities which you give to the Levites shall be forty-eight, with their pasture lands. [8]And as for the cities which you shall give from the possession of the people of Israel, from the larger tribes you shall take many, and from the smaller tribes you shall take few; each, in proportion to the inheritance which it inherits, shall give of its cities to the Levites."

CITIES OF REFUGE

9 And the LORD said to Moses, [10]"Say to the people of Israel, When you cross the Jordan into the land of Canaan, [11]then you shall select cities to be cities of refuge for you, that the manslayer who kills any person without intent may flee there. [12]The cities shall be for you a refuge from the avenger, that the manslayer may not die until he stands before the congregation for judgment. [13]And the cities which you give shall be your six cities of refuge. [14]You shall give three cities beyond the Jordan, and three cities in the land of Canaan, to be cities of refuge. [15]These six cities shall be for refuge for the people of Israel, and for the stranger and for the sojourner among them, that any one who kills any person without intent may flee there.

CONCERNING MURDER AND BLOOD REVENGE

16 "But if he struck him down with an instrument of iron, so that he died, he is a murderer; the murderer shall be put to death. [17]And if he struck him down with a stone in the hand, by which a man may die, and he died, he is a murderer; the murderer shall be put to death. [18]Or if he struck him down with a weapon of wood in the hand, by which a man may die, and he died, he is a murderer; the murderer shall be put to death. [19]The avenger of blood shall himself put the murderer to death; when he meets him, he shall put him to death. [20]And if he stabbed him from hatred, or hurled at him, lying in wait, so that he died, [21]or in enmity struck him down with his hand, so that he died, then he who struck the blow shall be put to death; he is a murderer; the avenger of blood shall put the murderer to death, when he meets him.

22 "But if he stabbed him suddenly without enmity, or hurled anything on him without lying in wait, [23]or used a stone, by which a man may die, and without seeing him cast it upon him, so that he died, though he was not his enemy, and did not seek his harm; [24]then the congregation shall judge between the manslayer and the avenger of blood, in accordance with these ordinances; [25]and the congregation shall rescue the manslayer from the hand of the avenger of blood, and the congregation shall restore him to his city of refuge, to which he had fled, and he shall live in it until the death of the high priest who was anointed with the holy oil. [26]But if the manslayer shall at any time go beyond the bounds of his city of refuge to which he fled, [27]and the avenger of blood finds him outside the bounds of his city of refuge, and the avenger of blood slays the manslayer, he shall not be guilty of blood. [28]For the man must remain in his city of refuge until the death of the high priest; but after the death of the high priest the manslayer may return to the *land* of his possession.

29 "And these things shall be for a statute and ordinance to you throughout your generations in all your dwellings. [30]If any one kills a person, the murderer shall be put to death on the

evidence of witnesses; but no person
shall be put to death on the testimony
of one witness. 31Moreover you shall
accept no ransom for the life of a murderer, who is guilty of death; but he
shall be put to death. 32And you shall
accept no ransom for him who has
fled to his city of refuge, that he may
return to dwell in the land before the
death of the high priest. 33You shall
not thus pollute the land in which you
live; for blood pollutes the land, and
no expiation can be made for the land,
for the blood that is shed in it, except
by the blood of him who shed it. 34You
shall not defile the land in which you
live, in the midst of which I dwell; for
I the LORD dwell in the midst of the
people of Israel."

MARRIAGE OF FEMALE HEIRS

36 The heads of the fathers' houses of the families of the sons
of Gilead the son of Machir, son of
Manas´seh, of the fathers' houses of
the sons of Joseph, came near and
spoke before Moses and before the
leaders, the heads of the fathers'
houses of the people of Israel; 2they
said, "The LORD commanded my
lord to give the land for inheritance
by lot to the people of Israel; and my
lord was commanded by the LORD tc
give the inheritance of Zeloph´ehac
our brother to his daughters. 3But i
they are married to any of the son
of the other tribes of the people c
Israel then their inheritance will b
taken from the inheritance of our f
thers, and added to the inheritan
of the tribe to which they belong;
it will be taken away from the lot
our inheritance. 4And when the ju
lee of the people of Israel comes, th
their inheritance will be added to the
inheritance of the tribe to which they
belong; and their inheritance will
be taken from the inheritance of the
tribe of our fathers."

5 And Moses commanded the people of Israel according to the word of
the LORD saying, "The tribe of the
sons of Joseph is right. 6This is what
the LORD commands concerning the
daughters of Zeloph´ehad, 'Let them
marry whom they think best; only,
they shall marry within the family of
the tribe of their father. 7The inheritance of the people of Israel shall
not be transferred from one tribe to
another; for every one of the people
of Israel shall cleave to the inheritance of the tribe of his fathers. 8And
every daughter who possesses an inheritance in any tribe of the people of
Israel shall be wife to one of the family of the tribe of her father, so that
every one of the people of Israel may
possess the inheritance of his fathers.
9So no inheritance shall be transferred
from one tribe to another; for each of
the tribes of the people of Israel shall
cleave to its own inheritance.'"

10 The daughters of Zeloph´ehad
did as the LORD commanded Moses;
11for Mahlah, Tirzah, Hoglah, Milcah, and Noah, the daughters of
Zeloph´ehad, were married to sons
of their father's brothers. 12They were
married into the families of the sons
of Manas´seh the son of Joseph, and
their inheritance remained in the
tribe of the family of their father.

13 These are the commandments
and the ordinances which the LORD
commanded by Moses to the people
of Israel in the plains of Moab by the
Jordan at Jericho.

THE FIFTH BOOK OF MOSES COMMONLY CALLED

DEUTERONOMY

EVENTS AT HOREB RECALLED

1 These are the words that Moses
spoke to all Israel beyond the Jordan
in the wilderness, in the Arabah
over against Suph, between Paran
and Tophel, Laban, Haze´roth, and
Di´zahab. 2It is eleven days' journey
from Horeb by the way of Mount
Se´ir to Ka´desh-bar´nea. 3And in the
fortieth year, on the first day of the
eleventh month, Moses spoke to the
people of Israel according to all that
the LORD had given him in command-
ment to them, 4after he had defeated
Sihon the king of the Amorites, who
lived in Heshbon, and Og the king of
Bashan, who lived in Ash´taroth and
in Ed´re-i. 5Beyond the Jordan, in the
land of Moab, Moses undertook to
explain this law, saying, 6"The LORD
our God said to us in Horeb, 'You have
stayed long enough at this mountain;
7turn and take your journey, and go to
the hill country of the Amorites, and
to all their neighbors in the Arabah,
in the hill country and in the low-
land, and in the Negeb, and by the
seacoast, the land of the Canaanites,
and Lebanon, as far as the great riv-
er, the river Euphra´tes. 8Behold, I
have set the land before you; go in
and take possession of the land which
the LORD swore to your fathers, to
Abraham, to Isaac, and to Jacob, to
give to them and to their descendants
after them.'

APPOINTMENT OF TRIBAL LEADERS

9 "At that time I said to you, 'I
am not able alone to bear you; 10the
LORD your God has multiplied you,
and behold, you are this day as the
stars of heaven for multitude. 11May
the LORD, the God of your fathers,
make you a thousand times as many
as you are, and bless you, as he has
promised you! 12How can I bear alone
the weight and burden of you and your
strife? 13Choose wise, understanding,
and experienced men, according to
your tribes, and I will appoint them
as your heads.' 14And you answered
me, 'The thing that you have spoken
is good for us to do.' 15So I took the
heads of your tribes, wise and expe-
rienced men, and set them as heads
over you, commanders of thousands,
commanders of hundreds, command-
ers of fifties, commanders of tens, and
officers, throughout your tribes. 16And
I charged your judges at that time,
'Hear the cases between your breth-
ren, and judge righteously between a
man and his brother or the alien that
is with him. 17You shall not be partial
in judgment; you shall hear the small
and the great alike; you shall not be
afraid of the face of man, for the judg-
ment is God's; and the case that is too
hard for you, you shall bring to me,
and I will hear it.' 18And I commanded
you at that time all the things that you
should do.

ISRAEL'S REFUSAL TO ENTER THE LAND

19 "And we set out from Horeb,
nd went through all that great and
rrible wilderness which you saw,
the way to the hill country of the
norites, as the LORD our God com-
nded us; and we came to Ka´desh-
´nea. 20And I said to you, 'You
e come to the hill country of the
orites, which the LORD our God
s us. 21Behold, the LORD your God
set the land before you; go up,
possession, as the LORD, the God
our fathers, has told you; do not
or be dismayed.' 22Then all of you
near me, and said, 'Let us send
before us, that they may explore
nd for us, and bring us word
of the way by which we must go
the cities into which we shall

come.' 23The thing seemed good to
me, and I took twelve men of you, one
man for each tribe; 24and they turned
and went up into the hill country, and
came to the Valley of Eshcol and spied
it out. 25And they took in their hands
some of the fruit of the land and
brought it down to us, and brought us
word again, and said, 'It is a good land
which the LORD our God gives us.'

26 "Yet you would not go up, but
rebelled against the command of the
LORD your God; 27and you murmured
in your tents, and said, 'Because the
LORD hated us he has brought us
forth out of the land of Egypt, to give
us into the hand of the Amorites,
to destroy us. 28Whither are we go-
ing up? Our brethren have made our
hearts melt, saying, "The people are
greater and taller than we; the cities
are great and fortified up to heaven;
and moreover we have seen the sons
of the Anakim there."' 29Then I said
to you, 'Do not be in dread or afraid of
them. 30The LORD your God who goes
before you will himself fight for you,
just as he did for you in Egypt before
your eyes, 31and in the wilderness,
where you have seen how the LORD
your God bore you, as a man bears his
son, in all the way that you went until
you came to this place.' 32Yet in spite
of this word you did not believe the
LORD your God, 33who went before
you in the way to seek you out a place
to pitch your tents, in fire by night, to
show you by what way you should go,
and in the cloud by day.

THE PENALTY FOR ISRAEL'S REBELLION

34 "And the LORD heard your
words, and was angered, and he
swore, 35'Not one of these men of this
evil generation shall see the good land
which I swore to give to your fathers,
36except Caleb the son of Jephun´neh;
he shall see it, and to him and to his
children I will give the land upon
which he has trodden, because he
has wholly followed the LORD!' 37The
LORD was angry with me also on your
account, and said, 'You also shall not
go in there; 38Joshua the son of Nun,
who stands before you, he shall en-
ter; encourage him, for he shall cause
Israel to inherit it. 39Moreover your
little ones, who you said would be-
come a prey, and your children, who
this day have no knowledge of good or
evil, shall go in there, and to them I
will give it, and they shall possess it.
40But as for you, turn, and journey into
the wilderness in the direction of the
Red Sea.'

41 "Then you answered me, 'We
have sinned against the LORD; we
will go up and fight, just as the LORD
our God commanded us.' And every
man of you girded on his weapons
of war, and thought it easy to go up
into the hill country. 42And the LORD
said to me, 'Say to them, Do not go up
or fight, for I am not in the midst of
you; lest you be defeated before your
enemies.' 43So I spoke to you, and you
would not hearken; but you rebelled
against the command of the LORD,
and were presumptuous and went
up into the hill country. 44Then the
Amorites who lived in that hill coun-
try came out against you and chased
you as bees do and beat you down
in Se´ir as far as Hormah. 45And you
returned and wept before the LORD;
but the LORD did not hearken to your
voice or give ear to you. 46So you re-
mained at Kadesh many days, the days
that you remained there.

THE DESERT YEARS

2 "Then we turned, and journeyed
into the wilderness in the direc-
tion of the Red Sea, as the LORD told
me; and for many days we went about
Mount Se´ir. 2Then the LORD said to
me, 3'You have been going about this
mountain country long enough; turn
northward. 4And command the peo-
ple, You are about to pass through the
territory of your brethren the sons
of Esau, who live in Se´ir; and they
will be afraid of you. So take good
heed; 5do not contend with them; for

I will not give you any of their land,
no, not so much as for the sole of the
foot to tread on, because I have given
Mount Se´ir to Esau as a possession.
6You shall purchase food from them
for money, that you may eat; and you
shall also buy water of them for mon-
ey, that you may drink. 7For the LORD
your God has blessed you in all the
work of your hands; he knows your
going through this great wilderness;
these forty years the LORD your God
has been with you; you have lacked
nothing.' 8So we went on, away from
our brethren the sons of Esau who live
in Se´ir, away from the Arabah road
from Elath and E´zion-ge´ber.

"And we turned and went in the
direction of the wilderness of Moab.
9And the LORD said to me, 'Do not
harass Moab or contend with them in
battle, for I will not give you any of
their land for a possession, because
I have given Ar to the sons of Lot
for a possession.' 10(The Emim for-
merly lived there, a people great and
many, and tall as the Anakim; 11like
the Anakim they are also known as
Reph´aim, but the Moabites call them
Emim. 12The Horites also lived in Se´ir
formerly, but the sons of Esau dis-
possessed them, and destroyed them
from before them, and settled in their
stead; as Israel did to the land of their
possession, which the LORD gave to
them.) 13'Now rise up, and go over
the brook Zered.' So we went over
the brook Zered. 14And the time from
our leaving Ka´desh-bar´nea until we
crossed the brook Zered was thir-
ty-eight years, until the entire gen-
eration, that is, the men of war, had
perished from the camp, as the LORD
had sworn to them. 15For indeed the
hand of the LORD was against them,
to destroy them from the camp, until
they had perished.

16 "So when all the men of war had
perished and were dead from among
the people, 17the LORD said to me,
18'This day you are to pass over the
boundary of Moab at Ar; 19and when
you approach the frontier of the sons
of Ammon, do not harass them or con-
tend with them, for I will not give you
any of the land of the sons of Ammon
as a possession, because I have given
it to the sons of Lot for a possession.'
20(That also is known as a land of
Reph´aim; Reph´aim formerly lived
there, but the Ammonites call them
Zamzum´mim, 21a people great and
many, and tall as the Anakim; but the
LORD destroyed them before them;
and they dispossessed them, and set-
tled in their stead; 22as he did for the
sons of Esau, who live in Se´ir, when
he destroyed the Horites before them,
and they dispossessed them, and set-
tled in their stead even to this day.
23As for the Avvim, who lived in villag-
es as far as Gaza, the Caph´torim, who
came from Caphtor, destroyed them
and settled in their stead.) 24'Rise up,
take your journey, and go over the val-
ley of the Arnon; behold, I have given
into your hand Sihon the Amorite,
king of Heshbon, and his land; begin
to take possession, and contend with
him in battle. 25This day I will begin
to put the dread and fear of you upon
the peoples that are under the whole
heaven, who shall hear the report of
you and shall tremble and be in an-
guish because of you.'

DEFEAT OF KING SIHON

26 "So I sent messengers from the
wilderness of Ked´emoth to Sihon
the king of Heshbon, with words of
peace, saying, 27'Let me pass through
your land; I will go only by the road,
I will turn aside neither to the right
nor to the left. 28You shall sell me food
for money, that I may eat, and give
me water for money, that I may drink;
only let me pass through on foot, 29as
the sons of Esau who live in Se´ir and
the Moabites who live in Ar did for
me, until I go over the Jordan into the
land which the LORD our God gives to
us.' 30But Sihon the king of Heshbon
would not let us pass by him; for the
LORD your God hardened his spirit

and made his heart obstinate, that he
might give him into your hand, as at
this day. 31And the LORD said to me,
'Behold, I have begun to give Sihon
and his land over to you; begin to take
possession, that you may occupy his
land.' 32Then Sihon came out against
us, he and all his people, to battle at
Jahaz. 33And the LORD our God gave
him over to us; and we defeated him
and his sons and all his people. 34And
we captured all his cities at that time
and utterly destroyed every city, men,
women, and children; we left none re-
maining; 35only the cattle we took as
spoil for ourselves, with the booty of
the cities which we captured. 36From
Aro´er, which is on the edge of the
valley of the Arnon, and from the city
that is in the valley, as far as Gilead,
there was not a city too high for us;
the LORD our God gave all into our
hands. 37Only to the land of the sons
of Ammon you did not draw near, that
is, to all the banks of the river Jabbok
and the cities of the hill country, and
wherever the LORD our God forbade
us.

DEFEAT OF KING OG

3 "Then we turned and went up the
way to Bashan; and Og the king of
Bashan came out against u, he and
all his people, to battle at Ede-i. 2But
the LORD said to me, 'Do notear him;
for I have given him and all h people
and his land into your hand;nd you
shall do to him as you did Sihon
the king of the Amorites, wl dwelt
at Heshbon.' 3So the LORD God
gave into our hand Og also, t king
of Bashan, and all his people; d we
smote him until no survivor left
to him. 4And we took all his cs at
that time—there was not a cityhich
we did not take from them—si cit-
ies, the whole region of Argohe
kingdom of Og in Bashan. 5All se
were cities fortified with high s,
gates, and bars, besides very y
unwalled villages. 6And we uy
destroyed them, as we did to Sihon
the king of Heshbon, destroying every
city, men, women, and children. 7But
all the cattle and the spoil of the cities
we took as our booty. 8So we took the
land at that time out of the hand of the
two kings of the Amorites who were
beyond the Jordan, from the valley
of the Arnon to Mount Hermon 9(the
Sido´nians call Hermon Sir´ion, while
the Amorites call it Senir), 10all the
cities of the tableland and all Gilead
and all Bashan, as far as Sal´ecah and
Ed´re-i, cities of the kingdom of Og
in Bashan. 11(For only Og the king of
Bashan was left of the remnant of the
Reph´aim; behold, his bedstead was a
bedstead of iron; is it not in Rabbah
of the Ammonites? Nine cubits was its
length, and four cubits its breadth, ac-
cording to the common cubit.[a])

12 "When we took possession of
this land at that time, I gave to the
Reubenites and the Gadites the terri-
tory beginning at Aro´er, which is on
the edge of the valley of the Arnon,
and half the hill country of Gilead
with its cities; 13the rest of Gilead,
and all Bashan, the kingdom of Og,
that is, all the region of Argob, I gave
to the half-tribe of Manas´seh. (The
whole of that Bashan is called the
land of Reph´aim. 14Ja´ir the Manas´-
site took all the region of Argob, that
is, Bashan, as far as the border of the
Gesh´urites and the Ma-ac´athites,
and called the villages after his own
name, Hav´voth-ja´ir, as it is to this
day.) 15To Machir I gave Gilead, 16and
to the Reubenites and the Gadites I
gave the territory from Gilead as far as
the valley of the Arnon, with the mid-
dle of the valley as a boundary, as far
over as the river Jabbok, the boundary
of the Ammonites; 17the Arabah also,
with the Jordan as the boundary, from
Chin´nereth as far as the sea of the
Arabah, the Salt Sea, under the slopes
of Pisgah on the east.

18 "And I commanded you at that
time, saying, 'The LORD your God has

[a]Heb *cubit of a man*

given you this land to possess; all your
men of valor shall pass over armed
before your brethren the people of
Israel. 19But your wives, your little
ones, and your cattle (I know that you
have many cattle) shall remain in the
cities which I have given you, 20until
the LORD gives rest to your brethren,
as to you, and they also occupy the
land which the LORD your God gives
them beyond the Jordan; then you
shall return every man to his posses-
sion which I have given you.' 21And I
commanded Joshua at that time, 'Your
eyes have seen all that the LORD your
God has done to these two kings; so
will the LORD do to all the kingdoms
into which you are going over. 22You
shall not fear them; for it is the LORD
your God who fights for you.'

MOSES VIEWS CANAAN FROM PISGAH

23 "And I besought the LORD at
that time, saying, 24'O Lord GOD, thou
hast only begun to show thy servant
thy greatness and thy mighty hand;
for what god is there in heaven or
on earth who can do such works and
mighty acts as thine? 25Let me go over,
I pray, and see the good land beyond
the Jordan, that goodly hill country,
and Lebanon.' 26But the LORD was
angry with me on your account, and
would not hearken to me; and the
LORD said to me, 'Let it suffice you;
speak no more to me of this matter.
27Go up to the top of Pisgah, and lift
up your eyes westward and northward
and southward and eastward, and be-
hold it with your eyes; for you shall
not go over this Jordan. 28But charge
Joshua, and encourage and strengthen
him; for he shall go over at the head of
this people, and he shall put them in
possession of the land which you shall
see.' 29So we remained in the valley
opposite Beth-pe'or.

MOSES COMMANDS OBEDIENCE

4 "And now, O Israel, give heed to the
statutes and the ordinances which I
teach you, and do them; that you may
live, and go in and take possession of
the land which the LORD, the God of
your fathers, gives you. 2You shall not
add to the word which I command
you, nor take from it; that you may
keep the commandments of the LORD
your God which I command you. 3Your
eyes have seen what the LORD did at
Ba'al-pe'or; for the LORD your God
destroyed from among you all the men
who followed the Ba'al of Pe'or; 4but
you who held fast to the LORD your
God are all alive this day. 5Behold, I
have taught you statutes and ordi-
nances, as the LORD my God com-
manded me, that you should do them
in the land which you are entering to
take possession of it. 6Keep them and
do them; for that will be your wisdom
and your understanding in the sight
of the peoples, who, when they hear
all these statutes, will say, 'Surely this
great nation is a wise and understand-
ing people.' 7For what great nation is
there that has a god so near to it as
the LORD our God is to us, whenev-
er we call upon him? 8And what great
nation is there, that has statutes and
ordinances so righteous as all this law
which I set before you this day?

9 "Only take heed, and keep your
soul diligently, lest you forget the
things which your eyes have seen, and
lest they epart from your heart all the
days of yur life; make them known to
your chilren and your children's chil-
dren 10hw on the day that you stood
before e LORD your God at Horeb,
the LO said to me, 'Gather the peo-
ple to , that I may let them hear my
words, that they may learn to fear
me alle days that they live upon the
earthd that they may teach their
childso.' 11And you came near and
stoo the foot of the mountain,
whie mountain burned with fire
to theart of heaven, wrapped in
darks, cloud, and gloom. 12Then
theRD spoke to you out of the
mif the fire; you heard the sound
of s, but saw no form; there was
onoice. 13And he declared to you

his covenant, which he commanded
you to perform, that is, the ten com-
mandments;[a] and he wrote them upon
two tables of stone. 14 And the LORD
commanded me at that time to teach
you statutes and ordinances, that you
might do them in the land which you
are going over to possess.

15 "Therefore take good heed to
yourselves. Since you saw no form
on the day that the LORD spoke to
you at Horeb out of the midst of the
fire, 16 beware lest you act corruptly by
making a graven image for yourselves,
in the form of any figure, the likeness
of male or female, 17 the likeness of any
beast that is on the earth, the likeness
of any winged bird that flies in the air,
18 the likeness of anything that creeps
on the ground, the likeness of any fish
that is in the water under the earth.
19 And beware lest you lift up your eyes
to heaven, and when you see the sun
and the moon and the stars, all the
host of heaven, you be drawn away
and worship them and serve them,
things which the LORD your God has
allotted to all the peoples under the
whole heaven. 20 But the LORD has tak-
en you, and brought you forth out of
the iron furnace, out of Egypt, to be
a people of his own possession, as at
this day. 21 Furthermore the LORD was
angry with me on your account, and
he swore that I should not cross the
Jordan, and that I should not enter the
good land which the LORD your God
gives you for an inheritance. 22 For I
must die in this land, I must not go
over the Jordan; but you shall go over
and take possession of that good land.
23 Take heed to yourselves, lest you
forget the covenant of the LORD your
God, which he made with you, and
make a graven image in the form of
anything which the LORD your God
has forbidden you. 24 For the LORD
your God is a devouring fire, a jealous
God.

25 "When you beget children and
children's children, and have grown
old in the land, if you act corruptly by
making a graven image in the form of
anything, and by doing what is evil in
the sight of the LORD your God, so as
to provoke him to anger, 26 I call heav-
en and earth to witness against you
this day, that you will soon utterly
perish from the land which you are
going over the Jordan to possess; you
will not live long upon it, but will be
utterly destroyed. 27 And the LORD will
scatter you among the peoples, and
you will be left few in number among
the nations where the LORD will drive
you. 28 And there you will serve gods
of wood and stone, the work of men's
hands, that neither see, nor hear, nor
eat, nor smell. 29 But from there you
will seek the LORD your God, and you
will find him, if you search after him
with all your heart and with all your
soul. 30 When you are in tribulation,
and all these things come upon you in
the latter days, you will return to the
LORD your God and obey his voice,
31 for the LORD your God is a merciful
God; he will not fail you or destroy
you or forget the covenant with your
fathers which he swore to them.

32 "For ask now of the days that
are past, which were before you, since
the day that God created man upon
the earth, and ask from one end of
heaven to the other, whether such a
great thing as this has ever happened
or was ever heard of. 33 Did any people
ever hear the voice of a god speaking
out of the midst of the fire, as you
have heard, and still live? 34 Or has any
god ever attempted to go and take a
nation for himself from the midst of
another nation, by trials, by signs,
by wonders, and by war, by a mighty
hand and an outstretched arm, and by
great terrors, according to all that the
LORD your God did for you in Egypt
before your eyes? 35 To you it was
shown, that you might know that the
LORD is God; there is no other besides
him. 36 Out of heaven he let you hear
his voice, that he might discipline you;

[a] Heb *words*

and on earth he let you see his great
fire, and you heard his words out of
the midst of the fire. 37And because
he loved your fathers and chose their
descendants after them, and brought
you out of Egypt with his own pres-
ence, by his great power, 38driving out
before you nations greater and might-
ier than yourselves, to bring you in, to
give you their land for an inheritance,
as at this day; 39know therefore this
day, and lay it to your heart, that the
LORD is God in heaven above and on
the earth beneath; there is no other.
40Therefore you shall keep his statutes
and his commandments, which I com-
mand you this day, that it may go well
with you, and with your children after
you, and that you may prolong your
days in the land which the LORD your
God gives you for ever."*

CITIES OF REFUGE EAST OF THE JORDAN

41*Then Moses set apart three
cities in the east beyond the Jordan,
42that the manslayer might flee there,
who kills his neighbor unintentional-
ly, without being at enmity with him
in time past, and that by fleeing to one
of these cities he might save his life:
43Bezer in the wilderness on the table-
land for the Reubenites, and Ramoth
in Gilead for the Gadites, and Golan in
Bashan for the Manas′sites.

TRANSITION TO THE SECOND ADDRESS

44 This is the law which Moses set
before the children of Israel; 45these
are the testimonies, the statutes, and
the ordinances, which Moses spoke to
the children of Israel when they came
out of Egypt, 46beyond the Jordan in
the valley opposite Beth-pe′or, in the
land of Sihon the king of the Amorites,
who lived at Heshbon, whom Moses
and the children of Israel defeated
when they came out of Egypt. 47And
they took possession of his land and
the land of Og the king of Bashan, the
two kings of the Amorites, who lived
to the east beyond the Jordan; 48from
Aro′er, which is on the edge of the
valley of the Arnon, as far as Mount
Sir′ion[a] (that is, Hermon), 49together
with all the Arabah on the east side
of the Jordan as far as the Sea of the
Arabah, under the slopes of Pisgah.

THE TEN COMMANDMENTS

5 And Moses summoned all Israel,
and said to them, "Hear, O Israel,
the statutes and the ordinances which
I speak in your hearing this day, and
you shall learn them and be careful to
do them. 2The LORD our God made a
covenant with us in Horeb. 3Not with
our fathers did the LORD make this
covenant, but with us, who are all
of us here alive this day. 4The LORD
spoke with you face to face at the
mountain, out of the midst of the fire,
5while I stood between the LORD and
you at that time, to declare to you the
word of the LORD; for you were afraid
because of the fire, and you did not go
up into the mountain. He said:

6 "'I am the LORD your God, who
brought you out of the land of Egypt,
out of the house of bondage.

7 "'You shall have no other gods
before[b] me.

8 "'You shall not make for your-
self a graven image, or any likeness of
anything that is in heaven above, or
that is on the earth beneath, or that
is in the water under the earth; 9you
shall not bow down to them or serve
them; for I the LORD your God am a
jealous God, visiting the iniquity of
the fathers upon the children to the
third and fourth generation of those
who hate me, 10but showing steadfast
love to thousands of those who love
me and keep my commandments.

11 "'You shall not take the name
of the LORD your God in vain: for the
LORD will not hold him guiltless who
takes his name in vain.

12 "'Observe the sabbath day, to
keep it holy, as the LORD your God

[a] Syr: Heb *Sion*
[b] Or *besides*

commanded you. 13 Six days you shall
labor, and do all your work; 14 but the
seventh day is a sabbath to the LORD
your God; in it you shall not do any
work, you, or your son, or your daughter, or your manservant, or your maidservant, or your ox, or your ass, or any
of your cattle, or the sojourner who is
within your gates, that your manservant and your maidservant may rest
as well as you. 15 You shall remember
that you were a servant in the land
of Egypt, and the LORD your God
brought you out thence with a mighty
hand and an outstretched arm; therefore the LORD your God commanded
you to keep the sabbath day.

16 "'Honor your father and your
mother, as the LORD your God commanded you; that your days may be
prolonged, and that it may go well
with you, in the land which the LORD
your God gives you.

17 "'You shall not kill.

18 "'Neither shall you commit
adultery.

19 "'Neither shall you steal.

20 "'Neither shall you bear false
witness against your neighbor.

21 "'Neither shall you covet your
neighbor's wife; and you shall not desire your neighbor's house, his field,
or his manservant, or his maidservant, his ox, or his ass, or anything
that is your neighbor's.'

MOSES THE MEDIATOR OF GOD'S WILL

22 "These words the LORD spoke
to all your assembly at the mountain
out of the midst of the fire, the cloud,
and the thick darkness, with a loud
voice; and he added no more. And he
wrote them upon two tables of stone,
and gave them to me. 23 And when you
heard the voice out of the midst of the
darkness, while the mountain was
burning with fire, you came near to
me, all the heads of your tribes, and
your elders; 24 and you said, 'Behold
the LORD our God has shown us hi
glory and greatness, and we hav
heard his voice out of the midst of th
fire; we have this day seen God speak
with man and man still live. 25 Now
therefore why should we die? For
this great fire will consume us; if we
hear the voice of the LORD our God
any more, we shall die. 26 For who is
there of all flesh, that has heard the
voice of the living God speaking out
of the midst of fire, as we have, and
has still lived? 27 Go near, and hear all
that the LORD our God will say; and
speak to us all that the LORD our God
will speak to you; and we will hear
and do it.'

28 "And the LORD heard your
words, when you spoke to me; and
the LORD said to me, 'I have heard
the words of this people, which they
have spoken to you; they have rightly
said all that they have spoken. 29 Oh
that they had such a mind as this
always, to fear me and to keep all
my commandments, that it might go
well with them and with their children for ever! 30 Go and say to them,
"Return to your tents." 31 But you,
stand here by me, and I will tell you
all the commandment and the statutes and the ordinances which you
shall teach them, that they may do
them in the land which I give them to
possess.' 32 You shall be careful to do
therefore as the LORD your God has
commanded you; you shall not turn
aside to the right hand or to the left.
33 You shall walk in all the way which
the LORD your God has commanded
you, that you may live, and that it
may go well with you, and that you
may live long in the land which you
shall possess.

THE GREAT COMMANDMENT

6 "Now this is the commandment, the
statutes and the ordinances which
the LORD your God commanded me
to teach you, that you may do them in
the land to which you are going over,
to possess it; 2 that you may fear the
LORD your God, you and your son and
your son's son, by keeping all his statutes and his commandments, which

I command you, all the days of your
life; and that your days may be pro-
longed. 3Hear therefore, O Israel, and
be careful to do them; that it may go
well with you, and that you may mul-
tiply greatly, as the LORD, the God of
your fathers, has promised you, in a
land flowing with milk and honey.

4 "Hear, O Israel: The LORD our
God is one LORD;[a] 5and you shall
love the LORD your God with all your
heart, and with all your soul, and
with all your might. 6And these words
which I command you this day shall
be upon your heart; 7and you shall
teach them diligently to your chil-
dren, and shall talk of them when you
sit in your house, and when you walk
by the way, and when you lie down,
and when you rise. 8And you shall
bind them as a sign upon your hand,
and they shall be as frontlets between
your eyes. 9And you shall write them
on the doorposts of your house and on
your gates.*

CAUTION AGAINST DISOBEDIENCE

10 "And when the LORD your God
brings you into the land which he
swore to your fathers, to Abraham, to
Isaac, and to Jacob, to give you, with
great and goodly cities, which you did
not build, 11and houses full of all good
things, which you did not fill, and
cisterns hewn out, which you did not
hew, and vineyards and olive trees,
which you did not plant, and when
you eat and are full, 12then take heed
lest you forget the LORD, who brought
you out of the land of Egypt, out of the
house of bondage. 13You shall fear the
LORD your God; you shall serve him,
and swear by his name. 14You shall not
go after other gods, of the gods of the
peoples who are round about you; 15for
the LORD your God in the midst of
you is a jealous God; lest the anger of
the LORD your God be kindled against
you, and he destroy you from off the
face of the earth.

16 "You shall not put the LORD
your God to the test, as you tested
him at Massah. 17You shall diligently
keep the commandments of the LORD
your God, and his testimonies, and his
statutes, which he has commanded
you. 18And you shall do what is right
and good in the sight of the LORD,
that it may go well with you, and that
you may go in and take possession of
the good land which the LORD swore
to give to your fathers 19by thrusting
out all your enemies from before you,
as the LORD has promised.

20 "When your son asks you in time
to come, 'What is the meaning of the
testimonies and the statutes and the
ordinances which the LORD our God
has commanded you?' 21then you shall
say to your son, 'We were Pharaoh's
slaves in Egypt; and the LORD brought
us out of Egypt with a mighty hand;
22and the LORD showed signs and
wonders, great and grievous, against
Egypt and against Pharaoh and all
his household, before our eyes; 23and
he brought us out from there, that he
might bring us in and give us the land
which he swore to give to our fathers.
24And the LORD commanded us to do
all these statutes, to fear the LORD
our God, for our good always, that he
might preserve us alive, as at this day.
25And it will be righteousness for us, if
we are careful to do all this command-
ment before the LORD our God, as he
has commanded us.'

A CHOSEN PEOPLE

7 "When the LORD your God brings
you into the land which you are
entering to take possession of it,
and clears away many nations before
you, the Hittites, the Gir´gashites,
the Amorites, the Canaanites, the
Per´izzites, the Hivites, and the
Jeb´usites, seven nations greater and
mightier than yourselves, 2and when
the LORD your God gives them over
to you, and you defeat them; then you

[a]*Or the LORD our God, the LORD is one / Or the LORD is our God, the LORD is one / Or the LORD is our God, the LORD alone*

must utterly destroy them; you shall
make no covenant with them, and
show no mercy to them. 3You shall
not make marriages with them, giving
your daughters to their sons or taking
their daughters for your sons. 4For
they would turn away your sons from
following me, to serve other gods;
then the anger of the LORD would be
kindled against you, and he would de-
stroy you quickly. 5But thus shall you
deal with them: you shall break down
their altars, and dash in pieces their
pillars, and hew down their Ashe′rim,
and burn their graven images with
fire.

6 "For you are a people holy to the
LORD your God; the LORD your God
has chosen you to be a people for his
own possession, out of all the peoples
that are on the face of the earth. 7It
was not because you were more in
number than any other people that
the LORD set his love upon you and
chose you, for you were the fewest
of all peoples; 8but it is because the
LORD loves you, and is keeping the
oath which he swore to your fathers,
that the LORD has brought you out
with a mighty hand, and redeemed
you from the house of bondage, from
the hand of Pharaoh king of Egypt.
9Know therefore that the LORD your
God is God, the faithful God who
keeps covenant and steadfast love
with those who love him and keep his
commandments, to a thousand gen-
erations, 10and requites to their face
those who hate him, by destroying
them; he will not be slack with him
who hates him, he will requite him to
his face. 11You shall therefore be care-
ful to do the commandment, and the
statutes, and the ordinances, which I
command you this day.

BLESSINGS FOR OBEDIENCE

12 "And because you hearken
to these ordinances, and keep and
do them, the LORD your God will
keep with you the covenant and the
steadfast love which he swore to your
fathers to keep; 13he will love you,
bless you, and multiply you; he will
also bless the fruit of your body and
the fruit of your ground, your grain
and your wine and your oil, the in-
crease of your cattle and the young of
your flock, in the land which he swore
to your fathers to give you. 14You shall
be blessed above all peoples; there
shall not be male or female barren
among you, or among your cattle.
15And the LORD will take away from
you all sickness; and none of the evil
diseases of Egypt, which you knew,
will he inflict upon you, but he will
lay them upon all who hate you. 16And
you shall destroy all the peoples that
the LORD your God will give over to
you, your eye shall not pity them; nei-
ther shall you serve their gods, for
that would be a snare to you.

17 "If you say in your heart, 'These
nations are greater than I; how can I
dispossess them?' 18you shall not be
afraid of them, but you shall remem-
ber what the LORD your God did to
Pharaoh and to all Egypt, 19the great
trials which your eyes saw, the signs,
the wonders, the mighty hand, and the
outstretched arm, by which the LORD
your God brought you out; so will the
LORD your God do to all the peoples
of whom you are afraid. 20Moreover
the LORD your God will send hornets
among them, until those who are left
and hide themselves from you are de-
stroyed. 21You shall not be in dread of
them; for the LORD your God is in the
midst of you, a great and terrible God.
22The LORD your God will clear away
these nations before you *little by lit-
tle;* you may not make an end of them
at once,[b] lest the wild beasts grow
too numerous for you. 23But the LORD
your God will give them over to you,
and throw them into great confusion,
until they are destroyed. 24And he
will give their kings into your hand,
and you shall make their name perish
from under heaven; not a man shall

[b] Or *quickly*

be able to stand against you, until you
have destroyed them. 25 The graven im-
ages of their gods you shall burn with
fire; you shall not covet the silver or
the gold that is on them, or take it for
yourselves, lest you be ensnared by it;
for it is an abomination to the LORD
your God. 26 And you shall not bring
an abominable thing into your house,
and become accursed like it; you shall
utterly detest and abhor it; for it is an
accursed thing.

A WARNING NOT TO FORGET GOD IN PROSPERITY

8 “All the commandment which I
command you this day you shall be
careful to do, that you may live and
multiply, and go in and possess the
land which the LORD swore to give to
your fathers. 2 And you shall remem-
ber all the way which the LORD your
God has led you these forty years in
the wilderness, that he might humble
you, testing you to know what was in
your heart, whether you would keep
his commandments, or not. 3 And he
humbled you and let you hunger and
fed you with manna, which you did
not know, nor did your fathers know;
that he might make you know that
man does not live by bread alone, but
that man lives by everything that pro-
ceeds out of the mouth of the LORD.
4 Your clothing did not wear out upon
you, and your foot did not swell, these
forty years. 5 Know then in your heart
that, as a man disciplines his son, the
LORD your God disciplines you. 6 So
you shall keep the commandments
of the LORD your God, by walking
in his ways and by fearing him. 7 For
the LORD your God is bringing you
into a good land, a land of brooks of
water, of fountains and springs, flow-
ing forth in valleys and hills, 8 a land
of wheat and barley, of vines and fig
trees and pomegranates, a land of ol-
ive trees and honey, 9 a land in which
you will eat bread without scarci-
ty, in which you will lack nothing, a
land whose stones are iron, and out of
whose hills you can dig copper. 10 And
you shall eat and be full, and you shall
bless the LORD your God for the good
land he has given you.

11 “Take heed lest you forget the
LORD your God, by not keeping his
commandments and his ordinances
and his statutes, which I command
you this day: 12 lest, when you have eat-
en and are full, and have built goodly
houses and live in them, 13 and when
your herds and flocks multiply, and
your silver and gold is multiplied, and
all that you have is multiplied, 14 then
your heart be lifted up, and you for-
get the LORD your God, who brought
you out of the land of Egypt, out of
the house of bondage, 15 who led you
through the great and terrible wilder-
ness, with its fiery serpents and scor-
pions and thirsty ground where there
was no water, who brought you water
out of the flinty rock, 16 who fed you
in the wilderness with manna which
your fathers did not know, that he
might humble you and test you, to
do you good in the end. 17 Beware lest
you say in your heart, ‘My power and
the might of my hand have gotten me
this wealth.’ 18 You shall remember the
LORD your God, for it is he who gives
you power to get wealth; that he may
confirm his covenant which he swore
to your fathers, as at this day. 19 And
if you forget the LORD your God and
go after other gods and serve them
and worship them, I solemnly warn
you this day that you shall surely per-
ish. 20 Like the nations that the LORD
makes to perish before you, so shall
you perish, because you would not
obey the voice of the LORD your God.

THE CONSEQUENCES OF REBELLING AGAINST GOD

9 “Hear, O Israel; you are to pass over
the Jordan this day, to go in to dis-
possess nations greater and mightier
than yourselves, cities great and forti-
fied up to heaven, 2 a people great and
tall, the sons of the Anakim, whom
you know, and of whom you have

heard it said, 'Who can stand before
the sons of Anak?' 3 Know therefore
this day that he who goes over before
you as a devouring fire is the LORD
your God; he will destroy them and
subdue them before you; so you shall
drive them out, and make them per-
ish quickly, as the LORD has promised
you.

4 "Do not say in your heart, after
the LORD your God has thrust them
out before you, 'It is because of my
righteousness that the LORD has
brought me in to possess this land';
whereas it is because of the wicked-
ness of these nations that the LORD is
driving them out before you. 5 Not be-
cause of your righteousness or the up-
rightness of your heart are you going
in to possess their land; but because
of the wickedness of these nations the
LORD your God is driving them out
from before you, and that he may con-
firm the word which the LORD swore
to your fathers, to Abraham, to Isaac,
and to Jacob.

6 "Know therefore, that the LORD
your God is not giving you this good
land to possess because of your righ-
teousness; for you are a stubborn peo-
ple. 7 Remember and do not forget how
you provoked the LORD your God to
wrath in the wilderness; from the day
you came out of the land of Egypt,
until you came to this place, you have
been rebellious against the LORD.
8 Even at Horeb you provoked the LORD
to wrath, and the LORD was so angry
with you that he was ready to destroy
you. 9 When I went up the mountain to
receive the tables of stone, the tables
of the covenant which the LORD made
with you, I remained on the mountain
forty days and forty nights; I neither
ate bread nor drank water. 10 And the
LORD gave me the two tables of stone
written with the finger of God; and
on them were all the words which
the LORD had spoken with you on the
mountain out of the midst of the fire
on the day of the assembly. 11 And at
the end of forty days and forty nights
the LORD gave me the two tables of
stone, the tables of the covenant.
12 Then the LORD said to me, 'Arise,
go down quickly from here; for your
people whom you have brought from
Egypt have acted corruptly; they have
turned aside quickly out of the way
which I commanded them; they have
made themselves a molten image.'

13 "Furthermore the LORD said
to me, 'I have seen this people, and
behold, it is a stubborn people; 14 let
me alone, that I may destroy them
and blot out their name from under
heaven; and I will make of you a na-
tion mightier and greater than they.'
15 So I turned and came down from
the mountain, and the mountain was
burning with fire; and the two ta-
bles of the covenant were in my two
hands. 16 And I looked, and behold,
you had sinned against the LORD
your God; you had made yourselves
a molten calf; you had turned aside
quickly from the way which the LORD
had commanded you. 17 So I took hold
of the two tables, and cast them out
of my two hands, and broke them be-
fore your eyes. 18 Then I lay prostrate
before the LORD as before, forty days
and forty nights; I neither ate bread
nor drank water, because of all the
sin which you had committed, in do-
ing what was evil in the sight of the
LORD, to provoke him to anger. 19 For
I was afraid of the anger and hot dis-
pleasure which the LORD bore against
you, so that he was ready to destroy
you. But the LORD hearkened to me
that time also. 20 And the LORD was so
angry with Aaron that he was ready to
destroy him; and I prayed for Aaron
also at the same time. 21 Then I took
the sinful thing, the calf which you
had made, and burned it with fire and
crushed it, grinding it very small, un-
til it was as fine as dust; and I threw
the dust of it into the brook that de-
scended out of the mountain.

22 "At Tab′erah also, and at
Massah, and at Kib′roth-hatta′avah,
you provoked the LORD to wrath.

23And when the LORD sent you from
Ka´desh-bar´nea, saying, 'Go up and
take possession of the land which I
have given you,' then you rebelled
against the commandment of the
LORD your God, and did not believe
him or obey his voice. 24You have been
rebellious against the LORD from the
day that I knew you.

25 "So I lay prostrate before the
LORD for these forty days and forty
nights, because the LORD had said he
would destroy you. 26And I prayed to
the LORD, 'O Lord GOD, destroy not
thy people and thy heritage, whom
thou hast redeemed through thy
greatness, whom thou hast brought
out of Egypt with a mighty hand.
27Remember thy servants, Abraham,
Isaac, and Jacob; do not regard the
stubbornness of this people, or their
wickedness, or their sin, 28lest the
land from which thou didst bring us
say, "Because the LORD was not able
to bring them into the land which he
promised them, and because he hated
them, he has brought them out to slay
them in the wilderness." 29For they
are thy people and thy heritage, whom
thou didst bring out by thy great pow-
er and by thy outstretched arm.'

THE SECOND PAIR OF TABLETS

10 "At that time the LORD said to me,
'Hew two tables of stone like the
first, and come up to me on the moun-
tain, and make an ark of wood. 2And
I will write on the tables the words
that were on the first tables which
you broke, and you shall put them in
the ark.' 3So I made an ark of acacia
wood, and hewed two tables of stone
like the first, and went up the moun-
tain with the two tables in my hand.
4And he wrote on the tables, as at the
first writing, the ten commandments[a]
which the LORD had spoken to you
on the mountain out of the midst of
the fire on the day of the assembly;
and the LORD gave them to me. 5Then
I turned and came down from the
mountain, and put the tables in the
ark which I had made; and there they
are, as the LORD commanded me.

6 (The people of Israel journeyed
from Be-er´oth Bene-ja´akan[b] to
Mose´rah. There Aaron died, and
there he was buried; and his son
Elea´zar ministered as priest in his
stead. 7From there they journeyed to
Gud´godah, and from Gud´godah to
Jot´bathah, a land with brooks of wa-
ter. 8At that time the LORD set apart
the tribe of Levi to carry the ark of
the covenant of the LORD, to stand
before the LORD to minister to him
and to bless in his name, to this day.
9Therefore Levi has no portion or in-
heritance with his brothers; the LORD
is his inheritance, as the LORD your
God said to him.)

10 "I stayed on the mountain, as
at the first time, forty days and forty
nights, and the LORD hearkened to me
that time also; the LORD was unwill-
ing to destroy you. 11And the LORD
said to me, 'Arise, go on your journey
at the head of the people, that they
may go in and possess the land, which
I swore to their fathers to give them.'

THE ESSENCE OF THE LAW

12 "And now, Israel, what does the
LORD your God require of you, but to
fear the LORD your God, to walk in
all his ways, to love him, to serve the
LORD your God with all your heart
and with all your soul, 13and to keep
the commandments and statutes of
the LORD, which I command you this
day for your good? 14Behold, to the
LORD your God belong heaven and
the heaven of heavens, the earth with
all that is in it; 15yet the LORD set his
heart in love upon your fathers and
chose their descendants after them,
you above all peoples, as at this day.
16Circumcise therefore the foreskin
of your heart, and be no longer stub-
born. 17For the LORD your God is God

[a]Heb *words*
[b]Or *the wells of the Bene-jaakan*

of gods and Lord of lords, the great, the mighty, and the terrible God, who is not partial and takes no bribe. 18He executes justice for the fatherless and the widow, and loves the sojourner, giving him food and clothing. 19Love the sojourner therefore; for you were sojourners in the land of Egypt. 20You shall fear the LORD your God; you shall serve him and cleave to him, and by his name you shall swear. 21He is your praise; he is your God, who has done for you these great and terrible things which your eyes have seen. 22Your fathers went down to Egypt seventy persons; and now the LORD your God has made you as the stars of heaven for multitude.

REWARDS FOR OBEDIENCE

11 "You shall therefore love the LORD your God, and keep his charge, his statutes, his ordinances, and his commandments always. 2And consider this day (since I am not speaking to your children who have not known or seen it), consider the discipline[c] of the LORD your God, his greatness, his mighty hand and his outstretched arm, 3his signs and his deeds which he did in Egypt to Pharaoh the king of Egypt and to all his land; 4and what he did to the army of Egypt, to their horses and to their chariots; how he made the water of the Red Sea overflow them as they pursued after you, and how the LORD has destroyed them to this day; 5and what he did to you in the wilderness, until you came to this place; 6and what he did to Dathan *and Abi'ram* the sons of Eli'ab, son of Reuben; how the earth opened its mouth and swallowed them up, with their households, their tents, and every living thing that followed them, in the midst of all Israel; 7for your eyes have seen all the great work of the LORD which he did.

8 "You shall therefore keep all the commandment which I command you this day, that you may be strong, and go in and take possession of the land which you are going over to possess, 9and that you may live long in the land which the LORD swore to your fathers to give to them and to their descendants, a land flowing with milk and honey. 10For the land which you are entering to take possession of it is not like the land of Egypt, from which you have come, where you sowed your seed and watered it with your feet, like a garden of vegetables; 11but the land which you are going over to possess is a land of hills and valleys, which drinks water by the rain from heaven, 12a land which the LORD your God cares for; the eyes of the LORD your God are always upon it, from the beginning of the year to the end of the year.

13 "And if you will obey my commandments which I command you this day, to love the LORD your God, and to serve him with all your heart and with all your soul, 14he[d] will give the rain for your land in its season, the early rain and the later rain, that you may gather in your grain and your wine and your oil. 15And he[e] will give grass in your fields for your cattle, and you shall eat and be full. 16Take heed lest your heart be deceived, and you turn aside and serve other gods and worship them, 17and the anger of the LORD be kindled against you, and he shut up the heavens, so that there be no rain, and the land yield no fruit, and you perish quickly off the good land which the LORD gives you.

18 "You shall therefore lay up these words of mine *in your heart and in* your soul; and you shall bind them as a sign upon your hand, and they shall be as frontlets between your eyes. 19And you shall teach them to your children, talking of them when you are sitting in your house, and when you are walking by the way, and when you lie down, and when

[c] Or *instruction*
[d] Sam Gk Vg: Heb *I*
[e] Sam Gk Vg: Heb *I*

you rise. 20 And you shall write them
upon the doorposts of your house and
upon your gates, 21 that your days and
the days of your children may be mul-
tiplied in the land which the LORD
swore to your fathers to give them,
as long as the heavens are above the
earth. 22 For if you will be careful to
do all this commandment which I
command you to do, loving the LORD
your God, walking in all his ways,
and cleaving to him, 23 then the LORD
will drive out all these nations before
you, and you will dispossess nations
greater and mightier than yourselves.
24 Every place on which the sole of your
foot treads shall be yours; your terri-
tory shall be from the wilderness and
Lebanon and from the River, the river
Euphra´tes, to the western sea. 25 No
man shall be able to stand against
you; the LORD your God will lay the
fear of you and the dread of you upon
all the land that you shall tread, as he
promised you.

26 "Behold, I set before you this day
a blessing and a curse: 27 the blessing,
if you obey the commandments of the
LORD your God, which I command you
this day, 28 and the curse, if you do not
obey the commandments of the LORD
your God, but turn aside from the way
which I command you this day, to go
after other gods which you have not
known. 29 And when the LORD your
God brings you into the land which
you are entering to take possession of
it, you shall set the blessing on Mount
Geri´zim and the curse on Mount Ebal.
30 Are they not beyond the Jordan, west
of the road, toward the going down of
the sun, in the land of the Canaanites
who live in the Arabah, over against
Gilgal, beside the oak[a] of Moreh? 31 For
you are to pass over the Jordan to go in
to take possession of the land which
the LORD your God gives you; and
when you possess it and live in it, 32 you
shall be careful to do all the statutes
and the ordinances which I set before
you this day.

[a] Gk Syr: See Gen 12:6. Heb *oaks* or *terebinths*

PAGAN SHRINES TO BE DESTROYED

12 "These are the statutes and ordi-
nances which you shall be careful
to do in the land which the LORD, the
God of your fathers, has given you
to possess, all the days that you live
upon the earth. 2 *You shall surely de-
stroy all the places where the nations
whom you shall dispossess served
their gods, upon the high mountains
and upon the hills and under every
green tree; 3 you shall tear down their
altars, and dash in pieces their pillars,
and burn their Ashe´rim with fire;
you shall hew down the graven im-
ages of their gods, and destroy their
name out of that place. 4 You shall not
do so to the LORD your God. 5 But you
shall seek the place which the LORD
your God will choose out of all your
tribes to put his name and make his
habitation there; thither you shall
go, 6 and thither you shall bring your
burnt offerings and your sacrifices,
your tithes and the offering that you
present, your votive offerings, your
freewill offerings, and the firstlings
of your herd and of your flock; 7 and
there you shall eat before the LORD
your God, and you shall rejoice, you
and your households, in all that you
undertake, in which the LORD your
God has blessed you. 8 You shall not
do according to all that we are doing
here this day, every man doing what-
ever is right in his own eyes; 9 for you
have not as yet come to the rest and
to the inheritance which the LORD
your God gives you. 10 But when you go
over the Jordan, and live in the land
which the LORD your God gives you
to inherit, and when he gives you rest
from all your enemies round about,
so that you live in safety, 11 then to
the place which the LORD your God
will choose, to make his name dwell
there, thither you shall bring all that
I command you: your burnt offerings
and your sacrifices, your tithes and
the offering that you present, and all
your votive offerings which you vow

to the LORD. 12And you shall rejoice
before the LORD your God, you and
your sons and your daughters, your
menservants and your maidservants,
and the Levite that is within your
towns, since he has no portion or in-
heritance with you. 13Take heed that
you do not offer your burnt offerings
at every place that you see; 14but at
the place which the LORD will choose
in one of your tribes, there you shall
offer your burnt offerings, and there
you shall do all that I am command-
ing you.

A PRESCRIBED PLACE OF WORSHIP

15 "However, you may slaugh-
ter and eat flesh within any of your
towns, as much as you desire, accord-
ing to the blessing of the LORD your
God which he has given you; the un-
clean and the clean may eat of it, as of
the gazelle and as of the hart. 16Only
you shall not eat the blood; you shall
pour it out upon the earth like water.
17You may not eat within your towns
the tithe of your grain or of your wine
or of your oil, or the firstlings of your
herd or of your flock, or any of your
votive offerings which you vow, or
your freewill offerings, or the offer-
ing that you present; 18but you shall
eat them before the LORD your God
in the place which the LORD your God
will choose, you and your son and
your daughter, your manservant and
your maidservant, and the Levite who
is within your towns; and you shall re-
joice before the LORD your God in all
that you undertake. 19Take heed that
you do not forsake the Levite as long
as you live in your land.

20 "When the LORD your God en-
larges your territory, as he has prom-
ised you, and you say, 'I will eat flesh,'
because you crave flesh, you may eat
as much flesh as you desire. 21If the
place which the LORD your God will
choose to put his name there is too
far from you, then you may kill any
of your herd or your flock, which the
LORD has given you, as I have com-
manded you; and you may eat within
your towns as much as you desire.
22Just as the gazelle or the hart is
eaten, so you may eat of it; the un-
clean and the clean alike may eat of
it. 23Only be sure that you do not eat
the blood; for the blood is the life,
and you shall not eat the life with the
flesh. 24You shall not eat it; you shall
pour it out upon the earth like water.
25You shall not eat it; that all may go
well with you and with your children
after you, when you do what is right in
the sight of the LORD. 26But the holy
things which are due from you, and
your votive offerings, you shall take,
and you shall go to the place which
the LORD will choose, 27and offer your
burnt offerings, the flesh and the
blood, on the altar of the LORD your
God; the blood of your sacrifices shall
be poured out on the altar of the LORD
your God, but the flesh you may eat.
28Be careful to heed all these words
which I command you, that it may go
well with you and with your children
after you for ever, when you do what
is good and right in the sight of the
LORD your God.

WARNING AGAINST IDOLATRY

29 "When the LORD your God cuts
off before you the nations whom you
go in to dispossess, and you dispos-
sess them and dwell in their land,
30take heed that you be not ensnared
to follow them, after they have been
destroyed before you, and that you do
not inquire about their gods, saying,
'How did these nations serve their
gods?—that I also may do likewise.'
31You shall not do so to the LORD
your God; for every abominable thing
which the LORD hates they have done
for their gods; for they even burn their
sons and their daughters in the fire to
their gods.

32 [b]"Everything that I command
you you shall be careful to do; you
shall not add to it or take from it.

[b]Ch 13.1 in Heb

13 "If a prophet arises among you,
or a dreamer of dreams, and gives
you a sign or a wonder, 2and the sign
or wonder which he tells you comes
to pass, and if he says, 'Let us go af-
ter other gods,' which you have not
known, 'and let us serve them,' 3you
shall not listen to the words of that
prophet or to that dreamer of dreams;
for the LORD your God is testing you,
to know whether you love the LORD
your God with all your heart and
with all your soul. 4You shall walk af-
ter the LORD your God and fear him,
and keep his commandments and
obey his voice, and you shall serve
him and cleave to him. 5But that
prophet or that dreamer of dreams
shall be put to death, because he has
taught rebellion against the LORD
your God, who brought you out of
the land of Egypt and redeemed you
out of the house of bondage, to make
you leave the way in which the LORD
your God commanded you to walk.
So you shall purge the evil from the
midst of you.

6 "If your brother, the son of your
mother, or your son, or your daughter,
or the wife of your bosom, or your
friend who is as your own soul, entic-
es you secretly, saying, 'Let us go and
serve other gods,' which neither you
nor your fathers have known, 7some of
the gods of the peoples that are round
about you, whether near you or far
off from you, from the one end of the
earth to the other, 8you shall not yield
to him or listen to him, nor shall your
eye pity him, nor shall you spare him,
nor shall you conceal him; 9but you
shall kill him; your hand shall be first
against him to put him to death, and
afterwards the hand of all the people.
10You shall stone him to death with
stones, because he sought to draw you
away from the LORD your God, who
brought you out of the land of Egypt,
out of the house of bondage. 11And all
Israel shall hear, and fear, and never
again do any such wickedness as this
among you.

12 "If you hear in one of your cit-
ies, which the LORD your God gives
you to dwell there, 13that certain base
fellows have gone out among you and
have drawn away the inhabitants of
the city, saying, 'Let us go and serve
other gods,' which you have not
known, 14then you shall inquire and
make search and ask diligently; and
behold, if it be true and certain that
such an abominable thing has been
done among you, 15you shall surely
put the inhabitants of that city to the
sword, destroying it utterly, all who
are in it and its cattle, with the edge
of the sword. 16You shall gather all its
spoil into the midst of its open square,
and burn the city and all its spoil with
fire, as a whole burnt offering to the
LORD your God; it shall be a heap for
ever, it shall not be built again. 17None
of the devoted things shall cleave to
your hand; that the LORD may turn
from the fierceness of his anger, and
show you mercy, and have compassion
on you, and multiply you, as he swore
to your fathers, 18if you obey the voice
of the LORD your God, keeping all his
commandments which I command
you this day, and doing what is right
in the sight of the LORD your God.

PAGAN PRACTICES FORBIDDEN

14 "You are the sons of the LORD
your God; you shall not cut your-
selves or make any baldness on your
foreheads for the dead. 2For you are
a people holy to the LORD your God,
and the LORD has chosen you to be a
people for his own possession, out of
all the peoples that are on the face of
the earth.

CLEAN AND UNCLEAN FOODS

3 "You shall not eat any abomina-
ble thing. 4These are the animals you
may eat: the ox, the sheep, the goat,
5the hart, the gazelle, the roebuck, the
wild goat, the ibex, the antelope, and
the mountain-sheep. 6Every animal
that parts the hoof and has the hoof
cloven in two, and chews the cud,

among the animals, you may eat. 7 Yet
of those that chew the cud or have the
hoof cloven you shall not eat these:
The camel, the hare, and the rock
badger, because they chew the cud but
do not part the hoof, are unclean for
you. 8 And the swine, because it parts
the hoof but does not chew the cud, is
unclean for you. Their flesh you shall
not eat, and their carcases you shall
not touch.

9 "Of all that are in the waters you
may eat these: Whatever has fins and
scales you may eat. 10 And whatever
does not have fins and scales you shall
not eat; it is unclean for you.

11 "You may eat all clean birds.
12 But these are the ones which you
shall not eat: the eagle, the vulture,
the osprey, 13 the buzzard, the kite, af-
ter their kinds; 14 every raven after its
kind; 15 the ostrich, the nighthawk, the
sea gull, the hawk, after their kinds;
16 the litle owl and the great owl, the
water hen 17 and the pelican, the car-
rion vulture and the cormorant, 18 the
stork, the heron, after their kinds; the
hoopoe and the bat. 19 And all winged
insects are unclean for you; they shall
not be eaten. 20 All clean winged things
you may eat.

21 "You shall not eat anything that
dies of itself; you may give it to the
alien who is within your towns, that
he may eat it, or you may sell it to a
foreigner; for you are a people holy to
the LORD your God. "You shall not
boil a kid in its mother's milk.

REGULATIONS CONCERNING TITHES

22 "You shall tithe all the yield of
your seed, which comes forth from
the field year by year. 23 And before the
LORD your God, in the place which he
will choose, to make his name dwell
there, you shall eat the tithe of your
grain, of your wine, and of your oil,
and the firstlings of your herd and
flock; that you may learn to fear the
LORD your God always. 24 And if the
way is too long for you, so that you are
not able to bring the tithe, when the
LORD your God blesses you, because
the place is too far from you, which
the LORD your God chooses, to set
his name there, 25 then you shall turn
it into money, and bind up the mon-
ey in your hand, and go to the place
which the LORD your God chooses,
26 and spend the money for whatever
you desire, oxen, or sheep, or wine or
strong drink, whatever your appetite
craves; and you shall eat there before
the LORD your God and rejoice, you
and your household. 27 And you shall
not forsake the Levite who is within
your towns, for he has no portion or
inheritance with you.

28 "At the end of every three years
you shall bring forth all the tithe of
your produce in the same year, and
lay it up within your towns; 29 and the
Levite, because he has no portion or
inheritance with you, and the sojourn-
er, the fatherless, and the widow, who
are within your towns, shall come and
eat and be filled; that the LORD your
God may bless you in all the work of
your hands that you do.

LAWS CONCERNING THE SABBATICAL YEAR

15 "At the end of every seven years
you shall grant a release. 2 And
this is the manner of the release: ev-
ery creditor shall release what he has
lent to his neighbor; he shall not exact
it of his neighbor, his brother, because
the LORD'S release has been pro-
claimed. 3 Of a foreigner you may exact
it; but whatever of yours is with your
brother your hand shall release. 4 But
there will be no poor among you (for
the LORD will bless you in the land
which the LORD your God gives you
for an inheritance to possess), 5 if only
you will obey the voice of the LORD
your God, being careful to do all this
commandment which I command you
this day. 6 For the LORD your God will
bless you, as he promised you, and you
shall lend to many nations, but you
shall not borrow; and you shall rule
over many nations, but they shall not
rule over you.

7 “If there is among you a poor
man, one of your brethren, in any of
your towns within your land which
the LORD your God gives you, you
shall not harden your heart or shut
your hand against your poor brother,
8but you shall open your hand to him,
and lend him sufficient for his need,
whatever it may be. 9Take heed lest
there be a base thought in your heart,
and you say, ‘The seventh year, the
year of release is near,’ and your eye
be hostile to your poor brother, and
you give him nothing, and he cry to
the LORD against you, and it be sin in
you. 10You shall give to him freely, and
your heart shall not be grudging when
you give to him; because for this the
LORD your God will bless you in all
your work and in all that you under-
take. 11For the poor will never cease
out of the land; therefore I command
you, You shall open wide your hand to
your brother, to the needy and to the
poor, in the land.

12 “If your brother, a Hebrew man,
or a Hebrew woman, is sold to you, he
shall serve you six years, and in the
seventh year you shall let him go free
from you. 13And when you let him go
free from you, you shall not let him go
empty-handed; 14you shall furnish him
liberally out of your flock, out of your
threshing floor, and out of your wine
press; as the LORD your God has bless-
ed you, you shall give to him. 15You
shall remember that you were a slave in
the land of Egypt, and the LORD your
God redeemed you; therefore I com-
mand you this today. 16But if he says to
you, ‘I will not go out from you,’ be-
cause he loves you and your household,
since he fares well with you, 17then you
shall take an awl, and thrust it through
his ear into the door, and he shall be
your bondman for ever. And to your
bondwoman you shall do likewise. 18It
shall not seem hard to you, when you
let him go free from you; for at half the
cost of a hired servant he has served
you six years. So the LORD your God
will bless you in all that you do.

THE FIRSTBORN OF LIVESTOCK

19 “All the firstling males that are
born of your herd and flock you shall
consecrate to the LORD your God; you
shall do no work with the firstling of
your herd, nor shear the firstling of
your flock. 20You shall eat it, you and
your household, before the LORD your
God year by year at the place which
the LORD will choose. 21But if it has
any blemish, if it is lame or blind, or
has any serious blemish whatever,
you shall not sacrifice it to the LORD
your God. 22You shall eat it within
your towns; the unclean and the clean
alike may eat it, as though it were a
gazelle or a hart. 23Only you shall not
eat its blood; you shall pour it out on
the ground like water.

THE PASSOVER REVIEWED

16 “Observe the month of Abib, and
keep the passover to the LORD
your God; for in the month of Abib
the LORD your God brought you out
of Egypt by night. 2And you shall of-
fer the passover sacrifice to the LORD
your God, from the flock or the herd,
at the place which the LORD will
choose, to make his name dwell there.
3You shall eat no leavened bread with
it; seven days you shall eat it with
unleavened bread, the bread of afflic-
tion—for you came out of the land of
Egypt in hurried flight—that all the
days of your life you may remember
the day when you came out of the land
of Egypt. 4No leaven shall be seen
with you in all your territory for seven
days; nor shall any of the flesh which
you sacrifice on the evening of the
first day remain all night until morn-
ing. 5You may not offer the passover
sacrifice within any of your towns
which the LORD your God gives you;
6but at the place which the LORD your
God will choose, to make his name
dwell in it, there you shall offer the
passover sacrifice, in the evening at
the going down of the sun, at the time
you came out of Egypt. 7And you shall
boil it and eat it at the place which the

LORD your God will choose; and in
the morning you shall turn and go to
your tents. 8For six days you shall eat
unleavened bread; and on the seventh
day there shall be a solemn assembly
to the LORD your God; you shall do no
work on it.

THE FESTIVAL OF WEEKS REVIEWED

9 "You shall count seven weeks;
begin to count the seven weeks from
the time you first put the sickle to
the standing grain. 10Then you shall
keep the feast of weeks to the LORD
your God with the tribute of a free-
will offering from your hand, which
you shall give as the LORD your God
blesses you; 11and you shall rejoice
before the LORD your God, you and
your son and your daughter, your
manservant and your maidservant,
the Levite who is within your towns,
the sojourner, the fatherless, and the
widow who are among you, at the
place which the LORD your God will
choose, to make his name dwell there.
12You shall remember that you were a
slave in Egypt; and you shall be care-
ful to observe these statutes.

THE FESTIVAL OF BOOTHS REVIEWED

13 "You shall keep the feast of
booths seven days, when you make
your ingathering from your threshing
floor and your wine press; 14you shall
rejoice in your feast, you and your son
and your daughter, your manservant
and your maidservant, the Levite, the
sojourner, the fatherless, and the wid-
ow who are within your towns. 15For
seven days you shall keep the feast to
the LORD your God at the place which
the LORD will choose; because the
LORD your God will bless you in all
your produce and in all the work of
your hands, so that you will be alto-
gether joyful.

16 "Three times a year all your
males shall appear before the LORD
your God at the place which he will
choose: at the feast of unleavened
bread, at the feast of weeks, and at
the feast of booths. They shall not ap-
pear before the LORD empty-handed;
17every man shall give as he is able,
according to the blessing of the LORD
your God which he has given you.

MUNICIPAL JUDGES AND OFFICERS

18 "You shall appoint judges and
officers in all your towns which the
LORD your God gives you, according
to your tribes; and they shall judge the
people with righteous judgment. 19You
shall not pervert justice; you shall not
show partiality; and you shall not take
a bribe, for a bribe blinds the eyes of
the wise and subverts the cause of the
righteous. 20Justice, and only justice,
you shall follow, that you may live and
inherit the land which the LORD your
God gives you.

FORBIDDEN FORMS OF WORSHIP

21 "You shall not plant any tree as
an Ashe´rah beside the altar of the
LORD your God which you shall make.
22And you shall not set up a pillar,
which the LORD your God hates.

17 "You shall not sacrifice to the
LORD your God an ox or a sheep in
which is a blemish, any defect what-
ever; for that is an abomination to the
LORD your God.

2 "If there is found among you,
within any of your towns which the
LORD your God gives you, a man or
woman who does what is evil in the
sight of the LORD your God, in trans-
gressing his covenant, 3and has gone
and served other gods and worshiped
them, or the sun or the moon or any
of the host of heaven, which I have
forbidden, 4and it is told you and you
hear of it; then you shall inquire dili-
gently, and if it is true and certain that
such an abominable thing has been
done in Israel, 5then you shall bring
forth to your gates that man or wom-
an who has done this evil thing, and
you shall stone that man or woman to
death with stones. 6On the evidence
of two witnesses or of three witnesses

he that is to die shall be put to death;
a person shall not be put to death
on the evidence of one witness. 7The
hand of the witnesses shall be first
against him to put him to death, and
afterward the hand of all the people.
So you shall purge the evil from the
midst of you.

LEGAL DECISIONS BY PRIESTS AND JUDGES

8 "If any case arises requiring
decision between one kind of homi-
cide and another, one kind of legal
right and another, or one kind of
assault and another, any case with-
in your towns which is too difficult
for you, then you shall arise and go
up to the place which the LORD your
God will choose, 9and coming to the
Levitical priests, and to the judge
who is in office in those days, you
shall consult them, and they shall
declare to you the decision. 10Then
you shall do according to what they
declare to you from that place which
the LORD will choose; and you shall
be careful to do according to all that
they direct you; 11according to the in-
structions which they give you, and
according to the decision which they
pronounce to you, you shall do; you
shall not turn aside from the verdict
which they declare to you, either to
the right hand or to the left. 12The
man who acts presumptuously, by
not obeying the priest who stands
to minister there before the LORD
your God, or the judge, that man
shall die; so you shall purge the evil
from Israel. 13And all the people shall
hear, and fear, and not act presump-
tuously again.

LIMITATIONS OF ROYAL AUTHORITY

14 "When you come to the land
which the LORD your God gives you,
and you possess it and dwell in it, and
then say, 'I will set a king over me, like
all the nations that are round about
me'; 15you may indeed set as king over
you him whom the LORD your God
will choose. One from among your
brethren you shall set as king over
you; you may not put a foreigner over
you, who is not your brother. 16Only he
must not multiply horses for himself,
or cause the people to return to Egypt
in order to multiply horses, since the
LORD has said to you, 'You shall never
return that way again.' 17And he shall
not multiply wives for himself, lest his
heart turn away; nor shall he greatly
multiply for himself silver and gold.

18 "And when he sits on the throne
of his kingdom, he shall write for
himself in a book a copy of this law,
from that which is in charge of the
Levitical priests; 19and it shall be with
him, and he shall read in it all the days
of his life, that he may learn to fear
the LORD his God, by keeping all the
words of this law and these statutes,
and doing them; 20that his heart may
not be lifted up above his brethren,
and that he may not turn aside from
the commandment, either to the right
hand or to the left; so that he may con-
tinue long in his kingdom, he and his
children, in Israel.

PRIVILEGES OF PRIESTS AND LEVITES

18 "The Levitical priests, that is, all
the tribe of Levi, shall have no
portion or inheritance with Israel;
they shall eat the offerings by fire to
the LORD, and his rightful dues. 2They
shall have no inheritance among their
brethren; the LORD is their inher-
itance, as he promised them. 3And
this shall be the priests' due from the
people, from those offering a sacri-
fice, whether it be ox or sheep: they
shall give to the priest the shoulder
and the two cheeks and the stomach.
4The first fruits of your grain, of your
wine and of your oil, and the first of
the fleece of your sheep, you shall give
him. 5For the LORD your God has cho-
sen him out of all your tribes, to stand
and minister in the name of the LORD,
him and his sons for ever.

6 "And if a Levite comes from any
of your towns out of all Israel, where
he lives—and he may come when he

desires—to the place which the LORD
will choose, 7then he may minister in
the name of the LORD his God, like all
his fellow Levites who stand to minis-
ter there before the LORD. 8They shall
have equal portions to eat, besides
what he receives from the sale of his
patrimony.[a]

CHILD-SACRIFICE, DIVINATION, AND MAGIC PROHIBITED

9 "When you come into the land
which the LORD your God gives
you, you shall not learn to follow
the abominable practices of those
nations. 10There shall not be found
among you any one who burns his son
or his daughter as an offering,[b] any
one who practices divination, a sooth-
sayer, or an augur, or a sorcerer, 11or
a charmer, or a medium, or a wizard,
or a necromancer. 12For whoever does
these things is an abomination to the
LORD; and because of these abomi-
nable practices the LORD your God
is driving them out before you. 13You
shall be blameless before the LORD
your God. 14For these nations, which
you are about to dispossess, give heed
to soothsayers and to diviners; but as
for you, the LORD your God has not
allowed you so to do.

A NEW PROPHET LIKE MOSES

15 "The LORD your God will raise
up for you a prophet like me from
among you, from your brethren—him
you shall heed—16just as you desired
of the LORD your God at Horeb on the
day of the assembly, when you said,
'Let me not hear again the voice of the
LORD my God, or see this great fire
any more, lest I die.' 17And the LORD
said to me, 'They have rightly said all
that they have spoken. 18I will raise
up for them a prophet* like you from
among their brethren; and I will put
my words in his mouth, and he shall
speak to them all that I command
him. 19And whoever will not give heed
to my words which he shall speak in
my name, I myself will require it of
him. 20But the prophet who presumes
to speak a word in my name which I
have not commanded him to speak, or
who speaks in the name of other gods,
that same prophet shall die.' 21And
if you say in your heart, 'How may
we know the word which the LORD
has not spoken?'—22when a prophet
speaks in the name of the LORD, if the
word does not come to pass or come
true, that is a word which the LORD
has not spoken; the prophet has spo-
ken it presumptuously, you need not
be afraid of him.

LAWS CONCERNING THE CITIES OF REFUGE

19 "When the LORD your God cuts
off the nations whose land the
LORD your God gives you, and you
dispossess them and dwell in their
cities and in their houses, 2you shall
set apart three cities for you in the
land which the LORD your God gives
you to possess. 3You shall prepare the
roads, and divide into three parts the
area of the land which the LORD your
God gives you as a possession, so that
any manslayer can flee to them.

4 "This is the provision for the
manslayer, who by fleeing there may
save his life. If any one kills his neigh-
bor unintentionally without having
been at enmity with him in time
past—5as when a man goes into the
forest with his neighbor to cut wood,
and his hand swings the axe to cut
down a tree, and the head slips from
the handle and strikes his neighbor
so that he dies—he may flee to one
of these cities and save his life; 6lest
the avenger of blood in hot anger pur-
sue the manslayer and overtake him,
because the way is long, and wound
him mortally, though the man did
not deserve to die, since he was not
at enmity with his neighbor in time
past. 7Therefore I command you, You
shall set apart three cities. 8And if the

[a]Heb obscure
[b]Heb *makes his son or his daughter pass through the fire*

LORD your God enlarges your border,
as he has sworn to your fathers, and
gives you all the land which he prom-
ised to give to your fathers 9provided
you are careful to keep all this com-
mandment, which I command you this
day, by loving the LORD your God and
by walking ever in his ways—then you
shall add three other cities to these
three, 10lest innocent blood be shed in
your land which the LORD your God
gives you for an inheritance, and so
the guilt of bloodshed be upon you.

11 “But if any man hates his neigh-
bor, and lies in wait for him, and at-
tacks him, and wounds him mortally
so that he dies, and the man flees into
one of these cities, 12then the elders
of his city shall send and fetch him
from there, and hand him over to
the avenger of blood, so that he may
die. 13Your eye shall not pity him, but
you shall purge the guilt of innocent
blood[a] from Israel, so that it may be
well with you.

PROPERTY BOUNDARIES

14 “In the inheritance which you will hold in the land that the LORD your God gives you to possess, you shall not remove your neighbor’s landmark, which the men of old have set.

LAW CONCERNING WITNESSES

15 “A single witness shall not pre-
vail against a man for any crime or
for any wrong in connection with any
offense that he has committed; only
on the evidence of two witnesses, or
of three witnesses, shall a charge be
sustained. 16If a malicious witness ris-
es against any man to accuse him of
wrongdoing, 17then both parties to the
dispute shall appear before the LORD,
before the priests and the judges who
are in office in those days; 18the judg-
es shall inquire diligently, and if the
witness is a false witness and has ac-
cused his brother falsely, 19then you
shall do to him as he had meant to do
to his brother; so you shall purge the
evil from the midst of you. 20And the
rest shall hear, and fear, and shall nev-
er again commit any such evil among
you. 21Your eye shall not pity; it shall
be life for life, eye for eye, tooth for
tooth, hand for hand, foot for foot.

RULES OF WARFARE

20 “When you go forth to war against
your enemies, and see horses and
chariots and an army larger than your
own, you shall not be afraid of them;
for the LORD your God is with you,
who brought you up out of the land
of Egypt. 2And when you draw near
to the battle, the priest shall come
forward and speak to the people, 3and
shall say to them, ‘Hear, O Israel, you
draw near this day to battle against
your enemies: let not your heart faint;
do not fear, or tremble, or be in dread
of them; 4for the LORD your God is he
that goes with you, to fight for you
against your enemies, to give you the
victory.’ 5Then the officers shall speak
to the people, saying, ‘What man is
there that has built a new house and
has not dedicated it? Let him go back
to his house, lest he die in the battle
and another man dedicate it. 6And
what man is there that has planted a
vineyard and has not enjoyed its fruit?
Let him go back to his house, lest he
die in the battle and another man en-
joy its fruit. 7And what man is there
that has betrothed a wife and has
not taken her? Let him go back to his
house, lest he die in the battle and an-
other man take her.’ 8And the officers
shall speak further to the people, and
say, ‘What man is there that is fearful
and fainthearted? Let him go back to
his house, lest the heart of his fellows
melt as his heart.’ 9And when the offi-
cers have make an end of speaking to
the people, then commanders shall be
appointed at the head of the people.

10 “When you draw near to a city
to fight against it, offer terms of peace
to it. 11And if its answer to you is peace

[a]Or *the blood of the innocent*

and it opens to you, then all the peo-
ple who are found in it shall do forced
labor for you and shall serve you. 12But
if it makes no peace with you, but
makes war against you, then you shall
besiege it; 13and when the LORD your
God gives it into your hand you shall
put all its males to the sword, 14but the
women and the little ones, the cattle,
and everything else in the city, all its
spoil, you shall take as booty for your-
selves; and you shall enjoy the spoil
of your enemies, which the LORD your
God has given you. 15Thus you shall do
to all the cities which are very far from
you, which are not cities of the nations
here. 16But in the cities of these peo-
ples that the LORD your God gives you
for an inheritance, you shall save alive
nothing that breathes, 17but you shall
utterly destroy them, the Hittites and
the Amorites, the Canaanites and
the Per′izzites, the Hivites and the
Jeb′usites, as the LORD your God has
commanded; 18that they may not teach
you to do according to all their abom-
inable practices which they have done
in the service of their gods, and so to
sin against the LORD your God.

19 "When you besiege a city for a
long time, making war against it in
order to take it, you shall not destroy
its trees by wielding an axe against
them; for you may eat of them, but
you shall not cut them down. Are
the trees in the field men that they
should be besieged by you? 20Only the
trees which you know are not trees
for food you may destroy and cut
down that you may build siegeworks
against the city that makes war with
you, until it falls.

LAW CONCERNING MURDER BY PERSONS UNKNOWN

21 "If in the land which the LORD
your God gives you to possess,
any one is found slain, lying in the
open country, and it is not known
who killed him, 2then your elders
and your judges shall come forth, and
they shall measure the distance to
the cities which are around him that
is slain; 3and the elders of the city
which is nearest to the slain man shall
take a heifer which has never been
worked and which has not pulled in
the yoke. 4And the elders of that city
shall bring the heifer down to a valley
with running water, which is neither
plowed nor sown, and shall break the
heifer's neck there in the valley. 5And
the priests the sons of Levi shall come
forward, for the LORD your God has
chosen them to minister to him and
to bless in the name of the LORD, and
by their word every dispute and every
assault shall be settled. 6And all the
elders of that city nearest to the slain
man shall wash their hands over the
heifer whose neck was broken in the
valley; 7and they shall testify, 'Our
hands did not shed this blood, neither
did our eyes see it shed. 8Forgive, O
LORD, thy people Israel, whom thou
hast redeemed, and set not the guilt
of innocent blood in the midst of thy
people Israel; but let the guilt of blood
be forgiven them.' 9So you shall purge
the guilt of innocent blood from your
midst, when you do what is right in
the sight of the LORD.

FEMALE CAPTIVES

10 "When you go forth to war
against your enemies, and the LORD
your God gives them into your hands,
and you take them captive, 11and see
among the captives a beautiful wom-
an, and you have desire for her and
would take her for yourself as wife,
12then you shall bring her home to
your house, and she shall shave her
head and pare her nails. 13And she
shall put off her captive's garb, and
shall remain in your house and be-
wail her father and her mother a full
month; after that you may go in to her,
and be her husband, and she shall be
your wife. 14Then, if you have no de-
light in her, you shall let her go where
she will; but you shall not sell her for
money, you shall not treat her as a
slave, since you have humiliated her.

THE RIGHT OF THE FIRSTBORN

15 "If a man has two wives, the
one loved and the other disliked, and
they have borne him children, both
the loved and the disliked, and if the
first-born son is hers that is disliked,
16then on the day when he assigns his
possessions as an inheritance to his
sons, he may not treat the son of the
loved as the first-born in preference
to the son of the disliked, who is the
first-born, 17but he shall acknowledge
the first-born, the son of the disliked,
by giving him a double portion of all
that he has, for he is the first issue
of his strength; the right of the first-
born is his.

A REBELLIOUS SON

18 "If a man has a stubborn and
rebellious son, who will not obey
the voice of his father or the voice
of his mother, and, though they
chastise him, will not give heed to
them, 19then his father and his moth-
er shall take hold of him and bring
him out to the elders of his city at
the gate of the place where he lives,
20and they shall say to the elders of
his city, 'This our son is stubborn
and rebellious, he will not obey our
voice; he is a glutton and a drunk-
ard.' 21Then all the men of the city
shall stone him to death with stones;
so you shall purge the evil from your
midst; and all Israel shall hear, and
fear.

MISCELLANEOUS LAWS

22 "And if a man has committed
a crime punishable by death and he
is put to death, and you hang him
on a tree, 23his body shall not re-
main all night upon the tree, but
you shall bury him the same day, for
a hanged man is accursed by God;
you shall not defile your land which
the LORD your God gives you for an
inheritance.

[a]Heb *hide yourself*
[b]Heb *hide yourself*
[c]Heb *become holy*

22 "You shall not see your brother's
ox or his sheep go astray, and
withhold your help[a] from them; you
shall take them back to your brother.
2And if he is not near you, or if you do
not know him, you shall bring it home
to your house, and it shall be with
you until your brother seeks it; then
you shall restore it to him. 3And so
you shall do with his ass; so you shall
do with his garment; so you shall do
with any lost thing of your brother's,
which he loses and you find; you may
not withhold your help. 4You shall not
see your brother's ass or his ox fallen
down by the way, and withhold your
help[b] from them; you shall help him
to lift them up again.

5 "A woman shall not wear any-
thing that pertains to a man, nor shall
a man put on a woman's garment;
for whoever does these things is an
abomination to the LORD your God.

6 "If you chance to come upon
a bird's nest, in any tree or on the
ground, with young ones or eggs and
the mother sitting upon the young or
upon the eggs, you shall not take the
mother with the young; 7you shall
let the mother go, but the young you
may take to yourself; that it may go
well with you, and that you may live
long.

8 "When you build a new house,
you shall make a parapet for your
roof, that you may not bring the guilt
of blood upon your house, if any one
fall from it.

9 "You shall not sow your vineyard
with two kinds of seed, lest the whole
yield be forfeited to the sanctuary,[c]
the crop which you have sown and the
yield of the vineyard. 10You shall not
plow with an ox and an ass together.
11You shall not wear a mingled stuff,
wool and linen together.

12 "You shall make yourself tassels
on the four corners of your cloak with
which you cover yourself.

LAWS CONCERNING SEXUAL RELATIONS

13 “If any man takes a wife, and
goes in to her, and then spurns her,
14and charges her with shameful con-
duct, and brings an evil name upon
her, saying, ‘I took this woman, and
when I came near her, I did not find in
her the tokens of virginity,’ 15then the
father of the young woman and her
mother shall take and bring out the
tokens of her virginity to the elders of
the city in the gate; 16and the father of
the young woman shall say to the el-
ders, ‘I gave my daughter to this man
to wife, and he spurns her; 17and lo,
he has made shameful charges against
her, saying, “I did not find in your
daughter the tokens of virginity.” And
yet these are the tokens of my daugh-
ter’s virginity.’ And they shall spread
the garment before the elders of the
city. 18Then the elders of that city shall
take the man and whip him; 19and
they shall fine him a hundred shekels
of silver, and give them to the father
of the young woman, because he has
brought an evil name upon a virgin
of Israel; and she shall be his wife;
he may not put her away all his days.
20But if the thing is true, that the to-
kens of virginity were not found in the
young woman, 21then they shall bring
out the young woman to the door of
her father’s house, and the men of
her city shall stone her to death with
stones, because she has wrought folly
in Israel by playing the harlot in her
father’s house; so you shall purge the
evil from the midst of you.

22 “If a man is found lying with
the wife of another man, both of them
shall die, the man who *lay with the*
woman, and the woman; so you shall
purge the evil from Israel.

23 “If there is a betrothed virgin,
and a man meets her in the city and
lies with her, 24then you shall bring
them both out to the gate of that city,
and you shall stone them to death with
stones, the young woman because she
did not cry for help though she was in
the city, and the man because he vio-
lated his neighbor’s wife; so you shall
purge the evil from the midst of you.

25 “But if in the open country a
man meets a young woman who is
betrothed, and the man seizes her
and lies with her, then only the man
who lay with her shall die. 26But to
the young woman you shall do noth-
ing; in the young woman there is no
offense punishable by death, for this
case is like that of a man attacking
and murdering his neighbor; 27because
he came upon her in the open coun-
try, and though the betrothed young
woman cried for help there was no
one to rescue her.

28 “If a man meets a virgin who is
not betrothed, and seizes her and lies
with her, and they are found, 29then
the man who lay with her shall give
to the father of the young woman fifty
shekels of silver, and she shall be his
wife, because he has violated her; he
may not put her away all his days.

30 [d]“A man shall not take his fa-
ther’s wife, nor shall he uncover her
who is his father’s.[e]

THOSE EXCLUDED FROM THE ASSEMBLY

23 “He whose testicles are crushed
or whose male member is cut off
shall not enter the assembly of the
LORD.

2 “No bastard shall enter the as-
sembly of the LORD; even to the tenth
generation none of his descendants
shall enter the assembly of the LORD.

3 “No Ammonite or Moabite shall
enter the assembly of the LORD; even
to the tenth generation none belong-
ing to them shall enter the assembly
of the LORD for ever; 4because they did
not meet you with bread and with wa-
ter on the way, when you came forth
out of Egypt, and because they hired
against you Balaam the son of Be´or
from Pethor of Mesopota´mia, to curse
you. 5Nevertheless the LORD your God

[d]Ch 23.1 in Heb
[e]Heb *uncover his father’s skirt*

would not hearken to Balaam; but the
LORD your God turned the curse into
a blessing for you, because the LORD
your God loved you. 6 You shall not
seek their peace or their prosperity all
your days for ever.
7 "You shall not abhor an E´do-
mite, for he is your brother; you shall
not abhor an Egyptian, because you
were a sojourner in his land. 8 The chil-
dren of the third generation that are
born to them may enter the assembly
of the LORD.

SANITARY, RITUAL, AND HUMANITARIAN PRECEPTS

9 "When you go forth against your
enemies and are in camp, then you
shall keep yourself from every evil
thing.
10 "If there is among you any man
who is not clean by reason of what
chances to him by night, then he shall
go outside the camp, he shall not
come within the camp; 11 but when eve-
ning comes on, he shall bathe himself
in water, and when the sun is down,
he may come within the camp.
12 "You shall have a place outside
the camp and you shall go out to it;
13 and you shall have a stick with your
weapons; and when you sit down out-
side, you shall dig a hole with it, and
turn back and cover up your excre-
ment. 14 Because the LORD your God
walks in the midst of your camp, to
save you and to give up your enemies
before you, therefore your camp must
be holy, that he may not see anything
indecent among you, and turn away
from you.
15 "You shall not give up to his
master a slave who has escaped from
his master to you; 16 he shall dwell
with you, in your midst, in the place
which he shall choose within *one of
your towns, where it* pleases him best;
you shall not oppress him.
17 "There shall be no cult prosti-
tute of the daughters of Israel, neither
shall there be a cult prostitute of the
sons of Israel. 18 You shall not bring the
hire of a harlot, or the wages of a dog,[a]
into the house of the LORD your God
in payment for any vow; for both of
these are an abomination to the LORD
your God.
19 "You shall not lend upon in-
terest to your brother, interest on
money, interest on victuals, interest
on anything that is lent for interest.
20 To a foreigner you may lend upon in-
terest, but to your brother you shall
not lend upon interest; that the LORD
your God may bless you in all that you
undertake in the land which you are
entering to take possession of it.
21 "When you make a vow to the
LORD your God, you shall not be slack
to pay it; for the LORD your God will
surely require it of you, and it would
be sin in you. 22 But if you refrain from
vowing, it shall be no sin in you. 23 You
shall be careful to perform what has
passed your lips, for you have volun-
tarily vowed to the LORD your God
what you have promised with your
mouth.
24 "When you go into your neigh-
bor's vineyard, you may eat your fill
of grapes, as many as you wish, but
you shall not put any in your vessel.
25 When you go into your neighbor's
standing grain, you may pluck the
ears with your hand, but you shall not
put a sickle to your neighbor's stand-
ing grain.

LAWS CONCERNING MARRIAGE AND DIVORCE

24 *"When a man takes a wife and
marries her, if then she finds no
favor in his eyes because he has found
some indecency in her, and he writes
her a bill of divorce and puts it in her
hand and sends her out of his house,
and she departs out of his house,
2 and if she goes and becomes anoth-
er man's wife, 3 and the latter husband
dislikes her and writes her a bill of
divorce and puts it in her hand and
sends her out of his house, or if the

[a] Or *sodomite*

latter husband dies, who took her to be his wife, [4]then her former husband, who sent her away, may not take her again to be his wife, after she has been defiled; for that is an abomination before the LORD, and you shall not bring guilt upon the land which the LORD your God gives you for an inheritance.

MISCELLANEOUS LAWS

5 "When a man is newly married, he shall not go out with the army or be charged with any business; he shall be free at home one year, to be happy with his wife whom he has taken.

6 "No man shall take a mill or an upper millstone in pledge; for he would be taking a life in pledge.

7 "If a man is found stealing one of his brethren, the people of Israel, and if he treats him as a slave or sells him, then that thief shall die; so you shall purge the evil from the midst of you.

8 "Take heed, in an attack of leprosy, to be very careful to do according to all that the Levitical priests shall direct you; as I commanded them, so you shall be careful to do. [9]Remember what the LORD your God did to Miriam on the way as you came forth out of Egypt.

10 "When you make your neighbor a loan of any sort, you sh ll not go into his house to fetch his ledge. [11]You shall stand outside, an the man to whom you make the loa shall bring the pledge out to you. [12]d if he is a poor man, you shall not eep in his pledge; [13]when the sun go down, you shall restore to him the p ge that he may sleep in his cloak a bless you; and it shall be righteou ss to you before the LORD your Go

14 "You shall not opp a hired servant who is poor needy, whether he is one of your thren or one of the sojourners who in your land within your towns; u shall give him his hire on the d e earns it, before the sun goes do or he is poor, and sets his heart u t); lest he cry against you to the L and it be sin in you.

16 "The fathers shall not be put to death for the children, nor shall the children be put to death for the fathers; every man shall be put to death for his own sin.

17 "You shall not pervert the justice due to the sojourner or to the fatherless, or take a widow's garment in pledge; [18]but you shall remember that you were a slave in Egypt and the LORD your God redeemed you from there; therefore I command you to do this.

19 "When you reap your harvest in your field, and have forgotten a sheaf in the field, you shall not go back to get it; it shall be for the sojourner, the fatherless, and the widow; that the LORD your God may bless you in all the work of your hands. [20]When you beat your olive trees, you shall not go over the boughs again; it shall be for the sojourner, the fatherless, and the widow. [21]When you gather the grapes of your vineyard, you shall not glean it afterward; it shall be for the sojourner, the fatherless, and the widow. [22]You shall remember that you were a slave in the land of Egypt; therefore I command you to do this.

25 "If there is a dispute between men, and they come into court, and the judges decide between them, acquitting the innocent and condemning the guilty, [2]then if the guilty man deserves to be beaten, the judge shall cause him to lie down and be beaten in his presence with a number of stripes in proportion to his offense. [3]Forty stripes may be given him, but not more; lest, if one should go on to beat him with more stripes than these, your brother be degraded in your sight.

4 "You shall not muzzle an ox when it treads out the grain.

LEVIRATE MARRIAGE

5 "If brothers dwell together, and one of them dies and has no son, the

wife of the dead shall not be married
outside the family to a stranger; her
husband's brother shall go in to her,
and take her as his wife, and per-
form the duty of a husband's brother
to her. 6And the first son whom she
bears shall succeed to the name of his
brother who is dead, that his name
may not be blotted out of Israel. 7And
if the man does not wish to take his
brother's wife, then his brother's wife
shall go up to the gate to the elders,
and say, 'My husband's brother refus-
es to perpetuate his brother's name in
Israel; he will not perform the duty of
a husband's brother to me.' 8Then the
elders of his city shall call him, and
speak to him: and if he persists, say-
ing, 'I do not wish to take her,' 9then
his brother's wife shall go up to him in
the presence of the elders, and pull his
sandal off his foot, and spit in his face;
and she shall answer and say, 'So shall
it be done to the man who does not
build up his brother's house.' 10And
the name of his house[a] shall be called
in Israel, The house of him that had
his sandal pulled off.

VARIOUS COMMANDS

11 "When men fight with one an-
other, and the wife of the one draws
near to rescue her husband from the
hand of him who is beating him, and
puts out her hand and seizes him by
the private parts, 12then you shall cut
off her hand; your eye shall have no
pity.

13 "You shall not have in your bag
two kinds of weights, a large and a
small. 14You shall not have in your
house two kinds of measures, a large
and a small. 15A full and just weight
you shall have, a full and just measure
you shall have; that your days may be
prolonged in the land which the LORD
your God gives you. 16For all who do
such things, all who act dishonestly,
are an abomination to the LORD your
God.

17 "Remember what Am'alek did
to you on the way as you came out of
Egypt, 18how he attacked you on the
way, when you were faint and weary,
and cut off at your rear all who lagged
behind you; and he did not fear God.
19Therefore when the LORD your God
has given you rest from all your ene-
mies round about, in the land which
the LORD your God gives you for an
inheritance to possess, you shall blot
out the remembrance of Am'alek from
under heaven; you shall not forget.

FIRST FRUITS AND TITHES

26 "When you come into the land
which the LORD your God gives
you for an inheritance, and have tak-
en possession of it, and live in it, 2you
shall take some of the first of all the
fruit of the ground, which you harvest
from your land that the LORD your
God gives you, and you shall put it
in a basket, and you shall go to the
place which the LORD your God will
choose, *to* make his name to dwell
there. 3And you shall go to the priest
who is in office at that time, and say
to him, 'I declare this day to the LORD
your God that I have come into the
land which the LORD swore to our
fathers to give us.' 4Then the priest
shall take the basket from your hand,
and set it down before the altar of the
LORD your God.

5 "And you shall make response
before the LORD your God, 'A wander-
ing Aramean was my father; and he
went dow into Egypt and sojourned
there, fe in number; and there he
became nation, great, mighty, and
populou And the Egyptians treated
us harsh and afflicted us, and laid
upon us rd bondage. 7Then we cried
to the RD the God of our fathers,
and th ORD heard our voice, and
saw o ffliction, our toil, and our
oppre n; 8and the LORD brought
us ou Egypt with a mighty hand
and a utstretched arm, with great
terro ith signs and wonders; 9and
he br ht us into this place and gave

[a]Heb *its name*

us this land, a land flowing with milk
and honey. 10 And behold, now I bring
the first of the fruit of the ground,
which thou, O LORD, hast given me.'
And you shall set it down before the
LORD your God, and worship before
the LORD your God; 11 and you shall
rejoice in all the good which the LORD
your God has given to you and to your
house, you, and the Levite, and the so-
journer who is among you.

12 "When you have finished pay-
ing all the tithe of your produce in the
third year, which is the year of tithing,
giving it to the Levite, the sojourner,
the fatherless, and the widow, that
they may eat within your towns and
be filled, 13 then you shall say before
the LORD your God, 'I have removed
the sacred portion out of my house,
and moreover I have given it to the
Levite, the sojourner, the fatherless,
and the widow, according to all thy
commandment which thou hast com-
manded me; I have not transgressed
any of thy commandments, neither
have I forgotten them; 14 I have not eat-
en of the tithe while I was mourning,
or removed any of it while I was un-
clean, or offered any of it to the dead;
I have obeyed the voice of the LORD
my God, I have done according to all
that thou hast commanded me. 15 Look
down from thy holy habitation, from
heaven, and bless thy people Israel
and the ground which thou hast given
us, as thou didst swear to our fathers,
a land flowing with milk and honey.'

CONCLUDING EXHORTATION

16 "This day the LORD your God
commands you to do these *statutes*
and ordinances; you shall therefore
be careful to do them with all your
heart and with all your soul. 17 You
have declared this day concerning the
LORD that he is your God, and that
you will walk in his ways, and keep
his statutes and his commandments
and his ordinances, and will obey his
voice; 18 and the LORD has declared
this day concerning you that you are
a people for his own possession, as he
has promised you, and that you are
to keep all his commandments, 19 that
he will set you high above all nations
that he has made, in praise and in
fame and in honor, and that you shall
be a people holy to the LORD your
God, as he has spoken."

THE INSCRIBED STONES AND ALTAR ON MOUNT EBAL

27 Now Moses and the elders of
Israel commanded the people,
saying, "Keep all the commandment
which I command you this day. 2 And
on the day you pass over the Jordan
to the land which the LORD your
God gives you, you shall set up large
stones, and plaster them with plaster;
3 and you shall write upon them all the
words of this law, when you pass over
to enter the land which the LORD your
God gives you, a land flowing with
milk and honey, as the LORD, the God
of your fathers, has promised you.
4 And when you have passed over the
Jordan, you shall set up these stones,
concerning which I command you this
day, on Mount Ebal, and you shall
plaster them with plaster. 5 And there
you shall build an altar to the LORD
your God, an altar of stones; you shall
lift up no iron tool upon them. 6 You
shall build an altar to the LORD your
God of unhewn[b] stones; and you shall
offer burnt offerings on it to the LORD
your God; 7 and you shall sacrifice
peace offerings, and shall eat there;
and you shall rejoice before the LORD
your God. 8 And you shall write upon
the stones *all the words* of this law
very plainly."

9 And Moses and the Levitical
priests said to all Israel, "Keep silence
and hear, O Israel: this day you have
become the people of the LORD your
God. 10 You shall therefore obey the
voice of the LORD your God, keeping
his commandments and his statutes,
which I command you this day."

[b] Heb *whole*

TWELVE CURSES

11 And Moses charged the people
the same day, saying, 12"When you
have passed over the Jordan, these
shall stand upon Mount Geri´zim to
bless the people: Simeon, Levi, Judah,
Is´sachar, Joseph, and Benjamin. 13And
these shall stand upon Mount Ebal
for the curse: Reuben, Gad, Asher,
Zeb´ulun, Dan, and Naph´tali. 14And
the Levites shall declare to all the men
of Israel with a loud voice:

15 "'Cursed be the man who makes
a graven or molten image, an abomi-
nation to the LORD, a thing made by
the hands of a craftsman, and sets it
up in secret.' And all the people shall
answer and say, 'Amen.'

16 "'Cursed be he who dishonors
his father or his mother.' And all the
people shall say, 'Amen.'

17 "'Cursed be he who removes
his neighbor's landmark.' And all the
people shall say, 'Amen.'

18 "'Cursed be he who misleads a
blind man on the road.' And all the
people shall say, 'Amen.'

19 "'Cursed be he who perverts the
justice due to the sojourner, the fa-
therless, and the widow.' And all the
people shall say, 'Amen.'

20 "'Cursed be he who lies with his
father's wife, because he has uncov-
ered her who is his father's.'[a] And all
the people shall say, 'Amen.'

21 "'Cursed be he who lies with any
kind of beast.' And all the people shall
say, 'Amen.'

22 "'Cursed be he who lies with
his sister, whether the daughter of his
father or the daughter of his mother.'
And all the people shall say, 'Amen.'

23 "'Cursed be he who lies with
his mother-in-law.' And all the people
shall say, 'Amen.'

24 "'Cursed be he who slays his
neighbor in secret.' And all the people
shall say, 'Amen.'

25 "'Cursed be he who takes a
bribe to slay an innocent person.' And
all the people shall say, 'Amen.'

26 "'Cursed be he who does not
confirm the words of this law by do-
ing them.' And all the people shall say,
'Amen.'

BLESSINGS FOR OBEDIENCE

28 "And if you obey the voice of the
LORD your God, being careful
to do all his commandments which I
command you this day, the LORD your
God will set you high above all the
nations of the earth. 2And all these
blessings shall come upon you and
overtake you, if you obey the voice
of the LORD your God. 3Blessed shall
you be in the city, and blessed shall
you be in the field. 4Blessed shall be
the fruit of your body, and the fruit
of your ground, and the fruit of your
beasts, the increase of your cattle,
and the young of your flock. 5Blessed
shall be your basket and your knead-
ing-trough. 6Blessed shall you be
when you come in, and blessed shall
you be when you go out.

7 "The LORD will cause your en-
emies who rise against you to be de-
feated before you; they shall come out
against you one way, and flee before
you seven ways. 8The LORD will com-
mand the blessing upon you in your
barns, and in all that you undertake;
and he will bless you in the land
which the LORD your God gives you.
9The LORD will establish you as a peo-
ple holy to himself, as he has sworn to
you, if you keep the commandments
of the LORD your God, and walk in
his ways. 10And all the peoples of the
earth shall see that you are called by
the name of the LORD; and they shall
be afraid of you. 11And the LORD will
make you abound in prosperity, in the
fruit of your body, and in the fruit of
your cattle, and in the fruit of your
ground, within the land which the
LORD swore to your fathers to give
you. 12The LORD will open to you his
good treasury the heavens, to give the
rain of your land in its season and
to bless all the work of your hands;

[a] Heb *uncovered his father's skirt*

and you shall lend to many nations,
but you shall not borrow. 13 And the
LORD will make you the head, and
not the tail; and you shall tend up-
ward only, and not downward; if you
obey the commandments of the LORD
your God, which I command you this
day, being careful to do them, 14 and if
you do not turn aside from any of the
words which I command you this day,
to the right hand or to the left, to go
after other gods to serve them.

WARNINGS AGAINST DISOBEDIENCE

15 "But if you will not obey the
voice of the LORD your God or be
careful to do all his commandments
and his statutes which I command
you this day, then all these curses
shall come upon you and overtake
you. 16 Cursed shall you be in the city,
and cursed shall you be in the field.
17 Cursed shall be your basket and your
kneading-trough. 18 Cursed shall be
the fruit of your body, and the fruit
of your ground, the increase of your
cattle, and the young of your flock.
19 Cursed shall you be when you come
in, and cursed shall you be when you
go out.

20 "The LORD will send upon you
curses, confusion, and frustration,
in all that you undertake to do, until
you are destroyed and perish quickly,
on account of the evil of your doings,
because you have forsaken me. 21 The
LORD will make the pestilence cleave
to you until he has consumed you
off the land which you are entering
to take possession of it. 22 The LORD
will smite you with consumption, and
with fever, inflammation, and fiery
heat, and with dought,[b] and with
blasting, and with ildew; they shall
pursue you until yo perish. 23 And the
heavens over your hd *shall* be brass,
and the earth undeou shall be iron.
24 The LORD will mal the rain of your
land powder and du from heaven it
shall come down up you until you
are destroyed.

25 "The LORD will cause you to
be defeated before your enemies; you
shall go out one way against them, and
flee seven ways before them; and you
shall be a horror to all the kingdoms
of the earth. 26 And your dead body
shall be food for all birds of the air,
and for the beasts of the earth; and
there shall be no one to frighten them
away. 27 The LORD will smite you with
the boils of Egypt, and with the ulcers
and the scurvy and the itch, of which
you cannot be healed. 28 The LORD will
smite you with madness and blind-
ness and confusion of mind; 29 and you
shall grope at noonday, as the blind
grope in darkness, and you shall not
prosper in your ways; and you shall be
only oppressed and robbed continual-
ly, and there shall be no one to help
you. 30 You shall betroth a wife, and an-
other man shall lie with her; you shall
build a house, and you shall not dwell
in it; you shall plant a vineyard, and
you shall not use the fruit of it. 31 Your
ox shall be slain before your eyes, and
you shall not eat of it; your ass shall be
violently taken away before your face,
and shall not be restored to you; your
sheep shall be given to your enemies,
and there shall be no one to help you.
32 Your sons and your daughters shall
be given to another people, while your
eyes look on and fail with longing for
them all the day; and it shall not be in
the power of your hand to prevent it.
33 A nation which you have not known
shall eat up the fruit of your ground
and of all your labors; and you shall
be only oppressed and crushed con-
tinually; 34 so that you shall be driven
mad by the sight which your eyes shall
see. 35 The LORD will smite you on the
knees and on the legs with grievous
boils of which you cannot be healed,
from the sole of your foot to the crown
of your head.

36 "The LORD will bring you, and
your king whom you set over you, to
a nation that neither you nor your fa-
thers have known; and there you shall

[b] Another reading is *swor*

serve other gods, of wood and stone.
37And you shall become a horror, a
proverb, and a byword, among all the
peoples where the LORD will lead you
away. 38You shall carry much seed into
the field, and shall gather little in;
for the locust shall consume it. 39You
shall plant vineyards and dress them,
but you shall neither drink of the wine
nor gather the grapes; for the worm
shall eat them. 40You shall have olive
trees throughout all your territory,
but you shall not anoint yourself with
the oil; for your olives shall drop off.
41You shall beget sons and daughters,
but they shall not be yours; for they
shall go into captivity. 42All your trees
and the fruit of your ground the locust
shall possess. 43The sojourner who is
among you shall mount above you
higher and higher; and you shall come
down lower and lower. 44He shall lend
to you, and you shall not lend to him;
he shall be the head, and you shall
be the tail. 45All these curses shall
come upon you and pursue you and
overtake you, till you are destroyed,
because you did not obey the voice of
the LORD your God, to keep his com-
mandments and his statutes which he
commanded you. 46They shall be upon
you as a sign and a wonder, and upon
your descendants for ever.

47 "Because you did not serve the
LORD your God with joyfulness and
gladness of heart, by reason of the
abundance of all things, 48therefore
you shall serve your enemies whom the
LORD will send against you, in hunger
and thirst, in nakedness, and in want
of all things; and he will put a yoke
of iron upon your neck, until he has
destroyed you. 49The LORD will bring
a nation against you from afar, from
the end of the earth, as swift as the
eagle flies, a nation whose language
you do not understand, 50a nation of
stern countenance, who shall not re-
gard the person of the old or show
favor to the young, 51and shall eat the
offspring of your cattle and the fruit of
your ground, until you are destroyed;
who also shall not leave you grain,
wine, or oil, the increase of your cattle
or the young of your flock, until they
have caused you to perish. 52They shall
besiege you in all your towns, until
your high and fortified walls, in which
you trusted, come down throughout
all your land; and they shall besiege
you in all your towns throughout all
your land, which the LORD your God
has given you. 53And you shall eat the
offspring of your own body, the flesh
of your sons and daughters, whom the
LORD your God has given you, in the
siege and in the distress with which
your enemies shall distress you. 54The
man who is the most tender and del-
icately bred among you will grudge
food to his brother, to the wife of his
bosom, and to the last of the children
who remain to him; 55so that he will
not give to any of them any of the flesh
of his children whom he is eating, be-
cause he has nothing left him, in the
siege and in the distress with which
your enemy shall distress you in all
your towns. 56The most tender and del-
icately bred woman among you, who
would not venture to set the sole of
her foot upon the ground because she
is so delicate and tender, will grudge
to the husband of her bosom, to her
son and to her daughter, 57her after-
birth that comes out from between her
feet and her children whom she bears,
because she will eat them secretly, for
want of all things, in the siege and in
the distress with which your enemy
shall distress you in your towns.

58 "If you are not careful to do all
the words of this law which are writ-
ten in this book, that you may fear
this glorious and awful name, the
LORD your God, 59then the LORD will
bring on you and your offspring ex-
traordinary afflicons, afflictions se-
vere and lasting, id sicknesses griev-
ous and lasting. And he will bring
upon you agai ll the diseases of
Egypt, which y were afraid of; and
they shall clea to you. 61Every sick-
ness also, and ery affliction which

is not recorded in the book of this law, the LORD will bring upon you, until you are destroyed. 62Whereas you were as the stars of heaven for multitude, you shall be left few in number; because you did not obey the voice of the LORD your God. 63And as the LORD took delight in doing you good and multiplying you, so the LORD will take delight in bringing ruin upon you and destroying you; and you shall be plucked off the land which you are entering to take possession of it. 64And the LORD will scatter you among all peoples, from one end of the earth to the other; and there you shall serve other gods, of wood and stone, which neither you nor your fathers have known. 65And among these nations you shall find no ease, and there shall be no rest for the sole of your foot; but the LORD will give you there a trembling heart, and failing eyes, and a languishing soul; 66your life shall hang in doubt before you; night and day you shall be in dread, and have no assurance of your life. 67In the morning you shall say, 'Would it were evening!' and at evening you shall say, 'Would it were morning!' because of the dread which your heart shall fear, and the sights which your eyes shall see. 68And the LORD will bring you back in ships to Egypt, a journey which I promised that you should never make again; and there you shall offer yourselves for sale to your enemies as male and female slaves, but no man will buy you."

29[a] These are the words of the covenant which the LORD commanded Moses to make *with the people of* Israel in the land of Moab, besides the covenant which he had made with them at Horeb.

THE COVENANT RENEWED IN MOAB

2[b] And Moses summoned all Israel and said to them: "You have seen all that the LORD did before your eyes in the land of Egypt, to Pharaoh and to all his servants and to all his land, 3the great trials which your eyes saw, the signs, and those great wonders; 4but to this day the LORD has not given you a mind to understand, or eyes to see, or ears to hear. 5I have led you forty years in the wilderness; your clothes have not worn out upon you, and your sandals have not worn off your feet; 6you have not eaten bread, and you have not drunk wine or strong drink; that you may know that I am the LORD your God. 7And when you came to this place, Sihon the king of Heshbon and Og the king of Bashan came out against us to battle, but we defeated them; 8we took their land, and gave it for an inheritance to the Reubenites, the Gadites, and the half-tribe of the Manas´sites. 9Therefore be careful to do the words of this covenant, that you may prosper[c] in all that you do.

10 "You stand this day all of you before the LORD your God; the heads of your tribes,[d] your elders, and your officers, all the men of Israel, 11your little ones, your wives, and the sojourner who is in your camp, both he who hews your wood and he who draws your water, 12that you may enter into the sworn covenant of the LORD your God, which the LORD your God makes with you this day; 13that he may establish you this day as his people, and that he may be your God, as he promised you, and as he swore to your fathers, to Abraham, to Isaac, and to Jacob. 14Nor is it with you only that I make this sworn covenant, 15but with him who is not here with us this day as well as with him *who stands* here with us this day before the LORD our God.

16 "You know how we dwelt in the land of Egypt, and how we came through the midst of the nations through which you passed; 17and you

[a]Ch 28.69 in Heb
[b]Ch 29.1 in Heb
[c]Or *deal wisely*
[d]Gk Syr: Heb *your heads, your tribes*

have seen their detestable things,
their idols of wood and stone, of
silver and gold, which were among
them. 18Beware lest there be among
you a man or woman or family or
tribe, whose heart turns away this
day from the LORD our God to go
and serve the gods of those nations;
lest there be among you a root bear-
ing poisonous and bitter fruit, 19one
who, when he hears the words of this
sworn covenant, blesses himself in his
heart, saying, 'I shall be safe, though I
walk in the stubbornness of my heart.'
This would lead to the sweeping away
of moist and dry alike. 20The LORD
would not pardon him, but rather the
anger of the LORD and his jealousy
would smoke against that man, and
the curses written in this book would
settle upon him, and the LORD would
blot out his name from under heaven.
21And the LORD would single him out
from all the tribes of Israel for calam-
ity, in accordance with all the curses
of the covenant written in this book
of the law. 22And the generation to
come, your children who rise up af-
ter you, and the foreigner who comes
from a far land, would say, when they
see the afflictions of that land and the
sicknesses with which the LORD has
made it sick—23the whole land brim-
stone and salt, and a burnt-out waste,
unsown, and growing nothing, where
no grass can sprout, an overthrow like
that of Sodom and Gomor´rah, Admah
and Zeboi´im, which the LORD over-
threw in his anger and wrath—24yea,
all the nations would say, 'Why has
the LORD done thus to this land?
What means the heat of this great an-
ger?' 25Then men would say, 'It is be-
cause they forsook the covenant of the
LORD, the God of their fathers, which
he made with them when he brought
them out of the land of Egypt, 26and
went and served other gods and wor-
shiped them, gods whom they had not
known and whom he had not allotted
to them; 27therefore the anger of the
LORD was kindled against this land,
bringing upon it all the curses written
in this book; 28and the LORD uproot-
ed them from their land in anger and
fury and great wrath, and cast them
into another land, as at this day.'

29 "The secret things belong to the
LORD our God; but the things that are
revealed belong to us and to our chil-
dren for ever, that we may do all the
words of this law.

GOD'S FIDELITY ASSURED

30 "And when all these things come
upon you, the blessing and the
curse, which I have set before you,
and you call them to mind among
all the nations where the LORD your
God has driven you, 2and return to the
LORD your God, you and your chil-
dren, and obey his voice in all that I
command you this day, with all your
heart and with all your soul; 3then the
LORD your God will restore your for-
tunes, and have compassion upon you,
and he will gather you again from all
the peoples where the LORD your God
has scattered you. 4If your outcasts
are in the uttermost parts of heaven,
from there the LORD your God will
gather you, and from there he will
fetch you; 5and the LORD your God
will bring you into the land which
your fathers possessed, that you may
possess it; and he will make you more
prosperous and numerous than your
fathers. 6And the LORD your God will
circumcise your heart and the heart
of your offspring, so that you will
love the LORD your God with all your
heart and with all your soul, that you
may live. 7And the LORD your God
will put all these curses upon your
foes and enemies who persecuted you.
8And you shall again obey the voice of
the LORD, and keep all his command-
ments which I command you this day.
9The LORD your God will make you
abundantly prosperous in all the work
of your hand, in the fruit of your body,
and in the fruit of your cattle, and in
the fruit of your ground; for the LORD
will again take delight in prospering

you, as he took delight in your fathers,
10if you obey the voice of the LORD
your God, to keep his commandments
and his statutes which are written in
this book of the law, if you turn to the
LORD your God with all your heart
and with all your soul.

EXHORTATION TO CHOOSE LIFE

11 "For this commandment which I
command you this day is not too hard
for you, neither is it far off. 12It is not
in heaven, that you should say, 'Who
will go up for us to heaven, and bring
it to us, that we may hear it and do it?'
13Neither is it beyond the sea, that you
should say, 'Who will go over the sea
for us, and bring it to us, that we may
hear it and do it?' 14But the word is
very near you; it is in your mouth and
in your heart, so that you can do it.

15 "See, I have set before you this
day life and good, death and evil. 16If
you obey the commandments of the
LORD your God[a] which I command
you this day, by loving the LORD your
God, by walking in his ways, and by
keeping his commandments and his
statutes and his ordinances, then you
shall live and multiply, and the LORD
your God will bless you in the land
which you are entering to take pos-
session of it. 17But if your heart turns
away, and you will not hear, but are
drawn away to worship other gods and
serve them, 18I declare to you this day,
that you shall perish; you shall not
live long in the land which you are go-
ing over the Jordan to enter and pos-
sess. 19I call heaven and earth to wit-
ness against you this day, that I have
set before you life and death, blessing
and curse; therefor choose life, that
you and your descndants may live,
20loving the LORD yur God, obeying
his voice, and cleavi to him; for that
means life to you ar length of days,
that you may dwell ithe land which
the LORD swore to our fathers, to
Abraham, to Isaac, d to Jacob, to
give them."

JOSHUA BECOMES MOSES' SUCCESSOR

31 So Moses continued to speak
these words to all Israel. 2And
he said to them, "I am a hundred and
twenty years old this day; I am no lon-
ger able to go out and come in. The
LORD has said to me, 'You shall not go
over this Jordan.' 3The LORD your God
himself will go over before you; he
will destroy these nations before you,
so that you shall dispossess them; and
Joshua will go over at your head, as
the LORD has spoken. 4And the LORD
will do to them as he did to Sihon and
Og, the kings of the Amorites, and to
their land, when he destroyed them.
5And the LORD will give them over to
you, and you shall do to them accord-
ing to all the commandment which I
have commanded you. 6Be strong and
of good courage, do not fear or be in
dread of them: for it is the LORD your
God who goes with you; he will not
fail you or forsake you."

7 Then Moses summoned Joshua,
and said to him in the sight of all
Israel, "Be strong and of good cour-
age; for you shall go with this people
into the land which the LORD has
sworn to their fathers to give them;
and you shall put them in possession
of it. 8It is the LORD who goes before
you; he will be with you, he will not
fail you or forsake you; do not fear or
be dismayed."

THE LAW TO BE READ EVERY SEVENTH YEAR

9 And Moses wrote this law, and
gave it to the priests the sons of Levi,
who carried the ark of the covenant
of the LORD, and to all the elders of
Israel. 10And Moses commanded them,
"At the end of every seven years, at
the set time of the year of release, at
the feast of booths, 11when all Israel
comes to appear before the LORD
your God at the place which he will
choose, you shall read this law before
all Israel in their hearing. 12Assemble
the people, men, women, and little

[a]Gk: Heb lacks *If you obe e commandments of the LORD your God*

ones, and the sojourner within your
towns, that they may hear and learn
to fear the LORD your God, and be
careful to do all the words of this law,
13and that their children, who have not
known it, may hear and learn to fear
the LORD your God, as long as you live
in the land which you are going over
the Jordan to possess."

MOSES AND JOSHUA RECEIVE GOD'S CHARGE

14 And the LORD said to Moses,
"Behold, the days approach when you
must die; call Joshua, and present
yourselves in the tent of meeting, that
I may commission him." And Moses
and Joshua went and presented them-
selves in the tent of meeting. 15And
the LORD appeared in the tent in a
pillar of cloud; and the pillar of cloud
stood by the door of the tent.

16 And the LORD said to Moses,
"Behold, you are about to sleep with
your fathers; then this people will rise
and play the harlot after the strange
gods of the land, where they go to be
among them, and they will forsake me
and break my covenant which I have
made with them. 17Then my anger will
be kindled against them in that day,
and I will forsake them and hide my
face from them, and they will be de-
voured; and many evils and troubles
will come upon them, so that they
will say in that day, 'Have not these
evils come upon us because our God
is not among us?' 18And I will surely
hide my face in that day on account of
all the evil which they have done, be-
cause they have turned to other gods.
19Now therefore write this song, and
teach it to the people of Israel; put it
in their mouths, that this song may be
a witness for me against the people of
Israel. 20For when I have brought them
into the land flowing with milk and
honey, which I swore to give to their
fathers, and they have eaten and are
full and grown fat, they will turn to
other gods and serve them, and de-
spise me and break my covenant.
21And when many evils and troubles
have come upon them, this song shall
confront them as a witness (for it will
live unforgotten in the mouths of their
descendants); for I know the purposes
which they are already forming, be-
fore I have brought them into the land
that I swore to give." 22So Moses wrote
this song the same day, and taught it
to the people of Israel.

23 And the LORD commissioned
Joshua the son of Nun and said, "Be
strong and of good courage; for you
shall bring the children of Israel into
the land which I swore to give them: I
will be with you."

24 When Moses had finished writ-
ing the words of this law in a book, to
the very end, 25Moses commanded the
Levites who carried the ark of the cov-
enant of the LORD, 26"Take this book
of the law, and put it by the side of
the ark of the covenant of the LORD
your God, that it may be there for a
witness against you. 27For I know how
rebellious and stubborn you are; be-
hold, while I am yet alive with you, to-
day you have been rebellious against
the LORD; how much more after my
death! 28Assemble to me all the elders
of your tribes, and your officers, that
I may speak these words in their ears
and call heaven and earth to witness
against them. 29For I know that after
my death you will surely act corruptly,
and turn aside from the way which I
have commanded you; and in the days
to come evil will befall you, because
you will do what is evil in the sight
of the LORD, provoking him to anger
through the work of your hands."

THE SON(OF MOSES

30 Then Mosesspoke the words of
this song until thy were finished, in
the ears of all thassembly of Israel:

32 "Give ear, Cheavens, and I will
speak;
and letıe earth hear the
ords of my mouth.
2May my teaing drop as the

rain,
my speech distil as the dew,
as the gentle rain upon the tender grass,
and as the showers upon the herb.
3For I will proclaim the name of the LORD.
Ascribe greatness to our God!
4"The Rock, his work is perfect;
for all his ways are justice.
A God of faithfulness and without iniquity,
just and right is he.
5They have dealt corruptly with him,
they are no longer his children because of their blemish;
they are a perverse and crooked generation.
6Do you thus requite the LORD,
you foolish and senseless people?
Is not he your father, who created you,
who made you and established you?
7Remember the days of old,
consider the years of many generations;
ask your father, and he will show you;
your elders, and they will tell you.
8When the Most High gave to the nations their inheritance,
when he separated the sons of men,
he fixed the bounds of the peoples
*according to the num*ber of the sons of God.[a]
9For the LORD'S portion is his people,
Jacob his allotted heritage.
10"He found him in a desert land,
and in the howling waste of the wilderness;
he encircled him, he cared for him,
he kept him as the apple of his eye.
11Like an eagle that stirs up its nest,
that flutters over its young,
spreading out its wings, catching them,
bearing them on its pinions,
12the LORD alone did lead him,
and there was no foreign god with him.
13He made him ride on the high places of the earth,
and he ate the produce of the field;
and he made him suck honey out of the rock,
and oil out of the flinty rock.
14Curds from the herd, and milk from the flock,
with fat of lambs and rams,
herds of Bashan and goats,
with the finest of the wheat—
and of the blood of the grape you drank wine.
15"But Jesh'urun waxed fat, and kicked;
you waxed fat, you grew thick, you became sleek;
then he forsook God who made him,
and scoffed at the Rock of his salvation.
16They stirred him to jealousy with strange gods;
with abominable practices they provoked him to anger.
17They sacrificed to demons which were no gods,
to gods they had never known,
to new gods that had come in of late,
whom your fathers had never dreaded.
18You were unmindful of the Rock that begot[b] you,

[a] Compare Gk: Heb *Israel*
[b] Or *bore*

and you forgot the God who
gave you birth.
19"The LORD saw it, and spurned
them,
because of the provocation
of his sons and his
daughters.
20And he said, 'I will hide my face
from them,
I will see what their end
will be,
For they are a perverse
generation,
children in whom is no
faithfulness.
21They have stirred me to jealousy
with what is no god;
they have provoked me with
their idols.
So I will stir them to jealousy
with those who are no
people;
I will provoke them with a
foolish nation.
22For a fire is kindled by my anger,
and it burns to the depths of
Sheol,
devours the earth and its
increase,
and sets on fire the
foundations of the
mountains.
23"'And I will heap evils upon
them;
I will spend my arrows upon
them;
24they shall be wasted with
hunger,
and devoured with burning
heat
and poisonous pestilence;
and I will send the teeth of
beasts against them,
with venom of crawling
things of the dust.
25In the open the sword shall
bereave,
and in the chambers shall be
terror,
destroying both young man and
virgin,
the sucking child with the
man of gray hairs.
26I would have said, "I will scatter
them afar,
I will make the remem-
brance of them cease
from among men,"
27had I not feared provocation by
the enemy,
lest their adversaries should
judge amiss,
lest they should say, "Our hand
is triumphant,
the LORD has not wrought
all this.'"
28"For they are a nation void of
counsel,
and there is no understand-
ing in them.
29If they were wise, they would
understand this,
they would discern their
latter end!
30How should one chase a
thousand,
and two put ten thousand to
flight,
unless their Rock had sold
them,
and the LORD had given
them up?
31For their rock is not as our Rock,
even our enemies themselves
being judges.
32For their vine comes from the
vine of Sodom,
and from the fields of
Gomor'rah;
their grapes are grapes of
poison,
their clusters are bitter;
33their wine is the poison of
serpents,
and the cruel venom of asps.
34"Is not this laid up in store with
me,
sealed up in my treasuries?
35*Vengeance* is mine, and
recompense,
for the time when their foot
shall slip;
for the day of their calamity is
at hand,

and their doom comes
swiftly.
36For the LORD will vindicate his
people
and have compassion on his
servants,
when he sees that their power
is gone,
and there is none remaining,
bond or free.
37Then he will say, 'Where are
their gods,
the rock in which they took
refuge,
38who ate the fat of their
sacrifices,
and drank the wine of their
drink offering?
Let them rise up and help you,
let them be your protection!
39"'See now that I, even I, am he,
and there is no god beside
me;
I kill and I make alive;
I wound and I heal;
and there is none that can
deliver out of my
hand.
40For I lift up my hand to heaven,
and swear, As I live for ever,
41if I whet my glittering sword,[a]
and my hand takes hold on
judgment,
I will take vengeance on my
adversaries,
and will requite those who
hate me.
42I will make my arrows drunk
with blood,
and my sword shall devour
flesh—
with the blood ofhe slain and
the captiv,
from the long-lired heads
of the emy.'
43"Praise his people, you
nations;
for he avenges blood of
his servs,
and takes vengeance on his
adversaries,
and makes expiation for the
land of his people."[b]

44 Moses came and recited all the
words of this song in the hearing of
the people, he and Joshua[c] the son of
Nun. 45And when Moses had finished
speaking all these words to all Israel,
46he said to them, "Lay to heart all the
words which I enjoin upon you this
day, that you may command them to
your children, that they may be care-
ful to do all the words of this law. 47For
it is no trifle for you, but it is your life,
and thereby you shall live long in the
land which you are going over the
Jordan to possess."

MOSES' DEATH FORETOLD

48 And the LORD said to Moses
that very day, 49"Ascend this mountain
of the Ab'arim, Mount Nebo, which is
in the land of Moab, opposite Jericho;
and view the land of Canaan, which I
give to the people of Israel for a pos-
session; 50and die on the mountain
which you ascend, and be gathered
to your people, as Aaron your brother
died in Mount Hor and was gathered
to his people; 51because you broke faith
with me in the midst of the people of
Israel at the waters of Mer'i-bath-
ka'desh, in the wilderness of Zin; be-
cause you did not revere me as holy in
the midst of the people of Israel. 52For
you shall see the land before you; but
you shall not go there, into the land
which I give to the people of Israel."

MOSES' FINAL BLESSING ON ISRAEL

33 This is the blessing with which
Moses the man of God blessed
the children of Israel before his death.
2He said,

"The LORD came from Sinai,
and dawned from Se'ir upon
us;[d]
he shone forth from Mount

[a] Heb *the lightning of my swor*
[b] Gk Vg: Heb *his land his peop*
[c] Gk Syr Vg: Heb *Hoshea*
[d] Gk Syr Vg: Heb *them*

Paran,
he came from the ten thousands of holy ones,
with flaming fire[a] at his right hand.
3 Yea, he loved his people;[b]
all those consecrated to him were in his[c] hand;
so they followed[d] in thy steps,
receiving direction from thee,
4 when Moses commanded us a law,
as a possession for the assembly of Jacob.
5 Thus the LORD became king in Jesh´urun,
when the heads of the people were gathered,
all the tribes of Israel together.
6 "Let Reuben live, and not die,
nor let his men be few."
7 And this he said of Judah:
"Hear, O LORD, the voice of Judah,
and bring him in to his people.
With thy hands contend[e] for him,
and be a help against his adversaries."
8 And of Levi he said,
"Give to Levi[f] thy Thummim,
and thy Urim to thy godly one,
whom thou didst test at Massah,
with whom thou didst strive at the waters of Mer´ibah;
9 who said of his father and mother,
'I regard them not';
he disowned his brothers,
and ignored his children.
For they observed thy word,
and kept thy covenant.
10 They shall teach Jacob thy ordinances,
and Israel thy law;
they shall put incense before thee,
and whole burnt offering upon thy altar.
11 Bless, O LORD, his substance,
and accept the work of his hands;
crush the loins of his adversaries,
of those that hate him, that they rise not again."
12 Of Benjamin he said,
"The beloved of the LORD,
he dwells in safety by him;
he encompasses him all the day long,
and makes his dwelling between his shoulders."
13 And of Joseph he said,
"Blessed by the LORD be his land,
with the choicest gifts of heaven above,[g]
and of the deep that couches beneath,
14 with the choicest fruits of the sun,
and the rich yield of the months,
15 with the finest produce of the ancient mountains,
and the abundance of the everlasting hills,
16 with the best gifts of the earth and its fulness,
and the favor of him that dwelt in the bush.
Let these come upon the head of Joseph,
and upon the crown of the head of him that is prince among his brothers.
17 His firstling bull has majesty,

[a] The meaning of the Hebrew word is uncertain
[b] Gk: Heb *peoples*
[c] Heb *thy*
[d] The meaning of the Hebrew word is uncertain
[e] Cn: Heb *with his hands he contended*
[f] Gk: Heb lacks *Give to Levi*
[g] Two Heb Mss and Tg: Heb *with the dew*

and his horns are the horns
of a wild ox;
with them he shall push the
peoples,
all of them, to the ends of
the earth;
such are the ten thousands of
E´phraim,
and such are the thousands
of Manas´seh."
18And of Zeb´ulun he said,
"Rejoice, Zeb´ulun, in your
going out;
and Is´sachar, in your tents.
19They shall call peoples to their
mountain;
there they offer right
sacrifices;
for they suck the affluence of
the seas
and the hidden treasures of
the sand."
20And of Gad he said,
"Blessed be he who enlarges
Gad!
Gad couches like a lion,
he tears the arm, and the
crown of the head.
21He chose the best of the land for
himself,
for there a commander's por-
tion was reserved;
and he came to the heads of the
people,
with Israel he executed the
commands
and just decrees of the
LORD."
22And of Dan he said,
"Dan is a lion's whelp,
that leaps forth from
Bashan."
23And of Naph´tali he said,
"O Naph´tali, satisfied with
favor,
and full of the blessing of
the LORD,
possess the lake and the
south."
24And of Asher he said,
"Blessed above sons be Asher;
let him be the favorite of his
brothers,
and let him dip his foot in
oil.
25Your bars shall be iron and
bronze;
and as your days, so shall
your strength be.
26"There is none like God, O
Jesh´urun,
who rides through the heav-
ens to your help,
and in his majesty through
the skies.
27The eternal God is your dwelling
place,
and underneath are the
everlasting arms.
And he thrust out the enemy
before you,
and said, Destroy.
28So Israel dwelt in safety,
the fountain of Jacob alone,
in a land of grain and wine;
yea, his heavens drop down
dew.
29Happy are you, O Israel! Who is
like you,
a people saved by the LORD,
the shield of your help,
and the sword of your
triumph!
Your enemies shall come fawn-
ing to you;
and you shall tread upon
their high places."

MOSES DIES AND IS BURIED IN THE LAND OF MOAB

34 And Moses went up from the
plains of Moab to Mount Nebo,
to the top of Pisgah, which is opposite
Jericho. *And the LORD showed him*
all the land, Gilead as far as Dan, 2all
Naph´tali, the land of E´phraim and
Manas´seh, all the land of Judah as far
as the western sea, 3the Negeb, and
the Plain, that is, the valley of Jericho
the city of palm trees, as far as Zo´ar.
4And the LORD said to him, "This is
the land of which I swore to Abraham,
to Isaac, and to Jacob, 'I will give it to
your descendants.' I have let you see

it with your eyes, but you shall not
go over there." 5So Moses the servant
of the LORD died there in the land of
Moab, according to the word of the
LORD, 6and he buried him in the val-
ley in the land of Moab opposite Beth-
pe´or; but no man knows the place of
his burial to this day. 7Moses was a
hundred and twenty years old when
he died; his eye was not dim, nor his
natural force abated. 8And the people
of Israel wept for Moses in the plains
of Moab thirty days; then the days
of weeping and mourning for Moses
were ended.

9 And Joshua the son of Nun was
full of the spirit of wisdom, for Moses
had laid his hands upon him; so the
people of Israel obeyed him, and did
as the LORD had commanded Moses.
10And there has not arisen a prophet
since in Israel like Moses, whom the
LORD knew face to face, 11none like
him for all the signs and the wonders
which the LORD sent him to do in the
land of Egypt, to Pharaoh and to all
his servants and to all his land, 12and
for all the mighty power and all the
great and terrible deeds which Moses
wrought in the sight of all Israel.

THE BOOK OF JOSHUA

GOD'S COMMISSION TO JOSHUA

1 After the death of Moses the ser-
vant of the LORD, the LORD said to
Joshua the son of Nun, Moses' minis-
ter, 2 "Moses my servant is dead; now
therefore arise, go over this Jordan,
you and all this people, into the land
which I am giving to them, to the
people of Israel. 3 Every place that
the sole of your foot will tread upon
I have given to you, as I promised to
Moses. 4 From the wilderness and this
Lebanon as far as the great river, the
river Euphra´tes, all the land of the
Hittites to the Great Sea toward the
going down of the sun shall be your
territory. 5 No man shall be able to
stand before you all the days of your
life; as I was with Moses, so I will be
with you; I will not fail you or forsake
you. 6 Be strong and of good courage;
for you shall cause this people to in-
herit the land which I swore to their
fathers to give them. 7 Only be strong
and very courageous, being careful
to do according to all the law which
Moses my servant commanded you;
turn not from it to the right hand or
to the left, that you may have good
success wherever you go. 8 This book
of the law shall not depart out of your
mouth, but you shall meditate on it
day and night, that you may be careful
to do according to all that is written
in it; for then you shall make your
way prosperous, and then you shall
have good success. 9 Have I not com-
manded you? Be strong and of good
courage; be not frightened, neither be
dismayed; for the LORD your God is
with you wherever you go."

PREPARATIONS FOR THE INVASION

10 Then Joshua commanded the
officers of the people, 11 "Pass through
the camp, and command the people,
'Prepare your provisions; for within
three days you are to pass over this
Jordan, to go in to take possession of
the land which the LORD your God
gives you to possess.'"

12 And to the Reubenites, the
Gadites, and the half-tribe of Ma-
nas´seh Joshua said, 13 "Remember the
word which Moses the servant of the
LORD commanded you, saying, 'The
LORD your God is providing you a
place of rest, and will give you this
land.' 14 Your wives, your little ones,
and your cattle shall remain in the
land which Moses gave you beyond
the Jordan; but all the men of val-
or among you shall pass over armed
before your brethren and shall help
them, 15 until the LORD gives rest to
your brethren as well as to you, and
they also take possession of the land
which the LORD your God is giving
them; then you shall return to the
land of your possession, and shall
possess it, the land which Moses the
servant of the LORD gave you beyond
the Jordan toward the sunrise." 16 And
they answered Joshua, "All that you
have commanded us we will do, and
wherever you send us we will go. 17 Just
as we obeyed Moses in all things, so
we will obey you; only may the LORD
your God be with you, as he was with
Moses! 18 Whoever rebels against your
commandment and disobeys your
words, whatever you command him,
shall be put to death. Only be strong
and of good courage."

SPIES SENT TO JERICHO

2 And Joshua the son of Nun sent two
men secretly from Shittim as spies,
saying, "Go, view the land, especial-
ly Jericho." And they went, and came
into the house of a harlot whose name
was Rahab, and lodged there. 2 And it
was told the king of Jericho, "Behold,
certain men of Israel have come here

tonight to search out the land." 3Then
the king of Jericho sent to Rahab, say-
ing, "Bring forth the men that have
come to you, who entered your house;
for they have come to search out all
the land." 4But the woman had taken
the two men and hidden them; and
she said, "True, men came to me, but
I did not know where they came from;
5and when the gate was to be closed,
at dark, the men went out; where the
men went I do not know; pursue them
quickly, for you will overtake them."
6But she had brought them up to the
roof, and hid them with the stalks of
flax which she had laid in order on the
roof. 7So the men pursued after them
on the way to the Jordan as far as the
fords; and as soon as the pursuers had
gone out, the gate was shut.

8 Before they lay down, she came
up to them on the roof, 9and said to
the men, "I know that the LORD has
given you the land, and that the fear
of you has fallen upon us, and that all
the inhabitants of the land melt away
before you. 10For we have heard how
the LORD dried up the water of the
Red Sea before you when you came
out of Egypt, and what you did to the
two kings of the Amorites that were
beyond the Jordan, to Sihon and Og,
whom you utterly destroyed. 11And as
soon as we heard it, our hearts melt-
ed, and there was no courage left in
any man, because of you; for the LORD
your God is he who is God in heaven
above and on earth beneath. 12Now
then, swear to me by the LORD that
as I have dealt kindly with you, you
also will deal kindly with my father's
house, and give me a sure sign, 13and
save alive my father and mother, my
brothers and sisters, and all who be-
long to them, and deliver our lives
from death." 14And the men said to
her, "Our life for yours! If you do not
tell this business of ours, then we will
deal kindly and faithfully with you
when the LORD gives us the land."

15 Then she let them down by a
rope through the window, for her
house was built into the city wall, so
that she dwelt in the wall. 16And she
said to them, "Go into the hills, lest
the pursuers meet you; and hide your-
selves there three days, until the pur-
suers have returned; then afterward
you may go your way." 17The men said
to her, "We will be guiltless with re-
spect to this oath of yours which you
have made us swear. 18Behold, when
we come into the land, you shall
bind this scarlet cord in the window
through which you let us down; and
you shall gather into your house
your father and mother, your broth-
ers, and all your father's household.
19If any one goes out of the doors of
your house into the street, his blood
shall be upon his head, and we shall
be guiltless; but if a hand is laid upon
any one who is with you in the house,
his blood shall be on our head. 20But if
you tell this business of ours, then we
shall be guiltless with respect to your
oath which you have made us swear."
21And she said, "According to your
words, so be it." Then she sent them
away, and they departed; and she
bound the scarlet cord in the window.

22 They departed, and went into
the hills, and remained there three
days, until the pursuers returned;
for the pursuers had made search
all along the way and found noth-
ing. 23Then the two men came down
again from the hills, and passed over
and came to Joshua the son of Nun;
and they told him all that had befall-
en them. 24And they said to Joshua,
"Truly the LORD has given all the land
into our hands; and moreover all the
inhabitants of the land are faintheart-
ed because of us."

ISRAEL CROSSES THE JORDAN

3Early in the morning Joshua rose
and set out from Shittim, with all
the people of Israel; and they came to
the Jordan, and lodged there before
they passed over. 2At the end of three
days the officers went through the
camp 3and commanded the people,

"When you see the ark of the covenant of the LORD your God being carried by the Levitical priests, then you shall set out from your place and follow it, 4that you may know the way you shall go, for you have not passed this way before. Yet there shall be a space between you and it, a distance of about two thousand cubits; do not come near it." 5And Joshua said to the people, "Sanctify yourselves; for tomorrow the LORD will do wonders among you." 6And Joshua said to the priests, "Take up the ark of the covenant, and pass on before the people." And they took up the ark of the covenant, and went before the people.

7 And the LORD said to Joshua, "This day I will begin to exalt you in the sight of all Israel, that they may know that, as I was with Moses, so I will be with you. 8And you shall command the priests who bear the ark of the covenant, 'When you come to the brink of the waters of the Jordan, you shall stand still in the Jordan.'" 9And Joshua said to the people of Israel, "Come hither, and hear the words of the LORD your God." 10And Joshua said, "Hereby you shall know that the living God is among you, and that he will without fail drive out from before you the Canaanites, the Hittites, the Hivites, the Per´izzites, the Gir´gashites, the Amorites, and the Jeb´usites. 11Behold, the ark of the covenant of the Lord of all the earth is to pass over before you into the Jordan. 12Now therefore take twelve men from the tribes of Israel, from each tribe a man. 13And when the soles of the feet of the priests who bear the ark of the LORD, the Lord of all the earth, shall rest in the waters of the Jordan, the waters of the Jordan shall be stopped from flowing, and the waters coming down from above shall stand in one heap."

14 So, when the people set out from their tents, to pass over the Jordan with the priests bearing the ark of the covenant before the people, 15and when those who bore the ark had come to the Jordan, and the feet of the priests bearing the ark were dipped in the brink of the water (the Jordan overflows all its banks throughout the time of harvest), 16the waters coming down from above stood and rose up in a heap far off, at Adam, the city that is beside Zar´ethan, and those flowing down toward the sea of the Arabah, the Salt Sea, were wholly cut off; and the people passed over opposite Jericho. 17And while all Israel were passing over on dry ground, the priests who bore the ark of the covenant of the LORD stood on dry ground in the midst of the Jordan, until all the nation finished passing over the Jordan.*

TWELVE STONES SET UP AT GILGAL

4 When all the nation had finished passing over the Jordan, the LORD said to Joshua, 2"Take twelve men from the people, from each tribe a man, 3and command them, 'Take twelve stones from here out of the midst of the Jordan, from the very place where the priests' feet stood, and carry them over with you, and lay them down in the place where you lodge tonight.'" 4Then Joshua called the twelve men from the people of Israel, whom he had appointed, a man from each tribe; 5and Joshua said to them, "Pass on before the ark of the LORD your God into the midst of the Jordan, and take up each of you a stone upon his shoulder, according to the number of the tribes of the people of Israel, 6that this may be a sign among you, when your children ask in time to come, 'What do those stones mean to you?' 7Then you shall tell them that the waters of the Jordan were cut off before the ark of the covenant of the LORD; when it passed over the Jordan, the waters of the Jordan were cut off. So these stones shall be to the people of Israel a memorial for ever."

8 And the men of Israel did as Joshua commanded, and took up twelve

stones out of the midst of the Jordan,
according to the number of the tribes
of the people of Israel, as the LORD
told Joshua; and they carried them
over with them to the place where
they lodged, and laid them down
there. 9And Joshua set up twelve
stones in the midst of the Jordan, in
the place where the feet of the priests
bearing the ark of the covenant had
stood; and they are there to this day.
10For the priests who bore the ark
stood in the midst of the Jordan, until everything was finished that the
LORD commanded Joshua to tell the
people, according to all that Moses
had commanded Joshua.

The people passed over in haste;
11and when all the people had finished
passing over, the ark of the LORD and
the priests passed over before the people. 12The sons of Reuben and the sons
of Gad and the half-tribe of Manas'seh
passed over armed before the people
of Israel, as Moses had bidden them;
13about forty thousand ready armed
for war passed over before the LORD
for battle, to the plains of Jericho. 14On
that day the LORD exalted Joshua in
the sight of all Israel; and they stood
in awe of him, as they had stood in
awe of Moses, all the days of his life.

15 And the LORD said to Joshua,
16"Command the priests who bear the
ark of the testimony to come up out
of the Jordan." 17Joshua therefore commanded the priests, "Come up out of
the Jordan." 18And when the priests
bearing the ark of the covenant of the
LORD came up from the midst of the
Jordan, and the soles of the priests'
feet were lifted up on dry ground, the
waters of the Jordan returned to their
place and overflowed all its banks, as
before.

19 The people came up out of the
Jordan on the tenth day of the first
month, and they encamped in Gilgal
on the east border of Jericho. 20And
those twelve stones, which they took
out of the Jordan, Joshua set up in
Gilgal. 21And he said to the people of
Israel, "When your children ask their
fathers in time to come, 'What do
these stones mean?' 22then you shall
let your children know, 'Israel passed
over this Jordan on dry ground.' 23For
the LORD your God dried up the waters of the Jordan for you until you
passed over, as the LORD your God
did to the Red Sea, which he dried up
for us until we passed over, 24so that
all the peoples of the earth may know
that the hand of the LORD is mighty;
that you may fear the LORD your God
for ever."

THE NEW GENERATION CIRCUMCISED

5 When all the kings of the Amorites
that were beyond the Jordan to
the west, and all the kings of the
Canaanites that were by the sea,
heard that the LORD had dried up the
waters of the Jordan for the people
of Israel until they had crossed over,
their heart melted, and there was no
longer any spirit in them, because of
the people of Israel.

2 At that time the LORD said to
Joshua, "Make flint knives and circumcise the people of Israel again the
second time." 3So Joshua made flint
knives, and circumcised the people of
Israel at Gib'eath-ha-ar'aloth.[a] 4And
this is the reason why Joshua circumcised them: all the males of the people
who came out of Egypt, all the men of
war, had died on the way in the wilderness after they had come out of Egypt.
5Though all the people who came out
had been circumcised, yet all the people that were born on the way in the
wilderness after they had come out of
Egypt had not been circumcised. 6For
the people of Israel walked forty years
in the wilderness, till all the nation,
the men of war that came forth out of
Egypt, perished, because they did not
hearken to the voice of the LORD; to
them the LORD swore that he would
not let them see the land which the
LORD had sworn to their fathers to

[a]That is *the hill of the foreskins*

give us, a land flowing with milk and
honey. 7So it was their children, whom
he raised up in their stead, that Joshua
circumcised; for they were uncircum-
cised, because they had not been cir-
cumcised on the way.
8 When the circumcising of all the
nation was done, they remained in their
places in the camp till they were healed.
9And the LORD said to Joshua, "This
day I have rolled away the reproach of
Egypt from you." And so the name of
that place is called Gilgal[b] to this day.

THE PASSOVER AT GILGAL

10 While the people of Israel were
encamped in Gilgal they kept the
passover on the fourteenth day of
the month at evening in the plains of
Jericho. 11And on the morrow after the
passover, on that very day, they ate of
the produce of the land, unleavened
cakes and parched grain. 12And the
manna ceased on the morrow, when
they ate of the produce of the land;
and the people of Israel had manna no
more, but ate of the fruit of the land of
Canaan that year.

JOSHUA'S VISION

13 When Joshua was by Jericho, he
lifted up his eyes and looked, and be-
hold, a man stood before him with his
drawn sword in his h:nd; and Joshua
went to him and sai to him, "Are
you for us, or for ou adversaries?"
14And he said, "No; buas commander
of the army of the LCD I have now
come." And Joshua febn his face to
the earth, and worshed, and said
to him, "What does n lord bid his
servant?" 15And the mmander of
the LORD's army said toshua, "Put
off your shoes from yofeet; for the
place where you stand holy." And
Joshua did so.

JERICHO TAKEN AND DROYED

6 *Now Jericho was s up from
within and from witt because
of the people of Israel; n went out,
and none came in. 2And the LORD
said to Joshua, "See, I have given into
your hand Jericho, with its king and
mighty men of valor. 3You shall march
around the city, all the men of war go-
ing around the city once. Thus shall
you do for six days. 4And seven priests
shall bear seven trumpets of rams'
horns before the ark; and on the sev-
enth day you shall march around the
city seven times, the priests blowing
the trumpets. 5And when they make a
long blast with the ram's horn, as soon
as you hear the sound of the trumpet,
then all the people shall shout with a
great shout; and the wall of the city
will fall down flat, and the people
shall go up every man straight before
him." 6So Joshua the son of Nun called
the priests and said to them, "Take up
the ark of the covenant, and let seven
priests bear seven trumpets of rams'
horns before the ark of the LORD."
7And he said to the people, "Go for-
ward; march around the city, and let
the armed men pass on before the ark
of the LORD."
8 And as Joshua had commanded
the people, the seven priests bearing
the seven trumpets of rams' horns
before the LORD went forward, blow-
ing the trumpets, with the ark of the
covenant of the LORD following them.
9And the armed men went before the
priests who blew the trumpets, and
the rear guard came after the ark,
while the trumpets blew continually.
10But Joshua commanded the people,
"You shall not shout or let your voice
be heard, neither shall any word go
out of your mouth, until the day I bid
you shout; then you shall shout." 11So
he caused the ark of the LORD to com-
pass the city, going about it once; and
they came into the camp, and spent
the night in the camp.
12 Then Joshua rose early in the
morning, and the priests took up
the ark of the LORD. 13And the seven
priests bearing the seven trumpets
of rams' horns before the ark of the

[b]From Heb *galal* to roll

LORD passed on, blowing the trum-
pets continually; and the armed men
went before them, and the rear guard
came after the ark of the LORD, while
the trumpets blew continually. 14And
the second day they marched around
the city once, and returned into the
camp. So they did for six days.

15 On the seventh day they rose
early at the dawn of day, and marched
around the city in the same manner
seven times: it was only on that day
that they marched around the city
seven times. 16And at the seventh
time, when the priests had blown the
trumpets, Joshua said to the people,
"Shout; for the LORD has given you
the city. 17And the city and all that
is within it shall be devoted to the
LORD for destruction;* only Rahab
the harlot and all who are with her in
her house shall live, because she hid
the messengers that we sent. 18But
you, keep yourselves from the things
devoted to destruction, lest when
you have devoted them you take any
of the devoted things and make the
camp of Israel a thing for destruction,
and bring trouble upon it. 19But all
silver and gold, and vessels of bronze
and iron, are sacred to the LORD;
they shall go into the treasury of the
LORD." 20So the people shouted, and
the trumpets were blown. As soon
as the people heard the sound of the
trumpet, the people raised a great
shout, and the wall fell down flat, so
that the people went up into the city,
every man straight before him, and
they took the city. 21Then they utterly
destroyed all in the city, both men and
women, young and old, oxen, sheep,
and asses, with the edge of the sword.

22 And Joshua said to the two men
who had spied out the land, "Go into
the harlot's house, and bring out from
it the woman, and all who belong to
her, as you swore to her." 23So the
young men who had been spies went
in, and brought out Rahab, and her
father and mother and brothers and
all who belonged to her; and they
brought all her kindred, and set them
outside the camp of Israel. 24And they
burned the city with fire, and all with-
in it; only the silver and gold, and the
vessels of bronze and of iron, they put
into the treasury of the house of the
LORD. 25But Rahab the harlot, and her
father's household, and all who be-
longed to her, Joshua saved alive; and
she dwelt in Israel to this day, because
she hid the messengers whom Joshua
sent to spy out Jericho.

26 Joshua laid an oath upon them
at that time, saying, "Cursed before
the LORD be the man that rises up and
rebuilds this city, Jericho.

At the cost of his first-born
shall he
lay its foundation,
and at the cost of his youngest
son
shall he set up its gates."

27 So the LORD was with Joshua;
and his fame was in all the land.

THE SIN OF ACHAN AND ITS PUNISHMENT

7 But the people of Israel broke faith
in regard to the devoted things; for
Achan the son of Carmi, son of Zabdi,
son of Zerah, of the tribe of Judah,
took some of the devoted things; and
the anger of the LORD burned against
the people of Israel.

2 Joshua sent men from Jericho
to Ai, which is near Beth-a'ven, east
of Bethel, and said to them, "Go up
and spy out the land." And the men
went up and spied out Ai. 3And they
returned to Joshua, and said to him,
"Let not all the people go up, but let
about two or three thousand men go
up and attack Ai; do not make the
whole people toil up there, for they
are but few." 4So about three thou-
sand went up there from the people;
and they fled before the men of Ai,
5and the men of Ai killed about thir-
ty-six men of them, and chased them
before the gate as far as Sheb'arim,
and slew them at the descent. And the
hearts of the people melted, and be-
came as water.

6 Then Joshua rent his clothes, and
fell to the earth upon his face before
the ark of the LORD until the eve-
ning, he and the elders of Israel; and
they put dust upon their heads. [7]And
Joshua said, "Alas, O Lord GOD, why
hast thou brought this people over the
Jordan at all, to give us into the hands
of the Amorites, to destroy us? Would
that we had been content to dwell be-
yond the Jordan! [8]O Lord, what can
I say, when Israel has turned their
backs before their enemies! [9]For the
Canaanites and all the inhabitants of
the land will hear of it, and will sur-
round us, and cut off our name from
the earth; and what wilt thou do for
thy great name?"

10 The LORD said to Joshua, "Arise,
why have you thus fallen upon your
face? [11]Israel has sinned; they have
transgressed my covenant which I
commanded them; they have taken
some of the devoted things; they have
stolen, and lied, and put them among
their own stuff. [12]Therefore the people
of Israel cannot stand before their ene-
mies; they turn their backs before their
enemies, because they have become
a thing for destruction. I will be with
you no more, unless you destroy the
devoted things from among you. [13]Up,
sanctify the people, and say, 'Sanctify
yourselves for tomorrow; for thus says
the LORD, God of Israel, "There are
devoted things in the midst of you, O
Israel; you cannot stand before your en-
emies, until you take away the devoted
things from among you." [14]In the morn-
ing therefore you shall be brought near
by your tribes; and the tribe which the
LORD takes shall come near by families;
and the family which the LORD takes
shall come near by households; and the
household which the LORD takes shall
come near man by man. [15]And he who is
taken with the devoted things shall be
burned with fire, he and all that he has,
because he has transgressed the cove-
nant of the LORD, and because he has
done a shameful thing in Israel.'"

16 So Joshua rose early in the morn-
ing, and brought Israel near tribe by
tribe, and the tribe of Judah was tak-
en; [17]and he brought near the fami-
lies of Judah, and the family of the
Zer´ahites was taken; and he brought
near the family of the Zer´ahites man
by man, and Zabdi was taken; [18]and
he brought near his household man by
man, and Achan the son of Carmi, son
of Zabdi, son of Zerah, of the tribe of
Judah, was taken. [19]Then Joshua said
to Achan, "My son, give glory to the
LORD God of Israel, and render praise
to him; and tell me now what you have
done; do not hide it from me." [20]And
Achan answered Joshua, "Of a truth I
have sinned against the LORD God of
Israel, and this is what I did: [21]when
I saw among the spoil a beautiful
mantle from Shinar, and two hundred
shekels of silver, and a bar of gold
weighing fifty shekels, then I covet-
ed them, and took them; and behold,
they are hidden in the earth inside my
tent, with the silver underneath."

22 So Joshua sent messengers, and
they ran to the tent; and behold, it
was hidden in his tent with the silver
underneath. [23]And they took them
out of the tent and brought them to
Joshua and all the people of Israel;
and they laid them down before the
LORD. [24]And Joshua and all Israel with
him took Achan the son of Zerah, and
the silver and the mantle and the bar
of gold, and his sons and daughters,
and his oxen and asses and sheep,
and his tent, and all that he had; and
they brought them up to the Valley of
Achor. [25]And Joshua said, "Why did
you bring trouble on us? The LORD
brings trouble on you today." And all
Israel stoned him with stones; they
burned them with fire, and stoned
them with stones. [26]And they raised
over him a great heap of stones that
remains to this day; then the LORD
turned from his burning anger.
Therefore to this day the name of that
place is called the Valley of Achor.[a]

[a]That is *Trouble*

AI CAPTURED BY A STRATAGEM AND DESTROYED

8 And the LORD said to Joshua, "Do not fear or be dismayed; take all the fighting men with you, and arise, go up to Ai; see, I have given into your hand the king of Ai, and his people, his city, and his land; 2 and you shall do to Ai and its king as you did to Jericho and its king; only its spoil and its cattle you shall take as booty for yourselves; lay an ambush against the city, behind it."

3 So Joshua arose, and all the fighting men, to go up to Ai; and Joshua chose thirty thousand mighty men of valor, and sent them forth by night. 4 And he commanded them, "Behold, you shall lie in ambush against the city, behind it; do not go very far from the city, but hold yourselves all in readiness; 5 and I, and all the people who are with me, will approach the city. And when they come out against us, as before, we shall flee before them; 6 and they will come out after us, till we have drawn them away from the city; for they will say, 'They are fleeing from us, as before.' So we will flee from them; 7 then you shall rise up from the ambush, and seize the city; for the LORD your God will give it into your hand. 8 And when you have taken the city, you shall set the city on fire, doing as the LORD has bidden; see, I have commanded you." 9 So Joshua sent them forth; and they went to the place of ambush, and lay between Bethel and Ai, to the west of Ai; but Joshua spent that night among the people.

10 And Joshua arose early in the morning and mustered the people, and went up, with the elders of Israel, before the people to Ai. 11 And all the fighting men who were with him went *up, and drew near before* the city, and encamped on the north side of Ai, with a ravine between them and Ai. 12 And he took about five thousand men, and set them in ambush between Bethel and Ai, to the west of the city. 13 So they stationed the forces, the main encampment which was north of the city and its rear guard west of the city. But Joshua spent that night in the valley. 14 And when the king of Ai saw this he and all his people, the men of the city, made haste and went out early to the descent[a] toward the Arabah to meet Israel in battle; but he did not know that there was an ambush against him behind the city. 15 And Joshua and all Israel made a pretense of being beaten before them, and fled in the direction of the wilderness. 16 So all the people who were in the city were called together to pursue them, and as they pursued Joshua they were drawn away from the city. 17 There was not a man left in Ai or Bethel, who did not go out after Israel; they left the city open, and pursued Israel.

18 Then the LORD said to Joshua, "Stretch out the javelin that is in your hand toward Ai; for I will give it into your hand." And Joshua stretched out the javelin that was in his hand toward the city. 19 And the ambush rose quickly out of their place, and as soon as he had stretched out his hand, they ran and entered the city and took it; and they made haste to set the city on fire. 20 So when the men of Ai looked back, behold, the smoke of the city went up to heaven; and they had no power to flee this way or that, for the people that fled to the wilderness turned back upon the pursuers. 21 And when Joshua and all Israel saw that the ambush had taken the city, and that the smoke of the city went up, then they turned back and smote the men of Ai. 22 And the others came forth from the city against them; so they were in the midst of Israel, some on this side, and some on that side; and Israel smote them, until *there* was left none that survived or escaped. 23 But the king of Ai they took alive, and brought him to Joshua.

24 When Israel had finished slaughtering all the inhabitants of Ai

[a] Cn: Heb *appointed time*

in the open wilderness where they
pursued them, and all of them to the
very last had fallen by the edge of the
sword, all Israel returned to Ai, and
smote it with the edge of the sword.
25And all who fell that day, both men
and women, were twelve thousand,
all the people of Ai. 26For Joshua did
not draw back his hand, with which
he stretched out the javelin, until he
had utterly destroyed all the inhabi-
tants of Ai. 27Only the cattle and the
spoil of that city Israel took as their
booty, according to the word of the
LORD which he commanded Joshua.
28So Joshua burned Ai, and made it
for ever a heap of ruins, as it is to this
day. 29And he hanged the king of Ai on
a tree until evening; and at the going
down of the sun Joshua commanded,
and they took his body down from
the tree, and cast it at the entrance of
the gate of the city, and raised over it
a great heap of stones, which stands
there to this day.

JOSHUA RENEWS THE COVENANT

30 Then Joshua built an altar on
Mount Ebal to the LORD, the God of
Israel, 31as Moses the servant of the
LORD had commanded the people of
Israel, as it is written in the book of
the law of Moses, "an altar of unhewn
stones, upon which no man has lifted
an iron tool"; and they offered on it
burnt offerings to the LORD, and sac-
rificed peace offerings. 32And there, in
the presence of the people of Israel,
he wrote upon the stones a copy of
the law of Moses, which he had writ-
ten. 33And all Israel, sojourner as well
as homeborn, with their elders and
officers and their judges, stood on
opposite sides of the ark before the
Levitical priests who carried the ark
of the covenant of the LORD, half of
them in front of Mount Geri´zim and
half of them in front of Mount Ebal,
as Moses the servant of the LORD
had commanded at the first, that
they should bless the people of Israel.
34And afterward he read all the words
of the law, the blessing and the curse,
according to all that is written in the
book of the law. 35There was not a
word of all that Moses commanded
which Joshua did not read before all
the assembly of Israel, and the wom-
en, and the little ones, and the so-
journers who lived among them.

THE GIBEONITES SAVE THEMSELVES BY TRICKERY

9 When all the kings who were be-
yond the Jordan in the hill coun-
try and in the lowland all along
the coast of the Great Sea toward
Lebanon, the Hittites, the Amorites,
the Canaanites, the Per´izzites, the
Hivites, and the Jeb´usites, heard of
this, 2they gathered together with one
accord to fight Joshua and Israel.
3 But when the inhabitants of
Gibeon heard what Joshua had done
to Jericho and to Ai, 4they on their
part acted with cunning, and went
and made ready provisions, and took
worn-out sacks upon their asses, and
wineskins, worn-out and torn and
mended, 5with worn-out, patched
sandals on their feet, and worn-
out clothes; and all their provisions
were dry and moldy. 6And they went
to Joshua in the camp at Gilgal, and
said to him and to the men of Israel,
"We have come from a far country; so
now make a covenant with us." 7But
the men of Israel said to the Hivites,
"Perhaps you live among us; then how
can we make a covenant with you?"
8They said to Joshua, "We are your
servants." And Joshua said to them,
"Who are you? And where do you
come from?" 9They said to him, "From
a very far country your servants have
come, because of the name of the
LORD your God; for we have heard
a report of him, and all that he did
in Egypt, 10and all that he did to the
two kings of the Amorites who were
beyond the Jordan, Sihon the king of
Heshbon, and Og king of Bashan, who
dwelt in Ash´taroth. 11And our elders
and all the inhabitants of our country

said to us, 'Take provisions in your
hand for the journey, and go to meet
them, and say to them, "We are your
servants; come now, make a covenant
with us."'" 12 Here is our bread; it was
still warm when we took it from our
houses as our food for the journey, on
the day we set forth to come to you,
but now, behold, it is dry and moldy;
13 these wineskins were new when
we filled them, and behold, they are
burst; and these garments and shoes
of ours are worn out from the very
long journey." 14 So the men partook of
their provisions, and did not ask di-
rection from the LORD. 15 And Joshua
made peace with them, and made a
covenant with them, to let them live;
and the leaders of the congregation
swore to them.

16 At the end of three days af-
ter they had made a covenant with
them, they heard that they were
their neighbors, and that they dwelt
among them. 17 And the people of
Israel set out and reached their cit-
ies on the third day. Now their cities
were Gibeon, Chephi´rah, Be-er´oth,
and Kir´iath-je´arim. 18 But the people
of Israel did not kill them, because
the leaders of the congregation had
sworn to them by the LORD, the God
of Israel. Then all the congregation
murmured against the leaders. 19 But
all the leaders said to all the congrega-
tion, "We have sworn to them by the
LORD, the God of Israel, and now we
may not touch them. 20 This we will do
to them, and let them live, lest wrath
be upon us, because of the oath which
we swore to them." 21 And the leaders
said to them, "Let them live." So they
became hewers of wood and drawers
of water for all the congregation, as
the leaders had said of them.

22 Joshua summoned them, and he
said to them, "Why did you deceive
us, saying, 'We are very far from you,'
when you dwell among us? 23 Now
therefore you are cursed, and some
of you shall always be slaves, hewers
of wood and drawers of water for the
house of my God." 24 They answered
Joshua, "Because it was told to your
servants for a certainty that the LORD
your God had commanded his servant
Moses to give you all the land, and to
destroy all the inhabitants of the land
from before you; so we feared greatly
for our lives because of you, and did
this thing. 25 And now, behold, we are
in your hand: do as it seems good and
right in your sight to do to us." 26 So he
did to them, and delivered them out of
the hand of the people of Israel; and
they did not kill them. 27 But Joshua
made them that day hewers of wood
and drawers of water for the congre-
gation and for the altar of the LORD,
to continue to this day, in the place
which he should choose.

THE SUN STANDS STILL

10 When Ado´ni-ze´dek king of
Jerusalem heard how Joshua had
taken Ai, and had utterly destroyed it,
doing to Ai and its king as he had done
to Jericho and its king, and how the
inhabitants of Gibeon had made peace
with Israel and were among them,
2 he[a] feared greatly, because Gibeon
was a great city, like one of the roy-
al cities, and because it was greater
than Ai, and all its men were mighty.
3 So Ado´ni-ze´dek king of Jerusalem
sent to Hoham king of Hebron, to
Piram king of Jarmuth, to Japhi´a
king of Lachish, and to Debir king of
Eglon, saying, 4 "Come up to me, and
help me, and let us smite Gibeon; for
it has made peace with Joshua and
with the people of Israel." 5 Then the
five kings of the Amorites, the king
of Jerusalem, the king of Hebron, the
king of Jarmuth, the king of Lachish,
and the king of Eglon, gathered their
forces, and went up with all their
armies and encamped against Gibeon,
and made war against it.

6 And the men of Gibeon sent to
Joshua at the camp in Gilgal, saying,
"Do not relax your hand from your

[a]Heb *they*

servants; come up to us quickly, and
save us, and help us; for all the kings
of the Amorites that dwell in the hill
country are gathered against us." 7So
Joshua went up from Gilgal, he and all
the people of war with him, and all the
mighty men of valor. 8And the LORD
said to Joshua, "Do not fear them, for
I have given them into your hands;
there shall not a man of them stand
before you." 9So Joshua came upon
them suddenly, having marched up
all night from Gilgal. 10And the LORD
threw them into a panic before Israel,
who slew them with a great slaugh-
ter at Gibeon, and chased them by
the way of the ascent of Beth-hor´on,
and smote them as far as Aze´kah and
Makke´dah. 11And as they fled before
Israel, while they were going down
the ascent of Beth-hor´on, the LORD
threw down great stones from heaven
upon them as far as Aze´kah, and they
died; there were more who died be-
cause of the hailstones than the men
of Israel killed with the sword.

12 Then spoke Joshua to the LORD
in the day when the LORD gave the
Amorites over to the men of Israel;
and he said in the sight of Israel,

"Sun, stand thou still at
Gibeon,
and thou Moon in the valley of
Ai´jalon."
13And the sun stood still, and
the moon stayed,
until the nation took vengeance
on their enemies.

Is this not written in the Book of
Jashar? The sun stayed in the midst
of heaven, and did not hasten to go
down for about a whole day. 14There
has been no day like it before or since,
when the LORD hearkened to the
voice of a man; for the LORD fought
for Israel.*

15 Then Joshua returned, and all
Israel with him, to the camp at Gilgal.

FIVE KINGS DEFEATED

16 These five kings fled, and hid
themselves in the cave at Makke´dah.
17And it was told Joshua, "The five
kings have been found, hidden in the
cave at Makke´dah." 18And Joshua
said, "Roll great stones against the
mouth of the cave, and set men by it
to guard them; 19but do not stay there
yourselves, pursue your enemies, fall
upon their rear, do not let them enter
their cities; for the LORD your God has
given them into your hand." 20When
Joshua and the men of Israel had fin-
ished slaying them with a very great
slaughter, until they were wiped out,
and when the remnant which remained
of them had entered into the fortified
cities, 21all the people returned safe to
Joshua in the camp at Makke´dah; not
a man moved his tongue against any of
the people of Israel.

22 Then Joshua said, "Open the
mouth of the cave, and bring those
five kings out to me from the cave."
23And they did so, and brought those
five kings out to him from the cave,
the king of Jerusalem, the king of
Hebron, the king of Jarmuth, the king
of Lachish, and the king of Eglon.
24And when they brought those kings
out to Joshua, Joshua summoned all
the men of Israel, and said to the
chiefs of the men of war who had gone
with him, "Come near, put your feet
upon the necks of these kings." Then
they came near, and put their feet
on their necks. 25And Joshua said to
them, "Do not be afraid or dismayed;
be strong and of good courage; for
thus the LORD will do to all your en-
emies against whom you fight." 26And
afterward Joshua smote them and put
them to death, and he hung them on
five trees. *And they hung upon* the
trees until evening; 27but at the time
of the going down of the sun, Joshua
commanded, and they took them
down from the trees, and threw them
into the cave where they had hidden
themselves, and they set great stones
against the mouth of the cave, which
remain to this very day.

28 And Joshua took Makke´dah
on that day, and smote it and its king

with the edge of the sword; he utterly
destroyed every person in it, he left
none remaining; and he did to the
king of Makke´dah as he had done to
the king of Jericho.

29 Then Joshua passed on from
Makke´dah, and all Israel with him,
to Libnah, and fought against Libnah;
30and the LORD gave it also and its
king into the hand of Israel; and he
smote it with the edge of the sword,
and every person in it; he left none re-
maining in it; and he did to its king
as he had done to the king of Jericho.

31 And Joshua passed on from
Libnah, and all Israel with him, to
Lachish, and laid siege to it, and
assaulted it: 32and the LORD gave
Lachish into the hand of Israel, and he
took it on the second day, and smote it
with the edge of the sword, and every
person in it, as he had done to Libnah.

33 Then Horam king of Gezer came
up to help Lachish; and Joshua smote
him and his people, until he left none
remaining.

34 And Joshua passed on with all
Israel from Lachish to Eglon; and they
laid siege to it, and assaulted it; 35and
they took it on that day, and smote it
with the edge of the sword; and every
person in it he utterly destroyed that
day, as he had done to Lachish.

36 Then Joshua went up with all
Israel from Eglon to Hebron; and they
assaulted it, 37and took it, and smote
it with the edge of the sword, and its
king and its towns, and every person
in it; he left none remaining, as he had
done to Eglon, and utterly destroyed it
with every person in it.

38 Then Joshua, with all Israel,
turned back to Debir and assaulted it,
39and he took it with its king and all
its towns; and they smote them with
the edge of the sword, and utterly de-
stroyed every person in it; he left none
remaining; as he had done to Hebron
and to Libnah and its king, so he did
to Debir and to its king.

40 So Joshua defeated the whole
land, the hill country and the Negeb
and the lowland and the slopes, and
all their kings; he left none remain-
ing, but utterly destroyed all that
breathed, as the LORD God of Israel
commanded. 41And Joshua defeated
them from Ka´desh-bar´nea to Gaza,
and all the country of Goshen, as far
as Gibeon. 42And Joshua took all these
kings and their land at one time, be-
cause the LORD God of Israel fought
for Israel. 43Then Joshua returned,
and all Israel with him, to the camp
at Gilgal.

THE UNITED KINGS OF NORTHERN CANAAN DEFEATED

11 When Jabin king of Hazor heard
of this, he sent to Jobab king of
Madon, and to the king of Shimron,
and to the king of Ach´shaph, 2and to
the kings who were in the northern
hill country, and in the Arabah south
of Chin´neroth, and in the lowland,
and in Naphoth-dor on the west, 3to
the Canaanites in the east and the
west, the Amorites, the Hittites, the
Per´izzites, and the Jeb´usites in the
hill country, and the Hivites under
Hermon in the land of Mizpah. 4And
they came out, with all their troops,
a great host, in number like the sand
that is upon the seashore, with very
many horses and chariots. 5And all
these kings joined their forces, and
came and encamped together at the
waters of Merom, to fight with Israel.

6 And the LORD said to Joshua,
"Do not be afraid of them, for tomor-
row at this time I will give over all of
them, slain, to Israel; you shall ham-
string their horses, and burn their
chariots with fire." 7So Joshua came
suddenly upon them with all his peo-
ple of war, by the waters of Merom,
and fell upon them. 8And the LORD
gave them into the hand of Israel, who
smote them and chased them as far as
Great Sidon and Mis´rephoth-ma´im,
and eastward as far as the valley of
Mizpeh; and they smote them, until
they left none remaining. 9And Joshua
did to them as the LORD bade him; he

hamstrung their horses, and burned
their chariots with fire.
10 And Joshua turned back at that
time, and took Hazor, and smote its
king with the sword; for Hazor former-
ly was the head of all those kingdoms.
11 And they put to the sword all who
were in it, utterly destroying them;
there was none left that breathed, and
he burned Hazor with fire. 12 And all
the cities of those kings, and all their
kings, Joshua took, and smote them
with the edge of the sword, utterly de-
stroying them, as Moses the servant of
the LORD had commanded. 13 But none
of the cities that stood on mounds did
Israel burn, except Hazor only; that
Joshua burned. 14 And all the spoil of
these cities and the cattle, the people
of Israel took for their booty; but ev-
ery man they smote with the edge of
the sword, until they had destroyed
them, and they did not leave any that
breathed. 15 As the LORD had com-
manded Moses his servant, so Moses
commanded Joshua, and so Joshua
did; he left nothing undone of all that
the LORD had commanded Moses.

SUMMARY OF JOSHUA'S CONQUESTS

16 So Joshua took all that land, the
hill country and all the Negeb and all
the land of Goshen and the lowland
and the Arabah and the hill country
of Israel and its lowland 17 from Mount
Halak, that rises toward Se'ir, as far
as Ba'al-gad in the valley of Lebanon
below Mount Hermon. And he took
all their kings, and smote them, and
put them to death. 18 Joshua made
war a long time with all those kings.
19 There was not a city that made peace
with the people of Israel, except the
Hivites, the inhabitants of Gibeon;
they took all in battle. 20 For it was the
LORD's doing to harden their hearts
that they should come against Israel
in battle, in order that they should be
utterly destroyed, and should receive
no mercy but be exterminated, as the
LORD commanded Moses.

21 And Joshua came at that time,
and wiped out the Anakim from
the hill country, from Hebron, from
Debir, from Anab, and from all the
hill country of Judah, and from all
the hill country of Israel; Joshua ut-
terly destroyed them with their cities.
22 There was none of the Anakim left
in the land of the people of Israel;
only in Gaza, in Gath, and in Ashdod,
did some remain. 23 So Joshua took
the whole land, according to all that
the LORD had spoken to Moses; and
Joshua gave it for an inheritance to
Israel according to their tribal allot-
ments. And the land had rest from
war.

THE KINGS CONQUERED BY MOSES

12 Now these are the kings of the
land, whom the people of Israel
defeated, and took possession of
their land beyond the Jordan toward
the sunrising, from the valley of the
Arnon to Mount Hermon, with all
the Arabah eastward: 2 Sihon king of
the Amorites who dwelt at Heshbon,
and ruled from Aro'er, which is on
the edge of the valley of the Arnon,
and from the middle of the valley as
far as the river Jabbok, the bound-
ary of the Ammonites, that is, half
of Gilead, 3 and the Arabah to the
Sea of Chin'neroth eastward, and in
the direction of Beth-jesh'imoth, to
the sea of the Arabah, the Salt Sea,
southward to the foot of the slopes of
Pisgah; 4 and Og[a] king of Bashan, one
of the remnant of the Reph'aim, who
dwelt at Ash'taroth and at Ed're-i
5 and ruled over Mount Hermon and
Sal'ecah and all Bashan to the bound-
ary of the Gesh'urites and the Ma-
ac'athites, and over half of Gilead
to the boundary of Sihon king of
Heshbon. 6 Moses, the servant of the
LORD, and the people of Israel defeat-
ed them; and Moses the servant of the
LORD gave their land for a possession
to the Reubenites and the Gadites and
the half-tribe of Manas'seh.

[a] Gk: Heb *the boundary of Og*

THE KINGS CONQUERED BY JOSHUA

7 And these are the kings of the
land whom Joshua and the people of
Israel defeated on the west side of
the Jordan, from Ba´al-gad in the val-
ley of Lebanon to Mount Halak, that
rises toward Se´ir (and Joshua gave
their land to the tribes of Israel as a
possession according to their allot-
ments, 8in the hill country, in the low-
land, in the Arabah, in the slopes, in
the wilderness, and in the Negeb, the
land of the Hittites, the Amorites,
the Canaanites, the Per´izzites, the
Hivites, and the Jeb´usites): 9the king
of Jericho, one; the king of Ai, which
is beside Bethel, one; 10the king of
Jerusalem, one; the king of Hebron,
one; 11the king of Jarmuth, one; the
king of Lachish, one; 12the king of
Eglon, one; the king of Gezer, one;
13the king of Debir, one; the king of
Geder, one; 14the king of Hormah,
one; the king of Arad, one; 15the king
of Libnah, one; the king of Adul´lam,
one; 16the king of Makke´dah, one;
the king of Bethel, one; 17the king of
Tap´pu-ah, one; the king of Hepher,
one; 18the king of Aphek, one; the king
of Lashar´on, one; 19the king of Madon,
one; the king of Hazor, one; 20the king
of Shim´ron-me´ron, one; the king of
Ach´shaph, one; 21the king of Ta´anach,
one; the king of Megid´do, one; 22the
king of Kedesh, one; the king of
Jok´ne-am in Carmel, one; 23the king
of Dor in Na´phath-dor, one; the king
of Goi´im in Galilee,[a] one; 24the king
of Tirzah, one: in all, thirty-one kings.

THE PARTS OF CANAAN STILL UNCONQUERED

13 *Now Joshua was old and ad-
vanced in years; and the LORD
said to him, "You are old and ad-
vanced in years, and there remains
yet very much land to be possessed.
2This is the land that yet remains: all
the regions of the Philistines, and
all those of the Gesh´urites 3(from
the Shihor, which is east of Egypt,
northward to the boundary of Ekron,
it is reckoned as Canaanite; there
are five rulers of the Philistines,
those of Gaza, Ashdod, Ash´kelon,
Gath, and Ekron), and those of the
Avvim, 4in the south, all the land of
the Canaanites, and Mear´ah which
belongs to the Sido´nians, to Aphek,
to the boundary of the Amorites, 5and
the land of the Geb´alites, and all
Lebanon, toward the sunrising, from
Ba´al-gad below Mount Hermon to the
entrance of Hamath, 6all the inhabi-
tants of the hill country from Lebanon
to Mis´rephoth-ma´im, even all the
Sido´nians. I will myself drive them
out from before the people of Israel;
only allot the land to Israel for an in-
heritance, as I have commanded you.
7Now therefore divide this land for an
inheritance to the nine tribes and half
the tribe of Manas´seh."

THE TERRITORY EAST OF THE JORDAN

8 With the other half of the tribe
of Manas´seh[b] the Reubenites and the
Gadites received their inheritance,
which Moses gave them, beyond the
Jordan eastward, as Moses the servant
of the LORD gave them: 9from Aro´er,
which is on the edge of the valley of
the Arnon, and the city that is in the
middle of the valley, and all the ta-
bleland of Med´eba as far as Dibon;
10and all the cities of Sihon king of the
Amorites, who reigned in Heshbon, as
far as the boundary of the Ammonites;
11and Gilead, and the region of the
Gesh´urites and Ma-ac´athites, and
all Mount Hermon, and all Bashan to
Sal´ecah; 12all the kingdom of Og in
Bashan, who reigned in Ash´taroth
and in Ed´re-i (he alone was left of
the remnant of the Reph´aim); these
Moses had defeated and driven out.
13Yet the people of Israel did not
drive out the Gesh´urites or the Ma-
ac´athites; but Geshur and Ma´acath
dwell in the midst of Israel to this day.

[a]Gk: Heb *Gilgal*
[b]Cn: Heb *With it*

14 To the tribe of Levi alone Moses
gave no inheritance; the offerings by
fire to the LORD God of Israel are
their inheritance, as he said to him.

THE TERRITORY OF REUBEN

15 And Moses gave an inheritance
to the tribe of the Reubenites accord-
ing to their families. 16So their ter-
ritory was from Aro´er, which is on
the edge of the valley of the Arnon,
and the city that is in the middle of
the valley, and all the tableland by
Med´eba; 17with Heshbon, and all its
cities that are in the tableland; Dibon,
and Ba´moth-ba´al, and Beth-ba´al-
me´on, 18and Jahaz, and Ked´emoth,
and Meph´a-ath, 19and Kiriatha´im,
and Sibmah, and Zer´eth-sha´har on
the hill of the valley, 20and Beth-pe´or,
and the slopes of Pisgah, and Beth-
jesh´imoth, 21that is, all the cities of
the tableland, and all the kingdom
of Sihon king of the Amorites, who
reigned in Heshbon, whom Moses
defeated with the leaders of Mid´ian,
Evi and Rekem and Zur and Hur and
Reba, the princes of Sihon, who dwelt
in the land. 22Balaam also, the son of
Be´or, the soothsayer, the people of
Israel killed with the sword among
the rest of their slain. 23And the bor-
der of the people of Reuben was the
Jordan as a boundary. This was the
inheritance of the Reubenites, accord-
ing to their families with their cities
and villages.

THE TERRITORY OF GAD

24 And Moses gave an inheritance
also to the tribe of the Gadites, ac-
cording to their families. 25Their ter-
ritory was Jazer, and all the cities
of Gilead, and half the land of the
Ammonites, to Aro´er, which is east
of Rabbah, 26and from Heshbon to
Ra´math-miz´peh and Bet´onim, and
from Mahana´im to the territory of
Debir,[c] 27and in the valley Beth-ha´ram,
Beth-nim´rah, Succoth, and Zaphon,
the rest of the kingdom of Sihon king
of Heshbon, having the Jordan as a
boundary, to the lower end of the Sea
of Chin´nereth, eastward beyond the
Jordan. 28This is the inheritance of the
Gadites according to their families,
with their cities and villages.

THE TERRITORY OF THE HALF-TRIBE OF MANASSEH (EAST)

29 And Moses gave an inheritance
to the half-tribe of Manas´seh; it
was allotted to the half-tribe of the
Manas´sites according to their fam-
ilies. 30Their region extended from
Mahana´im, through all Bashan, the
whole kingdom of Og king of Bashan,
and all the towns of Ja´ir, which are in
Bashan, sixty cities, 31and half Gilead,
and Ash´taroth, and Ed´re-i, the cit-
ies of the kingdom of Og in Bashan;
these were allotted to the people of
Machir the son of Manas´seh for the
half of the Machirites according to
their families.

32 These are the inheritances
which Moses distributed in the plains
of Moab, beyond the Jordan east of
Jericho. 33But to the tribe of Levi
Moses gave no inheritance; the LORD
God of Israel is their inheritance, as
he said to them.

THE DISTRIBUTION OF TERRITORY WEST OF THE JORDAN

14 And these are the inheritances
which the people of Israel re-
ceived in the land of Canaan, which
Elea´zar the priest, and Joshua the son
of Nun, and the heads of the fathers'
houses of the tribes of the people of
Israel distributed to them. 2Their in-
heritance was by lot, as the LORD had
commanded Moses for the nine and
one-half tribes. 3For Moses had given
an inheritance to the two and one-half
tribes beyond the Jordan; but to the
Levites he gave no inheritance among
them. 4For the people of Joseph were
two tribes, Manas´seh and E´phraim;
and no portion was given to the

[c] Gk Syr Vg: Heb *Lidebir*

Levites in the land, but only cities to
dwell in, with their pasture lands for
their cattle and their substance. 5The
people of Israel did as the LORD com-
manded Moses; they allotted the land.

HEBRON ALLOTTED TO CALEB

6 Then the people of Judah came
to Joshua at Gilgal; and Caleb the son
of Jephun´neh the Ken´izzite said to
him, "You know what the LORD said
to Moses the man of God in Ka´desh-
bar´nea concerning you and me. 7I
was forty years old when Moses the
servant of the LORD sent me from
Ka´desh-bar´nea to spy out the land;
and I brought him word again as it
was in my heart. 8But my brethren
who went up with me made the heart
of the people melt; yet I wholly fol-
lowed the LORD my God. 9And Moses
swore on that day, saying, 'Surely the
land on which your foot has trodden
shall be an inheritance for you and
your children for ever, because you
have wholly followed the LORD my
God.' 10And now, behold, the LORD
has kept me alive, as he said, these
forty-five years since the time that the
LORD spoke this word to Moses, while
Israel walked in the wilderness; and
now, lo, I am this day eighty-five years
old. 11I am still as strong to this day as
I was in the day that Moses sent me;
my strength now is as my strength
was then, for war, and for going and
coming. 12So now give me this hill
country of which the LORD spoke on
that day; for you heard on that day
how the Anakim were there, with
great fortified cities: it may be that
the LORD will be with me, and I shall
drive them out as the LORD said."

13 Then Joshua blessed him; and
he gave Hebron to Caleb the son of
Jephun´neh for an inheritance. 14So
Hebron became the inheritance of
Caleb the son of Jephun´neh the
Ken´izzite to this day, because he
wholly followed the LORD, the God
of Israel. 15Now the name of Hebron
formerly was Kir´iath-ar´ba;[a] this
Arba was the greatest man among the
Anakim. And the land had rest from
war.

THE TERRITORY OF JUDAH

15 The lot for the tribe of the people
of Judah according to their fami-
lies reached southward to the bound-
ary of Edom, to the wilderness of
Zin at the farthest south. 2And their
south boundary ran from the end of
the Salt Sea, from the bay that faces
southward; 3it goes out southward of
the ascent of Akrab´bim, passes along
to Zin, and goes up south of Ka´desh-
bar´nea, along by Hezron, up to Addar,
turns about to Karka, 4passes along
to Azmon, goes out by the Brook of
Egypt, and comes to its end at the sea.
This shall be your south boundary.
5And the east boundary is the Salt
Sea, to the mouth of the Jordan. And
the boundary on the north side runs
from the bay of the sea at the mouth
of the Jordan; 6and the boundary goes
up to Beth-hoglah, and passes along
north of Beth-arabah; and the bound-
ary goes up to the stone of Bohan
the son of Reuben; 7and the bound-
ary goes up to Debir from the Valley
of Achor, and so northward, turning
toward Gilgal, which is opposite the
ascent of Adum´mim, which is on
the south side of the valley; and the
boundary passes along to the waters
of En-she´mesh, and ends at En-ro´gel;
8then the boundary goes up by the val-
ley of the son of Hinnom at the south-
ern shoulder of the Jeb´usite (that is,
Jerusalem); and the boundary goes up
to the top of the mountain that lies
over against the valley of Hinnom, on
the west, at the northern end of the
valley of Reph´aim; 9then the bound-
ary extends from the top of the moun-
tain to the spring of the Waters of
Nephto´ah, and from there to the cit-
ies of Mount Ephron; then the bound-
ary bends round to Ba´alah (that is,
Kir´iath-je´arim); 10and the boundary

[a]That is *The city of Arba*

circles west of Ba´alah to Mount Se´ir,
passes along to the northern shoulder
of Mount Je´arim (that is, Ches´alon),
and goes down to Beth-she´mesh, and
passes along by Timnah; 11the bound-
ary goes out to the shoulder of the
hill north of Ekron, then the bound-
ary bends round to Shik´keron, and
passes along to Mount Ba´alah, and
goes out to Jabneel; then the bound-
ary comes to an end at the sea. 12And
the west boundary was the Great Sea
with its coast-line. This is the bound-
ary round about the people of Judah
according to their families.

CALEB OCCUPIES HIS PORTION

13 According to the commandment
of the LORD to Joshua, he gave to
Caleb the son of Jephun´neh a portion
among the people of Judah, Kir´iath-
ar´ba, that is, Hebron (Arba was the
father of Anak). 14And Caleb drove
out from there the three sons of Anak,
She´shai and Ahi´man and Talmai, the
descendants of Anak. 15And he went
up from there against the inhabitants
of Debir; now the name of Debir for-
merly was Kir´iath-se´pher. 16And
Caleb said, "Whoever smites Kir´iath-
se´pher, and takes it, to him will I give
Achsah my daughter as wife." 17And
Oth´ni-el the son of Kenaz, the broth-
er of Caleb, took it; and he gave him
Achsah his daughter as wife. 18When
she came to him, she urged him to ask
her father for a field; and she alight-
ed from her ass, and Caleb said to
her, "What do you wish?" 19She said
to him, "Give me a present; since you
have set me in the land of the Negeb,
give me also springs of water." And
Caleb gave her the upper springs and
the lower springs.

THE TOWNS OF JUDAH

20 This is the inheritance of the
tribe of the people of Judah accord-
ing to their families. 21The cities be-
longing to the tribe of the people of
Judah in the extreme South, toward
the boundary of Edom, were Kabzeel,
Eder, Jagur, 22Kinah, Dimo´nah,
Ada´dah, 23Kedesh, Hazor, Ithnan,
24Ziph, Telem, Be-a´loth, 25Ha´zor-
hadat´tah, Ker´i-oth-hezron (that is,
Hazor), 26Amam, Shema, Mola´dah,
27Ha´zar-gad´dah, Heshmon, Beth-
pel´et, 28Hazar-shu´al, Beer-sheba,
Biziothi´ah, 29Ba´alah, I´im, Ezem,
30Elto´lad, Chesil, Hormah, 31Ziklag,
Madman´nah, Sansan´nah, 32Leba´oth,
Shilhim, A´in, and Rimmon: in all,
twenty-nine cities, with their villages.

33 And in the lowland, Eshta´ol,
Zorah, Ashnah, 34Zano´ah, En-gan´nim,
Tap´pu-ah, Enam, 35Jarmuth, Adul´lam,
Socoh, Aze´kah, 36Sha-ara´im, Aditha´-
im, Gede´rah, Gederotha´im: fourteen
cities with their villages.

37 Zenan, Hadash´ah, Mig´dal-
gad, 38Di´lean, Mizpeh, Jok´theel,
39Lachish, Bozkath, Eglon, 40Cabbon,
Lahmam, Chitlish, 41Gede´roth, Beth-
da´gon, Na´amah, and Makke´dah:
sixteen cities with their villages.

42 Libnah, Ether, Ashan, 43Iphtah,
Ashnah, Nezib, 44Ke-i´lah, Achzib,
and Mare´shah: nine cities with their
villages.

45 Ekron, with its towns and its
villages; 46from Ekron to the sea, all
that were by the side of Ashdod, with
their villages.

47 Ashdod, its towns and its villag-
es; Gaza, its towns and its villages; to
the Brook of Egypt, and the Great Sea
with its coast-line.

48 And in the hill country, Sha-
mir, Jattir, Socoh, 49Dannah, Kir´iath-
san´nah (that is, Debir), 50Anab, Esh´-
temoh, Anim, 51Goshen, Holon, and
Giloh: eleven cities with their villages.

52 Arab, Dumah, Eshan, 53Janim,
Beth-Tap´puah, Aphe´kah, 54Humtah,
Kir´iath-ar´ba (that is, Hebron), and
Zi´or: nine cities with their villages.

55 Ma´on, Carmel, Ziph, Juttah,
56Jezreel, Jok´de-am, Zano´ah, 57Kain,
Gib´e-ah, and Timnah: ten cities with
their villages.

58 Halhul, Beth-zur, Gedor, 59Ma´-
arath, Beth-anoth, and El´tekon: six
cities with their villages.

60 Kir´iath-ba´al (that is, Kir´iath-
je´arim), and Rabbah: two cities with
their villages.

61 In the wilderness, Beth-arabah,
Middin, Seca´cah, 62Nibshan, the City
of Salt, and En-ged´i: six cities with
their villages.

63 But the Jeb´usites, the inhab-
itants of Jerusalem, the people of
Judah could not drive out; so the
Jeb´usites dwell with the people of
Judah at Jerusalem to this day.

THE TERRITORY OF EPHRAIM

16 The allotment of the descen-
dants of Joseph went from the
Jordan by Jericho, east of the waters
of Jericho, into the wilderness, going
up from Jericho into the hill country
to Bethel; 2then going from Bethel to
Luz, it passes along to At´aroth, the
territory of the Archites; 3then it goes
down westward to the territory of the
Japh´letites, as far as the territory of
Lower Beth-hor´on, then to Gezer,
and it ends at the sea.

4 The people of Joseph, Manas´-
seh and E´phraim, received their
inheritance.

5 The territory of the E´phraimites
by their families was as follows: the
boundary of their inheritance on the
east was At´aroth-ad´dar as far as
Upper Beth-hor´on, 6and the bound-
ary goes thence to the sea; on the
north is Michme´thath; then on the
east the boundary turns round toward
Ta´anath-shi´loh, and passes along
beyond it on the east to Jano´ah, 7then
it goes down from Jano´ah to At´aroth
and to Na´arah, and touches Jericho,
ending at the Jordan. 8From Tap´pu-
ah the boundary goes westward to
the brook Kanah, and ends at the sea.
Such is the inheritance of the tribe
of the E´phraimites by their families,
9together with the towns which were
set apart for the E´phraimites within
the inheritance of the Manas´sites,
all those towns with their villages.
10However they did not drive out the
Canaanites that dwelt in Gezer: so the
Canaanites have dwelt in the midst of
E´phraim to this day but have become
slaves to do forced labor.

THE OTHER HALF-TRIBE OF MANASSEH (WEST)

17 Then allotment was made to the
tribe of Manas´seh, for he was
the first-born of Joseph. To Machir
the first-born of Manas´seh, the fa-
ther of Gilead, were allotted Gilead
and Bashan, because he was a man of
war. 2And allotments were made to
the rest of the tribe of Manas´seh, by
their families, Abi-e´zer, Helek, As´ri-
el, Shechem, Hepher, and Shemi´da;
these were the male descendants of
Manas´seh the son of Joseph, by their
families.

3 Now Zeloph´ehad the son of
Hepher, son of Gilead, son of Machir,
son of Manas´seh, had no sons, but
only daughters; and these are the
names of his daughters: Mahlah,
Noah, Hoglah, Milcah, and Tirzah.
4They came before Elea´zar the priest
and Joshua the son of Nun and the
leaders, and said, "The LORD com-
manded Moses to give us an inher-
itance along with our brethren." So
according to the commandment of the
LORD he gave them an inheritance
among the brethren of their father.
5Thus there fell to Manas´seh ten por-
tions, besides the land of Gilead and
Bashan, which is on the other side
of the Jordan; 6because the daugh-
ters of Manas´seh received an inheri-
tance along with his sons. The land of
Gilead was allotted to the rest of the
Manas´sites.

7 The territory of Manas´seh
reached from Asher to Michme´thath,
which is east of Shechem; then the
boundary goes along southward to
the inhabitants of En-Tap´pu-ah.
8The land of Tap´pu-ah belonged to
Manas´seh, but the town of Tap´pu-
ah on the boundary of Manas´seh be-
longed to the sons of E´phraim. 9Then
the boundary went down to the brook
Kanah. The cities here, to the south

of the brook, among the cities of
Manas´seh, belong to E´phraim. Then
the boundary of Manas´seh goes on
the north side of the brook and ends
at the sea; 10the land to the south be-
ing E´phraim's and that to the north
being Manas´seh's, with the sea form-
ing its boundary; on the north Asher
is reached, and on the east Is´sachar.
11Also in Is´sachar and in Asher
Manas´seh had Beth-she´an and its
villages, and Ibleam and its villages,
and the inhabitants of Dor and its vil-
lages, and the inhabitants of En-dor
and its villages, and the inhabitants of
Ta´anach and its villages, and the in-
habitants of Megid´do and its villages;
the third is Naphath.[a] 12Yet the sons of
Manas´seh could not take possession
of those cities; but the Canaanites
persisted in dwelling in that land.
13But when the people of Israel grew
strong, they put the Canaanites to
forced labor, and did not utterly drive
them out.

THE TRIBE OF JOSEPH PROTESTS

14 And the tribe of Joseph spoke to
Joshua, saying, "Why have you given
me but one lot and one portion as an
inheritance, although I am a numer-
ous people, since hitherto the LORD
has blessed me?" 15And Joshua said to
them, "If you are a numerous people,
go up to the forest, and there clear
ground for yourselves in the land of
the Per´izzites and the Reph´aim,
since the hill country of E´phraim is
too narrow for you." 16The tribe of
Joseph said, "The hill country is not
enough for us; yet all the Canaanites
who dwell in the plain have chariots
of iron, both those in Beth-she´an and
its villages and those in the Valley of
Jezre´el." 17Then Joshua said to the
house of Joseph, to E´phraim and
Manas´seh, "You are a numerous peo-
ple, and have great power; you shall
not have one lot only, 18but the hill
country shall be yours, for though it is
a forest, you shall clear it and possess
it to its farthest borders; for you shall
drive out the Canaanites, though they
have chariots of iron, and though they
are strong."

THE TERRITORIES OF THE REMAINING TRIBES

18 Then the whole congregation of
the people of Israel assembled at
Shiloh, and set up the tent of meet-
ing there; the land lay subdued before
them.

2 There remained among the peo-
ple of Israel seven tribes whose inher-
itance had not yet been apportioned.
3So Joshua said to the people of Israel,
"How long will you be slack to go in
and take possession of the land, which
the LORD, the God of your fathers, has
given you? 4Provide three men from
each tribe, and I will send them out
that they may set out and go up and
down the land, writing a description
of it with a view to their inheritances,
and then come to me. 5They shall di-
vide it into seven portions, Judah con-
tinuing in his territory on the south,
and the house of Joseph in their terri-
tory on the north. 6And you shall de-
scribe the land in seven divisions and
bring the description here to me; and
I will cast lots for you here before the
LORD our God. 7The Levites have no
portion among you, for the priesthood
of the LORD is their heritage; and
Gad and Reuben and half the tribe of
Manas´seh have received their inher-
itance beyond the Jordan eastward,
which Moses the servant of the LORD
gave them."

8 So the men started on their way;
and Joshua charged *those who went to*
write the description of the land, say-
ing, "Go up and down and write a de-
scription of the land, and come again
to me; and I will cast lots for you here
before the LORD in Shiloh." 9So the
men went and passed up and down in
the land and set down in a book a de-
scription of it by towns in seven divi-
sions; then they came to Joshua in the

[a] Heb obscure

camp at Shiloh, 10and Joshua cast lots
for them in Shiloh before the LORD;
and there Joshua apportioned the
land to the people of Israel, to each
his portion.

THE TERRITORY OF BENJAMIN

11 The lot of the tribe of Benjamin
according to its families came up,
and the territory allotted to it fell be-
tween the tribe of Judah and the tribe
of Joseph. 12On the north side their
boundary began at the Jordan; then
the boundary goes up to the shoul-
der north of Jericho, then up through
the hill country westward; and it
ends at the wilderness of Beth-a´ven.
13From there the boundary passes
along southward in the direction of
Luz, to the shoulder of Luz (the same
is Bethel), then the boundary goes
down to At´aroth-ad´dar, upon the
mountain that lies south of Lower
Beth-hor´on. 14Then the boundary
goes in another direction, turning
on the western side southward from
the mountain that lies to the south,
opposite Beth-hor´on, and it ends
at Kir´iath-ba´al (that is, Kir´iath-
je´arim), a city belonging to the tribe
of Judah. This forms the western
side. 15And the southern side begins
at the outskirts of Kir´iath-je´arim;
and the boundary goes from there to
Ephron,[a] to the spring of the Waters
of Nephto´ah; 16then the boundary
goes down to the border of the moun-
tain that overlooks the valley of the
son of Hinnom, which is at the north
end of the valley of Reph´aim; and it
then goes down the valley of Hinnom,
south of the shoulder of the Jeb´usites,
and downward to En-ro´gel; 17then it
bends in a northerly direction going
on to En-she´mesh, and thence goes
to Geli´loth, which is opposite the
ascent of Adum´mim; then it goes
down to the stone of Bohan the son
of Reuben; 18and passing on to the
north of the shoulder of Beth-arabah[b]
it goes down to the Arabah; 19then the
boundary passes on to the north of
the shoulder of Beth-hoglah; and the
boundary ends at the northern bay of
the Salt Sea, at the south end of the
Jordan: this is the southern border.
20The Jordan forms its boundary on
the eastern side. This is the inher-
itance of the tribe of Benjamin, ac-
cording to its families, boundary by
boundary round about.

21 Now the cities of the tribe of
Benjamin according to their families
were Jericho, Beth-hoglah, Emek-ke´-
ziz, 22Beth-arabah, Zemara´im, Bethel,
23Avvim, Parah, Ophrah, 24Che´phar-
am´moni, Ophni, Geba—twelve cities
with their villages: 25Gibeon, Ramah, Be-
er´oth, 26Mizpeh, Chephi´rah, Mozah,
27Rekem, Irpeel, Tar´alah, 28Zela, Ha-
eleph, Jebus[c] (that is, Jerusalem), Gib´e-
ah[d] and Kir´iath-je´arim[e]—fourteen
cities with their villages. This is the
inheritance of the tribe of Benjamin ac-
cording to its families.

THE TERRITORY OF SIMEON

19 The second lot came out for
Simeon, for the tribe of Simeon,
according to its families; and its in-
heritance was in the midst of the
inheritance of the tribe of Judah.
2And it had for its inheritance Beer-
sheba, Sheba, Mola´dah, 3Hazar-
shu´al, Balah, Ezem, 4Elto´lad, Bethul,
Hormah, 5Ziklag, Beth-mar´caboth,
Ha´zar-su´sah, 6Beth-leba´oth, and
Sharu´hen—thirteen cities with their
villages; 7En-rimmon, Ether, and
Ashan—four cities with their villages;
8together with all the villages round
about these cities as far as Ba´alath-
beer, Ramah of the Negeb. This was
the inheritance of the tribe of Simeon
according to its families. 9The inher-
itance of the tribe of Simeon formed

[a] Cn See 15.9. Heb *westward*
[b] Gk: Heb *to the shoulder over against the Araba*
[c] Gk Syr Vg: Heb *the Jebusite*
[d] Heb *Gibeath*
[e] Gk: Heb *Kiriath*

part of the territory of Judah; because
the portion of the tribe of Judah was
too large for them, the tribe of Simeon
obtained an inheritance in the midst
of their inheritance.

THE TERRITORY OF ZEBULUN

10 The third lot came up for the
tribe of Zeb´ulun, according to its
families. And the territory of its in-
heritance reached as far as Sarid;
11then its boundary goes up west-
ward, and on to Mar´eal, and touches
Dab´besheth, then the brook which
is east of Jok´ne-am; 12from Sarid it
goes in the other direction eastward
toward the sunrise to the boundary
of Chis´loth-ta´bor; thence it goes to
Dab´erath, then up to Japhi´a; 13from
there it passes along on the east to-
ward the sunrise to Gath-hepher, to
Eth-kazin, and going on to Rimmon
it bends toward Ne´ah; 14then on the
north the boundary turns about to
Han´nathon, and it ends at the valley
of Iph´tahel; 15and Kattath, Na´halal,
Shimron, I´dalah, and Bethlehem—
twelve cities with their villages.
16This is the inheritance of the tribe of
Zeb´ulun, according to its families—
these cities with their villages.

THE TERRITORY OF ISSACHAR

17 The fourth lot came out for
Is´sachar, for the tribe of Is´sachar,
according to its families. 18Its terri-
tory included Jezre´el, Chesul´loth,
Shunem, 19Haph´ara-im, Shion, Ana´-
harath, 20Rabbith, Kish´ion, Ebez,
21Remeth, En-gan´nim, En-had´dah,
Beth-paz´zez; 22the boundary also
touches Tabor, Shahazu´mah, and
Beth-she´mesh, and its boundary ends
at the Jordan—sixteen cities with their
villages. 23This is the inheritance of the
tribe of Is´sachar, according to its fami-
lies—the cities with their villages.

THE TERRITORY OF ASHER

24 The fifth lot came out for the
tribe of Asher according to its families.
25Its territory included Helkath, Hali,
Beten, Ach´shaph, 26Allam´melech,
Amad, and Mishal; on the west it
touches Carmel and Shihor-lib´nath,
27then it turns eastward, it goes to
Beth-dagon, and touches Zeb´ulun
and the valley of Iph´tahel northward
to Beth-emek and Nei´el; then it con-
tinues in the north to Cabul, 28Ebron,
Rehob, Hammon, Kanah, as far as
Sidon the Great; 29then the boundary
turns to Ramah, reaching to the for-
tified city of Tyre; then the boundary
turns to Hosah, and it ends at the sea;
Mahalab,[f] Achzib, 30Ummah, Aphek
and Rehob—twenty-two cities with
their villages. 31This is the inheri-
tance of the tribe of Asher according
to its families—these cities with their
villages.

THE TERRITORY OF NAPHTALI

32 The sixth lot came out for the
tribe of Naph´tali, for the tribe of
Naph´tali, according to its families.
33And its boundary ran from Heleph,
from the oak in Za-anan´nim, and
Ad´ami-nekeb, and Jabneel, as far as
Lakkum; and it ended at the Jordan;
34then the boundary turns westward
to Az´noth-ta´bor, and goes from
there to Hukkok, touching Zeb´ulun
at the south, and Asher on the west,
and Judah on the east at the Jordan.
35The fortified cities are Ziddim, Zer,
Hammath, Rakkath, Chin´nereth,
36Ad´amah, Ramah, Hazor, 37Kedesh,
Ed´re-i, En-ha´zor, 38Yiron, Mig´dal-
el, Horem, Beth-anath, and Beth-
she´mesh—nineteen cities with their
villages. 39This is the inheritance of
the tribe of Naph´tali according to
its families—the cities with their
villages.

THE TERRITORY OF DAN

40 The seventh lot came out for
the tribe of Dan, according to its
families. 41And the territory of its in-
heritance included Zorah, Esh´ta-ol,
Ir-she´mesh, 42Sha-alab´bin, Ai´jalon,

[f]Cn Compare Gk: Heb *Mehebel*

Ithlah, 43Elon, Timnah, Ekron, 44El´te-
keh, Gib´bethon, Ba´alath, 45Jehud,
Bene-be´rak, Gath-rim´mon, 46and
Me-jar´kon and Rakkon with the ter-
ritory over against Joppa. 47When the
territory of the Danites was lost to
them, the Danites went up and fought
against Leshem, and after capturing
it and putting it to the sword they
took possession of it and settled in it,
calling Leshem, Dan, after the name
of Dan their ancestor. 48This is the in-
heritance of the tribe of Dan, accord-
ing to their families—these cities with
their villages.

JOSHUA'S INHERITANCE

49 When they had finished dis-
tributing the several territories of
the land as inheritances, the people
of Israel gave an inheritance among
them to Joshua the son of Nun.
50By command of the LORD they
gave him the city which he asked,
Tim´nath-se´rah in the hill country
of E´phraim; and he rebuilt the city,
and settled in it.

51 These are the inheritances
which Elea´zar the priest and Joshua
the son of Nun and the heads of the
fathers' houses of the tribes of the
people of Israel distributed by lot at
Shiloh before the LORD, at the door of
the tent of meeting. So they finished
dividing the land.

THE CITIES OF REFUGE

20 Then the LORD said to Joshua,
2"Say to the people of Israel,
'Appoint the cities of refuge, of which
I spoke to you through Moses, 3that
the manslayer who kills any person
without intent or unwittingly may
flee there; they shall be for you a ref-
uge from the avenger of blood. 4He
shall flee to one of these cities and
shall stand at the entrance of the gate
of the city, and explain his case to the
elders of that city; then they shall take
him into the city, and give him a place,
and he shall remain with them. 5And
if the avenger of blood pursues him,
they shall not give up the slayer into
his hand; because he killed his neigh-
bor unwittingly, having had no en-
mity against him in times past. 6And
he shall remain in that city until he
has stood before the congregation for
judgment, until the death of him who
is high priest at the time: then the
slayer may go again to his own town
and his own home, to the town from
which he fled.'"

7 So they set apart Kedesh
in Galilee in the hill country of
Naph´tali, and Shechem in the hill
country of E´phraim, and Kir´iath-
ar´ba (that is, Hebron) in the hill
country of Judah. 8And beyond the
Jordan east of Jericho, they appointed
Bezer in the wilderness on the table-
land, from the tribe of Reuben, and
Ramoth in Gilead, from the tribe of
Gad, and Golan in Bashan, from the
tribe of Manas´seh. 9These were the
cities designated for all the people of
Israel, and for the stranger sojourning
among them, that any one who killed
a person without intent could flee
there, so that he might not die by the
hand of the avenger of blood, till he
stood before the congregation.

CITIES ALLOTTED TO THE LEVITES

21 Then the heads of the fathers'
houses of the Levites came to
Elea´zar the priest and to Joshua the
son of Nun and to the heads of the fa-
thers' houses of the tribes of the peo-
ple of Israel; 2and they said to them
at Shiloh in the land of Canaan, "The
LORD commanded through Moses
that we be given cities to dwell in,
along with their pasture lands for our
cattle." 3So by command of the LORD
the people of Israel gave to the Levites
the following cities and pasture lands
out of their inheritance.

4 The lot came out for the families
of the Ko´hathites. So those Levites
who were descendants of Aaron the
priest received by lot from the tribes
of Judah, Simeon, and Benjamin, thir-
teen cities.

5 And the rest of the Ko´hathites
received by lot from the families of the
tribe of E´phraim, from the tribe of
Dan and the half-tribe of Manas´seh,
ten cities.

6 The Gershonites received by
lot from the families of the tribe of
Is´sachar, from the tribe of Asher,
from the tribe of Naph´tali, and from
the half-tribe of Manas´seh in Bashan,
thirteen cities.

7 The Merar´ites according to
their families received from the tribe
of Reuben, the tribe of Gad, and the
tribe of Zeb´ulun, twelve cities.

8 These cities and their pasture
lands the people of Israel gave by lot
to the Levites, as the LORD had com-
manded through Moses.

9 Out of the tribe of Judah and the
tribe of Simeon they gave the follow-
ing cities mentioned by name, 10 which
went to the descendants of Aaron,
one of the families of the Ko´hathites
who belonged to the Levites; since
the lot fell to them first. 11 They gave
them Kir´iath-ar´ba (Arba being the
father of Anak), that is Hebron, in the
hill country of Judah, along with the
pasture lands round about it. 12 But
the fields of the city and its villages
had been given to Caleb the son of
Jephun´neh as his possession.

13 And to the descendants of Aaron
the priest they gave Hebron, the city
of refuge for the slayer, with its pas-
ture lands, Libnah with its pasture
lands, 14 Jattir with its pasture lands,
Eshtemo´a with its pasture lands,
15 Holon with its pasture lands, Debir
with its pasture lands, 16 A´in with its
pasture lands, Juttah with its pasture
lands, Beth-she´mesh with its pas-
ture lands—nine cities out of these
two tribes; 17 then out of the tribe of
Benjamin, Gibeon with its pasture
lands, Geba with its pasture lands,
18 An´athoth with its pasture lands, and
Almon with its pasture lands—four
cities. 19 The cities of the descendants
of Aaron, the priests, were in all thir-
teen cities with their pasture lands.

20 As to the rest of the Ko´hathites
belonging to the Ko´hathite fami-
lies of the Levites, the cities allot-
ted to them were out of the tribe
of E´phraim. 21 To them were given
Shechem, the city of refuge for the
slayer, with its pasture lands in the
hill country of E´phraim, Gezer with
its pasture lands, 22 Kib´za-im with
its pasture lands, Beth-hor´on with
its pasture lands—four cities; 23 and
out of the tribe of Dan, El´teke with
its pasture lands, Gib´bethon with
its pasture lands, 24 Ai´jalon with its
pasture lands, Gath-rim´mon with its
pasture lands—four cities; 25 and out of
the half-tribe of Manas´seh, Ta´anach
with its pasture lands, and Gath-
rim´mon with its pasture lands—two
cities. 26 The cities of the families of
the rest of the Ko´hathites were ten in
all with their pasture lands.

27 And to the Gershonites, one of
the families of the Levites, were giv-
en out of the half-tribe of Manas´seh,
Golan in Bashan with its pasture
lands, the city of refuge for the slay-
er, and Be-esh´terah with its pasture
lands—two cities; 28 and out of the
tribe of Is´sachar, Kish´ion with its
pasture lands, Dab´erath with its pas-
ture lands, 29 Jarmuth with its pasture
lands, En-gan´nim with its pasture
lands—four cities; 30 and out of the
tribe of Asher, Mishal with its pasture
lands, Abdon with its pasture lands,
31 Helkath with its pasture lands,
and Rehob with its pasture lands—
four cities; 32 and out of the tribe of
Naph´tali, Kedesh in Galilee with its
pasture lands, the city of refuge for
the slayer, Ham´moth-dor with its
pasture lands, and Kartan with its
pasture lands—three cities. 33 The
cities of the several families of the
Gershonites were in all thirteen cities
with their pasture lands.

34 And to the rest of the Levites,
the Merar´ite families, were given out
of the tribe of Zeb´ulun, Jok´ne-am
with its pasture lands, Kartah with
its pasture lands, 35 Dimnah with its

pasture lands, Na´halal with its pas-
ture lands—four cities; 36and out of
the tribe of Reuben, Bezer with its
pasture lands, Jahaz with its pasture
lands, 37Ked´emoth with its pasture
lands, and Meph´a-ath with its pas-
ture lands—four cities; 38and out of
the tribe of Gad, Ramoth in Gilead
with its pasture lands, the city of ref-
uge for the slayer, Mahana´im with
its pasture lands, 39Heshbon with its
pasture lands, Jazer with its pasture
lands—four cities in all. 40As for the
cities of the several Merar´ite fami-
lies, that is, the remainder of the fam-
ilies of the Levites, those allotted to
them were in all twelve cities.

41 The cities of the Levites in the
midst of the possession of the people
of Israel were in all forty-eight cities
with their pasture lands. 42These cit-
ies had each its pasture lands round
about it; so it was with all these cities.

43 Thus the LORD gave to Israel
all the land which he swore to give to
their fathers; and having taken pos-
session of it, they settled there. 44And
the LORD gave them rest on every side
just as he had sworn to their fathers;
not one of all their enemies had with-
stood them, for the LORD had given all
their enemies into their hands. 45Not
one of all the good promises which
the LORD had made to the house of
Israel had failed; all came to pass.

THE EASTERN TRIBES RETURN TO THEIR TERRITORY

22 Then Joshua summoned the Reu-
benites, and the Gadites, and the
half-tribe of Manas´seh, 2and said to
them, "You have kept all that Moses
the servant of the LORD command-
ed you, and have obeyed my voice in
all that I have commanded you; 3you
have not forsaken your brethren these
many days, down to this day, but have
been careful to keep the charge of the
LORD your God. 4And now the LORD
your God has given rest to your breth-
ren, as he promised them; therefore
turn and go to your home in the land
where your possession lies, which
Moses the servant of the LORD gave
you on the other side of the Jordan.
5Take good care to observe the com-
mandment and the law which Moses
the servant of the LORD commanded
you, to love the LORD your God, and
to walk in all his ways, and to keep his
commandments, and to cleave to him,
and to serve him with all your heart
and with all your soul." 6So Joshua
blessed them, and sent them away;
and they went to their homes.

7 Now to the one half of the tribe
of Manas´seh Moses had given a pos-
session in Bashan; but to the other
half Joshua had given a possession
beside their brethren in the land west
of the Jordan. And when Joshua sent
them away to their homes and bless-
ed them, 8he said to them, "Go back
to your homes with much wealth,
and with very many cattle, with sil-
ver, gold, bronze, and iron, and with
much clothing; divide the spoil of
your enemies with your brethren."
9So the Reubenites and the Gadites
and the half-tribe of Manas´seh re-
turned home, parting from the people
of Israel at Shiloh, which is in the land
of Canaan, to go to the land of Gilead,
their own land of which they had pos-
sessed themselves by command of the
LORD through Moses.

A MEMORIAL ALTAR EAST OF THE JORDAN

10 And when they came to the re-
gion about the Jordan, that lies in
the land of Canaan, the Reubenites
and the Gadites and the half-tribe of
Manas´seh built there an altar by the
Jordan, an altar of great size. 11And the
people of Israel heard say, "Behold,
the Reubenites and the Gadites and
the half-tribe of Manas´seh have built
an altar at the frontier of the land
of Canaan, in the region about the
Jordan, on the side that belongs to the
people of Israel." 12And when the peo-
ple of Israel heard of it, the whole as-
sembly of the people of Israel gathered
at Shiloh, to make war against them.

13 Then the people of Israel sent
to the Reubenites and the Gadites
and the half-tribe of Manas´seh, in
the land of Gilead, Phin´ehas the
son of Elea´zar the priest, 14and with
him ten chiefs, one from each of the
tribal families of Israel, every one
of them the head of a family among
the clans of Israel. 15And they came
to the Reubenites, the Gadites, and
the half-tribe of Manas´seh, in the
land of Gilead, and they said to them,
16"Thus says the whole congregation
of the LORD, 'What is this treachery
which you have committed against the
God of Israel in turning away this day
from following the LORD, by building
yourselves an altar this day in rebel-
lion against the LORD? 17Have we not
had enough of the sin at Pe´or from
which even yet we have not cleansed
ourselves, and for which there came a
plague upon the congregation of the
LORD, 18that you must turn away this
day from following the LORD? And if
you rebel against the LORD today he
will be angry with the whole congre-
gation of Israel tomorrow. 19But now,
if your land is unclean, pass over into
the LORD's land where the LORD's
tabernacle stands, and take for your-
selves a possession among us; only do
not rebel against the LORD, or make
us as rebels by building yourselves an
altar other than the altar of the LORD
our God. 20Did not Achan the son of
Zerah break faith in the matter of the
devoted things, and wrath fell upon
all the congregation of Israel? And he
did not perish alone for his iniquity.'"

21 Then the Reubenites, the Gad-
ites, and the half-tribe of Manas´seh
said in answer to the heads of the
families of Israel, 22"The Mighty One,
God, the LORD! The Mighty One, God,
the LORD! He knows; and let Israel it-
self know! If it was in rebellion or in
breach of faith toward the LORD, spare
us not today 23for building an altar to
turn away from following the LORD;
or if we did so to offer burnt offerings
or cereal offerings or peace offerings
on it, may the LORD himself take ven-
geance. 24Nay, but we did it from fear
that in time to come your children
might say to our children, 'What have
you to do with the LORD, the God of
Israel? 25For the LORD has made the
Jordan a boundary between us and
you, you Reubenites and Gadites;
you have no portion in the LORD.'
So your children might make our
children cease to worship the LORD.
26Therefore we said, 'Let us now build
an altar, not for burnt offering, nor for
sacrifice, 27but to be a witness between
us and you, and between the genera-
tions after us, that we do perform the
service of the LORD in his presence
with our burnt offerings and sacrifices
and peace offerings; lest your children
say to our children in time to come,
"You have no portion in the LORD."'
28And we thought, If this should be
said to us or to our descendants in
time to come, we should say, 'Behold
the copy of the altar of the LORD,
which our fathers made, not for burnt
offerings, nor for sacrifice, but to be a
witness between us and you.' 29Far be
it from us that we should rebel against
the LORD, and turn away this day from
following the LORD by building an al-
tar for burnt offering, cereal offering,
or sacrifice, other than the altar of the
LORD our God that stands before his
tabernacle!"

30 When Phin´ehas the priest and
the chiefs of the congregation, the
heads of the families of Israel who
were with him, heard the words that
the Reubenites and the Gadites and
the Manas´sites spoke, it pleased
them well. 31And Phin´ehas the son
of Elea´zar the priest said to the
Reubenites and the Gadites and the
Manas´sites, "Today we know that the
LORD is in the midst of us, because
you have not committed this treach-
ery against the LORD; now you have
saved the people of Israel from the
hand of the LORD."

32 Then Phin´ehas the son of
Elea´zar the priest, and the chiefs,

returned from the Reubenites and
the Gadites in the land of Gilead to
the land of Canaan, to the people
of Israel, and brought back word to
them. 33And the report pleased the
people of Israel; and the people of
Israel blessed God and spoke no more
of making war against them, to de-
stroy the land where the Reubenites
and the Gadites were settled. 34The
Reubenites and the Gadites called the
altar Witness; "For," said they, "it is
a witness between us that the LORD
is God."

JOSHUA EXHORTS THE PEOPLE

23 A long time afterward, when the
LORD had given rest to Israel
from all their enemies round about,
and Joshua was old and well advanced
in years, 2Joshua summoned all Israel,
their elders and heads, their judges
and officers, and said to them, "I am
now old and well advanced in years;
3and you have seen all that the LORD
your God has done to all these nations
for your sake, for it is the LORD your
God who has fought for you. 4Behold, I
have allotted to you as an inheritance
for your tribes those nations that
remain, along with all the nations
that I have already cut off, from the
Jordan to the Great Sea in the west.
5The LORD your God will push them
back before you, and drive them out of
your sight; and you shall possess their
land, as the LORD your God prom-
ised you. 6Therefore be very steadfast
to keep and do all that is written in
the book of the law of Moses, turn-
ing aside from it neither to the right
hand nor to the left, 7that you may
not be mixed with these nations left
here among you, or make mention of
the names of their gods, or swear by
them, or serve them, or bow down
yourselves to them, 8but cleave to the
LORD your God as you have done to
this day. 9For the LORD has driven out
before you great and strong nations;
and as for you, no man has been able
to withstand you to this day. 10One
man of you puts to flight a thousand,
since it is the LORD your God who
fights for you, as he promised you.
11Take good heed to yourselves, there-
fore, to love the LORD your God. 12For
if you turn back, and join the remnant
of these nations left here among you,
and make marriages with them, so
that you marry their women and they
yours, 13know assuredly that the LORD
your God will not continue to drive
out these nations before you; but they
shall be a snare and a trap for you, a
scourge on your sides, and thorns in
your eyes, till you perish from off this
good land which the LORD your God
has given you.

14 "And now I am about to go the
way of all the earth, and you know
in your hearts and souls, all of you,
that not one thing has failed of all
the good things which the LORD your
God promised concerning you; all
have come to pass for you, not one of
them has failed. 15But just as all the
good things which the LORD your
God promised concerning you have
been fulfilled for you, so the LORD
will bring upon you all the evil things,
until he have destroyed you from off
this good land which the LORD your
God has given you, 16if you transgress
the covenant of the LORD your God,
which he commanded you, and go and
serve other gods and bow down to
them. Then the anger of the LORD will
be kindled against you, and you shall
perish quickly from off the good land
which he has given to you."

THE TRIBES RENEW THE COVENANT

24 *Then Joshua gathered all the
tribes of Israel to Shechem, and
summoned the elders, the heads,
the judges, and the officers of Israel;
and they presented themselves be-
fore God. 2And Joshua said to all the
people, "Thus says the LORD, the
God of Israel, 'Your fathers lived of
old beyond the Euphra'tes, Terah,
the father of Abraham and of Nahor;
and they served other gods. 3Then I

took your father Abraham from be-
yond the River and led him through
all the land of Canaan, and made
his offspring many. I gave him Isaac;
4and to Isaac I gave Jacob and Esau.
And I gave Esau the hill country of
Se´ir to possess, but Jacob and his
children went down to Egypt. 5And I
sent Moses and Aaron, and I plagued
Egypt with what I did in the midst of
it; and afterwards I brought you out.
6Then I brought your fathers out of
Egypt, and you came to the sea; and
the Egyptians pursued your fathers
with chariots and horsemen to the
Red Sea. 7And when they cried to the
LORD, he put darkness between you
and the Egyptians, and made the sea
come upon them and cover them; and
your eyes saw what I did to Egypt;
and you lived in the wilderness a long
time. 8Then I brought you to the land
of the Amorites, who lived on the
other side of the Jordan; they fought
with you, and I gave them into your
hand, and you took possession of their
land, and I destroyed them before you.
9Then Balak the son of Zippor, king
of Moab, arose and fought against
Israel; and he sent and invited Balaam
the son of Be´or to curse you, 10but I
would not listen to Balaam; therefore
he blessed you; so I delivered you out
of his hand. 11And you went over the
Jordan and came to Jericho, and the
men of Jericho fought against you,
and also the Amorites, the Per´izzites,
the Canaanites, the Hittites, the
Gir´gashites, the Hivites, and the
Jeb´usites; and I gave them into your
hand. 12And I sent the hornet before
you, which drove them out before you,
the two kings of the Amorites; it was
not by your sword or by your bow. 13I
gave you a land on which you had not
labored, and cities which you had not
built, and you dwell therein; you eat
the fruit of vineyards and oliveyards
which you did not plant.'

14 "Now therefore fear the LORD,
and serve him in sincerity and in
faithfulness; put away the gods which
your fathers served beyond the River,
and in Egypt, and serve the LORD.
15And if you be unwilling to serve the
LORD, choose this day whom you will
serve, whether the gods your fathers
served in the region beyond the River,
or the gods of the Amorites in whose
land you dwell; but as for me and my
house, we will serve the LORD."

16 Then the people answered, "Far
be it from us that we should forsake
the LORD, to serve other gods; 17for
it is the LORD our God who brought
us and our fathers up from the land
of Egypt, out of the house of bondage,
and who did those great signs in our
sight, and preserved us in all the way
that we went, and among all the peo-
ples through whom we passed; 18and
the LORD drove out before us all the
peoples, the Amorites who lived in
the land; therefore we also will serve
the LORD, for he is our God."

19 But Joshua said to the people,
"You cannot serve the LORD; for he
is a holy God; he is a jealous God;
he will not forgive your transgres-
sions or your sins. 20If you forsake
the LORD and serve foreign gods,
then he will turn and do you harm,
and consume you, after having done
you good." 21And the people said to
Joshua, "Nay; but we will serve the
LORD." 22Then Joshua said to the
people, "You are witnesses against
yourselves that you have chosen the
LORD, to serve him." And they said,
"We are witnesses." 23He said, "Then
put away the foreign gods which are
among you, and incline your heart to
the LORD, the God of Israel." 24And
the people *said to* Joshua, "The LORD
our God we will serve, and his voice
we will obey." 25So Joshua made a cov-
enant with the people that day, and
made statutes and ordinances for
them at Shechem. 26And Joshua wrote
these words in the book of the law of
God; and he took a great stone, and
set it up there under the oak in the
sanctuary of the LORD. 27And Joshua
said to all the people, "Behold, this

stone shall be a witness against us;
for it has heard all the words of the
LORD which he spoke to us; therefore
it shall be a witness against you, lest
you deal falsely with your God." 28So
Joshua sent the people away, every
man to his inheritance.

DEATH OF JOSHUA AND ELEAZAR

29 After these things Joshua the
son of Nun, the servant of the LORD,
died, being a hundred and ten years
old. 30And they buried him in his own
inheritance at Tim´nath-se´rah, which
is in the hill country of E´phraim,
north of the mountain of Ga´ash.

31 And Israel served the LORD all
the days of Joshua, and all the days
of the elders who outlived Joshua and
had known all the work which the
LORD did for Israel.

32 The bones of Joseph which
the people of Israel brought up from
Egypt were buried at Shechem, in the
portion of ground which Jacob bought
from the sons of Hamor the father of
Shechem for a hundred pieces of money;[a] it became an inheritance of the
descendants of Joseph.

33 And Elea´zar the son of Aaron
died; and they buried him at Gib´e-ah,
the town of Phin´ehas his son, which
had been given him in the hill country
of E´phraim.

[a] Heb *qesitah*

THE BOOK OF JUDGES

ISRAEL'S FAILURE TO COMPLETE THE CONQUEST OF CANAAN

1 *After the death of Joshua the people
of Israel inquired of the LORD, "Who
shall go up first for us against the
Canaanites, to fight against them?"
2The LORD said, "Judah shall go up;
behold, I have given the land into his
hand." 3And Judah said to Simeon his
brother, "Come up with me into the
territory alloted to me, that we may
fight against the Canaanites; and I
likewise will go with you into the
territory allotted to you." So Simeon
went with him. 4Then Judah went up
and the LORD gave the Canaanites and
the Per´izzites into their hand; and
they defeated ten thousand of them
at Bezek. 5They came upon Ado´ni-
be´zek at Bezek, and fought against
him, and defeated the Canaanites and
the Per´izzites. 6Ado´ni-be´zek fled;
but they pursued him, and caught
him, and cut off his thumbs and his
great toes. 7And Ado´ni-be´zek said,
"Seventy kings with their thumbs and
their great toes cut off used to pick up
scraps under my table; as I have done,
so God has requited me." And they
brought him to Jerusalem, and he died
there.

8 And the men of Judah fought
against Jerusalem, and took it, and
smote it with the edge of the sword,
and set the city on fire. 9And after-
ward the men of Judah went down
to fight against the Canaanites who
dwelt in the hill country, in the Negeb,
and in the lowland. 10And Judah went
against the Canaanites who dwelt in
Hebron (now the name of Hebron was
formerly Kir´iath-ar´ba); and they
defeated Sheshai and Ahi´man and
Talmai.

11 From there they went against
the inhabitants of Debir. The name of
Debir was formerly Kir´iath-se´pher.
12And Caleb said, "He who attacks
Kir´iath-se´pher and takes it, I will
give him Achsah my daughter as
wife." 13And Oth´ni-el the son of
Kenaz, Caleb's younger brother, took
it; and he gave him Achsah his daugh-
ter as wife. 14When she came to him,
she urged him to ask her father for a
field; and she alighted from her ass,
and Caleb said to her, "What do you
wish?" 15She said to him, "Give me
a present; since you have set me in
the land of the Negeb, give me also
springs of water." And Caleb gave
her the upper springs and the lower
springs.

16 And the descendants of the
Ken´ite, Moses' father-in-law, went
up with the people of Judah from the
city of palms into the wilderness of
Judah, which lies in the Negeb near
Arad; and they went and settled
with the people. 17And Judah went
with Simeon his brother, and they
defeated the Canaanites who inhab-
ited Zephath, and utterly destroyed
it. So the name of the city was called
Hormah. 18Judah also took Gaza with
its territory, and Ash´kelon with its
territory, and Ekron with its territory.
19And the LORD was with Judah, and
he took possession of the hill country,
but he could not drive out the inhab-
itants of the plain, because they had
chariots of iron. 20And Hebron was
given to Caleb, as Moses had said; and
he drove out from it the three sons of
Anak. 21But the people of Benjamin did
not drive out the Jeb´usites who dwelt
in Jerusalem; so the Jeb´usites have
dwelt with the people of Benjamin in
Jerusalem to this day.

22 The house of Joseph also went
up against Bethel; and the LORD was
with them. 23And the house of Joseph
sent to spy out Bethel. (Now the name
of the city was formerly Luz.) 24And
the spies saw a man coming out of

the city, and they said to him, "Pray, show us the way into the city, and we will deal kindly with you." 25 And he showed them the way into the city; and they smote the city with the edge of the sword, but they let the man and all his family go. 26 And the man went to the land of the Hittites and built a city, and called its name Luz; that is its name to this day.

27 Manas´seh did not drive out the inhabitants of Beth-she´an and its villages, or Ta´anach and its villages, or the inhabitants of Dor and its villages, or the inhabitants of Ib´leam and its villages, or the inhabitants of Megid´do and its villages; but the Canaanites persisted in dwelling in that land. 28 When Israel grew strong, they put the Canaanites to forced labor, but did not utterly drive them out.

29 And E´phraim did not drive out the Canaanites who dwelt in Gezer; but the Canaanites dwelt in Gezer among them.

30 Zeb´ulun did not drive out the inhabitants of Kitron, or the inhabitants of Na´halol; but the Canaanites dwelt among them, and became subject to forced labor.

31 Asher did not drive out the inhabitants of Acco, or the inhabitants of Sidon, or of Ahlab, or of Achzib, or of Helbah, or of Aphik, or of Rehob; 32 but the Asherites dwelt among the Canaanites, the inhabitants of the land; for they did not drive them out.

33 Naph´tali did not drive out the inhabitants of Beth-she´mesh, or the inhabitants of Beth-anath, but dwelt among the Canaanites, the inhabitants of the land; nevertheless the inhabitants of Beth-she´mesh and of Beth-anath became subject to forced labor for them.

34 The Amorites pressed the Danites back into the hill country, for they did not allow them to come down to the plain; 35 the Amorites persisted in dwelling in Har-heres, in Ai´jalon, and in Sha-al´bim, but the hand of the house of Joseph rested heavily upon them, and they became subject to forced labor. 36 And the border of the Amorites ran from the ascent of Akrab´bim, from Sela and upward.

ISRAEL'S DISOBEDIENCE

2 Now the angel of the LORD went up from Gilgal to Bochim. And he said, "I brought you up from Egypt, and brought you into the land which I swore to give to your fathers. I said, 'I will never break my covenant with you, 2 and you shall make no covenant with the inhabitants of this land; you shall break down their altars.' But you have not obeyed my command. What is this you have done? 3 So now I say, I will not drive them out before you; but they shall become adversaries[a] to you, and their gods shall be a snare to you." 4 When the angel of the LORD spoke these words to all the people of Israel, the people lifted up their voices and wept. 5 And they called the name of that place Bochim;[b] and they sacrificed there to the LORD.

DEATH OF JOSHUA

6 When Joshua dismissed the people, the people of Israel went each to his inheritance to take possession of the land. 7 And the people served the LORD all the days of Joshua, and all the days of the elders who outlived Joshua, who had seen all the great work which the LORD had done for Israel. 8 And Joshua the son of Nun, the servant of the LORD, died at the age of one hundred and ten years. 9 And they buried him within the bounds of his inheritance in Tim´nath-he´res, in the hill country of E´phraim, north of the mountain of Ga´ash. 10 And all that generation also were gathered to their fathers; and there arose another generation after them, who did not know the LORD or the work which he had done for Israel.

[a] Vg Old Latin Compare Gk: Heb *sides*
[b] That is *Weepers*

ISRAEL'S UNFAITHFULNESS

11 And the people of Israel did what
was evil in the sight of the LORD and
served the Ba´als; 12and they forsook
the LORD, the God of their fathers,
who had brought them out of the land
of Egypt; they went after other gods,
from among the gods of the peoples
who were round about them, and
bowed down to them; and they pro-
voked the LORD to anger. 13They for-
sook the LORD, and served the Ba´als
and the Ash´taroth. 14So the anger of
the LORD was kindled against Israel,
and he gave them over to plunderers,
who plundered them; and he sold
them into the power of their ene-
mies round about, so that they could
no longer withstand their enemies.
15Whenever they marched out, the
hand of the LORD was against them
for evil, as the LORD had warned, and
as the LORD had sworn to them; and
they were in sore straits.

16 Then the LORD raised up judg-
es, who saved them out of the power
of those who plundered them. 17And
yet they did not listen to their judg-
es; for they played the harlot after
other gods and bowed down to them;
they soon turned aside from the way
in which their fathers had walked,
who had obeyed the commandments
of the LORD, and they did not do so.
18Whenever the LORD raised up judg-
es for them, the LORD was with the
judge, and he saved them from the
hand of their enemies all the days of
the judge; for the LORD was moved
to pity by their groaning because of
those who afflicted and oppressed
them. 19But whenever the judge died,
they turned back and behaved worse
than their fathers, going after other
gods, serving them and bowing down
to them; they did not drop any of their
practices or their stubborn ways.* 20So
the anger of the LORD was kindled
against Israel; and he said, "Because
this people have transgressed my cov-
enant which I commanded their fa-
thers, and have not obeyed my voice,
21I will not henceforth drive out before
them any of the nations that Joshua
left when he died, 22that by them I
may test Israel, whether they will take
care to walk in the way of the LORD
as their fathers did, or not." 23So the
LORD left those nations, not driving
them out at once, and he did not give
them into the power of Joshua.

NATIONS REMAINING IN THE LAND

3 Now these are the nations which
the LORD left, to test Israel by
them, that is, all in Israel who had no
experience of any war in Canaan; 2it
was only that the generations of the
people of Israel might know war, that
he might teach war to such at least
as had not known it before. 3These
are the nations: the five lords of the
Philistines, and all the Canaanites,
and the Sido´nians, and the Hivites
who dwelt on Mount Lebanon, from
Mount Ba´al-her´mon as far as the
entrance of Hamath. 4They were for
the testing of Israel, to know whether
Israel would obey the commandments
of the LORD, which he commanded
their fathers by Moses. 5So the people
of Israel dwelt among the Canaanites,
the Hittites, the Amorites, the Per´-
izzites, the Hivites, and the Jeb´usites;
6and they took their daughters to
themselves for wives, and their own
daughters they gave to their sons; and
they served their gods.

OTHNIEL

7 And the people of Israel did what
was evil in the sight of the LORD,
forgetting the LORD their God, and
serving the Ba´als and the Ashe´roth.
8Therefore the anger of the LORD
was kindled against Israel, and he
sold them into the hand of Cu´shan-
rishatha´im king of Mesopota´mia;
and the people of Israel served
Cu´shan-rishatha´im eight years. 9But
when the people of Israel cried to the
LORD, the LORD raised up a deliverer
for the people of Israel, who delivered
them, Oth´ni-el the son of Kenaz,

Caleb's younger brother. 10 The Spirit of the LORD came upon him, and he judged Israel; he went out to war, and the LORD gave Cu´shan-rishatha´im king of Mesopota´mia into his hand; and his hand prevailed over Cu´shan-rishatha´im. 11 So the land had rest forty years. Then Oth´ni-el the son of Kenaz died.

EHUD

12 And the people of Israel again did what was evil in the sight of the LORD; and the LORD strengthened Eglon the king of Moab against Israel, because they had done what was evil in the sight of the LORD. 13 He gathered to himself the Ammonites and the Amal´ekites, and went and defeated Israel; and they took possession of the city of palms. 14 And the people of Israel served Eglon the king of Moab eighteen years.

15 But when the people of Israel cried to the LORD, the LORD raised up for them a deliverer, Ehud, the son of Gera, the Benjaminite, a left-handed man. The people of Israel sent tribute by him to Eglon the king of Moab. 16 And Ehud made for himself a sword with two edges, a cubit in length; and he girded it on his right thigh under his clothes. 17 And he presented the tribute to Eglon king of Moab. Now Eglon was a very fat man. 18 And when Ehud had finished presenting the tribute, he sent away the people that carried the tribute. 19 But he himself turned back at the sculptured stones near Gilgal, and said, "I have a secret message for you, O king." And he commanded, "Silence." And all his attendants went out from his presence. 20 And Ehud came to him, as he was sitting alone in his cool roof chamber. And Ehud said, "I have a message from God for you." And he arose from his seat. 21 And Ehud reached with his left hand, took the sword from his right thigh, and thrust it into his belly; 22 and the hilt also went in after the blade, and the fat closed over the blade, for he did not draw the sword out of his belly; and the dirt came out. 23 Then Ehud went out into the vestibule,[a] and closed the doors of the roof chamber upon him, and locked them.

24 When he had gone, the servants came; and when they saw that the doors of the roof chamber were locked, they thought, "He is only relieving himself in the closet of the cool chamber." 25 And they waited till they were utterly at a loss; but when he still did not open the doors of the roof chamber, they took the key and opened them; and there lay their lord dead on the floor.

26 Ehud escaped while they delayed, and passed beyond the sculptured stones, and escaped to Se-i´rah. 27 When he arrived, he sounded the trumpet in the hill country of E´phraim; and the people of Israel went down with him from the hill country, having him at their head. 28 And he said to them, "Follow after me; for the LORD has given your enemies the Moabites into your hand." So they went down after him, and seized the fords of the Jordan against the Moabites, and allowed not a man to pass over. 29 And they killed at that time about ten thousand of the Moabites, all strong, able-bodied men; not a man escaped. 30 So Moab was subdued that day under the hand of Israel. And the land had rest for eighty years.

SHAMGAR

31 After him was Shamgar the son of Anath, who killed six hundred of the Philistines with an oxgoad; and he too delivered Israel.

DEBORAH AND BARAK

4 And the people of Israel again did what was evil in the sight of the LORD, after Ehud died. 2 And the LORD sold them into the hand of Jabin king

[a] The meaning of the Hebrew word is unknown

of Canaan, who reigned in Hazor; the
commander of his army was Sis´era,
who dwelt in Haro´sheth-ha-goi´im.
3Then the people of Israel cried to the
LORD for help; for he had nine hun-
dred chariots of iron, and oppressed
the people of Israel cruelly for twenty
years.

4 Now Deb´orah, a prophetess,
the wife of Lap´pidoth, was judging
Israel at that time. 5She used to sit
under the palm of Deb´orah between
Ramah and Bethel in the hill country
of E´phraim; and the people of Israel
came up to her for judgment. 6She
sent and summoned Barak the son of
Abin´o-am from Kedesh in Naph´tali,
and said to him, "The LORD, the God
of Israel, commands you, 'Go, gather
your men at Mount Tabor, taking ten
thousand from the tribe of Naph´tali
and the tribe of Zeb´ulun. 7And I will
draw out Sis´era, the general of Jabin's
army, to meet you by the river Kishon
with his chariots and his troops; and I
will give him into your hand.'" 8Barak
said to her, "If you will go with me, I
will go; but if you will not go with me,
I will not go." 9And she said, "I will
surely go with you; nevertheless, the
road on which you are going will not
lead to your glory, for the LORD will
sell Sis´era into the hand of a wom-
an." Then Deb´orah arose, and went
with Barak to Kedesh. 10And Barak
summoned Zeb´ulun and Naph´tali to
Kedesh; and ten thousand men went
up at his heels; and Deb´orah went up
with him.

11 Now Heber the Ken´ite had
separated from the Ken´ites, the de-
scendants of Hobab the father-in-law
of Moses, and had pitched his tent as
far away as the oak in Za-anan´nim,
which is near Kedesh.

12 When Sis´era was told that
Barak the son of Abin´o-am had gone
up to Mount Tabor, 13Sis´era called out
all his chariots, nine hundred chari-
ots of iron, and all the men who were
with him, from Haro´sheth-ha-goi´im
to the river Kishon. 14And Deb´orah
said to Barak, "Up! For this is the day
in which the LORD has given Sis´era
into your hand. Does not the LORD go
out before you?" So Barak went down
from Mount Tabor with ten thousand
men following him. 15And the LORD
routed Sis´era and all his chariots
and all his army before Barak at the
edge of the sword; and Sis´era alight-
ed from his chariot and fled away on
foot. 16And Barak pursued the chari-
ots and the army to Haro´sheth-ha-
goi´im, and all the army of Sis´era fell
by the edge of the sword; not a man
was left.

17 But Sis´era fled away on foot
to the tent of Ja´el, the wife of Heber
the Ken´ite; for there was peace be-
tween Jabin the king of Hazor and
the house of Heber the Ken´ite. 18And
Ja´el came out to meet Sis´era, and
said to him, "Turn aside, my lord,
turn aside to me; have no fear." So he
turned aside to her into the tent, and
she covered him with a rug. 19And he
said to her, "Pray, give me a little wa-
ter to drink; for I am thirsty." So she
opened a skin of milk and gave him a
drink and covered him. 20And he said
to her, "Stand at the door of the tent,
and if any man comes and asks you,
'Is any one here?' say, No." 21But Ja´el
the wife of Heber took a tent peg, and
took a hammer in her hand, and went
softly to him and drove the peg into
his temple, till it went down into the
ground, as he was lying fast asleep
from weariness. So he died. 22And
behold, as Barak pursued Sis´era,
Ja´el went out to meet him, and said
to him, "Come, and I will show you
the man whom you are seeking." So
he went in to her tent; and there lay
Sis´era dead, with the tent peg in his
temple.

23 So on that day God subdued
Jabin the king of Canaan before the
people of Israel. 24And the hand of
the people of Israel bore harder and
harder on Jabin the king of Canaan,
until they destroyed Jabin king of
Canaan.

Mid´ianites and the Amal´ekites and
the people of the East would come up
and attack them; 4they would encamp
against them and destroy the produce
of the land, as far as the neighborhood
of Gaza, and leave no sustenance in
Israel, and no sheep or ox or ass. 5For
they would come up with their cattle
and their tents, coming like locusts
for number; both they and their cam-
els could not be counted; so that they
wasted the land as they came in. 6And
Israel was brought very low because
of Mid´ian; and the people of Israel
cried for help to the LORD.

7 When the people of Israel
cried to the LORD on account of the
Mid´ianites, 8the LORD sent a prophet
to the people of Israel; and he said to
them, "Thus says the LORD, the God
of Israel: I led you up from Egypt,
and brought you out of the house of
bondage; 9and I delivered you from the
hand of the Egyptians, and from the
hand of all who oppressed you, and
drove them out before you, and gave
you their land; 10and I said to you,
'I am the LORD your God; you shall
not pay reverence to the gods of the
Amorites, in whose land you dwell.'
But you have not given heed to my
voice."

THE CALL OF GIDEON

11 Now the angel of the LORD
came and sat under the oak at
Ophrah, which belonged to Jo´ash
the Abiez´rite, as his son Gideon was
beating out wheat in the wine press,
to hide it from the Mid´ianites. 12And
the angel of the LORD appeared to
him and said to him, "The LORD is
with you, you mighty man of valor."
13And Gideon said to him, "Pray, sir,
if the LORD is with us, why then has
all this befallen us? And where are all
his wonderful deeds which our fathers
recounted to us, saying, 'Did not the
LORD bring us up from Egypt?' But
now the LORD has cast us off, and giv-
en us into the hand of Mid´ian." 14And
the LORD turned to him and said,
"Go in this might of yours and deliv-
er Israel from the hand of Mid´ian;
do not I send you?" 15And he said to
him, "Pray, Lord, how can I deliver
Israel? Behold, my clan is the weak-
est in Manas´seh, and I am the least
in my family." 16And the LORD said
to him, "But I will be with you, and
you shall smite the Mid´ianites as one
man." 17And he said to him, "If now I
have found favor with thee, then show
me a sign that it is thou who speakest
with me. 18Do not depart from here,
I pray thee, until I come to thee, and
bring out my present, and set it before
thee." And he said, "I will stay till you
return."

19 So Gideon went into his house
and prepared a kid, and unleavened
cakes from an ephah of flour; the meat
he put in a basket, and the broth he
put in a pot, and brought them to him
under the oak and presented them.
20And the angel of God said to him,
"Take the meat and the unleavened
cakes, and put them on this rock, and
pour the broth over them." And he
did so. 21Then the angel of the LORD
reached out the tip of the staff that
was in his hand, and touched the meat
and the unleavened cakes; and there
sprang up fire from the rock and con-
sumed the flesh and the unleavened
cakes; and the angel of the LORD van-
ished from his sight. 22Then Gideon
perceived that he was the angel of the
LORD; and Gideon said, "Alas, O Lord
GOD! For now I have seen the angel of
the LORD face to face." 23But the LORD
said to him, "Peace be to you; do not
fear, you shall not die." 24Then Gideon
built an altar there to the LORD, and
called it, The LORD is peace. To this
day it still stands at Ophrah, which
belongs to the Abiez´rites.

25 That night the LORD said to
him, "Take your father's bull, the
second bull seven years old, and pull
down the altar of Ba´al which your fa-
ther has, and cut down the Ashe´rah
that is beside it; 26and build an altar
to the LORD your God on the top of

the stronghold here, with stones laid
in due order; then take the second
bull, and offer it as a burnt offering
with the wood of the Ashe´rah which
you shall cut down." 27So Gideon took
ten men of his servants, and did as the
LORD had told him; but because he
was too afraid of his family and the
men of the town to do it by day, he did
it by night.

GIDEON DESTROYS THE ALTAR OF BAAL

28 When the men of the town rose
early in the morning, behold, the al-
tar of Ba´al was broken down, and
the Ashe´rah beside it was cut down,
and the second bull was offered upon
the altar which had been built. 29And
they said to one another, "Who has
done this thing?" And after they had
made search and inquired, they said,
"Gideon the son of Jo´ash has done
this thing." 30Then the men of the
town said to Jo´ash, "Bring out your
son, that he may die, for he has pulled
down the altar of Ba´al and cut down
the Ashe´rah beside it." 31But Jo´ash
said to all who were arrayed against
him, "Will you contend for Ba´al? Or
will you defend his cause? Whoever
contends for him shall be put to death
by morning. If he is a god, let him con-
tend for himself, because his altar has
been pulled down." 32Therefore on that
day he was called Jerubba´al, that is to
say, "Let Ba´al contend against him,"
because he pulled down his altar.

33 Then all the Mid´ianites and
the Amal´ekites and the people of
the East came together, and cross-
ing the Jordan they encamped in the
Valley of Jezreel. 34But the Spirit of
the LORD took possession of Gideon;
and he sounded the trumpet, and the
Abiez´rites were called out to fol-
low him. 35And he sent messengers
throughout all Manas´seh; and they
too were called out to follow him.
And he sent messengers to Asher,
Zeb´ulun, and Naph´tali; and they
went up to meet them.

THE SIGN OF THE FLEECE

36 Then Gideon said to God, "If
thou wilt deliver Israel by my hand,
as thou hast said, 37behold, I am lay-
ing a fleece of wool on the threshing
floor; if there is dew on the fleece
alone, and it is dry on all the ground,
then I shall know that thou wilt de-
liver Israel by my hand, as thou hast
said." 38And it was so. When he rose
early next morning and squeezed the
fleece, he wrung enough dew from
the fleece to fill a bowl with water.
39Then Gideon said to God, "Let not
thy anger burn against me, let me
speak but this once; pray, let me make
trial only this once with the fleece;
pray, let it be dry only on the fleece,
and on all the ground let there be
dew." 40And God did so that night; for
it was dry on the fleece only, and on
all the ground there was dew.

GIDEON SURPRISES AND ROUTS THE MIDIANITES

7 Then Jerubba´al (that is, Gideon)
and all the people who were with
him rose early and encamped beside
the spring of Harod; and the camp of
Mid´ian was north of them, by the hill
of Moreh, in the valley.

2 The LORD said to Gideon, "The
people with you are too many for
me to give the Mid´ianites into their
hand, lest Israel vaunt themselves
against me, saying, 'My own hand has
delivered me.' 3Now therefore pro-
claim in the ears of the people, saying,
'Whoever is fearful and trembling, let
him return home.'" And Gideon test-
ed them;[a] twenty-two thousand re-
turned, and ten thousand remained.

4 And the LORD said to Gideon,
"The people are still too many; take
them down to the water and I will
test them for you there; and he of
whom I say to you, 'This man shall go
with you,' shall go with you; and any
of whom I say to you, 'This man shall
not go with you,' shall not go." 5So
he brought the people down to the

[a] Cn: Heb *and depart from Mount Gilead*

water; and the LORD said to Gideon,
"Every one that laps the water with
his tongue, as a dog laps, you shall
set by himself; likewise every one
that kneels down to drink." 6And the
number of those that lapped, putting
their hands to their mouths, was
three hundred men; but all the rest
of the people knelt down to drink
water. 7And the LORD said to Gideon,
"With the three hundred men that
lapped I will deliver you, and give
the Mid'ianites into your hand; and
let all the others go every man to his
home." 8So he took the jars of the
people from their hands,[a] and their
trumpets; and he sent all the rest of
Israel every man to his tent, but re-
tained the three hundred men; and
the camp of Mid'ian was below him
in the valley.

9 That same night the LORD said to
him, "Arise, go down against the camp;
for I have given it into your hand. 10But
if you fear to go down, go down to the
camp with Purah your servant; 11and
you shall hear what they say, and af-
terward your hands shall be strength-
ened to go down against the camp."
Then he went down with Purah his
servant to the outposts of the armed
men that were in the camp. 12And the
Mid'ianites and the Amal'ekites and
all the people of the East lay along the
valley like locusts for multitude; and
their camels were without number, as
the sand which is upon the seashore
for multitude. 13When Gideon came,
behold, a man was telling a dream to
his comrade; and he said, "Behold, I
dreamed a dream; and lo, a cake of
barley bread tumbled into the camp
of Mid'ian, and came to the tent, and
struck it so that it fell, and turned it
upside down, so that the tent lay flat."
14And his comrade answered, "This is
no other than the sword of Gideon the
son of Jo'ash, a man of Israel; into his
hand God has given Mid'ian and all
the host."

15 When Gideon heard the telling
of the dream and its interpretation,
he worshiped; and he returned to
the camp of Israel, and said, "Arise;
for the LORD has given the host of
Mid'ian into your hand." 16And he
divided the three hundred men into
three companies, and put trumpets
into the hands of all of them and
empty jars, with torches inside the
jars. 17And he said to them, "Look
at me, and do likewise; when I come
to the outskirts of the camp, do as I
do. 18When I blow the trumpet, I and
all who are with me, then blow the
trumpets also on every side of all the
camp, and shout, 'For the LORD and
for Gideon.'"

19 So Gideon and the hundred men
who were with him came to the out-
skirts of the camp at the beginning of
the middle watch, when they had just
set the watch; and they blew the trum-
pets and smashed the jars that were
in their hands. 20And the three compa-
nies blew the trumpets and broke the
jars, holding in their left hands the
torches, and in their right hands the
trumpets to blow; and they cried, "A
sword for the LORD and for Gideon!"
21They stood every man in his place
round about the camp, and all the
army ran; they cried out and fled.
22When they blew the three hundred
trumpets, the LORD set every man's
sword against his fellow and against
all the army; and the army fled as far
as Beth-shit'tah toward Zer'erah,[b] as
far as the border of A'bel-meho'lah,
by Tabbath. 23And the men of Israel
were called out from Naph'tali and
from Asher and from all Manas'seh,
and they pursued after Mid'ian.

24 And Gideon sent messen-
gers throughout all the hill country
of E'phraim, saying, "Come down
against the Mid'ianites and seize the
waters against them, as far as Beth-
bar'ah, and also the Jordan." So all
the men of E'phraim were called out,

[a]Cn: Heb *the people took provisions in their hands*
[b]Another reading is *Zeredah*

and they seized the waters as far as
Beth-bar´ah, and also the Jordan.
25 And they took the two princes of
Mid´ian, Oreb and Zeeb; they killed
Oreb at the rock of Oreb, and Zeeb
they killed at the wine press of Zeeb,
as they pursued Mid´ian; and they
brought the heads of Oreb and Zeeb
to Gideon beyond the Jordan.

GIDEON'S TRIUMPH AND VENGEANCE

8 And the men of E´phraim said to
him, "What is this that you have
done to us, not to call us when you
went to fight with Mid´ian?" And they
upbraided him violently. 2 And he said
to them, "What have I done now in
comparison with you? Is not the glean-
ing of the grapes of E´phraim better
than the vintage of Abi-e´zer? 3 God
has given into your hands the princes
of Mid´ian, Oreb and Zeeb; what have
I been able to do in comparison with
you?" Then their anger against him
was abated, when he had said this.

4 And Gideon came to the Jordan
and passed over, he and the three hun-
dred men who were with him, faint
yet pursuing. 5 So he said to the men of
Succoth, "Pray, give loaves of bread to
the people who follow me; for they are
faint, and I am pursuing after Zebah
and Zalmun´na, the kings of Mid´ian."
6 And the officials of Succoth said,
"Are Zebah and Zalmun´na already in
your hand, that we should give bread
to your army?" 7 And Gideon said,
"Well then, when the LORD has given
Zebah and Zalmun´na into my hand, I
will flail your flesh with the thorns of
the wilderness and with briers." 8 And
from there he went up to Penu´el, and
spoke to them in the same way; and
the men of Penu´el answered him as
the men of Succoth had answered.
9 And he said to the men of Penu´el,
"When I come again in peace, I will
break down this tower."

10 Now Zebah and Zalmun´na
were in Karkor with their army, about
fifteen thousand men, all who were
left of all the army of the people of the
East; for there had fallen a hundred
and twenty thousand men who drew
the sword. 11 And Gideon went up by
the caravan route east of Nobah and
Jog´behah, and attacked the army;
for the army was off its guard. 12 And
Zebah and Zalmun´na fled; and he
pursued them and took the two kings
of Mid´ian, Zebah and Zalmun´na,
and he threw all the army into a panic.

13 Then Gideon the son of Jo´ash
returned from the battle by the ascent
of Heres. 14 And he caught a young man
of Succoth, and questioned him; and
he wrote down for him the officials
and elders of Succoth, seventy-seven
men. 15 And he came to the men of
Succoth, and said, "Behold Zebah
and Zalmun´na, about whom you
taunted me, saying, 'Are Zebah and
Zalmun´na already in your hand, that
we should give bread to your men who
are faint?'" 16 And he took the elders
of the city and he took thorns of the
wilderness and briers and with them
taught the men of Succoth. 17 And he
broke down the tower of Penu´el, and
slew the men of the city.

18 Then he said to Zebah and Zal-
mun´na, "Where are the men whom
you slew at Tabor?" They answered,
"As you are, so were they, every one
of them; they resembled the sons of a
king." 19 And he said, "They were my
brothers, the sons of my mother; as
the LORD lives, if you had saved them
alive, I would not slay you." 20 And he
said to Jether his first-born, "Rise, and
slay them." But the youth did not draw
his sword; for he was afraid, because
he was still a youth. 21 Then Zebah and
Zalmun´na said, "Rise yourself, and
fall upon us; for as the man is, so is his
strength." And Gideon arose and slew
Zebah and Zalmun´na; and he took
the crescents that were on the necks
of their camels.

GIDEON'S IDOLATRY

22 Then the men of Israel said to
Gideon, "Rule over us, you and your
son and your grandson also; for you

have delivered us out of the hand of
Mid´ian." 23Gideon said to them, "I
will not rule over you, and my son
will not rule over you; the LORD will
rule over you."* 24And Gideon said
to them, "Let me make a request of
you; give me every man of you the
earrings of his spoil." (For they had
golden earrings, because they were
Ish´maelites.) 25And they answered,
"We will willingly give them." And
they spread a garment, and every man
cast in it the earrings of his spoil.
26And the weight of the golden ear-
rings that he requested was one thou-
sand seven hundred shekels of gold;
besides the crescents and the pen-
dants and the purple garments worn
by the kings of Mid´ian, and besides
the collars that were about the necks
of their camels. 27And Gideon made
an ephod of it and put it in his city,
in Ophrah; and all Israel played the
harlot after it there, and it became a
snare to Gideon and to his family. 28So
Mid´ian was subdued before the peo-
ple of Israel, and they lifted up their
heads no more. And the land had rest
forty years in the days of Gideon.

DEATH OF GIDEON

29 Jerubba´al the son of Jo´ash went
and dwelt in his own house. 30Now
Gideon had seventy sons, his own off-
spring, for he had many wives. 31And
his concubine who was in Shechem
also bore him a son, and he called his
name Abim´elech. 32And Gideon the
son of Jo´ash died in a good old age,
and was buried in the tomb of Jo´ash
his father, at Ophrah of the Abiez´rites.

33 As soon as Gideon died, the peo-
ple of Israel turned again and played
the harlot after the Ba´als, and made
Ba´al-be´rith their god. 34And the peo-
ple of Israel did not remember the
LORD their God, who had rescued them
from the hand of all their enemies on
every side; 35and they did not show
kindness to the family of Jerubba´al
(that is, Gideon) in return for all the
good that he had done to Israel.

ABIMELECH ATTEMPTS TO ESTABLISH A MONARCHY

9 Now Abim´elech the son of Je-
rubba´al went to Shechem to his
mother's kinsmen and said to them
and to the whole clan of his mother's
family, 2"Say in the ears of all the cit-
izens of Shechem, 'Which is better
for you, that all seventy of the sons
of Jerubba´al rule over you, or that
one rule over you?' Remember also
that I am your bone and your flesh."
3And his mother's kinsmen spoke all
these words on his behalf in the ears
of all the men of Shechem; and their
hearts inclined to follow Abim´elech,
for they said, "He is our brother."
4And they gave him seventy pieces
of silver out of the house of Ba´al-
be´rith with which Abim´elech hired
worthless and reckless fellows, who
followed him. 5And he went to his fa-
ther's house at Ophrah, and slew his
brothers the sons of Jerubba´al, seven-
ty men, upon one stone; but Jotham
the youngest son of Jerubba´al was
left, for he hid himself. 6And all the
citizens of Shechem came together,
and all Beth-millo, and they went and
made Abim´elech king, by the oak of
the pillar at Shechem.

THE PARABLE OF THE TREES

7 When it was told to Jotham, he
went and stood on the top of Mount
Geri´zim, and cried aloud and said
to them, "Listen to me, you men of
Shechem, that God may listen to you.
8The trees once went forth to anoint a
king over them; and they said to the
olive tree, 'Reign over us.' 9But the
olive tree said to them, 'Shall I leave
my fatness, by which gods and men
are honored, and go to sway over the
trees?' 10And the trees said to the fig
tree, 'Come you, and reign over us.'
11But the fig tree said to them, 'Shall
I leave my sweetness and my good
fruit, and go to sway over the trees?'
12And the trees said to the vine, 'Come
you, and reign over us.' 13But the vine

4And he had thirty sons who rode on
thirty asses; and they had thirty cit-
ies, called Hav´voth-ja´ir to this day,
which are in the land of Gilead. 5And
Ja´ir died, and was buried in Kamon.

OPPRESSION BY THE AMMONITES

6 And the people of Israel again
did what was evil in the sight of the
LORD, and served the Ba´als and the
Ash´taroth, the gods of Syria, the gods
of Sidon, the gods of Moab, the gods
of the Ammonites, and the gods of
the Philistines; and they forsook the
LORD, and did not serve him. 7And the
anger of the LORD was kindled against
Israel, and he sold them into the hand
of the Philistines and into the hand
of the Ammonites, 8and they crushed
and oppressed the children of Israel
that year. For eighteen years they op-
pressed all the people of Israel that
were beyond the Jordan in the land of
the Amorites, which is in Gilead. 9And
the Ammonites crossed the Jordan to
fight also against Judah and against
Benjamin and against the house of
E´phraim; so that Israel was sorely
distressed.

10 And the people of Israel cried
to the LORD, saying, "We have sinned
against thee, because we have for-
saken our God and have served the
Ba´als." 11And the LORD said to the
people of Israel, "Did I not deliver
you from the Egyptians and from the
Amorites, from the Ammonites and
from the Philistines? 12The Sido´nians
also, and the Amal´ekites, and the
Ma´onites, oppressed you; and you
cried to me, and I delivered you out
of their hand. 13Yet you have forsaken
me and served other gods; therefore I
will deliver you no more. 14Go and cry
to the gods whom you have chosen; let
them deliver you in the time of your
distress." 15And the people of Israel
said to the LORD, "We have sinned;
do to us whatever seems good to thee;
only deliver us, we pray thee, this
day." 16So they put away the foreign
gods from among them and served the
LORD; and he became indignant over
the misery of Israel.

17 Then the Ammonites were
called to arms, and they encamped
in Gilead; and the people of Israel
came together, and they encamp-
ed at Mizpah. 18And the people, the
leaders of Gilead, said one to anoth-
er, "Who is the man that will begin
to fight against the Ammonites? He
shall be head over all the inhabitants
of Gilead."

JEPHTHAH

11 Now Jephthah the Gileadite was
a mighty warrior, but he was the
son of a harlot. Gilead was the father
of Jephthah. 2And Gilead's wife also
bore him sons; and when his wife's
sons grew up, they thrust Jephthah
out, and said to him, "You shall not
inherit in our father's house; for you
are the son of another woman." 3Then
Jephthah fled from his brothers, and
dwelt in the land of Tob; and worth-
less fellows collected round Jephthah,
and went raiding with him.

4 After a time the Ammonites
made war against Israel. 5And when
the Ammonites made war against
Israel, the elders of Gilead went to
bring Jephthah from the land of Tob;
6and they said to Jephthah, "Come and
be our leader, that we may fight with
the Ammonites." 7But Jephthah said to
the elders of Gilead, "Did you not hate
me, and drive me out of my father's
house? Why have you come to me now
when you are in trouble?" 8And the el-
ders of Gilead said to Jephthah, "That
is why we have turned to you now,
that you may go with us and fight
with the Ammonites, and be our head
over all the inhabitants of Gilead."
9Jephthah said to the elders of Gilead,
"If you bring me home again to fight
with the Ammonites, and the LORD
gives them over to me, I will be your
head." 10And the elders of Gilead said
to Jephthah, "The LORD will be wit-
ness between us; we will surely do as
you say." 11So Jephthah went with the

JEPHTHAH'S DAUGHTER

34 Then Jephthah came to his home at Mizpah; and behold, his daughter came out to meet him with timbrels and with dances; she was his only child; beside her he had neither son nor daughter. 35 And when he saw her, he rent his clothes, and said, "Alas, my daughter! you have brought me very low, and you have become the cause of great trouble to me; for I have opened my mouth to the LORD, and I cannot take back my vow." 36 And she said to him, "My father, if you have opened your mouth to the LORD, do to me according to what has gone forth from your mouth, now that the LORD has avenged you on your enemies, on the Ammonites." 37 And she said to her father, "Let this thing be done for me; let me alone two months, that I may go and wander[a] on the mountains, and bewail my virginity, I and my companions." 38 And he said, "Go." And he sent her away for two months; and she departed, she and her companions, and bewailed her virginity upon the mountains. 39 And at the end of two months, she returned to her father, who did with her according to his vow which he had made.* She had never known a man. And it became a custom in Israel 40 that the daughters of Israel went year by year to lament the daughter of Jephthah the Gileadite four days in the year.

INTERTRIBAL DISSENSION

12 The men of E´phraim were called to arms, and they crossed to *Zaphon and said to Jephthah*, "Why did you cross over to fight against the Ammonites, and did not call us to go with you? We will burn your house over you with fire." 2 And Jephthah said to them, "I and my people had a great feud with the Ammonites; and when I called you, you did not deliver me from their hand. 3 And when I saw that you would not deliver me, I took my life in my hand, and crossed over against the Ammonites, and the LORD gave them into my hand; why then have you come up to me this day, to fight against me?" 4 Then Jephthah gathered all the men of Gilead and fought with E´phraim; and the men of Gilead smote E´phraim, because they said, "You are fugitives of E´phraim, you Gileadites, in the midst of E´phraim and Manas´seh." 5 And the Gileadites took the fords of the Jordan against the E´phraimites. And when any of the fugitives of E´phraim said, "Let me go over," the men of Gilead said to him, "Are you an E´phraimite?" When he said, "No," 6 they said to him, "Then say Shibboleth," and he said, "Sibboleth," for he could not pronounce it right; then they seized him and slew him at the fords of the Jordan. And there fell at that time forty-two thousand of the E´phraimites.

7 Jephthah judged Israel six years. Then Jephthah the Gileadite died, and was buried in his city in Gilead.[b]

IBZAN, ELON, AND ABDON

8 After him Ibzan of Bethlehem judged Israel. 9 He had thirty sons; and thirty daughters he gave in marriage outside his clan, and thirty daughters he brought in from outside for his sons. And he judged Israel seven years. 10 Then Ibzan died, and was buried at Bethlehem.

11 After him Elon the Zeb´ulunite judged Israel; and he judged Israel ten years. 12 Then Elon the Zeb´ulunite died, and was buried at Ai´jalon in the land of Zeb´ulun.

13 After him Abdon the son of Hillel the Pir´athonite judged Israel. 14 He had forty sons and thirty grandsons, who rode on seventy asses; and he judged Israel eight years. 15 Then Abdon the son of Hillel the Pir´athonite died, and was buried at Pir´athon in the land of E´phraim, in the hill country of the Amal´ekites.

[a] Cn: Heb *go down*
[b] Gk: Heb *in the cities of Gilead*

THE BIRTH OF SAMSON

13 *And the people of Israel again did what was evil in the sight of the LORD; and the LORD gave them into the hand of the Philistines for forty years.

2 And there was a certain man of Zorah, of the tribe of the Danites, whose name was Mano´ah; and his wife was barren and had no children. 3And the angel of the LORD appeared to the woman and said to her, "Behold, you are barren and have no children; but you shall conceive and bear a son. 4Therefore beware, and drink no wine or strong drink, and eat nothing unclean, 5for lo, you shall conceive and bear a son. No razor shall come upon his head, for the boy shall be a Nazirite to God from birth; and he shall begin to deliver Israel from the hand of the Philistines." 6Then the woman came and told her husband, "A man of God came to me, and his countenance was like the countenance of the angel of God, very terrible; I did not ask him whence he was, and he did not tell me his name; 7but he said to me, 'Behold, you shall conceive and bear a son; so then drink no wine or strong drink, and eat nothing unclean, for the boy shall be a Nazirite to God from birth to the day of his death.'"

8 Then Mano´ah entreated the LORD, and said, "O, LORD, I pray thee, let the man of God whom thou didst send come again to us, and teach us what we are to do with the boy that will be born." 9And God listened to the voice of Mano´ah, and the angel of God came again to the woman as she sat in the field; but Mano´ah her husband was not with her. 10And the woman ran in haste and told her husband, "Behold, the man who came to me the other day has appeared to me." 11And Mano´ah arose *and went after his wife,* and came to the man and said to him, "Are you the man who spoke to this woman?" And he said, "I am." 12And Mano´ah said, "Now when your words come true, what is to be the boy's manner of life, and what is he to do?" 13And the angel of the LORD said to Mano´ah, "Of all that I said to the woman let her beware. 14She may not eat of anything that comes from the vine, neither let her drink wine or strong drink, or eat any unclean thing; all that I commanded her let her observe."

15 Mano´ah said to the angel of the LORD, "Pray, let us detain you, and prepare a kid for you." 16And the angel of the LORD said to Mano´ah, "If you detain me, I will not eat of your food; but if you make ready a burnt offering, then offer it to the LORD." (For Mano´ah did not know that he was the angel of the LORD.) 17And Mano´ah said to the angel of the LORD, "What is your name, so that, when your words come true, we may honor you?" 18And the angel of the LORD said to him, "Why do you ask my name, seeing it is wonderful?" 19So Mano´ah took the kid with the cereal offering, and offered it upon the rock to the LORD, to him who works[a] wonders.[b] 20And when the flame went up toward heaven from the altar, the angel of the LORD ascended in the flame of the altar while Mano´ah and his wife looked on; and they fell on their faces to the ground.

21 The angel of the LORD appeared no more to Mano´ah and to his wife. Then Mano´ah knew that he was the angel of the LORD. 22And Mano´ah said to his wife, "We shall surely die, for we have seen God." 23But his wife said to him, "If the LORD had meant to kill us, he would not have accepted a burnt offering and a cereal offering at our hands or shown us all these things, or now announced to us such things as these." 24And the woman bore a son, and called his name Samson; and the boy grew, and the LORD blessed him. 25And the Spirit of the LORD began to stir him in Ma´haneh-dan, between Zorah and Esh´ta-ol.

[a] Gk Vg: Heb *and working*
[b] Heb *wonders, while Manoah and his wife looked on*

night at the gate of the city. They kept
quiet all night, saying, "Let us wait till
the light of the morning; then we will
kill him." 3But Samson lay till mid-
night, and at midnight he arose and
took hold of the doors of the gate of
the city and the two posts, and pulled
them up, bar and all, and put them on
his shoulders and carried them to the
top of the hill that is before Hebron.

4 After this he loved a woman
in the valley of Sorek, whose name
was Deli´lah. 5And the lords of the
Philistines came to her and said to
her, "Entice him, and see wherein
his great strength lies, and by what
means we may overpower him, that
we may bind him to subdue him; and
we will each give you eleven hundred
pieces of silver." 6And Deli´lah said
to Samson, "Please tell me wherein
your great strength lies, and how you
might be bound, that one could sub-
due you." 7And Samson said to her, "If
they bind me with seven fresh bow-
strings which have not been dried,
then I shall become weak, and be like
any other man." 8Then the lords of the
Philistines brought her seven fresh
bowstrings which had not been dried,
and she bound him with them. 9Now
she had men lying in wait in an inner
chamber. And she said to him, "The
Philistines are upon you, Samson!"
But he snapped the bowstrings, as a
string of tow snaps when it touches
the fire. So the secret of his strength
was not known.

10 And Deli´lah said to Samson,
"Behold, you have mocked me, and
told me lies; please tell me how you
might be bound." 11And he said to
her, "If they bind me with new ropes
that have not been used, then I shall
become weak, and be like any other
man." 12So Deli´lah took new ropes
and bound him with them, and said
to him, "The Philistines are upon
you, Samson!" And the men lying in
wait were in an inner chamber. But he
snapped the ropes off his arms like a
thread.

13 And Deli´lah said to Samson,
"Until now you have mocked me, and
told me lies; tell me how you might
be bound." And he said to her, "If
you weave the seven locks of my head
with the web and make it tight with
the pin, then I shall become weak, and
be like any other man." 14So while he
slept, Deli´lah took the seven locks of
his head and wove them into the web.[c]
And she made them tight with the
pin, and said to him, "The Philistines
are upon you, Samson!" But he awoke
from his sleep, and pulled away the
pin, the loom, and the web.

15 And she said to him, "How can
you say, 'I love you,' when your heart
is not with me? You have mocked me
these three times, and you have not
told me wherein your great strength
lies." 16And when she pressed him
hard with her words day after day, and
urged him, his soul was vexed to death.
17And he told her all his mind, and said
to her, "A razor has never come upon
my head; for I have been a Nazirite to
God from my mother's womb. If I be
shaved, then my strength will leave
me, and I shall become weak, and be
like any other man."

18 When Deli´lah saw that he had
told her all his mind, she sent and
called the lords of the Philistines,
saying, "Come up this once, for he
has told me all his mind." Then the
lords of the Philistines came up to
her, and brought the money in their
hands. 19She made him sleep upon
her knees; and she called a man, and
had him shave off the seven locks of
his head. Then she began to torment
him, and his strength left him. 20And
she said, "The Philistines are upon
you, Samson!" And he awoke from
his sleep, and said, "I will go out as at
other times, and shake myself free."
And he did not know that the LORD
had left him. 21And the Philistines
seized him and gouged out his eyes,
and brought him down to Gaza, and

[c] Compare Gk: Heb lacks *and make it tight. . . into the web*

bound him with bronze fetters; and he ground at the mill in the prison. 22But the hair of his head began to grow again after it had been shaved.

SAMSON'S DEATH

23 Now the lords of the Philistines gathered to offer a great sacrifice to Dagon their god, and to rejoice; for they said, "Our god has given Samson our enemy into our hand." 24And when the people saw him, they praised their god; for they said, "Our god has given our enemy into our hand, the ravager of our country, who has slain many of us." 25And when their hearts were merry, they said, "Call Samson, that he may make sport for us." So they called Samson out of the prison, and he made sport before them. They made him stand between the pillars; 26and Samson said to the lad who held him by the hand, "Let me feel the pillars on which the house rests, that I may lean against them." 27Now the house was full of men and women; all the lords of the Philistines were there, and on the roof there were about three thousand men and women, who looked on while Samson made sport.

28 Then Samson called to the LORD and said, "O Lord GOD, remember me, I pray thee, and strengthen me, I pray thee, only this once, O God, that I may be avenged upon the Philistines for one of my two eyes." 29And Samson grasped the two middle pillars upon which the house rested, and he leaned his weight upon them, his right hand on the one and his left hand on the other. 30And Samson said, "Let me die with the Philistines." Then he bowed with all his might; and the house fell upon the lords and upon all the people that were in it. So the dead whom he slew at his death were more than those whom he had slain during his life. 31Then his brothers and all his family came down and took him and brought him up and buried him between Zorah and Esh´ta-ol in the tomb of Mano´ah his father. He had judged Israel twenty years.

MICAH AND THE LEVITE

17 *There was a man of the hill country of E´phraim, whose name was Micah. 2And he said to his mother, "The eleven hundred pieces of silver which were taken from you, about which you uttered a curse, and also spoke it in my ears, behold, the silver is with me; I took it." And his mother said, "Blessed be my son by the LORD." 3And he restored the eleven hundred pieces of silver to his mother; and his mother said, "I consecrate the silver to the LORD from my hand for my son, to make a graven image and a molten image; now therefore I will restore it to you." 4So when he restored the money to his mother, his mother took two hundred pieces of silver, and gave it to the silversmith, who made it into a graven image and a molten image; and it was in the house of Micah. 5And the man Micah had a shrine, and he made an ephod and ter´aphim, and installed one of his sons, who became his priest. 6In those days there was no king in Israel; every man did what was right in his own eyes.

7 Now there was a young man of Bethlehem in Judah, of the family of Judah, who was a Levite; and he sojourned there. 8And the man departed from the town of Bethlehem in Judah, to live where he could find a place; and as he journeyed, he came to the hill country of E´phraim to the house of Micah. 9And Micah said to him, "From where do you come?" And he said to him, "I am a Levite of Bethlehem in Judah, and I am going to sojourn where I may find a place." 10And Micah said to him, "Stay with me, and be to me a father and a priest, and I will give you ten pieces of silver a year, and a suit of apparel, and your living."[a] 11And the Levite was content to dwell with the man; and the young man became to him like one

[a]Heb *living, and the Levite went*

of his sons. 12And Micah installed the
Levite, and the young man became his
priest, and was in the house of Micah.
13Then Micah said, "Now I know that
the LORD will prosper me, because I
have a Levite as priest."

THE MIGRATION OF DAN

18 In those days there was no king
in Israel. And in those days the
tribe of the Danites was seeking for
itself an inheritance to dwell in; for
until then no inheritance among the
tribes of Israel had fallen to them. 2So
the Danites sent five able men from
the whole number of their tribe, from
Zorah and from Esh´ta-ol, to spy
out the land and to explore it; and
they said to them, "Go and explore
the land." And they came to the hill
country of E´phraim, to the house of
Micah, and lodged there. 3When they
were by the house of Micah, they rec-
ognized the voice of the young Levite;
and they turned aside and said to
him, "Who brought you here? What
are you doing in this place? What is
your business here?" 4And he said
to them, "Thus and thus has Micah
dealt with me: he has hired me, and
I have become his priest." 5And they
said to him, "Inquire of God, we pray
thee, that we may know whether the
journey on which we are setting out
will succeed." 6And the priest said to
them, "Go in peace. The journey on
which you go is under the eye of the
LORD."

7 Then the five men departed,
and came to La´ish, and saw the peo-
ple who were there, how they dwelt
in security, after the manner of the
Sido´nians, quiet and unsuspecting,
lacking[b] nothing that is in the earth,
and possessing wealth, and how they
were far from the Sido´nians and had
no dealings with any one. 8And when
they came to their brethren at Zorah
and Esh´ta-ol, their brethren said to
them, "What do you report?" 9They
said, "Arise, and let us go up against
them; for we have seen the land, and
behold, it is very fertile. And will you
do nothing? Do not be slow to go, and
enter in and possess the land. 10When
you go, you will come to an unsus-
pecting people. The land is broad;
yea, God has given it into your hands,
a place where there is no lack of any-
thing that is in the earth."

11 And six hundred men of the
tribe of Dan, armed with weapons of
war, set forth from Zorah and Esh´ta-
ol, 12and went up and encamped at
Kir´iath-je´arim in Judah. On this ac-
count that place is called Ma´haneh-
dan[c] to this day; behold, it is west of
Kir´iath-je´arim. 13And they passed
on from there to the hill country of
E´phraim, and came to the house of
Micah.

14 Then the five men who had gone
to spy out the country of La´ish said to
their brethren, "Do you know that in
these houses there are an ephod, ter´-
aphim, a graven image, and a molten
image? Now therefore consider what
you will do." 15And they turned aside
thither, and came to the house of the
young Levite, at the home of Micah,
and asked him of his welfare. 16Now
the six hundred men of the Danites,
armed with their weapons of war,
stood by the entrance of the gate;
17and the five men who had gone to
spy out the land went up, and entered
and took the graven image, the ephod,
the ter´aphim, and the molten image,
while the priest stood by the entrance
of the gate with the six hundred men
armed with weapons of war. 18And
when these went into Micah's house
and took the graven image, the ephod,
the ter´aphim, and the molten image,
the priest said to them, "What are
you doing?" 19And they said to him,
"Keep quiet, put your hand upon your
mouth, and come with us, and be to
us a father and a priest. Is it better for
you to be priest to the house of one

[b]Cn Compare 18.10. The Hebrew text is uncertain
[c]That is *Camp of Dan*

man, or to be priest to a tribe and fam-
ily in Israel?" 20And the priest's heart
was glad; he took the ephod, and the
ter′aphim, and the graven image, and
went in the midst of the people.
21 So they turned and departed,
putting the little ones and the cat-
tle and the goods in front of them.
22When they were a good way from the
home of Micah, the men who were in
the houses near Micah's house were
called out, and they overtook the
Danites. 23And they shouted to the
Danites, who turned round and said
to Micah, "What ails you that you
come with such a company?" 24And he
said, "You take my gods which I made,
and the priest, and go away, and what
have I left? How then do you ask me,
'What ails you?'" 25And the Danites
said to him, "Do not let your voice be
heard among us, lest angry fellows fall
upon you, and you lose your life with
the lives of your household." 26Then
the Danites went their way; and when
Micah saw that they were too strong
for him, he turned and went back to
his home.

THE DANITES SETTLE IN LAISH

27 And taking what Micah had
made, and the priest who belonged
to him, the Danites came to La′ish,
to a people quiet and unsuspecting,
and smote them with the edge of the
sword, and burned the city with fire.
28And there was no deliverer because
it was far from Sidon, and they had no
dealings with any one. It was in the
valley which belongs to Beth-rehob.
And they rebuilt the city, and dwelt
in it. 29And they named the city Dan,
after the name of Dan their ancestor,
who was born to Israel; but the name
of the city was La′ish at the first.
30And the Danites set up the graven
image for themselves; and Jonathan
the son of Gershom, son of Moses,[a]
and his sons were priests to the tribe
of the Danites until the day of the
captivity of the land. 31So they set up
Micah's graven image which he made,
as long as the house of God was at
Shiloh.

THE LEVITE'S CONCUBINE

19 In those days, when there was no
king in Israel, a certain Levite was
sojourning in the remote parts of the
hill country of E′phraim, who took to
himself a concubine from Bethlehem
in Judah. 2And his concubine became
angry with[b] him, and she went away
from him to her father's house at
Bethlehem in Judah, and was there
some four months. 3Then her husband
arose and went after her, to speak
kindly to her and bring her back. He
had with him his servant and a couple
of asses. And he came[c] to her father's
house; and when the girl's father saw
him, he came with joy to meet him.
4And his father-in-law, the girl's fa-
ther, made him stay, and he remained
with him three days; so they ate and
drank, and lodged there. 5And on the
fourth day they arose early in the
morning, and he prepared to go; but
the girl's father said to his son-in-law,
"Strengthen your heart with a morsel
of bread, and after that you may go."
6So the two men sat and ate and drank
together; and the girl's father said to
the man, "Be pleased to spend the
night, and let your heart be merry."
7And when the man rose up to go, his
father-in-law urged him, till he lodged
there again. 8And on the fifth day he
arose early in the morning to depart;
and the girl's father said, "Strengthen
your heart, and tarry until the day
declines." So they ate, both of them.
9And when the man and his concubine
and his servant rose up to depart, his
father-in-law, the girl's father, said to
him, "Behold, now the day has waned
toward evening; pray tarry all night.
Behold, the day draws to its close;
lodge here and let your heart be mer-
ry; and tomorrow you shall arise early

[a] Another reading is *Manasseh*
[b] Gk Old Latin: Heb *played the harlot against*
[c] Gk: Heb *she brought him*

in the morning for your journey, and
go home."

10 But the man would not spend
the night; he rose up and departed,
and arrived opposite Jebus (that is,
Jerusalem). He had with him a couple
of saddled asses, and his concubine
was with him. 11When they were near
Jebus, the day was far spent, and the
servant said to his master, "Come
now, let us turn aside to this city of
the Jeb´usites, and spend the night
in it." 12And his master said to him,
"We will not turn aside into the city
of foreigners, who do not belong to
the people of Israel; but we will pass
on to Gib´e-ah." 13And he said to his
servant, "Come and let us draw near
to one of these places, and spend the
night at Gib´e-ah or at Ramah." 14So
they passed on and went their way;
and the sun went down on them near
Gib´e-ah, which belongs to Benjamin,
15and they turned aside there, to go
in and spend the night at Gib´e-ah.
And he went in and sat down in the
open square of the city; for no man
took them into his house to spend the
night.

16 And behold, an old man was
coming from his work in the field at
evening; the man was from the hill
country of E´phraim, and he was
sojourning in Gib´e-ah; the men of
the place were Benjaminites. 17And
he lifted up his eyes, and saw the
wayfarer in the open square of the
city; and the old man said, "Where
are you going? and whence do you
come?" 18And he said to him, "We
are passing from Bethlehem in Judah
to the remote parts of the hill coun-
try of E´phraim, from which I come.
I went to Bethlehem in Judah; and I
am going to my home;[d] and nobody
takes me into his house. 19We have
straw and provender for our asses,
with bread and wine for me and your
maidservant and the young man with
your servants; there is no lack of any-
thing." 20And the old man said, "Peace
be to you; I will care for all your
wants; only, do not spend the night in
the square." 21So he brought him into
his house, and gave the asses proven-
der; and they washed their feet, and
ate and drank.

GIBEAH'S CRIME

22 As they were making their
hearts merry, behold, the men of the
city, base fellows, beset the house
round about, beating on the door; and
they said to the old man, the master
of the house, "Bring out the man who
came into your house, that we may
know him." 23And the man, the mas-
ter of the house, went out to them and
said to them, "No, my brethren, do not
act so wickedly; seeing that this man
has come into my house, do not do
this vile thing. 24Behold, here are my
virgin daughter and his concubine; let
me bring them out now. Ravish them
and do with them what seems good to
you; but against this man do not do so
vile a thing." 25But the men would not
listen to him. So the man seized his
concubine, and put her out to them;
and they knew her, and abused her all
night until the morning. And as the
dawn began to break, they let her go.
26And as morning appeared, the wom-
an came and fell down at the door of
the man's house where her master
was, till it was light.

27 And her master rose up in the
morning, and when he opened the
doors of the house and went out to go
on his way, behold, there was his con-
cubine lying at the door of the house,
with her hands on the threshold. 28He
said to her, "Get up, let us be going."
But there was no answer. Then he put
her upon the ass; and the man rose
up and went away to his home. 29And
when he entered his house, he took a
knife, and laying hold of his concu-
bine he divided her, limb by limb, into
twelve pieces, and sent her through-
out all the territory of Israel. 30And
all who saw it said, "Such a thing has

[d] Gk Compare 19.29. Heb *to the house of the* LORD

never happened or been seen from the day that the people of Israel came up out of the land of Egypt until this day; consider it, take counsel, and speak."

THE OTHER TRIBES ATTACK BENJAMIN

20 Then all the people of Israel came out, from Dan to Beer-sheba, including the land of Gilead, and the congregation assembled as one man to the LORD at Mizpah. 2 And the chiefs of all the people, of all the tribes of Israel, presented themselves in the assembly of the people of God, four hundred thousand men on foot that drew the sword. 3 (Now the Benjaminites heard that the people of Israel had gone up to Mizpah.) And the people of Israel said, "Tell us, how was this wickedness brought to pass?" 4 And the Levite, the husband of the woman who was murdered, answered and said, "I came to Gib´e-ah that belongs to Benjamin, I and my concubine, to spend the night. 5 And the men of Gib´e-ah rose against me, and beset the house round about me by night; they meant to kill me, and they ravished my concubine, and she is dead. 6 And I took my concubine and cut her in pieces, and sent her throughout all the country of the inheritance of Israel; for they have committed abomination and wantonness in Israel. 7 Behold, you people of Israel, all of you, give your advice and counsel here."

8 And all the people arose as one man, saying, "We will not any of us go to his tent, and none of us will return to his house. 9 But now this is what we will do to Gib´e-ah: we will go up against it by lot, 10 and we will take ten men of a hundred throughout all the tribes of Israel, and a hundred of a thousand, and a thousand of ten thousand, to bring provisions for the people, that when they come they may requite Gib´e-ah of Benjamin, for all the wanton crime which they have committed in Israel." 11 So all the men of Israel gathered against the city, united as one man.

12 And the tribes of Israel sent men through all the tribe of Benjamin, saying, "What wickedness is this that has taken place among you? 13 Now therefore give up the men, the base fellows in Gib´e-ah, that we may put them to death, and put away evil from Israel." But the Benjaminites would not listen to the voice of their brethren, the people of Israel. 14 And the Benjaminites came together out of the cities to Gib´e-ah, to go out to battle against the people of Israel. 15 And the Benjaminites mustered out of their cities on that day twenty-six thousand men that drew the sword, besides the inhabitants of Gib´e-ah, who mustered seven hundred picked men. 16 Among all these were seven hundred picked men who were left-handed; every one could sling a stone at a hair, and not miss. 17 And the men of Israel, apart from Benjamin, mustered four hundred thousand men that drew sword; all these were men of war.

18 The people of Israel arose and went up to Bethel, and inquired of God, "Which of us shall go up first to battle against the Benjaminites?" And the LORD said, "Judah shall go up first."

19 Then the people of Israel rose in the morning, and encamped against Gib´e-ah. 20 And the men of Israel went out to battle against Benjamin; and the men of Israel drew up the battle line against them at Gib´e-ah. 21 The Benjaminites came out of Gib´e-ah, and felled to the ground on that day twenty-two thousand men of the Israelites. 22 But the people, the men of Israel, took courage, and again formed the battle line in the same place where they had formed it on the first day. 23 And the people of Israel went up and wept before the LORD until the evening; and they inquired of the LORD, "Shall we again draw near to battle against our brethren the Benjaminites?" And the LORD said, "Go up against them."

24 So the people of Israel came

near against the Benjamnites the sec-
ond day. 25And Benjamin went against
them out of Gib´e-ah the second day,
and felled to the ground eighteen
thousand men of the people of Israel;
all these were men who drew the
sword. 26Then all the people of Israel,
the whole army, went up and came to
Bethel and wept; they sat there before
the LORD, and fasted that day until
evening, and offered burnt offerings
and peace offerings before the LORD.
27And the people of Israel inquired of
the LORD (for the ark of the covenant
of God was there in those days, 28and
Phin´ehas the son of Elea´zar, son of
Aaron, ministered before it in those
days), saying, "Shall we yet again go
out to battle against our brethren the
Benjaminites, or shall we cease?" And
the LORD said, "Go up; for tomorrow I
will give them into your hand."

29 So Israel set men in ambush
round about Gib´e-ah. 30And the peo-
ple of Israel went up against the Ben-
jaminites on the third day, and set
themselves in array against Gib´e-
ah, as at other times. 31And the Ben-
jaminites went out against the people,
and were drawn away from the city;
and as at other times they began to
smite and kill some of the people, in
the highways, one of which goes up to
Bethel and the other to Gib´e-ah, and
in the open country, about thirty men
of Israel. 32And the Benjaminites said,
"They are routed before us, as at the
first." But the men of Israel said, "Let
us flee, and draw them away from
the city to the highways." 33And all
the men of Israel rose up out of their
place, and set themselves in array at
Ba´al-ta´mar; and the men of Israel
who were in ambush rushed out of
their place west[a] of Geba. 34And there
came against Gib´e-ah ten thousand
picked men out of all Israel, and the
battle was hard; but the Benjaminites
did not know that disaster was close
upon them. 35And the LORD defeated
Benjamin before Israel; and the men
of Israel destroyed twenty-five thou-
sand one hundred men of Benjamin
that day; all these were men who drew
the sword. 36So the Benjaminites saw
that they were defeated.

The men of Israel gave ground to
Benjamin, because they trusted to the
men in ambush whom they had set
against Gib´e-ah. 37And the men in
ambush made haste and rushed upon
Gib´e-ah; the men in ambush moved
out and smote all the city with the
edge of the sword. 38Now the appoint-
ed signal between the men of Israel
and the men in ambush was that when
they made a great cloud of smoke rise
up out of the city 39the men of Israel
should turn in battle. Now Benjamin
had begun to smite and kill about
thirty men of Israel; they said, "Surely
they are smitten down before us, as in
the first battle." 40But when the sig-
nal began to rise out of the city in a
column of smoke, the Benjaminites
looked behind them; and behold, the
whole of the city went up in smoke
to heaven. 41Then the men of Israel
turned, and the men of Benjamin were
dismayed, for they saw that disaster
was close upon them. 42Therefore they
turned their backs before the men of
Israel in the direction of the wilder-
ness; but the battle overtook them,
and those who came out of the cities
destroyed them in the midst of them.
43Cutting down[b] the Benjaminites,
they pursued them and trod them
down from Nohah[c] as far as opposite
Gib´e-ah on the east. 44Eighteen thou-
sand men of Benjamin fell, all of them
men of valor. 45And they turned and
fled toward the wilderness to the rock
of Rimmon; five thousand men of
them were cut down in the highways,
and they were pursued hard to Gidom,
and two thousand men of them were
slain. 46So all who fell that day of
Benjamin were twenty-five thousand
men that drew the sword, all of them

[a] Gk Vg: Heb *in the plain*
[b] Gk: Heb *surrounding*
[c] Gk: Heb *(at their) resting place*

men of valor. 47But six hundred men
turned and fled toward the wilderness
to the rock of Rimmon, and abode at
the rock of Rimmon four months.
48And the men of Israel turned back
against the Benjaminites, and smote
them with the edge of the sword, men
and beasts and all that they found.
And all the towns which they found
they set on fire.

THE BENJAMINITES SAVED FROM EXTINCTION

21 Now the men of Israel had sworn
at Mizpah, "No one of us shall
give his daughter in marriage to
Benjamin." 2And the people came to
Bethel, and sat there till evening be-
fore God, and they lifted up their voic-
es and wept bitterly. 3And they said,
"O LORD, the God of Israel, why has
this come to pass in Israel, that there
should be today one tribe lacking in
Israel?" 4And on the morrow the peo-
ple rose early, and built there an al-
tar, and offered burnt offerings and
peace offerings. 5And the people of
Israel said, "Which of all the tribes of
Israel did not come up in the assem-
bly to the LORD?" For they had taken
a great oath concerning him who did
not come up to the LORD to Mizpah,
saying, "He shall be put to death."
6And the people of Israel had compas-
sion for Benjamin their brother, and
said, "One tribe is cut off from Israel
this day. 7What shall we do for wives
for those who are left, since we have
sworn by the LORD that we will not
give them any of our daughters for
wives?"

8 And they said, "What one is
there of the tribes of Israel that did
not come up to the LORD to Mizpah?"
And behold, no one had come to the
camp from Ja´besh-gil´ead, to the as-
sembly. 9For when the people were
mustered, behold, not one of the
inhabitants of Ja´besh-gil´ead was
there. 10So the congregation sent
thither twelve thousand of their brav-
est men, and commanded them, "Go
and smite the inhabitants of Ja´besh-
gil´ead with the edge of the sword;
also the women and the little ones.
11This is what you shall do; every male
and every woman that has lain with a
male you shall utterly destroy." 12And
they found among the inhabitants of
Ja´besh-gil´ead four hundred young
virgins who had not known man by ly-
ing with him; and they brought them
to the camp at Shiloh, which is in the
land of Canaan.

13 Then the whole congregation
sent word to the Benjaminites who
were at the rock of Rimmon, and
proclaimed peace to them. 14And
Benjamin returned at that time; and
they gave them the women whom
they had saved alive of the women of
Ja´besh-gil´ead; but they did not suf-
fice for them. 15And the people had
compassion on Benjamin because the
LORD had made a breach in the tribes
of Israel.

16 Then the elders of the congrega-
tion said, "What shall we do for wives
for those who are left, since the wom-
en are destroyed out of Benjamin?"
17And they said, "There must be an
inheritance for the survivors of Ben-
jamin, that a tribe be not blotted out
from Israel. 18Yet we cannot give them
wives of our daughters." For the peo-
ple of Israel had sworn, "Cursed be he
who gives a wife to Benjamin." 19So
they said, "Behold, there is the year-
ly feast of the LORD at Shiloh, which
is north of Bethel, on the east of the
highway that goes up from Bethel to
Shechem, and south of Lebo´nah."
20And they commanded the Benja-
minites, saying, "Go and lie in wait
in the vineyards, 21and watch; if the
daughters of Shiloh come out to dance
in the dances, then come out of the
vineyards and seize each man his wife
from the daughters of Shiloh, and go
to the land of Benjamin. 22And when
their fathers or their brothers come to
complain to us, we will say to them,
'Grant them graciously to us; because
we did not take for each man of them

his wife in battle, neither did you give
them to them, else you would now be
guilty.'" 23And the Benjaminites did
so, and took their wives, according
to their number, from the dancers
whom they carried off; then they went
and returned to their inheritance,
and rebuilt the towns, and dwelt in
them. 24And the people of Israel de-
parted from there at that time, every
man to his tribe and family, and they
went out from there every man to his
inheritance.

25 In those days there was no king
in Israel; every man did what was
right in his own eyes.

THE BOOK OF

RUTH

ELIMELECH'S FAMILY GOES TO MOAB

1 In the days when the judges ruled
there was a famine in the land,
and a certain man of Bethlehem in
Judah went to sojourn in the coun-
try of Moab, he and his wife and his
two sons. 2The name of the man was
Elim´elech and the name of his wife
Na´omi, and the names of his two
sons were Mahlon and Chil´ion; they
were Eph´rathites from Bethlehem
in Judah. They went into the coun-
try of Moab and remained there. 3But
Elim´elech, the husband of Na´omi,
died, and she was left with her two
sons. 4These took Moabite wives;
the name of the one was Orpah and
the name of the other Ruth. They
lived there about ten years; 5and both
Mahlon and Chil´ion died, so that the
woman was bereft of her two sons and
her husband.

NA´OMI AND HER MOABITE DAUGHTERS-IN-LAW

6 Then she started with her daugh-
ters-in-law to return from the country
of Moab, for she had heard in the coun-
try of Moab that the LORD had visited
his people and given them food. 7So
she set out from the place where she
was, with her two daughters-in-law,
and they went on the way to return to
the land of Judah. 8But Na´omi said to
her two daughters-in-law, "Go, return
each of you to her mother's house. May
the LORD deal kindly with you, as you
have dealt with the dead and with me.
9The LORD grant that you may find a
home, each of you in the house of her
husband!" Then she kissed them, and
they lifted up their voices and wept.
10And they said to her, "No, we will
return with you to your people." 11But
Na´omi said, "Turn back, my daugh-
ters, why will you go with me? Have
I yet sons in my womb that they may
become your husbands? 12Turn back,
my daughters, go your way, for I am
too old to have a husband. If I should
say I have hope, even if I should have
a husband this night and should bear
sons, 13would you therefore wait till
they were grown? Would you there-
fore refrain from marrying? No, my
daughters, for it is exceedingly bitter
to me for your sake that the hand of
the LORD has gone forth against me."
14Then they lifted up their voices and
wept again; and Orpah kissed her
mother-in-law, but Ruth clung to her.

15 And she said, "See, your sister-
in-law has gone back to her people
and to her gods; return after your sis-
ter-in-law." 16But Ruth said, "Entreat
me not to leave you or to return from
following you; for where you go I will
go, and where you lodge I will lodge;
your people shall be my people, and
your God my God; 17where you die I
will die, and there will I be buried.
May the LORD do so to me and more
also if even death parts me from you."
18And when Na´omi saw that she was
determined to go with her, she said no
more.

19 So the two of them went on
until they came to Bethlehem. And
when they came to Bethlehem, the
whole town was stirred because of
them; and the women said, "Is this
Na´omi?" 20She said to them, "Do not
call me Na´omi,[a] call me Mara, for the
Almighty has dealt very bitterly with
me. 21I went away full, and the LORD
has brought[b] me back empty. Why
call me Na´omi, when the LORD has
afflicted[c] me and the Almighty has
brought calamity upon me?"

[a]That is *Pleasant*
[b]That is *Bitter*
[c]Gk Syr Vg: Heb *testified against*

22 So Na´omi returned, and Ruth
the Moabitess her daughter-in-law with
her, who returned from the country of
Moab. And they came to Bethlehem at
the beginning of barley harvest.

RUTH MEETS BOAZ

2 Now Na´omi had a kinsman of her
husband's, a man of wealth, of the
family of Elim´elech, whose name was
Bo´az. 2 And Ruth the Moabitess said
to Na´omi, "Let me go to the field, and
glean among the ears of grain after
him in whose sight I shall find favor."
And she said to her, "Go, my daugh-
ter." 3 So she set forth and went and
gleaned in the field after the reapers;
and she happened to come to the part
of the field belonging to Bo´az, who
was of the family of Elim´elech. 4 And
behold, Bo´az came from Bethlehem;
and he said to the reapers, "The LORD
be with you!" And they answered,
"The LORD bless you." 5 Then Bo´az
said to his servant who was in charge
of the reapers, "Whose maiden is
this?" 6 And the servant who was in
charge of the reapers answered, "It
is the Moabite maiden, who came
back with Na´omi from the coun-
try of Moab. 7 She said, 'Pray, let me
glean and gather among the sheaves
after the reapers.' So she came, and
she has continued from early morning
until now, without resting even for a
moment."[d]

8 Then Bo´az said to Ruth, "Now,
listen, my daughter, do not go to glean
in another field or leave this one, but
keep close to my maidens. 9 Let your
eyes be upon the field which they are
reaping, and go after them. Have I not
charged the young men not to molest
you? And when you are thirsty, go to
the vessels and drink what the young
men have drawn." 10 Then she fell on
her face, bowing to the ground, and
said to him, "Why have I found favor
in your eyes, that you should take no-
tice of me, when I am a foreigner?"
11 But Bo´az answered her, "All that
you have done for your mother-in-
law since the death of your husband
has been fully told me, and how you
left your father and mother and your
native land and came to a people that
you did not know before. 12 The LORD
recompense you for what you have
done, and a full reward be given you
by the LORD, the God of Israel, under
whose wings you have come to take
refuge!" 13 Then she said, "You are
most gracious to me, my lord, for you
have comforted me and spoken kindly
to your maidservant, though I am not
one of your maidservants."

14 And at mealtime Bo´az said to
her, "Come here, and eat some bread,
and dip your morsel in the wine." So
she sat beside the reapers, and he
passed to her parched grain; and she
ate until she was satisfied, and she
had some left over. 15 When she rose
to glean, Bo´az instructed his young
men, saying, "Let her glean even
among the sheaves, and do not re-
proach her. 16 And also pull out some
from the bundles for her, and leave
it for her to glean, and do not rebuke
her."

17 So she gleaned in the field un-
til evening; then she beat out what
she had gleaned, and it was about an
ephah of barley. 18 And she took it up
and went into the city; she showed her
mother-in-law what she had gleaned,
and she also brought out and gave
her what food she had left over after
being satisfied. 19 And her mother-in-
law said to her, "Where did you glean
today? And where have you worked?
Blessed be the man who took notice
of you." So she told her mother-in-law
with whom she had worked, and said,
"The man's name with whom I worked
today is Bo´az." 20 And Na´omi said to
her daughter-in-law, "Blessed be he by
the LORD, whose kindness has not for-
saken the living or the dead!" Na´omi
also said to her, "The man is a relative
of ours, one of our nearest kin." 21 And
Ruth the Moabitess said, "Besides, he

[d] Compare Gk Vg: the meaning of the Hebrew text is uncertain

said to me, 'You shall keep close by
my servants, till they have finished
all my harvest.'" 22And Na´omi said to
Ruth, her daughter-in-law, "It is well,
my daughter, that you go out with his
maidens, lest in another field you be
molested." 23So she kept close to the
maidens of Bo´az, gleaning until the
end of the barley and wheat harvests;
and she lived with her mother-in-law.

RUTH AND BOAZ AT THE THRESHING FLOOR

3 Then Na´omi her mother-in-law
said to her, "My daughter, should I
not seek a home for you, that it may
be well with you? 2Now is not Bo´az
our kinsman, with whose maidens
you were? See, he is winnowing barley
tonight at the threshing floor. 3Wash
therefore and anoint yourself, and put
on your best clothes and go down to
the threshing floor; but do not make
yourself known to the man until he
has finished eating and drinking. 4But
when he lies down, observe the place
where he lies; then, go and uncover
his feet and lie down; and he will tell
you what to do." 5And she replied, "All
that you say I will do."

6 So she went down to the thresh-
ing floor and did just as her mother-
in-law had told her. 7And when Bo´az
had eaten and drunk, and his heart
was merry, he went to lie down at the
end of the heap of grain. Then she
came softly, and uncovered his feet,
and lay down. 8At midnight the man
was startled, and turned over, and be-
hold, a woman lay at his feet! 9He said,
"Who are you?" And she answered, "I
am Ruth, your maidservant; spread
your skirt over your maidservant, for
you are next of kin." 10And he said,
"May you be blessed by the LORD,
my daughter; you have made this last
kindness greater than the first, in
that you have not gone after young
men, whether poor or rich. 11And now,
my daughter, do not fear, I will do for
you all that you ask, for all my fellow
townsmen know that you are a wom-
an of worth. 12And now it is true that
I am a near kinsman, yet there is a
kinsman nearer than I. 13Remain this
night, and in the morning, if he will
do the part of the next of kin for you,
well; let him do it; but if he is not will-
ing to do the part of the next of kin for
you, then, as the LORD lives, I will do
the part of the next of kin for you. Lie
down until the morning."

14 So she lay at his feet until the
morning, but arose before one could
recognize another; and he said, "Let
it not be known that the woman came
to the threshing floor." 15And he said,
"Bring the mantle you are wearing
and hold it out." So she held it, and
he measured out six measures of bar-
ley, and laid it upon her; then she went
into the city. 16And when she came to
her mother-in-law, she said, "How
did you fare, my daughter?" Then she
told her all that the man had done for
her, 17saying, "These six measures of
barley he gave to me, for he said, 'You
must not go back empty-handed to
your mother-in-law.'" 18She replied,
"Wait, my daughter, until you learn
how the matter turns out, for the man
will not rest, but will settle the matter
today."

THE MARRIAGE OF BOAZ AND RUTH

4 And Bo´az went up to the gate and
sat down there; and behold, the
next of kin, of whom Bo´az had spo-
ken, came by. So Bo´az said, "Turn
aside, friend; sit down here"; and he
turned aside and sat down. 2And he
took ten men of the elders of the city,
and said, "Sit down here"; so they
sat down. 3Then he said to the next
of kin, "Na´omi, who has come back
from the country of Moab, is selling
the parcel of land which belonged to
our kinsman Elim´elech. 4So I thought
I would tell you of it, and say, Buy it
in the presence of those sitting here,
and in the presence of the elders of my
people. If you will redeem it, redeem
it; but if you will not, tell me, that I
may know, for there is no one besides
you to redeem it, and I come after

you." And he said, "I will redeem it."
5Then Bo´az said, "The day you buy
the field from the hand of Na´omi, you
are also buying Ruth[a] the Moabitess,
the widow of the dead, in order to re-
store the name of the dead to his in-
heritance." 6Then the next of kin said,
"I cannot redeem it for myself, lest I
impair my own inheritance. Take my
right of redemption yourself, for I can-
not redeem it."

7 Now this was the custom in
former times in Israel concerning re-
deeming and exchanging: to confirm a
transaction, the one drew off his san-
dal and gave it to the other, and this
was the manner of attesting in Israel.
8So when the next of kin said to Bo´az,
"Buy it for yourself," he drew off his
sandal. 9Then Bo´az said to the elders
and all the people, "You are witnesses
this day that I have bought from the
hand of Na´omi all that belonged to
Elim´elech and all that belonged to
Chil´ion and to Mahlon. 10Also Ruth
the Moabitess, the widow of Mahlon,
I have bought to be my wife, to per-
petuate the name of the dead in his
inheritance, that the name of the
dead may not be cut off from among
his brethren and from the gate of his
native place; you are witnesses this
day." 11Then all the people who were
at the gate, and the elders, said, "We
are witnesses. May the LORD make
the woman, who is coming into your
house, like Rachel and Leah, who
together built up the house of Israel.
May you prosper in Eph´rathah and
be renowned in Bethlehem; 12and may
your house be like the house of Perez,
whom Tamar bore to Judah, because
of the children that the LORD will give
you by this young woman."

THE GENEALOGY OF DAVID

13 So Bo´az took Ruth and she be-
came his wife; and he went in to her,
and the LORD gave her conception,
and she bore a son. 14Then the wom-
en said to Na´omi, "Blessed be the
LORD, who has not left you this day
without next of kin; and may his name
be renowned in Israel! 15He shall be to
you a restorer of life and a nourisher
of your old age; for your daughter-in-
law who loves you, who is more to
you than seven sons, has borne him."
16Then Na´omi took the child and laid
him in her bosom, and became his
nurse. 17And the women of the neigh-
borhood gave him a name, saying, "A
son has been born to Na´omi." They
named him Obed; he was the father of
Jesse, the father of David.

18 Now these are the descen-
dants of Perez: Perez was the father
of Hezron, 19Hezron of Ram, Ram of
Ammin´adab, 20Ammin´adab of Nah-
shon, Nahshon of Salmon, 21Salmon of
Bo´az, Bo´az of Obed, 22Obed of Jesse,
and Jesse of David.

[a] Old Latin Vg: Heb *of Na´omi and from Ruth*

THE FIRST BOOK OF
SAMUEL

SAMUEL'S BIRTH AND DEDICATION

1 There was a certain man of Ramatha´im-zo´phim of the hill country of E´phraim, whose name was Elka´nah the son of Jero´ham, son of Eli´hu, son of Tohu, son of Zuph, an E´phraimite. 2 He had two wives; the name of the one was Hannah, and the name of the other Penin´nah. And Penin´nah had children, but Hannah had no children.

3 Now this man used to go up year by year from his city to worship and to sacrifice to the LORD of hosts at Shiloh,* where the two sons of Eli, Hophni and Phin´ehas, were priests of the LORD. 4 On the day when Elka´nah sacrificed, he would give portions to Penin´nah his wife and to all her sons and daughters; 5 and, although[a] he loved Hannah, he would give Hannah only one portion, because the LORD had closed her womb. 6 And her rival used to provoke her sorely, to irritate her, because the LORD had closed her womb. 7 So it went on year by year; as often as she went up to the house of the LORD, she used to provoke her. Therefore Hannah wept and would not eat. 8 And Elka´nah, her husband, said to her, "Hannah, why do you weep? And why do you not eat? And why is your heart sad? Am I not more to you than ten sons?"

9 After they had eaten and drunk in Shiloh, Hannah rose. Now Eli the priest was sitting on the seat beside the doorpost of the temple of the LORD. 10 She was deeply distressed and prayed to the LORD, and wept bitterly. 11 And she vowed a vow and said, "O LORD of hosts, if thou wilt indeed look on the affliction of thy maidservant, and remember me, and not forget thy maidservant, but wilt give to thy maidservant a son, then I will give him to the LORD all the days of his life, and no razor shall touch his head."

12 As she continued praying before the LORD, Eli observed her mouth. 13 Hannah was speaking in her heart; only her lips moved, and her voice was not heard; therefore Eli took her to be a drunken woman. 14 And Eli said to her, "How long will you be drunken? Put away your wine from you." 15 But Hannah answered, "No, my lord, I am a woman sorely troubled; I have drunk neither wine nor strong drink, but I have been pouring out my soul before the LORD. 16 Do not regard your maidservant as a base woman, for all along I have been speaking out of my great anxiety and vexation." 17 Then Eli answered, "Go in peace, and the God of Israel grant your petition which you have made to him." 18 And she said, "Let your maidservant find favor in your eyes." Then the woman went her way and ate, and her countenance was no longer sad.

19 They rose early in the morning and worshiped before the LORD; then they went back to their house at Ramah. And Elka´nah knew Hannah his wife, and the LORD remembered her; 20 and in due time Hannah conceived and bore a son, and she called his name Samuel, for she said, "I have asked him of the LORD."

21 And the man Elka´nah and all his house went up to offer to the LORD the yearly sacrifice, and to pay his vow. 22 But Hannah did not go up, for she said to her husband, "As soon as the child is weaned, I will bring him, that he may appear in the presence of the LORD, and abide there for ever." 23 Elka´nah her husband said to her, "Do what seems best to you, wait until you have weaned him; only, may the LORD establish his word." So the

[a] Gk: Heb obscure

woman remained and nursed her son,
until she weaned him. 24And when
she had weaned him, she took him up
with her, along with a three-year-old
bull,[b] an ephah of flour, and a skin
of wine; and she brought him to the
house of the LORD at Shiloh; and the
child was young. 25Then they slew the
bull, and they brought the child to Eli.
26And she said, "Oh, my lord! As you
live, my lord, I am the woman who
was standing here in your presence,
praying to the LORD. 27For this child
I prayed; and the LORD has granted
me my petition which I made to him.
28Therefore I have lent him to the
LORD; as long as he lives, he is lent to
the LORD."

And they[c] worshiped the LORD there.

HANNAH'S PRAYER

2 Hannah also prayed and said,*
"My heart exults in the LORD;
my strength is exalted in the LORD.
My mouth derides my enemies,
because I rejoice in thy salvation.
2"There is none holy like the LORD,
there is none besides thee;
there is no rock like our God.
3Talk no more so very proudly,
let not arrogance come from your mouth;
for the LORD is a God of knowledge,
and by him actions are weighed.
4The bows of the mighty are broken,
but the feeble gird on strength.
5Those who were full have hired themselves out for bread,
but those who were hungry have ceased to hunger.
The barren has borne seven,
but she who has many children is forlorn.
6The LORD kills and brings to life;
he brings down to Sheol and raises up.
7The LORD makes poor and makes rich;
he brings low, he also exalts.
8He raises up the poor from the dust;
he lifts the needy from the ash heap,
to make them sit with princes
and inherit a seat of honor.
For the pillars of the earth are the LORD'S,
and on them he has set the world.
9"He will guard the feet of his faithful ones;
but the wicked shall be cut off in darkness;
for not by might shall a man prevail.
10The adversaries of the LORD
shall be broken to pieces;
against them he will thunder in heaven.
The LORD will judge the ends of the earth;
he will give strength to his king,
and exalt the power of his anointed."

ELI'S WICKED SONS

11 Then Elka´nah went home to
Ramah. And the boy ministered to
the LORD, in the presence of Eli the
priest.

12 Now the sons of Eli were worth-
less men; they had no regard for the
LORD. 13The custom of the priests
with the people was that when any
man offered sacrifice, the priest's ser-
vant would come, while the meat was
boiling, with a three-pronged fork in
his hand, 14and he would thrust it into
the pan, or kettle, or caldron, or pot;

[b]Gk Syr: Heb *three bulls*
[c]Heb *he*

all that the fork brought up the priest would take for himself.[a] So they did at Shiloh to all the Israelites who came there. 15 Moreover, before the fat was burned, the priest's servant would come and say to the man who was sacrificing, "Give meat for the priest to roast; for he will not accept boiled meat from you, but raw." 16 And if the man said to him, "Let them burn the fat first, and then take as much as you wish," he would say, "No, you must give it now; and if not, I will take it by force." 17 Thus the sin of the young men was very great in the sight of the LORD; for the men treated the offering of the LORD with contempt.

THE CHILD SAMUEL AT SHILOH

18 Samuel was ministering before the LORD, a boy girded with a linen ephod.* 19 And his mother used to make for him a little robe and take it to him each year, when she went up with her husband to offer the yearly sacrifice. 20 Then Eli would bless Elka´nah and his wife, and say, "The LORD give you children by this woman for the loan which she lent to[b] The LORD"; so then they would return to their home.

21 And the LORD visited Hannah, and she conceived and bore three sons and two daughters. And the boy Samuel grew in the presence of the LORD.

PROPHECY AGAINST ELI'S HOUSEHOLD

22 Now Eli was very old, and he heard all that his sons were doing to all Israel, and how they lay with the women who served at the entrance to the tent of meeting. 23 And he said to them, "Why do you do such things? For I hear of your evil dealings from all the people. 24 No, my sons; it is no good report that I hear the people of the LORD spreading abroad. 25 If a man sins against a man, God will mediate for him; but if a man sins against the LORD, who can intercede for him?" But they would not listen to the voice of their father; for it was the will of the LORD to slay them.

26 Now the boy Samuel continued to grow both in stature and in favor with the LORD and with men.

27 And there came a man of God to Eli, and said to him, "Thus the LORD has said, 'I revealed[c] myself to the house of your father when they were in Egypt subject to the house of Pharaoh. 28 And I chose him out of all the tribes of Israel to be my priest, to go up to my altar, to burn incense, to wear an ephod before me; and I gave to the house of your father all my offerings by fire from the people of Israel. 29 Why then look with greedy eye at[d] my sacrifices and my offerings which I commanded, and honor your sons above me by fattening yourselves upon the choicest parts of every offering of my people Israel?' 30 Therefore the LORD the God of Israel declares: 'I promised that your house and the house of your father should go in and out before me for ever'; but now the LORD declares: 'Far be it from me; for those who honor me I will honor, and those who despise me shall be lightly esteemed. 31 Behold, the days are coming, when I will cut off your strength and the strength of your father's house, so that there will not be an old man in your house. 32 Then in distress you will look with envious eye on all the prosperity which shall be bestowed upon Israel; and there shall not be an old man in your house for ever. 33 The man of you whom I shall not cut off from my altar shall be spared to weep out his[e] eyes and grieve his[f] heart; and all the increase of your house shall die by the sword

[a] Gk Syr Vg: Heb *with it*
[b] Or *for the petition which she asked of*
[c] Gk Tg: Heb *Did I reveal*
[d] Or *treat with scorn* Gk: Heb *kick at*
[e] Gk: Heb *your*
[f] Gk: Heb *your*

of men.[g] 34And this which shall befall
your two sons, Hophni and Phin´ehas,
shall be the sign to you: both of them
shall die on the same day. 35And I will
raise up for myself a faithful priest,
who shall do according to what is in
my heart and in my mind; and I will
build him a sure house, and he shall
go in and out before my anointed for
ever. 36And every one who is left in
your house shall come to implore him
for a piece of silver or a loaf of bread,
and shall say, "Put me, I pray you, in
one of the priest's places, that I may
eat a morsel of bread.""'

SAMUEL'S CALLING AND PROPHETIC ACTIVITY

3 *Now the boy Samuel was minister-
ing to the LORD under Eli. And the
word of the LORD was rare in those
days; there was no frequent vision.
2 At that time Eli, whose eyesight
had begun to grow dim, so that he
could not see, was lying down in his
own place; 3the lamp of God had not
yet gone out, and Samuel was lying
down within the temple of the LORD,
where the ark of God was. 4Then the
LORD called, "Samuel! Samuel!"[h] and
he said, "Here I am!" 5and ran to Eli,
and said, "Here I am, for you called
me." But he said, "I did not call; lie
down again." So he went and lay
down. 6And the LORD called again,
"Samuel!" and Samuel arose and went
to Eli, and said, "Here I am, for you
called me." But he said, "I did not call,
my son; lie down again." 7Now Samuel
did not yet know the LORD, and the
word of the LORD had not yet been re-
vealed to him. 8And the LORD called
Samuel again the third time. And he
arose and went to Eli, and said, "Here
I am, for you called me." Then Eli per-
ceived that the LORD was calling the
boy. 9Therefore Eli said to Samuel,
"Go, lie down; and if he calls you,
you shall say, 'Speak, LORD, for thy
servant hears.'" So Samuel went and
lay down in his place.
10 And the LORD came and stood
forth, calling as at other times,
"Samuel! Samuel!" And Samuel said,
"Speak, for thy servant hears." 11Then
the LORD said to Samuel, "Behold, I
am about to do a thing in Israel, at
which the two ears of every one that
hears it will tingle. 12On that day I will
fulfil against Eli all that I have spoken
concerning his house, from beginning
to end. 13And I tell him that I am about
to punish his house for ever, for the
iniquity which he knew, because his
sons were blaspheming God,[i] and he
did not restrain them. 14Therefore I
swear to the house of Eli that the in-
iquity of Eli's house shall not be expi-
ated by sacrifice or offering for ever."
15 Samuel lay until morning; then
he opened the doors of the house of
the LORD. And Samuel was afraid to
tell the vision to Eli. 16But Eli called
Samuel and said, "Samuel, my son."
And he said, "Here I am." 17And Eli
said, "What was it that he told you?
Do not hide it from me. May God do so
to you and more also, if you hide any-
thing from me of all that he told you."
18So Samuel told him everything and
hid nothing from him. And he said, "It
is the LORD; let him do what seems
good to him."
19 And Samuel grew, and the
LORD was with him and let none of
his words fall to the ground. 20And
all Israel from Dan to Beer-sheba
knew that Samuel was established
as a prophet of the LORD. 21And the
LORD appeared again at Shiloh, for
the LORD revealed himself to Samuel
at Shiloh by the word of the LORD.
4 And the word of Samuel came to all
Israel.

THE ARK OF GOD CAPTURED *

Now Israel went out to battle
against the Philistines; they encamp-
ed at Ebene´zer, and the Philistines

[g] Gk: Heb *die as men*
[h] Gk See 3.10: Heb *the* Lord *called Samuel*
[i] Another reading is *for themselves*

encamped at Aphek. 2The Philistines drew up in line against Israel, and when the battle spread, Israel was defeated by the Philistines, who slew about four thousand men on the field of battle. 3And when the troops came to the camp, the elders of Israel said, "Why has the LORD put us to rout today before the Philistines? Let us bring the ark of the covenant of the LORD here from Shiloh, that he may come among us and save us from the power of our enemies." 4So the people sent to Shiloh, and brought from there the ark of the covenant of the LORD of hosts, who is enthroned on the cherubim; and the two sons of Eli, Hophni and Phin′ehas, were there with the ark of the covenant of God.

5 When the ark of the covenant of the LORD came into the camp, all Israel gave a mighty shout, so that the earth resounded. 6And when the Philistines heard the noise of the shouting, they said, "What does this great shouting in the camp of the Hebrews mean?" And when they learned that the ark of the LORD had come to the camp, 7the Philistines were afraid; for they said, "A god has come into the camp." And they said, "Woe to us! For nothing like this has happened before. 8Woe to us! Who can deliver us from the power of these mighty gods? These are the gods who smote the Egyptians with every sort of plague in the wilderness. 9Take courage, and acquit yourselves like men, O Philistines, lest you become slaves to the Hebrews as they have been to you; acquit yourselves like men and fight."

10 So the Philistines fought, and Israel was defeated, and they fled, every man to his home; and there was a very great slaughter, for there fell of Israel thirty thousand foot soldiers. 11And the ark of God was captured; and the two sons of Eli, Hophni and Phin′ehas, were slain.

DEATH OF ELI

12 A man of Benjamin ran from the battle line, and came to Shiloh the same day, with his clothes rent and with earth upon his head. 13When he arrived, Eli was sitting upon his seat by the road watching, for his heart trembled for the ark of God. And when the man came into the city and told the news, all the city cried out. 14When Eli heard the sound of the outcry, he said, "What is this uproar?" Then the man hastened and came and told Eli. 15Now Eli was ninety-eight years old and his eyes were set, so that he could not see. 16And the man said to Eli, "I am he who has come from the battle; I fled from the battle today." And he said, "How did it go, my son?" 17He who brought the tidings answered and said, "Israel has fled before the Philistines, and there has also been a great slaughter among the people; your two sons also, Hophni and Phin′ehas, are dead, and the ark of God has been captured." 18When he mentioned the ark of God, Eli fell over backward from his seat by the side of the gate; and his neck was broken and he died, for he was an old man, and heavy. He had judged Israel forty years.

19 Now his daughter-in-law, the wife of Phin′ehas, was with child, about to give birth. And when she heard the tidings that the ark of God was captured, and that her father-in-law and her husband were dead, she bowed and gave birth; for her pains came upon her. 20And about the time of her death the women attending her said to her, "Fear not, for you have borne a son." But she did not answer or give heed. 21And she named the child Ich′abod,* saying, "The glory has departed from Israel!" because the ark of God had been captured and because of her father-in-law and her husband. 22And she said, "The glory has departed from Israel, for the ark of God has been captured."

THE PHILISTINES AND THE ARK

5 When the Philistines captured the ark of God, they carried it

from Ebene´zer to Ashdod; 2then the
Philistines took the ark of God and
brought it into the house of Dagon
and set it up beside Dagon. 3And
when the people of Ashdod rose early
the next day, behold, Dagon had fall-
en face downward on the ground be-
fore the ark of the LORD. So they took
Dagon and put him back in his place.
4But when they rose early on the next
morning, behold, Dagon had fallen
face downward on the ground before
the ark of the LORD, and the head of
Dagon and both his hands were ly-
ing cut off upon the threshold; only
the trunk of Dagon was left to him.
5This is why the priests of Dagon and
all who enter the house of Dagon do
not tread on the threshold of Dagon in
Ashdod to this day.

6 The hand of the LORD was heavy
upon the people of Ashdod, and he ter-
rified and afflicted them with tumors,
both Ashdod and its territory. 7And
when the men of Ashdod saw how
things were, they said, "The ark of the
God of Israel must not remain with
us; for his hand is heavy upon us and
upon Dagon our god." 8So they sent
and gathered together all the lords
of the Philistines, and said, "What
shall we do with the ark of the God of
Israel?" They answered, "Let the ark
of the God of Israel be brought around
to Gath." So they brought the ark of
the God of Israel there. 9But after they
had brought it around, the hand of the
LORD was against the city, causing a
very great panic, and he afflicted the
men of the city, both young and old, so
that tumors broke out upon them. 10So
they sent the ark of God to Ekron. But
when the ark of God came to Ekron,
the people of Ekron cried out, "They
have brought around to us the ark of
the God of Israel to slay us and our
people." 11They sent therefore and
gathered together all the lords of the
Philistines, and said, "Send away the
ark of the God of Israel, and let it re-
turn to its own place, that it may not
slay us and our people." For there was
a deathly panic throughout the whole
city. The hand of God was very heavy
there; 12the men who did not die were
stricken with tumors, and the cry of
the city went up to heaven.

THE ARK RETURNED TO ISRAEL

6 The ark of the LORD was in the
country of the Philistines seven
months. 2And the Philistines called for
the priests and the diviners and said,
"What shall we do with the ark of the
LORD? Tell us with what we shall send
it to its place." 3They said, "If you send
away the ark of the God of Israel, do
not send it empty, but by all means
return him a guilt offering. Then you
will be healed, and it will be known to
you why his hand does not turn away
from you." 4And they said, "What is
the guilt offering that we shall return
to him?" They answered, "Five golden
tumors and five golden mice, accord-
ing to the number of the lords of the
Philistines; for the same plague was
upon all of you and upon your lords.
5So you must make images of your
tumors and images of your mice that
ravage the land, and give glory to the
God of Israel; perhaps he will lighten
his hand from off you and your gods
and your land. 6Why should you hard-
en your hearts as the Egyptians and
Pharaoh hardened their hearts? After
he had made sport of them, did not
they let the people go, and they de-
parted? 7Now then, take and prepare
a new cart and two milch cows upon
which there has never come a yoke,
and yoke the cows to the cart, but take
their calves home, away from them.
8And take the ark of the LORD and
place it on the cart, and put in a box at
its side the figures of gold, which you
are returning to him as a guilt offer-
ing. Then send it off, and let it go its
way. 9And watch; if it goes up on the
way to its own land, to Beth-she´mesh,
then it is he who has done us this great
harm; but if not, then we shall know
that it is not his hand that struck us, it
happened to us by chance."

10 The men did so, and took two milch cows and yoked them to the cart, and shut up their calves at home. 11And they put the ark of the LORD on the cart, and the box with the golden mice and the images of their tumors. 12And the cows went straight in the direction of Beth-she´mesh along one highway, lowing as they went; they turned neither to the right nor to the left, and the lords of the Philistines went after them as far as the border of Beth-she´mesh. 13Now the people of Beth-she´mesh were reaping their wheat harvest in the valley; and when they lifted up their eyes and saw the ark, they rejoiced to see it. 14The cart came into the field of Joshua of Beth-she´mesh, and stopped there. A great stone was there; and they split up the wood of the cart and offered the cows as a burnt offering to the LORD. 15And the Levites took down the ark of the LORD and the box that was beside it, in which were the golden figures, and set them upon the great stone; and the men of Beth-she´mesh offered burnt offerings and sacrificed sacrifices on that day to the LORD. 16And when the five lords of the Philistines saw it, they returned that day to Ekron.

17 These are the golden tumors, which the Philistines returned as a guilt offering to the LORD: one for Ashdod, one for Gaza, one for Ash´kelon, one for Gath, one for Ekron; 18also the golden mice, according to the number of all the cities of the Philistines belonging to the five lords, both fortified cities and unwalled villages. The great stone, beside which they set down the ark of the LORD, is a witness to this day in the field of Joshua of Beth-she´mesh.

THE ARK AT KIRIATH-JEARIM

19 And he slew some of the men of Beth-she´mesh, because they looked into the ark of the LORD; he slew seventy men of them,[a] and the people mourned because the LORD had made a great slaughter among the people. 20Then the men of Beth-she´mesh said, "Who is able to stand before the LORD, this holy God? And to whom shall he go up away from us?" 21So they sent messengers to the inhabitants of Kir´iath-je´arim, saying, "The Philistines have returned the ark of the LORD. Come down and take it up to you."

7 And the men of Kir´iath-je´arim came and took up the ark of the LORD, and brought it to the house of Abin´adab on the hill; and they consecrated his son, Elea´zar, to have charge of the ark of the LORD. 2From the day that the ark was lodged at Kir´iath-je´arim, a long time passed, some twenty years, and all the house of Israel lamented after the LORD.*

SAMUEL AS JUDGE

3 Then Samuel said to all the house of Israel, "If you are returning to the LORD with all your heart, then put away the foreign gods and the Ash´taroth from among you, and direct your heart to the LORD, and serve him only, and he will deliver you out of the hand of the Philistines." 4So Israel put away the Ba´als and the Ash´taroth, and they served the LORD only.

5 Then Samuel said, "Gather all Israel at Mizpah, and I will pray to the LORD for you." 6So they gathered at Mizpah, and drew water and poured it out before the LORD, and fasted on that day, and said there, "We have sinned against the LORD." And Samuel judged the people of Israel at Mizpah. 7Now when the Philistines heard that the people of Israel had gathered at Mizpah, the lords of the Philistines went up against Israel. And when the people of Israel heard of it they were afraid of the Philistines. 8And the people of Israel said to Samuel, "Do not cease to cry to the LORD our God for us, that he may save us from the hand of the Philistines." 9So Samuel took a sucking lamb and offered it as

[a]Cn: Heb *of the people seventy men, fifty thousand men*

a whole burnt offering to the LORD;
and Samuel cried to the LORD for
Israel, and the LORD answered him.
10As Samuel was offering up the burnt
offering, the Philistines drew near to
attack Israel; but the LORD thundered
with a mighty voice that day against
the Philistines and threw them into
confusion; and they were routed be-
fore Israel. 11And the men of Israel
went out of Mizpah and pursued the
Philistines, and smote them, as far as
below Beth-car.

12 Then Samuel took a stone and set
it up between Mizpah and Jesha´nah,[b]
and called its name Ebene´zer;[c] for he
said, "Hitherto the LORD has helped
us." 13So the Philistines were subdued
and did not again enter the territory
of Israel. And the hand of the LORD
was against the Philistines all the
days of Samuel. 14The cities which
the Philistines had taken from Israel
were restored to Israel, from Ekron to
Gath; and Israel rescued their territo-
ry from the hand of the Philistines.
There was peace also between Israel
and the Amorites.

15 Samuel judged Israel all the
days of his life. 16And he went on a
circuit year by year to Bethel, Gilgal,
and Mizpah; and he judged Israel in
all these places. 17Then he would come
back to Ramah, for his home was
there, and there also he administered
justice to Israel. And he built there an
altar to the LORD.

ISRAEL DEMANDS A KING

8 When Samuel became old, he made
his sons judges over Israel. 2The
name of his first-born son was Jo´el,
and the name of his second, Abi´jah;
they were judges in Beer-sheba. 3Yet
his sons did not walk in his ways,
but turned aside after gain; they took
bribes and perverted justice.

4 Then all the elders of Israel gath-
ered together and came to Samuel at
Ramah, 5and said to him, "Behold,
you are old and your sons do not walk
in your ways; now appoint for us a
king to govern us like all the nations."
6But the thing displeased Samuel
when they said, "Give us a king to
govern us." And Samuel prayed to the
LORD. 7And the LORD said to Samuel,
"Hearken to the voice of the people in
all that they say to you; for they have
not rejected you, but they have re-
jected me from being king over them.
8According to all the deeds which
they have done to me,[d] from the day
I brought them up out of Egypt even
to this day, forsaking me and serv-
ing other gods, so they are also doing
to you. 9Now then, hearken to their
voice; only, you shall solemnly warn
them, and show them the ways of the
king who shall reign over them."

10 So Samuel told all the words
of the LORD to the people who were
asking a king from him.* 11He said,
"These will be the ways of the king
who will reign over you: he will take
your sons and appoint them to his
chariots and to be his horsemen, and
to run before his chariots; 12and he
will appoint for himself command-
ers of thousands and commanders of
fifties, and some to plow his ground
and to reap his harvest, and to make
his implements of war and the equip-
ment of his chariots. 13He will take
your daughters to be perfumers and
cooks and bakers. 14He will take the
best of your fields and vineyards and
olive orchards and give them to his
servants. 15He will take the tenth
of your grain and of your vineyards
and give it to his officers and to his
servants. 16He will take your men-
servants and maidservants, and the
best of your cattle[e] and your asses,
and put them to his work. 17He will
take the tenth of your flocks, and you
shall be his slaves. 18And in that day
you will cry out because of your king,

[b]Gk Syr: Heb *Shen*
[c]That is *Stone of help*
[d]Gk: Heb lacks *to me*
[e]Gk: Heb *young men*

whom you have chosen for your-
selves; but the LORD will not answer
you in that day."

ISRAEL'S REQUEST FOR A KING GRANTED

19 But the people refused to listen
to the voice of Samuel; and they said,
"No! but we will have a king over us,
20that we also may be like all the na-
tions, and that our king may govern us
and go out before us and fight our bat-
tles." 21And when Samuel had heard
all the words of the people, he repeat-
ed them in the ears of the LORD. 22And
the LORD said to Samuel, "Hearken to
their voice, and make them a king."
Samuel then said to the men of Israel,
"Go every man to his city."

SAUL CHOSEN TO BE KING

9 There was a man of Benjamin
whose name was Kish, the son of
Abi´el, son of Zeror, son of Beco´rath,
son of Aphi´ah, a Benjaminite, a man
of wealth; 2and he had a son whose
name was Saul, a handsome young
man. There was not a man among the
people of Israel more handsome than
he; from his shoulders upward he was
taller than any of the people.

3 Now the asses of Kish, Saul's fa-
ther, were lost. So Kish said to Saul his
son, "Take one of the servants with
you, and arise, go and look for the
asses." 4And they[a] passed through the
hill country of E´phraim and passed
through the land of Shal´ishah, but
they did not find them. And they
passed through the land of Sha´alim,
but they were not there. Then they
passed through the land of Benjamin,
but did not find them.

5 When they came to the land of
Zuph, Saul said to his servant who
was with him, "Come, let us go back,
lest my father cease to care about the
asses and become anxious about us."
6But he said to him, "Behold, there is
a man of God in this city, and he is
a man that is held in honor; all that
he says comes true. Let us go there;
perhaps he can tell us about the jour-
ney on which we have set out." 7Then
Saul said to his servant, "But if we go,
what can we bring the man? For the
bread in our sacks is gone, and there
is no present to bring to the man of
God. What have we?" 8The servant
answered Saul again, "Here, I have
with me the fourth part of a shekel of
silver, and I will give it to the man of
God, to tell us our way." 9(Formerly
in Israel, when a man went to inquire
of God, he said, "Come, let us go to
the seer"; for he who is now called a
prophet was formerly called a seer.)
10And Saul said to his servant, "Well
said; come, let us go." So they went
to the city where the man of God was.

11 As they went up the hill to the
city, they met young maidens coming
out to draw water, and said to them,
"Is the seer here?" 12They answered,
"He is; behold, he is just ahead of you.
Make haste; he has come just now to
the city, because the people have a
sacrifice today on the high place. 13As
soon as you enter the city, you will
find him, before he goes up to the
high place* to eat; for the people will
not eat till he comes, since he must
bless the sacrifice; afterward those
eat who are invited. Now go up, for
you will meet him immediately." 14So
they went up to the city. As they were
entering the city, they saw Samuel
coming out toward them on his way
up to the high place.

15 Now the day before Saul came,
the LORD had revealed to Samuel:
16"Tomorrow about this time I will
send to you a man from the land of
Benjamin, and you shall anoint him
to be prince over my people Israel. He
shall save my people from the hand
of Philistines; for I have seen the af-
fliction of[b] my people, because their
cry has come to me." 17When Samuel
saw Saul, the LORD told him, "Here is
the man of whom I spoke to you! He

[a] Gk Vg: Heb *he*
[b] Gk: Heb lacks *the affliction of*

it is who shall rule over my people."
18 Then Saul approached Samuel in the
gate, and said, "Tell me where is the
house of the seer?" 19 Samuel answered
Saul, "I am the seer; go up before me
to the high place, for today you shall
eat with me, and in the morning I will
let you go and will tell you all that is
on your mind. 20 As for your asses that
were lost three days ago, do not set
your mind on them, for they have been
found. And for whom is all that is de-
sirable in Israel? Is it not for you and
for all your father's house?" 21 Saul an-
swered, "Am I not a Benjaminite, from
the least of the tribes of Israel? And
is not my family the humblest of all
the families of the tribe of Benjamin?
Why then have you spoken to me in
this way?"

22 Then Samuel took Saul and
his servant and brought them into
the hall and gave them a place at the
head of those who had been invited,
who were about thirty persons. 23 And
Samuel said to the cook, "Bring the
portion I gave you, of which I said to
you, 'Put it aside.'" 24 So the cook took
up the leg and the upper portion[c] and
set them before Saul; and Samuel
said, "See, what was kept is set before
you. Eat; because it was kept for you
until the hour appointed, that you
might eat with the guests."[d]

So Saul ate with Samuel that day.
25 And when they came down from the
high place into the city, a bed was
spread for Saul[e] upon the roof, and he
lay down to sleep. 26 Then at the break
of dawn[f] Samuel called to Saul upon
the roof, "Up, that I may send you on
your way." So Saul arose, and both he
and Samuel went out into the street.

SAMUEL ANOINTS SAUL

27 As they were going down to
the outskirts of the city, Samuel said
to Saul, "Tell the servant to pass on
before us, and when he has passed on
stop here yourself for a while, that I
may make known to you the word of
God."

10 Then Samuel took a vial of oil and
poured it on his head, and kissed
him and said, "Has not the LORD
anointed you to be prince over his peo-
ple Israel? And you shall reign over the
people of the LORD and you will save
them from the hand of their enemies
round about. And this shall be the
sign to you that the LORD has anoint-
ed you to be prince[g] over his heritage.
2 When you depart from me today you
will meet two men by Rachel's tomb
in the territory of Benjamin at Zelzah,
and they will say to you, 'The asses
which you went to seek are found, and
now your father has ceased to care
about the asses and is anxious about
you, saying, "What shall I do about
my son?"' 3 Then you shall go on from
there further and come to the oak of
Tabor; three men going up to God at
Bethel will meet you there, one carry-
ing three kids, another carrying three
loaves of bread, and another carrying
a skin of wine. 4 And they will greet
you and give you two loaves of bread,
which you shall accept from their
hand. 5 After that you shall come to
Gib´e-ath-elo´him,[h] where there is a
garrison of the Philistines; and there,
as you come to the city, you will meet
a band of prophets* coming down
from the high place with harp, tam-
bourine, flute, and lyre before them,
prophesying. 6 Then the spirit of the
LORD will come mightily upon you,
and you shall prophesy with them and
be turned into another man. 7 Now
when these signs meet you, do what-
ever your hand finds to do, for God
is with you. 8 And you shall go down
before me to Gilgal; and behold, I am

[c] Heb obscure
[d] Cn: Heb *saying, I have invited the people*
[e] Gk: Heb *and he spoke with Saul*
[f] Gk: Heb *and they arose early and at break of dawn*
[g] Gk: Heb lacks *over his people Israel? And you shall... to be prince*
[h] Or *the hill of God*

coming to you to offer burnt offerings
and to sacrifice peace offerings. Seven
days you shall wait, until I come to
you and show you what you shall do."

SAUL PROPHESIES

9 When he turned his back to leave
Samuel, God gave him another heart;
and all these signs came to pass that
day. 10When they came to Gib'e-ah,[a]
behold, a band of prophets met him;
and the spirit of God came mightily
upon him, and he prophesied among
them. 11And when all who knew him
before saw how he prophesied with
the prophets, the people said to one
another, "What has come over the
son of Kish? Is Saul also among the
prophets?" 12And a man of the place
answered, "And who is their father?"
Therefore it became a proverb, "Is
Saul also among the prophets?"
13When he had finished prophesying,
he came to the high place.

14 Saul's uncle said to him and to
his servant, "Where did you go?" And
he said, "To seek the asses; and when
we saw they were not to be found, we
went to Samuel." 15And Saul's uncle
said, "Pray, tell me what Samuel said
to you." 16And Saul said to his uncle,
"He told us plainly that the asses had
been found." But about the matter of
the kingdom, of which Samuel had
spoken, he did not tell him anything.

SAUL PROCLAIMED KING

17 Now Samuel called the people
together to the LORD at Mizpah; 18and
he said to the people of Israel, "Thus
says the LORD, the God of Israel, 'I
brought up Israel out of Egypt, and
I delivered you from the hand of the
Egyptians and from the hand of all
the kingdoms that were oppressing
you.' 19But you have this day rejected
your God, who saves you from all your
calamities and your distresses; and
you have said, 'No! but set a king over
us.' Now therefore present yourselves
before the LORD by your tribes and by
your thousands."

20 Then Samuel brought all the
tribes of Israel near, and the tribe
of Benjamin was taken by lot. 21He
brought the tribe of Benjamin near
by its families, and the family of the
Matrites was taken by lot; finally he
brought the family of the Matrites
near man by man,[b] and Saul the son of
Kish was taken by lot. But when they
sought him, he could not be found.
22So they inquired again of the LORD,
"Did the man come hither?"[c] and the
LORD said, "Behold, he has hidden
himself among the baggage." 23Then
they ran and fetched him from there;
and when he stood among the people,
he was taller than any of the people
from his shoulders upward. 24And
Samuel said to all the people, "Do you
see him whom the LORD has chosen?
There is none like him among all the
people." And all the people shouted,
"Long live the king!"

25 Then Samuel told the people the
rights and duties of the kingship; and
he wrote them in a book and laid it up
before the LORD. Then Samuel sent
all the people away, each one to his
home. 26Saul also went to his home at
Gib'e-ah, and with him went men of
valor whose hearts God had touched.
27But some worthless fellows said,
"How can this man save us?" And
they despised him, and brought him
no present. But he held his peace.

SAUL DEFEATS THE AMMONITES

11 Then Nahash the Ammonite went
up and besieged Ja'besh-gil'ead;
and all the men of Jabesh said to
Nahash, "Make a treaty with us, and
we will serve you." 2But Nahash the
Ammonite said to them, "On this
condition I will make a treaty with
you, that I gouge out all your right
eyes, and thus put disgrace upon all
Israel." 3The elders of Jabesh said to
him, "Give us seven days respite that

[a]Or *the hill*
[b]Gk: Heb lacks *finally. . . man by man*
[c]Gk: Heb *Is there yet a man to come hither?*

we may send messengers through all
the territory of Israel. Then, if there
is no one to save us, we will give our-
selves up to you." 4When the messen-
gers came to Gib´e-ah of Saul, they
reported the matter in the ears of the
people; and all the people wept aloud.
5 Now Saul was coming from the
field behind the oxen; and Saul said,
"What ails the people, that they are
weeping?" So they told him the tid-
ings of the men of Jabesh. 6And the
spirit of God came mightily upon Saul
when he heard these words, and his
anger was greatly kindled. 7He took a
yoke of oxen, and cut them in pieces
and sent them throughout all the ter-
ritory of Israel by the hand of messen-
gers, saying, "Whoever does not come
out after Saul and Samuel, so shall it
be done to his oxen!" Then the dread
of the LORD fell upon the people, and
they came out as one man. 8When he
mustered them at Bezek, the men of
Israel were three hundred thousand,
and the men of Judah thirty thou-
sand.* 9And they said to the messen-
gers who had come, "Thus shall you
say to the men of Ja´besh-gil´ead:
'Tomorrow, by the time the sun is
hot, you shall have deliverance.'"
When the messengers came and told
the men of Jabesh, they were glad.
10Therefore the men of Jabesh said,
"Tomorrow we will give ourselves up
to you, and you may do to us whatev-
er seems good to you." 11And on the
morrow Saul put the people in three
companies; and they came into the
midst of the camp in the morning
watch, and cut down the Ammonites
until the heat of the day; and those
who survived were scattered, so that
no two of them were left together.
12 Then the people said to Samuel,
"Who is it that said, 'Shall Saul reign
over us?' Bring the men, that we may
put them to death." 13But Saul said,
"Not a man shall be put to death this
day, for today the LORD has wrought
deliverance in Israel." 14Then Samuel
said to the people, "Come, let us go to
Gilgal and there renew the kingdom."
15So all the people went to Gilgal, and
there they made Saul king before the
LORD in Gilgal. There they sacrificed
peace offerings before the LORD, and
there Saul and all the men of Israel re-
joiced greatly.

SAMUEL'S FAREWELL ADDRESS

12 And Samuel said to all Israel,
"Behold, I have hearkened to your
voice in all that you have said to me,
and have made a king over you. 2And
now, behold, the king walks before
you; and I am old and gray, and be-
hold, my sons are with you; and I have
walked before you from my youth un-
til this day. 3Here I am; testify against
me before the LORD and before his
anointed. Whose ox have I taken?
Or whose ass have I taken? Or whom
have I defrauded? Whom have I op-
pressed? Or from whose hand have I
taken a bribe to blind my eyes with it?
Testify gainst me[d] and I will restore
it to you." 4They said, "You have not
defrauded us or oppressed us or taken
anything from any man's hand." 5And
he said to them, "The LORD is witness
against you, and his anointed is wit-
ness this day, that you have not found
anything in my hand." And they said,
"He is witness."
6 And Samuel said to the people,
"The LORD is witness,[e] who appoint-
ed Moses and Aaron and brought your
fathers up out of the land of Egypt.
7Now therefore stand still, that I may
plead with you before the LORD con-
cerning all the saving deeds of the
LORD which he performed for you and
for your fathers. 8When Jacob went
into Egypt and the Egyptians op-
pressed them,[f] then your fathers cried
to the LORD and the LORD sent Moses
and Aaron, who brought forth your
fathers out of Egypt, and made them
dwell in this place. 9But they forgot

[d]Gk: Heb lacks *Testify against me*
[e]Gk: Heb lacks *is witness*
[f]Gk: Heb lacks *and the Egyptians oppressed them*

the LORD their God; and he sold them
into the hand of Sis´era, commander of
the army of Jabin king of[a] Hazor, and
into the hand of the Philistines, and
into the hand of the king of Moab; and
they fought against them. 10And they
cried to the LORD, and said, 'We have
sinned, because we have forsaken the
LORD, and have served the Ba´als and
the Ash´taroth; but now deliver us
out of the hand of our enemies, and
we will serve thee.' 11And the LORD
sent Jerubba´al* and Barak,[b] and
Jephthah, and Samuel, and delivered
you out of the hand of your enemies
on every side; and you dwelt in safety.
12And when you saw that Nahash the
king of the Ammonites came against
you, you said to me, 'No, but a king
shall reign over us,' when the LORD
your God was your king. 13And now
behold the king whom you have cho-
sen, for whom you have asked; behold,
the LORD has set a king over you. 14If
you will fear the LORD and serve him
and hearken to his voice and not reb-
el against the commandment of the
LORD, and if both you and the king
who reigns over you will follow the
LORD your God, it will be well; 15but
if you will not hearken to the voice
of the LORD, but rebel against the
commandment of the LORD, then the
hand of the LORD will be against you
and your king.[c] 16Now therefore stand
still and see this great thing, which
the LORD will do before your eyes.
17Is it not wheat harvest today? I will
call upon the LORD, that he may send
thunder and rain; and you shall know
and see that your wickedness is great,
which you have done in the sight of
the LORD, in asking for yourselves a
king." 18So Samuel called upon the
LORD, and the LORD sent thunder and
rain that day; and all the people great-
ly feared the LORD and Samuel.

19 And all the people said to
Samuel, "Pray for your servants to
the LORD your God, that we may not
die; for we have added to all our sins
this evil, to ask for ourselves a king."
20And Samuel said to the people,
"Fear not; you have done all this evil,
yet do not turn aside from following
the LORD, but serve the LORD with
all your heart; 21and do not turn aside
after[d] vain things which cannot prof-
it or save, for they are vain. 22For the
LORD will not cast away his people,
for his great name's sake, because it
has pleased the LORD to make you a
people for himself. 23Moreover as for
me, far be it from me that I should sin
against the LORD by ceasing to pray
for you; and I will instruct you in the
good and the right way. 24Only fear the
LORD, and serve him faithfully with
all your heart; for consider what great
things he has done for you. 25But if you
still do wickedly, you shall be swept
away, both you and your king."*

SAUL'S UNLAWFUL SACRIFICE

13 Saul was . . .[e] years old when he
began to reign; and he reigned . . .
and two[f]* years over Israel.

2 Saul chose three thousand men
of Israel; two thousand were with
Saul in Michmash and the hill country
of Bethel, and a thousand were with
Jonathan in Gib´e-ah of Benjamin; the
rest of the people he sent home, every
man to his tent. 3Jonathan defeated
the garrison of the Philistines which
was at Geba; and the Philistines heard
of it. And Saul blew the trumpet
throughout all the land, saying, "Let
the Hebrews hear." 4And all Israel
heard it said that Saul had defeated
the garrison of the Philistines, and
also that Israel had become odious to
the Philistines. And the people were
called out to join Saul at Gilgal.

[a] Gk: Heb lacks *Jabin king of*
[b] Gk Syr: Heb *Bedan*
[c] Gk: Heb *fathers*
[d] Gk Syr Tg Vg: Heb *because after*
[e] The number is lacking in Heb
[f] *Two* is not the entire number. Something has dropped out.

5 And the Philistines mustered
to fight with Israel, thirty thousand
chariots, and six thousand horsemen,
and troops like the sand on the sea-
shore in multitude; they came up and
encamped in Michmash, to the east of
Beth-a′ven. 6When the men of Israel
saw that they were in straits (for the
people were hard pressed), the people
hid themselves in caves and in holes
and in rocks and in tombs and in
cisterns, 7or crossed the fords of the
Jordan[g] to the land of Gad and Gilead.
Saul was still at Gilgal, and all the
people followed him trembling.

8 He waited seven days, the time
appointed by Samuel; but Samuel did
not come to Gilgal, and the people
were scattering from him. 9So Saul
said, "Bring the burnt offering here to
me, and the peace offerings." And he
offered the burnt offering. 10As soon as
he had finished offering the burnt of-
fering, behold, Samuel came; and Saul
went out to meet him and salute him.
11Samuel said, "What have you done?"
And Saul said, "When I saw that the
people were scattering from me, and
that you did not come within the days
appointed, and that the Philistines
had mustered at Michmash, 12I said,
'Now the Philistines will come down
upon me at Gilgal, and I have not en-
treated the favor of the LORD'; so I
forced myself, and offered the burnt
offering." 13And Samuel said to Saul,
"You have done foolishly; you have
not kept the commandment of the
LORD your God, which he command-
ed you; for now the LORD would have
established your kingdom over Israel
for ever. 14But now your kingdom shall
not continue; the LORD has sought
out a man after his own heart; and the
LORD has appointed him to be prince
over his people, because you have not
kept what the LORD commanded you."
15And Samuel arose, and went up from
Gilgal to Gib′e-ah of Benjamin.

PREPARATIONS FOR BATTLE

And Saul numbered the people
who were present with him, about
six hundred men. 16And Saul, and
Jonathan his son, and the people who
were present with them, stayed in
Geba of Benjamin; but the Philistines
encamped in Michmash. 17And raid-
ers came out of the camp of the
Philistines in three companies; one
company turned toward Ophrah, to
the land of Shu′al, 18another compa-
ny turned toward Beth-hor′on, and
another company turned toward the
border that looks down upon the val-
ley of Zebo′im toward the wilderness.

19 Now there was no smith to
be found throughout all the land of
Israel; for the Philistines said, "Lest
the Hebrews make themselves swords
or spears"; 20but every one of the
Israelites went down to the Philistines
to sharpen his plowshare, his mat-
tock, his axe, or his sickle;[h] 21and the
charge was a pim for the plowshares
and for the mattocks, and a third of a
shekel for sharpening the axes and for
setting the goads.[i] 22So on the day of
the battle there was neither sword nor
spear found in the hand of any of the
people with Saul and Jonathan; but
Saul and Jonathan his son had them.
23And the garrison of the Philistines
went out to the pass of Michmash.

JONATHAN SURPRISES AND ROUTS THE PHILISTINES

14 One day Jonathan the son of Saul
said to the young man who bore
his armor, "Come, let us go over to the
Philistine garrison on yonder side."
But he did not tell his father. 2Saul was
staying in the outskirts of Gib′e-ah
under the pomegranate tree which is
at Migron; the people who were with
him were about six hundred men, 3and
Ahi′jah the son of Ahi′tub, Ich′abod's
brother, son of Phin′ehas, son of Eli,
the priest of the LORD in Shiloh,

[g] Cn: Heb *Hebrews crossed the Jordan*
[h] Gk: Heb *plowshare*
[i] The Heb of this verse is obscure

wearing an ephod. And the people did not know that Jonathan had gone. 4In the pass,[a] by which Jonathan sought to go over to the Philistine garrison, there was a rocky crag on the one side and a rocky crag on the other side; the name of the one was Bozez, and the name of the other Seneh. 5The one crag rose on the north in front of Michmash, and the other on the south in front of Geba.

6 And Jonathan said to the young man who bore his armor, "Come, let us go over to the garrison of these uncircumcised; it may be that the LORD will work for us; for nothing can hinder the LORD from saving by many or by few." 7And his armor-bearer said to him, "Do all that your mind inclines to;[b] behold, I am with you, as is your mind so is mine."[c] 8Then said Jonathan, "Behold, we will cross over to the men, and we will show ourselves to them. 9If they say to us, 'Wait until we come to you,' then we will stand still in our place, and we will not go up to them. 10But if they say, 'Come up to us,' then we will go up; for the LORD has given them into our hand. And this shall be the sign to us." 11So both of them showed themselves to the garrison of the Philistines; and the Philistines said, "Look, Hebrews are coming out of the holes where they have hid themselves." 12And the men of the garrison hailed Jonathan and his armor-bearer, and said, "Come up to us, and we will show you a thing." And Jonathan said to his armor-bearer, "Come up after me; for the LORD has given them into the hand of Israel." 13Then Jonathan climbed up on his hands and feet, and his armor-bearer after him. And they fell before Jonathan, and his armor-bearer killed them after him; 14and that first slaughter, which Jonathan and his armor-bearer made, was of about twenty men within as it were half a furrow's length in an acre[d] of land. 15And there was a panic in the camp, in the field, and among all the people; the garrison and even the raiders trembled; the earth quaked; and it became a very great panic.

16 And the watchmen of Saul in Gib´e-ah of Benjamin looked; and behold, the multitude was surging hither and thither.[e] 17Then Saul said to the people who were with him, "Number and see who has gone from us." And when they had numbered, behold, Jonathan and his armor-bearer were not there. 18And Saul said to Ahi´jah, "Bring hither the ark of God." For the ark of God went at that time with the people of Israel. 19And while Saul was talking to the priest, the tumult in the camp of the Philistines increased more and more; and Saul said to the priest, "Withdraw your hand." 20Then Saul and all the people who were with him rallied and went into the battle; and behold, every man's sword was against his fellow, and there was very great confusion. 21Now the Hebrews who had been with the Philistines before that time and who had gone up with them into the camp, even they also turned to be with[f] the Israelites who were with Saul and Jonathan. 22Likewise, when all the men of Israel who had hid themselves in the hill country of E´phraim heard that the Philistines were fleeing, they too followed hard after them in the battle. 23So the LORD delivered Israel that day; and the battle passed beyond Beth-a´ven.

SAUL'S RASH OATH

24 And the men of Israel were distressed that day; for Saul laid an oath on the people, saying, "Cursed be the

[a] Heb *between the passes*
[b] Gk: Heb *Do all that is in your mind.*
[c] Gk: Heb lacks *so is mine*
[d] Heb *yoke*
[e] Gk: Heb *they went and thither*
[f] Gk Syr Vg Tg: Heb *round about, they also, to be with*

man who eats food until it is evening
and I am avenged on my enemies." So
none of the people tasted food. 25 And
all the people[g] came into the forest;
and there was honey on the ground.
26 And when the people entered the
forest, behold, the honey was drop-
ping, but no man put his hand to his
mouth; for the people feared the oath.
27 But Jonathan had not heard his fa-
ther charge the people with the oath;
so he put forth the tip of the staff that
was in his hand, and dipped it in the
honeycomb, and put his hand to his
mouth; and his eyes became bright.
28 Then one of the people said, "Your
father strictly charged the people with
an oath, saying, 'Cursed be the man
who eats food this day.'" And the peo-
ple were faint. 29 Then Jonathan said,
"My father has troubled the land; see
how my eyes have become bright, be-
cause I tasted a little of this honey.
30 How much better if the people had
eaten freely today of the spoil of their
enemies which they found; for now
the slaughter among the Philistines
has not been great."

31 They struck down the Philistines
that day from Michmash to Ai´jalon.
And the people were very faint; 32 the
people flew upon the spoil, and took
sheep and oxen and calves, and slew
them on the ground; and the people
ate them with the blood. 33 Then they
told Saul, "Behold, the people are
sinning against the LORD, by eating
with the blood." And he said, "You
have dealt treacherously; roll a great
stone to me here."[h] 34 And Saul said,
"Disperse yourselves among the peo-
ple, and say to them, 'Let every man
bring his ox or his sheep, and slay
them here, and eat; and do not sin
against the LORD by eating with the
blood.'" So every one of the people
brought his ox with him that night,
and slew them there. 35 And Saul built
an altar to the LORD; it was the first
altar that he built to the LORD.

JONATHAN IN DANGER OF DEATH

36 Then Saul said, "Let us go down
after the Philistines by night and de-
spoil them until the morning light;
let us not leave a man of them." And
they said, "Do whatever seems good
to you." But the priest said, "Let us
draw near hither to God." 37 And Saul
inquired of God, "Shall I go down after
the Philistines? Wilt thou give them
into the hand of Israel?" But he did
not answer him that day. 38 And Saul
said, "Come hither, all you leaders of
the people; and know and see how this
sin has arisen today. 39 For as the LORD
lives who saves Israel, though it be in
Jonathan my son, he shall surely die."
But there was not a man among all the
people that answered him. 40 Then he
said to all Israel, "You shall be on one
side, and I and Jonathan my son will be
on the other side." And the people said
to Saul, "Do what seems good to you."
41 Therefore Saul said, "O LORD God of
Israel, why hast thou not answered thy
servant this day? If this guilt is in me
or in Jonathan my son, O LORD, God
of Israel, give Urim; but if this guilt is
in thy people Israel,[i] give Thummim."
And Jonathan and Saul were taken, but
the people escaped. 42 Then Saul said,
"Cast the lot between me and my son
Jonathan." And Jonathan was taken.*

43 Then Saul said to Jonathan,
"Tell me what you have done." And
Jonathan told him, "I tasted a little
honey with the tip of the staff that was
in my hand; here I am, I will die." 44 And
Saul said, "God do so to me and more
also; you shall surely die, Jonathan."
45 Then the people said to Saul, "Shall
Jonathan die, who has wrought this
great victory in Israel? Far from it! As
the LORD lives, there shall not one hair
of his head fall to the ground; for he
has wrought with God this day." So
the people ransomed Jonathan, that
he did not die. 46 Then Saul went up
from pursuing the Philistines; and the
Philistines went to their own place.

[g] Heb *land*
[h] Gk: Heb *this day*
[i] Vg Compare Gk: Heb *Saul said to the* Lord, *the God of Israel*

SAUL'S CONTINUING WARS

47 When Saul had taken the king-
ship over Israel, he fought against all
his enemies on every side, against
Moab, against the Ammonites, against
Edom, against the kings of Zobah,
and against the Philistines; wherever
he turned he put them to the worse.
48And he did valiantly, and smote the
Amal´ekites, and delivered Israel out
of the hands of those who plundered
them.

49 Now the sons of Saul were
Jonathan, Ishvi, and Mal´chishu´a;
and the names of his two daughters
were these: the name of the first-
born was Merab, and the name of the
younger Michal; 50and the name of
Saul's wife was Ahin´o-am the daugh-
ter of Ahim´a-az. And the name of the
commander of his army was Abner the
son of Ner, Saul's uncle; 51Kish was the
father of Saul, and Ner the father of
Abner was the son of Abi´el.

52 There was hard fighting against
the Philistines all the days of Saul;
and when Saul saw any strong man,
or any valiant man, he attached him
to himself.

SAUL DEFEATS THE AMALEKITES BUT SPARES THEIR KING

15 And Samuel said to Saul, "The
LORD sent me to anoint you king
over his people Israel; now therefore
hearken to the words of the LORD.
2Thus says the LORD of hosts, 'I will
punish what Am´alek did to Israel in
opposing them on the way, when they
came up out of Egypt. 3Now go and
smite Am´alek, and utterly destroy all
that they have; do not spare them, but
kill both man and woman, infant and
suckling, ox and sheep, camel and ass.'"

4 So Saul summoned the people,
and numbered them in Tela´im, two
hundred thousand men on foot, and
ten thousand men of Judah. 5And Saul
came to the city of Am´alek, and lay
in wait in the valley. 6And Saul said
to the Ken´ites, "Go, depart, go down
from among the Amal´ekites, lest I de-
stroy you with them; for you showed
kindness to all the people of Israel
when they came up out of Egypt." So
the Ken´ites departed from among the
Amal´ekites. 7And Saul defeated the
Amal´ekites, from Hav´ilah as far as
Shur, which is east of Egypt. 8And he
took Agag the king of the Amal´ekites
alive, and utterly destroyed all the
people with the edge of the sword.
9But Saul and the people spared
Agag, and the best of the sheep and
of the oxen and of the fatlings, and
the lambs, and all that was good, and
would not utterly destroy them; all
that was despised and worthless they
utterly destroyed.

SAUL REJECTED AS KING

10 The word of the LORD came to
Samuel: 11"I repent that I have made
Saul king; for he has turned back from
following me, and has not performed
my commandments." And Samuel
was angry; and he cried to the LORD
all night. 12And Samuel rose early to
meet Saul in the morning; and it was
told Samuel, "Saul came to Carmel,
and behold, he set up a monument
for himself and turned, and passed
on, and went down to Gilgal." 13And
Samuel came to Saul, and Saul said to
him, "Blessed be you to the LORD; I
have performed the commandment of
the LORD." 14And Samuel said, "What
then is this bleating of the sheep in
my ears, and the lowing of the oxen
which I hear?" 15Saul said, "They have
brought them from the Amal´ekites;
for the people spared the best of the
sheep and of the oxen, to sacrifice
to the LORD your God; and the rest
we have utterly destroyed." 16Then
Samuel said to Saul, "Stop! I will tell
you what the LORD said to me this
night." And he said to him, "Say on."

17 And Samuel said, "Though you
are little in your own eyes, are you
not the head of the tribes of Israel?
The LORD anointed you king over
Israel. 18And the LORD sent you on a

mission, and said, 'Go, utterly destroy
the sinners, the Amal'ekites, and
fight against them until they are con-
sumed.' 19Why then did you not obey
the voice of the LORD? Why did you
swoop on the spoil, and do what was
evil in the sight of the LORD?" 20And
Saul said to Samuel, "I have obeyed
the voice of the LORD, I have gone on
the mission on which the LORD sent
me, I have brought Agag the king of
Am'alek, and I have utterly destroyed
the Amal'ekites. 21But the people took
of the spoil, sheep and oxen, the best
of the things devoted to destruction,
to sacrifice to the LORD your God in
Gilgal." 22And Samuel said,

"Has the LORD as great delight
in burnt offerings and
sacrifices,
as in obeying the voice of the
LORD?
Behold, to obey is better than
sacrifice,
and to hearken than the fat
of rams.
23For rebellion is as the sin of
divination,
and stubbornness is as iniq-
uity and idolatry.
Because you have rejected the
word of the LORD,
he has also rejected you
from being king."*

24 And Saul said to Samuel, "I
have sinned; for I have transgressed
the commandment of the LORD and
your words, because I feared the
people and obeyed their voice. 25Now
therefore, I pray, pardon my sin, and
return with me, that I may worship
the LORD." 26And Samuel said to Saul,
"I will not return with you; for you
have rejected the word of the LORD,
and the LORD has rejected you from
being king over Israel." 27As Samuel
turned to go away, Saul laid hold upon
the skirt of his robe, and it tore. 28And
Samuel said to him, "The LORD has
torn the kingdom of Israel from you
this day, and has given it to a neighbor
of yours, who is better than you. 29And
also the Glory of Israel will not lie or
repent; for he is not a man, that he
should repent." 30Then he said, "I have
sinned; yet honor me now before the
elders of my people and before Israel,
and return with me, that I may wor-
ship the LORD your God." 31So Samuel
turned back after Saul; and Saul wor-
shiped the LORD.

32 Then Samuel said, "Bring here to
me Agag the king of the Amal'ekites."
And Agag came to him cheerfully.
Agag said, "Surely the bitterness of
death is past." 33And Samuel said, "As
your sword has made women child-
less, so shall your mother be childless
among women." And Samuel hewed
Agag in pieces before the LORD in
Gilgal.

34 Then Samuel went to Ramah;
and Saul went up to his house in
Gib'e-ah of Saul. 35And Samuel did
not see Saul again until the day of his
death, but Samuel grieved over Saul.
And the LORD repented that he had
made Saul king over Israel.

DAVID ANOINTED AS KING

16 The LORD said to Samuel, "How
long will you grieve over Saul,
seeing I have rejected him from being
king over Israel? Fill your horn with
oil, and go; I will send you to Jesse
the Bethlehemite, for I have provid-
ed for myself a king among his sons."
2And Samuel said, "How can I go? If
Saul hears it, he will kill me." And
the LORD said, "Take a heifer with
you, and say, 'I have come to sacrifice
to the LORD.' 3And invite Jesse to the
sacrifice, and I will show you what you
shall do; and you shall anoint for me
him whom I name to you." 4Samuel
did what the LORD commanded, and
came to Bethlehem. The elders of the
city came to meet him trembling, and
said, "Do you come peaceably?" 5And
he said, "Peaceably; I have come to
sacrifice to the LORD; consecrate your-
selves, and come with me to the sacri-
fice." And he consecrated Jesse and his
sons, and invited them to the sacrifice.

6 When they came, he looked on
Eli´ab and thought, "Surely the LORD's
anointed is before him." 7But the
LORD said to Samuel, "Do not look
on his appearance or on the height
of his stature, because I have reject-
ed him; for the LORD sees not as man
sees; man looks on the outward ap-
pearance, but the LORD looks on the
heart." 8Then Jesse called Abin´adab,
and made him pass before Samuel.
And he said, "Neither has the LORD
chosen this one." 9Then Jesse made
Shammah pass by. And he said,
"Neither has the LORD chosen this
one." 10And Jesse made seven of his
sons pass before Samuel. And Samuel
said to Jesse, "The LORD has not
chosen these." 11And Samuel said
to Jesse, "Are all your sons here?"
And he said, "There remains yet the
youngest, but behold, he is keeping
the sheep." And Samuel said to Jesse,
"Send and fetch him; for we will not
sit down till he comes here." 12And he
sent, and brought him in. Now he was
ruddy, and had beautiful eyes, and
was handsome. And the LORD said,
"Arise, anoint him; for this is he."
13Then Samuel took the horn of oil,
and anointed him in the midst of his
brothers; and the Spirit of the LORD
came mightily upon David from that
day forward. And Samuel rose up, and
went to Ramah.

DAVID PLAYS THE LYRE FOR SAUL

14 Now the Spirit of the LORD de-
parted from Saul, and an evil spirit
from the LORD tormented him. 15And
Saul's servants said to him, "Behold
now, an evil spirit from God is tor-
menting you. 16Let our lord now com-
mand your servants, who are before
you, to seek out a man who is skilful
in playing the lyre; and when the evil
spirit from God is upon you, he will
play it, and you will be well." 17So
Saul said to his servants, "Provide
for me a man who can play well, and
bring him to me." 18One of the young
men answered, "Behold, I have seen
a son of Jesse the Bethlehemite, who
is skilful in playing, a man of valor, a
man of war, prudent in speech, and a
man of good presence; and the LORD
is with him." 19Therefore Saul sent
messengers to Jesse, and said, "Send
me David your son, who is with the
sheep." 20And Jesse took an ass laden
with bread, and a skin of wine and a
kid, and sent them by David his son
to Saul. 21And David came to Saul,
and entered his service. And Saul
loved him greatly, and he became
his armor-bearer. 22And Saul sent to
Jesse, saying, "Let David remain in
my service, for he has found favor in
my sight." 23And whenever the evil
spirit from God was upon Saul, David
took the lyre and played it with his
hand; so Saul was refreshed, and
was well, and the evil spirit departed
from him.

DAVID AND GOLIATH

17 Now the Philistines gathered their
armies for battle; and they were
gathered at Socoh, which belongs to
Judah, and encamped between Socoh
and Aze´kah, in E´phes-dam´mim.
2And Saul and the men of Israel were
gathered, and encamped in the valley
of Elah, and drew up in line of bat-
tle against the Philistines. 3And the
Philistines stood on the mountain on
the one side, and Israel stood on the
mountain on the other side, with a
valley between them. 4And there came
out from the camp of the Philistines
a champion named Goliath, of Gath,
whose height was six cubits and a
span. 5He had a helmet of bronze
on his head, and he was armed with
a coat of mail, and the weight of
the coat was five thousand shekels
of bronze. 6And he had greaves of
bronze upon his legs, and a javelin of
bronze slung between his shoulders.
7And the shaft of his spear was like a
weaver's beam, and his spear's head
weighed six hundred shekels of iron;
and his shield-bearer went before
him. 8He stood and shouted to the

ranks of Israel, "Why have you come
out to draw up for battle? Am I not a
Philistine, and are you not servants
of Saul? Choose a man for yourselves,
and let him come down to me. 9If he
is able to fight with me and kill me,
then we will be your servants; but if I
prevail against him and kill him, then
you shall be our servants and serve
us." 10And the Philistine said, "I defy
the ranks of Israel this day; give me
a man, that we may fight together."
11When Saul and all Israel heard these
words of the Philistine, they were dis-
mayed and greatly afraid.

12 Now David was the son of an
Eph´rathite of Bethlehem in Judah,
named Jesse, who had eight sons. In
the days of Saul the man was already
old and advanced in years.[a] 13The three
eldest sons of Jesse had followed Saul
to the battle; and the names of his
three sons who went to the battle were
Eli´ab the first-born, and next to him
Abin´adab, and the third Shammah.
14David was the youngest; the three
eldest followed Saul, 15but David went
back and forth from Saul to feed his
father's sheep at Bethlehem. 16For
forty days the Philistine came for-
ward and took his stand, morning and
evening.

17 And Jesse said to David his son,
"Take for your brothers an ephah of
this parched grain, and these ten
loaves, and carry them quickly to the
camp to your brothers; 18also take
these ten cheeses to the command-
er of their thousand. See how your
brothers fare, and bring some token
from them."

19 Now Saul, and they, and all the
men of Israel, were in the valley of
Elah, fighting with the Philistines.
20And David rose early in the morn-
ing, and left the sheep with a keeper,
and took the provisions, and went,
as Jesse had commanded him; and he
came to the encampment as the host
was going forth to the battle line,
shouting the war cry. 21And Israel and
the Philistines drew up for battle,
army against army. 22And David left
the things in charge of the keeper of
the baggage, and ran to the ranks, and
went and greeted his brothers. 23As he
talked with them, behold, the champi-
on, the Philistine of Gath, Goliath by
name, came up out of the ranks of the
Philistines, and spoke the same words
as before. And David heard him.

24 All the men of Israel, when they
saw the man, fled from him, and were
much afraid. 25And the men of Israel
said, "Have you seen this man who
has come up? Surely he has come up
to defy Israel; and the man who kills
him, the king will enrich with great
riches, and will give him his daugh-
ter, and make his father's house free
in Israel." 26And David said to the
men who stood by him, "What shall
be done for the man who kills this
Philistine, and takes away the re-
proach from Israel? For who is this
uncircumcised Philistine, that he
should defy the armies of the living
God?" 27And the people answered him
in the same way, "So shall it be done
to the man who kills him."

28 Now Eli´ab his eldest brother
heard when he spoke to the men; and
Eli´ab's anger was kindled against
David, and he said, "Why have you
come down? And with whom have
you left those few sheep in the wil-
derness? I know your presumption,
and the evil of your heart; for you
have come down to see the battle."
29And David said, "What have I done
now? Was it not but a word?" 30And he
turned away from him toward anoth-
er, and spoke in the same way; and the
people answered him again as before.

31 When the words which Da-
vid spoke were heard, they repeat-
ed them before Saul; and he sent for
him. 32And David said to Saul, "Let
no man's heart fail because of him;
your servant will go and fight with
this Philistine." 33And Saul said to
David, "You are not able to go against

[a] Gk Syr: Heb *among men*

this Philistine to fight with him; for
you are but a youth, and he has been
a man of war from his youth." 34But
David said to Saul, "Your servant used
to keep sheep for his father; and when
there came a lion, or a bear, and took a
lamb from the flock, 35I went after him
and smote him and delivered it out of
his mouth; and if he arose against me,
I caught him by his beard, and smote
him and killed him. 36Your servant has
killed both lions and bears; and this
uncircumcised Philistine shall be like
one of them, seeing he has defied the
armies of the living God." 37And David
said, "The LORD who delivered me
from the paw of the lion and from the
paw of the bear, will deliver me from
the hand of this Philistine." And Saul
said to David, "Go, and the LORD be
with you!" 38Then Saul clothed David
with his armor; he put a helmet of
bronze on his head, and clothed him
with a coat of mail. 39And David gird-
ed his sword over his armor, and he
tried in vain to go, for he was not used
to them. Then David said to Saul, "I
cannot go with these; for I am not
used to them." And David put them
off. 40Then he took his staff in his
hand, and chose five smooth stones
from the brook, and put them in his
shepherd's bag or wallet; his sling was
in his hand, and he drew near to the
Philistine.

41 And the Philistine came on
and drew near to David, with his
shield-bearer in front of him. 42And
when the Philistine looked, and saw
David, he disdained him; for he was
but a youth, ruddy and comely in ap-
pearance. 43And the Philistine said to
David, "Am I a dog, that you come to
me with sticks?" And the Philistine
cursed David by his gods. 44The
Philistine said to David, "Come to
me, and I will give your flesh to the
birds of the air and to the beasts of
the field." 45Then David said to the
Philistine, "You come to me with a
sword and with a spear and with a
javelin; but I come to you in the name
of the LORD of hosts, the God of the
armies of Israel, whom you have de-
fied. 46This day the LORD will deliver
you into my hand, and I will strike you
down, and cut off your head; and I will
give the dead bodies of the host of the
Philistines this day to the birds of the
air and to the wild beasts of the earth;
that all the earth may know that there
is a God in Israel, 47and that all this as-
sembly may know that the LORD saves
not with sword and spear; for the bat-
tle is the LORD's and he will give you
into our hand."

48 When the Philistine arose and
came and drew near to meet David,
David ran quickly toward the bat-
tle line to meet the Philistine. 49And
David put his hand in his bag and took
out a stone, and slung it, and struck
the Philistine on his forehead; the
stone sank into his forehead, and he
fell on his face to the ground.

50 So David prevailed over the
Philistine with a sling and with a
stone, and struck the Philistine, and
killed him; there was no sword in the
hand of David. 51Then David ran and
stood over the Philistine, and took his
sword and drew it out of its sheath,
and killed him, and cut off his head
with it. When the Philistines saw that
their champion was dead, they fled.
52And the men of Israel and Judah
rose with a shout and pursued the
Philistines as far as Gath[a] and the
gates of Ekron, so that the wounded
Philistines fell on the way from Sha-
ara´im as far as Gath and Ekron. 53And
the Israelites came back from chasing
the Philistines, and they plundered
their camp. 54And David took the
head of the Philistine and brought it
to Jerusalem; but he put his armor in
his tent.

55 When Saul saw David go forth
against the Philistine, he said to
Abner, the commander of the army,
"Abner, whose son is this youth?"
And Abner said, "As your soul lives,

[a]Gk: Heb *Gai*

O king, I cannot tell." 56And the king
said, "Inquire whose son the stripling
is." 57And as David returned from the
slaughter of the Philistine, Abner took
him, and brought him before Saul
with the head of the Philistine in his
hand. 58And Saul said to him, "Whose
son are you, young man?" And David
answered, "I am the son of your ser-
vant Jesse the Bethlehemite."

JONATHAN'S COVENANT WITH DAVID

18 When he had finished speaking to
Saul, the soul of Jonathan was knit
to the soul of David, and Jonathan
loved him as his own soul. 2And Saul
took him that day, and would not
let him return to his father's house.
3Then Jonathan made a covenant
with David, because he loved him as
his own soul. 4And Jonathan stripped
himself of the robe that was upon
him, and gave it to David, and his ar-
mor, and even his sword and his bow
and his girdle. 5And David went out
and was successful wherever Saul sent
him; so that Saul set him over the men
of war. And this was good in the sight
of all the people and also in the sight
of Saul's servants.

6 As they were coming home,
when David returned from slaying
the Philistine, the women came out
of all the cities of Israel, singing and
dancing, to meet King Saul, with
timbrels, with songs of joy, and with
instruments[b] of music. 7And the wom-
en sang to one another as they made
merry,

"Saul has slain his
thousands,
and David his ten
thousands."

8And Saul was very angry, and this
saying displeased him; he said, "They
have ascribed to David ten thousands,
and to me they have ascribed thou-
sands; and what more can he have but
the kingdom?" 9And Saul eyed David
from that day on.

SAUL TRIES TO KILL DAVID

10 And on the morrow an evil
spirit from God rushed upon Saul,
and he raved within his house, while
David was playing the lyre, as he did
day by day. Saul had his spear in his
hand; 11and Saul cast the spear, for
he thought, "I will pin David to the
wall." But David evaded him twice.

12 Saul was afraid of David, be-
cause the LORD was with him but had
departed from Saul. 13So Saul removed
him from his presence, and made him
a commander of a thousand; and he
went out and came in before the peo-
ple. 14And David had success in all his
undertakings; for the LORD was with
him. 15And when Saul saw that he had
great success, he stood in awe of him.
16But all Israel and Judah loved David;
for he went out and came in before
them.

DAVID MARRIES MICHAL

17 Then Saul said to David, "Here
is my elder daughter Merab; I will give
her to you for a wife; only be valiant
for me and fight the LORD's battles."
For Saul thought, "Let not my hand
be upon him, but let the hand of the
Philistines be upon him." 18And David
said to Saul, "Who am I, and who
are my kinsfolk, my father's family
in Israel, that I should be son-in-law
to the king?" 19But at the time when
Merab, Saul's daughter, should have
been given to David, she was given to
A´driel the Meho´lathite for a wife.

20 Now Saul's daughter Michal
loved David; and they told Saul, and
the thing pleased him. 21Saul thought,
"Let me give her to him, that she may
be a snare for him, and that the hand
of the Philistines may be against him."
Therefore Saul said to David a second
time,[c] "You shall now be my son-in-
law." 22And Saul commanded his ser-
vants, "Speak to David in private and
say, 'Behold, the king has delight in
you, and all his servants love you; now

[b] Or *triangles*, or *three-stringed instruments*
[c] Heb *by two*

then become the king's son-in-law.'"
23And Saul's servants spoke those
words in the ears of David. And David
said, "Does it seem to you a little thing
to become the king's son-in-law, see-
ing that I am a poor man and of no re-
pute?" 24And the servants of Saul told
him, "Thus and so did David speak."
25Then Saul said, "Thus shall you say
to David, 'The king desires no mar-
riage present* except a hundred fore-
skins of the Philistines, that he may
be avenged of the king's enemies.'"
Now Saul thought to make David fall
by the hand of the Philistines. 26And
when his servants told David these
words, it pleased David well to be the
king's son-in-law. Before the time had
expired, 27David arose and went, along
with his men, and killed two hundred
of the Philistines; and David brought
their foreskins, which were given in
full number to the king, that he might
become the king's son-in-law. And
Saul gave him his daughter Michal for
a wife. 28But when Saul saw and knew
that the LORD was with David, and
that all Israel[a] loved him, 29Saul was
still more afraid of David. So Saul was
David's enemy continually.

30 Then the princes of the Philis-
tines came out to battle, and as often
as they came out David had more suc-
cess than all the servants of Saul; so
that his name was highly esteemed.

JONATHAN INTERCEDES FOR DAVID

19 And Saul spoke to Jonathan his
son and to all his servants, that
they should kill David. But Jonathan,
Saul's son, delighted much in David.
2And Jonathan told David, "Saul my
father seeks to kill you; therefore
take heed to yourself in the morn-
ing, stay in a secret place and hide
yourself; 3and I will go out and stand
beside my father in the field where
you are, and I will speak to my father
about you; and if I learn anything I
will tell you." 4And Jonathan spoke
well of David to Saul his father, and
said to him, "Let not the king sin
against his servant David; because
he has not sinned against you, and
because his deeds have been of good
service to you; 5for he took his life in
his hand and he slew the Philistine,
and the LORD wrought a great victory
for all Israel. You saw it, and rejoiced;
why then will you sin against inno-
cent blood by killing David without
cause?" 6And Saul hearkened to the
voice of Jonathan; Saul swore, "As
the LORD lives, he shall not be put to
death." 7And Jonathan called David,
and Jonathan showed him all these
things. And Jonathan brought David
to Saul, and he was in his presence
as before.

MICHAL HELPS DAVID ESCAPE FROM SAUL

8 And there was war again; and
David went out and fought with the
Philistines, and made a great slaugh-
ter among them, so that they fled be-
fore him. 9Then an evil spirit from the
LORD came upon Saul, as he sat in his
house with his spear in his hand; and
David was playing the lyre. 10And Saul
sought to pin David to the wall with
the spear; but he eluded Saul, so that
he struck the spear into the wall. And
David fled, and escaped.

11 That night Saul[b] sent messen-
gers to David's house to watch him,
that he might kill him in the morn-
ing. But Michal, David's wife, told
him, "If you do not save your life to-
night, tomorrow you will be killed."
12So Michal let David down through
the window; and he fled away and
escaped. 13Michal took an image[c] and
laid it on the bed and put a pillow[d] of
goats' hair at its head, and covered
it with the clothes. 14And when Saul
sent messengers to take David, she
said, "He is sick." 15Then Saul sent
the messengers to see David, saying,

[a] Gk: Heb *Michal, Saul's daughter*
[b] Gk Old Latin: Heb *escaped that night. 11And Saul*
[c] Heb *teraphim*
[d] The meaning of the Hebrew word is uncertain

"Bring him up to me in the bed, that
I may kill him." 16And when the mes-
sengers came in, behold, the image[e]
was in the bed, with the pillow[f] of
goats' hair at its head. 17Saul said to
Michal, "Why have you deceived me
thus, and let my enemy go, so that he
has escaped?" And Michal answered
Saul, "He said to me, 'Let me go; why
should I kill you?'"

DAVID JOINS SAMUEL IN RAMAH

18 Now David fled and escaped,
and he came to Samuel at Ramah,
and told him all that Saul had done
to him. And he and Samuel went and
dwelt at Nai´oth. 19And it was told
Saul, "Behold, David is at Nai´oth in
Ramah." 20Then Saul sent messengers
to take David; and when they saw the
company of the prophets prophesying,
and Samuel standing as head over
them, the Spirit of God came upon
the messengers of Saul, and they also
prophesied. 21When it was told Saul,
he sent other messengers, and they
also prophesied. And Saul sent mes-
sengers again the third time, and they
also prophesied. 22Then he himself
went to Ramah, and came to the great
well that is in Secu; and he asked,
"Where are Samuel and David?" And
one said, "Behold, they are at Nai´oth
in Ramah." 23And he went from[g] there
to Nai´oth in Ramah; and the Spirit of
God came upon him also, and as he
went he prophesied, until he came
to Nai´oth in Ramah. 24And he too
stripped off his clothes, and he too
prophesied before Samuel, and lay
naked all that day and all that night.
Hence it is said, "Is Saul also among
the prophets?"*

THE FRIENDSHIP OF DAVID AND JONATHAN

20 Then David fled from Nai´oth
in Ramah, and came and said
before Jonathan, "What have I done?
What is my guilt? And what is my
sin before your father, that he seeks
my life?" 2And he said to him, "Far
from it! You shall not die. Behold,
my father does nothing either great
or small without disclosing it to me;
and why should my father hide this
from me? It is not so." 3But David re-
plied,[h] "Your father knows well that
I have found favor in your eyes; and
he thinks, 'Let not Jonathan know
this, lest he be grieved.' But truly,
as the LORD lives and as your soul
lives, there is but a step between
me and death." 4Then said Jonathan
to David, "Whatever you say, I will
do for you." 5David said to Jonathan,
"Behold, tomorrow is the new moon,
and I should not fail to sit at table
with the king; but let me go, that I
may hide myself in the field till the
third day at evening. 6If your father
misses me at all, then say, 'David
earnestly asked leave of me to run
to Bethlehem his city; for there is a
yearly sacrifice there for all the fam-
ily.' 7If he says, 'Good!' it will be well
with your servant; but if he is angry,
then know that evil is determined by
him. 8Therefore deal kindly with your
servant, for you have brought your
servant into a sacred covenant[i] with
you. But if there is guilt in me, slay
me yourself; for why should you bring
me to your father?" 9And Jonathan
said, "Far be it from you! If I knew
that it was determined by my father
that evil should come upon you,
would I not tell you?" 10Then said
David to Jonathan, "Who will tell me
if your father answers you roughly?"
11And Jonathan said to David, "Come,
let us go out into the field." So they
both went out into the field.
12 And Jonathan said to David,
"The LORD, the God of Israel, be

[e] Heb *teraphim*
[f] The meaning of the Hebrew word is uncertain
[g] Gk: Heb lacks *from*
[h] Gk: Heb *swore again*
[i] Heb *a covenant of the LORD*

witness![a] When I have sounded my father, about this time tomorrow, or the third day, behold, if he is well disposed toward David, shall I not then send and disclose it to you? 13But should it please my father to do you harm, the LORD do so to Jonathan and more also, if I do not disclose it to you, and send you away, that you may go in safety. May the LORD be with you, as he has been with my father. 14If I am still alive, show me the loyal love of the LORD, that I may not die;[b] 15and do not cut off your loyalty from my house for ever. When the LORD cuts off every one of the enemies of David from the face of the earth, 16let not the name of Jonathan be cut off from the house of David.[c] And may the LORD take vengeance on David's enemies." 17And Jonathan made David swear again by his love for him; for he loved him as he loved his own soul.

18 Then Jonathan said to him, "Tomorrow is the new moon; and you will be missed, because your seat will be empty. 19And on the third day you will be greatly missed;[d] then go to the place where you hid yourself when the matter was in hand, and remain beside yonder stone heap.[e] 20And I will shoot three arrows to the side of it, as though I shot at a mark. 21And behold, I will send the lad, saying, 'Go, find the arrows.' If I say to the lad, 'Look, the arrows are on this side of you, take them,' then you are to come, for, as the LORD lives, it is safe for you and there is no danger. 22But if I say to the youth, 'Look, the arrows are beyond you,' then go; for the LORD has sent you away. 23And as for the matter of which you and I have spoken, behold, the LORD is between you and me for ever."

24 So David hid himself in the field; and when the new moon came, the king sat down to eat food. 25The king sat upon his seat, as at other times, upon the seat by the wall; Jonathan sat opposite,[f] and Abner sat by Saul's side, but David's place was empty.

26 Yet Saul did not say anything that day; for he thought, "Something has befallen him; he is not clean, surely he is not clean." 27But on the second day, the morrow after the new moon, David's place was empty. And Saul said to Jonathan his son, "Why has not the son of Jesse come to the meal, either yesterday or today?" 28Jonathan answered Saul, "David earnestly asked leave of me to go to Bethlehem; 29he said, 'Let me go; for our family holds a sacrifice in the city, and my brother has commanded me to be there. So now, if I have found favor in your eyes, let me get away, and see my brothers.' For this reason he has not come to the king's table."

30 Then Saul's anger was kindled against Jonathan, and he said to him, "You son of a perverse, rebellious woman, do I not know that you have chosen the son of Jesse to your own shame, and to the shame of your mother's nakedness? 31For as long as the son of Jesse lives upon the earth, neither you nor your kingdom shall be established. Therefore send and fetch him to me, for he shall surely die." 32Then Jonathan answered Saul his father, "Why should he be put to death? What has he done?" 33But Saul cast his spear at him to smite him; so Jonathan knew that his father was determined to put David to death. 34And Jonathan rose from the table in fierce anger and ate no food the second day of the month, for he was grieved for David, because his father had disgraced him.

35 In the morning Jonathan went out into the field to the appointment

[a] Heb lacks *be witness*
[b] Heb uncertain
[c] Gk: Heb *earth, and Jonathan made a covenant with the house of David*
[d] Gk: Heb *go down quickly*
[e] Gk: Heb *the stone Ezel*
[f] Cn See Gk: Heb *stood up*

with David, and with him a little lad.
36And he said to his lad, "Run and find
the arrows which I shoot." As the lad
ran, he shot an arrow beyond him.
37And when the lad came to the place
of the arrow which Jonathan had shot,
Jonathan called after the lad and said,
"Is not the arrow beyond you?" 38And
Jonathan called after the lad, "Hurry,
make haste, stay not." So Jonathan's
lad gathered up the arrows, and came
to his master. 39But the lad knew noth-
ing; only Jonathan and David knew the
matter. 40And Jonathan gave his weap-
ons to his lad, and said to him, "Go
and carry them to the city." 41And as
soon as the lad had gone, David rose
from beside the stone heap[g] and fell
on his face to the ground, and bowed
three times; and they kissed one an-
other, and wept with one another,
until David recovered himself.[h] 42Then
Jonathan said to David, "Go in peace,
forasmuch as we have sworn both of
us in the name of the LORD, saying,
'The LORD shall be between me and
you, and between my descendants and
your descendants, for ever.'" And he
rose and departed; and Jonathan went
into the city.[i]

DAVID AND THE HOLY BREAD

21[j] Then came David to Nob to
Ahim´elech the priest; and Ahim´-
elech came to meet David trembling,
and said to him, "Why are you alone,
and no one with you?" 2And David
said to Ahim´elech the priest, "The
king has charged me with a matter,
and said to me, 'Let no one know any-
thing of the matter about which I send
you, and with which I have charged
you.' I have made an appointment
with the young men for such and such
a place. 3Now then, what have you at
hand? Give me five loaves of bread,
or whatever is here." 4And the priest
answered David, "I have no common
bread at hand, but there is holy bread;
if only the young men have kept them-
selves from women." 5And David an-
swered the priest, "Of a truth wom-
en have been kept from us as always
when I go on an expedition; the ves-
sels of the young men are holy, even
when it is a common journey; how
much more today will their vessels be
holy?" 6So the priest gave him the holy
bread; for there was no bread there
but the bread of the Presence, which
is removed from before the LORD, to
be replaced by hot bread on the day it
is taken away.

7 Now a certain man of the ser-
vants of Saul was there that day, de-
tained before the LORD; his name was
Do´eg the E´domite, the chief of Saul's
herdsmen.

8 And David said to Ahim´elech,
"And have you not here a spear or a
sword at hand? For I have brought
neither my sword nor my weapons
with me, because the king's business
required haste." 9And the priest said,
"The sword of Goliath the Philistine,
whom you killed in the valley of Elah,
behold, it is here wrapped in a cloth
behind the ephod; if you will take
that, take it, for there is none but that
here." And David said, "There is none
like that; give it to me."

DAVID FLEES TO GATH

10 And David rose and fled that
day from Saul, and went to A´chish
the king of Gath. 11And the servants of
A´chish said to him, "Is not this David
the king of the land? Did they not sing
to one another of him in dances,

'Saul has slain his
thousands,
and David his ten
thousands'?"

12And David took these words to
heart, and was much afraid of A´chish
the king of Gath. 13So he changed his
behavior before them, and feigned
himself mad in their hands, and made

[g] Gk: Heb *from beside the south*
[h] Or *exceeded*
[i] This sentence is 21.1 in Heb
[j] Ch 21.2 in Heb

marks on the doors of the gate, and let
his spittle run down his beard. 14Then
said A´chish to his servants, "Lo, you
see the man is mad; why then have
you brought him to me? 15Do I lack
madmen, that you have brought this
fellow to play the madman in my pres-
ence? Shall this fellow come into my
house?"

DAVID AND HIS FOLLOWERS AT ADUL´LAM

22 David departed from there and
escaped to the cave of Adullam;
and when his brothers and all his fa-
ther's house heard it, they went down
there to him. 2And every one who was
in distress, and every one who was
in debt, and every one who was dis-
contented, gathered to him; and he
became captain over them. And there
were with him about four hundred
men.

3 And David went from there to
Mizpeh of Moab; and he said to the
king of Moab, "Pray let my father
and my mother stay[a] with you, till I
know what God will do for me." 4And
he left them with the king of Moab,
and they stayed with him all the time
that David was in the stronghold.
5Then the prophet Gad said to David,
"Do not remain in the stronghold; de-
part, and go into the land of Judah."
So David departed, and went into the
forest of Hereth.

SAUL SLAUGHTERS THE PRIESTS AT NOB

6 Now Saul heard that David was
discovered, and the men who were
with him. Saul was sitting at Gib´e-
ah, under the tamarisk tree on the
height, with his spear in his hand,
and all his servants were standing
about him. 7And Saul said to his ser-
vants who stood about him, "Hear
now, you Benjaminites; will the son
of Jesse give every one of you fields
and vineyards, will he make you all
commanders of thousands and com-
manders of hundreds, 8that all of you
have conspired against me? No one
discloses to me when my son makes
a league with the son of Jesse, none
of you is sorry for me or discloses to
me that my son has stirred up my ser-
vant against me, to lie in wait, as at
this day." 9Then answered Do´eg the
E´domite, who stood by the servants
of Saul, "I saw the son of Jesse coming
to Nob, to Ahim´elech the son of Ahi´-
tub, 10and he inquired of the LORD for
him, and gave him provisions, and
gave him the sword of Goliath the Phi-
listine." 11Then the king sent to sum-
mon Ahim´elech the priest, the son
of Ahi´tub, and all his father's house,
the priests who were at Nob; and all
of them came to the king. 12And Saul
said, "Hear now, son of Ahi´tub." And
he answered, "Here I am, my lord."
13And Saul said to him, "Why have you
conspired against me, you and the son
of Jesse, in that you have given him
bread and a sword, and have inquired
of God for him, so that he has risen
against me, to lie in wait, as at this
day?" 14Then Ahim´elech answered
the king, "And who among all your
servants is so faithful as David, who
is the king's son-in-law, and captain
over[b] your bodyguard, and honored in
your house? 15Is today the first time
that I have inquired of God for him?
No! Let not the king impute anything
to his servant or to all the house of
my father; for your servant has known
nothing of all this, much or little."
16And the king said, "You shall surely
die, Ahim´elech, you and all your fa-
ther's house." 17And the king said to
the guard who stood about him, "Turn
and kill the priests of the LORD; be-
cause their hand also is with David,
and they knew that he fled, and did
not disclose it to me." But the servants
of the king would not put forth their
hand to fall upon the priests of the
LORD. 18Then the king said to Do´eg,
"You turn and fall upon the priests."
And Do´eg the E´domite turned and

[a] Syr Vg: Heb *come out*
[b] Gk Tg: Heb *and has turned aside to*

fell upon the priests, and he killed on
that day eighty-five persons who wore
the linen ephod. 19And Nob, the city of
the priests, he put to the sword; both
men and women, children and suck-
lings, oxen, asses and sheep, he put to
the sword.

20 But one of the sons of Ahim′elech
the son of Ahi′tub, named Abi′athar,
escaped and fled after David. 21And
Abi′athar told David that Saul had
killed the priests of the LORD. 22And
David said to Abi′athar, "I knew on
that day, when Do′eg the E′domite
was there, that he would surely tell
Saul. I have occasioned the death of
all the persons of your father's house.
23Stay with me, fear not; for he that
seeks my life seeks your life; with me
you shall be in safekeeping."

DAVID SAVES THE CITY OF KEILAH

23 Now they told David, "Behold, the
Philistines are fighting against
Ke-i′lah, and are robbing the thresh-
ing floors." 2Therefore David inquired
of the LORD, "Shall I go and attack
these Philistines?" And the LORD
said to David, "Go and attack the
Philistines and save Ke-i′lah." 3But
David's men said to him, "Behold, we
are afraid here in Judah; how much
more then if we go to Ke-i′lah against
the armies of the Philistines?" 4Then
David inquired of the LORD again.
And the LORD answered him, "Arise,
go down to Ke-i′lah; for I will give
the Philistines into your hand." 5And
David and his men went to Ke-i′lah,
and fought with the Philistines, and
brought away their cattle, and made a
great slaughter among them. So David
delivered the inhabitants of Ke-i′lah.

6 When Abi′athar the son of
Ahim′elech fled to David to Ke-i′lah,
he came down with an ephod in his
hand. 7Now it was told Saul that David
had come to Ke-i′lah. And Saul said,
"God has given him into my hand; for
he has shut himself in by entering a
town that has gates and bars." 8And
Saul summoned all the people to war,
to go down to Ke-i′lah, to besiege
David and his men. 9David knew that
Saul was plotting evil against him;
and he said to Abi′athar the priest,
"Bring the ephod here." 10Then said
David, "O LORD, the God of Israel,
thy servant has surely heard that Saul
seeks to come to Ke-i′lah, to destroy
the city on my account. 11Will the men
of Ke-i′lah surrender me into his
hand? Will Saul come down, as thy
servant has heard? O LORD, the God
of Israel, I beseech thee, tell thy ser-
vant." And the LORD said, "He will
come down." 12Then said David, "Will
the men of Ke-i′lah surrender me and
my men into the hand of Saul?" And
the LORD said, "They will surrender
you." 13Then David and his men, who
were about six hundred, arose and de-
parted from Ke-i′lah, and they went
wherever they could go. When Saul
was told that David had escaped from
Ke-i′lah, he gave up the expedition.
14And David remained in the strong-
holds in the wilderness, in the hill
country of the Wilderness of Ziph.
And Saul sought him every day, but
God did not give him into his hand.

DAVID ELUDES SAUL IN THE WILDERNESS

15 And David was afraid because[c]
Saul had come out to seek his life.
David was in the Wilderness of Ziph
at Horesh. 16And Jonathan, Saul's son,
rose, and went to David at Horesh,
and strengthened his hand in God.
17And he said to him, "Fear not; for
the hand of Saul my father shall not
find you; you shall be king over Israel,
and I shall be next to you; Saul my fa-
ther also knows this." 18And the two
of them made a covenant before the
LORD; David remained at Horesh, and
Jonathan went home.

19 Then the Ziphites went up
to Saul at Gib′e-ah, saying, "Does
not David hide among us in the
strongholds at Horesh, on the hill
of Hachi′lah, which is south of

[c] Or *saw that*

Jeshi´mon? 20 Now come down, O king,
according to all your heart's desire to
come down; and our part shall be to
surrender him into the king's hand."
21 And Saul said, "May you be blessed
by the LORD; for you have had com-
passion on me. 22 Go, make yet more
sure; know and see the place where
his haunt is, and who has seen him
there; for it is told me that he is very
cunning. 23 See therefore, and take
note of all the lurking places where he
hides, and come back to me with sure
information. Then I will go with you;
and if he is in the land, I will search
him out among all the thousands of
Judah." 24 And they arose, and went to
Ziph ahead of Saul.

Now David and his men were
in the wilderness of Ma´on, in the
Arabah to the south of Jeshi´mon.
25 And Saul and his men went to seek
him. And David was told; therefore he
went down to the rock which is[a] in the
wilderness of Ma´on. And when Saul
heard that, he pursued after David
in the wilderness of Ma´on. 26 Saul
went on one side of the mountain,
and David and his men on the other
side of the mountain; and David was
making haste to get away from Saul,
as Saul and his men were closing in
upon David and his men to capture
them, 27 when a messenger came to
Saul, saying, "Make haste and come;
for the Philistines have made a raid
upon the land." 28 So Saul returned
from pursuing after David, and went
against the Philistines; therefore that
place was called the Rock of Escape.
29[b] And David went up from there, and
dwelt in the strongholds of En-ge´di.

DAVID SPARES SAUL'S LIFE

24 When Saul returned from follow-
ing the Philistines, he was told,
"Behold, David is in the wilderness
of En-ge´di." 2 Then Saul took three
thousand chosen men out of all Israel,
and went to seek David and his men
in front of the Wildgoats' Rocks. 3 And
he came to the sheepfolds by the way,
where there was a cave; and Saul went
in to relieve himself. Now David and
his men were sitting in the innermost
parts of the cave. 4 And the men of
David said to him, "Here is the day of
which the LORD said to you, 'Behold,
I will give your enemy into your
hand, and you shall do to him as it
shall seem good to you.'" Then David
arose and stealthily cut off the skirt
of Saul's robe. 5 And afterward David's
heart smote him, because he had cut
off Saul's skirt. 6 He said to his men,
"The LORD forbid that I should do this
thing to my lord, the LORD's anoint-
ed, to put forth my hand against him,
seeing he is the LORD's anointed." 7 So
David persuaded his men with these
words, and did not permit them to at-
tack Saul. And Saul rose up and left
the cave, and went upon his way.

8 Afterward David also arose, and
went out of the cave, and called after
Saul, "My lord the king!" And when
Saul looked behind him, David bowed
with his face to the earth, and did
obeisance. 9 And David said to Saul,
"Why do you listen to the words of
men who say, 'Behold, David seeks
your hurt'? 10 Lo, this day your eyes
have seen how the LORD gave you
today into my hand in the cave; and
some bade me kill you, but I[c] spared
you. I said, 'I will not put forth my
hand against my lord; for he is the
LORD's anointed.' 11 See, my father,
see the skirt of your robe in my hand;
for by the fact that I cut off the skirt
of your robe, and did not kill you,
you may know and see that there is
no wrong or treason in my hands. I
have not sinned against you, though
you hunt my life to take it. 12 May the
LORD judge between me and you, may
the LORD avenge me upon you; but my
hand shall not be against you. 13 As the
proverb of the ancients says, 'Out of
the wicked comes forth wickedness';

[a] Gk: Heb *and dwelt*
[b] Ch 24.1 in Heb
[c] Gk Syr Tg: Heb *you*

but my hand shall not be against you. 14After whom has the king of Israel come out? After whom do you pursue? After a dead dog! After a flea! 15May the LORD therefore be judge, and give sentence between me and you, and see to it, and plead my cause, and deliver me from your hand."

16 When David had finished speaking these words to Saul, Saul said, "Is this your voice, my son David?" And Saul lifted up his voice and wept. 17He said to David, "You are more righteous than I; for you have repaid me good, whereas I have repaid you evil. 18And you have declared this day how you have dealt well with me, in that you did not kill me when the LORD put me into your hands. 19For if a man finds his enemy, will he let him go away safe? So may the LORD reward you with good for what you have done to me this day. 20And now, behold, I know that you shall surely be king, and that the kingdom of Israel shall be established in your hand. 21Swear to me therefore by the LORD that you will not cut off my descendants after me, and that you will not destroy my name out of my father's house." 22And David swore this to Saul. Then Saul went home; but David and his men went up to the stronghold.

DEATH OF SAMUEL

25 Now Samuel died; and all Israel assembled and mourned for him, and they buried him in his house at Ramah.

DAVID AND THE WIFE OF NABAL

Then David rose and went down to the wilderness of Paran. 2And there was a man in Ma'on, whose business was in Carmel. The man was very rich; he had three thousand sheep and a thousand goats. He was shearing his sheep in Carmel. 3Now the name of the man was Nabal, and the name of his wife Ab'igail. The woman was of good understanding and beautiful, but the man was churlish and ill-behaved; he was a Ca'lebite. 4David heard in the wilderness that Nabal was shearing his sheep. 5So David sent ten young men; and David said to the young men, "Go up to Carmel, and go to Nabal, and greet him in my name. 6And thus you shall salute him: 'Peace be to you, and peace be to your house, and peace be to all that you have. 7I hear that you have shearers; now your shepherds have been with us, and we did them no harm, and they missed nothing, all the time they were in Carmel. 8Ask your young men, and they will tell you. Therefore let my young men find favor in your eyes; for we come on a feast day. Pray, give whatever you have at hand to your servants and to your son David.'"

9 When David's young men came, they said all this to Nabal in the name of David; and then they waited. 10And Nabal answered David's servants, "Who is David? Who is the son of Jesse? There are many servants nowadays who are breaking away from their masters. 11Shall I take my bread and my water and my meat that I have killed for my shearers, and give it to men who come from I do not know where?" 12So David's young men turned away, and came back and told him all this. 13And David said to his men, "Every man gird on his sword!" And every man of them girded on his sword; David also girded on his sword; and about four hundred men went up after David, while two hundred remained with the baggage.

14 But one of the young men told Ab'igail, Nabal's wife, "Behold, David sent messengers out of the wilderness to salute our master; and he railed at them. 15Yet the men were very good to us, and we suffered no harm, and we did not miss anything when we were in the fields, as long as we went with them; 16they were a wall to us both by night and by day, all the while we were with them keeping the sheep. 17Now therefore know this and consider what you should do; for evil is

determined against our master and
against all his house, and he is so
ill-natured that one cannot speak to
him."

18 Then Ab´igail made haste, and
took two hundred loaves, and two
skins of wine, and five sheep ready
dressed, and five measures of parched
grain, and a hundred clusters of rai-
sins, and two hundred cakes of figs,
and laid them on asses. 19And she said
to her young men, "Go on before me;
behold, I come after you." But she did
not tell her husband Nabal. 20And as
she rode on the ass, and came down
under cover of the mountain, behold,
David and his men came down toward
her; and she met them. 21Now David
had said, "Surely in vain have I guard-
ed all that this fellow has in the wil-
derness, so that nothing was missed
of all that belonged to him; and he has
returned me evil for good. 22God do so
to David[a] and more also, if by morning
I leave so much as one male of all who
belong to him."

23 When Ab´igail saw David, she
made haste, and alighted from the
ass, and fell before David on her face,
and bowed to the ground. 24She fell at
his feet and said, "Upon me alone, my
lord, be the guilt; pray let your hand-
maid speak in your ears, and hear the
words of your handmaid. 25Let not
my lord regard this ill-natured fel-
low, Nabal; for as his name is, so is
he; Nabal[b] is his name, and folly is
with him; but I your handmaid did
not see the young men of my lord,
whom you sent. 26Now then, my lord,
as the LORD lives, and as your soul
lives, seeing the LORD has restrained
you from bloodguilt, and from taking
vengeance with your own hand, now
then let your enemies and those who
seek to do evil to my lord be as Nabal.
27And now let this present which your
servant has brought to my lord be
given to the young men who follow
my lord. 28Pray forgive the trespass
of your handmaid; for the LORD will
certainly make my lord a sure house,
because my lord is fighting the bat-
tles of the LORD; and evil shall not be
found in you so long as you live. 29If
men rise up to pursue you and to seek
your life, the life of my lord shall be
bound in the bundle of the living in
the care of the LORD your God; and
the lives of your enemies he shall
sling out as from the hollow of a sling.
30And when the LORD has done to my
lord according to all the good that he
has spoken concerning you, and has
appointed you prince over Israel, 31my
lord shall have no cause of grief, or
pangs of conscience, for having shed
blood without cause or for my lord
taking vengeance himself. And when
the LORD has dealt well with my lord,
then remember your handmaid."

32 And David said to Ab´igail,
"Blessed be the LORD, the God of
Israel, who sent you this day to meet
me! 33Blessed be your discretion, and
blessed be you, who have kept me this
day from bloodguilt and from aveng-
ing myself with my own hand! 34For as
surely as the LORD the God of Israel
lives, who has restrained me from
hurting you, unless you had made
haste and come to meet me, truly by
morning there had not been left to
Nabal so much as one male." 35Then
David received from her hand what
she had brought him; and he said to
her, "Go up in peace to your house;
see, I have hearkened to your voice,
and I have granted your petition."

36 And Ab´igail came to Nabal;
and lo, he was holding a feast in his
house, like the feast of a king. And
Nabal's heart was merry within him,
for he was very drunk; so she told him
nothing at all until the morning light.
37And in the morning, when the wine
had gone out of Nabal, his wife told
him these things, and his heart died
within him, and he became as a stone.
38And about ten days later the LORD

[a]Gk Compare Syr: Heb *the enemies of David*
[b]That is *fool*

smote Nabal; and he died.
39 When David heard that Nabal
was dead, he said, "Blessed be the
LORD who has avenged the insult
I received at the hand of Nabal, and
has kept back his servant from evil;
the LORD has returned the evil-doing
of Nabal upon his own head." Then
David sent and wooed Ab´igail, to
make her his wife. 40And when the
servants of David came to Ab´igail at
Carmel, they said to her, "David has
sent us to you to take you to him as
his wife." 41And she rose and bowed
with her face to the ground, and said,
"Behold, your handmaid is a servant
to wash the feet of the servants of my
lord." 42And Ab´igail made haste and
rose and mounted on an ass, and her
five maidens attended her; she went
after the messengers of David, and be-
came his wife.
43 David also took Ahin´o-am of
Jezre´el; and both of them became
his wives. 44Saul had given Michal his
daughter, David's wife, to Palti the
son of La´ish, who was of Gallim.

DAVID SPARES SAUL'S LIFE A SECOND TIME

26 Then the Ziphites came to Saul
at Gib´e-ah, saying, "Is not
David hiding himself on the hill of
Hachi´lah, which is on the east of
Jeshi´mon?" 2So Saul arose and went
down to the wilderness of Ziph, with
three thousand chosen men of Israel,
to seek David in the wilderness of
Ziph. 3And Saul encamped on the hill
of Hachi´lah, which is beside the road
on the east of Jeshi´mon. But David
remained in the wilderness; and when
he saw that Saul came after him into
the wilderness, 4David sent out spies,
and learned of a certainty that Saul
had come. 5Then David rose and came
to the place where Saul had encamped;
and David saw the place where Saul
lay, with Abner the son of Ner, the
commander of his army; Saul was ly-
ing within the encampment, while the
army was encamped around him.
6 Then David said to Ahim´elech
the Hittite, and to Jo´ab's brother
Abi´shai the son of Zeru´iah, "Who
will go down with me into the camp
to Saul?" And Abi´shai said, "I will
go down with you." 7So David and
Abi´shai went to the army by night;
and there lay Saul sleeping within the
encampment, with his spear stuck in
the ground at his head; and Abner and
the army lay around him. 8Then said
Abi´shai to David, "God has given
your enemy into your hand this day;
now therefore let me pin him to the
earth with one stroke of the spear,
and I will not strike him twice." 9But
David said to Abi´shai, "Do not de-
stroy him; for who can put forth his
hand against the LORD's anointed, and
be guiltless?" 10And David said, "As
the LORD lives, the LORD will smite
him; or his day shall come to die; or
he shall go down into battle and per-
ish. 11The LORD forbid that I should
put forth my hand against the LORD's
anointed; but take now the spear that
is at his head, and the jar of water, and
let us go." 12So David took the spear
and the jar of water from Saul's head;
and they went away. No man saw it, or
knew it, nor did any awake; for they
were all asleep, because a deep sleep
from the LORD had fallen upon them.
13 Then David went over to the
other side, and stood afar off on the
top of the mountain, with a great
space between them; 14and David
called to the army, and to Abner the
son of Ner, saying, "Will you not an-
swer, Abner?" Then Abner answered,
"Who are you that calls to the king?"
15And David said to Abner, "Are you
not a man? Who is like you in Israel?
Why then have you not kept watch
over your lord the king? For one of
the people came in to destroy the king
your lord. 16This thing that you have
done is not good. As the LORD lives,
you deserve to die, because you have
not kept watch over your lord, the
LORD's anointed. And now see where
the king's spear is, and the jar of wa-
ter that was at his head."

17 Saul recognized David's voice,
and said, "Is this your voice, my son
David?" And David said, "It is my
voice, my lord, O king." 18And he said,
"Why does my lord pursue after his
servant? For what have I done? What
guilt is on my hands? 19Now therefore
let my lord the king hear the words of
his servant. If it is the LORD who has
stirred you up against me, may he ac-
cept an offering; but if it is men, may
they be cursed before the LORD, for
they have driven me out this day that
I should have no share in the heritage
of the LORD, saying, 'Go, serve other
gods.'* 20Now therefore, let not my
blood fall to the earth away from the
presence of the LORD; for the king of
Israel has come out to seek my life,[a]
like one who hunts a partridge in the
mountains."

21 Then Saul said, "I have done
wrong; return, my son David, for I will
no more do you harm, because my life
was precious in your eyes this day; be-
hold, I have played the fool, and have
erred exceedingly." 22And David made
answer, "Here is the spear, O king!
Let one of the young men come over
and fetch it. 23The LORD rewards ev-
ery man for his righteousness and his
faithfulness; for the LORD gave you
into my hand today, and I would not
put forth my hand against the LORD's
anointed. 24Behold, as your life was
precious this day in my sight, so may
my life be precious in the sight of the
LORD, and may he deliver me out of
all tribulation." 25Then Saul said to
David, "Blessed be you, my son David!
You will do many things and will suc-
ceed in them." So David went his way,
and Saul returned to his place.

DAVID SERVES KING ACHISH OF GATH

27 And David said in his heart, "I
shall now perish one day by the
hand of Saul; there is nothing better
for me than that I should escape to the
land of the Philistines; then Saul will
despair of seeking me any longer with-
in the borders of Israel, and I shall es-
cape out of his hand." 2So David arose
and went over, he and the six hundred
men who were with him, to A'chish
the son of Ma'och, king of Gath. 3And
David dwelt with A'chish at Gath, he
and his men, every man with his house-
hold, and David with his two wives,
Ahin'o-am of Jezre'el, and Ab'igail of
Carmel, Nabal's widow. 4And when it
was told Saul that David had fled to
Gath, he sought for him no more.

5 Then David said to A'chish, "If
I have found favor in your eyes, let a
place be given me in one of the coun-
try towns, that I may dwell there;
for why should your servant dwell in
the royal city with you?" 6So that day
A'chish gave him Ziklag; therefore
Ziklag has belonged to the kings of
Judah to this day. 7And the number of
the days that David dwelt in the coun-
try of the Philistines was a year and
four months.

8 Now David and his men went up,
and made raids upon the Gesh'urites,
the Gir'zites, and the Amal'ekites; for
these were the inhabitants of the land
from of old, as far as Shur, to the land of
Egypt. 9And David smote the land, and
left neither man nor woman alive, but
took away the sheep, the oxen, the ass-
es, the camels, and the garments, and
came back to A'chish. 10When A'chish
asked, "Against whom[b] have you made a
raid today?" David would say, "Against
the Negeb of Judah," or, "Against
the Negeb of the Jerah'meelites," or,
"Against the Negeb of the Ken'ites."
11And David saved neither man nor
woman alive, to bring tidings to Gath,
thinking, "Lest they should tell about
us, and say, 'So David has done.'" Such
was his custom all the while he dwelt
in the country of the Philistines. 12And
A'chish trusted David, thinking, "He
has made himself utterly abhorred by
his people Israel; therefore he shall be
my servant always."

[a]Gk: Heb *a flea* (as in 24. 14)
[b]Gk Vg: Heb lacks *whom*

28 In those days the Philistines
gathered their forces for war,
to fight against Israel. And A´chish
said to David, "Understand that you
and your men are to go out with me
in the army." 2David said to A´chish,
"Very well, you shall know what your
servant can do." And A´chish said to
David, "Very well, I will make you my
bodyguard for life."

SAUL CONSULTS A MEDIUM

3 Now Samuel had died, and all
Israel had mourned for him and
buried him in Ramah, his own city.
And Saul had put the mediums and
the wizards out of the land. 4The
Philistines assembled, and came and
encamped at Shunem; and Saul gath-
ered all Israel, and they encamped at
Gilbo´a. 5When Saul saw the army of
the Philistines, he was afraid, and his
heart trembled greatly. 6And when
Saul inquired of the LORD, the LORD
did not answer him, either by dreams,
or by Urim, or by prophets. 7Then Saul
said to his servants, "Seek out for me
a woman who is a medium, that I may
go to her and inquire of her." And his
servants said to him, "Behold, there is
a medium at Endor."

8 So Saul disguised himself and
put on other garments, and went, he
and two men with him; and they came
to the woman by night. And he said,
"Divine for me by a spirit, and bring
up for me whomever I shall name to
you." 9The woman said to him, "Surely
you know what Saul has done, how
he has cut off the mediums and the
wizards from the land. Why then are
you laying a snare for my life to bring
about my death?" 10But Saul swore
to her by the LORD, "As the LORD
lives, no punishment shall come upon
you for this thing." 11Then the wom-
an said, "Whom shall I bring up for
you?" He said, "Bring up Samuel for
me." 12When the woman saw Samuel,
she cried out with a loud voice; and
the woman said to Saul, "Why have
you deceived me? You are Saul." 13The
king said to her, "Have no fear; what
do you see?" And the woman said to
Saul, "I see a god coming up out of the
earth." 14He said to her, "What is his
appearance?" And she said, "An old
man is coming up; and he is wrapped
in a robe." And Saul knew that it was
Samuel, and he bowed with his face to
the ground, and did obeisance.

15 Then Samuel said to Saul, "Why
have you disturbed me by bringing
me up?" Saul answered, "I am in
great distress; for the Philistines are
warring against me, and God has
turned away from me and answers
me no more, either by prophets or by
dreams; therefore I have summoned
you to tell me what I shall do." 16And
Samuel said, "Why then do you ask
me, since the LORD has turned from
you and become your enemy? 17The
LORD has done to you as he spoke by
me; for the LORD has torn the king-
dom out of your hand, and given it to
your neighbor, David. 18Because you
did not obey the voice of the LORD,
and did not carry out his fierce wrath
against Am´alek, therefore the LORD
has done this thing to you this day.
19Moreover the LORD will give Israel
also with you into the hand of the
Philistines; and tomorrow you and
your sons shall be with me; the LORD
will give the army of Israel also into
the hand of the Philistines."

20 Then Saul fell at once full
length upon the ground, filled with
fear because of the words of Samuel;
and there was no strength in him,
for he had eaten nothing all day and
all night. 21And the woman came to
Saul, and when she saw that he was
terrified, she said to him, "Behold,
your handmaid has hearkened to you;
I have taken my life in my hand, and
have hearkened to what you have
said to me. 22Now therefore, you also
hearken to your handmaid; let me set
a morsel of bread before you; and eat,
that you may have strength when you
go on your way." 23He refused, and
said, "I will not eat." But his servants,

together with the woman, urged him;
and he hearkened to their words.
So he arose from the earth, and sat
upon the bed. 24Now the woman had
a fatted calf in the house, and she
quickly killed it, and she took flour,
and kneaded it and baked unleavened
bread of it, 25and she put it before Saul
and his servants; and they ate. Then
they rose and went away that night.

THE PHILISTINES REJECT DAVID

29 Now the Philistines gathered all
their forces at Aphek; and the
Israelites were encamped by the foun-
tain which is in Jezre´el. 2As the lords
of the Philistines were passing on by
hundreds and by thousands, and David
and his men were passing on in the
rear with A´chish, 3the commanders of
the Philistines said, "What are these
Hebrews doing here?" And A´chish said
to the commanders of the Philistines,
"Is not this David, the servant of Saul,
king of Israel, who has been with me
now for days and years, and since he
deserted to me I have found no fault in
him to this day." 4But the commanders
of the Philistines were angry with him;
and the commanders of the Philistines
said to him, "Send the man back, that
he may return to the place to which
you have assigned him; he shall not
go down with us to battle, lest in the
battle he become an adversary to us.
For how could this fellow reconcile
himself to his lord? Would it not be
with the heads of the men here? 5Is not
this David, of whom they sing to one
another in dances,

'Saul has slain his
thousands,
and David his ten
thousands'?"

6 Then A´chish called David and
said to him, "As the LORD lives, you
have been honest, and to me it seems
right that you should march out and
in with me in the campaign; for I have
found nothing wrong in you from the
day of your coming to me to this day.
Nevertheless the lords do not ap-
prove of you. 7So go back now; and go
peaceably, that you may not displease
the lords of the Philistines." 8And
David said to A´chish, "But what have
I done? What have you found in your
servant from the day I entered your
service until now, that I may not go
and fight against the enemies of my
lord the king?" 9And A´chish made
answer to David, "I know that you
are as blameless in my sight as an
angel of God; nevertheless the com-
manders of the Philistines have said,
'He shall not go up with us to the
battle.' 10Now then rise early in the
morning with the servants of your
lord who came with you; and start
early in the morning, and depart as
soon as you have light." 11So David
set out with his men early in the
morning, to return to the land of the
Philistines. But the Philistines went
up to Jezre´el.

DAVID AVENGES THE DESTRUCTION OF ZIKLAG

30 Now when David and his men
came to Ziklag on the third day,
the Amal´ekites had made a raid upon
the Negeb and upon Ziklag. They had
overcome Ziklag, and burned it with
fire, 2and taken captive the women
and all[a] who were in it, both small and
great; they killed no one, but carried
them off, and went their way. 3And
when David and his men came to the
city, they found it burned with fire,
and their wives and sons and daugh-
ters taken captive. 4Then David and the
people who were with him raised their
voices and wept, until they had no more
strength to weep. 5David's two wives
also had been taken captive, Ahin´o-
am of Jezre´el, and Ab´igail the widow
of Nabal of Carmel. 6And David was
greatly distressed; for the people spoke
of stoning him, because all the people
were bitter in soul, each for his sons
and daughters. But David strengthened
himself in the LORD his God.

[a]Gk: Heb lacks *and all*

7 And David said to Abi´athar the
priest, the son of Ahim´elech, "Bring
me the ephod." So Abi´athar brought
the ephod to David. 8And David in-
quired of the LORD, "Shall I pursue af-
ter this band? Shall I overtake them?"
He answered him, "Pursue; for you
shall surely overtake and shall surely
rescue." 9So David set out, and the six
hundred men who were with him, and
they came to the brook Besor, where
those stayed who were left behind.
10But David went on with the pursuit,
he and four hundred men; two hun-
dred stayed behind, who were too ex-
hausted to cross the brook Besor.

11 They found an Egyptian in
the open country, and brought him
to David; and they gave him bread
and he ate, they gave him water to
drink, 12and they gave him a piece
of a cake of figs and two clusters of
raisins. And when he had eaten, his
spirit revived; for he had not eaten
bread or drunk water for three days
and three nights. 13And David said to
him, "To whom do you belong? And
where are you from?" He said, "I am
a young man of Egypt, servant to an
Amal´ekite; and my master left me
behind because I fell sick three days
ago. 14We had made a raid upon the
Negeb of the Cher´ethites and upon
that which belongs to Judah and upon
the Negeb of Caleb; and we burned
Ziklag with fire." 15And David said
to him, "Will you take me down to
this band?" And he said, "Swear to
me by God, that you will not kill me,
or deliver me into the hands of my
master, and I will take you down to
this band."

16 And when he had taken him
down, behold, they were spread
abroad over all the land, eating and
drinking and dancing, because of all
the great spoil they had taken from
the land of the Philistines and from
the land of Judah. 17And David smote
them from twilight until the evening
of the next day; and not a man of
them escaped, except four hundred
young men, who mounted camels and
fled. 18David recovered all that the
Amal´ekites had taken; and David
rescued his two wives. 19Nothing was
missing, whether small or great, sons
or daughters, spoil or anything that
had been taken; David brought back
all. 20David also captured all the flocks
and herds; and the people drove those
cattle before him,[b] and said, "This is
David's spoil."

21 Then David came to the two
hundred men, who had been too ex-
hausted to follow David, and who had
been left at the brook Besor; and they
went out to meet David and to meet
the people who were with him; and
when David drew near to the people
he saluted them. 22Then all the wicked
and base fellows among the men who
had gone with David said, "Because
they did not go with us, we will not
give them any of the spoil which we
have recovered, except that each man
may lead away his wife and children,
and depart." 23But David said, "You
shall not do so, my brothers, with
what the LORD has given us; he has
preserved us and given into our hand
the band that came against us. 24Who
would listen to you in this matter? For
as his share is who goes down into
the battle, so shall his share be who
stays by the baggage; they shall share
alike." 25And from that day forward he
made it a statute and an ordinance for
Israel to this day.

26 When David came to Ziklag, he
sent part of the spoil to his friends,
the elders of Judah, saying, "Here is
a present for you from the spoil of
the enemies of the LORD"; 27it was
for those in Bethel, in Ramoth of
the Negeb, in Jattir, 28in Aro´er, in
Siphmoth, in Eshtemo´a, 29in Racal, in
the cities of the Jerah´meelites, in the
cities of the Ken´ites, 30in Hormah, in
Borash´an, in A´thach, 31in Hebron,
for all the places where David and his
men had roamed.

[b] Cn: Heb *they drove before those cattle*

THE DEATH OF SAUL AND HIS SONS

31 Now the Philistines fought against
Israel; and the men of Israel fled
before the Philistines, and fell slain
on Mount Gilbo´a. 2And the Philis-
tines overtook Saul and his sons; and
the Philistines slew Jonathan and
Abin´adab and Mal´chishu´a, the sons
of Saul. 3The battle pressed hard upon
Saul, and the archers found him; and
he was badly wounded by the archers.
4Then Saul said to his armor-bearer,
"Draw your sword, and thrust me
through with it, lest these uncircum-
cised come and thrust me through,
and make sport of me." But his ar-
mor-bearer would not; for he feared
greatly. Therefore Saul took his own
sword, and fell upon it. 5And when his
armor-bearer saw that Saul was dead,
he also fell upon his sword, and died
with him. 6Thus Saul died, and his
three sons, and his armor-bearer, and
all his men, on the same day togeth-
er. 7And when the men of Israel who
were on the other side of the valley
and those beyond the Jordan saw that
the men of Israel had fled and that
Saul and his sons were dead, they
forsook their cities and fled; and the
Philistines came and dwelt in them.

8 On the morrow, when the Phi-
listines came to strip the slain, they
found Saul and his three sons fallen on
Mount Gilbo´a. 9And they cut off his
head, and stripped off his armor, and
sent messengers throughout the land
of the Philistines, to carry the good
news to their idols[a] and to the people.
10They put his armor in the temple of
Ash´taroth; and they fastened his body
to the wall of Beth-shan. 11But when the
inhabitants of Ja´besh-gil´ead heard
what the Philistines had done to Saul,
12all the valiant men arose, and went
all night, and took the body of Saul
and the bodies of his sons from the
wall of Beth-shan; and they came to
Jabesh and burnt them there. 13And
they took their bones and buried them
under the tamarisk tree in Jabesh, and
fasted seven days.

[a] Gk Compare 1Chron 10. 9: Heb *to the house of their idols*

THE SECOND BOOK OF

SAMUEL

DAVID MOURNS FOR SAUL AND JONATHAN

1 After the death of Saul, when David
had returned from the slaughter of
the Amal´ekites, David remained two
days in Ziklag; 2and on the third day,
behold, a man came from Saul's camp,
with his clothes rent and earth upon
his head. And when he came to David,
he fell to the ground and did obei-
sance. 3David said to him, "Where
do you come from?" And he said to
him, "I have escaped from the camp of
Israel." 4And David said to him, "How
did it go? Tell me." And he answered,
"The people have fled from the bat-
tle, and many of the people also have
fallen and are dead; and Saul and his
son Jonathan are also dead." 5Then
David said to the young man who told
him, "How do you know that Saul and
his son Jonathan are dead?" 6And the
young man who told him said, "By
chance I happened to be on Mount
Gilbo´a; and there was Saul leaning
upon his spear; and lo, the chariots
and the horsemen were close upon
him. 7And when he looked behind
him, he saw me, and called to me. And
I answered, 'Here I am.' 8And he said
to me, 'Who are you?' I answered him,
'I am an Amal´ekite.' 9And he said to
me, 'Stand beside me and slay me; for
anguish has seized me, and yet my life
still lingers.' 10So I stood beside him,
and slew him, because I was sure that
he could not live after he had fallen;
and I took the crown which was on his
head and the armlet which was on his
arm, and I have brought them here to
my lord."

11 Then David took hold of his
clothes, and rent them; and so did
all the men who were with him; 12and
they mourned and wept and fasted un-
til evening for Saul and for Jonathan
his son and for the people of the LORD
and for the house of Israel, because
they had fallen by the sword. 13And
David said to the young man who told
him, "Where do you come from?" And
he answered, "I am the son of a so-
journer, an Amal´ekite." 14David said
to him, "How is it you were not afraid
to put forth your hand to destroy
the LORD's anointed?" 15Then David
called one of the young men and said,
"Go, fall upon him." And he smote
him so that he died. 16And David said
to him, "Your blood be upon your
head; for your own mouth has testi-
fied against you, saying, 'I have slain
the LORD's anointed.'"

17 And David lamented with this
lamentation over Saul and Jonathan
his son, 18and he said it[a] should be
taught to the people of Judah; behold,
it is written in the Book of Jashar.[b] He
said:

19"Thy glory, O Israel, is slain
upon thy high places!
How are the mighty fallen!
20Tell it not in Gath,
publish it not in the streets
of Ash´kelon;
lest the daughters of the
Philistines rejoice,
lest the daughters of the un-
circumcised exult.
21"Ye mountains of Gilbo´a,
let there be no dew or rain
upon you,
nor upsurging of the deep![c]
For there the shield of the
mighty was defiled,
the shield of Saul, not
anointed with oil.
22"From the blood of the slain,
from the fat of the mighty,
the bow of Jonathan turned not
back,

[a]Gk: Heb *the Bow*
[b]Or *The upright*
[c]Cn: Heb *fields of offerings*

and the sword of Saul re-
turned not empty.
23"Saul and Jonathan, beloved and
lovely!
In life and in death they
were not divided;
they were swifter than eagles,
they were stronger than
lions.
24"Ye daughters of Israel, weep
over Saul,
who clothed you daintily in
scarlet,
who put ornaments of gold
upon your apparel.
25"How are the mighty fallen
in the midst of the battle!
"Jonathan lies slain upon thy
high places.
26I am distressed for you, my
brother Jonathan;
very pleasant have you been
to me;
your love to me was
wonderful,
passing the love of women.*
27"How are the mighty fallen,
and the weapons of war
perished!"

DAVID ANOINTED KING OF JUDAH

2 After this David inquired of the
LORD, "Shall I go up into any of
the cities of Judah?" And the LORD
said to him, "Go up." David said, "To
which shall I go up?" And he said, "To
Hebron." 2So David went up there,
and his two wives also, Ahin´o-am
of Jezre´el, and Ab´igail the widow of
Nabal of Carmel. 3And David brought
up his men who were with him, ev-
ery one with his household; and they
dwelt in the towns of Hebron. 4And
the men of Judah came, and there they
anointed David king over the house of
Judah.

When they told David, "It was
the men of Ja´besh-gil´ead who bur-
ied Saul," 5David sent messengers to
the men of Ja´besh-gil´ead, and said
to them, "May you be blessed by the
LORD, because you showed this loyal-
ty to Saul your lord, and buried him!
6Now may the LORD show steadfast
love and faithfulness to you! And I
will do good to you because you have
done this thing. 7Now therefore let
your hands be strong, and be valiant;
for Saul your lord is dead, and the
house of Judah has anointed me king
over them."

ISHBAAL KING OF ISRAEL

8 Now Abner the son of Ner, com-
mander of Saul's army, had taken
Ish-bo´sheth* the son of Saul, and
brought him over to Mahana´im;
9and he made him king over Gilead
and the Ash´urites and Jezre´el and
E´phraim and Benjamin and all Israel.
10Ish-bo´sheth, Saul's son, was forty
years old when he began to reign over
Israel, and he reigned two years. But
the house of Judah followed David.
11And the time that David was king in
Hebron over the house of Judah was
seven years and six months.

THE BATTLE OF GIBEON

12 Abner the son of Ner, and the
servants of Ish-bo´sheth the son
of Saul, went out from Mahana´im
to Gibeon. 13And Jo´ab the son of
Zeru´iah, and the servants of David,
went out and met them at the pool of
Gibeon; and they sat down, the one on
the one side of the pool, and the oth-
er on the other side of the pool. 14And
Abner said to Jo´ab, "Let the young
men arise and play* before us." And
Jo´ab said, "Let them arise." 15Then
they arose and passed over by number,
twelve for Benjamin and Ish-bo´sheth
the son of Saul, and twelve of the ser-
vants of David. 16And each caught his
opponent by the head, and thrust his
sword in his opponent's side; so they
fell down together. Therefore that
place was called Hel´kath-hazzu´rim,[a]
which is at Gibeon. 17And the battle
was very fierce that day; and Abner
and the men of Israel were beaten

[a] That is *the field of sword-edges*

before the servants of David.
18 And the three sons of Zeru'iah
were there, Jo'ab, Abi'shai, and
As'ahel. Now As'ahel was as swift of
foot as a wild gazelle; 19and As'ahel
pursued Abner, and as he went he
turned neither to the right hand nor
to the left from following Abner.
20Then Abner looked behind him and
said, "Is it you, As'ahel?" And he an-
swered, "It is I." 21Abner said to him,
"Turn aside to your right hand or to
your left, and seize one of the young
men, and take his spoil." But As'ahel
would not turn aside from follow-
ing him. 22And Abner said again to
As'ahel, "Turn aside from following
me; why should I smite you to the
ground? How then could I lift up my
face to your brother Jo'ab?" 23But he
refused to turn aside; therefore Abner
smote him in the belly with the butt
of his spear, so that the spear came
out at his back; and he fell there, and
died where he was. And all who came
to the place where As'ahel had fallen
and died, stood still.
24 But Jo'ab and Abi'shai pursued
Abner; and as the sun was going down
they came to the hill of Ammah,
which lies before Gi'ah on the way to
the wilderness of Gibeon. 25And the
Benjaminites gathered themselves to-
gether behind Abner, and became one
band, and took their stand on the top
of a hill. 26Then Abner called to Jo'ab,
"Shall the sword devour for ever? Do
you not know that the end will be bit-
ter? How long will it be before you bid
your people turn from the pursuit of
their brethren?" 27And Jo'ab said, "As
God lives, if you had not spoken, sure-
ly the men would have given up the
pursuit of their brethren in the morn-
ing." 28So Jo'ab blew the trumpet; and
all the men stopped, and pursued
Israel no more, nor did they fight any
more.
29 And Abner and his men went
all that night through the Arabah;
they crossed the Jordan, and march-
ing the whole forenoon they came to
Mahana'im. 30Jo'ab returned from the
pursuit of Abner; and when he had
gathered all the people together,
there were missing of David's ser-
vants nineteen men besides As'ahel.
31But the servants of David had slain
of Benjamin three hundred and sixty
of Abner's men. 32And they took up
As'ahel, and buried him in the tomb
of his father, which was at Bethlehem.
And Jo'ab and his men marched all
night, and the day broke upon them
at Hebron.

ABNER DEFECTS TO DAVID

3 There was a long war between the
house of Saul and the house of
David; and David grew stronger and
stronger, while the house of Saul be-
came weaker and weaker.
2 And sons were born to David at
Hebron: his first-born was Amnon, of
Ahin'o-am of Jezre'el; 3and his sec-
ond, Chil'e-ab, of Ab'igail the widow
of Nabal of Carmel; and the third,
Ab'salom the son of Ma'acah the
daughter of Talmai king of Geshur;
4and the fourth, Adoni'jah the son of
Haggith; and the fifth, Shephati'ah
the son of Abi'tal; 5and the sixth,
Ith're-am, of Eglah, David's wife.
These were born to David in Hebron.
6 While there was war between
the house of Saul and the house of
David, Abner was making himself
strong in the house of Saul. 7Now
Saul had a concubine, whose name
was Rizpah, the daughter of Ai'ah;
and Ish-bo'sheth said to Abner, "Why
have you gone in to my father's con-
cubine?" 8Then Abner was very angry
over the words of Ish-bo'sheth, and
said, "Am I a dog's head of Judah?
This day I keep showing loyalty to
the house of Saul your father, to his
brothers, and to his friends, and have
not given you into the hand of David;
and yet you charge me today with a
fault concerning a woman. 9God do
so to Abner and more also, if I do not
accomplish for David what the LORD
has sworn to him, 10to transfer the

kingdom from the house of Saul, and
set up the throne of David over Israel
and over Judah, from Dan to Beer-
sheba." 11And Ish-bo´sheth could not
answer Abner another word, because
he feared him.

12 And Abner sent messengers to
David at Hebron,[a] saying, "To whom
does the land belong? Make your cov-
enant with me, and behold, my hand
shall be with you to bring over all
Israel to you." 13And he said, "Good;
I will make a covenant with you;
but one thing I require of you; that
is, you shall not see my face, unless
you first bring Michal, Saul's daugh-
ter, when you come to see my face."
14Then David sent messengers to Ish-
bo´sheth Saul's son, saying, "Give me
my wife Michal, whom I betrothed at
the price of a hundred foreskins of the
Philistines." 15And Ish-bo´sheth sent,
and took her from her husband Pal´ti-
el the son of La´ish. 16But her husband
went with her, weeping after her all
the way to Bahu´rim. Then Abner said
to him, "Go, return"; and he returned.

17 And Abner conferred with the
elders of Israel, saying, "For some
time past you have been seeking
David as king over you. 18Now then
bring it about; for the LORD has
promised David, saying, 'By the hand
of my servant David I will save my
people Israel from the hand of the
Philistines, and from the hand of all
their enemies.'" 19Abner also spoke
to Benjamin; and then Abner went to
tell David at Hebron all that Israel and
the whole house of Benjamin thought
good to do.

20 When Abner came with twenty
men to David at Hebron, David made a
feast for Abner and the men who were
with him. 21And Abner said to David,
"I will arise and go, and will gather all
Israel to my lord the king, that they
may make a covenant with you, and
that you may reign over all that your
heart desires." So David sent Abner
away; and he went in peace.

[a]Gk: Heb *where he was*

ABNER IS KILLED BY JOAB

22 Just then the servants of David
arrived with Jo´ab from a raid, bring-
ing much spoil with them. But Abner
was not with David at Hebron, for he
had sent him away, and he had gone in
peace. 23When Jo´ab and all the army
that was with him came, it was told
Jo´ab, "Abner the son of Ner came to
the king, and he has let him go, and
he has gone in peace." 24Then Jo´ab
went to the king and said, "What have
you done? Behold, Abner came to you;
why is it that you have sent him away,
so that he is gone? 25You know that
Abner the son of Ner came to deceive
you, and to know your going out and
your coming in, and to know all that
you are doing."

26 When Jo´ab came out from
David's presence, he sent messengers
after Abner, and they brought him back
from the cistern of Sirah; but David
did not know about it. 27And when
Abner returned to Hebron, Jo´ab took
him aside into the midst of the gate to
speak with him privately, and there he
smote him in the belly, so that he died,
for the blood of As´ahel his brother.
28Afterward, when David heard of it,
he said, "I and my kingdom are for ever
guiltless before the LORD for the blood
of Abner the son of Ner. 29May it fall
upon the head of Jo´ab, and upon all
his father's house; and may the house
of Jo´ab never be without one who has
a discharge, or who is leprous, or who
holds a spindle, or who is slain by the
sword, or who lacks bread!" 30So Jo´ab
and Abi´shai his brother slew Abner,
because he had killed their brother
As´ahel in the battle at Gibeon.

31 Then David said to Jo´ab and to all
the people who were with him, "Rend
your clothes, and gird on sackcloth,
and mourn before Abner." And King
David followed the bier. 32They buried
Abner at Hebron; and the king lifted
up his voice and wept at the grave of
Abner; and all the people wept. 33And
the king lamented for Abner, saying,

"Should Abner die as a fool dies?
34 Your hands were not bound,
your feet were not fettered;
as one falls before the wicked
you have fallen."

And all the people wept again over
him. 35 Then all the people came to
persuade David to eat bread while it
was yet day; but David swore, saying,
"God do so to me and more also, if I
taste bread or anything else till the
sun goes down!" 36 And all the peo-
ple took notice of it, and it pleased
them; as everything that the king did
pleased all the people. 37 So all the peo-
ple and all Israel understood that day
that it had not been the king's will to
slay Abner the son of Ner. 38 And the
king said to his servants, "Do you not
know that a prince and a great man
has fallen this day in Israel? 39 And I
am this day weak, though anointed
king; these men the sons of Zeru′iah
are too hard for me. The LORD re-
quite the evildoer according to his
wickedness!"

ISHBAAL ASSASSINATED

4 When Ish-bo′sheth, Saul's son, heard
that Abner had died at Hebron, his
courage failed, and all Israel was dis-
mayed. 2 Now Saul's son had two men
who were captains of raiding bands;
the name of the one was Ba′anah, and
the name of the other Rechab, sons of
Rimmon a man of Benjamin from Be-
er′oth (for Be-er′oth also is reckoned
to Benjamin; 3 the Be-er′othites fled
to Gitta′im, and have been sojourners
there to this day).

4 Jonathan, the son of Saul, had
a son who was crippled in his feet.
He was five years old when the news
about Saul and Jonathan came from
Jezre′el; and his nurse took him up,
and fled; and, as she fled in her haste,
he fell, and became lame. And his
name was Mephib′osheth.

5 Now the sons of Rimmon the Be-
er′othite, Rechab and Ba′anah, set out,
and about the heat of the day they came
to the house of Ish-bo′sheth, as he was
taking his noonday rest. 6 And behold,
the doorkeeper of the house had been
cleaning wheat, but she grew drowsy
and slept; so Rechab and Ba′anah his
brother slipped in.[b] 7 When they came
into the house, as he lay on his bed in
his bedchamber, they smote him, and
slew him, and beheaded him. They
took his head, and went by the way
of the Arabah all night, 8 and brought
the head of Ish-bo′sheth to David at
Hebron. And they said to the king,
"Here is the head of Ish-bo′sheth, the
son of Saul, your enemy, who sought
your life; the LORD has avenged my
lord the king this day on Saul and on
his offspring." 9 But David answered
Rechab and Ba′anah his brother, the
sons of Rimmon the Be-er′othite, "As
the LORD lives, who has redeemed my
life out of every adversity, 10 when one
told me, 'Behold, Saul is dead,' and
thought he was bringing good news,
I seized him and slew him at Ziklag,
which was the reward I gave him for
his news. 11 How much more, when
wicked men have slain a righteous man
in his own house upon his bed, shall I
not now require his blood at your hand,
and destroy you from the earth?" 12 And
David commanded his young men, and
they killed them, and cut off their
hands and feet, and hanged them be-
side the pool at Hebron. But they took
the head of Ish-bo′sheth, and buried it
in the tomb of Abner at Hebron.

DAVID ANOINTED KING OF ALL ISRAEL

5 *Then all the tribes of Israel came
to David at Hebron, and said,
"Behold, we are your bone and flesh.
2 In times past, when Saul was king
over us, it was you that led out and
brought in Israel; and the LORD said
to you, 'You shall be shepherd of my
people Israel, and you shall be prince
over Israel.'" 3 So all the elders of
Israel came to the king at Hebron;

[b] Gk: Heb *6 And hither they came into the midst of the house fetching wheat; and they smote him in the belly; and Rechab and Baanah his brother escaped*

and King David made a covenant with
them at Hebron before the LORD, and
they anointed David king over Israel.
4David was thirty years old when he
began to reign, and he reigned forty
years. 5At Hebron he reigned over
Judah seven years and six months; and
at Jerusalem he reigned over all Israel
and Judah thirty-three years.

JERUSALEM MADE CAPITAL OF THE UNITED KINGDOM

6 And the king and his men went to
Jerusalem against the Jeb´usites, the
inhabitants of the land, who said to
David, "You will not come in here, but
the blind and the lame* will ward you
off"—thinking, "David cannot come
in here." 7Nevertheless David took the
stronghold of Zion, that is, the city of
David. 8And David said on that day,
"Whoever would smite the Jeb´usites,
let him get up the water shaft to at-
tack the lame and the blind, who are
hated by David's soul." Therefore it
is said, "The blind and the lame shall
not come into the house." 9And David
dwelt in the stronghold, and called
it the city of David. And David built
the city round about from the Millo
inward. 10And David became greater
and greater, for the LORD, the God of
hosts, was with him.
11 And Hiram king of Tyre sent
messengers to David, and cedar trees,
also carpenters and masons who built
David a house. 12And David perceived
that the LORD had established him
king over Israel, and that he had ex-
alted his kingdom for the sake of his
people Israel.
13 And David took more concubines
and wives from Jerusalem, after he
came from Hebron; and more sons and
daughters were born to David. 14And
these are the names of those who were
born to him in Jerusalem: Sham´mu-a,
Shobab, Nathan, Solomon, 15Ibhar,
Eli´shu-a, Nepheg, Japhi´a, 16Elish´-
ama, Eli´ada, and Eliph´elet.

PHILISTINE ATTACK REPULSED

17 When the Philistines heard that
David had been anointed king over
Israel, all the Philistines went up in
search of David; but David heard of
it and went down to the stronghold.
18Now the Philistines had come and
spread out in the valley of Reph´aim.
19And David inquired of the LORD,
"Shall I go up against the Philistines?
Wilt thou give them into my hand?"
And the LORD said to David, "Go up;
for I will certainly give the Philistines
into your hand." 20And David came to
Ba´al-pera´zim, and David defeated
them there; and he said, "The LORD
has broken through[a] my enemies
before me, like a bursting flood."
Therefore the name of that place
is called Ba´al-pera´zim.[b] 21And the
Philistines left their idols there, and
David and his men carried them away.
22 And the Philistines came up
yet again, and spread out in the val-
ley of Reph´aim. 23And when David
inquired of the LORD, he said, "You
shall not go up; go around to their
rear, and come upon them opposite
the balsam trees. 24And when you hear
the sound of marching in the tops of
the balsam trees, then bestir your-
self; for then the LORD has gone out
before you to smite the army of the
Philistines." 25And David did as the
LORD commanded him, and smote the
Philistines from Geba to Gezer.

DAVID BRINGS THE ARK TO JERUSALEM

6 David again gathered all the cho-
sen men of Israel, thirty thousand.
2And David arose and went with all
the people who were with him from
Ba´ale-judah, to bring up from there
the ark of God, which is called by the
name of the LORD of hosts who sits
enthroned on the cherubim. 3And
they carried the ark of God upon a
new cart, and brought it out of the
house of Abin´adab which was on the
hill; and Uzzah and Ahi´o,[c] the sons

[a] Heb *paraz*
[b] That is *Lord of breaking through*
[c] Or *and his brother*

of Abin´adab, were driving the new
cart[d] 4 with the ark of God; and Ahi´o[e]
went before the ark. 5 And David and
all the house of Israel were making
merry before the LORD with all their
might, with songs[f] and lyres and
harps and tambourines and castanets
and cymbals.

6 And when they came to the
threshing floor of Nacon, Uzzah put
out his hand to the ark of God and
took hold of it, for the oxen stumbled.
7 And the anger of the LORD was kin-
dled against Uzzah; and God smote
him there because he put forth his
hand to the ark;[g] and he died there
beside the ark of God. 8 And David
was angry because the LORD had bro-
ken forth upon Uzzah; and that place
is called Pe´rez-uz´zah,[h] to this day.
9 And David was afraid of the LORD
that day; and he said, "How can the
ark of the LORD come to me?" 10 So
David was not willing to take the ark
of the LORD into the city of David;
but David took it aside to the house
of O´bed-e´dom the Gittite. 11 And
the ark of the LORD remained in the
house of O´bed-e´dom the Gittite
three months; and the LORD blessed
O´bed-e´dom and all his household.

12 And it was told King David,
"The LORD has blessed the household
of O´bed-e´dom and all that belongs
to him, because of the ark of God." So
David went and brought up the ark of
God from the house of O´bed-e´dom
to the city of David with rejoicing;
13 and when those who bore the ark of
the LORD had gone six paces, he sacri-
ficed an ox and a fatling. 14 And David
danced before the LORD with all his
might; and David was girded with a
linen ephod. 15 So David and all the
house of Israel brought up the ark of
the LORD with shouting, and with the
sound of the horn.

16 As the ark of the LORD came into
the city of David, Michal the daughter
of Saul looked out of the window, and
saw King David leaping and dancing
before the LORD; and she despised
him in her heart. 17 And they brought
in the ark of the LORD, and set it in its
place, inside the tent which David had
pitched for it; and David offered burnt
offerings and peace offerings before
the LORD. 18 And when David had fin-
ished offering the burnt offerings and
the peace offerings, he blessed the
people in the name of the LORD of
hosts, 19 and distributed among all the
people, the whole multitude of Israel,
both men and women, to each a cake
of bread, a portion of meat,[i] and a cake
of raisins. Then all the people depart-
ed, each to his house.

20 And David returned to bless his
household. But Michal the daughter
of Saul came out to meet David, and
said, "How the king of Israel honored
himself today, uncovering himself to-
day before the eyes of his servants'
maids, as one of the vulgar fellows
shamelessly uncovers himself!" 21 And
David said to Michal, "It was before
the LORD, who chose me above your
father, and above all his house, to
appoint me as prince over Israel, the
people of the LORD—and I will make
merry before the LORD. 22 I will make
myself yet more contemptible than
this, and I will be abased in your[j]
eyes; but by the maids of whom you
have spoken, by them I shall be held
in honor." 23 And Michal the daughter
of Saul had no child to the day of her
death.

GOD'S COVENANT WITH DAVID

7 Now when the king dwelt in his
house, and the LORD had given him
rest from all his enemies round about,
2 the king said to Nathan the prophet,

[d] Compare Gk: Heb *the new cart, and brought it out of the house of Abinadab which was on the hill*
[e] Or *and his brother*
[f] Gk 1Chron 13. 8: Heb *fir-trees*
[g] 1Chron 13. 10: Heb uncertain
[h] That is *The breaking forth upon Uzzah*
[i] Vg: Heb uncertain
[j] Gk: Heb *my*

"See now, I dwell in a house of cedar,
but the ark of God dwells in a tent."
3And Nathan said to the king, "Go, do
all that is in your heart; for the LORD
is with you."
4 But that same night the word of
the LORD came to Nathan, 5"Go and
tell my servant David, 'Thus says the
LORD: Would you build me a house to
dwell in? 6I have not dwelt in a house
since the day I brought up the people
of Israel from Egypt to this day, but
I have been moving about in a tent
for my dwelling. 7In all places where
I have moved with all the people of
Israel, did I speak a word with any
of the judges[a] of Israel, whom I com-
manded to shepherd my people Israel,
saying, "Why have you not built me a
house of cedar?"' 8Now therefore thus
you shall say to my servant David,
'Thus says the LORD of hosts, I took
you from the pasture, from following
the sheep, that you should be prince
over my people Israel; 9and I have
been with you wherever you went,
and have cut off all your enemies from
before you; and I will make for you a
great name, like the name of the great
ones of the earth. 10And I will appoint
a place for my people Israel, and will
plant them, that they may dwell in
their own place, and be disturbed no
more; and violent men shall afflict
them no more, as formerly, 11from the
time that I appointed judges over my
people Israel; and I will give you rest
from all your enemies. Moreover the
LORD declares to you that the LORD
will make you a house. 12When your
days are fulfilled and you lie down
with your fathers, I will raise up your
offspring after you, who shall come
forth from your body, and I will es-
tablish his kingdom. 13He shall build
a house for my name, and I will es-
tablish the throne of his kingdom for
ever. 14I will be his father, and he shall
be my son. When he commits iniqui-
ty, I will chasten him with the rod of
men, with the stripes of the sons of
men; 15but I will not take[b] my steadfast
love from him, as I took it from Saul,
whom I put away from before you.
16And your house and your kingdom
shall be made sure for ever before me;
your throne shall be established for
ever.'" 17In accordance with all these
words, and in accordance with all this
vision, Nathan spoke to David.

DAVID'S PRAYER

18 Then King David went in and
sat before the LORD, and said, "Who
am I, O Lord GOD, and what is my
house, that thou hast brought me thus
far? 19And yet this was a small thing
in thy eyes, O Lord GOD; thou hast
spoken also of thy servant's house for
a great while to come, and hast shown
me future generations,[c] O Lord GOD!
20And what more can David say to
thee? For thou knowest thy servant,
O Lord GOD! 21Because of thy promise,
and according to thy own heart, thou
hast wrought all this greatness, to
make thy servant know it. 22Therefore
thou art great, O LORD God; for there
is none like thee, and there is no God
besides thee, according to all that we
have heard with our ears. 23What oth-
er[d] nation on earth is like thy people
Israel, whom God went to redeem to
be his people, making himself a name,
and doing for them[e] great and terri-
ble things, by driving out[f] before his
people a nation and its gods?[g] 24And
thou didst establish for thyself thy
people Israel to be thy people for ever;
and thou, O LORD, didst become their
God. 25And now, O LORD God, confirm
for ever the word which thou hast spo-
ken concerning thy servant and con-
cerning his house, and do as thou hast

[a] 1Chron 17. 6: Heb *tribes*
[b] Gk Syr Vg 1Chron 17. 13: Heb *shall not depart*
[c] Cn: Heb *this is the law for man*
[d] Gk: Heb *one*
[e] Heb *you*
[f] Gk 1Chron 17. 21: Heb *for your land*
[g] Heb *before thy people, whom thou didst redeem for thyself from Egypt, nations and its gods*

spoken; 26and thy name will be mag-
nified for ever, saying, 'The LORD of
hosts is God over Israel,' and the house
of thy servant David will be estab-
lished before thee. 27For thou, O LORD
of hosts, the God of Israel, hast made
this revelation to thy servant, saying,
'I will build you a house'; therefore
thy servant has found courage to pray
this prayer to thee. 28And now, O Lord
GOD, thou art God, and thy words
are true, and thou hast promised this
good thing to thy servant; 29now there-
fore may it please thee to bless the
house of thy servant, that it may con-
tinue for ever before thee; for thou, O
Lord GOD, hast spoken, and with thy
blessing shall the house of thy servant
be blessed for ever."*

DAVID'S WARS

8 After this David defeated the Phil-
istines and subdued them, and
David took Meth'eg-am'mah out of
the hand of the Philistines.

2 And he defeated Moab, and mea-
sured them with a line, making them
lie down on the ground; two lines
he measured to be put to death, and
one full line to be spared. And the
Moabites became servants to David
and brought tribute.

3 David also defeated Hadade'zer
the son of Rehob, king of Zobah, as he
went to restore his power at the riv-
er Euphra'tes. 4And David took from
him a thousand and seven hundred
horsemen, and twenty thousand foot
soldiers; and David hamstrung all the
chariot horses, but left enough for
a hundred chariots. 5And when the
Syrians of Damascus came to help
Hadade'zer king of Zobah, David
slew twenty-two thousand men of the
Syrians. 6Then David put garrisons in
Aram of Damascus; and the Syrians
became servants to David and brought
tribute. And the LORD gave victory to
David wherever he went. 7And David
took the shields of gold which were
carried by the servants of Hadade'zer,
and brought them to Jerusalem. 8And
from Betah and from Bero'thai, cities
of Hadade'zer, King David took very
much bronze.

9 When To'i king of Hamath heard
that David had defeated the whole
army of Hadade'zer, 10To'i sent his
son Joram to King David, to greet
him, and to congratulate him because
he had fought against Hadade'zer and
defeated him; for Hadade'zer had of-
ten been at war with To'i. And Joram
brought with him articles of silver, of
gold, and of bronze; 11these also King
David dedicated to the LORD, together
with the silver and gold which he dedi-
cated from all the nations he subdued,
12from Edom, Moab, the Ammonites,
the Philistines, Am'alek, and from the
spoil of Hadade'zer the son of Rehob,
king of Zobah.

13 And David won a name for him-
self. When he returned, he slew eigh-
teen thousand E'domites[h] in the Valley
of Salt. 14And he put garrisons in Edom;
throughout all Edom he put garrisons,
and all the E'domites became David's
servants. And the LORD gave victory to
David wherever he went.

DAVID'S OFFICERS

15 So David reigned over all Israel;
and David administered justice and
equity to all his people. 16And Jo'ab
the son of Zeru'iah was over the
army; and Jehosh'aphat the son of
Ahi'lud was recorder; 17and Zadok
the son of Ahi'tub and Ahim'elech
the son of Abi'athar were priests; and
Serai'ah was secretary; 18and Benai'ah
the son of Jehoi'ada was over[i] the
Cher'ethites and the Pel'ethites; and
David's sons were priests.

DAVID'S KINDNESS TO MEPHIBOSHETH

9 *And David said, "Is there still any
one left of the house of Saul, that I
may show him kindness for Jonathan's
sake?" 2Now there was a servant of the

[h]Gk: Heb *returned from smiting eighteen thousand Syrians*
[i]Syr Tg Vg 20.23; 1Chron 18.17: Heb lacks *was over*

house of Saul whose name was Ziba,
and they called him to David; and the
king said to him, "Are you Ziba?" And
he said, "Your servant is he." 3And the
king said, "Is there not still some one
of the house of Saul, that I may show
the kindness of God to him?" Ziba
said to the king, "There is still a son
of Jonathan; he is crippled in his feet."
4The king said to him, "Where is he?"
And Ziba said to the king, "He is in
the house of Machir the son of Am´mi-
el, at Lo-debar." 5Then King David
sent and brought him from the house
of Machir the son of Am´mi-el, at Lo-
debar. 6And Mephib´osheth the son of
Jonathan, son of Saul, came to David,
and fell on his face and did obeisance.
And David said, "Mephib´osheth!"
And he answered, "Behold, your ser-
vant." 7And David said to him, "Do
not fear; for I will show you kindness
for the sake of your father Jonathan,
and I will restore to you all the land
of Saul your father; and you shall eat
at my table always." 8And he did obei-
sance, and said, "What is your ser-
vant, that you should look upon a dead
dog such as I?"

9 Then the king called Ziba, Saul's
servant, and said to him, "All that be-
longed to Saul and to all his house I
have given to your master's son. 10And
you and your sons and your servants
shall till the land for him, and shall
bring in the produce, that your mas-
ter's son may have bread to eat; but
Mephib´osheth your master's son
shall always eat at my table." Now
Ziba had fifteen sons and twenty ser-
vants. 11Then Ziba said to the king,
"According to all that my lord the
king commands his servant, so will
your servant do." So Mephib´osheth
ate at David's[a] table, like one of the
king's sons. 12And Mephib´osheth had
a young son, whose name was Mica.
And all who dwelt in Ziba's house be-
came Mephib´osheth's servants. 13So
Mephib´osheth dwelt in Jerusalem; for
he ate always at the king's table. Now
he was lame in both his feet.

THE AMMONITES AND ARAMEANS ARE DEFEATED

10 After this the king of the Am-
monites died, and Hanun his son
reigned in his stead. 2And David said,
"I will deal loyally with Hanun the
son of Nahash, as his father dealt loy-
ally with me." So David sent by his
servants to console him concerning
his father. And David's servants came
into the land of the Ammonites. 3But
the princes of the Ammonites said
to Hanun their lord, "Do you think,
because David has sent comforters to
you, that he is honoring your father?
Has not David sent his servants to you
to search the city, and to spy it out,
and to overthrow it?" 4So Hanun took
David's servants, and shaved off half
the beard of each, and cut off their
garments in the middle, at their hips,
and sent them away. 5When it was told
David, he sent to meet them, for the
men were greatly ashamed. And the
king said, "Remain at Jericho until
your beards have grown, and then
return."

6 When the Ammonites saw that
they had become odious to David,
the Ammonites sent and hired the
Syrians of Beth-re´hob, and the
Syrians of Zobah, twenty thousand
foot soldiers, and the king of Ma´acah
with a thousand men, and the men of
Tob, twelve thousand men. 7And when
David heard of it, he sent Jo´ab and
all the host of the mighty men. 8And
the Ammonites came out and drew
up in battle array at the entrance of
the gate; and the Syrians of Zobah
and of Rehob, and the men of Tob and
Ma´acah, were by themselves in the
open country.

9 When Jo´ab saw that the bat-
tle was set against him both in front
and in the rear, he chose some of the
picked men of Israel, and arrayed
them against the Syrians; 10the rest
of his men he put in the charge of

[a]Gk: Heb *my*

Abi´shai his brother, and he arrayed
them against the Ammonites. 11 And
he said, "If the Syrians are too strong
for me, then you shall help me; but if
the Ammonites are too strong for you,
then I will come and help you. 12 Be of
good courage, and let us play the man
for our people, and for the cities of
our God; and may the LORD do what
seems good to him." 13 So Jo´ab and
the people who were with him drew
near to battle against the Syrians; and
they fled before him. 14 And when the
Ammonites saw that the Syrians fled,
they likewise fled before Abi´shai, and
entered the city. Then Jo´ab returned
from fighting against the Ammonites,
and came to Jerusalem.

15 But when the Syrians saw that
they had been defeated by Israel,
they gathered themselves together.
16 And Hadade´zer sent, and brought
out the Syrians who were beyond the
Euphra´tes;[b] and they came to Helam,
with Shobach the commander of the
army of Hadade´zer at their head.
17 And when it was told David, he gath-
ered all Israel together, and crossed
the Jordan, and came to Helam.
And the Syrians arrayed themselves
against David, and fought with him.
18 And the Syrians fled before Israel;
and David slew of the Syrians the men
of seven hundred chariots, and for-
ty thousand horsemen, and wound-
ed Shobach the commander of their
army, so that he died there. 19 And
when all the kings who were servants
of Hadade´zer saw that they had been
defeated by Israel, they made peace
with Israel, and became subject to
them. So the Syrians feared to help
the Ammonites any more.

DAVID COMMITS ADULTERY WITH BATHSHEBA

11 *In the spring of the year, the
time when kings go forth to bat-
tle, David sent Jo´ab, and his servants
with him, and all Israel; and they rav-
aged the Ammonites, and besieged
Rabbah. But David remained at
Jerusalem.

2 It happened, late one afternoon,
when David arose from his couch
and was walking upon the roof of the
king's house, that he saw from the
roof a woman bathing; and the woman
was very beautiful. 3 And David sent
and inquired about the woman. And
one said, "Is not this Bathshe´ba, the
daughter of Eli´am, the wife of Uri´ah
the Hittite?" 4 So David sent messen-
gers, and took her; and she came to
him, and he lay with her. (Now she
was purifying herself from her un-
cleanness.) Then she returned to her
house. 5 And the woman conceived;
and she sent and told David, "I am
with child."

6 So David sent word to Jo´ab,
"Send me Uri´ah the Hittite." And
Jo´ab sent Uri´ah to David. 7 When
Uri´ah came to him, David asked how
Jo´ab was doing, and how the people
fared, and how the war prospered.
8 Then David said to Uri´ah, "Go down
to your house, and wash your feet."
And Uri´ah went out of the king's
house, and there followed him a pres-
ent from the king. 9 But Uri´ah slept at
the door of the king's house with all
the servants of his lord, and did not go
down to his house. 10 When they told
David, "Uri´ah did not go down to his
house," David said to Uri´ah, "Have
you not come from a journey? Why
did you not go down to your house?"
11 Uri´ah said to David, "The ark and
Israel and Judah dwell in booths; and
my lord Jo´ab and the servants of my
lord are camping in the open field;
shall I then go to my house, to eat and
to drink, and to lie with my wife?* As
you live, and as your soul lives, I will
not do this thing." 12 Then David said
to Uri´ah, "Remain here today also,
and tomorrow I will let you depart." So
Uri´ah remained in Jerusalem that day,
and the next. 13 And David invited him,
and he ate in his presence and drank,
so that he made him drunk; and in the

[b] Heb *river*

evening he went out to lie on his couch
with the servants of his lord, but he
did not go down to his house.

DAVID HAS URIAH KILLED

14 In the morning David wrote a
letter to Jo´ab, and sent it by the hand
of Uri´ah. 15In the letter he wrote, "Set
Uri´ah in the forefront of the hardest
fighting, and then draw back from
him, that he may be struck down, and
die." 16And as Jo´ab was besieging the
city, he assigned Uri´ah to the place
where he knew there were valiant
men. 17And the men of the city came
out and fought with Jo´ab; and some
of the servants of David among the
people fell. Uri´ah the Hittite was
slain also. 18Then Jo´ab sent and told
David all the news about the fight-
ing; 19and he instructed the messen-
ger, "When you have finished telling
all the news about the fighting to the
king, 20then, if the king's anger rises,
and if he says to you, 'Why did you
go so near the city to fight? Did you
not know that they would shoot from
the wall? 21Who killed Abim´elech
the son of Jerub´besheth? Did not a
woman cast an upper millstone upon
him from the wall, so that he died at
Thebez? Why did you go so near the
wall?' then you shall say, 'Your ser-
vant Uri´ah the Hittite is dead also.'"

22 So the messenger went, and
came and told David all that Jo´ab had
sent him to tell. 23The messenger said
to David, "The men gained an advan-
tage over us, and came out against us
in the field; but we drove them back
to the entrance of the gate. 24Then the
archers shot at your servants from
the wall; some of the king's servants
are dead; and your servant Uri´ah the
Hittite is dead also." 25David said to
the messenger, "Thus shall you say to
Jo´ab, 'Do not let this matter trouble
you, for the sword devours now one
and now another; strengthen your at-
tack upon the city, and overthrow it.'
And encourage him."

26 When the wife of Uri´ah heard
that Uri´ah her husband was dead,
she made lamentation for her hus-
band. 27And when the mourning was
over, David sent and brought her to
his house, and she became his wife,
and bore him a son. But the thing that
David had done displeased the LORD.

NATHAN CONDEMNS DAVID

12 And the LORD sent Nathan to
David. He came to him, and said
to him, "There were two men in a cer-
tain city, the one rich and the other
poor. 2The rich man had very many
flocks and herds; 3but the poor man
had nothing but one little ewe lamb,
which he had bought. And he brought
it up, and it grew up with him and
with his children; it used to eat of
his morsel, and drink from his cup,
and lie in his bosom, and it was like
a daughter to him. 4Now there came
a traveler to the rich man, and he was
unwilling to take one of his own flock
or herd to prepare for the wayfarer
who had come to him, but he took
the poor man's lamb, and prepared it
for the man who had come to him."
5Then David's anger was greatly kin-
dled against the man; and he said to
Nathan, "As the LORD lives, the man
who has done this deserves to die;
6and he shall restore the lamb four-
fold, because he did this thing, and
because he had no pity."

7 Nathan said to David, "You are
the man. Thus says the LORD, the
God of Israel, 'I anointed you king
over Israel, and I delivered you out
of the hand of Saul; 8and I gave you
your master's house, and your mas-
ter's wives into your bosom, and gave
you the house of Israel and of Judah;
and if this were too little, I would
add to you as much more. 9Why have
you despised the word of the LORD,
to do what is evil in his sight? You
have smitten Uri´ah the Hittite with
the sword, and have taken his wife
to be your wife, and have slain him
with the sword of the Ammonites.
10Now therefore the sword shall never

depart from your house, because you
have despised me, and have taken the
wife of Uri´ah the Hittite to be your
wife.' 11 Thus says the LORD, 'Behold,
I will raise up evil against you out of
your own house; and I will take your
wives before your eyes, and give them
to your neighbor, and he shall lie with
your wives in the sight of this sun.
12 For you did it secretly; but I will do
this thing before all Israel, and before
the sun.'" 13 David said to Nathan, "I
have sinned against the LORD." And
Nathan said to David, "The LORD also
has put away your sin; you shall not
die. 14 Nevertheless, because by this
deed you have utterly scorned the
LORD,[a] the child that is born to you
shall die." 15 Then Nathan went to his
house.

BATHSHEBA'S CHILD DIES

And the LORD struck the child that
Uri´ah's wife bore to David, and it be-
came sick. 16 David therefore besought
God for the child; and David fasted,
and went in and lay all night upon the
ground. 17 And the elders of his house
stood beside him, to raise him from
the ground; but he would not, nor
did he eat food with them. 18 On the
seventh day the child died. And the
servants of David feared to tell him
that the child was dead; for they said,
"Behold, while the child was yet alive,
we spoke to him, and he did not lis-
ten to us; how then can we say to him
the child is dead? He may do himself
some harm." 19 But when David saw
that his servants were whispering to-
gether, David perceived that the child
was dead; and David said to his ser-
vants, "Is the child dead?" They said,
"He is dead." 20 Then David arose from
the earth, and washed, and anointed
himself, and changed his clothes; and
he went into the house of the LORD,
and worshiped; he then went to his
own house; and when he asked, they
set food before him, and he ate. 21 Then
his servants said to him, "What is this
thing that you have done? You fasted
and wept for the child while it was
alive; but when the child died, you
arose and ate food." 22 He said, "While
the child was still alive, I fasted and
wept; for I said, 'Who knows wheth-
er the LORD will be gracious to me,
that the child may live?' 23 But now he
is dead; why should I fast? Can I bring
him back again? I shall go to him, but
he will not return to me."

SOLOMON IS BORN

24 Then David comforted his wife,
Bathshe´ba, and went in to her, and
lay with her; and she bore a son, and
he called his name Solomon. And the
LORD loved him, 25 and sent a message
by Nathan the prophet; so he called
his name Jedidi´ah,[b] because of the
LORD.

THE AMMONITES CRUSHED

26 Now Jo´ab fought against
Rabbah of the Ammonites, and took
the royal city. 27 And Jo´ab sent mes-
sengers to David, and said, "I have
fought against Rabbah; moreover, I
have taken the city of waters. 28 Now,
then, gather the rest of the people to-
gether, and encamp against the city,
and take it; lest I take the city, and
it be called by my name." 29 So David
gathered all the people together and
went to Rabbah, and fought against
it and took it. 30 And he took the
crown of their king[c] from his head;
the weight of it was a talent of gold,
and in it was a precious stone; and it
was placed on David's head. And he
brought forth the spoil of the city, a
very great amount. 31 And he brought
forth the people who were in it, and
set them to labor with saws and iron
picks and iron axes, and made them
toil at[d] the brickkilns; and thus he
did to all the cities of the Ammonites.

[a] Heb *the enemies of the LORD*
[b] That is *beloved of the LORD*
[c] Or *Milcom*. See Zeph 1. 5
[d] Cn: Heb *pass through*

Then David and all the people returned to Jerusalem.

AMNON AND TAMAR

13 *Now Ab´salom, David's son, had a beautiful sister, whose name was Tamar; and after a time Amnon, David's son, loved her. 2And Amnon was so tormented that he made himself ill because of his sister Tamar; for she was a virgin, and it seemed impossible to Amnon to do anything to her. 3But Amnon had a friend, whose name was Jon´adab, the son of Shim´e-ah, David's brother; and Jon´adab was a very crafty man. 4And he said to him, "O son of the king, why are you so haggard morning after morning? Will you not tell me?" Amnon said to him, "I love Tamar, my brother Ab´salom's sister." 5Jon´adab said to him, "Lie down on your bed, and pretend to be ill; and when your father comes to see you, say to him, 'Let my sister Tamar come and give me bread to eat, and prepare the food in my sight, that I may see it, and eat it from her hand.'" 6So Amnon lay down, and pretended to be ill; and when the king came to see him, Amnon said to the king, "Pray let my sister Tamar come and make a couple of cakes in my sight, that I may eat from her hand."

7 Then David sent home to Tamar, saying, "Go to your brother Amnon's house, and prepare food for him." 8So Tamar went to her brother Amnon's house, where he was lying down. And she took dough, and kneaded it, and made cakes in his sight, and baked the cakes. 9And she took the pan and emptied it out before him, but he refused to eat. And Amnon said, "Send out every one from me." So every one went out from him. 10Then Amnon said to Tamar, "Bring the food into the chamber, that I may eat from your hand." And Tamar took the cakes she had made, and brought them into the chamber to Amnon her brother. 11But when she brought them near him to eat, he took hold of her, and said to her, "Come, lie with me, my sister." 12She answered him, "No, my brother, do not force me; for such a thing is not done in Israel; do not do this wanton folly. 13As for me, where could I carry my shame? And as for you, you would be as one of the wanton fools in Israel. Now therefore, I pray you, speak to the king; for he will not withhold me from you." 14But he would not listen to her; and being stronger than she, he forced her, and lay with her.

15 Then Amnon hated her with very great hatred; so that the hatred with which he hated her was greater than the love with which he had loved her. And Amnon said to her, "Arise, be gone." 16But she said to him, "No, my brother; for this wrong in sending me away is greater than the other which you did to me."[a] But he would not listen to her. 17He called the young man who served him and said, "Put this woman out of my presence, and bolt the door after her." 18Now she was wearing a long robe with sleeves; for thus were the virgin daughters of the king clad of old.[b] So his servant put her out, and bolted the door after her. 19And Tamar put ashes on her head, and rent the long robe which she wore; and she laid her hand on her head, and went away, crying aloud as she went.

20 And her brother Ab´salom said to her, "Has Amnon your brother been with you? Now hold your peace, my sister; he is your brother; do not take this to heart." So Tamar dwelt, a desolate woman, in her brother Ab´salom's house. 21When King David heard of all these things, he was very angry. 22But Ab´salom spoke to Amnon neither good nor bad; for Ab´salom hated Amnon, because he had forced his sister Tamar.

[a] Cn Compare Gk Vg: Heb *No, for this great wrong in sending me away is (worse) than the other which you did to me*

[b] Cn: Heb *clad in robes*

ABSALOM AVENGES THE VIOLATION OF HIS SISTER

23 After two full years Ab´salom
had sheepshearers at Ba´al-ha´zor,
which is near E´phraim, and Ab´-
salom invited all the king's sons.
24 And Ab´salom came to the king,
and said, "Behold, your servant has
sheepshearers; pray let the king and
his servants go with your servant."
25 But the king said to Ab´salom, "No,
my son, let us not all go, lest we be
burdensome to you." He pressed him,
but he would not go but gave him his
blessing. 26 Then Ab´salom said, "If
not, pray let my brother Amnon go
with us." And the king said to him,
"Why should he go with you?" 27 But
Ab´salom pressed him until he let
Amnon and all the king's sons go with
him. 28 Then Ab´salom commanded
his servants, "Mark when Amnon's
heart is merry with wine, and when
I say to you, 'Strike Amnon,' then kill
him. Fear not; have I not commanded
you? Be courageous and be valiant."
29 So the servants of Ab´salom did to
Amnon as Ab´salom had commanded.
Then all the king's sons arose, and
each mounted his mule and fled.

30 While they were on the way,
tidings came to David, "Ab´salom
has slain all the king's sons, and not
one of them is left." 31 Then the king
arose, and rent his garments, and lay
on the earth; and all his servants who
were standing by rent their garments.
32 But Jon´adab the son of Shim´e-ah,
David's brother, said, "Let not my
lord suppose that they have killed
all the young men the king's sons,
for Amnon alone is dead, for by the
command of Ab´salom this has been
determined from the day he forced his
sister Tamar. 33 Now therefore let not
my lord the king so take it to heart as
to suppose that all the king's sons are
dead; for Amnon alone is dead."

34 But Ab´salom fled. And the
young man who kept the watch lifted
up his eyes, and looked, and behold,
many people were coming from the
Horona´im road[c] by the side of the
mountain. 35 And Jon´adab said to the
king, "Behold, the king's sons have
come; as your servant said, so it has
come about." 36 And as soon as he had
finished speaking, behold, the king's
sons came, and lifted up their voice
and wept; and the king also and all his
servants wept very bitterly.

37 But Ab´salom fled, and went to
Talmai the son of Ammi´hud, king of
Geshur. And David mourned for his
son day after day. 38 So Ab´salom fled,
and went to Geshur, and was there
three years. 39 And the spirit[d] of the
king longed to go forth to Ab´salom;
for he was comforted about Amnon,
seeing he was dead.

ABSALOM RETURNS TO JERUSALEM

14 Now Jo´ab the son of Zeru´iah per-
ceived that the king's heart went
out to Ab´salom. 2 And Jo´ab sent to
Teko´a, and fetched from there a wise
woman, and said to her, "Pretend to
be a mourner, and put on mourning
garments; do not anoint yourself with
oil, but behave like a woman who has
been mourning many days for the
dead; 3 and go to the king, and speak
thus to him." So Jo´ab put the words
in her mouth.

4 When the woman of Teko´a came
to the king, she fell on her face to the
ground, and did obeisance, and said,
"Help, O king." 5 And the king said
to her, "What is your trouble?" She
answered, "Alas, I am a widow; my
husband is dead. 6 And your handmaid
had two sons, and they quarreled with
one another in the field; there was no
one to part them, and one struck the
other and killed him. 7 And now the
whole family has risen against your
handmaid, and they say, 'Give up the
man who struck his brother, that we
may kill him for the life of his broth-
er whom he slew'; and so they would

[c] Cn Compare Gk: Heb *the road behind him*
[d] Gk: Heb *David*

destroy the heir also. Thus they would
quench my coal which is left, and
leave to my husband neither name nor
remnant upon the face of the earth."
8 Then the king said to the woman,
"Go to your house, and I will give or-
ders concerning you." 9And the wom-
an of Teko´a said to the king, "On me
be the guilt, my lord the king, and on
my father's house; let the king and
his throne be guiltless." 10The king
said, "If any one says anything to you,
bring him to me, and he shall never
touch you again." 11Then she said,
"Pray let the king invoke the LORD
your God, that the avenger of blood
slay no more, and my son be not de-
stroyed." He said, "As the LORD lives,
not one hair of your son shall fall to
the ground."
12 Then the woman said, "Pray
let your handmaid speak a word to
my lord the king." He said, "Speak."
13And the woman said, "Why then
have you planned such a thing against
the people of God? For in giving this
decision the king convicts himself, in-
asmuch as the king does not bring his
banished one home again. 14We must
all die, we are like water spilt on the
ground, which cannot be gathered up
again; but God will not take away the
life of him who devises[a] means not
to keep his banished one an outcast.
15Now I have come to say this to my
lord the king because the people have
made me afraid; and your handmaid
thought, 'I will speak to the king; it
may be that the king will perform the
request of his servant. 16For the king
will hear, and deliver his servant from
the hand of the man who would de-
stroy me and my son together from
the heritage of God.' 17And your hand-
maid thought, 'The word of my lord
the king will set me at rest'; for my
lord the king is like the angel of God
to discern good and evil. The LORD
your God be with you!"
18 Then the king answered the
woman, "Do not hide from me
anything I ask you." And the woman
said, "Let my lord the king speak."
19The king said, "Is the hand of Jo´ab
with you in all this?" The woman an-
swered and said, "As surely as you
live, my lord the king, one cannot turn
to the right hand or to the left from
anything that my lord the king has
said. It was your servant Jo´ab who
bade me; it was he who put all these
words in the mouth of your handmaid.
20In order to change the course of af-
fairs your servant Jo´ab did this. But
my lord has wisdom like the wisdom
of the angel of God to know all things
that are on the earth."
21 Then the king said to Jo´ab,
"Behold now, I grant this; go, bring
back the young man Ab´salom." 22And
Jo´ab fell on his face to the ground,
and did obeisance, and blessed the
king; and Jo´ab said, "Today your ser-
vant knows that I have found favor in
your sight, my lord the king, in that
the king has granted the request of his
servant." 23So Jo´ab arose and went to
Geshur, and brought Ab´salom to
Jerusalem. 24And the king said, "Let
him dwell apart in his own house;
he is not to come into my presence."
So Ab´salom dwelt apart in his own
house, and did not come into the
king's presence.

DAVID FORGIVES ABSALOM

25 Now in all Israel there was no
one so much to be praised for his beau-
ty as Ab´salom; from the sole of his
foot to the crown of his head there was
no blemish in him. 26And when he cut
the hair of his head (for at the end of
every year he used to cut it; when it was
heavy on him, he cut it), he weighed
the hair of his head, two hundred shek-
els by the king's weight. 27There were
born to Ab´salom three sons, and one
daughter whose name was Tamar; she
was a beautiful woman.
28 So Ab´salom dwelt two full years
in Jerusalem, without coming into the
king's presence. 29Then Ab´salom sent

[a]Cn: Heb *and he devises*

for Jo´ab, to send him to the king; but
Jo´ab would not come to him. And he
sent a second time, but Jo´ab would
not come. 30Then he said to his ser-
vants, "See, Jo´ab's field is next to
mine, and he has barley there; go and
set it on fire." So Ab´salom's servants
set the field on fire. 31Then Jo´ab arose
and went to Ab´salom at his house,
and said to him, "Why have your ser-
vants set my field on fire?" 32Ab´salom
answered Jo´ab, "Behold, I sent word
to you, 'Come here, that I may send
you to the king, to ask, "Why have I
come from Geshur? It would be better
for me to be there still." Now there-
fore let me go into the presence of the
king; and if there is guilt in me, let
him kill me.'" 33Then Jo´ab went to the
king, and told him; and he summoned
Ab´salom. So he came to the king,
and bowed himself on his face to the
ground before the king; and the king
kissed Ab´salom.

ABSALOM USURPS THE THRONE

15 After this Ab´salom got himself a
chariot and horses, and fifty men
to run before him. 2And Ab´salom
used to rise early and stand beside
the way of the gate; and when any
man had a suit to come before the
king for judgment, Ab´salom would
call to him, and say, "From what city
are you?" And when he said, "Your
servant is of such and such a tribe
in Israel," 3Ab´salom would say to
him, "See, your claims are good and
right; but there is no man deputed by
the king to hear you." 4Ab´salom said
moreover, "Oh that I were judge in the
land! Then every man with a suit or
cause might come to me, and I would
give him justice." 5And whenever a
man came near to do obeisance to
him, he would put out his hand, and
take hold of him, and kiss him. 6Thus
Ab´salom did to all of Israel who came
to the king for judgment; so Ab´salom
stole the hearts of the men of Israel.

7 And at the end of four[b] years
Ab´salom said to the king, "Pray let
me go and pay my vow, which I have
vowed to the LORD, in Hebron. 8For
your servant vowed a vow while I
dwelt at Geshur in Aram, saying, 'If
the LORD will indeed bring me back
to Jerusalem, then I will offer worship
to the LORD.'" 9The king said to him,
"Go in peace." So he arose, and went
to Hebron. 10But Ab´salom sent secret
messengers throughout all the tribes
of Israel, saying, "As soon as you hear
the sound of the trumpet, then say,
'Ab´salom is king at Hebron!'" 11With
Ab´salom went two hundred men from
Jerusalem who were invited guests,
and they went in their simplicity, and
knew nothing. 12And while Ab´salom
was offering the sacrifices, he sent
for[c] Ahith´ophel the Gi´lonite, David's
counselor, from his city Giloh. And the
conspiracy grew strong, and the peo-
ple with Ab´salom kept increasing.

DAVID FLEES FROM JERUSALEM

13 And a messenger came to David,
saying, "The hearts of the men of Israel
have gone after Ab´salom." 14Then
David said to all his servants who
were with him at Jerusalem, "Arise,
and let us flee; or else there will be
no escape for us from Ab´salom; go in
haste, lest he overtake us quickly, and
bring down evil upon us, and smite
the city with the edge of the sword."
15And the king's servants said to the
king, "Behold, your servants are ready
to do whatever my lord the king de-
cides." 16So the king went forth, and
all his household after him. And the
king left ten concubines to keep the
house. 17And the king went forth, and
all the people after him; and they
halted at the last house. 18And all his
servants passed by him; and all the
Cher´ethites, and all the Pel´ethites,
and all the six hundred Gittites who
had followed him from Gath, passed
on before the king.

[b] Gk Syr: Heb *forty*
[c] Or *sent*

19 Then the king said to It´tai the
Gittite, "Why do you also go with us?
Go back, and stay with the king; for
you are a foreigner, and also an ex-
ile from[a] your home. 20You came only
yesterday, and shall I today make you
wander about with us, seeing I go I
know not where? Go back, and take
your brethren with you; and may the
LORD show[b] steadfast love and faith-
fulness to you." 21But It´tai answered
the king, "As the LORD lives, and
as my lord the king lives, wherever
my lord the king shall be, whether
for death or for life, there also will
your servant be." 22And David said
to It´tai, "Go then, pass on." So It´tai
the Gittite passed on, with all his men
and all the little ones who were with
him. 23And all the country wept aloud
as all the people passed by, and the
king crossed the brook Kidron, and
all the people passed on toward the
wilderness.

24 And Abi´athar came up, and lo,
Zadok came also, with all the Levites,
bearing the ark of the covenant of God;
and they set down the ark of God, un-
til the people had all passed out of the
city. 25Then the king said to Zadok,
"Carry the ark of God back into the
city. If I find favor in the eyes of the
LORD, he will bring me back and let
me see both it and his habitation; 26but
if he says, 'I have no pleasure in you,'
behold, here I am, let him do to me
what seems good to him." 27The king
also said to Zadok the priest, "Look,[c]
go back to the city in peace, you
and Abi´athar,[d] with your two sons,
Ahim´a-az your son, and Jonathan the
son of Abi´athar. 28See, I will wait at
the fords of the wilderness, until word
comes from you to inform me." 29So
Zadok and Abi´athar carried the ark
of God back to Jerusalem; and they re-
mained there.

30 But David went up the ascent
of the Mount of Olives, weeping as
he went, barefoot and with his head
covered; and all the people who were
with him covered their heads, and
they went up, weeping as they went.
31And it was told David, "Ahith´ophel
is among the conspirators with
Ab´salom." And David said, "O
LORD, I pray thee, turn the counsel of
Ahith´ophel into foolishness."

HUSHAI BECOMES DAVID'S SPY

32 When David came to the sum-
mit, where God was worshiped, be-
hold, Hushai the Archite came to meet
him with his coat rent and earth upon
his head. 33David said to him, "If you
go on with me, you will be a burden
to me. 34But if you return to the city,
and say to Ab´salom, 'I will be your
servant, O king; as I have been your
father's servant in time past, so now I
will be your servant,' then you will de-
feat for me the counsel of Ahith´ophel.
35Are not Zadok and Abi´athar the
priests with you there? So whatever
you hear from the king's house, tell
it to Zadok and Abi´athar the priests.
36Behold, their two sons are with
them there, Ahim´a-az, Zadok's son,
and Jonathan, Abi´athar's son; and by
them you shall send to me everything
you hear." 37So Hushai, David's friend,
came into the city, just as Ab´salom
was entering Jerusalem.

DAVID'S ADVERSARIES

16 When David had passed a little
beyond the summit, Ziba the ser-
vant of Mephib´osheth met him, with
a couple of asses saddled, bearing two
hundred loaves of bread, a hundred
bunches of raisins, a hundred of sum-
mer fruits, and a skin of wine. 2And
the king said to Ziba, "Why have you
brought these?" Ziba answered, "The
asses are for the king's household to
ride on, the bread and summer fruit
for the young men to eat, and the wine
for those who faint in the wilderness

[a] Gk Syr Vg: Heb *to*
[b] Gk: Heb lacks *may the* Lord *show*
[c] Gk: Heb *Are you a seer?* or *Do you see?*
[d] Cn: Heb lacks *and Abiathar*

to drink." 3 And the king said, "And
where is your master's son?" Ziba
said to the king, "Behold, he remains
in Jerusalem; for he said, 'Today the
house of Israel will give me back the
kingdom of my father.'" 4 Then the
king said to Ziba, "Behold, all that
belonged to Mephib'osheth is now
yours." And Ziba said, "I do obei-
sance; let me ever find favor in your
sight, my lord the king."

SHIMEI CURSES DAVID

5 When King David came to
Bahu'rim, there came out a man
of the family of the house of Saul,
whose name was Shim'e-i, the son
of Gera; and as he came he cursed
continually. 6 And he threw stones at
David, and at all the servants of King
David; and all the people and all the
mighty men were on his right hand
and on his left. 7 And Shim'e-i said
as he cursed, "Begone, begone, you
man of blood, you worthless fellow!
8 The LORD has avenged upon you all
the blood of the house of Saul, in
whose place you have reigned; and
the LORD has given the kingdom into
the hand of your son Ab'salom. See,
your ruin is on you; for you are a man
of blood."

9 Then Abi'shai the son of Zeru'iah
said to the king, "Why should this
dead dog curse my lord the king? Let
me go over and take off his head."
10 But the king said, "What have I to
do with you, you sons of Zeru'iah? If
he is cursing because the LORD has
said to him, 'Curse David,' who then
shall say, 'Why have you done so?'"
11 And David said to Abi'shai and to
all his servants, "Behold, my own son
seeks my life; how much more now
may this Benjaminite! Let him alone,
and let him curse; for the LORD has
bidden him. 12 It may be that the LORD
will look upon my affliction,[e] and that
the LORD will repay me with good for
this cursing of me today." 13 So David
and his men went on the road, while
Shim'e-i went along on the hillside
opposite him and cursed as he went,
and threw stones at him and flung
dust. 14 And the king, and all the peo-
ple who were with him, arrived weary
at the Jordan;[f] and there he refreshed
himself.

THE COUNSEL OF AHITHOPHEL

15 Now Ab'salom and all the
people, the men of Israel, came to
Jerusalem, and Ahith'ophel with
him. 16 And when Hushai the Archite,
David's friend, came to Ab'salom,
Hushai said to Ab'salom, "Long live
the king! Long live the king!" 17 And
Ab'salom said to Hushai, "Is this your
loyalty to your friend? Why did you not
go with your friend?" 18 And Hushai
said to Ab'salom, "No; for whom the
LORD and this people and all the men
of Israel have chosen, his I will be, and
with him I will remain. 19 And again,
whom should I serve? Should it not be
his son? As I have served your father,
so I will serve you."

20 Then Ab'salom said to Ahith'-
ophel, "Give your counsel; what shall
we do?" 21 Ahith'ophel said to Ab'sa-
lom, "Go in to your father's concu-
bines, whom he has left to keep the
house; and all Israel will hear that you
have made yourself odious to your
father, and the hands of all who are
with you will be strengthened." 22 So
they pitched a tent for Ab'salom upon
the roof; and Ab'salom went in to his
father's concubines in the sight of all
Israel.* 23 Now in those days the coun-
sel which Ahith'ophel gave was as if
one consulted the oracle[g] of God; so
was all the counsel of Ahith'ophel
esteemed, both by David and by
Ab'salom.

17 Moreover Ahith'ophel said to
Ab'salom, "Let me choose twelve
thousand men, and I will set out and
pursue David tonight. 2 I will come
upon him while he is weary and

[e] Gk Vg: Heb *iniquity*
[f] Gk: Heb lacks *at the Jordan*
[g] Heb *word*

discouraged, and throw him into a
panic; and all the people who are with
him will flee. I will strike down the
king only, 3and I will bring all the peo-
ple back to you as a bride comes home
to her husband. You seek the life of
only one man,[a] and all the people will
be at peace." 4And the advice pleased
Ab´salom and all the elders of Israel.

THE COUNSEL OF HUSHAI

5 Then Ab´salom said, "Call
Hushai the Archite also, and let us
hear what he has to say." 6And when
Hushai came to Ab´salom, Ab´salom
said to him, "Thus has Ahith´ophel
spoken; shall we do as he advises? If
not, you speak." 7Then Hushai said
to Ab´salom, "This time the counsel
which Ahith´ophel has given is not
good." 8Hushai said moreover, "You
know that your father and his men
are mighty men, and that they are en-
raged, like a bear robbed of her cubs
in the field. Besides, your father is
expert in war; he will not spend the
night with the people. 9Behold, even
now he has hidden himself in one of
the pits, or in some other place. And
when some of the people fall[b] at the
first attack, whoever hears it will say,
'There has been a slaughter among
the people who follow Ab´salom.'
10Then even the valiant man, whose
heart is like the heart of a lion, will
utterly melt with fear; for all Israel
knows that your father is a mighty
man, and that those who are with him
are valiant men. 11But my counsel is
that all Israel be gathered to you, from
Dan to Beer-sheba, as the sand by the
sea for multitude, and that you go to
battle in person. 12So we shall come
upon him in some place where he is
to be found, and we shall light upon
him as the dew falls on the ground;
and of him and all the men with him
not one will be left. 13If he withdraws
into a city, then all Israel will bring
ropes to that city, and we shall drag it
into the valley, until not even a pebble
is to be found there." 14And Ab´salom
and all the men of Israel said, "The
counsel of Hushai the Archite is bet-
ter than the counsel of Ahith´ophel."
For the LORD had ordained to defeat
the good counsel of Ahith´ophel, so
that the LORD might bring evil upon
Ab´salom.

HUSHAI WARNS DAVID TO ESCAPE

15 Then Hushai said to Zadok and
Abi´athar the priests, "Thus and so
did Ahith´ophel counsel Ab´salom
and the elders of Israel; and thus and
so have I counseled. 16Now therefore
send quickly and tell David, 'Do not
lodge tonight at the fords of the wil-
derness, but by all means pass over;
lest the king and all the people who
are with him be swallowed up.'" 17Now
Jonathan and Ahim´a-az were wait-
ing at En-ro´gel; a maidservant used
to go and tell them, and they would
go and tell King David; for they must
not be seen entering the city. 18But
a lad saw them, and told Ab´salom;
so both of them went away quick-
ly, and came to the house of a man
at Bahu´rim, who had a well in his
courtyard; and they went down into
it. 19And the woman took and spread
a covering over the well's mouth, and
scattered grain upon it; and nothing
was known of it. 20When Ab´salom's
servants came to the woman at the
house, they said, "Where are Ahim´a-
az and Jonathan?" And the woman
said to them, "They have gone over
the brook[c] of water." And when they
had sought and could not find them,
they returned to Jerusalem.

21 After they had gone, the men
came up out of the well, and went and
told King David. They said to David,
"Arise, and go quickly over the wa-
ter; for thus and so has Ahith´ophel
counseled against you." 22Then
David arose, and all the people who
were with him, and they crossed the

[a] Gk: Heb *like the return of the whole] ([is]) [the man whom you seek*
[b] Or *when he falls upon them*
[c] The meaning of the Hebrew word is uncertain

Jordan; by daybreak not one was left
who had not crossed the Jordan.

23 When Ahith´ophel saw that his
counsel was not followed, he saddled
his ass, and went off home to his own
city. And he set his house in order,
and hanged himself; and he died, and
was buried in the tomb of his father.

24 Then David came to Mahana´im.
And Ab´salom crossed the Jordan with
all the men of Israel. 25Now Ab´salom
had set Ama´sa over the army instead
of Jo´ab. Ama´sa was the son of a man
named Ithra the Ish´maelite,[d] who
had married Ab´igal the daughter of
Nahash, sister of Zeru´iah, Jo´ab's
mother. 26And Israel and Ab´salom
encamped in the land of Gilead.

27 When David came to Maha-
na´im, Shobi the son of Nahash
from Rabbah of the Ammonites, and
Machir the son of Am´mi-el from Lo-
debar, and Barzil´lai the Gileadite
from Ro´gelim, 28brought beds, basins,
and earthen vessels, wheat, barley,
meal, parched grain, beans and len-
tils,[e] 29honey and curds and sheep and
cheese from the herd, for David and
the people with him to eat; for they
said, "The people are hungry and
weary and thirsty in the wilderness."

THE DEFEAT AND DEATH OF ABSALOM

18 Then David mustered the men
who were with him, and set over
them commanders of thousands and
commanders of hundreds. 2And David
sent forth the army, one third under
the command of Jo´ab, one third un-
der the command of Abi´shai the son
of Zeru´iah, Jo´ab's brother, and one
third under the command of It´tai the
Gittite. And the king said to the men,
"I myself will also go out with you."
3But the men said, "You shall not go
out. For if we flee, they will not care
about us. If half of us die, they will not
care about us. But you are worth ten
thousand of us;[f] therefore it is better
that you send us help from the city."
4The king said to them, "Whatever
seems best to you I will do." So the
king stood at the side of the gate,
while all the army marched out by
hundreds and by thousands. 5And the
king ordered Jo´ab and Abi´shai and
It´tai, "Deal gently for my sake with
the young man Ab´salom." And all
the people heard when the king gave
orders to all the commanders about
Ab´salom.

6 So the army went out into the
field against Israel; and the battle was
fought in the forest of E´phraim. 7And
the men of Israel were defeated there
by the servants of David, and the
slaughter there was great on that day,
twenty thousand men. 8The battle
spread over the face of all the country;
and the forest devoured more people
that day than the sword.

9 And Ab´salom chanced to meet
the servants of David. Ab´salom was
riding upon his mule, and the mule
went under the thick branches of a
great oak, and his head caught fast
in the oak, and he was left hanging[g]
between heaven and earth, while the
mule that was under him went on.
10And a certain man saw it, and told
Jo´ab, "Behold, I saw Ab´salom hang-
ing in an oak." 11Jo´ab said to the man
who told him, "What, you saw him!
Why then did you not strike him there
to the ground? I would have been glad
to give you ten pieces of silver and a
girdle." 12But the man said to Jo´ab,
"Even if I felt in my hand the weight
of a thousand pieces of silver, I would
not put forth my hand against the
king's son; for in our hearing the king
commanded you and Abi´shai and
It´tai, 'For my sake protect the young
man Ab´salom.' 13On the other hand,
if I had dealt treacherously against
his life[h] (and there is nothing hidden

[d] 1Chron 2. 17: Heb *Israelite*
[e] Heb *lentils and parched grain*
[f] Gk Vg Symmachus: Heb *for now there are ten thousand such as we*
[g] Gk Syr Tg: Heb *was put*
[h] Another reading is *at the risk of my life*

from the king), then you yourself would have stood aloof." 14 Jo´ab said, "I will not waste time like this with you." And he took three darts in his hand, and thrust them into the heart of Ab´salom, while he was still alive in the oak. 15 And ten young men, Jo´ab's armor-bearers, surrounded Ab´salom and struck him, and killed him.

16 Then Jo´ab blew the trumpet, and the troops came back from pursuing Israel; for Jo´ab restrained them. 17 And they took Ab´salom, and threw him into a great pit in the forest, and raised over him a very great heap of stones; and all Israel fled every one to his own home. 18 Now Ab´salom in his lifetime had taken and set up for himself the pillar which is in the King's Valley, for he said, "I have no son to keep my name in remembrance"; he called the pillar after his own name, and it is called Ab´salom's monument to this day.

DAVID HEARS OF ABSALOM'S DEATH

19 Then said Ahim´a-az the son of Zadok, "Let me run, and carry tidings to the king that the LORD has delivered him from the power of his enemies." 20 And Jo´ab said to him, "You are not to carry tidings today; you may carry tidings another day, but today you shall carry no tidings, because the king's son is dead." 21 Then Jo´ab said to the Cushite, "Go, tell the king what you have seen." The Cushite bowed before Jo´ab, and ran. 22 Then Ahim´a-az the son of Zadok said again to Jo´ab, "Come what may, let me also run after the Cushite." And Jo´ab said, "Why will you run, my son, seeing that you will have no reward for the tidings?" 23 "Come what may," he said, "I will run." So he said to him, "Run." Then Ahim´a-az ran by the way of the plain, and outran the Cushite.

24 Now David was sitting between the two gates; and the watchman went up to the roof of the gate by the wall, and when he lifted up his eyes and looked, he saw a man running alone. 25 And the watchman called out and told the king. And the king said, "If he is alone, there are tidings in his mouth." And he came apace, and drew near. 26 And the watchman saw another man running; and the watchman called to the gate and said, "See, another man running alone!" The king said, "He also brings tidings." 27 And the watchman said, "I think the running of the foremost is like the running of Ahim´a-az the son of Zadok." And the king said, "He is a good man, and comes with good tidings."

28 Then Ahim´a-az cried out to the king, "All is well." And he bowed before the king with his face to the earth, and said, "Blessed be the LORD your God, who has delivered up the men who raised their hand against my lord the king." 29 And the king said, "Is it well with the young man Ab´salom?" Ahim´a-az answered, "When Jo´ab sent your servant,[a] I saw a great tumult, but I do not know what it was." 30 And the king said, "Turn aside, and stand here." So he turned aside, and stood still.

DAVID MOURNS FOR ABSALOM

31 And behold, the Cushite came; and the Cushite said, "Good tidings for my lord the king! For the LORD has delivered you this day from the power of all who rose up against you." 32 The king said to the Cushite, "Is it well with the young man Ab´salom?" And the Cushite answered, "May the enemies of my lord the king, and all who rise up against you for evil, be like that young man." 33 [b] And the king was deeply moved, and went up to the chamber over the gate, and wept; and as he went, he said, "O my son Ab´salom, my son, my son Ab´salom! Would I had died instead of you, O Ab´salom, my son, my son!"

[a] Heb *the king's servant, your servant*
[b] Ch 19.1 in Heb

19 It was told Jo´ab, "Behold, the
king is weeping and mourning
for Ab´salom." 2So the victory that
day was turned into mourning for
all the people; for the people heard
that day, "The king is grieving for his
son." 3And the people stole into the
city that day as people steal in who
are ashamed when they flee in bat-
tle. 4The king covered his face, and
the king cried with a loud voice, "O
my son Ab´salom, O Ab´salom, my
son, my son!" 5Then Jo´ab came into
the house to the king, and said, "You
have today covered with shame the
faces of all your servants, who have
this day saved your life, and the lives
of your sons and your daughters, and
the lives of your wives and your con-
cubines, 6because you love those who
hate you and hate those who love you.
For you have made it clear today that
commanders and servants are noth-
ing to you; for today I perceive that
if Ab´salom were alive and all of us
were dead today, then you would be
pleased. 7Now therefore arise, go out
and speak kindly to your servants;
for I swear by the LORD, if you do
not go, not a man will stay with you
this night; and this will be worse for
you than all the evil that has come
upon you from your youth until now."
8Then the king arose, and took his
seat in the gate. And the people were
all told, "Behold, the king is sitting in
the gate"; and all the people came be-
fore the king.

DAVID RECALLED TO JERUSALEM

Now Israel had fled every man
to his own home. 9And all the peo-
ple were at strife throughout all the
tribes of Israel, saying, "The king de-
livered us from the hand of our ene-
mies, and saved us from the hand of
the Philistines; and now he has fled
out of the land from Ab´salom. 10But
Ab´salom, whom we anointed over us,
is dead in battle. Now therefore why
do you say nothing about bringing the
king back?"

11 And King David sent this mes-
sage to Zadok and Abi´athar the
priests, "Say to the elders of Judah,
'Why should you be the last to bring
the king back to his house, when the
word of all Israel has come to the
king?[c] 12You are my kinsmen, you
are my bone and my flesh; why then
should you be the last to bring back
the king?' 13And say to Ama´sa, 'Are
you not my bone and my flesh? God do
so to me and more also, if you are not
commander of my army henceforth in
place of Jo´ab.'" 14And he swayed the
heart of all the men of Judah as one
man; so that they sent word to the
king, "Return, both you and all your
servants." 15So the king came back to
the Jordan; and Judah came to Gilgal
to meet the king and to bring the king
over the Jordan.

DAVID'S MERCY TO SHIMEI

16 And Shim´e-i the son of Gera,
the Benjaminite, from Bahu´rim,
made haste to come down with the
men of Judah to meet King David;
17and with him were a thousand men
from Benjamin. And Ziba the servant
of the house of Saul, with his fifteen
sons and his twenty servants, rushed
down to the Jordan before the king,
18and they crossed the ford[d] to bring
over the king's household, and to do
his pleasure. And Shim´e-i the son of
Gera fell down before the king, as he
was about to cross the Jordan, 19and
said to the king, "Let not my lord hold
me guilty or remember how your ser-
vant did wrong on the day my lord
the king left Jerusalem; let not the
king bear it in mind. 20For your ser-
vant knows that I have sinned; there-
fore, behold, I have come this day,
the first of all the house of Joseph to
come down to meet my lord the king."
21Abi´shai the son of Zeru´iah an-
swered, "Shall not Shim´e-i be put to

[c] Gk: Heb *to the king, to his house*
[d] Cn: Heb *the ford crossed*

death for this, because he cursed the
LORD's anointed?" 22But David said,
"What have I to do with you, you sons
of Zeru'iah, that you should this day
be as an adversary to me? Shall any
one be put to death in Israel this day?
For do I not know that I am this day
king over Israel?" 23And the king said
to Shim'e-i, "You shall not die." And
the king gave him his oath.

DAVID AND MEPHIBOSHETH MEET

24 And Mephib'osheth the son of
Saul came down to meet the king;
he had neither dressed his feet, nor
trimmed his beard, nor washed his
clothes, from the day the king de-
parted until the day he came back
in safety. 25And when he came from[a]
Jerusalem to meet the king, the king
said to him, "Why did you not go with
me, Mephib'osheth?" 26He answered,
"My lord, O king, my servant deceived
me; for your servant said to him,
'Saddle an ass for me,[b] that I may ride
upon it and go with the king.' For your
servant is lame. 27He has slandered
your servant to my lord the king. But
my lord the king is like the angel of
God; do therefore what seems good to
you. 28For all my father's house were
but men doomed to death before my
lord the king; but you set your ser-
vant among those who eat at your ta-
ble. What further right have I, then,
to cry to the king?" 29And the king
said to him, "Why speak any more
of your affairs? I have decided: you
and Ziba shall divide the land." 30And
Mephib'osheth said to the king, "Oh,
let him take it all, since my lord the
king has come safely home."

DAVID'S KINDNESS TO BARZILLAI

31 Now Barzil'lai the Gileadite
had come down from Ro'gelim;
and he went on with the king to
the Jordan, to escort him over the
Jordan. 32Barzil'lai was a very aged
man, eighty years old; and he had
provided the king with food while
he stayed at Mahana'im; for he was
a very wealthy man. 33And the king
said to Barzil'lai, "Come over with
me, and I will provide for you with
me in Jerusalem." 34But Barzil'lai said
to the king, "How many years have I
still to live, that I should go up with
the king to Jerusalem? 35I am this day
eighty years old; can I discern what is
pleasant and what is not? Can your
servant taste what he eats or what he
drinks? Can I still listen to the voice
of singing men and singing women?
Why then should your servant be an
added burden to my lord the king?
36Your servant will go a little way over
the Jordan with the king. Why should
the king recompense me with such a
reward? 37Pray let your servant return,
that I may die in my own city, near the
grave of my father and my mother. But
here is your servant Chimham; let him
go over with my lord the king; and do
for him whatever seems good to you."
38And the king answered, "Chimham
shall go over with me, and I will do
for him whatever seems good to you;
and all that you desire of me I will do
for you." 39Then all the people went
over the Jordan, and the king went
over; and the king kissed Barzil'lai
and blessed him, and he returned to
his own home. 40The king went on to
Gilgal, and Chimham went on with
him; all the people of Judah, and also
half the people of Israel, brought the
king on his way.

41 Then all the men of Israel came
to the king, and said to the king, "Why
have our brethren the men of Judah
stolen you away, and brought the king
and his household over the Jordan,
and all David's men with him?" 42All
the men of Judah answered the men
of Israel, "Because the king is near
of kin to us. Why then are you angry
over this matter? Have we eaten at all
at the king's expense? Or has he given
us any gift?" 43And the men of Israel

[a]Heb *to*
[b]Gk Syr Vg: Heb *said, I will saddle an ass for myself*

answered the men of Judah, "We have
ten shares in the king, and in David
also we have more than you. Why
then did you despise us? Were we not
the first to speak of bringing back our
king?" But the words of the men of
Judah were fiercer than the words of
the men of Israel.

THE REBELLION OF SHEBA

20 Now there happened to be there
a worthless fellow, whose name
was Sheba, the son of Bichri, a
Benjaminite; and he blew the trumpet, and said,

"We have no portion in David,
and we have no inheritance
in the son of Jesse;
every man to his tents, O
Israel!"

2 So all the men of Israel withdrew
from David, and followed Sheba the
son of Bichri; but the men of Judah
followed their king steadfastly from
the Jordan to Jerusalem.

3 And David came to his house at
Jerusalem; and the king took the ten
concubines whom he had left to care
for the house, and put them in a house
under guard, and provided for them,
but did not go in to them. So they
were shut up until the day of their
death, living as if in widowhood.

4 Then the king said to Ama'sa,
"Call the men of Judah together to me
within three days, and be here yourself."
5 So Ama'sa went to summon
Judah; but he delayed beyond the set
time which had been appointed him.
6 And David said to Abi'shai, "Now
Sheba the son of Bichri will do us
more harm than Ab'salom; take your
lord's servants and pursue him, lest he
get himself fortified cities, and cause
us trouble."[c] 7 And there went out after
Abi'shai, Jo'ab[d] and the Cher'ethites
and the Pel'ethites, and all the mighty
men; they went out from Jerusalem to
pursue Sheba the son of Bichri. 8 When
they were at the great stone which is
in Gibeon, Ama'sa came to meet them.
Now Jo'ab was wearing a soldier's garment,
and over it was a girdle with a
sword in its sheath fastened upon his
loins, and as he went forward it fell
out. 9 And Jo'ab said to Ama'sa, "Is it
well with you, my brother?" And Jo'ab
took Ama'sa by the beard with his
right hand to kiss him. 10 But Ama'sa
did not observe the sword which was
in Jo'ab's hand; so Jo'ab struck him
with it in the body, and shed his bowels
to the ground, without striking a
second blow; and he died.* Then Jo'ab
and Abi'shai his brother pursued
Sheba the son of Bichri. 11 And one of
Jo'ab's men took his stand by Ama'sa,
and said, "Whoever favors Jo'ab, and
whoever is for David, let him follow
Jo'ab." 12 And Ama'sa lay wallowing in
his blood in the highway. And any one
who came by, seeing him, stopped;[e]
and when the man saw that all the
people stopped, he carried Ama'sa
out of the highway into the field, and
threw a garment over him. 13 When he
was taken out of the highway, all the
people went on after Jo'ab to pursue
Sheba the son of Bichri.

14 And Sheba passed through all
the tribes of Israel to Abel of Beth-ma'acah;[f]
and all the Bichrites[g] assembled,
and followed him in. 15 And
all the men who were with Jo'ab
came and besieged him in Abel of
Beth-ma'acah; they cast up a mound
against the city, and it stood against
the rampart; and they were battering
the wall, to throw it down. 16 Then a
wise woman called from the city,
"Hear! Hear! Tell Jo'ab, 'Come here,
that I may speak to you.'" 17 And he
came near her; and the woman said,
"Are you Jo'ab?" He answered, "I am."
Then she said to him, "Listen to the
words of your maidservant." And he

[c] Tg: Heb *snatch away our eyes*
[d] Cn Compare Gk: Heb *after him Joab's men*
[e] This clause is transposed from the end of the verse
[f] With 20.15: Heb *and Beth-maacah*
[g] Heb *Berites*

answered, "I am listening." 18Then
she said, "They were wont to say in
old time, 'Let them but ask counsel
at Abel'; and so they settled a matter.
19I am one of those who are peaceable
and faithful in Israel; you seek to de-
stroy a city which is a mother in Israel;
why will you swallow up the heritage
of the LORD?" 20Jo´ab answered, "Far
be it from me, far be it, that I should
swallow up or destroy! 21That is not
true. But a man of the hill country
of E´phraim, called Sheba the son of
Bichri, has lifted up his hand against
King David; give up him alone, and
I will withdraw from the city." And
the woman said to Jo´ab, "Behold, his
head shall be thrown to you over the
wall." 22Then the woman went to all
the people in her wisdom. And they
cut off the head of Sheba the son of
Bichri, and threw it out to Jo´ab. So he
blew the trumpet, and they dispersed
from the city, every man to his home.
And Jo´ab returned to Jerusalem to
the king.

23 Now Jo´ab was in command of
all the army of Israel; and Benai´ah the
son of Jehoi´ada was in command of
the Cher´ethites and the Pel´ethites;
24and Ador´am was in charge of the
forced labor; and Jehosh´aphat the
son of Ahi´lud was the recorder; 25and
Sheva was secretary; and Zadok and
Abi´athar were priests; 26and Ira the
Ja´irite was also David's priest.

DAVID AVENGES THE GIBEONITES

21 Now there was a famine in the
days of David for three years,
year after year; and David sought
the face of the LORD. And the LORD
said, "There is bloodguilt on Saul
and on his house, because he put
the Gib´eonites to death." 2So the
king called the Gib´eonites.[a] Now
the Gib´eonites were not of the peo-
ple of Israel, but of the remnant of
the Amorites; although the people of
Israel had sworn to spare them, Saul
had sought to slay them in his zeal
for the people of Israel and Judah.
3And David said to the Gib´eonites,
"What shall I do for you? And how
shall I make expiation, that you may
bless the heritage of the LORD?" 4The
Gib´eonites said to him, "It is not a
matter of silver or gold between us
and Saul or his house; neither is it for
us to put any man to death in Israel."
And he said, "What do you say that
I shall do for you?" 5They said to the
king, "The man who consumed us
and planned to destroy us, so that we
should have no place in all the terri-
tory of Israel, 6let seven of his sons be
given to us, so that we may hang them
up before the LORD at Gibeon on the
mountain of the LORD."[b] And the king
said, "I will give them."

7 But the king spared Mephib´o-
sheth, the son of Saul's son Jonathan,
because of the oath of the LORD which
was between them, between David
and Jonathan the son of Saul. 8The
king took the two sons of Rizpah the
daughter of Ai´ah, whom she bore to
Saul, Armo´ni and Mephib´osheth;
and the five sons of Merab[c] the daugh-
ter of Saul, whom she bore to A´dri-el
the son of Barzil´lai the Meho´lathite;
9and he gave them into the hands of
the Gib´eonites, and they hanged
them on the mountain before the
LORD, and the seven of them perished
together. They were put to death in
the first days of harvest, at the begin-
ning of barley harvest.

10 Then Rizpah the daughter of
Ai´ah took sackcloth, and spread
it for herself on the rock, from the
beginning of harvest until rain fell
upon them from the heavens; and she
did not allow the birds of the air to
come upon them by day, or the beasts
of the field by night. 11When David
was told what Rizpah the daugh-
ter of Ai´ah, the concubine of Saul,
had done, 12David went and took the
bones of Saul and the bones of his son

[a]Heb *the Gibeonites and said to them*
[b]Cn Compare Gk and 21.9: Heb *at Gibeah of Saul, the chosen of the* Lord
[c]Two Hebrew Mss Gk: Heb *Michal*

Jonathan from the men of Ja´besh-
gil´ead, who had stolen them from
the public square of Beth-shan, where
the Philistines had hanged them, on
the day the Philistines killed Saul
on Gilbo´a; 13and he brought up from
there the bones of Saul and the bones
of his son Jonathan; and they gathered
the bones of those who were hanged.
14And they buried the bones of Saul
and his son Jonathan in the land of
Benjamin in Zela, in the tomb of Kish
his father; and they did all that the
king commanded. And after that God
heeded supplications for the land.

EXPLOITS OF DAVID'S MEN

15 The Philistines had war again
with Israel, and David went down
together with his servants, and they
fought against the Philistines; and
David grew weary. 16And Ish´bi-
be´nob, one of the descendants of the
giants, whose spear weighed three
hundred shekels of bronze, and who
was girded with a new sword, thought
to kill David. 17But Abi´shai the son
of Zeru´iah came to his aid, and at-
tacked the Philistine and killed him.
Then David's men adjured him, "You
shall no more go out with us to battle,
lest you quench the lamp of Israel."

18 After this there was again war
with the Philistines at Gob; then
Sib´becai the Hu´shathite slew Saph,
who was one of the descendants of
the giants. 19And there was again
war with the Philistines at Gob; and
Elha´nan the son of Ja´are-or´egim,
the Bethlehemite, slew Goliath the
Gittite, the shaft of whose spear was
like a weaver's beam. 20And there was
again war at Gath, where there was
a man of great stature, who had six
fingers on each hand, and six toes
on each foot, twenty-four in number;
and he also was descended from the
giants. 21And when he taunted Israel,
Jonathan the son of Shim´e-i, David's
brother, slew him. 22These four were
descended from the giants in Gath;
and they fell by the hand of David and
by the hand of his servants.

DAVID'S SONG OF THANKSGIVING

22 And David spoke to the LORD
the words of this song on the day
when the LORD delivered him from
the hand of all his enemies, and from
the hand of Saul. 2He said,*

"The LORD is my rock, and
my fortress, and my
deliverer,
3my[d] God, my rock, in whom
I take refuge,
my shield and the horn of my
salvation,
my stronghold and my
refuge,
my savior; thou savest me
from violence.
4I call upon the LORD, who is
worthy to be praised,
and I am saved from my
enemies.

5"For the waves of death encom-
passed me,
the torrents of perdition
assailed me;
6the cords of Sheol entangled me,
the snares of death confront-
ed me.

7"In my distress I called upon the
LORD;
to my God I called.
From his temple he heard my
voice,
and my cry came to his ears.

8"Then the earth reeled and rocked;
the foundations of the heav-
ens trembled
and quaked, because he was
angry.
9Smoke went up from his nostrils,
and devouring fire from his
mouth;
glowing coals flamed forth
from him.
10He bowed the heavens, and came
down;
thick darkness was under
his feet.

[d]Gk Ps 18. 2: Heb lacks *my*

11He rode on a cherub, and flew;
he was seen upon the wings of the wind.
12He made darkness around him his canopy, thick clouds, a gathering of water.
13Out of the brightness before him coals of fire flamed forth.
14The LORD thundered from heaven,
and the Most High uttered his voice.
15And he sent out arrows, and scattered them;
lightning, and routed them.
16Then the channels of the sea were seen,
the foundations of the world were laid bare,
at the rebuke of the LORD,
at the blast of the breath of his nostrils.
17"He reached from on high, he took me,
he drew me out of many waters.
18He delivered me from my strong enemy,
from those who hated me;
for they were too mighty for me.
19They came upon me in the day of my calamity;
but the LORD was my stay.
20He brought me forth into a broad place;
he delivered me, because he delighted in me.
21"The LORD rewarded me according to my righteousness;
according to the cleanness of my hands he recompensed me.
22For I have kept the ways of the LORD,
and have not wickedly departed from my God.
23For all his ordinances were before me,
and from his statutes I did not turn aside.
24I was blameless before him,
and I kept myself from guilt.
25Therefore the LORD has recompensed me according to my righteousness,
according to my cleanness in his sight.
26"With the loyal thou dost show thyself loyal;
with the blameless man thou dost show thyself blameless;
27with the pure thou dost show thyself pure,
and with the crooked thou dost show thyself perverse.
28Thou dost deliver a humble people,
but thy eyes are upon the haughty to bring them down.
29Yea, thou art my lamp, O LORD,
and my God lightens my darkness.
30Yea, by thee I can crush a troop,
and by my God I can leap over a wall.
31This God—his way is perfect;
the promise of the LORD proves true;
he is a shield for all those who take refuge in him.
32"For who is God, but the LORD?
And who is a rock, except our God?
33This God is my strong refuge,
and has made[a] my[b] way safe.
34He made my[c] feet like hinds' feet,
and set me secure on the heights.
35He trains my hands for war,
so that my arms can bend a bow of bronze.
36Thou hast given me the shield of thy salvation,

[a] Ps 18. 32: Heb *set free*
[b] Another reading is *his*
[c] Another reading is *his*

and thy help[d] made me great.
37Thou didst give a wide place for
my steps under me,
and my feet[e] did not slip;
38I pursued my enemies and destroyed them,
and did not turn back until
they were consumed.
39I consumed them; I thrust them
through, so that they did
not rise;
they fell under my feet.
40For thou didst gird me with
strength for the battle;
thou didst make my assailants sink under me.
41Thou didst make my enemies
turn their backs to me,
those who hated me, and I
destroyed them.
42They looked, but there was none
to save;
they cried to the LORD, but
he did not answer
them.
43I beat them fine as the dust of
the earth,
I crushed them and stamped
them down like the
mire of the streets.
44"Thou didst deliver me from
strife with the peoples;[f]
thou didst keep me as the
head of the nations;
people whom I had not
known served me.
45Foreigners came cringing to me;
as soon as they heard of me,
they obeyed me.
46Foreigners lost heart,
and came trembling[g] out of
their fastnesses.
47"The LORD lives; and blessed be
my rock,
and exalted be my God, the
rock of my salvation,
48the God who gave me vengeance
and brought down peoples
under me,
49who brought me out from my
enemies;
thou didst exalt me above
my adversaries,
thou didst deliver me from
men of violence.
50"For this I will extol thee, O
LORD, among the nations,
and sing praises to thy name.
51Great triumphs he gives[h] to his
king,
and shows steadfast love to
his anointed,
to David, and his descendants for ever."

THE LAST WORDS OF DAVID

23 Now these are the last words of David:
The oracle of David, the son of
Jesse,
the oracle of the man who
was raised on high,
the anointed of the God of
Jacob,
the sweet psalmist of Israel:[i]
2"The Spirit of the LORD speaks
by me,
his word is upon my tongue.
3The God of Israel has spoken,
the Rock of Israel has said
to me:
When one rules justly over
men,
ruling in the fear of God,
4he dawns on them like the morning light,
like the sun shining forth
upon a cloudless
morning,
like rain[j] that makes grass
to sprout from the
earth.
5Yea, does not my house stand so
with God?

[d] Or *gentleness*
[e] Heb *ankles*
[f] Gk: Heb *from strife with my people*
[g] Ps 18. 45: Heb *girded themselves*
[h] Another reading is *He is a tower of salvation*
[i] Or *the favorite of the songs of Israel*
[j] Heb *from rain*

For he has made with me an
everlasting covenant,
ordered in all things and
secure.
For will he not cause to prosper
all my help and my desire?
6 But godless men[a] are all like
thorns that are thrown
away;
for they cannot be taken
with the hand;
7 but the man who touches them
arms himself with iron and
the shaft of a spear,
and they are utterly con-
sumed with fire."[b]

DAVID'S MIGHTY MEN

8 These are the names of the
mighty men whom David had: Josheb-
basshe´beth a Tah-che´monite; he
was chief of the three;[c] he wielded his
spear[d] against eight hundred whom he
slew at one time.

9 And next to him among the
three mighty men was Elea´zar the
son of Dodo, son of Aho´hi. He was
with David when they defied the
Philistines who were gathered there
for battle, and the men of Israel with-
drew. 10 He rose and struck down the
Philistines until his hand was weary,
and his hand cleaved to the sword;
and the LORD wrought a great victory
that day; and the men returned after
him only to strip the slain.

11 And next to him was Shammah,
the son of Agee the Har´arite. The
Philistines gathered together at Lehi,
where there was a plot of ground full
of lentils; and the men fled from the
Philistines. 12 But he took his stand in
the midst of the plot, and defended
it, and slew the Philistines; and the
LORD wrought a great victory.

13 And three of the thirty chief
men went down, and came about
harvest time to David at the cave of
Adul´lam, when a band of Philistines
was encamped in the valley of
Reph´aim. 14 David was then in the
stronghold; and the garrison of the
Philistines was then at Bethlehem.
15 And David said longingly, "O that
some one would give me water to
drink from the well of Bethlehem
which is by the gate!" 16 Then the three
mighty men broke through the camp
of the Philistines, and drew water out
of the well of Bethlehem which was by
the gate, and took and brought it to
David. But he would not drink of it; he
poured it out to the LORD, 17 and said,
"Far be it from me, O LORD, that I
should do this. Shall I drink the blood
of the men who went at the risk of
their lives?" Therefore he would not
drink it. These things did the three
mighty men.

18 Now Abi´shai, the brother of
Jo´ab, the son of Zeru´iah, was chief
of the thirty.[e] And he wielded his
spear against three hundred men and
slew them, and won a name beside the
three. 19 He was the most renowned
of the thirty,[f] and became their com-
mander; but he did not attain to the
three.

20 And Benai´ah the son of Jehoi´ada
was a valiant man[g] of Kabzeel, a doer
of great deeds; he smote two ariels[h] of
Moab. He also went down and slew a
lion in a pit on a day when snow had
fallen. 21 And he slew an Egyptian, a
handsome man. The Egyptian had a
spear in his hand; but Benai´ah went
down to him with a staff, and snatched
the spear out of the Egyptian's hand,
and slew him with his own spear.
22 These things did Benai´ah the son of
Jehoi´ada, and won a name beside the
three mighty men. 23 He was renowned

[a] Heb *worthlessness*
[b] Heb *fire in the sitting*
[c] Or *captains*
[d] 1Chron 11. 11: Heb obscure
[e] Two Hebrew Mss Syr: MT *three*
[f] 1Chron 11. 25: Heb *Was he the most renowned of the three?*
[g] Another reading is *the son of Ish-hai*
[h] The meaning of the word *ariel* is unknown

among the thirty, but he did not attain
to the three. And David set him over
his bodyguard.
24 As´ahel the brother of Jo´ab was
one of the thirty; Elha´nan the son
of Dodo of Bethlehem, 25 Shammah
of Harod, Eli´ka of Harod, 26 Helez
the Paltite, Ira the son of Ikkesh
of Teko´a, 27 Abie´zer, of An´athoth,
Mebun´nai the Hu´shathite, 28 Zalmon
the Aho´hite, Ma´harai of Netoph´ah,
29 Heleb the son of Ba´anah of Ne-
toph´ah, It´tai the son of Ri´bai of
Gib´e-ah of the Benjaminites, 30 Be-
nai´ah of Pira´thon, Hid´dai of the
brooks of Ga´ash, 31 Abi-al´bon the
Ar´bathite, Az´maveth of Bahu´rim,
32 Eli´ahba of Sha-al´bon, the sons
of Jashen, Jonathan, 33 Shammah the
Har´arite, Ahi´am the son of Sharar
the Har´arite, 34 Eliph´elet the son of
Ahas´bai of Ma´acah, Eli´am the son
of Ahith´ophel of Gilo, 35 Hezro[i] of
Carmel, Pa´arai the Arbite, 36 Igal the
son of Nathan of Zobah, Bani the
Gadite, 37 Zelek the Ammonite, Na´-
harai of Be-er´oth, the armor-bearer
of Jo´ab the son of Zeru´iah, 38 Ira the
Ithrite, Gareb the Ithrite, 39 Uri´ah the
Hittite: thirty-seven in all.

DAVID'S CENSUS OF ISRAEL AND JUDAH

24 Again the anger of the LORD was
kindled against Israel, and he in-
cited David against them, saying, "Go,
number Israel and Judah."* 2 So the
king said to Jo´ab and the commanders
of the army,[j] who were with him, "Go
through all the tribes of Israel, from
Dan to Beer-sheba, and number the
people, that I may know the number
of the people." 3 But Jo´ab said to the
king, "May the LORD your God add to
the people a hundred times as many
as they are, while the eyes of my lord
the king still see it; but why does my
lord the king delight in this thing?"
4 But the king's word prevailed against
Jo´ab and the commanders of the
army. So Jo´ab and the commanders of
the army went out from the presence
of the king to number the people of
Israel. 5 They crossed the Jordan, and
began from Aro´er,[k] and from the city
that is in the middle of the valley, to-
ward Gad and on to Jazer. 6 Then they
came to Gilead, and to Kadesh in the
land of the Hittites;[l] and they came to
Dan, and from Dan[m] they went around
to Sidon, 7 and came to the fortress of
Tyre and to all the cities of the Hivites
and Canaanites; and they went out
to the Negeb of Judah at Beer-sheba.
8 So when they had gone through all
the land, they came to Jerusalem at
the end of nine months and twenty
days. 9 And Jo´ab gave the sum of the
numbering of the people to the king:
in Israel there were eight hundred
thousand valiant men who drew the
sword, and the men of Judah were five
hundred thousand.

JUDGMENT ON DAVID'S SIN

10 But David's heart smote him
after he had numbered the people.
And David said to the LORD, "I have
sinned greatly in what I have done.
But now, O LORD, I pray thee, take
away the iniquity of thy servant; for I
have done very foolishly." 11 And when
David arose in the morning, the word
of the LORD came to the prophet Gad,
David's seer, saying, 12 "Go and say to
David, 'Thus says the LORD, Three
things I offer[n] you; choose one of
them, that I may do it to you.'" 13 So
Gad came to David and told him, and
said to him, "Shall three[o] years of
famine come to you in your land? Or
will you flee three months before your
foes while they pursue you? Or shall
there be three days' pestilence in your
land? Now consider, and decide what

[i] Another reading is *Hezrai*
[j] 1Chron 21. 2 Gk: Heb *to Joab the commander of the army*
[k] Gk: Heb *encamped in Aroer*
[l] Gk: Heb *to the land of Tahtim-hodshi*
[m] Cn Compare Gk: Heb *they came to Dan-jaan and*
[n] Or *hold over*
[o] 1Chron 21. 12 Gk: Heb *seven*

answer I shall return to him who sent
me." 14 Then David said to Gad, "I am
in great distress; let us fall into the
hand of the LORD, for his mercy is
great; but let me not fall into the hand
of man."

15 So the LORD sent a pestilence
upon Israel from the morning until
the appointed time; and there died
of the people from Dan to Beer-sheba
seventy thousand men. 16 And when
the angel stretched forth his hand
toward Jerusalem to destroy it, the
LORD repented of the evil, and said to
the angel who was working destruc-
tion among the people, "It is enough;
now stay your hand." And the angel
of the LORD was by the threshing
floor of Arau´nah the Jeb´usite. 17 Then
David spoke to the LORD when he saw
the angel who was smiting the peo-
ple, and said, "Lo, I have sinned, and
I have done wickedly; but these sheep,
what have they done? Let thy hand, I
pray thee, be against me and against
my father's house."

DAVID'S ALTAR ON THE THRESHING FLOOR

18 And Gad came that day to
David, and said to him, "Go up, rear
an altar to the LORD on the thresh-
ing floor of Arau´nah the Jeb´usite."
19 So David went up at Gad's word, as
the LORD commanded. 20 And when
Arau´nah looked down, he saw the
king and his servants coming on to-
ward him; and Arau´nah went forth,
and did obeisance to the king with his
face to the ground. 21 And Arau´nah
said, "Why has my lord the king come
to his servant?" David said, "To buy
the threshing floor of you, in order to
build an altar to the LORD, that the
plague may be averted from the peo-
ple." 22 Then Arau´nah said to David,
"Let my lord the king take and offer
up what seems good to him; here are
the oxen for the burnt offering, and
the threshing sledges and the yokes
of the oxen for the wood. 23 All this, O
king, Arau´nah gives to the king." And
Arau´nah said to the king, "The LORD
your God accept you." 24 But the king
said to Arau´nah, "No, but I will buy
it of you for a price; I will not offer
burnt offerings to the LORD my God
which cost me nothing." So David
bought the threshing floor and the
oxen for fifty shekels of silver. 25 And
David built there an altar to the LORD,
and offered burnt offerings and peace
offerings. So the LORD heeded suppli-
cations for the land, and the plague
was averted from Israel.

THE FIRST BOOK OF THE
KINGS

THE STRUGGLE FOR THE SUCCESSION

1 *Now King David was old and ad-
vanced in years; and although they
covered him with clothes, he could
not get warm. 2Therefore his servants
said to him, "Let a young maiden be
sought for my lord the king, and let
her wait upon the king, and be his
nurse; let her lie in your bosom, that
my lord the king may be warm." 3So
they sought for a beautiful maiden
throughout all the territory of Israel,
and found Ab´ishag the Shu´nammite,
and brought her to the king. 4The
maiden was very beautiful; and she
became the king's nurse and minis-
tered to him; but the king knew her
not.

5 Now Adoni´jah the son of Hag-
gith exalted himself, saying, "I will
be king";* and he prepared for him-
self chariots and horsemen, and fifty
men to run before him. 6His father
had never at any time displeased him
by asking, "Why have you done thus
and so?" He was also a very hand-
some man; and he was born next
after Ab´salom. 7He conferred with
Jo´ab the son of Zeru´iah and with
Abi´athar the priest; and they fol-
lowed Adoni´jah and helped him.
8But Zadok the priest, and Benai´ah
the son of Jehoi´ada, and Nathan the
prophet, and Shim´e-i, and Re´i, and
David's mighty men were not with
Adoni´jah.

9 Adoni´jah sacrificed sheep, oxen,
and fatlings by the Serpent's Stone,
which is beside En-ro´gel, and he in-
vited all his brothers, the king's sons,
and all the royal officials of Judah,
10but he did not invite Nathan the
prophet or Benai´ah or the mighty
men or Solomon his brother.

11 Then Nathan said to Bathshe´ba
the mother of Solomon, "Have you
not heard that Adoni´jah the son of
Haggith has become king and David
our lord does not know it? 12Now
therefore come, let me give you coun-
sel, that you may save your own life
and the life of your son Solomon. 13Go
in at once to King David, and say to
him, 'Did you not, my lord the king,
swear to your maidservant, saying,
"Solomon your son shall reign after
me, and he shall sit upon my throne"?
Why then is Adoni´jah king?' 14Then
while you are still speaking with the
king, I also will come in after you and
confirm your words."

15 So Bathshe´ba went to the
king into his chamber (now the
king was very old, and Ab´ishag the
Shu´nammite was ministering to the
king). 16Bathshe´ba bowed and did
obeisance to the king, and the king
said, "What do you desire?" 17She
said to him, "My lord, you swore to
your maidservant by the LORD your
God, saying, 'Solomon your son
shall reign after me, and he shall sit
upon my throne.' 18And now, behold,
Adoni´jah is king, although you, my
lord the king, do not know it. 19He has
sacrificed oxen, fatlings, and sheep
in abundance, and has invited all the
sons of the king, Abi´athar the priest,
and Jo´ab the commander of the army;
but Solomon your servant he has
not invited. 20And now, my lord the
king, the eyes of all Israel are upon
you, to tell them who shall sit on the
throne of my lord the king after him.
21Otherwise it will come to pass, when
my lord the king sleeps with his fa-
thers, that I and my son Solomon will
be counted offenders."

22 While she was still speaking
with the king, Nathan the prophet
came in. 23And they told the king,
"Here is Nathan the prophet." And
when he came in before the king, he
bowed before the king, with his face
to the ground. 24And Nathan said,

"My lord the king, have you said,
'Adoni´jah shall reign after me, and
he shall sit upon my throne'? 25 For
he has gone down this day, and has
sacrificed oxen, fatlings, and sheep
in abundance, and has invited all
the king's sons, Jo´ab the command-
er[a] of the army, and Abi´athar the
priest; and behold, they are eating
and drinking before him, and saying,
'Long live King Adoni´jah!' 26 But me,
your servant, and Zadok the priest,
and Benai´ah the son of Jehoi´ada,
and your servant Solomon, he has
not invited. 27 Has this thing been
brought about by my lord the king and
you have not told your servants who
should sit on the throne of my lord the
king after him?"

THE ACCESSION OF SOLOMON

28 Then King David answered,
"Call Bathshe´ba to me." So she came
into the king's presence, and stood
before the king. 29 And the king swore,
saying, "As the LORD lives, who has
redeemed my soul out of every adver-
sity, 30 as I swore to you by the LORD,
the God of Israel, saying, 'Solomon
your son shall reign after me, and he
shall sit upon my throne in my stead';
even so will I do this day." 31 Then
Bathshe´ba bowed with her face to the
ground, and did obeisance to the king,
and said, "May my lord King David
live for ever!"

32 King David said, "Call to me
Zadok the priest, Nathan the prophet,
and Benai´ah the son of Jehoi´ada."
So they came before the king. 33 And
the king said to them, "Take with you
the servants of your lord, and cause
Solomon my son to ride on my own
mule, and bring him down to Gihon;
34 and let Zadok the priest and Nathan
the prophet there anoint him king over
Israel; then blow the trumpet, and say,
'Long live King Solomon!' 35 You shall
then come up after him, and he shall
come and sit upon my throne; for he
shall be king in my stead; and I have
appointed him to be ruler over Israel
and over Judah." 36 And Benai´ah the
son of Jehoi´ada answered the king,
"Amen! May the LORD, the God of my
lord the king, say so. 37 As the LORD
has been with my lord the king, even
so may he be with Solomon, and make
his throne greater than the throne of
my lord King David."

38 So Zadok the priest, Nathan
the prophet, and Benai´ah the son of
Jehoi´ada, and the Cher´ethites and
the Pel´ethites, went down and caused
Solomon to ride on King David's mule,
and brought him to Gihon. 39 There
Zadok the priest took the horn of oil
from the tent, and anointed Solomon.
Then they blew the trumpet; and
all the people said, "Long live King
Solomon!" 40 And all the people went
up after him, playing on pipes, and
rejoicing with great joy, so that the
earth was split by their noise.

41 Adoni´jah and all the guests who
were with him heard it as they fin-
ished feasting. And when Jo´ab heard
the sound of the trumpet, he said,
"What does this uproar in the city
mean?" 42 While he was still speaking,
behold, Jonathan the son of Abi´athar
the priest came; and Adoni´jah said,
"Come in, for you are a worthy man
and bring good news." 43 Jonathan an-
swered Adoni´jah, "No, for our lord
King David has made Solomon king;
44 and the king has sent with him
Zadok the priest, Nathan the prophet,
and Benai´ah the son of Jehoi´ada, and
the Cher´ethites and the Pel´ethites;
and they have caused him to ride on
the king's mule; 45 and Zadok the priest
and Nathan the prophet have anoint-
ed him king at Gihon; and they have
gone up from there rejoicing, so that
the city is in an uproar. This is the
noise that you have heard. 46 Solomon
sits upon the royal throne. 47 Moreover
the king's servants came to congrat-
ulate our lord King David, saying,
'Your God make the name of Solomon
more famous than yours, and make

[a]Gk: Heb *commanders*

his throne greater than your throne.'
And the king bowed himself upon the
bed. 48 And the king also said, 'Blessed
be the LORD, the God of Israel, who
has granted one of my offspring[b] to sit
on my throne this day, my own eyes
seeing it.'"

49 Then all the guests of Adoni'jah
trembled, and rose, and each went
his own way. 50 And Adoni'jah feared
Solomon; and he arose, and went, and
caught hold of the horns of the altar.
51 And it was told Solomon, "Behold,
Adoni'jah fears King Solomon; for lo,
he has laid hold of the horns of the al-
tar, saying, 'Let King Solomon swear
to me first that he will not slay his ser-
vant with the sword.'" 52 And Solomon
said, "If he prove to be a worthy man,
not one of his hairs shall fall to the
earth; but if wickedness is found in
him, he shall die." 53 So King Solomon
sent, and they brought him down from
the altar. And he came and did obei-
sance to King Solomon; and Solomon
said to him, "Go to your house."

DAVID'S INSTRUCTION TO SOLOMON

2 When David's time to die drew
near, he charged Solomon his son,
saying, 2 "I am about to go the way
of all the earth. Be strong, and show
yourself a man, 3 and keep the charge
of the LORD your God, walking in his
ways and keeping his statutes, his
commandments, his ordinances, and
his testimonies, as it is written in the
law of Moses, that you may prosper
in all that you do and wherever you
turn; 4 that the LORD may establish his
word which he spoke concerning me,
saying, 'If your sons take heed to their
way, to walk before me in faithfulness
with all their heart and with all their
soul, there shall not fail you a man on
the throne of Israel.'

5 "Moreover you know also what
Jo'ab the son of Zeru'iah did to me,
how he dealt with the two command-
ers of the armies of Israel, Abner the
son of Ner, and Ama'sa the son of
Jether, whom he murdered, aveng-
ing[c] in time of peace blood which had
been shed in war, and putting inno-
cent blood[d] upon the girdle about
my[e] loins, and upon the sandals on
my[f] feet. 6 Act therefore according to
your wisdom, but do not let his gray
head go down to Sheol in peace. 7 But
deal loyally with the sons of Barzil'lai
the Gileadite, and let them be among
those who eat at your table, for with
such loyalty they met me when I fled
from Ab'salom your brother. 8 And
there is also with you Shim'e-i the
son of Gera, the Benjaminite from
Bahu'rim, who cursed me with a
grievous curse on the day when I
went to Mahana'im; but when he
came down to meet me at the Jordan,
I swore to him by the LORD, saying,
'I will not put you to death with the
sword.' 9 Now therefore hold him not
guiltless, for you are a wise man; you
will know what you ought to do to
him, and you shall bring his gray head
down with blood to Sheol."

DEATH OF DAVID

10 Then David slept with his fa-
thers, and was buried in the city of
David. 11 And the time that David
reigned over Israel was forty years;
he reigned seven years in Hebron, and
thirty-three years in Jerusalem. 12 So
Solomon sat upon the throne of David
his father; and his kingdom was firm-
ly established.

SOLOMON CONSOLIDATES HIS REIGN

13 Then Adoni'jah the son of Hag-
gith came to Bathshe'ba the mother of
Solomon. And she said, "Do you come
peaceably?" He said, "Peaceably."
14 Then he said, "I have something to
say to you." She said, "Say on." 15 He

[b] Gk: Heb *one*
[c] Gk: Heb *placing*
[d] Gk: Heb *blood of war*
[e] Gk: Heb *his*
[f] Gk: Heb *his*

said, "You know that the kingdom was mine, and that all Israel fully expected me to reign; however the kingdom has turned about and become my brother's, for it was his from the LORD. 16 And now I have one request to make of you; do not refuse me." She said to him, "Say on." 17 And he said, "Pray ask King Solomon—he will not refuse you—to give me Ab´ishag the Shu´nammite as my wife." 18 Bathshe´ba said, "Very well; I will speak for you to the king."

19 So Bathshe´ba went to King Solomon, to speak to him on behalf of Adoni´jah. And the king rose to meet her, and bowed down to her; then he sat on his throne, and had a seat brought for the king's mother; and she sat on his right. 20 Then she said, "I have one small request to make of you; do not refuse me." And the king said to her, "Make your request, my mother; for I will not refuse you." 21 She said, "Let Ab´ishag the Shu´nammite be given to Adoni´jah your brother as his wife." 22 King Solomon answered his mother, "And why do you ask Ab´ishag the Shu´nammite for Adoni´jah? Ask for him the kingdom also; for he is my elder brother, and on his side are Abi´athar[a] the priest and Jo´ab the son of Zeru´iah." 23 Then King Solomon swore by the LORD, saying, "God do so to me and more also if this word does not cost Adoni´jah his life! 24 Now therefore as the LORD lives, who has established me, and placed me on the throne of David my father, and who has made me a house, as he promised, Adoni´jah shall be put to death this day." 25 So King Solomon sent Benai´ah the son of Jehoi´ada; and he struck him down, and he died.

26 And to Abi´athar the priest the king said, "Go to An´athoth, to your estate; for you deserve death. But I will not at this time put you to death, because you bore the ark of the Lord GOD before David my father, and because you shared in all the affliction of my father." 27 So Solomon expelled Abi´athar from being priest to the LORD, thus fulfilling the word of the LORD which he had spoken concerning the house of Eli in Shiloh.

28 When the news came to Jo´ab—for Jo´ab had supported Adoni´jah although he had not supported Ab´salom—Jo´ab fled to the tent of the LORD and caught hold of the horns of the altar. 29 And when it was told King Solomon, "Jo´ab has fled to the tent of the LORD, and behold, he is beside the altar," Solomon sent Benai´ah the son of Jehoi´ada, saying, "Go, strike him down." 30 So Benai´ah came to the tent of the LORD, and said to him, "The king commands, 'Come forth.'" But he said, "No, I will die here." Then Benai´ah brought the king word again, saying, "Thus said Jo´ab, and thus he answered me." 31 The king replied to him, "Do as he has said, strike him down and bury him; and thus take away from me and from my father's house the guilt for the blood which Jo´ab shed without cause. 32 The LORD will bring back his bloody deeds upon his own head, because, without the knowledge of my father David, he attacked and slew with the sword two men more righteous and better than himself, Abner the son of Ner, commander of the army of Israel, and Ama´sa the son of Jether, commander of the army of Judah. 33 So shall their blood come back upon the head of Jo´ab and upon the head of his descendants for ever; but to David, and to his descendants, and to his house, and to his throne, there shall be peace from the LORD for evermore." 34 Then Benai´ah the son of Jehoi´ada went up, and struck him down and killed him; and he was buried in his own house in the wilderness. 35 The king put Benai´ah the son of Jehoi´ada over the army in place of Jo´ab, and the king put Zadok the priest in the place of Abi´athar.

36 Then the king sent and summoned Shim´e-i, and said to him,

[a] Gk Syr Vg: Heb *and for him and for Abiathar*

"Build yourself a house in Jerusalem,
and dwell there, and do not go forth
from there to any place whatever. 37For
on the day you go forth, and cross the
brook Kidron, know for certain that
you shall die; your blood shall be upon
your own head." 38And Shim'e-i said
to the king, "What you say is good;
as my lord the king has said, so will
your servant do." So Shim'e-i dwelt in
Jerusalem many days.

39 But it happened at the end of
three years that two of Shim'e-i's
slaves ran away to Achish, son of
Ma'acah, king of Gath. And when
it was told Shim'e-i, "Behold, your
slaves are in Gath," 40Shim'e-i arose
and saddled an ass, and went to
Gath to Achish, to seek his slaves;
Shim'e-i went and brought his slaves
from Gath. 41And when Solomon was
told that Shim'e-i had gone from
Jerusalem to Gath and returned, 42the
king sent and summoned Shim'e-i,
and said to him, "Did I not make you
swear by the LORD, and solemnly ad-
monish you, saying, 'Know for certain
that on the day you go forth and go
to any place whatever, you shall die'?
And you said to me, 'What you say is
good; I obey.' 43Why then have you not
kept your oath to the LORD and the
commandment with which I charged
you?" 44The king also said to Shim'e-i,
"You know in your own heart all the
evil that you did to David my father;
so the LORD will bring back your
evil upon your own head. 45But King
Solomon shall be blessed, and the
throne of David shall be established
before the LORD for ever." 46Then the
king commanded Benai'ah the son of
Jehoi'ada; and he went out and struck
him down, and he died.

So the kingdom was established in
the hand of Solomon.

SOLOMON'S PRAYER FOR WISDOM

3 *Solomon made a marriage alliance
with Pharaoh king of Egypt; he took
Pharaoh's daughter, and brought her
into the city of David, until he had
finished building his own house and
the house of the LORD and the wall
around Jerusalem. 2The people were
sacrificing at the high places, how-
ever, because no house had yet been
built for the name of the LORD.

3 Solomon loved the LORD, walk-
ing in the statutes of David his father;
only, he sacrificed and burnt incense at
the high places. 4And the king went to
Gibeon to sacrifice there, for that was
the great high place; Solomon used
to offer a thousand burnt offerings
upon that altar. 5At Gibeon the LORD
appeared to Solomon in a dream* by
night; and God said, "Ask what I shall
give you." 6And Solomon said, "Thou
hast shown great and steadfast love to
thy servant David my father, because
he walked before thee in faithfulness,
in righteousness, and in uprightness
of heart toward thee; and thou hast
kept for him this great and steadfast
love, and hast given him a son to sit on
his throne this day. 7And now, O LORD
my God, thou hast made thy servant
king in place of David my father, al-
though I am but a little child; I do not
know how to go out or come in. 8And
thy servant is in the midst of thy peo-
ple whom thou hast chosen, a great
people, that cannot be numbered or
counted for multitude. 9Give thy ser-
vant therefore an understanding mind
to govern thy people, that I may dis-
cern between good and evil; for who is
able to govern this thy great people?"

10 It pleased the Lord that Solomon
had asked this. 11And God said to
him, "Because you have asked this,
and have not asked for yourself long
life or riches or the life of your ene-
mies, but have asked for yourself un-
derstanding to discern what is right,
12behold, I now do according to your
word. Behold, I give you a wise and
discerning mind, so that none like you
has been before you and none like you
shall arise after you. 13I give you also
what you have not asked, both riches
and honor, so that no other king shall
compare with you, all your days. 14And

if you will walk in my ways, keeping
my statutes and my commandments,
as your father David walked, then I
will lengthen your days."
15 And Solomon awoke, and be-
hold, it was a dream. Then he came
to Jerusalem, and stood before the
ark of the covenant of the LORD, and
offered up burnt offerings and peace
offerings, and made a feast for all his
servants.

SOLOMON'S WISDOM IN JUDGMENT

16 Then two harlots came to the
king, and stood before him. 17 The one
woman said, "Oh, my lord, this woman
and I dwell in the same house; and I
gave birth to a child while she was in
the house. 18 Then on the third day after
I was delivered, this woman also gave
birth; and we were alone; there was no
one else with us in the house, only we
two were in the house. 19 And this wom-
an's son died in the night, because she
lay on it. 20 And she arose at midnight,
and took my son from beside me, while
your maidservant slept, and laid it in
her bosom, and laid her dead son in my
bosom. 21 When I rose in the morning
to nurse my child, behold, it was dead;
but when I looked at it closely in the
morning, behold, it was not the child
that I had borne." 22 But the other wom-
an said, "No, the living child is mine,
and the dead child is yours." The first
said, "No, the dead child is yours, and
the living child is mine." Thus they
spoke before the king.
23 Then the king said, "The one
says, 'This is my son that is alive,
and your son is dead'; and the other
says, 'No; but your son is dead, and
my son is the living one.'" 24 And the
king said, "Bring me a sword." So a
sword was brought before the king.
25 And the king said, "Divide the liv-
ing child in two, and give half to the
one, and half to the other." 26 Then the
woman whose son was alive said to
the king, because her heart yearned
for her son, "Oh, my lord, give her the
living child, and by no means slay it."
But the other said, "It shall be neither
mine nor yours; divide it." 27 Then the
king answered and said, "Give the liv-
ing child to the first woman, and by
no means slay it; she is its mother."
28 And all Israel heard of the judgment
which the king had rendered; and they
stood in awe of the king, because they
perceived that the wisdom of God was
in him, to render justice.

SOLOMON'S ADMINISTRATIVE OFFICERS

4 King Solomon was king over all
Israel, 2 and these were his high of-
ficials: Azari´ah the son of Zadok was
the priest; 3 Elihor´eph and Ahi´jah
the sons of Shisha were secretar-
ies; Jehosh´aphat the son of Ahi´lud
was recorder; 4 Benai´ah the son of
Jehoi´ada was in command of the
army; Zadok and Abi´athar were
priests; 5 Azari´ah the son of Nathan
was over the officers; Zabud the son of
Nathan was priest and king's friend;
6 Ahi´shar was in charge of the palace;
and Adoni´ram the son of Abda was in
charge of the forced labor.
7 Solomon had twelve officers
over all Israel, who provided food
for the king and his household; each
man had to make provision for one
month in the year. 8 These were their
names: Ben-hur, in the hill coun-
try of E´phraim; 9 Ben-deker, in Ma-
kaz, Sha-al´bim, Beth-she´mesh, and
E´lon-beth-ha´nan; 10 Ben-hesed, in
Arub´both (to him belonged Socoh
and all the land of Hepher); 11 Ben-
abin´adab, in all Naphath-dor (he had
Taphath the daughter of Solomon as
his wife); 12 Ba´ana the son of Ahi´lud,
in Ta´anach, Megid´do, and all Beth-
she´an which is beside Zarethan be-
low Jezre´el, and from Beth-she´an
to A´bel-meho´lah, as far as the oth-
er side of Jok´meam; 13 Ben-geber, in
Ra´moth-gil´ead (he had the villages
of Ja´ir the son of Manas´seh, which
are in Gilead, and he had the region
of Argob, which is in Bashan, sixty
great cities with walls and bronze
bars); 14 Ahin´adab the son of Iddo, in

Mahana´im; 15Ahim´a-az, in Naph´tali
(he had taken Bas´emath the daughter
of Solomon as his wife); 16Ba´ana the
son of Hushai, in Asher and Bealoth;
17Jehosh´aphat the son of Paru´ah, in
Is´sachar; 18Shim´e-i the son of Ela,
in Benjamin; 19Geber the son of Uri,
in the land of Gilead, the country of
Sihon king of the Amorites and of Og
king of Bashan. And there was one officer in the land of Judah.

MAGNIFICENCE OF SOLOMON'S RULE

20 Judah and Israel were as many
as the sand by the sea; they ate and
drank and were happy. 21[a] Solomon
ruled over all the kingdoms from
the Euphra´tes to the land of the
Philistines and to the border of Egypt;
they brought tribute and served
Solomon all the days of his life.

22 Solomon's provision for one
day was thirty cors of fine flour, and
sixty cors of meal, 23ten fat oxen, and
twenty pasture-fed cattle, a hundred
sheep, besides harts, gazelles, roebucks, and fatted fowl. 24For he had
dominion over all the region west
of the Euphra´tes from Tiphsah to
Gaza, over all the kings west of the
Euphra´tes; and he had peace on all
sides round about him. 25And Judah
and Israel dwelt in safety, from Dan
even to Beer-sheba, every man under
his vine and under his fig tree, all the
days of Solomon. 26Solomon also had
forty thousand stalls of horses for his
chariots, and twelve thousand horsemen. 27And those officers supplied
provisions for King Solomon, and for
all who came to King Solomon's table,
each one in his month; they let nothing be lacking. 28Barley also and straw
for the horses and swift steeds they
brought to the place where it was required, each according to his charge.

FAME OF SOLOMON'S WISDOM

29 And God gave Solomon wisdom
and understanding beyond measure,
and largeness of mind like the sand
on the seashore, 30so that Solomon's
wisdom surpassed the wisdom of all
the people of the east, and all the
wisdom of Egypt. 31For he was wiser
than all other men, wiser than Ethan
the Ez´rahite, and Heman, Calcol,
and Darda, the sons of Mahol; and
his fame was in all the nations round
about. 32He also uttered three thousand proverbs;* and his songs were a
thousand and five. 33He spoke of trees,
from the cedar that is in Lebanon to
the hyssop that grows out of the wall;
he spoke also of beasts, and of birds,
and of reptiles, and of fish. 34And men
came from all peoples to hear the
wisdom of Solomon, and from all the
kings of the earth, who had heard of
his wisdom.

PREPARATIONS AND MATERIALS FOR THE TEMPLE

5[b] Now Hiram king of Tyre sent his
servants to Solomon, when he heard
that they had anointed him king in
place of his father; for Hiram always
loved David. 2And Solomon sent word
to Hiram, 3"You know that David my
father could not build a house for the
name of the LORD his God because of
the warfare with which his enemies
surrounded him, until the LORD put
them under the soles of his feet. 4But
now the LORD my God has given me
rest on every side; there is neither
adversary nor misfortune. 5And so I
purpose to build a house for the name
of the LORD my God, as the LORD
said to David my father, 'Your son,
whom I will set upon your throne in
your place, shall build the house for
my name.' 6Now therefore command
that cedars of Lebanon be cut for me;
and my servants will join your servants, and I will pay you for your servants such wages as you set; for you
know that there is no one among us
who knows how to cut timber like the
Sido´nians."

[a]Ch 5.1 in Heb
[b]Ch 5.15 in Heb

7 When Hiram heard the words of
Solomon, he rejoiced greatly, and said,
"Blessed be the LORD this day, who
has given to David a wise son to be
over this great people." 8And Hiram
sent to Solomon, saying, "I have heard
the message which you have sent to
me; I am ready to do all you desire in
the matter of cedar and cypress tim-
ber. 9My servants shall bring it down
to the sea from Lebanon; and I will
make it into rafts to go by sea to the
place you direct, and I will have them
broken up there, and you shall receive
it; and you shall meet my wishes by
providing food for my household."
10So Hiram supplied Solomon with
all the timber of cedar and cypress
that he desired, 11while Solomon gave
Hiram twenty thousand cors of wheat
as food for his household, and twenty
thousand[a] cors of beaten oil. Solomon
gave this to Hiram year by year. 12And
the LORD gave Solomon wisdom, as
he promised him; and there was peace
between Hiram and Solomon; and the
two of them made a treaty.

13 King Solomon raised a levy of
forced labor out of all Israel; and the
levy numbered thirty thousand men.
14And he sent them to Lebanon, ten
thousand a month in relays; they
would be a month in Lebanon and two
months at home; Adoni′ram was in
charge of the levy. 15Solomon also had
seventy thousand burden-bearers and
eighty thousand hewers of stone in
the hill country, 16besides Solomon's
three thousand three hundred chief
officers who were over the work, who
had charge of the people who carried
on the work. 17At the king's com-
mand, they quarried out great, costly
stones in order to lay the foundation
of the house with dressed stones. 18So
Solomon's builders and Hiram's build-
ers and the men of Gebal did the hew-
ing and prepared the timber and the
stone to build the house.

SOLOMON BUILDS THE TEMPLE

6 In the four hundred and eightieth
year after the people of Israel came
out of the land of Egypt, in the fourth
year of Solomon's reign over Israel, in
the month of Ziv, which is the second
month, he began to build the house
of the LORD.* 2The house which King
Solomon built for the LORD was six-
ty cubits long, twenty cubits wide,
and thirty cubits high. 3The vestibule
in front of the nave of the house was
twenty cubits long, equal to the width
of the house, and ten cubits deep in
front of the house. 4And he made for
the house windows with recessed
frames. 5He also built a structure
against the wall of the house, running
round the walls of the house, both the
nave and the inner sanctuary; and he
made side chambers all around. 6The
lowest story[b] was five cubits broad,
the middle one was six cubits broad,
and the third was seven cubits broad;
for around the outside of the house he
made offsets on the wall in order that
the supporting beams should not be
inserted into the walls of the house.

7 When the house was built, it was
with stone prepared at the quarry; so
that neither hammer nor axe nor any
tool of iron was heard in the temple,
while it was being built.

8 The entrance for the lowest[c] sto-
ry was on the south side of the house;
and one went up by stairs to the mid-
dle story, and from the middle story to
the third. 9So he built the house, and
finished it; and he made the ceiling
of the house of beams and planks of
cedar. 10He built the structure against
the whole house, each story[d] five
cubits high, and it was joined to the
house with timbers of cedar.

11 Now the word of the LORD
came to Solomon, 12"Concerning
this house which you are building,
if you will walk in my statutes and
obey my ordinances and keep all my

[a] Gk: Heb *twenty*
[b] Gk: Heb *structure*
[c] Gk Tg: Heb *middle*
[d] Heb lacks *each story*

commandments and walk in them, then I will establish my word with you, which I spoke to David your father. 13 And I will dwell among the children of Israel, and will not forsake my people Israel."

14 So Solomon built the house, and finished it. 15 He lined the walls of the house on the inside with boards of cedar; from the floor of the house to the rafters[e] of the ceiling, he covered them on the inside with wood; and he covered the floor of the house with boards of cypress. 16 He built twenty cubits of the rear of the house with boards of cedar from the floor to the rafters,[f] and he built this within as an inner sanctuary, as the most holy place. 17 The house, that is, the nave in front of the inner sanctuary, was forty cubits long. 18 The cedar within the house was carved in the form of gourds and open flowers; all was cedar, no stone was seen. 19 The inner sanctuary he prepared in the innermost part of the house, to set there the ark of the covenant of the LORD. 20 The inner sanctuary[g] was twenty cubits long, twenty cubits wide, and twenty cubits high; and he overlaid it with pure gold. He also made[h] an altar of cedar. 21 And Solomon overlaid the inside of the house with pure gold, and he drew chains of gold across, in front of the inner sanctuary, and overlaid it with gold. 22 And he overlaid the whole house with gold, until all the house was finished. Also the whole altar that belonged to the inner sanctuary he overlaid with gold.

THE FURNISHINGS OF THE TEMPLE

23 In the inner sanctuary he made two cherubim of olivewood, each ten cubits high. 24 Five cubits was the length of one wing of the cherub, and five cubits the length of the other wing of the cherub; it was ten cubits from the tip of one wing to the tip of the other. 25 The other cherub also measured ten cubits; both cherubim had the same measure and the same form. 26 The height of one cherub was ten cubits, and so was that of the other cherub. 27 He put the cherubim in the innermost part of the house; and the wings of the cherubim were spread out so that a wing of one touched the one wall, and a wing of the other cherub touched the other wall; their other wings touched each other in the middle of the house. 28 And he overlaid the cherubim with gold.

29 He carved all the walls of the house round about with carved figures of cherubim and palm trees and open flowers, in the inner and outer rooms. 30 The floor of the house he overlaid with gold in the inner and outer rooms.

31 For the entrance to the inner sanctuary he made doors of olivewood; the lintel and the doorposts formed a pentagon.[i] 32 He covered the two doors of olivewood with carvings of cherubim, palm trees, and open flowers; he overlaid them with gold, and spread gold upon the cherubim and upon the palm trees.

33 So also he made for the entrance to the nave doorposts of olivewood, in the form of a square, 34 and two doors of cypress wood; the two leaves of the one door were folding, and the two leaves of the other door were folding. 35 On them he carved cherubim and palm trees and open flowers; and he overlaid them with gold evenly applied upon the carved work. 36 He built the inner court with three courses of hewn stone and one course of cedar beams.

37 In the fourth year the foundation of the house of the LORD was laid, in the month of Ziv. 38 And in the eleventh year, in the month of Bul,

[e] Gk: Heb *walls*
[f] Gk: Heb *walls*
[g] Vg: Heb *and before the inner sanctuary*
[h] Gk: Heb *covered*
[i] Heb obscure

which is the eighth month, the house
was finished in all its parts, and ac-
cording to all its specifications. He
was seven years in building it.

SOLOMON'S PALACE AND OTHER BUILDINGS

7 Solomon was building his own
house thirteen years, and he fin-
ished his entire house.

2 He built the House of the Forest
of Lebanon; its length was a hundred
cubits, and its breadth fifty cubits,
and its height thirty cubits, and it was
built upon three[a] rows of cedar pil-
lars, with cedar beams upon the pil-
lars. 3 And it was covered with cedar
above the chambers that were upon
the forty-five pillars, fifteen in each
row. 4 There were window frames in
three rows, and window opposite win-
dow in three tiers. 5 All the doorways
and windows[b] had square frames,
and window was opposite window in
three tiers.

6 And he made the Hall of Pillars;
its length was fifty cubits, and its
breadth thirty cubits; there was a
porch in front with pillars, and a can-
opy before them.

7 And he made the Hall of the
Throne where he was to pronounce
judgment, even the Hall of Judgment;
it was finished with cedar from floor
to rafters.[c]

8 His own house where he was
to dwell, in the other court back of
the hall, was of like workmanship.
Solomon also made a house like this
hall for Pharaoh's daughter whom he
had taken in marriage.

9 All these were made of costly
stones, hewn according to measure,
sawed with saws, back and front, even
from the foundation to the coping,
and from the court of the house of
the LORD[d] to the great court. 10 The
foundation was of costly stones, huge
stones, stones of eight and ten cubits.
11 And above were costly stones, hewn
according to measurement, and cedar.
12 The great court had three courses of
hewn stone round about, and a course
of cedar beams; so had the inner court
of the house of the LORD, and the ves-
tibule of the house.

PRODUCTS OF HIRAM THE BRONZEWORKER

13 And King Solomon sent and
brought Hiram from Tyre. 14 He was
the son of a widow of the tribe of
Naph´tali, and his father was a man of
Tyre, a worker in bronze; and he was
full of wisdom, understanding, and
skill, for making any work in bronze.
He came to King Solomon, and did all
his work.

15 He cast two pillars of bronze.
Eighteen cubits was the height of
one pillar, and a line of twelve cubits
measured its circumference; it was
hollow, and its thickness was four
fingers; the second pillar was the
same.[e] 16 He also made two capitals of
molten bronze, to set upon the tops
of the pillars; the height of the one
capital was five cubits, and the height
of the other capital was five cubits.
17 Then he made two[f] nets of checker
work with wreaths of chain work for
the capitals upon the tops of the pil-
lars; a net[g] for the one capital, and a
net[h] for the other capital. 18 Likewise
he made pomegranates;[i] in two rows
round about upon the one network,
to cover the capital that was upon the
top of the pillar; and he did the same
with the other capital. 19 Now the cap-
itals that were upon the tops of the

[a] Gk: Heb *four*
[b] Gk: Heb *posts*
[c] Syr Vg: Heb *floor*
[d] With 7.12: Heb *from the outside*
[e] Tg Syr Compare Gk and Jer 52. 21: Heb *and a line of twelve cubits measured the circumference of the second pillar*
[f] Gk: Heb lacks *he made two*
[g] Gk: Heb *seven*
[h] Gk: Heb *seven*
[i] With 2 Mss Compare Gk: Heb *pillars*

pillars in the vestibule were of lily-
work, four cubits. [20]The capitals were
upon the two pillars and also above
the rounded projection which was
beside the network; there were two
hundred pomegranates, in two rows
round about; and so with the other
capital. [21]He set up the pillars at the
vestibule of the temple; he set up the
pillar on the south and called its name
Jachin; and he set up the pillar on the
north and called its name Bo´az. [22]And
upon the tops of the pillars was lily-
work. Thus the work of the pillars was
finished.

23 Then he made the molten sea;
it was round, ten cubits from brim to
brim, and five cubits high, and a line
of thirty cubits measured its circum-
ference. [24]Under its brim were gourds,
for thirty[j] cubits, compassing the sea
round about; the gourds were in two
rows, cast with it when it was cast. [25]It
stood upon twelve oxen, three facing
north, three facing west, three facing
south, and three facing east; the sea
was set upon them, and all their hinder
parts were inward. [26]Its thickness was
a handbreadth; and its brim was made
like the brim of a cup, like the flower of
a lily; it held two thousand baths.

27 He also made the ten stands of
bronze; each stand was four cubits
long, four cubits wide, and three cu-
bits high. [28]This was the construction
of the stands: they had panels, and the
panels were set in the frames [29]and on
the panels that were set in the frames
were lions, oxen, and cherubim. Upon
the frames, both above and below the
lions and oxen, there were wreaths of
beveled work. [30]Moreover each stand
had four bronze wheels and axles of
bronze; and at the four corners were
supports for a laver. The supports
were cast, with wreaths at the side of
each. [31]Its opening was within a crown
which projected upward one cubit; its
opening was round, as a pedestal is
made, a cubit and a half deep. At its
opening there were carvings; and its
panels were square, not round. [32]And
the four wheels were underneath the
panels; the axles of the wheels were
of one piece with the stands; and the
height of a wheel was a cubit and a
half. [33]The wheels were made like a
chariot wheel; their axles, their rims,
their spokes, and their hubs, were all
cast. [34]There were four supports at
the four corners of each stand; the
supports were of one piece with the
stands. [35]And on the top of the stand
there was a round band half a cubit
high; and on the top of the stand its
stays and its panels were of one piece
with it. [36]And on the surfaces of its
stays and on its panels, he carved
cherubim, lions, and palm trees, ac-
cording to the space of each, with
wreaths round about. [37]After this
manner he made the ten stands; all
of them were cast alike, of the same
measure and the same form.

38 And he made ten lavers of
bronze; each laver held forty baths,
each laver measured four cubits, and
there was a laver for each of the ten
stands. [39]And he set the stands, five
on the south side of the house, and
five on the north side of the house;
and he set the sea at the southeast
corner of the house.

40 Hiram also made the pots, the
shovels, and the basins. So Hiram fin-
ished all the work that he did for King
Solomon on the house of the LORD:
[41]the two pillars, the two bowls of the
capitals that were on the tops of the
pillars, and the two networks to cov-
er the two bowls of the capitals that
were on the tops of the pillars; [42]and
the four hundred pomegranates for
the two networks, two rows of pome-
granates for each network, to cover
the two bowls of the capitals that were
upon the pillars; [43]the ten stands, and
the ten lavers upon the stands; [44]and
the one sea, and the twelve oxen un-
derneath the sea.

45 Now the pots, the shovels, and
the basins, all these vessels in the

[j]Heb *ten*

house of the LORD, which Hiram
made for King Solomon, were of bur-
nished bronze. 46In the plain of the
Jordan the king cast them, in the clay
ground between Succoth and Zare-
than. 47And Solomon left all the ves-
sels unweighed, because there were
so many of them; the weight of the
bronze was not found out.

48 So Solomon made all the vessels
that were in the house of the LORD:
the golden altar, the golden table for
the bread of the Presence, 49the lamp-
stands of pure gold, five on the south
side and five on the north, before
the inner sanctuary; the flowers, the
lamps, and the tongs, of gold; 50the
cups, snuffers, basins, dishes for in-
cense, and firepans, of pure gold; and
the sockets of gold, for the doors of
the innermost part of the house, the
most holy place, and for the doors of
the nave of the temple.

51 Thus all the work that King
Solomon did on the house of the LORD
was finished. And Solomon brought
in the things which David his father
had dedicated, the silver, the gold, and
the vessels, and stored them in the
treasuries of the house of the LORD.

DEDICATION OF THE TEMPLE

8 Then Solomon assembled the el-
ders of Israel and all the heads of
the tribes, the leaders of the fathers'
houses of the people of Israel, before
King Solomon in Jerusalem, to bring
up the ark of the covenant of the
LORD out of the city of David, which
is Zion. 2And all the men of Israel as-
sembled to King Solomon at the feast
in the month Eth'anim, which is the
seventh month. 3And all the elders
of Israel came, and the priests took
up the ark. 4And they brought up the
ark of the LORD, the tent of meeting,
and all the holy vessels that were in
the tent; the priests and the Levites
brought them up. 5And King Solomon
and all the congregation of Israel,
who had assembled before him, were
with him before the ark, sacrificing so
many sheep and oxen that they could
not be counted or numbered. 6Then
the priests brought the ark of the
covenant of the LORD to its place, in
the inner sanctuary of the house, in
the most holy place, underneath the
wings of the cherubim. 7For the cher-
ubim spread out their wings over the
place of the ark, so that the cherubim
made a covering above the ark and
its poles. 8And the poles were so long
that the ends of the poles were seen
from the holy place before the inner
sanctuary; but they could not be seen
from outside; and they are there to
this day. 9There was nothing in the ark
except the two tables of stone which
Moses put there at Horeb, where the
LORD made a covenant with the peo-
ple of Israel, when they came out of
the land of Egypt. 10And when the
priests came out of the holy place, a
cloud* filled the house of the LORD,
11so that the priests could not stand to
minister because of the cloud; for the
glory of the LORD filled the house of
the LORD.

12 Then Solomon said,
"The LORD has set the sun in
the heavens,
but[a] has said that he would
dwell in thick
darkness.
13I have built thee an exalted
house,
a place for thee to dwell in
for ever."

SOLOMON'S SPEECH

14Then the king faced about, and
blessed all the assembly of Israel,
while all the assembly of Israel stood.
15And he said, "Blessed be the LORD,
the God of Israel, who with his hand
has fulfilled what he promised with
his mouth to David my father, say-
ing, 16'Since the day that I brought my
people Israel out of Egypt, I chose no
city in all the tribes of Israel in which
to build a house, that my name might

[a] Gk: Heb lacks *has set the sun in the heavens, but*

be there; but I chose David to be over
my people Israel.' 17Now it was in the
heart of David my father to build a
house for the name of the LORD, the
God of Israel. 18But the LORD said to
David my father, 'Whereas it was in
your heart to build a house for my
name, you did well that it was in your
heart; 19nevertheless you shall not
build the house, but your son who
shall be born to you shall build the
house for my name.' 20Now the LORD
has fulfilled his promise which he
made; for I have risen in the place of
David my father, and sit on the throne
of Israel, as the LORD promised, and
I have built the house for the name
of the LORD, the God of Israel. 21And
there I have provided a place for the
ark, in which is the covenant of the
LORD which he made with our fa-
thers, when he brought them out of
the land of Egypt."

SOLOMON'S PRAYER OF DEDICATION

22 Then Solomon stood before the
altar of the LORD in the presence of
all the assembly of Israel, and spread
forth his hands toward heaven; 23and
said,* "O LORD, God of Israel, there
is no God like thee, in heaven above
or on earth beneath, keeping covenant
and showing steadfast love to thy ser-
vants who walk before thee with all
their heart; 24who hast kept with thy
servant David my father what thou
didst declare to him; yea, thou didst
speak with thy mouth, and with thy
hand hast fulfilled it this day. 25Now
therefore, O LORD, God of Israel,
keep with thy servant David my fa-
ther what thou hast promised him,
saying, 'There shall never fail you a
man before me to sit upon the throne
of Israel, if only your sons take heed
to their way, to walk before me as you
have walked before me.' 26Now there-
fore, O God of Israel, let thy word be
confirmed, which thou hast spoken to
thy servant David my father.

27 "But will God indeed dwell on
the earth? Behold, heaven and the
highest heaven cannot contain thee;
how much less this house which I
have built!* 28Yet have regard to the
prayer of thy servant and to his sup-
plication, O LORD my God, hearken-
ing to the cry and to the prayer which
thy servant prays before thee this day;
29that thy eyes may be open night and
day toward this house, the place of
which thou hast said, 'My name shall
be there,' that thou mayest hearken
to the prayer which thy servant offers
toward this place. 30And hearken thou
to the supplication of thy servant and
of thy people Israel, when they pray
toward this place; yea, hear thou in
heaven thy dwelling place; and when
thou hearest, forgive.

31 "If a man sins against his neigh-
bor and is made to take an oath, and
comes and swears his oath before
thine altar in this house, 32then hear
thou in heaven, and act, and judge
thy servants, condemning the guilty
by bringing his conduct upon his own
head, and vindicating the righteous
by rewarding him according to his
righteousness.

33 "When thy people Israel are de-
feated before the enemy because they
have sinned against thee, if they turn
again to thee, and acknowledge thy
name, and pray and make supplication
to thee in this house; 34then hear thou
in heaven, and forgive the sin of thy
people Israel, and bring them again
to the land which thou gavest to their
fathers.

35 "When heaven is shut up and
there is no rain because they have
sinned against thee, if they pray to-
ward this place, and acknowledge thy
name, and turn from their sin, when
thou dost afflict them, 36then hear
thou in heaven, and forgive the sin of
thy servants, thy people Israel, when
thou dost teach them the good way
in which they should walk; and grant
rain upon thy land, which thou hast
given to thy people as an inheritance.

37 "If there is famine in the land, if
there is pestilence or blight or mildew

or locust or caterpillar; if their enemy besieges them in any[a] of their cities; whatever plague, whatever sickness there is; 38 whatever prayer, whatever supplication is made by any man or by all thy people Israel, each knowing the affliction of his own heart and stretching out his hands toward this house; 39 then hear thou in heaven thy dwelling place, and forgive, and act, and render to each whose heart thou knowest, according to all his ways (for thou, thou only, knowest the hearts of all the children of men); 40 that they may fear thee all the days that they live in the land which thou gavest to our fathers.

41 "Likewise when a foreigner, who is not of thy people Israel, comes from a far country for thy name's sake 42 (for they shall hear of thy great name, and thy mighty hand, and of thy outstretched arm), when he comes and prays toward this house, 43 hear thou in heaven thy dwelling place, and do according to all for which the foreigner calls to thee; in order that all the peoples of the earth may know thy name and fear thee, as do thy people Israel, and that they may know that this house which I have built is called by thy name.

44 "If thy people go out to battle against their enemy, by whatever way thou shalt send them, and they pray to the LORD toward the city which thou hast chosen and the house which I have built for thy name, 45 then hear thou in heaven their prayer and their supplication, and maintain their cause.

46 "If they sin against thee—for there is no man who does not sin—and thou art angry with them, and dost give them to an enemy, so that they are carried away captive to the land of the enemy, far off or near; 47 yet if they lay it to heart in the land to which they have been carried captive, and repent, and make supplication to thee in the land of their captors, saying, 'We have sinned, and have acted perversely and wickedly'; 48 if they repent with all their mind and with all their heart in the land of their enemies, who carried them captive, and pray to thee toward their land, which thou gavest to their fathers, the city which thou hast chosen, and the house which I have built for thy name; 49 then hear thou in heaven thy dwelling place their prayer and their supplication, and maintain their cause 50 and forgive thy people who have sinned against thee, and all their transgressions which they have committed against thee; and grant them compassion in the sight of those who carried them captive, that they may have compassion on them 51 (for they are thy people, and thy heritage, which thou didst bring out of Egypt, from the midst of the iron furnace). 52 Let thy eyes be open to the supplication of thy servant, and to the supplication of thy people Israel, giving ear to them whenever they call to thee. 53 For thou didst separate them from among all the peoples of the earth, to be thy heritage, as thou didst declare through Moses, thy servant, when thou didst bring our fathers out of Egypt, O Lord GOD."

SOLOMON BLESSES THE ASSEMBLY

54 Now as Solomon finished offering all this prayer and supplication to the LORD, he arose from before the altar of the LORD, where he had knelt with hands outstretched toward heaven; 55 and he stood, and blessed all the assembly of Israel with a loud voice, saying, 56 "Blessed be the LORD who has given rest to his people Israel, according to all that he promised; not one word has failed of all his good promise, which he uttered by Moses his servant. 57 The LORD our God be with us, as he was with our fathers; may he not leave us or forsake us; 58 that he may incline our hearts to him, to walk in all his ways, and to keep his commandments, his statutes, and his ordinances, which

[a] Gk Syr: Heb *the land*

he commanded our fathers. 59 Let these
words of mine, wherewith I have made
supplication before the LORD, be near
to the LORD our God day and night,
and may he maintain the cause of his
servant, and the cause of his people
Israel, as each day requires; 60 that all
the peoples of the earth may know
that the LORD is God; there is no oth-
er. 61 Let your heart therefore be wholly
true to the LORD our God, walking in
his statutes and keeping his command-
ments, as at this day."

SOLOMON OFFERS SACRIFICES

62 Then the king, and all Israel
with him, offered sacrifice before the
LORD. 63 Solomon offered as peace of-
ferings to the LORD twenty-two thou-
sand oxen and a hundred and twen-
ty thousand sheep. So the king and
all the people of Israel dedicated the
house of the LORD. 64 The same day
the king consecrated the middle of the
court that was before the house of the
LORD; for there he offered the burnt
offering and the cereal offering and
the fat pieces of the peace offerings,
because the bronze altar that was be-
fore the LORD was too small to receive
the burnt offering and the cereal of-
fering and the fat pieces of the peace
offerings.

65 So Solomon held the feast at
that time, and all Israel with him, a
great assembly, from the entrance of
Hamath to the Brook of Egypt, be-
fore the LORD our God, seven days.[b]
66 On the eighth day he sent the people
away; and they blessed the king, and
went to their homes joyful and glad
of heart for all the goodness that the
LORD had shown to David his servant
and to Israel his people.

GOD APPEARS AGAIN TO SOLOMON

9 When Solomon had finished build-
ing the house of the LORD and the
king's house and all that Solomon
desired to build, 2 the LORD appeared
to Solomon a second time, as he had
appeared to him at Gibeon. 3 And the
LORD said to him,* "I have heard
your prayer and your supplication,
which you have made before me; I
have consecrated this house which
you have built, and put my name there
for ever; my eyes and my heart will
be there for all time. 4 And as for you,
if you will walk before me, as David
your father walked, with integrity of
heart and uprightness, doing accord-
ing to all that I have commanded you,
and keeping my statutes and my or-
dinances, 5 then I will establish your
royal throne over Israel for ever, as I
promised David your father, saying,
'There shall not fail you a man upon
the throne of Israel.' 6 But if you turn
aside from following me, you or your
children, and do not keep my com-
mandments and my statutes which I
have set before you, but go and serve
other gods and worship them, 7 then I
will cut off Israel from the land which
I have given them; and the house
which I have consecrated for my name
I will cast out of my sight; and Israel
will become a proverb and a byword
among all peoples. 8 And this house
will become a heap of ruins;[c] everyone
passing by it will be astonished, and
will hiss; and they will say, 'Why has
the LORD done thus to this land and
to this house?' 9 Then they will say,
'Because they forsook the LORD their
God who brought their fathers out of
the land of Egypt, and laid hold on
other gods, and worshiped them and
served them; therefore the LORD has
brought all this evil upon them.'"

10 At the end of twenty years, in
which Solomon had built the two
houses, the house of the LORD and
the king's house, 11 and Hiram king of
Tyre had supplied Solomon with cedar
and cypress timber and gold, as much
as he desired, King Solomon gave to
Hiram twenty cities in the land of
Galilee. 12 But when Hiram came from

[b] Gk: Heb *seven days and seven days, fourteen days*
[c] Syr Old Latin: Heb *high*

Tyre to see the cities which Solomon
had given him, they did not please
him. 13Therefore he said, "What kind
of cities are these which you have giv-
en me, my brother?" So they are called
the land of Cabul to this day. 14Hiram
had sent to the king one hundred and
twenty talents of gold.

OTHER ACTS OF SOLOMON

15 And this is the account of the
forced labor which King Solomon
levied to build the house of the LORD
and his own house and the Millo and
the wall of Jerusalem and Hazor and
Megid´do and Gezer 16(Pharaoh king
of Egypt had gone up and captured
Gezer and burnt it with fire, and had
slain the Canaanites who dwelt in
the city, and had given it as dowry
to his daughter, Solomon's wife; 17so
Solomon rebuilt Gezer) and Lower
Beth-hor´on 18and Ba´alath and Tamar
in the wilderness, in the land of
Judah,[a] 19and all the store-cities that
Solomon had, and the cities for his
chariots, and the cities for his horse-
men, and whatever Solomon desired
to build in Jerusalem, in Lebanon,
and in all the land of his dominion.
20All the people who were left of the
Amorites, the Hittites, the Per´izzites,
the Hivites, and the Jeb´usites, who
were not of the people of Israel 21their
descendants who were left after them
in the land, whom the people of Israel
were unable to destroy utterly—these
Solomon made a forced levy of slaves,
and so they are to this day. 22But of
the people of Israel Solomon made
no slaves; they were the soldiers, they
were his officials, his commanders,
his captains, his chariot commanders
and his horsemen.

23 These were the chief officers
who were over Solomon's work: five
hundred and fifty, who had charge of
the people who carried on the work.

24 But Pharaoh's daughter went
up from the city of David to her own
house which Solomon had built for
her; then he built the Millo.

25 Three times a year Solomon
used to offer up burnt offerings and
peace offerings upon the altar which
he built to the LORD, burning incense[b]
before the LORD. So he finished the
house.

SOLOMON'S COMMERCIAL ACTIVITY

26 King Solomon built a fleet of
ships at E´zion-ge´ber, which is near
Eloth on the shore of the Red Sea, in
the land of Edom. 27And Hiram sent
with the fleet his servants, seamen
who were familiar with the sea, to-
gether with the servants of Solomon;
28and they went to Ophir, and brought
from there gold, to the amount of four
hundred and twenty talents; and they
brought it to King Solomon.

VISIT OF THE QUEEN OF SHEBA

10 Now when the queen of Sheba*
heard of the fame of Solomon con-
cerning the name of the LORD, she
came to test him with hard questions.
2She came to Jerusalem with a very
great retinue, with camels bearing
spices, and very much gold, and pre-
cious stones; and when she came to
Solomon, she told him all that was on
her mind. 3And Solomon answered all
her questions; there was nothing hid-
den from the king which he could not
explain to her. 4And when the queen
of Sheba had seen all the wisdom of
Solomon, the house that he had built,
5the food of his table, the seating of
his officials, and the attendance of
his servants, their clothing, his cup-
bearers, and his burnt offerings which
he offered at the house of the LORD,
there was no more spirit in her.

6 And she said to the king, "The
report was true which I heard in my
own land of your affairs and of your
wisdom, 7but I did not believe the re-
ports until I came and my own eyes
had seen it; and behold, the half was

[a] Heb lacks *of Judah*
[b] Gk: Heb *burning incense with it which*

said to Ahi´jah, "Behold, the wife of Jerobo´am is coming to inquire of you concerning her son; for he is sick. Thus and thus shall you say to her."

When she came, she pretended to be another woman. 6But when Ahi´jah heard the sound of her feet, as she came in at the door, he said, "Come in, wife of Jerobo´am; why do you pretend to be another? For I am charged with heavy tidings for you. 7Go, tell Jerobo´am, 'Thus says the LORD, the God of Israel: "Because I exalted you from among the people, and made you leader over my people Israel, 8and tore the kingdom away from the house of David and gave it to you; and yet you have not been like my servant David, who kept my commandments, and followed me with all his heart, doing only that which was right in my eyes, 9but you have done evil above all that were before you and have gone and made for yourself other gods, and molten images, provoking me to anger, and have cast me behind your back; 10therefore behold, I will bring evil upon the house of Jerobo´am, and will cut off from Jerobo´am every male, both bond and free in Israel, and will utterly consume the house of Jerobo´am, as a man burns up dung until it is all gone. 11Any one belonging to Jerobo´am who dies in the city the dogs shall eat; and any one who dies in the open country the birds of the air shall eat; for the LORD has spoken it."' 12Arise therefore, go to your house. When your feet enter the city, the child shall die. 13And all Israel shall mourn for him, and bury him; for he only of Jerobo´am shall come to the grave, because in him there is found something pleasing to the LORD, the God of Israel, in the house of Jerobo´am. 14Moreover the LORD will raise up for himself a king over Israel, who shall cut off the house of Jerobo´am today. And henceforth[b] 15the LORD will smite Israel, as a reed is shaken in the water, and root up Israel out of this good land which he gave to their fathers, and scatter them beyond the Euphra´tes, because they have made their Ashe´rim, provoking the LORD to anger. 16And he will give Israel up because of the sins of Jerobo´am, which he sinned and which he made Israel to sin."

DEATH OF JEROBOAM

17 Then Jerobo´am's wife arose, and departed, and came to Tirzah. And as she came to the threshold of the house, the child died. 18And all Israel buried him and mourned for him, according to the word of the LORD, which he spoke by his servant Ahi´jah the prophet. 19Now the rest of the acts of Jerobo´am, how he warred and how he reigned, behold, they are written in the Book of the Chronicles of the Kings of Israel. 20And the time that Jerobo´am reigned was twenty-two years; and he slept with his fathers, and Nadab his son reigned in his stead.

REHOBOAM REIGNS OVER JUDAH

21 Now Rehobo´am the son of Solomon reigned in Judah. Rehobo´am was forty-one years old when he began to reign, and he reigned seventeen years in Jerusalem, the city which the LORD had chosen out of all the tribes of Israel, to put his name there. His mother's name was Na´amah the Ammonitess. 22And Judah did what was evil in the sight of the LORD, and they provoked him to jealousy with their sins which they committed, more than all that their fathers had done. 23For they also built for themselves high places, and pillars, and Ashe´rim on every high hill and under every green tree; 24and there were also male cult prostitutes in the land. They did according to all the abominations of the nations which the LORD drove out before the people of Israel.

25 In the fifth year of King Rehobo´am, Shishak king of Egypt

[b] Heb obscure

came up against Jerusalem; 26he took
away the treasures of the house of the
LORD and the treasures of the king's
house; he took away everything.
He also took away all the shields of
gold which Solomon had made; 27and
King Rehobo´am made in their stead
shields of bronze, and committed
them to the hands of the officers of
the guard, who kept the door of the
king's house. 28And as often as the
king went into the house of the LORD,
the guard bore them and brought
them back to the guardroom.

29 Now the rest of the acts of Reho-
bo´am, and all that he did, are they not
written in the Book of the Chronicles
of the Kings of Judah? 30And there
was war between Rehobo´am and
Jerobo´am continually. 31And Re-
hobo´am slept with his fathers and
was buried with his fathers in the city
of David. His mother's name was Na´-
amah the Ammonitess. And Abi´jam
his son reigned in his stead.

ABIJAM REIGNS OVER JUDAH: IDOLATRY AND WAR

15 Now in the eighteenth year of
King Jerobo´am the son of Ne-
bat, Abi´jam began to reign over Ju-
dah. 2He reigned for three years in
Jerusalem. His mother's name was
Ma´acah the daughter of Abish´alom.
3And he walked in all the sins which
his father did before him; and his
heart was not wholly true to the LORD
his God, as the heart of David his fa-
ther. 4Nevertheless for David's sake
the LORD his God gave him a lamp
in Jerusalem, setting up his son af-
ter him, and establishing Jerusalem;
5because David did what was right
in the eyes of the LORD, and did not
turn aside from anything that he
commanded him all the days of his
life, except in the matter of Uri´ah
the Hittite. 6Now there was war be-
tween Rehobo´am and Jerobo´am all
the days of his life. 7The rest of the
acts of Abi´jam, and all that he did,
are they not written in the Book of the
Chronicles of the Kings of Judah? And
there was war between Abi´jam and
Jerobo´am. 8And Abi´jam slept with
his fathers; and they buried him in the
city of David. And Asa his son reigned
in his stead.

ASA REIGNS OVER JUDAH

9 In the twentieth year of Jer-
obo´am king of Israel, Asa began to
reign over Judah, 10and he reigned for-
ty-one years in Jerusalem. His moth-
er's name was Ma´acah the daughter
of Abish´alom. 11And Asa did what
was right in the eyes of the LORD, as
David his father had done. 12He put
away the male cult prostitutes out of
the land, and removed all the idols
that his fathers had made. 13He also
removed Ma´acah his mother from be-
ing queen mother because she had an
abominable image made for Ashe´rah;
and Asa cut down her image and
burned it at the brook Kidron. 14But
the high places were not taken away.
Nevertheless the heart of Asa was
wholly true to the LORD all his days.
15And he brought into the house of the
LORD the votive gifts of his father and
his own votive gifts, silver, and gold,
and vessels.

ALLIANCE WITH ARAM AGAINST ISRAEL

16 And there was war between Asa
and Ba´asha king of Israel all their
days. 17Ba´asha king of Israel went up
against Judah, and built Ramah, that
he might permit no one to go out or
come in to Asa king of Judah. 18Then
Asa took all the silver and the gold that
were left in the treasures of the house
of the LORD and the treasures of the
king's house, and gave them into the
hands of his servants; and King Asa
sent them to Ben-ha´dad the son of
Tabrim´mon, the son of He´zi-on, king
of Syria, who dwelt in Damascus, say-
ing, 19"Let there be a league between
me and you, as between my father and
your father: behold, I am sending to
you a present of silver and gold; go,
break your league with Ba´asha king

of Israel, that he may withdraw from
me.” 20 And Ben-ha´dad hearkened to
King Asa, and sent the commanders of
his armies against the cities of Israel,
and conquered Ijon, Dan, A´bel-beth-
ma´acah, and all Chin´neroth, with
all the land of Naph´tali. 21 And when
Ba´asha heard of it, he stopped build-
ing Ramah, and he dwelt in Tirzah.
22 Then King Asa made a proclama-
tion to all Judah, none was exempt,
and they carried away the stones of
Ramah and its timber, with which
Ba´asha had been building; and with
them King Asa built Geba of Benjamin
and Mizpah. 23 Now the rest of all the
acts of Asa, all his might, and all that
he did, and the cities which he built,
are they not written in the Book of
the Chronicles of the Kings of Judah?
But in his old age he was diseased in
his feet. 24 And Asa slept with his fa-
thers, and was buried with his fathers
in the city of David his father; and
Jehosh´aphat his son reigned in his
stead.

NADAB REIGNS OVER ISRAEL

25 Nadab the son of Jerobo´am
began to reign over Israel in the sec-
ond year of Asa king of Judah; and
he reigned over Israel two years. 26 He
did what was evil in the sight of the
LORD, and walked in the way of his
father, and in his sin which he made
Israel to sin.

27 Ba´asha the son of Ahi´jah,
of the house of Is´sachar, conspired
against him; and Ba´asha struck
him down at Gib´bethon, which be-
longed to the Philistines; for Nadab
and all Israel were laying siege to
Gib´bethon. 28 So Ba´asha killed him
in the third year of Asa king of Judah,
and reigned in his stead. 29 And as soon
as he was king, he killed all the house
of Jerobo´am; he left to the house of
Jerobo´am not one that breathed, until
he had destroyed it, according to the
word of the LORD which he spoke by
his servant Ahi´jah the Shi´lonite; 30 it
was for the sins of Jerobo´am which
he sinned and which he made Israel
to sin, and because of the anger to
which he provoked the LORD, the God
of Israel.

31 Now the rest of the acts of
Nadab, and all that he did, are they not
written in the Book of the Chronicles
of the Kings of Israel? 32 And there was
war between Asa and Ba´asha king of
Israel all their days.

SECOND DYNASTY: BAASHA REIGNS OVER ISRAEL

33 In the third year of Asa king of
Judah, Ba´asha the son of Ahi´jah be-
gan to reign over all Israel at Tirzah,
and he reigned twenty-four years.
34 He did what was evil in the sight
of the LORD, and walked in the way
of Jerobo´am and in his sin which he
made Israel to sin.

16 And the word of the LORD came
to Jehu the son of Hana´ni against
Ba´asha, saying, 2 “Since I exalted you
out of the dust and made you leader
over my people Israel, and you have
walked in the way of Jerobo´am, and
have made my people Israel to sin,
provoking me to anger with their
sins, 3 behold, I will utterly sweep
away Ba´asha and his house, and I will
make your house like the house of
Jerobo´am the son of Nebat. 4 Any one
belonging to Ba´asha who dies in the
city the dogs shall eat; and any one of
his who dies in the field the birds of
the air shall eat.”

5 Now the rest of the acts of
Ba´asha, and what he did, and his
might, are they not written in the
Book of the Chronicles of the Kings
of Israel? 6 And Ba´asha slept with his
fathers, and was buried at Tirzah;
and Elah his son reigned in his stead.
7 Moreover the word of the LORD came
by the prophet Jehu the son of Hana´ni
against Ba´asha and his house, both
because of all the evil that he did in
the sight of the LORD, provoking him
to anger with the work of his hands, in
being like the house of Jerobo´am, and
also because he destroyed it.

ELAH REIGNS OVER ISRAEL

8 In the twenty-sixth year of Asa
king of Judah, Elah the son of Ba´asha
began to reign over Israel in Tirzah,
and he reigned two years. 9But his
servant Zimri, commander of half
his chariots, conspired against him.
When he was at Tirzah, drinking him-
self drunk in the house of Arza, who
was over the household in Tirzah,
10Zimri came in and struck him down
and killed him, in the twenty-seventh
year of Asa king of Judah, and reigned
in his stead.

11 When he began to reign, as
soon as he had seated himself on
his throne, he killed all the house of
Ba´asha; he did not leave him a single
male of his kinsmen or his friends.
12Thus Zimri destroyed all the house
of Ba´asha, according to the word of
the LORD, which he spoke against
Ba´asha by Jehu the prophet, 13for all
the sins of Ba´asha and the sins of
Elah his son which they sinned, and
which they made Israel to sin, provok-
ing the LORD God of Israel to anger
with their idols. 14Now the rest of the
acts of Elah, and all that he did, are
they not written in the Book of the
Chronicles of the Kings of Israel?

THIRD DYNASTY: ZIMRI REIGNS OVER ISRAEL

15 In the twenty-seventh year of
Asa king of Judah, Zimri reigned sev-
en days in Tirzah. Now the troops
were encamped against Gib´bethon,
which belonged to the Philistines,
16and the troops who were encamped
heard it said, "Zimri has conspired,
and he has killed the king"; therefore
all Israel made Omri, the commander
of the army, king over Israel that day
in the camp. 17So Omri went up from
Gib´bethon, and all Israel with him,
and they besieged Tirzah. 18And when
Zimri saw that the city was taken,
he went into the citadel of the king's
house, and burned the king's house
over him with fire, and died, 19because
of his sins which he committed, doing
evil in the sight of the LORD, walk-
ing in the way of Jerobo´am, and for
his sin which he committed, making
Israel to sin. 20Now the rest of the acts
of Zimri, and the conspiracy which
he made, are they not written in the
Book of the Chronicles of the Kings
of Israel?

FOURTH DYNASTY: OMRI REIGNS OVER ISRAEL

21 Then the people of Israel were
divided into two parts; half of the peo-
ple followed Tibni the son of Ginath,
to make him king, and half followed
Omri. 22But the people who followed
Omri overcame the people who fol-
lowed Tibni the son of Ginath; so Tibni
died, and Omri became king. 23In the
thirty-first year of Asa king of Judah,
Omri began to reign over Israel and he
reigned for twelve years; six years he
reigned in Tirzah. 24He bought the hill
of Samar´ia* from Shemer for two tal-
ents of silver; and he fortified the hill,
and called the name of the city which
he built, Samar´ia, after the name of
Shemer, the owner of the hill.

25 Omri did what was evil in the
sight of the LORD, and did more evil
than all who were before him. 26For he
walked in all the way of Jerobo´am the
son of Nebat, and in the sins which
he made Israel to sin, provoking the
LORD, the God of Israel, to anger by
their idols. 27Now the rest of the acts
of Omri which he did, and the might
that he showed, are they not writ-
ten in the Book of the Chronicles of
the Kings of Israel? 28And Omri slept
with his fathers, and was buried in
Samar´ia; and Ahab his son reigned
in his stead.

AHAB REIGNS OVER ISRAEL

29 In the thirty-eighth year of Asa
king of Judah, Ahab the son of Omri
began to reign over Israel, and Ahab
the son of Omri reigned over Israel
in Samar´ia twenty-two years. 30And

Ahab the son of Omri did evil in the
sight of the LORD more than all that
were before him. 31And as if it had
been a light thing for him to walk in
the sins of Jerobo´am the son of Nebat,
he took for wife Jez´ebel the daughter
of Ethba´al king of the Sido´nians,
and went and served Ba´al, and wor-
shiped him. 32He erected an altar for
Ba´al in the house of Ba´al, which he
built in Samar´ia. 33And Ahab made
an Ashe´rah. Ahab did more to pro-
voke the LORD, the God of Israel, to
anger than all the kings of Israel who
were before him. 34In his days Hi´el of
Bethel built Jericho; he laid its foun-
dation at the cost of Abi´ram his first-
born, and set up its gates at the cost of
his youngest son Segub, according to
the word of the LORD, which he spoke
by Joshua the son of Nun.

ELIJAH PREDICTS A DROUGHT

17 *Now Eli´jah the Tishbite, of
Tishbe[a] in Gilead, said to Ahab,
"As the LORD the God of Israel lives,
before whom I stand, there shall be
neither dew nor rain these years, ex-
cept by my word." 2And the word of
the LORD came to him, 3"Depart from
here and turn eastward, and hide
yourself by the brook Cherith, that
is east of the Jordan. 4You shall drink
from the brook, and I have command-
ed the ravens to feed you there." 5So
he went and did according to the word
of the LORD; he went and dwelt by
the brook Cherith that is east of the
Jordan. 6And the ravens brought him
bread and meat in the morning, and
bread and meat in the evening; and
he drank from the brook. 7And after
a while the brook dried up, because
there was no rain in the land.

THE WIDOW OF ZAREPHATH

8 Then the word of the LORD came
to him, 9"Arise, go to Zar´ephath,
which belongs to Sidon, and dwell
there. Behold, I have commanded
a widow there to feed you." 10So he
arose and went to Zar´ephath; and
when he came to the gate of the city,
behold, a widow was there gathering
sticks; and he called to her and said,
"Bring me a little water in a vessel,
that I may drink." 11And as she was
going to bring it, he called to her and
said, "Bring me a morsel of bread in
your hand." 12And she said, "As the
LORD your God lives, I have nothing
baked, only a handful of meal in a jar,
and a little oil in a cruse; and now, I
am gathering a couple of sticks, that
I may go in and prepare it for myself
and my son, that we may eat it, and
die." 13And Eli´jah said to her, "Fear
not; go and do as you have said; but
first make me a little cake of it and
bring it to me, and afterward make
for yourself and your son. 14For thus
says the LORD the God of Israel, 'The
jar of meal shall not be spent, and the
cruse of oil shall not fail, until the
day that the LORD sends rain upon
the earth.'" 15And she went and did as
Eli´jah said; and she, and he, and her
household ate for many days. 16The
jar of meal was not spent, neither did
the cruse of oil fail, according to the
word of the LORD which he spoke by
Eli´jah.

ELIJAH REVIVES THE WIDOW'S SON

17 After this the son of the wom-
an, the mistress of the house, became
ill; and his illness was so severe that
there was no breath left in him. 18And
she said to Eli´jah, "What have you
against me, O man of God? You have
come to me to bring my sin to remem-
brance, and to cause the death of my
son!" 19And he said to her, "Give me
your son." And he took him from her
bosom, and carried him up into the
upper chamber, where he lodged, and
laid him upon his own bed. 20And he
cried to the LORD, "O LORD my God,
hast thou brought calamity even upon
the widow with whom I sojourn, by
slaying her son?" 21Then he stretched
himself upon the child three times,

[a]Gk: Heb *of the settlers*

and cried to the LORD, "O LORD my
God, let this child's soul come into
him again." 22And the LORD hear-
kened to the voice of Eli´jah; and the
soul of the child came into him again,
and he revived. 23And Eli´jah took the
child, and brought him down from the
upper chamber into the house, and de-
livered him to his mother; and Eli´jah
said, "See, your son lives." 24And the
woman said to Eli´jah, "Now I know
that you are a man of God, and that
the word of the LORD in your mouth
is truth."

ELIJAH'S MESSAGE TO AHAB

18 After many days the word of the
LORD came to Eli´jah, in the third
year, saying, "Go, show yourself to
Ahab; and I will send rain upon the
earth." 2So Eli´jah went to show
himself to Ahab. Now the famine
was severe in Samar´ia. 3And Ahab
called Obadi´ah, who was over the
household. (Now Obadi´ah revered
the LORD greatly; 4and when Jez´ebel
cut off the prophets of the LORD,
Obadi´ah took a hundred prophets
and hid them by fifties in a cave, and
fed them with bread and water.) 5And
Ahab said to Obadi´ah, "Go through
the land to all the springs of water and
to all the valleys; perhaps we may find
grass and save the horses and mules
alive, and not lose some of the ani-
mals." 6So they divided the land be-
tween them to pass through it; Ahab
went in one direction by himself, and
Obadi´ah went in another direction by
himself.

7 And as Obadi´ah was on the
way, behold, Eli´jah met him; and
Obadi´ah recognized him, and fell on
his face, and said, "Is it you, my lord
Eli´jah?" 8And he answered him, "It
is I. Go, tell your lord, 'Behold, Eli´jah
is here.'" 9And he said, "Wherein have
I sinned, that you would give your
servant into the hand of Ahab, to kill
me? 10As the LORD your God lives,
there is no nation or kingdom whith-
er my lord has not sent to seek you;
and when they would say, 'He is not
here,' he would take an oath of the
kingdom or nation, that they had not
found you. 11And now you say, 'Go, tell
your lord, "Behold, Eli´jah is here."'
12And as soon as I have gone from you,
the Spirit of the LORD will carry you
whither I know not; and so, when I
come and tell Ahab and he cannot find
you, he will kill me, although I your
servant have revered the LORD from
my youth. 13Has it not been told my
lord what I did when Jez´ebel killed
the prophets of the LORD, how I hid a
hundred men of the LORD's prophets
by fifties in a cave, and fed them with
bread and water? 14And now you say,
'Go, tell your lord, "Behold, Eli´jah
is here"'; and he will kill me." 15And
Eli´jah said, "As the LORD of hosts
lives, before whom I stand, I will sure-
ly show myself to him today." 16So
Obadi´ah went to meet Ahab, and told
him; and Ahab went to meet Eli´jah.

17 When Ahab saw Eli´jah, Ahab
said to him, "Is it you, you troubler of
Israel?" 18And he answered, "I have
not troubled Israel; but you have, and
your father's house, because you have
forsaken the commandments of the
LORD and followed the Ba´als. 19Now
therefore send and gather all Israel
to me at Mount Carmel, and the four
hundred and fifty prophets of Ba´al[a]
and the four hundred prophets of
Ashe´rah, who eat at Jez´ebel's table."

ELIJAH'S TRIUMPH OVER THE PRIESTS OF BAAL

20 So Ahab sent to all the people of
Israel, and gathered the prophets to-
gether at Mount Carmel. 21And Eli´jah
came near to all the people, and said,
"How long will you go limping with
two different opinions? If the LORD
is God, follow him; but if Ba´al, then
follow him." And the people did not
answer him a word. 22Then Eli´jah
said to the people, "I, even I only,
am left a prophet of the LORD; but
Ba´al's prophets are four hundred and
fifty men. 23Let two bulls be given to

us; and let them choose one bull for
themselves, and cut it in pieces and
lay it on the wood, but put no fire to
it; and I will prepare the other bull
and lay it on the wood, and put no fire
to it. 24And you call on the name of
your god and I will call on the name
of the LORD; and the God who an-
swers by fire, he is God." And all the
people answered, "It is well spoken."
25Then Eli´jah said to the prophets
of Ba´al, "Choose for yourselves one
bull and prepare it first, for you are
many; and call on the name of your
god, but put no fire to it." 26And they
took the bull which was given them,
and they prepared it, and called on
the name of Ba´al from morning until
noon, saying, "O Ba´al, answer us!"
But there was no voice, and no one
answered. And they limped about the
altar which they had made. 27And at
noon Eli´jah mocked them, saying,
"Cry aloud, for he is a god; either he
is musing, or he has gone aside, or he
is on a journey, or perhaps he is asleep
and must be awakened." 28And they
cried aloud, and cut themselves after
their custom with swords and lances,
until the blood gushed out upon them.
29And as midday passed, they raved on
until the time of the offering of the
oblation, but there was no voice; no
one answered, no one heeded.

30 Then Eli´jah said to all the
people, "Come near to me"; and all
the people came near to him. And he
repaired the altar of the LORD that
had been thrown down; 31Eli´jah took
twelve stones, according to the num-
ber of the tribes of the sons of Jacob,
to whom the word of the LORD came,
saying, "Israel shall be your name";
32and with the stones he built an al-
tar in the name of the LORD. And he
made a trench about the altar, as great
as would contain two measures of
seed. 33And he put the wood in order,
and cut the bull in pieces and laid it on
the wood. And he said, "Fill four jars
with water, and pour it on the burnt
offering, and on the wood." 34And he
said, "Do it a second time"; and they
did it a second time. And he said, "Do
it a third time"; and they did it a third
time. 35And the water ran round about
the altar, and filled the trench also
with water.

36 And at the time of the offering
of the oblation, Eli´jah the prophet
came near and said, "O LORD, God of
Abraham, Isaac, and Israel, let it be
known this day that thou art God in
Israel, and that I am thy servant, and
that I have done all these things at
thy word. 37Answer me, O LORD, an-
swer me, that this people may know
that thou, O LORD, art God, and that
thou hast turned their hearts back."
38Then the fire of the LORD fell, and
consumed the burnt offering, and the
wood, and the stones, and the dust,
and licked up the water that was in
the trench. 39And when all the people
saw it, they fell on their faces; and
they said, "The LORD, he is God; the
LORD, he is God." 40And Eli´jah said
to them, "Seize the prophets of Ba´al;
let not one of them escape." And they
seized them; and Eli´jah brought
them down to the brook Kishon, and
killed them there.

THE DROUGHT ENDS

41 And Eli´jah said to Ahab, "Go
up, eat and drink; for there is a sound
of the rushing of rain." 42So Ahab
went up to eat and to drink. And
Eli´jah went up to the top of Carmel;
and he bowed himself down upon the
earth, and put his face between his
knees. 43And he said to his servant,
"Go up now, look toward the sea."
And he went up and looked, and said,
"There is nothing." And he said, "Go
again seven times." 44And at the sev-
enth time he said, "Behold, a little
cloud like a man's hand is rising out
of the sea." And he said, "Go up, say
to Ahab, 'Prepare your chariot and go
down, lest the rain stop you.'" 45And
in a little while the heavens grew
black with clouds and wind, and there
was a great rain. And Ahab rode and

went to Jezre´el. 46 And the hand of the
LORD was on Eli´jah; and he girded
up his loins and ran before Ahab to
the entrance of Jezre´el.

ELIJAH FLEES FROM JEZEBEL

19 Ahab told Jez´ebel all that Eli´jah
had done, and how he had slain all
the prophets with the sword. 2 Then
Jez´ebel sent a messenger to Eli´jah,
saying, "So may the gods do to me
and more also, if I do not make your
life as the life of one of them by this
time tomorrow." 3 Then he was afraid,
and he arose and went for his life, and
came to Beer-sheba, which belongs to
Judah, and left his servant there.

4 But he himself went a day's jour-
ney into the wilderness, and came and
sat down under a broom tree; and he
asked that he might die, saying, "It is
enough; now, O LORD, take away my
life; for I am no better than my fa-
thers." 5 And he lay down and slept un-
der a broom tree; and behold, an angel
touched him, and said to him, "Arise
and eat." 6 And he looked, and behold,
there was at his head a cake baked on
hot stones and a jar of water. And he
ate and drank, and lay down again.
7 And the angel of the LORD came
again a second time, and touched him,
and said, "Arise and eat, else the jour-
ney will be too great for you." 8 And he
arose, and ate and drank, and went in
the strength of that food forty days
and forty nights to Horeb* the mount
of God.

ELIJAH MEETS GOD AT HOREB

9 And there he came to a cave,
and lodged there; and behold, the
word of the LORD came to him, and
he said to him, "What are you doing
here, Eli´jah?" 10 He said, "I have been
very jealous for the LORD, the God
of hosts; for the people of Israel have
forsaken thy covenant, thrown down
thy altars, and slain thy prophets
with the sword; and I, even I only, am
left; and they seek my life, to take it
away." 11 And he said, "Go forth, and
stand upon the mount before the
LORD." And behold, the LORD passed
by, and a great and strong wind rent
the mountains, and broke in pieces
the rocks before the LORD, but the
LORD was not in the wind; and after
the wind an earthquake, but the LORD
was not in the earthquake; 12 and after
the earthquake a fire, but the LORD
was not in the fire; and after the fire
a still small voice. 13 And when Eli´jah
heard it, he wrapped his face in his
mantle and went out and stood at
the entrance of the cave. And behold,
there came a voice to him, and said,
"What are you doing here, Eli´jah?"
14 He said, "I have been very jealous
for the LORD, the God of hosts; for
the people of Israel have forsaken
thy covenant, thrown down thy al-
tars, and slain thy prophets with the
sword; and I, even I only, am left; and
they seek my life, to take it away."
15 And the LORD said to him, "Go, re-
turn on your way to the wilderness of
Damascus; and when you arrive, you
shall anoint Haz´ael to be king over
Syria; 16 and Jehu the son of Nimshi
you shall anoint to be king over Israel;
and Eli´sha the son of Shaphat of
A´bel-meho´lah you shall anoint to be
prophet in your place. 17 And him who
escapes from the sword of Haz´ael
shall Jehu slay; and him who escapes
from the sword of Jehu shall Eli´sha
slay. 18 Yet I will leave seven thousand
in Israel, all the knees that have not
bowed to Ba´al, and every mouth that
has not kissed him."

ELISHA BECOMES ELIJAH'S DISCIPLE

19 So he departed from there, and
found Eli´sha the son of Shaphat,
who was plowing, with twelve yoke
of oxen before him, and he was with
the twelfth. Eli´jah passed by him
and cast his mantle upon him. 20 And
he left the oxen, and ran after Eli´jah,
and said, "Let me kiss my father and
my mother, and then I will follow
you." And he said to him, "Go back
again; for what have I done to you?"

21 And he returned from following him, and took the yoke of oxen, and slew them, and boiled their flesh with the yokes of the oxen, and gave it to the people, and they ate. Then he arose and went after Eli′jah, and ministered to him.

AHAB'S WARS WITH THE ARAMEANS

20 Ben-ha′dad the king of Syria gathered all his army together; thirty-two kings were with him, and horses and chariots; and he went up and besieged Samar′ia, and fought against it. 2 And he sent messengers into the city to Ahab king of Israel, and said to him, "Thus says Ben-ha′dad: 3 'Your silver and your gold are mine; your fairest wives and children also are mine.'" 4 And the king of Israel answered, "As you say, my lord, O king, I am yours, and all that I have." 5 The messengers came again, and said, "Thus says Ben-ha′dad: 'I sent to you, saying, "Deliver to me your silver and your gold, your wives and your children"; 6 nevertheless I will send my servants to you tomorrow about this time, and they shall search your house and the houses of your servants, and lay hands on whatever pleases them,[a] and take it away.'"

7 Then the king of Israel called all the elders of the land, and said, "Mark, now, and see how this man is seeking trouble; for he sent to me for my wives and my children, and for my silver and my gold, and I did not refuse him." 8 And all the elders and all the people said to him, "Do not heed or consent." 9 So he said to the messengers of Ben-ha′dad, "Tell my lord the king, 'All that you first demanded of your servant I will do; but this thing I cannot do.'" And the messengers departed and brought him word again. 10 Ben-ha′dad sent to him and said, "The gods do so to me and more also, if the dust of Samar′ia shall suffice for handfuls for all the people who follow me." 11 And the king of Israel answered, "Tell him, 'Let not him that girds on his armor boast himself as he that puts it off.'" 12 When Ben-ha′dad heard this message as he was drinking with the kings in the booths, he said to his men, "Take your positions." And they took their positions against the city.

PROPHETIC OPPOSITION TO AHAB

13 And behold, a prophet came near to Ahab king of Israel and said, "Thus says the LORD, Have you seen all this great multitude? Behold, I will give it into your hand this day; and you shall know that I am the LORD." 14 And Ahab said, "By whom?" He said, "Thus says the LORD, By the servants of the governors of the districts." Then he said, "Who shall begin the battle?" He answered, "You." 15 Then he mustered the servants of the governors of the districts, and they were two hundred and thirty-two; and after them he mustered all the people of Israel, seven thousand.

16 And they went out at noon, while Ben-ha′dad was drinking himself drunk in the booths, he and the thirty-two kings who helped him. 17 The servants of the governors of the districts went out first. And Ben-ha′dad sent out scouts, and they reported to him, "Men are coming out from Samar′ia." 18 He said, "If they have come out for peace, take them alive; or if they have come out for war, take them alive."

19 So these went out of the city, the servants of the governors of the districts, and the army which followed them. 20 And each killed his man; the Syrians fled and Israel pursued them, but Ben-ha′dad king of Syria escaped on a horse with horsemen. 21 And the king of Israel went out, and captured[b] the horses and chariots, and killed the Syrians with a great slaughter.

22 Then the prophet came near to the king of Israel, and said to him,

[a] Gk Syr Vg: Heb *you*
[b] Gk: Heb *smote*

"Come, strengthen yourself, and con-
sider well what you have to do; for in
the spring the king of Syria will come
up against you."

THE ARAMEANS ARE DEFEATED

23 And the servants of the king
of Syria said to him, "Their gods are
gods of the hills, and so they were
stronger than we; but let us fight
against them in the plain, and surely
we shall be stronger than they. 24And
do this: remove the kings, each from
his post, and put commanders in their
places; 25and muster an army like the
army that you have lost, horse for
horse, and chariot for chariot; then
we will fight against them in the
plain, and surely we shall be stronger
than they." And he hearkened to their
voice, and did so.

26 In the spring Ben-ha´dad mus-
tered the Syrians, and went up to
Aphek, to fight against Israel. 27And
the people of Israel were mustered,
and were provisioned, and went
against them; the people of Israel
encamped before them like two little
flocks of goats, but the Syrians filled
the country. 28And a man of God came
near and said to the king of Israel,
"Thus says the LORD, 'Because the
Syrians have said, "The LORD is a god
of the hills but he is not a god of the
valleys," therefore I will give all this
great multitude into your hand, and
you shall know that I am the LORD.'"
29And they encamped opposite one an-
other seven days. Then on the seventh
day the battle was joined; and the
people of Israel smote of the Syrians a
hundred thousand foot soldiers in one
day. 30And the rest fled into the city of
Aphek; and the wall fell upon twen-
ty-seven thousand men that were left.

Ben-ha´dad also fled, and entered
an inner chamber in the city. 31And his
servants said to him, "Behold now, we
have heard that the kings of the house
of Israel are merciful kings; let us
put sackcloth on our loins and ropes
upon our heads, and go out to the
king of Israel; perhaps he will spare
your life." 32So they girded sackcloth
on their loins, and put ropes on their
heads, and went to the king of Israel
and said, "Your servant Ben-ha´dad
says, 'Pray, let me live.'" And he said,
"Does he still live? He is my broth-
er." 33Now the men were watching for
an omen, and they quickly took it up
from him and said, "Yes, your brother
Ben-ha´dad." Then he said, "Go and
bring him." Then Ben-ha´dad came
forth to him; and he caused him to
come up into the chariot. 34And Ben-
ha´dad said to him, "The cities which
my father took from your father I will
restore; and you may establish bazaars
for yourself in Damascus, as my father
did in Samar´ia." And Ahab said, "I
will let you go on these terms." So he
made a covenant with him and let him
go.

A PROPHET CONDEMNS AHAB

35 And a certain man of the sons of
the prophets said to his fellow at the
command of the LORD, "Strike me, I
pray." But the man refused to strike
him. 36Then he said to him, "Because
you have not obeyed the voice of the
LORD, behold, as soon as you have
gone from me, a lion shall kill you."
And as soon as he had departed from
him, a lion met him and killed him.
37Then he found another man, and
said, "Strike me, I pray." And the man
struck him, smiting and wounding
him. 38So the prophet departed, and
waited for the king by the way, dis-
guising himself with a bandage over
his eyes. 39And as the king passed,
he cried to the king and said, "Your
servant went out into the midst of the
battle; and behold, a soldier turned
and brought a man to me, and said,
'Keep this man; if by any means he be
missing, your life shall be for his life,
or else you shall pay a talent of silver.'
40And as your servant was busy here
and there, he was gone." The king of
Israel said to him, "So shall your judg-
ment be; you yourself have decided it."

41 Then he made haste to take the ban-
dage away from his eyes; and the king
of Israel recognized him as one of the
prophets. 42 And he said to him, "Thus
says the LORD, 'Because you have let
go out of your hand the man whom I
had devoted to destruction, therefore
your life shall go for his life, and your
people for his people.'" 43 And the king
of Israel went to his house resentful
and sullen, and came to Samar´ia.

NABOTH'S VINEYARD

21 Now Naboth the Jezre´elite had
a vineyard in Jezre´el, beside the
palace of Ahab king of Samar´ia. 2 And
after this Ahab said to Naboth, "Give
me your vineyard, that I may have it
for a vegetable garden, because it is
near my house; and I will give you a
better vineyard for it; or, if it seems
good to you, I will give you its value
in money." 3 But Naboth said to Ahab,
"The LORD forbid that I should give
you the inheritance of my fathers."
4 And Ahab went into his house vexed
and sullen because of what Naboth
the Jezre´elite had said to him; for he
had said, "I will not give you the in-
heritance of my fathers." And he lay
down on his bed, and turned away his
face, and would eat no food.

5 But Jez´ebel his wife came to
him, and said to him, "Why is your
spirit so vexed that you eat no food?"
6 And he said to her, "Because I spoke
to Naboth the Jezre´elite, and said
to him, 'Give me your vineyard for
money; or else, if it please you, I will
give you another vineyard for it'; and
he answered, 'I will not give you my
vineyard.'" 7 And Jez´ebel his wife said
to him, "Do you now govern Israel?
Arise, and eat bread, and let your
heart be cheerful; I will give you the
vineyard of Naboth the Jezre´elite."

8 So she wrote letters in Ahab's
name and sealed them with his seal,
and she sent the letters to the el-
ders and the nobles who dwelt with
Naboth in his city. 9 And she wrote in
the letters, "Proclaim a fast, and set
Naboth on high among the people;
10 and set two* base fellows opposite
him, and let them bring a charge
against him, saying, 'You have cursed
God and the king.' Then take him
out, and stone him to death." 11 And
the men of his city, the elders and the
nobles who dwelt in his city, did as
Jez´ebel had sent word to them. As it
was written in the letters which she
had sent to them, 12 they proclaimed a
fast, and set Naboth on high among
the people. 13 And the two base fellows
came in and sat opposite him; and the
base fellows brought a charge against
Naboth, in the presence of the people,
saying, "Naboth cursed God and the
king." So they took him outside the
city, and stoned him to death with
stones. 14 Then they sent to Jez´ebel,
saying, "Naboth has been stoned; he
is dead."

15 As soon as Jez´ebel heard that
Naboth had been stoned and was
dead, Jez´ebel said to Ahab, "Arise,
take possession of the vineyard of
Naboth the Jezre´elite, which he
refused to give you for money; for
Naboth is not alive, but dead." 16 And
as soon as Ahab heard that Naboth
was dead, Ahab arose to go down to
the vineyard of Naboth the Jezre´elite,
to take possession of it.

ELIJAH PRONOUNCES GOD'S SENTENCE

17 Then the word of the LORD
came to Eli´jah the Tishbite, saying,
18 "Arise, go down to meet Ahab king
of Israel, who is in Samar´ia; behold,
he is in the vineyard of Naboth, where
he has gone to take possession. 19 And
you shall say to him, 'Thus says the
LORD, "Have you killed, and also tak-
en possession?"' And you shall say
to him, 'Thus says the LORD: "In the
place where dogs licked up the blood
of Naboth shall dogs lick your own
blood."'"

20 Ahab said to Eli´jah, "Have
you found me, O my enemy?" He an-
swered, "I have found you, because
you have sold yourself to do what is

evil in the sight of the LORD. 21Behold,
I will bring evil upon you; I will ut-
terly sweep you away, and will cut off
from Ahab every male, bond or free,
in Israel; 22and I will make your house
like the house of Jerobo´am the son of
Nebat, and like the house of Ba´asha
the son of Ahi´jah, for the anger to
which you have provoked me, and
because you have made Israel to sin.
23And of Jez´ebel the LORD also said,
'The dogs shall eat Jez´ebel within the
bounds of Jezre´el.' 24Any one belong-
ing to Ahab who dies in the city the
dogs shall eat; and any one of his who
dies in the open country the birds of
the air shall eat."

25 (There was none who sold him-
self to do what was evil in the sight
of the LORD like Ahab, whom Jez´ebel
his wife incited. 26He did very abom-
inably in going after idols, as the
Amorites had done, whom the LORD
cast out before the people of Israel.)

27 And when Ahab heard those
words, he rent his clothes, and put
sackcloth upon his flesh, and fasted
and lay in sackcloth, and went about
dejectedly. 28And the word of the
LORD came to Eli´jah the Tishbite,
saying, 29"Have you seen how Ahab
has humbled himself before me?
Because he has humbled himself be-
fore me, I will not bring the evil in his
days; but in his son's days I will bring
the evil upon his house."*

JOINT CAMPAIGN WITH JUDAH AGAINST ARAM

22 For three years Syria and Israel
continued without war. 2But in
the third year Jehosh´aphat the king
of Judah came down to the king of
Israel. 3And the king of Israel said
to his servants, "Do you know that
Ra´moth-gil´ead belongs to us, and
we keep quiet and do not take it out
of the hand of the king of Syria?"
4And he said to Jehosh´aphat, "Will
you go with me to battle at Ra´moth-
gil´ead?" And Jehosh´aphat said to
the king of Israel, "I am as you are,
my people as your people, my horses
as your horses."

5 And Jehosh´aphat said to the
king of Israel, "Inquire first for the
word of the LORD." 6Then the king of
Israel gathered the prophets togeth-
er, about four hundred men, and said
to them, "Shall I go to battle against
Ra´moth-gil´ead, or shall I forbear?"
And they said, "Go up; for the Lord
will give it into the hand of the king."
7But Jehosh´aphat said, "Is there not
here another prophet of the LORD of
whom we may inquire?" 8And the king
of Israel said to Jehosh´aphat, "There
is yet one man by whom we may in-
quire of the LORD, Micai´ah the son
of Imlah; but I hate him, for he never
prophesies good concerning me, but
evil." And Jehosh´aphat said, "Let not
the king say so." 9Then the king of
Israel summoned an officer and said,
"Bring quickly Micai´ah the son of
Imlah." 10Now the king of Israel and
Jehosh´aphat the king of Judah were
sitting on their thrones, arrayed in
their robes, at the threshing floor at
the entrance of the gate of Samar´ia;
and all the prophets were prophesy-
ing before them. 11And Zedeki´ah the
son of Chena´anah made for himself
horns of iron, and said, "Thus says
the LORD, 'With these you shall push
the Syrians until they are destroyed.'"
12And all the prophets prophesied so,
and said, "Go up to Ra´moth-gil´ead
and triumph; the LORD will give it
into the hand of the king."

MICAIAH PREDICTS FAILURE

13 And the messenger who went
to summon Micai´ah said to him,
"Behold, the words of the prophets
with one accord are favorable to the
king; let your word be like the word
of one of them, and speak favor-
ably." 14But Micai´ah said, "As the
LORD lives, what the LORD says to
me, that I will speak." 15And when he
had come to the king, the king said
to him, "Micai´ah, shall we go to
Ra´moth-gil´ead to battle, or shall we

forbear?" And he answered him, "Go
up and triumph; the LORD will give it
into the hand of the king." 16But the
king said to him, "How many times
shall I adjure you that you speak to
me nothing but the truth in the name
of the LORD?" 17And he said, "I saw
all Israel scattered upon the moun-
tains, as sheep that have no shepherd;
and the LORD said, 'These have no
master; let each return to his home in
peace.'" 18And the king of Israel said
to Jehosh´aphat, "Did I not tell you
that he would not prophesy good con-
cerning me, but evil?" 19And Micai´ah
said, "Therefore hear the word of the
LORD: I saw the LORD sitting on his
throne, and all the host of heaven
standing beside him on his right hand
and on his left; 20and the LORD said,
'Who will entice Ahab, that he may
go up and fall at Ra´moth-gil´ead?'
And one said one thing, and anoth-
er said another. 21Then a spirit came
forward and stood before the LORD,
saying, 'I will entice him.' 22And the
LORD said to him, 'By what means?'
And he said, 'I will go forth, and will
be a lying spirit in the mouth of all
his prophets.' And he said, 'You are
to entice him, and you shall succeed;
go forth and do so.' 23Now therefore
behold, the LORD has put a lying
spirit in the mouth of all these your
prophets; the LORD has spoken evil
concerning you."

24 Then Zedeki´ah the son of
Chena´anah came near and struck
Micai´ah on the cheek, and said, "How
did the Spirit of the LORD go from me
to speak to you?" 25And Micai´ah said,
"Behold, you shall see on that day
when you go into an inner chamber
to hide yourself." 26And the king of
Israel said, "Seize Micai´ah, and take
him back to Amon the governor of the
city and to Jo´ash the king's son; 27and
say, 'Thus says the king, "Put this fel-
low in prison, and feed him with scant
fare of bread and water, until I come
in peace."'" 28And Micai´ah said, "If
you return in peace, the LORD has not
spoken by me." And he said, "Hear, all
you peoples!"

DEFEAT AND DEATH OF AHAB

29 So the king of Israel and
Jehosh´aphat the king of Judah went
up to Ra´moth-gil´ead. 30And the king
of Israel said to Jehosh´aphat, "I will
disguise myself and go into battle, but
you wear your robes." And the king of
Israel disguised himself and went into
battle. 31Now the king of Syria had
commanded the thirty-two captains
of his chariots, "Fight with neither
small nor great, but only with the king
of Israel." 32And when the captains of
the chariots saw Jehosh´aphat, they
said, "It is surely the king of Israel."
So they turned to fight against him;
and Jehosh´aphat cried out. 33And
when the captains of the chariots saw
that it was not the king of Israel, they
turned back from pursuing him. 34But
a certain man drew his bow at a ven-
ture, and struck the king of Israel be-
tween the scale armor and the breast-
plate; therefore he said to the driver
of his chariot, "Turn about, and carry
me out of the battle, for I am wound-
ed." 35And the battle grew hot that
day, and the king was propped up in
his chariot facing the Syrians, until at
evening he died; and the blood of the
wound flowed into the bottom of the
chariot. 36And about sunset a cry went
through the army, "Every man to his
city, and every man to his country!"

37 So the king died, and was
brought to Samar´ia; and they bur-
ied the king in Samar´ia. 38And they
washed the chariot by the pool of
Samar´ia, and the dogs licked up his
blood, and the harlots washed them-
selves in it, according to the word of
the LORD which he had spoken. 39Now
the rest of the acts of Ahab, and all
that he did, and the ivory house which
he built, and all the cities that he built,
are they not written in the Book of
the Chronicles of the Kings of Israel?
40So Ahab slept with his fathers; and
Ahazi´ah his son reigned in his stead.

JEHOSHAPHAT REIGNS OVER JUDAH

41 Jehosh´aphat the son of Asa
began to reign over Judah in the
fourth year of Ahab king of Israel.
42 Jehosh´aphat was thirty-five years
old when he began to reign, and
he reigned twenty-five years in
Jerusalem. His mother's name was
Azu´bah the daughter of Shilhi. 43 He
walked in all the way of Asa his fa-
ther; he did not turn aside from it,
doing what was right in the sight of
the LORD; yet the high places were
not taken away, and the people still
sacrificed and burned incense on the
high places. 44 Jehosh´aphat also made
peace with the king of Israel.

45 Now the rest of the acts of
Jehosh´aphat, and his might that
he showed, and how he warred, are
they not written in the Book of the
Chronicles of the Kings of Judah?
46 And the remnant of the male cult
prostitutes who remained in the days
of his father Asa, he exterminated
from the land.

47 There was no king in Edom;
a deputy was king. 48 Jehosh´aphat
made ships of Tarshish to go to
Ophir for gold; but they did not
go, for the ships were wrecked at
E´zion-ge´ber. 49 Then Ahazi´ah the
son of Ahab said to Jehosh´aphat,
"Let my servants go with your ser-
vants in the ships," but Jehosh´aphat
was not willing. 50 And Jehosh´aphat
slept with his fathers, and was bur-
ied with his fathers in the city of
David his father; and Jeho´ram his
son reigned in his stead.

AHAZIAH REIGNS OVER ISRAEL

51 Ahazi´ah the son of Ahab began
to reign over Israel in Samar´ia in the
seventeenth year of Jehosh´aphat
king of Judah, and he reigned two
years over Israel. 52 He did what was
evil in the sight of the LORD, and
walked in the way of his father, and
in the way of his mother, and in the
way of Jerobo´am the son of Nebat,
who made Israel to sin. 53 He served
Ba´al and worshiped him, and pro-
voked the LORD, the God of Israel,
to anger in every way that his father
had done.

THE SECOND BOOK OF THE
KINGS

ELIJAH DENOUNCES AHAZIAH

1 After the death of Ahab, Moab re-
belled against Israel.

2 Now Ahazi´ah fell through the
lattice in his upper chamber in Sa-
mar´ia, and lay sick; so he sent mes-
sengers, telling them, "Go, inquire
of Ba´al-ze´bub, the god of Ekron,
whether I shall recover from this
sickness." 3 But the angel of the LORD
said to Eli´jah the Tishbite, "Arise,
go up to meet the messengers of the
king of Samar´ia, and say to them,
'Is it because there is no God in Is-
rael that you are going to inquire of
Ba´al-ze´bub, the god of Ekron?' 4 Now
therefore thus says the LORD, 'You
shall not come down from the bed to
which you have gone, but you shall
surely die.'" So Eli´jah went.

5 The messengers returned to the
king, and he said to them, "Why have
you returned?" 6 And they said to him,
"There came a man to meet us, and
said to us, 'Go back to the king who
sent you, and say to him, Thus says
the LORD, Is it because there is no
God in Israel that you are sending
to inquire of Ba´al-ze´bub, the god of
Ekron? Therefore you shall not come
down from the bed to which you have
gone, but shall surely die.'" 7 He said
to them, "What kind of man was he
who came to meet you and told you
these things?" 8 They answered him,
"He wore a garment of haircloth,
with a girdle of leather about his
loins." And he said, "It is Eli´jah the
Tishbite."

9 Then the king sent to him a cap-
tain of fifty men with his fifty. He
went up to Eli´jah, who was sitting
on the top of a hill, and said to him,
"O man of God, the king says, 'Come
down.'" 10 But Eli´jah answered the
captain of fifty, "If I am a man of God,
let fire come down from heaven and
consume you and your fifty." Then
fire came down from heaven, and con-
sumed him and his fifty.

11 Again the king sent to him an-
other captain of fifty men with his
fifty. And he went up[a] and said to
him, "O man of God, this is the king's
order, 'Come down quickly!'" 12 But
Eli´jah answered them, "If I am a
man of God, let fire come down from
heaven and consume you and your fif-
ty." Then the fire of God came down
from heaven and consumed him and
his fifty.

13 Again the king sent the captain
of a third fifty with his fifty. And the
third captain of fifty went up, and
came and fell on his knees before
Eli´jah, and entreated him, "O man of
God, I pray you, let my life, and the
life of these fifty servants of yours, be
precious in your sight. 14 Lo, fire came
down from heaven, and consumed the
two former captains of fifty men with
their fifties; but now let my life be pre-
cious in your sight." 15 Then the angel
of the LORD said to Eli´jah, "Go down
with him; do not be afraid of him."
So he arose and went down with him
to the king, 16 and said to him, "Thus
says the LORD, 'Because you have sent
messengers to inquire of Ba´al-ze´bub,
the god of Ekron,—is it because there
is no God in Israel to inquire of his
word?—therefore you shall not come
down from the bed to which you have
gone, but you shall surely die.'"

DEATH OF AHAZIAH

17 So he died according to the word
of the LORD which Eli´jah had spo-
ken. Jehor´am, his brother,[b] became
king in his stead in the second year
of Jehor´am the son of Jehosh´aphat,
king of Judah, because Ahazi´ah had

[a] Gk Compare verses 9, 13: Heb *answered*
[b] Gk Syr: Heb lacks *his brother*

no son. 18 Now the rest of the acts of
Ahazi´ah which he did, are they not
written in the Book of the Chronicles
of the Kings of Israel?

ELIJAH ASCENDS TO HEAVEN

2 Now when the LORD was about
to take Eli´jah up to heaven by a
whirlwind, Eli´jah and Eli´sha were
on their way from Gilgal. 2 And Eli´jah
said to Eli´sha, "Tarry here, I pray
you; for the LORD has sent me as far
as Bethel." But Eli´sha said, "As the
LORD lives, and as you yourself live,
I will not leave you." So they went
down to Bethel. 3 And the sons of the
prophets who were in Bethel came out
to Eli´sha, and said to him, "Do you
know that today the LORD will take
away your master from over you?"
And he said, "Yes, I know it; hold your
peace."

4 Eli´jah said to him, "Eli´sha,
tarry here, I pray you; for the LORD
has sent me to Jericho." But he said,
"As the LORD lives, and as you yourself
live, I will not leave you." So they
came to Jericho. 5 The sons of the
prophets who were at Jericho drew
near to Eli´sha, and said to him, "Do
you know that today the LORD will
take away your master from over
you?" And he answered, "Yes, I know
it; hold your peace."

6 Then Eli´jah said to him, "Tarry
here, I pray you; for the LORD has sent
me to the Jordan." But he said, "As the
LORD lives, and as you yourself live, I
will not leave you." So the two of them
went on. 7 Fifty men of the sons of the
prophets also went, and stood at some
distance from them, as they both were
standing by the Jordan. 8 Then Eli´jah
took his mantle, and rolled it up, and
struck the water, and the water was
parted to the one side and to the other,
till the two of them could go over
on dry ground.

9 When they had crossed, Eli´jah
said to Eli´sha, "Ask what I shall do
for you, before I am taken from you."
And Eli´sha said, "I pray you, let me
inherit a double share of your spirit."
10 And he said, "You have asked
a hard thing; yet, if you see me as I
am being taken from you, it shall be
so for you; but if you do not see me,
it shall not be so." 11 And as they still
went on and talked, behold, a chariot
of fire and horses of fire separated the
two of them. And Eli´jah went up by a
whirlwind into heaven. 12 And Eli´sha
saw it and he cried, "My father, my
father! the chariots of Israel and its
horsemen!" And he saw him no more.

ELISHA SUCCEEDS ELIJAH

Then he took hold of his own
clothes and rent them in two pieces.
13 And he took up the mantle of Eli´jah
that had fallen from him, and went
back and stood on the bank of the
Jordan. 14 Then he took the mantle of
Eli´jah that had fallen from him, and
struck the water, saying, "Where is
the LORD, the God of Eli´jah?" And
when he had struck the water, the water
was parted to the one side and to
the other; and Eli´sha went over.

15 Now when the sons of the prophets
who were at Jericho saw him over
against them, they said, "The spirit
of Eli´jah rests on Eli´sha." And they
came to meet him, and bowed to the
ground before him. 16 And they said
to him, "Behold now, there are with
your servants fifty strong men; pray,
let them go, and seek your master; it
may be that the Spirit of the LORD
has caught him up and cast him upon
some mountain or into some valley."
And he said, "You shall not send."
17 But when they urged him till he was
ashamed, he said, "Send." They sent
therefore fifty men; and for three days
they sought him but did not find him.
18 And they came back to him, while he
tarried at Jericho, and he said to them,
"Did I not say to you, Do not go?"

ELISHA PERFORMS MIRACLES

19 Now the men of the city said
to Eli´sha, "Behold, the situation of
this city is pleasant, as my lord sees;

but the water is bad, and the land is
unfruitful." 20 He said, "Bring me a
new bowl, and put salt in it." So they
brought it to him. 21 Then he went to
the spring of water and threw salt in
it, and said, "Thus says the LORD, I
have made this water wholesome;
henceforth neither death nor miscar-
riage shall come from it." 22 So the wa-
ter has been wholesome to this day,
according to the word which Eli´sha
spoke.

23 He went up from there to Bethel;
and while he was going up on the way,
some small boys came out of the city
and jeered at him, saying, "Go up,
you baldhead! Go up, you baldhead!"
24 And he turned around, and when he
saw them, he cursed them in the name
of the LORD. And two she-bears came
out of the woods and tore forty-two
of the boys. 25 From there he went on
to Mount Carmel, and thence he re-
turned to Samar´ia.

JEHORAM REIGNS OVER ISRAEL

3 In the eighteenth year of Jehosh´-
aphat king of Judah, Jehor´am the
son of Ahab became king over Israel
in Samar´ia, and he reigned twelve
years. 2 He did what was evil in the
sight of the LORD, though not like his
father and mother, for he put away
the pillar of Ba´al which his father
had made. 3 Nevertheless he clung to
the sin of Jerobo´am the son of Nebat,
which he made Israel to sin; he did not
depart from it.

WAR WITH MOAB

4 *Now Mesha king of Moab was a
sheep breeder; and he had to deliver
annually[a] to the king of Israel a hun-
dred thousand lambs, and the wool
of a hundred thousand rams. 5 But
when Ahab died, the king of Moab
rebelled against the king of Israel.
6 So King Jehor´am marched out of
Samar´ia at that time and mustered
all Israel. 7 And he went and sent word
to Jehosh´aphat king of Judah, "The
king of Moab has rebelled against me;
will you go with me to battle against
Moab?" And he said, "I will go; I am
as you are, my people as your people,
my horses as your horses." 8 Then he
said, "By which way shall we march?"
Jehor´am answered, "By the way of
the wilderness of Edom."

9 So the king of Israel went with
the king of Judah and the king of
Edom. And when they had made a
circuitous march of seven days, there
was no water for the army or for the
beasts which followed them. 10 Then
the king of Israel said, "Alas! The
LORD has called these three kings
to give them into the hand of Moab."
11 And Jehosh´aphat said, "Is there no
prophet of the LORD here, through
whom we may inquire of the LORD?"
Then one of the king of Israel's ser-
vants answered, "Eli´sha the son
of Shaphat is here, who poured wa-
ter on the hands of Eli´jah." 12 And
Jehosh´aphat said, "The word of the
LORD is with him." So the king of
Israel and Jehosh´aphat and the king
of Edom went down to him.

13 And Eli´sha said to the king of
Israel, "What have I to do with you?
Go to the prophets of your father and
the prophets of your mother." But
the king of Israel said to him, "No;
it is the LORD who has called these
three kings to give them into the
hand of Moab." 14 And Eli´sha said,
"As the LORD of hosts lives, whom I
serve, were it not that I have regard
for Jehosh´aphat the king of Judah,
I would neither look at you, nor see
you. 15 But now bring me a minstrel."
And when the minstrel played, the
power of the LORD came upon him.
16 And he said, "Thus says the LORD, 'I
will make this dry stream-bed full of
pools.' 17 For thus says the LORD, 'You
shall not see wind or rain, but that
stream-bed shall be filled with water,
so that you shall drink, you, your cat-
tle, and your beasts.' 18 This is a light
thing in the sight of the LORD; he will

[a] Tg: Heb lacks *annually*

also give the Moabites into your hand,
19and you shall conquer every fortified
city, and every choice city, and shall
fell every good tree, and stop up all
springs of water, and ruin every good
piece of land with stones." 20The next
morning, about the time of offering
the sacrifice, behold, water came from
the direction of Edom, till the country
was filled with water.

21 When all the Moabites heard
that the kings had come up to fight
against them, all who were able to
put on armor, from the youngest to
the oldest, were called out, and were
drawn up at the frontier. 22And when
they rose early in the morning, and
the sun shone upon the water, the
Moabites saw the water opposite
them as red as blood. 23And they said,
"This is blood; the kings have surely
fought together, and slain one anoth-
er. Now then, Moab, to the spoil!"
24But when they came to the camp of
Israel, the Israelites rose and attacked
the Moabites, till they fled before
them; and they went forward, slaugh-
tering the Moabites as they went.[a]
25And they overthrew the cities, and
on every good piece of land every man
threw a stone, until it was covered;
they stopped every spring of water,
and felled all the good trees; till only
its stones were left in Kir-har´eseth,
and the slingers surrounded and con-
quered it. 26When the king of Moab
saw that the battle was going against
him, he took with him seven hun-
dred swordsmen to break through,
opposite the king of Edom; but they
could not. 27Then he took his eldest
son who was to reign in his stead, and
offered him for a burnt offering upon
the wall. And there came great wrath
upon Israel; and they withdrew from
him and returned to their own land.

ELISHA AND THE WIDOW'S OIL

4 Now the wife of one of the sons of
the prophets cried to Eli´sha, "Your
servant my husband is dead; and you
know that your servant feared the
LORD, but the creditor has come to
take my two children to be his slaves."
2And Eli´sha said to her, "What shall
I do for you? Tell me; what have you
in the house?" And she said, "Your
maidservant has nothing in the
house, except a jar of oil." 3Then he
said, "Go outside, borrow vessels of
all your neighbors, empty vessels and
not too few. 4Then go in, and shut the
door upon yourself and your sons, and
pour into all these vessels; and when
one is full, set it aside." 5So she went
from him and shut the door upon her-
self and her sons; and as she poured
they brought the vessels to her. 6When
the vessels were full, she said to her
son, "Bring me another vessel." And
he said to her, "There is not another."
Then the oil stopped flowing. 7She
came and told the man of God, and
he said, "Go, sell the oil and pay your
debts, and you and your sons can live
on the rest."

ELISHA RAISES THE SHUNAMMITE'S SON

8 One day Eli´sha went on to
Shunem, where a wealthy woman
lived, who urged him to eat some
food. So whenever he passed that way,
he would turn in there to eat food.
9And she said to her husband, "Behold
now, I perceive that this is a holy man
of God, who is continually passing our
way. 10Let us make a small roof cham-
ber with walls, and put there for him
a bed, a table, a chair, and a lamp, so
that whenever he comes to us, he can
go in there."

11 One day he came there, and he
turned into the chamber and rested
there. 12And he said to Geha´zi his
servant, "Call this Shu´nammite."
When he had called her, she stood
before him. 13And he said to him,
"Say now to her, See, you have taken
all this trouble for us; what is to be
done for you? Would you have a word
spoken on your behalf to the king or
to the commander of the army?" She

[a]Gk: Heb uncertain

answered, "I dwell among my own people." 14And he said, "What then is to be done for her?" Geha´zi answered, "Well, she has no son, and her husband is old." 15He said, "Call her." And when he had called her, she stood in the doorway. 16And he said, "At this season, when the time comes round, you shall embrace a son." And she said, "No, my lord, O man of God; do not lie to your maidservant." 17But the woman conceived, and she bore a son about that time the following spring, as Eli´sha had said to her.

18 When the child had grown, he went out one day to his father among the reapers. 19And he said to his father, "Oh, my head, my head!" The father said to his servant, "Carry him to his mother." 20And when he had lifted him, and brought him to his mother, the child sat on her lap till noon, and then he died. 21And she went up and laid him on the bed of the man of God, and shut the door upon him, and went out. 22Then she called to her husband, and said, "Send me one of the servants and one of the asses, that I may quickly go to the man of God, and come back again." 23And he said, "Why will you go to him today? It is neither new moon nor sabbath." She said, "It will be well." 24Then she saddled the ass, and she said to her servant, "Urge the beast on; do not slacken the pace for me unless I tell you." 25So she set out, and came to the man of God at Mount Carmel.

When the man of God saw her coming, he said to Geha´zi his servant, "Look, yonder is the Shu´nammite; 26run at once to meet her, and say to her, Is it well with you? Is it well with your husband? Is it well with the child?" And she answered, "It is well." 27And when she came to the mountain to the man of God, she caught hold of his feet. And Geha´zi came to thrust her away. But the man of God said, "Let her alone, for she is in bitter distress; and the LORD has hidden it from me, and has not told me." 28Then she said, "Did I ask my lord for a son? Did I not say, Do not deceive me?" 29He said to Geha´zi, "Gird up your loins, and take my staff in your hand, and go. If you meet any one, do not salute him; and if any one salutes you, do not reply; and lay my staff upon the face of the child." 30Then the mother of the child said, "As the LORD lives, and as you yourself live, I will not leave you." So he arose and followed her. 31Geha´zi went on ahead and laid the staff upon the face of the child, but there was no sound or sign of life. Therefore he returned to meet him, and told him, "The child has not awaked."

32 When Eli´sha came into the house, he saw the child lying dead on his bed. 33So he went in and shut the door upon the two of them, and prayed to the LORD. 34Then he went up and lay upon the child, putting his mouth upon his mouth, his eyes upon his eyes, and his hands upon his hands; and as he stretched himself upon him, the flesh of the child became warm. 35Then he got up again, and walked once to and fro in the house, and went up, and stretched himself upon him; the child sneezed seven times, and the child opened his eyes. 36Then he summoned Geha´zi and said, "Call this Shu´nammite." So he called her. And when she came to him, he said, "Take up your son." 37She came and fell at his feet, bowing to the ground; then she took up her son and went out.

ELISHA PURIFIES THE POT OF STEW

38 And Eli´sha came again to Gilgal when there was a famine in the land. And as the sons of the prophets were sitting before him, he said to his servant, "Set on the great pot, and boil pottage for the sons of the prophets." 39One of them went out into the field to gather herbs, and found a wild vine and gathered from it his lap full of wild gourds, and came and cut them up into the pot of pottage, not knowing what they were. 40And they poured out for the men to eat. But while they

were eating of the pottage, they cried
out, "O man of God, there is death in
the pot!" And they could not eat it.
41He said, "Then bring meal." And he
threw it into the pot, and said, "Pour
out for the men, that they may eat."
And there was no harm in the pot.

ELISHA FEEDS ONE HUNDRED MEN

42 A man came from Ba´al-
shal´ishah, bringing the man of God
bread of the first fruits, twenty loaves
of barley, and fresh ears of grain in
his sack. And Eli´sha said, "Give to
the men, that they may eat." 43But his
servant said, "How am I to set this
before a hundred men?" So he repeat-
ed, "Give them to the men, that they
may eat, for thus says the LORD, 'They
shall eat and have some left.'" 44So he
set it before them. And they ate, and
had some left, according to the word
of the LORD.

THE HEALING OF NAAMAN

5 Na´aman, commander of the army
of the king of Syria, was a great man
with his master and in high favor,
because by him the LORD had given
victory to Syria. He was a mighty man
of valor, but he was a leper. 2Now the
Syrians on one of their raids had car-
ried off a little maid from the land of
Israel, and she waited on Na´aman's
wife. 3She said to her mistress,
"Would that my lord were with the
prophet who is in Samar´ia! He would
cure him of his leprosy." 4So Na´aman
went in and told his lord, "Thus and
so spoke the maiden from the land of
Israel." 5And the king of Syria said,
"Go now, and I will send a letter to
the king of Israel." So he went, tak-
ing with him ten talents of silver, six
thousand shekels of gold, and ten fes-
tal garments. 6And he brought the let-
ter to the king of Israel, which read,
"When this letter reaches you, know
that I have sent to you Na´aman my
servant, that you may cure him of his
leprosy." 7And when the king of Israel
read the letter, he rent his clothes and
said, "Am I God, to kill and to make
alive, that this man sends word to me
to cure a man of his leprosy? Only
consider, and see how he is seeking a
quarrel with me."

8 But when Eli´sha the man of God
heard that the king of Israel had rent
his clothes, he sent to the king, say-
ing, "Why have you rent your clothes?
Let him come now to me, that he may
know that there is a prophet in Israel."
9So Na´aman came with his horses
and chariots, and halted at the door
of Eli´sha's house. 10And Eli´sha sent
a messenger to him, saying, "Go and
wash in the Jordan seven times, and
your flesh shall be restored, and you
shall be clean." 11But Na´aman was an-
gry, and went away, saying, "Behold,
I thought that he would surely come
out to me, and stand, and call on the
name of the LORD his God, and wave
his hand over the place, and cure the
leper. 12Are not Aba´na[a] and Pharpar,
the rivers of Damascus, better than all
the waters of Israel? Could I not wash
in them, and be clean?" So he turned
and went away in a rage. 13But his ser-
vants came near and said to him, "My
father, if the prophet had commanded
you to do some great thing, would you
not have done it? How much rather,
then, when he says to you, 'Wash,
and be clean'?" 14So he went down
and dipped himself seven times in
the Jordan, according to the word of
the man of God; and his flesh was re-
stored like the flesh of a little child,
and he was clean.

15 Then he returned to the man of
God, he and all his company, and he
came and stood before him; and he
said, "Behold, I know that there is no
God in all the earth but in Israel;* so
accept now a present from your ser-
vant." 16But he said, "As the LORD
lives, whom I serve, I will receive
none." And he urged him to take it,
but he refused. 17Then Na´aman said,
"If not, I pray you, let there be given

[a] Another reading is *Amana*

to your servant two mules' burden of earth; for henceforth your servant will not offer burnt offering or sacrifice to any god but the LORD. 18In this matter may the LORD pardon your servant: when my master goes into the house of Rimmon to worship there, leaning on my arm, and I bow myself in the house of Rimmon, when I bow myself in the house of Rimmon, the LORD pardon your servant in this matter." 19He said to him, "Go in peace."

GEHAZI'S GREED

But when Na'aman had gone from him a short distance, 20Geha'zi, the servant of Eli'sha the man of God, said, "See, my master has spared this Na'aman the Syrian, in not accepting from his hand what he brought. As the LORD lives, I will run after him, and get something from him." 21So Geha'zi followed Na'aman. And when Na'aman saw some one running after him, he alighted from the chariot to meet him, and said, "Is all well?" 22And he said, "All is well. My master has sent me to say, 'There have just now come to me from the hill country of E'phraim two young men of the sons of the prophets; pray, give them a talent of silver and two festal garments.'" 23And Na'aman said, "Be pleased to accept two talents." And he urged him, and tied up two talents of silver in two bags, with two festal garments, and laid them upon two of his servants; and they carried them before Geha'zi. 24And when he came to the hill, he took them from their hand, and put them in the house; and he sent the men away, and they departed. 25He went in, and stood before his master, and Eli'sha said to him, "Where have you been, Geha'zi?" And he said, "Your servant went nowhere." 26But he said to him, "Did I not go with you in spirit when the man turned from his chariot to meet you? Was it a time to accept money and garments, olive orchards and vineyards, sheep and oxen, menservants and maidservants? 27Therefore the leprosy of Na'aman shall cleave to you, and to your descendants for ever." So he went out from his presence a leper, as white as snow.

THE MIRACLE OF THE AX HEAD

6 Now the sons of the prophets said to Eli'sha, "See, the place where we dwell under your charge is too small for us. 2Let us go to the Jordan and each of us get there a log, and let us make a place for us to dwell there." And he answered, "Go." 3Then one of them said, "Be pleased to go with your servants." And he answered, "I will go." 4So he went with them. And when they came to the Jordan, they cut down trees. 5But as one was felling a log, his axe head fell into the water; and he cried out, "Alas, my master! It was borrowed." 6Then the man of God said, "Where did it fall?" When he showed him the place, he cut off a stick, and threw it in there, and made the iron float. 7And he said, "Take it up." So he reached out his hand and took it.

THE ARAMEAN ATTACK IS THWARTED

8 Once when the king of Syria was warring against Israel, he took counsel with his servants, saying, "At such and such a place shall be my camp." 9But the man of God sent word to the king of Israel, "Beware that you do not pass this place, for the Syrians are going down there." 10And the king of Israel sent to the place of which the man of God told him. Thus he used to warn him, so that he saved himself there more than once or twice.

11 And the mind of the king of Syria was greatly troubled because of this thing; and he called his servants and said to them, "Will you not show me who of us is for the king of Israel?" 12And one of his servants said, "None, my lord, O king; but Eli'sha, the prophet who is in Israel, tells the king of Israel the words that you speak in your bedchamber." 13And he

said, "Go and see where he is, that I
may send and seize him." It was told
him, "Behold, he is in Dothan." 14So
he sent there horses and chariots and
a great army; and they came by night,
and surrounded the city.

15 When the servant of the man
of God rose early in the morning and
went out, behold, an army with hors-
es and chariots was round about the
city. And the servant said, "Alas, my
master! What shall we do?" 16He said,
"Fear not, for those who are with us
are more than those who are with
them." 17Then Eli´sha prayed, and
said, "O LORD, I pray thee, open his
eyes that he may see." So the LORD
opened the eyes of the young man,
and he saw; and behold, the moun-
tain was full of horses and chariots of
fire round about Eli´sha. 18And when
the Syrians came down against him,
Eli´sha prayed to the LORD, and said,
"Strike this people, I pray thee, with
blindness." So he struck them with
blindness in accordance with the
prayer of Eli´sha. 19And Eli´sha said to
them, "This is not the way, and this
is not the city; follow me, and I will
bring you to the man whom you seek."
And he led them to Samar´ia.

20 As soon as they entered Sa-
mar´ia, Eli´sha said, "O LORD, open
the eyes of these men, that they may
see." So the LORD opened their eyes,
and they saw; and lo, they were in the
midst of Samar´ia. 21When the king
of Israel saw them he said to Eli´sha,
"My father, shall I slay them? Shall I
slay them?" 22He answered, "You shall
not slay them. Would you slay those
whom you have taken captive with
your sword and with your bow? Set
bread and water before them, that
they may eat and drink and go to their
master." 23So he prepared for them a
great feast; and when they had eaten
and drunk, he sent them away, and
they went to their master. And the
Syrians came no more on raids into
the land of Israel.

BEN-HADAD'S SIEGE OF SAMARIA

24 Afterward Ben-ha´dad king
of Syria mustered his entire army,
and went up, and besieged Samar´ia.
25And there was a great famine in
Samar´ia, as they besieged it, until an
ass's head was sold for eighty shekels
of silver, and the fourth part of a kab
of dove's dung for five shekels of sil-
ver. 26Now as the king of Israel was
passing by upon the wall, a woman
cried out to him, saying, "Help, my
lord, O king!" 27And he said, "If the
LORD will not help you, whence shall I
help you? From the threshing floor, or
from the wine press?" 28And the king
asked her, "What is your trouble?"
She answered, "This woman said to
me, 'Give your son, that we may eat
him today, and we will eat my son to-
morrow.' 29So we boiled my son, and
ate him. And on the next day I said
to her, 'Give your son, that we may
eat him'; but she has hidden her son."
30When the king heard the words of
the woman he rent his clothes—now
he was passing by upon the wall—and
the people looked, and behold, he had
sackcloth beneath upon his body 31and
he said, "May God do so to me and
more also, if the head of Eli´sha the
son of Shaphat remains on his shoul-
ders today."

32 Eli´sha was sitting in his house,
and the elders were sitting with him.
Now the king had dispatched a man
from his presence; but before the
messenger arrived Eli´sha said to the
elders, "Do you see how this murder-
er has sent to take off my head? Look,
when the messenger comes, shut the
door, and hold the door fast against
him. Is not the sound of his master's
feet behind him?" 33And while he was
still speaking with them, the king[a]
came down to him and said, "This
trouble is from the LORD! Why should
I wait for the LORD any longer?"
7 But Eli´sha said, "Hear the word
of the LORD: thus says the LORD,
Tomorrow about this time a measure

[a]See 7.2: Heb *messenger*

of fine meal shall be sold for a shek-
el, and two measures of barley for a
shekel, at the gate of Samar´ia." 2Then
the captain on whose hand the king
leaned said to the man of God, "If the
LORD himself should make windows
in heaven, could this thing be?" But
he said, "You shall see it with your
own eyes, but you shall not eat of it."

THE ARAMEANS FLEE

3 Now there were four men who
were lepers at the entrance to the gate;
and they said to one another, "Why do
we sit here till we die? 4If we say, 'Let
us enter the city,' the famine is in the
city, and we shall die there; and if we
sit here, we die also. So now come, let
us go over to the camp of the Syrians;
if they spare our lives we shall live,
and if they kill us we shall but die." 5So
they arose at twilight to go to the camp
of the Syrians; but when they came to
the edge of the camp of the Syrians,
behold, there was no one there. 6For
the Lord had made the army of the
Syrians hear the sound of chariots,
and of horses, the sound of a great
army, so that they said to one another,
"Behold, the king of Israel has hired
against us the kings of the Hittites and
the kings of Egypt to come upon us."
7So they fled away in the twilight and
forsook their tents, their horses, and
their asses, leaving the camp as it was,
and fled for their lives. 8And when
these lepers came to the edge of the
camp, they went into a tent, and ate
and drank, and they carried off silver
and gold and clothing, and went and
hid them; then they came back, and
entered another tent, and carried off
things from it, and went and hid them.

9 Then they said to one another,
"We are not doing right. This day is a
day of good news; if we are silent and
wait until the morning light, punish-
ment will overtake us; now therefore
come, let us go and tell the king's house-
hold." 10So they came and called to the
gatekeepers of the city, and told them,
"We came to the camp of the Syrians,
and behold, there was no one to be seen
or heard there, nothing but the horses
tied, and the asses tied, and the tents
as they were." 11Then the gatekeepers
called out, and it was told within the
king's household. 12And the king rose
in the night, and said to his servants, "I
will tell you what the Syrians have pre-
pared against us. They know that we
are hungry; therefore they have gone
out of the camp to hide themselves
in the open country, thinking, 'When
they come out of the city, we shall take
them alive and get into the city.'" 13And
one of his servants said, "Let some
men take five of the remaining horses,
seeing that those who are left here will
fare like the whole multitude of Israel
that have already perished; let us send
and see." 14So they took two mounted
men, and the king sent them after the
army of the Syrians, saying, "Go and
see." 15So they went after them as far
as the Jordan; and lo, all the way was
littered with garments and equipment
which the Syrians had thrown away
in their haste. And the messengers re-
turned, and told the king.

16 Then the people went out, and
plundered the camp of the Syrians. So
a measure of fine meal was sold for a
shekel, and two measures of barley for
a shekel, according to the word of the
LORD. 17Now the king had appointed
the captain on whose hand he leaned
to have charge of the gate; and the
people trod upon him in the gate, so
that he died, as the man of God had
said when the king came down to him.
18For when the man of God had said
to the king, "Two measures of barley
shall be sold for a shekel, and a mea-
sure of fine meal for a shekel, about
this time tomorrow in the gate of
Samar´ia," 19the captain had answered
the man of God, "If the LORD himself
should make windows in heaven,
could such a thing be?" And he had
said, "You shall see it with your own
eyes, but you shall not eat of it." 20And
so it happened to him, for the people
trod upon him in the gate and he died.

THE SHUNAMMITE WOMAN'S LAND RESTORED

8 Now Eli´sha had said to the wom-
an whose son he had restored to
life, "Arise, and depart with your
household, and sojourn wherever
you can; for the LORD has called for
a famine, and it will come upon the
land for seven years." 2So the woman
arose, and did according to the word
of the man of God; she went with her
household and sojourned in the land
of the Philistines seven years. 3And
at the end of the seven years, when
the woman returned from the land
of the Philistines, she went forth to
appeal to the king for her house and
her land. 4Now the king was talking
with Geha´zi the servant of the man
of God, saying, "Tell me all the great
things that Eli´sha has done." 5And
while he was telling the king how
Eli´sha had restored the dead to life,
behold, the woman whose son he
had restored to life appealed to the
king for her house and her land. And
Geha´zi said, "My lord, O king, here is
the woman, and here is her son whom
Eli´sha restored to life." 6And when
the king asked the woman, she told
him. So the king appointed an official
for her, saying, "Restore all that was
hers, together with all the produce of
the fields from the day that she left
the land until now."

DEATH OF BEN-HADAD

7 Now Eli´sha came to Damascus.
Ben-ha´dad the king of Syria was sick;
and when it was told him, "The man
of God has come here," 8the king said
to Haz´ael, "Take a present with you
and go to meet the man of God, and
inquire of the LORD through him,
saying, 'Shall I recover from this
sickness?'" 9So Haz´ael went to meet
him, and took a present with him, all
kinds of goods of Damascus, forty
camel loads. When he came and stood
before him, he said, "Your son Ben-
ha´dad king of Syria has sent me to
you, saying, 'Shall I recover from this
sickness?'" 10And Eli´sha said to him,
"Go, say to him, 'You shall certainly
recover'; but the LORD has shown me
that he shall certainly die." 11And he
fixed his gaze and stared at him, un-
til he was ashamed. And the man of
God wept. 12And Haz´ael said, "Why
does my lord weep?" He answered,
"Because I know the evil that you will
do to the people of Israel; you will
set on fire their fortresses, and you
will slay their young men with the
sword, and dash in pieces their little
ones, and rip up their women with
child." 13And Haz´ael said, "What is
your servant, who is but a dog, that
he should do this great thing?" Eli´sha
answered, "The LORD has shown me
that you are to be king over Syria."
14Then he departed from Eli´sha, and
came to his master, who said to him,
"What did Eli´sha say to you?" And he
answered, "He told me that you would
certainly recover." 15But on the mor-
row he took the coverlet and dipped
it in water and spread it over his face,
till he died. And Haz´ael became king
in his stead.

JEHORAM REIGNS OVER JUDAH

16 In the fifth year of Joram the son
of Ahab, king of Israel,[a] Jehor´am the
son of Jehosh´aphat, king of Judah,
began to reign. 17He was thirty-two
years old when he became king, and
he reigned eight years in Jerusalem.
18And he walked in the way of the
kings of Israel, as the house of Ahab
had done, for the daughter of Ahab
was his wife. And he did what was
evil in the sight of the LORD. 19Yet the
LORD would not destroy Judah, for
the sake of David his servant, since he
promised to give a lamp to him and to
his sons for ever.

20 In his days Edom revolted from
the rule of Judah, and set up a king
of their own. 21Then Joram passed
over to Za´ir with all his chariots, and
rose by night, and he and his chariot

[a]Gk Syr: Heb *Israel, Jehoshaphat being king of Judah*

commanders smote the E´domites
who had surrounded him; but his
army fled home. 22So Edom revolted
from the rule of Judah to this day.
Then Libnah revolted at the same
time. 23Now the rest of the acts of
Joram, and all that he did, are they not
written in the Book of the Chronicles
of the Kings of Judah? 24So Joram slept
with his fathers, and was buried with
his fathers in the city of David; and
Ahazi´ah his son reigned in his stead.

AHAZIAH REIGNS OVER JUDAH

25 In the twelfth year of Joram the
son of Ahab, king of Israel, Ahazi´-
ah the son of Jehor´am, king of Ju-
dah, began to reign. 26Ahazi´ah was
twenty-two years old when he began
to reign, and he reigned one year in
Jerusalem. His mother's name was
Athali´ah; she was a granddaughter of
Omri king of Israel. 27He also walked in
the way of the house of Ahab, and did
what was evil in the sight of the LORD,
as the house of Ahab had done, for he
was son-in-law to the house of Ahab.

28 He went with Joram the son of
Ahab to make war against Haz´ael
king of Syria at Ra´moth-gil´ead,
where the Syrians wounded Joram.
29And King Joram returned to be
healed in Jezre´el of the wounds which
the Syrians had given him at Ramah,
when he fought against Haz´ael king
of Syria. And Ahazi´ah the son of
Jehor´am king of Judah went down to
see Joram the son of Ahab in Jezre´el,
because he was sick.

ANOINTING OF JEHU

9 Then Eli´sha the prophet called one
of the sons of the prophets and said
to him, "Gird up your loins, and take
this flask of oil in your hand, and go
to Ra´moth-gil´ead. 2And when you
arrive, look there for Jehu the son
of Jehosh´aphat, son of Nimshi; and
go in and bid him rise from among
his fellows, and lead him to an inner
chamber. 3Then take the flask of oil,
and pour it on his head, and say, 'Thus
says the LORD, I anoint you king over
Israel.' Then open the door and flee;
do not tarry."

4 So the young man, the prophet,[b]
went to Ra´moth-gil´ead. 5And when
he came, behold, the commanders of
the army were in council; and he said,
"I have an errand to you, O command-
er." And Jehu said, "To which of us
all?" And he said, "To you, O com-
mander." 6So he arose, and went into
the house; and the young man poured
the oil on his head, saying to him,
"Thus says the LORD the God of Israel,
I anoint you king over the people of
the LORD, over Israel. 7And you shall
strike down the house of Ahab your
master, that I may avenge on Jez´ebel
the blood of my servants the proph-
ets, and the blood of all the servants
of the LORD. 8For the whole house of
Ahab shall perish; and I will cut off
from Ahab every male, bond or free,
in Israel. 9And I will make the house
of Ahab like the house of Jerobo´am
the son of Nebat, and like the house of
Ba´asha the son of Ahi´jah. 10And the
dogs shall eat Jez´ebel in the territory
of Jezre´el, and none shall bury her."
Then he opened the door, and fled.

11 When Jehu came out to the ser-
vants of his master, they said to him,
"Is all well? Why did this mad fellow
come to you?" And he said to them,
"You know the fellow and his talk."
12And they said, "That is not true; tell
us now." And he said, "Thus and so
he spoke to me, saying, 'Thus says the
LORD, I anoint you king over Israel.'"
13Then in haste every man of them took
his garment, and put it under him on
the bare[c] steps, and they blew the trum-
pet, and proclaimed, "Jehu is king."

JORAM OF ISRAEL KILLED

14 Thus Jehu the son of Jehosh´-
aphat the son of Nimshi conspired
against Joram. (Now Joram with all

[b]Gk Syr: Heb *the young man, the young man, the prophet*
[c]The meaning of the Hebrew word is uncertain

Israel had been on guard at Ra´moth-
gil´ead against Haz´ael king of Syria;
15 but King Joram had returned to be
healed in Jezre´el of the wounds which
the Syrians had given him, when he
fought with Haz´ael king of Syria.) So
Jehu said, "If this is your mind, then
let no one slip out of the city to go
and tell the news in Jezre´el." 16 Then
Jehu mounted his chariot, and went
to Jezre´el, for Joram lay there. And
Ahazi´ah king of Judah had come
down to visit Joram.

17 Now the watchman was stand-
ing on the tower in Jezre´el, and he
spied the company of Jehu as he came,
and said, "I see a company." And
Joram said, "Take a horseman, and
send to meet them, and let him say,
'Is it peace?'" 18 So a man on horse-
back went to meet him, and said,
"Thus says the king, 'Is it peace?'"
And Jehu said, "What have you to do
with peace? Turn round and ride be-
hind me." And the watchman report-
ed, saying, "The messenger reached
them, but he is not coming back."
19 Then he sent out a second horseman,
who came to them, and said, "Thus
the king has said, 'Is it peace?'" And
Jehu answered, "What have you to
do with peace? Turn round and ride
behind me." 20 Again the watchman
reported, "He reached them, but he
is not coming back. And the driving
is like the driving of Jehu the son of
Nimshi; for he drives furiously."

21 Joram said, "Make ready." And
they made ready his chariot. Then
Joram king of Israel and Ahazi´ah king
of Judah set out, each in his chariot,
and went to meet Jehu, and met him at
the property of Naboth the Jezre´elite.
22 And when Joram saw Jehu, he said,
"Is it peace, Jehu?" He answered,
"What peace can there be, so long
as the harlotries and the sorceries of
your mother Jez´ebel are so many?"
23 Then Joram reined about and fled,
saying to Ahazi´ah, "Treachery, O
Ahazi´ah!" 24 And Jehu drew his bow
with his full strength, and shot Joram
between the shoulders, so that the
arrow pierced his heart, and he sank
in his chariot.* 25 Jehu said to Bidkar
his aide, "Take him up, and cast him
on the plot of ground belonging to
Naboth the Jezre´elite; for remember,
when you and I rode side by side be-
hind Ahab his father, how the LORD
uttered this oracle against him: 26 'As
surely as I saw yesterday the blood of
Naboth and the blood of his sons—
says the LORD—I will requite you on
this plot of ground.' Now therefore
take him up and cast him on the plot
of ground, in accordance with the
word of the LORD."

AHAZIAH OF JUDAH KILLED

27 When Ahazi´ah the king of Judah
saw this, he fled in the direction of
Beth-haggan. And Jehu pursued him,
and said, "Shoot him also"; and they
shot him[a] in the chariot at the ascent
of Gur, which is by Ibleam. And he
fled to Megid´do, and died there. 28 His
servants carried him in a chariot to
Jerusalem, and buried him in his tomb
with his fathers in the city of David.

29 In the eleventh year of Joram the
son of Ahab, Ahazi´ah began to reign
over Judah.

JEZEBEL'S VIOLENT DEATH

30 When Jehu came to Jezre´el,
Jez´ebel heard of it; and she painted her
eyes, and adorned her head, and looked
out of the window. 31 And as Jehu en-
tered the gate, she said, "Is it peace, you
Zimri, murderer of your master?" 32 And
he lifted up his face to the window, and
said, "Who is on my side? Who?" Two
or three eunuchs looked out at him.
33 He said, "Throw her down." So they
threw her down; and some of her blood
spattered on the wall and on the hors-
es, and they trampled on her. 34 Then he
went in and ate and drank; and he said,
"See now to this cursed woman, and
bury her; for she is a king's daughter."
35 But when they went to bury her, they

[a] Syr Vg Compare Gk: Heb lacks *and they shot him*

found no more of her than the skull and
the feet and the palms of her hands.
36When they came back and told him,
he said, "This is the word of the LORD,
which he spoke by his servant Eli´jah
the Tishbite, 'In the territory of Jezre´el
the dogs shall eat the flesh of Jez´ebel;
37and the corpse of Jez´ebel shall be as
dung upon the face of the field in the
territory of Jezre´el, so that no one can
say, This is Jez´ebel.'"

MASSACRE OF AHAB'S DESCENDANTS

10 Now Ahab had seventy sons in
Samar´ia. So Jehu wrote letters,
and sent them to Samar´ia, to the
rulers of the city,[b] to the elders, and
to the guardians of the sons of Ahab,
saying, 2"Now then, as soon as this
letter comes to you, seeing your mas-
ter's sons are with you, and there are
with you chariots and horses, fortified
cities also, and weapons, 3select the
best and fittest of your master's sons
and set him on his father's throne,
and fight for your master's house."
4But they were exceedingly afraid,
and said, "Behold, the two kings
could not stand before him; how then
can we stand?" 5So he who was over
the palace, and he who was over the
city, together with the elders and the
guardians, sent to Jehu, saying, "We
are your servants, and we will do all
that you bid us. We will not make any
one king; do whatever is good in your
eyes." 6Then he wrote to them a sec-
ond letter, saying, "If you are on my
side, and if you are ready to obey me,
take the heads of your master's sons,
and come to me at Jezre´el tomorrow
at this time." Now the king's sons,
seventy persons, were with the great
men of the city, who were bringing
them up. 7And when the letter came
to them, they took the king's sons,
and slew them, seventy persons, and
put their heads in baskets, and sent
them to him at Jezre´el. 8When the
messenger came and told him, "They
have brought the heads of the king's
sons," he said, "Lay them in two
heaps at the entrance of the gate until
the morning." 9Then in the morning,
when he went out, he stood, and said
to all the people, "You are innocent.
It was I who conspired against my
master, and slew him; but who struck
down all these? 10Know then that
there shall fall to the earth nothing
of the word of the LORD, which the
LORD spoke concerning the house of
Ahab; for the LORD has done what he
said by his servant Eli´jah." 11So Jehu
slew all that remained of the house of
Ahab in Jezre´el, all his great men, and
his familiar friends, and his priests,
until he left him none remaining.

12 Then he set out and went to
Samar´ia. On the way, when he was
at Beth-eked of the Shepherds, 13Jehu
met the kinsmen of Ahazi´ah king of
Judah, and he said, "Who are you?"
And they answered, "We are the kins-
men of Ahazi´ah, and we came down
to visit the royal princes and the sons
of the queen mother." 14He said, "Take
them alive." And they took them alive,
and slew them at the pit of Beth-eked,
forty-two persons, and he spared none
of them.

15 And when he departed from
there, he met Jehon´adab the son of
Rechab coming to meet him; and he
greeted him, and said to him, "Is your
heart true to my heart as mine is to
yours?"[c] And Jehon´adab answered,
"It is." Jehu said,[d] "If it is, give me your
hand." So he gave him his hand. And
Jehu took him up with him into the
chariot. 16And he said, "Come with
me, and see my zeal for the LORD." So
he[e] had him ride in his chariot. 17And
when he came to Samar´ia, he slew all
that remained to Ahab in Samar´ia,
till he had wiped them out, accord-
ing to the word of the LORD which he
spoke to Eli´jah.

[b] Gk Vg: Heb *Jezre´el*
[c] Gk: Heb *Is it right with your heart, as my heart is with your heart?*
[d] Gk: Heb lacks *Jehu said*
[e] Gk Syr Tg: Heb *they*

SLAUGHTER OF WORSHIPERS OF BAAL

18 Then Jehu assembled all the peo-
ple, and said to them, "Ahab served
Ba´al a little; but Jehu will serve him
much. 19Now therefore call to me all
the prophets of Ba´al, all his worship-
ers and all his priests; let none be
missing, for I have a great sacrifice to
offer to Ba´al; whoever is missing shall
not live." But Jehu did it with cunning
in order to destroy the worshipers of
Ba´al. 20And Jehu ordered, "Sanctify
a solemn assembly for Ba´al." So they
proclaimed it. 21And Jehu sent through-
out all Israel; and all the worshipers
of Ba´al came, so that there was not a
man left who did not come. And they
entered the house of Ba´al, and the
house of Ba´al was filled from one end
to the other. 22He said to him who was
in charge of the wardrobe, "Bring out
the vestments for all the worshipers
of Ba´al." So he brought out the vest-
ments for them. 23Then Jehu went into
the house of Ba´al with Jehon´adab the
son of Rechab; and he said to the wor-
shipers of Ba´al, "Search, and see that
there is no servant of the LORD here
among you, but only the worshipers of
Ba´al." 24Then he[a] went in to offer sac-
rifices and burnt offerings.

Now Jehu had stationed eighty
men outside, and said, "The man who
allows any of those whom I give into
your hands to escape shall forfeit his
life." 25So as soon as he had made an
end of offering the burnt offering,
Jehu said to the guard and to the of-
ficers, "Go in and slay them; let not a
man escape." So when they put them
to the sword, the guard and the offi-
cers cast them out and went into the
inner room[b] of the house of Ba´al 26and
they brought out the pillar that was
in the house of Ba´al, and burned it.
27And they demolished the pillar of
Ba´al, and demolished the house of
Ba´al, and made it a latrine to this day.

28 Thus Jehu wiped out Ba´al from
Israel. 29But Jehu did not turn aside
from the sins of Jerobo´am the son of
Nebat, which he made Israel to sin,
the golden calves that were in Bethel,
and in Dan. 30And the LORD said to
Jehu, "Because you have done well
in carrying out what is right in my
eyes, and have done to the house of
Ahab according to all that was in my
heart, your sons of the fourth genera-
tion shall sit on the throne of Israel."
31But Jehu was not careful to walk in
the law of the LORD the God of Israel
with all his heart; he did not turn
from the sins of Jerobo´am, which he
made Israel to sin.

DEATH OF JEHU

32 In those days the LORD began
to cut off parts of Israel. Haz´ael de-
feated them throughout the territory
of Israel: 33from the Jordan eastward,
all the land of Gilead, the Gadites, and
the Reubenites, and the Manas´sites,
from Aro´er, which is by the valley of
the Arnon, that is, Gilead and Bashan.
34Now the rest of the acts of Jehu, and
all that he did, and all his might, are
they not written in the Book of the
Chronicles of the Kings of Israel? 35So
Jehu slept with his fathers, and they
buried him in Samar´ia. And Jeho´ahaz
his son reigned in his stead. 36The
time that Jehu reigned over Israel in
Samar´ia was twenty-eight years.

ATHALIAH REIGNS OVER JUDAH

11 Now when Athali´ah the moth-
er of Ahazi´ah saw that her son
was dead, she arose and destroyed
all the royal family. 2But Jehosh´eba,
the daughter of King Joram, sister
of Ahazi´ah, took Jo´ash the son of
Ahazi´ah, and stole him away from
among the king's sons who were about
to be slain, and she put[c] him and his
nurse in a bedchamber. Thus she[d] hid
him from Athali´ah, so that he was not
slain; 3and he remained with her six

[a] Gk Compare verse 25: Heb *they*
[b] Cn: Heb *city*
[c] With 2Chron 22. 11: Heb lacks *and she put*
[d] Gk Syr Vg Compare 2Chron 22. 11: Heb *they*

years, hid in the house of the LORD,
while Athali´ah reigned over the land.

JEHOIADA ANOINTS THE CHILD JOASH

4 But in the seventh year Jehoi´ada
sent and brought the captains of the
Carites and of the guards, and had
them come to him in the house of the
LORD; and he made a covenant with
them and put them under oath in the
house of the LORD, and he showed
them the king's son. 5And he com-
manded them, "This is the thing that
you shall do: one third of you, those
who come off duty on the sabbath and
guard the king's house 6(another third
being at the gate Sur and a third at the
gate behind the guards), shall guard
the palace; 7and the two divisions of
you, which come on duty in force on
the sabbath and guard the house of
the LORD,[e] 8shall surround the king,
each with his weapons in his hand;
and whoever approaches the ranks is
to be slain. Be with the king when he
goes out and when he comes in."

9 The captains did according to all
that Jehoi´ada the priest commanded,
and each brought his men who were
to go off duty on the sabbath, with
those who were to come on duty on
the sabbath, and came to Jehoi´ada
the priest. 10And the priest delivered
to the captains the spears and shields
that had been King David's, which
were in the house of the LORD; 11and
the guards stood, every man with his
weapons in his hand, from the south
side of the house to the north side of
the house, around the altar and the
house.[f] 12Then he brought out the
king's son, and put the crown upon
him, and gave him the testimony; and
they proclaimed him king, and anoint-
ed him; and they clapped their hands,
and said, "Long live the king!"

DEATH OF ATHALIAH

13 When Athali´ah heard the noise
of the guard and of the people, she
went into the house of the LORD to
the people; 14and when she looked,
there was the king standing by the pil-
lar, according to the custom, and the
captains and the trumpeters beside
the king, and all the people of the land
rejoicing and blowing trumpets. And
Athali´ah rent her clothes, and cried,
"Treason! Treason!" 15Then Jehoi´ada
the priest commanded the captains
who were set over the army, "Bring
her out between the ranks; and slay
with the sword any one who follows
her." For the priest said, "Let her not
be slain in the house of the LORD."
16So they laid hands on her; and she
went through the horses' entrance to
the king's house, and there she was
slain.

17 And Jehoi´ada made a cove-
nant between the LORD and the king
and people, that they should be the
LORD's people; and also between the
king and the people. 18Then all the
people of the land went to the house
of Ba´al, and tore it down; his altars
and his images they broke in pieces,
and they slew Mattan the priest of
Ba´al before the altars. And the priest
posted watchmen over the house of
the LORD. 19And he took the captains,
the Carites, the guards, and all the
people of the land; and they brought
the king down from the house of the
LORD, marching through the gate of
the guards to the king's house. And
he took his seat on the throne of the
kings. 20So all the people of the land
rejoiced; and the city was quiet after
Athali´ah had been slain with the
sword at the king's house.

21[g] Jeho´ash was seven years old
when he began to reign.

THE TEMPLE REPAIRED

12 In the seventh year of Jehu
Jeho´ash began to reign, and he
reigned forty years in Jerusalem. His
mother's name was Zib´iah of Beer-
sheba. 2And Jeho´ash did what was

[e] Heb *the* Lord *to the king*
[f] Heb *the house to the king*
[g] Ch 12.1 in Heb

right in the eyes of the LORD all his
days, because Jehoi´ada the priest in-
structed him. 3 Nevertheless the high
places were not taken away; the peo-
ple continued to sacrifice and burn
incense on the high places.

4 Jeho´ash said to the priests, "All
the money of the holy things which is
brought into the house of the LORD,
the money for which each man is
assessed—the money from the as-
sessment of persons—and the mon-
ey which a man's heart prompts him
to bring into the house of the LORD,
5 let the priests take, each from his
acquaintance; and let them repair the
house wherever any need of repairs is
discovered." 6 But by the twenty-third
year of King Jeho´ash the priests
had made no repairs on the house.
7 Therefore King Jeho´ash summoned
Jehoi´ada the priest and the other
priests and said to them, "Why are
you not repairing the house? Now
therefore take no more money from
your acquaintances, but hand it over
for the repair of the house." 8 So the
priests agreed that they should take
no more money from the people, and
that they should not repair the house.

9 Then Jehoi´ada the priest took a
chest, and bored a hole in the lid of it,
and set it beside the altar on the right
side as one entered the house of the
LORD; and the priests who guarded
the threshold put in it all the money
that was brought into the house of
the LORD. 10 And whenever they saw
that there was much money in the
chest, the king's secretary and the
high priest came up and they count-
ed and tied up in bags the money that
was found in the house of the LORD.
11 Then they would give the money
that was weighed out into the hands
of the workmen who had the over-
sight of the house of the LORD; and
they paid it out to the carpenters and
the builders who worked upon the
house of the LORD, 12 and to the ma-
sons and the stonecutters, as well as
to buy timber and quarried stone for
making repairs on the house of the
LORD, and for any outlay upon the
repairs of the house. 13 But there were
not made for the house of the LORD
basins of silver, snuffers, bowls, trum-
pets, or any vessels of gold, or of sil-
ver, from the money that was brought
into the house of the LORD, 14 for that
was given to the workmen who were
repairing the house of the LORD with
it. 15 And they did not ask an account-
ing from the men into whose hand
they delivered the money to pay out to
the workmen, for they dealt honestly.
16 The money from the guilt offerings
and the money from the sin offerings
was not brought into the house of the
LORD; it belonged to the priests.

HAZAEL THREATENS JERUSALEM

17 At that time Haz´ael king of Syria
went up and fought against Gath, and
took it. But when Haz´ael set his face
to go up against Jerusalem, 18 Jeho´ash
king of Judah took all the votive gifts
that Jehosh´aphat and Jehor´am and
Ahazi´ah, his fathers, the kings of
Judah, had dedicated, and his own
votive gifts, and all the gold that was
found in the treasuries of the house of
the LORD and of the king's house, and
sent these to Haz´ael king of Syria. Then
Haz´ael went away from Jerusalem.

DEATH OF JOASH

19 Now the rest of the acts of
Jo´ash, and all that he did, are they not
written in the Book of the Chronicles
of the Kings of Judah? 20 His servants
arose and made a conspiracy, and
slew Jo´ash in the house of Millo, on
the way that goes down to Silla. 21 It
was Jo´zacar the son of Shim´eath and
Jeho´zabad the son of Shomer, his ser-
vants, who struck him down, so that
he died. And they buried him with
his fathers in the city of David, and
Amazi´ah his son reigned in his stead.

JEHOAHAZ REIGNS OVER ISRAEL

13 In the twenty-third year of Jo´ash
the son of Ahazi´ah, king of Judah,

Jeho´ahaz the son of Jehu began to
reign over Israel in Samar´ia, and he
reigned seventeen years. 2He did what
was evil in the sight of the LORD, and
followed the sins of Jerobo´am the son
of Nebat, which he made Israel to sin;
he did not depart from them. 3And the
anger of the LORD was kindled against
Israel, and he gave them continual-
ly into the hand of Haz´ael king of
Syria and into the hand of Ben-ha´dad
the son of Haz´ael. 4Then Jeho´ahaz
besought the LORD, and the LORD
hearkened to him; for he saw the op-
pression of Israel, how the king of
Syria oppressed them. 5(Therefore the
LORD gave Israel a savior, so that they
escaped from the hand of the Syrians;
and the people of Israel dwelt in their
homes as formerly. 6Nevertheless they
did not depart from the sins of the
house of Jerobo´am, which he made
Israel to sin, but walked[a] in them;
and the Ashe´rah also remained in
Samar´ia.) 7For there was not left to
Jeho´ahaz an army of more than fifty
horsemen and ten chariots and ten
thousand footmen; for the king of
Syria had destroyed them and made
them like the dust at threshing. 8Now
the rest of the acts of Jeho´ahaz and
all that he did, and his might, are
they not written in the Book of the
Chronicles of the Kings of Israel? 9So
Jeho´ahaz slept with his fathers, and
they buried him in Samar´ia; and
Jo´ash his son reigned in his stead.

JEHOASH REIGNS OVER ISRAEL

10 In the thirty-seventh year of
Jo´ash king of Judah Jeho´ash the son
of Jeho´ahaz began to reign over Israel
in Samar´ia, and he reigned sixteen
years. 11He also did what was evil in
the sight of the LORD; he did not de-
part from all the sins of Jerobo´am the
son of Nebat, which he made Israel
to sin, but he walked in them. 12Now
the rest of the acts of Jo´ash, and
all that he did, and the might with
which he fought against Amazi´ah
king of Judah, are they not written
in the Book of the Chronicles of the
Kings of Israel? 13So Jo´ash slept with
his fathers, and Jerobo´am sat upon
his throne; and Jo´ash was buried in
Samar´ia with the kings of Israel.

DEATH OF ELISHA

14 Now when Eli´sha had fallen
sick with the illness of which he was
to die, Jo´ash king of Israel went down
to him, and wept before him, crying,
"My father, my father! The chariots
of Israel and its horsemen!" 15And
Eli´sha said to him, "Take a bow and
arrows"; so he took a bow and arrows.
16Then he said to the king of Israel,
"Draw the bow"; and he drew it.
And Eli´sha laid his hands upon the
king's hands. 17And he said, "Open
the window eastward"; and he opened
it. Then Eli´sha said, "Shoot"; and
he shot. And he said, "The LORD's
arrow of victory, the arrow of victo-
ry over Syria! For you shall fight the
Syrians in Aphek until you have made
an end of them." 18And he said, "Take
the arrows"; and he took them. And
he said to the king of Israel, "Strike
the ground with them"; and he struck
three times, and stopped. 19Then the
man of God was angry with him, and
said, "You should have struck five or
six times; then you would have struck
down Syria until you had made an end
of it, but now you will strike down
Syria only three times."

20 So Eli´sha died, and they buried
him. Now bands of Moabites used to
invade the land in the spring of the
year. 21And as a man was being buried,
lo, a marauding band was seen and the
man was cast into the grave of Eli´sha;
and as soon as the man touched the
bones of Eli´sha, he revived, and stood
on his feet.

ISRAEL RECAPTURES CITIES FROM ARAM

22 Now Haz´ael king of Syria op-
pressed Israel all the days of Jeho´a-
haz. 23But the LORD was gracious to

[a]Gk Syr Tg Vg: Heb *he walked*

them and had compassion on them,
and he turned toward them, because
of his covenant with Abraham, Isaac,
and Jacob, and would not destroy
them; nor has he cast them from his
presence until now.

24 When Haz´ael king of Syria
died, Ben-ha´dad his son became king
in his stead. 25Then Jeho´ash the son of
Jeho´ahaz took again from Ben-ha´dad
the son of Haz´ael the cities which he
had taken from Jeho´ahaz his father in
war. Three times Jo´ash defeated him
and recovered the cities of Israel.

AMAZIAH REIGNS OVER JUDAH

14 In the second year of Jo´ash the
son of Jo´ahaz, king of Israel,
Amazi´ah the son of Jo´ash, king of
Judah, began to reign. 2He was twen-
ty-five years old when he began to
reign, and he reigned twenty-nine
years in Jerusalem. His mother's
name was Jeho-ad´din of Jerusalem.
3And he did what was right in the eyes
of the LORD, yet not like David his
father; he did in all things as Jo´ash
his father had done. 4But the high
places were not removed; the people
still sacrificed and burned incense on
the high places. 5And as soon as the
royal power was firmly in his hand he
killed his servants who had slain the
king his father. 6But he did not put to
death the children of the murderers;
according to what is written in the
book of the law of Moses, where the
LORD commanded, "The fathers shall
not be put to death for the children,
or the children be put to death for the
fathers; but every man shall die for his
own sin."

7 He killed ten thousand E´domites
in the Valley of Salt and took Sela by
storm, and called it Jok´the-el, which
is its name to this day.

8 Then Amazi´ah sent messengers
to Jeho´ash the son of Jeho´ahaz, son
of Jehu, king of Israel, saying, "Come,
let us look one another in the face."
9And Jeho´ash king of Israel sent
word to Amazi´ah king of Judah, "A
thistle on Lebanon sent to a cedar on
Lebanon, saying, 'Give your daughter
to my son for a wife'; and a wild beast
of Lebanon passed by and trampled
down the thistle. 10You have indeed
smitten Edom, and your heart has lift-
ed you up. Be content with your glory,
and stay at home; for why should you
provoke trouble so that you fall, you
and Judah with you?"

11 But Amazi´ah would not listen.
So Jeho´ash king of Israel went up,
and he and Amazi´ah king of Judah
faced one another in battle at Beth-
she´mesh, which belongs to Judah.
12And Judah was defeated by Israel,
and every man fled to his home.
13And Jeho´ash king of Israel captured
Amazi´ah king of Judah, the son of
Jeho´ash, son of Ahazi´ah, at Beth-
she´mesh, and came to Jerusalem,
and broke down the wall of Jerusalem
for four hundred cubits, from the
E´phraim Gate to the Corner Gate.
14And he seized all the gold and silver,
and all the vessels that were found in
the house of the LORD and in the trea-
suries of the king's house, also hos-
tages, and he returned to Samar´ia.

15 Now the rest of the acts of
Jeho´ash which he did, and his might,
and how he fought with Amazi´ah
king of Judah, are they not written
in the Book of the Chronicles of the
Kings of Israel? 16And Jeho´ash slept
with his fathers, and was buried in
Samar´ia with the kings of Israel; and
Jerobo´am his son reigned in his stead.

17 Amazi´ah the son of Jo´ash, king
of Judah, lived fifteen years after the
death of Jeho´ash son of Jeho´ahaz,
king of Israel. 18Now the rest of the
deeds of Amazi´ah, are they not writ-
ten in the Book of the Chronicles of
the Kings of Judah? 19And they made a
conspiracy against him in Jerusalem,
and he fled to Lachish. But they
sent after him to Lachish, and slew
him there. 20And they brought him
upon horses; and he was buried in
Jerusalem with his fathers in the city
of David. 21And all the people of Judah

took Azari´ah,* who was sixteen years
old, and made him king instead of his
father Amazi´ah. 22 He built Elath and
restored it to Judah, after the king
slept with his fathers.

JEROBOAM II REIGNS OVER ISRAEL

23 In the fifteenth year of Amazi´ah
the son of Jo´ash, king of Judah,
Jerobo´am the son of Jo´ash, king of
Israel, began to reign in Samar´ia, and
he reigned forty-one years. 24 And he
did what was evil in the sight of the
LORD; he did not depart from all the
sins of Jerobo´am the son of Nebat,
which he made Israel to sin. 25 He re-
stored the border of Israel from the
entrance of Hamath as far as the Sea
of the Arabah, according to the word
of the LORD, the God of Israel, which
he spoke by his servant Jonah the son
of Amit´tai, the prophet, who was
from Gath-he´pher. 26 For the LORD
saw that the affliction of Israel was
very bitter, for there was none left,
bond or free, and there was none to
help Israel. 27 But the LORD had not
said that he would blot out the name
of Israel from under heaven, so he
saved them by the hand of Jerobo´am
the son of Jo´ash.

28 Now the rest of the acts of
Jerobo´am, and all that he did, and
his might, how he fought, and how
he recovered for Israel Damascus and
Hamath, which had belonged to Judah,
are they not written in the Book of
the Chronicles of the Kings of Israel?
29 And Jerobo´am slept with his fathers,
the kings of Israel, and Zechari´ah his
son reigned in his stead.

AZARIAH REIGNS OVER JUDAH

15 In the twenty-seventh year of
Jerobo´am king of Israel Azari´ah
the son of Amazi´ah, king of Judah,
began to reign. 2 He was sixteen years
old when he began to reign, and he
reigned fifty-two years in Jerusalem.
His mother's name was Jecoli´ah of
Jerusalem. 3 And he did what was right
in the eyes of the LORD, according
to all that his father Amazi´ah had
done. 4 Nevertheless the high places
were not taken away; the people still
sacrificed and burned incense on the
high places. 5 And the LORD smote the
king, so that he was a leper to the day
of his death, and he dwelt in a sepa-
rate house. And Jotham the king's son
was over the household, governing
the people of the land. 6 Now the rest
of the acts of Azari´ah, and all that
he did, are they not written in the
Book of the Chronicles of the Kings
of Judah? 7 And Azari´ah slept with
his fathers, and they buried him with
his fathers in the city of David, and
Jotham his son reigned in his stead.

ZECHARIAH REIGNS OVER ISRAEL

8 In the thirty-eighth year of
Azari´ah king of Judah Zechari´ah the
son of Jerobo´am reigned over Israel
in Samar´ia six months. 9 And he did
what was evil in the sight of the LORD,
as his fathers had done. He did not de-
part from the sins of Jerobo´am the son
of Nebat, which he made Israel to sin.
10 Shallum the son of Jabesh conspired
against him, and struck him down at
Ibleam,[a] and killed him, and reigned
in his stead. 11 Now the rest of the
deeds of Zechari´ah, behold, they are
written in the Book of the Chronicles
of the Kings of Israel. 12 (This was the
promise of the LORD which he gave
to Jehu, "Your sons shall sit upon the
throne of Israel to the fourth genera-
tion." And so it came to pass.)

SHALLUM REIGNS OVER ISRAEL

13 Shallum the son of Jabesh began
to reign in the thirty-ninth year of
Uzzi´ah king of Judah, and he reigned
one month in Samar´ia. 14 Then Men´-
ahem the son of Gadi came up from
Tirzah and came to Samar´ia, and he
struck down Shallum the son of Jabesh
in Samar´ia and slew him, and reigned
in his stead. 15 Now the rest of the
deeds of Shallum, and the conspiracy

[a] Gk Compare 9.27: Heb *before the people*

which he made, behold, they are writ-
ten in the Book of the Chronicles of
the Kings of Israel. 16At that time
Men'ahem sacked Tap'pu-ah[a] and all
who were in it and its territory from
Tirzah on; because they did not open
it to him, therefore he sacked it, and
he ripped up all the women in it who
were with child.

MENAHEM REIGNS OVER ISRAEL

17 In the thirty-ninth year of
Azari'ah king of Judah Men'ahem the
son of Gadi began to reign over Israel,
and he reigned ten years in Samar'ia.
18And he did what was evil in the sight
of the LORD; he did not depart all his
days from all the sins of Jerobo'am the
son of Nebat, which he made Israel to
sin. 19Pul the king of Assyria came
against the land; and Men'ahem gave
Pul* a thousand talents of silver, that
he might help him to confirm his hold
of the royal power. 20Men'ahem ex-
acted the money from Israel, that is,
from all the wealthy men, fifty shek-
els of silver from every man, to give
to the king of Assyria. So the king of
Assyria turned back, and did not stay
there in the land. 21Now the rest of
the deeds of Men'ahem, and all that
he did, are they not written in the
Book of the Chronicles of the Kings of
Israel? 22And Men'ahem slept with his
fathers, and Pekahi'ah his son reigned
in his stead.

PEKAHIAH REIGNS OVER ISRAEL

23 In the fiftieth year of Azari'ah
king of Judah Pekahi'ah the son of
Men'ahem began to reign over Israel
in Samar'ia, and he reigned two years.
24And he did what was evil in the sight
of the LORD; he did not turn away
from the sins of Jerobo'am the son of
Nebat, which he made Israel to sin.
25And Pekah the son of Remali'ah,
his captain, conspired against him
with fifty men of the Gileadites, and
slew him in Samar'ia, in the citadel
of the king's house;[b] he slew him, and
reigned in his stead. 26Now the rest of
the deeds of Pekahi'ah, and all that
he did, behold, they are written in the
Book of the Chronicles of the Kings
of Israel.

PEKAH REIGNS OVER ISRAEL

27 In the fifty-second year of
Azari'ah king of Judah Pekah the son
of Remali'ah began to reign over Israel
in Samar'ia, and he reigned twenty
years. 28And he did what was evil in
the sight of the LORD; he did not de-
part from the sins of Jerobo'am the son
of Nebat, which he made Israel to sin.
29 In the days of Pekah king of
Israel Tig'lath-pile'ser king of Assyria
came and captured I'jon, A'bel-beth-
ma'acah, Jan-o'ah, Kedesh, Hazor,
Gilead, and Galilee, all the land of
Naph'tali; and he carried the people
captive to Assyria. 30Then Hoshe'a the
son of Elah made a conspiracy against
Pekah the son of Remali'ah, and
struck him down, and slew him, and
reigned in his stead, in the twentieth
year of Jotham the son of Uzzi'ah.
31Now the rest of the acts of Pekah,
and all that he did, behold, they are
written in the Book of the Chronicles
of the Kings of Israel.

JOTHAM REIGNS OVER JUDAH

32 In the second year of Pekah
the son of Remali'ah, king of Israel,
Jotham the son of Uzzi'ah, king of
Judah, began to reign. 33He was twen-
ty-five years old when he began to
reign, and he reigned sixteen years
in Jerusalem. His mother's name was
Jeru'sha the daughter of Zadok. 34And
he did what was right in the eyes of
the LORD, according to all that his fa-
ther Uzzi'ah had done. 35Nevertheless
the high places were not removed; the
people still sacrificed and burned in-
cense on the high places. He built the
upper gate of the house of the LORD.
36Now the rest of the acts of Jotham,

[a] Compare Gk: Heb *Tiphsah*
[b] Heb adds *Argob and Arieh,* which probably belong to the list of places in verse 29

and all that he did, are they not written in the Book of the Chronicles of the Kings of Judah? 37 In those days the LORD began to send Rezin the king of Syria and Pekah the son of Remali´ah against Judah. 38 Jotham slept with his fathers, and was buried with his fathers in the city of David his father; and Ahaz his son reigned in his stead.

AHAZ REIGNS OVER JUDAH

16 In the seventeenth year of Pekah the son of Remali´ah, Ahaz the son of Jotham, king of Judah, began to reign. 2 Ahaz was twenty years old when he began to reign, and he reigned sixteen years in Jerusalem. And he did not do what was right in the eyes of the LORD his God, as his father David had done, 3 but he walked in the way of the kings of Israel. He even burned his son as an offering,[c] according to the abominable practices of the nations whom the LORD drove out before the people of Israel.* 4 And he sacrificed and burned incense on the high places, and on the hills, and under every green tree.

5 Then Rezin king of Syria and Pekah the son of Remali´ah, king of Israel, came up to wage war on Jerusalem, and they besieged Ahaz but could not conquer him. 6 At that time[d] the king of Edom[e] recovered Elath for Edom,[f] and drove the men of Judah from Elath; and the E´domites came to Elath, where they dwell to this day. 7 So Ahaz sent messengers to Tig´lath-pile´ser king of Assyria, saying, "I am your servant and your son. Come up, and rescue me from the hand of the king of Syria and from the hand of the king of Israel, who are attacking me." 8 Ahaz also took the silver and gold that was found in the house of the LORD and in the treasures of the king's house, and sent a present to the king of Assyria. 9 And the king of Assyria hearkened to him; the king of Assyria marched up against Damascus, and took it, carrying its people captive to Kir, and he killed Rezin.

10 When King Ahaz went to Damascus to meet Tig´lath-pile´ser king of Assyria, he saw the altar that was at Damascus. And King Ahaz sent to Uri´ah the priest a model of the altar, and its pattern, exact in all its details. 11 And Uri´ah the priest built the altar; in accordance with all that King Ahaz had sent from Damascus, so Uri´ah the priest made it, before King Ahaz arrived from Damascus. 12 And when the king came from Damascus, the king viewed the altar. Then the king drew near to the altar, and went up on it, 13 and burned his burnt offering and his cereal offering, and poured his drink offering, and threw the blood of his peace offerings upon the altar. 14 And the bronze altar which was before the LORD he removed from the front of the house, from the place between his altar and the house of the LORD, and put it on the north side of his altar. 15 And King Ahaz commanded Uri´ah the priest, saying, "Upon the great altar burn the morning burnt offering, and the evening cereal offering, and the king's burnt offering, and his cereal offering, with the burnt offering of all the people of the land, and their cereal offering, and their drink offering; and throw upon it all the blood of the burnt offering, and all the blood of the sacrifice; but the bronze altar shall be for me to inquire by." 16 Uri´ah the priest did all this, as King Ahaz commanded.

17 And King Ahaz cut off the frames of the stands, and removed the laver from them, and he took down the sea from off the bronze oxen that were under it, and put it upon a pediment of stone. 18 And the covered way for the sabbath which had been built inside the palace, and

[c] Or *made his son to pass through the fire*
[d] Heb *At that time Rezin*
[e] Heb *Aram* (Syria)
[f] Heb *Aram* (Syria)

the outer entrance for the king he removed from[a] the house of the LORD, because of the king of Assyria. 19 Now the rest of the acts of Ahaz which he did, are they not written in the Book of the Chronicles of the Kings of Judah? 20 And Ahaz slept with his fathers, and was buried with his fathers in the city of David; and Hezeki´ah his son reigned in his stead.

HOSHEA REIGNS OVER ISRAEL; ISRAEL CARRIED CAPTIVE TO ASSYRIA

17 In the twelfth year of Ahaz king of Judah Hoshe´a the son of Elah began to reign in Samar´ia over Israel, and he reigned nine years. 2 And he did what was evil in the sight of the LORD, yet not as the kings of Israel who were before him. 3 Against him came up Shalmane´ser king of Assyria; and Hoshe´a became his vassal, and paid him tribute. 4 But the king of Assyria found treachery in Hoshe´a; for he had sent messengers to So, king of Egypt, and offered no tribute to the king of Assyria, as he had done year by year; therefore the king of Assyria shut him up, and bound him in prison. 5 Then the king of Assyria invaded all the land and came to Samar´ia, and for three years he besieged it. 6 In the ninth year of Hoshe´a the king of Assyria captured Samar´ia, and he carried the Israelites away to Assyria, and placed them in Halah, and on the Habor, the river of Gozan, and in the cities of the Medes.

7 And this was so, because the people of Israel had sinned against the LORD their God, who had brought them up out of the land of Egypt from under the hand of Pharaoh king of Egypt, and had feared other gods 8 and walked in the customs of the nations whom the LORD drove out before the people of Israel, and in the customs which the kings of Israel had introduced.[b] 9 And the people of Israel did secretly against the LORD their God things that were not right. They built for themselves high places at all their towns, from watchtower to fortified city; 10 they set up for themselves pillars and Ashe´rim on every high hill and under every green tree; 11 and there they burned incense on all the high places, as the nations did whom the LORD carried away before them. And they did wicked things, provoking the LORD to anger, 12 and they served idols, of which the LORD had said to them, "You shall not do this." 13 Yet the LORD warned Israel and Judah by every prophet and every seer, saying, "Turn from your evil ways and keep my commandments and my statutes, in accordance with all the law which I commanded your fathers, and which I sent to you by my servants the prophets." 14 But they would not listen, but were stubborn, as their fathers had been, who did not believe in the LORD their God. 15 They despised his statutes, and his covenant that he made with their fathers, and the warnings which he gave them. They went after false idols, and became false, and they followed the nations that were round about them, concerning whom the LORD had commanded them that they should not do like them. 16 And they forsook all the commandments of the LORD their God, and made for themselves molten images of two calves; and they made an Ashe´rah, and worshiped all the host of heaven, and served Ba´al. 17 And they burned their sons and their daughters as offerings,[c] and used divination and sorcery, and sold themselves to do evil in the sight of the LORD, provoking him to anger. 18 Therefore the LORD was very angry with Israel, and removed them out of his sight; none was left but the tribe of Judah only.*

19 Judah also did not keep the commandments of the LORD their God, but walked in the customs which

[a] Cn: Heb *turned to*
[b] Heb obscure
[c] Or *made their sons and their daughters pass through the fire*

Israel had introduced. 20And the LORD
rejected all the descendants of Israel,
and afflicted them, and gave them
into the hand of spoilers, until he had
cast them out of his sight.

21 When he had torn Israel from the
house of David they made Jerobo'am
the son of Nebat king. And Jerobo'am
drove Israel from following the LORD
and made them commit great sin.
22The people of Israel walked in all
the sins which Jerobo'am did; they
did not depart from them, 23until the
LORD removed Israel out of his sight,
as he had spoken by all his servants
the prophets. So Israel was exiled
from their own land to Assyria until
this day.

ASSYRIA RESETTLES SAMARIA

24*And the king of Assyria brought
people from Babylon, Cuthah, Avva,
Hamath, and Sepharva'im, and placed
them in the cities of Samar'ia instead
of the people of Israel; and they took
possession of Samar'ia, and dwelt in
its cities. 25And at the beginning of
their dwelling there, they did not fear
the LORD; therefore the LORD sent
lions among them, which killed some
of them. 26So the king of Assyria was
told, "The nations which you have car-
ried away and placed in the cities of
Samar'ia do not know the law of the
god of the land; therefore he has sent
lions among them, and behold, they
are killing them, because they do not
know the law of the god of the land."
27Then the king of Assyria command-
ed, "Send there one of the priests
whom you carried away thence; and
let him[d] go and dwell there, and teach
them the law of the god of the land."
28So one of the priests whom they had
carried away from Samar'ia came and
dwelt in Bethel, and taught them how
they should fear the LORD.

29 But every nation still made
gods of its own, and put them in the
shrines of the high places which the
Samaritans had made, every nation
in the cities in which they dwelt;
30the men of Babylon made Suc'coth-
be'noth, the men of Cuth made
Nergal, the men of Hamath made
Ashi'ma, 31and the Av'vites made
Nibhaz and Tartak; and the Sephar'-
vites burned their children in the fire
to Adram'melech and Anam'melech,
the gods of Sepharva'im. 32They also
feared the LORD, and appointed from
among themselves all sorts of peo-
ple as priests of the high places, who
sacrificed for them in the shrines of
the high places. 33So they feared the
LORD but also served their own gods,
after the manner of the nations from
among whom they had been carried
away. 34To this day they do according
to the former manner.

They do not fear the LORD, and
they do not follow the statutes or the
ordinances or the law or the com-
mandment which the LORD com-
manded the children of Jacob, whom
he named Israel. 35The LORD made a
covenant with them, and commanded
them, "You shall not fear other gods
or bow yourselves to them or serve
them or sacrifice to them; 36but you
shall fear the LORD, who brought you
out of the land of Egypt with great
power and with an outstretched arm;
you shall bow yourselves to him, and
to him you shall sacrifice. 37And the
statutes and the ordinances and the
law and the commandment which he
wrote for you, you shall always be
careful to do. You shall not fear oth-
er gods, 38and you shall not forget the
covenant that I have made with you.
You shall not fear other gods, 39but
you shall fear the LORD your God, and
he will deliver you out of the hand
of all your enemies." 40However they
would not listen, but they did accord-
ing to their former manner.

41 So these nations feared the
LORD, and also served their graven
images; their children likewise, and
their children's children—as their fa-
thers did, so they do to this day.

[d] Syr Vg: Heb *them*

HEZEKIAH'S REIGN OVER JUDAH

18 In the third year of Hoshe´a son
of Elah, king of Israel, Hezeki´ah
the son of Ahaz, king of Judah, be-
gan to reign. 2He was twenty-five
years old when he began to reign,
and he reigned twenty-nine years in
Jerusalem. His mother's name was
Abi the daughter of Zechari´ah. 3And
he did what was right in the eyes of
the LORD, according to all that David
his father had done. 4He removed the
high places, and broke the pillars, and
cut down the Ashe´rah. And he broke
in pieces the bronze serpent that
Moses had made, for until those days
the people of Israel had burned in-
cense to it; it was called Nehush´tan.
5He trusted in the LORD the God of
Israel; so that there was none like
him among all the kings of Judah af-
ter him, nor among those who were
before him. 6For he held fast to the
LORD; he did not depart from follow-
ing him, but kept the commandments
which the LORD commanded Moses.
7And the LORD was with him; wher-
ever he went forth, he prospered. He
rebelled against the king of Assyria,
and would not serve him. 8He smote
the Philistines as far as Gaza and its
territory, from watchtower to forti-
fied city.

9 In the fourth year of King
Hezeki´ah, which was the seventh
year of Hoshe´a son of Elah, king of
Israel, Shalmane´ser king of Assyria
came up against Samar´ia and be-
sieged it 10and at the end of three
years he took it. In the sixth year of
Hezeki´ah, which was the ninth year
of Hoshe´a king of Israel, Samar´ia
was taken. 11The king of Assyria car-
ried the Israelites away to Assyria,
and put them in Halah, and on the
Habor, the river of Gozan, and in the
cities of the Medes, 12because they did
not obey the voice of the LORD their
God but transgressed his covenant,
even all that Moses the servant of the
LORD commanded; they neither lis-
tened nor obeyed.

SENNACHERIB INVADES JUDAH

13 In the fourteenth year of King
Hezeki´ah Sennach´erib king of As-
syria came up against all the fortified
cities of Judah and took them. 14And
Hezeki´ah king of Judah sent to the
king of Assyria at Lachish, saying,
"I have done wrong; withdraw from
me; whatever you impose on me I
will bear." And the king of Assyria
required of Hezeki´ah king of Judah
three hundred talents of silver and
thirty talents of gold. 15And Hezeki´ah
gave him all the silver that was found
in the house of the LORD, and in the
treasuries of the king's house. 16At
that time Hezeki´ah stripped the gold
from the doors of the temple of the
LORD, and from the doorposts which
Hezeki´ah king of Judah had overlaid
and gave it to the king of Assyria. 17And
the king of Assyria sent the Tartan,
the Rab´saris, and the Rab´shakeh
with a great army from Lachish to
King Hezeki´ah at Jerusalem. And
they went up and came to Jerusalem.
When they arrived, they came and
stood by the conduit of the upper
pool, which is on the highway to the
Fuller's Field. 18And when they called
for the king, there came out to them
Eli´akim the son of Hilki´ah, who was
over the household, and Shebnah the
secretary, and Jo´ah the son of Asaph,
the recorder.

19 And the Rab´shakeh said to
them, "Say to Hezeki´ah, 'Thus says
the great king, the king of Assyria:
On what do you rest this confidence
of yours? 20Do you think that mere
words are strategy and power for war?
On whom do you now rely, that you
have rebelled against me? 21Behold,
you are relying now on Egypt, that
broken reed of a staff, which will
pierce the hand of any man who leans
on it. Such is Pharaoh king of Egypt
to all who rely on him. 22But if you
say to me, "We rely on the LORD our
God," is it not he whose high places
and altars Hezeki´ah has removed,
saying to Judah and to Jerusalem,

are dismayed and
confounded,
and have become like plants of
the field,
and like tender grass,
like grass on the housetops;
blighted before it is grown?
27"But I know your sitting down
and your going out and
coming in,
and your raging against me.
28Because you have raged
against me
and your arrogance has
come into my ears,
I will put my hook in your nose
and my bit in your mouth,
and I will turn you back on
the way
by which you came.

29 "And this shall be the sign
for you: this year you shall eat what
grows of itself, and in the second year
what springs of the same; then in the
third year sow, and reap, and plant
vineyards, and eat their fruit. 30And
the surviving remnant of the house
of Judah shall again take root down-
ward, and bear fruit upward; 31for out
of Jerusalem shall go forth a remnant,
and out of Mount Zion a band of survi-
vors. The zeal of the LORD will do this.

32 "Therefore thus says the LORD
concerning the king of Assyria, He
shall not come into this city or shoot
an arrow there, or come before it with
a shield or cast up a siege mound
against it. 33By the way that he came,
by the same he shall return, and he
shall not come into this city, says the
LORD. 34For I will defend this city to
save it, for my own sake and for the
sake of my servant David."

SENNACHERIB'S DEFEAT AND DEATH

35 And that night the angel of the
LORD went forth, and slew a hundred
and eighty-five thousand in the camp
of the Assyrians;* and when men
arose early in the morning, behold,
these were all dead bodies. 36Then
Sennach´erib king of Assyria departed,
and went home, and dwelt at Nin´eveh.
37And as he was worshiping in the house
of Nisroch his god, Adram´melech and
Share´zer, his sons, slew him with
the sword, and escaped into the land
of Ar´arat. And Esarhad´don his son
reigned in his stead.

HEZEKIAH'S ILLNESS

20 In those days Hezeki´ah be-
came sick and was at the point
of death. And Isaiah the prophet the
son of Amoz came to him, and said to
him, "Thus says the LORD, 'Set your
house in order; for you shall die, you
shall not recover.'" 2Then Hezeki´ah
turned his face to the wall, and prayed
to the LORD, saying, 3"Remember
now, O LORD, I beseech thee, how
I have walked before thee in faith-
fulness and with a whole heart, and
have done what is good in thy sight."
And Hezeki´ah wept bitterly. 4And
before Isaiah had gone out of the
middle court, the word of the LORD
came to him: 5"Turn back, and say to
Hezeki´ah the prince of my people,
Thus says the LORD, the God of David
your father: I have heard your prayer,
I have seen your tears; behold, I will
heal you; on the third day you shall
go up to the house of the LORD. 6And
I will add fifteen years to your life. I
will deliver you and this city out of the
hand of the king of Assyria, and I will
defend this city for my own sake and
for my servant David's sake." 7And
Isaiah said, "Bring a cake of figs. And
let them take and lay it on the boil,
that he may recover."

8 And Hezeki´ah said to Isaiah,
"What shall be the sign that the LORD
will heal me, and that I shall go up to
the house of the LORD on the third
day?" 9And Isaiah said, "This is the
sign to you from the LORD, that the
LORD will do the thing that he has
promised: shall the shadow go for-
ward ten steps, or go back ten steps?"
10And Hezeki´ah answered, "It is an
easy thing for the shadow to length-
en ten steps; rather let the shadow

go back ten steps." 11And Isaiah the
prophet cried to the LORD; and he
brought the shadow back ten steps,
by which the sun[a] had declined on the
dial of Ahaz.

ENVOYS FROM BABYLON

12 At that time Mero′dach-bal′-
adan the son of Bal′adan, king of
Babylon, sent envoys with letters and
a present to Hezeki′ah; for he heard
that Hezeki′ah had been sick. 13And
Hezeki′ah welcomed them, and he
showed them all his treasure house,
the silver, the gold, the spices, the
precious oil, his armory, all that was
found in his storehouses; there was
nothing in his house or in all his
realm that Hezeki′ah did not show
them. 14Then Isaiah the prophet came
to King Hezeki′ah, and said to him,
"What did these men say? And whence
did they come to you?" And Hezeki′ah
said, "They have come from a far
country, from Babylon." 15He said,
"What have they seen in your house?"
And Hezeki′ah answered, "They have
seen all that is in my house; there is
nothing in my storehouses that I did
not show them."

16 Then Isaiah said to Hezeki′ah,
"Hear the word of the LORD: 17Behold,
the days are coming, when all that is
in your house, and that which your fa-
thers have stored up till this day, shall
be carried to Babylon; nothing shall
be left, says the LORD. 18And some of
your own sons, who are born to you,
shall be taken away; and they shall
be eunuchs in the palace of the king
of Babylon." 19Then said Hezeki′ah
to Isaiah, "The word of the LORD
which you have spoken is good." For
he thought, "Why not, if there will be
peace and security in my days?"

DEATH OF HEZEKIAH

20 The rest of the deeds of Hez-
eki′ah, and all his might, and how
he made the pool and the conduit
and brought water into the city, are
they not written in the Book of the
Chronicles of the Kings of Judah?
21And Hezeki′ah slept with his fa-
thers; and Manas′seh his son reigned
in his stead.

MANASSEH REIGNS OVER JUDAH

21 Manas′seh was twelve years old
when he began to reign, and he
reigned fifty-five years in Jerusalem.
His mother's name was Heph′zibah.
2And he did what was evil in the sight
of the LORD, according to the abom-
inable practices of the nations whom
the LORD drove out before the people
of Israel. 3For he rebuilt the high plac-
es which Hezeki′ah his father had de-
stroyed; and he erected altars for Ba′al,
and made an Ashe′rah, as Ahab king
of Israel had done, and worshiped all
the host of heaven, and served them.
4And he built altars in the house of the
LORD, of which the LORD had said, "In
Jerusalem will I put my name." 5And
he built altars for all the host of heav-
en in the two courts of the house of
the LORD. 6And he burned his son as
an offering, and practiced soothsaying
and augury, and dealt with mediums
and with wizards. He did much evil
in the sight of the LORD, provoking
him to anger. 7And the graven image
of Ashe′rah that he had made he set in
the house of which the LORD said to
David and to Solomon his son, "In this
house, and in Jerusalem, which I have
chosen out of all the tribes of Israel, I
will put my name for ever; 8and I will
not cause the feet of Israel to wander
any more out of the land which I gave
to their fathers, if only they will be
careful to do according to all that I
have commanded them, and according
to all the law that my servant Moses
commanded them." 9But they did not
listen, and Manas′seh seduced them
to do more evil than the nations had
done whom the LORD destroyed be-
fore the people of Israel.

10 And the LORD said by his
servants the prophets, 11"Because

[a] Syr See Is 38. 8 and Tg: Heb lacks *the sun*

Manas´seh king of Judah has commit-
ted these abominations, and has done
things more wicked than all that the
Amorites did, who were before him,
and has made Judah also to sin with
his idols; 12therefore thus says the
LORD, the God of Israel, Behold, I am
bringing upon Jerusalem and Judah
such evil that the ears of every one
who hears of it will tingle. 13And I will
stretch over Jerusalem the measuring
line of Samar´ia, and the plummet of
the house of Ahab; and I will wipe
Jerusalem as one wipes a dish, wiping
it and turning it upside down. 14And I
will cast off the remnant of my heri-
tage, and give them into the hand of
their enemies, and they shall become
a prey and a spoil to all their enemies,
15because they have done what is evil
in my sight and have provoked me to
anger, since the day their fathers came
out of Egypt, even to this day."

16 Moreover Manas´seh shed very
much innocent blood, till he had filled
Jerusalem from one end to another,
besides the sin which he made Judah
to sin so that they did what was evil in
the sight of the LORD.

17 Now the rest of the acts of
Manas´seh, and all that he did,
and the sin that he committed, are
they not written in the Book of the
Chronicles of the Kings of Judah?
18And Manas´seh slept with his fa-
thers, and was buried in the garden of
his house, in the garden of Uzza; and
Amon his son reigned in his stead.

AMON REIGNS OVER JUDAH

19 Amon was twenty-two years
old when he began to reign, and he
reigned two years in Jerusalem. His
mother's name was Meshul´lemeth
the daughter of Haruz of Jotbah.
20And he did what was evil in the
sight of the LORD, as Manas´seh his
father had done. 21He walked in all the
way in which his father walked, and
served the idols that his father served,
and worshiped them; 22he forsook the
LORD, the God of his fathers, and
did not walk in the way of the LORD.
23And the servants of Amon conspired
against him, and killed the king in his
house. 24But the people of the land
slew all those who had conspired
against King Amon, and the people of
the land made Josi´ah his son king in
his stead. 25Now the rest of the acts
of Amon which he did, are they not
written in the Book of the Chronicles
of the Kings of Judah? 26And he was
buried in his tomb in the garden of
Uzza; and Josi´ah his son reigned in
his stead.

JOSIAH REIGNS OVER JUDAH

22 Josi´ah was eight years old when
he began to reign, and he reigned
thirty-one years in Jerusalem. His
mother's name was Jedi´dah the
daughter of Adai´ah of Bozkath. 2And
he did what was right in the eyes of
the LORD, and walked in all the way of
David his father, and he did not turn
aside to the right hand or to the left.

HILKIAH FINDS THE BOOK OF THE LAW

3 In the eighteenth year of King
Josi´ah, the king sent Shaphan the son
of Azali´ah, son of Meshul´lam, the
secretary, to the house of the LORD,
saying, 4"Go up to Hilki´ah the high
priest, that he may reckon the amount
of the money which has been brought
into the house of the LORD, which
the keepers of the threshold have col-
lected from the people; 5and let it be
given into the hand of the workmen
who have the oversight of the house
of the LORD; and let them give it to
the workmen who are at the house of
the LORD, repairing the house, 6that
is, to the carpenters, and to the build-
ers, and to the masons, as well as for
buying timber and quarried stone to
repair the house. 7But no accounting
shall be asked from them for the mon-
ey which is delivered into their hand,
for they deal honestly."

8 And Hilki´ah the high priest
said to Shaphan the secretary, "I
have found the book of the law* in

the house of the LORD." And Hilki´ah
gave the book to Shaphan, and he read
it. 9And Shaphan the secretary came
to the king, and reported to the king,
"Your servants have emptied out the
money that was found in the house,
and have delivered it into the hand of
the workmen who have the oversight
of the house of the LORD." 10Then
Shaphan the secretary told the king,
"Hilki´ah the priest has given me a
book." And Shaphan read it before
the king.

11 And when the king heard the
words of the book of the law, he rent
his clothes. 12And the king command-
ed Hilki´ah the priest, and Ahi´kam
the son of Shaphan, and Achbor the
son of Micai´ah, and Shaphan the sec-
retary, and Asai´ah the king's servant,
saying, 13"Go, inquire of the LORD for
me, and for the people, and for all
Judah, concerning the words of this
book that has been found; for great is
the wrath of the LORD that is kindled
against us, because our fathers have
not obeyed the words of this book, to
do according to all that is written con-
cerning us."

14 So Hilki´ah the priest, and
Ahi´kam, and Achbor, and Shaphan,
and Asai´ah went to Huldah the
prophetess, the wife of Shallum the
son of Tikvah, son of Harhas, keep-
er of the wardrobe (now she dwelt in
Jerusalem in the Second Quarter); and
they talked with her. 15And she said to
them, "Thus says the LORD, the God
of Israel: 'Tell the man who sent you
to me, 16Thus says the LORD, Behold,
I will bring evil upon this place and
upon its inhabitants, all the words
of the book which the king of Judah
has read. 17Because they have forsak-
en me and have burned incense to
other gods, that they might provoke
me to anger with all the work of their
hands, therefore my wrath will be
kindled against this place, and it will
not be quenched. 18But as to the king
of Judah, who sent you to inquire of
the LORD, thus shall you say to him,
Thus says the LORD, the God of Israel:
Regarding the words which you have
heard, 19because your heart was pen-
itent, and you humbled yourself be-
fore the LORD, when you heard how
I spoke against this place, and against
its inhabitants, that they should be-
come a desolation and a curse, and
you have rent your clothes and wept
before me, I also have heard you, says
the LORD. 20Therefore, behold, I will
gather you to your fathers, and you
shall be gathered to your grave in
peace, and your eyes shall not see all
the evil which I will bring upon this
place.'" And they brought back word
to the king.

JOSIAH'S REFORMATION

23 Then the king sent, and all the
elders of Judah and Jerusalem
were gathered to him. 2And the king
went up to the house of the LORD, and
with him all the men of Judah and all
the inhabitants of Jerusalem, and the
priests and the prophets, all the peo-
ple, both small and great; and he read
in their hearing all the words of the
book of the covenant which had been
found in the house of the LORD. 3And
the king stood by the pillar and made
a covenant before the LORD, to walk
after the LORD and to keep his com-
mandments and his testimonies and
his statutes, with all his heart and
all his soul, to perform the words of
this covenant that were written in this
book; and all the people joined in the
covenant.

4 And the king commanded
Hilki´ah, the high priest, and the
priests of the second order, and the
keepers of the threshold, to bring out
of the temple of the LORD all the ves-
sels made for Ba´al, for Ashe´rah, and
for all the host of heaven; he burned
them outside Jerusalem in the fields
of the Kidron, and carried their ashes
to Bethel. 5And he deposed the idola-
trous priests whom the kings of Judah
had ordained to burn incense in the
high places at the cities of Judah and

round about Jerusalem; those also who
burned incense to Ba´al, to the sun,
and the moon, and the constellations,
and all the host of the heavens. 6And
he brought out the Ashe´rah from the
house of the LORD, outside Jerusalem,
to the brook Kidron, and burned it
at the brook Kidron, and beat it to
dust and cast the dust of it upon the
graves of the common people. 7And
he broke down the houses of the male
cult prostitutes which were in the
house of the LORD, where the women
wove hangings for the Ashe´rah. 8And
he brought all the priests out of the
cities of Judah, and defiled the high
places where the priests had burned
incense, from Geba to Beer-sheba; and
he broke down the high places of the
gates that were at the entrance of the
gate of Joshua the governor of the city,
which were on one's left at the gate of
the city. 9However, the priests of the
high places did not come up to the al-
tar of the LORD in Jerusalem, but they
ate unleavened bread among their
brethren. 10And he defiled To´pheth,
which is in the valley of the sons of
Hinnom, that no one might burn his
son or his daughter as an offering to
Molech. 11And he removed the horses
that the kings of Judah had dedicat-
ed to the sun, at the entrance to the
house of the LORD, by the chamber
of Nathan-melech the chamberlain,
which was in the precincts;[a] and he
burned the chariots of the sun with
fire. 12And the altars on the roof of
the upper chamber of Ahaz, which
the kings of Judah had made, and the
altars which Manas´seh had made in
the two courts of the house of the
LORD, he pulled down and broke in
pieces,[b] and cast the dust of them into
the brook Kidron. 13And the king de-
filed the high places that were east of
Jerusalem, to the south of the mount
of corruption, which Solomon the
king of Israel had built for Ash´toreth
the abomination of the Sido´nians,
and for Chemosh the abomination of
Moab, and for Milcom the abomina-
tion of the Ammonites. 14And he broke
in pieces the pillars, and cut down the
Ashe´rim, and filled their places with
the bones of men.

15 Moreover the altar at Bethel,
the high place erected by Jerobo´am
the son of Nebat, who made Israel to
sin, that altar with the high place he
pulled down and he broke in pieces its
stones,[c] crushing them to dust; also he
burned the Ashe´rah. 16And as Josi´ah
turned, he saw the tombs there on
the mount; and he sent and took the
bones out of the tombs, and burned
them upon the altar, and defiled it,
according to the word of the LORD
which the man of God proclaimed,
who had predicted these things.
17Then he said, "What is yonder mon-
ument that I see?" And the men of
the city told him, "It is the tomb of
the man of God who came from Judah
and predicted these things which you
have done against the altar at Bethel."
18And he said, "Let him be; let no man
move his bones." So they let his bones
alone, with the bones of the prophet
who came out of Samar´ia. 19And all
the shrines also of the high places
that were in the cities of Samar´ia,
which kings of Israel had made, pro-
voking the LORD to anger, Josi´ah re-
moved; he did to them according to all
that he had done at Bethel. 20And he
slew all the priests of the high places
who were there, upon the altars, and
burned the bones of men upon them.
Then he returned to Jerusalem.

THE PASSOVER CELEBRATED

21 And the king commanded all
the people, "Keep the passover to the
LORD your God, as it is written in
this book of the covenant." 22For no
such passover had been kept since the
days of the judges who judged Israel,
or during all the days of the kings of
Israel or of the kings of Judah; 23but

[a] The meaning of the Hebrew word is uncertain
[b] Heb *pieces from there*
[c] Gk: Heb *he burned the high place*

in the eighteenth year of King Josi´ah
this passover was kept to the LORD in
Jerusalem.
24 Moreover Josi´ah put away the
mediums and the wizards and the ter-
aphim and the idols and all the abom-
inations that were seen in the land of
Judah and in Jerusalem, that he might
establish the words of the law which
were written in the book that Hilki´ah
the priest found in the house of the
LORD. 25 Before him there was no king
like him, who turned to the LORD
with all his heart and with all his soul
and with all his might, according to all
the law of Moses; nor did any like him
arise after him.
26 Still the LORD did not turn from
the fierceness of his great wrath, by
which his anger was kindled against
Judah, because of all the provocations
with which Manas´seh had provoked
him. 27 And the LORD said, "I will re-
move Judah also out of my sight, as I
have removed Israel, and I will cast
off this city which I have chosen,
Jerusalem, and the house of which I
said, My name shall be there."

JOSIAH DIES IN BATTLE

28 Now the rest of the acts of
Josi´ah, and all that he did, are
they not written in the Book of the
Chronicles of the Kings of Judah? 29 In
his days Pharaoh Neco king of Egypt
went up to the king of Assyria to the
river Euphra´tes. King Josi´ah went
to meet him; and Pharaoh Neco slew
him at Megid´do, when he saw him.
30 And his servants carried him dead in
a chariot from Megid´do, and brought
him to Jerusalem, and buried him in
his own tomb. And the people of the
land took Jeho´ahaz the son of Josi´ah,
and anointed him, and made him king
in his father's stead.

REIGN AND CAPTIVITY OF JEHOAHAZ

31 Jeho´ahaz was twenty-three
years old when he began to reign, and
he reigned three months in Jerusalem.
His mother's name was Hamu´tal the
daughter of Jeremiah of Libnah. 32 And
he did what was evil in the sight of
the LORD, according to all that his fa-
thers had done. 33 And Pharaoh Neco
put him in bonds at Riblah in the land
of Hamath, that he might not reign in
Jerusalem, and laid upon the land a
tribute of a hundred talents of silver
and a talent of gold. 34 And Pharaoh
Neco made Eli´akim the son of Josi´ah
king in the place of Josi´ah his father,
and changed his name to Jehoi´akim.
But he took Jeho´ahaz away; and he
came to Egypt, and died there. 35 And
Jehoi´akim gave the silver and the
gold to Pharaoh, but he taxed the
land to give the money according to
the command of Pharaoh. He exacted
the silver and the gold of the people of
the land, from every one according to
his assessment, to give it to Pharaoh
Neco.

JEHOIAKIM REIGNS OVER JUDAH

36 Jehoi´akim was twenty-five
years old when he began to reign, and
he reigned eleven years in Jerusalem.
His mother's name was Zebi´dah the
daughter of Pedai´ah of Rumah. 37 And
he did what was evil in the sight of the
LORD, according to all that his fathers
had done.

JUDAH OVERRUN BY ENEMIES

24 In his days Nebuchadnez´zar
king of Babylon came up, and
Jehoi´akim became his servant three
years; then he turned and rebelled
against him. 2 And the LORD sent
against him bands of the Chalde´ans,
and bands of the Syrians, and bands
of the Moabites, and bands of the
Ammonites, and sent them against
Judah to destroy it, according to the
word of the LORD which he spoke by
his servants the prophets. 3 Surely this
came upon Judah at the command of
the LORD, to remove them out of his
sight, for the sins of Manas´seh, ac-
cording to all that he had done, 4 and
also for the innocent blood that he
had shed; for he filled Jerusalem with

innocent blood, and the LORD would
not pardon. 5Now the rest of the deeds
of Jehoi´akim, and all that he did, are
they not written in the Book of the
Chronicles of the Kings of Judah?
6So Jehoi´akim slept with his fathers,
and Jehoi´achin his son reigned in his
stead. 7And the king of Egypt did not
come again out of his land, for the king
of Babylon had taken all that belonged
to the king of Egypt from the Brook of
Egypt to the river Euphra´tes.

REIGN AND CAPTIVITY OF JEHOIACHIN

8 Jehoi´achin was eighteen years
old when he became king, and he
reigned three months in Jerusalem.
His mother's name was Nehush´ta the
daughter of Elna´than of Jerusalem.
9And he did what was evil in the sight
of the LORD, according to all that his
father had done.

CAPTURE OF JERUSALEM

10 At that time the servants of
Nebuchadnez´zar king of Babylon
came up to Jerusalem, and the city
was besieged. 11And Nebuchadnez´-
zar king of Babylon came to the
city, while his servants were besieg-
ing it; 12and Jehoi´achin the king of
Judah gave himself up to the king of
Babylon, himself, and his mother, and
his servants, and his princes, and his
palace officials. The king of Babylon
took him prisoner in the eighth year
of his reign, 13and carried off all the
treasures of the house of the LORD,
and the treasures of the king's house,
and cut in pieces all the vessels of
gold in the temple of the LORD, which
Solomon king of Israel had made, as
the LORD had foretold. 14He carried
away all Jerusalem, and all the princ-
es, and all the mighty men of valor, ten
thousand captives, and all the crafts-
men and the smiths; none remained,
except the poorest people of the land.
15And he carried away Jehoi´achin to
Babylon; the king's mother, the king's
wives, his officials, and the chief men
of the land, he took into captivity from
Jerusalem to Babylon. 16And the king
of Babylon brought captive to Babylon
all the men of valor, seven thousand,
and the craftsmen and the smiths,
one thousand, all of them strong and
fit for war. 17And the king of Babylon
made Mattani´ah, Jehoi´achin's uncle,
king in his stead, and changed his
name to Zedeki´ah.

ZEDEKIAH REIGNS OVER JUDAH

18 Zedeki´ah was twenty-one
years old when he became king, and
he reigned eleven years in Jerusalem.
His mother's name was Hamu´tal the
daughter of Jeremiah of Libnah. 19And
he did what was evil in the sight of the
LORD, according to all that Jehoi´akim
had done. 20For because of the anger
of the LORD it came to the point in
Jerusalem and Judah that he cast them
out from his presence.

THE FALL AND CAPTIVITY OF JUDAH

And Zedeki´ah rebelled against
the king of Babylon.
25 And in the ninth year of his reign,
in the tenth month, on the tenth
day of the month, Nebuchadnez´zar
king of Babylon came with all his
army against Jerusalem, and laid
siege to it; and they built siegeworks
against it round about. 2So the city
was besieged till the eleventh year of
King Zedeki´ah. 3On the ninth day of
the fourth month the famine was so
severe in the city that there was no
food for the people of the land. 4Then
a breach was made in the city; the
king with all the men of war fled[a] by
night by the way of the gate between
the two walls, by the king's garden,
though the Chalde´ans were around
the city. And they went in the direc-
tion of the Arabah. 5But the army of
the Chalde´ans pursued the king, and
overtook him in the plains of Jericho;
and all his army was scattered from
him. 6Then they captured the king,
and brought him up to the king of

[a]Gk Compare Jer 39. 4; 52.7: Heb lacks *the king* and *fled*

Babylon at Riblah, who passed sen-
tence upon him. 7They slew the sons
of Zedeki´ah before his eyes, and
put out the eyes of Zedeki´ah, and
bound him in fetters, and took him to
Babylon.
8 In the fifth month, on the sev-
enth day of the month—which
was the nineteenth year of King
Nebuchadnez´zar, king of Babylon—
Nebu´zarad´an, the captain of the
bodyguard, a servant of the king of
Babylon, came to Jerusalem. 9And he
burned the house of the LORD, and
the king's house and all the houses
of Jerusalem; every great house he
burned down. 10And all the army of
the Chalde´ans, who were with the
captain of the guard, broke down the
walls around Jerusalem. 11And the rest
of the people who were left in the city
and the deserters who had deserted to
the king of Babylon, together with the
rest of the multitude, Nebu´zarad´an
the captain of the guard carried into
exile. 12But the captain of the guard
left some of the poorest of the land to
be vinedressers and plowmen.
13 And the pillars of bronze that
were in the house of the LORD, and
the stands and the bronze sea that
were in the house of the LORD, the
Chalde´ans broke in pieces, and car-
ried the bronze to Babylon. 14And they
took away the pots, and the shovels,
and the snuffers, and the dishes for
incense and all the vessels of bronze
used in the temple service, 15the fire-
pans also, and the bowls. What was
of gold the captain of the guard took
away as gold, and what was of sil-
ver, as silver. 16As for the two pillars,
the one sea, and the stands, which
Solomon had made for the house of
the LORD, the bronze of all these ves-
sels was beyond weight. 17The height
of the one pillar was eighteen cubits,
and upon it was a capital of bronze;
the height of the capital was three
cubits; a network and pomegranates,
all of bronze, were upon the capital
round about. And the second pillar
had the like, with the network.
18 And the captain of the guard
took Serai´ah the chief priest, and
Zephani´ah the second priest, and the
three keepers of the threshold; 19and
from the city he took an officer who
had been in command of the men of
war, and five men of the king's council
who were found in the city; and the
secretary of the commander of the
army who mustered the people of the
land; and sixty men of the people of
the land who were found in the city.
20And Nebu´zarad´an the captain of
the guard took them, and brought
them to the king of Babylon at Riblah.
21And the king of Babylon smote them,
and put them to death at Riblah in the
land of Hamath. So Judah was taken
into exile out of its land.

GEDALIAH MADE GOVERNOR OF JUDAH

22 And over the people who re-
mained in the land of Judah, whom
Nebuchadnez´zar king of Babylon
had left, he appointed Gedali´ah the
son of Ahi´kam, son of Shaphan, gov-
ernor. 23Now when all the captains
of the forces in the open country[a]
and their men heard that the king
of Babylon had appointed Gedali´ah
governor, they came with their men
to Gedali´ah at Mizpah, namely,
Ish´mael the son of Nethani´ah, and
Joha´nan the son of Kare´ah, and
Serai´ah the son of Tan´humeth the
Netoph´athite, and Ja-azani´ah the
son of the Ma-ac´athite. 24And Gedali´-
ah swore to them and their men, say-
ing, "Do not be afraid because of the
Chalde´an officials; dwell in the land,
and serve the king of Babylon, and it
shall be well with you." 25But in the
seventh month, Ish´mael the son of
Nethani´ah, son of Elish´ama, of the
royal family, came with ten men, and
attacked and killed Gedali´ah and the
Jews and the Chalde´ans who were
with him at Mizpah. 26Then all the
people, both small and great, and the

[a]With Jer 40. 7: Heb lacks *in the open country*

captains of the forces arose, and went
to Egypt; for they were afraid of the
Chalde´ans.

JEHOIACHIN RELEASED FROM PRISON

27 And in the thirty-seventh year
of the exile of Jehoi´achin king of
Judah, in the twelfth month, on the
twenty-seventh day of the month,
Evil-mer´odach king of Babylon, in the
year that he began to reign, graciously
freed Jehoi´achin king of Judah from
prison; 28and he spoke kindly to him,
and gave him a seat above the seats
of the kings who were with him in
Babylon. 29So Jehoi´achin put off his
prison garments. And every day of his
life he dined regularly at the king's
table; 30and for his allowance, a reg-
ular allowance was given him by the
king, every day a portion, as long as
he lived.

THE FIRST BOOK OF THE
CHRONICLES

FROM ADAM TO ABRAHAM

1 *Adam, Seth, Enosh; 2 Kenan, Mahal´-
alel, Jared; 3 Enoch, Methu´selah, La-
mech; 4 Noah, Shem, Ham, and Japheth.
5 The sons of Japheth: Gomer,
Magog, Madai, Javan, Tubal, Meshech,
and Tiras. 6 The sons of Gomer: Ash´-
kenaz, Diphath, and Togar´mah. 7 The
sons of Javan: Eli´shah, Tarshish, Kit-
tim, and Ro´danim.
8 The sons of Ham: Cush, Egypt,
Put, and Canaan. 9 The sons of Cush:
Seba, Hav´ilah, Sabta, Ra´ama, and
Sab´teca. The sons of Ra´amah: Sheba
and Dedan. 10 Cush was the father of
Nimrod; he began to be a mighty one
in the earth.
11 Egypt was the father of Ludim, An´-
amim, Leha´bim, Naph´tuhim, 12 Pathru´-
sim, Caslu´him (whence came the Phi-
listines), and Caph´torim.
13 Canaan was the father of Sidon
his first-born, and Heth, 14 and the
Jeb´usites, the Amorites, the Gir´-
gashites, 15 the Hivites, the Arkites,
the Sinites, 16 the Ar´vadites, the
Zem´arites, and the Ha´mathites.
17 The sons of Shem: Elam, Asshur,
Arpach´shad, Lud, Aram, Uz, Hul,
Gether, and Meshech. 18 Arpach´shad
was the father of Shelah; and Shelah
was the father of Eber. 19 To Eber were
born two sons: the name of the one
was Peleg (for in his days the earth was
divided), and the name of his broth-
er Joktan. 20 Joktan was the father of
Almo´dad, Sheleph, Hazarma´veth,
Jerah, 21 Hador´am, Uzal, Diklah, 22 Ebal,
Abim´a-el, Sheba, 23 Ophir, Hav´ilah, and
Jobab; all these were the sons of Joktan.
24 Shem, Arpach´shad, Shelah;
25 Eber, Peleg, Re´u; 26 Serug, Nahor, Te-
rah; 27 Abram, that is, Abraham.

FROM ABRAHAM TO JACOB

28 The sons of Abraham: Isaac
and Ish´mael. 29 These are their
genealogies: the first-born of Ish´-
mael, Neba´ioth; and Kedar, Adbeel,
Mibsam, 30 Mishma, Dumah, Mas-
sa, Hadad, Tema, 31 Jetur, Naphish,
and Ked´emah. These are the sons
of Ish´mael. 32 The sons of Ketu´rah,
Abraham's concubine: she bore Zim-
ran, Jokshan, Medan, Mid´ian, Ish-
bak, and Shu´ah. The sons of Jokshan:
Sheba and Dedan. 33 The sons of Mid´-
ian: Ephah, Epher, Hanoch, Abi´da,
and Elda´ah. All these were the de-
scendants of Ketu´rah.
34 Abraham was the father of Isaac.
The sons of Isaac: Esau and Israel.
35 The sons of Esau: Eli´phaz, Reu´el,
Je´ush, Jalam, and Korah. 36 The sons
of Eli´phaz: Teman, Omar, Zephi,
Gatam, Kenaz, Timna, and Am´alek.
37 The sons of Reu´el: Nahath, Zerah,
Shammah, and Mizzah.
38 The sons of Se´ir: Lotan,
Shobal, Zib´eon, Anah, Dishon, Ezer,
and Dishan. 39 The sons of Lotan: Hori
and Homam; and Lotan's sister was
Timna. 40 The sons of Shobal: Al´ian,
Man´ahath, Ebal, Shephi, and Onam.
The sons of Zib´eon: A´iah and Anah.
41 The sons of Anah: Dishon. The sons
of Dishon: Hamran, Eshban, Ithran,
and Cheran. 42 The sons of Ezer: Bil-
han, Za´avan, and Ja´akan. The sons
of Dishan: Uz and Aran.
43 These are the kings who reigned
in the land of Edom before any king
reigned over the Israelites: Bela the son
of Be´or, the name of whose city was
Din´habah. 44 When Bela died, Jobab
the son of Zerah of Bozrah reigned in
his stead. 45 When Jobab died, Husham
of the land of the Te´manites reigned
in his stead. 46 When Husham died,
Hadad the son of Bedad, who defeat-
ed Mid´ian in the country of Moab,
reigned in his stead; and the name
of his city was Avith. 47 When Hadad
died, Samlah of Masre´kah reigned in
his stead. 48 When Samlah died, Sha´ul

of Reho´both on the Euphra´tes
reigned in his stead. 49When Sha´ul
died, Ba´al-ha´nan, the son of Achbor,
reigned in his stead. 50When Ba´al-
ha´nan died, Hadad reigned in his
stead; and the name of his city was
Pa´i, and his wife's name Mehet´abel
the daughter of Matred, the daughter
of Me´zahab. 51And Hadad died.

The chiefs of Edom were: chiefs
Timna, Al´iah, Jetheth, 52Oholiba´-
mah, Elah, Pinon, 53Kenaz, Teman,
Mibzar, 54Mag´di-el, and Iram; these
are the chiefs of Edom.

THE SONS OF ISRAEL AND THE DESCENDANTS OF JUDAH

2 These are the sons of Israel: Reuben,
Simeon, Levi, Judah, Is´sachar,
Zeb´ulun, 2Dan, Joseph, Benjamin,
Naph´tali, Gad, and Asher. 3The sons
of Judah: Er, Onan, and Shelah; these
three Bath-shu´a the Canaanitess bore
to him. Now Er, Judah's first-born,
was wicked in the sight of the LORD,
and he slew him. 4His daughter-in-law
Tamar also bore him Perez and Zerah.
Judah had five sons in all.

5 The sons of Perez: Hezron and
Hamul. 6The sons of Zerah: Zimri,
Ethan, Heman, Calcol, and Dara, five
in all. 7The sons of Carmi: Achar, the
troubler of Israel, who transgressed in
the matter of the devoted thing; 8and
Ethan's son was Azari´ah.

9 The sons of Hezron, that were
born to him: Jerah´meel, Ram, and
Chelu´bai. 10Ram was the father of
Ammin´adab, and Ammin´adab was
the father of Nahshon, prince of the
sons of Judah. 11Nahshon was the fa-
ther of Salma, Salma of Bo´az, 12Bo´az
of Obed, Obed of Jesse. 13Jesse was
the father of Eli´ab his first-born,
Abin´adab the second, Shim´e-a the
third, 14Nethan´el the fourth, Raddai
the fifth, 15Ozem the sixth, David
the seventh; 16and their sisters were
Zeru´iah and Ab´igail. The sons of
Zeru´iah: Abi´shai, Jo´ab, and As´ahel,
three. 17Ab´igail bore Ama´sa, and
the father of Ama´sa was Jether the
Ish´maelite.

18 Caleb the son of Hezron had
children by his wife Azu´bah, and
by Jer´ioth; and these were her sons:
Jesher, Shobab, and Ardon. 19When
Azu´bah died, Caleb married Ephrath,
who bore him Hur. 20Hur was the fa-
ther of Uri, and Uri was the father of
Bez´alel.

21 Afterward Hezron went in to
the daughter of Machir the father of
Gilead, whom he married when he
was sixty years old; and she bore him
Segub; 22and Segub was the father
of Ja´ir, who had twenty-three cities
in the land of Gilead. 23But Geshur
and Aram took from them Hav´voth-
ja´ir, Kenath and its villages, sixty
towns. All these were descendants of
Machir, the father of Gilead. 24After
the death of Hezron, Caleb went in to
Eph´rathah,[a] the wife of Hezron his
father, and she bore him Ashhur, the
father of Teko´a.

25 The sons of Jerah´meel, the
first-born of Hezron: Ram, his first-
born, Bunah, Oren, Ozem, and Ahi´-
jah. 26Jerah´meel also had another
wife, whose name was At´arah; she
was the mother of Onam. 27The sons
of Ram, the first-born of Jerah´meel:
Ma´az, Jamin, and Eker. 28The sons of
Onam: Sham´mai and Jada. The sons
of Sham´mai: Nadab and Abi´shur.
29The name of Abi´shur's wife was
Ab´ihail, and she bore him Ahban
and Molid. 30The sons of Nadab:
Seled and Ap´pa-im; and Seled died
childless. 31The sons of Ap´pa-im:
Ishi. The sons of Ishi: Sheshan. The
sons of Sheshan: Ahlai. 32The sons of
Jada, Sham´mai's brother: Jether and
Jonathan; and Jether died childless.
33The sons of Jonathan: Peleth and
Zaza. These were the descendants of
Jerah´meel. 34Now Sheshan had no
sons, only daughters; but Sheshan
had an Egyptian slave, whose name
was Jarha. 35So Sheshan gave his
daughter in marriage to Jarha his

[a]Gk Vg: Heb *in Caleb Ephrathah*

slave; and she bore him Attai. 36Attai
was the father of Nathan and Nathan
of Zabad. 37Zabad was the father of
Ephlal, and Ephlal of Obed. 38Obed
was the father of Jehu, and Jehu of
Azari´ah. 39Azari´ah was the father of
Helez, and Helez of Ele-a´sah. 40Ele-
a´sah was the father of Sismai, and
Sismai of Shallum. 41Shallum was the
father of Jekami´ah, and Jekami´ah of
Elish´ama.

42 The sons of Caleb the brother of
Jerah´meel: Mare´shah[a] his first-born,
who was the father of Ziph. The sons
of Mare´shah: Hebron.[b] 43The sons of
Hebron: Korah, Tap´pu-ah, Rekem,
and Shema. 44Shema was the father of
Raham, the father of Jor´ke-am; and
Rekem was the father of Sham´mai.
45The son of Sham´mai: Ma´on; and
Ma´on was the father of Beth-zur.
46Ephah also, Caleb's concubine, bore
Haran, Moza, and Gazez; and Haran
was the father of Gazez. 47The sons
of Jah´dai: Regem, Jotham, Geshan,
Pelet, Ephah, and Sha´aph. 48Ma´acah,
Caleb's concubine, bore Sheber and
Tir´hanah. 49She also bore Sha´aph
the father of Madman´nah, Sheva the
father of Machbe´nah and the father
of Gib´e-a; and the daughter of Caleb
was Achsah. 50These were the descen-
dants of Caleb. The sons[c] of Hur the
first-born of Eph´rathah: Shobal the
father of Kir´iath-je´arim, 51Salma,
the father of Bethlehem, and Hareph
the father of Beth-gader. 52Shobal the
father of Kir´iath-je´arim had other
sons: Haro´eh, half of the Menu´hoth.
53And the families of Kir´iath-
je´arim: the Ithrites, the Puthites, the
Shu´mathites, and the Mish´ra-ites;
from these came the Zor´athites and
the Esh´taolites. 54The sons of Salma:
Bethlehem, the Netoph´athites,
At´roth-beth-jo´ab, and half of the
Man´aha´thites, the Zorites. 55The
families also of the scribes that dwelt
at Jabez: the Ti´rathites, the Shim´e-
athites, and the Su´cathites. These
are the Ken´ites who came from
Hammath, the father of the house of
Rechab.

DESCENDANTS OF DAVID AND SOLOMON

3 These are the sons of David that
were born to him in Hebron: the
first-born Amnon, by Ahin´o-am
the Jez´reelitess; the second Daniel,
by Ab´igail the Car´melitess, 2the
third Ab´salom, whose mother was
Ma´acah, the daughter of Talmai,
king of Geshur; the fourth Adoni´jah,
whose mother was Haggith; 3the fifth
Shephati´ah, by Abi´tal; the sixth
Ith´ream, by his wife Eglah; 4six
were born to him in Hebron, where
he reigned for seven years and six
months. And he reigned thirty-three
years in Jerusalem. 5These were
born to him in Jerusalem: Shim´e-a,
Shobab, Nathan, and Solomon, four
by Bath-shu´a, the daughter of Am´mi-
el; 6then Ibhar, Elish´ama, Eliph´elet,
7Nogah, Nepheg, Japhi´a, 8Elish´ama,
Eli´ada, and Eliph´elet, nine. 9All
these were David's sons, besides the
sons of the concubines; and Tamar
was their sister.

10 The descendants of Solomon:
Rehobo´am, Abi´jah his son, Asa his
son, Jehosh´aphat his son, 11Joram
his son, Ahazi´ah his son, Jo´ash his
son, 12Amazi´ah his son, Azari´ah his
son, Jotham his son, 13Ahaz his son,
Hezeki´ah his son, Manas´seh his
son, 14Amon his son, Josi´ah his son.
15The sons of Josi´ah: Joha´nan the
first-born, the second Jehoi´akim, the
third Zedeki´ah, the fourth Shallum.
16The descendants of Jehoi´akim:
Jeconi´ah his son, Zedeki´ah his son;
17and the sons of Jeconi´ah, the cap-
tive: She-al´ti-el his son, 18Malchi´-
ram, Peda´iah, Shenaz´zar, Jekami´-
ah, Hosh´ama, and Nedabi´ah; 19and
the sons of Peda´iah: Zerub´babel
and Shim´e-i; and the sons of Zerub´-
babel: Meshul´lam and Hanani´ah,
and Shelo´mith was their sister; 20and

[a] Gk: Heb *Mesha*
[b] Heb *the father of Hebron*
[c] Gk Vg: Heb *son*

Hashu´bah, Ohel, Berechi´ah, Hasadi´ah, and Ju´shab-he´sed, five. 21 The sons of Hanani´ah: Pelati´ah and Jesha´iah, his son[d] Repha´iah, his son[e] Arnan, his son[f] Obadi´ah, his son[g] Shecani´ah. 22 The sons of Shecani´ah: Shemai´ah. And the sons of Shemai´ah: Hattush, Igal, Bari´ah, Neari´ah, and Shaphat, six. 23 The sons of Neari´ah: Eli-o-e´nai, Hizki´ah, and Azri´kam, three. 24 The sons of Eli-o-e´nai: Hodavi´ah, Eli´ashib, Pela´iah, Akkub, Joha´nan, Delai´ah, and Ana´ni, seven.

DESCENDANTS OF JUDAH

4 The sons of Judah: Perez, Hezron, Carmi, Hur, and Shobal. 2 Re-a´iah the son of Shobal was the father of Jahath, and Jahath was the father of Ahu´mai and Lahad. These were the families of the Zor´athites. 3 These were the sons[h] of Etam: Jezre´el, Ishma, and Idbash; and the name of their sister was Hazzelelpo´ni, 4 and Penu´el was the father of Gedor, and Ezer the father of Hushah. These were the sons of Hur, the first-born of Eph´rathah, the father of Bethlehem. 5 Ashhur, the father of Teko´a, had two wives, Helah and Na´arah; 6 Na´arah bore him Ahuz´zam, Hepher, Te´meni, and Ha-ahash´tari. These were the sons of Na´arah. 7 The sons of Helah: Zereth, Izhar, and Ethnan. 8 Koz was the father of Anub, Zobe´bah, and the families of Ahar´hel the son of Harum. 9 Jabez was more honorable than his brothers; and his mother called his name Jabez, saying, "Because I bore him in pain." 10 Jabez called on the God of Israel, saying, "Oh that thou wouldst bless me and enlarge my border, and that thy hand might be with me, and that thou wouldst keep me from harm so that it might not hurt me!" And God granted what he asked. 11 Chelub, the brother of Shuhah, was the father of Mehir, who was the father of Eshton. 12 Eshton was the father of Bethra´pha, Pase´ah, and Tehin´nah the father of Irna´hash. These are the men of Recah. 13 The sons of Kenaz: Oth´niel and Sera´iah; and the sons of Oth´niel: Hathath and Meo´nothai.[i] 14 Meo´nothai was the father of Ophrah; and Sera´iah was the father of Jo´ab the father of Gehar´ashim,[j] so-called because they were craftsmen. 15 The sons of Caleb the son of Jephun´neh: Iru, Elah, and Na´am; and the sons of Elah: Kenaz. 16 The sons of Jehal´lelel: Ziph, Ziphah, Tir´i-a, and As´arel. 17 The sons of Ezrah: Jether, Mered, Epher, and Jalon. These are the sons of Bith´i-ah, the daughter of Pharaoh, whom Mered married;[k] and she conceived and bore[l] Miriam, Sham´mai, and Ishbah, the father of Eshtemo´a. 18 And his Jewish wife bore Jered the father of Gedor, Heber the father of Soco, and Jeku´thiel the father of Zano´ah. 19 The sons of the wife of Hodi´ah, the sister of Naham, were the fathers of Ke´ilah the Garmite and Eshtemo´a the Maac´athite. 20 The sons of Shimon: Amnon, Rinnah, Ben-ha´nan, and Tilon. The sons of Ishi: Zoheth and Ben-zo´heth. 21 The sons of Shelah the son of Judah: Er the father of Lecah, La´adah the father of Mare´shah, and the families of the house of linen workers at Beth-ashbe´a; 22 and Jokim, and the men of Coze´ba, and Jo´ash, and Saraph, who ruled in Moab and returned to Lehem[m] (now the records[n]

[d] Gk Compare Syr Vg: Heb *sons of*
[e] Gk Compare Syr Vg: Heb *sons of*
[f] Gk Compare Syr Vg: Heb *sons of*
[g] Gk Compare Syr Vg: Heb *sons of*
[h] Gk Compare Vg: Heb [father]
[i] Gk Vg: Heb lacks *Meonothai*
[j] That is *Valley of craftsmen*
[k] The clause: *These are... married* is transposed from verse 18
[l] Heb lacks *and bore*
[m] Vg Compare Gk: Heb *and Jashubi-lahem*
[n] Or *matters*

are ancient). 23These were the pot-
ters and inhabitants of Neta´im and
Gede´rah; they dwelt there with the
king for his work.

DESCENDANTS OF SIMEON

24 The sons of Simeon: Nem´uel,
Jamin, Jarib, Zerah, Sha´ul; 25Shallum
was his son, Mibsam his son, Mishma
his son. 26The sons of Mishma:
Ham´mu-el his son, Zac´cur his son,
Shim´e-i his son. 27Shim´e-i had sixteen
sons and six daughters; but his brothers
had not many children, nor did all their
family multiply like the men of Judah.
28They dwelt in Ba, Mola´dah, Ha´zar-
shu´al, 29Bilhah, Ezem, Tolad, 30Bethu´-
el, Hormah, Ziklag, 31Beth-mar´caboth,
Ha´zar-su´sim, Beth-biri, and Sha-
ara´im. These were their cities until
David reigned. 32And their villages
were Etam, A´in, Rimmon, Tochen,
and Ashan, five cities, 33along with all
their villages which were round about
these cities as far as Ba´al. These were
their settlements, and they kept a ge-
nealogical record.

34 Mesho´bab, Jamlech, Joshah
the son of Amazi´ah, 35Jo´el, Jehu the
son of Joshibi´ah, son of Sera´iah, son
of As´i-el, 36Eli-o-e´nai, Ja-ako´bah,
Jeshohai´ah, Asa´iah, Ad´i-el, Jesim´i-
el, Bena´iah, 37Ziza the son of Shiphi,
son of Allon, son of Jeda´iah, son of
Shimri, son of Shemai´ah 38these men-
tioned by name were princes in their
families, and their fathers' houses in-
creased greatly. 39They journeyed to
the entrance of Gedor, to the east side
of the valley, to seek pasture for their
flocks, 40where they found rich, good
pasture, and the land was very broad,
quiet, and peaceful; for the former
inhabitants there belonged to Ham.
41These, registered by name, came in
the days of Hezeki´ah, king of Judah,
and destroyed their tents and the Me-
u´nim who were found there, and ex-
terminated them to this day, and set-
tled in their place, because there was
pasture there for their flocks. 42And
some of them, five hundred men of
the Simeonites, went to Mount Se´ir,
having as their leaders Pelati´ah,
Neari´ah, Repha´iah, and Uz´ziel, the
sons of Ishi; 43and they destroyed the
remnant of the Amal´ekites that had
escaped, and they have dwelt there to
this day.

DESCENDANTS OF REUBEN

5 The sons of Reuben the first-born
of Israel (for he was the first-born;
but because he polluted his father's
couch, his birthright was given to
the sons of Joseph the son of Israel,
so that he is not enrolled in the ge-
nealogy according to the birthright;
2though Judah became strong among
his brothers and a prince was from
him, yet the birthright belonged to
Joseph), 3the sons of Reuben, the
first-born of Israel: Hanoch, Pallu,
Hezron, and Carmi. 4The sons of
Jo´el: Shemai´ah his son, Gog his son,
Shim´e-i his son, 5Micah his son, Re-
a´iah his son, Ba´al his son, 6Be-er´ah
his son, whom Til´gath-pilne´ser king
of Assyria carried away into exile; he
was a chieftain of the Reubenites.
7And his kinsmen by their families,
when the genealogy of their genera-
tions was reckoned: the chief, Je-i´el,
and Zechari´ah, 8and Bela the son of
Azaz, son of Shema, son of Jo´el, who
dwelt in Aro´er, as far as Nebo and
Ba´al-me´on. 9He also dwelt to the east
as far as the entrance of the desert
this side of the Euphra´tes, because
their cattle had multiplied in the land
of Gilead. 10And in the days of Saul
they made war on the Hagrites, who
fell by their hand; and they dwelt in
their tents throughout all the region
east of Gilead.

DESCENDANTS OF GAD

11 The sons of Gad dwelt over
against them in the land of Bashan
as far as Sal´ecah: 12Jo´el the chief,
Shapham the second, Ja´nai, and
Shaphat in Bashan. 13And their kins-
men according to their fathers' hous-
es: Michael, Meshul´lam, Sheba,

Jo´rai, Jacan, Zi´a, and Eber, seven.
14These were the sons of Ab´ihail
the son of Huri, son of Jaro´ah, son
of Gilead, son of Michael, son of
Jeshish´ai, son of Jahdo, son of Buz;
15Ahi the son of Ab´di-el, son of Guni,
was chief in their fathers' houses;
16and they dwelt in Gilead, in Bashan
and in its towns, and in all the pasture
lands of Sharon to their limits. 17All of
these were enrolled by genealogies in
the days of Jotham king of Judah, and
in the days of Jerobo´am king of Israel.
18 The Reubenites, the Gadites,
and the half-tribe of Manas´seh had
valiant men, who carried shield and
sword, and drew the bow, expert in
war, forty-four thousand seven hun-
dred and sixty, ready for service.
19They made war upon the Hagrites,
Jetur, Naphish, and Nodab; 20and
when they received help against them,
the Hagrites and all who were with
them were given into their hands, for
they cried to God in the battle, and
he granted their entreaty because
they trusted in him. 21They carried off
their livestock: fifty thousand of their
camels, two hundred and fifty thou-
sand sheep, two thousand asses, and
a hundred thousand men alive. 22For
many fell slain, because the war was
of God. And they dwelt in their place
until the exile.

THE HALF-TRIBE OF MANASSEH

23 The members of the half-tribe
of Manas´seh dwelt in the land; they
were very numerous from Bashan
to Ba´al-her´mon, Senir, and Mount
Hermon. 24These were the heads of
their fathers' houses: Epher,[a] Ishi,
Eli´el, Az´riel, Jeremiah, Hodavi´ah,
and Jah´di-el, mighty warriors, fa-
mous men, heads of their fathers'
houses. 25But they transgressed
against the God of their fathers, and
played the harlot after the gods of
the peoples of the land, whom God
had destroyed before them. 26So the
God of Israel stirred up the spirit
of Pul king of Assyria, the spirit of
Til´gath-pilne´ser king of Assyria, and
he carried them away, namely, the
Reubenites, the Gadites, and the half-
tribe of Manas´seh, and brought them
to Halah, Habor, Hara, and the river
Gozan, to this day.

DESCENDANTS OF LEVI

6[b] The sons of Levi: Gershom,
Kohath, and Merar´i. 2The sons of
Kohath: Amram, Izhar, Hebron, and
Uz´ziel. 3The children of Amram:
Aaron, Moses, and Miriam. The sons
of Aaron: Nadab, Abi´hu, Elea´zar,
and Ith´amar. 4Elea´zar was the father
of Phin´ehas, Phin´ehas of Abishu´a,
5Abishu´a of Bukki, Bukki of Uzzi,
6Uzzi of Zerahi´ah, Zerahi´ah of
Mera´ioth, 7Mera´ioth of Amari´ah,
Amari´ah of Ahi´tub, 8Ahi´tub of
Zadok, Zadok of Ahim´a-az, 9Ahim´a-
az of Azari´ah, Azari´ah of Joha´nan,
10and Joha´nan of Azari´ah (it was
he who served as priest in the house
that Solomon built in Jerusalem).
11Azari´ah was the father of Amari´ah,
Amari´ah of Ahi´tub, 12Ahi´tub of
Zadok, Zadok of Shallum, 13Shallum
of Hilki´ah, Hilki´ah of Azari´ah,
14Azari´ah of Sera´iah, Sera´iah of
Jeho´zadak; 15and Jeho´zadak went
into exile when the LORD sent Judah
and Jerusalem into exile by the hand
of Nebuchadnez´zar.
16[c] The sons of Levi: Gershom,
Kohath, and Merar´i. 17And these are
the names of the sons of Gershom:
Libni and Shim´e-i. 18The sons of
Kohath: Amram, Izhar, Hebron, and
Uz´ziel. 19The sons of Merar´i: Mahli
and Mushi. These are the families of
the Levites according to their fathers.
20Of Gershom: Libni his son, Jahath
his son, Zimmah his son, 21Jo´ah his
son, Iddo his son, Zerah his son,
Je-ath´erai his son. 22The sons of Ko-
hath: Ammin´adab his son, Korah
his son, Assir his son, 23Elka´nah

[a] Gk Vg: Heb *and Epher*
[b] Ch 5.27 in Heb
[c] Ch 6.1 in Heb

his son, Ebi´asaph his son, Assir his
son, 24Tahath his son, U´riel his son,
Uzzi´ah his son, and Sha´ul his son.
25The sons of Elka´nah: Ama´sai and
Ahi´moth, 26Elka´nah his son, Zophai
his son, Nahath his son, 27Eli´ab his
son, Jero´ham his son, Elka´nah his
son. 28The sons of Samuel: Jo´el[a] his
first-born, the second Abi´jah.[b] 29The
sons of Merar´i: Mahli, Libni his
son, Shim´e-i his son, Uzzah his son,
30Shim´e-a his son, Haggi´ah his son,
and Asa´iah his son.

MUSICIANS APPOINTED BY DAVID

31 These are the men whom David
put in charge of the service of song in
the house of the LORD, after the ark
rested there. 32They ministered with
song before the tabernacle of the tent
of meeting, until Solomon had built
the house of the LORD in Jerusalem;
and they performed their service in
due order. 33These are the men who
served and their sons. Of the sons of
the Ko´hathites: Heman the singer
the son of Jo´el, son of Samuel, 34son
of Elka´nah, son of Jero´ham, son of
Eli´el, son of To´ah, 35son of Zuph,
son of Elka´nah, son of Mahath,
son of Ama´sai, 36son of Elka´nah,
son of Jo´el, son of Azari´ah, son of
Zephani´ah, 37son of Tahath, son of
Assir, son of Ebi´asaph, son of Korah,
38son of Izhar, son of Kohath, son of
Levi, son of Israel; 39and his brother
Asaph, who stood on his right hand,
namely, Asaph the son of Berechi´ah,
son of Shim´e-a, 40son of Michael, son
of Ba-ase´iah, son of Malchi´jah, 41son
of Ethni, son of Zerah, son of Ada´iah,
42son of Ethan, son of Zimmah, son
of Shim´e-i, 43son of Jahath, son of
Gershom, son of Levi. 44On the left
hand were their brethren the sons
of Merar´i: Ethan the son of Kishi,
son of Abdi, son of Malluch, 45son of
Hashabi´ah, son of Amazi´ah, son of
Hilki´ah, 46son of Amzi, son of Bani,
son of Shemer, 47son of Mahli, son of
Mushi, son of Merar´i, son of Levi;
48and their brethren the Levites were
appointed for all the service of the
tabernacle of the house of God.

49 But Aaron and his sons made of-
ferings upon the altar of burnt offer-
ing and upon the altar of incense for
all the work of the most holy place,
and to make atonement for Israel,
according to all that Moses the ser-
vant of God had commanded. 50These
are the sons of Aaron: Elea´zar his
son, Phin´ehas his son, Abishu´a his
son, 51Bukki his son, Uzzi his son,
Zerahi´ah his son, 52Mera´ioth his
son, Amari´ah his son, Ahi´tub his
son, 53Zadok his son, Ahim´a-az his
son.

SETTLEMENTS OF THE LEVITES

54 These are their dwelling places
according to their settlements within
their borders: to the sons of Aaron
of the families of Ko´hathites, for
theirs was the lot, 55to them they gave
Hebron in the land of Judah and its
surrounding pasture lands, 56but the
fields of the city and its villages they
gave to Caleb the son of Jephun´neh.
57To the sons of Aaron they gave the
cities of refuge: Hebron, Libnah with
its pasture lands, Jattir, Eshtemo´a
with its pasture lands, 58Hilen with
its pasture lands, Debir with its pas-
ture lands, 59Ashan with its pasture
lands, and Beth-she´mesh with its
pasture lands; 60and from the tribe
of Benjamin, Geba with its pasture
lands, Al´emeth with its pasture
lands, and An´athoth with its pasture
lands. All their cities throughout their
families were thirteen.

61 To the rest of the Ko´hathites
were given by lot out of the fami-
ly of the tribe, out of the half-tribe,
the half of Manas´seh, ten cities. 62To
the Gershomites according to their
families were allotted thirteen cities
out of the tribes of Is´sachar, Asher,
Naph´tali, and Manas´seh in Bashan.

[a] Gk Syr Compare verse 33 and 1Sam 8. 2: Heb lacks *Joel*
[b] Heb *and Abijah*

63To the Merar´ites according to their
families were allotted twelve cities
out of the tribes of Reuben, Gad, and
Zeb´ulun. 64So the people of Israel
gave the Levites the cities with their
pasture lands. 65They also gave them
by lot out of the tribes of Judah,
Simeon, and Benjamin these cities
which are mentioned by name.
66 And some of the families of the
sons of Kohath had cities of their ter-
ritory out of the tribe of E´phraim.
67They were given the cities of refuge:
Shechem with its pasture lands in the
hill country of E´phraim, Gezer with
its pasture lands, 68Jok´me-am with
its pasture lands, Beth-hor´on with its
pasture lands, 69Ai´jalon with its pas-
ture lands, Gath-rim´mon with its pas-
ture lands, 70and out of the half-tribe
of Manas´seh, Aner with its pasture
lands, and Bil´e-am with its pasture
lands, for the rest of the families of
the Ko´hathites.
71 To the Gershomites were giv-
en out of the half-tribe of Manas´seh:
Golan in Bashan with its pasture
lands and Ash´taroth with its pas-
ture lands; 72and out of the tribe of
Is´sachar: Kedesh with its pasture
lands, Dab´erath with its pasture
lands, 73Ramoth with its pasture lands,
and Anem with its pasture lands; 74out
of the tribe of Asher: Mashal with its
pasture lands, Abdon with its pasture
lands, 75Hukok with its pasture lands,
and Rehob with its pasture lands; 76and
out of the tribe of Naph´tali: Kedesh
in Galilee with its pasture lands,
Ham´mon with its pasture lands, and
Kiriatha´im with its pasture lands.
77To the rest of the Merar´ites were
allotted out of the tribe of Zeb´ulun:
Rim´mono with its pasture lands,
Tabor with its pasture lands, 78and
beyond the Jordan at Jericho, on the
east side of the Jordan, out of the
tribe of Reuben: Bezer in the steppe
with its pasture lands, Jahzah with
its pasture lands, 79Ked´emoth with
its pasture lands, and Meph´a-ath
with its pasture lands; 80and out of the
tribe of Gad: Ramoth in Gilead with
its pasture lands, Mahana´im with its
pasture lands, 81Heshbon with its pas-
ture lands, and Jazer with its pasture
lands.

DESCENDANTS OF ISSACHAR

7 The sons[c] of Is´sachar: Tola, Pu´ah,
Jashub, and Shimron, four. 2The
sons of Tola: Uzzi, Repha´iah, Je´ri-el,
Jah´mai, Ibsam, and Shem´uel, heads
of their fathers' houses, namely of
Tola, mighty warriors of their gen-
erations, their number in the days of
David being twenty-two thousand six
hundred. 3The sons of Uzzi: Izrahi´ah.
And the sons of Izrahi´ah: Michael,
Obadi´ah, Jo´el, and Isshi´ah, five, all
of them chief men; 4and along with
them, by their generations, according
to their fathers' houses, were units
of the army for war, thirty-six thou-
sand, for they had many wives and
sons. 5Their kinsmen belonging to all
the families of Is´sachar were in all
eighty-seven thousand mighty war-
riors, enrolled by genealogy.

DESCENDANTS OF BENJAMIN

6 The sons of Benjamin: Bela,
Becher, and Jedi´a-el, three. 7The
sons of Bela: Ezbon, Uzzi, Uz´ziel,
Jer´imoth, and Iri, five, heads of fa-
thers' houses, mighty warriors; and
their enrollment by genealogies was
twenty-two thousand and thirty-four.
8The sons of Becher: Zemi´rah, Jo´ash,
Elie´zer, Eli-o-e´nai, Omri, Jer´emoth,
Abi´jah, An´athoth, and Al´emeth. All
these were the sons of Becher; 9and
their enrollment by genealogies, ac-
cording to their generations, as heads
of their fathers' houses, mighty war-
riors, was twenty thousand two hun-
dred. 10The sons of Jedi´a-el: Bilhan.
And the sons of Bilhan: Je´ush,
Benjamin, Ehud, Chena´anah, Zethan,
Tarshish, and Ahish´ahar. 11All these
were the sons of Jedi´a-el according
to the heads of their fathers' houses,

[c] Syr Compare Vg: Heb *and to the sons*

mighty warriors, seventeen thousand
and two hundred, ready for service
in war. 12 And Shuppim and Huppim
were the sons of Ir, Hushim the sons
of Aher.

DESCENDANTS OF NAPHTALI

13 The sons of Naph´tali: Jah´zi-
el, Guni, Jezer, and Shallum, the off-
spring of Bilhah.

DESCENDANTS OF MANASSEH

14 The sons of Manas´seh: As´ri-el,
whom his Arame´an concubine bore;
she bore Machir the father of Gilead.
15 And Machir took a wife for Huppim
and for Shuppim. The name of his
sister was Ma´acah. And the name
of the second was Zeloph´ehad; and
Zeloph´ehad had daughters. 16 And
Ma´acah the wife of Machir bore a
son, and she called his name Peresh;
and the name of his brother was
Sheresh; and his sons were Ulam and
Rakem. 17 The sons of Ulam: Bedan.
These were the sons of Gilead the son
of Machir, son of Manas´seh. 18 And his
sister Hammo´lecheth bore Ishhod,
Abi-e´zer, and Mahlah. 19 The sons
of Shemi´da were Ahi´an, Shechem,
Likhi, and Ani´am.

DESCENDANTS OF EPHRAIM

20 The sons of E´phraim: Shuthe´-
lah, and Bered his son, Tahath his
son, Ele-a´dah his son, Tahath his son,
21 Zabad his son, Shuthe´lah his son,
and Ezer and E´le-ad, whom the men
of Gath who were born in the land slew,
because they came down to raid their
cattle. 22 And E´phraim their father
mourned many days, and his brothers
came to comfort him. 23 And E´phraim
went in to his wife, and she conceived
and bore a son; and he called his name
Beri´ah, because evil had befallen his
house. 24 His daughter was She´erah,
who built both Lower and Upper
Beth-hor´on, and Uz´zen-she´erah.
25 Rephah was his son, Resheph his son,
Telah his son, Tahan his son, 26 Ladan
his son, Ammi´hud his son, Elish´ama
his son, 27 Nun his son, Joshua his son.
28 Their possessions and settlements
were Bethel and its towns, and east-
ward Na´aran, and westward Gezer
and its towns, Shechem and its towns,
and Ayyah and its towns; 29 also along
the borders of the Manas´sites, Beth-
she´an and its towns, Ta´anach and its
towns, Megid´do and its towns, Dor
and its towns. In these dwelt the sons
of Joseph the son of Israel.

DESCENDANTS OF ASHER

30 The sons of Asher: Imnah,
Ishvah, Ishvi, Beri´ah, and their sis-
ter Serah. 31 The sons of Beri´ah:
Heber and Mal´chi-el, who was the
father of Bir´zaith. 32 Heber was the
father of Japhlet, Shomer, Hotham,
and their sister Shu´a. 33 The sons of
Japhlet: Pasach, Bimhal, and Ashvath.
These are the sons of Japhlet. 34 The
sons of Shemer his brother: Rohgah,
Jehub´bah, and Aram. 35 The sons of
Helem his brother: Zophah, Imna,
Shelesh, and Amal. 36 The sons of
Zophah: Su´ah, Har´nepher, Shu´al,
Beri, Imrah. 37 Bezer, Hod, Shamma,
Shilshah, Ithran, and Be-e´ra. 38 The
sons of Jether: Jephun´neh, Pispa,
and Ara. 39 The sons of Ulla: Arah,
Han´niel, and Rizi´a. 40 All of these
were men of Asher, heads of fathers'
houses, approved, mighty warriors,
chief of the princes. Their number
enrolled by genealogies, for service in
war, was twenty-six thousand men.

DESCENDANTS OF BENJAMIN

8 Benjamin was the father of Bela
his first-born, Ashbel the sec-
ond, Ahar´ah the third, 2 Nohah the
fourth, and Rapha the fifth. 3 And
Bela had sons: Addar, Gera, Abi´hud,
4 Abishu´a, Na´aman, Aho´ah, 5 Gera,
Shephu´phan, and Huram. 6 These are
the sons of Ehud (they were heads of
fathers' houses of the inhabitants of
Geba, and they were carried into exile
to Man´ahath): 7 Na´aman,[a] Ahi´jah,

[a] Heb *and Naaman*

and Gera, that is, Heglam,[b] who was
the father of Uzza and Ahi´hud. 8And
Shahara´im had sons in the country of
Moab after he had sent away Hushim
and Ba´ara his wives. 9He had sons
by Hodesh his wife: Jobab, Zib´ia,
Mesha, Malcam, 10Je´uz, Sachi´a, and
Mirmah. These were his sons, heads
of fathers' houses. 11He also had sons
by Hushim: Abi´tub and Elpa´al. 12The
sons of Elpa´al: Eber, Misham, and
Shemed, who built Ono and Lod with
its towns, 13and Beri´ah and Shema
(they were heads of fathers' houses
of the inhabitants of Ai´jalon, who
put to flight the inhabitants of Gath);
14and Ahi´o, Shashak, and Jer´emoth.
15Zebadi´ah, Arad, Eder, 16Michael,
Ishpah, and Joha were sons of Beri´ah.
17Zebadi´ah, Meshul´lam, Hizki, He-
ber, 18Ish´merai, Izli´ah, and Jobab
were the sons of Elpa´al. 19Jakim,
Zichri, Zabdi, 20Eli-e´nai, Zil´le-thai,
Eli´el, 21Ada´iah, Bera´iah, and Shim-
rath were the sons of Shim´e-i. 22Ish-
pan, Eber, Eli´el, 23Abdon, Zichri,
Hanan, 24Hanani´ah, Elam, Anthothi´-
jah, 25Iphde´iah, and Penu´el were
the sons of Shashak. 26Sham´sherai,
Shehari´ah, Athali´ah, 27Ja-areshi´ah,
Eli´jah, and Zichri were the sons of
Jero´ham. 28These were the heads of
fathers' houses, according to their
generations, chief men. These dwelt
in Jerusalem.

29 Je-i´el[c] the father of Gibeon
dwelt in Gibeon, and the name of his
wife was Ma´acah. 30His first-born son:
Abdon, then Zur, Kish, Ba´al, Nadab,
31Gedor, Ahi´o, Zecher, 32and Mikloth
(he was the father of Shim´e-ah). Now
these also dwelt opposite their kins-
men in Jerusalem, with their kinsmen.
33Ner was the father of Kish, Kish of
Saul, Saul of Jonathan, Mal´chishu´a,
Abin´adab, and Eshba´al; 34and the
son of Jonathan was Mer´ib-ba´al;
and Mer´ib-ba´al was the father of
Micah. 35The sons of Micah: Pithon,
Melech, Tar´e-a, and Ahaz. 36Ahaz was
the father of Jeho´addah; and Jeho´-
addah was the father of Al´emeth,
Az´maveth, and Zimri; Zimri was the
father of Moza. 37Moza was the fa-
ther of Bin´e-a; Raphah was his son,
Ele-a´sah his son, Azel his son. 38Azel
had six sons, and these are their
names: Azri´kam, Bo´cheru, Ish´mael,
She-ari´ah, Obadi´ah, and Hanan. All
these were the sons of Azel. 39The
sons of Eshek his brother: Ulam his
first-born, Je´ush the second, and
Eliph´elet the third. 40The sons of
Ulam were men who were mighty
warriors, bowmen, having many sons
and grandsons, one hundred and fifty.
All these were Benjaminites.

INHABITANTS OF JERUSALEM AFTER THE EXILE

9 So all Israel was enrolled by gene-
alogies; and these are written in
the Book of the Kings of Israel. And
Judah was taken into exile in Babylon
because of their unfaithfulness. 2Now
the first to dwell again in their pos-
sessions in their cities were Israel,
the priests, the Levites, and the tem-
ple servants. 3And some of the peo-
ple of Judah, Benjamin, E´phraim,
and Manas´seh dwelt in Jerusalem:
4Uthai the son of Ammi´hud, son of
Omri, son of Imri, son of Bani, from
the sons of Perez the son of Judah.
5And of the Shi´lonites: Asa´iah
the first-born, and his sons. 6Of the
sons of Zerah: Jeu´el and their kins-
men, six hundred and ninety. 7Of
the Benjaminites: Sallu the son of
Meshul´lam, son of Hodavi´ah, son
of Hassenu´ah, 8Ibne´iah the son of
Jero´ham, Elah the son of Uzzi, son
of Michri, and Meshul´lam the son
of Shephati´ah, son of Reu´el, son
of Ibni´jah; 9and their kinsmen ac-
cording to their generations, nine
hundred and fifty-six. All these were
heads of fathers' houses according to
their fathers' houses.

[b] Or *he carried them into exile*
[c] Compare 9.35: Heb lacks *Jeiel*

PRIESTLY FAMILIES

10 Of the priests: Jeda´iah, Jehoi´-
arib, Jachin, 11and Azari´ah the son of
Hilki´ah, son of Meshul´lam, son of
Zadok, son of Mera´ioth, son of Ahi´-
tub, the chief officer of the house of
God; 12and Ada´iah the son of Jero´-
ham, son of Pashhur, son of Malchi´-
jah, and Ma´asai the son of Ad´i-el,
son of Jah´zerah, son of Meshul´lam,
son of Meshil´lemith, son of Immer;
13besides their kinsmen, heads of their
fathers' houses, one thousand seven
hundred and sixty, very able men for
the work of the service of the house
of God.

LEVITICAL FAMILIES

14 Of the Levites: Shemai´ah the
son of Hasshub, son of Azri´kam, son
of Hashabi´ah, of the sons of Merar´i;
15and Bakbak´kar, Heresh, Galal, and
Mattani´ah the son of Mica, son of
Zichri, son of Asaph; 16and Obadi´ah
the son of Shemai´ah, son of Galal,
son of Jedu´thun, and Berechi´ah the
son of Asa, son of Elka´nah, who dwelt
in the villages of the Netoph´athites.

17 The gatekeepers were: Shallum,
Akkub, Talmon, Ahi´man, and their
kinsmen (Shallum being the chief),
18stationed hitherto in the king's
gate on the east side. These were
the gatekeepers of the camp of the
Levites. 19Shallum the son of Kor´e,
son of Ebi´asaph, son of Korah, and
his kinsmen of his fathers' house,
the Kor´ahites, were in charge of the
work of the service, keepers of the
thresholds of the tent, as their fathers
had been in charge of the camp of the
LORD, keepers of the entrance. 20And
Phin´ehas the son of Elea´zar was the
ruler over them in time past; the LORD
was with him. 21Zechari´ah the son of
Meshelemi´ah was gatekeeper at the
entrance of the tent of meeting. 22All
these, who were chosen as gatekeep-
ers at the thresholds, were two hun-
dred and twelve. They were enrolled
by genealogies in their villages. David
and Samuel the seer established them
in their office of trust. 23So they and
their sons were in charge of the gates
of the house of the LORD, that is, the
house of the tent, as guards. 24The
gatekeepers were on the four sides,
east, west, north, and south; 25and
their kinsmen who were in their vil-
lages were obliged to come in every
seven days, from time to time, to be
with these; 26for the four chief gate-
keepers, who were Levites, were in
charge of the chambers and the trea-
sures of the house of God. 27And they
lodged round about the house of God;
for upon them lay the duty of watch-
ing, and they had charge of opening it
every morning.

28 Some of them had charge
of the utensils of service, for they
were required to count them when
they were brought in and taken out.
29Others of them were appointed over
the furniture, and over all the holy
utensils, also over the fine flour, the
wine, the oil, the incense, and the
spices. 30Others, of the sons of the
priests, prepared the mixing of the
spices, 31and Mattithi´ah, one of the
Levites, the first-born of Shallum
the Kor´ahite, was in charge of mak-
ing the flat cakes. 32Also some of
their kinsmen of the Ko´hathites had
charge of the showbread, to prepare it
every sabbath.

33 Now these are the singers,
the heads of fathers' houses of the
Levites, dwelling in the chambers of
the temple free from other service,
for they were on duty day and night.
34These were heads of fathers' hous-
es of the Levites, according to their
generations, leaders, who lived in
Jerusalem.

THE FAMILY OF KING SAUL

35 In Gibeon dwelt the father of
Gibeon, Je-i´el, and the name of his
wife was Ma´acah, 36and his first-born
son Abdon, then Zur, Kish, Ba´al, Ner,
Nadab, 37Gedor, Ahi´o, Zechari´ah,
and Mikloth; 38and Mikloth was the
father of Shim´e-am; and these also

Saul." 4All the assembly agreed to do
so, for the thing was right in the eyes
of all the people.
5 So David assembled all Israel
from the Shihor of Egypt to the en-
trance of Hamath, to bring the ark
of God from Kir´iath-je´arim. 6And
David and all Israel went up to
Ba´alah, that is, to Kir´iath-je´arim
which belongs to Judah, to bring up
from there the ark of God, which is
called by the name of the LORD who
sits enthroned above the cherubim.
7And they carried the ark of God
upon a new cart, from the house of
Abin´adab, and Uzzah and Ahi´o[c]
were driving the cart. 8And David and
all Israel were making merry before
God with all their might, with song
and lyres and harps and tambourines
and cymbals and trumpets.
9 And when they came to the
threshing floor of Chidon, Uzzah put
out his hand to hold the ark, for the
oxen stumbled. 10And the anger of
the LORD was kindled against Uzzah;
and he smote him because he put
forth his hand to the ark; and he died
there before God. 11And David was
angry because the LORD had broken
forth upon Uzzah; and that place is
called Pe´rez-uz´za[d] to this day. 12And
David was afraid of God that day; and
he said, "How can I bring the ark of
God home to me?" 13So David did not
take the ark home into the city of
David, but took it aside to the house
of O´bed-e´dom the Gittite. 14And the
ark of God remained with the house-
hold of O´bed-e´dom in his house
three months; and the LORD blessed
the household of O´bed-e´dom and all
that he had.

DAVID ESTABLISHED AT JERUSALEM

14 And Hiram king of Tyre sent mes-
sengers to David, and cedar trees,
also masons and carpenters to build a
house for him. 2And David perceived
that the LORD had established him
king over Israel, and that his kingdom
was highly exalted for the sake of his
people Israel.
3 And David took more wives in
Jerusalem, and David begot more
sons and daughters. 4These are the
names of the children whom he had
in Jerusalem: Shammu´a, Shobab,
Nathan, Solomon, 5Ibhar, Eli´shu-a,
El´pelet, 6Nogah, Nepheg, Japhi´a,
7Elish´ama, Beeli´ada, and Eliph´elet.

DEFEAT OF THE PHILISTINES

8 When the Philistines heard that
David had been anointed king over
all Israel, all the Philistines went up
in search of David; and David heard of
it and went out against them. 9Now the
Philistines had come and made a raid in
the valley of Reph´aim. 10And David in-
quired of God, "Shall I go up against the
Philistines? Wilt thou give them into my
hand?" And the LORD said to him, "Go
up, and I will give them into your hand."
11And he went up to Ba´al-pera´zim, and
David defeated them there; and David
said, "God has broken through[e] my
enemies by my hand, like a bursting
flood." Therefore the name of that place
is called Ba´al-pera´zim.[f] 12And they left
their gods there, and David gave com-
mand, and they were burned.
13 And the Philistines yet again
made a raid in the valley. 14And when
David again inquired of God, God
said to him, "You shall not go up af-
ter them; go around and come upon
them opposite the balsam trees. 15And
when you hear the sound of marching
in the tops of the balsam trees, then
go out to battle; for God has gone out
before you to smite the army of the
Philistines." 16And David did as God
commanded him, and they smote the
Philistine army from Gibeon to Gezer.
17And the fame of David went out into
all lands, and the LORD brought the
fear of him upon all nations.

[c] Or *and his brother*
[d] That is *The breaking forth upon* Uzzah
[e] Heb *paraz*
[f] That is *Lord of breaking through*

THE ARK BROUGHT TO JERUSALEM

15 David built houses for himself in
the city of David; and he prepared
a place for the ark of God, and pitched
a tent for it. 2Then David said, "No one
but the Levites may carry the ark of
God, for the LORD chose them to carry
the ark of the LORD and to minister to
him for ever." 3And David assembled
all Israel at Jerusalem, to bring up the
ark of the LORD to its place, which he
had prepared for it. 4And David gath-
ered together the sons of Aaron and
the Levites: 5of the sons of Kohath,
U´riel the chief, with a hundred and
twenty of his brethren; 6of the sons
of Merar´i, Asa´iah the chief, with
two hundred and twenty of his breth-
ren; 7of the sons of Gershom, Jo´el the
chief, with a hundred and thirty of his
brethren; 8of the sons of Eli-za´phan,
Shemai´ah the chief, with two hun-
dred of his brethren; 9of the sons of
Hebron, Eli´el the chief, with eighty of
his brethren; 10of the sons of Uz´ziel,
Ammin´adab the chief, with a hundred
and twelve of his brethren. 11Then
David summoned the priests Zadok
and Abi´athar, and the Levites U´riel,
Asa´iah, Jo´el, Shemai´ah, Eli´el, and
Ammin´adab, 12and said to them, "You
are the heads of the fathers' houses
of the Levites; sanctify yourselves,
you and your brethren, so that you
may bring up the ark of the LORD, the
God of Israel, to the place that I have
prepared for it. 13Because you did not
carry it the first time,[a] the LORD our
God broke forth upon us, because we
did not care for it in the way that is
ordained." 14So the priests and the
Levites sanctified themselves to bring
up the ark of the LORD, the God of
Israel. 15And the Levites carried the
ark of God upon their shoulders with
the poles, as Moses had commanded
according to the word of the LORD.

16 David also commanded the
chiefs of the Levites to appoint their
brethren as the singers who should
play loudly on musical instruments, on
harps and lyres and cymbals, to raise
sounds of joy. 17So the Levites appoint-
ed Heman the son of Jo´el; and of his
brethren Asaph the son of Berechi´ah;
and of the sons of Merar´i, their
brethren, Ethan the son of Kusha´iah;
18and with them their brethren of the
second order, Zechari´ah, Ja-a´ziel,
Shemi´ramoth, Jehi´el, Unni, Eli´ab,
Bena´iah, Ma-ase´iah, Mattithi´ah,
Eliph´elehu, and Mikne´iah, and
the gatekeepers O´bed-e´dom and
Je-i´el. 19The singers, Heman, Asaph,
and Ethan, were to sound bronze
cymbals; 20Zechari´ah, A´zi-el, She-
mi´ramoth, Jehi´el, Unni, Eli´ab, Ma-
ase´iah, and Bena´iah were to play
harps according to Al´amoth; 21but
Mattithi´ah, Eliph´elehu, Mikne´iah,
O´bed-e´dom, Je-i´el, and Azazi´ah
were to lead with lyres according to
the Shem´inith. 22Chenani´ah, leader
of the Levites in music, should di-
rect the music, for he understood it.
23Berechi´ah and Elka´nah were to be
gatekeepers for the ark. 24Shebani´-
ah, Josh´aphat, Nethan´el, Ama´sai,
Zechari´ah, Bena´iah, and Elie´zer,
the priests, should blow the trumpets
before the ark of God. O´bed-e´dom
and Jehi´ah also were to be gatekeep-
ers for the ark.

25 So David and the elders of
Israel, and the commanders of thou-
sands, went to bring up the ark of the
covenant of the LORD from the house
of O´bed-e´dom with rejoicing. 26And
because God helped the Levites who
were carrying the ark of the covenant
of the LORD, they sacrificed seven
bulls and seven rams. 27David was
clothed with a robe of fine linen, as
also were all the Levites who were
carrying the ark, and the singers, and
Chenani´ah the leader of the music of
the singers; and David wore a linen
ephod. 28So all Israel brought up the
ark of the covenant of the LORD with
shouting, to the sound of the horn,
trumpets, and cymbals, and made
loud music on harps and lyres.

[a]The meaning of the Hebrew word is uncertain

29 And as the ark of the covenant
of the LORD came to the city of David,
Michal the daughter of Saul looked
out of the window, and saw King
David dancing and making merry; and
she despised him in her heart.

THE ARK PLACED IN THE TENT

16 And they brought in the ark of
God, and set it inside the tent
which David had pitched for it; and
they offered burnt offerings and peace
offerings before God. 2 And when
David had finished offering the burnt
offerings and the peace offerings, he
blessed the people in the name of the
LORD, 3 and distributed to all Israel,
both men and women, to each a loaf of
bread, a portion of meat,[b] and a cake
of raisins.
4 Moreover he appointed certain
of the Levites as ministers before the
ark of the LORD, to invoke, to thank,
and to praise the LORD, the God of
Israel. 5 Asaph was the chief, and sec-
ond to him were Zechari´ah, Je-i´el,
Shemi´ramoth, Jehi´el, Mattithi´ah,
Eli´ab, Bena´iah, O´bed-e´dom, and
Je-i´el, who were to play harps and
lyres; Asaph was to sound the cym-
bals, 6 and Bena´iah and Jaha´ziel the
priests were to blow trumpets contin-
ually, before the ark of the covenant
of God.

DAVID'S PSALM OF THANKSGIVING

7 Then on that day David first ap-
pointed that thanksgiving be sung to
the LORD by Asaph and his brethren.

8 O give thanks to the LORD, call
on his name,
make known his deeds
among the peoples!
9 Sing to him, sing praises to him,
tell of all his wonderful
works!
10 Glory in his holy name;
let the hearts of those
who seek the LORD
rejoice!
11 Seek the LORD and his strength,
seek his presence
continually!
12 Remember the wonderful works
that he has done,
the wonders he wrought, the
judgments he uttered,
13 O offspring of Abraham his
servant,
sons of Jacob, his chosen
ones!
14 He is the LORD our God;
his judgments are in all the
earth.
15 He is mindful of his covenant
for ever,
of the word that he com-
manded, for a thou-
sand generations,
16 the covenant which he made
with Abraham,
his sworn promise to Isaac,
17 which he confirmed as a statute
to Jacob,
as an everlasting covenant to
Israel,
18 saying, "To you I will give the
land of Canaan,
as your portion for an
inheritance."
19 When they were few in number,
and of little account, and
sojourners in it,
20 wandering from nation to
nation,
from one kingdom to anoth-
er people,
21 he allowed no one to oppress
them;
he rebuked kings on their
account,
22 saying, "Touch not my anointed
ones,
do my prophets no harm!"
23 Sing to the LORD, all the earth!
Tell of his salvation from day
to day.
24 Declare his glory among the
nations,
his marvelous works among
all the peoples!
25 For great is the LORD, and

[b] Compare Gk Syr Vg: Heb uncertain

greatly to be praised,
and he is to be held in awe
above all gods.
26For all the gods of the peoples
are idols;
but the LORD made the
heavens.
27Honor and majesty are before
him;
strength and joy are in his
place.
28Ascribe to the LORD, O families
of the peoples,
ascribe to the LORD glory
and strength!
29Ascribe to the LORD the glory
due his name;
bring an offering, and come
before him!
Worship the LORD in holy
array;
30tremble before him, all the
earth;
yea, the world stands firm,
never to be moved.
31Let the heavens be glad, and let
the earth rejoice,
and let them say among the
nations, "The LORD
reigns!"
32Let the sea roar, and all that
fills it,
let the field exult, and every-
thing in it!
33Then shall the trees of the wood
sing for joy
before the LORD, for he
comes to judge the
earth.
34O give thanks to the LORD, for
he is good;
for his steadfast love en-
dures for ever!
35Say also:
"Deliver us, O God of our
salvation,
and gather and save us from
among the nations,
that we may give thanks to thy
holy name,
and glory in thy praise.
36Blessed be the LORD, the God
of Israel,
from everlasting to
everlasting!"

REGULAR WORSHIP MAINTAINED

37 So David left Asaph and his
brethren there before the ark of the
covenant of the LORD to minister
continually before the ark as each
day required, 38and also O´bed-e´dom
and his[a] sixty-eight brethren; while
O´bed-e´dom, the son of Jedu´thun,
and Hosah were to be gatekeepers.
39And he left Zadok the priest and his
brethren the priests before the taber-
nacle of the LORD in the high place
that was at Gibeon, 40to offer burnt
offerings to the LORD upon the altar
of burnt offering continually morning
and evening, according to all that is
written in the law of the LORD which
he commanded Israel. 41With them
were Heman and Jedu´thun, and the
rest of those chosen and expressly
named to give thanks to the LORD,
for his steadfast love endures for ever.
42Heman and Jedu´thun had trumpets
and cymbals for the music and instru-
ments for sacred song. The sons of
Jedu´thun were appointed to the gate.
43 Then all the people departed
each to his house, and David went
home to bless his household.

GOD'S COVENANT WITH DAVID

17 Now when David dwelt in his
house, David said to Nathan the
prophet, "Behold, I dwell in a house
of cedar, but the ark of the covenant
of the LORD is under a tent." 2And
Nathan said to David, "Do all that is
in your heart, for God is with you."
3 But that same night the word of
the LORD came to Nathan, 4"Go and
tell my servant David, 'Thus says the
LORD: You shall not build me a house
to dwell in. 5For I have not dwelt in
a house since the day I led up Israel
to this day, but I have gone from tent
to tent and from dwelling to dwelling.

[a] Heb *their*

6In all places where I have moved with
all Israel, did I speak a word with
any of the judges of Israel, whom I
commanded to shepherd my people,
saying, "Why have you not built me
a house of cedar?"" 7Now therefore
thus shall you say to my servant
David, 'Thus says the LORD of hosts,
I took you from the pasture, from
following the sheep, that you should
be prince over my people Israel; 8and
I have been with you wherever you
went, and have cut off all your ene-
mies from before you; and I will make
for you a name, like the name of the
great ones of the earth. 9And I will ap-
point a place for my people Israel, and
will plant them, that they may dwell
in their own place, and be disturbed
no more; and violent men shall waste
them no more, as formerly, 10from the
time that I appointed judges over my
people Israel; and I will subdue all
your enemies. Moreover I declare to
you that the LORD will build you a
house. 11When your days are fulfilled
to go to be with your fathers, I will
raise up your offspring after you, one
of your own sons, and I will establish
his kingdom. 12He shall build a house
for me, and I will establish his throne
for ever. 13I will be his father, and he
shall be my son; I will not take my
steadfast love from him, as I took it
from him who was before you, 14but I
will confirm him in my house and in
my kingdom for ever and his throne
shall be established for ever.'" 15In
accordance with all these words, and
in accordance with all this vision,
Nathan spoke to David.

DAVID'S PRAYER

16 Then King David went in and sat
before the LORD, and said, "Who am
I, O LORD God, and what is my house,
that thou hast brought me thus far?
17And this was a small thing in thy
eyes, O God; thou hast also spoken of
thy servant's house for a great while
to come, and hast shown me future
generations,[b] O LORD God! 18And
what more can David say to thee for
honoring thy servant? For thou know-
est thy servant. 19For thy servant's
sake, O LORD, and according to thy
own heart, thou hast wrought all this
greatness, in making known all these
great things. 20There is none like thee,
O LORD, and there is no God besides
thee, according to all that we have
heard with our ears. 21What other[c] na-
tion on earth is like thy people Israel,
whom God went to redeem to be his
people, making for thyself a name for
great and terrible things, in driving
out nations before thy people whom
thou didst redeem from Egypt? 22And
thou didst make thy people Israel to
be thy people for ever; and thou, O
LORD, didst become their God. 23And
now, O LORD, let the word which thou
hast spoken concerning thy servant
and concerning his house be estab-
lished for ever, and do as thou hast
spoken; 24and thy name will be estab-
lished and magnified for ever, saying,
'The LORD of hosts, the God of Israel,
is Israel's God,' and the house of thy
servant David will be established be-
fore thee. 25For thou, my God, hast
revealed to thy servant that thou wilt
build a house for him; therefore thy
servant has found courage to pray be-
fore thee. 26And now, O LORD, thou
art God, and thou hast promised
this good thing to thy servant; 27now
therefore may it please thee to bless
the house of thy servant, that it may
continue for ever before thee; for what
thou, O LORD, hast blessed is blessed
for ever."

DAVID'S KINGDOM ESTABLISHED AND EXTENDED

18 After this David defeated the
Philistines and subdued them,
and he took Gath and its villages out
of the hand of the Philistines.

2 And he defeated Moab, and the

[b]Cn: Heb uncertain
[c]Gk Vg: Heb *one*

Mo´abites became servants to David
and brought tribute.
3 David also defeated Hadade´zer
king of Zobah, toward Hamath, as
he went to set up his monument[a] at
the river Euphra´tes. 4 And David took
from him a thousand chariots, sev-
en thousand horsemen, and twenty
thousand foot soldiers; and David
hamstrung all the chariot horses, but
left enough for a hundred chariots.
5 And when the Syrians of Damascus
came to help Hadade´zer king of
Zobah, David slew twenty-two thou-
sand men of the Syrians. 6 Then David
put garrisons[b] in Syria of Damascus;
and the Syrians became servants to
David, and brought tribute. And the
LORD gave victory to David wherever
he went. 7 And David took the shields
of gold which were carried by the
servants of Hadade´zer, and brought
them to Jerusalem. 8 And from Tibhath
and from Cun, cities of Hadade´zer,
David took very much bronze; with it
Solomon made the bronze sea and the
pillars and the vessels of bronze.
9 When To´u king of Hamath
heard that David had defeated the
whole army of Hadade´zer, king of
Zobah, 10 he sent his son Hador´am to
King David, to greet him, and to con-
gratulate him because he had fought
against Hadade´zer and defeated him;
for Hadade´zer had often been at war
with To´u. And he sent all sorts of ar-
ticles of gold, of silver, and of bronze;
11 these also King David dedicated to
the LORD, together with the silver and
gold which he had carried off from
all the nations, from Edom, Moab,
the Ammonites, the Philistines, and
Am´alek.
12 And Abi´shai, the son of
Zeru´iah, slew eighteen thousand
E´domites in the Valley of Salt. 13 And
he put garrisons in Edom; and all the
E´domites became David's servants.
And the LORD gave victory to David
wherever he went.

DAVID'S ADMINISTRATION

14 So David reigned over all Israel;
and he administered justice and eq-
uity to all his people. 15 And Jo´ab the
son of Zeru´iah was over the army;
and Jehosh´aphat the son of Ahi´lud
was recorder; 16 and Zadok the son of
Ahi´tub and Ahim´elech the son of
Abi´athar were priests; and Shavsha
was secretary; 17 and Benai´ah the son
of Jehoi´ada was over the Cher´ethites
and the Pel´ethites; and David's sons
were the chief officials in the service
of the king.

DEFEAT OF THE AMMONITES AND ARAME´ANS

19 Now after this Nahash the king
of the Ammonites died, and his
son reigned in his stead. 2 And David
said, "I will deal loyally with Hanun
the son of Nahash, for his father dealt
loyally with me." So David sent mes-
sengers to console him concerning his
father. And David's servants came to
Hanun in the land of the Ammonites,
to console him. 3 But the princes of the
Ammonites said to Hanun, "Do you
think, because David has sent com-
forters to you, that he is honoring your
father? Have not his servants come to
you to search and to overthrow and
to spy out the land?" 4 So Hanun took
David's servants, and shaved them,
and cut off their garments in the mid-
dle, at their hips, and sent them away;
5 and they departed. When David was
told concerning the men, he sent to
meet them, for the men were greatly
ashamed. And the king said, "Remain
at Jericho until your beards have
grown, and then return."
6 When the Ammonites saw that
they had made themselves odious to
David, Hanun and the Ammonites
sent a thousand talents of silver to
hire chariots and horsemen from
Mesopota´mia, from Aram-ma´acah,
and from Zobah. 7 They hired thir-
ty-two thousand chariots and the
king of Ma´acah with his army, who

[a] Heb *hand*
[b] Gk Vg 2Sam 8. 6. Compare Syr: Heb lacks *garrisons*

came and encamped before Med´eba.
And the Ammonites were mustered
from their cities and came to bat-
tle. 8 When David heard of it, he sent
Jo´ab and all the army of the mighty
men. 9 And the Ammonites came out
and drew up in battle array at the en-
trance of the city, and the kings who
had come were by themselves in the
open country.

10 When Jo´ab saw that the bat-
tle was set against him both in front
and in the rear, he chose some of the
picked men of Israel, and arrayed
them against the Syrians; 11 the rest
of his men he put in the charge of
Abi´shai his brother, and they were
arrayed against the Ammonites. 12 And
he said, "If the Syrians are too strong
for me, then you shall help me; but
if the Ammonites are too strong for
you, then I will help you. 13 Be of good
courage, and let us play the man for
our people, and for the cities of our
God; and may the LORD do what
seems good to him." 14 So Jo´ab and
the people who were with him drew
near before the Syrians for battle; and
they fled before him. 15 And when the
Ammonites saw that the Syrians fled,
they likewise fled before Abi´shai,
Jo´ab's brother, and entered the city.
Then Jo´ab came to Jerusalem.

16 But when the Syrians saw that
they had been defeated by Israel,
they sent messengers and brought
out the Syrians who were beyond the
Euphra´tes, with Shophach the com-
mander of the army of Hadade´zer
at their head. 17 And when it was told
David, he gathered all Israel together,
and crossed the Jordan, and came to
them, and drew up his forces against
them. And when David set the battle in
array against the Syrians, they fought
with him. 18 And the Syrians fled before
Israel; and David slew of the Syrians
the men of seven thousand chariots,
and forty thousand foot soldiers, and
killed also Shophach the commander
of their army. 19 And when the servants
of Hadade´zer saw that they had been
defeated by Israel, they made peace
with David, and became subject to
him. So the Syrians were not willing to
help the Ammonites any more.

SIEGE AND CAPTURE OF RABBAH

20 In the spring of the year, the time
when kings go forth to battle,
Jo´ab led out the army, and ravaged the
country of the Ammonites, and came
and besieged Rabbah. But David re-
mained at Jerusalem. And Jo´ab smote
Rabbah, and overthrew it. 2 And David
took the crown of their king[c] from his
head; he found that it weighed a talent
of gold, and in it was a precious stone;
and it was placed on David's head. And
he brought forth the spoil of the city,
a very great amount. 3 And he brought
forth the people who were in it, and
set them to labor[d] with saws and iron
picks and axes;[e] and thus David did to
all the cities of the Ammonites. Then
David and all the people returned to
Jerusalem.

EXPLOITS AGAINST THE PHILISTINES

4 And after this there arose war
with the Philistines at Gezer; then
Sib´becai the Hu´shathite slew Sip´pai,
who was one of the descendants of
the giants; and the Philistines were
subdued. 5 And there was again war
with the Philistines; and Elha´nan the
son of Ja´ir slew Lahmi the brother of
Goliath the Gittite, the shaft of whose
spear was like a weaver's beam. 6 And
there was again war at Gath, where
there was a man of great stature, who
had six fingers on each hand, and six
toes on each foot, twenty-four in num-
ber; and he also was descended from
the giants. 7 And when he taunted
Israel, Jonathan the son of Shim´e-a,
David's brother, slew him. 8 These
were descended from the giants in
Gath; and they fell by the hand of
David and by the hand of his servants.

[c] Or *Milcom*. See 1Kings 11. 5
[d] Compare 2Sam 12. 31: Heb *he sawed*
[e] Compare 2Sam 12. 31: Heb *saws*

THE CENSUS AND PLAGUE

21 *Satan stood up against Israel,
and incited David to number
Israel. 2So David said to Jo´ab and the
commanders of the army, "Go, num-
ber Israel, from Beer-sheba to Dan,
and bring me a report, that I may
know their number." 3But Jo´ab said,
"May the LORD add to his people a
hundred times as many as they are!
Are they not, my lord the king, all of
them my lord's servants? Why then
should my lord require this? Why
should he bring guilt upon Israel?"
4But the king's word prevailed against
Jo´ab. So Jo´ab departed and went
throughout all Israel, and came back
to Jerusalem. 5And Jo´ab gave the
sum of the numbering of the people
to David. In all Israel there were one
million one hundred thousand men
who drew the sword, and in Judah
four hundred and seventy thousand
who drew the sword. 6But he did not
include Levi and Benjamin in the
numbering, for the king's command
was abhorrent to Jo´ab.

7 But God was displeased with
this thing, and he smote Israel. 8And
David said to God, "I have sinned
greatly in that I have done this thing.
But now, I pray thee, take away the in-
iquity of thy servant; for I have done
very foolishly." 9And the LORD spoke
to Gad, David's seer, saying, 10"Go and
say to David, 'Thus says the LORD,
Three things I offer you; choose one
of them, that I may do it to you.'" 11So
Gad came to David and said to him,
"Thus says the LORD, 'Take which
you will: 12either three years of fam-
ine; or three months of devastation
by your foes, while the sword of your
enemies overtakes you; or else three
days of the sword of the LORD, pes-
tilence upon the land, and the angel
of the LORD destroying throughout
all the territory of Israel.' Now decide
what answer I shall return to him who
sent me." 13Then David said to Gad, "I
am in great distress; let me fall into
the hand of the LORD, for his mercy is
very great; but let me not fall into the
hand of man."

14 So the LORD sent a pestilence
upon Israel; and there fell seventy
thousand men of Israel. 15And God
sent the angel to Jerusalem to de-
stroy it; but when he was about to
destroy it, the LORD saw, and he re-
pented of the evil; and he said to the
destroying angel, "It is enough; now
stay your hand." And the angel of the
LORD was standing by the thresh-
ing floor of Ornan the Jeb´usite.
16And David lifted his eyes and saw
the angel of the LORD standing be-
tween earth and heaven, and in his
hand a drawn sword stretched out
over Jerusalem. Then David and the
elders, clothed in sackcloth, fell upon
their faces. 17And David said to God,
"Was it not I who gave command to
number the people? It is I who have
sinned and done very wickedly. But
these sheep, what have they done?
Let thy hand, I pray thee, O LORD my
God, be against me and against my
father's house; but let not the plague
be upon thy people."

DAVID'S ALTAR AND SACRIFICE

18 Then the angel of the LORD
commanded Gad to say to David
that David should go up and rear an
altar to the LORD on the threshing
floor of Ornan the Jeb´usite. 19So
David went up at Gad's word, which
he had spoken in the name of the
LORD. 20Now Ornan was threshing
wheat; he turned and saw the angel,
and his four sons who were with him
hid themselves. 21As David came to
Ornan, Ornan looked and saw David
and went forth from the threshing
floor, and did obeisance to David with
his face to the ground. 22And David
said to Ornan, "Give me the site of the
threshing floor that I may build on it
an altar to the LORD—give it to me
at its full price—that the plague may
be averted from the people." 23Then
Ornan said to David, "Take it; and let
my lord the king do what seems good

to him; see, I give the oxen for burnt offerings, and the threshing sledges for the wood, and the wheat for a cereal offering. I give it all." 24But King David said to Ornan, "No, but I will buy it for the full price; I will not take for the LORD what is yours, nor offer burnt offerings which cost me nothing." 25So David paid Ornan six hundred shekels of gold by weight for the site. 26And David built there an altar to the LORD and presented burnt offerings and peace offerings, and called upon the LORD, and he answered him with fire from heaven upon the altar of burnt offering. 27Then the LORD commanded the angel; and he put his sword back into its sheath.

THE PLACE CHOSEN FOR THE TEMPLE

28 At that time, when David saw that the LORD had answered him at the threshing floor of Ornan the Jeb´usite, he made his sacrifices there. 29For the tabernacle of the LORD, which Moses had made in the wilderness, and the altar of burnt offering were at that time in the high place at Gibeon; 30but David could not go before it to inquire of God, for he was afraid of the sword of the angel of the LORD.

22 1Then David said, "Here shall be the house of the LORD God and here the altar of burnt offering for Israel."

DAVID PREPARES TO BUILD THE TEMPLE

2 David commanded to gather together the aliens who were in the land of Israel, and he set stonecutters to prepare dressed stones for building the house of God. 3David also provided great stores of iron for nails for the doors of the gates and for clamps, as well as bronze in quantities beyond weighing, 4and cedar timbers without number; for the Sido´nians and Tyrians brought great quantities of cedar to David. 5For David said, "Solomon my son is young and inexperienced, and the house that is to be built for the LORD must be exceedingly magnificent, of fame and glory throughout all lands; I will therefore make preparation for it." So David provided materials in great quantity before his death.

DAVID'S CHARGE TO SOLOMON AND THE LEADERS

6 Then he called for Solomon his son, and charged him to build a house for the LORD, the God of Israel. 7David said to Solomon, "My son, I had it in my heart to build a house to the name of the LORD my God. 8But the word of the LORD came to me, saying, 'You have shed much blood and have waged great wars; you shall not build a house to my name, because you have shed so much blood before me upon the earth. 9Behold, a son shall be born to you; he shall be a man of peace. I will give him peace from all his enemies round about; for his name shall be Solomon, and I will give peace and quiet to Israel in his days. 10He shall build a house for my name. He shall be my son, and I will be his father, and I will establish his royal throne in Israel for ever.' 11Now, my son, the LORD be with you, so that you may succeed in building the house of the LORD your God, as he has spoken concerning you. 12Only, may the LORD grant you discretion and understanding, that when he gives you charge over Israel you may keep the law of the LORD your God. 13Then you will prosper if you are careful to observe the statutes and the ordinances which the LORD commanded Moses for Israel. Be strong, and of good courage. Fear not; be not dismayed. 14With great pains I have provided for the house of the LORD a hundred thousand talents of gold, a million talents of silver, and bronze and iron beyond weighing, for there is so much of it; timber and stone too I have provided. To these you must add. 15You have an abundance of workmen: stonecutters, masons, carpenters, and all kinds of

craftsmen without number, skilled
in working 16 gold, silver, bronze, and
iron. Arise and be doing! The LORD be
with you!"

17 David also commanded all the
leaders of Israel to help Solomon his
son, saying, 18 "Is not the LORD your
God with you? And has he not given
you peace on every side? For he has
delivered the inhabitants of the land
into my hand; and the land is sub-
dued before the LORD and his people.
19 Now set your mind and heart to seek
the LORD your God. Arise and build
the sanctuary of the LORD God, so
that the ark of the covenant of the
LORD and the holy vessels of God may
be brought into a house built for the
name of the LORD."

FAMILIES OF THE LEVITES AND THEIR FUNCTIONS

23 When David was old and full of
days, he made Solomon his son
king over Israel.

2 David assembled all the lead-
ers of Israel and the priests and the
Levites. 3 The Levites, thirty years old
and upward, were numbered, and the
total was thirty-eight thousand men.
4 "Twenty-four thousand of these,"
David said, "shall have charge of the
work in the house of the LORD, six
thousand shall be officers and judges,
5 four thousand gatekeepers, and four
thousand shall offer praises to the
LORD with the instruments which I
have made for praise." 6 And David or-
ganized them in divisions correspond-
ing to the sons of Levi: Gershom,
Kohath, and Merar'i.

7 The sons of Gershom[a] were
Ladan and Shim'e-i. 8 The sons of
Ladan: Jehi'el the chief, and Zetham,
and Jo'el, three. 9 The sons of Shim'e-i:
Shelo'moth, Ha'zi-el, and Haran,
three. These were the heads of the fa-
thers' houses of Ladan. 10 And the sons
of Shim'e-i: Jahath, Zina, and Je'ush,
and Beri'ah. These four were the sons
of Shim'e-i. 11 Jahath was the chief,
and Zizah the second; but Je'ush and
Beri'ah had not many sons, therefore
they became a fathers' house in one
reckoning.

12 The sons of Kohath: Amram,
Izhar, Hebron, and Uz'ziel, four. 13 The
sons of Amram: Aaron and Moses.
Aaron was set apart to consecrate the
most holy things, that he and his sons
for ever should burn incense before
the LORD, and minister to him and
pronounce blessings in his name for
ever. 14 But the sons of Moses the man
of God were named among the tribe
of Levi. 15 The sons of Moses: Gershom
and Elie'zer. 16 The sons of Gershom:
Sheb'uel the chief. 17 The sons of
Elie'zer: Rehabi'ah the chief; Elie'zer
had no other sons, but the sons of
Rehabi'ah were very many. 18 The
sons of Izhar: Shelo'mith the chief.
19 The sons of Hebron: Jeri'ah the
chief, Amari'ah the second, Jaha'ziel
the third, and Jekame'am the fourth.
20 The sons of Uz'ziel: Micah the chief
and Isshi'ah the second.

21 The sons of Merar'i: Mahli and
Mushi. The sons of Mahli: Elea'zar
and Kish. 22 Elea'zar died having no
sons, but only daughters; their kins-
men, the sons of Kish, married them.
23 The sons of Mushi: Mahli, Eder, and
Jer'emoth, three.

24 These were the sons of Levi by
their fathers' houses, the heads of
fathers' houses as they were regis-
tered according to the number of the
names of the individuals from twen-
ty years old and upward who were
to do the work for the service of the
house of the LORD. 25 For David said,
"The LORD, the God of Israel, has giv-
en peace to his people; and he dwells
in Jerusalem for ever. 26 And so the
Levites no longer need to carry the
tabernacle or any of the things for
its service" 27 for by the last words of
David these were the number of the
Levites from twenty years old and up-
ward 28 "but their duty shall be to as-
sist the sons of Aaron for the service

[a] Vg Compare Gk Syr: Heb *to the Gershonite*

of the house of the LORD, having the care of the courts and the chambers, the cleansing of all that is holy, and any work for the service of the house of God; [29]to assist also with the showbread, the flour for the cereal offering, the wafers of unleavened bread, the baked offering, the offering mixed with oil, and all measures of quantity or size. [30]And they shall stand every morning, thanking and praising the LORD, and likewise at evening, [31]and whenever burnt offerings are offered to the LORD on sabbaths, new moons, and feast days, according to the number required of them, continually before the LORD. [32]Thus they shall keep charge of the tent of meeting and the sanctuary, and shall attend the sons of Aaron, their brethren, for the service of the house of the LORD."

DIVISIONS OF THE PRIESTS

24 The divisions of the sons of Aaron were these. The sons of Aaron: Nadab, Abi´hu, Elea´zar, and Ith´amar. [2]But Nadab and Abi´hu died before their father, and had no children, so Elea´zar and Ith´amar became the priests. [3]With the help of Zadok of the sons of Elea´zar, and Ahim´elech of the sons of Ith´amar,* David organized them according to the appointed duties in their service. [4]Since more chief men were found among the sons of Elea´zar than among the sons of Ith´amar, they organized them under sixteen heads of fathers' houses of the sons of Elea´zar, and eight of the sons of Ith´amar. [5]They organized them by lot, all alike, for there were officers of the sanctuary and officers of God among both the sons of Elea´zar and the sons of Ith´amar. [6]And the scribe Shemai´ah the son of Nethan´el, a Levite, recorded them in the presence of the king, and the princes, and Zadok the priest, and Ahim´elech the son of Abi´athar, and the heads of the fathers' houses of the priests and of the Levites; one father's house being chosen for Elea´zar and one chosen for Ith´amar.

7 The first lot fell to Jehoi´arib, the second to Jeda´iah, [8]the third to Harim, the fourth to Se-o´rim, [9]the fifth to Malchi´jah, the sixth to Mij´amin, [10]the seventh to Hakkoz, the eighth to Abi´jah, [11]the ninth to Jeshua, the tenth to Shecani´ah, [12]the eleventh to Eli´ashib, the twelfth to Jakim, [13]the thirteenth to Huppah, the fourteenth to Jesheb´e-ab, [14]the fifteenth to Bilgah, the sixteenth to Immer, [15]the seventeenth to Hezir, the eighteenth to Hap´pizzez, [16]the nineteenth to Pethahi´ah, the twentieth to Jehez´kel, [17]the twenty-first to Jachin, the twenty-second to Gamul, [18]the twenty-third to Delai´ah, the twenty-fourth to Ma-azi´ah. [19]These had as their appointed duty in their service to come into the house of the LORD according to the procedure established for them by Aaron their father, as the LORD God of Israel had commanded him.

OTHER LEVITES

20 And of the rest of the sons of Levi: of the sons of Amram, Shu´ba-el; of the sons of Shu´ba-el, Jehde´iah. [21]Of Rehabi´ah: of the sons of Rehabi´ah, Isshi´ah the chief. [22]Of the Iz´harites, Shelo´moth; of the sons of Shelo´moth, Jahath. [23]The sons of Hebron:[b] Jeri´ah the chief,[c] Amari´ah the second, Jaha´ziel the third, Jekame´am the fourth. [24]The sons of Uz´ziel, Micah; of the sons of Micah, Shamir. [25]The brother of Micah, Isshi´ah; of the sons of Isshi´ah, Zechari´ah. [26]The sons of Merar´i: Mahli and Mushi. The sons of Ja-azi´ah: Beno. [27]The sons of Merar´i: of Ja-azi´ah, Beno, Shoham, Zaccur, and Ibri. [28]Of Mahli: Elea´zar, who had no sons. [29]Of Kish, the sons of Kish: Jerah´meel. [30]The sons of Mushi: Mahli, Eder, and Jer´imoth. These

[b]See 23.19: Heb lacks *Hebron*
[c]See 23.19: Heb lacks *the chief*

were the sons of the Levites accord-
ing to their fathers' houses. 31These
also, the head of each father's house
and his younger brother alike, cast
lots, just as their brethren the sons of
Aaron, in the presence of King David,
Zadok, Ahim´elech, and the heads of
fathers' houses of the priests and of
the Levites.

THE TEMPLE MUSICIANS

25 David and the chiefs of the ser-
vice also set apart for the service
certain of the sons of Asaph, and of
Heman, and of Jedu´thun, who should
prophesy with lyres, with harps, and
with cymbals. The list of those who
did the work and of their duties was:
2Of the sons of Asaph: Zaccur, Joseph,
Nethani´ah, and Ashare´lah, sons of
Asaph, under the direction of Asaph,
who prophesied under the direction
of the king. 3Of Jedu´thun, the sons
of Jedu´thun: Gedali´ah, Zeri, Jesh-
a´iah, Shim´e-i,[a] Hashabi´ah, and
Mattithi´ah, six, under the direction
of their father Jedu´thun, who proph-
esied with the lyre in thanksgiving
and praise to the LORD. 4Of Heman,
the sons of Heman: Bukki´ah, Mat-
tani´ah, Uz´ziel, Shebu´el, and Jer´-
imoth, Hanani´ah, Hana´ni, Eli´a-
thah, Giddal´ti, and Romam´ti-e´zer,
Joshbekash´ah, Mallo´thi, Hothir,
Maha´zi-oth. 5All these were the sons
of Heman the king's seer, according
to the promise of God to exalt him;
for God had given Heman fourteen
sons and three daughters. 6They were
all under the direction of their father
in the music in the house of the LORD
with cymbals, harps, and lyres for the
service of the house of God. Asaph,
Jedu´thun, and Heman were under
the order of the king. 7The number of
them along with their brethren, who
were trained in singing to the LORD,
all who were skilful, was two hun-
dred and eighty-eight. 8And they cast
lots for their duties, small and great,
teacher and pupil alike.

9 The first lot fell for Asaph to
Joseph; the second to Gedali´ah, to him
and his brethren and his sons, twelve;
10the third to Zaccur, his sons and his
brethren, twelve; 11the fourth to Izri,
his sons and his brethren, twelve;
12the fifth to Nethani´ah, his sons and
his brethren, twelve; 13the sixth to
Bukki´ah, his sons and his brethren,
twelve; 14the seventh to Jeshare´lah,
his sons and his brethren, twelve;
15the eighth to Jesha´iah, his sons and
his brethren, twelve; 16the ninth to
Mattani´ah, his sons and his brethren,
twelve; 17the tenth to Shim´e-i, his sons
and his brethren, twelve; 18the eleventh
to Az´arel, his sons and his brethren,
twelve; 19the twelfth to Hashabi´ah, his
sons and his brethren, twelve; 20to the
thirteenth, Shu´ba-el, his sons and his
brethren, twelve; 21to the fourteenth,
Mattithi´ah, his sons and his brethren,
twelve; 22to the fifteenth, to Jer´emoth,
his sons and his brethren, twelve; 23to
the sixteenth, to Hanani´ah, his sons
and his brethren, twelve; 24to the sev-
enteenth, to Joshbekash´ah, his sons
and his brethren, twelve; 25to the
eighteenth, to Hana´ni, his sons and
his brethren, twelve; 26to the nine-
teenth, to Mallo´thi, his sons and his
brethren, twelve; 27to the twentieth, to
Eli´athah, his sons and his brethren,
twelve; 28to the twenty-first, to Hothir,
his sons and his brethren, twelve; 29to
the twenty-second, to Giddal´ti, his
sons and his brethren, twelve; 30to the
twenty-third, to Maha´zi-oth, his sons
and his brethren, twelve; 31to the twen-
ty-fourth, to Romam´ti-e´zer, his sons
and his brethren, twelve.

THE GATEKEEPERS

26 As for the divisons of the gate-
keepers: of the Kor´ahites, Meshel-
emi´ah the son of Kor´e, of the sons of
Asaph. 2And Meshelemi´ah had sons:
Zechari´ah the first-born, Jedi´a-el the
second, Zebadi´ah the third, Jath´ni-
el the fourth, 3Elam the fifth, Jeho-
ha´nan the sixth, Eli-e-ho-e´nai the

[a]One Ms: Gk: Heb lacks *Shimei*

seventh. 4And O´bed-e´dom had sons:
Shemai´ah the first-born, Jeho´zabad
the second, Jo´ah the third, Sachar the
fourth, Nethan´el the fifth, 5Am´mi-el
the sixth, Is´sachar the seventh, Pe-
ul´lethai the eighth; for God blessed
him. 6Also to his son Shemai´ah were
sons born who were rulers in their
fathers' houses, for they were men of
great ability. 7The sons of Shemai´ah:
Othni, Reph´a-el, Obed, and Elza´bad,
whose brethren were able men, Eli´hu
and Semachi´ah. 8All these were of
the sons of O´bed-e´dom with their
sons and brethren, able men qualified
for the service; sixty-two of O´bed-
e´dom. 9And Meshelemi´ah had sons
and brethren, able men, eighteen.
10And Hosah, of the sons of Merar´i,
had sons: Shimri the chief (for though
he was not the first-born, his father
made him chief), 11Hilki´ah the sec-
ond, Tebali´ah the third, Zechari´ah
the fourth: all the sons and brethren
of Hosah were thirteen.

12 These divisions of the gate-
keepers, corresponding to their chief
men, had duties, just as their brethren
did, ministering in the house of the
LORD; 13and they cast lots by fathers'
houses, small and great alike, for
their gates. 14The lot for the east fell
to Shelemi´ah. They cast lots also for
his son Zechari´ah, a shrewd counsel-
or, and his lot came out for the north.
15O´bed-e´dom's came out for the
south, and to his sons was allotted the
storehouse. 16For Shuppim and Hosah
it came out for the west, at the gate
of Shal´lecheth on the road that goes
up. Watch corresponded to watch. 17On
the east there were six each day,[b] on
the north four each day, on the south
four each day, as well as two and two
at the storehouse; 18and for the parbar[c]
on the west there were four at the road
and two at the parbar. 19These were the
divisions of the gatekeepers among the
Kor´ahites and the sons of Merar´i.

THE TREASURERS, OFFICERS, AND JUDGES

20 And of the Levites, Ahi´jah had
charge of the treasuries of the house
of God and the treasuries of the ded-
icated gifts. 21The sons of Ladan, the
sons of the Gershonites belonging to
Ladan, the heads of the fathers' hous-
es belonging to Ladan the Gershonite:
Jehi´eli.[d]

22 The sons of Jehi´eli, Zetham
and Jo´el his brother, were in charge
of the treasuries of the house of
the LORD. 23Of the Am´ramites, the
Iz´harites, the He´bronites, and the
Uz´zielites 24and Sheb´uel the son of
Gershom, son of Moses, was chief of-
ficer in charge of the treasuries. 25His
brethren: from Elie´zer were his son
Rehabi´ah, and his son Jesha´iah, and
his son Joram, and his son Zichri, and
his son Shelo´moth. 26This Shelo´moth
and his brethren were in charge of all
the treasuries of the dedicated gifts
which David the king, and the heads
of the fathers' houses, and the officers
of the thousands and the hundreds,
and the commanders of the army, had
dedicated. 27From spoil won in battles
they dedicated gifts for the mainte-
nance of the house of the LORD. 28Also
all that Samuel the seer, and Saul the
son of Kish, and Abner the son of Ner,
and Jo´ab the son of Zeru´iah had ded-
icated—all dedicated gifts were in the
care of Shelo´moth[e] and his brethren.

29 Of the Iz´harites, Chenani´ah
and his sons were appointed to outside
duties for Israel, as officers and judg-
es. 30Of the He´bronites, Hashabi´ah
and his brethren, one thousand sev-
en hundred men of ability, had the
oversight of Israel westward of the
Jordan for all the work of the LORD
and for the service of the king. 31Of
the He´bronites, Jeri´jah was chief of
the He´bronites of whatever genealo-
gy or fathers' houses. (In the fortieth
year of David's reign search was made
and men of great ability among them

[b] Gk: Heb *Levites*
[c] The meaning of the word *parbar* is unknown
[d] The Hebrew text of verse 21 is confused
[e] Heb *Shelomith*

were found at Jazer in Gilead.) 32King
David appointed him and his breth-
ren, two thousand seven hundred men
of ability, heads of fathers' houses, to
have the oversight of the Reubenites,
the Gadites, and the half-tribe of the
Manas´sites for everything pertaining
to God and for the affairs of the king.

THE MILITARY DIVISIONS

27 This is the list of the people of
Israel, the heads of fathers' hous-
es, the commanders of thousands
and hundreds, and their officers who
served the king in all matters con-
cerning the divisions that came and
went, month after month throughout
the year, each division numbering
twenty-four thousand:
2 Jasho´beam the son of Zab´di-el
was in charge of the first division in
the first month; in his division were
twenty-four thousand. 3He was a de-
scendant of Perez, and was chief of all
the commanders of the army for the
first month. 4Dodai the Aho´hite[a] was
in charge of the division of the second
month; in his division were twenty-four
thousand. 5The third commander, for
the third month, was Bena´iah, the son
of Jehoi´ada the priest, as chief; in his
division were twenty-four thousand.
6This is the Bena´iah who was a mighty
man of the thirty and in command of
the thirty; Ammiz´abad his son was
in charge of his division.[b] 7As´ahel the
brother of Jo´ab was fourth, for the
fourth month, and his son Zebadi´ah
after him; in his division were twen-
ty-four thousand. 8The fifth command-
er, for the fifth month, was Shamhuth,
the Iz´rahite; in his division were
twenty-four thousand. 9Sixth, for
the sixth month, was Ira, the son of
Ikkesh the Teko´ite; in his division
were twenty-four thousand. 10Seventh,
for the seventh month, was Helez the
Pel´onite, of the sons of E´phraim; in
his division were twenty-four thou-
sand. 11Eighth, for the eighth month,
was Sib´becai the Hu´shathite, of the
Ze´rahites; in his division were twen-
ty-four thousand. 12Ninth, for the ninth
month, was Abi-e´zer of An´athoth, a
Benjaminite; in his division were twen-
ty-four thousand. 13Tenth, for the tenth
month, was Ma´harai of Neto´phah,
of the Ze´rahites; in his division were
twenty-four thousand. 14Eleventh, for
the eleventh month, was Bena´iah of
Pir´athon, of the sons of E´phraim; in
his division were twenty-four thousand.
15Twelfth, for the twelfth month, was
Heldai the Netoph´athite, of Oth´niel;
in his division were twenty-four
thousand.

LEADERS OF TRIBES

16 Over the tribes of Israel, for the
Reubenites Elie´zer the son of Zichri
was chief officer; for the Simeonites,
Shephati´ah the son of Ma´acah; 17for
Levi, Hashabi´ah the son of Kemu´el;
for Aaron, Zadok; 18for Judah, Eli´hu,
one of David's brothers; for Is´sachar,
Omri the son of Michael; 19for Zeb´-
ulun, Ishma´iah the son of Obadi´-
ah; for Naph´tali, Jer´emoth the son
of Az´riel; 20for the E´phraimites,
Hoshe´a the son of Azazi´ah; for the
half-tribe of Manas´seh, Jo´el the son
of Peda´iah; 21for the half-tribe of
Manas´seh in Gilead, Iddo the son of
Zechari´ah; for Benjamin, Ja-a´siel the
son of Abner; 22for Dan, Az´arel the
son of Jero´ham. These were the lead-
ers of the tribes of Israel. 23David did
not number those below twenty years
of age, for the LORD had promised to
make Israel as many as the stars of
heaven. 24Jo´ab the son of Zeru´iah be-
gan to number, but did not finish; yet
wrath came upon Israel for this, and
the number was not entered in the
chronicles of King David.

OTHER CIVIC OFFICIALS

25 Over the king's treasuries was
Az´maveth the son of Ad´i-el; and over
the treasuries in the country, in the

[a]Gk: Heb *Ahohite and his division and Mikloth the chief officer*
[b]Gk Vg: Heb *was his division*

cities, in the villages and in the tow-
ers, was Jonathan the son of Uzzi´ah;
26and over those who did the work of
the field for tilling the soil was Ezri
the son of Chelub; 27and over the vine-
yards was Shim´e-i the Ra´mathite;
and over the produce of the vineyards
for the wine cellars was Zabdi the
Shiphmite. 28Over the olive and syc-
amore trees in the Shephe´lah was
Ba´al-ha´nan the Gede´rite; and over
the stores of oil was Jo´ash. 29Over the
herds that pastured in Sharon was
Shitrai the Sha´ronite; over the herds
in the valleys was Shaphat the son of
Adlai. 30Over the camels was Obil the
Ish´maelite; and over the she-asses
was Jehde´iah the Meron´othite. Over
the flocks was Jaziz the Hagrite. 31All
these were stewards of King David's
property.

32 Jonathan, David's uncle, was a
counselor, being a man of understand-
ing and a scribe; he and Jehi´el the
son of Hach´moni attended the king's
sons. 33Ahith´ophel was the king's
counselor, and Hushai the Archite
was the king's friend. 34Ahith´ophel
was succeeded by Jehoi´ada the son
of Bena´iah, and Abi´athar. Jo´ab was
commander of the king's army.

SOLOMON INSTRUCTED TO BUILD THE TEMPLE

28 David assembled at Jerusalem all
the officials of Israel, the offi-
cials of the tribes, the officers of the
divisions that served the king, the
commanders of thousands, the com-
manders of hundreds, the stewards of
all the property and cattle of the king
and his sons, together with the palace
officials, the mighty men, and all the
seasoned warriors. 2Then King David
rose to his feet and said: "Hear me,
my brethren and my people. I had it
in my heart to build a house of rest for
the ark of the covenant of the LORD,
and for the footstool of our God; and
I made preparations for building. 3But
God said to me, 'You may not build
a house for my name, for you are a
warrior and have shed blood.' 4Yet the
LORD God of Israel chose me from
all my father's house to be king over
Israel for ever; for he chose Judah as
leader, and in the house of Judah my
father's house, and among my father's
sons he took pleasure in me to make
me king over all Israel. 5And of all my
sons (for the LORD has given me many
sons) he has chosen Solomon my son
to sit upon the throne of the kingdom
of the LORD over Israel. 6He said to
me, 'It is Solomon your son who shall
build my house and my courts, for I
have chosen him to be my son, and
I will be his father. 7I will establish
his kingdom for ever if he continues
resolute in keeping my command-
ments and my ordinances, as he is
today.' 8Now therefore in the sight of
all Israel, the assembly of the LORD,
and in the hearing of our God, observe
and seek out all the commandments
of the LORD your God; that you may
possess this good land, and leave it for
an inheritance to your children after
you for ever.

9 "And you, Solomon my son,
know the God of your father, and
serve him with a whole heart and with
a willing mind; for the LORD search-
es all hearts, and understands every
plan and thought. If you seek him, he
will be found by you; but if you for-
sake him, he will cast you off for ever.
10Take heed now, for the LORD has
chosen you to build a house for the
sanctuary; be strong, and do it."

11 Then David gave Solomon his son
the plan of the vestibule of the tem-
ple, and of its houses, its treasuries,
its upper rooms, and its inner cham-
bers, and of the room for the mercy
seat; 12and the plan of all that he had
in mind for the courts of the house of
the LORD, all the surrounding cham-
bers, the treasuries of the house of
God, and the treasuries for dedicated
gifts; 13for the divisions of the priests
and of the Levites, and all the work of
the service in the house of the LORD;
for all the vessels for the service in

the house of the LORD, 14 the weight of gold for all golden vessels for each service, the weight of silver vessels for each service, 15 the weight of the golden lampstands and their lamps, the weight of gold for each lampstand and its lamps, the weight of silver for a lampstand and its lamps, according to the use of each lampstand in the service, 16 the weight of gold for each table for the showbread, the silver for the silver tables, 17 and pure gold for the forks, the basins, and the cups; for the golden bowls and the weight of each; for the silver bowls and the weight of each; 18 for the altar of incense made of refined gold, and its weight; also his plan for the golden chariot of the cherubim that spread their wings and covered the ark of the covenant of the LORD. 19 All this he made clear by the writing from the hand of the LORD concerning it,[a] all the work to be done according to the plan.

20 Then David said to Solomon his son, "Be strong and of good courage, and do it. Fear not, be not dismayed; for the LORD God, even my God, is with you. He will not fail you or forsake you, until all the work for the service of the house of the LORD is finished. 21 And behold the divisions of the priests and the Levites for all the service of the house of God; and with you in all the work will be every willing man who has skill for any kind of service; also the officers and all the people will be wholly at your command."

OFFERINGS FOR BUILDING THE TEMPLE

29 And David the king said to all the assembly, "Solomon my son, whom alone God has chosen, is young and inexperienced, and the work is great; for the palace will not be for man but for the LORD God. 2 So I have provided for the house of my God, so far as I was able, the gold for the things of gold, the silver for the things of silver, and the bronze for the things of bronze, the iron for the things of iron, and wood for the things of wood, besides great quantities of onyx and stones for setting, antimony, colored stones, all sorts of precious stones, and marble. 3 Moreover, in addition to all that I have provided for the holy house, I have a treasure of my own of gold and silver, and because of my devotion to the house of my God I give it to the house of my God: 4 three thousand talents of gold, of the gold of Ophir, and seven thousand talents of refined silver, for overlaying the walls of the house, 5 and for all the work to be done by craftsmen, gold for the things of gold and silver for the things of silver. Who then will offer willingly, consecrating himself today to the LORD?"

6 Then the heads of fathers' houses made their freewill offerings, as did also the leaders of the tribes, the commanders of thousands and of hundreds, and the officers over the king's work. 7 They gave for the service of the house of God five thousand talents and ten thousand darics of gold, ten thousand talents of silver, eighteen thousand talents of bronze, and a hundred thousand talents of iron. 8 And whoever had precious stones gave them to the treasury of the house of the LORD, in the care of Jehi´el the Gershonite. 9 Then the people rejoiced because these had given willingly, for with a whole heart they had offered freely to the LORD; David the king also rejoiced greatly.

DAVID'S PRAISE TO GOD

10 Therefore David blessed the LORD in the presence of all the assembly; and David said: "Blessed art thou, O LORD, the God of Israel our father, for ever and ever. 11 Thine, O LORD, is the greatness, and the power, and the glory, and the victory, and the majesty; for all that is in the heavens and in the earth is thine; thine is the kingdom, O LORD, and thou art exalted

[a]Cn: Heb *upon me*

as head above all. 12Both riches and
honor come from thee, and thou rul-
est over all. In thy hand are power and
might; and in thy hand it is to make
great and to give strength to all. 13And
now we thank thee, our God, and
praise thy glorious name.

14 “But who am I, and what is my
people, that we should be able thus
to offer willingly? For all things come
from thee, and of thy own have we giv-
en thee. 15For we are strangers before
thee, and sojourners, as all our fathers
were; our days on the earth are like
a shadow, and there is no abiding.[b]
16O LORD our God, all this abundance
that we have provided for building
thee a house for thy holy name comes
from thy hand and is all thy own. 17I
know, my God, that thou triest the
heart, and hast pleasure in upright-
ness; in the uprightness of my heart
I have freely offered all these things,
and now I have seen thy people, who
are present here, offering freely and
joyously to thee. 18O LORD, the God
of Abraham, Isaac, and Israel, our fa-
thers, keep for ever such purposes and
thoughts in the hearts of thy people,
and direct their hearts toward thee.
19Grant to Solomon my son that with
a whole heart he may keep thy com-
mandments, thy testimonies, and thy
statutes, performing all, and that he
may build the palace for which I have
made provision.”

20 Then David said to all the as-
sembly, “Bless the LORD your God.”
And all the assembly blessed the
LORD, the God of their fathers, and
bowed their heads, and worshiped
the LORD, and did obeisance to the
king. 21And they performed sacrific-
es to the LORD, and on the next day
offered burnt offerings to the LORD, a
thousand bulls, a thousand rams, and
a thousand lambs, with their drink
offerings, and sacrifices in abundance
for all Israel; 22and they ate and drank
before the LORD on that day with
great gladness.

SOLOMON ANOINTED KING

And they made Solomon the son of
David king the second time, and they
anointed him as prince for the LORD,
and Zadok as priest.

23 Then Solomon sat on the throne
of the LORD as king instead of David
his father; and he prospered, and all
Israel obeyed him. 24All the leaders
and the mighty men, and also all the
sons of King David, pledged their al-
legiance to King Solomon. 25And the
LORD gave Solomon great repute in
the sight of all Israel, and bestowed
upon him such royal majesty as had
not been on any king before him in
Israel.

SUMMARY OF DAVID'S REIGN

26 Thus David the son of Jesse
reigned over all Israel. 27The time that
he reigned over Israel was forty years;
he reigned seven years in Hebron,
and thirty-three years in Jerusalem.
28Then he died in a good old age, full of
days, riches, and honor; and Solomon
his son reigned in his stead. 29Now
the acts of King David, from first to
last, are written in the Chronicles of
Samuel the seer, and in the Chronicles
of Nathan the prophet, and in the
Chronicles of Gad the seer, 30with ac-
counts of all his rule and his might
and of the circumstances that came
upon him and upon Israel, and upon
all the kingdoms of the countries.

[b]Gk Vg: Heb *hope*

THE SECOND BOOK OF THE

CHRONICLES

SOLOMON REQUESTS WISDOM

1 Solomon the son of David established himself in his kingdom, and the LORD his God was with him and made him exceedingly great.*

2 Solomon spoke to all Israel, to the commanders of thousands and of hundreds, to the judges, and to all the leaders in all Israel, the heads of fathers' houses. 3 And Solomon, and all the assembly with him, went to the high place that was at Gibeon; for the tent of meeting of God, which Moses the servant of the LORD had made in the wilderness, was there. 4 (But David had brought up the ark of God from Kir'iath-je'arim to the place that David had prepared for it, for he had pitched a tent for it in Jerusalem.) 5 Moreover the bronze altar that Bez'alel the son of Uri, son of Hur, had made, was there before the tabernacle of the LORD. And Solomon and the assembly sought the LORD. 6 And Solomon went up there to the bronze altar before the LORD, which was at the tent of meeting, and offered a thousand burnt offerings upon it.

7 In that night God appeared to Solomon, and said to him, "Ask what I shall give you." 8 And Solomon said to God, "Thou hast shown great and steadfast love to David my father, and hast made me king in his stead. 9 O LORD God, let thy promise to David my father be now fulfilled, for thou hast made me king over a people as many as the dust of the earth. 10 Give me now wisdom and knowledge to go out and come in before this people, for who can rule this thy people, that is so great?" 11 God answered Solomon, "Because this was in your heart, and you have not asked possessions, wealth, honor, or the life of those who hate you, and have not even asked long life, but have asked wisdom and knowledge for yourself that you may rule my people over whom I have made you king, 12 wisdom and knowledge are granted to you. I will also give you riches, possessions, and honor, such as none of the kings had who were before you, and none after you shall have the like." 13 So Solomon came from[a] the high place at Gibeon, from before the tent of meeting, to Jerusalem. And he reigned over Israel.

SOLOMON'S MILITARY AND COMMERCIAL ACTIVITY

14 Solomon gathered together chariots and horsemen; he had fourteen hundred chariots and twelve thousand horsemen, whom he stationed in the chariot cities and with the king in Jerusalem. 15 And the king made silver and gold as common in Jerusalem as stone, and he made cedar as plentiful as the sycamore of the Shephe'lah. 16 And Solomon's import of horses was from Egypt and Ku'e, and the king's traders received them from Ku'e for a price. 17 They imported a chariot from Egypt for six hundred shekels of silver, and a horse for a hundred and fifty; likewise through them these were exported to all the kings of the Hittites and the kings of Syria.

PREPARATIONS FOR BUILDING THE TEMPLE

2[b] Now Solomon purposed to build a temple for the name of the LORD, and a royal palace for himself. 2[c] And Solomon assigned seventy thousand men to bear burdens and eighty thousand to quarry in the hill country, and three thousand six hundred to oversee them. 3 And Solomon sent word to

[a] Gk Vg: Heb *to*
[b] Ch 1.18 in Heb
[c] Ch 2.1 in Heb

Huram the king of Tyre: "As you dealt
with David my father and sent him ce-
dar to build himself a house to dwell
in, so deal with me. [4]Behold, I am
about to build a house for the name
of the LORD my God and dedicate it
to him for the burning of incense of
sweet spices before him, and for the
continual offering of the showbread,
and for burnt offerings morning and
evening, on the sabbaths and the new
moons and the appointed feasts of
the LORD our God, as ordained for
ever for Israel. [5]The house which I am
to build will be great, for our God is
greater than all gods. [6]But who is able
to build him a house, since heaven,
even highest heaven, cannot contain
him? Who am I to build a house for
him, except as a place to burn incense
before him? [7]So now send me a man
skilled to work in gold, silver, bronze,
and iron, and in purple, crimson, and
blue fabrics, trained also in engraving,
to be with the skilled workers who
are with me in Judah and Jerusalem,
whom David my father provided.
[8]Send me also cedar, cypress, and al-
gum timber from Lebanon, for I know
that your servants know how to cut
timber in Lebanon. And my servants
will be with your servants, [9]to pre-
pare timber for me in abundance, for
the house I am to build will be great
and wonderful. [10]I will give for your
servants, the hewers who cut tim-
ber, twenty thousand cors of crushed
wheat, twenty thousand cors of bar-
ley, twenty thousand baths of wine,
and twenty thousand baths of oil."

11 Then Huram the king of Tyre
answered in a letter which he sent to
Solomon, "Because the LORD loves
his people he has made you king over
them." [12]Huram also said, "Blessed
be the LORD God of Israel, who made
heaven and earth, who has given King
David a wise son, endued with dis-
cretion and understanding, who will
build a temple for the LORD, and a
royal palace for himself.

13 "Now I have sent a skilled man,
endued with understanding, Huram-
abi, [14]the son of a woman of the
daughters of Dan, and his father was
a man of Tyre. He is trained to work
in gold, silver, bronze, iron, stone, and
wood, and in purple, blue, and crim-
son fabrics and fine linen, and to do
all sorts of engraving and execute any
design that may be assigned him, with
your craftsmen, the craftsmen of my
lord, David your father. [15]Now there-
fore the wheat and barley, oil and
wine, of which my lord has spoken, let
him send to his servants; [16]and we will
cut whatever timber you need from
Lebanon, and bring it to you in rafts
by sea to Joppa, so that you may take
it up to Jerusalem."

17 Then Solomon took a census of
all the aliens who were in the land of
Israel, after the census of them which
David his father had taken; and there
were found a hundred and fifty-three
thousand six hundred. [18]Seventy thou-
sand of them he assigned to bear bur-
dens, eighty thousand to quarry in
the hill country, and three thousand
six hundred as overseers to make the
people work.

SOLOMON BUILDS THE TEMPLE

3 Then Solomon began to build the
house of the LORD in Jerusalem
on Mount Mori´ah, where the LORD
had appeared to David his father, at
the place that David had appointed,
on the threshing floor of Ornan the
Jeb´usite. [2]He began to build in the
second month of the fourth year of his
reign. [3]These are Solomon's measure-
ments[d] for building the house of God:
the length, in cubits of the old stan-
dard, was sixty cubits, and the breadth
twenty cubits. [4]The vestibule in front
of the nave of the house was twenty
cubits long, equal to the width of the
house;[e] and its height was a hundred
and twenty cubits. He overlaid it on

[d]Syr: Heb *foundations*
[e]1Kings 6. 3: Heb uncertain

the inside with pure gold. 5The nave he lined with cypress, and covered it with fine gold, and made palms and chains on it. 6He adorned the house with settings of precious stones. The gold was gold of Parva′im. 7So he lined the house with gold—its beams, its thresholds, its walls, and its doors; and he carved cherubim on the walls.

8 And he made the most holy place; its length, corresponding to the breadth of the house, was twenty cubits, and its breadth was twenty cubits; he overlaid it with six hundred talents of fine gold. 9The weight of the nails was one shekel[a] to fifty shekels of gold. And he overlaid the upper chambers with gold.

10 In the most holy place he made two cherubim of wood[b] and overlaid[c] them with gold. 11The wings of the cherubim together extended twenty cubits: one wing of the one, of five cubits, touched the wall of the house, and its other wing, of five cubits, touched the wing of the other cherub; 12and of this cherub, one wing, of five cubits, touched the wall of the house, and the other wing, also of five cubits, was joined to the wing of the first cherub. 13The wings of these cherubim extended twenty cubits; the cherubim[d] stood on their feet, facing the nave. 14And he made the veil of blue and purple and crimson fabrics and fine linen, and worked cherubim on it.

15 In front of the house he made two pillars thirty-five cubits high, with a capital of five cubits on the top of each. 16He made chains like a necklace[e] and put them on the tops of the pillars; and he made a hundred pomegranates, and put them on the chains. 17He set up the pillars in front of the temple, one on the south, the other on the north; that on the south he called Jachin, and that on the north Bo′az.

FURNISHINGS OF THE TEMPLE

4 He made an altar of bronze, twenty cubits long, and twenty cubits wide, and ten cubits high. 2Then he made the molten sea; it was round, ten cubits from brim to brim, and five cubits high, and a line of thirty cubits measured its circumference. 3Under it were figures of gourds,[f] for thirty[g] cubits, compassing the sea round about; the gourds[h] were in two rows, cast with it when it was cast. 4It stood upon twelve oxen, three facing north, three facing west, three facing south, and three facing east; the sea was set upon them, and all their hinder parts were inward. 5Its thickness was a handbreadth; and its brim was made like the brim of a cup, like the flower of a lily; it held over three thousand baths. 6He also made ten lavers in which to wash, and set five on the south side, and five on the north side. In these they were to rinse off what was used for the burnt offering, and the sea was for the priests to wash in.

7 And he made ten golden lampstands as prescribed, and set them in the temple, five on the south side and five on the north. 8He also made ten tables, and placed them in the temple, five on the south side and five on the north. And he made a hundred basins of gold. 9He made the court of the priests, and the great court, and doors for the court, and overlaid their doors with bronze; 10and he set the sea at the southeast corner of the house.

11 Huram also made the pots, the shovels, and the basins. So Huram finished the work that he did for King Solomon on the house of God:

[a] Compare Gk: Heb lacks *one shekel*
[b] Gk: Heb uncertain
[c] Heb *they overlaid*
[d] Heb *they*
[e] Cn: Heb *in the inner sanctuary*
[f] 1Kings 7. 24: Heb *oxen*
[g] Compare verse 2: Heb *ten*
[h] 1Kings 7. 24: Heb *oxen*

12the two pillars, the bowls, and the two capitals on the top of the pillars; and the two networks to cover the two bowls of the capitals that were on the top of the pillars; 13and the four hundred pomegranates for the two networks, two rows of pomegranates for each network, to cover the two bowls of the capitals that were upon the pillars. 14He made the stands also, and the lavers upon the stands, 15and the one sea, and the twelve oxen underneath it. 16The pots, the shovels, the forks, and all the equipment for these Huram-abi made of burnished bronze for King Solomon for the house of the LORD. 17In the plain of the Jordan the king cast them, in the clay ground between Succoth and Zer′edah. 18Solomon made all these things in great quantities, so that the weight of the bronze was not ascertained.

19 So Solomon made all the things that were in the house of God: the golden altar, the tables for the bread of the Presence, 20the lampstands and their lamps of pure gold to burn before the inner sanctuary, as prescribed; 21the flowers, the lamps, and the tongs, of purest gold; 22the snuffers, basins, dishes for incense, and firepans, of pure gold; and the sockets[i] of the temple, for the inner doors to the most holy place and for the doors of the nave of the temple were of gold.

5 Thus all the work that Solomon did for the house of the LORD was finished. And Solomon brought in the things which David his father had dedicated, and stored the silver, the gold, and all the vessels in the treasuries of the house of God.

THE ARK BROUGHT INTO THE TEMPLE

2 Then Solomon assembled the elders of Israel and all the heads of the tribes, the leaders of the fathers' houses of the people of Israel, in Jerusalem, to bring up the ark of the covenant of the LORD out of the city of David, which is Zion. 3And all the men of Israel assembled before the king at the feast which is in the seventh month. 4And all the elders of Israel came, and the Levites took up the ark. 5And they brought up the ark, the tent of meeting, and all the holy vessels that were in the tent; the priests and the Levites brought them up. 6And King Solomon and all the congregation of Israel, who had assembled before him, were before the ark, sacrificing so many sheep and oxen that they could not be counted or numbered. 7So the priests brought the ark of the covenant of the LORD to its place, in the inner sanctuary of the house, in the most holy place, underneath the wings of the cherubim. 8For the cherubim spread out their wings over the place of the ark, so that the cherubim made a covering above the ark and its poles. 9And the poles were so long that the ends of the poles were seen from the holy place before the inner sanctuary; but they could not be seen from outside; and they are there to this day. 10There was nothing in the ark except the two tables which Moses put there at Horeb, where the LORD made a covenant with the people of Israel, when they came out of Egypt. 11Now when the priests came out of the holy place (for all the priests who were present had sanctified themselves, without regard to their divisions; 12and all the Levitical singers, Asaph, Heman, and Jedu′thun, their sons and kinsmen, arrayed in fine linen, with cymbals, harps, and lyres, stood east of the altar with a hundred and twenty priests who were trumpeters; 13and it was the duty of the trumpeters and singers to make themselves heard in unison in praise and thanksgiving to the LORD), and when the song was raised, with trumpets and cymbals and other musical instruments, in praise to the LORD,

[i] 1Kings 7. 50: Heb *the door of the house*

"For he is good,
for his steadfast love endures for ever,"
the house, the house of the LORD,
was filled with a cloud, 14so that the
priests could not stand to minister because of the cloud; for the glory of the
LORD filled the house of God.

DEDICATION OF THE TEMPLE

6 Then Solomon said,
"The LORD has said that he
would dwell in thick
darkness.
2I have built thee an exalted
house,
a place for thee to dwell in
for ever."
3Then the king faced about, and
blessed all the assembly of Israel,
while all the assembly of Israel stood.
4And he said, "Blessed be the LORD,
the God of Israel, who with his hand
has fulfilled what he promised with
his mouth to David my father, saying,
5'Since the day that I brought my people out of the land of Egypt, I chose
no city in all the tribes of Israel in
which to build a house, that my name
might be there, and I chose no man
as prince over my people Israel; 6but
I have chosen Jerusalem that my
name may be there and I have chosen
David to be over my people Israel.'
7Now it was in the heart of David my
father to build a house for the name
of the LORD, the God of Israel. 8But
the LORD said to David my father,
'Whereas it was in your heart to
build a house for my name, you did
well that it was in your heart; 9nevertheless you shall not build the house,
but your son who shall be born to you
shall build the house for my name.'
10Now the LORD has fulfilled his
promise which he made; for I have
risen in the place of David my father,
and sit on the throne of Israel, as the
LORD promised, and I have built the
house for the name of the LORD, the
God of Israel. 11And there I have set
the ark, in which is the covenant of
the LORD which he made with the
people of Israel."

SOLOMON'S PRAYER OF DEDICATION

12 Then Solomon stood before the
altar of the LORD in the presence of
all the assembly of Israel, and spread
forth his hands. 13Solomon had made
a bronze platform five cubits long,
five cubits wide, and three cubits
high, and had set it in the court; and
he stood upon it. Then he knelt upon
his knees in the presence of all the assembly of Israel, and spread forth his
hands toward heaven; 14and said, "O
LORD, God of Israel, there is no God
like thee, in heaven or on earth, keeping covenant and showing steadfast
love to thy servants who walk before
thee with all their heart; 15who hast
kept with thy servant David my father what thou didst declare to him;
yea, thou didst speak with thy mouth,
and with thy hand hast fulfilled it this
day. 16Now therefore, O LORD, God of
Israel, keep with thy servant David
my father what thou hast promised
him, saying, 'There shall never fail
you a man before me to sit upon the
throne of Israel, if only your sons take
heed to their way, to walk in my law
as you have walked before me.' 17Now
therefore, O LORD, God of Israel, let
thy word be confirmed, which thou
hast spoken to thy servant David.
18 "But will God dwell indeed with
man on the earth? Behold, heaven
and the highest heaven cannot contain thee; how much less this house
which I have built! 19Yet have regard
to the prayer of thy servant and to his
supplication, O LORD my God, hearkening to the cry and to the prayer
which thy servant prays before thee;
20that thy eyes may be open day and
night toward this house, the place
where thou hast promised to set thy
name, that thou mayest hearken to
the prayer which thy servant offers
toward this place. 21And hearken thou
to the supplications of thy servant and
of thy people Israel, when they pray

toward this place; yea, hear thou from
heaven* thy dwelling place; and when
thou hearest, forgive.

22 "If a man sins against his neigh-
bor and is made to take an oath, and
comes and swears his oath before
thy altar in this house, 23then hear
thou from heaven, and act, and judge
thy servants, requiting the guilty by
bringing his conduct upon his own
head, and vindicating the righteous
by rewarding him according to his
righteousness.

24 "If thy people Israel are defeated
before the enemy because they have
sinned against thee, when they turn
again and acknowledge thy name, and
pray and make supplication to thee
in this house, 25then hear thou from
heaven, and forgive the sin of thy peo-
ple Israel, and bring them again to the
land which thou gavest to them and to
their fathers.

26 "When heaven is shut up and
there is no rain because they have
sinned against thee, if they pray to-
ward this place, and acknowledge thy
name, and turn from their sin, when
thou dost afflict them, 27then hear
thou in heaven, and forgive the sin of
thy servants, thy people Israel, when
thou dost teach them the good way[a]
in which they should walk; and grant
rain upon thy land, which thou hast
given to thy people as an inheritance.

28 "If there is famine in the land,
if there is pestilence or blight or mil-
dew or locust or caterpillar; if their
enemies besiege them in any of their
cities; whatever plague, whatever
sickness there is; 29whatever prayer,
whatever supplication is made by any
man or by all thy people Israel, each
knowing his own affliction, and his
own sorrow and stretching out his
hands toward this house; 30then hear
thou from heaven thy dwelling place,
and forgive, and render to each whose
heart thou knowest, according to all
his ways (for thou, thou only, know-
est the hearts of the children of men);
31that they may fear thee and walk in
thy ways all the days that they live
in the land which thou gavest to our
fathers.

32 "Likewise when a foreigner,
who is not of thy people Israel, comes
from a far country for the sake of thy
great name, and thy mighty hand, and
thy outstretched arm, when he comes
and prays toward this house, 33hear
thou from heaven thy dwelling place,
and do according to all for which the
foreigner calls to thee; in order that
all the peoples of the earth may know
thy name and fear thee, as do thy peo-
ple Israel, and that they may know
that this house which I have built is
called by thy name.

34 "If thy people go out to battle
against their enemies, by whatever
way thou shalt send them, and they
pray to thee toward this city which
thou hast chosen and the house which
I have built for thy name, 35then hear
thou from heaven their prayer and
their supplication, and maintain their
cause.

36 "If they sin against thee—for
there is no man who does not sin—
and thou art angry with them, and
dost give them to an enemy, so that
they are carried away captive to a
land far or near; 37yet if they lay it to
heart in the land to which they have
been carried captive, and repent, and
make supplication to thee in the land
of their captivity, saying, 'We have
sinned, and have acted perversely
and wickedly'; 38if they repent with all
their mind and with all their heart in
the land of their captivity, to which
they were carried captive, and pray
toward their land, which thou gavest
to their fathers, the city which thou
hast chosen, and the house which I
have built for thy name, 39then hear
thou from heaven thy dwelling place
their prayer and their supplications,
and maintain their cause and forgive
thy people who have sinned against
thee. 40Now, O my God, let thy eyes be

[a]Gk Syr Vg: Heb *toward the good way*

open and thy ears attentive to a prayer
of this place.

41"And now arise, O LORD God,
and go to thy resting place,
thou and the ark of thy
might.
Let thy priests, O LORD
God, be clothed with
salvation,
and let thy saints rejoice in
thy goodness.
42O LORD God, do not turn away
the face of thy anointed
one!
Remember thy steadfast love
for David thy servant."

SOLOMON DEDICATES THE TEMPLE

7 When Solomon had ended his
prayer, fire came down* from heav-
en and consumed the burnt offering
and the sacrifices, and the glory of
the LORD filled the temple. 2And the
priests could not enter the house of
the LORD, because the glory of the
LORD filled the LORD's house. 3When
all the children of Israel saw the fire
come down and the glory of the LORD
upon the temple, they bowed down
with their faces to the earth on the
pavement, and worshiped and gave
thanks to the LORD, saying,

"For he is good,
for his steadfast love en-
dures for ever."

4 Then the king and all the peo-
ple offered sacrifice before the LORD.
5King Solomon offered as a sacrifice
twenty-two thousand oxen and a hun-
dred and twenty thousand sheep. So
the king and all the people dedicated
the house of God. 6The priests stood
at their posts; the Levites also, with
the instruments for music to the LORD
which King David had made for giving
thanks to the LORD—for his stead-
fast love endures for ever—whenever
David offered praises by their minis-
try; opposite them the priests sound-
ed trumpets; and all Israel stood.

7 And Solomon consecrated the
middle of the court that was before
the house of the LORD; for there he
offered the burnt offering and the fat
of the peace offerings, because the
bronze altar Solomon had made could
not hold the burnt offering and the ce-
real offering and the fat.

8 At that time Solomon held the
feast for seven days, and all Israel with
him, a very great congregation, from
the entrance of Hamath to the Brook
of Egypt. 9And on the eighth day they
held a solemn assembly; for they had
kept the dedication of the altar seven
days and the feast seven days. 10On
the twenty-third day of the seventh
month he sent the people away to
their homes, joyful and glad of heart
for the goodness that the LORD had
shown to David and to Solomon and
to Israel his people.

GOD'S SECOND APPEARANCE TO SOLOMON

11 Thus Solomon finished the
house of the LORD and the king's
house; all that Solomon had planned
to do in the house of the LORD and in
his own house he successfully accom-
plished. 12Then the LORD appeared to
Solomon in the night and said to him:
"I have heard your prayer, and have
chosen this place for myself as a house
of sacrifice. 13When I shut up the heav-
ens so that there is no rain, or com-
mand the locust to devour the land,
or send pestilence among my people,
14if my people who are called by my
name humble themselves, and pray
and seek my face, and turn from their
wicked ways, then I will hear from
heaven, and will forgive their sin and
heal their land. 15Now my eyes will
be open and my ears attentive to the
prayer that is made in this place. 16For
now I have chosen and consecrat-
ed this house that my name may be
there for ever; my eyes and my heart
will be there for all time. 17And as for
you, if you walk before me, as David
your father walked, doing according
to all that I have commanded you and
keeping my statutes and my ordinanc-
es, 18then I will establish your royal

throne, as I covenanted with David
your father, saying, 'There shall not
fail you a man to rule Israel.'

19 "But if you[a] turn aside and for-
sake my statutes and my command-
ments which I have set before you, and
go and serve other gods and worship
them, [20]then I will pluck you[b] up from
the land which I have given you;[c] and
this house, which I have consecrat-
ed for my name, I will cast out of my
sight, and will make it a proverb and
a byword among all peoples. [21]And at
this house, which is exalted, every
one passing by will be astonished, and
say, 'Why has the LORD done thus to
this land and to this house?' [22]Then
they will say, 'Because they forsook
the LORD the God of their fathers
who brought them out of the land of
Egypt, and laid hold on other gods,
and worshiped them and served them;
therefore he has brought all this evil
upon them.'"

VARIOUS ACTIVITIES OF SOLOMON

8 At the end of twenty years, in which
Solomon had built the house of the
LORD and his own house, [2]Solomon
rebuilt the cities which Huram had
given to him, and settled the people of
Israel in them.

3 And Solomon went to Ha´math-
zo´bah, and took it. [4]He built Tadmor in
the wilderness and all the store-cities
which he built in Hamath. [5]He also
built Upper Beth-hor´on and Lower
Beth-hor´on, fortified cities with walls,
gates, and bars, [6]and Ba´alath, and all
the store-cities that Solomon had, and
all the cities for his chariots, and the
cities for his horsemen, and whatever
Solomon desired to build in Jerusalem,
in Lebanon, and in all the land of his
dominion. [7]All the people who were
left of the Hittites, the Amorites,
the Per´izzites, the Hivites, and the
Jeb´usites, who were not of Israel,
[8]from their descendants who were left
after them in the land, whom the peo-
ple of Israel had not destroyed—these
Solomon made a forced levy and so
they are to this day. [9]But of the people
of Israel Solomon made no slaves for
his work; they were soldiers, and his of-
ficers, the commanders of his chariots,
and his horsemen. [10]And these were
the chief officers of King Solomon, two
hundred and fifty, who exercised au-
thority over the people.

11 Solomon brought Pharaoh's
daughter up from the city of David to
the house which he had built for her,
for he said, "My wife shall not live
in the house of David king of Israel,
for the places to which the ark of the
LORD has come are holy."

12 Then Solomon offered up burnt
offerings to the LORD upon the altar
of the LORD which he had built before
the vestibule, [13]as the duty of each day
required, offering according to the
commandment of Moses for the sab-
baths, the new moons, and the three
annual feasts—the feast of unleav-
ened bread, the feast of weeks, and
the feast of tabernacles. [14]According to
the ordinance of David his father, he
appointed the divisions of the priests
for their service, and the Levites for
their offices of praise and ministry
before the priests as the duty of each
day required, and the gatekeepers in
their divisions for the several gates;
for so David the man of God had com-
manded. [15]And they did not turn aside
from what the king had commanded
the priests and Levites concerning any
matter and concerning the treasuries.

16 Thus was accomplished all the
work of Solomon from[d] the day the
foundation of the house of the LORD
was laid until it was finished. So the
house of the LORD was completed.

17 Then Solomon went to E´zion-
ge´ber and Eloth on the shore of the
sea, in the land of Edom. [18]And Huram
sent him by his servants ships and

[a]The word *you* is plural here
[b]Heb *them*
[c]Heb *them*
[d]Gk Syr Vg: Heb *to*

servants familiar with the sea, and
they went to Ophir together with the
servants of Solomon, and fetched from
there four hundred and fifty talents of
gold and brought it to King Solomon.

VISIT OF THE QUEEN OF SHEBA

9 Now when the queen of Sheba heard
of the fame of Solomon she came to
Jerusalem to test him with hard ques-
tions, having a very great retinue and
camels bearing spices and very much
gold and precious stones. When she
came to Solomon, she told him all
that was on her mind. 2And Solomon
answered all her questions; there was
nothing hidden from Solomon which
he could not explain to her. 3And
when the queen of Sheba had seen the
wisdom of Solomon, the house that he
had built, 4the food of his table, the
seating of his officials, and the atten-
dance of his servants, and their cloth-
ing, his cupbearers, and their cloth-
ing, and his burnt offerings which
he offered at the house of the LORD,
there was no more spirit in her.
5 And she said to the king, "The
report was true which I heard in my
own land of your affairs and of your
wisdom, 6but I did not believe the[a] re-
ports until I came and my own eyes
had seen it; and behold, half the great-
ness of your wisdom was not told me;
you surpass the report which I heard.
7Happy are your wives![b] Happy are
these your servants, who continually
stand before you and hear your wis-
dom! 8Blessed be the LORD your God,
who has delighted in you and set you
on his throne as king for the LORD
your God! Because your God loved
Israel and would establish them for
ever, he has made you king over them,
that you may execute justice and righ-
teousness." 9Then she gave the king a
hundred and twenty talents of gold,
and a very great quantity of spices,
and precious stones: there were no
spices such as those which the queen
of Sheba gave to King Solomon.
10 Moreover the servants of Huram
and the servants of Solomon, who
brought gold from Ophir, brought al-
gum wood and precious stones. 11And
the king made of the algum wood
steps[c] for the house of the LORD and
for the king's house, lyres also and
harps for the singers; there never was
seen the like of them before in the
land of Judah.
12 And King Solomon gave to the
queen of Sheba all that she desired,
whatever she asked besides what she
had brought to the king. So she turned
and went back to her own land, with
her servants.

SOLOMON'S GREAT WEALTH

13 Now the weight of gold that
came to Solomon in one year was
six hundred and sixty-six talents of
gold, 14besides that which the traders
and merchants brought; and all the
kings of Arabia and the governors of
the land brought gold and silver to
Solomon. 15King Solomon made two
hundred large shields of beaten gold;
six hundred shekels of beaten gold
went into each shield. 16And he made
three hundred shields of beaten gold;
three hundred shekels of gold went
into each shield; and the king put
them in the House of the Forest of
Lebanon. 17The king also made a great
ivory throne, and overlaid it with pure
gold. 18The throne had six steps and a
footstool of gold, which were attached
to the throne, and on each side of the
seat were arm rests and two lions
standing beside the arm rests, 19while
twelve lions stood there, one on each
end of a step on the six steps. The like
of it was never made in any kingdom.
20All King Solomon's drinking vessels
were of gold, and all the vessels of the
House of the Forest of Lebanon were
of pure gold; silver was not considered
as anything in the days of Solomon.
21For the king's ships went to Tarshish

[a] Heb *their*
[b] Gk Compare 1Kings 10. 8: Heb *men*
[c] Gk Vg: The meaning of the Hebrew word is uncertain

with the servants of Huram; once ev-
ery three years the ships of Tarshish
used to come bringing gold, silver,
ivory, apes, and peacocks.[d]

22 Thus King Solomon excelled all
the kings of the earth in riches and
in wisdom. 23 And all the kings of the
earth sought the presence of Solomon
to hear his wisdom, which God had
put into his mind. 24 Every one of them
brought his present, articles of silver
and of gold, garments, myrrh, spices,
horses, and mules, so much year by
year. 25 And Solomon had four thou-
sand stalls for horses and chariots, and
twelve thousand horsemen, whom he
stationed in the chariot cities and with
the king in Jerusalem. 26 And he ruled
over all the kings from the Euphra´tes
to the land of the Philistines, and to
the border of Egypt. 27 And the king
made silver as common in Jerusalem
as stone, and cedar as plentiful as the
sycamore of the Shephe´lah. 28 And
horses were imported for Solomon
from Egypt and from all lands.

DEATH OF SOLOMON

29 Now the rest of the acts of
Solomon, from first to last, are they
not written in the history of Nathan
the prophet, and in the prophecy of
Ahi´jah the Shi´lonite, and in the
visions of Iddo the seer concerning
Jerobo´am the son of Nebat? 30 Solomon
reigned in Jerusalem over all Israel
forty years. 31 And Solomon slept with
his fathers, and was buried in the city
of David his father; and Rehobo´am
his son reigned in his stead.*

THE REVOLT AGAINST REHOBOAM

10 Rehobo´am went to Shechem, for
all Israel had come to Shechem to
make him king. 2 And when Jerobo´am
the son of Nebat heard of it (for he
was in Egypt, whither he had fled
from King Solomon), then Jerobo´am
returned from Egypt. 3 And they sent
and called him; and Jerobo´am and all
Israel came and said to Rehobo´am,
4 "Your father made our yoke heavy.
Now therefore lighten the hard ser-
vice of your father and his heavy yoke
upon us, and we will serve you." 5 He
said to them, "Come to me again in
three days." So the people went away.

6 Then King Rehobo´am took coun-
sel with the old men, who had stood
before Solomon his father while he
was yet alive, saying, "How do you ad-
vise me to answer this people?" 7 And
they said to him, "If you will be kind
to this people and please them, and
speak good words to them, then they
will be your servants for ever." 8 But
he forsook the counsel which the old
men gave him, and took counsel with
the young men who had grown up
with him and stood before him. 9 And
he said to them, "What do you advise
that we answer this people who have
said to me, 'Lighten the yoke that your
father put upon us'?" 10 And the young
men who had grown up with him said
to him, "Thus shall you speak to the
people who said to you, 'Your father
made our yoke heavy, but do you
lighten it for us'; thus shall you say to
them, 'My little finger is thicker than
my father's loins. 11 And now, whereas
my father laid upon you a heavy yoke,
I will add to your yoke. My father
chastised you with whips, but I will
chastise you with scorpions.'"

12 So Jerobo´am and all the people
came to Rehobo´am the third day, as
the king said, "Come to me again the
third day." 13 And the king answered
them harshly, and forsaking the coun-
sel of the old men, 14 King Rehobo´am
spoke to them according to the coun-
sel of the young men, saying, "My
father made your yoke heavy, but I
will add to it; my father chastised you
with whips, but I will chastise you
with scorpions." 15 So the king did not
hearken to the people; for it was a turn
of affairs brought about by God that
the LORD might fulfil his word, which
he spoke by Ahi´jah the Shi´lonite to
Jerobo´am the son of Nebat.

[d] Or *baboons*

16 And when all Israel saw that the
king did not hearken to them, the peo-
ple answered the king,

"What portion have we in
David?
We have no inheritance in
the son of Jesse.
Each of you to your tents, O
Israel!
Look now to your own
house, David."

17But Rehobo´am reigned over the
people of Israel who dwelt in the cit-
ies of Judah. 18Then King Rehobo´am
sent Hador´am, who was taskmaster
over the forced labor, and the people
of Israel stoned him to death with
stones. And King Rehobo´am made
haste to mount his chariot, to flee to
Jerusalem. 19So Israel has been in re-
bellion against the house of David to
this day.

JUDAH AND BENJAMIN FORTIFIED

11 When Rehobo´am came to Jeru-
salem, he assembled the house of
Judah, and Benjamin, a hundred and
eighty thousand chosen warriors, to
fight against Israel, to restore the
kingdom to Rehobo´am. 2But the
word of the LORD came to Shemai´ah
the man of God: 3"Say to Rehobo´am
the son of Solomon king of Judah, and
to all Israel in Judah and Benjamin,
4'Thus says the LORD, You shall not
go up or fight against your breth-
ren. Return every man to his home,
for this thing is from me.'" So they
hearkened to the word of the LORD,
and returned and did not go against
Jerobo´am.

5 Rehobo´am dwelt in Jerusalem,
and he built cities for defense in
Judah. 6He built Bethlehem, Etam,
Teko´a, 7Beth-zur, Soco, Adul´lam,
8Gath, Mare´shah, Ziph, 9Adora´im,
Lachish, Aze´kah, 10Zorah, Ai´jalon,
and Hebron, fortified cities which are
in Judah and in Benjamin. 11He made
the fortresses strong, and put com-
manders in them, and stores of food,
oil, and wine. 12And he put shields
and spears in all the cities, and made
them very strong. So he held Judah
and Benjamin.

PRIESTS AND LEVITES SUPPORT REHOBOAM

13 And the priests and the Levites
that were in all Israel resorted to
him from all places where they lived.
14For the Levites left their common
lands and their holdings and came
to Judah and Jerusalem, because
Jerobo´am and his sons cast them out
from serving as priests of the LORD,
15and he appointed his own priests
for the high places, and for the sa-
tyrs, and for the calves which he had
made. 16And those who had set their
hearts to seek the LORD God of Israel
came after them from all the tribes
of Israel to Jerusalem to sacrifice to
the LORD, the God of their fathers.
17They strengthened the kingdom of
Judah, and for three years they made
Rehobo´am the son of Solomon se-
cure, for they walked for three years
in the way of David and Solomon.

REHOBOAM'S MARRIAGES

18 Rehobo´am took as wife Ma´ha-
lath the daughter of Jer´imoth the son
of David, and of Ab´ihail the daugh-
ter of Eli´ab the son of Jesse; 19and she
bore him sons, Je´ush, Shemari´ah,
and Zaham. 20After her he took Ma´-
acah the daughter of Ab´salom, who
bore him Abi´jah, Attai, Ziza, and
Shelo´mith. 21Rehobo´am loved Ma´a-
cah the daughter of Ab´salom above
all his wives and concubines (he took
eighteen wives and sixty concubines,
and had twenty-eight sons and sixty
daughters); 22and Rehobo´am appoint-
ed Abi´jah the son of Ma´acah as chief
prince among his brothers, for he in-
tended to make him king. 23And he
dealt wisely, and distributed some of
his sons through all the districts of
Judah and Benjamin, in all the forti-
fied cities; and he gave them abundant

provisions, and procured wives for
them.[a]

EGYPT ATTACKS JUDAH

12 When the rule of Rehobo´am was
established and was strong, he
forsook the law of the LORD, and all
Israel with him. 2 In the fifth year of
King Rehobo´am, because they had
been unfaithful to the LORD, Shishak
king of Egypt came up against Jeru-
salem 3 with twelve hundred chariots
and sixty thousand horsemen. And
the people were without number who
came with him from Egypt—Libyans,
Suk´ki-im, and Ethiopians. 4 And he
took the fortified cities of Judah and
came as far as Jerusalem. 5 Then She-
mai´ah the prophet came to Rehobo´-
am and to the princes of Judah, who
had gathered at Jerusalem because
of Shishak, and said to them, "Thus
says the LORD, 'You abandoned me, so
I have abandoned you to the hand of
Shishak.'" 6 Then the princes of Israel
and the king humbled themselves and
said, "The LORD is righteous." 7 When
the LORD saw that they humbled
themselves, the word of the LORD
came to Shemai´ah: "They have hum-
bled themselves; I will not destroy
them, but I will grant them some de-
liverance, and my wrath shall not be
poured out upon Jerusalem by the
hand of Shishak. 8 Nevertheless they
shall be servants to him, that they
may know my service and the service
of the kingdoms of the countries."
9 So Shishak king of Egypt came
up against Jerusalem; he took away
the treasures of the house of the
LORD and the treasures of the king's
house; he took away everything. He
also took away the shields of gold
which Solomon had made; 10 and
King Rehobo´am made in their stead
shields of bronze, and committed
them to the hands of the officers of
the guard, who kept the door of the
king's house. 11 And as often as the
king went into the house of the LORD,
the guard came and bore them, and
brought them back to the guardroom.
12 And when he humbled himself the
wrath of the LORD turned from him,
so as not to make a complete destruc-
tion; moreover, conditions were good
in Judah.

DEATH OF REHOBOAM

13 So King Rehobo´am established
himself in Jerusalem and reigned. Re-
hobo´am was forty-one years old when
he began to reign, and he reigned se-
venteen years in Jerusalem, the city
which the LORD had chosen out of
all the tribes of Israel to put his name
there. His mother's name was Na´a-
mah the Ammonitess. 14 And he did
evil, for he did not set his heart to seek
the LORD.
15 Now the acts of Rehobo´am,
from first to last, are they not writ-
ten in the chronicles of Shemai´ah
the prophet and of Iddo the seer?[b]
There were continual wars between
Rehobo´am and Jerobo´am. 16 And
Rehobo´am slept with his fathers, and
was buried in the city of David; and
Abi´jah his son reigned in his stead.

ABIJAH REIGNS OVER JUDAH

13 In the eighteenth year of King
Jerobo´am Abi´jah began to reign
over Judah. 2 He reigned for three years
in Jerusalem. His mother's name was
Micai´ah the daughter of U´riel of
Gib´eah. Now there was war between
Abi´jah and Jerobo´am. 3 Abi´jah went
out to battle having an army of valiant
men of war, four hundred thousand
picked men; and Jerobo´am drew up
his line of battle against him with
eight hundred thousand picked mighty
warriors. 4 Then Abi´jah stood up on
Mount Zemara´im which is in the hill
country of E´phraim, and said, "Hear
me, O Jerobo´am and all Israel! 5 Ought
you not to know that the LORD God of
Israel gave the kingship over Israel for

[a] Cn: Heb *sought a multitude of wives*
[b] Heb *seer, to enroll oneself*

ever to David and his sons by a covenant of salt? 6Yet Jerobo´am the son of Nebat, a servant of Solomon the son of David, rose up and rebelled against his lord; 7and certain worthless scoundrels gathered about him and defied Rehobo´am the son of Solomon, when Rehobo´am was young and irresolute and could not withstand them.

8 "And now you think to withstand the kingdom of the LORD in the hand of the sons of David, because you are a great multitude and have with you the golden calves which Jerobo´am made you for gods. 9Have you not driven out the priests of the LORD, the sons of Aaron, and the Levites, and made priests for yourselves like the peoples of other lands? Whoever comes to consecrate himself with a young bull or seven rams becomes a priest of what are no gods. 10But as for us, the LORD is our God, and we have not forsaken him. We have priests ministering to the LORD who are sons of Aaron, and Levites for their service. 11They offer to the LORD every morning and every evening burnt offerings and incense of sweet spices, set out the showbread on the table of pure gold, and care for the golden lampstand that its lamps may burn every evening; for we keep the charge of the LORD our God, but you have forsaken him. 12Behold, God is with us at our head, and his priests with their battle trumpets to sound the call to battle against you. O sons of Israel, do not fight against the LORD, the God of your fathers; for you cannot succeed."

13 Jerobo´am had sent an ambush around to come on them from behind; thus his troops[a] were in front of Judah, and the ambush was behind them. 14And when Judah looked, behold, the battle was before and behind them; and they cried to the LORD, and the priests blew the trumpets. 15Then the men of Judah raised the battle shout. And when the men of Judah shouted, God defeated Jerobo´am and all Israel before Abi´jah and Judah. 16The men of Israel fled before Judah, and God gave them into their hand. 17Abi´jah and his people slew them with a great slaughter; so there fell slain of Israel five hundred thousand picked men. 18Thus the men of Israel were subdued at that time, and the men of Judah prevailed, because they relied upon the LORD, the God of their fathers. 19And Abi´jah pursued Jerobo´am, and took cities from him, Bethel with its villages and Jesha´nah with its villages and Ephron[b] with its villages. 20Jerobo´am did not recover his power in the days of Abi´jah; and the LORD smote him, and he died. 21But Abi´jah grew mighty. And he took fourteen wives, and had twenty-two sons and sixteen daughters. 22The rest of the acts of Abi´jah, his ways and his sayings, are written in the story of the prophet Iddo.

ASA REIGNS

14 [c] So Abi´jah slept with his fathers, and they buried him in the city of David; and Asa his son reigned in his stead. In his days the land had rest for ten years. 2[d]And Asa did what was good and right in the eyes of the LORD his God. 3He took away the foreign altars and the high places, and broke down the pillars and hewed down the Ashe´rim, 4and commanded Judah to seek the LORD, the God of their fathers, and to keep the law and the commandment. 5He also took out of all the cities of Judah the high places and the incense altars. And the kingdom had rest under him. 6He built fortified cities in Judah, for the land had rest. He had no war in those years, for the LORD gave him peace. 7And he said to Judah, "Let us build these cities, and surround them with walls and towers, gates and bars; the

[a] Heb *they*
[b] Another reading is *Ephrain*
[c] Ch 13.23 in Heb
[d] Ch 14.1 in Heb

land is still ours, because we have
sought the LORD our God; we have
sought him, and he has given us peace
on every side." So they built and pros-
pered. 8And Asa had an army of three
hundred thousand from Judah, armed
with bucklers and spears, and two
hundred and eighty thousand men
from Benjamin, that carried shields
and drew bows; all these were mighty
men of valor.

ETHIOPIAN INVASION REPULSED

9 Zerah the Ethiopian came out
against them with an army of a mil-
lion men and three hundred chariots,
and came as far as Mare´shah. 10And
Asa went out to meet him, and they
drew up their lines of battle in the val-
ley of Zeph´athah at Mare´shah. 11And
Asa cried to the LORD his God, "O
LORD, there is none like thee to help,
between the mighty and the weak.
Help us, O LORD our God, for we rely
on thee, and in thy name we have
come against this multitude. O LORD,
thou art our God; let not man prevail
against thee." 12So the LORD defeated
the Ethiopians before Asa and before
Judah, and the Ethiopians fled. 13Asa
and the people that were with him
pursued them as far as Gerar, and the
Ethiopians fell until none remained
alive; for they were broken before
the LORD and his army. The men of
Judah[e] carried away very much booty.
14And they smote all the cities round
about Gerar, for the fear of the LORD
was upon them. They plundered all
the cities, for there was much plunder
in them. 15And they smote the tents
of those who had cattle,[f] and carried
away sheep in abundance and camels.
Then they returned to Jerusalem.

15 The Spirit of God came upon
Azari´ah the son of Oded, 2and
he went out to meet Asa, and said to
him, "Hear me, Asa, and all Judah
and Benjamin: The LORD is with you,
while you are with him. If you seek
him, he will be found by you, but if
you forsake him, he will forsake you.
3For a long time Israel was without
the true God, and without a teaching
priest, and without law; 4but when
in their distress they turned to the
LORD, the God of Israel, and sought
him, he was found by them. 5In those
times there was no peace to him who
went out or to him who came in, for
great disturbances afflicted all the
inhabitants of the lands. 6They were
broken in pieces, nation against na-
tion and city against city, for God
troubled them with every sort of dis-
tress. 7But you, take courage! Do not
let you hands be weak, for your work
shall be rewarded."

8 When Asa heard these words,
the prophecy of Azari´ah the son of
Oded,[g] he took courage, and put away
the abominable idols from all the
land of Judah and Benjamin and from
the cities which he had taken in the
hill country of E´phraim, and he re-
paired the altar of the LORD that was
in front of the vestibule of the house
of the LORD.[h] 9And he gathered all
Judah and Benjamin, and those from
E´phraim, Manas´seh, and Simeon
who were sojourning with them, for
great numbers had deserted to him
from Israel when they saw that the
LORD his God was with him. 10They
were gathered at Jerusalem in the
third month of the fifteenth year of
the reign of Asa. 11They sacrificed to
the LORD on that day, from the spoil
which they had brought, seven hun-
dred oxen and seven thousand sheep.
12And they entered into a covenant to
seek the LORD, the God of their fa-
thers, with all their heart and with all
their soul; 13and that whoever would
not seek the LORD, the God of Israel,
should be put to death, whether young
or old, man or woman. 14They took
oath to the LORD with a loud voice,

[e] Heb *they*
[f] Heb obscure
[g] Compare Syr Vg: Heb *the prophecy, Oded the prophet*
[h] Heb *the vestibule of the* Lord

and with shouting, and with trum-
pets, and with horns. 15 And all Judah
rejoiced over the oath; for they had
sworn with all their heart, and had
sought him with their whole desire,
and he was found by them, and the
LORD gave them rest round about.
16 Even Ma´acah, his mother,
King Asa removed from being queen
mother because she had made an
abominable image for Ashe´rah. Asa
cut down her image, crushed it, and
burned it at the brook Kidron. 17 But
the high places were not taken out of
Israel. Nevertheless the heart of Asa
was blameless all his days. 18 And he
brought into the house of God the vo-
tive gifts of his father and his own vo-
tive gifts, silver, and gold, and vessels.
19 And there was no more war until the
thirty-fifth year of the reign of Asa.

ALLIANCE WITH ARAM CONDEMNED

16 In the thirty-sixth year of the
reign of Asa, Ba´asha king of Israel
went up against Judah, and built
Ramah, that he might permit no one
to go out or come in to Asa king of
Judah. 2 Then Asa took silver and gold
from the treasures of the house of the
LORD and the king's house, and sent
them to Ben-ha´dad king of Syria,
who dwelt in Damascus, saying, 3 "Let
there be a league between me and
you, as between my father and your
father; behold, I am sending to you
silver and gold; go, break your league
with Ba´asha king of Israel, that he
may withdraw from me." 4 And Ben-
ha´dad hearkened to King Asa, and
sent the commanders of his armies
against the cities of Israel, and they
conquered I´jon, Dan, A´bel-ma´im,
and all the store-cities of Naph´tali.
5 And when Ba´asha heard of it, he
stopped building Ramah, and let his
work cease. 6 Then King Asa took
all Judah, and they carried away the
stones of Ramah and its timber, with
which Ba´asha had been building, and
with them he built Geba and Mizpah.
7 At that time Hana´ni the seer
came to Asa king of Judah, and said
to him, "Because you relied on the
king of Syria, and did not rely on the
LORD your God, the army of the king
of Syria has escaped you. 8 Were not
the Ethiopians and the Libyans a huge
army with exceedingly many chariots
and horsemen? Yet because you relied
on the LORD, he gave them into your
hand. 9 For the eyes of the LORD run to
and fro throughout the whole earth,
to show his might in behalf of those
whose heart is blameless toward him.
You have done foolishly in this; for
from now on you will have wars."
10 Then Asa was angry with the seer,
and put him in the stocks, in prison,
for he was in a rage with him because
of this. And Asa inflicted cruelties
upon some of the people at the same
time.

ASA'S DISEASE AND DEATH

11 The acts of Asa, from first to last,
are written in the Book of the Kings of
Judah and Israel. 12 In the thirty-ninth
year of his reign Asa was diseased in
his feet, and his disease became se-
vere; yet even in his disease he did not
seek the LORD, but sought help from
physicians. 13 And Asa slept with his
fathers, dying in the forty-first year
of his reign. 14 They buried him in the
tomb which he had hewn out for him-
self in the city of David. They laid him
on a bier which had been filled with
various kinds of spices prepared by
the perfumer's art; and they made a
very great fire in his honor.

JEHOSHAPHAT'S REIGN

17 Jehosh´aphat his son reigned in
his stead, and strengthened him-
self against Israel. 2 He placed forces in
all the fortified cities of Judah, and set
garrisons in the land of Judah, and in
the cities of E´phraim which Asa his
father had taken. 3 The LORD was with
Jehosh´aphat, because he walked in
the earlier ways of his father;[a] he did

a Another reading is *his father David*

not seek the Ba´als, 4but sought the
God of his father and walked in his
commandments, and not according
to the ways of Israel. 5Therefore the
LORD established the kingdom in his
hand; and all Judah brought tribute to
Jehosh´aphat; and he had great riches
and honor. 6His heart was courageous
in the ways of the LORD; and further-
more he took the high places and the
Ashe´rim out of Judah.

7 In the third year of his reign he
sent his princes, Ben-hail, Obadi´ah,
Zechari´ah, Nethan´el, and Micai´ah,
to teach in the cities of Judah; 8and
with them the Levites, Shemai´ah,
Nethani´ah, Zebadi´ah, As´ahel, She-
mi´ramoth, Jehon´athan, Adoni´jah,
Tobi´jah, and Tobadoni´jah; and with
these Levites, the priests Elish´ama
and Jehor´am. 9And they taught in
Judah, having the book of the law of
the LORD with them; they went about
through all the cities of Judah and
taught among the people.

10 And the fear of the LORD fell
upon all the kingdoms of the lands
that were round about Judah, and they
made no war against Jehosh´aphat.
11Some of the Philistines brought
Jehosh´aphat presents, and silver for
tribute; and the Arabs also brought
him seven thousand seven hundred
rams and seven thousand seven hun-
dred he-goats. 12And Jehosh´aphat
grew steadily greater. He built in Ju-
dah fortresses and store-cities, 13and
he had great stores in the cities of
Judah. He had soldiers, mighty men
of valor, in Jerusalem. 14This was the
muster of them by fathers' houses: Of
Judah, the commanders of thousands:
Adnah the commander, with three
hundred thousand mighty men of val-
or, 15and next to him Jeho-ha´nan the
commander, with two hundred and
eighty thousand, 16and next to him
Amasi´ah the son of Zichri, a volun-
teer for the service of the LORD, with
two hundred thousand mighty men of
valor. 17Of Benjamin: Eli´ada, a mighty
man of valor, with two hundred
thousand men armed with bow and
shield, 18and next to him Jeho´zabad
with a hundred and eighty thousand
armed for war. 19These were in the
service of the king, besides those
whom the king had placed in the for-
tified cities throughout all Judah.

MICAIAH PREDICTS FAILURE

18 Now Jehosh´aphat had great
riches and honor; and he made a
marriage alliance with Ahab. 2After
some years he went down to Ahab in
Samar´ia. And Ahab killed an abun-
dance of sheep and oxen for him and
for the people who were with him,
and induced him to go up against
Ra´moth-gil´ead. 3Ahab king of Israel
said to Jehosh´aphat king of Judah,
"Will you go with me to Ra´moth-
gil´ead?" He answered him, "I am as
you are, my people as your people. We
will be with you in the war."

4 And Jehosh´aphat said to the
king of Israel, "Inquire first for the
word of the LORD." 5Then the king
of Israel gathered the prophets to-
gether, four hundred men, and said to
them, "Shall we go to battle against
Ra´moth-gil´ead, or shall I forbear?"
And they said, "Go up; for God will
give it into the hand of the king." 6But
Jehosh´aphat said, "Is there not here
another prophet of the LORD of whom
we may inquire?" 7And the king of
Israel said to Jehosh´aphat, "There
is yet one man by whom we may in-
quire of the LORD, Micai´ah the son
of Imlah; but I hate him, for he never
prophesies good concerning me, but
always evil." And Jehosh´aphat said,
"Let not the king say so." 8Then the
king of Israel summoned an officer
and said, "Bring quickly Micai´ah
the son of Imlah." 9Now the king of
Israel and Jehosh´aphat the king of
Judah were sitting on their thrones,
arrayed in their robes; and they were
sitting at the threshing floor at the
entrance of the gate of Samar´ia; and
all the prophets were prophesying
before them. 10And Zedeki´ah the

son of Chena´anah made for himself
horns of iron, and said, "Thus says
the LORD, 'With these you shall push
the Syrians until they are destroyed.'"
11 And all the prophets prophesied so,
and said, "Go up to Ra´moth-gil´ead
and triumph; the LORD will give it
into the hand of the king."
12 And the messenger who went
to summon Micai´ah said to him,
"Behold, the words of the prophets*
with one accord are favorable to the
king; let your word be like the word
of one of them, and speak favorably."
13 But Micai´ah said, "As the LORD
lives, what my God says, that I will
speak." 14 And when he had come
to the king, the king said to him,
"Micai´ah, shall we go to Ra´moth-
gil´ead to battle, or shall I forbear?"
And he answered, "Go up and tri-
umph; they will be given into your
hand." 15 But the king said to him,
"How many times shall I adjure you
that you speak to me nothing but
the truth in the name of the LORD?"
16 And he said, "I saw all Israel scat-
tered upon the mountains, as sheep
that have no shepherd; and the LORD
said, 'These have no master; let each
return to his home in peace.'" 17 And
the king of Israel said to Jehosh´aphat,
"Did I not tell you that he would not
prophesy good concerning me, but
evil?" 18 And Micai´ah said, "Therefore
hear the word of the LORD: I saw the
LORD sitting on his throne, and all the
host of heaven standing on his right
hand and on his left; 19 and the LORD
said, 'Who will entice Ahab the king
of Israel, that he may go up and fall
at Ra´moth-gil´ead?' And one said
one thing, and another said another.
20 Then a spirit came forward and stood
before the LORD, saying, 'I will entice
him.' And the LORD said to him, 'By
what means?' 21 And he said, 'I will
go forth, and will be a lying spirit in
the mouth of all his prophets.' And
he said, 'You are to entice him, and
you shall succeed; go forth and do so.'
22 Now therefore behold, the LORD has
put a lying spirit in the mouth of these
your prophets; the LORD has spoken
evil concerning you."
23 Then Zedeki´ah the son of
Chena´anah came near and struck
Micai´ah on the cheek, and said,
"Which way did the Spirit of the
LORD go from me to speak to you?"
24 And Micai´ah said, "Behold, you
shall see on that day when you go into
an inner chamber to hide yourself."
25 And the king of Israel said, "Seize
Micai´ah, and take him back to Amon
the governor of the city and to Jo´ash
the king's son; 26 and say, 'Thus says
the king, Put this fellow in prison, and
feed him with scant fare of bread and
water, until I return in peace.'" 27 And
Micai´ah said, "If you return in peace,
the LORD has not spoken by me." And
he said, "Hear, all you peoples!"

DEFEAT AND DEATH OF AHAB

28 So the king of Israel and
Jehosh´aphat the king of Judah went
up to Ra´moth-gil´ead. 29 And the king
of Israel said to Jehosh´aphat, "I will
disguise myself and go into battle, but
you wear your robes." And the king
of Israel disguised himself; and they
went into battle. 30 Now the king of
Syria had commanded the captains of
his chariots, "Fight with neither small
nor great, but only with the king of
Israel." 31 And when the captains of
the chariots saw Jehosh´aphat, they
said, "It is the king of Israel." So
they turned to fight against him; and
Jehosh´aphat cried out, and the LORD
helped him. God drew them away
from him, 32 for when the captains of
the chariots saw that it was not the
king of Israel, they turned back from
pursuing him. 33 But a certain man
drew his bow at a venture, and struck
the king of Israel between the scale
armor and the breastplate; therefore
he said to the driver of his chariot,
"Turn about, and carry me out of the
battle, for I am wounded." 34 And the
batle grew hot that day, and the king
of Israel propped himself up in his

chariot facing the Syrians until eve-
ning; then at sunset he died.

19 Jehosh´aphat the king of Judah
returned in safety to his house
in Jerusalem. 2But Jehu the son of
Hana´ni the seer went out to meet
him, and said to King Jehosh´aphat,
"Should you help the wicked and love
those who hate the LORD? Because
of this, wrath has gone out against
you from the LORD. 3Nevertheless
some good is found in you, for you de-
stroyed the Ashe´rahs out of the land,
and have set your heart to seek God."

THE REFORMS OF JEHOSHAPHAT

4 Jehosh´aphat dwelt at Jerusalem;
and he went out again among the peo-
ple, from Beer-sheba to the hill coun-
try of E´phraim, and brought them
back to the LORD, the God of their
fathers. 5He appointed judges in the
land in all the fortified cities of Judah,
city by city, 6and said to the judges,
"Consider what you do, for you judge
not for man but for the LORD; he is
with you in giving judgment. 7Now
then, let the fear of the LORD be upon
you; take heed what you do, for there
is no perversion of justice with the
LORD our God, or partiality, or taking
bribes."

8 Moreover in Jerusalem Jehosh´-
aphat appointed certain Levites and
priests and heads of families of Israel,
to give judgment for the LORD and to
decide disputed cases. They had their
seat at Jerusalem. 9And he charged
them: "Thus you shall do in the fear
of the LORD, in faithfulness, and with
your whole heart: 10whenever a case
comes to you from your brethren who
live in their cities, concerning blood-
shed, law or commandment, statutes
or ordinances, then you shall instruct
them, that they may not incur guilt
before the LORD and wrath may not
come upon you and your brethren.
Thus you shall do, and you will not in-
cur guilt. 11And behold, Amari´ah the
chief priest is over you in all matters
of the LORD; and Zebadi´ah the son
of Ish´mael, the governor of the house
of Judah, in all the king's matters; and
the Levites will serve you as officers.
Deal courageously, and may the LORD
be with the upright!"

INVASION FROM THE EAST

20 After this the Moabites and
Ammonites, and with them some
of the Me-u´nites,[a] came against
Jehosh´aphat for battle. 2Some men
came and told Jehosh´aphat, "A great
multitude is coming against you from
Edom,[b] from beyond the sea; and, be-
hold, they are in Haz´azon-ta´mar"
(that is, En-ged´i). 3Then Jehosh´aphat
feared, and set himself to seek the
LORD, and proclaimed a fast through-
out all Judah. 4And Judah assembled
to seek help from the LORD; from all
the cities of Judah they came to seek
the LORD.

JEHOSHAPHAT'S PRAYER AND VICTORY

5 And Jehosh´aphat stood in the
assembly of Judah and Jerusalem, in
the house of the LORD, before the
new court, 6and said, "O LORD, God
of our fathers, art thou not God in
heaven? Dost thou not rule over all
the kingdoms of the nations? In thy
hand are power and might, so that
none is able to withstand thee. 7Didst
thou not, O our God, drive out the in-
habitants of this land before thy peo-
ple Israel, and give it for ever to the
descendants of Abraham thy friend?
8And they have dwelt in it, and have
built thee in it a sanctuary for thy
name, saying, 9'If evil comes upon us,
the sword, judgment,[c] or pestilence,
or famine, we will stand before this
house, and before thee, for thy name
is in this house, and cry to thee in
our affliction, and thou wilt hear and
save.' 10And now behold, the men of
Ammon and Moab and Mount Se´ir,
whom thou wouldest not let Israel

[a] Compare 26.7: Heb *Ammonites*
[b] One Ms: Heb *Aram* (Syria)
[c] Or *the sword of judgment*

invade when they came from the land
of Egypt, and whom they avoided and
did not destroy 11behold, they reward
us by coming to drive us out of thy
possession, which thou hast given us
to inherit. 12O our God, wilt thou not
execute judgment upon them? For we
are powerless against this great multi-
tude that is coming against us. We do
not know what to do, but our eyes are
upon thee."

13 Meanwhile all the men of Judah
stood before the LORD, with their little
ones, their wives, and their children.
14And the Spirit of the LORD came
upon Jaha´ziel the son of Zechari´ah,
son of Benai´ah, son of Je-i´el, son of
Mattani´ah, a Levite of the sons of
Asaph, in the midst of the assembly.
15And he said, "Hearken, all Judah and
inhabitants of Jerusalem, and King
Jehosh´aphat: Thus says the LORD to
you, 'Fear not, and be not dismayed
at this great multitude; for the battle
is not yours but God's. 16Tomorrow go
down against them; behold, they will
come up by the ascent of Ziz; you will
find them at the end of the valley, east
of the wilderness of Jeru´el. 17You will
not need to fight in this battle; take
your position, stand still, and see the
victory of the LORD on your behalf, O
Judah and Jerusalem.' Fear not, and
be not dismayed; tomorrow go out
against them, and the LORD will be
with you."

18 Then Jehosh´aphat bowed his
head with his face to the ground,
and all Judah and the inhabitants
of Jerusalem fell down before the
LORD, worshiping the LORD. 19And
the Levites, of the Ko´hathites and
the Kor´ahites, stood up to praise the
LORD, the God of Israel, with a very
loud voice.

20 And they rose early in the
morning and went out into the wil-
derness of Teko´a; and as they went
out, Jehosh´aphat stood and said,
"Hear me, Judah and inhabitants of
Jerusalem! Believe in the LORD your
God, and you will be established;
believe his prophets, and you will
succeed." 21And when he had taken
counsel with the people, he appointed
those who were to sing to the LORD
and praise him in holy array, as they
went before the army, and say,

"Give thanks to the LORD,
for his steadfast love en-
dures for ever."

22And when they began to sing
and praise, the LORD set an ambush
against the men of Ammon, Moab,
and Mount Se´ir, who had come
against Judah, so that they were rout-
ed. 23For the men of Ammon and Moab
rose against the inhabitants of Mount
Se´ir, destroying them utterly, and
when they had made an end of the in-
habitants of Se´ir, they all helped to
destroy one another.

24 When Judah came to the watch-
tower of the wilderness, they looked
toward the multitude; and behold,
they were dead bodies lying on the
ground; none had escaped. 25When
Jehosh´aphat and his people came to
take the spoil from them, they found
cattle[a] in great numbers, goods, cloth-
ing, and precious things, which they
took for themselves until they could
carry no more. They were three days
in taking the spoil, it was so much.
26On the fourth day they assembled
in the Valley of Bera´cah,[b] for there
they blessed the LORD; therefore the
name of that place has been called the
Valley of Bera´cah to this day. 27Then
they returned, every man of Judah and
Jerusalem, and Jehosh´aphat at their
head, returning to Jerusalem with joy,
for the LORD had made them rejoice
over their enemies. 28They came to
Jerusalem, with harps and lyres and
trumpets, to the house of the LORD.
29And the fear of God came on all
the kingdoms of the countries when
they heard that the LORD had fought
against the enemies of Israel. 30So the

[a]Gk: Heb *among them*
[b]That is *Blessing*

realm of Jehosh´aphat was quiet, for
his God gave him rest round about.

THE END OF JEHOSHAPHAT'S REIGN

31 Thus Jehosh´aphat reigned over
Judah. He was thirty-five years old
when he began to reign, and he reigned
twenty-five years in Jerusalem. His
mother's name was Azu´bah the
daughter of Shilhi. 32He walked in the
way of Asa his father and did not turn
aside from it; he did what was right
in the sight of the LORD. 33The high
places, however, were not taken away;
the people had not yet set their hearts
upon the God of their fathers.

34 Now the rest of the acts of
Jehosh´aphat, from first to last, are
written in the chronicles of Jehu the
son of Hana´ni, which are recorded in
the Book of the Kings of Israel.

35 After this Jehosh´aphat king
of Judah joined with Ahazi´ah king
of Israel, who did wickedly. 36He
joined him in building ships to go
to Tarshish, and they built the ships
in E´zion-ge´ber. 37Then Elie´zer
the son of Dodav´ahu of Mare´shah
prophesied against Jehosh´aphat, say-
ing, "Because you have joined with
Ahazi´ah, the LORD will destroy what
you have made." And the ships were
wrecked and were not able to go to
Tarshish.

JEHORAM'S REIGN

21 Jehosh´aphat slept with his fa-
thers, and was buried with his
fathers in the city of David; and
Jehor´am his son reigned in his
stead. 2He had brothers, the sons
of Jehosh´aphat: Azari´ah, Jehi´el,
Zechari´ah, Azari´ah, Michael, and
Shephati´ah; all these were the sons
of Jehosh´aphat king of Judah. 3Their
father gave them great gifts, of silver,
gold, and valuable possessions, to-
gether with fortified cities in Judah;
but he gave the kingdom to Jehor´am,
because he was the first-born. 4When
Jehor´am had ascended the throne
of his father and was established, he
slew all his brothers with the sword,
and also some of the princes of Israel.
5Jehor´am was thirty-two years old
when he became king, and he reigned
eight years in Jerusalem. 6And he
walked in the way of the kings of
Israel, as the house of Ahab had done;
for the daughter of Ahab was his wife.
And he did what was evil in the sight
of the LORD. 7Yet the LORD would not
destroy the house of David, because of
the covenant which he had made with
David, and since he had promised to
give a lamp to him and to his sons for
ever.

REVOLT OF EDOM

8 In his days Edom revolted from
the rule of Judah, and set up a king
of their own. 9Then Jehor´am passed
over with his commanders and all
his chariots, and he rose by night
and smote the E´domites who had
surrounded him and his chariot com-
manders. 10So Edom revolted from the
rule of Judah to this day. At that time
Libnah also revolted from his rule, be-
cause he had forsaken the LORD, the
God of his fathers.

ELIJAH'S LETTER

11 Moreover he made high plac-
es in the hill country of Judah, and
led the inhabitants of Jerusalem into
unfaithfulness, and made Judah go
astray. 12And a letter came to him from
Eli´jah the prophet, saying, "Thus
says the LORD, the God of David your
father, 'Because you have not walked
in the ways of Jehosh´aphat your fa-
ther, or in the ways of Asa king of
Judah, 13but have walked in the way of
the kings of Israel, and have led Judah
and the inhabitants of Jerusalem into
unfaithfulness, as the house of Ahab
led Israel into unfaithfulness, and
also you have killed your brothers, of
your father's house, who were better
than yourself; 14behold, the LORD will
bring a great plague on your people,
your children, your wives, and all
your possessions, 15and you yourself

will have a severe sickness with a dis-
ease of your bowels, until your bowels
come out because of the disease, day
by day.'"
16 And the LORD stirred up against
Jehor'am the anger of the Philistines
and of the Arabs who are near the
Ethiopians; 17and they came up against
Judah, and invaded it, and carried
away all the possessions they found
that belonged to the king's house, and
also his sons and his wives, so that no
son was left to him except Jeho'ahaz,
his youngest son.

DISEASE AND DEATH OF JEHORAM

18 And after all this the LORD
smote him in his bowels with an in-
curable disease. 19In course of time,
at the end of two years, his bowels
came out because of the disease, and
he died in great agony. His people
made no fire in his honor, like the
fires made for his fathers. 20He was
thirty-two years old when he began
to reign, and he reigned eight years in
Jerusalem; and he departed with no
one's regret. They buried him in the
city of David, but not in the tombs of
the kings.

AHAZIAH'S REIGN

22 And the inhabitants of Jerusalem
made Ahazi'ah his youngest son
king in his stead; for the band of
men that came with the Arabs to the
camp had slain all the older sons. So
Ahazi'ah the son of Jehor'am king
of Judah reigned. 2Ahazi'ah was for-
ty-two years old when he began to
reign, and he reigned one year in
Jerusalem. His mother's name was
Athali'ah, the granddaughter of
Omri. 3He also walked in the ways of
the house of Ahab, for his mother was
his counselor in doing wickedly. 4He
did what was evil in the sight of the
LORD, as the house of Ahab had done;
for after the death of his father they
were his counselors, to his undoing.
5He even followed their counsel, and
went with Jehor'am the son of Ahab
king of Israel to make war against
Haz'ael king of Syria at Ra'moth-
gil'ead. And the Syrians wounded
Joram, 6and he returned to be healed
in Jezre'el of the wounds which he had
received at Ramah, when he fought
against Haz'ael king of Syria. And
Ahazi'ah the son of Jehor'am king of
Judah went down to see Joram the son
of Ahab in Jezre'el, because he was
sick.
7 But it was ordained by God that
the downfall of Ahazi'ah should
come about through his going to vis-
it Joram. For when he came there he
went out with Jehor'am to meet Jehu
the son of Nimshi, whom the LORD
had anointed to destroy the house
of Ahab. 8And when Jehu was exe-
cuting judgment upon the house of
Ahab, he met the princes of Judah
and the sons of Ahazi'ah's brothers,
who attended Ahazi'ah, and he killed
them. 9He searched for Ahazi'ah,
and he was captured while hiding in
Samar'ia, and he was brought to Jehu
and put to death. They buried him,
for they said, "He is the grandson of
Jehosh'aphat, who sought the LORD
with all his heart." And the house of
Ahazi'ah had no one able to rule the
kingdom.

ATHALIAH SEIZES THE THRONE

10 Now when Athali'ah the moth-
er of Ahazi'ah saw that her son was
dead, she arose and destroyed all the
royal family of the house of Judah.
11But Jeho-shab'e-ath, the daughter
of the king, took Jo'ash the son of
Ahazi'ah, and stole him away from
among the king's sons who were
about to be slain, and she put him
and his nurse in a bedchamber. Thus
Jeho-shab'e-ath, the daughter of King
Jehor'am and wife of Jehoi'ada the
priest, because she was a sister of
Ahazi'ah, hid him from Athali'ah, so
that she did not slay him; 12and he re-
mained with them six years, hid in the
house of God, while Athali'ah reigned
over the land.

23 But in the seventh year Jehoi´ada
took courage, and entered into a
compact with the commanders of hun-
dreds, Azari´ah the son of Jero´ham,
Ish´mael the son of Jeho-ha´nan,
Azari´ah the son of Obed, Ma-asei´ah
the son of Adai´ah, and Elisha´phat
the son of Zichri. 2And they went
about through Judah and gathered the
Levites from all the cities of Judah, and
the heads of fathers' houses of Israel,
and they came to Jerusalem. 3And all
the assembly made a covenant with
the king in the house of God. And
Jehoi´ada[a] said to them, "Behold, the
king's son! Let him reign, as the LORD
spoke concerning the sons of David.
4This is the thing that you shall do: of
you priests and Levites who come off
duty on the sabbath, one third shall
be gatekeepers, 5and one third shall
be at the king's house and one third
at the Gate of the Foundation; and
all the people shall be in the courts
of the house of the LORD. 6Let no one
enter the house of the LORD except
the priests and ministering Levites;
they may enter, for they are holy, but
all the people shall keep the charge of
the LORD. 7The Levites shall surround
the king, each with his weapons in his
hand; and whoever enters the house
shall be slain. Be with the king when
he comes in, and when he goes out."

JOASH CROWNED KING

8 The Levites and all Judah did ac-
cording to all that Jehoi´ada the priest
commanded. They each brought his
men, who were to go off duty on the
sabbath, with those who were to come
on duty on the sabbath; for Jehoi´ada
the priest did not dismiss the divi-
sions. 9And Jehoi´ada the priest de-
livered to the captains the spears and
the large and small shields that had
been King David's, which were in the
house of God; 10and he set all the peo-
ple as a guard for the king, every man
with his weapon in his hand, from the
south side of the house to the north
side of the house, around the altar and
the house. 11Then he brought out the
king's son, and put the crown upon
him, and gave him the testimony;
and they proclaimed him king, and
Jehoi´ada and his sons anointed him,
and they said, "Long live the king."

ATHALIAH MURDERED

12 When Athali´ah heard the noise
of the people running and praising the
king, she went into the house of the
LORD to the people; 13and when she
looked, there was the king standing
by his pillar at the entrance, and the
captains and the trumpeters beside
the king, and all the people of the
land rejoicing and blowing trumpets,
and the singers with their musical
instruments leading in the celebra-
tion. And Athali´ah rent her clothes,
and cried, "Treason! Treason!" 14Then
Jehoi´ada the priest brought out the
captains who were set over the army,
saying to them, "Bring her out be-
tween the ranks; any one who follows
her is to be slain with the sword."
For the priest said, "Do not slay her
in the house of the LORD." 15So they
laid hands on her; and she went into
the entrance of the horse gate of the
king's house, and they slew her there.
16 And Jehoi´ada made a covenant
between himself and all the people
and the king that they should be the
LORD's people. 17Then all the people
went to the house of Ba´al, and tore it
down; his altars and his images they
broke in pieces, and they slew Mattan
the priest of Ba´al before the altars.
18And Jehoi´ada posted watchmen for
the house of the LORD under the di-
rection of the Levitical priests and the
Levites whom David had organized to
be in charge of the house of the LORD,
to offer burnt offerings to the LORD,
as it is written in the law of Moses,
with rejoicing and with singing, ac-
cording to the order of David. 19He
stationed the gatekeepers at the gates
of the house of the LORD so that no

[a] Heb *he*

one should enter who was in any way
unclean. 20And he took the captains,
the nobles, the governors of the peo-
ple, and all the people of the land; and
they brought the king down from the
house of the LORD, marching through
the upper gate to the king's house.
And they set the king upon the royal
throne. 21So all the people of the land
rejoiced; and the city was quiet, af-
ter Athali´ah had been slain with the
sword.

JOASH REPAIRS THE TEMPLE

24 Jo´ash was seven years old when
he began to reign, and he reigned
forty years in Jerusalem; his mother's
name was Zib´iah of Beer-sheba. 2And
Jo´ash did what was right in the eyes
of the LORD all the days of Jehoi´ada
the priest. 3Jehoi´ada got for him two
wives, and he had sons and daughters.
4 After this Jo´ash decided to re-
store the house of the LORD. 5And he
gathered the priests and the Levites,
and said to them, "Go out to the cit-
ies of Judah, and gather from all Israel
money to repair the house of your God
from year to year; and see that you
hasten the matter." But the Levites
did not hasten it. 6So the king sum-
moned Jehoi´ada the chief, and said
to him, "Why have you not required
the Levites to bring in from Judah and
Jerusalem the tax levied by Moses, the
servant of the LORD, on[a] the congre-
gation of Israel for the tent of testimo-
ny?" 7For the sons of Athali´ah, that
wicked woman, had broken into the
house of God; and had also used all
the dedicated things of the house of
the LORD for the Ba´als.
8 So the king commanded, and
they made a chest, and set it out-
side the gate of the house of the
LORD. 9And proclamation was made
throughout Judah and Jerusalem, to
bring in for the LORD the tax that
Moses the servant of God laid upon
Israel in the wilderness. 10And all the
princes and all the people rejoiced
and brought their tax and dropped
it into the chest until they had fin-
ished. 11And whenever the chest was
brought to the king's officers by the
Levites, when they saw that there was
much money in it, the king's secre-
tary and the officer of the chief priest
would come and empty the chest and
take it and return it to its place. Thus
they did day after day, and collected
money in abundance. 12And the king
and Jehoi´ada gave it to those who
had charge of the work of the house
of the LORD, and they hired masons
and carpenters to restore the house
of the LORD, and also workers in iron
and bronze to repair the house of the
LORD. 13So those who were engaged
in the work labored, and the repair-
ing went forward in their hands, and
they restored the house of God to its
proper condition and strengthened it.
14And when they had finished, they
brought the rest of the money before
the king and Jehoi´ada, and with it
were made utensils for the house of
the LORD, both for the service and for
the burnt offerings, and dishes for in-
cense, and vessels of gold and silver.
And they offered burnt offerings in
the house of the LORD continually all
the days of Jehoi´ada.

APOSTASY OF JOASH

15 But Jehoi´ada grew old and full
of days, and died; he was a hundred
and thirty years old at his death.
16And they buried him in the city of
David among the kings, because he
had done good in Israel, and toward
God and his house.
17 Now after the death of Jehoi´ada
the princes of Judah came and did
obeisance to the king; then the king
harkened to them. 18And they forsook
the house of the LORD, the God of
their fathers, and served the Ashe´rim
and the idols. And wrath came upon
Judah and Jerusalem for this their
guilt. 19Yet he sent prophets among
them to bring them back to the LORD;

[a]Compare Vg: Heb *and*

father Amazi´ah. 2He built Eloth and
restored it to Judah, after the king
slept with his fathers. 3Uzzi´ah was
sixteen years old when he began to
reign, and he reigned fifty-two years
in Jerusalem. His mother's name
was Jecoli´ah of Jerusalem. 4And he
did what was right in the eyes of the
LORD, according to all that his father
Amazi´ah had done. 5He set himself to
seek God in the days of Zechari´ah,
who instructed him in the fear of God;
and as long as he sought the LORD,
God made him prosper.

6 He went out and made war
against the Philistines, and broke
down the wall of Gath and the wall of
Jabneh and the wall of Ashdod; and he
built cities in the territory of Ashdod
and elsewhere among the Philistines.
7God helped him against the
Philistines, and against the Arabs that
dwelt in Gurba´al, and against the Me-
u´nites. 8The Ammonites paid tribute
to Uzzi´ah, and his fame spread even
to the border of Egypt, for he became
very strong. 9Moreover Uzzi´ah built
towers in Jerusalem at the Corner
Gate and at the Valley Gate and at
the Angle, and fortified them. 10And
he built towers in the wilderness, and
hewed out many cisterns, for he had
large herds, both in the Shephe´lah
and in the plain, and he had farm-
ers and vinedressers in the hills and
in the fertile lands, for he loved the
soil. 11Moreover Uzzi´ah had an army
of soldiers, fit for war, in divisions ac-
cording to the numbers in the muster
made by Je-i´el the secretary and Ma-
asei´ah the officer, under the direc-
tion of Hanani´ah, one of the king's
commanders. 12The whole number of
the heads of fathers' houses of mighty
men of valor was two thousand six
hundred. 13Under their command was
an army of three hundred and seven
thousand five hundred, who could
make war with mighty power, to help
the king against the enemy. 14And
Uzzi´ah prepared for all the army
shields, spears, helmets, coats of mail,
bows, and stones for slinging. 15In
Jerusalem he made engines, invented
by skilful men, to be on the towers
and the corners, to shoot arrows and
great stones. And his fame spread far,
for he was marvelously helped, till he
was strong.

PRIDE AND APOSTASY

16 But when he was strong he grew
proud, to his destruction. For he was
false to the LORD his God, and en-
tered the temple of the LORD to burn
incense on the altar of incense. 17But
Azari´ah the priest went in after him,
with eighty priests of the LORD who
were men of valor; 18and they with-
stood King Uzzi´ah, and said to him,
"It is not for you, Uzzi´ah, to burn in-
cense to the LORD, but for the priests
the sons of Aaron, who are consecrat-
ed to burn incense. Go out of the sanc-
tuary; for you have done wrong, and
it will bring you no honor from the
LORD God." 19Then Uzzi´ah was an-
gry. Now he had a censer in his hand
to burn incense, and when he became
angry with the priests leprosy broke
out on his forehead, in the presence of
the priests in the house of the LORD,
by the altar of incense. 20And Azari´ah
the chief priest, and all the priests,
looked at him, and behold, he was lep-
rous in his forehead! And they thrust
him out quickly, and he himself has-
tened to go out, because the LORD had
smitten him. 21And King Uzzi´ah was
a leper to the day of his death, and be-
ing a leper dwelt in a separate house,
for he was excluded from the house
of the LORD. And Jotham his son was
over the king's household, governing
the people of the land.

22 Now the rest of the acts of
Uzzi´ah, from first to last, Isaiah
the prophet the son of Amoz wrote.
23And Uzzi´ah slept with his fathers,
and they buried him with his fathers
in the burial field which belonged to
the kings, for they said, "He is a lep-
er." And Jotham his son reigned in his
stead.

REIGN OF JOTHAM

27 Jotham was twenty-five years old when he began to reign, and he reigned sixteen years in Jerusalem. His mother's name was Jeru´shah the daughter of Zadok. 2 And he did what was right in the eyes of the LORD according to all that his father Uzzi´ah had done—only he did not invade the temple of the LORD. But the people still followed corrupt practices. 3 He built the upper gate of the house of the LORD, and did much building on the wall of Ophel. 4 Moreover he built cities in the hill country of Judah, and forts and towers on the wooded hills. 5 He fought with the king of the Ammonites and prevailed against them. And the Ammonites gave him that year a hundred talents of silver, and ten thousand cors of wheat and ten thousand of barley. The Ammonites paid him the same amount in the second and the third years. 6 So Jotham became mighty, because he ordered his ways before the LORD his God. 7 Now the rest of the acts of Jotham, and all his wars, and his ways, behold, they are written in the Book of the Kings of Israel and Judah. 8 He was twenty-five years old when he began to reign, and he reigned sixteen years in Jerusalem. 9 And Jotham slept with his fathers, and they buried him in the city of David; and Ahaz his son reigned in his stead.

REIGN OF AHAZ

28 Ahaz was twenty years old when he began to reign, and he reigned sixteen years in Jerusalem. And he did not do what was right in the eyes of the LORD, like his father David, 2 but walked in the ways of the kings of Israel. He even made molten images for the Ba´als; 3 and he burned incense in the valley of the son of Hinnom, and burned his sons as an offering, according to the abominable practices of the nations whom the LORD drove out before the people of Israel. 4 And he sacrificed and burned incense on the high places, and on the hills, and under every green tree.

ARAM AND ISRAEL DEFEAT JUDAH

5 Therefore the LORD his God gave him into the hand of the king of Syria, who defeated him and took captive a great number of his people and brought them to Damascus. He was also given into the hand of the king of Israel, who defeated him with great slaughter. 6 For Pekah the son of Remali´ah slew a hundred and twenty thousand in Judah in one day, all of them men of valor, because they had forsaken the LORD, the God of their fathers. 7 And Zichri, a mighty man of E´phraim, slew Ma-asei´ah the king's son and Azri´kam the commander of the palace and Elka´nah the next in authority to the king.

INTERVENTION OF ODED

8 The men of Israel took captive two hundred thousand of their kinsfolk, women, sons, and daughters; they also took much spoil from them and brought the spoil to Samar´ia. 9 But a prophet of the LORD was there, whose name was Oded; and he went out to meet the army that came to Samar´ia, and said to them, "Behold, because the LORD, the God of your fathers, was angry with Judah, he gave them into your hand, but you have slain them in a rage which has reached up to heaven. 10 And now you intend to subjugate the people of Judah and Jerusalem, male and female, as your slaves. Have you not sins of your own against the LORD your God? 11 Now hear me, and send back the captives from your kinsfolk whom you have taken, for the fierce wrath of the LORD is upon you." 12 Certain chiefs also of the men of E´phraim, Azari´ah the son of Joha´nan, Berechi´ah the son of Meshil´lemoth, Jehizki´ah the son of Shallum, and Ama´sa the son of Hadlai, stood up against those who were coming from the war, 13 and said to them, "You shall not bring the

captives in here, for you propose to
bring upon us guilt against the LORD
in addition to our present sins and
guilt. For our guilt is already great,
and there is fierce wrath against
Israel." 14 So the armed men left the
captives and the spoil before the
princes and all the assembly. 15 And
the men who have been mentioned by
name rose and took the captives, and
with the spoil they clothed all that
were naked among them; they clothed
them, gave them sandals, provided
them with food and drink, and anoint-
ed them; and carrying all the feeble
among them on asses, they brought
them to their kinsfolk at Jericho, the
city of palm trees. Then they returned
to Samar´ia.

ASSYRIA REFUSES TO HELP JUDAH

16 At that time King Ahaz sent
to the king[a] of Assyria for help. 17 For
the E´domites had again invaded and
defeated Judah, and carried away cap-
tives. 18 And the Philistines had made
raids on the cities in the Shephe´lah
and the Negeb of Judah, and had taken
Beth-she´mesh, Ai´jalon, Gede´roth,
Soco with its villages, Timnah with its
villages, and Gimzo with its villages;
and they settled there. 19 For the LORD
brought Judah low because of Ahaz
king of Israel, for he had dealt wan-
tonly in Judah and had been faithless
to the LORD. 20 So Til´gath-pilne´ser
king of Assyria came against him, and
afflicted him instead of strengthening
him. 21 For Ahaz took from the house
of the LORD and the house of the king
and of the princes, and gave tribute
to the king of Assyria; but it did not
help him.

APOSTASY AND DEATH OF AHAZ

22 In the time of his distress he be-
came yet more faithless to the LORD—
this same King Ahaz. 23 For he sacri-
ficed to the gods of Damascus which
had defeated him, and said, "Because
the gods of the kings of Syria helped
them, I will sacrifice to them that they
may help me." But they were the ruin
of him, and of all Israel. 24 And Ahaz
gathered together the vessels of the
house of God and cut in pieces the
vessels of the house of God, and he
shut up the doors of the house of the
LORD; and he made himself altars in
every corner of Jerusalem. 25 In every
city of Judah he made high places to
burn incense to other gods, provoking
to anger the LORD, the God of his fa-
thers. 26 Now the rest of his acts and
all his ways, from first to last, behold,
they are written in the Book of the
Kings of Judah and Israel. 27 And Ahaz
slept with his fathers, and they buried
him in the city, in Jerusalem, for they
did not bring him into the tombs of
the kings of Israel. And Hezeki´ah his
son reigned in his stead.

REIGN OF HEZEKIAH

29 Hezeki´ah began to reign when
he was twenty-five years old,
and he reigned twenty-nine years in
Jerusalem. His mother's name was
Abi´jah the daughter of Zechari´ah.
2 And he did what was right in the
eyes of the LORD, according to all that
David his father had done.

THE TEMPLE CLEANSED

3 In the first year of his reign, in
the first month, he opened the doors
of the house of the LORD, and repaired
them. 4 He brought in the priests and
the Levites, and assembled them in
the square on the east, 5 and said to
them, "Hear me, Levites! Now sancti-
fy yourselves, and sanctify the house
of the LORD, the God of your fathers,
and carry out the filth from the holy
place. 6 For our fathers have been un-
faithful and have done what was evil
in the sight of the LORD our God; they
have forsaken him, and have turned
away their faces from the habitation
of the LORD, and turned their backs.
7 They also shut the doors of the vesti-
bule and put out the lamps, and have

[a] Gk Syr Vg Compare 2Kings 16. 7: Heb *kings*

not burned incense or offered burnt
offerings in the holy place to the God
of Israel. 8Therefore the wrath of the
LORD came on Judah and Jerusalem,
and he has made them an object of
horror, of astonishment, and of hiss-
ing, as you see with your own eyes.
9For lo, our fathers have fallen by the
sword and our sons and our daughters
and our wives are in captivity for this.
10Now it is in my heart to make a cove-
nant with the LORD, the God of Israel,
that his fierce anger may turn away
from us. 11My sons, do not now be neg-
ligent, for the LORD has chosen you to
stand in his presence, to minister to
him, and to be his ministers and burn
incense to him."

12 Then the Levites arose, Mahath
the son of Ama´sai, and Jo´el the son
of Azari´ah, of the sons of the Ko´ha-
thites; and of the sons of Merar´i, Kish
the son of Abdi, and Azari´ah the son
of Jehal´lelel; and of the Gershonites,
Jo´ah the son of Zimmah, and Eden
the son of Jo´ah; 13and of the sons of
Eliza´phan, Shimri and Jeu´el; and
of the sons of Asaph, Zechari´ah
and Mattani´ah; 14and of the sons of
Heman, Jehu´el and Shim´e-i; and of
the sons of Jedu´thun, Shemai´ah and
Uz´ziel. 15They gathered their breth-
ren, and sanctified themselves, and
went in as the king had commanded,
by the words of the LORD, to cleanse
the house of the LORD. 16The priests
went into the inner part of the house
of the LORD to cleanse it, and they
brought out all the uncleanness that
they found in the temple of the LORD
into the court of the house of the
LORD; and the Levites took it and car-
ried it out to the brook Kidron. 17They
began to sanctify on the first day of
the first month, and on the eighth day
of the month they came to the vesti-
bule of the LORD; then for eight days
they sanctified the house of the LORD,
and on the sixteenth day of the first
month they finished. 18Then they went
in to Hezeki´ah the king and said,
"We have cleansed all the house of the
LORD, the altar of burnt offering and
all its utensils, and the table for the
showbread and all its utensils. 19All
the utensils which King Ahaz discard-
ed in his reign when he was faithless,
we have made ready and sanctified;
and behold, they are before the altar
of the LORD."

TEMPLE WORSHIP RESTORED

20 Then Hezeki´ah the king rose
early and gathered the officials of the
city, and went up to the house of the
LORD. 21And they brought seven bulls,
seven rams, seven lambs, and sev-
en he-goats for a sin offering for the
kingdom and for the sanctuary and for
Judah. And he commanded the priests
the sons of Aaron to offer them on
the altar of the LORD. 22So they killed
the bulls, and the priests received the
blood and threw it against the altar;
and they killed the rams and their
blood was thrown against the altar;
and they killed the lambs and their
blood was thrown against the altar.
23Then the he-goats for the sin offer-
ing were brought to the king and the
assembly, and they laid their hands
upon them, 24and the priests killed
them and made a sin offering with
their blood on the altar, to make
atonement for all Israel. For the king
commanded that the burnt offering
and the sin offering should be made
for all Israel.

25 And he stationed the Levites
in the house of the LORD with cym-
bals, harps, and lyres, according to
the commandment of David and of
Gad the king's seer and of Nathan the
prophet; for the commandment was
from the LORD through his proph-
ets. 26The Levites stood with the in-
struments of David, and the priests
with the trumpets. 27Then Hezeki´ah
commanded that the burnt offering
be offered on the altar. And when
the burnt offering began, the song to
the LORD began also, and the trum-
pets, accompanied by the instruments
of David king of Israel. 28The whole

assembly worshiped, and the singers
sang, and the trumpeters sounded; all
this continued until the burnt offering
was finished. 29When the offering was
finished, the king and all who were
present with him bowed themselves
and worshiped. 30And Hezeki´ah the
king and the princes commanded the
Levites to sing praises to the LORD
with the words of David and of Asaph
the seer. And they sang praises with
gladness, and they bowed down and
worshiped.
31 Then Hezeki´ah said, "You have
now consecrated yourselves to the
LORD; come near, bring sacrifices and
thank offerings to the house of the
LORD." And the assembly brought
sacrifices and thank offerings; and all
who were of a willing heart brought
burnt offerings. 32The number of the
burnt offerings which the assembly
brought was seventy bulls, a hundred
rams, and two hundred lambs; all
these were for a burnt offering to the
LORD. 33And the consecrated offer-
ings were six hundred bulls and three
thousand sheep. 34But the priests were
too few and could not flay all the
burnt offerings, so until other priests
had sanctified themselves their breth-
ren the Levites helped them, until the
work was finished—for the Levites
were more upright in heart than the
priests in sanctifying themselves.
35Besides the great number of burnt
offerings there was the fat of the
peace offerings, and there were the
libations for the burnt offerings. Thus
the service of the house of the LORD
was restored. 36And Hezeki´ah and all
the people rejoiced because of what
God had done for the people; for the
thing came about suddenly.

THE GREAT PASSOVER

30 Hezeki´ah sent to all Israel and
Judah, and wrote letters also to
E´phraim and Manas´seh, that they
should come to the house of the
LORD at Jerusalem, to keep the pass-
over* to the LORD the God of Israel.
2For the king and his princes and all
the assembly in Jerusalem had taken
counsel to keep the passover in the
second month 3for they could not
keep it in its time because the priests
had not sanctified themselves in suf-
ficient number, nor had the people
assembled in Jerusalem 4and the plan
seemed right to the king and all the
assembly. 5So they decreed to make
a proclamation throughout all Israel,
from Beer-sheba to Dan, that the peo-
ple should come and keep the pass-
over to the LORD the God of Israel,
at Jerusalem; for they had not kept it
in great numbers as prescribed. 6So
couriers went throughout all Israel
and Judah with letters from the king
and his princes, as the king had
commanded, saying, "O people of
Israel, return to the LORD, the God
of Abraham, Isaac, and Israel, that he
may turn again to the remnant of you
who have escaped from the hand of
the kings of Assyria. 7Do not be like
your fathers and your brethren, who
were faithless to the LORD God of
their fathers, so that he made them
a desolation, as you see. 8Do not now
be stiff-necked as your fathers were,
but yield yourselves to the LORD,
and come to his sanctuary, which he
has sanctified for ever, and serve the
LORD your God, that his fierce anger
may turn away from you. 9For if you
return to the LORD, your brethren
and your children will find compas-
sion with their captors, and return to
this land. For the LORD your God is
gracious and merciful, and will not
turn away his face from you, if you
return to him."
10 So the couriers went from
city to city through the country of
E´phraim and Manas´seh, and as far
as Zeb´ulun; but they laughed them
to scorn, and mocked them. 11Only a
few men of Asher, of Manas´seh, and
of Zeb´ulun humbled themselves and
came to Jerusalem. 12The hand of God
was also upon Judah to give them one
heart to do what the king and the

princes commanded by the word of
the LORD.
13 And many people came together
in Jerusalem to keep the feast of un-
leavened bread in the second month, a
very great assembly. 14They set to work
and removed the altars that were in
Jerusalem, and all the altars for burn-
ing incense they took away and threw
into the Kidron valley. 15And they
killed the passover lamb on the four-
teenth day of the second month. And
the priests and the Levites were put to
shame, so that they sanctified them-
selves, and brought burnt offerings
into the house of the LORD. 16They
took their accustomed posts accord-
ing to the law of Moses the man of
God; the priests sprinkled the blood
which they received from the hand of
the Levites. 17For there were many in
the assembly who had not sanctified
themselves; therefore the Levites had
to kill the passover lamb for every one
who was not clean, to make it holy
to the LORD. 18For a multitude of the
people, many of them from E´phraim,
Manas´seh, Is´sachar, and Zeb´ulun,
had not cleansed themselves, yet they
ate the passover otherwise than as
prescribed. For Hezeki´ah had prayed
for them, saying, "The good LORD
pardon every one 19who sets his heart
to seek God, the LORD the God of his
fathers, even though not according to
the sanctuary's rules of cleanness."
20And the LORD heard Hezeki´ah, and
healed the people. 21And the people of
Israel that were present at Jerusalem
kept the feast of unleavened bread
seven days with great gladness; and
the Levites and the priests praised
the LORD day by day, singing with
all their might[a] to the LORD. 22And
Hezeki´ah spoke encouragingly to all
the Levites who showed good skill in
the service of the LORD. So the people
ate the food of the festival for seven
days, sacrificing peace offerings and
giving thanks to the LORD the God of
their fathers.
23 Then the whole assembly agreed
together to keep the feast for anoth-
er seven days; so they kept it for an-
other seven days with gladness. 24For
Hezeki´ah king of Judah gave the as-
sembly a thousand bulls and seven
thousand sheep for offerings, and the
princes gave the assembly a thousand
bulls and ten thousand sheep. And the
priests sanctified themselves in great
numbers. 25The whole assembly of
Judah, and the priests and the Levites,
and the whole assembly that came out
of Israel, and the sojourners who came
out of the land of Israel, and the so-
journers who dwelt in Judah, rejoiced.
26So there was great joy in Jerusalem,
for since the time of Solomon the son
of David king of Israel there had been
nothing like this in Jerusalem. 27Then
the priests and the Levites arose and
blessed the people, and their voice
was heard, and their prayer came to
his holy habitation in heaven.

PAGAN SHRINES DESTROYED

31 Now when all this was finished,
all Israel who were present went
out to the cities of Judah and broke in
pieces the pillars and hewed down the
Ashe´rim and broke down the high
places and the altars throughout all
Judah and Benjamin, and in E´phraim
and Manas´seh, until they had de-
stroyed them all. Then all the people
of Israel returned to their cities, every
man to his possession.
2 And Hezeki´ah appointed the
divisions of the priests and of the
Levites, division by division, each
according to his service, the priests
and the Levites, for burnt offerings
and peace offerings, to minister in the
gates of the camp of the LORD and to
give thanks and praise. 3The contri-
bution of the king from his own pos-
sessions was for the burnt offerings:
the burnt offerings of morning and
evening, and the burnt offerings for
the sabbaths, the new moons, and the
appointed feasts, as it is written in the

[a]Compare 1Chron 13. 8: Heb *with instruments of might*

law of the LORD. 4And he commanded
the people who lived in Jerusalem to
give the portion due to the priests and
the Levites, that they might give them-
selves to the law of the LORD. 5As soon
as the command was spread abroad,
the people of Israel gave in abundance
the first fruits of grain, wine, oil, hon-
ey, and of all the produce of the field;
and they brought in abundantly the
tithe of everything. 6And the people of
Israel and Judah who lived in the cit-
ies of Judah also brought in the tithe
of cattle and sheep, and the dedicated
things[b] which had been consecrated
to the LORD their God, and laid them
in heaps. 7In the third month they be-
gan to pile up the heaps, and finished
them in the seventh month. 8When
Hezeki´ah and the princes came and
saw the heaps, they blessed the LORD
and his people Israel. 9And Hezeki´ah
questioned the priests and the Levites
about the heaps. 10Azari´ah the chief
priest, who was of the house of Za-
dok, answered him, "Since they began
to bring the contributions into the
house of the LORD we have eaten and
had enough and have plenty left; for
the LORD has blessed his people, so
that we have this great store left."

REORGANIZATION OF PRIESTS AND LEVITES

11 Then Hezeki´ah command-
ed them to prepare chambers in the
house of the LORD; and they prepared
them. 12And they faithfully brought
in the contributions, the tithes and
the dedicated things. The chief offi-
cer in charge of them was Conani´ah
the Levite, with Shim´e-i his brother
as second; 13while Jehi´el, Azazi´ah,
Nahath, As´ahel, Jer´imoth, Jo´zabad,
Eli´el, Ismachi´ah, Mahath, and Bena-
i´ah were overseers assisting Conan-
i´ah and Shim´e-i his brother, by the
appointment of Hezeki´ah the king
and Azari´ah the chief officer of the
house of God. 14And Kor´e the son of
Imnah the Levite, keeper of the east
gate, was over the freewill offerings to
God, to apportion the contribution re-
served for the LORD and the most holy
offerings. 15Eden, Mini´amin, Jeshua,
Shemai´ah, Amari´ah, and Shecani´ah
were faithfully assisting him in the
cities of the priests, to distribute the
portions to their brethren, old and
young alike, by divisions, 16except
those enrolled by genealogy, males
from three years old and upwards, all
who entered the house of the LORD as
the duty of each day required, for their
service according to their offices, by
their divisions. 17The enrollment of
the priests was according to their fa-
thers' houses; that of the Levites from
twenty years old and upwards was ac-
cording to their offices, by their divi-
sions. 18The priests were enrolled with
all their little children, their wives,
their sons, and their daughters, the
whole multitude; for they were faith-
ful in keeping themselves holy. 19And
for the sons of Aaron, the priests, who
were in the fields of common land be-
longing to their cities, there were men
in the several cities who were desig-
nated by name to distribute portions
to every male among the priests and
to every one among the Levites who
was enrolled.

20 Thus Hezeki´ah did through-
out all Judah; and he did what was
good and right and faithful before
the LORD his God. 21And every work
that he undertook in the service of
the house of God and in accordance
with the law and the commandments,
seeking his God, he did with all his
heart, and prospered.

SENNACHERIB'S INVASION

32 After these things and these acts
of faithfulness Sennach´erib king
of Assyria came and invaded Judah
and encamped against the fortified
cities, thinking to win them for him-
self. 2And when Hezeki´ah saw that
Sennach´erib had come and intended
to fight against Jerusalem, 3he planned
with his officers and his mighty men

[b]Heb *the tithe of the dedicated things*

to stop the water of the springs that
were outside the city; and they helped
him. 4 A great many people were gath-
ered, and they stopped all the springs
and the brook that flowed through the
land, saying, "Why should the kings
of Assyria come and find much wa-
ter?" 5 He set to work resolutely and
built up all the wall that was broken
down, and raised towers upon it,[a]
and outside it he built another wall;
and he strengthened the Millo in the
city of David. He also made weapons
and shields in abundance. 6 And he set
combat commanders over the people,
and gathered them together to him in
the square at the gate of the city and
spoke encouragingly to them, saying,
7 "Be strong and of good courage. Do
not be afraid or dismayed before the
king of Assyria and all the horde that
is with him; for there is one greater
with us than with him. 8 With him is
an arm of flesh; but with us is the
LORD our God, to help us and to fight
our battles." And the people took con-
fidence from the words of Hezeki´ah
king of Judah.

9 After this Sennach´erib king of
Assyria, who was besieging Lachish
with all his forces, sent his servants
to Jerusalem to Hezeki´ah king of
Judah and to all the people of Ju-
dah that were in Jerusalem, saying,
10 "Thus says Sennach´erib king of As-
syria, 'On what are you relying, that
you stand siege in Jerusalem? 11 Is not
Hezeki´ah misleading you, that he
may give you over to die by famine
and by thirst, when he tells you, "The
LORD our God will deliver us from
the hand of the king of Assyria"?
12 Has not this same Hezeki´ah taken
away his high places and his altars
and commanded Judah and Jeru-
salem, "Before one altar you shall
worship, and upon it you shall burn
your sacrifices"? 13 Do you not know
what I and my fathers have done to
all the peoples of other lands? Were
the gods of the nations of those lands
at all able to deliver their lands out of
my hand? 14 Who among all the gods
of those nations which my fathers ut-
terly destroyed was able to deliver his
people from my hand, that your God
should be able to deliver you from my
hand? 15 Now therefore do not let He-
zeki´ah deceive you or mislead you in
this fashion, and do not believe him,
for no god of any nation or kingdom
has been able to deliver his people
from my hand or from the hand of my
fathers. How much less will your God
deliver you out of my hand!'"

16 And his servants said still more
against the Lord GOD and against his
servant Hezeki´ah. 17 And he wrote
letters to cast contempt on the LORD
the God of Israel and to speak against
him, saying, "Like the gods of the na-
tions of the lands who have not deliv-
ered their people from my hands, so
the God of Hezeki´ah will not deliv-
er his people from my hand." 18 And
they shouted it with a loud voice in
the language of Judah to the people
of Jerusalem who were upon the wall,
to frighten and terrify them, in order
that they might take the city. 19 And
they spoke of the God of Jerusalem as
they spoke of the gods of the peoples
of the earth, which are the work of
men's hands.

SENNACHERIB'S DEFEAT AND DEATH

20 Then Hezeki´ah the king and
Isaiah the prophet, the son of Amoz,
prayed because of this and cried to
heaven. 21 And the LORD sent an an-
gel, who cut off all the mighty war-
riors and commanders and officers
in the camp of the king of Assyria.
So he returned with shame of face to
his own land. And when he came into
the house of his god, some of his own
sons struck him down there with the
sword. 22 So the LORD saved Hezeki´ah
and the inhabitants of Jerusalem from
the hand of Sennach´erib king of
Assyria and from the hand of all his
enemies; and he gave them rest on

[a] Vg: Heb *and raised upon the towers*

every side. 23And many brought gifts
to the LORD to Jerusalem and precious
things to Hezeki´ah king of Judah, so
that he was exalted in the sight of all
nations from that time onward.

HEZEKIAH'S SICKNESS

24 In those days Hezeki´ah became
sick and was at the point of death,
and he prayed to the LORD; and he
answered him and gave him a sign.
25But Hezeki´ah did not make return
according to the benefit done to him,
for his heart was proud. Therefore
wrath came upon him and Judah and
Jerusalem. 26But Hezeki´ah humbled
himself for the pride of his heart, both
he and the inhabitants of Jerusalem,
so that the wrath of the LORD did
not come upon them in the days of
Hezeki´ah.

HEZEKIAH'S PROSPERITY AND ACHIEVEMENTS

27 And Hezeki´ah had very great
riches and honor; and he made for
himself treasuries for silver, for gold,
for precious stones, for spices, for
shields, and for all kinds of costly ves-
sels; 28storehouses also for the yield of
grain, wine, and oil; and stalls for all
kinds of cattle, and sheepfolds. 29He
likewise provided cities for himself,
and flocks and herds in abundance;
for God had given him very great
possessions. 30This same Hezeki´ah
closed the upper outlet of the waters
of Gihon and directed them down to
the west side of the city of David. And
Hezeki´ah prospered in all his works.
31And so in the matter of the envoys
of the princes of Babylon, who had
been sent to him to inquire about the
sign that had been done in the land,
God left him to himself, in order to
try him and to know all that was in
his heart.

32 Now the rest of the acts of
Hezeki´ah, and his good deeds, be-
hold, they are written in the vision of
Isaiah the prophet the son of Amoz,
in the Book of the Kings of Judah and
Israel. 33And Hezeki´ah slept with his
fathers, and they buried him in the as-
cent of the tombs of the sons of David;
and all Judah and the inhabitants of
Jerusalem did him honor at his death.
And Manas´seh his son reigned in his
stead.

REIGN OF MANASSEH

33 Manas´seh was twelve years old
when he began to reign, and he
reigned fifty-five years in Jerusalem.
2He did what was evil in the sight of
the LORD, according to the abomina-
ble practices of the nations whom the
LORD drove out before the people of
Israel. 3For he rebuilt the high plac-
es which his father Hezeki´ah had
broken down, and erected altars to
the Ba´als, and made Ashe´rahs, and
worshiped all the host of heaven, and
served them. 4And he built altars in
the house of the LORD, of which the
LORD had said, "In Jerusalem shall
my name be for ever." 5And he built
altars for all the host of heaven in the
two courts of the house of the LORD.
6And he burned his sons as an offer-
ing in the valley of the son of Hinnom,
and practiced soothsaying and augury
and sorcery, and dealt with mediums
and with wizards. He did much evil
in the sight of the LORD, provoking
him to anger. 7And the image of the
idol which he had made he set in the
house of God, of which God said to
David and to Solomon his son, "In
this house, and in Jerusalem, which
I have chosen out of all the tribes of
Israel, I will put my name for ever;
8and I will no more remove the foot of
Israel from the land which I appointed
for your fathers, if only they will be
careful to do all that I have command-
ed them, all the law, the statutes, and
the ordinances given through Moses."
9Manas´seh seduced Judah and the in-
habitants of Jerusalem, so that they
did more evil than the nations whom
the LORD destroyed before the people
of Israel.

MANASSEH RESTORED AFTER REPENTANCE

10 The LORD spoke to Manas´seh
and to his people, but they gave no
heed. 11Therefore the LORD brought
upon them the commanders of the
army of the king of Assyria, who took
Manas´seh with hooks and bound him
with fetters of bronze and brought
him to Babylon.* 12And when he was
in distress he entreated the favor of
the LORD his God and humbled him-
self greatly before the God of his fa-
thers. 13He prayed to him, and God
received his entreaty and heard his
supplication and brought him again
to Jerusalem into his kingdom. Then
Manas´seh knew that the LORD was
God.

14 Afterwards he built an out-
er wall for the city of David west of
Gihon, in the valley, and for the en-
trance into the Fish Gate, and carried
it round Ophel, and raised it to a very
great height; he also put commanders
of the army in all the fortified cities
in Judah. 15And he took away the for-
eign gods and the idol from the house
of the LORD, and all the altars that
he had built on the mountain of the
house of the LORD and in Jerusalem,
and he threw them outside of the
city. 16He also restored the altar of
the LORD and offered upon it sacri-
fices of peace offerings and of thanks-
giving; and he commanded Judah to
serve the LORD the God of Israel.
17Nevertheless the people still sacri-
ficed at the high places, but only to
the LORD their God.

DEATH OF MANASSEH

18 Now the rest of the acts of
Manas´seh, and his prayer* to his
God, and the words of the seers
who spoke to him in the name of the
LORD the God of Israel, behold, they
are in the Chronicles of the Kings of
Israel. 19And his prayer, and how God
received his entreaty, and all his sin
and his faithlessness, and the sites
on which he built high places and
set up the Ashe´rim and the images,
before he humbled himself, behold,
they are written in the Chronicles of
the Seers.[a] 20So Manas´seh slept with
his fathers, and they buried him in his
house; and Amon his son reigned in
his stead.

AMON'S REIGN AND DEATH

21 Amon was twenty-two years
old when he began to reign, and he
reigned two years in Jerusalem. 22He
did what was evil in the sight of the
LORD, as Manas´seh his father had
done. Amon sacrificed to all the im-
ages that Manas´seh his father had
made, and served them. 23And he did
not humble himself before the LORD,
as Manas´seh his father had humbled
himself, but this Amon incurred guilt
more and more. 24And his servants
conspired against him and killed him
in his house. 25But the people of the
land slew all those who had conspired
against King Amon; and the people of
the land made Josi´ah his son king in
his stead.

REIGN OF JOSIAH

34 Josi´ah was eight years old when
he began to reign, and he reigned
thirty-one years in Jerusalem. 2He
did what was right in the eyes of the
LORD, and walked in the ways of
David his father; and he did not turn
aside to the right or to the left. 3For
in the eighth year of his reign, while
he was yet a boy, he began to seek the
God of David his father; and in the
twelfth year he began to purge Judah
and Jerusalem of the high places, the
Ashe´rim, and the graven and the mol-
ten images. 4And they broke down the
altars of the Ba´als in his presence;
and he hewed down the incense altars
which stood above them; and he broke
in pieces the Ashe´rim and the graven
and the molten images, and he made
dust of them and strewed it over the
graves of those who had sacrificed to
them. 5He also burned the bones of

[a]One Ms: Gk: Heb *of Hozai*

the priests on their altars, and purged
Judah and Jerusalem. 6And in the cities
of Manas´seh, E´phraim, and Simeon,
and as far as Naph´tali, in their ruins[b]
round about, 7he broke down the al-
tars, and beat the Ashe´rim and the
images into powder, and hewed down
all the incense altars throughout all
the land of Israel. Then he returned
to Jerusalem.

DISCOVERY OF THE BOOK OF THE LAW

8 Now in the eighteenth year of
his reign, when he had purged the
land and the house, he sent Shaphan
the son of Azali´ah, and Ma-asei´ah
the governor of the city, and Jo´ah
the son of Jo´ahaz, the recorder, to
repair the house of the LORD his
God. 9They came to Hilki´ah the high
priest and delivered the money that
had been brought into the house of
God, which the Levites, the keepers
of the threshold, had collected from
Manas´seh and E´phraim and from
all the remnant of Israel and from all
Judah and Benjamin and from the in-
habitants of Jerusalem. 10They deliv-
ered it to the workmen who had the
oversight of the house of the LORD;
and the workmen who were working
in the house of the LORD gave it for
repairing and restoring the house.
11They gave it to the carpenters and
the builders to buy quarried stone,
and timber for binders and beams
for the buildings which the kings of
Judah had let go to ruin. 12And the
men did the work faithfully. Over
them were set Jahath and Obadi´ah
the Levites, of the sons of Merar´i,
and Zechari´ah and Meshul´lam, of
the sons of the Ko´hathites, to have
oversight. The Levites, all who were
skilful with instruments of music,
13were over the burden bearers and
directed all who did work in every
kind of service; and some of the
Levites were scribes, and officials,
and gatekeepers.

14 While they were bringing out
the money that had been brought
into the house of the LORD, Hilki´ah
the priest found the book of the law
of the LORD given through Moses.
15Then Hilki´ah said to Shaphan
the secretary, "I have found the
book of the law in the house of the
LORD"; and Hilki´ah gave the book to
Shaphan. 16Shaphan brought the book
to the king, and further reported to
the king, "All that was committed to
your servants they are doing. 17They
have emptied out the money that was
found in the house of the LORD and
have delivered it into the hand of the
overseers and the workmen." 18Then
Shaphan the secretary told the king,
"Hilki´ah the priest has given me a
book." And Shaphan read it before
the king.

19 When the king heard the
words of the law he rent his clothes.
20And the king commanded Hilki´ah,
Ahi´kam the son of Shaphan, Abdon
the son of Micah, Shaphan the secre-
tary, and Asai´ah the king's servant,
saying, 21"Go, inquire of the LORD for
me and for those who are left in Israel
and in Judah, concerning the words
of the book that has been found; for
great is the wrath of the LORD that is
poured out on us, because our fathers
have not kept the word of the LORD,
to do according to all that is written
in this book."

THE PROPHET HULDAH CONSULTED

22 So Hilki´ah and those whom
the king had sent[c] went to Huldah the
prophetess, the wife of Shallum the
son of Tokhath, son of Hasrah, keep-
er of the wardrobe (now she dwelt
in Jerusalem in the Second Quarter)
and spoke to her to that effect. 23And
she said to them, "Thus says the
LORD, the God of Israel: 'Tell the man
who sent you to me, 24Thus says the
LORD, Behold, I will bring evil upon
this place and upon its inhabitants,

[b]Heb uncertain
[c]Syr Vg: Heb lacks *had sent*

all the curses that are written in the book which was read before the king of Judah. 25 Because they have forsaken me and have burned incense to other gods, that they might provoke me to anger with all the works of their hands, therefore my wrath will be poured out upon this place and will not be quenched. 26 But to the king of Judah, who sent you to inquire of the LORD, thus shall you say to him, Thus says the LORD, the God of Israel: Regarding the words which you have heard, 27 because your heart was penitent and you humbled yourself before God when you heard his words against this place and its inhabitants, and you have humbled yourself before me, and have rent your clothes and wept before me, I also have heard you, says the LORD. 28 Behold, I will gather you to your fathers, and you shall be gathered to your grave in peace, and your eyes shall not see all the evil which I will bring upon this place and its inhabitants.'" And they brought back word to the king.

THE COVENANT RENEWED

29 Then the king sent and gathered together all the elders of Judah and Jerusalem. 30 And the king went up to the house of the LORD, with all the men of Judah and the inhabitants of Jerusalem and the priests and the Levites, all the people both great and small; and he read in their hearing all the words of the book of the covenant which had been found in the house of the LORD. 31 And the king stood in his place and made a covenant before the LORD, to walk after the LORD and to keep his commandments and his testimonies and his statutes, with all his heart and all his soul, to perform the words of the covenant that were written in this book. 32 Then he made all who were present in Jerusalem and in Benjamin stand to it. And the inhabitants of Jerusalem did according to the covenant of God, the God of their fathers. 33 And Josi'ah took away all the abominations from all the territory that belonged to the people of Israel, and made all who were in Israel serve the LORD their God. All his days they did not turn away from following the LORD the God of their fathers.

CELEBRATION OF THE PASSOVER

35 Josi'ah kept a passover to the LORD in Jerusalem; and they killed the passover lamb on the fourteenth day of the first month. 2 He appointed the priests to their offices and encouraged them in the service of the house of the LORD. 3 And he said to the Levites who taught all Israel and who were holy to the LORD, "Put the holy ark in the house which Solomon the son of David, king of Israel, built; you need no longer carry it upon your shoulders. Now serve the LORD your God and his people Israel. 4 Prepare yourselves according to your fathers' houses by your divisions, following the directions of David king of Israel and the directions of Solomon his son. 5 And stand in the holy place according to the groupings of the fathers' houses of your brethren the lay people, and let there be for each a part of a father's house of the Levites.[a] 6 And kill the passover lamb, and sanctify yourselves, and prepare for your brethren, to do according to the word of the LORD by Moses."

7 Then Josi'ah contributed to the lay people, as passover offerings for all that were present, lambs and kids from the flock to the number of thirty thousand, and three thousand bulls; these were from the king's possessions. 8 And his princes contributed willingly to the people, to the priests, and to the Levites. Hilki'ah, Zechari'ah, and Jehi'el, the chief officers of the house of God, gave to the priests for the passover offerings two

[a] Heb obscure

thousand six hundred lambs and kids
and three hundred bulls. 9Conani´ah
also, and Shemai´ah and Nethan´el
his brothers, and Hashabi´ah and
Je-i´el and Jo´zabad, the chiefs of
the Levites, gave to the Levites for
the passover offerings five thousand
lambs and kids and five hundred
bulls.

10 When the service had been pre-
pared for, the priests stood in their
place, and the Levites in their divi-
sions according to the king's com-
mand. 11And they killed the passover
lamb, and the priests sprinkled the
blood which they received from them
while the Levites flayed the victims.
12And they set aside the burnt offer-
ings that they might distribute them
according to the groupings of the
fathers' houses of the lay people, to
offer to the LORD, as it is written in
the book of Moses. And so they did
with the bulls. 13And they roasted the
passover lamb with fire according to
the ordinance; and they boiled the
holy offerings in pots, in caldrons,
and in pans, and carried them quickly
to all the lay people. 14And afterward
they prepared for themselves and for
the priests, because the priests the
sons of Aaron were busied in offering
the burnt offerings and the fat parts
until night; so the Levites prepared
for themselves and for the priests the
sons of Aaron. 15The singers, the sons
of Asaph, were in their place accord-
ing to the command of David, and
Asaph, and Heman, and Jedu´thun
the king's seer; and the gatekeepers
were at each gate; they did not need
to depart from their service, for their
brethren the Levites prepared for
them.

16 So all the service of the LORD
was prepared that day, to keep the
passover and to offer burnt offerings
on the altar of the LORD, according to
the command of King Josi´ah. 17And
the people of Israel who were present
kept the passover at that time, and the
feast of unleavened bread seven days.
18No passover like it had been kept in
Israel since the days of Samuel the
prophet; none of the kings of Israel
had kept such a passover as was kept
by Josi´ah, and the priests and the
Levites, and all Judah and Israel who
were present, and the inhabitants of
Jerusalem. 19In the eighteenth year of
the reign of Josi´ah this passover was
kept.

DEFEAT BY PHARAOH NECO AND DEATH OF JOSIAH

20 After all this, when Josi´ah had
prepared the temple, Neco king of
Egypt went up to fight at Car´chemish
on the Euphra´tes and Josi´ah went
out against him. 21But he sent envoys
to him, saying, "What have we to do
with each other, king of Judah? I am
not coming against you this day, but
against the house with which I am
at war; and God has commanded me
to make haste. Cease opposing God,
who is with me, lest he destroy you."
22Nevertheless Josi´ah would not turn
away from him, but disguised himself
in order to fight with him. He did not
listen to the words of Neco from the
mouth of God, but joined battle in the
plain of Megid´do. 23And the archers
shot King Josi´ah; and the king said
to his servants, "Take me away, for I
am badly wounded." 24So his servants
took him out of the chariot and car-
ried him in his second chariot and
brought him to Jerusalem. And he
died, and was buried in the tombs of
his fathers. All Judah and Jerusalem
mourned for Josi´ah. 25Jeremiah also
uttered a lament for Josi´ah; and all
the singing men and singing wom-
en have spoken of Josi´ah in their
laments to this day. They made these
an ordinance in Israel; behold, they
are written in the Laments. 26Now the
rest of the acts of Josi´ah, and his good
deeds according to what is written in
the law of the LORD, 27and his acts,
first and last, behold, they are written
in the Book of the Kings of Israel and
Judah.

REIGN OF JEHOAHAZ

36 The people of the land took Jeho'ahaz the son of Josi'ah and made him king in his father's stead in Jerusalem. 2 Jeho'ahaz was twenty-three years old when he began to reign; and he reigned three months in Jerusalem. 3 Then the king of Egypt deposed him in Jerusalem and laid upon the land a tribute of a hundred talents of silver and a talent of gold. 4 And the king of Egypt made Eli'akim his brother king over Judah and Jerusalem, and changed his name to Jehoi'akim; but Neco took Jeho'ahaz his brother and carried him to Egypt.

REIGN AND CAPTIVITY OF JEHOIAKIM

5 Jehoi'akim was twenty-five years old when he began to reign, and he reigned eleven years in Jerusalem. He did what was evil in the sight of the LORD his God. 6 Against him came up Nebuchadnez'zar king of Babylon, and bound him in fetters to take him to Babylon. 7 Nebuchadnez'zar also carried part of the vessels of the house of the LORD to Babylon and put them in his palace in Babylon. 8 Now the rest of the acts of Jehoi'akim, and the abominations which he did, and what was found against him, behold, they are written in the Book of the Kings of Israel and Judah; and Jehoi'achin his son reigned in his stead.

REIGN AND CAPTIVITY OF JEHOIACHIN

9 Jehoi'achin was eight years old when he began to reign, and he reigned three months and ten days in Jerusalem. He did what was evil in the sight of the LORD. 10 In the spring of the year King Nebuchadnez'zar sent and brought him to Babylon, with the precious vessels of the house of the LORD, and made his brother Zedeki'ah king over Judah and Jerusalem.

REIGN OF ZEDEKIAH

11 Zedeki'ah was twenty-one years old when he began to reign, and he reigned eleven years in Jerusalem. 12 He did what was evil in the sight of the LORD his God. He did not humble himself before Jeremiah the prophet, who spoke from the mouth of the LORD. 13 He also rebelled against King Nebuchadnez'zar, who had made him swear by God; he stiffened his neck and hardened his heart against turning to the LORD, the God of Israel. 14 All the leading priests and the people likewise were exceedingly unfaithful, following all the abominations of the nations; and they polluted the house of the LORD which he had hallowed in Jerusalem.

THE FALL OF JERUSALEM

15 The LORD, the God of their fathers, sent persistently to them by his messengers, because he had compassion on his people and on his dwelling place; 16 but they kept mocking the messengers of God, despising his words, and scoffing at his prophets, till the wrath of the LORD rose against his people, till there was no remedy.

17 Therefore he brought up against them the king of the Chalde'ans, who slew their young men with the sword in the house of their sanctuary, and had no compassion on young man or virgin, old man or aged; he gave them all into his hand. 18 And all the vessels of the house of God, great and small, and the treasures of the house of the LORD, and the treasures of the king and of his princes, all these he brought to Babylon. 19 And they burned the house of God, and broke down the wall of Jerusalem, and burned all its palaces with fire, and destroyed all its precious vessels. 20 He took into exile in Babylon those who had escaped from the sword, and they became servants to him and to his sons until the establishment of the kingdom of Persia, 21 to fulfil the word of the LORD by the mouth of Jeremiah, until the land had enjoyed its sabbaths. All the days that it lay desolate it kept sabbath, to fulfil seventy years.

CYRUS PROCLAIMS LIBERTY FOR THE EXILES

22 Now in the first year of Cyrus
king of Persia, that the word of the
LORD by the mouth of Jeremiah
might be accomplished, the LORD
stirred up the spirit of Cyrus king of
Persia so that he made a proclamation throughout all his kingdom and
also put it in writing: 23"Thus says
Cyrus king of Persia, 'The LORD, the
God of heaven, has given me all the
kingdoms of the earth, and he has
charged me to build him a house at
Jerusalem, which is in Judah. Whoever is among you of all his people,
may the LORD his God be with him.
Let him go up.'"

THE BOOK OF
EZRA

END OF THE BABYLONIAN CAPTIVITY

1 In the first year of Cyrus king of
Persia, that the word of the LORD
by the mouth of Jeremiah might be
accomplished, the LORD stirred up
the spirit of Cyrus king of Persia so
that he made a proclamation through-
out all his kingdom and also put it in
writing:
2 "Thus says Cyrus king of Persia:*
The LORD, the God of heaven, has giv-
en me all the kingdoms of the earth,
and he has charged me to build him
a house at Jerusalem, which is in
Judah. 3Whoever is among you of all
his people, may his God be with him,
and let him go up to Jerusalem, which
is in Judah, and rebuild the house of
the LORD, the God of Israel—he is the
God who is in Jerusalem; 4and let each
survivor, in whatever place he so-
journs, be assisted by the men of his
place with silver and gold, with goods
and with beasts, besides freewill of-
ferings for the house of God which is
in Jerusalem."
5 Then rose up the heads of the fa-
thers' houses of Judah and Benjamin,
and the priests and the Levites, every
one whose spirit God had stirred to go
up to rebuild the house of the LORD
which is in Jerusalem; 6and all who
were about them aided them with ves-
sels of silver, with gold, with goods,
with beasts, and with costly wares,
besides all that was freely offered.
7Cyrus the king also brought out
the vessels of the house of the LORD
which Nebuchadnez'zar had carried
away from Jerusalem and placed in
the house of his gods. 8Cyrus king of
Persia brought these out in charge
of Mith'redath the treasurer, who
counted them out to Shesh-baz'zar
the prince of Judah. 9And this was the
number of them: a thousand[a] basins
of gold, a thousand basins of silver,
twenty-nine censers, 10thirty bowls of
gold, two thousand[b] four hundred and
ten bowls of silver, and a thousand
other vessels; 11all the vessels of gold
and of silver were five thousand four
hundred and sixty-nine.[c] All these did
Shesh-baz'zar bring up, when the ex-
iles were brought up from Babylonia
to Jerusalem.

LIST OF THE RETURNED EXILES

2 Now these were the people of
the province who came up out of
the captivity of those exiles whom
Nebuchadnez'zar the king of Babylon
had carried captive to Babylonia; they
returned to Jerusalem and Judah, each
to his own town. 2They came with
Zerub'babel, Jeshua, Nehemi'ah, Se-
rai'ah, Reel-ai'ah, Mor'decai, Bilshan,
Mispar, Big'vai, Rehum, and Ba'anah.
The number of the men of the
people of Israel: 3the sons of Parosh,
two thousand one hundred and sev-
enty-two. 4The sons of Shephati'ah,
three hundred and seventy-two. 5The
sons of Arah, seven hundred and
seventy-five. 6The sons of Pa'hath-
mo'ab, namely the sons of Jeshua and
Jo'ab, two thousand eight hundred
and twelve. 7The sons of Elam, one
thousand two hundred and fifty-four.
8The sons of Zattu, nine hundred
and forty-five. 9The sons of Zac'cai,
seven hundred and sixty. 10The sons
of Bani, six hundred and forty-two.
11The sons of Be'bai, six hundred and
twenty-three. 12The sons of Azgad,
one thousand two hundred and twen-
ty-two. 13The sons of Adoni'kam, six
hundred and sixty-six. 14The sons of
Big'vai, two thousand and fifty-six.
15The sons of Adin, four hundred and

[a] 1Esdras 2.13: Heb *thirty*
[b] 1Esdras 2.13: Heb *of a second sort*
[c] 1Esdras 2.14: Heb *five thousand four hundred*

fifty-four. **16**The sons of Ater, name-
ly of Hezeki´ah, ninety-eight. **17**The
sons of Be´zai, three hundred and
twenty-three. **18**The sons of Jorah,
one hundred and twelve. **19**The sons
of Hashum, two hundred and twen-
ty-three. **20**The sons of Gibbar, nine-
ty-five. **21**The sons of Bethlehem, one
hundred and twenty-three. **22**The men
of Neto´phah, fifty-six. **23**The men of
An´athoth, one hundred and twen-
ty-eight. **24**The sons of Az´maveth, for-
ty-two. **25**The sons of Kir´iathar´im,
Chephi´rah, and Be-er´oth, seven
hundred and forty-three. **26**The sons
of Ramah and Geba, six hundred and
twenty-one. **27**The men of Michmas,
one hundred and twenty-two. **28**The
men of Bethel and Ai, two hundred
and twenty-three. **29**The sons of Nebo,
fifty-two. **30**The sons of Magbish, one
hundred and fifty-six. **31**The sons of
the other Elam, one thousand two
hundred and fifty-four. **32**The sons of
Harim, three hundred and twenty.
33The sons of Lod, Hadid, and Ono,
seven hundred and twenty-five. **34**The
sons of Jericho, three hundred and
forty-five. **35**The sons of Sena´ah, three
thousand six hundred and thirty.

36 The priests: the sons of Jedai´ah,
of the house of Jeshua, nine hundred
and seventy-three. **37**The sons of
Immer, one thousand and fifty-two.
38The sons of Pashhur, one thousand
two hundred and forty-seven. **39**The
sons of Harim, one thousand and
seventeen.

40 The Levites: the sons of
Jeshua and Kad´mi-el, of the sons of
Hodavi´ah, seventy-four. **41**The sing-
ers: the sons of Asaph, one hundred
and twenty-eight. **42**The sons of the
gatekeepers: the sons of Shallum, the
sons of Ater, the sons of Talmon, the
sons of Akkub, the sons of Hati´ta,
and the sons of Sho´bai, in all one
hundred and thirty-nine.

43 The temple servants:[d] the sons
of Ziha, the sons of Hasu´pha, the
sons of Tabba´oth, **44**the sons of Keros,
the sons of Si´aha, the sons of Padon,
45the sons of Leba´nah, the sons of
Hag´abah, the sons of Akkub, **46**the
sons of Hagab, the sons of Shamlai,
the sons of Hanan, **47**the sons of
Giddel, the sons of Gahar, the sons of
Re-ai´ah, **48**the sons of Rezin, the sons
of Neko´da, the sons of Gazzam, **49**the
sons of Uzza, the sons of Pase´ah, the
sons of Besai, **50**the sons of Asnah,
the sons of Me-u´nim, the sons of
Nephi´sim, **51**the sons of Bakbuk, the
sons of Haku´pha, the sons of Harhur,
52the sons of Bazluth, the sons of
Mehi´da, the sons of Harsha, **53**the
sons of Barkos, the sons of Sis´era, the
sons of Temah, **54**the sons of Nezi´ah,
and the sons of Hati´pha.

55 The sons of Solomon's ser-
vants: the sons of So´tai, the sons of
Hasso´phereth, the sons of Peru´da,
56the sons of Ja´alah, the sons of
Darkon, the sons of Giddel, **57**the sons
of Shephati´ah, the sons of Hattil, the
sons of Po´chereth-hazzeba´im, and
the sons of Ami.

58 All the temple servants[e] and the
sons of Solomon's servants were three
hundred and ninety-two.

59 The following were those
who came up from Tel-me´lah, Tel-
har´sha, Cherub, Addan, and Immer,
though they could not prove their fa-
thers' houses or their descent, wheth-
er they belonged to Israel: **60**the sons
of Delai´ah, the sons of Tobi´ah, and
the sons of Neko´da, six hundred and
fifty-two. **61**Also, of the sons of the
priests: the sons of Habai´ah, the sons
of Hakkoz, and the sons of Barzil´lai
(who had taken a wife from the
daughters of Barzil´lai the Gileadite,
and was called by their name). **62**These
sought their registration among those
enrolled in the genealogies, but they
were not found there, and so they
were excluded from the priesthood as
unclean; **63**the governor told them that
they were not to partake of the most

[d] Heb *nethinim*
[e] Heb *nethinim*

holy food, until there should be a
priest to consult Urim and Thummim.
64 The whole assembly together
was forty-two thousand three hun-
dred and sixty, 65 besides their men-
servants and maidservants, of whom
there were seven thousand three hun-
dred and thirty-seven; and they had
two hundred male and female singers.
66 Their horses were seven hundred
and thirty-six, their mules were two
hundred and forty-five, 67 their camels
were four hundred and thirty-five,
and their asses were six thousand sev-
en hundred and twenty.

68 Some of the heads of families,
when they came to the house of the
LORD which is in Jerusalem, made
freewill offerings for the house of
God, to erect it on its site; 69 according
to their ability they gave to the trea-
sury of the work sixty-one thousand
darics of gold, five thousand minas
of silver, and one hundred priests'
garments.

70 The priests, the Levites, and
some of the people lived in Jerusalem
and its vicinity;[a] and the singers, the
gatekeepers, and the temple servants
lived in their towns, and all Israel in
their towns.

WORSHIP RESTORED AT JERUSALEM

3 When the seventh month came, and
the sons of Israel were in the towns,
the people gathered as one man to
Jerusalem. 2 Then arose Jeshua the son
of Jo´zadak, with his fellow priests,
and Zerub´babel the son of She-al´ti-
el with his kinsmen, and they built
the altar of the God of Israel, to offer
burnt offerings upon it, as it is written
in the law of Moses the man of God.
3 They set the altar in its place, for fear
was upon them because of the peoples
of the lands, and they offered burnt
offerings upon it to the LORD, burnt
offerings morning and evening. 4 And
they kept the feast of booths, as it is
written, and offered the daily burnt
offerings by number according to the
ordinance, as each day required, 5 and
after that the continual burnt offer-
ings, the offerings at the new moon
and at all the appointed feasts of the
LORD, and the offerings of every one
who made a freewill offering to the
LORD. 6 From the first day of the sev-
enth month they began to offer burnt
offerings to the LORD. But the foun-
dation of the temple of the LORD was
not yet laid. 7 So they gave money to
the masons and the carpenters, and
food, drink, and oil to the Sido´nians
and the Tyrians to bring cedar trees
from Lebanon to the sea, to Joppa, ac-
cording to the grant which they had
from Cyrus king of Persia.

FOUNDATION LAID FOR THE TEMPLE

8 Now in the second year of
their coming to the house of God
at Jerusalem, in the second month,
Zerub´babel the son of She-al´ti-el
and Jeshua the son of Jo´zadak made
a beginning, together with the rest
of their brethren, the priests and
the Levites and all who had come to
Jerusalem from the captivity. They
appointed the Levites, from twen-
ty years old and upward, to have the
oversight of the work of the house of
the LORD. 9 And Jeshua with his sons
and his kinsmen, and Kad´mi-el and
his sons, the sons of Judah, together
took the oversight of the workmen in
the house of God, along with the sons
of Hen´adad and the Levites, their
sons and kinsmen.

10 And when the builders laid
the foundation of the temple of the
LORD, the priests in their vestments
came forward with trumpets, and the
Levites, the sons of Asaph, with cym-
bals, to praise the LORD, according to
the directions of David king of Israel;
11 and they sang responsively, praising
and giving thanks to the LORD,

"For he is good,
for his steadfast love en-
dures for ever toward
Israel."

[a] 1Esdras 5.46: Heb lacks *lived in Jerusalem and its vicinity*

in the temple which is in Jerusalem,
and let the house of God be rebuilt
on its site." 16 Then this Shesh-baz´zar
came and laid the foundations of the
house of God which is in Jerusalem;
and from that time until now it has
been in building, and it is not yet fin-
ished.' 17 Therefore, if it seem good to
the king, let search be made in the
royal archives there in Babylon, to
see whether a decree was issued by
Cyrus the king for the rebuilding of
this house of God in Jerusalem. And
let the king send us his pleasure in
this matter."

THE DECREE OF DARI´US

6 Then Dari´us the king made a
decree, and search was made in
Babylonia, in the house of the ar-
chives where the documents were
stored. 2 And in Ecbat´ana, the capital
which is in the province of Media, a
scroll was found on which this was
written: "A record. 3 In the first year
of Cyrus the king, Cyrus the king is-
sued a decree: Concerning the house
of God at Jerusalem, let the house
be rebuilt, the place where sacrifices
are offered and burnt offerings are
brought; its height shall be sixty cu-
bits and its breadth sixty cubits, 4 with
three courses of great stones and one
course of timber; let the cost be paid
from the royal treasury. 5 And also let
the gold and silver vessels of the house
of God, which Nebuchadnez´zar took
out of the temple that is in Jerusalem
and brought to Babylon, be restored
and brought back to the temple which
is in Jerusalem, each to its place; you
shall put them in the house of God."

6 "Now therefore, Tat´tenai, gov-
ernor of the province Beyond the
River, She´thar-boz´enai, and your as-
sociates the governors who are in the
province Beyond the River, keep away;
7 let the work on this house of God
alone; let the governor of the Jews
and the elders of the Jews rebuild this
house of God on its site. 8 Moreover
I make a decree regarding what you
shall do for these elders of the Jews
for the rebuilding of this house of
God; the cost is to be paid to these
men in full and without delay from
the royal revenue, the tribute of the
province from Beyond the River. 9 And
whatever is needed—young bulls,
rams, or sheep for burnt offerings to
the God of heaven, wheat, salt, wine,
or oil, as the priests at Jerusalem re-
quire—let that be given to them day
by day without fail, 10 that they may
offer pleasing sacrifices to the God
of heaven, and pray for the life of the
king and his sons. 11 Also I make a de-
cree that if any one alters this edict, a
beam shall be pulled out of his house,
and he shall be impaled upon it, and
his house shall be made a dunghill.
12 May the God who has caused his
name to dwell there overthrow any
king or people that shall put forth a
hand to alter this, or to destroy this
house of God which is in Jerusalem. I
Dari´us make a decree; let it be done
with all diligence."

COMPLETION AND DEDICATION OF THE TEMPLE

13 Then, according to the word
sent by Dari´us the king, Tat´tenai,
the governor of the province Beyond
the River, She´thar-boz´enai, and
their associates did with all diligence
what Dari´us the king had ordered.
14 And the elders of the Jews built and
prospered, through the prophesying
of Hag´gai the prophet and Zechari´ah
the son of Iddo. They finished their
building by command of the God of
Israel and by decree of Cyrus and
Dari´us and Ar-ta-xerx´es king of
Persia; 15 and this house was finished
on the third day of the month of
Adar, in the sixth year of the reign of
Dari´us the king.

16 And the people of Israel, the
priests and the Levites, and the rest
of the returned exiles, celebrated the
dedication of this house of God with
joy. 17 They offered at the dedication
of this house of God one hundred

bulls, two hundred rams, four hun-
dred lambs, and as a sin offering for
all Israel twelve he-goats, according
to the number of the tribes of Israel.
18 And they set the priests in their divi-
sions and the Levites in their courses,
for the service of God at Jerusalem, as
it is written in the book of Moses.

THE PASSOVER CELEBRATED

19 On the fourteenth day of the
first month the returned exiles kept
the passover. 20 For the priests and the
Levites had purified themselves to-
gether; all of them were clean. So they
killed the passover lamb for all the re-
turned exiles, for their fellow priests,
and for themselves; 21 it was eaten by
the people of Israel who had returned
from exile, and also by every one who
had joined them and separated him-
self from the pollutions of the peoples
of the land to worship the LORD, the
God of Israel. 22 And they kept the
feast of unleavened bread seven days
with joy; for the LORD had made them
joyful, and had turned the heart of
the king of Assyria to them, so that he
aided them in the work of the house of
God, the God of Israel.

THE COMING AND WORK OF EZRA

7 *Now after this, in the reign of
Ar-ta-xerx´es king of Persia, Ezra
the son of Serai´ah, son of Azari´ah,
son of Hilki´ah, 2 son of Shallum,
son of Zadok, son of Ahi´tub, 3 son
of Amari´ah, son of Azari´ah, son of
Merai´oth, 4 son of Zerahi´ah, son of
Uzzi, son of Bukki, 5 son of Abi´shua,
son of Phin´ehas, son of Elea´zar, son
of Aaron the chief priest 6 this Ezra
went up from Babylonia. He was a
scribe skilled in the law of Moses
which the LORD the God of Israel
had given; and the king granted him
all that he asked, for the hand of the
LORD his God was upon him.
7 And there went up also to
Jerusalem, in the seventh year of
Ar-ta-xerx´es the king, some of the
people of Israel, and some of the
priests and Levites, the singers and
gatekeepers, and the temple servants.
8 And he came to Jerusalem in the fifth
month, which was in the seventh year
of the king; 9 for on the first day of the
first month he began[a] to go up from
Babylonia, and on the first day of the
fifth month he came to Jerusalem, for
the good hand of his God was upon
him. 10 For Ezra had set his heart to
study the law of the LORD, and to do
it, and to teach his statutes and ordi-
nances in Israel.

THE LETTER OF ARTAXERXES TO EZRA

11 This is a copy of the letter which
King Ar-ta-xerx´es gave to Ezra the
priest, the scribe, learned in matters
of the commandments of the LORD
and his statutes for Israel: 12 "Ar-ta-
xerx´es, king of kings, to Ezra the
priest, the scribe of the law of the God
of heaven.[b] And now 13 I make a decree
that any one of the people of Israel or
their priests or Levites in my kingdom,
who freely offers to go to Jerusalem,
may go with you. 14 For you are sent
by the king and his seven counselors
to make inquiries about Judah and
Jerusalem according to the law of your
God, which is in your hand, 15 and also
to convey the silver and gold which
the king and his counselors have free-
ly offered to the God of Israel, whose
dwelling is in Jerusalem, 16 with all the
silver and gold which you shall find
in the whole province of Babylonia,
and with the freewill offerings of the
people and the priests, vowed willing-
ly for the house of their God which is
in Jerusalem. 17 With this money, then,
you shall with all diligence buy bulls,
rams, and lambs, with their cereal of-
ferings and their drink offerings, and
you shall offer them upon the altar
of the house of your God which is in
Jerusalem. 18 Whatever seems good to
you and your brethren to do with the

[a] Vg See Syr: Heb *that was the foundation of the going up*
[b] Aramaic adds a word of uncertain meaning

rest of the silver and gold, you may
do, according to the will of your God.
19The vessels that have been given you
for the service of the house of your
God, you shall deliver before the God
of Jerusalem. 20And whatever else is
required for the house of your God,
which you have occasion to provide,
you may provide it out of the king's
treasury.

21 "And I, Ar-ta-xerx´es the king,
make a decree to all the treasurers
in the province Beyond the River:
Whatever Ezra the priest, the scribe
of the law of the God of heaven, re-
quires of you, be it done with all dil-
igence, 22up to a hundred talents of
silver, a hundred cors of wheat, a hun-
dred baths of wine, a hundred baths of
oil, and salt without prescribing how
much. 23Whatever is commanded by
the God of heaven, let it be done in
full for the house of the God of heav-
en, lest his wrath be against the realm
of the king and his sons. 24We also no-
tify you that it shall not be lawful to
impose tribute, custom, or toll upon
any one of the priests, the Levites, the
singers, the doorkeepers, the temple
servants, or other servants of this
house of God.

25 "And you, Ezra, according to the
wisdom of your God which is in your
hand, appoint magistrates and judges
who may judge all the people in the
province Beyond the River, all such as
know the laws of your God; and those
who do not know them, you shall
teach. 26Whoever will not obey the law
of your God and the law of the king,
let judgment be strictly executed upon
him, whether for death or for banish-
ment or for confiscation of his goods
or for imprisonment."

27 Blessed be the LORD, the God
of our fathers, who put such a thing
as this into the heart of the king, to
beautify the house of the LORD which
is in Jerusalem, 28and who extended to
me his steadfast love before the king
and his counselors, and before all the
king's mighty officers. I took courage,
for the hand of the LORD my God was
upon me, and I gathered leading men
from Israel to go up with me.

HEADS OF FAMILIES WHO RETURNED WITH EZRA

8 These are the heads of their fathers'
houses, and this is the genealogy
of those who went up with me from
Babylonia, in the reign of Ar-ta-xerx´es
the king: 2Of the sons of Phin´ehas,
Gershom. Of the sons of Ith´amar,
Daniel. Of the sons of David, Hattush,
3of the sons of Shecani´ah. Of the sons
of Parosh, Zechari´ah, with whom
were registered one hundred and fifty
men. 4Of the sons of Pa´hath-mo´ab,
Eli-e-ho-e´nai the son of Zerahi´ah,
and with him two hundred men. 5Of
the sons of Zattu,[c] Shecani´ah the
son of Jaha´ziel, and with him three
hundred men. 6Of the sons of Adin,
Ebed the son of Jonathan, and with
him fifty men. 7Of the sons of Elam,
Jeshai´ah the son of Athali´ah, and
with him seventy men. 8Of the sons
of Shephati´ah, Zebadi´ah the son of
Michael, and with him eighty men. 9Of
the sons of Jo´ab, Obadi´ah the son of
Jehi´el, and with him two hundred and
eighteen men. 10Of the sons of Bani,[d]
Shelo´mith the son of Josiphi´ah, and
with him a hundred and sixty men.
11Of the sons of Be´bai, Zechari´ah,
the son of Be´bai, and with him twen-
ty-eight men. 12Of the sons of Azgad,
Joha´nan the son of Hak´katan, and
with him a hundred and ten men.
13Of the sons of Adoni´kam, those
who came later, their names being
Eliph´elet, Jeu´el, and Shemai´ah, and
with them sixty men. 14Of the sons of
Big´vai, Uthai and Zaccur, and with
them seventy men.

SERVANTS FOR THE TEMPLE

15 I gathered them to the river
that runs to Aha´va, and there we

[c]Gk: 1Esdras 8.32: Heb lacks *of Zattu*
[d]Gk: 1Esdras 8.36: Heb lacks *Bani*

encamped three days. As I reviewed
the people and the priests, I found
there none of the sons of Levi. 16Then
I sent for Elie´zer, Ariel, Shemai´ah,
Elna´than, Jarib, Elna´than, Nathan,
Zechari´ah, and Meshul´lam, leading
men, and for Joi´arib and Elna´than,
who were men of insight, 17and sent
them to Iddo, the leading man at the
place Casiphi´a, telling them what to
say to Iddo and his brethren the tem-
ple servants[a] at the place Casiphi´a,
namely, to send us ministers for the
house of our God. 18And by the good
hand of our God upon us, they brought
us a man of discretion, of the sons of
Mahli the son of Levi, son of Israel,
namely Sherebi´ah with his sons and
kinsmen, eighteen; 19also Hashabi´ah
and with him Jeshai´ah of the sons of
Merar´i, with his kinsmen and their
sons, twenty; 20besides two hundred
and twenty of the temple servants,
whom David and his officials had set
apart to attend the Levites. These
were all mentioned by name.

FASTING AND PRAYER FOR PROTECTION

21 Then I proclaimed a fast there, at
the river Aha´va, that we might hum-
ble ourselves before our God, to seek
from him a straight way for ourselves,
our children, and all our goods. 22For
I was ashamed to ask the king for a
band of soldiers and horsemen to pro-
tect us against the enemy on our way;
since we had told the king, "The hand
of our God is for good upon all that
seek him, and the power of his wrath
is against all that forsake him." 23So
we fasted and besought our God for
this, and he listened to our entreaty.

GIFTS FOR THE TEMPLE

24 Then I set apart twelve of the
leading priests: Sherebi´ah, Hasha-
bi´ah, and ten of their kinsmen with
them. 25And I weighed out to them the
silver and the gold and the vessels,
the offering for the house of our God
which the king and his counselors and
his lords and all Israel there present
had offered; 26I weighed out into their
hand six hundred and fifty talents of
silver, and silver vessels worth a hun-
dred talents, and a hundred talents of
gold, 27twenty bowls of gold worth a
thousand darics, and two vessels of
fine bright bronze as precious as gold.
28And I said to them, "You are holy to
the LORD, and the vessels are holy;
and the silver and the gold are a free-
will offering to the LORD, the God of
your fathers. 29Guard them and keep
them until you weigh them before the
chief priests and the Levites and the
heads of fathers' houses in Israel at
Jerusalem, within the chambers of the
house of the LORD." 30So the priests
and the Levites took over the weight
of the silver and the gold and the ves-
sels, to bring them to Jerusalem, to
the house of our God.

THE RETURN TO JERUSALEM

31 Then we departed from the river
Aha´va on the twelfth day of the first
month, to go to Jerusalem; the hand of
our God was upon us, and he delivered
us from the hand of the enemy and
from ambushes by the way. 32We came
to Jerusalem, and there we remained
three days. 33On the fourth day, with-
in the house of our God, the silver
and the gold and the vessels were
weighed into the hands of Mer´emoth
the priest, son of Uri´ah, and with him
was Elea´zar the son of Phin´ehas, and
with them were the Levites, Jo´zabad
the son of Jeshua and No-adi´ah the
son of Bin´nui. 34The whole was count-
ed and weighed, and the weight of ev-
erything was recorded.

35 At that time those who had come
from captivity, the returned exiles,
offered burnt offerings to the God of
Israel, twelve bulls for all Israel, nine-
ty-six rams, seventy-seven lambs, and
as a sin offering twelve he-goats; all
this was a burnt offering to the LORD.
36They also delivered the king's com-
missions to the king's satraps and to

[a]Heb *nethinim*

the governors of the province Beyond
the River; and they aided the people
and the house of God.

DENUNCIATION OF MIXED MARRIAGES

9 *After these things had been done,
the officials approached me and
said, "The people of Israel and the
priests and the Levites have not sep-
arated themselves from the peoples
of the lands with their abominations,
from the Canaanites, the Hittites,
the Per´izzites, the Jeb´usites, the
Ammonites, the Moabites, the Egyp-
tians, and the Amorites. 2For they
have taken some of their daughters to
be wives for themselves and for their
sons; so that the holy race has mixed
itself with the peoples of the lands.
And in this faithlessness the hand of
the officials and chief men has been
foremost." 3When I heard this, I rent
my garments and my mantle, and
pulled hair from my head and beard,
and sat appalled. 4Then all who trem-
bled at the words of the God of Israel,
because of the faithlessness of the
returned exiles, gathered round me
while I sat appalled until the evening
sacrifice. 5And at the evening sacri-
fice I rose from my fasting, with my
garments and my mantle rent, and
fell upon my knees and spread out my
hands to the LORD my God, 6saying:

EZRA'S PRAYER

"O my God, I am ashamed and
blush to lift my face to thee, my God,
for our iniquities have risen high-
er than our heads, and our guilt has
mounted up to the heavens. 7From the
days of our fathers to this day we have
been in great guilt; and for our iniq-
uities we, our kings, and our priests
have been given into the hand of the
kings of the lands, to the sword, to
captivity, to plundering, and to utter
shame, as at this day. 8But now for a
brief moment favor has been shown
by the LORD our God, to leave us a
remnant, and to give us a secure hold[b]
within his holy place, that our God
may brighten our eyes and grant us a
little reviving in our bondage. 9For we
are bondmen; yet our God has not for-
saken us in our bondage, but has ex-
tended to us his steadfast love before
the kings of Persia, to grant us some
reviving to set up the house of our
God, to repair its ruins, and to give
us protection[c] in Judea and Jerusalem.
10 "And now, O our God, what
shall we say after this? For we have
forsaken thy commandments, 11which
thou didst command by thy servants
the prophets, saying, 'The land which
you are entering, to take possession
of it, is a land unclean with the pol-
lutions of the peoples of the lands,
with their abominations which have
filled it from end to end with their un-
cleanness. 12Therefore give not your
daughters to their sons, neither take
their daughters for your sons, and
never seek their peace or prosperity,
that you may be strong, and eat the
good of the land, and leave it for an
inheritance to your children for ever.'
13And after all that has come upon us
for our evil deeds and for our great
guilt, seeing that thou, our God, hast
punished us less than our iniquities
deserved and hast given us such a
remnant as this, 14shall we break thy
commandments again and intermarry
with the peoples who practice these
abominations? Wouldst thou not be
angry with us till thou wouldst con-
sume us, so that there should be no
remnant, nor any to escape? 15O LORD
the God of Israel, thou art just, for we
are left a remnant that has escaped, as
at this day. Behold, we are before thee
in our guilt, for none can stand before
thee because of this."

THE PEOPLE'S RESPONSE

10 While Ezra prayed and made con-
fession, weeping and casting him-
self down before the house of God, a

[b] Heb *nail* or *tent-pin*
[c] Heb *a wall*

very great assembly of men, women,
and children, gathered to him out of
Israel; for the people wept bitterly.
2And Shecani´ah the son of Jehi´el,
of the sons of Elam, addressed Ezra:
"We have broken faith with our God
and have married foreign women from
the peoples of the land, but even now
there is hope for Israel in spite of this.
3Therefore let us make a covenant
with our God to put away all these
wives and their children, according
to the counsel of my lord and of those
who tremble at the commandment of
our God; and let it be done according
to the law. 4Arise, for it is your task,
and we are with you; be strong and
do it." 5Then Ezra arose and made
the leading priests and Levites and all
Israel take oath that they would do as
had been said. So they took the oath.

FOREIGN WIVES AND THEIR CHILDREN REJECTED

6 Then Ezra withdrew from before
the house of God, and went to the
chamber of Jeho-ha´nan the son of
Eli´ashib, where he spent the night,[a]
neither eating bread nor drinking
water; for he was mourning over the
faithlessness of the exiles. 7And a
proclamation was made throughout
Judah and Jerusalem to all the re-
turned exiles that they should assem-
ble at Jerusalem, 8and that if any one
did not come within three days, by
order of the officials and the elders all
his property should be forfeited, and
he himself banned from the congrega-
tion of the exiles.

9 Then all the men of Judah and
Benjamin assembled at Jerusalem
within the three days; it was the ninth
month, on the twentieth day of the
month. And all the people sat in the
open square before the house of God,
trembling because of this matter and
because of the heavy rain. 10And Ezra
the priest stood up and said to them,
"You have trespassed and married
foreign women, and so increased the
guilt of Israel. 11Now then make con-
fession to the LORD the God of your
fathers, and do his will; separate your-
selves from the peoples of the land
and from the foreign wives." 12Then
all the assembly answered with a loud
voice, "It is so; we must do as you have
said. 13But the people are many, and
it is a time of heavy rain; we cannot
stand in the open. Nor is this a work
for one day or for two; for we have
greatly transgressed in this matter.
14Let our officials stand for the whole
assembly; let all in our cities who have
taken foreign wives come at appoint-
ed times, and with them the elders
and judges of every city, till the fierce
wrath of our God over this matter be
averted from us." 15Only Jonathan the
son of As´ahel and Jahzei´ah the son of
Tikvah opposed this, and Meshul´lam
and Shab´bethai the Levite supported
them.

16 Then the returned exiles did so.
Ezra the priest selected men,[b] heads
of fathers' houses, according to their
fathers' houses, each of them desig-
nated by name. On the first day of the
tenth month they sat down to exam-
ine the matter; 17and by the first day of
the first month they had come to the
end of all the men who had married
foreign women.

18 Of the sons of the priests who
had married foreign women were
found Ma-asei´ah, Elie´zer, Jarib,
and Gedali´ah, of the sons of Jeshua
the son of Jo´zadak and his brethren.
19They pledged themselves to put away
their wives, and their guilt offering
was a ram of the flock for their guilt.
20Of the sons of Immer: Hana´ni and
Zebadi´ah. 21Of the sons of Harim:
Ma-asei´ah, Eli´jah, Shemai´ah, Jehi´-
el, and Uzzi´ah. 22Of the sons of Pash-
hur: Eli-o-e´nai, Ma-asei´ah, Ish´mael,
Nethan´el, Jo´zabad, and Ela´sah.

23 Of the Levites: Jo´zabad,
Shim´e-i, Kelai´ah (that is, Keli´ta),

[a] 1Esdras 9.2: Heb *where he went*
[b] 1Esdras 9.16: Syr: Heb *and there were selected Ezra*, etc.

Petha-hi´ah, Judah, and Elie´zer. 24Of
the singers: Eli´ashib. Of the gate-
keepers: Shallum, Telem, and Uri.
25 And of Israel: of the sons of
Parosh: Rami´ah, Izzi´ah, Malchi´-
jah, Mi´jamin, Elea´zar, Hashabi´ah,[c]
and Benai´ah. 26Of the sons of Elam:
Mattani´ah, Zechari´ah, Jehi´el, Ab-
di, Jer´emoth, and Eli´jah. 27Of the
sons of Zattu: Eli-o-e´nai, Eli´ashib,
Mattani´ah, Jer´emoth, Zabad, and
Azi´za. 28Of the sons of Be´bai were
Jeho-ha´nan, Hanani´ah, Zab´bai, and
Ath´lai. 29Of the sons of Bani were
Meshul´lam, Malluch, Adai´ah, Ja-
shub, She´al, and Jer´emoth. 30Of the
sons of Pa´hath-mo´ab: Adna, Chelal,
Benai´ah, Ma-asei´ah, Mattani´ah,
Bez´alel, Bin´nui, and Manas´seh. 31Of
the sons of Harim: Elie´zer, Isshi´jah,
Malchi´jah, Shemai´ah, Shim´e-on,
32Benjamin, Malluch, and Shemari´ah.
33Of the sons of Hashum: Matte´nai,
Mat´tattah, Zabad, Eliph´elet, Jer´e-
mai, Manas´seh, and Shi´me-i. 34Of
the sons of Bani: Ma-ada´i, Amram,
Uel, 35Benai´ah, Bedei´ah, Chel´uhi,
36Vani´ah, Mer´emoth, Eli´ashib, 37Mat-
tani´ah, Matte´nai, Ja´asu. 38Of the
sons of Bin´nui:[d] Shi´me-i, 39Shelemi´-
ah, Nathan, Adai´ah, 40Machnad´ebai,
Shashai, Sha´rai, 41Az´arel, Shelemi´-
ah, Shemari´ah, 42Shallum, Amari´-
ah, and Joseph. 43Of the sons of Nebo:
Je-i´el, Mattithi´ah, Zabad, Zebi´na,
Jaddai, Jo´el, and Benai´ah. 44All these
had married foreign women, and they
put them away with their children.[e]

[c] 1Esdras 9.26: Gk: Heb *Malchijah*
[d] Gk: Heb *Bani, Binnui*
[e] 1Esdras 9.36: Heb obscure

THE BOOK OF

NEHEMIAH

NEHEMIAH PRAYS FOR HIS PEOPLE

1 The words of Nehemi´ah the son
of Hacali´ah. Now it happened in
the month of Chislev, in the twenti-
eth year, as I was in Susa the capital,
2that Hana´ni, one of my brethren,
came with certain men out of Judah;
and I asked them concerning the
Jews that survived, who had escaped
exile, and concerning Jerusalem.
3And they said to me, "The survivors
there in the province who escaped
exile are in great trouble and shame;
the wall of Jerusalem is broken
down, and its gates are destroyed by
fire."

4 When I heard these words I sat
down and wept, and mourned for
days; and I continued fasting and
praying before the God of heaven.
5And I said, "O LORD God of heav-
en, the great and terrible God who
keeps covenant and steadfast love
with those who love him and keep
his commandments; 6let thy ear be
attentive, and thy eyes open, to hear
the prayer of thy servant which I now
pray before thee day and night for the
people of Israel thy servants, confess-
ing the sins of the people of Israel,
which we have sinned against thee.
Yea, I and my father's house have
sinned. 7We have acted very corruptly
against thee, and have not kept the
commandments, the statutes, and
the ordinances which thou didst com-
mand thy servant Moses. 8Remember
the word which thou didst command
thy servant Moses, saying, 'If you are
unfaithful, I will scatter you among
the peoples; 9but if you return to me
and keep my commandments and do
them, though your dispersed be un-
der the farthest skies, I will gather
them thence and bring them to the
place which I have chosen, to make
my name dwell there.' 10They are thy
servants and thy people, whom thou
hast redeemed by thy great power and
by thy strong hand. 11O Lord, let thy
ear be attentive to the prayer of thy
servant, and to the prayer of thy ser-
vants who delight to fear thy name;
and give success to thy servant today,
and grant him mercy in the sight of
this man."

Now I was cupbearer to the king.

NEHEMIAH SENT TO JUDAH

2 In the month of Nisan, in the twen-
tieth year of King Ar-ta-xerx´es,
when wine was before him, I took
up the wine and gave it to the king.
Now I had not been sad in his pres-
ence. 2And the king said to me, "Why
is your face sad, seeing you are not
sick? This is nothing else but sadness
of the heart." Then I was very much
afraid. 3I said to the king, "Let the
king live for ever! Why should not my
face be sad, when the city, the place
of my fathers' sepulchres, lies waste,
and its gates have been destroyed
by fire?" 4Then the king said to me,
"For what do you make request?" So
I prayed to the God of heaven. 5And
I said to the king, "If it pleases the
king, and if your servant has found
favor in your sight, that you send me
to Judah, to the city of my fathers'
sepulchres, that I may rebuild it."
6And the king said to me (the queen
sitting beside him), "How long will
you be gone, and when will you re-
turn?" So it pleased the king to send
me; and I set him a time. 7And I said
to the king, "If it pleases the king, let
letters be given me to the governors
of the province Beyond the River, that
they may let me pass through until I
come to Judah; 8and a letter to Asaph,
the keeper of the king's forest, that he
may give me timber to make beams
for the gates of the fortress of the

temple, and for the wall of the city,
and for the house which I shall occu-
py." And the king granted me what I
asked, for the good hand of my God
was upon me.

9 Then I came to the governors of
the province Beyond the River, and
gave them the king's letters. Now
the king had sent with me officers of
the army and horsemen. 10But when
Sanbal′lat the Hor′onite and Tobi′ah
the servant, the Ammonite, heard
this, it displeased them greatly that
some one had come to seek the wel-
fare of the children of Israel.

NEHEMIAH'S INSPECTION OF THE WALLS

11 So I came to Jerusalem and was
there three days. 12Then I arose in the
night, I and a few men with me; and I
told no one what my God had put into
my heart to do for Jerusalem. There
was no beast with me but the beast
on which I rode. 13I went out by night
by the Valley Gate to the Jackal's Well
and to the Dung Gate, and I inspect-
ed the walls of Jerusalem which were
broken down and its gates which had
been destroyed by fire. 14Then I went
on to the Fountain Gate and to the
King's Pool; but there was no place for
the beast that was under me to pass.
15Then I went up in the night by the
valley and inspected the wall; and I
turned back and entered by the Valley
Gate, and so returned. 16And the offi-
cials did not know where I had gone
or what I was doing; and I had not yet
told the Jews, the priests, the nobles,
the officials, and the rest that were to
do the work.

DECISION TO RESTORE THE WALLS

17 Then I said to them, "You see
the trouble we are in, how Jerusalem
lies in ruins with its gates burned.
Come, let us build the wall of
Jerusalem, that we may no longer suf-
fer disgrace." 18And I told them of the
hand of my God which had been upon
me for good, and also of the words
which the king had spoken to me. And
they said, "Let us rise up and build."
So they strengthened their hands for
the good work. 19But when Sanbal′lat
the Hor′onite and Tobi′ah the ser-
vant, the Ammonite, and Geshem the
Arab heard of it, they derided us and
despised us and said, "What is this
thing that you are doing? Are you
rebelling against the king?" 20Then
I replied to them, "The God of heav-
en will make us prosper, and we his
servants will arise and build; but you
have no portion or right or memorial
in Jerusalem."

ORGANIZATION OF THE WORK

3 Then Eli′ashib the high priest rose
up with his brethren the priests
and they built the Sheep Gate. They
consecrated it and set its doors; they
consecrated it as far as the Tower of
the Hundred, as far as the Tower of
Hanan′el. 2And next to him the men
of Jericho built. And next to them[a]
Zaccur the son of Imri built.

3 And the sons of Hassena′ah built
the Fish Gate; they laid its beams and
set its doors, its bolts, and its bars.
4And next to them Mer′emoth the son
of Uri′ah, son of Hakkoz repaired.
And next to them Meshul′lam the son
of Berechi′ah, son of Meshez′abel re-
paired. And next to them Zadok the
son of Ba′ana repaired. 5And next to
them the Teko′ites repaired; but their
nobles did not put their necks to the
work of their LORD.[b]

6 And Joi′ada the son of Pase′ah
and Meshul′lam the son of Besodei′ah
repaired the Old Gate; they laid its
beams and set its doors, its bolts, and
its bars. 7And next to them repaired
Melati′ah the Gibeonite and Jadon
the Mero′nothite, the men of Gibeon
and of Mizpah, who were under the
jurisdiction of the governor of the
province Beyond the River. 8Next to
them Uz′ziel the son of Harhai′ah,

[a] Heb *him*
[b] Or *lords*

goldsmiths, repaired. Next to him
Hanani'ah, one of the perfumers, re-
paired; and they restored[a] Jerusalem
as far as the Broad Wall. 9Next to
them Rephai'ah the son of Hur, rul-
er of half the district of[b] Jerusalem,
repaired. 10Next to them Jedai'ah the
son of Haru'maph repaired opposite
his house; and next to him Hattush
the son of Hashabnei'ah repaired.
11Malchi'jah the son of Harim and
Hasshub the son of Pa'hath-mo'ab re-
paired another section and the Tower
of the Ovens. 12Next to him Shallum
the son of Hallo'hesh, ruler of half
the district of[a] Jerusalem, repaired, he
and his daughters.

13 Hanun and the inhabitants of
Zano'ah repaired the Valley Gate;
they rebuilt it and set its doors, its
bolts, and its bars, and repaired a
thousand cubits of the wall, as far as
the Dung Gate.

14 Malchi'jah the son of Rechab,
ruler of the district of[a] Beth-
hacche'rem, repaired the Dung Gate;
he rebuilt it and set its doors, its bolts,
and its bars.

15 And Shallum the son of
Colho'zeh, ruler of the district of[a]
Mizpah, repaired the Fountain Gate;
he rebuilt it and covered it and set its
doors, its bolts, and its bars; and he
built the wall of the Pool of Shelah of
the king's garden, as far as the stairs
that go down from the City of David.
16After him Nehemi'ah the son of
Azbuk, ruler of half the district of[a]
Beth-zur, repaired to a point opposite
the sepulchres of David, to the arti-
ficial pool, and to the house of the
mighty men. 17After him the Levites
repaired: Rehum the son of Bani; next
to him Hashabi'ah, ruler of half the
district of[a] Ke'ilah, repaired for his
district. 18After him their brethren re-
paired: Bav'vai the son of Hen'adad,
ruler of half the district of[a] Ke'ilah;
19next to him Ezer the son of Jeshua,
ruler of Mizpah, repaired another
section opposite the ascent to the
armory at the Angle. 20After him
Baruch the son of Zab'bai repaired
another section from the Angle to
the door of the house of Eli'ashib the
high priest. 21After him Mer'emoth
the son of Uri'ah, son of Hakkoz re-
paired another section from the door
of the house of Eli'ashib to the end
of the house of Eli'ashib. 22After him
the priests, the men of the Plain, re-
paired. 23After them Benjamin and
Hasshub repaired opposite their
house. After them Azari'ah the son of
Ma-asei'ah, son of Anani'ah repaired
beside his own house. 24After him
Bin'nui the son of Hen'adad repaired
another section, from the house of
Azari'ah to the Angle 25and to the
corner. Palal the son of Uzai repaired
opposite the Angle and the tower pro-
jecting from the upper house of the
king at the court of the guard. After
him Pedai'ah the son of Parosh 26and
the temple servants living[c] on Ophel
repaired to a point opposite the Water
Gate on the east and the projecting
tower. 27After him the Teko'ites re-
paired another section opposite the
great projecting tower as far as the
wall of Ophel.

28 Above the Horse Gate the priests
repaired, each one opposite his own
house. 29After them Zadok the son
of Immer repaired opposite his own
house. After him Shemai'ah the son
of Shecani'ah, the keeper of the East
Gate, repaired. 30After him Hanani'ah
the son of Shelemi'ah and Hanun the
sixth son of Zalaph repaired another
section. After him Meshul'lam the
son of Berechi'ah repaired opposite
his chamber. 31After him Malchi'jah,
one of the goldsmiths, repaired as far
as the house of the temple servants
and of the merchants, opposite the
Muster Gate,[d] and to the upper cham-
ber of the corner. 32And between the

[a] Or *abandoned*
[b] Or *foreman of half the portion assigned to*
[c] Cn: Heb *were living*
[d] Or *Hammiphkad Gate*

upper chamber of the corner and the
Sheep Gate the goldsmiths and the
merchants repaired.

HOSTILE PLOTS THWARTED

4[e] Now when Sanbal´lat heard that
we were building the wall, he was
angry and greatly enraged, and he rid-
iculed the Jews. 2And he said in the
presence of his brethren and of the
army of Samar´ia, "What are these
feeble Jews doing? Will they restore
things? Will they sacrifice? Will they
finish up in a day? Will they revive
the stones out of the heaps of rubbish,
and burned ones at that?" 3Tobi´ah
the Ammonite was by him, and he
said, "Yes, what they are building—if
a fox goes up on it he will break down
their stone wall!" 4Hear, O our God,
for we are despised; turn back their
taunt upon their own heads, and give
them up to be plundered in a land
where they are captives. 5Do not cov-
er their guilt, and let not their sin be
blotted out from thy sight; for they
have provoked thee to anger before
the builders.

6 So we built the wall; and all the
wall was joined together to half its
height. For the people had a mind to
work.

7[f] But when Sanbal´lat and Tobi´ah
and the Arabs and the Ammonites
and the Ash´dodites heard that the re-
pairing of the walls of Jerusalem was
going forward and that the breaches
were beginning to be closed, they
were very angry; 8and they all plotted
together to come and fight against
Jerusalem and to cause confusion in
it. 9And we prayed to our God, and set
a guard as a protection against them
day and night.

10 But Judah said, "The strength
of the burden-bearers is failing, and
there is much rubbish; we are not
able to work on the wall." 11And our
enemies said, "They will not know
or see till we come into the midst
of them and kill them and stop the
work." 12When the Jews who lived by
them came they said to us ten times,
"From all the places where they live[g]
they will come up against us."[h] 13So in
the lowest parts of the space behind
the wall, in open places, I stationed
the people according to their families,
with their swords, their spears, and
their bows. 14And I looked, and arose,
and said to the nobles and to the of-
ficials and to the rest of the people,
"Do not be afraid of them. Remember
the Lord, who is great and terrible,
and fight for your brethren, your sons,
your daughters, your wives, and your
homes."

15 When our enemies heard that
it was known to us and that God had
frustrated their plan, we all returned
to the wall, each to his work. 16From
that day on, half of my servants
worked on construction, and half
held the spears, shields, bows, and
coats of mail; and the leaders stood
behind all the house of Judah, 17who
were building on the wall. Those
who carried burdens were laden in
such a way that each with one hand
labored on the work and with the
other held his weapon. 18And each of
the builders had his sword girded at
his side while he built. The man who
sounded the trumpet was beside me.
19And I said to the nobles and to the
officials and to the rest of the peo-
ple, "The work is great and widely
spread, and we are separated on the
wall, far from one another. 20In the
place where you hear the sound of the
trumpet, rally to us there. Our God
will fight for us."

21 So we labored at the work, and
half of them held the spears from the
break of dawn till the stars came out.
22I also said to the people at that time,
"Let every man and his servant pass
the night within Jerusalem, that they

[e] Ch 3.33 in Heb
[f] Ch 4.1 in Heb
[g] Cn: Heb *you return*
[h] Compare Gk Syr: Heb uncertain

until the sun is hot; and while they
are still standing guard[a] let them
shut and bar the doors. Appoint
guards from among the inhabitants
of Jerusalem, each to his station and
each opposite his own house." 4The
city was wide and large, but the peo-
ple within it were few and no houses
had been built.

LISTS OF THE RETURNED EXILES

5 Then God put it into my mind to
assemble the nobles and the officials
and the people to be enrolled by ge-
nealogy. And I found the book of the
genealogy of those who came up at the
first, and I found written in it:

6 These were the people of the
province who came up out of the
captivity of those exiles whom Nebu-
chadnez´zar the king of Babylon had
carried into exile; they returned to Je-
rusalem and Judah, each to his town.
7They came with Zerub´babel, Jeshua,
Nehemi´ah, Azari´ah, Ra-ami´ah, Na-
ham´ani, Mor´decai, Bilshan, Mis´-
pereth, Big´vai, Nehum, Ba´anah.

The number of the men of the peo-
ple of Israel: 8the sons of Parosh, two
thousand a hundred and seventy-two.
9The sons of Shephati´ah, three hun-
dred and seventy-two. 10The sons
of Arah, six hundred and fifty-two.
11The sons of Pa´hath-mo´ab, name-
ly the sons of Jeshua and Jo´ab, two
thousand eight hundred and eighteen.
12The sons of Elam, a thousand two
hundred and fifty-four. 13The sons of
Zattu, eight hundred and forty-five.
14The sons of Zac´cai, seven hundred
and sixty. 15The sons of Bin´nui, six
hundred and forty-eight. 16The sons of
Be´bai, six hundred and twenty-eight.
17The sons of Azgad, two thousand
three hundred and twenty-two. 18The
sons of Adoni´kam, six hundred and
sixty-seven. 19The sons of Big´vai,
two thousand and sixty-seven. 20The
sons of Adin, six hundred and fif-
ty-five. 21The sons of Ater, namely
of Hezeki´ah, ninety-eight. 22The
sons of Hashum, three hundred and
twenty-eight. 23The sons of Be´zai,
three hundred and twenty-four.
24The sons of Hariph, a hundred and
twelve. 25The sons of Gibeon, nine-
ty-five. 26The men of Bethlehem and
Neto´phah, a hundred and eighty-
eight. 27The men of An´athoth, a hun-
dred and twenty-eight. 28The men
of Beth-az´maveth, forty-two. 29The
men of Kir´iath-je´arim, Chephi´rah,
and Be-er´oth, seven hundred and
forty-three. 30The men of Ramah and
Geba, six hundred and twenty-one.
31The men of Michmas, a hundred and
twenty-two. 32The men of Bethel and
Ai, a hundred and twenty-three. 33The
men of the other Nebo, fifty-two.
34The sons of the other Elam, a thou-
sand two hundred and fifty-four.
35The sons of Harim, three hundred
and twenty. 36The sons of Jericho,
three hundred and forty-five. 37The
sons of Lod, Hadid, and Ono, seven
hundred and twenty-one. 38The sons
of Sena´ah, three thousand nine hun-
dred and thirty.

39 The priests: the sons of Jedai´ah,
namely the house of Jeshua, nine hun-
dred and seventy-three. 40The sons
of Immer, a thousand and fifty-two.
41The sons of Pashhur, a thousand two
hundred and forty-seven. 42The sons
of Harim, a thousand and seventeen.

43 The Levites: the sons of Jeshua,
namely of Kad´mi-el of the sons of
Ho´devah, seventy-four. 44The sing-
ers: the sons of Asaph, a hundred and
forty-eight. 45The gatekeepers: the
sons of Shallum, the sons of Ater, the
sons of Talmon, the sons of Akkub,
the sons of Hati´ta, the sons of Sho´-
bai, a hundred and thirty-eight.

46 The temple servants:[b] the sons
of Ziha, the sons of Hasu´pha, the sons
of Tabba´oth, 47the sons of Keros, the
sons of Si´a, the sons of Padon, 48the
sons of Leba´na, the sons of Hag´aba,
the sons of Shalmai, 49the sons of

[a] Heb obscure
[b] Heb *nethinim*

Hanan, the sons of Giddel, the sons of
Gahar, 50the sons of Re-ai´ah, the sons
of Rezin, the sons of Neko´da, 51the
sons of Gazzam, the sons of Uzza, the
sons of Pase´ah, 52the sons of Besai,
the sons of Me-u´nim, the sons of
Nephush´esim, 53the sons of Bakbuk,
the sons of Haku´pha, the sons of
Harhur, 54the sons of Bazlith, the sons
of Mehi´da, the sons of Harsha, 55the
sons of Barkos, the sons of Sis´era, the
sons of Temah, 56the sons of Nezi´ah,
the sons of Hati´pha.

57 The sons of Solomon's ser-
vants: the sons of So´tai, the sons of
So´phereth, the sons of Peri´da, 58the
sons of Ja´ala, the sons of Darkon,
the sons of Giddel, 59the sons of
Shephati´ah, the sons of Hattil, the
sons of Po´chereth-hazzeba´im, the
sons of Amon.

60 All the temple servants and the
sons of Solomon's servants were three
hundred and ninety-two.

61 The following were those
who came up from Tel-me´lah, Tel-
har´sha, Cherub, Addon, and Immer,
but they could not prove their fathers'
houses nor their descent, whether
they belonged to Israel: 62the sons
of Delai´ah, the sons of Tobi´ah, the
sons of Neko´da, six hundred and for-
ty-two. 63Also, of the priests: the sons
of Hobai´ah, the sons of Hakkoz, the
sons of Barzil´lai (who had taken a
wife of the daughters of Barzil´lai
the Gileadite and was called by their
name). 64These sought their regis-
tration among those enrolled in the
genealogies, but it was not found
there, so they were excluded from the
priesthood as unclean; 65the gover-
nor told them that they were not to
partake of the most holy food, until
a priest with Urim and Thummim
should arise.

66 The whole assembly together
was forty-two thousand three hun-
dred and sixty, 67besides their men-
servants and maidservants, of whom
there were seven thousand three
hundred and thirty-seven; and they
had two hundred and forty-five sing-
ers, male and female. 68Their horses
were seven hundred and thirty-six,
their mules two hundred and for-
ty-five,[c] 69their camels four hundred
and thirty-five, and their asses six
thousand seven hundred and twenty.

70 Now some of the heads of fa-
thers' houses gave to the work. The
governor gave to the treasury a thou-
sand darics of gold, fifty basins, five
hundred and thirty priests' garments.
71And some of the heads of fathers'
houses gave into the treasury of the
work twenty thousand darics of gold
and two thousand two hundred minas
of silver. 72And what the rest of the
people gave was twenty thousand
darics of gold, two thousand minas
of silver, and sixty-seven priests'
garments.

73 So the priests, the Levites, the
gatekeepers, the singers, some of the
people, the temple servants, and all
Israel, lived in their towns.

EZRA SUMMONS THE PEOPLE TO OBEY THE LAW

And when the seventh month had
come, the children of Israel were in
their towns.*

8 And all the people gathered as one
man into the square before the
Water Gate; and they told Ezra the
scribe to bring the book of the law of
Moses which the LORD had given to
Israel. 2And Ezra the priest brought
the law before the assembly, both
men and women and all who could
hear with understanding, on the first
day of the seventh month. 3And he
read from it facing the square before
the Water Gate from early morning
until midday, in the presence of the
men and the women and those who
could understand; and the ears of
all the people were attentive to the
book of the law. 4And Ezra the scribe
stood on a wooden pulpit which
they had made for the purpose; and

[c] Ezra 2. 66 and the margins of some Hebrew Mss: Heb lacks *their horses. .. forty-five*

beside him stood Mattithi´ah, Shema,
Anai´ah, Uri´ah, Hilki´ah, and Ma-
asei´ah on his right hand; and Pedai´-
ah, Mish´a-el, Malchi´jah, Hashum,
Hash-bad´danah, Zechari´ah, and Me-
shul´lam on his left hand. 5And Ezra
opened the book in the sight of all the
people, for he was above all the peo-
ple; and when he opened it all the peo-
ple stood. 6And Ezra blessed the LORD,
the great God; and all the people an-
swered, "Amen, Amen," lifting up their
hands; and they bowed their heads and
worshiped the LORD with their faces
to the ground. 7Also Jeshua, Bani, She-
rebi´ah, Jamin, Akkub, Shab´bethai,
Hodi´ah, Ma-asei´ah, Keli´ta, Azari´-
ah, Jo´zabad, Hanan, Pelai´ah, the Le-
vites,[a] helped the people to understand
the law, while the people remained in
their places. 8And they read from the
book, from the law of God, clearly;[b] and
they gave the sense, so that the people
understood the reading.*

9 And Nehemi´ah, who was the
governor, and Ezra the priest and
scribe, and the Levites who taught
the people said to all the people,
"This day is holy to the LORD your
God; do not mourn or weep." For all
the people wept when they heard the
words of the law. 10Then he said to
them, "Go your way, eat the fat and
drink sweet wine and send portions
to him for whom nothing is prepared;
for this day is holy to our Lord; and
do not be grieved, for the joy of the
LORD is your strength." 11So the
Levites stilled all the people, saying,
"Be quiet, for this day is holy; do
not be grieved." 12And all the people
went their way to eat and drink and
to send portions and to make great
rejoicing, because they had under-
stood the words that were declared
to them.

THE FESTIVAL OF BOOTHS CELEBRATED

13 On the second day the heads of
fathers' houses of all the people, with
the priests and the Levites, came to-
gether to Ezra the scribe in order to
study the words of the law. 14And
they found it written in the law that
the LORD had commanded by Moses
that the people of Israel should dwell
in booths during the feast of the sev-
enth month, 15and that they should
publish and proclaim in all their
towns and in Jerusalem, "Go out to
the hills and bring branches of olive,
wild olive, myrtle, palm, and oth-
er leafy trees to make booths, as it
is written." 16So the people went out
and brought them and made booths
for themselves, each on his roof, and
in their courts and in the courts of
the house of God, and in the square
at the Water Gate and in the square
at the Gate of E´phraim. 17And all the
assembly of those who had returned
from the captivity made booths and
dwelt in the booths; for from the days
of Jeshua the son of Nun to that day
the people of Israel had not done so.
And there was very great rejoicing.
18And day by day, from the first day
to the last day, he read from the book
of the law of God. They kept the feast
seven days; and on the eighth day
there was a solemn assembly, accord-
ing to the ordinance.

NATIONAL CONFESSION

9 Now on the twenty-fourth day of
this month the people of Israel
were assembled with fasting and in
sackcloth, and with earth upon their
heads. 2And the Israelites separated
themselves from all foreigners, and
stood and confessed their sins and the
iniquities of their fathers. 3And they
stood up in their place and read from
the book of the law of the LORD their
God for a fourth of the day; for another
fourth of it they made confession and
worshiped the LORD their God. 4Upon
the stairs of the Levites stood Jeshua,
Bani, Kad´mi-el, Shebani´ah, Bunni,
Sherebi´ah, Bani, and Chena´ni; and

[a] 1Esdras 9.48 Vg: Heb *and the Levites*
[b] Or *with interpretation*

they cried with a loud voice to the
LORD their God. 5 Then the Levites,
Jeshua, Kad'miel, Bani, Hashabne-
i'ah, Sherebi'ah, Hodi'ah, Shebani'-
ah, and Pethahi'ah, said, "Stand up
and bless the LORD your God from
everlasting to everlasting. Blessed be
thy glorious name which is exalted
above all blessing and praise."

6 And Ezra said:[c] "Thou art the
LORD, thou alone; thou hast made
heaven, the heaven of heavens, with
all their host, the earth and all that is
on it, the seas and all that is in them;
and thou preservest all of them; and
the host of heaven worships thee.
7 Thou art the LORD, the God who
didst choose Abram and bring him
forth out of Ur of the Chalde'ans and
give him the name Abraham; 8 and
thou didst find his heart faithful be-
fore thee, and didst make with him
the covenant to give to his descen-
dants the land of the Canaanite, the
Hittite, the Amorite, the Per'izzite,
the Jeb'usite, and the Gir'gashite; and
thou hast fulfilled thy promise, for
thou art righteous.

9 "And thou didst see the afflic-
tion of our fathers in Egypt and hear
their cry at the Red Sea, 10 and didst
perform signs and wonders against
Pharaoh and all his servants and all
the people of his land, for thou knew-
est that they acted insolently against
our fathers; and thou didst get thee a
name, as it is to this day. 11 And thou
didst divide the sea before them, so
that they went through the midst of
the sea on dry land; and thou didst
cast their pursuers into the depths,
as a stone into mighty waters. 12 By a
pillar of cloud thou didst lead them
in the day, and by a pillar of fire in
the night to light for them the way in
which they should go. 13 Thou didst
come down upon Mount Sinai, and
speak with them from heaven and
give them right ordinances and true
laws, good statutes and command-
ments, 14 and thou didst make known
to them thy holy sabbath and com-
mand them commandments and stat-
utes and a law by Moses thy servant.
15 Thou didst give them bread from
heaven for their hunger and bring
forth water for them from the rock for
their thirst, and thou didst tell them
to go in to possess the land which
thou hadst sworn to give them.

16 "But they and our fathers acted
presumptuously and stiffened their
neck and did not obey thy command-
ments; 17 they refused to obey, and
were not mindful of the wonders
which thou didst perform among
them; but they stiffened their neck
and appointed a leader to return to
their bondage in Egypt. But thou art
a God ready to forgive, gracious and
merciful, slow to anger and abound-
ing in steadfast love, and didst not
forsake them. 18 Even when they had
made for themselves a molten calf
and said, 'This is your God who
brought you up out of Egypt,' and had
committed great blasphemies, 19 thou
in thy great mercies didst not forsake
them in the wilderness; the pillar of
cloud which led them in the way did
not depart from them by day, nor the
pillar of fire by night which light-
ed for them the way by which they
should go. 20 Thou gavest thy good
Spirit to instruct them, and didst
not withhold thy manna from their
mouth, and gavest them water for
their thirst. 21 Forty years didst thou
sustain them in the wilderness, and
they lacked nothing; their clothes
did not wear out and their feet did
not swell. 22 And thou didst give them
kingdoms and peoples, and didst al-
lot to them every corner; so they took
possession of the land of Sihon king
of Heshbon and the land of Og king
of Bashan. 23 Thou didst multiply their
descendants as the stars of heaven,
and thou didst bring them into the
land which thou hadst told their fa-
thers to enter and possess. 24 So the
descendants went in and possessed

[c] Gk: Heb lacks *and Ezra said*

the land, and thou didst subdue be-
fore them the inhabitants of the land,
the Canaanites, and didst give them
into their hands, with their kings
and the peoples of the land, that they
might do with them as they would.
25And they captured fortified cities
and a rich land, and took possession
of houses full of all good things, cis-
terns hewn out, vineyards, olive or-
chards and fruit trees in abundance;
so they ate, and were filled and be-
came fat, and delighted themselves in
thy great goodness.

26 "Nevertheless they were dis-
obedient and rebelled against thee
and cast thy law behind their back
and killed thy prophets, who had
warned them in order to turn them
back to thee, and they committed
great blasphemies. 27Therefore thou
didst give them into the hand of their
enemies, who made them suffer; and
in the time of their suffering they
cried to thee and thou didst hear
them from heaven; and according
to thy great mercies thou didst give
them saviors who saved them from
the hand of their enemies. 28But af-
ter they had rest they did evil again
before thee, and thou didst abandon
them to the hand of their enemies, so
that they had dominion over them;
yet when they turned and cried to
thee thou didst hear from heaven,
and many times thou didst deliver
them according to thy mercies. 29And
thou didst warn them in order to
turn them back to thy law. Yet they
acted presumptuously and did not
obey thy commandments, but sinned
against thy ordinances, by the obser-
vance of which a man shall live, and
turned a stubborn shoulder and stiff-
ened their neck and would not obey.
30Many years thou didst bear with
them, and didst warn them by thy
Spirit through thy prophets; yet they
would not give ear. Therefore thou
didst give them into the hand of the
peoples of the lands. 31Nevertheless
in thy great mercies thou didst not
make an end of them or forsake
them; for thou art a gracious and
merciful God.

32 "Now therefore, our God, the
great and mighty and terrible God,
who keepest covenant and steadfast
love, let not all the hardship seem
little to thee that has come upon
us, upon our kings, our princes, our
priests, our prophets, our fathers,
and all thy people, since the time of
the kings of Assyria until this day.
33Yet thou hast been just in all that
has come upon us, for thou hast dealt
faithfully and we have acted wickedly;
34our kings, our princes, our priests,
and our fathers have not kept thy law
or heeded thy commandments and thy
warnings which thou didst give them.
35They did not serve thee in their king-
dom, and in thy great goodness which
thou gavest them, and in the large and
rich land which thou didst set before
them; and they did not turn from their
wicked works. 36Behold, we are slaves
this day; in the land that thou gavest
to our fathers to enjoy its fruit and
its good gifts, behold, we are slaves.
37And its rich yield goes to the kings
whom thou hast set over us because
of our sins; they have power also
over our bodies and over our cattle
at their pleasure, and we are in great
distress."

THOSE WHO SIGNED THE COVENANT

38[a] Because of all this we make a
firm covenant and write it, and our
princes, our Levites, and our priests
set their seal to it.

10[b] Those who set their seal are
Nehemi´ah the governor, the son
of Hacali´ah, Zedeki´ah, 2Serai´ah,
Azari´ah, Jeremiah, 3Pashhur, Amari´-
ah, Malchi´jah, 4Hattush, Shebani´ah,
Malluch, 5Harim, Mer´emoth, Oba-
di´ah, 6Daniel, Gin´nethon, Baruch,
7Meshul´lam, Abi´jah, Mi´jamin,

[a]Ch 10.1 in Heb
[b]Ch 10.2 in Heb

TOBIT

1 The book of the acts[a] of Tobit the
son of To´biel, son of Anan´iel,
son of Ad´uel, son of Gab´ael, of the
descendants of As´iel and the tribe
of Naph´tali, 2who in the days of
Shalmane´ser,[b] king of the Assyrians,
was taken into captivity from Thisbe,
which is to the south of Kedesh
Naph´tali in Galilee above Asher.

TOBIT'S YOUTH AND VIRTUOUS LIFE

3 I, Tobit, walked in the ways of
truth and righteousness all the days of
my life, and I performed many acts of
charity to my brethren and country-
men who went with me into the land
of the Assyrians, to Nin´eveh. 4Now
when I was in my own country, in the
land of Israel, while I was still a young
man, the whole tribe of Naph´tali
my forefather deserted the house of
Jerusalem. This was the place which
had been chosen from among all the
tribes of Israel, where all the tribes
should sacrifice and where the temple
of the dwelling of the Most High was
consecrated and established for all
generations for ever.

5 All the tribes that joined in apos-
tasy used to sacrifice to the calf[c] Ba´al,
and so did the house of Naph´tali
my forefather. 6But I alone went of-
ten to Jerusalem for the feasts, as it
is ordained for all Israel by an ever-
lasting decree. Taking the first fruits
and the tithes of my produce and the
first shearings, I would give these to
the priests, the sons of Aaron, at the
altar. 7Of all my produce I would give
a tenth to the sons of Levi who min-
istered at Jerusalem; a second tenth I
would sell, and I would go and spend
the proceeds each year at Jerusalem;
8the third tenth I would give to those
to whom it was my duty, as Deb´orah
my father's mother had commanded
me, for I was left an orphan by my fa-
ther. 9When I became a man I married
Anna, a member of our family, and by
her I became the father of Tobi´as.

TAKEN CAPTIVE TO NINEVEH

10 Now when I was carried away
captive to Nin´eveh, all my brethren
and my relatives ate the food of the
Gentiles; 11but I kept myself from eat-
ing it, 12because I remembered God
with all my heart. 13Then the Most
High gave me favor and good appear-
ance in the sight of Shalmane´ser,[d]
and I was his buyer of provisions. 14So
I used to go into Media, and once at
Rages in Media I left ten talents of sil-
ver in trust with Gab´ael, the brother
of Gabri´as. 15But when Shalmane´ser[e]
died, Sennach´erib his son reigned in
his place; and under him the highways
were unsafe, so that I could no longer
go into Media.

COURAGE IN BURYING THE DEAD

16 In the days of Shalmane´ser[f] I
performed many acts of charity to my
brethren. 17I would give my bread to
the hungry and my clothing to the na-
ked; and if I saw any one of my people
dead and thrown out behind the wall
of Nin´eveh, I would bury him. 18And
if Sennach´erib the king put to death
any who came fleeing from Judea, I
buried them secretly. For in his anger
he put many to death. When the bod-
ies were sought by the king, they were
not found. 19Then one of the men of
Nin´eveh went and informed the king
about me, that I was burying them;
so I hid myself. When I learned that
I was being searched for, to be put
to death, I left home in fear. 20Then
all my property was confiscated and

[a] Gk *words*
[b] Gk *Enemessarus*
[c] Other authorities read *heifer*
[d] Gk *Enemessarus*
[e] Gk *Enemessarus*
[f] Gk *Enemessarus*

nothing was left to me except my wife
Anna and my son Tobi´as.
21 But not fifty[a] days passed be-
fore two of Sennach´erib's[b] sons killed
him, and they fled to the mountains of
Ar´arat. Then Esarhad´don,[c] his son,
reigned in his place; and he appointed
Ahi´kar, the son of my brother An´ael,
over all the accounts of his kingdom
and over the entire administration.
22 Ahi´kar interceded for me, and I re-
turned to Nin´eveh. Now Ahi´kar was
cupbearer, keeper of the signet, and
in charge of administration of the ac-
counts, for Esarhad´don[d] had appoint-
ed him second to himself.[e] He was my
nephew.

2 When I arrived home and my wife
Anna and my son Tobi´as were re-
stored to me, at the feast of Pentecost,
which is the sacred festival of the sev-
en weeks, a good dinner was prepared
for me and I sat down to eat. 2 Upon
seeing the abundance of food I said to
my son, "Go and bring whatever poor
man of our brethren you may find who
is mindful of the Lord, and I will wait
for you." 3 But he came back and said,
"Father, one of our people has been
strangled and thrown into the market
place." 4 So before I tasted anything I
sprang up and removed the body[f] to
a place of shelter until sunset. 5 And
when I returned I washed myself and
ate my food in sorrow. 6 Then I remem-
bered the prophecy of Amos, how he
said,

> "Your feasts shall be turned
> into mourning,
> and all your festivities into
> lamentation."

TOBIT BECOMES BLIND

7 When the sun had set I went and
dug a grave and buried the body.[g] 8 And
my neighbors laughed at me and said,
"He is no longer afraid that he will be
put to death for doing this; he once
ran away, and here he is burying the
dead again!" 9 On the same night I
returned from burying him, and be-
cause I was defiled I slept by the wall
of the courtyard, and my face was un-
covered. 10 I did not know that there
were sparrows on the wall and their
fresh droppings fell into my open eyes
and white films formed on my eyes. I
went to physicians, but they did not
help me. Ahi´kar, however, took care
of me until he[h] went to Elyma´is.*

TOBIT'S WIFE EARNS THEIR LIVELIHOOD

11 Then my wife Anna earned
money at women's work. 12 She used
to send the product to the owners.
Once when they paid her wages, they
also gave her a kid; 13 and when she
returned to me it began to bleat. So
I said to her, "Where did you get the
kid? It is not stolen, is it? Return it to
the owners; for it is not right to eat
what is stolen." 14 And she said, "It was
given to me as a gift in addition to my
wages." But I did not believe her, and
told her to return it to the owners; and
I blushed for her. Then she replied to
me, "Where are your charities and
your righteous deeds? You seem to
know everything!"

TOBIT'S PRAYER

3 Then in my grief I wept, and I prayed
in anguish, saying, 2 "Righteous art
thou, O Lord; all thy deeds and all
thy ways are mercy and truth, and
thou dost render true and righteous
judgment for ever. 3 Remember me and
look favorably upon me; do not punish
me for my sins and for my unwitting
offenses and those which my fathers
committed before thee. 4 For they dis-
obeyed thy commandments, and thou

[a] Other authorities read *fifty-five*
[b] Gk *his*
[c] Gk *Sacherdonus*
[d] Gk *Sacherdonus*
[e] Or *a second time*
[f] Gk *him*
[g] Gk *him*
[h] Other authorities read *I*

gavest us over to plunder, captivity,
and death; thou madest us a byword
of reproach in all the nations among
which we have been dispersed. 5And
now thy many judgments are true in
exacting penalty from me for my sins
and those of my fathers, because we
did not keep thy commandments. For
we did not walk in truth before thee.
6And now deal with me according to
thy pleasure; command my spirit to
be taken up, that I may depart and be-
come dust. For it is better for me to
die than to live, because I have heard
false reproaches, and great is the sor-
row within me. Command that I now
be released from my distress to go to
the eternal abode; do not turn thy face
away from me."

SARAH FALSELY ACCUSED

7 On the same day, at Ecbat´ana
in Media, it also happened that
Sarah, the daughter of Rag´uel, was
reproached by her father's maids,
8because she had been given to sev-
en husbands, and the evil demon
Asmode´us had slain each of them
before he had been with her as his
wife. So the maids[i] said to her, "Do
you not know that you strangle your
husbands? You already have had seven
and have had no benefit from[j] any of
them. 9Why do you beat us? If they are
dead, go with them! May we never see
a son or daughter of yours!"

SARAH'S PRAYER FOR DEATH

10 When she heard these things
she was deeply grieved, even to the
thought of hanging herself. But she
said, "I am the only child of my father;
if I do this, it will be a disgrace to him,
and I shall bring his old age down in
sorrow to the grave."[k] 11So she prayed
by her window and said, "Blessed art
thou, O Lord my God, and blessed is
thy holy and honored name for ever.
May all thy works praise thee for ever.
12And now, O Lord, I have turned
my eyes and my face toward thee.
13Command that I be released from
the earth and that I hear reproach no
more. 14Thou knowest, O Lord, that
I am innocent of any sin with man,
15and that I did not stain my name or
the name of my father in the land of
my captivity. I am my father's only
child, and he has no child to be his
heir, no near kinsman or kinsman's[l]
son for whom I should keep myself as
wife. Already seven husbands of mine
are dead. Why should I live? But if it
be not pleasing to thee to take my life,
command that respect be shown to me
and pity be taken upon me, and that I
hear reproach no more."*

AN ANSWER TO PRAYER

16 The prayer of both was heard
in the presence of the glory of the
great God. 17And Raph´ael[m] was sent
to heal the two of them: to scale away
the white films of Tobit's eyes; to give
Sarah the daughter of Rag´uel in mar-
riage to Tobi´as the son of Tobit, and
to bind Asmode´us the evil demon,
because Tobi´as was entitled to pos-
sess her. At that very moment Tobit
returned and entered his house and
Sarah the daughter of Rag´uel came
down from her upper room.

TOBIT GIVES INSTRUCTIONS TO HIS SON

4 On that day Tobit remembered the
money which he had left in trust
with Gab´ael at Rages in Media, and
he said to himself: 2"I have asked
for death. Why do I not call my son
Tobi´as so that I may explain to him
about the money[n] before I die?" 3So he
called him and said, "My son, when I
die, bury me, and do not neglect your
mother. Honor her all the days of your

[i] Gk *they*
[j] Other authorities read *have not borne the name of*
[k] Gk *to Hades*
[l] Gk *his*
[m] Other authorities read *the great Raph´ael. And he*
[n] Other authorities omit *about the money*

life; do what is pleasing to her, and do
not grieve her. 4 Remember, my son,
that she faced many dangers for you
while you were yet unborn. When she
dies, bury her beside me in the same
grave.

5 "Remember the Lord our God all
your days, my son, and refuse to sin
or to transgress his commandments.
Live uprightly all the days of your life,
and do not walk in the ways of wrong-
doing. 6 For if you do what is true, your
ways will prosper through your deeds.
7 Give alms from your possessions to
all who live uprightly, and do not let
your eye begrudge the gift when you
make it. Do not turn your face away
from any poor man, and the face of
God will not be turned away from
you. 8 If you have many possessions,
make your gift from them in propor-
tion; if few, do not be afraid to give ac-
cording to the little you have. 9 So you
will be laying up a good treasure for
yourself against the day of necessity.
10 For charity* delivers from death and
keeps you from entering the darkness;
11 and for all who practice it charity is
an excellent offering in the presence
of the Most High.

12 "Beware, my son, of all immoral-
ity.* First of all take a wife from among
the descendants of your fathers and
do not marry a foreign woman, who
is not of your father's tribe; for we are
the sons of the prophets. Remember,
my son, that Noah, Abraham, Isaac,
and Jacob, our fathers of old, all took
wives from among their brethren.
They were blessed in their children,
and their posterity will inherit the
land. 13 So now, my son, love your
brethren, and in your heart do not dis-
dain your brethren and the sons and
daughters of your people by refusing
to take a wife for yourself from among
them. For in pride there is ruin and
great confusion; and in shiftlessness
there is loss and great want, because
shiftlessness is the mother of famine.
14 Do not hold over till the next day the
wages of any man who works for you,
but pay him at once; and if you serve
God you will receive payment. "Watch
yourself, my son, in everything you do,
and be disciplined in all your conduct.
15 And what you hate, do not do to any
one. Do not drink wine to excess or
let drunkenness go with you on your
way. 16 Give of your bread to the hun-
gry, and of your clothing to the naked.
Give all your surplus to charity, and
do not let your eye begrudge the gift
when you made it. 17 Place your bread*
on the grave of the righteous, but give
none to sinners. 18 Seek advice from ev-
ery wise man, and do not despise any
useful counsel. 19 Bless the Lord God
on every occasion; ask him that your
ways may be made straight and that
all your paths and plans may prosper.
For none of the nations has under-
standing; but the Lord himself gives
all good things, and according to his
will he humbles whomever he wishes.

MONEY LEFT IN TRUST WITH GABAEL

"So, my son, remember my com-
mands, and do not let them be blot-
ted out of your mind. 20 And now let
me explain to you about the ten tal-
ents of silver which I left in trust with
Gab´ael the son of Gabri´as at Rages
in Media. 21 Do not be afraid, my son,
because we have become poor. You
have great wealth if you fear God and
refrain from every sin and do what is
pleasing in his sight."

THE ANGEL RAPH´AEL

5 Then Tobi´as answered him,
"Father, I will do everything that
you have commanded me; 2 but how
can I obtain the money when I do not
know the man?" 3 Then Tobit gave him
the receipt, and said to him, "Find a
man to go with you and I will pay him
wages as long as I live; and go and get
the money." 4 So he went to look for a
man; and he found Raph´ael, who was
an angel, 5 but Tobi´as[a] did not know

[a] Gk *he*

it. Tobi´as[b] said to him, "Can you go
with me to Rages in Media? Are you
acquainted with that region?" 6The
angel replied, "I will go with you; I
am familiar with the way, and I have
stayed with our brother Gab´ael."
7Then Tobi´as said to him, "Wait for
me, and I shall tell my father." 8And
he said to him, "Go, and do not delay."
So he went in and said to his father,
"I have found some one to go with
me." He said, "Call him to me, so that
I may learn to what tribe he belongs,
and whether he is a reliable man to go
with you."

9 So Tobi´as[c] invited him in; he
entered and they greeted each other.
10Then Tobit said to him, "My broth-
er, to what tribe and family do you
belong? Tell me." 11But he answered,
"Are you looking for a tribe and a fam-
ily or for a man whom you will pay to
go with your son?" And Tobit said to
him, "I should like to know, my broth-
er, your people and your name." 12He
replied, "I am Azari´as the son of the
great Anani´as, one of your relatives."
13Then Tobit said to him, "You are
welcome, my brother. Do not be angry
with me because I tried to learn your
tribe and family. You are a relative of
mine, of a good and noble lineage. For
I used to know Anani´as and Jathan,
the sons of the great Shema´iah, when
we went together to Jerusalem to wor-
ship and offered the first-born of our
flocks and the tithes of our produce.
They did not go astray in the error of
our brethren. My brother, you come of
good stock. 14But tell me, what wages
am I to pay you—a drachma a day, and
expenses for yourself as for my son?
15And besides, I will add to your wages
if you both return safe and sound." So
they agreed to these terms.

16 Then he said to Tobi´as, "Get
ready for the journey, and good suc-
cess to you both." So his son made
the preparations for the journey. And
his father said to him, "Go with this
man; God who dwells in heaven will
prosper your way, and may his angel
attend you." So they both went out
and departed, and the young man's
dog was with them.

17 But Anna,[d] his mother, began to
weep, and said to Tobit, "Why have
you sent our child away? Is he not the
staff of our hands as he goes in and
out before us? 18Do not add money
to money, but consider it as rubbish
as compared to our child. 19For the
life that is given to us by the Lord is
enough for us." 20And Tobit said to
her, "Do not worry, my sister; he will
return safe and sound, and your eyes
will see him. 21For a good angel will go
with him; his journey will be success-
ful, and he will come back safe and
sound." 22So she stopped weeping.

JOURNEY TO RAGES

6 Now as they proceeded on their
way they came at evening to the
Tigris river and camped there. 2Then
the young man went down to wash
himself. A fish leaped up from the
river and would have swallowed the
young man; 3and the angel said to
him, "Catch the fish." So the young
man seized the fish and threw it up on
the land. 4Then the angel said to him,
"Cut open the fish and take the heart
and liver and gall and put them away
safely." 5So the young man did as the
angel told him; and they roasted and
ate the fish. And they both continued
on their way until they came near to
Ecbat´ana. 6Then the young man said
to the angel, "Brother Azari´as, of
what use is the liver and heart and
gall of the fish?" 7He replied, "As for
the heart and the liver, if a demon or
evil spirit gives trouble to any one,
you make a smoke from these before
the man or woman, and that person
will never be troubled again. 8And as
for the gall, anoint with it a man who
has white films in his eyes, and he will
be cured."

[b] Gk *he*
[c] Gk *he*
[d] Other authorities omit *Anna*

RAPH´AEL'S INSTRUCTIONS

9 When they approached Ecbat´a-
na,[a] [10]the angel said to the young man,
"Brother, today we shall stay with
Rag´uel. He is your relative, and he
has an only daughter named Sarah. I
will suggest that she be given to you in
marriage, [11]because you are entitled to
her and to her inheritance, for you are
her only eligible kinsman. [12]The girl
is also beautiful and sensible. Now
listen to my plan. I will speak to her
father, and as soon as we return from
Rages we will celebrate the marriage.
For I know that Rag´uel, according to
the law of Moses, cannot give her to
another man without incurring the
penalty of death, because you rather
than any other man are entitled to the
inheritance."

13 Then the young man said to the
angel, "Brother Azari´as, I have heard
that the girl has been given to seven
husbands and that each died in the
bridal chamber. [14]Now I am the only
son my father has, and I am afraid
that if I go in I will die as those be-
fore me did, for a demon is in love
with her, and he harms no one except
those who approach her. So now I fear
that I may die and bring the lives of
my father and mother to the grave in
sorrow on my account. And they have
no other son to bury them."

15* But the angel said to him, "Do
you not remember the words with
which your father commanded you
to take a wife from among your own
people? Now listen to me, brother,
for she will become your wife; and do
not worry about the demon, for this
very night she will be given to you in
marriage. [16]When you enter the bridal
chamber, you shall take live ashes of
incense and lay upon them some of
the heart and liver of the fish so as to
make a smoke. [17]Then the demon will
smell it and flee away, and will never
again return. And when you approach
her, rise up, both of you, and cry out
to the merciful God, and he will save
you and have mercy on you. Do not be
afraid, for she was destined for you
from eternity. You will save her, and
she will go with you, and I suppose
that you will have children by her."
When Tobi´as heard these things, he
fell in love with her and yearned deep-
ly for her.

ARRIVAL AT HOME OF RAGUEL

7 When they reached Ecbat´ana and
arrived at the house of Rag´uel,
Sarah met them and greeted them.
They returned her greeting, and she
brought them into the house. [2]Then
Rag´uel said to his wife Edna, "How
much the young man resembles my
cousin Tobit!" [3]And Rag´uel asked
them, "Where are you from, breth-
ren?" They answered him, "We be-
long to the sons of Naph´tali, who
are captives in Nin´eveh." [4]So he said
to them, "Do you know our brother
Tobit?" And they said, "Yes, we do."
And he asked them, "Is he in good
health?" [5]They replied, "He is alive
and in good health." And Tobi´as
said, "He is my father." [6]Then Rag´uel
sprang up and kissed him and wept.
[7]And he blessed him and exclaimed,
"Son of that good and noble man!"
When he heard that Tobit had lost
his sight, he was stricken with grief
and wept. [8]And his wife Edna and his
daughter Sarah wept. They received
them very warmly; and they killed a
ram from the flock and set large serv-
ings of food before them.

MARRIAGE OF TOBIAS AND SARAH

Then Tobi´as said to Raph´ael,
"Brother Azari´as, speak of those
things which you talked about on the
journey, and let the matter be settled."
[9]So he communicated the proposal to
Rag´uel. And Rag´uel said to Tobi´as,
"Eat, drink, and be merry; [10]for it is
your right to take my child. But let
me explain the true situation to you.
[11]I have given my daughter to seven
husbands, and when each came to her

[a]Other authorities read *Rages*

he died in the night. But for the pres-
ent be merry." And Tobi´as said, "I
will eat nothing here until you make
a binding agreement with me." 12So
Rag´uel said, "Take her right now, in
accordance with the law. You are her
relative, and she is yours. The merci-
ful God will guide you both for the
best." 13Then he called his daughter
Sarah, and taking her by the hand he
gave her to Tobi´as to be his wife, say-
ing, "Here she is; take her according
to the law of Moses, and take her with
you to your father." And he blessed
them.* 14Next he called his wife Edna,
and took a scroll and wrote out the
contract; and they set their seals to it.
15Then they began to eat.

16 And Rag´uel called his wife
Edna and said to her, "Sister, make
up the other room, and take her into
it." 17So she did as he said, and took
her there; and the girl[b] began to weep.
But the mother[c] comforted her daugh-
ter in her tears, and said to her, 18"Be
brave, my child; the Lord of heaven
and earth grant you joy[d] in place of
this sorrow of yours. Be brave, my
daughter."

TOBIAS ROUTS THE DEMON

8 When they had finished eating,
they escorted Tobi´as in to her. 2As
he went he remembered the words of
Raph´ael, and he took the live ashes
of incense and put the heart and liv-
er of the fish upon them and made a
smoke. 3And when the demon smelled
the odor he fled to the remotest parts
of Egypt, and the angel bound him.
4*When the door was shut* and the two
were alone, Tobi´as got up from the
bed and said, "Sister, get up, and let
us pray that the Lord may have mercy
upon us."* 5And Tobi´as began to pray,

"Blessed art thou, O God of
our fathers,
and blessed be thy holy and
glorious name for
ever.
Let the heavens and all thy
creatures bless thee.
6Thou madest Adam and gavest
him Eve his wife
as a helper and support.
From them the race of man-
kind has sprung.
Thou didst say, 'It is not good
that the man should be
alone;
let us make a helper for him
like himself.'

7And now, O Lord, I am not taking
this sister of mine because of lust,
but with sincerity. Grant that I may
find mercy and may grow old togeth-
er with her." 8And she said with him,
"Amen." 9Then they both went to
sleep for the night. But Rag´uel arose
and went and dug a grave, 10with the
thought, "Perhaps he too will die."
11Then Rag´uel went into his house
12and said to his wife Edna, "Send
one of the maids to see whether he
is alive; and if he is not, let us bury
him without any one knowing about
it." 13So the maid opened the door and
went in, and found them both asleep.
14And she came out and told them that
he was alive. 15Then Rag´uel blessed
God and said,

"Blessed art thou, O God, with
every pure and holy
blessing.
Let thy saints and all thy
creatures bless thee;
let all thy angels and thy
chosen people bless
thee for ever.
16Blessed art thou, because thou
hast made me glad.
It has not happened to me as
I expected;
but thou hast treated us
according to thy great
mercy.
17Blessed art thou, because thou
hast had compassion on
two only children.
Show them mercy, O Lord;

[b]Gk *she*
[c]Gk *she*
[d]Other authorities read *favor*

and bring their lives to
fulfilment in health
and happiness and
mercy."
18 Then he ordered his servants to fill
in the grave.

WEDDING FEAST

19 After this he gave a wedding
feast for them which lasted fourteen
days. 20 And before the days of the
feast were over, Rag´uel declared by
oath to Tobi´as[a] that he should not
leave until the fourteen days of the
wedding feast were ended, 21 that then
he should take half of Rag´uel's[b] prop-
erty and return in safety to his father,
and that the rest would be his "when
my wife and I die."

THE MONEY RECOVERED

9 Then Tobi´as called Raph´ael and
said to him, 2 "Brother Azari´as,
take a servant and two camels with
you and go to Gab´ael at Rages in
Media and get the money for me;
and bring him to the wedding feast.
3 For Rag´uel has sworn that I should
not leave; 4 but my father is counting
the days, and if I delay long he will
be greatly distressed." 5 So Raph´ael
made the journey and stayed over
night with Gab´ael. He gave him the
receipt, and Gab´ael[c] brought out the
money bags with their seals intact
and gave them to him. 6 In the morning
they both got up early and came to the
wedding feast. And Gab´ael blessed
Tobi´as and his wife.[d]*

ANXIETY OF THE PARENTS

10 Now his father Tobit was count-
ing each day, and when the days
for the journey had expired and they
did not arrive, 2 he said, "Is it possi-
ble that he has been detained?[e] Or
is it possible that Gab´ael has died
and there is no one to give him the
money?" 3 And he was greatly dis-
tressed. 4 And his wife said to him,
"The lad has perished; his long delay
proves it." Then she began to mourn
for him, and said, 5 "Am I not dis-
tressed, my child, that I let you go,
you who are the light of my eyes?"
6 But Tobit said to her, "Be still and
stop worrying; he is well." 7 And she
answered him, "Be still and stop de-
ceiving me; my child has perished."
And she went out every day to the
road by which they had left; she ate
nothing in the daytime, and through-
out the nights she never stopped
mourning for her son Tobi´as, until
the fourteen days of the wedding
feast had expired which Rag´uel had
sworn that he should spend there.

TOBIAS AND SARAH START FOR HOME

At that time Tobi´as said to
Rag´uel, "Send me back, for my father
and mother have given up hope of ever
seeing me again." 8 But his father-in-
law said to him, "Stay with me, and I
will send messengers to your father,
and they will inform him how things
are with you." 9 Tobi´as replied, "No,
send me back to my father." 10 So
Rag´uel arose and gave him his wife
Sarah and half of his property in
slaves, cattle, and money. 11 And when
he had blessed them he sent them
away, saying, "The God of heaven
will prosper you, my children, before
I die." 12 He said also to his daughter,
"Honor your father-in-law and your
mother-in-law; they are now your
parents. Let me hear a good report of
you." And he kissed her. And Edna
said to Tobi´as, "The Lord of heaven
bring you back safely, dear brother,
and grant me to see your children by
my daughter Sarah, that I may rejoice
before the Lord. See, I am entrusting
my daughter to you; do nothing to
grieve her."

[a] Gk *him*
[b] Gk *his*
[c] Gk *he*
[d] Cn: Gk *And Tobi´as blessed his wife*
[e] One Gk Ms Lat: Gk *they are put to shame* or *they are disappointed*

HOMEWARD JOURNEY

11 After this Tobi´as went on his way,
praising God because he had made
his journey a success. And he bless-
ed Rag´uel and his wife Edna. So he
continued on his way until they came
near to Nin´eveh. 2Then Raph´ael said
to Tobi´as, "Are you not aware, broth-
er, of how you left your father? 3Let us
run ahead of your wife and prepare the
house. 4And take the gall of the fish
with you." So they went their way, and
the dog went along behind them.

5 Now Anna sat looking intently
down the road for her son. 6And she
caught sight of him coming, and said
to his father, "Behold, your son is
coming, and so is the man who went
with him!"

TOBIT'S SIGHT RESTORED

7 Raph´ael said, "I know, Tobi´as,
that your father will open his eyes.
8You therefore must anoint his eyes
with the gall; and when they smart
he will rub them, and will cause the
white films to fall away, and he will
see you."

9 Then Anna ran to meet them,
and embraced her son, and said to
him, "I have seen you, my child; now I
am ready to die." And they both wept.
10Tobit started toward the door, and
stumbled. But his son ran to him 11and
took hold of his father, and he sprin-
kled the gall upon his father's eyes,
saying, "Be of good cheer, father."
12And when his eyes began to smart
he rubbed them, 13and the white films
scaled off from the corners of his eyes.
14Then he saw his son and embraced
him, and he wept and said, "Blessed
art thou, O God, and blessed is thy
name for ever, and blessed are all thy
holy angels. 15For thou hast afflicted
me, but thou hast had mercy upon me;
here I see my son Tobi´as!" And his
son went in rejoicing, and he reported
to his father the great things that had
happened to him in Media.

16 Then Tobit went out to meet
his daughter-in-law at the gate of
Nin´eveh, rejoicing and praising
God. Those who saw him as he went
were amazed because he could see.
17And Tobit gave thanks before them
that God had been merciful to him.
When Tobit came near to Sarah his
daughter-in-law, he blessed her, say-
ing, "Welcome, daughter! Blessed
is God who has brought you to us,
and blessed are your father and
your mother." So there was rejoicing
among all his brethren in Nin´eveh.
18Ahi´kar and his nephew Nadab[f]
came, 19and Tobi´as' marriage was
celebrated for seven days with great
festivity.

RAPH´AEL'S WAGES

12 Tobit then called his son Tobi´as
and said to him, "My son, see
to the wages of the man who went
with you; and he must also be given
more." 2He replied, "Father, it would
do me no harm to give him half of
what I have brought back. 3For he has
led me back to you safely, he cured
my wife, he obtained the money for
me, and he also healed you." 4The
old man said, "He deserves it." 5So
he called the angel and said to him,
"Take half of all that you two have
brought back."

RAPH´AEL'S EXHORTATION

6 Then the angel[g] called the two
of them privately and said to them:
"Praise God and give thanks to him;
exalt him and give thanks to him
in the presence of all the living for
what he has done for you. It is good
to praise God and to exalt his name,
worthily declaring the works of God.
Do not be slow to give him thanks. 7It
is good to guard the secret of a king,
but gloriously to reveal the works of
God. Do good, and evil will not over-
take you. 8Prayer is good when accom-
panied by fasting, almsgiving, and

[f] Other authorities read *Nasbas*
[g] Gk *he*

righteousness. A little with righteous-
ness is better than much with wrong-
doing. It is better to give alms than
to treasure up gold. 9For almsgiving
delivers from death, and it will purge
away every sin. Those who perform
deeds of charity* and of righteousness
will have fulness of life; 10but those
who commit sin are the enemies of
their own lives.

RAPH´AEL DISCLOSES HIS IDENTITY

11 "I will not conceal anything
from you. I have said, 'It is good to
guard the secret of a king, but glo-
riously to reveal the works of God.'
12And so, when you and your daugh-
ter-in-law Sarah prayed, I brought a
reminder of your prayer before the
Holy One; and when you buried the
dead, I was likewise present with
you. 13When you did not hesitate to
rise and leave your dinner in order
to go and lay out the dead, your good
deed was not hidden from me, but
I was with you. 14So now God sent
me to heal you and your daughter-
in-law Sarah. 15I am Raph´ael, one of
the seven holy angels who present
the prayers of the saints and enter
into the presence of the glory of the
Holy One."

16 They were both alarmed; and
they fell upon their faces, for they
were afraid. 17But he said to them,
"Do not be afraid; you will be safe.
But praise God for ever. 18For I did
not come as a favor on my part, but
by the will of our God. Therefore
praise him for ever. 19All these days
I merely appeared to you and did not
eat or drink, but you were seeing a vi-
sion. 20And now give thanks to God,
for I am ascending to him who sent
me. Write in a book everything that
has happened." 21Then they stood up;
but they saw him no more. 22So they
confessed the great and wonderful
works of God, and acknowledged that
the angel of the Lord had appeared to
them.

TOBIT'S THANKSGIVING TO GOD

13 Then Tobit wrote a prayer of re-
joicing, and said:
"Blessed is God who lives for
ever,
and blessed is his kingdom.
2For he afflicts, and he shows
mercy;
he leads down to Hades, and
brings up again,
and there is no one who can
escape his hand.
3Acknowledge him before the
nations, O sons of Israel;
for he has scattered us
among them.
4Make his greatness known there,
and exalt him in the pres-
ence of all the living;
because he is our Lord and
God,
he is our Father for ever.
5He will afflict us for our
iniquities;
and again he will show
mercy,
and will gather us from all the
nations
among whom you[a] have been
scattered.
6If you turn to him with all your
heart and with all your
soul,
to do what is true before
him,
then he will turn to you
and will not hide his face
from you.
But see what he will do with
you;
give thanks to him with your
full voice.
Praise the Lord of
righteousness,
and exalt the King of the
ages.
I give him thanks in the land of
my captivity,
and I show his power and
majesty to a nation of
sinners.

[a]Other authorities read *we*

Turn back, you sinners, and do
right before him;
who knows if he will accept
you and have mercy
on you?
7I exalt my God;
my soul exalts the King of
heaven,
and will rejoice in his
majesty.
8Let all men speak,
and give him thanks in
Jerusalem.
9O Jerusalem, the holy city,
he will afflict you for the
deeds of your sons,
but again he will show mer-
cy to the sons of the
righteous.
10Give thanks worthily to the Lord,
and praise the King of the
ages,
that his tent may be raised
for you again with joy.
May he cheer those within you
who are captives,
and love those within you
who are distressed,
to all generations for ever.
11Many nations will come from
afar to the name of the
Lord God,
bearing gifts in their hands,
gifts for the King of
heaven.
Generations of generations will
give you joyful praise.
12Cursed are all who hate you;
blessed for ever will be all
who love you.
13Rejoice and be glad for the sons
of the righteous
for they will be gathered
together,
and will praise the Lord of
the righteous.
14How blessed are those who love
you!
They will rejoice in your
peace.
Blessed are those who grieved
over all your afflictions;
for they will rejoice for you
upon seeing all your
glory,
and they will be made glad
for ever.
15Let my soul praise God the great
King.
16For Jerusalem will be built with
sapphires and emeralds,
her[b] walls with precious
stones,
and her towers and battle-
ments with pure gold.
17The streets of Jerusalem will be
paved[c] with beryl and ruby
and stones of Ophir;
18all her lanes will cry
'Hallelujah!' and will
give praise,
saying, 'Blessed is God, who
has exalted you for
ever.'"

TOBIT'S FINAL COUNSEL

14 Here Tobit ended his words of
praise. 2He was fifty-eight years
old when he lost his sight, and after
eight years he regained it. He gave
alms, and he continued to fear the
Lord God and to praise him. 3When he
had grown very old he called his son
and grandsons, and said to him, "My
son, take your sons; behold, I have
grown old and am about to depart
this life. 4Go to Media, my son, for I
fully believe what Jonah the prophet
said about Nin′eveh, that it will be
overthrown. But in Media there will
be peace for a time. Our brethren will
be scattered over the earth from the
good land, and Jerusalem will be des-
olate. The house of God in it will be
burned down and will be in ruins for
a time. 5But God will again have mer-
cy on them, and bring them back into
their land; and they will rebuild the
house of God,[d] though it will not be
like the former one until the times of

[b]Gk *your*
[c]Or *inlaid*
[d]Gk [house]

the age are completed. After this they
will return from the places of their
captivity, and will rebuild Jerusalem
in splendor. And the house of God
will be rebuilt there with a glorious
building for all generations for ever,
just as the prophets said of it. [6]Then
all the Gentiles will turn to fear the
Lord God in truth, and will bury their
idols. [7]All the Gentiles will praise the
Lord, and his people will give thanks
to God, and the Lord will exalt his
people. And all who love the Lord God
in truth and righteousness will re-
joice, showing mercy to our brethren.
8 "So now, my son, leave Nin'eveh,
because what the prophet Jonah said
will surely happen. [9]But keep the law
and the commandments, and be mer-
ciful and just, so that it may be well
with you. [10]Bury me properly, and
your mother with me. And do not live
in Nin'eveh any longer. See, my son,
what Nadab[a] did to Ahi'kar who had
reared him, how he brought him from
light into darkness, and with what he
repaid him. But Ahi'kar was saved,
and the other received repayment as
he himself went down into the dark-
ness. Ahi'kar[b] gave alms and escaped
the deathtrap which Nadab[c] had set
for him; but Nadab[d] fell into the trap
and perished. [11]So now, my children,
consider what almsgiving accomplish-
es and how righteousness delivers."
As he said this he died in his bed. He
was a hundred and fifty-eight years
old; and Tobi'as[e] gave him a magnif-
icent funeral. [12]And when Anna died
he buried her with his father.

DEATH OF TOBIT AND ANNA

Then Tobi'as returned with his
wife and his sons to Ecbat'ana, to
Rag'uel his father-in-law. [13]He grew
old with honor, and he gave his fa-
ther-in-law and mother-in-law mag-
nificent funerals. He inherited their
property and that of his father Tobit.
[14]He died in Ecbat'ana of Media at the
age of a hundred and twenty-seven
years. [15]But before he died he heard
of the destruction of Nin'eveh, which
Nebuchadnez'zar and Ahasu-e'rus
had captured. Before his death he re-
joiced over Nin'eveh.

[a] Other authorities read *Aman*
[b] Other authorities read *Manasses*
[c] Gk *he*
[d] Other authorities read *Aman*
[e] Gk *he*

JUDITH

ARPHAXAD FORTIFIES ECBATANA

1 In the twelfth year of the reign of
Nebuchadnez´zar, who ruled over
the Assyrians in the great city of
Nin´eveh, in the days of Arphax´ad,
who ruled over the Medes in
Ecbat´ana— 2he is the king who built
walls about Ecbat´ana with hewn
stones three cubits thick and six cu-
bits long; he made the walls seventy
cubits high and fifty cubits wide; 3at
the gates he built towers a hundred
cubits high and sixty cubits wide at
the foundations; 4and he made its
gates, which were seventy cubits
high and forty cubits wide, so that
his armies could march out in force
and his infantry form their ranks—
5it was in those days that King
Nebuchadnez´zar made war against
King Arphax´ad in the great plain
which is on the borders of Ragae. 6He
was joined by all the people of the
hill country and all those who lived
along the Euphra´tes and the Tigris
and the Hydas´pes and in the plain
where Ar´ioch ruled the Elymae´ans.
Many nations joined the forces of the
Chalde´ans.

NEBUCHADNEZZAR ISSUES ULTIMATUM

7 Then Nebuchadnez´zar king of
the Assyrians sent to all who lived
in Persia and to all who lived in the
west, those who lived in Cili´cia
and Damas´cus and Leb´anon and
Antileb´anon and all who lived along
the seacoast, 8and those among the
nations of Carmel and Gil´ead, and
Upper Galilee and the great Plain
of Esdrae´lon, 9and all who were in
Samar´ia and its surrounding towns,
and beyond the Jordan as far as
Jerusalem and Bethany and Chel´ous
and Kadesh and the river of Egypt,
and Tah´panhes and Ra-am´ses and
the whole land of Goshen, 10even
beyond Tanis and Memphis, and all
who lived in Egypt as far as the bor-
ders of Ethiopia. 11But all who lived
in the whole region disregarded the
orders of Nebuchadnez´zar king of
the Assyrians, and refused to join
him in the war; for they were not
afraid of him, but looked upon him
as only one man,[a] and they sent back
his messengers empty-handed and
shamefaced.

ARPHAXAD IS DEFEATED

12 Then Nebuchadnez´zar was
very angry with this whole region,
and swore by his throne and kingdom
that he would surely take revenge on
the whole territory of Cili´cia and
Damas´cus and Syria, that he would
kill them by the sword, and also all
the inhabitants of the land of Moab,
and the people of Ammon, and all
Judea, and every one in Egypt, as far
as the coasts of the two seas. 13In the
seventeenth year he led his forces
against King Arphax´ad, and defeat-
ed him in battle, and overthrew the
whole army of Arphax´ad, and all his
cavalry and all his chariots. 14Thus
he took possession of his cities, and
came to Ecbat´ana, captured its tow-
ers, plundered its markets, and turned
its beauty into shame. 15He captured
Arphax´ad in the mountains of Ragae
and struck him down with hunting
spears; and he utterly destroyed him,
to this day. 16Then he returned with
them to Nin´eveh, he and all his com-
bined forces, a vast body of troops;
and there he and his forces rested and
feasted for one hundred and twenty
days.

THE EXPEDITION AGAINST THE WEST

2 In the eighteenth year, on the
twenty-second day of the first
month, there was talk in the pal-
ace of Nebuchadnez´zar king of the

[a] Or *a man*

Assyrians about carrying out his re-
venge on the whole region, just as
he said. 2He called together all his
officers and all his nobles and set
forth to them his secret plan and re-
counted fully, with his own lips, all
the wickedness of the region;[a] 3and
it was decided that every one who
had not obeyed his command should
be destroyed. 4When he had finished
setting forth his plan, Nebuchad-
nez´zar king of the Assyrians called
Holofer´nes, the chief general of his
army, second only to himself, and
said to him,

5 "Thus says the Great King, the
lord of the whole earth: When you
leave my presence, take with you
men confident in their strength,
to the number of one hundred and
twenty thousand foot soldiers and
twelve thousand cavalry. 6Go and at-
tack the whole west country, because
they disobeyed my orders. 7Tell them
to prepare earth and water, for I am
coming against them in my anger, and
will cover the whole face of the earth
with the feet of my armies, and will
hand them over to be plundered by
my troops,[b] 8till their wounded shall
fill their valleys, and every brook and
river shall be filled with their dead,
and overflow; 9and I will lead them
away captive to the ends of the whole
earth. 10You shall go and seize all their
territory for me in advance. They will
yield themselves to you, and you shall
hold them for me till the day of their
punishment. 11But if they refuse, your
eye shall not spare and you shall hand
them over to slaughter and plunder
throughout your whole region. 12For
as I live, and by the power of my king-
dom, what I have spoken my hand
will execute. 13And you—take care
not to transgress any of your sover-
eign's commands, but be sure to carry
them out just as I have ordered you;
and do not delay about it."

CAMPAIGN OF HOLOFERNES

14 So Holofer´nes left the pres-
ence of his master, and called to-
gether all the commanders, generals,
and officers of the Assyrian army,
15and mustered the picked troops
by divisions as his lord had ordered
him to do, one hundred and twen-
ty thousand of them, together with
twelve thousand archers on horse-
back, 16and he organized them as a
great army is marshaled for a cam-
paign. 17He collected a vast number
of camels and asses and mules for
transport, and innumerable sheep
and oxen and goats for provision;
18also plenty of food for every man,
and a huge amount of gold and silver
from the royal palace. 19So he set out
with his whole army, to go ahead of
King Nebuchadnez´zar and to cover
the whole face of the earth to the
west with their chariots and horse-
men and picked troops of infantry.
20Along with them went a mixed
crowd like a swarm of locusts, like
the dust of the earth—a multitude
that could not be counted.

21 They marched for three
days from Nin´eveh to the plain of
Becti´leth, and camped opposite
Becti´leth near the mountain which
is to the north of Upper Cili´cia.
22From there Holofer´nes[c] took his
whole army, his infantry, cavalry,
and chariots, and went up into the
hill country 23and ravaged Put and
Lud, and plundered all the people
of Rassis and the Ish´maelites who
lived along the desert, south of the
country of the Chel´leans. 24Then
he followed[d] the Euphra´tes and
passed through Mesopota´mia and
destroyed all the hilltop cities along
the brook Abron, as far as the sea.
25He also seized the territory of
Cili´cia, and killed every one who
resisted him, and came to the south-
ern borders of Japheth, fronting

[a] The meaning of the Greek of the last clause of this verse is uncertain
[b] Gk *them*
[c] Gk *he*
[d] Or *crossed*

toward Arabia. [26]He surrounded all
the Mid´ianites, and burned their
tents and plundered their sheepfolds.
[27]Then he went down into the plain
of Damas´cus during the wheat har-
vest, and burned all their fields and
destroyed their flocks and herds and
sacked their cities and ravaged their
lands and put to death all their young
men with the edge of the sword.

28 So fear and terror of him fell
upon all the people who lived along
the seacoast, at Sidon and Tyre, and
those who lived in Sur and Oci´na and
all who lived in Jam´nia. Those who
lived in Azo´tus and As´calon feared
him exceedingly.

ENTREATIES FOR PEACE

3 So they sent messengers to sue
for peace, and said, [2]"Behold, we
the servants of Nebuchadnez´zar,
the Great King, lie prostrate before
you. Do with us whatever you will.
[3]Behold, our buildings, and all our
land, and all our wheat fields, and our
flocks and herds, and all our sheep-
folds with their tents, lie before you;
do with them whatever you please.
[4]Our cities also and their inhabitants
are your slaves; come and deal with
them in any way that seems good to
you."

5 The men came to Holofer´nes
and told him all this. [6]Then he went
down to the seacoast with his army
and stationed garrisons in the hilltop
cities and took picked men from them
as his allies. [7]And these people and
all in the country round about wel-
comed him with garlands and dances
and tambourines. [8]And he demolished
all their shrines[e] and cut down their
sacred groves; for it had been given
to him to destroy all the gods of the
land, so that all nations should wor-
ship Nebuchadnez´zar only, and all
their tongues and tribes should call
upon him as god.

9 Then he came to the edge of
Esdrae´lon, near Dothan, fronting the
great ridge of Judea; [10]here he camped
between Geba and Scythop´olis, and
remained for a whole month in order
to assemble all the supplies for his
army.

JUDEA ON THE ALERT

4 By this time the people of Israel
living in Judea heard of every-
thing that Holofer´nes, the general
of Nebuchadnez´zar the king of the
Assyrians, had done to the nations,
and how he had plundered and de-
stroyed all their temples; [2]they were
therefore very greatly terrified at his
approach, and were alarmed both for
Jerusalem and for the temple of the
Lord their God. [3]For they had only
recently returned from the captivi-
ty, and all the people of Judea were
newly gathered together, and the
sacred vessels and the altar and the
temple had been consecrated after
their profanation. [4]So they sent to
every district of Samar´ia, and to
Kona and Beth-hor´on and Belma´in
and Jericho and to Choba and Aesor´a
and the valley of Salem, [5]and imme-
diately seized all the high hilltops
and fortified the villages on them
and stored up food in preparation for
war—since their fields had recently
been harvested. [6]And Jo´akim, the
high priest, who was in Jerusalem
at the time, wrote to the people of
Bethu´lia and Betomestha´im, which
faces Esdrae´lon opposite the plain
near Dothan, [7]ordering them to seize
the passes up into the hills, since by
them Judea could be invaded, and
it was easy to stop any who tried to
enter, for the approach was narrow,
only wide enough for two men at the
most.

PRAYER AND PENANCE

8 So the Israelites did as Jo´akim
the high priest and the senate of
the whole people of Israel, in ses-
sion at Jerusalem, had given order.
[9]And every man of Israel cried out

[e] Syr: Gk *borders*

to God with great fervor, and they
humbled themselves with much fast-
ing. 10They and their wives and their
children and their cattle and every
resident alien and hired laborer and
purchased slave—they all girded
themselves with sackcloth. 11And all
the men and women of Israel, and
their children, living at Jerusalem,
prostrated themselves before the
temple and put ashes on their heads
and spread out their sackcloth before
the Lord. 12They even surrounded the
altar with sackcloth and cried out in
unison, praying earnestly to the God
of Israel not to give up their infants
as prey and their wives as booty, and
the cities they had inherited to be
destroyed, and the sanctuary to be
profaned and desecrated to the ma-
licious joy of the Gentiles. 13So the
Lord heard their prayers and looked
upon their affliction; for the people
fasted many days throughout Judea
and in Jerusalem before the sanc-
tuary of the Lord Almighty. 14And
Jo´akim the high priest and all the
priests who stood before the Lord
and ministered to the Lord, with
their loins girded with sackcloth,
offered the continual burnt offerings
and the vows and freewill offerings
of the people. 15With ashes upon
their turbans, they cried out to the
Lord with all their might to look
with favor upon the whole house of
Israel.

COUNCIL AGAINST THE ISRAELITES

5 When Holofer´nes, the general of
the Assyrian army, heard that the
people of Israel had prepared for war
and had closed the passes in the hills
and fortified all the high hilltops
and set up barricades in the plains,
2he was very angry. So he called to-
gether *all the princes of Moab* and
the commanders of Ammon and
all the governors of the coastland,
3and said to them, "Tell me, you
Canaanites, what people is this that
lives in the hill country? What cities
do they inhabit? How large is their
army, and in what does their power
or strength consist? Who rules over
them as king, leading their army?
4And why have they alone, of all who
live in the west, refused to come out
and meet me?"

ACHIOR'S REPORT

5 Then Ach´ior, the leader of all
the Am´monites, said to him, "Let
my lord now hear a word from the
mouth of your servant, and I will tell
you the truth about this people that
dwells in the nearby mountain dis-
trict. No falsehood shall come from
your servant's mouth. 6This people is
descended from the Chalde´ans. 7At
one time they lived in Mesopota´mia,
because they would not follow the
gods of their fathers who were in
Chalde´a. 8For they had left the
ways of their ancestors, and they
worshiped the God of heaven, the
God they had come to know; hence
they drove them out from the pres-
ence of their gods; and they fled to
Mesopota´mia, and lived there for
a long time. 9Then their God com-
manded them to leave the place
where they were living and go to the
land of Canaan. There they settled,
and prospered, with much gold and
silver and very many cattle. 10When a
famine spread over Canaan they went
down to Egypt and lived there as
long as they had food; and there they
became a great multitude—so great
that they could not be counted. 11So
the king of Egypt became hostile to
them; he took advantage of them and
set them to making bricks, and hum-
bled them and made slaves of them.
12Then they cried out to their God,
and he afflicted the whole land of
Egypt with incurable plagues; and so
the Egyptians drove them out of their
sight. 13Then God dried up the Red
Sea before them, 14and he led them
by the way of Sinai and Ka´desh-
bar´nea, and drove out all the people
of the wilderness. 15So they lived in

the land of the Am´orites, and by
their might destroyed all the inhab-
itants of Heshbon; and crossing over
the Jordan they took possession of
all the hill country. 16And they drove
out before them the Canaanites and
the Per´izzites and the Jeb´usites
and the She´chemites and all the
Ger´gesites, and lived there a long
time. 17As long as they did not sin
against their God they prospered, for
the God who hates iniquity is with
them. 18But when they departed from
the way which he had appointed for
them, they were utterly defeated in
many battles and were led away cap-
tive to a foreign country; the temple
of their God was razed to the ground,
and their cities were captured by
their enemies. 19But now they have
returned to their God, and have come
back from the places to which they
were scattered, and have occupied
Jerusalem, where their sanctuary is,
and have settled in the hill country,
because it was uninhabited. 20Now
therefore, my master and lord, if
there is any unwitting error in this
people and they sin against their God
and we find out their offense, then
we will go up and defeat them. 21But
if there is no transgression in their
nation, then let my lord pass them
by; for their Lord will defend them,
and their God will protect them, and
we shall be put to shame before the
whole world."

22 When Ach´ior had finished
saying this, all the men standing
around the tent began to complain;
Holofer´nes' officers and all the men
from the seacoast and from Moab in-
sisted that he must be put to death.
23"For," they said, "we will not be
afraid of the Israelites; they are a
people with no strength or power for
making war. 24Therefore let us go up,
Lord Holofer´nes, and they will be de-
voured by your vast army."

ACHIOR HANDED OVER TO THE ISRAELITES

6 When the disturbance made by the
men outside the council died down,
Holofer´nes, the commander of the
Assyrian army, said to Ach´ior and
all the Mo´abites in the presence of all
the foreign contingents:

2 "And who are you, Ach´ior, and
you hirelings of E´phraim, to proph-
esy among us as you have done today
and tell us not to make war against
the people of Israel because their God
will defend them? Who is God except
Nebuchadnez´zar? 3He will send his
forces and will destroy them from
the face of the earth, and their God
will not deliver them—we the king's[a]
servants will destroy them as one
man. They cannot resist the might of
our cavalry. 4We will burn them up,[b]
and their mountains will be drunk
with their blood, and their fields will
be full of their dead. They[c] cannot
withstand us, but will utterly perish.
So says King Nebuchadnez´zar, the
lord of the whole earth. For he has
spoken; none of his words shall be
in vain.

5 "But you, Ach´ior, you Am´mo-
nite hireling, who have said these
words on the day of your iniqui-
ty, you shall not see my face again
from this day until I take revenge
on this race that came out of Egypt.
6Then the sword of my army and the
spear[d] of my servants shall pierce
your sides, and you shall fall among
their wounded, when I return. 7Now
my slaves are going to take you back
into the hill country and put you in
one of the cities beside the passes,
8*and you will* not die until you perish
along with them. 9If you really hope
in your heart that they will not be
taken, do not look downcast! I have
spoken and none of my words shall
fail."

10 Then Holofer´nes ordered his
slaves, who waited on him in his

[a] Gk *his*
[b] Other authorities add *with it*
[c] Gk *The track of their feet*
[d] Lat Syr: Gk *people*

tent, to seize Ach´ior and take him
to Bethu´lia and hand him over to
the men of Israel. 11 So the slaves took
him and led him out of the camp into
the plain, and from the plain they
went up into the hill country and
came to the springs below Bethu´lia.
12 When the men of the city saw
them,[a] they caught up their weap-
ons and ran out of the city to the
top of the hill, and all the slingers
kept them from coming up by casting
stones at them. 13 However, they got
under the shelter of the hill and they
bound Ach´ior and left him lying at
the foot of the hill, and returned to
their master.

14 Then the men of Israel came
down from their city and found him;
and they untied him and brought him
into Bethu´lia and placed him before
the magistrates of their city, 15 who in
those days were Uzzi´ah the son of
Micah, of the tribe of Sim´eon, and
Chabris the son of Gothon´iel, and
Charmis the son of Mel´chiel. 16 They
called together all the elders of the
city, and all their young men and
their women ran to the assembly; and
they set Ach´ior in the midst of all
their people, and Uzzi´ah asked him
what had happened. 17 He answered
and told them what had taken place
at the council of Holofer´nes, and
all that he had said in the presence
of the Assyrian leaders, and all that
Holofer´nes had said so boastfully
against the house of Israel. 18 Then the
people fell down and worshiped God,
and cried out to him, and said,

19 "O Lord God of heaven, behold
their arrogance, and have pity on the
humiliation of our people, and look
this day upon the faces of those who
are consecrated to thee."

20 Then they consoled Ach´ior, and
praised him greatly. 21 And Uzzi´ah
took him from the assembly to his
own house and gave a banquet for the
elders; and all that night they called
on the God of Israel for help.

[a]Other authorities add *on the top of the hill*

THE CAMPAIGN AGAINST BETHULIA

7 The next day Holofer´nes ordered
his whole army, and all the allies
who had joined him, to break camp
and move against Bethu´lia, and to
seize the passes up into the hill coun-
try and make war on the Israelites.
2 So all their warriors moved their
camp that day; their force of men of
war was one hundred and seventy
thousand infantry and twelve thou-
sand cavalry, together with the bag-
gage and the foot soldiers handling
it, a very great multitude. 3 They en-
camped in the valley near Bethu´lia,
beside the spring, and they spread
out in breadth over Dothan as far
as Balba´im and in length from Be-
thu´lia to Cy´amon, which faces
Esdrae´lon.

4 When the Israelites saw their
vast numbers they were greatly terri-
fied, and every one said to his neigh-
bor, "These men will now lick up
the face of the whole land; neither
the high mountains nor the valleys
nor the hills will bear their weight."
5 Then each man took up his weapons,
and when they had kindled fires on
their towers they remained on guard
all that night.

6 On the second day Holofer´nes
led out all his cavalry in full view of
the Israelites in Bethu´lia, 7 and ex-
amined the approaches to the city,
and visited the springs that supplied
their water, and seized them and set
guards of soldiers over them, and then
returned to his army.

8 Then all the chieftains of the
people of Esau and all the leaders of
the Mo´abites and the commanders
of the coastland came to him and
said, 9 "Let our lord hear a word, lest
his army be defeated. 10 For these
people, the Israelites, do not rely on
their spears but on the height of the
mountains where they live, for it is
not easy to reach the tops of their
mountains. 11 Therefore, my lord,
do not fight against them in battle

array, and not a man of your army
will fall. 12Remain in your camp,
and keep all the men in your forc-
es with you; only let your servants
take possession of the spring of wa-
ter that flows from the foot of the
mountain— 13for this is where all the
people of Bethu´lia get their water.
So thirst will destroy them, and they
will give up their city. We and our
people will go up to the tops of the
nearby mountains and camp there to
keep watch that not a man gets out
of the city. 14They and their wives
and children will waste away with
famine, and before the sword reach-
es them they will be strewn about
in the streets where they live. 15So
you will pay them back with evil,
because they rebelled and did not re-
ceive you peaceably."

16 These words pleased
Holofer´nes and all his servants, and
he gave orders to do as they had said.
17So the army of the Am´monites
moved forward, together with five
thousand Assyrians, and they en-
camped in the valley and seized the
water supply and the springs of the
Israelites. 18And the sons of Esau
and the sons of Ammon went up and
encamped in the hill country oppo-
site Dothan; and they sent some of
their men toward the south and the
east, toward Acr´aba, which is near
Chusi beside the brook Mochmur.
The rest of the Assyrian army en-
camped in the plain, and covered
the whole face of the land, and their
tents and supply trains spread out in
great number, and they formed a vast
multitude.

THE DISTRESS OF THE ISRAELITES

19 The people of Israel cried out
to the Lord their God, for their cour-
age failed, because all their enemies
had surrounded them and there was
no way of escape from them. 20The
whole Assyrian army, their infantry,
chariots, and cavalry, surrounded
them for thirty-four days, until all
the vessels of water belonging to
every inhabitant of Bethu´lia were
empty; 21their cisterns were going
dry, and they did not have enough
water to drink their fill for a single
day, because it was measured out to
them to drink. 22Their children lost
heart, and the women and young
men fainted from thirst and fell
down in the streets of the city and
in the passages through the gates;
there was no strength left in them
any longer.

23 Then all the people, the young
men, the women, and the children,
gathered about Uzzi´ah and the rul-
ers of the city and cried out with a
loud voice, and said before all the
elders, 24"God be judge between you
and us! For you have done us a great
injury in not making peace with the
Assyrians. 25For now we have no one
to help us; God has sold us into their
hands, to strew us on the ground
before them with thirst and utter
destruction. 26Now call them in and
surrender the whole city to the army
of Holofer´nes and to all his forces, to
be plundered. 27For it would be better
for us to be captured by them;[b] for we
will be slaves, but our lives will be
spared, and we shall not witness the
death of our babes before our eyes,
or see our wives and children draw
their last breath. 28We call to witness
against you heaven and earth and our
God, the Lord of our fathers, who
punishes us according to our sins and
the sins of our fathers. Let him not
do this day the things which we have
described!"

29 Then great and general lam-
entation arose throughout the as-
sembly, and they cried out to the
Lord God with a loud voice. 30And
Uzzi´ah said to them, "Have cour-
age, my brothers! Let us hold out
for five more days; by that time the
Lord our God will restore to us his
mercy, for he will not forsake us

[b]Other authorities add *than to die of thirst*

utterly. 31But if these days pass by,
and no help comes for us, I will do
what you say."

32 Then he dismissed the people
to their various posts, and they went
up on the walls and towers of their
city. The women and children he
sent home. And they were greatly depressed in the city.

THE CHARACTER OF JUDITH

8 At that time Judith heard about
these things: she was the daughter of Merar'i the son of Ox, son of
Joseph, son of O'ziel, son of Elki'ah,
son of Anani'as, son of Gid'eon,
son of Raph'a-im, son of Ahi'tub,
son of Eli'jah, son of Hilki'ah, son
of El'iab, son of Nathan'ael, son of
Salam'iel, son of Sarasad'ai, son of
Israel.* 2Her husband Manas'seh,
who belonged to her tribe and family, had died during the barley harvest. 3For as he stood overseeing
the men who were binding sheaves
in the field, he was overcome by
the burning heat, and took to his
bed and died in Bethu'lia his city.
So they buried him with his fathers
in the field between Dothan and
Bala'mon. 4Judith had lived at home
as a widow for three years and four
months. 5She set up a tent for herself
on the roof of her house, and girded
sackcloth about her loins and wore
the garments of her widowhood.
6She fasted all the days of her widowhood, except the day before the
sabbath and the sabbath itself, the
day before the new moon and the
day of the new moon, and the feasts
and days of rejoicing of the house of
Israel. 7She was beautiful in appearance, and had a very lovely face; and
her husband Manas'seh had left her
gold and silver, and men and women slaves, and cattle, and fields; and
she maintained this estate. 8No one
spoke ill of her, for she feared God
with great devotion.

JUDITH AND THE ELDERS

9 When Judith heard the wicked
words spoken by the people against
the ruler, because they were faint for
lack of water, and when she heard all
that Uzzi'ah said to them, and how
he promised them under oath to surrender the city to the Assyrians after
five days, 10she sent her maid, who
was in charge of all she possessed,
to summon[a] Chabris and Charmis,
the elders of her city. 11They came to
her, and she said to them, "Listen to
me, rulers of the people of Bethu'lia!
What you have said to the people today is not right; you have even sworn
and pronounced this oath between
God and you, promising to surrender
the city to our enemies unless the
Lord turns and helps us within so
many days. 12Who are you, that have
put God to the test this day, and are
setting yourselves up in the place of[b]
God among the sons of men? 13You
are putting the Lord Almighty to
the test—but you will never know
anything! 14You cannot plumb the
depths of the human heart, nor find
out what a man is thinking; how
do you expect to search out God,
who made all these things, and find
out his mind or comprehend his
thought? No, my brethren, do not
provoke the Lord our God to anger.
15For if he does not choose to help us
within these five days, he has power to protect us within any time he
pleases, or even to destroy us in the
presence of our enemies. 16Do not
try to bind the purposes of the Lord
our God; for God is not like man,
to be threatened, nor like a human
being, to be won over by pleading.
17Therefore, while we wait for his
deliverance, let us call upon him to
help us, and he will hear our voice, if
it pleases him.

18 "For never in our generation, nor
in these present days, has there been
any tribe or family or people or city

[a] Some authorities add *Uzzi'ah and* (See verses 28 and 35)
[b] Or *above*

of ours which worshiped gods made
with hands, as was done in days gone
by— 19and that was why our fathers
were handed over to the sword, and to
be plundered, and so they suffered a
great catastrophe before our enemies.
20But we know no other god but him,
and therefore we hope that he will not
disdain us or any of our nation. 21For
if we are captured all Judea will be
captured and our sanctuary will be
plundered; and he will exact of us[c] the
penalty for its desecration. 22And the
slaughter of our brethren and the cap-
tivity of the land and the desolation of
our inheritance—all this he will bring
upon our heads among the Gentiles,
wherever we serve as slaves; and we
shall be an offense and a reproach in
the eyes of those who acquire us. 23For
our slavery will not bring us into fa-
vor, but the Lord our God will turn it
to dishonor.

24 "Now therefore, brethren, let
us set an example to our brethren,
for their lives depend upon us, and
the sanctuary and the temple and
the altar rest upon us. 25In spite of
everything let us give thanks to
the Lord our God, who is putting
us to the test as he did our fore-
fathers. 26Remember what he did
with Abraham, and how he tested
Isaac, and what happened to Jacob
in Mesopota´mia in Syria, while he
was keeping the sheep of Laban, his
mother's brother. 27For he has not
tried us with fire, as he did them,
to search their hearts, nor has he
taken revenge upon us; but the Lord
scourges those who draw near to
him, in order to admonish them."

28 Then Uzzi´ah said to her, "All
that you have said has been spoken
out of a true heart, and there is no one
who can deny your words. 29Today is
not the first time your wisdom has
been shown, but from the beginning
of your life all the people have recog-
nized your understanding, for your
heart's disposition is right. 30But the
people were very thirsty, and they
compelled us to do for them what we
have promised, and made us take an
oath which we cannot break. 31So pray
for us, since you are a devout woman,
and the Lord will send us rain to fill
our cisterns and we will no longer be
faint."

32 Judith said to them, "Listen to
me. I am about to do a thing which
will go down through all generations
of our descendants. 33Stand at the city
gate tonight, and I will go out with my
maid; and within the days after which
you have promised to surrender the
city to our enemies, the Lord will de-
liver Israel by my hand. 34Only, do not
try to find out what I plan; for I will
not tell you until I have finished what
I am about to do."

35 Uzzi´ah and the rulers said to
her, "Go in peace, and may the Lord
God go before you, to take revenge
upon our enemies." 36So they returned
from the tent and went to their posts.

THE PRAYER OF JUDITH

9 Then Judith fell upon her face, and
put ashes on her head, and uncov-
ered the sackcloth she was wearing;
and at the very time when that eve-
ning's incense was being offered in
the house of God in Jerusalem, Judith
cried out to the Lord with a loud
voice, and said,

2 "O Lord God of my father
Sim´eon, to whom thou gavest a sword
to take revenge on the strangers who
had loosed the girdle[d] of a virgin to
defile her, and uncovered her thigh
to put her to shame, and polluted her
womb to disgrace her; for thou hast
said, 'It shall not be done'—yet they
did it. 3So thou gavest up their rulers
to be slain, and their bed, which was
ashamed of the deceit they had prac-
ticed, to be stained with blood, and
thou didst strike down slaves along
with princes, and princes on their

[c] Gk *our blood*
[d] Cn: Gk *womb*

thrones; 4and thou gavest their wives
for a prey and their daughters to cap-
tivity, and all their booty to be divid-
ed among thy beloved sons, who were
zealous for thee, and abhorred the
pollution of their blood, and called on
thee for help—O God, my God, hear
me also, a widow.

5 "For thou hast done these things
and those that went before and those
that followed; thou hast designed the
things that are now, and those that
are to come. Yea, the things thou didst
intend came to pass, 6and the things
thou didst will presented themselves
and said, 'Lo, we are here'; for all thy
ways are prepared in advance, and thy
judgment is with foreknowledge.

7 "Behold now, the Assyrians are
increased in their might; they are ex-
alted, with their horses and riders;
they glory in the strength of their
foot soldiers; they trust in shield
and spear, in bow and sling, and
know not that thou art the Lord who
crushest wars; the Lord is thy name.
8Break their strength by thy might,
and bring down their power in thy
anger; for they intend to defile thy
sanctuary, and to pollute the taber-
nacle where thy glorious name rests,
and to cast down the horn of thy altar
with the sword. 9Behold their pride,
and send thy wrath upon their heads;
give to me, a widow, the strength to
do what I plan. 10By the deceit of my
lips strike down the slave with the
prince and the prince with his ser-
vant; crush their arrogance by the
hand of a woman.

11 "For thy power depends not
upon numbers, nor thy might upon
men of strength; for thou art God of
the lowly, helper of the oppressed,
upholder of the weak, protector of
the forlorn, savior of those without
hope. 12Hear, O hear me, God of my
father, God of the inheritance of
Israel, Lord of heaven and earth,
Creator of the waters, King of all thy
creation, hear my prayer! 13Make my
deceitful words to be their wound
and stripe, for they have planned cru-
el things against thy covenant, and
against thy consecrated house, and
against the top of Zion, and against
the house possessed by thy children.
14And cause thy whole nation and
every tribe to know and understand
that thou art God, the God of all
power and might, and that there is
no other who protects the people of
Israel but thou alone!"

JUDITH PREPARES TO GO TO HOLOFERNES

10 When Judith[a] had ceased crying
out to the God of Israel, and had
ended all these words, 2she rose from
where she lay prostrate and called her
maid and went down into the house
where she lived on sabbaths and on
her feast days; 3and she removed the
sackcloth which she had been wear-
ing, and took off her widow's gar-
ments, and bathed her body with
water, and anointed herself with pre-
cious ointment, and combed her hair
and put on a tiara, and arrayed herself
in her gayest apparel, which she used
to wear while her husband Manas´seh
was living. 4And she put sandals on
her feet, and put on her anklets and
bracelets and rings, and her earrings
and all her ornaments,* and made her-
self very beautiful, to entice the eyes
of all men who might see her. 5And
she gave her maid a bottle of wine
and a flask of oil, and filled a bag with
parched grain and a cake of dried fruit
and fine bread; and she wrapped up
all her vessels and gave them to her
to carry.

6 Then they went out to the city
gate of Bethu´lia, and found Uzzi´ah
standing there with the elders of the
city, Chabris and Charmis. 7When
they saw her, and noted how her face
was altered and her clothing changed,
they greatly admired her beauty, and
said to her, 8"May the God of our fa-
thers grant you favor and fulfil your
plans, that the people of Israel may

[a]Gk *she*

glory and Jerusalem may be exalted."
And she worshiped God.
9 Then she said to them, "Order
the gate of the city to be opened for
me, and I will go out and accomplish
the things about which you spoke
with me." So they ordered the young
men to open the gate for her, as she
had said. 10When they had done this,
Judith went out, she and her maid
with her; and the men of the city
watched her until she had gone down
the mountain and passed through the
valley and they could no longer see
her.

JUDITH IS CAPTURED

11 The women[b] went straight on
through the valley; and an Assyrian
patrol met her 12and took her into
custody, and asked her, "To what
people do you belong, and where are
you coming from, and where are you
going?" She replied, "I am a daugh-
ter of the Hebrews, but I am fleeing
from them, for they are about to be
handed over to you to be devoured.
13I am on my way to the presence of
Holofer´nes the commander of your
army, to give him a true report; and I
will show him a way by which he can
go and capture all the hill country
without losing one of his men, cap-
tured or slain."
14 When the men heard her
words, and observed her face—she
was in their eyes marvelously beau-
tiful—they said to her, 15"You have
saved your life by hurrying down to
the presence of our lord. Go at once
to his tent; some of us will escort
you and hand you over to him. 16And
when you stand before him, do not be
afraid in your heart, but tell him just
what you have said, and he will treat
you well."
17 They chose from their number
a hundred men to accompany her
and her maid, and they brought them
to the tent of Holofer´nes. 18There
was great excitement in the whole
camp, for her arrival was reported
from tent to tent, and they came
and stood around her as she waited
outside the tent of Holofer´nes while
they told him about her. 19And they
marveled at her beauty, and admired
the Israelites, judging them by her,
and every one said to his neighbor,
"Who can despise these people, who
have women like this among them?
Surely not a man of them had bet-
ter be left alive, for if we let them
go they will be able to ensnare the
whole world!"

JUDITH IS BROUGHT BEFORE HOLOFERNES

20 Then Holofer´nes' companions
and all his servants came out and
led her into the tent. 21Holofer´nes
was resting on his bed, under a can-
opy which was woven with purple
and gold and emeralds and precious
stones. 22When they told him of her he
came forward to the front of the tent,
with silver lamps carried before him.
23And when Judith came into the pres-
ence of Holofer´nes[c] and his servants,
they all marveled at the beauty of her
face; and she prostrated herself and
made obeisance to him, and his slaves
raised her up.
11 Then Holofer´nes said to her,
"Take courage, woman, and do
not be afraid in your heart, for I have
never hurt any one who chose to serve
Nebuchadnez´zar, the king of all the
earth. 2And even now, if your people
who live in the hill country had not
slighted me, I would never have lift-
ed my spear against them; but they
have brought all this on themselves.
3And now tell me why you have fled
from them and have come over to
us—since you have come to safety.
4Have courage; you will live, tonight
and from now on. No one will hurt
you, but all will treat you well, as
they do the servants of my lord King
Nebuchadnezzar."

[b] Gk *They*
[c] Gk *him*

JUDITH EXPLAINS HER PRESENCE

5 Judith replied to him, "Accept
the words of your servant, and let
your maidservant speak in your
presence, and I will tell nothing
false to my lord this night. 6 And
if you follow out the words of your
maidservant, God will accomplish
something through you, and my lord
will not fail to achieve his purposes.
7 Nebuchadnez´zar the king of the
whole earth lives, and as his power
endures, who had sent you to direct
every living soul, not only do men
serve him because of you, but also
the beasts of the field and the cattle
and the birds of the air will live by
your power under Nebuchadnez´zar
and all his house. 8 For we have heard
of your wisdom and skill, and it is re-
ported throughout the whole world
that you are the one good man in the
whole kingdom, thoroughly informed
and marvelous in military strategy.

9 "Now as for the things Ach´ior
said in your council, we have heard
his words, for the men of Bethu´lia
spared him and he told them all he
had said to you. 10 Therefore, my lord
and master, do not disregard what
he said, but keep it in your mind,
for it is true: our nation cannot be
punished, nor can the sword prevail
against them, unless they sin against
their God.

11 "And now, in order that my
lord may not be defeated and his
purpose frustrated, death will fall
upon them, for a sin has overtaken
them by which they are about to pro-
voke their God to anger when they
do what is wrong. 12 Since their food
supply is exhausted and their wa-
ter has almost given out, they have
planned to kill their cattle and have
determined to use all that God by
his laws has forbidden them to eat.
13 They have decided to consume the
first fruits of the grain and the tithes
of the wine and oil, which they had
consecrated and set aside for the
priests who minister in the presence
of our God at Jerusalem—although it
is not lawful for any of the people so
much as to touch these things with
their hands. 14 They have sent men to
Jerusalem, because even the people
living there have been doing this, to
bring back to them permission from
the senate. 15 When the word reaches
them and they proceed to do this,
on that very day they will be handed
over to you to be destroyed.

16 "Therefore, when I, your ser-
vant, learned all this, I fled from
them; and God has sent me to ac-
complish with you things that will
astonish the whole world, as many
as shall hear about them. 17 For your
servant is religious, and serves the
God of heaven day and night; there-
fore, my lord, I will remain with you,
and every night your servant will go
out into the valley, and I will pray to
God and he will tell me when they
have committed their sins. 18 And I
will come and tell you, and then you
shall go out with your whole army,
and not one of them will withstand
you. 19 Then I will lead you through
the middle of Judea, till you come to
Jerusalem; and I will set your throne[a]
in the midst of it; and you will lead
them like sheep that have no shep-
herd, and not a dog will so much as
open its mouth to growl at you. For
this has been told me, by my fore-
knowledge; it was announced to me,
and I was sent to tell you."

20 Her words pleased Holofer´nes
and all his servants, and they mar-
veled at her wisdom and said,
21 "There is not such a woman from
one end of the earth to the other, ei-
ther for beauty of face or wisdom of
speech!" 22 And Holofer´nes said to
her, "God has done well to send you
before the people, to lend strength to
our hands and to bring destruction
upon those who have slighted my
lord. 23 You are not only beautiful in
appearance, but wise in speech; and

[a] Or *chariot*

if you do as you have said, your God
shall be my God, and you shall live in
the house of King Nebuchadnez´zar
and be renowned throughout the
whole world."

JUDITH AS A GUEST OF HOLOFERNES

12 Then he commanded them to
bring her in where his silver dish-
es were kept, and ordered them to
set a table for her with some of his
own food and to serve her with his
own wine. 2But Judith said, "I can-
not eat it, lest it be an offense; but
I will be provided from the things I
have brought with me." 3Holofer´nes
said to her, "If your supply runs out,
where can we get more like it for you?
For none of your people is here with
us." 4Judith replied, "As your soul
lives, my lord, your servant will not
use up the things I have with me be-
fore the Lord carries out by my hand
what he has determined to do."

5 Then the servants of Holofer´nes
brought her into the tent, and she
slept until midnight. Along toward
the morning watch she arose 6and
sent to Holofer´nes and said, "Let
my lord now command that your
servant be permitted to go out and
pray." 7So Holofer´nes commanded
his guards not to hinder her. And
she remained in the camp for three
days, and went out each night to the
valley of Bethu´lia, and bathed at
the spring in the camp.[b] 8When she
came up from the spring she prayed
the Lord God of Israel to direct her
way for the raising up of her people.
9So she returned clean and stayed in
the tent until she ate her food toward
evening.

JUDITH ATTENDS HOLOFERNES' BANQUET

10 On the fourth day Holofer´nes
held a banquet for his slaves only,
and did not invite any of his officers.
11And he said to Bago´as, the eunuch
who had charge of all his personal
affairs, "Go now and persuade the
Hebrew woman who is in your care
to join us and eat and drink with us.
12For it will be a disgrace if we let
such a woman go without enjoying
her company, for if we do not em-
brace her she will laugh at us." 13So
Bago´as went out from the presence of
Holofer´nes, and approached her and
said, "This beautiful maidservant will
please come to my lord and be hon-
ored in his presence, and drink wine
and be merry with us, and become to-
day like one of the daughters of the
Assyrians who serve in the house of
Nebuchadnez´zar." 14And Judith said,
"Who am I, to refuse my lord? Surely
whatever pleases him I will do at
once, and it will be a joy to me until
the day of my death!" 15So she got up
and arrayed herself in all her wom-
an's finery, and her maid went and
spread on the ground for her before
Holofer´nes the soft fleeces which
she had received from Bago´as for her
daily use, so that she might recline on
them when she ate.

16 Then Judith came in and lay
down, and Holofer´nes' heart was
ravished with her and he was moved
with great desire to possess her; for
he had been waiting for an opportu-
nity to deceive her, ever since the day
he first saw her. 17So Holofer´nes said
to her. "Drink now, and be merry
with us!" 18Judith said, "I will drink
now, my lord, because my life means
more to me today than in all the
days since I was born." 19Then she
took and ate and drank before him
what her maid had prepared. 20And
Holofer´nes was greatly pleased with
her, and drank a great quantity of
wine, much more than he had ever
drunk in any one day since he was
born.

JUDITH BEHEADS HOLOFERNES

13 When evening came, his slaves
quickly withdrew, and Bago´as
closed the tent from outside and
shut out the attendants from his

[b]Other authorities omit *in the camp*

master's presence; and they went
to bed, for they all were weary be-
cause the banquet had lasted long.
2 So Judith was left alone in the tent
, with Holofer´nes stretched out on
his bed, for he was overcome with
wine.

3 Now Judith had told her maid
to stand outside the bedchamber
and to wait for her to come out, as
she did every day; for she said she
would be going out for her prayers.
And she had said the same thing to
Bago´as. 4 So every one went out, and
no one, either small or great, was
left in the bedchamber. Then Judith,
standing beside his bed, said in her
heart, "O Lord God of all might,
look in this hour upon the work
of my hands for the exaltation of
Jerusalem. 5 For now is the time to
help thy inheritance, and to carry
out my undertaking for the destruc-
tion of the enemies who have risen
up against us."

6 She went up to the post at the
end of the bed, above Holofer´nes'
head, and took down his sword that
hung there. 7 She came close to his
bed and took hold of the hair of his
head, and said, "Give me strength
this day, O Lord God of Israel!" 8 And
she struck his neck twice with all her
might, and severed his head from his
body. 9 Then she tumbled his body off
the bed and pulled down the canopy
from the posts; after a moment she
went out, and gave Holofer´nes' head
to her maid, 10 who placed it in her
food bag.

JUDITH RETURNS TO BETHULIA

Then the two of them went out
together, as they were accustomed
to go for prayer; and they passed
through the camp and circled around
the valley and went up the mountain
to Bethu´lia and came to its gates.
11 Judith called out from afar to the
watchmen at the gates, "Open, open
the gate! God, our God, is still with
us, to show his power in Israel, and
his strength against our enemies,
even as he has done this day!"

12 When the men of her city
heard her voice, they hurried down
to the city gate and called together
the elders of the city. 13 They all ran
together, both small and great, for
it was unbelievable that she had re-
turned; they opened the gate and ad-
mitted them, and they kindled a fire
for light, and gathered around them.
14 Then she said to them with a loud
voice, "Praise God, O praise him!
Praise God, who has not withdrawn
his mercy from the house of Israel,
but has destroyed our enemies by my
hand this very night!"

15 Then she took the head out
of the bag and showed it to them,
and said, "See, here is the head of
Holofer´nes, the commander of the
Assyrian army, and here is the canopy
beneath which he lay in his drunken
stupor. The Lord has struck him down
by the hand of a woman. 16 As the Lord
lives, who has protected me in the way
I went, it was my face that tricked him
to his destruction, and yet he commit-
ted no act of sin with me, to defile and
shame me."

17 All the people were greatly as-
tonished, and bowed down and wor-
shiped God, and said with one accord,
"Blessed art thou, our God, who hast
brought into contempt this day the en-
emies of thy people."

18 And Uzzi´ah said to her, "O
daughter, you are blessed by the
Most High God above all women on
earth; and blessed be the Lord God,
who created the heavens and the
earth, who has guided you to strike
the head of the leader of our enemies.
19 Your hope will never depart from
the hearts of men, as they remember
the power of God. 20 May God grant
this to be a perpetual honor to you,
and may he visit you with blessings,
because you did not spare your own
life when our nation was brought low,
but have avenged our ruin, walking
in the straight path before our God."

And all the people said, "So be it, so
be it!"*

JUDITH'S COUNSEL

14 Then Judith said to them, "Listen
to me, my brethren, and take this
head and hang it upon the parapet of
your wall. 2And as soon as morning
comes and the sun rises, let every
valiant man take his weapons and go
out of the city, and set a captain over
them, as if you were going down to
the plain against the Assyrian out-
post; only do not go down. 3Then
they will seize their arms and go
into the camp and rouse the officers
of the Assyrian army; and they will
rush into the tent of Holofer´nes,
and will not find him. Then fear will
come over them, and they will flee
before you, 4and you and all who live
within the borders of Israel shall
pursue them and cut them down
as they flee. 5But before you do all
this, bring Ach´ior the Am´monite
to me, and let him see and recognize
the man who despised the house of
Israel and sent him to us as if to his
death."

6 So they summoned Ach´ior
from the house of Uzzi´ah. And
when he came and saw the head of
Holofer´nes in the hand of one of the
men at the gathering of the people,
he fell down on his face and his spir-
it failed him. 7And when they raised
him up he fell at Judith's feet, and
knelt before her, and said, "Blessed
are you in every tent of Judah! In ev-
ery nation those who hear your name
will be alarmed. 8Now tell me what
you have done during these days."
Then Judith described to him in the
presence of the people all that she
had done, from the day she left until
the moment of her speaking to them.
9And when she had finished, the
people raised a great shout and made
a joyful noise in their city. 10And
when Ach´ior saw all that the God
of Israel had done, he believed firm-
ly in God, and was circumcised, and
joined the house of Israel, remaining
so to this day.

HOLOFERNES' DEATH IS DISCOVERED

11 As soon as it was dawn they
hung the head of Holofer´nes on the
wall, and every man took his weap-
ons, and they went out in compa-
nies to the passes in the mountains.
12And when the Assyrians saw them
they sent word to their commanders,
and they went to the generals and
the captains and to all their officers.
13So they came to Holofer´nes' tent
and said to the steward in charge of
all his personal affairs, "Wake up
our lord, for the slaves have been so
bold as to come down against us to
give battle, in order to be destroyed
completely."

14 So Bago´as went in and knocked
at the door of the tent, for he sup-
posed that he was sleeping with
Judith. 15But when no one answered,
he opened it and went into the bed-
chamber and found him thrown
down on the platform dead, with his
head cut off and missing. 16And he
cried out with a loud voice and wept
and groaned and shouted, and rent
his garments. 17Then he went to the
tent where Judith had stayed, and
when he did not find her he rushed
out to the people and shouted, 18"The
slaves have tricked us! One Hebrew
woman has brought disgrace upon
the house of King Nebuchadnez´zar!
For look, here is Holofer´nes lying on
the ground, and his head is not on
him!"

19 When the leaders of the Assyrian
army heard this, they rent their tunics
and were greatly dismayed, and their
loud cries and shouts arose in the
midst of the camp.

THE ASSYRIANS FLEE IN PANIC

15 When the men in the tents heard
it, they were amazed at what had
happened. 2Fear and trembling came
over them, so that they did not wait
for one another, but with one impulse

all rushed out and fled by every path
across the plain and through the hill
country. 3Those who had camped in
the hills around Bethu´lia also took
to flight. Then the men of Israel, ev-
ery one that was a soldier, rushed out
upon them. 4And Uzzi´ah sent men
to Betomastha´im and Be´bai and
Choba and Kola, and to all the fron-
tiers of Israel, to tell what had taken
place and to urge all to rush out upon
their enemies to destroy them. 5And
when the Israelites heard it, with one
accord they fell upon the enemy,[a] and
cut them down as far as Choba. Those
in Jerusalem and all the hill country
also came, for they were told what had
happened in the camp of the enemy;
and those in Gil´ead and in Galilee
outflanked them with great slaugh-
ter, even beyond Damas´cus and its
borders. 6The rest of the people of
Bethu´lia fell upon the Assyrian camp
and plundered it, and were greatly en-
riched. 7And the Israelites, when they
returned from the slaughter, took
possession of what remained, and the
villages and towns in the hill country
and in the plain got a great amount of
booty, for there was a vast quantity
of it.

THE ISRAELITES CELEBRATE THEIR VICTORY

8 Then Jo´akim the high priest, and
the senate of the people of Israel who
lived at Jerusalem, came to witness
the good things which the Lord had
done for Israel, and to see Judith and
to greet her. 9And when they met her
they all blessed her with one accord
and said to her, "You are the exalta-
tion of Jerusalem,* you are the great
glory of Israel, you are the great pride
of our nation! 10You have done all this
singlehanded; you have done great
good to Israel, and God is well pleased
with it. May the Almighty Lord bless
you for ever!" And all the people said,
"So be it!"

11 So all the people plundered the
camp for thirty days. They gave Judith
the tent of Holofer´nes and all his sil-
ver dishes and his beds and his bowls
and all his furniture; and she took
them and loaded her mule and hitched
up her carts and piled the things on
them.

12 Then all the women of Israel
gathered to see her, and blessed her,
and some of them performed a dance
for her; and she took branches in her
hands and gave them to the women
who were with her; 13and they crowned
themselves with olive wreaths, she
and those who were with her; and
she went before all the people in the
dance, leading all the women, while
all the men of Israel followed, bearing
their arms and wearing garlands and
with songs on their lips.

JUDITH OFFERS HER HYMN OF PRAISE

16 Then Judith began this thanksgiv-
ing before all Israel, and all the
people loudly sang this song of praise.
2And Judith said,

Begin a song to my God with
tambourines,
sing to my Lord with
cymbals.
Raise to him a new psalm;[b]
exalt him, and call upon his
name.
3For God is the Lord who crushes
wars;
for he has delivered me out
of the hands of my
pursuers,
and brought me to his camp,
in the midst of the
people.
4The Assyrian came down from
the mountains of the
north;
he came with myriads of his
warriors;
their multitude blocked up the
valleys,
their cavalry covered the

[a] Gk *them*
[b] Other authorities read *a psalm and praise*

hills.
5He boasted that he would burn
up my territory,
and kill my young men with
the sword,
and dash my infants to the
ground
and seize my children as
prey,
and take my virgins as
booty.
6But the Lord Almighty has foiled
them
by the hand of a woman.
7For their mighty one did not fall
by the hands of the young
men,
nor did the sons of the
Titans smite him,
nor did tall giants set upon
him;
but Judith the daughter of
Merar´i undid him
with the beauty of her
countenance.
8For she took off her widow's
mourning
to exalt the oppressed in
Israel.
She anointed her face with
ointment
and fastened her hair with
a tiara
and put on a linen gown to
deceive him.
9Her sandal ravished his eyes,
her beauty captivated his
mind,
and the sword severed his
neck.
10The Persians trembled at her
boldness,
the Medes were daunted at
her daring.
11Then my oppressed people
shouted for joy;
my weak people shouted[c]
and the enemy[d]
trembled;
they lifted up their voices,
and the enemy[e] were
turned back.
12The sons of maidservants have
pierced them through;
they were wounded like the
children of fugitives,
they perished before the
army of my Lord.
13I will sing to my God a new
song:
O Lord, thou are great and
glorious,
wonderful in strength,
invincible.
14Let all thy creatures serve thee,
for thou didst speak, and
they were made.
Thou didst send forth thy
Spirit,[f] and it formed
them;
there is none that can resist
thy voice.
15For the mountains shall be shak-
en to their foundations
with the waters;
at thy presence the rocks
shall melt like wax,
but to those who fear thee
thou wilt continue to show
mercy.
16For every sacrifice as a fragrant
offering is a small thing,
and all fat for burnt offer-
ings to thee is a very
little thing,
but he who fears the Lord shall
be great for ever.
17Woe to the nations that rise up
against my people!
The Lord Almighty will take
vengeance on them in
the day of judgment;
fire and worms he will give to
their flesh;
they shall weep in pain for
ever.

18 When they arrived at Jerusalem
they worshiped God. As soon as the

[c] Other authorities read *feared*
[d] Gk *they*
[e] Gk *they*
[f] Or *breath*

people were purified, they offered
their burnt offerings, their freewill
offerings, and their gifts. 19 Judith
also dedicated to God all the vessels
of Holofer´nes, which the people had
given her; and the canopy which she
took for herself from his bedcham-
ber she gave as a votive offering to
the Lord. 20 So the people continued
feasting in Jerusalem before the sanc-
tuary for three months, and Judith re-
mained with them.

THE RENOWN AND DEATH OF JUDITH

21 After this every one returned
home to his own inheritance, and
Judith went to Bethu´lia, and re-
mained on her estate, and was hon-
ored in her time throughout the whole
country. 22 Many desired to marry her,
but she remained a widow all the days
of her life after Manas´seh her hus-
band died and was gathered to his
people. 23 She became more and more
famous, and grew old in her husband's
house, until she was one hundred and
five years old. She set her maid free.
She died in Bethu´lia, and they bur-
ied her in the cave of her husband
Manas´seh, 24 and the house of Israel
mourned for her seven days. Before
she died she distributed her property
to all those who were next of kin to
her husband Manas´seh, and to her
own nearest kindred. 25 And no one
ever again spread terror among the
people of Israel in the days of Judith,
or for a long time after her death.*

THE BOOK OF
ESTHER

MORDECAI'S DREAM

11 * 2*In the second year of the reign*
of Ahasu-e´rus[a] *the Great, on the*
first day of Nisan, Mor´decai the son
of Ja´ir, son of Shim´e-i, son of Kish, of
the tribe of Benjamin, had a dream. 3*He*
was a Jew, dwelling in the city of Susa,
a great man, serving in the court of the
king. 4*He was one of the captives whom*
Nebuchadnez´zar king of Babylon had
brought from Jerusalem with Jeconi´ah
king of Judea. And this was his dream:
5*Behold, noise*[b] *and confusion, thun-*
ders and earthquake, tumult upon the
earth! 6*And behold, two great dragons*
came forward, both ready to fight, and
they roared terribly. 7*And at their roar-*
ing every nation prepared for war, to fight
against the nation of the righteous. 8*And*
behold, a day of darkness and gloom,
tribulation and distress, affliction and
great tumult upon the earth! 9*And the*
whole righteous nation was troubled; they
feared the evils that threatened them, and
were ready to perish. 10*Then they cried to*
God; and from their cry, as though from a
tiny spring, there came a grect river, with
abundant water; 11*light came, nd the sun*
rose, and the lowly were exaltd and con-
sumed those held in honor.
12*Mor´decai saw in this d am what*
God had determined to do, an after he
awoke he had it on his mind a sought
all day to understand it in every tail.

A PLOT AGAINST THE KING

12 1*Now Mor´decai took his res n the*
courtyard with Gab´atha and rra,
the two eunuchs of the king wh kept
watch in the courtyard. 2*He ove ard*
their conversation and inquired int eir
purposes, and learned that they we e-
paring to lay hands upon Ahasu- sc
the king; and he informed the king con-
cerning them. 3*Then the king examined*
the two eunuchs, and when they con-
fessed they were led to execution. 4*The*
king made a permanent record of these
things, and Mor´decai wrote an account
of them. 5*And the king ordered Mor´decai*
to serve in the court and rewarded him
for these things. 6*But Haman, the son of*
Hammeda´tha, a Bougae´an, was in great
honor with the king, and he sought to in-
jure Mor´decai and his people because of
the two eunuchs of the king.

KING AHASU-ERUS DEPOSES QUEEN VASHTI

1 In the days of Ahasu-e´rus, the
Ahasu-e´rus who reigned from India
to Ethiopia over one hundred and
twenty-seven provinces, 2in those
days when King Ahasu-e´rus sat on
his royal throne in Susa the capital,
3in the third year of his reign he gave
a banquet for all his princes and ser-
vants, the army chiefs[d] of Persia and
Media and the nobles and governors
of the provinces being before him,
4while he showed the riches of his roy-
al glory and the splendor and pomp of
his majesty for many days, a hundred
and eighty days. 5And when these days
were completed, the king gave for all
the people present in Susa the cap-
ital, both great and small, a banquet
lasting for seven days, in the court of
the garden of the king's palace. 6There
were white cotton curtains and blue
hangings caught up with cords of fine
linen and purple to silver rings[e] and
marble pillars, and also couches of
gold and silver on a mosaic pavement
of porphyry, marble, mother-of-pearl
and precious stones. 7Drinks were
served in golden goblets, goblets of
different kinds, and the royal wine

[a]Gk *Artaxerxes*
[b]Or *voices*
[c]Gk *Artaxerxes*
[d]Heb *the army*
[e]Or *rods*

was lavished according to the bounty
of the king. 8And drinking was accord-
ing to the law, no one was compelled;
for the king had given orders to all the
officials of his palace to do as every
man desired. 9Queen Vashti also gave
a banquet for the women in the palace
which belonged to King Ahasu-e´rus.

10On the seventh day, when the
heart of the king was merry with wine,
he commanded Mehu´man, Biztha,
Harbo´na, Bigtha and Abag´tha,
Zethar and Carkas, the seven eunuchs
who served King Ahasu-e´rus as
chamberlains, 11to bring Queen Vashti
before the king with her royal crown,
in order to show the peoples and the
princes her beauty; for she was fair to
behold. 12But Queen Vashti refused to
come at the king's command conveyed
by the eunuchs. At this the king was
enraged, and his anger burned within
him.

13Then the king said to the wise
men who knew the times—for this
was the king's procedure toward all
who were versed in law and judgment,
14the men next to him being Carshe´na,
Shethar, Adma´tha, Tarshish, Meres,
Marse´na, and Memu´can, the seven
princes of Persia and Media, who saw
the king's face, and sat first in the
kingdom—: 15"According to the law,
what is to be done to Queen Vashti,
because she has not performed the
command of King Ahasu-e´rus con-
veyed by the eunuchs?" 16Then
Memu´can said in presence of the
king and the princes, "Not only to the
king has Queen Vashti done wrong,
but also to all the princes and all the
peoples who are in all the provinces
of King Ahasu-e´rus. 17For this deed
of the queen will be made known to
all women, causing them to look with
contempt upon their husbands, since
they will say, 'King Ahasu-e´rus com-
manded Queen Vashti to be brought
before him, and she did not come.'
18This very day the ladies of Persia
and Media who have heard of the
queen's behavior will be telling it to
all the king's princes, and there will
be contempt and wrath in plenty. 19If
it please the king, let a royal order go
forth from him, and let it be written
among the laws of the Persians and
the Medes so that it may not be al-
tered, that Vashti is to come no more
before King Ahasu-e´rus; and let the
king give her royal position to another
who is better than she. 20So when the
decree made by the king is proclaimed
throughout all his kingdom, vast as it
is, all women will give honor to their
husbands, high and low." 21This advice
pleased the king and the princes, and
the king did as Memu´can proposed;
22he sent letters to all the royal prov-
inces, to every province in its own
script and to every people in its own
language, that every man be lord in
his own house and speak according to
the language of his people.

ESTHER BECOMES QUEEN

2After these things, when the anger
of King Ahasu-e´rus had abated,
he remembered Vashti and what she
had done and what had been decreed
against her. 2Then the king's servants
who attended him said, "Let beautiful
young virgins be sought out for the
king. 3And let the king appoint offi-
cers in all the provinces of his king-
dom to gather all the beautiful young
virgins t the harem in Susa the capi-
tal, und custody of Hegai the king's
eunuch ho is in charge of the wom-
en; let eir ointments be given them.
4And l the maiden who pleases the
king b ueen instead of Vashti." This
please he king, and he did so.

5N there was a Jew in Susa the
capit whose name was Mor´decai,
the of Ja´ir, son of Shim´e-i, son
of , a Benjaminite, 6who had
bee arried away from Jerusalem
am the captives carried away
wit econi´ah king of Judah, whom
Ne hadnez´zar king of Babylon
ha rried away. 7He had brought up
H ´sah, that is Esther, the daughter
o uncle, for she had neither father

nor mother; the maiden was beautiful and lovely, and when her father and her mother died, Mor´decai adopted her as his own daughter. 8So when the king's order and his edict were proclaimed, and when many maidens were gathered in Susa the capital in custody of Hegai, Esther also was taken into the king's palace and put in custody of Hegai who had charge of the women. 9And the maiden pleased him and won his favor; and he quickly provided her with her ointments and her portion of food, and with seven chosen maids from the king's palace, and advanced her and her maids to the best place in the harem. 10Esther had not made known her people or kindred, for Mor´decai had charged her not to make it known. 11And every day Mor´decai walked in front of the court of the harem, to learn how Esther was and how she fared.

12Now when the turn came for each maiden to go in to King Ahasu-e´rus, after being twelve months under the regulations for the women, since this was the regular period of their beautifying, six months with oil of myrrh and six months with spices and ointments for women 13when the maiden went in to the king in this way she was given whatever she desired to take with her from the harem to the king's palace. 14In the evening she went, and in the morning she came back to the second harem in custody of Sha-ash´gaz the king's eunuch who was in charge of the concubines; she did not go in to the king again, unless the king delighted in her and she was summoned by name.

15When the turn came for Esther the daughter of Ab´ihail the uncle of Mor´decai, who had adopted her as his own daughter, to go in to the king, she asked for nothing except what Hegai the king's eunuch, who had charge of the women, advised. Now Esther found favor in the eyes of all who saw her. 16And when Esther was taken to King Ahasu-e´rus into his royal palace in the tenth month, which is the month of Tebeth, in the seventh year of his reign, 17the king loved Esther more than all the women, and she found grace and favor in his sight more than all the virgins, so that he set the royal crown on her head and made her queen instead of Vashti. 18Then the king gave a great banquet to all his princes and servants; it was Esther's banquet. He also granted a remission of taxes[a] to the provinces, and gave gifts with royal liberality.

MORDECAI DISCOVERS A PLOT

19When the virgins were gathered together the second time, Mor´decai was sitting at the king's gate. 20Now Esther had not made known her kindred or her people, as Mor´decai had charged her; for Esther obeyed Mor´decai just as when she was brought up by him. 21And in those days, as Mor´decai was sitting at the king's gate, Bigthan and Teresh, two of the king's eunuchs, who guarded the threshold, became angry and sought to lay hands on King Ahasu-e´rus. 22And this came to the knowledge of Mor´decai, and he told it to Queen Esther, and Esther told the king in the name of Mor´decai. 23When the affair was investigated and found to be so, the men were both hanged on the gallows. And it was recorded in the Book of the Chronicles in the presence of the king.

HAMAN UNDERTAKES TO DESTROY THE JEWS

3 After these things King Ahasu-e´rus promoted Haman the Ag´agite, the son of Hammeda´tha, and advanced him and set his seat above all the princes who were with him. 2And all the king's servants who were at the king's gate bowed down and did obeisance to Haman; for the king had so commanded concerning him. But Mor´decai did not bow down or do

[a]Or *a holiday*

obeisance. 3Then the king's servants
who were at the king's gate said to
Mor´decai, "Why do you transgress
the king's command?" 4And when
they spoke to him day after day and
he would not listen to them, they
told Haman, in order to see whether
Mor´decai's words would avail; for he
had told them that he was a Jew. 5And
when Haman saw that Mor´decai did
not bow down or do obeisance to him,
Haman was filled with fury. 6But he
disdained to lay hands on Mor´decai
alone. So, as they had made known to
him the people of Mor´decai, Haman
sought to destroy all the Jews, the
people of Mor´decai, throughout the
whole kingdom of Ahasu-e´rus.

7In the first month, which is the
month of Nisan, in the twelfth year of
King Ahasu-e´rus, they cast Pur, that
is the lot, before Haman day after day;
and they cast it month after month
till the twelfth month, which is the
month of Adar. 8Then Haman said to
King Ahasu-e´rus, "There is a certain
people scattered abroad and dispersed
among the peoples in all the provinces
of your kingdom; their laws are differ-
ent from those of every other people,
and they do not keep the king's laws,
so that it is not for the king's profit to
tolerate them. 9If it please the king, let
it be decreed that they be destroyed,
and I will pay ten thousand talents
of silver into the hands of those who
have charge of the king's business,
that they may put it into the king's
treasuries." 10So the king took his
signet ring from his hand and gave
it to Haman the Ag´agite, the son of
Hammeda´tha, the enemy of the Jews.
11And the king said to Haman, "The
money is given to you, the people also,
to do with them as it seems good to
you."

12Then the king's secretaries were
summoned on the thirteenth day of
the first month, and an edict, accord-
ing to all that Haman commanded,
was written to the king's satraps and
to the governors over all the prov-
inces and to the princes of all the
peoples, to every province in its own
script and every people in its own
language; it was written in the name
of King Ahasu-e´rus and sealed with
the king's ring. 13Letters were sent by
couriers to all the king's provinces,
to destroy, to slay, and to annihilate
all Jews, young and old, women and
children, in one day, the thirteenth
day of the twelfth month, which is the
month of Adar, and to plunder their
goods.

THE KING'S LETTER

13 *This is a copy of the letter: "The Great
King, Ahasu-e´rus,[a] to the rulers of
the hundred and twenty-seven provinces
from India to Ethiopia and to the gover-
nors under them, writes thus:*

*2"Having become ruler of many na-
tions and master of the whole world, not
elated with presumption of authority but
always acting reasonably and with kind-
ness, I have determined to settle the lives
of my subjects in lasting tranquillity and,
in order to make my kingdom peaceable
and open to travel throughout all its ex-
tent, to re-establish the peace which all
men desire.*

*3"When I asked my counselors how
this might be accomplished, Haman, who
excels among us in sound judgment, and
is distinguished for his unchanging good
will and steadfast fidelity, and has at-
tained the second place in the kingdom,
4pointed out to us that among all the
nations in the world there is scattered
a certain hostile people, who have laws
contrary to those of every nation and
continually disregard the ordinances of
the kings, so that the unifying of the king-
dom which we honorably intend cannot be
brought about. 5We understand that this
people, and it alone, stands constantly in
opposition to all men, perversely follow-
ing a strange manner of life and laws, and
is ill-disposed to our government, doing
all the harm they can so that our kingdom
may not attain stability.*

[a]Gk *Artaxerxes*

6“Therefore we have decreed that those
indicated to you in the letters of Haman,
who is in charge of affairs and is our sec-
ond father, shall all, with their wives and
children, be utterly destroyed by the sword
of their enemies, without pity or mercy, on
the fourteenth day of the twelfth month,
Adar, of this present year, 7so that those
who have long been and are now hostile
may in one day go down in violence to
Hades, and leave our government com-
pletely secure and untroubled hereafter.”

3 14A copy of the document was to be
issued as a decree in every province
by proclamation to all the peoples to
be ready for that day. 15The couriers
went in haste by order of the king,
and the decree was issued in Susa the
capital. And the king and Haman sat
down to drink; but the city of Susa
was perplexed.

ESTHER AGREES TO HELP THE JEWS

4 When Mor´decai learned all that
had been done, Mor´decai rent his
clothes and put on sackcloth and ash-
es, and went out into the midst of the
city, wailing with a loud and bitter
cry; 2he went up to the entrance of the
king’s gate, for no one might enter the
king’s gate clothed with sackcloth.
3And in every province, wherever the
king’s command and his decree came,
there was great mourning among the
Jews, with fasting and weeping and
lamenting, and most of them lay in
sackcloth and ashes.

4When Esther’s maids and her eu-
nuchs came and told her, the queen
was deeply distressed; she sent gar-
ments to clothe Mor´decai, so that he
might take off his sackcloth, but he
would not accept them. 5Then Esther
called for Hathach, one of the king’s
eunuchs, who had been appointed
to attend her, and ordered him to go
to Mor´decai to learn what this was
and why it was. 6Hathach went out
to Mor´decai in the open square of
the city in front of the king’s gate,
7and Mor´decai told him all that had
happened to him, and the exact sum
of money that Haman had promised to
pay into the king’s treasuries for the
destruction of the Jews. 8Mor´decai
also gave him a copy of the written de-
cree issued in Susa for their destruc-
tion, that he might show it to Esther
and explain it to her and charge her to
go to the king to make supplication to
him and entreat him for her people,*
“Remembering the days of your lowliness,
when you were cared for by me, because
Haman, who is next to the king, spoke
against us for our destruction. Beseech
the Lord and speak to the king concern-
ing us and deliver us from death.” 9And
Hathach went and told Esther what
Mor´decai had said. 10Then Esther
spoke to Hathach and gave him a
message for Mor´decai, saying, 11“All
the king’s servants and the people
of the king’s provinces know that if
any man or woman goes to the king
inside the inner court without being
called, there is but one law; all alike
are to be put to death, except the
one to whom the king holds out the
golden scepter that he may live. And
I have not been called to come in to
the king these thirty days.” 12And they
told Mor´decai what Esther had said.
13Then Mor´decai told them to return
answer to Esther, “Think not that in
the king’s palace you will escape any
more than all the other Jews. 14For if
you keep silence at such a time as this,
relief and deliverance will rise for the
Jews from another quarter, but you
and your father’s house will perish.
And who knows whether you have not
come to the kingdom for such a time
as this?” 15Then Esther told them to
reply to Mor´decai, 16“Go, gather all
the Jews to be found in Susa, and hold
a fast on my behalf, and neither eat
nor drink for three days, night or day.
I and my maids will also fast as you
do. Then I will go to the king, though
it is against the law; and if I perish,
I perish.” 17Mor´decai then went away
and did everything as Esther had or-
dered him.

MORDECAI'S PRAYER

13 [8]Then Mor′decai[a] prayed to the Lord,
calling to remembrance all the works
of the Lord. He said:
[9]"O Lord, Lord, King who rulest over
all things, for the universe is in thy power
and there is no one who can oppose thee if
it is thy will to save Israel. [10]For thou hast
made heaven and earth and every won-
derful thing under heaven, [11]and thou art
Lord of all, and there is no one who can re-
sist thee, who art the Lord. [12]Thou know-
est all things; thou knowest, O Lord, that
it was not in insolence or pride or for any
love of glory that I did this, and refused
to bow down to this proud Haman. [13]For
I would have been willing to kiss the soles
of his feet, to save Israel! [14]But I did this,
that I might not set the glory of man above
the glory of God, and I will not bow down
to any one but to thee, who art my Lord;
and I will not do these things in pride.
[15]And now, O Lord God and King, God of
Abraham, spare thy people; for the eyes
of our foes are upon us[b] to annihilate us,
and they desire to destroy the inheritance
that has been thine from the beginning.
[16]Do not neglect thy portion, which thou
didst redeem for thyself out of the land of
Egypt. [17]Hear my prayer, and have mercy
upon thy inheritance; turn our mourning
into feasting, that we may live and sing
praise to thy name, O Lord; do not destroy
the mouth of those who praise thee."
[18]And all Israel cried out mightily, for
their death was before their eyes.

ESTHER'S PRAYER

14 And Esther the queen, seized with
deathly anxiety, fled to the Lord; [2]she
took off her splendid apparel and put on
the garments of distress and mourning,
and instead of costly perfumes she covered
her head with ashes and dung, and she
utterly humbled her body, and every part
that she loved to adorn she covered with
her tangled hair. [3]And she prayed to the
Lord God of Israel, and said: "O my Lord,
thou only art our King; help me, who am
alone and have no helper but thee, [4]for my
danger is in my hand. [5]Ever since I was
born I have heard in the tribe of my family
that thou, O Lord, didst take Israel out
of all the nations, and our fathers from
among all their ancestors, for an ever-
lasting inheritance, and that thou didst
do for them all that thou didst promise.
[6]And now we have sinned before thee, and
thou hast given us into the hands of our
enemies, [7]because we glorified their gods.
Thou art righteous, O Lord! [8]And now
they are not satisfied that we are in bit-
ter slavery, but they have covenanted with
their idols [9]to abolish what thy mouth has
ordained and to destroy thy inheritance,
to stop the mouths of those who praise
thee and to quench thy altar and the glo-
ry of thy house, [10]to open the mouths of
the nations for the praise of vain idols,
and to magnify for ever a mortal king.
[11]O Lord, do not surrender thy scepter to
what has no being; and do not let them
mock at our downfall; but turn their plan
against themselves, and make an example
of the man who began this against us.
[12]Remember, O Lord; make thyself known
in this time of our affliction, and give me
courage, O King of the gods and Master of
all dominion! [13]Put eloquent speech in my
mouth before the lion, and turn his heart
to hate the man who is fighting against
us, so that there may be an end of him and
those who agree with him. [14]But save us
by thy hand, and help me, who am alone
and have no helper but thee, O Lord.
[15]Thou hast knowledge of all things; and
thou knowest that I hate the splendor of
the wicked and abhor the bed of the uncir-
cumcised and of any alien. [16]Thou know-
est my necessity—that I abhor the sign
of my proud position, which is upon my
head on the days when I appear in public.
I abhor it like a menstruous rag, and I
do not wear it on the days when I am at
leisure. [17]And thy servant has not eaten at
Haman's table, and I have not honored the
king's feast or drunk the wine of the liba-
tions. [18]Thy servant has had no joy since
the day that I was brought here until now,
except in thee, O Lord God of Abraham.

[a]Gk *he*
[b]Gk *for they are looking upon us*

[19]O God, whose might is over all, hear the
voice of the despairing, and save us from
the hands of evildoers. And save me from
my fear!"

ESTHER'S BANQUET

5 On the third day Esther put on her
royal robes and stood in the inner
court of the king's palace, opposite
the king's hall. The king was sitting
on his royal throne inside the palace
opposite the entrance to the palace;
[2]and when the king saw Queen Esther
standing in the court, she found favor
in his sight and he held out to Esther
the golden scepter that was in his
hand. Then Esther approached and
touched the top of the scepter.

ESTHER IS RECEIVED BY THE KING

15 **On the third day, when she ended*
her prayer, she took off the garments
in which she had worshiped, and arrayed
herself in splendid attire. [2]Then, majesti-
cally adorned, after invoking the aid of
the all-seeing God and Savior, she took
her two maids with her, [3]leaning daintily
on one, [4]while the other followed carrying
her train. [5]She was radiant with perfect
beauty, and she looked happy, as if be-
loved, but her heart was frozen with fear.
[6]When she had gone through all the doors,
she stood before the king. He was seated
on his royal throne, clothed in the full ar-
ray of his majesty, all covered with gold
and precious stones. And he was most
terrifying.

[7]Lifting his face, flushed with splen-
dor, he looked at her in fierce anger. And
the queen faltered, and turned pale and
faint, and collapsed upon the head of the
maid who went before her. [8]Then God
changed the spirit of the king to gentle-
ness, and in alarm he sprang from his
throne and took her in his arms until she
came to herself. And he comforted her with
soothing words, and said to her, [9]"What
is it, Esther? I am your brother. Take cour-
age; [10]you shall not die, for our law applies
only to the people.[c] Come near."

[11]Then he raised the golden scep-
ter and touched it to her neck; [12]and he
embraced her, and said, "Speak to me."
[13]And she said to him, "I saw you, my
lord, like an angel of God, and my heart
was shaken with fear at your glory. [14]For
you are wonderful, my lord, and your
countenance is full of grace." [15]But as she
was speaking, she fell fainting. [16]And the
king was agitated, and all his servants
sought to comfort her.

5 [3]And the king said to her, "What is
it, Queen Esther? What is your re-
quest? It shall be given you, even to
the half of my kingdom." [4]And Esther
said, "If it please the king, let the king
and Haman come this day to a dinner
that I have prepared for the king."
[5]Then said the king, "Bring Haman
quickly, that we may do as Esther de-
sires." So the king and Haman came to
the dinner that Esther had prepared.
[6]And as they were drinking wine, the
king said to Esther, "What is your pe-
tition? It shall be granted you. And
what is your request? Even to the half
of my kingdom, it shall be fulfilled."
[7]But Esther said, "My petition and my
request is: [8]If I have found favor in the
sight of the king, and if it please the
king to grant my petition and fulfil my
request, let the king and Haman come
tomorrow[d] to the dinner which I will
prepare for them, and tomorrow I will
do as the king has said."

HAMAN PLANS TO HAVE MORDECAI HANGED

[9]And Haman went out that day joy-
ful and glad of heart. But when Haman
saw Mor´decai in the king's gate, that
he neither rose nor trembled before
him, he was filled with wrath against
Mor´decai. [10]Nevertheless Haman
restrained himself, and went home;
and he sent and fetched his friends
and his wife Zeresh. [11]And Haman
recounted to them the splendor of
his riches, the number of his sons, all

[c]The meaning of the Greek text of this clause is obscure
[d]Gk: Heb lacks *tomorrow*

the promotions with which the king had honored him, and how he had advanced him above the princes and the servants of the king. 12And Haman added, "Even Queen Esther let no one come with the king to the banquet she prepared but myself. And tomorrow also I am invited by her together with the king. 13Yet all this does me no good, so long as I see Mor´decai the Jew sitting at the king's gate." 14Then his wife Zeresh and all his friends said to him, "Let a gallows fifty cubits high be made, and in the morning tell the king to have Mor´decai hanged upon it; then go merrily with the king to the dinner." This counsel pleased Haman, and he had the gallows made.

THE KING HONORS MORDECAI

6 On that night the king could not sleep; and he gave orders to bring the book of memorable deeds, the chronicles, and they were read before the king. 2And it was found written how Mor´decai had told about Bigthana and Teresh, two of the king's eunuchs, who guarded the threshold, and who had sought to lay hands upon King Ahasu-e´rus. 3And the king said, "What honor or dignity has been bestowed on Mor´decai for this?" The king's servants who attended him said, "Nothing has been done for him." 4And the king said, "Who is in the court?" Now Haman had just entered the outer court of the king's palace to speak to the king about having Mor´decai hanged on the gallows that he had prepared for him. 5So the king's servants told him, "Haman is there, standing in the court." And the king said, "Let him come in." 6So Haman came in, and the king said to him, "What shall be done *to the man whom the king delights to honor?*" And Haman said to himself, "Whom would the king delight to honor more than me?" 7And Haman said to the king, "For the man whom the king delights to honor, 8let royal robes be brought, which the king has worn, and the horse which the king has ridden, and on whose head a royal crown is set; 9and let the robes and the horse be handed over to one of the king's most noble princes; let him[a] array the man whom the king delights to honor, and let him[b] conduct the man on horseback through the open square of the city, proclaiming before him: 'Thus shall it be done to the man whom the king delights to honor.x 10Then the king said to Haman, "Make haste, take the robes and the horse, as you have said, and do so to Mor´decai the Jew who sits at the king's gate. Leave out nothing that you have mentioned." 11So Haman took the robes and the horse, and he arrayed Mor´decai and made him ride through the open square of the city, proclaiming, "Thus shall it be done to the man whom the king delights to honor."

12Then Mor´decai returned to the king's gate. But Haman hurried to his house, mourning and with his head covered. 13And Haman told his wife Zeresh and all his friends everything that had befallen him. Then his wise men and his wife Zeresh said to him, "If Mor´decai, before whom you have begun to fall, is of the Jewish people, you will not prevail against him but will surely fall before him."

HAMAN'S DOWNFALL AND MORDECAI'S ADVANCEMENT

14While they were yet talking with him, the king's eunuchs arrived and brought Haman in haste to the banquet that Esther had prepared.

7 So the king and Haman went in to *feast* with Queen Esther. 2And on the second day, as they were drinking wine, the king again said to Esther, "What is your petition, Queen Esther? It shall be granted you. And what is

[a]Heb *them*
[b]Heb *them*

your request? Even to the half of my
kingdom, it shall be fulfilled." 3Then
Queen Esther answered, "If I have
found favor in your sight, O king, and
if it please the king, let my life be giv-
en me at my petition, and my people at
my request. 4For we are sold, I and my
people, to be destroyed, to be slain,
and to be annihilated. If we had been
sold merely as slaves, men and women,
I would have held my peace; for our af-
fliction is not to be compared with the
loss to the king." 5Then King Ahasu-
e´rus said to Queen Esther, "Who is
he, and where is he, that would pre-
sume to do this?" 6And Esther said, "A
foe and enemy! This wicked Haman!"
Then Haman was in terror before the
king and the queen. 7And the king rose
from the feast in wrath and went into
the palace garden; but Haman stayed
to beg his life from Queen Esther,
for he saw that evil was determined
against him by the king. 8And the king
returned from the palace garden to
the place where they were drinking
wine, as Haman was falling on the
couch where Esther was; and the king
said, "Will he even assault the queen
in my presence, in my own house?" As
the words left the mouth of the king,
they covered Haman's face. 9Then said
Harbo´na, one of the eunuchs in at-
tendance on the king, "Moreover, the
gallows which Haman has prepared
for Mor´decai, whose word saved the
king, is standing in Haman's house,
fifty cubits high." 10And the king said,
"Hang him on that." So they hanged
Haman on the gallows which he had
prepared for Mor´decai. Then the an-
ger of the king abated.

8 On that day King Ahasu-e´rus
gave to Queen Esther the house of
Haman, the enemy of the Jews. And
Mor´decai came before the king, for
Esther had told what he was to her;
2and the king took off his signet ring,
which he had taken from Haman, and
gave it to Mor´decai. And Esther set
Mor´decai over the house of Haman.

ESTHER SAVES THE JEWS

3Then Esther spoke again to the
king; she fell at his feet and besought
him with tears to avert the evil de-
sign of Haman the Ag´agite and the
plot which he had devised against
the Jews. 4And the king held out the
golden scepter to Esther, 5and Esther
rose and stood before the king. And
she said, "If it please the king, and if
I have found favor in his sight, and if
the thing seem right before the king,
and I be pleasing in his eyes, let an
order be written to revoke the let-
ters devised by Haman the Ag´agite,
the son of Hammeda´tha, which he
wrote to destroy the Jews who are in
all the provinces of the king. 6For how
can I endure to see the calamity that
is coming to my people? Or how can
I endure to see the destruction of my
kindred?" 7Then King Ahasu-e´rus
said to Queen Esther and to Mor´decai
the Jew, "Behold, I have given Esther
the house of Haman, and they have
hanged him on the gallows, because
he would lay hands on the Jews. 8And
you may write as you please with re-
gard to the Jews, in the name of the
king, and seal it with the king's ring;
for an edict written in the name of the
king and sealed with the king's ring
cannot be revoked."

9The king's secretaries were
summoned at that time, in the third
month, which is the month of Sivan,
on the twenty-third day; and an edict
was written according to all that
Mor´decai commanded concerning
the Jews to the satraps and the gov-
ernors and the princes of the provinc-
es from India to Ethiopia, a hundred
and twenty-seven provinces, to every
province in its own script and to every
people in its own language, and also to
the Jews in their script and their lan-
guage. 10The writing was in the name
of King Ahasu-e´rus and sealed with
the king's ring, and letters were sent
by mounted couriers riding on swift
horses that were used in the king's
service, bred from the royal stud. 11By

these the king allowed the Jews who
were in every city to gather and de-
fend their lives, to destroy, to slay, and
to annihilate any armed force of any
people or province that might attack
them, with their children and women,
and to plunder their goods, 12upon one
day throughout all the provinces of
King Ahasu-e′rus, on the thirteenth
day of the twelfth month, which is the
month of Adar.

THE DECREE OF AHASU-ERUS

16 *The following is a copy of this letter:*
"The Great King, Ahasu-e′rus,[a] *to*
the rulers of the provinces from India to
Ethiopia, one hundred and twenty-seven
satrapies, and to those who are loyal to
our government, greeting.

2"The more often they are honored
by the too great kindness of their bene-
factors, the more proud do many men
become. 3They not only seek to injure our
subjects, but in their inability to stand
prosperity they even undertake to scheme
against their own benefactors. 4They not
only take away thankfulness from among
men, but, carried away by the boasts of
those who know nothing of goodness, they
suppose that they will escape the evil-hat-
ing justice of God, who always sees every-
thing. 5And often many of those who are
set in places of authority have been made
in part responsible for the shedding of in-
nocent blood, and have been involved in
irremediable calamities, by the persua-
sion of friends who have been entrusted
with the administration of public affairs,
6when these men by the false trickery of
their evil natures beguile the sincere good
will of their sovereigns.

7"What has been wickedly accom-
plished through the pestilent behavior of
those who exercise authority unworthily,
can be seen not so much from the more an-
cient records which we hand on as from
investigation of matters close at hand.
8For the future we will take care to ren-
der our kingdom quiet and peaceable for
all men, 9by changing our methods and
always judging what comes before our
eyes with more equitable consideration.
10For Haman, the son of Hammeda′tha,
a Macedo′nian (really an alien to the
Persian blood, and quite devoid of our
kindliness), having become our guest, 11so
far enjoyed the good will that we have for
every nation that he was called our fa-
ther and was continually bowed down to
by all as the person second to the royal
throne. 12But, unable to restrain his arro-
gance, he undertook to deprive us of our
kingdom and our life, 13and with intricate
craft and deceit asked for the destruction
of Mor′decai, our savior and perpetual
benefactor, and of Esther, the blameless
partner of our kingdom, together with
their whole nation. 14He thought that in
this way he would find us undefended
and would transfer the kingdom of the
Persians to the Macedo′nians.

15"But we find that the Jews, who were
consigned to annihilation by this thrice
accursed man, are not evildoers but are
governed by most righteous laws 16and are
sons of the Most High, the most mighty
living God, who has directed the kingdom
both for us and for our fathers in the most
excellent order.

17"You will therefore do well not to put
in execution the letters sent by Haman the
son of Hammeda′tha, 18because the man
himself who did these things has been
hanged at the gate of Susa, with all his
household. For God, who rules over all
things, has speedily inflicted on him the
punishment he deserved.

19"Therefore post a copy of this letter
publicly in every place, and permit the
Jews to live under their own laws. 20And
give them reinforcements, so that on the
thirteenth day of the twelfth month, Adar,
on that very day they may defend them-
selves against those who attack them at
the time of their affliction. 21For God,
who rules over all things, has made this
day to be a joy to his chosen people in-
stead of a day of destruction for them.

22"Therefore you shall observe
this with all good cheer as a notable
day among your commemorative festi-
vals, 23so that both now and hereafter

[a] Gk *Artaxerxes*

*it may mean salvation for us and the
loyal Persians, but that for those who
plot against us it may be a reminder of
destruction.*

*24"Every city and country, without
exception, which does not act accordingly,
shall be destroyed in wrath with spear and
fire. It shall be made not only impassable
for men, but also most hateful for all time
to beasts and birds."*

8 13A copy of what was written was
to be issued as a decree in every
province, and by proclamation to all
peoples, and the Jews were to be ready
on that day to avenge themselves
upon their enemies. 14So the couriers,
mounted on their swift horses that
were used in the king's service, rode
out in haste, urged by the king's com-
mand; and the decree was issued in
Susa the capital.

15Then Mor´decai went out from
the presence of the king in royal robes
of blue and white, with a great golden
crown and a mantle of fine linen and
purple, while the city of Susa shout-
ed and rejoiced. 16The Jews had light
and gladness and joy and honor. 17And
in every province and in every city,
wherever the king's command and his
edict came, there was gladness and
joy among the Jews, a feast and a holi-
day. And many from the peoples of the
country declared themselves Jews, for
the fear of the Jews had fallen upon
them.

DESTRUCTION OF THE ENEMIES OF THE JEWS

9 Now in the twelfth month, which
is the month of Adar, on the thir-
teenth day of the same, when the
king's command and edict were
about to be executed, on the very
day when the enemies of the Jews
hoped to get the mastery over them,
but which had been changed to a day
when the Jews should get the mas-
tery over their foes, 2the Jews gath-
ered in their cities throughout all
the provinces of King Ahasu-e´rus
to lay hands on such as sought their
hurt. And no one could make a stand
against them, for the fear of them
had fallen upon all peoples. 3All the
princes of the provinces and the sa-
traps and the governors and the roy-
al officials also helped the Jews, for
the fear of Mor´decai had fallen upon
them. 4For Mor´decai was great in
the king's house, and his fame spread
throughout all the provinces; for the
man Mor´decai grew more and more
powerful. 5So the Jews smote all their
enemies with the sword, slaughter-
ing, and destroying them, and did
as they pleased to those who hated
them. 6In Susa the capital itself the
Jews slew and destroyed five hundred
men, 7and also slew Parshan-da´tha
and Dalphon and Aspa´tha 8and
Pora´tha and Ada´lia and Arida´tha
9and Parmash´ta and Ar´isai and
Ar´idai and Vaiza´tha, 10the ten sons
of Haman the son of Hammeda´tha,
the enemy of the Jews; but they laid
no hand on the plunder.

11That very day the number of
those slain in Susa the capital was re-
ported to the king. 12And the king said
to Queen Esther, "In Susa the capital
the Jews have slain five hundred men
and also the ten sons of Haman. What
then have they done in the rest of the
king's provinces! Now what is your
petition? It shall be granted you. And
what further is your request? It shall
be fulfilled." 13And Esther said, "If it
please the king, let the Jews who are in
Susa be allowed tomorrow also to do
according to this day's edict. And let
the ten sons of Haman be hanged on
the gallows." 14So the king command-
ed this to be done; a decree was issued
in Susa, and the ten sons of Haman
were hanged. 15The Jews who were in
Susa gathered also on the fourteenth
day of the month of Adar and they
slew three hundred men in Susa; but
they laid no hands on the plunder.

16Now the other Jews who were in
the king's provinces also gathered to

defend their lives, and got relief from
their enemies, and slew seventy-five
thousand of those who hated them;
but they laid no hands on the plunder.
17This was on the thirteenth day of
the month of Adar, and on the four-
teenth day they rested and made that
a day of feasting and gladness. 18But
the Jews who were in Susa gathered
on the thirteenth day and on the four-
teenth, and rested on the fifteenth
day, making that a day of feasting
and gladness. 19Therefore the Jews
of the villages, who live in the open
towns, hold the fourteenth day of the
month of Adar as a day for gladness
and feasting and holiday-making, and
a day on which they send choice por-
tions to one another.

THE FEAST OF PURIM INAUGURATED

20And Mor´decai recorded these
things, and sent letters to all the
Jews who were in all the provinc-
es of King Ahasu-e´rus, both near
and far, 21enjoining them that they
should keep the fourteenth day of
the month Adar and also the fif-
teenth day of the same, year by year,
22as the days on which the Jews got
relief from their enemies, and as the
month that had been turned for them
from sorrow into gladness and from
mourning into a holiday; that they
should make them days of feast-
ing and gladness, days for sending
choice portions to one another and
gifts to the poor.

23So the Jews undertook to do as
they had begun, and as Mor´decai
had written to them. 24For Haman the
Ag´agite, the son of Hammeda´tha,
the enemy of all the Jews, had plot-
ted against the Jews to destroy them,
and had cast Pur, that is the lot, to
crush and destroy them; 25but when
Esther came before the king, he gave
orders in writing that his wicked
plot which he had devised against
the Jews should come upon his own
head, and that he and his sons should
be hanged on the gallows. 26Therefore
they called these days Purim, after
the term Pur. And therefore, be-
cause of all that was written in this
letter, and of what they had faced in
this matter, and of what had befallen
them, 27the Jews ordained and took
it upon themselves and their descen-
dants and all who joined them, that
without fail they would keep these
two days according to what was writ-
ten and at the time appointed every
year, 28that these days should be re-
membered and kept throughout ev-
ery generation, in every family, prov-
ince, and city, and that these days
of Purim should never fall into dis-
use among the Jews, nor should the
commemoration of these days cease
among their descendants.

29Then Queen Esther, the daughter
of Ab´ihail, and Mor´decai the Jew
gave full written authority, confirm-
ing this second letter about Purim.
30Letters were sent to all the Jews, to
the hundred and twenty-seven prov-
inces of the kingdom of Ahasu-e´rus,
in words of peace and truth, 31that
these days of Purim should be ob-
served at their appointed seasons, as
Mor´decai the Jew and Queen Esther
enjoined upon the Jews, and as they
had laid down for themselves and
for their descendants, with regard to
their fasts and their lamenting. 32The
command of Queen Esther fixed these
practices of Purim, and it was record-
ed in writing.

10King Ahasu-e´rus laid tribute on
the land and on the coastlands of
the sea. 2And all the acts of his pow-
er and might, and the full account of
the high honor of Mor´decai, to which
the king advanced him, are they not
written in the Book of the Chronicles
of the kings of Media and Persia? 3For
Mor´decai the Jew was next in rank to
King Ahasu-e´rus, and he was great
among the Jews and popular with
the multitude of his brethren, for he
sought the welfare of his people and
spoke peace to all his people.

MORDECAI'S DREAM FULFILLED

*And Mor´decai said, "These things
have come from God. 5For I remember the
dream that I had concerning these mat-
ters, and none of them has failed to be
fulfilled. 6The tiny spring which became
a river, and there was light and the sun
and abundant water—the river is Esther,
whom the king married and made queen.
7The two dragons are Haman and myself.
8The nations are those that gathered to
destroy the name of the Jews. 9And my na-
tion, this is Israel, who cried out to God
and were saved. The Lord has saved his
people; the Lord has delivered us from all
these evils; God has done great signs and
wonders, which have not occurred among
the nations. 10For this purpose he made
two lots, one for the people of God and
one for all the nations. 11And these two
lots came to the hour and moment and day
of decision before God and among all the
nations. 12And God remembered his peo-
ple and vindicated his inheritance. 13So
they will observe these days in the month
of Adar, on the fourteenth and fifteenth
of that month, with an assembly and joy
and gladness before God, from generation
to generation for ever among his people
Israel."*

POSTSCRIPT

11 *In the fourth year of the reign of
Ptol´emy and Cleopatra, Dosith´eus,
who said that he was a priest and a Levite,[a]
and Ptol´emy his son brought to Egypt[b]
the preceeding Letter of Purim, which they
said was genuine and had been translated
by Lysim´achus the son of Ptol´emy, one of
the residents of Jerusalem.*

[a] *Or priest, and Levitas*
[b] Cn: Gk *brought in*

THE BOOK OF

JOB

JOB AND HIS FAMILY

1 There was a man in the land of Uz, whose name was Job; and that man was blameless and upright, one who feared God, and turned away from evil. 2There were born to him seven sons and three daughters. 3He had seven thousand sheep, three thousand camels, five hundred yoke of oxen, and five hundred she-asses, and very many servants; so that this man was the greatest of all the people of the east. 4His sons used to go and hold a feast in the house of each on his day; and they would send and invite their three sisters to eat and drink with them. 5And when the days of the feast had run their course, Job would send and sanctify them, and he would rise early in the morning and offer burnt offerings according to the number of them all; for Job said, "It may be that my sons have sinned, and cursed God in their hearts." Thus Job did continually.

ATTACK ON JOB'S CHARACTER

6 Now there was a day when the sons of God came to present themselves before the LORD, and Satan[a] also came among them. 7The LORD said to Satan, "Whence have you come?" Satan answered the LORD, "From going to and fro on the earth, and from walking up and down on it." 8And the LORD said to Satan, "Have you considered my servant Job, that there is none like him on the earth, a blameless and upright man, who fears God and turns away from evil?" 9Then Satan answered the LORD, "Does Job fear God for nought? 10Hast thou not put a hedge about him and his house and all that he has, on every side? Thou hast blessed the work of his hands, and his possessions have increased in the land. 11But put forth thy hand now, and touch all that he has, and he will curse thee to thy face." 12And the LORD said to Satan, "Behold, all that he has is in your power; only upon himself do not put forth your hand." So Satan went forth from the presence of the LORD.

JOB LOSES PROPERTY AND CHILDREN

13 Now there was a day when his sons and daughters were eating and drinking wine in their eldest brother's house; 14and there came a messenger to Job, and said, "The oxen were plowing and the asses feeding beside them; 15and the Sabe´ans fell upon them and took them, and slew the servants with the edge of the sword; and I alone have escaped to tell you." 16While he was yet speaking, there came another, and said, "The fire of God fell from heaven and burned up the sheep and the servants, and consumed them; and I alone have escaped to tell you." 17While he was yet speaking, there came another, and said, "The Chalde´ans formed three companies, and made a raid upon the camels and took them, and slew the servants with the edge of the sword; and I alone have escaped to tell you." 18While he was yet speaking, there came another, and said, "Your sons and daughters were eating and drinking wine in their eldest brother's house; 19and behold, a great wind came across the wilderness, and struck the four corners of the house, and it fell upon the young people, and they are dead; and I alone have escaped to tell you."

20 Then Job arose, and rent his robe, and shavd his head, and fell upon the grond, and worshiped. 21And he said, "Naked I came from my mother's wmb, and naked shall I return; the LoD gave, and the LORD

[a]Heb *the adversary*

has taken away; blessed be the name
of the LORD."
22 In all this Job did not sin or
charge God with wrong.

ATTACK ON JOB'S HEALTH

2Again there was a day when the
sons of God came to present them-
selves before the LORD, and Satan also
came among them to present himself
before the LORD. 2And the LORD said
to Satan, "Whence have you come?"
Satan answered the LORD, "From go-
ing to and fro on the earth, and from
walking up and down on it." 3And the
LORD said to Satan, "Have you consid-
ered my servant Job, that there is none
like him on the earth, a blameless
and upright man, who fears God and
turns away from evil? He still holds
fast his integrity, although you moved
me against him, to destroy him with-
out cause." 4Then Satan answered the
LORD, "Skin for skin! All that a man
has he will give for his life. 5But put
forth thy hand now, and touch his
bone and his flesh, and he will curse
thee to thy face." 6And the LORD said
to Satan, "Behold, he is in your power;
only spare his life."
7 So Satan went forth from the
presence of the LORD, and afflicted
Job with loathsome sores from the
sole of his foot to the crown of his
head. 8And he took a potsherd with
which to scrape himself, and sat
among the ashes.
9 Then his wife said to him, "Do
you still hold fast your integrity?
Curse God, and die." 10But he said to
her, "You speak as one of the foolish
women would speak. Shall we receive
good at the hand of God, and shall we
not receive evil?" In all this Job did
not sin with his lips.

JOB'S THREE FRIENDS

11 Now when Job's three friends
heard of all this evil that had come
upon him, they came each from his
own place, Eli´phaz the Te´manite,
Bildad the Shuhite, and Zophar the
Na´amathite. They made an appoint-
ment together to come to condole
with him and comfort him. 12And
when they saw him from afar, they
did not recognize him; and they raised
their voices and wept; and they rent
their robes and sprinkled dust upon
their heads toward heaven. 13And they
sat with him on the ground seven days
and seven nights, and no one spoke a
word to him, for they saw that his suf-
fering was very great.

JOB CURSES THE DAY HE WAS BORN

3 After this Job opened his mouth and
cursed the day of his birth. 2And Job
said:

3"Let the day perish wherein I was born,
and the night which said,
'A man-child is conceived.'
4Let that day be darkness!
May God above not seek it,
nor light shine upon it.
5Let gloom and deep darkness claim it.
Let clouds dwell upon it;
let the blackness of the day terrify it.
6That night—let thick darkness seize it!
let it not rejoice among the days of the year,
let it not come into the number of the months.
7Yea, let that night be barren;
let no joyful cry be heard[b] in it.
8Let those curse it who curse the day,
who are skilled to rouse up Levi´athan.
9Let the stars of its dawn be dark;
let it hope for light, but have none,
nor see the eyelids of the morning;
10because it did not shut the doors of my mother's womb,
nor hide trouble from my eyes.

[b]Heb *come*

11 "Why did I not die at birth,
come forth from the womb
and expire?
12 Why did the knees receive me?
Or why the breasts, that I
should suck?
13 For then I should have lain down
and been quiet;
I should have slept; then I
should have been at
rest,
14 with kings and counselors of the
earth
who rebuilt ruins for
themselves,
15 or with princes who had gold,
who filled their houses with
silver.
16 Or why was I not as a hidden
untimely birth,
as infants that never see the
light?
17 There the wicked cease from
troubling,
and there the weary are at
rest.
18 There the prisoners are at ease
together;
they hear not the voice of
the taskmaster.
19 The small and the great are there,
and the slave is free from his
master.
20 "Why is light given to him that
is in misery,
and life to the bitter in soul,
21 who long for death, but it comes
not,
and dig for it more than for
hid treasures;
22 who rejoice exceedingly,
and are glad, when they find
the grave?
23 Why is light given to a man
whose way is hid,
whom God has hedged in?
24 For my *sighing* comes as[a] my
bread,
and my groanings are
poured out like water.
25 For the thing that I fear comes
upon me,
and what I dread befalls me.
26 I am not at ease, nor am I quiet;
I have no rest; but trouble
comes."

ELIPHAZ SPEAKS: JOB HAS SINNED

4 Then Eli´phaz the Te´manite
answered:
2 "If one ventures a word with you,
will you be offended?
Yet who can keep from
speaking?
3 Behold, you have instructed many,
and you have strengthened
the weak hands.
4 Your words have upheld him who
was stumbling,
and you have made firm the
feeble knees.
5 But now it has come to you, and
you are impatient;
it touches you, and you are
dismayed.
6 Is not your fear of God your
confidence,
and the integrity of your
ways your hope?
7 "Think now, who that was inno-
cent ever perished?
Or where were the upright
cut off?
8 As I have seen, those who plow
iniquity
and sow trouble reap the
same.
9 By the breath of God they perish,
and by the blast of his anger
they are consumed.
10 The roar of the lion, the voice of
the fierce lion,
the teeth of the young lions,
are broken.
11 The strong lion perishes for lack
of prey,
and the whelps of the lioness
are scattered.
12 "Now a word was brought to me
stealthily,
my ear received the whisper
of it.

[a] Heb *before*

13Amid thoughts from visions of
the night,
when deep sleep falls on
men,
14dread came upon me, and
trembling,
which made all my bones
shake.
15A spirit glided past my face;
the hair of my flesh stood
up.
16It stood still,
but I could not discern its
appearance.
A form was before my eyes;
there was silence, then I
heard a voice:
17'Can mortal man be righteous
before[b] God?
Can a man be pure before[c]
his Maker?
18Even in his servants he puts no
trust,
and his angels he charges
with error;
19how much more those who dwell
in houses of clay,
whose foundation is in the
dust,
who are crushed before the
moth.
20Between morning and evening
they are destroyed;
they perish for ever without
any regarding it.
21If their tent-cord is plucked up
within them,
do they not die, nd that
without vsdom?'

JOB IS CORRECTED BGOD

5 "Call now; is there any e who will
answer you?
To which of the holynes will
you turn?
2Surely vexation kills t fool,
and jealousy slayse simple.
3I have seen the fool taking root,
but suddenly I cursed his
dwelling.
4His sons are far from safety,
they are crushed in the gate,
and there is no one to deliv-
er them.
5His harvest the hungry eat,
and he takes it even out of
thorns;[d]
and the thirsty[e] pant after
his[f] wealth.
6For affliction does not come from
the dust,
nor does trouble sprout from
the ground;
7but man is born to trouble
as the sparks fly upward.
8"As for me, I would seek God,
and to God would I commit
my cause;
9who does great things and
unsearchable,
marvelous things without
number:
10he gives rain upon the earth
and sends waters upon the
fields;
11he sets on high those who are
lowly,
and those who mourn are
lifted to safety.
12He frustrates the devices of the
crafty,
so that their hands achieve
no success.
13He takes the wise in their own
craftiness;
and the schemes of the wily
are brought to a quick
end.
14They meet with darkness in the
daytime,
and grope at noonday as in
the night.
15But he saves the fatherless from
their mouth,[g]

[b] Or *more than*
[c] Or *more than*
[d] Heb obscure
[e] Aquila Symmachus Syr Vg: Heare
[f] Heb *their*
[g] Cn: Heb uncertain

the needy from the hand of
the mighty.
16So the poor have hope,
and injustice shuts her
mouth.
17"Behold, happy is the man whom
God reproves;
therefore despise not the
chastening of the
Almighty.
18For he wounds, but he binds up;
he smites, but his hands
heal.
19He will deliver you from six
troubles;
in seven there shall no evil
touch you.
20In famine he will redeem you
from death,
and in war from the power
of the sword.
21You shall be hid from the
scourge of the tongue,
and shall not fear destruc-
tion when it comes.
22At destruction and famine you
shall laugh,
and shall not fear the beasts
of the earth.
23For you shall be in league with
the stones of the field,
and the beasts of the field
shall be at peace with
you.
24You shall know that your tent
is safe,
and you shall inspect your
fold and miss nothing.
25You shall know also that your
descendants shall be many,
and your offspring as the
grass of the earth.
26You shall come to your grave in
ripe old age,
as a shock of grain comes up
to the threshing floor
in its season.
27Lo, this we have searched out; it
is true.
Hear, and know it for your
good."[a]

JOB REPLIES: MY COMPLAINT IS JUST

6 Then Job answered:
2"O that my vexation were
weighed,
and all my calamity laid in
the balances!
3For then it would be heavier than
the sand of the sea;
therefore my words have
been rash.
4For the arrows of the Almighty
are in me;
my spirit drinks their
poison;
the terrors of God are ar-
rayed against me.
5Does the wild ass bray when he
has grass,
or the ox low over his
fodder?
6Can that which is tasteless be
eaten without salt,
or is there any taste in
the slime of the
purslane?[b]
7My appetite refuses to touch
them;
they are as food that is
loathsome to me.[c]
8"O that I might have my request,
and that God would grant
my desire;
9that it vould please God to crush
ne,
tht he would let loose his
hand and cut me off!
10This ould be my consolation;
Iould even exult[d] in pain
unsparing;
r I have not denied the
words of the Holy
One.
11Whis my strength, that I
should wait?
nd what is my end, that I
should be patient?

[a] Heb *for yourself*
[b] The meaning of the Hebrew word is uncertain
[c] Heb obscure
[d] The meaning of the Hebrew word is uncertain

12Is my strength the strength of stones,
or is my flesh bronze?
13In truth I have no help in me,
and any resource is driven from me.
14"He who withholds[e] kindness from a friend
forsakes the fear of the Almighty.
15My brethren are treacherous as a torrent-bed,
as freshets that pass away,
16which are dark with ice,
and where the snow hides itself.
17In time of heat they disappear;
when it is hot, they vanish from their place.
18The caravans turn aside from their course;
they go up into the waste, and perish.
19The caravans of Tema look,
the travelers of Sheba hope.
20They are disappointed because they were confident;
they come thither and are confounded.
21Such you have now become to me;[f]
you see my calamity, and are afraid.
22Have I said, 'Make me a gift'?
Or, 'From your wealth offer a bribe for me'?
23Or, 'Deliver me from the adversary's hand'?
Or, 'Ransom me from the hand of oppressors'?
24"Teach me, and I will be silent;
make me understand how I have erred.
25How forceful are honest words!
But what does reproof from you reprove?
26Do you think that you can reprove words,
when the speech of a despairing man is wind?
27You would even cast lots over the fatherless,
and bargain over your friend.
28"But now, be pleased to look at me;
for I will not lie to your face.
29Turn, I pray, let no wrong be done.
Turn now, my vindication is at stake.
30Is there any wrong on my tongue?
Cannot my taste discern calamity?

JOB: MY SUFFERING IS WITHOUT END

7 "Has not man a hard service upon earth,
and are not his days like the days of a hireling?
2Like a slave who longs for the shadow,
and like a hireling who looks for his wages,
3so I am allotted months of emptiness,
and nights of misery are apportioned to me.
4When I lie down I say, 'When shall I arise?'
But the night is long,
and I am full of tossing till the dawn.
5My flesh is clothed with worms and dirt;
my skin hardens, then breaks out afresh.
6My days are swifter than a weaver's shuttle,
and come to their end without hope.
7"Remember that my life is a breath;
my eye will never again see good.
8The eye of him who sees me will behold me no more;
while thy eyes are upon me, I shall be gone.

[e] Syr Vg Compare Tg: Heb obscure
[f] Cn Compare Gk Syr: Heb obscure

9As the cloud fades and vanishes,
so he who goes down to Sheol
does not come up;
10he returns no more to his house,
nor does his place know him
any more.
11"Therefore I will not restrain my
mouth;
I will speak in the anguish
of my spirit;
I will complain in the bit-
terness of my soul.
12Am I the sea, or a sea monster,
that thou settest a guard
over me?
13When I say, 'My bed will comfort
me,
my couch will ease my
complaint,'
14then thou dost scare me with
dreams
and terrify me with visions,
15so that I would choose
strangling
and death rather than my
bones.
16I loathe my life; I would not live
for ever.
Let me alone, for my days
are a breath.
17What is man, that thou dost
make so much of him,
and that thou dost set thy
mind upon him,
18dost visit him every morning,
and test him every moment?
19How long wilt thou not look
away from me,
nor let me alone till I swal-
low my spittle?
20If I sin, what do I do to thee,
thou watcher of men?
Why hast thou made me thy
mark?
Why have I become a burden
to thee?
21Why dost thou not pardon my
transgression
and take away my iniquity?
For now I shall lie in the earth;
thou wilt seek me, but I
shall not be."

BILDAD SPEAKS: JOB SHOULD REPENT

8 Then Bildad the Shuhite answered:
2"How long will you say these
things,
and the words of your
mouth be a great
wind?
3Does God pervert justice?
Or does the Almighty per-
vert the right?
4If your children have sinned
against him,
he has delivered them into
the power of their
transgression.
5If you will seek God
and make supplication to the
Almighty,
6if you are pure and upright,
surely then he will rouse
himself for you
and reward you with a right-
ful habitation.
7And though your beginning was
small,
your latter days will be very
great.
8"For inquire, I pray you, of by-
gone ages,
and consider what the fa-
thers have found;
9for we are but of yesterday, and
know nothing,
for our days on earth are a
shadow.
10Will they not teach you, and tell
you,
and utter words out of their
understanding?
11"Can papyrus grow where there
is no marsh?
Can reeds flourish where
there is no water?
12While yet in flower and not cut
down,
they wither before any other
plant.
13Such are the paths of all who
forget God;
the hope of the godless man
shall perish.
14His confidence breaks in sunder,

and his trust is a spider's
web.[a]
15He leans against his house, but
it does not stand;
he lays hold of it, but it does
not endure.
16He thrives before the sun,
and his shoots spread over
his garden.
17His roots twine about the
stoneheap;
he lives among the rocks.[b]
18If he is destroyed from his place,
then it will deny him,
saying, 'I have never
seen you.'
19Behold, this is the joy of his way;
and out of the earth others
will spring.
20"Behold, God will not reject a
blameless man,
nor take the hand of
evildoers.
21He will yet fill your mouth with
laughter,
and your lips with shouting.
22Those who hate you will be
clothed with shame,
and the tent of the wicked
will be no more."

JOB REPLIES: THERE IS NO MEDIATOR

9 Then Job answered:
2"Truly I know that it is so:
But how can a man be just
before God?
3If one wished to contend with
him,
one could not answer him
once in a thousand
times.
4He is wise in heart, and mighty
in strength
—who has hardened him-
self against him, and
succeeded?—
5he who removes mountains, and
they know it not,
when he overturns them in
his anger;
6who shakes the earth out of its
place,
and its pillars tremble;
7who commands the sun, and it
does not rise;
who seals up the stars;
8who alone stretched out the
heavens,
and trampled the waves of
the sea;[c]
9who made the Bear and Orion,
the Plei'ades and the cham-
bers of the south;
10who does great things beyond
understanding,
and marvelous things with-
out number.
11Lo, he passes by me, and I see
him not;
he moves on, but I do not
perceive him.
12Behold, he snatches away; who
can hinder him?
Who will say to him, 'What
doest thou?'
13"God will not turn back his
anger;
beneath him bowed the
helpers of Rahab.
14How then can I answer him,
choosing my words with
him?
15Though I am innocent, I cannot
answer him;
I must appeal for mercy to
my accuser.[d]
16If I summoned him and he an-
swered me,
I would not believe that he
was listening to my
voice.
17For he crushes me with a
tempest,
and multiplies my wounds
without cause;
18he will not let me get my
breath,
but fills me with bitterness.

[a]Heb *house*
[b]Gk Vg: Heb uncertain
[c]Or *trampled the back of the sea dragon*
[d]Or *for my right*

19If it is a contest of strength,
behold him!
If it is a matter of justice,
who can summon
him?[a]
20Though I am innocent, my own
mouth would condemn me;
though I am blameless,
he would prove me
perverse.
21I am blameless; I regard not
myself;
I loathe my life.
22It is all one; therefore I say,
he destroys both the
blameless and the
wicked.
23When disaster brings sudden
death,
he mocks at the calamity[b] of
the innocent.
24The earth is given into the hand
of the wicked;
he covers the faces of its
judges—
if it is not he, who then is it?
25"My days are swifter than a
runner;
they flee away, they see no
good.
26They go by like skiffs of reed,
like an eagle swooping on
the prey.
27If I say, 'I will forget my
complaint,
I will put off my sad
countenance, and be
of good cheer,'
28I become afraid of all my
suffering,
for I know thou wilt not hold
me innocent.
29I shall be condemned;
why then do I labor in vain?
30If I wash myself with snow,
and cleanse my hands with
lye,
31yet thou wilt plunge me into a
pit,
and my own clothes will
abhor me.
32For he is not a man, as I am, that
I might answer him,
that we should come to trial
together.
33There is no[c] umpire between us,
who might lay his hand upon
us both.
34Let him take his rod away from
me,
and let not dread of him
terrify me.
35Then I would speak without fear
of him,
for I am not so in myself.

JOB: I LOATHE MY LIFE

10 "I loathe my life;
I will give free utterance to my
complaint;
I will speak in the bitterness
of my soul.
2I will say to God, Do not con-
demn me;
let me know why thou dost
contend against me.
3Does it seem good to thee to
oppress,
to despise the work of thy
hands
and favor the designs of the
wicked?
4Hast thou eyes of flesh?
Dost thou see as man sees?
5Are thy days as the days of man,
or thy years as man's years,
6that thou dost seek out my
iniquity
and search for my sin,
7although thou knowest that I am
not guilty,
and there is none to deliver
out of thy hand?
8Thy hands fashioned and made
me;
and now thou dost turn
about and destroy
me.[d]

[a] Compare Gk: Heb *me*. The text of the verse is uncertain
[b] The meaning of the Hebrew word is uncertain
[c] Another reading is *Would that there were*
[d] Cn Compare Gk Syr: Heb *made me together round about and thou dost destroy me*

9Remember that thou hast made
me of clay;[e]
and wilt thou turn me to
dust again?
10Didst thou not pour me out like
milk
and curdle me like cheese?
11Thou didst clothe me with skin
and flesh,
and knit me together with
bones and sinews.
12Thou hast granted me life and
steadfast love;
and thy care has preserved
my spirit.
13Yet these things thou didst hide
in thy heart;
I know that this was thy
purpose.
14If I sin, thou dost mark me,
and dost not acquit me of my
iniquity.
15If I am wicked, woe to me!
If I am righteous, I cannot
lift up my head,
for I am filled with disgrace
and look upon my
affliction.
16And if I lift myself up,[f] thou dost
hunt me like a lion,
and again work wonders
against me;
17thou dost renew thy witnesses
against me,
and increase thy vexation
toward me;
thou dost bring fresh hosts
against me.[g]
18"Why didst thou bring me forth
from the womb?
Would that I had died before
any eye had seen me,
19and were as though I had not
been,
carried from the womb to
the grave.
20Are not the days of my life few?[h]
Let me alone, that I may find
a little comfort[i]
21before I go whence I shall not
return,
to the land of gloom and
deep darkness,
22the land of gloom[j] and chaos,
where light is as darkness."

ZOPHAR SPEAKS: JOB'S GUILT DESERVES PUNISHMENT

11 Then Zophar the Na'amathite
answered:
2"Should a multitude of words go
unanswered,
and a man full of talk be
vindicated?
3Should your babble silence men,
and when you mock, shall no
one shame you?
4For you say, 'My doctrine is
pure,
and I am clean in God's
eyes.'
5But oh, that God would speak,
and open his lips to you,
6and that he would tell you the
secrets of wisdom!
For he is manifold in
understanding.[k]
Know then that God exacts of
you less than your guilt
deserves.
7"Can you find out the deep
things of God?
Can you find out the limit of
the Almighty?
8It is higher than heaven[l] —what
can you do?
Deeper than Sheol—what
can you know?
9Its measure is longer than the
earth,
and broader than the sea.

[e] Gk: Heb *like clay*
[f] Syr: Heb *he lifts himself up*
[g] Cn Compare Gk: Heb *changes and a host are with me*
[h] Cn Compare Gk Syr: Heb *Are not my days few? Let him cease*
[i] Heb *brighten up*
[j] Heb *gloom as darkness, deep darkness*
[k] Heb obscure
[l] Heb *The heights of heaven*

10If he passes through, and
imprisons,
and calls to judgment, who
can hinder him?
11For he knows worthless men;
when he sees iniquity, will
he not consider it?
12But a stupid man will get
understanding,
when a wild ass's colt is born
a man.
13"If you set your heart aright,
you will stretch out your
hands toward him.
14If iniquity is in your hand, put it
far away,
and let not wickedness dwell
in your tents.
15Surely then you will lift up your
face without blemish;
you will be secure, and will
not fear.
16You will forget your misery;
you will remember it as waters that have passed
away.
17And your life will be brighter
than the noonday;
its darkness will be like the
morning.
18And you will have confidence,
because there is hope;
you will be protected[a] and
take your rest in
safety.
19You will lie down, and none will
make you afraid;
many will entreat your
favor.
20But the eyes of the wicked will
fail;
all way of escape will be lost
to them,
and their hope is to breathe
their last."

JOB REPLIES: I AM A LAUGHINGSTOCK

12 Then Job answered:
2"No doubt you are the people,
and wisdom will die with
you.
3But I have understanding as well
as you;
I am not inferior to you.
Who does not know such
things as these?
4I am a laughingstock to my
friends;
I, who called upon God and
he answered me,
a just and blameless man,
am a laughingstock.
5In the thought of one who is at
ease there is contempt for
misfortune;
it is ready for those whose
feet slip.
6The tents of robbers are at
peace,
and those who provoke God
are secure,
who bring their god in their
hand.[b]
7"But ask the beasts, and they will
teach you;
the birds of the air, and they
will tell you;
8or the plants of the earth,[c] and
they will teach you;
and the fish of the sea will
declare to you.
9Who among all these does not
know
that the hand of the LORD
has done this?
10In his hand is the life of every
living thing
and the breath of all
mankind.
11Does not the ear try words
as the palate tastes food?
12Wisdom is with the aged,
and understanding in length
of days.
13"With God[d] are wisdom and
might;
he has counsel and
understanding.

[a] Or *you will look around*
[b] Hebrew uncertain
[c] Or *speak to the earth*
[d] Heb *him*

14If he tears down, none can rebuild;
if he shuts a man in, none can open.
15If he withholds the waters, they dry up;
if he sends them out, they overwhelm the land.
16With him are strength and wisdom;
the deceived and the deceiver are his.
17He leads counselors away stripped,
and judges he makes fools.
18He looses the bonds of kings,
and binds a waistcloth on their loins.
19He leads priests away stripped,
and overthrows the mighty.
20He deprives of speech those who are trusted,
and takes away the discernment of the elders.
21He pours contempt on princes,
and looses the belt of the strong.
22He uncovers the deeps out of darkness,
and brings deep darkness to light.
23He makes nations great, and he destroys them:
he enlarges nations, and leads them away.
24He takes away understanding from the chiefs of the people of the earth,
and makes them wander in a pathless waste.
25They grope in the dark without light;
and he makes them stagger like a drunken man.

13 "Lo, my eye has seen all this,
my ear has heard and understood it.
2What you know, I also know;
I am not inferior to you.
3But I would speak to the Almighty,
and I desire to argue my case with God.
4As for you, you whitewash with lies;
worthless physicians are you all.
5Oh that you would keep silent,
and it would be your wisdom!
6Hear now my reasoning,
and listen to the pleadings of my lips.
7Will you speak falsely for God,
and speak deceitfully for him?
8Will you show partiality toward him,
will you plead the case for God?
9Will it be well with you when he searches you out?
Or can you deceive him, as one deceives a man?
10He will surely rebuke you
if in secret you show partiality.
11Will not his majesty terrify you,
and the dread of him fall upon you?
12Your maxims are proverbs of ashes,
your defenses are defenses of clay.
13"Let me have silence, and I will speak,
and let come on me what may.
14I will take[e] my flesh in my teeth,
and put my life in my hand.
15Behold, he will slay me; I have no hope;
yet I will defend my ways to his face.
16This will be my salvation,
that a godless man shall not come before him.
17Listen carefully to my words,
and let my declaration be in your ears.
18Behold, I have prepared my case;

[e] Gk: Heb *Why should I take?*

I know that I shall be
vindicated.
19Who is there that will contend
with me?
For then I would be silent
and die.

JOB'S DESPONDENT PRAYER

20Only grant two things to me,
then I will not hide myself
from thy face:
21withdraw thy hand far from me,
and let not dread of thee
terrify me.
22Then call, and I will answer;
or let me speak, and do thou
reply to me.
23How many are my iniquities and
my sins?
Make me know my trans-
gression and my sin.
24Why dost thou hide thy face,
and count me as thy enemy?
25Wilt thou frighten a driven leaf
and pursue dry chaff?
26For thou writest bitter things
against me,
and makest me inherit the
iniquities of my
youth.
27Thou puttest my feet in the
stocks,
and watchest all my paths;
thou settest a bound to the
soles of my feet.
28Man[a] wastes away like a rotten
thing,
like a garment that is
moth-eaten.

14 "Man that is born of a woman
is of few days, and full of
trouble.
2He comes forth like a flower, and
withers;
he flees like a shadow and
continues not.
3*And dost thou open thy eyes*
upon such a one
and bring him[b] into judg-
ment with thee?
4Who can bring a clean thing out
of an unclean?
There is not one.
5Since his days are determined,
and the number of his
months is with thee,
and thou hast appointed
his bounds that he
cannot pass,
6look away from him, and desist,[c]
that he may enjoy, like a
hireling, his day.
7"For there is hope for a tree,
if it be cut down, that it will
sprout again,
and that its shoots will not
cease.
8Though its root grow old in the
earth,
and its stump die in the
ground,
9yet at the scent of water it will
bud
and put forth branches like a
young plant.
10But man dies, and is laid low;
man breathes his last, and
where is he?
11As waters fail from a lake,
and a river wastes away and
dries up,
12so man lies down and rises not
again;
till the heavens are no more
he will not awake,
or be roused out of his sleep.
13Oh that thou wouldest hide me
in Sheol,
that thou wouldest conceal
me until thy wrath
be past,
that thou wouldest appoint
me a set time, and
remember me!
14If a man die, shall he live again?
All the days of my service I
would wait,
till my release should come.
15Thou wouldest call, and I would
answer thee;

[a]Heb *He*
[b]Gk Syr Vg: Heb *me*
[c]Cn: Heb *that he may desist*

thou wouldest long for the
work of thy hands.
16For then thou wouldest number
my steps,
thou wouldest not keep
watch over my sin;
17my transgression would be
sealed up in a bag,
and thou wouldest cover
over my iniquity.
18"But the mountain falls and
crumbles away,
and the rock is removed
from its place;
19the waters wear away the
stones;
the torrents wash away the
soil of the earth;
so thou destroyest the hope
of man.
20Thou prevailest for ever against
him, and he passes;
thou changest his counte-
nance, and sendest
him away.
21His sons come to honor, and he
does not know it;
they are brought low, and he
perceives it not.
22He feels only the pain of his own
body,
and he mourns only for
himself."

ELIPHAZ SPEAKS: JOB UNDERMINES RELIGION

15 Then Eli´phaz the Te´manite answered:
2"Should a wise man answer with
windy knowledge,
and fill himself with the east
wind?
3Should he argue in unprofitable
talk,
or in words with which he
can do no good?
4But you are doing away with the
fear of God,
and hindering meditation
before God.
5For your iniquity teaches your
mouth,
and you choose the tongue
of the crafty.
6Your own mouth condemns you,
and not I;
your own lips testify against
you.
7"Are you the first man that was
born?
Or were you brought forth
before the hills?
8Have you listened in the council
of God?
And do you limit wisdom to
yourself?
9What do you know that we do
not know?
What do you understand
that is not clear to
us?
10Both the gray-haired and the
aged are among us,
older than your father.
11Are the consolations of God too
small for you,
or the word that deals gently
with you?
12Why does your heart carry you
away,
and why do your eyes flash,
13that you turn your spirit against
God,
and let such words go out of
your mouth?
14What is man, that he can be
clean?
Or he that is born of a wom-
an, that he can be
righteous?
15Behold, God puts no trust in his
holy ones,
and the heavens are not
clean in his sight;
16how much less one who is abom-
inable and corrupt,
a man who drinks iniquity
like water!
17"I will show you, hear me;
and what I have seen I will
declare
18(what wise men have told,
and their fathers have not
hidden,

19to whom alone the land was
given,
and no stranger passed
among them).
20The wicked man writhes in pain
all his days,
through all the years that
are laid up for the
ruthless.
21Terrifying sounds are in his ears;
in prosperity the destroyer
will come upon him.
22He does not believe that he will
return out of darkness,
and he is destined for the
sword.
23He wanders abroad for bread,
saying, 'Where is it?'
He knows that a day of
darkness is ready at
his hand;
24distress and anguish terrify him;
they prevail against him,
like a king prepared
for battle.
25Because he has stretched forth
his hand against God,
and bids defiance to the
Almighty,
26running stubbornly against him
with a thick-bossed shield;
27because he has covered his face
with his fat,
and gathered fat upon his
loins,
28and has lived in desolate cities,
in houses which no man
should inhabit,
which were destined to become heaps of ruins;
29he will not be rich, and his
wealth will not endure,
nor will he strike root in the
earth;[a]
30he will not escape from
darkness;
the flame will dry up his
shoots,
and his blossom[b] will be
swept away[c] by the
wind.
31Let him not trust in emptiness,
deceiving himself;
for emptiness will be his
recompense.
32It will be paid in full before his
time,
and his branch will not be
green.
33He will shake off his unripe
grape, like the vine,
and cast off his blossom, like
the olive tree.
34For the company of the godless
is barren,
and fire consumes the tents
of bribery.
35They conceive mischief and
bring forth evil
and their heart prepares
deceit."

JOB REAFFIRMS HIS INNOCENCE

16Then Job answered:
2"I have heard many such things;
miserable comforters are
you all.
3Shall windy words have an end?
Or what provokes you that
you answer?
4I also could speak as you do,
if you were in my place;
I could join words together
against you,
and shake my head at you.
5I could strengthen you with my
mouth,
and the solace of my lips
would assuage your
pain.
6"If I speak, my pain is not
assuaged,
and if I forbear, how much of
it leaves me?
7Surely now God has worn me
out;
he has[d] made desolate all my
company.

[a] Vg: Heb obscure
[b] Gk: Heb *mouth*
[c] Cn: Heb *will depart*
[d] Heb *thou hast*

8And he has[e] shriveled me up,
which is a witness against me;
and my leanness has risen up against me,
it testifies to my face.
9He has torn me in his wrath, and hated me;
he has gnashed his teeth at me;
my adversary sharpens his eyes against me.
10Men have gaped at me with their mouth,
they have struck me insolently upon the cheek,
they mass themselves together against me.
11God gives me up to the ungodly,
and casts me into the hands of the wicked.
12I was at ease, and he broke me asunder;
he seized me by the neck and dashed me to pieces;
he set me up as his target,
13his archers surround me.
He slashes open my kidneys, and does not spare;
he pours out my gall on the ground.
14He breaks me with breach upon breach;
he runs upon me like a warrior.
15I have sewed sackcloth upon my skin,
and have laid my strength in the dust.
16My face is red with weeping,
and on my eyelids is deep darkness;
17although there is no violence in my hands,
and my prayer is pure.
18"O earth, cover not my blood,
and let my cry find no resting place.
19Even now, behold, my witness is in heaven,
and he that vouches for me is on high.
20My friends scorn me;
my eye pours out tears to God,
21that he would maintain the right of a man with God,
like[f] that of a man with his neighbor.
22For when a few years have come
I shall go the way whence I shall not return.

JOB PRAYS FOR RELIEF

17 My spirit is broken, my days are extinct,
the grave is ready for me.
2Surely there are mockers about me,
and my eye dwells on their provocation.
3"Lay down a pledge for me with thyself;
who is there that will give surety for me?
4Since thou hast closed their minds to understanding,
therefore thou wilt not let them triumph.
5He who informs against his friends to get a share of their property,
the eyes of his children will fail.
6"He has made me a byword of the peoples,
and I am one before whom men spit.
7My eye has grown dim from grief,
and all my members are like a shadow.
8Upright men are appalled at this,
and the innocent stirs himself up against the godless.

[e] Heb *thou hast*
[f] Syr Vg Tg: Heb *and*

9Yet the righteous holds to his way,
and he that has clean hands grows stronger and stronger.
10But you, come on again, all of you,
and I shall not find a wise man among you.
11My days are past, my plans are broken off,
the desires of my heart.
12They make night into day;
'The light,' they say, 'is near to the darkness.'[a]
13If I look for Sheol as my house,
if I spread my couch in darkness,
14if I say to the pit, 'You are my father,'
and to the worm, 'My mother,' or 'My sister,'
15where then is my hope?
Who will see my hope?
16Will it go down to the bars of Sheol?
Shall we descend together into the dust?"

BILDAD SPEAKS: GOD PUNISHES THE WICKED

18 Then Bildad the Shuhite answered:
2"How long will you hunt for words?
Consider, and then we will speak.
3Why are we counted as cattle?
Why are we stupid in your sight?
4You who tear yourself in your anger,
shall the earth be forsaken for you,
or the rock be removed out of its place?
5"Yea, the light of the wicked is put out,
and the flame of his fire does not shine.
6The light is dark in his tent,
and his lamp above him is put out.
7His strong steps are shortened
and his own schemes throw him down.
8For he is cast into a net by his own feet,
and he walks on a pitfall.
9A trap seizes him by the heel,
a snare lays hold of him.
10A rope is hid for him in the ground,
a trap for him in the path.
11Terrors frighten him on every side,
and chase him at his heels.
12His strength is hunger-bitten,
and calamity is ready for his stumbling.
13By disease his skin is consumed,[b]
the first-born of death consumes his limbs.
14He is torn from the tent in which he trusted,
and is brought to the king of terrors.
15In his tent dwells that which is none of his;
brimstone is scattered upon his habitation.
16His roots dry up beneath,
and his branches wither above.
17His memory perishes from the earth,
and he has no name in the street.
18He is thrust from light into darkness,
and driven out of the world.
19He has no offspring or descendant among his people,
and no survivor where he used to live.
20They of the west are appalled at his day,
and horror seizes them of the east.
21Surely such are the dwellings of

[a] Heb *obscure*
[b] Cn: Heb *it consumes the limbs of his skin*

the ungodly,
such is the place of him who
knows not God."

JOB REPLIES: I KNOW THAT MY REDEEMER LIVES

19 Then Job answered:
2 "How long will you torment me,
and break me in pieces with
words?
3 These ten times you have cast
reproach upon me;
are you not ashamed to
wrong me?
4 And even if it be true that I have
erred,
my error remains with
myself.
5 If indeed you magnify yourselves
against me,
and make my humiliation an
argument against me,
6 know then that God has put me
in the wrong,
and closed his net about me.
7 Behold, I cry out, 'Violence!' but
I am not answered;
I call aloud, but there is no
justice.
8 He has walled up my way, so that
I cannot pass,
and he has set darkness
upon my paths.
9 He has stripped from me my
glory,
and taken the crown from
my head.
10 He breaks me down on every
side, and I am gone,
and my hope has he pulled
up *like* a tree.
11 He has kindled his wrath against
me,
and counts me as his
adversary.
12 His troops come on together;
they have cast up siege-
works[c] against me,
and encamp round about my
tent.

13 "He has put my brethren far
from me,
and my acquaintances are
wholly estranged
from me.
14 My kinsfolk and my close friends
have failed me;
15 the guests in my house
have forgotten me;
my maidservants count me as a
stranger;
I have become an alien in
their eyes.
16 I call to my servant, but he gives
me no answer;
I must beseech him with my
mouth.
17 I am repulsive to my wife,
loathsome to the sons of my
own mother.
18 Even young children despise
me;
when I rise they talk against
me.
19 All my intimate friends abhor
me,
and those whom I loved have
turned against me.
20 My bones cleave to my skin and
to my flesh,
and I have escaped by the
skin of my teeth.
21 Have pity on me, have pity on
me, O you my friends,
for the hand of God has
touched me!
22 Why do you, like God, pursue
me?
Why are you not satisfied
with my flesh?
23 "Oh that my words were
written!
Oh that they were inscribed
in a book!
24 Oh that with an iron pen and
lead
they were graven in the rock
for ever!
25 For I know that my Redeemer[d]
lives,

[c] Heb *their way*
[d] Or *Vindicator*

and at last he will stand
upon the earth;[a]
26and after my skin has been thus
destroyed,
then from[b] my flesh I shall
see God,[c]
27whom I shall see on my side,[d]
and my eyes shall behold,
and not another.
My heart faints within me!
28If you say, 'How we will pursue
him!'
and, 'The root of the matter
is found in him';
29be afraid of the sword,
for wrath brings the punishment of the sword,
that you may know there is a
judgment."

ZOPHAR SPEAKS: WICKEDNESS RECEIVES JUST RETRIBUTION

20 Then Zophar the Na′amathite
answered:
2"Therefore my thoughts answer
me,
because of my haste within
me.
3I hear censure which insults me,
and out of my understanding
a spirit answers me.
4Do you not know this from of
old,
since man was placed upon
earth,
5that the exulting of the wicked
is short,
and the joy of the godless
but for a moment?
6Though his height mount up to
the heavens,
and his head reach to the
clouds,
7he will perish for ever like his
own dung;
those who have seen him
will say, 'Where is
he?'
8He will fly away like a dream,
and not be found;
he will be chased away like a
vision of the night.
9The eye which saw him will see
him no more,
nor will his place any more
behold him.
10His children will seek the favor
of the poor,
and his hands will give back
his wealth.
11His bones are full of youthful
vigor,
but it will lie down with him
in the dust.
12"Though wickedness is sweet in
his mouth,
though he hides it under his
tongue,
13though he is loath to let it go,
and holds it in his mouth,
14yet his food is turned in his
stomach;
it is the gall of asps within
him.
15He swallows down riches and
vomits them up again;
God casts them out of his
belly.
16He will suck the poison of asps;
the tongue of a viper will
kill him.
17He will not look upon the rivers,
the streams flowing with
honey and curds.
18He will give back the fruit of
his toil,
and will not swallow it
down;
from the profit of his trading
he will get no enjoyment.
19For he has crushed and abandoned the poor,
he has seized a house which
he did not build.
20"Because his greed knew no rest,
he will not save anything in
which he delights.

[a] Or *dust*
[b] Or *without*
[c] The meaning of this verse is uncertain
[d] Or *for myself*

21There was nothing left after he
had eaten;
therefore his prosperity will
not endure.
22In the fulness of his sufficiency
he will be in straits;
all the force of misery will
come upon him.
23To fill his belly to the full
God[e] will send his fierce
anger into him,
and rain it upon him as his
food.[f]
24He will flee from an iron weapon;
a bronze arrow will strike
him through.
25It is drawn forth and comes out
of his body,
the glittering point comes
out of his gall;
terrors come upon him.
26Utter darkness is laid up for his
treasures;
a fire not blown upon will
devour him;
what is left in his tent will
be consumed.
27The heavens will reveal his
iniquity,
and the earth will rise up
against him.
28The possessions of his house
will be carried away,
dragged off in the day of
God's[g] wrath.
29This is the wicked man's portion
from God,
the heritage decreed for him
by God."

JOB REPLIES: THE WICKED OFTEN GO UNPUNISHED

21 Then Job answered:
2"Listen carefully to my words,
and let this b your
consoltion.
3Bear with me, and will speak,
and after I hav spoken,
mock o
4As for me, is my complaint
against man?
Why should I not be
impatient?
5Look at me, and be appalled,
and lay your hand upon your
mouth.
6When I think of it I am dismayed,
and shuddering seizes my
flesh.
7Why do the wicked live,
reach old age, and grow
mighty in power?
8Their children are established in
their presence,
and their offspring before
their eyes.
9Their houses are safe from fear,
and no rod of God is upon
them.
10Their bull breeds without fail;
their cow calves, and does
not cast her calf.
11They send forth their little ones
like a flock,
and their children dance.
12They sing to the tambourine and
the lyre,
and rejoice to the sound of
the pipe.
13They spend their days in
prosperity,
and in peace they go down
to Sheol.
14They say to God, 'Depart from
us!
We do not desire the knowl-
edge of thy ways.
15What is the Almighty, that we
should serve him?
And what profit do we get if
we pray to him?'
16Behold, is not their prosperity in
their hand?
The counsel of the wicked is
far from me.
17"How often is it that the lamp of
the wicked is put out?
That their calamity comes
upon them?

[e]Heb *he*
[f]Cn: Heb *in his flesh*
[g]Heb *his*

That God[a] distributes pains
in his anger?
18That they are like straw before
the wind,
and like chaff that the storm
carries away?
19You say, 'God stores up their
iniquity for their sons.'
Let him recompense it to
themselves, that they
may know it.
20Let their own eyes see their
destruction,
and let them drink of
the wrath of the
Almighty.
21For what do they care for their
houses after them,
when the number of their
months is cut off?
22Will any teach God knowledge,
seeing that he judges those
that are on high?
23One dies in full prosperity,
being wholly at ease and
secure,
24his body[b] full of fat
and the marrow of his bones
moist.
25Another dies in bitterness of
soul,
never having tasted of good.
26They lie down alike in the dust,
and the worms cover them.
27"Behold, I know your thoughts,
and your schemes to wrong
me.
28For you say, 'Where is the house
of the prince?
Where is the tent in which
the wicked dwelt?'
29Have you not asked those who
travel the roads,
and do you not accept their
testimony
30that the wicked man is spared in
the day of calamity,
that he is rescued in the day
of wrath?
31Who declares his way to his face,
and who requites him for
what he has done?
32When he is borne to the grave,
watch is kept over his tomb.
33The clods of the valley are sweet
to him;
all men follow after him,
and those who go before him
are innumerable.
34How then will you comfort me
with empty nothings?
There is nothing left of
your answers but
falsehood."

ELIPHAZ SPEAKS: JOB'S WICKEDNESS IS GREAT

22 Then Eli´phaz the Te´manite
answered:
2"Can a man be profitable to God?
Surely he who is wise is
profitable to himself.
3Is it any pleasure to the Almighty
if you are righteous,
or is it gain to him if you
make your ways
blameless?
4Is it for your fear of him that he
reproves you,
and enters into judgment
with you?
5Is not your wickedness great?
There is no end to your
iniquities.
6For you have exacted pledges of
your brothers for nothing,
and stripped the naked of
their clothing.
7You have given no water to the
weary to drink,
and you have withheld bread
from the hungry.
8The man with power possessed
the land,
and the favored man dwelt
in it.
9You have sent widows away
empty,
and the arms of the father-
less were crushed.

[a] Heb *he*
[b] The meaning of the Hebrew word is uncertain

10Therefore snares are round
about you,
and sudden terror over-
whelms you;
11your light is darkened, so that[c]
you cannot see,
and a flood of water covers
you.
12"Is not God high in the heavens?
See the highest stars, how
lofty they are!
13Therefore you say, 'What does
God know?
Can he judge through the
deep darkness?
14Thick clouds enwrap him, so
that he does not see,
and he walks on the vault of
heaven.'
15Will you keep to the old way
which wicked men have
trod?
16They were snatched away before
their time;
their foundation was washed
away.
17They said to God, 'Depart from
us,'
and 'What can the Almighty
do to us?'[d]
18Yet he filled their houses with
good things—
but the counsel of the wick-
ed is far from me.
19The righteous see it and are
glad;
the innocent laugh them to
scorn,
20saying, 'Surely our adversaries
are cut off,
and what they left the fire
has consumed.'
21"Agree with God, and be at
peace;
thereby good will come to
you.
22Receive instruction from his
mouth,
and lay up his words in your
heart.
23If you return to the Almighty
and humble yourself,[e]
if you remove unrighteous-
ness far from your
tents,
24if you lay gold in the dust,
and gold of Ophir among the
stones of the torrent
bed,
25and if the Almighty is your gold,
and your precious silver;
26then you will delight yourself in
the Almighty,
and lift up your face to God.
27You will make your prayer to
him, and he will hear you;
and you will pay your vows.
28You will decide on a matter, and
it will be established for
you,
and light will shine on your
ways.
29For God abases the proud,[f]
but he saves the lowly.
30He delivers the innocent man;[g]
you will be delivered
through the clean-
ness of your hands."

JOB REPLIES: MY COMPLAINT IS BITTER

23 Then Job answered:
2"Today also my complaint is
bitter,[h]
his[i] hand is heavy in spite of
my groaning.
3Oh, that I knew where I might
find him,
that I might come even to
his seat!
4I would lay my case before him
and fill my mouth with
arguments.
5I would learn what he would
answer me,

[c] Cn Compare Gk: Heb *or darkness*
[d] Gk Syr: Heb *them*
[e] Gk: Heb *you will be built up*
[f] Cn: Heb *when they abased you said, Proud*
[g] Gk Syr Vg: Heb *him that is not innocent*
[h] Syr Vg Tg: Heb *rebellious*
[i] Gk Syr: Heb *my*

and understand what he
would say to me.
6 Would he contend with me in the
greatness of his power?
No; he would give heed to
me.
7 There an upright man could
reason with him,
and I should be acquitted for
ever by my judge.
8 "Behold, I go forward, but he is
not there;
and backward, but I cannot
perceive him;
9 on the left hand I seek him,[a] but I
cannot behold him;
I[b] turn to the right hand, but
I cannot see him.
10 But he knows the way that I take;
when he has tried me, I shall
come forth as gold.
11 My foot has held fast to his
steps;
I have kept his way and have
not turned aside.
12 I have not departed from the
commandment of his lips;
I have treasured in[c] my bo-
som the words of his
mouth.
13 But he is unchangeable and who
can turn him?
What he desires, that he
does.
14 For he will complete what he
appoints for me;
and many such things are in
his mind.
15 Therefore I am terrified at his
presence;
when I consider, I am in
dread of him.
16 God has made my heart faint;
the Almighty has terrified
me;
17 for I am[d] hemmed in by
darkness,
and thick darkness covers
my face.[e]

JOB COMPLAINS OF VIOLENCE ON THE EARTH

24 "Why are not times of judgment
kept by the Almighty,
and why do those who know
him never see his
days?
2 Men remove landmarks;
they seize flocks and pasture
them.
3 They drive away the ass of the
fatherless;
they take the widow's ox for
a pledge.
4 They thrust the poor off the road;
the poor of the earth all hide
themselves.
5 Behold, like wild asses in the
desert
they go forth to their toil,
seeking prey in the wilderness
as food[f] for their children.
6 They gather their[g] fodder in the
field
and they glean the vineyard
of the wicked man.
7 They lie all night naked, without
clothing,
and have no covering in the
cold.
8 They are wet with the rain of the
mountains,
and cling to the rock for
want of shelter.
9 (There are those who snatch the
fatherless child from the
breast,
and take in pledge the infant
of the poor.)
10 They go about naked, without
clothing;
hungry, they carry the
sheaves;

[a] Compare Syr: Heb *on the left hand when he works*
[b] Syr Vg: Heb *he*
[c] Gk Vg: Heb *from*
[d] With one Ms: Heb *am not*
[e] Vg: Heb *from my face*
[f] Heb *food to him*
[g] Heb *his*

11among the olive rows of the
wicked[h] they make oil;
they tread the wine presses,
but suffer thirst.
12From out of the city the dying
groan,
and the soul of the wounded
cries for help;
yet God pays no attention to
their prayer.
13"There are those who rebel
against the light,
who are not acquainted with
its ways,
and do not stay in its paths.
14The murderer rises in the dark,[i]
that he may kill the poor and
needy;
and in the night he is as a
thief.
15The eye of the adulterer also
waits for the twilight,
saying, 'No eye will see me';
and he disguises his face.
16In the dark they dig through
houses;
by day they shut themselves
up;
they do not know the light.
17For deep darkness is morning to
all of them;
for they are friends with
the terrors of deep
darkness.
18"You say, 'They are swiftly car-
ried away uponthe face of
the waters;
their portion is crsed in the
land;
no treader turns ward
their vineyds.
19Drought and heat snah away
the snow waters
so does Sheol thosvho
have sinned
20The squares of the towforget
them;
their name[k] is no longer
remembered;
so wickedness is broken like
a tree.'
21"They feed on the barren child-
less woman,
and do no good to the
widow.
22Yet God[l] prolongs the life of the
mighty by his power;
they rise up when they
despair of life.
23He gives them security, and they
are supported;
and his eyes are upon their
ways.
24They are exalted a little while,
and then are gone;
they wither and fade like the
mallow;[m]
they are cut off like the
heads of grain.
25If it is not so, who will prove me
a liar,
and show that there is noth-
ing in what I say?"

BILDAD SPEAKS: HOW CAN A MORTAL BE RIGHTEOUS BEFORE GOD?

25 Then Bildad the Shuhite answered:
2"Dominion and fear are with
God; [n]
he makes peace in his high
heaven.
3Is there any number to his
armies?
Upon whom does his light
not arise?
4How then can man be righteous
before God?
How can he who is born of
woman be clean?
5Behold, even the moon is not
bright
and the stars are not clean
in his sight;

[h]Heb *their olive rows*
[i]Cn: Heb *at the light*
[j]Cn: Heb obscure
[k]Cn: Heb *a worm*
[l]Heb *he*
[m]Gk: Heb *all*
[n]Heb *him*

6how much less man, who is a
maggot,
and the son of man, who is a
worm!"

JOB REPLIES: GOD'S MAJESTY IS UNSEARCHABLE

26 Then Job answered:
2"How you have helped him who
has no power!
How you have saved the arm
that has no strength!
3How you have counseled him
who has no wisdom,
and plentifully declared
sound knowledge!
4With whose help have you ut-
tered words,
and whose spirit has come
forth from you?
5The shades below tremble,
the waters and their
inhabitants.
6Sheol is naked before God,
and Abaddon has no
covering.
7He stretches out the north over
the void,
and hangs the earth upon
nothing.
8He binds up the waters in his
thick clouds,
and the cloud is not rent
under them.
9He covers the face of the moon,[a]
and spreads over it his cloud.
10He has described a circle upon
the face of the waters
at the boundary between
light and darkness.
11The pillars of heaven tremble,
and are astounded at his
rebuke.
12By his power he stilled the sea;
by his understanding he
smote *Rahab*.
13By his wind the heavens were
made fair;
his hand pierced the fleeing
serpent.
14Lo, these are but the outskirts of
his ways;
and how small a whisper do
we hear of him!
But the thunder of his
power who can
understand?"

JOB MAINTAINS HIS INTEGRITY

27 And Job again took up his dis-
course, and said:
2"As God lives, who has taken
away my right,
and the Almighty, who has
made my soul bitter;
3as long as my breath is in me,
and the spirit of God is in
my nostrils;
4my lips will not speak falsehood,
and my tongue will not utter
deceit.
5Far be it from me to say that you
are right;
till I die I will not put away
my integrity from me.
6I hold fast my righteousness, and
will not let it go;
my heart does not reproach
me for any of my
days.
7"Let my enemy be as the wicked,
and let him that rises up
against me be as the
unrighteous.
8For what is the hope of the
godless when God cuts
him off,
wlen God takes away his
life?
9Will (od hear his cry,
ʹhen trouble comes upon
him?
10Wihe take delight in the
Almighty?
Will he call upon God at all
times?
11I ll teach you concerning the
hand of God;
what is with the Almighty I
will not conceal.
ʹhold, all of you have seen it
yourselves;

[a]Or *his throne*

why then have you become
altogether vain?
13"This is the portion of a wicked
man with God,
and the heritage which oppressors receive from
the Almighty:
14If his children are multiplied, it
is for the sword;
and his offspring have not
enough to eat.
15Those who survive him the
pestilence buries,
and their widows make no
lamentation.
16Though he heap up silver like
dust,
and pile up clothing like
clay;
17he may pile it up, but the just
will wear it,
and the innocent will divide
the silver.
18The house which he builds is
like a spider's web,[b]
like a booth which a watchman makes.
19He goes to bed rich, but will do
so no more;[c]
he opens his eyes, and his
wealth is gone.
20Terrors overtake him like a
flood;
in the night a whirlwind
carries him off.
21The east wind lifts him up and
he is gone;
it sweeps him out of his
place.
22It[d] hurls at him without pity;
*he flees from its[e] power in
headlong flight.*
23It[f] claps its[g] hands at him,
and hisses at him from its[h]
place.

INTERLUDE: WHERE WISDOM IS FOUND

28 "Surely there is a mine for silver,
and a place for gold which they
refine.
2Iron is taken out of the earth,
and copper is smelted from
the ore.
3Men put an end to darkness,
and search out to the farthest bound
the ore in gloom and deep
darkness.
4They open shafts in a valley away
from where men live;
they are forgotten by
travelers,
they hang afar from men,
they swing to and fro.
5As for the earth, out of it comes
bread;
but underneath it is turned
up as by fire.
6Its stones are the place of
sapphires,[i]
and it has dust of gold.
7"That path no bird of prey knows,
and the falcon's eye has not
seen it.
8The proud beasts have not trodden it;
the lion has not passed
over it.
9"Man puts his hand to the flinty
rock,
and overturns mountains by
the roots.
10He cuts out channels in the
rocks,
and his eye sees every precious thing.
11He binds up the streams so that
they do not trickle,
and the thing that is hid he
brings forth to light.
12"But where shall wisdom be
found?

[b] Cn Compare Gk Syr: Heb *He builds his house like the moth*
[c] Gk Compare Syr: Heb *shall not be gathered*
[d] Or *he* (that is God)
[e] Or *his*
[f] Or *he* (that is God)
[g] Or *his*
[h] Or *his*
[i] Or *lapis lazuli*

And where is the place of
understanding?
13Man does not know the way
to it,[a]
and it is not found in the
land of the living.
14The deep says, 'It is not in me,'
and the sea says, 'It is not
with me.'
15It cannot be gotten for gold,
and silver cannot be weighed
as its price.
16It cannot be valued in the gold
of Ophir,
in precious onyx or sapphire.[b]
17Gold and glass cannot equal it,
nor can it be exchanged for
jewels of fine gold.
18No mention shall be made of
coral or of crystal;
the price of wisdom is above
pearls.
19The topaz of Ethiopia cannot
compare with it,
nor can it be valued in pure
gold.
20"Whence then comes wisdom?
And where is the place of
understanding?
21It is hid from the eyes of all
living,
and concealed from the birds
of the air.
22Abaddon and Death say,
'We have heard a rumor of it
with our ears.'
23"God understands the way to it,
and he knows its place.
24For he looks to the ends of the
earth,
and sees everything under
the heavens.
25When he gave to the wind its
weight,
and meted out the waters by
measure;
26when he made a decree for the
rain,
and a way for the lightning
of the thunder;
27then he saw it and declared it;
he established it, and
searched it out.
28And he said to man,
'Behold, the fear of the Lord,
that is wisdom;
and to depart from evil is
understanding.'"

JOB FINISHES HIS DEFENSE

29 And Job again took up his discourse, and said:
2"Oh, that I were as in the months
of old,
as in the days when God
watched over me;
3when his lamp shone upon my
head,
and by his light I walked
through darkness;
4as I was in my autumn days,
when the friendship of God
was upon my tent;
5when the Almighty was yet with
me,
when my children were
about me;
6when my steps were washed with
milk,
and the rock poured out for
me streams of oil!
7When I went out to the gate of
the city,
when I prepared my seat in
the square,
8the young men saw me and
withdrew,
and the aged rose and stood;
9the princes refrained from talking,
and laid their hand on their
mouth;
10the voice of the nobles was
hushed,
and their tongue cleaved
to the roof of their
mouth.
11When the ear heard, it called me
blessed,
and when the eye saw, it
approved;

[a]Gk: Heb *its price*
[b]Or *lapis lazuli*

12because I delivered the poor who cried,
and the fatherless who had none to help him.
13The blessing of him who was about to perish came upon me,
and I caused the widow's heart to sing for joy.
14I put on righteousness, and it clothed me;
my justice was like a robe and a turban.
15I was eyes to the blind,
and feet to the lame.
16I was a father to the poor,
and I searched out the cause of him whom I did not know.
17I broke the fangs of the unrighteous,
and made him drop his prey from his teeth.
18Then I thought, 'I shall die in my nest,
and I shall multiply my days as the sand,
19my roots spread out to the waters,
with the dew all night on my branches,
20my glory fresh with me,
and my bow ever new in my hand.'
21"Men listened to me, and waited,
and kept silence for my counsel.
22After I spoke they did not speak again,
and my word dropped upon them.
23They waited for me as for the rain;
and they opened their mouths as for the spring rain.
24I smiled on them when they had no confidence;
and the light of my countenance they did not cast down.
25I chose their way, and sat as chief,
and I dwelt like a king among his troops,
like one who comforts mourners.

30 "But now they make sport of me,
men who are younger than I,
whose fathers I would have disdained
to set with the dogs of my flock.
2What could I gain from the strength of their hands,
men whose vigor is gone?
3Through want and hard hunger
they gnaw the dry and desolate ground;[c]
4they pick mallow and the leaves of bushes,
and to warm themselves the roots of the broom.
5They are driven out from among men;
they shout after them as after a thief.
6In the gullies of the torrents they must dwell,
in holes of the earth and of the rocks.
7Among the bushes they bray;
under the nettles they huddle together.
8A senseless, a disreputable brood,
they have been whipped out of the land.
9"And now I have become their song,
I am a byword to them.
10They abhor me, they keep aloof from me;
they do not hesitate to spit at the sight of me.
11Because God has loosed my cord and humbled me,
they have cast off restraint in my presence.
12On my right hand the rabble rise,
they drive me[d] forth,
they cast up against me their ways of destruction.

[c]Heb *ground yesterday waste*
[d]Heb *my feet*

13They break up my path,
they promote my calamity;
no one restrains[a] them.
14As through[b] a wide breach they come;
amid the crash they roll on.
15Terrors are turned upon me;
my honor is pursued as by the wind,
and my prosperity has passed away like a cloud.
16"And now my soul is poured out within me;
days of affliction have taken hold of me.
17The night racks my bones,
and the pain that gnaws me takes no rest.
18With violence it seizes my garment;[c]
it binds me about like the collar of my tunic.
19God has cast me into the mire,
and I have become like dust and ashes.
20I cry to thee and thou dost not answer me;
I stand, and thou dost not[d] heed me.
21Thou hast turned cruel to me;
with the might of thy hand thou dost persecute me.
22Thou liftest me up on the wind,
thou makest me ride on it,
and thou tossest me about in the roar of the storm.
23Yea, I know that thou wilt bring me to death,
and to the house appointed for all living.
24"Yet does not one in a heap of ruins stretch out his hand,
and in his disaster cry for help?[e]
25Did not I weep for him whose day was hard?
Was not my soul grieved for the poor?
26But when I looked for good, evil came;
and when I waited for light, darkness came.
27My heart is in turmoil, and is never still;
days of affliction come to meet me.
28I go about blackened, but not by the sun;
I stand up in the assembly, and cry for help.
29I am a brother of jackals,
and a companion of ostriches.
30My skin turns black and falls from me,
and my bones burn with heat.
31My lyre is turned to mourning,
and my pipe to the voice of those who weep.

31 "I have made a covenant with my eyes;
how then could I look upon a virgin?
2What would be my portion from God above,
and my heritage from the Almighty on high?
3Does not calamity befall the unrighteous,
and disaster the workers of iniquity?
4Does not he see my ways,
and number all my steps?
5"If I have walked with falsehood,
and my foot has hastened to deceit;
6(Let me be weighed in a just balance,
and let God know my integrity!)
7if my step has turned aside from the way,
and my heart has gone after my eyes,

[a]Cn: Heb *helps*
[b]Cn: Heb *like*
[c]Gk: Heb *my garment is disfigured*
[d]One Heb Ms and Vg: Heb lacks *not*
[e]Cn: Heb obscure

and if any spot has cleaved to my hands;
8then let me sow, and another eat;
and let what grows for me be rooted out.
9"If my heart has been enticed to a woman,
and I have lain in wait at my neighbor's door;
10then let my wife grind for another,
and let others bow down upon her.
11For that would be a heinous crime;
that would be an iniquity to be punished by the judges;
12for that would be a fire which consumes unto Abaddon,
and it would burn to the root all my increase.
13"If I have rejected the cause of my manservant or my maidservant,
when they brought a complaint against me;
14what then shall I do when God rises up?
When he makes inquiry, what shall I answer him?
15Did not he who made me in the womb make him?
And did not one fashion us in the womb?
16"If I have withheld anything that the poor desired,
or have caused the eyes of the widow to fail,
17or have eaten my morsel alone,
and the fatherless has not eaten of it
18(for from his youth I reared him as a father,
and from his mother's womb I guided him[f]);
19if I have seen any one perish for lack of clothing,
or a poor man without covering;
20if his loins have not blessed me,
and if he was not warmed with the fleece of my sheep;
21if I have raised my hand against the fatherless,
because I saw help in the gate;
22then let my shoulder blade fall from my shoulder,
and let my arm be broken from its socket.
23For I was in terror of calamity from God,
and I could not have faced his majesty.
24"If I have made gold my trust,
or called fine gold my confidence;
25if I have rejoiced because my wealth was great,
or because my hand had gotten much;
26if I have looked at the sun[g] when it shone,
or the moon moving in splendor,
27and my heart has been secretly enticed,
and my mouth has kissed my hand;
28this also would be an iniquity to be punished by the judges,
for I should have been false to God above.
29"If I have rejoiced at the ruin of him that hated me,
or exulted when evil overtook him
30(I have not let my mouth sin by asking for his life with a curse);
31if the men of my tent have not said,
'Who is there that has not been filled with his meat?'
32(the sojourner has not lodged in the street;
I have opened my doors to the wayfarer);

[f] Cn: Heb *for from my youth he grew up to me as a father, and from my mother's womb I guided her*
[g] Heb *the light*

33 if I have concealed my transgressions from men,[a]
by hiding my iniquity in my bosom,
34 because I stood in great fear of the multitude,
and the contempt of families terrified me,
so that I kept silence, and did not go out of doors—
35 Oh, that I had one to hear me!
(Here is my signature! let the Almighty answer me!)
Oh, that I had the indictment written by my adversary!
36 Surely I would carry it on my shoulder;
I would bind it on me as a crown;
37 I would give him an account of all my steps;
like a prince I would approach him.
38 "If my land has cried out against me,
and its furrows have wept together;
39 if I have eaten its yield without payment,
and caused the death of its owners;
40 let thorns grow instead of wheat,
and foul weeds instead of barley."

The words of Job are ended.

ELIHU REBUKES JOB'S FRIENDS

32 So these three men ceased to
answer Job, because he was righ-
teous in his own eyes. 2 Then Eli´hu
the son of Bar´achel the Buzite, of
the family of Ram, became angry. He
was angry at Job because he justified
himself rather than God; 3 he was an-
gry also at Job's three friends because
they had found no answer, although
they had declared Job to be in the
wrong. 4 Now Eli´hu had waited to
speak to Job because they were older
than he. 5 And when Eli´hu saw that
there was no answer in the mouth of
these three men, he became angry.

6 And Eli´hu the son of Bar´achel
the Buzite answered:

"I am young in years,
and you are aged;
therefore I was timid and afraid
to declare my opinion to you.
7 I said, 'Let days speak,
and many years teach wisdom.'
8 But it is the spirit in a man,
the breath of the Almighty, that makes him understand.
9 It is not the old[b] that are wise,
nor the aged that understand what is right.
10 Therefore I say, 'Listen to me;
let me also declare my opinion.'
11 "Behold, I waited for your words,
I listened for your wise sayings,
while you searched out what to say.
12 I gave you my attention,
and, behold, there was none that confuted Job,
or that answered his words, among you.
13 Beware lest you say, 'We have found wisdom;
God may vanquish him, not man.'
14 He has not directed his words against me,
and I will not answer him with your speeches.
15 "They are discomfited, they answer no more;
they have not a word to say.
16 And shall I wait, because they do not speak,

[a] Cn: Heb *like men* or *like Adam*
[b] Gk Syr Vg: Heb *many*

because they stand there,
and answer no more?
17I also will give my answer;
I also will declare my
opinion.
18For I am full of words,
the spirit within me con-
strains me.
19Behold, my heart is like wine
that has no vent;
like new wineskins, it is
ready to burst.
20I must speak, that I may find
relief;
I must open my lips and
answer.
21I will not show partiality to any
person
or use flattery toward any
man.
22For I do not know how to flatter,
else would my Maker soon
put an end to me.

ELIHU REBUKES JOB

33 "But now, hear my speech, O Job,
and listen to all my words.
2Behold, I open my mouth;
the tongue in my mouth
speaks.
3My words declare the upright-
ness of my heart,
and what my lips know they
speak sincerely.
4The spirit of God has made me,
and the breath of the
Almighty gives me
life.
5Answer me, if you can;
set your words in order
before me; take your
stand.
6Behold, I am toward God as you
are;
I too was formed from a
piece of clay.
7Behold, no fear of me need terrify
you;
my pressure will not be
heavy upon you.
8"Surely, you have spoken in my
hearing,
and I have heard the sound
of your words.
9You say, 'I am clean, without
transgression;
I am pure, and there is no
iniquity in me.
10Behold, he finds occasions
against me,
he counts me as his enemy;
11he puts my feet in the stocks,
and watches all my paths.'
12"Behold, in this you are not
right. I will answer you.
God is greater than man.
13Why do you contend against
him,
saying, 'He will answer none
of my[c] words'?
14For God speaks in one way,
and in two, though man does
not perceive it.
15In a dream, in a vision of the
night,
when deep sleep falls upon
men,
while they slumber on their
beds,
16then he opens the ears of men,
and terrifies them with
warnings,
17that he may turn man aside from
his deed,
and cut off[d] pride from
man;
18he keeps back his soul from the
Pit,
his life from perishing by the
sword.
19"Man is also chastened with
pain upon his bed,
and with continual strife in
his bones;
20so that his life loathes bread,
and his appetite dainty food.
21His flesh is so wasted away that
it cannot be seen;
and his bones which were
not seen stick out.

[c]Compare Gk: Heb *his*
[d]Cn: Heb *hide*

22His soul draws near the Pit,
and his life to those who bring death.
23If there be for him an angel,
a mediator, one of the thousand,
to declare to man what is right for him;
24and he is gracious to him, and says,
'Deliver him from going down into the Pit,
I have found a ransom;
25let his flesh become fresh with youth;
let him return to the days of his youthful vigor';
26then man prays to God, and he accepts him,
he comes into his presence with joy.
He recounts[a] to men his salvation,
27and he sings before men, and says:
'I sinned, and perverted what was right,
and it was not requited to me.
28He has redeemed my soul from going down into the Pit,
and my life shall see the light.'
29"Behold, God does all these things,
twice, three times, with a man,
30to bring back his soul from the Pit,
that he may see the light of life.[b]
31Give heed, O Job, listen to me;
be silent, and I will speak.
32If you have anything to say, answer me;
speak, for I desire to justify you.
33If not, listen to me;
be silent and I will teach you wisdom."

ELIHU PROCLAIMS GOD'S JUSTICE

34 Then Eli´hu said:
2"Hear my words, you wise men,
and give ear to me, you who know;
3for the ear tests words
as the palate tastes food.
4Let us choose what is right;
let us determine among ourselves what is good.
5For Job has said, 'I am innocent,
and God has taken away my right;
6in spite of my right I am counted a liar;
my wound is incurable,
though I am without transgression.'
7What man is like Job,
who drinks up scoffing like water,
8who goes in company with evildoers
and walks with wicked men?
9For he has said, 'It profits a man nothing
that he should take delight in God.'
10"Therefore, hear me, you men of understanding,
far be it from God that he should do wickedness,
and from the Almighty that he should do wrong.
11For according to the work of a man he will requite him,
and according to his ways he will make it befall him.
12Of a truth, God will not do wickedly,
and the Almighty will not pervert justice.
13Who gave him charge over the earth
and who laid on him[c] the whole world?

[a]Cn: Heb *returns*
[b]Syr: Heb *to be lighted with the light of life*
[c]Heb lacks *on him*

14If he should take back his spirit[d]
to himself,
and gather to himself his
breath,
15all flesh would perish together,
and man would return to
dust.
16"If you have understanding, hear
this;
listen to what I say.
17Shall one who hates justice
govern?
Will you condemn him who
is righteous and
mighty,
18who says to a king, 'Worthless
one,'
and to nobles, 'Wicked man';
19who shows no partiality to
princes,
nor regards the rich more
than the poor,
for they are all the work of
his hands?
20In a moment they die;
at midnight the people are
shaken and pass
away,
and the mighty are taken
away by no human
hand.
21"For his eyes are upon the ways
of a man,
and he sees all his steps.
22There is no gloom or deep
darkness
where evildoers may hide
themselves.
23For he has not appointed a time[e]
for any man
to go before God in
judgment.
24He shatters the mighty without
investigation,
and sets others in their
place.
25Thus, knowing their works,
he overturns them in the
night, and they are
crushed.
26He strikes them for their
wickedness
in the sight of men,
27because they turned aside from
following him,
and had no regard for any of
his ways,
28so that they caused the cry of
the poor to come to him,
and he heard the cry of the
afflicted—
29When he is quiet, who can
condemn?
When he hides his face, who
can behold him,
whether it be a nation or a
man?—
30that a godless man should not
reign,
that he should not ensnare
the people.
31"For has any one said to God,
'I have borne chastisement;
I will not offend any
more;
32teach me what I do not see;
if I have done iniquity, I will
do it no more'?
33Will he then make requital to
suit you,
because you reject it?
For you must choose, and
not I;
therefore declare what you
know.[f]
34Men of understanding will say
to me,
and the wise man who hears
me will say:
35'Job speaks without knowledge,
his words are without
insight.'
36Would that Job were tried to
the end,
because he answers like
wicked men.
37For he adds rebellion to his sin;
he claps his hands among us,
and multiplies his words
against God."

[d]Heb *his heart his spirit*
[e]Cn: Heb *yet*
[f]The Hebrew of verses 29-33 is obscure

ELIHU CONDEMNS SELF-RIGHTEOUSNESS

35 And Eli´hu said:
2"Do you think this to be just?
Do you say, 'It is my right before God,'
3that you ask, 'What advantage have I?
How am I better off than if I had sinned?'
4I will answer you
and your friends with you.
5Look at the heavens, and see;
and behold the clouds, which are higher than you.
6If you have sinned, what do you accomplish against him?
And if your transgressions are multiplied, what do you do to him?
7If you are righteous, what do you give to him;
or what does he receive from your hand?
8Your wickedness concerns a man like yourself,
and your righteousness a son of man.
9"Because of the multitude of oppressions people cry out;
they call for help because of the arm of the mighty.
10But none says, 'Where is God my Maker,
who gives songs in the night,
11who teaches us more than the beasts of the earth,
and makes us wiser than the birds of the air?'
12There they cry out, but he does not answer,
because of the pride of evil men.
13Surely God does not hear an *empty cry*,
nor does the Almighty regard it.
14How much less when you say that you do not see him,
that the case is before him, and you are waiting for him!
15And now, because his anger does not punish,
and he does not greatly heed transgression,[a]
16Job opens his mouth in empty talk,
he multiplies words without knowledge."

ELIHU EXALTS GOD'S GOODNESS

36 And Eli´hu continued, and said:
2"Bear with me a little, and I will show you,
for I have yet something to say on God's behalf.
3I will fetch my knowledge from afar,
and ascribe righteousness to my Maker.
4For truly my words are not false;
one who is perfect in knowledge is with you.
5"Behold, God is mighty, and does not despise any;
he is mighty in strength of understanding.
6He does not keep the wicked alive,
but gives the afflicted their right.
7He does not withdraw his eyes from the righteous,
but with kings upon the throne
he sets them for ever, and they are exalted.
8And if they are bound in fetters
and caught in the cords of affliction,
9then he declares to them their work
and their transgressions, that they are behaving arrogantly.
10He opens their ears to instruction,
and commands that they return from iniquity.

[a]Theodotion Symmachus Compare Vg: The meaning of the Hebrew word is uncertain

11If they hearken and serve him,
they complete their days in
prosperity,
and their years in
pleasantness.
12But if they do not hearken, they
perish by the sword,
and die without knowledge.
13"The godless in heart cherish
anger;
they do not cry for help
when he binds them.
14They die in youth,
and their life ends in
shame.[b]
15He delivers the afflicted by their
affliction,
and opens their ear by
adversity.
16He also allured you out of
distress
into a broad place where
there was no
cramping,
and what was set on your
table was full of
fatness.
17"But you are full of the judgment
on the wicked;
judgment and justice seize
you.
18Beware lest wrath entice you
into scoffing;
and let not the greatness of
the ransom turn you
aside.
19Will your cry avail to keep you
from distress,
or all the force f your
strengtl
20Do not long for theight,
when peoples e cut off in
their ple.
21Take heed, do not rn to
iniquity,
for this you hacho-
sen ratl than
afflictic
22Behold, God is exal in his
power;
who is a teacher like him?
23Who has prescribed for him his
way,
or who can say, 'Thou hast
done wrong'?

ELIHU PROCLAIMS GOD'S MAJESTY

24"Remember to extol his work,
of which men have sung.
25All men have looked on it;
man beholds it from afar.
26Behold, God is great, and we
know him not;
the number of his years is
unsearchable.
27For he draws up the drops of
water,
he[c] distils his mist in rain
28which the skies pour down,
and drop upon man
abundantly.
29Can any one understand the
spreading of the clouds,
the thunderings of his
pavilion?
30Behold, he scatters his lightning
about him,
and covers the roots of the
sea.
31For by these he judges peoples;
he gives food in abundance.
32He covers his hands with the
lightning,
and commands it to strike
the mark.
33Its crashing declares concerning
him,
who is jealous with anger
against iniquity.

37 "At this also my heart trembles,
and leaps out of its place.
2Hearken to the thunder of his
voice
and the rumbling that comes
from his mouth.
3Under the whole heaven he lets
it go,
and his lightning to the cor-
ners of the earth.
4After it his voice roars;

[b]Heb *among the cult prostitu*
[c]Cn: Heb *they distil*

he thunders with his majes-
tic voice
and he does not restrain the
lightnings[a] when his
voice is heard.
5God thunders wondrously with
his voice;
he does great things
which we cannot
comprehend.
6For to the snow he says, 'Fall on
the earth';
and to the shower and the
rain,[b] 'Be strong.'
7He seals up the hand of every
man,
that all men may know his
work.[c]
8Then the beasts go into their
lairs,
and remain in their dens.
9From its chamber comes the
whirlwind,
and cold from the scattering
winds.
10By the breath of God ice is given,
and the broad waters are fro-
zen fast.
11He loads the thick cloud with
moisture;
the clouds scatter his
lightning.
12They turn round and round by
his guidance,
to accomplish all that he
commands them
on the face of the habitable
world.
13Whether for correction, or for
his land,
or for love, he causes it to
happen.
14"Hear this, O Job;
stop and consider the won-
drous works of God.
15Do you know how God lays his
command upon them,
and causes the lightning of
his cloud to shine?
16Do you know the balancings of
the clouds,
the wondrous works of him
who is perfect in
knowledge,
17you whose garments are hot
when the earth is still
because of the south
wind?
18Can you, like him, spread out
the skies,
hard as a molten mirror?
19Teach us what we shall say to
him;
we cannot draw up our case
because of darkness.
20Shall it be told him that I would
speak?
Did a man ever wish that he
would be swallowed
up?
21"And now men cannot look on
the light
when it is bright in the skies,
when the wind has passed
and cleared them.
22Out of the north comes golden
splendor;
God is clothed with terrible
majesty.
23The Almighty—we cannot find
him;
he is great in power and
justice,
and abundant righteousness
he will not violate.
24Therefore men fear him;
he does not regard any who
are wise in their own
conceit."

THEORD ANSWERS JOB

38 Then tl Lord answered Job out
of the virlwind:
2"Who ihis that darkens
ansel by words without
owledge?
3Gird uour loins like a man,
I l question you, and you
shall declare to me.
4"Whewere you when I laid the

[a] Heb *them*
[b] Cn Compare Syr: Heb *shower of rain and shower of rains*
[c] Vg Compare Syr Tg: Heb *that all men whom he has made mayw it*

foundation of the earth?
Tell me, if you have understanding.
5 Who determined its measurements—surely you know!
Or who stretched the line upon it?
6 On what were its bases sunk,
or who laid its cornerstone,
7 when the morning stars sang together,
and all the sons of God shouted for joy?
8 "Or who shut in the sea with doors,
when it burst forth from the womb;
9 when I made clouds its garment,
and thick darkness its swaddling band,
10 and prescribed bounds for it,
and set bars and doors,
11 and said, 'Thus far shall you come, and no farther,
and here shall your proud waves be stayed'?
12 "Have you commanded the morning since your days began,
and caused the dawn to know its place,
13 that it might take hold of the skirts of the earth,
and the wicked be shaken out of it?
14 It is changed like clay under the seal,
and it is dyed[d] like a garment.
15 *From the wicked their* light is withheld,
and their uplifted arm is broken.
16 "Have you entered into the springs of the sea,
or walked in the recesses of the deep?
17 Have the gates of death been revealed to you,
or have you seen the gates of deep darkness?
18 Have you comprehended the expanse of the earth?
Declare, if you know all this.
19 "Where is the way to the dwelling of light,
and where is the place of darkness,
20 that you may take it to its territory
and that you may discern the paths to its home?
21 You know, for you were born then,
and the number of your days is great!
22 "Have you entered the storehouses of the snow,
or have you seen the storehouses of the hail,
23 which I have reserved for the time of trouble,
for the day of battle and war?
24 What is the way to the place where the light is distributed,
or where the east wind is scattered upon the earth?
25 "Who has cleft a channel for the torrents of rain,
and a way for the thunderbolt,
26 to bring rain on a land where no man is,
on the desert in which there is no man;
27 to satisfy the waste and desolate land,
and to make the ground put forth grass?
28 "Has the rain a father,
or who has begotten the drops of dew?
29 From whose womb did the ice come forth,
and who has given birth to the hoarfrost of heaven?
30 The waters become hard like stone,

[d] Cn: Heb *they stand forth*

and the face of the deep is
frozen.
31"Can you bind the chains of the
Plei´ades,
or loose the cords of Orion?
32Can you lead forth the
Maz´zaroth in their season,
or can you guide the Bear
with its children?
33Do you know the ordinances of
the heavens?
Can you establish their rule
on the earth?
34"Can you lift up your voice to
the clouds,
that a flood of waters may
cover you?
35Can you send forth lightnings,
that they may go
and say to you, 'Here we
are'?
36Who has put wisdom in the
clouds,[a]
or given understanding to
the mists?[b]
37Who can number the clouds by
wisdom?
Or who can tilt the water-
skins of the heavens,
38when the dust runs into a mass
and the clods cleave fast
together?
39"Can you hunt the prey for the
lion,
or satisfy the appetite of the
young lions,
40when they crouch in their dens,
or lie in wait in their covert?
41Who provides for the raven its
prey,
when its young ones cry to
God,
and wander about for lack
of food?

39 "Do you know when the moun-
tain goats bring forth?
Do you observe the calving
of the hinds?
2Can you number the months that
they fulfil,
and do you know the time
when they bring
forth,
3when they crouch, bring forth
their offspring,
and are delivered of their
young?
4Their young ones become strong,
they grow up in the open;
they go forth, and do not
return to them.
5"Who has let the wild ass go
free?
Who has loosed the bonds of
the swift ass,
6to whom I have given the steppe
for his home,
and the salt land for his
dwelling place?
7He scorns the tumult of the city;
he hears not the shouts of
the driver.
8He ranges the mountains as his
pasture,
and he searches after every
green thing.
9"Is the wild ox willing to serve
you?
Will he spend the night at
your crib?
10Can you bind him in the furrow
with ropes,
or will he harrow the valleys
after you?
11Will you depend on him because
his strength is great,
and will you leave to him
your labor?
12Do you have faith in him that he
will return,
and bring your grain to your
threshing floor?[c]
13"The wings of the ostrich wave
proudly;
but are they the pinions and
plumage of love?[d]
14For she leaves her eggs to the
earth,

[a] The meaning of the Hebrew word is uncertain
[b] The meaning of the Hebrew word is uncertain
[c] Heb *your grain and your threshing floor*
[d] Heb obscure

and lets them be warmed on
the ground,
15forgetting that a foot may crush
them,
and that the wild beast may
trample them.
16She deals cruelly with her young,
as if they were not hers;
though her labor be in vain,
yet she has no fear;
17because God has made her forget
wisdom,
and given her no share in
understanding.
18When she rouses herself to flee,[e]
she laughs at the horse and
his rider.
19"Do you give the horse his
might?
Do you clothe his neck with
strength?[f]
20Do you make him leap like the
locust?
His majestic snorting is
terrible.
21He paws[g] in the valley, and
exults in his strength;
he goes out to meet the
weapons.
22He laughs at fear, and is not
dismayed;
he does not turn back from
the sword.
23Upon him rattle the quiver,
the flashing spear and the
javelin.
24With fierceness and rage he
swallows the ground;
he cannot stand still at the
sound of the trumpet.
25*When the trumpet* sounds, he
says 'Aha!'
He smells the battle from
afar,
the thunder of the captains,
and the shouting.
26"Is it by your wisdom that the
hawk soars,
and spreads his wings to-
ward the south?
27Is it at your command that the
eagle mounts up
and makes his nest on high?
28On the rock he dwells and
makes his home
in the fastness of the rocky
crag.
29Thence he spies out the prey;
his eyes behold it afar off.
30His young ones suck up blood;
and where the slain are,
there is he."

40 And the LORD said to Job:
2"Shall a faultfinder contend
with the Almighty?
He who argues with God, let
him answer it."

JOB'S RESPONSE TO GOD

3Then Job answered the LORD:
4"Behold, I am of small account;
what shall I answer thee?
I lay my hand on my mouth.
5I have spoken once, and I will not
answer;
twice, but I will proceed no
further."

GOD'S CHALLENGE TO JOB

6 Then the LORD answered Job out
of the whirlwind:
7"Gird up your loins like a man;
I will question you, and you
declare to me.
8Will you even put me in the
wrong?
Will you condemn me that
you may be justified?
9Have you an arm like God,
and can you thunder with a
voice like his?
10"Deck yourself with majesty and
dignity;
clothe yourself with glory
and splendor.
11Pour forth the overflowings of
your anger,
and look on every one that
is proud, and abase
him.

[e] Heb obscure
[f] Tg: The meaning of the Hebrew word is obscure
[g] Gk Syr Vg: Heb *they dig*

12Look on every one that is proud,
and bring him low;
and tread down the wicked
where they stand.
13Hide them all in the dust
together;
bind their faces in the world
below.[a]
14Then will I also acknowledge
to you,
that your own right hand
can give you victory.
15"Behold, Be´hemoth,[b]
which I made as I made
you;
he eats grass like an ox.
16Behold, his strength in his loins,
and his power in the muscles
of his belly.
17He makes his tail stiff like a
cedar;
the sinews of his thighs are
knit together.
18His bones are tubes of bronze,
his limbs like bars of iron.
19"He is the first of the works[c] of
God;
let him who made him bring
near his sword!
20For the mountains yield food
for him
where all the wild beasts
play.
21Under the lotus plants he lies,
in the covert of the reeds
and in the marsh.
22For his shade the lotus trees
cover him;
the willows of the brook
surround him.
23Behold, if the river is turbulent
he is not frightened;
he is confident though
Jordan rushes against
his mouth.
24Can one take him with hooks,[d]
or pierce his nose with a
snare?

41 [e]"Can you draw out Levi´athan[f]
with a fishhook,
or press down his tongue
with a cord?
2Can you put a rope in his nose,
or pierce his jaw with a
hook?
3Will he make many supplications
to you?
Will he speak to you soft
words?
4Will he make a covenant with
you
to take him for your servant
for ever?
5Will you play with him as with
a bird,
or will you put him on leash
for your maidens?
6Will traders bargain over him?
Will they divide him
up among the
merchants?
7Can you fill his skin with
harpoons,
or his head with fishing
spears?
8Lay hands on him;
think of the battle; you will
not do it again!
9[g] Behold, the hope of a man is
disappointed;
he is laid low even at the
sight of him.
10No one is so fierce that he dares
to stir him up.
Who then is he that can
stand before me?
11Who has given to me,[h] that I
should repay him?
Whatever is under the whole
heaven is mine.
12"I will not keep silence concern-
ing his limbs,

[a] Heb *hidden place*
[b] Or *the hippopotamus*
[c] Heb *ways*
[d] Cn: Heb *in his eyes*
[e] Ch 40.25 in Heb
[f] Or *the crocodile*
[g] Ch 41.1 in Heb
[h] The meaning of the Hebrew is uncertain

or his mighty strength, or
his goodly frame.
13Who can strip off his outer
garment?
Who can penetrate his dou-
ble coat of mail?[i]
14Who can open the doors of his
face?
Round about his teeth is
terror.
15His back[j] is made of rows of
shields,
shut up closely as with a
seal.
16One is so near to another
that no air can come be-
tween them.
17They are joined one to another;
they clasp each other and
cannot be separated.
18His sneezings flash forth light,
and his eyes are like the eye-
lids of the dawn.
19Out of his mouth go flaming
torches;
sparks of fire leap forth.
20Out of his nostrils comes forth
smoke,
as from a boiling pot and
burning rushes.
21His breath kindles coals,
and a flame comes forth
from his mouth.
22In his neck abides strength,
and terror dances before
him.
23The folds of his flesh cleave
together,
firmly cast upon him and
immovable.
24*His heart* is hard as a stone,
hard as the nether millstone.
25When he raises himself up the
mighty[k] are afraid;
at the crashing they are
beside themselves.
26Though the sword reaches him,
it does not avail;
nor the spear, the dart, or
the javelin.
27He counts iron as straw,
and bronze as rotten wood.
28The arrow cannot make him
flee;
for him slingstones are
turned to stubble.
29Clubs are counted as stubble;
he laughs at the rattle of
javelins.
30His underparts are like sharp
potsherds;
he spreads himself like a
threshing sledge on
the mire.
31He makes the deep boil like a
pot;
he makes the sea like a pot
of ointment.
32Behind him he leaves a shining
wake;
one would think the deep to
be hoary.
33Upon earth there is not his like,
a creature without fear.
34He beholds everything that is
high;
he is king over all the sons
of pride."

JOB IS HUMBLED AND SATISFIED

42 Then Job answered the LORD:
2"I know that thou canst do all
things,
and that no purpose of thine
can be thwarted.
3'Who is this that hides counsel
without knowledge?'
Therefore I have uttered what I
did not understand,
things too wonderful for me,
which I did not know.
4'Hear, and I will speak;
I will question you, and you
declare to me.'
5I had heard of thee by the hear-
ing of the ear,
but now my eye sees thee;
6therefore I despise myself,
and repent in dust and
ashes."

[i]Gk: Heb *bridle*
[j]Cn Compare Gk Vg: Heb *pride*
[k]Or *gods*

JOB'S FRIENDS ARE HUMILIATED

7 After the LORD had spoken these words to Job, the LORD said to Eli´phaz the Te´manite: "My wrath is kindled against you and against your two friends; for you have not spoken of me what is right, as my servant Job has. 8 Now therefore take seven bulls and seven rams, and go to my servant Job, and offer up for yourselves a burnt offering; and my servant Job shall pray for you, for I will accept his prayer not to deal with you according to your folly; for you have not spoken of me what is right, as my servant Job has." 9 So Eli´phaz the Te´manite and Bildad the Shuhite and Zophar the Na´amathite went and did what the LORD had told them; and the LORD accepted Job's prayer.

JOB'S FORTUNES ARE RESTORED TWOFOLD

10 And the LORD restored the fortunes of Job, when he had prayed for his friends; and the LORD gave Job twice as much as he had before. 11 Then came to him all his brothers and sisters and all who had known him before, and ate bread with him in his house; and they showed him sympathy and comforted him for all the evil that the LORD had brought upon him; and each of them gave him a piece of money[a] and a ring of gold. 12 And the LORD blessed the latter days of Job more than his beginning; and he had fourteen thousand sheep, six thousand camels, a thousand yoke of oxen, and a thousand she-asses. 13 He had also seven sons and three daughters. 14 And he called the name of the first Jemi´mah; and the name of the second Kezi´ah; and the name of the third Ker´en-hap´puch. 15 And in all the land there were no women so fair as Job's daughters; and their father gave them inheritance among their brothers. 16 And after this Job lived a hundred and forty years, and saw his sons, and his sons' sons, four generations. 17 And Job died, an old man, and full of days.

[a] Heb *qesitah*

THE PSALMS

BOOK I

THE TWO WAYS

1 Blessed is the man
who walks not in the counsel
of the wicked,
nor stands in the way of
sinners,
nor sits in the seat of
scoffers;
2 but his delight is in the law of
the LORD,
and on his law he meditates
day and night.
3 He is like a tree
planted by streams of water,
that yields its fruit in its
season,
and its leaf does not wither.
In all that he does, he prospers.
4 The wicked are not so,
but are like chaff which the
wind drives away.
5 Therefore the wicked will not
stand in the judgment,
nor sinners in the congrega-
tion of the righteous;
6 for the LORD knows the way of
the righteous,
but the way of the wicked
will perish.

GOD'S PROMISE TO HIS ANOINTED

2 *Why do the nations conspire,
and the peoples plot in vain?
2 The kings of the earth set
themselves,
and the rulers take counsel
together,
against the LORD and his
anointed, saying,
3 "Let us burst their bonds
asunder,
and cast their cords from
us."
4 He who sits in the heavens
laughs;
the LORD has them in
derision.
5 Then he will speak to them in his
wrath,
and terrify them in his fury,
saying,
6 "I have set my king
on Zion, my holy hill."
7 I will tell of the decree of the
LORD:
He said to me, "You are my son,
today I have begotten you.
8 Ask of me, and I will make the
nations your heritage,
and the ends of the earth
your possession.
9 You shall break them with a rod
of iron,
and dash them in pieces like
a potter's vessel."
10 Now therefore, O kings, be wise;
be warned, O rulers of the
earth.
11 Serve the LORD with fear,
with trembling 12 kiss his feet,[a]
lest he be angry, and you perish
in the way;
for his wrath is quickly
kindled.
Blessed are all who take refuge
in him.

TRUST IN GOD UNDER ADVERSITY

A Psalm of David, when he
fled from Absalom his son.

3 O LORD, how many are my foes!
Many are rising against me;
2 many are saying of me,
there is no help for him in
God. *Selah*
3 But thou, O LORD, art a shield
about me,
my glory, and the lifter of
my head.
4 I cry aloud to the LORD,
and he answers me from his
holy hill. *Selah*

[a] Cn: The Hebrew of 11b and 12a is uncertain

5I lie down and sleep;
I wake again, for the LORD sustains me.
6I am not afraid of ten thousands of people
who have set themselves against me round about.
7Arise, O LORD!
Deliver me, O my God!
For thou dost smite all my enemies on the cheek,
thou dost break the teeth of the wicked.
8Deliverance belongs to the LORD;
thy blessing be upon thy people! *Selah*

CONFIDENT PLEA FOR DELIVERANCE FROM ENEMIES

To the choirmaster: with stringed instruments. A Psalm of David.

4 Answer me when I call, O God of my right!
Thou hast given me room when I was in distress.
Be gracious to me, and hear my prayer.
2O men, how long shall my honor suffer shame?
How long will you love vain words, and seek after lies? *Selah*
3But know that the LORD has set apart the godly for himself;
the LORD hears when I call to him.
4Be angry, but sin not;
commune with your own hearts on your beds, and be silent. *Selah*
5Offer right sacrifices,
and put your trust in the LORD.
6There are many who say, "O that we might see some good!
Lift up the light of thy countenance upon us, O LORD!"
7Thou hast put more joy in my heart
than they have when their grain and wine abound.
8In peace I will both lie down and sleep;
for thou alone, O LORD, makest me dwell in safety.

TRUST IN GOD FOR DELIVERANCE FROM ENEMIES

To the choirmaster: for the flutes. A Psalm of David.

5 Give ear to my words, O LORD;
give heed to my groaning.
2Hearken to the sound of my cry,
my King and my God,
for to thee do I pray.
3O LORD, in the morning thou dost hear my voice;
in the morning I prepare a sacrifice for thee, and watch.
4For thou art not a God who delights in wickedness;
evil may not sojourn with thee.
5The boastful may not stand before thy eyes;
thou hatest all evildoers.
6Thou destroyest those who speak lies;
the LORD abhors bloodthirsty and deceitful men.
7But I through the abundance of thy steadfast love
will enter thy house,
I will worship toward thy holy temple
in the fear of thee.
8Lead me, O LORD, in thy righteousness
because of my enemies;
make thy way straight before me.
9For there is no truth in their mouth;
their heart is destruction,
their throat is an open sepulchre,

I will tell of all thy wonderful deeds.
2I will be glad and exult in thee,
I will sing praise to thy name, O Most High.
3When my enemies turned back,
they stumbled and perished before thee.
4For thou hast maintained my just cause;
thou hast sat on the throne giving righteous judgment.
5Thou hast rebuked the nations,
thou hast destroyed the wicked;
thou hast blotted out their name for ever and ever.
6The enemy have vanished in everlasting ruins;
their cities thou hast rooted out;
the very memory of them has perished.
7But the LORD sits enthroned for ever,
he has established his throne for judgment;
8and he judges the world with righteousness,
he judges the peoples with equity.
9The LORD is a stronghold for the oppressed,
a stronghold in times of trouble.
10And those who know thy name put their trust in thee,
for thou, O LORD, hast not *forsaken those who* seek thee.
11Sing praises to the LORD, who dwells in Zion!
Tell among the peoples his deeds!
12For he who avenges blood is mindful of them;
he does not forget the cry of the afflicted.
13Be gracious to me, O LORD!
Behold what I suffer from those who hate me,
O thou who liftest me up from the gates of death,
14that I may recount all thy praises,
that in the gates of the daughter of Zion
I may rejoice in thy deliverance.
15The nations have sunk in the pit which they made;
in the net which they hid has their own foot been caught.
16The LORD has made himself known, he has executed judgment;
the wicked are snared in the work of their own hands. *Higgaion. Selah*
17The wicked shall depart to Sheol,
all the nations that forget God.
18For the needy shall not always be forgotten,
and the hope of the poor shall not perish for ever.
19Arise, O LORD! Let not man prevail;
let the nations be judged before thee!
20Put them in fear, O LORD!
Let the nations know that they are but men! *Selah*

PRAYER FOR DELIVERANCE FROM ENEMIES

10 Why dost thou stand afar off, O LORD?
Why dost thou hide thyself in times of trouble?
2In arrogance the wicked hotly pursue the poor;
let them be caught in the schemes which they have devised.
3For the wicked boasts of the desires of his heart,
and the man greedy for gain curses and renounces the LORD.

4In the pride of his countenance
the wicked does not seek
him;
all his thoughts are, "There
is no God."
5His ways prosper at all times;
thy judgments are on high,
out of his sight;
as for all his foes, he puffs
at them.
6He thinks in his heart, "I shall
not be moved;
throughout all generations
I shall not meet
adversity."
7His mouth is filled with cursing
and deceit and oppression;
under his tongue are mis-
chief and iniquity.
8He sits in ambush in the villages;
in hiding places he murders
the innocent.
His eyes stealthily watch for
the hapless,
9he lurks in secret like a lion in
his covert;
he lurks that he may seize the
poor,
he seizes the poor when he
draws him into his
net.
10The hapless is crushed, sinks
down,
and falls by his might.
11He thinks in his heart, "God has
forgotten,
he has hidden his face, he
will never see it."
12Arise, O LORD; O God, lift up
thy hand;
forget not the afflicted.
13Why does the wicked renounce
God,
and say in his heart, "Thou
wilt not call to
account"?
14Thou dost see; yea, *thou dost*
note trouble and vexation,
that thou mayst take it into
thy hands;
the hapless commits himself
to thee;
thou hast been the helper of
the fatherless.
15Break thou the arm of the wick-
ed and evildoer;
seek out his wickedness till
thou find none.
16The LORD is king for ever and
ever;
the nations shall perish from
his land.
17O LORD, thou wilt hear the
desire of the meek;
thou wilt strengthen their
heart, thou wilt
incline thy ear
18to do justice to the fatherless
and the oppressed,
so that man who is of the
earth may strike
terror no more.

SONG OF TRUST IN GOD

To the choirmaster. Of David.

11 In the LORD I take refuge;
how can you say to me,
"Flee like a bird to the
mountains;[a]
2for lo, the wicked bend the bow,
they have fitted their arrow
to the string,
to shoot in the dark at the
upright in heart;
3if the foundations are destroyed,
what can the righteous do"?
4The LORD is in his holy temple,
the LORD's throne is in
heaven;
his eyes behold, his eyelids
test, the children of
men.
5The LORD tests the righteous and
the wicked,
and his soul hates him that
loves violence.
6On the wicked he will rain coals
of fire and *brimstone*;
a scorching wind shall be
the portion of their
cup.

[a] Gk Syr Jerome Tg: Heb *flee to your mountain, O bird*

7For the LORD is righteous, he
loves righteous deeds;
the upright shall behold his
face.

PLEA FOR HELP IN EVIL TIMES

To the choirmaster: according to
The Sheminith. A Psalm of David.

12 Help, LORD; for there is no longer
any that is godly;
for the faithful have vanished from among the
sons of men.
2Every one utters lies to his
neighbor;
with flattering lips and a
double heart they
speak.
3May the LORD cut off all flattering lips,
the tongue that makes great
boasts,
4those who say, "With our tongue
we will prevail,
our lips are with us; who is
our master?"
5"Because the poor are despoiled,
because the needy groan,
I will now arise," says the
LORD;
"I will place him in the
safety for which he
longs."
6The promises of the LORD are
promises that are pure,
silver refined in a furnace on
the ground,
purified seven times.
7Do thou, O LORD, protect us,
guard us ever from this
generation.
8On every side the wicked prowl,
as vileness is exalted among
the sons of men.

PRAYER FOR DELIVERANCE FROM ENEMIES

To the choirmaster. A Psalm of David.

13 How long, O LORD? Wilt thou forget me for ever?
How long wilt thou hide thy
face from me?
2How long must I bear pain[b] in
my soul,
and have sorrow in my heart
all the day?
How long shall my enemy be
exalted over me?
3Consider and answer me, O
LORD my God;
lighten my eyes, lest I sleep
the sleep of death;
4lest my enemy say, "I have prevailed over him";
lest my foes rejoice because I
am shaken.
5But I have trusted in thy steadfast love;
my heart shall rejoice in thy
salvation.
6I will sing to the LORD,
because he has dealt bountifully with me.

DENUNCIATION OF GODLESSNESS

To the choirmaster. Of David.

14 The fool says in his heart, "There
is no God."
They are corrupt, they do
abominable deeds,
there is none that does good.
2The LORD looks down from
heaven upon the children
of men,
to see if there are any that
act wisely,
that seek after God.
3They have all gone astray, they
are all alike corrupt;
there is none that does good,
no, not one.
4Have they no knowledge, all the
evildoers
who eat up my people as
they eat bread,
and do not call upon the
LORD?
5There they shall be in great
terror,
for God is with the generation of the righteous.

[b] Syr: Heb *hold counsels*

6You would confound the plans of
the poor,
but the LORD is his refuge.
7O that deliverance for Israel
would come out of Zion!
When the LORD restores
the fortunes of his
people,
Jacob shall rejoice, Israel
shall be glad.

WHO SHALL ABIDE IN GOD'S SANCTUARY?

A Psalm of David.

15 O LORD, who shall sojourn in thy
tent?
Who shall dwell on thy holy
hill?
2He who walks blamelessly, and
does what is right,
and speaks truth from his
heart;
3who does not slander with his
tongue,
and does no evil to his
friend,
nor takes up a reproach
against his neighbor;
4in whose eyes a reprobate is
despised,
but who honors those who
fear the LORD;
who swears to his own hurt
and does not change;
5who does not put out his money
at interest,
and does not take a bribe
against the innocent.
He who does these things shall
never be moved.

SONG OF TRUST AND SECURITY IN GOD

A Miktam of David.

16 Preserve me, O God, for in thee I
take refuge.
2I say to the LORD, "Thou art my
Lord;
I have no good apart from
thee."[a]
3As for the saints in the land, they
are the noble,
in whom is all my delight.
4Those who choose another god
multiply their sorrows;[b]
their libations of blood I will
not pour out
or take their names upon
my lips.
5The LORD is my chosen portion
and my cup;
thou holdest my lot.
6The lines have fallen for me in
pleasant places;
yea, I have a goodly heritage.
7I bless the LORD who gives me
counsel;
in the night also my heart
instructs me.
8I keep the LORD always before
me;
because he is at my right
hand, I shall not be
moved.
9Therefore my heart is glad, and
my soul rejoices;
my body also dwells secure.
10For thou dost not give me up to
Sheol,
or let thy godly one see the
Pit.
11Thou dost show me the path of
life;
in thy presence there is
fulness of joy,
in thy right hand are plea-
sures for evermore.

PRAYER FOR DELIVERANCE FROM PERSECUTORS

A Prayer of David.

17 Hear a just cause, O LORD; attend
to my cry!
Give ear to my prayer from
lips free of deceit!
2From thee let my vindication
come!
Let thy eyes see the right!
3If thou triest my heart, if thou
visitest me by night,

[a]Jerome Tg: The meaning of the Hebrew is uncertain
[b]Cn: The meaning of the Hebrew is uncertain

if thou testest me, thou wilt
find no wickedness
in me;
my mouth does not
transgress.
4With regard to the works of men,
by the word of thy lips
I have avoided the ways of
the violent.
5My steps have held fast to thy
paths,
my feet have not slipped.
6I call upon thee, for thou wilt
answer me, O God;
incline thy ear to me, hear
my words.
7Wondrously show thy steadfast
love,
O savior of those who seek
refuge
from their adversaries at thy
right hand.
8Keep me as the apple of the eye;
hide me in the shadow of thy
wings,
9from the wicked who despoil me,
my deadly enemies who
surround me.
10They close their hearts to pity;
with their mouths they
speak arrogantly.
11They track me down; now they
surround me;
they set their eyes to cast me
to the ground.
12They are like a lion eager to tear,
as a young lion lurking in
ambush.
13Arise, O LORD! confront them,
overthrow them!
Deliver my life from the
wicked by thy sword,
14from men by thy hand, O LORD,
from men whose portion
life is of the worl
May their belly be filled wi
what thou hast store
up for them;
may their children have
more than enough
may they leave something
over to their babes

15As for me, I shall behold thy face
in righteousness;
when I awake, I shall be sat-
isfied with beholding
thy form.

ROYAL THANKSGIVING FOR VICTORY

To the choirmaster. A Psalm of David the servant of the LORD, who addressed the words of this song to the LORD on the day when the LORD delivered him from the hand of all his enemies, and from the hand of Saul. He said:

18 *I love thee, O LORD, my strength.
2The LORD is my rock, and my
fortress, and my deliverer,
my God, my rock, in whom I
take refuge,
my shield, and the horn of
my salvation, my
stronghold.
3I call upon the LORD, who is
worthy to be praised,
and I am saved from my
enemies.
4The cords of death encompassed
me,
the torrents of perdition
assailed me;
5the cords of Sheol entangled me,
the snares of death confront-
ed me.
6In my distress I called upon the
LORD;
to my God I cried for help.
From his temple he heard my
voice,
and my cry to him reached
his ears.
7Then the earth reeled and rocked;
the foundations also of the
mountains trembled
and quaked, because he was
angry.
8Smoke went up from his nostrils,
and devouring fire from his
mouth;
glowing coals flamed forth
from him.
9He bowed the heavens, and came
down;

thick darkness was under
his feet.
10He rode on a cherub, and flew;
he came swiftly upon the
wings of the wind.
11He made darkness his covering
around him,
his canopy thick clouds dark
with water.
12Out of the brightness before him
there broke through his
clouds
hailstones and coals of fire.
13The LORD also thundered in the
heavens,
and the Most High uttered
his voice,
hailstones and coals of fire.
14And he sent out his arrows, and
scattered them;
he flashed forth lightnings,
and routed them.
15Then the channels of the sea
were seen,
and the foundations of the
world were laid bare,
at thy rebuke, O LORD,
at the blast of the breath of
thy nostrils.
16He reached from on high, he
took me,
he drew me out of many
waters.
17He delivered me from my strong
enemy,
and from those who hated me;
for they were too mighty
for me.
18They came upon me in the day of
my calamity;
but the LORD was my stay.
19He brought me forth into a broad
place;
he delivered me, because he
delighted in me.
20The LORD rewarded me accord-
ing to my righteousness;
according to the cleanness of
my hands he recom-
pensed me.
21For I have kept the ways of the
LORD,
and have not wickedly
departed from my
God.
22For all his ordinances were
before me,
and his statutes I did not put
away from me.
23I was blameless before him,
and I kept myself from guilt.
24Therefore the LORD has recom-
pensed me according to my
righteousness,
according to the cleanness of
my hands in his sight.
25With the loyal thou dost show
thyself loyal;
with the blameless man thou
dost show thyself
blameless;
26with the pure thou dost show
thyself pure;
and with the crooked thou
dost show thyself
perverse.
27For thou dost deliver a humble
people;
but the haughty eyes thou
dost bring down.
28Yea, thou dost light my lamp;
the LORD my God lightens
my darkness.
29Yea, by thee I can crush a troop;
and by my God I can leap
over a wall.
30This God—his way is perfect;
the promise of the LORD
proves true;
he is a shield for all those
who take refuge in
him.
31r who is God, but the LORD?
And who is a rock, except
our God?—
e God who girded me with
strength,
and made my way safe.
e made my feet like hinds' feet,
and set me secure on the
heights.
le trains my hands for war,
so that my arms can bend a
bow of bronze.

35Thou hast given me the shield of
thy salvation,
and thy right hand supported me,
and thy help[a] made me great.
36Thou didst give a wide place for
my steps under me,
and my feet did not slip.
37I pursued my enemies and overtook them;
and did not turn back till
they were consumed.
38I thrust them through, so that
they were not able to rise;
they fell under my feet.
39For thou didst gird me with
strength for the battle;
thou didst make my assailants sink under me.
40Thou didst make my enemies
turn their backs to me,
and those who hated me I
destroyed.
41They cried for help, but there
was none to save,
they cried to the LORD, but
he did not answer
them.
42I beat them fine as dust before
the wind;
I cast them out like the mire
of the streets.
43Thou didst deliver me from
strife with the peoples;[b]
thou didst make me the head
of the nations;
people whom I had not
known served me.
44As soon as they heard of me they
obeyed me;
foreigners came cringing
to me.
45Foreigners lost heart,
and came trembling out of
their fastnesses.
46The LORD lives; and blessed be
my rock,
and exalted be the God of
my salvation,
47the God who gave me vengeance
and subdued peoples under
me;
48who delivered me from my
enemies;
yea, thou didst exalt
me above my
adversaries;
thou didst deliver me from
men of violence.
49For this I will extol thee, O
LORD, among the nations,
and sing praises to thy
name.
50Great triumphs he gives to his
king,
and shows steadfast love to
his anointed,
to David and his descendants for ever.

GOD'S GLORY IN CREATION AND THE LAW

To the choirmaster. A Psalm of David.

19 The heavens are telling the glory
of God;
and the firmament proclaims his handiwork.
2Day to day pours forth speech,
and night to night declares
knowledge.
3There is no speech, nor are there
words;
their voice is not heard;
4yet their voice[c] goes out through
all the earth,
and their words to the end of
the world.
In them he has set a tent for
the sun,
5which comes forth like a
bridegroom leaving his
chamber,
and like a strong man runs
its course with joy.
6Its rising is from the end of the
heavens,
and its circuit to the end of
them;
and there is nothing hid
from its heat.

[a] Or *gentleness*
[b] Gk Tg: Heb *people*
[c] Gk Jerome Compare Syr: Heb *line*

7The law of the LORD is perfect,
reviving the soul;
the testimony of the LORD is sure,
making wise the simple;
8the precepts of the LORD are right,
rejoicing the heart;
the commandment of the LORD is pure,
enlightening the eyes;
9the fear of the LORD is clean,
enduring for ever;
the ordinances of the LORD are true,
and righteous altogether.
10More to be desired are they than gold,
even much fine gold;
sweeter also than honey
and drippings of the honeycomb.
11Moreover by them is thy servant warned;
in keeping them there is great reward.
12But who can discern his errors?
Clear thou me from hidden faults.
13Keep back thy servant also from presumptuous sins;
let them not have dominion over me!
Then I shall be blameless,
and innocent of great transgression.
14Let the words of my mouth and the meditation of my heart
be acceptable in thy sight,
O LORD, my rock and my redeemer.

PRAYER FOR VICTORY

To the choirmaster. A Psalm of David.

20 The LORD answer you in the day *of trouble!*
The name of the God of Jacob protect you!
2May he send you help from the sanctuary,
and give you support from Zion!
3May he remember all your offerings,
and regard with favor your burnt sacrifices! *Selah*
4May he grant you your heart's desire,
and fulfil all your plans!
5May we shout for joy over your victory,
and in the name of our God set up our banners!
May the LORD fulfil all your petitions!
6Now I know that the LORD will help his anointed;
he will answer him from his holy heaven
with mighty victories by his right hand.
7Some boast of chariots, and some of horses;
but we boast of the name of the LORD our God.
8They will collapse and fall;
but we shall rise and stand upright.
9Give victory to the king, O LORD;
answer us when we call.[a]

THANKSGIVING FOR VICTORY

To the choirmaster. A Psalm of David.

21 In thy strength the king rejoices, O LORD;
and in thy help how greatly he exults!
2Thou hast given him his heart's desire,
and hast not withheld the request of his lips. *Selah*
3For thou dost meet him with goodly blessings;
thou dost set a crown of fine gold upon his head.
4He asked life of thee; thou gavest it to him,

[a] Gk: Heb *give victory, O Lord, let the King answer us when we call*

length of days for ever and
ever.
5His glory is great through thy
help;
splendor and majesty thou
dost bestow upon
him.
6Yea, thou dost make him most
blessed for ever;
thou dost make him glad
with the joy of thy
presence.
7For the king trusts in the LORD;
and through the steadfast
love of the Most
High he shall not be
moved.
8Your hand will find out all your
enemies;
your right hand will find out
those who hate you.
9You will make them as a blazing
oven
when you appear.
The LORD will swallow them
up in his wrath;
and fire will consume them.
10You will destroy their offspring
from the earth,
and their children from
among the sons of
men.
11If they plan evil against you,
if they devise mischief, they
will not succeed.
12For you will put them to flight;
you will aim at their faces
with your bows.
13Be exalted, O LORD, in thy
strength!
We will sing and raise thy
power.

PLEA FOR DELIVERANCEROM SUFFERING AND HOSTITY

To the choirmaster: accordg to The Hind of the Dawn. A Psalmf David.

22 *My God, my God, whyast thou
forsaken me?
Why art thou so farom
helping me, om
the words of my
groaning?
2O my God, I cry by day, but thou
dost not answer;
and by night, but find no
rest.
3Yet thou art holy,
enthroned on the praises of
Israel.
4In thee our fathers trusted;
they trusted, and thou didst
deliver them.
5To thee they cried, and were
saved;
in thee they trusted,
and were not
disappointed.
6But I am a worm, and no man;
scorned by men, and de-
spised by the people.
7All who see me mock at me,
they make mouths at me,
they wag their
heads;
8"He committed his cause to the
LORD; let him deliver him,
let him rescue him, for he
delights in him!"
9Yet thou art he who took me
from the womb;
thou didst keep me safe
upon my mother's
breasts.
10Upon thee was I cast from my
birth,
and since my mother bore
me thou hast been
my God.
11Be not far from me,
for trouble is near
and there is none to help.
12Many bulls encompass me,
strong bulls of Bashan sur-
round me;
13they open wide their mouths
at me,
like a ravening and roaring
lion.
14I am poured out like water,
and all my bones are out of
joint;
my heart is like wax,

it is melted within my breast;
15my strength is dried up like a potsherd,
and my tongue cleaves to my jaws;
thou dost lay me in the dust of death.
16Yea, dogs are round about me;
a company of evildoers encircle me;
they have pierced[a] my hands and feet—
17I can count all my bones—
they stare and gloat over me;
18they divide my garments among them,
and for my raiment they cast lots.
19But thou, O LORD, be not far off!
O thou my help, hasten to my aid!
20Deliver my soul from the sword,
my life[b] from the power of the dog!
21Save me from the mouth of the lion,
my afflicted soul[c] from the horns of the wild oxen!
22I will tell of thy name to my brethren;
in the midst of the congregation I will praise thee:
23You who fear the LORD, praise him!
all you sons of Jacob, glorify him,
and stand in awe of him, all you sons of Israel!
24For he has not despised or abhorred
the affliction of the afflicted;
and he has not hid his face from him,
but has heard, when he cried to him.
25From thee comes my praise in the great congregation;
my vows I will pay before those who fear him.
26The afflicted[d] shall eat and be satisfied;
those who seek him shall praise the LORD!
May your hearts live for ever!
27All the ends of the earth shall remember
and turn to the LORD;
and all the families of the nations
shall worship before him.[e]
28For dominion belongs to the LORD,
and he rules over the nations.
29Yea, to him[f] shall all the proud of the earth bow down;
before him shall bow all who go down to the dust,
and he who cannot keep himself alive.
30Posterity shall serve him;
men shall tell of the Lord to the coming generation,
31and proclaim his deliverance to a people yet unborn,
that he has wrought it.

THE DIVINE SHEPHERD

A Psalm of David.

23 The LORD is my shepherd, I shall not want;
2he makes me lie down in green pastures.
He leads me beside still waters;[g]

[a] Gk Syr Jerome: Heb *like a lion*
[b] Heb *my only one*
[c] Gk Syr: Heb *thou hast answered me*
[d] Or *poor*
[e] Gk Syr Jerome: Heb *thee*
[f] Cn: Heb *they have eaten and*
[g] Heb *the waters of rest*

3he restores my soul.[h]
He leads me in paths of
righteousness[i]
for his name's sake.
4Even though I walk through the
valley of the shadow of
death,[j]
I fear no evil;
for thou art with me;
thy rod and thy staff,
they comfort me.
5Thou preparest a table before me
in the presence of my
enemies;
thou anointest my head with oil,
my cup overflows.
6Surely[k] goodness and mercy[l]
shall follow me
all the days of my life;
and I shall dwell in the house
of the LORD
for ever.[m]

ENTRANCE INTO THE TEMPLE

A Psalm of David.

24The earth is the LORD's and the
fulness thereof,
the world and those who
dwell therein;
2for he has founded it upon the
seas,
and established it upon the
rivers.
3Who shall ascend the hill of the
LORD?
And who shall stand in his
holy place?
4He who has clean hands and a
pure heart,
who does not lift up his soul
to what is false,
and does not swear
deceitfully.
5He will receive blessing from the
LORD,
and vindication from the
God of his salvation.
6Such is the generation of those
who seek him,
who seek the face of the God
of Jacob.[n] *Selah*
7Lift up your heads, O gates!
and be lifted up, O ancient
doors!
that the King of glory may
come in.
8Who is the King of glory?
The LORD, strong and
mighty,
the LORD, mighty in battle!
9Lift up your heads, O gates!
and be lifted up,[o] O ancient
doors!
that the King of glory may
come in.
10Who is this King of glory?
The LORD of hosts,
he is the King of
glory! *Selah*

PRAYER FOR GUIDANCE AND FOR DELIVERANCE

A Psalm of David.

25To thee, O LORD, I lift up my soul.
2O my God, in thee I trust,
let me not be put to shame;
let not my enemies exult
over me.
3Yea, let none that wait for thee
be put to shame;
let them be ashamed
who are wantonly
treacherous.
4Make me to know thy ways, O
LORD;
teach me thy paths.
5Lead me in thy truth, and teach
me,
for thou art the God of my
salvation;

[h] Or *life*
[i] Or *right paths*
[j] Or *the valley of deep darkness*
[k] Or *Only*
[l] Or *kindness*
[m] Or *as long as I live*
[n] Gk Syr: Heb *thy face, O Jacob*
[o] Gk Syr Jerome Tg Compare verse 7: Heb *lift up*

for thee I wait all the day
long.
6Be mindful of thy mercy, O
LORD, and of thy steadfast
love,
for they have been from of
old.
7Remember not the sins
of my youth, or my
trangressions;
according to thy steadfast
love remember me,
for thy goodness' sake, O
LORD!
8Good and upright is the LORD;
therefore he instructs sin-
ners in the way.
9He leads the humble in what is
right,
and teaches the humble his
way.
10All the paths of the LORD
are steadfast love and
faithfulness,
for those who keep his
covenant and his
testimonies.
11For thy name's sake, O LORD,
pardon my guilt, for it is
great.
12Who is the man that fears the
LORD?
Him will he instruct in the
way that he should
choose.
13He himself shall abide in
prosperity,
and his children shall pos-
sess the land.
14The friendship of the LORD is for
those who fear him,
and he makes known to
them his covenant.
15My eyes are ever toward the
LORD,
for he will pluck my feet out
of the net.
16Turn thou to me, and be gracious
to me;
for I am lonely and
afflicted.
17Relieve the troubles of my heart,
and bring me[a] out of my
distresses.
18Consider my affliction and my
trouble,
and forgive all my sins.
19Consider how many are my
foes,
and with what violent hatred
they hate me.
20Oh guard my life, and deliver
me;
let me not be put to shame,
for I take refuge in
thee.
21May integrity and uprightness
preserve me,
for I wait for thee.
22Redeem Israel, O God,
out of all his troubles.

PLEA FOR JUSTICE AND DECLARATION OF RIGHTEOUSNESS

A Psalm of David.

26 Vindicate me, O LORD,
for I have walked in my
integrity,
and I have trusted in the
LORD without
wavering.
2Prove me, O LORD, and try me;
test my heart and my mind.
3For thy steadfast love is before
my eyes,
and I walk in faithfulness to
thee.[b]
4I do not sit with false men,
nor do I consort with
dissemblers;
5I hate the company of evildoers,
and I will not sit with the
wicked.
6I wash my hands in innocence,
and go about thy altar, O
LORD,
7singing aloud a song of
thanksgiving,
and telling all thy wondrous

[a] Or *The troubles of my heart are enlarged; bring me*
[b] Or *in thy faithfulness*

deeds.
8O LORD, I love the habitation of
thy house,
and the place where thy
glory dwells.
9Sweep me not away with
sinners,
nor my life with bloodthirsty
men,
10men in whose hands are evil
devices,
and whose right hands are
full of bribes.
11But as for me, I walk in my
integrity;
redeem me, and be gracious
to me.
12My foot stands on level ground;
in the great congregation I
will bless the LORD.

TRIUMPHANT SONG OF CONFIDENCE

A Psalm of David

27 The LORD is my light and my
salvation;
whom shall I fear?
The LORD is the stronghold[c] of
my life;
of whom shall I be afraid?
2When evildoers assail me,
uttering slanders against
me,[d]
my adversaries and foes,
they shall stumble and fall.
3Though a host encamp against
me,
my heart shall not fear;
though war arise against me,
yet I will be confident.
4One thing have asked of the
LORD,
that will I s ek after;
that I may dwe in the house of
the LOR
all the days my life,
to behold the b uty of the
LORD,
and to inquir n his
temple
5For he will hide m n his
shelter
in the day of trouble;
he will conceal me under the
cover of his tent,
he will set me high upon a
rock.
6And now my head shall be lifted
up
above my enemies round
about me;
and I will offer in his tent
sacrifices with shouts of
joy;
I will sing and make melody to
the LORD.
7Hear, O LORD, when I cry aloud,
be gracious to me and an-
swer me!
8Thou hast said, "Seek ye my
face."
My heart says to thee,
"Thy face, LORD, do I seek."
9Hide not thy face from me.
Turn not thy servant away in
anger,
thou who hast been my
help.
Cast me not off, forsake me
not,
O God of my salvation!
10For my father and my mother
have forsaken me,
but the LORD will take me
up.
11Teach me thy way, O LORD;
and lead me on a level path
because of my enemies.
12Give me not up to the will of my
adversaries;
for false witnesses have
risen against me,
and they breathe out
violence.
13I believe that I shall see the
goodness of the LORD
in the land of the living!
14Wait for the LORD;
be strong, and let your heart
take courage;
yea, wait for the LORD!

[c] Or *refuge*
[d] Heb *to eat up my flesh*

PRAYER FOR HELP AND THANKSGIVING FOR IT

A Psalm of David.

28 To thee, O LORD, I call;
my rock, be not deaf to me,
lest, if thou be silent to me,
I become like those who go
down to the Pit.
2 Hear the voice of my
supplication,
as I cry to thee for help,
as I lift up my hands
towards thy most holy
sanctuary.[a]
3 Take me not off with the
wicked,
with those who are workers
of evil,
who speak peace with their
neighbors,
while mischief is in their
hearts.
4 Requite them according to their
work,
and according to the evil of
their deeds;
requite them according to the
work of their hands;
render them their due
reward.
5 Because they do not regard the
works of the LORD,
or the work of his hands,
he will break them down and
build them up no more.
6 Blessed be the LORD!
for he has heard the voice of
my supplications.
7 The LORD is my strength and my
shield;
in him my heart trusts;
so I am helped, and my heart
exults,
and with my song I give
thanks to him.
8 *The LORD is the strength of his
people,*
he is the saving refuge of his
anointed.
9 O save thy people, and bless thy
heritage;
be thou their shepherd, and
carry them for ever.

THE VOICE OF GOD IN A GREAT STORM

A Psalm of David.

29 Ascribe to the LORD, O heavenly
beings,[b]
ascribe to the LORD glory
and strength.
2 Ascribe to the LORD the glory of
his name;
worship the LORD in holy
array.
3 The voice of the LORD is upon
the waters;
the God of glory thunders,
the LORD, upon many
waters.
4 The voice of the LORD is
powerful,
the voice of the LORD is full
of majesty.
5 The voice of the LORD breaks the
cedars,
the LORD breaks the cedars
of Lebanon.
6 He makes Lebanon to skip like
a calf,
and Sir′ion like a young
wild ox.
7 The voice of the LORD flashes
forth flames of fire.
8 The voice of the LORD shakes the
wilderness,
the LORD shakes the wilder-
ness of Kadesh.
9 The voice of the LORD makes the
oaks to whirl,[c]
and strips the forests bare;
and in his temple all cry,
"Glory!"
10 The LORD sits enthroned over
the flood;
the LORD sits enthroned as
king for ever.
11 May the LORD give strength to
his people!

[a] Heb *thy innermost sanctuary*
[b] Heb *sons of gods*
[c] Or *makes the hinds to calve*

May the LORD bless his people with peace!

THANKSGIVING FOR RECOVERY FROM GRAVE ILLNESS

A Psalm of David. A Song at the dedication of the Temple.

30 I will extol thee, O LORD, for thou hast drawn me up,
and hast not let my foes rejoice over me.
2 O LORD my God, I cried to thee for help,
and thou hast healed me.
3 O LORD, thou hast brought up my soul from Sheol,
restored me to life from among those gone down to the Pit.[d]
4 Sing praises to the LORD, O you his saints,
and give thanks to his holy name.
5 For his anger is but for a moment,
and his favor is for a lifetime.
Weeping may tarry for the night,
but joy comes with the morning.
6 As for me, I said in my prosperity,
"I shall never be moved."
7 By thy favor, O LORD,
thou hadst established me as a strong mountain;
thou didst hide thy face,
I was dismayed.
8 *To thee, O LORD, I cried*;
and to the LORD I made supplication:
9 "What profit is there in my death,
if I go down to the Pit?
Will the dust praise thee?
Will it tell of thy faithfulness?
10 Hear, O LORD, and be gracious to me!
O LORD, be thou my helper!"
11 Thou hast turned for me my mourning into dancing;
thou hast loosed my sackcloth
and girded me with gladness,
12 that my soul[e] may praise thee and not be silent.
O LORD my God, I will give thanks to thee for ever.

PRAYER AND PRAISE FOR DELIVERANCE FROM ENEMIES

To the choirmaster. A Psalm of David.

31 In thee, O LORD, do I seek refuge;
let me never be put to shame;
in thy righteousness deliver me!
2 Incline thy ear to me,
rescue me speedily!
Be thou a rock of refuge for me,
a strong fortress to save me!
3 Yea, thou art my rock and my fortress;
for thy name's sake lead me and guide me,
4 take me out of the net which is hidden for me,
for thou art my refuge.
5 Into thy hand I commit my spirit;
thou hast redeemed me, O LORD, faithful God.
6 Thou hatest[f] those who pay regard to vain idols;
but I trust in the LORD.
7 I will rejoice and be glad for thy steadfast love,
because thou hast seen my affliction,
thou hast taken heed of my adversities,
8 and hast not delivered me into the hand of the enemy;
thou hast set my feet in a broad place.

[d] Or *that I should not go down to the Pit*
[e] Heb *that glory*
[f] With one Heb Ms Gk Syr Jerome: Heb *I hate*

9Be gracious to me, O LORD, for I
am in distress;
my eye is wasted from grief,
my soul and my body also.
10For my life is spent with sorrow,
and my years with sighing;
my strength fails because of my
misery,[a]
and my bones waste away.
11I am the scorn of all my
adversaries,
a horror[b] to my neighbors,
an object of dread to my
acquaintances;
those who see me in the
street flee from me.
12I have passed out of mind like
one who is dead;
I have become like a broken
vessel.
13Yea, I hear the whispering of
many—
terror on every side!—
as they scheme together
against me,
as they plot to take my life.
14But I trust in thee, O LORD,
I say, "Thou art my God."
15My times are in thy hand;
deliver me from the hand
of my enemies and
persecutors!
16Let thy face shine on thy
servant;
save me in thy steadfast
love!
17Let me not be put to shame, O
LORD,
for I call on thee;
let the wicked be put to shame,
let them go dumbfounded to
Sheol.
18Let the lying lips be dumb,
which speak insolently
against the righteous
in pride and contempt.
19O how abundant is thy goodness,
which thou hast laid up for
those who fear thee,
and wrought for those who
take refuge in thee,
in the sight of the sons of
men!
20In the covert of thy presence
thou hidest them
from the plots of men;
thou holdest them safe under
thy shelter
from the strife of tongues.
21Blessed be the LORD,
for he has wondrously
shown his steadfast
love to me
when I was beset as in a
besieged city.
22I had said in my alarm,
"I am driven far[c] from thy
sight."
But thou didst hear my
supplications,
when I cried to thee for help.
23Love the LORD, all you his
saints!
The LORD preserves the
faithful,
but abundantly requites him
who acts haughtily.
24Be strong, and let your heart
take courage,
all you who wait for the
LORD!

THE JOY OF FORGIVENESS

A Psalm of David. A Maskil.

32 Blessed is he whose transgression
is forgiven,
whose sin is covered.
2Blessed is the man to whom the
LORD imputes no iniquity,
and in whose spirit there is
no deceit.
3When I declared not my sin, my
body wasted away
through my groaning all day
long.
4For day and night thy hand was
heavy upon me;

[a] Gk Syr: Heb *iniquity*
[b] Cn: Heb *exceedingly*
[c] Another reading is *cut off*

my strength was dried up[d]
as by the heat of
summer. *Selah*
5I acknowledged my sin to thee,
and I did not hide my
iniquity;
I said, "I will confess my transgressions to the LORD";
then thou didst forgive the
guilt of my sin. *Selah*
6Therefore let every one who is
godly
offer prayer to thee;
at a time of distress,[e] in the
rush of great waters,
they shall not reach him.
7Thou art a hiding place for me,
thou preservest me from
trouble;
thou dost encompass me with
deliverance.[f] *Selah*
8I will instruct you and teach you
the way you should go;
I will counsel you with my
eye upon you.
9Be not like a horse or a mule,
without understanding,
which must be curbed with
bit and bridle,
else it will not keep with
you.
10Many are the pangs of the
wicked;
but steadfast love surrounds
him who trusts in the
LORD.
11Be glad in the LORD, and rejoice,
O righteous,
and shout for joy, all you
upright in heart!

THE GREATNESS AND GOODNESS OF GOD

33 Rejoice in the LORD, O you
righteous!
Praise befits the upright.
2Praise the LORD with the lyre,
make melody to him with
the harp of ten
strings!
3Sing to him a new song,
play skilfully on the strings,
with loud shouts.
4For the word of the LORD is
upright;
and all his work is done in
faithfulness.
5He loves righteousness and
justice;
the earth is full of the steadfast love of the LORD.
6By the word of the LORD the
heavens were made,
and all their host by the
breath of his mouth.
7He gathered the waters of the sea
as in a bottle;
he put the deeps in
storehouses.
8Let all the earth fear the LORD,
let all the inhabitants of the
world stand in awe
of him!
9For he spoke, and it came to be;
he commanded, and it stood
forth.
10The LORD brings the counsel of
the nations to nought;
he frustrates the plans of the
peoples.
11The counsel of the LORD stands
for ever,
the thoughts of his heart to
all generations.
12Blessed is the nation whose God
is the LORD,
the people whom he has chosen as his heritage!
13The LORD looks down from
heaven,
he sees all the sons of men;
14from where he sits enthroned he
looks forth
on all the inhabitants of the
earth,
15he who fashions the hearts of
them all,
and observes all their deeds.
16A king is not saved by his great
army;

[d] Heb obscure
[e] Cn: Heb *at a time of finding only*
[f] Cn: Heb *shouts of deliverance*

a warrior is not delivered by
his great strength.
17The war horse is a vain hope for
victory,
and by its great might it
cannot save.
18Behold, the eye of the LORD is
on those who fear him,
on those who hope in his
steadfast love,
19that he may deliver their soul
from death,
and keep them alive in
famine.
20Our soul waits for the LORD;
he is our help and shield.
21Yea, our heart is glad in him,
because we trust in his holy
name.
22Let thy steadfast love, O LORD,
be upon us,
even as we hope in thee.

PRAISE FOR DELIVERANCE FROM TROUBLE

A Psalm of David, when he feigned madness before Abimelech, so that he drove him out, and he went away.

34 I will bless the LORD at all times;
his praise shall continually be
in my mouth.
2My soul makes its boast in the
LORD;
let the afflicted hear and be
glad.
3O magnify the LORD with me,
and let us exalt his name
together!
4I sought the LORD, and he an-
swered me,
and delivered me from all
my fears.
5Look to him, and be radiant;
so your[a] faces shall never be
ashamed.
6This poor man cried, and the
LORD heard him,
and saved him out of all his
troubles.
7The angel of the LORD encamps
around those who fear him,
and delivers them.
8O taste and see that the LORD is
good!
Happy is the man who takes
refuge in him!
9O fear the LORD, you his saints,
for those who fear him have
no want!
10The young lions suffer want and
hunger;
but those who seek the
LORD lack no good
thing.
11Come, O sons, listen to me,
I will teach you the fear of
the LORD.
12What man is there who desires
life,
and covets many days, that
he may enjoy good?
13Keep your tongue from evil,
and your lips from speaking
deceit.
14Depart from evil, and do good;
seek peace, and pursue it.
15The eyes of the LORD are toward
the righteous,
and his ears toward their
cry.
16The face of the LORD is against
evildoers,
to cut off the remembrance
of them from the
earth.
17When the righteous cry for help,
the LORD hears,
and delivers them out of all
their troubles.
18The LORD is near to the
brokenhearted,
and saves the crushed in
spirit.
19Many are the afflictions of the
righteous;
but the LORD delivers him
out of them all.
20He keeps all his bones;
not one of them is broken.
21Evil shall slay the wicked;
and those who hate the
righteous will be

[a] Gk Syr Jerome: Heb *their*

condemned.
22The LORD redeems the life of his servants;
none of those who take refuge in him will be condemned.

PRAYER FOR DELIVERANCE FROM ENEMIES

A Psalm of David.

35 Contend, O LORD, with those who contend with me;
fight against those who fight against me!
2Take hold of shield and buckler,
and rise for my help!
3Draw the spear and javelin against my pursuers!
Say to my soul,
"I am your deliverance!"
4Let them be put to shame and dishonor
who seek after my life!
Let them be turned back and confounded
who devise evil against me!
5Let them be like chaff before the wind,
with the angel of the LORD driving them on!
6Let their way be dark and slippery,
with the angel of the LORD pursuing them!
7For without cause they hid their net for me;
without cause they dug a pit[b] for my life.
8Let ruin come upon them unawares!
And let the net which they hid ensnare them;
let them fall therein to ruin!
9Then my soul shall rejoice in the LORD,
exulting in his deliverance.
10All my bones shall say,
"O LORD, who is like thee,
thou who deliverest the weak
from him who is too strong for him,
the weak and needy from him who despoils him?"
11Malicious witnesses rise up;
they ask me of things that I know not.
12They requite me evil for good;
my soul is forlorn.
13But I, when they were sick—
I wore sackcloth,
I afflicted myself with fasting.
I prayed with head bowed[c] on my bosom,
14as though I grieved for my friend or my brother;
I went about as one who laments his mother,
bowed down and in mourning.
15But at my stumbling they gathered in glee,
they gathered together against me;
cripples whom I knew not
slandered me without ceasing;
16they impiously mocked more and more,[d]
gnashing at me with their teeth.
17How long, O LORD, wilt thou look on?
Rescue me from their ravages,
my life from the lions!
18Then I will thank thee in the great congregation;
in the mighty throng I will praise thee.
19Let not those rejoice over me
who are wrongfully my foes,
and let not those wink the eye
who hate me without cause.
20For they do not speak peace,
but against those who are quiet in the land
they conceive words of deceit.

[b]The word *pit* is transposed from the preceding line
[c]Or *My prayer turned back*
[d]Cn Compare Gk: Heb *like the profanest of mockers of a cake*

21They open wide their mouths
against me;
they say, "Aha, Aha!
our eyes have seen it!"
22Thou hast seen, O LORD; be not
silent!
O Lord, be not far from me!
23Bestir thyself, and awake for my
right,
for my cause, my God and
my Lord!
24Vindicate me, O LORD, my
God, according to thy
righteousness;
and let them not rejoice over
me!
25Let them not say to themselves,
"Aha, we have our heart's
desire!"
Let them not say, "We have
swallowed him up."
26Let them be put to shame and
confusion altogether
who rejoice at my calamity!
Let them be clothed with
shame and dishonor
who magnify themselves
against me!
27Let those who desire my
vindication
shout for joy and be glad,
and say evermore,
"Great is the LORD,
who delights in the welfare
of his servant!"
28Then my tongue shall tell of thy
righteousness
and of thy praise all the day
long.

HUMAN WICKEDNESS AND DIVINE GOODNESS

To the choirmaster. A Psalm of David, the servant of the LORD.

36 Transgression speaks to the
wicked
deep in his heart;
there is no fear of God
before his eyes.
2For he flatters himself in his own
eyes
that his iniquity cannot be
found out and hated.
3The words of his mouth are mis-
chief and deceit;
he has ceased to act wisely
and do good.
4He plots mischief while on his
bed;
he sets himself in a way that
is not good;
he spurns not evil.
5Thy steadfast love, O LORD, ex-
tends to the heavens,
thy faithfulness to the
clouds.
6Thy righteousness is like the
mountains of God,
thy judgments are like the
great deep;
man and beast thou savest,
O LORD.
7How precious is thy steadfast
love, O God!
The children of men take
refuge in the shadow
of thy wings.
8They feast on the abundance of
thy house,
and thou givest them drink
from the river of thy
delights.
9For with thee is the fountain of
life;
in thy light do we see light.
10O continue thy steadfast love to
those who know thee,
and thy salvation to the
upright of heart!
11Let not the foot of arrogance
come upon me,
nor the hand of the wicked
drive me away.
12There the evildoers lie prostrate,
they are thrust down, unable
to rise.

EXHORTATION TO PATIENCE AND TRUST

A Psalm of David.

37 Fret not yourself because of the
wicked,
be not envious of

wrongdoers!
2For they will soon fade like the
grass,
and wither like the green
herb.
3Trust in the LORD, and do good;
so you will dwell in the land,
and enjoy security.
4Take delight in the LORD,
and he will give you the desires of your heart.
5Commit your way to the LORD;
trust in him, and he will act.
6He will bring forth your vindication as the light,
and your right as the
noonday.
7Be still before the LORD, and
wait patiently for him;
fret not yourself over him
who prospers in his
way,
over the man who carries
out evil devices!
8Refrain from anger, and forsake
wrath!
Fret not yourself; it tends
only to evil.
9For the wicked shall be cut off;
but those who wait for the
LORD shall possess
the land.
10Yet a little while, and the wicked
will be no more;
though you look well at his
place, he will not be
there.
11But the meek shall possess the
land,
and delight themselves in
abundant prosperity.
12*The wicked plots against the*
righteous,
and gnashes his teeth at
him;
13but the LORD laughs at the
wicked,
for he sees that his day is
coming.
14The wicked draw the sword and
bend their bows,
to bring down the poor and
needy,
to slay those who walk
uprightly;
15their sword shall enter their own
heart,
and their bows shall be
broken.
16Better is a little that the righteous has
than the abundance of many
wicked.
17For the arms of the wicked shall
be broken;
but the LORD upholds the
righteous.
18The LORD knows the days of the
blameless,
and their heritage will abide
for ever;
19they are not put to shame in evil
times,
in the days of famine they
have abundance.
20But the wicked perish;
the enemies of the LORD are
like the glory of the
pastures,
they vanish—like smoke
they vanish away.
21The wicked borrows, and cannot
pay back,
but the righteous is generous and gives;
22for those blessed by the LORD
shall possess the land,
but those cursed by him
shall be cut off.
23The steps of a man are from the
LORD,
and he establishes him
in whose way he
delights;
24though he fall, he shall not be
cast headlong,
for the LORD is the stay of
his hand.
25I have been young, and now am
old;
yet I have not seen the righteous forsaken
or his children begging
bread.

26 He is ever giving liberally and lending,
and his children become a blessing.
27 Depart from evil, and do good;
so shall you abide for ever.
28 For the LORD loves justice;
he will not forsake his saints.
The righteous shall be preserved for ever,
but the children of the wicked shall be cut off.
29 The righteous shall possess the land,
and dwell upon it for ever.
30 The mouth of the righteous utters wisdom,
and his tongue speaks justice.
31 The law of his God is in his heart;
his steps do not slip.
32 The wicked watches the righteous,
and seeks to slay him.
33 The LORD will not abandon him to his power,
or let him be condemned when he is brought to trial.
34 Wait for the LORD, and keep to his way,
and he will exalt you to possess the land;
you will look on the destruction of the wicked.
35 I have seen a wicked man overbearing,
and towering like a cedar of Lebanon.[a]
36 Again I[b] passed by, and lo, he was no more;
though I sought him, he could not be found.
37 Mark the blameless man, and behold the upright,
for there is posterity for the man of peace.
38 But transgressors shall be altogether destroyed;
the posterity of the wicked shall be cut off.
39 The salvation of the righteous is from the LORD;
he is their refuge in the time of trouble.
40 The LORD helps them and delivers them;
he delivers them from the wicked, and saves them,
because they take refuge in him.

A PENITENT SUFFERER'S PLEA FOR HEALING

A Psalm of David, for the memorial offering.

38 O LORD, rebuke me not in thy anger,
nor chasten me in thy wrath!
2 For thy arrows have sunk into me,
and thy hand has come down on me.
3 There is no soundness in my flesh
because of thy indignation;
there is no health in my bones
because of my sin.
4 For my iniquities have gone over my head;
they weigh like a burden too heavy for me.
5 My wounds grow foul and fester
because of my foolishness,
6 I am utterly bowed down and prostrate;
all the day I go about mourning.
7 For my loins are filled with burning,
and there is no soundness in my flesh.
8 I am utterly spent and crushed;
I groan because of the tumult of my heart.
9 Lord, all my longing is known

[a] Gk: Heb obscure
[b] Gk Syr Jerome: Heb *he*

to thee,
my sighing is not hidden from thee.
10 My heart throbs, my strength fails me;
and the light of my eyes—it also has gone from me.
11 My friends and companions stand aloof from my plague,
and my kinsmen stand afar off.
12 Those who seek my life lay their snares,
those who seek my hurt speak of ruin,
and meditate treachery all the day long.
13 But I am like a deaf man, I do not hear,
like a dumb man who does not open his mouth.
14 Yea, I am like a man who does not hear,
and in whose mouth are no rebukes.
15 But for thee, O LORD, do I wait;
it is thou, O LORD my God, who wilt answer.
16 For I pray, "Only let them not rejoice over me,
who boast against me when my foot slips!"
17 For I am ready to fall,
and my pain is ever with me.
18 I confess my iniquity,
I am sorry for my sin.
19 Those who are my foes without cause[c] are mighty,
and many are those who hate me wrongfully.
20 Those who render me evil for good
are my adversaries because I follow after good.
21 Do not forsake me, O LORD!
O my God, be not far from me!
22 Make haste to help me,
O Lord, my salvation!

[c] Cn: Heb *living*
[d] Heb *muzzle*
[e] Heb *hostility*

PRAYER FOR WISDOM AND FORGIVENESS

To the choirmaster: to Jeduthun.
A Psalm of David.

39 I said, "I will guard my ways,
that I may not sin with my tongue;
I will bridle[d] my mouth,
so long as the wicked are in my presence."
2 I was dumb and silent,
I held my peace to no avail;
my distress grew worse,
3 my heart became hot within me.
As I mused, the fire burned;
then I spoke with my tongue:
4 "LORD, let me know my end,
and what is the measure of my days;
let me know how fleeting my life is!
5 Behold, thou hast made my days a few handbreadths,
and my lifetime is as nothing in thy sight.
Surely every man stands as a mere breath! *Selah*
6 Surely man goes about as a shadow!
Surely for nought are they in turmoil;
man heaps up, and knows not who will gather!
7 "And now, Lord, for what do I wait?
My hope is in thee.
8 Deliver me from all my transgressions.
Make me not the scorn of the fool!
9 I am dumb, I do not open my mouth;
for it is thou who hast done it.
10 Remove thy stroke from me;
I am spent by the blows[e] of thy hand.
11 When thou dost chasten man
with rebukes for sin,

thou dost consume like a moth
what is dear to him;
surely every man is a mere
breath! *Selah*
12"Hear my prayer, O LORD,
and give ear to my cry;
hold not thy peace at my
tears!
For I am thy passing guest,
a sojourner, like all my
fathers.
13Look away from me, that I may
know gladness,
before I depart and be no
more!"

THANKSGIVING FOR DELIVERANCE AND PRAYER FOR HELP

To the choirmaster. A Psalm of David.

40 I waited patiently for the LORD;
he inclined to me and heard
my cry.
2He drew me up from the desolate
pit, [a]
out of the miry bog,
and set my feet upon a rock,
making my steps secure.
3He put a new song in my mouth,
a song of praise to our God.
Many will see and fear,
and put their trust in the
LORD.
4Blessed is the man who makes
the LORD his trust,
who does not turn to the
proud,
to those who go astray after
false gods!
5Thou hast multiplied, O LORD
my God,
thy wondrous deeds and thy
thoughts toward us;
none can compare with
thee!
Were I to proclaim and tell of
them,
they would be more than can
be numbered.
6Sacrifice and offering thou dost
not desire;
but thou hast given me an
open ear. [b]
Burnt offering and sin offering
thou hast not required.
7Then I said, "Lo, I come;
in the roll of the book it is
written of me;
8I delight to do thy will, O my
God;
thy law is within my heart."
9I have told the glad news of
deliverance
in the great congregation;
lo, I have not restrained my
lips,
as thou knowest, O LORD.
10I have not hid thy saving help
within my heart,
I have spoken of thy
faithfulness and thy
salvation;
I have not concealed thy
steadfast love and thy
faithfulness
from the great congregation.
11Do not thou, O LORD, withhold
thy mercy from me,
let thy steadfast love and thy
faithfulness
ever preserve me!
12For evils have encompassed me
without number;
my iniquities have overtaken
me,
till I cannot see;
they are more than the hairs of
my head;
my heart fails me.
13Be pleased, O LORD, to deliver
me!
O LORD, make haste to help
me!
14Let them be put to shame and
confusion altogether
who seek to snatch away
my life;
let them be turned back and
brought to dishonor
who desire my hurt!

[a] Cn: Heb *pit of tumult*
[b] Heb *ears thou hast dug for me*

15Let them be appalled because of their shame
who say to me, "Aha, Aha!"
16But may all who seek thee rejoice and be glad in thee;
may those who love thy salvation
say continually, "Great is the LORD!"
17As for me, I am poor and needy;
but the Lord takes thought for me.
Thou art my help and my deliverer;
do not tarry, O my God!

ASSURANCE OF GOD'S HELP AND A PLEA FOR HEALING

To the choirmaster. A Psalm of David.

41 Blessed is he who considers the poor![c]
The LORD delivers him in the day of trouble;
2the LORD protects him and keeps him alive;
he is called blessed in the land;
thou dost not give him up to the will of his enemies.
3The LORD sustains him on his sickbed;
in his illness thou healest all his infirmities.[d]
4As for me, I said, "O LORD, be gracious to me;
heal me, for I have sinned against thee!"
5My enemies say of me in malice:
"When will he die, and his name perish?"
6And when one comes to see me, he utters empty words,
while his heart gathers mischief;
when he goes out, he tells it abroad.
7All who hate me whisper together about me;
they imagine the worst for me.
8They say, "A deadly thing has fastened upon him;
he will not rise again from where he lies."
9Even my bosom friend in whom I trusted,
who ate of my bread, has lifted his heel against me.
10But do thou, O LORD, be gracious to me,
and raise me up, that I may requite them!
11By this I know that thou art pleased with me,
in that my enemy has not triumphed over me.
12But thou hast upheld me because of my integrity,
and set me in thy presence for ever.
13Blessed be the LORD, the God of Israel,
from everlasting to everlasting!
Amen and Amen.

BOOK II

LONGING FOR GOD AND HIS HELP IN DISTRESS

To the choirmaster. A Maskil of the Sons of Korah.

42 *As a hart longs for flowing streams,
so longs my soul for thee, O God.
2My soul thirsts for God, for the living God.
When shall I come and behold the face of God?
3My tears have been my food day and night,
while men say to me continually,
"Where is your God?"

[c] Or *weak*
[d] Heb *thou changest all his bed*

4 These things I remember,
as I pour out my soul:
how I went with the throng,
and led them in procession
to the house of God,
with glad shouts and songs of
thanksgiving,
a multitude keeping
festival.
5 Why are you cast down, O my
soul,
and why are you disquieted
within me?
Hope in God; for I shall again
praise him,
my help 6 and my God.
My soul is cast down within
me,
therefore I remember thee
from the land of Jordan and of
Hermon,
from Mount Mizar.
7 Deep calls to deep
at the thunder of thy
cataracts;
all thy waves and thy billows
have gone over me.
8 By day the LORD commands his
steadfast love;
and at night his song is with
me,
a prayer to the God of my
life.
9 I say to God, my rock:
"Why hast thou forgotten
me?
Why go I mourning
because of the oppression of
the enemy?"
10 As with a deadly wound in my
body,
my adversaries taunt me,
while they say to me
continually,
"Where is your God?"
11 Why are you cast down, O my
soul,
and why are you disquieted
within me?
Hope in God; for I shall again
praise him,
my help and my God.

PRAYER TO GOD IN TIME OF TROUBLE

43 Vindicate me, O God, and defend
my cause
against an ungodly people;
from deceitful and unjust men
deliver me!
2 For thou art the God in whom I
take refuge;
why hast thou cast me off?
Why go I mourning
because of the oppression of
the enemy?
3 Oh send out thy light and thy
truth;
let them lead me,
let them bring me to thy holy
hill
and to thy dwelling!
4 Then I will go to the altar of
God,
to God my exceeding joy;
and I will praise thee with the
lyre,
O God, my God.
5 Why are you cast down, O my
soul,
and why are you disquieted
within me?
Hope in God; for I shall again
praise him,
my help and my God.

NATIONAL LAMENT AND PRAYER FOR HELP

To the choirmaster. A Maskil
of the Sons of Korah.

44 We have heard with our ears, O
God,
our fathers have told us,
what deeds thou didst perform
in their days,
in the days of old:
2 thou with thy own hand didst
drive out the nations,
but them thou didst plant;
thou didst afflict the peoples,
but them thou didst set
free;
3 for not by their own sword did
they win the land,
nor did their own arm give
them victory;

but thy right hand, and thy arm,
and the light of thy countenance;
for thou didst delight in them.
4Thou art my King and my God,
who ordainest[a] victories for Jacob.
5Through thee we push down our foes;
through thy name we tread down our assailants.
6For not in my bow do I trust,
nor can my sword save me.
7But thou hast saved us from our foes,
and hast put to confusion those who hate us.
8In God we have boasted continually,
and we will give thanks to thy name for ever.
9Yet thou hast cast us off and abased us,
and hast not gone out with our armies.
10Thou hast made us turn back from the foe;
and our enemies have gotten spoil.
11Thou hast made us like sheep for slaughter,
and hast scattered us among the nations.
12Thou hast sold thy people for a trifle,
demanding no high price for them.
13Thou hast made us the taunt of our neighbors,
the derision and scorn of those about us.
14Thou hast made us a byword among the nations,
a laughingstock[b] among the peoples.
15All day long my disgrace is before me,
and shame has covered my face,
16at the words of the taunters and revilers,
at the sight of the enemy and the avenger.
17All this has come upon us,
though we have not forgotten thee,
or been false to thy covenant.
18Our heart has not turned back,
nor have our steps departed from thy way,
19that thou shouldst have broken us in the place of jackals,
and covered us with deep darkness.
20If we had forgotten the name of our God,
or spread forth our hands to a strange god,
21would not God discover this?
For he knows the secrets of the heart.
22Nay, for thy sake we are slain all the day long,
and accounted as sheep for the slaughter.
23Rouse thyself! Why sleepest thou, O Lord?
Awake! Do not cast us off for ever!
24Why dost thou hide thy face?
Why dost thou forget our affliction and oppression?
25For our soul is bowed down to the dust;
our body cleaves to the ground.
26Rise up, come to our help!
Deliver us for the sake of thy steadfast love!

ODE FOR A ROYAL WEDDING

To the choirmaster: according to Lilies. A Maskil of the Sons of Korah; a love song.

45 My heart overflows with a goodly theme;
I address my verses to the king;

[a] Gk Syr: Heb *Thou art my King, O God; ordain*
[b] Heb *a shaking of the head*

my tongue is like the pen of
a ready scribe.
2You are the fairest of the sons
of men;
grace is poured upon your
lips;
therefore God has blessed
you for ever.
3Gird your sword upon your thigh,
O mighty one,
in your glory and majesty!
4In your majesty ride forth
victoriously
for the cause of truth and to
defend[a] the right;
let your right hand teach you
dread deeds!
5Your arrows are sharp
in the heart of the king's
enemies;
the peoples fall under you.
6Your divine throne[b] endures for
ever and ever.
Your royal scepter is a scep-
ter of equity;
7you love righteousness and
hate wickedness.
Therefore God, your God, has
anointed you
with the oil of gladness
above your fellows;
8your robes are all fragrant
with myrrh and aloes
and cassia.
From ivory palaces stringed
instruments make you
glad;
9daughters of kings are
among your ladies of
honor;
at your right hand stands
the queen in gold of
Ophir.
10Hear, O daughter, consider, and
incline your ear;
forget your people and your
father's house;
11and the king will desire
your beauty.
Since he is your lord, bow to
him;
12the people[c] of Tyre will sue
your favor with gifts,
the richest of the people
13with all kinds of
wealth.
The princess is decked in her
chamber with gold-wo-
ven robes;[d]
14in many-colored robes she
is led to the king,
with her virgin companions,
her escort,[e] in her
train.
15With joy and gladness they are
led along
as they enter the palace of
the king.
16Instead of your fathers shall be
your sons;
you will make them princes
in all the earth.
17I will cause your name to be cel-
ebrated in all generations;
therefore the peoples will
praise you for ever
and ever.

GOD'S DEFENSE OF HIS CITY AND PEOPLE

To the choirmaster. A Psalm of
the Sons of Korah. According
to Alamoth. A Song.

46 God is our refuge and strength,
a very present[f] help in trouble.
2Therefore we will not fear though
the earth should change,
though the mountains shake
in the heart of the
sea;
3though its waters roar and foam,
though the mountains
tremble with its
tumult. Selah
4There is a river whose streams

[a]Cn: Heb *and the meekness of*
[b]Or *Your throne is a throne of God*, or *Thy throne, O God*
[c]Heb *daughter*
[d]Or *people. All glorious is the princess within, gold embroidery is her clothing*
[e]Heb *those brought to you*
[f]Or *well proved*

make glad the city of God,
the holy habitation of the Most High.
5God is in the midst of her, she shall not be moved;
God will help her right early.
6The nations rage, the kingdoms totter;
he utters his voice, the earth melts.
7The LORD of hosts is with us;
the God of Jacob is our refuge.[g] *Selah*
8Come, behold the works of the LORD,
how he has wrought desolations in the earth.
9He makes wars cease to the end of the earth;
he breaks the bow, and shatters the spear,
he burns the chariots with fire!
10"Be still, and know that I am God.
I am exalted among the nations,
I am exalted in the earth!"
11The LORD of hosts is with us;
the God of Jacob is our refuge.[h] *Selah*

GOD'S RULE OVER THE NATIONS

To the choirmaster. A Psalm of the Sons of Korah.

47 Clap your hands, all peoples!
Shout to God with loud songs of joy!
2For the LORD, the Most High, is terrible,
a great king over all the earth.
3He subdued peoples under us,
and nations under our feet.
4He chose our heritage for us,
the pride of Jacob whom he loves. *Selah*
5God has gone up with a shout,
the LORD with the sound of a trumpet.
6Sing praises to God, sing praises!
Sing praises to our King, sing praises!
7For God is the king of all the earth;
sing praises with a psalm![i]
8God reigns over the nations;
God sits on his holy throne.
9The princes of the peoples gather
as the people of the God of Abraham.
For the shields of the earth belong to God;
he is highly exalted!

THE GLORY AND STRENGTH OF ZION

A Song. A Psalm of the Sons of Korah.

48 Great is the LORD and greatly to be praised
in the city of our God!
His holy mountain, 2beautiful in elevation,
is the joy of all the earth,
Mount Zion, in the far north,
the city of the great King.
3Within her citadels God
has shown himself a sure defense.
4For lo, the kings assembled,
they came on together.
5As soon as they saw it, they were astounded,
they were in panic, they took to flight;
6trembling took hold of them there,
anguish as of a woman in travail.
7By the east wind thou didst shatter
the ships of Tarshish.
8As we have heard, so have we seen
in the city of the LORD of hosts,
in the city of our God,
which God establishes for ever. *Selah*
9We have thought on thy steadfast love, O God,
in the midst of thy temple.

[g] Or *fortress*
[h] Or *fortress*
[i] Heb *Maskil*

10As thy name, O God,
so thy praise reaches to the ends of the earth.
Thy right hand is filled with victory;
11let Mount Zion be glad!
Let the daughters of Judah rejoice
because of thy judgments!
12Walk about Zion, go round about her,
number her towers,
13consider well her ramparts,
go through her citadels;
that you may tell the next generation 14that this is God,
our God for ever and ever.
He will be our guide for ever.

THE FOLLY OF TRUST IN RICHES

To the choirmaster. A Psalm of the Sons of Korah.

49 Hear this, all peoples!
Give ear, all inhabitants of the world,
2both low and high,
rich and poor together!
3My mouth shall speak wisdom;
the meditation of my heart shall be understanding.
4I will incline my ear to a proverb;
I will solve my riddle to the music of the lyre.
5Why should I fear in times of trouble,
when the iniquity of my persecutors surrounds me,
6men who trust in their wealth
and boast of the abundance of their riches?
7Truly no man can ransom himself,[a]
or give to God the price of his life,
8for the ransom of his[b] life is costly,
and can never suffice,
9that he should continue to live on for ever,
and never see the Pit.
10Yea, he shall see that even the wise die,
the fool and the stupid alike must perish
and leave their wealth to others.
11Their graves[c] are their homes for ever,
their dwelling places to all generations,
though they named lands their own.
12Man cannot abide in his pomp,
he is like the beasts that perish.
13This is the fate of those who have foolish confidence,
the end of those[d] who are pleased with their portion. *Selah*
14Like sheep they are appointed for Sheol;
Death shall be their shepherd;
straight to the grave they descend,[e]
and their form shall waste away;
Sheol shall be their home.[f]
15But God will ransom my soul from the power of Sheol,
for he will receive me. *Selah*
16Be not afraid when one becomes rich,
when the glory[g] of his house increases.
17For when he dies he will carry nothing away;

[a]Another reading is *no man can ransom his brother*
[b]Gk: Heb *their*
[c]Gk Syr Compare Tg: Heb *their inward* (thought)
[d]Tg: Heb *after them*
[e]Cn: Heb *the upright shall have dominion over them in the morning*
[f]Heb uncertain
[g]Or *wealth*

his glory[h] will not go down
after him.
18Though, while he lives, he
counts himself happy,
and though a man gets
praise when he does
well for himself,
19he will go to the generation of
his fathers,
who will never more see the
light.
20Man cannot abide in his pomp,
he is like the beasts that
perish.

THE ACCEPTABLE SACRIFICE

A Psalm of Asaph.

50 The Mighty One, God the LORD,
speaks and summons the earth
from the rising of the sun to
its setting.
2Out of Zion, the perfection of
beauty,
God shines forth.
3Our God comes, he does not keep
silence,
before him is a devouring
fire,
round about him a mighty
tempest.
4He calls to the heavens above
and to the earth, that he may
judge his people:
5"Gather to me my faithful ones,
who made a covenant with
me by sacrifice!"
6The heavens declare his
righteousness,
for God himself is
judge! *Selah*
7"Hear, O my people, and I will
speak,
O Israel, I will testify
against you.
I am God, your God.
8I do not reprove you for your
sacrifices;
your burnt offerings are con-
tinually before me.
9I will accept no bull from your
house,
nor he-goat from your folds.
10For every beast of the forest is
mine,
the cattle on a thousand
hills.
11I know all the birds of the air,[i]
and all that moves in the
field is mine.
12"If I were hungry, I would not
tell you;
for the world and all that is
in it is mine.
13Do I eat the flesh of bulls,
or drink the blood of goats?
14Offer to God a sacrifice of
thanksgiving,[j]
and pay your vows to the
Most High;
15and call upon me in the day of
trouble;
I will deliver you, and you
shall glorify me."
16But to the wicked God says:
"What right have you to
recite my statutes,
or take my covenant on your
lips?
17For you hate discipline,
and you cast my words
behind you.
18If you see a thief, you are a
friend of his;
and you keep company with
adulterers.
19"You give your mouth free rein
for evil,
and your tongue frames
deceit.
20You sit and speak against your
brother;
you slander your own moth-
er's son.
21These things you have done and
I have been silent;
you thought that I was one
like yourself.
But now I rebuke you, and lay
the charge before you.

[h]Or *wealth*
[i]Gk Syr Tg: Heb *mountains*
[j]Or *make thanksgiving your sacrifice to God*

22"Mark this, then, you who forget
God,
lest I rend, and there be
none to deliver!
23He who brings thanksgiving as
his sacrifice honors me;
to him who orders his way
aright
I will show the salvation of
God!"

PRAYER FOR CLEANSING AND PARDON

To the choirmaster. A Psalm of David, when Nathan the prophet came to him, after he had gone in to Bathsheba.

51 *Have mercy on me, O God, according to thy steadfast
love;
according to thy abundant
mercy blot out my
transgressions.
2Wash me thoroughly from my
iniquity,
and cleanse me from my sin!
3For I know my transgressions,
and my sin is ever before me.
4Against thee, thee only, have I
sinned,
and done that which is evil
in thy sight,
so that thou art justified in thy
sentence
and blameless in thy
judgment.
5Behold, I was brought forth in
iniquity,
and in sin did my mother
conceive me.
6Behold, thou desirest truth in the
inward being;
therefore teach me wisdom
in my secret heart.
7Purge me with hyssop, and I shall
be clean;
wash me, and I shall be
whiter than snow.
8Fill[a] me with joy and gladness;
let the bones which thou
hast broken rejoice.
9Hide thy face from my sins,
and blot out all my
iniquities.
10Create in me a clean heart, O
God,
and put a new and right[b]
spirit within me.
11Cast me not away from thy
presence,
and take not thy holy Spirit
from me.
12Restore to me the joy of thy
salvation,
and uphold me with a willing spirit.
13Then I will teach transgressors
thy ways,
and sinners will return to
thee.
14Deliver me from bloodguiltiness,[c] O God,
thou God of my salvation,
and my tongue will
sing aloud of thy
deliverance.
15O Lord, open thou my lips,
and my mouth shall show
forth thy praise.
16For thou hast no delight in
sacrifice;
were I to give a burnt offering, thou wouldst not
be pleased.
17The sacrifice acceptable to God[d]
is a broken spirit;
a broken and contrite heart,
O God, thou wilt not
despise.
18Do good to Zion in thy good
pleasure;
rebuild the walls of
Jerusalem,
19then wilt thou delight in right
sacrifices,
in burnt offerings and whole
burnt offerings;
then bulls will be offered on
thy altar.

[a] Syr: Heb *Make to hear*
[b] Or *steadfast*
[c] Or *death*
[d] Or *My sacrifice, O God*

JUDGMENT ON THE DECEITFUL

To the choirmaster. A Maskil of David, when Doeg, the Edomite, came and told Saul, "David has come to the house of Ahimelech."

52 Why do you boast, O mighty man,
of mischief done against the godly?[e]
All the day [2]you are plotting destruction.
Your tongue is like a sharp razor,
you worker of treachery.
3 You love evil more than good,
and lying more than speaking the truth. *Selah*
4 You love all words that devour,
O deceitful tongue.
5 But God will break you down for ever;
he will snatch and tearyou from your tent;
he will uproot you from the land of the living. *Selah*
6 The righteous shall see, and fear,
and shall laugh at him, saying,
7 "See the man who would not make
God his refuge,
but trusted in the abundanc of his riches,
and sought refuge in his wealth!"[f]
8 But I am like a green olive tree
in the house of God.
I trust in the steadfast love of God
for ever and ever.
9 I will thank thee for ever,
because thou hast done it.
I will proclaim[g] thy name, for it is good,
in the presence of the godly.

DENUNCIATION OF GODLESSNESS

To the choirmaster: according to Mahalath. A Maskil of David.

53 The fool says in his heart,
"There is no God."
They are corrupt, doing abominable iniquity;
there is none that does good.
2 God looks down from heaven
upon the sons of men
to see if there are any that are wise,
that seek after God.
3 They have all fallen away;
they are all alike depraved;
there is none that does good,
no, not one.
4 Have those who work evil no understanding,
who eat up my people as they eat bread,
and do not call upon God?
5 There they are, in great terror,
in terror such as has not been!
For God will scatter the bones of the ungodly;[h]
they will be put to shame,[i]
for God has rejected them.
6 O that deliverance for Israel
would come from Zion!
When God restores the fortunes of his people,
Jacob will rejoice and Israel be glad.

PRAYER FOR VINDICATION

To the choirmaster: with stringed instruments. A Maskil of David, when the Ziphites went and told Saul, "David is in hiding among us."

54 Save me, O God, by thy name,
and vindicate me by thy might.
2 Hear my prayer, O God;
give ear to the words of my mouth.

[e] Cn Compare Syr: Heb *the kindness of God*
[f] Syr Tg: Heb *his destruction*
[g] Cn: Heb *wait for*
[h] Cn Compare Gk Syr: Heb *him who encamps against you*
[i] Gk: Heb *you will put to shame*

3For insolent men[a] have risen
against me,
ruthless men seek my life;
they do not set God before
them. *Selah*
4Behold, God is my helper;
the Lord is the upholder[b] of
my life.
5He will requite my enemies with
evil;
in thy faithfulness put an
end to them.
6With a freewill offering I will
sacrifice to thee;
I will give thanks to thy
name, O LORD, for it
is good.
7For thou hast delivered me from
every trouble,
and my eye has looked in tri-
umph on my enemies.

COMPLAINT ABOUT A FRIEND'S TREACHERY

To the choirmaster: with stringed instruments. A Maskil of David.

55 Give ear to my prayer, O God;
and hide not thyself from my
supplication!
2Attend to me, and answer me;
I am overcome by my
trouble.
I am distraught 3by the noise of
the enemy,
because of the oppression of
the wicked.
For they bring[c] trouble upon
me,
and in anger they cherish
enmity against me.
4My heart is in anguish within
me,
the terrors of death have
fallen upon me.
5Fear and trembling come upon
me,
and horror overwhelms me.
6And I say, "O that I had wings
like a dove!
I would fly away and be at
rest;
7yea, I would wander afar,
I would lodge in the
wilderness, *Selah*
8I would haste to find me a
shelter
from the raging wind and
tempest."
9Destroy their plans,[d] O Lord,
confuse their tongues;
for I see violence and strife
in the city.
10Day and night they go around it
on its walls;
and mischief and trouble are
within it,
11ruin is in its midst;
oppression and fraud
do not depart from its mar-
ket place.
12It is not an enemy who taunts
me—
then I could bear it;
it is not an adversary who
deals insolently with
me—
then I could hide from him.
But it is you, my equal,
my companion, my familiar
friend.
We used to hold sweet converse
together;
within God's house we
walked in fellowship.
15Let death[e] come upon them;
let them go down to Sheol
alive;
let them go away in terror
into their graves.[f]
16But I call upon God;
and the LORD will save me.
17Evening and morning and at
noon
I utter my complaint and
moan,

[a] Another reading is *strangers*
[b] Gk Syr Jerome: Heb *of* or *with those who uphold*
[c] Cn Compare Gk: Heb *they cause to totter*
[d] Tg: Heb lacks *their plans*
[e] Or *desolations*
[f] Cn: Heb *evils are in their habitation, in their midst*

and he will hear my voice.
18He will deliver my soul in
safety
from the battle that I wage,
for many are arrayed against
me.
19God will give ear, and humble
them,
he who is enthroned from
of old;
because they keep no law,[g]
and do not fear God. *Selah*
20My companion stretched out his
hand against his friends,
he violated his covenant.
21His speech was smoother than
butter,
yet war was in his heart;
his words were softer than oil,
yet they were drawn swords.
22Cast your burden[h] on the LORD,
and he will sustain you;
he will never permit
the righteous to be moved.
23But thou, O God, wilt cast them
down
into the lowest pit;
men of blood and treachery
shall not live out half their
days.
But I will trust in thee.

TRUST IN GOD UNDER PERSECUTION

To the choirmaster: according to The Dove on Far-off Terebinths. A Miktam of David, when the Philistines seized him in Gath.

56 Be gracious to me, O God,
for men trample upon me;
all day long foemen oppress
me;
2my enemies trample upon me all
day long,
for many fight against me
proudly.
3When I am afraid,
I put my trust in thee.
4In God, whose word I praise,
in God I trust without a
fear.
What can flesh do to me?
5All day long they seek to injure
my cause;
all their thoughts are against
me for evil.
6They band themselves together,
they lurk,
they watch my steps.
As they have waited for my
life,
7so recompense[i] them for
their crime;
in wrath cast down the peo-
ples, O God!
8Thou hast kept count of my
tossings;
put thou my tears in thy
bottle!
Are they not in thy book?
9Then my enemies will be turned
back
in the day when I call.
This I know, that[j] God is
for me.
10In God, whose word I praise,
in the LORD, whose word I
praise,
11in God I trust without a fear.
What can man do to me?
12My vows to thee I must perform,
O God;
I will render thank offerings
to thee.
13For thou hast delivered my soul
from death,
yea, my feet from falling,
that I may walk before God
in the light of life.

PRAISE AND ASSURANCE UNDER PERSECUTION

To the choirmaster: according to Do Not Destroy. A Miktam of David, when he fled from Saul, in the cave.

57 Be merciful to me, O God, be mer-
ciful to me,

[g] Or *do not change*
[h] Or *what he has given you*
[i] Cn: Heb *deliver*
[j] Or *because*

for in thee my soul takes refuge;
in the shadow of thy wings I will take refuge,
till the storms of destruction pass by.
2I cry to God Most High,
to God who fulfils his purpose for me.
3He will send from heaven and save me,
he will put to shame those who trample upon me. *Selah*
God will send forth his steadfast love and his faithfulness!
4I lie in the midst of lions
that greedily devour[a] the sons of men;
their teeth are spears and arrows,
their tongues sharp swords.
5Be exalted, O God, above the heavens!
Let thy glory be over all the earth!
6They set a net for my steps;
my soul was bowed down.
They dug a pit in my way,
but they have fallen into it themselves. *Selah*
7My heart is steadfast, O God,
my heart is steadfast!
I will sing and make melody!
8Awake, my soul!
Awake, O harp and lyre!
I will awake the dawn!
9I will give thanks to thee, O Lord, among the peoples;
I will sing praises to thee among the nations.
10For thy steadfast love is great to the heavens,
thy faithfulness to the clouds.
11Be exalted, O God, above the heavens!
Let thy glory be over all the earth!

PRAYER FOR VENGEANCE

To the choirmaster: according to Do Not Destroy. A Miktam of David.

58 Do you indeed decree what is right, you gods?[b]
Do you judge the sons of men uprightly?
2Nay, in your hearts you devise wrongs;
your hands deal out violence on earth.
3The wicked go astray from the womb,
they err from their birth, speaking lies.
4They have venom like the venom of a serpent,
like the deaf adder that stops its ear,
5so that it does not hear the voice of charmers
or of the cunning enchanter.
6O God, break the teeth in their mouths;
tear out the fangs of the young lions, O LORD!
7Let them vanish like water that runs away;
like grass let them be trodden down and wither.[c]
8Let them be like the snail which dissolves into slime,
like the untimely birth that never sees the sun.
9Sooner than your pots can feel the heat of thorns,
whether green or ablaze, may he sweep them away!
10The righteous will rejoice when he sees the vengeance;
he will bathe his feet in the blood of the wicked.
11Men will say, "Surely there is a reward for the righteous;
surely there is a God who judges on earth."

[a] Cn: Heb *are aflame*
[b] Or *mighty lords*
[c] Cn: Heb uncertain

PRAYER FOR DELIVERANCE FROM ENEMIES

To the choirmaster: according to Do Not Destroy. A Miktam of David, when Saul sent men to watch his house in order to kill him.

59 Deliver me from my enemies, O my God,
protect me from those who rise up against me,
2deliver me from those who work evil,
and save me from bloodthirsty men.
3For lo, they lie in wait for my life;
fierce men band themselves against me.
For no transgression or sin of mine, O LORD,
4for no fault of mine, they run and make ready.
Rouse thyself, come to my help, and see!
5Thou, LORD God of hosts, art God of Israel.
Awake to punish all the nations;
spare none of those who treacherously plot evil. *Selah*
6Each evening they come back,
howling like dogs
and prowling about the city.
7There they are, bellowing with their mouths,
and snarling with[d] their lips—
for "Who," they think, "will hear us?"
8But thou, O LORD, dost laugh at them;
thou dost hold all the nations in derision.
9O my Strength, I will sing praises to thee;[e]
for thou, O God, art my fortress.
10My God in his steadfast love will meet me;
my God will let me look in triumph on my enemies.
11Slay them not, lest my people forget;
make them totter by thy power, and bring them down,
O Lord, our shield!
12For the sin of their mouths, the words of their lips,
let them be trapped in their pride.
For the cursing and lies which they utter, 13consume them in wrath,
consume them till they are no more,
that men may know that God rules over Jacob
to the ends of the earth. *Selah*
14Each evening they come back,
howling like dogs
and prowling about the city.
15They roam about for food,
and growl if they do not get their fill.
16But I will sing of thy might;
I will sing aloud of thy steadfast love in the morning.
For thou hast been to me a fortress
and a refuge in the day of my distress.
17O my Strength, I will sing praises to thee,
for thou, O God, art my fortress,
the God who shows me steadfast love.

PRAYER FOR NATIONAL VICTORY AFTER DEFEAT

To the choirmaster: according to Shushan Eduth. A Miktam of David; for instruction; when he strove with Aram-naharaim and with Aram-zobah, and when Joab on his return killed twelve thousand of Edom in the Valley of Salt.

60 O God, thou hast rejected us, broken our defenses;

[d]Cn: Heb *swords in*
[e]Syr: Heb *I will watch for thee*

thou hast been angry; oh,
restore us.
2Thou hast made the land to quake,
thou hast rent it open;
repair its breaches, for it
totters.
3Thou hast made thy people suffer
hard things;
thou hast given us wine to
drink that made us
reel.
4Thou hast set up a banner for
those who fear thee,
to rally to it from the
bow.[a] *Selah*
5That thy beloved may be
delivered,
give victory by thy right
hand and answer us!
6God has spoken in his
sanctuary:[b]
"With exultation I will di-
vide up Shechem
and portion out the Vale of
Succoth.
7Gilead is mine; Manas´seh is mine;
E´phraim is my helmet;
Judah is my scepter.
8Moab is my washbasin;
upon Edom I cast my shoe;
over Philistia I shout in
triumph."
9Who will bring me to the forti-
fied city?
Who will lead me to Edom?
10Hast thou not rejected us, O God?
Thou dost not go forth, O
God, with our armies.
11O grant us help against the foe,
for vain is the help of man!
12With God we shall do valiantly;
it is he who will tread down
our foes.

ASSURANCE OF GOD'S PROTECTION

To the choirmaster: with stringed
instruments. A Psalm of David.

61 Hear my cry, O God,
listen to my prayer;
2from the end of the earth I call
to thee,
when my heart is faint.
Lead thou me
to the rock that is higher
than I;
3for thou art my refuge,
a strong tower against the
enemy.
4Let me dwell in thy tent for ever!
Oh to be safe under the
shelter of thy
wings! *Selah*
5For thou, O God, hast heard my
vows,
thou hast given me the
heritage of those who
fear thy name.
6Prolong the life of the king;
may his years endure to all
generations!
7May he be enthroned for ever
before God;
bid steadfast love and faith-
fulness watch over
him!
8So will I ever sing praises to thy
name,
as I pay my vows day after
day.

SONG OF TRUST IN GOD ALONE

To the choirmaster: according to
Jeduthun. A Psalm of David.

62 For God alone my soul waits in
silence;
from him comes my
salvation.
2He only is my rock and my
salvation,
my fortress; I shall not be
greatly moved.
3How long will you set upon a
man
to shatter him, all of you,
like a leaning wall, a totter-
ing fence?
4They only plan to thrust him
down from his eminence.
They take pleasure in
falsehood.

[a]Gk Syr Jerome: Heb *truth*
[b]Or *by his holiness*

They bless with their mouths,
but inwardly they
curse. *Selah*
5For God alone my soul waits in
silence,
for my hope is from him.
6He only is my rock and my
salvation,
my fortress; I shall not be
shaken.
7On God rests my deliverance and
my honor;
my mighty rock, my refuge
is God.
8Trust in him at all times, O
people;
pour out your heart before
him;
God is a refuge for us. *Selah*
9Men of low estate are but a breath,
men of high estate are a
delusion;
in the balances they go up;
they are together lighter
than a breath.
10Put no confidence in extortion,
set no vain hopes on
robbery;
if riches increase, set not
your heart on them.
11Once God has spoken;
twice have I heard this:
that power belongs to God;
12and that to thee, O Lord, be-
longs steadfast love.
For thou dost requite a man
according to his work.

COMFORT AND ASSURANCE IN GOD'S PRESENCE

A Psalm of David, when he was
in the Wilderness of Judah.

63 O God, thou art my God, I seek
thee,
my soul thirsts for thee;
my flesh faints for thee,
as in a dry and weary land
where no water is.
2So I have looked upon thee in the
sanctuary,
beholding thy power and
glory.
3Because thy steadfast love is
better than life,
my lips will praise thee.
4So I will bless thee as long as I
live;
I will lift up my hands and
call on thy name.
5My soul is feasted as with mar-
row and fat,
and my mouth praises thee
with joyful lips,
6when I think of thee upon my
bed,
and meditate on thee in the
watches of the night;
7for thou hast been my help,
and in the shadow of thy
wings I sing for joy.
8My soul clings to thee;
thy right hand upholds me.
9But those who seek to destroy
my life
shall go down into the
depths of the earth;
10they shall be given over to the
power of the sword,
they shall be prey for
jackals.
11But the king shall rejoice in God;
all who swear by him shall
glory;
for the mouths of liars will
be stopped.

PRAYER FOR PROTECTION FROM ENEMIES

To the choirmaster. A Psalm of David.

64 Hear my voice, O God, in my
complaint;
preserve my life from dread
of the enemy,
2hide me from the secret plots of
the wicked,
from the scheming of
evildoers,
3who whet their tongues like
swords,
who aim bitter words like
arrows,
4shooting from ambush at the
blameless,

shooting at him suddenly
and without fear.
5They hold fast to their evil
purpose;
they talk of laying snares
secretly,
thinking, "Who can see us?
[a]6Who can search out
our crimes?[b]
We have thought out a cunningly conceived plot."
For the inward mind and
heart of a man are
deep!
7But God will shoot his arrow at
them;
they will be wounded
suddenly.
8Because of their tongue he will
bring them to ruin;[c]
all who see them will wag
their heads.
9Then all men will fear;
they will tell what God has
wrought,
and ponder what he has
done.
10Let the righteous rejoice in the
LORD,
and take refuge in him!
Let all the upright in heart
glory!

THANKSGIVING FOR EARTH'S BOUNTY

To the choirmaster. A Psalm
of David. A Song.

65 Praise is due to thee,
O God, in Zion;
and to thee shall vows be
performed,
2O thou who hearest prayer!
To thee shall all flesh come 3on
account of sins.
When our transgressions prevail over us, [d]
thou dost forgive them.
4Blessed is he whom thou dost
choose and bring near,
to dwell in thy courts!
We shall be satisfied with the
goodness of thy house,
thy holy temple!
5By dread deeds thou dost answer
us with deliverance,
O God of our salvation,
who art the hope of all the
ends of the earth,
and of the farthest seas;
6who by thy strength hast established the mountains,
being girded with might;
7who dost still the roaring of the
seas,
the roaring of their waves,
the tumult of the peoples;
8so that those who dwell at earth's
farthest bounds
are afraid at thy signs;
thou makest the outgoings of
the morning and the
evening
to shout for joy.
9Thou visitest the earth and
waterest it,
thou greatly enrichest it;
the river of God is full of water;
thou providest their grain,
for so thou hast prepared it.
10Thou waterest its furrows
abundantly,
settling its ridges,
softening it with showers,
and blessing its growth.
11Thou crownest the year with thy
bounty;
the tracks of thy chariot drip
with fatness.
12The pastures of the wilderness
drip,
the hills gird themselves
with joy,
13the meadows clothe themselves
with flocks,
the valleys deck themselves
with grain,
they shout and sing together
for joy.

[a]Syr: Heb *them*
[b]Cn: Heb *they search out crimes*
[c]Cn: Heb *They will bring him to ruin, their tongue being against them*
[d]Gk: Heb *me*

PRAISE FOR GOD'S GOODNESS TO ISRAEL

To the choirmaster. A Song. A Psalm.

66 Make a joyful noise to God, all the
earth;
2sing the glory of his name;
give to him glorious praise!
3Say to God, "How terrible are thy
deeds!
So great is thy power that
thy enemies cringe
before thee.
4All the earth worships thee;
they sing praises to thee,
sing praises to thy
name." *Selah*
5Come and see what God has
done:
he is terrible in his deeds
among men.
6He turned the sea into dry land;
men passed through the
river on foot.
There did we rejoice in him,
7who rules by his might
for ever,
whose eyes keep watch on the
nations—
let not the rebellious exalt
themselves. *Selah*
8Bless our God, O peoples,
let the sound of his praise be
heard,
9who has kept us among the
living,
and has not let our feet slip.
10For thou, O God, hast tested us;
thou hast tried us as silver
is tried.
11Thou didst bring us into the
net;
thou didst lay affliction on
our loins;
12thou didst let men ride over our
heads;
we went through fire and
through water;
yet thou hast brought us forth
to a spacious place.[e]
13I will come into thy house with
burnt offerings;
I will pay thee my vows,
14that which my lips uttered
and my mouth promised
when I was in
trouble.
15I will offer to thee burnt offer-
ings of fatlings,
with the smoke of the sacri-
fice of rams;
I will make an offering of bulls
and goats. *Selah*
16Come and hear, all you who fear
God,
and I will tell what he has
done for me.
17I cried aloud to him,
and he was extolled with my
tongue.
18If I had cherished iniquity in my
heart,
the Lord would not have
listened.
19But truly God has listened;
he has given heed to the
voice of my prayer.
20Blessed be God,
because he has not rejected
my prayer
or removed his steadfast love
from me!

THE NATIONS CALLED TO PRAISE GOD

To the choirmaster: with stringed
instruments. A Psalm. A Song.

67 May God be gracious to us and
bless us
and make his face to shine
upon us, *Selah*
2that thy way may be known upon
earth,
thy saving power among all
nations.
3Let the peoples praise thee, O
God;
let all the peoples praise
thee!
4Let the nations be glad and sing
for joy,
for thou dost judge the peo-
ples with equity

[e]Cn Compare Gk Syr Jerome Tg: Heb *saturation*

and guide the nations upon
earth. *Selah*
5Let the peoples praise thee, O
God;
let all the peoples praise
thee!
6The earth has yielded its
increase;
God, our God, has blessed
us.
7God has blessed us;
let all the ends of the earth
fear him!

PRAISE AND THANKSGIVING

To the choirmaster. A Psalm
of David. A Song.

68 *Let God arise, let his enemies be
scattered;
let those who hate him flee
before him!
2As smoke is driven away, so drive
them away;
as wax melts before fire,
let the wicked perish before
God!
3But let the righteous be joyful;
let them exult before God;
let them be jubilant with joy!
4Sing to God, sing praises to his
name;
lift up a song to him who
rides upon the
clouds;[a]
his name is the LORD, exult
before him!
5Father of the fatherless and pro-
tector of widows
is God in his holy habitation.
6God gives the desolate a home to
dwell in;
he leads out the prisoners to
prosperity;
but the rebellious dwell in a
parched land.
7O God, when thou didst go forth
before thy people,
when thou didst march
through the
wilderness, *Selah*
8the earth quaked, the heavens
poured down rain,
at the presence of God;
yon Sinai quaked at the pres-
ence of God,
the God of Israel.
9Rain in abundance, O God, thou
didst shed abroad;
thou didst restore thy heri-
tage as it languished;
10thy flock found a dwelling in it;
in thy goodness, O God,
thou didst provide for
the needy.
11The Lord gives the command;
great is the host of those
who bore the tidings:
12"The kings of the
armies, they flee,
they flee!"
The women at home divide the
spoil,
13though they stay among the
sheepfolds—
the wings of a dove covered
with silver,
its pinions with green gold.
14When the Almighty scattered
kings there,
snow fell on Zalmon.
15O mighty mountain, mountain of
Bashan;
O many-peaked mountain,
mountain of Bashan!
16Why lookyou with envy, O ma-
ny-peaked mountain,
at the mount which God de-
sired for his abode,
yea, where the LORD will
dwell for ever?
17With mighty chariotry, twice ten
thousand,
thousands upon thousands,
the Lord came from Sinai
into the holy place.[b]
18Thou didst ascend the high
mount,
leading captives in thy train,
and receiving gifts among
men,

[a] Or *cast up a highway for him who rides through the deserts*
[b] Cn: Heb *The Lord among them Sinai in the holy place*

even among the rebellious,
that the LORD God may dwell there.
19Blessed be the Lord,
who daily bears us up;
God is our salvation. *Selah*
20Our God is a God of salvation;
and to GOD, the Lord,
belongs escape from death.
21But God will shatter the heads of his enemies,
the hairy crown of him who walks in his guilty ways.
22The Lord said,
"I will bring them back from Bashan,
I will bring them back from the depths of the sea,
23that you may bathe[c] your feet in blood,
that the tongues of your dogs may have their portion from the foe."
24Thy solemn processions are seen,[d] O God,
the processions of my God, my King, into the sanctuary—
25the singers in front, the minstrels last,
between them maidens playing timbrels:
26"Bless God in the great congregation,
the LORD, O you who are of Israel's fountain!"
27There is Benjamin, the least of them, in the lead,
the princes of Judah in their throng,
the princes of Zeb´ulun, the princes of Naph´tali.
28Summon thy might, O God;
show thy strength, O God, thou who hast wrought for us.
29Because of thy temple at Jerusalem
kings bear gifts to thee.
30Rebuke the beasts that dwell among the reeds,
the herd of bulls with the calves of the peoples.
Trample[e] under foot those who lust after tribute;
scatter the peoples who delight in war.[f]
31Let bronze be brought from Egypt;
let Ethiopia hasten to stretch out her hands to God.
32Sing to God, O kingdoms of the earth;
sing praises to the Lord, *Selah*
33to him who rides in the heavens, the ancient heavens;
lo, he sends forth his voice, his mighty voice.
34Ascribe power to God,
whose majesty is over Israel,
and his power is in the skies.
35Terrible is God in his[g] sanctuary,
the God of Israel,
he gives power and strength to his people.
Blessed be God!

PRAYER FOR DELIVERANCE FROM PERSECUTION

To the choirmaster: according to Lilies. A Psalm of David.

69 Save me, O God!
For the waters have come up to my neck.
2I sink in deep mire,
where there is no foothold;
I have come into deep waters,
and the flood sweeps over me.
3I am weary with my crying;
my throat is parched.
My eyes grow dim
with waiting for my God.

[c]Gk Syr Tg: Heb *shatter*
[d]Or *have been seen*
[e]Cn: Heb *trampling*
[f]The Hebrew of verse 30 is obscure
[g]Gk: Heb *from thy*

4More in number than the hairs of
my head
are those who hate me without cause;
mighty are those who would
destroy me,
those who attack me with
lies.
What I did not steal
must I now restore?
5O God, thou knowest my folly;
the wrongs I have done
are not hidden from
thee.
6Let not those who hope in thee
be put to shame through
me,
O Lord GOD of hosts;
let not those who seek thee
be brought to dishonor
through me,
O God of Israel.
7For it is for thy sake that I have
borne reproach,
that shame has covered my
face.
8I have become a stranger to my
brethren,
an alien to my mother's
sons.
9For zeal for thy house has consumed me,
and the insults of those
who insult thee have
fallen on me.
10When I humbled[a] my soul with
fasting,
it became my reproach.
11When I made sackcloth my
clothing,
I became a byword to them.
12I am the talk of those who sit in
the gate,
and the drunkards make
songs about me.
13But as for me, my prayer is to
thee, O LORD.
At an acceptable time, O
God,
in the abundance of thy
steadfast love answer me.
With thy faithful help
14rescue me
from sinking in the mire;
let me be delivered from my
enemies
and from the deep waters.
15Let not the flood sweep over
me,
or the deep swallow me up,
or the pit close its mouth
over me.
16Answer me, O LORD, for thy
steadfast love is good;
according to thy abundant
mercy, turn to me.
17Hide not thy face from thy
servant;
for I am in distress, make
haste to answer me.
18Draw near to me, redeem me,
set me free because of my
enemies!
19Thou knowest my reproach,
and my shame and my
dishonor;
my foes are all known to
thee.
20Insults have broken my heart,
so that I am in despair.
I looked for pity, but there was
none;
and for comforters, but I
found none.
21They gave me poison for food,
and for my thirst they gave
me vinegar to drink.
22Let their own table before them
become a snare;
let their sacrificial feasts[b] be
a trap.
23Let their eyes be darkened, so
that they cannot see;
and make their loins tremble
continually.
24Pour out thy indignation upon
them,
and let thy burning anger
overtake them.

[a]Gk Syr: Heb *I wept with fasting my soul* or *I made my soul mourn with fasting*
[b]Tg: Heb *for security*

[25]May their camp be a desolation,
let no one dwell in their tents.
[26]For they persecute him whom thou hast smitten,
and him[c] whom thou hast wounded, they afflict still more.[d]
[27]Add to them punishment upon punishment;
may they have no acquittal from thee.
[28]Let them be blotted out of the book of the living;
let them not be enrolled among the righteous.
[29]But I am afflicted and in pain;
let thy salvation, O God, set me on high!
[30]I will praise the name of God with a song;
I will magnify him with thanksgiving.
[31]This will please the LORD more than an ox
or a bull with horns and hoofs.
[32]Let the oppressed see it and be glad;
you who seek God, let your hearts revive.
[33]For the LORD hears the needy,
and does not despise his own that are in bonds.
[34]Let heaven and earth praise him,
the seas and everything that moves therein.
[35]For God will save Zion
and rebuild the cities of Judah;
and his servants shall dwell[e] there and possess it;
[36]the children of his servants shall inherit it,
and those who love his name shall dwell in it.

PRAYER FOR DELIVERANCE FROM ENEMIES

To the choirmaster. A Psalm of David, for the memorial offering.

70 Be pleased, O God, to deliver me!
O LORD, make haste to help me!
[2]Let them be put to shame and confusion
who seek my life!
Let them be turned back and brought to dishonor
who desire my hurt!
[3]Let them be appalled because of their shame
who say, "Aha, Aha!"
[4]May all who seek thee
rejoice and be glad in thee!
May those who love thy salvation
say evermore, "God is great!"
[5]But I am poor and needy;
hasten to me, O God!
Thou art my help and my deliverer;
O LORD, do not tarry!

PRAYER FOR LIFELONG PROTECTION AND HELP

71 In thee, O LORD, do I take refuge;
let me never be put to shame!
[2]In thy righteousness deliver me and rescue me;
incline thy ear to me, and save me!
[3]Be thou to me a rock of refuge,
a strong fortress,[f] to save me,
for thou art my rock and my fortress.
[4]Rescue me, O my God, from the hand of the wicked,
from the grasp of the unjust and cruel man.
[5]For thou, O Lord, art my hope,
my trust, O LORD, from my youth.

[c]One Ms Tg Compare Syr: Heb *those*
[d]Gk Syr: Heb *recount the pain of*
[e]Syr: Heb *and they shall dwell*
[f]Gk Compare 31.3: Heb *to come continually thou hast commanded*

6Upon thee I have leaned from my birth;
thou art he who took me from my mother's womb.
My praise is continually of thee.
7I have been as a portent to many;
but thou art my strong refuge.
8My mouth is filled with thy praise,
and with thy glory all the day.
9Do not cast me off in the time of old age;
forsake me not when my strength is spent.
10For my enemies speak concerning me,
those who watch for my life consult together,
11and say, "God has forsaken him;
pursue and seize him,
for there is none to deliver him."
12O God, be not far from me;
O my God, make haste to help me!
13May my accusers be put to shame and consumed;
with scorn and disgrace may they be covered
who seek my hurt.
14But I will hope continually,
and will praise thee yet more and more.
15My mouth will tell of thy righteous acts,
of thy deeds of salvation all the day,
for their number is past my knowledge.
16With the mighty deeds of the Lord GOD I will come,
I will praise thy righteousness, *thine alone.*
17O God, from my youth thou hast taught me,
and I still proclaim thy wondrous deeds.
18So even to old age and gray hairs,
O God, do not forsake me,
till I proclaim thy might
to all the generations to come.[a]
Thy power 19and thy righteousness, O God,
reach the high heavens.
Thou who hast done great things,
O God, who is like thee?
20Thou who hast made me see many sore troubles
wilt revive me again;
from the depths of the earth
thou wilt bring me up again.
21Thou wilt increase my honor,
and comfort me again.
22I will also praise thee with the harp
for thy faithfulness, O my God;
I will sing praises to thee with the lyre,
O Holy One of Israel.
23My lips will shout for joy,
when I sing praises to thee;
my soul also, which thou hast rescued.
24And my tongue will talk of thy righteous help
all the day long,
for they have been put to shame and disgraced
who sought to do me hurt.

PRAYER FOR GUIDANCE AND SUPPORT FOR THE KING

A Psalm of Solomon.

72 Give the king thy justice, O God,
and thy righteousness to the royal son!
2May he judge thy people with righteousness,
and thy poor with justice!
3Let the mountains bear prosperity for the people,
and the hills, in righteousness!
4May he defend the cause of the

[a]Gk Compare Syr: Heb *to a generation, to all that come*

poor of the people,
give deliverance to the needy,
and crush the oppressor!
5 May he live[b] while the sun endures,
and as long as the moon, throughout all generations!
6 May he be like rain that falls on the mown grass,
like showers that water the earth!
7 In his days may righteousness flourish,
and peace abound, till the moon be no more!
8 May he have dominion from sea to sea,
and from the River to the ends of the earth!
9 May his foes[c] bow down before him,
and his enemies lick the dust!
10 May the kings of Tarshish and of the isles
render him tribute,
may the kings of Sheba and Seba bring gifts!
11 May all kings fall down before him,
all nations serve him!
12 For he delivers the needy when he calls,
the poor and him who has no helper.
13 He has pity on the weak and the needy,
and saves the lives of the needy.
14 From oppression and violence he redeems their life;
and precious is their blood in his sight.
15 Long may he live,
may gold of Sheba be given to him!
May prayer be made for him continually,
and blessings invoked for him all the day!
16 May there be abundance of grain in the land;
on the tops of the mountains may it wave;
may its fruit be like Lebanon;
and may men blossom forth from the cities
like the grass of the field!
17 May his name endure for ever,
his fame continue as long as the sun!
May men bless themselves by him,
all nations call him blessed!
18 Blessed be the LORD, the God of Israel,
who alone does wondrous things.
19 Blessed be his glorious name for ever;
may his glory fill the whole earth!
20 Amen and Amen!The prayers of David, the son of Jesse, are ended.

BOOK III

PLEA FOR RELIEF FROM OPPRESSORS

A Psalm of Asaph.

73 Truly God is good to the upright,
to those who are pure in heart.[d]
2 But as for me, my feet had almost stumbled,
my steps had well nigh slipped.
3 For I was envious of the arrogant,
when I saw the prosperity of the wicked.
4 For they have no pangs;
their bodies are sound and sleek.
5 They are not in trouble as other men are;
they are not stricken like other men.
6 Therefore pride is their necklace;
violence covers them as a garment.

[b] Gk: Heb *may they fear thee*
[c] Cn: Heb *those who dwell in the wilderness*
[d] Or *Truly God is good to Israel, to those who are pure in heart*

7 Their eyes swell out with fatness,
their hearts overflow with follies.
8 They scoff and speak with malice;
loftily they threaten oppression.
9 They set their mouths against the heavens,
and their tongue struts through the earth.
10 Therefore the people turn and praise them;[a]
and find no fault in them.[b]
11 And they say, "How can God know?
Is there knowledge in the Most High?"
12 Behold, these are the wicked;
always at ease, they increase in riches.
13 All in vain have I kept my heart clean
and washed my hands in innocence.
14 For all the day long I have been stricken,
and chastened every morning.
15 If I had said, "I will speak thus,"
I would have been untrue to the generation of thy children.
16 But when I thought how to understand this,
it seemed to me a wearisome task,
17 until I went into the sanctuary of God;
then I perceived their end.
18 Truly thou dost set them in slippery places;
thou dost make them fall to ruin.
19 How they are destroyed in a moment,
swept away utterly by terrors!
20 They are[c] like a dream when one awakes,
on awaking you despise their phantoms.
21 When my soul was embittered,
when I was pricked in heart,
22 I was stupid and ignorant,
I was like a beast toward thee.
23 Nevertheless I am continually with thee;
thou dost hold my right hand.
24 Thou dost guide me with thy counsel,
and afterward thou wilt receive me to glory.[d]
25 Whom have I in heaven but thee?
And there is nothing upon earth that I desire besides thee.
26 My flesh and my heart may fail,
but God is the strength[e] of my heart and my portion for ever.
27 For lo, those who are far from thee shall perish;
thou dost put an end to those who are false to thee.
28 But for me it is good to be near God;
I have made the Lord GOD my refuge,
that I may tell of all thy works.

PLEA FOR HELP IN TIME OF NATIONAL HUMILIATION

A Maskil of Asaph.

74 O God, why dost thou cast us off for ever?
Why does thy anger smoke against the sheep of thy pasture?
2 Remember thy congregation,

[a] Cn: Heb *his people return hither*
[b] Cn: Heb *abundant waters are drained by them*
[c] Cn: Heb *Lord*
[d] Or *honor*
[e] Heb *rock*

which thou hast gotten
of old,
which thou hast redeemed
to be the tribe of thy
heritage!
Remember Mount Zion,
where thou hast
dwelt.
3Direct thy steps to the perpetual
ruins;
the enemy has destroyed
everything in the
sanctuary!
4Thy foes have roared in the midst
of thy holy place;
they set up their own signs
for signs.
5At the upper entrance they
hacked
the wooden trellis with
axes.[f]
6And then all its carved wood
they broke down with hatch-
ets and hammers.
7They set thy sanctuary on fire;
to the ground they desecrat-
ed the dwelling place
of thy name.
8They said to themselves, "We
will utterly subdue them";
they burned all the meeting
places of God in the
land.
9We do not see our signs;
there is no longer any
prophet,
and there is none among us
who knows how long.
10How long, O God is the foe to
scoff?
Is the enemy revile thy
name r ever?
11Why dost thou hd back thy
hand,
why dost thoteep thy right
hand i thy bosom?
12Yet God my King from of old,
working salvan in the
midst the earth.

13Thou didst divide the sea by thy
might;
thou didst break the heads
of the dragons on the
waters.
14Thou didst crush the heads of
Leviathan,
thou didst give him as food[h]
for the creatures of
the wilderness.
15Thou didst cleave open springs
and brooks;
thou didst dry up ever-flow-
ing streams.
16Thine is the day, thine also the
night;
thou hast established the
luminaries and the
sun.
17Thou hast fixed all the bounds
of the earth;
thou hast made summer and
winter.
18Remember this, O LORD, how
the enemy scoffs,
and an impious people
reviles thy name.
19Do not deliver the soul of thy
dove to the wild beasts;
do not forget the life of thy
poor for ever.
20Have regard for thy[i] covenant;
for the dark places of the
land are full of
the habitations of
violence.
21Let not the downtrodden be put
to shame;
let the poor and needy praise
thy name.
22Arise, O God, plead thy cause;
remember how the impious
scoff at thee all the
day!
23Do not forget the clamor of thy
foes,
the uproar of thy adversar-
ies which goes up
continually!

[f] Cn Compare Gk Syr: Heb certain
[g] Cn: Heb *consume thy right d from*
[h] Heb *food for the people*
[i] Gk Syr: Heb *the*

THANKSGIVING FOR GOD'S WONDROUS DEEDS

To the choirmaster: according to Do Not Destroy. A Psalm of Asaph. A Song.

75 We give thanks to thee, O God;
we give thanks;
we call on thy name and recount[a] thy wondrous deeds.
2 At the set time which I appoint
I will judge with equity.
3 When the earth totters, and all its inhabitants,
it is I who keep steady its pillars. *Selah*
4 I say to the boastful, "Do not boast,"
and to the wicked, "Do not lift up your horn;
5 do not lift up your horn on high,
or speak with insolent neck."
6 For not from the east or from the west
and not from the wilderness comes lifting up;
7 but it is God who executes judgment,
putting down one and lifting up another.
8 For in the hand of the LORD there is a cup,
with foaming wine, well mixed;
and he will pour a draught from it,
and all the wicked of the earth
shall drain it down to the dregs.
9 But I will rejoice[b] for ever,
I will sing praises to the God of Jacob.
10 All the horns of the wicked he[c] will cut off,
but the horns of the righteous shall be exalted.

ISRAEL'S GOD—JUDGE OF ALL THE EARTH

To the choirmaster: with stringed instruments. A Psalm of Asaph. A Song.

76 In Judah God is known,
his name is great in Israel.
2 His abode has been established in Salem,
his dwelling place in Zion.
3 There he broke the flashing arrows,
the shield, the sword, and the weapons of war. *Selah*
4 Glorious art thou, more majestic than the everlasting mountains.[d]
5 The stouthearted were stripped of their spoil;
they sank into sleep;
all the men of war
were unable to use their hands.
6 At thy rebuke, O God of Jacob,
both rider and horse lay stunned.
7 But thou, terrible art thou!
Who can stand before thee
when once thy anger is roused?
8 From the heavens thou didst utter judgment;
the earth feared and was still,
9 when God arose to establish judgment
to save all the oppressed of the earth. *Selah*
10 Surely the wrath of men shall praise thee;
the residue of wrath thou wilt gird upon thee.
11 Make your vows to the LORD your God, and perform them;
let all around him bring gifts
to him who is to be feared,
12 who cuts off the spirit of princes,
who is terrible to the kings of the earth.

[a] Syr Compare Gk: Heb *and near is thy name. They recount*
[b] Gk: Heb *declare*
[c] Heb *I*
[d] Gk: Heb *the mountains of prey*

GOD'S MIGHTY DEEDS RECALLED

To the choirmaster: according to Jeduthun. A Psalm of Asaph.

77 I cry aloud to God,
aloud to God, that he may hear me.
2 In the day of my trouble I seek the Lord;
in the night my hand is stretched out without wearying;
my soul refuses to be comforted.
3 I think of God, and I moan;
I meditate, and my spirit faints. *Selah*
4 Thou dost hold my eyelids from closing;
I am so troubled that I cannot speak.
5 I consider the days of old,
I remember the years long ago.
6 I commune[e] with my heart in the night;
I meditate and search my spirit:[f]
7 "Will the Lord spurn for ever,
and never again be favorable?
8 Has his steadfast love for ever ceased?
Are his promises at an end for all time?
9 Has God forgotten to be gracious?
Has he in anger shut up his compassion?" *Selah*
10 And I say, "It is my grief
that the right hand of the Most High has changed."
11 I will call to mind the deeds of the LORD;
yea, I will remember thy wonders of old.
12 I will meditate on all thy work,
and muse on thy mighty deeds.
13 Thy way, O God, is holy.
What god is great like our God?
14 Thou art the God who workest wonders,
who hast manifested thy might among the peoples.
15 Thou didst with thy arm redeem thy people,
the sons of Jacob and Joseph. *Selah*
16 When the waters saw thee, O God,
when the waters saw thee, they were afraid,
yea, the deep trembled.
17 The clouds poured out water;
the skies gave forth thunder;
thy arrows flashed on every side.
18 The crash of thy thunder was in the whirlwind;
thy lightnings lighted up the world;
the earth trembled and shook.
19 Thy way was through the sea,
thy path through the great waters;
yet thy footprints were unseen.
20 Thou didst lead thy people like a flock
by the hand of Moses and Aaron.

GOD'S GOODNESS AND ISRAEL'S INGRATITUDE

A Maskil of Asaph.

78 Give ear, O my people, to my teaching;
incline your ears to the words of my mouth!
2 I will open my mouth in a parable;
I will utter dark sayings from of old,
3 things that we have heard and known,
that our fathers have told us.

[e] Gk Syr: Heb *my music*
[f] Syr Jerome: Heb *my spirit searches*

4We will not hide them from their
children,
but tell to the coming
generation
the glorious deeds of the LORD,
and his might,
and the wonders which he
has wrought.
5He established a testimony in
Jacob,
and appointed a law in
Israel,
which he commanded our
fathers
to teach to their children;
6that the next generation might
know them,
the children yet unborn,
and arise and tell them to their
children,
7so that they should set their
hope in God,
and not forget the works of
God,
but keep his
commandments;
8and that they should not be like
their fathers,
a stubborn and rebellious
generation,
a generation whose heart was
not steadfast,
whose spirit was not faithful
to God.
9The E´phraimites, armed with[a]
the bow,
turned back on the day of
battle.
10They did not keep God's
covenant,
but refused to walk according
to his law.
11They forgot what he had done,
and the miracles that he had
shown them.
12In the sight of their fathers he
wrought marvels
in the land of Egypt, in the
fields of Zo´an.
13He divided the sea and let them
pass through it,
and made the waters stand
like a heap.
14In the daytime he led them with
a cloud,
and all the night with a fiery
light.
15He cleft rocks in the wilderness,
and gave them drink abundantly
as from the
deep.
16He made streams come out of
the rock,
and caused waters to flow
down like rivers.
17Yet they sinned still more
against him,
rebelling against the Most
High in the desert.
18They tested God in their heart
by demanding the food they
craved.
19They spoke against God, saying,
"Can God spread a table in
the wilderness?
20He smote the rock so that water
gushed out
and streams overflowed.
Can he also give bread,
or provide meat for his
people?"
21Therefore, when the LORD
heard, he was full of
wrath;
a fire was kindled against
Jacob,
his anger mounted against
Israel;
22because they had no faith in
God,
and did not trust his saving
power.
23Yet he commanded the skies
above,
and opened the doors of
heaven;
24and he rained down upon them
manna to eat,
and gave them the grain of
heaven.
25Man ate of the bread of the
angels;

[a]Heb *armed with shooting*

he sent them food in abundance.
26He caused the east wind to blow in the heavens,
and by his power he led out the south wind;
27he rained flesh upon them like dust,
winged birds like the sand of the seas;
28he let them fall in the midst of their camp,
all around their habitations.
29And they ate and were well filled,
for he gave them what they craved.
30But before they had sated their craving,
while the food was still in their mouths,
31the anger of God rose against them
and he slew the strongest of them,
and laid low the picked men of Israel.
32In spite of all this they still sinned;
despite his wonders they did not believe.
33So he made their days vanish like a breath,
and their years in terror.
34When he slew them, they sought for him;
they repented and sought God earnestly.
35They remembered that God was their rock,
the Most High God their redeemer.
36But they flattered him with their mouths;
they lied to him with their tongues.
37Their heart was not steadfast toward him;
they were not true to his covenant.
38Yet he, being compassionate, forgave their iniquity,
and did not destroy them;
he restrained his anger often,
and did not stir up all his wrath.
39He remembered that they were but flesh,
a wind that passes and comes not again.
40How often they rebelled against him in the wilderness
and grieved him in the desert!
41They tested him again and again,
and provoked the Holy One of Israel.
42They did not keep in mind his power,
or the day when he redeemed them from the foe;
43when he wrought his signs in Egypt,
and his miracles in the fields of Zo′an.
44He turned their rivers to blood,
so that they could not drink of their streams.
45He sent among them swarms of flies, which devoured them,
and frogs, which destroyed them.
46He gave their crops to the caterpillar,
and the fruit of their labor to the locust.
47He destroyed their vines with hail,
and their sycamores with frost.
48He gave over their cattle to the hail,
and their flocks to thunderbolts.
49He let loose on them his fierce anger,
wrath, indignation, and distress,
a company of destroying angels.
50He made a path for his anger;
he did not spare them from death,

but gave their lives over to
the plague.
51He smote all the first-born in
Egypt,
the first issue of their
strength in the tents
of Ham.
52Then he led forth his people like
sheep,
and guided them in the wil-
derness like a flock.
53He led them in safety, so that
they were not afraid;
but the sea overwhelmed
their enemies.
54And he brought them to his holy
land,
to the mountain which his
right hand had won.
55He drove out nations before
them;
he apportioned them for a
possession
and settled the tribes of
Israel in their tents.
56Yet they tested and rebelled
against the Most High
God,
and did not observe his
testimonies,
57but turned away and acted
treacherously like their
fathers;
they twisted like a deceitful
bow.
58For they provoked him to anger
with their high places;
they moved him to jealousy
with their graven
images.
59When God heard, he was full of
wrath,
and he utterly rejected
Israel.
60He forsook his dwelling at
Shiloh,
the tent where he dwelt
among men,
61and delivered his power to
captivity,
his glory to the hand of the
foe.
62He gave his people over to the
sword,
and vented his wrath on his
heritage.
63Fire devoured their young men,
and their maidens had no
marriage song.
64Their priests fell by the sword,
and their widows made no
lamentation.
65Then the Lord awoke as from
sleep,
like a strong man shouting
because of wine.
66And he put his adversaries to
rout;
he put them to everlasting
shame.
67He rejected the tent of Joseph,
he did not choose the tribe
of E´phraim;
68but he chose the tribe of Judah,
Mount Zion, which he loves.
69He built his sanctuary like the
high heavens,
like the earth, which he has
founded for ever.
70He chose David his servant,
and took him from the
sheepfolds;
71from tending the ewes that had
young he brought him
to be the shepherd of Jacob
his people,
of Israel his inheritance.
72With upright heart he tended
them,
and guided them with skilful
hand.

PLEA FOR MERCY FOR JERUSALEM

A Psalm of Asaph.

79 O God, the heathen have come
into thy inheritance;
they have defiled thy holy
temple;
they have laid Jerusalem in
ruins.
They have given the bodies of thy
servants
to the birds of the air for

food,
the flesh of thy saints to the
beasts of the earth.
3They have poured out their blood
like water
round about Jerusalem,
and there was none to bury
them.
4We have become a taunt to our
neighbors,
mocked and derided by
those round about us.
5How long, O LORD? Wilt thou be
angry for ever?
Will thy jealous wrath burn
like fire?
6Pour out thy anger on the nations
that do not know thee,
and on the kingdoms
that do not call on thy name!
7For they have devoured Jacob,
and laid waste his
habitation.
8Do not remember against us
the iniquities of our
forefathers;
let thy compassion come
speedily to meet us,
for we are brought very low.
9Help us, O God of our salvation,
for the glory of thy name;
deliver us, and forgive our sins,
for thy name's sake!
10Why should the nations say,
"Where is their God?"
Let the avenging of the out-
poured blood of thy
servants
be known among the nations
before our eyes!
11*Let the groans* of the prisoners
come before thee;
according to thy great
power preserve those
doomed to die!
12Return sevenfold into the bosom
of our neighbors
the taunts with which they
have taunted thee, O
Lord!
13Then we thy people, the flock of
thy pasture,
will give thanks to thee for
ever;
from generation to genera-
tion we will recount
thy praise.

PRAYER FOR ISRAEL'S RESTORATION

To the choirmaster: according to Lilies.
A Testimony of Asaph. A Psalm.

80 Give ear, O Shepherd of Israel,
thou who leadest Joseph like
a flock!
Thou who art enthroned upon
the cherubim, shine
forth
2before E´phraim and
Benjamin and
Manas´seh!
Stir up thy might,
and come to save us!
3Restore us, O God;
let thy face shine, that we
may be saved!
4O LORD God of hosts,
how long wilt thou be angry
with thy people's
prayers?
5Thou hast fed them with the
bread of tears,
and given them tears to
drink in full measure.
6Thou dost make us the scorn[a] of
our neighbors;
and our enemies laugh
among themselves.
7Restore us, O God of hosts;
let thy face shine, that we
may be saved!
8Thou didst bring a vine out of
Egypt;
thou didst drive out the na-
tions and plant it.
9Thou didst clear the ground for it;
it took deep root and filled
the land.
10The mountains were covered
with its shade,
the mighty cedars with its
branches;

[a]Syr: Heb *strife*

11it sent out its branches to the sea,
and its shoots to the River.
12Why then hast thou broken
down its walls,
so that all who pass along
the way pluck its
fruit?
13The boar from the forest ravages
it,
and all that move in the field
feed on it.
14Turn again, O God of hosts!
Look down from heaven,
and see;
have regard for this vine,
15the stock which thy right
hand planted.[a]
16They have burned it with fire,
they have cut it down;
may they perish at the
rebuke of thy
countenance!
17But let thy hand be upon the
man of thy right hand,
the son of man whom thou
hast made strong for
thyself!
18Then we will never turn back
from thee;
give us life, and we will call
on thy name!
19Restore us, O LORD God of
hosts!
let thy face shine, that we
may be saved!

GOD'S APPEAL TO STUBBORN ISRAEL

To the choirmaster: according to
The Gittith. A Psalm of Asaph.

81 Sing aloud to God our strength;
shout for joy to the God of
Jacob!
2Raise a song, sound the timbrel,
the sweet lyre with the harp.
3Blow the trumpet at the new
moon,
at the full moon, on our
feast day.
4For it is a statute for Israel,
an ordinance of the God of
Jacob.
5He made it a decree in Joseph,
when he went out over[b] the
land of Egypt.
I hear a voice I had not known:
6"I relieved your[c] shoulder of the
burden;
your[d] hands were freed from
the basket.
7In distress you called, and I deliv-
ered you;
I answered you in the secret
place of thunder;
I tested you at the waters of
Mer´ibah. *Selah*
8Hear, O my people, while I ad-
monish you!
O Israel, if you would but
listen to me!
9There shall be no strange god
among you;
you shall not bow down to a
foreign god.
10I am the LORD your God,
who brought you up out of
the land of Egypt.
Open your mouth wide, and
I will fill it.
11"But my people did not listen to
my voice;
Israel would have none of
me.
12So I gave them over to their
stubborn hearts,
to follow their own counsels.
13O that my people would listen
to me,
that Israel would walk in my
ways!
14I would soon subdue their
enemies,
and turn my hand against
their foes.
15Those who hate the LORD would
cringe toward him,
and their fate would last for
ever.

[a] Heb *planted and upon the son whom thou hast reared for thyself*
[b] Or *against*
[c] Heb *his*
[d] Heb *his*

16I would feed you[e] with the finest
of the wheat,
and with honey from the
rock I would satisfy
you."

A PLEA FOR JUSTICE

A Psalm of Asaph.

82 God has taken his place in the divine council;
in the midst of the gods he
holds judgment:
2"How long will you judge unjustly
and show partiality to the
wicked? *Selah*
3Give justice to the weak and the
fatherless;
maintain the right of the
afflicted and the
destitute.
4Rescue the weak and the needy;
deliver them from the hand
of the wicked."
5They have neither knowledge nor
understanding,
they walk about in darkness;
all the foundations of the
earth are shaken.
6I say, "You are gods,
sons of the Most High, all
of you;
7nevertheless, you shall die like
men,
and fall like any prince."[f]
8Arise, O God, judge the earth;
for to thee belong all the
nations!

PRAYER FOR JUDGMENT ON ISRAEL'S FOES

A Song. A Psalm of Asaph.

83 O God, do not keep silence;
do not hold thy peace or be
still, O God!
2For lo, thy enemies are in tumult;
those who hate thee have
raised their heads.
3They lay crafty plans against thy
people;
they consult together against
thy protected ones.
4They say, "Come, let us wipe
them out as a nation;
let the name of Israel be remembered no more!"
5Yea, they conspire with one
accord;
against thee they make a
covenant—
6the tents of Edom and the
Ish´maelites,
Moab and the Hagrites,
7Gebal and Ammon and Am´alek,
Philistia with the inhabitants of Tyre;
8Assyria also has joined them;
they are the strong arm
of the children of
Lot. *Selah*
9Do to them as thou didst to
Mid´ian,
as to Sis´era and Jabin at the
river Kishon,
10who were destroyed at En-dor,
who became dung for the
ground.
11Make their nobles like Oreb and
Zeeb,
all their princes like Zebah
and Zalmun´na,
12who said, "Let us take possession for ourselves
of the pastures of God."
13O my God, make them like
whirling dust,[g]
like chaff before the wind.
14As fire consumes the forest,
as the flame sets the mountains ablaze,
15so do thou pursue them with thy
tempest
and terrify them with thy
hurricane!
16Fill their faces with shame,
that they may seek thy
name, O LORD.
17Let them be put to shame and
dismayed for ever;
let them perish in disgrace.

[e]Cn Compare verse 16b: Heb *he would feed him*
[f]*Or fall as one man, O princes*
[g]*Or a tumbleweed*

18Let them know that thou alone,
whose name is the LORD,
art the Most High over all
the earth.

THE JOY OF WORSHIP IN THE TEMPLE

To the choirmaster: according to The Gittith. A Psalm of the Sons of Korah.

84 How lovely is thy dwelling place,
O LORD of hosts!
2My soul longs, yea, faints
for the courts of the LORD;
my heart and flesh sing for joy
to the living God.
3Even the sparrow finds a home,
and the swallow a nest for
herself,
where she may lay her
young,
at thy altars, O LORD of
hosts,
my King and my God.
4Blessed are those who dwell in
thy house,
ever singing thy
praise! *Selah*
5Blessed are the men whose
strength is in thee,
in whose heart are the high-
ways to Zion.[a]
6As they go through the valley of
Baca
they make it a place of
springs;
the early rain also covers it
with pools.
7They go from strength to
strength;
the God of gods will be seen
in Zion.
8O LORD God of hosts, hear my
prayer;
give ear, O God of
Jacob! *Selah*
9Behold our shield, O God;
look upon the face of thine
anointed!
10For a day in thy courts is better
than a thousand elsewhere.
I would rather be a doorkeeper
in the house of my God
than dwell in the tents of
wickedness.
11For the LORD God is a sun and
shield;
he bestows favor and
honor.
No good thing does the LORD
withhold
from those who walk
uprightly.
12O LORD of hosts,
blessed is the man who
trusts in thee!

PRAYER FOR THE RESTORATION OF GOD'S FAVOR

To the choirmaster. A Psalm of the Sons of Korah.

85 LORD, thou wast favorable to thy
land;
thou didst restore the for-
tunes of Jacob.
2Thou didst forgive the iniquity of
thy people;
thou didst pardon all their
sin. *Selah*
3Thou didst withdraw all thy
wrath;
thou didst turn from thy hot
anger.
4Restore s again, O God of our
sa/ation,
and ut away thy indigna-
tion toward us!
5Wilt th be angry with us for
er?
W thou prolong
thy anger to all
generations?
6Wilt t not revive us again,
t thy people may rejoice
in thee?
7Show thy steadfast love, O
RD,
grant us thy salvation.
8Let rear what God the LORD
ill speak,
he will speak peace to his
people,

[a]Heb lacks *to Zion*

to his saints, to those who
turn to him in their
hearts.[b]
9Surely his salvation is at hand for
those who fear him,
that glory may dwell in our
land.
10Steadfast love and faithfulness
will meet;
righteousness and peace will
kiss each other.
11Faithfulness will spring up from
the ground,
and righteousness will look
down from the sky.
12Yea, the LORD will give what is
good,
and our land will yield its
increase.
13Righteousness will go before
him,
and make his footsteps a
way.

SUPPLICATION FOR HELP AGAINST ENEMIES

A Prayer of David.

86 Incline thy ear, O LORD, and an-
swer me,
for I am poor and needy.
2Preserve my life, for I am godly;
save thy servant who trusts
in thee.
Thou art my God; 3be gracious
to me, O Lord,
for to thee do I cry all the
day.
4Gladden the soul of thy servant,
for to thee, O Lord, do I lift
up my soul.
5For thou, O Lord, art good and
forgiving,
abounding in steadfast love
to all who call on
thee.
6Give ear, O LORD, to my prayer;
hearken to my cry of
supplication.
7In the day of my trouble I call on
thee,
for thou dost answer me.
8There is none like thee among
the gods, O Lord,
nor are there any works like
thine.
9All the nations thou hast made
shall come
and bow down before thee,
O Lord,
and shall glorify thy name.
10For thou art great and doest
wondrous things,
thou alone art God.
11Teach me thy way, O LORD,
that I may walk in thy
truth;
unite my heart to fear thy
name.
12I give thanks to thee, O Lord
my God, with my whole
heart,
and I will glorify thy name
for ever.
13For great is thy steadfast love
toward me;
thou hast delivered my soul
from the depths of
Sheol.
14O God, insolent men have risen
up against me;
a band of ruthless men seek
my life,
and they do not set thee
before them.
15But thou, O Lord, art a God
merciful and gracious,
slow to anger and abounding
in steadfast love and
faithfulness.
16Turn to me and take pity on me;
give thy strength to thy
servant,
and save the son of thy
handmaid.
17Show me a sign of thy favor,
that those who hate me may
see and be put to
shame
because thou, LORD, hast
helped me and com-
forted me.

[b]Gk: Heb *but let them not turn back to folly*

THE JOY OF LIVING IN ZION

A Psalm of the Sons of Korah. A Song.

87 On the holy mount stands the city
he founded;
2the LORD loves the gates of Zion
more than all the dwelling
places of Jacob.
3Glorious things are spoken of
you,
O city of God. *Selah*
4Among those who know me
I mention Rahab and
Babylon;
behold, Philistia and Tyre,
with Ethiopia—
"This one was born there,"
they say.
5And of Zion it shall be said,
"This one and that one were
born in her";
for the Most High himself
will establish her.
6The LORD records as he registers
the peoples,
"This one was born
there." *Selah*
7Singers and dancers alike say,
"All my springs are in you."

PRAYER FOR HELP IN DESPONDENCY

A Song. A Psalm of the Sons of Korah. To the choirmaster: according to Mahalath Leannoth. A Maskil of Heman the Ezrahite.

88 O LORD, my God, I call for help[a]
by day;
I cry out in the night before
thee.
2Let my prayer come before thee,
incline thy ear to my cry!
3For my soul is full of troubles,
and my life draws near to
Sheol.
4I am reckoned among those who
go down to the Pit;
I am a man who has no
strength,
5like one forsaken among the
dead,
like the slain that lie in the
grave,
like those whom thou dost
remember no more,
for they are cut off from thy
hand.
6Thou hast put me in the depths
of the Pit,
in the regions dark and deep.
7Thy wrath lies heavy upon me,
and thou dost overwhelm
me with all thy
waves. *Selah*
8Thou hast caused my companions
to shun me;
thou hast made me a thing
of horror to them.
I am shut in so that I cannot
escape;
9my eye grows dim through
sorrow.
Every day I call upon thee, O
LORD;
I spread out my hands to
thee.
10Dost thou work wonders for the
dead?
Do the shades rise up to
praise thee? *Selah*
11Is thy steadfast love declared in
the grave,
or thy faithfulness in
Abaddon?
12Are thy wonders known in the
darkness,
or thy saving help in the
land of forgetfulness?
13But I, O LORD, cry to thee;
in the morning my prayer
comes before thee.
14O LORD, why dost thou cast me
off?
Why dost thou hide thy face
from me?
15Afflicted and close to death from
my youth up,
I suffer thy terrors; I am
helpless.[b]
16Thy wrath has swept over me;
thy dread assaults destroy

[a]Cn: Heb O Lord, *God of my salvation*
[b]The meaning of the Hebrew word is uncertain

me.
17They surround me like a flood
all day long;
they close in upon me
together.
18Thou hast caused lover and
friend to shun me;
my companions are in
darkness.

GOD'S COVENANT WITH DAVID

A Maskil of Ethan the Ezrahite.

89 I will sing of thy steadfast love, O
LORD,[c] for ever;
with my mouth I will pro-
claim thy faithfulness
to all generations.
2For thy steadfast love was estab-
lished for ever,
thy faithfulness is firm as
the heavens.
3Thou hast said, "I have made a
covenant with my chosen
one,
I have sworn to David my
servant:
4'I will establish your descendants
for ever,
and build your throne fo all
generations.'" Sdah
5Let the heavens praise thy wn-
ders, O LORD,
thy faithfulness in the
assembly of the hly
ones!
6For who in the skies can be cm-
pared to the LORD?
Who among the heavenl
beings[d] is like th
LORD,
7a God feared in the council ohe
holy ones,
great and terrible[e] abovel
that are round abt
him?
8O LORD God of hosts,
who is mighty as thou aD
LORD,
with thy faithfulness round
about thee?
9Thou dost rule the raging of the
sea;
when its waves rise, thou
stillest them.
10Thou didst crush Rahab like a
carcass,
thou didst scatter thy ene-
mies with thy mighty
arm.
11The heavens are thine, the earth
also is thine;
the world and all that is in
it, thou hast founded
them.
12The north and the south, thou
hast created them;
Tabor and Hermon joyously
praise thy name.
13Thou hast a mighty arm;
strong is thy hand, high thy
right hand.
14Righteousness and justice are
the foundation of thy
throne;
steadfast love and faithful-
ness go before thee.
15Blessed are the people who
know the festal shout,
who walk, O LORD, in
the light of thy
countenance,
16who exult in thy name all the
day,
and extol[f] thy righteousness.
17For thou art the glory of their
strength;
by thy favor our horn is
exalted.
18For our shield belongs to the
LORD,
our king to the Holy One of
Israel.
19Of old thou didst speak in a
vision
to thy faithful one, and say:

[c] Gk: Heb *the steadfast love of the Lord*
[d] Or *sons of gods*
[e] Gk Syr: Heb *greatly terrible*
[f] Cn: Heb *are exalted in*

"I have set the crown[a] upon
one who is mighty,
I have exalted one chosen
from the people.
20I have found David, my servant;
with my holy oil I have
anointed him;
21so that my hand shall ever abide
with him,
my arm also shall strength-
en him.
22The enemy shall not outwit him,
the wicked shall not humble
him.
23I will crush his foes before him
and strike down those who
hate him.
24My faithfulness and my steadfast
love shall be with him,
and in my name shall his
horn be exalted.
25I will set his hand on the sea
and his right hand on the
rivers.
26He shall cry to me, 'Thou art my
Father,
my God, and the Rock of my
salvation.'
27And I will make him the
first-born,
the highest of the kings of
the earth.
28My steadfast love I will keep for
him for ever,
and my covenant will stand
firm for him.
29I will establish his line for ever
and his throne as the days of
the heavens.
30If his children forsake my law
and do not walk according to
my ordinances,
31if they violate my statutes
and do not keep my
commandments,
32then I will punish their trans-
gression with the rod
and their iniquity with
scourges;
33but I will not remove from him
my steadfast love,
or be false to my
faithfulness.
34I will not violate my covenant,
or alter the word that went
forth from my lips.
35Once for all I have sworn by my
holiness;
I will not lie to David.
36His line shall endure for ever,
his throne as long as the sun
before me.
37Like the moon it shall be estab-
lished for ever;
it shall stand firm while the
skies endure."[b] *Selah*
38But now thou hast cast off and
rejected,
thou art full of wrath
against thy anointed.
39Thou hast renounced the cove-
nant with thy servant;
thou hast defiled his crown
in the dust.
40Thou hast breached all his walls;
thou hast laid his strong-
holds in ruins.
4All that pass by despoil him;
he has become the scorn of
his neighbors.
4Thou hast exalted the right hand
of his foes;
thou hast made all his ene-
mies rejoice.
4Yea, thou hast turned back the
edge of his sword,
and thou hast not made him
stand in battle.
Thou hast removed the scepter
from his hand,[c]
and cast his throne to the
ground.
hou hast cut short the days of
his youth;
thou hast covered him with
shame. *Selah*
ow long, O LORD? Wilt thou
hide thyself for ever?
How long will thy wrath
burn like fire?

[a]Cn: Heb *help*
[b]Cn: Heb *the witness in the skies is sure*
[c]Cn: Heb *removed his cleanness*

47Remember, O Lord,[d] what the
measure of life is,
for what vanity thou hast
created all the sons
of men!
48What man can live and never see
death?
Who can deliver his soul
from the power of
Sheol? *Selah*
49Lord, where is thy steadfast love
of old,
which by thy faithfulness
thou didst swear to
David?
50Remember, O Lord, how thy
servant is scorned;
how I bear in my bosom
the insults[e] of the
peoples,
51with which thy enemies taunt,
O LORD,
with which they mock the
footsteps of thy
anointed.
52Blessed be the LORD for ever!
Amen and Amen.

BOOK IV

GOD'S ETERNITY AND HUMAN FRAILTY

A Prayer of Moses, the man of God.

90 Lord, thou hast been our dwelling
place[f]
in all generations.
2Before the mountains were
brought forth,
or ever thou hadst formed
the earth and the
world,
from everlasting to everlast-
ing thou art God.
3Thou turnest man back to the
dust,
and sayest, "Turn back, O
children of men!"
4For a thousand years in thy sight
are but as yesterday when it
is past,
or as a watch in the night.
5Thou dost sweep men away; they
are like a dream,
like grass which is renewed
in the morning:
6in the morning it flourishes and
is renewed;
in the evening it fades and
withers.
7For we are consumed by thy
anger;
by thy wrath we are
overwhelmed.
8Thou hast set our iniquities
before thee,
our secret sins in the light of
thy countenance.
9For all our days pass away under
thy wrath,
our years come to an end[g]
like a sigh.
10The years of our life are three-
score and ten,
or even by reason of strength
fourscore;
yet their span[h] is but toil and
trouble;
they are soon gone, and we
fly away.
11Who considers the power of thy
anger,
and thy wrath according to
the fear of thee?
12So teach us to number our days
that we may get a heart of
wisdom.
13Return, O LORD! How long?
Have pity on thy servants!
14Satisfy us in the morning with
thy steadfast love,
that we may rejoice and be
glad all our days.
15Make us glad as many days as
thou hast afflicted us,
and as many years as we
have seen evil.

[d]Cn: Heb *I*
[e]Cn: Heb *all of many*
[f]Another reading is *refuge*
[g]Syr: Heb *we bring our years to an end*
[h]Cn Compare Gk Syr Jerome Tg: Heb *pride*

16 Let thy work be manifest to thy servants,
and thy glorious power to their children.
17 Let the favor of the Lord our God be upon us,
and establish thou the work of our hands upon us,
yea, the work of our hands establish thou it.

ASSURANCE OF GOD'S PROTECTION

91 He who dwells in the shelter of the Most High,
who abides in the shadow of the Almighty,
2 will say to the LORD, "My refuge and my fortress;
my God, in whom I trust."
3 For he will deliver you from the snare of the fowler
and from the deadly pestilence;
4 he will cover you with his pinions,
and under his wings you will find refuge;
his faithfulness is a shield and buckler.
5 You will not fear the terror of the night,
nor the arrow that flies by day,
6 nor the pestilence that stalks in darkness,
nor the destruction that wastes at noonday.
7 A thousand may fall at your side,
ten thousand at your right hand;
but it will not come near you.
8 You will only look with your eyes
and see the recompense of the wicked.
9 Because you have made the LORD your refuge,[a]
the Most High your habitation,
10 no evil shall befall you,
no scourge come near your tent.
11 For he will give his angels charge of you
to guard you in all your ways.
12 On their hands they will bear you up,
lest you dash your foot against a stone.
13 You will tread on the lion and the adder,
the young lion and the serpent you will trample under foot.
14 Because he cleaves to me in love, I will deliver him;
I will protect him, because he knows my name.
15 When he calls to me, I will answer him;
I will be with him in trouble,
I will rescue him and honor him.
16 With long life I will satisfy him,
and show him my salvation.

THANKSGIVING FOR VINDICATION

A Psalm. A Song for the Sabbath.

92 It is good to give thanks to the LORD,
to sing praises to thy name, O Most High;
2 to declare thy steadfast love in the morning,
and thy faithfulness by night,
3 to the music of the lute and the harp,
to the melody of the lyre.
4 For thou, O LORD, hast made me glad by thy work;
at the works of thy hands I sing for joy.
5 How great are thy works, O LORD!
Thy thoughts are very deep!

[a] Cn: Heb *Because thou,* Lord, *art my refuge; you have made*

6The dull man cannot know,
the stupid cannot understand this:
7that, though the wicked sprout like grass
and all evildoers flourish,
they are doomed to destruction for ever,
8but thou, O LORD, art on high for ever.
9For lo, thy enemies, O LORD,
for lo, thy enemies shall perish;
all evildoers shall be scattered.
10But thou hast exalted my horn like that of the wild ox;
thou hast poured over me[b] fresh oil.
11My eyes have seen the downfall of my enemies,
my ears have heard the doom of my evil assailants.
12The righteous flourish like the palm tree,
and grow like a cedar in Lebanon.
13They are planted in the house of the LORD,
they flourish in the courts of our God.
14They still bring forth fruit in old age,
they are ever full of sap and green,
15to show that the LORD is upright;
he is my rock, and there is no unrighteousness *in him.*

THE MAJESTY OF GOD'S RULE

93 *The LORD reigns; he is robed in majesty;
the LORD is robed, he is girded with strength.
Yea, the world is established; it shall never be moved;
2thy throne is established from of old;
thou art from everlasting.
3The floods have lifted up, O LORD,
the floods have lifted up their voice,
the floods lift up their roaring.
4Mightier than the thunders of many waters,
mightier than the waves[c] of the sea,
the LORD on high is mighty!
5Thy decrees are very sure;
holiness befits thy house,
O LORD, for evermore.

GOD THE AVENGER OF THE RIGHTEOUS

94 O LORD, thou God of vengeance,
thou God of vengeance, shine forth!
2Rise up, O judge of the earth;
render to the proud their deserts!
3O LORD, how long shall the wicked,
how long shall the wicked exult?
4They pour out their arrogant words,
they boast, all the evildoers.
5They crush thy people, O LORD,
and afflict thy heritage.
6They slay the widow and the sojourner,
and murder the fatherless;
7and they say, "The LORD does not see;
the God of Jacob does not perceive."
8Understand, O dullest of the people!
Fools, when will you be wise?
9He who planted the ear, does he not hear?
He who formed the eye, does he not see?
10He who chastens the nations,
does he not chastise?

[b]Syr: Heb uncertain
[c]Cn: Heb *mighty the waves*

He who teaches men
knowledge,
11the LORD, knows the
thoughts of man,
that they are but a breath.
12Blessed is the man whom thou
dost chasten, O LORD,
and whom thou dost teach
out of thy law
13to give him respite from days of
trouble,
until a pit is dug for the
wicked.
14For the LORD will not forsake
his people;
he will not abandon his
heritage;
15for justice will return to the
righteous,
and all the upright in heart
will follow it.
16Who rises up for me against the
wicked?
Who stands up for me
against evildoers?
17If the LORD had not been my
help,
my soul would soon have
dwelt in the land of
silence.
18When I thought, "My foot
slips,"
thy steadfast love, O LORD,
held me up.
19When the cares of my heart are
many,
thy consolations cheer my
soul.
20Can wicked rulers be allied with
thee,
who frame mischief by
statute?
21They band together against the
life of the righteous,
and condemn the innocent
to death.
22*But the LORD has become my*
stronghold,
and my God the rock of my
refuge.
23He will bring back on them their
iniquity
and wipe them out for their
wickedness;
the LORD our God will wipe
them out.

A CALL TO WORSHIP AND OBEDIENCE

95 O come, let us sing to the LORD;
let us make a joyful noise
to the rock of our
salvation!
2Let us come into his presence
with thanksgiving;
let us make a joyful noise
to him with songs of
praise!
3For the LORD is a great God,
and a great King above all
gods.
4In his hand are the depths of the
earth;
the heights of the mountains
are his also.
5The sea is his, for he made it;
for his hands formed the dry
land.
6O come, let us worship and bow
down,
let us kneel before the LORD,
our Maker!
7For he is our God,
and we are the people of his
pasture,
and the sheep of his hand.
O that today you would heark-
en to his voice!
8Harden not your hearts, as
at Mer´ibah,
as on the day at Massah in
the wilderness,
9when your fathers tested me,
and put me to the proof,
though they had seen
my work.
10For forty years I loathed that
generation
and said, "They are a people
who err in heart,
and they do not regard my
ways."
11Therefore I swore in my anger
that they should not enter
my rest.

PRAISE TO GOD WHO COMES IN JUDGMENT

96 O sing to the LORD a new song;
sing to the LORD, all the earth!
2 Sing to the LORD, bless his name;
tell of his salvation from day to day.
3 Declare his glory among the nations,
his marvelous works among all the peoples!
4 For great is the LORD, and greatly to be praised;
he is to be feared above all gods.
5 For all the gods of the peoples are idols;
but the LORD made the heavens.
6 Honor and majesty are before him;
strength and beauty are in his sanctuary.
7 Ascribe to the LORD, O families of the peoples,
ascribe to the LORD glory and strength!
8 Ascribe to the LORD the glory due his name;
bring an offering, and come into his courts!
9 Worship the LORD in holy array;
tremble before him, all the earth!
10 Say among the nations, "The LORD reigns!
Yea, the world is established, it shall never be moved;
he will judge the peoples with equity."
11 Let the heavens be glad, and let *the earth rejoice;*
let the sea roar, and all that fills it;
12 let the field exult, and everything in it!
Then shall all the trees of the wood sing for joy 13 before
the LORD, for he comes,
for he comes to judge the earth.
He will judge the world with righteousness,
and the peoples with his truth.

THE GLORY OF GOD'S REIGN

97 The LORD reigns; let the earth rejoice;
let the many coastlands be glad!
2 Clouds and thick darkness are round about him;
righteousness and justice are the foundation of his throne.
3 Fire goes before him,
and burns up his adversaries round about.
4 His lightnings lighten the world;
the earth sees and trembles.
5 The mountains melt like wax before the LORD,
before the Lord of all the earth.
6 The heavens proclaim his righteousness;
and all the peoples behold his glory.
7 All worshipers of images are put to shame,
who make their boast in worthless idols;
all gods bow down before him.
8 Zion hears and is glad,
and the daughters of Judah rejoice,
because of thy judgments, O God.
9 For thou, O LORD, art most high over all the earth;
thou art exalted far above all gods.
10 The LORD loves those who hate evil;[a]
he preserves the lives of his saints;
he delivers them from the hand of the wicked.
11 Light dawns[b] for the righteous,

[a] Cn: Heb *You who love the* Lord *hate evil*
[b] Gk Syr Jerome: Heb *is sown*

and joy for the upright in
heart.
12Rejoice in the LORD, O you
righteous,
and give thanks to his holy
name!

PRAISE THE JUDGE OF THE WORLD

A Psalm.

98O sing to the LORD a new song,
for he has done marvelous
things!
His right hand and his holy
arm
have gotten him victory.
2The LORD has made known his
victory,
he has revealed his vindica-
tion in the sight of
the nations.
3He has remembered his steadfast
love and faithfulness
to the house of Israel.
All the ends of the earth have
seen
the victory of our God.
4Make a joyful noise to the LORD,
all the earth;
break forth into joyous song
and sing praises!
5Sing praises to the LORD with
the lyre,
with the lyre and the sound
of melody!
6With trumpets and the sound of
the horn
make a joyful noise before
the King, the LORD!
7Let the sea roar, and all that
fills it;
the world and those who
dwell in it!
8Let the floods clap their hands;
let the hills sing for joy
together
9before the LORD, for he comes
to judge the earth.
He will judge the world with
righteousness,
and the peoples with equity.

PRAISE TO GOD FOR HIS HOLINESS

99The LORD reigns; let the peoples
tremble!
He sits enthroned upon the
cherubim; let the
earth quake!
2The LORD is great in Zion;
he is exalted over all the
peoples.
3Let them praise thy great and
terrible name!
Holy is he!
4Mighty King,[a] lover of justice,
thou hast established equity;
thou hast executed justice
and righteousness in Jacob.
5Extol the LORD our God;
worship at his footstool!
Holy is he!
6Moses and Aaron were among his
priests,
Samuel also was among
those who called on
his name.
They cried to the LORD, and
he answered them.
7He spoke to them in the pillar of
cloud;
they kept his testimonies,
and the statutes that he gave
them.
8O LORD our God, thou didst
answer them;
thou wast a forgiving God to
them,
but an avenger of their
wrongdoings.
9Extol the LORD our God,
and worship at his holy
mountain;
for the LORD our God is
holy!

ALL LANDS SUMMONED TO PRAISE GOD

A Psalm for the thank offering.

100Make a joyful noise to the LORD,
all the lands![b]
2Serve the LORD with gladness!
Come into his presence with
singing!

[a] Cn: Heb *and the king's strength*
[b] Heb *land* or *earth*

3Know that the LORD is God!
It is he that made us, and we are his;[c]
we are his people, and the sheep of his pasture.
4Enter his gates with thanksgiving,
and his courts with praise!
Give thanks to him, bless his name!
5For the LORD is good;
his steadfast love endures for ever,
and his faithfulness to all generations.

A SOVEREIGN'S PLEDGE OF INTEGRITY AND JUSTICE

A Psalm of David.

101 I will sing of loyalty and of justice;
to thee, O LORD, I will sing.
2I will give heed to the way that is blameless.
Oh when wilt thou come to me?
I will walk with integrity of heart
within my house;
3I will not set before my eyes
anything that is base.
I hate the work of those who fall away;
it shall not cleave to me.
4Perverseness of heart shall be far from me;
I will know nothing of evil.
5Him who slandershis neighbor secretly
I will destroy.
The man of haughty looks and arrogant eart
I will not endre.
6I will look with favr on the faithful in tḃ land,
that they maywell with me;
he who walks inhe way that is blameless
shall minster to me.
7No man who practices deceit
shall dwell in my house;
no man who utters lies
shall continue in my presence.
8Morning by morning I will destroy
all the wicked in the land,
cutting off all the evildoers
from the city of the LORD.

PRAYER TO THE ETERNAL KING FOR HELP

A prayer of one afflicted, when he is faint and pours out his complaint before the LORD.

102 Hear my prayer, O LORD;
let my cry come to thee!
2Do not hide thy face from me
in the day of my distress!
Incline thy ear to me;
answer me speedily in the day when I call!
3For my days pass away like smoke,
and my bones burn like a furnace.
4My heart is smitten like grass, and withered;
I forget to eat my bread.
5Because of my loud groaning
my bones cleave to my flesh.
6I am like a vulture[d] of the wilderness,
like an owl of the waste places;
7I lie awake,
I am like a lonely bird on the housetop.
8All the day my enemies taunt me,
those who deride me use my name for a curse.
9For I eat ashes like bread,
and mingle tears with my drink,
10because of thy indignation and anger;
for thou hast taken me up
and thrown me away.

[c]Another reading is *and nove ourselves*
[d]The meaning of the Hebr word is uncertain

11My days are like an evening
shadow;
I wither away like grass.
12But thou, O LORD, art enthroned
for ever;
thy name endures to all
generations.
13Thou wilt arise and have pity on
Zion;
it is the time to favor her;
the appointed time has
come.
14For thy servants hold her stones
dear,
and have pity on her dust.
15The nations will fear the name
of the LORD,
and all the kings of the earth
thy glory.
16For the LORD will build up Zion,
he will appear in his glory;
17he will regard the prayer of the
destitute,
and will not despise their
supplication.
18Let this be recorded for a genera-
tion to come,
so that a people yet unborn
may praise the LORD:
19that he looked down from his
holy height,
from heaven the LORD
looked at the earth,
20to hear the groans of the
prisoners,
to set free those who were
doomed to die;
21that men may declare in Zion
the name of the LORD,
and in Jerusalem his praise,
22when peoples gather together,
and kingdoms, to worship
the LORD.
23He has broken my strength in
midcourse;
he has shortened my days.
24"O my God," I say, "take me not
hence
in the midst of my days,
thou whose years endure
throughout all generations!"
25Of old thou didst lay the founda-
tion of the earth,
and the heavens are the
work of thy hands.
26They will perish, but thou dost
endure;
they will all wear out like a
garment.
Thou changest them like
raiment, and they pass
away;
27but thou art the same, and
thy years have no
end.
28The children of thy servants
shall dwell secure;
their posterity shall be es-
tablished before thee.

THANKSGIVING FOR GOD'S GOODNESS

A Psalm of David.

103 Bless the LORD, O my soul;
and all that is within me, bless
his holy name!
2Bless the LORD, O my soul,
and forget not all his
benefits,
3who forgives all your iniquity,
who heals all your diseases,
4who redeems your life from the
Pit,
who crowns you with stead-
fast love and mercy,
5who satisfies you with good as
long as you live[a]
so that your youth is
renewed like the
eagle's.
6The LORDworks vindication
and jıstice for all who are
oppressed.
7He made nown his ways to
Moes,
his ats to the people of
Israel.
8The LORI is merciful and
gr:ious,
slowo anger and abounding
in steadfast love.
9He will rt always chide,

[a]Heb uncertain

nor will he keep his anger
for ever.
10He does not deal with us according to our sins,
nor requite us according to
our iniquities.
11For as the heavens are high
above the earth,
so great is his steadfast love
toward those who
fear him;
12as far as the east is from the
west,
so far does he remove our
transgressions from
us.
13As a father pities his children,
so the LORD pities those
who fear him.
14For he knows our frame;
he remembers that we are
dust.
15As for man, his days are like
grass;
he flourishes like a flower of
the field;
16for the wind passes over it, and
it is gone,
and its place knows it no
more.
17But the steadfast love of the
LORD is from everlasting
to everlasting
upon those who fear him,
and his righteousness to
children's children,
18to those who keep his covenant
and remember to do his
commandments.
19The LORD has established his
throne in the heavens,
and his kingdom rules over
all.
20Bless the LORD, O you his
angels,
you mighty ones who do his
word,
hearkening to the voice of
his word!
21Bless the LORD, all his hosts,
his ministers that do his
will!
22Bless the LORD, all his works,
in all places of his
dominion.
Bless the LORD, O my soul!

GOD THE CREATOR AND PROVIDER

104 *Bless the LORD, O my soul!
O LORD my God, thou art very
great!
Thou art clothed with honor
and majesty,
2who coverest thyself with
light as with a
garment,
who hast stretched out the
heavens like a tent,
3who hast laid the beams of
thy chambers on the
waters,
who makest the clouds thy
chariot,
who ridest on the wings of
the wind,
4who makest the winds thy
messengers,
fire and flame thy ministers.
5Thou didst set the earth on its
foundations,
so that it should never be
shaken.
6Thou didst cover it with the deep
as with a garment;
the waters stood above the
mountains.
7At thy rebuke they fled;
at the sound of thy thunder
they took to flight.
8The mountains rose, the valleys
sank down
to the place which thou didst
appoint for them.
9Thou didst set a bound which
they should not pass,
so that they might not again
cover the earth.
10Thou makest springs gush forth
in the valleys;
they flow between the hills,
11they give drink to every beast of
the field;
the wild asses quench their
thirst.

12By them the birds of the air have their habitation;
they sing among the branches.
13From thy lofty abode thou waterest the mountains;
the earth is satisfied with the fruit of thy work.
14Thou dost cause the grass to grow for the cattle,
and plants for man to cultivate,[a]
that he may bring forth food from the earth,
15and wine to gladden the heart of man,
oil to make his face shine,
and bread to strengthen man's heart.
16The trees of the LORD are watered abundantly,
the cedars of Lebanon which he planted.
17In them the birds build their nests;
the stork has her home in the fir trees.
18The high mountains are for the wild goats;
the rocks are a refuge for the badgers.
19Thou hast made the moon to mark the seasons;
the sun knows its time for setting.
20Thou makest darkness, and it is night,
when all the beasts of the forest creep forth.
21The young lions roar for their prey,
seeking their food from God.
22When the sun rises, they get them away
and lie down in their dens.
23Man goes forth to his work
and to his labor until the evening.
24O LORD, how manifold are thy works!
In wisdom hast thou made them all;
the earth is full of thy creatures.
25Yonder is the sea, great and wide,
which teems with things innumerable,
living things both small and great.
26There go the ships,
and Leviathan which thou didst form to sport in it.
27These all look to thee,
to give them their food in due season.
28When thou givest to them, they gather it up;
when thou openest thy hand, they are filled with good things.
29When thou hidest thy face, they are dismayed;
when thou takest away their breath, they die
and return to their dust.
30When thou sendest forth thy Spirit,[b] they are created;
and thou renewest the face of the ground.
31May the glory of the LORD endure for ever,
may the LORD rejoice in his works,
32who looks on the earth and it trembles,
who touches the mountains and they smoke!
33I will sing to the LORD as long as I live;
I will sing praise to my God while I have being.
34May my meditation be pleasing to him,
for I rejoice in the LORD.
35Let sinners be consumed from the earth,

[a] Or *fodder for the animals that serve man*
[b] Or *breath*

and let the wicked be no
more!
Bless the LORD, O my soul!
Praise the LORD!

GOD'S FAITHFULNESS TO ISRAEL

105 O give thanks to the LORD,
call on his name,
make known his deeds
among the peoples!
2Sing to him, sing praises to him,
tell of all his wonderful
works!
3Glory in his holy name;
let the hearts of those
who seek the LORD
rejoice!
4Seek the LORD and his strength,
seek his presence
continually!
5Remember the wonderful works
that he has done,
his miracles, and the judg-
ments he uttered,
6O offspring of Abraham his
servant,
sons of Jacob, his chosen
ones!
7He is the LORD our God;
his judgments are in all the
earth.
8He is mindful of his covenant
for ever,
of the word that he
commanded,
for a thousand
generations,
9the covenant which he made with
Abraham,
his sworn promise to Isaac,
10which he confirmed to Jacob as
a statute,
to Israel as an everlasting
covenant,
11saying, "To you I will give the
land of Canaan
as your portion for an
inheritance."
12When they were few in number,
of little account, and so-
journers in it,
13wandering from nation to
nation,
from one kingdom to anoth-
er people,
14he allowed no one to oppress
them;
he rebuked kings on their
account,
15saying, "Touch not my anointed
ones,
do my prophets no harm!"
16When he summoned a famine on
the land,
and broke every staff of
bread,
17he had sent a man ahead of
them,
Joseph, who was sold as a
slave.
18His feet were hurt with fetters,
his neck was put in a collar
of iron;
19until what he had said came to
pass
the word of the LORD tested
him.
20The king sent and released
him,
the ruler of the peoples set
him free;
21he made him lord of his house,
and ruler of all his
possessions,
22to instruct[c] his princes at his
pleasure,
and to teach his elders
wisdom.
23Then Israel came to Egypt;
Jacob sojourned in the land
of Ham.
24And the LORD made his people
very fruitful,
and made them stronger
than their foes.
25He turned their hearts to hate
his people,
to deal craftily with his
servants.
26He sent Moses his servant,
and Aaron whom he had
chosen.

[c] Gk Syr Jerome: Heb *to bind*

27They wrought his signs among them,
and miracles in the land of Ham.
28He sent darkness, and made the land dark;
they rebelled[a] against his words.
29He turned their waters into blood,
and caused their fish to die.
30Their land swarmed with frogs,
even in the chambers of their kings.
31He spoke, and there came swarms of flies,
and gnats throughout their country.
32He gave them hail for rain,
and lightning that flashed through their land.
33He smote their vines and fig trees,
and shattered the trees of their country.
34He spoke, and the locusts came,
and young locusts without number;
35which devoured all the vegetation in their land,
and ate up the fruit of their ground.
36He smote all the first-born in their land,
the first issue of all their strength.
37Then he led forth Israel with silver and gold,
and there was none among his tribes who stumbled.
38Egypt was glad when they departed,
for dread of them had fallen upon it.
39He spread a cloud for a covering,
and fire to give light by night.
40They asked, and he brought quails,
and gave them bread from heaven in abundance.
41He opened the rock, and water gushed forth;
it flowed through the desert like a river.
42For he remembered his holy promise,
and Abraham his servant.
43So he led forth his people with joy,
his chosen ones with singing.
44And he gave them the lands of the nations;
and they took possession of the fruit of the peoples' toil,
45to the end that they should keep his statutes,
and observe his laws.
Praise the LORD!

A CONFESSION OF ISRAEL'S SINS

106 Praise the LORD!
O give thanks to the LORD, for he is good;
for his steadfast love endures for ever!
2Who can utter the mighty doings of the LORD,
or show forth all his praise?
3Blessed are they who observe justice,
who do righteousness at all times!
4Remember me, O LORD, when thou showest favor to thy people;
help me when thou deliverest them;
5that I may see the prosperity of thy chosen ones,
that I may rejoice in the gladness of thy nation,
that I may glory with thy heritage.
6Both we and our fathers have sinned;
we have committed

[a]Cn Compare Gk Syr: Heb *they did not rebel*

iniquity, we have
done wickedly.
7Our fathers, when they were in
Egypt,
did not consider thy wonderful works;
they did not remember the
abundance of thy steadfast love,
but rebelled against the
Most High[b]
at the Red Sea.
8Yet he saved them for his name's
sake,
that he might make known
his mighty power.
9He rebuked the Red Sea, and it
became dry;
and he led them through the
deep as through a
desert.
10So he saved them from the hand
of the foe,
and delivered them from the
power of the enemy.
11And the waters covered their
adversaries;
not one of them was left.
12Then they believed his words;
they sang his praise.
13But they soon forgot his works;
they did not wait for his
counsel.
14But they had a wanton craving in
the wilderness,
and put God to the test in
the desert;
15he gave them what they asked,
but sent a wasting disease
among them.
16*When men in the camp were*
jealous of Moses
and Aaron, the holy one of
the LORD,
17the earth opened and swallowed
up Dathan,
and covered the company of
Abi′ram.
18Fire also broke out in their
company;
the flame burned up the
wicked.
19They made a calf in Horeb
and worshiped a molten
image.
20They exchanged the glory of God
for the image of an ox that
eats grass.
21They forgot God, their Savior,
who had done great things
in Egypt,
22wondrous works in the land of
Ham,
and terrible things by the
Red Sea.
23Therefore he said he would
destroy them—
had not Moses, his chosen
one,
stood in the breach before him,
to turn away his wrath from
destroying them.
24Then they despised the pleasant
land,
having no faith in his
promise.
25They murmured in their tents,
and did not obey the voice of
the LORD.
26Therefore he raised his hand and
swore to them
that he would make
them fall in the
wilderness,
27and would disperse[c] their
descendants among the
nations,
scattering them over the
lands.
28Then they attached themselves
to the Ba′al of Pe′or,
and ate sacrifices offered to
the dead;
29they provoked the LORD to anger
with their doings,
and a plague broke out
among them.
30Then Phin′ehas stood up and
interposed,
and the plague was stayed.

[b] Cn Compare 78.17, 56: Heb *at the sea*
[c] Syr Compare Ezek 20. 23: Heb *cause to fall*

31And that has been reckoned to
him as righteousness
from generation to genera-
tion for ever.
32They angered him at the waters
of Mer′ibah,
and it went ill with Moses on
their account;
33for they made his spirit bitter,
and he spoke words that
were rash.
34They did not destroy the
peoples,
as the LORD commanded
them,
35but they mingled with the nations
and learned to do as they
did.
36They served their idols,
which became a snare to
them.
37They sacrificed their sons
and their daughters to the
demons;
38they poured out innocent blood,
the blood of their sons and
daughters,
whom they sacrificed to the
idols of Canaan;
and the land was polluted
with blood.
39Thus they became unclean by
their acts,
and played the harlot in
their doings.
40Then the anger of the LORD was
kindled against his people,
and he abhorred his
heritage;
41he gave them into the hand of
the nations,
so that those who hated
them ruled over
them.
42Their enemies oppressed them,
and they were brought into
subjection under
their power.
43Many times he delivered them,
but they were rebellious in
their purposes,
and were brought low
through their
iniquity.
44Nevertheless he regarded their
distress,
when he heard their cry.
45He remembered for their sake
his covenant,
and relented according to
the abundance of his
steadfast love.
46He caused them to be pitied
by all those who held them
captive.
47Save us, O LORD our God,
and gather us from among
the nations,
that we may give thanks to thy
holy name
and glory in thy praise.
48Blessed be the LORD, the God of
Israel,
from everlasting to
everlasting!
And let all the people say,
"Amen!"
Praise the LORD!

BOOK V

THANKSGIVING FOR DELIVERANCE FROM MANY TROUBLES

107 O give thanks to the LORD, for
he is good;
for his steadfast love en-
dures for ever!
2Let the redeemed of the LORD
say so,
whom he has redeemed from
trouble
3and gathered in from the lands,
from the east and from the
west,
from the north and from the
south.
4Some wandered in desert wastes,
finding no way to a city to
dwell in;
5hungry and thirsty,
their soul fainted within
them.
6Then they cried to the LORD in

their trouble,
and he delivered them from
their distress;
7 he led them by a straight way,
till they reached a city to
dwell in.
8 Let them thank the LORD for his
steadfast love,
for his wonderful works to
the sons of men!
9 For he satisfies him who is
thirsty,
and the hungry he fills with
good things.
10 Some sat in darkness and in
gloom,
prisoners in affliction and in
irons,
11 for they had rebelled against the
words of God,
and spurned the counsel of
the Most High.
12 Their hearts were bowed down
with hard labor;
they fell down, with none
to help.
13 Then they cried to the LORD in
their trouble,
and he delivered them from
their distress;
14 he brought them out of darkness
and gloom,
and broke their bonds
asunder.
15 Let them thank the LORD for his
steadfast love,
for his wonderful works to
the sons of men!
16 For he shatters the doors of
bronze,
and cuts in two the bars of
iron.
17 Some were sick[a] through their
sinful ways,
and because of their
iniquities suffered
affliction;
18 they loathed any kind of food,
and they drew near to the
gates of death.
19 Then they cried to the LORD in
their trouble,
and he delivered them from
their distress;
20 he sent forth his word, and
healed them,
and delivered them from
destruction.
21 Let them thank the LORD for his
steadfast love,
for his wonderful works to
the sons of men!
22 And let them offer sacrifices of
thanksgiving,
and tell of his deeds in songs
of joy!
23 Some went down to the sea in
ships,
doing business on the great
waters;
24 they saw the deeds of the LORD,
his wondrous works in the
deep.
25 For he commanded, and raised
the stormy wind,
which lifted up the waves of
the sea.
26 They mounted up to heaven,
they went down to the
depths;
their courage melted away in
their evil plight;
27 they reeled and staggered like
drunken men,
and were at their wits' end.
28 Then they cried to the LORD in
their trouble,
and he delivered them from
their distress;
29 he made the storm be still,
and the waves of the sea
were hushed.
30 Then they were glad because
they had quiet,
and he brought them to their
desired haven.
31 Let them thank the LORD for his
steadfast love,
for his wonderful works to
the sons of men!
32 Let them extol him in the con-
gregation of the people,

[a] Cn: Heb *fools*

and praise him in the
assembly of the
elders.
33 He turns rivers into a desert,
springs of water into thirsty
ground,
34 a fruitful land into a salty waste,
because of the wickedness of
its inhabitants.
35 He turns a desert into pools of
water,
a parched land into springs
of water.
36 And there he lets the hungry
dwell,
and they establish a city to
live in;
37 they sow fields, and plant
vineyards,
and get a fruitful yield.
38 By his blessing they multiply
greatly;
and he does not let their
cattle decrease.
39 When they are diminished and
brought low
through oppression, trouble,
and sorrow,
40 he pours contempt upon princes
and makes them wander in
trackless wastes;
41 but he raises up the needy out of
affliction,
and makes their families like
flocks.
42 The upright see it and are glad;
and all wickedness stops its
mouth.
43 Whoever is wise, let him give
heed to these things;
let men consider the stead-
fast love of the LORD.

PRAISE AND PRAYER FOR VICTORY

A Song. A Psalm of David.

108 *My heart is steadfast, O God,*
my heart is steadfast!
I will sing and make melody!
Awake, my soul!
2 Awake, O harp and lyre!
I will awake the dawn!
3 I will give thanks to thee, O
LORD, among the peoples,
I will sing praises to thee
among the nations.
4 For thy steadfast love is great
above the heavens,
thy faithfulness reaches to
the clouds.
5 Be exalted, O God, above the
heavens!
Let thy glory be over all the
earth!
6 That thy beloved may be
delivered,
give help by thy right hand,
and answer me!
7 God has promised in his
sanctuary:[a]
"With exultation I will di-
vide up Shechem,
and portion out the Vale of
Succoth.
8 Gilead is mine; Manas´seh is
mine;
E´phraim is my helmet;
Judah my scepter.
9 Moab is my washbasin;
upon Edom I cast my shoe;
over Philistia I shout in
triumph."
10 Who will bring me to the forti-
fied city?
Who will lead me to Edom?
11 Hast thou not rejected us, O
God?
Thou dost not go forth, O
God, with our armies.
12 O grant us help against the foe,
for vain is the help of man!
13 With God we shall do valiantly;
it is he who will tread down
our foes.

PRAYER FOR VINDICATION AND VENGEANCE

To the choirmaster. A Psalm of David.

109 Be not silent, O God of my
praise!
2 For wicked and deceitful mouths
are opened against me,

[a] Or *by his holiness*

speaking against me with
lying tongues.
3They beset me with words of
hate,
and attack me without
cause.
4In return for my love they accuse
me,
even as I make prayer for
them.[b]
5So they reward me evil for good,
and hatred for my love.
6Appoint a wicked man against
him;
let an accuser bring him to
trial.[c]
7When he is tried, let him come
forth guilty;
let his prayer be counted
as sin!
8May his days be few;
may another seize his goods!
9May his children be fatherless,
and his wife a widow!
10May his children wander about
and beg;
may they be driven out
of[d] the ruins they
inhabit!
11May the creditor seize all that
he has;
may strangers plunder the
fruits of his toil!
12Let there be none to extend
kindness to him,
nor any to pity his fatherless
children!
13May his posterity be cut off;
may his name be blotted
out in the second
generation!
14May the iniqu[...] of his fathers
be reme[...]ered before the
LORD,
and let no[...]e sin of his
mo[...]r be blotted
out
15Let them be be[...] the LORD
continual[...]

and may his[e] memory be cut
off from the earth!
16For he did not remember to
show kindness,
but pursued the poor and
needy
and the brokenhearted to
their death.
17He loved to curse; let curses
come on him!
He did not like blessing; may
it be far from him!
18He clothed himself with cursing
as his coat,
may it soak into his body
like water,
like oil into his bones!
19May it be like a garment which
he wraps round him,
like a belt with which he
daily girds himself!
20May this be the reward of my
accusers from the LORD,
of those who speak evil
against my life!
21But thou, O God my Lord,
deal on my behalf for thy
name's sake;
because thy steadfast love is
good, deliver me!
22For I am poor and needy,
and my heart is stricken
within me.
23I am gone, like a shadow at
evening;
I am shaken off like a locust.
24My knees are weak through
fasting;
my body has become gaunt.
25I am an object of scorn to my
accusers;
when they see me, they wag
their heads.
26Help me, O LORD my God!
Save me according to thy
steadfast love!
27Let them know that this is thy
hand;
thou, O LORD, hast done it!

[b] Syr: Heb *I prayer*
[c] Heb *stand at his right h[...]*
[d] Gk: Heb *and seek*
[e] Gk: Heb *their*

28 Let them curse, but do thou
bless!
Let my assailants be put
to shame;[a] may thy
servant be glad!
29 May my accusers be clothed with
dishonor;
may they be wrapped in
their own shame as in
a mantle!
30 With my mouth I will give great
thanks to the LORD;
I will praise him in the midst
of the throng.
31 For he stands at the right hand
of the needy,
to save him from those who
condemn him to
death.

ASSURANCE OF VICTORY FOR GOD'S PRIEST-KING

A Psalm of David.

110 *The LORD says to my lord:
"Sit at my right hand,
till I make your enemies your
footstool."
2 The LORD sends forth from Zion
your mighty scepter.
Rule in the midst of your
foes!
3 Your people will offer themselves
freely
on the day you lead your
host
upon the holy mountains.[b]
From the womb of the morning
like dew your youth[c] will
come to you.
4 The LORD has sworn
and will not change his
mind,
"You are a priest for ever
after the order of
Melchiz'edek."
5 The Lord is at your right hand;
he will shatter kings on the
day of his wrath.
6 He will execute judgment among
the nations,
filling them with corpses;
he will shatter chiefs[d]
over the wide earth.
7 He will drink from the brook by
the way;
therefore he will lift up his
head.

PRAISE FOR GOD'S WONDERFUL WORKS

111 Praise the LORD!
I will give thanks to the LORD
with my whole heart,
in the company of the
upright, in the
congregation.
2 Great are the works of the LORD,
studied by all who have
pleasure in them.
3 Full of honor and majesty is his
work,
and his righteousness en-
dures for ever.
4 He has caused his wonderful
works to be remembered;
the LORD is gracious and
merciful.
5 He provides food for those who
fear him;
he is ever mindful of his
covenant.
6 He has shown his people the
power of his works,
in giving them the heritage
of the nations.
7 The works of his hands are faith-
ful and just;
all his precepts are
trutworthy,
8 they are establhed for ever and
ever,
to be perfmed with
faifulness and
ughtness.
9 He sent redetion to his people;
he has cmanded his cove-
rt for ever.
Holy arerrible is his

[a] Gk: Heb *they have arisen and have been put to shame*
[b] Another reading is *in holy array*
[c] Cn: Heb *the dew of your youth*
[d] Or *the head*

name!
10The fear of the LORD is the
beginning of wisdom;
a good understanding have
all those who practice
it.
His praise endures for ever!

BLESSINGS OF THE RIGHTEOUS

112 Praise the LORD!
Blessed is the man who fears
the LORD,
who greatly delights in his
commandments!
2His descendants will be mighty
in the land;
the generation of the upright
will be blessed.
3Wealth and riches are in his
house;
and his righteousness en-
dures for ever.
4Light rises in the darkness for
the upright;
the LORD[e] is gracious, mer-
ciful, and righteous.
5It is well with the man who deals
generously and lends,
who conducts his affairs
with justice.
6For the righteous will never be
moved;
he will be remembered for
ever.
7He is not afraid of evil tidings;
his heart is firm, trusting in
the LORD.
8His heart is steady, he will not be
afraid,
until he sees his desire on
his adversaries.
9He has distributed freely, he has
given to the poor;
his righteousness endures
for ever;
his horn is exalted in honor.
10The wicked man sees it and is
angry;
he gnashes his teeth and
melts away;
the desire of the wicked man
comes to nought.

GOD THE HELPER OF THE NEEDY

113 Praise the LORD!
Praise, O servants of the
LORD,
praise the name of the
LORD!
2Blessed be the name of the LORD
from this time forth and for
evermore!
3From the rising of the sun to its
setting
the name of the LORD is to
be praised!
4The LORD is high above all
nations,
and his glory above the
heavens!
5Who is like the LORD our God,
who is seated on high,
6who looks far down
upon the heavens and the
earth?
7He raises the poor from the dust,
and lifts the needy from the
ash heap,
8to make them sit with princes,
with the princes of his
people.
9He gives the barren woman a
home,
making her the joyous moth-
er of children.
Praise the LORD!

GOD'S WONDERS AT THE EXODUS

114 When Israel went forth from
Egypt,
the house of Jacob from a
people of strange
language,
2Judah became his sanctuary,
Israel his dominion.
3The sea looked and fled,
Jordan turned back.
4The mountains skipped like
rams,
the hills like lambs.
5What ails you, O sea, that you
flee?

[e] Gk: Heb lacks *the* LORD

O Jordan, that you turn
back?
6O mountains, that you skip like
rams?
O hills, like lambs?
7Tremble, O earth, at the presence
of the LORD,
at the presence of the God of
Jacob,
8who turns the rock into a pool of
water,
the flint into a spring of
water.

THE IMPOTENCE OF IDOLS AND THE GREATNESS OF GOD

115 Not to us, O LORD, not to us,
but to thy name give glory,
for the sake of thy stead-
fast love and thy
faithfulness!
2Why should the nations say,
"Where is their God?"
3Our God is in the heavens;
he does whatever he pleases.
4Their idols are silver and gold,
the work of men's hands.
5They have mouths, but do not
speak;
eyes, but do not see.
6They have ears, but do not hear;
noses, but do not smell.
7They have hands, but do not feel;
feet, but do not walk;
and they do not make a
sound in their throat.
8Those who make them are like
them;
so are all who trust in them.
9O Israel, trust in the LORD!
He is their help and their
shield.
10O house of Aaron, put your trust
in the LORD!
He is their help and their
shield.
11You who fear the LORD, trust in
the LORD!
He is their help and their
shield.
12The LORD has been mindful of
us; he will bless us;
he will bless the house of
Israel;
he will bless the house of
Aaron;
13he will bless those who fear the
LORD,
both small and great.
14May the LORD give you increase,
you and your children!
15May you be blessed by the LORD,
who made heaven and earth!
16The heavens are the LORD's
heavens,
but the earth he has given to
the sons of men.
17The dead do not praise the
LORD,
nor do any that go down into
silence.
18But we will bless the LORD
from this time forth and for
evermore.
Praise the LORD!

THANKSGIVING FOR RECOVERY FROM ILLNESS

116 I love the LORD, because he has
heard
my voice and my
supplications.
2Because he inclined his ear to
me,
therefore I will call on him
as long as I live.
3The snares of death encompassed
me;
the pangs of Sheol laid hold
on me;
I suffered distress and
anguish.
4Then I called on the name of the
LORD:
"O LORD, I beseech thee,
save my life!"
5Gracious is the LORD, and
righteous;
our God is merciful.
6The LORD preserves the simple;
when I was brought low, he
saved me.
7Return, O my soul, to your rest;
for the LORD has dealt

bountifully with you.
8For thou hast delivered my soul
from death,
my eyes from tears,
my feet from stumbling;
9I walk before the LORD
in the land of the living.
10I kept my faith, even when I said,
"I am greatly afflicted";
11I said in my consternation,
"Men are all a vain hope."
12What shall I render to the LORD
for all his bounty to me?
13I will lift up the cup of salvation
and call on the name of the
LORD,
14I will pay my vows to the LORD
in the presence of all his
people.
15Precious in the sight of the LORD
is the death of his saints.
16O LORD, I am thy servant;
I am thy servant, the son of
thy handmaid.
Thou hast loosed my bonds.
17I will offer to thee the sacrifice
of thanksgiving
and call on the name of the
LORD.
18I will pay my vows to the LORD
in the presence of all his
people,
19in the courts of the house of the
LORD,
in your midst, O Jerusalem.
Praise the LORD!

UNIVERSAL CALL TO WORSHIP

117 Praise the LORD, all nations!
Extol him, all peoples!
2For great is his steadfast love
toward us;
and the faithfulness of the
LORD endures for
ever.
Praise the LORD!

A SONG OF VICTORY

118 O give thanks to the LORD, for
he is good;
his steadfast love endures
for ever!
2Let Israel say,
"His steadfast love endures
for ever."
3Let the house of Aaron say,
"His steadfast love endures
for ever."
4Let those who fear the LORD say,
"His steadfast love endures
for ever."
5Out of my distress I called on the
LORD;
the LORD answered me and
set me free.
6With the LORD on my side I do
not fear.
What can man do to me?
7The LORD is on my side to help
me;
I shall look in triumph on
those who hate me.
8It is better to take refuge in the
LORD
than to put confidence in
man.
9It is better to take refuge in the
LORD
than to put confidence in
princes.
10All nations surrounded me;
in the name of the LORD I
cut them off!
11They surrounded me, surround-
ed me on every side;
in the name of the LORD I
cut them off!
12They surrounded me like bees,
they blazed[a] like a fire of
thorns;
in the name of the LORD I
cut them off!
13I was pushed hard,[b] so that I was
falling,
but the LORD helped me.
14The LORD is my strength and
my song;
he has become my salvation.
15Hark, glad songs of victory
in the tents of the righteous:

[a] Gk: Heb *were extinguished*
[b] Gk Syr Jerome: Heb *thou didst push me hard*

"The right hand of the LORD
does valiantly,
16the right hand of the LORD
is exalted,
the right hand of the LORD
does valiantly!"
17I shall not die, but I shall live,
and recount the deeds of the
LORD.
18The LORD has chastened me
sorely,
but he has not given me over
to death.
19Open to me the gates of
righteousness,
that I may enter through
them
and give thanks to the
LORD.
20This is the gate of the LORD;
the righteous shall enter
through it.
21I thank thee that thou hast
answered me
and hast become my
salvation.
22The stone which the builders
rejected
has become the head of the
corner.
23This is the LORD's doing;
it is marvelous in our eyes.
24This is the day which the LORD
has made;
let us rejoice and be glad
in it.
25Save us, we beseech thee, O
LORD!
O LORD, we beseech thee,
give us success!
26Blessed be he who enters in the
name of the LORD!
We bless you from the house
of the LORD.
27The LORD is God,
and he has given us light.
Bind the festal procession with
branches,
up to the horns of the altar!
28Thou art my God, and I will give
thanks to thee;
thou art my God, I will extol
thee.
29O give thanks to the LORD, for
he is good;
for his steadfast love en-
dures for ever!

THE GLORIES OF GOD'S LAW

119 *Blessed are those whose way is
blameless,
who walk in the law of the
LORD!
2Blessed are those who keep his
testimonies,
who seek him with their
whole heart,
3who also do no wrong,
but walk in his ways!
4Thou hast commanded thy
precepts
to be kept diligently.
5O that my ways may be steadfast
in keeping thy statutes!
6Then I shall not be put to shame,
having my eyes fixed on all
thy commandments.
7I will praise thee with an upright
heart,
when I learn thy righteous
ordinances.
8I will observe thy statutes;
O forsake me not utterly!
9How can a young man keep his
way pure?
By guarding it according to
thy word.
10With my whole heart I seek thee;
let me not wander from thy
commandments!
11I have laid up thy word in my
heart,
that I might not sin against
thee.
12Blessed be thou, O LORD;
teach me thy statutes!
13With my lips I declare
all the ordinances of thy
mouth.
14In the way of thy testimonies I
delight
as much as in all riches.
15I will meditate on thy precepts,
and fix my eyes on thy ways.

16 I will delight in thy statutes;
I will not forget thy word.
17 Deal bountifully with thy
servant,
that I may live and observe
thy word.
18 Open my eyes, that I may behold
wondrous things out of thy
law.
19 I am a sojourner on earth;
hide not thy commandments
from me!
20 My soul is consumed with
longing
for thy ordinances at all
times.
21 Thou dost rebuke the insolent,
accursed ones,
who wander from thy
commandments;
22 take away from me their scorn
and contempt,
for I have kept thy
testimonies.
23 Even though princes sit plotting
against me,
thy servant will meditate on
thy statutes.
24 Thy testimonies are my delight,
they are my counselors.
25 My soul cleaves to the dust;
revive me according to thy
word!
26 When I told of my ways, thou
didst answer me;
teach me thy statutes!
27 Make me understand the way of
thy precepts,
and I will meditate on thy
wondrous works.
28 *My soul melts away* for sorrow;
strengthen me according to
thy word!
29 Put false ways far from me;
and graciously teach me thy
law!
30 I have chosen the way of
faithfulness,
I set thy ordinances before
me.
31 I cleave to thy testimonies, O
LORD;
let me not be put to shame!
32 I will run in the way of thy
commandments
when thou enlargest my
understanding!
33 Teach me, O LORD, the way of
thy statutes;
and I will keep it to the end.
34 Give me understanding, that I
may keep thy law
and observe it with my
whole heart.
35 Lead me in the path of thy
commandments,
for I delight in it.
36 Incline my heart to thy
testimonies,
and not to gain!
37 Turn my eyes from looking at
vanities;
and give me life in thy ways.
38 Confirm to thy servant thy
promise,
which is for those who fear
thee.
39 Turn away the reproach which
I dread;
for thy ordinances are
good.
40 Behold, I long for thy precepts;
in thy righteousness give
me life!
41 Let thy steadfast love come to
me, O LORD,
thy salvation according to
thy promise;
42 then shall I have an answer for
those who taunt me,
for I trust in thy word.
43 And take not the word of truth
utterly out of my mouth,
for my hope is in thy
ordinances.
44 I will keep thy law continually,
for ever and ever;
45 and I shall walk at liberty,
for I have sought thy
precepts.
46 I will also speak of thy testimo-
nies before kings,
and shall not be put to
shame;

47for I find my delight in thy
commandments,
which I love.
48I revere thy commandments,
which I love,
and I will meditate on thy
statutes.
49Remember thy word to thy
servant,
in which thou hast made me
hope.
50This is my comfort in my
affliction
that thy promise gives me
life.
51Godless men utterly deride me,
but I do not turn away from
thy law.
52When I think of thy ordinances
from of old,
I take comfort, O LORD.
53Hot indignation seizes me be-
cause of the wicked,
who forsake thy law.
54Thy statutes have been my songs
in the house of my
pilgrimage.
55I remember thy name in the
night, O LORD,
and keep thy law.
56This blessing has fallen to me,
that I have kept thy precepts.
57The LORD is my portion;
I promise to keep thy words.
58I entreat thy favor with all my
heart;
be gracious to me according
to thy promise.
59When I think of thy ways,
I turn my feet to thy
testimonies;
60I hasten and do not delay
to keep thy commandments.
61Though the cords of the wicked
ensnare me,
I do not forget thy law.
62At midnight I rise to praise thee,
because of thy righteous
ordinances.
63I am a companion of all who fear
thee,
of those who keep thy
precepts.
64The earth, O LORD, is full of thy
steadfast love;
teach me thy statutes!
65Thou hast dealt well with thy
servant,
O LORD, according to thy
word.
66Teach me good judgment and
knowledge,
for I believe in thy
commandments.
67Before I was afflicted I went
astray;
but now I keep thy word.
68Thou art good and doest good;
teach me thy statutes.
69The godless besmear me with
lies,
but with my whole heart I
keep thy precepts;
70their heart is gross like fat,
but I delight in thy law.
71It is good for me that I was
afflicted,
that I might learn thy
statutes.
72The law of thy mouth is better
to me
than thousands of gold and
silver pieces.
73Thy hands have made and fash-
ioned me;
give me understanding
that I may learn thy
commandments.
74Those who fear thee shall see me
and rejoice,
because I have hoped in thy
word.
75I know, O LORD, that thy judg-
ments are right,
and that in faithfulness thou
hast afflicted me.
76Let thy steadfast love be ready to
comfort me
according to thy promise to
thy servant.
77Let thy mercy come to me, that I
may live;
for thy law is my delight.
78Let the godless be put to shame,

because they have subverted
me with guile;
as for me, I will meditate on
thy precepts.
79Let those who fear thee turn
to me,
that they may know thy
testimonies.
80May my heart be blameless in
thy statutes,
that I may not be put to
shame!
81My soul languishes for thy
salvation;
I hope in thy word.
82My eyes fail with watching for
thy promise;
I ask, "When wilt thou com-
fort me?"
83For I have become like a wine-
skin in the smoke,
yet I have not forgotten thy
statutes.
84How long must thy servant
endure?
When wilt thou judge those
who persecute me?
85Godless men have dug pitfalls
for me,
men who do not conform to
thy law.
86All thy commandments are
sure;
they persecute me with
falsehood; help me!
87They have almost made an end
of me on earth;
but I have not forsaken thy
precepts.
88In thy steadfast love spare my
life,
that I may keep the testimo-
nies of thy mouth.
89For ever, O LORD, thy word
is firmly fixed in the
heavens.
90Thy faithfulness endures to all
generations;
thou hast established the
earth, and it stands
fast.
91By thy appointment they stand
this day;
for all things are thy
servants.
92If thy law had not been my
delight,
I should have perished in my
affliction.
93I will never forget thy precepts;
for by them thou hast given
me life.
94I am thine, save me;
for I have sought thy
precepts.
95The wicked lie in wait to destroy
me;
but I consider thy
testimonies.
96I have seen a limit to all
perfection,
but thy commandment is
exceedingly broad.
97Oh, how I love thy law!
It is my meditation all the
day.
98Thy commandment makes me
wiser than my enemies,
for it is ever with me.
99I have more understanding than
all my teachers,
for thy testimonies are my
meditation.
100I understand more than the
aged,
for I keep thy precepts.
101I hold back my feet from every
evil way,
in order to keep thy word.
102I do not turn aside from thy
ordinances,
for thou hast taught me.
103How sweet are thy words to my
taste,
sweeter than honey to my
mouth!
104Through thy precepts I get
understanding;
therefore I hate every false
way.
105Thy word is a lamp to my feet
and a light to my path.
106I have sworn an oath and con-
firmed it,

to observe thy righteous
ordinances.
107 I am sorely afflicted;
give me life, O LORD, according to thy word!
108 Accept my offerings of praise,
O LORD,
and teach me thy
ordinances.
109 I hold my life in my hand
continually,
but I do not forget thy law.
110 The wicked have laid a snare
for me,
but I do not stray from thy
precepts.
111 Thy testimonies are my heritage
for ever;
yea, they are the joy of my
heart.
112 I incline my heart to perform
thy statutes
for ever, to the end.
113 I hate double-minded men,
but I love thy law.
114 Thou art my hiding place and
my shield;
I hope in thy word.
115 Depart from me, you evildoers,
that I may keep the commandments of my
God.
116 Uphold me according to thy
promise, that I may live,
and let me not be put to
shame in my hope!
117 Hold me up, that I may be safe
and have regard for thy statutes continually!
118 Thou dost spurn all who go
astray from thy statutes;
yea, their cunning is in vain.
119 All the wicked of the earth thou
dost count as dross;
therefore I love thy
testimonies.
120 My flesh trembles for fear of
thee,
and I am afraid of thy
judgments.
121 I have done what is just and
right;
do not leave me to my
oppressors.
122 Be surety for thy servant for
good;
let not the godless oppress
me.
123 My eyes fail with watching for
thy salvation,
and for the fulfilment of thy
righteous promise.
124 Deal with thy servant according
to thy steadfast love,
and teach me thy statutes.
125 I am thy servant; give me
understanding,
that I may know thy
testimonies!
126 It is time for the LORD to act,
for thy law has been broken.
127 Therefore I love thy
commandments
above gold, above fine gold.
128 Therefore I direct my steps by
all thy precepts;[a]
I hate every false way.
129 Thy testimonies are wonderful;
therefore my soul keeps
them.
130 The unfolding of thy words
gives light;
it imparts understanding to
the simple.
131 With open mouth I pant,
because I long for thy
commandments.
132 Turn to me and be gracious to
me,
as is thy wont toward those
who love thy name.
133 Keep steady my steps according
to thy promise,
and let no iniquity get dominion over me.
134 Redeem me from man's
oppression,
that I may keep thy precepts.
135 Make thy face shine upon thy
servant,
and teach me thy statutes.
136 My eyes shed streams of tears,

[a] Gk Jerome: Heb uncertain

because men do not keep
thy law.
137Righteous art thou, O LORD,
and right are thy judgments.
138Thou hast appointed thy testimonies in righteousness
and in all faithfulness.
139My zeal consumes me,
because my foes forget thy words.
140Thy promise is well tried,
and thy servant loves it.
141I am small and despised,
yet I do not forget thy precepts.
142Thy righteousness is righteous for ever,
and thy law is true.
143Trouble and anguish have come upon me,
but thy commandments are my delight.
144Thy testimonies are righteous for ever;
give me understanding that I may live.
145With my whole heart I cry;
answer me, O LORD!
I will keep thy statutes.
146I cry to thee; save me,
that I may observe thy testimonies.
147I rise before dawn and cry for help;
I hope in thy words.
148My eyes are awake before the watches of the night,
that I may meditate upon thy promise.
149Hear my voice in thy steadfast love;
O LORD, in thy justice preserve my life.
150They draw near who persecute me with evil purpose;
they are far from thy law.
151But thou art near, O LORD,
and all thy commandments are true.
152Long have I known from thy testimonies
that thou hast founded them for ever.
153Look on my affliction and deliver me,
for I do not forget thy law.
154Plead my cause and redeem me;
give me life according to thy promise!
155Salvation is far from the wicked,
for they do not seek thy statutes.
156Great is thy mercy, O LORD;
give me life according to thy justice.
157Many are my persecutors and my adversaries,
but I do not swerve from thy testimonies.
158I look at the faithless with disgust,
because they do not keep thy commands.
159Consider how I love thy precepts!
Preserve my life according to thy steadfast love.
160The sum of thy word is truth;
and every one of thy righteous ordinances
endures for ever.
161Princes persecute me without cause,
but my heart stands in awe of thy words.
162I rejoice at thy word
like one who finds great spoil.
163I hate and abhor falsehood,
but I love thy law.
164Seven times a day I praise thee
for thy righteous ordinances.
165Great peace have those who love thy law;
nothing can make them stumble.
166I hope for thy salvation, O LORD,
and I do thy commandments.
167My soul keeps thy testimonies;
I love them exceedingly.
168I keep thy precepts and testimonies,

for all my ways are before thee.

169Let my cry come before thee, O LORD;
give me understanding according to thy word!

170Let my supplication come before thee;
deliver me according to thy word.

171My lips will pour forth praise
that thou dost teach me thy statutes.

172My tongue will sing of thy word,
for all thy commandments are right.

173Let thy hand be ready to help me,
for I have chosen thy precepts.

174I long for thy salvation, O LORD,
and thy law is my delight.

175Let me live, that I may praise thee,
and let thy ordinances help me.

176I have gone astray like a lost sheep; seek thy servant,
for I do not forget thy commandments.

PRAYER FOR DELIVERANCE FROM SLANDERERS

A Song of Ascents.

120 *In my distress I cry to the LORD,
that he may answer me:

2"Deliver me, O LORD,
from lying lips,
from a deceitful tongue."

3What shall be given to you?
And what more shall be done to you,
you deceitful tongue?

4A warrior's sharp arrows,
with glowing coals of the broom tree!

5Woe is me, that I sojourn in Meshech,
that I dwell among the tents of Kedar!

6Too long have I had my dwelling
among those who hate peace.

7I am for peace;
but when I speak,
they are for war!

ASSURANCE OF GOD'S PROTECTION

A Song of Ascents.

121 I lift up my eyes to the hills.
From whence does my help come?

2My help comes from the LORD,
who made heaven and earth.

3He will not let your foot be moved,
he who keeps you will not slumber.

4Behold, he who keeps Israel
will neither slumber nor sleep.

5The LORD is your keeper;
the LORD is your shade
on your right hand.

6The sun shall not smite you by day,
nor the moon by night.

7The LORD will keep you from all evil;
he will keep your life.

8The LORD will keep
your going out and your coming in
from this time forth and for evermore.

SONG OF PRAISE AND PRAYER FOR JERUSALEM

A Song of Ascents. Of David.

122 I was glad when they said to me,
"Let us go to the house of the LORD!"

2Our feet have been standing
within your gates, O Jerusalem!

3Jerusalem, built as a city
which is bound firmly together,

4to which the tribes go up,
the tribes of the LORD,
as was decreed for Israel,
to give thanks to the name
of the LORD.
5There thrones for judgment were
set,
the thrones of the house of
David.
6Pray for the peace of Jerusalem!
"May they prosper who love
you!
7Peace be within your walls,
and security within your
towers!"
8For my brethren and compan-
ions' sake
I will say, "Peace be within
you!"
9For the sake of the house of the
LORD our God,
I will seek your good.

SUPPLICATION FOR MERCY

A Song of Ascents.

123 To thee I lift up my eyes,
O thou who art enthroned in
the heavens!
2Behold, as the eyes of servants
look to the hand of their
master,
as the eyes of a maid
to the hand of her mistress,
so our eyes look to the LORD
our God,
till he have mercy upon us.
3Have mercy upon us, O LORD,
have mercy upon us,
for we have had more than
enough of contempt.
4Too long our soul has been
sated
with the scorn of those who
are at ease,
the contempt of the proud.

THANKSGIVING FOR ISRAEL'S DELIVERANCE

A Song of Ascents. Of David.

124 If it had not been the LORD who
was on our side,
let Israel now say—
2if it had not been the LORD who
was on our side,
when men rose up against
us,
3then they would have swallowed
us up alive,
when their anger was kin-
dled against us;
4then the flood would have swept
us away,
the torrent would have gone
over us;
5then over us would have gone
the raging waters.
6Blessed be the LORD,
who has not given us
as prey to their teeth!
7We have escaped as a bird
from the snare of the
fowlers;
the snare is broken,
and we have escaped!
8Our help is in the name of the
LORD,
who made heaven and earth.

THE SECURITY OF GOD'S PEOPLE

A Song of Ascents.

125 Those who trust in the LORD
are like Mount Zion,
which cannot be moved, but
abides for ever.
2As the mountains are round
about Jerusalem,
so the LORD is round about
his people,
from this time forth and for
evermore.
3For the scepter of wickedness
shall not rest
upon the land allotted to the
righteous,
lest the righteous put forth
their hands to do wrong.
4Do good, O LORD, to those who
are good,
and to those who are upright
in their hearts!
5But those who turn aside upon
their crooked ways

the LORD will lead away
with evildoers!
Peace be in Israel!

A HARVEST OF JOY

A Song of Ascents.

126 When the LORD restored the
fortunes of Zion,[a]
we were like those who
dream.
2 Then our mouth was filled with
laughter,
and our tongue with shouts
of joy;
then they said among the
nations,
"The LORD has done great
things for them."
3 The LORD has done great things
for us;
we are glad.
4 Restore our fortunes, O LORD,
like the watercourses in the
Negeb!
5 May those who sow in tears
reap with shouts of joy!
6 He that goes forth weeping,
bearing the seed for sowing,
shall come home with shouts
of joy,
bringing his sheaves with
him.

GOD'S BLESSINGS IN THE HOME

A Song of Ascents. Of Solomon.

127 Unless the LORD builds the
house,
those who build it labor in
vain.
Unless the LORD watches over
the city,
the watchman stays awake
in vain.
2 It is in vain that you rise up early
and go late to rest,
eating the bread of anxious
toil;
for[b] he gives to his beloved
sleep.
3 Lo, sons are a heritage from the
LORD,
the fruit of the womb a
reward.
4 Like arrows in the hand of a
warrior
are the sons of one's youth.
5 Happy is the man who has
his quiver full of them!
He shall not be put to shame
when he speaks with his
enemies in the gate.

THE HAPPY HOME OF THE FAITHFUL

A Song of Ascents.

128 Blessed is every one who fears
the LORD,
who walks in his ways!
2 You shall eat the fruit of the
labor of your hands;
you shall be happy, and it
shall be well with
you.
3 Your wife will be like a fruitful
vine
within your house;
your children will be like olive
shoots
around your table.
4 Lo, thus shall the man be blessed
who fears the LORD.
5 The LORD bless you from Zion!
May you see the prosperity
of Jerusalem
all the days of your life!
6 May you see your children's
children!
Peace be upon Israel!

PRAYER FOR THE DOWNFALL OF ISRAEL'S ENEMIES

A Song of Ascents.

129 "Sorely have they afflicted me
from my youth,"
let Israel now say—
2 "Sorely have they afflicted me
from my youth,
yet they have not prevailed
against me.

[a] Or *brought back those who returned to Zion*
[b] Another reading is *so*

3The plowers plowed upon my back;
they made long their furrows."
4The LORD is righteous;
he has cut the cords of the wicked.
5May all who hate Zion
be put to shame and turned backward!
6Let them be like the grass on the housetops,
which withers before it grows up,
7with which the reaper does not fill his hand
or the binder of sheaves his bosom,
8while those who pass by do not say,
"The blessing of the LORD be upon you!
We bless you in the name of the LORD!"

WAITING FOR DIVINE REDEMPTION

A Song of Ascents.

130 Out of the depths I cry to thee, O LORD! 2Lord, hear my voice!
Let thy ears be attentive
to the voice of my supplications!
3If thou, O LORD, shouldst mark iniquities,
Lord, who could stand?
4But there is forgiveness with thee,
that thou mayest be feared.
5I wait for the LORD, my soul waits,
and in his word I hope;
6my soul waits for the LORD
more than watchmen for the morning,
more than watchmen for the morning.
7O Israel, hope in the LORD!
For with the LORD there is steadfast love,
and with him is plenteous redemption.
8And he will redeem Israel
from all his iniquities.

SONG OF QUIET TRUST

A Song of Ascents. Of David.

131 O LORD, my heart is not lifted up,
my eyes are not raised too high;
I do not occupy myself with things
too great and too marvelous for me.
2But I have calmed and quieted my soul,
like a child quieted at its mother's breast;
like a child that is quieted is my soul.
3O Israel, hope in the LORD
from this time forth and for evermore.

THE ETERNAL DWELLING OF GOD IN ZION

A Song of Ascents.

132 Remember, O LORD, in David's favor,
all the hardships he endured;
2how he swore to the LORD
and vowed to the Mighty One of Jacob,
3"I will not enter my house
or get into my bed;
4I will not give sleep to my eyes
or slumber to my eyelids,
5until I find a place for the LORD,
a dwelling place for the Mighty One of Jacob."
6Lo, we heard of it in Eph′rathah,
we found it in the fields of Ja′ar.
7"Let us go to his dwelling place;
let us worship at his footstool!"
8Arise, O LORD, and go to thy resting place,
thou and the ark of thy might.

9Let thy priests be clothed with righteousness,
and let thy saints shout for joy.
10For thy servant David's sake
do not turn away the face of thy anointed one.
11The LORD swore to David a sure oath
from which he will not turn back:
"One of the sons of your body
I will set on your throne.
12If your sons keep my covenant
and my testimonies which I shall teach them,
their sons also for ever
shall sit upon your throne."
13For the LORD has chosen Zion;
he has desired it for his habitation:
14"This is my resting place for ever;
here I will dwell, for I have desired it.
15I will abundantly bless her provisions;
I will satisfy her poor with bread.
16Her priests I will clothe with salvation,
and her saints will shout for joy.
17There I will make a horn to sprout for David;
I have prepared a lamp for my anointed.
18His enemies I will clothe with shame,
but upon himself his crown will shed its luster."

THE BLESSEDNESS OF UNITY

A Song of Ascents.

133 Behold, how good and pleasant *it is*
when brothers dwell in unity!
2It is like the precious oil upon the head,
running down upon the beard,
upon the beard of Aaron,
running down on the collar of his robes!
3It is like the dew of Hermon,
which falls on the mountains of Zion!
For there the LORD has commanded the blessing,
life for evermore.

PRAISE IN THE NIGHT

A Song of Ascents.

134 Come, bless the LORD,
all you servants of the LORD,
who stand by night in the house of the LORD!
2Lift up your hands to the holy place,
and bless the LORD!
3May the LORD bless you from Zion,
he who made heaven and earth!

PRAISE FOR GOD'S GOODNESS AND MIGHT

135 Praise the LORD!
Praise the name of the LORD,
give praise, O servants of the LORD,
2you that stand in the house of the LORD,
in the courts of the house of our God!
3Praise the LORD, for the LORD is good;
sing to his name, for he is gracious!
4For the LORD has chosen Jacob for himself,
Israel as his own possession.
5For I know that the LORD is great,
and that our Lord is above all gods.
6Whatever the LORD pleases he does,
in heaven and on earth,
in the seas and all deeps.
7He it is who makes the clouds
rise at the end of the earth,

who makes lightnings for the rain
and brings forth the wind from his storehouses.
8He it was who smote the first-born of Egypt,
both of man and of beast;
9who in thy midst, O Egypt,
sent signs and wonders
against Pharaoh and all his servants;
10who smote many nations
and slew mighty kings,
11Sihon, king of the Amorites,
and Og, king of Bashan,
and all the kingdoms of Canaan,
12and gave their land as a heritage,
a heritage to his people Israel.
13Thy name, O LORD, endures for ever,
thy renown, O LORD,
throughout all ages.
14For the LORD will vindicate his people,
and have compassion on his servants.
15The idols of the nations are silver and gold,
the work of men's hands.
16They have mouths, but they speak not,
they have eyes, but they see not,
17they have ears, but they hear not,
nor is there any breath in their mouths.
18Like them be those who make them!—
yea, every one who trusts in them!
19O house of Israel, bless the LORD!
O house of Aaron, bless the LORD!
20O house of Levi, bless the LORD!
You that fear the LORD,
bless the LORD!
21Blessed be the LORD from Zion,
he who dwells in Jerusalem!
Praise the LORD!

GOD'S WORK IN CREATION AND IN HISTORY

136 O give thanks to the LORD, for he is good,
for his steadfast love endures for ever.
2O give thanks to the God of gods,
for his steadfast love endures for ever.
3O give thanks to the Lord of lords,
for his steadfast love endures for ever;
4to him who alone does great wonders,
for his steadfast love endures for ever;
5to him who by understanding made the heavens,
for his steadfast love endures for ever;
6to him who spread out the earth upon the waters,
for his steadfast love endures for ever;
7to him who made the great lights,
for his steadfast love endures for ever;
8the sun to rule over the day,
for his steadfast love endures for ever;
9the moon and stars to rule over the night,
for his steadfast love endures for ever;
10to him who smote the first-born of Egypt,
for his steadfast love endures for ever;
11and brought Israel out from among them,
for his steadfast love endures for ever;
12with a strong hand and an outstretched arm,
for his steadfast love endures for ever;

13to him who divided the Red Sea
in sunder,
for his steadfast love endures for ever;
14and made Israel pass through
the midst of it,
for his steadfast love endures for ever;
15but overthrew Pharaoh and his
host in the Red Sea,
for his steadfast love endures for ever;
16to him who led his people
through the wilderness,
for his steadfast love endures for ever;
17to him who smote great kings,
for his steadfast love endures for ever;
18and slew famous kings,
for his steadfast love endures for ever;
19Sihon, king of the Amorites,
for his steadfast love endures for ever;
20and Og, king of Bashan,
for his steadfast love endures for ever;
21and gave their land as a
heritage,
for his steadfast love endures for ever;
22a heritage to Israel his servant,
for his steadfast love endures for ever.
23It is he who remembered us in
our low estate,
for his steadfast love endures for ever;
24and rescued us from our foes,
for his steadfast love endures for ever;
25he who gives food to all flesh,
for his steadfast love endures for ever.
26O give thanks to the God of
heaven,
for his steadfast love endures for ever.

LAMENT OVER THE DESTRUCTION OF JERUSALEM

137 *By the waters[a] of Babylon,
there we sat down and wept,
when we remembered Zion.
2On the willows[b] there
we hung up our lyres.
3For there our captors
required of us songs,
and our tormentors, mirth,
saying,
"Sing us one of the songs of
Zion!"
4How shall we sing the LORD's
song
in a foreign land?
5If I forget you, O Jerusalem,
let my right hand wither!
6Let my tongue cleave to the roof
of my mouth,
if I do not remember you,
if I do not set Jerusalem
above my highest joy!
7Remember, O LORD, against the
E´domites
the day of Jerusalem,
how they said, "Raze it,
raze it!
Down to its foundations!"
8O daughter of Babylon, you
devastator![c]
Happy shall he be who
requites you
with what you have done
to us!
9Happy shall he be who takes your
little ones
and dashes them against the
rock!

THANKSGIVING AND PRAISE

A Psalm of David.

138 I give thee thanks, O LORD,
with my whole heart;
before the gods I sing thy
praise;
2I bow down toward thy holy
temple

[a]Heb *streams*
[b]Or *poplars*
[c]Or *you who are devastated*

and give thanks to thy name
for thy steadfast love
and thy faithfulness;
for thou hast exalted above
everything
thy name and thy word.[d]
3On the day I called, thou didst
answer me,
my strength of soul thou
didst increase.[e]
4All the kings of the earth shall
praise thee, O LORD,
for they have heard the
words of thy mouth;
5and they shall sing of the ways of
the LORD,
for great is the glory of the
LORD.
6For though the LORD is high, he
regards the lowly;
but the haughty he knows
from afar.
7Though I walk in the midst of
trouble,
thou dost preserve my life;
thou dost stretch out thy hand
against the wrath of my
enemies,
and thy right hand delivers
me.
8The LORD will fulfil his purpose
for me;
thy steadfast love, O LORD,
endures for ever.
Do not forsake the work of
thy hands.

THE INESCAPABLE GOD

To the choirmaster. A Psalm of David.

139 O LORD, thou hast searched me
and known me!
2Thou knowest when I sit down
and when I rise up;
thou discernest my thoughts
from afar.
3Thou searchest out my path and
my lying down,
and art acquainted with all
my ways.
4Even before a word is on my
tongue,
lo, O LORD, thou knowest it
altogether.
5Thou dost beset me behind and
before,
and layest thy hand upon
me.
6Such knowledge is too wonderful
for me;
it is high, I cannot attain it.
7Whither shall I go from thy
Spirit?
Or whither shall I flee from
thy presence?
8If I ascend to heaven, thou art
there!
If I make my bed in Sheol,
thou art there!
9If I take the wings of the
morning
and dwell in the uttermost
parts of the sea,
10even there thy hand shall lead
me,
and thy right hand shall hold
me.
11If I say, "Let only darkness cover
me,
and the light about me be
night,"
12even the darkness is not dark
to thee,
the night is bright as the
day;
for darkness is as light with
thee.
13For thou didst form my inward
parts,
thou didst knit me together
in my mother's
womb.
14I praise thee, for thou art fearful
and wonderful.[f]
Wonderful are thy works!
Thou knowest me right well;
15my frame was not hidden
from thee,
when I was being made in
secret,

[d]Cn: Heb *thou hast exalted thy word above all thy name*
[e]Syr Compare Gk Tg: Heb *thou didst make me arrogant in my soul with strength*
[f]Cn Compare Gk Syr Jerome: Heb *fearful things I am wonderful*

intricately wrought in the
depths of the earth.
16 Thy eyes beheld my unformed
substance;
in thy book were written,
every one of them,
the days that were formed for
me,
when as yet there was none
of them.
17 How precious to me are thy
thoughts, O God!
How vast is the sum of
them!
18 If I would count them, they are
more than the sand.
When I awake, I am still
with thee.[a]
19 O that thou wouldst slay the
wicked, O God,
and that men of blood would
depart from me,
20 men who maliciously defy thee,
who lift themselves up
against thee for evil![b]
21 Do I not hate them that hate
thee, O LORD?
And do I not loathe them
that rise up against
thee?
22 I hate them with perfect hatred;
I count them my enemies.
23 Search me, O God, and know my
heart!
Try me and know my
thoughts!
24 And see if there be any wicked[c]
way in me,
and lead me in the way
everlasting![d]

PRAYER FOR DELIVERANCE FROM ENEMIES

To the choirmaster. A Psalm of David.

140 Deliver me, O LORD, from evil
men;
preserve me from violent
men,
2 who plan evil things in their
heart,
and stir up wars continually.
3 They make their tongue sharp as
a serpent's,
and under their lips is
the poison of
vipers. *Selah*
4 Guard me, O LORD, from the
hands of the wicked;
preserve me from violent
men,
who have planned to trip up
my feet.
5 Arrogant men have hidden a trap
for me,
and with cords they have
spread a net,[e]
by the wayside they have set
snares for me. *Selah*
6 I say to the LORD, Thou art my
God;
give ear to the voice of my
supplications, O
LORD!
7 O LORD, my Lord, my strong
deliverer,
thou hast covered my head
in the day of battle.
8 Grant not, O LORD, the desires of
the wicked;
do not further his evil
plot! *Selah*
9 Those who surround me lift up
their head,[f]
let the mischief of their lips
overwhelm them!
10 Let burning coals fall upon
them!
Let them be cast into pits,
no more to rise!
11 Let not the slanderer be estab-
lished in the land;
let evil hunt down the vio-
lent man speedily!
12 I know that the LORD maintains
the cause of the afflicted,

[a] Or *were I to come to the end I would still be with thee*
[b] Cn: Heb uncertain
[c] Heb *hurtful*
[d] Or *the ancient way.* Compare Jer 6. 16
[e] Or *they have spread cords as a net*
[f] Cn Compare Gk: Heb *those who surround me are uplifted in head*

and executes justice for the needy.
13Surely the righteous shall give thanks to thy name;
the upright shall dwell in thy presence.

PRAYER FOR PRESERVATION FROM EVIL

A Psalm of David.

141 I call upon thee, O LORD; make haste to me!
Give ear to my voice, when I call to thee!
2Let my prayer be counted as incense before thee,
and the lifting up of my hands as an evening sacrifice!
3Set a guard over my mouth, O LORD,
keep watch over the door of my lips!
4Incline not my heart to any evil,
to busy myself with wicked deeds
in company with men who work iniquity;
and let me not eat of their dainties!
5Let a good man strike or rebuke me in kindness,
but let the oil of the wicked never anoint my head;[g]
for my prayer is continually[h] against their wicked deeds.
6When they are given over to those who shall condemn them,
then they shall learn that the word of the LORD is true.
7As a rock which one cleaves and shatters on the land,
so shall their bones be strewn at the mouth of Sheol.[i]
8But my eyes are toward thee, O LORD God;
in thee I seek refuge; leave me not defenseless!
9Keep me from the trap which they have laid for me,
and from the snares of evildoers!
10Let the wicked together fall into their own nets,
while I escape.

PRAYER FOR DELIVERANCE FROM PERSECUTORS

A Maskil of David, when he was in the cave. A Prayer.

142 I cry with my voice to the LORD,
with my voice I make supplication to the LORD,
2I pour out my complaint before him,
I tell my trouble before him.
3When my spirit is faint,
thou knowest my way!
In the path where I walk
they have hidden a trap for me.
4I look to the right and watch,[j]
but there is none who takes notice of me;
no refuge remains to me,
no man cares for me.
5I cry to thee, O LORD;
I say, Thou art my refuge,
my portion in the land of the living.
6Give heed to my cry;
for I am brought very low!
Deliver me from my persecutors;
for they are too strong for me!
7Bring me out of prison,
that I may give thanks to thy name!
The righteous will surround me;

[g] Gk: Heb obscure
[h] Cn: Heb *for continually and my prayer*
[i] The Hebrew of verses 5-7 is obscure
[j] Or *Look to the right and watch*

for thou wilt deal bountifully with me.

PRAYER FOR DELIVERANCE FROM ENEMIES

A Psalm of David.

143 Hear my prayer, O LORD;
give ear to my supplications!
In thy faithfulness answer me, in thy righteousness!
2Enter not into judgment with thy servant;
for no man living is righteous before thee.
3For the enemy has pursued me;
he has crushed my life to the ground;
he has made me sit in darkness like those long dead.
4Therefore my spirit faints within me;
my heart within me is appalled.
5I remember the days of old,
I meditate on all that thou hast done;
I muse on what thy hands have wrought.
6I stretch out my hands to thee;
my soul thirsts for thee like a parched land. *Selah*
7Make haste to answer me, O LORD!
My spirit fails!
Hide not thy face from me,
lest I be like those who go down to the Pit.
8Let me hear in the morning of thy steadfast love,
for in thee I put my trust.
Teach me the way I should go,
for to thee I lift up my soul.
9Deliver me, O LORD, from my enemies!
I have fled to thee for refuge![a]
10Teach me to do thy will,
for thou art my God!
Let thy good spirit lead me on a level path!
11For thy name's sake, O LORD,
preserve my life!
In thy righteousness bring me out of trouble!
12And in thy steadfast love cut off my enemies,
and destroy all my adversaries,
for I am thy servant.

PRAYER FOR NATIONAL DELIVERANCE AND SECURITY

A Psalm of David.

144 Blessed be the LORD, my rock,
who trains my hands for war,
and my fingers for battle;
2my rock[b] and my fortress,
my stronghold and my deliverer,
my shield and he in whom I take refuge,
who subdues the peoples under him.[c]
3O LORD, what is man that thou dost regard him,
or the son of man that thou dost think of him?
4Man is like a breath,
his days are like a passing shadow.
5Bow thy heavens, O LORD, and come down!
Touch the mountains that they smoke!
6Flash forth the lightning and scatter them,
send out thy arrows and rout them!
7Stretch forth thy hand from on high,
rescue me and deliver me from the many waters,
from the hand of aliens,
8whose mouths speak lies,
and whose right hand is

[a] One Heb Ms Gk: Heb *to thee I have hidden*
[b] With Ps 18. 2, 2Sam 22. 2: Heb *my steadfast love*
[c] Another reading is *my people under me*

a right hand of
falsehood.
9I will sing a new song to thee,
O God;
upon a ten-stringed harp I
will play to thee,
10who givest victory to kings,
who rescuest David thy[d]
servant.
11Rescue me from the cruel
sword,
and deliver me from the
hand of aliens,
whose mouths speak lies,
and whose right hand is
a right hand of
falsehood.
12May our sons in their youth
be like plants full grown,
our daughters like corner
pillars
cut for the structure of a
palace;
13may our garners be full,
providing all manner of
store;
may our sheep bring forth
thousands
and ten thousands in our
fields;
14may our cattle be heavy with
young,
suffering no mischance or
failure in bearing;
may there be no cry of distress
in our streets!
15Happy the people to whom such
blessings fall!
Happy the people whose
God is the LORD!

THE GREATNESS AND THE GOODNESS OF GOD

A Song of Praise. Of David.

145 I will extol thee, my God and
King,
and bless thy name for ever
and ever.
2Every day I will bless thee,
and praise thy name for ever
and ever.
3Great is the LORD, and greatly to
be praised,
and his greatness is
unsearchable.
4One generation shall laud thy
works to another,
and shall declare thy mighty
acts.
5On the glorious splendor of thy
majesty,
and on thy wondrous works,
I will meditate.
6Men shall proclaim the might of
thy terrible acts,
and I will declare thy
greatness.
7They shall pour forth the
fame of thy abundant
goodness,
and shall sing aloud of thy
righteousness.
8The LORD is gracious and
merciful,
slow to anger and abounding
in steadfast love.
9The LORD is good to all,
and his compassion is over
all that he has made.
10All thy works shall give thanks
to thee, O LORD
and tell of thy power,
12to make known to the sons of
men thy[e] mighty deeds,
and the glorious splendor of
thy[f] kingdom.
13Thy kingdom is an everlasting
kingdom,
and thy dominion endures
throughout all
generations.
The LORD is faithful in all his
words,
and gracious in all his
deeds.[g]
14The LORD upholds all who are
falling,

[d]Heb *his*
[e]Heb *his*
[f]Heb *his*
[g]These two lines are supplied by one Hebrew Ms, Gk and Syr

and raises up all who are
bowed down.
15The eyes of all look to thee,
and thou givest them their
food in due season.
16Thou openest thy hand,
thou satisfiest the desire of
every living thing.
17The LORD is just in all his ways,
and kind in all his doings.
18The LORD is near to all who call
upon him,
to all who call upon him in
truth.
19He fulfils the desire of all who
fear him,
he also hears their cry, and
saves them.
20The LORD preserves all who love
him;
but all the wicked he will
destroy.
21My mouth will speak the praise
of the LORD,
and let all flesh bless his holy
name for ever and
ever.

PRAISE FOR GOD'S HELP

146 Praise the LORD!
Praise the LORD, O my soul!
2I will praise the LORD as long as
I live;
I will sing praises to my God
while I have being.
3Put not your trust in princes,
in a son of man, in whom
there is no help.
4When his breath departs he
returns to his earth;
on that very day his plans
perish.
5Happy is he whose help is the
God of Jacob,
whose hope is in the LORD
his God,
6who made heaven and earth,
the sea, and all that is in
them;
who keeps faith for ever;
7who executes justice for the
oppressed;
who gives food to the
hungry.
The LORD sets the prisoners
free;
8the LORD opens the eyes of
the blind.
The LORD lifts up those who
are bowed down;
the LORD loves the
righteous.
9The LORD watches over the
sojourners,
he upholds the widow and
the fatherless;
but the way of the wicked he
brings to ruin.
10The LORD will reign for ever,
thy God, O Zion, to all
generations.
Praise the LORD!

PRAISE FOR GOD'S CARE FOR JERUSALEM

147 Praise the LORD!
For it is good to sing praises to
our God;
for he is gracious, and a song
of praise is seemly.
2The LORD builds up Jerusalem;
he gathers the outcasts of
Israel.
3He heals the brokenhearted,
and binds up their wounds.
4He determines the number of the
stars,
he gives to all of them their
names.
5Great is our LORD, and abundant
in power;
his understanding is beyond
measure.
6The LORD lifts up the
downtrodden,
he casts the wicked to the
ground.
7Sing to the LORD with
thanksgiving;
make melody to our God
upon the lyre!
8He covers the heavens with
clouds,
he prepares rain for the
earth,

he makes grass grow upon
the hills.
9He gives to the beasts their food,
and to the young ravens
which cry.
10His delight is not in the strength
of the horse,
nor his pleasure in the legs
of a man;
11but the LORD takes pleasure in
those who fear him,
in those who hope in his
steadfast love.
12Praise the LORD, O Jerusalem!
Praise your God, O Zion!
13For he strengthens the bars of
your gates;
he blesses your sons within
you.
14He makes peace in your borders;
he fills you with the finest of
the wheat.
15He sends forth his command to
the earth;
his word runs swiftly.
16He gives snow like wool;
he scatters hoarfrost like
ashes.
17He casts forth his ice like
morsels;
who can stand before his
cold?
18He sends forth his word, and
melts them;
he makes his wind blow, and
the waters flow.
19He declares his word to Jacob,
his statutes and ordinances
to Israel.
20He has not dealt thus with any
other nation;
they do not know his
ordinances.
Praise the LORD!

PRAISE FOR GOD'S UNIVERSAL GLORY

148 Praise the LORD!
Praise the LORD from the
heavens,
praise him in the heights!
2Praise him, all his angels,
praise him, all his host!
3Praise him, sun and moon,
praise him, all you shining
stars!
4Praise him, you highest heavens,
and you waters above the
heavens!
5Let them praise the name of the
LORD!
For he commanded and they
were created.
6And he established them for ever
and ever;
he fixed their bounds which
cannot be passed.[a]
7Praise the LORD from the earth,
you sea monsters and all
deeps,
8fire and hail, snow and frost,
stormy wind fulfilling his
command!
9Mountains and all hills,
fruit trees and all cedars!
10Beasts and all cattle,
creeping things and flying
birds!
11Kings of the earth and all
peoples,
princes and all rulers of the
earth!
12Young men and maidens
together,
old men and children!
13Let them praise the name of the
LORD,
for his name alone is
exalted;
his glory is above earth and
heaven.
14He has raised up a horn for his
people,
praise for all his saints,
for the people of Israel who
are near to him.
Praise the LORD!

PRAISE FOR GOD'S GOODNESS TO ISRAEL

149 Praise the LORD!
Sing to the LORD a new song,
his praise in the assembly of
the faithful!

[a]Or *he set a law which cannot pass away*

2Let Israel be glad in his Maker,
let the sons of Zion rejoice
in their King!
3Let them praise his name with
dancing,
making melody to him with
timbrel and lyre!
4For the LORD takes pleasure in
his people;
he adorns the humble with
victory.
5Let the faithful exult in glory;
let them sing for joy on their
couches.
6Let the high praises of God be in
their throats
and two-edged swords in
their hands,
7to wreak vengeance on the nations
and chastisement on the
peoples,
8to bind their kings with chains
and their nobles with fetters
of iron,
9to execute on them the judgment
written!
This is glory for all his faith-
ful ones.
Praise the LORD!

PRAISE FOR GOD'S SURPASSING GREATNESS

150 *Praise the LORD!
Praise God in his sanctuary;
praise him in his mighty
firmament!
2Praise him for his mighty deeds;
praise him according to his
exceeding greatness!
3Praise him with trumpet sound;
praise him with lute and
harp!
4Praise him with timbrel and
dance;
praise him with strings and
pipe!
5Praise him with sounding
cymbals;
praise him with loud clash-
ing cymbals!
6Let everything that breathes
praise the LORD!
Praise the LORD!

THE PROVERBS

1 The proverbs of Solomon, son of David, king of Israel:

PROLOGUE

2That men may know wisdom and
instruction,
understand words of
insight,
3receive instruction in wise
dealing,
righteousness, justice, and
equity;
4that prudence may be given to
the simple,
knowledge and discretion to
the youth—
5the wise man also may hear and
increase in learning,
and the man of understand-
ing acquire skill,
6to understand a proverb and a
figure,
the words of the wise and
their riddles.
7The fear of the LORD is the be-
ginning of knowledge;
fools despise wisdom and
instruction.

WARNINGS AGAINST EVIL COMPANIONS

8Hear, my son, your father's
instruction,
and reject not your mother's
teaching;
9for they are a fair garland for
your head,
and pendants for your neck.
10My son, if sinners entice you,
do not consent.
11If they say, "Come with us, let us
lie in wait for blood,
let us wantonly ambush the
innocent;
12like Sheol let us swallow them
alive
and whole, like those who go
down to the Pit;
13we shall find all precious goods,
we shall fill our houses with
spoil;
14throw in your lot among us,
we will all have one purse"—
15my son, do not walk in the way
with them,
hold back your foot from
their paths;
16for their feet run to evil,
and they make haste to shed
blood.
17For in vain is a net spread
in the sight of any bird;
18but these men lie in wait for
their own blood,
they set an ambush for their
own lives.
19Such are the ways of all who get
gain by violence;
it takes away the life of its
possessors.

THE CALL OF WISDOM

20Wisdom cries aloud in the
street;
in the markets she raises her
voice;
21on the top of the walls[a] she cries
out;
at the entrance of the city
gates she speaks:
22"How long, O simple ones, will
you love being simple?
How long will scoffers delight
in their scoffing
and fools hate knowledge?
23Give heed[b] to my reproof;
behold, I will pour out my
thoughts[c] to you;
I will make my words known
to you.
24Because I have called and you
refused to listen,
have stretched out my hand
and no one has
heeded,

[a]Heb uncertain
[b]Heb *Turn*
[c]Heb *spirit*

25 and you have ignored all my counsel
and would have none of my reproof,
26 I also will laugh at your calamity;
I will mock when panic strikes you,
27 when panic strikes you like a storm,
and your calamity comes like a whirlwind,
when distress and anguish come upon you.
28 Then they will call upon me, but I will not answer;
they will seek me diligently but will not find me.
29 Because they hated knowledge
and did not choose the fear of the LORD,
30 would have none of my counsel,
and despised all my reproof,
31 therefore they shall eat the fruit of their way
and be sated with their own devices.
32 For the simple are killed by their turning away,
and the complacence of fools destroys them;
33 but he who listens to me will dwell secure
and will be at ease, without dread of evil."

THE VALUE OF WISDOM

2 My son, if you receive my words
and treasure up my commandments with you,
2 making your ear attentive to wisdom
and inclining your heart to understanding;
3 yes, if you cry out for insight
and raise your voice for understanding,
4 if you seek it like silver
and search for it as for hidden treasures;
5 then you will understand the fear of the LORD
and find the knowledge of God.
6 For the LORD gives wisdom;
from his mouth come knowledge and understanding;
7 he stores up sound wisdom for the upright;
he is a shield to those who walk in integrity,
8 guarding the paths of justice
and preserving the way of his saints.
9 Then you will understand righteousness and justice
and equity, every good path;
10 for wisdom will come into your heart,
and knowledge will be pleasant to your soul;
11 discretion will watch over you;
understanding will guard you;
12 delivering you from the way of evil,
from men of perverted speech,
13 who forsake the paths of uprightness
to walk in the ways of darkness,
14 who rejoice in doing evil
and delight in the perverseness of evil;
15 men whose paths are crooked,
and who are devious in their ways.
16 You will be saved from the loose[a] woman,
from the adventuress[b] with her smooth words,
17 who forsakes the companion of her youth
and forgets the covenant of her God;
18 for her house sinks down to death,
and her paths to the shades;

[a] Heb *strange*
[b] Heb *foreign woman*

19none who go to her come back
nor do they regain the paths of life.
20So you will walk in the way of good men
and keep to the paths of the righteous.
21For the upright will inhabit the land,
and men of integrity will remain in it;
22but the wicked will be cut off from the land,
and the treacherous will be rooted out of it.

ADMONITION TO TRUST AND HONOR GOD

3 My son, do not forget my teaching,
but let your heart keep my commandments;
2for length of days and years of life
and abundant welfare will they give you.
3Let not loyalty and faithfulness forsake you;
bind them about your neck,
write them on the tablet of your heart.
4So you will find favor and good repute[c]
in the sight of God and man.
5Trust in the LORD with all your heart,
and do not rely on your own insight.
6In all your ways acknowledge him,
and he will make straight your paths.
7*Be not wise in your own* eyes;
fear the LORD, and turn away from evil.
8It will be healing to your flesh[d]
and refreshment[e] to your bones.
9Honor the LORD with your substance
and with the first fruits of all your produce;
10then your barns will be filled with plenty,
and your vats will be bursting with wine.
11My son, do not despise the LORD's discipline
or be weary of his reproof,
12for the LORD reproves him whom he loves,
as a father the son in whom he delights.

THE TRUE WEALTH

13Happy is the man who finds wisdom,
and the man who gets understanding,
14for the gain from it is better than gain from silver
and its profit better than gold.
15She is more precious than jewels,
and nothing you desire can compare with her.
16Long life is in her right hand;
in her left hand are riches and honor.
17Her ways are ways of pleasantness,
and all her paths are peace.
18She is a tree of life to those who lay hold of her;
those who hold her fast are called happy.

GOD'S WISDOM IN CREATION

19The LORD by wisdom founded the earth;
by understanding he established the heavens;
20by his knowledge the deeps broke forth,
and the clouds drop down the dew.

THE TRUE SECURITY

21My son, keep sound wisdom and discretion;

[c] Cn: Heb *understanding*
[d] Heb *navel*
[e] Or *medicine*

let them not escape from your sight,[a]
22and they will be life for your soul
and adornment for your neck.
23Then you will walk on your way securely
and your foot will not stumble.
24If you sit down,[b] you will not be afraid;
when you lie down, your sleep will be sweet.
25Do not be afraid of sudden panic,
or of the ruin[c] of the wicked, when it comes;
26for the LORD will be your confidence
and will keep your foot from being caught.
27Do not withhold good from those to whom it[d] is due,
when it is in your power to do it.
28Do not say to your neighbor, "Go, and come again,
tomorrow I will give it"— when you have it with you.
29Do not plan evil against your neighbor
who dwells trustingly beside you.
30Do not contend with a man for no reason,
when he has done you no harm.
31Do not envy a man of violence
and do not choose any of his ways;
32for the perverse man is an abomination to the LORD,
but the upright are in his confidence.
33The LORD's curse is on the house of the wicked,
but he blesses the abode of the righteous.
34Toward the scorners he is scornful,
but to the humble he shows favor.
35The wise will inherit honor,
but fools get[e] disgrace.

FATHERLY ADVICE

4 Hear, O sons, a father's instruction,
and be attentive, that you may gain[f] insight;
2for I give you good precepts:
do not forsake my teaching.
3When I was a son with my father,
tender, the only one in the sight of my mother,
4he taught me, and said to me,
"Let your heart hold fast my words;
keep my commandments, and live;
5do not forget, and do not turn away from the words of my mouth.
Get wisdom; get insight.[g]
6Do not forsake her, and she will keep you;
love her, and she will guard you.
7The beginning of wisdom is this: Get wisdom,
and whatever you get, get insight.
8Prize her highly,[h] and she will exalt you;
she will honor you if you embrace her.
9She will place on your head a fair garland;
she will bestow on you a beautiful crown."

[a] Reversing the order of the clauses
[b] Gk: Heb *lie down*
[c] Heb *storm*
[d] Heb *Do not withhold good from its owners*
[e] Cn: Heb *exalt*
[f] Heb *know*
[g] Reversing the order of the lines
[h] The meaning of the Hebrew is uncertain

ADMONITION TO KEEP TO THE RIGHT PATH

10Hear, my son, and accept my words,
that the years of your life may be many.
11I have taught you the way of wisdom;
I have led you in the paths of uprightness.
12When you walk, your step will not be hampered;
and if you run, you will not stumble.
13Keep hold of instruction, do not let go;
guard her, for she is your life.
14Do not enter the path of the wicked,
and do not walk in the way of evil men.
15Avoid it; do not go on it;
turn away from it and pass on.
16For they cannot sleep unless they have done wrong;
they are robbed of sleep unless they have made some one stumble.
17For they eat the bread of wickedness
and drink the wine of violence.
18But the path of the righteous is like the light of dawn,
which shines brighter and brighter until full day.
19The way of the wicked is like deep darkness;
they do not know over what they stumble.
20My son, be attentive to my words;
incline your ear to my sayings.
21Let them not escape from your sight;
keep them within your heart.
22For they are life to him who finds them,
and healing to all his flesh.
23Keep your heart with all vigilance;
for from it flow the springs of life.
24Put away from you crooked speech,
and put devious talk far from you.
25Let your eyes look directly forward,
and your gaze be straight before you.
26Take heed to[i] the path of your feet,
then all your ways will be sure.
27Do not swerve to the right or to the left;
turn your foot away from evil.

WARNING AGAINST IMPURITY AND INFIDELITY

5 My son, be attentive to my wisdom,
incline your ear to my understanding;
2that you may keep discretion,
and your lips may guard knowledge.
3For the lips of a loose woman drip honey,
and her speech[j] is smoother than oil;
4but in the end she is bitter as wormwood,
sharp as a two-edged sword.
5Her feet go down to death;
her steps follow the path to[k] Sheol;
6she does not take heed to[l] the path of life;
her ways wander, and she does not know it.
7And now, O sons, listen to me,

[i] The meaning of the Hebrew word is uncertain
[j] Heb *palate*
[k] Heb *lay hold of*
[l] The meaning of the Hebrew word is uncertain

and do not depart from the
words of my mouth.
8Keep your way far from her,
and do not go near the door
of her house;
9lest you give your honor to others
and your years to the
merciless;
10lest strangers take their fill of
your strength,[a]
and your labors go to the
house of an alien;
11and at the end of your life you
groan,
when your flesh and body
are consumed,
12and you say, "How I hated
discipline,
and my heart despised
reproof!
13I did not listen to the voice of my
teachers
or incline my ear to my
instructors.
14I was at the point of utter ruin
in the assembled
congregation."
15Drink water from your own
cistern,
flowing water from your
own well.
16Should your springs be scattered
abroad,
streams of water in the
streets?
17Let them be for yourself alone,
and not for strangers with
you.
18Let your fountain be blessed,
and rejoice in the wife of
your youth,
19a lovely hind, a graceful
doe.
Let her affection fill you at all
times with delight,
be infatuated always with
her love.
20Why should you be infatuated,
my son, with a loose
woman
and embrace the bosom of
an adventuress?
21For a man's ways are before the
eyes of the LORD,
and he watches[b] all his
paths.
22The iniquities of the wicked
ensnare him,
and he is caught in the toils
of his sin.
23He dies for lack of discipline,
and because of his great folly
he is lost.

PRACTICAL ADMONITIONS

6 My son, if you have become surety
for your neighbor,
have given your pledge for a
stranger;
2if you are snared in the utterance
of your lips,[c]
caught in the words of your
mouth;
3then do this, my son, and save
yourself,
for you have come into your
neighbor's power:
go, hasten,[d] and importune
your neighbor.
4Give your eyes no sleep
and your eyelids no slumber;
5save yourself like a gazelle from
the hunter,[e]
like a bird from the hand of
the fowler.
6Go to the ant, O sluggard;
consider her ways, and be
wise.
7Without having any chief,
officer or ruler,
8she prepares her food in summer,
and gathers her sustenance
in harvest.
9How long will you lie there, O
sluggard?
When will you arise from

[a] Or *wealth*
[b] The meaning of the Hebrew word is uncertain
[c] Cn Compare Gk Syr: Heb *the words of your mouth*
[d] Or *humble yourself*
[e] Cn: Heb *hand*

your sleep?
10 A little sleep, a little slumber,
a little folding of the hands
to rest,
11 and poverty will come upon you
like a vagabond,
and want like an armed
man.
12 A worthless person, a wicked
man,
goes about with crooked
speech,
13 winks with his eyes, scrapes[f]
with his feet,
points with his finger,
14 with perverted heart devises
evil,
continually sowing discord;
15 therefore calamity will come
upon him suddenly;
in a moment he will be bro-
ken beyond healing.
16 There are six things which the
LORD hates,
seven which are an abomina-
tion to him:
17 haughty eyes, a lying tongue,
and hands that shed inno-
cent blood,
18 a heart that devises wicked
plans,
feet that make haste to run
to evil,
19 a false witness who breathes
out lies,
and a man who sows discord
among brothers.
20 My son, keep your father's
commandment,
and forsake not your moth-
er's teaching.
21 Bind them upon your heart
always;
tie them about your neck.
22 When you walk, they[g] will lead
you;
when you lie down, they[h]
will watch over you;
and when you awake, they[i]
will talk with you.
23 For the commandment is a lamp
and the teaching a light,
and the reproofs of disci-
pline are the way of
life,
24 to preserve you from the evil
woman,
from the smooth tongue of
the adventuress.
25 Do not desire her beauty in your
heart,
and do not let her cap-
ture you with her
eyelashes;
26 for a harlot may be hired for a
loaf of bread,[j]
but an adulteress[k] stalks a
man's very life.
27 Can a man carry fire in his
bosom
and his clothes not be
burned?
28 Or can one walk upon hot coals
and his feet not be scorched?
29 So is he who goes in to his
neighbor's wife;
none who touches her will
go unpunished.
30 Do not men despise[l] a thief if
he steals
to satisfy his appetite when
he is hungry?
31 And if he is caught, he will pay
sevenfold;
he will give all the goods of
his house.
32 He who commits adultery has
no sense;
he who does it destroys
himself.
33 Wounds and dishonor will he
get,
and his disgrace will not be
wiped away.

[f] Or *taps*
[g] Heb *it*
[h] Heb *it*
[i] Heb *it*
[j] Cn Compare Gk Syr Vg Tg: Heb *for because of a harlot to a piece of bread*
[k] Heb *a man's wife*
[l] Or *Men do not despise*

34For jealousy makes a man
furious,
and he will not spare when
he takes revenge.
35He will accept no compensation,
nor be appeased though you
multiply gifts.

THE FALSE ATTRACTIONS OF ADULTERY

7 My son, keep my words
and treasure up my command-
ments with you;
2keep my commandments and
live,
keep my teachings as the
apple of your eye;
3bind them on your fingers,
write them on the tablet of
your heart.
4Say to wisdom, "You are my
sister,"
and call insight your inti-
mate friend;
5to preserve you from the loose
woman,
from the adventuress with
her smooth words.
6For at the window of my house
I have looked out through
my lattice,
7and I have seen among the
simple,
I have perceived among the
youths,
a young man without sense,
8passing along the street near her
corner,
taking the road to her house
9in the twilight, in the evening,
at the time of night and
darkness.
10And lo, a woman meets him,
dressed as a harlot, wily of
heart.[a]
11She is loud and wayward,
her feet do not stay at home;
12now in the street, now in the
market,
and at every corner she lies
in wait.
13She seizes him and kisses him,
and with impudent face she
says to him:
14"I had to offer sacrifices,
and today I have paid my
vows;
15so now I have come out to meet
you,
to seek you eagerly, and I
have found you.
16I have decked my couch with
coverings,
colored spreads of Egyptian
linen;
17I have perfumed my bed with
myrrh,
aloes, and cinnamon.
18Come, let us take our fill of love
till morning;
let us delight ourselves with
love.
19For my husband is not at home;
he has gone on a long
journey;
20he took a bag of money with
him;
at full moon he will come
home."
21With much seductive speech she
persuades him;
with her smooth talk she
compels him.
22All at once he follows her,
as an ox goes to the
slaughter,
or as a stag is caught fast[b]
23till an arrow pierces its
entrails;
as a bird rushes into a snare;
he does not know that it will
cost him his life.
24And now, O sons, listen to me,
and be attentive to the
words of my mouth.
25Let not your heart turn aside to
her ways,
do not stray into her paths;
26for many a victim has she laid
low;
yea, all her slain are a

[a]The meaning of the Hebrew is uncertain
[b]Cn Compare Gk: Heb uncertain

mighty host.
27Her house is the way to Sheol,
going down to the chambers
of death.

THE GIFTS OF WISDOM

8 Does not wisdom call,
does not understanding raise
her voice?
2On the heights beside the way,
in the paths she takes her
stand;
3beside the gates in front of the
town,
at the entrance of the portals she cries aloud:
4"To you, O men, I call,
and my cry is to the sons of
men.
5O simple ones, learn prudence;
O foolish men, pay attention.
6Hear, for I will speak noble
things,
and from my lips will come
what is right;
7for my mouth will utter truth;
wickedness is an abomination to my lips.
8All the words of my mouth are
righteous;
there is nothing twisted or
crooked in them.
9They are all straight to him who
understands
and right to those who find
knowledge.
10Take my instruction instead of
silver,
and knowledge rather than
choice gold;
11*for wisdom is better* than jewels,
and all that you may desire
cannot compare with
her.
12I, wisdom, dwell in prudence,[c]
and I find knowledge and
discretion.
13The fear of the LORD is hatred
of evil.
Pride and arrogance and the
way of evil
and perverted speech I hate.
14I have counsel and sound
wisdom,
I have insight, I have
strength.
15By me kings reign,
and rulers decree what is
just;
16by me princes rule,
and nobles govern[d] the
earth.
17I love those who love me,
and those who seek me diligently find me.
18Riches and honor are with me,
enduring wealth and
prosperity.
19My fruit is better than gold, even
fine gold,
and my yield than choice
silver.
20I walk in the way of
righteousness,
in the paths of justice,
21endowing with wealth those
who love me,
and filling their treasuries.

WISDOM'S PART IN CREATION

22The LORD created me at the
beginning of his work,[e]
the first of his acts of old.
23Ages ago I was set up,
at the first, before the beginning of the earth.
24When there were no depths I
was brought forth,
when there were no springs
abounding with
water.
25Before the mountains had been
shaped,
before the hills, I was
brought forth;
26before he had made the earth
with its fields,[f]

[c] Heb obscure
[d] Gk: Heb *all the governors of*
[e] Heb *way*
[f] The meaning of the Hebrew is uncertain

or the first of the dust[a] of
the world.
27When he established the heavens, I was there,
when he drew a circle on the
face of the deep,
28when he made firm the skies
above,
when he established[b] the
fountains of the deep,
29when he assigned to the sea its
limit,
so that the waters might
not transgress his
command,
when he marked out the foundations of the earth,
30then I was beside him, like
a master workman;[c]
and I was daily his[d] delight,
rejoicing before him always,
31rejoicing in his inhabited world
and delighting in the sons
of men.
32And now, my sons, listen to me:
happy are those who keep
my ways.
33Hear instruction and be wise,
and do not neglect it.
34Happy is the man who listens
to me,
watching daily at my gates,
waiting beside my doors.
35For he who finds me finds life
and obtains favor from the
LORD;
36but he who misses me injures
himself;
all who hate me love death."

WISDOM'S FEAST

9 Wisdom has built her house,
she has set up[e] her seven
pillars.
2She has slaughtered her beasts,
she has mixed her wine,
she has also set her table.
3She has sent out her maids to call
from the highest places in
the town,
4"Whoever is simple, let him turn
in here!"
To him who is without sense
she says,
5"Come, eat of my bread
and drink of the wine I have
mixed.
6Leave simpleness,[f] and live,
and walk in the way of
insight."

GENERAL MAXIMS

7He who corrects a scoffer gets
himself abuse,
and he who reproves a wicked man incurs injury.
8Do not reprove a scoffer, or he
will hate you;
reprove a wise man, and he
will love you.
9Give instruction[g] to a wise man,
and he will be still wiser;
teach a righteous man and
he will increase in
learning.
10The fear of the LORD is the
beginning of wisdom,
and the knowledge of the
Holy One is insight.
11For by me your days will be
multiplied,
and years will be added to
your life.
12If you are wise, you are wise for
yourself;
if you scoff, you alone will
bear it.

FOLLY'S INVITATION AND PROMISE

13A foolish woman is noisy;
she is wanton[h] and knows no

[a] The meaning of the Hebrew is uncertain
[b] The meaning of the Hebrew is uncertain
[c] Another reading is *little child*
[d] Gk: Heb lacks *his*
[e] Gk Syr Tg: Heb *hewn*
[f] Gk Syr Vg Tg: Heb *simple ones*
[g] Heb lacks *instruction*
[h] Cn Compare Syr Vg: The meaning of the Hebrew is uncertain

shame.[i]
14She sits at the door of her house,
she takes a seat on the high places of the town,
15calling to those who pass by,
who are going straight on their way,
16"Whoever is simple, let him turn in here!"
And to him who is without sense she says,
17"Stolen water is sweet,
and bread eaten in secret is pleasant."
18But he does not know that the dead[j] are there,
that her guests are in the depths of Sheol.

WISE SAYINGS OF SOLOMON

10 The proverbs of Solomon.
A wise son makes a glad father,
but a foolish son is a sorrow to his mother.
2Treasures gained by wickedness do not profit,
but righteousness delivers from death.
3The LORD does not let the righteous go hungry,
but he thwarts the craving of the wicked.
4A slack hand causes poverty,
but the hand of the diligent makes rich.
5A son who gathers in summer is prudent,
but a son who sleeps in harvest brings shame.
6Blessings are on the head of the *righteous,*
but the mouth of the wicked conceals violence.
7The memory of the righteous is a blessing,
but the name of the wicked will rot.
8The wise of heart will heed commandments,
but a prating fool will come to ruin.
9He who walks in integrity walks securely,
but he who perverts his ways will be found out.
10He who winks the eye causes trouble,
but he who boldly reproves makes peace.[k]
11The mouth of the righteous is a fountain of life,
but the mouth of the wicked conceals violence.
12Hatred stirs up strife,
but love covers all offenses.
13On the lips of him who has understanding wisdom is found,
but a rod is for the back of him who lacks sense.
14Wise men lay up knowledge,
but the babbling of a fool brings ruin near.
15A rich man's wealth is his strong city;
the poverty of the poor is their ruin.
16The wage of the righteous leads to life,
the gain of the wicked to sin.
17He who heeds instruction is on the path to life,
but he who rejects reproof goes astray.
18He who conceals hatred has lying lips,
and he who utters slander is a fool.
19When words are many, transgression is not lacking,
but he who restrains his lips is prudent.
20The tongue of the righteous is choice silver;
the mind of the wicked is of little worth.
21The lips of the righteous feed many,
but fools die for lack of sense.

[i] Gk Syr: The meaning of the Hebrew is uncertain
[j] Heb *shades*
[k] Gk: Heb *but a prating fool will come to ruin*

22The blessing of the LORD makes rich,
and he adds no sorrow with it.[a]
23It is like sport to a fool to do wrong,
but wise conduct is pleasure to a man of understanding.
24What the wicked dreads will come upon him,
but the desire of the righteous will be granted.
25When the tempest passes, the wicked is no more,
but the righteous is established for ever.
26Like vinegar to the teeth, and smoke to the eyes,
so is the sluggard to those who send him.
27The fear of the LORD prolongs life,
but the years of the wicked will be short.
28The hope of the righteous ends in gladness,
but the expectation of the wicked comes to nought.
29The LORD is a stronghold to him whose way is upright,
but destruction to evildoers.
30The righteous will never be removed,
but the wicked will not dwell in the land.
31The mouth of the righteous brings forth wisdom,
but the perverse tongue will be cut off.
32The lips of the righteous know what is acceptable,
but the mouth of the wicked, what is perverse.

11 A false balance is an abomination to the LORD,
but a just weight is his delight.
2When pride comes, then comes disgrace;
but with the humble is wisdom.
3The integrity of the upright guides them,
but the crookedness of the treacherous destroys them.
4Riches do not profit in the day of wrath,
but righteousness delivers from death.
5The righteousness of the blameless keeps his way straight,
but the wicked falls by his own wickedness.
6The righteousness of the upright delivers them,
but the treacherous are taken captive by their lust.
7When the wicked dies, his hope perishes,
and the expectation of the godless comes to nought.
8The righteous is delivered from trouble,
and the wicked gets into it instead.
9With his mouth the godless man would destroy his neighbor,
but by knowledge the righteous are delivered.
10When it goes well with the righteous, the city rejoices;
and when the wicked perish there are shouts of gladness.
11By the blessing of the upright a city is exalted,
but it is overthrown by the mouth of the wicked.
12He who belittles his neighbor lacks sense,
but a man of understanding remains silent.
13He who goes about as a talebearer reveals secrets,
but he who is trustworthy in spirit keeps a thing

[a] Or *and toil adds nothing to it*

hidden.

14Where there is no guidance, a people falls;
but in an abundance of counselors there is safety.

15He who gives surety for a stranger will smart for it,
but he who hates suretyship is secure.

16A gracious woman gets honor,
and violent men get riches.

17A man who is kind benefits himself,
but a cruel man hurts himself.

18A wicked man earns deceptive wages,
but one who sows righteousness gets a sure reward.

19He who is steadfast in righteousness will live,
but he who pursues evil will die.

20Men of perverse mind are an abomination to the LORD,
but those of blameless ways are his delight.

21Be assured, an evil man will not go unpunished,
but those who are righteous will be delivered.

22Like a gold ring in a swine's snout
is a beautiful woman without discretion.

23The desire of the righteous ends only in good;
the expectation of the wicked in wrath.

24One man gives freely, yet grows all the richer;
another withholds what he should give, and only suffers want.

25A liberal man will be enriched,
and one who waters will himself be watered.

26The people curse him who holds back grain,
but a blessing is on the head of him who sells it.

27He who diligently seeks good seeks favor,
but evil comes to him who searches for it.

28He who trusts in his riches will wither,[b]
but the righteous will flourish like a green leaf.

29He who troubles his household will inherit wind,
and the fool will be servant to the wise.

30The fruit of the righteous is a tree of life,
but lawlessness[c] takes away lives.

31If the righteous is requited on earth,
how much more the wicked and the sinner!

12 Whoever loves discipline loves knowledge,
but he who hates reproof is stupid.

2A good man obtains favor from the LORD,
but a man of evil devices he condemns.

3A man is not established by wickedness,
but the root of the righteous will never be moved.

4A good wife is the crown of her husband,
but she who brings shame is like rottenness in his bones.

5The thoughts of the righteous are just;
the counsels of the wicked are treacherous.

6The words of the wicked lie in wait for blood,
but the mouth of the upright delivers men.

7The wicked are overthrown and are no more,

[b]Cn: Heb *fall*
[c]Cn Compare Gk Syr: Heb *a wise man*

but the house of the righteous will stand.
8A man is commended according to his good sense,
but one of perverse mind is despised.
9Better is a man of humble standing who works for himself
than one who plays the great man but lacks bread.
10A righteous man has regard for the life of his beast,
but the mercy of the wicked is cruel.
11He who tills his land will have plenty of bread,
but he who follows worthless pursuits has no sense.
12The strong tower of the wicked comes to ruin,
but the root of the righteous stands firm.[a]
13An evil man is ensnared by the transgression of his lips,
but the righteous escapes from trouble.
14From the fruit of his words a man is satisfied with good,
and the work of a man's hand comes back to him.
15The way of a fool is right in his own eyes,
but a wise man listens to advice.
16The vexation of a fool is known at once,
but the prudent man ignores an insult.
17He who speaks the truth gives honest evidence,
but a false witness utters deceit.
18There is one whose rash words are like sword thrusts,
but the tongue of the wise brings healing.
19Truthful lips endure for ever,
but a lying tongue is but for a moment.
20Deceit is in the heart of those who devise evil,
but those who plan good have joy.
21No ill befalls the righteous,
but the wicked are filled with trouble.
22Lying lips are an abomination to the LORD,
but those who act faithfully are his delight.
23A prudent man conceals his knowledge,
but fools[b] proclaim their folly.
24The hand of the diligent will rule,
while the slothful will be put to forced labor.
25Anxiety in a man's heart weighs him down,
but a good word makes him glad.
26A righteous man turns away from evil,[c]
but the way of the wicked leads them astray.
27A slothful man will not catch his prey,[d]
but the diligent man will get precious wealth.[e]
28In the path of righteousness is life,
but the way of error leads to death.[f]

13 A wise son hears his father's instruction,
but a scoffer does not listen to rebuke.
2From the fruit of his mouth a good man eats good,
but the desire of the treacherous is for violence.
3He who guards his mouth

[a] Cn: The Hebrew of verse 12 is obscure
[b] Heb *the heart of fools*
[c] Cn: The meaning of the Hebrew is uncertain
[d] Cn Compare Gk Syr: The meaning of the Hebrew is uncertain
[e] Cn: The meaning of the Hebrew is uncertain
[f] Cn: The meaning of the Hebrew is uncertain

preserves his life;
he who opens wide his lips
comes to ruin.
4The soul of the sluggard craves,
and gets nothing,
while the soul of the diligent
is richly supplied.
5A righteous man hates falsehood,
but a wicked man acts
shamefully and
disgracefully.
6Righteousness guards him whose
way is upright,
but sin overthrows the
wicked.
7One man pretends to be rich, yet
has nothing;
another pretends to be poor,
yet has great wealth.
8The ransom of a man's life is his
wealth,
but a poor nan has
no neans of
redmption.[g]
9The light of th righteou
rejoices,
but he lap of e wicked
w be ut out.
10By insclencele leedless make
strife,
ut withose who take
vice is wisdom.
11Wlth hasy gotten[h] will
dwine,
but he ho gathers little by
ttle will increase it.
lope defeed makes the heart
sick,
but a sire fulfilled is a tree
of life.
13He who dspises the word brings
desuction on himself,
but h who respects the
commandment will
be rewarded.
14The teachng of the wise is a
fouain of life,
that oe may avoid the
snares of death.

15Good sense wins favor,
but the way of the faithless
is their ruin.[i]
16In everything a prudent man
acts with knowledge,
but a fool flaunts his folly.
17A bad messenger plunges men
into trouble,
but a faithful envoy brings
healing.
18Poverty and disgrace come
to him who ignores
instruction,
but he who heeds reproof is
honored.
19A desire fulfilled is sweet to the
soul;
but to turn away from evil
is an abomination to
fools.
20He who walks with wise men
becomes wise,
but the companion of fools
will suffer harm.
21Misfortune pursues sinners,
but prosperity rewards the
righteous.
22A good man leaves an inher-
itance to his children's
children,
but the sinner's wealth
is laid up for the
righteous.
23The fallow ground of the poor
yields much food,
but it is swept away through
injustice.
24He who spares the rod hates
his son,
but he who loves him is
diligent to discipline
him.
25The righteous has enough to
satisfy his appetite,
but the belly of the wicked
suffers want.

14 Wisdom[j] builds her house,
but folly with her own hands
tears it down.

[g]Cn: Heb *des not ear rebuke*
[h]Gk Vg: Heb *from anity*
[i]Cn Compare Gk Syr Vg Tg: Heb *is enduring*
[j]Heb *Wisdm of vomen*

2He who walks in uprightness
fears the LORD,
but he who is devious in his
ways despises him.
3The talk of a fool is a rod for his
back,[a]
but the lips of the wise will
preserve them.
4Where there are no oxen, there is
no[b] grain;
but abundant crops come
by the strength of
the ox.
5A faithful witness does not lie,
but a false witness breathes
out lies.
6A scoffer seeks wisdom in vain,
but knowledge is easy
for a man of
understanding.
7Leave the presence of a fool,
for there you do not meet
words of knowledge.
8The wisdom of a prudent man is
to discern his way,
but the folly of fools is
deceiving.
9God scorns the wicked,[c]
but the upright enjoy his
favor.
10The heart knows its own
bitterness,
and no stranger shares its
joy.
11The house of the wicked will be
destroyed,
but the tent of the upright
will flourish.
12There is a way which seems right
to a man,
but its end is the way to
death.[d]
13Even in laughter the heart is sad,
and the end of joy is grief.
14A perverse man will be filled
with the fruit of his ways,
and a good man with the
fruit of his deeds.[e]
15The simple believes everything,
but the prudent looks where
he is going.
16A wise man is cautious and
turns away from evil,
but a fool throws off
restraint and is
careless.
17A man of quick temper acts
foolishly,
but a man of discretion is
patient.[f]
18The simple acquire folly,
but the prudent are crowned
with knowledge.
19The evil bow down before the
good,
the wicked at the gates of
the righteous.
20The poor is dsliked even by his
neighbcr,
but the rih has many
frinds.
21He ho despis s his neighbor is
sinner,
but appy he ho is kind
to t poo.
22Do they not rhat evise evil?
Those who vise ood
mee yalt and
faithlness
23In all toil there profit
but mere tal ends y to
want.
24The crown of the ise is r
wisdom,[g]
but folly is th garland
fools.
25A truthful witness saves live
but one who u ers lies is
betraye
26In the fear of the RD one has
strong confience,
and his childrn will have a

[a] *Cn: Heb a rod of pride*
[b] Cn: Heb *a manger of*
[c] Cn: Heb obscure
[d] Heb *ways of death*
[e] Cn: Heb *from upon him*
[f] Gk: Heb *is hated*
[g] Cn Compare Gk: Heb *riches*
[h] Cn: Heb *folly*

refuge.
27The fear of the LORD is a fountain of life,
that one may avoid the snares of death.
28In a multitude of people is the glory of a king,
but without people a prince is ruined.
29He who is slow to anger has great understanding,
but he who has a hasty temper exalts folly.
30A tranquil mind gives life to the flesh,
but passion makes the bones rot.
31He who oppresses a poor man insults his Maker,
but he who is kind to the needy honors him.
32The wicked is overthrown through his evil-doing,
but the righteous finds refuge through his integrity.[i]
33Wisdom abides in the mind of a man of understanding,
but it is not[j] known in the heart of fools.
34Righteousness exalts a nation,
but sin is a reproach to any people.
35A servant who deals wisely has the king's favor,
but his wrath falls on one who acts shamefully.

15 A soft answer turns away wrath,
but a harsh word stirs up anger.
2The tongue of the wise dispenses *knowledge*,[k]
but the mouths of fools pour out folly.
3The eyes of the LORD are in every place,
keeping watch on the evil and the good.
4A gentle tongue is a tree of life,
but perverseness in it breaks the spirit.
5A fool despises his father's instruction,
but he who heeds admonition is prudent.
6In the house of the righteous there is much treasure,
but trouble befalls the income of the wicked.
7The lips of the wise spread knowledge;
not so the minds of fools.
8The sacrifice of the wicked is an abomination to the LORD,
but the prayer of the upright is his delight.
9The way of the wicked is an abomination to the LORD,
but he loves him who pursues righteousness.
10There is severe discipline for him who forsakes the way;
he who hates reproof will die.
11Sheol and Abaddon lie open before the LORD
how much more the hearts of men!
12A scoffer does not like to be reproved;
he will not go to the wise.
13A glad heart makes a cheerful countenance,
but by sorrow of heart the spirit is broken.
14The mind of him who has understanding seeks knowledge,
but the mouths of fools feed on folly.
15All the days of the afflicted are evil,
but a cheerful heart has a *continual feast*.
16Better is a little with the fear of the LORD
than great treasure and trouble with it.
17Better is a dinner of herbs where love is
than a fatted ox and hatred with it.

[i] Gk Syr: Heb *in his death*
[j] Gk Syr: Heb lacks *not*
[k] Cn: Heb *makes knowledge good*

18 A hot-tempered man stirs up
strife,
but he who is slow to anger
quiets contention.
19 The way of a sluggard is over-
grown with thorns,
but the path of the upright is
a level highway.
20 A wise son makes a glad father,
but a foolish man despises
his mother.
21 Folly is a joy to him who has no
sense,
but a man of understanding
walks aright.
22 Without counsel plans go wrong,
but with many advisers they
succeed.
23 To make an apt answer is a joy
to a man,
and a word in season, how
good it is!
24 The wise man's path leads up-
ward to life,
that he may avoid Sheol
beneath.
25 The LORD tears down the house
of the proud,
but maintains the widow's
boundaries.
26 The thoughts of the wicked are an
abomination to the LORD,
the words of the pure are
pleasing to him.[a]
27 He who is greedy for unjust
gain makes trouble for his
household,
but he who hates bribes will
live.
28 The mind of the righteous pon-
ders how to answer,
but the mouth of the wicked
pours out evil things.
29 The LORD is far from the
wicked,
but he hears the prayer of
the righteous.
30 The light of the eyes rejoices the
heart,
and good news refreshes[b] the
bones.
31 He whose ear heeds wholesome
admonition
will abide among the wise.
32 He who ignores instruction
despises himself,
but he who heeds ad-
monition gains
understanding.
33 The fear of the LORD is instruc-
tion in wisdom,
and humility goes before
honor.

16 The plans of the mind belong to
man,
but the answer of the tongue
is from the LORD.
2 All the ways of a man are pure in
his own eyes,
but the LORD weighs the
spirit.
3 Commit your work to the LORD,
and your plans will be
established.
4 The LORD has made everything
for its purpose,
even the wicked for the day
of trouble.
5 Every one who is arrogant is an
abomination to the LORD;
be assured, he will not go
unpunished.
6 By loyalty and faithfulness iniq-
uity is atoned for,
and by the fear of the LORD
a man avoids evil.
7 When a man's ways please the
LORD,
he makes even his enemies
to be at peace with
him.
8 Better is a little with
righteousness
than great revenues with
injustice.
9 A man's mind plans his way,
but the LORD directs his
steps.
10 Inspired decisions are on the lips
of a king;

[a] Cn Compare Gk: Heb *pleasant words are pure*
[b] Heb *makes fat*

18 He who is estranged[a] seeks pretexts[b]
to break out against all
sound judgment.
2 A fool takes no pleasure in
understanding,
but only in expressing his
opinion.
3 When wickedness comes, con-
tempt comes also;
and with dishonor comes
disgrace.
4 The words of a man's mouth are
deep waters;
the fountain of wisdom is a
gushing stream.
5 It is not good to be partial to a
wicked man,
or to deprive a righteous
man of justice.
6 A fool's lips bring strife,
and his mouth invites a
flogging.
7 A fool's mouth is his ruin,
and his lips are a snare to
himself.
8 The words of a whisperer are like
delicious morsels;
they go down into the inner
parts of the body.
9 He who is slack in his work
is a brother to him who
destroys.
10 The name of the LORD is a
strong tower;
the righteous man runs into
it and is safe.
11 A rich man's wealth is his strong
city,
and like a high wall protect-
ing him.[c]
12 Before destruction *a man's* heart
is haughty,
but humility goes before
honor.
13 If one gives answer before he
hears,
it is his folly and shame.
14 A man's spirit will endure
sickness;
but a broken spirit who can
bear?
15 An intelligent mind acquires
knowledge,
and the ear of the wise seeks
knowledge.
16 A man's gift makes room for him
and brings him before great
men.
17 He who states his case first
seems right,
until the other comes and
examines him.
18 The lot puts an end to disputes
and decides between power-
ful contenders.
19 A brother helped is like a strong
city,[d]
but quarreling is like the
bars of a castle.
20 From the fruit of his mouth a
man is satisfied;
he is satisfied by the yield of
his lips.
21 Death and life are in the power
of the tongue,
and those who love it will
eat its fruits.
22 He who finds a wife finds a good
thing,
and obtains favor from the
LORD.
23 The poor use entreaties,
but the rich answer roughly.
24 There are[e] friends who pretend
to be friends,[f]
but there is a friend who
sticks closer than a
brother.

19 Better is a poor man who walks in
his integrity
than a man who is perverse in
speech, and is a fool.
2 It is not good for a man to be
without knowledge,

[a] Heb *separated*
[b] Gk Vg: Heb *desire*
[c] Or *in his imagination*
[d] Gk Syr Vg Tg: The meaning of the Hebrew is uncertain
[e] Syr Tg: Heb *A man of*
[f] Cn Compare Syr Vg Tg: Heb *to be broken*

and he who makes haste
with his feet misses
his way.
3When a man's folly brings his
way to ruin,
his heart rages against the
LORD.
4Wealth brings many new friends,
but a poor man is deserted
by his friend.
5A false witness will not go
unpunished,
and he who utters lies will
not escape.
6Many seek the favor of a gener-
ous man,
and every one is a friend
to a man who gives
gifts.
7All a poor man's brothers hate
him;
how much more do his
friends go far from
him!
He pursues them with words,
but does not have
them.[a]
8He who gets wisdom loves
himself;
he who keeps understanding
will prosper.
9A false witness will not go
unpunished,
and he who utters lies will
perish.
10It is not fitting for a fool to live
in luxury,
much less for a slave to rule
over princes.
11Good sense makes a man slow
to anger,
and it is his glory to over-
look an offense.
12A king's wrath is like the growl-
ing of a lion,
but his favor is like dew
upon the grass.
13A foolish son is ruin to his
father,
and a wife's quarreling is a
continual dripping
of rain.
14House and wealth are inherited
from fathers,
but a prudent wife is from
the LORD.
15Slothfulness casts into a deep
sleep,
and an idle person will suf-
fer hunger.
16He who keeps the command-
ment keeps his life;
he who despises the word[b]
will die.
17He who is kind to the poor lends
to the LORD,
and he will repay him for his
deed.
18Discipline your son while there
is hope;
do not set your heart on his
destruction.
19A man of great wrath will pay
the penalty;
for if you deliver him, you
will only have to do it
again.[c]
20Listen to advice and accept
instruction,
that you may gain wisdom
for the future.
21Many are the plans in the mind
of a man,
but it is the purpose of the
LORD that will be
established.
22What is desired in a man is
loyalty,
and a poor man is better
than a liar.
23The fear of the LORD leads to
life;
and he who has it rests
satisfied;
he will not be visited by
harm.
24The sluggard buries his hand in
the dish,
and will not even bring it
back to his mouth.

[a] Heb uncertain
[b] Cn Compare 13.13: Heb *his ways*
[c] Heb obscure

25 Strike a scoffer, and the simple
will learn prudence;
reprove a man of understanding, and he will gain knowledge.
26 He who does violence to his
father and chases away his mother
is a son who causes shame
and brings reproach.
27 Cease, my son, to hear
instruction
only to stray from the words
of knowledge.
28 A worthless witness mocks at
justice,
and the mouth of the wicked
devours iniquity.
29 Condemnation is ready for
scoffers,
and flogging for the backs
of fools.

20 Wine is a mocker, strong drink a
brawler;
and whoever is led astray by
it is not wise.
2 The dread wrath of a king is like
the growling of a lion;
he who provokes him to anger forfeits his life.
3 It is an honor for a man to keep
aloof from strife;
but every fool will be
quarreling.
4 The sluggard does not plow in
the autumn;
he will seek at harvest and
have nothing.
5 The purpose in a man's mind is
like deep water,
but a man of understanding
will draw it out.
6 Many a man proclaims his own
loyalty,
but a faithful man who can
find?
7 A righteous man who walks in
his integrity—
blessed are his sons after
him!
8 A king who sits on the throne of
judgment
winnows all evil with his
eyes.
9 Who can say, "I have made my
heart clean;
I am pure from my sin"?
10 Diverse weights and diverse
measures
are both alike an abomination to the LORD.
11 Even a child makes himself
known by his acts,
whether what he does is
pure and right.
12 The hearing ear and the seeing
eye,
the LORD has made them
both.
13 Love not sleep, lest you come to
poverty;
open your eyes, and you will
have plenty of bread.
14 "It is bad, it is bad," says the
buyer;
but when he goes away, then
he boasts.
15 There is gold, and abundance of
costly stones;
but the lips of knowledge are
a precious jewel.
16 Take a man's garment when
he has given surety for a
stranger,
and hold him in pledge when
he gives surety for
foreigners.
17 Bread gained by deceit is sweet
to a man,
but afterward his mouth will
be full of gravel.
18 Plans are established by counsel;
by wise guidance wage war.
19 He who goes about gossiping
reveals secrets;
therefore do not associate
with one who speaks
foolishly.
20 If one curses his father or his
mother,
his lamp will be put out in
utter darkness.
21 An inheritance gotten hastily in
the beginning

will in the end not be
blessed.
22Do not say, "I will repay evil";
wait for the LORD, and he
will help you.
23Diverse weights are an abomination to the LORD,
and false scales are not
good.
24A man's steps are ordered by the
LORD;
how then can man understand his way?
25It is a snare for a man to say
rashly, "It is holy,"
and to reflect only after
making his vows.
26A wise king winnows the
wicked,
and drives the wheel over
them.
27The spirit of man is the lamp of
the LORD,
searching all his innermost
parts.
28Loyalty and faithfulness preserve the king,
and his throne is upheld by
righteousness.[a]
29The glory of young men is their
strength,
but the beauty of old men is
their gray hair.
30Blows that wound cleanse away
evil;
strokes make clean the
innermost parts.

21 The king's heart is a stream of
water in the hand of the
LORD;
he turns it wherever he will.
2Every way of a man is right in his
own eyes,
but the LORD weighs the
heart.
3To do righteousness and justice
is more acceptable to the
LORD than sacrifice.
4Haughty eyes and a proud heart,
the lamp of the wicked, are
sin.

[a]Gk: Heb *loyalty*

5The plans of the diligent lead
surely to abundance,
but every one who is hasty
comes only to want.
6The getting of treasures by a
lying tongue
is a fleeting vapor and a
snare of death.
7The violence of the wicked will
sweep them away,
because they refuse to do
what is just.
8The way of the guilty is crooked,
but the conduct of the pure
is right.
9It is better to live in a corner of
the housetop
than in a house shared with
a contentious woman.
10The soul of the wicked desires
evil;
his neighbor finds no mercy
in his eyes.
11When a scoffer is punished, the
simple becomes wise;
when a wise man is instructed, he gains
knowledge.
12The righteous observes the
house of the wicked;
the wicked are cast down to
ruin.
13He who closes his ear to the cry
of the poor
will himself cry out and not
be heard.
14A gift in secret averts anger;
and a bribe in the bosom,
strong wrath.
15When justice is done, it is a joy
to the righteous,
but dismay to evildoers.
16A man who wanders from the
way of understanding
will rest in the assembly of
the dead.
17He who loves pleasure will be a
poor man;
he who loves wine and oil
will not be rich.
18The wicked is a ransom for the

righteous,
and the faithless for the upright.

19 It is better to live in a desert land
than with a contentious and fretful woman.

20 Precious treasure remains[b] in a wise man's dwelling,
but a foolish man devours it.

21 He who pursues righteousness and kindness
will find life[c] and honor.

22 A wise man scales the city of the mighty
and brings down the stronghold in which they trust.

23 He who keeps his mouth and his tongue
keeps himself out of trouble.

24 "Scoffer" is the name of the proud, haughty man
who acts with arrogant pride.

25 The desire of the sluggard kills him
for his hands refuse to labor.

26 All day long the wicked covets,[d]
but the righteous gives and does not hold back.

27 The sacrifice of the wicked is an abomination;
how much more when he brings it with evil intent.

28 A false witness vill perish,
but the wordof *a man who* hearswill endure.

29 A wicked man ps on a bold face,
but an uprig man considerse[e] ḃ ways.

30 No wisdom, no derstanding,
no counse
can avail agast the LORD.

31 The horse is ma ready for the day of bat,
but the vict belongs to the LORD.

22 A good name is to be chosen rather than great riches,
and favor is better than silver or gold.

2 The rich and the poor meet together;
the LORD is the maker of them all.

3 A prudent man sees danger and hides himself;
but the simple go on, and suffer for it.

4 The reward for humility and fear of the LORD
is riches and honor and life.

5 Thorns and snares are in the way of the perverse;
he who guards himself will keep far from them.

6 Train up a child in the way he should go,
and when he is old he will not depart from it.

7 The rich rules over the poor,
and the borrower is the slave of the lender.

8 He who sows injustice will reap calamity,
and the rod of his fury will fail.

9 He who has a bountiful eye will be blessed,
for he shares his bread with the poor.

10 Drive out a scoffer, and strife will go out,
and quarreling and abuse will cease.

11 He who loves purity of heart,
and whose speech is gracious, will have the king as his friend.

12 The eyes of the LORD keep watch over knowledge,
but he overthrows the words of the faithless.

13 The sluggard says, "There is a lion outside!

[b] Gk: Heb *and oil*
[c] Gk: Heb *life and righteoess*
[d] Gk: Heb *all day long hets covetously*
[e] Another reading is *estahes*

I shall be slain in the
streets!"
14The mouth of a loose woman is a
deep pit;
he with whom the LORD is
angry will fall into it.
15Folly is bound up in the heart of
a child,
but the rod of discipline
drives it far from
him.
16He who oppresses the poor to
increase his own wealth,
or gives to the rich, will only
come to want.

SAYINGS OF THE WISE

17Incline your ear, and hear the
words of the wise,
and apply your mind to my
knowledge;
18for it will be pleasant if you keep
them within you,
if all of them are ready on
your lips.
19That your trust may be in the
LORD,
I have made them known to
you today, even to
you.
20Have I not written for you thirty
sayings
of admonition and
knowledge,
21to show you what is right and
true,
that you may give a true
answer to those who
sent you?
22Do not rob the poor, because he
is poor,
or crush the afflicted at the
gate;
23for the LORD will plead their
cause
and despoil of life those who
despoil them.
24Make no friendship with a man
given to anger,
nor go with a wrathful man,
25lest you learn his ways
and entangle yourself in a
snare.
26Be not one of those who give
pledges,
who become surety for
debts.
27If you have nothing with which
to pay,
why should your bed be tak-
en from under you?
28Remove not the ancient landmark
which your fathers have set.
29Do you see a man skilful in his
work?
he will stand before kings;
he will not stand before
obscure men.

23When you sit down to eat with a
ruler,
observe carefully what[a] is
before you;
2and put a knife to your throat
if you are a man given to
appetite.
3Do not desire his delicacies,
for they are deceptive food.
4Do not toil to acquire wealth;
be wise enough to desist.
5When your eyes light upon it, it
is gone;
for suddenly it takes to itself
wings,
flying like an eagle toward
heaven.
6Do not eat the bread of a man
who is stingy;
do not desire his delicacies;
7for he is lik one who is inwardly
reckning.[b]
"Eat ad drink!" he says to
you;
but hiheart is not with you.
8You will vnit up the morsels
whi you have eaten,
and wste your pleasant
words.
9Do not spk in the hearing of
a fc,
for hvill despise the

[a]Or *who*
[b]Heb obscure

wisdom of your
words.
10Do not remove an ancient
landmark
or enter the fields of the
fatherless;
11for their Redeemer is strong;
he will plead their cause
against you.
12Apply your mind to instruction
and your ear to words of
knowledge.
13Do not withhold discipline from
a child;
if you beat him with a rod,
he will not die.
14If you beat him with the rod
you will save his life from
Sheol.
15My son, if your heart is wise,
my heart too will be glad.
16My soul will rejoice
when your lips speak what
is right.
17Let not your heart envy sinners,
but continue in the fear of
the LORD all the day.
18Surely there is a future,
and your hope will not be
cut off.
19Hear, my son, and be wise,
and direct your mind in the
way.
20Be not among winebibbers,
or among gluttonous eaters
of meat;
21for the drunkard and the glutton
will come to poverty,
and drowsiness will clothe a
man with rags.
22Hearken to your father who
begot you,
and do not despise your
mother when she is
old.
23Buy truth, and do not sell it;
buy wisdom, instruction,
and understanding.
24The father of the righteous will
greatly rejoice;
he who begets a wise son
will be glad in him.
25Let your father and mother be
glad,
let her who bore you rejoice.
26My son, give me your heart,
and let your eyes observe[c]
my ways.
27For a harlot is a deep pit;
an adventuress is a narrow
well.
28She lies in wait like a robber
and increases the faithless
among men.
29Who has woe? Who has sorrow?
Who has strife? Who has
complaining?
Who has wounds without
cause?
Who has redness of eyes?
30Those who tarry long over wine,
those who go to try mixed
wine.
31Do not look at wine when it is
red,
when it sparkles in the cup
and goes down smoothly.
32At the last it bites like a serpent,
and stings like an adder.
33Your eyes will see strange
things,
and your mind utter per-
verse things.
34You will be like one who lies
down in the midst of the
sea,
like one who lies on the top
of a mast.[d]
35"They struck me," you will
say,[e] "but I was not hurt;
they beat me, but I did not
feel it.
When shall I awake?
I will seek another drink."

24 Be not envious of evil men,
nor desire to be with them;
2for their minds devise violence,
and their lips talk of
mischief.
3By wisdom a house is built,

[c] Another reading is *delight in*
[d] Heb obscure
[e] Gk Syr Vg Tg: Heb lacks *you will say*

and by understanding it is
established;
4by knowledge the rooms are
filled
with all precious and pleasant riches.
5A wise man is mightier than a
strong man,[a]
and a man of knowledge
than he who has
strength;
6for by wise guidance you can
wage your war,
and in abundance of counselors there is victory.
7Wisdom is too high for a fool;
in the gate he does not open
his mouth.
8He who plans to do evil
will be called a
mischief-maker.
9The devising of folly is sin,
and the scoffer is an abomination to men.
10If you faint in the day of
adversity,
your strength is small.
11Rescue those who are being
taken away to death;
hold back those who are
stumbling to the
slaughter.
12If you say, "Behold, we did not
know this,"
does not he who weighs the
heart perceive it?
Does not he who keeps watch
over your soul know it,
and will he not requite man
according to his
work?
13My son, eat honey, for it is good,
and the drippings of the
honeycomb are sweet
to your taste.
14Know that wisdom is such to
your soul;
if you find it, there will be a
future,
and your hope will not be
cut off.
15Lie not in wait as a wicked man
against the dwelling of the
righteous;
do not violence to his home;
16for a righteous man falls seven
times, and rises again;
but the wicked are overthrown by calamity.
17Do not rejoice when your enemy
falls,
and let not your heart
be glad when he
stumbles;
18lest the LORD see it, and be
displeased,
and turn away his anger
from him.
19Fret not yourself because of
evildoers,
and be not envious of the
wicked;
20for the evil man has no future;
the lamp of the wicked will
be put out.
21My son, fear the LORD and the
king,
and do not disobey either of
them;[b]
22for disaster from them will rise
suddenly,
and who knows the ruin that
will come from them
both?

FURTHER SAYINGS OF THE WISE

23These also are sayings of the
wise.
Partiality in judging is not good.
24He who says to the wicked, "You
are innocent,"
will be cursed by peoples,
abhorred by nations;
25but those who rebuke the wicked will have delight,
and a good blessing will be
upon them.
26He who gives a right answer
kisses the lips.
27Prepare your work outside,

[a]Gk Compare Syr Tg: Heb *is in strength*
[b]Gk: Heb *do not associate with those who change*

get everything ready for you
in the field;
and after that build your
house.
28Be not a witness against your
neighbor without cause,
and do not deceive with your
lips.
29Do not say, "I will do to him as
he has done to me;
I will pay the man back for
what he has done."
30I passed by the field of a sluggard,
by the vineyard of a man
without sense;
31and lo, it was all overgrown with
thorns;
the ground was covered with
nettles,
and its stone wall was broken down.
32Then I saw and considered it;
I looked and received
instruction.
33A little sleep, a little slumber,
a little folding of the hands
to rest,
34and poverty will come upon you
like a robber,
and want like an armed
man.

FURTHER WISE SAYINGS OF SOLOMON

25These also are proverbs of
Solomon which the men of
Hezekiah king of Judah copied.
2It is the glory of God to conceal
things,
but the glory of kings is to
search things out.
3*As the heavens for* height, and
the earth for depth,
so the mind of kings is
unsearchable.
4Take away the dross from the
silver,
and the smith has material
for a vessel;
5take away the wicked from the
presence of the king,
and his throne will be
established in
righteousness.
6Do not put yourself forward in
the king's presence
or stand in the place of the
great;
7for it is better to be told, "Come
up here,"
than to be put lower in
the presence of the
prince.
What your eyes have seen
8do not hastily bring into
court;
for[c] what will you do in the
end,
when your neighbor puts you
to shame?
9Argue your case with your neighbor himself,
and do not disclose another's secret;
10lest he who hears you bring
shame upon you,
and your ill repute have no
end.
11A word fitly spoken
is like apples of gold in a
setting of silver.
12Like a gold ring or an ornament
of gold
is a wise reprover to a listening ear.
13Like the cold of snow in the time
of harvest
is a faithful messenger to
those who send him,
he refreshes the spirit of his
masters.
14Like clouds and wind without
rain
is a man who boasts of a gift
he does not give.
15With patience a ruler may be
persuaded,
and a soft tongue will break
a bone.
16If you have found honey, eat only
enough for you,
lest you be sated with it and
vomit it.

[c] Cn: Heb *lest*

17Let your foot be seldom in your
neighbor's house,
lest he become weary of you
and hate you.
18A man who bears false witness
against his neighbor
is like a war club, or a sword,
or a sharp arrow.
19Trust in a faithless man in time
of trouble
is like a bad tooth or a foot
that slips.
20He who sings songs to a heavy
heart
is like one who takes off a
garment on a cold
day,
and like vinegar on a
wound.[a]
21If your enemy is hungry, give
him bread to eat;
and if he is thirsty, give him
water to drink;
22for you will heap coals of fire on
his head,
and the LORD will reward
you.
23The north wind brings forth rain;
and a backbiting tongue,
angry looks.
24It is better to live in a corner of
the housetop
than in a house shared with
a contentious woman.
25Like cold water to a thirsty soul,
so is good news from a far
country.
26Like a muddied spring or a pol-
luted fountain
is a righteous man who
gives way before the
wicked.
27It is not good to eat much honey,
so be sparing of compli-
mentary words.[b]
28A man without self-control
is like a city broken into and
left without walls.

26 Like snow in summer or rain in
harvest,
so honor is not fitting for
a fool.
2Like a sparrow in its flitting, like
a swallow in its flying,
a curse that is causeless does
not alight.
3A whip for the horse, a bridle for
the ass,
and a rod for the back of
fools.
4Answer not a fool according to
his folly,
lest you be like him yourself.
5Answer a fool according to his
folly,
lest he be wise in his own
eyes.
6He who sends a message by the
hand of a fool
cuts off his own feet and
drinks violence.
7Like a lame man's legs, which
hang useless,
is a proverb in the mouth of
fools.
8Like one who binds the stone in
the sling
is he who gives honor to a
fool.
9Like a thorn that goes up into the
hand of a drunkard
is a proverb in the mouth of
fools.
10Like an archer who wounds
everybody
is he who hires a passing
fool or drunkard.[c]
11Like a dog that returns to his
vomit
is a fool that repeats his
folly.
12Do you see a man who is wise in
his own eyes?
There is more hope for a fool
than for him.
13The sluggard says, "There is a
lion in the road!
There is a lion in the
streets!"
14As a door turns on its hinges,

[a] Gk: Heb *lye*
[b] Cn Compare Gk Syr Tg: Heb *searching out their glory is glory*
[c] The Hebrew text of this verse is uncertain

so does a sluggard on his
bed.
15The sluggard buries his hand in
the dish;
it wears him out to bring it
back to his mouth.
16The sluggard is wiser in his own
eyes
than seven men who can
answer discreetly.
17He who meddles in a quarrel not
his own
is like one who takes a pass-
ing dog by the ears.
18Like a madman who throws
firebrands,
arrows, and death,
19is the man who deceives his
neighbor
and says, "I am only joking!"
20For lack of wood the fire goes
out;
and where there is no
whisperer, quarreling
ceases.
21As charcoal to hot embers and
wood to fire,
so is a quarrelsome man for
kindling strife.
22The words of a whisperer are
like delicious morsels;
they go down into the inner
parts of the body.
23Like the glaze[d] covering an
earthen vessel
are smooth[e] lips with an evil
heart.
24He who hates, dissembles with
his lips
and harbors deceit in his
heart;
25when he speaks graciously,
believe him not,
for there are seven abomina-
tions in his heart;
26though his hatred be covered
with guile,
his wickedness will be
exposed in the
assembly.
27He who digs a pit will fall into it,
and a stone will come back
upon him who starts
it rolling.
28A lying tongue hates its victims,
and a flattering mouth
works ruin.

27 Do not boast about tomorrow,
for you do not know what a day
may bring forth.
2Let another praise you, and not
your own mouth;
a stranger, and not your own
lips.
3A stone is heavy, and sand is
weighty,
but a fool's provocation is
heavier than both.
4Wrath is cruel, anger is
overwhelming;
but who can stand before
jealousy?
5Better is open rebuke
than hidden love.
6Faithful are the wounds of a
friend;
profuse are the kisses of an
enemy.
7He who is sated loathes honey,
but to one who is hungry
everything bitter is
sweet.
8Like a bird that strays from its
nest,
is a man who strays from his
home.
9Oil and perfume make the heart
glad,
but the soul is torn by
trouble.[f]
10Your friend, and your father's
friend, do not forsake;
and do not go to your broth-
er's house in the day
of your calamity.
Better is a neighbor who is near
than a brother who is far
away.
11Be wise, my son, and make my
heart glad,

[d]Cn: Heb *silver of dross*
[e]Gk: Heb *burning*
[f]Gk: Heb *the sweetness of his friend from hearty counsel*

that I may answer him who
reproaches me.
12A prudent man sees danger and
hides himself;
but the simple go on, and
suffer for it.
13Take a man's garment when
he has given surety for a
stranger,
and hold him in pledge when
he gives surety for
foreigners.[a]
14He who blesses his neighbor
with a loud voice,
rising early in the morning,
will be counted as cursing.
15A continual dripping on a rainy
day
and a contentious woman
are alike;
16to restrain her is to restrain the
wind[b]
or to grasp oil in one's right
hand.
17Iron sharpens iron,
and one man sharpens
another.
18He who tends a fig tree will eat
its fruit,
and he who guards his mas-
ter will be honored.
19As in water face answers to face,
so the mind of man reflects
the man.
20Sheol and Abaddon are never
satisfied,
and never satisfied are the
eyes of man.
21The crucible is for silver, and the
furnace is for gold,
and a man is judged by his
praise.
22Crush a fool in a mortar with a
pestle
along with crushed grain,
yet his folly will not depart
from him.
23Know well the condition of your
flocks,
and give attention to your
herds;
24for riches do not last for ever;
and does a crown endure to
all generations?
25When the grass is gone, and the
new growth appears,
and the herbage of the
mountains is
gathered,
26the lambs will provide your
clothing,
and the goats the price of a
field;
27there will be enough goats' milk
for your food,
for the food of your
household
and maintenance for your
maidens.

28The wicked flee when no one
pursues,
but the righteous are bold as
a lion.
2When a land transgresses
it has many rulers;
but with men of understanding
and knowledge
its stability will long
continue.
3A poor man who oppresses the
poor
is a beating rain that leaves
no food.
4Those who forsake the law praise
the wicked,
but those who keep the law
strive against them.
5Evil men do not understand
justice,
but those who seek the
LORD understand it
completely.
6Better is a poor man who walks
in his integrity
than a rich man who is per-
verse in his ways.
7He who keeps the law is a wise
son,
but a companion of gluttons
shames his father.

[a] Vg and 20.16: Heb *a foreign woman*
[b] Heb obscure

8He who augments his wealth by
interest and increase
gathers it for him who is
kind to the poor.
9If one turns away his ear from
hearing the law,
even his prayer is an
abomination.
10He who misleads the upright
into an evil way
will fall into his own pit;
but the blameless will have a
goodly inheritance.
11A rich man is wise in his own
eyes,
but a poor man who has
understanding will
find him out.
12When the righteous triumph,
there is great glory;
but when the wicked rise,
men hide themselves.
13He who conceals his transgressions will not prosper,
but he who confesses and
forsakes them will
obtain mercy.
14Blessed is the man who fears the
LORD always;
but he who hardens his
heart will fall into
calamity.
15Like a roaring lion or a charging
bear
is a wicked ruler over a poor
people.
16A ruler who lacks understanding
is a cruel oppressor;
but he who hates unjust gain
will prolong his days.
17*If a man is burdened with the*
blood of another,
let him be a fugitive until
death;
let no one help him.
18He who walks in integrity will
be delivered,
but he who is perverse in
his ways will fall into
a pit.[c]
19He who tills his land will have
plenty of bread,
but he who follows
worthless pursuits
will have plenty of
poverty.
20A faithful man will abound with
blessings,
but he who hastens to be
rich will not go
unpunished.
21To show partiality is not good;
but for a piece of bread a
man will do wrong.
22A miserly man hastens after
wealth,
and does not know that
want will come upon
him.
23He who rebukes a man will afterward find more favor
than he who flatters with
his tongue.
24He who robs his father or his
mother
and says, "That is no
transgression,"
is the companion of a man
who destroys.
25A greedy man stirs up strife,
but he who trusts in
the LORD will be
enriched.
26He who trusts in his own mind
is a fool;
but he who walks in wisdom
will be delivered.
27He who gives to the poor will
not want,
but he who hides his eyes
will get many a curse.
28When the wicked rise, men hide
themselves,
but when they perish, the
righteous increase.

29He who is often reproved, yet
stiffens his neck,
will suddenly be broken
beyond healing.
2When the righteous are in
authority, the people
rejoice;

[c] Syr: Heb *in one*

but when the wicked rule,
the people groan.
3He who loves wisdom makes his father glad,
but one who keeps company with harlots squanders his substance.
4By justice a king gives stability to the land,
but one who exacts gifts ruins it.
5A man who flatters his neighbor
spreads a net for his feet.
6An evil man is ensnared in his transgression,
but a righteous man sings and rejoices.
7A righteous man knows the rights of the poor;
a wicked man does not understand such knowledge.
8Scoffers set a city aflame,
but wise men turn away wrath.
9If a wise man has an argument with a fool,
the fool only rages and laughs, and there is no quiet.
10Bloodthirsty men hate one who is blameless,
and the wicked[a] seek his life.
11A fool gives full vent to his anger,
but a wise man quietly holds it back.
12If a ruler listens to falsehood,
all his officials will be wicked.
13The poor man and the oppressor meet together;
the LORD gives light to the eyes of both.
14If a king judges the poor with equity
his throne will be established for ever.
15The rod and reproof give wisdom,
but a child left to himself brings shame to his mother.
16When the wicked are in authority, transgression increases;
but the righteous will look upon their downfall.
17Discipline your son, and he will give you rest;
he will give delight to your heart.
18Where there is no prophecy the people cast off restraint,
but blessed is he who keeps the law.
19By mere words a servant is not disciplined,
for though he understands, he will not give heed.
20Do you see a man who is hasty in his words?
There is more hope for a fool than for him.
21He who pampers his servant from childhood,
will in the end find him his heir.[b]
22A man of wrath stirs up strife,
and a man given to anger causes much transgression.
23A man's pride will bring him low,
but he who is lowly in spirit will obtain honor.
24The partner of a thief hates his own life;
he hears the curse, but discloses nothing.
25The fear of man lays a snare,
but he who trusts in the LORD is safe.
26Many seek the favor of a ruler,
but from the LORD a man gets justice.
27An unjust man is an abomination to the righteous,
but he whose way is straight is an abomination to the wicked.

[a]Cn: Heb *upright*
[b]The meaning of the Hebrew word is uncertain

SAYINGS OF AGUR

30 The words of Agur son of Jakeh of Massa.[c]
The man says to Ith´i-el,
to Ith´i-el and Ucal:[d]
2 Surely I am too stupid to be a man.
I have not the understanding of a man.
3 I have not learned wisdom,
nor have I knowledge of the Holy One.
4 Who has ascended to heaven and come down?
Who has gathered the wind in his fists?
Who has wrapped up the waters in a garment?
Who has established all the ends of the earth?
What is his name, and what is his son's name?
Surely you know!
5 Every word of God proves true;
he is a shield to those who take refuge in him.
6 Do not add to his words,
lest he rebuke you, and you be found a liar.
7 Two things I ask of thee;
deny them not to me before I die:
8 Remove far from me falsehood and lying;
give me neither poverty nor riches;
feed me with the food that is needful for me,
9 lest I be full, and deny thee,
and say, "Who is the LORD?"
or lest I be poor, and steal,
and profane the name of my God.
10 Do not slander a servant to his master,
lest he curse you, and you be held guilty.
11 There are those who curse their fathers
and do not bless their mothers.
12 There are those who are pure in their own eyes
but are not cleansed of their filth.
13 There are those—how lofty are their eyes,
how high their eyelids lift!
14 There are those whose teeth are swords,
whose teeth are knives,
to devour the poor from off the earth,
the needy from among men.
15 The leech[e] has two daughters;
"Give, give," they cry.
Three things are never satisfied;
four never say, "Enough":
16 Sheol, the barren womb,
the earth ever thirsty for water,
and the fire which never says, "Enough."[f]
17 The eye that mocks a father
and scorns to obey a mother
will be picked out by the ravens of the valley
and eaten by the vultures.
18 Three things are too wonderful for me;
four I do not understand:
19 the way of an eagle in the sky,
the way of a serpent on a rock,
the way of a ship on the high seas,
and the way of a man with a maiden.
20 This is the way of an adulteress:
she eats, and wipes her mouth,
and says, "I have done no wrong."
21 Under three things the earth trembles;
under four it cannot bear up:
22 a slave when he becomes king,

[c] Or *the oracle*
[d] The Hebrew of this verse is obscure
[e] The meaning of the Hebrew word is uncertain
[f] Heb obscure

and a fool when he is filled
with food;
23an unloved woman when she
gets a husband,
and a maid when she succeeds her mistress.
24Four things on earth are small,
but they are exceedingly
wise:
25the ants are a people not strong,
yet they provide their food
in the summer;
26the badgers are a people not
mighty,
yet they make their homes in
the rocks;
27the locusts have no king,
yet all of them march in
rank;
28the lizard you can take in your
hands,
yet it is in kings' palaces.
29Three things are stately in their
tread;
four are stately in their
stride:
30the lion, which is mightiest
among beasts
and does not turn back
before any;
31the strutting cock,[a] the he-goat,
and a king striding before[b]
his people.
32If you have been foolish, exalting yourself,
or if you have been devising
evil,
put your hand on your
mouth.
33For pressing milk produces curds,
pressing the nose produces
blood,
and pressing anger produces
strife.

THE TEACHING OF KING LEMUEL'S MOTHER

31 *The words of Lemuel, king of Massa,*[c] *which his mother taught him:*
2What, my son? What, son of my
womb?
What, son of my vows?
3Give not your strength to women,
your ways to those who
destroy kings.
4It is not for kings, O Lemuel,
it is not for kings to drink
wine,
or for rulers to desire[d] strong
drink;
5lest they drink and forget what
has been decreed,
and pervert the rights of all
the afflicted.
6Give strong drink to him who is
perishing,
and wine to those in bitter
distress;
7let them drink and forget their
poverty,
and remember their misery
no more.
8Open your mouth for the dumb,
for the rights of all who are
left desolate.[e]
9Open your mouth, judge
righteously,
maintain the rights of the
poor and needy.

ODE TO A CAPABLE WIFE

10A good wife who can find?
She is far more precious
than jewels.
11The heart of her husband trusts
in her,
and he will have no lack of
gain.
12She does him good, and not
harm,
all the days of her life.
13She seeks wool and flax,
and works with willing
hands.
14She is like the ships of the
merchant,

[a] Gk Syr Tg Compare Vg: Heb obscure
[b] The meaning of the Hebrew is uncertain
[c] Or *King Lemuel, the oracle*
[d] Cn: Heb *where*
[e] Heb *are sons of passing away*

she brings her food from
afar.
15 She rises while it is yet night
and provides food for her
household
and tasks for her maidens.
16 She considers a field and buys it;
with the fruit of her hands
she plants a vineyard.
17 She girds her loins with strength
and makes her arms strong.
18 She perceives that her merchan-
dise is profitable.
Her lamp does not go out at
night.
19 She puts her hands to the distaff,
and her hands hold the
spindle.
20 She opens her hand to the poor,
and reaches out her hands to
the needy.
21 She is not afraid of snow for her
household,
for all her household are
clothed in scarlet.
22 She makes herself coverings;
her clothing is fine linen and
purple.
23 Her husband is known in the
gates,
when he sits among the
elders of the land.
24 She makes linen garments and
sells them;
she delivers girdles to the
merchant.
25 Strength and dignity are her
clothing,
and she laughs at the time to
come.
26 She opens her mouth with
wisdom,
and the teaching of kindness
is on her tongue.
27 She looks well to the ways of her
household,
and does not eat the bread of
idleness.
28 Her children rise up and call her
blessed;
her husband also, and he
praises her:
29 "Many women have done
excellently,
but you surpass them all."
30 Charm is deceitful, and beauty
is vain,
but a woman who fears the
LORD is to be praised.
31 Give her of the fruit of her hands,
and let her works praise her
in the gates.

ECCLESIASTES
OR THE PREACHER

REFLECTIONS OF A ROYAL PHILOSOPHER

1 The words of the Preacher,[a] the son of David, king in Jerusalem.

2 Vanity of vanities, says the Preacher,
vanity of vanities! All is vanity.
3 What does man gain by all the toil
at which he toils under the sun?
4 A generation goes, and a generation comes,
but the earth remains for ever.
5 The sun rises and the sun goes down,
and hastens to the place where it rises.
6 The wind blows to the south,
and goes round to the north;
round and round goes the wind,
and on its circuits the wind returns.
7 All streams run to the sea,
but the sea is not full;
to the place where the streams flow,
there they flow again.
8 All things are full of weariness;
a man cannot utter it;
the eye is not satisfied with seeing,
nor the ear filled with hearing.
9 What has been is what will be,
and what has been done is what will be done;
and there is nothing new under the sun.
10 Is there a thing of which it is said,
"See, this is new"?
It has been already,
in the ages before us.
11 There is no remembrance of former things,
nor will there be any remembrance
of later things yet to happen
among those who come after.

THE FUTILITY OF SEEKING WISDOM

12 I the Preacher have been king
over Israel in Jerusalem. 13 And I ap-
plied my mind to seek and to search
out by wisdom all that is done under
heaven; it is an unhappy business that
God has given to the sons of men to
be busy with. 14 I have seen everything
that is done under the sun; and be-
hold, all is vanity and a striving after
wind.[b]

15 What is crooked cannot be made straight,
and what is lacking cannot be numbered.

16 I said to myself, "I have acquired
great wisdom, surpassing all who
were over Jerusalem before me; and
my mind has had great experience of
wisdom and knowledge." 17 And I ap-
plied my mind to know wisdom and to
know madness and folly. I perceived
that this also is but a striving after
wind.

18 For in much wisdom is much vexation,
and he who increases knowledge increases sorrow.

THE FUTILITY OF SELF-INDULGENCE

2 I said to myself, "Come now, I will
make a test of pleasure; enjoy your-
self." But behold, this also was van-
ity. 2 I said of laughter, "It is mad,"

[a] Heb *Qoheleth*
[b] Or *a feeding on wind*. See Hos 12. 1

and of pleasure, "What use is it?" 3I searched with my mind how to cheer my body with wine—my mind still guiding me with wisdom—and how to lay hold on folly, till I might see what was good for the sons of men to do under heaven during the few days of their life. 4I made great works; I built houses and planted vineyards for myself; 5I made myself gardens and parks, and planted in them all kinds of fruit trees. 6I made myself pools from which to water the forest of growing trees. 7I bought male and female slaves, and had slaves who were born in my house; I had also great possessions of herds and flocks, more than any who had been before me in Jerusalem. 8I also gathered for myself silver and gold and the treasure of kings and provinces; I got singers, both men and women, and many concubines,[c] man's delight.

9 So I became great and surpassed all who were before me in Jerusalem; also my wisdom remained with me. 10And whatever my eyes desired I did not keep from them; I kept my heart from no pleasure, for my heart found pleasure in all my toil, and this was my reward for all my toil. 11Then I considered all that my hands had done and the toil I had spent in doing it, and behold, all was vanity and a striving after wind, and there was nothing to be gained under the sun.

WISDOM AND JOY GIVEN TO ONE WHO PLEASES GOD

12 So I turned to consider wisdom and madness and folly; for what can the man do who comes after the king? Only what he has already done. 13Then I saw that wisdom excels folly as light excels darkness. 14The wise man has his eyes in his head, but the fool walks in darkness; and yet I perceived that one fate comes to all of them. 15Then I said to myself, "What befalls the fool will befall me also; why then have I been so very wise?" And I said to myself that this also is vanity. 16For of the wise man as of the fool there is no enduring remembrance, seeing that in the days to come all will have been long forgotten. How the wise man dies just like the fool! 17So I hated life, because what is done under the sun was grievous to me; for all is vanity and a striving after wind.

18 I hated all my toil in which I had toiled under the sun, seeing that I must leave it to the man who will come after me; 19and who knows whether he will be a wise man or a fool? Yet he will be master of all for which I toiled and used my wisdom under the sun. This also is vanity. 20So I turned about and gave my heart up to despair over all the toil of my labors under the sun, 21because sometimes a man who has toiled with wisdom and knowledge and skill must leave all to be enjoyed by a man who did not toil for it. This also is vanity and a great evil. 22What has a man from all the toil and strain with which he toils beneath the sun? 23For all his days are full of pain, and his work is a vexation; even in the night his mind does not rest. This also is vanity.

24 There is nothing better for a man than that he should eat and drink and find enjoyment in his toil. This also, I saw, is from the hand of God; 25for apart from him[d] who can eat or who can have enjoyment? 26For to the man who pleases him God gives wisdom and knowledge and joy; but to the sinner he gives the work of gathering and heaping, only to give to one who pleases God. This also is vanity and a striving after wind.

EVERYTHING HAS ITS TIME

3 For everything there is a season, and a time for every matter under heaven:

[c]The meaning of the Hebrew word is uncertain
[d]Gk Syr: Heb *apart from me*

2 a time to be born, and a time to
  die;
a time to plant, and a time
  to pluck up what is
  planted;
3 a time to kill, and a time to heal;
a time to break down, and a
  time to build up;
4 a time to weep, and a time to
  laugh;
a time to mourn, and a time to
  dance;
5 a time to cast away stones, and a
  time to gather
  stones together;
a time to embrace, and a
  time to refrain from
  embracing;
6 a time to seek, and a time to lose;
a time to keep, and a time to
  cast away;
7 a time to rend, and a time to sew;
a time to keep silence, and a
  time to speak;
8 a time to love, and a time to hate;
a time for war, and a time for
  peace.

THE GOD-GIVEN TASK

9 What gain has the worker from
  his toil?

10 I have seen the business that
God has given to the sons of men to
be busy with. 11 He has made every-
thing beautiful in its time; also he has
put eternity into man's mind, yet so
that he cannot find out what God has
done from the beginning to the end.
12 I know that there is nothing better
for them than to be happy and enjoy
themselves as long as they live; 13 also
that it is God's gift to man that every
one should eat and drink and take
pleasure in all his toil. 14 I know that
whatever God does endures for ever;
nothing can be added to it, nor any-
thing taken from it; God has made it
so, in order that men should fear be-
fore him. 15 That which is, already has
been; that which is to be, already has
been; and God seeks what has been
driven away.

JUDGMENT AND THE FUTURE BELONG TO GOD

16 Moreover I saw under the sun
that in the place of justice, even there
was wickedness, and in the place of
righteousness, even there was wick-
edness. 17 I said in my heart, God will
judge the righteous and the wicked,
for he has appointed a time for every
matter, and for every work. 18 I said
in my heart with regard to the sons
of men that God is testing them to
show them that they are but beasts.
19 For the fate of the sons of men and
the fate of beasts is the same; as one
dies, so dies the other. They all have
the same breath, and man has no
advantage over the beasts; for all is
vanity. 20 All go to one place; all are
from the dust, and all turn to dust
again. 21 Who knows whether the
spirit of man goes upward and the
spirit of the beast goes down to the
earth? 22 So I saw that there is noth-
ing better than that a man should
enjoy his work, for that is his lot;
who can bring him to see what will
be after him?

4 Again I saw all the oppressions that
are practiced under the sun. And
behold, the tears of the oppressed,
and they had no one to comfort them!
On the side of their oppressors there
was power, and there was no one to
comfort them. 2 And I thought the
dead who are already dead more for-
tunate than the living who are still
alive; 3 but better than both is he who
has not yet been, and has not seen
the evil deeds that are done under
the sun.

4 Then I saw that all toil and all
skill in work come from a man's envy
of his neighbor. This also is vanity and
a striving after wind.

5 The fool folds his hands, and eats
his own flesh.

6 Better is a handful of quietness
than two hands full of toil and a striv-
ing after wind.

7 Again, I saw vanity under the
sun: 8 a person who has no one, either

son or brother, yet there is no end
to all his toil, and his eyes are never
satisfied with riches, so that he never
asks, "For whom am I toiling and de-
priving myself of pleasure?" This also
is vanity and an unhappy business.

THE VALUE OF A FRIEND

9 Two are better than one, be-
cause they have a good reward for
their toil. 10For if they fall, one will
lift up his fellow; but woe to him
who is alone when he falls and has
not another to lift him up. 11Again, if
two lie together, they are warm; but
how can one be warm alone? 12And
though a man might prevail against
one who is alone, two will withstand
him. A threefold cord is not quickly
broken.

13 Better is a poor and wise youth
than an old and foolish king, who will
no longer take advice, 14even though
he had gone from prison to the throne
or in his own kingdom had been born
poor. 15I saw all the living who move
about under the sun, as well as that[a]
youth, who was to stand in his place;
16there was no end of all the people;
he was over all of them. Yet those
who come later will not rejoice in him.
Surely this also is vanity and a striv-
ing after wind.

REVERENCE, HUMILITY, AND CONTENTMENT

5[b] Guard your steps when you go to
the house of God; to draw near to
listen is better than to offer the sac-
rifice of fools; for they do not know
that they are doing evil. 2[c] Be not rash
with your mouth, nor let your heart be
hasty to utter a word before God, for
God is in heaven, and you upon earth;
therefore let your words be few.

3 For a dream comes with much
business, and a fool's voice with many
words.

4 When you vow a vow to God,
do not delay paying it; for he has no
pleasure in fools. Pay what you vow.
5It is better that you should not vow
than that you should vow and not
pay. 6Let not your mouth lead you
into sin, and do not say before the
messenger[d] that it was a mistake;
why should God be angry at your
voice, and destroy the work of your
hands?

7 For when dreams increase, emp-
ty words grow many:[e] but do you fear
God.

8 If you see in a province the poor
oppressed and justice and right vio-
lently taken away, do not be amazed
at the matter; for the high official is
watched by a higher, and there are yet
higher ones over them. 9But in all, a
king is an advantage to a land with
cultivated fields.[f]

10 He who loves money will not
be satisfied with money; nor he who
loves wealth, with gain: this also is
vanity.

11 When goods increase, they in-
crease who eat them; and what gain
has their owner but to see them with
his eyes?

12 Sweet is the sleep of a laborer,
whether he eats little or much; but
the surfeit of the rich will not let him
sleep.

13 There is a grievous evil which I
have seen under the sun: riches were
kept by their owner to his hurt, 14and
those riches were lost in a bad ven-
ture; and he is father of a son, but he
has nothing in his hand. 15As he came
from his mother's womb he shall go
again, naked as he came, and shall
take nothing for his toil, which he
may carry away in his hand. 16This
also is a grievous evil: just as he
came, so shall he go; and what gain

[a] Heb *the second*
[b] Ch 4.17 in Heb
[c] Ch 5.1 in Heb
[d] Or *angel*
[e] Or *For in a multitude of dreams there is futility, and ruin in a flood of words*
[f] Or *The profit of the land is among all of them; a cultivated field has a king*

has he that he toiled for the wind,
17and spent all his days in darkness
and grief,[a] in much vexation and sick-
ness and resentment?
18 Behold, what I have seen to be
good and to be fitting is to eat and
drink and find enjoyment in all the
toil with which one toils under the
sun the few days of his life which
God has given him, for this is his lot.
19Every man also to whom God has
given wealth and possessions and
power to enjoy them, and to accept his
lot and find enjoyment in his toil—
this is the gift of God. 20For he will
not much remember the days of his
life because God keeps him occupied
with joy in his heart.

THE FRUSTRATION OF DESIRES

6 There is an evil which I have seen
under the sun, and it lies heavy
upon men: 2a man to whom God
gives wealth, possessions, and hon-
or, so that he lacks nothing of all
that he desires, yet God does not
give him power to enjoy them, but a
stranger enjoys them; this is vanity;
it is a sore affliction. 3If a man begets
a hundred children, and lives many
years, so that the days of his years
are many, but he does not enjoy life's
good things, and also has no burial,
I say that an untimely birth is better
off than he. 4For it comes into vanity
and goes into darkness, and in dark-
ness its name is covered; 5moreover
it has not seen the sun or known
anything; yet it finds rest rather
than he. 6Even though he should live
a thousand years twice told, yet en-
joy no good—do not all go to the one
place?
7 All the toil of man is for his
mouth, yet his appetite is not sat-
isfied. 8For what advantage has the
wise man over the fool? And what
does the poor man have who knows
how to conduct himself before the
living? 9Better is the sight of the eyes
than the wandering of desire; this
also is vanity and a striving after
wind.
10 Whatever has come to be has
already been named, and it is known
what man is, and that he is not able
to dispute with one stronger than he.
11The more words, the more vanity,
and what is man the better? 12For who
knows what is good for man while
he lives the few days of his vain life,
which he passes like a shadow? For
who can tell man what will be after
him under the sun?

A DISILLUSIONED VIEW OF LIFE

7 A good name is better than precious
ointment;
and the day of death, than
the day of birth.
2It is better to go to the house of
mourning
than to go to the house of
feasting;
for this is the end of all men,
and the living will lay it to
heart.
3Sorrow is better than laughter,
for by sadness of counte-
nance the heart is
made glad.
4The heart of the wise is in the
house of mourning;
but the heart of fools is in
the house of mirth.
5It is better for a man to hear the
rebuke of the wise
than to hear the song of
fools.
6For as the crackling of thorns
under a pot,
so is the laughter of the
fools;
this also is vanity.
7Surely oppression makes the
wise man foolish,
and a bribe corrupts the
mind.
8Better is the end of a thing than
its beginning;
and the patient in spirit is
better than the proud

[a]Gk: Heb *all his days also he eats in darkness*

in spirit.
9Be not quick to anger,
for anger lodges in the bosom of fools.
10Say not, "Why were the former days better than these?"
For it is not from wisdom that you ask this.
11Wisdom is good with an inheritance,
an advantage to those who see the sun.
12For the protection of wisdom is like the protection of money;
and the advantage of knowledge is that wisdom preserves the life of him who has it.
13Consider the work of God;
who can make straight what he has made crooked?

14 In the day of prosperity be joy-
ful, and in the day of adversity con-
sider; God has made the one as well
as the other, so that man may not
find out anything that will be after
him.

THE RIDDLES OF LIFE

15 In my vain life I have seen ev-
erything; there is a righteous man
who perishes in his righteousness,
and there is a wicked man who pro-
longs his life in his evil-doing. 16Be
not righteous overmuch, and do not
make yourself overwise; why should
you destroy yourself? 17Be not wick-
ed overmuch, neither be a fool; why
should you die before your time? 18It
is good that you should take hold of
this, and from that withhold not your
hand; for he who fears God shall come
forth from them all.

19 Wisdom gives strength to the
wise man more than ten rulers that
are in a city.

20 Surely there is not a righteous
man on earth who does good and
never sins.

21 Do not give heed to all the things
that men say, lest you hear your ser-
vant cursing you; 22your heart knows
that many times you have yourself
cursed others.

23 All this I have tested by wis-
dom; I said, "I will be wise"; but it
was far from me. 24That which is,
is far off, and deep, very deep; who
can find it out? 25I turned my mind
to know and to search out and to
seek wisdom and the sum of things,
and to know the wickedness of folly
and the foolishness which is mad-
ness. 26And I found more bitter than
death the woman whose heart is
snares and nets, and whose hands
are fetters; he who pleases God es-
capes her, but the sinner is taken by
her. 27Behold, this is what I found,
says the Preacher, adding one thing
to another to find the sum, 28which
my mind has sought repeatedly, but
I have not found. One man among
a thousand I found, but a woman
among all these I have not found.
29Behold, this alone I found, that
God made man upright, but they
have sought out many devices.

OBEY THE KING AND ENJOY YOURSELF

8 Who is like the wise man?
And who knows the interpretation of a thing?
A man's wisdom makes his face shine,
and the hardness of his countenance is changed.

2 Keep[b] the king's command, and
because of your sacred oath be not
dismayed; 3go from his presence, do
not delay when the matter is unpleas-
ant, for he does whatever he pleases.
4For the word of the king is supreme,
and who may say to him, "What are
you doing?" 5He who obeys a com-
mand will meet no harm, and the
mind of a wise man will know the
time and way. 6For every matter has

[b]Heb inserts an *I*

its time and way, although man's trou-
ble lies heavy upon him. 7For he does
not know what is to be, for who can
tell him how it will be? 8No man has
power to retain the spirit, or author-
ity over the day of death; there is no
discharge from war, nor will wicked-
ness deliver those who are given to
it. 9All this I observed while applying
my mind to all that is done under the
sun, while man lords it over man to
his hurt.

GOD'S WAYS ARE INSCRUTABLE

10 Then I saw the wicked buried;
they used to go in and out of the holy
place, and were praised in the city
where they had done such things.
This also is vanity. 11Because sentence
against an evil deed is not execut-
ed speedily, the heart of the sons of
men is fully set to do evil. 12Though a
sinner does evil a hundred times and
prolongs his life, yet I know that it
will be well with those who fear God,
because they fear before him; 13but
it will not be well with the wicked,
neither will he prolong his days like
a shadow, because he does not fear
before God.

14 There is a vanity which takes
place on earth, that there are righ-
teous men to whom it happens ac-
cording to the deeds of the wicked,
and there are wicked men to whom
it happens according to the deeds of
the righteous. I said that this also is
vanity. 15And I commend enjoyment,
for man has no good thing under the
sun but to eat and drink and enjoy
himself, for this will go with him in
his toil through the days of life which
God gives him under the sun.

16 When I applied my mind to
know wisdom, and to see the business
that is done on earth, how neither day
nor night one's eyes see sleep; 17then
I saw all the work of God, that man
cannot find out the work that is done
under the sun. However much man
may toil in seeking, he will not find it
out; even though a wise man claims to
know, he cannot find it out.

TAKE LIFE AS IT COMES

9 But all this I laid to heart, exam-
ining it all, how the righteous and
the wise and their deeds are in the
hand of God; whether it is love or
hate man does not know. Everything
before them is vanity,[a] 2since one fate
comes to all, to the righteous and the
wicked, to the good and the evil,[b] to
the clean and the unclean, to him who
sacrifices and him who does not sac-
rifice. As is the good man, so is the
sinner; and he who swears is as he
who shuns an oath. 3This is an evil
in all that is done under the sun, that
one fate comes to all; also the hearts
of men are full of evil, and madness
is in their hearts while they live, and
after that they go to the dead. 4But he
who is joined with all the living has
hope, for a living dog is better than
a dead lion. 5For the living know that
they will die, but the dead know noth-
ing, and they have no more reward;
but the memory of them is lost. 6Their
love and their hate and their envy
have already perished, and they have
no more for ever any share in all that
is done under the sun.

7 Go, eat your bread with enjoy-
ment, and drink your wine with a
merry heart; for God has already ap-
proved what you do.

8 Let your garments be always
white; let not oil be lacking on your
head.

9 Enjoy life with the wife whom
you love, all the days of your vain
life which he has given you under the
sun, because that is your portion in
life and in your toil at which you toil
under the sun. 10Whatever your hand
finds to do, do it with your might; for
there is no work or thought or knowl-
edge or wisdom in Sheol, to which
you are going.

[a] Syr Compare Gk: Heb *Everything before them is everything*
[b] Gk Syr Vg: Heb lacks *and the evil*

11 Again I saw that under the sun
the race is not to the swift, nor the bat-
tle to the strong, nor bread to the wise,
nor riches to the intelligent, nor favor
to the men of skill; but time and chance
happen to them all. 12For man does not
know his time. Like fish which are tak-
en in an evil net, and like birds which
are caught in a snare, so the sons of
men are snared at an evil time, when it
suddenly falls upon them.

WISDOM SUPERIOR TO FOLLY

13 I have also seen this example of
wisdom under the sun, and it seemed
great to me. 14There was a little city
with few men in it; and a great king
came against it and besieged it, build-
ing great siegeworks against it. 15But
there was found in it a poor wise man,
and he by his wisdom delivered the
city. Yet no one remembered that poor
man. 16But I say that wisdom is better
than might, though the poor man's
wisdom is despised, and his words are
not heeded.

17 The words of the wise heard in
quiet are better than the shouting of a
ruler among fools. 18Wisdom is better
than weapons of war, but one sinner
destroys much good.

MISCELLANEOUS OBSERVATIONS

10 Dead flies make the perfumer's
ointment give off an evil
odor;
so a little folly outweighs
wisdom and honor.
2A wise man's heat inclines him
toward theight,
but a fool's hrt toward the
left.
3Even when the fo walks on the
road, he lac sense,
and he says t every one that
he is a ol.
4If the anger of the ler rises
against you, not leave
your place,
for deference v make
amends great
offenses

5 There is an evil which I have
seen under the sun, as it were an error
proceeding from the ruler: 6folly is set
in many high places, and the rich sit
in a low place. 7I have seen slaves on
horses, and princes walking on foot
like slaves.
8He who digs a pit will fall into it;
and a serpent will bite him
who breaks through
a wall.
9He who quarries stones is hurt
by them;
and he who splits logs is en-
dangered by them.
10If the iron is blunt, and one does
not whet the edge,
he must put forth more
strength;
but wisdom helps one to
succeed.
11If the serpent bites before it is
charmed,
there is no advantage in a
charmer.
12The words of a wise man's
mouth win him favor,
but the lips of a fool con-
sume him.
13The beginning of the words of
his mouth is foolishness,
and the end of his talk is
wicked madness.
14A fool multiplies words,
though no man knows what
is to be,
and who can tell him what
will be after him?
15The toil of a fool wearies him,
so that he does not know the
way to the city.
16Woe to you, O land, when your
king is a child,
and your princes feast in the
morning!
17Happy are you, O land, when
your king is the son of free
men,
and your princes feast at the
proper time,
for strength, and not for
drunkenness!

18 Through sloth the roof sinks in,
and through indolence the
house leaks.
19 Bread is made for laughter,
and wine gladdens life,
and money answers
everything.
20 Even in your thought, do not
curse the king,
nor in your bedchamber
curse the rich;
for a bird of the air will carry
your voice,
or some winged creature tell
the matter.

THE VALUE OF DILIGENCE

11 Cast your bread upon the waters,
for you will find it after many
days.
2 Give a portion to seven, or even
to eight,
for you know not what
evil may happen on
earth.
3 If the clouds are full of rain,
they empty themselves on
the earth;
and if a tree falls to the south
or to the north,
in the place where the tree
falls, there it will lie.
4 He who observes the wind will
not sow;
and he who regards the
clouds will not reap.

5 As you do not know how the spir-
it comes to the bones in the womb[a] of
a woman with child, so you do not
know the work of God who makes
everything.

6 In the morning sow your seed,
and at evening withhold not your
hand; for you do not know which will
prosper, this or that, or whether both
alike will be good.

YOUTH AND OLD AGE

7 Light is sweet, and it is pleasant
for the eyes to behold the sun.

8 For if a man lives many years, let
him rejoice in them all; but let him re-
member that the days of darkness will
be many. All that comes is vanity.

9 Rejoice, O young man, in your
youth, and let your heart cheer you
in the days of your youth; walk in
the ways of your heart and the sight
of your eyes. But know that for all
these things God will bring you into
judgment.

10 Remove vexation from your
mind, and put away pain from your
body; for youth and the dawn of life
are vanity.

12 Remember also your Creator in
the days of your youth, before the
evil days come, and the years draw
nigh, when you will say, "I have no
pleasure in them"; 2 before the sun
and the light and the moon and the
stars are darkened and the clouds re-
turn after the rain; 3 in the day when
the keepers of the house tremble,
and the strong men are bent, and the
grinders cease because they are few,
and those that look through the win-
dows are dimmed, 4 and the doors on
the street are shut; when the sound
of the grinding is low, and one rises
up at the voice of a bird, and all the
daughters of song are brought low;
5 they are afraid also of what is high,
and terrors are in the way; the almond
tree blossoms, the grasshopper drags
itself along[b] and desire fails; because
man goes to his eternal home, and
the mourners go about the streets;
6 before the sil er cord is snapped,[c]
or the golden owl is broken, or the
pitcher is broen at the fountain, or
the wheel broen at the cistern, 7 and
the dust retns to the earth as it
was, and th spirit returns to God
who gave it Vanity of vanities, says
the Preache all is vanity.

EPILOGUE

9 Besid being wise, the Preacher
also taug the people knowledge,

[a] Or *As you do not know the way of the wind, or how the bones g in the womb*
[b] Or *is a burden*
[c] Syr Vg Compare Gk: Heb *is removed*

weighing and studying and arrang-
ing proverbs with great care. 10The
Preacher sought to find pleasing
words, and uprightly he wrote words
of truth.

11 The sayings of the wise are like
goads, and like nails firmly fixed are
the collected sayings which are given
by one Shepherd. 12My son, beware of
anything beyond these. Of making
many books there is no end, and much
study is a weariness of the flesh.

13 The end of the matter; all has
been heard. Fear God, and keep his
commandments; for this is the whole
duty of man.[d] 14For God will bring ev-
ery deed into judgment, with[e] every
secret thing, whether good or evil.

[d] Or *the duty of all men*
[e] Or *into the judgment on*

THE SONG OF SOLOMON

1 The Song of Songs, which is Solomon's.

COLLOQUY OF BRIDE AND FRIENDS

2 O that you[a] would kiss me with
the kisses of your[b] mouth!
For your love is better than
wine,
3 your anointing oils are
fragrant,
your name is oil poured out;
therefore the maidens love
you.
4 Draw me after you, let us make
haste.
The king has brought me
into his chambers.
We will exult and rejoice in
you;
we will extol your love more
than wine;
rightly do they love you.
5 I am very dark, but comely,
O daughters of Jerusalem,
like the tents of Kedar,
like the curtains of
Solomon.
6 Do not gaze at me because I am
swarthy,
because the sun has
scorched me.
My mother's sons were angry
with me,
they made me keeper of the
vineyards;
but, my own vineyard I have
not kept!
7 Tell me, you whom my soul loves,
where you pasture your
flock,
where you make it lie down
at noon;
for why should I be like one
who wanders[c]
beside the flocks of your
companions?
8 If you do not know,
O fairest among women,
follow in the tracks of the
flock,
and pasture your kids
beside the shepherds' tents.

COLLOQUY OF BRIDEGROOM, FRIENDS, AND BRIDE

9 I compare you, my love,
to a mare of Pharaoh's
chariots.
10 Your cheeks are comely with
ornaments,
your neck with strings of
jewels.
11 We will make you ornaments of
gold,
studded with silver.
12 While the king was on his couch,
my nard gave forth its
fragrance.
13 My beloved is to me a bag of
myrrh,
that lies between my
breasts.
14 My beloved is to me a cluster of
henna blossoms
in the vineyards of
En-ged′i.
15 Behold, you are beautiful, my
love;
behold, you are beautiful;
your eyes are doves.
16 Behold, you are beautiful, my
beloved,
truly lovely.
Our couch is green;
17 the beams of our house are
cedar,
our rafters[d] are pine.

[a] Heb *he*
[b] Heb *his*
[c] Gk Syr Vg: Heb *is veiled*
[d] The meaning of the Hebrew word is uncertain

2 I am a rose[e] of Sharon,
a lily of the valleys.
2 As a lily among brambles,
so is my love among maidens.
3 As an apple tree among the trees of the wood,
so is my beloved among young men.
With great delight I sat in his shadow,
and his fruit was sweet to my taste,
4 He brought me to the banqueting house,
and his banner over me was love.
5 Sustain me with raisins,
refresh me with apples;
for I am sick with love.
6 O that his left hand were under my head,
and that his right hand embraced me!
7 I adjure you, O daughters of Jerusalem,
by the gazelles or the hinds of the field,
that you stir not up nor awaken love
until it please.

SPRINGTIME RHAPSODY

8 The voice of my beloved!
Behold, he comes,
leaping upon the mountains,
bounding over the hills.
9 My beloved is like a gazelle,
or a young stag.
Behold, there he stands
behind *our wall,*
gazing in at the windows,
looking through the lattice.
10 My beloved speaks and says to me:
"Arise, my love, my fair one,
and come away;
11 for lo, the winter is past,
the rain is over and gone.
12 The flowers appear on the earth,
the time of singing has come,
and the voice of the turtledove
is heard in our land.
13 The fig tree puts forth its figs,
and the vines are in blossom;
they give forth fragrance.
Arise, my love, my fair one,
and come away.
14 O my dove, in the clefts of the rock,
in the covert of the cliff,
let me see your face,
let me hear your voice,
for your voice is sweet,
and your face is comely.
15 Catch us the foxes,
the little foxes,
that spoil the vineyards,
for our vineyards are in blossom."
16 My beloved is mine and I am his,
he pastures his flock among the lilies.
17 Until the day breathes
and the shadows flee,
turn, my beloved, be like a gazelle,
or a young stag upon rugged[f] mountains.

LOVE'S DREAM

3 Upon my bed by night
I sought him whom my soul loves;
I sought him, but found him not;
I called him, but he gave no answer.[g]
2 "I will rise now and go about the city,
in the streets and in the squares;
I will seek him whom my soul loves."
I sought him, but found him not.
3 The watchmen found me,

[e] Heb *crocus*
[f] The meaning of the Hebrew word is unknown
[g] Gk: Heb lacks this line

as they went about in the
city.
"Have you seen him whom my
soul loves?"
4Scarcely had I passed them,
when I found him whom my
soul loves.
I held him, and would not let
him go
until I had brought him into
my mother's house,
and into the chamber of her
that conceived me.
5I adjure you, O daughters of
Jerusalem,
by the gazelles or the hinds
of the field,
that you stir not up nor awaken
love
until it please.

THE GROOM AND HIS PARTY APPROACH

6What is that coming up from the
wilderness,
like a column of smoke,
perfumed with myrrh and
frankincense,
with all the fragrant
powders of the
merchant?
7Behold, it is the litter of
Solomon!
About it are sixty mighty men
of the mighty men of Israel,
8all girt with swords
and expert in war,
each with his sword at his
thigh,
against alarms by night.
9King Solomon made himself a
palanquin
from the wood of Lebanon.
10He made its posts of silver,
its back of gold, its seat of
purple;
it was lovingly wrought within[a]
by the daughters of
Jerusalem.
11Go forth, O daughters of Zion,
and behold King Solomon,
with the crown with which his
mother crowned him
on the day of his wedding,
on the day of the gladness of
his heart.

THE BRIDE'S BEAUTY EXTOLLED

4 Behold, you are beautiful, my love,
behold, you are beautiful!
Your eyes are doves
behind your veil.
Your hair is like a flock of
goats,
moving down the slopes of
Gilead.
2Your teeth are like a flock of
shorn ewes
that have come up from the
washing,
all of which bear twins,
and not one among them is
bereaved.
3Your lips are like a scarlet
thread,
and your mouth is lovely.
Your cheeks are like halves of a
pomegranate
behind your veil.
4Your neck is like the tower of
David,
built for an arsenal,[b]
whereon hang a thousand
bucklers,
all of them shields of
warriors.
5Your two breasts are like two
fawns,
twins of a gazelle,
that feed among the lilies.
6Until the day breathes
and the shadows flee,
I will hie me to the mountain
of myrrh
and the hill of frankincense.
7You are all fair, my love;
there is no flaw in you.
8Come with me from Lebanon, my
bride;
come with me from
Lebanon.

[a]The meaning of the Hebrew is uncertain
[b]The meaning of the Hebrew word is uncertain

Depart[c] from the peak of
Ama´na,
from the peak of Senir and
Hermon,
from the dens of lions,
from the mountains of
leopards.
9You have ravished my heart, my
sister, my bride,
you have ravished my heart
with a glance of your
eyes,
with one jewel of your
necklace.
10How sweet is your love, my
sister, my bride!
how much better is your love
than wine,
and the fragrance of your
oils than any spice!
11Your lips distil nectar, my bride;
honey and milk are under
your tongue;
the scent of your garments
is like the scent of
Lebanon.
12A garden locked is my sister, my
bride,
a garden locked, a fountain
sealed.
13Your shoots are an orchard of
pomegranates
with all choicest fruits,
henna with nard,
14nard and saffron, calamus and
cinnamon,
with all trees of
frankincense,
myrrh and aloes,
with all chief spices—
15a garden fountain, *a well of
living* water,
and flowing streams from
Lebanon.
16Awake, O north wind,
and come, O south wind!
Blow upon my garden,
let its fragrance be wafted
abroad.
Let my beloved come to his
garden,
and eat its choicest fruits.

5 I come to my garden, my sister, my
bride,
I gather my myrrh with my
spice,
I eat my honeycomb with my
honey,
I drink my wine with my
milk.
Eat, O friends, and drink:
drink deeply, O lovers!

ANOTHER DREAM

2I slept, but my heart was awake.
Hark! my beloved is knocking.
"Open to me, my sister, my
love,
my dove, my perfect one;
for my head is wet with dew,
my locks with the drops of
the night."
3I had put off my garment,
how could I put it on?
I had bathed my feet,
how could I soil them?
4My beloved put his hand to the
latch,
and my heart was thrilled
within me.
5I arose to open to my beloved,
and my hands dripped with
myrrh,
my fingers with liquid myrrh,
upon the handles of the bolt.
6I opened to my beloved,
but my beloved had turned
and gone.
My soul failed me when he
spoke.
I sought him, but found him
not;
I called him, but he gave no
answer.
7The watchmen found me,
as they went about in the
city;
they beat me, they wounded
me,
they took away my mantle,
those watchmen of the
walls.

[c] Or *Look*

8I adjure you, O daughters of
Jerusalem,
if you find my beloved,
that you tell him
I am sick with love.

COLLOQUY OF FRIENDS AND BRIDE

9What is your beloved more than
another beloved,
O fairest among women?
What is your beloved more
than another beloved,
that you thus adjure us?
10My beloved is all radiant and
ruddy,
distinguished among ten
thousand.
11His head is the finest gold;
his locks are wavy,
black as a raven.
12His eyes are like doves
beside springs of water,
bathed in milk,
fitly set.[a]
13His cheeks are like beds of
spices,
yielding fragrance.
His lips are lilies,
distilling liquid myrrh.
14His arms are rounded gold,
set with jewels.
His body is ivory work,[b]
encrusted with sapphires.[c]
15His legs are alabaster columns,
set upon bases of gold.
His appearance is like
Lebanon,
choice as the cedars.
16His speech is most sweet,
and he is altogether
desirable.
This is my beloved and this is
my friend,
O daughters of Jerusalem.

6 Whither has your beloved gone,
O fairest among women?
Whither has your beloved
turned,
that we may seek him with
you?
2My beloved has gone down to his
garden,
to the beds of spices,
to pasture his flock in the
gardens,
and to gather lilies.
3I am my beloved's and my be-
loved is mine;
he pastures his flock among
the lilies.

THE BRIDE'S MATCHLESS BEAUTY

4You are beautiful as Tirzah, my
love,
comely as Jerusalem,
terrible as an army with
banners.
5Turn away your eyes from me,
for they disturb me—
Your hair is like a flock of
goats,
moving down the slopes of
Gilead.
6Your teeth are like a flock of
ewes,
that have come up from the
washing,
all of them bear twins,
not one among them is
bereaved.
7Your cheeks are like halves of a
pomegranate
behind your veil.
8There are sixty queens and
eighty concubines,
and maidens without
number.
9My dove, my perfect one, is only
one,
the darling of her mother,
flawless to her that bore her.
The maidens saw her and
called her happy;
the queens and concubines
also, and they praised
her.
10"Who is this that looks forth
like the dawn,
fair as the moon, bright as
the sun,

[a]The meaning of the Hebrew is uncertain
[b]The meaning of the Hebrew word is uncertain
[c]Heb *lapis lazuli*

**weighing and studying and arrang-
ing proverbs with great care. 10The
Preacher sought to find pleasing
words, and uprightly he wrote words
of truth.**

**11 The sayings of the wise are like
goads, and like nails firmly fixed are
the collected sayings which are given
by one Shepherd. 12My son, beware of
anything beyond these. Of making
many books there is no end, and much
study is a weariness of the flesh.**

**13 The end of the matter; all has
been heard. Fear God, and keep his
commandments; for this is the whole
duty of man.[d] 14For God will bring ev-
ery deed into judgment, with[e] every
secret thing, whether good or evil.**

[d]Or *the duty of all men*
[e]Or *into the judgment on*

THE SONG OF SOLOMON

1 The Song of Songs, which is Solomon's.

COLLOQUY OF BRIDE AND FRIENDS

2 O that you[a] would kiss me with
the kisses of your[b] mouth!
For your love is better than
wine,
3 your anointing oils are
fragrant,
your name is oil poured out;
therefore the maidens love
you.
4 Draw me after you, let us make
haste.
The king has brought me
into his chambers.
We will exult and rejoice in
you;
we will extol your love more
than wine;
rightly do they love you.
5 I am very dark, but comely,
O daughters of Jerusalem,
like the tents of Kedar,
like the curtains of
Solomon.
6 Do not gaze at me because I am
swarthy,
because the sun has
scorched me.
My mother's sons were angry
with me,
they made me keeper of the
vineyards;
but, my own vineyard I have
not kept!
7 Tell me, you whom my soul loves,
where you pasture your
flock,
where you make it lie down
at noon;
for why should I be like one
who wanders[c]
beside the flocks of your
companions?
8 If you do not know,
O fairest among women,
follow in the tracks of the
flock,
and pasture your kids
beside the shepherds' tents.

COLLOQUY OF BRIDEGROOM, FRIENDS, AND BRIDE

9 I compare you, my love,
to a mare of Pharaoh's
chariots.
10 Your cheeks are comely with
ornaments,
your neck with strings of
jewels.
11 We will make you ornaments of
gold,
studded with silver.
12 While the king was on his couch,
my nard gave forth its
fragrance.
13 My beloved is to me a bag of
myrrh,
that lies between my
breasts.
14 My beloved is to me a cluster of
henna blossoms
in the vineyards of
En-ged´i.
15 Behold, you are beautiful, my
love;
behold, you are beautiful;
your eyes are doves.
16 Behold, you are beautiful, my
beloved,
truly lovely.
Our couch is green;
17 the beams of our house are
cedar,
our rafters[d] are pine.

[a] Heb *he*
[b] Heb *his*
[c] Gk Syr Vg: Heb *is veiled*
[d] The meaning of the Hebrew word is uncertain

terrible as an army with
banners?"
11I went down to the nut orchard,
to look at the blossoms of
the valley,
to see whether the vines had
budded,
whether the pomegranates
were in bloom.
12Before I was aware, my fancy
set me
in a chariot beside my
prince.[d]
13[e] Return, return, O Shu´lammite,
return, return, that we may
look upon you.
Why should you look upon the
Shu´lammite,
as upon a dance before two
armies?[f]

EXPRESSIONS OF PRAISE

7 How graceful are your feet in
sandals,
O queenly maiden!
Your rounded thighs are like
jewels,
the work of a master hand.
2Your navel is a rounded bowl
that never lacks mixed wine.
Your belly is a heap of wheat,
encircled with lilies.
3Your two breasts are like two
fawns,
twins of a gazelle.
4Your neck is like an ivory tower.
Your eyes are pools in
Heshbon,
by the gate of Bth-rab´bim.
Your nose is like tower of
Lebanon,
overlooking Daascus.
5Your head crowns yclike
Carmel,
and your flowinocks are
like purple;
a king is held captive in the
tresses.[g]
6How fair and pleasant you are,
O loved one, delectable
maiden![h]
7You are stately[i] as a palm tree,
and your breasts are like its
clusters.
8I say I will climb the palm tree
and lay hold of its branches.
Oh, may your breasts be like
clusters of the vine,
and the scent of your breath
like apples,
9and your kisses[j] like the best
wine
that goes down[k] smoothly,
gliding over lips and teeth.[l]
10I am my beloved's,
and his desire is for me.
11Come, my beloved,
let us go forth into the
fields,
and lodge in the villages;
12let us go out early to the
vineyards,
and see whether the vines
have budded,
whether the grape blossoms
have opened
and the pomegranates are in
bloom.
There I will give you my love.
13The mandrakes give forth
fragrance,
and over our doors are all
choice fruits,
new as well as old,
which I have laid up for you,
O my beloved.

8 O that you were like a brother to
me,
that nursed at my mother's
breast!

[d]Cn: The meaning of the Heb is uncertain
[e]Ch 7.1 in Heb
[f]Or *dance of Mahanaim*
[g]The meaning of the Hebrew d is uncertain
[h]Syr: Heb *in delights*
[i]Heb *This your stature is*
[j] Heb *palate*
[k]Heb *down for my lover*
[l]Gk Syr Vg: Heb *lips of sleepers*

If I met you outside, I would
kiss you,
and none would despise me.
2I would lead you and bring you
into the house of my
mother,
and into the chamber of her
that conceived me.[a]
I would give you spiced wine to
drink,
the juice of my
pomegranates.
3O that his left hand were under
my head,
and that his right hand em-
braced me!
4I adjure you, O daughters of
Jerusalem,
that you stir not up nor
awaken love
until it please.

HOMECOMING

5Who is that coming up from the
wilderness,
leaning upon her beloved?
Under the apple tree I awak-
ened you.
There your mother was in
travail with you,
there she who bore you was
in travail.
6Set me as a seal upon your heart,
as a seal upon your arm;
for love is strong as death,
jealousy is cruel as the
grave.
Its flashes are flashes of fire,
a most vehement flame.
7Many waters cannot quench love,
neither can floods drown it.
If a man offered for love
all the wealth of his house,
it would be utterly scorned.
8We have a little sister,
and she has no breasts.
What shall we do for our sister,
on the day when she is spo-
ken for?
9If she is a wall,
we will build upon her a bat-
tlement of silver;
but if she is a door,
we will enclose her with
boards of cedar.
10I was a wall,
and my breasts were like
towers;
then I was in his eyes
as one who brings[b] peace.
11Solomon had a vineyard at
Ba´al-ha´mon;
he let out the vineyard to
keepers;
each one was to bring for
its fruit a thousand
pieces of silver.
12My vineyard, my very own, is for
myself;
you, O Solomon, may have
the thousand,
and the keepers of the fruit
two hundred.
13O you who dwell in the gardens,
my companions are listening
for your voice;
let me hear it.
14Make haste, my beloved,
and be like a gazelle
or a young stag
upon the mountains of
spices.

[a]Gk Syr: Heb *mother; she* (or *you*) *will teach me*
[b]Or *finds*

THE WISDOM OF SOLOMON

EXHORTATION TO UPRIGHTNESS

1 Love righteousness, you rulers of
the earth,
think of the Lord with
uprightness,
and seek him with sincerity of
heart;
2because he is found by those who
do not put him to the test,
and manifests himself to those
who do not distrust
him.
3For perverse thoughts separate
men from God,
and when his power is tested, it
convicts the foolish;
4because wisdom will not enter a
deceitful soul,
nor dwell in a body enslaved
to sin.
5For a holy and disciplined spirit*
will flee from deceit,
and will rise and depart from
foolish thoughts,
and will be ashamed at
the approach of
unrighteousness.
6For wisdom is a kindly spirit
and will not free a blasphemer
from the guilt of his
words;
because God is witness of his
inmost feelings,
and a true observer of his
heart, and a hearer of
his tongue.
7Because the Spirit of the Lord
has filled the world,
and that which holds all things
together knows what
is said;
8therefore no one who utters
unrighteous things will
escape notice,
and justice, when it punishes,
will not pass him by.
9For inquiry will be made into
the counsels of an ungodly
man,
and a report of his words will
come to the Lord,
to convict him of his lawless
deeds;
10because a jealous ear hears all
things,
and the sound of murmurings
does not go unheard.
11Beware then of useless
murmuring,
and keep your tongue from
slander;
because no secret word is with-
out result,[a]
and a lying mouth destroys the
soul.
12Do not invite death by the error
of your life,
nor bring on destruction by the
works of your hands;
13because God did not make
death,
and he does not delight in the
death of the living.
14For he created all things that
they might exist,
and the generative forces[b]
of the world are
wholesome,
and there is no destructive
poison in them;
and the dominion[c] of Hades is
not on earth.
15For righteousness is immortal.

LIFE AS THE UNGODLY SEE IT

16But ungodly men by their words
and deeds summoned
death;[d]

[a] Or *will go unpunished*
[b] Or *the creatures*
[c] Or *palace*
[d] Gk *him*

considering him a friend, they pined away,
and they made a covenant with him,
because they are fit to belong to his party.

2 For they reasoned unsoundly, saying to themselves,
"Short and sorrowful is our life,
and there is no remedy when a man comes to his end,
and no one has been known to return from Hades.
2Because we were born by mere chance,
and hereafter we shall be as though we had never been;
because the breath in our nostrils is smoke,
and reason is a spark kindled by the beating of our hearts.
3When it is extinguished, the body will turn to ashes,
and the spirit will dissolve like empty air.
4Our name will be forgotten in time,
and no one will remember our works;
our life will pass away like the traces of a cloud,
and be scattered like mist
that is chased by the rays of the sun
and overcome by its heat.
5For our allotted time is the passing of a shadow,
and there is no return from our death,
because it is sealed up and no one turns back.
6"Come, therefore, let us enjoy the good things that exist,
and make use of the creation to *the full* as in youth.
7Let us take our fill of costly wine and *perfumes*,
and let no flower of spring pass by us.
8Let us crown ourselves with rosebuds before they wither.
9Let none of us fail to share in our revelry,
everywhere let us leave signs of enjoyment,
because this is our portion, and this our lot.
10Let us oppress the righteous poor man;
let us not spare the widow
nor regard the gray hairs of the aged.
11But let our might be our law of right,
for what is weak proves itself to be useless.
12"Let us lie in wait for the righteous man,
because he is inconvenient to us and opposes our actions;
he reproaches us for sins against the law,
and accuses us of sins against our training.
13He professes to have knowledge of God,
and calls himself a child[a] of the Lord.
14He became to us a reproof of our thoughts;
15the very sight of him is a burden to us,
because his manner of life is unlike that of others,
and his ways are strange.
16We are considered by him as something base,
and he avoids our ways as unclean;
he calls the last end of the righteous happy,
and boasts that God is his father.
17Let us see if his words are true,
and let us test what will happen at the end of his life;
18for if the righteous man is God's son, he will help him,
and will deliver him from the hand of his adversaries.

[a] Or *servant*

19Let us test him with insult and
torture,
that we may find out how gen-
tle he is,
and make trial of his
forbearance.
20Let us condemn him to a shame-
ful death,
for, according to what he says,
he will be protected."

ERROR OF THE WICKED

21Thus they reasoned, but they
were led astray,
for their wickedness blinded
them,
22and they did not know the secret
purposes of God,
nor hope for the wages of
holiness,
nor discern the prize for blame-
less souls;
23for God created man for
incorruption,
and made him in the image of
his own eternity,[b]
24but through the devil's envy
death entered the world,
and those who belong to his
party experience it.

THE DESTINY OF THE RIGHTEOUS

3 But the souls of the righteous are
in the hand of God,
and no torment will ever touch
them.
2In the eyes of the foolish they
seemed to have died,
and their departure was
thought to be an
affliction,
3and their going from us to be
their destruction;
but they are at peace.
4For though in the sight of men
they were punished,
their hope is full of immortality.
5Having been disciplined a little,
they will receive great good,
because God tested them and
found them worthy of
himself;
6like gold in the furnace he tried
them,
and like a sacrificial burnt
offering he accepted
them.
7In the time of their visitation
they will shine forth,
and will run like sparks
through the stubble.
8They will govern nations and rule
over peoples,
and the Lord will reign over
them for ever.
9Those who trust in him will
understand truth,
and the faithful will abide with
him in love,
because grace and mercy are
upon his elect,
and he watches over his holy
ones.[c]

THE DESTINY OF THE UNGODLY

10But the ungodly will be pun-
ished as their reasoning
deserves,
who disregarded the righteous
man[d] and rebelled
against the Lord;
11for whoever despises wis-
dom and instruction is
miserable.
Their hope is vain, their labors
are unprofitable,
and their works are useless.
12Their wives are foolish, and
their children evil;
13their offspring are accursed.

ON CHILDLESSNESS

For blessed is the barren wom-
an who is undefiled,
who has not entered into a
sinful union;
she will have fruit when God
examines souls.

[b] Other ancient authorities read *nature*
[c] The text of this line is uncertain, and it is omitted here by some ancient authorities. Compare 4.15
[d] Or *what is right*

14Blessed also is the eunuch
whose hands have done no
lawless deed,
and who has not devised wicked
things against the Lord;
for special favor will be shown
him for his faithfulness,
and a place of great delight in
the temple of the Lord.
15For the fruit of good labors is
renowned,
and the root of understanding
does not fail.
16But children of adulterers will
not come to maturity,
and the offspring of an unlawful
union will perish.
17Even if they live long they will
be held of no account,
and finally their old age will be
without honor.
18If they die young, they will have
no hope
and no consolation in the day
of decision.
19For the end of an unrighteous
generation is grievous.

4 Better than this is childlessness
with virtue,
for in the memory of virtue[a] is
immortality,
because it is known both by
God and by men.
2When it is present, men imitate[b]
it,
and they long for it when it has
gone;
and throughout all time it
marches crowned in
triumph,
victor in the contest for prizes
that are undefiled.
3But the prolific brood of the ungodly
will be of no use,
and none of their illegitimate
seedlings will strike a
deep root
or take a firm hold.
4For even if they put forth boughs
for a while,
standing insecurely they will
be shaken by the wind,
and by the violence of the winds
they will be uprooted.
5The branches will be broken
off before they come to
maturity,
and their fruit will be useless,
not ripe enough to eat, and
good for nothing.
6For children born of unlawful
unions
are witnesses of evil against
their parents when God
examines them.[c]
7But the righteous man, though he
die early, will be at rest.
8For old age is not honored for
length of time,
nor measured by number of
years;
9but understanding is gray hair
for men,
and a blameless life is ripe old
age.
10There was one who pleased God
and was loved by him,
and while living among sinners
he was taken up.
11He was caught up lest evil
change his understanding
or guile deceive his soul.
12For the fascination of wickedness
obscures what is good,
and roving desire perverts the
innocent mind.
13Being perfected in a short time,
he fulfilled long years;
14for his soul was pleasing to the
Lord,
therefore he took him quickly
from the midst of
wickedness.
15Yet the peoples saw and did not
understand,
nor take such a thing to heart,
that God's grace and mercy are
with his elect,
and he watches over his holy
ones.

[a] Gk *it*
[b] Other ancient authorities read *honor*
[c] Gk *at their examination*

THE TRIUMPH OF THE RIGHTEOUS

16The righteous man who has died
will condemn the ungodly
who are living,
and youth that is quickly perfected[d] will condemn the
prolonged old age of the
unrighteous man.
17For they will see the end of the
wise man,
and will not understand what
the Lord purposed for
him,
and for what he kept him safe.
18They will see, and will have
contempt for him,
but the Lord will laugh them
to scorn.
After this they will become
dishonored corpses,
and an outrage among the dead
for ever;
19because he will dash them
speechless to the ground,
and shake them from the
foundations;
they will be left utterly dry and
barren,
and they will suffer anguish,
and the memory of them will
perish.

THE FINAL JUDGMENT

20They will come with dread when
their sins are reckoned up,
and their lawless deeds will convict them to their face.
5 Then the righteous man will stand
with great confidence
in the presence of those who
have afflicted him,
and those *who make light of*
his labors.
2When they see him, they will be
shaken with dreadful fear,
and they will be amazed at his
unexpected salvation.
3They will speak to one another in
repentance,
and in anguish of spirit they
will groan, and say,
4"This is the man whom we once
held in derision
and made a byword of
reproach—we fools!
We thought that his life was
madness
and that his end was without
honor.
5Why has he been numbered
among the sons of God?
And why is his lot among the
saints?
6So it was we who strayed from
the way of truth,
and the light of righteousness
did not shine on us,
and the sun did not rise upon
us.
7We took our fill of the paths
of lawlessness and
destruction,
and we journeyed through
trackless deserts,
but the way of the Lord we
have not known.
8What has our arrogance profited
us?
And what good has our boasted
wealth brought us?
9"All those things have vanished
like a shadow,
and like a rumor that passes
by;
10like a ship that sails through the
billowy water,
and when it has passed no
trace can be found,
nor track of its keel in the
waves;
11or as, when a bird flies through
the air,
no evidence of its passage is
found;
the light air, lashed by the beat
of its pinions
and pierced by the force of its
rushing flight,
is traversed by the movement
of its wings,
and afterward no sign of its
coming is found there;

[d]Or *ended*

12or as, when an arrow is shot at
a target,
the air, thus divided, comes
together at once,
so that no one knows its
pathway.
13So we also, as soon as we were
born, ceased to be,
and we had no sign of virtue to
show,
but were consumed in our
wickedness."*
14Because the hope of the ungodly
man is like chaff[a] carried
by the wind,
and like a light hoarfrost[b] driv-
en away by a storm;
it is dispersed like smoke be-
fore the wind,
and it passes like the remem-
brance of a guest who
stays but a day.

THE REWARD OF THE RIGHTEOUS

15But the righteous live for ever,
and their reward is with the
Lord;
the Most High takes care of
them.
16Therefore they will receive a
glorious crown
and a beautiful diadem from
the hand of the Lord,
because with his right hand he
will cover them,
and with his arm he will shield
them.
17The Lord[c] will take his zeal as
his whole armor,
and will arm all creation to
repel[d] his enemies;
18he will put on righteousness as a
breastplate,
and wear impartial justice as a
helmet;
19he will take holiness as an invin-
cible shield,
20and sharpen stern wrath for a
sword,
and creation will join with
him to fight against the
madmen.
21Shafts of lightning will fly with
true aim,
and will leap to the target as
from a well-drawn bow
of clouds,
22and hailstones full of wrath
will be hurled as from a
catapult;
the water of the sea will rage
against them,
and rivers will relentlessly
overwhelm them;
23a mighty wind will rise against
them,
and like a tempest it will win-
now them away.
Lawlessness will lay waste the
whole earth,
and evil-doing will overturn
the thrones of rulers.

KINGS SHOULD SEEK WISDOM

6 Listen therefore, O kings, and
understand;
learn, O judges of the ends of
the earth.
2Give ear, you that rule over
multitudes,
and boast of many nations.
3For your dominion was given you
from the Lord,
and your sovereignty from the
Most High,
who will search out your works
and inquire into your
plans.
4Because as servants of his
kingdom you did not rule
rightly,
nor keep the law,
nor walk according to the pur-
pose of God,
5he will come upon you terribly
and swiftly,
because severe judgment falls
on those in high places.

[a]Or *dust*
[b]Other authorities read *spider's web*
[c]Gk *He*
[d]Or *punish*

6For the lowliest man may be
pardoned in mercy,
but mighty men will be mighti-
ly tested.*
7For the Lord of all will not stand
in awe of any one,
nor show deference to
greatness;
because he himself made both
small and great,
and he takes thought for all
alike.
8But a strict inquiry is in store for
the mighty.
9To you then, O monarchs, my
words are directed,
that you may learn wisdom and
not transgress.
10For they will be made holy who
observe holy things in
holiness,
and those who have been taught
them will find a defense.
11Therefore set your desire on my
words;
long for them, and you will be
instructed.

DESCRIPTION OF WISDOM

12Wisdom is radiant and unfading,
and she is easily discerned by
those who love her,
and is found by those who seek
her.
13She hastens to make herself
known to those who desire
her.
14He who rises early to seek her
will have no difficulty,
for he will find her sitting at
his gates.
15To fix one's thought on her is
perfect understanding,
and he who is vigilant on her
account will soon be
free from care,
16because she goes about seeking
those worthy of her,
and she graciously appears to
them in their paths,
and meets them in every
thought.
17The beginning of wisdom[e] is the
most sincere desire for
instruction,
and concern for instruction is
love of her,
18and love of her is the keeping of
her laws,
and giving heed to her
laws is assurance of
immortality,
19and immortality brings one near
to God;
20so the desire for wisdom leads to
a kingdom.
21Therefore if you delight in
thrones and scepters, O
monarchs over the peoples,
honor wisdom, that you may
reign for ever.
22I will tell you what wisdom is
and how she came to be,
and I will hide no secrets from
you,
but I will trace her course
from the beginning of
creation,
and make knowledge of her
clear,
and I will not pass by the truth;
23neither will I travel in the com-
pany of sickly envy,
for envy[f] does not associate
with wisdom.
24A multitude of wise men is the
salvation of the world,
and a sensible king is the sta-
bility of his people.
25Therefore be instructed by my
words, and you will profit.

SOLOMON LIKE OTHER MORTALS

7 I also am mortal, like all men,
a descendant of the first-
formed child of earth;
and in the womb of a mother I
was molded into flesh,
2within the period of ten months,
compacted with blood,

[e]Gk *Her beginning*
[f]Gk *this*

from the seed of a man and the
pleasure of marriage.
3And when I was born, I began to
breathe the common air,
and fell upon the kindred earth,
and my first sound was a cry,
like that of all.
4I was nursed with care in swad-
dling cloths.
5For no king has had a different
beginning of existence;
6there is for all mankind one
entrance into life, and a
common departure.

SOLOMON'S RESPECT FOR WISDOM

7Therefore I prayed, and under-
standing was given me;
I called upon God, and the
spirit of wisdom came
to me.
8I preferred her to scepters and
thrones,
and I accounted wealth as
nothing in comparison
with her.
9Neither did I liken to her any
priceless gem,
because all gold is but a little
sand in her sight,
and silver will be accounted as
clay before her.
10I loved her more than health and
beauty,
and I chose to have her rather
than light,
because her radiance never
ceases.
11All good things came to me
along with her,
and in her hands uncounted
wealth.
12I rejoiced in them all, because
wisdom leads them;
but I did not know that she was
their mother.
13I learned without guile and I
impart without grudging;
I do not hide her wealth,
14for it is an unfailing treasure for
men;
those who get it obtain friend-
ship with God,
commended for the gifts that
come from instruction.

SOLOMON PRAYS FOR WISDOM

15May God grant that I speak with
judgment
and have thoughts worthy of
what I have received,
for he is the guide even of
wisdom
and the corrector of the wise.
16For both we and our words are
in his hand,
as are all understanding and
skill in crafts.
17For it is he who gave me unerring
knowledge of what exists,
to know the structure of the
world and the activity of
the elements;
18the beginning and end and mid-
dle of times,
the alternations of the solstices
and the changes of the
seasons,
19the cycles of the year and the
constellations of the stars,
20the natures of animals and the
tempers of wild beasts,
the powers of spirits[a] and the
reasonings of men,
the varieties of plants and the
virtues of roots;
21I learned both what is secret and
what is manifest,
22for wisdom, the fashioner of all
things, taught me.

THE NATURE OF WISDOM

For in her there is a spirit that
is intelligent, holy,
unique, manifold, subtle,
mobile, clear, unpolluted,
distinct, invulnerable, loving
the good, keen,
irresistible, 23beneficent,
humane,
steadfast, sure, free from
anxiety,

[a]Or *winds*

all-powerful, overseeing all,
and penetrating through all
spirits
that are intelligent and pure
and most subtle.
24For wisdom is more mobile than
any motion;
because of her pureness she
pervades and penetrates
all things.
25For she is a breath of the power
of God,
and a pure emanation of the
glory of the Almighty;
therefore nothing defiled gains
entrance into her.
26For she is a reflection of eternal
light,
a spotless mirror of the work-
ing of God,
and an image of his goodness.
27Though she is but one, she can
do all things,
and while remaining in herself,
she renews all things;
in every generation she passes
into holy souls
and makes them friends of
God, and prophets;
28for God loves nothing so much
as the man who lives with
wisdom.
29For she is more beautiful than
the sun,
and excels every constellation
of the stars.
Compared with the light she is
found to be superior,
30for it is succeeded by the night,
but against wisdom evil does
not prevail.

8 She reaches mightily from one end
of the earth to the other,
and she orders all things well.

SOLOMON'S LOVE FOR WISDOM

2I loved her and sought her from
my youth,
and I desired to take her for my
bride,
and I became enamored of her
beauty.
3She glorifies her noble birth by
living with God,
and the Lord of all loves her.
4For she is an initiate in the
knowledge of God,
and an associate in his works.
5If riches are a desirable posses-
sion in life,
what is richer than wisdom
who effects all things?
6And if understanding is effective,
who more than she is fashioner
of what exists?
7And if any one loves
righteousness,
her labors are virtues;
for she teaches self-control and
prudence,
justice and courage;
nothing in life is more profit-
able for men than these.
8And if any one longs for wide
experience,
she knows the things of old,
and infers the things to
come;
she understands turns of
speech and the solutions
of riddles;
she has foreknowledge of signs
and wonders
and of the outcome of seasons
and times.

WISDOM INDISPENSIBLE TO RULERS

9Therefore I determined to take
her to live with me,
knowing that she would give
me good counsel
and encouragement in cares
and grief.
10Because of her I shall have glory
among the multitudes
and honor in the presence of
the elders, though I am
young.
11I shall be found keen in
judgment,
and in the sight of rulers I shall
be admired.
12When I am silent they will wait
for me,

and when I speak they will give heed;
and when I speak at greater length
they will put their hands on their mouths.
13Because of her I shall have immortality,
and leave an everlasting remembrance to those who come after me.
14I shall govern peoples,
and nations will be subject to me;
15dread monarchs will be afraid of me when they hear of me;
among the people I shall show myself capable, and courageous in war.
16When I enter my house, I shall find rest with her,
for companionship with her has no bitterness,
and life with her has no pain,
but gladness and joy.
17When I considered these things inwardly,
and thought upon them in my mind,
that in kinship with wisdom there is immortality,
18and in friendship with her, pure delight,
and in the labors of her hands, unfailing wealth,
and in the experience of her company, understanding,
and renown in sharing her words,
I went about seeking how to get her for myself.
19As a child I was by nature well endowed,
and a good soul fell to my lot;
20or rather, being good, I entered an undefiled body.
21But I perceived that I would not possess wisdom unless God gave her to me—
and it was a mark of insight to know whose gift she was—
so I appealed to the Lord and besought him,
and with my whole heart I said:

SOLOMON'S PRAYER FOR WISDOM

9 "O God of my fathers and Lord of mercy,
who hast made all things by thy word,
2and by thy wisdom hast formed man,
to have dominion over the creatures thou hast made,
3and rule the world in holiness and righteousness,
and pronounce judgment in uprightness of soul,
4give me the wisdom that sits by thy throne,
and do not reject me from among thy servants.
5For I am thy slave and the son of thy maidservant,
a man who is weak and short-lived,
with little understanding of judgment and laws;
6for even if one is perfect among the sons of men,
yet without the wisdom that comes from thee he will be regarded as nothing.
7Thou hast chosen me to be king of thy people
and to be judge over thy sons and daughters.
8Thou hast given command to build a temple on thy holy mountain,
and an altar in the city of thy habitation,
a copy of the holy tent which thou didst prepare from the beginning.
9With thee is wisdom, who knows thy works
and was present when thou didst make the world,
and who understand what is pleasing in thy sight

and what is right according to
thy commandments.
10Send her forth from the holy
heavens,
and from the throne of thy
glory send her,
that she may be with me and
toil,
and that I may learn what is
pleasing to thee.
11For she knows and understands
all things,
and she will guide me wisely in
my actions
and guard me with her glory.
12Then my works will be
acceptable,
and I shall judge thy people
justly,
and shall be worthy of the
throne[a] of my father.
13For what man can learn the
counsel of God?
Or who can discern what the
Lord wills?
14For the reasoning of mortals is
worthless,
and our designs are likely to
fail,
15for a perishable body weighs
down the soul,
and this earthy tent burdens
the thoughtful[b] mind.
16We can hardly guess at what is
on earth,
and what is at hand we find
with labor;
but who has traced out what is
in the heavens?
17Who has learned thy counsel,
unless thou hast given
wisdom
and sent thy holy Spirit from
on high?
18And thus the paths of those on
earth were set right,
and men were taught what
pleases thee,
and were saved by wisdom."

THE WORK OF WISDOM FROM ADAM TO MOSES

10 Wisdom[c] protected the first-formed
father of the world,
when he alone had been
created;
she delivered him from his
transgression,
2and gave him strength to rule all
things.
3But when an unrighteous man
departed from her in his
anger,
he perished because in rage he
slew his brother.
4When the earth was flooded
because of him, wisdom
again saved it,
steering the righteous man by a
paltry piece of wood.
5Wisdom[d] also, when the nations
in wicked agreement had
been confounded,
recognized the righteous man
and preserved him
blameless before God,
and kept him strong in the face
of his compassion for
his child.
6Wisdom[e] rescued a righteous
man when the ungodly
were perishing;
he escaped the fire that de-
scended on the Five
Cities.[f]
7Evidence of their wickedness still
remains:
a continually smoking
wasteland,
plants bearing fruit that does
not ripen,
and a pillar of salt standing
as a monument to an
unbelieving soul.

[a] Gk *thrones*
[b] Or *anxious*
[c] Gk *She*
[d] Gk *She*
[e] Gk *She*
[f] Or *Pentapolis*

8For because they passed wisdom by,
they not only were hindered from recognizing the good,
but also left for mankind a reminder of their folly,
so that their failures could never go unnoticed.
9Wisdom rescued from troubles those who served her.
10When a righteous man fled from his brother's wrath,
she guided him on straight paths;
she showed him the kingdom of God,
and gave him knowledge of angels;[a]
she prospered him in his labors,
and increased the fruit of his toil.
11When his oppressors were covetous,
she stood by him and made him rich.
12She protected him from his enemies,
and kept him safe from those who lay in wait for him;
in his arduous contest she gave him the victory,
so that he might learn that godliness is more powerful than anything.
13When a righteous man was sold, wisdom[b] did not desert him,
but delivered him from sin.
She descended with him into the dungeon,
14and when he was in prison she did not leave him,
until she brought him the scepter of a kingdom
and authority over his masters.
Those who accused him she showed to be false,
and she gave him everlasting honor.

WISDOM LED THE ISRAELITES OUT OF EGYPT

15A holy people and blameless race wisdom[c] delivered from a nation of oppressors.
16She entered the soul of a servant of the Lord,
and withstood dread kings with wonders and signs.
17She gave holy men the reward of their labors;
she guided them along a marvelous way,
and became a shelter to them by day,
and a starry flame through the night.
18She brought them over the Red Sea,
and led them through deep waters;
19but she drowned their enemies,
and cast them up from the depth of the sea.
20Therefore the righteous plundered the ungodly;
they sang hymns, O Lord, to thy holy name,
and praised with one accord thy defending hand,
21because wisdom opened the mouth of the dumb,
and made the tongues of babes speak clearly.

WISDOM LED THE ISRAELITES THROUGH THE DESERT

11 Wisdom[d] prospered their works by the hand of a holy prophet.
2They journeyed through an uninhabited wilderness,
and pitched their tents in untrodden places.
3They withstood their enemies
and fought off their foes.

[a] Or *of holy things*
[b] Gk *she*
[c] Gk *she*
[d] Gk *She*

4When they thirsted they called
upon thee,
and water was given them out
of flinty rock,
and slaking of thirst from hard
stone.
5For through the very things by
which their enemies were
punished,
they themselves received bene-
fit in their need.
6Instead of the fountain of an
ever-flowing river,
stirred up and defiled with
blood
7in rebuke for the decree to slay
the infants,
thou gavest them abundant
water unexpectedly,
8showing by their thirst at that
time
how thou didst punish their
enemies.
9For when they were tried, though
they were being disciplined
in mercy,
they learned how the ungodly
were tormented when
judged in wrath.
10For thou didst test them as a
father does in warning,
but thou didst examine the
ungodly[e] as a stern king
does in condemnation.
11Whether absent or present, they
were equally distressed,
12for a twofold grief possessed
them,
and a groaning at the memory
of what had occurred.
13For when they heard that through
their own punishments
the righteous[f] had received
benefit, they perceived
it was the Lord's doing.
14For though they had mockingly
rejected him who long
before had been cast out
and exposed,
at the end of the events they
marveled at him,
for their thirst was not like
that of the righteous.

PUNISHMENT OF THE WICKED

15In return for their foolish and
wicked thoughts,
which led them astray to wor-
ship irrational serpents
and worthless animals,
thou didst send upon them a
multitude of irrational
creatures to punish
them,
16that they might learn that one
is punished by the very
things by which he sins.
17For thy all-powerful hand,
which created the world out of
formless matter,
did not lack the means to send
upon them a multitude
of bears, or bold lions,
18or newly created unknown
beasts full of rage,
or such as breathe out fiery
breath,
or belch forth a thick pall of
smoke,
or flash terrible sparks from
their eyes;
19not only could their damage
exterminate men,[g]
but the mere sight of them
could kill by fright.
20Even apart from these, men[h]
could fall at a single
breath
when pursued by justice
and scattered by the breath of
thy power.
But thou hast arranged all
things by measure and
number and weight.

GOD IS POWERFUL AND MERCIFUL

21For it is always in thy power to
show great strength,

[e]Gk *those*
[f]Gk *they*
[g]Gk *them*
[h]Gk *they*

and who can withstand the
might of thy arm?
22Because the whole world before
thee is like a speck that
tips the scales,
and like a drop of morning
dew that falls upon the
ground.
23But thou art merciful to all, for
thou canst do all things,
and thou dost overlook men's
sins, that they may
repent.
24For thou lovest all things that
exist,
and hast loathing for none of
the things which thou
hast made,
for thou wouldst not have made
anything if thou hadst
hated it.
25How would anything have
endured if thou hadst not
willed it?
Or how would anything not
called forth by thee have
been preserved?
26Thou sparest all things, for they
are thine, O Lord who
lovest the living.*

12 For thy immortal spirit is in all
things.
2Therefore thou dost correct little
by little those who trespass,
and dost remind and warn
them of the things
wherein they sin,
that they may be freed from
wickedness and put
their trust in thee, O
Lord.

THE SINS OF THE CANAANITES

3Those who dwelt of old in thy
holy land
4thou didst hate for their detest-
able practices,
their works of sorcery and
unholy rites,
5their merciless slaughter[a] of
children,
and their sacrificial feasting on
human flesh and blood.
These initiates from the midst
of a heathen cult,[b]
6these parents who murder help-
less lives,
thou didst will to destroy by the
hands of our fathers,
7that the land most precious of all
to thee
might receive a worthy colony
of the servants[c] of God.
8But even these thou didst spare,
since they were but men,
and didst send wasps[d] as fore-
runners of thy army,
to destroy them little by little,
9though thou wast not unable to
give the ungodly into the
hands of the righteous in
battle,
or to destroy them at one blow
by dread wild beasts or
thy stern word.
10But judging them little by little
thou gavest them a chance
to repent,
though thou wast not unaware
that their origin[e] was
evil
and their wickedness inborn,
and that their way of thinking
would never change.
11For they were an accursed race
from the beginning,
and it was not through fear of
any one that thou didst
leave them unpunished
for their sins.

GOD IS SOVEREIGN

12For who will say, "What hast
thou done?"
Or will resist thy judgment?
Who will accuse thee for the

[a] Cn: Gk *slaughterers*
[b] The Greek text of this line is uncertain
[c] Or *children*
[d] Or *hornets*
[e] Or *nature*

destruction of nations
which thou didst make?
Or who will come before thee
to plead as an advocate
for unrighteous men?
13For neither is there any god
besides thee, whose care is
for all men,[f]
to whom thou shouldst prove
that thou hast not
judged unjustly;
14nor can any king or monarch
confront thee about those
whom thou hast punished.
15Thou art righteous and rulest all
things righteously,
deeming it alien to thy power
to condemn him who does not
deserve to be punished.
16For thy strength is the source of
righteousness,
and thy sovereignty over all
causes thee to spare all.
17For thou dost show thy strength
when men doubt the com-
pleteness of thy power,
and dost rebuke any insolence
among those who know
it.[g]
18Thou who art sovereign in
strength dost judge with
mildness,
and with great forbearance
thou dost govern us;
for thou hast power to act
whenever thou dost
choose.

GOD'S LESSONS FOR ISRA

19Through such works thou has
taught thy people
that the righteous man n st
be kind,
and thou hast filled thy so
with good hope,
because thou givest repent e
for sins.
20For if thou didst punish with s
great care and indulgence[h]
the enemies of thy servants[i]
and those deserving of
death,
granting them time and oppor-
tunity to give up their
wickedness,
21with what strictness thou hast
judged thy sons,
to whose fathers thou gavest
oaths and covenants full
of good promises!
22So while chastening us thou
scourgest our enemies ten
thousand times more,
so that we may meditate upon
thy goodness when we
judge,
and when we are judged we
may expect mercy.

THE PUNISHMENT OF THE EGYPTIANS

23Therefore those who in folly of
life lived unrighteously
thou didst torment through
their own abominations.
24For they went far astray on the
paths of error,
accepting as gods those ani-
mals which even their
enemies[j] despised;
they were deceived like foolish
babes.
25Therefore, as to thoughtless
children,
thou didst send thy judgment
to mock them.
26But those who have not heeded
the warning of light
rebukes
will experience the deserved
judgment of God.
27For when in their suffering they
became incensed
at those creatures which they
had thought to be gods,
being punished by
means of them,

[f] Or *all things*
[g] The Greek text of this line is uncertain
[h] Some ancient authorities omit *and indulg*; others read *and entreaty*
[i] Or *children*
[j] Gk *they*

they saw and recognized as the true God him whom they had before refused to know.
Therefore the utmost condemnation came upon them.

THE FOOLISHNESS OF NATURE WORSHIP

13 For all men who were ignorant of God were foolish by nature;
and they were unable from the good things that are seen to know him who exists,
nor did they recognize the craftsman while paying heed to his works;
2 but they supposed that either fire or wind or swift air,
or the circle of the stars, or turbulent water,
or the luminaries of heaven were the gods that rule the world.
3 If through delight in the beauty of these things men[a] assumed them to be gods,
let them know how much better than these is their Lord,
for the author of beauty created them.
4 And if men[b] were amazed at their power and working,
let them perceive from them
how much more powerful is he who formed them.
5 For from the greatness and beauty of created things
comes a corresponding perception of their Creator.
6 Yet these men are little to be blamed,
for perhaps they go astray
while seeking God and desiring to find him.
7 For as they live among his works they keep searching,
and they trust in what they see, because the things that are seen are beautiful.
8 Yet again, not even they are to be excused;
9 for if they had the power to know so much
that they could investigate the world,
how did they fail to find sooner the Lord of these things?

THE FOOLISHNESS OF IDOLATRY

10 But miserable, with their hopes set on dead things, are the men
who give the name "gods" to the works of men's hands,
gold and silver fashioned with skill,
and likenesses of animals,
or a useless stone, the work of an ancient hand.
11 A skilled woodcutter may saw down a tree easy to handle
and skilfully strip off all its bark,
and then with pleasing workmanship
make a useful vessel that serves life's needs,
12 and burn the castoff pieces of his work
to prepare his food, and eat his fill.
13 But a castoff piece from among them, useful for nothing,
a stick crooked and full of knots,
he takes and carves with care in his leisure,
and shapes it with skill gained in idleness;[c]
he forms it like the image of a man,
or makes it like some worthless animal,
giving it a coat of red paint and coloring its surface red
and covering every blemish in

[a] Gk *they*
[b] Gk *they*
[c] Other authorities read *with intelligent skill*

it with paint;
15then he makes for it a niche that befits it,
and sets it in the wall, and fastens it there with iron.
16So he takes thought for it, that it may not fall,
because he knows that it cannot help itself,
for it is only an image and has need of help.
17When he prays about possessions and his marriage and children,
he is not ashamed to address a lifeless thing.
18For health he appeals to a thing that is weak;
for life he prays to a thing that is dead;
for aid he entreats a thing that is utterly inexperienced;
for a prosperous journey, a thing that cannot take a step;
19for money-making and work and success with his hands
he asks strength of a thing whose hands have no strength.

FOLLY OF A NAVIGATOR PRAYING TO AN IDOL

14 Again, one preparing to sail and about to voyage over raging waves
calls upon a piece of wood more fragile than the ship which carries him.
2For it was desire for gain that *planned that vessel,*
and wisdom was the craftsman who built it;
3but it is thy providence, O Father, that steers its course,
because thou hast given it a path in the sea,
and a safe way through the waves,
4showing that thou canst save from every danger,
so that even if a man lacks skill, he may put to sea.
5It is thy will that works of thy wisdom should not be without effect;
therefore men trust their lives even to the smallest piece of wood,
and passing through the billows on a raft they come safely to land.
6For even in the beginning, when arrogant giants were perishing,
the hope of the world took refuge on a raft,
and guided by thy hand left to the world the seed of a new generation.
7For blessed is the wood by which righteousness comes.
8But the idol made with hands is accursed, and so is he who made it;
because he did the work, and the perishable thing was named a god.
9For equally hateful to God are the ungodly man and his ungodliness,
10for what was done will be punished together with him who did it.
11Therefore there will be a visitation also upon the heathen idols,
because, though part of what God created, they became an abomination,
and became traps for the souls of men
and a snare to the feet of the foolish.

THE ORIGIN AND EVILS OF IDOLATRY

12For the idea of making idols was the beginning of fornication,
and the invention of them was the corruption of life,
13for neither have they existed from the beginning
nor will they exist for ever.

14For through the vanity of men
they entered the world,
and therefore their speedy end
has been planned.
15For a father, consumed with
grief at an untimely
bereavement,
made an image of his child,
who had been suddenly
taken from him;
and he now honored as a god
what was once a dead
human being,
and handed on to his dependents secret rites and
initiations.
16Then the ungodly custom, grown
strong with time, was kept
as a law,
and at the command of monarchs graven images
were worshiped.
17When men could not honor
monarchs[a] in their presence, since they lived at a
distance,
they imagined their appearance
far away,
and made a visible image of
the king whom they
honored,
so that by their zeal they might
flatter the absent one as
though present.
18Then the ambition of the craftsman impelled
even those who did not know
the king to intensify
their worship.
19For he, perhaps wishing to
please his ruler,
skilfully forced the likeness
to take more beautiful
form,
20and the multitude, attracted by
the charm of his work,
now regarded as an object of
worship the one whom
shortly before they had
honored as a man.
21And this became a hidden trap
for mankind,
because men, in bondage to
misfortune or to royal
authority,
bestowed on objects of stone
or wood the name that
ought not to be shared.
22Afterward it was not enough
for them to err about the
knowledge of God,
but they live in great strife due
to ignorance,
and they call such great evils
peace.
23For whether they kill children in
their initiations, or celebrate secret mysteries,
or hold frenzied revels with
strange customs,
24they no longer keep either their
lives or their marriages pure,
but they either treacherously
kill one another, or
grieve one another by
adultery,
25and all is a raging riot of blood
and murder, theft and deceit, corruption, faithlessness, tumult, perjury,
26confusion over what is good,
forgetfulness of favors,
pollution of souls, sex
perversion,
disorder in marriage, adultery,
and debauchery.
27For the worship of idols not to
be named
is the beginning and cause and
end of every evil.
28For their worshipers[b] either rave in
exultation, or prophesy lies,
or live unrighteously, or readily
commit perjury;
29for because they trust in lifeless
idols
they swear wicked oaths and
expect to suffer no harm.
30But just penalties will overtake
them on two counts:

[a]Gk *them*
[b]Gk *they*

because they thought wickedly
of God in devoting
themselves to idols,
and because in deceit they
swore unrighteously
through contempt for
holiness.
31 For it is not the power of the
things by which men swear,[c]
but the just penalty for those
who sin,
that always pursues the
transgression of the
unrighteous.

BENEFITS OF WORSHIPING THE TRUE GOD

15 But thou, our God, art kind and
true,
patient, and ruling all things[d]
in mercy.
2 For even if we sin we are thine,
knowing thy power;
but we will not sin, because
we know that we are
accounted thine.
3 For to know thee is complete
righteousness,
and to know thy power is the
root of immortality.
4 For neither has the evil intent of
human art misled us,
nor the fruitless toil of painters,
a figure stained with varied
colors,
5 whose appearance arouses yearn-
ing in fools,
so that they desire[e] the lifeless
form of a lead image.
6 Lovers of evil thin$ and fit for
such objects[f] hope[f]
are those who ei er make or
desire or rship them.

THE FOOLISHNEOF WORSHIPING CLAYDLS

7 For when a potter kds the
soft earth
and laboriously m each
vessel for our service,
he fashions out of the same
clay
both the vessels that serve
clean uses
and those for contrary uses,
making all in like
manner;
but which shall be the use of
each of these
the worker in clay decides.
8 With misspent toil, he forms a
futile god from the same
clay—
this man who was made of
earth a short time
before
and after a little while goes to
the earth from which he
was taken,
when he is required to return
the soul that was lent
him.
9 But he is not concerned that he is
destined to die
or that his life is brief,
but he competes with workers
in gold and silver,
and imitates workers in copper;
and he counts it his glory that
he molds counterfeit
gods.
10 His heart is ashes, his hope is
cheaper than dirt,
and his life is of less worth
than clay,
11 because he failed to know the
one who formed him
and inspired him with an active
soul
and breathed into him a living
spirit.
12 But he[g] considered our existence
an idle game,
and life a festival held for profit,
for he says one must get money
however one can, even
by base means.

[c] Or *of the oaths men swear*
[d] Or *ruling the universe*
[e] Gk *and he desires*
[f] Gk *such hopes*
[g] Other authorities read *they*

13For this man, more than all others, knows that he sins
when he makes from earthy matter fragile vessels
and graven images.
14But most foolish, and more miserable than an infant,
are all the enemies who oppressed thy people.
15For they thought that all their heathen idols were gods,
though these have neither the use of their eyes to see with,
nor nostrils with which to draw breath,
nor ears with which to hear,
nor fingers to feel with,
and their feet are of no use for walking.
16For a man made them,
and one whose spirit is borrowed formed them;
for no man can form a god which is like himself.
17He is mortal, and what he makes with lawless hands is dead,
for he is better than the objects he worships,
since[a] he has life, but they never have.

SERPENTS IN THE DESERT

18The enemies of thy people[b] worship even the most hateful animals,
which are worse than all others, when judged by their lack of intelligence;
19and even as animals they are not so beautiful in appearance that one would desire them,
but they have escaped both the praise of God and his blessing.

16 Therefore those men were deservedly punished through such creatures,
and were tormented by a multitude of animals.
2Instead of this punishment thou didst show kindness to thy people,
and thou didst prepare quails to eat,
a delicacy to satisfy the desire of appetite;
3in order that those men, when they desired food,
might lose the least remnant of appetite[c]
because of the odious creatures sent to them,
while thy people,[d] after suffering want a short time,
might partake of delicacies.
4For it was necessary that upon those oppressors inexorable want should come,
while to these it was merely shown how their enemies were being tormented.
5For when the terrible rage of wild beasts came upon thy people[e]
and they were being destroyed by the bites of writhing serpents,
thy wrath did not continue to the end;
6they were troubled for a little while as a warning,
and received a token of deliverance to remind them of
ny law's command.
7For he wo turned toward it was
s ed, not by what he saw,
but b hee, the Savior of all.
8And by his also thou didst con-
nce our enemies
tha is thou who deliverest
from every evil.
9For t were killed by the bites
f locusts and flies,

[a] Other authorities read *of which*
[b] Gk *They*
[c] Gk *loathe the necessary appetite*
[d] Gk *they*
[e] Gk *them*

and no healing was found for them,
because they deserved to be punished by such things;
10but thy sons were not conquered even by the teeth of venomous serpents,
for thy mercy came to their help and healed them.
11To remind them of thy oracles they were bitten,
and then were quickly delivered,
lest they should fall into deep forgetfulness
and become unresponsive[f] to thy kindness.
12For neither herb nor poultice cured them,
but it was thy word, O Lord, which heals all men.
13For thou hast power over life and death;
thou dost lead men down to the gates of Hades and back again.
14A man in his wickedness kills another,
but he cannot bring back the departed spirit,
nor set free the imprisoned soul.

DISASTROUS STORMS STRIKE EGYPT

15To escape from thy hand is impossible;
16for the ungodly, refusing to know thee,
were scourged by the strength of thy arm,
pursued by unusual rains and hail and relentless storms,
and utterly consumed by fire.
17For—most incredible of all—in the water, which quenches all things,
the fire had still greater effect,
for the universe defends the righteous.
18At one time the flame was restrained,
so that it might not consume the creatures sent against the ungodly,
but that seeing this they might know
that they were being pursued by the judgment of God;
19and at another time even in the midst of water it burned more intensely than fire,
to destroy the crops of the unrighteous land.

THE ISRAELITES RECEIVE MANNA

20Instead of these things thou didst give thy people food of angels,
and without their toil thou didst supply them from heaven with bread ready to eat,
providing every pleasure and suited to every taste.
21For thy sustenance manifested thy sweetness toward thy children;
and the bread, ministering[g] to the desire of the one who took it,
was changed to suit every one's liking.
22Snow and ice withstood fire without melting,
so that they might know that the crops of their enemies
were being destroyed by the fire that blazed in the hail
and flashed in the showers of rain;
23whereas the fire,[h] in order that the righteous might be fed,
even forgot its native power.
24For creation, serving thee who hast made it,
exerts itself to punish the unrighteous,

[f]The meaning of the Greek is obscure
[g]Gk *and it, ministering*
[h]Gk *this*

and in kindness relaxes on behalf of those who trust in thee.
25Therefore at that time also, changed into all forms,
it served thy all-nourishing bounty,
according to the desire of those who had need,[a]
26so that thy sons, whom thou didst love, O Lord, might learn
that it is not the production of crops that feeds man,
but that thy word preserves those who trust in thee.
27For what was not destroyed by fire
was melted when simply warmed by a fleeting ray of the sun,
28to make it known that one must rise before the sun to give thee thanks,
and must pray to thee at the dawning of the light;
29for the hope of an ungrateful man will melt like wintry frost,
and flow away like waste water.

TERROR STRIKES THE EGYPTIANS AT NIGHT

17 Great are thy judgments and hard to describe;
therefore uninstructed souls have gone astray.
2For when lawless men supposed that they held the holy nation in their power,
they themselves lay as captives of darkness and prisoners of long night,
shut in under their roofs, exiles from eternal providence.
3For thinking that in their secret sins they were unobserved
behind a dark curtain of forgetfulness,
they were scattered, terribly[b] alarmed,
and appalled by specters.
4For not even the inner chamber that held them protected them from fear,
but terrifying sounds rang out around them,
and dismal phantoms with gloomy faces appeared.
5And no power of fire was able to give light,
nor did the brilliant flames of the stars
avail to illumine that hateful night.
6Nothing was shining through to them
except a dreadful, self-kindled fire,
and in terror they deemed the things which they saw
to be worse than that unseen appearance.
7The delusions of their magic art lay humbled,
and their boasted wisdom was scornfully rebuked.
8For those who promised to drive off the fears and disorders of a sick soul
were sick themselves with ridiculous fear.
9For even if nothing disturbing frightened them,
yet, scared by the passing of beasts and the hissing of serpents,
10they perished in trembling fear,
refusing to look even at the air, though it nowhere could be avoided.
11For wickedness is a cowardly thing, condemned by its own testimony;[c]
distressed by conscience, it has always exaggerated[d] the difficulties.
12For fear is nothing but surrender of the helps that come

[a]Or *who made supplication*
[b]Or, with other authorities, *unobserved, they were darkened behind a dark curtain of forgetfulness, terribly*
[c]The Greek text of this line is uncertain and probably corrupt
[d]Other ancient authorities read *anticipated*

from reason;
13and the inner expectation of
help, being weak,
prefers ignorance of what causes the torment.
14But throughout the night, which
was really powerless,
and which beset them from the
recesses of powerless
Hades,
they all slept the same sleep,
15and now were driven by monstrous specters,
and now were paralyzed by
their souls' surrender,
for sudden and unexpected fear
overwhelmed them.
16And whoever was there fell
down,
and thus was kept shut up in a
prison not made of iron;
17for whether he was a farmer or a
shepherd
or a workman who toiled in the
wilderness,
he was seized, and endured the
inescapable fate;
for with one chain of darkness
they all were bound.
18Whether there came a whistling
wind,
or a melodious sound of birds
in wide-spreading
branches,
or the rhythm of violently rushing water,
19or the harsh crash of rocks
hurled down,
or the unseen running of leaping animals,
or the *sound of the most savage*
roaring beasts,
or an echo thrown back
from a hollow of the
mountains,
it paralyzed them with terror.
20For the whole world was illumined with brilliant light,
and was engaged in unhindered
work,
21while over those men alone
heavy night was spread,
an image of the darkness that
was destined to receive
them;
but still heavier than darkness
were they to themselves.

LIGHT SHINES ON THE ISRAELITES

18 But for thy holy ones there was
very great light.
Their enemies[e] heard their
voices but did not see
their forms,
and counted them happy for
not having suffered,
2and were thankful that thy holy
ones,[f] though previously
wronged, were doing them
no injury;
and they begged their pardon
for having been at variance with them.[g]
3Therefore thou didst provide a
flaming pillar of fire
as a guide for thy people's[h]
unknown journey,
and a harmless sun for their
glorious wandering.
4For their enemies[i] deserved to
be deprived of light and
imprisoned in darkness,
those who had kept thy sons
imprisoned,
through whom the imperishable light of the law was
to be given to the world.

THE DEATH OF THE EGYPTIAN FIRSTBORN

5When they had resolved to kill
the babes of thy holy ones,
and one child had been exposed and rescued,
thou didst in punishment take
away a multitude of
their children;

[e] Gk *they*
[f] Gk *they*
[g] The meaning of the Greek of this line is uncertain
[h] Gk *their*
[i] Gk *those men*

and thou didst destroy them
all together by a mighty
flood.
6That night was made known beforehand to our fathers,
so that they might rejoice in
sure knowledge of the
oaths in which they
trusted.
7The deliverance of the righteous
and the destruction of
their enemies
were expected by thy people.
8For by the same means by which
thou didst punish our
enemies
thou didst call us to thyself and
glorify us.
9For in secret the holy children of
good men offered sacrifices,
and with one accord agreed to
the divine law,
that the saints would share
alike the same things,
both blessings and dangers;
and already they were singing
the praises of the
fathers.[a]
10But the discordant cry of their
enemies echoed back,
and their piteous lament for
their children was
spread abroad.
11The slave was punished with the
same penalty as the master,
and the common man suffered
the same loss as the
king;
12and they all together, by the one
form of death,
had corpses too many to count.
For the living were not sufficient even to bury them,
since in one instant their most
valued children had
been destroyed.
13For though they had disbelieved
everything because of their
magic arts,
yet, when their first-born
were destroyed, they
acknowledged thy people to be God's son.
14For while gentle silence enveloped all things,
and night in its swift course
was now half gone,
15thy all-powerful word leaped
from heaven, from the
royal throne,
into the midst of the land that
was doomed,
a stern warrior 16carrying the
sharp sword of thy
authentic command,
and stood and filled all things
with death,
and touched heaven while
standing on the earth.
17Then at once apparitions in
dreadful dreams greatly
troubled them,
and unexpected fears assailed
them;
18and one here and another there,
hurled down half dead,
made known why they were
dying;
19for the dreams which disturbed
them forewarned them of
this,
so that they might not perish
without knowing why
they suffered.

THREAT OF ANNIHILATION IN THE DESERT

20The experience of death touched
also the righteous,
and a plague came upon the
multitude in the desert,
but the wrath did not long
continue.
21For a blameless man was quick
to act as their champion;
he brought forward the shield
of his ministry,
prayer and propitiation by
incense;
he withstood the anger and put
an end to the disaster,
showing that he was thy
servant.

[a] Other authorities read *dangers, the fathers already leading the songs of praise*

22He conquered the wrath[b] not by strength of body,
and not by force of arms,
but by his word he subdued the punisher,
appealing to the oaths and covenants given to our fathers.
23For when the dead had already fallen on one another in heaps,
he intervened and held back the wrath,
and cut off its way to the living.
24For upon his long robe the whole world was depicted,
and the glories of the fathers were engraved on the four rows of stones,
and thy majesty on the diadem upon his head.
25To these the destroyer yielded, these he[c] feared;
for merely to test the wrath was enough.

THE RED SEA

19 But the ungodly were assailed to the end by pitiless anger,
for God[d] knew in advance even their future actions,
2that, though they themselves had permitted[e] thy people to depart
and hastily sent them forth,
they would change their minds and pursue them.
3For while they were still busy at mourning,
and were lamenting at the graves of their dead,
they reached another foolish decision,
and pursued as fugitives those whom they had begged and compelled to depart.
4For the fate they deserved drew them on to this end,
and made them forget what had happened,
in order that they might fill up the punishment which their torments still lacked,
5and that thy people might experience[f] an incredible journey,
but they themselves might meet a strange death.

GOD GUIDES AND PROTECTS HIS PEOPLE

6For the whole creation in its nature was fashioned anew,
complying with thy commands,
that thy children[g] might be kept unharmed.
7The cloud was seen overshadowing the camp,
and dry land emerging where water had stood before,
an unhindered way out of the Red Sea,
and a grassy plain out of the raging waves,
8where those protected by thy hand passed through as one nation,
after gazing on marvelous wonders.
9For they ranged like horses,
and leaped like lambs,
praising thee, O Lord, who didst deliver them.
10For they still recalled the events of their sojourn,
how instead of producing animals the earth brought forth gnats,
and instead of fish the river spewed out vast numbers of frogs.
11Afterward they saw also a new kind[h] of birds,

[b] Cn: Gk *multitude*
[c] Other authorities read *they*
[d] Gk *he*
[e] Other authorities read *had changed their minds to permit*
[f] Other authorities read *accomplish*
[g] Or *servants*
[h] Or *production*

when desire led them to ask for luxurious food;
12for, to give them relief, quails came up from the sea.

THE PUNISHMENT OF THE EGYPTIANS

13The punishments did not come upon the sinners
without prior signs in the violence of thunder,
for they justly suffered because of their wicked acts;
for they practiced a more bitter hatred of strangers.
14Others had refused to receive strangers when they came to them,
but these made slaves of guests who were their benefactors.
15And not only so, but punishment of some sort will come upon the former
for their hostile reception of the aliens;
16but the latter, after receiving them with festal celebrations,
afflicted with terrible sufferings
those who had already shared the same rights.
17They were stricken also with loss of sight—
just as were those at the door of the righteous man—
when, surrounded by yawning darkness,
each tried to find the way through his own door.

A NEW HARMONY IN NATURE

18For the elements changed[a] places with one another,
as on a harp the notes vary the nature of the rhythm,
while each note remains the same.[b]
This may be clearly inferred from the sight of what took place.
19For land animals were transformed into water creatures,
and creatures that swim moved over to the land.
20Fire even in water retained its normal power,
and water forgot its fire-quenching nature.
21Flames, on the contrary, failed to consume
the flesh of perishable creatures that walked among them,
nor did they melt[c] the crystalline, easily melted kind of heavenly food.

CONCLUSION

22For in everything, O Lord, thou hast exalted and glorified thy people;
and thou hast not neglected to help them at all times and in all places.

[a] Gk *changing*
[b] The meaning of this verse is uncertain
[c] Cn: Gk *nor could be melted*

ECCLESIASTICUS,

OR THE WISDOM OF JESUS THE SON OF

SIRACH

Whereas many great teachings have been given to us through the law and the prophets and the others that followed them, on account of which we should praise Israel for instruction and wisdom; and since it is necessary not only that the readers themselves should acquire understanding but also that those who love learning should be able to help the outsiders by both speaking and writing, my grandfather Jesus, after devoting himself especially to the reading of the law and the prophets and the other books of our fathers, and after acquiring considerable proficiency in them, was himself also led to write something pertaining to instruction and wisdom, in order that, by becoming conversant with this also, those who love learning should make even greater progress in living according to the law. You are urged therefore to read with good will and attention, and to be indulgent[a] in cases where, despite out diligent labor in translating, we may seem to have rendered some phrases imperfectly. For what was originally expressed in Hebrew does not have exactly the same sense when translated into another language. Not only this work, but even the law itself, the prophecies, and the rest of the books differ not a little as originally expressed. When I came to Egypt in the thirty-eighth year of the reign of Eu-er´getes and stayed for some time, I found opportunity for no little instruction.[b] It seemed highly necessary that I should myself devote some pains and labor to the translation of the following book, using in that period of time great watchfulness and skill in order to complete and publish the book for those living abroad who wished to gain learning, being prepared in character to live according to the law.

IN PRAISE OF WISDOM

1 All wisdom comes from the Lord
and is with him for ever.
2 The sand of the sea, the drops of rain,
and the days of eternity—
who can count them?
3 The height of heaven, the breadth of the earth,
the abyss, and wisdom—who can search them out?
4 Wisdom was created before all things,
and prudent understanding from eternity.[c]
6 The root of wisdom—to whom has it been revealed?
Her clever devices—who knows them?[d]
8 There is One who is wise, greatly to be feared,
sitting upon his throne.
9 The Lord himself created wisdom;[e]
he saw her and apportioned her,
he poured her out upon all his works.
10 She dwells with all flesh according to his gift,
and he supplied her to those who love him.

[a] Or *Please read therefore ith good will and attention, and be indulgent*
[b] Other authorities read *copy affording no little instruction*
[c] Other authorities add verse 5, *The source of wisdom is God's word in the highest heaven, and her ways are the eternal commandments.*
[d] Other authorities add verse 7, *The knowledge of wisdom—to whom was it manifested? And her abundant experience—who has understood it?*
[e] Gk *her*

FEAR OF THE LORD IS TRUE WISDOM

11 The fear of the Lord is glory and exultation,
and gladness and a crown of rejoicing.
12 The fear of the Lord delights the heart,
and gives gladness and joy and long life.
13 With him who fears the Lord it will go well at the end;
on the day of his death he will be blessed.
14 To fear the Lord is the beginning of wisdom;
she is created with the faithful in the womb.
15 She made[a] among men an eternal foundation,
and among their descendants she will be trusted.
16 To fear the Lord is wisdom's full measure;
she satisfies[b] men with her fruits;
17 she fills their whole house with desirable goods,
and their storehouses with her produce.
18 The fear of the Lord is the crown of wisdom,
making peace and perfect health to flourish.
19 He saw her and apportioned her;
he rained down knowledge and discerning comprehension,
and he exalted the glory of those who held her fast.
20 To fear the Lord is the root of wisdom,
and her branches are long life.[c]
22 *Unrighteous anger cannot be justified,*
for a man's anger tips the scale to his ruin.
23 A patient man will endure until the right moment,
and then joy will burst forth for him.
24 He will hide his words until the right moment,
and the lips of many will tell of his good sense.
25 In the treasuries of wisdom are wise sayings,
but godliness is an abomination to a sinner.
26 If you desire wisdom, keep the commandments,
and the Lord will supply it for you.
27 For the fear of the Lord is wisdom and instruction,
and he delights in fidelity and meekness.
28 Do not disobey the fear of the Lord;
do not approach him with a divided mind.
29 Be not a hypocrite in men's sight,[d]
and keep watch over your lips.
30 Do not exalt yourself lest you fall,
and thus bring dishonor upon yourself.
The Lord will reveal your secrets
and cast you down in the midst of the congregation,
because you did not come in the fear of the Lord,
and your heart was full of deceit.

DUTIES TOWARD GOD

2 My son, if you come forward to serve the Lord,
prepare yourself for

[a] Gk *made as nest*
[b] Gk *intoxicates*
[c] Other authorities add as verse 21, *The fear of the Lord drives away sin and where it abides, it will turn away all anger.*
[d] Syr: Gk *in the mouths of men*

temptation.[e]
2Set your heart right and be steadfast,
and do not be hasty in time of calamity.
3Cleave to him and do not depart,
that you may be honored at the end of your life.
4Accept whatever is brought upon you,
and in changes that humble you be patient.
5For gold is tested in the fire,
and acceptable men in the furnace of humiliation.
6Trust in him, and he will help you;
make your ways straight, and hope in him.
7You who fear the Lord, wait for his mercy;
and turn not aside, lest you fall.
8You who fear the Lord, trust in him,
and your reward will not fail;
9you who fear the Lord, hope for good things,
for everlasting joy and mercy.
10Consider the ancient generations and see:
who ever trusted in the Lord and was put to shame?
Or who ever persevered in the fear of the Lord[f] and was forsaken?
Or who ever called upon him and was overlooked?
11For the Lord is compassionate and merciful;
he forgives sins and saves in time of affliction.
12Woe to timid hearts and to slack hands,
and to the sinner who walks along two ways!
13Woe to the faint heart, for it has no trust!
Therefore it will not be sheltered.
14Woe to you who have lost your endurance!
What will you do when the Lord punishes you?
15Those who fear the Lord will not disobey his words,
and those who love him will keep his ways.
16Those who fear the Lord will seek his approval,
and those who love him will be filled with the law.
17Those who fear the Lord will prepare their hearts,
and will humble themselves before him.
18Let us fall[g] into the hands of the Lord,
but not into the hands of men;
for as his majesty is,
so also is his mercy.

DUTIES TOWARD PARENTS

3 Listen to me your father, O children;
and act accordingly, that you may be kept in safety.
2For the Lord honored the father above the children,
and he confirmed the right of the mother over her sons.
3Whoever honors his father atones for sins,
4and whoever glorifies his mother is like one who lays up treasure.
5Whoever honors his father will be gladdened by his own children,
and when he prays he will be heard.

[e]Or *trials*
[f]Gk *of him*
[g]Gk *We shall fall*

6Whoever glorifies his father will
have long life,
and whoever obeys the
Lord will refresh his
mother;
7he will serve his parents as
his masters.[a]
8Honor your father by word and
deed,
that a blessing from him may
come upon you.
9For a father's blessing strength-
ens the houses of the
children,
but a mother's curse uproots
their foundations.
10Do not glorify yourself by dis-
honoring your father,
for your father's dishonor is
no glory to you.
11For a man's glory comes from
honoring his father,
and it is a disgrace for chil-
dren not to respect
their mother.
12O son, help your father in his
old age,
and do not grieve him as
long as he lives;
13even if he is lacking in un-
derstanding, show
forbearance;
in all your strength do not
despise him.
14For kindness to a father will not
be forgotten,
and against your sins it will
be credited to you;
15in the day of your affliction it
will be remembered in
your favor;
as frost in fair weather, your
sins will melt away.
16Whoever forsakes his father is
like a blasphemer,
and whoever angers his
mother is cursed by
the Lord.

HUMILITY

17My son, perform your tasks in
meekness;
then you will be loved by
those whom God
accepts.
18The greater you are, the more
you must humble yourself;
so you will find favor in the
sight of the Lord.[b]
20For great is the might of the
Lord;
he is glorified by the
humble.
21Seek not what is too difficult
for you,
nor investigate what is be-
yond your power.
22Reflect upon what has been
assigned to you,
for you do not need what is
hidden.
23Do not meddle in what is beyond
your tasks,
for matters too great for hu-
man understanding
have been shown you.
24For their hasty judgment has led
many astray,
and wrong opinion has
caused their thoughts
to slip.[c]
26A stubborn mind will be afflict-
ed at the end,
and whoever loves danger
will perish by it.
27A stubborn mind will be bur-
dened by troubles,
and the sinner will heap sin
upon sin.
28The affliction of the proud has
no healing,
for a plant of wickedness has
taken root in him.
29The mind of the intelligent man
will ponder a parable,
and an attentive ear is the
wise man's desire.

[a]In other authorities this line is preceded by *Whoever fears the Lord will honor his father,*
[b]Other authorities add as verse 19, *Many are lofty and renowned, but to the meek he reveals his secrets.*
[c]Other authorities add as verse 25, *If you have no eyes you will be without light; if you lack knowledge do not profess to have it.*

ALMS FOR THE POOR

30Water extinguishes a blazing
fire:
so almsgiving atones for sin.
31Whoever requites favors gives
thought to the future;
at the moment of his falling
he will find support.

DUTIES TOWARD THE POOR AND THE OPPRESSED

4 My son, deprive not the poor of
his living,
and do not keep needy eyes
waiting.
2Do not grieve the one who is
hungry,
nor anger a man in want.
3Do not add to the troubles of an
angry mind,
nor delay your gift to a
beggar.
4Do not reject an afflicted
suppliant,
nor turn your face away from
the poor.
5Do not avert your eye from the
needy,
nor give a man occasion to
curse you;
6for if in bitterness of soul he calls
down a curse upon you,
his Creator will hear his
prayer.
7Make yourself beloved in the
congregation;
bow your head low to a great
man.
8Incline your ear to the poor,
and answer him peaceably
and gently.
9Deliver him who is wonged from
the hand of thewrongdoer;
and do not be faithearted
in judging case.
10Be like a father to orpans,
and instead of a hsband to
their mothr;
you will then be like son of
the Most High,
and he will love you more
than does your
mother.

THE REWARDS OF WISDOM

11Wisdom exalts her sons
and gives help to those who
seek her.
12Whoever loves her loves life,
and those who seek her early
will be filled with joy.
13Whoever holds her fast will
obtain glory,
and the Lord will bless the
place she[d] enters.
14Those who serve her will minis-
ter to the Holy One;[e]
the Lord loves those who
love her.
15He who obeys her will judge the
nations,
and whoever gives heed to
her will dwell secure.
16If he has faith in her he will
obtain her;
and his descendants will
remain in possession
of her.
17For at first she will walk with
him on tortuous paths,
she will bring fear and cow-
ardice upon him,
and will torment him by her
discipline
until she trusts him,
and she will test him with her
ordinances.
18Then she will come straight back
to him and gladden him,
and will reveal her secrets
to him.
19If he goes astray she will forsake
him,
and hand him over to his
ruin.
20Observe the right time, and
beware of evil;[f]
and do not bring shame on
yourself.

[d] Or *he*
[e] Or *at the holy place*
[f] Or *an evil man*

21For there is a shame which
brings sin,
and there is a shame which
is glory and favor.
22Do not show partiality, to your
own harm,
or deference, to your
downfall.
23Do not refrain from speaking at
the crucial time,[a]
and do not hide your
wisdom.[b]
24For wisdom is known through
speech,
and education through the
words of the tongue.
25Never speak against the truth,
but be mindful of your
ignorance.
26Do not be ashamed to confess
your sins,
and do not try to stop the
current of a river.
27Do not subject yourself to a
foolish fellow,
nor show partiality to a
ruler.
28Strive even to death for the truth
and the Lord God will fight
for you.
29Do not be reckless in your
speech,
or sluggish and remiss in
your deeds.
30Do not be like a lion in your
home,
nor be a faultfinder with
your servants.
31Let not your hand be extended
to receive,
but withdrawn when it is
time to repay.

PRECEPTS FOR EVERYDAY LIVING

5 Do not set your heart on your
wealth,
nor say, "I have enough."
2Do not follow your inclination
and strength,
walking according to the
desires of your heart.
3Do not say, "Who will have pow-
er over me?"
for the Lord will surely
punish you.
4Do not say, "I sinned, and what
happened to me?"
for the Lord is slow to anger.
5Do not be so confident of
atonement
that you add sin to sin.
6Do not say, "His mercy is great,
he will forgive[c] the multi-
tude of my sins,"
for both mercy and wrath are
with him,
and his anger rests on
sinners.
7Do not delay to turn to the Lord,
nor postpone it from day to
day;
for suddenly the wrath of the
Lord will go forth,
and at the time of punish-
ment you will perish.
8Do not depend on dishonest
wealth,
for it will not benefit you in
the day of calamity.
9Do not winnow with every wind,
nor follow every path:
the double-tongued sinner
does that.
10Be steadfast in your
understanding,
and let your speech be
consistent.
11Be quick to hear,
and be deliberate in
answering.
12If you have understanding, an-
swer your neighbor;
but if not, put your hand on
your mouth.
13Glory and dishonor come from
speaking,
and a man's tongue is his
downfall.
14Do not be called a slanderer,
and do not lie in ambush

[a]Cn: Gk *at a time of salvation*
[b]So some Gk Mss and Heb Syr Vg: other Gk Mss omit *and do not hide your wisdom*
[c]Heb: Gk *he* (or *it*) *will atone for*

with your tongue;
for shame comes to the thief,
and severe condemnation to the double-tongued.
15In great and small matters do not act amiss,
and do not become an enemy instead of a friend;
6 for a bad name incurs shame and reproach:
so fares the double-tongued sinner.
2Do not exalt yourself through our soul's counsel,
lest your soul be torn in pieces like a bull.[d]
3You will devour your leaves and destroy your fruit,
and will be left like a withered tree.
4An evil soul will destroy him who has it,
and make him the laughingstock of his enemies.

FRIENDSHIP, FALSE AND TRUE

5A pleasant voice multiplies friends,
and a gracious tongue multiplies courtesies.
6Let those that are at peace with you be many,
but let your advisers be one in a thousand.
7When you gain a friend, gain him through testing,
and do not trust him hastily.
8For there is a friend who is such at his own convenience,
but will not stand by you in your day of trouble.
9And there is a friend who changes into an enemy,
and will disclose a quarrel to your disgrace.
10And there is a friend who is a table companion,
but will not stand by you in your day of trouble.
11In your prosperity he will make himself your equal,
and be bold with your servants;
12but if you are brought low he will turn against you,
and will hide himself from your presence.
13Keep yourself far from your enemies,
and be on guard toward your friends.
14A faithful friend is a sturdy shelter:
he that has found one has found a treasure.
15There is nothing so precious as a faithful friend,
and no scales can measure his excellence.
16A faithful friend is an elixir of life;
and those who fear the Lord will find him.
17Whoever fears the Lord directs his friendship aright,
for as he is, so is his neighbor also.

BLESSINGS OF WISDOM

18My son, from your youth up choose instruction,
and until you are old you will keep finding wisdom.
19Come to her like one who plows and sows,
and wait for her good harvest.
For in her service you will toil a little while,
and soon you will eat of her produce.
20She seems very harsh to the uninstructed;
a weakling will not remain with her.
21She will weigh him down like a heavy testing stone,
and he will not be slow to cast her off.
22For wisdom is like her name,
and is not manifest to many.

[d]The meaning of the Greek of this verse is obscure

23Listen, my son, and accept my
judgment;
do not reject my counsel.
24Put your feet into her fetters,
and your neck into her
collar.
25Put your shoulder under her and
carry her,
and do not fret under her
bonds.
26Come to her with all your soul,
and keep her ways with all
your might.
27Search out and seek, and she
will become known to you;
and when you get hold of
her, do not let her go.
28For at last you will find the rest
she gives,
and she will be changed into
joy for you.
29Then her fetters will become for
you a strong protection,
and her collar a glorious
robe.
30Her yoke[a] is a golden ornament,
and her bonds are a cord of
blue.
31You will wear her like a glorious
robe,
and put her on like a crown
of gladness.
32If you are willing, my son, you
will be taught,
and if you apply yourself you
will become clever.
33If you love to listen you will gain
knowledge,
and if you incline your ear
you will become wise.
34Stand in the assembly of the
elders.
Who is wise? Cleave to him.
35Be ready to listen to every[b]
narrative,
and do not let wise proverbs
escape you.
36*If you see an intelligent man,*
visit him early;
let your foot wear out his
doorstep.
37Reflect on the statutes of the
Lord,
and meditate at all times on
his commandments.
It is he who will give insight to[c]
your mind,
and your desire for wisdom
will be granted.

MISCELLANEOUS ADVICE

7 Do no evil, and evil will never
befall you.
2Stay away from wrong, and
it will turn away from
you.
3My son, do not sow the furrows
of injustice,
and you will not reap a sev-
enfold crop.
4Do not seek from the Lord the
highest office,
nor the seat of honor from
the king.
5Do not assert your righteousness
before the Lord,
nor display your wisdom
before the king.
6Do not seek to become a judge,
lest you be unable to remove
iniquity,
lest you be partial to a power-
ful man,
and thus put a blot on your
integrity.
7Do not offend against the public,
and do not disgrace yourself
among the people.
8Do not commit a sin twice;
even for one you will not go
unpunished.
9Do not say, "He will consider the
multitude of my gifts,
and when I make an offering
to the Most High God
he will accept it."
10Do not be fainthearted in your
prayer,
nor neglect to give alms.
11Do not ridicule a man who is

[a] Heb: Gk *Upon her*
[b] Heb: Gk adds *divine*
[c] Heb: Gk *will confirm*

bitter in soul,
for there is One who abases
and exalts.
12Do not devise[d] a lie against your
brother,
nor do the like to a friend.
13Refuse to utter any lie,
for the habit of lying serves
no good.
14Do not prattle in the assembly of
the elders,
nor repeat yourself in your
prayer.
15Do not hate toilsome labor,
or farm work, which were
created by the Most
High.
16Do not count yourself among the
crowd of sinners;
remember that wrath does
not delay.
17Humble yourself greatly,
for the punishment of the
ungodly is fire and
worms.[e]

RELATIONS WITH OTHERS

18Do not exchange a friend for
money,
or a real brother for the gold
of Ophir.
19Do not deprive yourself of a wise
and good wife,
for her charm is worth more
than gold.
20Do not abuse a servant who per-
forms his work faithfully,
or a hired laborer who de-
votes himself to you.
21Let your soul love[f] an intelligent
servant;
do not withhold from him
his freedom.
22Do you have cattle? Look after
them;
if they are profitable to you,
keep them.
23Do you have children? Discipline
them,
and make them obedient[g]
from their youth.
24Do you have daughters? Be con-
cerned for their chastity,[h]
and do not show yourself too
indulgent with them.
25Give a daughter in marriage; you
will have finished a great
task.
But give her to a man of
understanding.
26If you have a wife who pleases
you,[i] do not cast her out;
but do not trust yourself to
one whom you detest.
27With all your heart honor your
father,
and do not forget the birth
pangs of your mother.
28Remember that through your
parents[j] you were born;
and what can you give back
to them that equals
their gift to you?
29With all your soul fear the Lord,
and honor his priests.
30With all your might love your
Maker,
and do not forsake his
ministers.
31Fear the Lord and honor the
priest,
and give him his portion, as
is commanded you:
the first fruits, the guilt
offering, the gift of the
shoulders,
the sacrifice of sanctifica-
tion, and the first
fruits of the holy
things.
32Stretch forth your hand to the
poor,
so that your blessing may be
complete.

[d]Heb: Gk *plow*
[e]The Hebrew text reads *for the expectation of man is worms*
[f]The Hebrew text reads *Love like yourself*
[g]Gk *bend their necks*
[h]Gk *body*
[i]Heb Syr omit *who pleases you*
[j]Gk *them*

33Give graciously to all the living,
and withhold not kindness from the dead.
34Do not fail those who weep,
but mourn with those who mourn.
35Do not shrink from visiting a sick man,
because for such deeds you will be loved.
36In all you do, remember the end of your life,
and then you will never sin.

PRUDENCE AND COMMON SENSE

8 Do not contend with a powerful man,
lest you fall into his hands.
2Do not quarrel with a rich man,
lest his resources outweigh yours;
for gold has ruined many,
and has perverted the minds of kings.
3Do not argue with a chatterer,
nor heap wood on his fire.
4Do not jest with an ill-bred person,
lest your ancestors be disgraced.
5Do not reproach a man who is turning away from sin;
remember that we all deserve punishment.
6Do not disdain a man when he is old,
for some of us are growing old.
7Do not rejoice over any one's death;
remember that we all must die.
8Do not slight the discourse of the sages,
but busy yourself with their *maxims;*
because from them you will gain instruction
and learn how to serve great men.
9Do not disregard the discourse of the aged,
for they themselves learned from their fathers;
because from them you will gain understanding
and learn how to give an answer in time of need.
10Do not kindle the coals of a sinner,
lest you be burned in his flaming fire.
11Do not get up and leave an insolent fellow,
lest he lie in ambush against your words.
12Do not lend to a man who is stronger than you;
but if you do lend anything, be as one who has lost it.
13Do not give surety beyond your means,
but if you give surety, be concerned as one who must pay.
14Do not go to law against a judge,
for the decision will favor him because of his standing.
15Do not travel on the road with a foolhardy fellow,
lest he be burdensome to you;
for he will act as he pleases,
and through his folly you will perish with him.
16Do not fight with a wrathful man,
and do not cross the wilderness with him;
because blood is as nothing in his sight,
and where no help is at hand, he will strike you down.
17Do not consult with a fool,
for he will not be able to keep a secret.
18In the presence of a stranger do nothing that is to be kept

secret,
for you do not know what he will divulge.[a]
19Do not reveal your thoughts to every one,
lest you drive away your good luck.[b]

ADVICE CONCERNING WOMEN

9 Do not be jealous of the wife of your bosom,
and do not teach her an evil lesson to your own hurt.
2Do not give yourself to a woman
so that she gains mastery over your strength.
3Do not go to meet a loose woman,
lest you fall into her snares.
4Do not associate with a woman singer,
lest you be caught in her intrigues.
5Do not look intently at a virgin,
lest you stumble and incur penalties for her.
6Do not give yourself to harlots
lest you lose your inheritance.
7Do not look around in the streets of a city,
nor wander about in its deserted sections.
8Turn away your eyes from a shapely woman,
and do not look intently at beauty belonging to another;
many have been misled by a woman's beauty,
and by it passion is kindled like a fire.
9Never dine with another man's wife,
nor revel with her at wine;
lest your heart turn aside to her,
and in blood[c] you be plunged into destruction.

CHOICE OF FRIENDS

10Forsake not an old friend,
for a new one does not compare with him.
A new friend is like new wine;
when it has aged you will drink it with pleasure.
11Do not envy the honors of a sinner,
for you do not know what his end will be.
12Do not delight in what pleases the ungodly;
remember that they will not be held guiltless as long as they live.
13Keep far from a man who has the power to kill,
and you will not be worried by the fear of death.
But if you approach him, make no misstep,
lest he rob you of your life.
Know that you are walking in the midst of snares,
and that you are going about on the city battlements.
14As much as you can, aim to know your neighbors,
and consult with the wise.
15Let your conversation be with men of understanding,
and let all your discussion be about the law of the Most High.
16Let righteous men be your dinner companions,
and let your glorying be in the fear of the Lord.

CONCERNING RULERS

17A work will be praised for the skill of the craftsmen;
so a people's leader is proved wise by his words.

[a]Or *it will bring forth*
[b]Heb: Gk *let him not return a favor to you*
[c]Heb: Gk *by your spirit*

18 A babbler is feared in his city,
and the man who is reckless in speech will be hated.

10 A wise magistrate will educate his people,
and the rule of an understanding man will be well ordered.
2 Like the magistrate of the people, so are his officials;
and like the ruler of the city, so are all its inhabitants.
3 An undisciplined king will ruin his people,
but a city will grow through the understanding of its rulers.
4 The government of the earth is in the hands of the Lord,
and over it he will raise up the right man for the time.
5 The success of a man is in the hands of the Lord,
and he confers his honor upon the person of the scribe.[a]

THE SIN OF PRIDE

6 Do not be angry with your neighbor for any injury,
and do not attempt anything by acts of insolence.
7 Arrogance is hateful before the Lord and before men,
and injustice is outrageous to both.
8 Sovereignty passes from nation to nation
on account of injustice and insolence and wealth.
9 How can he who is dust and ashes be proud?
for even in life his bowels decay.[b]
10 A long illness baffles the physician;[c]
the king of today will die tomorrow.
11 For when a man is dead,
he will inherit creeping things, and wild beasts, and worms.
12 The beginning of man's pride is to depart from the Lord;
his heart has forsaken his Maker.
13 For the beginning of pride is sin,
and the man who clings to it pours out abominations.
Therefore the Lord brought upon them extraordinary afflictions,
and destroyed them utterly.
14 The Lord has cast down the thrones of rulers,
and has seated the lowly in their place.
15 The Lord has plucked up the roots of the nations,[d]
and has planted the humble in their place.
16 The Lord has overthrown the lands of the nations,
and has destroyed them to the foundations of the earth.
17 He has removed some of them and destroyed them,
and has extinguished the memory of them from the earth.
18 Pride was not created for men,
nor fierce anger for those born of women.

PERSONS DESERVING HONOR

19 What race is worthy of honor? The human race.
What race is worthy of honor? Those who fear the Lord.
What race is unworthy of

[a] Or *the official*
[b] Heb: Gk is obscure
[c] Heb Vg: Gk is uncertain
[d] Some authorities read *proud nations*

honor? The human race.
What race is unworthy
of honor? Those
who transgress the
commandments.
20Among brothers their leader is
worthy of honor,
and those who fear the Lord
are worthy of honor
in his eyes.[e]
22The rich, and the eminent, and
the poor—
their glory is the fear of the
Lord.
23It is not right to despise an intel-
ligent poor man,
nor is it proper to honor a
sinful man.
24The nobleman, and the judge,
and the ruler will be
honored,
but none of them is greater
than the man who
fears the Lord.
25Free men will be at the service
of a wise servant,
and a man of understanding
will not grumble.

CONCERNING HUMILITY

26Do not make a dislay of your
wisdom whe you do your
work,
nor glorify yorself at a
time wen you are in
want.
27Better is a man wh works
and has an andance of
everything,
than one who es about
boastinbut lacks
bread.
28My son, glorify yoelf with
humility,
and ascribe to rself hon-
or accorg to your
worth.
29Who will justify than that
sins against elf?
And who will hr the man
that dishonors his
own life?
30A poor man is honored for his
knowledge,
while a rich man is honored
for his wealth.
31A man honored in poverty, how
much more in wealth!
And a man dishonored in
wealth, how much
more in poverty!

THE DECEPTIVENESS OF APPEARANCES

11 The wisdom of a humble man will
lift up his head,
and will seat him among the
great.
2Do not praise a man for his good
looks,
nor loathe a man because of
his appearance.
3The bee is small among flying
creatures,
but her product is the best of
sweet things.
4Do not boast about wearing fine
clothes,
nor exalt yourself in the
day that you are
honored;
for the works of the Lord are
wonderful,
and his works are concealed
from men.
5Many kings have had to sit on the
ground,
but one who was never
thought of has worn
a crown.
6Many rulers have been greatly
disgraced,
and illustrious men have
been handed over to
others.

DELIBERATION AND CAUTION

7Do not find fault before you
investigate;
first consider, and then
reprove.

[e] Other authorities add as vel, *The fear of the Lord is the beginning of acceptance; obduracy and pride are the beginning of ion.*

8 Do not answer before you have
heard,
nor interrupt a speaker
in the midst of his
words.
9 Do not argue about a matter
which does not concern
you,
nor sit with sinners when
they judge a case.
10 My son, do not busy yourself
with many matters;
if you multiply activities
you will not go
unpunished,
and if you pursue you will not
overtake,
and by fleeing you will not
escape.
11 There is a man who works, and
toils, and presses on,
but is so much the more in
want.
12 There is another who is slow and
needs help,
who lacks strength and
abounds in poverty;
but the eyes of the Lord look
upon him for his good;
he lifts him out of his low
estate
13 and raises up his head,
so that many are amazed at
him.
14 Good things and bad, life and
death,
poverty and wealth, come
from the Lord.[a]
17 The gift of the Lord endures for
those who are godly,
and what he approves will
have lasting success.
18 There is a man who is rich
through his diligence and
self-denial,
and this is the reward allot-
ted to him:
19 when he says, "I have found
rest,
and now I shall enjoy[b] my
goods!"
he does not know how much
time will pass
until he leaves them to oth-
ers and dies.
20 Stand by your covenant[c] and
attend to it,
and grow old in your work.
21 Do not wonder at the works of
a sinner,
but trust in the Lord and
keep at your toil;
for it is easy in the sight of the
Lord
to enrich a poor man quickly
and suddenly.
22 The blessing of the Lord is[d] the
reward of the godly,
and quickly God causes his
blessing to flourish.
23 Do not say, "What do I need,
and what prosperity could be
mine in the future?"
24 Do not say, "I have enough,
and what calamity could
happen to me in the
future?"
25 In the day of prosperity, adversi-
ty i forgotten,
and i the day of adversity,
prosperity is not
remembered.
26 For it isasy in the sight of the
Ld
to ward a man on the day
of death according to
his conduct.
27 The mery of an hour makes
e forget luxury,
a at the close of a man's
life his deeds will be
revealed.
28 Call one happy before his
eath;

[a] Other authorities add as verses 15 and 16, [15] *Wisdom, undnding, and knowledge of the law come from the Lord; affection and the ways of good works come him.* [16] *Error and darkness were created with sinners; evil will grow old with those who take primalice.*
[b] Gk *eat of*
[c] Heb *task*
[d] Gk *is in*

a man will be known
through his children.

CARE IN CHOOSING FRIENDS

29Do not bring every man into
your home,
for many are the wiles of the
crafty.
30Like a decoy partridge in a cage,
so is the mind of a proud
man,
and like a spy he observes
your weakness;[e]
31for he lies in wait, turning good
into evil,
and to worthy actions he
will attach blame.
32From a spark of fire come many
burning coals,
and a sinner lies in wait to
shed blood.
33Beware of a scoundrel, for he
devises evil,
lest he give you a lasting
blemish.
34Receive a stranger into your
home and he will upset
you with commotion,
and will estrange you from
your family.

12If you do a kindness, know to
whom you do it,
and you will be thanked for
your good deeds.
2Do good to a godly man, and you
will be repaid—
if not by him, certainly by
the Most High.
3No good will come to the man
who persists in evil
or to him who does not give
alms.
4Give to the godly man, but do not
help the sinner.
5Do good to the humble, but
do not give to the
ungodly;
hold back his bread, and do not
give it to him,
lest by means of it he subdue
you;
for you will receive twice as
much evil
for all the good which you
do to him.
6For the Most High also hates
sinners
and will inflict punishment
on the ungodly.[f]
7Give to the good man, but do not
help the sinner.
8A friend will not be known[g] in
prosperity,
nor will an enemy be hidden
in adversity.
9A man's enemies are grieved
when he prospers,
and in his adversity even his
friend will separate
from him.
10Never trust your enemy,
for like the rusting of
copper, so is his
wickedness.
11Even if he humbles himself and
goes about cringing,
watch yourself, and be on
your guard against
him;
and you will be to him like
one who has polished
a mirror,
and you will know that it
was not hopelessly
tarnished.
12Do not put him next to you,
lest he overthrow you and
take your place;
do not have him sit at your
right,
lest he try to take your seat
of honor,
and at last you will realize the
truth of my words,
and be stung by what I have
said.
13Who will pity a snake charmer
bitten by a serpent,
or any who go near wild
beasts?

[e] Heb: Gk *downfall*
[f] Other authorities add *and he is keeping them for the mighty day of their punishment*
[g] Other authorities read *punished*

14 So no one will pity a man who
associates with a sinner
and becomes involved in his
sins.
15 He will stay with you for a
time,
but if you falter, he will not
stand by you.
16 An enemy will speak sweetly
with his lips,
but in his mind he will plan
to throw you into
a pit;
an enemy will weep with his
eyes,
but if he finds an opportuni-
ty his thirst for blood
will be insatiable.
17 If calamity befalls you, you will
find him there ahead of
you;
and while pretending to help
you, he will trip you
by the heel;
18 he will shake his head, and clap
his hands,
and whisper much,
and change his
expression.

CAUTION REGARDING ASSOCIATES

13 Whoever touches pitch will be
defiled,
and whoever associates with
a proud man will
become like him.
2 Do not lift a weight beyond your
strength,
nor associate with a man
mightier and richer
than you.
How can the clay pot associate
with the iron kettle?
The pot will strike against
it, and will itself be
broken.
3 *A rich man does wrong*, and he
even adds reproaches;
a poor man suffers wrong,
and he must add
apologies.
4 A rich man[a] will exploit you if
you can be of use to him,
but if you are in need he will
forsake you.
5 If you own something, he will
live with you;
he will drain your resources
and he will not care.
6 When he needs you he will de-
ceive you,
he will smile at you and give
you hope.
He will speak to you kindly
and say, "What do you
need?"
7 He will shame you with his
foods,
until he has drained you two
or three times;
and finally he will deride
you.
Should he see you afterwards,
he will forsake you,
and shake his head at you.
8 Take care not to be led astray,
and not to be humiliated in
your feasting.[b]
9 When a powerful man invites
you, be reserved;
and he will invite you the
more often.
10 Do not push forward, lest you be
repulsed;
and do not remain at a
distance, lest you be
forgotten.
11 Do not try to treat him as an
equal,
nor trust his abundance of
words;
for he will test you through
much talk,
and while he smiles he will
be examining you.
12 Cruel is he who does not keep
words to himself;
he will not hesitate
to injure or to
imprison.

[a] Gk *He*
[b] Other authorities read *folly*

13Keep words to yourself and be
very watchful,
for you are walking about
with your own
downfall.[c]
15Every creature loves its like,
and every person his
neighbor;
16all living beings associate by
species,
and a man clings to one like
himself.
17What fellowship has a wolf with
a lamb?
No more has a sinner with a
godly man.
18What peace is there between a
hyena and a dog?
And what peace between a
rich man and a poor
man?
19Wild asses in the wilderness are
the prey of lions;
likewise the poor are pas-
tures for the rich.
20Humility is an abomination to a
proud man;
likewise a poor man is an
abomination to a rich
one.
21When a rich man totters, he is
steadied by frieds,
but when a humle man
falls, he ieven
pushed away by
friends.
22If a rich man slips, hhelpers
are many;
he speaks unseey words,
and they tify him.
If a humble man sl, they
even reproahim;
he speaks sensiland re-
ceives ncention.
23When the rich man aks all
are silent,
and they extol te clouds
what he .
When the poor maeaks
they say, "is this
fellow?"
And should he stumble,
they even push him
down.
24Riches are good if they are free
from sin,
and poverty is evil in the
opinion of the
ungodly.
25A man's heart changes his
countenance,
either for good or for evil.[d]
26The mark of a happy heart is a
cheerful face,
but to devise proverbs
requires painful
thinking.

14 Blessed is the man who does not
blunder with his lips
and need not suffer grief
for sin.
2Blessed is he whose heart does
not condemn him,
and who has not given up
his hope.

RESPONSIBLE USE OF WEALTH

3Riches are not seemly for a stin-
gy man;
and of what use is property
to an envious man?
4Whoever accumulates by depriv-
ing himself, accumulates
for others;
and others will live in luxury
on his goods.
5If a man is mean to himself, to
whom will he be generous?
He will not enjoy his own
riches.
6No one is meaner than the man
who is grudging to himself,
and this is the retribution
for his baseness;
7even if he does good, he does it
unintentionally,
and betrays his baseness in
the end.
8Evil is the man with a grudging
eye;

[c] Other authorities add *Whenear these things in your sleep, wake up! 14During all your life love the Lord, and call on him for salvation.*
[d] Other authorities add *and aheart makes a cheerful countenance*

he averts his face and disregards people.
9A greedy man's eye is not satisfied with a portion,
and mean injustice withers the soul.
10A stingy man's eye begrudges bread,
and it is lacking at his table.
11My son, treat yourself well, according to your means,
and present worthy offerings to the Lord.
12Remember that death will not delay,
and the decree[a] of Hades has not been shown to you.
13Do good to a friend before you die,
and reach out and give to him as much as you can.
14Do not deprive yourself of a happy day;
let not your share of desired good pass by you.
15Will you not leave the fruit of your labors to another,
and what you acquired by toil to be divided by lot?
16Give, and take, and beguile yourself,
because in Hades one cannot look for luxury.
17All living beings become old like a garment,
for the decree[b] from of old is, "You must surely die!"
18Like flourishing leaves on a spreading tree
which sheds some and puts forth others,
so are the generations of flesh and blood:
one dies and another is born.
19Every product decays and ceases to exist,
and the man who made it will pass away with it.

THE HAPPINESS OF SEEKING WISDOM

20Blessed is the man who meditates on[c] wisdom
and who reasons intelligently.
21He who reflects in his mind on her ways
will also ponder her secrets.
22Pursue wisdom[d] like a hunter,
and lie in wait on her paths.
23He who peers through her windows
will also listen at her doors;
24he who encamps near her house
will also fasten his tent peg to her walls;
25he will pitch his tent near her,
and will lodge in an excellent lodging place;
26he will place his children under her shelter,
and will camp under her boughs;
27he will be sheltered by her from the heat,
and will dwell in the midst of her glory.

15 The man who fears the Lord will do this,
and he who holds to the law will obtain wisdom.[e]
2She will come to meet him like a mother,
and like the wife of his youth she will welcome him.
3She will feed him with the bread of understanding,
and give him the water of wisdom to drink.

[a] Gk *covenant*
[b] Gk *covenant*
[c] Other authorities read *dies in*
[d] Gk *her*
[e] Gk *her*

4He will lean on her and will not
fall,
and he will rely on her and
will not be put to
shame.
5She will exalt him above his
neighbors,
and will open his mouth
in the midst of the
assembly.
6He will find gladness and a
crown of rejoicing,
and will acquire an everlast-
ing name.
7Foolish men will not obtain her,
and sinful men will not see
her.
8She is far from men of pride,
and liars will never think
of her.
9A hymn of praise is not fitting on
the lips of a sinner,
for it has not been sent from
the Lord.
10For a hymn of praise should be
uttered in wisdom,
and the Lord will prosper it.

FREEDOM OF CHOICE

11Do not say, "Because of the Lord
I left the right way";
for he[f] will not do what he
hates.
12Do not say, "It was he who led
me astray";
for he had no need of a sin-
ful man.
13The Lord hates all abominations,
and they are not loved by
those who fear him.
14*It was he who* created man in
the beginning,
and he left him in the
power of his own
inclination.
15If you will, you can keep the
commandments,
and to act faithfully is a
matter of your own
choice.
16He has placed before you fire
and water:
stretch out your hand for
whichever you wish.
17Before a man[g] are life and
death,
and whichever he chooses
will be given to him.
18For great is the wisdom of the
Lord;
he is mighty in power and
sees everything;
19his eyes are on those who fear
him,
and he knows every deed of
man.
20He has not commanded any one
to be ungodly,
and he has not given any one
permission to sin.

GOD'S PUNISHMENT OF SINNERS

16 Do not desire a multitude of use-
less children,
nor rejoice in ungodly sons.
2If they multiply, do not rejoice in
them,
unless the fear of the Lord is
in them.
3Do not trust in their survival,
and do not rely on their
multitude;
for one is better than a
thousand,[h]
and to die childless is better
than to have ungodly
children.
4For through one man of under-
standing a city will be
filled with people,
but through a tribe of
lawless men *it will* be
made desolate.
5Many such things my eye has
seen,
and my ear has heard things
more striking than
these.
6In an assembly of sinners a fire
will be kindled,

[f]Heb: Gk *you*
[g]Gk *men*
[h]The text of this line is uncertain

and in a disobedient nation
wrath was kindled.
7He was not propitiated for the
ancient giants
who revolted in their might.
8He did not spare the neighbors
of Lot,
whom he loathed on account
of their insolence.
9He showed no pity for a nation
devoted to destruction,
for those destroyed in their
sins;
10nor for the six hundred thou-
sand men on foot,
who rebelliously assembled
in their stubbornness.
11Even if there is only one stiff-
necked person,
it will be a wonder if he re-
mains unpunished.
For mercy and wrath are with
the Lord;[a]
he is mighty to forgive, and
he pours out wrath.
12As great as his mercy, so great is
also his reproof;
he judges a man according to
his deeds.
13The sinner will not escape with
his plunder,
and the patience of the godly
will not be frustrated.
14He will make room for every act
of mercy;
every one will receive in
accordance with his
deeds.[b]
17Do not say, "I shall be hidden
from the Lord,
and who from on high will
remember me?
Among so many people I shall
not be known,
for what is my soul in the
boundless creation?
18Behold, heaven and the highest
heaven,
the abyss and the earth,
will tremble at his
visitation.
19The mountains also and the
foundations of the earth
shake with trembling when
he looks upon them.
20And no mind will reflect on this.
Who will ponder his ways?
21Like a tempest which no man
can see,
so most of his works are
concealed.
22Who will announce his acts of
justice?
Or who will await them?
For the covenant is
far off."
23This is what one devoid of un-
derstanding thinks;
a senseless and misguided
man thinks foolishly.

GOD'S WISDOM SEEN IN CREATION

24Listen to me, my son, and ac-
quire knowledge,
and pay close attention to
my words.
25I will impart instruction by
weight,
and declare knowledge
accurately.
26The works of the Lord have
existed from the beginning
by his creation,[c]
and when he made them,
he determined their
divisions.
27He arranged his works in an
eternal order,
and their dominion[d] for all[e]
generations;
they neither hunger nor grow
weary,
and they do not cease from
their labors.

[a] Gk *him*
[b] Other authorities add *15The Lord hardened Pharaoh up so that he did not know him; in order that his works might be known under heaven. 16His mercy is manifest to the whole of creation, and he divided his light and darkness with a plumb line.*
[c] Heb: Gk *judgment*
[d] Or *elements*
[e] Gk *their*

28They do not crowd one another
aside,
and they will never disobey
his word.
29After this the Lord looked upon
the earth,
and filled it with his good
things;
30with all kinds of living beings he
covered its surface,
and to it they return.

17 The Lord created man out of
earth,
and turned him back to it
again.
2He gave to men[f] few days, a
limited time,
but granted them authority
over the things upon
the earth.[g]
3He endowed them with strength
like his own,[h]
and made them in his own
image.
4He placed the fear of them[i] in all
living beings,
and granted them domin-
ion over beasts and
birds.[j]
6He made for them[k] tongue and
eyes;
he gave them ears and a
mind for thinking.
7He filled them with knowledge
and understanding,
and showed them good and
evil.
8He set his eye upon their hearts
to show them the majesty of
his works.[l]
10And they will praise his holy
name,
to proclaim the grandeur of
his works.
11He bestowed knowledge upon
them,
and allotted to them the law
of life.
12He established with them an
eternal covenant,
and showed them his
judgments.
13Their eyes saw his glorious
majesty,
and their ears heard the
glory of his voice.
14And he said to them, "Beware of
all unrighteousness."[m]
And he gave command-
ment to each of
them concerning his
neighbor.
15Their ways are always before
him,
they will not be hid from his
eyes.[n]
17He appointed a ruler for every
nation,
but Israel is the Lord's own
portion.[o]
19All their works are as the sun
before him,
and his eyes are continually
upon their ways.
20Their iniquities are not hidden
from him,
and all their sins are before
the Lord.[p]

[f] Gk *them*
[g] Gk *it*
[h] Cn: Gk *proper to them*
[i] Syr: Gk *him*
[j] Other authorities add *They obtained the use of the five operatiois of the Lord; as sixth he distributed to them the giftf mind, and as seventh reason, the interprter of his operations.*
[k] Syr: Gk *Inclination an*
[l] Other authorities add *and he gave them to boast of his marvels for ever*
[m] Or *every unrighteous m*
[n] Other authorities ad *Their ways from youth tend toward evil, anl they are unable to make for themselves hearts of flesn place of their stony hearts. 17For in the divsion of the nations of the whole earth*
[o] Other authorities ad *whom, being his first-born, he brings up wit discipline, and allotting to him the light of his love, does not neglect him.*
[p] Other authorities ad *But the Lord, who is gracious and knows his reatures, has neither left nor abandoned them, bwared them*

22A man's almsgiving is like a signet with the Lord,[a]
and he will keep a person's kindness like the apple of his eye.
23Afterward he will arise and requite them,
and he will bring their recompense on their heads.
24Yet to those who repent he grants a return,
and he encourages those whose endurance is failing.

A CALL TO REPENTANCE

25Turn to the Lord and forsake your sins;
pray in his presence and lessen your offenses.
26Return to the Most High and turn away from iniquity,[b]
and hate abominations intensely.
27Who will sing praises to the Most High in Hades,
as do those who are alive and give thanks?
28From the dead, as from one who does not exist, thanksgiving has ceased;
he who is alive and well sings the Lord's praises.
29How great is the mercy of the Lord,
and his forgiveness for those who turn to him!
30For all things cannot be in men,[c]
since a son of man is not immortal.
31What is brighter than the sun? Yet its light fails.[d]
So flesh and blood devise evil.
32He marshals the host of the height of heaven;
but all men are dust and ashes.

THE MAJESTY OF GOD

18 He who lives for ever created the whole universe;
2the Lord alone will be declared righteous.[e]
4To none has he given power to proclaim his works;
and who can search out his mighty deeds?
5Who can measure his majestic power?
And who can fully recount his mercies?
6It is not possible to diminish or increase them,
nor is it possible to trace the wonders of the Lord.
7When a man has finished, he is just beginning,
and when he stops, he will be at a loss.
8What is man, and of what use is he?
What is his good and what is his evil?
9The number of a man's days is great if he reaches a hundred years.
10Like a drop of water from the sea and a grain[f] of sand
so are a few years in the day of eternity.
11Therefore the Lord is patient with them
and pours out his mercy upon them.
12He sees and recognizes that their end will be evil;
therefore he grants them forgiveness in abundance.

[a] Gk *him*
[b] Other authorities add *for he will lead you out of darkness to the light of health*
[c] The Greek text of this line is uncertain
[d] Or *suffers eclipse*
[e] Other authorities add *and there is no other beside him; 3he steers the wo with the span of his hand, and all things obey his will; for he is king of all things, by his power arating among them the holy things from the profane.*
[f] Gk *pebble*

[13]The compassion of man is for his neighbor,
but the compassion of the Lord is for all living beings.
He rebukes and trains and teaches them,
and turns them back, as a shepherd his flock.
[14]He has compassion on those who accept his discipline
and who are eager for his judgments.

THE RIGHT SPIRIT IN GIVING ALMS

[15]My son, do not mix reproach with your good deeds,
nor cause grief by your words when you present a gift.
[16]Does not the dew assuage the scorching heat?
So a word is better than a gift.
[17]Indeed, does not a word surpass a good gift?
Both are to be found in a gracious man.
[18]A fool is ungracious and abusive,
and the gift of a grudging man makes the eyes dim.

THE NEED OF REFLECTION AND SELF-CONTROL

[19]Before you speak, learn,
and before you fall ill, take care of your health.
[20]Before judgment, examine yourself,
and in the hour of visitation you will find forgiveness.
[21]Before falling ill, humble yourself,
and when you are on the point of sinning, turn back.
[22]Let nothing hinder you from paying a vow promptly,
and do not wait until death to be released from it.
[23]Before making a vow,[g] prepare yourself;
and do not be like a man who tempts the Lord.
[24]Think of his wrath on the day of death,
and of the moment of vengeance when he turns away his face.
[25]In the time of plenty think of the time of hunger;
in the days of wealth think of poverty and need.
[26]From morning to evening conditions change,
and all things move swiftly before the Lord.
[27]A wise man is cautious in everything,
and in days of sin he guards against wrongdoing.
[28]Every intelligent man knows wisdom,
and he praises the one who finds her.
[29]Those who understand sayings become skilled themselves,
and pour forth apt proverbs.
[30]Do not follow your base desires,
but restrain your appetites.
[31]If you allow your soul to take pleasure in base desire,
it will make you the laughingstock of your enemies.
[32]Do not revel in great luxury,
lest you become impoverished by its expense.
[33]Do not become a beggar by feasting with borrowed money,
when you have nothing in your purse.

19 A workman who is a drunkard will not become rich;
he who despises small things will fail little by little.
[2]Wine and women lead intelligent men astray,

[g] Or *offering a prayer*

and the man who consorts
with harlots is very
reckless.
3Decay and worms will inherit
him,
and the reckless soul will be
snatched away.

AGAINST LOOSE TALK

4One who trusts others too quick-
ly is lightminded,
and one who sins does
wrong to himself.
5One who rejoices in wickedness[a]
will be condemned,[b]
6and for one who hates gos-
sip evil is lessened.
7Never repeat a conversation,
and you will lose nothing
at all.
8With friend or foe do not report
it,
and unless it would be a
sin for you, do not
disclose it;
9for some one has heard you and
watched you,
and when the time comes he
will hate you.
10Have you heard a word? Let it
die with you.
Be brave! It will not make
you burst!
11With such a word a fool will
suffer pangs
like a woman in labor with
a child.
12Like an arrow stuck in the flesh
of the thigh,
so is a word inside a fool.
13Question a friend, perhaps he
did not do it;
but if he did anything, so
that he may do it no
more.
14Question a neighbor, perhaps he
did not say it;
but if he said it, so that he
may not say it again.
15Question a friend, for often it is
slander;
so do not believe everything
you hear.
16A person may make a slip with-
out intending it.
Who has never sinned with
his tongue?
17Question your neighbor before
you threaten him;
and let the law of the Most
High take its course.[c]

TRUE AND FALSE WISDOM

20All wisdom is the fear of the
Lord,
and in all wisdom there is
the fulfilment of the
law.[d]
22But the knowledge of wicked-
ness is not wisdom,
nor is there prudence where
sinners take counsel.
23There is a cleverness which is
abominable,
but there is a fool who mere-
ly lacks wisdom.
24Better is the God-fearing man
who lacks intelligence,
than the highly prudent man
who transgresses the
law.
25There is a cleverness which is
scrupulous but unjust,
and there are people who
distort kindness to
gain a verdict.
26There is a rascal bowed down in
mourning,[e]
but inwardly he is full of
deceit.

[a] Other authorities read *heart*

[b] *Other authorities add but he who withstands pleasures crowns his life.* [6]*He who controls his tongue will live without strife,*

[c] Other authorities add *and do not be angry.* [18]*The fear of the Lord is the beginning of acceptance, and wisdom obtains his love.* [19]*The knowledge of the Lord's commandments is life-giving discipline; and those who do what is pleasing to him enjoy the fruit of the tree of immortality.*

[d] Other authorities add *and the knowledge of his omnipotence.* [21]*When a servant says to his master, "I will not act as you wish," even if later he does it, he angers the one who supports him.*

[e] Gk *blackness*

27He hides his face and pretends
not to hear;
but where no one notices, he
will forestall you.
28And if by lack of strength he is
prevented from sinning,
he will do evil when he finds
an opportunity.
29A man is known by his
appearance,
and a sensible man is known
by his face, when you
meet him.
30A man's attire and open-
mouthed laughter,
and a man's manner of walk-
ing, show what he is.

SILENCE AND SPEECH

20 There is a reproof which is not
timely;
and there is a man who
keeps silent but is
wise.
2How much better it is to reprove
than to stay angry!
And the one who confesses
his fault will be kept
from loss.*f*
4Like a eunuch's desire to violate
a maiden
is a man who executes judg-
ments by violence.
5There is one who by keeping
silent is found wise,
while another is detested for
being too talkative.
6There is one who keeps silent
because le *has* no answer,
while anoter *keeps silent*
becıse *he* knows
wh to *speak.*
7A wise man wibe *silent* until
the rightoment,
but a brag·t and fool goes
beyd the right
mont.
8Whoever uses many words
will be lhed,
and whoeusurps the
right to speak will be
hated.

PARADOXES

9There may be good fortune for a
man in adversity,
and a windfall may result in
a loss.
10There is a gift that profits you
nothing,
and there is a gift that
brings a double
return.
11There are losses because of
glory,
and there are men who
have raised their
heads from humble
circumstances.
12There is a man who buys much
for a little,
but pays for it seven times
over.
13The wise man makes himself
beloved through his words,
but the courtesies of fools
are wasted.
14A fool's gift will profit you
nothing,
for he has many eyes instead
of one.
15He gives little and upbraids
much,
he opens his mouth like a
herald;
today he lends and tomorrow
he asks it back;
such a one is a hateful man.
16A fool will say, "I have no
friend,
and there is no gratitude for
my good deeds;
those who eat my bread
speak unkindly."
17How many will ridicule him, and
how often!

INAPPROPRIATE SPEECH

18A slip on the pavement is better
than a slip of the tongue;

*f*Other authorities adow *good it is to show repentance when you are reproved, for so you will escape deliberate sin!*

so the downfall of the
wicked will occur
speedily.
19An ungracious man is like a
story told at the wrong
time,
which is continually on the
lips of the ignorant.
20A proverb from a fool's lips will
be rejected,
for he does not tell it at its
proper time.
21A man may be prevented from
sinning by his poverty,
so when he rests he feels no
remorse.
22A man may lose his life through
shame,
or lose it because of his
foolish look.
23A man may for shame make
promises to a friend,
and needlessly make him an
enemy.

LYING

24A lie is an ugly blot on a man;
it is continually on the lips
of the ignorant.
25A thief is preferable to a habitual
liar,
but the lot of both is ruin.
26The disposition of a liar brings
disgrace,
and his shame is ever with
him.
27He who speaks wisely will ad-
vance himself,
and a sensible man will
please great men.
28Whoever cultivates the soil will
heap up his harvest,
and whoever pleases great
men will atone for
injustice.
29Presents and gifts blind the eyes
of the wise;
like a muzzle on the mouth
they avert reproofs.
30Hidden wisdom and unseen
treasure,
what advantage is there in
either of them?
31Better is the man who hides his
folly
than the man who hides his
wisdom.[a]

VARIOUS SINS

21 Have you sinned, my son? Do so
no more,
but pray about your former
sins.
2Flee from sin as from a snake;
for if you approach sin, it
will bite you.
Its teeth are lion's teeth,
and destroy the souls of
men.
3All lawlessness is like a two-
edged sword;
there is no healing for its
wound.
4Terror and violence will lay waste
riches;
thus the house of the proud
will be laid waste.
5The prayer of a poor man goes
from his lips to the ears
of God,[b]
and his judgment comes
speedily.
6Whoever hates reproof walks in
the steps of the sinner,
but he that fears the Lord
will repent in his
heart.
7He who is mighty in speech is
known rom afar;
but the sosible man, when
helips, is aware
of.
8A man who bids his house with
other pple's money
is like orvho gathers
stes for his burial
mnd.[c]
9An assembly he wicked is like

[a]Other authorities add *32Unwearied patience in seeking the Lord is betten a masterless charioteer of one's own life.*
[b]Gk *his ears*
[c]Other authorities read *for the winter*

tow gathered together,
and their end is a flame of fire.
10The way of sinners is smoothly paved with stones,
but at its end is the pit of Hades.

WISDOM AND FOOLISHNESS

11Whoever keeps the law controls his thoughts,
and wisdom is the fulfilment of the fear of the Lord.
12He who is not clever cannot be taught,
but there is a cleverness which increases bitterness.
13The knowledge of a wise man will increase like a flood,
and his counsel like a flowing spring.
14The mind of a fool is like a broken jar;
it will hold no knowledge.
15When a man of understanding hears a wise saying,
he will praise it and add to it;
when a reveler hears it, he dislikes it
and casts it behind his back.
16A fool's narration is like a burden on a journey,
but delight will be found in the speech of the intelligent.
17The utterance of a sensible man will be sought in the *assembly,*
and they will ponder his words in their minds.
18Like a house that has vanished, so is wisdom to a fool;
and the knowledge of the ignorant is unexamined talk.
19To a senseless man education is fetters on his feet,
and like manacles on his right hand.
20A fool raises his voice when he laughs,
but a clever man smiles quietly.
21To a sensible man education is like a golden ornament,
and like a bracelet on the right arm.
22The foot of a fool rushes into a house,
but a man of experience stands respectfully before it.
23A boor peers into the house from the door,
but a cultivated man remains outside.
24It is ill-mannered for a man to listen at a door,
and a discreet man is grieved by the disgrace.
25The lips of strangers will speak of these things,[d]
but the words of the prudent will be weighed in the balance.
26The mind of fools is in their mouth,
but the mouth of wise men is in[e] their mind.
27When an ungodly man curses his adversary,[f]
he curses his own soul.
28A whisperer defiles his own soul
and is hated in his neighborhood.

THE IDLER

22 The indolent may be compared to a filthy stone,
and every one hisses at his disgrace.
2The indolent may be compared to the filth of dunghills;
any one that picks it up will shake it off his hand.

[d]The Greek text of this line is uncertain
[e]Other authorities omit *in*
[f]Or *curses Satan*

DEGENERATE CHILDREN

3It is a disgrace to be the father of
an undisciplined son,
and the birth of a daughter
is a loss.
4A sensible daughter obtains her
husband,
but one who acts shamefully
brings grief to her
father.
5An impudent daughter disgraces
father and husband,
and will be despised by
both.
6Like music in mourning is a tale
told at the wrong time,
but chastising and discipline
are wisdom at all
times.

WISDOM AND FOLLY

7He who teaches a fool is like
one who glues potsherds
together,
or who rouses a sleeper from
deep slumber.
8He who tells a story to a fool tells
it to a drowsy man;
and at the end he will say,
"What is it?"[a]
11Weep for the dead, for he lacks
the light;
and weep for the fool, for he
lacks intelligence;
weep less bitterly for the
dead, for he has attained rest;
but the life of the fool is
worse than death.
12Mourning for the dead lasts
seven days,
but for a fool or an ungodly
man it lasts all his
life.
13Do not talk much with a foolish
man,
and do not visit an unintelligent man;
guard yourself from him to
escape trouble,
and you will not be soiled
when he shakes himself off;
avoid him and you will find
rest,
and you will never be wearied by his madness.
14What is heavier than lead?
And what is its name except
"Fool"?
15Sand, salt, and a piece of iron
are easier to bear than a
stupid man.
16A wooden beam firmly bonded
into a building
will not be torn loose by an
earthquake;
so the mind firmly fixed on a
reasonable counsel
will not be afraid in a
crisis.
17A mind settled on an intelligent
thought
is like the stucco decoration on the wall of a
colonnade.[b]
18Fences set on a high place
will not stand firm against
the wind;
so a timid heart with a fool's
purpose
will not stand firm against
any fear.

THE PRESERVATION OF FRIENDSHIP

19A man who pricks an eye will
make tears fall,
and one who pricks the
heart makes it show
feeling.
20One who throws a stone at birds
scares them away,
and one who reviles a friend
will break off the
friendship.
21Even if you have drawn your
sword against a friend,
do not despair, for a renewal
of friendship is
possible.

[a] Other authorities add *9Children who are brought up in a good life, conceal the lowly birth of their parents. 10Children who are disdainfully and boorishly haughty stain the nobility of their kindred.*
[b] Or *on a smooth wall*

who lacks good
sense.
3You have gathered nothing in
your youth;
how then can you find
anything in your old
age?
4What an attractive thing is
judgment in gray-haired
men,
and for the aged to possess
good counsel!
5How attractive is wisdom in the
aged,
and understanding and
counsel in honorable
men!
6Rich experience is the crown of
the aged,
and their boast is the fear of
the Lord.
7With nine thoughts I have gladdened my heart,
and a tenth I shall tell with
my tongue:
a man rejoicing in his
children;
a man who lives to see the
downfall of his foes;
8happy is he who lives with an
intelligent wife,
and he who has not made a
slip with his tongue,
and he who has not served
a man inferior to
himself;
9happy is he who has gained good
sense,
and he who speaks to attentive listeners.
10*How great is he who has gained*
wisdom!
But there is no one superior
to him who fears the
Lord.
11The fear of the Lord surpasses
everything;
to whom shall be likened
the one who holds it
fast?[e]

SOME EXTREME FORMS OF EVIL

13Any wound, but not a wound of
the heart!
Any wickedness, but not
the wickedness of a
wife!
14Any attack, but not an attack
from those who hate!
And any vengeance, but
not the vengeance of
enemies!
15There is no venom[f] worse than a
snake's venom,[g]
and no wrath worse than an
enemy's wrath.

THE EVIL OF A WICKED WOMAN

16I would rather dwell with a lion
and a dragon
than dwell with an evil
wife.
17The wickedness of a wife changes her appearance,
and darkens her face like
that of a bear.
18Her husband takes his meals
among the neighbors,
and he cannot help sighing[h]
bitterly.
19Any iniquity is insignificant
compared to a wife's
iniquity;
may a sinner's lot befall
her!
20A sandy ascent for the feet of
the aged—
such is a garrulous wife for a
quiet husband.
21Do not be ensnared by a woman's beauty,
and do not desire a
woman for her
possessions.[i]

[e] Other authorities add *12The fear of the Lord is the beginning of love for him, and faith is the beginning of clinging to him.*
[f] Cn: Gk *head*
[g] Cn: Gk *head*
[h] Other authorities read *and listening he sighs*
[i] Heb Syr: Some Gk authorities read *for her beauty*

22There is wrath and impudence
and great disgrace
when a wife supports her
husband.
23A dejected mind, a gloomy face,
and a wounded heart are
caused by an evil
wife.
Drooping hands and weak
knees
are caused by the wife who
does not make her
husband happy.
24From a woman sin had its
beginning,
and because of her we all
die.
25Allow no outlet to water,
and no boldness of speech in
an evil wife.
26If she does not go as you direct,
separate her from yourself.

THE JOY OF A GOOD WIFE

26 Happy is the husband of a good
wife;
the number of his days will
be doubled.
2A loyal wife rejoices her husband,
and he will complete his
years in peace.
3A good wife is a great blessing;
she will be granted among
the blessings of the
man who fears the
Lord.
4Whether rich or poor, his heart
is glad,
and at all times his face is
cheerful.

THE WORST OF EVILS: A WICKED WIFE

5Of three things my heart is
afraid,
and of a fourth I am
frightened:[a]
The slander of a *city*, the gath-
ering of a mob,
and false accusation—all
these are worse than
death.
6There is grief of heart and sorrow
when a wife is envious of
a rival,
and a tongue-lashing makes
it known to all.
7An evil wife is an ox yoke which
chafes;
taking hold of her is like
grasping a scorpion.
8There is great anger when a wife
is drunken;
she will not hide her shame.
9A wife's harlotry shows in her
lustful eyes,
and she is known by her
eyelids.
10Keep strict watch over a head-
strong daughter,
lest, when she finds liberty,
she use it to her
hurt.
11Be on guard against her impu-
dent eye,
and do not wonder if she
sins against you.
12As a thirsty wayfarer opens his
mouth
and drinks from any water
near him,
so will she sit in front of every
post
and open her quiver to the
arrow.

THE BLESSING OF A GOOD WIFE

13A wife's charm delights her
husband,
and her skill puts fat on his
bones.
14A silent wife is a gift of the
Lord,
and there is nothing so pre-
cious as a disciplined
soul.
15A modest wife adds charm to
charm,
and no balance can weigh
the value of a chaste
soul.
16Like the sun rising in the heights
of the Lord,

[a]The Greek of this line is uncertain

so is the beauty of a good
wife in her well-ordered home.
17Like the shining lamp on the
holy lampstand,
so is a beautiful face on a
stately figure.
18Like pillars of gold on a base of
silver,
so are beautiful feet with a
steadfast heart.[b]

THREE DEPRESSING THINGS

28At two things my heart is
grieved,
and because of a third anger
comes over me:
a warrior in want through
poverty,
and intelligent men
who are treated
contemptuously;
a man who turns back from
righteousness to sin—
the Lord will prepare him
for the sword!

THE TEMPTATIONS OF COMMERCE

29A merchant can hardly keep
from wrongdoing,
and a tradesman will not
be declared innocent
of sin.
27 Many have committed sin for a
trifle,[c]
and whoever seeks to get
rich will avert his
eyes.
2As a stake is driven firmly into a
fissure between stones,
so sin is wedged in between
selling and buying.
3If a man is not steadfast and
zealous in the fear of the
Lord,
his house will be quickly
overthrown.

TESTS IN LIFE

4When a sieve is shaken, the
refuse remains;
so a man's filth remains in
his thoughts.
5The kiln tests the potter's
vessels;
so the test of a man is in his
reasoning.
6The fruit discloses the cultivation of a tree;
so the expression of a
thought discloses the
cultivation of a man's
mind.
7Do not praise a man before you
hear him reason,
for this is the test of men.

REWARD AND RETRIBUTION

8If you pursue justice, you will
attain it
and wear it as a glorious
robe.
9Birds flock with their kind;
so truth returns to those
who practice it.
10A lion lies in wait for prey;
so does sin for the workers
of iniquity.

VARIETIES OF SPEECH

11The talk of the godly man is
always wise,
but the fool changes like the
moon.

[b]Other authorities add verses 19-27: *19My son, keep sound the bloom of your youth, and do not give your strength to strangers. 20Seek a fertile field within the whole plain, and sow it with your own seed, trusting in your fine stock. 21So your offspring will survive and, having confidence in their good descent, will grow great. 22A harlot is regarded as spittle, and a married woman as a tower of death to her lovers. 23A godless wife is given as a portion to a lawless man, but a pious wife is given to the man who fears the Lord. 24A shameless woman constantly acts disgracefully, but a modest daughter will even be embarrassed before her husband. 25A headstrong wife is regarded as a dog, but one who has a sense of shame will fear the Lord. 26A wife honoring her husband will seem wise to all, but is she dishonors him in her pride she will be known to all as ungodly. Happy is the husband of a good wife; for the number of his years will be doubled. 27A loud-voiced and garrulous wife is regarded as a war trumpet for putting the enemy to flight, and every person like this lives in the anarchy of war.*
[c]One ancient authority reads *gain*

12Among stupid people watch for a chance to leave,
but among thoughtful people stay on.
13The talk of fools is offensive,
and their laughter is wantonly sinful.
14The talk of men given to swearing makes one's hair stand on end,
and their quarrels make a man stop his ears.
15The strife of the proud leads to bloodshed,
and their abuse is grievous to hear.

BETRAYING SECRETS

16Whoever betrays secrets destroys confidence,
and he will never find a congenial friend.
17Love your friend and keep faith with him;
but if you betray his secrets, do not run after him.
18For as a man destroys his enemy,
so you have destroyed the friendship of your neighbor.
19And as you allow a bird to escape from your hand,
so you have let your neighbor go, and will not catch him again.
20Do not go after him, for he is too far off,
and has escaped like a gazelle from a snare.
21For a wound may be bandaged,
and there is reconciliation after abuse,
but whoever has betrayed secrets is without hope.

HYPOCRISY AND RETRIBUTION

22Whoever winks his eye plans evil deeds,
and no one can keep him from them.
23In your presence his mouth is all sweetness,
and he admires your words;
but later he will twist his speech
and with your own words he will give offense.
24I have hated many things, but none to be compared to him;
even the Lord will hate him.
25Whoever throws a stone straight up throws it on his own head;
and a treacherous blow opens up wounds.
26He who digs a pit will fall into it,
and he who sets a snare will be caught in it.
27If a man does evil, it will roll back upon him,
and he will not know where it came from.
28Mockery and abuse issue from the proud man,[a]
but vengeance lies in wait for him like a lion.
29Those who rejoice in the fall of the godly will be caught in a snare,
and pain will consume them before their death.

ANGER AND VENGEANCE

30Anger and wrath, these also are abominations,
and the sinful man will possess them.

28 He that takes vengeance will suffer vengeance from the Lord,
and he will firmly establish[b] his sins.
2Forgive your neighbor the wrong he has done,
and then your sins will be pardoned when you pray.
3Does a man harbor anger against another,

[a]Other authorities read *proud men*
[b]Other authorities read *closely observe*

and yet seek for healing
from the Lord?
4Does he have no mercy toward a
man like himself,
and yet pray for his own
sins?
5If he himself, being flesh, maintains wrath,
who will make expiation for
his sins?
6Remember the end of your life,
and cease from enmity,
remember destruction and
death, and be true to
the commandments.
7Remember the commandments,
and do not be angry with
your neighbor;
remember the covenant of
the Most High, and
overlook ignorance.
8Refrain from strife, and you will
lessen sins;
for a man given to anger will
kindle strife,
9and a sinful man will disturb
friends
and inject enmity among
those who are at
peace.
10In proportion to the fuel for
the fire, so will be the
burning,
and in proportion to the obstinacy of strife will
be the burning;[c]
in proportion to the strength
of the man will be his
anger,
and in proportion to his
wealth he will heighten his wrath.
11A hasty quarrel kindles fire,
and urgent strife sheds
blood.

THE EVIL TOGUE

12If you blow on a sark, it will
glow;
if you spit on it, it will be
put out;
and both come out of your
mouth.
13Curse the whisperer and
deceiver,
for he has destroyed many
who were at peace.
14Slander[d] has shaken many,
and scattered them from
nation to nation,
and destroyed strong cities,
and overturned the houses
of great men.
15Slander[e] has driven away courageous women,
and deprived them of the
fruit of their toil.
16Whoever pays heed to slander[f]
will not find rest,
nor will he settle down in
peace.
17The blow of a whip raises a welt,
but a blow of the tongue
crushes the bones.
18Many have fallen by the edge of
the sword,
but not so many as have
fallen because of the
tongue.
19Happy is the man who is protected from it,
who has not been exposed to
its anger,
who has not borne its yoke,
and has not been bound with
its fetters;
20for its yoke is a yoke of iron,
and its fetters are fetters of
bronze;
21its death is an evil death,
and Hades is preferable
to it.
22It will not be master over the
godly,
and they will not be burned
in its flame.
23Those who forsake the Lord will
fall into its power;

[c] Other authorities place tl line at the end of the verse, or omit it
[d] Gk *a third tongue*
[e] Gk *a third tongue*
[f] Gk *it*

it will burn among them
and will not be put
out.
It will be sent out against them
like a lion;
like a leopard it will mangle
them.
24 See that you fence in your prop-
erty with thorns,
lock up your silver and
gold,
25 make balances and scales for
your words,
and make a door and a bolt
for your mouth.
26 Beware lest you err with your
tongue,[a]
lest you fall before him who
lies in wait.

ON LENDING AND BORROWING

29 He that shows mercy will lend to
his neighbor,
and he that strength-
ens him with his
hand keeps the
commandments.
2 Lend to your neighbor in the
time of his need;
and in turn, repay your
neighbor promptly.
3 Confirm your word and keep
faith with him,
and on every occasion you
will find what you
need.
4 Many persons regard a loan as a
windfall,
and cause trouble to those
who help them.
5 A man will kiss another's hands
until he gets a loan,
and will lower his voice in
speaking of his neigh-
bor's money;
but at the time for repayment
he will delay,
and will pay in words of
unconcern,
and will find fault with the
time.
6 If the lender[b] exert pressure, he
will hardly get back half,
and will regard that as a
windfall.
If he does not, the borrower[c]
has robbed him of his
money,
and he has needlessly made
him his enemy;
he will repay him with curses
and reproaches,
and instead of glory will
repay him with
dishonor.
7 Because of such wickedness,
therefore,[d] many have
refused to lend;
they have been afraid of
being defrauded
needlessly.
8 Nevertheless, be patient
with a man in humble
circumstances,
and do not make him wait
for your alms.
9 Help a poor man for the com-
mandment's sake,
and because of his need do
not send him away
empty.
10 Lose your silver for the sake of a
brother or a friend,
and do not let it rust under a
stone and be lost.
11 Lay up your treasure according
to the commandments of
the Most High,
and it will profit you more
than gold.
12 Store up almsgiving in your
treasury,
and it will rescue you from
all affliction;
13 more than a mighty shield and
more than a heavy spear,
it will fight on your behalf
against your enemy.

[a] Gk *with it*
[b] Gk *he*
[c] Gk *he*
[d] Other authorities read *It is not because of wickedness that*

ON GUARANTEEING DEBTS

14A good man will be surety for
his neighbor,
but a man who has lost his
sense of shame will
fail him.
15Do not forget all the kindness of
your surety,
for he has given his life for
you.
16A sinner will overthrow the
prosperity of his surety,
17and one who does not feel
grateful will abandon his
rescuer.
18Being surety has ruined many
men who were prosperous,
and has shaken them like a
wave of the sea;
it has driven men of power into
exile,
and they have wandered
among foreign
nations.
19The sinner who has fallen into
suretyship
and pursues gain will fall
into lawsuits.
20Assist your neighbor according
to your ability,
but take heed to yourself lest
you fall.

HOME AND HOSPITALITY

21The essentials for life are water
and bread
and clothing and a house
to cover one's
nakedness.
22Better is the life of a poor man
under the shelter of his
roof
than sumptuous food in an-
other man's house.
23Be content with little or much.[e]
24It is a miserable life to go from
house to house,
and where you are a stranger
you may not open
your mouth;
25you will play the host and pro-
vide drink without being
thanked,
and besides this you will
hear bitter words:
26"Come here, stranger, prepare
the table,
and if you have anything at
hand, let me have it
to eat."
27"Give place, stranger, to an hon-
ored person;
my brother has come to stay
with me; I need my
house."
28These things are hard to bear for
a man who has feeling:
scolding about lodging[f] and
the reproach of the
moneylender.

30 He who loves his son will whip
him often,
in order that he may rejoice
at the way he turns
out.
2He who disciplines his son will
profit by him,
and will boast of him among
acquaintances.
3He who teaches his son will
make his enemies envious,
and will glory in him in the
presence of friends.
4The[g] father may die, and yet he is
not dead,
for he has left behind him
one like himself;
5while alive he saw and rejoiced,
and when he died he was not
grieved;
6he has left behind him an aveng-
er against his enemies,
and one to repay the kind-
ness of his friends.
7He who spoils his son will bind
up his wounds,
and his feelings will be trou-
bled at every cry.
8A horse that is untamed turns
out to be stubborn,

[e] Other authorities add *and you will not hear reproach for your sojourning.*
[f] Or *from the household,* or (Syr) *from the host*
[g] Gk *His*

and a son unrestrained turns
out to be wilful.
9Pamper a child, and he will
frighten you;
play with him, and he will
give you grief.
10Do not laugh with him, lest you
have sorrow with him,
and in the end you will
gnash your teeth.
11Give him no authority in his
youth,
and do not ignore his
errors.
12Bow down his neck in his
youth,[a]
and beat his sides while he is
young,
lest he become stubborn and
disobey you,
and you have sorrow of soul
from him.[b]
13Discipline your son and take
pains with him,
that you may not be
offended by his
shamelessness.
14Better off is a poor man who
is well and strong in
constitution
than a rich man who is
severely afflicted in
body.
15Health and soundness are better
than all gold,
and a robust body than
countless riches.
16There is no wealth better than
health of body,
and there is no gladness
above joy of heart.
17Death is better than a miserable
life,
and eternal rest[c] than chron-
ic sickness.
18Good things poured out upon a
mouth that is closed
are like offerings of food
placed upon a grave.
19Of what use to an idol is an
offering of fruit?
For it can neither eat nor
smell.
So is he who is afflicted by the
Lord;
20he sees with his eyes and
groans,
like a eunuch who embraces
a maiden and groans.
21Do not give yourself over to
sorrow,
and do not afflict yourself
deliberately.
22Gladness of heart is the life of
man,
and the rejoicing of a man is
length of days.
23Delight your soul and comfort
your heart,
and remove sorrow far from
you,
for sorrow has destroyed
many,
and there is no profit in it.
24Jealousy and anger shorten life,
and anxiety brings on old
age too soon.
25A man of cheerful and good
heart
will give heed to the food
he eats.

RIGHT ATTITUDE TOWARD RICHES

31 Wakefulness over wealth wastes
away one's flesh,
and anxiety about it removes
sleep.
2Wakeful anxiety prevents
slumber,
and a severe illness carries
off sleep.[d]
3The rich man toils as his wealth
accumulates,
and when he rests he fills
himself with his
dainties.
4The poor man toils as his liveli-
hood diminishes,

[a] Other authorities omit this line and the preceding line
[b] Other authorities omit this line
[c] Some authorities omit *eternal rest*
[d] Other authorities read *sleep carries off a severe illness*

and when he rests he becomes needy.
5He who loves gold will not be justified,
and he who pursues money will be led astray[e] by it.
6Many have come to ruin because of gold,
and their destruction has met them face to face.
7It is a stumbling block to those who are devoted to it,
and every fool will be taken captive by it.
8Blessed is the rich man who is found blameless,
and who does not go after gold.
9Who is he? And we will call him blessed,
for he has done wonderful things among his people.
10Who has been tested by it and been found perfect?
Let it be for him a ground for boasting.
Who has had the power to transgress and did not transgress,
and to do evil and did not do it?
11His prosperity will be established,
and the assembly will relate his acts of charity.

TABLE ETIQUETTE

12Are you seated at the table of a great man?[f]
Do not be greedy[g] at it,
and do not say, "There is certainly much upon it!"
13Remember that a greedy[h] eye is a bad thing.
What has been created more greedy[i] than the eye?
Therefore it sheds tears from every face.
14Do not reach out your hand for everything you see,
and do not crowd your neighbor[j] at the dish.
15Judge your neighbor's feelings by your own,
and in every matter be thoughtful.
16Eat like a human being what is set before you,
and do not chew greedily, lest you be hated.
17Be the first to stop eating, for the sake of good manners,
and do not be insatiable, lest you give offense.
18If you are seated among many persons,
do not reach out your hand before they do.
19How ample a little is for a well-disciplined man!
He does not breathe heavily upon his bed.
20Healthy sleep depends on moderate eating;
he rises early, and feels fit.[k]
The distress of sleeplessness and of nausea
and colic are with the glutton.
21If you are overstuffed with food,
get up in the middle of the meal, and you will have relief.
22Listen to me, my son, and do not disregard me,
and in the end you will appreciate my words.
In all your work be industrious,

[e] Heb Syr: Gk *will be filled*
[f] Heb Syr: Gk *at a great table*
[g] Gk *open your throat*
[h] Gk *evil*
[i] Gk *evil*
[j] Gk *him*
[k] Gk *his soul is with him*

and no sickness will overtake you.
23Men will praise the one who is liberal with food,
and their testimony to his excellence is trustworthy.
24The city will complain of the one who is niggardly with food,
and their testimony to his niggardliness is accurate.

TEMPERANCE IN DRINKING WINE

25Do not aim to be valiant over wine,
for wine has destroyed many.
26Fire and water prove[a] the temper of steel,
so wine tests hearts in the strife of the proud.
27Wine is like life to men,
if you drink it in moderation.
What is life to a man who is without wine?
It has been created to make men glad.
28Wine drunk in season and temperately
is rejoicing of heart and gladness of soul.
29Wine drunk to excess is bitterness of soul,
with provocation and stumbling.
30Drunkenness increases the anger of a fool to his injury,
reducing his strength and adding wounds.
31Do not reprove your neighbor at a banquet of wine,
and do not despise him in his merrymaking;
speak no word of reproach to him,
and do not afflict him by making demands of him.

ETIQUETTE AT A BANQUET

32 If they make you master of the feast, do not exalt yourself;
be among them as one of them;
take good care of them and then be seated;
2when you have fulfilled your duties, take your place,
that you may be merry on their account
and receive a wreath for your excellent leadership.
3Speak, you who are older, for it is fitting that you should,
but with accurate knowledge, and do not interrupt the music.
4Where there is entertainment, do not pour out talk;
do not display your cleverness out of season.
5A ruby seal in a setting of gold
is a concert of music at a banquet of wine.
6A seal of emerald in a rich setting of gold
is the melody of music with good wine.
7Speak, young man, if there is need of you,
but no more than twice, and only if asked.
8Speak concisely, say much in few words;
be as one who knows and yet holds his tongue.
9Among the great do not act as their equal;
and when another is speaking, do not babble.
10Lightning speeds before the thunder,
and approval precedes a modest man.
11Leave in good time and do not be the last;
go home quickly and do not linger.

[a]Gk *The furnace by dipping proves*

[12]Amuse yourself there, and do
what you have in mind,
but do not sin through proud
speech.
[13]And for these things bless him
who made you
and satisfies you with his
good gifts.

THE PROVIDENCE OF GOD

[14]He who fears the Lord will
accept his discipline,
and those who rise early to
seek him[b] will find
favor.
[15]He who seeks the law will be
filled with it,
but the hypocrite will stum-
ble at it.
[16]Those who fear the Lord will
form true judgments,
and like a light they will
kindle righteous
deeds.
[17]A sinful man will shun reproof,
and will find a decision
according to his
liking.
[18]A man of judgment will not
overlook an idea,
and an insolent[c] and proud
man will not cower
in fear.[d]
[19]Do nothing without
deliberation;
and when you have acted, do
not regret it.
[20]Do not go on a path full of
hazards,
and do not stumble over
stony ground.
[21]Do not be overconfident on a
smooth[e] way,
[22]and give good heed to your
paths.[f]
[23]Guard[g] yourself in every act,
for this is the keeping of the
commandments.
[24]He who believes the law
gives heed to the
commandments,
and he who trusts the Lord
will not suffer loss.

33 No evil will befall the man who
fears the Lord,
but in trial he will deliver
him again and again.
[2]A wise man will not hate the
law,
but he who is hypocritical
about it is like a boat
in a storm.
[3]A man of understanding will
trust in the law;
for him the law is as
dependable as an
inquiry by means of
Urim.
[4]Prepare what to say, and thus you
will be heard;
bind together your instruc-
tion, and make your
answer.
[5]The heart of a fool is like a cart
wheel,
and his thoughts like a turn-
ing axle.
[6]A stallion is like a mocking
friend;
he neighs under every one
who sits on him.

DIFFERENCES IN NATURE AND IN MANKIND

[7]Why is any day better than
another,
when all the daylight in the
year is from the sun?
[8]By the Lord's decision they were
distinguished,
and he appointed the dif-
ferent seasons and
feasts;
[9]some of them he exalted and
hallowed,

[b]Other authorities omit *to seek him*
[c]Heb: Gk *alien*
[d]The meaning of this line is uncertain. Other authorities add the phrases *and after acting, with him, without deliberation*
[e]Or *an unexplored*
[f]Syr Vg: Gk *and beware of your children*
[g]Heb Syr: Gk *Trust*

and some of them he made
ordinary days.
10All men are from the ground,
and Adam was created of the
dust.
11In the fulness of his knowledge
the Lord distinguished
them
and appointed their different
ways;
12some of them he blessed and
exalted,
and some of them he made
holy and brought near
to himself;
but some of them he cursed
and brought low,
and he turned them out of
their place.
13As clay in the hand of the
potter—
for all his ways are as he
pleases—
so men are in the hand of him
who made them,
to give them as he decides.
14Good is the opposite of evil,
and life the opposite of
death;
so the sinner is the opposite
of the godly.
15Look upon all the works of the
Most High;
they likewise are in pairs,
one the opposite of
the other.
16I was the last on watch;
I was like one who
gleans after the
grape-gatherers;
by the blessing of the Lord I
excelled,
and like a grape-gatherer I
filled my wine press.
17Consider that I have not labored
for myself alone,
but for all who seek
instruction.
18Hear me, you who are great
among the people,
and you leaders of the con-
gregation, hearken.

THE ADVANTAGE OF INDEPENDENCE

19To son or wife, to brother or
friend,
do not give power over
yourself, as long as
you live;
and do not give your property
to another,
lest you change your mind
and must ask for it.
20While you are still alive and
have breath in you,
do not let any one take your
place.
21For it is better that your
children should ask from
you
than that you should look
to the hand of you
sons.
22Excel in all that you do;
bring no stain upon your
honor.
23At the time when you end the
days of your life,
in the hour of death,
distribute your
inheritance.

THE TREATMENT OF SLAVES

24Fodder and a stick and burdens
for an ass;
bread and discipline and
work for a servant.
25Set your slave to work, and you
will find rest;
leave his hands idle, and he
will seek liberty.
26Yoke and thong will bow the
neck,
and for a wicked servant
there are racks and
tortures.
27Put him to work, that he may
not be idle,
for idleness teaches much
evil.
28Set him to work, as is fitting for
him,
and if he does not obey,
make his fetters
heavy.

29Do not act immoderately toward
anybody,
and do nothing without
discretion.
30If you have a servant, let him be
as yourself,
because you have bought
him with blood.
31If you have a servant, treat him
as a brother,
for as your own soul you will
need him.
If you ill-treat him, and he
leaves and runs away,
which way will you go to
seek him?

DREAMS MEAN NOTHING

34 A man of no understanding has
vain and false hopes,
and dreams give wings to
fools.
2As one who catches at a shadow
and pursues the wind,
so is he who gives heed to
dreams.
3The vision of dreams is this
against that,
the likeness of a face con-
fronting a face.
4From an unclean thing what will
be made clean?
And from something false
what will be true?
5Divinations and omens and
dreams are folly,
and like a woman in tra-
vail the mind has
fancies.
6Unless they are sent from the
Most High as a visitation,
do not give your mind to
them.
7For dreams have deceived many,
and those who put their
hope in them have
failed.
8Without such deceptions the law
will be fulfilled,
and wisdom is made perfect
in truthful lips.

EXPERIENCE AS A TEACHER

9An educated[a] man knows many
things,
and one with much experi-
ence will speak with
understanding.
10He that is inexperienced knows
few things,
but he that has traveled
acquires much
cleverness.
11I have seen many things in my
travels,
and I understand more than
I can express.
12I have often been in danger of
death,
but have escaped because of
these experiences.

FEAR THE LORD

13The spirit of those who fear the
Lord will live,
for their hope is in him who
saves them.
14He who fears the Lord will not
be timid,
nor play the coward, for he is
his hope.
15Blessed is the soul of the man
who fears the Lord!
To whom does he look? And
who is his support?
16The eyes of the Lord are upon
those who love him,
a mighty protection and
strong support,
a shelter from the hot wind and
a shade from noonday
sun,
a guard against stumbling
and a defense against
falling.
17He lifts up the soul and gives
light to the eyes;
he grants healing, life, and
blessing.

OFFERING SACRIFICES

18If one sacrifices from what has
been wrongfully obtained,

[a]Other authorities read *A traveled*

the offering is blemished;[a]
the gifts[b] of the lawless are
not acceptable.
19The Most High is not pleased
with the offerings of the
ungodly;
and he is not propitiated for
sins by a multitude of
sacrifices.
20Like one who kills a son before
his father's eyes
is the man who offers a
sacrifice from the
property of the poor.
21The bread of the needy is the life
of the poor;
whoever deprives them of it
is a man of blood.
22To take away a neighbor's living
is to murder him;
to deprive an employee of
his wages is to shed
blood.
23When one builds and another
tears down,
what do they gain but toil?
24When one prays and another
curses,
to whose voice will the Lord
listen?
25If a man washes after touching
a dead body, and touches
it again,
what has he gained by his
washing?
26So if a man fasts for his sins,
and goes again and does the
same things,
who will listen to his prayer?
And what has he gained by
humbling himself?

THE LAW AND SACRIFICES

35 He who keeps the law makes
many offerings;
he who heeds the command-
ments sacrifices a
peace offering.
2He who returns a kindness offers
fine flour,
and he who gives alms
sacrifices a thank
offering.
3To keep from wickedness is
pleasing to the Lord,
and to forsake unrighteous-
ness is atonement.
4Do not appear before the Lord
empty-handed,
5for all these things are to be
done because of the
commandment.
6The offering of a righteous man
anoints the altar,
and its pleasing odor rises
before the Most
High.
7The sacrifice of a righteous man
is acceptable,
and the memory of it will
not be forgotten.
8Glorify the Lord generously,
and do not stint the first
fruits of your hands.
9With every gift show a cheerful
face,
and dedicate your tithe with
gladness.
10Give to the Most High as he has
given,
and as generously as your
hand has found.
11For the Lord is the one who
repays,
and he will repay you
sevenfold.

DIVINE JUSTICE

12Do not offer him a bribe, for he
will not accept it;
and do not trust to an un-
righteous sacrifice;
for the Lord is the judge,
and with him is no
partiality.
13He will not show partiality in
the case of a poor man;
and he will listen to the
prayer of one who is
wronged.

[a]Other authorities read *is made in mockery*
[b]Other authorities read *mockeries*

14He will not ignore the
supplication of the
fatherless,
nor the widow when she
pours out her story.
15Do not the tears of the widow
run down her cheek
as she cries out against him
who has caused them
to fall?
16He whose service is pleasing to
the Lord will be accepted,
and his prayer will reach to
the clouds.
17The prayer of the humble pierces
the clouds,
and he will not be consoled
until it reaches the
Lord;[c]
he will not desist until the
Most High visits him,
and does justice for the righ-
teous, and executes
judgment.
18And the Lord will not delay,
neither will he be patient
with them,
till he crushes the loins of the
unmerciful
and repays vengeance on the
nations;
till he takes away the
multitude of the
insolent,
and breaks the scepters of
the unrighteous;
19till he repays man according to
his deeds,
and the works of men
according to their
devices;
till he judges the case of his
people
and makes them rejoice in
his mercy.
20Mercy is as welcome when he
afflicts them
as clouds of rain in the time
of drought.

A PRAYER FOR GOD'S PEOPLE

36 Have mercy upon us, O Lord,
the God of all, and look
upon us,
2and cause the fear of thee
to fall upon all the
nations.
3Lift up thy hand against foreign
nations
and let them see thy might.
4As in us thou hast been sancti-
fied before them,
so in them be thou magni-
fied before us;
5and let them know thee, as we
have known
that there is not God but
thee, O Lord.
6Show signs anew, and work fur-
ther wonders;
make thy hand and thy right
arm glorious.
7Rouse thy anger and pour out thy
wrath;
destroy the adversary and
wipe out the enemy.
8Hasten the day, and remember
the appointed time,[d]
and let people recount thy
mighty deeds.
9Let him who survives be con-
sumed in the fiery wrath,
and may those who harm
thy people meet
destruction.
10Crush the heads of the rulers of
the enemy,
who say, "There is no one
but ourselves."
11Gather all the tribes of Jacob,
and give[e] them their in-
heritance, as at the
beginning.
12Have mercy, O Lord, upon
the people called by thy
name,
upon Israel, whom thou hast
likened to a[f] first-
born son.

[c] Or *until the Lord draws near*
[d] Other authorities read *remember thy oath*
[e] Other authorities read *I gave*
[f] Other authorities read *hast named thy*

13Have pity on the city of thy
sanctuary,[a]
Jerusalem, the place of thy
rest.
14Fill Zion with the celebration of
thy wondrous deeds,
and thy temple[b] with thy
glory.
15Bear witness to those whom
thou didst create in the
beginning,
and fulfil the prophecies
spoken in thy name.
16Reward those who wait for thee,
and let thy prophets be
found trustworthy.
17Hearken, O Lord, to the prayer
of thy servants,
according to the blessing of
Aaron for thy people,
and all who are on the earth
will know
that thou art the Lord, the
God of the ages.

CONCERNING DISCRIMINATION

18The stomach will take any food,
yet one food is better than
another.
19As the palate tastes the kinds
of game,
so an intelligent mind detects false words.
20A perverse mind will cause grief,
but a man of experience will
pay him back.
21A woman will accept any man,
but one daughter is better
than another.
22A woman's beauty gladdens the
countenance,
and surpasses every human
desire.
23If kindness and humility mark
her speech,
her husband is not like other
men.
24He who acquires a wife gets his
best possession,[c]
a helper fit for him and a
pillar of support.[d]
25Where there is no fence, the
property will be plundered;
and where there is no wife,
a man will wander
about and sigh.
26For who will trust a nimble
robber
that skips from city to city?
So who will trust a man that
has no home,
and lodges wherever night
finds him?

FALSE FRIENDS

37 Every friend will say, "I too am a
friend";
but some friends are friends
only in name.
2Is it not a grief to the death
when a companion and
friend turns to
enmity?
3O evil imagination, why were you
formed
to cover the land with
deceit?
4Some companions rejoice in the
happiness of a friend,
but in time of trouble are
against him.
5Some companions help a friend
for their stomach's sake,
and in the face of battle take
up the shield.
6Do not forget a friend in your
heart,
and be not unmindful of him
in your wealth.

CAUTION IN TAKING ADVICE

7Every counselor praises counsel,
but some give counsel in
their own interest.
8Be wary of a counselor,
and learn first what is his
interest—
for he will take thought for

[a] Or *on thy holy city*
[b] Heb Syr: Gk Vg *people*
[c] Heb: Gk *enters upon a possession*
[d] Heb: Gk *rest*

himself—
lest he cast the lot against you
9and tell you, "Your way is good,"
and then stand aloof to see what will happen to you.
10Do not consult the one who looks at you suspiciously;
hide your counsel from those who are jealous of you.
11Do not consult with a woman about her rival
or with a coward about war,
with a merchant about barter
or with a buyer about selling,
with a grudging man about gratitude
or with a merciless man about kindness,
with an idler about any work
or with a man hired for a year about completing his work,
with a lazy servant about a big task—
pay no attention to these in any matter of counsel.
12But stay constantly with a godly man
whom you know to be a keeper of the commandments,
whose soul is in accord with your soul,
and who will sorrow with you if you fail.
13And establish the counsel of your own heart,
for no one is more faithful to you than it is.
14For a man's soul sometimes keeps him better informed
than seven watchmen sitting high on a watchtower.
15And besides all this pray to the Most High
that he may direct your way in truth.

TRUE AND FALSE WISDOM

16Reason is the beginning of every work,
and counsel precedes every undertaking.
17As a clue to changes of heart
18four turns of fortune appear,
good and evil, life and death;
and it is the tongue that continually rules them.
19A man may be shrewd and the teacher of many,
and yet be unprofitable to himself.
20A man skilled in words may be hated;
he will be destitute of all food,
21for grace was not given him by the Lord,
since he is lacking in all wisdom.
22A man may be wise to his own advantage,
and the fruits of his understanding may be trustworthy on his lips.
23A wise man will instruct his own people,
and the fruits of his understanding will be trustworthy.
24A wise man will have praise heaped upon him,
and all who see him will call him happy.
25The life of a man is numbered by days,
but the days of Israel are without number.
26He who is wise among his people will inherit confidence,[e]
and his name will live for ever.

[e]Other authorities read *honor*

CONCERNING MODERATION

27My son, test your soul while you live;
see what is bad for it and do not give it that.
28For not everything is good for every one,
and not every person enjoys everything.
29Do not have an insatiable appetite for any luxury,
and do not give yourself up to food;
30for overeating brings sickness,
and gluttony leads to nausea.
31Many have died of gluttony,
but he who is careful to avoid it prolongs his life.

CONCERNING PHYSICIANS AND HEALTH

38 Honor the physician with the honor due him,[a] according to your need of him,
for the Lord created him;
2for healing comes from the Most High,
and he will receive a gift from the king.
3The skill of the physician lifts up his head,
and in the presence of great men he is admired.
4The Lord created medicines from the earth,
and a sensible man will not despise them.
5Was not water made sweet with a tree
in order that his[b] power might be known?
6And he gave skill to men
that he[c] might be glorified in his marvelous works.
7By them he heals and takes away pain;
8the pharmacist makes of them a compound.
His works will never be finished;
and from him health[d] is upon the face of the earth.
9My son, when you are sick do not be negligent,
but pray to the Lord, and he will heal you.
10Give up your faults and direct your hands aright,
and cleanse your heart from all sin.
11Offer a sweet-smelling sacrifice,
and a memorial portion of fine flour,
and pour oil on your offering, as much as you can afford.[e]
12And give the physician his place,
for the Lord created him;
let him not leave you, for there is need of him.
13There is a time when success lies in the hands of physicians,[f]
14for they too will pray to the Lord
that he should grant them success in diagnosis[g]
and in healing, for the sake of preserving life.
15He who sins before his Maker,
may he fall into the care[h] of a physician.

ON MOURNING FOR THE DEAD

16My son, let your tears fall for the dead,
and as one who is suffering grievously begin the lament.
Lay out his body with the

[a] Other authorities omit *with the honor due him*
[b] Or *its*
[c] Or *they*
[d] Or *peace*
[e] Heb: Vulgate omits *as much as you can afford;* Greek is obscure
[f] Gk *in their hands*
[g] Heb: Gk *rest*
[h] Gk *hands*

honor due him,
and do not neglect his
burial.
17Let your weeping be bitter and
your wailing fervent;
observe the mourning
according to his
merit,
for one day, or two, to avoid
criticism;
then be comforted for your
sorrow.
18For sorrow results in death,
and sorrow of heart saps
one's strength.
19In calamity sorrow continues,
and the life of the poor man
weighs down his
heart.
20Do not give your heart to
sorrow;
drive it away, remembering
the end of life.
21Do not forget, there is no coming
back;
you do the dead[i] no good,
and you injure
yourself.
22"Remember my doom, for yours
is like it:
yesterday it was mine, and
today it is yours."
23When the dead is at rest, let his
remembrance cease,
and be comforted for him
when his spirit has
departed.

TRADES AND CRAFTS

24The wisdom of the scribe depends on the opportunity
of leisure;
and he who has little business may become
wise.
25How can he become wise who
handles the plow,
and who glories in the shaft
of a goad,
who drives oxen and is
occupied with their
work,
and whose talk is about[j]
bulls?
26He sets his heart on plowing
furrows,
and he is careful about fodder for the heifers.
27So too is every craftsman and
master workman
who labors by night as well
as by day;
those who cut the signets of
seals,
each is diligent in making a
great variety;
he sets his heart on painting a
lifelike image,
and he is careful to finish
his work.
28So too is the smith sitting by the
anvil,
intent upon his handiwork
in iron;
the breath of the fire melts his
flesh,
and he wastes away in[k] the
heat of the furnace;
he inclines his ear to the sound
of the hammer,[l]
and his eyes are on the pattern of the object.
He sets his heart on finishing
his handiwork,
and he is careful to complete
its decoration.
29So too is the potter sitting at his
work
and turning the wheel with
his feet;
he is always deeply concerned
over his work,
and all his output is by
number.
30He moulds the clay with his
arm
and makes it pliable with
his feet;

[i]Gk *him*
[j]Or *among*
[k]Cn Compare Syr: Gk *contends with*
[l]Cn: Gk *the sound of the hammer renews his ear*

he sets his heart to finish the
glazing,
and he is careful to clean the
furnace.
31All these rely upon their hands,
and each is skilful in his
own work.
32Without them a city cannot be
established,
and men can neither sojourn
nor live there.
33Yet they are not sought out for
the council of the people,
nor do they attain emi-
nence in the public
assembly.
They do not sit in the judge's
seat,
nor do they understand the
sentence of judgment;
they cannot expound discipline
or judgment,
and they are not found using
proverbs.
34But they keep stable the fabric of
the world,
and their prayer is in the
practice of their
trade.

THE ACTIVITY OF THE SCRIBE

39 On the other hand he who de-
votes himself
to the study of the law of the
Most High
will seek out the wisdom of all
the ancients,
and will be concerned with
prophecies;
2he will preserve the discourse of
notable men
and penetrate the subtleties
of parables;
3he will seek out the hidden
meanings of proverbs
and be at home with the ob-
scurities of parables.
4He will serve among great men
and appear before rulers;
he will travel through the lands
of foreign nations,
for he tests the good and the
evil among men.
5He will set his heart to rise early
to seek the Lord who made
him,
and will make supplication
before the Most
High;
he will open his mouth in
prayer
and make supplication for
his sins.
6If the great Lord is willing,
he will be filled with
the spirit of
understanding;
he will pour forth words[a] of
wisdom
and give thanks to the Lord
in prayer.
7He will direct his counsel and
knowledge aright,
and meditate on his secrets.
8He will reveal instruction in his
teaching,
and will glory in the law of
the Lord's covenant.
9Many will praise his
understanding,
and it will never be blotted
out;
his memory will not
disappear,
and his name will live
through all
generations.
10Nations will declare his wisdom,
and the congregation will
proclaim his praise;
11if he lives long, he will leave
a name greater than a
thousand,
and if he goes to rest, it is
enough[b] for him.

A HYMN OF PRAISE TO GOD

12I have yet more to say, which I
have thought upon,
and I am filled, like the

[a]Other authorities read *his words*
[b]Cn: the meaning of the Greek is uncertain

moon at the full.
13Listen to me, O you holy sons,
and bud like a rose growing
by a stream of water;
14send forth fragrance like
frankincense,
and put forth blossoms like
a lily.
Scatter the fragrance, and sing
a hymn of praise;
bless the Lord for all his
works;
15ascribe majesty to his name
and give thanks to him with
praise,
with songs on your lips, and
with lyres;
and this you shall say in
thanksgiving:
16"All things are the works of the
Lord, for they are very
good,
and whatever he commands
will be done in his
time."
17No one can say, "What is
this?" "Why is that?"
for in God's[c] time all things
will be sought after.
At his word the waters stood in
a heap,
and the reservoirs of water
at the word of his
mouth.
18At his command whatever pleas-
es him is done,
and none can limit his sav-
ing power.
19The works of all flesh are before
him,
and nothing can be hid from
his eyes.
20From everlasting to everlasting
he beholds them,
and nothing is marvelous
to him.
21No one can say, "What is
this?" "Why is that?"
for everything has been
created for its use.
22His blessing covers the dry land
like a river,
and drenches it like a flood.
23The nations will incur his wrath,
just as he turns fresh water
into salt.
24To the holy his ways are
straight,
just as they are obstacles to
the wicked.
25From the beginning good things
were created for good
people,
just as evil things for
sinners.
26Basic to all the needs of man's
life
are water and fire and iron
and salt
and wheat flour and milk and
honey,
the blood of the grape, and
oil and clothing.
27All these are for good to the
godly,
just as they turn into evils
for sinners.
28There are winds that have been
created for vengeance,
and in their anger they
scourge heavily;
in the time of consummation
they will pour out their
strength
and calm the anger of their
Maker.
29Fire and hail and famine and
pestilence,
all these have been created
for vengeance;
30the teeth of wild beasts, and
scorpions and vipers,
and the sword that punishes
the ungodly with
destruction;
31they will rejoice in his
commands,
and be made ready on earth
for their service,
and when their times come
they will not trans-
gress his word.

[c] Gk *his*

[32]Therefore from the beginning I
have been convinced,
and have thought this out
and left it in writing:
[33]The works of the Lord are all
good,
and he will supply every
need in its hour.
[34]And no one can say, "This is
worse than that,"
for all things will prove good
in their season.
[35]So now sing praise with all your
heart and voice,
and bless the name of the
Lord.

HUMAN WRETCHEDNESS

40 Much labor was created for every
man,
and a heavy yoke is upon the
sons of Adam,
from the day they come forth
from their mother's
womb
till the day they return to[a]
the mother of all.
[2]Their perplexities and fear of
heart—
their anxious thought is the
day of death,
[3]from the man who sits on a
splendid throne
to the one who is humbled in
dust and ashes,
[4]from the man who wears purple
and a crown
to the one who is clothed in
burlap;
[5]there is anger and envy and trou-
ble and unrest,
and fear of death, and fury
and strife.
And when one rests upon his
bed,
his sleep at night confuses
his mind.
[6]He gets little or no rest,
and afterward in his sleep,
as though he were on
watch,
he is troubled by the visions of
his mind
like one who has es-
caped from the
battle-front;
[7]at the moment of his rescue he
wakes up,
and wonders that his fear
came to nothing.
[8]With all flesh, both man and
beast,
and upon sinners seven
times more,
[9]are death and bloodshed and
strife and sword,
calamities, famine and af-
fliction and plague.
[10]All these were created for the
wicked,
and on their account the
flood came.
[11]All things that are from the
earth turn back to the
earth,
and what is from the waters
returns to the sea.

INJUSTICE WILL NOT PROSPER

[12]All bribery and injustice will be
blotted out,
but good faith will stand for
ever.
[13]The wealth of the unjust will dry
up like a torrent,
and crash like a loud clap of
thunder in a rain.
[14]A generous man will be made
glad;
likewise transgressors will
utterly fail.
[15]The children of the ungodly
will not put forth many
branches;
they are unhealthy roots
upon sheer rock.
[16]The reeds by any water or river
bank
will be plucked up before
any grass.
[17]Kindness is like a garden of
blessings,

[a]Other authorities read *are buried in*

Then you will show proper shame,
and will find favor with every man.

42 Of the following things do not be ashamed,
and do not let partiality lead you to sin:
2of the law of the Most High and his covenant,
and of rendering judgment to acquit the ungodly;
3of keeping accounts with a partner or with traveling companions,
and of dividing the inheritance of friends;
4of accuracy with scales and weights,
and of acquiring much or little;
5of profit from dealing with merchants,
and of much discipline of children,
and of whipping a wicked servant severely.[b]
6Where there is an evil wife, a seal is a good thing;
and where there are many hands, lock things up.
7Whatever you deal out, let it be by number and weight,
and make a record of all that you give out or take in.
8Do not be ashamed to instruct the stupid or foolish
or the aged man who quarrels with the young.
Then you will be truly instructed,
and will be approved before all men.

DAUGHTERS AND FATHERS

9A daughter keeps her father secretly wakeful,
and worry over her robs him of sleep;
when she is young, lest she do not marry,
or if married, lest she be hated;
10while a virgin, lest she be defiled
or become pregnant in her father's house;
or having a husband, lest she prove unfaithful,
or, though married, lest she be barren.
11Keep strict watch over a headstrong daughter,
lest she make you a laughingstock to your enemies,
a byword in the city and notorious[c] among the people,
and put you to shame before the great multitude.
12Do not look upon any one for beauty,
and do not sit in the midst of women;
13for from garments comes the moth,
and from a woman comes woman's wickedness.
14Better is the wickedness of a man than a woman who does good;
and it is a woman who brings shame and disgrace.

THE WORKS OF GOD IN NATURE

15I will now call to mind the works of the Lord,
and will declare what I have seen.
By the words of the Lord his works are done.
16The sun looks down on everything with its light,
and the work of the Lord is full of his glory.
17The Lord has not enabled his holy ones
to recount all his marvelous works,

[b] Gk *making the side of a wicked servant bleed*
[c] Gk *called out*

which the Lord the Almighty
has established
that the universe may stand
firm in his glory.
18He searches out the abyss, and
the hearts of men,[a]
and considers their crafty
devices.
For the Most High knows all
that may be known,
and he looks into the signs[b]
of the age.
19He declares what has been and
what is to be,
and he reveals the tracks of
hidden things.
20No thought escapes him,
and not one word is hidden
from him.
21He has ordained the splendors of
his wisdom,
and he is from everlasting
and to everlasting.
Nothing can be added or taken
away,
and he needs no one to be
his counselor.
22How greatly to be desired are all
his works,
and how sparkling they are
to see![c]
23All these things live and remain
for ever
for every need, and are all
obedient.
24All things are twofold, one
opposite the other,
and he has made nothing
incomplete.
25One confirms the good things of
the other,
and who can have enough of
beholding his glory?

THE SPLENDOR OF THE SUN

43 The pride of the heavenly heights
is the clear firmament,
the appearance of heaven in
a spectacle of glory.
2The sun, when it appears, mak-
ing proclamation as it goes
forth,
is a marvelous instrument,
the work of the Most
High.
3At noon it parches the land;
and who can withstand its
burning heat?
4A man tending[d] a furnace works
in burning heat,
but the sun burns the moun-
tains three times as
much;
it breathes out fiery vapors,
and with bright beams it
blinds the eyes.
5Great is the Lord who made it;
and at his command it has-
tens on its course.

THE SPLENDOR OF THE MOON

6He made the moon also, to serve
in its season[e]
to mark the times and to be
an everlasting sign.
7From the moon comes the sign
for feast days,
a light that wanes when it
has reached the full.
8The month is named for the
moon,
increasing marvelously in its
phases,
an instrument of the hosts on
high
shining forth in the firma-
ment of heaven.

THE GLORY OF THE STARS AND THE RAINBOW

9The glory of the stars is the beau-
ty of heaven,
a gleaming array in the
heights of the Lord.
10At the command of the Holy One
they stand as ordered,

[a] Gk *and the heart*
[b] Gk *sign*
[c] The Greek of this line is uncertain
[d] Other authorities read *blowing*
[e] The Greek text of this line is uncertain

they never relax in their
watches.
11 Look upon the rainbow, and
praise him who made it,
exceedingly beautiful in its
brightness.
12 It encircles the heaven with its
glorious arc;
the hands of the Most High
have stretched it out.

THE MARVELS OF NATURE

13 By his command he sends the
driving snow
and speeds the lightnings of
his judgment.
14 Therefore the storehouses are
opened,
and the clouds fly forth like
birds.
15 In his majesty he amasses the
clouds,
and the hailstones are bro-
ken in pieces.
16 At his appearing the mountains
are shaken;
at his will the south wind
blows.
17 The voice of his thunder rebukes
the earth;
so do the tempest from
the north and the
whirlwind.
He scatters the snow like birds
flying down,
and its descent is like lo-
custs alighting.
18 The eye marvels at the beauty of
its whiteness,
and the mind is amazed at
its falling.
19 He pours the hoarfrost upon the
earth like salt,
and when it freezes, it
becomes pointed
thorns.
20 The cold north wind blows,
and ice freezes over the
water;
it rests upon every pool of
water,
and the water puts it on like
a breastplate.
21 He consumes the mountains and
burns up the wilderness,
and withers the tender grass
like fire.
22 A mist quickly heals all things;
when the dew appears, it
refreshes from the
heat.
23 By his counsel he stilled the
great deep
and planted islands in it.
24 Those who sail the sea tell of its
dangers,
and we marvel at what we
hear.
25 for in it are strange and marvel-
ous works,
all kinds of living things,
and huge creatures of
the sea.
26 Because of him his messenger
finds the way,
and by his word all things
hold together.
27 Though we speak much we can-
not reach the end,
and the sum of our words is:
"He is the all."
28 Where shall we find strength to
praise him?
For he is greater than all his
works.
29 Terrible is the Lord and very
great,
and marvelous is his power.
30 When you praise the Lord, exalt
him as much as you can;
for he will surpass even that.
When you exalt him, put forth
all your strength,
and do not grow weary, for
you cannot praise
him enough.
31 Who has seen him and can
describe him?
Or who can extol him as
he is?
32 Many things greater than these
lie hidden,
for we have seen but few of
his works.

33For the Lord has made all
things,
and to the godly he has
granted wisdom.

44 Let us now praise famous men,
and our fathers in their
generations.
2The Lord apportioned to them[a]
great glory,
his majesty from the
beginning.
3There were those who ruled in
their kingdoms,
and were men renowned for
their power,
giving counsel by their
understanding,
and proclaiming prophecies;
4leaders of the people in their
deliberations
and in understanding of
learning for the
people,
wise in their words of
instruction;
5those who composed musical
tunes,
and set forth verses in
writing;
6rich men furnished with
resources,
living peaceably in their
habitations—
7all these were honored in their
generations,
and were the glory of their
times.
8There are some of them who have
left a name,
so that men declare their
praise.
9And there are some who have no
memorial,
who have perished as though
they had not lived;
they have become as though
they had not been born,
and so have their children
after them.
10But these were men of mercy,
whose righteous deeds have
not been forgotten;
11their prosperity will remain with
their descendants,
and their inheritance to
their children's
children.[b]
12Their descendants stand by the
covenants;
their children also, for their
sake.
13Their posterity will continue
for ever,
and their glory will not be
blotted out.
14Their bodies were buried in
peace,
and their name lives to all
generations.
15Peoples will declare their
wisdom,
and the congregation pro-
claims their praise.

ENOCH

16Enoch pleased the Lord, and was
taken up;
he was an example of
repentance to all
generations.

NOAH

17Noah was found perfect and
righteous;
in the time of wrath he was
taken in exchange;
therefore a remnant was left to
the earth
when the flood came.
18Everlasting covenants were
made with him
that all flesh should not
be blotted out by a
flood.

ABRAHAM

19Abraham was the great father of
a multitude of nations,
and no one has been found
like him in glory;

[a]Heb: Gk *created*
[b]Heb Compare Vg Syr: The Greek of this verse is uncertain

20he kept the law of the Most
High,
and was taken into covenant
with him;
he established the covenant in
his flesh,
and when he was tested he
was found faithful.
21Therefore the Lord[c] assured him
by an oath
that the nations would be
blessed through his
posterity;
that he would multiply him like
the dust of the earth,
and exalt his posterity like
the stars,
and cause them to inherit from
sea to sea
and from the River to the
ends of the earth.

ISAAC AND JACOB

22To Isaac also he gave the same
assurance
for the sake of Abraham his
father.
23The blessing of all men and the
covenant
he made to rest upon the
head of Jacob;
he acknowledged him with his
blessings,
and gave him his
inheritance;[d]
he determined his portions,
and distributed them among
twelve tribes.

MOSES

45 From his descendants the Lord[e]
brought forth a man of
mercy,
who found favor in the sight
of all flesh
and was beloved by God and
man,
Moses, whose memory is
blessed.
2He made him equal in glory to
the holy ones,
and made him great in the
fears of his enemies.
3By his words he caused signs to
cease;
the Lord[f] glorified him
in the presence of
kings.
He gave him commands for his
people,
and showed him part of his
glory.
4He sanctified him through faith-
fulness and meekness;
he chose him out of all
mankind.
5He made him hear his voice,
and led him into the thick
darkness,
and gave him the command-
ments face to face,
the law of life and
knowledge,
to teach Jacob the covenant,
and Israel his judgments.

AARON

6He exalted Aaron, the brother of
Moses,[g]
a holy man like him, of the
tribe of Levi.
7He made an everlasting covenant
with him,
and gave him the priesthood
of the people.
He blessed him with splendid
vestments,
and put a glorious robe upon
him.
8He clothed him with superb
perfection,
and strengthened him
with the symbols of
authority,
the linen breeches, the long
robe, and the ephod.

[c] Gk *he*
[d] Heb: Gk *by inheritance*
[e] Gk *he*
[f] Gk *he*
[g] Gk *him*

9And he encircled him with pomegranates,
with very many golden bells round about,
to send forth a sound as he walked,
to make their ringing heard in the temple
as a reminder to the sons of his people;
10with a holy garment, of gold and blue
and purple, the work of an embroiderer;
with the oracle of judgment, Urim and Thummim;
11with twisted scarlet, the work of a craftsman;
with precious stones engraved like signets,
in a setting of gold, the work of a jeweler,
for a reminder, in engraved letters,
according to the number of the tribes of Israel;
12with a gold crown upon his turban,
inscribed like a signet with "Holiness,"
a distinction to be prized, the work of an expert,
the delight of the eyes, richly adorned.
13Before his time there never were such beautiful things.
No outsider ever put them on,
but only his sons
and his descendants perpetually.
14His sacrifices shall be wholly burned
twice every day continually.
15Moses ordained him,
and anointed him with holy oil;
it was an everlasting covenant for him
and for his descendants all the days of heaven,
to minister to the Lord[a] and serve as priest
and bless his people in his name.
16He chose him out of all the living
to offer sacrifice to the Lord,
incense and a pleasing odor as a memorial portion,
to make atonement for the people.[b]
17In his commandments he gave him
authority and statutes and[c] judgments,
to teach Jacob the testimonies,
and to enlighten Israel with his law.
18Outsiders conspired against him,
and envied him in the wilderness,
Dathan and Abi′ram and their men
and the company of Korah, in wrath and anger.
19The Lord saw it and was not pleased,
and in the wrath of his anger they were destroyed;
he wrought wonders against them
to consume them in flaming fire.
20He added glory to Aaron
and gave him a heritage;
he allotted to him the first of the first fruits,
he prepared bread of first fruits in abundance;
21for they eat the sacrifices to the Lord,
which he gave to him and his descendants.
22But in the land of the people he has no inheritance,
and he has no portion among the people;

[a]Gk *him*
[b]Other authorities read *thy people*
[c]Heb: Gk *in covenants of*

for the Lord[d] himself is
his[e] portion and
inheritance.

PHINEHAS

23Phin´ehas the son of Elea´zar is
the third in glory,
for he was zealous in the
fear of the Lord,
and stood fast, when the peo-
ple turned away,
in the ready goodness of his
soul,
and made atonement for
Israel.
24Therefore a covenant of peace
was established with him,
that he should be leader of
the sanctuary and of
his people,
that he and his descendants
should have
the dignity of the priesthood
for ever.
25A covenant was also established
with David,
the son of Jesse, of the tribe
of Judah:
the heritage of the king is from
son to son only;
so the heritage of Aaron is
for his descendants.
26May the Lord[f] grant you wisdom
in your heart
to judge his people in
righteousness,
so that their prosperity may
not vanish,
and that their glory may en-
dure throughout their
generations.[g]

JOSHUA AND CALEB

46 Joshua the son of Nun was
mighty in war,
and was the
successor of Moses in
prophesying.
He became, in accordance with
his name,
a great savior of God's[h]
elect,
to take vengeance on the ene-
mies that rose against
them,
so that he might give Israel
its inheritance.
2How glorious he was when he
lifted his hands
and stretched out his sword
against the cities!
3Who before him ever stood so
firm?
For he waged the wars of the
Lord.
4Was not the sun held back by his
hand?
And did not one day become
as long as two?
5He called upon the Most High,
the Mighty One,
when enemies pressed him
on every side,
6and the great Lord answered him
with hailstones of mighty
power.
He hurled down war upon that
nation,
and at the descent of Beth-
hor´on[i] he destroyed
those who resisted,
so that the nations might know
his armament,
that he was fighting in the
sight of the Lord;
for he wholly followed the
Mighty One.
7And in the days of Moses he did a
loyal deed,
he and Caleb the son of
Jephun´neh:
they withstood the
congregation,[j]

[d] Gk *he*
[e] Other authorities read *your*
[f] Gk *he*
[g] The Greek of this line is obscure
[h] Gk *his*
[i] Compare Joshua 10.11: Greek lacks *of Beth-horon*
[j] Other authorities read *the enemy*

restrained the people from sin,
and stilled their wicked murmuring.
8And these two alone were preserved
out of six hundred thousand people on foot,
to bring them into their inheritance,
into a land flowing with milk and honey.
9And the Lord gave Caleb strength,
which remained with him to old age,
so that he went up to the hill country,
and his children obtained it for an inheritance;
10so that all the sons of Israel might see
that it is good to follow the Lord.

THE JUDGES

11The judges also, with their respective names,
those whose hearts did not fall into idolatry
and who did not turn away from the Lord—
may their memory be blessed!
12May their bones revive from where they lie,
and may the name of those who have been honored
live again in their sons!
13Samuel, beloved by his Lord,
a prophet of the Lord, established the kingdom
and anointed rulers over his people.
14By the law of the Lord he judged the congregation,
and the Lord watched over Jacob.
15By his faithfulness he was proved to be a prophet,
and by his words he became known as a trustworthy seer.
16He called upon the Lord, the Mighty One,
when his enemies pressed him on every side,
and he offered in sacrifice a sucking lamb.
17Then the Lord thundered from heaven,
and made his voice heard with a mighty sound;
18and he wiped out the leaders of the people of Tyre
and all the rulers of the Philistines.
19Before the time of his eternal sleep,
Samuel[a] called men to witness before the Lord and his anointed:
"I have not taken any one's property,
not so much as a pair of shoes."
And no man accused him.
20Even after he had fallen asleep he prophesied
and revealed to the king his death,
and lifted up his voice out of the earth in prophecy,
to blot out the wickedness of the people.

NATHAN

47 And after him Nathan rose up to prophesy in the days of David.

DAVID

2As the fat is selected from the peace offering,
so David was selected from the sons of Israel.
3He played with lions as with young goats,
and with bears as with lambs of the flock.
4In his youth did he not kill a

[a]Gk *he*

giant,
and take away reproach from the people,
when he lifted his hand with a stone in the sling
and struck down the boasting of Goliath?
5For he appealed to the Lord, the Most High,
and he gave him strength in his right hand
to slay a man mighty in war,
to exalt the power[b] of his people.
6So they glorified him for his ten thousands,
and praised him for the blessings of the Lord,
when the glorious diadem was bestowed upon him.
7For he wiped out his enemies on every side,
and annihilated his adversaries the Philistines;
he crushed their power[c] even to this day.
8In all that he did he gave thanks to the Holy One, the Most High, with ascriptions of glory;
he sang praise with all his heart,
and he loved his Maker.
9He placed singers before the altar,
to make sweet melody with their voices.
10He gave beauty to the feasts,
and arranged their times throughout the year,[d]
while they praised God's[e] holy name,
and the sanctuary resounded from early morning.
11The Lord took away his sins,
and exalted his power[f] for ever;
he gave him the covenant of kings
and a throne of glory in Israel.

SOLOMON

12After him rose up a wise son
who fared amply[g] because of him;
13Solomon reigned in days of peace,
and God gave him rest on every side,
that he might build a house for his name
and prepare a sanctuary to stand for ever.
14How wise you became in your youth!
You overflowed like a river with understanding.
15Your soul covered the earth,
and you filled it with parables and riddles.
16Your name reached to far-off islands,
and you were loved for your peace.
17For your songs and proverbs and parables,
and for your interpretations,
the countries marveled at you.
18In the name of the Lord God,
who is called the God of Israel,
you gathered gold like tin
and amassed silver like lead.
19But you laid your loins beside women,
and through your body you were brought into subjection.

[b] Gk *horn*
[c] Gk *horn*
[d] Gk *to completion*
[e] Gk *his*
[f] Gk *horn*
[g] Gk *lived in a broad place*

20You put a stain upon your honor,
and defiled your posterity,
so that you brought wrath upon your children
and they were grieved[a] at your folly,
21so that the sovereignty was divided
and a disobedient kingdom arose out of E´phraim.
22But the Lord will never give up his mercy,
nor cause any of his works to perish;
he will never blot out the descendants of his chosen one,
nor destroy the posterity of him who loved him;
so he gave a remnant to Jacob,
and to David a root of his stock.

REHOBOAM AND JEROBOAM

23Solomon rested with his fathers,
and left behind him one of his sons,
ample in[b] folly and lacking in understanding,
Rehobo´am, whose policy caused the people to revolt.
Also Jerobo´am the son of Nebat, who caused Israel to sin
and gave to E´phraim a sinful way.
24Their sins became exceedingly many,
so as to remove them from their land.
25For they sought out every sort of wickedness,
till vengeance came upon them.

ELIJAH

48 Then the prophet Eli´jah arose like a fire,
and his word burned like a torch.
2He brought a famine upon them,
and by his zeal he made them few in number.
3By the word of the Lord he shut up the heavens,
and also three times brought down fire.
4How glorious you were, O Eli´jah, in your wondrous deeds!
And who has the right to boast which you have?
5You who raised a corpse from death
and from Hades, by the word of the Most High;
6who brought kings down to destruction,
and famous men from their beds;
7who heard rebuke at Sinai
and judgments of vengeance at Horeb;
8who anointed kings to inflict retribution,
and prophets to succeed you.[c]
9You who were taken up by a whirlwind of fire,
in a chariot with horses of fire;
10you who are ready[d] at the appointed time, it is written,
to calm the wrath of God before it breaks out in fury,
to turn the heart of the father to the son,
and to restore the tribes of Jacob.
11Blessed are those who saw you,
and those who have been

[a]Other authorities read *I was grieved*
[b]Heb (with a play on the name Rehoboam) Syr: Gk *the people's*
[c]Heb: Gk *him*
[d]Heb: Gk *are for reproofs*

adorned[e] in love;
for we also shall surely live.[f]

ELISHA

12It was Eli´jah who was covered
by the whirlwind,
and Eli´sha was filled with
his spirit;
in all his days he did not trem-
ble before any ruler,
and no one brought him into
subjection.
13Nothing was too hard for him,
and when he was dead his
body prophesied.
14As in his life he did wonders,
so in death his deeds were
marvelous.
15For all this the people did not
repent,
and they did not forsake
their sins,
till they were carried away cap-
tive from their land
and were scattered over all
the earth;
the people were left very few in
number,
but with rulers from the
house of David.
16Some of them did what was
pleasing to God,[g]
but others multiplied sins.

HEZEKIAH

17Hezeki´ah fortified his city,
and brought water into the
midst of it;
he tunneled the sheer rock
with iron
and built pools for water.
18In his days Sennach´erib came
up,
and sent the Rab´shakeh;[h]
he lifted up his hand against
Zion
and made great boasts in his
arrogance.
19Then their hearts were shaken
and their hands trembled,
and they were in anguish,
like women in
travail.
20But they called upon the Lord
who is merciful,
spreading forth their hands
toward him;
and the Holy One quickly heard
them from heaven,
and delivered them by the
hand of Isaiah.
21The Lord[i] smote the camp of the
Assyrians,
and his angel wiped them
out.
22For Hezeki´ah did what was
pleasing to the Lord,
and he held strongly to the
ways of David his
father,
which Isaiah the prophet
commanded,
who was great and faithful
in his vision.

ISAIAH

23In his days the sun went
backward,
and he lengthened the life of
the king.
24By the spirit of might he saw the
last things,
and comforted those who
mourned in Zion.
25He revealed what was to occur
to the end of time,
and the hidden things before
they came to pass.

JOSIAH AND OTHER WORTHIES

49 The memory of Josi´ah is like a
blending of incense
prepared by the art of the
perfumer;
it is sweet as honey to every
mouth,

[e]Other authorities read *who have died*
[f]The text and meaning of this verse are uncertain
[g]Gk lacks *to God*
[h]Other authorities add *and departed*
[i]Gk *he*

and like music at a banquet
of wine.
2He was led aright in converting
the people,
and took away the abominations of iniquity.
3He set his heart upon the Lord;
in the days of wicked men
he strengthened
godliness.
4Except David and Hezeki´ah and
Josi´ah
they all sinned greatly,
for they forsook the law of the
Most High;
the kings of Judah came to
an end;
5for they gave their power to
others,
and their glory to a foreign
nation,
6who set fire to the chosen city of
the sanctuary,
and made her streets
desolate,
according to the word[a] of
Jeremiah.
7For they had afflicted him;
yet he had been consecrated in the womb as
prophet,
to pluck up and afflict and
destroy,
and likewise to build and to
plant.
8It was Ezekiel who saw the vision
of glory
which God[b] showed him
above the chariot of
the cherubim.
9For God[c] remembered his enemies with storm,
and did good to those who
directed their ways
aright.[d]
10May the bones of the twelve
prophets
revive from where they lie,
for they comforted the people
of Jacob
and delivered them with
confident hope.
11How shall we magnify
Zerub´babel?
He was like a signet on the
right hand,
12and so was Jeshua the son
of Jo´zadak;
in their days they built the
house
and raised a temple[e] holy to
the Lord,
prepared for everlasting
glory.
13The memory of Nehemi´ah also
is lasting;
he raised for us the walls
that had fallen,
and set up the gates and bars
and rebuilt our ruined
houses.

RETROSPECT

14No one like Enoch has been
created on earth,
for he was taken up from the
earth.
15And no man like Joseph[f] has
been born,
and his bones are cared for.
16Shem and Seth were honored
among men,
and Adam above every living
being in the creation.

SIMON SON OF ONIAS

50 The leader of his brethren and
the pride of his people[g]
was Simon the high priest,
son of Onias,
who in his life repaired the
house,
and in his time fortified the

[a] Gk *by the hand*
[b] Gk *he*
[c] Gk *he*
[d] The text and meaning of this verse are uncertain
[e] Other authorities read *people*
[f] Heb Syr: Greek adds *the leader of his brothers, the support of the people*
[g] Heb Syr: Greek lacks this line. Compare 49.15

temple.
2He laid the foundations for the
high double walls,[h]
the high retaining walls for
the temple enclosure.
3In his days a cistern for water
was quarried out,[i]
a reservoir like the sea in
circumference.
4He considered how to save his
people from ruin,
and fortified the city to
withstand a siege.
5How glorious he was when the
people gathered round him
as he came out of the inner
sanctuary![j]
6Like the morning star among the
clouds,
like the moon when it is full;
7like the sun shining upon the
temple of the Most High,
and like the rainbow
gleaming in glorious
clouds;
8like roses in the days of the first
fruits,
like lilies by a spring of
water,
like a green shoot on
Leb´anon[k] on a sum-
mer day;
9like fire and incense in the
censer,
like a vessel of hammered
gold
adorned with all kinds of
precious stones;
10like an olive tree putting forth
its fruit,
and like a cypress towering
in the clouds.
11When he put on his glorious
robe
and clothed himself with
superb perfection
and went up to the holy altar,
he made the court of the
sanctuary glorious.
12And when he received the por-
tions from the hands of the
priests,
as he stood by the hearth of
the altar
with a garland of brethren
around him,
he was like a young cedar on
Leb´anon;
and they surrounded him like
the trunks of palm
trees,
13all the sons of Aaron in
their splendor
with the Lord's offering in
their hands,
before the whole congrega-
tion of Israel.
14Finishing the service at the
altars,
and arranging the offering
to the Most High, the
Almighty,
15he reached out his hand to the
cup
and poured a libation of the
blood of the grape;
he poured it out at the foot of
the altar,
a pleasing odor to the Most
High, the King of all.
16Then the sons of Aaron shouted,
they sounded the trumpets
of hammered work,
they made a great noise to be
heard
for remembrance before the
Most High.
17Then all the people together
made haste
and fell to the ground upon
their faces
to worship their Lord,
the Almighty, God Most
High.
18And the singers praised him
with their voices

[h]The meaning of this phrase is obscure
[i]Cn Compare Heb: Gk *was diminished*
[j]Gk the house of the veil
[k]Or *a sprig of frankincense*

in sweet and full-toned
melody.[a]
19And the people besought the
Lord Most High
in prayer before him who is
merciful,
till the order of worship of the
Lord was ended;
so they completed his
service.
20Then Simon[b] came down, and
lifted up his hands
over the whole congrega-
tion of the sons of
Israel,
to pronounce the blessing of
the Lord with his lips,
and to glory in his name;
21and they bowed down in worship
a second time,
to receive the blessing from
the Most High.

A BENEDICTION

22And now bless the God of all,
who in every way does great
things;
who exalts our days from
birth,
and deals with us according
to his mercy.
23May he give us[c] gladness of
heart,
and grant that peace may
be in our days in
Israel,
as in the days of old.
24May he entrust to us his mercy!
And let him deliver us in
our[d] days!

EPILOGUE

25With two nations my soul is
vexed,
and the third is no nation:
26Those who live on Mount Se´ir,[e]
and the Philistines,
and the foolish people that
dwell in Shechem.
27Instruction in understanding
and knowledge
I have written in this book,
Jesus the son of Sirach, son of
Elea´zar,[f] of Jerusalem,
who out of his heart poured
forth wisdom.
28Blessed is he who concerns him-
self with these things,
and he who lays them to
heart will become
wise.
29For if he does them, he will be
strong for all things,
for the light of the Lord is
his path.

51 I will give thanks to thee, O Lord
and King,
and will praise thee as God
my Savior.
I give thanks to thy name,
2for thou hast been my pro-
tector and helper
and hast delivered my body
from destruction
and from the snare of a slan-
derous tongue,
from lips that utter lies.
Before those who stood by
thou wast my helper,
3and didst deliver me,
in the greatness of thy mercy
and of thy name,
from the gnashings of teeth
about to devour me,[g]
from the hand of those who
sought my life,
from the many afflictions
that I endured,
4from choking fire on every side
and from the midst of fire
which I did not
kindle,
5from the depths of the belly of

[a] Other authorities read *in sweet melody throughout the house*
[b] Gk *he*
[c] Other authorities read *you*
[d] Other authorities read *his*
[e] Heb Vg: Gk *on the mountain of Samaria*
[f] The text of this line is uncertain
[g] Cn Compare Vg: Gk *when I was about to be devoured*

Hades,
from an unclean tongue and lying words—
6the slander of an unrighteous tongue to the king.
My soul drew near to death,
and my life was very near to Hades beneath.
7They surrounded me on every side,
and there was no one to help me;
I looked for the assistance of men,
and there was none.
8Then I remembered thy mercy, O Lord,
and thy work from of old,
that thou dost deliver those who wait for thee
and dost save them from the hand of their enemies.
9And I sent up my supplication from the earth,
and prayed for deliverance from death.
10I appealed to the Lord, the Father of my lord,
not to forsake me in the days of affliction,
at the time when there is no help against the proud.
11I will praise thy name continually,
and will sing praise with thanksgiving.
My prayer was heard,
12for thou didst save me from destruction
and rescue me from an evil plight.
Therefore I will give thanks to thee and praise thee,
and I will bless the name of the Lord.

AUTOBIOGRAPHICAL POEM ON WISDOM

13While I was still young, before I went on my travels,
I sought wisdom openly in my prayer.
14Before the temple I asked for her,
and I will search for her to the last.
15From blossom to[h] ripening grape
my heart delighted in her;
my foot entered upon the straight path;
from my youth I followed her steps.
16I inclined my ear a little and received her,
and I found for myself much instruction.
17I made progress therein;
to him who gives wisdom I will give glory.
18For I resolved to live according to wisdom,[i]
and I was zealous for the good;
and I shall never be put to shame.
19My soul grappled with wisdom,[j]
and in my conduct I was strict;[k]
I spread out my hands to the heavens,
and lamented my ignorance of her.
20I directed my soul to her,
and through purification I found her.
I gained understanding[l] with her from the first,
therefore I will not be forsaken.
21My heart was stirred to seek her,
therefore I have gained a good possession.
22The Lord gave me a tongue as my reward,
and I will praise him with it.

[h] Other authorities read *As from*
[i] Gk *her*
[j] Gk *her*
[k] The Greek text of this line is uncertain
[l] Gk *heart*

23Draw near to me, you who are
untaught,
and lodge in my school.
24Why do you say you are lacking
in these things,[a]
and why are your souls very
thirsty?
25I opened my mouth and said,
Get these things[b] for
yourselves without
money.
26Put your neck under the yoke,
and let your souls receive
instruction;
it is to be found close by.
27See with your eyes that I have
labored little
and found for myself much
rest.
28Get instruction with a large sum
of silver,
and you will gain by it much
gold.
29May your soul rejoice in his
mercy,
and may you not be put to
shame when you
praise him.
30Do your work before the ap-
pointed time,
and in God's[c] time he will
give you your reward.

[a]Cn Compare Heb Syr: The Greek text of this line is uncertain
[b]Greek lacks *these things*
[c]Gk *his*

THE BOOK OF

ISAIAH

1 The vision of Isaiah the son of Amoz,
which he saw concerning Judah and
Jerusalem in the days of Uzzi´ah, Jo-
tham, Ahaz, and Hezeki´ah, kings of
Judah.

THE WICKEDNESS OF JUDAH

2Hear, O heavens, and give ear, O
earth;
for the LORD has spoken:
"Sons have I reared and
brought up,
but they have rebelled
against me.
3The ox knows its owner,
and the ass its master's
crib;
but Israel does not know,
my people does not
understand."
4Ah, sinful nation,
a people laden with
iniquity,
offspring of evildoers,
sons who deal corruptly!
They have forsaken the LORD,
they have despised the Holy
One of Israel,
they are utterly estranged.
5Why will you still be smitten,
that you continue to rebel?
The whole head is sick,
and the whole heart faint.
6From the sole of the foot even to
the head,
there is no soundness in it,
but bruises and sores
and bleeding wounds;
they are not pressed out, or
bound up,
or softened with oil.
7Your country lies desolate,
your cities are burned with
fire;
in your very presence
aliens devour your land;
it is desolate, as overthrown
by aliens.
8And the daughter of Zion is left
like a booth in a vineyard,
like a lodge in a cucumber
field,
like a besieged city.
9If the LORD of hosts
had not left us a few
survivors,
we should have been like
Sodom,
and become like Gomor´rah.
10Hear the word of the LORD,
you rulers of Sodom!
Give ear to the teaching of our
God,
you people of Gomor´rah!
11"What to me is the multitude of
your sacrifices?
says the LORD;
I have had enough of burnt
offerings of rams
and the fat of fed beasts;
I do not delight in the blood of
bulls,
or of lambs, or of he-goats.
12"When you come to appear
before me,
who requires of you
this trampling of my
courts?
13Bring no more vain offerings;
incense is an abomination
to me.
New moon and sabbath
and the calling of
assemblies—
I cannot endure iniq-
uity and solemn
assembly.
14Your new moons and your ap-
pointed feasts
my soul hates;
they have become a burden
to me,
I am weary of bearing them.
15When you spread forth your
hands,
I will hide my eyes from you;

even though you make many prayers,
I will not listen;
your hands are full of blood.
16 Wash yourselves; make yourselves clean;
remove the evil of your doings
from before my eyes;
cease to do evil,
17 learn to do good;
seek justice,
correct oppression;
defend the fatherless,
plead for the widow.
18 "Come now, let us reason together,
says the LORD:
though your sins are like scarlet,
they shall be as white as snow;
though they are red like crimson,
they shall become like wool.
19 If you are willing and obedient,
you shall eat the good of the land;
20 but if you refuse and rebel,
you shall be devoured by the sword;
for the mouth of the LORD has spoken."

THE DEGENERATE CITY

21 How the faithful city
has become a harlot,
she that was full of justice!
Righteousness lodged in her,
but now murderers.
22 Your silver has become dross,
your wine mixed with water.
23 Your princes are rebels
and companions of thieves.
Every one loves a bribe
and runs after gifts.
They do not defend the fatherless,
and the widow's cause does not come to them.
24 Therefore the Lord says,
the LORD of hosts,
the Mighty One of Israel:
"Ah, I will vent my wrath on my enemies,
and avenge myself on my foes.
25 I will turn my hand against you
and will smelt away your dross as with lye
and remove all your alloy.
26 And I will restore your judges as at the first,
and your counselors as at the beginning.
Afterward you shall be called the city of righteousness,
the faithful city."
27 Zion shall be redeemed by justice,
and those in her who repent, by righteousness.
28 But rebels and sinners shall be destroyed together,
and those who forsake the LORD shall be consumed.
29 For you shall be ashamed of the oaks
in which you delighted;
and you shall blush for the gardens
which you have chosen.
30 For you shall be like an oak
whose leaf withers,
and like a garden without water.
31 And the strong shall become tow,
and his work a spark,
and both of them shall burn together,
with none to quench them.

THE FUTURE HOUSE OF GOD

2 The word which Isaiah the son of Amoz saw concerning Judah and Jerusalem.
2 It shall come to pass in the latter days

that the mountain of the
house of the LORD
shall be established as
the highest of the
mountains,
and shall be raised above the
hills;
and all the nations shall flow
to it,
3and many peoples shall
come, and say:
"Come, let us go up to the
mountain of the LORD,
to the house of the God of
Jacob;
that he may teach us his ways
and that we may walk in his
paths."
For out of Zion shall go forth
the law,
and the word of the LORD
from Jerusalem.
4He shall judge between the
nations,
and shall decide for many
peoples;
and they shall beat
their swords into
plowshares,
and their spears into prun-
ing hooks;
nation shall not lift up sword
against nation,
neither shall they learn war
any more.*

JUDGMENT PRONOUNCED ON ARROGANCE

5O house of Jacob,
come, let us walk
in the light of the LORD.
6For thou hast rejected thy
people,
the house of Jacob,
because they are full of divin-
ers[a] from the east
and of soothsayers like the
Philistines,
and they strike hands with
foreigners.
7Their land is filled with silver
and gold,
and there is no end to their
treasures;
their land is filled with horses,
and there is no end to their
chariots.
8Their land is filled with idols;
they bow down to the work
of their hands,
to what their own fingers
have made.
9So man is humbled,
and men are brought low—
forgive them not!
10Enter into the rock,
and hide in the dust
from before the terror of the
LORD,
and from the glory of his
majesty.
11The haughty looks of man shall
be brought low,
and the pride of men shall
be humbled;
and the LORD alone will be
exalted
in that day.
12For the LORD of hosts has a day
against all that is proud and
lofty,
against all that is lifted up
and high;[b]
13against all the cedars of
Lebanon,
lofty and lifted up;
and against all the oaks of
Bashan;
14against all the high mountains,
and against all the lofty
hills;
15against every high tower,
and against every fortified
wall;
16against all the ships of Tarshish,
and against all the beautiful
craft.
17And the haughtiness of man
shall be humbled,
and the pride of men shall
be brought low;

[a]Cn: Heb lacks *of diviners*
[b]Cn Compare Gk: Heb *low*

and the LORD alone will be
exalted in that day.
18And the idols shall utterly pass
away.
19And men shall enter the caves of
the rocks
and the holes of the
ground,
from before the terror of the
LORD,
and from the glory of his
majesty,
when he rises to terrify the
earth.
20In that day men will cast forth
their idols of silver and their
idols of gold,
which they made for them-
selves to worship,
to the moles and to the
bats,
21to enter the caverns of the
rocks
and the clefts of the cliffs,
from before the terror of the
LORD,
and from the glory of his
majesty,
when he rises to terrify the
earth.
22Turn away from man
in whose nostrils is breath,
for of what account is he?

3 For, behold, the Lord, the LORD
of hosts,
is taking away from
Jerusalem and from
Judah
stay and staff,
the whole stay of bread,
and the whole stay of
water;
2the mighty man and the soldier,
the judge and the prophet,
the diviner and the elder,
3the captain of fifty
and the man of rank,
the counselor and the skilful
magician
and the expert in charms.
4And I will make boys their
princes,
and babes shall rule over
them.
5And the people will oppress one
another,
every man his fellow
and every man his
neighbor;
the youth will be insolent to
the elder,
and the base fellow to the
honorable.
6When a man takes hold of his
brother
in the house of his father,
saying:
"You have a mantle;
you shall be our leader,
and this heap of ruins
shall be under your rule";
7in that day he will speak out,
saying:
"I will not be a healer;
in my house there is neither
bread nor mantle;
you shall not make me
leader of the people."
8For Jerusalem has stumbled,
and Judah has fallen;
because their speech and their
deeds are against the
LORD,
defying his glorious
presence.
9Their partiality witnesses against
them;
they proclaim their sin like
Sodom,
they do not hide it.
Woe to them!
For they have brought evil
upon themselves.
10Tell the righteous that it shall be
well with them,
for they shall eat the fruit of
their deeds.
11Woe to the wicked! It shall be ill
with him,
for what his hands have
done shall be done
to him.
12My people—children are their
oppressors,

and women rule over them.
O my people, your leaders
mislead you,
and confuse the course of
your paths.
13The LORD has taken his place to
contend,
he stands to judge his
people.[a]
14The LORD enters into judgment
with the elders and princes
of his people:
"It is you who have devoured
the vineyard,
the spoil of the poor is in
your houses.
15What do you mean by crushing
my people,
by grinding the face of the poor?"
says the Lord GOD of
hosts.
16The LORD said:
Because the daughters of Zion
are haughty
and walk with outstretched
necks,
glancing wantonly with their
eyes,
mincing along as they go,
tinkling with their feet;
17the Lord will smite with a scab
the heads of the daughters
of Zion,
and the LORD will lay bare
their secret parts.

18 In that day the Lord will take
away the finery of the anklets, the
headbands, and the crescents; 19the
pendants, the bracelets, and the
scarfs; 20the headdresses, the arm-
lets, the sashes, the perfume boxes,
and the amulets; 21the signet rings
and nose rings; 22the festal robes, the
mantles, the cloaks, and the hand-
bags; 23the garments of gauze, the
linen garments, the turbans, and the
veils.

24Instead of perfume there will be
rottenness;
and instead of a girdle, a
rope;
and instead of well-set hair,
baldness;
and instead of a rich robe, a
girding of sackcloth;
instead of beauty, shame.[b]
25Your men shall fall by the
sword
and your mighty men in
battle.
26And her gates shall lament and
mourn;
ravaged, she shall sit upon
the ground.

4 And seven women shall take hold
of one man in that day, saying,
"We will eat our own bread and
wear our own clothes, only let us be
called by your name; take away our
reproach."

THE FUTURE GLORY OF THE SURVIVORS IN ZION

2 In that day the branch of the
LORD shall be beautiful and glorious,
and the fruit of the land shall be the
pride and glory of the survivors of
Israel. 3And he who is left in Zion and
remains in Jerusalem will be called
holy, every one who has been record-
ed for life in Jerusalem, 4when the
Lord shall have washed away the filth
of the daughters of Zion and cleansed
the bloodstains of Jerusalem from its
midst by a spirit of judgment and by
a spirit of burning. 5Then the LORD
will create over the whole site of
Mount Zion and over her assemblies
a cloud by day, and smoke and the
shining of a flaming fire by night;
for over all the glory there will be a
canopy and a pavilion. 6It will be for
a shade by day from the heat, and for
a refuge and a shelter from the storm
and rain.

THE SONG OF THE UNFRUITFUL VINEYARD

5 *Let me sing for my beloved
a love song concerning his
vineyard:

[a]Gk Syr: Heb *judge peoples*
[b]One ancient Ms: Heb lacks *shame*

My beloved had a vineyard
on a very fertile hill.
2He digged it and cleared it of stones,
and planted it with choice vines;
he built a watchtower in the midst of it,
and hewed out a wine vat in it;
and he looked for it to yield grapes,
but it yielded wild grapes.
3And now, O inhabitants of Jerusalem
and men of Judah,
judge, I pray you, between me
and my vineyard.
4What more was there to do for my vineyard,
that I have not done in it?
When I looked for it to yield grapes,
why did it yield wild grapes?
5And now I will tell you
what I will do to my vineyard.
I will remove its hedge,
and it shall be devoured;
I will break down its wall,
and it shall be trampled down.
6I will make it a waste;
it shall not be pruned or hoed,
and briers and thorns shall grow up;
I will also command the clouds
that they rain no rain upon it.
7For the vineyard of the LORD of hosts
is the house of Israel,
and the men of Judah
are his pleasant planting;
and he looked for justice,
but behold, bloodshed;
for righteousness,
but behold, a cry!

SOCIAL INJUSTICE DENOUNCED

8Woe to those who join house to house,
who add field to field,
until there is no more room,
and you are made to dwell alone
in the midst of the land.
9The LORD of hosts has sworn in my hearing:
"Surely many houses shall be desolate,
large and beautiful houses,
without inhabitant.
10For ten acres of vineyard shall yield but one bath,
and a homer of seed shall yield but an ephah."
11Woe to those who rise early in the morning,
that they may run after strong drink,
who tarry late into the evening
till wine inflames them!
12They have lyre and harp,
timbrel and flute and wine at their feasts;
but they do not regard the deeds of the LORD,
or see the work of his hands.
13Therefore my people go into exile
for want of knowledge;
their honored men are dying of hunger,
and their multitude is parched with thirst.
14Therefore Sheol has enlarged its appetite
and opened its mouth beyond measure,
and the nobility of Jerusalem[a]
and her multitude go down,
her throng and he who exults in her.
15Man is bowed down, and men are brought low,
and the eyes of the haughty

[a] Heb *her nobility*

are humbled.
16But the LORD of hosts is exalted
in justice,
and the Holy God shows
himself holy in
righteousness.
17Then shall the lambs graze as in
their pasture,
fatlings and kids[b] shall
feed among the
ruins.
18Woe to those who draw
iniquity with cords of
falsehood,
who draw sin as with cart
ropes,
19who say: "Let him make haste,
let him speed his work
that we may see it;
let the purpose of the Holy
One of Israel draw
near,
and let it come, that we may
know it!"
20Woe to those who call evil
good
and good evil,
who put darkness for light
and light for darkness,
who put bitter for sweet
and sweet for bitter!
21Woe to those who are wise in
their own eyes,
and shrewd in their own
sight!
22Woe to those who are heroes at
drinking wine,
and valiant men in mixing
strong drink,
23who acquit the guilty for a
bribe,
and deprive the innocent of
his right!

FOREIGN INVASION PREDICTED

24Therefore, as the tongue of fire
devours the stubble,
and as dry grass sinks down
in the flame,
so their root will be as
rottenness,
and their blossom go up like
dust;
for they have rejected the law
of the LORD of hosts,
and have despised the word
of the Holy One of
Israel.
25Therefore the anger of the LORD
was kindled against his
people,
and he stretched out his
hand against them
and smote them,
and the mountains quaked;
and their corpses were as
refuse
in the midst of the streets.
For all this his anger is not
turned away
and his hand is stretched
out still.
26He will raise a signal for a na-
tion afar off,
and whistle for it from the
ends of the earth;
and lo, swiftly, speedily it
comes!
27None is weary, none stumbles,
none slumbers or sleeps,
not a waistcloth is loose,
not a sandal-thong broken;
28their arrows are sharp,
all their bows bent,
their horses' hoofs seem like
flint,
and their wheels like the
whirlwind.
29Their roaring is like a lion,
like young lions they roar;
they growl and seize their
prey,
they carry it off, and none
can rescue.
30They will growl over it on that
day,
like the roaring of the sea.
And if one look to the land,
behold, darkness and
distress;
and the light is darkened by its
clouds.

[b] Cn Compare Gk: Heb *aliens*

A VISION OF GOD IN THE TEMPLE

6 *In the year that King Uzzi´ah
died I saw the Lord sitting upon a
throne, high and lifted up; and his
train filled the temple. 2Above him
stood the seraphim; each had six
wings: with two he covered his face,
and with two he covered his feet, and
with two he flew. 3And one called to
another and said:

"Holy, holy, holy is the LORD
of hosts;
the whole earth is full of his
glory."

4And the foundations of the
thresholds shook at the voice of him
who called, and the house was filled
with smoke. 5And I said: "Woe is me!
For I am lost; for I am a man of un-
clean lips, and I dwell in the midst
of a people of unclean lips; for my
eyes have seen the King, the LORD of
hosts!"

6 Then flew one of the seraphim
to me, having in his hand a burning
coal which he had taken with tongs
from the altar. 7And he touched my
mouth, and said: "Behold, this has
touched your lips; your guilt is taken
away, and your sin forgiven." 8And I
heard the voice of the Lord saying,
"Whom shall I send, and who will
go for us?" Then I said, "Here am I!
Send me." 9And he said, "Go, and say
to this people:

'Hear and hear, but do not
understand;
see and see, but do not
perceive.'
10Make the heart of this people
fat,
and their ears heavy,
and shut their eyes;
lest they see with their eyes,
and hear with their ears,
and understand with their
hearts,
and turn and be healed."

11Then I said, "How long, O
Lord?"
And he said:

"Until cities lie waste
without inhabitant,
and houses without men,
and the land is utterly
desolate,
12and the LORD removes men far
away,
and the forsaken places are
many in the midst of
the land.
13And though a tenth remain
in it,
it will be burned again,
like a terebinth or an oak,
whose stump remains
standing
when it is felled."
The holy seed is its stump.

ISAIAH REASSURES KING AHAZ

7 In the days of Ahaz the son of
Jotham, son of Uzzi´ah, king of
Judah, Rezin the king of Syria and
Pekah the son of Remali´ah the king
of Israel came up to Jerusalem to
wage war against it, but they could
not conquer it. 2When the house of
David was told, "Syria is in league
with E´phraim," his heart and the
heart of his people shook as the
trees of the forest shake before the
wind.

3 And the LORD said to Isaiah,
"Go forth to meet Ahaz, you and
She´ar-jash´ub[a] your son, at the end
of the conduit of the upper pool on
the highway to the Fuller's Field, 4and
say to him, 'Take heed, be quiet, do
not fear, and do not let your heart be
faint because of these two smoldering
stumps of firebrands, at the fierce
anger of Rezin and Syria and the son
of Remali´ah. 5Because Syria, with
E´phraim and the son of Remali´ah,
has devised evil against you, saying,
6"Let us go up against Judah and ter-
rify it, and let us conquer it for our-
selves, and set up the son of Ta´be-el
as king in the midst of it," 7thus says
the Lord GOD:

[a]That is *A remnant shall return*

It shall not stand,
and it shall not come to pass.
8For the head of Syria is Damascus,
and the head of Damascus is Rezin.
(Within sixty-five years E´phraim will be broken to pieces so that it will no longer be a people.)
9And the head of E´phraim is Samar´ia,
and the head of Samar´ia is the son of Remali´ah.
If you will not believe,
surely you shall not be established.'"

ISAIAH GIVES AHAZ THE SIGN OF IMMANUEL

10 Again the LORD spoke to Ahaz,
11"Ask a sign of the LORD your God; let
it be deep as Sheol or high as heaven."
12But Ahaz said, "I will not ask, and
I will not put the LORD to the test."
13And he said, "Hear then, O house of
David! Is it too little for you to wea-
ry men, that you weary my God also?
14Therefore the Lord himself will give
you a sign. Behold, a young wom-
an[b]* shall conceive and bear[c] a son,
and shall call his name Imman´u-el.[d]
15He shall eat curds and honey when
he knows how to refuse the evil and
choose the good. 16For before the
child knows how to refuse the evil
and choose the good, the land before
whose two kings you are in dread will
be deserted. 17The LORD will bring
upon you and upon your people and
upon your father's house such days
as have not come since the day that
E´phraim departed from Judah—the
king of Assyria."

18 In that day the LORD will whis-
tle for the fly which is at the sources
of the streams of Egypt, and for the
bee which is in the land of Assyria.
19And they will all come and settle in
the steep ravines, and in the clefts of
the rocks, and on all the thornbushes,
and on all the pastures.

20 In that day the Lord will shave with a razor which is hired beyond the River—with the king of Assyria—the head and the hair of the feet, and it will sweep away the beard also.

21 In that day a man will keep alive
a young cow and two sheep; 22and be-
cause of the abundance of milk which
they give, he will eat curds; for every
one that is left in the land will eat
curds and honey.

23 In that day every place where
there used to be a thousand vines,
worth a thousand shekels of silver,
will become briers and thorns. 24With
bow and arrows men will come there,
for all the land will be briers and
thorns; 25and as for all the hills which
used to be hoed with a hoe, you will
not come there for fear of briers and
thorns; but they will become a place
where cattle are let loose and where
sheep tread.

ISAIAH'S SON A SIGN OF THE ASSYRIAN INVASION

8 Then the LORD said to me, "Take
a large tablet and write upon it in
common characters, 'Belonging to
Ma´her-shal´al-hash´baz.'"[e] 2And
I got reliable witnesses, Uri´ah the
priest and Zechari´ah the son of
Jeberechi´ah, to attest for me. 3And
I went to the prophetess, and she
conceived and bore a son. Then the
LORD said to me, "Call his name
Ma´her-shal´al-hash´baz; 4for before
the child knows how to cry 'My fa-
ther' or 'My mother,' the wealth of
Damascus and the spoil of Samar´ia
will be carried away before the king
of Assyria."

[b]Or *virgin*
[c]Or *is with child and shall bear*
[d]That is *God is with us*
[e]That is *The spoil speeds, the prey hastes*

5 The LORD spoke to me again:
6"Because this people have refused
the waters of Shilo´ah that flow gen-
tly, and melt in fear before[a] Rezin
and the son of Remali´ah; 7there-
fore, behold, the Lord is bringing
up against them the waters of the
River, mighty and many, the king
of Assyria and all his glory; and it
will rise over all its channels and
go over all its banks; 8and it will
sweep on into Judah, it will over-
flow and pass on, reaching even to
the neck; and its outspread wings
will fill the breadth of your land, O
Imman´u-el."

9Be broken, you peoples, and be dismayed;
give ear, all you far countries;
gird yourselves and be dismayed;
gird yourselves and be dismayed.
10Take counsel together, but it will come to nought;
speak a word, but it will not stand,
for God is with us.[b]

11 For the LORD spoke thus to
me with his strong hand upon me,
and warned me not to walk in the
way of this people, saying: 12"Do not
call conspiracy all that this people
call conspiracy, and do not fear what
they fear, nor be in dread. 13But the
LORD of hosts, him you shall re-
gard as holy; let him be your fear,
and let him be your dread. 14And
he will become a sanctuary, and a
stone of offense, and a rock of stum-
bling to both houses of Israel, a trap
and a snare to the inhabitants of
Jerusalem. 15And many shall stum-
ble thereon; they shall fall and be
broken; they shall be snared and
taken."

DISCIPLES OF ISAIAH

16 Bind up the testimony, seal the
teaching among my disciples. 17I will
wait for the LORD, who is hiding his
face from the house of Jacob, and I
will hope in him. 18Behold, I and
the children whom the LORD has
given me are signs and portents in
Israel from the LORD of hosts, who
dwells on Mount Zion. 19And when
they say to you, "Consult the medi-
ums and the wizards who chirp and
mutter," should not a people consult
their God? Should they consult the
dead on behalf of the living? 20To
the teaching and to the testimo-
ny! Surely for this word which they
speak there is no dawn. 21They will
pass through the land,[c] greatly dis-
tressed and hungry; and when they
are hungry, they will be enraged
and will curse[d] their king and their
God, and turn their faces upward;
22and they will look to the earth, but
behold, distress and darkness, the
gloom of anguish; and they will be
thrust into thick darkness.

THE RIGHTEOUS REIGN OF THE COMING KING

9[e] But there will be no gloom for
her that was in anguish. In the for-
mer time he brought into contempt
the land of Zeb´ulun and the land of
Naph´tali, but in the latter time he
will make glorious the way of the sea,
the land beyond the Jordan, Galilee of
the nations.

2[f] The people who walked in darkness
have seen a great light;
those who dwelt in a land of deep darkness,
on them has light shined.
3Thou hast multiplied the nation,
thou hast increased its joy;
they rejoice before thee

[a]Cn: Heb *rejoices in*
[b]Heb *immanu el*
[c]Heb *it*
[d]Or *curse by*
[e]Ch 8.23 in Heb
[f]Ch 9.1 in Heb

as with joy at the harvest,
as men rejoice when they
divide the spoil.
4For the yoke of his burden,
and the staff for his
shoulder,
the rod of his oppressor,
thou hast broken as on the
day of Mid´ian.
5For every boot of the tramping
warrior in battle tumult
and every garment rolled in
blood
will be burned as fuel for
the fire.
6For to us a child is born,
to us a son is given;
and the government will be
upon his shoulder,
and his name will be called
"Wonderful Counselor, Mighty
God,
Everlasting Father, Prince of
Peace."*
7Of the increase of his govern-
ment and of peace
there will be no end,
upon the throne of David, and
over his kingdom,
to establish it, and to
uphold it
with justice and with
righteousness
from this time forth and for
evermore.
The zeal of the LORD of hosts
will do this.

JUDGMENT ON ARROGANCE AND OPPRESSION

8The Lord has sent a word against
Jacob,
and it will light upon
Israel;
9and all the people will know,
E´phraim and the inhabi-
tants of Samar´ia,
who say in pride and in arro-
gance of heart:
10"The bricks have fallen,
but we will build with
dressed stones;
the sycamores have been cut
down,
but we will put cedars in
their place."
11So the LORD raises adversaries[g]
against them,
and stirs up their enemies.
12The Syrians on the east and the
Philistines on the west
devour Israel with open
mouth.
For all this his anger is not
turned away
and his hand is stretched
out still.
13The people did not turn to him
who smote them,
nor seek the LORD of hosts.
14So the LORD cut off from Israel
head and tail,
palm branch and reed in one
day—
15the elder and honored man is
the head,
and the prophet who teaches
lies is the tail;
16for those who lead this people
lead them astray,
and those who are led by
them are swallowed
up.
17Therefore the Lord does not
rejoice over their young
men,
and has no compassion on
their fatherless and
widows;
for every one is godless and an
evildoer,
and every mouth speaks
folly.
For all this his anger is not
turned away
and his hand is stretched
out still.
18For wickedness burns like a fire,
it consumes briers and
thorns;
it kindles the thickets of the
forest,

gCn: Heb *the adversaries of Rezin*

and they roll upward in a
column of smoke.
19Through the wrath of the LORD
of hosts
the land is burned,
and the people are like fuel for
the fire;
no man spares his brother.
20They snatch on the right, but are
still hungry,
and they devour on the left,
but are not satisfied;
each devours his neighbor's[a]
flesh,
21Manas'seh E'phraim, and
E'phraim Manas'seh,
and together they are
against Judah.
For all this his anger is not
turned away
and his hand is stretched
out still.

10 Woe to those who decree iniqui-
tous decrees,
and the writers who keep
writing oppression,
2to turn aside the needy from
justice
and to rob the poor of my
people of their right,
that widows may be their
spoil,
and that they may make
the fatherless their
prey!
3What will you do on the day of
punishment,
in the storm which will
come from afar?
To whom will you flee for
help,
and where will you leave
your wealth?
4Nothing remains but to crouch
among the prisoners
or fall among the slain.
For all this his anger is not
turned away
and his hand is stretched
out still.

ARROGANT ASSYRIA ALSO JUDGED

5Ah, Assyria, the rod of my
anger,
the staff of my fury![b]
6Against a godless nation I send
him,
and against the people of
my wrath I command
him,
to take spoil and seize
plunder,
and to tread them down
like the mire of the
streets.
7But he does not so intend,
and his mind does not so
think;
but it is in his mind to
destroy,
and to cut off nations not
a few;
8for he says:
"Are not my commanders all
kings?
9Is not Calno like Car'chemish?
Is not Hamath like
Arpad?
Is not Samar'ia like
Damascus?
10As my hand has reached to the
kingdoms of the idols
whose graven images were
greater than those
of Jerusalem and
Samar'ia,
11shall I not do to Jerusalem and
her idols
as I have done to Samar'ia
and her images?"
12 When the Lord has finished
all his work on Mount Zion and on
Jerusalem he[c] will punish the arrogant
boasting of the king of Assyria and his
haughty pride. 13For he says:
"By the strength of my hand I
have done it,
and by my wisdom, for I
have understanding;
I have removed the boundaries
of peoples,

[a] Tg Compare Gk: Heb *the flesh of his arm*
[b] Heb *a staff it is in their hand my fury*
[c] Heb *I*

and have plundered their
treasures;
like a bull I have brought
down those who sat
on thrones.
14My hand has found like a nest
the wealth of the peoples;
and as men gather eggs that
have been forsaken
so I have gathered all the
earth;
and there was none that moved
a wing,
or opened the mouth, or
chirped."
15Shall the axe vaunt itself over
him who hews with it,
or the saw magnify itself
against him who
wields it?
As if a rod should wield him
who lifts it,
or as if a staff should lift
him who is not
wood!
16Therefore the Lord, the LORD
of hosts,
will send wasting sickness
among his stout
warriors,
and under his glory a burning
will be kindled,
like the burning of fire.
17The light of Israel will become
a fire,
and his Holy One a
flame;
and it will burn and devour
his thorns and briers in one
day.
18The glory of his forest and of his
fruitful land
the LORD will destroy, both
soul and body,
and it will be as when a
sick man wastes
away.
19The remnant of the trees of his
forest will be so few
that a child can write them
down.

THE REPENTANT REMNANT OF ISRAEL

20 In that day the remnant of Israel
and the survivors of the house of Jacob
will no more lean upon him that smote
them, but will lean upon the LORD,
the Holy One of Israel, in truth. 21A
remnant will return, the remnant of
Jacob, to the mighty God. 22For though
your people Israel be as the sand of
the sea, only a remnant of them will
return. Destruction is decreed, over-
flowing with righteousness. 23For the
Lord, the LORD of hosts, will make a
full end, as decreed, in the midst of
all the earth.

24 Therefore thus says the Lord,
the LORD of hosts: "O my people, who
dwell in Zion, be not afraid of the
Assyrians when they smite with the
rod and lift up their staff against you
as the Egyptians did. 25For in a very
little while my indignation will come
to an end, and my anger will be di-
rected to their destruction. 26And the
LORD of hosts will wield against them
a scourge, as when he smote Mid´ian
at the rock of Oreb; and his rod will
be over the sea, and he will lift it as
he did in Egypt. 27And in that day his
burden will depart from your shoul-
der, and his yoke will be destroyed
from your neck."

He has gone up from
Rimmon,[d]
28he has come to Ai´ath;
he has passed through
Migron,
at Michmash he stores his
baggage;
29they have crossed over the
pass,
at Geba they lodge for the
night;
Ramah trembles,
Gib´e-ah of Saul has fled.
30Cry aloud, O daughter of Gallim!
Hearken, O La´ishah!
Answer her, O An´athoth!
31Madme´nah is in flight,
the inhabitants of Gebim
flee for safety.

[d]Cn: Heb *and his yoke from your neck, and a yoke will be destroyed because of fatness*

32This very day he will halt at Nob,
he will shake his fist
at the mount of the daughter of Zion,
the hill of Jerusalem.
33Behold, the Lord, the LORD of hosts
will lop the boughs with terrifying power;
the great in height will be hewn down,
and the lofty will be brought low.
34He will cut down the thickets of the forest with an axe,
and Lebanon with its majestic trees[a] will fall.

THE PEACEFUL KINGDOM

11 *There shall come forth a shoot from the stump of Jesse,
and a branch shall grow out of his roots.
2And the Spirit of the LORD shall rest upon him,
the spirit of wisdom and understanding,
the spirit of counsel and might,
the spirit of knowledge and the fear of the LORD.*
3And his delight shall be in the fear of the LORD.
He shall not judge by what his eyes see,
or decide by what his ears hear;
4but with righteousness he shall judge the poor,
and decide with equity for the meek of the earth;
and he shall smite the earth with the rod of his mouth,
and with the breath of his lips he shall slay the wicked.
5Righteousness shall be the girdle of his waist,
and faithfulness the girdle of his loins.
6The wolf shall dwell with the lamb,
and the leopard shall lie down with the kid,
and the calf and the lion and the fatling together,
and a little child shall lead them.
7The cow and the bear shall feed;
their young shall lie down together;
and the lion shall eat straw like the ox.
8The sucking child shall play over the hole of the asp,
and the weaned child shall put his hand on the adder's den.
9They shall not hurt or destroy
in all my holy mountain;
for the earth shall be full of the knowledge of the LORD
as the waters cover the sea.

RETURN OF THE REMNANT OF ISRAEL AND JUDAH

10 In that day the root of Jesse shall
stand as an ensign to the peoples; him
shall the nations seek, and his dwell-
ings shall be glorious.
11 In that day the Lord will extend
his hand yet a second time to recover
the remnant which is left of his peo-
ple, from Assyria, from Egypt, from
Pathros, from Ethiopia, from Elam,
from Shinar, from Hamath, and from
the coastlands of the sea.
12He will raise an ensign for the nations,
and will assemble the outcasts of Israel,
and gather the dispersed of Judah
from the four corners of the earth.
13The jealousy of E´phraim shall

[a] Cn Compare Gk Vg: Heb *with a majestic one*

depart,
and those who harass Judah
shall be cut off;
E´phraim shall not be jealous
of Judah,
and Judah shall not harass
E´phraim.
14But they shall swoop down
upon the shoulder of the
Philistines in the west,
and together they shall
plunder the people of
the east.
They shall put forth their
hand against Edom and
Moab,
and the Ammonites shall
obey them.
15And the LORD will utterly
destroy
the tongue of the sea of
Egypt;
and will wave his hand over the
River
with his scorching wind,
and smite it into seven
channels
that men may cross
dryshod.
16And there will be a highway
from Assyria
for the remnant which is left
of his people,
as there was for Israel
when they came up from the
land of Egypt.

THANKSGIVING AND PRAISE

12 You will say in that day:
"I will give thanks to thee,
O LORD,
for though thou wast angry
with me,
thy anger turned away,
and thou didst comfort me.
2"Behold, God is my salvation;
I will trust, and will not be
afraid;
for the LORD GOD is my
strength and my song,
and he has become my
salvation."
3 With joy you will draw water
from the wells of salvation. 4And you
will say in that day:
"Give thanks to the LORD,
call upon his name;
make known his deeds among
the nations,
proclaim that his name is
exalted.
5"Sing praises to the LORD, for he
has done gloriously;
let this be known[b] in all the
earth.
6Shout, and sing for joy, O inhabi-
tant of Zion,
for great in your midst is
the Holy One of
Israel."

PROCLAMATION AGAINST BABYLON

13 The oracle concerning Babylon
which Isaiah the son of Amoz saw.
2On a bare hill raise a signal,
cry aloud to them;
wave the hand for them to
enter
the gates of the nobles.
3I myself have commanded my
consecrated ones,
have summoned my mighty
men to execute my
anger,
my proudly exulting ones.
4Hark, a tumult on the
mountains
as of a great multitude!
Hark, an uproar of kingdoms,
of nations gathering
together!
The LORD of hosts is
mustering
a host for battle.
5They come from a distant land,
from the end of the
heavens,
the LORD and the weapons of
his indignation,
to destroy the whole earth.
6Wail, for the day of the LORD is
near;

[b] Or *this is made known*

as destruction from the
Almighty it will
come!
7Therefore all hands will be
feeble,
and every man's heart will
melt,
8and they will be dismayed.
Pangs and agony will seize
them;
they will be in anguish like a
woman in travail.
They will look aghast at one
another;
their faces will be aflame.
9Behold, the day of the LORD
comes,
cruel, with wrath and fierce
anger,
to make the earth a desolation
and to destroy its sinners
from it.
10For the stars of the heavens and
their constellations
will not give their light;
the sun will be dark at its
rising
and the moon will not shed
its light.
11I will punish the world for its
evil,
and the wicked for their
iniquity;
I will put an end to the pride of
the arrogant,
and lay low the haughtiness
of the ruthless.
12I will make men more rare than
fine gold,
and mankind than the gold
of Ophir.
13Therefore I will make the heav-
ens tremble,
and the earth will be shaken
out of its place,
at the wrath of the LORD of
hosts
in the day of his fierce
anger.
14And like a hunted gazelle,
or like sheep with none to
gather them,
every man will turn to his own
people,
and every man will flee to
his own land.
15Whoever is found will be thrust
through,
and whoever is caught will
fall by the sword.
16Their infants will be dashed in
pieces
before their eyes;
their houses will be plundered
and their wives ravished.
17Behold, I am stirring up the
Medes against them,
who have no regard for
silver
and do not delight in gold.
18Their bows will slaughter the
young men;
they will have no mercy
on the fruit of the
womb;
their eyes will not pity
children.
19And Babylon, the glory of
kingdoms,
the splendor and pride of the
Chalde´ans,
will be like Sodom and
Gomor´rah
when God overthrew them.
20It will never be inhabited
or dwelt in for all
generations;
no Arab will pitch his tent
there,
no shepherds will make
their flocks lie down
there.
21But wild beasts will lie down
there,
and its houses will be full of
howling creatures;
there ostriches will dwell,
and there satyrs will dance.
22Hyenas will cry in its towers,
and jackals in the pleasant
palaces;
its time is close at hand
and its days will not be
prolonged.

RESTORATION OF JUDAH

14 The LORD will have compassion
on Jacob and will again choose
Israel, and will set them in their own
land, and aliens will join them and
will cleave to the house of Jacob. 2And
the peoples will take them and bring
them to their place, and the house of
Israel will possess them in the LORD's
land as male and female slaves; they
will take captive those who were their
captors, and rule over those who oppressed them.

DOWNFALL OF THE KING OF BABYLON

3 When the LORD has given you
rest from your pain and turmoil and
the hard service with which you
were made to serve, 4you will take
up this taunt against the king of
Babylon:

"How the oppressor has
ceased,
the insolent fury[a] ceased!
5The LORD has broken the staff of
the wicked,
the scepter of rulers,
6that smote the peoples in wrath
with unceasing blows,
that ruled the nations in
anger
with unrelenting
persecution.
7The whole earth is at rest and
quiet;
they break forth into
singing.
8The cypresses rejoice at you,
the cedars of Lebanon,
saying,
'Since you were laid low,
no hewer comes up against
us.'
9Sheol beneath is stirred up
to meet you when you
come;
it rouses the shades to greet
you,
all who were leaders of the
earth;
it raises from their thrones
all who were kings of the
nations.
10All of them will speak
and say to you:
'You too have become as weak
as we!
You have become like us!'
11Your pomp is brought down to
Sheol,
the sound of your harps;
maggots are the bed beneath
you,
and worms are your
covering.
12"How you are fallen from
heaven,
O Day Star, son of Dawn!
How you are cut down to the
ground,
you who laid the nations
low!
13You said in your heart,
'I will ascend to heaven;
above the stars of God
I will set my throne on high;
I will sit on the mount of
assembly
in the far north;
14I will ascend above the heights
of the clouds,
I will make myself like the
Most High.'
15But you are brought down to
Sheol,
to the depths of the Pit.
16Those who see you will stare
at you,
and ponder over you:
'Is this the man who made the
earth tremble,
who shook kingdoms,
17who made the world like a
desert
and overthrew its cities,
who did not let his prisoners
go home?'
18All the kings of the nations lie
in glory,
each in his own tomb;
19but you are cast out, away from
your sepulchre,

[a] One ancient Ms Compare Gk Syr Vg: The meaning of the Hebrew word is uncertain

like a loathed untimely birth,[a]
clothed with the slain, those pierced by the sword,
who go down to the stones of the Pit,
like a dead body trodden under foot.
20You will not be joined with them in burial,
because you have destroyed your land,
you have slain your people.
"May the descendants of evildoers
nevermore be named!
21Prepare slaughter for his sons
because of the guilt of their fathers,
lest they rise and possess the earth,
and fill the face of the world with cities."

22 "I will rise up against them,"
says the LORD of hosts, "and will
cut off from Babylon name and rem-
nant, offspring and posterity, says the
LORD. 23And I will make it a posses-
sion of the hedgehog, and pools of
water, and I will sweep it with the
broom of destruction, says the LORD
of hosts."

AN ORACLE CONCERNING ASSYRIA

24The LORD of hosts has sworn:
"As I have planned,
so shall it be,
and as I have purposed,
so shall it stand,
25that I will break the Assyrian in my land,
and upon my mountains trample him under foot;
and his yoke shall depart from them,
and his burden from their shoulder."
26This is the purpose that is purposed
concerning the whole earth;
and this is the hand that is stretched out
over all the nations.
27For the LORD of hosts has purposed,
and who will annul it?
His hand is stretched out,
and who will turn it back?

AN ORACLE CONCERNING PHILISTIA

28In the year that King Ahaz died
came this oracle:
29"Rejoice not, O Philistia, all of you,
that the rod which smote you is broken,
for from the serpent's root will come forth an adder,
and its fruit will be a flying serpent.
30And the first-born of the poor will feed,
and the needy lie down in safety;
but I will kill your root with famine,
and your remnant I[b] will slay.
31Wail, O gate; cry, O city;
melt in fear, O Philistia, all of you!
For smoke comes out of the north,
and there is no straggler in his ranks."
32What will one answer the messengers of the nation?
"The LORD has founded Zion,
and in her the afflicted of his people find refuge."

AN ORACLE CONCERNING MOAB

15 An oracle concerning Moab.
Because Ar is laid waste in a night
Moab is undone;
because Kir is laid waste in a

[a]Cn Compare Tg Symmachus: Heb *a loathed branch*
[b]One ancient Ms Vg: Heb *he*

night
Moab is undone.
2The daughter of Dibon[c] has gone up
to the high places to weep;
over Nebo and over Med´eba
Moab wails.
On every head is baldness,
every beard is shorn;
3in the streets they gird on sackcloth;
on the housetops and in the squares
every one wails and melts in tears.
4Heshbon and Elea´leh cry out,
their voice is heard as far as Jahaz;
therefore the armed men of Moab cry aloud;
his soul trembles.
5My heart cries out for Moab;
his fugitives flee to Zo´ar,
to Eg´lath-shelish´iyah.
For at the ascent of Luhith
they go up weeping;
on the road to Horona´im
they raise a cry of destruction;
6the waters of Nimrim
are a desolation;
the grass is withered, the new growth fails,
the verdure is no more.
7Therefore the abundance they have gained
and what they have laid up
they carry away
over the Brook of the Willows.
8For a cry has gone
round the land of Moab;
the wailing reaches to Egla´im,
the wailing reaches to Beer-e´lim.
9For the waters of Dibon[d] are full of blood;
yet I will bring upon Dibon[e] even more,
a lion for those of Moab who escape,
for the remnant of the land.

16 They have sent lambs
to the ruler of the land,
from Sela, by way of the desert,
to the mount of the daughter of Zion.
2Like fluttering birds,
like scattered nestlings,
so are the daughters of Moab
at the fords of the Arnon.
3"Give counsel,
grant justice;
make your shade like night
at the height of noon;
hide the outcasts,
betray not the fugitive;
4let the outcasts of Moab
sojourn among you;
be a refuge to them
from the destroyer.
When the oppressor is no more,
and destruction has ceased,
and he who tramples under foot
has vanished from the land,
5then a throne will be established
in steadfast love
and on it will sit in faithfulness
in the tent of David
one who judges and seeks justice
and is swift to do righteousness."
6We have heard of the pride of Moab,
how proud he was;
of his arrogance, his pride, and his insolence—
his boasts are false.
7Therefore let Moab wail,
let every one wail for Moab.
Mourn, utterly stricken,
for the raisin-cakes of Kir-har´eseth.
8For the fields of Heshbon
languish,

[c] Cn: Heb *the house and Dibon*
[d] One ancient Ms Vg Compare Syr: Heb *Dimon*
[e] One ancient Ms Vg Compare Syr: Heb *Dimon*

and the vine of Sibmah;
the lords of the nations
have struck down its branches,
which reached to Jazer
and strayed to the desert;
its shoots spread abroad
and passed over the sea.
9 Therefore I weep with the weeping of Jazer
for the vine of Sibmah;
I drench you with my tears,
O Heshbon and Elea′leh;
for upon your fruit and your harvest
the battle shout has fallen.
10 And joy and gladness are taken away
from the fruitful field;
and in the vineyards no songs are sung,
no shouts are raised;
no treader treads out wine in the presses;
the vintage shout is hushed.[a]
11 Therefore my soul moans like a lyre for Moab,
and my heart for Kir-he′res.

12 And when Moab presents him-
self, when he wearies himself upon
the high place, when he comes to
his sanctuary to pray, he will not
prevail.

13 This is the word which the LORD
spoke concerning Moab in the past.
14 But now the LORD says, "In three
years, like the years of a hireling, the
glory of Moab will be brought into
contempt, in spite of all his great multitude, and those who survive will be
very few and feeble."

AN ORACLE CONCERNING DAMASCUS

17 An oracle concerning Damascus.
Behold, Damascus will cease to be a city,
and will become a heap of ruins.
2 Her cities will be deserted for ever;[b]
they will be for flocks,
which will lie down, and none will make them afraid.
3 The fortress will disappear from E′phraim,
and the kingdom from Damascus;
and the remnant of Syria will be
like the glory of the children of Israel, says the LORD of hosts.
4 And in that day
the glory of Jacob will be brought low,
and the fat of his flesh will grow lean.
5 And it shall be as when the reaper gathers standing grain
and his arm harvests the ears,
and as when one gleans the ears of grain
in the Valley of Reph′aim.
6 Gleanings will be left in it,
as when an olive tree is beaten—
two or three berries
in the top of the highest bough,
four or five
on the branches of a fruit tree, says the LORD God of Israel.

7 In that day men will regard their
Maker, and their eyes will look to
the Holy One of Israel; 8 they will not
have regard for the altars, the work
of their hands, and they will not look
to what their own fingers have made,
either the Ashe′rim or the altars of
incense.

9 In that day their strong cities
will be like the deserted places of the
Hivites and the Amorites,[c] which they
deserted because of the children of
Israel, and there will be desolation.

[a] Gk: Heb *I have hushed*
[b] Cn Compare Gk: Heb *the cities of Aroer are deserted*
[c] Cn Compare Gk: Heb *the wood and the highest bough*

10For you have forgotten the God
of your salvation,
and have not remembered
the Rock of your
refuge;
therefore, though you plant
pleasant plants
and set out slips of an alien
god,
11though you make them grow
on the day that you plant
them,
and make them blossom in
the morning that you
sow;
yet the harvest will flee away
in a day of grief and incur-
able pain.
12Ah, the thunder of many
peoples,
they thunder like the thun-
dering of the sea!
Ah, the roar of nations,
they roar like the roaring of
mighty waters!
13The nations roar like the roaring
of many waters,
but he will rebuke them,
and they will flee far
away,
chased like chaff on the
mountains before the
wind
and whirling dust before the
storm.
14At evening time, behold,
terror!
Before morning, they are no
more!
This is the portion of those
who despoil us,
and the lot of those who
plunder us.

AN ORACLE CONCERNING ETHIOPIA

18 Ah, land of whirring wings
which is beyond the rivers of
Ethiopia;
2which sends ambassadors by the
Nile,
in vessels of papyrus upon
the waters!
Go, you swift messengers,
to a nation, tall and
smooth,
to a people feared near and
far,
a nation mighty and
conquering,
whose land the rivers
divide.
3All you inhabitants of the
world,
you who dwell on the earth,
when a signal is raised on the
mountains, look!
When a trumpet is blown,
hear!
4For thus the LORD said to me:
"I will quietly look from my
dwelling
like clear heat in sunshine,
like a cloud of dew in the
heat of harvest."
5For before the harvest, when the
blossom is over,
and the flower becomes a
ripening grape,
he will cut off the shoots with
pruning hooks,
and the spreading branches
he will hew away.
6They shall all of them be left
to the birds of prey of the
mountains
and to the beasts of the
earth.
And the birds of prey will sum-
mer upon them,
and all the beasts of the
earth will winter
upon them,
7 At that time gifts will be brought
to the LORD of hosts
from a people tall and
smooth,
from a people feared near
and far,
a nation mighty and
conquering,
whose land the rivers
divide,
to Mount Zion, the place of the name
of the LORD of Hosts.

AN ORACLE CONCERNING EGYPT

19 An oracle concerning Egypt.
Behold, the LORD is riding on a swift cloud
and comes to Egypt;
and the idols of Egypt will tremble at his presence,
and the heart of the Egyptians will melt within them.
2 And I will stir up Egyptians against Egyptians,
and they will fight, every man against his brother
and every man against his neighbor,
city against city, kingdom against kingdom;
3 and the spirit of the Egyptians within them will be emptied out,
and I will confound their plans;
and they will consult the idols and the sorcerers,
and the mediums and the wizards;
4 and I will give over the Egyptians into the hand of a hard master;
and a fierce king will rule over them,
says the Lord, the LORD of hosts.
5 And the waters of the Nile will be dried up,
and the river will be parched and dry;
6 and its canals will become foul,
and the branches of Egypt's Nile will diminish and dry up,
reeds and rushes will rot away.
7 There will be bare places by the Nile,
on the brink of the Nile,
and all that is sown by the Nile will dry up,
be driven away, and be no more.
8 The fishermen will mourn and lament,
all who cast hook in the Nile;
and they will languish who spread nets upon the water.
9 The workers in combed flax will be in despair,
and the weavers of white cotton.
10 Those who are the pillars of the land will be crushed,
and all who work for hire will be grieved.
11 The princes of Zo´an are utterly foolish;
the wise counselors of Pharaoh give stupid counsel.
How can you say to Pharaoh,
"I am a son of the wise,
a son of ancient kings"?
12 Where then are your wise men?
Let them tell you and make known
what the LORD of hosts has purposed against Egypt.
13 The princes of Zo´an have become fools,
and the princes of Memphis are deluded;
those who are the cornerstones of her tribes
have led Egypt astray.
14 The LORD has mingled within her a spirit of confusion;
and they have made Egypt stagger in all her doings
as a drunken man staggers in his vomit.
15 And there will be nothing for Egypt
which head or tail, palm branch or reed, may do.

16 In that day the Egyptians will
be like women, and tremble with
fear before the hand which the
LORD of hosts shakes over them.

17And the land of Judah will become
a terror to the Egyptians; every one
to whom it is mentioned will fear
because of the purpose which the
LORD of hosts has purposed against
them.

EGYPT, ASSYRIA, AND ISRAEL BLESSED

18 In that day there will be five cit-
ies in the land of Egypt which speak
the language of Canaan and swear
allegiance to the LORD of hosts. One
of these will be called the City of the
Sun.

19 In that day there will be an altar
to the LORD in the midst of the land
of Egypt, and a pillar to the LORD at
its border. 20It will be a sign and a wit-
ness to the LORD of hosts in the land
of Egypt; when they cry to the LORD
because of oppressors he will send
them a savior, and will defend and de-
liver them. 21And the LORD will make
himself known to the Egyptians; and
the Egyptians will know the LORD
in that day and worship with sacri-
fice and burnt offering, and they will
make vows to the LORD and perform
them. 22And the LORD will smite
Egypt, smiting and healing, and they
will return to the LORD, and he will
heed their supplications and heal
them.

23 In that day there will be a
highway from Egypt to Assyria, and
the Assyrian will come into Egypt,
and the Egyptian into Assyria, and
the Egyptians will worship with the
Assyrians.

24 In that day Israel will be the
third with Egypt and Assyria, a bless-
ing in the midst of the earth, 25whom
the LORD of hosts has blessed, saying,
"Blessed be Egypt my people, and
Assyria the work of my hands, and
Israel my heritage."

ISAIAH DRAMATIZES THE CONQUEST OF EGYPT AND ETHIOPIA

20 In the year that the commander
in chief, who was sent by Sargon
the king of Assyria, came to Ashdod
and fought against it and took it,
2at that time the LORD had spoken
by Isaiah the son of Amoz, saying,
"Go, and loose the sackcloth from
your loins and take off your shoes
from your feet," and he had done
so, walking naked and barefoot 3the
LORD said, "As my servant Isaiah has
walked naked and barefoot for three
years as a sign and a portent against
Egypt and Ethiopia, 4so shall the king
of Assyria lead away the Egyptians
captives and the Ethiopians exiles,
both the young and the old, naked
and barefoot, with buttocks uncov-
ered, to the shame of Egypt. 5Then
they shall be dismayed and con-
founded because of Ethiopia their
hope and of Egypt their boast. 6And
the inhabitants of this coastland
will say in that day, 'Behold, this is
what has happened to those in whom
we hoped and to whom we fled for
help to be delivered from the king
of Assyria! And we, how shall we
escape?'"

ORACLES CONCERNING BABYLON, EDOM, AND ARABIA

21 The oracle concerning the wilder-
ness of the sea.

As whirlwinds in the Negeb
sweep on,
it comes from the desert,
from a terrible land.
2A stern vision is told to me;
the plunderer plunders,
and the destroyer destroys.
Go up, O Elam,
lay siege, O Media;
all the sighing she has caused
I bring to an end.
3Therefore my loins are filled with
anguish;
pangs have seized me,
like the pangs of a woman in
travail;
I am bowed down so that I
cannot hear,
I am dismayed so that I
cannot see.

4My mind reels, horror has appalled me;
the twilight I longed for
has been turned for me into trembling.
5They prepare the table,
they spread the rugs,
they eat, they drink.
Arise, O princes,
oil the shield!
6For thus the Lord said to me:
"Go, set a watchman,
let him announce what he sees.
7When he sees riders, horsemen in pairs,
riders on asses, riders on camels,
let him listen diligently,
very diligently."
8Then he who saw[a] cried:
"Upon a watchtower I stand, O Lord,
continually by day,
and at my post I am stationed
whole nights.
9And behold, here come riders,
horsemen in pairs!"
And he answered,
"Fallen, fallen is Babylon;
and all the images of her gods
he has shattered to the ground."
10O my threshed and winnowed one,
what I have heard from the LORD of hosts,
the God of Israel, I announce to you.
11The oracle concerning Dumah.
One is calling to me from Se´ir,
"Watchman, what of the night?
Watchman, what of the night?"
12The watchman says:
"Morning comes, and also the night.
If you will inquire, inquire;
come back again."
13The oracle concerning Arabia.
In the thickets in Arabia you will lodge,
O caravans of De´danites.
14To the thirsty bring water,
meet the fugitive with bread,
O inhabitants of the land of Tema.
15For they have fled from the swords,
from the drawn sword,
from the bent bow,
and from the press of battle.

16 For thus the Lord said to me,
"Within a year, according to the years
of a hireling, all the glory of Kedar
will come to an end; 17and the remainder of the archers of the mighty
men of the sons of Kedar will be few;
for the LORD, the God of Israel, has
spoken."

A WARNING OF DESTRUCTION OF JERUSALEM

22 The oracle concerning the valley of vision.
What do you mean that you have gone up,
all of you, to the housetops,
2you who are full of shoutings,
tumultuous city, exultant town?
Your slain are not slain with the sword
or dead in battle.
3All your rulers have fled together,
without the bow they were captured.
All of you who were found were captured,
though they had fled far away.[b]
4Therefore I said:
"Look away from me,
let me weep bitter tears;
do not labor to comfort me

[a]One ancient Ms: Heb *a lion*
[b]Gk Syr Vg: Heb *from far away*

for the destruction of the
daughter of my
people."
5For the Lord GOD of hosts has
a day
of tumult and trampling and
confusion
in the valley of vision,
a battering down of walls
and a shouting to the
mountains.
6And Elam bore the quiver
with chariots and
horsemen,[c]
and Kir uncovered the
shield.
7Your choicest valleys were full of
chariots,
and the horsemen took
their stand at the
gates.
8He has taken away the covering
of Judah.
In that day you looked to the weap-
ons of the House of the Forest, 9and
you saw that the breaches of the city
of David were many, and you collected
the waters of the lower pool, 10and you
counted the houses of Jerusalem, and
you broke down the houses to fortify
the wall. 11You made a reservoir be-
tween the two walls for the water of
the old pool. But you did not look to
him who did it, or have regard for him
who planned it long ago.
12In that day the Lord GOD of hosts
called to weeping and
mourning,
to baldness and girding with
sackcloth;
13and behold, joy and gladness,
slaying oxen and killing
sheep,
eating flesh and drinking
wine.
"Let us eat and drink,
for tomorrow we die."
14The LORD of hosts has revealed
himself in my ears:
"Surely this iniquity will not be
forgiven you
till you die,"
says the Lord GOD of hosts.

DENUNCIATION OF SELF-SEEKING OFFICIALS

15 Thus says the Lord GOD of hosts,
"Come, go to this steward, to Shebna,
who is over the household, and say
to him: 16What have you to do here
and whom have you here, that you
have hewn here a tomb for yourself,
you who hew a tomb on the height,
and carve a habitation for yourself
in the rock? 17Behold, the LORD will
hurl you away violently, O you strong
man. He will seize firm hold on you,
18and whirl you round and round, and
throw you like a ball into a wide land;
there you shall die, and there shall be
your splendid chariots, you shame of
your master's house. 19I will thrust
you from your office, and you will be
cast down from your station. 20In that
day I will call my servant Eli'akim the
son of Hilki'ah, 21and I will clothe him
with your robe, and will bind your gir-
dle on him, and will commit your au-
thority to his hand; and he shall be a
father to the inhabitants of Jerusalem
and to the house of Judah. 22And I will
place on his shoulder the key of the
house of David; he shall open, and
none shall shut; and he shall shut,
and none shall open. 23And I will fas-
ten him like a peg in a sure place, and
he will become a throne of honor to
his father's house. 24And they will
hang on him the whole weight of his
father's house, the offspring and is-
sue, every small vessel, from the cups
to all the flagons. 25In that day, says
the LORD of hosts, the peg that was
fastened in a sure place will give way;
and it will be cut down and fall, and
the burden that was upon it will be
cut off, for the LORD has spoken."

AN ORACLE CONCERNING TYRE

23 The oracle concerning Tyre.
Wail, O ships of Tarshish,
for Tyre is laid waste, with-
out house or haven!

[c]The Hebrew of this line is obscure

From the land of Cyprus
it is revealed to them.
2Be still, O inhabitants of the coast,
O merchants of Sidon;
your messengers passed over the sea[a]
3and were on many waters;
your revenue was the grain of Shihor,
the harvest of the Nile;
you were the merchant of the nations.
4Be ashamed, O Sidon, for the sea has spoken,
the stronghold of the sea, saying:
"I have neither travailed nor given birth,
I have neither reared young men
nor brought up virgins."
5When the report comes to Egypt,
they will be in anguish over the report about Tyre.
6Pass over to Tarshish,
wail, O inhabitants of the coast!
7Is this your exultant city
whose origin is from days of old,
whose feet carried her
to settle afar?
8Who has purposed this
against Tyre, the bestower of crowns,
whose merchants were princes,
whose traders were the honored of the earth?
9The LORD of hosts has purposed it,
to defile the pride of all glory,
to dishonor all the honored of the earth.
10Overflow your land like the Nile,
O daughter of Tarshish;
there is no restraint any more.
11He has stretched out his hand over the sea,
he has shaken the kingdoms;
the LORD has given command concerning Canaan
to destroy its strongholds.
12And he said:
"You will no more exult,
O oppressed virgin daughter of Sidon;
arise, pass over to Cyprus,
even there you will have no rest."

13 Behold the land of the
Chalde´ans! This is the people; it was
not Assyria. They destined Tyre for
wild beasts. They erected their siege
towers, they razed her palaces, they
made her a ruin.[b]

14Wail, O ships of Tarshish,
for your stronghold is laid waste.

15In that day Tyre will be forgotten
for seventy years, like the days of one
king. At the end of seventy years, it
will happen to Tyre as in the song of
the harlot:

16"Take a harp,
go about the city,
O forgotten harlot!
Make sweet melody,
sing many songs,
that you may be remembered."

17At the end of seventy years, the
LORD will visit Tyre, and she will re-
turn to her hire, and will play the har-
lot with all the kingdoms of the world
upon the face of the earth. 18Her mer-
chandise and her hire will be dedicat-
ed to the LORD; it will not be stored
or hoarded, but her merchandise will
supply abundant food and fine cloth-
ing for those who dwell before the
LORD.

[a] One ancient Ms: Heb *who passed over the sea, they replenished you*
[b] The Hebrew of this verse is obscure

IMPENDING JUDGMENT ON THE EARTH

24 Behold, the LORD will lay waste
the earth and make it
desolate,
and he will twist its surface
and scatter its
inhabitants.
2And it shall be, as with the people, so with the priest;
as with the slave, so with his
master;
as with the maid, so with
her mistress;
as with the buyer, so with the
seller;
as with the lender, so with
the borrower;
as with the creditor, so with
the debtor.
3The earth shall be utterly
laid waste and utterly
despoiled;
for the LORD has spoken
this word.
4The earth mourns and withers,
the world languishes and
withers;
the heavens languish
together with the
earth.
5The earth lies polluted
under its inhabitants;
for they have transgressed the
laws,
violated the statutes,
broken the everlasting
covenant.
6Therefore a curse devours the
earth,
and its inhabitants suffer for
their guilt;
therefore the inhabitants of the
earth are scorched,
and few men are left.
7The wine mourns,
the vine languishes,
all the merry-hearted sigh.
8The mirth of the timbrels is
stilled,
the noise of the jubilant has
ceased,
the mirth of the lyre
is stilled.
9No more do they drink wine with
singing;
strong drink is bitter to
those who drink it.
10The city of chaos is broken
down,
every house is shut up so
that none can enter.
11There is an outcry in the streets
for lack of wine;
all joy has reached its
eventide;
the gladness of the earth is
banished.
12Desolation is left in the city,
the gates are battered into
ruins.
13For thus it shall be in the midst
of the earth
among the nations,
as when an olive tree is beaten,
as at the gleaning when the
vintage is done.
14They lift up their voices, they
sing for joy;
over the majesty of the LORD
they shout from the
west.
15Therefore in the east give glory
to the LORD;
in the coastlands of the sea,
to the name of the
LORD, the God of
Israel.
16From the ends of the earth we
hear songs of praise,
of glory to the Righteous
One.
But I say, "I pine away,
I pine away. Woe is me!
For the treacherous deal
treacherously,
the treacherous deal very
treacherously."
17Terror, and the pit, and the
snare
are upon you, O inhabitant
of the earth!
18He who flees at the sound of the
terror
shall fall into the pit;

and he who climbs out of the
pit
shall be caught in the
snare.
For the windows of heaven are
opened,
and the foundations of the
earth tremble.
19The earth is utterly broken,
the earth is rent asunder,
the earth is violently
shaken.
20The earth staggers like a drunk-
en man,
it sways like a hut;
its transgression lies heavy
upon it,
and it falls, and will not rise
again.
21On that day the LORD will
punish
the host of heaven, in
heaven,
and the kings of the earth,
on the earth.
22They will be gathered together
as prisoners in a pit;
they will be shut up in a
prison,
and after many days they
will be punished.
23Then the moon will be
confounded,
and the sun ashamed;
for the LORD of hosts will reign
on Mount Zion and in
Jerusalem
and before his elders he will
manifest his glory.

PRAISE FOR DELIVERANCE FROM OPPRESSION

25 O LORD, thou art my God;
I will exalt thee, I will praise
thy name;
for thou hast done wonderful
things,
plans formed of old, faithful
and sure.
2For thou hast made the city a
heap,
the fortified city a ruin;
the palace of aliens is a city no
more,
it will never be rebuilt.
3Therefore strong peoples will
glorify thee;
cities of ruthless nations will
fear thee.
4For thou hast been a stronghold
to the poor,
a stronghold to the needy in
his distress,
a shelter from the storm
and a shade from the
heat;
for the blast of the ruthless is
like a storm against a
wall,
5like heat in a dry place.
Thou dost subdue the noise of
the aliens;
as heat by the shade of a
cloud,
so the song of the ruthless is
stilled.

6 On this mountain the LORD of
hosts will make for all peoples a feast
of fat things, a feast of wine on the
lees, of fat things full of marrow, of
wine on the lees well refined. 7And
he will destroy on this mountain the
covering that is cast over all peo-
ples, the veil that is spread over all
nations. 8He will swallow up death
for ever, and the Lord GOD will wipe
away tears from all faces, and the re-
proach of his people he will take away
from all the earth; for the LORD has
spoken.

9 It will be said on that day, "Lo,
this is our God; we have waited for
him, that he might save us. This is
the LORD; we have waited for him;
let us be glad and rejoice in his
salvation."

10 For the hand of the LORD will
rest on this mountain, and Moab
shall be trodden down in his place,
as straw is trodden down in a dung-
pit. 11And he will spread out his
hands in the midst of it as a swim-
mer spreads his hands out to swim;

but the LORD will lay low his pride
together with the skill[a] of his hands.
12And the high fortifications of his
walls he will bring down, lay low,
and cast to the ground, even to the
dust.

JUDAH'S SONG OF VICTORY

26 In that day this song will be sung
in the land of Judah:
"We have a strong city;
he sets up salvation
as walls and bulwarks.
2Open the gates,
that the righteous nation
which keeps faith
may enter in.
3Thou dost keep him in perfect
peace,
whose mind is stayed on
thee,
because he trusts in thee.
4Trust in the LORD for ever,
for the LORD GOD
is an everlasting rock.
5For he has brought low
the inhabitants of the
height,
the lofty city.
He lays it low, lays it low to the
ground,
casts it to the dust.
6The foot tramples it,
the feet of the poor,
the steps of the needy."
7The way of the righteous is
level;
thou[b] dost make smooth the
path of the righteous.
8In the path of thy judgments,
O LORD, we wait for thee;
thy memorial name
is the desire of our soul.
9My soul yearns for thee in the
night,
my spirit within me earnest-
ly seeks thee.
For when thy judgments are in
the earth,
the inhabitants of the world
learn righteousness.
10If favor is shown to the wicked,
he does not learn
righteousness;
in the land of uprightness he
deals perversely
and does not see the majesty
of the LORD.
11O LORD, thy hand is lifted up,
but they see it not.
Let them see thy zeal for
thy people, and be
ashamed.
Let the fire for thy adversar-
ies consume them.
12O LORD, thou wilt ordain peace
for us,
thou hast wrought for us all
our works.
13O LORD our God,
other lords besides thee have
ruled over us,
but thy name alone we
acknowledge.
14They are dead, they will not
live;
they are shades, they will
not arise;
to that end thou hast visited
them with destruction
and wiped out all remem-
brance of them.
15But thou hast increased the
nation, O LORD,
thou hast increased the
nation; thou art
glorified;
thou hast enlarged all the
borders of the land.
16O LORD, in distress they sought
thee,
they poured out a prayer[c]
when thy chastening was
upon them.
17Like a woman with child,
who writhes and cries out in
her pangs,
when she is near her time,
so were we because of thee, O
LORD;

[a] The meaning of the Hebrew word is uncertain
[b] Cn Compare Gk: Heb *thou (that art) upright*
[c] Heb uncertain

18we were with child, we writhed,
we have as it were brought forth wind.
We have wrought no deliverance in the earth,
and the inhabitants of the world have not fallen.
19Thy dead shall live, their bodies[a] shall rise.
O dwellers in the dust, awake and sing for joy!
For thy dew is a dew of light,
and on the land of the shades thou wilt let it fall.
20Come, my people, enter your chambers,
and shut your doors behind you;
hide yourselves for a little while
until the wrath is past.
21For behold, the LORD is coming forth out of his place
to punish the inhabitants of the earth for their iniquity,
and the earth will disclose the blood shed upon her,
and will no more cover her slain.

ISRAEL'S REDEMPTION

27 In that day the LORD with his
hard and great and strong sword
will punish Levi´athan the fleeing ser-
pent, Levi´athan the twisting serpent,
and he will slay the dragon that is in
the sea.

2In that day:
"A pleasant vineyard, sing of it!
3I, the LORD, am its keeper;
every moment I water it.
Lest any one harm it,
I guard it night and day;
4I have no wrath.
Would that I had thorns and briers to battle!
I would set out against them,
I would burn them up together.
5Or let them lay hold of my protection,
let them make peace with me,
let them make peace with me."
6In days to come[b] Jacob shall take root,
Israel shall blossom and put forth shoots,
and fill the whole world with fruit.
7Has he smitten them as he smote those who smote them?
Or have they been slain as their slayers were slain?
8Measure by measure,[c] by exile thou didst contend with them;
he removed them with his fierce blast in the day of the east wind.
9Therefore by this the guilt of Jacob will be expiated,
and this will be the full fruit of the removal of his sin:
when he makes all the stones of the altars
like chalkstones crushed to pieces,
no Ashe´rim or incense altars will remain standing.
10For the fortified city is solitary,
a habitation deserted and forsaken, like the wilderness;
there the calf grazes,
there he lies down, and strips its branches.
11When its boughs are dry, they

[a] Cn Compare Syr Tg: Heb *my body*
[b] Heb *Those to come*
[c] Compare Syr Vg Tg: The meaning of the Hebrew word is unknown

are broken;
women come and make a fire of them.
For this is a people without discernment;
therefore he who made them will not have compassion on them,
he that formed them will show them no favor.

12 In that day from the river
Euphra´tes to the Brook of Egypt the
LORD will thresh out the grain, and
you will be gathered one by one, O
people of Israel. 13And in that day
a great trumpet will be blown, and
those who were lost in the land of
Assyria and those who were driven
out to the land of Egypt will come and
worship the LORD on the holy moun-
tain at Jerusalem.

JUDGMENT ON CORRUPT RULERS, PRIESTS, AND PROPHETS

28 Woe to the proud crown of the drunkards of E´phraim,
and to the fading flower of its glorious beauty,
which is on the head of the rich valley of those overcome with wine!
2Behold, the Lord has one who is mighty and strong;
like a storm of hail, a destroying tempest,
like a storm of mighty, overflowing waters,
he will cast down to the earth with violence.
3The proud crown of the drunkards of E´phraim
will be trodden under foot;
4and the fading flower of its glorious beauty,
which is on the head of the rich valley,
will be like a first-ripe fig before the summer:
when a man sees it, he eats it up
as soon as it is in his hand.
5In that day the LORD of hosts
will be a crown of glory,
and a diadem of beauty, to the remnant of his people;
6and a spirit of justice to him who sits in judgment,
and strength to those who turn back the battle at the gate.
7These also reel with wine
and stagger with strong drink;
the priest and the prophet reel with strong drink,
they are confused with wine,
they stagger with strong drink;
they err in vision,
they stumble in giving judgment.
8For all tables are full of vomit,
no place is without filthiness.
9"Whom will he teach knowledge,
and to whom will he explain the message?
Those who are weaned from the milk,
those taken from the breast?
10For it is precept upon precept,
precept upon precept,
line upon line, line upon line,
here a little, there a little."
11Nay, but by men of strange lips
and with an alien tongue
the LORD will speak to this people,
12to whom he has said,
"This is rest;
give rest to the weary;
and this is repose";
yet they would not hear.
13Therefore the word of the LORD
will be to them
precept upon precept, precept upon precept,
line upon line, line upon line,

here a little, there a little;
that they may go, and fall backward,
and be broken, and snared, and taken.
14 Therefore hear the word of the LORD, you scoffers,
who rule this people in Jerusalem!
15 Because you have said, "We have made a covenant with death,
and with Sheol we have an agreement;
when the overwhelming scourge passes through
it will not come to us;
for we have made lies our refuge,
and in falsehood we have taken shelter";
16 therefore thus says the Lord GOD,
"Behold, I am laying in Zion for a foundation
a stone, a tested stone,
a precious cornerstone, of a sure foundation:
'He who believes will not be in haste.'
17 And I will make justice the line,
and righteousness the plummet;
and hail will sweep away the refuge of lies,
and waters will overwhelm the shelter."
18 Then your covenant with death will be annulled,
and your agreement with Sheol will not stand;
when the overwhelming scourge passes through
you will be beaten down by it.
19 As often as it passes through it will take you;
for morning by morning it will pass through,
by day and by night;
and it will be sheer terror
to understand the message.
20 For the bed is too short to stretch oneself on it,
and the covering too narrow to wrap oneself in it.
21 For the LORD will rise up as on Mount Pera'zim,
he will be wroth as in the valley of Gibeon;
to do his deed—strange is his deed!
and to work his work—alien is his work!
22 Now therefore do not scoff,
lest your bonds be made strong;
for I have heard a decree of destruction
from the Lord GOD of hosts upon the whole land.
23 Give ear, and hear my voice;
hearken, and hear my speech.
24 Does he who plows for sowing plow continually?
does he continually open and harrow his ground?
25 When he has leveled its surface,
does he not scatter dill, sow cummin,
and put in wheat in rows
and barley in its proper place,
and spelt as the border?
26 For he is instructed aright;
his God teaches him.
27 Dill is not threshed with a threshing sledge,
nor is a cart wheel rolled over cummin;
but dill is beaten out with a stick,
and cummin with a rod.
28 Does one crush bread grain?
No, he does not thresh it for ever;
when he drives his cart wheel over it

with his horses, he does not
crush it.
29This also comes from the LORD
of hosts;
he is wonderful in counsel,
and excellent in wisdom.

THE SIEGE OF JERUSALEM

29 Ho Ariel, Ariel,
the city where David
encamped!
Add year to year;
let the feasts run their
round.
2Yet I will distress Ariel,
and there shall be moaning
and lamentation,
and she shall be to me like
an Ariel.
3And I will encamp against you
round about,
and will besiege you with
towers
and I will raise siegeworks
against you.
4Then deep from the earth you
shall speak,
from low in the dust your
words shall come;
your voice shall come from the
ground like the voice of
a ghost,
and your speech shall whis-
per out of the dust.
5But the multitude of your foes[a]
shall be like small dust,
and the multitude of the
ruthless like passing
chaff.
And in an instant, suddenly,
6you will be visited by the
LORD of hosts
with thunder and with earth-
quake and great noise,
with whirlwind and tempest,
and the flame of a
devouring fire.
7And the multitude of all the
nations that fight against
Ariel,
all that fight against her and
her stronghold and
distress her,
shall be like a dream, a
vision of the night.
8As when a hungry man dreams
he is eating
and awakes with his hunger
not satisfied,
or as when a thirsty man
dreams he is drinking
and awakes faint, with his
thirst not quenched,
so shall the multitude of all the
nations be
that fight against Mount
Zion.
9Stupefy yourselves and be in a
stupor,
blind yourselves and be
blind!
Be drunk, but not with wine;
stagger, but not with strong
drink!
10For the LORD has poured out
upon you
a spirit of deep sleep,
and has closed your eyes, the
prophets,
and covered your heads, the
seers.

11 And the vision of all this has be-
come to you like the words of a book
that is sealed. When men give it to one
who can read, saying, "Read this," he
says, "I cannot, for it is sealed." 12And
when they give the book to one who
cannot read, saying, "Read this," he
says, "I cannot read."

13And the Lord said:
"Because this people draw near
with their mouth
and honor me with their
lips,
while their hearts are far
from me,
and their fear of me is a
commandment of men
learned by rote;
14therefore, behold, I will again
do marvelous things with
this people,

[a] Cn: Heb *strangers*

wonderful and marvelous;
and the wisdom of their wise men shall perish,
and the discernment of their discerning men shall be hid."

15 Woe to those who hide deep from the LORD their counsel,
whose deeds are in the dark,
and who say, "Who sees us? Who knows us?"

16 You turn things upside down!
Shall the potter be regarded as the clay;
that the thing made should say of its maker,
"He did not make me";
or the thing formed say of him who formed it,
"He has no understanding"?

HOPE FOR THE FUTURE

17 Is it not yet a very little while
until Lebanon shall be turned into a fruitful field,
and the fruitful field shall be regarded as a forest?

18 In that day the deaf shall hear the words of a book,
and out of their gloom and darkness
the eyes of the blind shall see.

19 The meek shall obtain fresh joy in the LORD,
and the poor among men shall exult in the Holy One of Israel.

20 For the ruthless shall come to nought and the scoffer cease,
and all who watch to do evil shall be cut off,

21 who by a word make a man out to be an offender,
and lay a snare for him who reproves in the gate,
and with an empty plea turn aside him who is in the right.

22 Therefore thus says the LORD,
who redeemed Abraham, concerning
the house of Jacob:
"Jacob shall no more be ashamed,
no more shall his face grow pale.

23 For when he sees his children,
the work of my hands, in his midst,
they will sanctify my name;
they will sanctify the Holy One of Jacob,
and will stand in awe of the God of Israel.

24 And those who err in spirit will come to understanding,
and those who murmur will accept instruction."

THE FUTILITY OF RELIANCE ON EGYPT

30 "Woe to the rebellious children," says the LORD,
"who carry out a plan, but not mine;
and who make a league, but not of my spirit,
that they may add sin to sin;

2 who set out to go down to Egypt,
without asking for my counsel,
to take refuge in the protection of Pharaoh,
and to seek shelter in the shadow of Egypt!

3 Therefore shall the protection of Pharaoh turn to your shame,
and the shelter in the shadow of Egypt to your humiliation.

4 For though his officials are at Zo′an
and his envoys reach Ha′nes,

5 every one comes to shame
through a people that cannot profit them,
that brings neither help nor profit,

but shame and disgrace."
6An oracle on the beasts of the Negeb.
Through a land of trouble and anguish,
from where come the lioness and the lion,
the viper and the flying serpent,
they carry their riches on the backs of asses,
and their treasures on the humps of camels,
to a people that cannot profit them.
7For Egypt's help is worthless and empty,
therefore I have called her
"Rahab who sits still."

A REBELLIOUS PEOPLE

8And now, go, write it before them on a tablet,
and inscribe it in a book,
that it may be for the time to come
as a witness for ever.
9For they are a rebellious people,
lying sons,
sons who will not hear
the instruction of the LORD;
10who say to the seers, "See not";
and to the prophets,
"Prophesy not to us what is right;
speak to us smooth things,
prophesy illusions,
11leave the way, turn aside from the path,
let us hear no more of the Holy One of Israel."
12Therefore thus says the Holy One of Israel,
"Because you despise this word,
and trust in oppression and perverseness,
and rely on them;
13therefore this iniquity shall be to you
like a break in a high wall,
bulging out, and about to collapse,
whose crash comes suddenly, in an instant;
14and its breaking is like that of a potter's vessel
which is smashed so ruthlessly
that among its fragments not a sherd is found
with which to take fire from the hearth,
or to dip up water out of the cistern."
15For thus said the Lord GOD, the Holy One of Israel,
"In returning and rest you shall be saved;
in quietness and in trust shall be your strength."
And you would not, 16but you said,
"No! We will speed upon horses,"
therefore you shall speed away;
and, "We will ride upon swift steeds,"
therefore your pursuers shall be swift.
17A thousand shall flee at the threat of one,
at the threat of five you shall flee,
till you are left
like a flagstaff on the top of a mountain,
like a signal on a hill.

GOD'S PROMISE TO ZION

18Therefore the LORD waits to be gracious to you;
therefore he exalts himself to show mercy to you.
For the LORD is a God of justice;
blessed are all those who wait for him.

19 Yea, O people in Zion who
dwell at Jerusalem; you shall weep
no more. He will surely be gracious

to you at the sound of your cry; when
he hears it, he will answer you. 20And
though the Lord give you the bread
of adversity and the water of afflic-
tion, yet your Teacher will not hide
himself any more, but your eyes
shall see your Teacher. 21And your
ears shall hear a word behind you,
saying, "This is the way, walk in it,"
when you turn to the right or when
you turn to the left. 22Then you will
defile your silver-covered graven
images and your gold-plated molten
images. You will scatter them as un-
clean things; you will say to them,
"Begone!"

23 And he will give rain for the
seed with which you sow the ground,
and grain, the produce of the ground,
which will be rich and plenteous.
In that day your cattle will graze in
large pastures; 24and the oxen and
the asses that till the ground will
eat salted provender, which has been
winnowed with shovel and fork.
25And upon every lofty mountain and
every high hill there will be brooks
running with water, in the day of
the great slaughter, when the towers
fall. 26Moreover the light of the moon
will be as the light of the sun, and
the light of the sun will be sevenfold,
as the light of seven days, in the day
when the LORD binds up the hurt of
his people, and heals the wounds in-
flicted by his blow.

JUDGMENT ON ASSYRIA

27Behold, the name of the LORD
comes from far,
burning with his anger,
and in thick rising
smoke;
his lips are full of indignation,
and his tongue is like a
devouring fire;
28his breath is like an overflowing
stream
that reaches up to the neck;
to sift the nations with the
sieve of destruction,
and to place on the jaws of
the peoples a bridle
that leads astray.

29 You shall have a song as in
the night when a holy feast is kept;
and gladness of heart, as when one
sets out to the sound of the flute to
go to the mountain of the LORD, to
the Rock of Israel. 30And the LORD
will cause his majestic voice to be
heard and the descending blow of
his arm to be seen, in furious anger
and a flame of devouring fire, with
a cloudburst and tempest and hail-
stones. 31The Assyrians will be ter-
ror-stricken at the voice of the LORD,
when he smites with his rod. 32And
every stroke of the staff of punish-
ment which the LORD lays upon them
will be to the sound of timbrels and
lyres; battling with brandished arm
he will fight with them. 33For a burn-
ing place[a] has long been prepared;
yea, for the king[b] it is made ready, its
pyre made deep and wide, with fire
and wood in abundance; the breath of
the LORD, like a stream of brimstone,
kindles it.

ALLIANCE WITH EGYPT IS FUTILE

31 Woe to those who go down to
Egypt for help
and rely on horses,
who trust in chariots because
they are many
and in horsemen because
they are very strong,
but do not look to the Holy
One of Israel
or consult the LORD!
2And yet he is wise and brings
disaster,
he does not call back his
words,
but will arise against the house
of the evildoers,
and against the helpers
of those who work
iniquity.

[a]Or *Topheth*
[b]Or *Molech*

3The Egyptians are men, and not
God;
and their horses are flesh,
and not spirit.
When the LORD stretches out
his hand,
the helper will stumble, and
he who is helped will
fall,
and they will all perish
together.
4For thus the LORD said to me,
As a lion or a young lion growls
over his prey,
and when a band of shep-
herds is called forth
against him
is not terrified by their
shouting
or daunted at their noise,
so the LORD of hosts will come
down
to fight upon Mount Zion
and upon its hill.
5Like birds hovering, so the LORD
of hosts
will protect Jerusalem;
he will protect and deliver it,
he will spare and rescue it.
6 Turn to him from whom you[c]
have deeply revolted, O people of
Israel. 7For in that day every one shall
cast away his idols of silver and his
idols of gold, which your hands have
sinfully made for you.
8"And the Assyrian shall fall by a
sword, not of man;
and a sword, not of man,
shall devour him;
and he shall flee from the
sword,
and his young men shall be
put to forced labor.
9His rock shall pass away in
terror,
and his officers desert the
standard in panic,"
says the LORD, whose fire is
in Zion,
and whose furnace is in
Jerusalem.

[c]Heb *they*

GOVERNMENT WITH JUSTICE PREDICTED

32 Behold, a king will reign in
righteousness,
and princes will rule in
justice.
2Each will be like a hiding place
from the wind,
a covert from the tempest,
like streams of water in a dry
place,
like the shade of a great rock
in a weary land.
3Then the eyes of those who see
will not be closed,
and the ears of those who
hear will hearken.
4The mind of the rash will have
good judgment,
and the tongue of the
stammerers will
speak readily and
distinctly.
5The fool will no more be called
noble,
nor the knave said to be
honorable.
6For the fool speaks folly,
and his mind plots iniquity:
to practice ungodliness,
to utter error concerning the
LORD,
to leave the craving of the hun-
gry unsatisfied,
and to deprive the thirsty of
drink.
7The knaveries of the knave are
evil;
he devises wicked devices
to ruin the poor with lying
words,
even when the plea of the
needy is right.
8But he who is noble devises noble
things,
and by noble things he
stands.

COMPLACENT WOMEN WARNED OF DISASTER

9Rise up, you women who are at
ease, hear my voice;

you complacent daughters, give ear to my speech.
10In little more than a year
you will shudder, you complacent women;
for the vintage will fail,
the fruit harvest will not come.
11Tremble, you women who are at ease,
shudder, you complacent ones;
strip, and make yourselves bare,
and gird sackcloth upon your loins.
12Beat upon your breasts for the pleasant fields,
for the fruitful vine,
13for the soil of my people
growing up in thorns and briers;
yea, for all the joyous houses
in the joyful city.
14For the palace will be forsaken,
the populous city deserted;
the hill and the watchtower
will become dens for ever,
a joy of wild asses,
a pasture of flocks;
15until the Spirit is poured upon us from on high,
and the wilderness becomes a fruitful field,
and the fruitful field is deemed a forest.

THE PEACE OF GOD'S REIGN

16Then justice will dwell in the wilderness,
and righteousness abide in the fruitful field.
17And the effect of righteousness will be peace,
and the result of righteousness, quietness and trust for ever.
18My people will abide in a peaceful habitation,
in secure dwellings, and in quiet resting places.
19And the forest will utterly go down,[a]
and the city will be utterly laid low.
20Happy are you who sow beside all waters,
who let the feet of the ox and the ass range free.

A PROPHECY OF DELIVERANCE FROM FOES

33 Woe to you, destroyer,
who yourself have not been destroyed;
you treacherous one,
with whom none has dealt treacherously!
When you have ceased to destroy,
you will be destroyed;
and when you have made an end of dealing treacherously,
you will be dealt with treacherously.
2O LORD, be gracious to us; we wait for thee.
Be our arm every morning,
our salvation in the time of trouble.
3At the thunderous noise peoples flee,
at the lifting up of thyself nations are scattered;
4and spoil is gathered as the caterpillar gathers;
as locusts leap, men leap upon it.
5The LORD is exalted, for he dwells on high;
he will fill Zion with justice and righteousness;
6and he will be the stability of your times,
abundance of salvation, wisdom, and knowledge;
the fear of the LORD is his treasure.

[a]Cn: Heb *And it will hail when the forest comes down*

7Behold, the valiant ones[b] cry
without;
the envoys of peace weep
bitterly.
8The highways lie waste,
the wayfaring man ceases.
Covenants are broken,
witnesses[c] are despised,
there is no regard for man.
9The land mourns and
languishes;
Lebanon is confounded and
withers away;
Sharon is like a desert;
and Bashan and Carmel
shake off their
leaves.
10"Now I will arise," says the
LORD,
"now I will lift myself up;
now I will be exalted.
11You conceive chaff, you bring
forth stubble;
your breath is a fire that will
consume you.
12And the peoples will be as if
burned to lime,
like thorns cut down, that
are burned in the
fire."
13Hear, you who are far off, what I
have done;
and you who are near,
acknowledge my
might.
14The sinners in Zion are afraid;
trembling has seized the
godless:
"Who among us can dwell
with the devouring
fire?
Who among us can dwell
with everlasting
burnings?"
15He who walks righteously and
speaks uprightly,
who despises the gain of
oppressions,
who shakes his hands, lest they
hold a bribe,
who stops his ears from
hearing of bloodshed
and shuts his eyes from
looking upon evil,
16he will dwell on the heights;
his place of defense will
be the fortresses of
rocks;
his bread will be given him,
his water will be
sure.

THE LAND OF THE MAJESTIC KING

17Your eyes will see the king in his
beauty;
they will behold a land that
stretches afar.
18Your mind will muse on the
terror:
"Where is he who counted,
where is he who
weighed the tribute?
Where is he who counted
the towers?"
19You will see no more the inso-
lent people,
the people of an obscure
speech which you
cannot comprehend,
stammering in a tongue
which you cannot
understand.
20Look upon Zion, the city of our
appointed feasts!
Your eyes will see Jerusalem,
a quiet habitation, an im-
movable tent,
whose stakes will never be
plucked up,
nor will any of its cords be
broken.
21But there the LORD in majesty
will be for us
a place of broad rivers and
streams,
where no galley with oars can
go,
nor stately ship can pass.
22For the LORD is our judge, the
LORD is our ruler,

[b] The meaning of the Hebrew word is uncertain
[c] One ancient Ms: Heb *cities*

the LORD is our king; he will
save us.
23Your tackle hangs loose;
it cannot hold the mast firm
in its place,
or keep the sail spread out.
Then prey and spoil in
abundance will be
divided;
even the lame will take the
prey.
24And no inhabitant will say, "I
am sick";
the people who dwell there
will be forgiven their
iniquity.

JUDGMENT ON THE NATIONS

34 Draw near, O nations, to hear,
and hearken, O peoples!
Let the earth listen, and all
that fills it;
the world, and all that comes
from it.
2For the LORD is enraged against
all the nations,
and furious against all their
host,
he has doomed them, has
given them over for
slaughter.
3Their slain shall be cast out,
and the stench of their
corpses shall rise;
the mountains shall flow
with their blood.
4All the host of heaven shall rot
away,
and the skies roll up like a
scroll.
All their host shall fall,
as leaves fall from the vine,
like leaves falling from the
fig tree.
5For my sword has drunk its fill in
the heavens;
behold, it descends for
judgment upon
Edom,
upon the people I have
doomed.
6The LORD has a sword; it is sated
with blood,
it is gorged with fat,
with the blood of lambs and
goats,
with the fat of the kidneys
of rams.
For the LORD has a sacrifice in
Bozrah,
a great slaughter in the land
of Edom.
7Wild oxen shall fall with them,
and young steers with the
mighty bulls.
Their land shall be soaked with
blood,
and their soil made rich with
fat.
8For the LORD has a day of
vengeance,
a year of recompense for the
cause of Zion.
9And the streams of Edom[a] shall
be turned into pitch,
and her soil into brimstone;
her land shall become burn-
ing pitch.
10Night and day it shall not be
quenched;
its smoke shall go up for
ever.
From generation to generation
it shall lie waste;
none shall pass through it
for ever and ever.
11But the hawk and the porcupine
shall possess it,
the owl and the raven shall
dwell in it.
He shall stretch the line of
confusion over it,
and the plummet of chaos
over[b] its nobles.
12They shall name it No Kingdom
There,
and all its princes shall be
nothing.
13Thorns shall grow over its
strongholds,

[a] Heb *her streams*
[b] Heb lacks *over*

nettles and thistles in its
fortresses.
It shall be the haunt of
jackals,
an abode for ostriches.
14And wild beasts shall meet with
hyenas,
the satyr shall cry to his
fellow;
yea, there shall the night hag
alight,
and find for herself a resting
place.
15There shall the owl nest and
lay
and hatch and gather her
young in her shadow;
yea, there shall the kites be
gathered,
each one with her mate.
16Seek and read from the book of
the LORD:
Not one of these shall be
missing;
none shall be without her
mate.
For the mouth of the LORD has
commanded,
and his Spirit has gathered
them.
17He has cast the lot for them,
his hand has portioned it
out to them with the
line;
they shall possess it for ever,
from generation to genera-
tion they shall dwell
in it.

THE RETURN OF THE REDEEMED TO ZION

35 The wilderness and the dry land
shall be glad,
the desert shall rejoice and
blossom;
like the crocusit shall blossom
abundantly,
and rejoice with joy and
singing.
The glory of Lebanon shall be
given to it,
the majesty of Carmel and
Sharon.
They shall see the glory of the
LORD,
the majesty of our God.
3Strengthen the weak hands,
and make firm the feeble
knees.
4Say to those who are of a fearful
heart,
"Be strong, fear not!
Behold, your God
will come with vengeance,
with the recompense of God.
He will come and save
you."
5Then the eyes of the blind shall
be opened,
and the ears of the deaf
unstopped;
6then shall the lame man leap like
a hart,
and the tongue of the dumb
sing for joy.
For waters shall break forth in
the wilderness,
and streams in the desert;
7the burning sand shall become
a pool,
and the thirsty ground
springs of water;
the haunt of jackals shall be-
come a swamp,[c]
the grass shall become reeds
and rushes.
8And a highway shall be there,
and it shall be called the
Holy Way;
the unclean shall not pass over
it,[d]
and fools shall not err
therein.
9No lion shall be there,
nor shall any ravenous beast
come up on it;
they shall not be found there,
but the redeemed shall walk
there.
10And the ransomed of the LORD
shall return,

[c] Cn: Heb *in the haunt of jackals is her resting place*
[d] Heb *it and he is for them a wayfarer*

and come to Zion with
singing;
everlasting joy shall be upon
their heads;
they shall obtain joy and
gladness,
and sorrow and sighing shall
flee away.

SENNACHERIB THREATENS JERUSALEM

36 In the fourteenth year of King Hezeki´ah, Sennach´erib king of Assyria came up against all the fortified cities of Judah and took them. 2And the king of Assyria sent the Rab´shakeh from Lachish to King Hezeki´ah at Jerusalem, with a great army. And he stood by the conduit of the upper pool on the highway to the Fuller's Field. 3And there came out to him Eli´akim the son of Hilki´ah, who was over the household, and Shebna the secretary, and Jo´ah the son of Asaph, the recorder.

4 And the Rab´shakeh said to them, "Say to Hezeki´ah, 'Thus says the great king, the king of Assyria: On what do you rest this confidence of yours? 5Do you think that mere words are strategy and power for war? On whom do you now rely, that you have rebelled against me? 6Behold, you are relying on Egypt, that broken reed of a staff, which will pierce the hand of any man who leans on it. Such is Pharaoh king of Egypt to all who rely on him. 7But if you say to me, "We rely on the LORD our God," is it not he whose high places and altars Hezeki´ah has removed, saying to Judah and to Jerusalem, "You shall worship before this altar"? 8Come now, make a wager with my master the king of Assyria: I will give you two thousand horses, if you are able on your part to set riders upon them. 9How then can you repulse a single captain among the least of my master's servants, when you rely on Egypt for chariots and for horsemen? 10Moreover, is it without the LORD that I have come up against this land to destroy it? The LORD said to me, Go up against this land, and destroy it.'"

11 Then Eli´akim, Shebna, and Jo´ah said to the Rab´shakeh, "Pray, speak to your servants in Aramaic, for we understand it; do not speak to us in the language of Judah within the hearing of the people who are on the wall." 12But the Rab´shakeh said, "Has my master sent me to speak these words to your master and to you, and not to the men sitting on the wall, who are doomed with you to eat their own dung and drink their own urine?"

13 Then the Rab´shakeh stood and called out in a loud voice in the language of Judah: "Hear the words of the great king, the king of Assyria! 14Thus says the king: 'Do not let Hezeki´ah deceive you, for he will not be able to deliver you. 15Do not let Hezeki´ah make you rely on the LORD by saying, "The LORD will surely deliver us; this city will not be given into the hand of the king of Assyria." 16Do not listen to Hezeki´ah; for thus says the king of Assyria: Make your peace with me and come out to me; then every one of you will eat of his own vine, and every one of his own fig tree, and every one of you will drink the water of his own cistern; 17until I come and take you away to a land like your own land, a land of grain and wine, a land of bread and vineyards. 18Beware lest Hezeki´ah mislead you by saying, "The LORD will deliver us." Has any of the gods of the nations delivered his land out of the hand of the king of Assyria? 19Where are the gods of Hamath and Arpad? Where are the gods of Sepharva´im? Have they delivered Samar´ia out of my hand? 20Who among all the gods of these countries have delivered their countries out of my hand, that the LORD should deliver Jerusalem out of my hand?'"

21 But they were silent and an-
swered him not a word, for the king's
command was, "Do not answer him."
22Then Eli´akim the son of Hilki´ah,
who was over the household, and
Shebna the secretary, and Jo´ah the
son of Asaph, the recorder, came to
Hezeki´ah with their clothes rent, and
told him the words of the Rab´shakeh.

HEZEKIAH CONSULTS ISAIAH

37 When King Hezeki´ah heard it,
he rent his clothes, and covered
himself with sackcloth, and went into
the house of the LORD. 2And he sent
Eli´akim, who was over the house-
hold, and Shebna the secretary, and
the senior priests, clothed with sack-
cloth, to the prophet Isaiah the son of
Amoz. 3They said to him, "Thus says
Hezeki´ah, 'This day is a day of dis-
tress, of rebuke, and of disgrace; chil-
dren have come to the birth, and there
is no strength to bring them forth.
4It may be that the LORD your God
heard the words of the Rab´shakeh,
whom his master the king of Assyria
has sent to mock the living God, and
will rebuke the words which the LORD
your God has heard; therefore lift up
your prayer for the remnant that is
left.'"

5 When the servants of King
Hezeki´ah came to Isaiah, 6Isaiah
said to them, "Say to your master,
'Thus says the LORD: Do not be
afraid because of the words that you
have heard, with which the servants
of the king of Assyria have reviled
me. 7Behold, I will put a spirit in
him, so that he shall hear a rumor,
and return to his own land; and I will
make him fall by the sword in his
own land.'"

8 The Rab´shakeh returned, and
found the king of Assyria fighting
against Libnah; for he had heard that
the king had left Lachish. 9Now the
king heard concerning Tirha´kah
king of Ethiopia, "He has set out
to fight against you." And when
he heard it, he sent messengers to
Hezeki´ah, saying, 10"Thus shall you
speak to Hezeki´ah king of Judah:
'Do not let your God on whom you
rely deceive you by promising that
Jerusalem will not be given into the
hand of the king of Assyria. 11Behold,
you have heard what the kings of
Assyria have done to all lands, de-
stroying them utterly. And shall
you be delivered? 12Have the gods of
the nations delivered them, the na-
tions which my fathers destroyed,
Gozan, Haran, Rezeph, and the peo-
ple of Eden who were in Telas´sar?
13Where is the king of Hamath, the
king of Arpad, the king of the city
of Sepharva´im, the king of Hena, or
the king of Ivvah?'"

HEZEKIAH'S PRAYER

14 Hezeki´ah received the letter
from the hand of the messengers,
and read it; and Hezeki´ah went up
to the house of the LORD, and spread
it before the LORD. 15And Hezeki´ah
prayed to the LORD: 16"O LORD of
hosts, God of Israel, who art en-
throned above the cherubim, thou art
the God, thou alone, of all the king-
doms of the earth; thou hast made
heaven and earth. 17Incline thy ear,
O LORD, and hear; open thy eyes, O
LORD, and see; and hear all the words
of Sennach´erib, which he has sent to
mock the living God. 18Of a truth,
O LORD, the kings of Assyria have
laid waste all the nations and their
lands, 19and have cast their gods into
the fire; for they were no gods, but
the work of men's hands, wood and
stone; therefore they were destroyed.
20So now, O LORD our God, save us
from his hand, that all the kingdoms
of the earth may know that thou
alone art the LORD."

21 Then Isaiah the son of Amoz
sent to Hezeki´ah, saying, "Thus says
the LORD, the God of Israel: Because
you have prayed to me concerning
Sennach´erib king of Assyria, 22this
is the word that the LORD has spoken
concerning him:

'She despises you, she scorns
you—
the virgin daughter of Zion;
she wags her head behind
you—
the daughter of Jerusalem.
23'Whom have you mocked and
reviled?
Against whom have you
raised your voice
and haughtily lifted your
eyes?
Against the Holy One of
Israel!
24By your servants you have
mocked the Lord,
and you have said, With my
many chariots
I have gone up the heights of
the mountains,
to the far recesses of
Lebanon;
I felled its tallest cedars,
its choicest cypresses;
I came to its remotest height,
its densest forest.
25I dug wells
and drank waters,
and I dried up with the sole of
my foot
all the streams of Egypt.
26'Have you not heard
that I determined it long
ago?
I planned from days of old
what now I bring to pass,
that you should make fortified
cities
crash into heaps of ruins,
27while their inhabitants, shorn of
strength,
are dismayed and
confounded,
and have become like plants of
the field
and like tender grass,
like grass on the housetops,
blighted[a] before it is grown.
28'I know your sitting down
and your going out and
coming in,
and your raging against me.
29Because you have raged against
me
and your arrogance has
come to my ears,
I will put my hook in your
nose
and my bit in your mouth,
and I will turn you back on
the way
by which you came.'

30 "And this shall be the sign for
you: this year eat what grows of itself,
and in the second year what springs of
the same; then in the third year sow
and reap, and plant vineyards, and
eat their fruit. 31And the surviving
remnant of the house of Judah shall
again take root downward, and bear
fruit upward; 32for out of Jerusalem
shall go forth a remnant, and out of
Mount Zion a band of survivors. The
zeal of the LORD of hosts will accom-
plish this.

33 "Therefore thus says the LORD
concerning the king of Assyria: He
shall not come into this city, or
shoot an arrow there, or come before
it with a shield, or cast up a siege
mound against it. 34By the way that
he came, by the same he shall re-
turn, and he shall not come into this
city, says the LORD. 35For I will de-
fend this city to save it, for my own
sake and for the sake of my servant
David."

SENNACHERIB'S DEFEAT AND DEATH

36 And the angel of the LORD
went forth, and slew a hundred and
eighty-five thousand in the camp
of the Assyrians; and when men
arose early in the morning, behold,
these were all dead bodies. 37Then
Sennach′erib king of Assyria de-
parted, and went home and dwelt at
Nin′eveh. 38And as he was worship-
ing in the house of Nisroch his god,
Adram′melech and Share′zer, his
sons, slew him with the sword, and
escaped into the land of Ar′arat. And

[a] With 2Kings 19. 26: Heb *field*

E´sar-had´don his son reigned in his
stead.

HEZEKIAH'S ILLNESS

38 In those days Hezeki´ah be-
came sick and was at the point
of death. And Isaiah the prophet the
son of Amoz came to him, and said
to him, "Thus says the LORD: Set
your house in order; for you shall
die, you shall not recover." 2Then
Hezeki´ah turned his face to the
wall, and prayed to the LORD, 3and
said, "Remember now, O LORD, I
beseech thee, how I have walked be-
fore thee in faithfulness and with a
whole heart, and have done what is
good in thy sight." And Hezeki´ah
wept bitterly. 4Then the word of the
LORD came to Isaiah: 5"Go and say
to Hezeki´ah, Thus says the LORD,
the God of David your father: I have
heard your prayer, I have seen your
tears; behold, I will add fifteen years
to your life. 6I will deliver you and
this city out of the hand of the king
of Assyria, and defend this city.

7 "This is the sign to you from the
LORD, that the LORD will do this thing
that he has promised: 8Behold, I will
make the shadow cast by the declin-
ing sun on the dial of Ahaz turn back
ten steps." So the sun turned back on
the dial the ten steps by which it had
declined.[b]

9 A writing of Hezeki´ah king of
Judah, after he had been sick and had
recovered from his sickness:

10I said, In the noontide of my days
I must depart;
I am consigned to the gates of Sheol
for the rest of my years.
11I said, I shall not see the LORD
in the land of the living;
I shall look upon man no more
among the inhabitants of the world.
12My dwelling is plucked up and removed from me
like a shepherd's tent;
like a weaver I have rolled up my life;
he cuts me off from the loom;
from day to night thou dost bring me to an end;[c]
13I cry for help[d] until morning;
like a lion he breaks all my bones;
from day to night thou dost bring me to an end.[e]
14Like a swallow or a crane[f] I clamor,
I moan like a dove.
My eyes are weary with looking upward.
O Lord, I am oppressed; be thou my security!
15But what can I say? For he has spoken to me,
and he himself has done it.
All my sleep has fled[g]
because of the bitterness of my soul.
16O Lord, by these things men live,
and in all these is the life of my spirit.[h]
Oh, restore me to health and make me live!
17Lo, it was for my welfare
that I had great bitterness;
but thou hast held back[i] my life
from the pit of destruction,
for thou hast cast all my sins
behind thy back.
18For Sheol cannot thank thee,
death cannot praise thee;

[b]The Hebrew of this verse is obscure
[c] Heb uncertain
[d]Cn: Heb obscure
[e] Heb uncertain
[f]Heb uncertain
[g]Cn Compare Syr: Heb *I will walk slowly all my years*
[h] Heb uncertain
[i]Cn Compare Gk Vg: Heb *loved*

those who go down to the pit
cannot hope
for thy faithfulness.
19The living, the living, he thanks
thee,
as I do this day;
the father makes known to the
children
thy faithfulness.
20The LORD will save me,
and we will sing to stringed
instruments[a]
all the days of our life,
at the house of the LORD.

21 Now Isaiah had said, "Let
them take a cake of figs, and apply
it to the boil, that he may recover."
22Hezeki′ah also had said, "What is
the sign that I shall go up to the house
of the LORD?"

ENVOYS FROM BABYLON WELCOMED

39 At that time Mero′dach-bal′adan
the son of Bal′adan, king of
Babylon, sent envoys with letters
and a present to Hezeki′ah, for he
heard that he had been sick and
had recovered. 2And Hezeki′ah wel-
comed them; and he showed them
his treasure house, the silver, the
gold, the spices, the precious oil, his
whole armory, all that was found in
his storehouses. There was nothing
in his house or in all his realm that
Hezeki′ah did not show them. 3Then
Isaiah the prophet came to King
Hezeki′ah, and said to him, "What
did these men say? And whence
did they come to you?" Hezeki′ah
said, "They have come to me from
a far country, from Babylon." 4He
said, "What have they seen in your
house?" Hezeki′ah answered, "They
have seen all that is in my house;
there is nothing in my storehouses
that I did not show them."

5 Then Isaiah said to Hezeki′ah,
"Hear the word of the LORD of
hosts: 6Behold, the days are coming,
when all that is in your house, and
that which your fathers have stored
up till this day, shall be carried to
Babylon; nothing shall be left, says
the LORD. 7And some of your own
sons, who are born to you, shall be
taken away; and they shall be eu-
nuchs in the palace of the king of
Babylon." 8Then said Hezeki′ah
to Isaiah, "The word of the LORD
which you have spoken is good." For
he thought, "There will be peace and
security in my days."

GOD'S PEOPLE ARE COMFORTED

40 *Comfort, comfort my people,
says your God.
2Speak tenderly to Jerusalem,
and cry to her
that her warfare[b] is ended,
that her iniquity is
pardoned,
that she has received from the
LORD's hand
double for all her sins.
3A voice cries:
"In the wilderness prepare the
way of the LORD,
make straight in the desert
a highway for our
God.
4Every valley shall be lifted up,
and every mountain and hill
be made low;
the uneven ground shall be-
come level,
and the rough places a
plain.
5And the glory of the LORD shall
be revealed,
and all flesh shall see it
together,
for the mouth of the LORD
has spoken."
6A voice says, "Cry!"
And I said, "What shall I
cry?"
All flesh is grass,
and all its beauty is like the
flower of the field.
7The grass withers, the flower

[a] Heb *my stringed instruments*
[b] Or *time of service*

fades,
when the breath of the LORD blows upon it;
surely the people is grass.
8The grass withers, the flower fades;
but the word of our God will stand for ever.
9Get you up to a high mountain,
O Zion, herald of good tidings;[c]
lift up your voice with strength,
O Jerusalem, herald of good tidings,[d]
lift it up, fear not;
say to the cities of Judah,
"Behold your God!"
10Behold, the Lord GOD comes with might,
and his arm rules for him;
behold, his reward is with him,
and his recompense before him.
11He will feed his flock like a shepherd,
he will gather the lambs in his arms,
he will carry them in his bosom,
and gently lead those that are with young.
12Who has measured the waters in the hollow of his hand
and marked off the heavens with a span,
enclosed the dust of the earth in a measure
and weighed the mountains in scales
and the hills in a balance?
13Who has directed the Spirit of the LORD,
or as his counselor has instructed him?
14Whom did he consult for his enlightenment,
and who taught him the path of justice,
and taught him knowledge,
and showed him the way of understanding?
15Behold, the nations are like a drop from a bucket,
and are accounted as the dust on the scales;
behold, he takes up the isles like fine dust.
16Lebanon would not suffice for fuel,
nor are its beasts enough for a burnt offering.
17All the nations are as nothing before him,
they are accounted by him as less than nothing and emptiness.
18To whom then will you liken God,
or what likeness compare with him?
19The idol! a workman casts it,
and a goldsmith overlays it with gold,
and casts for it silver chains.
20He who is impoverished[e] chooses for an offering
wood that will not rot;
he seeks out a skilful craftsman
to set up an image that will not move.
21Have you not known? Have you not heard?
Has it not been told you from the beginning?
Have you not understood from the foundations of the earth?
22It is he who sits above the circle of the earth,
and its inhabitants are like grasshoppers;
who stretches out the heavens like a curtain,
and spreads them like a tent to dwell in;
23who brings princes to nought,

[c] Or *O herald of good tidings to Zion*
[d] Or *O herald of good tidings to Jerusalem*
[e] Heb uncertain

and makes the rulers of the
earth as nothing.
24Scarcely are they planted,
scarcely sown,
scarcely has their stem taken
root in the earth,
when he blows upon them, and
they wither,
and the tempest car-
ries them off like
stubble.
25To whom then will you compare
me,
that I should be like him?
says the Holy One.
26Lift up your eyes on high and
see:
who created these?
He who brings out their host
by number,
calling them all by name;
by the greatness of his might,
and because he is strong in
power
not one is missing.
27Why do you say, O Jacob,
and speak, O Israel,
"My way is hid from the
LORD,
and my right is disregarded
by my God"?
28Have you not known? Have you
not heard?
The LORD is the everlasting
God,
the Creator of the ends of
the earth.
He does not faint or grow
weary,
his understanding is
unsearchable.
29He gives power to the faint,
and to him who has no
might he increases
strength.
30Even youths shall faint and be
weary,
and young men shall fall
exhausted;
31but they who wait for the
LORD shall renew their
strength,
they shall mount up with
wings like eagles,
they shall run and not be
weary,
they shall walk and not
faint.

ISRAEL ASSURED OF GOD'S HELP

41 Listen to me in silence, O
coastlands;
let the peoples renew their
strength;
let them approach, then let
them speak;
let us together draw near for
judgment.
2Who stirred up one from the
east
whom victory meets at every
step?
He gives up nations before
him,
so that he tramples kings
under foot;
he makes them like dust with
his sword,
like driven stubble with his
bow.
3He pursues them and passes on
safely,
by paths his feet have not
trod.
4Who has performed and done
this,
calling the generations from
the beginning?
I, the LORD, the first,
and with the last; I am He.
5The coastlands have seen and are
afraid,
the ends of the earth
tremble;
they have drawn near and
come.
6Every one helps his neighbor,
and says to his brother,
"Take courage!"
7The craftsman encourages the
goldsmith,
and he who smooths with
the hammer him
who strikes the

anvil,
saying of the soldering, "It is good";
and they fasten it with nails so that it cannot be moved.
8But you, Israel, my servant,
Jacob, whom I have chosen,
the offspring of Abraham, my friend;
9you whom I took from the ends of the earth,
and called from its farthest corners,
saying to you, "You are my servant,
I have chosen you and not cast you off";
10fear not, for I am with you,
be not dismayed, for I am your God;
I will strengthen you, I will help you,
I will uphold you with my victorious right hand.
11Behold, all who are incensed against you
shall be put to shame and confounded;
those who strive against you
shall be as nothing and shall perish.
12You shall seek those who contend with you,
but you shall not find them;
those who war against you
shall be as nothing at all.
13For I, the LORD your God,
hold your right hand;
it is I who say to you, "Fear not,
I will help you."
14Fear not, you worm Jacob,
you men of Israel!
I will help you, says the LORD;
your Redeemer is the Holy One of Israel.
15Behold, I will make of you a threshing sledge,
new, sharp, and having teeth;
you shall thresh the mountains and crush them,
and you shall make the hills like chaff;
16you shall winnow them and the wind shall carry them away,
and the tempest shall scatter them.
And you shall rejoice in the LORD;
in the Holy One of Israel you shall glory.
17When the poor and needy seek water,
and there is none,
and their tongue is parched with thirst,
I the LORD will answer them,
I the God of Israel will not forsake them.
18I will open rivers on the bare heights,
and fountains in the midst of the valleys;
I will make the wilderness a pool of water,
and the dry land springs of water.
19I will put in the wilderness the cedar,
the acacia, the myrtle, and the olive;
I will set in the desert the cypress,
the plane and the pine together;
20that men may see and know,
may consider and understand together,
that the hand of the LORD has done this,
the Holy One of Israel has created it.

THE FUTILITY OF IDOLS

21Set forth your case, says the LORD;
bring your proofs, says the King of Jacob.
22Let them bring them, and tell us what is to happen.

Tell us the former things, what they are,
that we may consider them,
that we may know their outcome;
or declare to us the things to come.
23Tell us what is to come hereafter,
that we may know that you are gods;
do good, or do harm,
that we may be dismayed and terrified.
24Behold, you are nothing,
and your work is nought;
an abomination is he who chooses you.
25I stirred up one from the north, and he has come,
from the rising of the sun, and he shall call on my name;
he shall trample[a] on rulers as on mortar,
as the potter treads clay.
26Who declared it from the beginning, that we might know,
and beforetime, that we might say, "He is right"?
There was none who declared it, none who proclaimed,
none who heard your words.
27I first have declared it to Zion,[b]
and I give to Jerusalem a herald of good tidings.
28But when I look there is no one;
among these there is no counselor
who, when I ask, gives an answer.
29Behold, they are all a delusion;
their works are nothing;
their molten images are empty wind.

THE SERVANT, A LIGHT TO THE NATIONS

42 *Behold my servant, whom I uphold,
my chosen, in whom my soul delights;
I have put my Spirit upon him,
he will bring forth justice to the nations.
2He will not cry or lift up his voice,
or make it heard in the street;
3a bruised reed he will not break,
and a dimly burning wick he will not quench;
he will faithfully bring forth justice.
4He will not fail[c] or be discouraged[d]
till he has established justice in the earth;
and the coastlands wait for his law.
5Thus says God, the LORD,
who created the heavens and stretched them out,
who spread forth the earth and what comes from it,
who gives breath to the people upon it
and spirit to those who walk in it:
6"I am the LORD, I have called you in righteousness,
I have taken you by the hand and kept you;
I have given you as a covenant to the people,
a light to the nations,
7to open the eyes that are blind,
to bring out the prisoners from

[a]Cn: Heb *come*
[b]Cn: Heb *first to Zion, Behold, behold them*
[c]Or *burn dimly*
[d]Or *bruised*

the dungeon,
from the prison those who
sit in darkness.
8I am the LORD, that is my name;
my glory I give to no other,
nor my praise to graven
images.
9Behold, the former things have
come to pass,
and new things I now
declare;
before they spring forth
I tell you of them."

A HYMN OF PRAISE

10Sing to the LORD a new song,
his praise from the end of
the earth!
Let the sea roar[e] and all that
fills it,
the coastlands and their
inhabitants.
11Let the desert and its cities lift
up their voice,
the villages that Kedar
inhabits;
let the inhabitants of Sela sing
for joy,
let them shout from the top
of the mountains.
12Let them give glory to the
LORD,
and declare his praise in the
coastlands.
13The LORD goes forth like a
mighty man,
like a man of war he stirs up
his fury;
he cries out, he shouts aloud,
he shows himself mighty
against his foes.
14For a long time I have held my
peace,
I have kept still and re-
strained myself;
now I will cry out like a woman
in travail,
I will gasp and pant.
15I will lay waste mountains and
hills,
and dry up all their
herbage;
I will turn the rivers into
islands,
and dry up the pools.
16And I will lead the blind
in a way that they know
not,
in paths that they have not
known
I will guide them.
I will turn the darkness before
them into light,
the rough places into level
ground.
These are the things I will do,
and I will not forsake them.
17They shall be turned back and
utterly put to shame,
who trust in graven images,
who say to molten images,
"You are our gods."
18Hear, you deaf;
and look, you blind, that you
may see!
19Who is blind but my servant,
or deaf as my messenger
whom I send?
Who is blind as my dedicated
one,
or blind as the servant of the
LORD?
20He sees[f] many things, but does
not observe them;
his ears are open, but he
does not hear.

ISRAEL'S DISOBEDIENCE

21The LORD was pleased, for his
righteousness' sake,
to magnify his law and make
it glorious.
22But this is a people robbed and
plundered,
they are all of them trapped
in holes
and hidden in prisons;
they have become a prey with
none to rescue,
a spoil with none to say,

[e] Cn Compare Ps 96. 11; 98.7: Heb *Those who go down to the sea*
[f] Heb *you see*

"Restore!"
23Who among you will give ear
to this,
will attend and listen for the
time to come?
24Who gave up Jacob to the
spoiler,
and Israel to the robbers?
Was it not the LORD, against
whom we have sinned,
in whose ways they would
not walk,
and whose law they would
not obey?
25So he poured upon him the heat
of his anger
and the might of battle;
it set him on fire round
about, but he did not
understand;
it burned him, but he did not
take it to heart.

RESTORATION AND PROTECTION PROMISED

43 But now thus says the LORD,
he who created you, O Jacob,
he who formed you, O
Israel:
"Fear not, for I have redeemed
you;
I have called you by name,
you are mine.
2When you pass through the wa-
ters I will be with you;
and through the rivers, they
shall not overwhelm
you;
when you walk through
fire you shall not be
burned,
and the flame shall not
consume you.
3For I am the LORD your God,
the Holy One of Israel, your
Savior.
I give Egypt as your ransom,
Ethiopia and Seba in ex-
change for you.
4Because you are precious in my
eyes,
and honored, and I love
you,
I give men in return for you,
peoples in exchange for your
life.
5Fear not, for I am with you;
I will bring your offspring
from the east,
and from the west I will
gather you;
6I will say to the north, Give up,
and to the south, Do not
withhold;
bring my sons from afar
and my daughters from the
end of the earth,
7every one who is called by my
name,
whom I created for my
glory,
whom I formed and made."
8Bring forth the people who are
blind, yet have eyes,
who are deaf, yet have ears!
9Let all the nations gather
together,
and let the peoples
assemble.
Who among them can declare
this,
and show us the former
things?
Let them bring their witnesses
to justify them,
and let them hear and say, It
is true.
10"You are my witnesses," says the
LORD,
"and my servant whom I
have chosen,
that you may know and believe
me
and understand that I am
He.
Before me no god was formed,
nor shall there be any after
me.
11I, I am the LORD,
and besides me there is no
savior.
12I declared and saved and
proclaimed,
when there was no strange

god among you;
and you are my witnesses,"
says the LORD.
13"I am God, and also henceforth
I am He;
there is none who can deliver from my hand;
I work and who can hinder
it?"
14Thus says the LORD,
your Redeemer, the Holy One
of Israel:
"For your sake I will send to
Babylon
and break down all the
bars,
and the shouting of the
Chalde´ans will
be turned to
lamentations.[a]
15I am the LORD, your Holy One,
the Creator of Israel, your
King."
16Thus says the LORD,
who makes a way in the sea,
a path in the mighty waters,
17who brings forth chariot and
horse,
army and warrior;
they lie down, they cannot
rise,
they are extinguished,
quenched like a
wick:
18"Remember not the former
things,
nor consider the things of
old.
19Behold, I am doing a new thing;
now it springs forth, do you
not perceive it?
I will make a way in the
wilderness
and rivers in the desert.
20The wild beasts will honor me,
the jackals and the
ostriches;
for I give water in the
wilderness,
rivers in the desert,
to give drink to my chosen
people,
21the people whom I formed
for myself
that they might declare my
praise.
22"Yet you did not call upon me,
O Jacob;
but you have been weary of
me, O Israel!
23You have not brought me your
sheep for burnt offerings,
or honored me with your
sacrifices.
I have not burdened you with
offerings,
or wearied you with
frankincense.
24You have not bought me sweet
cane with money,
or satisfied me with the fat
of your sacrifices.
But you have burdened me with
your sins,
you have wearied me with
your iniquities.
25"I, I am He
who blots out your transgressions for my own
sake,
and I will not remember
your sins.
26Put me in remembrance, let us
argue together;
set forth your case, that
you may be proved
right.
27Your first father sinned,
and your mediators transgressed against me.
28Therefore I profaned the princes
of the sanctuary,
I delivered Jacob to utter
destruction
and Israel to reviling.

GOD'S BLESSING ON ISRAEL

44 "But now hear, O Jacob my
servant,
Israel whom I have chosen!
2Thus says the LORD who made
you,

[a]Heb obscure

who formed you from the
womb and will help
you:
Fear not, O Jacob my servant,
Jesh´urun whom I have
chosen.
3For I will pour water on the
thirsty land,
and streams on the dry
ground;
I will pour my Spirit upon your
descendants,
and my blessing on your
offspring.
4They shall spring up like grass
amid waters,[a]
like willows by flowing
streams.
5This one will say, 'I am the
LORD's,'
another will call himself by
the name of Jacob,
and another will write on his
hand, 'The LORD's,'
and surname himself by the
name of Israel."
6Thus says the LORD, the King of
Israel
and his Redeemer, the LORD
of hosts:
"I am the first and I am the
last;
besides me there is no god.
7Who is like me? Let him pro-
claim it,
let him declare and set it
forth before me.
Who has announced from
of old the things to
come?[b]
Let them tell us[c] what is yet
to be.
8Fear not, nor be afraid;
have I not told you from of
old and declared it?
And you are my witnesses!
Is there a God besides me?
There is no Rock; I know not
any."

THE ABSURDITY OF IDOL WORSHIP

9 All who make idols are nothing,
and the things they delight in do not
profit; their witnesses neither see
nor know, that they may be put to
shame. 10Who fashions a god or casts
an image, that is profitable for noth-
ing? 11Behold, all his fellows shall
be put to shame, and the craftsmen
are but men; let them all assemble,
let them stand forth, they shall be
terrified, they shall be put to shame
together.

12 The ironsmith fashions it[d] and
works it over the coals; he shapes it
with hammers, and forges it with his
strong arm; he becomes hungry and
his strength fails, he drinks no water
and is faint. 13The carpenter stretch-
es a line, he marks it out with a pen-
cil; he fashions it with planes, and
marks it with a compass; he shapes
it into the figure of a man, with the
beauty of a man, to dwell in a house.
14He cuts down cedars; or he choos-
es a holm tree or an oak and lets it
grow strong among the trees of the
forest; he plants a cedar and the rain
nourishes it. 15Then it becomes fuel
for a man; he takes a part of it and
warms himself, he kindles a fire and
bakes bread; also he makes a god and
worships it, he makes it a graven im-
age and falls down before it. 16Half of
it he burns in the fire; over the half
he eats flesh, he roasts meat and is
satisfied; also he warms himself
and says, "Aha, I am warm, I have
seen the fire!" 17And the rest of it he
makes into a god, his idol; and falls
down to it and worships it; he prays
to it and says, "Deliver me, for thou
art my god!"

18 They know not, nor do they
discern; for he has shut their eyes, so
that they cannot see, and their minds,
so that they cannot understand. 19No
one considers, nor is there knowledge
or discernment to say, "Half of it I

[a]Gk Compare Tg: Heb *They shall spring up in among grass*
[b]Cn: Heb *from my placing an eternal people and things to come*
[c]Tg: Heb *them*
[d]Cn: Heb *an axe*

burned in the fire, I also baked bread
on its coals, I roasted flesh and have
eaten; and shall I make the residue of
it an abomination? Shall I fall down
before a block of wood?" 20He feeds
on ashes; a deluded mind has led him
astray, and he cannot deliver himself
or say, "Is there not a lie in my right
hand?"

ISRAEL IS NOT FORGOTTEN

21Remember these things, O Jacob,
and Israel, for you are my servant;
I formed you, you are my servant;
O Israel, you will not be forgotten by me.
22I have swept away your transgressions like a cloud,
and your sins like mist;
return to me, for I have redeemed you.
23Sing, O heavens, for the LORD has done it;
shout, O depths of the earth;
break forth into singing, O mountains,
O forest, and every tree in it!
For the LORD has redeemed Jacob,
and will be glorified in Israel.
24Thus says the LORD, your Redeemer,
who formed you from the womb:
"I am the LORD, who made all things,
who stretched out the heavens alone,
who spread out the earth—Who was with me?[e]—
25who frustrates the omens of liars,
and makes fools of diviners;
who turns wise men back,
and makes their knowledge foolish;
26who confirms the word of his servant,
and performs the counsel of his messengers;
who says of Jerusalem, 'She shall be inhabited,'
and of the cities of Judah, 'They shall be built,
and I will raise up their ruins';
27who says to the deep, 'Be dry,
I will dry up your rivers';
28who says of Cyrus, 'He is my shepherd,
and he shall fulfil all my purpose';
saying of Jerusalem, 'She shall be built,'
and of the temple, 'Your foundation shall be laid.'"

CYRUS, GOD'S INSTRUMENT

45 Thus says the LORD to his anointed, to Cyrus,
whose right hand I have grasped,
to subdue nations before him
and ungird the loins of kings,
to open doors before him
that gates may not be closed:
2"I will go before you
and level the mountains,[f]
I will break in pieces the doors of bronze
and cut asunder the bars of iron,
3I will give you the treasures of darkness
and the hoards in secret places,
that you may know that it is I, the LORD,
the God of Israel, who call you by your name.

[e] Another reading is *who spread out the earth by myself*
[f] One ancient Ms Gk: Heb *the swellings*

4For the sake of my servant
Jacob,
and Israel my chosen,
I call you by your name,
I surname you, though you
do not know me.
5I am the LORD, and there is no
other,
besides me there is no God;
I gird you, though you do
not know me,
6that men may know, from the
rising of the sun
and from the west, that
there is none besides
me;
I am the LORD, and there is
no other.
7I form light and create
darkness,
I make weal and create
woe,
I am the LORD, who do all
these things.
8"Shower, O heavens, from
above,
and let the skies rain down
righteousness;
let the earth open, that salva-
tion may sprout forth,[a]
and let it cause righteous-
ness to spring up
also;
I the LORD have created it.
9"Woe to him who strives with his
Maker,
an earthen vessel with the
potter![b]
Does the clay say to him who
fashions it, 'What are
you making?'
or 'Your work has no
handles'?
10Woe to him who says to a
father, 'What are you
begetting?'
or to a woman, 'With what
are you in travail?'"
11Thus says the LORD,
the Holy One of Israel, and
his Maker:
"Will you question me[c] about
my children,
or command me concern-
ing the work of my
hands?
12I made the earth,
and created man upon it;
it was my hands that
stretched out the
heavens,
and I commanded all their
host.
13I have aroused him in
righteousness,
and I will make straight all
his ways;
he shall build my city
and set my exiles free,
not for price or reward,"
says the LORD of hosts.
14Thus says the LORD:
"The wealth of Egypt and
the merchandise of
Ethiopia,
and the Sabe´ans, men of
stature,
shall come over to you and be
yours,
they shall follow you;
they shall come over in
chains and bow down
to you.
They will make supplication to
you, saying:
'God is with you only, and
there is no other,
no god besides him.'"
15Truly, thou art a God who hidest
thyself,
O God of Israel, the Savior.
16All of them are put to shame and
confounded,
the makers of idols go in
confusion together.
17But Israel is saved by the LORD
with everlasting salvation;
you shall not be put to shame
or confounded
to all eternity.

[a] One ancient Ms: Heb *that they may bring forth salvation*
[b] Cn: Heb *potsherds* or *potters*
[c] Cn: Heb *Ask me of things to come*

18For thus says the LORD,
who created the heavens
(he is God!),
who formed the earth and
made it
(he established it;
he did not create it a chaos,
he formed it to be
inhabited!):
"I am the LORD, and there is no
other.
19I did not speak in secret,
in a land of darkness;
I did not say to the offspring of
Jacob,
'Seek me in chaos.'
I the LORD speak the truth,
I declare what is right.

IDOLS CANNOT SAVE BABYLON

20"Assemble yourselves and
come,
draw near together,
you survivors of the
nations!
They have no knowledge
who carry about their wood-
en idols,
and keep on praying to a god
that cannot save.
21Declare and present your case;
let them take counsel
together!
Who told this long ago?
Who declared it of old?
Was it not I, the LORD?
And there is no other god
besides me,
a righteous God and a Savior;
there is none besides me.
22"Turn to me and be saved,
all the ends of the earth!
For I am God, and there is
no other.
23By myself I have sworn,
from my mouth has
gone forth in
righteousness
a word that shall not
return:
'To me every knee shall bow,
every tongue shall swear.'
24"Only in the LORD, it shall be
said of me,
are righteousness and
strength;
to him shall come and be
ashamed,
all who were incensed
against him.
25In the LORD all the offspring of
Israel
shall triumph and glory."

46 Bel bows down, Nebo stoops,
their idols are on beasts and
cattle;
these things you carry are
loaded
as burdens on weary beasts.
2They stoop, they bow down
together,
they cannot save the burden,
but themselves go into
captivity.
3"Hearken to me, O house of
Jacob,
all the remnant of the house
of Israel,
who have been borne by me
from your birth,
carried from the womb;
4even to your old age I am He,
and to gray hairs I will carry
you.
I have made, and I will bear;
I will carry and will save.
5"To whom will you liken me and
make me equal,
and compare me, that we
may be alike?
6Those who lavish gold from the
purse,
and weigh out silver in the
scales,
hire a goldsmith, and he makes
it into a god;
then they fall down and
worship!
7They lift it upon their shoulders,
they carry it,
they set it in its place, and
its stands there;
it cannot move from its
place.

If one cries to it, it does not answer
or save him from his trouble.
8"Remember this and consider,
recall it to mind, you transgressors,
9remember the former things of old;
for I am God, and there is no other;
I am God, and there is none like me,
10declaring the end from the beginning
and from ancient times things not yet done,
saying, 'My counsel shall stand,
and I will accomplish all my purpose,'
11calling a bird of prey from the east,
the man of my counsel from a far country.
I have spoken, and I will bring it to pass;
I have purposed, and I will do it.
12"Hearken to me, you stubborn of heart,
you who are far from deliverance:
13I bring near my deliverance, it is not far off,
and my salvation will not tarry;
I will put salvation in Zion,
for Israel my glory."

THE HUMILIATION OF BABYLON

47 Come down and sit in the dust,
O virgin daughter of Babylon;
sit on the ground without a throne,
O daughter of the Chalde´ans!
For you shall no more be called
tender and delicate.
2Take the millstones and grind meal,
put off your veil,
strip off your robe, uncover your legs,
pass through the rivers.
3Your nakedness shall be uncovered,
and your shame shall be seen.
I will take vengeance,
and I will spare no man.
4Our Redeemer—the LORD of hosts is his name—
is the Holy One of Israel.
5Sit in silence, and go into darkness,
O daughter of the Chalde´ans;
for you shall no more be called
the mistress of kingdoms.
6I was angry with my people,
I profaned my heritage;
I gave them into your hand,
you showed them no mercy;
on the aged you made your yoke
exceedingly heavy.
7You said, "I shall be mistress for ever,"
so that you did not lay these things to heart
or remember their end.
8Now therefore hear this, you lover of pleasures,
who sit securely,
who say in your heart,
"I am, and there is no one besides me;
I shall not sit as a widow
or know the loss of children":
9These two things shall come to you
in a moment, in one day;
the loss of children and widowhood
shall come upon you in full measure,
in spite of your many sorceries
and the great power of your enchantments.
10You felt secure in your

wickedness,
you said, "No one sees me";
your wisdom and your knowledge
led you astray,
and you said in your heart,
"I am, and there is no one besides me."
11But evil shall come upon you,
for which you cannot atone;
disaster shall fall upon you,
which you will not be able to expiate;
and ruin shall come on you suddenly,
of which you know nothing.
12Stand fast in your enchantments
and your many sorceries,
with which you have labored from your youth;
perhaps you may be able to succeed,
perhaps you may inspire terror.
13You are wearied with your many counsels;
let them stand forth and save you,
those who divide the heavens,
who gaze at the stars,
who at the new moons predict
what[a] shall befall you.
14Behold, they are like stubble,
the fire consumes them;
they cannot deliver themselves
from the power of the flame.
No coal for warming oneself is this,
no fire to sit before!
15Such to you are those with whom you have labored,
who have trafficked with you from your youth;
they wander about each in his own direction;
there is no one to save you.

GOD THE CREATOR AND REDEEMER

48 Hear this, O house of Jacob,
who are called by the name of Israel,
and who came forth from the loins[b] of Judah;
who swear by the name of the LORD,
and confess the God of Israel,
but not in truth or right.
2For they call themselves after the holy city,
and stay themselves on the God of Israel;
the LORD of hosts is his name.
3"The former things I declared of old,
they went forth from my mouth and I made them known;
then suddenly I did them and they came to pass.
4Because I know that you are obstinate,
and your neck is an iron sinew
and your forehead brass,
5I declared them to you from of old,
before they came to pass I announced them to you,
lest you should say, 'My idol did them,
my graven image and my molten image commanded them.'
6"You have heard; now see all this;
and will you not declare it?
From this time forth I make you hear new things,
hidden things which you have not known.
7They are created now, not long ago;
before today you have never heard of them,

[a] Gk Syr Compare Vg: Heb *from what*
[b] Cn: Heb *waters*

lest you should say,
'Behold, I knew
them.'
8You have never heard, you have
never known,
from of old your ear has not
been opened.
For I knew that you would deal
very treacherously,
and that from birth you were
called a rebel.
9"For my name's sake I defer my
anger,
for the sake of my praise I
restrain it for you,
that I may not cut you off.
10Behold, I have refined you, but
not like[a] silver;
I have tried you in the fur-
nace of affliction.
11For my own sake, for my own
sake, I do it,
for how should my name[b] be
profaned?
My glory I will not give to
another.
12"Hearken to me, O Jacob,
and Israel, whom I called!
I am He, I am the first,
and I am the last.
13My hand laid the foundation of
the earth,
and my right hand spread
out the heavens;
when I call to them,
they stand forth together.
14"Assemble, all of you, and hear!
who among them has de-
clared these things?
The LORD loves him;
he shall perform his purpose
on Babylon,
and his arm shall be against
the Chalde'ans.
15I, even I, have spoken and called
him,
I have brought him, and he
will prosper in his
way.
16Draw near to me, hear this:
from the beginning I have
not spoken in secret,
from the time it came to be I
have been there."
And now the Lord GOD has
sent me and his Spirit.
17Thus says the LORD,
your Redeemer, the Holy
One of Israel:
"I am the LORD your God,
who teaches you to profit,
who leads you in the way
you should go.
18O that you had hearkened to my
commandments!
Then your peace would
have been like a
river,
and your righteousness like
the waves of the sea;
19your offspring would have been
like the sand,
and your descendants like its
grains;
their name would never be
cut off
or destroyed from before
me."
20Go forth from Babylon, flee from
Chalde'a,
declare this with a shout of
joy, proclaim it,
send it forth to the end of the
earth;
say, "The LORD has re-
deemed his servant
Jacob!"
21They thirsted not when he led
them through the deserts;
he made water flow for them
from the rock;
he cleft the rock and the
water gushed out.
22"There is no peace," says the
LORD, "for the wicked."

THE SERVANT'S MISSION

49 Listen to me, O coastlands,
and hearken, you peoples from
afar.

[a]Cn: Heb *with*
[b]Gk Old Latin: Heb lacks *my name*

The LORD called me from the womb,
from the body of my mother he named my name.
2He made my mouth like a sharp sword,
in the shadow of his hand he hid me;
he made me a polished arrow,
in his quiver he hid me away.
3And he said to me, "You are my servant,
Israel, in whom I will be glorified."
4But I said, "I have labored in vain,
I have spent my strength for nothing and vanity;
yet surely my right is with the LORD,
and my recompense with my God."
5And now the LORD says,
who formed me from the womb to be his servant,
to bring Jacob back to him,
and that Israel might be gathered to him,
for I am honored in the eyes of the LORD,
and my God has become my strength—
6he says:
"It is too light a thing that you should be my servant
to raise up the tribes of Jacob
and to restore the preserved of Israel;
I will give you as a light to the nations,
that my salvation may reach to the end of the earth."
7Thus says the LORD,
the Redeemer of Israel and his Holy One,
to one deeply despised, abhorred by the nations,
the servant of rulers:
"Kings shall see and arise;
princes, and they shall prostrate themselves;
because of the LORD, who is faithful,
the Holy One of Israel, who has chosen you."

ZION'S CHILDREN TO BE BROUGHT HOME

8Thus says the LORD:
"In a time of favor I have answered you,
in a day of salvation I have helped you;
I have kept you and given you
as a covenant to the people,
to establish the land,
to apportion the desolate heritages;
9saying to the prisoners, 'Come forth,'
to those who are in darkness, 'Appear.'
They shall feed along the ways,
on all bare heights shall be their pasture;
10they shall not hunger or thirst,
neither scorching wind nor sun shall smite them,
for he who has pity on them will lead them,
and by springs of water will guide them.
11And I will make all my mountains a way,
and my highways shall be raised up.
12Lo, these shall come from afar,
and lo, these from the north and from the west,
and these from the land of Syenne."[c]
13Sing for joy, O heavens, and exult, O earth;

[c]Cn: Heb *Sinim*

break forth, O mountains,
into singing!
For the LORD has comforted
his people,
and will have compassion on
his afflicted.
14But Zion said, "The LORD has
forsaken me,
my Lord has forgotten me."
15"Can a woman forget her suck-
ing child,
that she should have no com-
passion on the son of
her womb?
Even these may forget,
yet I will not forget you.
16Behold, I have graven you on the
palms of my hands;
your walls are continually
before me.
17Your builders outstrip your
destroyers,
and those who laid you
waste go forth from
you.
18Lift up your eyes round about
and see;
they all gather, they come
to you.
As I live, says the LORD,
you shall put them all on as
an ornament,
you shall bind them on as a
bride does.
19"Surely your waste and your
desolate places
and your devastated land—
surely now you will be too
narrow for your
inhabitants,
and those who swallowed
you up will be far
away.
20The children born in the time of
your bereavement
will yet say in your ears:
'The place is too narrow for
me;
make room for me to dwell
in.'
21Then you will say in your
heart:
'Who has borne me these?
I was bereaved and barren,
exiled and put away,
but who has brought up
these?
Behold, I was left alone;
whence then have these
come?'"
22Thus says the Lord GOD:
"Behold, I will lift up my hand
to the nations,
and raise my signal to the
peoples;
and they shall bring your sons
in their bosom,
and your daughters shall
be carried on their
shoulders.
23Kings shall be your foster
fathers,
and their queens your nurs-
ing mothers.
With their faces to the ground
they shall bow down
to you,
and lick the dust of your
feet.
Then you will know that I am
the LORD;
those who wait for me
shall not be put to
shame."
24Can the prey be taken from the
mighty,
or the captives of a tyrant[a]
be rescued?
25Surely, thus says the LORD:
"Even the captives of the
mighty shall be taken,
and the prey of the tyrant be
rescued,
for I will contend with those
who contend with you,
and I will save your
children.
26I will make your oppressors eat
their own flesh,
and they shall be drunk with
their own blood as
with wine.

[a]One ancient Ms Syr Vg: Heb *righteous man*

Then all flesh shall know
that I am the LORD your Savior,
and your Redeemer, the Mighty One of Jacob."

50 Thus says the LORD:
"Where is your mother's bill of divorce,
with which I put her away?
Or which of my creditors is it
to whom I have sold you?
Behold, for your iniquities you were sold,
and for your transgressions your mother was put away.
2Why, when I came, was there no man?
When I called, was there no one to answer?
Is my hand shortened, that it cannot redeem?
Or have I no power to deliver?
Behold, by my rebuke I dry up the sea,
I make the rivers a desert;
their fish stink for lack of water,
and die of thirst.
3I clothe the heavens with blackness,
and make sackcloth their covering."

THE SERVANT'S HUMILIATION AND VINDICATION

4The Lord GOD has given me
the tongue of those who are taught,
that I may know how to sustain with a word
him that is weary.
Morning by morning he wakens,
he wakens my ear
to hear as those who are taught.
5The Lord GOD has opened my ear,
and I was not rebellious,
I turned not backward.
6I gave my back to the smiters,
and my cheeks to those who pulled out the beard;
I hid not my face
from shame and spitting.
7For the Lord GOD helps me;
therefore I have not been confounded;
therefore I have set my face like a flint,
and I know that I shall not be put to shame;
8he who vindicates me is near.
Who will contend with me?
Let us stand up together.
Who is my adversary?
Let him come near to me.
9Behold, the Lord GOD helps me;
who will declare me guilty?
Behold, all of them will wear out like a garment;
the moth will eat them up.
10Who among you fears the LORD
and obeys the voice of his servant,
who walks in darkness
and has no light,
yet trusts in the name of the LORD
and relies upon his God?
11Behold, all you who kindle a fire,
who set brands alight![b]
Walk by the light of your fire,
and by the brands which you have kindled!
This shall you have from my hand:
you shall lie down in torment.

BLESSINGS IN STORE FOR GOD'S PEOPLE

51 "Hearken to me, you who pursue deliverance,
you who seek the LORD;
look to the rock from which you were hewn,

[b]Syr: Heb *gird yourselves with brands*

and to the quarry from
which you were
digged.
2Look to Abraham your father
and to Sarah who bore you;
for when he was but one I
called him,
and I blessed him and made
him many.
3For the LORD will comfort Zion;
he will comfort all her waste
places,
and will make her wilderness
like Eden,
her desert like the garden of
the LORD;
joy and gladness will be found
in her,
thanksgiving and the voice
of song.
4"Listen to me, my people,
and give ear to me, my
nation;
for a law will go forth from
me,
and my justice for a light to
the peoples.
5My deliverance draws near
speedily,
my salvation has gone
forth,
and my arms will rule the
peoples;
the coastlands wait for me,
and for my arm they hope.
6Lift up your eyes to the
heavens,
and look at the earth
beneath;
for the heavens will vanish like
smoke,
the earth will wear out like a
garment,
and they who dwell in it will
die like gnats;[a]
but my salvation will be for
ever,
and my deliverance will
never be ended.
7"Hearken to me, you who know
righteousness,
the people in whose heart is
my law;
fear not the reproach of men,
and be not dismayed at their
revilings.
8For the moth will eat them up
like a garment,
and the worm will eat them
like wool;
but my deliverance will be for
ever,
and my salvation to all
generations."
9Awake, awake, put on strength,
O arm of the LORD;
awake, as in days of old,
the generations of long ago.
Was it not thou that didst cut
Rahab in pieces,
that didst pierce the
dragon?
10Was it not thou that didst dry up
the sea,
the waters of the great
deep;
that didst make the depths of
the sea a way
for the redeemed to pass
over?
11And the ransomed of the LORD
shall return,
and come to Zion with
singing;
everlasting joy shall be upon
their heads;
they shall obtain joy and
gladness,
and sorrow and sighing shall
flee away.
12"I, I am he that comforts you;
who are you that you are
afraid of man who
dies,
of the son of man who is
made like grass,
13and have forgotten the LORD,
your Maker,
who stretched out the
heavens
and laid the foundations of
the earth,

[a]Or *in like manner*

and fear continually all the day
because of the fury of the oppressor,
when he sets himself to destroy?
And where is the fury of the oppressor?
14He who is bowed down shall speedily be released;
he shall not die and go down to the Pit,
neither shall his bread fail.
15For I am the LORD your God,
who stirs up the sea so that its waves roar—
the LORD of hosts is his name.
16And I have put my words in your mouth,
and hid you in the shadow of my hand,
stretching out[b] the heavens
and laying the foundations of the earth,
and saying to Zion, 'You are my people.'"
17Rouse yourself, rouse yourself,
stand up, O Jerusalem,
you who have drunk at the hand of the LORD
the cup of his wrath,
who have drunk to the dregs
the bowl of staggering.
18There is none to guide her
among all the sons she has borne;
there is none to take her by the hand
among all the sons she has brought up.
19These two things have befallen you—
who will condole with you?—
devastation and destruction,
famine and sword;
who will comfort you?[c]
20Your sons have fainted,
they lie at the head of every street
like an antelope in a net;
they are full of the wrath of the LORD,
the rebuke of your God.
21Therefore hear this, you who are afflicted,
who are drunk, but not with wine:
22Thus says your Lord, the LORD,
your God who pleads the cause of his people:
"Behold, I have taken from your hand
the cup of staggering;
the bowl of my wrath
you shall drink no more;
23and I will put it into the hand of your tormentors,
who have said to you,
'Bow down, that we may pass over';
and you have made your back like the ground
and like the street for them to pass over."

LET ZION REJOICE

52 Awake, awake,
put on your strength, O Zion;
put on your beautiful garments,
O Jerusalem, the holy city;
for there shall no more come into you
the uncircumcised and the unclean.
2Shake yourself from the dust, arise,
O captive[d] Jerusalem;
loose the bonds from your neck,
O captive daughter of Zion.
3 For thus says the LORD: "You
were sold for nothing, and you shall
be redeemed without money. 4For
thus says the Lord GOD: My people
went down at the first into Egypt
to sojourn there, and the Assyrian
oppressed them for nothing. 5Now

[b] Syr: Heb *plant*
[c] One ancient Ms Gk Syr Vg: Heb *how may I comfort you*
[d] Cn: Heb *sit*

therefore what have I here, says the
LORD, seeing that my people are tak-
en away for nothing? Their rulers
wail, says the LORD, and continual-
ly all the day my name is despised.
6Therefore my people shall know
my name; therefore in that day they
shall know that it is I who speak;
here am I."

7How beautiful upon the mountains
are the feet of him who brings good tidings,
who publishes peace, who brings good tidings of good,
who publishes salvation,
who says to Zion, "Your God reigns."
8Hark, your watchmen lift up their voice,
together they sing for joy;
for eye to eye they see
the return of the LORD to Zion.
9Break forth together into singing,
you waste places of Jerusalem;
for the LORD has comforted his people,
he has redeemed Jerusalem.
10The LORD has bared his holy arm
before the eyes of all the nations;
and all the ends of the earth shall see
the salvation of our God.
11Depart, depart, go out thence,
touch no unclean thing;
go out from the midst of her,
purify yourselves,
you who bear the vessels of the LORD.
12For you shall not go out in haste,
and you shall not go in flight,
for the LORD will go before you,
and the God of Israel will be your rear guard.

THE SUFFERING SERVANT

13Behold, my servant shall prosper,
he shall be exalted and lifted up,
and shall be very high.
14As many were astonished at him[a] —
his appearance was so marred, beyond human semblance,
and his form beyond that of the sons of men—
15so shall he startle[b] many nations;
kings shall shut their mouths because of him;
for that which has not been told them they shall see,
and that which they have not heard they shall understand.

53 Who has believed what we have heard?
And to whom has the arm of the LORD been revealed?
2For he grew up before him like a young plant,
and like a root out of dry ground;
he had no form or comeliness that we should look at him,
and no beauty that we should desire him.
3He was despised and rejected[c] by men;
a man of sorrows,[d] and acquainted with

[a]Syr Tg: Heb *you*
[b]The meaning of the Hebrew word is uncertain
[c]Or *forsaken*
[d]Or *pains*

grief;[e]
and as one from whom men
hide their faces
he was despised, and we
esteemed him not.
4Surely he has borne our griefs[f]
and carried our sorrows;[g]
yet we esteemed him stricken,
smitten by God, and
afflicted.
5But he was wounded for our
transgressions,
he was bruised for our
iniquities;
upon him was the chastise-
ment that made us
whole,
and with his stripes we are
healed.
6All we like sheep have gone
astray;
we have turned every one to
his own way;
and the LORD has laid on him
the iniquity of us all.*
7He was oppressed, and he was
afflicted,
yet he opened not his
mouth;
like a lamb that is led to the
slaughter,
and like a sheep that before
its shearers is dumb,
so he opened not his
mouth.
8By oppression and judgment he
was taken away;
and as for his generation,
who considered
that he was cut off out of the
land of the living,
stricken for the transgres-
sion of my people?
9And they made his grave with
the wicked
and with a rich man in his
death,
although he had done no
violence,
and there was no deceit in
his mouth.
10Yet it was the will of the LORD
to bruise him;
he has put him to grief;[h]
when he makes himself[i] an
offering for sin,
he shall see his offspring,
he shall prolong his
days;
the will of the LORD shall pros-
per in his hand;
11he shall see the fruit of the
travail of his soul and
be satisfied;
by his knowledge shall the
righteous one, my
servant,
make many to be accounted
righteous;
and he shall bear their
iniquities.
12Therefore I will divide him a
portion with the great,
and he shall divide the
spoil with the
strong;
because he poured out his soul
to death,
and was numbered with the
transgressors;
yet he bore the sin of many,
and made intercession for
the transgressors.

THE ETERNAL COVENANT OF PEACE

54 "Sing, O barren one, who did not
bear;
break forth into singing and
cry aloud,
you who have not been in
travail!
For the children of the desolate
one will be more
than the children of her that
is married, says the
LORD.

[e] Or *sickness*
[f] Or *sicknesses*
[g] Or *pains*
[h] Heb *made him sick*
[i] Vg: Heb *thou makest his soul*

2Enlarge the place of your tent,
and let the curtains of your habitations be stretched out;
hold not back, lengthen your cords
and strengthen your stakes.
3For you will spread abroad to the right and to the left,
and your descendants will possess the nations
and will people the desolate cities.
4"Fear not, for you will not be ashamed;
be not confounded, for you will not be put to shame;
for you will forget the shame of your youth,
and the reproach of your widowhood you will remember no more.
5For your Maker is your husband,
the LORD of hosts is his name;
and the Holy One of Israel is your Redeemer,
the God of the whole earth he is called.
6For the LORD has called you
like a wife forsaken and grieved in spirit,
like a wife of youth when she is cast off,
says your God.
7For a brief moment I forsook you,
but with great compassion I will gather you.
8In overflowing wrath for a moment
I hid my face from you,
but with everlasting love I will have compassion on you,
says the LORD, your Redeemer.
9"For this is like the days of Noah to me:
as I swore that the waters of Noah
should no more go over the earth,
so I have sworn that I will not be angry with you
and will not rebuke you.
10For the mountains may depart
and the hills be removed,
but my steadfast love shall not depart from you,
and my covenant of peace shall not be removed,
says the LORD, who has compassion on you.
11"O afflicted one, storm-tossed, and not comforted,
behold, I will set your stones in antimony,
and lay your foundations with sapphires.[a]
12I will make your pinnacles of agate,
your gates of carbuncles,
and all your wall of precious stones.
13All your sons shall be taught by the LORD,
and great shall be the prosperity of your sons.
14In righteousness you shall be established;
you shall be far from oppression, for you shall not fear;
and from terror, for it shall not come near you.
15If any one stirs up strife,
it is not from me;
whoever stirs up strife with you
shall fall because of you.
16Behold, I have created the smith
who blows the fire of coals,
and produces a weapon for its purpose.
I have also created the ravager to destroy;
17no weapon that is

[a]Or *lapis lazuli*

fashioned against you
shall prosper,
and you shall confute
every tongue that
rises against you in
judgment.
This is the heritage of the servants of the LORD
and their vindication from
me, says the LORD."

AN INVITATION TO ABUNDANT LIFE

55 "Ho, every one who thirsts,
come to the waters;
and he who has no money,
come, buy and eat!
Come, buy wine and milk
without money and without
price.
2 Why do you spend your money
for that which is not
bread,
and your labor for that
which does not
satisfy?
Hearken diligently to me, and
eat what is good,
and delight yourselves in
fatness.
3 Incline your ear, and come to
me;
hear, that your soul may
live;
and I will make with you an
everlasting covenant,
my steadfast, sure love for
David.
4 Behold, I made him a witness to
the peoples,
a leader and commander for
the peoples.
5 Behold, you shall call nations
that you know not,
and nations that knew you
not shall run to you,
because of the LORD your God,
and of the Holy One of
Israel,
for he has glorified you.
6 "Seek the LORD while he may be
found,
call upon him while he is
near;
7 let the wicked forsake his way,
and the unrighteous man his
thoughts;
let him return to the LORD,
that he may have mercy
on him,
and to our God, for he will
abundantly pardon.
8 For my thoughts are not your
thoughts,
neither are your ways my
ways, says the LORD.
9 For as the heavens are higher
than the earth,
so are my ways higher than
your ways
and my thoughts than your
thoughts.
10 "For as the rain and the snow
come down from heaven,
and return not thither but
water the earth,
making it bring forth and
sprout,
giving seed to the sower and
bread to the eater,
11 so shall my word be that goes
forth from my mouth;
it shall not return to me
empty,
but it shall accomplish that
which I purpose,
and prosper in the thing for
which I sent it.
12 "For you shall go out in joy,
and be led forth in peace;
the mountains and the hills
before you
shall break forth into
singing,
and all the trees of the
field shall clap their
hands.
13 Instead of the thorn shall come
up the cypress;
instead of the brier shall
come up the myrtle;
and it shall be to the LORD for
a memorial,
for an everlasting sign which
shall not be cut off."

THE COVENANT EXTENDED TO ALL WHO OBEY

56 *Thus says the LORD:
"Keep justice, and do righteousness,
for soon my salvation will come,
and my deliverance be revealed.
2Blessed is the man who does this,
and the son of man who holds it fast,
who keeps the sabbath, not profaning it,
and keeps his hand from doing any evil."
3Let not the foreigner who has joined himself to the LORD say,
"The LORD will surely separate me from his people";
and let not the eunuch say,
"Behold, I am a dry tree."
4For thus says the LORD:
"To the eunuchs who keep my sabbaths,
who choose the things that please me
and hold fast my covenant,
5I will give in my house and within my walls
a monument and a name
better than sons and daughters;
I will give them an everlasting name
which shall not be cut off.
6"And the foreigners who join themselves to the LORD,
to minister to him, to love the name of the LORD,
and to be his servants,
every one who keeps the sabbath, and does not profane it,
and holds fast my covenant—
7these I will bring to my holy mountain,
and make them joyful in my house of prayer;
their burnt offerings and their sacrifices
will be accepted on my altar;
for my house shall be called a house of prayer
for all peoples.
8Thus says the Lord GOD,
who gathers the outcasts of Israel,
I will gather yet others to him
besides those already gathered."[a]

THE CORRUPTION OF ISRAEL'S RULERS

9All you beasts of the field, come to devour—
all you beasts in the forest.
10His watchmen are blind,
they are all without knowledge;
they are all dumb dogs,
they cannot bark;
dreaming, lying down,
loving to slumber.
11The dogs have a mighty appetite;
they never have enough.
The shepherds also have no understanding;
they have all turned to their own way,
each to his own gain, one and all.
12"Come," they say, "let us[b] get wine,
let us fill ourselves with strong drink;
and tomorrow will be like this day,
great beyond measure."

ISRAEL'S FUTILE IDOLATRY

57 The righteous man perishes,
and no one lays it to heart;
devout men are taken away,
while no one understands.
For the righteous man is taken away from calamity,
2he enters into peace;

[a]Heb *his gathered ones*
[b]One ancient Ms Syr Vg Tg: Heb *me*

they rest in their beds
who walk in their
uprightness.
3But you, draw near hither,
sons of the sorceress,
offspring of the adulterer
and the harlot.
4Of whom are you making sport?
Against whom do you open
your mouth wide
and put out your tongue?
Are you not children of
transgression,
the offspring of deceit,
5you who burn with lust among
the oaks,
under every green tree;
who slay your children in the
valleys,
under the clefts of the
rocks?
6Among the smooth stones of the
valley is your portion;
they, they, are your lot;
to them you have poured out a
drink offering,
you have brought a cereal
offering.
Shall I be appeased for these
things?
7Upon a high and lofty mountain
you have set your bed,
and thither you went up to
offer sacrifice.
8Behind the door and the
doorpost
you have set up your symbol;
for, deserting me, you have
uncovered your bed,
you have gone up to it,
you have made it wide;
and you have made a bargain
for yourself with them,
you have loved their bed,
you have looked on
nakedness.[c]
9You journeyed to Molech[d] with
oil
and multiplied your
perfumes;
you sent your envoys far off,
and sent down even to
Sheol.
10You were wearied with the
length of your way,
but you did not say, "It is
hopeless";
you found new life for your
strength,
and so you were not faint.
11Whom did you dread and fear,
so that you lied,
and did not remember me,
did not give me a thought?
Have I not held my peace, even
for a long time,
and so you do not fear me?
12I will tell of your righteousness
and your doings,
but they will not help you.
13When you cry out, let your
collection of idols deliver
you!
The wind will carry them
off,
a breath will take them
away.
But he who takes refuge in me
shall possess the land,
and shall inherit my holy
mountains.

A PROMISE OF HELP AND HEALING

14And it shall be said,
"Build up, build up, prepare
the way,
remove every obstruction
from my people's
way."
15For thus says the high and lofty
One
who inhabits eternity, whose
name is Holy:
"I dwell in the high and holy
place,
and also with him who is of
a contrite and humble
spirit,
to revive the spirit of the
humble,

[c]The meaning of the Hebrew is uncertain
[d]Or *the king*

and to revive the heart of the
contrite.
16For I will not contend for ever,
nor will I always be angry;
for from me proceeds the spirit,
and I have made the breath
of life.
17Because of the iniquity of his
covetousness I was angry,
I smote him, I hid my face
and was angry;
but he went on backsliding
in the way of his own
heart.
18I have seen his ways, but I will
heal him;
I will lead him and requite
him with comfort,
creating for his mourners
the fruit of the lips.
19Peace, peace, to the far and to
the near, says the LORD;
and I will heal him.
20But the wicked are like the
tossing sea;
for it cannot rest,
and its waters toss up mire
and dirt.
21There is no peace, says my God,
for the wicked."

FALSE AND TRUE WORSHIP

58 "Cry aloud, spare not,
lift up your voice like a
trumpet;
declare to my people their
transgression,
to the house of Jacob their
sins.
2Yet they seek me daily,
and delight to know my
ways,
as if they were a nation that did
righteousness
and did not forsake the ordi-
nance of their God;
they ask of me righteous
judgments,
they delight to draw near to
God.
3'Why have we fasted, and thou
seest it not?
Why have we humbled
ourselves, and thou
takest no knowledge
of it?'
Behold, in the day of your
fast you seek your own
pleasure,[a]
and oppress all your
workers.
4Behold, you fast only to quarrel
and to fight
and to hit with wicked fist.
Fasting like yours this day
will not make your voice to
be heard on high.
5Is such the fast that I choose,
a day for a man to humble
himself?
Is it to bow down his head like
a rush,
and to spread sackcloth and
ashes under him?
Will you call this a fast,
and a day acceptable to the
LORD?
6"Is not this the fast that I choose:
to loose the bonds of
wickedness,
to undo the thongs of the
yoke,
to let the oppressed go free,
and to break every yoke?
7Is it not to share your bread with
the hungry,
and bring the homeless poor
into your house;
when you see the naked, to
cover him,
and not to hide yourself
from your own flesh?
8Then shall your light break forth
like the dawn,
and your healing shall spring
up speedily;
your righteousness shall go
before you,
the glory of the LORD shall
be your rear guard.
9Then you shall call, and the
LORD will answer;

[a]Or *pursue your own business*

you shall cry, and he will
say, Here I am.
"If you take away from the
midst of you the yoke,
the pointing of the finger,
and speaking
wickedness,
10if you pour yourself out for the
hungry
and satisfy the desire of the
afflicted,
then shall your light rise in the
darkness
and your gloom be as the
noonday.
11And the LORD will guide you
continually,
and satisfy your desire with
good things,[b]
and make your bones strong;
and you shall be like a watered
garden,
like a spring of water,
whose waters fail not.
12And your ancient ruins shall be
rebuilt;
you shall raise up the
foundations of many
generations;
you shall be called the repairer
of the breach,
the restorer of streets to
dwell in.
13"If you turn back your foot from
the sabbath,
from doing your pleasure[c] on
my holy day,
and call the sabbath a delight
and the holy day of the LORD
honorable;
if you honor it, not going your
own ways,
or seeking your own plea-
sure,[d] or talking idly;
14then you shall take delight in
the LORD,
and I will make you ride
upon the heights of
the earth;
I will feed you with the
heritage of Jacob your
father,
for the mouth of the LORD
has spoken."

INJUSTICE AND OPPRESSION TO BE PUNISHED

59 Behold, the LORD's hand is not
shortened, that it cannot
save,
or his ear dull, that it cannot
hear;
2but your iniquities have made a
separation
between you and your God,
and your sins have hid his face
from you
so that he does not hear.
3For your hands are defiled with
blood
and your fingers with
iniquity;
your lips have spoken lies,
your tongue mutters
wickedness.
4No one enters suit justly,
no one goes to law honestly;
they rely on empty pleas, they
speak lies,
they conceive mischief and
bring forth iniquity.
5They hatch adders' eggs,
they weave the spider's web;
he who eats their eggs dies,
and from one which is
crushed a viper is
hatched.
6Their webs will not serve as
clothing;
men will not cover them-
selves with what they
make.
Their works are works of
iniquity,
and deeds of violence are in
their hands.
7Their feet run to evil,
and they make haste to shed
innocent blood;

[b] The meaning of the Hebrew word is uncertain
[c] Or *business*
[d] Or *pursuing your own business*

their thoughts are thoughts of
iniquity,
desolation and destruction
are in their highways.
8The way of peace they know not,
and there is no justice in
their paths;
they have made their roads
crooked,
no one who goes in them
knows peace.
9Therefore justice is far from us,
and righteousness does not
overtake us;
we look for light, and behold,
darkness,
and for brightness, but we
walk in gloom.
10We grope for the wall like the
blind,
we grope like those who
have no eyes;
we stumble at noon as in the
twilight,
among those in full vigor we
are like dead men.
11We all growl like bears,
we moan and moan like
doves;
we look for justice, but there
is none;
for salvation, but it is far
from us.
12For our transgressions are multi-
plied before thee,
and our sins testify against
us;
for our transgressions are with
us,
and we know our iniquities:
13transgressing, and denying the
LORD,
and turning away from fol-
lowing our God,
speaking oppression and revolt,
conceiving and uttering from
the heart lying words.
14Justice is turned back,
and righteousness stands
afar off;
for truth has fallen in the pub-
lic squares,
and uprightness cannot
enter.
15Truth is lacking,
and he who departs from
evil makes himself
a prey.
The LORD saw it, and it dis-
pleased him
that there was no justice.
16He saw that there was no man,
and wondered that there was
no one to intervene;
then his own arm brought him
victory,
and his righteousness upheld
him.
17He put on righteousness as a
breastplate,
and a helmet of salvation
upon his head;
he put on garments of ven-
geance for clothing,
and wrapped himself in fury
as a mantle.
18According to their deeds, so will
he repay,
wrath to his adversaries, re-
quital to his enemies;
to the coastlands he will
render requital.
19So they shall fear the name of
the LORD from the west,
and his glory from the rising
of the sun;
for he will come like a rushing
stream,
which the wind of the LORD
drives.
20"And he will come to Zion as
Redeemer,
to those in Jacob who turn
from transgression,
says the LORD.
21"And as for me, this is my cov-
enant with them, say the LORD: my
spirit which is upon you, and my
words which I have put in your mouth,
shall not depart out of your mouth, or
out of the mouth of your children, or
out of the mouth of your children's
children, says the LORD, from this
time forth and for evermore."

THE INGATHERING OF THE DISPERSED

60 Arise, shine; for your light has
come,
and the glory of the LORD
has risen upon you.
2For behold, darkness shall cover
the earth,
and thick darkness the
peoples;
but the LORD will arise upon
you,
and his glory will be seen
upon you.
3And nations shall come to your
light,
and kings to the brightness
of your rising.
4Lift up your eyes round about,
and see;
they all gather together, they
come to you;
your sons shall come from far,
and your daughters shall be
carried in the arms.
5Then you shall see and be
radiant,
your heart shall thrill and
rejoice;[a]
because the abundance of the
sea shall be turned to
you,
the wealth of the nations
shall come to you.
6A multitude of camels shall cover
you,
the young camels of Mid´ian
and Ephah;
all those from Sheba shall
come.
They shall bring gold and
frankincense,
and shall proclaim the praise
of the LORD.
7All the flocks of Kedar shall be
gathered to you,
the rams of Nebai´oth shall
minister to you;
they shall come up with accep-
tance on my altar,
and I will glorify my glorious
house.
8Who are these that fly like a
cloud,
and like doves to their
windows?
9For the coastlands shall wait
for me,
the ships of Tarshish first,
to bring your sons from far,
their silver and gold with
them,
for the name of the LORD your
God,
and for the Holy One of
Israel,
because he has glorified you.
10Foreigners shall build up your
walls,
and their kings shall minis-
ter to you;
for in my wrath I smote you,
but in my favor I have had
mercy on you.
11Your gates shall be open
continually;
day and night they shall not
be shut;
that men may bring to you the
wealth of the nations,
with their kings led in
procession.
12For the nation and kingdom
that will not serve you shall
perish;
those nations shall be utter-
ly laid waste.
13The glory of Lebanon shall come
to you,
the cypress, the plane, and
the pine,
to beautify the place of my
sanctuary;
and I will make the place of
my feet glorious.
14The sons of those who oppressed
you
shall come bending low to
you;
and all who despised you
shall bow down at your feet;
they shall call you the City of
the LORD,

[a]Heb *be enlarged*

the Zion of the Holy One of
Israel.
15Whereas you have been forsaken
and hated,
with no one passing
through,
I will make you majestic for
ever,
a joy from age to age.
16You shall suck the milk of
nations,
you shall suck the breast of
kings;
and you shall know that I, the
LORD, am your Savior
and your Redeemer, the
Mighty One of Jacob.
17Instead of bronze I will bring
gold,
and instead of iron I will
bring silver;
instead of wood, bronze,
instead of stones, iron.
I will make your overseers
peace
and your taskmasters
righteousness.
18Violence shall no more be heard
in your land,
devastation or destruction
within your borders;
you shall call your walls
Salvation,
and your gates Praise.

GOD THE GLORY OF ZION

19The sun shall be no more
your light by day,
nor for brightness shall the
moon
give light to you by night;[a]
but the LORD will be your
everlasting light,
and your God will be your
glory.
20Your sun shall no more go down,
nor your moon withdraw
itself;
for the LORD will be your ever-
lasting light,
and your days of mourning
shall be ended.
21Your people shall all be
righteous;
they shall possess the land
for ever,
the shoot of my planting, the
work of my hands,
that I might be glorified.
22The least one shall become a
clan,
and the smallest one a
mighty nation;
I am the LORD;
in its time I will hasten it.

THE GOOD NEWS OF DELIVERANCE

61 *The Spirit of the Lord GOD is
upon me,
because the LORD has
anointed me
to bring good tidings to the
afflicted;[b]
he has sent me to bind up
the brokenhearted,
to proclaim liberty to the
captives,
and the opening of the pris-
on[c] to those who are
bound;
2to proclaim the year of the
LORD's favor,
and the day of vengeance of
our God;
to comfort all who mourn;
3to grant to those who mourn in
Zion—
to give them a garland in-
stead of ashes,
the oil of gladness instead of
mourning,
the mantle of praise instead
of a faint spirit;
that they may be called oaks of
righteousness,
the planting of the LORD,
that he may be
glorified.
4They shall build up the ancient
ruins,

[a]One ancient Ms Gk Old Latin Tg: Heb lacks *by night*
[b]Or *poor*
[c]Or *the opening of the eyes:* Heb *the opening*

they shall raise up the former devastations;
they shall repair the ruined cities,
the devastations of many generations.
5Aliens shall stand and feed your flocks,
foreigners shall be your plowmen and vinedressers;
6but you shall be called the priests of the LORD,
men shall speak of you as the ministers of our God;
you shall eat the wealth of the nations,
and in their riches you shall glory.
7Instead of your shame you shall have a double portion,
instead of dishonor you[d] shall rejoice in your[e] lot;
therefore in your[f] land you[g] shall possess a double portion;
yours[h] shall be everlasting joy.
8For I the LORD love justice,
I hate robbery and wrong;[i]
I will faithfully give them their recompense,
and I will make an everlasting covenant with them.
9Their descendants shall be known among the nations,
and their offspring in the midst of the peoples;
all who see them shall acknowledge them,
that they are a people whom the LORD has blessed.
10I will greatly rejoice in the LORD,
my soul shall exult in my God;
for he has clothed me with the garments of salvation,
he has covered me with the robe of righteousness,
as a bridegroom decks himself with a garland,
and as a bride adorns herself with her jewels.
11For as the earth brings forth its shoots,
and as a garden causes what is sown in it to spring up,
so the Lord GOD will cause righteousness and praise
to spring forth before all the nations.

THE VINDICATION AND SALVATION OF ZION

62 For Zion's sake I will not keep silent,
and for Jerusalem's sake I will not rest,
until her vindication goes forth as brightness,
and her salvation as a burning torch.
2The nations shall see your vindication,
and all the kings your glory;
and you shall be called by a new name
which the mouth of the LORD will give.
3You shall be a crown of beauty in the hand of the LORD,
and a royal diadem in the hand of your God.
4You shall no more be termed Forsaken,[j]
and your land shall no more be termed Desolate;[k]

[d] Heb *they*
[e] Heb *their*
[f] Heb *their*
[g] Heb *they*
[h] Heb *theirs*
[i] Or *robbery with a burnt offering*
[j] Heb *Azubah*
[k] Heb *Shemamah*

but you shall be called My
delight is in her, [a]
and your land Married;[b]
for the LORD delights in you,
and your land shall be
married.
5For as a young man marries a
virgin,
so shall your sons marry
you,
and as the bridegroom rejoices
over the bride,
so shall your God rejoice
over you.
6Upon your walls, O Jerusalem,
I have set watchmen;
all the day and all the night
they shall never be silent.
You who put the LORD in
remembrance,
take no rest,
7and give him no rest
until he establishes
Jerusalem
and makes it a praise in the
earth.
8The LORD has sworn by his right
hand
and by his mighty arm:
"I will not again give your
grain
to be food for your enemies,
and foreigners shall not drink
your wine
for which you have labored;
9but those who garner it shall
eat it
and praise the LORD,
and those who gather it shall
drink it
in the courts of my
sanctuary."
10Go through, go through the
gates,
prepare the way for the
people;
build up, build up the highway,
clear it of stones,
lift up an ensign over the
peoples.
11Behold, the LORD has
proclaimed
to the end of the earth:
Say to the daughter of Zion,
"Behold, your salvation
comes;
behold, his reward is with him,
and his recompense before
him."
12And they shall be called The
holy people,
The redeemed of the LORD;
and you shall be called Sought
out,
a city not forsaken.

VENGEANCE ON EDOM

63 Who is this that comes from
Edom,
in crimsoned garments from
Bozrah,
he that is glorious in his
apparel,
marching in the greatness of
his strength?
"It is I, announcing
vindication,
mighty to save."
2Why is thy apparel red,
and thy garments like his
that treads in the
wine press?
3"I have trodden the wine press
alone,
and from the peoples no one
was with me;
I trod them in my anger
and trampled them in my
wrath;
their lifeblood is sprinkled
upon my garments,
and I have stained all my
raiment.
4For the day of vengeance was in
my heart,
and my year of redemption[c]
has come.
5I looked, but there was no one
to help;
I was appalled, but there was

[a] Heb *Hephzibah*
[b] Heb *Beulah*
[c] Or *the year of my redeemed*

no one to uphold;
so my own arm brought me victory,
and my wrath upheld me.
6I trod down the peoples in my anger,
I made them drunk in my wrath,
and I poured out their lifeblood on the earth."

GOD'S MERCY REMEMBERED

7I will recount the steadfast love of the LORD,
the praises of the LORD,
according to all that the LORD has granted us,
and the great goodness to the house of Israel
which he has granted them according to his mercy,
according to the abundance of his steadfast love.
8For he said, Surely they are my people,
sons who will not deal falsely;
and he became their Savior.
9In all their affliction he was afflicted,[d]
and the angel of his presence saved them;
in his love and in his pity he redeemed them;
he lifted them up and carried them all the days of old.
10But they rebelled
and grieved his holy Spirit;
therefore he turned to be their enemy,
and himself fought against them.
11Then he remembered the days of old,
of Moses his servant.
Where is he who brought up out of the sea
the shepherds of his flock?
Where is he who put in the midst of them
his holy Spirit,
12who caused his glorious arm
to go at the right hand of Moses,
who divided the waters before them
to make for himself an everlasting name,
13who led them through the depths?
Like a horse in the desert,
they did not stumble.
14Like cattle that go down into the valley,
the Spirit of the LORD gave them rest.
So thou didst lead thy people,
to make for thyself a glorious name.

A PRAYER OF PENITENCE

15Look down from heaven and see,
from thy holy and glorious habitation.
Where are thy zeal and thy might?
The yearning of thy heart and thy compassion
are withheld from me.
16For thou art our Father,
though Abraham does not know us
and Israel does not acknowledge us;
thou, O LORD, art our Father,
our Redeemer from of old is thy name.
17O LORD, why dost thou make us err from thy ways
and harden our heart, so that we fear thee not?
Return for the sake of thy servants,
the tribes of thy heritage.
18Thy holy people possessed thy sanctuary a little while;
our adversaries have trodden it down.

[d]Another reading is *he did not afflict*

19We have become like those over
whom thou hast never
ruled,
like those who are not called
by thy name.

64 O that thou wouldst rend the
heavens and come down,
that the mountains might
quake at thy
presence—
2a as when fire kindles brushwood
and the fire causes water to
boil—
to make thy name known to
thy adversaries,
and that the nations might
tremble at thy
presence!
3When thou didst terrible things
which we looked not for,
thou camest down, the
mountains quaked at
thy presence.
4From of old no one has heard
or perceived by the ear,
no eye has seen a God besides
thee,
who works for those who
wait for him.
5Thou meetest him that joyfully
works righteousness,
those that remember thee in
thy ways.
Behold, thou wast angry, and
we sinned;
in our sins we have been a
long time, and shall
we be saved?[b]
6We have all become like one who
is unclean,
and all our righteous deeds
are like a polluted
garment.
We all fade like a leaf,
and our iniquities, like the
wind, take us away.
7There is no one that calls upon
thy name,
that bestirs himself to take
hold of thee;
for thou hast hid thy face
from us,
and hast delivered[c] us into
the hand of our
iniquities.
8Yet, O LORD, thou art our
Father;
we are the clay, and thou art
our potter;
we are all the work of thy
hand.
9Be not exceedingly angry, O
LORD,
and remember not iniquity
for ever.
Behold, consider, we are all
thy people.
10Thy holy cities have become a
wilderness,
Zion has become a
wilderness,
Jerusalem a desolation.
11Our holy and beautiful house,
where our fathers praised
thee,
has been burned by fire,
and all our pleasant places
have become ruins.
12Wilt thou restrain thyself at
these things, O LORD?
Wilt thou keep silent, and
afflict us sorely?

THE RIGHTEOUSNESS OF GOD'S JUDGMENT

65 I was ready to be sought by those
who did not ask for me;
I was ready to be found by
those who did not
seek me.
I said, "Here am I, here am I, "
to a nation that did not call
on my name.
2I spread out my hands all the day
to a rebellious people,
who walk in a way that is not
good,
following their own devices;
3a people who provoke me
to my face continually,
sacrificing in gardens

[a]Ch 64.1 in Heb
[b]Hebrew obscure
[c]Gk Syr Old Latin Tg: Heb *melted*

and burning incense upon
bricks;
4who sit in tombs,
and spend the night in secret
places;
who eat swine's flesh,
and broth of abominable
things is in their
vessels;
5who say, "Keep to yourself,
do not come near me, for
I am set apart from
you."
These are a smoke in my
nostrils,
a fire that burns all the day.
6Behold, it is written before me:
"I will not keep silent, but I
will repay,
yea, I will repay into their
bosom
7their[d] iniquities and their[e]
fathers' iniquities
together,
says the LORD;
because they burned incense
upon the mountains
and reviled me upon the
hills,
I will measure into their bosom
payment for their former
doings."
8Thus says the LORD:
"As the wine is found in the
cluster,
and they say, 'Do not destroy
it,
for there is a blessing in it,'
so I will do for my servants'
sake,
and not destroy them all.
9I will bring forth descendants
from Jacob,
and from Judah inheritors of
my mountains;
my chosen shall inherit it,
and my servants shall dwell
there.
10Sharon shall become a pasture
for flocks,
and the Valley of Achor a
place for herds to lie
down,
for my people who have
sought me.
11But you who forsake the LORD,
who forget my holy
mountain,
who set a table for Fortune
and fill cups of mixed wine
for Destiny;
12I will destine you to the sword,
and all of you shall bow
down to the
slaughter;
because, when I called, you did
not answer,
when I spoke, you did not
listen,
but you did what was evil in
my eyes,
and chose what I did not
delight in."
13Therefore thus says the Lord
GOD:
"Behold, my servants shall eat,
but you shall be hungry;
behold, my servants shall
drink,
but you shall be thirsty;
behold, my servants shall
rejoice,
but you shall be put to
shame;
14behold, my servants shall sing
for gladness of heart,
but you shall cry out for pain
of heart,
and shall wail for anguish of
spirit.
15You shall leave your name to my
chosen for a curse,
and the Lord GOD will slay
you;
but his servants he will call
by a different name.
16So that he who blesses himself
in the land
shall bless himself by the
God of truth,

[d]Gk Syr: Heb *your*
[e]Gk Syr: Heb *your*

and he who takes an oath in
the land
shall swear by the God of
truth;
because the former troubles are
forgotten
and are hid from my eyes.

THE GLORIOUS NEW CREATION

17"For behold, I create new
heavens
and a new earth;
and the former things shall not
be remembered
or come into mind.
18But be glad and rejoice for ever
in that which I create;
for behold, I create Jerusalem a
rejoicing,
and her people a joy.
19I will rejoice in Jerusalem,
and be glad in my people;
no more shall be heard in it the
sound of weeping
and the cry of distress.
20No more shall there be in it
an infant that lives but a few
days,
or an old man who does not
fill out his days,
for the child shall die a hun-
dred years old,
and the sinner a hundred
years old shall be
accursed.
21They shall build houses and
inhabit them;
they shall plant vineyards
and eat their fruit.
22They shall not build and another
inhabit;
they shall not plant and
another eat;
for like the days of a tree shall
the days of my people
be,
and my chosen shall long
enjoy the work of
their hands.
23They shall not labor in vain,
or bear children for
calamity;[a]
for they shall be the offspring
of the blessed of the
LORD,
and their children with
them.
24Before they call I will answer,
while they are yet speaking I
will hear.
25The wolf and the lamb shall feed
together,
the lion shall eat straw like
the ox;
and dust shall be the ser-
pent's food.
They shall not hurt or destroy
in all my holy mountain,
says the LORD."

THE WORSHIP GOD DEMANDS

66 Thus says the LORD:
"Heaven is my throne
and the earth is my
footstool;
what is the house which you
would build for me,
and what is the place of my
rest?
2All these things my hand has
made,
and so all these things are
mine,[b]
says the LORD.
But this is the man to whom I
will look,
he that is humble and con-
trite in spirit,
and trembles at my word.
3"He who slaughters an ox is like
him who kills a man;
he who sacrifices a lamb,
like him who breaks a
dog's neck;
he who presents a cereal offer-
ing, like him who offers
swine's blood;
he who makes a memorial
offering of frankin-
cense, like him who

[a] Or *sudden terror*
[b] Gk Syr: Heb *came to be*

blesses an idol.
These have chosen their own ways,
and their soul delights in their abominations;
4I also will choose affliction for them,
and bring their fears upon them;
because, when I called, no one answered,
when I spoke they did not listen;
but they did what was evil in my eyes,
and chose that in which I did not delight."

THE LORD VINDICATES ZION

5Hear the word of the LORD,
you who tremble at his word:
"Your brethren who hate you
and cast you out for my name's sake
have said, 'Let the LORD be glorified,
that we may see your joy';
but it is they who shall be put to shame.
6"Hark, an uproar from the city!
A voice from the temple!
The voice of the LORD,
rendering recompense to his enemies!
7"Before she was in labor
she gave birth;
before her pain came upon her
she was delivered of a son.
8Who has heard such a thing?
Who has seen such things?
Shall a land be born in one day?
Shall a nation be brought forth in one moment?
For as soon as Zion was in labor
she brought forth her sons.
9Shall I bring to the birth and not cause to bring forth?
says the LORD;
shall I, who cause to bring forth, shut the womb?
says your God.
10"Rejoice with Jerusalem, and be glad for her,
all you who love her;
rejoice with her in joy,
all you who mourn over her;
11that you may suck and be satisfied
with her consoling breasts;
that you may drink deeply with delight
from the abundance of her glory."
12For thus says the LORD:
"Behold, I will extend prosperity to her like a river,
and the wealth of the nations like an overflowing stream;
and you shall suck, you shall be carried upon her hip,
and dandled upon her knees.
13As one whom his mother comforts,
so I will comfort you;
you shall be comforted in Jerusalem.

THE REIGN AND INDIGNATION OF GOD

14You shall see, and your heart shall rejoice;
your bones shall flourish like the grass;
and it shall be known that the hand of the LORD is with his servants,
and his indignation is against his enemies.
15"For behold, the LORD will come in fire,
and his chariots like the stormwind,
to render his anger in fury,
and his rebuke with flames of fire.
16For by fire will the LORD execute judgment,
and by his sword, upon all flesh;
and those slain by the LORD shall be many.

17 "Those who sanctify and purify themselves to go into the gardens, following one in the midst, eating swine's flesh and the abomination and mice, shall come to an end together, says the LORD.

18 "For I know[a] their works and their thoughts, and I am[b] coming to gather all nations and tongues; and they shall come and shall see my glory,
19and I will set a sign among them. And from them I will send survivors to the nations, to Tarshish, Put,[c] and Lud, who draw the bow, to Tubal and Javan, to the coastlands afar off, that have not heard my fame or seen my glory; and they shall declare my glory among the nations.
20And they shall bring all your brethren from all the nations as an offering to the LORD, upon horses, and in chariots, and in litters, and upon mules, and upon dromedaries, to my holy mountain Jerusalem, says the LORD, just as the Israelites bring their cereal offering in a clean vessel to the house of the LORD.
21And some of them also I will take for priests and for Levites, says the LORD.

22"For as the new heavens and the new earth
which I will make
shall remain before me, says the LORD;
so shall your descendants and your name remain.
23From new moon to new moon,
and from sabbath to sabbath,
all flesh shall come to worship before me,
says the LORD.

24 "And they shall go forth and look on the dead bodies of the men that have rebelled against me; for their worm shall not die, their fire shall not be quenched, and they shall be an abhorrence to all flesh."

[a]Gk Syr: Heb lacks *know*
[b]Gk Syr Vg Tg: Heb *it is*
[c]Gk: Heb *Pul*

THE BOOK OF

JEREMIAH

1 The words of Jeremiah, the son of Hilki´ah, of the priests who were in An´athoth in the land of Benjamin,
2to whom the word of the LORD came in the days of Josi´ah the son of Amon, king of Judah, in the thirteenth year of his reign.
3It came also in the days of Jehoi´akim the son of Josi´ah, king of Judah, and until the end of the eleventh year of Zedeki´ah, the son of Josi´ah, king of Judah, until the captivity of Jerusalem in the fifth month.

JEREMIAH'S CALL AND COMMISSION

4 Now the word of the LORD came
to me saying,
5"Before I formed you in the
womb I knew you,
and before you were born I
consecrated you;
I appointed you a prophet to
the nations."
6Then I said, "Ah, Lord
GOD! Behold, I do
not know how to
speak, for I am only a
youth."*
7But the LORD said to me,
"Do not say, 'I am only a
youth';
for to all to whom I send you
you shall go,
and whatever I command you
you shall speak.
8Be not afraid of them,
for I am with you to deliver
you,
says the LORD."
9Then the LORD put forth his
hand and touched my
mouth; and the LORD
said to me,
"Behold, I have put my words
in your mouth.
10See, I have set you this day
over nations and over
kingdoms,
to pluck up and to break
down,
to destroy and to overthrow,
to build and to plant."

11 And the word of the LORD came
to me, saying, "Jeremiah, what do you
see?" And I said, "I see a rod of al-
mond."[a] 12Then the LORD said to me,
"You have seen well, for I am watch-
ing[b] over my word to perform it."
13 The word of the LORD came to
me a second time, saying, "What do
you see?" And I said, "I see a boil-
ing pot, facing away from the north."
14Then the LORD said to me, "Out
of the north evil shall break forth
upon all the inhabitants of the land.
15For lo, I am calling all the tribes
of the kingdoms of the north, says
the LORD; and they shall come and
every one shall set his throne at the
entrance of the gates of Jerusalem,
against all its walls round about, and
against all the cities of Judah. 16And
I will utter my judgments against
them, for all their wickedness in
forsaking me; they have burned in-
cense to other gods, and worshiped
the works of their own hands. 17But
you, gird up your loins; arise, and say
to them everything that I command
you. Do not be dismayed by them,
lest I dismay you before them. 18And
I, behold, I make you this day a for-
tified city, an iron pillar, and bronze
walls, against the whole land, against
the kings of Judah, its princes, its
priests, and the people of the land.
19They will fight against you; but
they shall not prevail against you,
for I am with you, says the LORD, to
deliver you."

[a] Heb *shaqed*
[b] Heb *shoqed*

GOD PLEADS WITH ISRAEL TO REPENT

2 The word of the LORD came to me, saying, 2"Go and proclaim in the hearing of Jerusalem, Thus says the LORD,

I remember the devotion of your youth,
your love as a bride,
how you followed me in the wilderness,
in a land not sown.
3Israel was holy to the LORD,
the first fruits of his harvest.
All who ate of it became guilty;
evil came upon them,
says the LORD."

4 Hear the word of the LORD, O house of Jacob, and all the families of the house of Israel. 5Thus says the LORD:

"What wrong did your fathers find in me
that they went far from me,
and went after worthlessness,
and became worthless?
6They did not say, 'Where is the LORD
who brought us up from the land of Egypt,
who led us in the wilderness,
in a land of deserts and pits,
in a land of drought and deep darkness,
in a land that none passes through,
where no man dwells?'
7And I brought you into a plentiful land
to enjoy its fruits and its good things.
But when you came in you defiled my land,
and made my heritage an abomination.
8The priests did not say, 'Where is the LORD?'
Those who handle the law did not know me;
the rulers[a] transgressed against me;
the prophets prophesied by Ba´al,
and went after things that do not profit.
9"Therefore I still contend with you,
says the LORD,
and with your children's children I will contend.
10For cross to the coasts of Cyprus and see,
or send to Kedar and examine with care;
see if there has been such a thing.
11Has a nation changed its gods,
even though they are no gods?
But my people have changed their glory
for that which does not profit.
12Be appalled, O heavens, at this,
be shocked, be utterly desolate,
says the LORD,
13for my people have committed two evils:
they have forsaken me,
the fountain of living waters,
and hewed out cisterns for themselves,
broken cisterns,
that can hold no water.
14"Is Israel a slave? Is he a homeborn servant?
Why then has he become a prey?
15The lions have roared against him,
they have roared loudly.
They have made his land a waste;
his cities are in ruins, without inhabitant.
16Moreover, the men of Memphis and Tah´panhes
have broken the crown of

[a] Heb *shepherds*

your head.
17Have you not brought this upon yourself
by forsaking the LORD your God,
when he led you in the way?
18And now what do you gain by going to Egypt,
to drink the waters of the Nile?
Or what do you gain by going to Assyria,
to drink the waters of the Euphra´tes?
19Your wickedness will chasten you,
and your apostasy will reprove you.
Know and see that it is evil and bitter
for you to forsake the LORD your God;
the fear of me is not in you,-
says the Lord GOD of hosts.
20"For long ago you broke your yoke
and burst your bonds;
and you said, 'I will not serve.'
Yea, upon every high hill
and under every green tree
you bowed down as a harlot.
21Yet I planted you a choice vine,
wholly of pure seed.
How then have you turned degenerate
and become a wild vine?
22Though you wash yourself with lye
and use much soap,
the stain of your guilt is still before me,
says the Lord GOD.
23How can you say, 'I am not defiled,
I have not gone after the Ba´als'?
Look at your way in the valley;
know what you have done—
a restive young camel interlacing her tracks,
24a wild ass used to the wilderness,
in her heat sniffing the wind!
Who can restrain her lust?
None who seek her need weary themselves;
in her month they will find her.
25Keep your feet from going unshod
and your throat from thirst.
But you said, 'It is hopeless,
for I have loved strangers,
and after them I will go.'
26"As a thief is shamed when caught,
so the house of Israel shall be shamed:
they, their kings, their princes,
their priests, and their prophets,
27who say to a tree, 'You are my father,'
and to a stone, 'You gave me birth.'
For they have turned their back to me,
and not their face.
But in the time of their trouble they say,
'Arise and save us!'
28But where are your gods
that you made for yourself?
Let them arise, if they can save you,
in your time of trouble;
for as many as your cities
are your gods, O Judah.
29"Why do you complain against me?
You have all rebelled against me,
says the LORD.
30In vain have I smitten your children,
they took no correction;
your own sword devoured your prophets
like a ravening lion.

31And you, O generation, heed the
word of the LORD.
Have I been a wilderness to
Israel,
or a land of thick darkness?
Why then do my people say,
'We are free,
we will come no more to
thee'?
32Can a maiden forget her
ornaments,
or a bride her attire?
Yet my people have forgotten
me
days without number.
33"How well you direct your
course
to seek lovers!
So that even to wicked women
you have taught your ways.
34Also on your skirts is found
the lifeblood of guiltless
poor;
you did not find them breaking
in.
Yet in spite of all these
things
35you say, 'I am innocent;
surely his anger has turned
from me.'
Behold, I will bring you to
judgment
for saying, 'I have not
sinned.'
36How lightly you gad about,
changing your way!
You shall be put to shame by
Egypt
as you were put to shame by
Assyria.
37From it too you will come away
with your hands upon your
head,
for the LORD has rejected those
in whom you trust,
and you will not prosper by
them.

UNFAITHFUL ISRAEL

3 "If[a] a man divorces his wife
and she goes from him
and becomes another man's
wife,
will he return to her?
Would not that land be greatly
polluted?
You have played the harlot with
many lovers;
and would you return to
me?
says the LORD.
2Lift up your eyes to the bare
heights, and see!
Where have you not been
lain with?
By the waysides you have sat
awaiting lovers
like an Arab in the
wilderness.
You have polluted the land
with your vile harlotry.
3Therefore the showers have been
withheld,
and the spring rain has not
come;
yet you have a harlot's brow,
you refuse to be ashamed.
4Have you not just now called to
me,
'My father, thou art the
friend of my youth—
5will he be angry for ever,
will he be indignant to the
end?'
Behold, you have spoken,
but you have done all the
evil that you could."

A CALL TO REPENTANCE

6 The LORD said to me in the
days of King Josi´ah: "Have you seen
what she did, that faithless one,
Israel, how she went up on every
high hill and under every green tree,
and there played the harlot? 7And I
thought, 'After she has done all this
she will return to me'; but she did
not return, and her false sister Judah
saw it. 8She saw that for all the adul-
teries of that faithless one, Israel, I
had sent her away with a decree of
divorce; yet her false sister Judah did

[a]Gk Syr: Heb *Saying, If*

not fear, but she too went and played
the harlot. 9Because harlotry was so
light to her, she polluted the land,
committing adultery with stone and
tree. 10Yet for all this her false sister
Judah did not return to me with her
whole heart, but in pretense, says the
LORD."

11 And the LORD said to me,
"Faithless Israel has shown herself
less guilty than false Judah. 12Go,
and proclaim these words toward the
north, and say,

'Return, faithless Israel,
says the LORD.
I will not look on you in
anger,
for I am merciful,
says the LORD;
I will not be angry for ever.
13Only acknowledge your guilt,
that you rebelled against the
LORD your God
and scattered your favors
among strangers under
every green tree,
and that you have not
obeyed my voice,
says the LORD.
14Return, O faithless children,
says the LORD;
for I am your master;
I will take you, one from a
city and two from a
family,
and I will bring you to
Zion.

15 "'And I will give you shepherds
after my own heart, who will feed
you with knowledge and understand-
ing. 16And when you have multiplied
and increased in the land, in those
days, says the LORD, they shall no
more say, "The ark of the covenant
of the LORD." It shall not come to
mind, or be remembered, or missed;
it shall not be made again.* 17At that
time Jerusalem shall be called the
throne of the LORD, and all nations
shall gather to it, to the presence
of the LORD in Jerusalem, and they
shall no more stubbornly follow their
own evil heart. 18In those days the
house of Judah shall join the house
of Israel, and together they shall
come from the land of the north to
the land that I gave your fathers for
a heritage.

19"'I thought
how I would set you among
my sons,
and give you a pleasant land,
a heritage most beauteous of
all nations.
And I thought you would call
me, My Father,
and would not turn from
following me.
20Surely, as a faithless wife leaves
her husband,
so have you been faithless
to me, O house of
Israel,
says the LORD.'"
21A voice on the bare heights is
heard,
the weeping and pleading of
Israel's sons
because they have perverted
their way,
they have forgotten the
LORD their God.
22"Return, O faithless sons,
I will heal your
faithlessness."
"Behold, we come to thee;
for thou art the LORD our
God.
23Truly the hills are a delusion,
the orgies on the
mountains.
Truly in the LORD our God
is the salvation of Israel.

24 "But from our youth the shame-
ful thing has devoured all for which
our fathers labored, their flocks and
their herds, their sons and their
daughters. 25Let us lie down in our
shame, and let our dishonor cover us;
for we have sinned against the LORD
our God, we and our fathers, from our
youth even to this day; and we have
not obeyed the voice of the LORD our
God."

4 "If you return, O Israel,
says the LORD,
to me you should return.
If you remove your abominations from my presence,
and do not waver,
2and if you swear, 'As the LORD lives,'
in truth, in justice, and in uprightness,
then nations shall bless themselves in him,
and in him shall they glory."

3 For thus says the LORD to the
men of Judah and to the inhabitants
of Jerusalem:
"Break up your fallow ground,
and sow not among thorns.
4Circumcise yourselves to the LORD,
remove the foreskin of your hearts,
O men of Judah and inhabitants of Jerusalem;
lest my wrath go forth like fire,
and burn with none to quench it,
because of the evil of your doings."

INVASION AND DESOLATION OF JUDAH THREATENED

5 Declare in Judah, and proclaim in
Jerusalem, and say,
"Blow the trumpet through the land;
cry aloud and say,
'Assemble, and let us go
into the fortified cities!'
6Raise a standard toward Zion,
flee for safety, stay not,
for I bring evil from the north,
and great destruction.
7A lion has gone up from his thicket,
a destroyer of nations has set out;
he has gone forth from his place
to make your land a waste;
your cities will be ruins
without inhabitant.
8For this gird you with sackcloth,
lament and wail;
for the fierce anger of the LORD
has not turned back from us."

9"In that day, says the LORD, cour-
age shall fail both king and princes;
the priests shall be appalled and the
prophets astounded." 10Then I said,
"Ah, Lord GOD, surely thou hast utter-
ly deceived this people and Jerusalem,
saying, 'It shall be well with you';
whereas the sword has reached their
very life."

11 At that time it will be said to
this people and to Jerusalem, "A hot
wind from the bare heights in the
desert toward the daughter of my
people, not to winnow or cleanse, 12a
wind too full for this comes for me.
Now it is I who speak in judgment
upon them."

13Behold, he comes up like clouds,
his chariots like the whirlwind;
his horses are swifter than eagles—
woe to us, for we are ruined!
14O Jerusalem, wash your heart from wickedness,
that you may be saved.
How long shall your evil thoughts
lodge within you?
15For a voice declares from Dan
and proclaims evil from Mount E′phraim.
16Warn the nations that he is coming;
announce to Jerusalem,
"Besiegers come from a distant land;
they shout against the cities of Judah.
17Like keepers of a field are they

against her round about,
because she has rebelled
against me,
says the LORD.
18 Your ways and your doings
have brought this upon you.
This is your doom, and it is
bitter;
it has reached your very
heart."

SORROW FOR A DOOMED NATION

19 My anguish, my anguish! I
writhe in pain!
Oh, the walls of my heart!
My heart is beating wildly;
I cannot keep silent;
for I hear the sound of the
trumpet,
the alarm of war.
20 Disaster follows hard on
disaster,
the whole land is laid
waste.
Suddenly my tents are
destroyed,
my curtains in a moment.
21 How long must I see the
standard,
and hear the sound of the
trumpet?
22 "For my people are foolish,
they know me not;
they are stupid children,
they have no
understanding.
They are skilled in doing evil,
but how to do good they
know not."
23 I looked on the earth, and lo, it
was waste and void;
and to the heavens, and they
had no light.
24 I looked on the mountains, and
lo, they were quaking,
and all the hills moved to
and fro.
25 I looked, and lo, there was no
man,
and all the birds of the air
had fled.
26 I looked, and lo, the fruitful land
was a desert,
and all its cities were laid in
ruins
before the LORD, before his
fierce anger.

27 For thus says the LORD, "The
whole land shall be a desolation; yet I
will not make a full end.

28 For this the earth shall mourn,
and the heavens above be
black;
for I have spoken, I have
purposed;
I have not relented nor will I
turn back."
29 At the noise of horseman and
archer
every city takes to flight;
they enter thickets; they climb
among rocks;
all the cities are forsaken,
and no man dwells in them.
30 And you, O desolate one,
what do you mean that you
dress in scarlet,
that you deck yourself with
ornaments of gold,
that you enlarge your eyes
with paint?
In vain you beautify yourself.
Your lovers despise you;
they seek your life.
31 For I heard a cry as of a woman
in travail,
anguish as of one bringing
forth her first child,
the cry of the daughter of Zion
gasping for breath,
stretching out her hands,
"Woe is me! I am fainting
before murderers."

THE UTTER CORRUPTION OF GOD'S PEOPLE

5 Run to and fro through the
streets of Jerusalem,
look and take note!
Search her squares to see
if you can find a man,
one who does justice
and seeks truth;
that I may pardon her.

2Though they say, "As the LORD
lives,"
yet they swear falsely.
3O LORD, do not thy eyes look for
truth?
Thou hast smitten them,
but they felt no anguish;
thou hast consumed them,
but they refused to take
correction.
They have made their faces
harder than rock;
they have refused to
repent.
4Then I said, "These are only the
poor,
they have no sense;
for they do not know the way
of the LORD,
the law of their God.
5I will go to the great,
and will speak to them;
for they know the way of the
LORD,
the law of their God."
But they all alike had broken
the yoke,
they had burst the bonds.
6Therefore a lion from the forest
shall slay them,
a wolf from the desert shall
destroy them.
A leopard is watching against
their cities,
every one who goes out of
them shall be torn in
pieces;
because their transgressions
are many,
their apostasies are great.
7"How can I pardon you?
Your children have
forsaken me,
and have sworn by those
who are no gods.
When I fed them to the full,
they committed adultery
and trooped to the houses of
harlots.
8They were well-fed lusty
stallions,
each neighing for his neigh-
bor's wife.
9Shall I not punish them for these
things?
says the LORD;
and shall I not avenge
myself
on a nation such as this?
10"Go up through her vine-rows
and destroy,
but make not a full end;
strip away her branches,
for they are not the LORD's.
11For the house of Israel and the
house of Judah
have been utterly faithless
to me,
says the LORD.
12They have spoken falsely of the
LORD,
and have said, 'He will do
nothing;
no evil will come upon us,
nor shall we see sword or
famine.
13The prophets will become
wind;
the word is not in them.
Thus shall it be done to
them!'"
14Therefore thus says the LORD,
the God of hosts:
"Because they[a] have spoken
this word,
behold, I am making my
words in your mouth
a fire,
and this people wood, and
the fire shall devour
them.
15Behold, I am bringing upon you
a nation from afar, O house
of Israel,
says the LORD.
It is an enduring nation,
it is an ancient nation,
a nation whose language you
do not know,
nor can you understand
what they say.
16Their quiver is like an open

[a] Heb *you*

tomb,
they are all mighty men.
17They shall eat up your harvest
and your food;
they shall eat up your sons
and your daughters;
they shall eat up your flocks
and your herds;
they shall eat up your vines
and your fig trees;
your fortified cities in which
you trust
they shall destroy with the
sword."
18 "But even in those days, says
the LORD, I will not make a full end
of you. 19And when your people say,
'Why has the LORD our God done all
these things to us?' you shall say to
them, 'As you have forsaken me and
served foreign gods in your land, so
you shall serve strangers in a land
that is not yours.'"
20Declare this in the house of
Jacob,
proclaim it in Judah:
21"Hear this, O foolish and senseless people,
who have eyes, but see not,
who have ears, but hear
not.
22Do you not fear me? says the
LORD;
Do you not tremble before
me?
I placed the sand as the bound
for the sea,
a perpetual barrier which it
cannot pass;
though the waves toss, they
cannot prevail,
though they roar, they cannot pass over it.
23But this people has a stubborn
and rebellious heart;
they have turned aside and
gone away.
24They do not say in their hearts,
'Let us fear the LORD our
God,
who gives the rain in its
season,
the autumn rain and the
spring rain,
and keeps for us
the weeks appointed for the
harvest.'
25Your iniquities have turned
these away,
and your sins have kept good
from you.
26For wicked men are found
among my people;
they lurk like fowlers lying
in wait.[b]
They set a trap;
they catch men.
27Like a basket full of birds,
their houses are full of
treachery;
therefore they have become
great and rich,
28they have grown fat and
sleek.
They know no bounds in deeds
of wickedness;
they judge not with justice
the cause of the fatherless, to
make it prosper,
and they do not defend the
rights of the needy.
29Shall I not punish them for these
things?
says the LORD,
and shall I not avenge
myself
on a nation such as this?"
30An appalling and horrible
thing
has happened in the land:
31the prophets prophesy falsely,
and the priests rule at their
direction;
my people love to have it so,
but what will you do when
the end comes?

THE IMMINENCE AND HORROR OF THE INVASION

6 Flee for safety, O people of
Benjamin,
from the midst of Jerusalem!

[b]Heb uncertain

Blow the trumpet in Teko´a,
and raise a signal on
Beth-hacche´rem;
for evil looms out of the
north,
and great destruction.
2The comely and delicately bred I
will destroy,
the daughter of Zion.
3Shepherds with their flocks shall
come against her;
they shall pitch their tents
around her,
they shall pasture, each in
his place.
4"Prepare war against her;
up, and let us attack at
noon!"
"Woe to us, for the day
declines,
for the shadows of evening
lengthen!"
5"Up, and let us attack by night,
and destroy her palaces!"
6For thus says the LORD of
hosts:
"Hew down her trees;
cast up a siege mound
against Jerusalem.
This is the city which must be
punished;
there is nothing but
oppression within
her.
7As a well keeps its water fresh,
so she keeps fresh her
wickedness;
violence and destruction are
heard within her;
sickness and wounds are
ever before me.
8Be warned, O Jerusalem,
lest I be alienated from
you;
lest I make you a desolation,
an uninhabited land."
9Thus says the LORD of hosts:
"Glean[a] thoroughly as a vine
the remnant of Israel;
like a grape-gatherer pass your
hand again
over its branches."
10To whom shall I speak and give
warning,
that they may hear?
Behold, their ears are closed,[b]
they cannot listen;
behold, the word of the LORD
is to them an object of
scorn,
they take no pleasure in it.
11Therefore I am full of the wrath
of the LORD;
I am weary of holding it in.
"Pour it out upon the children
in the street,
and upon the gatherings of
young men, also;
both husband and wife shall be
taken,
the old folk and the very
aged.
12Their houses shall be turned
over to others,
their fields and wives
together;
for I will stretch out my hand
against the inhabitants of the
land,"
says the LORD.
13"For from the least to the great-
est of them,
every one is greedy for un-
just gain;
and from prophet to priest,
every one deals falsely.
14They have healed the wound of
my people lightly,
saying, 'Peace, peace,'
when there is no peace.
15Were they ashamed when they
committed abomination?
No, they were not at all
ashamed;
they did not know how to
blush.
Therefore they shall fall among
those who fall;
at the time that I punish
them, they shall be

[a] Cn: Heb *they shall glean*
[b] Heb *uncircumcised*

overthrown,"
says the LORD.
16Thus says the LORD:
"Stand by the roads, and look,
and ask for the ancient paths,
where the good way is; and walk in it,
and find rest for your souls.
But they said, 'We will not walk in it.'
17I set watchmen over you, saying,
'Give heed to the sound of the trumpet!'
But they said, 'We will not give heed.'
18Therefore hear, O nations,
and know, O congregation,
what will happen to them.
19Hear, O earth; behold, I am bringing evil upon this people,
the fruit of their devices,
because they have not given heed to my words;
and as for my law, they have rejected it.
20To what purpose does frankincense come to me from Sheba,
or sweet cane from a distant land?
Your burnt offerings are not acceptable,
nor your sacrifices pleasing to me.
21Therefore thus says the LORD:
'Behold, I will lay before this people
stumbling blocks against which they shall stumble;
fathers and sons together,
neighbor and friend shall perish.'"
22Thus says the LORD:
"Behold, a people is coming from the north country,
a great nation is stirring from the farthest parts of the earth.
23They lay hold on bow and spear,
they are cruel and have no mercy,
the sound of them is like the roaring sea;
they ride upon horses,
set in array as a man for battle,
against you, O daughter of Zion!"
24We have heard the report of it,
our hands fall helpless;
anguish has taken hold of us,
pain as of a woman in travail.
25Go not forth into the field,
nor walk on the road;
for the enemy has a sword,
terror is on every side.
26O daughter of my people, gird on sackcloth,
and roll in ashes;
make mourning as for an only son,
most bitter lamentation;
for suddenly the destroyer will come upon us.
27"I have made you an assayer and tester among my people,
that you may know and assay their ways.
28They are all stubbornly rebellious,
going about with slanders;
they are bronze and iron,
all of them act corruptly.
29The bellows blow fiercely,
the lead is consumed by the fire;
in vain the refining goes on,
for the wicked are not removed.
30Refuse silver they are called,
for the LORD has rejected them."

JEREMIAH PROCLAIMS GOD'S JUDGMENT ON THE NATION

7The word that came to Jeremiah
from the LORD: 2"Stand in the gate

of the LORD's house, and proclaim
there this word, and say, Hear the
word of the LORD, all you men of
Judah who enter these gates to wor-
ship the LORD. 3Thus says the LORD
of hosts, the God of Israel, Amend
your ways and your doings, and I
will let you dwell in this place. 4Do
not trust in these deceptive words:
'This is the temple of the LORD, the
temple of the LORD, the temple of the
LORD.'*

5 "For if you truly amend your
ways and your doings, if you truly ex-
ecute justice one with another, 6if you
do not oppress the alien, the father-
less or the widow, or shed innocent
blood in this place, and if you do not
go after other gods to your own hurt,
7then I will let you dwell in this place,
in the land that I gave of old to your
fathers for ever.

8 "Behold, you trust in decep-
tive words to no avail. 9Will you
steal, murder, commit adultery,
swear falsely, burn incense to Ba´-
al, and go after other gods that you
have not known, 10and then come
and stand before me in this house,
which is called by my name, and
say, 'We are delivered!'—only to go
on doing all these abominations?
11Has this house, which is called by
my name, become a den of robbers
in your eyes? Behold, I myself have
seen it, says the LORD. 12Go now to
my place that was in Shiloh, where I
made my name dwell at first, and see
what I did to it for the wickedness
of my people Israel. 13And now, be-
cause you have done all these things,
says the LORD, and when I spoke to
you persistently you did not listen,
and when I called you, you did not
answer, 14therefore I will do to the
house which is called by my name,
and in which you trust, and to the
place which I gave to you and to
your fathers, as I did to Shiloh. 15And
I will cast you out of my sight, as I
cast out all your kinsmen, all the off-
spring of E´phraim.

THE PEOPLE'S DISOBEDIENCE

16 "As for you, do not pray for
this people, or lift up cry or prayer
for them, and do not intercede with
me, for I do not hear you. 17Do you
not see what they are doing in the
cities of Judah and in the streets of
Jerusalem? 18The children gather
wood, the fathers kindle fire, and
the women knead dough, to make
cakes for the queen of heaven; and
they pour out drink offerings to
other gods, to provoke me to anger.
19Is it I whom they provoke? says the
LORD. Is it not themselves, to their
own confusion? 20Therefore thus says
the Lord GOD: Behold, my anger and
my wrath will be poured out on this
place, upon man and beast, upon
the trees of the field and the fruit of
the ground; it will burn and not be
quenched."

21 Thus says the LORD of hosts,
the God of Israel: "Add your burnt
offerings to your sacrifices, and
eat the flesh. 22For in the day that
I brought them out of the land of
Egypt, I did not speak to your fa-
thers or command them concerning
burnt offerings and sacrifices. 23But
this command I gave them, 'Obey my
voice, and I will be your God, and
you shall be my people; and walk
in all the way that I command you,
that it may be well with you.' 24But
they did not obey or incline their ear,
but walked in their own counsels
and the stubbornness of their evil
hearts, and went backward and not
forward. 25From the day that your fa-
thers came out of the land of Egypt
to this day, I have persistently sent
all my servants the prophets to them,
day after day; 26yet they did not listen
to me, or incline their ear, but stiff-
ened their neck. They did worse than
their fathers.

27 "So you shall speak all these
words to them, but they will not listen
to you. You shall call to them, but they
will not answer you. 28And you shall
say to them, 'This is the nation that

did not obey the voice of the LORD
their God, and did not accept disci-
pline; truth has perished; it is cut off
from their lips.

29 Cut off your hair and cast it
away;
raise a lamentation on the
bare heights,
for the LORD has rejected and
forsaken
the generation of his
wrath.'

30 "For the sons of Judah have
done evil in my sight, says the LORD;
they have set their abominations
in the house which is called by my
name, to defile it. 31 And they have
built the high place[a] of To´pheth,
which is in the valley of the son of
Hinnom, to burn their sons and their
daughters in the fire; which I did not
command, nor did it come into my
mind. 32 Therefore, behold, the days
are coming, says the LORD, when it
will no more be called To´pheth, or
the valley of the son of Hinnom, but
the valley of Slaughter: for they will
bury in To´pheth, because there is
no room elsewhere. 33 And the dead
bodies of this people will be food for
the birds of the air, and for the beasts
of the earth; and none will frighten
them away. 34 And I will make to cease
from the cities of Judah and from
the streets of Jerusalem the voice of
mirth and the voice of gladness, the
voice of the bridegroom and the voice
of the bride; for the land shall become
a waste.

8 "At that time, says the LORD, the
bones of the kings of Judah, the
bones of its princes, the bones of
the priests, the bones of the proph-
ets, and the bones of the inhabitants
of Jerusalem shall be brought out
of their tombs; 2 and they shall be
spread before the sun and the moon
and all the host of heaven, which
they have loved and served, which
they have gone after, and which they
have sought and worshiped; and they
shall not be gathered or buried; they
shall be as dung on the surface of the
ground. 3 Death shall be preferred to
life by all the remnant that remains
of this evil family in all the places
where I have driven them, says the
LORD of hosts.

THE BLIND PERVERSITY OF THE WHOLE NATION

4 "You shall say to them, Thus says
the LORD:
When men fall, do they not rise
again?
If one turns away, does he
not return?
5 Why then has this people turned
away
in perpetual backsliding?
They hold fast to deceit,
they refuse to return.
6 I have given heed and listened,
but they have not spoken
aright;
no man repents of his
wickedness,
saying, 'What have I done?'
Every one turns to his own
course,
like a horse plunging head-
long into battle.
7 Even the stork in the heavens
knows her times;
and the turtledove, swallow,
and crane[b]
keep the time of their
coming;
but my people know not
the ordinance of the LORD.*
8 "How can you say, 'We are wise,
and the law of the LORD is
with us'?
But behold, the false pen of the
scribes
has made it into a lie.
9 The wise men shall be put to
shame,
they shall be dismayed and
taken;

[a] Gk Tg: Heb *high places*
[b] The meaning of the Hebrew word is uncertain

lo, they have rejected the word
of the LORD,
and what wisdom is in
them?
10Therefore I will give their wives
to others
and their fields to
conquerors,
because from the least to the
greatest
every one is greedy for unjust gain;
from prophet to priest
every one deals falsely.
11They have healed the wound of
my people lightly,
saying, 'Peace, peace,'
when there is no peace.
12Were they ashamed when they
committed abomination?
No, they were not at all
ashamed;
they did not know how to
blush.
Therefore they shall fall among
the fallen;
when I punish them, they
shall be overthrown,
says the LORD.
13When I would gather them, says
the LORD,
there are no grapes on the
vine,
nor figs on the fig tree;
even the leaves are withered,
and what I gave them has
passed away from
them."[a]
14Why do we sit still?
Gather together, let us go into
the fortified cities
and perish there;
for the LORD our God has
doomed us to perish,
and has given us poisoned
water to drink,
because we have sinned
against the LORD.
15We looked for peace, but no
good came,
for a time of healing, but
behold, terror.
16"The snorting of their horses is
heard from Dan;
at the sound of the neighing
of their stallions
the whole land quakes.
They come and devour the
land and all that
fills it,
the city and those who dwell
in it.
17For behold, I am sending among
you serpents,
adders which cannot be
charmed,
and they shall bite you,"
says the LORD.

THE PROPHET MOURNS FOR THE PEOPLE

18My grief is beyond healing,[b]
my heart is sick within me.
19Hark, the cry of the daughter of
my people
from the length and breadth
of the land:
"Is the LORD not in Zion?
Is her King not in her?"
"Why have they provoked me
to anger with their graven images,
and with their foreign
idols?"
20"The harvest is past, the summer is ended,
and we are not saved."
21For the wound of the daughter
of my people is my heart
wounded,
I mourn, and dismay has
taken hold on me.
22Is there no balm in Gilead?
Is there no physician there?
Why then has the health of
the daughter of my
people
not been restored?

9[c] O that my head were waters,
and my eyes a fountain of
tears,

[a]Heb uncertain
[b]Cn: Compare Gk: Heb uncertain
[c]Ch 8.23 in Heb

that I might weep day and
night
for the slain of the daughter
of my people!
2[d] O that I had in the desert
a wayfarers' lodging place,
that I might leave my people
and go away from them!
For they are all adulterers,
a company of treacherous
men.
3They bend their tongue like a
bow;
falsehood and not truth has
grown strong[e] in the
land;
for they proceed from evil to
evil,
and they do not know me,
says the LORD.
4Let every one beware of his
neighbor,
and put no trust in any
brother;
for every brother is a
supplanter,
and every neighbor goes
about as a slanderer.
5Every one deceives his
neighbor,
and no one speaks the
truth;
they have taught their tongue
to speak lies;
they commit iniquity and
are too weary to
repent.[f]
6Heaping oppression upon oppression, and deceit upon
deceit,
they refuse to know me, says
the LORD.

7Therefore thus says the LORD of
hosts:

"Behold, I will refine them and
test them,
for what else can I do,
because of my
people?
8Their tongue is a deadly arrow;
it speaks deceitfully;
with his mouth each speaks
peaceably to his
neighbor,
but in his heart he plans an
ambush for him.
9Shall I not punish them for these
things? says the LORD;
and shall I not avenge
myself
on a nation such as this?
10"Take up[g] weeping and wailing
for the mountains,
and a lamentation for the
pastures of the
wilderness,
because they are laid waste
so that no one passes
through,
and the lowing of cattle is
not heard;
both the birds of the air and
the beasts
have fled and are gone.
11I will make Jerusalem a heap of
ruins,
a lair of jackals;
and I will make the cities of
Judah a desolation,
without inhabitant."

12 Who is the man so wise that he
can understand this? To whom has
the mouth of the LORD spoken, that
he may declare it? Why is the land
ruined and laid waste like a wilderness, so that no one passes through?
13And the LORD says: "Because they
have forsaken my law which I set before them, and have not obeyed my
voice, or walked in accord with it,
14but have stubbornly followed their
own hearts and have gone after the
Ba'als, as their fathers taught them.
15Therefore thus says the LORD of
hosts, the God of Israel: Behold, I
will feed this people with wormwood,
and give them poisonous water to
drink. 16I will scatter them among the

[d]Ch 9.1 in Heb
[e]Gk: Heb *and not for truth they have grown strong*
[f]Cn Compare Gk: Heb *your dwelling*
[g]Gk Syr: Heb *I will take up*

nations whom neither they nor their
fathers have known; and I will send
the sword after them, until I have
consumed them."

THE PEOPLE MOURN IN JUDGMENT

17Thus says the LORD of hosts:
"Consider, and call for the
mourning women to
come;
send for the skilful women
to come;
18let them make haste and raise a
wailing over us,
that our eyes may run down
with tears,
and our eyelids gush with
water.
19For a sound of wailing is heard
from Zion:
'How we are ruined!
We are utterly shamed,
because we have left the land,
because they have cast down
our dwellings.'"
20Hear, O women, the word of the
LORD,
and let your ear receive the
word of his mouth;
teach to your daughters a
lament,
and each to her neighbor a
dirge.
21For death has come up into our
windows,
it has entered our palaces,
cutting off the children from
the streets
and the young men from the
squares.
22Speak, "Thus says the LORD:
'The dead bodies of men shall
fall
like dung upon the open
field,
like sheaves after the reaper,
and none shall gather
them.'"
23 Thus says the LORD: "Let not
the wise man glory in his wisdom,
let not the mighty man glory in his
might, let not the rich man glory in
his riches; 24but let him who glories
glory in this, that he understands
and knows me, that I am the LORD
who practice steadfast love, justice,
and righteousness in the earth; for
in these things I delight, says the
LORD."*
25 "Behold, the days are coming,
says the LORD, when I will punish
all those who are circumcised but yet
uncircumcised 26Egypt, Judah, Edom,
the sons of Ammon, Moab, and all
who dwell in the desert that cut the
corners of their hair; for all these na-
tions are uncircumcised, and all the
house of Israel is uncircumcised in
heart."

IDOLATRY HAS BROUGHT RUIN ON ISRAEL

10 Hear the word which the LORD
speaks to you, O house of
Israel.
2Thus says the LORD:
"Learn not the way of the
nations,
nor be dismayed at the signs
of the heavens
because the nations are
dismayed at them,
3for the customs of the peoples
are false.
A tree from the forest is cut
down,
and worked with an axe
by the hands of a
craftsman.
4Men deck it with silver and
gold;
they fasten it with hammer
and nails
so that it cannot move.
5Their idols[a] are like scarecrows
in a cucumber field,
and they cannot speak;
they have to be carried,
for they cannot walk.
Be not afraid of them,
for they cannot do evil,
neither is it in them to do
good."

[a]Heb *They*

6There is none like thee, O
LORD;
thou art great, and thy
name is great in
might.
7Who would not fear thee, O King
of the nations?
For this is thy due;
for among all the wise ones of
the nations
and in all their kingdoms
there is none like thee.
8They are both stupid and
foolish;
the instruction of idols is
but wood!
9Beaten silver is brought from
Tarshish,
and gold from Uphaz.
They are the work of the crafts-
man and of the hands of
the goldsmith;
their clothing is violet and
purple;
they are all the work of
skilled men.
10But the LORD is the true God;
he is the living God and the
everlasting King.
At his wrath the earth quakes,
and the nations can-
not endure his
indignation.
11 Thus shall you say to them:
"The gods who did not make the
heavens and the earth shall perish
from the earth and from under the
heavens."[b]
12It is he who made the earth by
his power,
who established the world
by his wisdom,
and by his understanding
stretched out the
heavens.
13When he utters his voice there
is a tumult of waters in the
heavens,
and he makes the mist rise
from the ends of the
earth.
He makes lightnings for the
rain,
and he brings forth the
wind from his
storehouses.
14Every man is stupid and without
knowledge;
every goldsmith is put to
shame by his idols;
for his images are false,
and there is no breath in
them.
15They are worthless, a work of
delusion;
at the time of their pun-
ishment they shall
perish.
16Not like these is he who is the
portion of Jacob,
for he is the one who formed
all things,
and Israel is the tribe of his
inheritance;
the LORD of hosts is his
name.

THE COMING EXILE

17Gather up your bundle from the
ground,
O you who dwell under
siege!
18For thus says the LORD:
"Behold, I am slinging out the
inhabitants of the land
at this time,
and I will bring distress on
them,
that they may feel it."
19Woe is me because of my hurt!
My wound is grievous.
But I said, "Truly this is an
affliction,
and I must bear it."
20My tent is destroyed,
and all my cords are
broken;
my children have gone from
me,
and they are not;
there is no one to spread my
tent again,

[b]This verse is in Aramaic

and to set up my curtains.
21For the shepherds are stupid,
and do not inquire of the LORD;
therefore they have not prospered,
and all their flock is scattered.
22Hark, a rumor! Behold, it comes!—
a great commotion out of the north country
to make the cities of Judah a desolation,
a lair of jackals.
23I know, O LORD, that the way of man is not in himself,
that it is not in man who walks to direct his steps.
24Correct me, O LORD, but in just measure;
not in thy anger, lest thou bring me to nothing.
25Pour out thy wrath upon the nations that know thee not,
and upon the peoples that call not on thy name;
for they have devoured Jacob;
they have devoured him and consumed him,
and have laid waste his habitation.

ISRAEL AND JUDAH HAVE BROKEN THE COVENANT

11 The word that came to Jeremiah
from the LORD: 2"Hear the words
of this covenant, and speak to the
men of Judah and the inhabitants of
Jerusalem. 3You shall say to them,
Thus says the LORD, the God of
Israel: Cursed be the man who does
not heed the words of this covenant
4which I commanded your fathers
when I brought them out of the land
of Egypt, from the iron furnace, say-
ing, Listen to my voice, and do all that
I command you. So shall you be my
people, and I will be your God, 5that
I may perform the oath which I swore
to your fathers, to give them a land
flowing with milk and honey, as at
this day." Then I answered, "So be it,
LORD."

6 And the LORD said to me,
"Proclaim all these words in the
cities of Judah, and in the streets of
Jerusalem: Hear the words of this
covenant and do them. 7For I sol-
emnly warned your fathers when I
brought them up out of the land of
Egypt, warning them persistently,
even to this day, saying, Obey my
voice. 8Yet they did not obey or in-
cline their ear, but every one walked
in the stubbornness of his evil heart.
Therefore I brought upon them all
the words of this covenant, which I
commanded them to do, but they did
not."

9 Again the LORD said to me,
"There is revolt among the men
of Judah and the inhabitants of
Jerusalem. 10They have turned back
to the iniquities of their forefathers,
who refused to hear my words; they
have gone after other gods to serve
them; the house of Israel and the
house of Judah have broken my cove-
nant which I made with their fathers.
11Therefore, thus says the LORD,
Behold, I am bringing evil upon them
which they cannot escape; though
they cry to me, I will not listen to
them. 12Then the cities of Judah and
the inhabitants of Jerusalem will go
and cry to the gods to whom they
burn incense, but they cannot save
them in the time of their trouble.
13For your gods have become as many
as your cities, O Judah; and as many
as the streets of Jerusalem are the al-
tars you have set up to shame, altars
to burn incense to Ba′al.

14 "Therefore do not pray for this
people, or lift up a cry or prayer on
their behalf, for I will not listen when
they call to me in the time of their
trouble. 15What right has my beloved
in my house, when she has done vile

deeds? Can vows[a] and sacrificial
flesh avert your doom? Can you then
exult? 16The LORD once called you,
'A green olive tree, fair with goodly
fruit'; but with the roar of a great
tempest he will set fire to it, and its
branches will be consumed. 17The
LORD of hosts, who planted you, has
pronounced evil against you, because
of the evil which the house of Israel
and the house of Judah have done,
provoking me to anger by burning in-
cense to Ba'al."

JEREMIAH'S LIFE THREATENED

18The LORD made it known to me
and I knew;
then thou didst show me
their evil deeds.
19But I was like a gentle lamb
led to the slaughter.
I did not know it was against
me
they devised schemes,
saying,
"Let us destroy the tree with
its fruit,
let us cut him off from the
land of the living,
that his name be remem-
bered no more."
20But, O LORD of hosts, who judg-
est righteously,
who triest the heart and the
mind,
let me see thy vengeance upon
them,
for to thee have I committed
my cause.

21 Therefore thus says the LORD
concerning the men of An'athoth, who
seek your life, and say, "Do not proph-
esy in the name of the LORD, or you
will die by our hand" 22therefore thus
says the LORD of hosts: "Behold, I will
punish them; the young men shall die
by the sword; their sons and their
daughters shall die by famine; 23and
none of them shall be left. For I will
bring evil upon the men of An'athoth,
the year of their punishment."

[a]Gk: Heb *many*

JEREMIAH COMPLAINS TO GOD

12 Righteous art thou, O LORD,
when I complain to thee;
yet I would plead my case
before thee.
Why does the way of the wick-
ed prosper?
Why do all who are treacher-
ous thrive?
2Thou plantest them, and they
take root;
they grow and bring forth
fruit;
thou art near in their mouth
and far from their heart.
3But thou, O LORD, knowest me;
thou seest me, and triest
my mind toward
thee.
Pull them out like sheep for the
slaughter,
and set them apart for the
day of slaughter.
4How long will the land mourn,
and the grass of every field
wither?
For the wickedness of those
who dwell in it
the beasts and the birds are
swept away,
because men said, "He will
not see our latter
end."

GOD REPLIES TO JEREMIAH

5"If you have raced with men on
foot, and they have wea-
ried you,
how will you compete with
horses?
And if in a safe land you fall
down,
how will you do in the jungle
of the Jordan?
6For even your brothers and the
house of your father,
even they have dealt treach-
erously with you;
they are in full cry after
you;
believe them not,

though they speak fair
words to you."
7"I have forsaken my house,
I have abandoned my
heritage;
I have given the beloved of my
soul
into the hands of her
enemies.
8My heritage has become to me
like a lion in the forest,
she has lifted up her voice
against me;
therefore I hate her.
9Is my heritage to me like a speck-
led bird of prey?
Are the birds of prey against
her round about?
Go, assemble all the wild
beasts;
bring them to devour.
10Many shepherds have destroyed
my vineyard,
they have trampled down my
portion,
they have made my pleasant
portion
a desolate wilderness.
11They have made it a desolation;
desolate, it mourns to me.
The whole land is made
desolate,
but no man lays it to heart.
12Upon all the bare heights in the
desert
destroyers have come;
for the sword of the LORD
devours
from one end of the land to
the other;
no flesh has peace.
13They have sown wheat and have
reaped thorns,
they have tired them-
selves out but profit
nothing.
They shall be ashamed of their[a]
harvests
because of the fierce anger
of the LORD."

14 Thus says the LORD concerning
all my evil neighbors who touch the
heritage which I have given my peo-
ple Israel to inherit: "Behold, I will
pluck them up from their land, and
I will pluck up the house of Judah
from among them. 15And after I have
plucked them up, I will again have
compassion on them, and I will bring
them again each to his heritage and
each to his land. 16And it shall come
to pass, if they will diligently learn
the ways of my people, to swear by
my name, 'As the LORD lives,' even
as they taught my people to swear
by Ba'al, then they shall be built up
in the midst of my people. 17But if any
nation will not listen, then I will ut-
terly pluck it up and destroy it, says
the LORD."

THE LINEN LOINCLOTH

13 *Thus says the LORD to me, "Go
and buy a linen waistcloth, and
put it on your loins, and do not dip
it in water." 2So I bought a waist-
cloth according to the word of the
LORD, and put it on my loins. 3And
the word of the LORD came to me
a second time, 4"Take the waist-
cloth which you have bought, which
is upon your loins, and arise, go to
the Euphra'tes, and hide it there in
a cleft of the rock." 5So I went, and
hid it by the Euphra'tes, as the LORD
commanded me. 6And after many
days the LORD said to me, "Arise,
go to the Euphra'tes, and take from
there the waistcloth which I com-
manded you to hide there." 7Then I
went to the Euphra'tes, and dug, and
I took the waistcloth from the place
where I had hidden it. And behold,
the waistcloth was spoiled; it was
good for nothing.

8 Then the word of the LORD
came to me: 9"Thus says the LORD:
Even so will I spoil the pride of Judah
and the great pride of Jerusalem.
10This evil people, who refuse to hear
my words, who stubbornly follow
their own heart and have gone after

[a]Heb *your*

other gods to serve them and worship them, shall be like this waistcloth, which is good for nothing.
11For as the waistcloth clings to the
loins of a man, so I made the whole house of Israel and the whole house of Judah cling to me, says the LORD, that they might be for me a people, a name, a praise, and a glory, but they would not listen.

SYMBOL OF THE WINE-JARS

12 "You shall speak to them this
word: 'Thus says the LORD, the God of Israel, "Every jar shall be filled with wine."'" And they will say to you, 'Do we not indeed know that every jar will be filled with wine?'
13Then you shall say to them, 'Thus
says the LORD: Behold, I will fill with drunkenness all the inhabitants of this land: the kings who sit on David's throne, the priests, the prophets, and all the inhabitants of Jerusalem.
14And I will dash them one against
another, fathers and sons together, says the LORD. I will not pity or spare or have compassion, that I should not destroy them.'"

EXILE THREATENED

15Hear and give ear; be not
proud,
for the LORD has spoken.
16Give glory to the LORD your
God
before he brings darkness,
before your feet stumble
on the twilight mountains,
and while you look for light
he turns it into gloom
and makes it deep
darkness.
17But if you will not listen,
my soul will weep in secret
for your pride;
my eyes will weep bitterly and
run down with tears,
because the LORD's flock
has been taken
captive.
18Say to the king and the queen
mother:
"Take a lowly seat,
for your beautiful crown
has come down from your
head."[b]
19The cities of the Negeb are
shut up,
with none to open them;
all Judah is taken into exile,
wholly taken into exile.
20"Lift up your eyes and see
those who come from the
north.
Where is the flock that was
given you,
your beautiful flock?
21What will you say when they set
as head over you
those whom you yourself
have taught
to be friends to you?
Will not pangs take hold of
you,
like those of a woman in
travail?
22And if you say in your heart,
'Why have these things
come upon me?'
it is for the greatness of your
iniquity
that your skirts are
lifted up,
and you suffer violence.
23Can the Ethiopian change his
skin
or the leopard his spots?
Then also you can do good
who are accustomed to do
evil.
24I will scatter you[c] like chaff
driven by the wind from the
desert.
25This is your lot,
the portion I have measured
out to you, says the
LORD,
because you have forgotten me
and trusted in lies.

[b] Gk Syr Vg: Heb obscure
[c] Heb *them*

26I myself will lift up your skirts
over your face,
and your shame will be
seen.
27I have seen your abominations,
your adulteries and neighings, your lewd
harlotries,
on the hills in the field.
Woe to you, O Jerusalem!
How long will it be
before you are made
clean?"

THE GREAT DROUGHT

14 The word of the LORD which came to Jeremiah concerning the drought:
2"Judah mourns
and her gates languish;
her people lament on the
ground,
and the cry of Jerusalem
goes up.
3Her nobles send their servants
for water;
they come to the cisterns,
they find no water,
they return with their vessels empty;
they are ashamed and
confounded
and cover their heads.
4Because of the ground which is
dismayed,
since there is no rain on the
land,
the farmers are ashamed,
they cover their heads.
5Even the hind in the field forsakes her newborn calf
because there is no grass.
6The wild asses stand on the bare
heights,
they pant for air like
jackals;
their eyes fail
because there is no
herbage.
7"Though our iniquities testify
against us,
act, O LORD, for thy name's
sake;
for our backslidings are many,
we have sinned against
thee.
8O thou hope of Israel,
its savior in time of
trouble,
why shouldst thou be like a
stranger in the land,
like a wayfarer who turns
aside to tarry for a
night?
9Why shouldst thou be like a man
confused,
like a mighty man who cannot save?
Yet thou, O LORD, art in the
midst of us,
and we are called by thy
name;
leave us not."
10Thus says the LORD concerning
this people:
"They have loved to wander
thus,
they have not restrained
their feet;
therefore the LORD does not
accept them
now he will remember their
iniquity
and punish their sins."

11 The LORD said to me: "Do not
pray for the welfare of this people.
12Though they fast, I will not hear
their cry, and though they offer burnt
offering and cereal offering, I will
not accept them; but I will consume
them by the sword, by famine, and by
pestilence."

DENUNCIATION OF LYING PROPHETS

13 Then I said: "Ah, Lord GOD,
behold, the prophets say to them,
'You shall not see the sword, nor
shall you have famine, but I will give
you assured peace in this place.'"
14And the LORD said to me: "The
prophets are prophesying lies in
my name; I did not send them, nor
did I command them or speak to
them. They are prophesying to you

a lying vision, worthless divination,
and the deceit of their own minds.
15Therefore thus says the LORD con-
cerning the prophets who prophesy
in my name although I did not send
them, and who say, 'Sword and fam-
ine shall not come on this land': By
sword and famine those prophets
shall be consumed. 16And the people
to whom they prophesy shall be cast
out in the streets of Jerusalem, vic-
tims of famine and sword, with none
to bury them—them, their wives,
their sons, and their daughters. For I
will pour out their wickedness upon
them.

17"You shall say to them this
word:
'Let my eyes run down with
tears night and day,
and let them not cease,
for the virgin daughter of my
people is smitten with a
great wound,
with a very grievous blow.
18If I go out into the field,
behold, those slain by the
sword!
And if I enter the city,
behold, the diseases of
famine!
For both prophet and priest ply
their trade through the
land,
and have no knowledge.'"

THE PEOPLE PLEAD FOR MERCY

19Hast thou utterly rejected
Judah?
Does thy soul loathe Zion?
Why hast thou smitten us
so that there is no healing
for us?
We looked for peace, but no
good came;
for a time of healing, but
behold, terror.
20We acknowledge our wicked-
ness, O LORD,
and the iniquity of our
fathers,
for we have sinned against
thee.
21Do not spurn us, for thy name's
sake;
do not dishonor thy glorious
throne;
remember and do not
break thy covenant
with us.
22Are there any among the false
gods of the nations that
can bring rain?
Or can the heavens give
showers?
Art thou not he, O LORD our
God?
We set our hope on thee,
for thou doest all these
things.

PUNISHMENT IS INEVITABLE

15 Then the LORD said to me,
"Though Moses and Samuel stood
before me, yet my heart would not
turn toward this people. Send them
out of my sight, and let them go! 2And
when they ask you, 'Where shall we
go?' you shall say to them, 'Thus says
the LORD:
"Those who are for pestilence,
to pestilence,
and those who are for
the sword, to the
sword;
those who are for famine, to
famine,
and those who are for
captivity, to
captivity."

3"I will appoint over them four
kinds of destroyers, says the LORD:
the sword to slay, the dogs to tear,
and the birds of the air and the
beasts of the earth to devour and
destroy.4And I will make them a hor-
ror to all the kingdoms of the earth
because of what Manas´seh the son
of Hezeki´ah, king of Judah, did in
Jerusalem.

5"Who will have pity on you, O
Jerusalem,
or who will bemoan you?
Who will turn aside

to ask about your welfare?
6You have rejected me, says the LORD,
you keep going backward;
so I have stretched out my hand against you and destroyed you;—
I am weary of relenting.
7I have winnowed them with a winnowing fork
in the gates of the land;
I have bereaved them, I have destroyed my people;
they did not turn from their ways.
8I have made their widows more in number
than the sand of the seas;
I have brought against the mothers of young men
a destroyer at noonday;
I have made anguish and terror
fall upon them suddenly.
9She who bore seven has languished;
she has swooned away;
her sun went down while it was yet day;
she has been shamed and disgraced.
And the rest of them I will give to the sword
before their enemies,
says the LORD."

JEREMIAH COMPLAINS AGAIN AND IS REASSURED

10 Woe is me, my mother, that you
bore me, a man of strife and conten-
tion to the whole land! I have not lent,
nor have I borrowed, yet all of them
curse me. 11So let it be, O LORD,[a] if
I have not entreated[b] thee for their
good, if I have not pleaded with thee
on behalf of the enemy in the time of
trouble and in the time of distress!
12Can one break iron, iron from the
north, and bronze?
13 "Your wealth and your
treasures I will give as spoil, without
price, for all your sins, throughout
all your territory. 14I will make you
serve your enemies in a land which
you do not know, for in my anger a
fire is kindled which shall burn for
ever."

15O LORD, thou knowest;
remember me and visit me,
and take vengeance for me on my persecutors.
In thy forbearance take me not away;
know that for thy sake I bear reproach.
16Thy words were found, and I ate them,
and thy words became to me a joy
and the delight of my heart;
for I am called by thy name,
O LORD, God of hosts.
17I did not sit in the company of merrymakers,
nor did I rejoice;
I sat alone, because thy hand was upon me,
for thou hadst filled me with indignation.
18Why is my pain unceasing,
my wound incurable,
refusing to be healed?
Wilt thou be to me like a deceitful brook,
like waters that fail?
19Therefore thus says the LORD:
"If you return, I will restore you,
and you shall stand before me.
If you utter what is precious, and not what is worthless,
you shall be as my mouth.
They shall turn to you,
but you shall not turn to them.
20And I will make you to this people

[a]Gk Old Latin: Heb *the Lord said*
[b]Cn: Heb obscure

a fortified wall of bronze;
they will fight against you,
but they shall not prevail
over you,
for I am with you
to save you and deliver you,
says the LORD.
21 I will deliver you out of the hand
of the wicked,
and redeem you from
the grasp of the
ruthless."

JEREMIAH'S CELIBACY AND MESSAGE

16 The word of the LORD came to
me: 2 "You shall not take a wife,
nor shall you have sons or daugh-
ters in this place. 3 For thus says
the LORD concerning the sons and
daughters who are born in this place,
and concerning the mothers who
bore them and the fathers who begot
them in this land: 4 They shall die of
deadly diseases. They shall not be
lamented, nor shall they be buried;
they shall be as dung on the surface
of the ground. They shall perish by
the sword and by famine, and their
dead bodies shall be food for the
birds of the air and for the beasts of
the earth.

5 "For thus says the LORD: Do
not enter the house of mourning, or
go to lament, or bemoan them; for I
have taken away my peace from this
people, says the LORD, my stead-
fast love and mercy. 6 Both great and
small shall die in this land; they
shall not be buried, and no one shall
lament for them or cut himself or
make himself bald for them. 7 No one
shall break bread for the mourner, to
comfort him for the dead; nor shall
any one give him the cup of conso-
lation to drink for his father or his
mother. 8 You shall not go into the
house of feasting to sit with them,
to eat and drink. 9 For thus says the
LORD of hosts, the God of Israel:
Behold, I will make to cease from
this place, before your eyes and in
your days, the voice of mirth and
the voice of gladness, the voice of
the bridegroom and the voice of the
bride.

10 "And when you tell this peo-
ple all these words, and they say to
you, 'Why has the LORD pronounced
all this great evil against us? What
is our iniquity? What is the sin
that we have committed against the
LORD our God?' 11 then you shall say
to them: 'Because your fathers have
forsaken me, says the LORD, and
have gone after other gods and have
served and worshiped them, and
have forsaken me and have not kept
my law, 12 and because you have done
worse than your fathers, for behold,
every one of you follows his stub-
born evil will, refusing to listen to
me; 13 therefore I will hurl you out of
this land into a land which neither
you nor your fathers have known,
and there you shall serve other gods
day and night, for I will show you no
favor.'

GOD WILL RESTORE ISRAEL

14 "Therefore, behold, the days are
coming, says the LORD, when it shall
no longer be said, 'As the LORD lives
who brought up the people of Israel
out of the land of Egypt,' 15 but 'As the
LORD lives who brought up the people
of Israel out of the north country and
out of all the countries where he had
driven them.' For I will bring them
back to their own land which I gave to
their fathers.

16 "Behold, I am sending for many
fishers, says the LORD, and they shall
catch them; and afterwards I will
send for many hunters, and they shall
hunt them from every mountain and
every hill, and out of the clefts of the
rocks. 17 For my eyes are upon all their
ways; they are not hid from me, nor
is their iniquity concealed from my
eyes. 18 And[c] I will doubly recompense
their iniquity and their sin, because
they have polluted my land with the

[c] Gk: Heb *And first*

carcasses of their detestable idols, and have filled my inheritance with their abominations."

19 O LORD, my strength and my stronghold,
my refuge in the day of trouble,
to thee shall the nations come
from the ends of the earth and say:
"Our fathers have inherited nought but lies,
worthless things in which there is no profit.
20 Can man make for himself gods?
Such are no gods!"

21 "Therefore, behold, I will make them know, this once I will make them know my power and my might, and they shall know that my name is the LORD."

JUDAH'S SIN AND PUNISHMENT

17 "The sin of Judah is written with
a pen of iron; with a point of diamond it is engraved on the tablet of
their heart, and on the horns of their
altars, 2 while their children remem-
ber their altars and their Ashe′rim,
beside every green tree, and on the
high hills, 3 on the mountains in the
open country. Your wealth and all
your treasures I will give for spoil
as the price of your sin[a] throughout
all your territory. 4 You shall loosen
your hand[b] from your heritage which
I gave to you, and I will make you
serve your enemies in a land which
you do not know, for in my anger a
fire is kindled which shall burn for
ever."

5 Thus says the LORD:
"Cursed is the man who trusts in man
and makes flesh his arm,
whose heart turns away from the LORD.
6 He is like a shrub in the desert,
and shall not see any good come.
He shall dwell in the parched places of the wilderness,
in an uninhabited salt land.
7 "Blessed is the man who trusts in the LORD,
whose trust is the LORD.
8 He is like a tree planted by water,
that sends out its roots by the stream,
and does not fear when heat comes,
for its leaves remain green,
and is not anxious in the year of drought,
for it does not cease to bear fruit."
9 The heart is deceitful above all things,
and desperately corrupt;
who can understand it?
10 "I the LORD search the mind
and try the heart,
to give every man according to his ways,
according to the fruit of his doings."
11 Like the partridge that gathers a brood which she did not hatch,
so is he who gets riches but not by right;
in the midst of his days they will leave him,
and at his end he will be a fool.
12 A glorious throne set on high from the beginning
is the place of our sanctuary.
13 O LORD, the hope of Israel,
all who forsake thee shall be put to shame;
those who turn away from thee[c] shall be written in the earth,
for they have forsaken the

[a] Cn: Heb *your high places for sin*
[b] Cn: Heb *and in you*
[c] Heb *me*

LORD, the fountain of
living water.

JEREMIAH PRAYS FOR VINDICATION

14Heal me, O LORD, and I shall be
healed;
save me, and I shall be
saved;
for thou art my praise.
15Behold, they say to me,
"Where is the word of the
LORD?
Let it come!"
16I have not pressed thee to send
evil,
nor have I desired the day of
disaster,
thou knowest;
that which came out of
my lips
was before thy face.
17Be not a terror to me;
thou art my refuge in the
day of evil.
18Let those be put to shame who
persecute me,
but let me not be put to
shame;
let them be dismayed,
but let me not be dismayed;
bring upon them the day of
evil;
destroy them with double
destruction!

HALLOW THE SABBATH DAY

19 Thus said the LORD to me: "Go
and stand in the Benjamin[d] Gate, by
which the kings of Judah enter and
by which they go out, and in all the
gates of Jerusalem, 20and say: 'Hear
the word of the LORD, you kings of
Judah, and all Judah, and all the in-
habitants of Jerusalem, who enter by
these gates. 21Thus says the LORD:
Take heed for the sake of your lives,
and do not bear a burden on the sab-
bath day or bring it in by the gates of
Jerusalem. 22And do not carry a bur-
den out of your houses on the sabbath
or do any work, but keep the sab-
bath day holy, as I commanded your
fathers. 23Yet they did not listen or
incline their ear, but stiffened their
neck, that they might not hear and
receive instruction.

24 "'But if you listen to me, says
the LORD, and bring in no burden
by the gates of this city on the sab-
bath day, but keep the sabbath day
holy and do no work on it, 25then
there shall enter by the gates of this
city kings[e] who sit on the throne
of David, riding in chariots and on
horses, they and their princes, the
men of Judah and the inhabitants of
Jerusalem; and this city shall be in-
habited for ever. 26And people shall
come from the cities of Judah and
the places round about Jerusalem,
from the land of Benjamin, from the
Shephe´lah, from the hill country,
and from the Negeb, bringing burnt
offerings and sacrifices, cereal of-
ferings and frankincense, and bring-
ing thank offerings to the house of
the LORD. 27But if you do not listen
to me, to keep the sabbath day holy,
and not to bear a burden and enter
by the gates of Jerusalem on the sab-
bath day, then I will kindle a fire
in its gates, and it shall devour the
palaces of Jerusalem and shall not be
quenched.'"

THE POTTER AND THE CLAY

18 The word that came to Jeremiah
from the LORD: 2"Arise, and go
down to the potter's house, and there
I will let you hear my words." 3So I
went down to the potter's house, and
there he was working at his wheel.
4And the vessel he was making of
clay was spoiled in the potter's hand,
and he reworked it into another ves-
sel, as it seemed good to the potter
to do.

5 Then the word of the LORD
came to me: 6"O house of Israel, can
I not do with you as this potter has

[d]Cn: Heb *sons of people*
[e]Cn: Heb *kings and princes*

done? says the LORD. Behold, like
the clay in the potter's hand, so are
you in my hand, O house of Israel.
7If at any time I declare concerning a
nation or a kingdom, that I will pluck
up and break down and destroy it,
8and if that nation, concerning which
I have spoken, turns from its evil, I
will repent of the evil that I intended
to do to it. 9And if at any time I de-
clare concerning a nation or a king-
dom that I will build and plant it,
10and if it does evil in my sight, not
listening to my voice, then I will re-
pent of the good which I had intend-
ed to do to it. 11Now, therefore, say to
the men of Judah and the inhabitants
of Jerusalem: 'Thus says the LORD,
Behold, I am shaping evil against
you and devising a plan against
you. Return, every one from his evil
way, and amend your ways and your
doings.'

ISRAEL'S STUBBORN IDOLATRY

12 "But they say, 'That is in vain!
We will follow our own plans, and will
every one act according to the stub-
bornness of his evil heart.'

13"Therefore thus says the LORD:
Ask among the nations,
who has heard the like of this?
The virgin Israel
has done a very horrible thing.
14Does the snow of Lebanon leave
the crags of Sir´ion?[a]
Do the mountain[b] waters run dry,[c]
the cold flowing streams?
15But my people have forgotten me,
they burn incense to false gods;
they have stumbled[d] in their ways,
in the ancient roads,
and have gone into bypaths,
not the highway,
16making their land a horror,
a thing to be hissed at for ever.
Every one who passes by it is horrified
and shakes his head.
17Like the east wind I will scatter them
before the enemy.
I will show them my back, not my face,
in the day of their calamity."

A PLOT AGAINST JEREMIAH

18 Then they said, "Come, let us
make plots against Jeremiah, for the
law shall not perish from the priest,
nor counsel from the wise, nor the
word from the prophet. Come, let us
smite him with the tongue, and let us
not heed any of his words."

19Give heed to me, O LORD,
and hearken to my plea.[e]
20Is evil a recompense for good?
Yet they have dug a pit for my life.
Remember how I stood before thee
to speak good for them,
to turn away thy wrath from them.
21Therefore deliver up their children to famine;
give them over to the power of the sword,
let their wives become childless and widowed.
May their men meet death by pestilence,
their youths be slain by the sword in battle.
22May a cry be heard from their houses,
when thou bringest the

[a] Cn: Heb *the field*
[b] Cn: Heb *foreign*
[c] Cn: Heb *Are.. plucked up?*
[d] Gk Syr Vg: Heb *they made them stumble*
[e] Gk Compare Syr Tg: Heb *my adversaries*

marauder suddenly
upon them!
For they have dug a pit to
take me,
and laid snares for my feet.
23Yet, thou, O LORD, knowest
all their plotting to
slay me.
Forgive not their iniquity,
nor blot out their sin from
thy sight.
Let them be overthrown before
thee;
deal with them in the time
of thine anger.

THE BROKEN EARTHENWARE JUG

19 Thus said the LORD, "Go, buy
a potter's earthen flask, and
take some of the elders of the peo-
ple and some of the senior priests,
2and go out to the valley of the son of
Hinnom at the entry of the Potsherd
Gate, and proclaim there the words
that I tell you. 3You shall say, 'Hear
the word of the LORD, O kings of
Judah and inhabitants of Jerusalem.
Thus says the LORD of hosts, the
God of Israel, Behold, I am bring-
ing such evil upon this place that
the ears of every one who hears of it
will tingle. 4Because the people have
forsaken me, and have profaned this
place by burning incense in it to oth-
er gods whom neither they nor their
fathers nor the kings of Judah have
known; and because they have filled
this place with the blood of inno-
cents, 5and have built the high places
of Ba´al to burn their sons in the fire
as burnt offerings to Ba´al, which I
did not command or decree, nor did
it come into my mind; 6therefore,
behold, days are coming, says the
LORD, when this place shall no more
be called To´pheth, or the valley of
the son of Hinnom, but the valley of
Slaughter. 7And in this place I will
make void the plans of Judah and
Jerusalem, and will cause their peo-
ple to fall by the sword before their
enemies, and by the hand of those
who seek their life. I will give their
dead bodies for food to the birds of
the air and to the beasts of the earth.
8And I will make this city a horror, a
thing to be hissed at; every one who
passes by it will be horrified and
will hiss because of all its disasters.
9And I will make them eat the flesh
of their sons and their daughters,
and every one shall eat the flesh of
his neighbor in the siege and in the
distress, with which their enemies
and those who seek their life afflict
them.'

10 "Then you shall break the flask
in the sight of the men who go with
you, 11and shall say to them, 'Thus
says the LORD of hosts: So will I
break this people and this city, as
one breaks a potter's vessel, so that it
can never be mended. Men shall bury
in To´pheth because there will be no
place else to bury. 12Thus will I do
to this place, says the LORD, and to
its inhabitants, making this city like
To´pheth. 13The houses of Jerusalem
and the houses of the kings of
Judah—all the houses upon whose
roofs incense has been burned to all
the host of heaven, and drink offer-
ings have been poured out to other
gods—shall be defiled like the place
of To´pheth.'"

14 Then Jeremiah came from
To´pheth, where the LORD had sent
him to prophesy, and he stood in the
court of the LORD's house, and said to
all the people: 15"Thus says the LORD
of hosts, the God of Israel, Behold, I
am bringing upon this city and upon
all its towns all the evil that I have
pronounced against it, because they
have stiffened their neck, refusing to
hear my words."

JEREMIAH PERSECUTED BY PASHHUR

20 Now Pashhur the priest, the son
of Immer, who was chief offi-
cer in the house of the LORD, heard
Jeremiah prophesying these things.
2Then Pashhur beat Jeremiah the
prophet, and put him in the stocks

that were in the upper Benjamin
Gate of the house of the LORD. 3On
the morrow, when Pashhur released
Jeremiah from the stocks, Jeremiah
said to him, "The LORD does not call
your name Pashhur, but Terror on
every side. 4For thus says the LORD:
Behold, I will make you a terror to
yourself and to all your friends. They
shall fall by the sword of their ene-
mies while you look on. And I will
give all Judah into the hand of the
king of Babylon; he shall carry them
captive to Babylon, and shall slay
them with the sword. 5Moreover, I
will give all the wealth of the city,
all its gains, all its prized belong-
ings, and all the treasures of the
kings of Judah into the hand of their
enemies, who shall plunder them,
and seize them, and carry them to
Babylon. 6And you, Pashhur, and all
who dwell in your house, shall go
into captivity; to Babylon you shall
go; and there you shall die, and there
you shall be buried, you and all your
friends, to whom you have prophe-
sied falsely."

JEREMIAH DENOUNCES HIS PERSECUTORS

7O LORD, thou hast deceived me,
and I was deceived;
thou art stronger than I,
and thou hast prevailed.
I have become a laughingstock
all the day;
every one mocks me.
8For whenever I speak, I cry out,
I shout, "Violence and
destruction!"
For the word of the LORD has
become for me
a reproach and derision all
day long.
9If I say, "I will not mention him,
or speak any more in his
name,"
there is in my heart as it were a
burning fire
shut up in my bones,
and I am weary with holding
it in,
and I cannot.
10For I hear many whispering.
Terror is on every side!
"Denounce him! Let us de-
nounce him!"
say all my familiar friends,
watching for my fall.
"Perhaps he will be deceived,
then we can overcome him,
and take our revenge on
him."
11But the LORD is with me as a
dread warrior;
therefore my persecutors
will stumble,
they will not overcome me.
They will be greatly shamed,
for they will not succeed.
Their eternal dishonor
will never be forgotten.
12O LORD of hosts, who triest the
righteous,
who seest the heart and the
mind,
let me see thy vengeance upon
them,
for to thee have I committed
my cause.
13Sing to the LORD;
praise the LORD!
For he has delivered the life of
the needy
from the hand of evildoers.
14Cursed be the day
on which I was born!
The day when my mother bore
me,
let it not be blessed!
15Cursed be the man
who brought the news to my
father,
"A son is born to you,"
making him very glad.
16Let that man be like the cities
which the LORD overthrew
without pity;
let him hear a cry in the
morning
and an alarm at noon,
17because he did not kill me in the
womb;

so my mother would have
been my grave,
and her womb for ever
great.
18 Why did I come forth from the
womb
to see toil and sorrow,
and spend my days in
shame?

JERUSALEM WILL FALL TO NEBUCHADREZZAR

21 This is the word which came to
Jeremiah from the LORD, when
King Zedeki´ah sent to him Pashhur
the son of Malchi´ah and Zephani´ah
the priest, the son of Ma-asei´ah, say-
ing, 2 "Inquire of the LORD for us, for
Nebuchadrez´zar king of Babylon is
making war against us; perhaps the
LORD will deal with us according
to all his wonderful deeds, and will
make him withdraw from us."
3 Then Jeremiah said to them:
4 "Thus you shall say to Zedeki´ah,
'Thus says the LORD, the God of
Israel: Behold, I will turn back the
weapons of war which are in your
hands and with which you are fight-
ing against the king of Babylon and
against the Chalde´ans who are be-
sieging you outside the walls; and
I will bring them together into the
midst of this city. 5 I myself will fight
against you with outstretched hand
and strong arm, in anger, and in
fury, and in great wrath. 6 And I will
smite the inhabitants of this city,
both man and beast; they shall die of
a great pestilence. 7 Afterward, says
the LORD, I will give Zedeki´ah king
of Judah, and his servants, and the
people in this city who survive the
pestilence, sword, and famine, into
the hand of Nebuchadrez´zar king of
Babylon and into the hand of their
enemies, into the hand of those who
seek their lives. He shall smite them
with the edge of the sword; he shall
not pity them, or spare them, or have
compassion.'
8 "And to this people you shall say:
'Thus says the LORD: Behold, I set be-
fore you the way of life and the way of
death. 9 He who stays in this city shall
die by the sword, by famine, and by
pestilence; but he who goes out and
surrenders to the Chalde´ans who
are besieging you shall live and shall
have his life as a prize of war. 10 For I
have set my face against this city for
evil and not for good, says the LORD:
it shall be given into the hand of the
king of Babylon, and he shall burn it
with fire.'

MESSAGE TO THE HOUSE OF DAVID

11 "And to the house of the king
of Judah say, 'Hear the word of the
LORD, 12 O house of David! Thus says
the LORD:

"'Execute justice in the
morning,
and deliver from the hand of
the oppressor
him who has been robbed,
lest my wrath go forth like
fire,
and burn with none to
quench it,
because of your evil
doings.'"
13 "Behold, I am against you, O
inhabitant of the valley,
O rock of the plain,
says the LORD;
you who say, 'Who shall come
down against us,
or who shall enter our
habitations?'
14 I will punish you according to
the fruit of your doings,
says the LORD;
I will kindle a fire in her
forest,
and it shall devour all that is
round about her."

EXHORTATION TO REPENT

22 Thus says the LORD: "Go down
to the house of the king of
Judah, and speak there this word,
2 and say, 'Hear the word of the
LORD, O King of Judah, who sit on

the throne of David, you, and your
servants, and your people who enter
these gates.
3Thus says the LORD: Do
justice and righteousness, and deliver from the hand of the oppressor
him who has been robbed. And do no
wrong or violence to the alien, the
fatherless, and the widow, nor shed
innocent blood in this place.
4For if
you will indeed obey this word, then
there shall enter the gates of this
house kings who sit on the throne
of David, riding in chariots and on
horses, they, and their servants, and
their people.
5But if you will not
heed these words, I swear by myself,
says the LORD, that this house shall
become a desolation.
6For thus says
the LORD concerning the house of
the king of Judah:

"'You are as Gilead to me,
as the summit of Lebanon,
yet surely I will make you a
desert,
an uninhabited city.[a]
7I will prepare destroyers against
you,
each with his weapons;
and they shall cut down your
choicest cedars,
and cast them into the fire.

8 "'And many nations will pass by
this city, and every man will say to his
neighbor, "Why has the LORD dealt
thus with this great city?"
9And they
will answer, "Because they forsook
the covenant of the LORD their God,
and worshiped other gods and served
them."'"

10Weep not for him who is dead,
nor bemoan him;
but weep bitterly for him who
goes away,
for he shall return no more
to see his native land.

MESSAGE TO THE SONS OF JOSIAH

11 For thus says the LORD concerning Shallum the son of Josi´ah, king of
Judah, who reigned instead of Josi´ah
his father, and who went away from
this place: "He shall return here no
more,
12but in the place where they
have carried him captive, there shall
he die, and he shall never see this land
again."

13"Woe to him who builds his
house by unrighteousness,
and his upper rooms by
injustice;
who makes his neighbor serve
him for nothing,
and does not give him his
wages;
14who says, 'I will build myself a
great house
with spacious upper
rooms,'
and cuts out windows for it,
paneling it with cedar,
and painting it with
vermilion.
15Do you think you are a king
because you compete in
cedar?
Did not your father eat and
drink
and do justice and
righteousness?
Then it was well with him.
16He judged the cause of the poor
and needy;
then it was well.
Is not this to know me?
says the LORD.
17But you have eyes and heart
only for your dishonest
gain,
for shedding innocent blood,
and for practicing oppression and violence."

18 Therefore thus says the LORD
concerning Jehoi´akim the son of
Josi´ah, king of Judah:

"They shall not lament for him,
saying,
'Ah my brother!' or 'Ah
sister!'
They shall not lament for him,
saying,
'Ah lord!' or 'Ah his
majesty!'

[a]Cn: Heb *cities*

19With the burial of an ass he shall
be buried,
dragged and cast forth
beyond the gates of
Jerusalem."
20"Go up to Lebanon, and cry
out,
and lift up your voice in
Bashan;
cry from Ab´arim,
for all your lovers are
destroyed.
21I spoke to you in your
prosperity,
but you said, 'I will not
listen.'
This has been your way from
your youth,
that you have not obeyed my
voice.
22The wind shall shepherd all your
shepherds,
and your lovers shall go into
captivity;
then you will be ashamed and
confounded
because of all your
wickedness.
23O inhabitant of Lebanon,
nested among the cedars,
how you will groan[b] when
pangs come upon you,
pain as of a woman in
travail!"

JUDGMENT ON CONIAH (JEHOIACHIN)

24 "As I live, says the LORD, though
Coni´ah the son of Jehoi´akim, king
of Judah, were the signet ring on my
right hand, yet I would tear you off
25and give you into the hand of those
who seek your life, into the hand of
those of whom you are afraid, even
into the hand of Nebuchadrez´zar
king of Babylon and into the hand of
the Chalde´ans. 26I will hurl you and
the mother who bore you into anoth-
er country, where you were not born,
and there you shall die. 27But to the
land to which they will long to return,
there they shall not return."

[b]Gk Vg Syr: Heb *be pitied*

28Is this man Coni´ah a despised,
broken pot,
a vessel no one cares for?
Why are he and his children
hurled and cast
into a land which they do
not know?
29O land, land, land,
hear the word of the LORD!
30Thus says the LORD:
"Write this man down as
childless,
a man who shall not succeed
in his days;
for none of his offspring shall
succeed
in sitting on the throne of
David,
and ruling again in Judah."

RESTORATION AFTER EXILE

23 "Woe to the shepherds who
destroy and scatter the sheep
of my pasture!" says the LORD.
2Therefore thus says the LORD, the
God of Israel, concerning the shep-
herds who care for my people: "You
have scattered my flock, and have
driven them away, and you have not
attended to them. Behold, I will at-
tend to you for your evil doings, says
the LORD. 3Then I will gather the
remnant of my flock out of all the
countries where I have driven them,
and I will bring them back to their
fold, and they shall be fruitful and
multiply. 4I will set shepherds over
them who will care for them, and
they shall fear no more, nor be dis-
mayed, neither shall any be missing,
says the LORD.

THE RIGHTEOUS BRANCH OF DAVID

5 "Behold, the days are coming,
says the LORD, when I will raise up
for David a righteous Branch, and he
shall reign as king and deal wisely,
and shall execute justice and righ-
teousness in the land. 6In his days
Judah will be saved, and Israel will
dwell securely. And this is the name

by which he will be called: 'The LORD
is our righteousness.'
7 "Therefore, behold, the days are
coming, says the LORD, when men
shall no longer say, 'As the LORD lives
who brought up the people of Israel
out of the land of Egypt,' 8but 'As the
LORD lives who brought up and led
the descendants of the house of Israel
out of the north country and out of all
the countries where he[a] had driven
them.' Then they shall dwell in their
own land."

FALSE PROPHETS OF HOPE DENOUNCED

9 Concerning the prophets:
My heart is broken within me,
all my bones shake;
I am like a drunken man,
like a man overcome by
wine,
because of the LORD
and because of his holy
words.
10For the land is full of
adulterers;
because of the curse the land
mourns,
and the pastures of the
wilderness are
dried up.
Their course is evil,
and their might is not right.
11"Both prophet and priest are
ungodly;
even in my house I have found
their wickedness, says the
LORD.
12Therefore their way shall be to
them
like slippery paths in the
darkness,
into which they shall be
driven and fall;
for I will bring evil upon them
in the year of their punishment,
says the LORD.
13In the prophets of Samar´ia
I saw an unsavory thing:
they prophesied by Ba´al
and led my people Israel
astray.
14But in the prophets of
Jerusalem
I have seen a horrible thing:
they commit adultery and walk
in lies;
they strengthen the hands of
evildoers,
so that no one turns from
his wickedness;
all of them have become like
Sodom to me,
and its inhabitants like
Gomor´rah."
15 Therefore thus says the LORD of
hosts concerning the prophets:
"Behold, I will feed them with
wormwood,
and give them poisoned
water to drink;
for from the prophets of
Jerusalem
ungodliness has gone forth
into all the land."
16 Thus says the LORD of hosts:
"Do not listen to the words of the
prophets who prophesy to you, fill-
ing you with vain hopes; they speak
visions of their own minds, not from
the mouth of the LORD. 17They say
continually to those who despise
the word of the LORD, 'It shall be
well with you'; and to every one who
stubbornly follows his own heart,
they say, 'No evil shall come upon
you.'"
18For who among them has stood
in the council of the LORD
to perceive and to hear his
word,
or who has given heed
to his word and
listened?
19Behold, the storm of the LORD!
Wrath has gone forth,
a whirling tempest;
it will burst upon the head
of the wicked.
20The anger of the LORD will not
turn back
until he has executed and

[a] Gk: Heb *I*

accomplished
the intents of his mind.
In the latter days you will understand it clearly.

21 "I did not send the prophets,
yet they ran;
I did not speak to them,
yet they prophesied.
22 But if they had stood in my council,
then they would have proclaimed my words to my people,
and they would have turned them from their evil way,
and from the evil of their doings.

23 "Am I a God at hand, says the
LORD, and not a God afar off? 24 Can
a man hide himself in secret plac-
es so that I cannot see him? says
the LORD. Do I not fill heaven and
earth? says the LORD. 25 I have heard
what the prophets have said who
prophesy lies in my name, saying,
'I have dreamed, I have dreamed!'
26 How long shall there be lies[b] in the
heart of the prophets who prophesy
lies, and who prophesy the deceit of
their own heart, 27 who think to make
my people forget my name by their
dreams which they tell one another,
even as their fathers forgot my name
for Ba´al? 28 Let the prophet who has
a dream tell the dream, but let him
who has my word speak my word
faithfully. What has straw in com-
mon with wheat? says the LORD. 29 Is
not my word like fire, says the LORD,
and like a hammer which breaks the
rock in pieces? 30 Therefore, behold,
I am against the prophets, says the
LORD, who steal my words from
one another. 31 Behold, I am against
the prophets, says the LORD, who
use their tongues and say, 'Says the
LORD.' 32 Behold, I am against those
who prophesy lying dreams, says the
LORD, and who tell them and lead
my people astray by their lies and
their recklessness, when I did not
send them or charge them; so they
do not profit this people at all, says
the LORD.

33 "When one of this people,
or a prophet, or a priest asks you,
'What is the burden of the LORD?'
you shall say to them, 'You are the
burden,[c] and I will cast you off, says
the LORD.' 34 And as for the proph-
et, priest, or one of the people who
says, 'The burden of the LORD,' I will
punish that man and his household.
35 Thus shall you say, every one to his
neighbor and every one to his broth-
er, 'What has the LORD answered?'
or 'What has the LORD spoken?'
36 But 'the burden of the LORD' you
shall mention no more, for the bur-
den is every man's own word, and
you pervert the words of the living
God, the LORD of hosts, our God.
37 Thus you shall say to the prophet,
'What has the LORD answered you?'
or 'What has the LORD spoken?'
38 But if you say, 'The burden of the
LORD,' thus says the LORD, 'Because
you have said these words, "The
burden of the LORD," when I sent
to you, saying, "You shall not say,
'The burden of the LORD,'" 39 there-
fore, behold, I will surely lift you up
and cast you away from my presence,
you and the city which I gave to you
and your fathers. 40 And I will bring
upon you everlasting reproach and
perpetual shame, which shall not be
forgotten.'"

THE GOOD AND THE BAD FIGS

24 After Nebuchadrez´zar king of
Babylon had taken into exile
from Jerusalem Jeconi´ah the son of
Jehoi´akim, king of Judah, togeth-
er with the princes of Judah, the
craftsmen, and the smiths, and had
brought them to Babylon, the LORD
showed me this vision: Behold, two
baskets of figs placed before the

[b] Cn Compare Syr: Heb obscure
[c] Gk Vg: Heb *What burden*

temple of the LORD. 2One basket had
very good figs, like first-ripe figs, but
the other basket had very bad figs,
so bad that they could not be eaten.
3And the LORD said to me, "What do
you see, Jeremiah?" I said, "Figs, the
good figs very good, and the bad figs
very bad, so bad that they cannot be
eaten."

4 Then the word of the LORD came
to me: 5"Thus says the LORD, the
God of Israel: Like these good figs,
so I will regard as good the exiles
from Judah, whom I have sent away
from this place to the land of the
Chaldé'ans. 6I will set my eyes upon
them for good, and I will bring them
back to this land. I will build them
up, and not tear them down; I will
plant them, and not uproot them. 7I
will give them a heart to know that
I am the LORD; and they shall be my
people and I will be their God, for
they shall return to me with their
whole heart.

8 "But thus says the LORD: Like
the bad figs which are so bad they
cannot be eaten, so will I treat
Zedeki'ah the king of Judah, his
princes, the remnant of Jerusalem
who remain in this land, and those
who dwell in the land of Egypt. 9I will
make them a horror[a] to all the king-
doms of the earth, to be a reproach,
a byword, a taunt, and a curse in all
the places where I shall drive them.
10And I will send sword, famine, and
pestilence upon them, until they
shall be utterly destroyed from the
land which I gave to them and their
fathers."

THE BABYLONIAN CAPTIVITY FORETOLD

25 The word that came to Jeremiah
concerning all the people
of Judah, in the fourth year of
Jehoi'akim the son of Josi'ah, king
of Judah (that was the first year of
Nebuchadrez'zar king of Babylon),
2which Jeremiah the prophet spoke
to all the people of Judah and all
the inhabitants of Jerusalem: 3"For
twenty-three years, from the thir-
teenth year of Josi'ah the son of
Amon, king of Judah, to this day, the
word of the LORD has come to me,
and I have spoken persistently to
you, but you have not listened. 4You
have neither listened nor inclined
your ears to hear, although the LORD
persistently sent to you all his ser-
vants the prophets, 5saying, 'Turn
now, every one of you, from his evil
way and wrong doings, and dwell
upon the land which the LORD has
given to you and your fathers from
of old and for ever; 6do not go af-
ter other gods to serve and worship
them, or provoke me to anger with
the work of your hands. Then I will
do you no harm.' 7Yet you have not
listened to me, says the LORD, that
you might provoke me to anger with
the work of your hands to your own
harm.

8 "Therefore thus says the LORD
of hosts: Because you have not
obeyed my words, 9behold, I will send
for all the tribes of the north, says
the LORD, and for Nebuchadrez'zar
the king of Babylon, my servant, and
I will bring them against this land
and its inhabitants, and against all
these nations round about; I will ut-
terly destroy them, and make them a
horror, a hissing, and an everlasting
reproach.[b] 10Moreover, I will banish
from them the voice of mirth and
the voice of gladness, the voice of
the bridegroom and the voice of the
bride, the grinding of the millstones
and the light of the lamp. 11This
whole land shall become a ruin and
a waste, and these nations shall
serve the king of Babylon seventy
years. 12Then after seventy years are
completed, I will punish the king of
Babylon and that nation, the land
of the Chalde'ans, for their iniqui-
ty, says the LORD, making the land

[a]Compare Gk: Heb *horror for evil*
[b]Gk Compare Syr: Heb *desolations*

an everlasting waste. 13I will bring
upon that land all the words which
I have uttered against it, everything
written in this book, which Jeremiah
prophesied against all the nations.
14For many nations and great kings
shall make slaves even of them; and
I will recompense them according
to their deeds and the work of their
hands."

THE CUP OF GOD'S WRATH

15 Thus the LORD, the God of
Israel, said to me: "Take from my
hand this cup of the wine of wrath,
and make all the nations to whom I
send you drink it. 16They shall drink
and stagger and be crazed because of
the sword which I am sending among
them."

17 So I took the cup from the
LORD's hand, and made all the na-
tions to whom the LORD sent me
drink it: 18Jerusalem and the cit-
ies of Judah, its kings and princes,
to make them a desolation and a
waste, a hissing and a curse, as at
this day; 19Pharaoh king of Egypt,
his servants, his princes, all his peo-
ple, 20and all the foreign folk among
them; all the kings of the land of Uz
and all the kings of the land of the
Philistines (Ash′kelon, Gaza, Ekron,
and the remnant of Ashdod); 21Edom,
Moab, and the sons of Ammon; 22all
the kings of Tyre, all the kings of
Sidon, and the kings of the coastland
across the sea; 23Dedan, Tema, Buz,
and all who cut the corners of their
hair; 24all the kings of Arabia and all
the kings of the mixed tribes that
dwell in the desert; 25all the kings
of Zimri, all the kings of Elam, and
all the kings of Media; 26all the kings
of the north, far and near, one after
another, and all the kingdoms of the
world which are on the face of the
earth. And after them the king of
Babylon[c] shall drink.

27 "Then you shall say to them,
'Thus says the LORD of hosts, the God
of Israel: Drink, be drunk and vomit,
fall and rise no more, because of the
sword which I am sending among
you.'

28 "And if they refuse to accept
the cup from your hand to drink,
then you shall say to them, 'Thus
says the LORD of hosts: You must
drink! 29For behold, I begin to work
evil at the city which is called by my
name, and shall you go unpunished?
You shall not go unpunished, for I
am summoning a sword against all
the inhabitants of the earth, says the
LORD of hosts.'

30 "You, therefore, shall prophesy
against them all these words, and say
to them:

'The LORD will roar from on high,
and from his holy habitation utter his voice;
he will roar mightily against his fold,
and shout, like those who tread grapes,
against all the inhabitants of the earth.
31The clamor will resound to the ends of the earth,
for the LORD has an indictment against the nations;
he is entering into judgment with all flesh,
and the wicked he will put to the sword,
says the LORD.'

32"Thus says the LORD of hosts:
Behold, evil is going forth from nation to nation,
and a great tempest is stirring from the farthest parts of the earth!

33 "And those slain by the LORD on
that day shall extend from one end of
the earth to the other. They shall not
be lamented, or gathered, or buried;
they shall be dung on the surface of
the ground.

34"Wail, you shepherds, and cry,

[c] Heb *Sheshach*, a cipher for Babylon

and roll in ashes, you lords
of the flock,
for the days of your slaughter
and dispersion have
come,
and you shall fall like choice
rams.[a]
35No refuge will remain for the
shepherds,
nor escape for the lords of
the flock.
36Hark, the cry of the shepherds,
and the wail of the lords of
the flock!
For the LORD is despoiling
their pasture,
37and the peaceful folds are
devastated,
because of the fierce anger
of the LORD.
38Like a lion he has left his
covert,
for their land has become a
waste
because of the sword of the
oppressor,
and because of his fierce
anger."

JEREMIAH'S PROPHECIES IN THE TEMPLE

26 In the beginning of the reign of
Jehoi′akim the son of Josi′ah,
king of Judah, this word came from
the LORD, 2"Thus says the LORD:
Stand in the court of the LORD's
house, and speak to all the cities of
Judah which come to worship in the
house of the LORD all the words that
I command you to speak to them; do
not hold back a word. 3It may be they
will listen, and every one turn from
his evil way, that I may repent of the
evil which I intend to do to them be-
cause of their evil doings. 4You shall
say to them, 'Thus says the LORD: If
you will not listen to me, to walk in
my law which I have set before you,
5and to heed the words of my ser-
vants the prophets whom I send to
you urgently, though you have not
heeded, 6then I will make this house
like Shiloh, and I will make this city
a curse for all the nations of the
earth.'"

7 The priests and the prophets
and all the people heard Jeremiah
speaking these words in the house of
the LORD. 8And when Jeremiah had
finished speaking all that the LORD
had commanded him to speak to all
the people, then the priests and the
prophets and all the people laid hold
of him, saying, "You shall die! 9Why
have you prophesied in the name of
the LORD, saying, 'This house shall be
like Shiloh, and this city shall be des-
olate, without inhabitant'?" And all
the people gathered about Jeremiah in
the house of the LORD.

10 When the princes of Judah heard
these things, they came up from the
king's house to the house of the LORD
and took their seat in the entry of the
New Gate of the house of the LORD.
11Then the priests and the prophets
said to the princes and to all the peo-
ple, "This man deserves the sentence
of death, because he has prophesied
against this city, as you have heard
with your own ears."

12 Then Jeremiah spoke to all
the princes and all the people, say-
ing, "The LORD sent me to prophesy
against this house and this city all the
words you have heard. 13Now there-
fore amend your ways and your do-
ings, and obey the voice of the LORD
your God, and the LORD will repent
of the evil which he has pronounced
against you. 14But as for me, behold,
I am in your hands. Do with me as
seems good and right to you. 15Only
know for certain that if you put me
to death, you will bring innocent
blood upon yourselves and upon this
city and its inhabitants, for in truth
the LORD sent me to you to speak all
these words in your ears."

16 Then the princes and all the
people said to the priests and the
prophets, "This man does not de-
serve the sentence of death, for he has

[a] Gk: Heb *a choice vessel*

spoken to us in the name of the LORD
our God." 17And certain of the elders
of the land arose and spoke to all the
assembled people, saying, 18"Micah of
Mo'resheth prophesied in the days of
Hezeki'ah king of Judah, and said to
all the people of Judah: 'Thus says the
LORD of hosts,

> Zion shall be plowed as a
> field;
> Jerusalem shall become a
> heap of ruins,
> and the mountain of the
> house a wooded
> height.'

19Did Hezeki'ah king of Judah
and all Judah put him to death? Did
he not fear the LORD and entreat the
favor of the LORD, and did not the
LORD repent of the evil which he
had pronounced against them? But
we are about to bring great evil upon
ourselves."

20 There was another man who
prophesied in the name of the LORD,
Uri'ah the son of Shemai'ah from
Kir'iath-je'arim. He prophesied against
this city and against this land in
words like those of Jeremiah. 21And
when King Jehoi'akim, with all his
warriors and all the princes, heard
his words, the king sought to put him
to death; but when Uri'ah heard of it,
he was afraid and fled and escaped to
Egypt. 22Then King Jehoi'akim sent to
Egypt certain men, Elna'than the son
of Achbor and others with him, 23and
they fetched Uri'ah from Egypt and
brought him to King Jehoi'akim, who
slew him with the sword and cast his
dead body into the burial place of the
common people.

24 But the hand of Ahi'kam the
son of Shaphan was with Jeremiah so
that he was not given over to the peo-
ple to be put to death.

THE SIGN OF THE YOKE

27 In the beginning of the reign of
Zedeki'ah[b] the son of Josi'ah,
king of Judah, this word came to
Jeremiah from the LORD. 2Thus
the LORD said to me: "Make your-
self thongs and yoke-bars, and put
them on your neck. 3Send word[c] to
the king of Edom, the king of Moab,
the king of the sons of Ammon, the
king of Tyre, and the king of Sidon
by the hand of the envoys who have
come to Jerusalem to Zedeki'ah king
of Judah. 4Give them this charge for
their masters: 'Thus says the LORD
of hosts, the God of Israel: This is
what you shall say to your masters:
5"It is I who by my great power and
my outstretched arm have made the
earth, with the men and animals
that are on the earth, and I give it
to whomever it seems right to me.
6Now I have given all these lands
into the hand of Nebuchadnez'zar,
the king of Babylon, my servant, and
I have given him also the beasts of
the field to serve him. 7All the na-
tions shall serve him and his son and
his grandson, until the time of his
own land comes; then many nations
and great kings shall make him their
slave.

8 "'"But if any nation or kingdom
will not serve this Nebuchadnez'zar
king of Babylon, and put its neck un-
der the yoke of the king of Babylon,
I will punish that nation with the
sword, with famine, and with pesti-
lence, says the LORD, until I have con-
sumed it by his hand. 9So do not listen
to your prophets, your diviners, your
dreamers,[d] your soothsayers, or your
sorcerers, who are saying to you, 'You
shall not serve the king of Babylon.'
10For it is a lie which they are prophe-
sying to you, with the result that you
will be removed far from your land,
and I will drive you out, and you will
perish. 11But any nation which will
bring its neck under the yoke of the
king of Babylon and serve him, I will
leave on its own land, to till it and
dwell there, says the LORD."'"

[b] Another reading is *Jehoiakim*
[c] Cn: Heb *send them*
[d] Gk Syr Vg: Heb *dreams*

12 To Zedeki´ah king of Judah I
spoke in like manner: "Bring your
necks under the yoke of the king of
Babylon, and serve him and his peo-
ple, and live. 13Why will you and your
people die by the sword, by famine,
and by pestilence, as the LORD has
spoken concerning any nation which
will not serve the king of Babylon?
14Do not listen to the words of the
prophets who are saying to you, 'You
shall not serve the king of Babylon,'
for it is a lie which they are prophe-
sying to you. 15I have not sent them,
says the LORD, but they are prophesy-
ing falsely in my name, with the result
that I will drive you out and you will
perish, you and the prophets who are
prophesying to you."

16 Then I spoke to the priests
and to all this people, saying, "Thus
says the LORD: Do not listen to the
words of your prophets who are
prophesying to you, saying, 'Behold,
the vessels of the LORD's house will
now shortly be brought back from
Babylon,' for it is a lie which they are
prophesying to you. 17Do not listen to
them; serve the king of Babylon and
live. Why should this city become a
desolation? 18If they are prophets,
and if the word of the LORD is with
them, then let them intercede with
the LORD of hosts, that the vessels
which are left in the house of the
LORD, in the house of the king of
Judah, and in Jerusalem may not go
to Babylon. 19For thus says the LORD
of hosts concerning the pillars, the
sea, the stands, and the rest of the
vessels which are left in this city,
20which Nebuchadnez´zar king of
Babylon did not take away, when
he took into exile from Jerusalem
to Babylon Jeconi´ah the son of
Jehoi´akim, king of Judah, and all the
nobles of Judah and Jerusalem 21thus
says the LORD of hosts, the God of
Israel, concerning the vessels which
are left in the house of the LORD, in
the house of the king of Judah, and in
Jerusalem: 22They shall be carried to
Babylon and remain there until the
day when I give attention to them,
says the LORD. Then I will bring
them back and restore them to this
place."

HANANIAH OPPOSES JEREMIAH AND DIES

28 In that same year, at the begin-
ning of the reign of Zedeki´ah
king of Judah, in the fifth month of
the fourth year, Hanani´ah the son
of Azzur, the prophet from Gib´eon,
spoke to me in the house of the
LORD, in the presence of the priests
and all the people, saying, 2"Thus
says the LORD of hosts, the God of
Israel: I have broken the yoke of the
king of Babylon. 3Within two years I
will bring back to this place all the
vessels of the LORD's house, which
Nebuchadnez´zar king of Babylon
took away from this place and car-
ried to Babylon. 4I will also bring
back to this place Jeconi´ah the
son of Jehoi´akim, king of Judah,
and all the exiles from Judah who
went to Babylon, says the LORD, for
I will break the yoke of the king of
Babylon."

5 Then the prophet Jeremiah
spoke to Hanani´ah the prophet in
the presence of the priests and all
the people who were standing in the
house of the LORD; 6and the proph-
et Jeremiah said, "Amen! May the
LORD do so; may the LORD make
the words which you have proph-
esied come true, and bring back to
this place from Babylon the vessels
of the house of the LORD, and all
the exiles. 7Yet hear now this word
which I speak in your hearing and in
the hearing of all the people. 8The
prophets who preceded you and
me from ancient times prophesied
war, famine, and pestilence against
many countries and great kingdoms.
9As for the prophet who prophesies
peace, when the word of that proph-
et comes to pass, then it will be
known that the LORD has truly sent
the prophet."

10 Then the prophet Hanani´ah
took the yoke-bars from the neck
of Jeremiah the prophet, and broke
them. 11And Hanani´ah spoke in the
presence of all the people, saying,
"Thus says the LORD: Even so will I
break the yoke of Nebuchadnez´zar
king of Babylon from the neck of all
the nations within two years." But
Jeremiah the prophet went his way.

12 Sometime after the prophet
Hanani´ah had broken the yoke-bars
from off the neck of Jeremiah the
prophet, the word of the LORD came
to Jeremiah: 13"Go, tell Hanani´ah,
'Thus says the LORD: You have bro-
ken wooden bars, but I[a] will make
in their place bars of iron. 14For thus
says the LORD of hosts, the God of
Israel: I have put upon the neck of
all these nations an iron yoke of ser-
vitude to Nebuchadnez´zar king of
Babylon, and they shall serve him, for
I have given to him even the beasts of
the field.'" 15And Jeremiah the proph-
et said to the prophet Hanani´ah,
"Listen, Hanani´ah, the LORD has
not sent you, and you have made this
people trust in a lie. 16Therefore thus
says the LORD: 'Behold, I will remove
you from the face of the earth. This
very year you shall die, because you
have uttered rebellion against the
LORD.'"

17 In that same year, in the sev-
enth month, the prophet Hanani´ah
died.

JEREMIAH'S LETTER TO THE EXILES IN BABYLON

29 These are the words of the let-
ter which Jeremiah the prophet
sent from Jerusalem to the elders[b]
of the exiles, and to the priests, the
prophets, and all the people, whom
Nebuchadnez´zar had taken into
exile from Jerusalem to Babylon.
2This was after King Jeconi´ah, and
the queen mother, the eunuchs, the
princes of Judah and Jerusalem, the
craftsmen, and the smiths had de-
parted from Jerusalem. 3The letter
was sent by the hand of Ela´sah the
son of Shaphan and Gemari´ah the
son of Hilki´ah, whom Zedeki´ah
king of Judah sent to Babylon to
Nebuchadnez´zar king of Babylon. It
said: 4"Thus says the LORD of hosts,
the God of Israel, to all the exiles
whom I have sent into exile from
Jerusalem to Babylon: 5Build houses
and live in them; plant gardens and
eat their produce. 6Take wives and
have sons and daughters; take wives
for your sons, and give your daugh-
ters in marriage, that they may bear
sons and daughters; multiply there,
and do not decrease. 7But seek the
welfare of the city where I have sent
you into exile, and pray to the LORD
on its behalf, for in its welfare you
will find your welfare. 8For thus says
the LORD of hosts, the God of Israel:
Do not let your prophets and your
diviners who are among you deceive
you, and do not listen to the dreams
which they dream,[c] 9for it is a lie
which they are prophesying to you in
my name; I did not send them, says
the LORD.

10 "For thus says the LORD: When
seventy years are completed for
Babylon, I will visit you, and I will ful-
fil to you my promise and bring you
back to this place. 11For I know the
plans I have for you, says the LORD,
plans for welfare and not for evil, to
give you a future and a hope. 12Then
you will call upon me and come and
pray to me, and I will hear you. 13You
will seek me and find me; when you
seek me with all your heart, 14I will
be found by you, says the LORD, and
I will restore your fortunes and gath-
er you from all the nations and all the
places where I have driven you, says
the LORD, and I will bring you back to
the place from which I sent you into
exile.

[a] Gk: Heb *you*
[b] Gk: Heb *the rest of the elders*
[c] Cn: Heb *your dreams which you cause to dream*

15 "Because you have said, 'The
LORD has raised up prophets for us
in Babylon,'—16Thus says the LORD
concerning the king who sits on the
throne of David, and concerning all
the people who dwell in this city,
your kinsmen who did not go out
with you into exile: 17'Thus says the
LORD of hosts, Behold, I am sending
on them sword, famine, and pes-
tilence, and I will make them like
vile figs which are so bad they can-
not be eaten. 18I will pursue them
with sword, famine, and pestilence,
and will make them a horror to all
the kingdoms of the earth, to be a
curse, a terror, a hissing, and a re-
proach among all the nations where I
have driven them, 19because they did
not heed my words, says the LORD,
which I persistently sent to you by
my servants the prophets, but you
would not listen, says the LORD.'—
20Hear the word of the LORD, all
you exiles whom I sent away from
Jerusalem to Babylon: 21'Thus says
the LORD of hosts, the God of Israel,
concerning Ahab the son of Kolai´ah
and Zedeki´ah the son of Ma-asei´ah,
who are prophesying a lie to you in
my name: Behold, I will deliver them
into the hand of Nebuchadrez´zar
king of Babylon, and he shall slay
them before your eyes. 22Because of
them this curse shall be used by all
the exiles from Judah in Babylon:
"The LORD make you like Zedeki´ah
and Ahab, whom the king of Babylon
roasted in the fire," 23because they
have committed folly in Israel, they
have committed adultery with their
neighbors' wives, and they have spo-
ken in my name lying words which I
did not command them. I am the one
who knows, and I am witness, says
the LORD.'"

THE LETTER OF SHEMAIAH

24 To Shemai´ah of Nehel´am you
shall say: 25"Thus says the LORD of
hosts, the God of Israel: You have
sent letters in your name to all the
people who are in Jerusalem, and to
Zephani´ah the son of Ma-asei´ah the
priest, and to all the priests, saying,
26'The LORD has made you priest in-
stead of Jehoi´ada the priest, to have
charge in the house of the LORD
over every madman who prophesies,
to put him in the stocks and collar.
27Now why have you not rebuked
Jeremiah of An´athoth who is proph-
esying to you? 28For he has sent to
us in Babylon, saying, "Your exile
will be long; build houses and live in
them, and plant gardens and eat their
produce."'"

29 Zephani´ah the priest read
this letter in the hearing of Jeremiah
the prophet. 30Then the word of the
LORD came to Jeremiah: 31"Send to
all the exiles, saying, 'Thus says
the LORD concerning Shemai´ah of
Nehel´am: Because Shemai´ah had
prophesied to you when I did not
send him, and has made you trust in
a lie, 32therefore thus says the LORD:
Behold, I will punish Shemai´ah of
Nehel´am and his descendants; he
shall not have any one living among
this people to see[a] the good that I
will do to my people, says the LORD,
for he has talked rebellion against
the LORD.'"

RESTORATION PROMISED FOR ISRAEL AND JUDAH

30 The word that came to Jeremiah
from the LORD: 2"Thus says the
LORD, the God of Israel: Write in a
book all the words that I have spoken
to you. 3For behold, days are coming,
says the LORD, when I will restore
the fortunes of my people, Israel and
Judah, says the LORD, and I will bring
them back to the land which I gave to
their fathers, and they shall take pos-
session of it."

4 These are the words which the
LORD spoke concerning Israel and
Judah:

5"Thus says the LORD:

[a] Gk: Heb *and he shall not see*

We have heard a cry of panic,
of terror, and no peace.
6Ask now, and see,
can a man bear a child?
Why then do I see every man
with his hands on his loins
like a woman in
labor?
Why has every face turned
pale?
7Alas! that day is so great
there is none like it;
it is a time of distress for
Jacob;
yet he shall be saved out
of it.

8 "And it shall come to pass in
that day, says the LORD of hosts, that
I will break the yoke from off their[b]
neck, and I will burst their[c] bonds,
and strangers shall no more make
servants of them.[d]* 9But they shall
serve the LORD their God and David
their king, whom I will raise up for
them.

10"Then fear not, O Jacob my servant, says the LORD,
nor be dismayed, O Israel;
for lo, I will save you from
afar,
and your offspring from
the land of their
captivity.
Jacob shall return and have
quiet and ease,
and none shall make him
afraid.
11For I am with you to save you,
says the LORD;
I will make a full end of all the
nations
among whom I scattered
you,
but of you I will not make a
full end.
I will chasten you in just
measure,
and I will by no means
leave you
unpunished.

[b]Gk Old Latin: Heb *your*
[c]Gk Old Latin: Heb *your*
[d]Heb *make a servant of him*

12"For thus says the LORD:
Your hurt is incurable,
and your wound is
grievous.
13There is none to uphold your
cause,
no medicine for your
wound,
no healing for you.
14All your lovers have forgotten
you;
they care nothing for you;
for I have dealt you the blow of
an enemy,
the punishment of a merciless foe,
because your guilt is great,
because your sins are
flagrant.
15Why do you cry out over your
hurt?
Your pain is incurable.
Because your guilt is great,
because your sins are
flagrant,
I have done these things to
you.
16Therefore all who devour you
shall be devoured,
and all your foes, every one
of them, shall go into
captivity;
those who despoil you shall
become a spoil,
and all who prey on you I
will make a prey.
17For I will restore health to you,
and your wounds I will
heal,
says the LORD,
because they have called you an
outcast:
'It is Zion, for whom no one
cares!'
18"Thus says the LORD:
Behold, I will restore the
fortunes of the tents of
Jacob,
and have compassion on his
dwellings;

the city shall be rebuilt upon
its mound,
and the palace shall stand
where it used to be.
19Out of them shall come songs of
thanksgiving,
and the voices of those who
make merry.
I will multiply them, and they
shall not be few;
I will make them honored,
and they shall not be
small.
20Their children shall be as they
were of old,
and their congregation
shall be established
before me;
and I will punish all who
oppress them.
21Their prince shall be one of
themselves,
their ruler shall come forth
from their midst;
I will make him draw near,
and he shall approach
me,
for who would dare of
himself to approach
me?
says the LORD.
22And you shall be my people,
and I will be your God."
23Behold the storm of the LORD!
Wrath has gone forth,
a whirling tempest;
it will burst upon the head
of the wicked.
24The fierce anger of the LORD
will not turn back
until he has executed and
accomplished
the intents of his mind.
In the latter days you will
understand this.

THE JOYFUL RETURN OF THE EXILES

31 "At that time, says the LORD, I
will be the God of all the fami-
lies of Israel, and they shall be my
people."

2Thus says the LORD:
"The people who survived the
sword
found grace in the
wilderness;
when Israel sought for rest,
3the LORD appeared to him[a]
from afar.
I have loved you with an ever-
lasting love;
therefore I have continued
my faithfulness to
you.
4Again I will build you, and you
shall be built,
O virgin Israel!
Again you shall adorn yourself
with timbrels,
and shall go forth in
the dance of the
merrymakers.
5Again you shall plant vineyards
upon the mountains of
Samar´ia;
the planters shall plant,
and shall enjoy the fruit.
6For there shall be a day when
watchmen will call
in the hill country of
E´phraim:
'Arise, and let us go up to
Zion,
to the LORD our God.'"
7For thus says the LORD:
"Sing aloud with gladness for
Jacob,
and raise shouts for the chief
of the nations;
proclaim, give praise, and say,
'The LORD has saved his
people,
the remnant of Israel.'
8Behold, I will bring them from
the north country,
and gather them from the
farthest parts of the
earth,
among them the blind and the
lame,
the woman with child and
her who is in travail,

[a]Gk: Heb *me*

together;
a great company, they shall
return here.
9With weeping they shall come,
and with consolations[b] I will
lead them back,
I will make them walk by
brooks of water,
in a straight path in which
they shall not
stumble;
for I am a father to Israel,
and E´phraim is my
first-born.
10"Hear the word of the LORD, O
nations,
and declare it in the coast-
lands afar off;
say, 'He who scattered Israel
will gather him,
and will keep him as a
shepherd keeps his
flock.'
11For the LORD has ransomed
Jacob,
and has redeemed him from
hands too strong for
him.
12They shall come and sing aloud
on the height of Zion,
and they shall be radiant
over the goodness of
the LORD,
over the grain, the wine, and
the oil,
and over the young of the
flock and the herd;
their life shall be like a watered
garden,
and they shall languish no
more.
13Then shall the maidens rejoice
in the dance,
and the young men and the
old shall be merry.
I will turn their mourning into
joy,
I will comfort them, and give
them gladness for
sorrow.
14I will feast the soul of the priests
with abundance,
and my people shall be
satisfied with my
goodness,
says the LORD."
15Thus says the LORD:
"A voice is heard in Ramah,
lamentation and bitter
weeping.
Rachel is weeping for her
children;
she refuses to be comforted
for her children,
because they are not."*
16Thus says the LORD:
"Keep your voice from
weeping,
and your eyes from tears;
for your work shall be
rewarded,
says the LORD,
and they shall come back
from the land of the
enemy.
17There is hope for your future,
says the LORD,
and your children shall come
back to their own
country.
18I have heard E´phraim
bemoaning,
'Thou hast chastened me, and I
was chastened,
like an untrained calf;
bring me back that I may be
restored,
for thou art the LORD my
God.
19For after I had turned away I
repented;
and after I was instructed,
I smote upon my
thigh;
I was ashamed, and I was
confounded,
because I bore the disgrace
of my youth.'
20Is E´phraim my dear son?
Is he my darling child?
For as often as I speak against
him,

[b]Gk Compare Vg Tg: Heb *supplications*

I do remember him still.
Therefore my heart yearns for him;
I will surely have mercy on him,
says the LORD.
21 "Set up waymarks for yourself,
make yourself guideposts;
consider well the highway,
the road by which you went.
Return, O virgin Israel,
return to these your cities.
22 How long will you waver,
O faithless daughter?
For the LORD has created
a new thing on the earth:
a woman protects a man."

23 Thus says the LORD of hosts, the
God of Israel: "Once more they shall
use these words in the land of Judah
and in its cities, when I restore their
fortunes:

'The LORD bless you,
O habitation of righteousness,
O holy hill!'

24 And Judah and all its cities shall
dwell there together, and the farmers
and those who wander[a] with their
flocks. 25 For I will satisfy the weary
soul, and every languishing soul I will
replenish."

26 Thereupon I awoke and looked,
and my sleep was pleasant to me.

INDIVIDUAL RETRIBUTION

27 "Behold, the days are coming,
says the LORD, when I will sow the
house of Israel and the house of Judah
with the seed of man and the seed of
beast. 28 And it shall come to pass that
as I have watched over them to pluck
up and break down, to overthrow, de-
stroy, and bring evil, so I will watch
over them to build and to plant, says
the LORD. 29 In those days they shall
no longer say:

'The fathers have eaten sour grapes,
and the children's teeth are
set on edge.'

30 But every one shall die for his
own sin; each man who eats sour
grapes, his teeth shall be set on
edge.

A NEW COVENANT

31* "Behold, the days are coming,
says the LORD, when I will make
a new covenant with the house of
Israel and the house of Judah, 32 not
like the covenant which I made with
their fathers when I took them by the
hand to bring them out of the land
of Egypt, my covenant which they
broke, though I was their husband,
says the LORD. 33 But this is the cov-
enant which I will make with the
house of Israel after those days, says
the LORD: I will put my law within
them, and I will write it upon their
hearts; and I will be their God, and
they shall be my people. 34 And no lon-
ger shall each man teach his neighbor
and each his brother, saying, 'Know
the LORD,' for they shall all know me,
from the least of them to the greatest,
says the LORD; for I will forgive their
iniquity, and I will remember their
sin no more."

35 Thus says the LORD,
who gives the sun for light by day
and the fixed order of the
moon and the stars
for light by night,
who stirs up the sea so that its
waves roar—
the LORD of hosts is his name:
36 "If this fixed order departs
from before me, says the LORD,
then shall the descendants of
Israel cease
from being a nation before
me for ever."
37 Thus says the LORD:
"If the heavens above can be
measured,
and the foundations of the

[a] Cn Compare Syr Vg Tg: Heb *and they shall wander*

earth below can be
explored,
then I will cast off all the de-
scendants of Israel
for all that they have done,
says the LORD."

JERUSALEM TO BE ENLARGED

38 "Behold, the days are coming
says the LORD, when the city shall be
rebuilt for the LORD from the tow-
er of Hanan'el to the Corner Gate.
39 And the measuring line shall go out
farther, straight to the hill Gareb,
and shall then turn to Go'ah. 40 The
whole valley of the dead bodies and
the ashes, and all the fields as far as
the brook Kidron, to the corner of
the Horse Gate toward the east, shall
be sacred to the LORD. It shall not
be uprooted or overthrown any more
for ever."

JEREMIAH BUYS A FIELD DURING THE SIEGE

32 The word that came to Jeremiah
from the LORD in the tenth
year of Zedeki'ah king of Judah,
which was the eighteenth year of
Nebuchadrez'zar. 2 At that time the
army of the king of Babylon was be-
sieging Jerusalem, and Jeremiah the
prophet was shut up in the court of
the guard which was in the palace
of the king of Judah. 3 For Zedeki'ah
king of Judah had imprisoned him,
saying, "Why do you prophesy and
say, 'Thus says the LORD: Behold,
I am giving this city into the hand
of the king of Babylon, and he shall
take it; 4 Zedeki'ah king of Judah shall
not escape out of the hand of the
Chalde'ans, but shall surely be given
into the hand of the king of Babylon,
and shall speak with him face to
face and see him eye to eye; 5 and he
shall take Zedeki'ah to Babylon, and
there he shall remain until I visit
him, says the LORD; though you fight
against the Chalde'ans, you shall not
succeed'?"

6 Jeremiah said, "The word of the
LORD came to me: 7 Behold, Han'amel
the son of Shallum your uncle will
come to you and say, 'Buy my field
which is at An'athoth, for the right
of redemption by purchase is yours.'
8 Then Han'amel my cousin came to
me in the court of the guard, in accor-
dance with the word of the LORD, and
said to me, 'Buy my field which is at
An'athoth in the land of Benjamin, for
the right of possession and redemp-
tion is yours; buy it for yourself.' Then
I knew that this was the word of the
LORD.

9 "And I bought the field at
An'athoth from Han'amel my cous-
in, and weighed out the money to
him, seventeen shekels of silver.
10 I signed the deed, sealed it, got
witnesses, and weighed the money
on scales. 11 Then I took the sealed
deed of purchase, containing the
terms and conditions, and the open
copy; 12 and I gave the deed of pur-
chase to Baruch the son of Neri'ah
son of Mahsei'ah, in the presence of
Han'amel my cousin, in the presence
of the witnesses who signed the deed
of purchase, and in the presence
of all the Jews who were sitting in
the court of the guard. 13 I charged
Baruch in their presence, saying,
14 'Thus says the LORD of hosts, the
God of Israel: Take these deeds, both
this sealed deed of purchase and this
open deed, and put them in an earth-
enware vessel, that they may last for
a long time. 15 For thus says the LORD
of hosts, the God of Israel: Houses
and fields and vineyards shall again
be bought in this land.'

JEREMIAH PRAYS FOR UNDERSTANDING

16 "After I had given the deed
of purchase to Baruch the son of
Neri'ah, I prayed to the LORD, say-
ing: 17 'Ah Lord GOD! It is thou who
hast made the heavens and the earth
by thy great power and by thy out-
stretched arm! Nothing is too hard
for thee, 18 who showest steadfast

love to thousands, but dost requite
the guilt of fathers to their children
after them, O great and mighty God
whose name is the LORD of hosts,
19great in counsel and mighty in
deed; whose eyes are open to all the
ways of men, rewarding every man
according to his ways and accord-
ing to the fruit of his doings; 20who
hast shown signs and wonders in
the land of Egypt, and to this day in
Israel and among all mankind, and
hast made thee a name, as at this
day. 21Thou didst bring thy people
Israel out of the land of Egypt with
signs and wonders, with a strong
hand and outstretched arm, and with
great terror; 22and thou gavest them
this land, which thou didst swear
to their fathers to give them, a land
flowing with milk and honey; 23and
they entered and took possession of
it. But they did not obey thy voice
or walk in thy law; they did noth-
ing of all thou didst command them
to do. Therefore thou hast made all
this evil come upon them. 24Behold,
the siege mounds have come up to
the city to take it, and because of
sword and famine and pestilence the
city is given into the hands of the
Chalde´ans who are fighting against
it. What thou didst speak has come
to pass, and behold, thou seest it.
25Yet thou, O Lord GOD, hast said to
me, "Buy the field for money and get
witnesses"—though the city is given
into the hands of the Chalde´ans.'"

GOD'S ASSURANCE OF THE PEOPLE'S RETURN

26 The word of the LORD came to
Jeremiah: 27"Behold, I am the LORD,
the God of all flesh; is anything too
hard for me? 28Therefore, thus says
the LORD: Behold, I am giving this
city into the hands of the Chalde´ans
and into the hand of Nebuchadrez´zar
king of Babylon, and he shall take
it. 29The Chalde´ans who are fight-
ing against this city shall come and
set this city on fire, and burn it,
with the houses on whose roofs in-
cense has been offered to Ba´al and
drink offerings have been poured
out to other gods, to provoke me to
anger. 30For the sons of Israel and
the sons of Judah have done noth-
ing but evil in my sight from their
youth; the sons of Israel have done
nothing but provoke me to anger by
the work of their hands, says the
LORD. 31This city has aroused my
anger and wrath, from the day it
was built to this day, so that I will
remove it from my sight 32because
of all the evil of the sons of Israel
and the sons of Judah which they did
to provoke me to anger—their kings
and their princes, their priests and
their prophets, the men of Judah and
the inhabitants of Jerusalem. 33They
have turned to me their back and not
their face; and though I have taught
them persistently they have not lis-
tened to receive instruction. 34They
set up their abominations in the
house which is called by my name, to
defile it. 35They built the high places
of Ba´al in the valley of the son of
Hinnom, to offer up their sons and
daughters to Molech, though I did
not command them, nor did it en-
ter into my mind, that they should
do this abomination, to cause Judah
to sin.

36 "Now therefore thus says the
LORD, the God of Israel, concern-
ing this city of which you say, 'It is
given into the hand of the king of
Babylon by sword, by famine, and
by pestilence': 37Behold, I will gather
them from all the countries to which
I drove them in my anger and my
wrath and in great indignation; I will
bring them back to this place, and I
will make them dwell in safety. 38And
they shall be my people, and I will be
their God. 39I will give them one heart
and one way, that they may fear me
for ever, for their own good and the
good of their children after them. 40I
will make with them an everlasting
covenant, that I will not turn away

from doing good to them; and I will put the fear of me in their hearts, that they may not turn from me. 41I will rejoice in doing them good, and I will plant them in this land in faithfulness, with all my heart and all my soul.

42 "For thus says the LORD: Just as I have brought all this great evil upon this people, so I will bring upon them all the good that I promise them. 43Fields shall be bought in this land of which you are saying, It is a desolation, without man or beast; it is given into the hands of the Chalde´ans. 44Fields shall be bought for money, and deeds shall be signed and sealed and witnessed, in the land of Benjamin, in the places about Jerusalem, and in the cities of Judah, in the cities of the hill country, in the cities of the Shephe´lah, and in the cities of the Negeb; for I will restore their fortunes, says the LORD."

HEALING AFTER PUNISHMENT

33 The word of the LORD came to Jeremiah a second time, while he was still shut up in the court of the guard: 2"Thus says the LORD who made the earth,[a] the LORD who formed it to establish it—the LORD is his name: 3Call to me and I will answer you, and will tell you great and hidden things which you have not known. 4For thus says the LORD, the God of Israel, concerning the houses of this city and the houses of the kings of Judah which were torn down to make a defense against the siege mounds and before the sword:[b] 5The Chalde´ans are coming in to fight[c] and to fill them with the dead bodies of men whom I shall smite in my anger and my wrath, for I have hidden my face from this city because of all their wickedness. 6Behold, I will bring to it health and healing, and I will heal them and reveal to them abundance[d] of prosperity and security. 7I will restore the fortunes of Judah and the fortunes of Israel, and rebuild them as they were at first. 8I will cleanse them from all the guilt of their sin against me, and I will forgive all the guilt of their sin and rebellion against me. 9And this city[e] shall be to me a name of joy, a praise and a glory before all the nations of the earth who shall hear of all the good that I do for them; they shall fear and tremble because of all the good and all the prosperity I provide for it.

10 "Thus says the LORD: In this place of which you say, 'It is a waste without man or beast,' in the cities of Judah and the streets of Jerusalem that are desolate, without man or inhabitant or beast, there shall be heard again 11the voice of mirth and the voice of gladness, the voice of the bridegroom and the voice of the bride, the voices of those who sing, as they bring thank offerings to the house of the LORD:

'Give thanks to the LORD of hosts,
for the LORD is good,
for his steadfast love endures for ever!'

12 "Thus says the LORD of hosts: In this place which is waste, without man or beast, and in all of its cities, there shall again be habitations of shepherds resting their flocks. 13In the cities of the hill country, in the cities of the Shephe´lah, and in the cities of the Negeb, in the land of Benjamin, the places about Jerusalem, and in the cities of Judah, flocks shall again pass under the hands of the one who counts them, says the LORD.

[a]Gk: Heb *it*
[b]Heb obscure
[c]Cn: Heb *They are coming in to fight against the Chaldeans*
[d]Heb uncertain
[e]Heb *and it*

THE RIGHTEOUS BRANCH AND THE COVENANT WITH DAVID

14 "Behold, the days are coming,
says the LORD, when I will fulfil the
promise I made to the house of Israel
and the house of Judah. 15In those
days and at that time I will cause
a righteous Branch to spring forth
for David;* and he shall execute jus-
tice and righteousness in the land.
16In those days Judah will be saved
and Jerusalem will dwell secure-
ly. And this is the name by which
it will be called: 'The LORD is our
righteousness.'

17 "For thus says the LORD: David
shall never lack a man to sit on the
throne of the house of Israel, 18and
the Levitical priests shall never lack a
man in my presence to offer burnt of-
ferings, to burn cereal offerings, and
to make sacrifices for ever."

19 The word of the LORD came to
Jeremiah: 20"Thus says the LORD: If
you can break my covenant with the
day and my covenant with the night,
so that day and night will not come at
their appointed time, 21then also my
covenant with David my servant may
be broken, so that he shall not have
a son to reign on his throne, and my
covenant with the Levitical priests
my ministers. 22As the host of heaven
cannot be numbered and the sands of
the sea cannot be measured, so I will
multiply the descendants of David my
servant, and the Levitical priests who
minister to me."

23 The word of the LORD came to
Jeremiah: 24"Have you not observed
what these people are saying, 'The
LORD has rejected the two families
which he chose'? Thus they have de-
spised my people so that they are no
longer a nation in their sight. 25Thus
says the LORD: If I have not estab-
lished my covenant with day and
night and the ordinances of heaven
and earth, 26then I will reject the de-
scendants of Jacob and David my ser-
vant and will not choose one of his
descendants to rule over the seed of
Abraham, Isaac, and Jacob. For I will
restore their fortunes, and will have
mercy upon them."

DEATH IN CAPTIVITY PREDICTED FOR ZEDEKIAH

34 The word which came to Je-
remiah from the LORD, when
Nebuchadrez′zar king of Babylon and
all his army and all the kingdoms of
the earth under his dominion and
all the peoples were fighting against
Jerusalem and all of its cities: 2"Thus
says the LORD, the God of Israel: Go
and speak to Zedeki′ah king of Judah
and say to him, 'Thus says the LORD:
Behold, I am giving this city into the
hand of the king of Babylon, and he
shall burn it with fire. 3You shall
not escape from his hand, but shall
surely be captured and delivered into
his hand; you shall see the king of
Babylon eye to eye and speak with
him face to face; and you shall go to
Babylon.' 4Yet hear the word of the
LORD, O Zedeki′ah king of Judah!
Thus says the LORD concerning you:
'You shall not die by the sword.
5You shall die in peace. And as spic-
es were burned for your fathers, the
former kings who were before you,
so men shall burn spices for you and
lament for you, saying, "Alas, lord!"'
For I have spoken the word, says the
LORD."

6 Then Jeremiah the prophet spoke
all these words to Zedeki′ah king of
Judah, in Jerusalem, 7when the army
of the king of Babylon was fight-
ing against Jerusalem and against
all the cities of Judah that were left,
Lachish and Aze′kah; for these were
the only fortified cities of Judah that
remained.

TREACHEROUS TREATMENT OF SLAVES

8 The word which came to
Jeremiah from the LORD, after King
Zedeki′ah had made a covenant with
all the people in Jerusalem to make
a proclamation of liberty to them,

9that every one should set free his
Hebrew slaves, male and female, so
that no one should enslave a Jew,
his brother. 10And they obeyed, all
the princes and all the people who
had entered into the covenant that
every one would set free his slave,
male or female, so that they would
not be enslaved again; they obeyed
and set them free. 11But afterward
they turned around and took back
the male and female slaves they had
set free, and brought them into sub-
jection as slaves. 12The word of the
LORD came to Jeremiah from the
LORD: 13"Thus says the LORD, the
God of Israel: I made a covenant with
your fathers when I brought them out
of the land of Egypt, out of the house
of bondage, saying, 14'At the end of
six[a] years each of you must set free
the fellow Hebrew who has been sold
to you and has served you six years;
you must set him free from your ser-
vice.' But your fathers did not listen
to me or incline their ears to me.
15You recently repented and did what
was right in my eyes by proclaiming
liberty, each to his neighbor, and you
made a covenant before me in the
house which is called by my name;
16but then you turned around and
profaned my name when each of you
took back his male and female slaves,
whom you had set free according to
their desire, and you brought them
into subjection to be your slaves.
17Therefore, thus says the LORD: You
have not obeyed me by proclaiming
liberty, every one to his brother and
to his neighbor; behold, I proclaim
to you liberty to the sword, to pesti-
lence, and to famine, says the LORD.
I will make you a horror to all the
kingdoms of the earth. 18And the
men who transgressed my covenant
and did not keep the terms of the
covenant which they made before
me, I will make like[b] the calf which
they cut in two and passed between
its parts 19the princes of Judah, the
princes of Jerusalem, the eunuchs,
the priests, and all the people of the
land who passed between the parts
of the calf; 20and I will give them into
the hand of their enemies and into
the hand of those who seek their
lives. Their dead bodies shall be
food for the birds of the air and the
beasts of the earth. 21And Zedeki´ah
king of Judah, and his princes I will
give into the hand of their enemies
and into the hand of those who seek
their lives, into the hand of the army
of the king of Babylon which has
withdrawn from you. 22Behold, I will
command, says the LORD, and will
bring them back to this city; and
they will fight against it, and take it,
and burn it with fire. I will make the
cities of Judah a desolation without
inhabitant."

THE RECHABITES COMMENDED

35 *The word which came to
Jeremiah from the LORD in the
days of Jehoi´akim the son of Josi´ah,
king of Judah: 2"Go to the house of
the Rech´abites, and speak with
them, and bring them to the house of
the LORD, into one of the chambers;
then offer them wine to drink." 3So I
took Ja-azani´ah the son of Jeremiah,
son of Habazzini´ah, and his broth-
ers, and all his sons, and the whole
house of the Rech´abites. 4I brought
them to the house of the LORD into
the chamber of the sons of Hanan
the son of Igdali´ah, the man of God,
which was near the chamber of the
princes, above the chamber of Ma-
asei´ah the son of Shallum, keeper
of the threshold. 5Then I set before
the Rech´abites pitchers full of wine,
and cups; and I said to them, "Drink
wine." 6But they answered, "We will
drink no wine, for Jon´adab the son
of Rechab, our father, commanded
us, 'You shall not drink wine, nei-
ther you nor your sons for ever; 7you

[a]Gk: Heb *seven*
[b]Cn: Heb lacks *like*

shall not build a house; you shall
not sow seed; you shall not plant or
have a vineyard; but you shall live
in tents all your days, that you may
live many days in the land where you
sojourn.' 8We have obeyed the voice
of Jon´adab the son of Rechab, our
father, in all that he commanded us,
to drink no wine all our days, our-
selves, our wives, our sons, or our
daughters, 9and not to build houses
to dwell in. We have no vineyard or
field or seed; 10but we have lived in
tents, and have obeyed and done all
that Jon´adab our father command-
ed us. 11But when Nebuchadrez´zar
king of Babylon came up against the
land, we said, 'Come, and let us go
to Jerusalem for fear of the army
of the Chalde´ans and the army
of the Syrians.' So we are living in
Jerusalem."

12 Then the word of the LORD
came to Jeremiah: 13"Thus says the
LORD of hosts, the God of Israel: Go
and say to the men of Judah and the
inhabitants of Jerusalem, Will you
not receive instruction and listen
to my words? says the LORD. 14The
command which Jon´adab the son of
Rechab gave to his sons, to drink no
wine, has been kept; and they drink
none to this day, for they have obeyed
their father's command. I have spo-
ken to you persistently, but you have
not listened to me. 15I have sent to
you all my servants the prophets,
sending them persistently, saying,
'Turn now every one of you from his
evil way, and amend your doings,
and do not go after other gods to
serve them, and then you shall dwell
in the land which I gave to you and
your fathers.' But you did not incline
your ear or listen to me. 16The sons of
Jon´adab the son of Rechab have kept
the command which their father gave
them, but this people has not obeyed
me. 17Therefore, thus says the LORD,
the God of hosts, the God of Israel:
Behold, I am bringing on Judah and
all the inhabitants of Jerusalem
all the evil that I have pronounced
against them; because I have spoken
to them and they have not listened, I
have called to them and they have not
answered."

18 But to the house of the Rech´-
abites Jeremiah said, "Thus says the
LORD of hosts, the God of Israel:
Because you have obeyed the com-
mand of Jon´adab your father, and
kept all his precepts, and done all
that he commanded you, 19therefore
thus says the LORD of hosts, the God
of Israel: Jon´adab the son of Rechab
shall never lack a man to stand be-
fore me."

THE SCROLL READ IN THE TEMPLE

36 In the fourth year of Jehoi´akim
the son of Josi´ah, king of Judah,
this word came to Jeremiah from the
LORD: 2"Take a scroll and write on it
all the words that I have spoken to
you against Israel and Judah and all
the nations, from the day I spoke to
you, from the days of Josi´ah until
today. 3It may be that the house of
Judah will hear all the evil which I
intend to do to them, so that every
one may turn from his evil way, and
that I may forgive their iniquity and
their sin."

4 Then Jeremiah called Baruch
the son of Neri´ah, and Baruch wrote
upon a scroll at the dictation of
Jeremiah all the words of the LORD
which he had spoken to him. 5And
Jeremiah ordered Baruch, saying, "I
am debarred from going to the house
of the LORD; 6so you are to go, and
on a fast day in the hearing of all the
people in the LORD's house you shall
read the words of the LORD from the
scroll which you have written at my
dictation. You shall read them also in
the hearing of all the men of Judah
who come out of their cities. 7It may
be that their supplication will come
before the LORD, and that every one
will turn from his evil way, for great
is the anger and wrath that the LORD
has pronounced against this people."

8And Baruch the son of Neri′ah did
all that Jeremiah the prophet ordered
him about reading from the scroll
the words of the LORD in the LORD's
house.

9 In the fifth year of Jehoi′akim
the son of Josi′ah, king of Judah, in
the ninth month, all the people in
Jerusalem and all the people who
came from the cities of Judah to
Jerusalem proclaimed a fast before
the LORD. 10Then, in the hearing of
all the people, Baruch read the words
of Jeremiah from the scroll, in the
house of the LORD, in the chamber
of Gemari′ah the son of Shaphan the
secretary, which was in the upper
court, at the entry of the New Gate of
the LORD's house.

THE SCROLL READ IN THE PALACE

11 When Micai′ah the son of
Gemari′ah, son of Shaphan, heard
all the words of the LORD from
the scroll, 12he went down to the
king's house, into the secretary's
chamber; and all the princes were
sitting there: Elish′ama the secre-
tary, Delai′ah the son of Shemai′ah,
Elna′than the son of Achbor,
Gemari′ah the son of Shaphan,
Zedeki′ah the son of Hanani′ah,
and all the princes. 13And Micai′ah
told them all the words that he had
heard, when Baruch read the scroll
in the hearing of the people. 14Then
all the princes sent Jehu′di the son
of Nethani′ah, son of Shelemi′ah,
son of Cushi, to say to Baruch, "Take
in your hand the scroll that you read
in the hearing of the people, and
come." So Baruch the son of Neri′ah
took the scroll in his hand and came
to them. 15And they said to him, "Sit
down and read it." So Baruch read it
to them. 16When they heard all the
words, they turned one to anoth-
er in fear; and they said to Baruch,
"We must report all these words to
the king." 17Then they asked Baruch,
"Tell us, how did you write all these
words? Was it at his dictation?"
18Baruch answered them, "He dic-
tated all these words to me, while I
wrote them with ink on the scroll."
19Then the princes said to Baruch,
"Go and hide, you and Jeremiah, and
let no one know where you are."

JEHOIAKIM BURNS THE SCROLL

20 So they went into the court
to the king, having put the scroll in
the chamber of Elish′ama the secre-
tary; and they reported all the words
to the king. 21Then the king sent
Jehu′di to get the scroll, and he took
it from the chamber of Elish′ama
the secretary; and Jehu′di read it
to the king and all the princes who
stood beside the king. 22It was the
ninth month, and the king was sit-
ting in the winter house and there
was a fire burning in the brazier
before him. 23As Jehu′di read three
or four columns, the king would cut
them off with a penknife and throw
them into the fire in the brazier, un-
til the entire scroll was consumed
in the fire that was in the brazier.
24Yet neither the king, nor any of his
servants who heard all these words,
was afraid, nor did they rend their
garments. 25Even when Elna′than
and Delai′ah and Gemari′ah urged
the king not to burn the scroll, he
would not listen to them. 26And the
king commanded Jerah′meel the
king's son and Serai′ah the son of
Az′ri-el and Shelemi′ah the son of
Abdeel to seize Baruch the secretary
and Jeremiah the prophet, but the
LORD hid them.

JEREMIAH DICTATES ANOTHER

27 Now, after the king had burned
the scroll with the words which
Baruch wrote at Jeremiah's dicta-
tion, the word of the LORD came
to Jeremiah: 28"Take another scroll
and write on it all the former words
that were in the first scroll, which
Jehoi′akim the king of Judah has
burned. 29And concerning Jehoi′akim
king of Judah you shall say, 'Thus

says the LORD, You have burned this
scroll, saying, "Why have you writ-
ten in it that the king of Babylon
will certainly come and destroy this
land, and will cut off from it man
and beast?" 30Therefore thus says the
LORD concerning Jehoi´akim king of
Judah, He shall have none to sit upon
the throne of David, and his dead
body shall be cast out to the heat by
day and the frost by night. 31And I
will punish him and his offspring and
his servants for their iniquity; I will
bring upon them, and upon the in-
habitants of Jerusalem, and upon the
men of Judah, all the evil that I have
pronounced against them, but they
would not hear.'"

32 Then Jeremiah took another
scroll and gave it to Baruch the scribe,
the son of Neri´ah, who wrote on it
at the dictation of Jeremiah all the
words of the scroll which Jehoi´akim
king of Judah had burned in the fire;
and many similar words were added
to them.

ZEDEKIAH'S VAIN HOPE

37 Zedeki´ah the son of Josi´ah,
whom Nebuchadrez´zar king of
Babylon made king in the land of Ju-
dah, reigned instead of Coni´ah the
son of Jehoi´akim. 2But neither he
nor his servants nor the people of the
land listened to the words of the LORD
which he spoke through Jeremiah the
prophet.

3 King Zedeki´ah sent Jehu´cal
the son of Shelemi´ah, and Zeph-
ani´ah the priest, the son of Ma-
asei´ah, to Jeremiah the prophet,
saying, "Pray for us to the LORD
our God." 4Now Jeremiah was still
going in and out among the people,
for he had not yet been put in prison.
5The army of Pharaoh had come out
of Egypt; and when the Chalde´ans
who were besieging Jerusalem heard
news of them, they withdrew from
Jerusalem.

6 Then the word of the LORD came
to Jeremiah the prophet: 7"Thus says
the LORD, God of Israel: Thus shall
you say to the king of Judah who sent
you to me to inquire of me, 'Behold,
Pharaoh's army which came to help
you is about to return to Egypt, to its
own land. 8And the Chalde´ans shall
come back and fight against this city;
they shall take it and burn it with fire.
9Thus says the LORD, Do not deceive
yourselves, saying, "The Chalde´ans
will surely stay away from us," for
they will not stay away. 10For even if
you should defeat the whole army of
Chalde´ans who are fighting against
you, and there remained of them only
wounded men, every man in his tent,
they would rise up and burn this city
with fire.'"

JEREMIAH IS IMPRISONED

11 Now when the Chalde´an army
had withdrawn from Jerusalem at
the approach of Pharaoh's army, 12Je-
remiah set out from Jerusalem to go
to the land of Benjamin to receive
his portion[a] there among the peo-
ple. 13When he was at the Benjamin
Gate, a sentry there named Iri´jah
the son of Shelemi´ah, son of Hana-
ni´ah, seized Jeremiah the prophet,
saying, "You are deserting to the
Chalde´ans." 14And Jeremiah said,
"It is false; I am not deserting to
the Chalde´ans." But Iri´jah would
not listen to him, and seized Jere-
miah and brought him to the princ-
es. 15And the princes were enraged
at Jeremiah, and they beat him and
imprisoned him in the house of Jo-
nathan the secretary, for it had been
made a prison.

16 When Jeremiah had come to the
dungeon cells, and remained there
many days, 17King Zedeki´ah sent
for him, and received him. The king
questioned him secretly in his house,
and said, "Is there any word from
the LORD?" Jeremiah said, "There
is." Then he said, "You shall be de-
livered into the hand of the king of

[a]Heb obscure

Babylon." 18 Jeremiah also said to King
Zedeki´ah, "What wrong have I done
to you or your servants or this peo-
ple, that you have put me in prison?
19 Where are your prophets who proph-
esied to you, saying, 'The king of
Babylon will not come against you and
against this land'? 20 Now hear, I pray
you, O my lord the king: let my humble
plea come before you, and do not send
me back to the house of Jonathan the
secretary, lest I die there." 21 So King
Zedeki´ah gave orders, and they com-
mitted Jeremiah to the court of the
guard; and a loaf of bread was given
him daily from the bakers' street, un-
til all the bread of the city was gone.
So Jeremiah remained in the court of
the guard.

JEREMIAH IN THE CISTERN

38 Now Shephati´ah the son of Mat-
tan, Gedali´ah the son of Pash-
hur, Jucal the son of Shelemi´ah, and
Pashhur the son of Malchi´ah heard
the words that Jeremiah was saying
to all the people, 2 "Thus says the
LORD, He who stays in this city shall
die by the sword, by famine, and by
pestilence; but he who goes out to
the Chalde´ans shall live; he shall
have his life as a prize of war, and
live. 3 Thus says the LORD, This city
shall surely be given into the hand of
the army of the king of Babylon and
be taken." 4 Then the princes said to
the king, "Let this man be put to
death, for he is weakening the hands
of the soldiers who are left in this
city, and the hands of all the people,
by speaking such words to them.
For this man is not seeking the wel-
fare of this people, but their harm."
5 King Zedeki´ah said, "Behold, he is
in your hands; for the king can do
nothing against you." 6 So they took
Jeremiah and cast him into the cis-
tern of Malchi´ah, the king's son,
which was in the court of the guard,
letting Jeremiah down by ropes. And
there was no water in the cistern,
but only mire, and Jeremiah sank in
the mire.

JEREMIAH IS RESCUED BY EBED-MELECH

7 When E´bed-mel´ech the Ethi-
opian, a eunuch, who was in the
king's house, heard that they had put
Jeremiah into the cistern—the king
was sitting in the Benjamin Gate
8 E´bed-mel´ech went from the king's
house and said to the king, 9 "My
lord the king, these men have done
evil in all that they did to Jeremiah
the prophet by casting him into the
cistern; and he will die there of hun-
ger, for there is no bread left in the
city." 10 Then the king commanded
E´bed-mel´ech, the Ethiopian, "Take
three men with you from here, and
lift Jeremiah the prophet out of the
cistern before he dies." 11 So E´bed-
mel´ech took the men with him and
went to the house of the king, to a
wardrobe of[b] the storehouse, and
took from there old rags and worn-
out clothes, which he let down to
Jeremiah in the cistern by ropes.
12 Then E´bed-mel´ech the Ethiopian
said to Jeremiah, "Put the rags and
clothes between your armpits and
the ropes." Jeremiah did so. 13 Then
they drew Jeremiah up with ropes
and lifted him out of the cistern. And
Jeremiah remained in the court of the
guard.

ZEDEKIAH CONSULTS JEREMIAH AGAIN

14 King Zedeki´ah sent for Jeremi-
ah the prophet and received him at
the third entrance of the temple of
the LORD. The king said to Jeremi-
ah, "I will ask you a question; hide
nothing from me." 15 Jeremiah said to
Zedeki´ah, "If I tell you, will you not
be sure to put me to death? And if I
give you counsel, you will not listen
to me." 16 Then King Zedeki´ah swore
secretly to Jeremiah, "As the LORD

[b] Cn: Heb *to under*

lives, who made our souls, I will not
put you to death or deliver you into
the hand of these men who seek your
life."

17 Then Jeremiah said to Zede-
ki´ah, "Thus says the LORD, the
God of hosts, the God of Israel, If
you will surrender to the princes of
the king of Babylon, then your life
shall be spared, and this city shall
not be burned with fire, and you and
your house shall live. 18But if you
do not surrender to the princes of
the king of Babylon, then this city
shall be given into the hand of the
Chalde´ans, and they shall burn it
with fire, and you shall not escape
from their hand." 19King Zedeki´ah
said to Jeremiah, "I am afraid of
the Jews who have deserted to the
Chalde´ans, lest I be handed over to
them and they abuse me." 20Jeremiah
said, "You shall not be given to
them. Obey now the voice of the
LORD in what I say to you, and it
shall be well with you, and your life
shall be spared. 21But if you refuse to
surrender, this is the vision which
the LORD has shown to me: 22Behold,
all the women left in the house of
the king of Judah were being led out
to the princes of the king of Babylon
and were saying,

'Your trusted friends have
deceived you
and prevailed against you;
now that your feet are sunk in
the mire,
they turn away from you.'

23All your wives and your sons
shall be led out to the Chalde´ans, and
you yourself shall not escape from
their hand, but shall be seized by the
king of Babylon; and this city shall be
burned with fire."

24 Then Zedeki´ah said to
Jeremiah, "Let no one know of these
words and you shall not die. 25If the
princes hear that I have spoken with
you and come to you and say to you,
'Tell us what you said to the king
and what the king said to you; hide
nothing from us and we will not
put you to death,' 26then you shall
say to them, 'I made a humble plea
to the king that he would not send
me back to the house of Jonathan
to die there.'" 27Then all the princ-
es came to Jeremiah and asked him,
and he answered them as the king
had instructed him. So they left off
speaking with him, for the conversa-
tion had not been overheard. 28And
Jeremiah remained in the court of the
guard until the day that Jerusalem
was taken.

THE FALL OF JERUSALEM

39 In the ninth year of Zedeki´ah
king of Judah, in the tenth
month, Nebuchadrez´zar king of
Babylon and all his army came
against Jerusalem and besieged it;
2in the eleventh year of Zedeki´ah,
in the fourth month, on the ninth
day of the month, a breach was made
in the city. 3When Jerusalem was
taken,[a] all the princes of the king of
Babylon came and sat in the middle
gate: Ner´gal-share´zer, Sam´gar-
ne´bo, Sar´sechim the Rab´saris,
Ner´gal-share´zer the Rabmag, with
all the rest of the officers of the
king of Babylon. 4When Zedeki´ah
king of Judah and all the soldiers
saw them, they fled, going out of
the city at night by way of the king's
garden through the gate between
the two walls; and they went to-
ward the Arabah. 5But the army of
the Chalde´ans pursued them, and
overtook Zedeki´ah in the plains
of Jericho; and when they had tak-
en him, they brought him up to
Nebuchadrez´zar king of Babylon, at
Riblah, in the land of Hamath; and
he passed sentence upon him. 6The
king of Babylon slew the sons of
Zedeki´ah at Riblah before his eyes;
and the king of Babylon slew all the
nobles of Judah. 7He put out the eyes

[a]This clause has been transposed from the end of Chapter 38

of Zedeki´ah, and bound him in fet-
ters to take him to Babylon. 8The
Chalde´ans burned the king's house
and the house of the people, and
broke down the walls of Jerusalem.
9Then Nebu´zarad´an, the captain
of the guard, carried into exile to
Babylon the rest of the people who
were left in the city, those who had
deserted to him, and the people who
remained. 10Nebu´zarad´an, the cap-
tain of the guard, left in the land of
Judah some of the poor people who
owned nothing, and gave them vine-
yards and fields at the same time.

JEREMIAH, SET FREE, REMEMBERS EBED-MELECH

11 Nebuchadrez´zar king of Bab-
ylon gave command concerning Je-
remiah through Nebu´zarad´an, the
captain of the guard, saying, 12"Take
him, look after him well and do him
no harm, but deal with him as he
tells you." 13So Nebu´zarad´an the
captain of the guard, Nebushaz´ban
the Rab´saris, Ner´gal-share´zer
the Rabmag, and all the chief of-
ficers of the king of Babylon 14sent
and took Jeremiah from the court
of the guard. They entrusted him
to Gedali´ah the son of Ahi´kam,
son of Shaphan, that he should take
him home. So he dwelt among the
people.

15 The word of the LORD came to
Jeremiah while he was shut up in the
court of the guard: 16"Go, and say to
E´bed-mel´ech the Ethiopian, 'Thus
says the LORD of hosts, the God of
Israel: Behold, I will fulfil my words
against this city for evil and not
for good, and they shall be accom-
plished before you on that day. 17But
I will deliver you on that day, says
the LORD, and you shall not be given
into the hand of the men of whom
you are afraid. 18For I will surely
save you, and you shall not fall by
the sword; but you shall have your
life as a prize of war, because you
have put your trust in me, says the
LORD.'"

JEREMIAH WITH GEDALIAH THE GOVERNOR

40 The word that came to Jeremi-
ah from the LORD after Nebu´-
zarad´an the captain of the guard
had let him go from Ramah, when
he took him bound in chains along
with all the captives of Jerusalem
and Judah who were being exiled to
Babylon. 2The captain of the guard
took Jeremiah and said to him, "The
LORD your God pronounced this evil
against this place; 3the LORD has
brought it about, and has done as
he said. Because you sinned against
the LORD, and did not obey his voice,
this thing has come upon you. 4Now,
behold, I release you today from the
chains on your hands. If it seems
good to you to come with me to Bab-
ylon, come, and I will look after you
well; but if it seems wrong to you
to come with me to Babylon, do not
come. See, the whole land is before
you; go wherever you think it good
and right to go. 5If you remain,[b] then
return to Gedali´ah the son of Ahi´-
kam, son of Shaphan, whom the king
of Babylon appointed governor of the
cities of Judah, and dwell with him
among the people; or go wherever
you think it right to go." So the cap-
tain of the guard gave him an allow-
ance of food and a present, and let
him go. 6Then Jeremiah went to Ge-
dali´ah the son of Ahi´kam, at Miz-
pah, and dwelt with him among the
people who were left in the land.

7 When all the captains of the
forces in the open country and their
men heard that the king of Babylon
had appointed Gedali´ah the son of
Ahi´kam governor in the land, and
had committed to him men, women,
and children, those of the poorest
of the land who had not been tak-
en into exile to Babylon, 8they went
to Gedali´ah at Mizpah—Ish´mael

[b] Syr: Heb obscure

the son of Nethani´ah, Joha´nan the
son of Kare´ah, Serai´ah the son
of Tanhu´meth, the sons of Ephai
the Netoph´athite, Jezani´ah the
son of the Ma-ac´athite, they and
their men. 9Gedali´ah the son of
Ahi´kam, son of Shaphan, swore to
them and their men, saying, "Do not
be afraid to serve the Chalde´ans.
Dwell in the land, and serve the
king of Babylon, and it shall be well
with you. 10As for me, I will dwell
at Mizpah, to stand for you before
the Chalde´ans who will come to us;
but as for you, gather wine and sum-
mer fruits and oil, and store them in
your vessels, and dwell in your cit-
ies that you have taken." 11Likewise,
when all the Jews who were in Moab
and among the Ammonites and in
Edom and in other lands heard that
the king of Babylon had left a rem-
nant in Judah and had appointed
Gedali´ah the son of Ahi´kam, son
of Shaphan, as governor over them,
12then all the Jews returned from
all the places to which they had
been driven and came to the land
of Judah, to Gedali´ah at Mizpah;
and they gathered wine and summer
fruits in great abundance.

13 Now Joha´nan the son of
Kare´ah and all the leaders of the
forces in the open country came
to Gedali´ah at Mizpah 14and said
to him, "Do you know that Ba´alis
the king of the Ammonites has sent
Ish´mael the son of Nethani´ah to
take your life?" But Gedali´ah the
son of Ahi´kam would not believe
them. 15Then Joha´nan the son of
Kare´ah spoke secretly to Gedali´ah
at Mizpah, "Let me go and slay
Ish´mael the son of Nethani´ah, and
no one will know it. Why should
he take your life, so that all the
Jews who are gathered about you
would be scattered, and the rem-
nant of Judah would perish?" 16But
Gedali´ah the son of Ahi´kam said
to Joha´nan the son of Kare´ah, "You
shall not do this thing, for you are
speaking falsely of Ish´mael."

INSURRECTION AGAINST GEDALIAH

41 In the seventh month, Ish´mael
the son of Nethani´ah, son of
Elish´ama, of the royal family, one of
the chief officers of the king, came
with ten men to Gedali´ah the son of
Ahi´kam, at Mizpah. As they ate bread
together there at Mizpah, 2Ish´mael
the son of Nethani´ah and the ten
men with him rose up and struck
down Gedali´ah the son of Ahi´kam,
son of Shaphan, with the sword, and
killed him, whom the king of Babylon
had appointed governor in the land.
3Ish´mael also slew all the Jews who
were with Gedali´ah at Mizpah, and
the Chalde´an soldiers who happened
to be there.

4 On the day after the murder of
Gedali´ah, before any one knew of it,
5eighty men arrived from Shechem
and Shiloh and Samar´ia, with their
beards shaved and their clothes torn,
and their bodies gashed, bringing
cereal offerings and incense to pres-
ent at the temple of the LORD. 6And
Ish´mael the son of Nethani´ah came
out from Mizpah to meet them, weep-
ing as he came. As he met them, he
said to them, "Come in to Gedali´ah
the son of Ahi´kam." 7When they
came into the city, Ish´mael the son
of Nethani´ah and the men with him
slew them, and cast them into a cis-
tern. 8But there were ten men among
them who said to Ish´mael, "Do not
kill us, for we have stores of wheat,
barley, oil, and honey hidden in the
fields." So he refrained and did not
kill them with their companions.

9 Now the cistern into which
Ish´mael cast all the bodies of the
men whom he had slain was the large
cistern[a] which King Asa had made for
defense against Ba´asha king of Israel;
Ish´mael the son of Nethani´ah filled
it with the slain. 10Then Ish´mael took
captive all the rest of the people who

[a]Gk: Heb *he had slain by the hand of Gedaliah*

to captivity, and to the sword those
who are doomed to the sword. 12He[b]
shall kindle a fire in the temples of
the gods of Egypt; and he shall burn
them and carry them away captive;
and he shall clean the land of Egypt,
as a shepherd cleans his cloak of
vermin; and he shall go away from
there in peace. 13He shall break the
obelisks of Heliop´olis which is in
the land of Egypt; and the temples
of the gods of Egypt he shall burn
with fire.'"

DENUNCIATION OF PERSISTENT IDOLATRY

44 The word that came to Jeremiah
concerning all the Jews that
dwelt in the land of Egypt, at Migdol,
at Tah´panhes, at Memphis, and in
the land of Pathros, 2"Thus says the
LORD of hosts, the God of Israel: You
have seen all the evil that I brought
upon Jerusalem and upon all the cit-
ies of Judah. Behold, this day they
are a desolation, and no one dwells
in them, 3because of the wickedness
which they committed, provoking me
to anger, in that they went to burn
incense and serve other gods that
they knew not, neither they, nor you,
nor your fathers. 4Yet I persistent-
ly sent to you all my servants the
prophets, saying, 'Oh, do not do this
abominable thing that I hate!' 5But
they did not listen or incline their
ear, to turn from their wickedness
and burn no incense to other gods.
6Therefore my wrath and my anger
were poured forth and kindled in the
cities of Judah and in the streets of
Jerusalem; and they became a waste
and a desolation, as at this day. 7And
now thus says the LORD God of
hosts, the God of Israel: Why do you
commit this great evil against your-
selves, to cut off from you man and
woman, infant and child, from the
midst of Judah, leaving you no rem-
nant? 8Why do you provoke me to
anger with the works of your hands,
burning incense to other gods in
the land of Egypt where you have
come to live, that you may be cut
off and become a curse and a taunt
among all the nations of the earth?
9Have you forgotten the wickedness
of your fathers, the wickedness of
the kings of Judah, the wickedness
of their[c] wives, your own wicked-
ness, and the wickedness of your
wives, which they committed in the
land of Judah and in the streets of
Jerusalem? 10They have not humbled
themselves even to this day, nor have
they feared, nor walked in my law
and my statutes which I set before
you and before your fathers.

11 "Therefore thus says the LORD
of hosts, the God of Israel: Behold, I
will set my face against you for evil,
to cut off all Judah. 12I will take the
remnant of Judah who have set their
faces to come to the land of Egypt to
live, and they shall all be consumed;
in the land of Egypt they shall fall; by
the sword and by famine they shall
be consumed; from the least to the
greatest, they shall die by the sword
and by famine; and they shall become
an execration, a horror, a curse, and
a taunt. 13I will punish those who
dwell in the land of Egypt, as I have
punished Jerusalem, with the sword,
with famine, and with pestilence,
14so that none of the remnant of
Judah who have come to live in the
land of Egypt shall escape or survive
or return to the land of Judah, to
which they desire to return to dwell
there; for they shall not return, ex-
cept some fugitives."

15 Then all the men who knew
that their wives had offered incense
to other gods, and all the women who
stood by, a great assembly, all the
people who dwelt in Pathros in the
land of Egypt, answered Jeremiah:
16"As for the word which you have
spoken to us in the name of the
LORD, we will not listen to you. 17But

[b] Gk Syr Vg: Heb *I*
[c] Heb *his*

we will do everything that we have vowed, burn incense to the queen of heaven and pour out libations to her, as we did, both we and our fathers, our kings and our princes, in the cities of Judah and in the streets of Jerusalem; for then we had plenty of food, and prospered, and saw no evil. 18But since we left off burning incense to the queen of heaven and pouring out libations to her, we have lacked everything and have been consumed by the sword and by famine." 19And the women said,[a] "When we burned incense to the queen of heaven and poured out libations to her, was it without our husbands' approval that we made cakes for her bearing her image and poured out libations to her?"

20 Then Jeremiah said to all the people, men and women, all the people who had given him this answer: 21"As for the incense that you burned in the cities of Judah and in the streets of Jerusalem, you and your fathers, your kings and your princes, and the people of the land, did not the LORD remember it?[b] Did it not come into his mind? 22The LORD could no longer bear your evil doings and the abominations which you committed; therefore your land has become a desolation and a waste and a curse, without inhabitant, as it is this day. 23It is because you burned incense, and because you sinned against the LORD and did not obey the voice of the LORD or walk in his law and in his statutes and in his testimonies, that this evil has befallen you, as at this day."

24 Jeremiah said to all the people and all the women, "Hear the word of the LORD, all you of Judah who are in the land of Egypt, 25Thus says the LORD of hosts, the God of Israel: You and your wives have declared with your mouths, and have fulfilled it with your hands, saying, 'We will surely perform our vows that we have made, to burn incense to the queen of heaven and to pour out libations to her.' Then confirm your vows and perform your vows! 26Therefore hear the word of the LORD, all you of Judah who dwell in the land of Egypt: Behold, I have sworn by my great name, says the LORD, that my name shall no more be invoked by the mouth of any man of Judah in all the land of Egypt, saying, 'As the Lord GOD lives.' 27Behold, I am watching over them for evil and not for good; all the men of Judah who are in the land of Egypt shall be consumed by the sword and by famine, until there is an end of them. 28And those who escape the sword shall return from the land of Egypt to the land of Judah, few in number; and all the remnant of Judah, who came to the land of Egypt to live, shall know whose word will stand, mine or theirs. 29This shall be the sign to you, says the LORD, that I will punish you in this place, in order that you may know that my words will surely stand against you for evil: 30Thus says the LORD, Behold, I will give Pharaoh Hophra king of Egypt into the hand of his enemies and into the hand of those who seek his life, as I gave Zedeki´ah king of Judah into the hand of Nebuchadrez´zar king of Babylon, who was his enemy and sought his life."

A WORD OF COMFORT TO BARUCH

45 The word that Jeremiah the prophet spoke to Baruch the son of Neri´ah, when he wrote these words in a book at the dictation of Jeremiah, in the fourth year of Jehoi´akim the son of Josi´ah, king of Judah: 2"Thus says the LORD, the God of Israel, to you, O Baruch: 3You said, 'Woe is me! for the LORD has added sorrow to my pain; I am weary with my groaning, and I find no rest.'

[a]Compare Syr: Heb lacks *And the women said*
[b]Syr: Heb *them*

4 Thus shall you say to him, Thus says
the LORD: Behold, what I have built
I am breaking down, and what I have
planted I am plucking up—that is,
the whole land. 5 And do you seek
great things for yourself? Seek them
not; for behold, I am bringing evil
upon all flesh, says the LORD; but I
will give you your life as a prize of
war in all places to which you may
go."

JUDGMENT ON EGYPT

46 The word of the LORD which
came to Jeremiah the prophet
concerning the nations.

2 About Egypt. Concerning the
army of Pharaoh Neco, king of Egypt,
which was by the river Euphra´tes at
Car´chemish and which Nebuchad-
rez´zar king of Babylon defeated in the
fourth year of Jehoi´akim the son of
Josi´ah, king of Judah:

3 "Prepare buckler and shield,
and advance for battle!
4 Harness the horses;
mount, O horsemen!
Take your stations with your
helmets,
polish your spears,
put on your coats of mail!
5 Why have I seen it?
They are dismayed
and have turned backward.
Their warriors are beaten
down,
and have fled in haste;
they look not back—
terror on every side!
says the LORD.
6 The swift cannot flee away,
nor the warrior escape;
in the north by the river
Euphra´tes
they have stumbled and
fallen.
7 "Who is this, rising like the
Nile,
like rivers whose waters
surge?
8 Egypt rises like the Nile,
like rivers whose waters
surge.
He said, I will rise, I will cover
the earth,
I will destroy cities and their
inhabitants.
9 Advance, O horses,
and rage, O chariots!
Let the warriors go forth:
men of Ethiopia and Put
who handle the
shield,
men of Lud, skilled in han-
dling the bow.
10 That day is the day of the Lord
GOD of hosts,
a day of vengeance,
to avenge himself on his
foes.
The sword shall devour and be
sated,
and drink its fill of their
blood.
For the Lord GOD of hosts
holds a sacrifice
in the north coun-
try by the river
Euphra´tes.
11 Go up to Gilead, and take
balm,
O virgin daughter of Egypt!
in vain you have used many
medicines;
there is no healing for you.
12 The nations have heard of your
shame,
and the earth is full of your
cry;
for warrior has stumbled
against warrior;
they have both fallen
together."

BABYLONIA WILL STRIKE EGYPT

13 The word which the LORD
spoke to Jeremiah the prophet about
the coming of Nebuchadrez´zar
king of Babylon to smite the land of
Egypt:

14 "Declare in Egypt, and proclaim
in Migdol;
proclaim in Memphis and
Tah´panhes;

Say, 'Stand ready and be prepared,
for the sword shall devour round about you.'
15 Why has Apis fled?[a]
Why did not your bull stand?
Because the LORD thrust him down.
16 Your multitude stumbled[b] and fell,
and they said one to another,
'Arise, and let us go back to our own people
and to the land of our birth,
because of the sword of the oppressor.'
17 Call the name of Pharaoh, king of Egypt,
'Noisy one who lets the hour go by.'
18 "As I live, says the King,
whose name is the LORD of hosts,
like Tabor among the mountains,
and like Carmel by the sea, shall one come.
19 Prepare yourselves baggage for exile,
O inhabitants of Egypt!
For Memphis shall become a waste,
a ruin, without inhabitant.
20 "A beautiful heifer is Egypt,
but a gadfly from the north has come upon her.
21 Even her hired soldiers in her midst
are like fatted calves;
yea, they have turned and fled together,
they did not stand;
for the day of their calamity has come upon them,
the time of their punishment.
22 "She makes a sound like a serpent gliding away;
for her enemies march in force,
and come against her with axes,
like those who fell trees.
23 They shall cut down her forest, says the LORD,
though it is impenetrable,
because they are more numerous than locusts;
they are without number.
24 The daughter of Egypt shall be put to shame,
she shall be delivered into the hand of a people from the north."
25 The LORD of hosts, the God of
Israel, said: "Behold, I am bringing
punishment upon Amon of Thebes,
and Pharaoh, and Egypt and her
gods and her kings, upon Pharaoh
and those who trust in him. 26 I will
deliver them into the hand of those
who seek their life, into the hand of
Nebuchadrez´zar king of Babylon and
his officers. Afterward Egypt shall be
inhabited as in the days of old, says
the LORD.

GOD WILL SAVE ISRAEL

27 "But fear not, O Jacob my servant,
nor be dismayed, O Israel;
for lo, I will save you from afar,
and your offspring from the land of their captivity.
Jacob shall return and have quiet and ease,
and none shall make him afraid.
28 Fear not, O Jacob my servant, says the LORD,
for I am with you.
I will make a full end of all the nations
to which I have driven you,
but of you I will not make a

[a] Gk: Heb *Why was it swept away*
[b] Gk: Heb *He made many stumble*

full end.
I will chasten you in just
measure,
and I will by no means
leave you
unpunished."

JUDGMENT ON THE PHILISTINES

47 The word of the LORD that came
to Jeremiah the prophet concern-
ing the Philistines, before Pharaoh
smote Gaza.
2 "Thus says the LORD:
Behold, waters are rising out of
the north,
and shall become an over-
flowing torrent;
they shall overflow the land
and all that fills it,
the city and those who dwell
in it.
Men shall cry out,
and every inhabitant of the
land shall wail.
3 At the noise of the stamping of
the hoofs of his stallions,
at the rushing of his chari-
ots, at the rumbling
of their wheels,
the fathers look not back to
their children,
so feeble are their hands,
4 because of the day that is coming
to destroy
all the Philistines,
to cut off from Tyre and Sidon
every helper that remains.
For the LORD is destroying the
Philistines,
the remnant of the coastland
of Caphtor.
5 Baldness has come upon Gaza,
Ash´kelon has perished.
O remnant of the Anakim,[c]
how long will you gash
yourselves?
6 Ah, sword of the LORD!
How long till you are quiet?
Put yourself into your
scabbard,
rest and be still!
7 How can it[d] be quiet,
when the LORD has given it
a charge?
Against Ash´kelon and against
the seashore
he has appointed it."

JUDGMENT ON MOAB

48 Concerning Moab.
Thus says the LORD of hosts,
the God of Israel:
"Woe to Nebo, for it is laid
waste!
Kiriatha´im is put to shame,
it is taken;
the fortress is put to
shame and broken
down;
2 the renown of Moab is no
more.
In Heshbon they planned evil
against her:
'Come, let us cut her
off from being a
nation!'
You also, O Madmen, shall be
brought to silence;
the sword shall pursue you.
3 "Hark! a cry from Horona´im,
'Desolation and great
destruction!'
4 Moab is destroyed;
a cry is heard as far as
Zo´ar.[e]
5 For at the ascent of Luhith
they go up weeping;[f]
for at the descent of
Horona´im
they have heard the cry[g] of
destruction.
6 Flee! Save yourselves!
Be like a wild ass[h] in the
desert!

[c] Gk: Heb *their valley*
[d] Gk Vg: Heb *you*
[e] Gk: Heb *her little ones*
[f] Cn: Heb *weeping goes up with weeping*
[g] Gk Compare Is 15. 5: Heb *the distress of the cry*
[h] Gk Aquila: Heb *like Aroer*

7For, because you trusted in your
strongholds[a] and your
treasures,
you also shall be taken;
and Chemosh shall go forth
into exile,
with his priests and his
princes.
8The destroyer shall come upon
every city,
and no city shall escape;
the valley shall perish,
and the plain shall be
destroyed,
as the LORD has spoken.
9"Give wings to Moab,
for she would fly away;
her cities shall become a
desolation,
with no inhabitant in them.

10 "Cursed is he who does the
work of the LORD with slackness; and
cursed is he who keeps back his sword
from bloodshed.

11"Moab has been at ease from his
youth
and has settled on his lees;
he has not been emptied from
vessel to vessel,
nor has he gone into exile;
so his taste remains in him,
and his scent is not
changed.

12 "Therefore, behold, the days are
coming, says the LORD, when I shall
send to him tilters who will tilt him,
and empty his vessels, and break his[b]
jars in pieces. 13Then Moab shall be
ashamed of Chemosh, as the house
of Israel was ashamed of Bethel, their
confidence.

14"How do you say, 'We are
heroes
and mighty men of war'?
15The destroyer of Moab and his
cities has come up,
and the choicest of his young
men have gone down
to slaughter,
says the King, whose name
is the LORD of hosts.
16The calamity of Moab is near at
hand
and his affliction hastens
apace.
17Bemoan him, all you who are
round about him,
and all who know his name;
say, 'How the mighty scepter is
broken,
the glorious staff.'
18"Come down from your glory,
and sit on the parched
ground,
O inhabitant of Dibon!
For the destroyer of Moab has
come up against you;
he has destroyed your
strongholds.
19Stand by the way and watch,
O inhabitant of Aro′er!
Ask him who flees and her who
escapes;
say, 'What has happened?'
20Moab is put to shame, for it is
broken;
wail and cry!
Tell it by the Arnon,
that Moab is laid waste.

21 "Judgment has come upon the
tableland, upon Holon, and Jahzah,
and Meph′a-ath, 22and Dibon, and Ne-
bo, and Beth-diblatha′im, 23and Kiri-
atha′im, and Beth-ga′mul, and Beth-
me′on, 24and Ker′i-oth, and Bozrah,
and all the cities of the land of Moab,
far and near. 25The horn of Moab is cut
off, and his arm is broken, says the
LORD.

26 "Make him drunk, because he
magnified himself against the LORD;
so that Moab shall wallow in his vom-
it, and he too shall be held in derision.
27Was not Israel a derision to you? Was
he found among thieves, that whenev-
er you spoke of him you wagged your
head?

28"Leave the cities, and dwell in
the rock,
O inhabitants of Moab!

[a]Gk: Heb *works*
[b]Gk Aquila: Heb *their*

Be like the dove that nests
in the sides of the mouth of a gorge.
29We have heard of the pride of Moab—
he is very proud—
of his loftiness, his pride, and his arrogance,
and the haughtiness of his heart.
30I know his insolence, says the LORD;
his boasts are false,
his deeds are false.
31Therefore I wail for Moab;
I cry out for all Moab;
for the men of Kir-he´res I mourn.
32More than for Jazer I weep for you,
O vine of Sibmah!
Your branches passed over the sea,
reached as far as Jazer;[c]
upon your summer fruits and your vintage
the destroyer has fallen.
33Gladness and joy have been taken away
from the fruitful land of Moab;
I have made the wine cease
from the wine presses;
no one treads them with shouts of joy;
the shouting is not the shout of joy.

34 "Heshbon and Elea´leh cry
out;[d] as far as Jahaz they utter their
voice, from Zo´ar to Horona´im and
Eg´lath-shelish´iyah. For the waters
of Nimrim also have become desolate.
35And I will bring to an end in Moab,
says the LORD, him who offers sacri-
fice in the high place and burns in-
cense to his god. 36Therefore my heart
moans for Moab like a flute, and my
heart moans like a flute for the men
of Kir-he´res; therefore the riches they
gained have perished.

37 "For every head is shaved and
every beard cut off; upon all the hands
are gashes, and on the loins is sack-
cloth. 38On all the housetops of Moab
and in the squares there is nothing
but lamentation; for I have broken
Moab like a vessel for which no one
cares, says the LORD. 39How it is bro-
ken! How they wail! How Moab has
turned his back in shame! So Moab
has become a derision and a horror
to all that are round about him." 40For
thus says the LORD:

"Behold, one shall fly swiftly like an eagle,
and spread his wings against Moab;
41the cities shall be taken
and the strongholds seized.
The heart of the warriors of Moab shall be in that day
like the heart of a woman in her pangs;
42Moab shall be destroyed and be no longer a people,
because he magnified himself against the LORD.
43Terror, pit, and snare
are before you, O inhabitant of Moab! says the LORD.
44He who flees from the terror
shall fall into the pit,
and he who climbs out of the pit
shall be caught in the snare.
For I will bring these things[e] upon Moab
in the year of their punishment,
says the LORD.
45"In the shadow of Heshbon
fugitives stop without strength;
for a fire has gone forth from Heshbon,
a flame from the house of Sihon;

[c] Cn: Heb *the sea of Jazer*
[d] Cn: Heb *From the cry of Heshbon to Elealeh*
[e] Gk Syr: Heb *to her*

it has destroyed the forehead
of Moab,
the crown of the sons of
tumult.
46Woe to you, O Moab!
The people of Chemosh is
undone;
for your sons have been taken
captive,
and your daughters into
captivity.
47Yet I will restore the fortunes
of Moab
in the latter days, says the
LORD."
Thus far is the judgment on
Moab.

JUDGMENT ON THE AMMONITES

49 Concerning the Ammonites.
Thus says the LORD:
"Has Israel no sons?
Has he no heir?
Why then has Milcom dispos-
sessed Gad,
and his people settled in its
cities?
2Therefore, behold, the days are
coming,
says the LORD,
when I will cause the battle cry
to be heard
against Rabbah of the
Ammonites;
it shall become a desolate
mound,
and its villages shall be
burned with fire;
then Israel shall dispossess
those who dispossessed
him,
says the LORD.
3"Wail, O Heshbon, for Ai is laid
waste!
Cry, O daughters of
Rabbah!
Gird yourselves with
sackcloth,
lament, and run to and fro
among the hedges!
For Milcom shall go into
exile,
with his priests and his
princes.
4Why do you boast of your
valleys,[a]
O faithless daughter,
who trusted in her treasures,
saying,
'Who will come against
me?'
5Behold, I will bring terror upon
you,
says the Lord GOD of hosts,
from all who are round
about you,
and you shall be driven out,
every man straight
before him,
with none to gather the
fugitives.
6 But afterward I will restore the
fortunes of the Ammonites, says the
LORD."

JUDGMENT ON EDOM

7Concerning Edom.
Thus says the LORD of hosts:
"Is wisdom no more in
Teman?
Has counsel perished from
the prudent?
Has their wisdom
vanished?
8Flee, turn back, dwell in the
depths,
O inhabitants of Dedan!
For I will bring the calamity of
Esau upon him,
the time when I punish
him.
9If grape-gatherers came to you,
would they not leave
gleanings?
If thieves came by night,
would they not destroy
only enough for
themselves?
10But I have stripped Esau bare,
I have uncovered his hiding
places,
and he is not able to conceal

[a]Heb *valleys, your valley flows*

himself.
His children are destroyed, and
his brothers,
and his neighbors; and he is
no more.
11 Leave your fatherless children, I
will keep them alive;
and let your widows trust
in me."

12 For thus says the LORD: "If
those who did not deserve to drink
the cup must drink it, will you go
unpunished? You shall not go un-
punished, but you must drink. 13 For
I have sworn by myself, says the
LORD, that Bozrah shall become a
horror, a taunt, a waste, and a curse;
and all her cities shall be perpetual
wastes."

14 I have heard tidings from the
LORD,
and a messenger has been
sent among the
nations:
"Gather yourselves together
and come against her,
and rise up for battle!"
15 For behold, I will make you
small among the nations,
despised among men.
16 The horror you inspire has de-
ceived you,
and the pride of your heart,
you who live in the clefts of the
rock,[b]
who hold the height of the
hill.
Though you make your nest as
high as the eagle's,
I will bring you down from
there,
says the LORD.

17 "Edom shall become a horror;
every one who passes by it will be
horrified and will hiss because of all
its disasters. 18 As when Sodom and
Gomor'rah and their neighbor cities
were overthrown, says the LORD, no
man shall dwell there, no man shall
sojourn in her. 19 Behold, like a lion
coming up from the jungle of the
Jordan against a strong sheepfold, I
will suddenly make them[c] run away
from her; and I will appoint over
her whomever I choose. For who
is like me? Who will summon me?
What shepherd can stand before me?
20 Therefore hear the plan which the
LORD has made against Edom and
the purposes which he has formed
against the inhabitants of Teman:
Even the little ones of the flock shall
be dragged away; surely their fold
shall be appalled at their fate. 21 At
the sound of their fall the earth shall
tremble; the sound of their cry shall
be heard at the Red Sea. 22 Behold,
one shall mount up and fly swiftly
like an eagle, and spread his wings
against Bozrah, and the heart of the
warriors of Edom shall be in that
day like the heart of a woman in her
pangs."

JUDGMENT ON DAMASCUS

23 Concerning Damascus.
"Hamath and Arpad are
confounded,
for they have heard evil
tidings;
they melt in fear, they are trou-
bled like the sea[d]
which cannot be quiet.
24 Damascus has become feeble,
she turned to flee,
and panic seized her;
anguish and sorrows have
taken hold of her,
as of a woman in travail.
25 How the famous city is
forsaken,[e]
the joyful city![f]
26 Therefore her young men shall
fall in her squares,
and all her soldiers shall be
destroyed in that day,

[b] Or *Sela*
[c] Gk Syr: Heb *him*
[d] Cn: Heb *there is trouble in the sea*
[e] Vg: Heb *not forsaken*
[f] Syr Vg Tg: Heb *city of my joy*

says the LORD of hosts.
27And I will kindle a fire in the wall of Damascus,
and it shall devour the strongholds of Ben-ha´dad."

JUDGMENT ON KEDAR AND HAZOR

28Concerning Kedar and the kingdoms of Hazor which Nebuchadrez´zar king of Babylon smote. Thus says the LORD:
"Rise up, advance against Kedar!
Destroy the people of the east!
29Their tents and their flocks shall be taken,
their curtains and all their goods;
their camels shall be borne away from them,
and men shall cry to them:
'Terror on every side!'
30Flee, wander far away, dwell in the depths,
O inhabitants of Hazor!
says the LORD.
For Nebuchadrez´zar king of Babylon
has made a plan against you,
and formed a purpose against you.
31"Rise up, advance against a nation at ease,
that dwells securely,
says the LORD,
that has no gates or bars,
that dwells alone.
32Their camels shall become booty,
their herds of cattle a spoil.
I will scatter to every wind
those who cut the corners of their hair,
and I will bring their calamity
from every side of them,
says the LORD.
33Hazor shall become a haunt of jackals,
an everlasting waste;
no man shall dwell there,
no man shall sojourn in her."

JUDGMENT ON ELAM

34 The word of the LORD that came
to Jeremiah the prophet concerning
Elam, in the beginning of the reign of
Zedeki´ah king of Judah.
35 Thus says the LORD of hosts:
"Behold, I will break the bow of
Elam, the mainstay of their might;
36and I will bring upon Elam the four
winds from the four quarters of heaven; and I will scatter them to all those
winds, and there shall be no nation
to which those driven out of Elam
shall not come. 37I will terrify Elam
before their enemies, and before
those who seek their life; I will bring
evil upon them, my fierce anger, says
the LORD. I will send the sword after
them, until I have consumed them;
38and I will set my throne in Elam,
and destroy their king and princes,
says the LORD.
39 "But in the latter days I will restore the fortunes of Elam, says the
LORD."

JUDGMENT ON BABYLON

50 The word which the LORD spoke concerning Babylon, concerning the land of the Chalde´ans, by Jeremiah the prophet:
2"Declare among the nations and proclaim,
set up a banner and proclaim,
conceal it not, and say:
'Babylon is taken,
Bel is put to shame,
Mer´odach is dismayed.
Her images are put to shame,
her idols are dismayed.'
3 "For out of the north a nation has
come up against her, which shall make
her land a desolation, and none shall
dwell in it; both man and beast shall
flee away.

4 "In those days and in that time,
says the LORD, the people of Israel
and the people of Judah shall come
together, weeping as they come; and
they shall seek the LORD their God.
5They shall ask the way to Zion, with
faces turned toward it, saying, 'Come,
let us join ourselves to the LORD in an
everlasting covenant which will never
be forgotten.'

6 "My people have been lost sheep;
their shepherds have led them astray,
turning them away on the mountains;
from mountain to hill they have gone,
they have forgotten their fold. 7All
who found them have devoured them,
and their enemies have said, 'We
are not guilty, for they have sinned
against the LORD, their true habi-
tation, the LORD, the hope of their
fathers.'

8 "Flee from the midst of
Babylon, and go out of the land of
the Chalde´ans, and be as he-goats
before the flock. 9For behold, I am
stirring up and bringing against
Babylon a company of great nations,
from the north country; and they
shall array themselves against her;
from there she shall be taken. Their
arrows are like a skilled warrior
who does not return empty-handed.
10Chalde´a shall be plundered; all
who plunder her shall be sated, says
the LORD.

11"Though you rejoice, though you
exult,
O plunderers of my
heritage,
though you are wanton as a
heifer at grass,
and neigh like stallions,
12your mother shall be utterly
shamed,
and she who bore you shall
be disgraced.
Lo, she shall be the last of the
nations,
a wilderness dry and
desert.
13Because of the wrath of the
LORD she shall not be
inhabited,
but shall be an utter
desolation;
every one who passes by
Babylon shall be
appalled,
and hiss because of all her
wounds.
14Set yourselves in array against
Babylon round about,
all you that bend the bow;
shoot at her, spare no arrows,
for she has sinned against
the LORD.
15Raise a shout against her round
about,
she has surrendered;
her bulwarks have fallen,
her walls are thrown down.
For this is the vengeance of the
LORD:
take vengeance on her,
do to her as she has done.
16Cut off from Babylon the sower,
and the one who handles
the sickle in time of
harvest;
because of the sword of the
oppressor,
every one shall turn to his
own people,
and every one shall flee to
his own land.

17 "Israel is a hunted sheep driven
away by lions. First the king of As-
syria devoured him, and now at last
Nebuchadrez´zar king of Babylon has
gnawed his bones. 18Therefore, thus
says the LORD of hosts, the God of
Israel: Behold, I am bringing pun-
ishment on the king of Babylon and
his land, as I punished the king of
Assyria. 19I will restore Israel to his
pasture, and he shall feed on Carmel
and in Bashan, and his desire shall be
satisfied on the hills of E´phraim and
in Gilead. 20In those days and in that
time, says the LORD, iniquity shall
be sought in Israel, and there shall
be none; and sin in Judah, and none
shall be found; for I will pardon those
whom I leave as a remnant.

21"Go up against the land of
Meratha´im,[a]
and against the inhabitants
of Pekod.[b]
Slay, and utterly destroy after
them,
says the LORD,
and do all that I have commanded you.
22The noise of battle is in the
land,
and great destruction!
23How the hammer of the whole
earth
is cut down and broken!
How Babylon has become
a horror among the
nations!
24I set a snare for you and you
were taken, O Babylon,
and you did not know it;
you were found and caught,
because you strove against
the LORD.
25The LORD has opened his
armory,
and brought out the weapons of his wrath,
for the Lord GOD of hosts has a
work to do
in the land of the
Chalde´ans.
26Come against her from every
quarter;
open her granaries;
pile her up like heaps of
grain, and destroy her
utterly;
let nothing be left of her.
27Slay all her bulls,
let them go down to the
slaughter.
Woe to them, for their day has
come,
the time of their
punishment.

28 "Hark! they flee and escape
from the land of Babylon, to declare in
Zion the vengeance of the LORD our
God, vengeance for his temple.

29 "Summon archers against Babylon, all those who bend the bow.
Encamp round about her; let no one
escape. Requite her according to her
deeds, do to her according to all that
she has done; for she has proudly defied the LORD, the Holy One of Israel.
30Therefore her young men shall fall
in her squares, and all her soldiers
shall be destroyed on that day, says
the LORD.

31"Behold, I am against you, O
proud one,
says the Lord GOD of hosts;
for your day has come,
the time when I will punish
you.
32The proud one shall stumble
and fall,
with none to raise him up,
and I will kindle a fire in his
cities,
and it will devour all that is
round about him.

33 "Thus says the LORD of hosts:
The people of Israel are oppressed,
and the people of Judah with them; all
who took them captive have held them
fast, they refuse to let them go. 34Their
Redeemer is strong; the LORD of hosts
is his name. He will surely plead their
cause, that he may give rest to the
earth, but unrest to the inhabitants of
Babylon.

35"A sword upon the Chalde´ans,
says the LORD,
and upon the inhabitants of
Babylon,
and upon her princes and
her wise men!
36A sword upon the diviners,
that they may become
fools!
A sword upon her warriors,
that they may be destroyed!
37A sword upon her horses and
upon her chariots,
and upon all the foreign
troops in her midst,
that they may become

[a] Or *Double Rebellion*
[b] Or *Punishment*

women!
A sword upon all her treasures,
that they may be plundered!
38A drought upon her waters,
that they may be dried up!
For it is a land of images,
and they are mad over
idols.

39 "Therefore wild beasts shall
dwell with hyenas in Babylon, and
ostriches shall dwell in her; she shall
be peopled no more for ever, nor
inhabited for all generations. 40As
when God overthrew Sodom and
Gomor'rah and their neighbor cit-
ies, says the LORD, so no man shall
dwell there, and no son of man shall
sojourn in her.

41"Behold, a people comes from
the north;
a mighty nation and many
kings
are stirring from the far-
thest parts of the
earth.
42They lay hold of bow and spear;
they are cruel, and have no
mercy.
The sound of them is like the
roaring of the sea;
they ride upon horses,
arrayed as a man for battle
against you, O daughter of
Babylon!
43"The king of Babylon heard the
report of them,
and his hands fell helpless;
anguish seized him,
pain as of a woman in
travail.

44 "Behold, like a lion coming up
from the jungle of the Jordan against
a strong sheepfold, I will suddenly
make them run away from her; and
I will appoint over her whomever
I choose. For who is like me? Who
will summon me? What shepherd can
stand before me? 45Therefore hear
the plan which the LORD has made
against Babylon, and the purposes
which he has formed against the land
of the Chalde'ans: Surely the little
ones of their flock shall be dragged
away; surely their fold shall be ap-
palled at their fate. 46At the sound of
the capture of Babylon the earth shall
tremble, and her cry shall be heard
among the nations."

51 Thus says the LORD:
"Behold, I will stir up the spirit
of a destroyer
against Babylon,
against the inhabitants of
Chalde'a;[c]
2and I will send to Babylon
winnowers,
and they shall winnow her,
and they shall empty her land,
when they come against her
from every side
on the day of trouble.
3Let not the archer bend his bow,
and let him not stand up in
his coat of mail.
Spare not her young men;
utterly destroy all her host.
4They shall fall down slain in the
land of the Chalde'ans,
and wounded in her
streets.
5For Israel and Judah have not
been forsaken
by their God, the LORD of
hosts;
but the land of the
Chalde'ans[d] is full of
guilt
against the Holy One of
Israel.
6"Flee from the midst of
Babylon,
let every man save his life!
Be not cut off in her
punishment,
for this is the time of the
LORD's vengeance,
the requital he is rendering
her.
7Babylon was a golden cup in the
LORD's hand,

[c] Heb *Leb-qamai,* a cipher for Chaldea
[d] Heb *their land*

making all the earth
drunken;
the nations drank of her wine,
therefore the nations went
mad.
8Suddenly Babylon has fallen and
been broken;
wail for her!
Take balm for her pain;
perhaps she may be healed.
9We would have healed Babylon,
but she was not healed.
Forsake her, and let us go
each to his own country;
for her judgment has reached
up to heaven
and has been lifted up even
to the skies.
10The LORD has brought forth our
vindication;
come, let us declare in Zion
the work of the LORD our
God.
11"Sharpen the arrows!
Take up the shields!
12Set up a standard against the
walls of Babylon;
make the watch strong;
set up watchmen;
prepare the ambushes;
for the LORD has both planned
and done
what he spoke concerning
the inhabitants of
Babylon.
13O you who dwell by many
waters,
rich in treasures,
your end has come,
the thread of your life is
cut.
14The LORD of hosts has sworn by
himself:
Surely I will fill you with men,
as many as locusts,
and they shall raise the
shout of victory over
you.
15"It is he who made the earth by
his power,
who established the world
by his wisdom,
and by his understanding
stretched out the heavens.
16When he utters his voice there
is a tumult of waters in the
heavens,
and he makes the mist rise
from the ends of the
earth.
He makes lightnings for the
rain,
and he brings forth the
wind from his
storehouses.
17Every man is stupid and without
knowledge;
every goldsmith is put to
shame by his idols;
for his images are false,
and there is no breath in
them.
18They are worthless, a work of
delusion;
at the time of their pun-
ishment they shall
perish.
19Not like these is he who is the
portion of Jacob,
for he is the one who formed
all things,
and Israel is the tribe of his
inheritance;
the LORD of hosts is his
name.

ISRAEL THE CREATOR'S INSTRUMENT

20"You are my hammer and weap-
on of war:
with you I break nations in
pieces;
with you I destroy
kingdoms;
21with you I break in pieces the
horse and his rider;
with you I break in pieces
the chariot and the
charioteer;
22with you I break in pieces man
and woman;
with you I break in pieces
the old man and the
youth;
with you I break in pieces the

young man and the
maiden;
23with you I break in pieces
the shepherd and his
flock;
with you I break in pieces the
farmer and his team;
with you I break in pieces
governors and
commanders.

THE DOOM OF BABYLON

24 "I will requite Babylon and all
the inhabitants of Chalde´a before
your very eyes for all the evil that they
have done in Zion, says the LORD.
25"Behold, I am against you, O
destroying mountain,
says the LORD,
which destroys the whole
earth;
I will stretch out my hand
against you,
and roll you down from the
crags,
and make you a burnt
mountain.
26No stone shall be taken from
you for a corner
and no stone for a
foundation,
but you shall be a perpetual
waste,
says the LORD.
27"Set up a standard on the
earth,
blow the trumpet among the
nations;
prepare the nations for war
against her,
summon against her the
kingdoms,
Ar´arat, Minni, and
Ash´kenaz;
appoint a marshal against her,
bring up horses like bristling
locusts.
28Prepare the nations for war
against her,
the kings of the Medes, with
their governors and
deputies,
and every land under their
dominion.
29The land trembles and writhes
in pain,
for the LORD's purposes
against Babylon
stand,
to make the land of Babylon a
desolation,
without inhabitant.
30The warriors of Babylon have
ceased fighting,
they remain in their
strongholds;
their strength has failed,
they have become women;
her dwellings are on fire,
her bars are broken.
31One runner runs to meet
another,
and one messenger to meet
another,
to tell the king of Babylon
that his city is taken on
every side;
32the fords have been seized,
the bulwarks are burned
with fire,
and the soldiers are in
panic.
33For thus says the LORD of hosts,
the God of Israel:
The daughter of Babylon is like
a threshing floor
at the time when it is
trodden;
yet a little while
and the time of her harvest
will come."
34"Nebuchadrez´zar the king of
Babylon has devoured me,
he has crushed me;
he has made me an empty
vessel,
he has swallowed me like a
monster;
he has filled his belly with my
delicacies,
he has rinsed me out.
35The violence done to me and
to my kinsmen be upon
Babylon,"

let the inhabitant of Zion
say.
"My blood be upon the
inhabitants of
Chalde´a,"
let Jerusalem say.
36Therefore thus says the LORD:
"Behold, I will plead your cause
and take vengeance for
you.
I will dry up her sea
and make her fountain dry;
37and Babylon shall become a heap
of ruins,
the haunt of jackals,
a horror and a hissing,
without inhabitant.
38"They shall roar together like
lions;
they shall growl like lions'
whelps.
39While they are inflamed I will
prepare them a feast
and make them drunk, till
they swoon away[a]
and sleep a perpetual sleep
and not wake, says the
LORD.
40I will bring them down like
lambs to the slaughter,
like rams and he-goats.
41"How Babylon[b] is taken,
the praise of the whole earth
seized!
How Babylon has become
a horror among the
nations!
42The sea has come up on Babylon;
she is covered with its tu-
multuous waves.
43Her cities have become a horror,
a land of drought and a
desert,
a land in which no one dwells,
and through which no son of
man passes.
44And I will punish Bel in
Babylon,
and take out of his mouth
what he has
swallowed.
The nations shall no longer
flow to him;
the wall of Babylon has
fallen.
45"Go out of the midst of her, my
people!
Let every man save his life
from the fierce anger of the
LORD!
46Let not your heart faint, and be
not fearful
at the report heard in the
land,
when a report comes in one
year
and afterward a report in
another year,
and violence is in the land,
and ruler is against ruler.
47"Therefore, behold, the days are
coming
when I will punish the imag-
es of Babylon;
her whole land shall be put to
shame,
and all her slain shall fall in
the midst of her.
48Then the heavens and the
earth,
and all that is in them,
shall sing for joy over
Babylon;
for the destroyers shall come
against them out of the
north,
says the LORD.
49Babylon must fall for the slain
of Israel,
as for Babylon have fallen
the slain of all the
earth.
50"You that have escaped from the
sword,
go, stand not still!
Remember the LORD from
afar,
and let Jerusalem come into
your mind:
51'We are put to shame, for we

[a]Gk Vg: Heb *rejoice*
[b]Heb *Sheshach,* a cipher for Babylon

have heard reproach;
dishonor has covered our
face,
for aliens have come
into the holy places of the
LORD's house.'
52"Therefore, behold, the days
are coming, says the
LORD,
when I will execute
judgment upon her
images,
and through all her land
the wounded shall groan.
53Though Babylon should mount
up to heaven,
and though she should
fortify her strong
height,
yet destroyers would come
from me upon her,
says the LORD.
54"Hark! a cry from Babylon!
The noise of great destruc-
tion from the land of
the Chalde´ans!
55For the LORD is laying Babylon
waste,
and stilling her mighty
voice.
Their waves roar like many
waters,
the noise of their voice is
raised;
56for a destroyer has come upon
her,
upon Babylon;
her warriors are taken,
their bows are broken in
pieces;
for the LORD is a God of
recompense,
he will surely requite.
57I will make drunk her princes
and her wise men,
her governors, her com-
manders, and her
warriors;
they shall sleep a perpetual
sleep and not wake,
says the King, whose name
is the LORD of hosts.
58"Thus says the LORD of hosts:
The broad wall of Babylon
shall be leveled to the
ground
and her high gates
shall be burned with fire.
The peoples labor for nought,
and the nations weary
themselves only for
fire."

JEREMIAH'S COMMAND TO SERAIAH

59 The word which Jeremiah the
prophet commanded Serai´ah the
son of Neri´ah, son of Mahsei´ah,
when he went with Zedeki´ah king
of Judah to Babylon, in the fourth
year of his reign. Serai´ah was the
quartermaster. 60Jeremiah wrote in
a book all the evil that should come
upon Babylon, all these words that
are written concerning Babylon.
61And Jeremiah said to Serai´ah:
"When you come to Babylon, see
that you read all these words, 62and
say, 'O LORD, thou hast said con-
cerning this place that thou wilt cut
it off, so that nothing shall dwell in
it, neither man nor beast, and it shall
be desolate for ever.' 63When you fin-
ish reading this book, bind a stone
to it, and cast it into the midst of the
Euphra´tes, 64and say, 'Thus shall
Babylon sink, to rise no more, be-
cause of the evil that I am bringing
upon her.'"[c]

Thus far are the words of Jeremiah.

THE DESTRUCTION OF JERUSALEM REVIEWED

52* Zedeki´ah was twenty-one years
old when he became king; and he
reigned eleven years in Jerusalem.
His mother's name was Hamu´tal the
daughter of Jeremiah of Libnah. 2And
he did what was evil in the sight of the
LORD, according to all that Jehoi´akim
had done. 3Surely because of the an-
ger of the LORD things came to such
a pass in Jerusalem and Judah that he

[c] Gk: Heb *upon her. And they shall weary themselves*

cast them out from his presence. And
Zedeki´ah rebelled against the king of
Babylon. 4And in the ninth year of his
reign, in the tenth month, on the tenth
day of the month, Nebuchadrez´zar
king of Babylon came with all his
army against Jerusalem, and they
laid siege to it and built siegeworks
against it round about. 5So the city
was besieged till the eleventh year of
King Zedeki´ah. 6On the ninth day of
the fourth month the famine was so
severe in the city, that there was no
food for the people of the land. 7Then
a breach was made in the city; and all
the men of war fled and went out from
the city by night by the way of a gate
between the two walls, by the king's
garden, while the Chalde´ans were
round about the city. And they went in
the direction of the Arabah. 8But the
army of the Chalde´ans pursued the
king, and overtook Zedeki´ah in the
plains of Jericho; and all his army was
scattered from him. 9Then they cap-
tured the king, and brought him up to
the king of Babylon at Riblah in the
land of Hamath, and he passed sen-
tence upon him. 10The king of Babylon
slew the sons of Zedeki´ah before his
eyes, and also slew all the princes of
Judah at Riblah. 11He put out the eyes
of Zedeki´ah, and bound him in fet-
ters, and the king of Babylon took him
to Babylon, and put him in prison till
the day of his death.

12 In the fifth month, on the tenth
day of the month—which was the nine-
teenth year of King Nebuchadrez´zar,
king of Babylon—Nebu´zarad´an
the captain of the bodyguard who
served the king of Babylon, entered
Jerusalem. 13And he burned the house
of the LORD, and the king's house
and all the houses of Jerusalem; every
great house he burned down. 14And
all the army of the Chalde´ans, who
were with the captain of the guard,
broke down all the walls round about
Jerusalem. 15And Nebu´zarad´an the
captain of the guard carried away
captive some of the poorest of the
people and the rest of the people
who were left in the city and the de-
serters who had deserted to the king
of Babylon, together with the rest of
the artisans. 16But Nebu´zarad´an the
captain of the guard left some of the
poorest of the land to be vinedressers
and plowmen.

17 And the pillars of bronze that
were in the house of the LORD, and
the stands and the bronze sea that
were in the house of the LORD, the
Chalde´ans broke in pieces, and car-
ried all the bronze to Babylon. 18And
they took away the pots, and the shov-
els, and the snuffers, and the basins,
and the dishes for incense, and all the
vessels of bronze used in the temple
service; 19also the small bowls, and the
firepans, and the basins, and the pots,
and the lampstands, and the dishes
for incense, and the bowls for liba-
tion. What was of gold the captain of
the guard took away as gold, and what
was of silver, as silver. 20As for the two
pillars, the one sea, the twelve bronze
bulls which were under the sea,[a] and
the stands, which Solomon the king
had made for the house of the LORD,
the bronze of all these things was be-
yond weight. 21As for the pillars, the
height of the one pillar was eighteen
cubits, its circumference was twelve
cubits, and its thickness was four fin-
gers, and it was hollow. 22Upon it was
a capital of bronze; the height of the
one capital was five cubits; a network
and pomegranates, all of bronze, were
upon the capital round about. And the
second pillar had the like, with pome-
granates. 23There were ninety-six
pomegranates on the sides; all the
pomegranates were a hundred upon
the network round about.

24 And the captain of the guard
took Serai´ah the chief priest, and
Zephani´ah the second priest, and the
three keepers of the threshold; 25and
from the city he took an officer who
had been in command of the men of

[a] Heb lacks *the sea*

war, and seven men of the king's coun-
cil, who were found in the city; and
the secretary of the commander of the
army who mustered the people of the
land; and sixty men of the people of
the land, who were found in the midst
of the city. 26 And Nebu´zarad´an the
captain of the guard took them, and
brought them to the king of Babylon
at Riblah. 27 And the king of Babylon
smote them, and put them to death
at Riblah in the land of Hamath. So
Judah was carried captive out of its
land.

28 This is the number of the peo-
ple whom Nebuchadrez´zar carried
away captive: in the seventh year,
three thousand and twenty-three
Jews; 29 in the eighteenth year of
Nebuchadrez´zar he carried away cap-
tive from Jerusalem eight hundred
and thirty-two persons; 30 in the twen-
ty-third year of Nebuchadrez´zar,
Nebu´zarad´an the captain of the
guard carried away captive of the Jews
seven hundred and forty-five persons;
all the persons were four thousand
and six hundred.

JEHOIACHIN FAVORED IN CAPTIVITY

31 And in the thirty-seventh year
of the captivity of Jehoi´achin king of
Judah, in the twelfth month, on the
twenty-fifth day of the month, Evil-
me´rodach king of Babylon, in the
year that he became king, lifted up
the head of Jehoi´achin king of Judah
and brought him out of prison; 32 and
he spoke kindly to him, and gave him
a seat above the seats of the kings
who were with him in Babylon. 33 So
Jehoi´achin put off his prison gar-
ments. And every day of his life he
dined regularly at the king's table; 34 as
for his allowance, a regular allowance
was given him by the king according
to his daily need, until the day of his
death as long as he lived.

THE LAMENTATIONS
OF JEREMIAH

THE DESERTED CITY

1 How lonely sits the city
that was full of people!
How like a widow has she
become,
she that was great among
the nations!
She that was a princess among
the cities
has become a vassal.
2 She weeps bitterly in the night,
tears on her cheeks;
among all her lovers
she has none to comfort her;
all her friends have dealt
treacherously with her,
they have become her
enemies.
3 Judah has gone into exile because
of affliction
and hard servitude;
she dwells now among the
nations,
but finds no resting place;
her pursuers have all overtak-
en her
in the midst of her distress.
4 The roads to Zion mourn,
for none come to the ap-
pointed feasts;
all her gates are desolate,
her priests groan;
her maidens have been dragged
away,[a]
and she herself suffers
bitterly.
5 Her foes have become the head,
her enemies prosper,
because the LORD has made
her suffer
for the multitude of her
transgressions;
her children have gone away,
captives before the foe.
6 From the daughter of Zion has
departed
all her majesty.
Her princes have become like
harts
that find no pasture;
they fled without strength
before the pursuer.
7 Jerusalem remembers
in the days of her affliction
and bitterness[b]
all the precious things
that were hers from days
of old.
When her people fell into the
hand of the foe,
and there was none to help
her,
the foe gloated over her,
mocking at her downfall.
8 Jerusalem sinned grievously,
therefore she became filthy;
all who honored her despise
her,
for they have seen her
nakedness;
yea, she herself groans,
and turns her face away.
9 Her uncleanness was in her
skirts;
she took no thought of her
doom;
therefore her fall is terrible,
she has no comforter.
"O LORD, behold my affliction,
for the enemy has
triumphed!"
10 The enemy has stretched out his
hands
over all her precious things;
yea, she has seen the nations
invade her sanctuary,
those whom thou didst forbid
to enter thy congregation.
11 All her people groan
as they search for bread;
they trade their treasures for

[a] Gk Old Latin: Heb *afflicted*
[b] Cn: Heb *wandering*

food
to revive their strength.
"Look, O LORD, and behold,
for I am despised."
12"Is it nothing to you,[c] all you
who pass by?
Look and see
if there is any sorrow like my
sorrow
which was brought upon me,
which the LORD inflicted
on the day of his fierce
anger.
13"From on high he sent fire;
into my bones[d] he made it
descend;
he spread a net for my feet;
he turned me back;
he has left me stunned,
faint all the day long.
14"My transgressions were bound[e]
into a yoke;
by his hand they were fas-
tened together;
they were set upon my neck;
he caused my strength to
fail;
the Lord gave me into the
hands
of those whom I cannot
withstand.
15"The Lord flouted all my mighty
men
in the midst of me;
he summoned an assembly
against me
to crush my young men;
the Lord has trodden as in a
wine press
the virgin daughter of Judah.
16"For these things I weep;
my eyes flow with tears;
for a comforter is far from me,
one to revive my courage;
my children are desolate,
for the enemy has
prevailed."
17Zion stretches out her hands,
but there is none to comfort
her;
the LORD has commanded
against Jacob
that his neighbors should be
his foes;
Jerusalem has become
a filthy thing among them.
18"The LORD is in the right,
for I have rebelled against
his word;
but hear, all you peoples,
and behold my suffering;
my maidens and my young men
have gone into captivity.
19"I called to my lovers
but they deceived me;
my priests and elders
perished in the city,
while they sought food
to revive their strength.
20"Behold, O LORD, for I am in
distress,
my soul is in tumult,
my heart is wrung within me,
because I have been very
rebellious.
In the street the sword
bereaves;
in the house it is like death.
21"Hear[f] how I groan;
there is none to comfort me.
All my enemies have heard of
my trouble;
they are glad that thou hast
done it.
Bring thou[g] the day thou hast
announced,
and let them be as I am.
22"Let all their evil-doing come
before thee;
and deal with them
as thou hast dealt with me
because of all my
transgressions;
for my groans are many
and my heart is faint."

[c] Heb uncertain
[d] Gk: Heb *bones and*
[e] Cn: Heb uncertain
[f] Gk Syr: Heb *they heard*
[g] Syr: Heb *thou hast brought*

GOD'S WARNINGS FULFILLED

2 How the Lord in his anger
has set the daughter of Zion
under a cloud!
He has cast down from heaven
to earth
the splendor of Israel;
he has not remembered his
footstool
in the day of his anger.
2The Lord has destroyed without
mercy
all the habitations of Jacob;
in his wrath he has broken
down
the strongholds of the
daughter of Judah;
he has brought down to the
ground in dishonor
the kingdom and its rulers.
3He has cut down in fierce anger
all the might of Israel;
he has withdrawn from them
his right hand
in the face of the enemy;
he has burned like a flaming
fire in Jacob,
consuming all around.
4He has bent his bow like an
enemy,
with his right hand set like
a foe;
and he has slain all the pride of
our eyes
in the tent of the daughter
of Zion;
he has poured out his fury like
fire.
5The Lord has become like an
enemy,
he has destroyed Israel;
he has destroyed all its palaces,
laid in ruins its strongholds;
and he has multiplied in the
daughter of Judah
mourning and lamentation.
6He has broken down his booth
like that of a garden,
laid in ruins the place of his
appointed feasts;
the LORD has brought to an
end in Zion
appointed feast and sabbath,
and in his fierce indignation
has spurned
king and priest.
7The Lord has scorned his altar,
disowned his sanctuary;
he has delivered into the hand
of the enemy
the walls of her palaces;
a clamor was raised in the
house of the LORD
as on the day of an appoint-
ed feast.
8The LORD determined to lay in
ruins
the wall of the daughter of
Zion;
he marked it off by the line;
he restrained not his hand
from destroying;
he caused rampart and wall to
lament,
they languish together.
9Her gates have sunk into the
ground;
he has ruined and broken
her bars;
her king and princes are among
the nations;
the law is no more,
and her prophets obtain
no vision from the LORD.
10The elders of the daughter of
Zion
sit on the ground in silence;
they have cast dust on their
heads
and put on sackcloth;
the maidens of Jerusalem
have bowed their heads to
the ground.
11My eyes are spent with weeping;
my soul is in tumult;
my heart is poured out in grief[a]
because of the destruction
of the daughter of my
people,
because infants and babes faint
in the streets of the city.
12They cry to their mothers,

[a] Heb *to the ground*

"Where is bread and wine?"
as they faint like wounded men
in the streets of the city,
as their life is poured out
on their mothers' bosom.
13What can I say for you, to what
compare you,
O daughter of Jerusalem?
What can I liken to you, that I
may comfort you,
O virgin daughter of Zion?
For vast as the sea is your ruin;
who can restore you?
14Your prophets have seen for you
false and deceptive visions;
they have not exposed your
iniquity
to restore your fortunes,
but have seen for you oracles
false and misleading.
15All who pass along the way
clap their hands at you;
they hiss and wag their heads
at the daughter of Jerusalem;
"Is this the city which was
called
the perfection of beauty,
the joy of all the earth?"
16All your enemies
rail against you;
they hiss, they gnash their
teeth,
they cry: "We have de-
stroyed her!
Ah, this is the day we longed
for;
now we have it; we see it!"
17The LORD has done what he
purposed,
has carried out his threat;
as he ordained long ago,
he has demolished without
pity;
he has made the enemy rejoice
over you,
and exalted the might of
your foes.
18Cry aloud[b] to the Lord!
O[c] daughter of Zion!
Let tears stream down like a
torrent
day and night!
Give yourself no rest,
your eyes no respite!
19Arise, cry out in the night,
at the beginning of the
watches!
Pour out your heart like water
before the presence of the
Lord!
Lift your hands to him
for the lives of your children,
who faint for hunger
at the head of every street.
20Look, O LORD, and see!
With whom hast thou dealt
thus?
Should women eat their
offspring,
the children of their tender
care?
Should priest and prophet be
slain
in the sanctuary of the Lord?
21In the dust of the streets
lie the young and the old;
my maidens and my young men
have fallen by the sword;
in the day of thy anger thou
hast slain them,
slaughtering without mercy.
22Thou didst invite as to the day of
an appointed feast
my terrors on every side;
and on the day of the anger of
the LORD
none escaped or survived;
those whom I dandled and
reared
my enemy destroyed.

GOD'S STEADFAST LOVE ENDURES

3 I am the man who has seen
affliction
under the rod of his wrath;
2he has driven and brought me
into darkness without any
light;
3surely against me he turns his
hand

[b]Cn: Heb *Their heart cried*
[c]Cn: Heb *O wall of*

again and again the whole
day long.
4He has made my flesh and my
skin waste away,
and broken my bones;
5he has besieged and enveloped
me
with bitterness and
tribulation;
6he has made me dwell in
darkness
like the dead of long ago.
7He has walled me about so that I
cannot escape;
he has put heavy chains on
me;
8though I call and cry for help,
he shuts out my prayer;
9he has blocked my ways with
hewn stones,
he has made my paths
crooked.
10He is to me like a bear lying in
wait,
like a lion in hiding;
11he led me off my way and tore
me to pieces;
he has made me desolate;
12he bent his bow and set me
as a mark for his arrow.
13He drove into my heart
the arrows of his quiver;
14I have become the laughingstock
of all peoples,
the burden of their songs all
day long.
15He has filled me with bitterness,
he has sated me with
wormwood.
16He has made my teeth grind on
gravel,
and made me cower in ashes;
17my soul is bereft of peace,
I have forgotten what happi-
ness is;
18so I say, "Gone is my glory,
and my expectation from the
LORD."
19Remember my affliction and my
bitterness,[a]
the wormwood and the gall!
20My soul continually thinks of it
and is bowed down within
me.
21But this I call to mind,
and therefore I have hope:
22The steadfast love of the LORD
never ceases,[b]
his mercies never come to
an end;
23they are new every morning;
great is thy faithfulness.
24"The LORD is my portion," says
my soul,
"therefore I will hope in
him."
25The LORD is good to those who
wait for him,
to the soul that seeks him.
26It is good that one should wait
quietly
for the salvation of the
LORD.
27It is good for a man that he bear
the yoke in his youth.
28Let him sit alone in silence
when he has laid it on him;
29let him put his mouth in the
dust—
there may yet be hope;
30let him give his cheek to the
smiter,
and be filled with insults.
31For the Lord will not
cast off for ever,
32but, though he cause grief, he
will have compassion
according to the abundance
of his steadfast love;
33for he does not willingly afflict
or grieve the sons of men.
34To crush under foot
all the prisoners of the
earth,
35to turn aside the right of a man
in the presence of the Most
High,
36to subvert a man in his cause,
the Lord does not approve.
37Who has commanded and it

[a] Cn: Heb *wandering*
[b] Syr Tg: Heb *we are not cut off*

came to pass,
unless the Lord has ordained it?
38Is it not from the mouth of the Most High
that good and evil come?
39Why should a living man complain,
a man, about the punishment of his sins?
40Let us test and examine our ways,
and return to the Lord!
41Let us lift up our hearts and hands
to God in heaven:
42"We have transgressed and rebelled,
and thou hast not forgiven.
43"Thou hast wrapped thyself with anger and pursued us,
slaying without pity;
44thou hast wrapped thyself with a cloud
so that no prayer can pass through.
45Thou hast made us offscouring and refuse
among the peoples.
46"All our enemies
rail against us;
47panic and pitfall have come upon us,
devastation and destruction;
48my eyes flow with rivers of tears
because of the destruction of the daughter of my people.
49"My eyes will flow without ceasing,
without respite,
50until the LORD from heaven
looks down and sees;
51my eyes cause me grief
at the fate of all the maidens of my city.
52"I have been hunted like a bird
by those who were my enemies without cause;
53they flung me alive into the pit
and cast stones on me;
54water closed over my head;
I said, 'I am lost.'
55"I called on thy name, O LORD,
from the depths of the pit;
56thou didst hear my plea, 'Do not close
thine ear to my cry for help!'[c]
57Thou didst come near when I called on thee;
thou didst say, 'Do not fear!'
58"Thou hast taken up my cause, O Lord,
thou hast redeemed my life.
59Thou hast seen the wrong done to me, O LORD;
judge thou my cause.
60Thou hast seen all their vengeance, all their devices against me.
61"Thou hast heard their taunts, O LORD,
all their devices against me.
62The lips and thoughts of my assailants
are against me all the day long.
63Behold their sitting and their rising;
I am the burden of their songs.
64"Thou wilt requite them, O LORD,
according to the work of their hands.
65Thou wilt give them dullness of heart;
thy curse will be on them.
66Thou wilt pursue them in anger and destroy them
from under thy heavens, O LORD."[d]

THE PUNISHMENT OF ZION

4 How the gold has grown dim,
how the pure gold is changed!
The holy stones lie scattered
at the head of every street.
2The precious sons of Zion,

[c] Heb uncertain
[d] Syr Compare Gk Vg: Heb *the heavens of the* Lord

worth their weight in fine gold,
how they are reckoned as earthen pots,
the work of a potter's hands!
3Even the jackals give the breast
and suckle their young,
but the daughter of my people has become cruel,
like the ostriches in the wilderness.
4The tongue of the nursling cleaves
to the roof of its mouth for thirst;
the children beg for food,
but no one gives to them.
5Those who feasted on dainties
perish in the streets;
those who were brought up in purple
lie on ash heaps.
6For the chastisement[a] of the daughter of my people has been greater
than the punishment[b] of Sodom,
which was overthrown in a moment,
no hand being laid on it.[c]
7Her princes were purer than snow,
whiter than milk;
their bodies were more ruddy than coral,
the beauty of their form[d] was like sapphire.[e]
8Now their visage is blacker than soot,
they are not recognized in the streets;
their skin has shriveled upon their bones,
it has become as dry as wood.
9Happier were the victims of the sword
than the victims of hunger,
who pined away, stricken
by want of the fruits of the field.
10The hands of compassionate women
have boiled their own children;
they became their food
in the destruction of the daughter of my people.
11The LORD gave full vent to his wrath,
he poured out his hot anger;
and he kindled a fire in Zion,
which consumed its foundations.
12The kings of the earth did not believe,
or any of the inhabitants of the world,
that foe or enemy could enter
the gates of Jerusalem.
13This was for the sins of her prophets
and the iniquities of her priests,
who shed in the midst of her
the blood of the righteous.
14They wandered, blind, through the streets,
so defiled with blood
that none could touch
their garments.
15"Away! Unclean!" men cried at them;
"Away! Away! Touch not!"
So they became fugitives and wanderers;
men said among the nations,
"They shall stay with us no longer."
16The LORD himself has scattered them,
he will regard them no more;
no honor was shown to the priests,
no favor to the elders.

[a]Or *iniquity*
[b]Or *sin*
[c]Heb uncertain
[d]Heb uncertain
[e]Heb *lapis lazuli*

17Our eyes failed, ever watching
vainly for help;
in our watching[f] we watched
for a nation which could not
save.
18Men dogged our steps
so that we could not walk in
our streets;
our end drew near; our days
were numbered;
for our end had come.
19Our pursuers were swifter
than the vultures in the
heavens;
they chased us on the
mountains,
they lay in wait for us in the
wilderness.
20The breath of our nostrils, the
LORD's anointed,
was taken in their pits,
he of whom we said, "Under
his shadow
we shall live among the
nations."
21Rejoice and be glad, O daughter
of Edom,
dweller in the land of Uz;
but to you also the cup shall
pass;
you shall become drunk and
strip yourself bare.
22The punishment of your iniqui-
ty, O daughter of Zion, is
accomplished,
he will keep you in exile no
longer;
but your iniquity, O daughter
of Edom, he will punish,
he will uncover your sins.

A PLEA FOR MERCY

5 Remember, O LORD, what has
befallen us;
behold, and see our disgrace!
2Our inheritance has been turned
over to strangers,
our homes to aliens.
3We have become orphans,
fatherless;
our mothers are like
widows.
4We must pay for the water we
drink,
the wood we get must be
bought.
5With a yoke[g] on our necks we are
hard driven;
we are weary, we are given
no rest.
6We have given the hand to
Egypt,
and to Assyria, to get bread
enough.
7Our fathers sinned, and are no
more;
and we bear their
iniquities.
8Slaves rule over us;
there is none to deliver us
from their hand.
9We get our bread at the peril of
our lives,
because of the sword in the
wilderness.
10Our skin is hot as an oven
with the burning heat of
famine.
11Women are ravished in Zion,
virgins in the towns of
Judah.
12Princes are hung up by their
hands;
no respect is shown to the
elders.
13Young men are compelled to
grind at the mill;
and boys stagger under loads
of wood.
14The old men have quit the city
gate,
the young men their music.
15The joy of our hearts has
ceased;
our dancing has been turned
to mourning.
16The crown has fallen from our
head;
woe to us, for we have
sinned!

[f]Heb uncertain
[g]Symmachus: Heb lacks *with a yoke*

17For this our heart has become sick,
for these things our eyes have grown dim,
18for Mount Zion which lies desolate;
jackals prowl over it.
19But thou, O LORD, dost reign for ever;
thy throne endures to all generations.
20Why dost thou forget us for ever,
why dost thou so long forsake us?
21Restore us to thyself, O LORD,
that we may be restored!
Renew our days as of old!
22Or hast thou utterly rejected us?
Art thou exceedingly angry with us?

BARUCH

BARUCH AND THE JEWS IN BABYLON

1 These are the words of the book
which Baruch the son of Nera´iah,
son of Mahse´iah, son of Zedeki´ah,
son of Hasadi´ah, son of Hilki´ah,
wrote in Babylon, 2in the fifth year,
on the seventh day of the month, at
the time when the Chalde´ans took
Jerusalem and burned it with fire.
3And Baruch read the words of this
book in the hearing of Jeconi´ah the
son of Jehoi´akim, king of Judah, and
in the hearing of all the people who
came to hear the book, 4and in the
hearing of the mighty men and the
princes, and in the hearing of the el-
ders, and in the hearing of all the peo-
ple, small and great, all who dwelt in
Babylon by the river Sud.
5 Then they wept, and fasted, and
prayed before the Lord; 6and they col-
lected money, each giving what he
could; 7and they sent it to Jerusalem
to Jehoi´akim the high priest,[a] the son
of Hilki´ah, son of Shallum, and to the
priests, and to all the people who were
present with him in Jerusalem. 8At the
same time, on the tenth day of Sivan,
Baruch[b] took the vessels of the house
of the Lord, which had been car-
ried away from the temple, to return
them to the land of Judah—the silver
vessels which Zedeki´ah the son of
Josi´ah, king of Judah, had made, 9af-
ter Nebuchadnez´zar king of Babylon
had carried away from Jerusalem
Jeconi´ah and the princes and the
prisoners and the mighty men and the
people of the land, and brought them
to Babylon.

A LETTER TO JERUSALEM

10 And they said: "Herewith
we send you money; so buy with
the money burnt offerings and sin
offerings and incense, and prepare a
cereal offering, and offer them upon
the altar of the Lord our God; 11and
pray for the life of Nebuchadnez´zar
king of Babylon, and for the life of
Belshaz´zar his son, that their days
on earth may be like the days of
heaven. 12And the Lord will give us
strength, and he will give light to
our eyes, and we shall live under the
protection[c] of Nebuchadnez´zar king
of Babylon, and under the protec-
tion[d] of Belshaz´zar his son, and we
shall serve them many days and find
favor in their sight. 13And pray for
us to the Lord our God, for we have
sinned against the Lord our God, and
to this day the anger of the Lord and
his wrath have not turned away from
us. 14And you shall read this book
which we are sending you, to make
your confession in the house of the
Lord on the days of the feasts and at
appointed seasons.

CONFESSION OF SINS

15 "And you shall say: 'Righ-
teousness belongs to the Lord our
God, but confusion of face, as at this
day, to us, to the men of Judah, to the
inhabitants of Jerusalem, 16and to our
kings and our princes and our priests
and our prophets and our fathers,
17because we have sinned before the
Lord, 18and have disobeyed him, and
have not heeded the voice of the Lord
our God, to walk in the statutes of the
Lord which he set before us. 19From
the day when the Lord brought our fa-
thers out of the land of Egypt until to-
day, we have been disobedient to the
Lord our God, and we have been neg-
ligent, in not heeding his voice. 20So to
this day there have clung to us the ca-
lamities and the curse which the Lord
declared through Moses his servant at

[a]Gk *the priest*
[b]Gk *he*
[c]Gk *in the shadow*
[d]Gk *in the shadow*

the time when he brought our fathers
out of the land of Egypt to give to us
a land flowing with milk and honey.
21 We did not heed the voice of the Lord
our God in all the words of the proph-
ets whom he sent to us, but we each
followed the intent of his own wicked
heart by serving other gods and doing
what is evil in the sight of the Lord
our God.

2 "'So the Lord confirmed his word,
which he spoke against us, and
against our judges who judged Israel,
and against our kings and against our
princes and against the men of Israel
and Judah. 2 Under the whole heaven
there has not been done the like of
what he has done in Jerusalem, in ac-
cordance with what is written in the
law of Moses, 3 that we should eat, one
the flesh of his son and another the
flesh of his daughter. 4 And he gave
them into subjection to all the king-
doms around us, to be a reproach and
a desolation among all the surround-
ing peoples, where the Lord has scat-
tered them. 5 They were brought low
and not raised up, because we sinned
against the Lord our God, in not heed-
ing his voice.

6 "'Righteousness belongs to the
Lord our God, but confusion of face
to us and our fathers, as at this day.
7 All those calamities with which the
Lord threatened us have come upon
us. 8 Yet we have not entreated the
favor of the Lord by turning away,
each of us, from the thoughts of his
wicked heart. 9 And the Lord has kept
the calamities ready, and the Lord has
brought them upon us, for the Lord
is righteous in all his works which
he has commanded us to do. 10 Yet we
have not obeyed his voice, to walk in
the statutes of the Lord which he set
before us.

PRAYER FOR DELIVERANCE

11 "'And now, O Lord God of
Israel, who didst bring thy peo-
ple out of the land of Egypt with a
mighty hand and with signs and
wonders and with great power and
outstretched arm, and hast made
thee a name, as at this day, 12 we have
sinned, we have been ungodly, we
have done wrong, O Lord our God,
against all thy ordinances. 13 Let thy
anger turn away from us, for we are
left, few in number, among the na-
tions where thou hast scattered us.
14 Hear, O Lord, our prayer and our
supplication, and for thy own sake
deliver us, and grant us favor in the
sight of those who have carried us
into exile; 15 that all the earth may
know that thou art the Lord our
God, for Israel and his descendants
are called by thy name. 16 O Lord,
look down from thy holy habitation,
and consider us. Incline thy ear, O
Lord, and hear; 17 open thy eyes, O
Lord, and see; for the dead who are
in Hades, whose spirit has been tak-
en from their bodies, will not ascribe
glory or justice to the Lord, 18 but the
person that is greatly distressed,[a]
that goes about bent over and feeble,
and the eyes that are failing, and the
person that hungers, will ascribe
to thee glory and righteousness, O
Lord. 19 For it is not because of any
righteous deeds of our fathers or our
kings that we bring before thee our
prayer for mercy, O Lord our God.
20 For thou hast sent thy anger and
thy wrath upon us, as thou didst de-
clare by thy servants the prophets,
saying: 21 "Thus says the Lord: Bend
your shoulders and serve the king
of Babylon, and you will remain in
the land which I gave to your fathers.
22 But if you will not obey the voice of
the Lord and will not serve the king
of Babylon, 23 I will make to cease
from the cities of Judah and from
the region about Jerusalem the voice
of mirth and the voice of gladness,
the voice of the bridegroom and the
voice of the bride, and the whole
land will be a desolation without
inhabitants."

[a] The meaning of the Greek is uncertain

24 "'But we did not obey thy voice,
to serve the king of Babylon; and thou
hast confirmed thy words, which thou
didst speak by thy servants the proph-
ets, that the bones of our kings and the
bones of our fathers would be brought
out of their graves;[b] 25and behold, they
have been cast out to the heat of day
and the frost of night. They perished
in great misery, by famine and sword
and pestilence. 26And the house which
is called by thy name thou hast made
as it is today, because of the wicked-
ness of the house of Israel and the
house of Judah.

GOD'S PROMISE RECALLED

27 "'Yet thou hast dealt with us, O
Lord our God, in all thy kindness and
in all thy great compassion, 28as thou
didst speak by thy servant Moses on
the day when thou didst command
him to write thy law in the presence
of the people of Israel, saying, 29"If
you will not obey my voice, this very
great multitude will surely turn into
a small number among the nations,
where I will scatter them. 30For I
know that they will not obey me, for
they are a stiff-necked people. But in
the land of their exile they will come
to themselves, 31and they will know
that I am the Lord their God. I will
give them a heart that obeys and ears
that hear; 32and they will praise me
in the land of their exile, and will
remember my name, 33and will turn
from their stubbornness and their
wicked deeds; for they will remember
the ways of their fathers, who sinned
before the Lord. 34I will bring them
again into the land which I swore to
give to their fathers, to Abraham and
to Isaac and to Jacob, and they will
rule over it; and I will increase them,
and they will not be diminished. 35I
will make an everlasting covenant
with them to be their God and they
shall be my people; and I will never
again remove my people Israel from
the land which I have given them."

[b]Gk *their place*

3 "'O Lord Almighty, God of Israel,
the soul in anguish and the wea-
ried spirit cry out to thee. 2Hear, O
Lord, and have mercy, for we have
sinned before thee. 3For thou art en-
throned for ever, and we are perish-
ing for ever. 4O Lord Almighty, God
of Israel, hear now the prayer of the
dead of Israel and of the sons of those
who sinned before thee, who did not
heed the voice of the Lord their God,
so that calamities have clung to us.
5Remember not the iniquities of our
fathers, but in this crisis remember
thy power and thy name. 6For thou art
the Lord our God, and thee, O Lord,
will we praise. 7For thou hast put the
fear of thee in our hearts in order that
we should call upon thy name; and
we will praise thee in our exile, for
we have put away from our hearts all
the iniquity of our fathers who sinned
before thee. 8Behold, we are today in
our exile where thou hast scattered
us, to be reproached and cursed and
punished for all the iniquities of our
fathers who forsook the Lord our
God.'"

IN PRAISE OF WISDOM

9Hear the commandments of life,
O Israel;
give ear, and learn wisdom!
10Why is it, O Israel, why is it that
you are in the land of your
enemies,
that you are growing old in a
foreign country,
that you are defiled with the
dead,
11that you are counted among
those in Hades?
12You have forsaken the fountain
of wisdom.
13If you had walked in the way of
God,
you would be dwelling in
peace for ever.
14Learn where there is wisdom,
where there is strength,
where there is understanding,

that you may at the same time
discern
where there is length of
days, and life,
where there is light for the
eyes, and peace.
15Who has found her place?
And who has entered her
storehouses?
16Where are the princes of the
nations,
and those who rule over the
beasts on earth;
17those who have sport with the
birds of the air,
and who hoard up silver and
gold,
in which men trust,
and there is no end to their
getting;
18those who scheme to get silver,
and are anxious,
whose labors are beyond
measure?
19They have vanished and gone
down to Hades,
and others have arisen in
their place.
20Young men have seen the light
of day,
and have dwelt upon the
earth;
but they have not learned the
way to knowledge,
nor understood her paths,
nor laid hold of her.
21Their sons have strayed far from
her[a] way.
22She has not been heard of in
Canaan,
nor seen in Teman;
23the sons of Hagar, who seek
for understanding on the
earth,
the merchants of Merran
and Teman,
the story-tellers and
the seekers for
understanding,
have not learned the way to
wisdom,
nor given thought to her
paths.
24O Israel, how great is the house
of God!
And how vast the territory
that he possesses!
25It is great and has no bounds;
it is high and
immeasurable.
26The giants were born there, who
were famous of old,
great in stature, expert in
war.
27God did not choose them,
nor give them the way to
knowledge;
28so they perished because they
had no wisdom,
they perished through their
folly.
29Who has gone up into heaven,
and taken her,
and brought her down from
the clouds?
30Who has gone over the sea, and
found her,
and will buy her for pure
gold?
31No one knows the way to her,
or is concerned about the
path to her.
32But he who knows all things
knows her,
he found her by his
understanding.
He who prepared the earth for
all time
filled it with four-footed
creatures;
33he who sends forth the light,
and it goes,
called it, and it obeyed him
in fear;
34the stars shone in their watches,
and were glad;
he called them, and they
said, "Here we are!"
They shone with gladness
for him who made
them.
35This is our God;

[a] Other authorities read *their*

no other can be compared
to him!
36He found the whole way to
knowledge,
and gave her to Jacob his
servant
and to Israel whom he
loved.
37Afterward she appeared upon
earth
and lived among men.
4 She is the book of the commandments of God,
and the law that endures for
ever.
All who hold her fast will live,
and those who forsake her
will die.
2Turn, O Jacob, and take her;
walk toward the shining of
her light.
3Do not give your glory to
another,
or your advantages to an
alien people.
4Happy are we, O Israel,
for we know what is pleasing
to God.

ENCOURAGEMENT FOR ISRAEL

5Take courage, my people,
O memorial of Israel!
6It was not for destruction
that you were sold to the
nations,
but you were handed over to
your enemies
because you angered God.
7For you provoked him who made
you,
by sacrificing to demons and
not to God.
8You forgot the everlasting God,
who brought you up,
and you grieved Jerusalem,
who reared you.
9For she saw the wrath that came
upon you from God,
and she said:
"Hearken, you neighbors of
Zion,
God has brought great
sorrow upon me;
10for I have seen the captivity of
my sons and daughters,
which the Everlasting
brought upon them.
11With joy I nurtured them,
but I sent them away with
weeping and sorrow.
12Let no one rejoice over me, a
widow
and bereaved of many;
I was left desolate because of
the sins of my children,
because they turned away
from the law of God.
13They had no regard for his
statutes;
they did not walk in the
ways of God's
commandments,
nor tread the paths of
discipline in his
righteousness.
14Let the neighbors of Zion come;
remember the capture
of my sons and
daughters,
which the Everlasting
brought upon them.
15For he brought against them a
nation from afar,
a shameless nation, of a
strange language,
who had no respect for an old
man,
and had no pity for a child.
16They led away the widow's
beloved sons,
and bereaved the lonely woman of her
daughters.
17"But I, how can I help you?
18For he who brought these calamities upon you
will deliver you from
the hand of your
enemies.
19Go, my children, go;
for I have been left
desolate.
20I have taken off the robe of
peace

and put on the sackcloth of
my supplication;
I will cry to the Everlasting
all my days.
21"Take courage, my children, cry
to God,
and he will deliver you from
the power and hand
of the enemy.
22For I have put my hope in the
Everlasting to save you,
and joy has come to me from
the Holy One,
because of the mercy which
soon will come to you
from your everlasting
Savior.[a]
23For I sent you out with sorrow
and weeping,
but God will give you back
to me with joy and
gladness for ever.
24For as the neighbors of Zion
have now seen your
capture,
so they soon will see your
salvation by God,
which will come to you with
great glory
and with the splendor of the
Everlasting.
25My children, endure with pa-
tience the wrath that has
come upon you from God.
Your enemy has overtaken
you,
but you will soon see their
destruction
and will tread upon their
necks.
26My tender sons have traveled
rough roads;
they were taken away like a
flock carried off by
the enemy.
27"Take courage, my children, and
cry to God,
for you will be remembered
by him who brought
this upon you.
28For just as you purposed to go
astray from God,
return with tenfold zeal to
seek him.
29For he who brought these calam-
ities upon you
will bring you everlast-
ing joy with your
salvation."

JERUSALEM IS ASSURED OF HELP

30Take courage, O Jerusalem,
for he who named you will
comfort you.
31Wretched will be those who
afflicted you
and rejoiced at your fall.
32Wretched will be the cities
which your children served
as slaves;
wretched will be the city
which received your
sons.
33For just as she rejoiced at your
fall
and was glad for your ruin,
so she will be grieved at her
own desolation.
34And I will take away her pride in
her great population,
and her insolence will be
turned to grief.
35For fire will come upon her from
the Everlasting for many
days,
and for a long time she
will be inhabited by
demons.
36Look toward the east, O
Jerusalem,
and see the joy that is com-
ing to you from God!
37Behold, your sons are coming,
whom you sent away;
they are coming, gathered
from east and west,
at the word of the Holy One,
rejoicing in the glory of
God.

5 Take off the garment of your
sorrow and affliction, O
Jerusalem,

[a] Or *from the Everlasting, your Savior*

and put on for ever the
beauty of the glory
from God.
2Put on the robe of the righteous-
ness from God;
put on your head the diadem
of the glory of the
Everlasting.
3For God will show your splen-
dor everywhere under
heaven.
4For your name will for ever be
called by God,
"Peace of righteousness and
glory of godliness."
5Arise, O Jerusalem, stand upon
the height
and look toward the east,
and see your children gathered
from west and east,
at the word of the Holy
One,
rejoicing that God has re-
membered them.
6For they went forth from you on
foot,
led away by their enemies;
but God will bring them back
to you,
carried in glory, as on a royal
throne.
7For God has ordered that every
high mountain and the
everlasting hills be made
low
and the valleys filled up, to
make level ground,
so that Israel may walk
safely in the glory of
God.
8The woods and every fragrant
tree
have shaded Israel at God's
command.
9For God will lead Israel with
joy,
in the light of his glory,
with the mercy and righ-
teousness that come
from him.

THE LETTER OF JEREMIAH

6 A copy of a letter which Jeremiah
sent to those who were to be tak-
en to Babylon as captives by the king
of the Babylonians, to give them the
message which God had commanded
him.

THE PEOPLE FACE A LONG CAPTIVITY

2 Because of the sins which you
have committed before God, you
will be taken to Babylon as captives
by Nebuchadnez´zar, king of the
Babylonians. 3Therefore when you
have come to Babylon you will re-
main there for many years, for a long
time, up to seven generations; after
that I will bring you away from there
in peace. 4Now in Babylon you will
see gods made of silver and gold and
wood, which are carried on men's
shoulders and inspire fear in the hea-
then. 5So take care not to become at
all like the foreigners or to let fear for
these gods[b] possess you, when you
see the multitude before and behind
them worshiping them. 6But say in
your heart, "It is thou, O Lord, whom
we must worship." 7For my angel is
with you, and he is watching your
lives.

THE HELPLESSNESS OF IDOLS

8 Their tongues are smoothed by
the craftsman, and they themselves
are overlaid with gold and silver;
but they are false and cannot speak.
9People[c] take gold and make crowns
for the heads of their gods, as they
would for a girl who loves ornaments;
10and sometimes the priests secretly
take gold and silver from their gods
and spend it upon themselves, 11and
even give some of it to the harlots in
the brothel. They deck their gods[d]
out with garments like men—these
gods of silver and gold and wood,
12which cannot save themselves from
rust and corrosion. When they have
been dressed in purple robes, 13their

[b] Gk *for them*
[c] Gk *They*
[d] Gk *them*

faces are wiped because of the dust
from the temple, which is thick upon
them. 14Like a local ruler the god[a]
holds a scepter, though unable to de-
stroy any one who offends it. 15It has
a dagger in its right hand, and has
an axe; but it cannot save itself from
war and robbers. 16Therefore they ev-
idently are not gods; so do not fear
them.

17 For just as one's dish is useless
when it is broken, so are the gods of
the heathen,[b] when they have been
set up in the temples. Their eyes are
full of the dust raised by the feet of
those who enter. 18And just as the
gates are shut on every side upon
a man who has offended a king, as
though he were sentenced to death,
so the priests make their temples
secure with doors and locks and
bars, in order that they may not be
plundered by robbers. 19They light
lamps, even more than they light for
themselves, though their gods[c] can
see none of them. 20They are[d] just
like a beam of the temple, but men
say their hearts have melted, when
worms from the earth devour them
and their robes. They do not notice
21when their faces have been black-
ened by the smoke of the temple.
22Bats, swallows, and birds light on
their bodies and heads; and so do
cats. 23From this you will know that
they are not gods; so do not fear
them.

24 As for the gold which they wear
for beauty—they will not shine un-
less some one wipes off the rust; for
even when they were being cast, they
had no feeling. 25They are bought at
any cost, but there is no breath in
them. 26Having no feet, they are car-
ried on men's shoulders, revealing to
mankind their worthlessness. 27And
those who serve them are ashamed
because through them these gods[e]
are made to stand, lest they fall to the
ground. If any one sets one of them
upright, it cannot move itself; and if
it is tipped over, it cannot straighten
itself; but gifts are placed before them
just as before the dead. 28The priests
sell the sacrifices that are offered to
these gods[f] and use the money; and
likewise their wives preserve some
with salt, but give none to the poor or
helpless. 29Sacrifices to them may be
touched by women in menstruation or
at childbirth. Since you know by these
things that they are not gods, do not
fear them.

30 For why should they be called
gods? Women serve meals for gods
of silver and gold and wood; 31and in
their temples the priests sit with their
clothes rent, their heads and beards
shaved, and their heads uncovered.
32They howl and shout before their
gods as some do at a funeral feast
for a man who has died. 33The priests
take some of the clothing of their
gods[g] to clothe their wives and chil-
dren. 34Whether one does evil to them
or good, they will not be able to re-
pay it. They cannot set up a king or
depose one. 35Likewise they are not
able to give either wealth or money;
if one makes a vow to them and does
not keep it, they will not require it.
36They cannot save a man from death
or rescue the weak from the strong.
37They cannot restore sight to a blind
man; they cannot rescue a man who
is in distress. 38They cannot take pity
on a widow or do good to an orphan.
39These things that are made of wood
and overlaid with gold and silver are
like stones from the mountain, and
those who serve them will be put
to shame. 40Why then must any one
think that they are gods, or call them
gods?

[a] Gk *he*
[b] Gk *of them*
[c] Gk *they*
[d] Gk *It is*
[e] Gk *they*
[f] Gk *to them*
[g] Gk *them*

THE FOOLISHNESS OF WORSHIPING IDOLS

Besides, even the Chalde´ans them-
selves dishonor them; 41for when
they see a dumb man, who cannot
speak, they bring him and pray Bel[h]
that the man may speak, as though
Bel[i] were able to understand. 42Yet
they themselves cannot perceive this
and abandon them, for they have no
sense. 43And the women, with cords
about them, sit along the passage-
ways, burning bran for incense; and
when one of them is led off by one
of the passers-by and is lain with,
she derides the woman next to her,
because she was not as attractive as
herself and her cord was not broken.
44Whatever is done for them is false.
Why then must any one think that
they are gods, or call them gods?

45 They are made by carpenters
and goldsmiths; they can be nothing
but what the craftsmen wish them to
be. 46The men that make them will
certainly not live very long them-
selves; how then can the things that
are made by them be gods? 47They
have left only lies and reproach for
those who come after. 48For when war
or calamity comes upon them, the
priests consult together as to where
they can hide themselves and their
gods.[j] 49How then can one fail to see
that these are not gods, for they can-
not save themselves from war or ca-
lamity? 50Since they are made of wood
and overlaid with gold and silver, it
will afterward be known that they are
false. 51It will be manifest to all the
nations and kings that they are not
gods but the work of men's hands, and
that there is no work of God in them.
52Who then can fail to know that they
are not gods?[k]

53 For they cannot set up a king
over a country or give rain to men.
54They cannot judge their own cause or
deliver one who is wronged, for they
have no power; they are like crows
between heaven and earth. 55When
fire breaks out in a temple of wooden
gods overlaid with gold or silver, their
priests will flee and escape, but the
gods[l] will be burnt in two like beams.
56Besides, they can offer no resistance
to a king or any enemies. Why then
must any one admit or think that they
are gods?

57 Gods made of wood and over-
laid with silver and gold are not able
to save themselves from thieves and
robbers. 58Strong men will strip them
of their gold and silver and of the
robes they wear, and go off with this
booty, and they will not be able to
help themselves. 59So it is better to
be a king who shows his courage, or a
household utensil that serves its own-
er's need, than to be these false gods;
better even the door of a house that
protects its contents, than these false
gods; better also a wooden pillar in a
palace, than these false gods.

60 For sun and moon and stars,
shining and sent forth for service,
are obedient. 61So also the lightning,
when it flashes, is widely seen; and
the wind likewise blows in every land.
62When God commands the clouds to
go over the whole world, they carry
out his command. 63And the fire sent
from above to consume mountains
and woods does what it is ordered.
But these idols[m] are not to be com-
pared with them in appearance or
power. 64Therefore one must not think
that they are gods nor call them gods,
for they are not able either to decide a
case or to do good to men. 65Since you
know then that they are not gods, do
not fear them.

66 For they can neither curse
nor bless kings; 67they cannot show
signs in the heavens and[n] among the

[h] Or *they bring Bel and pray*
[i] Gk *he*
[j] Gk *them*
[k] The Greek text of this verse is uncertain
[l] Gk *they*
[m] Gk *these things*
[n] Other ancient authorities omit *and*

nations, or shine like the sun or give
light like the moon. 68The wild beasts
are better than they are, for they can
flee to cover and help themselves. 69So
we have no evidence whatever that
they are gods; therefore do not fear
them.

70 Like a scarecrow in a cucumber
bed, that guards nothing, so are their
gods of wood, overlaid with gold and
silver. 71In the same way, their gods of
wood, overlaid with gold and silver,
are like a thorn bush in a garden, on
which every bird sits; or like a dead
body cast out in the darkness. 72By the
purple and linen[a] that rot upon them
you will know that they are not gods;
and they will finally themselves be
consumed, and be a reproach in the
land. 73Better therefore is a just man
who has no idols, for he will be far
from reproach.

[a]Cn: Gk *marble*, Syr *silk*

THE BOOK OF

EZEKIEL

THE VISION OF THE CHARIOT

1 In the thirtieth year, in the fourth
month, on the fifth day of the month,
as I was among the exiles by the riv-
er Chebar, the heavens were opened,
and I saw visions of God. 2On the fifth
day of the month (it was the fifth year
of the exile of King Jehoi´achin), 3the
word of the LORD came to Ezekiel the
priest, the son of Buzi, in the land of
the Chalde´ans by the river Chebar;
and the hand of the LORD was upon
him there.

4 As I looked, behold, a stormy
wind came out of the north, and a
great cloud, with brightness round
about it, and fire flashing forth con-
tinually, and in the midst of the fire,
as it were gleaming bronze. 5And
from the midst of it came the likeness
of four living creatures.* And this
was their appearance: they had the
form of men, 6but each had four fac-
es, and each of them had four wings.
7Their legs were straight, and the
soles of their feet were like the sole
of a calf's foot; and they sparkled like
burnished bronze. 8Under their wings
on their four sides they had human
hands. And the four had their faces
and their wings thus: 9their wings
touched one another; they went ev-
ery one straight forward, without
turning as they went. 10As for the
likeness of their faces, each had the
face of a man in front;[a] the four had
the face of a lion on the right side,
the four had the face of an ox on the
left side, and the four had the face
of an eagle at the back.[b] 11Such were
their faces. And their wings were
spread out above; each creature had
two wings, each of which touched
the wing of another, while two cov-
ered their bodies. 12And each went
straight forward; wherever the spirit
would go, they went, without turning
as they went. 13In the midst of[c] the
living creatures there was something
that looked like burning coals of fire,
like torches moving to and fro among
the living creatures; and the fire was
bright, and out of the fire went forth
lightning. 14And the living creatures
darted to and fro, like a flash of
lightning.

15 Now as I looked at the living
creatures, I saw a wheel upon the
earth beside the living creatures, one
for each of the four of them.[d] 16As for
the appearance of the wheels and
their construction: their appearance
was like the gleaming of a chrysolite;
and the four had the same likeness,
their construction being as it were a
wheel within a wheel. 17When they
went, they went in any of their four
directions[e] without turning as they
went. 18The four wheels had rims and
they had spokes;[f] and their rims were
full of eyes round about. 19And when
the living creatures went, the wheels
went beside them; and when the liv-
ing creatures rose from the earth, the
wheels rose. 20Wherever the spirit
would go, they went, and the wheels
rose along with them; for the spirit of
the living creatures was in the wheels.
21When those went, these went; and
when those stood, these stood; and
when those rose from the earth, the
wheels rose along with them; for the
spirit of the living creatures was in
the wheels.

22 Over the heads of the living
creatures there was the likeness of

[a] Cn: Heb lacks *in front*
[b] Cn: Heb lacks *at the back*
[c] Gk Old Latin: Heb *And the likeness of*
[d] Heb *of their faces*
[e] Heb *on their four sides*
[f] Cn: Heb uncertain

a firmament, shining like crystal,[a]
spread out above their heads. 23And
under the firmament their wings
were stretched out straight, one
toward another; and each creature
had two wings covering its body.*
24And when they went, I heard the
sound of their wings like the sound
of many waters, like the thunder of
the Almighty, a sound of tumult like
the sound of a host; when they stood
still, they let down their wings.
25And there came a voice from above
the firmament over their heads;
when they stood still, they let down
their wings.

26 And above the firmament over
their heads there was the likeness
of a throne, in appearance like sap-
phire;[b] and seated above the likeness
of a throne was a likeness as it were
of a human form. 27And upward from
what had the appearance of his loins
I saw as it were gleaming bronze, like
the appearance of fire enclosed round
about; and downward from what had
the appearance of his loins I saw as it
were the appearance of fire, and there
was brightness round about him.[c]
28Like the appearance of the bow that
is in the cloud on the day of rain, so
was the appearance of the brightness
round about.

Such was the appearance of the
likeness of the glory of the LORD.*
And when I saw it, I fell upon my face,
and I heard the voice of one speaking.

THE VISION OF THE SCROLL

2And he said to me, "Son of man,
stand upon your feet, and I will
speak with you." 2And when he
spoke to me, the Spirit entered into
me and set me upon my feet; and I
heard him speaking to me. 3And he
said to me, "Son of man, I send you
to the people of Israel, to a nation[d]
of rebels, who have rebelled against
me; they and their fathers have
transgressed against me to this very
day. 4The people also are impudent
and stubborn: I send you to them;
and you shall say to them, 'Thus says
the Lord GOD.' 5And whether they
hear or refuse to hear (for they are
a rebellious house) they will know
that there has been a prophet among
them. 6And you, son of man, be not
afraid of them, nor be afraid of their
words, though briers and thorns are
with you and you sit upon scorpions;
be not afraid of their words, nor be
dismayed at their looks, for they are
a rebellious house. 7And you shall
speak my words to them, whether
they hear or refuse to hear; for they
are a rebellious house.

8 "But you, son of man, hear
what I say to you; be not rebellious
like that rebellious house; open your
mouth, and eat what I give you." 9And
when I looked, behold, a hand was
stretched out to me, and lo, a writ-
ten scroll was in it; 10and he spread
it before me; and it had writing on
the front and on the back, and there
were written on it words of lam-
entation and mourning and woe.
3And he said to me, "Son of man,
eat what is offered to you; eat this
scroll, and go, speak to the house of
Israel." 2So I opened my mouth, and
he gave me the scroll to eat. 3And he
said to me, "Son of man, eat this scroll
that I give you and fill your stomach
with it." Then I ate it; and it was in my
mouth as sweet as honey.

4 And he said to me, "Son of man,
go, get you to the house of Israel, and
speak with my words to them. 5For
you are not sent to a people of for-
eign speech and a hard language, but
to the house of Israel 6not to many
peoples of foreign speech and a hard
language, whose words you cannot
understand. Surely, if I sent you to
such, they would listen to you. 7But
the house of Israel will not listen to

[a] Gk: Heb *awesome crystal*
[b] Heb *lapis lazuli*
[c] Or *it*
[d] Syr: Heb *nations*

you; for they are not willing to lis-
ten to me; because all the house of
Israel are of a hard forehead and of
a stubborn heart. 8Behold, I have
made your face hard against their
faces, and your forehead hard against
their foreheads. 9Like adamant hard-
er than flint have I made your fore-
head; fear them not, nor be dismayed
at their looks, for they are a rebel-
lious house." 10Moreover he said to
me, "Son of man, all my words that
I shall speak to you receive in your
heart, and hear with your ears. 11And
go, get you to the exiles, to your peo-
ple, and say to them, 'Thus says the
Lord GOD'; whether they hear or re-
fuse to hear."

EZEKIEL AT THE RIVER CHEBAR

12 Then the Spirit lifted me up,
and as the glory of the LORD arose[e]
from its place, I heard behind me the
sound of a great earthquake; 13it was
the sound of the wings of the living
creatures as they touched one anoth-
er, and the sound of the wheels beside
them, that sounded like a great earth-
quake. 14The Spirit lifted me up and
took me away, and I went in bitterness
in the heat of my spirit, the hand of
the LORD being strong upon me; 15and
I came to the exiles at Tel-a´bib, who
dwelt by the river Chebar.[f] And I sat
there overwhelmed among them sev-
en days.

16 And at the end of seven days,
the word of the LORD came to me:
17"Son of man, I have made you a
watchman for the house of Israel;
whenever you hear a word from my
mouth, you shall give them warning
from me. 18If I say to the wicked, 'You
shall surely die,' and you give him no
warning, nor speak to warn the wick-
ed from his wicked way, in order to
save his life, that wicked man shall
die in his iniquity; but his blood I
will require at your hand. 19But if you
warn the wicked, and he does not
turn from his wickedness, or from
his wicked way, he shall die in his in-
iquity; but you will have saved your
life. 20Again, if a righteous man turns
from his righteousness and commits
iniquity, and I lay a stumbling block
before him, he shall die; because you
have not warned him, he shall die for
his sin, and his righteous deeds which
he has done shall not be remembered;
but his blood I will require at your
hand. 21Nevertheless if you warn the
righteous man not to sin, and he does
not sin, he shall surely live, because
he took warning; and you will have
saved your life."

EZEKIEL ISOLATED AND SILENCED

22 And the hand of the LORD was
there upon me; and he said to me,
"Arise, go forth into the plain,[g] and
there I will speak with you." 23So I
arose and went forth into the plain;[h]
and lo, the glory of the LORD stood
there, like the glory which I had seen
by the river Chebar; and I fell on my
face. 24But the Spirit entered into me,
and set me upon my feet; and he spoke
with me and said to me, "Go, shut
yourself within your house. 25And
you, O son of man, behold, cords will
be placed upon you, and you shall be
bound with them, so that you cannot
go out among the people; 26and I will
make your tongue cleave to the roof of
your mouth, so that you shall be dumb
and unable to reprove them; for they
are a rebellious house. 27But when
I speak with you, I will open your
mouth, and you shall say to them,
'Thus says the Lord GOD'; he that will
hear, let him hear; and he that will re-
fuse to hear, let him refuse; for they
are a rebellious house.

THE SIEGE OF JERUSALEM PORTRAYED

4 "And you, O son of man, take a
brick and lay it before you, and

[e]Cn: Heb *blessed be the glory of the* Lord
[f]Heb *Chebar, and to where they dwelt.* Another reading is *Chebar, and I sat where they sat*
[g]Or *valley*
[h]Or *valley*

portray upon it a city, even Jerusalem;
2and put siegeworks against it, and
build a siege wall against it, and cast
up a mound against it; set camps also
against it, and plant battering rams
against it round about. 3And take
an iron plate, and place it as an iron
wall between you and the city; and
set your face toward it, and let it be
in a state of siege, and press the siege
against it. This is a sign for the house
of Israel.

4 "Then lie upon your left side,
and I will lay the punishment of the
house of Israel upon you;[a] for the
number of the days that you lie upon
it, you shall bear their punishment.
5For I assign to you a number of
days, three hundred and ninety days,
equal to the number of the years of
their punishment; so long shall you
bear the punishment of the house of
Israel. 6And when you have complet-
ed these, you shall lie down a sec-
ond time, but on your right side, and
bear the punishment of the house of
Judah; forty days I assign you, a day
for each year. 7And you shall set your
face toward the siege of Jerusalem,
with your arm bared; and you shall
prophesy against the city. 8And be-
hold, I will put cords upon you, so
that you cannot turn from one side to
the other, till you have completed the
days of your siege.

9 "And you, take wheat and bar-
ley, beans and lentils, millet and
spelt, and put them into a single ves-
sel, and make bread of them. During
the number of days that you lie upon
your side, three hundred and ninety
days, you shall eat it. 10And the food
which you eat shall be by weight,
twenty shekels a day; once a day you
shall eat it. 11And water you shall
drink by measure, the sixth part of a
hin; once a day you shall drink. 12And
you shall eat it as a barley cake, bak-
ing it in their sight on human dung."
13And the LORD said, "Thus shall the
people of Israel eat their bread un-
clean, among the nations whither I
will drive them." 14Then I said, "Ah
Lord GOD! behold, I have never de-
filed myself; from my youth up till
now I have never eaten what died
of itself or was torn by beasts, nor
has foul flesh come into my mouth."
15Then he said to me, "See, I will let
you have cow's dung instead of hu-
man dung, on which you may prepare
your bread." 16Moreover he said to
me, "Son of man, behold, I will break
the staff of bread in Jerusalem; they
shall eat bread by weight and with
fearfulness; and they shall drink
water by measure and in dismay. 17I
will do this that they may lack bread
and water, and look at one another in
dismay, and waste away under their
punishment.

A SWORD AGAINST JERUSALEM

5 "And you, O son of man, take a
sharp sword; use it as a barber's
razor and pass it over your head
and your beard; then take balances
for weighing, and divide the hair.
2A third part you shall burn in the
fire in the midst of the city, when
the days of the siege are completed;
and a third part you shall take and
strike with the sword round about
the city; and a third part you shall
scatter to the wind, and I will un-
sheathe the sword after them. 3And
you shall take from these a small
number, and bind them in the skirts
of your robe. 4And of these again you
shall take some, and cast them into
the fire, and burn them in the fire;
from there a fire will come forth into
all the house of Israel. 5Thus says the
Lord GOD: This is Jerusalem; I have
set her in the center of the nations,
with countries round about her. 6And
she has wickedly rebelled against
my ordinances[b] more than the na-
tions, and against my statutes more
than the countries round about her,

[a] Cn: Heb *you shall lay .. upon it*
[b] Or *changed my ordinances into wickedness*

by rejecting my ordinances and not
walking in my statutes. 7Therefore
thus says the Lord GOD: Because you
are more turbulent than the nations
that are round about you, and have
not walked in my statutes or kept my
ordinances, but have acted[c] according
to the ordinances of the nations that
are round about you; 8therefore thus
says the Lord GOD: Behold, I, even
I, am against you; and I will execute
judgments in the midst of you in the
sight of the nations. 9And because
of all your abominations I will do
with you what I have never yet done,
and the like of which I will never do
again. 10Therefore fathers shall eat
their sons in the midst of you, and
sons shall eat their fathers; and I will
execute judgments on you, and any
of you who survive I will scatter to
all the winds. 11Wherefore, as I live,
says the Lord GOD, surely, because
you have defiled my sanctuary with
all your detestable things and with
all your abominations, therefore I
will cut you down;[d] my eye will not
spare, and I will have no pity. 12A
third part of you shall die of pesti-
lence and be consumed with famine
in the midst of you; a third part shall
fall by the sword round about you;
and a third part I will scatter to all
the winds and will unsheathe the
sword after them.

13 "Thus shall my anger spend
itself, and I will vent my fury upon
them and satisfy myself; and they
shall know that I, the LORD, have
spoken in my jealousy, when I spend
my fury upon them. 14Moreover I will
make you a desolation and an object
of reproach among the nations round
about you and in the sight of all that
pass by. 15You shall be[e] a reproach
and a taunt, a warning and a hor-
ror, to the nations round about you,
when I execute judgments on you
in anger and fury, and with furious
chastisements—I, the LORD, have
spoken 16when I loose against you[f]
my deadly arrows of famine, arrows
for destruction, which I will loose
to destroy you, and when I bring
more and more famine upon you,
and break your staff of bread. 17I will
send famine and wild beasts against
you, and they will rob you of your
children; pestilence and blood shall
pass through you; and I will bring
the sword upon you. I, the LORD,
have spoken."

JUDGMENT ON IDOLATROUS ISRAEL

6 The word of the LORD came to me:
2"Son of man, set your face toward
the mountains of Israel, and prophe-
sy against them, 3and say, You moun-
tains of Israel, hear the word of the
Lord GOD! Thus says the Lord GOD
to the mountains and the hills, to the
ravines and the valleys: Behold, I,
even I, will bring a sword upon you,
and I will destroy your high places.
4Your altars shall become desolate,
and your incense altars shall be bro-
ken; and I will cast down your slain
before your idols. 5And I will lay the
dead bodies of the people of Israel
before their idols; and I will scatter
your bones round about your altars.
6Wherever you dwell your cities shall
be waste and your high places ru-
ined, so that your altars will be waste
and ruined,[g] your idols broken and
destroyed, your incense altars cut
down, and your works wiped out.
7And the slain shall fall in the midst
of you, and you shall know that I am
the LORD.

8 "Yet I will leave some of you
alive. When you have among the na-
tions some who escape the sword,
and when you are scattered through
the countries, 9then those of you who
escape will remember me among the

[c] Another reading is *and have not acted*
[d] Another reading is *I will withdraw*
[e] Gk Syr Vg Tg: Heb *And it shall be*
[f] Heb *them*
[g] Syr Vg Tg: Heb *and be made guilty*

nations where they are carried captive, when I have broken[a] their wanton heart which has departed from me, and blinded their eyes which turn wantonly after their idols; and they will be loathsome in their own sight for the evils which they have committed, for all their abominations. 10And they shall know that I am the LORD; I have not said in vain that I would do this evil to them."

11 Thus says the Lord GOD: "Clap your hands, and stamp your foot, and say, Alas! because of all the evil abominations of the house of Israel; for they shall fall by the sword, by famine, and by pestilence. 12He that is far off shall die of pestilence; and he that is near shall fall by the sword; and he that is left and is preserved shall die of famine. Thus I will spend my fury upon them. 13And you shall know that I am the LORD, when their slain lie among their idols round about their altars, upon every high hill, on all the mountain tops, under every green tree, and under every leafy oak, wherever they offered pleasing odor to all their idols. 14And I will stretch out my hand against them, and make the land desolate and waste, throughout all their habitations, from the wilderness to Riblah.[b] Then they will know that I am the LORD."

IMPENDING DISASTER

7 The word of the LORD came to me: 2"And you, O son of man, thus says the Lord GOD to the land of Israel: An end! The end has come upon the four corners of the land. 3Now the end is upon you, and I will let loose my anger upon you, and will judge you according to your ways; and I will punish you for all your abominations. 4And my eye will not spare you, nor will I have pity; but I will punish you for your ways, while your abominations are in your midst. Then you will know that I am the LORD.

5 "Thus says the Lord GOD: Disaster after disaster! Behold, it comes. 6An end has come, the end has come; it has awakened against you. Behold, it comes. 7Your doom[c] has come to you, O inhabitant of the land; the time has come, the day is near, a day of tumult, and not of joyful shouting upon the mountains. 8Now I will soon pour out my wrath upon you, and spend my anger against you, and judge you according to your ways; and I will punish you for all your abominations. 9And my eye will not spare, nor will I have pity; I will punish you according to your ways, while your abominations are in your midst. Then you will know that I am the LORD, who smite.

10 "Behold, the day! Behold, it comes! Your doom[d] has come, injustice[e] has blossomed, pride has budded. 11Violence has grown up into a rod of wickedness; none of them shall remain, nor their abundance, nor their wealth; neither shall there be pre-eminence among them.[f] 12The time has come, the day draws near. Let not the buyer rejoice, nor the seller mourn, for wrath is upon all their multitude. 13For the seller shall not return to what he has sold, while they live. For wrath[g] is upon all their multitude; it shall not turn back; and because of his iniquity, none can maintain his life.[h]

14 "They have blown the trumpet and made all ready; but none goes to battle, for my wrath is upon all their multitude. 15The sword is without,

[a] Syr Vg Tg: Heb *I have been broken*
[b] Another reading is *Diblah*
[c] The meaning of the Hebrew word is uncertain
[d] The meaning of the Hebrew word is uncertain
[e] Or *the rod*
[f] The Hebrew of verse 11 is uncertain
[g] Cn: Heb *vision*
[h] Heb obscure

pestilence and famine are within; he that is in the field dies by the sword; and him that is in the city famine and pestilence devour. 16And if any survivors escape, they will be on the mountains, like doves of the valleys, all of them moaning, every one over his iniquity. 17All hands are feeble, and all knees weak as water. 18They gird themselves with sackcloth, and horror covers them; shame is upon all faces, and baldness on all their heads. 19They cast their silver into the streets, and their gold is like an unclean thing; their silver and gold are not able to deliver them in the day of the wrath of the LORD; they cannot satisfy their hunger or fill their stomachs with it. For it was the stumbling block of their iniquity. 20Their[i] beautiful ornament they used for vainglory, and they made their abominable images and their detestable things of it; therefore I will make it an unclean thing to them. 21And I will give it into the hands of foreigners for a prey, and to the wicked of the earth for a spoil; and they shall profane it. 22I will turn my face from them, that they may profane my precious[j] place; robbers shall enter and profane it, 23and make a desolation.[k] "Because the land is full of bloody crimes and the city is full of violence, 24I will bring the worst of the nations to take possession of their houses; I will put an end to their proud might, and their holy places shall be profaned. 25When anguish comes, they will seek peace, but there shall be none. 26Disaster comes upon disaster, rumor follows rumor; they seek a vision from the prophet, but the law perishes from the priest, and counsel from the elders. 27The king mourns, the prince is wrapped in despair, and the hands of the people of the land are palsied by terror. According to their way I will do to them, and according to their own judgments I will judge them; and they shall know that I am the LORD."

ABOMINATIONS IN THE TEMPLE

8 In the sixth year, in the sixth month, on the fifth day of the month, as I sat in my house, with the elders of Judah sitting before me, the hand of the Lord GOD fell there upon me. 2Then I beheld, and lo, a form that had the appearance of a man;[l] below what appeared to be his loins it was fire, and above his loins it was like the appearance of brightness, like gleaming bronze. 3He put forth the form of a hand, and took me by a lock of my head; and the Spirit lifted me up between earth and heaven, and brought me in visions of God to Jerusalem, to the entrance of the gateway of the inner court that faces north, where was the seat of the image of jealousy, which provokes to jealousy. 4And behold, the glory of the God of Israel was there, like the vision that I saw in the plain.

5 Then he said to me, "Son of man, lift up your eyes now in the direction of the north." So I lifted up my eyes toward the north, and behold, north of the altar gate, in the entrance, was this image of jealousy. 6And he said to me, "Son of man, do you see what they are doing, the great abominations that the house of Israel are committing here, to drive me far from my sanctuary? But you will see still greater abominations."

7 And he brought me to the door of the court; and when I looked, behold, there was a hole in the wall. 8Then said he to me, "Son of man, dig in the wall"; and when I dug in the wall, lo, there was a door. 9And he said to me, "Go in, and see the vile abominations that they are committing here." 10So I went in and saw;

[i]Syr Symmachus: Heb *Its*
[j]Or *secret*
[k]Cn: Heb *make the chain*
[l]Gk: Heb *fire*

and there, portrayed upon the wall
round about, were all kinds of creep-
ing things, and loathsome beasts,
and all the idols of the house of
Israel. 11And before them stood sev-
enty men of the elders of the house
of Israel, with Ja-azani´ah the son of
Shaphan standing among them. Each
had his censer in his hand, and the
smoke of the cloud of incense went
up. 12Then he said to me, "Son of
man, have you seen what the elders
of the house of Israel are doing in the
dark, every man in his room[a] of pic-
tures? For they say, 'The LORD does
not see us, the LORD has forsaken
the land.'" 13He said also to me, "You
will see still greater abominations
which they commit."

14 Then he brought me to the en-
trance of the north gate of the house
of the LORD; and behold, there sat
women weeping for Tammuz.* 15Then
he said to me, "Have you seen this, O
son of man? You will see still greater
abominations than these."

16 And he brought me into the in-
ner court of the house of the LORD;
and behold, at the door of the tem-
ple of the LORD, between the porch
and the altar, were about twenty-five
men, with their backs to the temple
of the LORD, and their faces toward
the east, worshiping the sun toward
the east. 17Then he said to me, "Have
you seen this, O son of man? Is it
too slight a thing for the house of
Judah to commit the abominations
which they commit here, that they
should fill the land with violence,
and provoke me further to anger?
Lo, they put the branch to their nose.
18Therefore I will deal in wrath; my
eye will not spare, nor will I have
pity; and though they cry in my ears
with a loud voice, I will not hear
them."

THE SLAUGHTER OF THE IDOLATERS

9 Then he cried in my ears with a
loud voice, saying, "Draw near, you
executioners of the city, each with
his destroying weapon in his hand."
2And lo, six men came from the di-
rection of the upper gate, which faces
north, every man with his weapon for
slaughter in his hand, and with them
was a man clothed in linen, with a
writing case at his side. And they
went in and stood beside the bronze
altar.

3 Now the glory of the God of
Israel had gone up from the cherubim
on which it rested to the threshold of
the house; and he called to the man
clothed in linen, who had the writ-
ing case at his side. 4And the LORD
said to him, "Go through the city,
through Jerusalem, and put a mark
upon the foreheads of the men who
sigh and groan over all the abomina-
tions that are committed in it." 5And
to the others he said in my hearing,
"Pass through the city after him, and
smite; your eye shall not spare, and
you shall show no pity; 6slay old men
outright, young men and maidens,
little children and women, but touch
no one upon whom is the mark. And
begin at my sanctuary." So they be-
gan with the elders who were before
the house. 7Then he said to them,
"Defile the house, and fill the courts
with the slain. Go forth." So they
went forth, and smote in the city.
8And while they were smiting, and
I was left alone, I fell upon my face,
and cried, "Ah Lord GOD! wilt thou
destroy all that remains of Israel in
the outpouring of thy wrath upon
Jerusalem?"

9 Then he said to me, "The guilt
of the house of Israel and Judah is
exceedingly great; the land is full of
blood, and the city full of injustice;
for they say, 'The LORD has forsaken
the land, and the LORD does not see.'
10As for me, my eye will not spare, nor
will I have pity, but I will requite their
deeds upon their heads."

11 And lo, the man clothed in lin-
en, with the writing case at his side,

[a]Gk Syr Vg Tg: Heb *rooms*

brought back word, saying, "I have
done as thou didst command me."

GOD'S GLORY LEAVES JERUSALEM

10 Then I looked, and behold, on
the firmament that was over
the heads of the cherubim there
appeared above them something
like a sapphire, in form resembling
a throne. 2And he said to the man
clothed in linen, "Go in among the
whirling wheels underneath the
cherubim; fill your hands with burn-
ing coals from between the cheru-
bim, and scatter them over the city."
And he went in before my eyes. 3Now
the cherubim were standing on the
south side of the house, when the
man went in; and a cloud filled the
inner court. 4And the glory of the
LORD went up from the cherubim to
the threshold of the house; and the
house was filled with the cloud, and
the court was full of the brightness
of the glory of the LORD. 5And the
sound of the wings of the cherubim
was heard as far as the outer court,
like the voice of God Almighty when
he speaks.

6 And when he commanded the
man clothed in linen, "Take fire from
between the whirling wheels, from
between the cherubim," he went in
and stood beside a wheel. 7And a cher-
ub stretched forth his hand from be-
tween the cherubim to the fire that
was between the cherubim, and took
some of it, and put it into the hands
of the man clothed in linen, who took
it and went out. 8The cherubim ap-
peared to have the form of a human
hand under their wings.

9 And I looked, and behold, there
were four wheels beside the cher-
ubim, one beside each cherub; and
the appearance of the wheels was
like sparkling chrysolite. 10And as
for their appearance, the four had
the same likeness, as if a wheel were
within a wheel. 11When they went,
they went in any of their four di-
rections[b] without turning as they
went, but in whatever direction the
front wheel faced the others followed
without turning as they went. 12And[c]
their rims, and their spokes,[d] and
the wheels were full of eyes round
about—the wheels that the four of
them had. 13As for the wheels, they
were called in my hearing the whirl-
ing wheels. 14And every one had four
faces: the first face was the face of
the cherub, and the second face was
the face of a man, and the third the
face of a lion, and the fourth the face
of an eagle.

15 And the cherubim mounted
up. These were the living creatures
that I saw by the river Chebar.
16And when the cherubim went,
the wheels went beside them; and
when the cherubim lifted up their
wings to mount up from the earth,
the wheels did not turn from beside
them. 17When they stood still, these
stood still, and when they mounted
up, these mounted up with them; for
the spirit of the living creatures[e] was
in them.

18 Then the glory of the LORD
went forth from the threshold of
the house, and stood over the cher-
ubim. 19And the cherubim lifted up
their wings and mounted up from
the earth in my sight as they went
forth, with the wheels beside them;
and they stood at the door of the east
gate of the house of the LORD; and
the glory of the God of Israel was
over them.

20 These were the living crea-
tures that I saw underneath the God
of Israel by the river Chebar; and I
knew that they were cherubim. 21Each
had four faces, and each four wings,
and underneath their wings the sem-
blance of human hands. 22And as for
the likeness of their faces, they were

[b] Heb *on their four sides*
[c] Gk: Heb *And their whole body and*
[d] Heb *spokes and their wings*
[e] Or *of life*

the very faces whose appearance I had
seen by the river Chebar. They went
every one straight forward.

JUDGMENT ON WICKED COUNSELORS

11 The Spirit lifted me up, and
brought me to the east gate of the
house of the LORD, which faces east.
And behold, at the door of the gate-
way there were twenty-five men; and
I saw among them Ja-azani´ah the
son of Azzur, and Pelati´ah the son of
Benai´ah, princes of the people. 2And
he said to me, "Son of man, these are
the men who devise iniquity and who
give wicked counsel in this city; 3who
say, 'The time is not near[a] to build
houses; this city is the caldron, and
we are the flesh.' 4Therefore proph-
esy against them, prophesy, O son of
man."

5 And the Spirit of the LORD fell
upon me, and he said to me, "Say,
Thus says the LORD: So you think, O
house of Israel; for I know the things
that come into your mind. 6You have
multiplied your slain in this city, and
have filled its streets with the slain.
7Therefore thus says the Lord GOD:
Your slain whom you have laid in the
midst of it, they are the flesh, and
this city is the caldron; but you shall
be brought forth out of the midst of
it. 8You have feared the sword; and I
will bring the sword upon you, says
the Lord GOD. 9And I will bring you
forth out of the midst of it, and give
you into the hands of foreigners, and
execute judgments upon you. 10You
shall fall by the sword; I will judge
you at the border of Israel; and you
shall know that I am the LORD. 11This
city shall not be your caldron, nor
shall you be the flesh in the midst
of it; I will judge you at the border of
Israel; 12and you shall know that I am
the LORD; for you have not walked
in my statutes, nor executed my
ordinances, but have acted according
to the ordinances of the nations that
are round about you."

13 And it came to pass, while I was
prophesying, that Pelati´ah the son
of Benai´ah died. Then I fell down
upon my face, and cried with a loud
voice, and said, "Ah Lord GOD! wilt
thou make a full end of the remnant
of Israel?"

GOD WILL RESTORE ISRAEL

14 And the word of the LORD
came to me: 15"Son of man, your
brethren, even your brethren, your
fellow exiles,[b] the whole house
of Israel, all of them, are those of
whom the inhabitants of Jerusalem
have said, 'They have gone far from
the LORD; to us this land is given
for a possession.' 16Therefore say,
'Thus says the Lord GOD: Though I
removed them far off among the na-
tions, and though I scattered them
among the countries, yet I have been
a sanctuary to them for a while[c] in
the countries where they have gone.'
17Therefore say, 'Thus says the Lord
GOD: I will gather you from the peo-
ples, and assemble you out of the
countries where you have been scat-
tered, and I will give you the land of
Israel.' 18And when they come there,
they will remove from it all its de-
testable things and all its abomina-
tions. 19And I will give them one[d]
heart, and put a new spirit within
them; I will take the stony heart out
of their flesh and give them a heart
of flesh, 20that they may walk in my
statutes and keep my ordinances
and obey them; and they shall be my
people, and I will be their God. 21But
as for those[e] whose heart goes after
their detestable things and their
abominations, I will requite their
deeds upon their own heads, says
the Lord GOD."

[a] Or *Is not the time near. . .?*
[b] Gk Syr: Heb *men of your kindred*
[c] Or *in small measure*
[d] Another reading is *a new*
[e] Cn: Heb *To the heart of their detestable things and their abominations their heart goes*

22 Then the cherubim lifted up
their wings, with the wheels be-
side them; and the glory of the God
of Israel was over them. 23And the
glory of the LORD went up from the
midst of the city, and stood upon the
mountain which is on the east side
of the city. 24And the Spirit lifted
me up and brought me in the vision
by the Spirit of God into Chalde´a,
to the exiles. Then the vision that I
had seen went up from me. 25And I
told the exiles all the things that the
LORD had showed me.

JUDAH'S CAPTIVITY PORTRAYED

12 The word of the LORD came to
me: 2"Son of man, you dwell in the
midst of a rebellious house, who have
eyes to see, but see not, who have ears
to hear, but hear not; 3for they are a
rebellious house. Therefore, son of
man, prepare for yourself an exile's
baggage, and go into exile by day in
their sight; you shall go like an exile
from your place to another place in
their sight. Perhaps they will under-
stand, though[f] they are a rebellious
house. 4You shall bring out your bag-
gage by day in their sight, as bag-
gage for exile; and you shall go forth
yourself at evening in their sight, as
men do who must go into exile. 5Dig
through the wall in their sight, and
go[g] out through it. 6In their sight you
shall lift the baggage upon your shoul-
der, and carry it out in the dark; you
shall cover your face, that you may
not see the land; for I have made you a
sign for the house of Israel."

7 And I did as I was commanded.
I brought out my baggage by day, as
baggage for exile, and in the evening
I dug through the wall with my own
hands; I went forth in the dark, car-
rying my outfit upon my shoulder in
their sight.

8 In the morning the word of the
LORD came to me: 9"Son of man,
has not the house of Israel, the re-
bellious house, said to you, 'What
are you doing?' 10Say to them, 'Thus
says the Lord GOD: This oracle con-
cerns the prince in Jerusalem and
all the house of Israel who are in
it.'[h] 11Say, 'I am a sign for you: as
I have done, so shall it be done to
them; they shall go into exile, into
captivity.' 12And the prince who is
among them shall lift his baggage
upon his shoulder in the dark, and
shall go forth; he[i] shall dig through
the wall and go[j] out through it; he
shall cover his face, that he may not
see the land with his eyes. 13And I
will spread my net over him, and he
shall be taken in my snare; and I will
bring him to Babylon in the land of
the Chalde´ans, yet he shall not see
it; and he shall die there. 14And I will
scatter toward every wind all who
are round about him, his helpers[k]
and all his troops; and I will un-
sheathe the sword after them. 15And
they shall know that I am the LORD,
when I disperse them among the na-
tions and scatter them through the
countries. 16But I will let a few of
them escape from the sword, from
famine and pestilence, that they
may confess all their abominations
among the nations where they go,
and may know that I am the LORD."

JUDGMENT NOT POSTPONED

17 Moreover the word of the LORD
came to me: 18"Son of man, eat your
bread with quaking, and drink water
with trembling and with fearfulness;
19and say of the people of the land,
Thus says the Lord GOD concerning
the inhabitants of Jerusalem in the
land of Israel: They shall eat their
bread with fearfulness, and drink

[f] Or *will see that*
[g] Gk Syr Vg Tg: Heb *bring*
[h] Heb *in the midst of them*
[i] Gk Syr: Heb *they*
[j] Gk Syr Tg: Heb *bring*
[k] Gk Syr Tg: Heb *his help*

water in dismay, because their land
will be stripped of all it contains, on
account of the violence of all those
who dwell in it. 20 And the inhabited
cities shall be laid waste, and the land
shall become a desolation; and you
shall know that I am the LORD."
21 And the word of the LORD
came to me: 22 "Son of man, what
is this proverb that you have about
the land of Israel, saying, 'The days
grow long, and every vision comes
to nought'? 23 Tell them therefore,
'Thus says the Lord GOD: I will put
an end to this proverb, and they shall
no more use it as a proverb in Israel.'
But say to them, The days are at
hand, and the fulfilment[a] of every vi-
sion. 24 For there shall be no more any
false vision or flattering divination
within the house of Israel. 25 But I the
LORD will speak the word which I
will speak, and it will be performed.
It will no longer be delayed, but in
your days, O rebellious house, I will
speak the word and perform it, says
the Lord GOD."
26 Again the word of the LORD
came to me: 27 "Son of man, behold,
they of the house of Israel say, 'The
vision that he sees is for many days
hence, and he prophesies of times far
off.' 28 Therefore say to them, Thus
says the Lord GOD: None of my words
will be delayed any longer, but the
word which I speak will be performed,
says the Lord GOD."

FALSE PROPHETS CONDEMNED

13 The word of the LORD came to
me: 2 "Son of man, prophesy
against the prophets of Israel, proph-
esy[b] and say to those who prophesy
out of their own minds: 'Hear the
word of the LORD!' 3 Thus says the
Lord GOD, Woe to the foolish proph-
ets who follow their own spirit, and
have seen nothing! 4 Your prophets
have been like foxes among ruins,
O Israel. 5 You have not gone up into
the breaches, or built up a wall for
the house of Israel, that it might
stand in battle in the day of the
LORD. 6 They have spoken falsehood
and divined a lie; they say, 'Says the
LORD,' when the LORD has not sent
them, and yet they expect him to ful-
fil their word. 7 Have you not seen a
delusive vision, and uttered a lying
divination, whenever you have said,
'Says the LORD,' although I have not
spoken?"
8 Therefore thus says the Lord
GOD: "Because you have uttered de-
lusions and seen lies, therefore be-
hold, I am against you, says the Lord
GOD. 9 My hand will be against the
prophets who see delusive visions
and who give lying divinations; they
shall not be in the council of my
people, nor be enrolled in the regis-
ter of the house of Israel, nor shall
they enter the land of Israel; and you
shall know that I am the Lord GOD.
10 Because, yea, because they have
misled my people, saying, 'Peace,'
when there is no peace; and because,
when the people build a wall, these
prophets daub it with whitewash;
11 say to those who daub it with
whitewash that it shall fall! There
will be a deluge of rain,[c] great hail-
stones will fall, and a stormy wind
break out; 12 and when the wall falls,
will it not be said to you, 'Where is
the daubing with which you daubed
it?' 13 Therefore thus says the Lord
GOD: I will make a stormy wind
break out in my wrath; and there
shall be a deluge of rain in my an-
ger, and great hailstones in wrath to
destroy it. 14 And I will break down
the wall that you have daubed with
whitewash, and bring it down to
the ground, so that its foundation
will be laid bare; when it falls, you
shall perish in the midst of it; and
you shall know that I am the LORD.
15 Thus will I spend my wrath upon
the wall, and upon those who have

[a] Heb *word*
[b] Gk: Heb *who prophesy*
[c] Heb *rain and you*

daubed it with whitewash; and I will
say to you, The wall is no more, nor
those who daubed it, 16the prophets
of Israel who prophesied concerning
Jerusalem and saw visions of peace
for her, when there was no peace,
says the Lord GOD.

17 "And you, son of man, set your
face against the daughters of your
people, who prophesy out of their own
minds; prophesy against them 18and
say, Thus says the Lord GOD: Woe
to the women who sew magic bands
upon all wrists, and make veils for
the heads of persons of every stature,
in the hunt for souls! Will you hunt
down souls belonging to my people,
and keep other souls alive for your
profit? 19You have profaned me among
my people for handfuls of barley and
for pieces of bread, putting to death
persons who should not die and keep-
ing alive persons who should not live,
by your lies to my people, who listen
to lies.

20 "Wherefore thus says the Lord
GOD: Behold, I am against your mag-
ic bands with which you hunt the
souls,[d] and I will tear them from
your arms; and I will let the souls
that you hunt go free[e] like birds.
21Your veils also I will tear off, and
deliver my people out of your hand,
and they shall be no more in your
hand as prey; and you shall know
that I am the LORD. 22Because you
have disheartened the righteous
falsely, although I have not disheart-
ened him, and you have encouraged
the wicked, that he should not turn
from his wicked way to save his life;
23therefore you shall no more see
delusive visions nor practice divina-
tion; I will deliver my people out of
your hand. Then you will know that I
am the LORD."

GOD'S JUDGMENTS JUSTIFIED

14 Then came certain of the elders
of Israel to me, and sat before me.
2And the word of the LORD came to
me: 3"Son of man, these men have
taken their idols into their hearts,
and set the stumbling block of their
iniquity before their faces; should
I let myself be inquired of at all by
them? 4Therefore speak to them, and
say to them, Thus says the Lord GOD:
Any man of the house of Israel who
takes his idols into his heart and sets
the stumbling block of his iniquity
before his face, and yet comes to the
prophet, I the LORD will answer him
myself[f] because of the multitude of
his idols, 5that I may lay hold of the
hearts of the house of Israel, who are
all estranged from me through their
idols.

6 "Therefore say to the house
of Israel, Thus says the Lord GOD:
Repent and turn away from your
idols; and turn away your faces from
all your abominations. 7For any
one of the house of Israel, or of the
strangers that sojourn in Israel, who
separates himself from me, taking his
idols into his heart and putting the
stumbling block of his iniquity before
his face, and yet comes to a prophet
to inquire for himself of me, I the
LORD will answer him myself; 8and I
will set my face against that man, I
will make him a sign and a byword
and cut him off from the midst of my
people; and you shall know that I am
the LORD. 9And if the prophet be de-
ceived and speak a word, I, the LORD,
have deceived that prophet, and I will
stretch out my hand against him, and
will destroy him from the midst of my
people Israel. 10And they shall bear
their punishment—the punishment
of the prophet and the punishment of
the inquirer shall be alike 11that the
house of Israel may go no more astray
from me, nor defile themselves any
more with all their transgressions,
but that they may be my people and
I may be their God, says the Lord
GOD."

[d] Gk Syr: Heb *souls for birds*
[e] Cn: Heb *the souls*
[f] Cn Compare Tg: Heb uncertain

12*And the word of the LORD
came to me: 13"Son of man, when
a land sins against me by acting
faithlessly, and I stretch out my
hand against it, and break its staff
of bread and send famine upon it,
and cut off from it man and beast,
14even if these three men, Noah,
Daniel,* and Job, were in it, they
would deliver but their own lives by
their righteousness, says the Lord
GOD. 15If I cause wild beasts to pass
through the land, and they ravage
it, and it be made desolate, so that
no man may pass through because
of the beasts; 16even if these three
men were in it, as I live, says the
Lord GOD, they would deliver nei-
ther sons nor daughters; they alone
would be delivered, but the land
would be desolate. 17Or if I bring a
sword upon that land, and say, Let a
sword go through the land; and I cut
off from it man and beast; 18though
these three men were in it, as I live,
says the Lord GOD, they would de-
liver neither sons nor daughters,
but they alone would be delivered.
19Or if I send a pestilence into that
land, and pour out my wrath upon
it with blood, to cut off from it man
and beast; 20even if Noah, Daniel,
and Job were in it, as I live, says the
Lord GOD, they would deliver nei-
ther son nor daughter; they would
deliver but their own lives by their
righteousness.

21 "For thus says the Lord GOD:
How much more when I send upon
Jerusalem my four sore acts of judg-
ment, sword, famine, evil beasts,
and pestilence, to cut off from it
man and beast! 22Yet, if there should
be left in it any survivors to lead out
sons and daughters, when they come
forth to you, and you see their ways
and their doings, you will be con-
soled for the evil that I have brought
upon Jerusalem, for all that I have
brought upon it. 23They will console
you, when you see their ways and
their doings; and you shall know
that I have not done without cause
all that I have done in it, says the
Lord GOD."

THE USELESS VINE

15 And the word of the LORD came
to me: 2"Son of man, how does
the wood of the vine surpass any
wood, the vine branch which is
among the trees of the forest? 3Is
wood taken from it to make any-
thing? Do men take a peg from it
to hang any vessel on? 4Lo, it is
given to the fire for fuel; when the
fire has consumed both ends of it,
and the middle of it is charred, is it
useful for anything? 5Behold, when
it was whole, it was used for noth-
ing; how much less, when the fire
has consumed it and it is charred,
can it ever be used for anything!
6Therefore thus says the Lord GOD:
Like the wood of the vine among
the trees of the forest, which I have
given to the fire for fuel, so will I
give up the inhabitants of Jerusalem.
7And I will set my face against them;
though they escape from the fire, the
fire shall yet consume them; and you
will know that I am the LORD, when
I set my face against them. 8And I
will make the land desolate, because
they have acted faithlessly, says the
Lord GOD."

GOD'S FAITHLESS BRIDE

16 Again the word of the LORD
came to me: 2"Son of man, make
known to Jerusalem her abomina-
tions, 3and say, Thus says the Lord
GOD to Jerusalem: Your origin and
your birth are of the land of the
Canaanites; your father was an
Amorite, and your mother a Hittite.
4And as for your birth, on the day you
were born your navel string was not
cut, nor were you washed with water
to cleanse you, nor rubbed with salt,
nor swathed with bands. 5No eye pit-
ied you, to do any of these things to
you out of compassion for you; but
you were cast out on the open field,

for you were abhorred, on the day
that you were born.
6 "And when I passed by you, and
saw you weltering in your blood, I
said to you in your blood, 'Live, 7and
grow up[a] like a plant of the field.'
And you grew up and became tall and
arrived at full maidenhood;[b] your
breasts were formed, and your hair
had grown; yet you were naked and
bare.
8 "When I passed by you again
and looked upon you, behold, you
were at the age for love; and I spread
my skirt over you, and covered your
nakedness: yea, I plighted my troth
to you and entered into a covenant
with you, says the Lord GOD, and
you became mine. 9Then I bathed you
with water and washed off your blood
from you, and anointed you with oil.
10I clothed you also with embroidered
cloth and shod you with leather, I
swathed you in fine linen and cov-
ered you with silk. 11And I decked
you with ornaments, and put brace-
lets on your arms, and a chain on
your neck. 12And I put a ring on your
nose, and earrings in your ears, and
a beautiful crown upon your head.
13Thus you were decked with gold
and silver; and your raiment was of
fine linen, and silk, and embroidered
cloth; you ate fine flour and honey
and oil. You grew exceedingly beau-
tiful, and came to regal estate. 14And
your renown went forth among the
nations because of your beauty, for
it was perfect through the splendor
which I had bestowed upon you, says
the Lord GOD.
15 "But you trusted in your beau-
ty, and played the harlot because of
your renown, and lavished your har-
lotries on any passer-by. 16You took
some of your garments, and made for
yourself gaily decked shrines, and on
them played the harlot; the like has
never been, nor ever shall be. 17You
also took your fair jewels of my gold
and of my silver, which I had given
you, and made for yourself images
of men, and with them played the
harlot; 18and you took your embroi-
dered garments to cover them, and
set my oil and my incense before
them. 19Also my bread which I gave
you—I fed you with fine flour and oil
and honey—you set before them for
a pleasing odor, says the Lord GOD.[c]
20And you took your sons and your
daughters, whom you had borne to
me, and these you sacrificed to them
to be devoured. Were your harlotries
so small a matter 21that you slaugh-
tered my children and delivered them
up as an offering by fire to them?
22And in all your abominations and
your harlotries you did not remem-
ber the days of your youth, when you
were naked and bare, weltering in
your blood.
23 "And after all your wicked-
ness (woe, woe to you! says the Lord
GOD), 24you built yourself a vaulted
chamber, and made yourself a lofty
place in every square; 25at the head
of every street you built your lofty
place and prostituted your beauty, of-
fering yourself to any passer-by, and
multiplying your harlotry. 26You also
played the harlot with the Egyptians,
your lustful neighbors, multiplying
your harlotry, to provoke me to anger.
27Behold, therefore, I stretched out
my hand against you, and diminished
your allotted portion, and delivered
you to the greed of your enemies,
the daughters of the Philistines,
who were ashamed of your lewd be-
havior. 28You played the harlot also
with the Assyrians, because you
were insatiable; yea, you played the
harlot with them, and still you were
not satisfied. 29You multiplied your
harlotry also with the trading land
of Chalde'a; and even with this you
were not satisfied.
30 "How lovesick is your heart,
says the Lord GOD, seeing you did

[a] Gk Syr: Heb *I made you a myriad*
[b] Cn: Heb *ornament of ornaments*
[c] Syr: Heb *and it was, says the Lord* God

all these things, the deeds of a bra-
zen harlot; 31building your vaulted
chamber at the head of every street,
and making your lofty place in ev-
ery square. Yet you were not like a
harlot, because you scorned hire.
32Adulterous wife, who receives
strangers instead of her husband!
33Men give gifts to all harlots; but
you gave your gifts to all your lovers,
bribing them to come to you from ev-
ery side for your harlotries. 34So you
were different from other women in
your harlotries: none solicited you
to play the harlot; and you gave hire,
while no hire was given to you; there-
fore you were different.

35 "Wherefore, O harlot, hear
the word of the LORD: 36Thus says
the Lord GOD, Because your shame
was laid bare and your nakedness
uncovered in your harlotries with
your lovers, and because of all your
idols, and because of the blood of
your children that you gave to them,
37therefore, behold, I will gather all
your lovers, with whom you took
pleasure, all those you loved and
all those you loathed; I will gather
them against you from every side,
and will uncover your nakedness
to them, that they may see all your
nakedness. 38And I will judge you as
women who break wedlock and shed
blood are judged, and bring upon
you the blood of wrath and jealousy.
39And I will give you into the hand
of your lovers, and they shall throw
down your vaulted chamber and
break down your lofty places; they
shall strip you of your clothes and
take your fair jewels, and leave you
naked and bare. 40They shall bring
up a host against you, and they shall
stone you and cut you to pieces with
their swords. 41And they shall burn
your houses and execute judgments
upon you in the sight of many wom-
en; I will make you stop playing the
harlot, and you shall also give hire
no more. 42So will I satisfy my fury
on you, and my jealousy shall depart
from you; I will be calm, and will no
more be angry. 43Because you have
not remembered the days of your
youth, but have enraged me with
all these things; therefore, behold,
I will requite your deeds upon your
head, says the Lord GOD. "Have you
not committed lewdness in addition
to all your abominations? 44Behold,
every one who uses proverbs will
use this proverb about you, 'Like
mother, like daughter.' 45You are
the daughter of your mother, who
loathed her husband and her chil-
dren; and you are the sister of your
sisters, who loathed their husbands
and their children. Your mother was
a Hittite and your father an Amorite.
46And your elder sister is Samar´ia,
who lived with her daughters to the
north of you; and your younger sis-
ter, who lived to the south of you,
is Sodom with her daughters. 47Yet
you were not content to walk in
their ways, or do according to their
abominations; within a very little
time you were more corrupt than
they in all your ways. 48As I live, says
the Lord GOD, your sister Sodom
and her daughters have not done as
you and your daughters have done.
49Behold, this was the guilt of your
sister Sodom: she and her daughters
had pride, surfeit of food, and pros-
perous ease, but did not aid the poor
and needy. 50They were haughty, and
did abominable things before me;
therefore I removed them, when I
saw it. 51Samar´ia has not committed
half your sins; you have committed
more abominations than they, and
have made your sisters appear righ-
teous by all the abominations which
you have committed. 52Bear your dis-
grace, you also, for you have made
judgment favorable to your sisters;
because of your sins in which you
acted more abominably than they,
they are more in the right than you.
So be ashamed, you also, and bear
your disgrace, for you have made
your sisters appear righteous.

53 "I will restore their fortunes,
both the fortunes of Sodom and
her daughters, and the fortunes of
Samar´ia and her daughters, and I
will restore your own fortunes in the
midst of them, 54that you may bear
your disgrace and be ashamed of all
that you have done, becoming a con-
solation to them. 55As for your sis-
ters, Sodom and her daughters shall
return to their former estate, and
Samar´ia and her daughters shall re-
turn to their former estate; and you
and your daughters shall return to
your former estate. 56Was not your
sister Sodom a byword in your mouth
in the day of your pride, 57before your
wickedness was uncovered? Now
you have become like her[a] an ob-
ject of reproach for the daughters
of Edom[b] and all her neighbors, and
for the daughters of the Philistines,
those round about who despise you.
58You bear the penalty of your lewd-
ness and your abominations, says the
LORD.

AN EVERLASTING COVENANT

59 "Yea, thus says the Lord GOD:
I will deal with you as you have
done, who have despised the oath in
breaking the covenant, 60yet I will
remember my covenant with you in
the days of your youth, and I will
establish with you an everlasting
covenant. 61Then you will remember
your ways, and be ashamed when I[c]
take your sisters, both your elder and
your younger, and give them to you as
daughters, but not on account of the
covenant with you. 62I will establish
my covenant with you, and you shall
know that I am the LORD, 63that you
may remember and be confounded,
and never open your mouth again be-
cause of your shame, when I forgive
you all that you have done, says the
Lord GOD."

[a]Cn: Heb uncertain
[b]Another reading is *Aram*
[c]Syr: Heb *you*
[d]Cn: Heb *it was transplanted*
[e]Cn: Heb *fruit*

THE TWO EAGLES AND THE VINE

17 The word of the LORD came to
me: 2*"Son of man, propound
a riddle, and speak an allegory to
the house of Israel; 3say, Thus says
the Lord GOD: A great eagle with
great wings and long pinions, rich
in plumage of many colors, came to
Lebanon and took the top of the ce-
dar; 4he broke off the topmost of its
young twigs and carried it to a land
of trade, and set it in a city of mer-
chants. 5Then he took of the seed of
the land and planted it in fertile soil;
he placed it beside abundant waters.
He set it like a willow twig, 6and it
sprouted and became a low spread-
ing vine, and its branches turned
toward him, and its roots remained
where it stood. So it became a vine,
and brought forth branches and put
forth foliage.

7 "But there was another great
eagle with great wings and much
plumage; and behold, this vine bent
its roots toward him, and shot forth
its branches toward him that he
might water it. From the bed where
it was planted 8he transplanted it[d] to
good soil by abundant waters, that
it might bring forth branches, and
bear fruit, and become a noble vine.
9Say, Thus says the Lord GOD: Will it
thrive? Will he not pull up its roots
and cut off its branches,[e] so that
all its fresh sprouting leaves with-
er? It will not take a strong arm or
many people to pull it from its roots.
10Behold, when it is transplanted,
will it thrive? Will it not utterly
wither when the east wind strikes
it—wither away on the bed where it
grew?"

11 Then the word of the LORD
came to me: 12"Say now to the re-
bellious house, Do you not know
what these things mean? Tell them,
Behold, the king of Babylon came to

Jerusalem, and took her king and her
princes and brought them to him to
Babylon. 13And he took one of the
seed royal and made a covenant with
him,putting him under oath. (The
chief men of the land he had taken
away, 14that the kingdom might be
humble and not lift itself up, and
that by keeping his covenant it might
stand.) 15But he rebelled against him
by sending ambassadors to Egypt,
that they might give him horses and
a large army. Will he succeed? Can a
man escape who does such things?
Can he break the covenant and yet
escape? 16As I live, says the Lord
GOD, surely in the place where the
king dwells who made him king,
whose oath he despised, and whose
covenant with him he broke, in
Babylon he shall die. 17Pharaoh with
his mighty army and great compa-
ny will not help him in war, when
mounds are cast up and siege walls
built to cut off many lives. 18Because
he despised the oath and broke the
covenant, because he gave his hand
and yet did all these things, he shall
not escape. 19Therefore thus says
the Lord GOD: As I live, surely my
oath which he despised, and my cov-
enant which he broke, I will requite
upon his head. 20I will spread my net
over him, and he shall be taken in
my snare, and I will bring him to
Babylon and enter into judgment
with him there for the treason he
has committed against me. 21And all
the pick[a] of his troops shall fall by
the sword, and the survivors shall
be scattered to every wind; and you
shall know that I, the LORD, have
spoken."

ISRAEL EXALTED AT LAST

22 Thus says the Lord GOD: "I my-
self will take a sprig from the lofty
top of the cedar, and will set it out;
I will break off from the topmost of
its young twigs a tender one, and I
myself will plant it upon a high and
lofty mountain; 23on the mountain
height of Israel will I plant it, that
it may bring forth boughs and bear
fruit, and become a noble cedar;
and under it will dwell all kinds of
beasts;[b] in the shade of its branches
birds of every sort will nest. 24And all
the trees of the field shall know that
I the LORD bring low the high tree,
and make high the low tree, dry up
the green tree, and make the dry tree
flourish. I the LORD have spoken, and
I will do it."

INDIVIDUAL RETRIBUTION

18 The word of the LORD came to me
again: 2"What do you mean by re-
peating this proverb concerning the
land of Israel, 'The fathers have eaten
sour grapes, and the children's teeth
are set on edge'? 3As I live, says the
Lord GOD, this proverb shall no more
be used by you in Israel. 4Behold, all
souls are mine; the soul of the father
as well as the soul of the son is mine:
the soul that sins shall die.

5 "If a man is righteous and does
what is lawful and right 6if he does
not eat upon the mountains or lift up
his eyes to the idols of the house of
Israel, does not defile his neighbor's
wife or approach a woman in her
time of impurity, 7does not oppress
any one, but restores to the debtor
his pledge, commits no robbery, gives
his bread to the hungry and covers
the naked with a garment, 8does not
lend at interest or take any increase,
withholds his hand from iniquity,
executes true justice between man
and man, 9walks in my statutes, and
is careful to observe my ordinances[c]
—he is righteous, he shall surely live,
says the Lord GOD.

10 "If he begets a son who is a rob-
ber, a shedder of blood,[d] 11who does
none of these duties, but eats upon

[a] Another reading is *fugitives*
[b] Gk: Heb lacks *all kinds of beasts*
[c] Gk: Heb *has kept my ordinances, to deal truly*
[d] Heb *blood, and he does any one of these things*

the mountains, defiles his neighbor's
wife, 12oppresses the poor and needy,
commits robbery, does not restore the
pledge, lifts up his eyes to the idols,
commits abomination, 13lends at inter-
est, and takes increase; shall he then
live? He shall not live. He has done
all these abominable things; he shall
surely die; his blood shall be upon
himself.

14 "But if this man begets a son
who sees all the sins which his father
has done, and fears, and does not do
likewise, 15who does not eat upon the
mountains or lift up his eyes to the
idols of the house of Israel, does not
defile his neighbor's wife, 16does not
wrong any one, exacts no pledge, com-
mits no robbery, but gives his bread
to the hungry and covers the naked
with a garment, 17withholds his hand
from iniquity,[e] takes no interest or in-
crease, observes my ordinances, and
walks in my statutes; he shall not die
for his father's iniquity; he shall sure-
ly live. 18As for his father, because he
practiced extortion, robbed his broth-
er, and did what is not good among
his people, behold, he shall die for his
iniquity.

19 "Yet you say, 'Why should not
the son suffer for the iniquity of the
father?' When the son has done what
is lawful and right, and has been care-
ful to observe all my statutes, he shall
surely live. 20The soul that sins shall
die. The son shall not suffer for the
iniquity of the father, nor the father
suffer for the iniquity of the son; the
righteousness of the righteous shall
be upon himself, and the wickedness
of the wicked shall be upon himself.

21 "But if a wicked man turns away
from all his sins which he has com-
mitted and keeps all my statutes and
does what is lawful and right, he shall
surely live; he shall not die. 22None of
the transgressions which he has com-
mitted shall be remembered against
him; for the righteousness which he
has done he shall live. 23Have I any
pleasure in the death of the wicked,
says the Lord GOD, and not rath-
er that he should turn from his way
and live? 24But when a righteous
man turns away from his righteous-
ness and commits iniquity and does
the same abominable things that the
wicked man does, shall he live? None
of the righteous deeds which he has
done shall be remembered; for the
treachery of which he is guilty and
the sin he has committed, he shall
die.

25 "Yet you say, 'The way of the
Lord is not just.' Hear now, O house
of Israel: Is my way not just? Is it not
your ways that are not just? 26When
a righteous man turns away from his
righteousness and commits iniqui-
ty, he shall die for it; for the iniqui-
ty which he has committed he shall
die. 27Again, when a wicked man
turns away from the wickedness he
has committed and does what is law-
ful and right, he shall save his life.
28Because he considered and turned
away from all the transgressions
which he had committed, he shall
surely live, he shall not die. 29Yet the
house of Israel says, 'The way of the
Lord is not just.' O house of Israel, are
my ways not just? Is it not your ways
that are not just?

30 "Therefore I will judge you, O
house of Israel, every one according to
his ways, says the Lord GOD. Repent
and turn from all your transgressions,
lest iniquity be your ruin.[f] 31Cast away
from you all the transgressions which
you have committed against me, and
get yourselves a new heart and a new
spirit! Why will you die, O house of
Israel? 32For I have no pleasure in the
death of any one, says the Lord GOD;
so turn, and live."

ISRAEL DEGRADED

19 And you, take up a lamentation for
the princes of Israel, 2and say:

[e]Gk: Heb *the poor*
[f]Or *so that they shall not be a stumbling block of iniquity to you*

What a lioness was your mother
among lions!
She couched in the midst of young lions,
rearing her whelps.
3And she brought up one of her whelps;
he became a young lion,
and he learned to catch prey;
he devoured men.
4The nations sounded an alarm against him;
he was taken in their pit;
and they brought him with hooks
to the land of Egypt.
5When she saw that she was baffled,[a]
that her hope was lost,
she took another of her whelps
and made him a young lion.
6He prowled among the lions;
he became a young lion,
and he learned to catch prey;
he devoured men.
7And he ravaged their strongholds,[b]
and laid waste their cities;
and the land was appalled and all who were in it
at the sound of his roaring.
8Then the nations set against him
snares[c] on every side;
they spread their net over him;
he was taken in their pit.
9With hooks they put him in a cage,
and brought him to the king of Babylon;
they brought him into custody,
that his voice should no more be heard
upon the mountains of Israel.

10Your mother was like a vine in a vineyard[d]
transplanted by the water,
fruitful and full of branches
by reason of abundant water.
11Its strongest stem became
a ruler's scepter;
it towered aloft
among the thick boughs;
it was seen in its height
with the mass of its branches.
12But the vine was plucked up in fury,
cast down to the ground;
the east wind dried it up;
its fruit was stripped off,
its strong stem was withered;
the fire consumed it.
13Now it is transplanted in the wilderness,
in a dry and thirsty land.
14And fire has gone out from its stem,
has consumed its branches and fruit,
so that there remains in it no strong stem,
no scepter for a ruler.

This is a lamentation, and has become a lamentation.

ISRAEL'S CONTINUING REBELLION

20 In the seventh year, in the fifth
month, on the tenth day of the
month, certain of the elders of Israel
came to inquire of the LORD, and
sat before me. 2And the word of the
LORD came to me: 3"Son of man,
speak to the elders of Israel, and say
to them, Thus says the Lord GOD, Is
it to inquire of me that you come?
As I live, says the Lord GOD, I will
not be inquired of by you. 4Will you
judge them, son of man, will you
judge them? Then let them know
the abominations of their fathers,
5and say to them, Thus says the Lord

[a] Heb *had waited*
[b] Tg Compare Theodotion: Heb *knew his widows*
[c] Cn: Heb *from the provinces*
[d] Cn: Heb *in your blood*

GOD: On the day when I chose Israel,
I swore to the seed of the house of
Jacob, making myself known to them
in the land of Egypt, I swore to them,
saying, I am the LORD your God. 6 On
that day I swore to them that I would
bring them out of the land of Egypt
into a land that I had searched out for
them, a land flowing with milk and
honey, the most glorious of all lands.
7 And I said to them, Cast away the
detestable things your eyes feast on,
every one of you, and do not defile
yourselves with the idols of Egypt;
I am the LORD your God. 8 But they
rebelled against me and would not
listen to me; they did not every man
cast away the detestable things their
eyes feasted on, nor did they forsake
the idols of Egypt.

"Then I thought I would pour
out my wrath upon them and spend
my anger against them in the midst
of the land of Egypt. 9 But I acted for
the sake of my name, that it should
not be profaned in the sight of the
nations among whom they dwelt, in
whose sight I made myself known
to them in bringing them out of the
land of Egypt. 10 So I led them out of
the land of Egypt and brought them
into the wilderness. 11 I gave them my
statutes and showed them my ordi-
nances, by whose observance man
shall live. 12 Moreover I gave them my
sabbaths, as a sign between me and
them, that they might know that I the
LORD sanctify them. 13 But the house
of Israel rebelled against me in the
wilderness; they did not walk in my
statutes but rejected my ordinanc-
es, by whose observance man shall
live; and my sabbaths they greatly
profaned.

"Then I thought I would pour
out my wrath upon them in the wil-
derness, to make a full end of them.
14 But I acted for the sake of my name,
that it should not be profaned in the
sight of the nations, in whose sight
I had brought them out. 15 Moreover I
swore to them in the wilderness that
I would not bring them into the land
which I had given them, a land flow-
ing with milk and honey, the most
glorious of all lands, 16 because they
rejected my ordinances and did not
walk in my statutes, and profaned
my sabbaths; for their heart went af-
ter their idols. 17 Nevertheless my eye
spared them, and I did not destroy
them or make a full end of them in
the wilderness.

18 "And I said to their children in
the wilderness, Do not walk in the
statutes of your fathers, nor observe
their ordinances, nor defile your-
selves with their idols. 19 I the LORD
am your God; walk in my statutes, and
be careful to observe my ordinances,
20 and hallow my sabbaths that they
may be a sign between me and you,
that you may know that I the LORD
am your God. 21 But the children re-
belled against me; they did not walk
in my statutes, and were not careful to
observe my ordinances, by whose ob-
servance man shall live; they profaned
my sabbaths.

"Then I thought I would pour out
my wrath upon them and spend my
anger against them in the wilder-
ness. 22 But I withheld my hand, and
acted for the sake of my name, that
it should not be profaned in the sight
of the nations, in whose sight I had
brought them out. 23 Moreover I swore
to them in the wilderness that I would
scatter them among the nations and
disperse them through the countries,
24 because they had not executed my
ordinances, but had rejected my stat-
utes and profaned my sabbaths, and
their eyes were set on their fathers'
idols. 25 Moreover I gave them statutes
that were not good and ordinances by
which they could not have life; 26 and I
defiled them through their very gifts
in making them offer by fire all their
first-born, that I might horrify them; I
did it that they might know that I am
the LORD.

27 "Therefore, son of man, speak
to the house of Israel and say to

them, Thus says the Lord GOD: In
this again your fathers blasphemed
me, by dealing treacherously with
me. 28For when I had brought them
into the land which I swore to give
them, then wherever they saw any
high hill or any leafy tree, there they
offered their sacrifices and present-
ed the provocation of their offer-
ing; there they sent up their sooth-
ing odors, and there they poured
out their drink offerings. 29(I said
to them, What is the high place to
which you go? So its name is called
Bamah[a] to this day.) 30Wherefore say
to the house of Israel, Thus says the
Lord GOD: Will you defile yourselves
after the manner of your fathers
and go astray after their detestable
things? 31When you offer your gifts
and sacrifice your sons by fire, you
defile yourselves with all your idols
to this day. And shall I be inquired of
by you, O house of Israel? As I live,
says the Lord GOD, I will not be in-
quired of by you.

32 "What is in your mind shall
never happen—the thought, 'Let us
be like the nations, like the tribes of
the countries, and worship wood and
stone.'

GOD WILL RESTORE ISRAEL

33 "As I live, says the Lord GOD,
surely with a mighty hand and an
outstretched arm, and with wrath
poured out, I will be king over you.
34I will bring you out from the peo-
ples and gather you out of the coun-
tries where you are scattered, with
a mighty hand and an outstretched
arm, and with wrath poured out;
35and I will bring you into the wilder-
ness of the peoples, and there I will
enter into judgment with you face
to face. 36As I entered into judgment
with your fathers in the wilderness of
the land of Egypt, so I will enter into
judgment with you, says the Lord
GOD. 37I will make you pass under the
rod, and I will let you go in by num-
ber.[b] 38I will purge out the rebels from
among you, and those who trans-
gress against me; I will bring them
out of the land where they sojourn,
but they shall not enter the land of
Israel. Then you will know that I am
the LORD.

39 "As for you, O house of Israel,
thus says the Lord GOD: Go serve
every one of you his idols, now and
hereafter, if you will not listen to me;
but my holy name you shall no more
profane with your gifts and your
idols.

40 "For on my holy mountain,
the mountain height of Israel, says
the Lord GOD, there all the house of
Israel, all of them, shall serve me in
the land; there I will accept them,
and there I will require your con-
tributions and the choicest of your
gifts, with all your sacred offerings.
41As a pleasing odor I will accept
you, when I bring you out from the
peoples, and gather you out of the
countries where you have been scat-
tered; and I will manifest my holi-
ness among you in the sight of the
nations. 42And you shall know that
I am the LORD, when I bring you
into the land of Israel, the country
which I swore to give to your fathers.
43And there you shall remember your
ways and all the doings with which
you have polluted yourselves; and
you shall loathe yourselves for all
the evils that you have committed.
44And you shall know that I am the
LORD, when I deal with you for my
name's sake, not according to your
evil ways, nor according to your cor-
rupt doings, O house of Israel, says
the Lord GOD."

A PROPHECY AGAINST THE NEGEB

45[c] And the word of the LORD
came to me: 46"Son of man, set
your face toward the south, preach
against the south, and prophesy

[a]That is *High Place*
[b]Gk: Heb *bring you into the bond of the covenant*
[c]Ch 21.1 in Heb

against the forest land in the Negeb;
47say to the forest of the Negeb, Hear
the word of the LORD: Thus says the
Lord GOD, Behold, I will kindle a
fire in you, and it shall devour ev-
ery green tree in you and every dry
tree; the blazing flame shall not be
quenched, and all faces from south
to north shall be scorched by it. 48All
flesh shall see that I the LORD have
kindled it; it shall not be quenched."
49Then I said, "Ah Lord GOD! they
are saying of me, 'Is he not a maker
of allegories?'"

THE DRAWN SWORD OF GOD

21 [d] The word of the LORD came to
me: 2"Son of man, set your face
toward Jerusalem and preach against
the sanctuaries; prophesy against the
land of Israel 3and say to the land of
Israel, Thus says the LORD: Behold, I
am against you, and will draw forth
my sword out of its sheath, and will
cut off from you both righteous
and wicked. 4Because I will cut off
from you both righteous and wick-
ed, therefore my sword shall go out
of its sheath against all flesh from
south to north; 5and all flesh shall
know that I the LORD have drawn my
sword out of its sheath; it shall not
be sheathed again. 6Sigh therefore,
son of man; sigh with breaking heart
and bitter grief before their eyes.
7And when they say to you, 'Why do
you sigh?' you shall say, 'Because of
the tidings. When it comes, every
heart will melt and all hands will be
feeble, every spirit will faint and all
knees will be weak as water. Behold,
it comes and it will be fulfilled,'"
says the Lord GOD.

8 And the word of the LORD came
to me: 9"Son of man, prophesy and
say, Thus says the Lord, Say:

A sword, a sword is
sharpened
and also polished,
10sharpened for slaughter,
polished to flash like
lightning!

Or do we make mirth? You have
despised the rod, my son, with ev-
erything of wood. 11So the sword is
given to be polished, that it may be
handled; it is sharpened and polished
to be given into the hand of the slay-
er. 12Cry and wail, son of man, for it
is against my people; it is against all
the princes of Israel; they are deliv-
ered over to the sword with my peo-
ple. Smite therefore upon your thigh.
13For it will not be a testing—what
could it do if you despise the rod?"
says the Lord GOD.

14 "Prophesy therefore, son of
man; clap your hands and let the
sword come down twice, yea thrice,
the sword for those to be slain; it is
the sword for the great slaughter,
which encompasses them, 15that their
hearts may melt, and many fall at all
their gates. I have given the glittering
sword; ah! it is made like lightning, it
is polished[e] for slaughter. 16Cut sharp-
ly to right[f] and left where your edge is
directed. 17I also will clap my hands,
and I will satisfy my fury; I the LORD
have spoken."

18 The word of the LORD came to
me again: 19"Son of man, mark two
ways for the sword of the king of
Babylon to come; both of them shall
come forth from the same land. And
make a signpost, make it at the head
of the way to a city; 20mark a way
for the sword to come to Rabbah of
the Ammonites and to Judah and
to[g] Jerusalem the fortified. 21For the
king of Babylon stands at the part-
ing of the way, at the head of the two
ways, to use divination; he shakes
the arrows, he consults the teraphim,
he looks at the liver. 22Into his right
hand comes the lot for Jerusalem,[h]

[d] Ch 21.6 in Heb
[e] Tg: Heb *wrapped up*
[f] Gk Syr Vg: Heb *right, set*
[g] Gk Syr: Heb *in*
[h] Heb *Jerusalem, to set battering rams*

to open the mouth with a cry,[a] to lift
up the voice with shouting, to set
battering rams against the gates, to
cast up mounds, to build siege tow-
ers. 23But to them it will seem like a
false divination; they have sworn sol-
emn oaths; but he brings their guilt
to remembrance, that they may be
captured.

24 "Therefore thus says the Lord
GOD: Because you have made your
guilt to be remembered, in that your
transgressions are uncovered, so that
in all your doings your sins appear—
because you have come to remem-
brance, you shall be taken in them.[b]
25And you, O unhallowed wicked one,
prince of Israel, whose day has come,
the time of your final punishment,
26thus says the Lord GOD: Remove
the turban, and take off the crown;
things shall not remain as they are;
exalt that which is low, and abase
that which is high. 27A ruin, ruin,
ruin I will make it; there shall not
be even a trace[c] of it until he comes
whose right it is; and to him I will
give it.

28 "And you, son of man, prophe-
sy, and say, Thus says the Lord GOD
concerning the Ammonites, and con-
cerning their reproach; say, A sword,
a sword is drawn for the slaughter,
it is polished to glitter[d] and to flash
like lightning 29while they see for you
false visions, while they divine lies for
you—to be laid on the necks of the
unhallowed wicked, whose day has
come, the time of their final punish-
ment. 30Return it to its sheath. In the
place where you were created, in the
land of your origin, I will judge you.
31And I will pour out my indignation
upon you; I will blow upon you with
the fire of my wrath; and I will deliv-
er you into the hands of brutal men,
skilful to destroy. 32You shall be fuel
for the fire; your blood shall be in
the midst of the land; you shall be
no more remembered; for I the LORD
have spoken."

THE BLOODY CITY

22 Moreover the word of the LORD
came to me, saying, 2"And you,
son of man, will you judge, will you
judge the bloody city? Then declare
to her all her abominable deeds. 3You
shall say, Thus says the Lord GOD:
A city that sheds blood in the midst
of her, that her time may come, and
that makes idols to defile herself!
4You have become guilty by the blood
which you have shed, and defiled by
the idols which you have made; and
you have brought your day near, the
appointed time[e] of your years has
come. Therefore I have made you a re-
proach to the nations, and a mocking
to all the countries. 5Those who are
near and those who are far from you
will mock you, you infamous one, full
of tumult.

6 "Behold, the princes of Israel in
you, every one according to his pow-
er, have been bent on shedding blood.
7Father and mother are treated with
contempt in you; the sojourner suf-
fers extortion in your midst; the fa-
therless and the widow are wronged
in you. 8You have despised my holy
things, and profaned my sabbaths.
9There are men in you who slander
to shed blood, and men in you who
eat upon the mountains; men com-
mit lewdness in your midst. 10In you
men uncover their fathers' naked-
ness; in you they humble women who
are unclean in their impurity. 11One
commits abomination with his neigh-
bor's wife; another lewdly defiles
his daughter-in-law; another in you
defiles his sister, his father's daugh-
ter. 12In you men take bribes to shed
blood; you take interest and increase
and make gain of your neighbors by

[a] Gk: Heb *with slaughter*
[b] Gk: Heb *with the hand*
[c] Cn: Heb *not even this*
[d] Cn: Heb *to contain*
[e] Two Mss Gk Syr Vg Tg: Heb *until*

extortion; and you have forgotten me,
says the Lord GOD.

13 "Behold, therefore, I strike my
hands together at the dishonest gain
which you have made, and at the
blood which has been in the midst
of you. 14Can your courage endure, or
can your hands be strong, in the days
that I shall deal with you? I the LORD
have spoken, and I will do it. 15I will
scatter you among the nations and
disperse you through the countries,
and I will consume your filthiness
out of you. 16And I[f] shall be profaned
through you in the sight of the na-
tions; and you shall know that I am
the LORD."

17 And the word of the LORD
came to me: 18"Son of man, the
house of Israel has become dross to
me; all of them, silver[g] and bronze
and tin and iron and lead in the fur-
nace, have become dross. 19Therefore
thus says the Lord GOD: Because you
have all become dross, therefore,
behold, I will gather you into the
midst of Jerusalem. 20As men gather
silver and bronze and iron and lead
and tin into a furnace, to blow the
fire upon it in order to melt it; so I
will gather you in my anger and in
my wrath, and I will put you in and
melt you. 21I will gather you and blow
upon you with the fire of my wrath,
and you shall be melted in the midst
of it. 22As silver is melted in a fur-
nace, so you shall be melted in the
midst of it; and you shall know that I
the LORD have poured out my wrath
upon you."

23 And the word of the LORD
came to me: 24"Son of man, say
to her, You are a land that is not
cleansed, or rained upon in the day
of indignation. 25Her princes[h] in the
midst of her are like a roaring lion
tearing the prey; they have devoured
human lives; they have taken trea-
sure and precious things; they have
made many widows in the midst of
her. 26Her priests have done violence
to my law and have profaned my holy
things; they have made no distinc-
tion between the holy and the com-
mon, neither have they taught the
difference between the unclean and
the clean, and they have disregarded
my sabbaths, so that I am profaned
among them. 27Her princes in the
midst of her are like wolves tearing
the prey, shedding blood, destroying
lives to get dishonest gain. 28And
her prophets have daubed for them
with whitewash, seeing false visions
and divining lies for them, saying,
'Thus says the Lord GOD,' when the
LORD has not spoken. 29The people
of the land have practiced extortion
and committed robbery; they have
oppressed the poor and needy, and
have extorted from the sojourn-
er without redress. 30And I sought
for a man among them who should
build up the wall and stand in the
breach before me for the land, that
I should not destroy it; but I found
none. 31Therefore I have poured out
my indignation upon them; I have
consumed them with the fire of
my wrath; their way have I requit-
ed upon their heads, says the Lord
GOD."

OHOLAH AND OHOLIBAH

23 The word of the LORD came to
me: 2"Son of man, there were
two women, the daughters of one
mother; 3they played the harlot in
Egypt; they played the harlot in
their youth; there their breasts were
pressed and their virgin bosoms
handled. 4Oho′lah was the name of
the elder and Ohol′ibah the name of
her sister. They became mine, and
they bore sons and daughters. As for
their names, Oho′lah is Samar′ia,
and Ohol′ibah is Jerusalem.

5 "Oho′lah played the harlot
while she was mine; and she dot-
ed on her lovers the Assyrians,

[f] Gk Syr Vg: Heb *you*
[g] Transposed from the end of the verse. Compare verse 20
[h] Gk: Heb *a conspiracy of her prophets*

6warriors clothed in purple, gover-
nors and commanders, all of them
desirable young men, horsemen rid-
ing on horses. 7She bestowed her
harlotries upon them, the choicest
men of Assyria all of them; and she
defiled herself with all the idols of
every one on whom she doted. 8She
did not give up her harlotry which
she had practiced since her days
in Egypt; for in her youth men had
lain with her and handled her vir-
gin bosom and poured out their lust
upon her. 9Therefore I delivered her
into the hands of her lovers, into
the hands of the Assyrians, upon
whom she doted. 10These uncovered
her nakedness; they seized her sons
and her daughters; and her they slew
with the sword; and she became a by-
word among women, when judgment
had been executed upon her.

11 "Her sister Ohol´ibah saw this,
yet she was more corrupt than she in
her doting and in her harlotry, which
was worse than that of her sister.
12She doted upon the Assyrians, gov-
ernors and commanders, warriors
clothed in full armor, horsemen rid-
ing on horses, all of them desirable
young men. 13And I saw that she was
defiled; they both took the same way.
14But she carried her harlotry further;
she saw men portrayed upon the
wall, the images of the Chalde´ans
portrayed in vermilion, 15girded with
belts on their loins, with flowing
turbans on their heads, all of them
looking like officers, a picture of
Babylonians whose native land was
Chalde´a. 16When she saw them she
doted upon them, and sent messen-
gers to them in Chalde´a. 17And the
Babylonians came to her into the bed
of love, and they defiled her with
their lust; and after she was pollut-
ed by them, she turned from them in
disgust. 18When she carried on her
harlotry so openly and flaunted her
nakedness, I turned in disgust from
her, as I had turned from her sister.
19Yet she increased her harlotry, re-
membering the days of her youth,
when she played the harlot in the
land of Egypt 20and doted upon her
paramours there, whose members
were like those of asses, and whose
issue was like that of horses. 21Thus
you longed for the lewdness of your
youth, when the Egyptians[a] handled
your bosom and pressed[b] your young
breasts."

22 Therefore, O Ohol´ibah, thus
says the Lord GOD: "Behold, I will
rouse against you your lovers from
whom you turned in disgust, and
I will bring them against you from
every side: 23the Babylonians and
all the Chalde´ans, Pekod and Sho´a
and Ko´a, and all the Assyrians with
them, desirable young men, gover-
nors and commanders all of them,
officers and warriors,[c] all of them
riding on horses. 24And they shall
come against you from the north[d]
with chariots and wagons and a host
of peoples; they shall set themselves
against you on every side with buck-
ler, shield, and helmet, and I will
commit the judgment to them, and
they shall judge you according to
their judgments. 25And I will direct
my indignation against you, that
they may deal with you in fury. They
shall cut off your nose and your ears,
and your survivors shall fall by the
sword. They shall seize your sons
and your daughters, and your survi-
vors shall be devoured by fire. 26They
shall also strip you of your clothes
and take away your fine jewels.
27Thus I will put an end to your lewd-
ness and your harlotry brought from
the land of Egypt; so that you shall
not lift up your eyes to the Egyptians
or remember them any more. 28For
thus says the Lord GOD: Behold,
I will deliver you into the hands of

[a]Two Mss: Heb *from Egypt*
[b]Cn: Heb *for the sake of*
[c]Compare verses 6 and 12: Heb *called*
[d]Gk: The meaning of the Hebrew word is unknown

those whom you hate, into the hands
of those from whom you turned in
disgust; 29and they shall deal with
you in hatred, and take away all the
fruit of your labor, and leave you
naked and bare, and the nakedness
of your harlotry shall be uncovered.
Your lewdness and your harlotry
30have brought this upon you, be-
cause you played the harlot with the
nations, and polluted yourself with
their idols. 31You have gone the way
of your sister; therefore I will give
her cup into your hand. 32Thus says
the Lord GOD:

"You shall drink your sister's
cup
which is deep and large;
you shall be laughed at and
held in derision,
for it contains much;
33you will be filled with drunken-
ness and sorrow.
A cup of horror and
desolation,
is the cup of your sister
Samar´ia;
34you shall drink it and drain it
out,
and pluck out your hair,[e]
and tear your breasts;

for I have spoken, says the Lord
GOD. 35Therefore thus says the Lord
GOD: Because you have forgotten me
and cast me behind your back, there-
fore bear the consequences of your
lewdness and harlotry."

36 The LORD said to me: "Son of
man, will you judge Oho´lah and
Ohol´ibah? Then declare to them
their abominable deeds. 37For they
have committed adultery, and blood
is upon their hands; with their idols
they have committed adultery; and
they have even offered up to them
for food the sons whom they had
borne to me. 38Moreover this they
have done to me: they have defiled
my sanctuary on the same day and
profaned my sabbaths. 39For when
they had slaughtered their children
in sacrifice to their idols, on the
same day they came into my sanc-
tuary to profane it. And lo, this is
what they did in my house. 40They
even sent for men to come from far,
to whom a messenger was sent, and
lo, they came. For them you bathed
yourself, painted your eyes, and
decked yourself with ornaments;
41you sat upon a stately couch, with
a table spread before it on which
you had placed my incense and my
oil. 42The sound of a carefree mul-
titude was with her; and with men
of the common sort drunkards[f] were
brought from the wilderness; and
they put bracelets upon the hands
of the women, and beautiful crowns
upon their heads.

43 "Then I said, Do not men now
commit adultery[g] when they practice
harlotry with her? 44For they have
gone in to her, as men go in to a har-
lot. Thus they went in to Oho´lah and
to Ohol´ibah to commit lewdness.[h]
45But righteous men shall pass judg-
ment on them with the sentence of
adulteresses, and with the sentence of
women that shed blood; because they
are adulteresses, and blood is upon
their hands."

46 For thus says the Lord GOD:
"Bring up a host against them, and
make them an object of terror and
a spoil. 47And the host shall stone
them and dispatch them with their
swords; they shall slay their sons
and their daughters, and burn up
their houses. 48Thus will I put an
end to lewdness in the land, that all
women may take warning and not
commit lewdness as you have done.
49And your lewdness shall be requit-
ed upon you, and you shall bear the
penalty for your sinful idolatry; and
you shall know that I am the Lord
GOD."

[e] Compare Syr: Heb *gnaw its sherds*
[f] Heb uncertain
[g] Compare Gk: Heb obscure
[h] Gk: Heb *a woman of lewdness*

THE BOILING POT

24 In the ninth year, in the tenth
month, on the tenth day of the
month, the word of the LORD came
to me: 2"Son of man, write down
the name of this day, this very day.
The king of Babylon has laid siege to
Jerusalem this very day. 3And utter
an allegory to the rebellious house
and say to them, Thus says the Lord
GOD:

Set on the pot, set it on,
pour in water also;
4put in it the pieces of flesh,
all the good pieces, the thigh
and the shoulder;
fill it with choice bones.
5Take the choicest one of the
flock,
pile the logs[a] under it;
boil its pieces,[b]
seethe[c] also its bones in it.

6 "Therefore thus says the Lord
GOD: Woe to the bloody city, to the
pot whose rust is in it, and whose
rust has not gone out of it! Take
out of it piece after piece, without
making any choice.[d] 7For the blood
she has shed is still in the midst
of her; she put it on the bare rock,
she did not pour it upon the ground
to cover it with dust. 8To rouse my
wrath, to take vengeance, I have set
on the bare rock the blood she has
shed, that it may not be covered.
9Therefore thus says the Lord GOD:
Woe to the bloody city! I also will
make the pile great. 10Heap on the
logs, kindle the fire, boil well the
flesh, and empty out the broth,[e] and
let the bones be burned up. 11Then
set it empty upon the coals, that it
may become hot, and its copper may
burn, that its filthiness may be melt-
ed in it, its rust consumed. 12In vain
I have wearied myself;[f] its thick rust
does not go out of it by fire. 13Its
rust is your filthy lewdness. Because
I would have cleansed you and you
were not cleansed from your filthi-
ness, you shall not be cleansed any
more till I have satisfied my fury
upon you. 14I the LORD have spoken;
it shall come to pass, I will do it; I
will not go back, I will not spare, I
will not repent; according to your
ways and your doings I will judge
you, says the Lord GOD."

EZEKIEL'S BEREAVEMENT

15 Also the word of the LORD
came to me: 16"Son of man, behold, I
am about to take the delight of your
eyes away from you at a stroke; yet
you shall not mourn or weep nor shall
your tears run down. 17Sigh, but not
aloud; make no mourning for the
dead. Bind on your turban, and put
your shoes on your feet; do not cover
your lips, nor eat the bread of mourn-
ers."[g] 18So I spoke to the people in the
morning, and at evening my wife died.
And on the next morning I did as I
was commanded.

19 And the people said to me,
"Will you not tell us what these
things mean for us, that you are
acting thus?" 20Then I said to them,
"The word of the LORD came to me:
21'Say to the house of Israel, Thus
says the Lord GOD: Behold, I will
profane my sanctuary, the pride of
your power, the delight of your eyes,
and the desire of your soul; and your
sons and your daughters whom you
left behind shall fall by the sword.
22And you shall do as I have done;
you shall not cover your lips, nor eat
the bread of mourners.[h] 23Your tur-
bans shall be on your heads and your
shoes on your feet; you shall not
mourn or weep, but you shall pine

[a] Compare verse 10: Heb *the bones*
[b] Two Mss: Heb *its boilings*
[c] Cn: Heb *its bones seethe*
[d] Heb *no lot has fallen upon it*
[e] Compare Gk: Heb *mix the spices*
[f] Cn: Heb uncertain
[g] Vg Tg: Heb *men*
[h] Vg Tg: Heb *men*

away in your iniquities and groan to
one another. 24 Thus shall Ezekiel be
to you a sign; according to all that
he has done you shall do. When this
comes, then you will know that I am
the Lord GOD.'

25 "And you, son of man, on the
day when I take from them their
stronghold, their joy and glory, the
delight of their eyes and their heart's
desire, and also their sons and daugh-
ters, 26 on that day a fugitive will come
to you to report to you the news. 27 On
that day your mouth will be opened to
the fugitive, and you shall speak and
be no longer dumb. So you will be a
sign to them; and they will know that
I am the LORD."

PROCLAMATION AGAINST AMMON

25 The word of the LORD came
to me: 2 "Son of man, set your
face toward the Ammonites, and
prophesy against them. 3 Say to the
Ammonites, Hear the word of the
Lord GOD: Thus says the Lord GOD,
Because you said, 'Aha!' over my
sanctuary when it was profaned,
and over the land of Israel when it
was made desolate, and over the
house of Judah when it went into
exile; 4 therefore I am handing you
over to the people of the East for a
possession, and they shall set their
encampments among you and make
their dwellings in your midst; they
shall eat your fruit, and they shall
drink your milk. 5 I will make Rabbah
a pasture for camels and the cities
of the Ammonites[i] a fold for flocks.
Then you will know that I am the
LORD. 6 For thus says the Lord GOD:
Because you have clapped your
hands and stamped your feet and re-
joiced with all the malice within you
against the land of Israel, 7 therefore,
behold, I have stretched out my hand
against you, and will hand you over
as spoil to the nations; and I will cut
you off from the peoples and will
make you perish out of the coun-
tries; I will destroy you. Then you
will know that I am the LORD.

PROCLAMATION AGAINST MOAB

8 "Thus says the Lord GOD: Because
Moab[j] said, Behold, the house of Judah
is like all the other nations, 9 therefore
I will lay open the flank of Moab from
the cities[k] on its frontier, the glory of
the country, Beth-jesh´imoth, Ba´al-
me´on, and Kiriatha´im. 10 I will give it
along with the Ammonites to the peo-
ple of the East as a possession, that it[l]
may be remembered no more among
the nations, 11 and I will execute judg-
ments upon Moab. Then they will
know that I am the LORD.

PROCLAMATION AGAINST EDOM

12 "Thus says the Lord GOD:
Because Edom acted revengefully
against the house of Judah and has
grievously offended in taking ven-
geance upon them, 13 therefore thus
says the Lord GOD, I will stretch out
my hand against Edom, and cut off
from it man and beast; and I will make
it desolate; from Teman even to Dedan
they shall fall by the sword. 14 And I
will lay my vengeance upon Edom by
the hand of my people Israel; and they
shall do in Edom according to my an-
ger and according to my wrath; and
they shall know my vengeance, says
the Lord GOD.

PROCLAMATION AGAINST PHILISTIA

15 "Thus says the Lord GOD:
Because the Philistines acted re-
vengefully and took vengeance
with malice of heart to destroy in
never-ending enmity; 16 therefore
thus says the Lord GOD, Behold, I
will stretch out my hand against
the Philistines, and I will cut off the
Cher´ethites, and destroy the rest of
the seacoast. 17 I will execute great

[i] Cn: Heb lacks *the cities of*
[j] Gk Old Latin: Heb *Moab and Seir*
[k] Heb *cities from its cities*
[l] Cn: Heb *the Ammonites*

vengeance upon them with wrathful
chastisements. Then they will know
that I am the LORD, when I lay my
vengeance upon them."

PROCLAMATION AGAINST TYRE

26 *In the eleventh year, on the
first day of the month, the word
of the LORD came to me: 2"Son of
man, because Tyre said concerning
Jerusalem, 'Aha, the gate of the peo-
ples is broken, it has swung open to
me; I shall be replenished, now that
she is laid waste,' 3therefore thus
says the Lord GOD: Behold, I am
against you, O Tyre, and will bring
up many nations against you, as the
sea brings up its waves. 4They shall
destroy the walls of Tyre, and break
down her towers; and I will scrape
her soil from her, and make her a
bare rock. 5She shall be in the midst
of the sea a place for the spreading
of nets; for I have spoken, says the
Lord GOD; and she shall become a
spoil to the nations; 6and her daugh-
ters on the mainland shall be slain by
the sword. Then they will know that
I am the LORD.

7 "For thus says the Lord GOD:
Behold, I will bring upon Tyre from
the north Nebuchadrez'zar king of
Babylon, king of kings, with horses
and chariots, and with horsemen
and a host of many soldiers. 8He will
slay with the sword your daughters
on the mainland; he will set up a
siege wall against you, and throw
up a mound against you, and raise
a roof of shields against you. 9He
will direct the shock of his battering
rams against your walls, and with
his axes he will break down your
towers. 10His horses will be so many
that their dust will cover you; your
walls will shake at the noise of the
horsemen and wagons and chariots,
when he enters your gates as one en-
ters a city which has been breached.
11With the hoofs of his horses he will
trample all your streets; he will slay
your people with the sword; and
your mighty pillars will fall to the
ground. 12They will make a spoil of
your riches and a prey of your mer-
chandise; they will break down your
walls and destroy your pleasant
houses; your stones and timber and
soil they will cast into the midst of
the waters. 13And I will stop the mu-
sic of your songs, and the sound of
your lyres shall be heard no more. 14I
will make you a bare rock; you shall
be a place for the spreading of nets;
you shall never be rebuilt; for I the
LORD have spoken, says the Lord
GOD.

15 "Thus says the Lord GOD to
Tyre: Will not the coastlands shake
at the sound of your fall, when the
wounded groan, when slaughter is
made in the midst of you? 16Then all
the princes of the sea will step down
from their thrones, and remove their
robes, and strip off their embroidered
garments; they will clothe themselves
with trembling; they will sit upon the
ground and tremble every moment,
and be appalled at you. 17And they will
raise a lamentation over you, and say
to you,

'How you have vanished[a] from
the seas,
O city renowned,
that was mighty on the sea,
you and your inhabitants,
who imposed your terror
on all the mainland![b]
18Now the isles tremble
on the day of your fall;
yea, the isles that are in the
sea
are dismayed at your
passing.'

19 "For thus says the Lord GOD:
When I make you a city laid waste,
like the cities that are not inhab-
ited, when I bring up the deep over
you, and the great waters cover you,
20then I will thrust you down with

[a]Gk Old Latin Aquila: Heb *vanished, O inhabited one*
[b]Cn: Heb *her inhabitants*

those who descend into the Pit, to
the people of old, and I will make you
to dwell in the nether world, among
primeval ruins, with those who go
down to the Pit, so that you will not
be inhabited or have a place[c] in the
land of the living. 21I will bring you
to a dreadful end, and you shall be
no more; though you be sought for,
you will never be found again, says
the Lord GOD."

LAMENTATION OVER TYRE

27 The word of the LORD came to
me: 2"Now you, son of man, raise
a lamentation over Tyre, 3and say to
Tyre, who dwells at the entrance to
the sea, merchant of the peoples on
many coastlands, thus says the Lord
GOD:

"O Tyre, you have said,
'I am perfect in beauty.'
4Your borders are in the heart of
the seas;
your builders made perfect
your beauty.
5They made all your planks
of fir trees from Senir;
they took a cedar from
Lebanon
to make a mast for you.
6Of oaks of Bashan
they made your oars;
they made your deck of pines
from the coasts of Cyprus,
inlaid with ivory.
7Of fine embroidered linen from
Egypt
was your sail,
serving as your ensign;
blue and purple from the coasts
of Eli´shah
was your awning.
8The inhabitants of Sidon and
Arvad
were your rowers;
skilled men of Zemer[d] were
in you,
they were your pilots.
9The elders of Gebal and her
skilled men were in you,
caulking your seams;
all the ships of the sea with
their mariners were in
you,
to barter for your wares.

10 "Persia and Lud and Put were
in your army as your men of war;
they hung the shield and helmet in
you; they gave you splendor. 11The
men of Arvad and Helech[e] were upon
your walls round about, and men of
Gamad were in your towers; they
hung their shields upon your walls
round about; they made perfect your
beauty.

12 "Tarshish trafficked with you
because of your great wealth of every
kind; silver, iron, tin, and lead they
exchanged for your wares. 13Javan,
Tubal, and Meshech traded with you;
they exchanged the persons of men
and vessels of bronze for your mer-
chandise. 14Beth-togar´mah exchanged
for your wares horses, war horses, and
mules. 15The men of Rhodes[f] traded
with you; many coastlands were your
own special markets, they brought
you in payment ivory tusks and eb-
ony. 16Edom[g] trafficked with you be-
cause of your abundant goods; they
exchanged for your wares emeralds,
purple, embroidered work, fine lin-
en, coral, and agate. 17Judah and the
land of Israel traded with you; they
exchanged for your merchandise
wheat, olives and early figs,[h] hon-
ey, oil, and balm. 18Damascus traf-
ficked with you for your abundant
goods, because of your great wealth
of every kind; wine of Helbon, and
white wool, 19and wine[i] from Uzal
they exchanged for your wares;
wrought iron, cassia, and calamus

[c] Gk: Heb *I will give beauty*
[d] Compare Gen 10. 18: Heb *your skilled men, O Tyre*
[e] Or *and your army*
[f] Gk: Heb *Dedan*
[g] Another reading is *Aram*
[h] Cn: Heb *wheat of minnith and pannag*
[i] Gk: Heb *Vedan and Javan*

were bartered for your merchandise.
[20]Dedan traded with you in saddle-
cloths for riding. [21]Arabia and all the
princes of Kedar were your favored
dealers in lambs, rams, and goats; in
these they trafficked with you. [22]The
traders of Sheba and Ra´amah traded
with you; they exchanged for your
wares the best of all kinds of spic-
es, and all precious stones, and gold.
[23]Haran, Canneh, Eden,[a] Asshur, and
Chilmad traded with you. [24]These
traded with you in choice garments,
in clothes of blue and embroidered
work, and in carpets of colored stuff,
bound with cords and made secure;
in these they traded with you.[b] [25]The
ships of Tarshish traveled for you
with your merchandise.[c]

"So you were filled and heavily
laden
in the heart of the seas.
[26]Your rowers have brought you
out
into the high seas.
The east wind has wrecked
you
in the heart of the seas.
[27]Your riches, your wares, your
merchandise,
your mariners and your
pilots,
your caulkers, your dealers in
merchandise,
and all your men of war who
are in you,
with all your company
that is in your midst,
sink into the heart of the seas
on the day of your ruin.
[28]At the sound of the cry of your
pilots
the countryside shakes,
[29]and down from their ships
come all that handle the oar.
The mariners and all the pilots
of the sea
stand on the shore
[30]and wail aloud over you,
and cry bitterly.
They cast dust on their heads
and wallow in ashes;
[31]they make themselves bald for
you,
and gird themselves with
sackcloth,
and they weep over you in
bitterness of soul,
with bitter mourning.
[32]In their wailing they raise a
lamentation for you,
and lament over you:
'Who was ever destroyed[d] like
Tyre
in the midst of the sea?
[33]When your wares came from the
seas,
you satisfied many peoples;
with your abundant wealth and
merchandise
you enriched the kings of
the earth.
[34]Now you are wrecked by the
seas,
in the depths of the waters;
your merchandise and all your
crew
have sunk with you.
[35]All the inhabitants of the
coastlands
are appalled at you;
and their kings are horribly
afraid,
their faces are convulsed.
[36]The merchants among the peo-
ples hiss at you;
you have come to a dreadful
end
and shall be no more for
ever.'"

PROCLAMATION AGAINST THE KING OF TYRE

28 The word of the LORD came to me:
[2]"Son of man, say to the prince of
Tyre, Thus says the Lord GOD:
"Because your heart is proud,

[a]Cn: Heb *Eden the traders of Sheba*
[b]Cn: Heb *in your market*
[c]Cn: Heb *your travelers your merchandise*
[d]Tg Vg: Heb *like silence*

and you have said, 'I am a
god,
I sit in the seat of the gods,
in the heart of the seas,'
yet you are but a man, and no
god,
though you consider yourself
as wise as a god—
3you are indeed wiser than
Daniel;
no secret is hidden from you;
4by your wisdom and your
understanding
you have gotten wealth for
yourself,
and have gathered gold and
silver
into your treasuries;
5by your great wisdom in trade
you have increased your
wealth,
and your heart has become
proud in your
wealth—
6therefore thus says the Lord
GOD:
"Because you consider yourself
as wise as a god,
7therefore, behold, I will bring
strangers upon you,
the most terrible of the
nations;
and they shall draw their
swords against the
beauty of your wisdom
and defile your splendor.
8They shall thrust you down into
the Pit,
and you shall die the death
of the slain
in the heart of the seas.
9Will you still say, 'I am a god,'
in the presence of those who
slay you,
though you are but a man, and
no god,
in the hands of those who
wound you?
10You shall die the death of the
uncircumcised
by the hand of foreigners;
for I have spoken, says the
Lord GOD."

LAMENTATION OVER THE KING OF TYRE

11 Moreover the word of the LORD
came to me: 12"Son of man, raise a
lamentation over the king of Tyre, and
say to him, Thus says the Lord GOD:
"You were the signet of
perfection,[e]
full of wisdom
and perfect in beauty.
13You were in Eden, the garden
of God;
every precious stone was
your covering,
carnelian, topaz, and jasper,
chrysolite, beryl, and onyx,
sapphire,[f] carbuncle, and
emerald;
and wrought in gold were
your settings
and your engravings.[g]
On the day that you were
created
they were prepared.
14With an anointed guardian cher-
ub I placed you;[h]
you were on the holy moun-
tain of God;
in the midst of the stones of
fire you walked.
15You were blameless in your
ways
from the day you were
created,
till iniquity was found in
you.
16In the abundance of your trade
you were filled with
violence, and you
sinned;
so I cast you as a profane thing
from the mountain of
God,
and the guardian cherub
drove you out

[e] Heb obscure
[f] Or *lapis lazuli*
[g] Heb uncertain
[h] Heb uncertain

from the midst of the stones
of fire.
17Your heart was proud because of
your beauty;
you corrupted your wisdom
for the sake of your
splendor.
I cast you to the ground;
I exposed you before kings,
to feast their eyes on you.
18By the multitude of your
iniquities,
in the unrighteousness of
your trade
you profaned your
sanctuaries;
so I brought forth fire from the
midst of you;
it consumed you,
and I turned you to ashes upon
the earth
in the sight of all who saw
you.
19All who know you among the
peoples
are appalled at you;
you have come to a dreadful
end
and shall be no more for
ever."

PROCLAMATION AGAINST SIDON

20 The word of the LORD came to
me: 21"Son of man, set your face to-
ward Sidon, and prophesy against her
22and say, Thus says the Lord GOD:
"Behold, I am against you, O
Sidon,
and I will manifest my glory
in the midst of you.
And they shall know that I am
the LORD
when I execute judgments
in her,
and manifest my holiness
in her;
23for I will send pestilence into
her,
and blood into her streets;
and the slain shall fall in the
midst of her,
by the sword that is against
her on every side.
Then they will know that I am
the LORD.
24 "And for the house of Israel
there shall be no more a brier to
prick or a thorn to hurt them among
all their neighbors who have treated
them with contempt. Then they will
know that I am the Lord GOD.

FUTURE BLESSING FOR ISRAEL

25 "Thus says the Lord GOD: When
I gather the house of Israel from the
peoples among whom they are scat-
tered, and manifest my holiness in
them in the sight of the nations, then
they shall dwell in their own land
which I gave to my servant Jacob.
26And they shall dwell securely in it,
and they shall build houses and plant
vineyards. They shall dwell secure-
ly, when I execute judgments upon
all their neighbors who have treated
them with contempt. Then they will
know that I am the LORD their God."

PROCLAMATION AGAINST EGYPT

29 In the tenth year, in the tenth
month, on the twelfth day of the
month, the word of the LORD came
to me: 2"Son of man, set your face
against Pharaoh king of Egypt, and
prophesy against him and against all
Egypt; 3speak, and say, Thus says the
Lord GOD:
"Behold, I am against you,
Pharaoh king of Egypt,
the great dragon that lies
in the midst of his streams,
that says, 'My Nile is my own;
I made it.'[a]
4I will put hooks in your jaws,
and make the fish of your
streams stick to your
scales;
and I will draw you up out
of the midst of your
streams,
with all the fish of your
streams

[a] Syr Compare Gk: Heb *I have made mysel*

which stick to your scales.
5And I will cast you forth into the
wilderness,
you and all the fish of your
streams;
you shall fall upon the open
field,
and not be gathered and
buried.
To the beasts of the earth and
to the birds of the air
I have given you as food.

6 "Then all the inhabitants of
Egypt shall know that I am the LORD.
Because you[b] have been a staff of
reed to the house of Israel; 7when
they grasped you with the hand, you
broke, and tore all their shoulders;
and when they leaned upon you, you
broke, and made all their loins to
shake;[c] 8therefore thus says the Lord
GOD: Behold, I will bring a sword
upon you, and will cut off from you
man and beast; 9and the land of Egypt
shall be a desolation and a waste.
Then they will know that I am the
LORD. "Because you[d] said, 'The Nile
is mine, and I made it,' 10therefore,
behold, I am against you, and against
your streams, and I will make the
land of Egypt an utter waste and des-
olation, from Migdol to Syene, as far
as the border of Ethiopia. 11No foot
of man shall pass through it, and no
foot of beast shall pass through it;
it shall be uninhabited forty years.
12And I will make the land of Egypt
a desolation in the midst of desolat-
ed countries; and her cities shall be
a desolation forty years among cities
that are laid waste. I will scatter the
Egyptians among the nations, and
disperse them through the countries.

13 "For thus says the Lord GOD:
At the end of forty years I will gather
the Egyptians from the peoples among
whom they were scattered; 14and I will
restore the fortunes of Egypt, and
bring them back to the land of Pathros,
the land of their origin; and there they
shall be a lowly kingdom. 15It shall be
the most lowly of the kingdoms, and
never again exalt itself above the na-
tions; and I will make them so small
that they will never again rule over the
nations. 16And it shall never again be
the reliance of the house of Israel, re-
calling their iniquity, when they turn
to them for aid. Then they will know
that I am the Lord GOD."

BABYLONIA WILL PLUNDER EGYPT

17 In the twenty-seventh year, in
the first month, on the first day of the
month, the word of the LORD came to
me: 18"Son of man, Nebuchadrez'zar
king of Babylon made his army labor
hard against Tyre; every head was
made bald and every shoulder was
rubbed bare; yet neither he nor his
army got anything from Tyre to pay
for the labor that he had performed
against it. 19Therefore thus says the
Lord GOD: Behold, I will give the land
of Egypt to Nebuchadrez'zar king of
Babylon; and he shall carry off its
wealth[e] and despoil it and plunder it;
and it shall be the wages for his army.
20I have given him the land of Egypt as
his recompense for which he labored,
because they worked for me, says the
Lord GOD.

21 "On that day I will cause a horn
to spring forth to the house of Israel,
and I will open your lips among them.
Then they will know that I am the
LORD."

LAMENTATION FOR EGYPT

30 The word of the LORD came to
me: 2"Son of man, prophesy, and
say, Thus says the Lord GOD:

"Wail, 'Alas for the day!'
3For the day is near,
the day of the LORD is near;
it will be a day of clouds,
a time of doom for the
nations.

[b] Gk Syr Vg: Heb *they*
[c] Syr: Heb *stand*
[d] Gk Syr Vg: Heb *he*
[e] Or *multitude*

4A sword shall come upon Egypt,
and anguish shall be in Ethiopia,
when the slain fall in Egypt,
and her wealth is carried away,
and her foundations are torn down.
5Ethiopia, and Put, and Lud, and
all Arabia, and Libya,[a] and the people
of the land that is in league, shall fall
with them by the sword.
6"Thus says the LORD:
Those who support Egypt shall fall,
and her proud might shall come down;
from Migdol to Syene
they shall fall within her by the sword,
says the Lord GOD.
7And she[b] shall be desolated in the midst of desolated countries
and her cities shall be in the midst of cities that are laid waste.
8Then they will know that I am the LORD,
when I have set fire to Egypt,
and all her helpers are broken.
9 "On that day swift[c] messengers
shall go forth from me to terrify the
unsuspecting Ethiopians; and anguish
shall come upon them on the day of
Egypt's doom; for, lo, it comes!
10 "Thus says the Lord GOD:
I will put an end to the wealth[d] of Egypt,
by the hand of Nebuchadrez'zar king of Babylon.
11He and his people with him,
the most terrible of the nations,
shall be brought in to destroy the land;
and they shall draw their swords against Egypt,
and fill the land with the slain.
12And I will dry up the Nile,
and will sell the land into the hand of evil men;
I will bring desolation upon the land and everything in it,
by the hand of foreigners;
I, the LORD, have spoken.
13 "Thus says the Lord GOD:
I will destroy the idols,
and put an end to the images, in Memphis;
there shall no longer be a prince in the land of Egypt;
so I will put fear in the land of Egypt.
14I will make Pathros a desolation,
and will set fire to Zo'an,
and will execute acts of judgment upon Thebes.
15And I will pour my wrath upon Pelusium,
the stronghold of Egypt,
and cut off the multitude of Thebes.
16And I will set fire to Egypt;
Pelusium shall be in great agony;
Thebes shall be breached,
and its walls broken down.[e]
17The young men of On and of Pibe'seth shall fall by the sword;
and the women shall go into captivity.
18At Tehaph'nehes the day shall be dark,
when I break there the dominion of Egypt,
and her proud might shall come

[a]Gk Compare Syr Vg: Heb *Cub*
[b]Gk: Heb *they*
[c]Gk Syr: Heb *in ships*
[d]Or *multitude*
[e]Cn: Heb *and Memphis, distresses by day*

to an end;
she shall be covered by a cloud,
and her daughters shall go into captivity.
19 Thus I will execute acts of judgment upon Egypt.
Then they will know that I am the LORD."

PROCLAMATION AGAINST PHARAOH

20 In the eleventh year, in the first
month, on the seventh day of the
month, the word of the LORD came
to me: 21 "Son of man, I have broken
the arm of Pharaoh king of Egypt;
and lo, it has not been bound up, to
heal it by binding it with a bandage,
so that it may become strong to wield
the sword. 22 Therefore thus says
the Lord GOD: Behold, I am against
Pharaoh king of Egypt, and will break
his arms, both the strong arm and the
one that was broken; and I will make
the sword fall from his hand. 23 I will
scatter the Egyptians among the na-
tions, and disperse them through the
countries. 24 And I will strengthen the
arms of the king of Babylon, and put
my sword in his hand; but I will break
the arms of Pharaoh, and he will
groan before him like a man mortally
wounded. 25 I will strengthen the arms
of the king of Babylon, but the arms
of Pharaoh shall fall; and they shall
know that I am the LORD. When I put
my sword into the hand of the king of
Babylon, he shall stretch it out against
the land of Egypt; 26 and I will scatter
the Egyptians among the nations and
disperse them throughout the coun-
tries. Then they will know that I am
the LORD."

THE LOFTY CEDAR

31 In the eleventh year, in the third
month, on the first day of the
month, the word of the LORD came to
me: 2 "Son of man, say to Pharaoh king
of Egypt and to his multitude:

"Whom are you like in your greatness?
3 Behold, I will liken you to[f] a cedar in Lebanon,
with fair branches and forest shade,
and of great height,
its top among the clouds.[g]
4 The waters nourished it,
the deep made it grow tall,
making its rivers flow[h]
round the place of its planting,
sending forth its streams
to all the trees of the forest.
5 So it towered high
above all the trees of the forest;
its boughs grew large
and its branches long,
from abundant water in its shoots.
6 All the birds of the air
made their nests in its boughs;
under its branches all the beasts of the field
brought forth their young;
and under its shadow
dwelt all great nations.
7 It was beautiful in its greatness,
in the length of its branches;
for its roots went down
to abundant waters.
8 The cedars in the garden of God
could not rival it,
nor the fir trees equal its boughs;
the plane trees were as nothing
compared with its branches;
no tree in the garden of God
was like it in beauty.
9 I made it beautiful
in the mass of its branches,
and all the trees of Eden envied it,
that were in the garden of God.

[f] Cn: Heb *Behold, Assyria*
[g] Gk: Heb *thick boughs*
[h] Gk: Heb *going*

10 "Therefore thus says the Lord
God: Because it[a] towered high and
set its top among the clouds,[b] and its
heart was proud of its height, 11I will
give it into the hand of a mighty one of
the nations; he shall surely deal with
it as its wickedness deserves. I have
cast it out. 12Foreigners, the most ter-
rible of the nations, will cut it down
and leave it. On the mountains and
in all the valleys its branches will
fall, and its boughs will lie broken in
all the watercourses of the land; and
all the peoples of the earth will go
from its shadow and leave it. 13Upon
its ruin will dwell all the birds of the
air, and upon its branches will be all
the beasts of the field. 14All this is in
order that no trees by the waters may
grow to lofty height or set their tops
among the clouds,[c] and that no trees
that drink water may reach up to them
in height; for they are all given over
to death, to the nether world among
mortal men, with those who go down
to the Pit.

15 "Thus says the Lord God: When
it goes down to Sheol I will make the
deep mourn for[d] it, and restrain its riv-
ers, and many waters shall be stopped;
I will clothe Lebanon in gloom for it,
and all the trees of the field shall faint
because of it. 16I will make the nations
quake at the sound of its fall, when I
cast it down to Sheol with those who
go down to the Pit; and all the trees of
Eden, the choice and best of Lebanon,
all that drink water, will be comforted
in the nether world. 17They also shall
go down to Sheol with it, to those
who are slain by the sword; yea, those
who dwelt under its shadow among
the nations shall perish.[e] 18Whom are
you thus like in glory and in greatness
among the trees of Eden? You shall
be brought down with the trees of
Eden to the nether world; you shall lie
among the uncircumcised, with those
who are slain by the sword. "This is
Pharaoh and all his multitude, says
the Lord God."

LAMENTATION OVER PHARAOH AND EGYPT

32 In the twelfth year, in the twelfth
month, on the first day of the
month, the word of the LORD came to
me: 2"Son of man, raise a lamentation
over Pharaoh king of Egypt, and say
to him:

"You consider yourself a lion
among the nations,
but you are like a dragon in
the seas;
you burst forth in your rivers,
trouble the waters with your
feet,
and foul their rivers.
3Thus says the Lord God:
I will throw my net over you
with a host of many peoples;
and I[f] will haul you up in my
dragnet.
4And I will cast you on the
ground,
on the open field I will fling
you,
and will cause all the birds of
the air to settle on you,
and I will gorge the beasts of
the whole earth with
you.
5I will strew your flesh upon the
mountains,
and fill the valleys with your
carcass.[g]
6I will drench the land even to the
mountains
with your flowing blood;
and the watercourses will be
full of you.
7When I blot you out, I will cover
the heavens,
and make their stars dark;
I will cover the sun with a

[a] Syr Vg: Heb *you*
[b] Gk: Heb *thick boughs*
[c] Gk: Heb *thick boughs*
[d] Gk: Heb *mourn for, I have covered*
[e] Compare Gk: Heb obscure
[f] Gk Vg: Heb *they*
[g] Symmachus Syr Vg: Heb *your height*

cloud,
and the moon shall not give
its light.
8All the bright lights of heaven
will I make dark over you,
and put darkness upon your
land,
says the Lord GOD.

9 "I will trouble the hearts of many
peoples, when I carry you captive[h]
among the nations, into the countries
which you have not known. 10I will
make many peoples appalled at you,
and their kings shall shudder because
of you, when I brandish my sword be-
fore them; they shall tremble every
moment, every one for his own life,
on the day of your downfall. 11For thus
says the Lord GOD: The sword of the
king of Babylon shall come upon you.
12I will cause your multitude to fall by
the swords of mighty ones, all of them
most terrible among the nations.

"They shall bring to nought the
pride of Egypt,
and all its multitude shall
perish.
13I will destroy all its beasts
from beside many waters;
and no foot of man shall trou-
ble them any more,
nor shall the hoofs of beasts
trouble them.
14Then I will make their waters
clear,
and cause their rivers to run
like oil,
says the Lord GOD.
15When I make the land of Egypt
desolate
and when the land is
stripped of all that
fills it,
when I smite all who dwell
in it,
then they will know that I
am the LORD.

16This is a lamentation which
shall be chanted; the daughters of
the nations shall chant it; over Egypt,
and over all her multitude, shall they
chant it, says the Lord GOD."

DIRGE OVER EGYPT

17 In the twelfth year, in the first
month,[i] on the fifteenth day of the
month, the word of the LORD came to
me: 18"Son of man, wail over the mul-
titude of Egypt, and send them down,
her and the daughters of majestic na-
tions, to the nether world, to those
who have gone down to the Pit:

19'Whom do you surpass in
beauty?
Go down, and be laid with
the uncircumcised.'

20They shall fall amid those who
are slain by the sword,[j] and with her
shall lie all her multitudes.[k] 21The
mighty chiefs shall speak of them,
with their helpers, out of the midst of
Sheol: 'They have come down, they lie
still, the uncircumcised, slain by the
sword.'

22 "Assyria is there, and all her
company, their graves round about
her, all of them slain, fallen by the
sword; 23whose graves are set in the
uttermost parts of the Pit, and her
company is round about her grave;
all of them slain, fallen by the sword,
who spread terror in the land of the
living.

24 "Elam is there, and all her mul-
titude about her grave; all of them
slain, fallen by the sword, who went
down uncircumcised into the neth-
er world, who spread terror in the
land of the living, and they bear their
shame with those who go down to the
Pit. 25They have made her a bed among
the slain with all her multitude, their
graves round about her, all of them
uncircumcised, slain by the sword;
for terror of them was spread in the
land of the living, and they bear their
shame with those who go down to the
Pit; they are placed among the slain.

[h] Gk: Heb *bring your destruction*
[i] Gk: Heb lacks *in the first month*
[j] Gk Syr: Heb *sword, the sword is delivered*
[k] Gk: Heb *they have drawn her away and all her multitudes*

26 "Meshech and Tubal are there, and all their multitude, their graves round about them, all of them uncircumcised, slain by the sword; for they spread terror in the land of the living. 27 And they do not lie with the fallen mighty men of old[a] who went down to Sheol with their weapons of war, whose swords were laid under their heads, and whose shields[b] are upon their bones; for the terror of the mighty men was in the land of the living. 28 So you shall be broken and lie among the uncircumcised, with those who are slain by the sword.

29 "Edom is there, her kings and all her princes, who for all their might are laid with those who are slain by the sword; they lie with the uncircumcised, with those who go down to the Pit.

30 "The princes of the north are there, all of them, and all the Sido′nians, who have gone down in shame with the slain, for all the terror which they caused by their might; they lie uncircumcised with those who are slain by the sword, and bear their shame with those who go down to the Pit.

31 "When Pharaoh sees them, he will comfort himself for all his multitude, Pharaoh and all his army, slain by the sword, says the Lord GOD 32 For he[c] spread terror in the land of the living; therefore he shall be laid among the uncircumcised, with those who are slain by the sword, Pharaoh and all his multitude, says the Lord GOD."

EZEKIEL ISRAEL'S SENTRY

33 The word of the LORD came to me: 2 "Son of man, speak to your people and say to them, If I bring the sword upon a land, and the people of the land take a man from among them, and make him their watchman; 3 and if he sees the sword coming upon the land and blows the trumpet and warns the people; 4 then if any one who hears the sound of the trumpet does not take warning, and the sword comes and takes him away, his blood shall be upon his own head. 5 He heard the sound of the trumpet, and did not take warning; his blood shall be upon himself. But if he had taken warning, he would have saved his life. 6 But if the watchman sees the sword coming and does not blow the trumpet, so that the people are not warned, and the sword comes, and takes any one of them; that man is taken away in his iniquity, but his blood I will require at the watchman's hand.

7 "So you, son of man, I have made a watchman for the house of Israel; whenever you hear a word from my mouth, you shall give them warning from me. 8 If I say to the wicked, O wicked man, you shall surely die, and you do not speak to warn the wicked to turn from his way, that wicked man shall die in his iniquity, but his blood I will require at your hand. 9 But if you warn the wicked to turn from his way, and he does not turn from his way; he shall die in his iniquity, but you will have saved your life.

GOD'S JUSTICE AND MERCY

10 "And you, son of man, say to the house of Israel, Thus have you said: 'Our transgressions and our sins are upon us, and we waste away because of them; how then can we live?' 11 Say to them, As I live, says the Lord GOD, I have no pleasure in the death of the wicked, but that the wicked turn from his way and live; turn back, turn back from your evil ways; for why will you die, O house of Israel? 12 And you, son of man, say to your people, The righteousness of the righteous shall not deliver him when he transgresses; and as for the wickedness of the wicked, he shall not fall by it when he turns from his wickedness; and

[a] Gk Old Latin: Heb *of the uncircumcised*
[b] Cn: Heb *iniquities*
[c] Cn: Heb *I*

the righteous shall not be able to live
by his righteousness[d] when he sins.
13Though I say to the righteous that
he shall surely live, yet if he trusts in
his righteousness and commits iniqui-
ty, none of his righteous deeds shall
be remembered; but in the iniquity
that he has committed he shall die.
14Again, though I say to the wicked,
'You shall surely die,' yet if he turns
from his sin and does what is lawful
and right, 15if the wicked restores the
pledge, gives back what he has taken
by robbery, and walks in the stat-
utes of life, committing no iniquity;
he shall surely live, he shall not die.
16None of the sins that he has commit-
ted shall be remembered against him;
he has done what is lawful and right,
he shall surely live.

17 "Yet your people say, 'The way
of the Lord is not just'; when it is their
own way that is not just. 18When the
righteous turns from his righteous-
ness, and commits iniquity, he shall
die for it. 19And when the wicked
turns from his wickedness, and does
what is lawful and right, he shall live
by it. 20Yet you say, 'The way of the
Lord is not just.' O house of Israel, I
will judge each of you according to his
ways."

THE FALL OF JERUSALEM

21 In the twelfth year of our exile,
in the tenth month, on the fifth day
of the month, a man who had escaped
from Jerusalem came to me and said,
"The city has fallen." 22Now the hand
of the LORD had been upon me the
evening before the fugitive came; and
he had opened my mouth by the time
the man came to me in the morning;
so my mouth was opened, and I was
no longer dumb.

THE SURVIVORS IN JUDAH

23 The word of the LORD came to
me: 24"Son of man, the inhabitants
of these waste places in the land of
Israel keep saying, 'Abraham was
only one man, yet he got possession
of the land; but we are many; the
land is surely given us to possess.'
25Therefore say to them, Thus says
the Lord GOD: You eat flesh with
the blood, and lift up your eyes to
your idols, and shed blood; shall you
then possess the land? 26You resort
to the sword, you commit abomi-
nations and each of you defiles his
neighbor's wife; shall you then pos-
sess the land? 27Say this to them,
Thus says the Lord GOD: As I live,
surely those who are in the waste
places shall fall by the sword; and
him that is in the open field I will
give to the beasts to be devoured;
and those who are in strongholds
and in caves shall die by pestilence.
28And I will make the land a deso-
lation and a waste; and her proud
might shall come to an end; and the
mountains of Israel shall be so des-
olate that none will pass through.
29Then they will know that I am the
LORD, when I have made the land a
desolation and a waste because of all
their abominations which they have
committed.

30 "As for you, son of man, your
people who talk together about you
by the walls and at the doors of the
houses, say to one another, each to
his brother, 'Come, and hear what
the word is that comes forth from
the LORD.' 31And they come to you
as people come, and they sit before
you as my people, and they hear
what you say but they will not do it;
for with their lips they show much
love, but their heart is set on their
gain. 32And lo, you are to them like
one who sings love songs[e] with a
beautiful voice and plays well on an
instrument, for they hear what you
say, but they will not do it. 33When
this comes—and come it will!—then
they will know that a prophet has
been among them."

[d]Heb *by it*
[e]Cn: Heb *like a love song*

ISRAEL'S FALSE SHEPHERDS

34 The word of the LORD came
to me: 2"Son of man, prophe-
sy against the shepherds of Israel,*
prophesy, and say to them, even to the
shepherds, Thus says the Lord GOD:
Ho, shepherds of Israel who have been
feeding yourselves! Should not shep-
herds feed the sheep? 3You eat the fat,
you clothe yourselves with the wool,
you slaughter the fatlings; but you
do not feed the sheep. 4The weak you
have not strengthened, the sick you
have not healed, the crippled you have
not bound up, the strayed you have
not brought back, the lost you have
not sought, and with force and harsh-
ness you have ruled them. 5So they
were scattered, because there was no
shepherd; and they became food for
all the wild beasts. 6My sheep were
scattered, they wandered over all the
mountains and on every high hill; my
sheep were scattered over all the face
of the earth, with none to search or
seek for them.

7 "Therefore, you shepherds, hear
the word of the LORD: 8As I live, says
the Lord GOD, because my sheep have
become a prey, and my sheep have
become food for all the wild beasts,
since there was no shepherd; and be-
cause my shepherds have not searched
for my sheep, but the shepherds have
fed themselves, and have not fed my
sheep; 9therefore, you shepherds, hear
the word of the LORD: 10Thus says the
Lord GOD, Behold, I am against the
shepherds; and I will require my sheep
at their hand, and put a stop to their
feeding the sheep; no longer shall the
shepherds feed themselves. I will res-
cue my sheep from their mouths, that
they may not be food for them.

GOD, THE TRUE SHEPHERD

11 "For thus says the Lord GOD:
Behold, I, I myself will search for my
sheep, and will seek them out. 12As
a shepherd seeks out his flock when
some of his sheep[a] have been scat-
tered abroad, so will I seek out my
sheep; and I will rescue them from all
places where they have been scattered
on a day of clouds and thick darkness.
13And I will bring them out from the
peoples, and gather them from the
countries, and will bring them into
their own land; and I will feed them on
the mountains of Israel, by the foun-
tains, and in all the inhabited places
of the country. 14I will feed them with
good pasture, and upon the mountain
heights of Israel shall be their pas-
ture; there they shall lie down in good
grazing land, and on fat pasture they
shall feed on the mountains of Israel.
15I myself will be the shepherd of my
sheep, and I will make them lie down,
says the Lord GOD. 16I will seek the
lost, and I will bring back the strayed,
and I will bind up the crippled, and I
will strengthen the weak, and the fat
and the strong I will watch over;[b] I
will feed them in justice.

17 "As for you, my flock, thus says
the Lord GOD: Behold, I judge be-
tween sheep and sheep, rams and he-
goats. 18Is it not enough for you to feed
on the good pasture, that you must
tread down with your feet the rest of
your pasture; and to drink of clear wa-
ter, that you must foul the rest with
your feet? 19And must my sheep eat
what you have trodden with your feet,
and drink what you have fouled with
your feet?

20 "Therefore, thus says the Lord
GOD to them: Behold, I, I myself will
judge between the fat sheep and the
lean sheep. 21Because you push with
side and shoulder, and thrust at all
the weak with your horns, till you
have scattered them abroad, 22I will
save my flock, they shall no longer be
a prey; and I will judge between sheep
and sheep. 23*And I will set up over
them one shepherd, my servant David,
and he shall feed them: he shall feed
them and be their shepherd. 24And I,

[a] Cn: Heb *when he is among his sheep*
[b] Gk Syr Vg: Heb *destroy*

the LORD, will be their God, and my
servant David shall be prince among
them; I, the LORD, have spoken.
25 "I will make with them a cove-
nant of peace and banish wild beasts
from the land, so that they may dwell
securely in the wilderness and sleep
in the woods. 26And I will make them
and the places round about my hill
a blessing; and I will send down the
showers in their season; they shall be
showers of blessing. 27And the trees of
the field shall yield their fruit, and the
earth shall yield its increase, and they
shall be secure in their land; and they
shall know that I am the LORD, when
I break the bars of their yoke, and de-
liver them from the hand of those who
enslaved them. 28They shall no more
be a prey to the nations, nor shall the
beasts of the land devour them; they
shall dwell securely, and none shall
make them afraid. 29And I will pro-
vide for them prosperous[c] plantations
so that they shall no more be con-
sumed with hunger in the land, and
no longer suffer the reproach of the
nations. 30And they shall know that
I, the LORD their God, am with them,
and that they, the house of Israel, are
my people, says the Lord GOD. 31And
you are my sheep, the sheep of my
pasture,[d] and I am your God, says the
Lord GOD."

JUDGMENT ON MOUNT SEIR

35 The word of the LORD came to
me: 2"Son of man, set your face
against Mount Se´ir, and prophesy
against it, 3and say to it, Thus says the
Lord GOD: Behold, I am against you,
Mount Se´ir, and I will stretch out
my hand against you, and I will make
you a desolation and a waste. 4I will
lay your cities waste, and you shall
become a desolation; and you shall
know that I am the LORD. 5Because
you cherished perpetual enmity, and
gave over the people of Israel to the
power of the sword at the time of
their calamity, at the time of their fi-
nal punishment; 6therefore, as I live,
says the Lord GOD, I will prepare
you for blood, and blood shall pursue
you; because you are guilty of blood,[e]
therefore blood shall pursue you. 7I
will make Mount Se´ir a waste and a
desolation; and I will cut off from it
all who come and go. 8And I will fill
your mountains with the slain; on
your hills and in your valleys and in
all your ravines those slain with the
sword shall fall. 9I will make you a
perpetual desolation, and your cities
shall not be inhabited. Then you will
know that I am the LORD.
10 "Because you said, 'These two
nations and these two countries shall
be mine, and we will take possession
of them,'—although the LORD was
there 11therefore, as I live, says the
Lord GOD, I will deal with you ac-
cording to the anger and envy which
you showed because of your hatred
against them; and I will make myself
known among you,[f] when I judge you.
12And you shall know that I, the LORD,
have heard all the revilings which
you uttered against the mountains of
Israel, saying, 'They are laid desolate,
they are given us to devour.' 13And
you magnified yourselves against me
with your mouth, and multiplied your
words against me; I heard it. 14Thus
says the Lord GOD: For the rejoicing of
the whole earth I will make you deso-
late. 15As you rejoiced over the inheri-
tance of the house of Israel, because it
was desolate, so I will deal with you;
you shall be desolate, Mount Se´ir,
and all Edom, all of it. Then they will
know that I am the LORD.

BLESSING ON ISRAEL

36 "And you, son of man, prophesy
to the mountains of Israel, and
say, O mountains of Israel, hear the
word of the LORD. 2Thus says the Lord

[c] Gk Syr Old Latin: Heb *for renown*
[d] Gk Old Latin: Heb *pasture you are men*
[e] Gk: Heb *you have hated blood*
[f] Gk: Heb *them*

God: Because the enemy said of you,
'Aha!' and, 'The ancient heights have
become our possession,' 3therefore
prophesy, and say, Thus says the Lord
God: Because, yea, because they made
you desolate, and crushed you from all
sides, so that you became the posses-
sion of the rest of the nations, and
you became the talk and evil gossip of
the people; 4therefore, O mountains
of Israel, hear the word of the Lord
God: Thus says the Lord God to the
mountains and the hills, the ravines
and the valleys, the desolate wastes
and the deserted cities, which have
become a prey and derision to the rest
of the nations round about; 5therefore
thus says the Lord God: I speak in my
hot jealousy against the rest of the na-
tions, and against all Edom, who gave
my land to themselves as a posses-
sion with wholehearted joy and utter
contempt, that they might possess[a] it
and plunder it. 6Therefore prophesy
concerning the land of Israel, and say
to the mountains and hills, to the ra-
vines and valleys, Thus says the Lord
God: Behold, I speak in my jealous
wrath, because you have suffered the
reproach of the nations; 7therefore
thus says the Lord God: I swear that
the nations that are round about you
shall themselves suffer reproach.

8 "But you, O mountains of Israel,
shall shoot forth your branches, and
yield your fruit to my people Israel;
for they will soon come home. 9For
behold, I am for you, and I will turn
to you, and you shall be tilled and
sown; 10and I will multiply men upon
you, the whole house of Israel, all of
it; the cities shall be inhabited and the
waste places rebuilt; 11and I will multi-
ply upon you man and beast; and they
shall increase and be fruitful; and I
will cause you to be inhabited as in
your former times, and will do more
good to you than ever before. Then
you will know that I am the Lord.
12Yea, I will let men walk upon you,
even my people Israel; and they shall
possess you, and you shall be their
inheritance, and you shall no lon-
ger bereave them of children. 13Thus
says the Lord God: Because men say
to you, 'You devour men, and you be-
reave your nation of children,' 14there-
fore you shall no longer devour men
and no longer bereave your nation of
children, says the Lord God; 15and I
will not let you hear any more the re-
proach of the nations, and you shall
no longer bear the disgrace of the peo-
ples and no longer cause your nation
to stumble, says the Lord God."

THE RENEWAL OF ISRAEL

16 The word of the Lord came to
me: 17"Son of man, when the house of
Israel dwelt in their own land, they
defiled it by their ways and their do-
ings; their conduct before me was like
the uncleanness of a woman in her
impurity. 18So I poured out my wrath
upon them for the blood which they
had shed in the land, for the idols with
which they had defiled it. 19I scattered
them among the nations, and they
were dispersed through the countries;
in accordance with their conduct
and their deeds I judged them. 20But
when they came to the nations, wher-
ever they came, they profaned my
holy name, in that men said of them,
'These are the people of the Lord,
and yet they had to go out of his land.'
21But I had concern for my holy name,
which the house of Israel caused to be
profaned among the nations to which
they came.

22 "Therefore say to the house of
Israel, Thus says the Lord God: It is
not for your sake, O house of Israel,
that I am about to act, but for the
sake of my holy name, which you
have profaned among the nations to
which you came. 23And I will vindi-
cate the holiness of my great name,
which has been profaned among the
nations, and which you have pro-
faned among them; and the nations
will know that I am the Lord, says

[a]One Ms: Heb *drive out*

the Lord God, when through you I
vindicate my holiness before their
eyes. 24For I will take you from the
nations, and gather you from all the
countries, and bring you into your
own land. 25I will sprinkle clean wa-
ter upon you, and you shall be clean
from all your uncleannesses, and
from all your idols I will cleanse you.
26A new heart I will give you, and a
new spirit I will put within you; and
I will take out of your flesh the heart
of stone and give you a heart of flesh.
27And I will put my spirit within you,
and cause you to walk in my statutes
and be careful to observe my ordi-
nances. 28You shall dwell in the land
which I gave to your fathers; and you
shall be my people, and I will be your
God. 29And I will deliver you from all
your uncleannesses; and I will sum-
mon the grain and make it abundant
and lay no famine upon you. 30I will
make the fruit of the tree and the in-
crease of the field abundant, that you
may never again suffer the disgrace
of famine among the nations. 31Then
you will remember your evil ways,
and your deeds that were not good;
and you will loathe yourselves for
your iniquities and your abominable
deeds. 32It is not for your sake that I
will act, says the Lord God; let that
be known to you. Be ashamed and
confounded for your ways, O house
of Israel.

33 "Thus says the Lord God: On
the day that I cleanse you from all
your iniquities, I will cause the cities
to be inhabited, and the waste places
shall be rebuilt. 34And the land that
was desolate shall be tilled, instead
of being the desolation that it was in
the sight of all who passed by. 35And
they will say, 'This land that was des-
olate has become like the garden of
Eden; and the waste and desolate and
ruined cities are now inhabited and
fortified.' 36Then the nations that are
left round about you shall know that
I, the Lord, have rebuilt the ruined
places, and replanted that which was
desolate; I, the Lord, have spoken,
and I will do it.

37 "Thus says the Lord God: This
also I will let the house of Israel ask
me to do for them: to increase their
men like a flock. 38Like the flock for
sacrifices,[b] like the flock at Jerusalem
during her appointed feasts, so shall
the waste cities be filled with flocks
of men. Then they will know that I am
the Lord."

THE VALLEY OF DRY BONES

37 The hand of the Lord was upon
me, and he brought me out by
the Spirit of the Lord, and set me
down in the midst of the valley;[c] it
was full of bones.* 2And he led me
round among them; and behold, there
were very many upon the valley;[d] and
lo, they were very dry. 3And he said
to me, "Son of man, can these bones
live?" And I answered, "O Lord God,
thou knowest." 4Again he said to me,
"Prophesy to these bones, and say to
them, O dry bones, hear the word of
the Lord. 5Thus says the Lord God
to these bones: Behold, I will cause
breath[e] to enter you, and you shall
live. 6And I will lay sinews upon you,
and will cause flesh to come upon
you, and cover you with skin, and put
breath[f] in you, and you shall live; and
you shall know that I am the Lord."

7 So I prophesied as I was com-
manded; and as I prophesied, there
was a noise, and behold, a rattling;
and the bones came together, bone
to its bone. 8And as I looked, there
were sinews on them, and flesh had
come upon them, and skin had cov-
ered them; but there was no breath in
them. 9Then he said to me, "Prophesy
to the breath, prophesy, son of man,

[b] Heb *flock of holy things*
[c] Or *plain*
[d] Or *plain*
[e] Or *spirit*
[f] Or *spirit*

and say to the breath,[a] Thus says the
Lord GOD: Come from the four winds,
O breath,[b] and breathe upon these
slain, that they may live." 10So I proph-
esied as he commanded me, and the
breath came into them, and they lived,
and stood upon their feet, an exceed-
ingly great host.

11 Then he said to me, "Son of
man, these bones are the whole house
of Israel. Behold, they say, 'Our bones
are dried up, and our hope is lost; we
are clean cut off.' 12Therefore proph-
esy, and say to them, Thus says the
Lord GOD: Behold, I will open your
graves, and raise you from your
graves, O my people; and I will bring
you home into the land of Israel. 13And
you shall know that I am the LORD,
when I open your graves, and raise
you from your graves, O my people.
14And I will put my Spirit within you,
and you shall live, and I will place you
in your own land; then you shall know
that I, the LORD, have spoken, and I
have done it, says the LORD."

THE TWO STICKS

15 The word of the LORD came to
me: 16"Son of man, take a stick and
write on it, 'For Judah, and the chil-
dren of Israel associated with him';
then take another stick and write
upon it, 'For Joseph (the stick of
E´phraim) and all the house of Israel
associated with him'; 17and join them
together into one stick, that they may
become one in your hand. 18And when
your people say to you, 'Will you not
show us what you mean by these?'
19say to them, Thus says the Lord
GOD: Behold, I am about to take the
stick of Joseph (which is in the hand
of E´phraim) and the tribes of Israel
associated with him; and I will join[c]
with it the stick of Judah, and make
them one stick, that they may be
one in my hand. 20When the sticks
on which you write are in your hand
before their eyes, 21then say to them,
Thus says the Lord GOD: Behold, I
will take the people of Israel from the
nations among which they have gone,
and will gather them from all sides,
and bring them to their own land;
22and I will make them one nation
in the land, upon the mountains of
Israel; and one king shall be king over
them all; and they shall be no longer
two nations, and no longer divided
into two kingdoms. 23They shall not
defile themselves any more with their
idols and their detestable things, or
with any of their transgressions; but
I will save them from all the backslid-
ings in which they have sinned, and
will cleanse them; and they shall be
my people, and I will be their God.

24 "My servant David shall be king
over them; and they shall all have one
shepherd. They shall follow my ordi-
nances and be careful to observe my
statutes. 25They shall dwell in the land
where your fathers dwelt that I gave
to my servant Jacob; they and their
children and their children's children
shall dwell there for ever; and David
my servant shall be their prince for
ever. 26I will make a covenant of peace
with them; it shall be an everlasting
covenant with them; and I will bless[d]
them and multiply them, and will set
my sanctuary in the midst of them for
evermore. 27My dwelling place shall be
with them; and I will be their God,
and they shall be my people. 28Then
the nations will know that I the LORD
sanctify Israel, when my sanctuary is
in the midst of them for evermore."

INVASION BY GOG

38 *The word of the LORD came to
me: 2"Son of man, set your face
toward Gog, of the land of Magog, the
chief prince of Meshech and Tubal,
and prophesy against him 3and say,
Thus says the Lord GOD: Behold, I
am against you, O Gog, chief prince of

[a] Or *wind* or *spirit*
[b] Or *wind* or *spirit*
[c] Heb *join them*
[d] Tg: Heb *give*

Meshech and Tubal; 4and I will turn
you about, and put hooks into your
jaws, and I will bring you forth, and all
your army, horses and horsemen, all
of them clothed in full armor, a great
company, all of them with buckler
and shield, wielding swords; 5Persia,
Cush, and Put are with them, all of
them with shield and helmet; 6Gomer
and all his hordes; Beth-togar′mah
from the uttermost parts of the north
with all his hordes—many peoples are
with you.

7 "Be ready and keep ready, you
and all the hosts that are assembled
about you, and be a guard for them.
8After many days you will be mus-
tered; in the latter years you will go
against the land that is restored from
war, the land where people were gath-
ered from many nations upon the
mountains of Israel, which had been
a continual waste; its people were
brought out from the nations and now
dwell securely, all of them. 9You will
advance, coming on like a storm, you
will be like a cloud covering the land,
you and all your hordes, and many
peoples with you.

10 "Thus says the Lord God: On
that day thoughts will come into your
mind, and you will devise an evil
scheme 11and say, 'I will go up against
the land of unwalled villages; I will
fall upon the quiet people who dwell
securely, all of them dwelling without
walls, and having no bars or gates';
12to seize spoil and carry off plun-
der; to assail the waste places which
are now inhabited, and the people
who were gathered from the nations,
who have gotten cattle and goods,
who dwell at the center of the earth.
13Sheba and Dedan and the merchants
of Tarshish and all its villages will say
to you, 'Have you come to seize spoil?
Have you assembled your hosts to car-
ry off plunder, to carry away silver and
gold, to take away cattle and goods, to
seize great spoil?'

14 "Therefore, son of man, prophe-
sy, and say to Gog, Thus says the Lord
God: On that day when my people
Israel are dwelling securely, you will
bestir yourself[e] 15and come from your
place out of the uttermost parts of the
north, you and many peoples with
you, all of them riding on horses, a
great host, a mighty army; 16you will
come up against my people Israel, like
a cloud covering the land. In the latter
days I will bring you against my land,
that the nations may know me, when
through you, O Gog, I vindicate my
holiness before their eyes.

JUDGMENT ON GOG

17 "Thus says the Lord God: Are
you he of whom I spoke in former days
by my servants the prophets of Israel,
who in those days prophesied for
years that I would bring you against
them? 18But on that day, when Gog
shall come against the land of Israel,
says the Lord God, my wrath will be
roused. 19For in my jealousy and in my
blazing wrath I declare, On that day
there shall be a great shaking in the
land of Israel; 20the fish of the sea, and
the birds of the air, and the beasts of
the field, and all creeping things that
creep on the ground, and all the men
that are upon the face of the earth,
shall quake at my presence, and the
mountains shall be thrown down,
and the cliffs shall fall, and every wall
shall tumble to the ground. 21I will
summon every kind of terror[f] against
Gog,[g] says the Lord God; every man's
sword will be against his brother.
22With pestilence and bloodshed I will
enter into judgment with him; and I
will rain upon him and his hordes and
the many peoples that are with him,
torrential rains and hailstones, fire
and brimstone. 23So I will show my
greatness and my holiness and make
myself known in the eyes of many na-
tions. Then they will know that I am
the Lord.

[e]Gk: Heb *will you not know?*
[f]Gk: Heb *a sword to all my mountains*
[g]Heb *him*

GOG'S ARMIES DESTROYED

39 "And you, son of man, prophesy
against Gog, and say, Thus says
the Lord GOD: Behold, I am against
you, O Gog, chief prince of Meshech
and Tubal; 2and I will turn you about
and drive you forward, and bring you
up from the uttermost parts of the
north, and lead you against the moun-
tains of Israel; 3then I will strike your
bow from your left hand, and will
make your arrows drop out of your
right hand. 4You shall fall upon the
mountains of Israel, you and all your
hordes and the peoples that are with
you; I will give you to birds of prey of
every sort and to the wild beasts to be
devoured. 5You shall fall in the open
field; for I have spoken, says the Lord
GOD. 6I will send fire on Magog and on
those who dwell securely in the coast-
lands; and they shall know that I am
the LORD.

7 "And my holy name I will make
known in the midst of my people
Israel; and I will not let my holy name
be profaned any more; and the na-
tions shall know that I am the LORD,
the Holy One in Israel. 8Behold, it is
coming and it will be brought about,
says the Lord GOD. That is the day of
which I have spoken.

9 "Then those who dwell in the
cities of Israel will go forth and make
fires of the weapons and burn them,
shields and bucklers, bow and arrows,
handpikes and spears, and they will
make fires of them for seven years;
10so that they will not need to take
wood out of the field or cut down any
out of the forests, for they will make
their fires of the weapons; they will
despoil those who despoiled them,
and plunder those who plundered
them, says the Lord GOD.

THE BURIAL OF GOG

11 "On that day I will give to Gog
a place for burial in Israel, the Valley
of the Travelers[a] east of the sea; it
will block the travelers, for there Gog
and all his multitude will be buried;
it will be called the Valley of Hamon-
gog.[b] 12For seven months the house of
Israel will be burying them, in order
to cleanse the land. 13All the people
of the land will bury them; and it will
redound to their honor on the day
that I show my glory, says the Lord
GOD. 14They will set apart men to
pass through the land continually and
bury[c] those remaining upon the face
of the land, so as to cleanse it; at the
end of seven months they will make
their search. 15And when these pass
through the land and any one sees a
man's bone, then he shall set up a sign
by it, till the buriers have buried it
in the Valley of Hamon-gog. 16(A city
Hamo'nah[d] is there also.) Thus shall
they cleanse the land.

17 "As for you, son of man, thus
says the Lord GOD: Speak to the birds
of every sort and to all beasts of the
field, 'Assemble and come, gather
from all sides to the sacrificial feast
which I am preparing for you, a great
sacrificial feast upon the mountains
of Israel, and you shall eat flesh and
drink blood. 18You shall eat the flesh
of the mighty, and drink the blood
of the princes of the earth—of rams,
of lambs, and of goats, of bulls, all of
them fatlings of Bashan. 19And you
shall eat fat till you are filled, and
drink blood till you are drunk, at the
sacrificial feast which I am preparing
for you. 20And you shall be filled at
my table with horses and riders, with
mighty men and all kinds of warriors,'
says the Lord GOD.

ISRAEL RESTORED TO THE LAND

21 "And I will set my glory among
the nations; and all the nations shall
see my judgment which I have execut-
ed, and my hand which I have laid on
them. 22The house of Israel shall know

[a] Or *Abarim*
[b] That is *the multitude of Gog*
[c] Gk Syr: Heb *bury the travelers*
[d] That is *Multitude*

that I am the LORD their God, from
that day forward. 23And the nations
shall know that the house of Israel
went into captivity for their iniquity,
because they dealt so treacherously
with me that I hid my face from them
and gave them into the hand of their
adversaries, and they all fell by the
sword. 24I dealt with them according
to their uncleanness and their trans-
gressions, and hid my face from them.

25 "Therefore thus says the Lord
GOD: Now I will restore the for-
tunes of Jacob, and have mercy upon
the whole house of Israel; and I will
be jealous for my holy name. 26They
shall forget their shame, and all the
treachery they have practiced against
me, when they dwell securely in their
land with none to make them afraid,
27when I have brought them back from
the peoples and gathered them from
their enemies' lands, and through
them have vindicated my holiness in
the sight of many nations. 28Then they
shall know that I am the LORD their
God because I sent them into exile
among the nations, and then gathered
them into their own land. I will leave
none of them remaining among the
nations any more; 29and I will not hide
my face any more from them, when I
pour out my Spirit upon the house of
Israel, says the Lord GOD."

THE VISION OF THE NEW TEMPLE

40 *In the twenty-fifth year of our
exile, at the beginning of the year,
on the tenth day of the month, in the
fourteenth year after the city was con-
quered, on that very day, the hand of
the LORD was upon me, 2and brought
me in the visions of God into the land
of Israel, and set me down upon a very
high mountain, on which was a struc-
ture like a city opposite me.[e] 3When
he brought me there, behold, there
was a man, whose appearance was
like bronze, with a line of flax and a
measuring reed in his hand; and he
was standing in the gateway. 4And the
man said to me, "Son of man, look
with your eyes, and hear with your
ears, and set your mind upon all that I
shall show you, for you were brought
here in order that I might show it to
you; declare all that you see to the
house of Israel."

5 And behold, there was a wall all
around the outside of the temple area,
and the length of the measuring reed
in the man's hand was six long cubits,
each being a cubit and a handbreadth
in length; so he measured the thick-
ness of the wall, one reed; and the
height, one reed. 6Then he went into
the gateway facing east, going up its
steps, and measured the threshold of
the gate, one reed deep;[f] 7and the side
rooms, one reed long, and one reed
broad; and the space between the side
rooms, five cubits; and the threshold
of the gate by the vestibule of the gate
at the inner end, one reed. 8Then he
measured the vestibule of the gate-
way, eight cubits; 9and its jambs, two
cubits; and the vestibule of the gate
was at the inner end. 10And there were
three side rooms on either side of the
east gate; the three were of the same
size; and the jambs on either side were
of the same size. 11Then he measured
the breadth of the opening of the gate-
way, ten cubits; and the breadth of the
gateway, thirteen cubits. 12There was a
barrier before the side rooms, one cu-
bit on either side; and the side rooms
were six cubits on either side. 13Then
he measured the gate from the back[g]
of the one side room to the back[h] of
the other, a breadth of five and twenty
cubits, from door to door. 14He mea-
sured also the vestibule, twenty cu-
bits; and round about the vestibule of
the gateway was the court.[i] 15From the
front of the gate at the entrance to the

[e] Gk: Heb *on the south*
[f] Heb *deep, and one threshold, one reed deep*
[g] Compare Gk: Heb *roof*
[h] Compare Gk: Heb *roof*
[i] Compare Gk: Heb *and he made the jambs sixty cubits, and to the jamb of the court was the gate-*

end of the inner vestibule of the gate was fifty cubits. 16And the gateway had windows round about, narrowing inwards into their jambs in the side rooms, and likewise the vestibule had windows round about inside, and on the jambs were palm trees.

17 Then he brought me into the outer court; and behold, there were chambers and a pavement, round about the court; thirty chambers fronted on the pavement. 18And the pavement ran along the side of the gates, corresponding to the length of the gates; this was the lower pavement. 19Then he measured the distance from the inner front of[a] the lower gate to the outer front of the inner court, a hundred cubits. Then he went before me to the north, 20and behold, there was a gate[b] which faced toward the north, belonging to the outer court. He measured its length and its breadth. 21Its side rooms, three on either side, and its jambs and its vestibule were of the same size as those of the first gate; its length was fifty cubits, and its breadth twenty-five cubits. 22And its windows, its vestibule, and its palm trees were of the same size as those of the gate which faced toward the east; and seven steps led up to it; and its vestibule was on the inside. 23And opposite the gate on the north, as on the east, was a gate to the inner court; and he measured from gate to gate, a hundred cubits.

24 And he led me toward the south, and behold, there was a gate on the south; and he measured its jambs and its vestibule; they had the same size as the others. 25And there were windows round about in it and in its vestibule, like the windows of the others; its length was fifty cubits, and its breadth twenty-five cubits. 26And there were seven steps leading up to it, and its vestibule was on the inside; and it had palm trees on its jambs, one on either side. 27And there was a gate on the south of the inner court; and he measured from gate to gate toward the south, a hundred cubits.

28 Then he brought me to the inner court by the south gate, and he measured the south gate; it was of the same size as the others. 29Its side rooms, its jambs, and its vestibule were of the same size as the others; and there were windows round about in it and in its vestibule; its length was fifty cubits, and its breadth twenty-five cubits. 30And there were vestibules round about, twenty-five cubits long and five cubits broad. 31Its vestibule faced the outer court, and palm trees were on its jambs, and its stairway had eight steps.

32 Then he brought me to the inner court on the east side, and he measured the gate; it was of the same size as the others. 33Its side rooms, its jambs, and its vestibule were of the same size as the others; and there were windows round about in it and in its vestibule; its length was fifty cubits, and its breadth twenty-five cubits. 34Its vestibule faced the outer court, and it had palm trees on its jambs, one on either side; and its stairway had eight steps.

35 Then he brought me to the north gate, and he measured it; it had the same size as the others. 36Its side rooms, its jambs, and its vestibule were of the same size as the others;[c] and it had windows round about; its length was fifty cubits, and its breadth twenty-five cubits. 37Its vestibule[d] faced the outer court, and it had palm trees on its jambs, one on either side; and its stairway had eight steps.

way round about
[a] Compare Gk: Heb *from before*
[b] Gk: Heb *a hundred cubits on the east and on the north. And the gate*
[c] One Ms Compare verses 29 and 33: Heb lacks *were of the same size as the others*
[d] Gk Vg Compare verses 26, 31, 34: Heb *jambs*

38 There was a chamber with its
door in the vestibule of the gate,[e]
where the burnt offering was to be
washed. 39And in the vestibule of the
gate were two tables on either side,
on which the burnt offering and the
sin offering and the guilt offering
were to be slaughtered. 40And on
the outside of the vestibule[f] at the
entrance of the north gate were two
tables; and on the other side of the
vestibule of the gate were two tables.
41Four tables were on the inside, and
four tables on the outside of the side
of the gate, eight tables, on which
the sacrifices were to be slaughtered.
42And there were also four tables of
hewn stone for the burnt offering,
a cubit and a half long, and a cubit
and a half broad, and one cubit high,
on which the instruments were to be
laid with which the burnt offerings
and the sacrifices were slaughtered.
43And hooks, a handbreadth long,
were fastened round about within.
And on the tables the flesh of the offering was to be laid.

44 Then he brought me from
without into the inner court, and
behold, there were two chambers[g]
in the inner court, one[h] at the side
of the north gate facing south, the
other at the side of the south[i] gate
facing north. 45And he said to me,
This chamber which faces south is
for the priests who have charge of
the temple, 46and the chamber which
faces north is for the priests who
have charge of the altar; these are
the sons of Zadok, who alone among
the sons of Levi may come near to
the LORD to minister to him. 47And
he measured the court, a hundred
cubits long, and a hundred cubits
broad, foursquare; and the altar was in front of the temple.

THE TEMPLE

48 Then he brought me to the vestibule of the temple and measured the
jambs of the vestibule, five cubits on
either side; and the breadth of the gate
was fourteen cubits; and the sidewalls
of the gate were three cubits[j] on either side. 49The length of the vestibule
was twenty cubits, and the breadth
twelve[k] cubits; and ten steps led up[l]
to it; and there were pillars beside the jambs on either side.

41 Then he brought me to the nave,
and measured the jambs; on each
side six cubits was the breadth of the
jambs.[m] 2And the breadth of the entrance was ten cubits; and the sidewalls of the entrance were five cubits
on either side; and he measured the
length of the nave forty cubits, and its
breadth, twenty cubits. 3Then he went
into the inner room and measured
the jambs of the entrance, two cubits; and the breadth of the entrance,
six cubits; and the sidewalls[n] of the
entrance, seven cubits. 4And he measured the length of the room, twenty
cubits, and its breadth, twenty cubits,
beyond the nave. And he said to me,
"This is the most holy place."

5 Then he measured the wall of
the temple, six cubits thick; and the
breadth of the side chambers, four
cubits, round about the temple. 6And
the side chambers were in three stories, one over another, thirty in each
story. There were offsets[o] all around
the wall of the temple to serve as
supports for the side chambers, so
that they should not be supported

[e] Cn: Heb *at the jambs of the gates*
[f] Cn: Heb *to him who goes up*
[g] Gk: Heb *and from without to the inner gate were chambers for singers*
[h] Gk: Heb *which*
[i] Gk: Heb *east*
[j] Gk: Heb *and the breadth of the gate was three cubits*
[k] Gk: Heb *eleven*
[l] Gk: Heb *and by steps which went up*
[m] Compare Gk: Heb *tent*
[n] Gk: Heb *breadth*
[o] Gk Compare 1Kings 6. 6: Heb *they entered*

by the wall of the temple. 7And the side chambers became broader as they rose[a] from story to story, corresponding to the enlargement of the offset[b] from story to story round about the temple; on the side of the temple a stairway led upward, and thus one went up from the lowest story to the top story through the middle story. 8I saw also that the temple had a raised platform round about; the foundations of the side chambers measured a full reed of six long cubits. 9The thickness of the outer wall of the side chambers was five cubits; and the part of the platform which was left free was five cubits.[c] Between the platform[d] of the temple and the 10chambers of the court was a breadth of twenty cubits round about the temple on every side. 11And the doors of the side chambers opened on the part of the platform that was left free, one door toward the north, and another door toward the south; and the breadth of the part that was left free was five cubits round about.

12 The building that was facing the temple yard on the west side was seventy cubits broad; and the wall of the building was five cubits thick round about, and its length ninety cubits.

13 Then he measured the temple, a hundred cubits long; and the yard and the building with its walls, a hundred cubits long; 14also the breadth of the east front of the temple and the yard, a hundred cubits.

15 Then he measured the length of the building facing the yard which was at the west and its walls[e] on either side, a hundred cubits. The nave of the temple and the inner room and the outer[f] vestibule 16were paneled[g] and round about all three had windows with recessed[h] frames. Over against the threshold the temple was paneled with wood round about, from the floor up to the windows (now the windows were covered), 17to the space above the door, even to the inner room, and on the outside. And on all the walls round about in the inner room and the nave were carved likenesses[i] 18of cherubim and palm trees, a palm tree between cherub and cherub. Every cherub had two faces: 19the face of a man toward the palm tree on the one side, and the face of a young lion toward the palm tree on the other side. They were carved on the whole temple round about; 20from the floor to above the door cherubim and palm trees were carved on the wall.[j]

21 The doorposts of the nave were squared; and in front of the holy place was something resembling 22an altar of wood, three cubits high, two cubits long, and two cubits broad;[k] its corners, its base,[l] and its walls were of wood. He said to me, "This is the table which is before the LORD." 23The nave and the holy place had each a double door. 24The doors had two leaves apiece, two swinging leaves for each door. 25And on the doors of the nave were carved cherubim and palm trees, such as were carved on the walls; and there was a canopy of wood in front of the vestibule outside. 26And there were recessed windows and palm trees on either side, on the sidewalls of the vestibule.[m]

[a] Cn: Heb *it was surrounded*
[b] Gk: Heb *for the encompassing of the temple*
[c] Syr: Heb lacks *five cubits*
[d] Cn: Heb *house of the side chambers*
[e] Cn: The meaning of the Hebrew term is unknown
[f] Gk: Heb *of the court*
[g] Gk: Heb *the thresholds*
[h] Cn Compare Gk 1Kings 6. 4: The meaning of the Hebrew term is unknown
[i] Cn: Heb *measures and carved*
[j] Cn Compare verse 25: Heb *and the wall*
[k] Gk: Heb lacks *two cubits broad*
[l] Gk: Heb *length*
[m] Cn: Heb *vestibule. And the side chambers of the temple and the canopies*

THE HOLY CHAMBERS AND THE OUTER WALL

42 Then he led me out into the in-
ner[n] court, toward the north, and
he brought me to the chambers which
were opposite the temple yard and
opposite the building on the north.
2 The length of the building which was
on the north side[o] was[p] a hundred
cubits, and the breadth fifty cubits.
3 Adjoining the twenty cubits which
belonged to the inner court, and fac-
ing the pavement which belonged to
the outer court, was gallery[q] against
gallery[r] in three stories. 4 And before
the chambers was a passage inward,
ten cubits wide and a hundred cu-
bits long,[s] and their doors were on
the north. 5 Now the upper chambers
were narrower, for the galleries[t] took
more away from them than from the
lower and middle chambers in the
building. 6 For they were in three sto-
ries, and they had no pillars like the
pillars of the outer[u] court; hence the
upper chambers were set back from
the ground more than the lower and
the middle ones. 7 And there was a
wall outside parallel to the cham-
bers, toward the outer court, oppo-
site the chambers, fifty cubits long.
8 For the chambers on the outer court
were fifty cubits long, while those
opposite the temple were a hundred
cubits long. 9 Below these chambers
was an entrance on the east side, as
one enters them from the outer court,
10 where the outside wall begins.[v] On
the south[w] also, opposite the yard
and opposite the building, there were
chambers 11 with a passage in front of
them; they were similar to the cham-
bers on the north, of the same length
and breadth, with the same exits[x] and
arrangements and doors. 12 And below
the south chambers was an entrance
on the east side, where one enters the
passage, and opposite them was a di-
viding wall.[y]

13 Then he said to me, "The north
chambers and the south chambers
opposite the yard are the holy cham-
bers, where the priests who approach
the LORD shall eat the most holy of-
ferings; there they shall put the most
holy offerings—the cereal offering,
the sin offering, and the guilt offer-
ing, for the place is holy. 14 When the
priests enter the holy place, they shall
not go out of it into the outer court
without laying there the garments
in which they minister, for these are
holy; they shall put on other garments
before they go near to that which is
for the people."

15 Now when he had finished
measuring the interior of the temple
area, he led me out by the gate which
faced east, and measured the temple
area round about. 16 He measured the
east side with the measuring reed,
five hundred cubits by the measur-
ing reed. 17 Then he turned and mea-
sured[z] the north side, five hundred
cubits by the measuring reed. 18 Then
he turned and measured[aa] the south
side, five hundred cubits by the mea-
suring reed. 19 Then he turned to the
west side and measured, five hundred
cubits by the measuring reed. 20 He

[n] Gk: Heb outer court
[o] Gk: Heb *door*
[p] Gk: Heb *before the length*
[q] The meaning of the Hebrew word is unknown
[r] The meaning of the Hebrew word is unknown
[s] Gk Syr: Heb *a way of one cubit*
[t] The meaning of the Hebrew word is unknown
[u] Gk: Heb lacks *outer*
[v] Cn Compare Gk: Heb *in the breadth of the wall of the court*
[w] Gk: Heb *east*
[x] Heb *and all their exits*
[y] Cn: Heb *And according to the entrances of the chambers that were toward the south was an entrance at the head of the way, the way before the dividing wall toward the east as one enters them*
[z] Gk: Heb *measuring reed round about. He measured*
[aa] Gk: Heb *measuring reed round about. He measured*

measured it on the four sides. It had
a wall around it, five hundred cubits
long and five hundred cubits broad, to
make a separation between the holy
and the common.

THE DIVINE GLORY RETURNS TO THE TEMPLE

43 Afterward he brought me to the
gate, the gate facing east. 2And
behold, the glory of the God of Israel
came from the east; and the sound
of his coming was like the sound of
many waters; and the earth shone
with his glory. 3And[a] the vision I saw
was like the vision which I had seen
when he came to destroy the city, and[b]
like the vision which I had seen by the
river Chebar; and I fell upon my face.
4As the glory of the LORD entered the
temple by the gate facing east, 5the
Spirit lifted me up, and brought me
into the inner court; and behold, the
glory of the LORD filled the temple.

6 While the man was standing be-
side me, I heard one speaking to me
out of the temple; 7and he said to me,
"Son of man, this is the place of my
throne and the place of the soles of my
feet, where I will dwell in the midst of
the people of Israel for ever. And the
house of Israel shall no more defile
my holy name, neither they, nor their
kings, by their harlotry, and by the
dead bodies[c] of their kings, 8by setting
their threshold by my threshold and
their doorposts beside my doorposts,
with only a wall between me and
them. They have defiled my holy name
by their abominations which they
have committed, so I have consumed
them in my anger. 9Now let them put
away their idolatry and the dead bod-
ies[d] of their kings far from me, and I
will dwell in their midst for ever.

10 "And you, son of man, describe
to the house of Israel the temple and
its appearance and plan,[e] that they
may be ashamed of their iniquities.
11And if they are ashamed of all that
they have done, portray[f] the temple,
its arrangement, its exits and its en-
trances, and its whole form; and make
known to them all its ordinances and
all its laws; and write it down in their
sight, so that they may observe and
perform all its laws[g] and all its ordi-
nances. 12This is the law of the tem-
ple: the whole territory round about
upon the top of the mountain shall be
most holy. Behold, this is the law of
the temple.

THE ALTAR

13 "These are the dimensions of
the altar by cubits (the cubit being
a cubit and a handbreadth): its base
shall be one cubit high,[h] and one cubit
broad, with a rim of one span around
its edge. And this shall be the height[i]
of the altar: 14from the base on the
ground to the lower ledge, two cubits,
with a breadth of one cubit; and from
the smaller ledge to the larger ledge,
four cubits, with a breadth of one cu-
bit; 15and the altar hearth, four cubits;
and from the altar hearth projecting
upward, four horns, one cubit high.[j]
16The altar hearth shall be square,
twelve cubits long by twelve broad.
17The ledge also shall be square, four-
teen cubits long by fourteen broad,
with a rim around it half a cubit broad,
and its base one cubit round about.
The steps of the altar shall face east."

18 And he said to me, "Son of man,
thus says the Lord GOD: These are the
ordinances for the altar: On the day

[a] Gk: Heb *And like the vision*
[b] Syr: Heb *and the visions*
[c] Or *the monuments*
[d] Or *the monuments*
[e] Gk: Heb *the temple that they may measure the pattern*
[f] Gk: Heb *the form of*
[g] Compare Gk: Heb *its whole form*
[h] Gk: Heb lacks *high*
[i] Gk: Heb *back*
[j] Gk: Heb lacks *one cubit high*

when it is erected for offering burnt
offerings upon it and for throwing
blood against it, 19you shall give to
the Levitical priests of the family of
Zadok, who draw near to me to min-
ister to me, says the Lord GOD, a bull
for a sin offering. 20And you shall take
some of its blood, and put it on the
four horns of the altar, and on the four
corners of the ledge, and upon the rim
round about; thus you shall cleanse
the altar and make atonement for it.
21You shall also take the bull of the
sin offering, and it shall be burnt in
the appointed place belonging to the
temple, outside the sacred area. 22And
on the second day you shall offer a he-
goat without blemish for a sin offer-
ing; and the altar shall be cleansed, as
it was cleansed with the bull. 23When
you have finished cleansing it, you
shall offer a bull without blemish and
a ram from the flock without blemish.
24You shall present them before the
LORD, and the priests shall sprinkle
salt upon them and offer them up as a
burnt offering to the LORD. 25For sev-
en days you shall provide daily a goat
for a sin offering; also a bull and a
ram from the flock, without blemish,
shall be provided. 26Seven days shall
they make atonement for the altar and
purify it, and so consecrate it. 27And
when they have completed these days,
then from the eighth day onward the
priests shall offer upon the altar your
burnt offerings and your peace offer-
ings; and I will accept you, says the
Lord GOD."

THE CLOSED GATE

44 Then he brought me back to the
outer gate of the sanctuary, which
faces east; and it was shut. 2And he[k]
said to me, "This gate shall remain
shut; it shall not be opened, and no
one shall enter by it; for the LORD, the
God of Israel, has entered by it; there-
fore it shall remain shut. 3Only the
prince may sit in it to eat bread before
the LORD; he shall enter by way of the
vestibule of the gate, and shall go out
by the same way."

ADMISSION TO THE TEMPLE

4 Then he brought me by way
of the north gate to the front of the
temple; and I looked, and behold, the
glory of the LORD filled the temple
of the LORD; and I fell upon my face.
5And the LORD said to me, "Son of
man, mark well, see with your eyes,
and hear with your ears all that I shall
tell you concerning all the ordinances
of the temple of the LORD and all its
laws; and mark well those who may
be admitted to[l] the temple and all
those who are to be excluded from the
sanctuary. 6And say to the rebellious
house,[m] to the house of Israel, Thus
says the Lord GOD: O house of Israel,
let there be an end to all your abom-
inations, 7in admitting foreigners, un-
circumcised in heart and flesh, to be
in my sanctuary, profaning it,[n] when
you offer to me my food, the fat and
the blood. You[o] have broken my cove-
nant, in addition to all your abomina-
tions. 8And you have not kept charge
of my holy things; but you have set
foreigners to keep my charge in my
sanctuary.

9 "Therefore[p] thus says the Lord
GOD: No foreigner, uncircumcised in
heart and flesh, of all the foreigners
who are among the people of Israel,
shall enter my sanctuary. 10But the
Levites who went far from me, going
astray from me after their idols when
Israel went astray, shall bear their
punishment. 11They shall be minis-
ters in my sanctuary, having oversight
at the gates of the temple, and serv-
ing in the temple; they shall slay the

[k] Cn: Heb *the* Lord
[l] Cn: Heb *the entrance of*
[m] Gk: Heb lacks *house*
[n] Gk: Heb it my *temple*
[o] Gk Syr Vg: Heb *they*
[p] Gk: Heb *for you*

burnt offering and the sacrifice for the
people, and they shall attend on the
people, to serve them. 12Because they
ministered to them before their idols
and became a stumbling block of iniq-
uity to the house of Israel, therefore I
have sworn concerning them, says the
Lord GOD, that they shall bear their
punishment. 13They shall not come
near to me, to serve me as priest, nor
come near any of my sacred things
and the things that are most sacred;
but they shall bear their shame, be-
cause of the abominations which they
have committed. 14Yet I will appoint
them to keep charge of the temple, to
do all its service and all that is to be
done in it.

THE LEVITICAL PRIESTS

15 "But the Levitical priests, the
sons of Zadok, who kept the charge
of my sanctuary when the people of
Israel went astray from me, shall come
near to me to minister to me; and they
shall attend on me to offer me the fat
and the blood, says the Lord GOD;
16they shall enter my sanctuary, and
they shall approach my table, to min-
ister to me, and they shall keep my
charge. 17When they enter the gates of
the inner court, they shall wear linen
garments; they shall have nothing of
wool on them, while they minister at
the gates of the inner court, and with-
in. 18They shall have linen turbans
upon their heads, and linen breeches
upon their loins; they shall not gird
themselves with anything that caus-
es sweat. 19And when they go out into
the outer court to the people, they
shall put off the garments in which
they have been ministering, and lay
them in the holy chambers; and they
shall put on other garments, lest they
communicate holiness to the people
with their garments. 20They shall not
shave their heads or let their locks
grow long; they shall only trim the
hair of their heads. 21No priest shall
drink wine, when he enters the inner
court. 22They shall not marry a wid-
ow, or a divorced woman, but only
a virgin of the stock of the house of
Israel, or a widow who is the widow
of a priest. 23They shall teach my peo-
ple the difference between the holy
and the common, and show them how
to distinguish between the unclean
and the clean. 24In a controversy they
shall act as judges, and they shall
judge it according to my judgments.
They shall keep my laws and my stat-
utes in all my appointed feasts, and
they shall keep my sabbaths holy.
25They shall not defile themselves by
going near to a dead person; howev-
er, for father or mother, for son or
daughter, for brother or unmarried
sister they may defile themselves.
26After he is defiled,[a] he shall count
for himself seven days, and then he
shall be clean.[b] 27And on the day that
he goes into the holy place, into the
inner court, to minister in the holy
place, he shall offer his sin offering,
says the Lord GOD.

28 "They shall have no[c] inheri-
tance; I am their inheritance: and
you shall give them no possession in
Israel; I am their possession. 29They
shall eat the cereal offering, the sin
offering, and the guilt offering; and
every devoted thing in Israel shall be
theirs. 30And the first of all the first
fruits of all kinds, and every offering
of all kinds from all your offerings,
shall belong to the priests; you shall
also give to the priests the first of
your coarse meal, that a blessing may
rest on your house. 31The priests shall
not eat of anything, whether bird or
beast, that has died of itself or is torn.

THE HOLY DISTRICT

45 "When you allot the land as a
possession, you shall set apart
for the LORD a portion of the land

[a]Syr: Heb *cleansed*
[b]Syr: Heb lacks *and then he shall be clean*
[c]Vg: Heb *as an*

as a holy district, twenty-five thou-
sand cubits long and twenty[d] thou-
sand cubits broad; it shall be holy
throughout its whole extent. 2Of this
a square plot of five hundred by five
hundred cubits shall be for the sanc-
tuary, with fifty cubits for an open
space around it. 3And in the holy dis-
trict you shall measure off a section
twenty-five thousand cubits long and
ten thousand broad, in which shall be
the sanctuary, the most holy place. 4It
shall be the holy portion of the land;
it shall be for the priests, who minis-
ter in the sanctuary and approach the
LORD to minister to him; and it shall
be a place for their houses and a holy
place for the sanctuary. 5Another sec-
tion, twenty-five thousand cubits long
and ten thousand cubits broad, shall
be for the Levites who minister at the
temple, as their possession for cities
to live in.[e]

6 "Alongside the portion set apart
as the holy district you shall assign
for the possession of the city an area
five thousand cubits broad, and twen-
ty-five thousand cubits long; it shall
belong to the whole house of Israel.

7 "And to the prince shall be-
long the land on both sides of the
holy district and the property of the
city, alongside the holy district and
the property of the city, on the west
and on the east, corresponding in
length to one of the tribal portions,
and extending from the western to
the eastern boundary of the land. 8It
is to be his property in Israel. And
my princes shall no more oppress my
people; but they shall let the house
of Israel have the land according to
their tribes.

9 "Thus says the Lord GOD:
Enough, O princes of Israel! Put away
violence and oppression, and execute
justice and righteousness; cease your
evictions of my people, says the Lord
GOD.

WEIGHTS AND MEASURES

10 "You shall have just balances,
a just ephah, and a just bath. 11The
ephah and the bath shall be of the
same measure, the bath containing
one tenth of a homer, and the ephah
one tenth of a homer; the homer
shall be the standard measure. 12The
shekel shall be twenty gerahs; five
shekels shall be five shekels, and
ten shekels shall be ten shekels, and
your mina shall be fifty shekels.[f]

OFFERINGS

13 "This is the offering which you
shall make: one sixth of an ephah
from each homer of wheat, and one
sixth of an ephah from each homer
of barley, 14and as the fixed portion
of oil,[g] one tenth of a bath from each
cor (the cor,[h] like the homer, contains
ten baths); 15and one sheep from every
flock of two hundred, from the fami-
lies[i] of Israel. This is the offering for
cereal offerings, burnt offerings, and
peace offerings, to make atonement
for them, says the Lord GOD. 16All the
people of the land shall give[j] this of-
fering to the prince in Israel. 17It shall
be the prince's duty to furnish the
burnt offerings, cereal offerings, and
drink offerings, at the feasts, the new
moons, and the sabbaths, all the ap-
pointed feasts of the house of Israel:
he shall provide the sin offerings,
cereal offerings, burnt offerings, and
peace offerings, to make atonement
for the house of Israel.

FESTIVALS

18 "Thus says the Lord GOD: In
the first month, on the first day of
the month, you shall take a young

[d]Gk: Heb *ten*
[e]Gk: Heb *twenty chambers*
[f]Gk: Heb *twenty shekels, twenty-five shekels, fifteen shekels shall be your mina*
[g]Cn: Heb *oil, the bath the oil*
[h]Vg: Heb *homer*
[i]Gk: Heb *watering places*
[j]Gk Compare Syr: Heb *shall be to*

bull without blemish, and cleanse
the sanctuary. 19 The priest shall take
some of the blood of the sin offering
and put it on the doorposts of the
temple, the four corners of the ledge
of the altar, and the posts of the gate
of the inner court. 20 You shall do the
same on the seventh day of the month
for any one who has sinned through
error or ignorance; so you shall make
atonement for the temple.

21 "In the first month, on the four-
teenth day of the month, you shall cel-
ebrate the feast of the passover, and
for seven days unleavened bread shall
be eaten. 22 On that day the prince shall
provide for himself and all the people
of the land a young bull for a sin of-
fering. 23 And on the seven days of the
festival he shall provide as a burnt of-
fering to the LORD seven young bulls
and seven rams without blemish, on
each of the seven days; and a he-goat
daily for a sin offering. 24 And he shall
provide as a cereal offering an ephah
for each bull, an ephah for each ram,
and a hin of oil to each ephah. 25 In the
seventh month, on the fifteenth day
of the month and for the seven days
of the feast, he shall make the same
provision for sin offerings, burnt of-
ferings, and cereal offerings, and for
the oil.

MISCELLANEOUS REGULATIONS

46 "Thus says the Lord GOD: The
gate of the inner court that faces
east shall be shut on the six working
days; but on the sabbath day it shall
be opened and on the day of the new
moon it shall be opened. 2 The prince
shall enter by the vestibule of the gate
from without, and shall take his stand
by the post of the gate. The priests
shall offer his burnt offering and his
peace offerings, and he shall worship
at the threshold of the gate. Then he
shall go out, but the gate shall not be
shut until evening. 3 The people of the
land shall worship at the entrance
of that gate before the LORD on the
sabbaths and on the new moons. 4 The
burnt offering that the prince offers to
the LORD on the sabbath day shall be
six lambs without blemish and a ram
without blemish; 5 and the cereal of-
fering with the ram shall be an ephah,
and the cereal offering with the lambs
shall be as much as he is able, togeth-
er with a hin of oil to each ephah. 6 On
the day of the new moon he shall offer
a young bull without blemish, and six
lambs and a ram, which shall be with-
out blemish; 7 as a cereal offering he
shall provide an ephah with the bull
and an ephah with the ram, and with
the lambs as much as he is able, to-
gether with a hin of oil to each ephah.
8 When the prince enters, he shall go
in by the vestibule of the gate, and he
shall go out by the same way.

9 "When the people of the land
come before the LORD at the appoint-
ed feasts, he who enters by the north
gate to worship shall go out by the
south gate; and he who enters by the
south gate shall go out by the north
gate: no one shall return by way of the
gate by which he entered, but each
shall go out straight ahead. 10 When
they go in, the prince shall go in with
them; and when they go out, he shall
go out.

11 "At the feasts and the appoint-
ed seasons the cereal offering with
a young bull shall be an ephah, and
with a ram an ephah, and with the
lambs as much as one is able to give,
together with a hin of oil to an ephah.
12 When the prince provides a freewill
offering, either a burnt offering or
peace offerings as a freewill offering
to the LORD, the gate facing east shall
be opened for him; and he shall offer
his burnt offering or his peace offer-
ings as he does on the sabbath day.
Then he shall go out, and after he has
gone out the gate shall be shut.

13 "He shall provide a lamb a year
old without blemish for a burnt of-
fering to the LORD daily; morning by
morning he shall provide it. 14 And he
shall provide a cereal offering with it
morning by morning, one sixth of an

ephah, and one third of a hin of oil to
moisten the flour, as a cereal offering
to the LORD; this is the ordinance for
the continual burnt offering.[a] 15Thus
the lamb and the meal offering and
the oil shall be provided, morning
by morning, for a continual burnt
offering.

16 "Thus says the Lord GOD: If
the prince makes a gift to any of his
sons out of[b] his inheritance, it shall
belong to his sons, it is their proper-
ty by inheritance. 17But if he makes
a gift out of his inheritance to one
of his servants, it shall be his to the
year of liberty; then it shall revert to
the prince; only his sons may keep a
gift from his inheritance. 18The prince
shall not take any of the inheritance
of the people, thrusting them out of
their property; he shall give his sons
their inheritance out of his own prop-
erty, so that none of my people shall
be dispossessed of his property."

19 Then he brought me through
the entrance, which was at the side of
the gate, to the north row of the holy
chambers for the priests; and there I
saw a place at the extreme western
end of them. 20And he said to me,
"This is the place where the priests
shall boil the guilt offering and the
sin offering, and where they shall
bake the cereal offering, in order not
to bring them out into the outer court
and so communicate holiness to the
people."

21 Then he brought me forth to the
outer court, and led me to the four cor-
ners of the court; and in each corner
of the court there was a court 22in the
four corners of the court were small[c]
courts, forty cubits long and thirty
broad; the four were of the same size.
23On the inside, around each of the
four courts was a row of masonry,
with hearths made at the bottom of
the rows round about. 24Then he said
to me, "These are the kitchens where
those who minister at the temple shall
boil the sacrifices of the people."

WATER FLOWING FROM THE TEMPLE

47 Then he brought me back to the
door of the temple; and behold,
water was issuing from below the
threshold of the temple toward the
east (for the temple faced east); and
the water was flowing down from be-
low the south end of the threshold of
the temple, south of the altar. 2Then
he brought me out by way of the north
gate, and led me round on the outside
to the outer gate, that faces toward
the east;[d] and the water was coming
out on the south side.

3 Going on eastward with a line in
his hand, the man measured a thou-
sand cubits, and then led me through
the water; and it was ankle-deep.
4Again he measured a thousand, and
led me through the water; and it was
knee-deep. Again he measured a thou-
sand, and led me through the water;
and it was up to the loins. 5Again he
measured a thousand, and it was a
river that I could not pass through,
for the water had risen; it was deep
enough to swim in, a river that could
not be passed through. 6And he said to
me, "Son of man, have you seen this?"
Then he led me back along the bank
of the river. 7As I went back, I saw
upon the bank of the river very many
trees on the one side and on the other.
8And he said to me, "This water flows
toward the eastern region and goes
down into the Arabah; and when it
enters the stagnant waters of the sea,[e]
the water will become fresh. 9And
wherever the river[f] goes every living
creature which swarms will live, and
there will be very many fish; for this
water goes there, that the waters of

[a] Cn: Heb *perpetual ordinances continually*
[b] Gk: Heb *it is his inheritance*
[c] Gk Syr Vg: The meaning of the Hebrew word is uncertain
[d] Heb obscure
[e] Compare Syr: Heb *into the sea to the sea those that were made to issue forth*
[f] Gk Syr Vg Tg: Heb *two rivers*

the sea[a] may become fresh; so every-
thing will live where the river goes.
10Fishermen will stand beside the sea;
from En-ge´di to En-eg´laim it will be
a place for the spreading of nets; its
fish will be of very many kinds, like
the fish of the Great Sea. 11But its
swamps and marshes will not become
fresh; they are to be left for salt. 12And
on the banks, on both sides of the riv-
er, there will grow all kinds of trees
for food. Their leaves will not wither
nor their fruit fail, but they will bear
fresh fruit every month, because the
water for them flows from the sanc-
tuary. Their fruit will be for food, and
their leaves for healing."

THE NEW BOUNDARIES OF THE LAND

13 Thus says the Lord GOD: "These
are the boundaries by which you shall
divide the land for inheritance among
the twelve tribes of Israel. Joseph
shall have two portions. 14And you
shall divide it equally; I swore to give
it to your fathers, and this land shall
fall to you as your inheritance.

15 "This shall be the boundary of
the land: On the north side, from the
Great Sea by way of Hethlon to the en-
trance of Hamath, and on to Zedad,[b]
16Bero´thah, Sib´raim (which lies on
the border between Damascus and
Hamath), as far as Hazer-hatticon,
which is on the border of Hauran. 17So
the boundary shall run from the sea to
Hazar-e´non, which is on the northern
border of Damascus, with the border
of Hamath to the north.[c] This shall be
the north side.

18 "On the east side, the boundary
shall run from Hazar-e´non[d] between
Hauran and Damascus;[e] along the
Jordan between Gilead and the land
of Israel; to the eastern sea and as far
as Tamar.[f] This shall be the east side.

19 "On the south side, it shall run
from Tamar as far as the waters of
Meri´bath-ka´desh, thence along the
Brook of Egypt to the Great Sea. This
shall be the south side.

20 "On the west side, the Great Sea
shall be the boundary to a point op-
posite the entrance of Hamath. This
shall be the west side.

21 "So you shall divide this land
among you according to the tribes of
Israel. 22You shall allot it as an inheri-
tance for yourselves and for the aliens
who reside among you and have be-
gotten children among you. They shall
be to you as native-born sons of Israel;
with you they shall be allotted an in-
heritance among the tribes of Israel.
23In whatever tribe the alien resides,
there you shall assign him his inheri-
tance, says the Lord GOD.

THE TRIBAL PORTIONS

48 "These are the names of the
tribes: Beginning at the north-
ern border, from the sea by way[g] of
Hethlon to the entrance of Hamath,
as far as Hazar-e´non (which is on the
northern border of Damascus over
against Hamath), and[h] extending from
the east side to the west,[i] Dan, one
portion. 2Adjoining the territory of
Dan, from the east side to the west,
Asher, one portion. 3Adjoining the
territory of Asher, from the east side
to the west, Naph´tali, one portion.
4Adjoining the territory of Naph´tali,
from the east side to the west, Manas´-
seh, one portion. 5Adjoining the terri-
tory of Manas´seh, from the east side
to the west, E´phraim, one portion.
6Adjoining the territory of E´phraim,
from the east side to the west, Reuben,
one portion. 7Adjoining the territory

[a] Compare Syr: Heb lacks *the waters of the sea*
[b] Gk: Heb *the entrance of Zedad, Hamath*
[c] Heb obscure
[d] Cn: Heb lacks *Hazar-enon*
[e] Heb obscure
[f] Compare Syr: Heb *you shall measure*
[g] Compare 47.15: Heb *by the side of the way*
[h] Cn: Heb *and they shall be his*
[i] Gk Compare Verses 2-8: Heb *the east side the west*

of Reuben, from the east side to the
west, Judah, one portion.
8 "Adjoining the territory of Judah,
from the east side to the west, shall
be the portion which you shall set
apart, twenty-five thousand cubits in
breadth, and in length equal to one of
the tribal portions, from the east side
to the west, with the sanctuary in the
midst of it. 9The portion which you
shall set apart for the LORD shall be
twenty-five thousand cubits in length,
and twenty[j] thousand in breadth.
10These shall be the allotments of the
holy portion: the priests shall have
an allotment measuring twenty-five
thousand cubits on the northern side,
ten thousand cubits in breadth on the
western side, ten thousand in breadth
on the eastern side, and twenty-five
thousand in length on the southern
side, with the sanctuary of the LORD
in the midst of it. 11This shall be for
the consecrated priests, the sons[k] of
Zadok, who kept my charge, who did
not go astray when the people of Israel
went astray, as the Levites did. 12And
it shall belong to them as a special
portion from the holy portion of the
land, a most holy place, adjoining the
territory of the Levites. 13And along-
side the territory of the priests, the
Levites shall have an allotment twen-
ty-five thousand cubits in length and
ten thousand in breadth. The whole
length shall be twenty-five thousand
cubits and the breadth twenty[l] thou-
sand. 14They shall not sell or exchange
any of it; they shall not alienate this
choice portion of the land, for it is
holy to the LORD.
15 "The remainder, five thousand
cubits in breadth and twenty-five
thousand in length, shall be for or-
dinary use for the city, for dwellings
and for open country. In the midst of
it shall be the city; 16and these shall
be its dimensions: the north side four
thousand five hundred cubits, the
south side four thousand five hun-
dred, the east side four thousand
five hundred, and the west side four
thousand five hundred. 17And the city
shall have open land: on the north
two hundred and fifty cubits, on the
south two hundred and fifty, on the
east two hundred and fifty, and on
the west two hundred and fifty. 18The
remainder of the length alongside the
holy portion shall be ten thousand cu-
bits to the east, and ten thousand to
the west, and it shall be alongside the
holy portion. Its produce shall be food
for the workers of the city. 19And the
workers of the city, from all the tribes
of Israel, shall till it. 20The whole por-
tion which you shall set apart shall be
twenty-five thousand cubits square,
that is, the holy portion together with
the property of the city.
21 "What remains on both sides of
the holy portion and of the property
of the city shall belong to the prince.
Extending from the twenty-five thou-
sand cubits of the holy portion to the
east border, and westward from the
twenty-five thousand cubits to the
west border, parallel to the tribal por-
tions, it shall belong to the prince.
The holy portion with the sanctuary
of the temple in its midst, 22and the
property of the Levites and the prop-
erty of the city,[m] shall be in the midst
of that which belongs to the prince.
The portion of the prince shall lie be-
tween the territory of Judah and the
territory of Benjamin.
23 "As for the rest of the tribes:
from the east side to the west,
Benjamin, one portion. 24Adjoining
the territory of Benjamin, from the
east side to the west, Simeon, one
portion. 25Adjoining the territory of
Simeon, from the east side to the west,
Is´sachar, one portion. 26Adjoining
the territory of Is´sachar, from the
east side to the west, Zeb´ulun, one
portion. 27Adjoining the territory of

[j] Compare 45.1: Heb *ten*
[k] One Ms Gk: Heb *of the sons*
[l] Gk: Heb *ten*
[m] Cn: Heb *and from the property of the Levites and from the property of the city*

Zeb´ulun, from the east side to the
west, Gad, one portion. 28And ad-
joining the territory of Gad to the
south, the boundary shall run from
Tamar to the waters of Meri´bath-
ka´desh, thence along the Brook of
Egypt to the Great Sea. 29This is the
land which you shall allot as an inher-
itance among the tribes of Israel, and
these are their several portions, says
the Lord GOD.

30 "These shall be the exits of the
city: On the north side, which is to
be four thousand five hundred cubits
by measure, 31three gates, the gate
of Reuben, the gate of Judah, and
the gate of Levi, the gates of the city
being named after the tribes of Israel.
32On the east side, which is to be four
thousand five hundred cubits, three
gates, the gate of Joseph, the gate of
Benjamin, and the gate of Dan. 33On
the south side, which is to be four
thousand five hundred cubits by mea-
sure, three gates, the gate of Simeon,
the gate of Is´sachar, and the gate of
Zeb´ulun. 34On the west side, which
is to be four thousand five hundred
cubits, three gates,[a] the gate of Gad,
the gate of Asher, and the gate of
Naph´tali. 35The circumference of the
city shall be eighteen thousand cubits.
And the name of the city henceforth
shall be, The LORD is there."

[a] One Ms Gk Syr: Heb *their gates three*

THE BOOK OF
DANIEL

FOUR YOUNG ISRAELITES AT THE BABYLONIAN COURT

1 In the third year of the reign of
Jehoi´akim king of Judah, Nebu-
chadnez´zar king of Babylon came
to Jerusalem and besieged it. 2And
the Lord gave Jehoi´akim king of
Judah into his hand, with some of
the vessels of the house of God;
and he brought them to the land of
Shinar, to the house of his god, and
placed the vessels in the treasury of
his god. 3Then the king command-
ed Ash´penaz, his chief eunuch, to
bring some of the people of Israel,
both of the royal family and of the
nobility, 4youths without blemish,
handsome and skilful in all wisdom,
endowed with knowledge, under-
standing learning, and competent
to serve in the king's palace, and
to teach them the letters and lan-
guage of the Chalde´ans. 5The king
assigned them a daily portion of
the rich food which the king ate,
and of the wine which he drank.
They were to be educated for three
years, and at the end of that time
they were to stand before the king.
6Among these were Daniel, Hanani´-
ah, Mish´a-el, and Azari´ah of the
tribe of Judah. 7And the chief of the
eunuchs gave them names: Daniel he
called Belteshaz´zar, Hanani´ah he
called Shadrach, Mish´a-el he called
Meshach, and Azari´ah he called
Abed´nego.

8 But Daniel resolved that he
would not defile himself* with the
king's rich food, or with the wine
which he drank; therefore he asked
the chief of the eunuchs to allow
him not to defile himself. 9And God
gave Daniel favor and compassion
in the sight of the chief of the eu-
nuchs; 10and the chief of the eunuchs
said to Daniel, "I fear lest my lord
the king, who appointed your food
and your drink, should see that you
were in poorer condition than the
youths who are of your own age. So
you would endanger my head with
the king." 11Then Daniel said to the
steward whom the chief of the eu-
nuchs had appointed over Daniel,
Hanani´ah, Mish´a-el, and Azari´ah,
12"Test your servants for ten days;
let us be given vegetables to eat and
water to drink. 13Then let our ap-
pearance and the appearance of the
youths who eat the king's rich food
be observed by you, and according
to what you see deal with your ser-
vants." 14So he hearkened to them in
this matter, and tested them for ten
days. 15At the end of ten days it was
seen that they were better in appear-
ance and fatter in flesh than all the
youths who ate the king's rich food.
16So the steward took away their rich
food and the wine they were to drink,
and gave them vegetables.

17 As for these four youths, God
gave them learning and skill in all
letters and wisdom; and Daniel had
understanding in all visions and
dreams. 18At the end of the time,
when the king had commanded that
they should be brought in, the chief
of the eunuchs brought them in be-
fore Nebuchadnez´zar. 19And the
king spoke with them, and among
them all none was found like Daniel,
Hanani´ah, Mish´a-el, and Azari´ah;
therefore they stood before the king.
20And in every matter of wisdom and
understanding concerning which
the king inquired of them, he found
them ten times better than all the
magicians and enchanters that were
in all his kingdom. 21And Daniel con-
tinued until the first year of King
Cyrus.

NEBUCHADNEZZAR'S DREAM

2 In the second year of the reign of
Nebuchadnez´zar, Nebuchadnez´-
zar had dreams; and his spirit was
troubled, and his sleep left him.
2Then the king commanded that the
magicians, the enchanters, the sor-
cerers, and the Chalde´ans be sum-
moned, to tell the king his dreams.
So they came in and stood before the
king. 3And the king said to them, "I
had a dream, and my spirit is trou-
bled to know the dream." 4Then the
Chalde´ans said to the king,[a] "O
king, live for ever! Tell your servants
the dream, and we will show the in-
terpretation." 5The king answered
the Chalde´ans, "The word from me
is sure: if you do not make known to
me the dream and its interpretation,
you shall be torn limb from limb, and
your houses shall be laid in ruins.
6But if you show the dream and its in-
terpretation, you shall receive from
me gifts and rewards and great hon-
or. Therefore show me the dream and
its interpretation." 7They answered a
second time, "Let the king tell his
servants the dream, and we will
show its interpretation." 8The king
answered, "I know with certainty
that you are trying to gain time, be-
cause you see that the word from me
is sure 9that if you do not make the
dream known to me, there is but one
sentence for you. You have agreed to
speak lying and corrupt words before
me till the times change. Therefore
tell me the dream, and I shall know
that you can show me its interpreta-
tion." 10The Chalde´ans answered the
king, "There is not a man on earth
who can meet the king's demand;
for no great and powerful king has
asked such a thing of any magician or
enchanter or Chalde´an. 11The thing
that the king asks is difficult, and
none can show it to the king except
the gods, whose dwelling is not with
flesh."

12 Because of this the king was
angry and very furious, and com-
manded that all the wise men of
Babylon be destroyed. 13So the de-
cree went forth that the wise men
were to be slain, and they sought
Daniel and his companions, to slay
them. 14Then Daniel replied with
prudence and discretion to Ar´i-och,
the captain of the king's guard, who
had gone out to slay the wise men
of Babylon; 15he said to Ar´i-och, the
king's captain, "Why is the decree of
the king so severe?" Then Ar´i-och
made the matter known to Daniel.
16And Daniel went in and besought
the king to appoint him a time,
that he might show to the king the
interpretation.

GOD REVEALS NEBUCHADNEZZAR'S DREAM

17 Then Daniel went to his house
and made the matter known to
Hanani´ah, Mish´a-el, and Azari´ah,
his companions, 18and told them to
seek mercy of the God of heaven con-
cerning this mystery, so that Daniel
and his companions might not per-
ish with the rest of the wise men of
Babylon. 19Then the mystery was
revealed to Daniel in a vision of the
night. Then Daniel blessed the God of
heaven. 20Daniel said:

"Blessed be the name of God
for ever and ever,
to whom belong wisdom and
might.
21He changes times and seasons;
he removes kings and sets
up kings;
he gives wisdom to the wise
and knowledge to
those who have
understanding;
22he reveals deep and mysterious
things;
he knows what is in the
darkness,
and the light dwells with

[a]Heb adds *in Aramaic,* indicating that the text from this point to the end of chapter 7 is in Aramaic

him.
23To thee, O God of my fathers,
I give thanks and praise,
for thou hast given me wisdom
and strength,
and hast now made known
to me what we asked
of thee,
for thou hast made known
to us the king's
matter."

DANIEL INTERPRETS THE DREAM

24 Therefore Daniel went in to
Ar′i-och, whom the king had ap-
pointed to destroy the wise men of
Babylon; he went and said thus to
him, "Do not destroy the wise men
of Babylon; bring me in before the
king, and I will show the king the
interpretation."

25 Then Ar′i-och brought in
Daniel before the king in haste, and
said thus to him: "I have found among
the exiles from Judah a man who can
make known to the king the inter-
pretation." 26The king said to Daniel,
whose name was Belteshaz′zar, "Are
you able to make known to me the
dream that I have seen and its in-
terpretation?" 27Daniel answered
the king, "No wise men, enchant-
ers, magicians, or astrologers can
show to the king the mystery which
the king has asked, 28but there is a
God in heaven who reveals myster-
ies, and he has made known to King
Nebuchadnez′zar what will be in the
latter days. Your dream and the vi-
sions of your head as you lay in bed
are these: 29To you, O king, as you lay
in bed came thoughts of what would
be hereafter, and he who reveals mys-
teries made known to you what is to
be. 30But as for me, not because of
any wisdom that I have more than
all the living has this mystery been
revealed to me, but in order that the
interpretation may be made known to
the king, and that you may know the
thoughts of your mind.

31 "You saw, O king, and behold,
a great image. This image, mighty
and of exceeding brightness, stood
before you, and its appearance was
frightening. 32The head of this im-
age was of fine gold, its breast and
arms of silver, its belly and thighs
of bronze, 33its legs of iron, its feet
partly of iron and partly of clay. 34As
you looked, a stone was cut out by
no human hand, and it smote the im-
age on its feet of iron and clay, and
broke them in pieces; 35then the iron,
the clay, the bronze, the silver, and
the gold, all together were broken
in pieces, and became like the chaff
of the summer threshing floors; and
the wind carried them away, so that
not a trace of them could be found.
But the stone that struck the image
became a great mountain and filled
the whole earth.

36 "This was the dream; now we
will tell the king its interpretation.
37You, O king, the king of kings, to
whom the God of heaven has giv-
en the kingdom, the power, and the
might, and the glory, 38and into whose
hand he has given, wherever they
dwell, the sons of men, the beasts
of the field, and the birds of the air,
making you rule over them all—you
are the head of gold. 39After you
shall arise another kingdom inferior
to you, and yet a third kingdom of
bronze, which shall rule over all the
earth. 40And there shall be a fourth
kingdom, strong as iron, because
iron breaks to pieces and shatters all
things; and like iron which crushes, it
shall break and crush all these. 41And
as you saw the feet and toes partly
of potter's clay and partly of iron, it
shall be a divided kingdom; but some
of the firmness of iron shall be in it,
just as you saw iron mixed with the
miry clay. 42And as the toes of the
feet were partly iron and partly clay,
so the kingdom shall be partly strong
and partly brittle. 43As you saw the
iron mixed with miry clay, so they

will mix with one another in mar-
riage,[a] but they will not hold togeth-
er, just as iron does not mix with clay.
44And in the days of those kings the
God of heaven will set up a kingdom
which shall never be destroyed, nor
shall its sovereignty be left to anoth-
er people. It shall break in pieces all
these kingdoms and bring them to an
end, and it shall stand for ever; 45just
as you saw that a stone was cut from
a mountain by no human hand, and
that it broke in pieces the iron, the
bronze, the clay, the silver, and the
gold. A great God has made known to
the king what shall be hereafter. The
dream is certain, and its interpreta-
tion sure."

DANIEL AND HIS FRIENDS PROMOTED

46 Then King Nebuchadnez'zar
fell upon his face, and did homage
to Daniel, and commanded that an
offering and incense be offered up
to him. 47The king said to Daniel,
"Truly, your God is God of gods and
Lord of kings, and a revealer of mys-
teries, for you have been able to re-
veal this mystery." 48Then the king
gave Daniel high honors and many
great gifts, and made him ruler
over the whole province of Babylon,
and chief prefect over all the wise
men of Babylon. 49Daniel made re-
quest of the king, and he appointed
Shadrach, Meshach, and Abed'nego
over the affairs of the province of
Babylon; but Daniel remained at the
king's court.

THE GOLDEN IMAGE

3 King Nebuchadnez'zar made an
image of gold, whose height was
sixty cubits and its breadth six cu-
bits. He set it up on the plain of
Dura, in the province of Babylon.
2Then King Nebuchadnez'zar sent
to assemble the satraps, the pre-
fects, and the governors, the coun-
selors, the treasurers, the justices,
the magistrates, and all the offi-
cials of the provinces to come to
the dedication of the image which
King Nebuchadnez'zar had set up.
3Then the satraps, the prefects, and
the governors, the counselors, the
treasurers, the justices, the mag-
istrates, and all the officials of the
provinces, were assembled for the
dedication of the image that King
Nebuchadnez'zar had set up; and
they stood before the image that
Nebuchadnez'zar had set up. 4And
the herald proclaimed aloud, "You
are commanded, O peoples, nations,
and languages, 5that when you hear
the sound of the horn, pipe, lyre, tri-
gon, harp, bagpipe, and every kind
of music, you are to fall down and
worship the golden image that King
Nebuchadnez'zar has set up; 6and
whoever does not fall down and wor-
ship shall immediately be cast into
a burning fiery furnace." 7Therefore,
as soon as all the peoples heard the
sound of the horn, pipe, lyre, tri-
gon, harp, bagpipe, and every kind
of music, all the peoples, nations,
and languages fell down and wor-
shiped the golden image which King
Nebuchadnez'zar had set up.

8 Therefore at that time certain
Chalde'ans came forward and mali-
ciously accused the Jews. 9They said
to King Nebuchadnez'zar, "O king,
live for ever! 10You, O king, have
made a decree, that every man who
hears the sound of the horn, pipe,
lyre, trigon, harp, bagpipe, and ev-
ery kind of music, shall fall down
and worship the golden image; 11and
whoever does not fall down and wor-
ship shall be cast into a burning fi-
ery furnace. 12There are certain Jews
whom you have appointed over the
affairs of the province of Babylon:
Shadrach, Meshach, and Abed'nego.
These men, O king, pay no heed to
you; they do not serve your gods or
worship the golden image which you
have set up."

[a] Aramaic *by the seed of men*

13 Then Nebuchadnez´zar in furi-
ous rage commanded that Shadrach,
Meshach, and Abed´nego be brought.
Then they brought these men before
the king. 14Nebuchadnez´zar said
to them, "Is it true, O Shadrach,
Meshach, and Abed´nego, that you
do not serve my gods or worship the
golden image which I have set up?
15Now if you are ready when you hear
the sound of the horn, pipe, lyre, tri-
gon, harp, bagpipe, and every kind
of music, to fall down and worship
the image which I have made, well
and good; but if you do not worship,
you shall immediately be cast into a
burning fiery furnace; and who is the
god that will deliver you out of my
hands?"

16 Shadrach, Meshach, and
Abed´nego answered the king, "O
Nebuchadnez´zar, we have no need
to answer you in this matter. 17If it
be so, our God whom we serve is
able to deliver us from the burning
fiery furnace; and he will deliver
us out of your hand, O king.[b] 18But
if not, be it known to you, O king,
that we will not serve your gods or
worship the golden image which you
have set up."

THE FIERY FURNACE

19 Then Nebuchadnez´zar was
full of fury, and the expression of his
face was changed against Shadrach,
Meshach, and Abed´nego. He or-
dered the furnace heated seven times
more than it was wont to be heat-
ed. 20And he ordered certain mighty
men of his army to bind Shadrach,
Meshach, and Abed´nego, and to
cast them into the burning fiery fur-
nace. 21Then these men were bound
in their mantles,[c] their tunics,[d] their
hats, and their other garments, and
they were cast into the burning fiery
furnace. 22Because the king's order
was strict and the furnace very hot,
the flame of the fire slew those men
who took up Shadrach, Meshach, and
Abed´nego. 23And these three men,
Shadrach, Meshach, and Abed´nego,
fell bound into the burning fiery
furnace.*

THE PRAYER OF AZARIAH IN THE FURNACE

1 *And they walked about in the midst*
of the flames, singing hymns to God and
blessing the Lord. 2*Then Azari´ah stood*
and offered this prayer; in the midst of the
fire he opened his mouth and said:

3*"Blessed art thou, O Lord, God of*
our fathers, and worthy of
praise;
and thy name is glorified for
ever.
4*For thou art just in all that thou*
hast done to us,
and all thy works are true and
thy ways right,
and all thy judgments are
truth.
5*Thou hast executed true judgments*
in all that thou hast brought
upon us
and upon Jerusalem, the holy
city of our fathers,
for in truth and justice thou
hast brought all this
upon us because of our
sins.
6*For we have sinfully and lawlessly*
departed from thee,
and have sinned in all things
and have not obeyed thy
commandments;
7*we have not observed them or done*
them,
as thou hast commanded us
that it might go well
with us.
8*So all that thou hast brought upon*
us,
and all that thou hast done
to us,
thou hast done in true
judgment.

[b]Or *Behold, our God... king.* Or *If our God is able to deliver us, he will deliver us from the burning fiery furnace and out of your hand, O king.*
[c]The meaning of the Aramaic word is uncertain
[d]The meaning of the Aramaic word is uncertain

9Thou hast given us into the hands of
lawless enemies, most hateful
rebels,
and to an unjust king, the
most wicked in all the
world.
10And now we cannot open our
mouths;
shame and disgrace have befallen
thy servants and
worshipers.
11For thy name's sake do not give us
up utterly,
and do not break thy
covenant,
12and do not withdraw thy mercy
from us,
for the sake of Abraham thy
beloved
and for the sake of Isaac thy
servant
and Israel thy holy one,
13to whom thou didst promise
to make their descendants as
many as the stars of
heaven
and as the sand on the shore of
the sea.
14For we, O Lord, have become fewer
than any nation,
and are brought low this day in
all the world because of
our sins.
15And at this time there is no prince,
or prophet, or leader,
no burnt offering, or sacrifice,
or oblation, or incense,
no place to make an offering
before thee or to find
mercy.
16Yet with a contrite heart and a
humble spirit may we be
accepted,
as though it were with burnt
offerings of rams and
bulls,
and with tens of thousands of
fat lambs;
17such may our sacrifice be in thy
sight this day,
and may we wholly follow
thee,
for there will be no shame
for those who trust
in thee.
18And now with all our heart we
follow thee,
we fear thee and seek thy face.
19Do not put us to shame,
but deal with us in thy
forbearance
and in thy abundant mercy.
20Deliver us in accordance with thy
marvelous works,
and give glory to thy name, O
Lord!
Let all who do harm to thy servants
be put to shame;
21let them be disgraced and deprived
of all power and dominion,
and let their strength be
broken.
22Let them know that thou art the
Lord, the only God,
glorious over the whole
world."

THE SONG OF THE THREE JEWS

23 Now the king's servants who
threw them in did not cease feeding the
furnace fires with naphtha, pitch, tow,
and brush. 24And the flame streamed
out above the furnace forty-nine cubits,
25and it broke through and burned those
of the Chalde´ans whom it caught about
the furnace. 26But the angel of the Lord
came down into the furnace to be with
Azari´ah and his companions, and drove
the fiery flame out of the furnace, and
made the midst of the furnace like a
moist whistling wind, so that the fire did
not touch them at all or hurt or trouble
them.
28 Then the three, as with one mouth,
praised and glorified and blessed God in
the furnace, saying:
29"Blessed art thou, O Lord, God of
our fathers,
and to be praised and highly
exalted for ever;
30And blessed is thy glorious, holy
name
and to be highly praised and
highly exalted for ever;

[31]*Blessed art thou in the temple of thy holy glory*
and to be extolled and highly glorified for ever.
[32]*Blessed art thou, who sittest upon cherubim and lookest upon the deeps,*
and to be praised and highly exalted for ever.
[33]*Blessed art thou upon the throne of thy kingdom*
and to be extolled and highly exalted for ever.
[34]*Blessed art thou in the firmament of heaven*
and to be sung and glorified for ever.
[35]*"Bless the Lord, all works of the Lord,*
sing praise to him and highly exalt him for ever.
[36]*Bless the Lord, you heavens,*
sing praise to him and highly exalt him for ever.
[37]*Bless the Lord, you angels of the Lord,*
sing praise to him and highly exalt him for ever.
[38]*Bless the Lord, all waters above the heaven,*
sing praise to him and highly exalt him for ever.
[39]*Bless the Lord, all powers,*
sing praise to him and highly exalt him for ever.
[40]*Bless the Lord, sun and moon,*
sing praise to him and highly exalt him for ever.
[41]*Bless the Lord, stars of heaven,*
sing praise to him and highly exalt him for ever.
[42]*Bless the Lord, all rain and dew,*
sing praise to him and highly exalt him for ever.
[43]*Bless the Lord, all winds,*
sing praise to him and highly exalt him for ever.
[44]*Bless the Lord, fire and heat,*
sing praise to him and highly exalt him for ever.
[45]*Bless the Lord, winter cold and summer heat,*
sing praise to him and highly exalt him for ever.
[46]*Bless the Lord, dews and snows,*
sing praise to him and highly exalt him for ever.
[47]*Bless the Lord, nights and days,*
sing praise to him and highly exalt him for ever.
[48]*Bless the Lord, light and darkness,*
sing praise to him and highly exalt him for ever.
[49]*Bless the Lord, ice and cold,*
sing praise to him and highly exalt him for ever.
[50]*Bless the Lord, frosts and snows,*
sing praise to him and highly exalt him for ever.
[51]*Bless the Lord, lightnings and clouds,*
sing praise to him and highly exalt him for ever.
[52]*Let the earth bless the Lord;*
let it sing praise to him and highly exalt him for ever.
[53]*Bless the Lord, mountains and hills,*
sing praise to him and highly exalt him for ever.
[54]*Bless the Lord, all things that grow on the earth,*
sing praise to him and highly exalt him for ever.
[55]*Bless the Lord, you springs,*
sing praise to him and highly exalt him for ever.
[56]*Bless the Lord, seas and rivers,*
sing praise to him and highly exalt him for ever.
[57]*Bless the Lord, you whales and all creatures that move in the waters,*
sing praise to him and highly exalt him for ever.
[58]*Bless the Lord, all birds of the air,*
sing praise to him and highly exalt him for ever.
[59]*Bless the Lord, all beasts and cattle,*
sing praise to him and highly exalt him for ever.
[60]*Bless the Lord, you sons of men,*

sing praise to him and highly
exalt him for ever.
61*Bless the Lord, O Israel,*
sing praise to him and highly
exalt him for ever.
62*Bless the Lord, you priests of the*
Lord,
sing praise to him and highly
exalt him for ever.
63*Bless the Lord, you servants of the*
Lord,
sing praise to him and highly
exalt him for ever.
64*Bless the Lord, spirits and souls of*
the righteous,
sing praise to him and highly
exalt him for ever.
65*Bless the Lord, you who are holy*
and humble in heart,
sing praise to him and highly
exalt him for ever.
66*Bless the Lord, Hanani´ah,*
Azari´ah, and Mish´ael,
sing praise to him and highly
exalt him for ever;
for he has rescued us from Hades
and saved us from the
hand of death,
and delivered us from the midst
of the burning fiery
furnace;
from the midst of the fire he
has delivered us.
67*Give thanks to the Lord, for he is*
good,
for his mercy endures for ever.
68*Bless him, all who worship the*
Lord, the God of gods,
sing praise to him and give
thanks to him,
for his mercy endures for
*ever."**

24 Then King Nebuchadnez´zar
was astonished and rose up in haste.
He said to his counselors, "Did we not
cast three men bound into the fire?"
They answered the king, "True, O
king." 25He answered, "But I see four
men loose, walking in the midst of the
fire, and they are not hurt; and the
appearance of the fourth is like a son
of the gods."
26 Then Nebuchadnez´zar came
near to the door of the burning fi-
ery furnace and said, "Shadrach,
Meshach, and Abed´nego, servants
of the Most High God, come forth,
and come here!" Then Shadrach,
Meshach, and Abed´nego came out
from the fire. 27And the satraps, the
prefects, the governors, and the king's
counselors gathered together and saw
that the fire had not had any power
over the bodies of those men; the
hair of their heads was not singed,
their mantles[a] were not harmed, and
no smell of fire had come upon them.
28Nebuchadnez´zar said, "Blessed be
the God of Shadrach, Meshach, and
Abed´nego, who has sent his angel
and delivered his servants, who trust-
ed in him, and set at nought the king's
command, and yielded up their bodies
rather than serve and worship any god
except their own God. 29Therefore I
make a decree: Any people, nation, or
language that speaks anything against
the God of Shadrach, Meshach, and
Abed´nego shall be torn limb from
limb, and their houses laid in ruins;
for there is no other god who is able
to deliver in this way." 30Then the king
promoted Shadrach, Meshach, and
Abed´nego in the province of Babylon.

NEBUCHADNEZZAR'S SECOND DREAM

4[b]* King Nebuchadnez´zar to all peo-
ples, nations, and languages, that
dwell in all the earth: Peace be mul-
tiplied to you! 2It has seemed good
to me to show the signs and wonders
that the Most High God has wrought
toward me.

3How great are his signs,
how mighty his wonders!
His kingdom is an everlasting
kingdom,
and his dominion is from
generation to
generation.

[a]The meaning of the Aramaic word is uncertain
[b]Ch 3. 31 in Aramaic

4 [c] I, Nebuchadnez´zar, was at
ease in my house and prospering
in my palace. 5I had a dream which
made me afraid; as I lay in bed the
fancies and the visions of my head
alarmed me. 6Therefore I made
a decree that all the wise men of
Babylon should be brought before
me, that they might make known to
me the interpretation of the dream.
7Then the magicians, the enchant-
ers, the Chalde´ans, and the astrol-
ogers came in; and I told them the
dream, but they could not make
known to me its interpretation. 8At
last Daniel came in before me—he
who was named Belteshaz´zar* after
the name of my god, and in whom
is the spirit of the holy gods[d]—and
I told him the dream, saying, 9"O
Belteshaz´zar, chief of the magi-
cians, because I know that the spirit
of the holy gods[e] is in you and that
no mystery is difficult for you, here
is[f] the dream which I saw; tell me its
interpretation. 10The visions of my
head as I lay in bed were these: I saw,
and behold, a tree in the midst of the
earth; and its height was great. 11The
tree grew and became strong, and
its top reached to heaven, and it was
visible to the end of the whole earth.
12Its leaves were fair and its fruit
abundant, and in it was food for all.
The beasts of the field found shade
under it, and the birds of the air
dwelt in its branches, and all flesh
was fed from it.

13 "I saw in the visions of my head
as I lay in bed, and behold, a watch-
er, a holy one,* came down from
heaven. 14He cried aloud and said
thus, 'Hew down the tree and cut
off its branches, strip off its leaves
and scatter its fruit; let the beasts
flee from under it and the birds from
its branches. 15But leave the stump
of its roots in the earth, bound with
a band of iron and bronze, amid the
tender grass of the field. Let him be
wet with the dew of heaven; let his
lot be with the beasts in the grass of
the earth; 16let his mind be changed
from a man's, and let a beast's mind
be given to him; and let seven times
pass over him. 17The sentence is by
the decree of the watchers, the de-
cision by the word of the holy ones,
to the end that the living may know
that the Most High rules the king-
dom of men, and gives it to whom
he will, and sets over it the lowli-
est of men.' 18This dream I, King
Nebuchadnez´zar, saw. And you, O
Belteshaz´zar, declare the interpre-
tation, because all the wise men of
my kingdom are not able to make
known to me the interpretation, but
you are able, for the spirit of the holy
gods[g] is in you."

DANIEL INTERPRETS THE SECOND DREAM

19 Then Daniel, whose name was
Belteshaz´zar, was dismayed for a
moment, and his thoughts alarmed
him. The king said, "Belteshaz´zar,
let not the dream or the interpreta-
tion alarm you." Belteshaz´zar an-
swered, "My lord, may the dream
be for those who hate you and its
interpretation for your enemies!
20The tree you saw, which grew
and became strong, so that its top
reached to heaven, and it was vis-
ible to the end of the whole earth;
21whose leaves were fair and its fruit
abundant, and in which was food for
all; under which beasts of the field
found shade, and in whose branch-
es the birds of the air dwelt 22it is
you, O king, who have grown and
become strong. Your greatness has
grown and reaches to heaven, and
your dominion to the ends of the
earth. 23And whereas the king saw
a watcher, a holy one, coming down

[c] Ch 4.1 in Aramaic
[d] Or *Spirit of the holy God*
[e] Or *Spirit of the holy God*
[f] Cn: Aramaic *visions of*
[g] Or *Spirit of the holy God*

from heaven and saying, 'Hew down
the tree and destroy it, but leave the
stump of its roots in the earth, bound
with a band of iron and bronze, in
the tender grass of the field; and let
him be wet with the dew of heaven;
and let his lot be with the beasts of
the field, till seven times pass over
him'; 24this is the interpretation, O
king: It is a decree of the Most High,
which has come upon my lord the
king, 25that you shall be driven from
among men, and your dwelling shall
be with the beasts of the field; you
shall be made to eat grass like an ox,
and you shall be wet with the dew of
heaven, and seven times shall pass
over you, till you know that the Most
High rules the kingdom of men, and
gives it to whom he will. 26And as it
was commanded to leave the stump
of the roots of the tree, your king-
dom shall be sure for you from the
time that you know that Heaven
rules. 27Therefore, O king, let my
counsel be acceptable to you; break
off your sins by practicing righteous-
ness, and your iniquities by showing
mercy to the oppressed, that there
may perhaps be a lengthening of
your tranquillity."

NEBUCHADNEZZAR'S HUMILIATION

28 All this came upon King Neb-
uchadnez'zar. 29At the end of twelve
months he was walking on the roof of
the royal palace of Babylon, 30and the
king said, "Is not this great Babylon,
which I have built by my mighty pow-
er as a royal residence and for the
glory of my majesty?" 31While the
words were still in the king's mouth,
there fell a voice from heaven, "O
King Nebuchadnez'zar, to you it is
spoken: The kingdom has departed
from you, 32and you shall be driven
from among men, and your dwelling
shall be with the beasts of the field;
and you shall be made to eat grass
like an ox; and seven times shall pass
over you, until you have learned that
the Most High rules the kingdom of
men and gives it to whom he will."
33Immediately the word was fulfilled
upon Nebuchadnez'zar. He was driv-
en from among men, and ate grass
like an ox, and his body was wet with
the dew of heaven till his hair grew as
long as eagles' feathers, and his nails
were like birds' claws.

NEBUCHADNEZZAR PRAISES GOD

34 At the end of the days I,
Nebuchadnez'zar, lifted my eyes to
heaven, and my reason returned to
me, and I blessed the Most High, and
praised and honored him who lives for
ever;

for his dominion is an everlast-
  ing dominion,
 and his kingdom endures
  from generation to
  generation;
35all the inhabitants of the earth
  are accounted as nothing;
 and he does according to his
  will in the host of
  heaven
 and among the inhabitants
  of the earth;
and none can stay his hand
 or say to him, "What doest
  thou?"

36At the same time my reason re-
turned to me; and for the glory of my
kingdom, my majesty and splendor
returned to me. My counselors and
my lords sought me, and I was estab-
lished in my kingdom, and still more
greatness was added to me. 37Now I,
Nebuchadnez'zar, praise and extol
and honor the King of heaven; for all
his works are right and his ways are
just; and those who walk in pride he is
able to abase.

BELSHAZZAR'S FEAST

5 King Belshaz'zar* made a great
feast for a thousand of his lords, and
drank wine in front of the thousand.
2 Belshaz'zar, when he tast-
ed the wine, commanded that the
vessels of gold and of silver which
Nebuchadnez'zar his father had

taken out of the temple in Jerusalem
be brought, that the king and his lords,
his wives, and his concubines might
drink from them. 3Then they brought
in the golden and silver vessels[a] which
had been taken out of the temple, the
house of God in Jerusalem; and the
king and his lords, his wives, and his
concubines drank from them. 4They
drank wine, and praised the gods of
gold and silver, bronze, iron, wood,
and stone.

THE WRITING ON THE WALL

5 Immediately the fingers of a
man's hand appeared and wrote on
the plaster of the wall of the king's
palace, opposite the lampstand; and
the king saw the hand as it wrote.
6Then the king's color changed,
and his thoughts alarmed him;
his limbs gave way, and his knees
knocked together. 7The king cried
aloud to bring in the enchanters,
the Chalde'ans, and the astrologers.
The king said to the wise men of
Babylon, "Whoever reads this writ-
ing, and shows me its interpretation,
shall be clothed with purple, and
have a chain of gold about his neck,
and shall be the third ruler in the
kingdom." 8Then all the king's wise
men came in, but they could not read
the writing or make known to the
king the interpretation. 9Then King
Belshaz'zar was greatly alarmed,
and his color changed; and his lords
were perplexed.

10 The queen, because of the words
of the king and his lords, came into
the banqueting hall; and the queen
said, "O king, live for ever! Let not
your thoughts alarm you or your color
change. 11There is in your kingdom a
man in whom is the spirit of the holy
gods.[b] In the days of your father light
and understanding and wisdom, like
the wisdom of the gods, were found in
him, and King Nebuchadnez'zar, your
father, made him chief of the magi-
cians, enchanters, Chalde'ans, and as-
trologers,[c] 12because an excellent spirit,
knowledge, and understanding to inter-
pret dreams, explain riddles, and solve
problems were found in this Daniel,
whom the king named Belteshaz'zar.
Now let Daniel be called, and he will
show the interpretation."

THE WRITING ON THE WALL INTERPRETED

13 Then Daniel was brought in be-
fore the king. The king said to Daniel,
"You are that Daniel, one of the exiles
of Judah, whom the king my father
brought from Judah. 14I have heard of
you that the spirit of the holy gods[d] is
in you, and that light and understand-
ing and excellent wisdom are found in
you. 15Now the wise men, the enchant-
ers, have been brought in before me to
read this writing and make known to
me its interpretation; but they could
not show the interpretation of the
matter. 16But I have heard that you can
give interpretations and solve prob-
lems. Now if you can read the writing
and make known to me its interpreta-
tion, you shall be clothed with purple,
and have a chain of gold about your
neck, and shall be the third ruler in
the kingdom."

17 Then Daniel answered before
the king, "Let your gifts be for your-
self, and give your rewards to another;
nevertheless I will read the writing
to the king and make known to him
the interpretation. 18O king, the Most
High God gave Nebuchadnez'zar your
father kingship and greatness and
glory and majesty; 19and because of
the greatness that he gave him, all
peoples, nations, and languages trem-
bled and feared before him; whom he
would he slew, and whom he would he
kept alive; whom he would he raised
up, and whom he would he put down.
20But when his heart was lifted up and
his spirit was hardened so that he

[a] Theodotion Vg: Aramaic *golden vessels*
[b] Or *Spirit of the holy God*
[c] Aramaic repeats *the king your father*
[d] Or *Spirit of the holy God*

dealt proudly, he was deposed from
his kingly throne, and his glory was
taken from him; 21 he was driven from
among men, and his mind was made
like that of a beast, and his dwelling
was with the wild asses; he was fed
grass like an ox, and his body was wet
with the dew of heaven, until he knew
that the Most High God rules the king-
dom of men, and sets over it whom he
will. 22 And you his son, Belshaz′zar,
have not humbled your heart, though
you knew all this, 23 but you have lifted
up yourself against the Lord of heav-
en; and the vessels of his house have
been brought in before you, and you
and your lords, your wives, and your
concubines have drunk wine from
them; and you have praised the gods of
silver and gold, of bronze, iron, wood,
and stone, which do not see or hear or
know, but the God in whose hand is
your breath, and whose are all your
ways, you have not honored.

24 "Then from his presence the
hand was sent, and this writing was
inscribed. 25 And this is the writing
that was inscribed: MENE, MENE, TE-
KEL, and PARSIN. 26 This is the inter-
pretation of the matter: MENE, God
has numbered the days of your king-
dom and brought it to an end; 27 TEKEL,
you have been weighed in the balanc-
es and found wanting; 28 PERES, your
kingdom is divided and given to the
Medes and Persians."

29 Then Belshaz′zar commanded,
and Daniel was clothed with purple, a
chain of gold was put about his neck,
and proclamation was made concern-
ing him, that he should be the third
ruler in the kingdom.

30 That very night Belshaz′zar
the Chalde′an king was slain. 31 And
Darius the Mede* received the king-
dom, being about sixty-two years old.

THE PLOT AGAINST DANIEL

6 It pleased Darius to set over the
kingdom a hundred and twenty
satraps, to be throughout the whole
kingdom; 2 and over them three pres-
idents, of whom Daniel was one, to
whom these satraps should give ac-
count, so that the king might suffer
no loss. 3 Then this Daniel became
distinguished above all the other
presidents and satraps, because an
excellent spirit was in him; and the
king planned to set him over the
whole kingdom. 4 Then the presidents
and the satraps sought to find a
ground for complaint against Daniel
with regard to the kingdom; but they
could find no ground for complaint
or any fault, because he was faith-
ful, and no error or fault was found
in him. 5 Then these men said, "We
shall not find any ground for com-
plaint against this Daniel unless we
find it in connection with the law of
his God."

6 Then these presidents and sa-
traps came by agreement[a] to the king
and said to him, "O King Darius, live
for ever! 7 All the presidents of the
kingdom, the prefects and the sa-
traps, the counselors and the gover-
nors are agreed that the king should
establish an ordinance and enforce
an interdict, that whoever makes
petition to any god or man for thir-
ty days, except to you, O king, shall
be cast into the den of lions. 8 Now,
O king, establish the interdict and
sign the document, so that it cannot
be changed, according to the law of
the Medes and the Persians, which
cannot be revoked." 9 Therefore King
Darius signed the document and
interdict.

DANIEL IN THE LIONS' DEN

10 When Daniel knew that the
document had been signed, he went
to his house where he had windows
in his upper chamber open toward
Jerusalem; and he got down upon his
knees three times a day and prayed
and gave thanks before his God, as

[a] Or *thronging*

he had done previously. 11 Then these
men came by agreement[b] and found
Daniel making petition and suppli-
cation before his God. 12 Then they
came near and said before the king,
concerning the interdict, "O king!
Did you not sign an interdict, that
any man who makes petition to any
god or man within thirty days except
to you, O king, shall be cast into the
den of lions?" The king answered,
"The thing stands fast, according to
the law of the Medes and Persians,
which cannot be revoked." 13 Then
they answered before the king, "That
Daniel, who is one of the exiles from
Judah, pays no heed to you, O king,
or the interdict you have signed,
but makes his petition three times
a day."

14 Then the king, when he heard
these words, was much distressed,
and set his mind to deliver Daniel;
and he labored till the sun went
down to rescue him. 15 Then these
men came by agreement[c] to the king,
and said to the king, "Know, O king,
that it is a law of the Medes and
Persians that no interdict or ordi-
nance which the king establishes can
be changed."

16 Then the king commanded, and
Daniel was brought and cast into the
den of lions. The king said to Daniel,
"May your God, whom you serve con-
tinually, deliver you!" 17 And a stone
was brought and laid upon the mouth
of the den, and the king sealed it
with his own signet and with the
signet of his lords, that nothing
might be changed concerning Daniel.
18 Then the king went to his palace,
and spent the night fasting; no diver-
sions were brought to him, and sleep
fled from him.

DANIEL SAVED FROM THE LIONS

19 Then, at break of day, the king
arose and went in haste to the den of
lions. 20 When he came near to the den
where Daniel was, he cried out in a
tone of anguish and said to Daniel, "O
Daniel, servant of the living God, has
your God, whom you serve continual-
ly, been able to deliver you from the
lions?" 21 Then Daniel said to the king,
"O king, live for ever! 22 My God sent
his angel and shut the lions' mouths,
and they have not hurt me, because I
was found blameless before him; and
also before you, O king, I have done
no wrong." 23 Then the king was ex-
ceedingly glad, and commanded that
Daniel be taken up out of the den. So
Daniel was taken up out of the den,
and no kind of hurt was found upon
him, beause he had trusted in his
God. 24 And the king commanded, and
those men who had accused Daniel
were brought and cast into the den of
lions—they, their children, and their
wives; and before they reached the
bottom of the den the lions overpow-
ered them and broke all their bones
in pieces.

25 Then King Darius wrote to all
the peoples, nations, and languages
that dwell in all the earth: "Peace be
multiplied to you. 26 I make a decree,
that in all my royal dominion men
tremble and fear before the God of
Daniel,

for he is the living God,
enduring for ever;
his kingdom shall never be
destroyed,
and his dominion shall be to
the end.
27 He delivers and rescues,
he works signs and wonders
in heaven and on earth,
he who has saved Daniel
from the power of the lions."

28 So this Daniel prospered during
the reign of Darius and the reign of
Cyrus the Persian.

VISIONS OF THE FOUR BEASTS

7 In the first year of Belshaz´zar king
of Babylon, Daniel had a dream

[b] Or *thronging*
[c] Or *thronging*

and visions of his head as he lay in
his bed. Then he wrote down the
dream, and told the sum of the mat-
ter. 2Daniel said, "I saw in my vision
by night, and behold, the four winds
of heaven were stirring up the great
sea. 3And four great beasts came up
out of the sea, different from one an-
other. 4The first was like a lion and
had eagles' wings. Then as I looked
its wings were plucked off, and it was
lifted up from the ground and made
to stand upon two feet like a man;
and the mind of a man was given
to it. 5And behold, another beast, a
second one, like a bear. It was raised
up on one side; it had three ribs in
its mouth between its teeth; and it
was told, 'Arise, devour much flesh.'
6After this I looked, and lo, another,
like a leopard, with four wings of a
bird on its back; and the beast had
four heads; and dominion was given
to it. 7After this I saw in the night
visions, and behold, a fourth beast,
terrible and dreadful and exceeding-
ly strong; and it had great iron teeth;
it devoured and broke in pieces, and
stamped the residue with its feet. It
was different from all the beasts that
were before it; and it had ten horns.
8I considered the horns, and behold,
there came up among them another
horn, a little one,* before which three
of the first horns were plucked up by
the roots; and behold, in this horn
were eyes like the eyes of a man, and
a mouth speaking great things. 9As I
looked,

JUDGMENT BEFORE THE ANCIENT ONE

thrones were placed
and one that was ancient of
days took his seat;
his raiment was white as
snow,
and the hair of his head like
pure wool;
his throne was fiery flames,
its wheels were burning
fire.
10A stream of fire issued
and came forth from before
him;
a thousand thousands served
him,
and ten thousand times
ten thousand stood
before him;
the court sat in judgment,
and the books were opened.

11 I looked then because of the
sound of the great words which the
horn was speaking. And as I looked,
the beast was slain, and its body de-
stroyed and given over to be burned
with fire. 12As for the rest of the
beasts, their dominion was taken
away, but their lives were prolonged
for a season and a time. 13I saw in the
night visions,

and behold, with the clouds of
heaven
there came one like a son of
man,*
and he came to the Ancient of
Days
and was presented before
him.
14And to him was given dominion
and glory and kingdom,
that all peoples, nations, and
languages
should serve him;
his dominion is an everlasting
dominion,
which shall not pass away,
and his kingdom one
that shall not be destroyed.

DANIEL'S VISIONS INTERPRETED

15 "As for me, Daniel, my spir-
it within me was anxious and the
visions of my head alarmed me. 16I
approached one of those who stood
there and asked him the truth con-
cerning all this. So he told me, and
made known to me the interpreta-
tion of the things. 17'These four great
beasts are four kings who shall arise
out of the earth. 18But the saints of the
Most High shall receive the kingdom,
and possess the kingdom for ever, for
ever and ever.'

27 And I, Daniel, was overcome
and lay sick for some days; then I rose
and went about the king's business;
but I was appalled by the vision and
did not understand it.

DANIEL'S PRAYER FOR THE PEOPLE

9 In the first year of Darius the son
of Ahasu-e'rus, by birth a Mede,
who became king over the realm of
the Chalde'ans 2in the first year of his
reign, I, Daniel, perceived in the books
the number of years which, according
to the word of the LORD to Jeremiah
the prophet, must pass before the end
of the desolations of Jerusalem, name-
ly, seventy years.

3 Then I turned my face to the
Lord God, seeking him by prayer
and supplications with fasting and
sackcloth and ashes. 4I prayed to the
LORD my God and made confession,
saying, "O Lord, the great and ter-
rible God, who keeps covenant and
steadfast love with those who love
him and keep his commandments,
5we have sinned and done wrong and
acted wickedly and rebelled, turning
aside from thy commandments and
ordinances; 6we have not listened
to thy servants the prophets, who
spoke in thy name to our kings, our
princes, and our fathers, and to all
the people of the land. 7To thee, O
Lord, belongs righteousness, but to
us confusion of face, as at this day, to
the men of Judah, to the inhabitants
of Jerusalem, and to all Israel, those
that are near and those that are far
away, in all the lands to which thou
hast driven them, because of the
treachery which they have committed
against thee. 8To us, O Lord, belongs
confusion of face, to our kings, to our
princes, and to our fathers, because
we have sinned against thee. 9To the
Lord our God belong mercy and for-
giveness; because we have rebelled
against him, 10and have not obeyed
the voice of the LORD our God by fol-
lowing his laws, which he set before
us by his servants the prophets. 11All
Israel has transgressed thy law and
turned aside, refusing to obey thy
voice. And the curse and oath which
are written in the law of Moses the
servant of God have been poured
out upon us, because we have sinned
against him. 12He has confirmed his
words, which he spoke against us
and against our rulers who ruled us,
by bringing upon us a great calami-
ty; for under the whole heaven there
has not been done the like of what
has been done against Jerusalem.
13As it is written in the law of Moses,
all this calamity has come upon us,
yet we have not entreated the favor
of the LORD our God, turning from
our iniquities and giving heed to thy
truth. 14Therefore the LORD has kept
ready the calamity and has brought
it upon us; for the LORD our God is
righteous in all the works which he
has done, and we have not obeyed
his voice. 15And now, O Lord our
God, who didst bring thy people out
of the land of Egypt with a mighty
hand, and hast made thee a name, as
at this day, we have sinned, we have
done wickedly. 16O Lord, according to
all thy righteous acts, let thy anger
and thy wrath turn away from thy
city Jerusalem, thy holy hill; because
for our sins, and for the iniquities of
our fathers, Jerusalem and thy people
have become a byword among all who
are round about us. 17Now therefore,
O our God, hearken to the prayer of
thy servant and to his supplications,
and for thy own sake, O Lord,[g] cause
thy face to shine upon thy sanctuary,
which is desolate. 18O my God, incline
thy ear and hear; open thy eyes and
behold our desolations, and the city
which is called by thy name; for we
do not present our supplications be-
fore thee on the ground of our righ-
teousness, but on the ground of thy
great mercy. 19O LORD, hear; O LORD,
forgive; O LORD, give heed and act;
delay not, for thy own sake, O my

[g]Theodotion Vg Compare Syr: Heb *for the Lord's sake*

God, because thy city and thy people
are called by thy name."

THE SEVENTY WEEKS

20 While I was speaking and
praying, confessing my sin and the
sin of my people Israel, and pre-
senting my supplication before the
LORD my God for the holy hill of
my God; 21while I was speaking in
prayer, the man Gabriel, whom I had
seen in the vision at the first, came
to me in swift flight at the time of
the evening sacrifice. 22He came[a]
and he said to me, "O Daniel, I have
now come out to give you wisdom
and understanding. 23At the begin-
ning of your supplications a word
went forth, and I have come to tell
it to you, for you are greatly beloved;
therefore consider the word and un-
derstand the vision.

24*"Seventy weeks of years are
decreed concerning your people and
your holy city, to finish the trans-
gression, to put an end to sin, and
to atone for iniquity, to bring in ev-
erlasting righteousness, to seal both
vision and prophet, and to anoint a
most holy place.[b] 25Know therefore
and understand that from the going
forth of the word to restore and build
Jerusalem to the coming of an anoint-
ed one, a prince, there shall be seven
weeks. Then for sixty-two weeks it
shall be built again with squares and
moat, but in a troubled time. 26And
after the sixty-two weeks, an anoint-
ed one shall be cut off, and shall have
nothing; and the people of the prince
who is to come shall destroy the city
and the sanctuary. Its[c] end shall come
with a flood, and to the end there
shall be war; desolations are decreed.
27And he shall make a strong cove-
nant with many for one week; and
for half of the week he shall cause
sacrifice and offering to cease; and
upon the wing of abominations shall
come one who makes desolate, until
the decreed end is poured out on the
desolator."

CONFLICT OF NATIONS AND HEAVENLY POWERS

10 *In the third year of Cyrus king
of Persia a word was revealed to
Daniel, who was named Belteshaz'zar.
And the word was true, and it was a
great conflict. And he understood the
word and had understanding of the
vision.

2 In those days I, Daniel, was
mourning for three weeks. 3I ate no
delicacies, no meat or wine entered
my mouth, nor did I anoint my-
self at all, for the full three weeks.
4On the twenty-fourth day of the
first month, as I was standing on
the bank of the great river, that is,
the Tigris, 5I lifted up my eyes and
looked, and behold, a man clothed in
linen, whose loins were girded with
gold of Uphaz. 6His body was like
beryl, his face like the appearance
of lightning, his eyes like flaming
torches, his arms and legs like the
gleam of burnished bronze, and the
sound of his words like the noise of a
multitude. 7And I, Daniel, alone saw
the vision, for the men who were
with me did not see the vision, but a
great trembling fell upon them, and
they fled to hide themselves. 8So I
was left alone and saw this great vi-
sion, and no strength was left in me;
my radiant appearance was fearfully
changed, and I retained no strength.
9Then I heard the sound of his words;
and when I heard the sound of his
words, I fell on my face in deep sleep
with my face to the ground.

10 And behold, a hand touched
me and set me trembling on my
hands and knees. 11And he said to
me, "O Daniel, man greatly beloved,
give heed to the words that I speak
to you, and stand upright, for now
I have been sent to you." While he

[a] Gk Syr: Heb *made to understand*
[b] Or *thing* or *one*
[c] Or *his*

was speaking this word to me, I
stood up trembling. 12Then he said
to me, "Fear not, Daniel, for from
the first day that you set your mind
to understand and humbled yourself
before your God, your words have
been heard, and I have come be-
cause of your words. 13The prince of
the kingdom of Persia withstood me
twenty-one days; but Michael, one of
the chief princes, came to help me,
so I left him there with the prince
of the kingdom of Persia[d] 14and came
to make you understand what is
to befall your people in the latter
days. For the vision is for days yet
to come."

15 When he had spoken to me
according to these words, I turned
my face toward the ground and was
dumb. 16And behold, one in the like-
ness of the sons of men touched my
lips; then I opened my mouth and
spoke. I said to him who stood before
me, "O my lord, by reason of the vi-
sion pains have come upon me, and
I retain no strength. 17How can my
lord's servant talk with my lord? For
now no strength remains in me, and
no breath is left in me."

18 Again one having the ap-
pearance of a man touched me and
strengthened me. 19And he said, "O
man greatly beloved, fear not, peace
be with you; be strong and of good
courage." And when he spoke to me,
I was strengthened and said, "Let my
lord speak, for you have strengthened
me." 20Then he said, "Do you know
why I have come to you? But now I
will return to fight against the prince
of Persia; and when I am through
with him, lo, the prince of Greece will
come. 21But I will tell you what is in-
scribed in the book of truth: there is
none who contends by my side against
these except Michael, your prince.

11 And as for me, in the first year
of Darius the Mede, I stood up to
confirm and strengthen him.

2 "And now I will show you the
truth. Behold, three more kings
shall arise in Persia; and a fourth
shall be far richer than all of them;
and when he has become strong
through his riches, he shall stir up
all against the kingdom of Greece.
3Then a mighty king shall arise, who
shall rule with great dominion and
do according to his will. 4And when
he has arisen, his kingdom shall be
broken and divided toward the four
winds of heaven, but not to his pos-
terity, nor according to the dominion
with which he ruled; for his kingdom
shall be plucked up and go to others
besides these.

5 "Then the king of the south shall
be strong, but one of his princes shall
be stronger than he and his dominion
shall be a great dominion. 6After some
years they shall make an alliance, and
the daughter of the king of the south
shall come to the king of the north to
make peace; but she shall not retain
the strength of her arm, and he and
his offspring shall not endure; but she
shall be given up, and her attendants,
her child, and he who got possession
of[e] her.

7 "In those times a branch[f] from
her roots shall arise in his place; he
shall come against the army and enter
the fortress of the king of the north,
and he shall deal with them and shall
prevail. 8He shall also carry off to
Egypt their gods with their molten
images and with their precious ves-
sels of silver and of gold; and for some
years he shall refrain from attacking
the king of the north. 9Then the latter
shall come into the realm of the king
of the south but shall return into his
own land.

10 "His sons shall wage war and
assemble a multitude of great forces,
which shall come on and overflow
and pass through, and again shall
carry the war as far as his fortress.
11Then the king of the south, moved

[d]Theodotion Compare Gk: Heb *I was left there with the kings of Persia*
[e]Or *supported*
[f]Gk: Heb *from a branch*

with anger, shall come out and fight
with the king of the north; and he
shall raise a great multitude, but it
shall be given into his hand. 12And
when the multitude is taken, his
heart shall be exalted, and he shall
cast down tens of thousands, but he
shall not prevail. 13For the king of
the north shall again raise a multi-
tude, greater than the former; and
after some years[a] he shall come on
with a great army and abundant
supplies.

14 "In those times many shall
rise against the king of the south;
and the men of violence among your
own people shall lift themselves
up in order to fulfil the vision; but
they shall fail. 15Then the king of the
north shall come and throw up siege-
works, and take a well-fortified city.
And the forces of the south shall not
stand, or even his picked troops, for
there shall be no strength to stand.
16But he who comes against him shall
do according to his own will, and
none shall stand before him; and he
shall stand in the glorious land, and
all of it shall be in his power. 17He
shall set his face to come with the
strength of his whole kingdom, and
he shall bring terms of peace[b] and
perform them. He shall give him the
daughter of women to destroy the
kingdom;[c] but it shall not stand or
be to his advantage. 18Afterward he
shall turn his face to the coastlands,
and shall take many of them; but a
commander shall put an end to his
insolence; indeed[d] he shall turn his
insolence back upon him. 19Then he
shall turn his face back toward the
fortresses of his own land; but he
shall stumble and fall, and shall not
be found.

20 "Then shall arise in his place
one who shall send an exactor of
tribute through the glory of the
kingdom; but within a few days he
shall be broken, neither in anger nor
in battle. 21In his place shall arise a
contemptible person to whom royal
majesty has not been given; he shall
come in without warning and obtain
the kingdom by flatteries. 22Armies
shall be utterly swept away before
him and broken, and the prince of
the covenant also. 23And from the
time that an alliance is made with
him he shall act deceitfully; and he
shall become strong with a small
people. 24Without warning he shall
come into the richest parts[e] of the
province; and he shall do what nei-
ther his fathers nor his fathers' fa-
thers have done, scattering among
them plunder, spoil, and goods. He
shall devise plans against strong-
holds, but only for a time. 25And he
shall stir up his power and his cour-
age against the king of the south
with a great army; and the king of
the south shall wage war with an
exceedingly great and mighty army;
but he shall not stand, for plots shall
be devised against him. 26Even those
who eat his rich food shall be his un-
doing; his army shall be swept away,
and many shall fall down slain. 27And
as for the two kings, their minds
shall be bent on mischief; they shall
speak lies at the same table, but to no
avail; for the end is yet to be at the
time appointed. 28And he shall return
to his land with great substance, but
his heart shall be set against the holy
covenant. And he shall work his will,
and return to his own land.

29 "At the time appointed he shall
return and come into the south; but
it shall not be this time as it was
before. 30For ships of Kittim shall
come against him, and he shall be
afraid and withdraw, and shall turn
back and be enraged and take action
against the holy covenant. He shall

[a] Heb *at the end of the times years*
[b] Gk: Heb *upright ones*
[c] Heb *her* or *it*
[d] Heb obscure
[e] Or *among the richest men*

turn back and give heed to those who
forsake the holy covenant. 31Forces
from him shall appear and profane
the temple and fortress, and shall
take away the continual burnt offer-
ing. And they shall set up the abom-
ination that makes desolate. 32He
shall seduce with flattery those who
violate the covenant; but the people
who know their God shall stand firm
and take action. 33And those among
the people who are wise shall make
many understand, though they shall
fall by sword and flame, by captivity
and plunder, for some days. 34When
they fall, they shall receive a little
help. And many shall join themselves
to them with flattery; 35and some
of those who are wise shall fall, to
refine and to cleanse them[f] and to
make them white, until the time
of the end, for it is yet for the time
appointed.

36 "And the king shall do accord-
ing to his will; he shall exalt himself
and magnify himself above every
god, and shall speak astonishing
things against the God of gods. He
shall prosper till the indignation
is accomplished; for what is deter-
mined shall be done. 37He shall give
no heed to the gods of his fathers,
or to the one beloved by women; he
shall not give heed to any other god,
for he shall magnify himself above
all. 38He shall honor the god of for-
tresses instead of these; a god whom
his fathers did not know he shall
honor with gold and silver, with pre-
cious stones and costly gifts. 39He
shall deal with the strongest for-
tresses by the help of a foreign god;
those who acknowledge him he shall
magnify with honor. He shall make
them rulers over many and shall di-
vide the land for a price.

THE TIME OF THE END

40 "At the time of the end the king
of the south shall attack[g] him; but
the king of the north shall rush upon
him like a whirlwind, with chariots
and horsemen, and with many ships;
and he shall come into countries and
shall overflow and pass through. 41He
shall come into the glorious land.
And tens of thousands shall fall,
but these shall be delivered out of
his hand: Edom and Moab and the
main part of the Ammonites. 42He
shall stretch out his hand against the
countries, and the land of Egypt shall
not escape. 43He shall become ruler
of the treasures of gold and of silver,
and all the precious things of Egypt;
and the Libyans and the Ethiopians
shall follow in his train. 44But tidings
from the east and the north shall
alarm him, and he shall go forth with
great fury to exterminate and utter-
ly destroy many. 45And he shall pitch
his palatial tents between the sea
and the glorious holy mountain; yet
he shall come to his end, with none
to help him.

THE RESURRECTION OF THE DEAD

12 "At that time shall arise Michael,
the great prince who has charge
of your people. And there shall be
a time of trouble, such as never
has been since there was a nation
till that time; but at that time your
people shall be delivered, every one
whose name shall be found written
in the book. 2And many of those who
sleep in the dust of the earth shall
awake, some to everlasting life, and
some to shame and everlasting con-
tempt. 3And those who are wise shall
shine like the brightness of the fir-
mament; and those who turn many
to righteousness, like the stars for
ever and ever. 4But you, Daniel, shut
up the words, and seal the book, un-
til the time of the end. Many shall
run to and fro, and knowledge shall
increase."

5 Then I Daniel looked, and be-
hold, two others stood, one on this

[f] Gk: Heb *among them*
[g] Heb *thrust at*

bank of the stream and one on that bank of the stream. 6And I[a] said to the man clothed in linen, who was above the waters of the stream, "How long shall it be till the end of these wonders?" 7The man clothed in linen, who was above the waters of the stream, raised his right hand and his left hand toward heaven; and I heard him swear by him who lives for ever that it would be for a time, two times, and half a time; and that when the shattering of the power of the holy people comes to an end all these things would be accomplished. 8I heard, but I did not understand. Then I said, "O my lord, what shall be the issue of these things?" 9He said, "Go your way, Daniel, for the words are shut up and sealed until the time of the end. 10Many shall purify themselves, and make themselves white, and be refined; but the wicked shall do wickedly; and none of the wicked shall understand; but those who are wise shall understand. 11And from the time that the continual burnt offering is taken away, and the abomination that makes desolate is set up, there shall be a thousand two hundred and ninety days. 12Blessed is he who waits and comes to the thousand three hundred and thirty-five days. 13But go your way till the end; and you shall rest, and shall stand in your allotted place at the end of the days."

SUSANNA'S BEAUTY ATTRACTS TWO ELDERS

13 *There was a man living in Babylon whose name was Jo´akim. 2And he took a wife named Susanna, the daughter of Hilki´ah, a very beautiful woman and one who feared the Lord. 3Her parents were righteous, and had taught their daughter according to the law of Moses. 4Jo´akim was very rich, and had a spacious garden adjoining his house; and the Jews used to come to him because he was the most honored of them all.

5 In that year two elders from the people were appointed as judges. Concerning them the Lord had said: "Iniquity came forth from Babylon, from elders who were judges, who were supposed to govern the people." 6These men were frequently at Jo´akim's house, and all who had suits at law came to them.

7 When the people departed at noon, Susanna would go into her husband's garden to walk. 8The two elders used to see her every day, going in and walking about, and they began to desire her. 9And they perverted their minds and turned away their eyes from looking to Heaven or remembering righteous judgments. 10Both were overwhelmed with passion for her, but they did not tell each other of their distress, 11for they were ashamed to disclose their lustful desire to possess her. 12And they watched eagerly, day after day, to see her.

13 They said to each other, "Let us go home, for it is mealtime." 14And when they went out, they parted from each other. But turning back, they met again; and when each pressed the other for the reason, they confessed their lust. And then together they arranged for a time when they could find her alone.

THE ELDERS ATTEMPT TO SEDUCE SUSANNA

15 Once, while they were watching for an opportune day, she went in as before with only two maids, and wished to bathe in the garden, for it was very hot. 16And no one was there except the two elders, who had hid themselves and were watching her. 17She said to her maids, "Bring me oil and ointments, and shut the garden doors so that I may bathe." 18They did as she said, shut the garden doors, and went out by the side doors to

[a] Gk Vg: Heb *he*

bring what they had been command-
ed; and they did not see the elders,
because they were hidden.
19 When the maids had gone out,
the two elders rose and ran to her,
and said: 20“Look, the garden doors
are shut, no one sees us, and we are
in love with you; so give your consent,
and lie with us. 21If you refuse, we will
testify against you that a young man
was with you, and this was why you
sent your maids away.”
22 Susanna sighed deeply, and said,
“I am hemmed in on every side. For
if I do this thing, it is death for me;
and if I do not, I shall not escape your
hands. 23I choose not to do it and to
fall into your hands, rather than to sin
in the sight of the Lord.”
24 Then Susanna cried out with a
loud voice, and the two elders shout-
ed against her. 25And one of them ran
and opened the garden doors. 26When
the household servants heard the
shouting in the garden, they rushed
in at the side door to see what had
happened to her. 27And when the
elders told their tale, the servants
were greatly ashamed, for nothing
like this had ever been said about
Susanna.

THE ELDERS TESTIFY AGAINST SUSANNA

28 The next day, when the people
gathered at the house of her husband
Jo´akim, the two elders came, full of
their wicked plot to have Susanna put
to death. 29They said before the peo-
ple, “Send for Susanna, the daugh-
ter of Hilki´ah, who is the wife of
Jo´akim.” 30So they sent for her. And
she came, with her parents, her chil-
dren, and all her kindred.
31 Now Susanna was a woman of
great refinement, and beautiful in
appearance. 32As she was veiled, the
wicked men ordered her to be un-
veiled, that they might feed upon her
beauty. 33But her family and friends
and all who saw her wept.
34 Then the two elders stood up
in the midst of the people, and laid
their hands upon her head. 35And
she, weeping, looked up toward heav-
en, for her heart trusted in the Lord.
36The elders said, “As we were walk-
ing in the garden alone, this woman
came in with two maids, shut the gar-
den doors, and dismissed the maids.
37Then a young man, who had been
hidden, came to her and lay with her.
38We were in a corner of the garden,
and when we saw this wickedness we
ran to them. 39We saw them embrac-
ing, but we could not hold the man,
for he was too strong for us, and he
opened the doors and dashed out.
40So we seized this woman and asked
her who the young man was, but she
would not tell us. These things we
testify.”
41 The assembly believed them, be-
cause they were elders of the people
and judges; and they condemned her
to death.
42 Then Susanna cried out with a
loud voice, and said, “O eternal God,
who dost discern what is secret,
who art aware of all things before
they come to be, 43thou knowest that
these men have borne false witness
against me. And now I am to die! Yet
I have done none of the things that
they have wickedly invented against
me!”
44 The Lord heard her cry. 45And
as she was being led away to be put
to death, God aroused the holy spirit
of a young lad named Daniel; 46and he
cried with a loud voice, “I am innocent
of the blood of this woman.”

DANIEL RESCUES SUSANNA

47 All the people turned to him,
and said, “What is this that you
have said?” 48Taking his stand in
the midst of them, he said, “Are you
such fools, you sons of Israel? Have
you condemned a daughter of Israel
without examination and without
learning the facts? 49Return to the
place of judgment. For these men
have borne false witness against
her.”

50 Then all the people returned
in haste. And the elders said to him,
"Come, sit among us and inform us,
for God has given you that right."
51And Daniel said to them, "Separate
them far from each other, and I will
examine them."

52 When they were separated from
each other, he summoned one of
them and said to him, "You old relic
of wicked days, your sins have now
come home, which you have commit-
ted in the past, 53pronouncing unjust
judgments, condemning the innocent
and letting the guilty go free, though
the Lord said, 'Do not put to death
an innocent and righteous person.'
54Now then, if you really saw her, tell
me this: Under what tree did you see
them being intimate with each oth-
er?" He answered, "Under a mastic
tree."[a] 55And Daniel said, "Very well!
You have lied against your own head,
for the angel of God has received the
sentence from God and will immedi-
ately cut[b] you in two."

56 Then he put him aside, and
commanded them to bring the other.
And he said to him, "You offspring of
Canaan and not of Judah, beauty has
deceived you and lust has perverted
your heart. 57This is how you both
have been dealing with the daughters
of Israel, and they were intimate with
you through fear; but a daughter of
Judah would not endure your wicked-
ness. 58Now then, tell me: Under what
tree did you catch them being inti-
mate with each other?" He answered,
"Under an evergreen oak."[c] 59And
Daniel said to him, "Very well! You
also have lied against your own head,
for the angel of God is waiting with
his sword to saw[d] you in two, that he
may destroy you both."

60 Then all the assembly shout-
ed loudly and blessed God, who
saves those who hope in him. 61And
they rose against the two elders, for
out of their own mouths Daniel had
convicted them of bearing false wit-
ness; 62and they did to them as they
had wickedly planned to do to their
neighbor; acting in accordance with
the law of Moses, they put them to
death. Thus innocent blood was saved
that day.

63 And Hilki'ah and his wife
praised God for their daughter
Susanna, and so did Jo'akim her hus-
band and all her kindred, because
nothing shameful was found in her.
64And from that day onward Daniel
had a great reputation among the
people.

DANIEL AND THE PRIESTS OF BEL

14 *When King Asty'ages was
laid with his fathers, Cyrus the
Persian received his kingdom. 2And
Daniel was a companion of the king,
and was the most honored of his
friends.

3 Now the Babylonians had an idol
called Bel, and every day they spent
on it twelve bushels of fine flour and
forty sheep and fifty gallons of wine.
4The king revered it and went every
day to worship it. But Daniel wor-
shiped his own God.

5 And the king said to him, "Why
do you not worship Bel?" He an-
swered, "Because I do not revere man-
made idols, but the living God, who
created heaven and earth and has do-
minion over all flesh."

6 The king said to him, "Do you
not think that Bel is a living God?
Do you not see how much he eats
and drinks every day?" 7Then Daniel
laughed, and said, "Do not be de-
ceived, O king; for this is but clay in-
side and brass outside, and it never ate
or drank anything."

[a] The Greek words for *mastic tree* and *cut* are so similar that the use of *cut* is ironic wordplay
[b] The Greek words for *mastic tree* and *cut* are so similar that the use of *cut* is ironic wordplay
[c] The Greek words for *evergreen oak* and *saw* are so similar that the use of *saw* is ironic wordplay
[d] The Greek words for *evergreen oak* and *saw* are so similar that the use of *saw* is ironic wordplay

8 Then the king was angry, and he
called his priests and said to them,
"If you do not tell me who is eating
these provisions, you shall die. 9But
if you prove that Bel is eating them,
Daniel shall die, because he blas-
phemed against Bel." And Daniel said
to the king, "Let it be done as you
have said."

10 Now there were seventy priests
of Bel, besides their wives and chil-
dren. And the king went with Daniel
into the temple of Bel. 11And the
priests of Bel said, "Behold, we are
going outside; you yourself, O king,
shall set forth the food and mix and
place the wine, and shut the door and
seal it with your signet. 12And when
you return in the morning, if you do
not find that Bel has eaten it all, we
will die; or else Daniel will, who is
telling lies about us." 13They were
unconcerned, for beneath the table
they had made a hidden entrance,
through which they used to go in
regularly and consume the provi-
sions. 14When they had gone out, the
king set forth the food for Bel. Then
Daniel ordered his servants to bring
ashes and they sifted them through-
out the whole temple in the presence
of the king alone. Then they went
out, shut the door and sealed it with
the king's signet, and departed. 15In
the night the priests came with their
wives and children, as they were ac-
customed to do, and ate and drank
everything.

16 Early in the morning the king
rose and came, and Daniel with him.
17And the king said, "Are the seals
unbroken, Daniel?" He answered,
"They are unbroken, O king." 18As
soon as the doors were opened, the
king looked at the table, and shouted
in a loud voice, "You are great, O Bel;
and with you there is no deceit, none
at all."

19 Then Daniel laughed, and re-
strained the king from going in, and
said, "Look at the floor, and notice
whose footsteps these are." 20The king
said, "I see the footsteps of men and
women and children."

21 Then the king was enraged, and
he seized the priests and their wives
and children; and they showed him
the secret doors through which they
were accustomed to enter and devour
what was on the table. 22Therefore the
king put them to death, and gave Bel
over to Daniel, who destroyed it and
its temple.

DANIEL KILLS THE DRAGON

23 There was also a great drag-
on, which the Babylonians revered.
24And the king said to Daniel, "You
cannot deny that this is a living god;
so worship him." 25Daniel said, "I
will worship the Lord my God, for
he is the living God. 26But if you,
O king, will give me permission, I
will slay the dragon without sword
or club." The king said, "I give you
permission."

27 Then Daniel took pitch, fat, and
hair, and boiled them together and
made cakes, which he fed to the drag-
on. The dragon ate them, and burst
open. And Daniel said, "See what you
have been worshiping!"

28 When the Babylonians heard
it, they were very indignant and
conspired against the king, saying,
"The king has become a Jew; he has
destroyed Bel, and slain the dragon,
and slaughtered the priests." 29Going
to the king, they said, "Hand Daniel
over to us, or else we will kill you and
your household." 30The king saw that
they were pressing him hard, and un-
der compulsion he handed Daniel over
to them.

DANIEL IN THE LIONS' DEN

31 They threw Daniel into the
lions' den, and he was there for six
days. 32There were seven lions in the
den, and every day they had been
given two human bodies and two
sheep; but these were not given to
them now, so that they might devour
Daniel.

33 Now the prophet Hab´akkuk was in Judea. He had boiled pottage and had broken bread into a bowl, and was going into the field to take it to the reapers. 34But the angel of the Lord said to Hab´akkuk, "Take the dinner which you have to Babylon, to Daniel, in the lions' den." 35Hab´akkuk said, "Sir, I have never seen Babylon, and I know nothing about the den." 36Then the angel of the Lord took him by the crown of his head, and lifted him by his hair and set him down in Babylon, right over the den, with the rushing sound of the wind itself.

37 Then Hab´akkuk shouted, "Daniel, Daniel! Take the dinner which God has sent you." 38And Daniel said, "Thou hast remembered me, O God, and hast not forsaken those who love thee." 39So Daniel arose and ate. And the angel of God immediately returned Hab´akkuk to his own place.

40 On the seventh day the king came to mourn for Daniel. When he came to the den he looked in, and there sat Daniel. 41And the king shouted with a loud voice, "Thou art great, O Lord God of Daniel, and there is no other besides thee." 42And he pulled Daniel[a] out, and threw into the den the men who had attempted his destruction, and they were devoured immediately before his eyes.

[a] Gk *him*

THE BOOK OF

HOSEA

1 The word of the LORD that came
to Hose´a the son of Be-e´ri, in the
days of Uzzi´ah, Jotham, Ahaz, and
Hezeki´ah, kings of Judah, and in the
days of Jerobo´am the son of Jo´ash,
king of Israel.

THE FAMILY OF HOSEA

2 When the LORD first spoke
through Hose´a, the LORD said to
Hose´a, "Go, take to yourself a wife
of harlotry and have children of har-
lotry, for the land commits great har-
lotry by forsaking the LORD." 3So he
went and took Gomer the daughter of
Dibla´im, and she conceived and bore
him a son.

4 And the LORD said to him, "Call
his name Jezreel; for yet a little while,
and I will punish the house of Jehu
for the blood of Jezreel, and I will put
an end to the kingdom of the house
of Israel. 5And on that day, I will
break the bow of Israel in the valley
of Jezreel."

6 She conceived again and bore a
daughter. And the LORD said to him,
"Call her name Not pitied, for I will no
more have pity on the house of Israel,
to forgive them at all. 7But I will have
pity on the house of Judah, and I will
deliver them by the LORD their God;
I will not deliver them by bow, nor by
sword, nor by war, nor by horses, nor
by horsemen."

8 When she had weaned Not pit-
ied, she conceived and bore a son.
9And the LORD said, "Call his name
Not my people, for you are not my
people and I am not your God."[a]

THE RESTORATION OF ISRAEL

10[b] Yet the number of the people
of Israel shall be like the sand of
the sea, which can be neither mea-
sured nor numbered; and in the
place where it was said to them,
"You are not my people," it shall
be said to them, "Sons of the liv-
ing God." 11And the people of Judah
and the people of Israel shall be
gathered together, and they shall
appoint for themselves one head;
and they shall go up from the land,
for great shall be the day of Jezreel.

2 [c] Say to your brother,[d] "My people,"
and to your sister,[e] "She has ob-
tained pity."

ISRAEL'S INFIDELITY, PUNISHMENT, AND REDEMPTION

2"Plead with your mother,
plead—
for she is not my wife,
and I am not her husband—
that she put away her harlotry
from her face,
and her adultery from be-
tween her breasts;
3lest I strip her naked
and make her as in the day
she was born,
and make her like a
wilderness,
and set her like a parched
land,
and slay her with thirst.
4Upon her children also I will
have no pity,
because they are children of
harlotry.
5For their mother has played the
harlot;
she that conceived
them has acted
shamefully.
For she said, 'I will go after my
lovers,

[a] Heb *I am not yours*
[b] Ch 2.1 in Heb
[c] Ch 2.3 in Heb
[d] Gk: Heb *brothers*
[e] Gk Vg:Heb *sisters*

who give me my bread and
my water,
my wool and my flax, my oil
and my drink.'
6Therefore I will hedge up her[a]
way with thorns;
and I will build a wall
against her,
so that she cannot find her
paths.
7She shall pursue her lovers,
but not overtake them;
and she shall seek them,
but shall not find them.
Then she shall say, 'I will go
and return to my first
husband,
for it was better with me
then than now.'
8And she did not know
that it was I who gave her
the grain, the wine, and
the oil,
and who lavished upon her
silver
and gold which they used for
Ba'al.
9Therefore I will take back
my grain in its time,
and my wine in its season;
and I will take away my wool
and my flax,
which were to cover her
nakedness.
10Now I will uncover her
lewdness
in the sight of her lovers,
and no one shall rescue her
out of my hand.
11And I will put an end to all her
mirth,
her feasts, her new moons,
her sabbaths,
and all her appointed feasts.
12And I will lay waste her vines
and her fig trees,
of which she said,
'These are my hire,
which my lovers have given
me.'
I will make them a forest,
and the beasts of the field
shall devour them.
13And I will punish her for the
feast days of the Ba'als
when she burned incense to
them
and decked herself with her
ring and jewelry,
and went after her lovers,
and forgot me, says the
LORD.
14"Therefore, behold, I will allure
her,
and bring her into the
wilderness,
and speak tenderly to her.
15And there I will give her her
vineyards,
and make the Valley of
Achor a door of
hope.
And there she shall answer
as in the days of her
youth,
as at the time when she
came out of the land
of Egypt.

16"And in that day, says the LORD,
you will call me, 'My husband,' and
no longer will you call me, 'My Ba'al.'
17For I will remove the names of the
Ba'als from her mouth, and they
shall be mentioned by name no more.
18And I will make for you[b] a cove-
nant on that day with the beasts of
the field, the birds of the air, and the
creeping things of the ground; and I
will abolish[c] the bow, the sword, and
war from the land; and I will make
you lie down in safety. 19And I will
betroth you to me for ever; I will be-
troth you to me in righteousness and
in justice, in steadfast love, and in
mercy. 20I will betroth you to me in
faithfulness; and you shall know the
LORD.

21"And in that day, says the
LORD,
I will answer the heavens

[a] Gk Syr: Heb *your*
[b] Heb *them*
[c] Heb *break*

and they shall answer the
earth;
22and the earth shall answer the
grain, the wine, and the
oil,
and they shall answer
Jezreel;[d]
23and I will sow him[e] for
myself in the land.
And I will have pity on Not
pitied,
and I will say to Not my
people, 'You are my
people';
and he shall say, 'Thou art
my God.'"

FURTHER ASSURANCES OF GOD'S REDEEMING LOVE

3 And the LORD said to me, "Go
again, love a woman who is be-
loved of a paramour and is an adul-
teress; even as the LORD loves the
people of Israel, though they turn
to other gods and love cakes of rai-
sins." 2So I bought her for fifteen
shekels of silver and a homer and a
lethech of barley. 3And I said to her,
"You must dwell as mine for many
days; you shall not play the harlot,
or belong to another man; so will I
also be to you." 4For the children of
Israel shall dwell many days without
king or prince, without sacrifice or
pillar, without ephod or teraphim.
5Afterward the children of Israel
shall return and seek the LORD their
God, and David their king; and they
shall come in fear to the LORD and to
his goodness in the latter days.

GOD ACCUSES ISRAEL

4 Hear the word of the LORD,
O people of Israel;
for the LORD has a con-
troversy with the
inhabitants of the
land.
There is no faithfulness or
kindness,
and no knowledge of God in
the land;
2there is swearing, lying, killing,
stealing, and committing
adultery;
they break all bounds and
murder follows
murder.
3Therefore the land mourns,
and all who dwell in it
languish,
and also the beasts of the
field,
and the birds of the air;
and even the fish of the sea
are taken away.
4Yet let no one contend,
and let none accuse,
for with you is my conten-
tion, O priest.[f]
5You shall stumble by day,
the prophet also shall
stumble with you by
night;
and I will destroy your
mother.
6My people are destroyed for lack
of knowledge;
because you have rejected
knowledge,
I reject you from being a
priest to me.
And since you have forgotten
the law of your God,
I also will forget your
children.
7The more they increased,
the more they sinned against
me;
I will change their glory into
shame.
8They feed on the sin of my
people;
they are greedy for their
iniquity.
9And it shall be like people, like
priest;
I will punish them for their
ways,

[d]That is *God sows*
[e]Cn: Heb *her*
[f]Cn: Heb uncertain

and requite them for their
deeds.
10They shall eat, but not be
satisfied;
they shall play the harlot,
but not multiply;
because they have forsaken the
LORD
to cherish harlotry.

THE IDOLATRY OF ISRAEL

11Wine and new wine
take away the
understanding.
12My people inquire of a thing of
wood,
and their staff gives them
oracles.
For a spirit of harlotry has led
them astray,
and they have left their God
to play the harlot.
13They sacrifice on the tops of the
mountains,
and make offerings upon the
hills,
under oak, poplar, and
terebinth,
because their shade is
good.
Therefore your daughters play
the harlot,
and your brides commit
adultery.
14I will not punish your daugh-
ters when they play the
harlot,
nor your brides when they
commit adultery;
for the men themselves go
aside with harlots,
and sacrifice with cult
prostitutes,
and a people without under-
standing shall come to
ruin.
15Though you play the harlot, O
Israel,
let not Judah become guilty.
Enter not into Gilgal,
nor go up to Beth-a´ven,
and swear not, "As the LORD
lives."
16Like a stubborn heifer,
Israel is stubborn;
can the LORD now feed them
like a lamb in a broad
pasture?
17E´phraim is joined to idols,
let him alone.
18A band[a] of drunkards, they give
themselves to harlotry;
they love shame more than
their glory.[b]
19A wind has wrapped them[c] in its
wings,
and they shall be ashamed
because of their
altars.[d]

IMPENDING JUDGMENT ON ISRAEL AND JUDAH

5 Hear this, O priests!
Give heed, O house of Israel!
Hearken, O house of the king!
For the judgment pertains
to you;
for you have been a snare at
Mizpah,
and a net spread upon
Tabor.
2And they have made deep the pit
of Shittim;[e]
but I will chastise all of
them.
3I know E´phraim,
and Israel is not hid from
me;
for now, O E´phraim, you have
played the harlot,
Israel is defiled.
4Their deeds do not permit them
to return to their God.
For the spirit of harlotry is
within them,
and they know not the

[a]Cn: Heb uncertain
[b]Cn Compare Gk: Heb of this line uncertain
[c]Heb *her*
[d]Gk Syr: Heb *sacrifices*
[e]Cn: Heb uncertain

LORD.
5The pride of Israel testifies to
his face;
E´phraim[f] shall stumble in
his guilt;
Judah also shall stumble
with them.
6With their flocks and herds they
shall go
to seek the LORD,
but they will not find him;
he has withdrawn from
them.
7They have dealt faithlessly with
the LORD;
for they have borne alien
children.
Now the new moon shall
devour them with
their fields.
8Blow the horn in Gib´e-ah,
the trumpet in Ramah.
Sound the alarm at
Beth-a´ven;
tremble,[g] O Benjamin!
9E´phraim shall become a
desolation
in the day of punishment;
among the tribes of Israel
I declare what is sure.
10The princes of Judah have
become
like those who remove the
landmark;
upon them I will pour out
my wrath like water.
11E´phraim is oppressed, crushed
in judgment,
because he was determined
to go after vanity.[h]
12Therefore I am like a moth to
E´phraim,
and like dry rot to the house
of Judah.
13When E´phraim saw his
sickness,
and Judah his wound,
then E´phraim went to
Assyria,
and sent to the great king.[i]
But he is not able to cure you
or heal your wound.
14For I will be like a lion to
E´phraim,
and like a young lion to the
house of Judah.
I, even I, will rend and go
away,
I will carry off, and none
shall rescue.
15I will return again to my place,
until they acknowledge their
guilt and seek my
face,
and in their distress they
seek me, saying,

A CALL TO REPENTANCE

6 "Come, let us return to the LORD;
for he has torn, that he may
heal us;
he has stricken, and he will
bind us up.
2After two days he will revive us;
on the third day he will raise
us up,
that we may live before
him.
3Let us know, let us press on to
know the LORD;
his going forth is sure as the
dawn;
he will come to us as the
showers,
as the spring rains that
water the earth."

IMPENITENCE OF ISRAEL AND JUDAH

4What shall I do with you, O
E´phraim?
What shall I do with you, O
Judah?
Your love is like a morning
cloud,
like the dew that goes early
away.
5Therefore I have hewn them by
the prophets,

[f]Heb *Israel and Ephraim*
[g]Cn Compare Gk: Heb *after you*
[h]Gk: Heb *a command*
[i]Cn: Heb *a king that will contend*

I have slain them by the
words of my mouth,
and my judgment goes forth
as the light.[a]
6For I desire steadfast love and
not sacrifice,
the knowledge of God,
rather than burnt
offerings.
7But at[b] Adam they transgressed
the covenant;
there they dealt faithlessly
with me.
8Gilead is a city of evildoers,
tracked with blood.
9As robbers lie in wait[c] for a
man,
so the priests are banded
together;[d]
they murder on the way to
Shechem,
yea, they commit villainy.
10In the house of Israel I have seen
a horrible thing;
E´phraim's harlotry is there,
Israel is defiled.
11For you also, O Judah, a harvest
is appointed.
When I would restore the for-
tunes of my people,
7 when I would heal Israel,
the corruption of E´phraim is
revealed,
and the wicked deeds of
Samar´ia;
for they deal falsely,
the thief breaks in,
and the bandits raid
without.
2But they do not consider
that I remember all their evil
works.
Now their deeds encompass
them,
they are before my face.
3By their wickedness they make
the king glad,
and the princes by their
treachery.
4They are all adulterers;
they are like a heated oven,
whose baker ceases to stir the
fire,
from the kneading of the
dough until it is
leavened.
5On the day of our king the
princes
became sick with the heat
of wine;
he stretched out his hand
with mockers.
6For like an oven their hearts
burn[e] with intrigue;
all night their anger
smolders;
in the morning it blazes like
a flaming fire.
7All of them are hot as an oven,
and they devour their
rulers.
All their kings have fallen;
and none of them calls upon
me.
8E´phraim mixes himself with the
peoples;
E´phraim is a cake not
turned.
9Aliens devour his strength,
and he knows it not;
gray hairs are sprinkled upon
him,
and he knows it not.
10The pride of Israel witnesses
against him;
yet they do not return to the
LORD their God,
nor seek him, for all this.

FUTILE RELIANCE ON THE NATIONS

11E´phraim is like a dove,
silly and without sense,
calling to Egypt, going to
Assyria.
12As they go, I will spread over
them my net;

[a] Gk Syr: Heb *thy judgment goes forth*
[b] Cn: Heb *like*
[c] Cn: Heb uncertain
[d] Syr: Heb *a company*
[e] Gk Syr: Heb *brought near*

I will bring them down like
birds of the air;
I will chastise them for their
wicked deeds.[f]
13Woe to them, for they have
strayed from me!
Destruction to them, for
they have rebelled
against me!
I would redeem them,
but they speak lies against
me.
14They do not cry to me from the
heart,
but they wail upon their
beds;
for grain and wine they gash
themselves,
they rebel against me.
15Although I trained and strength-
ened their arms,
yet they devise evil against
me.
16They turn to Ba´al;[g]
they are like a treacherous
bow,
their princes shall fall by the
sword
because of the insolence of
their tongue.
This shall be their derision in
the land of Egypt.

ISRAEL'S APOSTASY

8 Set the trumpet to your lips,
for[h] a vulture is over the house
of the LORD,
because they have broken my
covenant,
and transgressed my law.
2To me they cry,
My God, we Israel know
thee.
3Israel has spurned the good;
the enemy shall pursue
him.
4They made kings, but not
through me.
They set up princes,
but without my
knowledge.
With their silver and gold they
made idols
for their own destruction.
5[i] spurned your calf, O Samar´ia.
My anger burns against
them.
How long will it be
till they are pure
6in Israel?[j]
A workman made it;
it is not God.
The calf of Samar´ia
shall be broken to pieces.[k]
7For they sow the wind,
and they shall reap the
whirlwind.
The standing grain has no
heads,
it shall yield no meal;
if it were to yield,
aliens would devour it.
8Israel is swallowed up;
already they are among the
nations
as a useless vessel.
9For they have gone up to
Assyria,
a wild ass wandering alone;
E´phraim has hired lovers.
10Though they hire allies among
the nations,
I will soon gather them up.
And they shall cease[l] for a little
while
from anointing[m] king and
princes.
11Because E´phraim has
multiplied altars for
sinning,
they have become to him
altars for sinning.

[f]Cn: Heb *according to the report to their congregation*
[g]Cn: Heb uncertain
[h]Cn: Heb *as*
[i]I haveHeb *He has*
[j]Gk: Heb *for from Israel*
[k]Or *shall go up in flames*
[l]Gk: Heb *begin*
[m]Gk: Heb *burden*

12Were I to write for him my laws
by ten thousands,
they would be regarded as a
strange thing.
13They love sacrifice;[a]
they sacrifice flesh and
eat it;
but the LORD has no delight
in them.
Now he will remember their
iniquity,
and punish their sins;
they shall return to Egypt.
14For Israel has forgotten his
Maker,
and built palaces;
and Judah has multiplied forti-
fied cities;
but I will send a fire upon
his cities,
and it shall devour his
strongholds.

PUNISHMENT FOR ISRAEL'S SIN

9 Rejoice not, O Israel!
Exult not[b] like the peoples;
for you have played the harlot,
forsaking your God.
You have loved a harlot's
hire
upon all threshing floors.
2Threshing floor and winevat
shall not feed them,
and the new wine shall fail
them.
3They shall not remain in the land
of the LORD;
but E´phraim shall return to
Egypt,
and they shall eat unclean
food in Assyria.
4They shall not pour libations of
wine to the LORD;
and they shall not please
him with their
sacrifices.
Their bread[c] shall be like
mourners' bread;
all who eat of it shall be
defiled;
for their bread shall be for their
hunger only;
it shall not come to the
house of the LORD.
5What will you do on the day of
appointed festival,
and on the day of the feast of
the LORD?
6For behold, they are going to
Assyria;[d]
Egypt shall gather them,
Memphis shall bury them.
Nettles shall possess their pre-
cious things of silver;
thorns shall be in their
tents.
7The days of punishment have
come,
the days of recompense have
come;
Israel shall know it.
The prophet is a fool,
the man of the spirit is
mad,
because of your great iniquity
and great hatred.
8The prophet is the watchman of
E´phraim,
the people of my God,
yet a fowler's snare is on all his
ways,
and hatred in the house of
his God.
9They have deeply corrupted
themselves
as in the days of Gib´e-ah:
he will remember their
iniquity,
he will punish their sins.
10Like grapes in the wilderness,
I found Israel.
Like the first fruit on the fig
tree,
in its first season,
I saw your fathers.
But they came to Ba´al-pe´or,
and consecrated themselves

[a]Cn: Heb uncertain
[b]Gk: Heb *to exultation*
[c]Cn: Heb *to them*
[d]Cn: Heb *from destruction*

to Ba´al,[e]
and became detestable like
the thing they loved.
11E´phraim's glory shall fly away
like a bird—
no birth, no pregnancy, no
conception!
12Even if they bring up children,
I will bereave them till none
is left.
Woe to them
when I depart from them!
13E´phraim's sons, as I have seen,
are destined for a prey;[f]
E´phraim must lead forth his
sons to slaughter.
14Give them, O LORD—
what wilt thou give?
Give them a miscarrying
womb
and dry breasts.
15Every evil of theirs is in Gilgal;
there I began to hate them.
Because of the wickedness of
their deeds
I will drive them out of my
house.
I will love them no more;
all their princes are rebels.
16E´phraim is stricken,
their root is dried up,
they shall bear no fruit.
Even though they bring forth,
I will slay their beloved
children.
17My God will cast them off,
because they have not hear-
kened to him;
they shall be wanderers
among the nations.

ISRAEL'S SIN AND CAPTIVITY

10 Israel is a luxuriant vine
that yields its fruit.
The more his fruit increased
the more altars he built;
as his country improved
he improved his pillars.
2Their heart is false;
now they must bear their
guilt.
The LORD[g] will break down
their altars,
and destroy their pillars.
3For now they will say:
"We have no king,
for we fear not the LORD,
and a king, what could he do
for us?"
4They utter mere words;
with empty oaths they make
covenants;
so judgment springs up like
poisonous weeds
in the furrows of the field.
5The inhabitants of Samar´ia
tremble
for the calf[h] of Beth-a´ven.
Its people shall mourn for it,
and its idolatrous priests
shall wail[i] over it,
over its glory which has
departed from it.
6Yea, the thing itself shall be
carried to Assyria,
as tribute to the great
king.[j]
E´phraim shall be put to
shame,
and Israel shall be ashamed
of his idol.[k]
7Samar´ia's king shall perish,
like a chip on the face of the
waters.
8The high places of Aven, the sin
of Israel,
shall be destroyed.
Thorn and thistle shall grow
up
on their altars;
and they shall say to the moun-
tains, Cover us,
and to the hills, Fall upon
us.

[e] Heb *shame*
[f] Cn Compare Gk: Heb uncertain
[g] Heb *he*
[h] Gk Syr: Heb *calves*
[i] Cn: Heb *exult*
[j] Cn: Heb *a king that will contend*
[k] Cn: Heb *counsel*

9From the days of Gib´e-ah, you
have sinned, O Israel;
there they have continued.
Shall not war overtake them
in Gib´e-ah?
10I will come[a] against the way-
ward people to chastise
them;
and nations shall be gath-
ered against them
when they are chastised[b]
for their double
iniquity.
11E´phraim was a trained heifer
that loved to thresh,
and I spared her fair neck;
but I will put E´phraim to the
yoke,
Judah must plow,
Jacob must harrow for
himself.
12Sow for yourselves
righteousness,
reap the fruit[c] of steadfast
love;
break up your fallow
ground,
for it is the time to seek the
LORD,
that he may come and rain
salvation upon you.
13You have plowed iniquity,
you have reaped injustice,
you have eaten the fruit of
lies.
Because you have trusted in
your chariots[d]
and in the multitude of your
warriors,
14therefore the tumult of war
shall arise among your
people,
and all your fortresses shall
be destroyed,
as Shalman destroyed Beth-
ar´bel on the day of
battle;
mothers were dashed in
pieces with their
children.
15Thus it shall be done to you, O
house of Israel,[e]
because of your great
wickedness.
In the storm[f] the king of
Israel
shall be utterly cut off.

GOD'S COMPASSION DESPITE ISRAEL'S INGRATITUDE

11 When Israel was a child,
I loved him,
and out of Egypt I called my
son.
2The more I[g] called them,
the more they went from
me;[h]
they kept sacrificing to the
Ba´als,
and burning incense to
idols.
3Yet it was I who taught E´phraim
to walk,
I took them up in my[i] arms;
but they did not know that I
healed them.
4I led them with cords of
compassion,[j]
with the bands of love,
and I became to them as one
who eases the yoke on their
jaws,
and I bent down to them and
fed them.
5They shall return to the land of
Egypt,
and Assyria shall be their
king,

[a] Cn Compare Gk: Heb *in my desire*
[b] Gk: Heb *bound*
[c] Gk: Heb *according to*
[d] Gk: Heb *way*
[e] Gk: Heb *O Bethel*
[f] Cn: Heb *dawn*
[g] Gk: Heb *they*
[h] Gk: Heb *them*
[i] Gk Syr Vg: Heb *his*
[j] Heb *man*

because they have refused to
return to me.
6The sword shall rage against
their cities,
consume the bars of their
gates,
and devour them in their
fortresses.[k]
7My people are bent on turning
away from me;[l]
so they are appointed to the
yoke,
and none shall remove it.
8How can I give you up, O
E´phraim!
How can I hand you over, O
Israel!
How can I make you like
Admah!
How can I treat you like
Zeboi´im!
My heart recoils within me,
my compassion grows warm
and tender.
9I will not execute my fierce
anger,
I will not again destroy
E´phraim;
for I am God and not man,
the Holy One in your
midst,
and I will not come to
destroy.[m]
10They shall go after the LORD,
he will roar like a lion;
yea, he will roar,
and his sons shall come
trembling from the
west;
11they shall come trembling like
birds from Egypt,
and like doves from the land
of Assyria;
and I will return them to
their homes, says the
LORD.
12[n] E´phraim has encompassed me
with lies,
and the house of Israel with
deceit;
but Judah is still known by[o]
God,
and is faithful to the Holy
One.

12 E´phraim herds the wind,
and pursues the east wind all
day long;
they multiply falsehood and
violence;
they make a bargain with
Assyria,
and oil is carried to Egypt.

THE LONG HISTORY OF REBELLION

2The LORD has an indictment
against Judah,
and will punish Jacob ac-
cording to his ways,
and requite him according to
his deeds.
3In the womb he took his brother
by the heel,
and in his manhood he
strove with God.
4He strove with the angel and
prevailed,
he wept and sought his
favor.
He met God at Bethel,
and there God spoke with
him[p]—
5the LORD the God of hosts,
the LORD is his name:
6"So you, by the help of your God,
return,
hold fast to love and justice,
and wait continually for your
God."
7A trader, in whose hands are
false balances,
he loves to oppress.
8E´phraim has said, "Ah, but I am
rich,
I have gained wealth for

[k] Cn: Heb *counsels*
[l] The meaning of the Hebrew is uncertain
[m] Cn: Heb *into the city*
[n] Ch 12.1 in Heb
[o] Cn Compare Gk: Heb *roams with*
[p] Gk Syr: Heb *us*

myself";
but all his riches can never
offset[a]
the guilt he has incurred.
9I am the LORD your God
from the land of Egypt;
I will again make you dwell in
tents,
as in the days of the appointed feast.
10I spoke to the prophets;
it was I who multiplied
visions,
and through the prophets
gave parables.
11If there is iniquity in Gilead
they shall surely come to
nought;
if in Gilgal they sacrifice
bulls,
their altars also shall be like
stone heaps
on the furrows of the field.
12(Jacob fled to the land of
Aram,
there Israel did service for
a wife,
and for a wife he herded
sheep.)
13By a prophet the LORD brought
Israel up from Egypt,
and by a prophet he was
preserved.
14E´phraim has given bitter
provocation;
so his LORD will leave his
bloodguilt upon
him,
and will turn back upon him
his reproaches.

RELENTLESS JUDGMENT ON ISRAEL

13 When E´phraim spoke,
men trembled;
he was exalted in Israel;
but he incurred guilt
through Ba´al and
died.
2And now they sin more and
more,
and make for themselves
molten images,
idols skilfully made of their
silver,
all of them the work of
craftsmen.
Sacrifice to these, they say.[b]
Men kiss calves!
3Therefore they shall be like the
morning mist
or like the dew that goes
early away,
like the chaff that swirls
from the threshing
floor
or like smoke from a
window.
4I am the LORD your God
from the land of Egypt;
you know no God but me,
and besides me there is no
saviour.
5It was I who knew you in the
wilderness,
in the land of drought;
6but when they had fed[c] to the
full,
they were filled, and their
heart was lifted up;
therefore they forgot me.
7So I will be to them like a lion,
like a leopard I will lurk
beside the way.
8I will fall upon them like a bear
robbed of her cubs,
I will tear open their
breast,
and there I will devour them
like a lion,
as a wild beast would rend
them.
9I will destroy you, O Israel;
who[d] can help you?
10Where[e] now is your king, to save
you;

[a] Cn Compare Gk: Heb obscure
[b] Gk: Heb *to these they say sacrifices of*
[c] Cn: Heb *according to their pasture*
[d] Gk Syr: Heb *for in me*
[e] Gk Syr Vg: Heb *I will be*

where are all[f] your princes,[g]
to defend you[h]—
those of whom you said,
"Give me a king and
princes"?
11I have given you kings in my
anger,
and I have taken them away
in my wrath.
12The iniquity of E´phraim is
bound up,
his sin is kept in store.
13The pangs of childbirth come
for him,
but he is an unwise son;
for now he does not present
himself
at the mouth of the womb.
14Shall I ransom them from the
power of Sheol?
Shall I redeem them from
Death?
O Death, where[i] are your
plagues?
O Sheol, where[j] is your
destruction?
Compassion is hid from my
eyes.
15Though he may flourish as the
reed plant,[k]
the east wind, the wind
of the LORD, shall
come,
rising from the wilderness;
and his fountain shall dry up,
his spring shall be parched;
it shall strip his treasury
of every precious thing.
16[l] Samar´ia shall bear her guilt,
because she has rebelled
against her God;
they shall fall by the sword,
their little ones shall be
dashed in pieces,
and their pregnant women
ripped open.

A PLEA FOR REPENTANCE

14 Return, O Israel, to the LORD
your God,
for you have stumbled
because of your
iniquity.
2Take with you words
and return to the LORD;
say to him,
"Take away all iniquity;
accept that which is good
and we will render
the fruit[m] of our lips.
3Assyria shall not save us,
we will not ride upon
horses;
and we will say no more, 'Our
God,'
to the work of our hands.
In thee the orphan finds
mercy."

ASSURANCE OF FORGIVENESS

4I will heal their faithlessness;
I will love them freely,
for my anger has turned
from them.
5I will be as the dew to Israel;
he shall blossom as the lily,
he shall strike root as the
poplar;[n]
6his shoots shall spread out;
his beauty shall be like the
olive,
and his fragrance like
Lebanon.
7They shall return and dwell
beneath my[o] shadow,
they shall flourish as a
garden;[p]

[f]Cn: Heb *in all*
[g]Cn: Heb *cities*
[h]Cn Compare Gk: Heb *and your judges*
[i]Gk Syr: Heb *I will be*
[j]Gk Syr: Heb *I will be*
[k]Cn: Heb *among brothers*
[l]Ch 14.1 in Heb
[m]Gk Syr: Heb *bulls*
[n]Cn: Heb Lebanon
[o]Heb *his*
[p]Cn: Heb *they shall grow grain*

they shall blossom as the
vine,
their fragrance shall be like
the wine of Lebanon.
8O E´phraim, what have I to do
with idols?
It is I who answer and look
after you.[a]
I am like an evergreen cypress,
from me comes your fruit.

9Whoever is wise, let him
understand these things;
whoever is discerning, let
him know them;
for the ways of the LORD are
right,
and the upright walk in
them,
but transgressors stumble in
them.

[a]Heb *him*

THE BOOK OF

JOEL

1 The word of the LORD that came to Joel, the son of Pethu′el:

LAMENT OVER THE RUIN OF THE COUNTRY

2 Hear this, you aged men,
give ear, all inhabitants of the land!
Has such a thing happened in your days,
or in the days of your fathers?
3 Tell your children of it,
and let your children tell their children,
and their children another generation.
4 What the cutting locust left,
the swarming locust has eaten.
What the swarming locust left,
the hopping locust has eaten,
and what the hopping locust left,
the destroying locust has eaten.
5 Awake, you drunkards, and weep;
and wail, all you drinkers of wine,
because of the sweet wine,
for it is cut off from your mouth.
6 For a nation has come up against my land,
powerful and without number;
its teeth are lions' teeth,
and it has the fangs of a lioness.
7 It has laid waste my vines,
and splintered my fig trees;
it has stripped off their bark
and thrown it down;
their branches are made white.
8 Lament like a virgin girded with sackcloth
for the bridegroom of her youth.
9 The cereal offering and the drink offering are cut off
from the house of the LORD.
The priests mourn,
the ministers of the LORD.
10 The fields are laid waste,
the ground mourns;
because the grain is destroyed,
the wine fails,
the oil languishes.
11 Be confounded, O tillers of the soil,
wail, O vinedressers,
for the wheat and the barley;
because the harvest of the field has perished.
12 The vine withers,
the fig tree languishes.
Pomegranate, palm, and apple,
all the trees of the field are withered;
and gladness fails
from the sons of men.

A CALL TO REPENTANCE AND PRAYER

13 Gird on sackcloth and lament, O priests,
wail, O ministers of the altar.
Go in, pass the night in sackcloth,
O ministers of my God!
Because cereal offering and drink offering
are withheld from the house of your God.
14 Sanctify a fast,
call a solemn assembly.
Gather the elders
and all the inhabitants of the land
to the house of the LORD your God;
and cry to the LORD.

15Alas for the day!
For the day of the LORD is near,
and as destruction from the Almighty it comes.
16Is not the food cut off
before our eyes,
joy and gladness
from the house of our God?
17The seed shrivels under the clods,[a]
the storehouses are desolate;
the granaries are ruined
because the grain has failed.
18How the beasts groan!
The herds of cattle are perplexed
because there is no pasture for them;
even the flocks of sheep are dismayed.
19Unto thee, O LORD, I cry.
For fire has devoured
the pastures of the wilderness,
and flame has burned
all the trees of the field.
20Even the wild beasts cry to thee
because the water brooks are dried up,
and fire has devoured
the pastures of the wilderness.

2 Blow the trumpet in Zion;
sound the alarm on my holy mountain!
Let all the inhabitants of the land tremble,
for the day of the LORD is coming, it is near,
2a day of darkness and gloom,
a day of clouds and thick darkness!
Like blackness there is spread upon the mountains
a great and powerful people;
their like has never been from of old,
nor will be again after them
through the years of all generations.
3Fire devours before them,
and behind them a flame burns.
The land is like the garden of Eden before them,
but after them a desolate wilderness,
and nothing escapes them.
4Their appearance is like the appearance of horses,
and like war horses they run.
5As with the rumbling of chariots,
they leap on the tops of the mountains,
like the crackling of a flame of fire
devouring the stubble,
like a powerful army
drawn up for battle.
6Before them peoples are in anguish,
all faces grow pale.
7Like warriors they charge,
like soldiers they scale the wall.
They march each on his way,
they do not swerve[b] from their paths.
8They do not jostle one another,
each marches in his path;
they burst through the weapons
and are not halted.
9They leap upon the city,
they run upon the walls;
they climb up into the houses,
they enter through the windows like a thief.
10The earth quakes before them,
the heavens tremble.
The sun and the moon are darkened,
and the stars withdraw their shining.
11The LORD utters his voice
before his army,

[a] Heb uncertain
[b] Gk Syr Vg: Heb *take a pledge*

for his host is exceedingly
great;
he that executes his word is
powerful.
For the day of the LORD is
great and very terrible;
who can endure it?
12"Yet even now," says the LORD,
"return to me with all your
heart,
with fasting, with weeping, and
with mourning;
13and rend your hearts and
not your garments."
Return to the LORD, your
God,
for he is gracious and
merciful,
slow to anger, and abounding
in steadfast love,
and repents of evil.
14Who knows whether he will not
turn and repent,
and leave a blessing behind
him,
a cereal offering and a drink
offering
for the LORD, your God?
15Blow the trumpet in Zion;
sanctify a fast;
call a solemn assembly;
16gather the people.
Sanctify the congregation;
assemble the elders;
gather the children,
even nursing infants.
Let the bridegroom leave his
room,
and the bride her chamber.
17Between the vestibule and the
altar
let the priests, the ministers
of the LORD, weep
and say, "Spare thy people, O
LORD,
and make not thy heritage a
reproach,
a byword among the
nations.
Why should they say among
the peoples,
'Where is their God?'"

GOD'S RESPONSE AND PROMISE

18Then the LORD became jealous
for his land,
and had pity on his people.
19The LORD answered and said to
his people,
"Behold, I am sending to you
grain, wine, and oil,
and you will be satisfied;
and I will no more make you
a reproach among the
nations.
20"I will remove the northerner far
from you,
and drive him into a parched
and desolate land,
his front into the eastern sea,
and his rear into the western
sea;
the stench and foul smell of
him will rise,
for he has done great
things.
21"Fear not, O land;
be glad and rejoice,
for the LORD has done great
things!
22Fear not, you beasts of the
field,
for the pastures of the wil-
derness are green;
the tree bears its fruit,
the fig tree and vine give
their full yield.
23"Be glad, O sons of Zion,
and rejoice in the LORD,
your God;
for he has given the early rain
for your vindication,
he has poured down for you
abundant rain,
the early and the latter rain,
as before.
24"The threshing floors shall be
full of grain,
the vats shall overflow with
wine and oil.
25I will restore to you the years
which the swarming locust
has eaten,
the hopper, the destroyer, and
the cutter,

my great army, which I sent
among you.
26"You shall eat in plenty and be
satisfied,
and praise the name of the
LORD your God,
who has dealt wondrously
with you.
And my people shall never
again be put to shame.
27You shall know that I am in the
midst of Israel,
and that I, the LORD, am
your God and there is
none else.
And my people shall never
again
be put to shame.

GOD'S SPIRIT POURED OUT

28[a]"And it shall come to pass
afterward,
that I will pour out my spirit
on all flesh;
your sons and your daughters
shall prophesy,
your old men shall dream
dreams,
and your young men shall
see visions.
29Even upon the menservants and
maidservants
in those days, I will pour out
my spirit.

30 "And I will give portents in the
heavens and on the earth, blood and
fire and columns of smoke. 31The sun
shall be turned to darkness, and the
moon to blood, before the great and
terrible day of the LORD comes. 32And
it shall come to pass that all who call
upon the name of the LORD shall be
delivered; for in Mount Zion and in
Jerusalem there shall be those who
escape, as the LORD has said, and
among the survivors shall be those
whom the LORD calls.

3 [b]"For behold, in those days and at
that time, when I restore the for-
tunes of Judah and Jerusalem, 2I will
gather all the nations and bring them
down to the valley of Jehosh´aphat,
and I will enter into judgment with
them there, on account of my people
and my heritage Israel, because they
have scattered them among the na-
tions, and have divided up my land,
3and have cast lots for my people, and
have given a boy for a harlot, and have
sold a girl for wine, and have drunk it.

4 "What are you to me, O Tyre and
Sidon, and all the regions of Philistia?
Are you paying me back for some-
thing? If you are paying me back, I
will requite your deed upon your own
head swiftly and speedily. 5For you
have taken my silver and my gold,
and have carried my rich treasures
into your temples.[c] 6You have sold the
people of Judah and Jerusalem to the
Greeks, removing them far from their
own border. 7But now I will stir them
up from the place to which you have
sold them, and I will requite your
deed upon your own head. 8I will sell
your sons and your daughters into the
hand of the sons of Judah, and they
will sell them to the Sabe´ans, to a na-
tion far off; for the LORD has spoken."

JUDGMENT IN THE VALLEY OF JEHOSHAPHAT

9Proclaim this among the nations:
Prepare war,
stir up the mighty men.
Let all the men of war draw
near,
let them come up.
10Beat your plowshares into
swords,
and your pruning hooks into
spears;
let the weak say, "I am a
warrior."
11Hasten and come,
all you nations round about,
gather yourselves there.
Bring down thy warriors, O
LORD.

[a]Ch 3.1 in Heb
[b]Ch 4.1 in Heb
[c]Or *palaces*

12Let the nations bestir
themselves,
and come up to the valley of
Jehosh′aphat;
for there I will sit to judge
all the nations round about.
13Put in the sickle,
for the harvest is ripe.
Go in, tread,
for the wine press is full.
The vats overflow,
for their wickedness is great.
14Multitudes, multitudes,
in the valley of decision!
For the day of the LORD is near
in the valley of decision.
15The sun and the moon are
darkened,
and the stars withdraw their
shining.
16And the LORD roars from Zion,
and utters his voice from
Jerusalem,
and the heavens and the
earth shake.
But the LORD is a refuge to his
people,
a stronghold to the people of
Israel.

THE GLORIOUS FUTURE OF JUDAH

17"So you shall know that I am the
LORD your God,
who dwell in Zion, my holy
mountain.
And Jerusalem shall be holy
and strangers shall never
again pass through it.
18"And in that day
the mountains shall drip sweet
wine,
and the hills shall flow with
milk,
and all the stream beds of
Judah
shall flow with water;
and a fountain shall come forth
from the house of the
LORD
and water the valley of
Shittim.
19"Egypt shall become a
desolation
and Edom a desolate
wilderness,
for the violence done to the
people of Judah,
because they have shed in-
nocent blood in their
land.
20But Judah shall be inhabited for
ever,
and Jerusalem to all
generations.
21I will avenge their blood, and I
will not clear the guilty,[d]
for the LORD dwells in
Zion."

[d] Gk Syr: Heb *I will hold innocent their blood which I have not held innocent*

THE BOOK OF

AMOS

1 The words of Amos, who was among
the shepherds of Teko´a, which he
saw concerning Israel in the days of
Uzzi´ah king of Judah and in the days
of Jerobo´am the son of Jo´ash, king
of Israel, two years[a] before the earth-
quake. 2 And he said:

JUDGMENT ON ISRAEL'S NEIGHBORS

"The LORD roars from Zion,
and utters his voice from Jerusalem;
the pastures of the shepherds mourn,
and the top of Carmel withers."

3 Thus says the LORD:
"For three transgressions of Damascus,
and for four, I will not revoke the punishment;[b]
because they have threshed Gilead
with threshing sledges of iron.
4 So I will send a fire upon the house of Haz´ael,
and it shall devour the strongholds of Ben-ha´dad.
5 I will break the bar of Damascus,
and cut off the inhabitants from the Valley of Aven,[c]
and him that holds the scepter from Beth-e´den;
and the people of Syria shall go into exile to Kir,"
says the LORD.

6 Thus says the LORD:
"For three transgressions of Gaza,
and for four, I will not revoke the punishment;[d]
because they carried into exile a whole people
to deliver them up to Edom.
7 So I will send a fire upon the wall of Gaza,
and it shall devour her strongholds.
8 I will cut off the inhabitants from Ashdod,
and him that holds the scepter from Ash´kelon;
I will turn my hand against Ekron;
and the remnant of the Philistines shall perish,"
says the Lord GOD.

9 Thus says the LORD:
"For three transgressions of Tyre,
and for four, I will not revoke the punishment;[e]
because they delivered up a whole people to Edom,
and did not remember the covenant of brotherhood.
10 So I will send a fire upon the wall of Tyre,
and it shall devour her strongholds."

11 Thus says the LORD:
"For three transgressions of Edom,
and for four, I will not revoke the punishment;[f]

[a] Or *during two years*
[b] Heb *cause it to return*
[c] Or *On*
[d] Heb *cause it to return*
[e] Heb *cause it to return*
[f] Heb *cause it to return*

because he pursued his brother
with the sword,
and cast off all pity,
and his anger tore perpetually,
and he kept his wrath[g] for
ever.
12So I will send a fire upon Teman,
and it shall devour the
strongholds of
Bozrah."
13Thus says the LORD:
"For three transgressions of
the Ammonites,
and for four, I will
not revoke the
punishment;[h]
because they have ripped up
women with child in
Gilead,
that they might enlarge their
border.
14So I will kindle a fire in the wall
of Rabbah,
and it shall devour her
strongholds,
with shouting in the day of
battle,
with a tempest in the day of
the whirlwind;
15and their king shall go into
exile,
he and his princes together,"
says the LORD.

2 Thus says the LORD:
"For three transgressions of
Moab,
and for four, I will
not revoke the
punishment;[i]
because he burned to lime
the bones of the king of
Edom.
2So I will send a fire upon Moab,
and it shall devour the
strongholds of
Ker´ioth,
and Moab shall die amid
uproar,
amid shouting and the
sound of the trumpet;
3I will cut off the ruler from its
midst,
and will slay all its princes
with him,"
says the LORD.

JUDGMENT ON JUDAH

4Thus says the LORD:
"For three transgressions of
Judah,
and for four, I will
not revoke the
punishment;[j]
because they have rejected the
law of the LORD,
and have not kept his
statutes,
but their lies have led them
astray,
after which their fathers
walked.
5So I will send a fire upon Judah,
and it shall devour the
strongholds of
Jerusalem."

JUDGMENT ON ISRAEL

6Thus says the LORD:
"For three transgressions of
Israel,
and for four, I will
not revoke the
punishment;[k]
because they sell the righteous
for silver,
and the needy for a pair of
shoes—
7they that trample the head of the
poor into the dust of the
earth,
and turn aside the way of
the afflicted;
a man and his father go in to
the same maiden,
so that my holy name is
profaned;

[g] Gk Syr Vg: Heb *his wrath kept*
[h] Heb *cause it to return*
[i] Heb *cause it to return*
[j] Heb *cause it to return*
[k] Heb *cause it to return*

8they lay themselves down beside
every altar
upon garments taken in
pledge;
and in the house of their God
they drink
the wine of those who have
been fined.
9"Yet I destroyed the Amorite
before them,
whose height was like the
height of the cedars,
and who was as strong as
the oaks;
I destroyed his fruit above,
and his roots beneath.
10Also I brought you up out of the
land of Egypt,
and led you forty years in
the wilderness,
to possess the land of the
Amorite.
11And I raised up some of your
sons for prophets,
and some of your young men
for Nazirites.
Is it not indeed so, O people
of Israel?"
says the LORD.
12"But you made the Nazirites
drink wine,
and commanded the
prophets,
saying, 'You shall not
prophesy.'
13"Behold, I will press you down
in your place,
as a cart full of sheaves
presses down.
14Flight shall perish from the
swift,
and the strong shall not
retain his strength,
nor shall the mighty save
his life;
15he who handles the bow shall
not stand,
and he who is swift of
foot shall not save
himself,
nor shall he who rides the
horse save his life;
16and he who is stout of heart
among the mighty
shall flee away naked in that
day,"
says the LORD.

ISRAEL'S GUILT AND PUNISHMENT

3Hear this word that the LORD
has spoken against you, O people
of Israel, against the whole family
which I brought up out of the land of
Egypt:
2"You only have I known
of all the families of the
earth;
therefore I will punish you
for all your iniquities.
3"Do two walk together,
unless they have made an
appointment?
4Does a lion roar in the forest,
when he has no prey?
Does a young lion cry out from
his den,
if he has taken nothing?
5Does a bird fall in a snare on the
earth,
when there is no trap for it?
Does a snare spring up from
the ground,
when it has taken nothing?
6Is a trumpet blown in a city,
and the people are not
afraid?
Does evil befall a city,
unless the LORD has done it?
7Surely the Lord GOD does
nothing,
without revealing his secret
to his servants the prophets.
8The lion has roared;
who will not fear?
The Lord GOD has spoken;
who can but prophesy?"
9Proclaim to the strongholds in
Assyria,[a]
and to the strongholds in the
land of Egypt,
and say, "Assemble yourselves
upon the mountains of

[a]Gk: Heb *Ashdod*

Samar´ia,
and see the great tumults
within her,
and the oppressions in her
midst."
10"They do not know how to do
right," says the LORD,
"those who store up violence
and robbery in their
strongholds."
11Therefore thus says the Lord GOD:
"An adversary shall surround
the land,
and bring down your defens-
es from you,
and your strongholds shall
be plundered."
12 Thus says the LORD: "As the
shepherd rescues from the mouth
of the lion two legs, or a piece of an
ear, so shall the people of Israel who
dwell in Samar´ia be rescued, with
the corner of a couch and part[b] of a
bed."
13"Hear, and testify against the
house of Jacob,"
says the Lord GOD, the God
of hosts,
14"that on the day I punish Israel
for his transgressions,
I will punish the altars of
Bethel,
and the horns of the altar shall
be cut off
and fall to the ground.
15I will smite the winter house
with the summer house;
and the houses of ivory shall
perish,
and the great houses[c] shall
come to an end,"
says the LORD.

4 "Hear this word, you cows of
Bashan,
who are in the mountain of
Samar´ia,
who oppress the poor, who
crush the needy,
who say to their husbands,
'Bring, that we may
drink!'
2The Lord GOD has sworn by his
holiness
that, behold, the days are
coming upon you,
when they shall take you away
with hooks,
even the last of you with
fishhooks.
3And you shall go out through the
breaches,
every one straight before
her;
and you shall be cast forth
into Harmon,"
says the LORD.
4"Come to Bethel, and transgress;
to Gilgal, and multiply
transgression;
bring your sacrifices every
morning,
your tithes every three days;
5offer a sacrifice of thanksgiving
of that which is leavened,
and proclaim freewill offer-
ings, publish them;
for so you love to do, O peo-
ple of Israel!"
says the Lord GOD.

ISRAEL REJECTS CORRECTION

6"I gave you cleanness of teeth in
all your cities,
and lack of bread in all your
places,
yet you did not return to me,"
says the LORD.
7"And I also withheld the rain
from you
when there were yet three
months to the
harvest;
I would send rain upon one
city,
and send no rain upon an-
other city;
one field would be rained upon,
and the field on which it did
not rain withered;

[b]The meaning of the Hebrew word is uncertain
[c]Or *many houses*

[8]so two or three cities wandered
to one city
to drink water, and were not
satisfied;
yet you did not return to me,"
says the LORD.
[9]"I smote you with blight and
mildew;
I laid waste[a] your gardens
and your vineyards;
your fig trees and your
olive trees the locust
devoured;
yet you did not return to me,"
says the LORD.
[10]"I sent among you a pestilence
after the manner of Egypt;
I slew your young men with
the sword;
I carried away your horses;[b]
and I made the stench of
your camp go up into
your nostrils;
yet you did not return to me,"
says the LORD.
[11]"I overthrew some of you,
as when God over-
threw Sodom and
Gomor´rah,
and you were as a brand
plucked out of the
burning;
yet you did not return to me,"
says the LORD.
[12]"Therefore thus I will do to you,
O Israel;
because I will do this to you,
prepare to meet your God, O
Israel!"
[13]For lo, he who forms the moun-
tains, and creates the
wind,
and declares to man what is
his thought;
who makes the morning
darkness,
and treads on the heights of
the earth—
the LORD, the God of hosts, is
his name!

[a]Cn: Heb *the multitude of*
[b]Heb *with the captivity of your horses*

A LAMENT FOR ISRAEL'S SIN

5 Hear this word which I take up
over you in lamentation, O house of
Israel:
[2]"Fallen, no more to rise,
is the virgin Israel;
forsaken on her land,
with none to raise her up."
[3]For thus says the Lord GOD:
"The city that went forth a
thousand
shall have a hundred left,
and that which went forth a
hundred
shall have ten left
to the house of Israel."
[4]For thus says the LORD to the
house of Israel:
"Seek me and live;
[5]but do not seek Bethel,
and do not enter into Gilgal
or cross over to Beer-sheba;
for Gilgal shall surely go into
exile,
and Bethel shall come to
nought."
[6]Seek the LORD and live,
lest he break out like fire in
the house of Joseph,
and it devour, with none to
quench it for Bethel,
[7]O you who turn justice to
wormwood,
and cast down righteousness
to the earth!
[8]He who made the Pleiades and
Orion,
and turns deep darkness
into the morning,
and darkens the day into
night,
who calls for the waters of the
sea,
and pours them out upon
the surface of the
earth,
the LORD is his name,
[9]who makes destruction flash
forth against the strong,
so that destruction comes

upon the fortress.
10They hate him who reproves in the gate,
and they abhor him who speaks the truth.
11Therefore because you trample upon the poor
and take from him exactions of wheat,
you have built houses of hewn stone,
but you shall not dwell in them;
you have planted pleasant vineyards,
but you shall not drink their wine.
12For I know how many are your transgressions,
and how great are your sins—
you who afflict the righteous, who take a bribe,
and turn aside the needy in the gate.
13Therefore he who is prudent will keep silent in such a time;
for it is an evil time.
14Seek good, and not evil,
that you may live;
and so the LORD, the God of hosts, will be with you,
as you have said.
15Hate evil, and love good,
and establish justice in the gate;
it may be that the LORD, the God of hosts,
will be gracious to the remnant of Joseph.

16Therefore thus says the LORD,
the God of hosts, the Lord:
"In all the squares there shall be wailing;
and in all the streets they shall say, 'Alas! alas!'
They shall call the farmers to mourning
and to wailing those who are skilled in lamentation,
17and in all vineyards there shall be wailing,
for I will pass through the midst of you,"
says the LORD.

THE DAY OF THE LORD A DARK DAY

18Woe to you who desire the day of the LORD!
Why would you have the day of the LORD?
It is darkness, and not light;
19as if a man fled from a lion,
and a bear met him;
or went into the house and leaned with his hand against the wall,
and a serpent bit him.
20Is not the day of the LORD darkness, and not light,
and gloom with no brightness in it?
21"I hate, I despise your feasts,
and I take no delight in your solemn assemblies.
22Even though you offer me your burnt offerings and cereal offerings,
I will not accept them,
and the peace offerings of your fatted beasts
I will not look upon.
23Take away from me the noise of your songs;
to the melody of your harps I will not listen.
24But let justice roll down like waters,
and righteousness like an everflowing stream.

25 "Did you bring to me sacrifices
and offerings the forty years in the
wilderness, O house of Israel? 26You
shall take up Sakkuth your king, and
Kaiwan your star-god, your imag-
es,[c] which you made for yourselves;
27therefore I will take you into exile
beyond Damascus," says the LORD,
whose name is the God of hosts.

[c]Heb *your images, your star-god*

COMPLACENT SELF-INDULGENCE WILL BE PUNISHED

6 "Woe to those who are at ease in Zion,
and to those who feel secure on the mountain of Samar′ia,
the notable men of the first of the nations,
to whom the house of Israel come!
2 Pass over to Calneh, and see;
and thence go to Hamath the great;
then go down to Gath of the Philistines.
Are they better than these kingdoms?
Or is their territory greater than your territory,
3 O you who put far away the evil day,
and bring near the seat of violence?
4 "Woe to those who lie upon beds of ivory,
and stretch themselves upon their couches,
and eat lambs from the flock,
and calves from the midst of the stall;
5 who sing idle songs to the sound of the harp,
and like David invent for themselves instruments of music;
6 who drink wine in bowls,
and anoint themselves with the finest oils,
but are not grieved over the ruin of Joseph!
7 Therefore they shall now be the first of those to go into exile,
and the revelry of those who stretch themselves shall pass away."
8 The Lord GOD has sworn by himself (says the LORD, the God of hosts):
"I abhor the pride of Jacob,
and hate his strongholds;
and I will deliver up the city and all that is in it."
9 And if ten men remain in one
house, they shall die. 10 And when a
man's kinsman, he who burns him,[a]
shall take him up to bring the bones
out of the house, and shall say to him
who is in the innermost parts of the
house, "Is there still any one with
you?" he shall say, "No"; and he shall
say, "Hush! We must not mention the
name of the LORD."
11 For behold, the LORD commands,
and the great house shall be smitten into fragments,
and the little house into bits.
12 Do horses run upon rocks?
Does one plow the sea with oxen?
But you have turned justice into poison
and the fruit of righteousness into wormwood—
13 you who rejoice in Lo-debar,[b]
who say, "Have we not by our own strength
taken Karnaim[c] for ourselves?"
14 "For behold, I will raise up against you a nation,
O house of Israel," says the LORD, the God of hosts;
"and they shall oppress you from the entrance of Hamath
to the Brook of the Arabah."

LOCUSTS, FIRE, AND A PLUMB LINE

7 Thus the Lord GOD showed me:
behold, he was forming locusts in
the beginning of the shooting up of
the latter growth; and lo, it was the

[a] Or *who makes a burning for him*
[b] Or *a thing of nought*
[c] Or *horns*

THE BOOK OF

OBADIAH

PROUD EDOM WILL BE BROUGHT LOW

1The vision of Obadi′ah.
Thus says the Lord God concerning Edom:
We have heard tidings from the Lord,
and a messenger has been sent among the nations:
"Rise up! let us rise against her for battle!"
2Behold, I will make you small among the nations,
you shall be utterly despised.
3The pride of your heart has deceived you,
you who live in the clefts of the rock,[a]
whose dwelling is high,
who say in your heart,
"Who will bring me down to the ground?"
4Though you soar aloft like the eagle,.
though your nest is set among the stars,
thence I will bring you down,
says the Lord.

PILLAGE AND SLAUGHTER WILL REPAY EDOM'S CRUELTY

5If thieves came to you,
if plunderers by night—
how you have been destroyed!—
would they not steal only enough for themselves?
If grape gatherers came to you,
would they not leave gleanings?
6How Esau has been pillaged,
his treasures sought out!
7All your allies have deceived you,
they have driven you to the border;
your confederates have prevailed against you;
your trusted friends have set a trap under you—
there is no understanding of it.
8Will I not on that day, says the Lord ,
destroy the wise men out of Edom,
and understanding out of Mount Esau?
9And your mighty men shall be dismayed, O Teman,
so that every man from Mount Esau will be cut off by slaughter.

EDOM MISTREATED HIS BROTHER

10For the violence done to your brother Jacob,
shame shall cover you,
and you shall be cut off for ever.
11On the day that you stood aloof,
on the day that strangers carried off his wealth,
and foreigners entered his gates
and cast lots for Jerusalem,
you were like one of them.
12But you should not have gloated over the day of your brother
in the day of his misfortune;
you should not have rejoiced over the people of Judah
in the day of their ruin;
you should not have boasted
in the day of distress.
13You should not have entered the gate of my people
in the day of his calamity;
you should not have gloated over his disaster
in the day of his calamity;

[a]Or *Sela*

you should not have looted his goods
in the day of his calamity.
14You should not have stood at the parting of the ways
to cut off his fugitives;
you should not have delivered up his survivors
in the day of distress.
15For the day of the LORD is near upon all the nations.
As you have done, it shall be done to you,
your deeds shall return on your own head.
16For as you have drunk upon my holy mountain,
all the nations round about shall drink;
they shall drink, and stagger,[a]
and shall be as though they had not been.

ISRAEL'S FINAL TRIUMPH

17But in Mount Zion there shall be those that escape,
and it shall be holy;
and the house of Jacob shall possess their own possessions.
18The house of Jacob shall be a fire,
and the house of Joseph a flame,
and the house of Esau stubble;
they shall burn them and consume them,
and there shall be no survivor to the house of Esau;
for the LORD has spoken.
19Those of the Negeb shall possess Mount Esau,
and those of the Shephe´lah the land of the Philistines;
they shall possess the land of E´phraim and the land of Samar´ia
and Benjamin shall possess Gilead.

20The exiles in Halah[b] who are of the people of Israel
shall possess[c] Phoenicia as far as Zar´ephath;
and the exiles of Jerusalem who are in Sephar´ad
shall possess the cities of the Negeb.
21Saviors shall go up to Mount Zion
to rule Mount Esau;
and the kingdom shall be the LORD's.

[a]Cn: Heb *swallow*
[b]Cn: Heb *this army*
[c]Cn: Heb *which*

THE BOOK OF

JONAH

JONAH TRIES TO RUN AWAY FROM GOD

1 Now the word of the LORD came to
Jonah the son of Amit´tai, saying,
2"Arise, go to Nin´eveh, that great
city, and cry against it; for their wick-
edness has come up before me." 3But
Jonah rose to flee to Tarshish from
the presence of the LORD. He went
down to Joppa and found a ship going
to Tarshish; so he paid the fare, and
went on board, to go with them to
Tarshish, away from the presence of
the LORD.

4 But the LORD hurled a great
wind upon the sea, and there was a
mighty tempest on the sea, so that
the ship threatened to break up.
5Then the mariners were afraid, and
each cried to his god; and they threw
the wares that were in the ship into
the sea, to lighten it for them. But
Jonah had gone down into the inner
part of the ship and had lain down,
and was fast asleep. 6So the captain
came and said to him, "What do
you mean, you sleeper? Arise, call
upon your god! Perhaps the god will
give a thought to us, that we do not
perish."

7 And they said to one anoth-
er, "Come, let us cast lots, that we
may know on whose account this
evil has come upon us." So they cast
lots, and the lot fell upon Jonah.
8Then they said to him, "Tell us on
whose account this evil has come
upon us. What is your occupation?
And whence do you come? What is
your country? And of what people
are you?" 9And he said to them, "I
am a Hebrew; and I fear the LORD,
the God of heaven, who made the
sea and the dry land." 10Then the
men were exceedingly afraid, and
said to him, "What is this that you
have done!" For the men knew that
he was fleeing from the presence of
the LORD, because he had told them.

11 Then they said to him, "What
shall we do to you, that the sea
may quiet down for us?" For the
sea grew more and more tempes-
tuous. 12He said to them, "Take me
up and throw me into the sea; then
the sea will quiet down for you; for
I know it is because of me that this
great tempest has come upon you."
13Nevertheless the men rowed hard
to bring the ship back to land, but
they could not, for the sea grew more
and more tempestuous against them.
14Therefore they cried to the LORD,
"We beseech thee, O LORD, let us
not perish for this man's life, and lay
not on us innocent blood; for thou, O
LORD, hast done as it pleased thee."
15So they took up Jonah and threw
him into the sea; and the sea ceased
from its raging. 16Then the men
feared the LORD exceedingly, and
they offered a sacrifice to the LORD
and made vows.

17[a] And the LORD appointed a
great fish to swallow up Jonah; and
Jonah was in the belly of the fish three
days and three nights.

A PSALM OF THANKSGIVING

2 Then Jonah prayed to the LORD
his God from the belly of the fish,
2saying,

"I called to the LORD, out of
my distress,
and he answered me;
out of the belly of Sheol I
cried,
and thou didst hear my
voice.
3For thou didst cast me into the
deep,
into the heart of the seas,
and the flood was round
about me;

[a]Ch 2.1 in Heb

all thy waves and thy billows
passed over me.
4Then I said, 'I am cast out
from thy presence;
how shall I again look
upon thy holy temple?'
5The waters closed in over me,
the deep was round about
me;
weeds were wrapped about my
head
6at the roots of the
mountains.
I went down to the land
whose bars closed upon me
for ever;
yet thou didst bring up my life
from the Pit,
O Lord my God.
7When my soul fainted within
me,
I remembered the Lord;
and my prayer came to thee,
into thy holy temple.
8Those who pay regard to vain
idols
forsake their true loyalty.
9But I with the voice of
thanksgiving
will sacrifice to thee;
what I have vowed I will pay.
Deliverance belongs to the
Lord!"
10And the Lord spoke to the fish,
and it vomited out Jonah upon the dry
land.

CONVERSION OF NINEVEH

3 Then the word of the Lord came
to Jonah the second time, saying,
2"Arise, go to Nin'eveh, that great city,
and proclaim to it the message that I
tell you." 3So Jonah arose and went to
Nin'eveh, according to the word of the
Lord. Now Nin'eveh was an exceed-
ingly great city, three days' journey in
breadth. 4Jonah began to go into the
city, going a day's journey. And he
cried, "Yet forty days, and Nin'eveh
shall be overthrown!" 5And the peo-
ple of Nin'eveh believed God; they
proclaimed a fast, and put on sack-
cloth, from the greatest of them to the
least of them.
6 Then tidings reached the king
of Nin'eveh, and he arose from his
throne, removed his robe, and covered
himself with sackcloth, and sat in ash-
es. 7And he made proclamation and
published through Nin'eveh, "By the
decree of the king and his nobles: Let
neither man nor beast, herd nor flock,
taste anything; let them not feed, or
drink water, 8but let man and beast be
covered with sackcloth, and let them
cry mightily to God; yea, let every one
turn from his evil way and from the
violence which is in his hands. 9Who
knows, God may yet repent and turn
from his fierce anger, so that we per-
ish not?"
10 When God saw what they did,
how they turned from their evil way,
God repented of the evil which he had
said he would do to them; and he did
not do it.

JONAH'S ANGER

4 But it displeased Jonah exceedingly,
and he was angry. 2And he prayed
to the Lord and said, "I pray thee,
Lord, is not this what I said when I
was yet in my country? That is why
I made haste to flee to Tarshish; for
I knew that thou art a gracious God
and merciful, slow to anger, and
abounding in steadfast love, and re-
pentest of evil. 3Therefore now, O
Lord, take my life from me, I beseech
thee, for it is better for me to die than
to live." 4And the Lord said, "Do you
do well to be angry?" 5Then Jonah
went out of the city and sat to the
east of the city, and made a booth for
himself there. He sat under it in the
shade, till he should see what would
become of the city.

JONAH IS REPROVED

6 And the Lord God appointed
a plant,[a] and made it come up over
Jonah, that it might be a shade over

[a]Heb *qiqayon*, probably *the castor oil plant*

his head, to save him from his dis-
comfort. So Jonah was exceedingly
glad because of the plant.[b] 7But when
dawn came up the next day, God ap-
pointed a worm which attacked the
plant,[c] so that it withered. 8When the
sun rose, God appointed a sultry east
wind, and the sun beat upon the head
of Jonah so that he was faint; and he
asked that he might die, and said, "It
is better for me to die than to live."
9But God said to Jonah, "Do you do
well to be angry for the plant?"[d] And
he said, "I do well to be angry, angry
enough to die." 10And the LORD said,
"You pity the plant,[e] for which you did
not labor, nor did you make it grow,
which came into being in a night, and
perished in a night. 11And should not I
pity Nin′eveh, that great city, in which
there are more than a hundred and
twenty thousand persons who do not
know their right hand from their left,
and also much cattle?"

[b] Heb *qiqayon,* probably *the castor oil plant*
[c] Heb *qiqayon,* probably *the castor oil plant*
[d] Heb *qiqayon,* probably *the castor oil plant*
[e] Heb *qiqayon,* probably *the castor oil plant*

THE BOOK OF MICAH

1 The word of the LORD that came to
Micah of Mo´resheth in the days of
Jotham, Ahaz, and Hezeki´ah, kings
of Judah, which he saw concerning
Samar´ia and Jerusalem.

JUDGMENT PRONOUNCED AGAINST SAMARIA

2 Hear, you peoples, all of you;
hearken, O earth, and all that is in it;
and let the Lord GOD be a witness against you,
the Lord from his holy temple.
3 For behold, the LORD is coming forth out of his place,
and will come down and tread upon the high places of the earth.
4 And the mountains will melt under him
and the valleys will be cleft,
like wax before the fire,
like waters poured down a steep place.
5 All this is for the transgression of Jacob
and for the sins of the house of Israel.
What is the transgression of Jacob?
Is it not Samar´ia?
And what is the sin of the house[a] of Judah?
Is it not Jerusalem?
6 Therefore I will make Samar´ia a heap in the open country,
a place for planting vineyards;
and I will pour down her stones into the valley,
and uncover her foundations.
7 All her images shall be beaten to pieces,
all her hires shall be burned with fire,
and all her idols I will lay waste;
for from the hire of a harlot she gathered them,
and to the hire of a harlot they shall return.

THE DOOM OF THE CITIES OF JUDAH

8 For this I will lament and wail;
I will go stripped and naked;
I will make lamentation like the jackals,
and mourning like the ostriches.
9 For her wound[b] is incurable;
and it has come to Judah,
it has reached to the gate of my people,
to Jerusalem.
10 Tell it not in Gath,
weep not at all;
in Beth-le-aph´rah
roll yourselves in the dust.
11 Pass on your way,
inhabitants of Shaphir,
in nakedness and shame;
the inhabitants of Za´anan
do not come forth;
the wailing of Beth-e´zel
shall take away from you its standing place.
12 For the inhabitants of Maroth
wait anxiously for good,
because evil has come down from the LORD
to the gate of Jerusalem.
13 Harness the steeds to the chariots,
inhabitants of Lachish;
you were[c] the beginning of sin
to the daughter of Zion,
for in you were found
the transgressions of Israel.
14 Therefore you shall give parting

[a] Gk Tg Compare Syr: Heb *what are the high places*
[b] Gk Syr Vg: Heb *wounds*
[c] Cn: Heb *it was*

gifts
to Mo´resheth-gath;
the houses of Achzib shall be a deceitful thing
to the kings of Israel.
15I will again bring a conqueror upon you,
inhabitants of Mare´shah;
the glory of Israel
shall come to Adul´lam.
16Make yourselves bald and cut off your hair,
for the children of your delight;
make yourselves as bald as the eagle,
for they shall go from you into exile.

SOCIAL EVILS DENOUNCED

2 Woe to those who devise wickedness
and work evil upon their beds!
When the morning dawns, they perform it,
because it is in the power of their hand.
2They covet fields, and seize them;
and houses, and take them away;
they oppress a man and his house,
a man and his inheritance.
3Therefore thus says the LORD:
Behold, against this family I am devising evil,
from which you cannot remove your necks;
and you shall not walk haughtily,
for it will be an evil time.
4In that day they shall take up a taunt song against you,
and wail with bitter lamentation,
and say, "We are utterly ruined;
he changes the portion of my people;
how he removes it from me!
Among our captors[d] he divides our fields."
5Therefore you will have none to cast the line by lot
in the assembly of the LORD.
6"Do not preach"—thus they preach—
"one should not preach of such things;
disgrace will not overtake us."
7Should this be said, O house of Jacob?
Is the Spirit of the LORD impatient?
Are these his doings?
Do not my words do good
to him who walks uprightly?
8But you rise against my people[e] as an enemy;
you strip the robe from the peaceful,[f]
from those who pass by trustingly
with no thought of war.
9The women of my people you drive out
from their pleasant houses;
from their young children you take away
my glory for ever.
10Arise and go,
for this is no place to rest;
because of uncleanness that destroys
with a grievous destruction.
11If a man should go about and utter wind and lies,
saying, "I will preach to you of wine and strong drink,"
he would be the preacher for this people!

A PROMISE FOR THE REMNANT OF ISRAEL

12I will surely gather all of you, O Jacob,
I will gather the remnant of

[d]Cn: Heb *the rebellious*
[e]Cn: Heb *yesterday my people rose*
[f]Cn: Heb *from before a garment*

Israel;
I will set them together
like sheep in a fold,
like a flock in its pasture,
a noisy multitude of men.
13He who opens the breach will go
up before them;
they will break through and
pass the gate,
going out by it.
Their king will pass on before
them,
the LORD at their head.

WICKED RULERS AND PROPHETS

3 And I said:
Hear, you heads of Jacob
and rulers of the house of
Israel!
Is it not for you to know
justice?—
2you who hate the good and
love the evil,
who tear the skin from off my
people,
and their flesh from off their
bones;
3who eat the flesh of my people,
and flay their skin from off
them,
and break their bones in pieces,
and chop them up like meat[a]
in a kettle,
like flesh in a caldron.
4Then they will cry to the LORD,
but he will not answer them;
he will hide his face from them
at that time,
because they have made
their deeds evil.
5Thus says the LORD concerning
the prophets
who lead my people astray,
who cry "Peace"
when they have something
to eat,
but declare war against him
who puts nothing into their
mouths.
6Therefore it shall be night to you,
without vision,
and darkness to you, with-
out divination.
The sun shall go down upon
the prophets,
and the day shall be black
over them;
7the seers shall be disgraced,
and the diviners put to
shame;
they shall all cover their lips,
for there is no answer from
God.
8But as for me, I am filled with
power,
with the Spirit of the LORD,
and with justice and might,
to declare to Jacob his
transgression
and to Israel his sin.
9Hear this, you heads of the house
of Jacob
and rulers of the house of
Israel,
who abhor justice
and pervert all equity,
10who build Zion with blood
and Jerusalem with wrong.
11Its heads give judgment for a
bribe,
its priests teach for hire,
its prophets divine for
money;
yet they lean upon the LORD
and say,
"Is not the LORD in the
midst of us?
No evil shall come upon us."
12Therefore because of you
Zion shall be plowed as a
field;
Jerusalem shall become a heap
of ruins,
and the mountain of the
house a wooded
height.

PEACE AND SECURITY THROUGH OBEDIENCE

4 It shall come to pass in the latter
days
that the mountain of the

[a] Gk: Heb *as*

house of the LORD
shall be established as
the highest of the
mountains,
and shall be raised up above
the hills;
and peoples shall flow to it,
2and many nations shall
come, and say:
"Come, let us go up to the
mountain of the LORD,
to the house of the God of
Jacob;
that he may teach us his ways
and we may walk in his
paths."
For out of Zion shall go forth
the law,
and the word of the LORD
from Jerusalem.
3He shall judge between many
peoples,
and shall decide for strong
nations afar off;
and they shall beat their
swords into plowshares,
and their spears into prun-
ing hooks;
nation shall not lift up sword
against nation,
neither shall they learn war
any more;
4but they shall sit every man
under his vine and under
his fig tree,
and none shall make them
afraid;
for the mouth of the LORD of
hosts has spoken.
5For all the peoples walk
each in the name of its god,
but we will walk in the name of
the LORD our God
for ever and ever.

RESTORATION PROMISED AFTER EXILE

6In that day, says the LORD,
I will assemble the lame
and gather those who have
been driven away,
and those whom I have
afflicted;
7and the lame I will make the
remnant;
and those who were cast off,
a strong nation;
and the LORD will reign over
them in Mount Zion
from this time forth and for
evermore.
8And you, O tower of the flock,
hill of the daughter of Zion,
to you shall it come,
the former dominion shall
come,
the kingdom of the daughter
of Jerusalem.
9Now why do you cry aloud?
Is there no king in you?
Has your counselor perished,
that pangs have seized you
like a woman in
travail?
10Writhe and groan,[b] O daughter
of Zion,
like a woman in travail;
for now you shall go forth from
the city
and dwell in the open
country;
you shall go to Babylon.
There you shall be rescued,
there the LORD will redeem
you
from the hand of your
enemies.
11Now many nations
are assembled against you,
saying, "Let her be profaned,
and let our eyes gaze upon
Zion."
12But they do not know
the thoughts of the LORD,
they do not understand his
plan,
that he has gathered them as
sheaves to the thresh-
ing floor.
13Arise and thresh,
O daughter of Zion,
for I will make your horn iron
and your hoofs bronze;

[b] Heb uncertain

you shall beat in pieces many peoples,
and shall[a] devote their gain to the LORD,
their wealth to the Lord of the whole earth.

5 [b] Now you are walled about with a wall;[c]
siege is laid against us;
with a rod they strike upon the cheek
the ruler of Israel.

THE RULER FROM BETHLEHEM

2[d] But you, O Bethlehem Eph´rathah,
who are little to be among the clans of Judah,
from you shall come forth for me
one who is to be ruler in Israel,
whose origin is from of old,
from ancient days.
3Therefore he shall give them up until the time
when she who is in travail has brought forth;
then the rest of his brethren shall return
to the people of Israel.
4And he shall stand and feed his flock in the strength of the LORD,
in the majesty of the name of the LORD his God.
And they shall dwell secure, for now he shall be great
to the ends of the earth.
5And this shall be peace,
when the Assyrian comes into our land
and treads upon our soil,[e]
that we will raise against him seven shepherds
and eight princes of men;
6they shall rule the land of Assyria with the sword,
and the land of Nimrod with the drawn sword;[f]
and they[g] shall deliver us from the Assyrian
when he comes into our land
and treads within our border.

THE FUTURE ROLE OF THE REMNANT

7Then the remnant of Jacob shall be
in the midst of many peoples
like dew from the LORD,
like showers upon the grass,
which tarry not for men
nor wait for the sons of men.
8And the remnant of Jacob shall be among the nations,
in the midst of many peoples,
like a lion among the beasts of the forest,
like a young lion among the flocks of sheep,
which, when it goes through, treads down
and tears in pieces, and there is none to deliver.
9Your hand shall be lifted up over your adversaries,
and all your enemies shall be cut off.
10And in that day, says the LORD,
I will cut off your horses from among you
and will destroy your chariots;
11and I will cut off the cities of your land
and throw down all your strongholds;
12and I will cut off sorceries from your hand,
and you shall have no more soothsayers;

[a] Gk Syr Tg: Heb *I will*
[b] Ch 4.14 in Heb
[c] Cn Compare Gk: Heb obscure
[d] Ch 5.1 in Heb
[e] Gk: Heb *in our palaces*
[f] Cn: Heb *in its entrances*
[g] Heb *he*

13and I will cut off your images
and your pillars from among you,
and you shall bow down no more
to the work of your hands;
14and I will root out your Ashe´rim from among you
and destroy your cities.
15And in anger and wrath I will execute vengeance
upon the nations that did not obey.

GOD CHALLENGES ISRAEL

6 Hear what the LORD says:
Arise, plead your case before the mountains,
and let the hills hear your voice.
2Hear, you mountains, the controversy of the LORD,
and you enduring foundations of the earth;
for the LORD has a controversy with his people,
and he will contend with Israel.
3"O my people, what have I done to you?
In what have I wearied you? Answer me!
4For I brought you up from the land of Egypt,
and redeemed you from the house of bondage;
and I sent before you Moses, Aaron, and Miriam.
5O my people, remember what Balak king of Moab devised,
and what Balaam the son of Be´or answered him,
and what happened from Shittim to Gilgal,
that you may know the saving acts of the LORD."

WHAT GOD REQUIRES

6"With what shall I come before the LORD,
and bow myself before God on high?
Shall I come before him with burnt offerings,
with calves a year old?
7Will the LORD be pleased with thousands of rams,
with ten thousands of rivers of oil?
Shall I give my first-born for my transgression,
the fruit of my body for the sin of my soul?"
8He has showed you, O man, what is good;
and what does the LORD require of you
but to do justice, and to love kindness,[h]
and to walk humbly with your God?

CHEATING AND VIOLENCE TO BE PUNISHED

9The voice of the LORD cries to the city—
and it is sound wisdom to fear thy name:
"Hear, O tribe and assembly of the city![i]
10Can I forget[j] the treasures of wickedness in the house of the wicked,
and the scant measure that is accursed?
11Shall I acquit the man with wicked scales
and with a bag of deceitful weights?
12Your[k] rich men are full of violence;
your[l] inhabitants speak lies,
and their tongue is deceitful in their mouth.

[h] Or *steadfast love*
[i] Cn Compare Gk: Heb *and who has appointed it yet*
[j] Cn: Heb uncertain
[k] Heb *whose*
[l] Heb *whose*

13Therefore I have begun[a] to smite you,
making you desolate because of your sins.
14You shall eat, but not be satisfied,
and there shall be hunger in your inward parts;
you shall put away, but not save,
and what you save I will give to the sword.
15You shall sow, but not reap;
you shall tread olives, but not anoint yourselves with oil;
you shall tread grapes, but not drink wine.
16For you have kept the statutes of Omri,[b]
and all the works of the house of Ahab;
and you have walked in their counsels;
that I may make you a desolation, and your[c] inhabitants a hissing;
so you shall bear the scorn of the peoples."[d]

THE TOTAL CORRUPTION OF THE PEOPLE

7 Woe is me! For I have become
as when the summer fruit has been gathered,
as when the vintage has been gleaned:
there is no cluster to eat,
no first-ripe fig which my soul desires.
2The godly man has perished from the earth,
and there is none upright among men;
they all lie in wait for blood,
and each hunts his brother with a net.
3*Their hands are upon* what is evil, to do it diligently;
the prince and the judge ask for a bribe,
and the great man utters the evil desire of his soul;
thus they weave it together.
4The best of them is like a brier,
the most upright of them a thorn hedge.
The day of their[e] watchmen, of their[f] punishment, has come;
now their confusion is at hand.
5Put no trust in a neighbor,
have no confidence in a friend;
guard the doors of your mouth
from her who lies in your bosom;
6for the son treats the father with contempt,
the daughter rises up against her mother,
the daughter-in-law against her mother-in-law;
a man's enemies are the men of his own house.
7But as for me, I will look to the LORD,
I will wait for the God of my salvation;
my God will hear me.

PENITENCE AND TRUST IN GOD

8Rejoice not over me, O my enemy;
when I fall, I shall rise;
when I sit in darkness,
the LORD will be a light to me.
9I will bear the indignation of the LORD
because I have sinned against him,
until he pleads my cause
and executes judgment for

[a] Gk Syr Vg: Heb *have made sick*
[b] Gk Syr Vg Tg: Heb *the statutes of Omri are kept*
[c] Heb *its*
[d] Gk: Heb *my people*
[e] Heb *your*
[f] Heb *your*

me.
He will bring me forth to the light;
I shall behold his deliverance.
10Then my enemy will see,
and shame will cover her who said to me,
"Where is the LORD your God?"
My eyes will gloat over her;
now she will be trodden down
like the mire of the streets.

A PROPHECY OF RESTORATION

11A day for the building of your walls!
In that day the boundary shall be far extended.
12In that day they will come to you,
from Assyria to[g] Egypt,
and from Egypt to the River,
from sea to sea and from mountain to mountain.
13But the earth will be desolate
because of its inhabitants,
for the fruit of their doings.
14Shepherd thy people with thy staff,
the flock of thy inheritance,
who dwell alone in a forest
in the midst of a garden land;
let them feed in Bashan and Gilead
as in the days of old.
15As in the days when you came out of the land of Egypt
I will show them[h] marvelous things.
16The nations shall see and be ashamed of all their might;
they shall lay their hands on their mouths;
their ears shall be deaf;
17they shall lick the dust like a serpent,
like the crawling things of the earth;
they shall come trembling out of their strongholds,
they shall turn in dread to the LORD our God,
and they shall fear because of thee.

GOD'S COMPASSION AND STEADFAST LOVE

18Who is a God like thee, pardoning iniquity
and passing over transgression
for the remnant of his inheritance?
He does not retain his anger for ever
because he delights in steadfast love.
19He will again have compassion upon us,
he will tread our iniquities under foot.
Thou wilt cast all our[i] sins
into the depths of the sea.
20Thou wilt show faithfulness to Jacob
and steadfast love to Abraham,
as thou hast sworn to our fathers
from the days of old.

[g] Cn: Heb *and cities of*
[h] Heb *him*
[i] Gk Syr Vg Tg: Heb *their*

THE BOOK OF
NAHUM

1 An oracle concerning Nin′eveh. The book of the vision of Nahum of Elkosh.

THE CONSUMING WRATH OF GOD

2 The LORD is a jealous God and avenging,
the LORD is avenging and wrathful;
the LORD takes vengeance on his adversaries
and keeps wrath for his enemies.
3 The LORD is slow to anger and of great might,
and the LORD will by no means clear the guilty.
His way is in whirlwind and storm,
and the clouds are the dust of his feet.
4 He rebukes the sea and makes it dry,
he dries up all the rivers;
Bashan and Carmel wither,
the bloom of Lebanon fades.
5 The mountains quake before him,
the hills melt;
the earth is laid waste before him,
the world and all that dwell therein.
6 Who can stand before his indignation?
Who can endure the heat of his anger?
His wrath is poured out like fire,
and the rocks are broken asunder by him.
7 The LORD is good,
a stronghold in the day of trouble;
he knows those who take refuge in him.
8 But with an overflowing flood
he will make a full end of his adversaries,[a]
and will pursue his enemies into darkness.
9 What do you plot against the LORD?
He will make a full end;
he will not take vengeance[b] twice on his foes.[c]
10 Like entangled thorns they are consumed,[d]
like dry stubble.
11 Did one not[e] come out from you,
who plotted evil against the LORD,
and counseled villainy?

GOOD NEWS FOR JUDAH

12 Thus says the LORD,
"Though they be strong and many,[f]
they will be cut off and pass away.
Though I have afflicted you,
I will afflict you no more.
13 And now I will break his yoke from off you
and will burst your bonds asunder."
14 The LORD has given commandment about you:
"No more shall your name be perpetuated;
from the house of your gods I will cut off

[a] Gk: Heb *her place*
[b] Gk: Heb *rise up*
[c] Cn: Heb *distress*
[d] Heb *are consumed, drunken as with their drink*
[e] Cn: Heb *fully*
[f] Heb uncertain

the graven image and the
molten image.
I will make your grave, for you
are vile."
15[g] Behold, on the mountains the
feet of him
who brings good tidings,
who proclaims peace!
Keep your feasts, O Judah,
fulfil your vows,
for never again shall the wick-
ed come against you,
he is utterly cut off.

THE DESTRUCTION OF THE WICKED CITY

2 The shatterer has come up against
you.
Man the ramparts;
watch the road;
gird your loins;
collect all your strength.
2(For the LORD is restoring the
majesty of Jacob
as the majesty of Israel,
for plunderers have stripped
them
and ruined their branches.)
3The shield of his mighty men is
red,
his soldiers are clothed in
scarlet.
The chariots flash like flame[h]
when mustered in array;
the chargers[i] prance.
4The chariots rage in the
streets,
they rush to and fro through
the squares;
they gleam like torches,
they dart like lightning.
5The officers are summoned,
they stumble as they go,
they hasten to the wall,
the mantelet is set up.
6The river gates are opened,
the palace is in dismay;
7its mistress[j] is stripped, she is
carried off,
her maidens lamenting,
moaning like doves,
and beating their breasts.
8Nin´eveh is like a pool
whose waters[k] run away.
"Halt! Halt!" they cry;
but none turns back.
9Plunder the silver,
plunder the gold!
There is no end of treasure,
or wealth of every precious
thing.
10Desolate! Desolation and ruin!
Hearts faint and knees
tremble,
anguish is on all loins,
all faces grow pale!
11Where is the lions' den,
the cave[l] of the young
lions,
where the lion brought his
prey,
where his cubs were, with
none to disturb?
12The lion tore enough for his
whelps
and strangled prey for his
lionesses;
he filled his caves with prey
and his dens with torn
flesh.

13 Behold, I am against you, says
the LORD of hosts, and I will burn
your[m] chariots in smoke, and the
sword shall devour your young lions;
I will cut off your prey from the earth,
and the voice of your messengers shall
no more be heard.

RUIN IMMINENT AND INEVITABLE

3 Woe to the bloody city,
all full of lies and booty—
no end to the plunder!

[g] Ch 2.1 in Heb
[h] Cn: The meaning of the Hebrew word is uncertain
[i] Cn Compare Gk Syr: Heb *cypresses*
[j] The meaning of the Hebrew is uncertain
[k] Cn Compare Gk: Heb *from the days that she has become, and they*
[l] Cn: Heb *pasture*
[m] Heb *her*

2The crack of whip, and rumble of wheel,
galloping horse and bounding chariot!
3Horsemen charging,
flashing sword and glittering spear,
hosts of slain,
heaps of corpses,
dead bodies without end—
they stumble over the bodies!
4And all for the countless harlotries of the harlot,
graceful and of deadly charms,
who betrays nations with her harlotries,
and peoples with her charms.
5Behold, I am against you,
says the LORD of hosts,
and will lift up your skirts over your face;
and I will let nations look on your nakedness
and kingdoms on your shame.
6I will throw filth at you
and treat you with contempt,
and make you a gazingstock.
7And all who look on you will shrink from you and say,
Wasted is Nin′eveh; who will bemoan her?
whence shall I seek comforters for her?[a]
8Are you better than Thebes[b]
that sat by the Nile,
with water around her,
her rampart a sea,
and water her wall?
9Ethiopia was her strength,
Egypt too, and that without *limit;*
Put and the Libyans were her[c] helpers.
10Yet she was carried away,
she went into captivity;
her little ones were dashed in pieces
at the head of every street;
for her honored men lots were cast,
and all her great men were bound in chains.
11You also will be drunken,
you will be dazed;
you will seek
a refuge from the enemy.
12All your fortresses are like fig trees
with first-ripe figs—
if shaken they fall
into the mouth of the eater.
13Behold, your troops
are women in your midst.
The gates of your land
are wide open to your foes;
fire has devoured your bars.
14Draw water for the siege,
strengthen your forts;
go into the clay,
tread the mortar,
take hold of the brick mold!
15There will the fire devour you,
the sword will cut you off.
It will devour you like the locust.
Multiply yourselves like the locust,
multiply like the grasshopper!
16You increased your merchants
more than the stars of the heavens.
The locust spreads its wings
and flies away.
17Your princes are like grasshoppers,
your scribes[d] like clouds of locusts
settling on the fences

[a] Gk: Heb *you*
[b] Heb *No-amon*
[c] Gk: Heb *your*
[d] Or *marshals*

in a day of cold—
when the sun rises, they fly away;
no one knows where they are.
18 Your shepherds are asleep,
O king of Assyria;
your nobles slumber.
Your people are scattered on the mountains
with none to gather them.
19 There is no assuaging your hurt,
your wound is grievous.
All who hear the news of you
clap their hands over you.
For upon whom has not come
your unceasing evil?

THE BOOK OF

HABAKKUK

1 The oracle of God which Habak´kuk
the prophet saw.

THE PROPHET'S COMPLAINT

2O LORD, how long shall I cry for
help,
and thou wilt not hear?
Or cry to thee "Violence!"
and thou wilt not save?
3Why dost thou make me see
wrongs
and look upon trouble?
Destruction and violence are
before me;
strife and contention arise.
4So the law is slacked
and justice never goes
forth.
For the wicked surround the
righteous,
so justice goes forth
perverted.
5Look among the nations, and
see;
wonder and be astounded.
For I am doing a work in your
days
that you would not believe
if told.
6For lo, I am rousing the
Chalde´ans,
that bitter and hasty
nation,
who march through the
breadth of the earth,
to seize habitations not their
own.
7Dread and terrible are they;
their justice and dignity
proceed from
themselves.
8Their horses are swifter than
leopards,
more fierce than the evening
wolves;
their horsemen press
proudly on.
Yea, their horsemen come from
afar;
they fly like an eagle swift to
devour.
9They all come for violence;
terror[a] of them goes before
them.
They gather captives like
sand.
10At kings they scoff,
and of rulers they make
sport.
They laugh at every fortress,
for they heap up earth and
take it.
11Then they sweep by like the
wind and go on,
guilty men, whose own
might is their god!
12Art thou not from everlasting,
O LORD my God, my Holy
One?
We shall not die.
O LORD, thou hast ordained
them as a judgment;
and thou, O Rock, hast
established them for
chastisement.
13Thou who art of purer eyes than
to behold evil
and canst not look on
wrong,
why dost thou look on faithless
men,
and art silent when the
wicked swallows up
the man more righteous
than he?
14For thou makest men like the
fish of the sea,
like cravling things that
have no ruler.
15He brings all of them up with a
hook,
he drags them out with his
net,
he gathers them in his seine;

[a]Cn: Heb uncertain

so he rejoices and exults.
16Therefore he sacrifices to his net
and burns incense to his seine;
for by them he lives in luxury,[b]
and his food is rich.
17Is he then to keep on emptying his net,
and mercilessly slaying nations for ever?

GOD'S REPLY TO THE PROPHET'S COMPLAINT

2 I will take my stand to watch,
and station myself on the tower,
and look forth to see what he will say to me,
and what I will answer concerning my complaint.
2And the LORD answered me:
"Write the vision;
make it plain upon tablets,
so he may run who reads it.
3For still the vision awaits its time;
it hastens to the end—it will not lie.
If it seem slow, wait for it;
it will surely come, it will not delay.
4Behold, he whose soul is not upright in him shall fail,[c]
but the righteous shall live by his faith.[d]
5Moreover, wine is treacherous;
the arrogant man shall not *abide.*[e]
His greed is as wide as Sheol;
like death he has never enough.
He gathers for himself all nations,
and collects as his own all peoples."

[b]Heb *his portion is fat*
[c]Cn: Heb *is puffed up*
[d]Or *faithfulness*
[e]The Hebrew of these two lines is obscure

THE WOES OF THE WICKED

6Shall not all these take up their
taunt against him, in scoffing derision
of him, and say,
"Woe to him who heaps up what is not his own—
for how long?—
and loads himself with pledges!"
7Will not your debtors suddenly arise,
and those awake who will make you tremble?
Then you will be booty for them.
8Because you have plundered many nations,
all the remnant of the peoples shall plunder you,
for the blood of men and violence to the earth,
to cities and all who dwell therein.
9Woe to him who gets evil gain for his house,
to set his nest on high,
to be safe from the reach of harm!
10You have devised shame to your house
by cutting off many peoples;
you have forfeited your life.
11For the stone will cry out from the wall,
and the beam from the woodwork respond.
12Woe to him who builds a town with blood,
and founds a city on *iniquity!*
13Behold, is it not from the LORD of hosts
that peoples labor only for fire,
and nations weary themselves for nought?

14For the earth will be filled
with the knowledge of the
glory of the LORD,
as the waters cover the sea.
15Woe to him who makes his
neighbors drink
of the cup of his wrath,[a]
and makes them
drunk,
to gaze on their shame!
16You will be sated with contempt
instead of glory.
Drink, yourself, and
stagger![b]
The cup in the LORD'S right
hand
will come around to you,
and shame will come upon
your glory!
17The violence done to Lebanon
will overwhelm you;
the destruction of the
beasts will terrify
you,[c]
for the blood of men and
violence to the
earth,
to cities and all who dwell
therein.
18What profit is an idol
when its maker has shaped
it,
a metal image, a teacher of
lies?
For the workman trusts in his
own creation
when he makes dumb
idols!
19Woe to him who says to a wood-
en thing, Awake;
to a dumb stone, Arise!
Can this give revelation?
Behold, it is overlaid with gold
and silver,
and there is no breath at all
in it.
20But the LORD *is in his holy*
temple;
let all the earth keep silence
before him.

[a]Cn: Heb *joining to your wrath*
[b]Cn Compare Gk Syr: Heb *be uncircumcised*
[c]Gk Syr: Heb *them*

3 A prayer of Habak'kuk the prophet,
according to Shigion'oth.

THE PROPHET'S PRAYER

2O LORD, I have heard the report
of thee,
and thy work, O LORD, do
I fear.
In the midst of the years renew
it;
in the midst of the years
make it known;
in wrath remember mercy.
3God came from Teman,
and the Holy One from
Mount Paran.
His glory covered the heavens,
and the earth was full of his
praise.
Selah
4His brightness was like the
light,
rays flashed from his hand;
and there he veiled his
power.
5Before him went pestilence,
and plague followed close
behind.
6He stood and measured the
earth;
he looked and shook the
nations;
then the eternal mountains
were scattered,
the everlasting hills sank
low.
His ways were as of old.
7I saw the tents of Cushan in
affliction;
the curtains of the land of
Mid'ian did tremble.
8Was thy wrath against the rivers,
O LORD?
Was thy anger against the
rivers,
or thy indignation against
the sea,
when thou didst ride upon thy
horses,
upon thy chariot of victory?

9Thou didst strip the sheath from
thy bow,
and put the arrows to the
string.[d]
Selah
Thou didst cleave the earth
with rivers.
10The mountains saw thee, and
writhed;
the raging waters swept on;
the deep gave forth its voice,
it lifted its hands on high.
11The sun and moon stood still in
their habitation[e]
at the light of thine arrows
as they sped,
at the flash of thy glittering
spear.
12Thou didst bestride the earth
in fury,
thou didst trample the nations in anger.
13Thou wentest forth for the salvation of thy people,
for the salvation of thy
anointed.
Thou didst crush the head of
the wicked,[f]
laying him bare from thigh
to neck.[g]
Sela
14Thou didst pierce with thy[h]
shafts the head of his
warriors,[i]
who came like a whirlwind
to scatter me,
rejoicing as if to devour the
poor in secret.
15Thou didst trample the sea with
thy horses,
the surging of mighty
waters.
16I hear, and my body trembles,
my lips quiver at the sound;
rottenness enters into my
bones,
my steps totter[j] beneath me.
I will quietly wait for the day of
trouble
to come upon people who
invade us.

TRUST AND JOY IN THE MIDST OF TROUBLE

17Though the fig tree do not
blossom,
nor fruit be on the vines,
the produce of the olive fail
and the fields yield no food,
the flock be cut off from the
fold
and there be no herd in the
stalls,
18yet I will rejoice in the LORD,
I will joy in the God of my
salvation.
19God, the Lord, is my strength;
he makes my feet like hinds'
feet,
he makes me tread upon my
high places.
To the choirmaster: with
stringed[k] instruments.

[d]Cn: Heb obscure
[e]Heb uncertain
[f]Cn: Heb *head from the house of the wicked*
[g]Heb obscure
[h]Heb *his*
[i]Vg Compare Gk Syr: Heb uncertain
[j]Cn Compare Gk: Heb *I tremble because*
[k]Heb *my stringed*

THE BOOK OF
ZEPHANIAH

1 The word of the LORD which came
to Zephani´ah the son of Cushi, son
of Gedali´ah, son of Amari´ah, son of
Hezeki´ah, in the days of Josi´ah the
son of Amon, king of Judah.

THE COMING JUDGMENT ON JUDAH

2"I will utterly sweep away
everything
from the face of the earth,"
says the LORD.
3"I will sweep away man and
beast;
I will sweep away the birds
of the air
and the fish of the sea.
I will overthrow[a] the wicked;
I will cut off mankind
from the face of the earth,"
says the LORD.
4"I will stretch out my hand
against Judah,
and against all the inhabi-
tants of Jerusalem;
and I will cut off from this
place the remnant of
Ba´al
and the name of the idola-
trous priests;[b]
5those who bow down on the
roofs
to the host of the heavens;
those who bow down and
swear to the LORD
and yet swear by Milcom;
6those who have turned back from
following the LORD,
who do not seek the LORD or
inquire of him."
7Be silent before the Lord GOD!
For the day of the LORD is
at hand;
the LORD has prepared a
sacrifice
and consecrated his guests.
8And on the day of the LORD's
sacrifice—

[a]Cn: Heb *the stumbling blocks*
[b]Compare Gk: Heb *idolatrous priests with the priest*

"I will punish the officials and
the king's sons
and all who array them-
selves in foreign
attire.
9On that day I will punish
every one who leaps over the
threshold,
and those who fill their mas-
ter's house
with violence and fraud."
10"On that day," says the LORD,
"a cry will be heard from the
Fish Gate,
a wail from the Second
Quarter,
a loud crash from the hills.
11Wail, O inhabitants of the
Mortar!
For all the traders are no
more;
all who weigh out silver are
cut off.
12At that time I will search
Jerusalem with lamps,
and I will punish the men
who are thickening upon their
lees,
those who say in their
hearts,
'The LORD will not do good,
nor will he do ill.'
13Their goods shall be plundered,
and their houses laid
waste.
Though they build houses,
they shall not inhabit
them;
though they plant vineyards,
they shall not drink wine
from them."

THE GREAT DAY OF THE LORD

14The great day of the LORD is
near,
near and hastening fast;
the sound of the day of the

LORD is bitter,
the mighty man cries aloud
there.
15A day of wrath is that day,
a day of distress and
anguish,
a day of ruin and devastation,
a day of darkness and
gloom,
a day of clouds and thick
darkness,
16a day of trumpet blast and
battle cry
against the fortified cities
and against the lofty
battlements.
17I will bring distress on men,
so that they shall walk like
the blind,
because they have sinned
against the LORD;
their blood shall be poured out
like dust,
and their flesh like dung.
18Neither their silver nor their
gold
shall be able to deliver
them
on the day of the wrath of
the LORD.
In the fire of his jealous
wrath,
all the earth shall be
consumed;
for a full, yea, sudden end
he will make of all the
inhabitants of the
earth.

JUDGMENT ON ISRAEL'S ENEMIES

2 Come together and hold
assembly,
O shameless nation,
2before you are driven away
like the drifting chaff,[c]
before there comes upon you
the fierce anger of the
LORD,
before there comes upon you
the day of the wrath of the
LORD.
3Seek the LORD, all you humble of
the land,
who do his commands;
seek righteousness, seek
humility;
perhaps you may be hidden
on the day of the wrath of
the LORD.
4For Gaza shall be deserted,
and Ash´kelon shall become
a desolation;
Ashdod's people shall be driven
out at noon,
and Ekron shall be
uprooted.
5Woe to you inhabitants of the
seacoast,
you nation of the
Cher´ethites!
The word of the LORD is
against you,
O Canaan, land of the
Philistines;
and I will destroy you till no
inhabitant is left.
6And you, O seacoast, shall be
pastures,
meadows for shepherds
and folds for flocks.
7The seacoast shall become the
possession
of the remnant of the house
of Judah,
on which they shall
pasture,
and in the houses of
Ash´kelon
they shall lie down at
evening.
For the LORD their God will be
mindful of them
and restore their fortunes.
8"I have heard the taunts of Moab
and the revilings of the
Ammonites,
how they have taunted my
people
and made boasts against
their territory.
9Therefore, as I live," says the
LORD of hosts,

[c]Cn Compare Gk Syr: Heb *before a decree is born; like chaff a day has passed away*

the God of Israel,
"Moab shall become like Sodom,
and the Ammonites like Gomor´rah,
a land possessed by nettles and salt pits,
and a waste for ever.
The remnant of my people shall plunder them,
and the survivors of my nation shall possess them."
10This shall be their lot in return for their pride,
because they scoffed and boasted
against the people of the LORD of hosts.
11The LORD will be terrible against them;
yea, he will famish all the gods of the earth,
and to him shall bow down,
each in its place,
all the lands of the nations.
12You also, O Ethiopians,
shall be slain by my sword.
13And he will stretch out his hand against the north,
and destroy Assyria;
and he will make Nin´eveh a desolation,
a dry waste like the desert.
14Herds shall lie down in the midst of her,
all the beasts of the field;[a]
the vulture[b] and the hedgehog
shall lodge in her capitals;
the owl[c] shall hoot in the window,
the raven[d] croak on the threshold;
for her cedar work will be laid bare.
15This is the exultant city
that *dwelt secure,*
that said to herself,
"I am and there is none else."
What a desolation she has become,
a lair for wild beasts!
Every one who passes by her
hisses and shakes his fist.

THE WICKEDNESS OF JERUSALEM

3 Woe to her that is rebellious and defiled,
the oppressing city!
2She listens to no voice,
she accepts no correction.
She does not trust in the LORD,
she does not draw near to her God.
3Her officials within her
are roaring lions;
her judges are evening wolves
that leave nothing till the morning.
4Her prophets are wanton,
faithless men;
her priests profane what is sacred,
they do violence to the law.
5The LORD within her is righteous,
he does no wrong;
every morning he shows forth his justice,
each dawn he does not fail;
but the unjust knows no shame.
6"I have cut off nations;
their battlements are in ruins;
I have laid waste their streets
so that none walks in them;
their cities have been made desolate,
without a man, without an inhabitant.
7I said, 'Surely she will fear me,
she will accept correction;
she will not lose sight[e]
of all that I have enjoined

[a]Tg Compare Gk: Heb *nation*
[b]The meaning of the Hebrew word is uncertain
[c]Cn: Heb *a voice*
[d]Gk Vg: Heb *desolation*
[e]Gk Syr: Heb *and her dwelling will not be cut off*

upon her.'
But all the more they were
eager
to make all their deeds
corrupt."

PUNISHMENT AND CONVERSION OF THE NATIONS

8"Therefore wait for me," says the
LORD,
"for the day when I arise as
a witness.
For my decision is to gather
nations,
to assemble kingdoms,
to pour out upon them my
indignation,
all the heat of my anger;
for in the fire of my jealous
wrath
all the earth shall be
consumed.
9"Yea, at that time I will change
the speech of the peoples
to a pure speech,
that all of them may call on the
name of the LORD
and serve him with one
accord.
10From beyond the rivers of
Ethiopia
my suppliants, the daugter
of my dispersed
ones,
shall bring my offering.
11"On that day you shall not be
put to shame
because of the deeds by
which you have re-
belled against me;
for then I will remove from
your midst
your proudly exultant one
and you shall no longer be
haughty
in my holy mountain.
12For I will leave in the midst of
you
a people humble and lowly
They shall seek refuge in the
name of the LORD,
13those who are left in
Israel;
they shall do no wrong
and utter no lies,
nor shall there be found in
their mouth
a deceitful tongue.
For they shall pasture and lie
down,
and none shall make them
afraid."

A SONG OF JOY

14Sing aloud, O daughter of Zion;
shout, O Israel!
Rejoice and exult with all your
heart,
O daughter of Jerusalem!
15The LORD has taken away the
judgments against you,
he has cast out your
enemies.
The King of Israel, the LORD, is
in your midst;
you shall fear evil no more.
16On that day it shall be said to
Jerusalem:
"Do not fear, O Zion;
let not your hands grow
weak.
17The LORD your God is in your
midst,
a warrior who gives victory;
he will rejoice over you with
gladness,
he will renew you[f] in his
love;
he will exult over you with
loud singing
18as on a day of festival.[g]
"I will remove disaster[h] from
you,
so that you will not bear
reproach for it.
19Behold, at that time I will deal
with all your oppressors.
And I will save the lame
and gather the outcast,

[f]Gk Syr: Heb *he will be silent*
[g]Gk Syr: Heb obscure
[h]Cn: Heb *they were*

and I will change their shame
into praise
and renown in all the earth.
20 At that time I will bring you
home,
at the time when I gather
you together;
yea, I will make you renowned
and praised
among all the peoples of the
earth,
when I restore your fortunes
before your eyes," says the
LORD.

THE BOOK OF

HAGGAI

THE COMMAND TO REBUILD THE TEMPLE

1 In the second year of Dari´us the
king, in the sixth month, on the
first day of the month, the word of the
LORD came by Haggai the prophet to
Zerub´babel the son of She-al´ti-el,
governor of Judah, and to Joshua the
son of Jeho´zadak, the high priest,
2 "Thus says the LORD of hosts: This
people say the time has not yet come
to rebuild the house of the LORD."
3 Then the word of the LORD came by
Haggai the prophet, 4 "Is it a time for
you yourselves to dwell in your pan-
eled houses, while this house lies in
ruins? 5 Now therefore thus says the
LORD of hosts: Consider how you
have fared. 6 You have sown much, and
harvested little; you eat, but you never
have enough; you drink, but you never
have your fill; you clothe yourselves,
but no one is warm; and he who earns
wages earns wages to put them into a
bag with holes.

7 "Thus says the LORD of hosts:
Consider how you have fared. 8 Go up
to the hills and bring wood and build
the house, that I may take pleasure in
it and that I may appear in my glory,
says the LORD. 9 You have looked for
much, and lo, it came to little; and
when you brought it home, I blew it
away. Why? says the LORD of hosts.
Because of my house that lies in ru-
ins, while you busy yourselves each
with his own house. 10 Therefore the
heavens above you have withheld
the dew, and the earth has withheld
its produce. 11 And I have called for a
drought upon the land and the hills,
upon the grain, the new wine, the oil,
upon what the ground brings forth,
upon men and cattle, and upon all
their labors."

12 Then Zerub´babel the son of
She-al´ti-el, and Joshua the son of
Jeho´zadak, the high priest, with all
the remnant of the people, obeyed the
voice of the LORD their God, and the
words of Haggai the prophet, as the
LORD their God had sent him; and the
people feared before the LORD. 13 Then
Haggai, the messenger of the LORD,
spoke to the people with the LORD's
message, "I am with you, says the
LORD." 14 And the LORD stirred up the
spirit of Zerub´babel the son of She-
al´ti-el, governor of Judah, and the
spirit of Joshua the son of Jeho´zadak,
the high priest, and the spirit of all
the remnant of the people; and they
came and worked on the house of the
LORD of hosts, their God, 15 on the
twenty-fourth day of the month, in
the sixth month.

THE FUTURE GLORY OF THE TEMPLE

2 In the second year of Dari´us the
king, 1 in the seventh month, on the
twenty-first day of the month, the
word of the LORD came by Haggai the
prophet, 2 "Speak now to Zerub´babel
the son of She-al´ti-el, governor
of Judah, and to Joshua the son of
Jeho´zadak, the high priest, and to all
the remnant of the people, and say,
3 'Who is left among you that saw this
house in its former glory? How do
you see it now? Is it not in your sight
as nothing? 4 Yet now take courage,
O Zerub´babel, says the LORD; take
courage, O Joshua, son of Jeho´zadak,
the high priest; take courage, all you
people of the land, says the LORD;
work, for I am with you, says the LORD
of hosts, 5 according to the promise
that I made you when you came out
of Egypt. My Spirit abides among you;
fear not. 6 For thus says the LORD of
hosts: Once again, in a little while, I
will shake the heavens and the earth
and the sea and the dry land; 7 and I
will shake all nations, so that the trea-
sures of all nations shall come in, and

I will fill this house with splendor, says the LORD of hosts. 8The silver is mine, and the gold is mine, says the LORD of hosts. 9The latter splendor of this house shall be greater than the former, says the LORD of hosts; and in this place I will give prosperity, says the LORD of hosts.'"

A REBUKE AND A PROMISE

10 On the twenty-fourth day of the ninth month, in the second year of Dari′us, the word of the LORD came by Haggai the prophet, 11"Thus says the LORD of hosts: Ask the priests to decide this question, 12'If one carries holy flesh in the skirt of his garment, and touches with his skirt bread, or pottage, or wine, or oil, or any kind of food, does it become holy?'" The priests answered, "No." 13Then said Haggai, "If one who is unclean by contact with a dead body touches any of these, does it become unclean?" The priests answered, "It does become unclean." 14Then Haggai said, "So is it with this people, and with this nation before me, says the LORD; and so with every work of their hands; and what they offer there is unclean. 15Pray now, consider what will come to pass from this day onward. Before a stone was placed upon a stone in the temple of the LORD, 16how did you fare?[a] When one came to a heap of twenty measures, there were but ten; when one came to the winevat to draw fifty measures, there were but twenty. 17I smote you and all the products of your toil with blight and mildew and hail; yet you did not return to me, says the LORD. 18Consider from this day onward, from the twenty-fourth day of the ninth month. Since the day that the foundation of the LORD's temple was laid, consider: 19Is the seed yet in the barn? Do the vine, the fig tree, the pomegranate, and the olive tree still yield nothing? From this day on I will bless you."

GOD'S PROMISE TO ZERUBBABEL

20 The word of the LORD came a second time to Haggai on the twenty-fourth day of the month, 21"Speak to Zerub′babel, governor of Judah, saying, I am about to shake the heavens and the earth, 22and to overthrow the throne of kingdoms; I am about to destroy the strength of the kingdoms of the nations, and overthrow the chariots and their riders; and the horses and their riders shall go down, every one by the sword of his fellow. 23On that day, says the LORD of hosts, I will take you, O Zerub′babel my servant, the son of She-al′ti-el, says the LORD, and make you like a signet ring; for I have chosen you, says the LORD of hosts."

[a]Gk: Heb *since they were*

THE BOOK OF

ZECHARIAH

ISRAEL URGED TO REPENT

1 In the eighth month, in the second
year of Dari´us, the word of the
LORD came to Zechari´ah the son of
Berechi´ah, son of Iddo, the proph-
et, saying, 2"The LORD was very an-
gry with your fathers. 3Therefore
say to them, Thus says the LORD of
hosts: Return to me, says the LORD
of hosts, and I will return to you, says
the LORD of hosts. 4Be not like your
fathers, to whom the former proph-
ets cried out, 'Thus says the LORD
of hosts, Return from your evil ways
and from your evil deeds.' But they
did not hear or heed me, says the
LORD. 5Your fathers, where are they?
And the prophets, do they live for
ever? 6But my words and my statutes,
which I commanded my servants the
prophets, did they not overtake your
fathers? So they repented and said,
As the LORD of hosts purposed to
deal with us for our ways and deeds,
so has he dealt with us."

FIRST VISION: THE HORSEMEN

7 On the twenty-fourth day of the
eleventh month which is the month
of Shebat, in the second year of
Dari´us, the word of the LORD came
to Zechari´ah the son of Berechi´ah,
son of Iddo, the prophet; and
Zechari´ah said, 8"I saw in the night,
and behold, a man riding upon a red
horse! He was standing among the
myrtle trees in the glen; and *behind*
him were red, sorrel, and white hors-
es. 9Then I said, 'What are these, my
lord?' The angel who talked with me
said to me, 'I will show you what they
are.' 10So the man who was standing
among the myrtle trees answered,
'These are they whom the LORD has
sent to patrol the earth.' 11And they
answered the angel of the LORD who
was standing among the myrtle trees,
'We have patrolled the earth, and be-
hold, all the earth remains at rest.'
12Then the angel of the LORD said,
'O LORD of hosts, how long wilt thou
have no mercy on Jerusalem and the
cities of Judah, against which thou
hast had indignation these seven-
ty years?' 13And the LORD answered
gracious and comforting words to
the angel who talked with me. 14So
the angel who talked with me said
to me, 'Cry out, Thus says the LORD
of hosts: I am exceedingly jealous
for Jerusalem and for Zion. 15And I
am very angry with the nations that
are at ease; for while I was angry
but a little they furthered the disas-
ter. 16Therefore, thus says the LORD,
I have returned to Jerusalem with
compassion; my house shall be built
in it, says the LORD of hosts, and the
measuring line shall be stretched out
over Jerusalem. 17Cry again, Thus
says the LORD of hosts: My cities
shall again overflow with prosperi-
ty, and the LORD will again comfort
Zion and again choose Jerusalem.'"

SECOND VISION: THE HORNS AND THE SMITHS

18[a] And I lifted my eyes and saw,
and behold, four horns! 19And I said to
the angel who talked with me, "What
are these?" And he answered me,
"These are the horns which have scat-
tered Judah, Israel, and Jerusalem."
20Then the LORD showed me four
smiths. 21And I said, "What are these
coming to do?" He answered, "These
are the horns which scattered Judah,
so that no man raised his head; and
these have come to terrify them, to
cast down the horns of the nations
who lifted up their horns against the
land of Judah to scatter it."

[a] Ch 2.1 in Heb

THIRD VISION: THE MAN WITH A MEASURING LINE

2[a] And I lifted my eyes and saw, and
behold, a man with a measuring line
in his hand! 2Then I said, "Where are
you going?" And he said to me, "To
measure Jerusalem, to see what is its
breadth and what is its length." 3And
behold, the angel who talked with
me came forward, and another angel
came forward to meet him, 4and said
to him, "Run, say to that young man,
'Jerusalem shall be inhabited as vil-
lages without walls, because of the
multitude of men and cattle in it. 5For
I will be to her a wall of fire round
about, says the LORD, and I will be the
glory within her.'"

INTERLUDE: AN APPEAL TO THE EXILES

6 Ho! ho! Flee from the land of
the north, says the LORD; for I have
spread you abroad as the four winds
of the heavens, says the LORD. 7Ho!
Escape to Zion, you who dwell with
the daughter of Babylon. 8For thus
said the LORD of hosts, after his
glory sent me to the nations who
plundered you, for he who touch-
es you touches the apple of his eye:
9"Behold, I will shake my hand over
them, and they shall become plunder
for those who served them. Then you
will know that the LORD of hosts has
sent me. 10Sing and rejoice, O daugh-
ter of Zion; for lo, I come and I will
dwell in the midst of you, says the
LORD. 11And many nations shall join
themselves to the LORD in that day,
and shall be my people; and I will
dwell in the midst of you, and you
shall know that the LORD of hosts
has sent me to you. 12And the LORD
will inherit Judah as his portion in
the holy land, and will again choose
Jerusalem."

13 Be silent, all flesh, before the
LORD; for he has roused himself from
his holy dwelling.

[a]Ch 2.5 in Heb

FOURTH VISION: JOSHUA AND SATAN

3 Then he showed me Joshua the high
priest standing before the angel of
the LORD, and Satan standing at his
right hand to accuse him. 2And the
LORD said to Satan, "The LORD re-
buke you, O Satan! The LORD who has
chosen Jerusalem rebuke you! Is not
this a brand plucked from the fire?"
3Now Joshua was standing before the
angel, clothed with filthy garments.
4And the angel said to those who
were standing before him, "Remove
the filthy garments from him." And
to him he said, "Behold, I have tak-
en your iniquity away from you, and
I will clothe you with rich apparel."
5And I said, "Let them put a clean tur-
ban on his head." So they put a clean
turban on his head and clothed him
with garments; and the angel of the
LORD was standing by.

6 And the angel of the LORD en-
joined Joshua, 7"Thus says the LORD
of hosts: If you will walk in my ways
and keep my charge, then you shall
rule my house and have charge of my
courts, and I will give you the right of
access among those who are standing
here. 8Hear now, O Joshua the high
priest, you and your friends who sit
before you, for they are men of good
omen: behold, I will bring my servant
the Branch. 9For behold, upon the
stone which I have set before Joshua,
upon a single stone with seven facets,
I will engrave its inscription, says the
LORD of hosts, and I will remove the
guilt of this land in a single day. 10In
that day, says the LORD of hosts, ev-
ery one of you will invite his neighbor
under his vine and under his fig tree."

FIFTH VISION: THE LAMPSTAND AND OLIVE TREES

4 And the angel who talked with me
came again, and waked me, like a
man that is wakened out of his sleep.
2And he said to me, "What do you

see?" I said, "I see, and behold, a lampstand all of gold, with a bowl on the top of it, and seven lamps on it, with seven lips on each of the lamps which are on the top of it. 3And there are two olive trees by it, one on the right of the bowl and the other on its left." 4And I said to the angel who talked with me, "What are these, my lord?" 5Then the angel who talked with me answered me, "Do you not know what these are?" I said, "No, my lord." 6Then he said to me, "This is the word of the LORD to Zerub´babel: Not by might, nor by power, but by my Spirit, says the LORD of hosts. 7What are you, O great mountain? Before Zerub´babel you shall become a plain; and he shall bring forward the top stone amid shouts of 'Grace, grace to it!'" 8Moreover the word of the LORD came to me, saying, 9"The hands of Zerub´babel have laid the foundation of this house; his hands shall also complete it. Then you will know that the LORD of hosts has sent me to you. 10For whoever has despised the day of small things shall rejoice, and shall see the plummet in the hand of Zerub´babel. "These seven are the eyes of the LORD, which range through the whole earth." 11Then I said to him, "What are these two olive trees on the right and the left of the lampstand?" 12And a second time I said to him, "What are these two branches of the olive trees, which are beside the two golden pipes from which the oil[b] is poured out?" 13He said to me, "Do you not know what these are?" I said, "No, my lord." 14Then he said, "These are the two anointed who stand by the Lord of the whole earth."

SIXTH VISION: THE FLYING SCROLL

5 Again I lifted my eyes and saw, and behold, a flying scroll! 2And he said to me, "What do you see?" I answered, "I see a flying scroll; its length is twenty cubits, and its breadth ten cubits." 3Then he said to me, "This is the curse that goes out over the face of the whole land; for every one who steals shall be cut off henceforth according to it, and every one who swears falsely shall be cut off henceforth according to it. 4I will send it forth, says the LORD of hosts, and it shall enter the house of the thief, and the house of him who swears falsely by my name; and it shall abide in his house and consume it, both timber and stones."

SEVENTH VISION: THE WOMAN IN A BASKET

5 Then the angel who talked with me came forward and said to me, "Lift your eyes, and see what this is that goes forth." 6And I said, "What is it?" He said, "This is the ephah that goes forth." And he said, "This is their iniquity[c] in all the land." 7And behold, the leaden cover was lifted, and there was a woman sitting in the ephah! 8And he said, "This is Wickedness." And he thrust her back into the ephah, and thrust down the leaden weight upon its mouth. 9Then I lifted my eyes and saw, and behold, two women coming forward! The wind was in their wings; they had wings like the wings of a stork, and they lifted up the ephah between earth and heaven. 10Then I said to the angel who talked with me, "Where are they taking the ephah?" 11He said to me, "To the land of Shinar, to build a house for it; and when this is prepared, they will set the ephah down there on its base."

EIGHTH VISION: FOUR CHARIOTS

6 And again I lifted my eyes and saw, and behold, four chariots came out from between two mountains; and the mountains were mountains of bronze. 2The first chariot had red horses, the second black horses, 3the third white horses, and the fourth chariot dappled

[b]Cn: Heb *gold*
[c]Gk Compare Syr: Heb *eye*

gray[a] horses. 4Then I said to the angel
who talked with me, "What are these,
my lord?" 5And the angel answered
me, "These are going forth to the
four winds of heaven, after present-
ing themselves before the Lord of all
the earth. 6The chariot with the black
horses goes toward the north country,
the white ones go toward the west
country,[b] and the dappled ones go to-
ward the south country." 7When the
steeds came out, they were impatient
to get off and patrol the earth. And he
said, "Go, patrol the earth." So they
patrolled the earth. 8Then he cried to
me, "Behold, those who go toward the
north country have set my Spirit at
rest in the north country."

THE CORONATION OF THE BRANCH

9 And the word of the LORD came
to me: 10"Take from the exiles Heldai,
Tobi´jah, and Jedai´ah, who have ar-
rived from Babylon; and go the same
day to the house of Josi´ah, the son of
Zephani´ah. 11Take from them silver
and gold, and make a crown,[c] and set
it upon the head of Joshua, the son of
Jeho´zadak, the high priest; 12and say
to him, 'Thus says the LORD of hosts,
"Behold, the man whose name is the
Branch: for he shall grow up in his
place, and he shall build the temple
of the LORD. 13It is he who shall build
the temple of the LORD, and shall
bear royal honor, and shall sit and
rule upon his throne. And there shall
be a priest by his throne, and peaceful
understanding shall be between them
both."' 14And the crown[d] shall be in
the temple of the LORD as a remind-
er to Heldai,[e] Tobi´jah, Jedai´ah, and
Josi´ah[f] the son of Zephani´ah.

15 "And those who are far off shall
come and help to build the temple of
the LORD; and you shall know that
the LORD of hosts has sent me to you.
And this shall come to pass, if you will
diligently obey the voice of the LORD
your God."

HYPOCRITICAL FASTING CONDEMNED

7 In the fourth year of King Dari´us,
the word of the LORD came to
Zechari´ah on the fourth day of
the ninth month, which is Chislev.
2Now the people of Bethel had sent
Share´zer and Reg´em-mel´ech and
their men, to entreat the favor of the
LORD, 3and to ask the priests of the
house of the LORD of hosts and the
prophets, "Should I mourn and fast in
the fifth month, as I have done for so
many years?" 4Then the word of the
LORD of hosts came to me: 5"Say to all
the people of the land and the priests,
When you fasted and mourned in the
fifth month and in the seventh, for
these seventy years, was it for me that
you fasted? 6And when you eat and
when you drink, do you not eat for
yourselves and drink for yourselves?
7When Jerusalem was inhabited and
in prosperity, with her cities round
about her, and the South and the low-
land were inhabited, were not these
the words which the LORD proclaimed
by the former prophets?"

PUNISHMENT FOR REJECTING GOD'S DEMANDS

8 And the word of the LORD came
to Zechari´ah, saying, 9"Thus says
the LORD of hosts, Render true judg-
ments, show kindness and mercy each
to his brother, 10do not oppress the
widow, the fatherless, the sojourner,
or the poor; and let none of you de-
vise evil against his brother in your
heart." 11But they refused to hearken,
and turned a stubborn shoulder, and
stopped their ears that they might not
hear. 12They made their hearts like
adamant lest they should hear the

[a] Compare Gk: The meaning of the Hebrew word is uncertain
[b] Cn: Heb *after them*
[c] Gk Mss: Heb *crowns*
[d] Gk: Heb *crowns*
[e] With verse 10: Heb *Helem*
[f] With verse 10: Heb *Hen*

law and the words which the LORD of
hosts had sent by his Spirit through
the former prophets. Therefore great
wrath came from the LORD of hosts.
13 "As I called, and they would not
hear, so they called, and I would not
hear," says the LORD of hosts, 14 "and
I scattered them with a whirlwind
among all the nations which they had
not known. Thus the land they left
was desolate, so that no one went to
and fro, and the pleasant land was
made desolate."

GOD'S PROMISES TO ZION

8 And the word of the LORD of hosts
came to me, saying, 2 "Thus says the
LORD of hosts: I am jealous for Zion
with great jealousy, and I am jealous
for her with great wrath. 3 Thus says
the LORD: I will return to Zion, and
will dwell in the midst of Jerusalem,
and Jerusalem shall be called the
faithful city, and the mountain of the
LORD of hosts, the holy mountain.
4 Thus says the LORD of hosts: Old men
and old women shall again sit in the
streets of Jerusalem, each with staff in
hand for very age. 5 And the streets of
the city shall be full of boys and girls
playing in its streets. 6 Thus says the
LORD of hosts: If it is marvelous in
the sight of the remnant of this people
in these days, should it also be mar-
velous in my sight, says the LORD of
hosts? 7 Thus says the LORD of hosts:
Behold, I will save my people from the
east country and from the west coun-
try; 8 and I will bring them to dwell in
the midst of Jerusalem; and they shall
be my people and I will be their God,
in faithfulness and in righteousness."
9 Thus says the LORD of hosts:
"Let your hands be strong, you who
in these days have been hearing these
words from the mouth of the proph-
ets, since the day that the foundation
of the house of the LORD of hosts was
laid, that the temple might be built.
10 For before those days there was no
wage for man or any wage for beast,
neither was there any safety from the
foe for him who went out or came in;
for I set every man against his fel-
low. 11 But now I will not deal with
the remnant of this people as in the
former days, says the LORD of hosts.
12 For there shall be a sowing of peace;
the vine shall yield its fruit, and the
ground shall give its increase, and
the heavens shall give their dew; and
I will cause the remnant of this peo-
ple to possess all these things. 13 And
as you have been a byword of cursing
among the nations, O house of Judah
and house of Israel, so will I save you
and you shall be a blessing. Fear not,
but let your hands be strong."
14 For thus says the LORD of hosts:
"As I purposed to do evil to you, when
your fathers provoked me to wrath,
and I did not relent, says the LORD
of hosts, 15 so again have I purposed
in these days to do good to Jerusalem
and to the house of Judah; fear not.
16 These are the things that you shall
do: Speak the truth to one another,
render in your gates judgments that
are true and make for peace, 17 do not
devise evil in your hearts against one
another, and love no false oath, for all
these things I hate, says the LORD."

JOYFUL FASTING

18 And the word of the LORD of
hosts came to me, saying, 19 "Thus
says the LORD of hosts: The fast of
the fourth month, and the fast of the
fifth, and the fast of the seventh, and
the fast of the tenth, shall be to the
house of Judah seasons of joy and
gladness, and cheerful feasts; there-
fore love truth and peace.

MANY PEOPLES DRAWN TO JERUSALEM

20 "Thus says the LORD of hosts:
Peoples shall yet come, even the in-
habitants of many cities; 21 the inhab-
itants of one city shall go to another,
saying, 'Let us go at once to entreat
the favor of the LORD, and to seek the
LORD of hosts; I am going.' 22 Many
peoples and strong nations shall
come to seek the LORD of hosts in

Jerusalem, and to entreat the favor
of the LORD. 23Thus says the LORD
of hosts: In those days ten men from
the nations of every tongue shall take
hold of the robe of a Jew, saying, 'Let
us go with you, for we have heard that
God is with you.'"

JUDGMENT ON ISRAEL'S ENEMIES

9 **An Oracle**

The word of the LORD is
against the land of
Hadrach
and will rest upon
Damascus.
For to the LORD belong the
cities of Aram,[a]
even as all the tribes of
Israel;
2Hamath also, which borders
thereon,
Tyre and Sidon, though they
are very wise.
3Tyre has built herself a rampart,
and heaped up silver like
dust,
and gold like the mud of the
streets.
4But lo, the Lord will strip her of
her possessions
and hurl her wealth into the
sea,
and she shall be devoured
by fire.
5Ash´kelon shall see it, and be
afraid;
Gaza too, and shall writhe in
anguish;
Ekron also, because
its hopes are
confounded.
The king shall perish from
Gaza;
Ash´kelon shall be
uninhabited;
6a mongrel people shall dwell in
Ashdod;
and I will make an end of
the pride of Philistia.
7I will take away its blood from its
mouth,
and its abominations from
between its teeth;
it too shall be a remnant for
our God;
it shall be like a clan in
Judah,
and Ekron shall be like the
Jeb´usites.
8Then I will encamp at my house
as a guard,
so that none shall march to
and fro;
no oppressor shall again over-
run them,
for now I see with my own
eyes.

THE COMING RULER OF GOD'S PEOPLE

9Rejoice greatly, O daughter of
Zion!
Shout aloud, O daughter of
Jerusalem!
Lo, your king comes to you;
triumphant and victorious
is he,
humble and riding on an ass,
on a colt the foal of an ass.
10I will cut off the chariot from
E´phraim
and the war horse from
Jerusalem;
and the battle bow shall be
cut off,
and he shall command peace
to the nations;
his dominion shall be from sea
to sea,
and from the River to the
ends of the earth.
11As for you also, because of the
blood of my covenant with
you,
I will set your captives free
from the waterless
pit.
12Return to your stronghold, O
prisons of hope;
today I declare that I will
restore to you double.
13For I have bent Judah as my bow;
I have made E´phraim its

[a]Cn: Heb *the eye of Adam* (or *man*)

arrow.
I will brandish your sons, O
Zion,
over your sons, O Greece,
and wield you like a warrior's sword.
14 Then the LORD will appear over
them,
and his arrow go forth like
lightning;
the Lord GOD will sound the
trumpet,
and march forth in the
whirlwinds of the
south.
15 The LORD of hosts will protect
them,
and they shall devour and
tread down the
slingers;[b]
and they shall drink their
blood[c] like wine,
and be full like a bowl,
drenched like the corners of
the altar.
16 On that day the LORD their God
will save them
for they are the flock of his
people;
for like the jewels of a crown
they shall shine on his land.
17 Yea, how good and how fair it
shall be!
Grain shall make the young
men flourish,
and new wine the maidens.

RESTORATION OF JUDAH AND ISRAEL

10 Ask rain from the LORD
in the season of the spring
rain,
from the LORD *who makes* the
storm clouds,
who gives men showers of
rain,
to every one the vegetation
in the field.
2 For the teraphim utter nonsense,
and the diviners see lies;
the dreamers tell false dreams,
and give empty consolation.
Therefore the people wander
like sheep;
they are afflicted for want of
a shepherd.
3 "My anger is hot against the
shepherds,
and I will punish the
leaders;[d]
for the LORD of hosts cares for
his flock, the house of
Judah,
and will make them like his
proud steed in battle.
4 Out of them shall come the
cornerstone,
out of them the tent peg,
out of them the battle bow,
out of them every ruler.
5 Together they shall be like
mighty men in battle,
trampling the foe in the mud
of the streets;
they shall fight because the
LORD is with them,
and they shall confound the
riders on horses.
6 "I will strengthen the house of
Judah,
and I will save the house of
Joseph.
I will bring them back because
I have compassion on
them,
and they shall be as though
I had not rejected
them;
for I am the LORD their God
and I will answer
them.
7 Then E´phraim shall become like
a mighty warrior,
and *their hearts shall* be
glad as with wine.
Their children shall see it and
rejoice,
their hearts shall exult in
the LORD.
8 "I will signal for them and gather
them in,

[b] Cn: Heb *the slingstones*
[c] Gk: Heb *be turbulent*
[d] Or *he-goats*

for I have redeemed them,
and they shall be as many as
of old.
9 Though I scattered them among
the nations,
yet in far countries they
shall remember me,
and with their children they
shall live and return.
10 I will bring them home from the
land of Egypt,
and gather them from
Assyria;
and I will bring them to the
land of Gilead and to
Lebanon,
till there is no room for
them.
11 They shall pass through the sea
of Egypt,[a]
and the waves of the sea
shall be smitten,
and all the depths of the
Nile dried up.
The pride of Assyria shall be
laid low,
and the scepter of Egypt
shall depart.
12 I will make them strong in the
LORD
and they shall glory[b] in his
name,"
says the LORD.

11 Open your doors, O Lebanon,
that the fire may devour your
cedars!
2 Wail, O cypress, for the cedar has
fallen,
for the glorious trees are
ruined!
Wail, oaks of Bashan,
for the thick forest has been
felled!
3 Hark, the wail of the shepherds,
for their glory is despoiled!
Hark, the roar of the lions,
for the *jungle of the Jordan*
is laid waste!

TWO KINDS OF SHEPHERDS

4 Thus said the LORD my God:
"Become shepherd of the flock
doomed to slaughter. 5 Those who buy
them slay them and go unpunished;
and those who sell them say, 'Blessed
be the LORD, I have become rich'; and
their own shepherds have no pity on
them. 6 For I will no longer have pity
on the inhabitants of this land, says
the LORD. Lo, I will cause men to fall
each into the hand of his shepherd,
and each into the hand of his king;
and they shall crush the earth, and I
will deliver none from their hand."

7 So I became the shepherd of the
flock doomed to be slain for those
who trafficked in the sheep. And I
took two staffs; one I named Grace,
the other I named Union. And I
tended the sheep. 8 In one month I
destroyed the three shepherds. But
I became impatient with them, and
they also detested me. 9 So I said, "I
will not be your shepherd. What is to
die, let it die; what is to be destroyed,
let it be destroyed; and let those that
are left devour the flesh of one an-
other." 10 And I took my staff Grace,
and I broke it, annulling the cove-
nant which I had made with all the
peoples. 11 So it was annulled on that
day, and the traffickers in the sheep,
who were watching me, knew that it
was the word of the LORD. 12 Then I
said to them, "If it seems right to you,
give me my wages; but if not, keep
them." And they weighed out as my
wages thirty shekels of silver. 13 Then
the LORD said to me, "Cast it into the
treasury"[c]—the lordly price at which
I was paid off by them. So I took the
thirty shekels of silver and cast them
into the treasury[d] in the house of the
LORD. 14 Then I broke my second staff
Union, annulling the brotherhood be-
tween Judah and Israel.

15 Then the LORD said to me,
"Take once more the implements of

[a] Cn: Heb *distress*
[b] Gk: Heb *walk*
[c] Syr: Heb *to the potter*
[d] Syr: Heb *to the potter*

a worthless shepherd. 16 For lo, I am
raising up in the land a shepherd
who does not care for the perishing,
or seek the wandering,[e] or heal the
maimed, or nourish the sound, but de-
vours the flesh of the fat ones, tearing
off even their hoofs.

17 Woe to my worthless shepherd,
who deserts the flock!
May the sword smite his arm
and his right eye!
Let his arm be wholly
withered,
his right eye utterly
blinded!"

JERUSALEM'S VICTORY

An Oracle

12 The word of the LORD con-
cerning Israel: Thus says the LORD,
who stretched out the heavens and
founded the earth and formed the
spirit of man within him: 2 "Lo, I am
about to make Jerusalem a cup of reel-
ing to all the peoples round about; it
will be against Judah also in the siege
against Jerusalem. 3 On that day I will
make Jerusalem a heavy stone for all
the peoples; all who lift it shall griev-
ously hurt themselves. And all the
nations of the earth will come togeth-
er against it. 4 On that day, says the
LORD, I will strike every horse with
panic, and its rider with madness. But
upon the house of Judah I will open
my eyes, when I strike every horse of
the peoples with blindness. 5 Then the
clans of Judah shall say to themselves,
'The inhabitants of Jerusalem have
strength through the LORD of hosts,
their God.'

6 "On that day I will make the
clans of Judah like a blazing pot in the
midst of wood, like a flaming torch
among sheaves; and they shall de-
vour to the right and to the left all the
peoples round about, while Jerusalem
shall still be inhabited in its place, in
Jerusalem.

7 "And the LORD will give victory
to the tents of Judah first, that the
glory of the house of David and the
glory of the inhabitants of Jerusalem
may not be exalted over that of Judah.
8 On that day the LORD will put a shield
about the inhabitants of Jerusalem so
that the feeblest among them on that
day shall be like David, and the house
of David shall be like God, like the an-
gel of the LORD, at their head. 9 And on
that day I will seek to destroy all the
nations that come against Jerusalem.

MOURNING FOR THE PIERCED ONE

10 "And I will pour out on the
house of David and the inhabitants of
Jerusalem a spirit of compassion and
supplication, so that, when they look
on him whom they have pierced, they
shall mourn for him, as one mourns
for an only child, and weep bitterly
over him, as one weeps over a first-
born. 11 On that day the mourning
in Jerusalem will be as great as the
mourning for Ha´dad-rim´mon in the
plain of Megid´do. 12 The land shall
mourn, each family by itself; the fam-
ily of the house of David by itself, and
their wives by themselves; the family
of the house of Nathan by itself, and
their wives by themselves; 13 the family
of the house of Levi by itself, and their
wives by themselves; the family of the
Shim´e-ites by itself, and their wives
by themselves; 14 and all the families
that are left, each by itself, and their
wives by themselves.

13 "On that day there shall be a
fountain opened for the house
of David and the inhabitants of
Jerusalem to cleanse them from sin
and uncleanness.

IDOLATRY CUT OFF

2 "And on that day, says the LORD
of hosts, I will cut off the names of the
idols from the land, so that they shall
be remembered no more; and also I
will remove from the land the proph-
ets and the unclean spirit. 3 And if any
one again appears as a prophet, his
father and mother who bore him will

[e] Syr Compare Gk Vg: Heb *the youth*

say to him, 'You shall not live, for you
speak lies in the name of the LORD';
and his father and mother who bore
him shall pierce him through when
he prophesies. 4On that day every
prophet will be ashamed of his vision
when he prophesies; he will not put
on a hairy mantle in order to deceive,
5but he will say, 'I am no prophet, I
am a tiller of the soil; for the land has
been my possession[a] since my youth.'
6And if one asks him, 'What are these
wounds on your back?' he will say,
'The wounds I received in the house
of my friends.'"

THE SHEPHERD STRUCK, THE FLOCK SCATTERED

7"Awake, O sword, against my
shepherd,
against the man who stands
next to me,"
says the LORD of hosts.
"Strike the shepherd, that the
sheep may be scattered;
I will turn my hand against
the little ones.
8In the whole land, says the LORD,
two thirds shall be cut off
and perish,
and one third shall be left
alive.
9And I will put this third into the
fire,
and refine them as one
refines silver,
and test them as gold is
tested.
They will call on my name,
and I will answer them.
I will say, 'They are my people';
and they will say, 'The LORD
is my God.'"

FUTURE WARFARE AND FINAL VICTORY

14 *Behold, a day of the LORD is com-*
ing, when the spoil taken from
you will be divided in the midst of
you. 2For I will gather all the nations
against Jerusalem to battle, and the
city shall be taken and the houses
plundered and the women ravished;
half of the city shall go into exile,
but the rest of the people shall not be
cut off from the city. 3Then the LORD
will go forth and fight against those
nations as when he fights on a day
of battle. 4On that day his feet shall
stand on the Mount of Olives which
lies before Jerusalem on the east; and
the Mount of Olives shall be split in
two from east to west by a very wide
valley; so that one half of the Mount
shall withdraw northward, and the
other half southward. 5And the valley
of my mountains shall be stopped up,
for the valley of the mountains shall
touch the side of it; and you shall flee
as you fled from the earthquake in the
days of Uzzi'ah king of Judah. Then
the LORD your[b] God will come, and all
the holy ones with him. [c]

6 On that day there shall be nei-
ther cold nor frost.[d] 7And there shall
be continuous day (it is known to the
LORD), not day and not night, for at
evening time there shall be light.

8 On that day living waters shall
flow out from Jerusalem, half of them
to the eastern sea and half of them to
the western sea; it shall continue in
summer as in winter.

9 And the LORD will become king
over all the earth; on that day the
LORD will be one and his name one.

10 The whole land shall be turned
into a plain from Geba to Rimmon
south of Jerusalem. But Jerusalem
shall remain aloft upon its site from
the Gate of Benjamin to the place of
the former gate, to the Corner Gate,
and from the Tower of Hanan'el to
the king's wine presses. 11And it shall
be inhabited, for there shall be no
more curse;[e] Jerusalem shall dwell in
security.

[a] Cn: Heb *for man has caused me to possess*
[b] Heb *my*
[c] Gk Syr Vg Tg: Heb *you*
[d] Compare Gk Syr Vg Tg: Heb uncertain
[e] Or *ban of utter destruction*

12 And this shall be the plague with
which the LORD will smite all the peo-
ples that wage war against Jerusalem:
their flesh shall rot while they are
still on their feet, their eyes shall rot
in their sockets, and their tongues
shall rot in their mouths. 13And on
that day a great panic from the LORD
shall fall on them, so that each will lay
hold on the hand of his fellow, and the
hand of the one will be raised against
the hand of the other; 14even Judah
will fight against Jerusalem. And the
wealth of all the nations round about
shall be collected, gold, silver, and
garments in great abundance. 15And
a plague like this plague shall fall on
the horses, the mules, the camels, the
asses, and whatever beasts may be in
those camps.

16 Then every one that survives of
all the nations that have come against
Jerusalem shall go up year after year
to worship the King, the LORD of
hosts, and to keep the feast of booths.
17And if any of the families of the
earth do not go up to Jerusalem to
worship the King, the LORD of hosts,
there will be no rain upon them. 18And
if the family of Egypt do not go up and
present themselves, then upon them
shall[f] come the plague with which
the LORD afflicts the nations that do
not go up to keep the feast of booths.
19This shall be the punishment to
Egypt and the punishment to all the
nations that do not go up to keep the
feast of booths.

20 And on that day there shall be
inscribed on the bells of the horses,
"Holy to the LORD." And the pots in
the house of the LORD shall be as the
bowls before the altar; 21and every pot
in Jerusalem and Judah shall be sacred
to the LORD of hosts, so that all who
sacrifice may come and take of them
and boil the flesh of the sacrifice in
them. And there shall no longer be
a trader in the house of the LORD of
hosts on that day.

[f] Gk Syr: Heb *shall not*

THE BOOK OF

MALACHI

1 The oracle of the word of the LORD
to Israel by Mal´achi.[a]

ISRAEL PREFERRED TO EDOM

2 "I have loved you," says the
LORD. But you say, "How hast thou
loved us?""Is not Esau Jacob's broth-
er?" says the LORD. "Yet I have loved
Jacob 3but I have hated Esau; I have
laid waste his hill country and left
his heritage to jackals of the desert."
4If Edom says, "We are shattered but
we will rebuild the ruins," the LORD
of hosts says, "They may build, but
I will tear down, till they are called
the wicked country, the people with
whom the LORD is angry for ever."
5Your own eyes shall see this, and you
shall say, "Great is the LORD, beyond
the border of Israel!"

CORRUPTION OF THE PRIESTHOOD

6 "A son honors his father, and
a servant his master. If then I am a
father, where is my honor? And if I
am a master, where is my fear? says
the LORD of hosts to you, O priests,
who despise my name. You say, 'How
have we despised thy name?' 7By of-
fering polluted food upon my altar.
And you say, 'How have we pollut-
ed it?'[b] By thinking that the LORD's
table may be despised. 8When you
offer blind animals in sacrifice, is
that no evil? And when you offer
those that are lame or sick, is that no
evil? Present that to your governor;
will he be pleased with you or show
you favor? says the LORD of hosts.
9'And now entreat the favor of God,
that he may be gracious to us.' With
such a gift from your hand, will he
show favor to any of you? says the
LORD of hosts. 10Oh, that there were
one among you who would shut the
doors, that you might not kindle
fire upon my altar in vain! I have no
pleasure in you, says the LORD of
hosts, and I will not accept an offer-
ing from your hand. 11For from the
rising of the sun to its setting my
name is great among the nations,
and in every place incense is offered
to my name, and a pure offering;
for my name is great among the na-
tions, says the LORD of hosts. 12But
you profane it when you say that the
LORD's table is polluted, and the
food for it[c] may be despised. 13'What
a weariness this is,' you say, and you
sniff at me,[d] says the LORD of hosts.
You bring what has been taken by
violence or is lame or sick, and this
you bring as your offering! Shall
I accept that from your hand? says
the LORD. 14Cursed be the cheat who
has a male in his flock, and vows it,
and yet sacrifices to the Lord what
is blemished; for I am a great King,
says the LORD of hosts, and my name
is feared among the nations.

2 "And now, O priests, this command
is for you. 2If you will not listen,
if you will not lay it to heart to give
glory to my name, says the LORD of
hosts, then I will send the curse upon
you and I will curse your blessings;
indeed I have already cursed them,
because you do not lay it to heart.
3Behold, I will rebuke your offspring,
and spread dung upon your faces,
the dung of your offerings, and I
will put you out of my presence.[e] 4So
shall you know that I have sent this
command to you, that my covenant
with Levi may hold, says the LORD
of hosts. 5My covenant with him was
a covenant of life and peace, and I

[a] Or *my messenger*
[b] Gk: Heb *thee*
[c] Heb *its fruit, its food*
[d] Another reading is *it*
[e] Cn Compare Gk Syr: Heb *and he shall bear you to it*

gave them to him, that he might fear;
and he feared me, he stood in awe of
my name. 6True instruction[f] was in
his mouth, and no wrong was found
on his lips. He walked with me in
peace and uprightness, and he turned
many from iniquity. 7For the lips of a
priest should guard knowledge, and
men should seek instruction[g] from
his mouth, for he is the messenger
of the LORD of hosts. 8But you have
turned aside from the way; you have
caused many to stumble by your in-
struction;[h] you have corrupted the
covenant of Levi, says the LORD of
hosts, 9and so I make you despised
and abased before all the people, in-
asmuch as you have not kept my ways
but have shown partiality in your
instruction."[i]

THE COVENANT PROFANED BY JUDAH

10 Have we not all one father? Has
not one God created us? Why then are
we faithless to one another, profaning
the covenant of our fathers? 11Judah
has been faithless, and abomination
has been committed in Israel and in
Jerusalem; for Judah has profaned
the sanctuary of the LORD, which he
loves, and has married the daughter
of a foreign god. 12May the LORD cut
off from the tents of Jacob, for the
man who does this, any to witness[j] or
answer, or to bring an offering to the
LORD of hosts!

13 And this again you do. You cov-
er the LORD's altar with tears, with
weeping and groaning because he
no longer regards the offering or ac-
cepts it with favor at your hand. 14You
ask, "Why does he not?" Because the
LORD was witness to the covenant be-
tween you and the wife of your youth,
to whom you have been faithless,
though she is your companion and
your wife by covenant. 15Has not the
one God made[k] and sustained for us
the spirit of life?[l] And what does he
desire? Godly offspring. So take heed
to yourselves, and let none be faith-
less to the wife of his youth. 16"For I
hate[m] divorce, says the LORD the God
of Israel, and covering one's garment
with violence, says the LORD of hosts.
So take heed to yourselves and do not
be faithless."

17 You have wearied the LORD with
your words. Yet you say, "How have
we wearied him?" By saying, "Every
one who does evil is good in the sight
of the LORD, and he delights in them."
Or by asking, "Where is the God of
justice?"

THE COMING MESSENGER

3 "Behold, I send my messenger to
prepare the way before me, and the
Lord whom you seek will suddenly
come to his temple; the messenger of
the covenant in whom you delight, be-
hold, he is coming, says the LORD of
hosts. 2But who can endure the day of
his coming, and who can stand when
he appears? "For he is like a refiner's
fire and like fullers' soap; 3he will
sit as a refiner and purifier of silver,
and he will purify the sons of Levi
and refine them like gold and silver,
till they present right offerings to the
LORD. 4Then the offering of Judah
and Jerusalem will be pleasing to the
LORD as in the days of old and as in
former years.

5 "Then I will draw near to you
for judgment; I will be a swift wit-
ness against the sorcerers, against
the adulterers, against those who
swear falsely, against those who op-
press the hireling in his wages, the
widow and the orphan, against those
who thrust aside the sojourner, and

[f] Or *law*
[g] Or *law*
[h] Or *law*
[i] Or *law*
[j] Cn Compare Gk: Heb *arouse*
[k] Or *has he not made one?*
[l] Cn: Heb *and a remnant of spirit was his*
[m] Cn: Heb *he hates*

do not fear me, says the LORD of
hosts.

DO NOT ROB GOD

6 "For I the LORD do not change;
therefore you, O sons of Jacob, are
not consumed. 7From the days of
your fathers you have turned aside
from my statutes and have not kept
them. Return to me, and I will return
to you, says the LORD of hosts. But
you say, 'How shall we return?' 8Will
man rob God? Yet you are robbing
me. But you say, 'How are we robbing
thee?' In your tithes and offerings.
9You are cursed with a curse, for you
are robbing me; the whole nation of
you. 10Bring the full tithes into the
storehouse, that there may be food in
my house; and thereby put me to the
test, says the LORD of hosts, if I will
not open the windows of heaven for
you and pour down for you an over-
flowing blessing. 11I will rebuke the
devourer[a] for you, so that it will not
destroy the fruits of your soil; and
your vine in the field shall not fail to
bear, says the LORD of hosts. 12Then
all nations will call you blessed, for
you will be a land of delight, says the
LORD of hosts.

13 "Your words have been stout
against me, says the LORD. Yet you
say, 'How have we spoken against
thee?' 14You have said, 'It is vain to
serve God. What is the good of our
keeping his charge or of walking as in
mourning before the LORD of hosts?
15Henceforth we deem the arrogant
blessed; evildoers not only prosper
but when they put God to the test they
escape.'"

THE REWARD OF THE FAITHFUL

16 Then those who feared the LORD
spoke with one another; the LORD
heeded and heard them, and a book of
remembrance was written before him
of those who feared the LORD and
thought on his name. 17"They shall
be mine, says the LORD of hosts, my
special possession on the day when
I act, and I will spare them as a man
spares his son who serves him. 18Then
once more you shall distinguish be-
tween the righteous and the wicked,
between one who serves God and one
who does not serve him.

THE GREAT DAY OF THE LORD

4 [b]"For behold, the day comes, burn-
ing like an oven, when all the arro-
gant and all evildoers will be stubble;
the day that comes shall burn them up,
says the LORD of hosts, so that it will
leave them neither root nor branch.
2But for you who fear my name the
sun of righteousness shall rise, with
healing in its wings. You shall go forth
leaping like calves from the stall. 3And
you shall tread down the wicked, for
they will be ashes under the soles of
your feet, on the day when I act, says
the LORD of hosts.

4 "Remember the law of my ser-
vant Moses, the statutes and ordi-
nances that I commanded him at
Horeb for all Israel.

5 "Behold, I will send you Eli´jah
the prophet before the great and ter-
rible day of the LORD comes. 6And he
will turn the hearts of fathers to their
children and the hearts of children to
their fathers, lest I come and smite the
land with a curse."[c]

[a] Or *devouring locust*
[b] Ch 4.1-6 are Ch 3.19-24 in the Hebrew
[c] Or *ban of utter destruction*

THE FIRST BOOK OF THE

MACCABEES

ALEXANDER THE GREAT

1 After Alexander son of Philip, the
Macedonian, who came from the
land of Kittim, had defeated[a] Dari´us,
king of the Persians and the Medes,
he succeeded him as king. (He had
previously become king of Greece.)
2 He fought many battles, conquered
strongholds, and put to death the
kings of the earth. 3 He advanced to
the ends of the earth, and plundered
many nations. When the earth be-
came quiet before him, he was exalt-
ed, and his heart was lifted up. 4 He
gathered a very strong army and ruled
over countries, nations, and princes,
and they became tributary to him.

5 After this he fell sick and per-
ceived that he was dying. 6 So he sum-
moned his most honored officers,
who had been brought up with him
from youth, and divided his kingdom
among them while he was still alive.
7 And after Alexander had reigned
twelve years, he died.

8 Then his officers began to rule,
each in his own place. 9 They all put
on crowns after his death, and so did
their sons after them for many years;
and they caused many evils on the
earth.

ANTIOCHUS EPIPHANES AND RENEGADE JEWS

10 From them came forth a sinful
root, Anti´ochus Epiph´anes, son of
Anti´ochus the king; he had been a
hostage in Rome. He began to reign
in the one hundred and thirty-seventh
year of the kingdom of the Greeks.[b]

11 In those days lawless men came
forth from Israel, and misled many,
saying, "Let us go and make a cove-
nant with the Gentiles round about
us, for since we separated from them
many evils have come upon us." 12 This
proposal pleased them, 13 and some of
the people eagerly went to the king.
He authorized them to observe the
ordinances of the Gentiles. 14 So they
built a gymnasium in Jerusalem, ac-
cording to Gentile custom, 15 and re-
moved the marks of circumcision, and
abandoned the holy covenant. They
joined with the Gentiles and sold
themselves to do evil.

ANTIOCHUS IN EGYPT

16 When Anti´ochus saw that his
kingdom was established, he deter-
mined to become king of the land of
Egypt, that he might reign over both
kingdoms. 17 So he invaded Egypt with
a strong force, with chariots and ele-
phants and cavalry and with a large
fleet. 18 He engaged Ptol´emy king of
Egypt in battle, and Ptol´emy turned
and fled before him, and many were
wounded and fell. 19 And they cap-
tured the fortified cities in the land
of Egypt, and he plundered the land
of Egypt.

PERSECUTION OF THE JEWS

20 After subduing Egypt, Anti´o-
chus returned in the one hundred and
forty-third year.[c] He went up against
Israel and came to Jerusalem with a
strong force. 21 He arrogantly entered
the sanctuary and took the golden al-
tar, the lampstand for the light, and
all its utensils. 22 He took also the ta-
ble for the bread of the Presence, the
cups for drink offerings, the bowls,
the golden censers, the curtain, the
crowns, and the gold decoration on
the front of the temple; he stripped
it all off. 23 He took the silver and the
gold, and the costly vessels; he took

[a] Greek adds and he defeated
[b] 175 b. c.
[c] 169 b. c.

also the hidden treasures which he
found. 24Taking them all, he departed
to his own land.

He committed deeds of murder,
and spoke with great
arrogance.
25Israel mourned deeply in every
community,
26rulers and elders groaned,
maidens and young men became faint,
the beauty of the women
faded.
27Every bridegroom took up the
lament;
she who sat in the bridal chamber was
mourning.
28Even the land shook for its
inhabitants,
and all the house of Jacob
was clothed with
shame.

THE OCCUPATION OF JERUSALEM

29 Two years later the king sent
to the cities of Judah a chief collector
of tribute, and he came to Jerusalem
with a large force. 30Deceitfully he
spoke peaceable words to them, and
they believed him; but he sudden-
ly fell upon the city, dealt it a severe
blow, and destroyed many people of
Israel. 31He plundered the city, burned
it with fire, and tore down its houses
and its surrounding walls. 32And they
took captive the women and children,
and seized the cattle. 33Then they for-
tified the city of David with a great
strong wall and strong towers, and it
became their citadel. 34And they sta-
tioned there a sinful people, lawless
men. These strengthened their posi-
tion; 35they stored up arms and food,
and collecting the spoils of Jerusalem
they stored them there, and became a
great snare.

36It became an ambush against the
sanctuary,
an evil adversary of Israel
continually.
37On every side of the sanctuary
they shed innocent blood;
they even defiled the
sanctuary.
38Because of them the residents of
Jerusalem fled;
she became a dwelling of
strangers;
she became strange to her
offspring,
and her children forsook her.
39Her sanctuary became desolate
as a desert;
her feasts were turned into
mourning,
her sabbaths into a reproach,
her honor into contempt.
40Her dishonor now grew as great
as her glory;
her exaltation was turned
into mourning.

INSTALLATION OF GENTILE CULTS

41 Then the king wrote to his
whole kingdom that all should be one
people, 42and that each should give
up his customs. 43All the Gentiles
accepted the command of the king.
Many even from Israel gladly adopted
his religion; they sacrificed to idols
and profaned the sabbath. 44And the
king sent letters by messengers to
Jerusalem and the cities of Judah;
he directed them to follow customs
strange to the land, 45to forbid burnt
offerings and sacrifices and drink
offerings in the sanctuary, to pro-
fane sabbaths and feasts, 46to defile
the sanctuary and the priests, 47to
build altars and sacred precincts and
shrines for idols, to sacrifice swine
and unclean animals, 48and to leave
their sons uncircumcised. They were
to make themselves abominable by
everything unclean and profane, 49so
that they should forget the law and
change all the ordinances. 50"And
whoever does not obey the command
of the king shall die."

51 In such words he wrote to his
whole kingdom. And he appointed
inspectors over all the people and
commanded the cities of Judah to

offer sacrifice, city by city. 52 Many of
the people, every one who forsook the
law, joined them, and they did evil in
the land; 53 they drove Israel into hid-
ing in every place of refuge they had.
54 Now on the fifteenth day of
Chislev, in the one hundred and for-
ty-fifth year,[a] they erected a desolat-
ing sacrilege upon the altar of burnt
offering. They also built altars in the
surrounding cities of Judah, 55 and
burned incense at the doors of the
houses and in the streets. 56 The books
of the law which they found they
tore to pieces and burned with fire.
57 Where the book of the covenant was
found in the possession of any one,
or if any one adhered to the law, the
decree of the king condemned him
to death. 58 They kept using violence
against Israel, against those found
month after month in the cities. 59 And
on the twenty-fifth day of the month
they offered sacrifice on the altar
which was upon the altar of burnt of-
fering. 60 According to the decree, they
put to death the women who had their
children circumcised, 61 and their fam-
ilies and those who circumcised them;
and they hung the infants from their
mothers' necks.
62 But many in Israel stood firm
and were resolved in their hearts not
to eat unclean food. 63 They chose to
die rather than to be defiled by food
or to profane the holy covenant; and
they did die. 64 And very great wrath
came upon Israel.

MATTATHIAS AND HIS SONS

2 *In those days Mattathi´as* the son of
John, son of Sim´eon, a priest of the
sons of Jo´arib, moved from Jerusalem
and settled in Mo´de-in. 2 He had
five sons, John surnamed Gaddi,
3 Simon called Thassi, 4 Judas called
Maccabe´us, 5 Elea´zar called Av´aran,
and Jonathan called Apphus. 6 He saw
the blasphemies being committed in
Judah and Jerusalem, 7 and said,

"Alas! Why was I born to see
this,
the ruin of my people, the
ruin of the holy city,
and to dwell there when it was
given over to the enemy,
the sanctuary given over to
aliens?
8 Her temple has become like a
man without honor;[b]
9 her glorious vessels have
been carried into
captivity.
Her babes have been killed in
her streets,
her youths by the sword of
the foe.
10 What nation has not inherited
her palaces[c]
and has not seized her
spoils?
11 All her adornment has been
taken away;
no longer free, she has be-
come a slave.
12 And behold, our holy place, our
beauty,
and our glory have been laid
waste;
the Gentiles have profaned it.
13 Why should we live any
longer?"

14 And Mattathi´as and his sons
rent their clothes, put on sackcloth,
and mourned greatly.

PAGAN WORSHIP REFUSED

15 Then the king's officers who
were enforcing the apostasy came to
the city of Mo´de-in to make them of-
fer sacrifice. 16 Many from Israel came
to them; and Mattathi´as and *his sons*
were assembled. 17 Then the king's of-
ficers spoke to Mattathi´as as follows:
"You are a leader, honored and great
in this city, and supported by sons and
brothers. 18 Now be the first to come
and do what the king commands, as
all the Gentiles and the men of Judah
and those that are left in Jerusalem

[a] 167 b. c.
[b] The text of this verse is uncertain
[c] Other authorities read *has not had a part in her kingdom*

have done. Then you and your sons
will be numbered among the friends
of the king, and you and your sons
will be honored with silver and gold
and many gifts."

19 But Mattathi´as answered and
said in a loud voice: "Even if all the
nations that live under the rule of the
king obey him, and have chosen to do
his commandments, departing each
one from the religion of his fathers,
20 yet I and my sons and my brothers
will live by the covenant of our fa-
thers. 21 Far be it from us to desert the
law and the ordinances. 22 We will not
obey the king's words by turning aside
from our religion to the right hand or
to the left."

23 When he had finished speaking
these words, a Jew came forward in
the sight of all to offer sacrifice upon
the altar in Mo´de-in, according to the
king's command. 24 When Mattathi´as
saw it, be burned with zeal and his
heart was stirred. He gave vent to
righteous anger; he ran and killed
him upon the altar. 25 At the same
time he killed the king's officer who
was forcing them to sacrifice, and he
tore down the altar. 26 Thus he burned
with zeal for the law, as Phin´ehas did
against Zimri the son of Salu.

27 Then Mattathi´as cried out in
the city with a loud voice, saying: "Let
every one who is zealous for the law
and supports the covenant come out
with me!" 28 And he and his sons fled
to the hills and left all that they had
in the city.

29 Then many who were seeking
righteousness and justice went down
to the wilderness to dwell there,
30 they, their sons, their wives, and
their cattle, because evils pressed
heavily upon them. 31 And it was re-
ported to the king's officers, and to
the troops in Jerusalem the city of
David, that men who had rejected the
king's command had gone down to
the hiding places in the wilderness.
32 Many pursued them, and overtook
them; they encamped opposite them
and prepared for battle against them
on the sabbath day. 33 And they said
to them, "Enough of this! Come out
and do what the king commands,
and you will live." 34 But they said,
"We will not come out, nor will we
do what the king commands and so
profane the sabbath day." 35 Then the
enemy[a] hastened to attack them.
36 But they did not answer them or
hurl a stone at them or block up their
hiding places, 37 for they said, "Let us
all die in our innocence; heaven and
earth testify for us that you are kill-
ing us unjustly." 38 So they attacked
them on the sabbath, and they died,
with their wives and children and
cattle, to the number of a thousand
persons.

39 When Mattathi´as and his
friends learned of it, they mourned
for them deeply. 40 And each said to his
neighbor: "If we all do as our breth-
ren have done and refuse to fight with
the Gentiles for our lives and for our
ordinances, they will quickly destroy
us from the earth." 41 So they made
this decision that day: "Let us fight
against every man who comes to at-
tack us on the sabbath day; let us not
all die as our brethren died in their
hiding places."

COUNTER-ATTACK

42 Then there united with them a
company of Haside´ans, mighty war-
riors of Israel, every one who offered
himself willingly for the law. 43 And all
who became fugitives to escape their
troubles joined them and reinforced
them. 44 They organized an army, and
struck down sinners in their anger
and lawless men in their wrath; the
survivors fled to the Gentiles for safe-
ty. 45 And Mattathi´as and his friends
went about and tore down the altars;
46 they forcibly circumcised all the
uncircumcised boys that they found
within the borders of Israel. 47 They
hunted down the arrogant men, and

[a] Gk *they*

the work prospered in their hands.
48They rescued the law out of the
hands of the Gentiles and kings, and
they never let the sinner gain the up-
per hand.

THE LAST WORDS OF MATTATHIAS

49 Now the days drew near for
Mattathi´as to die, and he said to his
sons: "Arrogance and reproach have
now become strong; it is a time of ruin
and furious anger. 50Now, my children,
show zeal for the law, and give your
lives for the covenant of our fathers.

51 "Remember the deeds of the
fathers, which they did in their gen-
erations; and receive great honor
and an everlasting name. 52Was not
Abraham found faithful when tested,
and it was reckoned to him as righ-
teousness? 53Joseph in the time of his
distress kept the commandment, and
became lord of Egypt. 54Phin´ehas our
father, because he was deeply zealous,
received the covenant of everlasting
priesthood. 55Joshua, because he ful-
filled the command, became a judge in
Israel. 56Caleb, because he testified in
the assembly, received an inheritance
in the land. 57David, because he was
merciful, inherited the throne of the
kingdom for ever. 58Eli´jah because
of great zeal for the law was taken up
into heaven. 59Hanani´ah, Azari´ah,
and Mish´a-el believed and were saved
from the flame. 60Daniel because of
his innocence was delivered from the
mouth of the lions.

61 "And so observe, from genera-
tion to generation, that none who put
their trust in him will lack strength.
62Do not fear the words of a sinner, for
his splendor will turn into dung and
worms. 63Today he will be exalted, but
tomorrow he will not be found, be-
cause he has returned to the dust, and
his plans will perish. 64My children,
be courageous and grow strong in the
law, for by it you will gain honor.

65 "Now behold, I know that
Sim´eon your brother is wise in coun-
sel; always listen to him; he shall be
your father. 66Judas Maccabe´us has
been a mighty warrior from his youth;
he shall command the army for you
and fight the battle against the peo-
ples.[b] 67You shall rally about you all
who observe the law, and avenge the
wrong done to your people. 68Pay back
the Gentiles in full, and heed what the
law commands."

69 Then he blessed them, and was
gathered to his fathers. 70He died in the
one hundred and forty-sixth year[c] and
was buried in the tomb of his fathers
at Mo´de-in. And all Israel mourned
for him with great lamentation.

THE EARLY VICTORIES OF JUDAS

3 Then Judas his son, who was called
Maccabe´us, took command in his
place. 2All his brothers and all who
had joined his father helped him; they
gladly fought for Israel.

3He extended the glory of his
people.
Like a giant he put on his
breastplate;
he girded on his armor of war
and waged battles,
protecting the host by his
sword.
4He was like a lion in his deeds,
like a lion's cub roaring for
prey.
5He searched out and pursued the
lawless;
he burned those who trou-
bled his people.
6Lawless men shrank back for fear
of him;
all the evildoers were
confounded;
and deliverance prospered
by his hand.
7He embittered many kings,
but he made Jacob glad by
his deeds,
and his memory is blessed
for ever.

[b] Or *of the people*
[c] 166 B. C.

8 He went through the cities of
Judah;
he destroyed the ungodly
out of the land;[a]
thus he turned away wrath
from Israel.
9 He was renowned to the ends of
the earth;
he gathered in those who
were perishing.

10 But Apollo´nius gathered to-
gether Gentiles and a large force
from Samar´ia to fight against Israel.
11 When Judas learned of it, he went
out to meet him, and he defeated and
killed him. Many were wounded and
fell, and the rest fled. 12 Then they
seized their spoils; and Judas took the
sword of Apollo´nius, and used it in
battle the rest of his life.

13 Now when Seron, the com-
mander of the Syrian army, heard
that Judas had gathered a large com-
pany, including a body of faithful men
who stayed with him and went out to
battle, 14 he said, "I will make a name
for myself and win honor in the king-
dom. I will make war on Judas and
his companions, who scorn the king's
command." 15 And again a strong army
of ungodly men went up with him to
help him, to take vengeance on the
sons of Israel.

16 When he approached the ascent
of Beth-hor´on, Judas went out to
meet him with a small company. 17 But
when they saw the army coming to
meet them, they said to Judas, "How
can we, few as we are, fight against
so great and strong a multitude? And
we are faint, for we have eaten noth-
ing today." 18 Judas replied, "It is easy
for many to be hemmed in by few, for
in the sight of Heaven there is no dif-
ference between saving by many or
by few. 19 It is not on the size of the
army that victory in battle depends,
but strength comes from Heaven.
20 They come against us in great pride
and lawlessness to destroy us and our
wives and our children, and to despoil
us; 21 but we fight for our lives and our
laws. 22 He himself will crush them be-
fore us; as for you, do not be afraid of
them."

23 When he finished speaking,
he rushed suddenly against Seron
and his army, and they were crushed
before him. 24 They pursued them[b]
down the descent of Beth-hor´on
to the plain; eight hundred of them
fell, and the rest fled into the land of
the Philistines. 25 Then Judas and his
brothers began to be feared, and ter-
ror fell upon the Gentiles round about
them. 26 His fame reached the king,
and the Gentiles talked of the battles
of Judas.

THE POLICY OF ANTIOCHUS

27 When king Anti´ochus heard
these reports, he was greatly an-
gered; and he sent and gathered all
the forces of his kingdom, a very
strong army. 28 And he opened his
coffers and gave a year's pay to his
forces, and ordered them to be ready
for any need. 29 Then he saw that the
money in the treasury was exhaust-
ed, and that the revenues from the
country were small because of the
dissension and disaster which he
had caused in the land by abolish-
ing the laws that had existed from
the earliest days. 30 He feared that he
might not have such funds as he had
before for his expenses and for the
gifts which he used to give more lav-
ishly than preceding kings. 31 He was
greatly perplexed in mind, and de-
termined to go to Persia and collect
the revenues from those regions and
raise a large fund.

32 He left Lys´ias, a distin-
guished man of royal lineage, in
charge of the king's affairs from
the river Euphra´tes to the borders
of Egypt. 33 Lys´ias was also to take
care of Anti´ochus his son until he
returned. 34 And he turned over to

[a] Gk *it*
[b] Other authorities read *him*

Lys´ias[c] half of his troops and the el-
ephants, and gave him orders about
all that he wanted done. As for the
residents of Judea and Jerusalem,
35Lys´ias was to send a force against
them to wipe out and destroy the
strength of Israel and the remnant
of Jerusalem; he was to banish the
memory of them from the place,
36settle aliens in all their territory,
and distribute their land. **37**Then the
king took the remaining half of his
troops and departed from Antioch
his capital in the one hundred and
forty-seventh year.[d] He crossed the
Euphra´tes river and went through
the upper provinces.

PREPARATIONS FOR BATTLE

38 Lys´ias chose Ptol´emy the son
of Dorym´enes, and Nica´nor and
Gor´gias, mighty men among the
friends of the king, **39**and sent with
them forty thousand infantry and
seven thousand cavalry to go into
the land of Judah and destroy it, as
the king had commanded. **40**So they
departed with their entire force, and
when they arrived they encamped
near Emma´us in the plain. **41**When the
traders of the region heard what was
said of them, they took silver and gold
in immense amounts, and fetters,[e]
and went to the camp to get the sons
of Israel for slaves. And forces from
Syria and the land of the Philistines
joined with them.

42 Now Judas and his brothers
saw that misfortunes had increased
and that the forces were encamped in
their territory. They also learned what
the king had commanded to do to the
people to cause their final destruc-
tion. **43**But they said to one another,
"Let us repair the destruction of our
people, and fight for our people and
the sanctuary." **44**And the congrega-
tion assembled to be ready for battle,
and to pray and ask for mercy and
compassion.

45Jerusalem was uninhabited like
a wilderness;
not one of her children went
in or out.
The sanctuary was trampled
down,
and the sons of aliens held
the citadel;
it was a lodging place for the
Gentiles.
Joy was taken from Jacob;
the flute and the harp
ceased to play.

46 So they assembled and went to
Mizpah, opposite Jerusalem, because
Israel formerly had a place of prayer in
Mizpah. **47**They fasted that day, put on
sackcloth and sprinkled ashes on their
heads, and rent their clothes. **48**And
they opened the book of the law to in-
quire into those matters about which
the Gentiles were consulting the im-
ages of their idols. **49**They also brought
the garments of the priesthood and
the first fruits and the tithes, and
they stirred up the Naz´irites who had
completed their days; **50**and they cried
aloud to Heaven, saying,
"What shall we do with these?
Where shall we take them?
51Thy sanctuary is trampled down
and profaned,
and thy priests mourn in
humiliation.
52And behold, the Gentiles are
assembled against us to
destroy us;
thou knowest what they plot
against us.
53How will we be able to with-
stand them,
if thou dost not help us?"

54 Then they sounded the trum-
pets and gave a loud shout. **55**After this
Judas appointed leaders of the people,
in charge of thousands and hundreds
and fifties and tens. **56**And he said
to those who were building houses,
or were betrothed, or were planting
vineyards, or were fainthearted, that

[c] Gk *him*
[d] 165 b. c.
[e] Syr: Gk *slaves*

each should return to his home, ac-
cording to the law. 57Then the army
marched out and encamped to the
south of Emma´us.

58 And Judas said, "Gird your-
selves and be valiant. Be ready early
in the morning to fight with these
Gentiles who have assembled against
us to destroy us and our sanctuary. 59It
is better for us to die in battle than to
see the misfortunes of our nation and
of the sanctuary. 60But as his will in
heaven may be, so he will do."

THE BATTLE AT EMMAUS

4 Now Gor´gias took five thousand
infantry and a thousand picked
cavalry, and this division moved out
by night 2to fall upon the camp of
the Jews and attack them suddenly.
Men from the citadel were his guides.
3But Judas heard of it, and he and his
mighty men moved out to attack the
king's force in Emma´us 4while the di-
vision was still absent from the camp.
5When Gor´gias entered the camp of
Judas by night, he found no one there,
so he looked for them in the hills, be-
cause he said, "These men are fleeing
from us."

6 At daybreak Judas appeared in
the plain with three thousand men,
but they did not have armor and
swords such as they desired. 7And
they saw the camp of the Gentiles,
strong and fortified, with cavalry
round about it; and these men were
trained in war. 8But Judas said to the
men who were with him, "Do not
fear their numbers or be afraid when
they charge. 9Remember how our
fathers were saved at the Red Sea,
when Pharaoh with his forces pursued
them. 10And now let us cry to Heaven,
to see whether he will favor us and re-
member his covenant with our fathers
and crush this army before us today.
11Then all the Gentiles will know that
there is one who redeems and saves
Israel."

12 When the foreigners looked up
and saw them coming against them,
13they went forth from their camp to
battle. Then the men with Judas blew
their trumpets 14and engaged in bat-
tle. The Gentiles were crushed and
fled into the plain, 15and all those
in the rear fell by the sword. They
pursued them to Gazar´a, and to the
plains of Idume´a, and to Azo´tus and
Jam´nia; and three thousand of them
fell. 16Then Judas and his force turned
back from pursuing them, 17and he
said to the people, "Do not be greedy
for plunder, for there is a battle before
us; 18Gor´gias and his force are near us
in the hills. But stand now against our
enemies and fight them, and after-
ward seize the plunder boldly."

19 Just as Judas was finishing this
speech, a detachment appeared, com-
ing out of the hills. 20They saw that
their army[a] had been put to flight,
and that the Jews[b] were burning the
camp, for the smoke that was seen
showed what had happened. 21When
they perceived this they were greatly
frightened, and when they also saw
the army of Judas drawn up in the
plain for battle, 22they all fled into the
land of the Philistines. 23Then Judas
returned to plunder the camp, and
they seized much gold and silver, and
cloth dyed blue and sea purple, and
great riches. 24On their return they
sang hymns and praises to Heaven,
for he is good, for his mercy endures
for ever. 25Thus Israel had a great de-
liverance that day.

FIRST CAMPAIGN OF LYSIAS

26 Those of the foreigners who es-
caped went and reported to Lys´ias all
that had happened. 27When he heard it,
he was perplexed and discouraged, for
things had not happened to Israel as
he had intended, nor had they turned
out as the king had commanded him.
28But the next year he mustered six-
ty thousand picked infantrymen and

[a] Gk *they*
[b] Gk *they*

five thousand cavalry to subdue them.
29 They came into Idume´a and en-
camped at Beth-zur,* and Judas met
them with ten thousand men.

30 When he saw that the army was
strong, he prayed, saying, "Blessed
art thou, O Savior of Israel, who didst
crush the attack of the mighty warrior
by the hand of thy servant David, and
didst give the camp of the Philistines
into the hands of Jonathan, the son of
Saul, and of the man who carried his
armor. 31 So do thou hem in this army
by the hand of thy people Israel, and
let them be ashamed of their troops
and their cavalry. 32 Fill them with
cowardice; melt the boldness of their
strength; let them tremble in their
destruction. 33 Strike them down with
the sword of those who love thee, and
let all who know thy name praise thee
with hymns."

34 Then both sides attacked, and
there fell of the army of Lys´ias five
thousand men; they fell in action.[c]
35 And when Lys´ias saw the rout of
his troops and observed the boldness
which inspired those of Judas, and
how ready they were either to live or
to die nobly, he departed to Antioch
and enlisted mercenaries, to invade
Judea again with an even larger army.

CLEANSING AND DEDICATION OF THE TEMPLE

36 Then said Judas and his broth-
ers, "Behold, our enemies are crushed;
let us go up to cleanse the sanctuary
and dedicate it." 37 So all the army as-
sembled and they went up to Mount
Zion. 38 *And they saw* the sanctuary
desolate, the altar profaned, and the
gates burned. In the courts they saw
bushes sprung up as in a thicket, or
as on one of the mountains. They saw
also the chambers of the priests in
ruins. 39 Then they rent their clothes,
and mourned with great lamentation,
and sprinkled themselves with ashes.
40 They fell face down on the ground,
and sounded the signal on the trum-
pets, and cried out to Heaven. 41 Then
Judas detailed men to fight against
those in the citadel until he had
cleansed the sanctuary.

42 He chose blameless priests de-
voted to the law, 43 and they cleansed
the sanctuary and removed the defiled
stones to an unclean place. 44 They de-
liberated what to do about the altar
of burnt offering, which had been
profaned. 45 And they thought it best
to tear it down, lest it bring reproach
upon them, for the Gentiles had de-
filed it. So they tore down the altar,
46 and stored the stones in a convenient
place on the temple hill until there
should come a prophet to tell what
to do with them. 47 Then they took
unhewn[d] stones, as the law directs,
and built a new altar like the former
one. 48 They also rebuilt the sanctuary
and the interior of the temple, and
consecrated the courts. 49 They made
new holy vessels, and brought the
lampstand, the altar of incense, and
the table into the temple. 50 Then they
burned incense on the altar and light-
ed the lamps on the lampstand, and
these gave light in the temple. 51 They
placed the bread on the table and hung
up the curtains. Thus they finished all
the work they had undertaken.

52 Early in the morning on the
twenty-fifth day of the ninth month,
which is the month of Chislev, in the
one hundred and forty-eighth year,[e]
53 they rose and offered sacrifice, as
the law directs, on the new altar of
burnt offering which they had built.
54 At the very season and on the very
day that the Gentiles had profaned
it, it was dedicated with songs and
harps and lutes and cymbals. 55 All
the people fell on their faces and wor-
shiped and blessed Heaven, who had
prospered them. 56 So they celebrated
the dedication of the altar for eight
days, and offered burnt offerings with

[c] Or *and some fell on the opposite side*
[d] Gk *whole*
[e] 164 b. c.

gladness; they offered a sacrifice of
deliverance and praise. 57 They dec-
orated the front of the temple with
golden crowns and small shields; they
restored the gates and the chambers
for the priests, and furnished them
with doors. 58 There was very great
gladness among the people, and the
reproach of the Gentiles was removed.
59 Then Judas and his brothers and
all the assembly of Israel determined
that every year at that season the days
of the dedication of the altar should
be observed with gladness and joy for
eight days, beginning with the twen-
ty-fifth day of the month of Chislev.
60 At that time they fortified Mount
Zion with high walls and strong tow-
ers round about, to keep the Gentiles
from coming and trampling them
down as they had done before. 61 And
he stationed a garrison there to hold
it. He also[a] fortified Beth-zur, so that
the people might have a stronghold
that faced Idume´a.

WARS WITH NEIGHBORING PEOPLES

5 When the Gentiles round about
heard that the altar had been built
and the sanctuary dedicated as it
was before, they became very an-
gry, 2 and they determined to destroy
the descendants of Jacob who lived
among them. So they began to kill
and destroy among the people. 3 But
Judas made war on the sons of Esau
in Idume´a, at Akrabatte´ne, because
they kept lying in wait for Israel. He
dealt them a heavy blow and humbled
them and despoiled them. 4 He also re-
membered the wickedness of the sons
of Baean, who were a trap and a snare
to the people and ambushed them on
the highways. 5 They were shut up by
him in their towers; and he encamp-
ed against them, vowed their com-
plete destruction, and burned with
fire their[b] towers and all who were
in them. 6 Then he crossed over to at-
tack the Am´monites, where he found
a strong band and many people with
Timothy as their leader. 7 He engaged
in many battles with them and they
were crushed before him; he struck
them down. 8 He also took Jazer and
its villages; then he returned to Judea.

LIBERATION OF GALILEAN JEWS

9 Now the Gentiles in Gil´ead gath-
ered together against the Israelites
who lived in their territory, and
planned to destroy them. But they fled
to the stronghold of Dath´ema, 10 and
sent to Judas and his brothers a let-
ter which said, "The Gentiles around
us have gathered together against us
to destroy us. 11 They are preparing to
come and capture the stronghold to
which we have fled, and Timothy is
leading their forces. 12 Now then come
and rescue us from their hands, for
many of us have fallen, 13 and all our
brethren who were in the land of Tob
have been killed; the enemy[c] have cap-
tured their wives and children and
goods, and have destroyed about a
thousand men there."
14 While the letter was still be-
ing read, behold, other messengers,
with their garments rent, came from
Galilee and made a similar report;
15 they said that against them had
gathered together men of Ptolema´is
and Tyre and Sidon, and all Galilee
of the Gentiles,[d] "to annihilate us."
16 When Judas and the people heard
these messages, a great assembly was
called to determine what they should
do for their brethren who were in
distress and were being attacked by
enemies.[e] 17 Then Judas said to Simon
his brother, "Choose your men and go
and rescue your brethren in Galilee;
I and Jonathan my brother will go to
Gil´ead." 18 But he left Joseph, the son
of Zechari´ah, and Azari´ah, a leader

[a] Gk adds *to hold it*
[b] Gk *her*
[c] Gk *they*
[d] Gk *aliens*
[e] Gk *them*

of the people, with the rest of the forc-
es, in Judea to guard it; 19and he gave
them this command, "Take charge of
this people, but do not engage in bat-
tle with the Gentiles until we return."
20Then three thousand men were as-
signed to Simon to go to Galilee, and
eight thousand to Judas for Gil´ead.

21 so Simon went to Galilee and
fought many battles against the
Gentiles, and the Gentiles were
crushed before him. 22He pursued
them to the gate of Ptolema´is, and
as many as three thousand of the
Gentiles fell, and he despoiled them.
23Then he took the Jews[f] of Galilee
and Arbat´ta, with their wives and
children, and all they possessed, and
led them to Judea with great rejoicing.

JUDAS AND JONATHAN IN GILEAD

24 Judas Maccabe´us and Jonathan
his brother crossed the Jordan and
went three days' journey into the
wilderness. 25They encountered the
Nabate´ans, who met them peaceably
and told them all that had happened
to their brethren in Gil´ead: 26"Many
of them have been shut up in Bozrah
and Bosor, in Al´ema and Chaspho,
Maked and Car´naim"—all these cit-
ies were strong and large—27"and
some have been shut up in the other
cities of Gil´ead; the enemy[g] are get-
ting ready to attack the strongholds
tomorrow and take and destroy all
these men in one day."

28 Then Judas and his rmy quick-
ly turned back by the wild·rness road
to Bozrah; and he took th city, and
killed every male by the e·ge of the
sword; then he seized all its ·poils and
burned it with fire. 29He dep··ed from
there at night, and they we· all the
way to the stronghold of Da´ema.[h]
30At dawn they looked up, an· ·ehold,
a large company, that could ·ot be
counted, carrying ladders and ·gines
of war to capture the stronghold, and
attacking the Jews within.[i] 31So Judas
saw that the battle had begun and that
the cry of the city went up to Heaven
with trumpets and loud shouts, 32and
he said to the men of his forces, "Fight
today for your brethren!" 33Then he
came up behind them in three com-
panies, who sounded their trumpets
and cried aloud in prayer. 34And when
the army of Timothy realized that it
was Maccabe´us, they fled before him,
and he dealt them a heavy blow. As
many as eight thousand of them fell
that day.

35 Next he turned aside to
Al´ema,[j]* and fought against it and
took it; and he killed every male in it,
plundered it, and burned it with fire.
36From there he marched on and took
Chaspho, Maked, and Bosor, and the
other cities of Gil´ead.

37 After these things Timothy
gathered another army and encamped
opposite Raphon, on the other side
of the stream. 38Judas sent men to
spy out the camp, and they reported
to him, "All the Gentiles around us
have gathered to him; it is a very large
force. 39They also have hired Arabs
to help them, and they are encamped
across the stream, ready to come and
fight against you." And Judas went to
meet them.

40 Now as Judas and his army
drew near to the stream of water,
Timothy said to the officers of his
forces, "If he crosses over to us first,
we will not be able to resist him, for
he will surely defeat us. 41But if he
shows fear and camps on the other
side of the river, we will cross over
to him and defeat him." 42When Judas
approached the stream of water, he
stationed the scribes of the people at
the stream and gave them this com-
mand, "Permit no man to encamp,
but make them all enter the battle."

[f] Gk *those*
[g] Gk *they*
[h] Greek lacks *of Dathema*. See verse 9
[i] Gk *and they were attacking them*
[j] The name is uncertain

43 Then he crossed over against them
first, and the whole army followed
him. All the Gentiles were defeat-
ed before him, and they threw away
their arms and fled into the sacred
precincts at Car´naim. 44 But he took
the city and burned the sacred pre-
cincts with fire, together with all
who were in them. Thus Car´naim
was conquered; they could stand be-
fore Judas no longer.

THE RETURN TO JERUSALEM

45 Then Judas gathered togeth-
er all the Israelites in Gil´ead, the
small and the great, with their
wives and children and goods, a very
large company, to go to the land of
Judah. 46 So they came to Ephron.
This was a large and very strong city
on the road, and they could not go
round it to the right or to the left;
they had to go through it. 47 But the
men of the city shut them out and
blocked up the gates with stones.
48 And Judas sent them this friendly
message, "Let us pass through your
land to get to our land. No one will
do you harm; we will simply pass by
on foot." But they refused to open
to him. 49 Then Judas ordered proc-
lamation to be made to the army
that each should encamp where he
was. 50 So the men of the forces en-
camped, and he fought against the
city all that day and all the night,
and the city was delivered into his
hands. 51 He destroyed every male by
the edge of the sword, and razed and
plundered the city. Then he passed
through the city over the slain.

52 And they crossed the Jordan
into the large plain before Beth-shan.
53 And Judas kept rallying the laggards
and encouraging the people all the
way till he came to the land of Judah.
54 So they went up to Mount Zion with
gladness and joy, and offered burnt
offerings, because not one of them
had fallen before they returned in
safety.

JOSEPH AND AZARIAH DEFEATED

55 Now while Judas and Jonathan
were in Gil´ead and Simon his broth-
er was in Galilee before Ptolema´is,
56 Joseph, the son of Zechari´ah, and
Azari´ah, the commanders of the
forces, heard of their brave deeds
and of the heroic war they had
fought. 57 So they said, "Let us also
make a name for ourselves; let us
go and make war on the Gentiles
around us." 58 And they issued orders
to the men of the forces that were
with them, and they marched against
Jam´nia. 59 And Gor´gias and his men
came out of the city to meet them in
battle. 60 Then Joseph and Azari´ah
were routed, and were pursued to
the borders of Judea; as many as two
thousand of the people of Israel fell
that day. 61 Thus the people suffered
a great rout because, thinking to do
a brave deed, they did not listen to
Judas and his brothers. 62 But they did
not belong to the family of those men
through whom deliverance was given
to Israel.

63 The man Judas and his broth-
ers were greatly honored in all Israel
and among all the Gentiles, wherever
their name was heard. 64 Men gathered
to them and praised them.

SUCCESS AT HEBRON AND PHILISTIA

65 Then Judas and his brothers
went forth and fought the sons of Esau
in the land to the south. He struck
Hebron and its villages and tore down
its strongholds and burned its towers
round about. 66 Then he marched off
to go into the land of the Philistines,
and passed through Mar´isa.[a]* 67 On
that day some priests, who wished
to do a brave deed, fell in battle, for
they went out to battle unwisely. 68 But
Judas turned aside to Azo´tus in the
land of the Philistines;* he tore down
their altars, and the graven images
of their gods he burned with fire; he
plundered the cities and returned to
the land of Judah.

[a] Other authorities read *Samaria*

THE LAST DAYS OF ANTIOCHUS EPIPHANES

6 King Anti´ochus was going through
the upper provinces when he heard
that Elyma´is in Persia was a city
famed for its wealth in silver and gold.
2Its temple was very rich, contain-
ing golden shields, breastplates, and
weapons left there by Alexander, the
son of Philip, the Macedonian king
who first reigned over the Greeks.
3So he came and tried to take the city
and plunder it, but he could not, be-
cause his plan became known to the
men of the city 4and they withstood
him in battle. So he fled and in great
grief departed from there to return to
Babylon.

5 Then some one came to him in
Persia and reported that the armies
which had gone into the land of Judah
had been routed; 6that Lys´ias had
gone first with a strong force, but had
turned and fled before the Jews;[b] that
the Jews[c] had grown strong from the
arms, supplies, and abundant spoils
which they had taken from the armies
they had cut down; 7that they had torn
down the abomination which he had
erected upon the altar in Jerusalem;
and that they had surrounded the
sanctuary with high walls as before,
and also Beth-zur, his city.

8 When the king heard this news,
he was astounded and badly shaken.
He took to his bed and became sick
from grief, because things had not
turned out for him as he had planned.
9He lay there for many days, because
deep grief continually gripped him,
and he concluded that he was dying.
10So he called all his friends and said
to them, "Sleep departs from my eyes
and I am downhearted with worry. 11I
said to myself, 'To what distress I have
come! And into what a great flood I
now am plunged! For I was kind and
beloved in my power.' 12But now I re-
member the evils I did in Jerusalem.
I seized all her vessels of silver and
gold; and I sent to destroy the inhab-
itants of Judah without good reason.
13I know that it is because of this that
these evils have come upon me; and
behold, I am perishing of deep grief in
a strange land."

14 Then he called for Philip, one
of his friends, and made him ruler
over all his kingdom. 15He gave him
the crown and his robe and the sig-
net, that he might guide Anti´ochus
his son and bring him up to be king.
16Thus Anti´ochus the king died there
in the one hundred and forty-ninth
year.[d] 17And when Lys´ias learned
that the king was dead, he set up
Anti´ochus the king's[e] son to reign.
Lys´ias[f] had brought him up as a boy,
and he named him Eu´pator.

RENEWED ATTACKS FROM SYRIA

18 Now the men in the citadel kept
hemming Israel in around the sanc-
tuary. They were trying in every way
to harm them and strengthen the
Gentiles. 19So Judas decided to destroy
them, and assembled all the people
to besiege them. 20They gathered to-
gether and besieged the citadel[g] in the
one hundred and fiftieth year;[h] and he
built siege towers and other engines
of war. 21But some of the garrison es-
caped from the siege and some of the
ungodly Israelites joined them. 22They
went to the king and said, "How
long will you fail to do justice and to
avenge our brethren? 23We were happy
to serve your father, to live by what
he said and to follow his commands.
24For this reason the sons of our peo-
ple besieged the citadel[i] and became
hostile to us; moreover, they have put
to death as many of us as they have

[b] Gk *them*
[c] Gk *they*
[d] 163 b. c.
[e] Gk *his*
[f] Gk *he*
[g] Gk *it*
[h] 162 b. c.
[i] The Greek text underlying *the sons ... the citadel* is uncertain

caught, and they have seized our inheritances. 25And not against us alone have they stretched out their hands, but also against all the lands on their borders. 26And behold, today they have encamped against the citadel in Jerusalem to take it; they have fortified both the sanctuary and Beth-zur; 27and unless you quickly prevent them, they will do still greater things, and you will not be able to stop them."

28 The king was enraged when he heard this. He assembled all his friends, the commanders of his forces and those in authority.[a] 29And mercenary forces came to him from other kingdoms and from islands of the seas. 30The number of his forces was a hundred thousand foot soldiers, twenty thousand horsemen, and thirty-two elephants accustomed to war. 31They came through Idume´a and encamped against Beth-zur, and for many days they fought and built engines of war; but the Jews[b] sallied out and burned these with fire, and fought manfully.

THE BATTLE AT BETH-ZECHARIAH

32 Then Judas marched away from the citadel and encamped at Beth-zechari´ah, opposite the camp of the king. 33Early in the morning the king rose and took his army by a forced march along the road to Beth-zechari´ah, and his troops made ready for battle and sounded their trumpets. 34They showed the elephants the juice of grapes and mulberries, to arouse them for battle. 35And they distributed the beasts among the phalanxes; with each elephant they stationed a thousand men armed with coats of mail, and with brass helmets on their heads; and five hundred picked horsemen were assigned to each beast. 36These took their position beforehand wherever the beast *was; wherever it* went *they went* with it, and they never left it. 37And upon the elephants[c] were wooden towers, strong and covered; they were fastened upon each beast by special harness, and upon each were four[d] armed men who fought from there, and also its Indian driver. 38The rest of the horsemen were stationed on either side, on the two flanks of the army, to harass the enemy while being themselves protected by the phalanxes. 39When the sun shone upon the shields of gold and brass, the hills were ablaze with them and gleamed like flaming torches.

40 Now a part of the king's army was spread out on the high hills, and some troops were on the plain, and they advanced steadily and in good order. 41All who heard the noise made by their multitude, by the marching of the multitude and the clanking of their arms, trembled, for the army was very large and strong. 42But Judas and his army advanced to the battle, and six hundred men of the king's army fell. 43And Elea´zar, called Av´aran, saw that one of the beasts was equipped with royal armor. It was taller than all the others, and he supposed that the king was upon it. 44So he gave his life to save his people and to win for himself an everlasting name. 45He courageously ran into the midst of the phalanx to reach it; he killed men right and left, and they parted before him on both sides. 46He got under the elephant, stabbed it from beneath, and killed it; but it fell to the ground upon him and there he died. 47And when the Jews[e] saw the royal might and the fierce attack of the forces, they turned away in flight.

THE SIEGE OF THE TEMPLE

48 The soldiers of the king's army *went up* to Jerusalem against them, and the king encamped in Judea and at Mount Zion. 49He made peace with the

[a] Gk *those over the reins*
[b] Gk *they*
[c] Gk *them*
[d] Cn: Some authorities read *thirty*; others *thirty-two*
[e] Gk *they*

men of Beth-zur, and they evacuated
the city, because they had no provi-
sions there to withstand a siege, since
it was a sabbatical year for the land.
50So the king took Beth-zur and sta-
tioned a guard there to hold it. 51Then
he encamped before the sanctuary for
many days. He set up siege towers, en-
gines of war to throw fire and stones,
machines to shoot arrows, and cata-
pults. 52The Jews[f] also made engines
of war to match theirs, and fought for
many days. 53But they had no food in
storage,[g] because it was the seventh
year; those who found safety in Judea
from the Gentiles had consumed the
last of the stores. 54Few men were left
in the sanctuary, because famine had
prevailed over the rest and they had
been scattered, each to his own place.

SYRIA OFFERS TERMS

55 Then Lys´ias heard that Philip,
whom King Anti´ochus while still
living had appointed to bring up
Anti´ochus his son to be king, 56had
returned from Persia and Media with
the forces that had gone with the king,
and that he was trying to seize control
of the government. 57So he quickly
gave orders to depart, and said to the
king, to the commanders of the forc-
es, and to the men, "We daily grow
weaker, our food supply is scant, the
place against which we are fighting is
strong, and the affairs of the kingdom
press urgently upon us. 58Now then let
us come to terms with these men, and
make peace with them and with all
their nation, 59and agree to let them
live by their laws as they did before;
for it was on account of their laws
which we abolished that they became
angry and did all these things."

60 The speech pleased the king
and the commanders, and he sent to
the Jews[h] an offer of peace, and they
accepted it. 61So the king and the
commanders gave them their oath.
On these conditions the Jews[i] evacu-
ated the stronghold. 62But when the
king entered Mount Zion and saw
what a strong fortress the place was,
he broke the oath he had sworn and
gave orders to tear down the wall all
around. 63Then he departed with haste
and returned to Antioch. He found
Philip in control of the city, but he
fought against him, and took the city
by force.

EXPEDITION OF BACCHIDES AND ALCIMUS

7 In the one hundred and fifty-first
year[j] Deme´trius the son of Seleu´cus
set forth from Rome, sailed with a few
men to a city by the sea, and there be-
gan to reign. 2As he was entering the
royal palace of his fathers, the army
seized Anti´ochus and Lys´ias to bring
them to him. 3But when this act be-
came known to him, he said, "Do not
let me see their faces!" 4So the army
killed them, and Deme´trius took his
seat upon the throne of his kingdom.

5 Then there came to him all the
lawless and ungodly men of Israel;
they were led by Al´cimus, who want-
ed to be high priest. 6And they brought
to the king this accusation against the
people: "Judas and his brothers have
destroyed all your friends, and have
driven us out of our land. 7Now then
send a man whom you trust; let him
go and see all the ruin which Judas[k]
has brought upon us and upon the
land of the king, and let him punish
them and all who help them."

8 So the king chose Bac´chides, one
of the king's friends, governor of the
province Beyond the River; he was a
great man in the kingdom and was
faithful to the king. 9And he sent him,
and with him the ungodly Al´cimus,
whom he made high priest; and he

[f] Gk *they*
[g] Other authorities read *in the sanctuary*
[h] Gk *them*
[i] Gk *they*
[j] 161 b. c.
[k] Gk *he*

commanded him to take vengeance on
the sons of Israel. 10 So they marched
away and came with a large force into
the land of Judah; and he sent mes-
sengers to Judas and his brothers with
peaceable but treacherous words.
11 But they paid no attention to their
words, for they saw that they had
come with a large force.

12 Then a group of scribes ap-
peared in a body before Al´cimus and
Bac´chides to ask for just terms. 13 The
Haside´ans were first among the sons
of Israel to seek peace from them,
14 for they said, "A priest of the line of
Aaron has come with the army, and
he will not harm us." 15 And he spoke
peaceable words to them and swore
this oath to them, "We will not seek
to injure you or your friends." 16 So
they trusted him; but he seized sixty
of them and killed them in one day, in
accordance with the word which was
written,

17 "The flesh of thy saints and
their blood
they poured out round about
Jerusalem,
and there was none to bury
them."

18 Then the fear and dread of them
fell upon all the people, for they said,
"There is no truth or justice in them,
for they have violated the agreement
and the oath which they swore."

19 Then Bac´chides departed from
Jerusalem and encamped in Beth-
zaith. And he sent and seized many
of the men who had deserted to him,[a]
and some of the people, and killed
them and threw them into the great
pit. 20 He placed Al´cimus in charge of
the country and left with him a force
to help him; then Bac´chides went
back to the king.

21 Al´cimus strove for the high
priesthood, 22 and all who were trou-
bling their people joined him. They
gained control of the land of Judah
and did great damage in Israel. 23 And
Judas saw all the evil that Al´cimus
and those with him had done among
the sons of Israel; it was more than
the Gentiles had done. 24 So Judas[b]
went out into all the surrounding
parts of Judea, and took vengeance
on the men who had deserted, and he
prevented those in the city[c] from going
out into the country. 25 When Al´cimus
saw that Judas and those with him
had grown strong, and realized that
he could not withstand them, he re-
turned to the king and brought wick-
ed charges against them.

NICANOR IN JUDEA

26 Then the king sent Nica´nor,
one of his honored princes, who
hated and detested Israel, and he
commanded him to destroy the peo-
ple. 27 So Nica´nor came to Jerusalem
with a large force, and treacherously
sent to Judas and his brothers this
peaceable message, 28 "Let there be
no fighting between me and you; I
shall come with a few men to see you
face to face in peace." 29 So he came to
Judas, and they greeted one another
peaceably. But the enemy were ready
to seize Judas. 30 It became known to
Judas that Nica´nor[d] had come to him
with treacherous intent, and he was
afraid of him and would not meet
him again. 31 When Nica´nor learned
that his plan had been disclosed, he
went out to meet Judas in battle near
Capharsal´ama. 32 About five hundred
men of the army of Nica´nor fell, and
the rest[e] fled into the city of David.

NICANOR THREATENS THE TEMPLE

33 After these events Nica´nor went
up to Mount Zion. Some of the priests
came out of the sanctuary, and some
of the elders of the people, to greet
him peaceably and to show him the

[a] Or *many of his men who had deserted*
[b] Gk *he*
[c] Gk *they were prevented*
[d] Gk *he*
[e] Gk *they*

burnt offering that was being offered
for the king. 34But he mocked them
and derided them and defiled them
and spoke arrogantly, 35and in anger
he swore this oath, "Unless Judas and
his army are delivered into my hands
this time, then if I return safely I will
burn up this house." And he went out
in great anger. 36Then the priests went
in and stood before the altar and the
temple, and they wept and said,

37"Thou didst choose this house
to be called by thy name,
and to be for thy people a
house of prayer and
supplication.
38Take vengeance on this man and
on his army,
and let them fall by the
sword;
remember their blasphemies,
and let them live no longer."

THE DEATH OF NICANOR

39 Now Nica´nor went out from
Jerusalem and encamped in Beth-
hor´on, and the Syrian army joined
him. 40And Judas encamped in Ad´asa
with three thousand men. Then Judas
prayed and said, 41"When the messen-
gers from the king spoke blasphemy,
thy angel went forth and struck down
one hundred and eighty-five thousand
of the Assyrians.[f] 42So also crush this
army before us today; let the rest learn
that Nica´nor[g] has spoken wickedly
against thy sanctuary, and judge him
according to this wickedness." 43So
the armies met in battle on the thir-
teenth day of the month of Adar. The
army of Nica´nor was crushed, and he
himself was the first to fall in the bat-
tle. 44When his army saw that Nica´nor
had fallen, they threw down their
arms and fled. 45The Jews[h] pursued
them a day's journey, from Ad´asa as
far as Gazar´a, and as they followed
kept sounding the battle call on the
trumpets. 46And men came out of all
the villages of Judea round about,
and they out-flanked the enemy[i] and
drove them back to their pursuers,[j]
so that they all fell by the sword; not
even one of them was left. 47Then the
Jews[k] seized the spoils and the plun-
der, and they cut off Nica´nor's head
and the right hand which he had so
arrogantly stretched out, and brought
them and displayed them just out-
side Jerusalem. 48The people rejoiced
greatly and celebrated that day as a
day of great gladness. 49And they de-
creed that this day should be celebrat-
ed each year on the thirteenth day of
Adar. 50So the land of Judah had rest
for a few days.

A EULOGY OF THE ROMANS

8 Now Judas heard of the fame of
the Romans, that they were very
strong and were well-disposed to-
ward all who made an alliance with
them, that they pledged friendship to
those who came to them, 2and that
they were very strong. Men told him
of their wars and of the brave deeds
which they were doing among the
Gauls, how they had defeated them
and forced them to pay tribute, 3and
what they had done in the land of
Spain to get control of the silver and
gold mines there, 4and how they had
gained control of the whole region
by their planning and patience, even
though the place was far distant from
them. They also subdued the kings
who came against them from the ends
of the earth, until they crushed them
and inflicted great disaster upon
them; the rest paid them tribute every
year. 5Philip, and Per´seus king of the
Macedonians,[l] and the others who
rose up against them, they crushed
in battle and conquered. 6They also

[f] Gk *of them*
[g] Gk *he*
[h] Gk *they*
[i] Gk *them*
[j] Gk *these*
[k] Gk *they*
[l] Or *Kittim*

defeated Anti´ochus the Great, king of Asia, who went to fight against them with a hundred and twenty elephants and with cavalry and chariots and a very large army. He was crushed by them; 7 they took him alive and decreed that he and those who should reign after him should pay a heavy tribute and give hostages and surrender some of their best provinces, 8 the country of India and Media and Lydia. These they took from him and gave to Eu´menes the king. 9 The Greeks planned to come and destroy them, 10 but this became known to them, and they sent a general against the Greeks[a] and attacked them. Many of them were wounded and fell, and the Romans[b] took captive their wives and children; they plundered them, conquered the land, tore down their strongholds, and enslaved them to this day. 11 The remaining kingdoms and islands, as many as ever opposed them, they destroyed and enslaved; 12 but with their friends and those who rely on them they have kept friendship. They have subdued kings far and near, and as many as have heard of their fame have feared them. 13 Those whom they wish to help and to make kings, they make kings, and those whom they wish they depose; and they have been greatly exalted. 14 Yet for all this not one of them has put on a crown or worn purple as a mark of pride, 15 but they have built for themselves a senate chamber, and every day three hundred and twenty senators constantly deliberate concerning the people, to govern them well. 16 They trust one man each year to rule over them and to control all their land; they all heed the one man, and there is no envy or jealousy among them.

AN ALLIANCE WITH ROME

17 So Judas chose Eupol´emus the son of John, son of Accos, and Jason the son of Elea´zar, and sent them to Rome to establish friendship and alliance, 18 and to free themselves from the yoke; for they saw that the kingdom of the Greeks was completely enslaving Israel. 19 They went to Rome, a very long journey; and they entered the senate chamber and spoke as follows: 20 "Judas, who is also called Maccabe´us, and his brothers and the people of the Jews have sent us to you to establish alliance and peace with you, that we may be enrolled as your allies and friends." 21 The proposal pleased them, 22 and this is a copy of the letter which they wrote in reply, on bronze tablets, and sent to Jerusalem to remain with them there as a memorial of peace and alliance:

23 "May all go well with the Romans and with the nation of the Jews at sea and on land for ever, and may sword and enemy be far from them. 24 If war comes first to Rome or to any of their allies in all their dominion, 25 the nation of the Jews shall act as their allies wholeheartedly, as the occasion may indicate to them. 26 And to the enemy who makes war they shall not give or supply grain, arms, money, or ships, as Rome has decided; and they shall keep their obligations without receiving any return. 27 In the same way, if war comes first to the nation of the Jews, the Romans shall willingly act as their allies, as the occasion may indicate to them. 28 And to the enemy allies shall be given no grain, arms, money, or ships, as Rome has decided; and they shall keep these obligations and do so without deceit. 29 Thus on these terms the Romans make a treaty with the Jewish people. 30 If after these terms are in effect both parties shall determine to add or delete anything, they shall do so at their discretion, and any addition or deletion that they may make shall be valid.

31 "And concerning the wrongs

[a] Gk *them*
[b] Gk *they*

which King Deme´trius is doing to
them we have written to him as fol-
lows, 'Why have you made your yoke
heavy upon our friends and allies the
Jews? 32If now they appeal again for
help against you, we will defend their
rights and fight you on sea and on
land.'"

BACCHIDES RETURNS TO JUDEA

9 When Deme´trius heard that
Nica´nor and his army had fall-
en in battle, he sent Bac´chides and
Al´cimus into the land of Judah a
second time, and with them the right
wing of the army. 2They went by the
road which leads to Gilgal and en-
camped against Mes´aloth in Arbe´la,
and they took it and killed many peo-
ple. 3In the first month of the one
hundred and fifty-second year[c] they
encamped against Jerusalem; 4then
they marched off and went to Berea
with twenty thousand foot soldiers
and two thousand cavalry.

5 Now Judas was encamped in
El´asa, and with him were three thou-
sand picked men. 6When they saw
the huge number of the enemy forc-
es, they were greatly frightened, and
many slipped away from the camp,
until no more than eight hundred of
them were left.

7 When Judas saw that his army
had slipped away and the battle was
imminent, he was crushed in spirit,
for he had no time to assemble them.
8He became faint, but he said to those
who were left, "Let us rise and go up
against our enemies. We may be able
to *fight them*." 9But they tried to dis-
suade him, saying, "We are not able.
Let us rather save our own lives now,
and let us come back with our breth-
ren and fight them; we are too few."
10But Judas said, "Far be it from us to
do such a thing as to flee from them.
If our time has come, let us die bravely
for our brethren, and leave no cause to
question our honor."

THE LAST BATTLE OF JUDAS

11 Then the army of Bac´chides[d]
marched out from the camp and took
its stand for the encounter. The cav-
alry was divided into two companies,
and the slingers and the archers went
ahead of the army, as did all the chief
warriors. 12Bac´chides was on the right
wing. Flanked by the two companies,
the phalanx advanced to the sound of
the trumpets; and the men with Judas
also blew their trumpets. 13The earth
was shaken by the noise of the armies,
and the battle raged from morning till
evening.

14 Judas saw that Bac´chides and
the strength of his army were on the
right; then all the stouthearted men
went with him, 15and they crushed the
right wing, and he pursued them as
far as Mount Azo´tus. 16When those
on the left wing saw that the right
wing was crushed, they turned and
followed close behind Judas and his
men. 17The battle became desperate,
and many on both sides were wound-
ed and fell. 18Judas also fell, and the
rest fled.

19 Then Jonathan and Simon took
Judas their brother and buried him in
the tomb of their fathers at Mo´de-
in, 20and wept for him. And all Israel
made great lamentation for him; they
mourned many days and said, 21"How
is the mighty fallen,
the savior of Israel!"

22Now the rest of the acts of Judas,
and his wars and the brave deeds
that he did, and his greatness, have
not been recorded, for they were very
many.

JONATHAN SUCCEEDS JUDAS

23 After the death of Judas, the
lawless emerged in all parts of Israel;
all the doers of injustice appeared.
24In those days a very great famine oc-
curred, and the country deserted with
them to the enemy. 25And Bac´chides
chose the ungodly and put them in

[c]160 b. c.
[d]Gk *the army*

charge of the country. 26 They sought
and searched for the friends of Judas,
and brought them to Bac´chides, and
he took vengeance on them and made
sport of them. 27 Thus there was great
distress in Israel, such as had not been
since the time that prophets ceased to
appear among them.

28 Then all the friends of Judas as-
sembled and said to Jonathan, 29 "Since
the death of your brother Judas there
has been no one like him to go against
our enemies and Bac´chides, and to
deal with those of our nation who
hate us. 30 So now we have chosen you
today to take his place as our ruler
and leader, to fight our battle." 31 And
Jonathan at that time accepted the
leadership and took the place of Judas
his brother.

THE CAMPAIGNS OF JONATHAN

32 When Bac´chides learned
of this, he tried to kill him. 33 But
Jonathan and Simon his brother and
all who were with him heard of it, and
they fled into the wilderness of Teko´a
and camped by the water of the pool
of Asphar. 34 Bac´chides found this out
on the sabbath day, and he with all his
army crossed the Jordan.

35 And Jonathan[a] sent his brother
as leader of the multitude and begged
the Nabate´ans, who were his friends,
for permission to store with them the
great amount of baggage which they
had. 36 But the sons of Jambri from
Me´deba came out and seized John
and all that he had, and departed with
it.

37 After these things it was report-
ed to Jonathan and Simon his brother,
"The sons of Jambri are celebrating a
great wedding, and are conducting the
bride, a daughter of one of the great
nobles of Canaan, from Nad´abath*
with a large escort." 38 *And* they re-
membered the blood of John their
brother, and went up and hid under
cover of the mountain. 39 They raised
their eyes and looked, and saw a tu-
multuous procession with much bag-
gage; and the bridegroom came out
with his friends and his brothers to
meet them with tambourines and
musicians and many weapons. 40 Then
they rushed upon them from the am-
bush and began killing them. Many
were wounded and fell, and the rest
fled to the mountain; and they took
all their goods. 41 Thus the wedding
was turned into mourning and the
voice of their musicians into a funer-
al dirge. 42 And when they had fully
avenged the blood of their brother,
they returned to the marshes of the
Jordan.

43 When Bac´chides heard of
this, he came with a large force on
the sabbath day to the banks of the
Jordan. 44 And Jonathan said to those
with him, "Let us rise up now and
fight for our lives, for today things
are not as they were before. 45 For
look! the battle is in front of us and
behind us; the water of the Jordan is
on this side and on that, with marsh
and thicket; there is no place to turn.
46 Cry out now to Heaven that you may
be delivered from the hands of our
enemies." 47 So the battle began, and
Jonathan stretched out his hand to
strike Bac´chides, but he eluded him
and went to the rear. 48 Then Jonathan
and the men with him leaped into the
Jordan and swam across to the other
side, and the enemy[b] did not cross the
Jordan to attack them. 49 And about
one thousand of Bac´chides' men fell
that day.

BACCHIDES BUILDS FORTIFICATIONS

50 Bac´chides[c] then returned
to Jerusalem and built strong cit-
ies in Judea: the fortress in Jericho,
and Emma´us, and Beth-hor´on,
and Bethel, and Timnath, and[d]
Phar´athon, and Tephon, with high

[a] Gk *he*
[b] Gk *they*
[c] Gk *he*
[d] Some authorities omit *and*

walls and gates and bars. 51 And he
placed garrisons in them to harass
Israel. 52 He also fortified the city of
Beth-zur, and Gazar´a, and the cit-
adel, and in them he put troops and
stores of food. 53 And he took the sons
of the leading men of the land as hos-
tages and put them under guard in
the citadel at Jerusalem.

54 In the one hundred and fif-
ty-third year,[e] in the second month,
Al´cimus gave orders to tear down
the wall of the inner court of the
sanctuary. He tore down the work of
the prophets! 55 But he only began to
tear it down, for at that time Al´cimus
was stricken and his work was hin-
dered; his mouth was stopped and
he was paralyzed, so that he could no
longer say a word or give commands
concerning his house. 56 And Al´cimus
died at that time in great agony.
57 When Bac´chides saw that Al´cimus
was dead, he returned to the king,
and the land of Judah had rest for two
years.

THE END OF THE WAR

58 Then all the lawless plotted and
said, "See! Jonathan and his men are
living in quiet and confidence. So now
let us bring Bac´chides back, and he
will capture them all in one night."
59 And they went and consulted with
him. 60 He started to come with a large
force, and secretly sent letters to all
his allies in Judea, telling them to
seize Jonathan and his men; but they
were unable to do it, because their
plan became known. 61 And Jonathan's
men[f] seized about fifty of the men of
the country who were leaders in this
treachery, and killed them.

62 Then Jonathan with his men,
and Simon, withdrew to Beth-ba´si in
the wilderness; he rebuilt the parts
of it that had been demolished, and
they fortified it. 63 When Bac´chides
learned of this, he assembled all his
forces, and sent orders to the men of
Judea. 64 Then he came and encamped
against Beth-ba´si; he fought against
it for many days and made machines
of war.

65 But Jonathan left Simon his
brother in the city, while he went
out into the country; and he went
with only a few men. 66 He struck
down Odome´ra and his brothers and
the sons of Phasi´ron in their tents.
67 Then he[g] began to attack and went
into battle with his forces; and Simon
and his men sallied out from the city
and set fire to the machines of war.
68 They fought with Bac´chides, and
he was crushed by them. They dis-
tressed him greatly, for his plan and
his expedition had been in vain. 69 So
he was greatly enraged at the lawless
men who had counseled him to come
into the country, and he killed many
of them. Then he decided to depart to
his own land.

70 When Jonathan learned of this,
he sent ambassadors to him to make
peace with him and obtain release of
the captives. 71 He agreed, and did as
he said; and he swore to Jonathan[h]
that he would not try to harm him as
long as he lived. 72 He restored to him
the captives whom he had formerly
taken from the land of Judah; then he
turned and departed to his own land,
and came no more into their territory.
73 Thus the sword ceased from Israel.
And Jonathan dwelt in Michmash.
And Jonathan began to judge the peo-
ple, and he destroyed the ungodly out
of Israel.

REVOLT OF ALEXANDER EPIPHANES

10 In the one hundred and sixtieth
year[i] Alexander Epiph´anes, the
son of Anti´ochus, landed and oc-
cupied Ptolema´is. They welcomed
him, and there he began to reign.

[e] 159 b. c.
[f] Gk *they*
[g] Other authorities read *they*
[h] Gk *him*
[i] 152 b. c.

2 When Deme´trius the king heard of
it, he assembled a very large army and
marched out to meet him in battle.
3 And Deme´trius sent Jonathan a let-
ter in peaceable words to honor him;
4 for he said, "Let us act first to make
peace with him[a] before he makes
peace with Alexander against us,
5 for he will remember all the wrongs
which we did to him and to his broth-
ers and his nation." 6 So Deme´trius[b]
gave him authority to recruit troops,
to equip them with arms, and to be-
come his ally; and he commanded that
the hostages in the citadel should be
released to him.

7 Then Jonathan came to Jerusalem
and read the letter in the hearing of
all the people and of the men in the
citadel. 8 They were greatly alarmed
when they heard that the king had
given him authority to recruit troops.
9 But the men in the citadel released
the hostages to Jonathan, and he re-
turned them to their parents.

10 And Jonathan dwelt in Jerusalem
and began to rebuild and restore the
city. 11 He directed those who were
doing the work to build the walls and
encircle Mount Zion with squared
stones, for better fortification; and
they did so.

12 Then the foreigners who were
in the strongholds that Bac´chides
had built fled; 13 each left his place
and departed to his own land. 14 Only
in Beth-zur did some remain who
had forsaken the law and the com-
mandments, for it served as a place
of refuge.

15 Now Alexander the king heard
of all the promises which Deme´trius
had sent to Jonathan, and men told
him of the battles that Jonathan[c] and
his brothers had fought, of the brave
deeds that they had done, and of the
troubles that they had endured. 16 So
he said, "Shall we find another such
man? Come now, we will make him
our friend and ally." 17 And he wrote a
letter and sent it to him, in the follow-
ing words:

JONATHAN BECOMES HIGH PRIEST

18 "King Alexander to his brother
Jonathan, greeting. 19 We have heard
about you, that you are a mighty
warrior and worthy to be our friend.
20 And so we have appointed you to-
day to be the high priest of your na-
tion; you are to be called the king's
friend" (and he sent him a purple
robe and a golden crown) "and you
are to take our side and keep friend-
ship with us."

21 So Jonathan put on the holy
garments in the seventh month of the
one hundred and sixtieth year,[d] at the
feast of tabernacles, and he recruited
troops and equipped them with arms
in abundance. 22 When Deme´trius
heard of these things he was grieved
and said, 23 "What is this that we have
done? Alexander has gotten ahead of
us in forming a friendship with the
Jews to strengthen himself. 24 I also
will write them words of encourage-
ment and promise them honor and
gifts, that I may have their help." 25 So
he sent a message to them in the fol-
lowing words:

A LETTER FROM DEMETRIUS TO JONATHAN

"King Deme´trius to the nation of
the Jews, greeting. 26 Since you have
kept your agreement with us and have
continued your friendship with us,
and have not sided with our enemies,
we have heard of it and rejoiced. 27 And
now continue still to keep faith with
us, and we will repay you with good
for what you do for us. 28 We will grant
you many immunities and give you
gifts.

29 "And now I free you and exempt
all the Jews from payment of tribute
and salt tax and crown levies, 30 and
instead of collecting the third of the

[a] Gk *them*
[b] Gk *he*
[c] Gk *he*
[d] 152 b. c.

grain and the half of the fruit of the trees that I should receive, I release them from this day and henceforth. I will not collect them from the land of Judah or from the three districts added to it from Samar´ia and Galilee, from this day and for all time. 31And let Jerusalem and her environs, her tithes and her revenues, be holy and free from tax. 32I release also my control of the citadel in Jerusalem and give it to the high priest, that he may station in it men of his own choice to guard it. 33And every one of the Jews taken as a captive from the land of Judah into any part of my kingdom, I set free without payment; and let all officials cancel also the taxes on their cattle.

34 "And all the feasts and sabbaths and new moons and appointed days, and the three days before a feast and the three after a feast—let them all be days of immunity and release for all the Jews who are in my kingdom. 35No one shall have authority to exact anything from them or annoy any of them about any matter.

36 "Let Jews be enrolled in the king's forces to the number of thirty thousand men, and let the maintenance be given them that is due to all the forces of the king. 37Let some of them be stationed in the great strongholds of the king, and let some of them be put in positions of trust in the kingdom. Let their officers and leaders be of their own number, and let them live by their own laws, just as the king has commande in the land *of Judah.*

38 "As for the three istricts that have been added to Juda from the country of Samar´ia, let hem be so annexed to Judea that theare considered to be under one rul and obey no other authority but theigh priest. 39Ptolema´is and the land ljoining it I have given as a gift to the sanctuary in Jerusalem, to meet the necessary expenses of the sanctuary. 40I also grant fifteen thousand shekels of silver yearly out of the king's revenues from appropriate places. 41And all the additional funds which the government officials have not paid as they did in the first years,[e] they shall give from now on for the service of the temple.[f] 42Moreover, the five thousand shekels of silver which my officials[g] have received every year from the income of the services of the temple, this too is canceled, because it belongs to the priests who minister there. 43And whoever takes refuge at the temple in Jerusalem, or in any of its precincts, because he owes money to the king or has any debt, let him be released and receive back all his property in my kingdom.

44 "Let the cost of rebuilding and restoring the structures of the sanctuary be paid from the revenues of the king. 45And let the cost of rebuilding the walls of Jerusalem and fortifying it round about, and the cost of rebuilding the walls in Judea, also be paid from the revenues of the king."

DEATH OF DEMETRIUS

46 When Jonathan and the people heard these words, they did not believe or accept them, because they remembered the great wrongs which Deme´trius[h] had done in Israel and how he had greatly oppressed them. 47They favored Alexander, because he had been the first to speak peaceable words to them, and they remained his allies all his days.

48 Now Alexander the king assembled large forces and encamped opposite Deme´trius. 49The two kings met in battle, and the army of Deme´trius fled, and Alexander[i] pursued him and defeated them. 50He pressed the

[e]The Greek text of this verse iuncertain
[f]Gk *house*
[g]Gk *they*
[h]Gk *he*
[i]Other authorities read *Alexarr fled, and Demetrius*

battle strongly until the sun set, and
Deme´trius fell on that day.

TREATY OF PTOLEMY AND ALEXANDER

51 Then Alexander sent ambassa-
dors to Ptol´emy king of Egypt with
the following message: **52**"Since I have
returned to my kingdom and have
taken my seat on the throne of my
fathers, and established my rule—for
I crushed Deme´trius and gained con-
trol of our country; **53**I met him in bat-
tle, and he and his army were crushed
by us, and we have taken our seat on
the throne of his kingdom— **54**now
therefore let us establish friendship
with one another; give me now your
daughter as my wife, and I will be-
come your son-in-law, and will make
gifts to you and to her in keeping with
your position."

55 Ptol´emy the king replied and
said, "Happy was the day on which
you returned to the land of your fa-
thers and took your seat on the throne
of their kingdom. **56**And now I will do
for you as you wrote, but meet me at
Ptolema´is, so that we may see one
another, and I will become your fa-
ther-in-law, as you have said."

57 So Ptol´emy set out from Egypt,
he and Cleopatra his daughter, and
came to Ptolema´is in the one hundred
and sixty-second year.[a] **58**Alexander
the king met him, and Ptol´emy[b] gave
him Cleopatra his daughter in mar-
riage, and celebrated her wedding at
Ptolema´is with great pomp, as kings
do.

59 Then Alexander the king wrote
to Jonathan to come to meet him. **60**So
he went with pomp to Ptolema´is
and met the two kings; he gave them
and their friends silver and gold and
many gifts, and found favor with
them. **61**A group of pestilent men from
Israel, lawless men, gathered togeth-
er against him to accuse him; but the
king paid no attention to them. **62**The
king gave orders to take off Jonathan's
garments and to clothe him in purple,
and they did so. **63**The king also seat-
ed him at his side; and he said to his
officers, "Go forth with him into the
middle of the city and proclaim that
no one is to bring charges against him
about any matter, and let no one an-
noy him for any reason." **64**And when
his accusers saw the honor that was
paid him, in accordance with the
proclamation, and saw him clothed in
purple, they all fled. **65**Thus the king
honored him and enrolled him among
his chief friends, and made him gener-
al and governor of the province. **66**And
Jonathan returned to Jerusalem in
peace and gladness.

APOLLONIUS IS DEFEATED BY JONATHAN

67 In the one hundred and six-
ty-fifth year[c] Deme´trius the son
of Deme´trius came from Crete
to the land of his fathers. **68**When
Alexander the king heard of it, he
was greatly grieved and returned
to Antioch. **69**And Deme´trius ap-
pointed Apollo´nius the governor of
Coelesyria, and he assembled a large
force and encamped against Jam´nia.
Then he sent the following message to
Jonathan the high priest:

70 "You are the only one to rise up
against us, and I have become a laugh-
ingstock and reproach because of you.
Why do you assume authority against
us in the hill country? **71**If you now
have confidence in your forces, come
down to the plain to meet us, and let
us match strength with each other
there, for I have with me the power of
the cities. **72**Ask and learn who I am
and who the others are that are help-
ing us. Men will tell you that you can-
not stand before us, for your fathers
were twice *put to flight* in their own
land. **73**And now you will not be able
to withstand my cavalry and such an
army in the plain, where there is no
stone or pebble, or place to flee."

74 When Jonathan heard the

[a] 150 b. c.
[b] Gk *he*
[c] 147 b. c.

words of Apollo´nius, his spirit was
aroused. He chose ten thousand
men and set out from Jerusalem, and
Simon his brother met him to help
him. 75He encamped before Joppa,
but the men of the city closed its
gates, for Apollo´nius had a garrison
in Joppa. 76So they fought against it,
and the men of the city became afraid
and opened the gates, and Jonathan
gained possession of Joppa.

77 When Apollo´nius heard of it, he
mustered three thousand cavalry and
a large army, and went to Azo´tus as
though he were going farther. At the
same time he advanced into the plain,
for he had a large troop of cavalry and
put confidence in it. 78Jonathan[d] pur-
sued him to Azo´tus, and the armies
engaged in battle. 79Now Apollo´nius
had secretly left a thousand cavalry
behind them. 80Jonathan learned that
there was an ambush behind him, for
they surrounded his army and shot
arrows at his men from early morning
till late afternoon. 81But his men stood
fast, as Jonathan commanded, and the
enemy's[e] horses grew tired.

82 Then Simon brought forward
his force and engaged the phalanx in
battle (for the cavalry was exhausted);
they were overwhelmed by him and
fled, 83and the cavalry was dispersed
in the plain. They fled to Azo´tus and
entered Beth-da´gon, the temple of
their idol, for safety. 84But Jonathan
burned Azo´tus and the surrounding
towns and plundered them; and the
temple of Dagon, and those who had
taken refuge in it he burned with fire.
85The number of those who fell by the
sword, with those burned alive, came
to eight thousand men.

86 Then Jonathan departed from
there and encamped against As´kalon,
and the men of the city came out to
meet him with great pomp. 87And
Jonathan and those with him returned
to Jerusalem with much booty. 88When
Alexander the king heard of these
things, he honored Jonathan still
more; 89and he sent to him a golden
buckle, such as it is the custom to give
to the kinsmen of kings. He also gave
him Ekron and all its environs as his
possession.

PTOLEMY INVADES SYRIA

11 Then the king of Egypt gathered
great forces, like the sand by the
seashore, and many ships; and he
tried to get possession of Alexander's
kingdom by trickery and add it to his
own kingdom. 2He set out for Syria
with peaceable words, and the people
of the cities opened their gates to him
and went to meet him, for Alexander
the king had commanded them to
meet him, since he was Alexander's[f]
father-in-law. 3But when Ptol´emy en-
tered the cities he stationed forces as
a garrison in each city.

4 When he[g] approached Azo´tus,
they showed him the temple of Dagon
burned down, and Azo´tus and its
suburbs destroyed, and the corpses
lying about, and the charred bodies
of those whom Jonathan[h] had burned
in the war, for they had piled them in
heaps along his route. 5They also told
the king what Jonathan had done, to
throw blame on him; but the king kept
silent. 6Jonathan met the king at Joppa
with pomp, and they greeted one an-
other and spent the night there. 7And
Jonathan went with the king as far as
the river called Eleu´therus; then he
returned to Jerusalem.

8 So King Ptol´emy gained control
of the coastal cities as far as Seleu´cia
by the sea, and he kept devising evil
designs against Alexander. 9He sent
envoys to Deme´trius the king, say-
ing, "Come, let us make a covenant
with each other, and I will give you
in marriage my daughter who was

[d] Gk *he*
[e] Gk *their*
[f] Gk *his*
[g] Other ancient authorities read *they*
[h] Gk *he*

Alexander's wife, and you shall reign
over your father's kingdom. 10For I
now regret that I gave him my daugh-
ter, for he has tried to kill me." 11He
threw blame on Alexander[a] because
he coveted his kingdom. 12So he took
his daughter away from him and gave
her to Deme´trius. He was estranged
from Alexander, and their enmity be-
came manifest.

13 Then Ptol´emy entered Antioch
and put on the crown of Asia. Thus
he put two crowns upon his head, the
crown of Egypt and that of Asia. 14Now
Alexander the king was in Cili´cia at
that time, because the people of that
region were in revolt. 15And Alexander
heard of it and came against him in
battle. Ptol´emy marched out and
met him with a strong force, and put
him to flight. 16So Alexander fled into
Arabia to find protection there, and
King Ptol´emy was exalted. 17And
Zab´diel the Arab cut off the head
of Alexander and sent it to Ptol´emy.
18But King Ptol´emy died three days
later, and his troops in the strong-
holds were killed by the inhabitants
of the strongholds. 19So Deme´trius
became king in the one hundred and
sixty-seventh year.[b]

JONATHAN'S DIPLOMACY

20 In those days Jonathan assem-
bled the men of Judea to attack the
citadel in Jerusalem, and he built
many engines of war to use against
it. 21But certain lawless men who
hated their nation went to the king
and reported to him that Jonathan
was besieging the citadel. 22When he
heard this he was angry, and as soon
as he heard it he set out and came to
Ptolema´is; and he wrote Jonathan
not to continue the siege, but to meet
him for a conference at Ptolema´is as
quickly as possible.

23 When Jonathan heard this, he
gave orders to continue the siege;
and he chose some of the elders of
Israel and some of the priests, and
put himself in danger, 24for he went
to the king at Ptolema´is, taking sil-
ver and gold and clothing and numer-
ous other gifts. And he won his fa-
vor. 25Although certain lawless men
of his nation kept making complaints
against him, 26the king treated him
as his predecessors had treated him;
he exalted him in the presence of all
his friends. 27He confirmed him in
the high priesthood and in as many
other honors as he had formerly had,
and made him to be regarded as one
of his chief friends. 28Then Jonathan
asked the king to free Judea and the
three districts of Samar´ia[c] from
tribute, and promised him three hun-
dred talents. 29The king consented,
and wrote a letter to Jonathan about
all these things; its contents were as
follows:

30 "King Deme´trius to Jonathan
his brother and to the nation of the
Jews, greeting. 31This copy of the let-
ter which we wrote concerning you
to Las´thenes our kinsman we have
written to you also, so that you may
know what it says. 32'King Deme´trius
to Las´thenes his father, greeting. 33To
the nation of the Jews, who are our
friends and fulfil their obligations to
us, we have determined to do good,
because of the good will they show to-
ward us. 34We have confirmed as their
possession both the territory of Judea
and the three districts of Aphair´ema
and Lydda and Rath´amin; the latter,
with all the region bordering them,
were added to Judea from Samar´ia.
To all those who offer sacrifice in
Jerusalem, we have granted release
from[d] the royal taxes which the king
formerly received from them each
year, from the crops of the land and
the fruit of the trees. 35And the oth-
er payments henceforth due to us of
the tithes, and the taxes due to us,

[a] Gk *him*
[b] 145 b. c.
[c] Cn: Gk *the three districts and Samaria*
[d] Or *Samaria, for all those who offer sacrifice in Jerusalem, in place of*

and the salt pits and the crown tax-
es due to us—from all these we shall
grant them release. 36And not one of
these grants shall be canceled from
this time forth for ever. 37Now there-
fore take care to make a copy of this,
and let it be given to Jonathan and put
up in a conspicuous place on the holy
mountain.'"

THE INTRIGUE OF TRYPHO

38 Now when Deme´trius the king
saw that the land was quiet before
him and that there was no opposition
to him, he dismissed all his troops,
each man to his own place, except the
foreign troops which he had recruited
from the islands of the nations. So all
the troops who had served his fathers
hated him. 39Now Trypho had former-
ly been one of Alexander's support-
ers. He saw that all the troops were
murmuring against Deme´trius. So he
went to Imalku´e the Arab, who was
bringing up Anti´ochus, the young
son of Alexander, 40and insistently
urged him to hand Anti´ochus[e] over
to him, to become king in place of his
father. He also reported to Imalku´e[f]
what Deme´trius had done and told
of the hatred which the troops of
Deme´trius[g] had for him; and he
stayed there many days.

41 Now Jonathan sent to
Deme´trius the king the request that
he remove the troops of the citadel
from Jerusalem, and the troops in the
strongholds; for they kept fighting
against Israel. 42And Deme´trius sent
this message to Jonathan, "Not only
will I do these things for you and your
nation, but I will confer great honor
on you and your nation, if I find an
opportunity. 43Now then you will do
well to send me men who will help
me, for all my troops have revolted."
44So Jonathan sent three thousand
stalwart men to him at Antioch, and
when they came to the king, the king
rejoiced at their arrival.

45 Then the men of the city assem-
bled within the city, to the number of
a hundred and twenty thousand, and
they wanted to kill the king. 46But
the king fled into the palace. Then
the men of the city seized the main
streets of the city and began to fight.
47So the king called the Jews to his
aid, and they all rallied about him and
then spread out through the city; and
they killed on that day as many as a
hundred thousand men. 48They set
fire to the city and seized much spoil
on that day, and they saved the king.
49When the men of the city saw that
the Jews had gained control of the city
as they pleased, their courage failed
and they cried out to the king with
this entreaty, 50"Grant us peace, and
make the Jews stop fighting against us
and our city." 51And they threw down
their arms and made peace. So the
Jews gained glory in the eyes of the
king and of all the people in his king-
dom, and they returned to Jerusalem
with much spoil.

52 So Deme´trius the king sat on
the throne of his kingdom, and the
land was quiet before him. 53But he
broke his word about all that he had
promised; and he became estranged
from Jonathan and did not repay the
favors which Jonathan[h] had done him,
but oppressed him greatly.

TRYPHO SEIZES POWER

54 After this Trypho returned, and
with him the young boy Anti´ochus,
who began to reign and put on the
crown. 55All the troops that Deme´trius
had cast off gathered around him, and
they fought against Deme´trius,[i] and
he fled and was routed. 56And Trypho
captured the elephants[j] and gained

[e] Gk *him*
[f] Gk *him*
[g] Gk *him*
[h] Gk *he*
[i] Gk *him*
[j] Gk *beasts*

control of Antioch. 57Then the young
Anti´ochus wrote to Jonathan, saying,
"I confirm you in the high priesthood
and set you over the four districts and
make you one of the friends of the
king." 58And he sent him gold plate
and a table service, and granted him
the right to drink from gold cups and
dress in purple and wear a gold buck-
le. 59Simon his brother he made gov-
ernor from the Ladder of Tyre to the
borders of Egypt.

CAMPAIGNS OF JONATHAN AND SIMON

60 Then Jonathan set forth and
traveled beyond the river and among
the cities, and all the army of Syria
gathered to him as allies. When he
came to As´kalon, the people of the
city met him and paid him honor.
61From there he departed to Gaza,
but the men of Gaza shut him out.
So he besieged it and burned its sub-
urbs with fire and plundered them.
62Then the people of Gaza pleaded
with Jonathan, and he made peace
with them, and took the sons of their
rulers as hostages and sent them to
Jerusalem. And he passed through the
country as far as Damas´cus.

63 Then Jonathan heard that the
officers of Deme´trius had come to
Kadesh in Galilee with a large army,
intending to remove him from office.
64He went to meet them, but left his
brother Simon in the country. 65Simon
encamped before Beth-zur and fought
against it for many days and hemmed
it in. 66Then they asked him to grant
them terms of peace, and he did so. He
removed them from there, took pos-
session of the city, and set a garrison
over it.

67 Jonathan and his army encamp-
ed by the waters of Gennes´aret. Early
in the morning they marched to the
plain of Hazor, 68and behold, the army
of the foreigners met him in the plain;
they had set an ambush against him
in the mountains, but they themselves
met him face to face. 69Then the men
in ambush emerged from their plac-
es and joined battle. 70All the men
with Jonathan fled; not one of them
was left except Mattathi´as the son
of Ab´salom and Judas the son of
Chalphi, commanders of the forces of
the army. 71Jonathan rent his garments
and put dust on his head, and prayed.
72Then he turned back to the battle
against the enemy[a] and routed them,
and they fled. 73When his men who
were fleeing saw this, they returned
to him and joined him in the pursuit
as far as Kadesh, to their camp, and
there they encamped. 74As many as
three thousand of the foreigners fell
that day. And Jonathan returned to
Jerusalem.

ALLIANCES WITH ROME AND SPARTA

12 Now when Jonathan saw that the
time was favorable for him, he
chose men and sent them to Rome
to confirm and renew the friendship
with them. 2He also sent letters to the
same effect to the Spartans and to
other places. 3So they went to Rome
and entered the senate chamber and
said, "Jonathan the high priest and
the Jewish nation have sent us to re-
new the former friendship and alli-
ance with them." 4And the Romans[b]
gave them letters to the people in ev-
ery place, asking them to provide for
the envoys[c] safe conduct to the land
of Judah.

5 This is a copy of the letter which
Jonathan wrote to the Spartans:
6"Jonathan the high priest, the senate
of the nation, the priests, and the rest
of the Jewish people to their brethren
the Spartans, greeting. 7Already in
time past a letter was sent to Oni´as
the high priest from Ari´us,[d] who
was king among you, stating that
you are our brethren, as the append-
ed copy shows. 8Oni´as welcomed the

[a] Gk *them*
[b] Gk *they*
[c] Gk *them*
[d] Vg Compare verse 20: Gk *Dari´us*

envoy with honor, and received the
letter, which contained a clear dec-
laration of alliance and friendship.
9 Therefore, though we have no need
of these things, since we have as en-
couragement the holy books which
are in our hands, 10 we have under-
taken to send to renew our brother-
hood and friendship with you, so that
we may not become estranged from
you, for considerable time has passed
since you sent your letter to us. 11 We
therefore remember you constantly
on every occasion, both in our feasts
and on other appropriate days, at the
sacrifices which we offer and in our
prayers, as it is right and proper to
remember brethren. 12 And we rejoice
in your glory. 13 But as for ourselves,
many afflictions and many wars have
encircled us; the kings round about us
have waged war against us. 14 We were
unwilling to annoy you and our oth-
er allies and friends with these wars,
15 for we have the help which comes
from Heaven for our aid; and we were
delivered from our enemies and our
enemies were humbled. 16 We there-
fore have chosen Nume´nius the son
of Anti´ochus and Antip´ater the son
of Jason, and have sent them to Rome
to renew our former friendship and
alliance with them. 17 We have com-
manded them to go also to you and
greet you and deliver to you this letter
from us concerning the renewal of our
brotherhood. 18 And now please send
us a reply to this."

19 This is a copy of the letter which
they sent to Oni´as: 20 "Ari´us, king
of the Spartans, to Oni´as the high
priest, greeting. 21 *It has been* found in
writing concerning the Spartans and
the Jews that they are brethren and
are of the family of Abraham. 22 And
now that we have learned this, please
write us concerning your welfare; 23 we
on our part write to you that your cat-
tle and your property belong to us,
and ours belong to you. We therefore
command that our envoys[e] report to
you accordingly."

FURTHER CAMPAIGNS OF JONATHAN AND SIMON

24 Now Jonathan heard that the
commanders of Deme´trius had re-
turned, with a larger force than be-
fore, to wage war against him. 25 So
he marched away from Jerusalem and
met them in the region of Hamath, for
he gave them no opportunity to in-
vade his own country. 26 He sent spies
to their camp, and they returned and
reported to him that the enemy[f] were
being drawn up in formation to fall
upon the Jews[g] by night. 27 So when
the sun set, Jonathan commanded his
men to be alert and to keep their arms
at hand so as to be ready all night
for battle, and he stationed outposts
around the camp. 28 When the ene-
my heard that Jonathan and his men
were prepared for battle, they were
afraid and were terrified at heart; so
they kindled fires in their camp and
withdrew.[h] 29 But Jonathan and his
men did not know it until morning,
for they saw the fires burning. 30 Then
Jonathan pursued them, but he did not
overtake them, for they had crossed
the Eleu´therus river. 31 So Jonathan
turned aside against the Arabs who
are called Zabade´ans, and he crushed
them and plundered them. 32 Then he
broke camp and went to Damas´cus,
and marched through all that region.

33 Simon also went forth and
marched through the country as
far as As´kalon and the neighbor-
ing strongholds. He turned aside to
Joppa and took it by surprise, 34 *for*
he had heard that they were ready to
hand over the stronghold to the men
whom Deme´trius had sent. And he
stationed a garrison there to guard it.

35 When Jonathan returned he

[e] Gk *they*
[f] Gk *they*
[g] Gk *them*
[h] Other ancient authorities omit *and withdrew*

convened the elders of the people and
planned with them to build strong-
holds in Judea, 36to build the walls of
Jerusalem still higher, and to erect a
high barrier between the citadel and
the city to separate it from the city, in
order to isolate it so that its garrison[a]
could neither buy nor sell. 37So they
gathered together to build up the city;
part of the wall on the valley to the
east had fallen, and he repaired the
section called Chaphena´tha. 38And
Simon built Ad´ida in the Shephe´lah;
he fortified it and installed gates with
bolts.

TRYPHO CAPTURES JONATHAN

39 Then Trypho attempted to be-
come king of Asia and put on the
crown, and to raise his hand against
Anti´ochus the king. 40He feared that
Jonathan might not permit him to
do so, but might make war on him,
so he kept seeking to seize and kill
him, and he marched forth and came
to Beth-shan. 41Jonathan went out to
meet him with forty thousand picked
fighting men, and he came to Beth-
shan. 42When Trypho saw that he
had come with a large army, he was
afraid to raise his hand against him.
43So he received him with honor and
commended him to all his friends, and
he gave him gifts and commanded his
friends and his troops to obey him as
they would himself. 44Then he said to
Jonathan, "Why have you wearied all
these people when we are not at war?
45Dismiss them now to their homes
and choose for yourself a few men
to stay with you, and come with me
to Ptolema´is. I will hand it over to
you as well as the other strongholds
and the remaining troops and all the
officials, and will turn round and go
home. For that is why I am here."

46 Jonathan[b] *trusted him and did
as he* said; he sent away the troops,
and they returned to the land of
Judah. 47He kept with himself three
thousand men, two thousand of
whom he left in Galilee, while a thou-
sand accompanied him. 48But when
Jonathan entered Ptolema´is, the
men of Ptolema´is closed the gates
and seized him, and all who had en-
tered with him they killed with the
sword.

49 Then Trypho sent troops and
cavalry into Galilee and the Great
Plain to destroy all Jonathan's
soldiers. 50But they realized that
Jonathan[c] had been seized and had
perished along with his men, and
they encouraged one another and
kept marching in close formation,
ready for battle. 51When their pursu-
ers saw that they would fight for their
lives, they turned back. 52So they all
reached the land of Judah safely, and
they mourned for Jonathan and his
companions and were in great fear;
and all Israel mourned deeply. 53And
all the nations round about them
tried to destroy them, for they said,
"They have no leader or helper. Now
therefore let us make war on them
and blot out the memory of them
from among men."

SIMON TAKES COMMAND

13 Simon heard that Trypho had as-
sembled a large army to invade
the land of Judah and destroy it, 2and
he saw that the people were trem-
bling and fearful. So he went up to
Jerusalem, and gathering the people
together 3he encouraged them, say-
ing to them, "You yourselves know
what great things I and my brothers
and the house of my father have done
for the laws and the sanctuary; you
know also the wars and the difficul-
ties which we have seen. 4By reason
of this all my brothers have perished
for the sake of Israel, and I alone am
left. 5And now, far be it from me to
spare my life in any time of distress,
for I am not better than my brothers.
6But I will avenge my nation and the

[a]Gk *they*
[b]Gk *he*
[c]Gk *he*

sanctuary and your wives and chil-
dren, for all the nations have gathered
together out of hatred to destroy us."
7 The spirit of the people was
rekindled when they heard these
words, 8and they answered in a loud
voice, "You are our leader in place
of Judas and Jonathan your brother.
9Fight our battles, and all that you
say to us we will do." 10So he assem-
bled all the warriors and hastened
to complete the walls of Jerusalem,
and he fortified it on every side. 11He
sent Jonathan the son of Ab´salom to
Joppa, and with him a considerable
army; he drove out its occupants and
remained there.

DECEIT AND TREACHERY OF TRYPHO

12 Then Trypho departed from
Ptolema´is with a large army to in-
vade the land of Judah, and Jonathan
was with him under guard. 13And
Simon encamped in Ad´ida, facing the
plain. 14Trypho learned that Simon
had risen up in place of Jonathan his
brother, and that he was about to join
battle with him, so he sent envoys to
him and said, 15"It is for the money
that Jonathan your brother owed the
royal treasury, in connection with the
offices he held, that we are detaining
him. 16Send now a hundred talents of
silver and two of his sons as hostag-
es, so that when released he will not
revolt against us, and we will release
him."
17 Simon knew that they were
speaking deceitfully to him, but he
sent to get the money and the sons,
lest he arouse great hostility among
the people, who might say, 18"Because
Simon[d] did not send him the money
and the sons, he perished." 19So he
sent the sons and the hundred talents,
but Trypho[e] broke his word and did
not release Jonathan.
20 After this Trypho came to in-
vade the country and destroy it,
and he circled around by the way to
Ador´a. But Simon and his army kept
marching along opposite him to ev-
ery place he went. 21Now the men in
the citadel kept sending envoys to
Trypho urging him to come to them
by way of the wilderness and to send
them food. 22So Trypho got all his
cavalry ready to go, but that night a
very heavy snow fell, and he did not
go because of the snow. He marched
off and went into the land of Gil´ead.
23When he approached Bas´kama, he
killed Jonathan, and he was buried
there. 24Then Trypho turned back and
departed to his own land.

JONATHAN'S TOMB

25 And Simon sent and took the
bones of Jonathan his brother, and
buried him in Mo´de-in, the city of
his fathers. 26All Israel bewailed him
with great lamentation, and mourned
for him many days. 27And Simon built
a monument over the tomb of his fa-
ther and his brothers; he made it high
that it might be seen, with polished
stone at the front and back. 28He also
erected seven pyramids, opposite one
another, for his father and mother
and four brothers. 29And for the pyra-
mids[f] he devised an elaborate setting,
erecting about them great columns,
and upon the columns he put suits of
armor for a permanent memorial, and
beside the suits of armor carved ships,
so that they could be seen by all who
sail the sea. 30This is the tomb which
he built in Mo´de-in; it remains to this
day.

JUDEA GAINS INDEPENDENCE

31 Trypho dealt treacherously with
the young king Anti´ochus; he killed
him 32and became king in his place,
putting on the crown of Asia; and he
brought great calamity upon the land.
But Simon built up the strongholds
of Judea and walled them all around,
with high towers and great walls and
gates and bolts, and he stored food in

[d]Gk *I*
[e]Gk *he*
[f]Gk *for these*

the strongholds. 34Simon also chose
men and sent them to Deme´trius the
king with a request to grant relief to
the country, for all that Trypho did
was to plunder. 35Deme´trius the king
sent him a favorable reply to this re-
quest, and wrote him a letter as fol-
lows, 36"King Deme´trius to Simon,
the high priest and friend of kings,
and to the elders and nation of the
Jews, greeting. 37We have received
the gold crown and the palm branch
which you[a] sent, and we are ready to
make a general peace with you and
to write to our officials to grant you
release from tribute. 38All the grants
that we have made to you remain
valid, and let the strongholds that
you have built be your possession.
39We pardon any errors and offenses
committed to this day, and cancel the
crown tax which you owe; and what-
ever other tax has been collected in
Jerusalem shall be collected no lon-
ger. 40And if any of you are qualified
to be enrolled in our bodyguard,[b] let
them be enrolled, and let there be
peace between us."

41 In the one hundred and seventi-
eth year[c] the yoke of the Gentiles was
removed from Israel, 42and the people
began to write in their documents and
contracts, "In the first year of Simon
the great high priest and commander
and leader of the Jews."

THE CAPTURE OF GAZARA BY SIMON

43 In those days Simon[d] encamped
against Gazar´a[e] and surrounded it
with troops. He made a siege engine,
brought it up to the city, and battered
and captured one tower. 44The men
in the siege engine leaped out into
the city, and a great tumult arose in
the city. 45The men in the city, with
their wives and children, went up on
the wall with their clothes rent, and
they cried out with a loud voice, ask-
ing Simon to make peace with them;
46they said, "Do not treat us accord-
ing to our wicked acts but according
to your mercy." 47So Simon reached
an agreement with them and stopped
fighting against them. But he expelled
them from the city and cleansed
the houses in which the idols were,
and then entered it with hymns and
praise. 48He cast out of it all unclean-
ness, and settled in it men who ob-
served the law. He also strengthened
its fortifications and built in it a house
for himself.

SIMON REGAINS THE CITADEL AT JERUSALEM

49 The men in the citadel at
Jerusalem were prevented from go-
ing out to the country and back to
buy and sell. So they were very hun-
gry, and many of them perished from
famine. 50Then they cried to Simon
to make peace with them, and he
did so. But he expelled them from
there and cleansed the citadel from
its pollutions. 51On the twenty-third
day of the second month, in the one
hundred and seventy-first year,[f] the
Jews[g] entered it with praise and palm
branches, and with harps and cymbals
and stringed instruments, and with
hymns and songs, because a great en-
emy had been crushed and removed
from Israel. 52And Simon[h] decreed
that every year they should celebrate
this day with rejoicing. He strength-
ened the fortifications of the temple
hill alongside the citadel, and he and
his men dwelt there. 53And Simon saw
that John his son had reached man-
hood, so he made him commander of
all the forces, and he dwelt in Gazar´a.

[a] The word *you* in verses 37-40 is plural
[b] Or *court*
[c] 142 b. c.
[d] Gk *he*
[e] Cn: Gk *Gaza*
[f] 141 b. c.
[g] Gk *they*
[h] Gk *he*

CAPTURE OF DEMETRIUS

14 In the one hundred and seventy-second year[i] Deme´trius the king assembled his forces and marched into Media to secure help, so that he could make war against Trypho. 2When Ar´saces the king of Persia and Media heard that Deme´trius had invaded his territory, he sent one of his commanders to take him alive. 3And he went and defeated the army of Deme´trius, and seized him and took him to Ar´saces, who put him under guard.

EULOGY OF SIMON

4The land[j] had rest all the days of
Simon.
He sought the good of his
nation;
his rule was pleasing to them,
as was the honor shown
him, all his days.
5To crown all his honors he took
Joppa for a harbor,
and opened a way to the
isles of the sea.
6He extended the borders of his
nation,
and gained full control of
the country.
7He gathered a host of captives;
he ruled over Gazar´a and
Beth-zur and the
citadel,
and he removed its uncleanness
from it;
and there was none to oppose him.
8They tilled their land in peace;
the ground gave its increase,
and the trees of the plains
their fruit.
9Old men sat in the streets;
they all talked together of
good things;
and the youths donned the
glories and garments
of war.
10He supplied the cities with food,
and furnished them with the
means of defense,
till his renown spread to the
ends of the earth.
11He established peace in the land,
and Israel rejoiced with
great joy.
12Each man sat under his vine and
his fig tree,
and there was none to make
them afraid.
13No one was left in the land to
fight them,
and the kings were crushed
in those days.
14He strengthened all the humble
of his people;
he sought out the law,
and did away with every
lawless and wicked
man.
15He made the sanctuary glorious,
and added to the vessels of
the sanctuary.

DIPLOMACY WITH ROME AND SPARTA

16 It was heard in Rome, and as
far away as Sparta, that Jonathan had
died, and they were deeply grieved.
17When they heard that Simon his
brother had become high priest in
his place, and that he was ruling over
the country and the cities in it, 18they
wrote to him on bronze tablets to
renew with him the friendship and
alliance which they had established
with Judas and Jonathan his brothers.
19And these were read before the assembly in Jerusalem.
20 This is a copy of the letter which
the Spartans sent: "The rulers and the
city of the Spartans to Simon the high
priest and to the elders and the priests
and the rest of the Jewish people, our
brethren, greeting. 21The envoys who
were sent to our people have told us
about your glory and honor, and we
rejoiced at their coming. 22And what
they said we have recorded in our public decrees, as follows, 'Nume´nius the

[i] 140 b. c.
[j] Other authorities add *of Judah*

son of Anti´ochus and Antip´ater the
son of Jason, envoys of the Jews, have
come to us to renew their friendship
with us. 23It has pleased our people to
receive these men with honor and to
put a copy of their words in the pub-
lic archives, so that the people of the
Spartans may have a record of them.
And they have sent a copy of this to
Simon the high priest.'"

24 After this Simon sent Nume´nius
to Rome with a large gold shield
weighing a thousand minas, to con-
firm the alliance with the Romans.[a]

OFFICIAL HONORS FOR SIMON

25 When the people heard these
things they said, "How shall we thank
Simon and his sons? 26For he and his
brothers and the house of his father
have stood firm; they have fought and
repulsed Israel's enemies and estab-
lished its freedom." 27So they made
a record on bronze tablets and put it
upon pillars on Mount Zion. This is
a copy of what they wrote: "On the
eighteenth day of Elul, in the one
hundred and seventy-second year,[b]
which is the third year of Simon the
great high priest, 28in As´aramel,[c] in
the great assembly of the priests and
the people and the rulers of the nation
and the elders of the country, the fol-
lowing was proclaimed to us:

29 "Since wars often occurred
in the country, Simon the son of
Mattathi´as, a priest of the sons[d] of
Jo´arib, and his brothers, exposed
themselves to danger and resisted the
enemies of their nation, in order that
their sanctuary and the law might be
perserved; and they brought great glo-
ry to their nation. 30Jonathan rallied
the[e] nation, and became their high
priest, and was gathered to his peo-
ple. 31And when their enemies decided
to invade their country and lay hands
on their sanctuary, 32then Simon rose
up and fought for his nation. He spent
great sums of his own money; he
armed the men of his nation's forces
and paid them wages. 33He fortified
the cities of Judea, and Beth-zur on the
borders of Judea, where formerly the
arms of the enemy had been stored,
and he placed there a garrison of Jews.
34He also fortified Joppa, which is by
the sea, and Gazar´a, which is on the
borders of Azo´tus, where the enemy
formerly dwelt. He settled Jews there,
and provided in those cities[f] whatever
was necessary for their restoration.

35 "The people saw Simon's faith-
fulness[g] and the glory which he had
resolved to win for his nation, and
they made him their leader and high
priest, because he had done all these
things and because of the justice and
loyalty which he had maintained to-
ward his nation. He sought in every
way to exalt his people. 36And in his
days things prospered in his hands, so
that the Gentiles were put out of the[h]
country, as were also the men in the
city of David in Jerusalem, who had
built themselves a citadel from which
they used to sally forth and defile the
environs of the sanctuary and do great
damage to its purity. 37He settled Jews
in it, and fortified it for the safety of
the country and of the city, and built
the walls of Jerusalem higher.

38 "In view of these things King
Deme´trius confirmed him in the high
priesthood, 39and he made him one of
the king's[i] friends and paid him high
honors. 40For he had heard that the
Jews were addressed by the Romans

[a] Gk *them*
[b] 140 b. c.
[c] *This word resembles the Hebrew words for the court of the people of God or the prince of the people of God*
[d] The Greek text of this phrase is uncertain
[e] Gk *their*
[f] Gk *them*
[g] Other authorities read *conduct*
[h] Gk *their*
[i] Gk *his*

as friends and allies and brethren, and
that the Romans[j] had received the en-
voys of Simon with honor.

41 "And[k] the Jews and their priests
decided that Simon should be their
leader and high priest for ever, until
a trustworthy prophet should arise,
42and that he should be governor over
them and that he should take charge
of the sanctuary and appoint men
over its tasks and over the country
and the weapons and the strongholds,
and that he should take charge of the
sanctuary, 43and that he should be
obeyed by all, and that all contracts in
the country should be written in his
name, and that he should be clothed
in purple and wear gold.

44 "And none of the people or
priests shall be permitted to nullify
any of these decisions or to oppose
what he says, or to convene an assem-
bly in the country without his per-
mission, or to be clothed in purple or
put on a gold buckle. 45Whoever acts
contrary to these decisions or nul-
lifies any of them shall be liable to
punishment."

46 And all the people agreed to
grant Simon the right to act in accord
with these decisions. 47So Simon ac-
cepted and agreed to be high priest,
to be commander and ethnarch of the
Jews and priests, and to be protector
of them all.[l] 48And they gave orders to
inscribe this decree upon bronze tab-
lets, to put them up in a conspicuous
place in the precincts of the sanctu-
ary, 49and to deposit copies of them in
the treasury, so that Simon and his
sons might have them.

LETTER OF ANTIOCHUS VII

15 Anti´ochus, the son of Deme´trius
the king, sent a letter from the is-
lands of the sea to Simon, the priest
and ethnarch of the Jews, and to all
the nation; 2its contents were as fol-
lows: "King Anti´ochus to Simon the
high priest and ethnarch and to the
nation of the Jews, greeting. 3Whereas
certain pestilent men have gained con-
trol of the kingdom of our fathers, and
I intend to lay claim to the kingdom
so that I may restore it as it formerly
was, and have recruited a host of mer-
cenary troops and have equipped war-
ships, 4and intend to make a landing
in the country so that I may proceed
against those who have destroyed our
country and those who have devastat-
ed many cities in my kingdom, 5now
therefore I confirm to you all the tax
remissions that the kings before me
have granted you, and release from all
the other payments from which they
have released you. 6I permit you to
mint your own coinage as money for
your country, 7and I grant freedom to
Jerusalem and the sanctuary. All the
weapons which you have prepared and
the strongholds which you have built
and now hold shall remain yours.
8Every debt you owe to the royal trea-
sury and any such future debts shall
be canceled for you from henceforth
and for all time. 9When we gain con-
trol of our kingdom, we will bestow
great honor upon you and your nation
and the temple, so that your glory will
become manifest in all the earth."

10 In the one hundred and seven-
ty-fourth year[m] Anti´ochus set out and
invaded the land of his fathers. All the
troops rallied to him, so that there
were few with Trypho. 11Anti´ochus
pursued him, and he came in his
flight to Dor, which is by the sea; 12for
he knew that troubles had converged
upon him, and his troops had de-
serted him. 13So Anti´ochus encamp-
ed against Dor, and with him were a
hundred and twenty thousand war-
riors and eight thousand cavalry. 14He
surrounded the city, and the ships
joined battle from the sea; he pressed
the city hard from land and sea, and
permitted no one to leave or enter it.

[j] Gk *they*
[k] Gk *honor; and that*
[l] Or *to preside over them all*
[m] 138 b. c.

ROME SUPPORTS THE JEWS

15 Then Nume´nius and his com-
panions arrived from Rome, with
letters to the kings and countries,
in which the following was written:
16"Lucius, consul of the Romans, to
King Ptol´emy, greeting. 17The envoys
of the Jews have come to us as our
friends and allies to renew our ancient
friendship and alliance. They had
been sent by Simon the high priest
and by the people of the Jews, 18and
have brought a gold shield weighing a
thousand minas. 19We therefore have
decided to write to the kings and
countries that they should not seek
their harm or make war against them
and their cities and their country, or
make alliance with those who war
against them. 20And it has seemed
good to us to accept the shield from
them. 21Therefore if any pestilent men
have fled to you from their country,
hand them over to Simon the high
priest, that he may punish them ac-
cording to their law."

22 The consul[a] wrote the same
thing to Deme´trius the king and to
At´talus and Ariar´athes and Ar´saces,
23and to all the countries, and to
Sam´psames,[b] and to the Spartans,
and to Delos, and to Myndos, and to
Sic´yon, and to Ca´ria, and to Samos,
and to Pamphyl´ia, and to Lyc´ia, and
to Halicarnas´sus, and to Rhodes,
and to Phase´lis, and to Cos, and to
Side, and to Ar´adus and Gorty´na
and Cnidus and Cyprus and Cyre´ne.
24They also sent a copy of these things
to Simon the high priest.

ANTIOCHUS VII THREATENS SIMON

25 Anti´ochus the king besieged
Dor anew,[c] continually throwing
his forces against it and making en-
gines of war; and he shut Trypho up
and kept him from going out or in.
26And Simon sent to Anti´ochus two
thousand picked men, to fight for him,
and silver and gold and much military
equipment. 27But he refused to receive
them, and he broke all the agreements
he formerly had made with Simon,[d]
and became estranged from him.
28He sent to him Athenob´ius, one of
his friends, to confer with him, say-
ing, "You hold control of Joppa and
Gazar´a and the citadel in Jerusalem;
they are cities of my kingdom. 29You
have devastated their territory, you
have done great damage in the land,
and you have taken possession of
many places in my kingdom. 30Now
then, hand over the cities which you
have seized and the tribute money of
the places which you have conquered
outside the borders of Judea; 31or else
give me for them five hundred talents
of silver, and for the destruction that
you have caused and the tribute mon-
ey of the cities, five hundred talents
more. Otherwise we will come and
conquer you."

32 So Athenob´ius the friend of
the king came to Jerusalem, and
when he saw the splendor of Simon,
and the sideboard with its gold and
silver plate, and his great magnifi-
cence, he was amazed. He reported
to him the words of the king, 33but
Simon gave him this reply: "We
have neither taken foreign land nor
seized foreign property, but only the
inheritance of our fathers, which at
one time had been unjustly taken by
our enemies. 34Now that we have the
opportunity, we are firmly holding
the inheritance of our fathers. 35As
for Joppa and Gazar´a, which you
demand, they were causing great
damage among the people and to our
land; for them we will give a hun-
dred talents." Athenob´ius[e] did not
answer him a word, 36but returned
in wrath to the king and reported to
him these words and the splendor of

[a] Gk *He*
[b] The name is uncertain
[c] Or *on the second day*
[d] Gk *him*
[e] Gk *he*

Simon and all that he had seen. And
the king was greatly angered.

VICTORY OVER CENDEBEUS

37 Now Trypho embarked on a ship
and escaped to Ortho´sia. 38Then the
king made Cendebe´us command-
er-in-chief of the coastal country,
and gave him troops of infantry and
cavalry. 39He commanded him to en-
camp against Judea, and commanded
him to build up Kedron and fortify its
gates, and to make war on the people;
but the king pursued Trypho. 40So
Cendebe´us came to Jam´nia and be-
gan to provoke the people and invade
Judea and take the people captive and
kill them. 41He built up Kedron and
stationed there horsemen and troops,
so that they might go out and make
raids along the highways of Judea, as
the king had ordered him.

16 John went up from Gazar´a and
reported to Simon his father what
Cendebe´us had done. 2And Simon
called in his two older sons Judas and
John, and said to them: "I and my
brothers and the house of my father
have fought the wars of Israel from
our youth until this day, and things
have prospered in our hands so that
we have delivered Israel many times.
3But now I have grown old, and you by
His mercy are mature in years. Take
my place and my brother's, and go
out and fight for our nation, and may
the help which comes from Heaven be
with you."

4 So John[f] chose out of the coun-
try twenty thousand warriors and
horsemen, and they marched against
Cendebe´us and camped for *the night*
in Mo´de-in. 5Early in the morning
they arose and marched into the
plain, and behold, a large force of in-
fantry and horsemen was coming to
meet them; and a stream lay between
them. 6Then he and his army lined
up against them. And he saw that
the soldiers were afraid to cross the
stream, so he crossed over first; and
when his men saw him, they crossed
over after him. 7Then he divided the
army and placed the horsemen in the
midst of the infantry, for the cavalry
of the enemy were very numerous.
8And they sounded the trumpets,
and Cendebe´us and his army were
put to flight, and many of them were
wounded and fell; the rest fled into
the stronghold. 9At that time Judas
the brother of John was wounded, but
John pursued them until Cendebe´us[g]
reached Kedron, which he had built.
10They also fled into the towers that
were in the fields of Azo´tus, and
John[h] burned it with fire, and about
two thousand of them fell. And he re-
turned to Judea safely.

MURDER OF SIMON AND HIS SONS

11 Now Ptol´emy the son of
Abu´bus had been appointed gov-
ernor over the plain of Jericho, and
he had much silver and gold, 12for he
was son-in-law of the high priest.
13His heart was lifted up; he deter-
mined to get control of the country,
and made treacherous plans against
Simon and his sons, to do away with
them. 14Now Simon was visiting the
cities of the country and attending
to their needs, and he went down to
Jericho with Mattathi´as and Judas
his sons, in the one hundred and sev-
enty-seventh year,[i] in the eleventh
month, which is the month of Shebat.
15The son of Abu´bus received them
treacherously in the little stronghold
called Dok, which he had built; he
gave them a great banquet, and hid
men there. 16When Simon and his
sons were drunk, Ptol´emy and his
men rose up, took their weapons,
and rushed in against Simon in the
banquet hall, and they killed him
and his two sons and some of his
servants. 17So he committed an act

[f] Other authorities read *he*
[g] Gk *he*
[h] Gk *he*
[i] 134 b. c.

of great treachery and returned evil
for good.

JOHN SUCCEEDS SIMON

18 Then Ptol´emy wrote a report
about these things and sent it to the
king, asking him to send troops to
aid him and to turn over to him the
cities and the country. 19He sent oth-
er men to Gazar´a to do away with
John; he sent letters to the captains
asking them to come to him so that
he might give them silver and gold
and gifts; 20and he sent other men to
take possession of Jerusalem and the
temple hill. 21But some one ran ahead
and reported to John at Gazar´a that
his father and brothers had perished,
and that "he has sent men to kill you
also." 22When he heard this, he was
greatly shocked; and he seized the
men who came to destroy him and
killed them, for he had found out that
they were seeking to destroy him.

23 The rest of the acts of John and
his wars and the brave deeds which
he did, and the building of the walls
which he built, and his achieve-
ments, 24behold, they are written in
the chronicles of his high priesthood,
from the time that he became high
priest after his father.

THE SECOND BOOK OF THE

MACCABEES

A LETTER TO THE JEWS IN EGYPT

1 The Jewish brethren in Jerusalem and those in the land of Judea, To their Jewish brethren in Egypt, Greeting, and good peace.

2 May God do good to you, and may he remember his covenant with Abraham and Isaac and Jacob, his faithful servants. 3 May he give you all a heart to worship him and to do his will with a strong heart and a willing spirit. 4 May he open your heart to his law and his commandments, and may he bring peace. 5 May he hear your prayers and be reconciled to you, and may he not forsake you in time of evil. 6 We are now praying for you here.

7 In the reign of Deme´trius, in the one hundred and sixty-ninth year,[a] we Jews wrote to you, in the critical distress which came upon us in those years after Jason and his company revolted from the holy land and the kingdom 8 and burned the gate and shed innocent blood. We besought the Lord and we were heard, and we offered sacrifice and cereal offering, and we lighted the lamps and we set out the loaves. 9 And now see that you keep the feast of booths in the month of Chislev, in the one hundred and eighty-eighth year.[b]

A LETTER TO ARISTOBULUS

10 Those in Jerusalem and those *in* Judea and the senate and Judas, To Aristobu´lus, *who is of the family* of the anointed priests, teacher of Ptol´emy the king, and to the Jews in Egypt, Greeting, and good health.

11 Having been saved by God out of grave dangers we thank him greatly for taking our side against the king.[c] 12 For he drove out those who fought against the holy city. 13 For when the leader reached Persia with a force that seemed irresistible, they were cut to pieces in the temple of Nane´a by a deception employed by the priests of Nane´a. 14 For under pretext of intending to marry her, Anti´ochus came to the place together with his friends, to secure most of its treasures as a dowry. 15 When the priests of the temple of Nane´a had set out the treasures and Anti´ochus had come with a few men inside the wall of the sacred precinct, they closed the temple as soon as he entered it. 16 Opening the secret door in the ceiling, they threw stones and struck down the leader and his men, and dismembered them and cut off their heads and threw them to the people outside. 17 Blessed in every way be our God, who has brought judgment upon those who have behaved impiously.

FIRE CONSUMES NEHEMIAH'S SACRIFICE

18 Since on the twenty-fifth day of Chislev we shall celebrate the purification of the temple, we thought it necessary to notify you, in order that you also may celebrate the feast of booths and the feast of the fire given when Nehemi´ah, who built the temple and altar, offered sacrifices.

19 For when our fathers were being led captive to Persia, the pious priests of that time took some of the fire of the altar and secretly hid it in the hollow of a dry cistern, where they took such precautions *that the* place was unknown to any one. 20 But after many years had passed, when it pleased God, Nehemi´ah, having been commissioned by the king of Persia, sent the descendants of the priests who had hidden the fire to get it. And when they reported to us that they

[a] 143 b. c.
[b] 124 b. c.
[c] Cn: Gk *as those who array themselves against a king*

had not found fire but thick liquid, he
ordered them to dip it out and bring it.
21 And when the materials for the sac-
rifices were presented, Nehemi'ah or-
dered the priests to sprinkle the liquid
on the wood and what was laid upon
it. 22 When this was done and some
time had passed and the sun, which
had been clouded over, shone out, a
great fire blazed up, so that all mar-
veled. 23 And while the sacrifice was
being consumed, the priests offered
prayer—the priests and every one.
Jonathan led, and the rest respond-
ed, as did Nehemi'ah. 24 The prayer
was to this effect: "O Lord, Lord
God, Creator of all things, who art
awe-inspiring and strong and just and
merciful, who alone art King and art
kind, 25 who alone art bountiful, who
alone art just and almighty and eter-
nal, who dost rescue Israel from every
evil, who didst choose the fathers and
consecrate them, 26 accept this sacri-
fice on behalf of all thy people Israel
and preserve thy portion and make it
holy. 27 Gather together our scattered
people, set free those who are slaves
among the Gentiles, look upon those
who are rejected and despised, and
let the Gentiles know that thou art
our God. 28 Afflict those who oppress
and are insolent with pride. 29 Plant
thy people in thy holy place, as Moses
said."

30 Then the priests sang the hymns.
31 And when the materials of the sac-
rifice were consumed, Nehemi'ah
ordered that the liquid that was left
should be poured upon large stones.
32 When this was done, a flame blazed
up; but when the light from the altar
shone back, it went out. 33 When this
matter became known, and it was
reported to the king of the Persians
that, in the place where the exiled
priests had hidden the fire, the liquid
had appeared with which Nehemi'ah
and his associates had burned the
materials of the sacrifice, 34 the king
investigated the matter, and enclosed
the place and made it sacred. 35 And
with those persons whom the king
favored he exchanged many excellent
gifts. 36 Nehemi'ah and his associates
called this "nephthar," which means
purification, but by most people it is
called naphtha.[a]

JEREMIAH HIDES THE TENT, ARK, AND ALTAR

2 One finds in the records that
Jeremiah the prophet ordered those
who were being deported to take
some of the fire, as has been told, 2 and
that the prophet after giving them the
law instructed those who were being
deported not to forget the command-
ments of the Lord, nor to be led astray
in their thoughts upon seeing the gold
and silver statues and their adorn-
ment. 3 And with other similar words
he exhorted them that the law should
not depart from their hearts.

4 It was also in the writing that the
prophet, having received an oracle, or-
dered that the tent and the ark should
follow with him, and that he went out
to the mountain where Moses had
gone up and had seen the inheritance
of God. 5 And Jeremiah came and found
a cave, and he brought there the tent
and the ark and the altar of incense,
and he sealed up the entrance. 6 Some
of those who followed him came up to
mark the way, but could not find it.
7 When Jeremiah learned of it, he re-
buked them and declared: "The place
shall be unknown until God gathers
his people together again and shows
his mercy. 8 And then the Lord will
disclose these things, and the glory of
the Lord and the cloud will appear, as
they were shown in the case of Moses,
and as Solomon asked that the place
should be specially consecrated."

9 It was also made clear that be-
ing possessed of wisdom Solomon[b]
offered sacrifice for the dedication
and completion of the temple. 10 Just

[a] Gk *nephthai*
[b] Gk *he*

as Moses prayed to the Lord, and
fire came down from heaven and de-
voured the sacrifices, so also Solomon
prayed, and the fire came down and
consumed the whole burnt offerings.
11And Moses said, "They were con-
sumed because the sin offering had
not been eaten." 12Likewise Solomon
also kept the eight days.

13 The same things are reported
in the records and in the memoirs of
Nehemi´ah, and also that he found-
ed a library and collected the books
about the kings and prophets, and
the writings of David, and letters of
kings about votive offerings. 14In the
same way Judas also collected all the
books that had been lost on account of
the war which had come upon us, and
they are in our possession. 15So if you
have need of them, send people to get
them for you.

16 Since, therefore, we are about
to celebrate the purification, we write
to you. Will you therefore please keep
the days? 17It is God who has saved
all his people, and has returned the
inheritance to all, and the kingship
and priesthood and consecration, 18as
he promised through the law. For we
have hope in God that he will soon
have mercy upon us and will gather us
from everywhere under heaven into
his holy place, for he has rescued us
from great evils and has purified the
place.

THE COMPILER'S PREFACE

19 The story of Judas Maccabe´us
and his brothers, and the purification
of the great temple, and the dedi-
cation of the altar, 20and further the
wars against Anti´ochus Epiph´anes
and his son Eu´pator, 21and the ap-
pearances which came from heaven
to those who strove zealously on be-
half of Judaism, so that though few
in number they seized the whole land
and pursued the barbarian hordes,
22and recovered the temple famous
throughout the world and freed the
city and restored the laws that were
about to be abolished, while the Lord
with great kindness became gracious
to them—23all this, which has been set
forth by Jason of Cyre´ne in five vol-
umes, we shall attempt to condense
into a single book. 24For considering
the flood of numbers involved and the
difficulty there is for those who wish
to enter upon the narratives of history
because of the mass of material, 25we
have aimed to please those who wish
to read, to make it easy for those who
are inclined to memorize, and to prof-
it all readers. 26For us who have un-
dertaken the toil of abbreviating, it is
no light matter but calls for sweat and
loss of sleep, 27just as it is not easy for
one who prepares a banquet and seeks
the benefit of others. However, to
secure the gratitude of many we will
gladly endure the uncomfortable toil,
28leaving the responsibility for exact
details to the compiler, while devoting
our effort to arriving at the outlines of
the condensation. 29For as the master
builder of a new house must be con-
cerned with the whole construction,
while the one who undertakes its
painting and decoration has to consid-
er only what is suitable for its adorn-
ment, such in my judgment is the case
with us. 30It is the duty of the original
historian to occupy the ground and to
discuss matters from every side and
to take trouble with details, 31but the
one who recasts the narrative should
be allowed to strive for brevity of
expression and to forego exhaustive
treatment. 32At this point therefore let
us begin our narrative, adding only so
much to what has already been said;
for it is foolish to lengthen the preface
while cutting short the history itself.

ARRIVAL OF HELIODORUS IN JERUSALEM

3 While the holy city was inhabited in
unbroken peace and the laws were
very well observed because of the pi-
ety of the high priest Oni´as and his
hatred of wickedness, 2it came about
that the kings themselves honored
the place and glorified the temple

with the finest presents, 3so that even
Seleu´cus, the king of Asia, defrayed
from his own revenues all the expens-
es connected with the service of the
sacrifices. 4But a man named Simon,
of the tribe of Benjamin, who had been
made captain of the temple, had a dis-
agreement with the high priest about
the administration of the city mar-
ket; 5and when he could not prevail
over Oni´as he went to Apollo´nius of
Tarsus,[a] who at that time was gover-
nor of Coelesyria and Phoenic´ia. 6He
reported to him that the treasury in
Jerusalem was full of untold sums
of money, so that the amount of the
funds could not be reckoned, and that
they did not belong to the account of
the sacrifices, but that it was possible
for them to fall under the control of
the king. 7When Apollo´nius met the
king, he told him of the money about
which he had been informed. The
king[b] chose Heliodor´us, who was in
charge of his affairs, and sent him
with commands to effect the removal
of the aforesaid money. 8Heliodor´us
at once set out on his journey, ostensi-
bly to make a tour of inspection of the
cities of Coelesyria and Phoenic´ia,
but in fact to carry out the king's
purpose.

9 When he had arrived at Jerusalem
and had been kindly welcomed by the
high priest of[c] the city, he told about
the disclosure that had been made
and stated why he had come, and he
inquired whether this really was the
situation. 10The high priest explained
that there were some deposits be-
longing to widows and orphans, 11and
also some money of Hyrca´nus, son of
Tobi´as, a man of very prominent po-
sition, and that it totaled in all four
hundred talents of silver and two hun-
dred of gold. To such an extent the im-
pious Simon had misrepresented the
facts. 12And he said that it was utterly
impossible that wrong should be done
to those people who had trusted in
the holiness of the place and in the
sanctity and inviolability of the tem-
ple which is honored throughout the
whole world. 13But Heliodor´us, be-
cause of the king's commands which
he had, said that this money must in
any case be confiscated for the king's
treasury. 14So he set a day and went in
to direct the inspection of these funds.
There was no little distress through-
out the whole city. 15The priests pros-
trated themselves before the altar in
their priestly garments and called to-
ward heaven upon him who had given
the law about deposits, that he should
keep them safe for those who had de-
posited them. 16To see the appearance
of the high priest was to be wounded
at heart, for his face and the change in
his color disclosed the anguish of his
soul. 17For terror and bodily trembling
had come over the man, which plainly
showed to those who looked at him
the pain lodged in his heart. 18People
also hurried out of their houses in
crowds to make a general supplication
because the holy place was about to
be brought into contempt. 19Women,
girded with sackcloth under their
breasts, thronged the streets. Some
of the maidens who were kept indoors
ran together to the gates, and some to
the walls, while others peered out of
the windows. 20And holding up their
hands to heaven, they all made en-
treaty. 21There was something pitiable
in the prostration of the whole popu-
lace and the anxiety of the high priest
in his great anguish.

THE LORD PROTECTS HIS TEMPLE

22 While they were calling upon
the Almighty Lord that he would keep
what had been entrusted safe and se-
cure for those who had entrusted it,
23Heliodor´us went on with what had
been decided. 24But when he arrived
at the treasury with his bodyguard,
then and there the Sovereign of spir-
its and of all authority caused so great

[a]Gk *Apollonius son of Tharseas*
[b]Gk *He*
[c]Some authorities read *and*

a manifestation that all who had been
so bold as to accompany him were
astounded by the power of God, and
became faint with terror. 25For there
appeared to them a magnificently ca-
parisoned horse, with a rider of fright-
ening mien, and it rushed furiously at
Heliodor´us and struck at him with its
front hoofs. Its rider was seen to have
armor and weapons of gold. 26Two
young men also appeared to him, re-
markably strong, gloriously beautiful
and splendidly dressed, who stood on
each side of him and scourged him
continuously, inflicting many blows
on him. 27When he suddenly fell to the
ground and deep darkness came over
him, his men took him up and put him
on a stretcher 28and carried him away,
this man who had just entered the
aforesaid treasury with a great retinue
and all his bodyguard but was now
unable to help himself; and they rec-
ognized clearly the sovereign power of
God. 29While he lay prostrate, speech-
less because of the divine intervention
and deprived of any hope of recovery,
30they praised the Lord who had acted
marvelously for his own place. And
the temple, which a little while before
was full of fear and disturbance, was
filled with joy and gladness, now that
the Almighty Lord had appeared.

ONIAS PRAYS FOR HELIODORUS

31 Quickly some of Heliodor´us'
friends asked Oni´as to call upon the
Most High and to grant life to one
who was lying quite at his last breath.
32And the high priest, fearing that the
king might get the notion that some
foul play had been perpetrated by
the Jews with regard to Heliodor´us,
offered sacrifice for the man's re-
covery. 33While the high priest was
making the offering of atonement,
the same young men appeared again
to Heliodor´us, dressed in the same
clothing, and they stood and said, "Be
very grateful to Oni´as the high priest,
since for his sake the Lord has granted
you your life. 34And see that you, who
have been scourged by heaven, report
to all men the majestic power of God."
Having said this they vanished.

THE CONVERSION OF HELIODORUS

35 Then Heliodor´us offered sacri-
fice to the Lord and made very great
vows to the Savior of his life, and
having bidden Oni´as farewell, he
marched off with his forces to the
king. 36And he bore testimony to all
men of the deeds of the supreme God,
which he had seen with his own eyes.
37When the king asked Heliodor´us
what sort of person would be suit-
able to send on another mission to
Jerusalem, he replied, 38"If you have
any enemy or plotter against your gov-
ernment, send him there, for you will
get him back thoroughly scourged, if
he escapes at all, for there certainly is
about the place some power of God.
39For he who has his dwelling in heav-
en watches over that place himself
and brings it aid, and he strikes and
destroys those who come to do it in-
jury." 40This was the outcome of the
episode of Heliodor´us and the protec-
tion of the treasury.

SIMON ACCUSES ONIAS

4 The previously mentioned Simon,
who had informed about the mon-
ey against[d] his own country, slan-
dered Oni´as, saying that it was he
who had incited Heliodor´us and had
been the real cause of the misfortune.
2He dared to designate as a plotter
against the government the man who
was the benefactor of the city, the
protector of his fellow countrymen,
and a zealot for the laws. 3When his
hatred progressed to such a degree
that even murders were committed
by one of Simon's approved agents,
4Oni´as recognized that the rivalry
was serious and that Apollo´nius, the
son of Menes´theus[e] and governor of

[d] Gk *and*
[e] Vg Compare verse 21: Greek uncertain

Coelesyria and Phoenic´ia, was inten-
sifying the malice of Simon. 5So he be-
took himself to the king, not accusing
his fellow citizens but having in view
the welfare, both public and private,
of all the people. 6For he saw that
without the king's attention public af-
fairs could not again reach a peaceful
settlement, and that Simon would not
stop his folly.

JASON'S REFORMS

7 When Seleu´cus died and
Anti´ochus who was called Epiph´anes
succeeded to the kingdom, Jason the
brother of Oni´as obtained the high
priesthood by corruption, 8promis-
ing the king at an interview[a] three
hundred and sixty talents of silver
and, from another source of revenue,
eighty talents. 9In addition to this he
promised to pay one hundred and fif-
ty more if permission were given to
establish by his authority a gymnasi-
um and a body of youth for it, and to
enrol the men of Jerusalem as citizens
of Antioch. 10When the king assent-
ed and Jason[b] came to office, he at
once shifted his countrymen over to
the Greek way of life. 11He set aside
the existing royal concessions to the
Jews, secured through John the fa-
ther of Eupole´mus, who went on the
mission to establish friendship and
alliance with the Romans; and he de-
stroyed the lawful ways of living and
introduced new customs contrary to
the law. 12For with alacrity he found-
ed a gymnasium right under the cit-
adel, and he induced the noblest of
the young men[c] to wear the Greek
hat. 13There was such an extreme of
Hellenization and increase in the
adoption of foreign ways because of
the surpassing wickedness of Jason,
who was ungodly and no high priest,
14that the priests were no longer in-
tent upon their service at the altar.
Despising the sanctuary and neglect-
ing the sacrifices, they hastened to
take part in the unlawful proceedings
in the wrestling arena after the call
to the discus, 15disdaining the honors
prized by their fathers and putting
the highest value upon Greek forms
of prestige. 16For this reason heavy
disaster overtook them, and those
whose ways of living they admired
and wished to imitate completely
became their enemies and punished
them. 17For it is no light thing to show
irreverence to the divine laws—a fact
which later events will make clear.

JASON INTRODUCES GREEK CUSTOMS

18 When the quadrennial games
were being held at Tyre and the king
was present, 19the vile Jason sent en-
voys, chosen as being Antioch´ian cit-
izens from Jerusalem, to carry three
hundred silver drachmas for the sac-
rifice to Her´cules. Those who carried
the money, however, thought best not
to use it for sacrifice, because that
was inappropriate, but to expend it
for another purpose. 20So this money
was intended by the sender for the
sacrifice to Her´cules, but by the de-
cision of its carriers it was applied to
the construction of triremes.

21 When Apollo´nius the son of
Menes´theus was sent to Egypt for the
coronation[d] of Philome´tor as king,
Anti´ochus learned that Philome´tor[e]
had become hostile to his govern-
ment, and he took measures for his
own security. Therefore upon arriving
at Joppa he proceeded to Jerusalem.
22He was welcomed magnificently by
Jason and the city, and ushered in with
a blaze of torches and with shouts.
Then he marched into Phoenic´ia.

MENELAUS BECOMES HIGH PRIEST

23 After a period of three years
Jason sent Menela´us, the brother of

[a] Or *by a petition*
[b] Gk *he*
[c] Some authorities add *subjecting them*
[d] The exact meaning of the Greek word is uncertain
[e] Gk *he*

the previously mentioned Simon, to
carry the money to the king and to
complete the records of essential busi-
ness. 24But he, when presented to the
king, extolled him with an air of au-
thority, and secured the high priest-
hood for himself, outbidding Jason
by three hundred talents of silver.
25After receiving the king's orders he
returned, possessing no qualification
for the high priesthood, but having
the hot temper of a cruel tyrant and
the rage of a savage wild beast. 26So
Jason, who after supplanting his own
brother was supplanted by another
man, was driven as a fugitive into the
land of Ammon. 27And Menela´us held
the office, but he did not pay regular-
ly any of the money promised to the
king. 28When So´stratus the captain
of the citadel kept requesting pay-
ment, for the collection of the reve-
nue was his responsibility, the two
of them were summoned by the king
on account of this issue. 29Menela´us
left his own brother Lysim´achus as
deputy in the high priesthood, while
So´stratus left Crates, the commander
of the Cyprian troops.*

THE MURDER OF ONIAS

30 While such was the state of af-
fairs, it happened that the people of
Tarsus and of Mallus revolted because
their cities had been given as a present
to Anti´ochis, the king's concubine.
31So the king went hastily to settle the
trouble, leaving Androni´cus, a man of
high rank, to act as his deputy. 32But
Menela´us, thinking he had obtained
a suitable opportunity, stole some of
the gold vessels of the temple and gave
them to Androni´cus; other vessels, as
it happened, he had sold to Tyre and
the neighboring cities. 33When Oni´as
became fully aware of these acts he
publicly exposed them, having first
withdrawn to a place of sanctuary
at Daphne near Antioch. 34Therefore
Menela´us, taking Androni´cus aside,
urged him to kill Oni´as. Androni´-
cus[f] came to Oni´as, and resorting to
treachery offered him sworn pledges
and gave him his right hand, and in
spite of his suspicion persuaded Oni´-
as[g] to come out from the place of sanc-
tuary; then, with no regard for justice,
he immediately put him out of the
way.* 35For this reason not only Jews,
but many also of other nations, were
grieved and displeased at the unjust
murder of the man. 36When the king
returned from the region of Cilic´ia,
the Jews in the city[h] appealed to him
with regard to the unreasonable mur-
der of Oni´as, and the Greeks shared
their hatred of the crime. 37Therefore
Anti´ochus was grieved at heart and
filled with pity, and wept because of
the moderation and good conduct of
the deceased; 38and inflamed with an-
ger, he immediately stripped off the
purple robe from Androni´cus, tore
off his garments, and led him about
the whole city to that very place where
he had committed the outrage against
Oni´as, and there he dispatched the
bloodthirsty fellow. The Lord thus
repaid him with the punishment he
deserved.

UNPOPULARITY OF LYSIMACHUS AND MENELAUS

39 When many acts of sacrilege
had been committed in the city by
Lysim´achus with the connivance of
Menela´us, and when report of them
had spread abroad, the populace gath-
ered against Lysim´achus, because
many of the gold vessels had already
been stolen. 40And since the crowds
were becoming aroused and filled
with anger, Lysim´achus armed about
three thousand men and launched an
unjust attack, under the leadership of
a certain Aura´nus,* a man advanced
in years and no less advanced in folly.

[f] Gk *He*
[g] Gk *him*
[h] Or in each city

41But when the Jews[a] became aware
of Lysim´achus' attack, some picked
up stones, some blocks of wood, and
others took handfuls of the ashes that
were lying about, and threw them in
wild confusion at Lysim´achus and
his men. 42As a result, they wounded
many of them, and killed some, and
put them all to flight; and the temple
robber himself they killed close by the
treasury.

43 Charges were brought against
Menela´us about this incident. 44When
the king came to Tyre, three men
sent by the senate presented the
case before him. 45But Menela´us, al-
ready as good as beaten, promised
a substantial bribe to Ptol´emy son
of Dorym´enes to win over the king.
46Therefore Ptol´emy, taking the king
aside into a colonnade as if for re-
freshment, induced the king to change
his mind. 47Menela´us, the cause of all
the evil, he acquitted of the charges
against him, while he sentenced to
death those unfortunate men, who
would have been freed uncondemned
if they had pleaded even before
Scyth´ians. 48And so those who had
spoken for the city and the villages[b]
and the holy vessels quickly suffered
the unjust penalty. 49Therefore even
the Tyr´ians, showing their hatred
of the crime, provided magnificent-
ly for their funeral. 50But Menela´us,
because of the cupidity of those in
power, remained in office, growing in
wickedness, having become the chief
plotter against his fellow citizens.

JASON TRIES TO REGAIN CONTROL

5 About this time Anti´ochus made
his second invasion of Egypt. 2And it
happened that over all the city, for al-
most forty days, there appeared gold-
en-clad horsemen charging through
the air, in companies fully armed with
lances and drawn swords—3troops
of horsemen drawn up, attacks and
counterattacks made on this side and
on that, brandishing of shields, mass-
ing of spears, hurling of missiles, the
flash of golden trappings, and armor
of all sorts. 4Therefore all men prayed
that the apparition might prove to
have been a good omen.

5 When a false rumor arose that
Anti´ochus was dead, Jason took no
less than a thousand men and sud-
denly made an assault upon the city.
When the troops upon the wall had
been forced back and at last the city
was being taken, Menela´us took ref-
uge in the citadel. 6But Jason kept
relentlessly slaughtering his fellow
citizens, not realizing that success at
the cost of one's kindred is the great-
est misfortune, but imagining that he
was setting up trophies of victory over
enemies and not over fellow country-
men. 7He did not gain control of the
government, however; and in the end
got only disgrace from his conspiracy,
and fled again into the country of the
Am´monites. 8Finally he met a miser-
able end. Accused[c] before Ar´etas the
ruler of the Arabs, fleeing from city
to city, pursued by all men, hated as
a rebel against the laws, and abhorred
as the executioner of his country and
his fellow citizens, he was cast ashore
in Egypt; 9and he who had driven
many from their own country into
exile died in exile, having embarked
to go to the Lacedaemo´nians in hope
of finding protection because of their
kinship. 10He who had cast out many
to lie unburied had no one to mourn
for him; he had no funeral of any
sort and no place in the tomb of his
fathers.

11 When news of what had hap-
pened reached the king, he took it
to mean that Judea was in revolt. So,
raging inwardly, he left Egypt and
took the city by storm. 12And he com-
manded his soldiers to cut down re-
lentlessly every one they met and to
slay those who went into the houses.
13Then there was killing of young and

[a] Gk *they*
[b] Other authorities read *the people*
[c] Cn: Gk *Imprisoned*

old, destruction of boys, women, and
children, and slaughter of virgins and
infants. 14Within the total of three
days eighty thousand were destroyed,
forty thousand in hand-to-hand fight-
ing; and as many were sold into slav-
ery as were slain.

PILLAGE OF THE TEMPLE

15 Not content with this, Anti´och-
us[d] dared to enter the most holy tem-
ple in all the world, guided by Mene-
la´us, who had become a traitor both
to the laws and to his country. 16He
took the holy vessels with his pollut-
ed hands, and swept away with pro-
fane hands the votive offerings which
other kings had made to enhance the
glory and honor of the place. 17Anti´-
ochus was elated in spirit, and did not
perceive that the Lord was angered
for a little while because of the sins of
those who dwelt in the city, and that
therefore he was disregarding the
holy place. 18But if it had not happened
that they were involved in many sins,
this man would have been scourged
and turned back from his rash act as
soon as he came forward, just as Heli-
odor´us was, whom Seleu´cus the king
sent to inspect the treasury. 19But the
Lord did not choose the nation for the
sake of the holy place, but the place
for the sake of the nation. 20Therefore
the place itself shared in the misfor-
tunes that befell the nation and after-
ward participated in its benefits; and
what was forsaken in the wrath of the
Almighty was restored again in all
its glory when the great Lord became
reconciled.

21 So Anti´ochus carried off eigh-
teen hundred talents from the temple,
and hurried away to Antioch, think-
ing in his arrogance that he could sail
on the land and walk on the sea, be-
cause his mind was elated. 22And he
left governors to afflict the people: at
Jerusalem, Philip, by birth a Phryg´ian
and in character more barbarous than
the man who appointed him; 23and
at Geri´zim, Androni´cus; and be-
sides these Menela´us, who lorded it
over his fellow citizens worse than
the others did. In his malice toward
the Jewish citizens,[e] 24Anti´ochus[f]
sent Apollo´nius, the captain of the
My´sians, with an army of twenty-two
thousand, and commanded him to
slay all the grown men and to sell the
women and boys as slaves. 25When this
man arrived in Jerusalem, he pretend-
ed to be peaceably disposed and wait-
ed until the holy sabbath day; then,
finding the Jews not at work, he or-
dered his men to parade under arms.
26He put to the sword all those who
came out to see them, then rushed
into the city with his armed men and
killed great numbers of people.

27 But Judas Maccabe´us, with
about nine others, got away to the
wilderness, and kept himself and his
companions alive in the mountains
as wild animals do; they continued to
live on what grew wild, so that they
might not share in the defilement.

THE SUPPRESSION OF JUDAISM

6 Not long after this, the king sent
an Athenian[g] senator[h] to compel
the Jews to forsake the laws of their
fathers and cease to live by the laws
of God, 2and also to pollute the tem-
ple in Jerusalem and call it the temple
of Olympian Zeus, and to call the one
in Geri´zim the temple of Zeus the
Friend of Strangers, as did the people
who dwelt in that place.

3 Harsh and utterly grievous was
the onslaught of evil. 4For the tem-
ple was filled with debauchery and
reveling by the Gentiles, who dallied
with harlots and had intercourse
with women within the sacred pre-
cincts, and besides brought in things

[d]Gk *he*
[e]Or *worse than the others did in his malice toward the Jewish citizens.*
[f]Gk *he*
[g]Some authorities read *Antiochian*
[h]Or *Geron an Athenian*

for sacrifice that were unfit. 5 The al-
tar was covered with abominable of-
ferings which were forbidden by the
laws. 6 A man could neither keep the
sabbath, nor observe the feasts of his
fathers, nor so much as confess him-
self to be a Jew.

7 On the monthly celebration of
the king's birthday, the Jews[a] were
taken, under bitter constraint, to par-
take of the sacrifices; and when the
feast of Diony´sus came, they were
compelled to walk in the procession in
honor of Diony´sus, wearing wreaths
of ivy. 8 At the suggestion of Ptol´emy a
decree was issued to the neighboring
Greek cities, that they should adopt
the same policy toward the Jews and
make them partake of the sacrifices,
9 and should slay those who did not
choose to change over to Greek cus-
toms. One could see, therefore, the
misery that had come upon them. 10 For
example, two women were brought in
for having circumcised their children.
These women they publicly parad-
ed about the city, with their babies
hung at their breasts, then hurled
them down headlong from the wall.
11 Others who had assembled in the
caves near by, to observe the seventh
day secretly, were betrayed to Philip
and were all burned together, because
their piety kept them from defending
themselves, in view of their regard for
that most holy day.

PROVIDENTIAL SIGNIFICANCE OF THE PERSECUTION

12 Now I urge those who read this
book not to be depressed by such ca-
lamities, but to recognize that these
punishments were designed not to de-
stroy but to discipline our people. 13 In
fact, not to let the impious alone for
long, but to punish them immediate-
ly, is a sign of great kindness. 14 For in
the case of the other nations the Lord
waits patiently to punish them until
they have reached the full measure of
their sins; but he does not deal in this
way with us, 15 in order that he may
not take vengeance on us afterward
when our sins have reached their
height. 16 Therefore he never with-
draws his mercy from us. Though he
disciplines us with calamities, he does
not forsake his own people. 17 Let what
we have said serve as a reminder; we
must go on briefly with the story.

THE MARTYRDOM OF ELEAZAR

18 Elea´zar, one of the scribes in
high position, a man now advanced
in age and of noble presence, was be-
ing forced to open his mouth to eat
swine's flesh. 19 But he, welcoming
death with honor rather than life with
pollution, went up to the the rack of
his own accord, spitting out the flesh,
20 as men ought to go who have the
courage to refuse things that it is not
right to taste, even for the natural love
of life.

21 Those who were in charge of
that unlawful sacrifice took the man
aside, because of their long acquain-
tance with him, and privately urged
him to bring meat of his own provid-
ing, proper for him to use, and pre-
tend that he was eating the flesh of
the sacrificial meal which had been
commanded by the king, 22 so that by
doing this he might be saved from
death, and be treated kindly on ac-
count of his old friendship with them.
23 But making a high resolve, worthy
of his years and the dignity of his old
age and the gray hairs which he had
reached with distinction and his ex-
cellent life even from childhood, and
moreover according to the holy God-
given law, he declared himself quick-
ly, telling them to send him to Hades.

24 "Such pretense is not worthy of
our time of life," he said, "lest many
of the young should suppose that
Elea´zar in his ninetieth year has gone
over to an alien religion, 25 and through
my pretense, for the sake of living a
brief moment longer, they should be
led astray because of me, while I defile

[a] Gk *they*

and disgrace my old age. 26For even if
for the present I should avoid the pun-
ishment of men, yet whether I live or
die I shall not escape the hands of the
Almighty. 27Therefore, by manfully
giving up my life now, I will show my-
self worthy of my old age 28and leave to
the young a noble example of how to
die a good death willingly and nobly
for the revered and holy laws." When
he had said this, he went[b] at once to
the rack. 29And those who a little be-
fore had acted toward him with good
will now changed to ill will, because
the words he had uttered were in their
opinion sheer madness.[c] 30When he
was about to die under the blows, he
groaned aloud and said: "It is clear to
the Lord in his holy knowledge that,
though I might have been saved from
death, I am enduring terrible suffer-
ings in my body under this beating,
but in my soul I am glad to suffer
these things because I fear him."

31 So in this way he died, leaving
in his death an example of nobility
and a memorial of courage, not only
to the young but to the great body of
his nation.

THE MARTYRDOM OF SEVEN BROTHERS

7 It happened also that seven broth-
ers and their mother were arrested
and were being compelled by the king,
under torture with whips and cords,
to partake of unlawful swine's flesh.
2One of them, acting as their spokes-
man, said, "What do you intend to ask
and learn from us? For we are ready to
die rather than transgress the laws of
our fathers."

3 The king fell into a rage, and
gave orders that pans and caldrons
be heated. 4These were heated imme-
diately, and he commanded that the
tongue of their spokesman be cut out
and that they scalp him and cut off
his hands and feet, while the rest of
the brothers and the mother looked
on. 5When he was utterly helpless,
the king[d] ordered them to take him
to the fire, still breathing, and to fry
him in a pan. The smoke from the pan
spread widely, but the brothers[e] and
their mother encouraged one another
to die nobly, saying, 6"The Lord God
is watching over us and in truth has
compassion on us, as Moses declared
in his song which bore witness against
the people to their faces, when he
said, 'And he will have compassion on
his servants.'"

7 After the first brother had died
in this way, they brought forward the
second for their sport. They tore off
the skin of his head with the hair,
and asked him, "Will you eat rather
than have your body punished limb by
limb?" 8He replied in the language of
his fathers, and said to them, "No."
Therefore he in turn underwent tor-
tures as the first brother had done.
9And when he was at his last breath,
he said, "You accursed wretch, you
dismiss us from this present life, but
the King of the universe will raise us
up to an everlasting renewal of life,*
because we have died for his laws."

10 After him, the third was the
victim of their sport. When it was de-
manded, he quickly put out his tongue
and courageously stretched forth his
hands, 11and said nobly, "I got these
from Heaven, and because of his laws
I disdain them, and from him I hope
to get them back again." 12As a result
the king himself and those with him
were astonished at the young man's
spirit, for he regarded his sufferings
as nothing.

13 When he too had died, they
maltreated and tortured the fourth
in the same way. 14And when he was
near death, he said, "One cannot but
choose to die at the hands of men and
to cherish the hope that God gives of
being raised again by him. But for you
there will be no resurrection to life!"

[b] Other authorities read *was dragged*
[c] The Greek text of this verse is uncertain
[d] Gk *he*
[e] Gk *they*

15 Next they brought forward
the fifth and maltreated him. 16 But
he looked at the king,[a] and said,
"Because you have authority among
men, mortal though you are, you do
what you please. But do not think that
God has forsaken our people. 17 Keep
on, and see how his mighty power will
torture you and your descendants!"

18 After him they brought forward
the sixth. And when he was about to
die, he said, "Do not deceive yourself
in vain. For we are suffering these
things on our own account, because
of our sins against our own God.
Therefore[b] astounding things have
happened. 19 But do not think that you
will go unpunished for having tried to
fight against God!"

20 The mother was especially ad-
mirable and worthy of honorable
memory. Though she saw her seven
sons perish within a single day, she
bore it with good courage because of
her hope in the Lord. 21 She encouraged
each of them in the language of their
fathers. Filled with a noble spirit, she
fired her woman's reasoning with a
man's courage, and said to them, 22 "I
do not know how you came into be-
ing in my womb. It was not I who gave
you life and breath, nor I who set in
order the elements within each of you.
23 Therefore the Creator of the world,
who shaped the beginning of man and
devised the origin of all things, will in
his mercy give life and breath back to
you again, since you now forget your-
selves for the sake of his laws."

24 Anti´ochus felt that he was be-
ing treated with contempt, and he was
suspicious of her reproachful tone.
The youngest brother being still alive,
Anti´ochus[c] not only appealed to him
in words, but promised with oaths
that he would make him rich and en-
viable if he would turn from the ways
of his fathers, and that he would take
him for his friend and entrust him
with public affairs. 25 Since the young
man would not listen to him at all,
the king called the mother to him and
urged her to advise the youth to save
himself. 26 After much urging on his
part, she undertook to persuade her
son. 27 But, leaning close to him, she
spoke in their native tongue as fol-
lows, deriding the cruel tyrant: "My
son, have pity on me. I carried you
nine months in my womb, and nursed
you for three years, and have reared
you and brought you up to this point
in your life, and have taken care of
you.[d] 28 I beseech you, my child, to look
at the heaven and the earth and see
everything that is in them, and rec-
ognize that God did not make them
out of things that existed.[e] Thus also
mankind comes into being. 29 Do not
fear this butcher, but prove worthy of
your brothers. Accept death, so that in
God's mercy I may get you back again
with your brothers."

30 While she was still speaking,
the young man said, "What are you[f]
waiting for? I will not obey the king's
command, but I obey the command of
the law that was given to our fathers
through Moses. 31 But you,[g] who have
contrived all sorts of evil against the
Hebrews, will certainly not escape the
hands of God. 32 For we are suffering
because of our own sins. 33 And if our
living Lord is angry for a little while,
to rebuke and discipline us, he will
again be reconciled with his own ser-
vants. 34 But you, unholy wretch, you
most defiled of all men, do not be
elated in vain and puffed up by uncer-
tain hopes, when you raise your hand
against the children of heaven. 35 You
have not yet escaped the judgment
of the almighty, all-seeing God. 36 For
our brothers after enduring a brief

[a] Gk *him*
[b] Lat: other authorities omit *Therefore*
[c] Gk *he*
[d] Or *have borne the burden of your education*
[e] Or *God made them out of things that did not exist*
[f] The Greek here for *you* is plural
[g] The Greek here for *you* is singular

suffering have drunk[h] of everflowing
life under God's covenant; but you,
by the judgment of God, will receive
just punishment for your arrogance.
37 I, like my brothers, give up body and
life for the laws of our fathers, appeal-
ing to God to show mercy soon to our
nation and by afflictions and plagues
to make you confess that he alone is
God, 38 and through me and my broth-
ers to bring to an end the wrath of the
Almighty which has justly fallen on
our whole nation."

39 The king fell into a rage, and
handled him worse than the others,
being exasperated at his scorn. 40 So he
died in his integrity, putting his whole
trust in the Lord.

41 Last of all, the mother died, af-
ter her sons.

42 Let this be enough, then, about
the eating of sacrifices and the ex-
treme tortures.

THE REVOLT OF JUDAS MACCABEUS

8 But Judas, who was also called
Maccabe´us, and his companions
secretly entered the villages and
summoned their kinsmen and enlist-
ed those who had continued in the
Jewish faith, and so they gathered
about six thousand men. 2 They be-
sought the Lord to look upon the peo-
ple who were oppressed by all, and
to have pity on the temple which had
been profaned by ungodly men, 3 and
to have mercy on the city which was
being destroyed and about to be lev-
eled to the ground, and to hearken to
the blood that cried out to him, 4 and
to remember also the lawless destruc-
tion of the innocent babies and the
blasphemies committed against his
name, and to show his hatred of evil.

5 As soon as Maccabe´us got his
army organized, the Gentiles could
not withstand him, for the wrath
of the Lord had turned to mercy.
6 Coming without warning, he would
set fire to towns and villages. He
captured strategic positions and put
to flight not a few of the enemy. 7 He
found the nights most advantageous
for such attacks. And talk of his valor
spread everywhere.

8 When Philip saw that the man
was gaining ground little by little,
and that he was pushing ahead with
more frequent successes, he wrote to
Ptol´emy, the governor of Coelesyria
and Phoenic´ia, for aid to the king's
government. 9 And Ptol´emy[i] prompt-
ly appointed Nica´nor the son of
Patroc´lus, one of the king's chief
friends, and sent him, in command
of no fewer than twenty thousand
Gentiles of all nations, to wipe out
the whole race of Judea. He associat-
ed with him Gor´gias, a general and
a man of experience in military ser-
vice. 10 Nica´nor determined to make
up for the king the tribute due to the
Romans, two thousand talents, by
selling the captured Jews into slavery.
11 And he immediately sent to the cit-
ies on the seacoast, inviting them to
buy Jewish slaves and promising to
hand over ninety slaves for a talent,
not expecting the judgment from the
Almighty that was about to overtake
him.

PREPARATION FOR BATTLE

12 Word came to Judas concern-
ing Nica´nor's invasion; and when he
told his companions of the arrival of
the army, 13 those who were cowardly
and distrustful of God's justice ran
off and got away. 14 Others sold all
their remaining property, and at the
same time besought the Lord to res-
cue those who had been sold by the
ungodly Nica´nor before he ever met
them, 15 if not for their own sake, yet
for the sake of the covenants made
with their fathers, and because he had
called them by his holy and glorious
name. 16 But Maccabe´us gathered his
men together, to the number of six
thousand, and exhorted them not to

[h] Cn: Gk *fallen*
[i] Gk *he*

be frightened by the enemy and not
to fear the great multitude of Gentiles
who were wickedly coming against
them, but to fight nobly, 17keeping
before their eyes the lawless outrage
which the Gentiles[a] had committed
against the holy place, and the tor-
ture of the derided city, and besides,
the overthrow of their ancestral way
of life. 18"For they trust to arms and
acts of daring," he said, "but we trust
in the Almighty God, who is able with
a single nod to strike down those who
are coming against us and even the
whole world."

19 Moreover, he told them of the
times when help came to their ances-
tors; both the time of Sennach′erib,
when one hundred and eighty-five
thousand perished, 20and the time
of the battle with the Galatians that
took place in Babylonia, when eight
thousand in all went into the affair,
with four thousand Macedonians;
and when the Macedonians were hard
pressed, the eight thousand, by the
help that came to them from heaven,
destroyed one hundred and twenty
thousand and took much booty.

JUDAS DEFEATS NICANOR

21 With these words he filled them
with good courage and made them
ready to die for their laws and their
country; then he divided his army into
four parts. 22He appointed his brothers
also, Simon and Joseph and Jonathan,
each to command a division, putting
fifteen hundred men under each.
23Besides, he appointed Elea′zar to
read aloud[b] from the holy book, and
gave the watchword, "God's help";
then, leading the first division him-
self, he joined battle with Nica′nor.

24 With the Almighty as their ally,
they slew more than nine thousand of
the enemy, and wounded and disabled
most of Nica′nor's army, and forced
them all to flee. 25They captured the
money of those who had come to buy
them as slaves. After pursuing them
for some distance, they were obliged
to return because the hour was late.
26For it was the day before the sab-
bath, and for that reason they did not
continue their pursuit. 27And when
they had collected the arms of the en-
emy and stripped them of their spoils,
they kept the sabbath, giving great
praise and thanks to the Lord, who
had preserved them for that day and
allotted it to them as the beginning
of mercy. 28After the sabbath they
gave some of the spoils to those who
had been tortured and to the widows
and orphans, and distributed the rest
among themselves and their children.
29When they had done this, they made
common supplication and besought
the merciful Lord to be wholly recon-
ciled with his servants.

JUDAS DEFEATS TIMOTHY AND BACCHIDES

30 In encounters with the forc-
es of Timothy and Bac′chides they
killed more than twenty thousand of
them and got possession of some ex-
ceedingly high strongholds, and they
divided very much plunder, giving to
those who had been tortured and to
the orphans and widows, and also to
the aged, shares equal to their own.
31Collecting the arms of the enemy,[c]
they stored them all carefully in stra-
tegic places, and carried the rest of
the spoils to Jerusalem. 32They killed
the commander of Timothy's forc-
es, a most unholy man, and one who
had greatly troubled the Jews. 33While
they were celebrating the victory in
the city of their fathers, they burned
those who had set fire to the sacred
gates, Callis′thenes and some others,
who had fled into one little house; so
these received the proper recompense
for their impiety.[d]

34 The thrice-accursed Nica′nor,
who had brought the thousand mer-

[a] Gk *they*
[b] The Greek text of this clause is uncertain
[c] Gk *their arms*
[d] The Greek text of this verse is uncertain

chants to buy the Jews, 35 having been
humbled with the help of the Lord by
opponents whom he regarded as of
the least account, took off his splen-
did uniform and made his way alone
like a runaway slave across the coun-
try till he reached Antioch, having
succeeded chiefly in the destruction
of his own army! 36 Thus he who had
undertaken to secure tribute for the
Romans by the capture of the people
of Jerusalem proclaimed that the Jews
had a Defender, and that therefore the
Jews were invulnerable, because they
followed the laws ordained by him.

THE LAST CAMPAIGN OF ANTIOCHUS EPIPHANES

9 About that time, as it happened,
Anti´ochus had retreated in disor-
der from the region of Persia. 2 For he
had entered the city called Persep´olis,
and attempted to rob the temples and
control the city. Therefore the people
rushed to the rescue with arms, and
Anti´ochus and his men were defeat-
ed,[e] with the result that Anti´ochus
was put to flight by the inhabitants
and beat a shameful retreat. 3 While he
was in Ecbat´ana, news came to him
of what had happened to Nica´nor and
the forces of Timothy. 4 Transported
with rage, he conceived the idea of
turning upon the Jews the injury done
by those who had put him to flight;
so he ordered his charioteer to drive
without stopping until he completed
the journey. But the judgment of heav-
en rode with him! For in his arrogance
he said, "When I get there I will make
Jerusalem a *cemetery of Jews."*

5 But the all-seeing Lord, the God
of Israel, struck him an incurable and
unseen blow. As soon as he ceased
speaking he was seized with a pain in
his bowels for which there was no re-
lief and with sharp internal tortures—
6 and that very justly, for he had tor-
tured the bowels of others with many
and strange inflictions. 7 Yet he did
not in any way stop his insolence, but
was even more filled with arrogance,
breathing fire in his rage against the
Jews, and giving orders to hasten the
journey. And so it came about that he
fell out of his chariot as it was rush-
ing along, and the fall was so hard
as to torture every limb of his body.
8 Thus he who had just been thinking
that he could command the waves of
the sea, in his superhuman arrogance,
and imagining that he could weigh
the high mountains in a balance, was
brought down to earth and carried
in a litter, making the power of God
manifest to all. 9 And so the ungodly
man's body swarmed with worms, and
while he was still living in anguish
and pain, his flesh rotted away, and
because of his stench the whole army
felt revulsion at his decay. 10 Because of
his intolerable stench no one was able
to carry the man who a little while
before had thought that he could
touch the stars of heaven. 11 Then it
was that, broken in spirit, he began
to lose much of his arrogance and to
come to his senses under the scourge
of God, for he was tortured with pain
every moment. 12 And when he could
not endure his own stench, he uttered
these words: "It is right to be subject
to God, and no mortal should think
that he is equal to God."[f]

ANTIOCHUS MAKES A PROMISE TO GOD

13 Then the abominable fellow
made a vow to the Lord, who would
no longer have mercy on him, stating
14 that the holy city, which he was has-
tening to level to the ground and to
make a cemetery, he was now declar-
ing to be free; 15 and the Jews, whom he
had not considered worth burying but
had planned to throw out with their
children to the beasts, for the birds
to pick, he would make, all of them,
equal to citizens of Athens; 16 and the
holy sanctuary, which he had formerly
plundered, he would adorn with the

[e] Gk *they were defeated*
[f] Or *think thoughts proper only to God*

finest offerings; and the holy ves-
sels he would give back, all of them,
many times over; and the expenses
incurred for the sacrifices he would
provide from his own revenues; 17 and
in addition to all this he also would
become a Jew and would visit every
inhabited place to proclaim the power
of God. 18 But when his sufferings did
not in any way abate, for the judgment
of God had justly come upon him, he
gave up all hope for himself and wrote
to the Jews the following letter, in the
form of a supplication. This was its
content:

ANTIOCHUS'S LETTER AND DEATH

19 "To his worthy Jewish citizens,
Anti´ochus their king and gener-
al sends hearty greetings and good
wishes for their health and prosperi-
ty. 20 If you and your children are well
and your affairs are as you wish, I am
glad. As my hope is in heaven, 21 I re-
member with affection your esteem
and good will. On my way back from
the region of Persia I suffered an an-
noying illness, and I have deemed it
necessary to take thought for the gen-
eral security of all. 22 I do not despair
of my condition, for I have good hope
of recovering from my illness, 23 but I
observed that my father, on the oc-
casions when he made expeditions
into the upper country, appointed his
successor, 24 so that, if anything unex-
pected happened or any unwelcome
news came, the people throughout
the realm would not be troubled, for
they would know to whom the gov-
ernment was left. 25 Moreover, I under-
stand how the princes along the bor-
ders and the neighbors to my kingdom
keep watching for opportunities and
waiting to see what will happen. So I
have appointed my son Anti´ochus to
be king, whom I have often entrusted
and commended to most of you when
I hastened off to the upper provinc-
es; and I have written to him what is
written here. 26 I therefore urge and
beseech you to remember the public
and private services rendered to you
and to maintain your present good
will, each of you, toward me and my
son. 27 For I am sure that he will fol-
low my policy and will treat you with
moderation and kindness."

28 So the murderer and blasphem-
er, having endured the most intense
suffering, such as he had inflicted
on others, came to the end of his life
by a most pitiable fate, among the
mountains in a strange land. 29 And
Philip, one of his courtiers, took his
body home; then, fearing the son
of Anti´ochus, he betook himself to
Ptol´emy Philome´tor in Egypt.

PURIFICATION OF THE TEMPLE

10 Now Maccabe´us and his follow-
ers, the Lord leading them on,
recovered the temple and the city;
2 and they tore down the altars which
had been built in the public square
by the foreigners, and also destroyed
the sacred precincts. 3 They purified
the sanctuary, and made another al-
tar of sacrifice; then, striking fire
out of flint, they offered sacrifices,
after a lapse of two years, and they
burned incense and lighted lamps
and set out the bread of the Presence.
4 And when they had done this, they
fell prostrate and besought the Lord
that they might never again fall into
such misfortunes, but that, if they
should ever sin, they might be disci-
plined by him with forbearance and
not be handed over to blasphemous
and barbarous nations. 5 It happened
that on the same day on which the
sanctuary had been profaned by the
foreigners, the purification of the
sanctuary took place, that is, on the
twenty-fifth day of the same month,
which was Chislev. 6 And they cele-
brated it for eight days with rejoicing,
in the manner of the feast of booths,
remembering how not long before,
during the feast of booths, they had
been wandering in the mountains and
caves like wild animals. 7 Therefore
bearing ivy-wreathed wands and

beautiful branches and also fronds of
palm, they offered hymns of thanks-
giving to him who had given success
to the purifying of his own holy place.
8They decreed by public ordinance and
vote that the whole nation of the Jews
should observe these days every year.

9 Such then was the end of Anti´-
ochus, who was called Epiph´anes.

ACCESSION OF ANTIOCHUS EUPATOR

10 Now we will tell what took
place under Anti´ochus Eu´pator,
who was the son of that ungodly
man, and will give a brief summary of
the principal calamities of the wars.
11This man, when he succeeded to the
kingdom, appointed one Lys´ias to
have charge of the government and
to be chief governor of Coelesyria
and Phoenic´ia. 12Ptol´emy, who was
called Macron, took the lead in show-
ing justice to the Jews because of the
wrong that had been done to them,
and attempted to maintain peaceful
relations with them. 13As a result
he was accused before Eu´pator by
the king's friends. He heard him-
self called a traitor at every turn,
because he had abandoned Cyprus,
which Philome´tor had entrusted to
him, and had gone over to Anti´ochus
Epiph´anes. Unable to command the
respect due his office,[a] he took poi-
son and ended his life.

CAMPAIGN IN IDUMEA

14 When Gor´gias became gov-
ernor of the region, h maintained
a force of mercenaries,and at every
turn kept on warringagainst the
Jews. 15Besides this, th Idume´ans,
who had control of impcant strong-
holds, were harassing tl Jews; they
received those who we banished
from Jerusalem, and enavored to
keep up the war. 16But Mabe´us and
his men, after making soln suppli-
cation and beseeching Go fight on
their side, rushed to the ongholds
of the Idume´ans. 17Attag them
vigorously, they gained possession of
the places, and beat off all who fought
upon the wall, and slew those whom
they encountered, killing no fewer
than twenty thousand.

18 When no less than nine thou-
sand took refuge in two very strong
towers well equipped to withstand
a siege, 19Maccabe´us left Simon and
Joseph, and also Zacchae´us and his
men, a force sufficient to besiege
them; and he himself set off for places
where he was more urgently needed.
20But the men with Simon, who were
money-hungry, were bribed by some
of those who were in the towers,
and on receiving seventy thousand
drachmas let some of them slip away.
21When word of what had happened
came to Maccabe´us, he gathered the
leaders of the people, and accused
these men of having sold their breth-
ren for money by setting their ene-
mies free to fight against them. 22Then
he slew these men who had turned
traitor, and immediately captured the
two towers. 23Having success at arms
in everything he undertook, he de-
stroyed more than twenty thousand
in the two strongholds.

JUDAS DEFEATS TIMOTHY

24 Now Timothy, who had been de-
feated by the Jews before, gathered a
tremendous force of mercenaries and
collected the cavalry from Asia in no
small number. He came on, intend-
ing to take Judea by storm. 25As he
drew near, Maccabe´us and his men
sprinkled dust upon their heads and
girded their loins with sackcloth, in
supplication to God. 26Falling upon
the steps before the altar, they be-
sought him to be gracious to them
and to be an enemy to their enemies
and an adversary to their adversaries,
as the law declares. 27And rising from
their prayer they took up their arms
and advanced a considerable distance
from the city; and when they came
near to the enemy they halted. 28Just

[a]Cn: the Greek text here is unc in

as dawn was breaking, the two armies
joined battle, the one having as pledge
of success and victory not only their
valor but their reliance upon the Lord,
while the other made rage their leader
in the fight.
29 When the battle became fierce,
there appeared to the enemy from
heaven five resplendent men on
horses with golden bridles, and they
were leading the Jews. 30 Surrounding
Maccabe´us and protecting him with
their own armor and weapons, they
kept him from being wounded. And
they showered arrows and thun-
derbolts upon the enemy, so that,
confused and blinded, they were
thrown into disorder and cut to piec-
es. 31 Twenty thousand five hundred
were slaughtered, besides six hundred
horsemen.
32 Timothy himself fled to a
stronghold called Gazar´a, especial-
ly well garrisoned, where Chae´reas
was commander. 33 Then Maccabe´us
and his men were glad, and they be-
sieged the fort for four days. 34 The
men within, relying on the strength
of the place, blasphemed terribly and
hurled out wicked words. 35 But at
dawn of the fifth day, twenty young
men in the army of Maccabe´us, fired
with anger because of the blasphe-
mies, bravely stormed the wall and
with savage fury cut down every one
they met. 36 Others who came up in
the same way wheeled around against
the defenders and set fire to the tow-
ers; they kindled fires and burned
the blasphemers alive. Others broke
open the gates and let in the rest
of the force, and they occupied the
city. 37 They killed Timothy, who was
hidden in a cistern, and his broth-
er Chae´reas, and Apolloph´anes.
38 When they had accomplished these
things, with hymns and thanksgiv-
ings they blessed the Lord who shows
great kindness to Israel and gives
them the victory.

LYS´IAS BESIEGES BETH-ZUR

11 Very soon after this, Lys´ias, the
king's guardian and kinsman,
who was in charge of the government,
being vexed at what had happened,
2 gathered about eighty thousand men
and all his cavalry and came against
the Jews. He intended to make the city
a home for Greeks, 3 and to levy tribute
on the temple as he did on the sacred
places of the other nations, and to put
up the high priesthood for sale every
year. 4 He took no account whatever of
the power of God, but was elated with
his ten thousands of infantry, and his
thousands of cavalry, and his eighty
elephants. 5 Invading Judea, he ap-
proached Beth-zur, which was a for-
tified place about five leagues[a] from
Jerusalem, and pressed it hard.
6 When Maccabe´us and his men
got word that Lys´ias[b] was besieg-
ing the strongholds, they and all the
people, with lamentations and tears,
besought the Lord to send a good an-
gel to save Israel. 7 Maccabe´us him-
self was the first to take up arms,
and he urged the others to risk their
lives with him to aid their brethren.
Then they eagerly rushed off togeth-
er. 8 And there, while they were still
near Jerusalem, a horseman appeared
at their head, clothed in white and
brandishing weapons of gold. 9 And
they all together praised the merciful
God, and were strengthened in heart,
ready to assail not only men but the
wildest beasts or walls of iron. 10 They
advanced in battle order, having their
heavenly ally, for the Lord had mercy
on them. 11 They hurled themselves
like lions against the enemy, and slew
eleven thousand of them and sixteen
hundred horsemen, and forced all the
rest to flee. 12 Most of them got away
stripped and wounded, and Lys´ias
himself escaped by disgraceful flight.
13 And as he was not without intelli-
gence, he pondered over the defeat
which had befallen him, and realized

[a] About twenty miles. The text is uncertain here
[b] Gk *he*

that the Hebrews were invincible be-
cause the mighty God fought on their
side. So he sent to them 14and persuad-
ed them to settle everything on just
terms, promising that he would per-
suade the king, constraining him to
be their friend.[c] 15Maccabe´us, having
regard for the common good, agreed
to all that Lys´ias urged. For the king
granted every request in behalf of the
Jews which Maccabe´us delivered to
Lys´ias in writing.

LYS´IAS MAKES PEACE WITH THE JEWS

16 The letter written to the Jews
by Lys´ias was to this effect: "Lys´ias
to the people of the Jews, greeting.
17John and Ab´salom, who were sent
by you, have delivered your signed
communication and have asked about
the matters indicated therein. 18I have
informed the king of everything that
needed to be brought before him, and
he has agreed to what was possible.
19If you will maintain your good will
toward the government, I will en-
deavor for the future to help promote
your welfare. 20And concerning these
matters and their details, I have or-
dered these men and my representa-
tives to confer with you. 21Farewell.
The one hundred and forty-eighth
year,[d] Dioscorin´thius twenty-fourth."

22 The king's letter ran thus: "King
Anti´ochus to his brother Lys´ias,
greeting. 23Now that our father has
gone on to the gods, we desire that
the subjects of the kingdom be un-
disturbed in caring for their own
affairs. 24We have heard that the
Jews do not consent to our father's
change to Greek customs but prefer
their own way of living and ask that
their own customs be allowed them.
25Accordingly, since we choose that
this nation also be free from distur-
bance, our decision is that their tem-
ple be restored to them and that they
live according to the customs of their
ancestors. 26You will do well, there-
fore, to send word to them and give
them pledges of friendship, so that
they may know our policy and be of
good cheer and go on happily in the
conduct of their own affairs."

27 To the nation the king's letter
was as follows: "King Anti´ochus to
the senate of the Jews and to the other
Jews, greeting. 28If you are well, it is as
we desire. We also are in good health.
29Menela´us has informed us that you
wish to return home and look after
your own affairs. 30Therefore those
who go home by the thirtieth day of
Xan´thicus will have our pledge of
friendship and full permission 31for
the Jews to enjoy their own food and
laws, just as formerly, and none of
them shall be molested in any way for
what he may have done in ignorance.
32And I have also sent Menela´us
to encourage you. 33Farewell. The
one hundred and forty-eighth year,[e]
Xan´thicus fifteenth."

34 The Romans also sent them
a letter, which read thus: "Quintus
Mem´mius and Titus Man´ius, envoys
of the Romans, to the people of the
Jews, greeting. 35With regard to what
Lys´ias the kinsman of the king has
granted you, we also give consent.
36But as to the matters which he de-
cided are to be referred to the king,
as soon as you have considered them,
send some one promptly, so that we
may make proposals appropriate for
you. For we are on our way to Antioch.
37Therefore make haste and send some
men, so that we may have your judg-
ment. 38Farewell. The one hundred
and forty-eighth year,[f] Xan´thicus
fifteenth."

INCIDENTS AT JOPPA AND JAMNIA

12 When this agreement had been
reached, Lys´ias returned to the
king, and the Jews went about their
farming.

[c] The Greek text here is corrupt
[d] 164 b. c.
[e] 164 b. c.
[f] 164 b. c.

2 But some of the governors in var-
ious places, Timothy and Apollo´nius
the son of Gennae´us, as well as
Hiero´nymus and De´mophon, and in
addition to these Nica´nor the gover-
nor of Cyprus, would not let them live
quietly and in peace. 3And some men
of Joppa did so ungodly a deed as this:
they invited the Jews who lived among
them to embark, with their wives and
children, on boats which they had
provided, as though there were no ill
will to the Jews;[a] 4and this was done
by public vote of the city. And when
they accepted, because they wished to
live peaceably and suspected nothing,
the men of Joppa[b] took them out to
sea and drowned them, not less than
two hundred. 5When Judas heard of
the cruelty visited on his country-
men, he gave orders to his men 6and,
calling upon God the righteous Judge,
attacked the murderers of his breth-
ren. He set fire to the harbor by night,
and burned the boats, and massacred
those who had taken refuge there.
7Then, because the city's gates were
closed, he withdrew, intending to
come again and root out the whole
community of Joppa. 8But learning
that the men in Jam´nia meant in the
same way to wipe out the Jews who
were living among them, 9he attacked
the people of Jam´nia by night and set
fire to the harbor and the fleet, so
that the glow of the light was seen in
Jerusalem, thirty miles[c] distant.

THE CAMPAIGN IN GILEAD

10 When they had gone more than
a mile[d] from there, on their march
against Timothy, not less than five
thousand Arabs with five hundred
horsemen attacked them. 11After a
hard fight Judas and his men won
the victory, by the help of God. The
defeated nomads besought Judas to
grant them pledges of friendship,
promising to give him cattle and to
help his people[e] in all other ways.
12Judas, thinking that they might re-
ally be useful in many ways, agreed
to make peace with them; and after
receiving his pledges they departed to
their tents.

13 He also attacked a certain city
which was strongly fortified with
earthworks[f] and walls, and inhabit-
ed by all sorts of Gentiles. Its name
was Caspin. 14And those who were
within, relying on the strength of the
walls and on their supply of provi-
sions, behaved most insolently toward
Judas and his men, railing at them and
even blaspheming and saying unholy
things. 15But Judas and his men, call-
ing upon the great Sovereign of the
world, who without battering-rams or
engines of war overthrew Jericho in
the days of Joshua, rushed furiously
upon the walls. 16They took the city
by the will of God, and slaughtered
untold numbers, so that the adjoining
lake, a quarter of a mile[g] wide, ap-
peared to be running over with blood.

JUDAS DEFEATS TIMOTHY'S ARMY

17 When they had gone nine-
ty-five miles[h] from there, they came
to Charax, to the Jews who are called
Toubia´ni. 18They did not find Timothy
in that region, for he had by then de-
parted from the region without ac-
complishing anything, though in one
place he had left a very strong garri-
son. 19Dosith´eus and Sosip´ater, who
were captains under Maccabe´us,
marched out and destroyed those
whom Timothy had left in the strong-
hold, more than ten thousand men.

[a] Gk *them*
[b] Gk they
[c] Gk *two hundred and forty stadia*
[d] Gk *nine stadia*
[e] Gk *them*
[f] The Greek text here is uncertain
[g] Gk *two stadia*
[h] Gk *seven hundred and fifty stadia*

20But Maccabe´us arranged his army
in divisions, set men[i] in command
of the divisions, and hastened after
Timothy, who had with him a hun-
dred and twenty thousand infantry
and two thousand five hundred cav-
alry. 21When Timothy learned of the
approach of Judas, he sent off the
women and the children and also the
baggage to a place called Car´naim;
for that place was hard to besiege and
difficult of access because of the nar-
rowness of all the approaches. 22But
when Judas' first division appeared,
terror and fear came over the enemy
at the manifestation to them of him
who sees all things; and they rushed
off in flight and were swept on, this
way and that, so that often they were
injured by their own men and pierced
by the points of their swords. 23And
Judas pressed the pursuit with the ut-
most vigor, putting the sinners to the
sword, and destroyed as many as thir-
ty thousand men.

24 Timothy himself fell into the
hands of Dosith´eus and Sosip´ater
and their men. With great guile he be-
sought them to let him go in safety,
because he held the parents of most of
them and the brothers of some and no
consideration would be shown them.
25And when with many words he had
confirmed his solemn promise to re-
store them unharmed, they let him go,
for the sake of saving their brethren.

JUDAS WINS OTHER VICTORIES

26 Then Judas[j] marched against
Car´naim and the temple of Atar´gatis,
and slaughtered twenty-five thousand
people. 27After the rout and destruc-
tion of these, he marched also against
Ephron, a fortified city where Lys´ias
dwelt with multitudes of people of all
nationalities.[k] Stalwart young men
took their stand before the walls and
made a vigorous defense; and great
stores of war engines and missiles
were there. 28But the Jews[l] called
upon the Sovereign who with power
shatters the might of his enemies, and
they got the city into their hands, and
killed as many as twenty-five thou-
sand of those who were within it.

29 Setting out from there, they
hastened to Scythop´olis, which is
seventy-five miles[m] from Jerusalem.
30But when the Jews who dwelt there
bore witness to the good will which
the people of Scythop´olis had shown
them and their kind treatment of
them in times of misfortune, 31they
thanked them and exhorted them to
be well disposed to their race in the
future also. Then they went up to
Jerusalem, as the feast of weeks was
close at hand.

JUDAS DEFEATS GORGIAS

32 After the feast called Pentecost,
they hastened against Gor´gias, the
governor of Idume´a. 33And he came
out with three thousand infantry
and four hundred cavalry. 34When
they joined battle, it happened that
a few of the Jews fell. 35But a certain
Dosith´eus, one of Bace´nor's men,
who was on horseback and was a
strong man, caught hold of Gor´gias,
and grasping his cloak was dragging
him off by main strength, wishing to
take the accursed man alive, when
one of the Thracian horsemen bore
down upon him and cut off his arm;
so Gor´gias escaped and reached
Mar´isa.

36 As Esdris and his men had been
fighting for a long time and were
weary, Judas called upon the Lord
to show himself their ally and lead-
er in the battle. 37In the language of
their fathers he raised the battle cry,
with hymns; then he charged against
Gor´gias' men when they were not ex-
pecting it, and put them to flight.

[i] Gk *them*
[j] Gk *he*
[k] The Greek text ofthis sentence is uncertain
[l] Gk *they*
[m] Gk *six hundred stadia*

PRAYERS FOR THOSE KILLED IN BATTLE

38 Then Judas assembled his army
and went to the city of Adul´lam. As
the seventh day was coming on, they
purified themselves according to the
custom, and they kept the sabbath
there.

39 On the next day, as by that time
it had become necessary, Judas and
his men went to take up the bodies of
the fallen and to bring them back to
lie with their kinsmen in the sepul-
chres of their fathers. 40Then under
the tunic of every one of the dead
they found sacred tokens of the idols
of Jam´nia, which the law forbids the
Jews to wear. And it became clear to
all that this was why these men had
fallen. 41So they all blessed the ways of
the Lord, the righteous Judge, who re-
veals the things that are hidden; 42and
they turned to prayer, beseeching
that the sin which had been commit-
ted might be wholly blotted out. And
the noble Judas exhorted the people
to keep themselves free from sin, for
they had seen with their own eyes
what had happened because of the sin
of those who had fallen. 43He also took
up a collection, man by man, to the
amount of two thousand drachmas of
silver, and sent it to Jerusalem to pro-
vide for a sin offering. In doing this he
acted very well and honorably, taking
account of the resurrection. 44For if
he were not expecting that those who
had fallen would rise again, it would
have been superfluous and foolish to
pray for the dead. 45But if he was look-
ing to the splendid reward that is laid
up for those who fall asleep in godli-
ness, it was a holy and pious thought.
Therefore he made atonement for the
dead, that they might be delivered
from their sin.*

MENELAUS IS PUT TO DEATH

13 In the one hundred and forty-ninth
year[a] word came to Judas and his
men that Anti´ochus Eu´pator was
coming with a great army against Ju-
dea, 2and with him Lys´ias, his guard-
ian, who had charge of the govern-
ment. Each of them had a Greek force
of one hundred and ten thousand in-
fantry, five thousand three hundred
cavalry, twenty-two elephants, and
three hundred chariots armed with
scythes.

3 Menela´us also joined them and
with utter hypocrisy urged Anti´ochus
on, not for the sake of his country's
welfare, but because he thought that
he would be established in office. 4But
the King of kings aroused the anger
of Anti´ochus against the scoundrel;
and when Lys´ias informed him that
this man was to blame for all the trou-
ble, he ordered them to take him to
Beroe´a and to put him to death by
the method which is the custom in
that place. 5For there is a tower in that
place, fifty cubits high, full of ashes,
and it has a rim running around it
which on all sides inclines precipi-
tously into the ashes. 6There they all
push to destruction any man guilty
of sacrilege or notorious for other
crimes. 7By such a fate it came about
that Menela´us the lawbreaker died,
without even burial in the earth. 8And
this was eminently just; because he
had committed many sins against the
altar whose fire and ashes were holy,
he met his death in ashes.

A BATTLE NEAR THE CITY OF MODEIN

9 The king with barbarous arro-
gance was coming to show to the Jews
things far worse than those that had
been done[b] in his father's time. 10But
when Judas heard of this, he ordered
the people to call upon the Lord day
and night, now if ever to help those
who were on the point of being de-
prived of the law and their country
and the holy temple, 11and not to let
the people who had just begun to re-
vive fall into the hands of the blas-
phemous Gentiles. 12When they had

[a] 163 B. C.
[b] Or *the worst of the things that had been done*

all joined in the same petition and
had besought the merciful Lord with
weeping and fasting and lying pros-
trate for three days without ceasing,
Judas exhorted them and ordered
them to stand ready.
13 After consulting privately with
the elders, he determined to march
out and decide the matter by the help
of God before the king's army could
enter Judea and get possession of the
city. 14So, committing the decision to
the Creator of the world and exhort-
ing his men to fight nobly to the death
for the laws, temple, city, country, and
commonwealth, he pitched his camp
near Mo´de-in. 15He gave his men the
watchword, "God's victory," and with
a picked force of the bravest young
men, he attacked the king's pavilion at
night and slew as many as two thou-
sand men in the camp. He stabbed[c]
the leading elephant and its rider.
16In the end they filled the camp with
terror and confusion and withdrew in
triumph. 17This happened, just as day
was dawning, because the Lord's help
protected him.

ANTIOCHUS MAKES A TREATY WITH THE JEWS

18 The king, having had a taste of
the daring of the Jews, tried strate-
gy in attacking their positions. 19He
advanced against Beth-zur, a strong
fortress of the Jews, was turned back,
attacked again,[d] and was defeated.
20Judas sent in to the garrison what-
ever was necessary. 21But Rhod´ocus,
a man from the ranks of the Jews,
gave secret information to the enemy;
he was sought for, caught, and put in
prison. 22The king negotiated a second
time with the people in Beth-zur, gave
pledges, received theirs, withdrew, at-
tacked Judas and his men, was defeat-
ed; 23he got word that Philip, who had
been left in charge of the government,
had revolted in Antioch; he was dis-
mayed, called in the Jews, yielded and
swore to observe all their rights, set-
tled with them and offered sacrifice,
honored the sanctuary and showed
generosity to the holy place. 24He re-
ceived Maccabe´us, left Hegemon´ides
as governor from Ptolema´is to Gerar,
25and went to Ptolema´is. The peo-
ple of Ptolema´is were indignant
over the treaty; in fact they were so
angry that they wanted to annul its
terms.[e] 26Lys´ias took the public plat-
form, made the best possible defense,
convinced them, appeased them,
gained their good will, and set out for
Antioch. This is how the king's attack
and withdrawal turned out.

AL´CIMUS SPEAKS AGAINST JUDAS

14 Three years later, word came to
Judas and his men that Deme´trius,
the son of Seleu´cus, had sailed into
the harbor of Trip´olis with a strong
army and a fleet, 2and had taken pos-
session of the country, having made
away with Anti´ochus and his guard-
ian Lys´ias.
3 Now a certain Al´cimus, who
had formerly been high priest but had
wilfully defiled himself in the times
of separation, realized that there was
no way for him to be safe or to have
access again to the holy altar, 4and
went to King Deme´trius in about the
one hundred and fifty-first year,[f] pre-
senting to him a crown of gold and a
palm, and besides these some of the
customary olive branches from the
temple. During that day he kept quiet.
5But he found an opportunity that fur-
thered his mad purpose when he was
invited by Deme´trius to a meeting of
the council and was asked about the
disposition and intentions of the Jews.
He answered:
6 "Those of the Jews who are
called Haside´ans, whose leader is
Judas Maccabe´us, are keeping up war

[c]The Greek text here is uncertain
[d]Or *faltered*
[e]The Greek text of this clause is uncertain
[f]161 b. c.

and stirring up sedition, and will not
let the kingdom attain tranquillity.
7 Therefore I have laid aside my an-
cestral glory—I mean the high priest-
hood—and have now come here, 8 first
because I am genuinely concerned for
the interests of the king, and second
because I have regard also for my fel-
low citizens. For through the folly of
those whom I have mentioned our
whole nation is now in no small mis-
fortune. 9 Since you are acquainted, O
king, with the details of this matter,
deign to take thought for our country
and our hard-pressed nation with the
gracious kindness which you show to
all. 10 For as long as Judas lives, it is
impossible for the government to find
peace."

11 When he had said this, the
rest of the king's friends, who were
hostile to Judas, quickly inflamed
Deme´trius still more. 12 And he im-
mediately chose Nica´nor, who had
been in command of the elephants,
appointed him governor of Judea, and
sent him off 13 with orders to kill Judas
and scatter his men, and to set up
Al´cimus as high priest of the greatest
temple. 14 And the Gentiles through-
out Judea, who had fled before[a] Judas,
flocked to join Nica´nor, thinking that
the misfortunes and calamities of
the Jews would mean prosperity for
themselves.

NICANOR MAKES FRIENDS WITH JUDAS

15 When the Jews[b] heard of
Nica´nor's coming and the gather-
ing of the Gentiles, they sprinkled
dust upon their heads and prayed to
him who established his own people
for ever and always upholds his own
heritage by manifesting himself. 16 At
the command of the leader, they[c]
set out from there immediately and
engaged them in battle at a village
called Dessau.[d] 17 Simon, the brother
of Judas, had encountered Nica´nor,
but had been temporarily[e] checked
because of the sudden consternation
created by the enemy.

18 Nevertheless Nica´nor, hear-
ing of the valor of Judas and his men
and their courage in battle for their
country, shrank from deciding the
issue by bloodshed. 19 Therefore he
sent Posido´nius and Theod´otus and
Mattathi´as to give and receive pledg-
es of friendship. 20 When the terms had
been fully considered, and the leader
had informed the people, and it had
appeared that they were of one mind,
they agreed to the covenant. 21 And the
leaders[f] set a day on which to meet by
themselves. A chariot came forward
from each army; seats of honor were
set in place; 22 Judas posted armed
men in readiness at key places to pre-
vent sudden treachery on the part
of the enemy; they held the proper
conference.

23 Nica´nor stayed on in Jerusalem
and did nothing out of the way, but
dismissed the flocks of people that
had gathered. 24 And he kept Judas al-
ways in his presence; he was warmly
attached to the man. 25 And he urged
him to marry and have children; so he
married, settled down, and shared the
common life.

NICANOR TURNS AGAINST JUDAS

26 But when Al´cimus noticed their
good will for one another, he took the
covenant that had been made and went
to Deme´trius. He told him that Nica´-
nor was disloyal to the government,
for he had appointed that conspirator
against the kingdom, Judas, to be his
successor. 27 The king became excited
and, provoked by the false accusations
of that depraved man, wrote to Nica´-
nor, stating that he was displeased

[a] The Greek text is uncertain
[b] Gk *they*
[c] Gk *he*
[d] The name is uncertain
[e] Other authorities read *slowly*
[f] Gk *they*

with the covenant and commanding
him to send Maccabe´us to Antioch as
a prisoner without delay.

28 When this message came to
Nica´nor, he was troubled and grieved
that he had to annul their agreement
when the man had done no wrong.
29 Since it was not possible to oppose
the king, he watched for an oppor-
tunity to accomplish this by a strata-
gem. 30 But Maccabe´us, noticing that
Nica´nor was more austere in his deal-
ings with him and was meeting him
more rudely than had been his cus-
tom, concluded that this austerity did
not spring from the best motives. So
he gathered not a few of his men, and
went into hiding from Nica´nor.

31 When the latter became aware
that he had been cleverly outwitted
by the man, he went to the great[g] and
holy temple while the priests were of-
fering the customary sacrifices, and
commanded them to hand the man
over. 32 And when they declared on
oath that they did not know where
the man was whom he sought, 33 he
stretched out his right hand toward
the sanctuary, and swore this oath: "If
you do not hand Judas over to me as a
prisoner, I will level this precinct of
God to the ground and tear down the
altar, and I will build here a splendid
temple to Diony´sus."

34 Having said this, he went away.
Then the priests stretched forth their
hands toward heaven and called upon
the constant Defender of our na-
tion, in these words: 35 "O Lord of all,
who hast need of nothing, thou wast
pleased that there be a temple for thy
habitation among us; 36 so now, O holy
One, Lord of all holiness, keep unde-
filed for ever this house that has been
so recently purified."

RAZIS DIES FOR HIS COUNTRY

37 A certain Razis, one of the el-
ders of Jerusalem, was denounced
to Nica´nor as a man who loved his
fellow citizens and was very well
thought of and for his good will was
called father of the Jews. 38 For in for-
mer times, when there was no min-
gling with the Gentiles, he had been
accused of Judaism, and for Judaism
he had with all zeal risked body and
life. 39 Nica´nor, wishing to exhibit the
enmity which he had for the Jews,
sent more than five hundred soldiers
to arrest him; 40 for he thought that by
arresting[h] him he would do them an
injury. 41 When the troops were about
to capture the tower and were forc-
ing the door of the courtyard, they
ordered that fire be brought and the
doors burned. Being surrounded,
Razis[i] fell upon his own sword, 42 pre-
ferring to die nobly rather than to fall
into the hands of sinners and suffer
outrages unworthy of his noble birth.
43 But in the heat of the struggle he did
not hit exactly, and the crowd was
now rushing in through the doors.
He bravely ran up on the wall, and
manfully threw himself down into
the crowd. 44 But as they quickly drew
back, a space opened and he fell in the
middle of the empty space. 45 Still alive
and aflame with anger, he rose, and
though his blood gushed forth and his
wounds were severe he ran through
the crowd; and standing upon a steep
rock, 46 with his blood now complete-
ly drained from him, he tore out his
entrails, took them with both hands
and hurled them at the crowd, calling
upon the Lord of life and spirit to give
them back to him again. This was the
manner of his death.

NICANOR'S ARROGANCE

15 When Nica´nor heard that Judas
and his men were in the region
of Samar´ia, he made plans to attack
them with complete safety on the day
of rest. 2 And when the Jews who were
compelled to follow him said, "Do not
destroy so savagely and barbarously,
but show respect for the day which

[g] Gk *greatest*
[h] The Greek text here is uncertain
[i] Gk *he*

he who sees all things has honored
and hallowed above other days," 3the
thrice-accursed wretch asked if there
were a sovereign in heaven who had
commanded the keeping of the sab-
bath day. 4And when they declared,
"It is the living Lord himself, the
Sovereign in heaven, who ordered us
to observe the seventh day," 5he re-
plied, "And I am a sovereign also, on
earth, and I command you to take up
arms and finish the king's business."
Nevertheless, he did not succeed in
carrying out his abominable design.

JUDAS PREPARES THE JEWS FOR BATTLE

6 This Nica′nor in his utter boast-
fulness and arrogance had deter-
mined to erect a public monument of
victory over Judas and his men. 7But
Maccabe′us did not cease to trust
with all confidence that he would get
help from the Lord. 8And he exhort-
ed his men not to fear the attack of
the Gentiles, but to keep in mind the
former times when help had come to
them from heaven, and now to look
for the victory which the Almighty
would give them. 9Encouraging them
from the law and the prophets, and
reminding them also of the struggles
they had won, he made them the more
eager. 10And when he had aroused
their courage, he gave his orders, at
the same time pointing out the perfi-
dy of the Gentiles and their violation
of oaths. 11He armed each of them not
so much with confidence in shields
and spears as with the inspiration of
brave words, and he cheered them all
by relating a dream, a sort of vision,[a]
which was worthy of belief.

12 What he saw was this: Oni′as,
who had been high priest, a noble
and good man, of modest bearing
and gentle manner, one who spoke
fittingly and had been trained from
childhood in all that belongs to excel-
lence, was praying with outstretched
hands for the whole body of the Jews.
13Then likewise a man appeared, dis-
tinguished by his gray hair and dig-
nity, and of marvelous majesty and
authority. 14And Oni′as spoke, saying,
"This is a man who loves the breth-
ren and prays much for the people and
the holy city, Jeremiah, the prophet
of God." 15Jeremiah stretched out his
right hand and gave to Judas a golden
sword, and as he gave it he addressed
him thus: 16"Take this holy sword, a
gift from God, with which you will
strike down your adversaries."

17 Encouraged by the words of
Judas, so noble and so effective in
arousing valor and awaking manliness
in the souls of the young, they deter-
mined not to carry on a campaign but
to attack bravely, and to decide the
matter, by fighting hand to hand with
all courage, because the city and the
sanctuary and the temple were in dan-
ger. 18Their concern for wives and chil-
dren, and also for brethren and rela-
tives, lay upon them less heavily; their
greatest and first fear was for the con-
secrated sanctuary. 19And those who
had to remain in the city were in no
little distress, being anxious over the
encounter in the open country.

THE DEFEAT AND DEATH OF NICANOR

20 When all were now looking for-
ward to the coming decision, and the
enemy was already close at hand with
their army drawn up for battle, the
elephants strategically stationed and
the cavalry deployed on the flanks,
21Maccabe′us, perceiving the hosts
that were before him and the varied
supply of arms and the savagery of the
elephants,[b] stretched out his hands
toward heaven and called upon the
Lord who works wonders; for he knew
that it is not by arms, but as the Lord[c]
decides, that he gains the victory for
those who deserve it. 22And he called
upon him in these words: "O Lord,
thou didst send thy angel in the time
of Hezeki′ah king of Judea, and he

[a]The Greek text here is uncertain
[b]Gk *beasts*
[c]Gk *he*

slew fully a hundred and eighty-five
thousand in the camp of Sennach´erib.
23So now, O Sovereign of the heavens,
send a good angel to carry terror and
trembling before us. 24By the might
of thy arm may these blasphemers
who come against thy holy people be
struck down." With these words he
ended his prayer.

25 Nica´nor and his men advanced
with trumpets and battle songs;
26and Judas and his men met the en-
emy in battle with invocation to God
and prayers. 27So, fighting with their
hands and praying to God in their
hearts, they laid low no less than thir-
ty-five thousand men, and were great-
ly gladdened by God's manifestation.

28 When the action was over and
they were returning with joy, they
recognized Nica´nor, lying dead, in
full armor. 29Then there was shout-
ing and tumult, and they blessed the
Sovereign Lord in the language of
their fathers. 30And the man who was
ever in body and soul the defender
of his fellow citizens, the man who
maintained his youthful good will to-
ward his countrymen, ordered them
to cut off Nica´nor's head and arm and
carry them to Jerusalem. 31And when
he arrived there and had called his
countrymen together and stationed
the priests before the altar, he sent
for those who were in the citadel.
32He showed them the vile Nica´nor's
head and that profane man's arm,
which had been boastfully stretched
out against the holy house of the
Almighty; 33and he cut out the tongue
of the ungodly Nica´nor and said that
he would give it piecemeal to the birds
and hang up these rewards of his folly
opposite the sanctuary. 34And they all,
looking to heaven, blessed the Lord
who had manifested himself, say-
ing, "Blessed is he who has kept his
own place undefiled." 35And he hung
Nica´nor's head from the citadel, a
clear and conspicuous sign to every
one of the help of the Lord. 36And
they all decreed by public vote never
to let this day go unobserved, but to
celebrate the thirteenth day of the
twelfth month—which is called Adar
in the Syrian language—the day be-
fore Mor´decai's day.

THE COMPILER'S EPILOGUE

37 This, then, is how matters
turned out with Nica´nor. And from
that time the city has been in the pos-
session of the Hebrews. So I too will
here end my story. 38If it is well told
and to the point, that is what I myself
desired; if it is poorly done and medio-
cre, that was the best I could do. 39For
just as it is harmful to drink wine
alone, or, again, to drink water alone,
while wine mixed with water is sweet
and delicious and enhances one's en-
joyment, so also the style of the story
delights the ears of those who read
the work. And here will be the end.

slew fully a hundred and eighty-five
thousand in the camp of Sennacherib.
23 So now, O Sovereign of the heavens,
send a good angel to carry terror and
trembling before us. 24 By the might
of thy arm may these blasphemers
who come against thy holy people be
struck down." With these words he
ended his prayer.
25 Nicanor and his men advanced
with trumpets and battle songs;
26 and Judas and his men met the en-
emy in battle with invocation to God
and prayers. 27 So, fighting with their
hands and praying to God in their
hearts, they laid low no less than thir-
ty-five thousand men, and were great-
ly gladdened by God's manifestation.
28 When the action was over and
they were returning with joy, they
recognized Nicanor, lying dead, in
full armor. 29 Then there was shout-
ing and tumult, and they blessed the
Sovereign Lord in the language of
their fathers. 30 And the man who was
ever in body and soul the defender
of his fellow citizens, the man who
maintained his youthful good will to-
ward his countrymen, ordered them
to cut off Nicanor's head and arm and
carry them to Jerusalem. 31 And when
he arrived there and had called his
countrymen together and stationed
the priests before the altar, he sent
for those who were in the citadel.
32 He showed them the vile Nicanor's
head and that profane man's arm,
which had been boastfully stretched
out against the holy house of the
Almighty; 33 and he cut out the tongue
of the ungodly Nicanor and said that
he would give it piecemeal to the birds
and hang up these rewards of his folly
opposite the sanctuary. 34 And they all,
looking to heaven, blessed the Lord
who had manifested himself, say-
ing, "Blessed is he who has kept his
own place undefiled." 35 And he hung
Nicanor's head from the citadel, a
clear and conspicuous sign to every
one of the help of the Lord. 36 And
they all decreed by public vote never
to let this day go unobserved, but to
celebrate the thirteenth day of the
twelfth month—which is called Adar
in the Syrian language—the day be-
fore Mordecai's day.

THE COMPILER'S EPILOGUE

37 This, then, is how matters
turned out with Nicanor. And from
that time the city has been in the pos-
session of the Hebrews. So I too will
here end my story. 38 If it is well told
and to the point, that is what I myself
desired; if it is poorly done and medio-
cre, that was the best I could do. 39 For
just as it is harmful to drink wine
alone, or, again, to drink water alone,
while wine mixed with water is sweet
and delicious and enhances one's en-
joyment, so also the style of the story
delights the ears of those who read
the work. And here will be the end.

NEW TESTAMENT

THE GOSPEL ACCORDING TO
MATTHEW

THE GENEALOGY OF JESUS THE MESSIAH

1 The book of the genealogy of Jesus
Christ, the son of David, the son of
Abraham.*

2 Abraham was the father of
Isaac, and Isaac the father of Jacob,
and Jacob the father of Judah and his
brothers, 3and Judah the father of
Perez and Zerah by Tamar, and Perez
the father of Hezron, and Hezron the
father of Ram,[a] 4and Ram[b] the father
of Ammin´adab, and Ammin´adab the
father of Nahshon, and Nahshon the
father of Salmon, 5and Salmon the
father of Bo´az by Rahab, and Bo´az
the father of Obed by Ruth, and Obed
the father of Jesse, 6and Jesse the fa-
ther of David the king. And David
was the father of Solomon by the
wife of Uri´ah, 7and Solomon the fa-
ther of Rehobo´am, and Rehobo´am
the father of Abi´jah, and Abi´jah the
father of Asa,[c] 8and Asa[d] the father
of Jehosh´aphat, and Jehosh´aphat
the father of Joram, and Joram the
father of Uzzi´ah, 9and Uzzi´ah the
father of Jotham, and Jotham the fa-
ther of Ahaz, and Ahaz the father of
Hezeki´ah, 10and Hezeki´ah the father
of Manas´seh, and Manas´seh the fa-
ther of Amos,[e] and Amos[f] the father
of Josi´ah, 11and Josi´ah the father of
Jechoni´ah and his brothers, at the
time of the deportation to Babylon.

12 And after the deportation
to Babylon: Jechoni´ah was the fa-
ther of She-al´ti-el,[g] and She-al´ti-
el[h] the father of Zerub´babel, 13and
Zerub´babel the father of Abi´ud,
and Abi´ud the father of Eli´akim,
and Eli´akim the father of Azor, 14and
Azor the father of Zadok, and Zadok
the father of Achim, and Achim the
father of Eli´ud, 15and Eli´ud the fa-
ther of Elea´zar, and Elea´zar the fa-
ther of Matthan, and Matthan the fa-
ther of Jacob, 16and Jacob the father of
Joseph the husband of Mary, of whom
Jesus was born, who is called Christ.*

17 So all the generations from
Abraham to David were fourteen
generations, and from David to the
deportation to Babylon fourteen gen-
erations, and from the deportation
to Babylon to the Christ fourteen
generations.

THE BIRTH OF JESUS THE MESSIAH

18 Now the birth of Jesus Christ[i]
took place in this way. When his
mother Mary had been betrothed to
Joseph, before they came together
she was found to be with child of the
Holy Spirit; 19and her husband Joseph,
being a just man and unwilling to put
her to shame, resolved to send her
away quietly. 20But as he considered
this, behold, an angel of the Lord
appeared to him in a dream, saying,
"Joseph, son of David, do not fear to
take Mary your wife, for that which is
conceived in her is of the Holy Spirit;
21she will bear a son, and you shall call
his name Jesus, for he will save his
people from their sins." 22All this took
place to fulfil what the Lord had spo-
ken by the prophet:

23"Behold, a virgin shall conceive
and bear a son,
and his name shall be called
Emman´u-el"

[a]Greek *Aram*
[b]Greek *Aram*
[c]Greek *Asaph*
[d]Greek *Asaph*
[e]Other authorities read *Amon*
[f]Other authorities read *Amon*
[g]Greek *Salathiel*
[h]Greek *Salathiel*
[i]Other ancient authorities read *of the Christ*

24When Joseph woke from sleep, he
did as the angel of the Lord command-
ed him; he took his wife, 25but knew
her not until she had borne a son;*
and he called his name Jesus.

THE VISIT OF THE WISE MEN

2 Now when Jesus was born in
Bethlehem of Judea in the days of
Herod the king, behold, wise men
from the East came to Jerusalem, say-
ing, 2"Where is he who has been born
king of the Jews? For we have seen
his star in the East, and have come to
worship him." 3When Herod the king
heard this, he was troubled, and all
Jerusalem with him; 4and assembling
all the chief priests and scribes of the
people, he inquired of them where the
Christ was to be born. 5They told him,
"In Bethlehem of Judea; for so it is
written by the prophet:

6'And you, O Bethlehem, in the
land of Judah,
are by no means least among
the rulers of Judah;
for from you shall come a ruler
who will govern my people
Israel.'"

7 Then Herod summoned the wise
men secretly and ascertained from
them what time the star appeared;
8and he sent them to Bethlehem, say-
ing, "Go and search diligently for the
child, and when you have found him
bring me word, that I too may come
and worship him." 9When they had
heard the king they went their way;
and lo, the star which they had seen in
the East went before them, till it came
to rest over the place where the child
was. 10When they saw the star, they
rejoiced exceedingly with great joy;
11and going into the house they saw
the child with Mary his mother, and
they fell down and worshiped him.
Then, opening their treasures, they
offered him gifts, gold and frankin-
cense and myrrh. 12And being warned
in a dream not to return to Herod,
they departed to their own country by
another way.

THE ESCAPE TO EGYPT

13 Now when they had departed,
behold, an angel of the Lord appeared
to Joseph in a dream and said, "Rise,
take the child and his mother, and flee
to Egypt, and remain there till I tell
you; for Herod is about to search for
the child, to destroy him." 14And he
rose and took the child and his moth-
er by night, and departed to Egypt,
15and remained there until the death
of Herod. This was to fulfil what the
Lord had spoken by the prophet, "Out
of Egypt have I called my son."

THE MASSACRE OF THE INFANTS

16 Then Herod, when he saw
that he had been tricked by the wise
men, was in a furious rage, and he
sent and killed all the male children
in Bethlehem and in all that region
who were two years old or under, ac-
cording to the time which he had as-
certained from the wise men. 17Then
was fulfilled what was spoken by the
prophet Jeremiah:

18"A voice was heard in Ramah,
wailing and loud lamentation,
Rachel weeping for her
children;
she refused to be consoled,
because they were no more."

THE RETURN FROM EGYPT

19 But when Herod died, behold,
an angel of the Lord appeared in a
dream to Joseph in Egypt, saying,
20"Rise, take the child and his moth-
er, and go to the land of Israel, for
those who sought the child's life are
dead." 21And he rose and took the
child and his mother, and went to the
land of Israel. 22But when he heard
that Archela´us reigned over Judea
in place of his father Herod, he was
afraid to go there, and being warned
in a dream he withdrew to the district
of Galilee. 23And he went and dwelt
in a city called Nazareth, that what
was spoken by the prophets might
be fulfilled, "He shall be called a
Nazarene."

THE PROCLAMATION OF JOHN THE BAPTIST

3 In those days came John the Baptist,
preaching in the wilderness of
Judea, 2"Repent,* for the kingdom of
heaven is at hand." 3For this is he who
was spoken of by the prophet Isaiah
when he said,

"The voice of one crying in the
wilderness:
Prepare the way of the Lord,
make his paths straight."

4Now John wore a garment of
camel's hair, and a leather girdle
around his waist; and his food was
locusts and wild honey. 5Then went
out to him Jerusalem and all Judea
and all the region about the Jordan,
6and they were baptized by him in
the river Jordan, confessing their
sins.*

7 But when he saw many of the
Pharisees and Sad´ducees coming
for baptism, he said to them, "You
brood of vipers! Who warned you
to flee from the wrath to come?
8Bear fruit that befits repentance,
9and do not presume to say to your-
selves, 'We have Abraham as our fa-
ther'; for I tell you, God is able from
these stones to raise up children to
Abraham. 10Even now the axe is laid
to the root of the trees; every tree
therefore that does not bear good
fruit is cut down and thrown into
the fire.

11 "I baptize you withwater for re-
pentance, but he who is coming after
me is mightier than I, whose sandals
I am not worthy to carry; he will bap-
tize you with the Holy Spirit and with
fire. 12*His winn*owing fok is in his
hand, and he will clear hi threshing
floor and gather his whet into the
granary, but the chaff hewill burn
with unquenchable fire."

THE BAPTISM OF JESU

13 Then Jesus came fro Galilee
to the Jordan to John, to bbaptized
by him. 14John would have evented
him, saying, "I need to be baptized by
you, and do you come to me?" 15But
Jesus answered him, "Let it be so now;
for thus it is fitting for us to fulfil all
righteousness." Then he consented.*
16And when Jesus was baptized, he
went up immediately from the water,
and behold, the heavens were opened[a]
and he saw the Spirit of God descend-
ing like a dove, and alighting on him;
17and lo, a voice from heaven, saying,
"This is my beloved Son,[b] with whom
I am well pleased."

THE TEMPTATION OF JESUS

4 Then Jesus was led up by the Spirit
into the wilderness to be tempted
by the devil. 2And he fasted forty days
and forty nights, and afterward he
was hungry. 3And the tempter came
and said to him, "If you are the Son
of God, command these stones to
become loaves of bread." 4But he an-
swered, "It is written,

'Man shall not live by bread
alone,
but by every word that pro-
ceeds from the mouth of
God.'"

5Then the devil took him to the
holy city, and set him on the pinnacle
of the temple, 6and said to him, "If you
are the Son of God, throw yourself
down; for it is written,

'He will give his angels charge
of you,'
'On their hands they will bear
you up,
lest you strike your foot against
a stone.'"

7Jesus said to him, "Again it is
written, 'You shall not tempt the Lord
your God.'" 8Again, the devil took him
to a very high mountain, and showed
him all the kingdoms of the world and
the glory of them; 9and he said to him,
"All these I will give you, if you will
fall down and worship me." 10Then
Jesus said to him, "Begone, Satan! for
it is written,

[a]Other ancient authorities add ton
[b]Or *my Son, my* (or *the*) *Beloved*

'You shall worship the Lord
your God
and him only shall you serve.'"
11Then the devil left him, and be-
hold, angels came and ministered to
him.

JESUS BEGINS HIS MINISTRY IN GALILEE

12 Now when he heard that John
had been arrested, he withdrew into
Galilee; 13and leaving Nazareth he
went and dwelt in Caper′na-um by the
sea, in the territory of Zeb′ulun and
Naph′tali, 14that what was spoken by
the prophet Isaiah might be fulfilled:
15"The land of Zeb′ulun and the
land of Naph′tali,
toward the sea, across the
Jordan,
Galilee of the Gentiles—
16the people who sat in darkness
have seen a great light,
and for those who sat in the
region and shadow of
death
light has dawned."
17From that time Jesus began to
preach, saying, "Repent, for the king-
dom of heaven is at hand."

JESUS CALLS THE FIRST DISCIPLES

18 As he walked by the Sea of
Galilee, he saw two brothers, Simon
who is called Peter and Andrew his
brother, casting a net into the sea; for
they were fishermen. 19And he said to
them, "Follow me, and I will make
you fishers of men." 20Immediately
they left their nets and followed him.
21And going on from there he saw
two other brothers, James the son
of Zeb′edee and John his brother, in
the boat with Zeb′edee their father,
mending their nets, and he called
them. 22Immediately they left the boat
and their father, and followed him.

JESUS MINISTERS TO CROWDS OF PEOPLE

23 And he went about all Galilee,
teaching in their synagogues and
preaching the gospel of the kingdom
and healing every disease and every
infirmity among the people. 24So his
fame spread throughout all Syria,
and they brought him all the sick,
those afflicted with various diseas-
es and pains, demoniacs, epileptics,
and paralytics, and he healed them.
25And great crowds followed him
from Galilee and the Decap′olis and
Jerusalem and Judea and from beyond
the Jordan.

THE BEATITUDES

5 Seeing the crowds, he went up on
the mountain, and when he sat
down his disciples came to him. 2And
he opened his mouth and taught
them, saying:
3 "Blessed are the poor in spirit,
for theirs is the kingdom of heaven.
4 "Blessed are those who mourn,
for they shall be comforted.
5 "Blessed are the meek, for they
shall inherit the earth.
6 "Blessed are those who hunger
and thirst for righteousness, for they
shall be satisfied.
7 "Blessed are the merciful, for
they shall obtain mercy.
8 "Blessed are the pure in heart,
for they shall see God.
9 "Blessed are the peacemakers,
for they shall be called sons of God.
10 "Blessed are those who are per-
secuted for righteousness' sake, for
theirs is the kingdom of heaven.
11 "Blessed are you when men re-
vile you and persecute you and utter
all kinds of evil against you falsely
on my account. 12Rejoice and be glad,
for your reward is great in heaven, for
so men persecuted the prophets who
were before you.

SALT AND LIGHT

13 "You are the salt of the earth;
but if salt has lost its taste, how shall
its saltness be restored? It is no longer
good for anything except to be thrown
out and trodden under foot by men.
14 "You are the light of the world.
A city set on a hill cannot be hid. 15Nor
do men light a lamp and put it under

a bushel, but on a stand, and it gives
light to all in the house. 16Let your
light so shine before men, that they
may see your good works and give
glory to your Father who is in heaven.

THE LAW AND THE PROPHETS

17 "Think not that I have come
to abolish the law and the prophets;
I have come not to abolish them but
to fulfil them.* 18For truly, I say to
you, till heaven and earth pass away,
not an iota, not a dot, will pass from
the law until all is accomplished.
19Whoever then relaxes one of the
least of these commandments and
teaches men so, shall be called least
in the kingdom of heaven; but he who
does them and teaches them shall be
called great in the kingdom of heaven.
20For I tell you, unless your righteous-
ness exceeds that of the scribes and
Pharisees, you will never enter the
kingdom of heaven.

CONCERNING ANGER

21 "You have heard that it was said
to the men of old, 'You shall not kill;
and whoever kills shall be liable to
judgment.' 22But I say to you that ev-
ery one who is angry with his brother[a]
shall be liable to judgment; whoever
insults[b] his brother shall be liable to
the council, and whoever says, 'You
fool!' shall be liable to the hell[c] of fire.
23So if you are offering your gift at the
altar, and there remember that your
brother has something against you,
24leave your gift there before the al-
tar and go; first be reconciled to your
brother, and then come and offer your
gift. 25Make friends quickly with your
accuser, while you are going with him
to court, lest your accuser hand you
over to the judge, and the judge to the
guard, and you be put in prison; 26tru-
ly, I say to you, you will never get out
till you have paid the last penny.

CONCERNING ADULTERY

27 "You have heard that it was said,
'You shall not commit adultery.' 28But
I say to you that every one who looks
at a woman lustfully has already com-
mitted adultery with her in his heart.
29If your right eye causes you to sin,
pluck it out and throw it away; it is
better that you lose one of your mem-
bers than that your whole body be
thrown into hell.[d]* 30And if your right
hand causes you to sin, cut it off and
throw it away; it is better that you lose
one of your members than that your
whole body go into hell.[e]

CONCERNING DIVORCE

31 "It was also said, 'Whoever di-
vorces his wife, let him give her a cer-
tificate of divorce.' 32But I say to you
that every one who divorces his wife,
except on the ground of unchastity,*
makes her an adulteress; and whoever
marries a divorced woman commits
adultery.

CONCERNING OATHS

33 "Again you have heard that it
was said to the men of old, 'You shall
not swear falsely, but shall perform to
the Lord what you have sworn.' 34But I
say to you, Do not swear at all, either
by heaven, for it is the throne of God,
35or by the earth, for it is his footstool,
or by Jerusalem, for it is the city of
the great King. 36And do not swear by
your head, for you cannot make one
hair white or black. 37Let what you say
be simply 'Yes' or 'No'; anything more
than this comes from evil.[f]

CONCERNING RETALIATION

38 "You have heard that it was said,
'An eye for an eye and a tooth for a
tooth.' 39But I say to you, Do not resist

[a] Other ancient authorities insert *without cause*
[b] Greek *says Raca to* (an obscure term of abuse)
[c] Greek *Gehenna*
[d] Greek *Gehenna*
[e] Greek *Gehenna*
[f] Or *the evil one*

one who is evil. But if any one strikes
you on the right cheek, turn to him
the other also; 40and if any one would
sue you and take your coat, let him
have your cloak as well; 41and if any
one forces you to go one mile, go with
him two miles. 42Give to him who begs
from you, and do not refuse him who
would borrow from you.

LOVE FOR ENEMIES

43 "You have heard that it was
said, 'You shall love your neighbor
and hate your enemy.' 44But I say to
you, Love your enemies and pray for
those who persecute you, 45so that you
may be sons of your Father who is in
heaven; for he makes his sun rise on
the evil and on the good, and sends
rain on the just and on the unjust.
46For if you love those who love you,
what reward have you? Do not even
the tax collectors do the same? 47And
if you salute only your brethren, what
more are you doing than others? Do
not even the Gentiles do the same?
48You, therefore, must be perfect, as
your heavenly Father is perfect.

CONCERNING ALMSGIVING

6 "Beware of practicing your piety
before men in order to be seen by
them; for then you will have no reward
from your Father who is in heaven.

2 "Thus, when you give alms,
sound no trumpet before you, as
the hypocrites do in the synagogues
and in the streets, that they may be
praised by men. Truly, I say to you,
they have their reward. 3But when you
give alms, do not let your left hand
know what your right hand is doing,
4so that your alms may be in secret;
and your Father who sees in secret
will reward you.

CONCERNING PRAYER

5 "And when you pray, you must
not be like the hypocrites; for they
love to stand and pray in the syna-
gogues and at the street corners, that
they may be seen by men. Truly, I say
to you, they have their reward. 6But
when you pray, go into your room and
shut the door and pray to your Father
who is in secret; and your Father who
sees in secret will reward you.*

7 "And in praying do not heap up
empty phrases as the Gentiles do; for
they think that they will be heard for
their many words. 8Do not be like
them, for your Father knows what you
need before you ask him. 9Pray then
like this:

Our Father who art in heaven,
Hallowed be thy name.
10Thy kingdom come,
Thy will be done,
On earth as it is in heaven.
11Give us this day our daily
bread;[a]
12And forgive us our debts,
As we also have forgiven our
debtors;
13And lead us not into temptation,
But deliver us from evil.[b]

14For if you forgive men their tres-
passes, your heavenly Father also will
forgive you; 15but if you do not forgive
men their trespasses, neither will
your Father forgive your trespasses.

CONCERNING FASTING

16 "And when you fast, do not look
dismal, like the hypocrites, for they
disfigure their faces that their fast-
ing may be seen by men. Truly, I say
to you, they have their reward. 17But
when you fast, anoint your head and
wash your face, 18that your fasting may
not be seen by men but by your Father
who is in secret; and your Father who
sees in secret will reward you.

CONCERNING TREASURES

19 "Do not lay up for yourselves
treasures on earth, where moth and
rust[c] consume and where thieves

[a] Or *our bread for the morrow*
[b] Or *the evil one.* Other authorities, some ancient, add, in some form, *For thine is the kingdom and the power and the glory, for ever. Amen.*
[c] Or *worm*

break in and steal, 20but lay up for
yourselves treasures in heaven, where
neither moth nor rust[d] consumes and
where thieves do not break in and
steal. 21For where your treasure is,
there will your heart be also.

THE SOUND EYE

22 "The eye is the lamp of the body.
So, if your eye is sound, your whole
body will be full of light; 23but if your
eye is not sound, your whole body will
be full of darkness. If then the light
in you is darkness, how great is the
darkness!

SERVING TWO MASTERS

24 "No one can serve two masters;
for either he will hate the one and love
the other, or he will be devoted to the
one and despise the other. You cannot
serve God and mammon.*

DO NOT WORRY

25 "Therefore I tell you, do not
be anxious about your life, what you
shall eat or what you shall drink,
nor about your body, what you shall
put on. Is not life more than food,
and the body more than clothing?
26Look at the birds of the air: they
neither sow nor reap nor gather into
barns, and yet your heavenly Father
feeds them. Are you not of more val-
ue than they? 27And which of you by
being anxious can add one cubit to
his span of life?[e] 28And why are you
anxious about clothing? Consider the
lilies of the field, how they grow; they
neither toil nor spin; 29yet I tell you,
even Solomon in all his glory was
not arrayed like one of these. 30But if
God so clothes the grass of the field,
which today is alive and tomorrow
is thrown into the oven, will he not
much more clothe you, O men of lit-
tle faith? 31Therefore do not be anx-
ious, saying, 'What shall we eat?' or
'What shall we drink?' or 'What shall
we wear?' 32For the Gentiles seek
all these things; and your heavenly
Father knows that you need them all.
33But seek first his kingdom and his
righteousness, and all these things
shall be yours as well.

34 "Therefore do not be anxious
about tomorrow, for tomorrow will be
anxious for itself. Let the day's own
trouble be sufficient for the day.

JUDGING OTHERS

7 "Judge not, that you be not judged.
2For with the judgment you pro-
nounce you will be judged, and the
measure you give will be the measure
you get. 3Why do you see the speck
that is in your brother's eye, but do
not notice the log that is in your own
eye? 4Or how can you say to your
brother, 'Let me take the speck out
of your eye,' when there is the log in
your own eye? 5You hypocrite, first
take the log out of your own eye, and
then you will see clearly to take the
speck out of your brother's eye.

PROFANING THE HOLY

6 "Do not give dogs what is holy;
and do not throw your pearls before
swine, lest they trample them under
foot and turn to attack you.

ASK, SEARCH, KNOCK

7 "Ask, and it will be given you;
seek, and you will find; knock, and
it will be opened to you. 8For every
one who asks receives, and he who
seeks finds, and to him who knocks
it will be opened. 9Or what man of
you, if his son asks him for bread,
will give him a stone? 10Or if he asks
for a fish, will give him a serpent?
11If you then, who are evil, know how
to give good gifts to your children,
how much more will your Father
who is in heaven give good things
to those who ask him! 12So whatever
you wish that men would do to you,
do so to them; for this is the law and
the prophets.

[d]Or *worm*
[e]Or *to his stature*

THE NARROW GATE

13 "Enter by the narrow gate; for
the gate is wide and the way is easy,[a]
that leads to destruction, and those
who enter by it are many. 14For the
gate is narrow and the way is hard,
that leads to life, and those who find
it are few.

A TREE AND ITS FRUIT

15 "Beware of false prophets, who
come to you in sheep's clothing but in-
wardly are ravenous wolves. 16You will
know them by their fruits. Are grapes
gathered from thorns, or figs from
thistles? 17So, every sound tree bears
good fruit, but the bad tree bears evil
fruit. 18A sound tree cannot bear evil
fruit, nor can a bad tree bear good
fruit. 19Every tree that does not bear
good fruit is cut down and thrown
into the fire. 20Thus you will know
them by their fruits.

CONCERNING SELF-DECEPTION

21 "Not every one who says to me,
'Lord, Lord,' shall enter the kingdom
of heaven, but he who does the will of
my Father who is in heaven. 22On that
day many will say to me, 'Lord, Lord,
did we not prophesy in your name,
and cast out demons in your name,
and do many mighty works in your
name?' 23And then will I declare to
them, 'I never knew you; depart from
me, you evildoers.'

HEARERS AND DOERS

24 "Every one then who hears
these words of mine and does them
will be like a wise man who built his
house upon the rock; 25and the rain
fell, and the floods came, and the
winds blew and beat upon that house,
but it did not fall, because it had been
founded on the rock. 26And every one
who hears these words of mine and
does not do them will be like a fool-
ish man who built his house upon
the sand; 27and the rain fell, and the
floods came, and the winds blew and
beat against that house, and it fell;
and great was the fall of it."

28 And when Jesus finished these
sayings, the crowds were astonished
at his teaching, 29for he taught them
as one who had authority, and not as
their scribes.

JESUS CLEANSES A LEPER

8 When he came down from the
mountain, great crowds followed
him; 2and behold, a leper came to him
and knelt before him, saying, "Lord,
if you will, you can make me clean."
3And he stretched out his hand and
touched him, saying, "I will; be
clean." And immediately his leprosy
was cleansed.* 4And Jesus said to him,
"See that you say nothing to any one;
but go, show yourself to the priest,
and offer the gift that Moses com-
manded, for a proof to the people."[b]

JESUS HEALS A CENTURION'S SERVANT

5 As he entered Caper'na-um, a
centurion came forward to him, be-
seeching him 6and saying, "Lord, my
servant is lying paralyzed at home, in
terrible distress." 7And he said to him,
"I will come and heal him." 8But the
centurion answered him, "Lord, I am
not worthy to have you come under
my roof; but only say the word, and
my servant will be healed. 9For I am
a man under authority, with soldiers
under me; and I say to one, 'Go,' and
he goes, and to another, 'Come,' and
he comes, and to my slave, 'Do this,'
and he does it." 10When Jesus heard
him, he marveled, and said to those
who followed him, "Truly, I say to
you, not even[c] in Israel have I found
such faith 11I tell you, many will come
from east and west and sit at table
with Abraham, Isaac, and Jacob in the
kingdom of heaven, 12while the sons of
the kingdom will be thrown into the
outer darkness; there men will weep

[a] Other ancient authorities read *for the way is wide and easy*
[b] Greek *to them*
[c] Other ancient authorities read *with no one*

and gnash their teeth." 13And to the
centurion Jesus said, "Go; be it done
for you as you have believed." And
the servant was healed at that very
moment.

JESUS HEALS MANY AT PETER'S HOUSE

14 And when Jesus entered Peter's
house, he saw his mother-in-law ly-
ing sick with a fever; 15he touched
her hand, and the fever left her, and
she rose and served him. 16That eve-
ning they brought to him many who
were possessed with demons; and he
cast out the spirits with a word, and
healed all who were sick. 17This was to
fulfil what was spoken by the prophet
Isaiah, "He took our infirmities and
bore our diseases."

WOULD-BE FOLLOWERS OF JESUS

18 Now when Jesus saw great
crowds around him, he gave orders to
go over to the other side. 19And a scribe
came up and said to him, "Teacher, I
will follow you wherever you go."
20And Jesus said to him, "Foxes have
holes, and birds of the air have nests;
but the Son of man has nowhere to lay
his head." 21Another of the disciples
said to him, "Lord, let me first go and
bury my father." 22But Jesus said to
him, "Follow me, and leave the dead
to bury their own dead."

JESUS STILLS THE STORM

23 And when he got into the boat,
his disciples followed him. 24And be-
hold, there arose a great storm on
the sea, so that the boat was being
swamped by the waves; but he was
asleep. 25And they went and woke
him, saying, "Save, Lord; we are per-
ishing." 26And he said to them, "Why
are you afraid, O men of little faith?"
Then he rose and rebuked the winds
and the sea; and there was a great
calm. 27And the men marveled, saying,
"What sort of man is this, that even
winds and sea obey him?"

JESUS HEALS THE GADARENE DEMONIACS

28 And when he came to the
other side, to the country of the
Gadarenes,[d] two demoniacs met
him, coming out of the tombs, so
fierce that no one could pass that
way. 29And behold, they cried out,
"What have you to do with us, O Son
of God? Have you come here to tor-
ment us before the time?"* 30Now a
herd of many swine was feeding at
some distance from them. 31And the
demons begged him, "If you cast us
out, send us away into the herd of
swine." 32And he said to them, "Go."
So they came out and went into the
swine; and behold, the whole herd
rushed down the steep bank into
the sea, and perished in the waters.
33The herdsmen fled, and going into
the city they told everything, and
what had happened to the demoni-
acs. 34And behold, all the city came
out to meet Jesus; and when they saw
him, they begged him to leave their
neighborhood.

JESUS HEALS A PARALYTIC

9 And getting into a boat he crossed
over and came to his own city.
2And behold, they brought to him a
paralytic, lying on his bed; and when
Jesus saw their faith he said to the
paralytic, "Take heart, my son; your
sins are forgiven." 3And behold,
some of the scribes said to them-
selves, "This man is blaspheming."
4But Jesus, knowing[e] their thoughts,
said, "Why do you think evil in your
hearts? 5For which is easier, to say,
'Your sins are forgiven,' or to say,
'Rise and walk'? 6But that you may
know that the Son of man has au-
thority on earth to forgive sins"—he
then said to the paralytic—"Rise,
take up your bed and go home." 7And
he rose and went home. 8When the
crowds saw it, they were afraid, and
they glorified God, who had given
such authority to men.

[d]Other ancient authorities read *Gergesenes*; some, *Gerasenes*
[e]Other ancient authorities read *seeing*

THE CALL OF MATTHEW

9 As Jesus passed on from there,
he saw a man called Matthew sitting
at the tax office; and he said to him,
"Follow me." And he rose and fol-
lowed him.

10 And as he sat at table[a] in the
house, behold, many tax collectors
and sinners came and sat down with
Jesus and his disciples. 11And when
the Pharisees saw this, they said to his
disciples, "Why does your teacher eat
with tax collectors and sinners?" 12But
when he heard it, he said, "Those who
are well have no need of a physician,
but those who are sick. 13Go and learn
what this means, 'I desire mercy, and
not sacrifice.' For I came not to call
the righteous, but sinners."

THE QUESTION ABOUT FASTING

14 Then the disciples of John came
to him, saying, "Why do we and the
Pharisees fast,[b] but your disciples do
not fast?" 15And Jesus said to them,
"Can the wedding guests mourn as
long as the bridegroom is with them?
The days will come, when the bride-
groom is taken away from them, and
then they will fast. 16And no one puts
a piece of unshrunk cloth on an old
garment, for the patch tears away
from the garment, and a worse tear is
made. 17Neither is new wine put into
old wineskins; if it is, the skins burst,
and the wine is spilled, and the skins
are destroyed; but new wine is put
into fresh wineskins, and so both are
preserved."

A GIRL RESTORED TO LIFE AND A WOMAN HEALED

18 While he was thus speaking
to them, behold, a ruler came in and
knelt before him, saying, "My daugh-
ter has just died; but come and lay your
hand on her, and she will live." 19And
Jesus rose and followed him, with his
disciples. 20And behold, a woman who
had suffered from a hemorrhage for
twelve years came up behind him and
touched the fringe of his garment; 21for
she said to herself, "If I only touch his
garment, I shall be made well." 22Jesus
turned, and seeing her he said, "Take
heart, daughter; your faith has made
you well." And instantly the wom-
an was made well. 23And when Jesus
came to the ruler's house, and saw the
flute players, and the crowd making a
tumult, 24he said, "Depart; for the girl
is not dead but sleeping." And they
laughed at him. 25But when the crowd
had been put outside, he went in and
took her by the hand, and the girl
arose. 26And the report of this went
through all that district.

JESUS HEALS TWO BLIND MEN

27 And as Jesus passed on from
there, two blind men followed him,
crying aloud, "Have mercy on us,
Son of David." 28When he entered the
house, the blind men came to him;
and Jesus said to them, "Do you be-
lieve that I am able to do this?" They
said to him, "Yes, Lord." 29Then he
touched their eyes, saying, "According
to your faith be it done to you." 30And
their eyes were opened. And Jesus
sternly charged them, "See that no
one knows it." 31But they went away
and spread his fame through all that
district.

JESUS HEALS ONE WHO WAS MUTE

32 As they were going away, be-
hold, a dumb demoniac was brought
to him. 33And when the demon had
been cast out, the dumb man spoke;
and the crowds marveled, saying,
"Never was anything like this seen
in Israel." 34But the Pharisees said,
"He casts out demons by the prince of
demons."

THE HARVEST IS GREAT, THE LABORERS FEW

35 And Jesus went about all the
cities and villages, teaching in their

[a] Greek *reclined*
[b] Other ancient authorities add *much* or *often*

synagogues and preaching the gospel
of the kingdom, and healing every dis-
ease and every infirmity. 36When he
saw the crowds, he had compassion
for them, because they were harassed
and helpless, like sheep without a
shepherd. 37Then he said to his disci-
ples, "The harvest is plentiful, but the
laborers are few; 38pray therefore the
Lord of the harvest to send out labor-
ers into his harvest."

THE TWELVE APOSTLES

10 And he called to him his twelve
disciples and gave them authority
over unclean spirits, to cast them out,
and to heal every disease and every
infirmity. 2The names of the twelve
apostles are these: first, Simon, who is
called Peter, and Andrew his brother;
James the son of Zeb′edee, and John
his brother; 3Philip and Bartholomew;
Thomas and Matthew the tax collec-
tor; James the son of Alphaeus, and
Thaddaeus;[c] 4Simon the Cananaean,
and Judas Iscariot, who betrayed him.

THE MISSION OF THE TWELVE

5 These twelve Jesus sent out,
charging them, "Go nowhere among
the Gentiles, and enter no town of
the Samaritans,* 6but go rather to
the lost sheep of the house of Israel.
7And preach as you go, saying, 'The
kingdom of heaven is at hand.' 8Heal
the sick, raise the dead, cleanse lep-
ers, cast out demons. You received
without pay, give without pay. 9Take
no gold, nor silver, nor copper in your
belts, 10no bag for your journey, nor
two tunics, nor sandals, nor a staff;
for the laborer deserves his food.
11And whatever town or village you
enter, find out who is worthy in it, and
stay with him until you depart. 12As
you enter the house, salute it. 13And
if the house is worthy, let your peace
come upon it; but if it is not worthy,
let your peace return to you. 14And if
any one will not receive you or listen
to your words, shake off the dust from
your feet as you leave that house or
town. 15Truly, I say to you, it shall be
more tolerable on the day of judgment
for the land of Sodom and Gomor′rah
than for that town.

COMING PERSECUTIONS

16 "Behold, I send you out as sheep
in the midst of wolves; so be wise
as serpents and innocent as doves.
17Beware of men; for they will deliv-
er you up to councils, and flog you in
their synagogues, 18and you will be
dragged before governors and kings
for my sake, to bear testimony before
them and the Gentiles. 19When they
deliver you up, do not be anxious how
you are to speak or what you are to
say; for what you are to say will be
given to you in that hour; 20for it is
not you who speak, but the Spirit of
your Father speaking through you.
21Brother will deliver up brother to
death, and the father his child, and
children will rise against parents and
have them put to death; 22and you will
be hated by all for my name's sake.
But he who endures to the end will be
saved. 23When they persecute you in
one town, flee to the next; for truly,
I say to you, you will not have gone
through all the towns of Israel, before
the Son of man comes.

24 "A disciple is not above his
teacher, nor a servant[d] above his mas-
ter; 25it is enough for the disciple to
be like his teacher, and the servant[e]
like his master. If they have called the
master of the house Be-el′zebul, how
much more will they malign those of
his household.

WHOM TO FEAR

26 "So have no fear of them; for
nothing is covered that will not be
revealed, or hidden that will not
be known. 27What I tell you in the
dark, utter in the light; and what you
hear whispered, proclaim upon the

[c] Other ancient authorities read *Lebbaeus* or *Lebbaeus called Thaddaeus*
[d] Or *slave*
[e] Or *slave*

housetops. 28And do not fear those
who kill the body but cannot kill the
soul; rather fear him who can destroy
both soul and body in hell.[a] 29Are not
two sparrows sold for a penny? And
not one of them will fall to the ground
without your Father's will. 30But even
the hairs of your head are all num-
bered. 31Fear not, therefore; you are
of more value than many sparrows.
32So every one who acknowledges me
before men, I also will acknowledge
before my Father who is in heaven;
33but whoever denies me before men,
I also will deny before my Father who
is in heaven.

NOT PEACE, BUT A SWORD

34 "Do not think that I have come
to bring peace on earth; I have not
come to bring peace, but a sword.
35For I have come to set a man against
his father, and a daughter against her
mother, and a daughter-in-law against
her mother-in-law; 36and a man's foes
will be those of his own household.
37He who loves father or mother more
than me is not worthy of me; and he
who loves son or daughter more than
me is not worthy of me; 38and he who
does not take his cross and follow me
is not worthy of me. 39He who finds
his life will lose it, and he who loses
his life for my sake will find it.

REWARDS

40 "He who receives you receives
me, and he who receives me receives
him who sent me. 41He who receives a
prophet because he is a prophet shall
receive a prophet's reward, and he
who receives a righteous man because
he is a righteous man shall receive a
righteous man's reward. 42And who-
ever gives to one of these little ones
even a cup of cold water because he is
a disciple, truly, I say to you, he shall
not lose his reward."

11 And when Jesus had finished in-
structing his twelve disciples,
he went on from there to teach and
preach in their cities.

MESSENGERS FROM JOHN THE BAPTIST

2 Now when John heard in prison
about the deeds of the Christ, he sent
word by his disciples 3and said to him,
"Are you he who is to come, or shall
we look for another?"* 4And Jesus an-
swered them, "Go and tell John what
you hear and see: 5the blind receive
their sight and the lame walk, lepers
are cleansed and the deaf hear, and
the dead are raised up, and the poor
have good news preached to them.
6And blessed is he who takes no of-
fense at me."

JESUS PRAISES JOHN THE BAPTIST

7 As they went away, Jesus began to
speak to the crowds concerning John:
"What did you go out into the wilder-
ness to behold? A reed shaken by the
wind? 8Why then did you go out? To
see a man[b] clothed in soft raiment?
Behold, those who wear soft raiment
are in kings' houses. 9Why then did
you go out? To see a prophet?[c] Yes,
I tell you, and more than a prophet.
10This is he of whom it is written,

'Behold I send my messenger
before thy face,
who shall prepare thy way
before thee.'

11Truly, I say to you, among those
born of women there has risen no one
greater than John the Baptist; yet he
who is least in the kingdom of heaven
is greater than he. 12From the days of
John the Baptist until now the king-
dom of heaven has suffered violence,[d]
and men of violence take it by force.
13For all the prophets and the law
prophesied until John; 14and if you are
willing to accept it, he is Eli'jah who
is to come. 15He who has ears to hear,[e]

[a] Greek *Gehenna*
[b] Or *What then did you go out to see? A man...*
[c] Other ancient authorities read *What then did you go out to see? A prophet?*
[d] Or *has been coming violently*
[e] Other ancient authorities omit *to hear*

let him hear.
16 "But to what shall I compare
this generation? It is like children sit-
ting in the market places and calling
to their playmates,
17'We piped to you, and you did
not dance;
we wailed, and you did not
mourn.'
18For John came neither eating nor
drinking, and they say, 'He has a de-
mon'; 19the Son of man came eating
and drinking, and they say, 'Behold, a
glutton and a drunkard, a friend of tax
collectors and sinners!' Yet wisdom is
justified by her deeds."[f]

WOES TO UNREPENTANT CITIES

20 Then he began to upbraid the
cities where most of his mighty works
had been done, because they did not
repent. 21"Woe to you, Chora´zin! woe
to you, Beth-sa´ida! for if the mighty
works done in you had been done in
Tyre and Sidon, they would have re-
pented long ago in sackcloth and ash-
es. 22But I tell you, it shall be more
tolerable on the day of judgment for
Tyre and Sidon than for you. 23And
you, Caper´na-um, will you be exalted
to heaven? You shall be brought down
to Hades. For if the mighty works
done in you had been done in Sodom,
it would have remained until this day.
24But I tell you that it shall be more
tolerable on the day of judgment for
the land of Sodom than for you."

JESUS THANKS HIS FATHER

25 At that time Jesus declared,
"*I thank thee,* Father, Lord of heav-
en and earth, that thou hast hidden
these things from the wise and un-
derstanding and revealed them to
babes; 26yea, Father, for such was thy
gracious will.[g] 27All things have been
delivered to me by my Father; and no
one knows the Son except the Father,
and no one knows the Father except
the Son and any one to whom the Son
chooses to reveal him.* 28Come to me,
all who labor and are heavy laden, and
I will give you rest. 29Take my yoke
upon you, and learn from me; for I am
gentle and lowly in heart, and you will
find rest for your souls. 30For my yoke
is easy, and my burden is light."

PLUCKING GRAIN ON THE SABBATH

12 At that time Jesus went through
the grainfields on the sabbath; his
disciples were hungry, and they be-
gan to pluck ears of grain and to eat.
2But when the Pharisees saw it, they
said to him, "Look, your disciples are
doing what is not lawful to do on the
sabbath." 3He said to them, "Have you
not read what David did, when he was
hungry, and those who were with him:
4how he entered the house of God and
ate the bread of the Presence, which
it was not lawful for him to eat nor
for those who were with him, but
only for the priests? 5Or have you not
read in the law how on the sabbath
the priests in the temple profane the
sabbath, and are guiltless? 6I tell you,
something greater than the temple is
here. 7And if you had known what this
means, 'I desire mercy, and not sacri-
fice,' you would not have condemned
the guiltless. 8For the Son of man is
lord of the sabbath."

THE MAN WITH A WITHERED HAND

9 And he went on from there, and
entered their synagogue. 10And be-
hold, there was a man with a with-
ered hand. And they asked him, "Is
it lawful to heal on the sabbath?" so
that they might accuse him. 11He said
to them, "What man of you, if he has
one sheep and it falls into a pit on the
sabbath, will not lay hold of it and lift
it out? 12Of how much more value is a
man than a sheep! So it is lawful to do
good on the sabbath." 13Then he said
to the man, "Stretch out your hand."
And the man stretched it out, and it
was restored, whole like the other.

[f] Other ancient authorities read *children* (Lk 7. 35)
[g] Or *so it was well-pleasing before thee*

14But the Pharisees went out and took
counsel against him, how to destroy
him.*

GOD'S CHOSEN SERVANT

15 Jesus, aware of this, withdrew
from there. And many followed him,
and he healed them all, 16and ordered
them not to make him known. 17This
was to fulfil what was spoken by the
prophet Isaiah:

18"Behold, my servant whom I
have chosen,
my beloved with whom my
soul is well pleased.
I will put my Spirit upon him,
and he shall proclaim justice
to the Gentiles.
19He will not wrangle or cry aloud,
nor will any one hear his
voice in the streets;
20he will not break a bruised reed
or quench a smoldering
wick,
till he brings justice to victory;
21and in his name will the
Gentiles hope."

JESUS AND BEELZEBUL

22 Then a blind and dumb de-
moniac was brought to him, and he
healed him, so that the dumb man
spoke and saw. 23And all the people
were amazed, and said, "Can this be
the Son of David?" 24But when the
Pharisees heard it they said, "It is
only by Be-el′zebul,* the prince of
demons, that this man casts out de-
mons." 25Knowing their thoughts, he
said to them, "Every kingdom divided
against itself is laid waste, and no city
or house divided against itself will
stand; 26and if Satan casts out Satan,
he is divided against himself; how
then will his kingdom stand? 27And if
I cast out demons by Be-el′zebul, by
whom do your sons cast them out?
Therefore they shall be your judges.
28But if it is by the Spirit of God that
I cast out demons, then the kingdom
of God has come upon you. 29Or how
can one enter a strong man's house
and plunder his goods, unless he first
binds the strong man? Then indeed
he may plunder his house. 30He who
is not with me is against me, and he
who does not gather with me scatters.
31Therefore I tell you, every sin and
blasphemy will be forgiven men, but
the blasphemy against the Spirit will
not be forgiven.* 32And whoever says
a word against the Son of man will be
forgiven; but whoever speaks against
the Holy Spirit will not be forgiven, ei-
ther in this age or in the age to come.

A TREE AND ITS FRUIT

33 "Either make the tree good, and
its fruit good; or make the tree bad,
and its fruit bad; for the tree is known
by its fruit. 34You brood of vipers! how
can you speak good, when you are
evil? For out of the abundance of the
heart the mouth speaks. 35The good
man out of his good treasure brings
forth good, and the evil man out of his
evil treasure brings forth evil. 36I tell
you, on the day of judgment men will
render account for every careless word
they utter; 37for by your words you will
be justified, and by your words you
will be condemned."

THE SIGN OF JONAH

38 Then some of the scribes and
Pharisees said to him, "Teacher, we
wish to see a sign from you." 39But he
answered them, "An evil and adulter-
ous generation seeks for a sign; but no
sign shall be given to it except the sign
of the prophet Jonah. 40For as Jonah
was three days and three nights in the
belly of the whale, so will the Son of
man be three days and three nights in
the heart of the earth. 41The men of
Nin′eveh will arise at the judgment
with this generation and condemn it;
for they repented at the preaching of
Jonah, and behold, something great-
er than Jonah is here. 42The queen of
the South will arise at the judgment
with this generation and condemn
it; for she came from the ends of the
earth to hear the wisdom of Solomon,

and behold, something greater than
Solomon is here.

THE RETURN OF THE UNCLEAN SPIRIT

43 "When the unclean spirit has
gone out of a man, he passes through
waterless places seeking rest, but he
finds none. 44Then he says, 'I will re-
turn to my house from which I came.'
And when he comes he finds it emp-
ty, swept, and put in order. 45Then he
goes and brings with him seven other
spirits more evil than himself, and
they enter and dwell there; and the
last state of that man becomes worse
than the first. So shall it be also with
this evil generation."

THE TRUE KINDRED OF JESUS

46 While he was still speaking to
the people, behold, his mother and
his brethren* stood outside, asking to
speak to him.[a] 48But he replied to the
man who told him, "Who is my moth-
er, and who are my brethren?"* 49And
stretching out his hand toward his
disciples, he said, "Here are my moth-
er and my brethren! 50For whoever
does the will of my Father in heaven
is my brother, and sister, and mother."

THE PARABLE OF THE SOWER

13 That same day Jesus went out of
the house and sat beside the sea.
2And great crowds gathered about
him, so that he got into a boat and sat
there; and the whole crowd stood on
the beach. 3And he told them many
things in parables, saying: "A sower
went out to sow. 4And as he sowed,
some seeds fell along the path, and
the birds came and devoured them.
5Other seeds fell on rocky ground,
where they had not much soil, and
immediately they sprang up, since
they had no depth of soil, 6but when
the sun rose they were scorched; and
since they had no root they withered
away. 7Other seeds fell upon thorns,
and the thorns grew up and choked
them. 8Other seeds fell on good soil
and brought forth grain, some a hun-
dredfold, some sixty, some thirty. 9He
who has ears,[b] let him hear."

THE PURPOSE OF THE PARABLES

10 Then the disciples came and said
to him, "Why do you speak to them in
parables?" 11And he answered them,
"To you it has been given to know the
secrets of the kingdom of heaven, but
to them it has not been given. 12For to
him who has will more be given, and
he will have abundance; but from him
who has not, even what he has will be
taken away.* 13This is why I speak to
them in parables, because seeing they
do not see, and hearing they do not
hear, nor do they understand. 14With
them indeed is fulfilled the prophecy
of Isaiah which says:

'You shall indeed hear but
never understand,
and you shall indeed see but
never perceive.
15For this people's heart has
grown dull,
and their ears are heavy of
hearing,
and their eyes they have
closed,
lest they should perceive with
their eyes,
and hear with their ears,
and understand with their
heart,
and turn for me to heal
them.'

16But blessed are your eyes, for
they see, and your ears, for they hear.
17Truly, I say to you, many prophets
and righteous men longed to see what
you see, and did not see it, and to hear
what you hear, and did not hear it.

THE PARABLE OF THE SOWER EXPLAINED

18 "Hear then the parable of the
sower. 19When any one hears the
word of the kingdom and does not

[a] Other ancient authorities insert verse 47, *Some one told him, "Your mother and your brethren* are standing outside, asking to speak to you"*
[b] Other ancient authorities add here and in verse 43 *to hear*

understand it, the evil one comes and
snatches away what is sown in his
heart; this is what was sown along
the path. 20As for what was sown on
rocky ground, this is he who hears
the word and immediately receives
it with joy; 21yet he has no root in
himself, but endures for a while, and
when tribulation or persecution aris-
es on account of the word, immedi-
ately he falls away.[a] 22As for what was
sown among thorns, this is he who
hears the word, but the cares of the
world and the delight in riches choke
the word, and it proves unfruitful.
23As for what was sown on good soil,
this is he who hears the word and
understands it; he indeed bears fruit,
and yields, in one case a hundred-
fold, in another sixty, and in another
thirty."

THE PARABLE OF WEEDS AMONG THE WHEAT

24 Another parable he put before
them, saying, "The kingdom of heav-
en may be compared to a man who
sowed good seed in his field; 25but
while men were sleeping, his enemy
came and sowed weeds among the
wheat, and went away. 26So when the
plants came up and bore grain, then
the weeds appeared also. 27And the
servants[b] of the householder came
and said to him, 'Sir, did you not sow
good seed in your field? How then
has it weeds?' 28He said to them, 'An
enemy has done this.' The servants[c]
said to him, 'Then do you want us to
go and gather them?' 29But he said,
'No; lest in gathering the weeds you
root up the wheat along with them.
30Let both grow together until the
harvest; and at harvest time I will
tell the reapers, Gather the weeds
first and bind them in bundles to be
burned, but gather the wheat into my
barn.'"

THE PARABLE OF THE MUSTARD SEED

31 Another parable he put before
them, saying, "The kingdom of heaven
is like a grain of mustard seed which a
man took and sowed in his field; 32it is
the smallest of all seeds, but when it
has grown it is the greatest of shrubs
and becomes a tree, so that the birds
of the air come and make nests in its
branches."

THE PARABLE OF THE YEAST

33 He told them another parable.
"The kingdom of heaven is like leav-
en which a woman took and hid in
three measures of meal, till it was all
leavened."

THE USE OF PARABLES

34 All this Jesus said to the crowds
in parables; indeed he said nothing
to them without a parable. 35This
was to fulfil what was spoken by the
prophet:[d]

"I will open my mouth in
parables,
I will utter what has been hid-
den since the foundation
of the world."

JESUS EXPLAINS THE PARABLE OF THE WEEDS

36 Then he left the crowds and
went into the house. And his disci-
ples came to him, saying, "Explain
to us the parable of the weeds of the
field." 37He answered, "He who sows
the good seed is the Son of man; 38the
field is the world, and the good seed
means the sons of the kingdom; the
weeds are the sons of the evil one,
39and the enemy who sowed them is
the devil; the harvest is the close of
the age, and the reapers are angels.
40Just as the weeds are gathered and
burned with fire, so will it be at the
close of the age. 41The Son of man will
send his angels, and they will gather

[a] Or *stumbles*
[b] Or *slaves*
[c] Or *slaves*
[d] Other ancient authorities read *the prophet Isaiah*

out of his kingdom all causes of sin
and all evildoers, 42and throw them
into the furnace of fire; there men will
weep and gnash their teeth. 43Then
the righteous will shine like the sun
in the kingdom of their Father. He
who has ears, let him hear.

THREE PARABLES

44 "The kingdom of heaven is like
treasure hidden in a field, which a
man found and covered up; then in his
joy he goes and sells all that he has
and buys that field.

45 "Again, the kingdom of heaven
is like a merchant in search of fine
pearls, 46who, on finding one pearl of
great value, went and sold all that he
had and bought it.

47 "Again, the kingdom of heaven
is like a net which was thrown into
the sea and gathered fish of every
kind; 48when it was full, men drew it
ashore and sat down and sorted the
good into vessels but threw away the
bad. 49So it will be at the close of the
age. The angels will come out and
separate the evil from the righteous,
50and throw them into the furnace of
fire; there men will weep and gnash
their teeth.

TREASURES NEW AND OLD

51 "Have you understood all this?"
They said to him, "Yes." 52And he said
to them, "Therefore every scribe who
has been trained for the kingdom of
heaven is like a householder who
brings out of his treasure what is new
and what is old."*

THE REJECTION OF JESUS AT NAZARETH

53 And when Jesus had finished
these parables, he went away from
there, 54and coming to his own coun-
try he taught them in their syna-
gogue, so that they were astonished,
and said, "Where did this man get
this wisdom and these mighty works?
55Is not this the carpenter's son? Is
not his mother called Mary? And are
not his brethren* James and Joseph
and Simon and Judas? 56And are not
all his sisters with us? Where then
did this man get all this?" 57And they
took offense at him. But Jesus said to
them, "A prophet is not without honor
except in his own country and in his
own house." 58And he did not do many
mighty works there, because of their
unbelief.

THE DEATH OF JOHN THE BAPTIST

14 At that time Herod the tetrarch
heard about the fame of Jesus; 2and
he said to his servants, "This is John
the Baptist, he has been raised from
the dead; that is why these powers
are at work in him." 3For Herod had
seized John and bound him and put
him in prison, for the sake of Hero´di-
as, his brother Philip's wife;[e] 4because
John said to him, "It is not lawful
for you to have her." 5And though he
wanted to put him to death, he feared
the people, because they held him to
be a prophet. 6But when Herod's birth-
day came, the daughter of Hero´di-
as danced before the company, and
pleased Herod, 7so that he promised
with an oath to give her whatever she
might ask. 8Prompted by her mother,
she said, "Give me the head of John
the Baptist here on a platter." 9And
the king was sorry; but because of his
oaths and his guests he commanded
it to be given; 10he sent and had John
beheaded in the prison, 11and his head
was brought on a platter and given
to the girl, and she brought it to her
mother. 12And his disciples came and
took the body and buried it; and they
went and told Jesus.

FEEDING THE FIVE THOUSAND

13 Now when Jesus heard this,
he withdrew from there in a boat to
a lonely place apart. But when the
crowds heard it, they followed him
on foot from the towns. 14As he went
ashore he saw a great throng; and he
had compassion on them, and healed

[e] Other ancient authorities read *his brother's wife*

their sick. 15When it was evening, the
disciples came to him and said, "This
is a lonely place, and the day is now
over; send the crowds away to go into
the villages and buy food for them-
selves." 16Jesus said, "They need not
go away; you give them something
to eat." 17They said to him, "We have
only five loaves here and two fish."
18And he said, "Bring them here to
me." 19Then he ordered the crowds to
sit down on the grass; and taking the
five loaves and the two fish he looked
up to heaven, and blessed, and broke
and gave the loaves to the disciples,
and the disciples gave them to the
crowds. 20And they all ate and were
satisfied. And they took up twelve
baskets full of the broken pieces left
over. 21And those who ate were about
five thousand men, besides women
and children.

JESUS WALKS ON THE WATER

22 Then he made the disciples get
into the boat and go before him to
the other side, while he dismissed the
crowds. 23And after he had dismissed
the crowds, he went up into the hills
by himself to pray. When evening
came, he was there alone, 24but the
boat by this time was many furlongs
distant from the land,[a] beaten by the
waves; for the wind was against them.
25And in the fourth watch of the night
he came to them, walking on the sea.
26But when the disciples saw him
walking on the sea, they were terri-
fied, saying, "It is a ghost!" And they
cried out for fear. 27But immediately
he spoke to them, saying, "Take heart,
it is I; have no fear."

28 And Peter answered him, "Lord,
if it is you, bid me come to you on the
water." 29He said, "Come." So Peter
got out of the boat and walked on the
water and came to Jesus; 30but when
he saw the wind,[b] he was afraid, and
beginning to sink he cried out, "Lord,
save me." 31Jesus immediately reached
out his hand and caught him, saying
to him, "O man of little faith, why did
you doubt?" 32And when they got into
the boat, the wind ceased. 33And those
in the boat worshiped him, saying,
"Truly you are the Son of God."*

JESUS HEALS THE SICK IN GENNESARET

34 And when they had crossed over,
they came to land at Gennes´aret.
35And when the men of that place
recognized him, they sent round to
all that region and brought to him
all that were sick, 36and besought
him that they might only touch the
fringe of his garment; and as many as
touched it were made well.

THE TRADITION OF THE ELDERS

15 Then Pharisees and scribes came
to Jesus from Jerusalem and said,
2"Why do your disciples transgress
the tradition of the elders? For they
do not wash their hands when they
eat." 3He answered them, "And why
do you transgress the commandment
of God for the sake of your tradition?
4For God commanded, 'Honor your fa-
ther and your mother,' and, 'He who
speaks evil of father or mother, let
him surely die.' 5But you say, 'If any
one tells his father or his mother,
What you would have gained from me
is given to God,[c] he need not honor his
father.'* 6So, for the sake of your tra-
dition, you have made void the word[d]
of God. 7You hypocrites! Well did
Isaiah prophesy of you, when he said:

8'This people honors me with
their lips,
but their heart is far from me;
9in vain do they worship me,
teaching as doctrines the pre-
cepts of men.'"

THINGS THAT DEFILE

10 And he called the people to
him and said to them, "Hear and

[a] Other ancient authorities read *was out on the sea*
[b] Other ancient authorities read *strong wind*
[c] Or *an offering*
[d] Other ancient authorities read *law*

understand: 11not what goes into the
mouth defiles a man, but what comes
out of the mouth, this defiles a man."
12Then the disciples came and said to
him, "Do you know that the Pharisees
were offended when they heard this
saying?" 13He answered, "Every plant
which my heavenly Father has not
planted will be rooted up. 14Let them
alone; they are blind guides. And if a
blind man leads a blind man, both will
fall into a pit." 15But Peter said to him,
"Explain the parable to us." 16And he
said, "Are you also still without un-
derstanding? 17Do you not see that
whatever goes into the mouth pass-
es into the stomach, and so passes
on?[e] 18But what comes out of the mouth
proceeds from the heart, and this
defiles a man. 19For out of the heart
come evil thoughts, murder, adultery,
fornication, theft, false witness, slan-
der. 20These are what defile a man; but
to eat with unwashed hands does not
defile a man."

THE CANAANITE WOMAN'S FAITH

21 And Jesus went away from there
and withdrew to the district of Tyre
and Sidon. 22And behold, a Canaanite
woman from that region came out and
cried, "Have mercy on me, O Lord,
Son of David; my daughter is severely
possessed by a demon." 23But he did
not answer her a word. And his dis-
ciples came and begged him, saying,
"Send her away, for she is crying af-
ter us." 24He answered, "I was sent
only to the lost sheep f the house
of Israel."* 25But she car and knelt
before him, saying, "Lor help me."
26And he answered, "It is not fair to
take the children's bread nd throw
it to the dogs." 27She said, 'es, Lord,
yet even the dogs eat the cmbs that
fall from their master's tab" 28Then
Jesus answered her, "O won, great
is your faith! Be it done for as you
desire." And her daughter w healed
instantly.

JESUS CURES MANY PEOPLE

29 And Jesus went on from there
and passed along the Sea of Galilee.
And he went up into the hills, and sat
down there. 30And great crowds came
to him, bringing with them the lame,
the maimed, the blind, the dumb, and
many others, and they put them at his
feet, and he healed them, 31so that the
throng wondered, when they saw the
dumb speaking, the maimed whole,
the lame walking, and the blind see-
ing; and they glorified the God of
Israel.

FEEDING THE FOUR THOUSAND

32 Then Jesus called his disciples
to him and said, "I have compassion
on the crowd, because they have been
with me now three days, and have
nothing to eat; and I am unwilling
to send them away hungry, lest they
faint on the way." 33And the disci-
ples said to him, "Where are we to
get bread enough in the desert to
feed so great a crowd?" 34And Jesus
said to them, "How many loaves have
you?" They said, "Seven, and a few
small fish." 35And commanding the
crowd to sit down on the ground, 36he
took the seven loaves and the fish,
and having given thanks he broke
them and gave them to the disciples,
and the disciples gave them to the
crowds. 37And they all ate and were
satisfied; and they took up seven
baskets full of the broken pieces left
over. 38Those who ate were four thou-
sand men, besides women and chil-
dren. 39And sending away the crowds,
he got into the boat and went to the
region of Mag´adan.

THE DEMAND FOR A SIGN

16 And the Pharisees and Sad´ducees
came, and to test him they asked
him to show them a sign from heaven.
2He answered them,[f] "When it is eve-
ning, you say, 'It will be fair weath-
er; for the sky is red.' 3And in the

[e] Or *is evacuated*
[f] Other ancient authorities omit th llowing words to the end of verse 3

morning, 'It will be stormy today, for
the sky is red and threatening.' You
know how to interpret the appearance
of the sky, but you cannot interpret
the signs of the times. 4An evil and
adulterous generation seeks for a sign,
but no sign shall be given to it except
the sign of Jonah." So he left them and
departed.

THE YEAST OF THE PHARISEES AND SADDUCEES

5 When the disciples reached
the other side, they had forgotten
to bring any bread. 6Jesus said to
them, "Take heed and beware of the
leaven of the Pharisees and Sad´du-
cees." 7And they discussed it among
themselves, saying, "We brought no
bread." 8But Jesus, aware of this,
said, "O men of little faith, why do
you discuss among yourselves the
fact that you have no bread? 9Do
you not yet perceive? Do you not re-
member the five loaves of the five
thousand, and how many baskets
you gathered? 10Or the seven loaves
of the four thousand, and how many
baskets you gathered? 11How is it
that you fail to perceive that I did
not speak about bread? Beware of
the leaven of the Pharisees and Sad´-
ducees." 12Then they understood that
he did not tell them to beware of the
leaven of bread, but of the teaching
of the Pharisees and Sad´ducees.

PETER'S DECLARATION ABOUT JESUS

13 Now when Jesus came into
the district of Caesare´a Philippi, he
asked his disciples, "Who do men say
that the Son of man is?" 14And they
said, "Some say John the Baptist, oth-
ers say Eli´jah, and others Jeremiah
or one of the prophets."* 15He said
to them, "But who do you say that
I am?" 16Simon Peter replied, "You
are the Christ, the Son of the living
God."* 17And Jesus answered him,
"Blessed are you, Simon Bar-Jona!
For flesh and blood has not revealed
this to you, but my Father who is
in heaven. 18And I tell you, you are
Peter,[a] and on this rock[b] I will build
my church, and the powers of death[c]
shall not prevail against it.* 19I will
give you the keys of the kingdom of
heaven,* and whatever you bind on
earth shall be bound in heaven, and
whatever you loose on earth shall be
loosed in heaven." 20Then he strictly
charged the disciples to tell no one
that he was the Christ.

JESUS FORETELLS HIS DEATH AND RESURRECTION

21 From that time Jesus began to
show his disciples that he must go
to Jerusalem and suffer many things
from the elders and chief priests and
scribes, and be killed, and on the
third day be raised. 22And Peter took
him and began to rebuke him, saying,
"God forbid, Lord! This shall never
happen to you." 23But he turned and
said to Peter, "Get behind me, Satan!
You are a hindrance[d] to me; for you
are not on the side of God, but of
men."

THE CROSS AND SELF-DENIAL

24 Then Jesus told his disciples, "If
any man would come after me, let him
deny himself and take up his cross
and follow me. 25For whoever would
save his life will lose it, and whoev-
er loses his life for my sake will find
it. 26For what will it profit a man, if
he gains the whole world and forfeits
his life?* Or what shall a man give in
return for his life?* 27For the Son of
man is to come with his angels in the
glory of his Father, and then he will
repay every man for what he has done.
28Truly, I say to you, there are some
standing here who will not taste death

[a] Greek *Petros*
[b] Greek *petra*
[c] Greek *the gates of Hades*
[d] Greek *stumbling block*

before they see the Son of man coming
in his kingdom."

THE TRANSFIGURATION

17 And after six days Jesus took with
him Peter and James and John his
brother, and led them up a high moun-
tain apart. 2And he was transfigured
before them, and his face shone like
the sun, and his garments became
white as light. 3And behold, there
appeared to them Moses and Eli´jah,
talking with him. 4And Peter said to
Jesus, "Lord, it is well that we are
here; if you wish, I will make three
booths here, one for you and one for
Moses and one for Eli´jah."* 5He was
still speaking, when lo, a bright cloud
overshadowed them, and a voice from
the cloud said, "This is my beloved
Son,[e] with whom I am well pleased;
listen to him." 6When the disciples
heard this, they fell on their faces, and
were filled with awe. 7But Jesus came
and touched them, saying, "Rise, and
have no fear." 8And when they lifted
up their eyes, they saw no one but
Jesus only.

9 And as they were coming down
the mountain, Jesus commanded
them, "Tell no one the vision, until
the Son of man is raised from the
dead." 10And the disciples asked him,
"Then why do the scribes say that
first Eli´jah must come?" 11He re-
plied, "Eli´jah does come, and he is
to restore all things; 12but I tell you
that Eli´jah has already come, and
they did not know him, but did to
him whatever they pleased. So also
the Son of man will suffer at their
hands." 13Then the disciples under-
stood that he was speaking to them of
John the Baptist.

JESUS CURES A BOY WITH A DEMON

14 And when they came to the
crowd, a man came up to him and
kneeling before him said, 15"Lord,
have mercy on my son, for he is an
epileptic and he suffers terribly; for
often he falls into the fire, and often
into the water. 16And I brought him
to your disciples, and they could not
heal him." 17And Jesus answered, "O
faithless and perverse generation,
how long am I to be with you? How
long am I to bear with you? Bring him
here to me." 18And Jesus rebuked him,
and the demon came out of him, and
the boy was cured instantly. 19Then
the disciples came to Jesus privately
and said, "Why could we not cast it
out?" 20He said to them, "Because of
your little faith. For truly, I say to you,
if you have faith as a grain of mustard
seed, you will say to this mountain,
'Move from hence to yonder place,'
and it will move; and nothing will be
impossible to you."[f]

JESUS AGAIN FORETELLS HIS DEATH AND RESURRECTION

22 As they were gathering[g] in
Galilee, Jesus said to them, "The Son
of man is to be delivered into the
hands of men, 23and they will kill him,
and he will be raised on the third day."
And they were greatly distressed.

JESUS AND THE TEMPLE TAX

24 When they came to Caper´na-
um, the collectors of the half-shekel
tax went up to Peter and said, "Does
not your teacher pay the tax?" 25He
said, "Yes." And when he came home,
Jesus spoke to him first, saying,
"What do you think, Simon? From
whom do kings of the earth take toll
or tribute? From their sons or from
others?" 26And when he said, "From
others," Jesus said to him, "Then the
sons are free. 27However, not to give
offense to them, go to the sea and
cast a hook, and take the first fish
that comes up, and when you open
its mouth you will find a shekel; take

[e] Or *my Son, my* (or *the*) *Beloved*

[f] Other ancient authorities insert verse 21, *"But this kind never comes out except by prayer and fasting"*

[g] Other ancient authorities read *abode*

that and give it to them for me and for
yourself."

TRUE GREATNESS

18 At that time the disciples came to
Jesus, saying, "Who is the great-
est in the kingdom of heaven?" 2And
calling to him a child, he put him in
the midst of them, 3and said, "Truly,
I say to you, unless you turn and be-
come like children, you will never en-
ter the kingdom of heaven. 4Whoever
humbles himself like this child, he is
the greatest in the kingdom of heaven.

TEMPTATIONS TO SIN

5 "Whoever receives one such child
in my name receives me; 6but whoev-
er causes one of these little ones who
believe in me to sin,[a] it would be bet-
ter for him to have a great millstone
fastened round his neck and to be
drowned in the depth of the sea.

7 "Woe to the world for tempta-
tions to sin![b] For it is necessary that
temptations come, but woe to the man
by whom the temptation comes! 8And
if your hand or your foot causes you to
sin,[c] cut it off and throw it from you; it
is better for you to enter life maimed
or lame than with two hands or two
feet to be thrown into the eternal fire.
9And if your eye causes you to sin,[d]
pluck it out and throw it from you; it
is better for you to enter life with one
eye than with two eyes to be thrown
into the hell[e]* of fire.

THE PARABLE OF THE LOST SHEEP

10 "See that you do not despise one
of these little ones; for I tell you that
in heaven their angels always behold
the face of my Father who is in heav-
en.[f] 12What do you think? If a man
has a hundred sheep, and one of them
has gone astray, does he not leave
the ninety-nine on the hills and go in
search of the one that went astray?
13And if he finds it, truly, I say to you,
he rejoices over it more than over the
ninety-nine that never went astray.
14So it is not the will of my[g] Father
who is in heaven that one of these lit-
tle ones should perish.

REPROVING ANOTHER WHO SINS

15 "If your brother sins against
you, go and tell him his fault, be-
tween you and him alone. If he listens
to you, you have gained your brother.
16But if he does not listen, take one
or two others along with you, that
every word may be confirmed by the
evidence of two or three witnesses.
17If he refuses to listen to them, tell
it to the church; and if he refuses to
listen even to the church, let him be
to you as a Gentile and a tax collec-
tor. 18Truly, I say to you, whatever you
bind on earth shall be bound in heav-
en, and whatever you loose on earth
shall be loosed in heaven.* 19Again
I say to you, if two of you agree on
earth about anything they ask, it will
be done for them by my Father in
heaven. 20For where two or three are
gathered in my name, there am I in
the midst of them."

FORGIVENESS

21 Then Peter came up and said
to him, "Lord, how often shall my
brother sin against me, and I forgive
him? As many as seven times?" 22Jesus
said to him, "I do not say to you seven
times, but seventy times seven.[h]

THE PARABLE OF THE UNFORGIVING SERVANT

23 "Therefore the kingdom of
heaven may be compared to a king

[a] Greek *causes... to stumble*
[b] Greek *stumbling blocks*
[c] Greek *causes... to stumble*
[d] Greek *causes... to stumble*
[e] Greek *Gehenna*
[f] Other ancient authorities add verse 11, *For the Son of man came to save the lost*
[g] Other ancient authorities read *your*
[h] Or *seventy-seven times*

who wished to settle accounts with
his servants. 24When he began the
reckoning, one was brought to him
who owed him ten thousand talents;[i]
25and as he could not pay, his lord or-
dered him to be sold, with his wife
and children and all that he had, and
payment to be made. 26So the ser-
vant fell on his knees, imploring him,
'Lord, have patience with me, and I
will pay you everything.' 27And out
of pity for him the lord of that ser-
vant released him and forgave him
the debt. 28But that same servant, as
he went out, came upon one of his
fellow servants who owed him a hun-
dred denarii;[j] and seizing him by the
throat he said, 'Pay what you owe.'
29So his fellow servant fell down and
besought him, 'Have patience with
me, and I will pay you.' 30He refused
and went and put him in prison till
he should pay the debt. 31When his
fellow servants saw what had taken
place, they were greatly distressed,
and they went and reported to their
lord all that had taken place. 32Then
his lord summoned him and said to
him, 'You wicked servant! I forgave
you all that debt because you be-
sought me; 33and should not you have
had mercy on your fellow servant, as I
had mercy on you?' 34And in anger his
lord delivered him to the jailers,[k] till
he should pay all his debt. 35So also
my heavenly Father will do to every
one of you, if you do not forgive your
brother from your heart."

TEACHING ABOUT DIVORCE

19 *Now when Jesus* had finished
these sayings, he went away from
Galilee and entered the region of
Judea beyond the Jordan; 2and large
crowds followed him, and he healed
them there.

3 And Pharisees came up to him
and tested him by asking, "Is it lawful
to divorce one's wife for any cause?"
4He answered, "Have you not read
that he who made them from the be-
ginning made them male and female,
5and said, 'For this reason a man shall
leave his father and mother and be
joined to his wife, and the two shall
become one'?[l] 6So they are no longer
two but one.[m] What therefore God
has joined together, let not man put
asunder." 7They said to him, "Why
then did Moses command one to give
a certificate of divorce, and to put her
away?" 8He said to them, "For your
hardness of heart Moses allowed you
to divorce your wives, but from the
beginning it was not so. 9And I say to
you: whoever divorces his wife, ex-
cept for unchastity,[n] and marries an-
other, commits adultery; and he who
marries a divorced woman, commits
adultery."[o]*

10 The disciples said to him, "If
such is the case of a man with his
wife, it is not expedient to marry."
11But he said to them, "Not all men
can receive this precept, but only
those to whom it is given. 12For there
are eunuchs who have been so from
birth, and there are eunuchs who
have been made eunuchs by men,
and there are eunuchs who have
made themselves eunuchs for the
sake of the kingdom of heaven. He
who is able to receive this, let him
receive it."*

JESUS BLESSES LITTLE CHILDREN

13 Then children were brought to
him that he might lay his hands on
them and pray. The disciples rebuked
the people; 14but Jesus said, "Let the
children come to me, and do not hin-
der them; for to such belongs the

[i] This talent was more than fifteen years' wages of a laborer
[j] The denarius was a day's wage for a laborer
[k] Greek *torturers*
[l] Greek *one flesh*
[m] Greek *one flesh*
[n] Other ancient authorities, after *unchastity,* read *makes her commit adultery*
[o] Other ancient authorities omit *and he who marries a divorced woman, commits adultery*

kingdom of heaven." 15And he laid his
hands on them and went away.

THE RICH YOUNG MAN

16 And behold, one came up to
him, saying, "Teacher, what good
deed must I do, to have eternal life?"
17And he said to him, "Why do you ask
me about what is good? One there is
who is good. If you would enter life,
keep the commandments." 18He said
to him, "Which?" And Jesus said,
"You shall not kill, You shall not com-
mit adultery, You shall not steal, You
shall not bear false witness, 19Honor
your father and mother, and, You shall
love your neighbor as yourself." 20The
young man said to him, "All these I
have observed; what do I still lack?"
21Jesus said to him, "If you would be
perfect, go, sell what you possess and
give to the poor, and you will have
treasure in heaven; and come, follow
me." 22When the young man heard
this he went away sorrowful; for he
had great possessions.

23 And Jesus said to his disciples,
"Truly, I say to you, it will be hard for
a rich man to enter the kingdom of
heaven. 24Again I tell you, it is easier
for a camel to go through the eye of
a needle than for a rich man to en-
ter the kingdom of God." 25When the
disciples heard this they were greatly
astonished, saying, "Who then can
be saved?" 26But Jesus looked at them
and said to them, "With men this is
impossible, but with God all things
are possible." 27Then Peter said in re-
ply, "Lo, we have left everything and
followed you. What then shall we
have?" 28Jesus said to them, "Truly, I
say to you, in the new world, when
the Son of man shall sit on his glo-
rious throne, you who have followed
me will also sit on twelve thrones,
judging the twelve tribes of Israel.
29And every one who has left hous-
es or brothers or sisters or father or
mother or children or lands, for my
name's sake, will receive a hundred-
fold,[a] and inherit eternal life. 30But
many that are first will be last, and
the last first.

THE LABORERS IN THE VINEYARD

20 "For the kingdom of heaven is
like a householder who went out
early in the morning to hire laborers
for his vineyard. 2After agreeing with
the laborers for a denarius[b] a day, he
sent them into his vineyard. 3And go-
ing out about the third hour he saw
others standing idle in the market
place; 4and to them he said, 'You go
into the vineyard too, and whatever
is right I will give you.' So they went.
5Going out again about the sixth hour
and the ninth hour, he did the same.
6Andabout the eleventh hour he went
out and found others standing; and
he said to them, 'Why do you stand
here idle all day?' 7They said to him,
'Because no one has hired us.' He
said to them, 'You go into the vine-
yard too.' 8And when evening came,
the owner of the vineyard said to his
steward, 'Call the laborers and pay
them their wages, beginning with
the last, up to the first.' 9And when
those hired about the eleventh hour
came, each of them received a denar-
ius. 10Now when the first came, they
thought they would receive more; but
each of them also received a denarius.
11And on receiving it they grumbled
at the householder, 12saying, 'These
last worked only one hour, and you
have made them equal to us who have
borne the burden of the day and the
scorching heat.' 13But he replied to one
of them, Friend, I am doing you no
wrong; did you not agree with me for a
denarius? 14Take what belongs to you,
and go; I choose to give to this last as
I give to you. 15Am I not allowed to do
what I choose with what belongs to
me? Or do you begrudge my generosi-
ty?'[c] 16So the last will be first, and the
first last."

[a] Other ancient authorities read *manifold*
[b] The denarius was a day's wage for a laborer
[c] Or *is your eye evil because I am good?*

A THIRD TIME JESUS FORETELLS HIS DEATH AND RESURRECTION

17 And as Jesus was going up to
Jerusalem, he took the twelve disci-
ples aside, and on the way he said to
them, 18"Behold, we are going up to
Jerusalem; and the Son of man will
be delivered to the chief priests and
scribes, and they will condemn him
to death, 19and deliver him to the
Gentiles to be mocked and scourged
and crucified, and he will be raised on
the third day."

THE REQUEST OF THE MOTHER OF JAMES AND JOHN

20 Then the mother of the sons
of Zeb´edee came up to him, with
her sons, and kneeling before him
she asked him for something. 21And
he said to her, "What do you want?"
She said to him, "Command that
these two sons of mine may sit, one
at your right hand and one at your
left, in your kingdom." 22But Jesus an-
swered, "You do not know what you
are asking. Are you able to drink the
cup that I am to drink?" They said
to him, "We are able." 23He said to
them, "You will drink my cup, but to
sit at my right hand and at my left is
not mine to grant, but it is for those
for whom it has been prepared by my
Father." 24And when the ten heard it,
they were indignant at the two broth-
ers. 25But Jesus called them to him and
said, "You know that the rulers of the
Gentiles lord it over them, and their
great men exercise authority over
them. 26It shall not be so among you;
but whoever would be great among
you must be your servant, 27and who-
ever would be first among you must be
your slave; 28even as the Son of man
came not to be served but to serve, and
to give his life as a ransom for many."

JESUS HEALS TWO BLIND MEN

29 And as they went out of Jericho,
a great crowd followed him. 30And
behold, two blind men sitting by the
roadside, when they heard that Jesus
was passing by, cried out,[d]"Have
mercy on us, Son of David!" 31The
crowd rebuked them, telling them
to be silent; but they cried out the
more, "Lord, have mercy on us, Son
of David!" 32And Jesus stopped and
called them, saying, "What do you
want me to do for you?" 33They said to
him, "Lord, let our eyes be opened."
34And Jesus in pity touched their eyes,
and immediately they received their
sight and followed him.

JESUS' TRIUMPHAL ENTRY INTO JERUSALEM

21 And when they drew near to
Jerusalem and came to Beth´-
phage, to the Mount of Olives, then
Jesus sent two disciples, 2saying to
them, "Go into the village opposite
you, and immediately you will find
an ass tied, and a colt with her; un-
tie them and bring them to me. 3If any
one says anything to you, you shall
say, 'The Lord has need of them,' and
he will send them immediately." 4This
took place to fulfil what was spoken
by the prophet, saying,

5"Tell the daughter of Zion,
Behold, your king is coming
to you,
humble, and mounted on an
ass,
and on a colt, the foal of an
ass."

6The disciples went and did
as Jesus had directed them; 7they
brought the ass and the colt, and put
their garments on them, and he sat
thereon. 8Most of the crowd spread
their garments on the road, and oth-
ers cut branches from the trees and
spread them on the road. 9And the
crowds that went before him and
that followed him shouted, "Hosanna
to the Son of David! Blessed is he
who comes in the name of the Lord!
Hosanna in the highest!"* 10And when
he entered Jerusalem, all the city was

[d]Other ancient authorities insert *Lord*

stirred, saying, "Who is this?" 11 And the crowds said, "This is the prophet Jesus from Nazareth of Galilee."

JESUS CLEANSES THE TEMPLE

12 And Jesus entered the temple of God[a] and drove out all who sold and bought in the temple, and he overturned the tables of the money-changers and the seats of those who sold pigeons. 13 He said to them, "It is written, 'My house shall be called a house of prayer'; but you make it a den of robbers."

14 And the blind and the lame came to him in the temple, and he healed them. 15 But when the chief priests and the scribes saw the wonderful things that he did, and the children crying out in the temple, "Hosanna to the Son of David!" they were indignant; 16 and they said to him, "Do you hear what these are saying?" And Jesus said to them, "Yes; have you never read,

'Out of the mouth of babes and
sucklings
thou hast brought perfect
praise'?"

17 And leaving them, he went out of the city to Bethany and lodged there.

JESUS CURSES THE FIG TREE

18 In the morning, as he was returning to the city, he was hungry. 19 And seeing a fig tree by the wayside he went to it, and found nothing on it but leaves only. And he said to it, "May no fruit ever come from you again!" And the fig tree withered at once. 20 When the disciples saw it they marveled, saying, "How did the fig tree wither at once?" 21 And Jesus answered them, "Truly, I say to you, if you have faith and never doubt, you will not only do what has been done to the fig tree, but even if you say to this mountain, 'Be taken up and cast into the sea,' it will be done. 22 And whatever you ask in prayer, you will receive, if you have faith."

[a] Other ancient authorities omit *of God*

THE AUTHORITY OF JESUS QUESTIONED

23 And when he entered the temple, the chief priests and the elders of the people came up to him as he was teaching, and said, "By what authority are you doing these things, and who gave you this authority?"* 24 Jesus answered them, "I also will ask you a question; and if you tell me the answer, then I also will tell you by what authority I do these things. 25 The baptism of John, whence was it? From heaven or from men?" And they argued with one another, "If we say, 'From heaven,' he will say to us, 'Why then did you not believe him?' 26 But if we say, 'From men,' we are afraid of the multitude; for all hold that John was a prophet." 27 So they answered Jesus, "We do not know." And he said to them, "Neither will I tell you by what authority I do these things.

THE PARABLE OF THE TWO SONS

28 "What do you think? A man had two sons; and he went to the first and said, 'Son, go and work in the vineyard today.' 29 And he answered, 'I will not'; but afterward he repented and went. 30 And he went to the second and said the same; and he answered, 'I go, sir,' but did not go. 31 Which of the two did the will of his father?" They said, "The first." Jesus said to them, "Truly, I say to you, the tax collectors and the harlots go into the kingdom of God before you. 32 For John came to you in the way of righteousness, and you did not believe him, but the tax collectors and the harlots believed him; and even when you saw it, you did not afterward repent and believe him.

THE PARABLE OF THE WICKED TENANTS

33 "Hear another parable.* There was a householder who planted a vineyard, and set a hedge around it, and dug a wine press in it, and built a tower, and let it out to tenants, and went into another country. 34 When

the season of fruit drew near, he
sent his servants to the tenants, to
get his fruit; 35and the tenants took
his servants and beat one, killed an-
other, and stoned another. 36Again he
sent other servants, more than the
first; and they did the same to them.
37Afterward he sent his son to them,
saying, 'They will respect my son.'
38But when the tenants saw the son,
they said to themselves, 'This is the
heir; come, let us kill him and have
his inheritance.' 39And they took him
and cast him out of the vineyard,
and killed him. 40When therefore the
owner of the vineyard comes, what
will he do to those tenants?" 41They
said to him, "He will put those
wretches to a miserable death, and
let out the vineyard to other tenants
who will give him the fruits in their
seasons."

42 Jesus said to them, "Have you
never read in the scriptures:

'The very stone which the
builders rejected
has become the head of the
corner;
this was the Lord's doing,
and it is marvelous in our
eyes'?

43Therefore I tell you, the king-
dom of God will be taken away from
you and given to a nation producing
the fruits of it. 44And he who falls on
this stone will be brokento pieces; but
when it falls on any one, it will crush
him."[b]

45 When the chief prsts and the
Pharisees heard his pables, they
perceived that he was spking about
them. 46But when they trd to arrest
him, they feared the mutudes, be-
cause they held him to beprophet.

THE PARABLE OF THE WEDDI BANQUET

22 And again Jesus spo to them
in parables, saying, 'he king-
dom of heaven may be cpared to
a king who gave a marriafeast for
his son, 3and sent his servs to call
those who were invited to the mar-
riage feast; but they would not come.
4Again he sent other servants, saying,
'Tell those who are invited, Behold, I
have made ready my dinner, my oxen
and my fat calves are killed, and ev-
erything is ready; come to the mar-
riage feast.' 5But they made light of it
and went off, one to his farm, another
to his business, 6while the rest seized
his servants, treated them shame-
fully, and killed them. 7The king
was angry, and he sent his troops
and destroyed those murderers and
burned their city. 8Then he said to his
servants, 'The wedding is ready, but
those invited were not worthy. 9Go
therefore to the thoroughfares, and
invite to the marriage feast as many
as you find.' 10And those servants
went out into the streets and gath-
ered all whom they found, both bad
and good; so the wedding hall was
filled with guests.

11 "But when the king came in
to look at the guests, he saw there a
man who had no wedding garment;*
12and he said to him, 'Friend, how
did you get in here without a wed-
ding garment?' And he was speech-
less. 13Then the king said to the at-
tendants, 'Bind him hand and foot,
and cast him into the outer darkness;
there men will weep and gnash their
teeth.' 14For many are called, but few
are chosen."

THE QUESTION ABOUT PAYING TAXES

15 Then the Pharisees went and
took counsel how to entangle him in
his talk. 16And they sent their disci-
ples to him, along with the Hero´di-
ans, saying, "Teacher, we know that
you are true, and teach the way of
God truthfully, and care for no man;
for you do not regard the position of
men. 17Tell us, then, what you think.
Is it lawful to pay taxes to Caesar,
or not?" 18But Jesus, aware of their
malice, said, "Why put me to the
test, you hypocrites? 19Show me the

[b]Other ancient authorities omirse 44

money for the tax." And they brought
him a coin.[a] 20And Jesus said to them,
"Whose likeness and inscription is
this?" 21They said, "Caesar's." Then
he said to them, "Render there-
fore to Caesar the things that are
Caesar's, and to God the things that
are God's." 22When they heard it,
they marveled; and they left him and
went away.

THE QUESTION ABOUT THE RESURRECTION

23 The same day Sad´ducees came
to him, who say that there is no res-
urrection; and they asked him a ques-
tion, 24saying, "Teacher, Moses said,
'If a man dies, having no children,
his brother must marry the widow,
and raise up children for his broth-
er.' 25Now there were seven broth-
ers among us; the first married, and
died, and having no children left his
wife to his brother. 26So too the sec-
ond and third, down to the seventh.
27After them all, the woman died. 28In
the resurrection, therefore, to which
of the seven will she be wife? For they
all had her."

29 But Jesus answered them, "You
are wrong, because you know neither
the scriptures nor the power of God.
30For in the resurrection they neither
marry nor are given in marriage, but
are like angels[b] in heaven. 31And as
for the resurrection of the dead, have
you not read what was said to you
by God, 32'I am the God of Abraham,
and the God of Isaac, and the God of
Jacob'? He is not God of the dead, but
of the living." 33And when the crowd
heard it, they were astonished at his
teaching.

THE GREATEST COMMANDMENT

34 But when the Pharisees heard
that he had silenced the Sad´ducees,
they came together. 35And one of
them, a lawyer, asked him a question,
to test him. 36"Teacher, which is the
great commandment in the law?"
37And he said to him, "You shall love
the Lord your God with all your heart,
and with all your soul, and with all
your mind. 38This is the great and
first commandment. 39And a second
is like it, You shall love your neighbor
as yourself. 40On these two command-
ments depend all the law and the
prophets."

THE QUESTION ABOUT DAVID'S SON

41 Now while the Pharisees were
gathered together, Jesus asked them
a question, 42saying, "What do you
think of the Christ? Whose son is he?"
They said to him, "The son of David."
43He said to them, "How is it then that
David, inspired by the Spirit,[c] calls
him Lord, saying,

44'The Lord said to my Lord,
Sit at my right hand,
till I put thy enemies under thy
feet'?

45If David thus calls him Lord, how
is he his son?" 46And no one was able
to answer him a word, nor from that
day did any one dare to ask him any
more questions.

JESUS DENOUNCES SCRIBES AND PHARISEES

23 Then said Jesus to the crowds and
to his disciples, 2"The scribes and
the Pharisees sit on Moses' seat; 3so
practice and observe whatever they
tell you, but not what they do; for they
preach, but do not practice. 4They
bind heavy burdens, hard to bear,[d] and
lay them on men's shoulders; but they
themselves will not move them with
their finge 5They do all their deeds
to be seen y men; for they make their
phylacteri* broad and their fringes
long, 6and hey love the place of hon-
or at fea and the best seats in the
synagog, 7and salutations in the
market ces, and being called rabbi
by men. ut you are not to be called
rabbi, f you have one teacher, and

[a] Greek *a denarius*
[b] Other ancient authorities add *of God*
[c] Or *David in the Spirit*
[d] Other ancient authorities omit *hard to bear*

you are all brethren. 9 And call no man
your father on earth, for you have one
Father, who is in heaven.* 10 Neither
be called masters, for you have one
master, the Christ. 11 He who is great-
est among you shall be your servant;
12 whoever exalts himself will be hum-
bled, and whoever humbles himself
will be exalted.

13 "But woe to you, scribes and
Pharisees, hypocrites! because you
shut the kingdom of heaven against
men; for you neither enter yourselves,
nor allow those who would enter
to go in.[e] 15 Woe to you, scribes and
Pharisees, hypocrites! for you traverse
sea and land to make a single prose-
lyte, and when he becomes a prose-
lyte, you make him twice as much a
child of hell[f] as yourselves.

16 "Woe to you, blind guides, who
say, 'If any one swears by the temple,
it is nothing; but if any one swears by
the gold of the temple, he is bound by
his oath.' 17 You blind fools! For which
is greater, the gold or the temple that
has made the gold sacred? 18 And you
say, 'If any one swears by the altar,
it is nothing; but if any one swears
by the gift that is on the altar, he is
bound by his oath.' 19 You blind men!
For which is greater, the gift or the
altar that makes the gift sacred? 20 So
he who swears by the altar, swears
by it and by everything on it; 21 and he
who swears by the temple, swears by
it and by him who dwells in it; 22 and
he who swears by heaven, swears by
the throne of God and by him who sits
upon it.

23 "Woe to you, scribes and
Pharisees, hypocrites! for you tithe
mint and dill and cummin, and have
neglected the weightier matters of the
law, justice and mercy and faith; these
you ought to have done, without ne-
glecting the others. 24 You blind guides,
straining out a gnat and swallowing a
camel!

25 "Woe to you, scribes and
Pharisees, hypocrites! for you cleanse
the outside of the cup and of the plate,
but inside they are full of extortion
and rapacity. 26 You blind Pharisee!
first cleanse the inside of the cup and
of the plate, that the outside also may
be clean.

27 "Woe to you, scribes and Phar-
isees, hypocrites! for you are like
whitewashed tombs, which outward-
ly appear beautiful, but within they
are full of dead men's bones and all
uncleanness. 28 So you also outwardly
appear righteous to men, but within
you are full of hypocrisy and iniquity.

29 "Woe to you, scribes and Phar-
isees, hypocrites! for you build the
tombs of the prophets and adorn the
monuments of the righteous, 30 saying,
'If we had lived in the days of our fa-
thers, we would not have taken part
with them in shedding the blood of
the prophets.' 31 Thus you witness
against yourselves, that you are sons
of those who murdered the prophets.
32 Fill up, then, the measure of your fa-
thers. 33 You serpents, you brood of vi-
pers, how are you to escape being sen-
tenced to hell?[g] 34 Therefore I send you
prophets and wise men and scribes,
some of whom you will kill and cruci-
fy, and some you will scourge in your
synagogues and persecute from town
to town, 35 that upon you may come all
the righteous blood shed on earth,
from the blood of innocent Abel to
the blood of Zechari´ah the son of
Barachi´ah, whom you murdered be-
tween the sanctuary and the altar.
36 Truly, I say to you, all this will come
upon this generation.

THE LAMENT OVER JERUSALEM

37 "O Jerusalem, Jerusalem, killing
the prophets and stoning those who
are sent to you! How often would I

[e] Other authorities add here (or after verse 12) verse 14, *Woe to you, scribes and Pharisees, hypocrites! for you devour widows' houses and for a pretense you make long prayers; therefore you will receive the greater condemnation*

[f] Greek *Gehenna*

[g] Greek *Gehenna*

have gathered your children together
as a hen gathers her brood under her
wings, and you would not! 38Behold,
your house is forsaken and desolate.[a]
39For I tell you, you will not see me
again, until you say, 'Blessed is he
who comes in the name of the Lord.'"

THE DESTRUCTION OF THE TEMPLE FORETOLD

24 Jesus left the temple and was go-
ing away, when his disciples came
to point out to him the buildings of
the temple.* 2But he answered them,
"You see all these, do you not? Truly,
I say to you, there will not be left here
one stone upon another, that will not
be thrown down."

SIGNS OF THE END OF THE AGE

3 As he sat on the Mount of Olives,
the disciples came to him privately,
saying, "Tell us, when will this be,
and what will be the sign of your com-
ing and of the close of the age?" 4And
Jesus answered them, "Take heed that
no one leads you astray. 5For many will
come in my name, saying, 'I am the
Christ,' and they will lead many astray.
6And you will hear of wars and rumors
of wars; see that you are not alarmed;
for this must take place, but the end
is not yet. 7For nation will rise against
nation, and kingdom against kingdom,
and there will be famines and earth-
quakes in various places: 8all this is but
the beginning of the sufferings.

PERSECUTIONS FORETOLD

9 "Then they will deliver you up to
tribulation, and put you to death; and
you will be hated by all nations for my
name's sake. 10And then many will fall
away,[b] and betray one another, and
hate one another. 11And many false
prophets will arise and lead many
astray. 12And because wickedness is
multiplied, most men's love will grow
cold. 13But he who endures to the end
will be saved. 14And this gospel of the
kingdom will be preached throughout
the whole world, as a testimony to all
nations; and then the end will come.

THE DESOLATING SACRILEGE

15 "So when you see the desolat-
ing sacrilege spoken of by the proph-
et Daniel, standing in the holy place
(let the reader understand), 16then
let those who are in Judea flee to the
mountains; 17let him who is on the
housetop not go down to take what
is in his house; 18and let him who is
in the field not turn back to take his
mantle. 19And alas for those who are
with child and for those who give suck
in those days! 20Pray that your flight
may not be in winter or on a sabbath.
21For then there will be great tribula-
tion, such as has not been from the
beginning of the world until now,
no, and never will be. 22And if those
days had not been shortened, no hu-
man being would be saved; but for
the sake of the elect those days will
be shortened. 23Then if any one says to
you, 'Lo, here is the Christ!' or 'There
he is!' do not believe it. 24For false
Christs and false prophets will arise
and show great signs and wonders, so
as to lead astray, if possible, even the
elect. 25Lo, I have told you beforehand.
26So, if they say to you, 'Lo, he is in the
wilderness,' do not go out; if they say,
'Lo, he is in the inner rooms,' do not
believe it. 27For as the lightning comes
from the east and shines as far as the
west, so will be the coming of the Son
of man. 28Wherever the body is, there
the eagles[c] will be gathered together.

THE COMING OF THE SON OF MAN

29 "Immediately after the tribu-
lation of those days the sun will be
darkened, and the moon will not give
its light, and the stars will fall from
heaven, and the powers of the heavens

[a] Other ancient authorities omit *and desolate*
[b] Or *stumble*
[c] Or *vultures*

will be shaken; 30then will appear the
sign of the Son of man in heaven, and
then all the tribes of the earth will
mourn, and they will see the Son of
man coming on the clouds of heaven
with power and great glory; 31and he
will send out his angels with a loud
trumpet call, and they will gather his
elect from the four winds, from one
end of heaven to the other.

THE LESSON OF THE FIG TREE

32 "From the fig tree learn its les-
son: as soon as its branch becomes
tender and puts forth its leaves, you
know that summer is near. 33So also,
when you see all these things, you
know that he is near, at the very
gates. 34Truly, I say to you, this gener-
ation will not pass away till all these
things take place. 35Heaven and earth
will pass away, but my words will not
pass away.

THE NECESSITY FOR WATCHFULNESS

36 "But of that day and hour no one
knows, not even the angels of heaven,
nor the Son,[d] but the Father only. 37As
were the days of Noah, so will be the
coming of the Son of man. 38For as in
those days before the flood they were
eating and drinking, marrying and
giving in marriage, until the day when
Noah entered the ark, 39and they did
not know until the flood came and
swept them all away, so will be the
coming of the Son of man. 40Then two
men will be in the field; one is taken
and one is left. 41Two women will be
grinding at the mill; one is taken and
one is left. 42Watch therefore, for you
do not know on what day your Lord
is coming. 43But know this, that if the
householder had known in what part
of the night the thief was coming, he
would have watched and would not
have let his house be broken into.
44Therefore you also must be ready;
for the Son of man is coming at an
hour you do not expect.

THE FAITHFUL OR THE UNFAITHFUL SLAVE

45 "Who then is the faithful and
wise servant, whom his master has set
over his household, to give them their
food at the proper time? 46Blessed is
that servant whom his master when
he comes will find so doing. 47Truly,
I say to you, he will set him over all
his possessions. 48But if that wicked
servant says to himself, 'My master
is delayed,' 49and begins to beat his
fellow servants, and eats and drinks
with the drunken, 50the master of that
servant will come on a day when he
does not expect him and at an hour
he does not know, 51and will punish[e]
him, and put him with the hypocrites;
there men will weep and gnash their
teeth.

THE PARABLE OF THE TEN BRIDESMAIDS

25 "Then the kingdom of heaven
shall be compared to ten maidens
who took their lamps and went to meet
the bridegroom.[f] 2Five of them were
foolish, and five were wise. 3For when
the foolish took their lamps, they took
no oil with them; 4but the wise took
flasks of oil with their lamps. 5As
the bridegroom was delayed, they all
slumbered and slept. 6But at midnight
there was a cry, 'Behold, the bride-
groom! Come out to meet him.' 7Then
all those maidens rose and trimmed
their lamps. 8And the foolish said to
the wise, 'Give us some of your oil,
for our lamps are going out.' 9But
the wise replied, 'Perhaps there will
not be enough for us and for you; go
rather to the dealers and buy for your-
selves.' 10And while they went to buy,
the bridegroom came, and those who
were ready went in with him to the
marriage feast; and the door was shut.
11Afterward the other maidens came
also, saying, 'Lord, lord, open to us.'
12But he replied, 'Truly, I say to you, I
do not know you.' 13Watch therefore,
for you know neither the day nor the
hour.

[d] Other ancient authorities omit *nor the Son*
[e] Or *cut him in pieces*
[f] Other ancient authorities add *and the bride*

THE PARABLE OF THE TALENTS

14 "For it will be as when a man
going on a journey called his servants
and entrusted to them his property;
15to one he gave five talents,[a] to anoth-
er two, to another one, to each accord-
ing to his ability. Then he went away.
16He who had received the five talents
went at once and traded with them;
and he made five talents more. 17So
also, he who had the two talents made
two talents more. 18But he who had re-
ceived the one talent went and dug in
the ground and hid his master's mon-
ey. 19Now after a long time the master
of those servants came and settled
accounts with them. 20And he who
had received the five talents came for-
ward, bringing five talents more, say-
ing, 'Master, you delivered to me five
talents; here I have made five talents
more.' 21His master said to him, 'Well
done, good and faithful servant; you
have been faithful over a little, I will
set you over much; enter into the joy
of your master.' 22And he also who had
the two talents came forward, say-
ing, 'Master, you delivered to me two
talents; here I have made two talents
more.' 23His master said to him, 'Well
done, good and faithful servant; you
have been faithful over a little, I will
set you over much; enter into the joy
of your master.' 24He also who had re-
ceived the one talent came forward,
saying, 'Master, I knew you to be a
hard man, reaping where you did not
sow, and gathering where you did not
winnow; 25so I was afraid, and I went
and hid your talent in the ground.
Here you have what is yours.' 26But his
master answered him, 'You wicked
and slothful servant! You knew that
I reap where I have not sowed, and
gather where I have not winnowed?
27Then you ought to have invested my
money with the bankers, and at my
coming I should have received what
was my own with interest. 28So take
the talent from him, and give it to him
who has the ten talents. 29For to every
one who has will more be given, and
he will have abundance; but from him
who has not, even what he has will be
taken away.* 30And cast the worthless
servant into the outer darkness; there
men will weep and gnash their teeth.'

THE JUDGMENT OF THE NATIONS

31 "When the Son of man comes
in his glory, and all the angels with
him, then he will sit on his glorious
throne. 32Before him will be gathered
all the nations, and he will separate
them one from another as a shepherd
separates the sheep from the goats,
33and he will place the sheep at his
right hand, but the goats at the left.
34Then the King will say to those at
his right hand, 'Come, O blessed of
my Father, inherit the kingdom pre-
pared for you from the foundation of
the world; 35for I was hungry and you
gave me food, I was thirsty and you
gave me drink, I was a stranger and
you welcomed me, 36I was naked and
you clothed me, I was sick and you
visited me, I was in prison and you
came to me.' 37Then the righteous will
answer him, 'Lord, when did we see
thee hungry and feed thee, or thirsty
and give thee drink? 38And when did
we see thee a stranger and welcome
thee, or naked and clothe thee? 39And
when did we see thee sick or in prison
and visit thee?' 40And the King will
answer them, 'Truly, I say to you, as
you did it to one of the least of these
my brethren, you did it to me.' 41Then
he will say to those at his left hand,
'Depart from me, you cursed, into
the eternal fire prepared for the devil
and his angels; 42for I was hungry and
you gave me no food, I was thirsty
and you gave me no drink, 43I was a
stranger and you did not welcome
me, naked and you did not clothe me,
sick and in prison and you did not vis-
it me.' 44Then they also will answer,
'Lord, when did we see thee hungry
or thirsty or a stranger or naked or
sick or in prison, and did not minister

[a]This talent was more than fifteen years' wages of a laborer

to thee?' 45 Then he will answer them,
'Truly, I say to you, as you did it not
to one of the least of these, you did
it not to me.' 46 And they will go away
into eternal punishment, but the righ-
teous into eternal life."

THE PLOT TO KILL JESUS

26 When Jesus had finished all
these sayings, he said to his dis-
ciples, 2 "You know that after two
days the Passover is coming, and the
Son of man will be delivered up to be
crucified."

3 Then the chief priests and the el-
ders of the people gathered in the pal-
ace of the high priest, who was called
Ca′iaphas, 4 and took counsel together
in order to arrest Jesus by stealth and
kill him. 5 But they said, "Not during
the feast, lest there be a tumult among
the people."

THE ANOINTING AT BETHANY

6 Now when Jesus was at Bethany
in the house of Simon the leper, 7 a
woman came up to him with an ala-
baster jar of very expensive ointment,
and she poured it on his head, as he
sat at table. 8 But when the disciples
saw it, they were indignant, saying,
"Why this waste? 9 For this ointment
might have been sold for a large sum,
and given to the poor." 10 But Jesus,
aware of this, said to them, "Why do
you trouble the woman? For she has
done a beautiful thing to me. 11 For
you always have the poor with you,
but you will not always have me. 12 In
pouring this ointment on my body she
has done it to prepare me for burial.
13 Truly, I say to you, wherever this
gospel is preached in the whole world,
what she has done will be told in
memory of her."

JUDAS AGREES TO BETRAY JESUS

14 Then one of the twelve, who was
called Judas Iscariot, went to the chief
priests 15 and said, "What will you give
me if I deliver him to you?" And they
paid him thirty pieces of silver. 16 And
from that moment he sought an op-
portunity to betray him.

THE PASSOVER WITH THE DISCIPLES

17 Now on the first day of
Unleavened Bread the disciples came
to Jesus, saying, "Where will you have
us prepare for you to eat the pass-
over?"* 18 He said, "Go into the city
to such a one, and say to him, 'The
Teacher says, My time is at hand; I
will keep the passover at your house
with my disciples.'" 19 And the disci-
ples did as Jesus had directed them,
and they prepared the passover.

20 When it was evening, he sat at
table with the twelve disciples;[b] 21 and
as they were eating, he said, "Truly, I
say to you, one of you will betray me."
22 And they were very sorrowful, and
began to say to him one after anoth-
er, "Is it I, Lord?" 23 He answered, "He
who has dipped his hand in the dish
with me, will betray me. 24 The Son of
man goes as it is written of him, but
woe to that man by whom the Son of
man is betrayed! It would have been
better for that man if he had not been
born." 25 Judas, who betrayed him,
said, "Is it I, Master?"[c] He said to him,
"You have said so."

THE INSTITUTION OF THE LORD'S SUPPER

26 Now as they were eating,* Jesus
took bread, and blessed, and broke it,
and gave it to the disciples and said,
"Take, eat; this is my body." 27 And
he took a cup, and when he had giv-
en thanks he gave it to them, *saying*,
"Drink of it, all of you; 28 for this is
my blood of the[d] covenant, which is
poured out for many for the forgive-
ness of sins. 29 I tell you I shall not
drink again of this fruit of the vine
until that day when I drink it new
with you in my Father's kingdom."

[b] Other authorities omit *disciples*
[c] Or *Rabbi*
[d] Other ancient authorities insert *new*

PETER'S DENIAL FORETOLD

30 And when they had sung a hymn, they went out to the Mount of Olives. 31 Then Jesus said to them, "You will all fall away because of me this night; for it is written, 'I will strike the shepherd, and the sheep of the flock will be scattered.' 32 But after I am raised up, I will go before you to Galilee." 33 Peter declared to him, "Though they all fall away because of you, I will never fall away." 34 Jesus said to him, "Truly, I say to you, this very night, before the cock crows, you will deny me three times." 35 Peter said to him, "Even if I must die with you, I will not deny you." And so said all the disciples.

JESUS PRAYS IN GETHSEMANE

36 Then Jesus went with them to a place called Gethsem´ane, and he said to his disciples, "Sit here, while I go yonder and pray." 37 And taking with him Peter and the two sons of Zeb´edee, he began to be sorrowful and troubled. 38 Then he said to them, "My soul is very sorrowful, even to death; remain here, and watch[a] with me." 39 And going a little farther he fell on his face and prayed, "My Father, if it be possible, let this cup pass from me; nevertheless, not as I will, but as thou wilt." 40 And he came to the disciples and found them sleeping; and he said to Peter, "So, could you not watch[b] with me one hour? 41 Watch[c] and pray that you may not enter into temptation; the spirit indeed is willing, but the flesh is weak." 42 Again, for the second time, he went away and prayed, "My Father, if this cannot pass unless I drink it, thy will be done." 43 And again he came and found them sleeping, for their eyes were heavy. 44 So, leaving them again, *he went away and* prayed for the third time, saying the same words. 45 Then he came to the disciples and said to them, "Are you still sleeping and taking your rest? Behold, the hour is at hand, and the Son of man is betrayed into the hands of sinners. 46 Rise, let us be going; see, my betrayer is at hand."

THE BETRAYAL AND ARREST OF JESUS

47 While he was still speaking, Judas came, one of the twelve, and with him a great crowd with swords and clubs, from the chief priests and the elders of the people. 48 Now the betrayer had given them a sign, saying, "The one I shall kiss is the man; seize him." 49 And he came up to Jesus at once and said, "Hail, Master!"[d] And he kissed him. 50 Jesus said to him, "Friend, why are you here?"[e] Then they came up and laid hands on Jesus and seized him. 51 And behold, one of those who were with Jesus stretched out his hand and drew his sword, and struck the slave of the high priest, and cut off his ear.* 52 Then Jesus said to him, "Put your sword back into its place; for all who take the sword will perish by the sword. 53 Do you think that I cannot appeal to my Father, and he will at once send me more than twelve legions of angels? 54 But how then should the scriptures be fulfilled, that it must be so?" 55 At that hour Jesus said to the crowds, "Have you come out as against a robber, with swords and clubs to capture me? Day after day I sat in the temple teaching, and you did not seize me. 56 But all this has taken place, that the scriptures of the prophets might be fulfilled." Then all the disciples forsook him and fled.

JESUS BEFORE THE HIGH PRIEST

57 Then those who had seized Jesus led him to Ca´iaphas the high priest, where the scribes and the elders had gathered. 58 But Peter followed him at a distance, as far as the courtyard of

[a] Or *keep awake*
[b] Or *keep awake*
[c] Or *keep awake*
[d] Or *Rabbi*
[e] Or *do that for which you have come*

the high priest, and going inside he
sat with the guards to see the end.
59Now the chief priests and the whole
council sought false testimony against
Jesus that they might put him to
death,* 60but they found none, though
many false witnesses came forward.
At last two came forward 61and said,
"This fellow said, 'I am able to de-
stroy the temple of God, and to build
it in three days.'" 62And the high priest
stood up and said, "Have you no an-
swer to make? What is it that these
men testify against you?" 63But Jesus
was silent. And the high priest said to
him, "I adjure you by the living God,
tell us if you are the Christ, the Son
of God." 64Jesus said to him, "You
have said so. But I tell you, hereafter
you will see the Son of man seated at
the right hand of Power, and coming
on the clouds of heaven." 65Then the
high priest tore his robes, and said,
"He has uttered blasphemy. Why do
we still need witnesses? You have
now heard his blasphemy.* 66What is
your judgment?" They answere "He
deserves death." 67Then they sat in
his face, and struck him; andsome
slapped him, 68saying, "Prophy to
us, you Christ! Who is it that ruck
you?"

PETER'S DENIAL OF JESUS

69 Now Peter was sitting tside
in the courtyard. And a maicame
up to him, and said, "You alswere
with Jesus the Galilean." 70 he
denied it before them all, sag, "I
do not know what you mean.And
when he went out to the por an-
other maid saw him, and ssaid
to the bystanders, "This mwas
with Jesus of Nazareth." 72Angain
he denied it with an oath, "I not
know the man." 73After a litthile
the bystanders came up andl to
Peter, "Certainly you are alse of
them, for your accent betrayu."
74Then he began to invoke a c on
himself and to swear, "I do now
the man." And immediately tock
crowed. 75And Peter remembered
the saying of Jesus, "Before the cock
crows, you will deny me three times."
And he went out and wept bitterly.

JESUS BROUGHT BEFORE PILATE

27 When morning came, all the chief
priests and the elders of the peo-
ple took counsel against Jesus to put
him to death; 2and they bound him
and led him away and delivered him
to Pilate the governor.

THE SUICIDE OF JUDAS

3 When Judas, his betrayer, saw
that he was condemned, he repented
and brought back the thirty pieces
of silver to the chief priests and the
elders, 4saying, "I have sinned in be-
traying innocent blood." They said,
"What is that to us? See to it your-
self." 5And throwing down the pieces
of silver in the temple, he departed;
and he went and hanged himself. 6But
the chief priests, taking the pieces of
silver, said, "It is not lawful to put
them into the treasury, since they are
blood money." 7So they took counsel,
and bought with them the potter's
field, to bury strangers in. 8Therefore
that field has been called the Field of
Blood to this day. 9Then was fulfilled
what had been spoken by the prophet
Jeremiah, saying, "And they took the
thirty pieces of silver, the price of him
on whom a price had been set by some
of the sons of Israel, 10and they gave
them for the potter's field, as the Lord
directed me."

PILATE QUESTIONS JESUS

11 Now Jesus stood before the gov-
ernor; and the governor asked him,
"Are you the King of the Jews?" Jesus
said to him, "You have said so." 12But
when he was accused by the chief
priests and elders, he made no answer.
13Then Pilate said to him, "Do you not
hear how many things they testify
against you?" 14But he gave him no an-
swer, not even to a single charge; so
that the governor wondered greatly.

BARABBAS OR JESUS?

15 Now at the feast the governor
was accustomed to release for the
crowd any one prisoner whom they
wanted. 16And they had then a notori-
ous prisoner, called Barab´bas.[a] 17So
when they had gathered, Pilate said
to them, "Whom do you want me to
release for you, Barab´bas[b] or Jesus
who is called Christ?" 18For he knew
that it was out of envy that they had
delivered him up. 19Besides, while he
was sitting on the judgment seat, his
wife sent word to him, "Have noth-
ing to do with that righteous man,
for I have suffered much over him
today in a dream." 20Now the chief
priests and the elders persuaded the
people to ask for Barab´bas and de-
stroy Jesus. 21The governor again said
to them, "Which of the two do you
want me to release for you?" And
they said, "Barab´bas." 22Pilate said
to them, "Then what shall I do with
Jesus who is called Christ?" They all
said, "Let him be crucified." 23And he
said, "Why, what evil has he done?"
But they shouted all the more, "Let
him be crucified."

PILATE HANDS JESUS OVER TO BE CRUCIFIED

24 So when Pilate saw that he
was gaining nothing, but rather
that a riot was beginning, he took
water and washed his hands before
the crowd, saying, "I am innocent of
this righteous man's blood;[c] see to
it yourselves." 25And all the people
answered, "His blood be on us and
on our children!" 26Then he released
for them Barab´bas, and having
scourged Jesus, delivered him to be
crucified.

THE SOLDIERS MOCK JESUS

27 Then the soldiers of the gov-
ernor took Jesus into the praetori-
um, and they gathered the whole
battalion before him. 28And they
stripped him and put a scarlet robe
upon him, 29and plaiting a crown of
thorns they put it on his head, and
put a reed in his right hand. And
kneeling before him they mocked
him, saying, "Hail, King of the Jews!"
30And they spat upon him, and took
the reed and struck him on the head.
31And when they had mocked him,
they stripped him of the robe, and
put his own clothes on him, and led
him away to crucify him.

THE CRUCIFIXION OF JESUS

32 As they were marching out,
they came upon a man of Cyre´ne,
Simon by name; this man they com-
pelled to carry his cross. 33And when
they came to a place called Gol´gotha
(which means the place of a skull),
34they offered him wine to drink,
mingled with gall; but when he tast-
ed it, he would not drink it. 35And
when they had crucified him, they
divid d his garments among them by
castig lots; 36then they sat down and
kept atch over him there. 37And over
his hd they put the charge against
him, hich read, "This is Jesus the
King f the Jews." 38Then two rob-
bers re crucified with him, one on
the rht and one on the left. 39And
those ho passed by derided him,
wagg their heads 40and saying,
"You o would destroy the temple
and bd it in three days, save your-
self! ou are the Son of God, come
down om the cross." 41So also the
chief iests, with the scribes and
elder mocked him, saying, 42"He
saved hers; he cannot save him-
self. s the King of Israel; let him
come n now from the cross, and
we believe in him. 43He trusts
in G et God deliver him now, if
he des him; for he said, 'I am the
Son od.'" 44And the robbers who
were ified with him also reviled
him e same way.

[a] Other ancient authorities read *Jesus Barabbas*
[b] Other ancient authorities read *Jesus Barabbas*
[c] Other authorities omit *righteous* or *man's*

THE DEATH OF JESUS

45 Now from the sixth hour there
was darkness over all the land[d] until
the ninth hour. 46And about the ninth
hour Jesus cried with a loud voice,
"Eli, Eli, la´ma sabach-tha´ni?" that
is, "My God, my God, why hast thou
forsaken me?"* 47And some of the by-
standers hearing it said, "This man
is calling Eli´jah." 48And one of them
at once ran and took a sponge, filled
it with vinegar, and put it on a reed,
and gave it to him to drink. 49But the
others said, "Wait, let us see whether
Eli´jah will come to save him."[e] 50And
Jesus cried again with a loud voice and
yielded up his spirit.

51 And behold, the curtain of the
temple was torn in two, from top to
bottom; and the earth shook, and
the rocks were split; 52the tombs also
were opened, and many bodies of the
saints who had fallen asleep were
raised, 53and coming out of the tombs
after his resurrection they went into
the holy city and appeared to many.
54When the centurion and those who
were with him, keeping watch over
Jesus, saw the earthquake and what
took place, they were filled with awe,
and said, "Truly this was the Son[f] of
God!"

55 There were also many women
there, looking on from afar, who had
followed Jesus from Galilee, minister-
ing to him; 56among whom were Mary
Mag´dalene, and Mary the mother of
James and Joseph, and the mother of
the sons of Zeb´edee.

THE BURIAL OF JESUS

57 When it was evening, there
came a rich man from Arimathe´a,
named Joseph, who also was a disciple
of Jesus. 58He went to Pilate and asked
for the body of Jesus. Then Pilate
ordered it to be given to him. 59And
Joseph took the body, and wrapped it
in a clean linen shroud, 60and laid it
in his own new tomb, which he had
hewn in the rock; and he rolled a great
stone to the door of the tomb, and de-
parted. 61Mary Mag´dalene and the
other Mary were there, sitting oppo-
site the sepulchre.

THE GUARD AT THE TOMB

62 Next day, that is, after the day of
Preparation, the chief priests and the
Pharisees gathered before Pilate 63and
said, "Sir, we remember how that im-
poster said, while he was still alive,
'After three days I will rise again.'
64Therefore order the sepulchre to be
made secure until the third day, lest
his disciples go and steal him away,
and tell the people, 'He has risen from
the dead,' and the last fraud will be
worse than the first." 65Pilate said to
them, "You have a guard[g] of soldiers;
go, make it as secure as you can."66So
they went and made the sepulchre se-
cure by sealing the stone and setting
a guard.*

THE RESURRECTION OF JESUS

28 *Now after the sabbath, toward
the dawn of the first day of the
week, Mary Mag´dalene and the other
Mary went to see the sepulchre. 2And
behold, there was a great earthquake;
for an angel of the Lord descend-
ed from heaven and came and rolled
back the stone, and sat upon it. 3His
appearance was like lightning, and
his raiment white as snow. 4And for
fear of him the guards trembled and
became like dead men. 5But the angel
said to the women, "Do not be afraid;
for I know that you seek Jesus who
was crucified. 6He is not here; for he
has risen, as he said. Come, see the
place where he[h] lay. 7Then go quickly
and tell his disciples that he has risen

[d] Or *earth*
[e] Other ancient authorities insert *And another took a spear and pierced his side, and out came water and blood*
[f] Or *a son*
[g] Or *Take a guard*
[h] Other ancient authorities read *the Lord*

from the dead, and behold, he is go-
ing before you to Galilee; there you
will see him. Lo, I have told you." 8So
they departed quickly from the tomb
with fear and great joy, and ran to tell
his disciples. 9And behold, Jesus met
them and said, "Hail!" And they came
up and took hold of his feet and wor-
shiped him. 10Then Jesus said to them,
"Do not be afraid; go and tell my
brethren to go to Galilee, and there
they will see me."

THE REPORT OF THE GUARD

11 While they were going, be-
hold, some of the guard went into
the city and told the chief priests
all that had taken place. 12And when
they had assembled with the elders
and taken counsel, they gave a sum
of money to the soldiers 13and said,
"Tell people, 'His disciples came by
night and stole him away while we
were asleep.' 14And if this comes to
the governor's ears, we will satisfy
him and keep you out of trouble."
15So they took the money and did as
they were directed; and this story
has been spread among the Jews to
this day.

THE COMMISSIONING OF THE DISCIPLES

16 Now the eleven disciples went
to Galilee, to the mountain to which
Jesus had directed them. 17And when
they saw him they worshiped him;
but some doubted. 18And Jesus came
and said to them, "All authority in
heaven and on earth has been given to
me. 19Go therefore and make disciples
of all nations, baptizing them in the
name of the Father and of the Son and
of the Holy Spirit, 20teaching them to
observe all that I have commanded
you; and lo, I am with you always, to
the close of the age."

THE GOSPEL ACCORDING TO
MARK

THE PROCLAMATION OF JOHN THE BAPTIST

1 The beginning of the gospel of Jesus
Christ, the Son of God.[a]
2 As it is written in Isaiah the
prophet,[b]

> "Behold, I send my messenger
> before thy face,
> who shall prepare thy way;
> 3 the voice of one crying in the
> wilderness:
> Prepare the way of the Lord,
> make his paths straight—"

4 John the baptizer appeared[c] in the
wilderness, preaching a baptism of re-
pentance for the forgiveness of sins.
5 And there went out to him all the
country of Judea, and all the people
of Jerusalem; and they were baptized
by him in the river Jordan, confessing
their sins. 6 Now John was clothed with
camel's hair, and had a leather girdle
around his waist, and ate locusts and
wild honey. 7 And he preached, saying,
"After me comes he who is mightier
than I, the thong of whose sandals I am
not worthy to stoop down and untie. 8 I
have baptized you with water; but he
will baptize you with the Holy Spirit."

THE BAPTISM OF JESUS

9 In those days Jesus came from
Nazareth of Galilee and was baptized
by John in the Jordan. 10 And when he
came up out of the water, immedi-
ately he saw the heavens opened and
the Spirit descending upon him like a
dove; 11 and a voice came from heaven,
"Thou art my beloved Son;[d] with thee
I am well pleased."

THE TEMPTATION OF JESUS

12 The Spirit immediately drove
him out into the wilderness. 13 And
he was in the wilderness forty days,
tempted by Satan; and he was with
the wild beasts; and the angels min-
istered to him.

THE BEGINNING OF THE GALILEAN MINISTRY

14 Now after John was arrested,
Jesus came into Galilee, preaching the
gospel of God, 15 and saying, "The time
is fulfilled, and the kingdom of God
is at hand; repent, and believe in the
gospel."

JESUS CALLS THE FIRST DISCIPLES

16 And passing along by the Sea
of Galilee, he saw Simon and Andrew
the brother of Simon casting a net
in the sea; for they were fishermen.
17 And Jesus said to them, "Follow me
and I will make you become fishers
of men." 18 And immediately they left
their nets and followed him. 19 And go-
ing on a little farther, he saw James
the son of Zeb´edee and John his
brother, who were in their boat mend-
ing the nets. 20 And immediately he
called them; and they left their father
Zeb´edee in the boat with the hired
servants, and followed him.

THE MAN WITH AN UNCLEAN SPIRIT

21 And they went into Caper´na-
um; and immediately on the sab-
bath he entered the synagogue and
taught. 22 And they were astonished
at his teaching, for he taught them
as one who had authority, and not as
the scribes. 23 And immediately there
was in their synagogue a man with
an unclean spirit; 24 and he cried out,
"What have you to do with us, Jesus of
Nazareth? Have you come to destroy
us? I know who you are, the Holy One
of God." 25 But Jesus rebuked him, say-
ing, "Be silent, and come out of him!"

[a] Other ancient authorities omit *the Son of God*
[b] Other ancient authorities read *in the prophets*
[c] Other ancient authorities read *John was baptizing*
[d] Or *my Son, my* (or *the*) *Beloved*

26 And the unclean spirit, convulsing
him and crying with a loud voice,
came out of him. 27 And they were
all amazed, so that they questioned
among themselves, saying, "What is
this? A new teaching! With authority
he commands even the unclean spirits,
and they obey him." 28 And at once his
fame spread everywhere throughout
all the surrounding region of Galilee.

JESUS HEALS MANY AT SIMON'S HOUSE

29 And immediately he[a] left the
synagogue, and entered the house of
Simon and Andrew, with James and
John. 30 Now Simon's mother-in-law
lay sick with a fever, and immediate-
ly they told him of her. 31 And he came
and took her by the hand and lifted
her up, and the fever left her; and she
served them.

32 That evening, at sundown, they
brought to him all who were sick or
possessed with demons. 33 And the
whole city was gathered together
about the door. 34 And he healed many
who were sick with various diseas-
es, and cast out many demons; and
he would not permit the demons to
speak, because they knew him.*

A PREACHING TOUR IN GALILEE

35 And in the morning, a great
while before day, he rose and went out
to a lonely place, and there he prayed.
36 And Simon and those who were with
him followed him, 37 and they found
him and said to him, "Every one is
searching for you." 38 And he said to
them, "Let us go on to the next towns,
that I may preach there also; for that
is why I came out." 39 And he went
throughout all Galilee, preaching
in their synagogues and casting out
demons.

JESUS CLEANSES A LEPER

40 And a leper came to him be-
seeching him, and kneeling said to
him, "If you will, you can make me
clean." 41 Moved with pity, he stretched
out his hand and touched him, and
said to him, "I will; be clean." 42 And
immediately the leprosy left him, and
he was made clean. 43 And he sternly
charged him, and sent him away at
once, 44 and said to him, "See that you
say nothing to any one; but go, show
yourself to the priest, and offer for
your cleansing what Moses command-
ed, for a proof to the people."[b] 45 But
he went out and began to talk freely
about it, and to spread the news, so
that Jesus[c] could no longer openly en-
ter a town, but was out in the country;
and people came to him from every
quarter.

JESUS HEALS A PARALYTIC

2 And when he returned to Caper´na-
um after some days, it was reported
that he was at home. 2 And many were
gathered together, so that there was
no longer room for them, not even
about the door; and he was preaching
the word to them. 3 And they came,
bringing to him a paralytic carried by
four men. 4 And when they could not
get near him because of the crowd,
they removed the roof above him;
and when they had made an opening,
they let down the pallet on which the
paralytic lay. 5 And when Jesus saw
their faith, he said to the paralyt-
ic, "My son, your sins are forgiven."
6 Now some of the scribes were sitting
there, questioning in their hearts,
7 "Why does this man speak thus? It is
blasphemy! Who can forgive sins but
God alone?" 8 And immediately Jesus,
perceiving in his spirit that they thus
questioned within themselves, said to
them, "Why do you question thus in
your hearts? 9 Which is easier, to say to
the paralytic, 'Your sins are forgiven,'
or to say, 'Rise, take up your pallet
and walk'? 10 But that you may know
that the Son of man has authority on
earth to forgive sins"—he said to the

[a]Other ancient authorities read *they*
[b]Greek *to them*
[c]Greek *he*

paralytic 11"I say to you, rise, take up your pallet and go home." 12And he rose, and immediately took up the pallet and went out before them all; so that they were all amazed and glorified God, saying, "We never saw anything like this!"

JESUS CALLS LEVI

13 He went out again beside the sea; and all the crowd gathered about him, and he taught them. 14And as he passed on, he saw Levi* the son of Alphaeus sitting at the tax office, and he said to him, "Follow me." And he rose and followed him.

15 And as he sat at table in his house, many tax collectors and sinners were sitting with Jesus and his disciples; for there were many who followed him. 16And the scribes of[d] the Pharisees, when they saw that he was eating with sinners and tax collectors, said to his disciples, "Why does he eat[e] with tax collectors and sinners?" 17And when Jesus heard it, he said to them, "Those who are well have no need of a physician, but those who are sick; I came not to call the righteous, but sinners."

THE QUESTION ABOUT FASTING

18 Now John's disciples and the Pharisees were fasting; and people came and said to him, "Why do John's disciples and the disciples of the Pharisees fast, but your disciples do not fast?" 19And Jesus said to them, "Can the wedding guests fast while the bridegroom is with them? As long *as they have the* bridegroom with them, they cannot fast. 20The days will come, when the bridegroom is taken away from them, and then they will fast in that day. 21No one sews a piece of unshrunk cloth on an old garment; if he does, the patch tears away from it, the new from the old, and a worse tear is made. 22And no one puts new wine into old wineskins; if he does, the wine will burst the skins, and the wine is lost, and so are the skins; but new wine is for fresh skins."[f]

PRONOUNCEMENT ABOUT THE SABBATH

23 One sabbath he was going through the grainfields; and as they made their way his disciples began to pluck ears of grain. 24And the Pharisees said to him, "Look, why are they doing what is not lawful on the sabbath?" 25And he said to them, "Have you never read what David did, when he was in need and was hungry, he and those who were with him: 26how he entered the house of God, when Abi´athar was high priest, and ate the bread of the Presence, which it is not lawful for any but the priests to eat, and also gave it to those who were with him?" 27And he said to them, "The sabbath was made for man, not man for the sabbath; 28so the Son of man is lord even of the sabbath."

THE MAN WITH A WITHERED HAND

3 Again he entered the synagogue, and a man was there who had a withered hand. 2And they watched him, to see whether he would heal him on the sabbath, so that they might accuse him. 3And he said to the man who had the withered hand, "Come here." 4And he said to them, "Is it lawful on the sabbath to do good or to do harm, to save life or to kill?" But they were silent. 5And he looked around at them with anger, grieved at their hardness of heart, and said to the man, "Stretch out your hand." He stretched it out, and his hand was restored. 6The Pharisees went out, and immediately held counsel with the Hero´di-ans against him, how to destroy him.

A MULTITUDE AT THE SEASIDE

7 Jesus withdrew with his disciples to the sea, and a great multitude from Galilee followed; also from Judea 8and

[d] Other ancient authorities read *and*
[e] Other ancient authorities add *and drink*
[f] Other ancient authorities omit *but new wine is for fresh skins*

Jerusalem and Idume´a and from be-
yond the Jordan and from about Tyre
and Sidon a great multitude, hearing
all that he did, came to him. 9And he
told his disciples to have a boat ready
for him because of the crowd, lest they
should crush him; 10for he had healed
many, so that all who had diseases
pressed upon him to touch him. 11And
whenever the unclean spirits beheld
him, they fell down before him and
cried out, "You are the Son of God."
12And he strictly ordered them not to
make him known.

JESUS APPOINTS THE TWELVE

13 And he went up into the hills,
and called to him those whom he de-
sired; and they came to him. 14And he
appointed twelve,[a] to be with him,
and to be sent out to preach 15and
have authority to cast out demons:
16Simon whom he surnamed Peter;
17James the son of Zeb´edee and
John the brother of James, whom he
surnamed Bo-aner´ges, that is, sons
of thunder; 18Andrew, and Philip,
and Bartholomew, and Matthew,
and Thomas, and James the son of
Alphaeus, and Thaddaeus, and Simon
the Cananaean, 19and Judas Iscariot,
who betrayed him.

JESUS AND BEELZEBUL

Then he went home; 20and the
crowd came together again, so that
they could not even eat. 21And when
his friends heard it, they went out to
seize him, for they said, "He is be-
side himself." 22And the scribes who
came down from Jerusalem said, "He
is possessed by Be-el´zebul, and by
the prince of demons he casts out
the demons." 23And he called them
to him, and said to them in parables,
"How can Satan cast out Satan? 24If
a kingdom is divided against itself,
that kingdom cannot stand. 25And if
a house is divided against itself, that
house will not be able to stand. 26And
if Satan has risen up against himself
and is divided, he cannot stand, but
is coming to an end. 27But no one can
enter a strong man's house and plun-
der his goods, unless he first binds the
strong man; then indeed he may plun-
der his house.

28 "Truly, I say to you, all sins
will be forgiven the sons of men, and
whatever blasphemies they utter;
29but whoever blasphemes against the
Holy Spirit never has forgiveness, but
is guilty of an eternal sin" 30for they
had said, "He has an unclean spirit."

THE TRUE KINDRED OF JESUS

31 And his mother and his breth-
ren* came; and standing outside they
sent to him and called him. 32And a
crowd was sitting about him; and they
said to him, "Your mother and your
brethren[b] are outside, asking for you."
33And he replied, "Who are my moth-
er and my brethren?" 34And looking
around on those who sat about him,
he said, "Here are my mother and my
brethren! 35Whoever does the will of
God is my brother, and sister, and
mother."

THE PARABLE OF THE SOWER

4Again he began to teach beside the
sea. And a very large crowd gath-
ered about him, so that he got into
a boat and sat in it on the sea; and
the whole crowd was beside the sea
on the land. 2And he taught them
many things in parables, and in his
teaching he said to them: 3"Listen!
A sower went out to sow. 4And as he
sowed, some seed fell along the path,
and the birds came and devoured it.
5Other seed fell on rocky ground,
where it had not much soil, and im-
mediately it sprang up, since it had no
depth of soil; 6and when the sun rose
it was scorched, and since it had no
root it withered away. 7Other seed fell
among thorns and the thorns grew up
and choked it, and it yielded no grain.

[a] Other ancient authorities add *whom also he named apostles*
[b] Other early authorities add *and your sisters*

8And other seeds fell into good soil
and brought forth grain, growing up
and increasing and yielding thirty-
fold and sixtyfold and a hundredfold."
9And he said, "He who has ears to
hear, let him hear."

THE PURPOSE OF THE PARABLES

10 And when he was alone, those
who were about him with the twelve
asked him concerning the parables.
11And he said to them, "To you has
been given the secret of the kingdom
of God, but for those outside every-
thing is in parables; 12so that* they
may indeed see but not perceive, and
may indeed hear but not understand;
lest they should turn again, and be
forgiven." 13And he said to them, "Do
you not understand this parable?
How then will you understand all
the parables? 14The sower sows the
word. 15And these are the ones along
the path, where the word is sown;
when they hear, Satan immediately
comes and takes away the word which
is sown in them. 16And these in like
manner are the ones sown upon rocky
ground, who, when they hear the
word, immediately receive it with joy;
17and they have no root in themselves,
but endure for a while; then, when
tribulation or persecution arises on
account of the word, immediately they
fall away.[c] 18And others are the ones
sown among thorns; they are those
who hear the word, 19but the cares of
the world, and the delight in riches,
and the desire for other things, enter
in and choke the word, and it proves
unfruitful. 20But those that were sown
upon the good soil are the ones who
hear the word and accept it and bear
fruit, thirtyfold and sixtyfold and a
hundredfold."

A LAMP UNDER A BUSHEL BASKET

21 And he said to them, "Is a lamp
brought in to be put under a bushel,
or under a bed, and not on a stand?
22For there is nothing hid, except to be
made manifest; nor is anything secret,
except to come to light. 23If any man
has ears to hear, let him hear." 24And
he said to them, "Take heed what you
hear; the measure you give will be the
measure you get, and still more will
be given you. 25For to him who has
will more be given; and from him who
has not, even what he has will be tak-
en away."

THE PARABLE OF THE GROWING SEED

26 And he said, "The kingdom of
God is as if a man should scatter seed
upon the ground, 27and should sleep
and rise night and day, and the seed
should sprout and grow, he knows not
how. 28The earth produces of itself,
first the blade, then the ear, then the
full grain in the ear. 29But when the
grain is ripe, at once he puts in the
sickle, because the harvest has come."

THE PARABLE OF THE MUSTARD SEED

30 And he said, "With what can we
compare the kingdom of God, or what
parable shall we use for it? 31It is like
a grain of mustard seed, which, when
sown upon the ground, is the smallest
of all the seeds on earth; 32yet when it
is sown it grows up and becomes the
greatest of all shrubs, and puts forth
large branches, so that the birds of the
air can make nests in its shade."

THE USE OF PARABLES

33 With many such parables he
spoke the word to them, as they were
able to hear it; 34he did not speak to
them without a parable, but private-
ly to his own disciples he explained
everything.

JESUS STILLS A STORM

35 On that day, when evening had
come, he said to them, "Let us go
across to the other side." 36And leaving
the crowd, they took him with them,
just as he was, in the boat. And oth-
er boats were with him. 37And a great
storm of wind arose, and the waves

[c]Or *stumble*

beat into the boat, so that the boat
was already filling. 38But he was in the
stern, asleep on the cushion; and they
woke him and said to him, "Teacher,
do you not care if we perish?" 39And
he awoke and rebuked the wind, and
said to the sea, "Peace! Be still!" And
the wind ceased, and there was a great
calm. 40He said to them, "Why are you
afraid? Have you no faith?" 41And they
were filled with awe, and said to one
another, "Who then is this, that even
wind and sea obey him?"

JESUS HEALS THE GERASENE DEMONIAC

5 They came to the other side of
the sea, to the country of the
Ger'asenes.[a] 2And when he had come
out of the boat, there met him out
of the tombs a man with an unclean
spirit, 3who lived among the tombs;
and no one could bind him any more,
even with a chain; 4for he had often
been bound with fetters and chains,
but the chains he wrenched apart,
and the fetters he broke in pieces; and
no one had the strength to subdue
him. 5Night and day among the tombs
and on the mountains he was always
crying out, and bruising himself with
stones. 6And when he saw Jesus from
afar, he ran and worshiped him; 7and
crying out with a loud voice, he said,
"What have you to do with me, Jesus,
Son of the Most High God? I adjure
you by God, do not torment me." 8For
he had said to him, "Come out of the
man, you unclean spirit!" 9And Jesus[b]
asked him, "What is your name?"
He replied, "My name is Legion; for
we are many." 10And he begged him
eagerly not to send them out of the
country. 11Now a great herd of swine
was feeding there on the hillside;
12and they begged him, "Send us to
the swine, let us enter them." 13So
he gave them leave. And the un-
clean spirits came out, and entered
the swine; and the herd, numbering
about two thousand, rushed down
the steep bank into the sea, and were
drowned in the sea.

14 The herdsmen fled, and told it in
the city and in the country. And peo-
ple came to see what it was that had
happened. 15And they came to Jesus,
and saw the demoniac sitting there,
clothed and in his right mind, the man
who had had the legion; and they were
afraid. 16And those who had seen it
told what had happened to the demo-
niac and to the swine. 17And they be-
gan to beg Jesus[c] to depart from their
neighborhood. 18And as he was getting
into the boat, the man who had been
possessed with demons begged him
that he might be with him. 19But he
refused, and said to him, "Go home to
your friends, and tell them how much
the Lord has done for you, and how he
has had mercy on you." 20And he went
away and began to proclaim in the
Decap'olis how much Jesus had done
for him; and all men marveled.

A GIRL RESTORED TO LIFE AND A WOMAN HEALED

21 And when Jesus had crossed
again in the boat to the other side, a
great crowd gathered about him; and
he was beside the sea. 22Then came
one of the rulers of the synagogue,
Ja'irus by name; and seeing him, he
fell at his feet, 23and besought him,
saying, "My little daughter is at the
point of death. Come and lay your
hands on her, so that she may be made
well, and live." 24And he went with
him. And a great crowd followed him
and thronged about him. 25And there
was a woman who had had a flow of
blood for twelve years, 26and who had
suffered much under many physi-
cians, and had spent all that she had,
and was no better but rather grew
worse. 27She had heard the reports
about Jesus, and came up behind him
in the crowd and touched his garment.
28For she said, "If I touch even his

[a] Other ancient authorities read *Gergesenes,* some *Gadarenes*
[b] Greek *he*
[c] Greek *him*

garments, I shall be made well." 29And immediately the hemorrhage ceased; and she felt in her body that she was healed of her disease. 30And Jesus, perceiving in himself that power had gone forth from him, immediately turned about in the crowd, and said, "Who touched my garments?" 31And his disciples said to him, "You see the crowd pressing around you, and yet you say, 'Who touched me?'" 32And he looked around to see who had done it. 33But the woman, knowing what had been done to her, came in fear and trembling and fell down before him, and told him the whole truth. 34And he said to her, "Daughter, your faith has made you well; go in peace, and be healed of your disease."

35 While he was still speaking, there came from the ruler's house some who said, "Your daughter is dead. Why trouble the Teacher any further?" 36But ignoring[d] what they said, Jesus said to the ruler of the synagogue, "Do not fear, only believe." 37And he allowed no one to follow him except Peter and James and John the brother of James. 38When they came to the house of the ruler of the synagogue, he saw a tumult, and people weeping and wailing loudly. 39And when he had entered, he said to them, "Why do you make a tumult and weep? The child is not dead but sleeping." 40And they laughed at him. But he put them all outside, and took the child's father and mother and those who were with him, and went in where the child was. 41Taking her *by the hand* he said to her, "Tal´itha cu´mi"; which means, "Little girl, I say to you, arise." 42And immediately the girl got up and walked; for she was twelve years old. And immediately they were overcome with amazement. 43And he strictly charged them that no one should know this,* and told them to give her something to eat.

THE REJECTION OF JESUS AT NAZARETH

6 He went away from there and came to his own country; and his disciples followed him. 2And on the sabbath he began to teach in the synagogue; and many who heard him were astonished, saying, "Where did this man get all this? What is the wisdom given to him? What mighty works are wrought by his hands! 3Is not this the carpenter, the son of Mary and brother of James and Joses and Judas and Simon, and are not his sisters here with us?" And they took offense[e] at him. 4And Jesus said to them, "A prophet is not without honor, except in his own country, and among his own kin, and in his own house." 5And he could do no mighty work there, except that he laid his hands upon a few sick people and healed them. 6And he marveled because of their unbelief. And he went about among the villages teaching.

THE MISSION OF THE TWELVE

7 And he called to him the twelve, and began to send them out two by two, and gave them authority over the unclean spirits. 8He charged them to take nothing for their journey except a staff; no bread, no bag, no money in their belts; 9but to wear sandals and not put on two tunics. 10And he said to them, "Where you enter a house, stay there until you leave the place. 11And if any place will not receive you and they refuse to hear you, when you leave, shake off the dust that is on your feet for a testimony against them." 12So they went out and preached that men *should* repent. 13And they cast out many demons, and anointed with oil many that were sick and healed them.

THE DEATH OF JOHN THE BAPTIST

14 King Herod heard of it; for Jesus'[f] name had become known.

[d]Or overhearing. Other ancient authorities read hearing
[e]Or *stumbled*
[f]Greek *his*

Some[a] said, "John the baptizer has
been raised from the dead; that is why
these powers are at work in him." 15But
others said, "It is Eli´jah." And others
said, "It is a prophet, like one of the
prophets of old." 16But when Herod
heard of it he said, "John, whom I be-
headed, has been raised." 17For Herod
had sent and seized John, and bound
him in prison for the sake of Hero´di-
as, his brother Philip's wife; because
he had married her. 18For John said to
Herod, "It is not lawful for you to have
your brother's wife." 19And Hero´di-as
had a grudge against him, and want-
ed to kill him. But she could not, 20for
Herod feared John, knowing that he
was a righteous and holy man, and
kept him safe. When he heard him, he
was much perplexed; and yet he heard
him gladly. 21But an opportunity came
when Herod on his birthday gave a
banquet for his courtiers and officers
and the leading men of Galilee. 22For
when Hero´di-as' daughter came in
and danced, she pleased Herod and
his guests; and the king said to the
girl, "Ask me for whatever you wish,
and I will grant it." 23And he vowed to
her, "Whatever you ask me, I will give
you, even half of my kingdom." 24And
she went out, and said to her moth-
er, "What shall I ask?" And she said,
"The head of John the baptizer." 25And
she came in immediately with haste to
the king, and asked, saying, "I want
you to give me at once the head of
John the Baptist on a platter." 26And
the king was exceedingly sorry; but
because of his oaths and his guests
he did not want to break his word to
her. 27And immediately the king sent a
soldier of the guard and gave orders to
bring his head. He went and beheaded
him in the prison, 28and brought his
head on a platter, and gave it to the
girl; and the girl gave it to her mother.
29When his disciples heard of it, they
came and took his body, and laid it in
a tomb.

FEEDING THE FIVE THOUSAND

30 The apostles returned to Jesus,
and told him all that they had done and
taught. 31And he said to them, "Come
away by yourselves to a lonely place,
and rest a while." For many were com-
ing and going, and they had no leisure
even to eat. 32And they went away in
the boat to a lonely place by them-
selves. 33Now many saw them going,
and knew them, and they ran there on
foot from all the towns, and got there
ahead of them. 34As he landed he saw
a great throng, and he had compassion
on them, because they were like sheep
without a shepherd; and he began to
teach them many things. 35And when
it grew late, his disciples came to
him and said, "This is a lonely place,
and the hour is now late; 36send them
away, to go into the country and vil-
lages round about and buy themselves
something to eat." 37But he answered
them, "You give them something to
eat." And they said to him, "Shall
we go and buy two hundred denarii[b]
worth of bread, and give it to them
to eat?" 38And he said to them, "How
many loaves have you? Go and see."
And when they had found out, they
said, "Five, and two fish." 39Then he
commanded them all to sit down by
companies upon the green grass. 40So
they sat down in groups, by hundreds
and by fifties. 41And taking the five
loaves and the two fish he looked up
to heaven, and blessed, and broke the
loaves, and gave them to the disciples
to set before the people; and he divid-
ed the two fish among them all. 42And
they all ate and were satisfied. 43And
they took up twelve baskets full of
broken pieces and of the fish. 44And
those who ate the loaves were five
thousand men.

JESUS WALKS ON THE WATER

45 Immediately he made his disci-
ples get into the boat and go before
him to the other side, to Beth-sa´ida,

[a] Other ancient authorities read *he*
[b] The denarius was a day's wage for a laborer

while he dismissed the crowd. 46And
after he had taken leave of them, he
went up into the hills to pray. 47And
when evening came, the boat was out
on the sea, and he was alone on the
land. 48And he saw that they were dis-
tressed in rowing, for the wind was
against them. And about the fourth
watch of the night he came to them,
walking on the sea. He meant to pass
by them, 49but when they saw him
walking on the sea they thought it
was a ghost, and cried out; 50for they
all saw him, and were terrified. But
immediately he spoke to them and
said, "Take heart, it is I; have no fear."
51And he got into the boat with them
and the wind ceased. And they were
utterly astounded, 52for they did not
understand about the loaves, but their
hearts were hardened.

HEALING THE SICK IN GENNESARET

53 And when they had crossed over,
they came to land at Gennes′aret, and
moored to the shore. 54And when they
got out of the boat, immediately the
people recognized him, 55and ran
about the whole neighborhood and
began to bring sick people on their
pallets to any place where they heard
he was. 56And wherever he came, in
villages, cities, or country, they laid
the sick in the market places, and
besought him that they might touch
even the fringe of his garment; and as
many as touched it were made well.

THE TRADITION OF THE ELDERS

7 Now when the Pharisees gath-
ered together to him, with some
of the scribes, who had come from
Jerusalem, 2they saw that some of his
disciples ate with hands defiled, that
is, unwashed. 3(For the Pharisees,
and all the Jews, do not eat unless
they wash their hands,[c] observing the
tradition of the elders;* 4and when
they come from the market place, they
do not eat unless they purify[d] them-
selves; and there are many other tra-
ditions which they observe, the wash-
ing of cups and pots and vessels of
bronze.)[e] 5And the Pharisees and the
scribes asked him, "Why do your dis-
ciples not live[f] according to the tradi-
tion of the elders, but eat with hands
defiled?" 6And he said to them, "Well
did Isaiah prophesy of you hypocrites,
as it is written,

'This people honors me with
their lips,
but their heart is far from me;
7in vain do they worship me,
teaching as doctrines the pre-
cepts of men.'

8You leave the commandment of
God, and hold fast the tradition of
men."

9 And he said to them, "You have
a fine way of rejecting the command-
ment of God, in order to keep your tra-
dition! 10For Moses said, 'Honor your
father and your mother'; and, 'He who
speaks evil of father or mother, let
him surely die'; 11but you say, 'If a man
tells his father or his mother, What
you would have gained from me is
Corban' (that is, given to God)[g] 12then
you no longer permit him to do any-
thing for his father or mother, 13thus
making void the word of God through
your tradition which you hand on.
And many such things you do."

14 And he called the people to him
again, and said to them, "Hear me,
all of you, and understand: 15there is
nothing outside a man which by go-
ing into him can defile him; but the
things which come out of a man are
what defile him."[h] 17And when he had
entered the house, and left the peo-
ple, his disciples asked him about the
parable. 18And he said to them, "Then

[c] One Greek word is of uncertain meaning and is not translated
[d] Other ancient authorities read *baptize*
[e] Other ancient authorities add *and beds*
[f] Greek *walk*
[g] Or *an offering*
[h] Other ancient authorities add verse 16, *"If any man has ears to hear, let him hear"*

are you also without understanding? Do you not see that whatever goes into a man from outside cannot defile him, 19since it enters, not his heart but his stomach, and so passes on?"[a] (Thus he declared all foods clean.) 20And he said, "What comes out of a man is what defiles a man. 21For from within, out of the heart of man, come evil thoughts, fornication, theft, murder, adultery, 22coveting, wickedness, deceit, licentiousness, envy, slander, pride, foolishness. 23All these evil things come from within, and they defile a man."

THE SYROPHOENICIAN WOMAN'S FAITH

24 And from there he arose and went away to the region of Tyre and Sidon.[b] And he entered a house, and would not have any one know it; yet he could not be hid. 25But immediately a woman, whose little daughter was possessed by an unclean spirit, heard of him, and came and fell down at his feet. 26Now the woman was a Greek, a Syrophoeni´cian by birth. And she begged him to cast the demon out of her daughter. 27And he said to her, "Let the children first be fed, for it is not right to take the children's bread and throw it to the dogs." 28But she answered him, "Yes, Lord; yet even the dogs under the table eat the children's crumbs." 29And he said to her, "For this saying you may go your way; the demon has left your daughter." 30And she went home, and found the child lying in bed, and the demon gone.

JESUS CURES A DEAF MAN

31 Then he returned from the region of Tyre, and went through Sidon to the Sea of Galilee, through the region of the Decap´olis. 32And they brought to him a man who was deaf *and had an impediment* in his speech; and they besought him to lay his hand upon him. 33And taking him aside from the multitude privately, he put his fingers into his ears, and he spat and touched his tongue; 34and looking up to heaven, he sighed, and said to him, "Eph´phatha," that is, "Be opened." 35And his ears were opened, his tongue was released, and he spoke plainly. 36And he charged them to tell no one; but the more he charged them, the more zealously they proclaimed it. 37And they were astonished beyond measure, saying, "He has done all things well; he even makes the deaf hear and the dumb speak."

FEEDING THE FOUR THOUSAND

8 In those days, when again a great crowd had gathered, and they had nothing to eat, he called his disciples to him, and said to them, 2"I have compassion on the crowd, because they have been with me now three days, and have nothing to eat; 3and if I send them away hungry to their homes, they will faint on the way; and some of them have come a long way." 4And his disciples answered him, "How can one feed these men with bread here in the desert?" 5And he asked them, "How many loaves have you?" They said, "Seven." 6And he commanded the crowd to sit down on the ground; and he took the seven loaves, and having given thanks he broke them and gave them to his disciples to set before the people; and they set them before the crowd. 7And they had a few small fish; and having blessed them, he commanded that these also should be set before them. 8And they ate, and were satisfied; and they took up the broken pieces left over, seven baskets full. 9And there were about four thousand people. 10And he sent them away; and immediately he got into the boat with his disciples, and went to the district of Dalmanu´tha.[c]

THE DEMAND FOR A SIGN

11 The Pharisees came and began to argue with him, seeking from him

[a] Or *is evacuated*
[b] Other ancient authorities omit *and Sidon*
[c] Other ancient authorities read *Magadan* or *Magdala*

a sign from heaven, to test him. 12And
he sighed deeply in his spirit, and
said, "Why does this generation seek
a sign? Truly, I say to you, no sign
shall be given to this generation."
13And he left them, and getting into
the boat again he departed to the oth-
er side.

THE YEAST OF THE PHARISEES AND OF HEROD

14 Now they had forgotten to
bring bread; and they had only one
loaf with them in the boat. 15And he
cautioned them, saying, "Take heed,
beware of the leaven of the Pharisees
and the leaven of Herod."[d] 16And they
discussed it with one another, say-
ing, "We have no bread." 17And being
aware of it, Jesus said to them, "Why
do you discuss the fact that you have
no bread? Do you not yet perceive or
understand? Are your hearts hard-
ened? 18Having eyes do you not see,
and having ears do you not hear? And
do you not remember? 19When I broke
the five loaves for the five thousand,
how many baskets full of broken
pieces did you take up?" They said to
him, "Twelve." 20"And the seven for
the four thousand, how many bas-
kets full of broken pieces did you take
up?" And they said to him, "Seven."
21And he said to them, "Do you not yet
understand?"

JESUS CURES A BLIND MAN AT BETHSAIDA

22 And they came to Beth-sa´ida.
And some people brought to him a
blind man, and begged him to touch
him. 23And he took the blind man
by the hand, and led him out of the
village; and when he had spit on his
eyes and laid his hands upon him, he
asked him, "Do you see anything?"
24And he looked up and said, "I see
men; but they look like trees, walk-
ing." 25Then again he laid his hands
upon his eyes; and he looked intently
and was restored, and saw everything
clearly. 26And he sent him away to his
home, saying, "Do not even enter the
village."

PETER'S DECLARATION ABOUT JESUS

27 And Jesus went on with his
disciples, to the villages of Caesare´a
Philippi; and on the way he asked his
disciples, "Who do men say that I
am?" 28And they told him, "John the
Baptist; and others say, Eli´jah; and
others one of the prophets." 29And he
asked them, "But who do you say that
I am?" Peter answered him, "You are
the Christ." 30And he charged them to
tell no one about him.

JESUS FORETELLS HIS DEATH AND RESURRECTION

31 And he began to teach them
that the Son of man must suffer many
things, and be rejected by the elders
and the chief priests and the scribes,
and be killed, and after three days
rise again. 32And he said this plainly.
And Peter took him, and began to re-
buke him. 33But turning and seeing his
disciples, he rebuked Peter, and said,
"Get behind me, Satan! For you are
not on the side of God, but of men."

34 And he called to him the mul-
titude with his disciples, and said to
them, "If any man would come after
me, let him deny himself and take
up his cross and follow me. 35For
whoever would save his life will lose
it; and whoever loses his life for my
sake and the gospel's will save it.
36For what does it profit a man, to
gain the whole world and forfeit his
life?* 37For what can a man give in
return for his life? 38For whoever is
ashamed of me and of my words in
this adulterous and sinful generation,
of him will the Son of man also be
ashamed, when he comes in the glory
of his Father with the holy angels."

9 And he said to them, "Truly, I say to
you, there are some standing here
who will not taste death before they
see the kingdom of God come with
power."

[d]Other ancient authorities read *the Herodians*

THE TRANSFIGURATION

2 And after six days Jesus took
with him Peter and James and John,
and led them up a high mountain
apart by themselves; and he was
transfigured before them, 3and his
garments became glistening, in-
tensely white, as no fuller on earth
could bleach them. 4And there ap-
peared to them Eli´jah with Moses;
and they were talking to Jesus. 5And
Peter said to Jesus, "Master,[a] it is
well that we are here; let us make
three booths, one for you and one
for Moses and one for Eli´jah." 6For
he did not know what to say, for
they were exceedingly afraid. 7And
a cloud overshadowed them, and a
voice came out of the cloud, "This
is my beloved Son;[b] listen to him."
8And suddenly looking around they
no longer saw any one with them but
Jesus only.

THE COMING OF ELIJAH

9 And as they were coming down
the mountain, he charged them to
tell no one what they had seen, un-
til the Son of man should have ris-
en from the dead. 10So they kept
the matter to themselves, question-
ing what the rising from the dead
meant. 11And they asked him, "Why
do the scribes say that first Eli´jah
must come?" 12And he said to them,
"Eli´jah does come first to restore
all things; and how is it written of
the Son of man, that he should suf-
fer many things and be treated with
contempt? 13But I tell you that Eli´jah
has come,* and they did to him what-
ever they pleased, as it is written of
him."

THE HEALING OF A BOY WITH A SPIRIT

14 And when they came to the dis-
ciples, they saw a great crowd about
them, and scribes arguing with them.
15And immediately all the crowd,
when they saw him, were greatly
amazed, and ran up to him and greet-
ed him. 16And he asked them, "What
are you discussing with them?" 17And
one of the crowd answered him,
"Teacher, I brought my son to you, for
he has a dumb spirit; 18and wherever
it seizes him, it dashes him down; and
he foams and grinds his teeth and be-
comes rigid; and I asked your disci-
ples to cast it out, and they were not
able." 19And he answered them, "O
faithless generation, how long am I to
be with you? How long am I to bear
with you? Bring him to me." 20And
they brought the boy to him; and
when the spirit saw him, immediate-
ly it convulsed the boy, and he fell on
the ground and rolled about, foaming
at the mouth. 21And Jesus[c] asked his
father, "How long has he had this?"
And he said, "From childhood. 22And
it has often cast him into the fire and
into the water, to destroy him; but if
you can do anything, have pity on us
and help us." 23And Jesus said to him,
"If you can! All things are possible
to him who believes." 24Immediately
the father of the child cried out[d] and
said, "I believe; help my unbelief!"
25And when Jesus saw that a crowd
came running together, he rebuked
the unclean spirit, saying to it, "You
dumb and deaf spirit, I command
you, come out of him, and never en-
ter him again." 26And after crying out
and convulsing him terribly, it came
out, and the boy was like a corpse; so
that most of them said, "He is dead."
27But Jesus took him by the hand and
lifted him up, and he arose. 28And
when he had entered the house, his
disciples asked him privately, "Why
could we not cast it out?" 29And he
said to them, "This kind cannot be
driven out by anything but prayer and
fasting."[e]

[a] Or *Rabbi*
[b] Or *my Son, my* (or *the*) *Beloved*
[c] Greek *he*
[d] Other ancient authorities add *with tears*
[e] Other ancient authorities omit *and fasting*

JESUS AGAIN FORETELLS HIS DEATH AND RESURRECTION

30 They went on from there and
passed through Galilee. And he would
not have any one know it; 31for he was
teaching his disciples, saying to them,
"The Son of man will be delivered into
the hands of men, and they will kill
him; and when he is killed, after three
days he will rise." 32But they did not
understand the saying, and they were
afraid to ask him.

WHO IS THE GREATEST?

33 And they came to Caper′na-
um; and when he was in the house
he asked them, "What were you dis-
cussing on the way?" 34But they were
silent; for on the way they had dis-
cussed with one another who was the
greatest. 35And he sat down and called
the twelve; and he said to them, "If
any one would be first, he must be
last of all and servant of all." 36And he
took a child, and put him in the midst
of them; and taking him in his arms,
he said to them, 37"Whoever receives
one such child in my name receives
me; and whoever receives me, receives
not me but him who sent me."

ANOTHER EXORCIST

38 John said to him, "Teacher, we
saw a man casting out demons in your
name,[f] and we forbade him, because
he was not following us." 39But Jesus
said, "Do not forbid him; for no one
who does a mighty work in my name
will be able soon after to speak evil
of me. 40For he that is not against
us is for us. 41For truly, I say to you,
whoever gives you a cup of water to
drink because you bear the name
of Christ, will by no means lose his
reward.

TEMPTATIONS TO SIN

42 "Whoever causes one of these
little ones who believe in me to sin,[g]
it would be better for him if a great
millstone were hung round his neck
and he were thrown into the sea.
43And if your hand causes you to sin,[h]
cut it off; it is better for you to enter
life maimed than with two hands to
go to hell,[i] to the unquenchable fire.[j]
45And if your foot causes you to sin,[k]
cut it off; it is better for you to enter
life lame than with two feet to be
thrown into hell.[l,m] 47And if your eye
causes you to sin,[n] pluck it out; it is
better for you to enter the kingdom of
God with one eye than with two eyes
to be thrown into hell,[o] 48where their
worm does not die, and the fire is not
quenched. 49For every one will be salt-
ed with fire.[p] 50Salt is good; but if the
salt has lost its saltness, how will you
season it? Have salt in yourselves, and
be at peace with one another."

TEACHING ABOUT DIVORCE

10 And he left there and went to the
region of Judea and beyond the
Jordan, and crowds gathered to him
again; and again, as his custom was,
he taught them.

2 And Pharisees came up and in
order to test him asked, "Is it lawful
for a man to divorce his wife?" 3He
answered them, "What did Moses
command you?" 4They said, "Moses
allowed a man to write a certificate

[f]Other ancient authorities add *who does not follow us*
[g]Greek *stumble*
[h]Greek *stumble*
[i]Greek *Gehenna*
[j]Verses 44 and 46 (which are identical with verse 48) are omitted by the best ancient authorities
[k]Greek *stumble*
[l]Greek *Gehenna*
[m]Verses 44 and 46 (which are identical with verse 48) are omitted by the best ancient authorities
[n]Greek *stumble*
[o]Greek *Gehenna*
[p]Other ancient authorities add *and every sacrifice will be salted with salt*

of divorce, and to put her away." 5But
Jesus said to them, "For your hard-
ness of heart he wrote you this com-
mandment. 6But from the beginning
of creation, 'God made them male and
female.' 7'For this reason a man shall
leave his father and mother and be
joined to his wife,[a] 8and the two shall
become one.'[b] So they are no longer
two but one.[c] 9What therefore God
has joined together, let not man put
asunder."

10 And in the house the disciples
asked him again about this matter.
11And he said to them, "Whoever di-
vorces his wife and marries another,
commits adultery against her; 12and if
she divorces her husband and marries
another, she commits adultery."

JESUS BLESSES LITTLE CHILDREN

13 And they were bringing children
to him, that he might touch them;
and the disciples rebuked them. 14But
when Jesus saw it he was indignant,
and said to them, "Let the children
come to me, do not hinder them; for
to such belongs the kingdom of God.
15Truly, I say to you, whoever does
not receive the kingdom of God like a
child shall not enter it." 16And he took
them in his arms and blessed them,
laying his hands upon them.

THE RICH MAN

17 And as he was setting out on
his journey, a man ran up and knelt
before him, and asked him, "Good
Teacher, what must I do to inherit
eternal life?" 18And Jesus said to him,
"Why do you call me good? No one is
good but God alone. 19You know the
commandments: 'Do not kill, Do not
commit adultery, Do not steal, Do not
bear false witness, Do not defraud,
Honor your father and mother.'"
20And he said to him, "Teacher, all
these I have observed from my youth."
21And Jesus looking upon him loved
him, and said to him, "You lack one
thing; go, sell what you have, and give
to the poor, and you will have treasure
in heaven; and come, follow me." 22At
that saying his countenance fell, and
he went away sorrowful; for he had
great possessions.

23 And Jesus looked around and
said to his disciples, "How hard it will
be for those who have riches to enter
the kingdom of God!" 24And the disci-
ples were amazed at his words.* But
Jesus said to them again, "Children,
how hard it is for those who trust in
riches[d] to enter the kingdom of God!
25It is easier for a camel to go through
the eye of a needle than for a rich man
to enter the kingdom of God." 26And
they were exceedingly astonished,
and said to him,[e] "Then who can be
saved?" 27Jesus looked at them and
said, "With men it is impossible, but
not with God; for all things are possi-
ble with God." 28Peter began to say to
him, "Lo, we have left everything and
followed you." 29Jesus said, "Truly, I
say to you, there is no one who has left
house or brothers or sisters or moth-
er or father or children or lands, for
my sake and for the gospel, 30who will
not receive a hundredfold now in this
time, houses and brothers and sisters
and mothers and children and lands,
with persecutions, and in the age to
come eternal life.* 31But many that are
first will be last, and the last first."

A THIRD TIME JESUS FORETELLS HIS DEATH AND RESURRECTION

32 And they were on the road, go-
ing up to Jerusalem, and Jesus was
walking ahead of them; and they were
amazed, and those who followed were
afraid. And taking the twelve again,
he began to tell them what was to
happen to him, 33saying, "Behold, we
are going up to Jerusalem; and the Son

[a] Other ancient authorities omit *and be joined to his wife*
[b] Greek *one flesh*
[c] Greek *one flesh*
[d] Other ancient authorities omit *for those who trust in riches*
[e] Other ancient authorities read *to one another*

of man will be delivered to the chief
priests and the scribes, and they will
condemn him to death, and deliver
him to the Gentiles; 34and they will
mock him, and spit upon him, and
scourge him, and kill him; and after
three days he will rise."

THE REQUEST OF JAMES AND JOHN

35 And James and John, the sons
of Zeb´edee, came forward to him,
and said to him, "Teacher, we want
you to do for us whatever we ask of
you." 36And he said to them, "What
do you want me to do for you?" 37And
they said to him, "Grant us to sit,
one at your right hand and one at
your left, in your glory." 38But Jesus
said to them, "You do not know what
you are asking. Are you able to drink
the cup that I drink, or to be bap-
tized with the baptism with which
I am baptized?" 39And they said to
him, "We are able." And Jesus said
to them, "The cup that I drink you
will drink; and with the baptism with
which I am baptized, you will be bap-
tized; 40but to sit at my right hand or
at my left is not mine to grant, but it
is for those for whom it has been pre-
pared." 41And when the ten heard it,
they began to be indignant at James
and John. 42And Jesus called them
to him and said to them, "You know
that those who are supposed to rule
over the Gentiles lord it over them,
and their great men exercise author-
ity over them. 43But it shall not be so
among you; but whoever would be
great among you must be your ser-
vant, 44and whoever would be first
among you must be slave of all. 45For
the Son of man also came not to be
served but to serve, and to give his
life as a ransom for many."

THE HEALING OF BLIND BARTIMAEUS

46 And they came to Jericho;
and as he was leaving Jericho with
his disciples and a great multitude,
Bartimae´us, a blind beggar, the son of
Timae´us, was sitting by the roadside.
47And when he heard that it was Jesus
of Nazareth, he began to cry out and
say, "Jesus, Son of David, have mer-
cy on me!" 48And many rebuked him,
telling him to be silent; but he cried
out all the more, "Son of David, have
mercy on me!" 49And Jesus stopped
and said, "Call him." And they called
the blind man, saying to him, "Take
heart; rise, he is calling you." 50And
throwing off his mantle he sprang up
and came to Jesus. 51And Jesus said to
him, "What do you want me to do for
you?" And the blind man said to him,
"Master,[f] let me receive my sight."
52And Jesus said to him, "Go your way;
your faith has made you well." And
immediately he received his sight and
followed him on the way.

JESUS' TRIUMPHAL ENTRY INTO JERUSALEM

11 And when they drew near to
Jerusalem, to Beth´phage and
Bethany, at the Mount of Olives, he
sent two of his disciples, 2and said to
them, "Go into the village opposite
you, and immediately as you enter it
you will find a colt tied, on which no
one has ever sat; untie it and bring
it. 3If any one says to you, 'Why are
you doing this?' say, 'The Lord has
need of it and will send it back here
immediately.'" 4And they went away,
and found a colt tied at the door out
in the open street; and they untied it.
5And those who stood there said to
them, "What are you doing, untying
the colt?" 6And they told them what
Jesus had said; and they let them go.
7And they brought the colt to Jesus,
and threw their garments on it; and
he sat upon it. 8And many spread their
garments on the road, and others
spread leafy branches which they had
cut from the fields. 9And those who
went before and those who followed
cried out, "Hosanna! Blessed is he
who comes in the name of the Lord!
10Blessed is the kingdom of our father

[f] Or *Rabbi*

David that is coming! Hosanna in the
highest!"

11 And he entered Jerusalem, and
went into the temple; and when he
had looked round at everything, as
it was already late, he went out to
Bethany with the twelve.

JESUS CURSES THE FIG TREE

12 On the following day, when they
came from Bethany, he was hungry.
13And seeing in the distance a fig tree
in leaf, he went to see if he could find
anything on it. When he came to it,
he found nothing but leaves, for it was
not the season for figs. 14And he said
to it, "May no one ever eat fruit from
you again." And his disciples heard it.

JESUS CLEANSES THE TEMPLE

15 And they came to Jerusalem.
And he entered the temple and be-
gan to drive out those who sold and
those who bought in the temple, and
he overturned the tables of the mon-
ey-changers and the seats of those
who sold pigeons; 16and he would
not allow any one to carry anything
through the temple. 17And he taught,
and said to them, "Is it not written,
'My house shall be called a house of
prayer for all the nations'? But you
have made it a den of robbers." 18And
the chief priests and the scribes heard
it and sought a way to destroy him; for
they feared him, because all the mul-
titude was astonished at his teaching.
19And when evening came they[a] went
out of the city.

THE LESSON FROM THE WITHERED FIG TREE

20 As they passed by in the morn-
ing, they saw the fig tree withered
away to its roots. 21And Peter re-
membered and said to him, "Master,[b]
look! The fig tree which you cursed
has withered." 22And Jesus answered
them, "Have faith in God. 23Truly,
I say to you, whoever says to this
mountain, 'Be taken up and cast into
the sea,' and does not doubt in his
heart, but believes that what he says
will come to pass, it will be done for
him. 24Therefore I tell you, whatever
you ask in prayer, believe that you re-
ceive it, and you will. 25And whenever
you stand praying, forgive, if you have
anything against any one; so that your
Father also who is in heaven may for-
give you your trespasses."[c]

JESUS' AUTHORITY IS QUESTIONED

27 And they came again to
Jerusalem. And as he was walking in
the temple, the chief priests and the
scribes and the elders came to him,
28and they said to him, "By what au-
thority are you doing these things,
or who gave you this authority to
do them?" 29Jesus said to them, "I
will ask you a question; answer me,
and I will tell you by what authority
I do these things. 30Was the baptism
of John from heaven or from men?
Answer me." 31And they argued with
one another, "If we say, 'From heav-
en,' he will say, 'Why then did you not
believe him?' 32But shall we say, 'From
men'?"—they were afraid of the peo-
ple, for all held that John was a real
prophet. 33So they answered Jesus,
"We do not know." And Jesus said to
them, "Neither will I tell you by what
authority I do these things."

THE PARABLE OF THE WICKED TENANTS

12 And he began to speak to them in
parables. "A man planted a vine-
yard, and set a hedge around it, and
dug a pit for the wine press, and built
a tower, and let it out to tenants, and
went into another country. 2When the
time came, he sent a servant to the
tenants, to get from them some of
the fruit of the vineyard. 3And they
took him and beat him, and sent him
away empty-handed. 4Again he sent
to them another servant, and they

[a]Other ancient authorities read *he*
[b]Or *Rabbi*
[c]Other ancient authorities add verse 26, *"But if you do not forgive, neither will your Father who is in heaven forgive your trespasses"*

wounded him in the head, and treated
him shamefully. 5And he sent another,
and him they killed; and so with many
others, some they beat and some
they killed. 6He had still one other,
a beloved son; finally he sent him to
them, saying, 'They will respect my
son.' 7But those tenants said to one
another, 'This is the heir; come, let us
kill him, and the inheritance will be
ours.' 8And they took him and killed
him, and cast him out of the vineyard.
9What will the owner of the vineyard
do? He will come and destroy the ten-
ants, and give the vineyard to others.
10Have you not read this scripture:

'The very stone which the
builders rejected
has become the head of the
corner;
11this was the Lord's doing,
and it is marvelous in our
eyes'?"

12 And they tried to arrest him,
but feared the multitude, for they
perceived that he had told the para-
ble against them; so they left him and
went away.

THE QUESTION ABOUT PAYING TAXES

13 And they sent to him some of the
Pharisees and some of the Hero´di-
ans, to entrap him in his talk. 14And
they came and said to him, "Teacher,
we know that you are true, and care
for no man; for you do not regard the
position of men, but truly teach the
way of God. Is it lawful to pay taxes to
Caesar, or not? 15Should we pay them,
or should we not?" But knowing their
hypocrisy, he said t(them, "Why put
me to the test? Brin me a coin,[d] and
let me look at it." 16 nd they brought
one. And he said t them, "Whose
likeness and inscntion is this?"
They said to him, "aesar's." 17Jesus
said to them, "Rend to Caesar the
things that are Caes's, and to God
the things that are Gd's." And they
were amazed at him.

THE QUESTION ABOUT THE RESURRECTION

18 And Sad´ducees came to him,
who say that there is no resurrection;
and they asked him a question, say-
ing, 19"Teacher, Moses wrote for us
that if a man's brother dies and leaves
a wife, but leaves no child, the man[e]
must take the wife, and raise up chil-
dren for his brother. 20There were sev-
en brothers; the first took a wife, and
when he died left no children; 21and
the second took her, and died, leaving
no children; and the third likewise;
22and the seven left no children. Last
of all the woman also died. 23In the
resurrection whose wife will she be?
For the seven had her as wife."

24 Jesus said to them, "Is not this
why you are wrong, that you know
neither the scriptures nor the pow-
er of God? 25For when they rise from
the dead, they neither marry nor are
given in marriage, but are like angels
in heaven. 26And as for the dead be-
ing raised, have you not read in the
book of Moses, in the passage about
the bush, how God said to him, 'I am
the God of Abraham, and the God of
Isaac, and the God of Jacob'? 27He is
not God of the dead, but of the living;
you are quite wrong."

THE FIRST COMMANDMENT

28 And one of the scribes came up
and heard them disputing with one
another, and seeing that he answered
them well, asked him, "Which com-
mandment is the first of all?" 29Jesus
answered, "The first is, 'Hear, O
Israel: The Lord our God, the Lord is
one; 30and you shall love the Lord your
God with all your heart, and with all
your soul, and with all your mind, and
with all your strength.' 31The second
is this, 'You shall love your neighbor
as yourself.' There is no other com-
mandment greater than these." 32And
the scribe said to him, "You are right,
Teacher; you have truly said that he
is one, and there is no other but he;

[d]Greek *a denarius*
[e]Greek *his brother*

33and to love him with all the heart,
and with all the understanding, and
with all the strength, and to love one's
neighbor as oneself, is much more
than all whole burnt offerings and
sacrifices." 34And when Jesus saw that
he answered wisely, he said to him,
"You are not far from the kingdom of
God." And after that no one dared to
ask him any question.

THE QUESTION ABOUT DAVID'S SON

35 And as Jesus taught in the tem-
ple, he said, "How can the scribes say
that the Christ is the son of David?
36David himself, inspired by[a] the Holy
Spirit, declared,

> 'The Lord said to my Lord,
> Sit at my right hand,
> till I put thy enemies under thy
> feet.'

37David himself calls him Lord;
so how is he his son?" And the great
throng heard him gladly.

JESUS DENOUNCES THE SCRIBES

38 And in his teaching he said,
"Beware of the scribes, who like to go
about in long robes, and to have salu-
tations in the market places 39and the
best seats in the synagogues and the
places of honor at feasts, 40who devour
widows' houses and for a pretense
make long prayers. They will receive
the greater condemnation."

THE WIDOW'S OFFERING

41 And he sat down opposite the
treasury, and watched the multitude
putting money into the treasury.
Many rich people put in large sums.
42And a poor widow came, and put in
two copper coins, which make a pen-
ny. 43And he called his disciples to
him, and said to them, "Truly, I say to
you, this poor widow has put in more
than all those who are contributing to
the treasury. 44For they all contributed
out of their abundance; but she out of
her poverty has put in everything she
had, her whole living."

THE DESTRUCTION OF THE TEMPLE FORETOLD

13And as he came out of the tem-
ple, one of his disciples said to
him, "Look, Teacher, what wonderful
stones and what wonderful build-
ings!" 2And Jesus said to him, "Do you
see these great buildings? There will
not be left here one stone upon anoth-
er, that will not be thrown down."

3 And as he sat on the Mount of
Olives opposite the temple, Peter and
James and John and Andrew asked
him privately, 4"Tell us, when will
this be, and what will be the sign
when these things are all to be accom-
plished?" 5And Jesus began to say to
them, "Take heed that no one leads
you astray. 6Many will come in my
name, saying, 'I am he!' and they will
lead many astray. 7And when you hear
of wars and rumors of wars, do not
be alarmed; this must take place, but
the end is not yet. 8For nation will rise
against nation, and kingdom against
kingdom; there will be earthquakes
in various places, there will be fam-
ines; this is but the beginning of the
sufferings.

PERSECUTION FORETOLD

9 "But take heed to yourselves;
for they will deliver you up to coun-
cils; and you will be beaten in syn-
agogues; and you will stand before
governors and kings for my sake, to
bear testimony before them. 10And
the gospel must first be preached to
all nations. 11And when they bring
you to trial and deliver you up, do
not be anxious beforehand what you
are to say; but say whatever is giv-
en you in that hour, for it is not you
who speak, but the Holy Spirit. 12And
brother will deliver up brother to
death, and the father his child, and
children will rise against parents and
have them put to death; 13and you
will be hated by all for my name's
sake. But he who endures to the end
will be saved.

[a]Or *himself, in*

THE DESOLATING SACRILEGE

14 "But when you see the desolat-
ing sacrilege set up where it ought
not to be (let the reader understand),
then let those who are in Judea flee
to the mountains; 15let him who is on
the housetop not go down, nor enter
his house, to take anything away;
16and let him who is in the field not
turn back to take his mantle. 17And
alas for those who are with child and
for those who give suck in those days!
18Pray that it may not happen in win-
ter. 19For in those days there will be
such tribulation as has not been from
the beginning of the creation which
God created until now, and nev-
er will be. 20And if the Lord had not
shortened the days, no human being
would be saved; but for the sake of the
elect, whom he chose, he shortened
the days. 21And then if any one says
to you, 'Look, here is the Christ!' or
'Look, there he is!' do not believe it.
22False Christs and false prophets will
arise and show signs and wonders, to
lead astray, if possible, the elect. 23But
take heed; I have told you all things
beforehand.

THE COMING OF THE SON OF MAN

24 "But in those days, after that
tribulation, the sun will be darkened,
and the moon will not give its light,
25and the stars will be falling from
heaven, and the powers in the heavens
will be shaken. 26And then they will
see the Son of man coming in clouds
with great power and glory. 27And
then he will send out the angels, and
gather his elect from the four winds,
from the ends of the earth to the ends
of heaven.

THE LESSON OF THE FIG TREE

28 "From the fig tree learn its les-
son: as soon as its branch becomes
tender and puts forth its leaves, you
know that summer is near. 29So also,
when you see these things taking
place, you know that he is near, at the
very gates. 30Truly, I say to you, this
generation will not pass away before
all these things take place. 31Heaven
and earth will pass away, but my
words will not pass away.

THE NECESSITY FOR WATCHFULNESS

32 "But of that day or that hour
no one knows, not even the angels
in heaven, nor the Son, but only the
Father. 33Take heed, watch and pray;[b]
for you do not know when the time
will come. 34It is like a man going on
a journey, when he leaves home and
puts his servants in charge, each with
his work, and commands the door-
keeper to be on the watch. 35Watch
therefore—for you do not know when
the master of the house will come,
in the evening, or at midnight, or at
cockcrow, or in the morning 36lest he
come suddenly and find you asleep.
37And what I say to you I say to all:
Watch."

THE PLOT TO KILL JESUS

14 It was now two days before
the Passover and the feast of
Unleavened Bread. And the chief
priests and the scribes were seeking
how to arrest him by stealth, and kill
him; 2for they said, "Not during the
feast, lest there be a tumult of the
people."

THE ANOINTING AT BETHANY

3 And while he was at Bethany in
the house of Simon the leper, as he
sat at table, a woman came with an
alabaster jar of ointment of pure nard,
very costly, and she broke the jar and
poured it over his head. 4But there
were some who said to themselves
indignantly, "Why was the ointment
thus wasted? 5For this ointment might
have been sold for more than three
hundred denarii,[c] and given to the
poor." And they reproached her. 6But
Jesus said, "Let her alone; why do you

[b]Other ancient authorities omit *and pray*
[c]The denarius was a day's wage for a laborer

trouble her? She has done a beautiful
thing to me. 7For you always have the
poor with you, and whenever you will,
you can do good to them; but you will
not always have me. 8She has done
what she could; she has anointed my
body beforehand for burying. 9And
truly, I say to you, wherever the gospel
is preached in the whole world, what
she has done will be told in memory
of her."

JUDAS AGREES TO BETRAY JESUS

10 Then Judas Iscariot, who was
one of the twelve, went to the chief
priests in order to betray him to them.
11And when they heard it they were
glad, and promised to give him mon-
ey. And he sought an opportunity to
betray him.

THE PASSOVER WITH THE DISCIPLES

12 And on the first day of Unleav-
ened Bread, when they sacrificed the
passover lamb, his disciples said to
him, "Where will you have us go and
prepare for you to eat the passover?"
13And he sent two of his disciples,
and said to them, "Go into the city,
and a man carrying a jar of water will
meet you; follow him,* 14and wherev-
er he enters, say to the householder,
'The Teacher says, Where is my guest
room, where I am to eat the passover
with my disciples?' 15And he will show
you a large upper room furnished and
ready; there prepare for us." 16And the
disciples set out and went to the city,
and found it as he had told them; and
they prepared the passover.

17 And when it was evening he
came with the twelve. 18And as they
were at table eating, Jesus said, "Truly,
I say to you, one of you will betray me,
one who is eating with me." 19They be-
gan to be sorrowful, and to say to him
one after another, "Is it I?" 20He said
to them, "It is one of the twelve, one
who is dipping bread in the same dish
with me. 21For the Son of man goes as
it is written of him, but woe to that
man by whom the Son of man is be-
trayed! It would have been better for
that man if he had not been born."

THE INSTITUTION OF THE LORD'S SUPPER

22 And as they were eating, he took
bread, and blessed, and broke it, and
gave it to them, and said, "Take; this
is my body." 23And he took a cup, and
when he had given thanks he gave it
to them, and they all drank of it. 24And
he said to them, "This is my blood of
the[a] covenant, which is poured out for
many. 25Truly, I say to you, I shall not
drink again of the fruit of the vine un-
til that day when I drink it new in the
kingdom of God."

PETER'S DENIAL FORETOLD

26 And when they had sung a
hymn, they went out to the Mount
of Olives. 27And Jesus said to them,
"You will all fall away; for it is writ-
ten, 'I will strike the shepherd, and
the sheep will be scattered.' 28But
after I am raised up, I will go before
you to Galilee." 29Peter said to him,
"Even though they all fall away, I will
not." 30And Jesus said to him, "Truly,
I say to you, this very night, before
the cock crows twice, you will deny
me three times." 31But he said vehe-
mently, "If I must die with you, I will
not deny you." And they all said the
same.

JESUS PRAYS IN GETHSEMANE

32 And they went to a place which
was called Gethsem´ane; and he said
to his disciples, "Sit here, while I
pray." 33And he took with him Peter
and James and John, and began to be
greatly distressed and troubled. 34And
he said to them, "My soul is very sor-
rowful, even to death; remain here,
and watch."[b] 35And going a little far-
ther, he fell on the ground and prayed
that, if it were possible, the hour
might pass from him. 36And he said,

[a]Other ancient authorities insert *new*
[b]Or *keep awake*

"Abba, Father, all things are possible
to thee; remove this cup from me; yet
not what I will, but what thou wilt."
37And he came and found them sleep-
ing, and he said to Peter, "Simon, are
you asleep? Could you not watch[c] one
hour? 38Watch[d] and pray that you may
not enter into temptation; the spir-
it indeed is willing, but the flesh is
weak." 39And again he went away and
prayed, saying the same words. 40And
again he came and found them sleep-
ing, for their eyes were very heavy;
and they did not know what to answer
him. 41And he came the third time,
and said to them, "Are you still sleep-
ing and taking your rest? It is enough;
the hour has come; the Son of man is
betrayed into the hands of sinners.
42Rise, let us be going; see, my betray-
er is at hand."

THE BETRAYAL AND ARREST OF JESUS

43 And immediately, while he
was still speaking, Judas came, one
of the twelve, and with him a crowd
with swords and clubs, from the chief
priests and the scribes and the elders.
44Now the betrayer had given them a
sign, saying, "The one I shall kiss is
the man; seize him and lead him away
safely." 45And when he came, he went
up to him at once, and said, "Master!"[e]
And he kissed him. 46And they laid
hands on him and seized him. 47But
one of those who stood by drew his
sword, and struck the slave of the high
priest and cut off his ear. 48And Jesus
said to them, "Have you come out as
against a robber, with swords and
clubs to capture me? 49Day after day I
was with you in the temple teaching,
and you did not seize me. But let the
scriptures be fulfilled." 50And they all
forsook him, and fled.

51 And a young man followed him,
with nothing but a linen cloth about
his body; and they seized him, 52but
he left the linen cloth and ran away
naked.*

[c] Or *keep awake*
[d] Or *keep awake*
[e] Or *Rabbi*

JESUS BEFORE THE COUNCIL

53 And they led Jesus to the high
priest; and all the chief priests and
the elders and the scribes were assem-
bled. 54And Peter had followed him at
a distance, right into the courtyard
of the high priest; and he was sitting
with the guards, and warming himself
at the fire. 55Now the chief priests and
the whole council sought testimony
against Jesus to put him to death; but
they found none. 56For many bore false
witness against him, and their wit-
ness did not agree. 57And some stood
up and bore false witness against him,
saying, 58"We heard him say, 'I will
destroy this temple that is made with
hands, and in three days I will build
another, not made with hands.'" 59Yet
not even so did their testimony agree.
60And the high priest stood up in the
midst, and asked Jesus, "Have you no
answer to make? What is it that these
men testify against you?" 61But he was
silent and made no answer. Again
the high priest asked him, "Are you
the Christ, the Son of the Blessed?"
62And Jesus said, "I am; and you will
see the Son of man sitting at the right
hand of Power, and coming with the
clouds of heaven." 63And the high
priest tore his mantle, and said, "Why
do we still need witnesses? 64You have
heard his blasphemy. What is your
decision?" And they all condemned
him as deserving death. 65And some
began to spit on him, and to cover his
face, and to strike him, saying to him,
"Prophesy!" And the guards received
him with blows.

PETER DENIES JESUS

66 And as Peter was below in the
courtyard, one of the maids of the
high priest came; 67and seeing Peter
warming himself, she looked at him,
and said, "You also were with the
Nazarene, Jesus." 68But he denied it,
saying, "I neither know nor under-
stand what you mean." And he went

out into the gateway.[a] 69And the maid
saw him, and began again to say to
the bystanders, "This man is one of
them." 70But again he denied it. And
after a little while again the bystand-
ers said to Peter, "Certainly you are
one of them; for you are a Galilean."
71But he began to invoke a curse on
himself and to swear, "I do not know
this man of whom you speak." 72And
immediately the cock crowed a sec-
ond time. And Peter remembered how
Jesus had said to him, "Before the
cock crows twice, you will deny me
three times." And he broke down and
wept.

JESUS BEFORE PILATE

15 And as soon as it was morning the
chief priests, with the elders and
scribes, and the whole council held
a consultation; and they bound Jesus
and led him away and delivered him
to Pilate.* 2And Pilate asked him, "Are
you the King of the Jews?" And he an-
swered him, "You have said so." 3And
the chief priests accused him of many
things. 4And Pilate again asked him,
"Have you no answer to make? See
how many charges they bring against
you." 5But Jesus made no further an-
swer, so that Pilate wondered.

PILATE HANDS JESUS OVER TO BE CRUCIFIED

6 Now at the feast he used to re-
lease for them one prisoner whom
they asked. 7And among the rebels in
prison, who had committed murder
in the insurrection, there was a man
called Barab´bas. 8And the crowd
came up and began to ask Pilate to do
as he was wont to do for them. 9And he
answered them, "Do you want me to
release for you the King of the Jews?"
10For he perceived that it was out of
envy that the chief priests had deliv-
ered him up. 11But the chief priests
stirred up the crowd to have him
release for them Barab´bas instead.
12And Pilate again said to them, "Then
what shall I do with the man whom
you call the King of the Jews?" 13And
they cried out again, "Crucify him."
14And Pilate said to them, "Why, what
evil has he done?" But they shout-
ed all the more, "Crucify him." 15So
Pilate, wishing to satisfy the crowd,
released for them Barab´bas; and hav-
ing scourged Jesus, he delivered him
to be crucified.

THE SOLDIERS MOCK JESUS

16 And the soldiers led him away
inside the palace (that is, the praeto-
rium); and they called together the
whole battalion. 17And they clothed
him in a purple cloak, and plaiting a
crown of thorns they put it on him.
18And they began to salute him, "Hail,
King of the Jews!" 19And they struck
his head with a reed, and spat upon
him, and they knelt down in homage
to him. 20And when they had mocked
him, they stripped him of the purple
cloak, and put his own clothes on
him. And they led him out to crucify
him.

THE CRUCIFIXION OF JESUS

21 And they compelled a passer-by,
Simon of Cyre´ne, who was coming
in from the country, the father of
Alexander and Rufus, to carry his
cross. 22And they brought him to the
place called Gol´gotha (which means
the place of a skull). 23And they of-
fered him wine mingled with myrrh;
but he did not take it. 24And they cru-
cified him, and divided his garments
among them, castng lots for them, to
decide what each hould take. 25And it
was the third hor, when they cruci-
fied him. 26And e inscription of the
charge against m read, "The King
of the Jews." 27Ad with him they cru-
cified two robbrs, one on his right
and one on his ft.[b] 29And those who
passed by derid him, wagging their

[a] Or *fore-court*. Other ancient authorities add *and the cock crowed*
[b] Other ancient authorities insert verse 28, *And the scripture was filled which says, "He was reckoned with the transgressors"*

heads, and saying, "Aha! You who
would destroy the temple and build
it in three days, 30 save yourself, and
come down from the cross!" 31 So also
the chief priests mocked him to one
another with the scribes, saying, "He
saved others; he cannot save himself.
32 Let the Christ, the King of Israel,
come down now from the cross, that
we may see and believe." Those who
were crucified with him also reviled
him.

THE DEATH OF JESUS

33 And when the sixth hour had
come, there was darkness over the
whole land[c] until the ninth hour.
34 And at the ninth hour Jesus cried
with a loud voice, "E´lo-i, E´lo-i, la´-
ma sabach-tha´ni?" which means, "My
God, my God, why hast thou forsaken
me?" 35 And some of the bystanders
hearing it said, "Behold, he is calling
Eli´jah." 36 And one ran and, filling a
sponge full of vinegar, put it on a reed
and gave it to him to drink, saying,
"Wait, let us see whether Eli´jah will
come to take him down." 37 And Jesus
uttered a loud cry, and breathed his
last. 38 And the curtain of the temple
was torn in two, from top to bottom.
39 And when the centurion, who stood
facing him, saw that he thus[d] breathed
his last, he said, "Truly this man was
the Son[e] of God!"

40 There were also women look-
ing on from afar, among whom were
Mary Mag´dalene, and Mary the
mother of James the younger* and
of Joses, and Salo´me, 41 who, when
he was in Galilee, followed him, and
ministered to him; and also many
other women who came up with him
to Jerusalem.

THE BURIAL OF JESUS

42 And when evening had come,
since it was the day of Preparation,
that is, the day before the sabbath,
43 Joseph of Arimathe´a, a respected
member of the council, who was also
himself looking for the kingdom of
God, took courage and went to Pilate,
and asked for the body of Jesus. 44 And
Pilate wondered if he were already
dead; and summoning the centurion,
he asked him whether he was already
dead.[f] 45 And when he learned from
the centurion that he was dead, he
granted the body to Joseph. 46 And he
bought a linen shroud, and taking
him down, wrapped him in the linen
shroud, and laid him in a tomb which
had been hewn out of the rock; and he
rolled a stone against the door of the
tomb. 47 Mary Mag´dalene and Mary
the mother of Joses saw where he was
laid.

THE RESURRECTION OF JESUS

16 And when the sabbath was past,
Mary Mag´dalene, and Mary
the mother of James, and Salo´me,
bought spices, so that they might go
and anoint him.* 2 And very early on
the first day of the week they went
to the tomb when the sun had risen.
3 And they were saying to one anoth-
er, "Who will roll away the stone
for us from the door of the tomb?"
4 And looking up, they saw that the
stone was rolled back; for it was very
large. 5 And entering the tomb, they
saw a young man sitting on the right
side, dressed in a white robe; and
they were amazed. 6 And he said to
them, "Do not be amazed; you seek
Jesus of Nazareth, who was cruci-
fied. He has risen, he is not here; see
the place where they laid him. 7 But
go, *tell his disciples and* Peter that
he is going before you to Galilee;
there you will see him, as he told
you." 8 And they went out and fled
from the tomb; for trembling and
astonishment had come upon them;
and they said nothing to any one, for
they were afraid.

[c] Or *earth*
[d] Other ancient authorities insert *cried out and*
[e] Or *a son*
[f] Other ancient authorities read *whether he had been some time dead*

JESUS APPEARS TO MARY MAGDALENE

9 Now when he rose early on the
first day of the week, he appeared
first to Mary Mag´dalene, from whom
he had cast out seven demons. 10She
went out and told those who had been
with him, as they mourned and wept.
11But when they heard that he was
alive and had been seen by her, they
would not believe it.

JESUS APPEARS TO TWO DISCIPLES

12 After this he appeared in anoth-
er form to two of them, as they were
walking into the country. 13And they
went back and told the rest, but they
did not believe them.

JESUS COMMISSIONS THE DISCIPLES

14 Afterward he appeared to the
eleven themselves as they sat at table;
and he upbraided them for their un-
belief and hardness of heart, because
they had not believed those who saw
him after he had risen. 15And he said
to them, "Go into all the world and
preach the gospel to the whole cre-
ation. 16He who believes and is bap-
tized will be saved; but he who does
not believe will be condemned. 17And
these signs will accompany those who
believe: in my name they will cast
out demons; they will speak in new
tongues; 18they will pick up serpents,
and if they drink any deadly thing,
it will not hurt them; they will lay
their hands on the sick, and they will
recover."

THE ASCENSION OF JESUS

19 So then the Lord Jesus, after
he had spoken to them, was taken
up into heaven, and sat down at the
right hand of God. 20And they went
forth and preached everywhere, while
the Lord worked with them and con-
firmed the message by the signs that
attended it. Amen.[a]*

[a]Other ancient authorities omit verses 9-20. Some ancient authorities conclude Mark instead with the following: *But they reported briefly to Peter and those with him all that they had been told. And after this, Jesus himself sent out by means of them, from east to west, the sacred and imperishable proclamation of eternal salvation.*

THE GOSPEL ACCORDING TO

LUKE

DEDICATION TO THEOPHILUS

1 Inasmuch as many have under-
taken to compile a narrative of
the things which have been accom-
plished among us, 2just as they were
delivered to us by those who from
the beginning were eyewitnesses
and ministers of the word, 3it seemed
good to me also, having followed all
things closely[a] for some time past,
to write an orderly account for you,
most excellent Theoph´ilus,* 4that
you may know the truth concerning
the things of which you have been
informed.

THE BIRTH OF JOHN THE BAPTIST FORETOLD

5*In the days of Herod, king of
Judea, there was a priest named Zech-
ari´ah,[b] of the division of Abi´jah;
and he had a wife of the daughters of
Aaron, and her name was Elizabeth.
6And they were both righteous before
God, walking in all the command-
ments and ordinances of the Lord
blameless. 7But they had no child, be-
cause Elizabeth was barren, and both
were advanced in years.

8 Now while he was serving as
priest before God when his division
was on duty, 9according to the cus-
tom of the priesthood, it fell to him
by lot to enter the temple of the Lord
and burn incense. 10A d the whole
multitude of the people vere praying
outside at the hour of i ense. 11And
there appeared to him an ngel of the
Lord standing on the righ side of the
altar of incense. 12And echari´ah
was troubled when he sa him, and
fear fell upon him. 13Bu the an-
gel said to him, "Do not afraid,
Zechari´ah, for your praye s heard,
and your wife Elizabeth wil ear you
a son, and you shall call name
John.

14And you will have joy and
gladness,
and many will rejoice at his
birth;
15for he will be great before the
Lord,
and he shall drink no wine nor
strong drink,
and he will be filled with the
Holy Spirit,
even from his mother's womb.
16And he will turn many of the
sons of Israel to the Lord
their God,
17and he will go before him in the
spirit and power of Eli´jah,
to turn the hearts of the fa-
thers to the children,
and the disobedient to the
wisdom of the just,
to make ready for the Lord a
people prepared."

18And Zechari´ah said to the an-
gel, "How shall I know this? For I am
an old man, and my wife is advanced
in years." 19And the angel answered
him, "I am Gabriel, who stand in the
presence of God; and I was sent to
speak to you, and to bring you this
good news. 20And behold, you will
be silent and unable to speak until
the day that these things come to
pass, because you did not believe my
words, which will be fulfilled in their
time." 21And the people were waiting
for Zechari´ah, and they wondered at
his delay in the temple. 22And when he
came out, he could not speak to them,
and they perceived that he had seen
a vision in the temple; and he made
signs to them and remained dumb.
23And when his time of service was
ended, he went to his home.

24 After these days his wife
Elizabeth conceived, and for five
months she hid herself, saying,

[a] Or *accurately*
[b] Greek *Zacharias*

25"Thus the Lord has done to me in the
days when he looked on me, to take
away my reproach among men."

THE BIRTH OF JESUS FORETOLD

26 In the sixth month the angel
Gabriel was sent from God to a city
of Galilee named Nazareth, 27to a vir-
gin betrothed to a man whose name
was Joseph, of the house of David; and
the virgin's name was Mary. 28And he
came to her and said, "Hail, full of
grace,[a] the Lord is with you!"[b] 29But
she was greatly troubled at the saying,
and considered in her mind what sort
of greeting this might be. 30And the
angel said to her,* "Do not be afraid,
Mary, for you have found favor with
God. 31And behold, you will conceive
in your womb and bear a son, and you
shall call his name Jesus.

32He will be great, and will be
called the Son of the Most
High;
and the Lord God will give to
him the throne of his
father David,
33and he will reign over the house
of Jacob for ever;
and of his kingdom there will
be no end."

34And Mary said to the angel,
"How can this be, since I have no hus-
band?" 35And the angel said to her,

"The Holy Spirit will come
upon you,
and the power of the Most
High will overshadow
you;
therefore the child to be born[c]
will be called holy,
the Son of God.

36And behold, your kinswom-
an Elizabeth in her old age has also
conceived a son; and this is the sixth
month with her who was called bar-
ren. 37For with God nothing will be im-
possible." 38And Mary said, "Behold, I
am the handmaid of the Lord; let it be
to me according to your word." And
the angel departed from her.

MARY VISITS ELIZABETH

39 In those days Mary arose and
went with haste into the hill country,
to a city of Judah, 40and she entered
the house of Zechari´ah and greet-
ed Elizabeth. 41And when Elizabeth
heard the greeting of Mary, the babe
leaped in her womb; and Elizabeth
was filled with the Holy Spirit
42and she exclaimed with a loud cry,
"Blessed are you among women, and
blessed is the fruit of your womb!
43And why is this granted me, that
the mother of my Lord should come
to me? 44For behold, when the voice
of your greeting came to my ears, the
babe in my womb leaped for joy. 45And
blessed is she who believed that there
would be[d] a fulfilment of what was
spoken to her from the Lord." 46And
Mary said,

MARY'S SONG OF PRAISE

"My soul magnifies the Lord,
47and my spirit rejoices in God my
Savior,
48for he has regarded the low es-
tate of his handmaiden.
For behold, henceforth all
generations will call me
blessed;
49for he who is mighty has done
great things for me,
and holy is his name.
50And his mercy is on those who
fear him
from generation to generation.
51He has shown strength with his
arm,
he has scattered the proud in
the imagination of their
hearts,
52he has put down the mighty
from their thrones,
and exalted those of low
degree;

[a] Or *O favored one*
[b] Other ancient authorities add *"Blessed are you among women!"*
[c] Other ancient authorities add *of you*
[d] Or *believed, for there will be*

53 he has filled the hungry with
good things,
and the rich he has sent empty
away.
54 He has helped his servant Israel,
in remembrance of his mercy,
55 as he spoke to our fathers,
to Abraham and to his posteri-
ty for ever."*
56 And Mary remained with her about
three months, and returned to her
home.

THE BIRTH OF JOHN THE BAPTIST

57 Now the time came for Eliz-
abeth to be delivered, and she gave
birth to a son. 58 And her neighbors
and kinsfolk heard that the Lord
had shown great mercy to her, and
they rejoiced with her. 59 And on the
eighth day they came to circumcise
the child; and they would have named
him Zechari´ah after his father, 60 but
his mother said, "Not so; he shall be
called John." 61 And they said to her,
"None of your kindred is called by
this name." 62 And they made signs to
his father, inquiring what he would
have him called. 63 And he asked for a
writing tablet, and wrote, "His name
is John." And they all marveled. 64 And
immediately his mouth was opened
and his tongue loosed, and he spoke,
blessing God. 65 And fear came on all
their neighbors. And all these things
were talked about through all the hill
country of Judea; 66 and all who heard
them laid them up in their hearts,
saying, "What then will this child
be?" For the hand of the Lord was
with him.

ZECHARIAH'S PROPHECY

67 And his father Zechari´ah was
filled with the Holy Spirit, and proph-
esied, saying,
68 "Blessed be the Lord God of
Israel,
for he has visited and redeemed
his people,
69 and has raised up a horn of
salvation* for us
in the house of his servant
David,
70 as he spoke by the mouth of his
holy prophets from of old,
71 that we should be saved from
our enemies,
and from the hand of all who
hate us;
72 to perform the mercy promised
to our fathers,
and to remember his holy
covenant,
73 the oath which he swore to our
father Abraham,
74 to grant us
that we, being delivered
from the hand of our
enemies,
might serve him without fear,
75 in holiness and righteousness
before him all the days of
our life.
76 And you, child, will be called the
prophet of the Most High;
for you will go before the Lord
to prepare his ways,
77 to give knowledge of salvation to
his people
in the forgiveness of their sins,
78 through the tender mercy of our
God,
when the day shall dawn upon[e]
us from on high
79 to give light to those who sit in
darkness and in the shad-
ow of death,
to guide our feet into the way
of peace."
80 And the child grew and became
strong in spirit, and he was in the wil-
derness till the day of his manifesta-
tion to Israel.

THE BIRTH OF JESUS

2 In those days a decree went out
from Caesar Augustus that all the
world should be enrolled. 2 This was
the first enrollment, when Quirin´i-us

[e] Or *whereby the dayspring will visit.* Other ancient authorities read *since the dayspring has visited*

was governor of Syria. 3And all went
to be enrolled, each to his own city.
4And Joseph also went up from
Galilee, from the city of Nazareth, to
Judea, to the city of David, which is
called Bethlehem, because he was of
the house and lineage of David, 5to
be enrolled with Mary, his betrothed,
who was with child. 6And while they
were there, the time came for her to
be delivered. 7And she gave birth to
her first-born* son and wrapped him
in swaddling cloths, and laid him in
a manger, because there was no place
for them in the inn.

THE SHEPHERDS AND THE ANGELS

8 And in that region there were
shepherds out in the field, keep-
ing watch over their flock by night.
9And an angel of the Lord appeared
to them, and the glory of the Lord
shone around them, and they were
filled with fear. 10And the angel said
to them, "Be not afraid; for behold,
I bring you good news of a great joy
which will come to all the people;
11for to you is born this day in the city
of David a Savior, who is Christ the
Lord. 12And this will be a sign for you:
you will find a babe wrapped in swad-
dling cloths and lying in a manger."
13And suddenly there was with the
angel a multitude of the heavenly host
praising God and saying,

14"Glory to God in the highest,
and on earth peace among
men with whom he is
pleased!"[a]

15 When the angels went away
from them into heaven, the shepherds
said to one another, "Let us go over to
Bethlehem and see this thing that has
happened, which the Lord has made
known to us." 16And they went with
haste, and found Mary and Joseph,
and the babe lying in a manger. 17And
when they saw it they made known
the saying which had been told them
concerning this child; 18and all who
heard it wondered at what the shep-
herds told them. 19But Mary kept all
these things, pondering them in her
heart. 20And the shepherds returned,
glorifying and praising God for all
they had heard and seen, as it had
been told them.

JESUS IS NAMED

21 And at the end of eight days,
when he was circumcised, he was
called Jesus, the name given by the
angel before he was conceived in the
womb.

JESUS IS PRESENTED IN THE TEMPLE

22 And when the time came for
their purification according to the
law of Moses, they brought him up
to Jerusalem to present him to the
Lord 23(as it is written in the law of
the Lord, "Every male that opens
the womb shall be called holy to the
Lord") 24and to offer a sacrifice ac-
cording to what is said in the law of
the Lord, "a pair of turtledoves, or
two young pigeons." 25Now there was
a man in Jerusalem, whose name was
Simeon, and this man was righteous
and devout, looking for the conso-
lation of Israel, and the Holy Spirit
was upon him. 26And it had been re-
vealed to him by the Holy Spirit that
he should not see death before he had
seen the Lord's Christ. 27And inspired
by the Spirit[b] he came into the tem-
ple; and when the parents brought in
the child Jesus, to do for him accord-
ing to the custom of the law, 28he took
him up in his arms and blessed God
and said,

29"Lord, now lettest thou thy ser-
vant depart in peace,
according to thy word;
30for mine eyes have seen thy
salvation
31which thou hast prepared in the
presence of all peoples,
32a light for revelation to the
Gentiles,

[a] Other ancient authorities read *peace, good will among men*
[b] Or *in the Spirit*

and for glory to thy people
Israel."

33 And his father and his mother
marveled at what was said about him;
34and Simeon blessed them and said to
Mary his mother,

"Behold, this child is set for
the fall* and rising of
many in Israel,
and for a sign that is spoken
against
35(and a sword will pierce through
your own soul also),
that thoughts out of many
hearts may be revealed."

36 And there was a prophetess,
Anna, the daughter of Phan′u-el, of
the tribe of Asher; she was of a great
age, having lived with her husband
seven years from her virginity, 37and
as a widow till she was eighty-four.
She did not depart from the temple,
worshiping with fasting and prayer
night and day. 38And coming up at
that very hour she gave thanks to
God, and spoke of him to all who
were looking for the redemption of
Jerusalem.

THE RETURN TO NAZARETH

39 And when they had performed
everything according to the law of
the Lord, they returned into Galilee,
to their own city, Nazareth. 40And the
child grew and became strong, filled
with wisdom; and the favor of God
was upon him.

THE BOY JESUS IN THE TEMPLE

41 Now his parents went to
Jerusalem every year at the feast of the
Passover. 42And when he was twelve
years old, they went up according
to custom; 43and when the feast was
ended, as they were returning, the
boy Jesus stayed behind in Jerusalem.
His parents did not know it, 44but
supposing him to be in the company
they went a day's journey, and they
sought him among their kinsfolk
and acquaintances; 45and when they
did not find him, they returned to
Jerusalem, seeking him. 46After three
days they found him in the temple,
sitting among the teachers, listening
to them and asking them questions;
47and all who heard him were amazed
at his understanding and his answers.
48And when they saw him they were
astonished; and his mother said to
him, "Son, why have you treated us
so? Behold, your father and I have
been looking for you anxiously." 49And
he said to them, "How is it that you
sought me? Did you not know that
I must be in my Father's house?"*
50And they did not understand the
saying which he spoke to them. 51And
he went down with them and came to
Nazareth, and was obedient to them;
and his mother kept all these things
in her heart.

52 And Jesus increased in wisdom
and in stature,[c] and in favor with God
and man.

THE PROCLAMATION OF JOHN THE BAPTIST

3 In the fifteenth year of the reign
of Tibe′ri-us Caesar, Pontius Pilate
being governor of Judea, and Herod
being tetrarch of Galilee, and his
brother Philip tetrarch of the region
of Iturae′a and Trachoni′tis, and
Lysa′ni-as tetrarch of Abile′ne, 2in
the high-priesthood of Annas and
Ca′iaphas,* the word of God came
to John the son of Zechari′ah in the
wilderness; 3and he went into all the
region about the Jordan, preaching
a baptism of repentance for the for-
giveness of sins. 4As it is written in
the book of the words of Isaiah the
prophet,

"The voice of one crying in the
wilderness:
Prepare the way of the Lord,
make his paths straight.
5Every valley shall be filled,
and every mountain and hill
shall be brought low,
and the crooked shall be made
straight,

[c] Or *years*

and the rough ways shall be
made smooth;
6and all flesh shall see the salva-
tion of God."
7 He said therefore to the multi-
tudes that came out to be baptized
by him, "You brood of vipers!* Who
warned you to flee from the wrath
to come? 8Bear fruits that befit re-
pentance, and do not begin to say
to yourselves, 'We have Abraham
as our father'; for I tell you, God is
able from these stones to raise up
children to Abraham. 9Even now the
axe is laid to the root of the trees; ev-
ery tree therefore that does not bear
good fruit is cut down and thrown
into the fire."
10 And the multitudes asked him,
"What then shall we do?" 11And he
answered them, "He who has two
coats, let him share with him who
has none; and he who has food, let
him do likewise." 12Tax collectors also
came to be baptized, and said to him,
"Teacher, what shall we do?" 13And he
said to them, "Collect no more than is
appointed you." 14Soldiers also asked
him, "And we, what shall we do?" And
he said to them, "Rob no one by vi-
olence or by false accusation, and be
content with your wages."
15 As the people were in expecta-
tion, and all men questioned in their
hearts concerning John, whether per-
haps he were the Christ, 16John an-
swered them all, "I baptize you with
water; but he who is mightier than I
is coming, the thong of whose san-
dals I am not worthy to untie; he will
baptize you with the Holy Spirit and
with fire. 17His winnowing fork is in
his hand, to clear his threshing floor,
and to gather the wheat into his gra-
nary, but the chaff he will burn with
unquenchable fire."
18 So, with many other exhorta-
tions, he preached good news to the
people. 19But Herod the tetrarch,
who had been reproved by him for
Hero´di-as, his brother's wife, and
for all the evil things that Herod had
done, 20added this to them all, that he
shut up John in prison.

THE BAPTISM OF JESUS

21 Now when all the people were
baptized, and when Jesus also had
been baptized and was praying, the
heaven was opened, 22and the Holy
Spirit descended upon him in bodily
form, as a dove, and a voice came from
heaven, "Thou art my beloved Son;[a]
with thee I am well pleased."[b]

THE ANCESTORS OF JESUS

23 Jesus, when he began his min-
istry, was about thirty years of age,
being the son (as was supposed) of
Joseph,* the son of Heli, 24the son of
Matthat, the son of Levi, the son
of Melchi, the son of Jan´na-i, the son
of Joseph, 25the son of Mattathi´as,
the son of Amos, the son of Nahum,
the son of Esli, the son of Nag´ga-i,
26the son of Ma´ath, the son of
Mattathi´as, the son of Sem´e-in, the
son of Josech, the son of Joda, 27the
son of Jo-an´an, the son of Rhesa,
the son of Zerub´babel, the son of
She-al´ti-el,[c] the son of Neri, 28the
son of Melchi, the son of Addi, the
son of Cosam, the son of Elma´dam,
the son of Er, 29the son of Joshua, the
son of Elie´zer, the son of Jorim,
the son of Matthat, the son of Levi,
30the son of Simeon, the son of
Judah, the son of Joseph, the son of
Jonam, the son of Eli´akim, 31the son
of Me´le-a, the son of Menna, the son
of Mat´tatha, the son of Nathan, the
son of David, 32the son of Jesse, the
son of Obed, the son of Bo´az, the son
of Sala, the son of Nahshon, 33the son
of Ammin´adab, the son of Admin,
the son of Arni, the son of Hezron,
the son of Perez, the son of Judah,
34the son of Jacob, the son of Isaac,
the son of Abraham, the son of Terah,
the son of Nahor, 35the son of Serug,

[a] Or *my Son, my* (or *the*) *Beloved*
[b] Other ancient authorities read *today I have begotten thee*
[c] Greek *Salathiel*

the son of Re´u, the son of Peleg, the
son of Eber, the son of Shelah, 36the
son of Ca-i´nan, the son of Arphax´ad,
the son of Shem, the son of Noah,
the son of Lamech, 37the son of
Methu´selah, the son of Enoch, the
son of Jared, the son of Maha´lale-el,
the son of Ca-i´nan, 38the son of Enos,
the son of Seth, the son of Adam, the
son of God.

THE TEMPTATION OF JESUS

4 And Jesus, full of the Holy Spirit, re-
turned from the Jordan, and was led
by the Spirit 2for forty days in the wil-
derness, tempted by the devil. And he
ate nothing in those days; and when
they were ended, he was hungry. 3The
devil said to him, "If you are the Son
of God, command this stone to be-
come bread." 4And Jesus answered
him, "It is written, 'Man shall not
live by bread alone.'" 5And the devil
took him up, and showed him all the
kingdoms of the world in a moment
of time, 6and said to him, "To you I
will give all this authority and their
glory; for it has been delivered to me,
and I give it to whom I will. 7If you,
then, will worship me, it shall all be
yours." 8And Jesus answered him, "It
is written,

'You shall worship the Lord
your God,
and him only shall you serve.'"

9And he took him to Jerusalem,
and set him on the pinnacle of the
temple, and said to him, "If you are
the Son of God, throw yourself down
from here; 10for it is written,

'He will give his angels charge
of you, to guard you,'

11and

'On their hands they will bear
you up,
lest you strike your foot against
a stone.'"

12And Jesus answered him, "It is
said, 'You shall not tempt the Lord
your God.'" 13And when the devil had
ended every temptation, he departed
from him until an opportune time.

THE BEGINNING OF THE GALILEAN MINISTRY

14 And Jesus returned in the power
of the Spirit into Galilee, and a report
concerning him went out through all
the surrounding country. 15And he
taught in their synagogues, being glo-
rified by all.

THE REJECTION OF JESUS AT NAZARETH

16 And he came to Nazareth, where
he had been brought up; and he went
to the synagogue, as his custom was,
on the sabbath day.* And he stood up
to read; 17and there was given to him
the book of the prophet Isaiah. He
opened the book and found the place
where it was written,

18"The Spirit of the Lord is upon
me,
because he has anointed me to
preach good news to the
poor.
He has sent me to proclaim
release to the captives
and recovering of sight to the
blind,
to set at liberty those who are
oppressed,
19to proclaim the acceptable year
of the Lord."

20And he closed the book, and gave
it back to the attendant, and sat down;
and the eyes of all in the synagogue
were fixed on him. 21And he began to
say to them, "Today this scripture has
been fulfilled in your hearing." 22And
all spoke well of him, and wondered
at the gracious words which proceed-
ed out of his mouth; and they said, "Is
not this Joseph's son?" 23And he said
to them, "Doubtless you will quote
to me this proverb, *'Physician,* heal
yourself; what we have heard you did
at Caper´na-um, do here also in your
own country.'" 24And he said, "Truly,
I say to you, no prophet is acceptable
in his own country. 25But in truth, I
tell you, there were many widows in
Israel in the days of Eli´jah, when the
heaven was shut up three years and
six months, when there came a great
famine over all the land; 26and Eli´jah

was sent to none of them but only to
Zar´ephath, in the land of Sidon, to a
woman who was a widow. 27And there
were many lepers in Israel in the time
of the prophet Eli´sha; and none of
them was cleansed, but only Na´aman
the Syrian." 28When they heard this,
all in the synagogue were filled with
wrath. 29And they rose up and put
him out of the city, and led him to the
brow of the hill on which their city
was built, that they might throw him
down headlong. 30But passing through
the midst of them he went away.

THE MAN WITH AN UNCLEAN SPIRIT

31 And he went down to Caper´na-
um, a city of Galilee. And he was
teaching them on the sabbath; 32and
they were astonished at his teaching,
for his word was with authority. 33And
in the synagogue there was a man who
had the spirit of an unclean demon;
and he cried out with a loud voice,
34"Ah![a] What have you to do with us,
Jesus of Nazareth? Have you come to
destroy us? I know who you are, the
Holy One of God." 35But Jesus rebuked
him, saying, "Be silent, and come out
of him!" And when the demon had
thrown him down in the midst, he
came out of him, having done him
no harm. 36And they were all amazed
and said to one another, "What is this
word? For with authority and power
he commands the unclean spirits, and
they come out." 37And reports of him
went out into every place in the sur-
rounding region.

HEALINGS AT SIMON'S HOUSE

38 And he arose and left the syn-
agogue, and entered Simon's house.
Now Simon's mother-in-law was ill
with a high fever, and they besought
him for her. 39And he stood over her
and rebuked the fever, and it left her;
and immediately she rose and served
them.

40 Now when the sun was setting,
all those who had any that were sick
with various diseases brought them to
him; and he laid his hands on every
one of them and healed them. 41And
demons also came out of many, cry-
ing, "You are the Son of God!" But he
rebuked them, and would not allow
them to speak, because they knew
that he was the Christ.

JESUS PREACHES IN THE SYNAGOGUES

42 And when it was day he depart-
ed and went into a lonely place. And
the people sought him and came to
him, and would have kept him from
leaving them; 43but he said to them,
"I must preach the good news of the
kingdom of God to the other cities
also; for I was sent for this purpose."
44And he was preaching in the syna-
gogues of Judea.[b]

JESUS CALLS THE FIRST DISCIPLES

5 While the people pressed upon him
to hear the word of God, he was
standing by the lake of Gennes´aret.
2And he saw two boats by the lake;
but the fishermen had gone out of
them and were washing their nets.
3Getting into one of the boats, which
was Simon's, he asked him to put out
a little from the land. And he sat down
and taught the people from the boat.
4And when he had ceased speaking, he
said to Simon, "Put out into the deep
and let down your nets for a catch."
5And Simon answered, "Master, we
toiled all night and took nothing! But
at your word I will let down the nets."
6And when they had done this, they
enclosed a great shoal of fish; and as
their nets were breaking, 7they beck-
oned to their partners in the other
boat to come and help them. And they
came and filled both the boats, so that
they began to sink. 8But when Simon
Peter saw it, he fell down at Jesus'
knees, saying, "Depart from me, for
I am a sinful man, O Lord." 9For he
was astonished, and all that were with

[a]Or *Let us alone*
[b]Other ancient authorities read *Galilee*

him, at the catch of fish which they
had taken; 10and so also were James
and John, sons of Zeb´edee, who were
partners with Simon. And Jesus said
to Simon, "Do not be afraid; hence-
forth you will be catching men." 11And
when they had brought their boats
to land, they left everything and fol-
lowed him.

JESUS CLEANSES A LEPER

12 While he was in one of the cit-
ies, there came a man full of leprosy;
and when he saw Jesus, he fell on
his face and besought him, "Lord, if
you will, you can make me clean."
13And he stretched out his hand,
and touched him, saying, "I will; be
clean." And immediately the leprosy
left him. 14And he charged him to tell
no one; but "go and show yourself to
the priest, and make an offering for
your cleansing, as Moses command-
ed, for a proof to the people."[c] 15But so
much the more the report went abroad
concerning him; and great multitudes
gathered to hear and to be healed of
their infirmities. 16But he withdrew to
the wilderness and prayed.

JESUS HEALS A PARALYTIC

17 On one of those days, as he was
teaching, there were Pharisees and
teachers of the law sitting by, who had
come from every village of Galilee and
Judea and from Jerusalem; and the
power of the Lord was with him to he-
al.[d] 18And behold, men were bringing
on a bed a man who was paralyzed,
and they sought to bring him in and
lay him before Jesus;[e] 19*but* finding no
way to bring him in, because of the
crowd, they went up on the roof and
let him down with his bed through the
tiles into the midst before Jesus. 20And
when he saw their faith he said, "Man,
your sins are forgiven you." 21And the
scribes and the Pharisees began to
question, saying, "Who is this that
speaks blasphemies? Who can for-
give sins but God only?" 22When Jesus
perceived their questionings, he an-
swered them, "Why do you question
in your hearts? 23Which is easier, to
say, 'Your sins are forgiven you,' or
to say, 'Rise and walk'? 24But that you
may know that the Son of man has
authority on earth to forgive sins"—
he said to the man who was para-
lyzed—"I say to you, rise, take up your
bed and go home." 25And immediately
he rose before them, and took up that
on which he lay, and went home, glo-
rifying God. 26And amazement seized
them all, and they glorified God and
were filled with awe, saying, "We
have seen strange things today."

JESUS CALLS LEVI

27 After this he went out, and saw
a tax collector, named Levi, sitting
at the tax office; and he said to him,
"Follow me." 28And he left everything,
and rose and followed him.

29 And Levi made him a great feast
in his house; and there was a large
company of tax collectors and others
sitting at table[f] with them. 30And the
Pharisees and their scribes murmured
against his disciples, saying, "Why do
you eat and drink with tax collectors
and sinners?" 31And Jesus answered
them, "Those who are well have no
need of a physician, but those who are
sick; 32I have not come to call the righ-
teous, but sinners to repentance."

THE QUESTION ABOUT FASTING

33 And they said to him, "The
disciples of John fast often and offer
prayers, and so do the disciples of the
Pharisees, but yours eat and drink."
34And Jesus said to them, "Can you
make wedding guests fast while the
bridegroom is with them? 35The days
will come, when the bridegroom is
taken away from them, and then they
will fast in those days." 36He told them

[c] Greek *to them*
[d] Other ancient authorities read *was present to heal them*
[e] Greek *him*
[f] Greek *reclining*

a parable also: "No one tears a piece
from a new garment and puts it upon
an old garment; if he does, he will tear
the new, and the piece from the new
will not match the old. 37And no one
puts new wine into old wineskins; if
he does, the new wine will burst the
skins and it will be spilled, and the
skins will be destroyed. 38But new
wine must be put into fresh wine-
skins. 39And no one after drinking old
wine desires new; for he says, 'The old
is good.'"[a]

THE QUESTION ABOUT THE SABBATH

6 On a sabbath,[b] while he was going
through the grainfields, his dis-
ciples plucked and ate some ears of
grain, rubbing them in their hands.
2But some of the Pharisees said, "Why
are you doing what is not lawful to
do on the sabbath?" 3And Jesus an-
swered, "Have you not read what
David did when he was hungry, he and
those who were with him: 4how he en-
tered the house of God, and took and
ate the bread of the Presence, which
it is not lawful for any but the priests
to eat, and also gave it to those with
him?" 5And he said to them, "The Son
of man is lord of the sabbath."

THE MAN WITH A WITHERED HAND

6 On another sabbath, when he
entered the synagogue and taught,
a man was there whose right hand
was withered. 7And the scribes and
the Pharisees watched him, to see
whether he would heal on the sab-
bath, so that they might find an accu-
sation against him. 8But he knew their
thoughts, and he said to the man who
had the withered hand, "Come and
stand here." And he rose and stood
there. 9And Jesus said to them, "I ask
you, is it lawful on the sabbath to do
good or to do harm, to save life or to
destroy it?" 10And he looked around
on them all, and said to him, "Stretch
out your hand." And he did so, and
his hand was restored. 11But they were
filled with fury and discussed with
one another what they might do to
Jesus.

JESUS CHOOSES THE TWELVE APOSTLES

12 In these days he went out into
the hills to pray; and all night he con-
tinued in prayer to God. 13And when
it was day, he called his disciples, and
chose from them twelve, whom he
named apostles; 14Simon, whom he
named Peter, and Andrew his broth-
er, and James and John, and Philip,
and Bartholomew, 15and Matthew,
and Thomas, and James the son of
Alphaeus, and Simon who was called
the Zealot, 16and Judas the son of
James, and Judas Iscariot, who be-
came a traitor.

JESUS TEACHES AND HEALS

17 And he came down with them
and stood on a level place, with a
great crowd of his disciples and a
great multitude of people from all
Judea and Jerusalem and the sea-
coast of Tyre and Sidon, who came
to hear him and to be healed of their
diseases; 18and those who were trou-
bled with unclean spirits were cured.
19And all the crowd sought to touch
him, for power came forth from him
and healed them all.

BLESSINGS AND WOES

20 And he lifted up his eyes on his
disciples, and said:* "Blessed are you
poor, for yours is the kingdom of God.

21 "Blessed are you that hun-
ger now, for you shall be satisfied.
"Blessed are you that weep now, for
you shall laugh.

22 "Blessed are you when men hate
you, and when they exclude you and
revile you, and cast out your name as
evil, on account of the Son of man!
23Rejoice in that day, and leap for joy,
for behold, your reward is great in

[a] Other ancient authorities read *better*
[b] Other ancient authorities read *On the second first sabbath* (on the second sabbath after the first)

heaven; for so their fathers did to the
prophets.
24 "But woe to you that are rich, for
you have received your consolation.
25 "Woe to you that are full now,
for you shall hunger. "Woe to you that
laugh now, for you shall mourn and
weep.
26 "Woe to you, when all men
speak well of you, for so their fathers
did to the false prophets.

LOVE FOR ENEMIES

27 "But I say to you that hear, Love
your enemies, do good to those who
hate you, 28bless those who curse you,
pray for those who abuse you. 29To
him who strikes you on the cheek, of-
fer the other also; and from him who
takes away your cloak do not withhold
your coat as well. 30Give to every one
who begs from you; and of him who
takes away your goods do not ask
them again. 31And as you wish that
men would do to you, do so to them.
32 "If you love those who love you,
what credit is that to you? For even
sinners love those who love them.
33And if you do good to those who
do good to you, what credit is that to
you? For even sinners do the same.
34And if you lend to those from whom
you hope to receive, what credit is
that to you? Even sinners lend to sin-
ners, to receive as much again. 35But
love your enemies, and do good, and
lend, expecting nothing in return;[c]
and your reward will be great, and you
will be sons of the Most High; for he is
kind to the ungrateful and the selfish.
36Be merciful, even as your Father is
merciful.

JUDGING OTHERS

37 "Judge not, and you will not be
judged; condemn not, and you will not
be condemned; forgive, and you will
be forgiven; 38give, and it will be given
to you; good measure, pressed down,
shaken together, running over, will
be put into your lap. For the measure
you give will be the measure you get
back."
39 He also told them a parable:
"Can a blind man lead a blind man?
Will they not both fall into a pit? 40A
disciple is not above his teacher, but
every one when he is fully taught will
be like his teacher. 41Why do you see
the speck that is in your brother's eye,
but do not notice the log that is in
your own eye? 42Or how can you say to
your brother, 'Brother, let me take out
the speck that is in your eye,' when
you yourself do not see the log that is
in your own eye? You hypocrite, first
take the log out of your own eye, and
then you will see clearly to take out
the speck that is in your brother's eye.

A TREE AND ITS FRUIT

43 "For no good tree bears bad
fruit, nor again does a bad tree bear
good fruit; 44for each tree is known by
its own fruit. For figs are not gathered
from thorns, nor are grapes picked
from a bramble bush. 45The good man
out of the good treasure of his heart
produces good, and the evil man out
of his evil treasure produces evil; for
out of the abundance of the heart his
mouth speaks.

THE TWO FOUNDATIONS

46 "Why do you call me 'Lord,
Lord,' and not do what I tell you?
47Every one who comes to me and
hears my words and does them, I will
show you what he is like: 48he is like a
man building a house, who dug deep,
and laid the foundation upon rock;
and when a flood arose, the stream
broke against that house, and could
not shake it, because it had been
well built.[d] 49But he who hears and
does not do them is like a man who
built a house on the ground without a
foundation; against which the stream
broke, and immediately it fell, and the
ruin of that house was great."

[c]Other ancient authorities read *despairing of no man*
[d]Other ancient authorities read *founded upon the rock*

JESUS HEALS A CENTURION'S SERVANT

7 After he had ended all his sayings
in the hearing of the people he en-
tered Caper′na-um. 2Now a centurion
had a slave who was dear[a] to him, who
was sick and at the point of death.
3When he heard of Jesus, he sent to
him elders of the Jews, asking him to
come and heal his slave. 4And when
they came to Jesus, they besought him
earnestly, saying, "He is worthy to
have you do this for him, 5for he loves
our nation, and he built us our syn-
agogue." 6And Jesus went with them.
When he was not far from the house,
the centurion sent friends to him,
saying to him, "Lord, do not trouble
yourself, for I am not worthy to have
you come under my roof; 7therefore I
did not presume to come to you. But
say the word, and let my servant be
healed. 8For I am a man set under au-
thority, with soldiers under me: and I
say to one, 'Go,' and he goes; and to
another, 'Come,' and he comes; and
to my slave, 'Do this,' and he does it."
9When Jesus heard this he marveled at
him, and turned and said to the multi-
tude that followed him, "I tell you, not
even in Israel have I found such faith."
10And when those who had been sent
returned to the house, they found the
slave well.

JESUS RAISES THE WIDOW'S SON AT NAIN

11 Soon afterward[b] he went to a
city called Na′in, and his disciples and
a great crowd went with him. 12As he
drew near to the gate of the city, be-
hold, a man who had died was being
carried out, the only son of his moth-
er, and she was a widow; and a large
crowd from the city was with her.
13And when the Lord saw her, he had
compassion on her and said to her, "Do
not weep." 14And he came and touched
the bier, and the bearers stood still.
And he said, "Young man, I say to you,
arise." 15And the dead man sat up, and
began to speak. And he gave him to
his mother. 16Fear seized them all; and
they glorified God, saying, "A great
prophet has arisen among us!" and
"God has visited his people!" 17And
this report concerning him spread
through the whole of Judea and all the
surrounding country.

MESSENGERS FROM JOHN THE BAPTIST

18 The disciples of John told him of
all these things. 19And John, calling to
him two of his disciples, sent them to
the Lord, saying, "Are you he who is to
come, or shall we look for another?"
20And when the men had come to him,
they said, "John the Baptist has sent
us to you, saying, 'Are you he who is to
come, or shall we look for another?'"
21In that hour he cured many of dis-
eases and plagues and evil spirits, and
on many that were blind he bestowed
sight. 22And he answered them, "Go
and tell John what you have seen and
heard: the blind receive their sight,
the lame walk, lepers are cleansed,
and the deaf hear, the dead are raised
up, the poor have good news preached
to them. 23And blessed is he who takes
no offense at me."

24 When the messengers of John
had gone, he began to speak to the
crowds concerning John: "What did
you go out into the wilderness to
behold? A reed shaken by the wind?
25What then did you go out to see? A
man clothed in soft raiment? Behold,
those who are gorgeously appareled
and live in luxury are in kings' courts.
26What then did you go out to see?
A prophet? Yes, I tell you, and more
than a prophet. 27This is he of whom
it is written,

'Behold, I send my messenger
before thy face,
who shall prepare thy way
before thee.'

28I tell you, among those born of
women none is greater than John; yet
he who is least in the kingdom of God
is greater than he."* 29(When they

[a]Or *valuable*
[b]Other ancient authorities read *Next day*

heard this all the people and the tax
collectors justified God, having been
baptized with the baptism of John;
30but the Pharisees and the lawyers
rejected the purpose of God for them-
selves, not having been baptized by
him.)

31 "To what then shall I compare
the men of this generation, and what
are they like? 32They are like children
sitting in the market place and calling
to one another,

'We piped to you, and you did
not dance;
we wailed, and you did not
weep.'

33For John the Baptist has come
eating no bread and drinking no
wine; and you say, 'He has a demon.'
34The Son of man has come eating and
drinking; and you say, 'Behold, a glut-
ton and a drunkard, a friend of tax
collectors and sinners!' 35Yet wisdom
is justified by all her children."

A SINFUL WOMAN FORGIVEN

36 One of the Pharisees asked him
to eat with him, and he went into the
Pharisee's house, and sat at table.
37And behold, a woman of the city,
who was a sinner, when she learned
that he was sitting at table in the
Pharisee's house, brought an alabas-
ter flask of ointment, 38and standing
behind him at his feet, weeping, she
began to wet his feet with her tears,
and wiped them with the hair of her
head, and kissed his feet, and anoint-
ed them with the ointment. 39Now
when the Pharisee who had invited
him saw it, he said to himself, "If this
man were a prophet, he would have
known who and what sort of woman
this is who is touching him, for she is a
sinner." 40And Jesus answering said to
him, "Simon, I have something to say
to you." And he answered, "What is
it, Teacher?" 41"A certain creditor had
two debtors; one owed five hundred
denarii, and the other fifty. 42When
they could not pay, he forgave them
both. Now which of them will love
him more?" 43Simon answered, "The
one, I suppose, to whom he forgave
more." And he said to him, "You have
judged rightly." 44Then turning toward
the woman he said to Simon, "Do you
see this woman? I entered your house,
you gave me no water for my feet, but
she has wet my feet with her tears and
wiped them with her hair. 45You gave
me no kiss, but from the time I came
in she has not ceased to kiss my feet.
46You did not anoint my head with oil,
but she has anointed my feet with
ointment. 47Therefore I tell you, her
sins, which are many, are forgiven, for
she loved much; but he who is forgiv-
en little, loves little."* 48And he said to
her, "Your sins are forgiven." 49Then
those who were at table with him be-
gan to say among themselves, "Who
is this, who even forgives sins?" 50And
he said to the woman, "Your faith has
saved you; go in peace."

SOME WOMEN ACCOMPANY JESUS

8 Soon afterward he went on through
cities and villages, preaching and
bringing the good news of the king-
dom of God. And the twelve were
with him, 2and also some women who
had been healed of evil spirits and
infirmities: Mary, called Mag´dalene,
from whom seven demons had gone
out, 3and Jo-an´na, the wife of Chu´za,
Herod's steward, and Susanna, and
many others, who provided for them[c]
out of their means.

THE PARABLE OF THE SOWER

4 And when a great crowd came
together and people from town after
town came to him, he said in a par-
able: 5"A sower went out to sow his
seed; and as he sowed, some fell along
the path, and was trodden under foot,
and the birds of the air devoured it.
6And some fell on the rock; and as it
grew up, it withered away, because
it had no moisture. 7And some fell
among thorns; and the thorns grew

[c]Other ancient authorities read *him*

with it and choked it. 8 And some fell
into good soil and grew, and yielded
a hundredfold." As he said this, he
called out, "He who has ears to hear,
let him hear."

THE PURPOSE OF THE PARABLES

9 And when his disciples asked
him what this parable meant, 10 he
said, "To you it has been given to
know the secrets of the kingdom of
God; but for others they are in para-
bles, so that seeing they may not see,
and hearing they may not understand.
11 Now the parable is this: The seed is
the word of God. 12 The ones along the
path are those who have heard; then
the devil comes and takes away the
word from their hearts, that they may
not believe and be saved. 13 And the
ones on the rock are those who, when
they hear the word, receive it with joy;
but these have no root, they believe
for a while and in time of temptation
fall away. 14 And as for what fell among
the thorns, they are those who hear,
but as they go on their way they are
choked by the cares and riches and
pleasures of life, and their fruit does
not mature. 15 And as for that in the
good soil, they are those who, hearing
the word, hold it fast in an honest and
good heart, and bring forth fruit with
patience.

A LAMP UNDER A JAR

16 "No one after lighting a lamp
covers it with a vessel, or puts it under
a bed, but puts it on a stand, that those
who enter may see the light. 17 For
nothing is hid that shall not be made
manifest, nor anything secret that
shall not be known and come to light.
18 Take heed then how you hear; for to
him who has will more be given, and
from him who has not, even what he
thinks that he has will be taken away."

THE TRUE KINDRED OF JESUS

19 Then his mother and his breth-
ren* came to him, but they could not
reach him for the crowd. 20 And he was
told, "Your mother and your breth-
ren are standing outside, desiring to
see you." 21 But he said to them, "My
mother and my brethren are those
who hear the word of God and do it."

JESUS CALMS A STORM

22 One day he got into a boat with
his disciples, and he said to them,
"Let us go across to the other side
of the lake." So they set out, 23 and
as they sailed he fell asleep. And a
storm of wind came down on the lake,
and they were filling with water, and
were in danger. 24 And they went and
woke him, saying, "Master, Master,
we are perishing!" And he awoke
and rebuked the wind and the raging
waves; and they ceased, and there was
a calm. 25 He said to them, "Where is
your faith?" And they were afraid, and
they marveled, saying to one another,
"Who then is this, that he commands
even wind and water, and they obey
him?"

JESUS HEALS THE GERASENE DEMONIAC

26 Then they arrived at the country
of the Ger′asenes,*a* which is opposite
Galilee. 27 And as he stepped out on
land, there met him a man from the
city who had demons; for a long time
he had worn no clothes, and he lived
not in a house but among the tombs.
28 When he saw Jesus, he cried out and
fell down before him, and said with a
loud voice, "What have you to do with
me, Jesus, Son of the Most High God?
I beseech you, do not torment me."
29 For he had commanded the unclean
spirit to come out of the man. (For
many a time it had seized him; he was
kept under guard, and bound with
chains and fetters, but he broke the
bonds and was driven by the demon
into the desert.) 30 Jesus then asked
him, "What is your name?" And he
said, "Legion"; for many demons had
entered him. 31 And they begged him
not to command them to depart into

a Other ancient authorities read *Gadarenes*, others *Gergesenes*

the abyss. 32Now a large herd of swine
was feeding there on the hillside; and
they begged him to let them enter
these. So he gave them leave. 33Then
the demons came out of the man
and entered the swine, and the herd
rushed down the steep bank into the
lake and were drowned.

34 When the herdsmen saw what
had happened, they fled, and told it
in the city and in the country. 35Then
people went out to see what had hap-
pened, and they came to Jesus, and
found the man from whom the de-
mons had gone, sitting at the feet of
Jesus, clothed and in his right mind;
and they were afraid. 36And those
who had seen it told them how he
who had been possessed with de-
mons was healed. 37Then all the peo-
ple of the surrounding country of the
Ger′asenes[b] asked him to depart from
them; for they were seized with great
fear; so he got into the boat and re-
turned. 38The man from whom the de-
mons had gone begged that he might
be with him; but he sent him away,
saying, 39"Return to your home, and
declare how much God has done for
you." And he went away, proclaiming
throughout the whole city how much
Jesus had done for him.*

A GIRL RESTORED TO LIFE AND A WOMAN HEALED

40 Now when Jesus returned, the
crowd welcomed him, for they were
all waiting for him. 41And there came
a man named Ja′irus, who was a ruler
of the synagogue; and falling at Jesus'
feet he besought him to come to his
house, 42for he had an only daughter,
about twelve years of age, and she was
dying. As he went, the people pressed
round him. 43And a woman who had
had a flow of blood for twelve years
and had spent all her living upon phy-
sicians[c] and could not be healed by
any one, 44came up behind him, and
touched the fringe of his garment;
and immediately her flow of blood
ceased. 45And Jesus said, "Who was it
that touched me?" When all denied it,
Peter[d] said, "Master, the multitudes
surround you and press upon you!"
46But Jesus said, "Some one touched
me; for I perceive that power has gone
forth from me." 47And when the wom-
an saw that she was not hidden, she
came trembling, and falling down be-
fore him declared in the presence of
all the people why she had touched
him, and how she had been imme-
diately healed. 48And he said to her,
"Daughter, your faith has made you
well; go in peace."

49 While he was still speaking, a
man from the ruler's house came and
said, "Your daughter is dead; do not
trouble the Teacher any more." 50But
Jesus on hearing this answered him,
"Do not fear; only believe, and she
shall be well." 51And when he came
to the house, he permitted no one to
enter with him, except Peter and John
and James, and the father and moth-
er of the child. 52And all were weep-
ing and bewailing her; but he said,
"Do not weep; for she is not dead but
sleeping." 53And they laughed at him,
knowing that she was dead. 54But tak-
ing her by the hand he called, saying,
"Child, arise." 55And her spirit re-
turned, and she got up at once; and
he directed that something should
be given her to eat. 56And her parents
were amazed; but he charged them to
tell no one what had happened.

THE MISSION OF THE TWELVE

9 And he called the twelve together
and gave them power and authority
over all demons and to cure diseases,
2and he sent them out to preach the
kingdom of God and to heal. 3And he
said to them, "Take nothing for your
journey, no staff, nor bag, nor bread,
nor money; and do not have two tu-
nics. 4And whatever house you enter,

[b] Other ancient authorities read *Gadarenes*, others *Gergesenes*
[c] Other ancient authorities omit *and had spent all her living upon physicians*
[d] Other ancient authorities add *and those who were with him*

stay there, and from there depart.
5And wherever they do not receive
you, when you leave that town shake
off the dust from your feet as a tes-
timony against them." 6And they de-
parted and went through the villag-
es, preaching the gospel and healing
everywhere.

HEROD'S PERPLEXITY

7 Now Herod the tetrarch heard
of all that was done, and he was per-
plexed, because it was said by some
that John had been raised from the
dead, 8by some that Eli′jah had ap-
peared, and by others that one of the
old prophets had risen. 9Herod said,
"John I beheaded; but who is this
about whom I hear such things?" And
he sought to see him.

FEEDING THE FIVE THOUSAND

10 On their return the apostles
told him what they had done. And
he took them and withdrew apart to
a city called Beth-sa′ida. 11When the
crowds learned it, they followed him;
and he welcomed them and spoke
to them of the kingdom of God, and
cured those who had need of healing.
12Now the day began to wear away;
and the twelve came and said to him,
"Send the crowd away, to go into the
villages and country round about, to
lodge and get provisions; for we are
here in a lonely place." 13But he said
to them, "You give them something
to eat." They said, "We have no more
than five loaves and two fish—unless
we are to go and buy food for all these
people." 14For there were about five
thousand men. And he said to his dis-
ciples, "Make them sit down in com-
panies, about fifty each." 15And they
did so, and made them all sit down.
16And taking the five loaves and the
two fish he looked up to heaven, and
blessed and broke them, and gave
them to the disciples to set before the
crowd. 17And all ate and were satis-
fied. And they took up what was left
over, twelve baskets of broken pieces.

PETER'S DECLARATION ABOUT JESUS

18 Now it happened that as he was
praying alone the disciples were with
him; and he asked them, "Who do
the people say that I am?" 19And they
answered, "John the Baptist; but oth-
ers say, Eli′jah; and others, that one
of the old prophets has risen." 20And
he said to them, "But who do you say
that I am?" And Peter answered, "The
Christ of God." 21But he charged and
commanded them to tell this to no
one, 22saying, "The Son of man must
suffer many things, and be rejected
by the elders and chief priests and
scribes, and be killed, and on the third
day be raised."

23 And he said to all, "If any man
would come after me, let him deny
himself and take up his cross daily
and follow me. 24For whoever would
save his life will lose it; and whoev-
er loses his life for my sake, he will
save it. 25For what does it profit a man
if he gains the whole world and los-
es or forfeits himself? 26For whoever
is ashamed of me and of my words, of
him will the Son of man be ashamed
when he comes in his glory and the
glory of the Father and of the holy
angels. 27But I tell you truly, there are
some standing here who will not taste
death before they see the kingdom of
God."

THE TRANSFIGURATION

28 Now about eight days after
these sayings he took with him Peter
and John and James, and went up on
the mountain to pray. 29And as he was
praying, the appearance of his coun-
tenance was altered, and his raiment
became dazzling white. 30And behold,
two men talked with him, Moses and
Eli′jah, 31who appeared in glory and
spoke of his departure, which he was
to accomplish at Jerusalem. 32Now
Peter and those who were with him
were heavy with sleep but kept awake,
and they saw his glory and the two
men who stood with him. 33And as
the men were parting from him, Peter

said to Jesus, "Master, it is well that
we are here; let us make three booths,
one for you and one for Moses and one
for Eli´jah"—not knowing what he
said. 34As he said this, a cloud came
and overshadowed them; and they
were afraid as they entered the cloud.
35And a voice came out of the cloud,
saying, "This is my Son, my Chosen;[a]
listen to him!" 36And when the voice
had spoken, Jesus was found alone.
And they kept silence and told no one
in those days anything of what they
had seen.

JESUS HEALS A BOY WITH A DEMON

37 On the next day, when they
had come down from the mountain, a
great crowd met him. 38And behold, a
man from the crowd cried, "Teacher,
I beg you to look upon my son, for he
is my only child; 39and behold, a spir-
it seizes him, and he suddenly cries
out; it convulses him till he foams,
and shatters him, and will hardly
leave him. 40And I begged your dis-
ciples to cast it out, but they could
not." 41Jesus answered, "O faithless
and perverse generation, how long
am I to be with you and bear with
you? Bring your son here." 42While he
was coming, the demon tore him and
convulsed him. But Jesus rebuked the
unclean spirit, and healed the boy,
and gave him back to his father. 43And
all were astonished at the majesty of
God.

JESUS AGAIN FORETELLS HIS DEATH

But while they were all marvel-
ing at everything he did, he said to
his disciples, 44"Let these words sink
into your ears; for the Son of man is to
be delivered into the hands of men."
45But they did not understand this say-
ing, and it was concealed from them,
that they should not perceive it; and
they were afraid to ask him about this
saying.

TRUE GREATNESS

46 And an argument arose among
them as to which of them was the
greatest. 47But when Jesus perceived
the thought of their hearts, he took
a child and put him by his side, 48and
said to them, "Whoever receives this
child in my name receives me, and
whoever receives me receives him who
sent me; for he who is least among you
all is the one who is great."

ANOTHER EXORCIST

49 John answered, "Master, we
saw a man casting out demons in your
name, and we forbade him, because he
does not follow with us." 50But Jesus
said to him, "Do not forbid him; for
he that is not against you is for you."

A SAMARITAN VILLAGE REFUSES TO RECEIVE JESUS

51 When the days drew near for
him to be received up,* he set his face
to go to Jerusalem.* 52And he sent mes-
sengers ahead of him, who went and
entered a village of the Samaritans, to
make ready for him; 53but the people
would not receive him, because his
face was set toward Jerusalem.* 54And
when his disciples James and John saw
it, they said, "Lord, do you want us to
bid fire come down from heaven and
consume them?"[b] 55But he turned and
rebuked them.[c] 56And they went on to
another village.

WOULD-BE FOLLOWERS OF JESUS

57 As they were going along the
road, a man said to him, "I will follow
you wherever you go." 58And Jesus said
to him, "Foxes have holes, and birds
of the air have nests; but the Son of
man has nowhere to lay his head." 59To
another he said, "Follow me." But he
said, "Lord, let me first go and bury my
father." 60But he said to him, "Leave
the dead to bury their own dead; but

[a] Other ancient authorities read *my Beloved*
[b] Other ancient authorities add *as Elijah did*
[c] Other ancient authorities add *and he said, "You do not know what manner of spirit you are of; for the Son of man came not to destroy men's lives but to save them"*

as for you, go and proclaim the king-
dom of God." 61Another said, "I will
follow you, Lord; but let me first say
farewell to those at my home." 62Jesus
said to him, "No one who puts his
hand to the plow and looks back is fit
for the kingdom of God."

THE MISSION OF THE SEVENTY

10 After this the Lord appointed
seventy[a] others, and sent them
on ahead of him, two by two, into ev-
ery town and place where he himself
was about to come. 2And he said to
them, "The harvest is plentiful, but
the laborers are few; pray therefore
the Lord of the harvest to send out la-
borers into his harvest. 3Go your way;
behold, I send you out as lambs in the
midst of wolves. 4Carry no purse, no
bag, no sandals; and salute no one on
the road. 5Whatever house you enter,
first say, 'Peace be to this house!'
6And if a son of peace is there, your
peace shall rest upon him; but if not,
it shall return to you. 7And remain in
the same house, eating and drinking
what they provide, for the laborer
deserves his wages; do not go from
house to house. 8Whenever you enter
a town and they receive you, eat what
is set before you; 9heal the sick in it
and say to them, 'The kingdom of God
has come near to you.' 10But whenev-
er you enter a town and they do not
receive you, go into its streets and
say, 11'Even the dust of your town that
clings to our feet, we wipe off against
you; nevertheless know this, that the
kingdom of God has come near.' 12I tell
you, it shall be more tolerable on that
day for Sodom than for that town.

WOES TO UNREPENTANT CITIES

13 "Woe to you, Chora´zin! woe
to you, Beth-sa´ida! for if the mighty
works done in you had been done in
Tyre and Sidon, they would have re-
pented long ago, sitting in sackcloth
and ashes. 14But it shall be more
tolerable in the judgment for Tyre
and Sidon than for you. 15And you,
Caper´na-um, will you be exalted to
heaven? You shall be brought down
to Hades.

16 "He who hears you hears me,
and he who rejects you rejects me,
and he who rejects me rejects him
who sent me."

THE RETURN OF THE SEVENTY

17 The seventy[b] returned with joy,
saying, "Lord, even the demons are
subject to us in your name!" 18And
he said to them, "I saw Satan fall
like lightning from heaven.* 19Behold,
I have given you authority to tread
upon serpents and scorpions, and over
all the power of the enemy; and noth-
ing shall hurt you. 20Nevertheless do
not rejoice in this, that the spirits are
subject to you; but rejoice that your
names are written in heaven."

JESUS REJOICES

21 In that same hour he rejoiced
in the Holy Spirit and said, "I thank
thee, Father, Lord of heaven and
earth, that thou hast hidden these
things from the wise and understand-
ing and revealed them to babes; yea,
Father, for such was thy gracious
will.[c] 22All things have been delivered
to me by my Father; and no one knows
who the Son is except the Father, or
who the Father is except the Son and
any one to whom the Son chooses to
reveal him."

23 Then turning to the disciples he
said privately, "Blessed are the eyes
which see what you see! 24For I tell
you that many prophets and kings de-
sired to see what you see, and did not
see it, and to hear what you hear, and
did not hear it."

THE PARABLE OF THE GOOD SAMARITAN

25 And behold, a lawyer stood up to
put him to the test, saying, "Teacher,

[a]Other ancient authorities read *seventy-two*
[b]Other ancient authorities read *seventy-two*
[c]Or *so it was well-pleasing before thee*

what shall I do to inherit eternal life?" 26 He said to him, "What is written in the law? How do you read?" 27 And he answered, "You shall love the Lord your God with all your heart, and with all your soul, and with all your strength, and with all your mind; and your neighbor as yourself." 28 And he said to him, "You have answered right; do this, and you will live."

29 But he, desiring to justify himself, said to Jesus, "And who is my neighbor?" 30 Jesus replied, "A man was going down from Jerusalem to Jericho, and he fell among robbers, who stripped him and beat him, and departed, leaving him half dead. 31 Now by chance a priest was going down that road; and when he saw him he passed by on the other side. 32 So likewise a Levite, when he came to the place and saw him, passed by on the other side. 33 But a Samaritan, as he journeyed, came to where he was; and when he saw him, he had compassion, 34 and went to him and bound up his wounds, pouring on oil and wine; then he set him on his own beast and brought him to an inn, and took care of him. 35 And the next day he took out two denarii[d] and gave them to the innkeeper, saying, 'Take care of him; and whatever more you spend, I will repay you when I come back.' 36 Which of these three, do you think, proved neighbor to the man who fell among the robbers?" 37 He said, "The one who showed mercy on him." And Jesus said to him, "Go and do likewise."

JESUS VISITS MARTHA AND MARY

38 Now as they went on their way, he entered a village; and a woman named Martha received him into her house. 39 And she had a sister called Mary, who sat at the Lord's feet and listened to his teaching. 40 But Martha was distracted with much serving; and she went to him and said, "Lord, do you not care that my sister has left me to serve alone? Tell her then to help me." 41 But the Lord answered her, "Martha, Martha, you are anxious and troubled about many things; 42 one thing is needful.[e] Mary has chosen the good portion, which shall not be taken away from her."

THE LORD'S PRAYER

11 He was praying in a certain place, and when he ceased, one of his disciples said to him, "Lord, teach us to pray, as John taught his disciples." 2 And he said to them, "When you pray, say:

"Father, hallowed be thy name. Thy kingdom come. 3 Give us each day our daily bread;[f] 4 and forgive us our sins, for we ourselves forgive every one who is indebted to us; and lead us not into temptation."

PERSEVERANCE IN PRAYER

5 And he said to them, "Which of you who has a friend will go to him at midnight and say to him, 'Friend, lend me three loaves; 6 for a friend of mine has arrived on a journey, and I have nothing to set before him'; 7 and he will answer from within, 'Do not bother me; the door is now shut, and my children are with me in bed; I cannot get up and give you anything'? 8 I tell you, though he will not get up and give him anything because he is his friend, yet because of his importunity he will rise and give him whatever he needs. 9 And I tell you, Ask, and it will be given you; seek, and you will find; knock, and it will be opened to you. 10 For every one who asks receives, and he who seeks finds, and to him who knocks it will be opened. 11 What father among you, if his son asks for[g] a fish, will instead of a fish give him a serpent; 12 or if he asks for an egg, will give him a scorpion? 13 If you then, who are evil, know how to give good

[d] The denarius was a day's wage for a laborer
[e] Other ancient authorities read *few things are needful, or only one*
[f] Or *our bread for the morrow*
[g] Other ancient authorities insert *bread, will give him a stone; or if he asks for*

gifts to your children, how much more
will the heavenly Father give the Holy
Spirit to those who ask him!"

JESUS AND BEELZEBUL

14 Now he was casting out a demon
that was dumb; when the demon had
gone out, the dumb man spoke, and the
people marveled. 15But some of them
said, "He casts out demons by Be-
el´zebul, the prince of demons"; 16while
others, to test him, sought from him
a sign from heaven. 17But he, knowing
their thoughts, said to them, "Every
kingdom divided against itself is laid
waste, and house falls upon house.
18And if Satan also is divided against
himself, how will his kingdom stand?
For you say that I cast out demons by
Be-el´zebul. 19And if I cast out demons
by Be-el´zebul, by whom do your sons
cast them out? Therefore they shall be
your judges. 20But if it is by the finger
of God that I cast out demons, then
the kingdom of God has come upon
you. 21When a strong man, fully armed,
guards his own palace, his goods are
in peace; 22but when one stronger than
he assails him and overcomes him, he
takes away his armor in which he trust-
ed, and divides his spoil. 23He who is
not with me is against me, and he who
does not gather with me scatters.

THE RETURN OF THE UNCLEAN SPIRIT

24 "When the unclean spirit has
gone out of a man, he passes through
waterless places seeking rest; and
finding none he says, 'I will return to
my house from which I came.' 25And
when he comes he finds it swept
and put in order. 26Then he goes and
brings seven other spirits more evil
than himself, and they enter and
dwell there; and the last state of that
man becomes worse than the first."

TRUE BLESSEDNESS

27 As he said this, a woman in the
crowd raised her voice and said to
him, "Blessed is the womb that bore
you, and the breasts that you sucked!"
28But he said, "Blessed rather are
those who hear the word of God and
keep it!"

THE SIGN OF JONAH

29 When the crowds were increas-
ing, he began to say, "This generation
is an evil generation; it seeks a sign,
but no sign shall be given to it except
the sign of Jonah. 30For as Jonah be-
came a sign to the men of Nin´eveh,
so will the Son of man be to this gen-
eration. 31The queen of the South will
arise at the judgment with the men of
this generation and condemn them;
for she came from the ends of the
earth to hear the wisdom of Solomon,
and behold, something greater
than Solomon is here. 32The men of
Nin´eveh will arise at the judgment
with this generation and condemn it;
for they repented at the preaching of
Jonah, and behold, something greater
than Jonah is here.

THE LIGHT OF THE BODY

33 "No one after lighting a lamp
puts it in a cellar or under a bushel,
but on a stand, that those who enter
may see the light. 34Your eye is the
lamp of your body; when your eye is
sound, your whole body is full of light;
but when it is not sound, your body is
full of darkness. 35Therefore be care-
ful lest the light in you be darkness.
36If then your whole body is full of
light, having no part dark, it will be
wholly bright, as when a lamp with its
rays gives you light."

JESUS DENOUNCES PHARISEES AND LAWYERS

37 While he was speaking, a
Pharisee asked him to dine with him;
so he went in and sat at table. 38The
Pharisee was astonished to see that
he did not first wash before dinner.
39And the Lord said to him, "Now you
Pharisees cleanse the outside of the

cup and of the dish, but inside you
are full of extortion and wickedness.
40You fools! Did not he who made the
outside make the inside also? 41But
give for alms those things which are
within; and behold, everything is
clean for you.

42 "But woe to you Pharisees! for
you tithe mint and rue and every herb,
and neglect justice and the love of
God; these you ought to have done,
without neglecting the others. 43Woe
to you Pharisees! for you love the
best seat in the synagogues and sal-
utations in the market places. 44Woe
to you! for you are like graves which
are not seen, and men walk over them
without knowing it."

45 One of the lawyers answered
him, "Teacher, in saying this you re-
proach us also." 46And he said, "Woe
to you lawyers also! for you load men
with burdens hard to bear, and you
yourselves do not touch the burdens
with one of your fingers. 47Woe to you!
for you build the tombs of the proph-
ets whom your fathers killed. 48So
you are witnesses and consent to the
deeds of your fathers; for they killed
them, and you build their tombs.
49Therefore also the Wisdom of God
said, 'I will send them prophets and
apostles, some of whom they will kill
and persecute,' 50that the blood of all
the prophets, shed from the founda-
tion of the world, may be required of
this generation, 51from the blood of
Abel to the blood of Zechari´ah, who
perished between the altar and the
sanctuary. Yes, I tell you, it shall be
required of this generation. 52Woe to
you lawyers! for you have taken away
the key of knowlege; you did not
enter yourselves, and you hindered
those who were entering."

53 As he went away from there,
the scribes and the Pharisees began
to press him hard and to provoke
him to speak of many things, 54lying
in wait for him, to catch at something
he might say.

A WARNING AGAINST HYPOCRISY

12 In the meantime, when so many
thousands of the multitude had
gathered together that they trod upon
one another, he began to say to his
disciples first, "Beware of the leaven
of the Pharisees, which is hypocrisy.
2Nothing is covered up that will not
be revealed, or hidden that will not
be known. 3Whatever you have said in
the dark shall be heard in the light,
and what you have whispered in pri-
vate rooms shall be proclaimed upon
the housetops.

EXHORTATION TO FEARLESS CONFESSION

4 "I tell you, my friends, do not fear
those who kill the body, and after that
have no more that they can do. 5But I
will warn you whom to fear: fear him
who, after he has killed, has power
to cast into hell;[a] yes, I tell you, fear
him! 6Are not five sparrows sold for
two pennies? And not one of them is
forgotten before God. 7Why, even the
hairs of your head are all numbered.
Fear not; you are of more value than
many sparrows.

8 "And I tell you, every one who
acknowledges me before men, the Son
of man also will acknowledge before
the angels of God; 9but he who denies
me before men will be denied before
the angels of God. 10And every one
who speaks a word against the Son
of man will be forgiven; but he who
blasphemes against the Holy Spirit
will not be forgiven. 11And when they
bring you before the synagogues and
the rulers and the authorities, do not
be anxious how or what you are to an-
swer or what you are to say; 12for the
Holy Spirit will teach you in that very
hour what you ought to say."

THE PARABLE OF THE RICH FOOL

13 One of the multitude said to
him, "Teacher, bid my brother divide
the inheritance with me." 14But he
said to him, "Man, who made me a
judge or divider over you?" 15And he

[a]Greek *Gehenna*

said to them, "Take heed, and beware
of all covetousness; for a man's life
does not consist in the abundance of
his possessions." 16And he told them
a parable, saying, "The land of a rich
man brought forth plentifully; 17and
he thought to himself, 'What shall
I do, for I have nowhere to store my
crops?' 18And he said, 'I will do this:
I will pull down my barns, and build
larger ones; and there I will store all
my grain and my goods. 19And I will
say to my soul, Soul, you have ample
goods laid up for many years; take
your ease, eat, drink, be merry.' 20But
God said to him, 'Fool! This night
your soul is required of you; and the
things you have prepared, whose will
they be?' 21So is he who lays up trea-
sure for himself, and is not rich to-
ward God."

DO NOT WORRY

22 And he said to his disciples,
"Therefore I tell you, do not be anx-
ious about your life, what you shall
eat, nor about your body, what you
shall put on. 23For life is more than
food, and the body more than cloth-
ing. 24Consider the ravens: they nei-
ther sow nor reap, they have neither
storehouse nor barn, and yet God
feeds them. Of how much more value
are you than the birds! 25And which of
you by being anxious can add a cubit
to his span of life?[a] 26If then you are
not able to do as small a thing as that,
why are you anxious about the rest?
27Consider the lilies, how they grow;
they neither toil nor spin;[b] yet I tell
you, even Solomon in all his glory was
not arrayed like one of these. 28But
if God so clothes the grass which is
alive in the field today and tomorrow
is thrown into the oven, how much
more will he clothe you, O men of
little faith! 29And do not seek what
you are to eat and what you are to
drink, nor be of anxious mind. 30For
all the nations of the world seek these
things; and your Father knows that
you need them. 31Instead, seek his[c]
kingdom, and these things shall be
yours as well.

32 "Fear not, little flock, for it is
your Father's good pleasure to give
you the kingdom. 33Sell your posses-
sions, and give alms; provide your-
selves with purses that do not grow
old, with a treasure in the heavens
that does not fail, where no thief ap-
proaches and no moth destroys. 34For
where your treasure is, there will your
heart be also.

WATCHFUL SLAVES

35 "Let your loins be girded and
your lamps burning, 36and be like
men who are waiting for their mas-
ter to come home from the marriage
feast, so that they may open to him
at once when he comes and knocks.
37Blessed are those servants whom
the master finds awake when he
comes; truly, I say to you, he will gird
himself and have them sit at table,
and he will come and serve them. 38If
he comes in the second watch, or in
the third, and finds them so, blessed
are those servants! 39But know this,
that if the householder had known at
what hour the thief was coming, he
would have been awake and[d] would
not have left his house to be broken
into. 40You also must be ready; for the
Son of man is coming at an hour you
do not expect."

THE FAITHFUL OR THE UNFAITHFUL SLAVE

41 Peter said, "Lord, are you tell-
ing this parable for us or for all?"
42And the Lord said, "Who then is the
faithful and wise steward, whom his
master will set over his household, to
give them their portion of food at the
proper time? 43Blessed is that servant
whom his master when he comes will
find so doing. 44Truly, I tell you, he

[a] Or *to his stature*
[b] Other ancient authorities read *Consider the lilies; they neither spin nor weave*
[c] Other ancient authorities read *God's*
[d] Other ancient authorities omit *would have been awake and*

will set him over all his possessions.
45 But if that servant says to himself,
'My master is delayed in coming,'
and begins to beat the menservants
and the maidservants, and to eat and
drink and get drunk, 46 the master of
that servant will come on a day when
he does not expect him and at an hour
he does not know, and will punish[e]
him, and put him with the unfaith-
ful. 47 And that servant who knew his
master's will, but did not make ready
or act according to his will, shall re-
ceive a severe beating. 48 But he who
did not know, and did what deserved
a beating, shall receive a light beating.
Every one to whom much is given, of
him will much be required; and of him
to whom men commit much they will
demand the more.

JESUS THE CAUSE OF DIVISION

49 "I came to cast fire upon the
earth; and would that it were already
kindled! 50 I have a baptism to be bap-
tized with; and how I am constrained
until it is accomplished! 51 Do you
think that I have come to give peace
on earth? No, I tell you, but rath-
er division; 52 for henceforth in one
house there will be five divided, three
against two and two against three;
53 they will be divided, father against
son and son against father, mother
against daughter and daughter against
her mother, mother-in-law against her
daughter-in-law and daughter-in-law
against her mother-in-law."

INTERPRETING THE TIME

54 *He also said to the multitudes,*
"When you see a cloud rising in the
west, you say at once, 'A shower is
coming'; and so it happens. 55 And
when you see the south wind blow-
ing, you say, 'There will be scorching
heat'; and it happens. 56 You hypo-
crites! You know how to interpret the
appearance of earth and sky; but why
do you not know how to interpret the
present time?

SETTLING WITH YOUR OPPONENT

57 "And why do you not judge for
yourselves what is right? 58 As you go
with your accuser before the magis-
trate, make an effort to settle with
him on the way, lest he drag you to
the judge, and the judge hand you over
to the officer, and the officer put you
in prison. 59 I tell you, you will never
get out till you have paid the very last
copper."

REPENT OR PERISH

13 There were some present at that
very time who told him of the
Galileans whose blood Pilate had
mingled with their sacrifices. 2 And he
answered them, "Do you think that
these Galileans were worse sinners
than all the other Galileans, because
they suffered thus? 3 I tell you, No; but
unless you repent you will all likewise
perish. 4 Or those eighteen upon whom
the tower in Silo´am fell and killed
them, do you think that they were
worse offenders than all the others
who dwelt in Jerusalem? 5 I tell you,
No; but unless you repent you will all
likewise perish."

THE PARABLE OF THE BARREN FIG TREE

6 And he told this parable: "A man
had a fig tree planted in his vineyard;
and he came seeking fruit on it and
found none. 7 And he said to the vine-
dresser, 'Lo, these three years I have
come seeking fruit on this fig tree,
and I find none. Cut it down; why
should it use up the ground?' 8 And he
answered him, 'Let it alone, sir, this
year also, till I dig about it and put
on manure. 9 And if it bears fruit next
year, well and good; but if not, you can
cut it down.'"

JESUS HEALS A CRIPPLED WOMAN

10 Now he was teaching in one of
the synagogues on the sabbath. 11 And
there was a woman who had had a
spirit of infirmity for eighteen years;
she was bent over and could not fully

[e] Or *cut him in pieces*

straighten herself. 12And when Jesus
saw her, he called her and said to her,
"Woman, you are freed from your in-
firmity." 13And he laid his hands upon
her, and immediately she was made
straight, and she praised God. 14But
the ruler of the synagogue, indig-
nant because Jesus had healed on the
sabbath, said to the people, "There
are six days on which work ought to
be done; come on those days and be
healed, and not on the sabbath day."
15Then the Lord answered him, "You
hypocrites! Does not each of you on
the sabbath untie his ox or his ass
from the manger, and lead it away to
water it? 16And ought not this woman,
a daughter of Abraham whom Satan
bound for eighteen years, be loosed
from this bond on the sabbath day?"
17As he said this, all his adversaries
were put to shame; and all the people
rejoiced at all the glorious things that
were done by him.

THE PARABLE OF THE MUSTARD SEED

18 He said therefore, "What is the
kingdom of God like? And to what
shall I compare it? 19It is like a grain of
mustard seed which a man took and
sowed in his garden; and it grew and
became a tree, and the birds of the air
made nests in its branches."

THE PARABLE OF THE YEAST

20 And again he said, "To what
shall I compare the kingdom of God?
21It is like leaven which a woman took
and hid in three measures of meal, till
it was all leavened."

THE NARROW DOOR

22 He went on his way through
towns and villages, teaching, and
journeying toward Jerusalem. 23And
some one said to him, "Lord, will
those who are saved be few?" And
he said to them, 24"Strive to enter by
the narrow door; for many, I tell you,
will seek to enter and will not be able.
25When once the householder has
risen up and shut the door, you will
begin to stand outside and to knock
at the door, saying, 'Lord, open to us.'
He will answer you, 'I do not know
where you come from.' 26Then you
will begin to say, 'We ate and drank
in your presence, and you taught in
our streets.' 27But he will say, 'I tell
you, I do not know where you come
from; depart from me, all you work-
ers of iniquity!' 28There you will weep
and gnash your teeth, when you see
Abraham and Isaac and Jacob and all
the prophets in the kingdom of God
and you yourselves thrust out. 29And
men will come from east and west,
and from north and south, and sit at
table in the kingdom of God. 30And
behold, some are last who will be
first, and some are first who will be
last."

THE LAMENT OVER JERUSALEM

31 At that very hour some
Pharisees came, and said to him, "Get
away from here, for Herod wants to
kill you." 32And he said to them, "Go
and tell that fox, 'Behold, I cast out
demons and perform cures today and
tomorrow, and the third day I finish
my course. 33Nevertheless I must go
on my way today and tomorrow and
the day following; for it cannot be that
a prophet should perish away from
Jerusalem.' 34O Jerusalem, Jerusalem,
killing the prophets and stoning those
who are sent to you! How often would
I have gathered your children together
as a hen gathers her brood under her
wings, and you would not! 35Behold,
your house is forsaken. And I tell
you, you will not see me until you say,
'Blessed is he who comes in the name
of the Lord!'"

JESUS HEALS THE MAN WITH DROPSY

14 One sabbath when he went to
dine at the house of a ruler who
belonged to the Pharisees, they were
watching him. 2And behold, there was
a man before him who had dropsy.
3And Jesus spoke to the lawyers and
Pharisees, saying, "Is it lawful to heal

on the sabbath, or not?" 4But they
were silent. Then he took him and
healed him, and let him go. 5And he
said to them, "Which of you, having
an ass[a] or an ox that has fallen into
a well, will not immediately pull him
out on a sabbath day?" 6And they
could not reply to this.

HUMILITY AND HOSPITALITY

7 Now he told a parable to those
who were invited, when he marked
how they chose the places of honor,
saying to them, 8"When you are invit-
ed by any one to a marriage feast, do
not sit down in a place of honor, lest
a more eminent man than you be in-
vited by him; 9and he who invited you
both will come, and say to you, 'Give
place to this man,' and then you will
begin with shame to take the lowest
place. 10But when you are invited, go
and sit in the lowest place, so that
when your host comes he may say to
you, 'Friend, go up higher'; then you
will be honored in the presence of all
who sit at table with you. 11For every
one who exalts himself will be hum-
bled, and he who humbles himself will
be exalted."

12 He said also to the man who
had invited him, "When you give
a dinner or a banquet, do not invite
your friends or your brothers or your
kinsmen or rich neighbors, lest they
also invite you in return, and you be
repaid. 13But when you give a feast, in-
vite the poor, the maimed, thelame,
the blind, 14and you will be bssed,
because they cannot repay yo You
*will be repaid at the resurrecon of
the just."*

THE PARABLE OF THE GREAT DIER

15 When one of those whsat at
table with him heard this, said
to him, "Blessed is he who ıll eat
bread in the kingdom of Go 16But
he said to him, "A man o gave
a great banquet, and invitenany;
17and at the time for the baet he
sent his servant to say to those who
had been invited, 'Come; for all is now
ready.' 18But they all alike began to
make excuses. The first said to him,
'I have bought a field, and I must go
out and see it; I pray you, have me
excused.' 19And another said, 'I have
bought five yoke of oxen, and I go to
examine them; I pray you, have me
excused.' 20And another said, 'I have
married a wife, and therefore I can-
not come.' 21So the servant came and
reported this to his master. Then the
householder in anger said to his ser-
vant, 'Go out quickly to the streets
and lanes of the city, and bring in the
poor and maimed and blind and lame.'
22And the servant said, 'Sir, what you
commanded has been done, and still
there is room.' 23And the master said
to the servant, 'Go out to the high-
ways and hedges, and compel people
to come in, that my house may be
filled. 24For I tell you, none of those
men who were invited shall taste my
banquet.'"

THE COST OF DISCIPLESHIP

25 Now great multitudes accom-
panied him; and he turned and said
to them, 26"If any one comes to me
and does not hate his own father and
mother and wife and children and
brothers and sisters, yes, and even his
own life, he cannot be my disciple.*
27Whoever does not bear his own cross
and come after me, cannot be my dis-
ciple. 28For which of you, desiring to
build a tower, does not first sit down
and count the cost, whether he has
enough to complete it? 29Otherwise,
when he has laid a foundation, and is
not able to finish, all who see it be-
gin to mock him, 30saying, 'This man
began to build, and was not able to
finish.' 31Or what king, going to en-
counter another king in war, will
not sit down first and take counsel
whether he is able with ten thousand
to meet him who comes against him
with twenty thousand? 32And if not,

[a]Other ancient authorities read *a*

while the other is yet a great way off,
he sends an embassy and asks terms
of peace. 33So therefore, whoever of
you does not renounce all that he has
cannot be my disciple.

ABOUT SALT

34 "Salt is good; but if salt has
lost its taste, how shall its saltness
be restored? 35It is fit neither for the
land nor for the dunghill; men throw
it away. He who has ears to hear, let
him hear."

THE PARABLE OF THE LOST SHEEP

15 Now the tax collectors and sinners were all drawing near to
hear him. 2And the Pharisees and the
scribes murmured, saying, "This man
receives sinners and eats with them."

3 So he told them this parable:
4"What man of you, having a hundred
sheep, if he has lost one of them, does
not leave the ninety-nine in the wilderness, and go after the one which is
lost, until he finds it? 5And when he
has found it, he lays it on his shoulders, rejoicing. 6And when he comes
home, he calls together his friends
and his neighbors, saying to them,
'Rejoice with me, for I have found my
sheep which was lost.' 7Just so, I tell
you, there will be more joy in heaven
over one sinner who repents than over
ninety-nine righteous persons who
need no repentance.

THE PARABLE OF THE LOST COIN

8 "Or what woman, having ten silver coins,[a] if she loses one coin, does
not light a lamp and sweep the house
and seek diligently until she finds it?
9And when she has found it, she calls
together her friends and neighbors,
saying, 'Rejoice with me, for I have
found the coin which I had lost.' 10Just
so, I tell you, there is joy before the
angels of God over one sinner who
repents."

THE PARABLE OF THE PRODIGAL AND HIS BROTHER

11 And he said, "There was a man
who had two sons; 12and the younger
of them said to his father, 'Father,
give me the share of property that
falls to me.' And he divided his living
between them. 13Not many days later,
the younger son gathered all he had
and took his journey into a far country, and there he squandered his property in loose living. 14And when he had
spent everything, a great famine arose
in that country, and he began to be in
want. 15So he went and joined himself
to one of the citizens of that country,
who sent him into his fields to feed
swine. 16And he would gladly have fed
on[b] the pods that the swine ate; and
no one gave him anything. 17But when
he came to himself he said, 'How
many of my father's hired servants
have bread enough and to spare, but I
perish here with hunger! 18I will arise
and go to my father, and I will say to
him, "Father, I have sinned against
heaven and before you; 19I am no longer worthy to be called your son; treat
me as one of your hired servants."'
20And he arose and came to his father.
But while he was yet at a distance,
his father saw him and had compassion, and ran and embraced him and
kissed him. 21And the son said to him,
'Father, I have sinned against heaven
and before you; I am no longer worthy
to becalled your son.'[c] 22But the father
said b his servants, 'Bring quickly the
best obe, and put it on him; and put
a rin on his hand, and shoes on his
feet; 3and bring the fatted calf and
kill i and let us eat and make merry;
24for is my son was dead, and is alive
agai he was lost, and is found.' And
theygan to make merry.

2Now his elder son was in the
field nd as he came and drew near to
the use, he heard music and dancing. nd he called one of the servants

[a] The drachma, rendered here by *silver coin*, was aboulay's wage for a laborer
[b] Other ancient authorities read *filled his belly with*
[c] Other ancient authorities add *treat me as one of your l servants*

and asked what this meant. 27And he
said to him, 'Your brother has come,
and your father has killed the fatted
calf, because he has received him safe
and sound.' 28But he was angry and re-
fused to go in. His father came out and
entreated him, 29but he answered his
father, 'Lo, these many years I have
served you, and I never disobeyed
your command; yet you never gave me
a kid, that I might make merry with
my friends. 30But when this son of
yours came, who has devoured your
living with harlots, you killed for him
the fatted calf!' 31And he said to him,
'Son, you are always with me, and all
that is mine is yours. 32It was fitting to
make merry and be glad, for this your
brother was dead, and is alive; he was
lost, and is found.'"

THE PARABLE OF THE DISHONEST MANAGER

16 He also said to the disciples,
"There was a rich man who had
a steward, and charges were brought
to him that this man was wasting his
goods. 2And he called him and said to
him, 'What is this that I hear about
you? Turn in the account of your
stewardship, for you can no longer
be steward.' 3And the steward said
to himself, 'What shall I do, since my
master is taking the stewardship away
from me? I am not strong enough to
dig, and I am ashamed to beg. 4I have
decided what to do, so that people
may receive me into their houses
when I am put out of the stewardship.'
5So, summoning his master's debtors
one by one, he said to the first, 'How
much do *you owe my master?*' 6*He
said,* 'A hundred measures of oil.' And
he said to him, 'Take your bill, and sit
down quickly and write fifty.' 7Then
he said to another, 'And how much
do you owe?' He said, 'A hundred
measures of wheat.' He said to him,
'Take your bill, and write eighty.' 8The
master commended the dishonest
steward for his prudence; for the sons
of this world[d] are wiser in their own
generation than the sons of light.*
9And I tell you, make friends for your-
selves by means of unrighteous mam-
mon, so that when it fails they may re-
ceive you into the eternal habitations.

10 "He who is faithful in a very
little is faithful also in much; and
he who is dishonest in a very little is
dishonest also in much. 11If then you
have not been faithful in the unrigh-
teous mammon, who will entrust
to you the true riches? 12And if you
have not been faithful in that which
is another's, who will give you that
which is your own? 13No servant can
serve two masters; for either he will
hate the one and love the other, or he
will be devoted to the one and despise
the other. You cannot serve God and
mammon."

THE LAW AND THE KINGDOM OF GOD

14 The Pharisees, who were lov-
ers of money, heard all this, and they
scoffed at him. 15But he said to them,
"You are those who justify yourselves
before men, but God knows your
hearts; for what is exalted among men
is an abomination in the sight of God.

16 "The law and the prophets were
until John; since then the good news
of the kingdom of God is preached,
and every one enters it violently. 17But
it is easier for heaven and earth to
pass away, than for one dot of the law
to become void.

18 "Every one who divorces his
wife and marries another commits
adultery, and he who marries a wom-
an divorced from her husband com-
mits adultery.

THE RICH MAN AND LAZARUS

19 "There was a rich man, who
was clothed in purple and fine linen
and who feasted sumptuously every
day. 20And at his gate lay a poor man
named Laz´arus, full of sores, 21who
desired to be fed with what fell from
the rich man's table; moreover the
dogs came and licked his sores. 22The

[d]Greek *age*

poor man died and was carried by the angels to Abraham's bosom. The rich man also died and was buried; 23and in Hades, being in torment, he lifted up his eyes, and saw Abraham far off and Laz′arus in his bosom. 24And he called out, 'Father Abraham, have mercy upon me, and send Laz′arus to dip the end of his finger in water and cool my tongue; for I am in anguish in this flame.' 25But Abraham said, 'Son, remember that you in your lifetime received your good things, and Laz′arus in like manner evil things; but now he is comforted here, and you are in anguish. 26And besides all this, between us and you a great chasm has been fixed, in order that those who would pass from here to you may not be able, and none may cross from there to us.' 27And he said, 'Then I beg you, father, to send him to my father's house, 28for I have five brothers, so that he may warn them, lest they also come into this place of torment.' 29But Abraham said, 'They have Moses and the prophets; let them hear them.' 30And he said, 'No, father Abraham; but if some one goes to them from the dead, they will repent.' 31He said to him, 'If they do not hear Moses and the prophets, neither will they be convinced if some one should rise from the dead.'"

SOME SAYINGS OF JESUS

17 And he said to his disciples, "Temptations to sin[a] are sure to come; but woe to him by whom they come! 2It would be better for him if a millstone were hung round his neck and he were cast into the sea, than that he should cause one of these little ones to sin.[b] 3Take heed to yourselves; if your brother sins, rebuke him, and if he repents, forgive him; 4and if he sins against you seven times in the day, and turns to you seven times, and says, 'I repent,' you must forgive him."

5 The apostles said to the Lord, "Increase our faith!" 6And the Lord said, "If you had faith as a grain of mustard seed, you could say to this sycamine tree, 'Be rooted up, and be planted in the sea,' and it would obey you.

7 "Will any one of you, who has a servant plowing or keeping sheep, say to him when he has come in from the field, 'Come at once and sit down at table'? 8Will he not rather say to him, 'Prepare supper for me, and gird yourself and serve me, till I eat and drink; and afterward you shall eat and drink'? 9Does he thank the servant because he did what was commanded? 10So you also, when you have done all that is commanded you, say, 'We are unworthy servants; we have only done what was our duty.'"

JESUS CLEANSES TEN LEPERS

11 On the way to Jerusalem he was passing along between Samar′ia and Galilee. 12And as he entered a village, he was met by ten lepers, who stood at a distance 13and lifted up their voices and said, "Jesus, Master, have mercy on us." 14When he saw them he said to them, "Go and show yourselves to the priests." And as they went they were cleansed. 15Then one of them, when he saw that he was healed, turned back, praising God with a loud voice; 16and he fell on his face at Jesus' feet, giving him thanks. Now he was a Samaritan. 17Then said Jesus, "Were not ten cleansed? Where are the nine? 18Was no one found to return and give praise to God except this foreigner?" 19And he said to him, "Rise and go your way; your faith has made you well."

THE COMING OF THE KINGDOM

20 Being asked by the Pharisees when the kingdom of God was coming, he answered them, "The kingdom of God is not coming with signs to be observed;* 21nor will they say, 'Lo, here it is!' or 'There!' for behold,

[a]Greek *stumbling blocks*
[b]Greek *stumble*

the kingdom of God is in the midst of
you."[c]

22 And he said to the disciples,
"The days are coming when you will
desire to see one of the days of the
Son of man, and you will not see it.
23And they will say to you, 'Lo, there!'
or 'Lo, here!' Do not go, do not follow
them. 24For as the lightning flashes
and lights up the sky from one side to
the other, so will the Son of man be
in his day.[d] 25But first he must suffer
many things and be rejected by this
generation. 26As it was in the days of
Noah, so will it be in the days of the
Son of man. 27They ate, they drank,
they married, they were given in
marriage, until the day when Noah
entered the ark, and the flood came
and destroyed them all. 28Likewise as
it was in the days of Lot—they ate,
they drank, they bought, they sold,
they planted, they built, 29but on the
day when Lot went out from Sodom
fire and brimstone rained from heav-
en and destroyed them all 30so will it
be on the day when the Son of man is
revealed. 31On that day, let him who is
on the housetop, with his goods in the
house, not come down to take them
away; and likewise let him who is in
the field not turn back. 32Remember
Lot's wife. 33Whoever seeks to gain
his life will lose it, but whoever los-
es his life will preserve it. 34I tell you,
in that night there will be two men
in one bed; one will be taken and the
other left. 35There will be two women
grinding together; one will be taken
and the other left."[e] 37And they said to
him, "Where, Lord?" He said to them,
"Where the body is, there the eagles[f]
will be gathered together."

THE PARABLE OF THE WIDOW AND THE UNJUST JUDGE

18 And he told them a parable, to the
effect that they ought always to
pray and not lose heart. 2He said, "In
a certain city there was a judge who
neither feared God nor regarded man;
3and there was a widow in that city
who kept coming to him and saying,
'Vindicate me against my adversary.'
4For a while he refused; but afterward
he said to himself, 'Though I neither
fear God nor regard man, 5yet because
this widow bothers me, I will vindi-
cate her, or she will wear me out by
her continual coming.'" 6And the Lord
said, "Hear what the unrighteous
judge says. 7And will not God vindi-
cate his elect, who cry to him day and
night? Will he delay long over them?
8I tell you, he will vindicate them
speedily. Nevertheless, when the Son
of man comes, will he find faith on
earth?"

THE PARABLE OF THE PHARISEE AND THE TAX COLLECTOR

9 He also told this parable to some
who trusted in themselves that they
were righteous and despised others:
10"Two men went up into the temple
to pray, one a Pharisee and the other
a tax collector. 11The Pharisee stood
and prayed thus with himself, 'God,
I thank thee that I am not like other
men, extortioners, unjust, adulterers,
or even like this tax collector. 12I fast
twice a week, I give tithes of all that
I get.' 13But the tax collector, standing
far off, would not even lift up his eyes
to heaven, but beat his breast, saying,
'God, be merciful to me a sinner!' 14I
tell you, this man went down to his
house justified rather than the other;
for every one who exalts himself will
be humbled, but he who humbles him-
self will be exalted."

JESUS BLESSES LITTLE CHILDREN

15 Now they were bringing even
infants to him that he might touch
them; and when the disciples saw it,

[c] Or *within you*
[d] Other ancient authorities omit *in his day*
[e] Other ancient authorities add verse 36, *"Two men will be in the field; one will be taken and the other left"*
[f] Or *vultures*

they rebuked them. 16But Jesus called
them to him, saying, "Let the children
come to me, and do not hinder them;
for to such belongs the kingdom of
God. 17Truly, I say to you, whoever
does not receive the kingdom of God
like a child shall not enter it."

THE RICH RULER

18 And a ruler asked him, "Good
Teacher, what shall I do to inherit
eternal life?" 19And Jesus said to him,
"Why do you call me good? No one
is good but God alone. 20You know
the commandments: 'Do not commit
adultery, Do not kill, Do not steal, Do
not bear false witness, Honor your
father and mother.'" 21And he said,
"All these I have observed from my
youth." 22And when Jesus heard it, he
said to him, "One thing you still lack.
Sell all that you have and distribute to
the poor, and you will have treasure
in heaven; and come, follow me." 23But
when he heard this he became sad,
for he was very rich. 24Jesus looking
at him said, "How hard it is for those
who have riches to enter the kingdom
of God! 25For it is easier for a camel to
go through the eye of a needle than
for a rich man to enter the kingdom
of God." 26Those who heard it said,
"Then who can be saved?" 27But he
said, "What is impossible with men
is possible with God." 28And Peter
said, "Lo, we have left our homes and
followed you." 29And he said to them,
"Truly, I say to you, there is no man
who has left house or wife or brothers
or parents or children, for the sake of
the kingdom of God, 30who will not re-
ceive manifold more in this time, and
in the age to come eternal life."

A THIRD TIME JESUS FORETELLS HIS DEATH AND RESURRECTION

31 And taking the twelve, he said
to them, "Behold, we are going up
to Jerusalem, and everything that
is written of the Son of man by the
prophets will be accomplished. 32For
he will be delivered to the Gentiles,
and will be mocked and shameful-
ly treated and spit upon; 33they will
scourge him and kill him, and on the
third day he will rise." 34But they un-
derstood none of these things; this
saying was hid from them, and they
did not grasp what was said.

JESUS HEALS A BLIND BEGGAR NEAR JERICHO

35 As he drew near to Jericho, a
blind man was sitting by the roadside
begging; 36and hearing a multitude go-
ing by, he inquired what this meant.
37They told him, "Jesus of Nazareth
is passing by." 38And he cried, "Jesus,
Son of David, have mercy on me!"
39And those who were in front re-
buked him, telling him to be silent;
but he cried out all the more, "Son
of David, have mercy on me!" 40And
Jesus stopped, and commanded him
to be brought to him; and when he
came near, he asked him, 41"What do
you want me to do for you?" He said,
"Lord, let me receive my sight." 42And
Jesus said to him, "Receive your sight;
your faith has made you well." 43And
immediately he received his sight and
followed him, glorifying God; and all
the people, when they saw it, gave
praise to God.

JESUS AND ZACCHAEUS

19 He entered Jericho and was pass-
ing through. 2And there was a man
named Zacchae'us; he was a chief tax
collector, and rich. 3And he sought to
see who Jesus was, but could not, on
account of the crowd, because he was
small of stature. 4So he ran on ahead
and climbed up into a sycamore tree
to see him, for he was to pass that
way. 5And when Jesus came to the
place, he looked up and said to him,
"Zacchae'us, make haste and come
down; for I must stay at your house
today." 6So he made haste and came
down, and received him joyfully. 7And
when they saw it they all murmured,

"He has gone in to be the guest of a
man who is a sinner." 8And Zacchae´us
stood and said to the Lord, "Behold,
Lord, the half of my goods I give to
the poor; and if I have defrauded any
one of anything, I restore it fourfold."
9And Jesus said to him, "Today salva-
tion has come to this house, since he
also is a son of Abraham. 10For the Son
of man came to seek and to save the
lost."

THE PARABLE OF THE TEN POUNDS

11 As they heard these things, he
proceeded to tell a parable, because
he was near to Jerusalem, and because
they supposed that the kingdom of
God was to appear immediately. 12He
said therefore, "A nobleman went into
a far country to receive kingly power[a]
and then return. 13Calling ten of his
servants, he gave them ten pounds,[b]
and said to them, 'Trade with these
till I come.' 14But his citizens hated
him and sent an embassy after him,
saying, 'We do not want this man to
reign over us.' 15When he returned,
having received the kingly power,[c] he
commanded these servants, to whom
he had given the money, to be called
to him, that he might know what they
had gained by trading. 16The first
came before him, saying, 'Lord, your
pound has made ten pounds more.'
17And he said to him, 'Well done, good
servant! Because you have been faith-
ful in a very little, you shall have au-
thority over ten cities.' 18And the sec-
ond came, saying, 'Lord, your pound
has made five pounds.' 19And he said
to him, 'And you are to be over five
cities.' 20Then another came, saying,
'Lord, here is your pound, which I
kept laid away in a napkin; 21for I
was afraid of you, because you are
a severe man; you take up what you
did not lay down, and reap what you
did not sow.' 22He said to him, 'I will
condemn you out of your own mouth,
you wicked servant! You knew that
I was a severe man, taking up what
I did not lay down and reaping what I
did not sow? 23Why then did you not
put my money into the bank, and at
my coming I should have collected it
with interest?' 24And he said to those
who stood by, 'Take the pound from
him, and give it to him who has the
ten pounds.' 25(And they said to him,
'Lord, he has ten pounds!') 26'I tell
you, that to every one who has will
more be given; but from him who has
not, even what he has will be taken
away. 27But as for these enemies of
mine, who did not want me to reign
over them, bring them here and slay
them before me.'"

JESUS' TRIUMPHAL ENTRY INTO JERUSALEM

28 And when he had said this, he
went on ahead, going up to Jerusalem.
29When he drew near to Beth´phage
and Bethany, at the mount that is
called Olivet, he sent two of the dis-
ciples, 30saying, "Go into the village
opposite, where on entering you will
find a colt tied, on which no one has
ever yet sat; untie it and bring it here.
31If any one asks you, 'Why are you un-
tying it?' you shall say this, 'The Lord
has need of it.'" 32So those who were
sent went away and found it as he had
told them. 33And as they were unty-
ing the colt, its owners said to them,
"Why are you untying the colt?"
34And they said, "The Lord has need
of it." 35And they brought it to Jesus,
and throwing their garments on the
colt they set Jesus upon it. 36And as
he rode along, they spread their gar-
ments on the road. 37As he was now
drawing near, at the descent of the
Mount of Olives, the whole multitude
of the disciples began to rejoice and
praise God with a loud voice for all
the mighty works that they had seen,
38saying, "Blessed is the King who
comes in the name of the Lord! Peace

[a] Greek *a kingdom*
[b] The mina, rendered here by *pound*, was about three months' wages for a laborer
[c] Greek *a kingdom*

in heaven and glory in the highest!"
39And some of the Pharisees in the
multitude said to him, "Teacher, re-
buke your disciples." 40He answered,
"I tell you, if these were silent, the
very stones would cry out."

JESUS WEEPS OVER JERUSALEM

41 And when he drew near and
saw the city he wept over it, 42saying,
"Would that even today you knew the
things that make for peace! But now
they are hid from your eyes. 43For the
days shall come upon you, when your
enemies will cast up a bank about
you and surround you, and hem you
in on every side, 44and dash you to the
ground, you and your children with-
in you, and they will not leave one
stone upon another in you; because
you did not know the time of your
visitation."*

JESUS CLEANSES THE TEMPLE

45 And he entered the temple and
began to drive out those who sold,
46saying to them, "It is written, 'My
house shall be a house of prayer'; but
you have made it a den of robbers."

47 And he was teaching daily in
the temple. The chief priests and the
scribes and the principal men of the
people sought to destroy him; 48but
they did not find anything they could
do, for all the people hung upon his
words.

THE AUTHORITY OF JESUS QUESTIONED

20 One day, as he was teaching the
people in the temple and preach-
ing the gospel, the chief priests and
the scribes with the elders came up
2and said to him, "Tell us by what
authority you do these things, or
who it is that gave you this authori-
ty." 3He answered them, "I also will
ask you a question; now tell me, 4Was
the baptism of John from heaven or
from men?" 5And they discussed it
with one another, saying, "If we say,
'From heaven,' he will say, 'Why did
you not believe him?' 6But if we say,
'From men,' all the people will stone
us; for they are convinced that John
was a prophet." 7So they answered
that they did not know whence it was.
8And Jesus said to them, "Neither will
I tell you by what authority I do these
things."

THE PARABLE OF THE WICKED TENANTS

9 And he began to tell the people
this parable: "A man planted a vine-
yard, and let it out to tenants, and
went into another country for a long
while. 10When the time came, he sent
a servant to the tenants, that they
should give him some of the fruit of
the vineyard; but the tenants beat him,
and sent him away empty-handed.
11And he sent another servant; him
also they beat and treated shameful-
ly, and sent him away empty-handed.
12And he sent yet a third; this one
they wounded and cast out. 13Then
the owner of the vineyard said, 'What
shall I do? I will send my beloved son;
it may be they will respect him.' 14But
when the tenants saw him, they said
to themselves, 'This is the heir; let us
kill him, that the inheritance may be
ours.' 15And they cast him out of the
vineyard and killed him. What then
will the owner of the vineyard do to
them? 16He will come and destroy
those tenants, and give the vineyard
to others." When they heard this, they
said, "God forbid!" 17But he looked at
them and said, "What then is this that
is written:

'The very stone which the
builders rejected
has become the head of the
corner'?

18Every one who falls on that stone
will be broken to pieces; but when it
falls on any one it will crush him."

THE QUESTION ABOUT PAYING TAXES

19 The scribes and the chief priests
tried to lay hands on him at that very
hour, but they feared the people;
for they perceived that he had told
this parable against them. 20So they

watched him, and sent spies, who pre-
tended to be sincere, that they might
take hold of what he said, so as to de-
liver him up to the authority and juris-
diction of the governor. 21They asked
him, "Teacher, we know that you
speak and teach rightly, and show no
partiality, but truly teach the way of
God. 22Is it lawful for us to give tribute
to Caesar, or not?" 23But he perceived
their craftiness, and said to them,
24"Show me a coin.[a] Whose likeness
and inscription has it?" They said,
"Caesar's." 25He said to them, "Then
render to Caesar the things that are
Caesar's, and to God the things that
are God's." 26And they were not able
in the presence of the people to catch
him by what he said; but marveling at
his answer they were silent.

THE QUESTION ABOUT THE RESURRECTION

27 There came to him some
Sad´ducees, those who say that there
is no resurrection, 28and they asked
him a question, saying, "Teacher,
Moses wrote for us that if a man's
brother dies, having a wife but no
children, the man[b] must take the wife
and raise up children for his brother.
29Now there were seven brothers; the
first took a wife, and died without
children; 30and the second 31and the
third took her, and likewise all seven
left no children and died. 32Afterward
the woman also died. 33In the resur-
rection, therefore, whose wife will the
woman be? For the seven had her as
wife."

34 And Jesus said to them, "The
sons of this age marry and are giv-
en in marriage; 35but those who are
accounted worthy to attain to that
age and to the resurrection from the
dead neither marry nor are given in
marriage, 36for they cannot die any
more, because they are equal to an-
gels and are sons of God, being sons
of the resurrection. 37But that the
dead are raised, even Moses showed,
in the passage about the bush, where
he calls the Lord the God of Abraham
and the God of Isaac and the God of
Jacob.* 38Now he is not God of the
dead, but of the living; for all live to
him." 39And some of the scribes an-
swered, "Teacher, you have spoken
well." 40For they no longer dared to
ask him any question.

THE QUESTION ABOUT DAVID'S SON

41 But he said to them, "How can
they say that the Christ is David's
son? 42For David himself says in the
Book of Psalms,

'The Lord said to my Lord,
Sit at my right hand,
43till I make thy enemies a stool
for thy feet.'

44David thus calls him Lord; so
how is he his son?"

JESUS DENOUNCES THE SCRIBES

45 And in the hearing of all the peo-
ple he said to his disciples, 46"Beware
of the scribes, who like to go about
in long robes, and love salutations in
the market places and the best seats
in the synagogues and the places of
honor at feasts, 47who devour widows'
houses and for a pretense make long
prayers. They will receive the greater
condemnation."

THE WIDOW'S OFFERING

21 He looked up and saw the rich
putting their gifts into the trea-
sury; 2and he saw a poor widow put in
two copper coins. 3And he said, "Truly
I tell you, this poor widow has put in
more than all of them; 4for they all
contributed out of their abundance,
but she out of her poverty put in all
the living that she had."

THE DESTRUCTION OF THE TEMPLE FORETOLD

5 And as some spoke of the tem-
ple, how it was adorned with noble

[a] Greek *denarius*
[b] Greek *his brother*

stones and offerings, he said, 6"As
for these things which you see, the
days will come when there shall not
be left here one stone upon another
that will not be thrown down." 7And
they asked him, "Teacher, when will
this be, and what will be the sign
when this is about to take place?"
8And he said, "Take heed that you are
not led astray; for many will come in
my name, saying, 'I am he!' and, 'The
time is at hand!' Do not go after them.
9And when you hear of wars and tu-
mults, do not be terrified; for this
must first take place, but the end will
not be at once."

SIGNS AND PERSECUTIONS

10 Then he said to them, "Nation
will rise against nation, and king-
dom against kingdom; 11there will
be great earthquakes, and in various
places famines and pestilences; and
there will be terrors and great signs
from heaven. 12But before all this they
will lay their hands on you and per-
secute you, delivering you up to the
synagogues and prisons, and you will
be brought before kings and gover-
nors for my name's sake. 13This will
be a time for you to bear testimony.
14Settle it therefore in your minds, not
to meditate beforehand how to an-
swer; 15for I will give you a mouth and
wisdom, which none of your adversar-
ies will be able to withstand or con-
tradict. 16You will be delivered up even
by parents and brothers and kinsmen
and friends, and some of you they will
put to death; 17you will be hated by all
for my name's sake. 18But not a hair of
your head will perish. 19By your endur-
ance you will gain your lives.

THE DESTRUCTION OF JERUSALEM FORETOLD

20 "But when you see Jerusalem
surrounded by armies, then know
that its desolation has come near.
21Then let those who are in Judea flee
to the mountains, and let those who
are inside the city depart, and let not
those who are out in the country enter
it; 22for these are days of vengeance,
to fulfil all that is written. 23Alas for
those who are with child and for those
who give suck in those days! For great
distress shall be upon the earth and
wrath upon this people; 24they will
fall by the edge of the sword, and be
led captive among all nations; and
Jerusalem will be trodden down by
the Gentiles, until the times of the
Gentiles* are fulfilled.

THE COMING OF THE SON OF MAN

25 "And there will be signs in sun
and moon and stars, and upon the
earth distress of nations in perplex-
ity at the roaring of the sea and the
waves, 26men fainting with fear and
with foreboding of what is coming
on the world; for the powers of the
heavens will be shaken. 27And then
they will see the Son of man coming
in a cloud with power and great glory.
28Now when these things begin to take
place, look up and raise your heads,
because your redemption is drawing
near."

THE LESSON OF THE FIG TREE

29 And he told them a parable:
"Look at the fig tree, and all the
trees; 30as soon as they come out in
leaf, you see for yourselves and know
that the summer is already near. 31So
also, when you see these things taking
place, you know that the kingdom of
God is near. 32Truly, I say to you, this
generation will not pass away till all
has taken place. 33Heaven and earth
will pass away, but my words will not
pass away.

EXHORTATION TO WATCH

34 "But take heed to yourselves
lest your hearts be weighed down
with dissipation and drunkenness
and cares of this life, and that day
come upon you suddenly like a snare;
35for it will come upon all who dwell
upon the face of the whole earth. 36But

watch at all times, praying that you may have strength to escape all these things that will take place, and to stand before the Son of man."

37 And every day he was teaching in the temple, but at night he went out and lodged on the mount called Olivet. 38 And early in the morning all the people came to him in the temple to hear him.

THE PLOT TO KILL JESUS

22 Now the feast of Unleavened Bread drew near, which is called the Passover. 2 And the chief priests and the scribes were seeking how to put him to death; for they feared the people.

3 Then Satan entered into Judas called Iscariot, who was of the number of the twelve; 4 he went away and conferred with the chief priests and captains how he might betray him to them. 5 And they were glad, and engaged to give him money. 6 So he agreed, and sought an opportunity to betray him to them in the absence of the multitude.

THE PREPARATION OF THE PASSOVER

7 Then came the day of Unleavened Bread, on which the passover lamb had to be sacrificed. 8 So Jesus[a] sent Peter and John, saying, "Go and prepare the passover for us, that we may eat it." 9 They said to him, "Where will you have us prepare it?" 10 He said to them, "Behold, when you have entered the city, a man carrying a jar of water will meet you; follow him into *the house which he enters,* 11 and tell the householder, 'The Teacher says to you, Where is the guest room, where I am to eat the passover with my disciples?' 12 And he will show you a large upper room furnished; there make ready." 13 And they went, and found it as he had told them; and they prepared the passover.

THE INSTITUTION OF THE LORD'S SUPPER

14 And when the hour came, he sat at table, and the apostles with him. 15 And he said to them, "I have earnestly desired to eat this passover with you before I suffer; 16 for I tell you I shall not eat it[b] until it is fulfilled in the kingdom of God." 17 And he took a cup, and when he had given thanks he said, "Take this, and divide it among yourselves; 18 for I tell you that from now on I shall not drink of the fruit of the vine until the kingdom of God comes." 19 And he took bread, and when he had given thanks he broke it and gave it to them, saying, "This is my body which is given for you. Do this in remembrance of me." 20 And likewise the cup after supper, saying, "This cup which is poured out for you is the new covenant in my blood.[c] 21 But behold the hand of him who betrays me is with me on the table. 22 For the Son of man goes as it has been determined; but woe to that man by whom he is betrayed!" 23 And they began to question one another, which of them it was that would do this.

THE DISPUTE ABOUT GREATNESS

24 A dispute also arose among them, which of them was to be regarded as the greatest. 25 And he said to them, "The kings of the Gentiles exercise lordship over them; and those in authority over them are called benefactors. 26 But not so with you; rather let the greatest among you become as the youngest, and the leader as one who serves. 27 For which is the greater, one who sits at table, or one who serves? Is it not the one who sits at table? But I am among you as one who serves.

28 "You are those who have continued with me in my trials; 29 as my Father appointed a kingdom for me, so do I appoint for you 30 that you may eat and drink at my table in my kingdom,

[a] Greek *he*
[b] Other ancient authorities read *never eat it again*
[c] Other authorities omit *which is given for you. Do this in remebrance of me." 20 And likewise the cup after supper, saying, "This cup which is poured out for you is the new covenant in my blood.*

and sit on thrones judging the twelve
tribes of Israel.

JESUS PREDICTS PETER'S DENIAL

31 “Simon, Simon, behold, Satan
demanded to have you,[a] that he might
sift you[b] like wheat, 32but I have
prayed for you that your faith may not
fail; and when you have turned again,
strengthen your brethren.” 33And
he said to him, “Lord, I am ready to
go with you to prison and to death.”
34He said, “I tell you, Peter, the cock
will not crow this day, until you three
times deny that you know me.”

PURSE, BAG, AND SWORD

35 And he said to them, “When I
sent you out with no purse or bag or
sandals, did you lack anything?” They
said, “Nothing.” 36He said to them,
“But now, let him who has a purse
take it, and likewise a bag. And let
him who has no sword sell his mantle
and buy one. 37For I tell you that this
scripture must be fulfilled in me, ‘And
he was reckoned with transgressors’;
for what is written about me has its
fulfilment.” 38And they said, “Look,
Lord, here are two swords.” And he
said to them, “It is enough.”

JESUS PRAYS ON THE MOUNT OF OLIVES

39 And he came out, and went,
as was his custom, to the Mount of
Olives; and the disciples followed
him. 40And when he came to the place
he said to them, “Pray that you may
not enter into temptation.” 41And he
withdrew from them about a stone's
throw, and knelt down and prayed,
42“Father, if thou art willing, remove
this cup from me; nevertheless not my
will, but thine, be done.” 43And there
appeared to him an angel from heav-
en, strengthening him. 44And being
in an agony he prayed more earnest-
ly; and his sweat became like great
drops of blood falling down upon the
ground.[c] 45And when he rose from
prayer, he came to the disciples and
found them sleeping for sorrow, 46and
he said to them, “Why do you sleep?
Rise and pray that you may not enter
into temptation.”

THE BETRAYAL AND ARREST OF JESUS

47 While he was still speaking,
there came a crowd, and the man
called Judas, one of the twelve, was
leading them. He drew near to Jesus
to kiss him; 48but Jesus said to him,
“Judas, would you betray the Son of
man with a kiss?” 49And when those
who were about him saw what would
follow, they said, “Lord, shall we
strike with the sword?” 50And one
of them struck the slave of the high
priest and cut off his right ear. 51But
Jesus said, “No more of this!” And
he touched his ear and healed him.
52Then Jesus said to the chief priests
and captains of the temple and el-
ders, who had come out against him,*
“Have you come out as against a rob-
ber, with swords and clubs? 53When
I was with you day after day in the
temple, you did not lay hands on me.
But this is your hour, and the power
of darkness.”

PETER DENIES JESUS

54 Then they seized him and led
him away, bringing him into the high
priest's house. Peter followed at a dis-
tance; 55and when they had kindled a
fire in the middle of the courtyard and
sat down together, Peter sat among
them. 56Then a maid, seeing him as
he sat in the light and gazing at him,
said, “This man also was with him.”
57But he denied it, saying, “Woman, I
do not know him.” 58And a little lat-
er some one else saw him and said,
“You also are one of them.” But Peter
said, “Man, I am not.” 59And after an
interval of about an hour still anoth-
er insisted, saying, “Certainly this
man also was with him; for he is a

[a] The Greek word for *you* here is plural; in verse 32 it is singular
[b] The Greek word for *you* here is plural; in verse 32 it is singular
[c] Other ancient authorities omit verses 43 and 44

Galilean." 60But Peter said, "Man, I do
not know what you are saying." And
immediately, while he was still speak-
ing, the cock crowed. 61And the Lord
turned and looked at Peter. And Peter
remembered the word of the Lord,
how he had said to him, "Before the
cock crows today, you will deny me
three times." 62And he went out and
wept bitterly.

THE MOCKING AND BEATING OF JESUS

63 Now the men who were hold-
ing Jesus mocked him and beat him;
64they also blindfolded him and asked
him, "Prophesy! Who is it that struck
you?" 65And they spoke many other
words against him, reviling him.

JESUS BEFORE THE COUNCIL

66 When day came, the assembly of
the elders of the people gathered to-
gether, both chief priests and scribes;
and they led him away to their council,
and they said, 67"If you are the Christ,
tell us." But he said to them, "If I tell
you, you will not believe; 68and if I ask
you, you will not answer. 69But from
now on the Son of man shall be seat-
ed at the right hand of the power of
God." 70And they all said, "Are you
the Son of God, then?" And he said to
them, "You say that I am." 71And they
said, "What further testimony do we
need? We have heard it ourselves from
his own lips."

JESUS BEFORE PILATE

23 Then the whole compny of them
arose, and brought im before
Pilate. 2And they began to cuse him,
saying, "We found this m pervert-
ing our nation, and forbidng us to
give tribute to Caesar, and ving that
he himself is Christ a kir"* 3And
Pilate asked him, "Are youe King
of the Jews?" And he answd him,
"You have said so." 4And Pil said to
the chief priests and the mtudes,
"I find no crime in this m" 5But
they were urgent, saying, "He stirs
up the people, teaching throughout
all Judea, from Galilee even to this
place."

JESUS BEFORE HEROD

6 When Pilate heard this, he asked
whether the man was a Galilean. 7And
when he learned that he belonged
to Herod's jurisdiction, he sent him
over to Herod, who was himself in
Jerusalem at that time. 8When Herod
saw Jesus, he was very glad, for he had
long desired to see him, because he
had heard about him, and he was hop-
ing to see some sign done by him. 9So
he questioned him at some length; but
he made no answer. 10The chief priests
and the scribes stood by, vehemently
accusing him. 11And Herod with his
soldiers treated him with contempt
and mocked him; then, arraying him
in gorgeous apparel, he sent him back
to Pilate. 12And Herod and Pilate be-
came friends with each other that
very day, for before this they had been
at enmity with each other.

JESUS SENTENCED TO DEATH

13 Pilate then called together
the chief priests and the rulers and
the people, 14and said to them, "You
brought me this man as one who
was perverting the people; and after
examining him before you, behold, I
did not find this man guilty of any of
your charges against him;* 15neither
did Herod, for he sent him back to us.
Behold, nothing deserving death has
been done by him; 16I will therefore
chastise him and release him."[d]

18 But they all cried out together,
"Away with this man, and release to
us Barab´bas"; 19a man who had been
thrown into prison for an insurrection
started in the city, and for murder.
20Pilate addressed them once more,
desiring to release Jesus; 21but they
shouted out, "Crucify, crucify him!"
22A third time he said to them, "Why,

[d]Here, or after verse 19, other ant authorities add verse 17, *Now he was obliged to release one man to them at the festival*

what evil has he done? I have found
in him no crime deserving death; I
will therefore chastise him and re-
lease him." 23But they were urgent,
demanding with loud cries that he
should be crucified. And their voices
prevailed. 24So Pilate gave sentence
that their demand should be granted.
25He released the man who had been
thrown into prison for insurrection
and murder, whom they asked for; but
Jesus he delivered up to their will.

THE CRUCIFIXION OF JESUS

26 And as they led him away, they
seized one Simon of Cyre′ne, who
was coming in from the country, and
laid on him the cross, to carry it be-
hind Jesus. 27And there followed him
a great multitude of the people, and
of women who bewailed and lament-
ed him. 28But Jesus turning to them
said, "Daughters of Jerusalem, do
not weep for me, but weep for your-
selves and for your children. 29For be-
hold, the days are coming when they
will say, 'Blessed are the barren, and
the wombs that never bore, and the
breasts that never gave suck!' 30Then
they will begin to say to the moun-
tains, 'Fall on us'; and to the hills,
'Cover us.' 31For if they do this when
the wood is green, what will happen
when it is dry?"*

32 Two others also, who were crim-
inals, were led away to be put to death
with him. 33And when they came to
the place which is called The Skull,
there they crucified him, and the
criminals, one on the right and one
on the left. 34And Jesus said, "Father,
forgive them; for they know not what
they do."[a] And they cast lots to divide
his garments. 35And the people stood
by, watching; but the rulers scoffed at
him, saying, "He saved others; let him
save himself, if he is the Christ of God,
his Chosen One!" 36The soldiers also
mocked him, coming up and offering
him vinegar, 37and saying, "If you are
the King of the Jews, save yourself!"
38There was also an inscription over
him, [b] "This is the King of the Jews."

39 One of the criminals who were
hanged railed at him, saying, "Are you
not the Christ? Save yourself and us!"
40But the other rebuked him, saying,
"Do you not fear God, since you are
under the same sentence of condem-
nation? 41And we indeed justly; for we
are receiving the due reward of our
deeds; but this man has done nothing
wrong." 42And he said, "Jesus, remem-
ber me when you come in your kingly
power."[c] 43And he said to him, "Truly,
I say to you, today you will be with me
in Paradise."

THE DEATH OF JESUS

44 It was now about the sixth
hour, and there was darkness over
the whole land[d] until the ninth hour,
45while the sun's light failed;[e] and the
curtain of the temple was torn in two.
46Then Jesus, crying with a loud voice,
said, "Father, into thy hands I com-
mit my spirit!" And having said this
he breathed his last. 47Now when the
centurion saw what had taken place,
he praised God, and said, "Certainly
this man was innocent!" 48And all the
multitudes who assembled to see the
sight, when they saw what had taken
place, returned home beating their
breasts. 49And all his acquaintances
and the women who had followed him
from Galilee stood at a distance and
saw these things.

THE BURIAL OF JESUS

50 N w there was a man named
Joseph rom the Jewish town of
Arimat ́a. He was a member of the
counc a good and righteous man,
51who d not consented to their pur-
pose d deed, and he was looking

[a] Other ancient authorities omit the sentence *And Jesu what they do*
[b] Other ancient authorities add *in letters of Greek and L and Hebrew*
[c] Greek *kingdom*
[d] Or *earth*
[e] Or *the sun was eclipsed*. Other ancient authorities re *e sun was darkened*

for the kingdom of God. 52This man
went to Pilate and asked for the body
of Jesus. 53Then he took it down and
wrapped it in a linen shroud, and laid
him in a rock-hewn tomb, where no
one had ever yet been laid. 54It was the
day of Preparation, and the sabbath
was beginning.[f] 55The women who had
come with him from Galilee followed,
and saw the tomb, and how his body
was laid; 56then they returned, and
prepared spices and ointments. On
the sabbath they rested according to
the commandment.

THE RESURRECTION OF JESUS

24 But on the first day of the week,
at early dawn, they went to the
tomb, taking the spices which they
had prepared. 2And they found the
stone rolled away from the tomb,
3but when they went in they did not
find the body.[g] 4While they were
perplexed about this, behold, two
men stood by them in dazzling ap-
parel; 5and as they were frightened
and bowed their faces to the ground,
the men said to them, "Why do you
seek the living among the dead? He is
not here, but has risen.[h] 6Remember
how he told you, while he was still
in Galilee, 7that the Son of man must
be delivered into the hands of sinful
men, and be crucified, and on the
third day rise." 8And they remem-
bered his words, 9and returning from
the tomb they told all this to the elev-
en and to all the rest. 10Now it was
Mary Mag´dalene and Jo-an´na and
Mary the mother of James and the
other women with them who told
this to the apostles; 11but these words
seemed to them an idle tale, and they
did not believe them. 12But Peter rose
and ran to the tomb; stooping and
looking in, he saw the linen cloths by
themselves; and he went home won-
dering at what had happened.[i]

THE WALK TO EMMAUS

13 That very day two of them were
going to a village named Emma´us,
about seven miles[j] from Jerusalem,
14and talking with each other about
all these things that had happened.
15While they were talking and dis-
cussing together, Jesus himself drew
near and went with them. 16But their
eyes were kept from recognizing him.
17And he said to them, "What is this
conversation which you are holding
with each other as you walk?" And
they stood still, looking sad. 18Then
one of them, named Cle´opas, an-
swered him, "Are you the only visitor
to Jerusalem who does not know the
things that have happened there in
these days?" 19And he said to them,
"What things?" And they said to
him, "Concerning Jesus of Nazareth,
who was a prophet mighty in deed
and word before God and all the
people, 20and how our chief priests
and rulers delivered him up to be
condemned to death, and crucified
him. 21But we had hoped that he was
the one to redeem Israel. Yes, and
besides all this, it is now the third
day since this happened. 22Moreover,
some women of our company amazed
us. They were at the tomb early in
the morning 23and did not find his
body; and they came back saying that
they had even seen a vision of angels,
who said that he was alive. 24Some of
those who were with us went to the
tomb, and found it just as the women
had said; but him they did not see."
25And he said to them, "O foolish
men, and slow of heart to believe
all that the prophets have spoken!
26Was it not necessary that the Christ
should suffer these things and enter
into his glory?" 27And beginning with
Moses and all the prophets, he inter-
preted to them in all the scriptures
the things concerning himself.

[f] Greek *was dawning*
[g] Other ancient authorities add *of the Lord Jesus*
[h] Other ancient authorities omit *He is not here, but has risen*
[i] Other ancient authorities omit verse 12
[j] Greek *sixty stadia;* some ancient authorities read *a hundred and sixty stadia*

28 So they drew near to the vil-
lage to which they were going. He
appeared to be going further, 29but
they constrained him, saying, "Stay
with us, for it is toward evening and
the day is now far spent." So he went
in to stay with them. 30When he was
at table with them, he took the bread
and blessed, and broke it, and gave it
to them. 31And their eyes were opened
and they recognized him; and he van-
ished out of their sight. 32They said
to each other, "Did not our hearts
burn within us while he talked to us
on the road, while he opened to us
the scriptures?" 33And they rose that
same hour and returned to Jerusalem;
and they found the eleven gathered
together and those who were with
them, 34who said, "The Lord has risen
indeed, and has appeared to Simon!"
35Then they told what had happened
on the road, and how he was known
to them in the breaking of the bread.

JESUS APPEARS TO HIS DISCIPLES

36 As they were saying this, Jesus
himself stood among them, and said
to them, "Peace to you."[a] 37But they
were startled and frightened, and sup-
posed that they saw a spirit. 38And he
said to them, "Why are you troubled,
and why do questionings rise in your
hearts?* 39See my hands and my feet,
that it is I myself; handle me, and see;
for a spirit has not flesh and bones as
you see that I have." 40And when he
had said this, he showed them his
hands and his feet.[b] 41And while they
still disbelieved for joy, and wondered,
he said to them, "Have you anything
here to eat?" 42They gave him a piece
of broiled fish, 43and he took it and ate
before them.

44 Then he said to them, "These
are my words which I spoke to you,
while I was still with you, that ev-
erything written about me in the law
of Moses and the prophets and the
psalms must be fulfilled." 45Then he
opened their minds to understand the
scriptures, 46and said to them, "Thus
it is written, that the Christ should
suffer and on the third day rise from
the dead, 47and that repentance and
forgiveness of sins should be preached
in his name to all nations,[c] beginning
from Jerusalem. 48You are witnesses of
these things. 49And behold, I send the
promise of my Father upon you; but
stay in the city, until you are clothed
with power from on high.

THE ASCENSION OF JESUS

50 Then he led them out as far as
Bethany, and lifting up his hands he
blessed them. 51While he blessed them,
he parted from them and was carried
up into heaven.[d] 52And they worshiped
him, and[e] returned to Jerusalem with
great joy, 53and were continually in the
temple blessing God.

[a] Other ancient authorities omit *and said to them, "Peace to you."*
[b] Other ancient authorities omit verse 40
[c] Or *nations. Beginning from Jerusalem you are witnesses*
[d] Other ancient authorities omit *and was carried up into heaven*
[e] Other ancient authorities omit *worshiped him, and*

THE GOSPEL ACCORDING TO
JOHN

THE WORD BECAME FLESH

1 In the beginning was the Word, and
the Word was with God, and the
Word was God.* 2He was in the begin-
ning with God; 3all things were made
through him, and without him was not
anything made that was made. 4In him
was life,[a] and the life was the light of
men. 5The light shines in the darkness,*
and the darkness has not overcome it.

6 There was a man sent from God,
whose name was John. 7He came for
testimony, to bear witness to the
light, that all might believe through
him. 8He was not the light, but came
to bear witness to the light.

9 The true light that enlightens ev-
ery man was coming into the world.
10He was in the world, and the world
was made through him, yet the world
knew him not. 11He came to his own
home, and his own people received
him not. 12But to all who received him,
who believed in his name, he gave
power to become children of God;
13who were born, not of blood nor of
the will of the flesh nor of the will of
man, but of God.

14 And the Word became flesh and
dwelt among us, full of grace and truth;
we have beheld his glory, glory as of
the only Son from the Father. 15(John
bore witness to him, and cried, "This
was he of whom I said, 'He who comes
after me ranks before me, for he was
before me.'") 16And from his fulness
have we all received, grace upon grace.
17For the law was given through Moses;
grace and truth came through Jesus
Christ. 18No one has ever seen God; the
only Son,[b] who is in the bosom of the
Father, he has made him known.

THE TESTIMONY OF JON THE BAPTIST

19 And this is t testimony of
John, when the Jews ent priests and
Levites from Jerusalem to ask him,
"Who are you?" 20He confessed, he did
not deny, but confessed, "I am not the
Christ." 21And they asked him, "What
then? Are you Eli´jah?" He said, "I
am not.""Are you the prophet?" And
he answered, "No." 22They said to him
then, "Who are you? Let us have an
answer for those who sent us. What
do you say about yourself?" 23He said,
"I am the voice of one crying in the
wilderness, 'Make straight the way of
the Lord,' as the prophet Isaiah said."

24 Now they had been sent from
the Pharisees. 25They asked him,
"Then why are you baptizing, if you
are neither the Christ, nor Eli´jah,
nor the prophet?" 26John answered
them, "I baptize with water; but
among you stands one whom you do
not know, 27even he who comes after
me, the thong of whose sandal I am
not worthy to untie." 28This took place
in Bethany beyond the Jordan, where
John was baptizing.

THE LAMB OF GOD

29 The next day he saw Jesus com-
ing toward him, and said, "Behold,
the Lamb of God, who takes away the
sin of the world!* 30This is he of whom
I said, 'After me comes a man who
ranks before me, for he was before
me.' 31I myself did not know him; but
for this I came baptizing with water,
that he might be revealed to Israel."
32And John bore witness, "I saw the
Spirit descend as a dove from heaven,
and it remained on him. 33I myself did
not know him; but he who sent me to
baptize with water said to me, 'He on
whom you see the Spirit descend and
remain, this is he who baptizes with
the Holy Spirit.' 34And I have seen and
have borne witness that this is the
Son of God."

[a] Or *was not anything madThat which has been made was life in him*
[b] Other ancient authoritiread *God*

THE FIRST DISCIPLES OF JESUS

35 The next day again John was
standing with two of his disciples;
36 and he looked at Jesus as he walked,
and said, "Behold, the Lamb of God!"
37 The two disciples heard him say
this, and they followed Jesus. 38 Jesus
turned, and saw them following, and
said to them, "What do you seek?"
And they said to him, "Rabbi" (which
means Teacher), "where are you stay-
ing?" 39 He said to them, "Come and
see." They came and saw where he
was staying; and they stayed with him
that day, for it was about the tenth
hour. 40 One of the two who heard John
speak, and followed him, was Andrew,
Simon Peter's brother. 41 He first found
his brother Simon, and said to him,
"We have found the Messiah" (which
means Christ). 42 He brought him to
Jesus. Jesus looked at him, and said,
"So you are Simon the son of John?
You shall be called Cephas" (which
means Peter[a]).

JESUS CALLS PHILIP AND NATHANAEL

43 The next day Jesus decided to
go to Galilee. And he found Philip
and said to him, "Follow me." 44 Now
Philip was from Beth-sa´ida, the city
of Andrew and Peter. 45 Philip found
Nathan´a-el, and said to him, "We
have found him of whom Moses in
the law and also the prophets wrote,
Jesus of Nazareth, the son of Joseph."
46 Nathan´a-el said to him, "Can any-
thing good come out of Nazareth?"
Philip said to him, "Come and see."
47 Jesus saw Nathan´a-el coming to
him, and said of him, "Behold, an
Israelite indeed, in whom is no guile!"
48 Nathan´a-el said to him, "How do
you know me?" Jesus answered him,
"Before Philip called you, when you
were under the fig tree, I saw you."
49 Nathan´a-el answered him, "Rabbi,
you are the Son of God! You are the
King of Israel!" 50 Jesus answered him,
"Because I said to you, I saw you under
the fig tree, do you believe? You shall
see greater things than these." 51 And
he said to him, "Truly, truly, I say to
you, you will see heaven opened, and
the angels of God ascending and de-
scending upon the Son of man."

THE WEDDING AT CANA

2 On the third day there was a mar-
riage at Cana in Galilee, and the
mother of Jesus was there; 2 Jesus also
was invited to the marriage, with his
disciples. 3 When the wine failed, the
mother of Jesus said to him, "They
have no wine." 4 And Jesus said to
her, "O woman, what have you to do
with me?* My hour has not yet come."
5 His mother said to the servants,
"Do whatever he tells you." 6 Now six
stone jars were standing there, for the
Jewish rites of purification, each hold-
ing twenty or thirty gallons. 7 Jesus
said to them, "Fill the jars with wa-
ter." And they filled them up to the
brim. 8 He said to them, "Now draw
some out, and take it to the steward
of the feast." So they took it. 9 When
the steward of the feast tasted the
water now become wine, and did not
know where it came from (though the
servants who had drawn the water
knew), the steward of the feast called
the bridegroom 10 and said to him,
"Every man serves the good wine
first; and when men have drunk free-
ly, then the poor wine; but you have
kept the good wine until now." 11 This,
the first of his signs, Jesus did at Cana
in Galilee, and manifested his glory;
and his disciples believed in him.

12 After this he went down to
Caper´na-um, with his mother and his
brethren* and his disciples; and there
they stayed for a few days.

JESUS CLEANSES THE TEMPLE

13 The Passover of the Jews was at
hand, and Jesus went up to Jerusalem.
14 In the temple he found those who
were selling oxen and sheep and pi-
geons, and the money-changers at
their business. And making a whip

[a] From the word for *rock* in Aramaic and Greek, respectively

of cords, he drove them all, with the
sheep and oxen, out of the temple;
and he poured out the coins of the
money-changers and overturned their
tables. 16And he told those who sold
the pigeons, "Take these things away;
you shall not make my Father's house
a house of trade." 17His disciples re-
membered that it was written, "Zeal
for thy house will consume me." 18The
Jews then said to him, "What sign
have you to show us for doing this?"
19Jesus answered them, "Destroy this
temple, and in three days I will raise it
up." 20The Jews then said, "It has tak-
en forty-six years to build this temple,
and will you raise it up in three days?"
21But he spoke of the temple of his
body. 22When therefore he was raised
from the dead, his disciples remem-
bered that he had said this; and they
believed the scripture and the word
which Jesus had spoken.

23 Now when he was in Jerusalem
at the Passover feast, many believed
in his name when they saw the signs
which he did; 24but Jesus did not trust
himself to them, 25because he knew all
men and needed no one to bear wit-
ness of man; for he himself knew what
was in man.

NICODEMUS VISITS JESUS

3 Now there was a man of the
Pharisees, named Nicode´mus, a
ruler of the Jews. 2This man came
to Jesus[b] by night and said to him,
"Rabbi, we know that you are a teach-
er come from God; for no one can do
these signs that you do, unless God
is with him." 3Jesus answered him,
"Truly, truly, I say to you, unless one
is born anew,[c] he cannot see the king-
dom of God." 4Nicode´mus said to
him, "How can a man be born when
he is old? Can he enter a second time
into his mother's womb and be born?"
5Jesus answered, "Truly, truly, I say to
you, unless one is born of water and
the Spirit, he cannot enter the king-
dom of God. 6That which is born of
the flesh is flesh, and that which is
born of the Spirit is spirit.[d] 7Do not
marvel that I said to you, 'You must
be born anew.'[e] 8The wind[f] blows
where it wills, and you hear the sound
of it, but you do not know whence it
comes or whither it goes; so it is with
every one who is born of the Spirit."
9Nicode´mus said to him, "How can
this be?" 10Jesus answered him, "Are
you a teacher of Israel, and yet you
do not understand this? 11Truly, tru-
ly, I say to you, we speak of what we
know, and bear witness to what we
have seen; but you do not receive our
testimony. 12If I have told you earth-
ly things and you do not believe, how
can you believe if I tell you heavenly
things? 13No one has ascended into
heaven but he who descended from
heaven, the Son of man.[g] 14And as
Moses lifted up the serpent in the wil-
derness, so must the Son of man be
lifted up, 15that whoever believes in
him may have eternal life."[h]

16 For God so loved the world that
he gave his only Son, that whoever
believes in him should not perish but
have eternal life. 17For God sent the
Son into the world, not to condemn
the world, but that the world might be
saved through him. 18He who believes
in him is not condemned; he who does
not believe is condemned already, be-
cause he has not believed in the name
of the only Son of God. 19And this is
the judgment, that the light has come
into the world, and men loved dark-
ness rather than light, because their
deeds were evil. 20For every one who
does evil hates the light, and does
not come to the light, lest his deeds
should be exposed. 21But he who does

[b] Greek *him*
[c] Or *from above*
[d] The same Greek word means both *wind* and *spirit*
[e] Or *from above*
[f] The same Greek word means both *wind* and *spirit*
[g] Other ancient authorities add *who is in heaven*
[h] Some interpreters hold that the quotation continues through verse 21

what is true comes to the light, that it may be clearly seen that his deeds have been wrought in God.

JESUS AND JOHN THE BAPTIST

22 After this Jesus and his disciples went into the land of Judea; there he remained with them and baptized.* 23John also was baptizing at Ae´non near Salim, because there was much water there; and people came and were baptized. 24For John had not yet been put in prison.*

25 Now a discussion arose between John's disciples and a Jew over purifying. 26And they came to John, and said to him, "Rabbi, he who was with you beyond the Jordan, to whom you bore witness, here he is, baptizing, and all are going to him." 27John answered, "No one can receive anything except what is given him from heaven. 28You yourselves bear me witness, that I said, I am not the Christ, but I have been sent before him. 29He who has the bride is the bridegroom; the friend of the bridegroom, who stands and hears him, rejoices greatly at the bridegroom's voice; therefore this joy of mine is now full. 30He must increase, but I must decrease."[a]

THE ONE WHO COMES FROM HEAVEN

31 He who comes from above is above all; he who is of the earth belongs to the earth, and of the earth he speaks; he who comes from heaven is above all. 32He bears witness to what he has seen and heard, yet no one receives his testimony; 33he who receives his testimony sets his seal to this, that God is true. 34For he whom God has sent utters the words of God, for it is not by measure that he gives *the Spirit;* 35the Father loves the Son, and has given all things into his hand. 36He who believes in the Son has eternal life; he who does not obey the Son shall not see life, but the wrath of God rests upon him.

JESUS AND THE WOMAN OF SAMARIA

4 Now when the Lord knew that the Pharisees had heard that Jesus was making and baptizing more disciples than John 2(although Jesus himself did not baptize, but only his disciples), 3he left Judea and departed again to Galilee. 4He had to pass through Samar´ia. 5So he came to a city of Samar´ia, called Sy´char, near the field that Jacob gave to his son Joseph. 6Jacob's well was there, and so Jesus, wearied as he was with his journey, sat down beside the well. It was about the sixth hour.

7 There came a woman of Samar´ia to draw water. Jesus said to her, "Give me a drink." 8For his disciples had gone away into the city to buy food. 9The Samaritan woman said to him, "How is it that you, a Jew, ask a drink of me, a woman of Samar´ia?" For Jews have no dealings with Samaritans. 10Jesus answered her, "If you knew the gift of God, and who it is that is saying to you, 'Give me a drink,' you would have asked him, and he would have given you living water." 11The woman said to him, "Sir, you have nothing to draw with, and the well is deep; where do you get that living water? 12Are you greater than our father Jacob, who gave us the well, and drank from it himself, and his sons, and his cattle?" 13Jesus said to her, "Every one who drinks of this water will thirst again, 14but whoever drinks of the water that I shall give him will never thirst; the water that I shall give him will become in him a spring of water welling up to eternal life." 15The woman said to him, "Sir, give me this water, that I may not thirst, nor come here to draw."

16 Jesus said to her, "Go, call your husband, and come here." 17The woman answered him, "I have no husband." Jesus said to her, "You are right in saying, 'I have no husband'; 18for you have had five husbands, and he whom you now have is not your

[a] Some interpreters hold that the quotation continues through verse 36

husband; this you said truly." 19The
woman said to him, "Sir, I perceive
that you are a prophet. 20Our fathers
worshiped on this mountain;* and
you say that in Jerusalem is the place
where men ought to worship." 21Jesus
said to her, "Woman, believe me, the
hour is coming when neither on this
mountain nor in Jerusalem will you
worship the Father. 22You worship
what you do not know; we worship
what we know, for salvation is from
the Jews. 23But the hour is coming, and
now is, when the true worshipers will
worship the Father in spirit and truth,
for such the Father seeks to worship
him. 24God is spirit, and those who
worship him must worship in spirit
and truth." 25The woman said to him,
"I know that Messiah is coming (he
who is called Christ); when he comes,
he will show us all things." 26Jesus
said to her, "I who speak to you am
he."

27 Just then his disciples came.
They marveled that he was talking
with a woman, but none said, "What
do you wish?" or, "Why are you
talking with her?" 28So the woman left
her water jar, and went away into the
city, and said to the people, 29"Come,
see a man who told me all that I ever
did. Can this be the Christ?" 30They
went out of the city and were coming
to him.

31 Meanwhile the disciples be-
sought him, saying, "Rabbi, eat." 32But
he said to them, "I have food to eat of
which you do not know." 33So the dis-
ciples said to one another, "Has any
one brought him food?" 34Jesus said
to them, "My food is :o do the will of
him who sent me, ard to accomplish
his work. 35Do you nc say, 'There are
yet four months, theicomes the har-
vest'? I tell you, lift u your eyes, and
see how the fields a: already white
for harvest. 36He wh reaps receives
wages, and gathers iit for eternal
life, so that sower anreaper may re-
joice together. 37For :re the saying
holds true, 'One so and another
reaps.' 38I sent you to reap that for
which you did not labor; others have
labored, and you have entered into
their labor."

39 Many Samaritans from that city
believed in him because of the wom-
an's testimony, "He told me all that I
ever did." 40So when the Samaritans
came to him, they asked him to stay
with them; and he stayed there two
days. 41And many more believed be-
cause of his word. 42They said to the
woman, "It is no longer because of
your words that we believe, for we
have heard for ourselves, and we
know that this is indeed the Savior of
the world."

JESUS RETURNS TO GALILEE

43 After the two days he departed
to Galilee. 44For Jesus himself testified
that a prophet has no honor in his own
country. 45So when he came to Galilee,
the Galileans welcomed him, having
seen all that he had done in Jerusalem
at the feast, for they too had gone to
the feast.

JESUS HEALS AN OFFICIAL'S SON

46 So he came again to Cana in
Galilee, where he had made the water
wine. And at Caper´na-um there was
an official whose son was ill. 47When
he heard that Jesus had come from
Judea to Galilee, he went and begged
him to come down and heal his son,
for he was at the point of death. 48Jesus
therefore said to him, "Unless you see
signs and wonders you will not be-
lieve." 49The official said to him, "Sir,
come down before my child dies."
50Jesus said to him, "Go; your son will
live." The man believed the word that
Jesus spoke to him and went his way.
51As he was going down, his servants
met him and told him that his son was
living. 52So he asked them the hour
when he began to mend, and they
said to him, "Yesterday at the seventh
hour the fever left him." 53The father
knew that was the hour when Jesus
had said to him, "Your son will live";

and he himself believed, and all his
household. 54This was now the second
sign that Jesus did when he had come
from Judea to Galilee.

JESUS HEALS ON THE SABBATH

5 After this there was a feast of
the Jews, and Jesus went up to
Jerusalem.
2 Now there is in Jerusalem by the
Sheep Gate a pool, in Hebrew called
Beth-za´tha,[a] which has five porti-
coes. 3In these lay a multitude of in-
valids, blind, lame, paralyzed.[b] 5One
man was there, who had been ill for
thirty-eight years. 6When Jesus saw
him and knew that he had been lying
there a long time, he said to him, "Do
you want to be healed?" 7The sick man
answered him, "Sir, I have no man to
put me into the pool when the water
is troubled, and while I am going an-
other steps down before me." 8Jesus
said to him, "Rise, take up your pal-
let, and walk." 9And at once the man
was healed, and he took up his pallet
and walked. Now that day was the
sabbath. 10So the Jews said to the man
who was cured, "It is the sabbath,
it is not lawful for you to carry your
pallet." 11But he answered them, "The
man who healed me said to me, 'Take
up your pallet, and walk.'" 12They
asked him, "Who is the man who
said to you, 'Take up your pallet, and
walk'?" 13Now the man who had been
healed did not know who it was, for
Jesus had withdrawn, as there was a
crowd in the place. 14Afterward, Jesus
found him in the temple, and said to
him, "See, you are well! Sin no more,
that nothing worse befall you." 15The
man went away and told the Jews
that it was Jesus who had healed him.
16And this was why the Jews persecut-
ed Jesus, because he did this on the
sabbath. 17But Jesus answered them,
"My Father is working still, and I am
working." 18This was why the Jews
sought all the more to kill him, be-
cause he not only broke the sabbath*
but also called God his Father, making
himself equal with God.

THE AUTHORITY OF THE SON

19 Jesus said to them, "Truly, truly,
I say to you, the Son can do nothing
of his own accord, but only what he
sees the Father doing; for whatever he
does, that the Son does likewise. 20For
the Father loves the Son, and shows
him all that he himself is doing; and
greater works than these will he show
him, that you may marvel. 21For as the
Father raises the dead and gives them
life, so also the Son gives life to whom
he will. 22The Father judges no one,
but has given all judgment to the Son,
23that all may honor the Son, even as
they honor the Father. He who does
not honor the Son does not honor the
Father who sent him. 24Truly, truly, I
say to you, he who hears my word and
believes him who sent me, has eternal
life; he does not come into judgment,
but has passed from death to life.
25 "Truly, truly, I say to you, the
hour is coming, and now is, when the
dead will hear the voice of the Son of
God, and those who hear will live.
26For as the Father has life in himself,
so he has granted the Son also to have
life in himself, 27and has given him au-
thority to execute judgment, because
he is the Son of man. 28Do not marvel
at this; for the hour is coming when
all who are in the tombs will hear
his voice 29and come forth, those who
have done good, to the resurrection of
life, and those who have done evil, to
the resurrection of judgment.

WITNESES TO JESUS

30 "I can do nothing on my own
authority; as I hear, I judge; and my
judgment is just, because I seek not
my own will but the will of him who
sent me. 31If I bear witness to myself,

[a] Other ancient authorities read *Bethesda*, others *Bethsaida*
[b] Other ancient authorities insert, wholly or in part, *waiting for the moving of the water; 4for an angel of the Lord went down at certain seasons into the pool, and troubled the water: whoever stepped in first after the troubling of the water was healed of whatever disease he had*

my testimony is not true; 32there is
another who bears witness to me,
and I know that the testimony which
he bears to me is true. 33You sent to
John, and he has borne witness to
the truth. 34Not that the testimony
which I receive is from man; but I say
this that you may be saved. 35He was
a burning and shining lamp, and you
were willing to rejoice for a while in
his light. 36But the testimony which I
have is greater than that of John; for
the works which the Father has grant-
ed me to accomplish, these very works
which I am doing, bear me witness
that the Father has sent me. 37And the
Father who sent me has himself borne
witness to me. His voice you have
never heard, his form you have never
seen; 38and you do not have his word
abiding in you, for you do not believe
him whom he has sent. 39You search
the scriptures, because you think that
in them you have eternal life; and it
is they that bear witness to me; 40yet
you refuse to come to me that you may
have life. 41I do not receive glory from
men. 42But I know that you have not
the love of God within you. 43I have
come in my Father's name, and you
do not receive me; if another comes in
his own name, him you will receive.
44How can you believe, who receive
glory from one another and do not
seek the glory that comes from the
only God? 45Do not think that I shall
accuse you to the Father; it is Moses
who accuses you, on whom you set
your hope. 46If you believed Moses,
you would believe me, for he wrote
of me. 47But if you do not believe his
writings, how will you believe my
words?"

FEEDING THE FIVE THOUSAND

6 After this Jesus went to the other
side of the Sea of Galilee, which is
the Sea of Tibe´ri-as. 2And a multitude
followed him, because they saw the
signs which he did on those who were
diseased. 3Jesus went up into the hills,
and there sat down with his disciples.
4Now the Passover, the feast of the
Jews, was at hand. 5Lifting up his eyes,
then, and seeing that a multitude was
coming to him, Jesus said to Philip,
"How are we to buy bread, so that
these people may eat?" 6This he said
to test him, for he himself knew what
he would do. 7Philip answered him,
"Two hundred denarii[c] would not buy
enough bread for each of them to get a
little." 8One of his disciples, Andrew,
Simon Peter's brother, said to him,
9"There is a lad here who has five bar-
ley loaves and two fish; but what are
they among so many?" 10Jesus said,
"Make the people sit down." Now
there was much grass in the place; so
the men sat down, in number about
five thousand. 11Jesus then took the
loaves, and when he had given thanks,
he distributed them to those who
were seated; so also the fish, as much
as they wanted. 12And when they had
eaten their fill, he told his disciples,
"Gather up the fragments left over,
that nothing may be lost." 13So they
gathered them up and filled twelve
baskets with fragments from the five
barley loaves, left by those who had
eaten. 14When the people saw the sign
which he had done, they said, "This
is indeed the prophet who is to come
into the world!"

15 Perceiving then that they were
about to come and take him by force
to make him king, Jesus withdrew
again to the hills by himself.

JESUS WALKS ON THE WATER

16 When evening came, his disci-
ples went down to the sea, 17got into
a boat, and started across the sea
to Caper´na-um. It was now dark,
and Jesus had not yet come to them.
18The sea rose because a strong wind
was blowing. 19When they had rowed
about three or four miles,[d] they saw
Jesus walking on the sea and drawing

[c] The denarius was a day's wage for a laborer
[d] Greek *twenty-five or thirty stadia*

near to the boat. They were fright-
ened, 20but he said to them, "It is I; do
not be afraid." 21Then they were glad
to take him into the boat, and imme-
diately the boat was at the land to
which they were going.

THE BREAD FROM HEAVEN

22 On the next day the people
who remained on the other side of
the sea saw that there had been only
one boat there, and that Jesus had
not entered the boat with his disci-
ples, but that his disciples had gone
away alone. 23However, boats from
Tibe´ri-as came near the place where
they ate the bread after the Lord had
given thanks. 24So when the people
saw that Jesus was not there, nor his
disciples, they themselves got into
the boats and went to Caper´na-um,
seeking Jesus.

25 When they found him on the
other side of the sea, they said to him,
"Rabbi, when did you come here?"
26Jesus answered them, "Truly, truly,
I say to you, you seek me, not because
you saw signs, but because you ate
your fill of the loaves. 27Do not labor
for the food which perishes, but for
the food which endures to eternal life,
which the Son of man will give to you;
for on him has God the Father set his
seal." 28Then they said to him, "What
must we do, to be doing the works of
God?" 29Jesus answered them, "This
is the work of God, that you believe
in him whom he has sent." 30So they
said to him, "Then what sign do you
do, that we may see, and believe you?
What work do you perform? 31Our fa-
thers ate the manna in the wilderness;
as it is written, 'He gave them bread
from heaven to eat.'" 32Jesus then said
to them, "Truly, truly, I say to you,
it was not Moses who gave you the
bread from heaven; my Father gives
you the true bread from heaven. 33For
the bread of God is that which comes
down from heaven, and gives life to
the world." 34They said to him, "Lord,
give us this bread always."

35 Jesus said to them, "I am the
bread of life; he who comes to me shall
not hunger, and he who believes in me
shall never thirst. 36But I said to you
that you have seen me and yet do not
believe. 37All that the Father gives me
will come to me; and him who comes
to me I will not cast out. 38For I have
come down from heaven, not to do my
own will, but the will of him who sent
me; 39and this is the will of him who
sent me, that I should lose nothing of
all that he has given me, but raise it
up at the last day. 40For this is the will
of my Father, that every one who sees
the Son and believes in him should
have eternal life; and I will raise him
up at the last day."

41 The Jews then murmured at
him, because he said, "I am the bread
which came down from heaven."
42They said, "Is not this Jesus, the son
of Joseph, whose father and mother we
know? How does he now say, 'I have
come down from heaven'?" 43Jesus an-
swered them, "Do not murmur among
yourselves. 44No one can come to me
unless the Father who sent me draws
him; and I will raise him up at the
last day. 45It is written in the proph-
ets, 'And they shall all be taught by
God.' Every one who has heard and
learned from the Father comes to me.
46Not that any one has seen the Father
except him who is from God; he has
seen the Father. 47Truly, truly, I say to
you, he who believes has eternal life.
48I am the bread of life. 49Your fathers
ate the manna in the wilderness, and
they died. 50This is the bread which
comes down from heaven, that a man
may eat of it and not die. 51I am the
living bread* which came down from
heaven; if any one eats of this bread,
he will live for ever; and the bread
which I shall give for the life of the
world is my flesh."

52 The Jews then disputed among
themselves, saying, "How can this
man give us his flesh to eat?"* 53So
Jesus said to them, "Truly, truly, I say
to you, unless you eat the flesh of the

Son of man and drink his blood, you
have no life in you; 54he who eats my
flesh and drinks my blood has eternal
life, and I will raise him up at the last
day. 55For my flesh is food indeed, and
my blood is drink indeed. 56He who
eats my flesh and drinks my blood
abides in me, and I in him. 57As the liv-
ing Father sent me, and I live because
of the Father, so he who eats me will
live because of me. 58This is the bread
which came down from heaven, not
such as the fathers ate and died; he
who eats this bread will live for ever."
59This he said in the synagogue, as he
taught at Caper´na-um.

THE WORDS OF ETERNAL LIFE

60 Many of his disciples, when they
heard it, said, "This is a hard saying;
who can listen to it?" 61But Jesus,
knowing in himself that his disciples
murmured at it, said to them, "Do
you take offense at this? 62Then what
if you were to see the Son of man as-
cending where he was before?* 63It is
the spirit that gives life, the flesh is of
no avail; the words that I have spoken
to you are spirit and life. 64But there
are some of you that do not believe."
For Jesus knew from the first who
those were that did not believe, and
who it was that should betray him.
65And he said, "This is why I told you
that no one can come to me unless it is
granted him by the Father."

66 After this many of his disciples
drew back and no longer went about
with him. 67Jesus said to the twelve,
"Will you also go away?" 68Simon
Peter answered him, "Lord, to whom
shall we go? You have the words of
eternal life; 69and we have believed,
and have come to know, that you are
the Holy One of God." 70Jesus an-
swered them, "Did I not choose you,
the twelve, and one of you is a devil?"
71He spoke of Judas the son of Simon
Iscariot, for he, one of the twelve, was
to betray him.

THE UNBELIEF OF JESUS' BRETHREN

7 After this Jesus went about in
Galilee; he would not go about
in Judea, because the Jews[a] sought
to kill him. 2Now the Jews' feast of
Tabernacles was at hand. 3So his
brethren* said to him, "Leave here
and go to Judea, that your disciples
may see the works you are doing. 4For
no man works in secret if he seeks
to be known openly. If you do these
things, show yourself to the world."
5For even his brethren did not believe
in him. 6Jesus said to them, "My time
has not yet come, but your time is
always here. 7The world cannot hate
you, but it hates me because I testify
of it that its works are evil. 8Go to the
feast yourselves; I am not[b] going up
to this feast, for my time has not yet
fully come." 9So saying, he remained
in Galilee.

JESUS AT THE FESTIVAL OF BOOTHS

10 But after his brethren had gone
up to the feast, then he also went up,
not publicly but in private. 11The Jews
were looking for him at the feast,
and saying, "Where is he?" 12And
there was much muttering about him
among the people. While some said,
"He is a good man," others said, "No,
he is leading the people astray." 13Yet
for fear of the Jews no one spoke
openly of him.

14 About the middle of the feast
Jesus went up into the temple and
taught. 15The Jews marveled at it,
saying, "How is it that this man has
learning,[c] when he has never stud-
ied?" 16So Jesus answered them, "My
teaching is not mine, but his who sent
me; 17if any man's will is to do his will,
he shall know whether the teaching
is from God or whether I am speak-
ing on my own authority. 18He who
speaks on his own authority seeks his
own glory; but he who seeks the glory
of him who sent him is true, and in
him there is no falsehood. 19Did not

[a] Or *Judeans*
[b] Other ancient authorities add *yet*
[c] Or *this man knows his letters*

Moses give you the law? Yet none of you keeps the law. Why do you seek to kill me?" 20The people answered, "You have a demon! Who is seeking to kill you?" 21Jesus answered them, "I did one deed, and you all marvel at it. 22Moses gave you circumcision (not that it is from Moses, but from the fathers), and you circumcise a man upon the sabbath. 23If on the sabbath a man receives circumcision, so that the law of Moses may not be broken, are you angry with me because on the sabbath I made a man's whole body well? 24Do not judge by appearances, but judge with right judgment."

IS THIS THE CHRIST?

25 Some of the people of Jerusalem therefore said, "Is not this the man whom they seek to kill? 26And here he is, speaking openly, and they say nothing to him! Can it be that the authorities really know that this is the Christ? 27Yet we know where this man comes from; and when the Christ appears, no one will know where he comes from." 28So Jesus proclaimed, as he taught in the temple, "You know me, and you know where I come from? But I have not come of my own accord; he who sent me is true, and him you do not know. 29I know him, for I come from him, and he sent me." 30So they sought to arrest him; but no one laid hands on him, because his hour had not yet come. 31Yet many of the people believed in him; they said, "When the Christ appears, will he do more signs than this man has done?"

OFFICERS ARE SENT TO ARREST JESUS

32 The Pharisees heard the crowd thus muttering about him, and the chief priests and Pharisees sent officers to arrest him. 33Jesus then said, "I shall be with you a little longer, and then I go to him who sent me; 34you will seek me and you will not find me; where I am you cannot come." 35The Jews said to one another, "Where does this man intend to go that we shall not find him? Does he intend to go to the Dispersion among the Greeks and teach the Greeks? 36What does he mean by saying, 'You will seek me and you will not find me,' and, 'Where I am you cannot come'?"

RIVERS OF LIVING WATER

37 On the last day of the feast, the great day, Jesus stood up and proclaimed, "If any one thirst, let him come to me and drink. 38He who believes in me, as[a] the scripture has said, 'Out of his heart shall flow rivers of living water.'" 39Now this he said about the Spirit, which those who believed in him were to receive; for as yet the Spirit had not been given, because Jesus was not yet glorified.

DIVISION AMONG THE PEOPLE

40 When they heard these words, some of the people said, "This is really the prophet." 41Others said, "This is the Christ." But some said, "Is the Christ to come from Galilee? 42Has not the scripture said that the Christ is descended from David, and comes from Bethlehem, the village where David was?" 43So there was a division among the people over him. 44Some of them wanted to arrest him, but no one laid hands on him.

THE UNBELIEF OF THOSE IN AUTHORITY

45 The officers then went back to the chief priests and Pharisees, who said to them, "Why did you not bring him?" 46The officers answered, "No man ever spoke like this man!" 47The Pharisees answered them, "Are you led astray, you also? 48Have any of the authorities or of the Pharisees believed in him? 49But this crowd, who do not know the law, are accursed." 50Nicode′mus, who had gone to him before, and who was one of them, said to them, 51"Does our law judge a man without first giving him a hearing and learning what he does?" 52They replied, "Are you from

[a] Or *let him come to me, and let him who believes in me drink. As*

Galilee too? Search and you will see
that no prophet is to rise from Galilee."
53They went each to his own house,
8 but Jesus went to the Mount of
Olives. 2Early in the morning he
came again to the temple; all the peo-
ple came to him, and he sat down and
taught them. 3The scribes and the
Pharisees brought a woman who had
been caught in adultery, and placing
her in the midst 4they said to him,
"Teacher, this woman has been caught
in the act of adultery. 5Now in the law
Moses commanded us to stone such.
What do you say about her?" 6This
they said to test him, that they might
have some charge to bring against
him. Jesus bent down and wrote with
his finger on the ground. 7And as they
continued to ask him, he stood up and
said to them, "Let him who is without
sin among you be the first to throw a
stone at her." 8And once more he bent
down and wrote with his finger on
the ground. 9But when they heard it,
they went away, one by one, beginning
with the eldest, and Jesus was left
alone with the woman standing be-
fore him. 10Jesus looked up and said to
her, "Woman, where are they? Has no
one condemned you?" 11She said, "No
one, Lord." And Jesus said, "Neither
do I condemn you; go, and do not sin
again."[b]*

JESUS THE LIGHT OF THE WORLD

12 Again Jesus spoke to them, say-
ing, "I am the light of the world; he
who follows me will not walk in dark-
ness, but will have the light of life."
13The Pharisees then said to him,
"You are bearing witness to yourself;
your testimony is not true." 14Jesus
answered, "Even if I do bear witness
to myself, my testimony is true, for I
know whence I have come and whith-
er I am going, but you do not know
whence I come or whither I am going.
15You judge according to the flesh, I
judge no one. 16Yet even if I do judge,
my judgment is true, for it is not I
alone that judge, but I and he[c] who
sent me. 17In your law it is written that
the testimony of two men is true; 18I
bear witness to myself, and the Father
who sent me bears witness to me."
19They said to him therefore, "Where
is your Father?" Jesus answered, "You
know neither me nor my Father; if you
knew me, you would know my Father
also." 20These words he spoke in the
treasury, as he taught in the temple;
but no one arrested him, because his
hour had not yet come.

JESUS FORETELLS HIS DEATH

21 Again he said to them, "I go
away, and you will seek me and die in
your sin;* where I am going, you can-
not come." 22Then said the Jews, "Will
he kill himself, since he says, 'Where
I am going, you cannot come'?" 23He
said to them, "You are from below, I
am from above; you are of this world,
I am not of this world. 24I told you that
you would die in your sins, for you will
die in your sins unless you believe that
I am he." 25They said to him, "Who are
you?" Jesus said to them, "Even what
I have told you from the beginning.[d]
26I have much to say about you and
much to judge; but he who sent me is
true, and I declare to the world what I
have heard from him." 27They did not
understand that he spoke to them of
the Father. 28So Jesus said, "When you
have lifted up the Son of man, then
you will know that I am he, and that
I do nothing on my own authority but
speak thus as the Father taught me.
29And he who sent me is with me; he
has not left me alone, for I always do
what is pleasing to him." 30As he spoke
thus, many believed in him.

TRUE DISCIPLES

31 Jesus then said to the Jews who
had believed in him, "If you continue

[b] Some ancient authorities insert 7.53—8.11 either at the end of this gospel or after Luke 21.38, with variations of text. Others omit it altogether.
[c] Other ancient authorities read *the Father*
[d] Or *Why do I talk to you at all?*

in my word, you are truly my disciples,
32and you will know the truth, and
the truth will make you free." 33They
answered him, "We are descendants
of Abraham, and have never been in
bondage to any one. How is it that you
say, 'You will be made free'?"

34 Jesus answered them, "Truly,
truly, I say to you, every one who com-
mits sin is a slave to sin. 35The slave
does not continue in the house for
ever; the son continues for ever. 36So
if the Son makes you free, you will
be free indeed. 37I know that you are
descendants of Abraham; yet you seek
to kill me, because my word finds no
place in you. 38I speak of what I have
seen with my Father, and you do what
you have heard from your father."

JESUS AND ABRAHAM

39 They answered him, "Abraham
is our father." Jesus said to them, "If
you were Abraham's children, you
would do what Abraham did, 40but
now you seek to kill me, a man who
has told you the truth which I heard
from God; this is not what Abraham
did. 41You do what your father did."
They said to him, "We were not born
of fornication; we have one Father,
even God."* 42Jesus said to them, "If
God were your Father, you would
love me, for I proceeded and came
forth from God; I came not of my
own accord, but he sent me. 43Why do
you not understand what I say? It is
because you cannot bear to hear my
word. 44You are of your father the dev-
il, and your will is to do your father's
desires. He was a murderer from the
beginning, and has nothing to do with
the truth, because there is no truth in
him. When he lies, he speaks accord-
ing to his own nature, for he is a liar
and the father of lies. 45But, because I
tell the truth, you do not believe me.
46Which of you convicts me of sin? If
I tell the truth, why do you not be-
lieve me? 47He who is of God hears the
words of God; the reason why you do
not hear them is that you are not of
God."

48 The Jews answered him, "Are
we not right in saying that you are a
Samaritan and have a demon?" 49Jesus
answered, "I have not a demon; but
I honor my Father, and you dishonor
me. 50Yet I do not seek my own glo-
ry; there is One who seeks it and he
will be the judge. 51Truly, truly, I say
to you, if any one keeps my word,
he will never see death." 52The Jews
said to him, "Now we know that you
have a demon. Abraham died, as did
the prophets; and you say, 'If any one
keeps my word, he will never taste
death.' 53Are you greater than our
father Abraham, who died? And the
prophets died! Who do you claim to
be?" 54Jesus answered, "If I glorify
myself, my glory is nothing; it is my
Father who glorifies me, of whom you
say that he is your God. 55But you have
not known him; I know him. If I said, I
do not know him, I should be a liar like
you; but I do know him and I keep his
word. 56Your father Abraham rejoiced
that he was to see my day; he saw it*
and was glad." 57The Jews then said to
him, "You are not yet fifty years old,
and have you seen Abraham?"[a] 58Jesus
said to them, "Truly, truly, I say to
you, before Abraham was, I am."* 59So
they took up stones to throw at him;
but Jesus hid himself, and went out of
the temple.

A MAN BORN BLIND RECEIVES SIGHT

9 As he passed by, he saw a man blind
from his birth. 2And his disciples
asked him, "Rabbi, who sinned, this
man or his parents, that he was born
blind?" 3Jesus answered, "It was not
that this man sinned, or his parents,
but that the works of God might be
made manifest in him.* 4We must
work the works of him who sent me,
while it is day; night comes, when no
one can work. 5As long as I am in the
world, I am the light of the world."
6As he said this, he spat on the ground

[a] Other ancient authorities read *has Abraham seen you?*

and made clay of the spittle and
anointed the man's eyes with the clay,
7 saying to him, "Go, wash in the pool
of Silo´am" (which means Sent). So he
went and washed and came back see-
ing. 8 The neighbors and those who had
seen him before as a beggar, said, "Is
not this the man who used to sit and
beg?" 9 Some said, "It is he"; others
said, "No, but he is like him." He said,
"I am the man." 10 They said to him,
"Then how were your eyes opened?"
11 He answered, "The man called Jesus
made clay and anointed my eyes and
said to me, 'Go to Silo´am and wash';
so I went and washed and received my
sight." 12 They said to him, "Where is
he?" He said, "I do not know."

THE PHARISEES INVESTIGATE THE HEALING

13 They brought to the Pharisees
the man who had formerly been blind.
14 Now it was a sabbath day when Jesus
made the clay and opened his eyes.
15 The Pharisees again asked him how
he had received his sight. And he said
to them, "He put clay on my eyes,
and I washed, and I see." 16 Some of
the Pharisees said, "This man is not
from God, for he does not keep the
sabbath." But others said, "How can
a man who is a sinner do such signs?"
There was a division among them.
17 So they again said to the blind man,
"What do you say about him, since he
has opened your eyes?" He said, "He
is a prophet."

18 The Jews did not believe that he
had been blind and had received his
sight, until they called the parents of
the man who had received his sight,
19 *and asked them, "Is this your son,*
who you say was born blind? How
then does he now see?" 20 His parents
answered, "We know that this is our
son, and that he was born blind; 21 but
how he now sees we do not know, nor
do we know who opened his eyes.
Ask him; he is of age, he will speak
for himself." 22 His parents said this
because they feared the Jews, for the
Jews had already agreed that if any
one should confess him to be Christ,
he was to be put out of the synagogue.
23 Therefore his parents said, "He is of
age, ask him."

24 So for the second time they
called the man who had been blind,
and said to him, "Give God the praise;
we know that this man is a sinner."
25 He answered, "Whether he is a sin-
ner, I do not know; one thing I know,
that though I was blind, now I see."
26 They said to him, "What did he do
to you? How did he open your eyes?"
27 He answered them, "I have told you
already, and you would not listen.
Why do you want to hear it again? Do
you too want to become his disciples?"
28 And they reviled him, saying, "You
are his disciple, but we are disciples of
Moses. 29 We know that God has spo-
ken to Moses, but as for this man, we
do not know where he comes from."
30 The man answered, "Why, this is a
marvel! You do not know where he
comes from, and yet he opened my
eyes. 31 We know that God does not lis-
ten to sinners, but if any one is a wor-
shiper of God and does his will, God
listens to him. 32 Never since the world
began has it been heard that any one
opened the eyes of a man born blind.
33 If this man were not from God, he
could do nothing." 34 They answered
him, "You were born in utter sin, and
would you teach us?" And they cast
him out.

SPIRITUAL BLINDNESS

35 Jesus heard that they had cast
him out, and having found him he
said, "Do you believe in the Son of
man?"[b] 36 He answered, "And who is
he, sir, that I may believe in him?"
37 Jesus said to him, "You have seen
him, and it is he who speaks to you."
38 He said, "Lord, I believe"; and he
worshiped him. 39 Jesus said, "For
judgment I came into this world,
that those who do not see may see,
and that those who see may become

[b] Other ancient authorities read *the Son of God*

blind." 40 Some of the Pharisees near
him heard this, and they said to him,
"Are we also blind?" 41 Jesus said to
them, "If you were blind, you would
have no guilt; but now that you say,
'We see,' your guilt remains.

JESUS THE GOOD SHEPHERD

10 "Truly, truly, I say to you, he who
does not enter the sheepfold by
the door but climbs in by another
way, that man is a thief and a rob-
ber; 2 but he who enters by the door
is the shepherd of the sheep. 3 To him
the gatekeeper opens; the sheep hear
his voice, and he calls his own sheep
by name and leads them out. 4 When
he has brought out all his own, he
goes before them, and the sheep fol-
low him, for they know his voice. 5 A
stranger they will not follow, but they
will flee from him, for they do not
know the voice of strangers." 6 This
figure Jesus used with them, but they
did not understand what he was say-
ing to them.

7 So Jesus again said to them,
"Truly, truly, I say to you, I am the
door of the sheep. 8 All who came be-
fore me are thieves and robbers; but
the sheep did not heed them. 9 I am the
door; if any one enters by me, he will
be saved, and will go in and out and
find pasture. 10 The thief comes only to
steal and kill and destroy; I came that
they may have life, and have it abun-
dantly. 11 I am the good shepherd. The
good shepherd lays down his life for
the sheep. 12 He who is a hireling and
not a shepherd, whose own the sheep
are not, sees the wolf coming and
leaves the sheep and flees; and the
wolf snatches them and scatters them.
13 He flees because he is a hireling and
cares nothing for the sheep. 14 I am
the good shepherd;* I know my own
and my own know me, 15 *as the Father*
knows me and I know the Father; and
I lay down my life for the sheep. 16 And
I have other sheep, that are not of this
fold; I must bring them also, and they
will heed my voice. So there shall be
one flock, one shepherd. 17 For this
reason the Father loves me, because
I lay down my life, that I may take it
again. 18 No one takes it from me, but
I lay it down of my own accord. I have
power to lay it down, and I have pow-
er to take it again; this charge I have
received from my Father."*

19 There was again a division
among the Jews because of these
words. 20 Many of them said, "He has
a demon, and he is mad; why listen
to him?" 21 Others said, "These are
not the sayings of one who has a de-
mon. Can a demon open the eyes of
the blind?"

JESUS IS REJECTED BY THE JEWS

22 It was the feast of the Dedication
at Jerusalem; 23 it was winter, and
Jesus was walking in the temple, in
the portico of Solomon. 24 So the Jews
gathered round him and said to him,
"How long will you keep us in sus-
pense? If you are the Christ, tell us
plainly." 25 Jesus answered them, "I
told you, and you do not believe. The
works that I do in my Father's name,
they bear witness to me; 26 but you do
not believe, because you do not belong
to my sheep 27 My sheep hear my voice,
and I know them, and they follow me;
28 and I give them eternal life, and they
shall never perish, and no one shall
snatch them out of my hand. 29 My
Father, who has given them to me,[a] is
greater than all, and no one is able to
snatch them out of the Father's hand.
30 I and the Father are one."

31 The Jews took up stones again
to stone him. 32 Jesus answered them,
"I have shown you many good works
from the Father; for which of these do
you stone me?" 33 The Jews answered
him, "We stone you for no good work
but for blasphemy; because you, being
a man, make yourself God." 34 Jesus
answered them, "Is it not written in
your law, 'I said, you are gods'? 35 If he
called them gods to whom the word

[a] Other ancient authorities read *What my Father has given to me*

of God came (and scripture cannot be
broken), 36do you say of him whom the
Father consecrated and sent into the
world, 'You are blaspheming,' because
I said, 'I am the Son of God'? 37If I am
not doing the works of my Father,
then do not believe me; 38but if I do
them, even though you do not believe
me, believe the works, that you may
know and understand that the Father
is in me and I am in the Father."
39Again they tried to arrest him, but
he escaped from their hands.

40 He went away again across the
Jordan to the place where John at
first baptized, and there he remained.
41And many came to him; and they
said, "John did no sign, but every-
thing that John said about this man
was true." 42And many believed in
him there.

THE DEATH OF LAZARUS

11 Now a certain man was ill,
Laz'arus of Bethany, the village of
Mary and her sister Martha. 2It was
Mary who anointed the Lord with
ointment and wiped his feet with her
hair, whose brother Laz'arus was ill.
3So the sisters sent to him, saying,
"Lord, he whom you love is ill." 4But
when Jesus heard it he said, "This ill-
ness is not unto death; it is fc the glo-
ry of God, so that the Son ofGod may
be glorified by means of it."

5 Now Jesus loved Marth and her
sister and Laz'arus. 6So whene heard
that he was ill, he stayed twdays lon-
ger* in the place where he ws. 7Then
after this he said to the discles, "Let
us go into Judea again." 8Thdisciples
said to him, "Rabbi, the Jewvere but
now seeking to stone you, a are you
going there again?" 9Jesus swered,
"Are there not twelve hot in the
day? If any one walks in t day, he
does not stumble, because bees the
light of this world. 10But any one
walks in the night, he stules, be-
cause the light is not in hi' 11Thus
he spoke, and then he said to them,
"Our friend Laz'arus has fallen asleep,
but I go to awake him out of sleep."
12The disciples said to him, "Lord, if
he has fallen asleep, he will recover."
13Now Jesus had spoken of his death,
but they thought that he meant taking
rest in sleep. 14Then Jesus told them
plainly, "Laz'arus is dead; 15and for
your sake I am glad that I was not
there, so that you may believe. But let
us go to him." 16Thomas, called the
Twin, said to his fellow disciples, "Let
us also go, that we may die with him."

JESUS THE RESURRECTION AND THE LIFE

17 Now when Jesus came, he found
that Laz'arus[b] had already been in the
tomb four days. 18Bethany was near
Jerusalem, about two miles[c] off, 19and
many of the Jews had come to Martha
and Mary to console them concerning
their brother. 20When Martha heard
that Jesus was coming, she went and
met him, while Mary sat in the house.
21Martha said to Jesus, "Lord, if you
had been here, my brother would not
have died. 22And even now I know that
whatever you ask from God, God will
give you." 23Jesus said to her, "Your
brother will rise again." 24Martha said
to him, "I know that he will rise again
in the resurrection at the last day."
25Jesus said to her, "I am the resurrec-
tion and the life;[d] he who believes in
me, though he die, yet shall he live,
26and whoever lives and believes in
me shall never die. Do you believe
this?" 27She said to him, "Yes, Lord;
I believe that you are the Christ, the
Son of God, he who is coming into the
world."

JESUS WEEPS

28 When she had said this, she
went and called her sister Mary, say-
ing quietly, "The Teacher is here and
is calling for you." 29And when she
heard it, she rose quickly and went to
him. 30Now Jesus had not yet come to

[b] Greek *he*
[c] Greek *fifteen stadia*
[d] Other ancient authorities omit *the life*

the village, but was still in the place
where Martha had met him. 31When
the Jews who were with her in the
house, consoling her, saw Mary rise
quickly and go out, they followed
her, supposing that she was going to
the tomb to weep there. 32Then Mary,
when she came where Jesus was and
saw him, fell at his feet, saying to him,
"Lord, if you had been here, my broth-
er would not have died." 33When Jesus
saw her weeping, and the Jews who
came with her also weeping, he was
deeply moved in spirit and troubled;
34and he said, "Where have you laid
him?" They said to him, "Lord, come
and see." 35Jesus wept. 36So the Jews
said, "See how he loved him!" 37But
some of them said, "Could not he who
opened the eyes of the blind man have
kept this man from dying?"

JESUS RAISES LAZARUS TO LIFE

38 Then Jesus, deeply moved again,
came to the tomb; it was a cave, and a
stone lay upon it. 39Jesus said, "Take
away the stone." Martha, the sister of
the dead man, said to him, "Lord, by
this time there will be an odor, for he
has been dead four days." 40Jesus said
to her, "Did I not tell you that if you
would believe you would see the glo-
ry of God?" 41So they took away the
stone. And Jesus lifted up his eyes and
said, "Father, I thank thee that thou
hast heard me. 42I knew that thou
hearest me always, but I have said this
on account of the people standing by,
that they may believe that thou didst
send me." 43When he had said this,
he cried with a loud voice, "Laz´arus,
come out." 44The dead man came out,
his hands and feet bound with ban-
dages, and his face wrapped with a
cloth. Jesus said to them, "Unbind
him, and let him go."

THE PLOT TO KILL JESUS

45 Many of the Jews therefore, who
had come with Mary and had seen
what he did, believed in him; 46but
some of them went to the Pharisees
and told them what Jesus had done.
47So the chief priests and the Pharisees
gathered the council, and said, "What
are we to do? For this man performs
many signs. 48If we let him go on thus,
every one will believe in him, and the
Romans will come and destroy both
our holy place[a] and our nation." 49But
one of them, Ca´iaphas, who was high
priest that year, said to them, "You
know nothing at all; 50you do not un-
derstand that it is expedient for you
that one man should die for the peo-
ple, and that the whole nation should
not perish."* 51He did not say this of
his own accord, but being high priest
that year he prophesied that Jesus
should die for the nation, 52and not for
the nation only, but to gather into one
the children of God who are scattered
abroad. 53So from that day on they
took counsel how to put him to death.

54 Jesus therefore no longer went
about openly among the Jews, but
went from there to the country near
the wilderness, to a town called
E´phraim; and there he stayed with
the disciples.

55 Now the Passover of the Jews
was at hand, and many went up from
the country to Jerusalem before the
Passover, to purify themselves. 56They
were looking for Jesus and saying to
one another as they stood in the tem-
ple, "What do you think? That he will
not come to the feast?" 57Now the chief
priests and the Pharisees had given
orders that if any one knew where he
was, he should let them know, so that
they might arrest him.

MARY ANOINTS JESUS

12 *Six days before the Passover,
Jesus came to Bethany, where
Laz´arus was, whom Jesus had raised
from the dead. 2There they made him
a supper; Martha served, and Laz´arus
was one of those at table with him.
3Mary took a pound of costly ointment
of pure nard and anointed the feet of

[a]Greek *our place*

this my Father is glorified, that you
bear much fruit, and so prove to be my
disciples. 9As the Father has loved me,
so have I loved you; abide in my love.
10If you keep my commandments, you
will abide in my love, just as I have
kept my Father's commandments and
abide in his love. 11These things I have
spoken to you, that my joy may be in
you, and that your joy may be full.

12 "This is my commandment, that
you love one another as I have loved
you. 13Greater love has no man than
this, that a man lay down his life for
his friends. 14You are my friends if you
do what I command you. 15No longer
do I call you servants,[b] for the servant[c]
does not know what his master is do-
ing; but I have called you friends, for
all that I have heard from my Father
I have made known to you. 16You did
not choose me, but I chose you and
appointed you that you should go and
bear fruit and that your fruit should
abide; so that whatever you ask the
Father in my name, he may give it to
you. 17This I command you, to love one
another.

THE WORLD'S HATRED

18 "If the world hates you, know
that it has hated me before it hated
you.* 19If you were of the world, the
world would love its own; but be-
cause you are not of the world, but I
chose you out of the world, therefore
the world hates you. 20Remember the
word that I said to you, 'A servant[d] is
not greater than his master.' If they
persecuted me, they will persecute
you; if they kept my word, they will
keep yours also. 21But all this they will
do to you on my account, because they
do not know him who sent me. 22If I
had not come and spoken to them,
they would not have sin; but now they
have no excuse for their sin. 23He who
hates me hates my Father also. 24If I
had not done among them the works
which no one else did, they would not
have sin; but now they have seen and
hated both me and my Father. 25It is to
fulfil the word that is written in their
law, 'They hated me without a cause.'
26But when the Counselor comes,
whom I shall send to you from the
Father, even the Spirit of truth, who
proceeds from the Father, he will bear
witness to me; 27and you also are wit-
nesses, because you have been with
me from the beginning.

16 "I have said all this to you to keep
you from falling away. 2They will
put you out of the synagogues; in-
deed, the hour is coming when who-
ever kills you will think he is offer-
ing service to God. 3And they will do
this because they have not known the
Father, nor me. 4But I have said these
things to you, that when their hour
comes you may remember that I told
you of them.

THE WORK OF THE SPIRIT

"I did not say these things to you
from the beginning, because I was
with you. 5But now I am going to him
who sent me; yet none of you asks me,
'Where are you going?' 6But because I
have said these things to you, sorrow
has filled your hearts. 7Nevertheless I
tell you the truth: it is to your advan-
tage that I go away, for if I do not go
away, the Counselor will not come to
you; but if I go, I will send him to you.
8And when he comes, he will convince
the world of sin and of righteousness
and of judgment: 9of sin, because they
do not believe in me; 10of righteous-
ness, because I go to the Father, and
you will see me no more;* 11of judg-
ment, because the ruler of this world
is judged.

12 "I have yet many things to say to
you, but you cannot bear them now.
13When the Spirit of truth comes, he
will guide you into all the truth; for he
will not speak on his own authority,
but whatever he hears he will speak,
and he will declare to you the things

[b] Or *slaves*
[c] Or *slave*
[d] Or *slave*

that are to come. 14He will glorify me,
for he will take what is mine and de-
clare it to you. 15All that the Father
has is mine; therefore I said that he
will take what is mine and declare it
to you.

SORROW WILL TURN INTO JOY

16 "A little while, and you will see
me no more; again a little while, and
you will see me." 17Some of his disci-
ples said to one another, "What is this
that he says to us, 'A little while, and
you will not see me, and again a lit-
tle while, and you will see me'; and,
'because I go to the Father'?" 18They
said, "What does he mean by 'a lit-
tle while'? We do not know what he
means." 19Jesus knew that they wanted
to ask him; so he said to them, "Is this
what you are asking yourselves, what
I meant by saying, 'A little while, and
you will not see me, and again a little
while, and you will see me'? 20Truly,
truly, I say to you, you will weep and
lament, but the world will rejoice; you
will be sorrowful, but your sorrow
will turn into joy. 21When a woman
is in travail she has sorrow, because
her hour has come; but when she is
delivered of the child, she no longer
remembers the anguish, for joy that a
child[a] is born into the world. 22So you
have sorrow now, but I will see you
again and your hearts will rejoice, and
no one will take your joy from you.
23In that day you will ask nothing of
me. Truly, truly, I say to you, if you
ask anything of the Father, he will
give it to you in my name. 24Hitherto
you have asked nothing in my name;
ask, and you will receive, that your joy
may be full.

PEACE FOR THE DISCIPLES

25 "I have said this to you in fig-
ures; the hour is coming when I shall
no longer speak to you in figures but
tell you plainly of the Father. 26In that
day you will ask in my name; and I
do not say to you that I shall pray the
Father for you; 27for the Father him-
self loves you, because you have loved
me and have believed that I came from
the Father. 28I came from the Father
and have come into the world; again, I
am leaving the world and going to the
Father."

29 His disciples said, "Ah, now you
are speaking plainly, not in any fig-
ure! 30Now we know that you know
all things, and need none to question
you; by this we believe that you came
from God." 31Jesus answered them,
"Do you now believe? 32The hour is
coming, indeed it has come, when you
will be scattered, every man to his
home, and will leave me alone; yet I
am not alone, for the Father is with
me. 33I have said this to you, that in me
you may have peace. In the world you
have tribulation; but be of good cheer,
I have overcome the world."

JESUS PRAYS FOR HIS DISCIPLES

17 When Jesus had spoken these
words, he lifted up his eyes to
heaven and said,* "Father, the hour
has come; glorify thy Son that the
Son may glorify thee, 2since thou hast
given him power over all flesh, to give
eternal life to all whom thou hast giv-
en him. 3And this is eternal life, that
they know thee the only true God, and
Jesus Christ whom thou hast sent. 4I
glorified thee on earth, having accom-
plished the work which thou gavest
me to do; 5and now, Father, glorify
thou me in thy own presence with the
glory which I had with thee before the
world was made.*

6 "I have manifested thy name to
the men whom thou gavest me out of
the world; thine they were, and thou
gavest them to me, and they have kept
thy word. 7Now they know that every-
thing that thou hast given me is from
thee; 8for I have given them the words
which thou gavest me, and they have
received them and know in truth that
I came from thee; and they have be-
lieved that thou didst send me. 9I am

[a]Greek *a human being*

praying for them; I am not praying for
the world but for those whom thou
hast given me, for they are thine; 10all
mine are thine, and thine are mine,
and I am glorified in them. 11And
now I am no more in the world, but
they are in the world, and I am com-
ing to thee. Holy Father, keep them
in thy name, which thou hast given
me, that they may be one, even as
we are one. 12While I was with them,
I kept them in thy name, which thou
hast given me; I have guarded them,
and none of them is lost but the son
of perdition, that the scripture might
be fulfilled. 13But now I am coming
to thee; and these things I speak in
the world, that they may have my joy
fulfilled in themselves. 14I have given
them thy word; and the world has hat-
ed them because they are not of the
world, even as I am not of the world.
15I do not pray that thou shouldst take
them out of the world, but that thou
shouldst keep them from the evil one.[b]
16They are not of the world, even as I
am not of the world. 17Sanctify them
in the truth; thy word is truth. 18As
thou didst send me into the world, so
I have sent them into the world. 19And
for their sake I consecrate myself, that
they also may be consecrated in truth.

20 "I do not pray for these only,
but also for those who believe in me
through their word, 21that they may
all be one; even as thou, Father, art in
me, and I in thee, that they also may
be in us, so that the world may believe
that thou hast sent me. 22The glory
which thou hast given me I have giv-
en to them, that they may be one even
as we are one, 23I in them and thou in
me, that they may become perfectly
one, so that the world may know that
thou hast sent me and hast loved them
even as thou hast loved me. 24Father, I
desire that they also, whom thou hast
given me, may be with me where I am,
to behold my glory which thou hast
given me in thy love for me before the
foundation of the world. 25O righteous
Father, the world has not known thee,
but I have known thee; and these
know that thou hast sent me. 26I made
known to them thy name, and I will
make it known, that the love with
which thou hast loved me may be in
them, and I in them."

THE BETRAYAL AND ARREST OF JESUS

18 When Jesus had spoken these
words, he went forth with his dis-
ciples across the Kidron valley, where
there was a garden, which he and his
disciples entered. 2Now Judas, who
betrayed him, also knew the place; for
Jesus often met there with his disci-
ples. 3So Judas, procuring a band of
soldiers and some officers from the
chief priests and the Pharisees, went
there with lanterns and torches and
weapons. 4Then Jesus, knowing all
that was to befall him, came forward
and said to them, "Whom do you
seek?" 5They answered him, "Jesus
of Nazareth." Jesus said to them, "I
am he." Judas, who betrayed him, was
standing with them. 6When he said to
them, "I am he," they drew back and
fell to the ground. 7Again he asked
them, "Whom do you seek?" And they
said, "Jesus of Nazareth." 8Jesus an-
swered, "I told you that I am he; so, if
you seek me, let these men go." 9This
was to fulfil the word which he had
spoken, "Of those whom thou gavest
me I lost not one." 10Then Simon Peter,
having a sword, drew it and struck the
high priest's slave and cut off his right
ear. The slave's name was Malchus.
11Jesus said to Peter, "Put your sword
into its sheath; shall I not drink the
cup which the Father has given me?"

JESUS BEFORE THE HIGH PRIEST

12 So the band of soldiers and their
captain and the officers of the Jews
seized Jesus and bound him. 13First
they led him to Annas; for he was
the father-in-law of Ca´iaphas, who
was high priest that year.* 14It was
Ca´iaphas who had given counsel to

[b] Or *from evil*

the Jews that it was expedient that
one man should die for the people.

PETER DENIES JESUS

15 Simon Peter followed Jesus, and
so did another disciple. As this disci-
ple was known to the high priest, he
entered the court of the high priest
along with Jesus, 16 while Peter stood
outside at the door. So the other dis-
ciple, who was known to the high
priest, went out and spoke to the maid
who kept the door, and brought Peter
in. 17 The maid who kept the door said
to Peter, "Are not you also one of this
man's disciples?" He said, "I am not."
18 Now the servants[a] and officers had
made a charcoal fire, because it was
cold, and they were standing and
warming themselves; Peter also was
with them, standing and warming
himself.

THE HIGH PRIEST QUESTIONS JESUS

19 The high priest then ques-
tioned Jesus about his disciples and
his teaching. 20 Jesus answered him,
"I have spoken openly to the world; I
have always taught in synagogues and
in the temple, where all Jews come
together; I have said nothing secretly.
21 Why do you ask me? Ask those who
have heard me, what I said to them;
they know what I said." 22 When he had
said this, one of the officers standing
by struck Jesus with his hand, say-
ing, "Is that how you answer the high
priest?" 23 Jesus answered him, "If I
have spoken wrongly, bear witness to
the wrong; but if I have spoken right-
ly, why do you strike me?" 24 Annas
then sent him bound to Ca´iaphas the
high priest.

PETER DENIES JESUS AGAIN

25 Now Simon Peter was stand-
ing and warming himself. They said
to him, "Are not you also one of his
disciples?" He denied it and said, "I
am not." 26 One of the servants[b] of the
high priest, a kinsman of the man
whose ear Peter had cut off, asked,
"Did I not see you in the garden with
him?" 27 Peter again denied it; and at
once the cock crowed.

JESUS BEFORE PILATE

28 Then they led Jesus from the
house of Ca´iaphas to the praetori-
um. It was early. They themselves did
not enter the praetorium, so that they
might not be defiled, but might eat
the passover.* 29 So Pilate went out to
them and said, "What accusation do
you bring against this man?"* 30 They
answered him, "If this man were not
an evildoer, we would not have hand-
ed him over." 31 Pilate said to them,
"Take him yourselves and judge him
by your own law." The Jews said to
him, "It is not lawful for us to put any
man to death."* 32 This was to fulfil
the word which Jesus had spoken to
show by what death he was to die.

33 Pilate entered the praetorium
again and called Jesus, and said to
him, "Are you the King of the Jews?"
34 Jesus answered, "Do you say this of
your own accord, or did others say it
to you about me?" 35 Pilate answered,
"Am I a Jew? Your own nation and
the chief priests have handed you
over to me; what have you done?"
36 Jesus answered, "My kingship is not
of this world; if my kingship were of
this world, my servants would fight,
that I might not be handed over to the
Jews; but my kingship is not from the
world." 37 Pilate said to him, "So you
are a king?" Jesus answered, "You
say that I am a king. For this I was
born, and for this I have come into the
world, to bear witness to the truth.
Every one who is of the truth hears
my voice." 38 Pilate said to him, "What
is truth?"

JESUS SENTENCED TO DEATH

After he had said this, he went out
to the Jews again, and told them, "I

[a] Or *slaves*
[b] Or *slaves*

find no crime in him. 39But you have
a custom that I should release one
man for you at the Passover; will you
have me release for you the King of
the Jews?" 40They cried out again,
"Not this man, but Barab´bas!" Now
Barab´bas was a robber.

19 Then Pilate took Jesus and
scourged him. 2And the soldiers
plaited a crown of thorns, and put it
on his head, and arrayed him in a pur-
ple robe; 3they came up to him, saying,
"Hail, King of the Jews!" and struck
him with their hands. 4Pilate went out
again, and said to them, "Behold, I am
bringing him out to you, that you may
know that I find no crime in him." 5So
Jesus came out, wearing the crown of
thorns and the purple robe. Pilate said
to them, "Here is the man!" 6When
the chief priests and the officers saw
him, they cried out, "Crucify him, cru-
cify him!" Pilate said to them, "Take
him yourselves and crucify him, for I
find no crime in him." 7The Jews an-
swered him, "We have a law, and by
that law he ought to die, because he
has made himself the Son of God."*
8When Pilate heard these words, he
was the more afraid; 9he entered the
praetorium again and said to Jesus,
"Where are you from?"* But Jesus
gave no answer. 10Pilate therefore said
to him, "You will not speak to me? Do
you not know that I have power to re-
lease you, and power to crucify you?"
11Jesus answered him, "You would
have no power over me unless it had
been given you from above; therefore
he who delivered me to you has the
greater sin."

12 Upon this Pilate sought to re-
lease him, but the Jews cried out,
"If you release this man, you are not
Caesar's friend; every one who makes
himself a king sets himself against
Caesar." 13When Pilate heard these
words, he brought Jesus out and sat
down on the judgment seat at a place
called The Pavement, and in Hebrew,
Gab´batha. 14Now it was the day of
Preparation of the Passover; it was
about the sixth hour. He said to the
Jews, "Here is your King!" 15They
cried out, "Away with him, away with
him, crucify him!" Pilate said to them,
"Shall I crucify your King?" The chief
priests answered, "We have no king
but Caesar." 16Then he handed him
over to them to be crucified.

THE CRUCIFIXION OF JESUS

17 So they took Jesus, and he went
out, bearing his own cross, to the place
called the place of a skull, which is
called in Hebrew Gol´gotha. 18There
they crucified him, and with him two
others, one on either side, and Jesus
between them. 19Pilate also wrote a
title and put it on the cross; it read,
"Jesus of Nazareth, the King of the
Jews." 20Many of the Jews read this ti-
tle, for the place where Jesus was cruci-
fied was near the city; and it was writ-
ten in Hebrew, in Latin, and in Greek.
21The chief priests of the Jews then said
to Pilate, "Do not write, 'The King of
the Jews,' but, 'This man said, I am
King of the Jews.'" 22Pilate answered,
"What I have written I have written."

23 When the soldiers had cruci-
fied Jesus they took his garments and
made four parts, one for each soldier;
also his tunic. But the tunic was with-
out seam, woven from top to bottom;
24so they said to one another, "Let us
not tear it, but cast lots for it to see
whose it shall be." This was to fulfil
the scripture,

"They parted my garments
among them,
and for my clothing they cast
lots."

25 So the soldiers did this. But
standing by the cross of Jesus were
his mother, and his mother's sister,
Mary the wife of Clopas, and Mary
Mag´dalene. 26When Jesus saw his
mother, and the disciple whom he
loved standing near, he said to his
mother, "Woman, behold, your son!"
27Then he said to the disciple, "Behold,
your mother!" And from that hour the
disciple took her to his own home.*

28 After this Jesus, knowing that
all was now finished, said (to fulfil
the scripture), "I thirst." 29A bowl full
of vinegar stood there; so they put a
sponge full of the vinegar on hyssop
and held it to his mouth. 30When Jesus
had received the vinegar, he said, "It
is finished"; and he bowed his head
and gave up his spirit.

JESUS' SIDE IS PIERCED

31 Since it was the day of
Preparation, in order to prevent the
bodies from remaining on the cross
on the sabbath (for that sabbath was
a high day), the Jews asked Pilate that
their legs might be broken, and that
they might be taken away. 32So the sol-
diers came and broke the legs of the
first, and of the other who had been
crucified with him; 33but when they
came to Jesus and saw that he was
already dead, they did not break his
legs. 34But one of the soldiers pierced
his side with a spear, and at once
there came out blood and water. 35He
who saw it has borne witness—his
testimony is true, and he knows that
he tells the truth—that you also may
believe. 36For these things took place
that the scripture might be fulfilled,
"Not a bone of him shall be broken."
37And again another scripture says,
"They shall look on him whom they
have pierced."

THE BURIAL OF JESUS

38 After this Joseph of Arimathe´a,
who was a disciple of Jesus, but secret-
ly, for fear of the Jews, asked Pilate
that he might take away the body
of Jesus, and Pilate gave him leave.
So he came and took away his body.
39Nicode´mus also, who had at first
come to him by night, came bringing
a mixture of myrrh and aloes, about a
hundred pounds' weight. 40They took
the body of Jesus, and bound it in
linen cloths with the spices, as is the
burial custom of the Jews. 41Now in
the place where he was crucified there
was a garden, and in the garden a new
tomb where no one had ever been
laid. 42So because of the Jewish day of
Preparation, as the tomb was close at
hand, they laid Jesus there.

THE RESURRECTION OF JESUS

20 Now on the first day of the week
Mary Mag´dalene came to the
tomb early, while it was still dark,
and saw that the stone had been tak-
en away from the tomb. 2So she ran,
and went to Simon Peter and the oth-
er disciple, the one whom Jesus loved,
and said to them, "They have taken
the Lord out of the tomb, and we do
not know where they have laid him."
3Peter then came out with the other
disciple, and they went toward the
tomb. 4They both ran, but the other
disciple outran Peter and reached the
tomb first; 5and stooping to look in, he
saw the linen cloths lying there, but
he did not go in. 6Then Simon Peter
came, following him, and went into
the tomb; he saw the linen cloths ly-
ing, 7and the napkin, which had been
on his head, not lying with the linen
cloths but rolled up in a place by itself.
8Then the other disciple, who reached
the tomb first, also went in, and he
saw and believed; 9for as yet they did
not know the scripture, that he must
rise from the dead. 10Then the disci-
ples went back to their homes.

JESUS APPEARS TO MARY MAGDALENE

11 But Mary stood weeping outside
the tomb, and as she wept she stooped
to look into the tomb; 12and she saw
two angels in white, sitting where
the body of Jesus had lain, one at the
head and one at the feet. 13They said
to her, "Woman, why are you weep-
ing?" She said to them, "Because they
have taken away my Lord, and I do
not know where they have laid him."
14Saying this, she turned round and
saw Jesus standing, but she did not
know that it was Jesus. 15Jesus said to
her, "Woman, why are you weeping?
Whom do you seek?" Supposing him
to be the gardener, she said to him,

"Sir, if you have carried him away, tell
me where you have laid him, and I will
take him away." 16Jesus said to her,
"Mary." She turned and said to him in
Hebrew, "Rab-bo′ni!" (which means
Teacher). 17Jesus said to her, "Do not
hold me, for I have not yet ascended
to the Father; but go to my brethren
and say to them, I am ascending to
my Father and your Father, to my God
and your God."* 18Mary Mag′dalene
went and said to the disciples, "I have
seen the Lord"; and she told them that
he had said these things to her.

JESUS APPEARS TO THE DISCIPLES

19 On the evening of that day, the
first day of the week, the doors be-
ing shut where the disciples were, for
fear of the Jews, Jesus came and stood
among them and said to them, "Peace
be with you." 20When he had said
this, he showed them his hands and
his side. Then the disciples were glad
when they saw the Lord. 21Jesus said
to them again, "Peace be with you. As
the Father has sent me, even so I send
you." 22And when he had said this, he
breathed on them, and said to them,
"Receive the Holy Spirit. 23If you for-
give the sins of any, they are forgiven;
if you retain the sins of any, they are
retained."

JESUS AND THOMAS

24 Now Thomas, one of the twelve,
called the Twin, was not with them
when Jesus came. 25So the other dis-
ciples told him, "We have seen the
Lord." But he said to them, "Unless I
see in his hands the print of the nails,
and place my finger in the mark of the
nails, and place my hand in his side, I
will not believe."

26 Eight days later, his disciples
were again in the house, and Thomas
was with them. The doors were shut,
but Jesus came and stood among
them, and said, "Peace be with you."
27Then he said to Thomas, "Put your
finger here, and see my hands; and
put out your hand, and place it in my
side; do not be faithless, but believ-
ing." 28Thomas answered him, "My
Lord and my God!" 29Jesus said to him,
"Have you believed because you have
seen me? Blessed are those who have
not seen and yet believe."

THE PURPOSE OF THIS BOOK

30 Now Jesus did many other signs
in the presence of the disciples, which
are not written in this book; 31but
these are written that you may believe
that Jesus is the Christ, the Son of
God, and that believing you may have
life in his name.

JESUS APPEARS TO SEVEN DISCIPLES

21 *After this Jesus revealed himself
again to the disciples by the Sea
of Tibe′ri-as; and he revealed himself
in this way. 2Simon Peter, Thomas
called the Twin, Nathan′a-el of Cana
in Galilee, the sons of Zeb′edee, and
two others of his disciples were to-
gether. 3Simon Peter said to them, "I
am going fishing." They said to him,
"We will go with you." They went out
and got into the boat; but that night
they caught nothing.

4 Just as day was breaking, Jesus
stood on the beach; yet the disci-
ples did not know that it was Jesus.
5Jesus said to them, "Children, have
you any fish?" They answered him,
"No." 6He said to them, "Cast the net
on the right side of the boat, and you
will find some." So they cast it, and
now they were not able to haul it in,
for the quantity of fish. 7That disciple
whom Jesus loved* said to Peter, "It
is the Lord!" When Simon Peter heard
that it was the Lord, he put on his
clothes, for he was stripped for work,
and sprang into the sea. 8But the oth-
er disciples came in the boat, dragging
the net full of fish, for they were not
far from the land, but about a hundred
yards[a] off.

9 When they got out on land, they
saw a charcoal fire there, with fish

[a]Greek *two hundred cubits*

lying on it, and bread. [10]Jesus said to
them, "Bring some of the fish that
you have just caught." [11]So Simon
Peter went aboard and hauled the net
ashore, full of large fish, a hundred
and fifty-three of them; and although
there were so many, the net was not
torn. [12]Jesus said to them, "Come and
have breakfast." Now none of the dis-
ciples dared ask him, "Who are you?"
They knew it was the Lord. [13]Jesus
came and took the bread and gave it
to them, and so with the fish. [14]This
was now the third time that Jesus was
revealed to the disciples after he was
raised from the dead.

JESUS AND PETER

15 When they had finished break-
fast, Jesus said to Simon Peter,
"Simon, son of John, do you love me
more than these?" He said to him,
"Yes, Lord; you know that I love you."
He said to him, "Feed my lambs." [16]A
second time he said to him, "Simon,
son of John, do you love me?" He said
to him, "Yes, Lord; you know that I
love you." He said to him, "Tend my
sheep." [17]He said to him the third time,
"Simon, son of John, do you love me?"
Peter was grieved because he said to
him the third time, "Do you love me?"
And he said to him, "Lord, you know
everything; you know that I love you."
Jesus said to him, "Feed my sheep.*
[18]Truly, truly, I say to you, when you
were young, you girded yourself and
walked where you would; but when
you are old, you will stretch out your
hands, and another will gird you and
carry you where you do not wish to
go." [19](This he said to show by what
death he was to glorify God.) And af-
ter this he said to him, "Follow me."

JESUS AND THE BELOVED DISCIPLE

20 Peter turned and saw following
them the disciple whom Jesus loved,
who had lain close to his breast at the
supper and had said, "Lord, who is it
that is going to betray you?" [21]When
Peter saw him, he said to Jesus,
"Lord, what about this man?" [22]Jesus
said to him, "If it is my will that he
remain until I come, what is that to
you? Follow me!" [23]The saying spread
abroad among the brethren that this
disciple was not to die; yet Jesus did
not say to him that he was not to die,
but, "If it is my will that he remain
until I come, what is that to you?"

24 This is the disciple who is bear-
ing witness to these things, and who
has written these things; and we
know that his testimony is true.

25 But there are also many other
things which Jesus did; were every
one of them to be written, I suppose
that the world itself could not contain
the books that would be written.

THE

ACTS OF THE APOSTLES

THE PROMISE OF THE HOLY SPIRIT

1 In the first book,* O Theoph´ilus, I
have dealt with all that Jesus began
to do and teach, 2until the day when he
was taken up, after he had given com-
mandment through the Holy Spirit to
the apostles whom he had chosen. 3To
them he presented himself alive after
his passion by many proofs, appearing
to them during forty days, and speak-
ing of the kingdom of God. 4And while
staying[a] with them he charged them
not to depart from Jerusalem, but to
wait for the promise of the Father,
which, he said, "you heard from me,
5for John baptized with water, but be-
fore many days you shall be baptized
with the Holy Spirit."

THE ASCENSION OF JESUS

6 So when they had come togeth-
er, they asked him, "Lord, will you
at this time restore the kingdom to
Israel?" 7He said to them, "It is not for
you to know times or seasons which
the Father has fixed by his own au-
thority. 8But you shall receive power
when the Holy Spirit has come upon
you; and you shall be my witness-
es in Jerusalem and in all Judea and
Samar´ia and to the end of the earth."
9And when he had said this, as they
were looking on, he was lifted up, and
a cloud took him out of their sight.
10And while they were gazing into
heaven as he went, behold, two men
stood by them in white robes, 11and
said, "Men of Galilee, why do you
stand looking into heaven? This Jesus,
who was taken up from you into heav-
en, will come in the same way as you
saw him go into heaven."

MATTHIAS CHOSEN TO REPLACE JUDAS

12 Then they returned to Jerusalem
from the mount called Olivet, which
is near Jerusalem, a sabbath day's
journey away; 13and when they had
entered, they went up to the upper
room, where they were staying, Peter
and John and James and Andrew,
Philip and Thomas, Bartholomew and
Matthew, James the son of Alphaeus
and Simon the Zealot and Judas the
son of James. 14All these with one ac-
cord devoted themselves to prayer,
together with the women and Mary
the mother of Jesus, and with his
brethren.*

15 In those days Peter stood up
among the brethren (the company of
persons was in all about a hundred
and twenty), and said, 16"Brethren,
the scripture had to be fulfilled,
which the Holy Spirit spoke be-
forehand by the mouth of David,
concerning Judas who was guide to
those who arrested Jesus. 17For he
was numbered among us, and was
allotted his share in this ministry.
18(Now this man bought a field with
the reward of his wickedness; and
falling headlong[b] he burst open in
the middle and all his bowels gushed
out. 19And it became known to all
the inhabitants of Jerusalem, so that
the field was called in their language
Akel´dama, that is, Field of Blood.)
20For it is written in the book of
Psalms,

'Let his habitation become
desolate,
and let there be no one to live
in it';
'His office let another take.'

21So one of the men who have ac-
companied us during all the time that
the Lord Jesus went in and out among
us, 22beginning from the baptism of
John until the day when he was tak-
en up from us—one of these men
must become with us a witness to his

[a] Or *eating*
[b] Or *swelling up*

resurrection."* 23And they put for-
ward two, Joseph called Barsab´bas,
who was surnamed Justus, and
Matthi´as. 24And they prayed and
said, "Lord, who knowest the hearts
of all men, show which one of these
two thou hast chosen 25to take the
place in this ministry and apostle-
ship from which Judas turned aside,
to go to his own place." 26And they
cast lots for them, and the lot fell on
Matthi´as; and he was enrolled with
the eleven apostles.

THE COMING OF THE HOLY SPIRIT

2 When the day of Pentecost had
come, they were all together in one
place. 2And suddenly a sound came
from heaven like the rush of a mighty
wind, and it filled all the house
where they were sitting. 3And there
appeared to them tongues as of fire,
distributed and resting on each one of
them. 4And they were all filled with
the Holy Spirit and began to speak in
other tongues, as the Spirit gave them
utterance.

5 Now there were dwelling in Je-
rusalem Jews, devout men from every
nation under heaven. 6And at this
sound the multitude came together,
and they were bewildered, because
each one heard them speaking in
his own language. 7And they were
amazed and wondered, saying, "Are
not all these who are speaking Gal-
ileans? 8And how is it that we hear,
each of us in his own native language?
9Par´thians and Medes and E´lamites
and residents of Mesopota´mia, Judea
and Cappado´cia, Pontus and Asia,
10Phryg´ia and Pamphyl´ia, Egypt
and the parts of Libya belonging to
Cyre´ne, and visitors from Rome,
both Jews and proselytes, 11Cretans
and Arabians, we hear them telling in
our own tongues the mighty works of
God." 12And all were amazed and per-
plexed, saying to one another, "What
does this mean?" 13But others mock-
ing said, "They are filled with new
wine."

PETER ADDRESSES THE CROWD

14 But Peter,* standing with the
eleven, lifted up his voice and ad-
dressed them, "Men of Judea and
all who dwell in Jerusalem, let this
be known to you, and give ear to my
words. 15For these men are not drunk,
as you suppose, since it is only the
third hour of the day; 16but this is
what was spoken by the prophet Joel:

17'And in the last days it shall be,
God declares,
that I will pour out my Spirit
upon all flesh,
and your sons and your daugh-
ters shall prophesy,
and your young men shall see
visions,
and your old men shall dream
dreams;
18yea, and on my menservants and
my maidservants in those
days
I will pour out my Spirit; and
they shall prophesy.
19And I will show wonders in the
heaven above
and signs on the earth
beneath,
blood, and fire, and vapor of
smoke;
20the sun shall be turned into
darkness
and the moon into blood,
before the day of the Lord
comes,
the great and manifest day.
21And it shall be that whoever
calls on the name of the
Lord shall be saved.'

22 "Men of Israel, hear these
words: Jesus of Nazareth, a man at-
tested to you by God with mighty
works and wonders and signs which
God did through him in your midst,
as you yourselves know 23this Jesus,
delivered up according to the definite
plan and foreknowledge of God, you
crucified and killed by the hands of
lawless men. 24But God raised him up,
having loosed the pangs of death, be-
cause it was not possible for him to be

held by it. 25For David says concerning
him,

'I saw the Lord always before
me,
for he is at my right hand that I
may not be shaken;
26therefore my heart was glad, and
my tongue rejoiced;
moreover my flesh will dwell
in hope.
27For thou wilt not abandon my
soul to Hades,
nor let thy Holy One see
corruption.
28Thou hast made known to me
the ways of life;
thou wilt make me full of glad-
ness with thy presence.'

29 "Brethren, I may say to you con-
fidently of the patriarch David that
he both died and was buried, and his
tomb is with us to this day. 30Being
therefore a prophet, and knowing
that God had sworn with an oath to
him that he would set one of his de-
scendants upon his throne, 31he fore-
saw and spoke of the resurrection
of the Christ, that he was not aban-
doned to Hades, nor did his flesh see
corruption. 32This Jesus God raised
up, and of that we all are witnesses.
33Being therefore exalted at the right
hand of God, and having received
from the Father the promise of the
Holy Spirit, he has poured out this
which you see and hear. 34For David
did not ascend into the heavens; but
he himself says,

'The Lord said to my Lord, Sit
at my right hand,
35till I make thy enemies a stool
for thy feet.'

36Let all the house of Israel there-
fore know assuredly that God has
made him both Lord and Christ, this
Jesus whom you crucified."

THE FIRST CONVERTS

37 Now when they heard this
they were cut to the heart, and said
to Peter and the rest of the apostles,
"Brethren, what shall we do?" 38And
Peter said to them, "Repent, and be
baptized every one of you in the name
of Jesus Christ for the forgiveness of
your sins; and you shall receive the
gift of the Holy Spirit. 39For the prom-
ise is to you and to your children and
to all that are far off, every one whom
the Lord our God calls to him." 40And
he testified with many other words
and exhorted them, saying, "Save
yourselves from this crooked gener-
ation." 41So those who received his
word were baptized, and there were
added that day about three thousand
souls. 42And they devoted themselves
to the apostles' teaching and fellow-
ship, to the breaking of bread and the
prayers.

LIFE AMONG THE BELIEVERS

43 And fear came upon every soul;
and many wonders and signs were
done through the apostles. 44And all
who believed were together and had
all things in common; 45and they sold
their possessions and goods and dis-
tributed them to all, as any had need.
46And day by day, attending the temple
together and breaking bread in their
homes, they partook of food with glad
and generous hearts, 47praising God
and having favor with all the people.
And the Lord added to their num-
ber day by day those who were being
saved.

PETER HEALS A CRIPPLED BEGGAR

3 Now Peter and John were going
up to the temple at the hour of
prayer, the ninth hour.* 2And a man
lame from birth was being carried,
whom they laid daily at that gate of
the temple which is called Beautiful
to ask alms of those who entered the
temple. 3Seeing Peter and John about
to go into the temple, he asked for
alms. 4And Peter directed his gaze
at him, with John, and said, "Look at
us." 5And he fixed his attention upon
them, expecting to receive something
from them. 6But Peter said, "I have no
silver and gold, but I give you what I

have; in the name of Jesus Christ of
Nazareth, walk." 7And he took him by
the right hand and raised him up; and
immediately his feet and ankles were
made strong. 8And leaping up he stood
and walked and entered the temple
with them, walking and leaping and
praising God. 9And all the people saw
him walking and praising God, 10and
recognized him as the one who sat for
alms at the Beautiful Gate of the tem-
ple; and they were filled with wonder
and amazement at what had happened
to him.

PETER SPEAKS IN SOLOMON'S PORTICO

11 While he clung to Peter and
John, all the people ran together to
them in the portico called Solomon's,
astounded. 12And when Peter saw
it he addressed the people, "Men of
Israel, why do you wonder at this, or
why do you stare at us, as though by
our own power or piety we had made
him walk? 13The God of Abraham and
of Isaac and of Jacob, the God of our
fathers, glorified his servant[a] Jesus,
whom you delivered up and denied in
the presence of Pilate, when he had
decided to release him. 14But you de-
nied the Holy and Righteous One, and
asked for a murderer to be granted to
you, 15and killed the Author of life,
whom God raised from the dead. To
this we are witnesses. 16And his name,
by faith in his name, has made this
man strong whom you see and know;
and the faith which is through Jesus[b]
has given the man this perfect health
in the presence of you all.

17 "And now, brethren, I know that
you acted in ignorance, as did also
your rulers. 18But what God foretold
by the mouth of all the prophets, that
his Christ should suffer, he thus ful-
filled. 19Repent therefore, and turn
again, that your sins may be blotted
out, that times of refreshing may
come from the presence of the Lord,
20and that he may send the Christ
appointed for you, Jesus, 21whom
heaven must receive until the time for
establishing all that God spoke by the
mouth of his holy prophets from of
old. 22Moses said, 'The Lord God will
raise up for you a prophet from your
brethren as he raised me up. You shall
listen to him in whatever he tells you.
23And it shall be that every soul that
does not listen to that prophet shall
be destroyed from the people.' 24And
all the prophets who have spoken,
from Samuel and those who came af-
terwards, also proclaimed these days.
25You are the sons of the prophets and
of the covenant which God gave to
your fathers, saying to Abraham, 'And
in your posterity shall all the families
of the earth be blessed.' 26God, having
raised up his servant,[c] sent him to you
first, to bless you in turning every one
of you from your wickedness."

PETER AND JOHN BEFORE THE COUNCIL

4 And as they were speaking to the
people, the priests and the captain
of the temple and the Sad´ducees
came upon them, 2annoyed because
they were teaching the people and
proclaiming in Jesus the resurrection
from the dead.* 3And they arrested
them and put them in custody until
the morrow, for it was already eve-
ning. 4But many of those who heard
the word believed; and the num-
ber of the men came to about five
thousand.

5 On the morrow their rulers and
elders and scribes were gathered to-
gether in Jerusalem, 6with Annas the
high priest and Ca´iaphas and John
and Alexander, and all who were of
the high-priestly family. 7And when
they had set them in the midst, they
inquired, "By what power or by what
name did you do this?" 8Then Peter,
filled with the Holy Spirit, said to
them, "Rulers of the people and el-
ders, 9if we are being examined to-
day concerning a good deed done to

[a] Or *child*
[b] Greek *him*
[c] Or *child*

a cripple, by what means this man
has been healed, 10be it known to you
all, and to all the people of Israel,
that by the name of Jesus Christ of
Nazareth, whom you crucified, whom
God raised from the dead, by him
this man is standing before you well.
11This is the stone which was reject-
ed by you builders, but which has
become the head of the corner. 12And
there is salvation in no one else, for
there is no other name under heaven
given among men by which we must
be saved."
13 Now when they saw the bold-
ness of Peter and John, and perceived
that they were uneducated, common
men, they wondered; and they recog-
nized that they had been with Jesus.
14But seeing the man that had been
healed standing beside them, they
had nothing to say in opposition. 15But
when they had commanded them to
go aside out of the council, they con-
ferred with one another, 16saying,
"What shall we do with these men?
For that a notable sign has been per-
formed through them is manifest to
all the inhabitants of Jerusalem, and
we cannot deny it. 17But in order that
it may spread no further among the
people, let us warn them to speak no
more to any one in this name." 18So
they called them and charged them
not to speak or teach at all in the
name of Jesus. 19But Peter and John
answered them, "Whether it is right
in the sight of God to listen to you
rather than to God, you must judge;
20for we cannot but speak of what we
have seen and heard." 21And when
they had further threatened them,
they let them go, finding no way to
punish them, because of the people;
for all men praised God for what had
happened. 22For the man on whom
this sign of healing was performed
was more than forty years old.

THE BELIEVERS PRAY FOR BOLDNESS

23 When they were released they
went to their friends and reported
what the chief priests and the elders
had said to them. 24And when they
heard it, they lifted their voices to-
gether to God and said, "Sovereign
Lord, who didst make the heaven and
the earth and the sea and everything
in them, 25who by the mouth of our fa-
ther David, thy servant,[d] didst say by
the Holy Spirit,

'Why did the Gentiles rage,
and the peoples imagine vain
things?
26The kings of the earth set them-
selves in array,
and the rulers were gathered
together,
against the Lord and against
his Anointed'—[e]

27for truly in this city there were
gathered together against thy holy ser-
vant[f] Jesus, whom thou didst anoint,
both Herod and Pontius Pilate, with
the Gentiles and the peoples of Israel,
28to do whatever thy hand and thy plan
had predestined to take place. 29And
now, Lord, look upon their threats,
and grant to thy servants[g] to speak
thy word with all boldness, 30while
thou stretchest out thy hand to heal,
and signs and wonders are performed
through the name of thy holy servant[h]
Jesus." 31And when they had prayed,
the place in which they were gathered
together was shaken; and they were
all filled with the Holy Spirit and
spoke the word of God with boldness.

THE BELIEVERS SHARE THEIR POSSESSIONS

32 Now the company of those
who believed were of one heart and
soul, and no one said that any of
the things which he possessed was
his own, but they had everything in
common.* 33And with great power
the apostles gave their testimony to

[d] Or *child*
[e] Or *Christ*
[f] Or *child*
[g] Or *slaves*
[h] Or *child*

the resurrection of the Lord Jesus,
and great grace was upon them all.
34There was not a needy person among
them, for as many as were possessors
of lands or houses sold them, and
brought the proceeds of what was
sold 35and laid it at the apostles' feet;
and distribution was made to each as
any had need. 36Thus Joseph who was
surnamed by the apostles Barnabas
(which means, Son of encourage-
ment), a Levite, a native of Cyprus,
37sold a field which belonged to him,
and brought the money and laid it at
the apostles' feet.

ANANIAS AND SAPPHIRA

5 But a man named Anani´as with his
wife Sapphi´ra sold a piece of prop-
erty, 2and with his wife's knowledge
he kept back some of the proceeds,
and brought only a part and laid it
at the apostles' feet. 3But Peter said,
"Anani´as, why has Satan filled your
heart to lie to the Holy Spirit and to
keep back part of the proceeds of the
land? 4While it remained unsold, did
it not remain your own? And after it
was sold, was it not at your disposal?
How is it that you have contrived this
deed in your heart? You have not lied
to men but to God." 5When Anani´as
heard these words, he fell down and
died. And great fear came upon all
who heard of it. 6The young men rose
and wrapped him up and carried him
out and buried him.

7 After an interval of about three
hours his wife came in, not knowing
what had happened. 8And Peter said
to her, "Tell me whether you sold
the land for so much." And she said,
"Yes, for so much." 9But Peter said to
her, "How is it that you have agreed
together to tempt the Spirit of the
Lord? Hark, the feet of those that
have buried your husband are at the
door, and they will carry you out."
10Immediately she fell down at his feet
and died. When the young men came
in they found her dead, and they car-
ried her out and buried her beside her
husband. 11And great fear came upon
the whole church,* and upon all who
heard of these things.

THE APOSTLES HEAL MANY

12 Now many signs and wonders
were done among the people by the
hands of the apostles. And they were
all together in Solomon's Portico.
13None of the rest dared join them, but
the people held them in high honor.
14And more than ever believers were
added to the Lord, multitudes both of
men and women, 15so that they even
carried out the sick into the streets,
and laid them on beds and pallets,
that as Peter came by at least his shad-
ow might fall on some of them. 16The
people also gathered from the towns
around Jerusalem, bringing the sick
and those afflicted with unclean spir-
its, and they were all healed.

THE APOSTLES ARE PERSECUTED

17 But the high priest rose up and
all who were with him, that is, the
party of the Sad´ducees, and filled
with jealousy 18they arrested the apos-
tles and put them in the common pris-
on. 19But at night an angel of the Lord
opened the prison doors and brought
them out and said, 20"Go and stand in
the temple and speak to the people all
the words of this Life."* 21And when
they heard this, they entered the
temple at daybreak and taught. Now
the high priest came and those who
were with him and called together the
council and all the senate of Israel,
and sent to the prison to have them
brought. 22But when the officers came,
they did not find them in the prison,
and they returned and reported, 23"We
found the prison securely locked and
the sentries standing at the doors, but
when we opened it we found no one
inside." 24Now when the captain of
the temple and the chief priests heard
these words, they were much per-
plexed about them, wondering what
this would come to. 25And some one
came and told them, "The men whom

you put in prison are standing in the
temple and teaching the people."
26Then the captain with the officers
went and brought them, but without
violence, for they were afraid of being
stoned by the people.

27 And when they had brought
them, they set them before the coun-
cil. And the high priest questioned
them, 28saying, "We strictly charged
you not to teach in this name, yet
here you have filled Jerusalem with
your teaching and you intend to bring
this man's blood upon us." 29But Peter
and the apostles answered, "We must
obey God rather than men. 30The God
of our fathers raised Jesus whom
you killed by hanging him on a tree.
31God exalted him at his right hand as
Leader and Savior, to give repentance
to Israel and forgiveness of sins. 32And
we are witnesses to these things, and
so is the Holy Spirit whom God has
given to those who obey him."

33 When they heard this they were
enraged and wanted to kill them.
34But a Pharisee in the council named
Gama´li-el,* a teacher of the law, held
in honor by all the people, stood up
and ordered the men to be put outside
for a while. 35And he said to them,
"Men of Israel, take care what you
do with these men. 36For before these
days Theu´das arose, giving himself
out to be somebody, and a number of
men, about four hundred, joined him;
but he was slain and all who followed
him were dispersed and came to noth-
ing. 37After him Judas the Galilean
arose in the days of the census and
drew away some of the people after
him; he also perished, and all who
followed him were scattered. 38So in
the present case I tell you, keep away
from these men and let them alone;
for if this plan or this undertaking
is of men, it will fail; 39but if it is of
God, you will not be able to overthrow
them. You might even be found oppos-
ing God!"

40 So they took his advice, and
when they had called in the apostles,
they beat them and charged them not
to speak in the name of Jesus, and let
them go. 41Then they left the presence
of the council, rejoicing that they were
counted worthy to suffer dishonor for
the name. 42And every day in the tem-
ple and at home they did not cease
teaching and preaching Jesus as the
Christ.

SEVEN CHOSEN TO SERVE

6 Now in these days when the disci-
ples were increasing in number, the
Hellenists* murmured against the
Hebrews because their widows were
neglected in the daily distribution.
2And the twelve summoned the body
of the disciples and said, "It is not
right that we should give up preach-
ing the word of God to serve tables.
3Therefore, brethren, pick out from
among you seven men of good repute,
full of the Spirit and of wisdom, whom
we may appoint to this duty. 4But we
will devote ourselves to prayer and to
the ministry of the word." 5And what
they said pleased the whole multi-
tude, and they chose Stephen, a man
full of faith and of the Holy Spirit,
and Philip, and Proch´orus, and
Nica´nor, and Timon, and Par´menas,
and Nicola´us, a proselyte of Antioch.
6These they set before the apostles,
and they prayed and laid their hands
upon them.

7 And the word of God increased;
and the number of the disciples multi-
plied greatly in Jerusalem, and a great
many of the priests were obedient to
the faith.

THE ARREST OF STEPHEN

8 And Stephen, full of grace and
power, did great wonders and signs
among the people. 9Then some of
those who belonged to the syna-
gogue of the Freedmen (as it was
called), and of the Cyre´nians, and of
the Alexandrians, and of those from
Cili´cia and Asia, arose and disputed
with Stephen. 10But they could not
withstand the wisdom and the Spirit

with which he spoke. 11Then they
secretly instigated men, who said,
"We have heard him speak blasphe-
mous words against Moses and God."
12And they stirred up the people and
the elders and the scribes, and they
came upon him and seized him and
brought him before the council, 13and
set up false witnesses who said,
"This man never ceases to speak
words against this holy place and the
law; 14for we have heard him say that
this Jesus of Nazareth will destroy
this place, and will change the cus-
toms which Moses delivered to us."
15And gazing at him, all who sat in
the council saw that his face was like
the face of an angel.

STEPHEN'S SPEECH TO THE COUNCIL

7 And the high priest said, "Is this
so?" 2And Stephen said: "Brethren
and fathers, hear me. The God of glo-
ry appeared to our father Abraham,
when he was in Mesopota´mia, before
he lived in Haran, 3and said to him,
'Depart from your land and from your
kindred and go into the land which
I will show you.' 4Then he departed
from the land of the Chalde´ans, and
lived in Haran. And after his father
died, God removed him from there
into this land in which you are now
living; 5yet he gave him no inheri-
tance in it, not even a foot's length,
but promised to give it to him in
possession and to his posterity after
him, though he had no child. 6And
God spoke to this effect, that his
posterity would be aliens in a land
belonging to others, who would en-
slave them and ill-treat them four
hundred years. 7'But I will judge the
nation which they serve,' said God,
'and after that they shall come out
and worship me in this place.' 8And
he gave him the covenant of circum-
cision. And so Abraham became the
father of Isaac, and circumcised him
on the eighth day; and Isaac became
the father of Jacob, and Jacob of the
twelve patriarchs.

9"And the patriarchs, jealous of
Joseph, sold him into Egypt; but God
was with him, 10and rescued him out
of all his afflictions, and gave him fa-
vor and wisdom before Pharaoh, king
of Egypt, who made him governor
over Egypt and over all his household.
11Now there came a famine through-
out all Egypt and Canaan, and great
affliction, and our fathers could find
no food. 12But when Jacob heard that
there was grain in Egypt, he sent forth
our fathers the first time. 13And at
the second visit Joseph made himself
known to his brothers, and Joseph's
family became known to Pharaoh.
14And Joseph sent and called to him
Jacob his father and all his kindred,
seventy-five souls; 15and Jacob went
down into Egypt. And he died, him-
self and our fathers, 16and they were
carried back to Shechem and laid in
the tomb that Abraham had bought
for a sum of silver from the sons of
Hamor in Shechem.

17 "But as the time of the prom-
ise drew near, which God had grant-
ed to Abraham, the people grew and
multiplied in Egypt 18till there arose
over Egypt another king who had
not known Joseph. 19He dealt craftily
with our race and forced our fathers
to expose their infants, that they
might not be kept alive. 20At this time
Moses was born, and was beautiful
before God. And he was brought up
for three months in his father's house;
21and when he was exposed, Pharaoh's
daughter adopted him and brought
him up as her own son. 22And Moses
was instructed in all the wisdom of
the Egyptians, and he was mighty in
his words and deeds.

23 "When he was forty years old,
it came into his heart to visit his
brethren, the sons of Israel. 24And
seeing one of them being wronged,
he defended the oppressed man and
avenged him by striking the Egyptian.
25He supposed that his brethren un-
derstood that God was giving them
deliverance by his hand, but they did

not understand. [26]And on the follow-
ing day he appeared to them as they
were quarreling and would have rec-
onciled them, saying, ‘Men, you are
brethren, why do you wrong each oth-
er?’ [27]But the man who was wronging
his neighbor thrust him aside, saying,
‘Who made you a ruler and a judge
over us? [28]Do you want to kill me as
you killed the Egyptian yesterday?’
[29]At this retort Moses fled, and be-
came an exile in the land of Mid′ian,
where he became the father of two
sons.

30 “Now when forty years had
passed, an angel appeared to him in
the wilderness of Mount Sinai, in a
flame of fire in a bush. [31]When Moses
saw it he wondered at the sight; and
as he drew near to look, the voice of
the Lord came, [32]‘I am the God of your
fathers, the God of Abraham and of
Isaac and of Jacob.’ And Moses trem-
bled and did not dare to look. [33]And the
Lord said to him, ‘Take off the shoes
from your feet, for the place where
you are standing is holy ground. [34]I
have surely seen the ill-treatment of
my people that are in Egypt and heard
their groaning, and I have come down
to deliver them. And now come, I will
send you to Egypt.’

35 “This Moses whom they re-
fused, saying, ‘Who made you a ruler
and a judge?’ God sent as both ruler
and deliverer by the hand of the an-
gel that appeared to him in the bush.
[36]He led them out, having performed
wonders and signs in Egypt and at
the Red Sea, and in the wilderness
for forty years. [37]This is the Moses
who said to the Israelites, ‘God will
raise up for you a prophet from your
brethren as he raised me up.’ [38]This is
he who was in the congregation in the
wilderness with the angel who spoke
to him at Mount Sinai, and with our
fathers; and he received living oracles
to give to us. [39]Our fathers refused to
obey him, but thrust him aside, and
in their hearts they turned to Egypt,
[40]saying to Aaron, ‘Make for us gods
to go before us; as for this Moses who
led us out from the land of Egypt,
we do not know what has become
of him.’ [41]And they made a calf in
those days, and offered a sacrifice
to the idol and rejoiced in the works
of their hands. [42]But God turned and
gave them over to worship the host of
heaven, as it is written in the book of
the prophets:

‘Did you offer to me slain
beasts and sacrifices,
forty years in the wilderness, O
house of Israel?
[43]And you took up the tent of
Moloch,
and the star of the god Rephan,
the figures which you made to
worship;
and I will remove you beyond
Babylon.’

44 “Our fathers had the tent of wit-
ness in the wilderness, even as he who
spoke to Moses directed him to make
it, according to the pattern that he had
seen. [45]Our fathers in turn brought
it in with Joshua when they dispos-
sessed the nations which God thrust
out before our fathers. So it was until
the days of David, [46]who found favor
in the sight of God and asked leave
to find a habitation for the God of
Jacob. [47]But it was Solomon who built
a house for him. [48]Yet the Most High
does not dwell in houses made with
hands; as the prophet says,

[49]‘Heaven is my throne,
and earth my footstool.
What house will you build for
me, says the Lord,
or what is the place of my res
[50]Did not my hand make all these
things?’

51 “You stiff-necked people, un-
circumcised in heart and ears, you
always resist the Holy Spirit. As your
fathers did, so do you. [52]Which of the
prophets did not your fathers perse-
cute? And they killed those who an-
nounced beforehand the coming of
the Righteous One, whom you have
now betrayed and murdered, [53]you

who received the law as delivered by
angels and did not keep it."

THE STONING OF STEPHEN

54 Now when they heard these
things they were enraged, and they
ground their teeth against him. 55 But
he, full of the Holy Spirit, gazed into
heaven and saw the glory of God, and
Jesus standing at the right hand of
God; 56 and he said, "Behold, I see the
heavens opened, and the Son of man
standing at the right hand of God."
57 But they cried out with a loud voice
and stopped their ears and rushed to-
gether upon him. 58 Then they cast him
out of the city and stoned him; and the
witnesses laid down their garments
at the feet of a young man named
Saul. 59 And as they were stoning Ste-
phen, he prayed, "Lord Jesus, receive
my spirit." 60 And he knelt down and
cried with a loud voice, "Lord, do
not hold this sin against them." And
when he had said this, he fell asleep.
8 And Saul was consenting to his
death.

SAUL PERSECUTES THE CHURCH

And on that day a great persecution
arose against the church in Jerusalem;
and they were all scattered through-
out the region of Judea and Samar´ia,
except the apostles. 2 Devout men bur-
ied Stephen, and made great lamen-
tation over him. 3 But Saul laid waste
the church, and entering house after
house, he dragged off men and women
and committed them to prison.

PHILIP PREACHES IN SAMARIA

4 Now those who were scat-
tered went about preaching the
word. 5 Philip went down to a city of
Samar´ia, and proclaimed to them the
Christ. 6 And the multitudes with one
accord gave heed to what was said by
Philip, when they heard him and saw
the signs which he did. 7 For unclean
spirits came out of many who were
possessed, crying with a loud voice;
and many who were paralyzed or lame
were healed. 8 So there was much joy
in that city.

9 But there was a man named
Simon who had previously practiced
magic in the city and amazed the
nation of Samar´ia, saying that he
himself was somebody great. 10 They
all gave heed to him, from the least
to the greatest, saying, "This man
is that power of God which is called
Great." 11 And they gave heed to him,
because for a long time he had amazed
them with his magic. 12 But when they
believed Philip as he preached good
news about the kingdom of God and
the name of Jesus Christ, they were
baptized, both men and women.
13 Even Simon himself believed, and af-
ter being baptized he continued with
Philip. And seeing signs and great
miracles performed, he was amazed.

14 Now when the apostles at
Jerusalem heard that Samar´ia had
received the word of God, they sent
to them Peter and John, 15 who came
down and prayed for them that they
might receive the Holy Spirit; 16 for it
had not yet fallen on any of them, but
they had only been baptized in the
name of the Lord Jesus. 17 Then they
laid their hands on them and they
received the Holy Spirit. 18 Now when
Simon saw that the Spirit was given
through the laying on of the apostles'
hands, he offered them money, 19 say-
ing, "Give me also this power, that
any one on whom I lay my hands may
receive the Holy Spirit." 20 But Peter
said to him, "Your silver perish with
you, because you thought you could
obtain the gift of God with money!*
21 You have neither part nor lot in this
matter, for your heart is not right be-
fore God. 22 Repent therefore of this
wickedness of yours, and pray to the
Lord that, if possible, the intent of
your heart may be forgiven you. 23 For
I see that you are in the gall of bit-
terness and in the bond of iniquity."
24 And Simon answered, "Pray for me
to the Lord, that nothing of what you
have said may come upon me."

25 Now when they had testified
and spoken the word of the Lord,
they returned to Jerusalem, preach-
ing the gospel to many villages of the
Samaritans.

PHILIP AND THE ETHIOPIAN EUNUCH

26 But an angel of the Lord said
to Philip, "Rise and go toward the
south[a] to the road that goes down
from Jerusalem to Gaza." This is a
desert road. 27And he rose and went.
And behold, an Ethiopian, a eunuch,
a minister of the Canda´ce the queen
of the Ethiopians, in charge of all her
treasure, had come to Jerusalem to
worship 28and was returning; seat-
ed in his chariot, he was reading the
prophet Isaiah. 29And the Spirit said
to Philip, "Go up and join this chari-
ot." 30So Philip ran to him, and heard
him reading Isaiah the prophet, and
asked, "Do you understand what you
are reading?" 31And he said, "How can
I, unless some one guides me?" And
he invited Philip to come up and sit
with him. 32Now the passage of the
scripture which he was reading was
this:

"As a sheep led to the slaughter
or a lamb before its shearer is
dumb,
so he opens not his mouth.
33In his humiliation justice was
denied him.
Who can describe his
generation?
For his life is taken up from the
earth."

34And the eunuch said to Philip,
"About whom, pray, does the proph-
et say this, about himself or about
some one else?" 35Then Philip opened
his mouth, and beginning with this
scripture he told him the good news
of Jesus. 36And as they went along
the road they came to some water,
and the eunuch said, "See, here is
water! What is to prevent my being
baptized?"[b] 38And he commanded the
chariot to stop, and they both went
down into the water, Philip and the
eunuch, and he baptized him. 39And
when they came up out of the water,
the Spirit of the Lord caught up Philip;
and the eunuch saw him no more, and
went on his way rejoicing. 40But Philip
was found at Azo´tus, and passing
on he preached the gospel to all the
towns till he came to Caesare´a.

THE CONVERSION OF SAUL

9 But Saul, still breathing threats
and murder against the disciples
of the Lord, went to the high priest
2and asked him for letters to the syn-
agogues at Damascus, so that if he
found any belonging to the Way, men
or women, he might bring them bound
to Jerusalem. 3Now as he journeyed he
approached Damascus, and suddenly
a light from heaven flashed about him.
4And he fell to the ground and heard a
voice saying to him, "Saul, Saul, why
do you persecute me?" 5And he said,
"Who are you, Lord?" And he said, "I
am Jesus, whom you are persecuting;*
6but rise and enter the city, and you
will be told what you are to do." 7The
men who were traveling with him
stood speechless, hearing the voice
but seeing no one. 8Saul arose from
the ground; and when his eyes were
opened, he could see nothing; so they
led him by the hand and brought him
into Damascus. 9And for three days he
was without sight, and neither ate nor
drank.

10 Now there was a disciple at
Damascus named Anani´as. The Lord
said to him in a vision, "Anani´as."
And he said, "Here I am, Lord." 11And
the Lord said to him, "Rise and go
to the street called Straight, and in-
quire in the house of Judas for a man
of Tarsus named Saul; for behold, he
is praying, 12and he has seen a man
named Anani´as come in and lay his
hands on him so that he might regain
his sight." 13But Anani´as answered,

[a] Or *at noon*

[b] Other ancient authorities add all or most of verse 37, *And Philip said, "If you believe with all your heart, you may." And he replied, "I believe that Jesus Christ is the Son of God."*

"Lord, I have heard from many about
this man, how much evil he has done
to thy saints* at Jerusalem; 14and here
he has authority from the chief priests
to bind all who call upon thy name."
15But the Lord said to him, "Go, for
he is a chosen instrument of mine to
carry my name before the Gentiles
and kings and the sons of Israel; 16for
I will show him how much he must
suffer for the sake of my name." 17So
Anani´as departed and entered the
house. And laying his hands on him
he said, "Brother Saul, the Lord Jesus
who appeared to you on the road by
which you came, has sent me that you
may regain your sight and be filled
with the Holy Spirit." 18And immedi-
ately something like scales fell from
his eyes and he regained his sight.
Then he rose and was baptized, 19and
took food and was strengthened.

SAUL PREACHES IN DAMASCUS

For several days he was with the
disciples at Damascus. 20And in the
synagogues immediately he pro-
claimed Jesus, saying, "He is the Son
of God." 21And all who heard him were
amazed, and said, "Is not this the man
who made havoc in Jerusalem of those
who called on this name? And he has
come here for this purpose, to bring
them bound before the chief priests."
22But Saul increased all the more in
strength, and confounded the Jews
who lived in Damascus by proving
that Jesus was the Christ.

SAUL ESCAPES FROM THE JEWS

23 When many days had passed,
the Jews plotted to kill him, 24but their
plot became known to Saul. They were
watching the gates day and night, to
kill him; 25but his disciples took him
by night and let him down over the
wall, lowering him in a basket.

SAUL IN JERUSALEM

26 And when he had come to
Jerusalem he attempted to join the
disciples; and they were all afraid of
him, for they did not believe that he
was a disciple. 27But Barnabas took
him, and brought him to the apostles,
and declared to them how on the road
he had seen the Lord, who spoke to
him, and how at Damascus he had
preached boldly in the name of Jesus.
28So he went in and out among them
at Jerusalem, 29preaching boldly in
the name of the Lord. And he spoke
and disputed against the Hellenists;
but they were seeking to kill him.
30And when the brethren knew it, they
brought him down to Caesare´a, and
sent him off to Tarsus.

31 So the church throughout all
Judea and Galilee and Samar´ia had
peace and was built up; and walking in
the fear of the Lord and in the comfort
of the Holy Spirit it was multiplied.

THE HEALING OF AENEAS

32 Now as Peter went here and
there among them all, he came
down also to the saints that lived at
Lydda. 33There he found a man named
Aene´as, who had been bedridden for
eight years and was paralyzed. 34And
Peter said to him, "Aene´as, Jesus
Christ heals you; rise and make your
bed." And immediately he rose. 35And
all the residents of Lydda and Sharon
saw him, and they turned to the Lord.

PETER IN LYDDA AND JOPPA

36 Now there was at Joppa a dis-
ciple named Tabitha, which means
Dorcas or Gazelle. She was full of
good works and acts of charity. 37In
those days she fell sick and died; and
when they had washed her, they laid
her in an upper room. 38Since Lydda
was near Joppa, the disciples, hearing
that Peter was there, sent two men
to him entreating him, "Please come
to us without delay." 39So Peter rose
and went with them. And when he
had come, they took him to the upper
room. All the widows stood beside
him weeping, and showing coats and
garments which Dorcas made while
she was with them. 40But Peter put

them all outside and knelt down and
prayed; then turning to the body he
said, "Tabitha, rise." And she opened
her eyes, and when she saw Peter she
sat up. 41And he gave her his hand and
lifted her up. Then calling the saints
and widows he presented her alive.
42And it became known throughout all
Joppa, and many believed in the Lord.
43And he stayed in Joppa for many
days with one Simon, a tanner.

PETER AND CORNELIUS

10 At Caesare´a there was a man
named Cornelius, a centurion of
what was known as the Italian Cohort,
2a devout man who feared God with
all his household, gave alms liberally
to the people, and prayed constantly
to God. 3About the ninth hour of the
day he saw clearly in a vision an angel
of God coming in and saying to him,
"Cornelius." 4And he stared at him in
terror, and said, "What is it, Lord?"
And he said to him, "Your prayers and
your alms have ascended as a memo-
rial before God. 5And now send men
to Joppa, and bring one Simon who
is called Peter; 6he is lodging with
Simon, a tanner, whose house is by
the seaside." 7When the angel who
spoke to him had departed, he called
two of his servants and a devout sol-
dier from among those that waited on
him, 8and having related everything to
them, he sent them to Joppa.

9 The next day, as they were on
their journey and coming near the city,
Peter went up on the housetop to pray,
about the sixth hour. 10And he became
hungry and desired something to eat;
but while they were preparing it, he
fell into a trance 11and saw the heaven
opened, and something descending,
like a great sheet, let down by four
corners upon the earth. 12In it were all
kinds of animals and reptiles and birds
of the air. 13And there came a voice to
him, "Rise, Peter; kill and eat." 14But
Peter said, "No, Lord; for I have nev-
er eaten anything that is common or
unclean." 15And the voice came to him
again a second time, "What God has
cleansed, you must not call common."
16This happened three times, and the
thing was taken up at once to heaven.*

17 Now while Peter was inwardly
perplexed as to what the vision which
he had seen might mean, behold, the
men that were sent by Cornelius, hav-
ing made inquiry for Simon's house,
stood before the gate 18and called out
to ask whether Simon who was called
Peter was lodging there. 19And while
Peter was pondering the vision, the
Spirit said to him, "Behold, three
men are looking for you. 20Rise and
go down, and accompany them with-
out hesitation; for I have sent them."
21And Peter went down to the men and
said, "I am the one you are looking
for; what is the reason for your com-
ing?" 22And they said, "Cornelius, a
centurion, an upright and God-fearing
man, who is well spoken of by the
whole Jewish nation, was directed by
a holy angel to send for you to come to
his house, and to hear what you have
to say." 23So he called them in to be
his guests. The next day he rose and
went off with them, and some of the
brethren from Joppa accompanied
him. 24And on the following day they
entered Caesare´a. Cornelius was ex-
pecting them and had called together
his kinsmen and close friends. 25When
Peter entered, Cornelius met him and
fell down at his feet and worshiped
him. 26But Peter lifted him up, saying,
"Stand up; I too am a man." 27And as
he talked with him, he went in and
found many persons gathered; 28and
he said to them, "You yourselves
know how unlawful it is for a Jew to
associate with or to visit any one of
another nation; but God has shown
me that I should not call any man
common or unclean. 29So when I was
sent for, I came without objection. I
ask then why you sent for me."

30 And Cornelius said, "Four days
ago, about this hour, I was keeping
the ninth hour of prayer in my house;
and behold, a man stood before me in

bright apparel, 31saying, 'Cornelius,
your prayer has been heard and your
alms have been remembered before
God. 32Send therefore to Joppa and
ask for Simon who is called Peter; he
is lodging in the house of Simon, a
tanner, by the seaside.' 33So I sent to
you at once, and you have been kind
enough to come. Now therefore we
are all here present in the sight of
God, to hear all that you have been
commanded by the Lord."

GENTILES HEAR THE GOOD NEWS

34 And Peter opened his mouth
and said: "Truly I perceive that God
shows no partiality, 35but in every
nation any one who fears him and
does what is right is acceptable to
him. 36You know the word which he
sent to Israel, preaching good news of
peace by Jesus Christ (he is Lord of
all), 37the word which was proclaimed
throughout all Judea, beginning from
Galilee after the baptism which John
preached: 38how God anointed Jesus
of Nazareth with the Holy Spirit and
with power; how he went about do-
ing good and healing all that were
oppressed by the devil, for God was
with him. 39And we are witnesses
to all that he did both in the coun-
try of the Jews and in Jerusalem.
They put him to death by hanging
him on a tree; 40but God raised him
on the third day and made him man-
ifest; 41not to all the people but to us
who were chosen by God as witness-
es, who ate and drank with him af-
ter he rose from the dead. 42And he
commanded us to preach to the peo-
ple, and to testify that he is the one
ordained by God to be judge of the
living and the dead. 43To him all the
prophets bear witness that every one
who believes in him receives forgive-
ness of sins through his name."

GENTILES RECEIVE THE HOLY SPIRIT

44 While Peter was still saying
this, the Holy Spirit fell on all who
heard the word. 45And the believers
from among the circumcised who
came with Peter were amazed, be-
cause the gift of the Holy Spirit had
been poured out even on the Gentiles.
46For they heard them speaking in
tongues and extolling God. Then
Peter declared, 47"Can any one forbid
water for baptizing these people who
have received the Holy Spirit just as
we have?" 48And he commanded them
to be baptized in the name of Jesus
Christ. Then they asked him to re-
main for some days.

PETER'S REPORT TO THE CHURCH AT JERUSALEM

11 Now the apostles and the breth-
ren who were in Judea heard that
the Gentiles also had received the
word of God. 2So when Peter went
up to Jerusalem, the circumcision
party criticized him, 3saying, "Why
did you go to uncircumcised men
and eat with them?" 4But Peter be-
gan and explained to them in order:
5"I was in the city of Joppa praying;
and in a trance I saw a vision, some-
thing descending, like a great sheet,
let down from heaven by four corners;
and it came down to me. 6Looking
at it closely I observed animals and
beasts of prey and reptiles and birds
of the air. 7And I heard a voice saying
to me, 'Rise, Peter; kill and eat.' 8But
I said, 'No, Lord; for nothing com-
mon or unclean has ever entered my
mouth.' 9But the voice answered a sec-
ond time from heaven, 'What God has
cleansed you must not call common.'
10This happened three times, and all
was drawn up again into heaven. 11At
that very moment three men arrived
at the house in which we were, sent
to me from Caesare´a. 12And the Spirit
told me to go with them, making no
distinction. These six brethren also
accompanied me, and we entered the
man's house. 13And he told us how he
had seen the angel standing in his
house and saying, 'Send to Joppa and
bring Simon called Peter; 14he will de-
clare to you a message by which you

will be saved, you and all your house-
hold.' 15As I began to speak, the Holy
Spirit fell on them just as on us at the
beginning. 16And I remembered the
word of the Lord, how he said, 'John
baptized with water, but you shall
be baptized with the Holy Spirit.' 17If
then God gave the same gift to them
as he gave to us when we believed in
the Lord Jesus Christ, who was I that
I could withstand God?" 18When they
heard this they were silenced. And
they glorified God, saying, "Then to
the Gentiles also God has granted re-
pentance unto life."

THE CHURCH IN ANTIOCH

19 Now those who were scat-
tered because of the persecution
that arose over Stephen traveled as
far as Phoeni´cia and Cyprus and
Antioch, speaking the word to none
except Jews. 20But there were some
of them, men of Cyprus and Cyre´ne,
who on coming to Antioch spoke to
the Greeks[a] also, preaching the Lord
Jesus. 21And the hand of the Lord was
with them, and a great number that
believed turned to the Lord. 22News
of this came to the ears of the church
in Jerusalem, and they sent Barnabas
to Antioch. 23When he came and saw
the grace of God, he was glad; and he
exhorted them all to remain faithful
to the Lord with steadfast purpose;
24for he was a good man, full of the
Holy Spirit and of faith. And a large
company was added to the Lord. 25So
Barnabas went to Tarsus to look for
Saul; 26and when he had found him, he
brought him to Antioch. For a whole
year they met with[b] the church, and
taught a large company of people; and
in Antioch the disciples were for the
first time called Christians.

27 Now in these days proph-
ets came down from Jerusalem to
Antioch. 28And one of them named
Ag´abus stood up and foretold by the
Spirit that there would be a great
famine over all the world; and this
took place in the days of Claudius.
29And the disciples determined, ev-
ery one according to his ability, to
send relief to the brethren who lived
in Judea; 30and they did so, sending it
to the elders by the hand of Barnabas
and Saul.

JAMES KILLED AND PETER IMPRISONED

12 About that time Herod the king
laid violent hands upon some
who belonged to the church.* 2He
killed James the brother of John with
the sword; 3and when he saw that it
pleased the Jews, he proceeded to ar-
rest Peter also. This was during the
days of Unleavened Bread. 4And when
he had seized him, he put him in pris-
on, and delivered him to four squads
of soldiers to guard him, intending
after the Passover to bring him out
to the people. 5So Peter was kept in
prison; but earnest prayer for him was
made to God by the church.

PETER DELIVERED FROM PRISON

6 The very night when Herod
was about to bring him out, Peter
was sleeping between two soldiers,
bound with two chains, and sentries
before the door were guarding the
prison; 7and behold, an angel of the
Lord appeared, and a light shone in
the cell; and he struck Peter on the
side and woke him, saying, "Get up
quickly." And the chains fell off his
hands. 8And the angel said to him,
"Dress yourself and put on your san-
dals." And he did so. And he said to
him, "Wrap your mantle around you
and follow me." 9And he went out
and followed him; he did not know
that what was done by the angel was
real, but thought he was seeing a vi-
sion. 10When they had passed the first
and the second guard, they came to
the iron gate leading into the city. It
opened to them of its own accord, and
they went out and passed on through

[a]Other ancient authorities read *Hellenists*
[b]Or *were guests of*

one street; and immediately the angel
left him. 11And Peter came to him-
self, and said, "Now I am sure that
the Lord has sent his angel and res-
cued me from the hand of Herod and
from all that the Jewish people were
expecting."

12 When he realized this, he went
to the house of Mary, the mother of
John whose other name was Mark,
where many were gathered togeth-
er and were praying. 13And when he
knocked at the door of the gateway, a
maid named Rhoda came to answer.
14Recognizing Peter's voice, in her joy
she did not open the gate but ran in
and told that Peter was standing at
the gate. 15They said to her, "You are
mad." But she insisted that it was
so. They said, "It is his angel!" 16But
Peter continued knocking; and when
they opened, they saw him and were
amazed. 17But motioning to them with
his hand to be silent, he described to
them how the Lord had brought him
out of the prison. And he said, "Tell
this to James and to the brethren."
Then he departed and went to anoth-
er place.

18 Now when day came, there was
no small stir among the soldiers over
what had become of Peter. 19And when
Herod had sought for him and could
not find him, he examined the sen-
tries and ordered that they should be
put to death. Then he went down from
Judea to Caesare´a, and remained
there.

THE DEATH OF HEROD

20 Now Herod was angry with the
people of Tyre and Sidon; and they
came to him in a body, and having
persuaded Blastus, the king's cham-
berlain, they asked for peace, because
their country depended on the king's
country for food. 21On an appointed
day Herod put on his royal robes, took
his seat upon the throne, and made
an oration to them. 22And the people
shouted, "The voice of a god, and not
of man!" 23Immediately an angel of the
Lord smote him, because he did not
give God the glory; and he was eaten
by worms and died.

24 But the word of God grew and
multiplied.

25 And Barnabas and Saul returned
from[a] Jerusalem when they had ful-
filled their mission, bringing with
them John whose other name was
Mark.

BARNABAS AND SAUL COMMISSIONED

13 Now in the church at Antioch
there were prophets and teachers,
Barnabas, Symeon who was called
Niger, Lucius of Cyre´ne, Man´a-en
a member of the court of Herod the
tetrarch, and Saul. 2While they were
worshiping the Lord and fasting, the
Holy Spirit said, "Set apart for me
Barnabas and Saul for the work to
which I have called them." 3Then af-
ter fasting and praying they laid their
hands on them and sent them off.

THE APOSTLES PREACH IN CYPRUS

4 So, being sent out by the Holy
Spirit, they went down to Seleu´cia;
and from there they sailed to Cyprus.
5When they arrived at Sal´amis, they
proclaimed the word of God in the
synagogues of the Jews. And they had
John to assist them. 6When they had
gone through the whole island as far as
Paphos, they came upon a certain ma-
gician, a Jewish false prophet, named
Bar-Jesus. 7He was with the procon-
sul, Sergius Paulus, a man of intelli-
gence, who summoned Barnabas and
Saul and sought to hear the word of
God. 8But El´ymas the magician (for
that is the meaning of his name) with-
stood them, seeking to turn away the
proconsul from the faith. 9But Saul,
who is also called Paul, filled with
the Holy Spirit, looked intently at him
10and said, "You son of the devil, you
enemy of all righteousness, full of all
deceit and villainy, will you not stop
making crooked the straight paths of

[a] Other ancient authorities read *to*

the Lord? 11And now, behold, the hand
of the Lord is upon you, and you shall
be blind and unable to see the sun for
a time." Immediately mist and dark-
ness fell upon him and he went about
seeking people to lead him by the
hand. 12Then the proconsul believed,
when he saw what had occurred, for
he was astonished at the teaching of
the Lord.

PAUL AND BARNABAS IN ANTIOCH OF PISIDIA

13 Now Paul and his company
set sail from Paphos, and came to
Perga in Pamphyl´ia. And John left
them and returned to Jerusalem;
14but they passed on from Perga and
came to Antioch of Pisid´ia. And on
the sabbath day they went into the
synagogue and sat down. 15After the
reading of the law and the prophets,
the rulers of the synagogue sent to
them, saying, "Brethren, if you have
any word of exhortation for the peo-
ple, say it." 16So Paul stood up, and
motioning with his hand said:* "Men
of Israel, and you that fear God, lis-
ten. 17The God of this people Israel
chose our fathers and made the peo-
ple great during their stay in the land
of Egypt, and with uplifted arm he
led them out of it. 18And for about
forty years he bore with[b] them in the
wilderness. 19And when he had de-
stroyed seven nations in the land of
Canaan, he gave them their land as
an inheritance, for about four hun-
dred and fifty years. 20And after that
he gave them judges until Samuel the
prophet. 21Then they asked for a king;
and God gave them Saul the son of
Kish, a man of the tribe of Benjamin,
for forty years. 22And when he had
removed him, he raised up David to
be their king; of whom he testified
and said, 'I have found in David the
son of Jesse a man after my heart,
who will do all my will.' 23Of this
man's posterity God has brought to
Israel a Savior, Jesus, as he prom-
ised. 24Before his coming John had
preached a baptism of repentance to
all the people of Israel. 25And as John
was finishing his course, he said,
'What do you suppose that I am? I
am not he. No, but after me one is
coming, the sandals of whose feet I
am not worthy to untie.'

26 "Brethren, sons of the family
of Abraham, and those among you
that fear God, to us has been sent the
message of this salvation. 27For those
who live in Jerusalem and their rul-
ers, because they did not recognize
him nor understand the utterances
of the prophets which are read every
sabbath, fulfilled these by condemn-
ing him. 28Though they could charge
him with nothing deserving death, yet
they asked Pilate to have him killed.
29And when they had fulfilled all that
was written of him, they took him
down from the tree, and laid him in
a tomb. 30But God raised him from the
dead; 31and for many days he appeared
to those who came up with him from
Galilee to Jerusalem, who are now
his witnesses to the people. 32And we
bring you the good news that what
God promised to the fathers, 33this he
has fulfilled to us their children by
raising Jesus; as also it is written in
the second psalm,

'Thou art my Son,
today I have begotten thee.'

34And as for the fact that he raised
him from the dead, no more to return
to corruption, he spoke in this way,

'I will give you the holy and
sure blessings of David.'

35Therefore he says also in another
psalm,

'Thou wilt not let thy Holy One
see corruption.'

36For David, after he had served
the counsel of God in his own genera-
tion, fell asleep, and was laid with his
fathers, and saw corruption; 37but he
whom God raised up saw no corrup-
tion. 38Let it be known to you there-
fore, brethren, that through this man
forgiveness of sins is proclaimed to

[b]Other ancient authorities read *cared for* (Deut 1. 31)

you, 39 and by him every one that be-
lieves is freed from everything from
which you could not be freed by the
law of Moses. 40 Beware, therefore, lest
there come upon you what is said in
the prophets:

41 'Behold, you scoffers, and won-
der, and perish;
for I do a deed in your days,
a deed you will never believe,
if one declares it to
you.'"

42 As they went out, the people
begged that these things might be told
them the next sabbath. 43 And when
the meeting of the synagogue broke
up, many Jews and devout converts to
Judaism followed Paul and Barnabas,
who spoke to them and urged them to
continue in the grace of God.

44 The next sabbath almost the
whole city gathered together to hear
the word of God. 45 But when the Jews
saw the multitudes, they were filled
with jealousy, and contradicted what
was spoken by Paul, and reviled him.
46 And Paul and Barnabas spoke out
boldly, saying, "It was necessary that
the word of God should be spoken
first to you. Since you thrust it from
you, and judge yourselves unworthy
of eternal life, behold, we turn to the
Gentiles. 47 For so the Lord has com-
manded us, saying,

'I have set you to be a light for
the Gentiles,
that you may bring salvation to
the uttermost parts of
the earth.'"

48 And when the Gentiles heard
this, they were glad and glorified the
word of God; and as many as were or-
dained to eternal life believed. 49 And
the word of the Lord spread through-
out all the region. 50 But the Jews incit-
ed the devout women of high standing
and the leading men of the city, and
stirred up persecution against Paul
and Barnabas, and drove them out of
their district. 51 But they shook off the
dust from their feet against them, and
went to Ico'nium. 52 And the disciples
were filled with joy and with the Holy
Spirit.

PAUL AND BARNABAS IN ICONIUM

14 Now at Ico'nium they entered to-
gether into the Jewish synagogue,
and so spoke that a great company
believed, both of Jews and of Greeks.
2 But the unbelieving Jews stirred
up the Gentiles and poisoned their
minds against the brethren. 3 So they
remained for a long time, speaking
boldly for the Lord, who bore witness
to the word of his grace, granting
signs and wonders to be done by their
hands. 4 But the people of the city were
divided; some sided with the Jews,
and some with the apostles. 5 When
an attempt was made by both Gentiles
and Jews, with their rulers, to molest
them and to stone them, 6 they learned
of it and fled to Lystra and Derbe, cit-
ies of Lycao'nia, and to the surround-
ing country; 7 and there they preached
the gospel.

PAUL AND BARNABAS IN LYSTRA AND DERBE

8 Now at Lystra there was a man
sitting, who could not use his feet; he
was a cripple from birth, who had nev-
er walked. 9 He listened to Paul speak-
ing; and Paul, looking intently at him
and seeing that he had faith to be made
well, 10 said in a loud voice, "Stand up-
right on your feet." And he sprang up
and walked. 11 And when the crowds
saw what Paul had done, they lifted
up their voices, saying in Lycao'nian,
"The gods have come down to us in
the likeness of men!" 12 Barnabas they
called Zeus, and Paul, because he was
the chief speaker, they called Hermes.
13 And the priest of Zeus, whose temple
was in front of the city, brought oxen
and garlands to the gates and want-
ed to offer sacrifice with the people.
14 But when the apostles Barnabas and
Paul heard of it, they tore their gar-
ments and rushed out among the mul-
titude, crying, 15 "Men, why are you

doing this? We also are men, of like
nature with you, and bring you good
news, that you should turn from these
vain things to a living God who made
the heaven and the earth and the sea
and all that is in them. 16In past gen-
erations he allowed all the nations to
walk in their own ways; 17yet he did
not leave himself without witness, for
he did good and gave you from heaven
rains and fruitful seasons, satisfying
your hearts with food and gladness."
18With these words they scarcely re-
strained the people from offering sac-
rifice to them.

THE RETURN TO ANTIOCH IN SYRIA

19 But Jews came there from
Antioch and Ico´nium; and having
persuaded the people, they stoned
Paul and dragged him out of the city,
supposing that he was dead. 20But
when the disciples gathered about
him, he rose up and entered the city;
and on the next day he went on with
Barnabas to Derbe. 21When they had
preached the gospel to that city and
had made many disciples, they re-
turned to Lystra and to Ico´nium and
to Antioch, 22strengthening the souls
of the disciples, exhorting them to
continue in the faith, and saying that
through many tribulations we must
enter the kingdom of God. 23And when
they had appointed elders for them in
every church, with prayer and fasting,
they committed them to the Lord in
whom they believed.

24 Then they passed through Pi-
sid´ia, and came to Pamphyl´ia. 25And
when they had spoken the word in
Perga, they went down to Attali´a;
26and from there they sailed to An-
tioch, where they had been commend-
ed to the grace of God for the work
which they had fulfilled. 27And when
they arrived, they gathered the church
together and declared all that God
had done with them, and how he had
opened a door of faith to the Gentiles.
28And they remained no little time
with the disciples.

THE COUNCIL AT JERUSALEM

15 But some men came down from
Judea and were teaching the
brethren, "Unless you are circumcised
according to the custom of Moses, you
cannot be saved." 2And when Paul and
Barnabas had no small dissension and
debate with them, Paul and Barnabas
and some of the others were appoint-
ed to go up to Jerusalem to the apos-
tles and the elders about this ques-
tion. 3So, being sent on their way by
the church, they passed through both
Phoeni´cia and Samar´ia, reporting
the conversion of the Gentiles, and
they gave great joy to all the breth-
ren. 4When they came to Jerusalem,
they were welcomed by the church
and the apostles and the elders, and
they declared all that God had done
with them. 5But some believers who
belonged to the party of the Pharisees
rose up, and said, "It is necessary to
circumcise them, and to charge them
to keep the law of Moses."

6 The apostles and the elders were
gathered together to consider this
matter. 7And after there had been
much debate, Peter rose and said to
them, "Brethren, you know that in the
early days God made choice among
you, that by my mouth the Gentiles
should hear the word of the gospel
and believe. 8And God who knows the
heart bore witness to them, giving
them the Holy Spirit just as he did to
us; 9and he made no distinction be-
tween us and them, but cleansed their
hearts by faith. 10Now therefore why
do you make trial of God by putting
a yoke upon the neck of the disciples
which neither our fathers nor we have
been able to bear? 11But we believe
that we shall be saved through the
grace of the Lord Jesus, just as they
will."

12 And all the assembly kept si-
lence; and they listened to Barnabas
and Paul as they related what signs
and wonders God had done through
them among the Gentiles. 13After
they finished speaking, James replied,

"Brethren, listen to me. 14Symeon
has related how God first visited the
Gentiles, to take out of them a peo-
ple for his name. 15And with this the
words of the prophets agree, as it is
written,

16'After this I will return,
and I will rebuild the dwelling
of David, which has
fallen;
I will rebuild its ruins,
and I will set it up,
17that the rest of men may seek
the Lord,
and all the Gentiles who are
called by my name,
18says the Lord, who has made
these things known from
of old.'

19Therefore my judgment is that
we should not trouble those of the
Gentiles who turn to God, 20but
should write to them to abstain from
the pollutions of idols and from un-
chastity and from what is strangled[a]
and from blood. 21For from early gen-
erations Moses has had in every city
those who preach him, for he is read
every sabbath in the synagogues."

THE COUNCIL'S LETTER TO GENTILE BELIEVERS

22 Then it seemed good to the apos-
tles and the elders, with the whole
church, to choose men from among
them and send them to Antioch with
Paul and Barnabas. They sent Judas
called Barsab´bas, and Silas, leading
men among the brethren, 23with the
following letter: "The brethren, both
the apostles and the elders, to the
brethren who are of the Gentiles in
Antioch and Syria and Cili´cia, greet-
ing. 24Since we have heard that some
persons from us have troubled you
with words, unsettling your minds, al-
though we gave them no instructions,
25it has seemed good to us in assembly
to choose men and send them to you
with our beloved Barnabas and Paul,
26men who have risked their lives for
the sake of our Lord Jesus Christ. 27We
have therefore sent Judas and Silas,
who themselves will tell you the same
things by word of mouth. 28For it has
seemed good to the Holy Spirit and to
us to lay upon you no greater burden
than these necessary things: 29that
you abstain from what has been sacri-
ficed to idols and from blood and from
what is strangled[b] and from unchasti-
ty. If you keep yourselves from these,
you will do well. Farewell."

30 So when they were sent off, they
went down to Antioch; and having
gathered the congregation together,
they delivered the letter. 31And when
they read it, they rejoiced at the ex-
hortation. 32And Judas and Silas, who
were themselves prophets, exhorted
the brethren with many words and
strengthened them. 33And after they
had spent some time, they were sent
off in peace by the brethren to those
who had sent them.[c]35But Paul and
Barnabas remained in Antioch, teach-
ing and preaching the word of the
Lord, with many others also.

PAUL AND BARNABAS SEPARATE

36 And after some days Paul said
to Barnabas, "Come, let us return and
visit the brethren in every city where
we proclaimed the word of the Lord,
and see how they are." 37And Barnabas
wanted to take with them John called
Mark. 38But Paul thought best not to
take with them one who had with-
drawn from them in Pamphyl´ia, and
had not gone with them to the work.
39And there arose a sharp contention,
so that they separated from each oth-
er; Barnabas took Mark with him and
sailed away to Cyprus, 40but Paul chose
Silas and departed, being commended
by the brethren to the grace of the
Lord. 41And he went through Syria and
Cili´cia, strengthening the churches.

[a]Other early authorities omit *and from what is strangled*
[b]Other early authorities omit *and from what is strangled*
[c]Other ancient authorities insert verse 34, *But it seemed good to Silas to remain there*

TIMOTHY JOINS PAUL AND SILAS

16 And he came also to Derbe and
to Lystra. A disciple was there,
named Timothy, the son of a Jewish
woman who was a believer; but his
father was a Greek. 2 He was well spo-
ken of by the brethren at Lystra and
Ico′nium. 3 Paul wanted Timothy to
accompany him; and he took him and
circumcised him because of the Jews
that were in those places, for they
all knew that his father was a Greek.
4 As they went on their way through
the cities, they delivered to them for
observance the decisions which had
been reached by the apostles and el-
ders who were at Jerusalem. 5 So the
churches were strengthened in the
faith, and they increased in numbers
daily.

PAUL'S VISION OF THE MAN OF MACEDONIA

6 And they went through the re-
gion of Phry′gia and Galatia, having
been forbidden by the Holy Spirit to
speak the word in Asia. 7 And when
they had come opposite My′sia, they
attempted to go into Bithyn′ia, but the
Spirit of Jesus did not allow them; 8 so,
passing by My′sia, they went down to
Tro′as. 9 And a vision appeared to Paul
in the night: a man of Macedo′nia was
standing beseeching him and saying,
"Come over to Macedo′nia and help
us." 10 And when he had seen the vi-
sion, immediately we sought to go on
into Macedo′nia, concluding that God
had called us to preach the gospel to
them.*

THE CONVERSION OF LYDIA

11 Setting sail therefore from
Tro′as, we made a direct voyage to
Sam′othrace, and the following day
to Ne-ap′olis, 12 and from there to
Philippi, which is the leading city
of the district[d] of Macedo′nia, and a
Roman colony. We remained in this
city some days; 13 and on the sabbath
day we went outside the gate to the
riverside, where we supposed there
was a place of prayer;* and we sat
down and spoke to the women who
had come together. 14 One who heard
us was a woman named Lydia, from
the city of Thyati′ra, a seller of purple
goods, who was a worshiper of God.
The Lord opened her heart to give
heed to what was said by Paul. 15 And
when she was baptized, with her
household, she besought us, saying,
"If you have judged me to be faithful
to the Lord, come to my house and
stay." And she prevailed upon us.

PAUL AND SILAS IN PRISON

16 As we were going to the place
of prayer, we were met by a slave girl
who had a spirit of divination and
brought her owners much gain by
soothsaying. 17 She followed Paul and
us, crying, "These men are servants of
the Most High God, who proclaim to
you the way of salvation." 18 And this
she did for many days. But Paul was
annoyed, and turned and said to the
spirit, "I charge you in the name of
Jesus Christ to come out of her." And
it came out that very hour.

19 But when her owners saw that
their hope of gain was gone, they
seized Paul and Silas and dragged
them into the market place before the
rulers; 20 and when they had brought
them to the magistrates they said,
"These men are Jews and they are
disturbing our city. 21 They advocate
customs which it is not lawful for us
Romans to accept or practice." 22 The
crowd joined in attacking them; and
the magistrates tore the garments off
them and gave orders to beat them
with rods. 23 And when they had in-
flicted many blows upon them, they
threw them into prison, charging the
jailer to keep them safely. 24 Having re-
ceived this charge, he put them into
the inner prison and fastened their
feet in the stocks.

25 But about midnight Paul and
Silas were praying and singing hymns
to God, and the prisoners were

[d] The Greek text is uncertain

listening to them, 26and suddenly there was a great earthquake, so that the foundations of the prison were shaken; and immediately all the doors were opened and every one's fetters were unfastened. 27When the jailer woke and saw that the prison doors were open, he drew his sword and was about to kill himself, supposing that the prisoners had escaped. 28But Paul cried with a loud voice, "Do not harm yourself, for we are all here." 29And he called for lights and rushed in, and trembling with fear he fell down before Paul and Silas, 30and brought them out and said, "Men, what must I do to be saved?" 31And they said, "Believe in the Lord Jesus, and you will be saved, you and your household." 32And they spoke the word of the Lord to him and to all that were in his house. 33And he took them the same hour of the night, and washed their wounds, and he was baptized at once, with all his family. 34Then he brought them up into his house, and set food before them; and he rejoiced with all his household that he had believed in God.

35 But when it was day, the magistrates sent the police, saying, "Let those men go." 36And the jailer reported the words to Paul, saying, "The magistrates have sent to let you go; now therefore come out and go in peace." 37But Paul said to them, "They have beaten us publicly, uncondemned, men who are Roman citizens, and have thrown us into prison; and do they now cast us out secretly? No! let them come themselves and take us out." 38The police reported these words to the magistrates, and they were afraid when they heard that they were Roman citizens; 39so they came and apologized to them. And they took them out and asked them to leave the city. 40So they went out of the prison, and visited Lydia; and when they had seen the brethren, they exhorted them and departed.

THE UPROAR IN THESSALONICA

17 Now when they had passed through Amphip´olis and Apollo´nia, they came to Thessaloni´ca, where there was a synagogue of the Jews. 2And Paul went in, as was his custom, and for three weeks[a] he argued with them from the scriptures, 3explaining and proving that it was necessary for the Christ to suffer and to rise from the dead, and saying, "This Jesus, whom I proclaim to you, is the Christ." 4And some of them were persuaded, and joined Paul and Silas; as did a great many of the devout Greeks and not a few of the leading women. 5But the Jews were jealous, and taking some wicked fellows of the rabble, they gathered a crowd, set the city in an uproar, and attacked the house of Jason, seeking to bring them out to the people. 6And when they could not find them, they dragged Jason and some of the brethren before the city authorities, crying, "These men who have turned the world upside down have come here also, 7and Jason has received them; and they are all acting against the decrees of Caesar, saying that there is another king, Jesus." 8And the people and the city authorities were disturbed when they heard this. 9And when they had taken security from Jason and the rest, they let them go.

PAUL AND SILAS IN BEROEA

10 The brethren immediately sent Paul and Silas away by night to Beroe´a; and when they arrived they went into the Jewish synagogue. 11Now these Jews were more noble than those in Thessaloni´ca, for they received the word with all eagerness, examining the scriptures daily to see if these things were so. 12Many of them therefore believed, with not a few Greek women of high standing as well as men. 13But when the Jews of Thessaloni´ca learned that the word of God was proclaimed by Paul

[a] Or *sabbaths*

at Beroe´a also, they came there too,
stirring up and inciting the crowds.
14 Then the brethren immediately sent
Paul off on his way to the sea, but
Silas and Timothy remained there.
15 Those who conducted Paul brought
him as far as Athens; and receiving
a command for Silas and Timothy to
come to him as soon as possible, they
departed.

PAUL IN ATHENS

16 Now while Paul was waiting for
them at Athens, his spirit was pro-
voked within him as he saw that the
city was full of idols. 17 So he argued
in the synagogue with the Jews and
the devout persons, and in the mar-
ket place every day with those who
chanced to be there. 18 Some also of the
Epicurean and Stoic philosophers met
him. And some said, "What would
this babbler say?" Others said, "He
seems to be a preacher of foreign di-
vinities"—because he preached Jesus
and the resurrection. 19 And they took
hold of him and brought him to the
Are-op´agus, saying, "May we know
what this new teaching is which you
present? 20 For you bring some strange
things to our ears; we wish to know
therefore what these things mean."
21 Now all the Athenians and the for-
eigners who lived there spent their
time in nothing except telling or hear-
ing something new.

22 So Paul, standing in the mid-
dle of the Are-op´agus, said: "Men
of Athens, I perceive that in every
way you are very religious. 23 For as I
passed along, and observed the ob-
jects of your worship, I found also
an altar with this inscription, 'To
an unknown god.' What therefore
you worship as unknown, this I pro-
claim to you. 24 The God who made
the world and everything in it, being
Lord of heaven and earth, does not
live in shrines made by man, 25 nor is
he served by human hands, as though
he needed anything, since he himself
gives to all men life and breath and
everything. 26 And he made from one
every nation of men to live on all the
face of the earth, having determined
allotted periods and the boundaries
of their habitation, 27 that they should
seek God, in the hope that they might
feel after him and find him. Yet he is
not far from each one of us, 28 for

'In him we live and move and
have our being';
'For we are indeed his
offspring.'

29 Being then God's offspring, we
ought not to think that the Deity is
like gold, or silver, or stone, a repre-
sentation by the art and imagination
of man. 30 The times of ignorance God
overlooked, but now he commands all
men everywhere to repent, 31 because
he has fixed a day on which he will
judge the world in righteousness by a
man whom he has appointed, and of
this he has given assurance to all men
by raising him from the dead."

32 Now when they heard of the res-
urrection of the dead, some mocked;
but others said, "We will hear you
again about this." 33 So Paul went out
from among them. 34 But some men
joined him and believed, among them
Dionys´ius the Are-op´agite and a
woman named Dam´aris and others
with them.

PAUL IN CORINTH

18 After this he left Athens and went
to Corinth. 2 And he found a Jew
named Aquila, a native of Pontus,
lately come from Italy with his wife
Priscilla, because Claudius had com-
manded all the Jews to leave Rome.
And he went to see them; 3 and be-
cause he was of the same trade he
stayed with them, and they worked,
for by trade they were tentmakers.
4 And he argued in the synagogue ev-
ery sabbath, and persuaded Jews and
Greeks.

5 When Silas and Timothy arrived
from Macedo´nia, Paul was occupied
with preaching, testifying to the
Jews that the Christ was Jesus. 6 And

when they opposed and reviled him,
he shook out his garments and said
to them, "Your blood be upon your
heads! I am innocent. From now on I
will go to the Gentiles." 7And he left
there and went to the house of a man
named Titius[a] Justus, a worshiper of
God; his house was next door to the
synagogue. 8Crispus, the ruler of the
synagogue, believed in the Lord, to-
gether with all his household; and
many of the Corinthians hearing Paul
believed and were baptized. 9And
the Lord said to Paul one night in a
vision, "Do not be afraid, but speak
and do not be silent; 10for I am with
you, and no man shall attack you to
harm you; for I have many people in
this city." 11And he stayed a year and
six months, teaching the word of God
among them.

12 But when Gallio was proconsul
of Acha´ia, the Jews made a united
attack upon Paul and brought him be-
fore the tribunal, 13saying, "This man
is persuading men to worship God
contrary to the law." 14But when Paul
was about to open his mouth, Gallio
said to the Jews, "If it were a matter of
wrongdoing or vicious crime, I should
have reason to bear with you, O Jews;
15but since it is a matter of questions
about words and names and your own
law, see to it yourselves; I refuse to
be a judge of these things." 16And he
drove them from the tribunal. 17And
they all seized Sos´thenes, the ruler of
the synagogue, and beat him in front
of the tribunal. But Gallio paid no at-
tention to this.

PAUL'S RETURN TO ANTIOCH

18 After this Paul stayed many
days longer, and then took leave of the
brethren and sailed for Syria, and with
him Priscilla and Aquila. At Cen´chre-
ae he cut his hair, for he had a vow.
19And they came to Ephesus, and he
left them there; but he himself went
into the synagogue and argued with
the Jews. 20When they asked him to
stay for a longer period, he declined;
21but on taking leave of them he said,
"I will return to you if God wills," and
he set sail from Ephesus.

22 When he had landed at
Caesare´a, he went up and greeted
the church, and then went down to
Antioch. 23After spending some time
there he departed and went from
place to place through the region of
Galatia and Phryg´ia, strengthening
all the disciples.

MINISTRY OF APOLLOS

24 Now a Jew named Apol´los, a na-
tive of Alexandria, came to Ephesus.
He was an eloquent man, well versed
in the scriptures. 25He had been in-
structed in the way of the Lord; and
being fervent in spirit, he spoke and
taught accurately the things concern-
ing Jesus, though he knew only the
baptism of John. 26He began to speak
boldly in the synagogue; but when
Priscilla and Aquila heard him, they
took him and expounded to him the
way of God more accurately. 27And
when he wished to cross to Acha´ia,
the brethren encouraged him, and
wrote to the disciples to receive him.
When he arrived, he greatly helped
those who through grace had be-
lieved, 28for he powerfully confuted
the Jews in public, showing by the
scriptures that the Christ was Jesus.

PAUL IN EPHESUS

19 While Apol´los was at Corinth,
Paul passed through the upper
country and came to Ephesus. There
he found some disciples. 2And he said
to them, "Did you receive the Holy
Spirit when you believed?" And they
said, "No, we have never even heard
that there is a Holy Spirit." 3And he
said, "Into what then were you bap-
tized?" They said, "Into John's bap-
tism." 4And Paul said, "John baptized
with the baptism of repentance, tell-
ing the people to believe in the one
who was to come after him, that is,

[a] Other early authorities read *Titus*

Jesus." 5On hearing this, they were
baptized in the name of the Lord
Jesus. 6And when Paul had laid his
hands upon them, the Holy Spirit
came on them; and they spoke with
tongues and prophesied. 7There were
about twelve of them in all.

8 And he entered the synagogue
and for three months spoke boldly,
arguing and pleading about the king-
dom of God; 9but when some were
stubborn and disbelieved, speaking
evil of the Way before the congrega-
tion, he withdrew from them, taking
the disciples with him, and argued
daily in the hall of Tyran´nus.[b] 10This
continued for two years, so that all
the residents of Asia heard the word
of the Lord, both Jews and Greeks.

THE SONS OF SCEVA

11 And God did extraordinary mir-
acles by the hands of Paul, 12so that
handkerchiefs or aprons were carried
away from his body to the sick, and
diseases left them and the evil spir-
its came out of them. 13Then some of
the itinerant Jewish exorcists under-
took to pronounce the name of the
Lord Jesus over those who had evil
spirits, saying, "I adjure you by the
Jesus whom Paul preaches." 14Seven
sons of a Jewish high priest named
Sceva were doing this. 15But the evil
spirit answered them, "Jesus I know,
and Paul I know; but who are you?"
16And the man in whom the evil spirit
was leaped on them, mastered all of
them, and overpowered them, so that
they fled out of that house naked and
wounded. 17And this became known
to all residents of Ephesus, both Jews
and Greeks; and fear fell upon them
all; and the name of the Lord Jesus
was extolled. 18Many also of those
who were now believers came, con-
fessing and divulging their practices.
19And a number of those who prac-
ticed magic arts brought their books
together and burned them in the sight
of all; and they counted the value of
them and found it came to fifty thou-
sand pieces of silver. 20So the word of
the Lord grew and prevailed mightily.

THE RIOT IN EPHESUS

21 Now after these events Paul re-
solved in the Spirit to pass through
Macedo´nia and Acha´ia and go to
Jerusalem, saying, "After I have been
there, I must also see Rome." 22And
having sent into Macedo´nia two of
his helpers, Timothy and Eras´tus, he
himself stayed in Asia for a while.

23 About that time there arose no
little stir concerning the Way. 24For
a man named Deme´trius, a silver-
smith, who made silver shrines of
Ar´temis, brought no little business
to the craftsmen. 25These he gath-
ered together, with the workmen of
like occupation, and said, "Men, you
know that from this business we have
our wealth. 26And you see and hear
that not only at Ephesus but almost
throughout all Asia this Paul has per-
suaded and turned away a consider-
able company of people, saying that
gods made with hands are not gods.
27And there is danger not only that this
trade of ours may come into disrepute
but also that the temple of the great
goddess Ar´temis may count for noth-
ing, and that she may even be deposed
from her magnificence, she whom all
Asia and the world worship."

28 When they heard this they
were enraged, and cried out, "Great
is Ar´temis of the Ephesians!" 29So
the city was filled with the confusion;
and they rushed together into the the-
ater, dragging with them Ga´ius and
Aristar´chus, Macedo´nians who were
Paul's companions in travel. 30Paul
wished to go in among the crowd,
but the disciples would not let him;
31some of the A´si-archs also, who
were friends of his, sent to him and
begged him not to venture into the
theater. 32Now some cried one thing,
some another; for the assembly was
in confusion, and most of them did

[b] Other ancient authorities add *from the fifth hour to the tenth*

not know why they had come togeth-
er. 33Some of the crowd prompted
Alexander, whom the Jews had put
forward. And Alexander motioned
with his hand, wishing to make a de-
fense to the people. 34But when they
recognized that he was a Jew, for
about two hours they all with one
voice cried out, "Great is Ar´temis
of the Ephesians!" 35And when the
town clerk had quieted the crowd,
he said, "Men of Ephesus, what man
is there who does not know that the
city of the Ephesians is temple keeper
of the great Ar´temis, and of the sa-
cred stone* that fell from the sky?[a]
36Seeing then that these things cannot
be contradicted, you ought to be quiet
and do nothing rash. 37For you have
brought these men here who are nei-
ther sacrilegious nor blasphemers of
our goddess. 38If therefore Deme´trius
and the craftsmen with him have a
complaint against any one, the courts
are open, and there are proconsuls;
let them bring charges against one
another. 39But if you seek anything
further,[b] it shall be settled in the reg-
ular assembly. 40For we are in danger
of being charged with rioting today,
there being no cause that we can give
to justify this commotion." 41And
when he had said this, he dismissed
the assembly.

PAUL GOES TO MACEDONIA AND GREECE

20 After the uproar ceased, Paul
sent for the disciples and having
exhorted them took leave of them
and departed for Macedo´nia. 2When
he had gone through these parts and
had given them much encourage-
ment, he came to Greece. 3There he
spent three months, and when a plot
was made against him by the Jews as
he was about to set sail for Syria, he
determined to return through Mace-
do´nia. 4Sop´ater of Beroe´a, the son
of Pyrrhus, accompanied him; and of
the Thessalo´nians, Aristar´chus and
Secun´dus; and Ga´ius of Derbe, and
Timothy; and the Asians, Tych´icus
and Troph´imus. 5These went on and
were waiting for us at Tro´as, 6but we
sailed away from Philippi after the
days of Unleavened Bread, and in five
days we came to them at Tro´as, where
we stayed for seven days.

PAUL'S FAREWELL VISIT TO TROAS

7 On the first day of the week,
when we were gathered together to
break bread,* Paul talked with them,
intending to depart on the morrow;
and he prolonged his speech until
midnight. 8There were many lights
in the upper chamber where we were
gathered. 9And a young man named
Eu´tychus was sitting in the window.
He sank into a deep sleep as Paul
talked still longer; and being over-
come by sleep, he fell down from the
third story and was taken up dead.
10But Paul went down and bent over
him, and embracing him said, "Do
not be alarmed, for his life is in him."
11And when Paul had gone up and
had broken bread and eaten, he con-
versed with them a long while, until
daybreak, and so departed. 12And they
took the lad away alive, and were not
a little comforted.

THE VOYAGE FROM TROAS TO MILETUS

13 But going ahead to the ship, we
set sail for Assos, intending to take
Paul aboard there; for so he had ar-
ranged, intending himself to go by
land. 14And when he met us at Assos,
we took him on board and came to
Mityle´ne. 15And sailing from there
we came the following day opposite
Chi´os; the next day we touched at
Samos; and[c] the day after that we
came to Mile´tus. 16For Paul had de-
cided to sail past Ephesus, so that
he might not have to spend time in
Asia; for he was hastening to be at
Jerusalem, if possible, on the day of
Pentecost.

[a]The meaning of the Greek is uncertain
[b]Other ancient authorities read *about other matters*
[c]Other ancient authorities add *after remaining at Trogyllium*

PAUL SPEAKS TO THE EPHESIAN ELDERS

17 And from Mile´tus he sent to
Ephesus and called to him the elders
of the church. 18And when they came
to him, he said to them:

PAUL'S JOURNEY TO JERUSALEM

"You yourselves know how I lived
among you all the time from the first
day that I set foot in Asia, 19serving
the Lord with all humility and with
tears and with trials which befell me
through the plots of the Jews; 20how
I did not shrink from declaring to
you anything that was profitable,
and teaching you in public and from
house to house, 21testifying both to
Jews and to Greeks of repentance to
God and of faith in our Lord Jesus
Christ. 22And now, behold, I am going
to Jerusalem, bound in the Spirit, not
knowing what shall befall me there;
23except that the Holy Spirit testifies
to me in every city that imprisonment
and afflictions await me. 24But I do
not account my life of any value nor
as precious to myself, if only I may ac-
complish my course and the ministry
which I received from the Lord Jesus,
to testify to the gospel of the grace
of God. 25And now, behold, I know
that all you among whom I have gone
about preaching the kingdom will see
my face no more. 26Therefore I testi-
fy to you this day that I am innocent
of the blood of all of you, 27for I did
not shrink from declaring to you the
whole counsel of God. 28Take heed
to yourselves and to all the flock, in
which the Holy Spirit has made you
guardians, to feed the church of the
Lord[d] which he obtained with his own
blood.[e] 29I know that after my depar-
ture fierce wolves will come in among
you, not sparing the flock; 30and from
among your own selves will arise
men speaking perverse things, to
draw away the disciples after them.
31Therefore be alert, remembering that
for three years I did not cease night or
day to admonish every one with tears.
32And now I commend you to God and
to the word of his grace, which is able
to build you up and to give you the
inheritance among all those who are
sanctified. 33I coveted no one's silver
or gold or apparel. 34You yourselves
know that these hands ministered to
my necessities, and to those who were
with me.* 35In all things I have shown
you that by so toiling one must help
the weak, remembering the words of
the Lord Jesus, how he said, 'It is more
blessed to give than to receive.'"

36 And when he had spoken thus,
he knelt down and prayed with them
all. 37And they all wept and embraced
Paul and kissed him, 38sorrowing most
of all because of the word he had spo-
ken, that they should see his face no
more. And they brought him to the
ship.

21 And when we had parted from
them and set sail, we came by a
straight course to Cos, and the next
day to Rhodes, and from there to
Pat´ara.[f] 2And having found a ship
crossing to Phoeni´cia, we went
aboard, and set sail. 3When we had
come in sight of Cyprus, leaving it on
the left we sailed to Syria, and land-
ed at Tyre; for there the ship was to
unload its cargo. 4And having sought
out the disciples, we stayed there for
seven days. Through the Spirit they
told Paul not to go* on to Jerusalem.
5And when our days there were ended,
we departed and went on our journey;
and they all, with wives and children,
brought us on our way till we were
outside the city; and kneeling down
on the beach we prayed and bade
one another farewell. 6Then we went
on board the ship, and they returned
home.

7 When we had finished the voyage
from Tyre, we arrived at Ptolema´is;
and we greeted the brethren and
stayed with them for one day. 8On
the morrow we departed and came to

[d] Other ancient authorities read *of God*
[e] Or *with the blood of his Own*
[f] Other ancient authorities add *and Myra*

Caesare´a; and we entered the house of
Philip the evangelist, who was one of
the seven, and stayed with him. 9 And
he had four unmarried daughters,
who prophesied. 10 While we were stay-
ing for some days, a prophet named
Ag´abus came down from Judea. 11 And
coming to us he took Paul's girdle and
bound his own feet and hands, and
said, "Thus says the Holy Spirit, 'So
shall the Jews at Jerusalem bind the
man who owns this girdle and deliver
him into the hands of the Gentiles.'"
12 When we heard this, we and the
people there begged him not to go up
to Jerusalem. 13 Then Paul answered,
"What are you doing, weeping and
breaking my heart? For I am ready not
only to be imprisoned but even to die
at Jerusalem for the name of the Lord
Jesus." 14 And when he would not be
persuaded, we ceased and said, "The
will of the Lord be done."

15 After these days we made ready
and went up to Jerusalem. 16 And some
of the disciples from Caesare´a went
with us, bringing us to the house of
Mnason of Cyprus, an early disciple,
with whom we should lodge.

PAUL VISITS JAMES AT JERUSALEM

17 When we had come to Jerusalem,
the brethren received us gladly. 18 On
the following day Paul went in with
us to James; and all the elders were
present. 19 After greeting them, he re-
lated one by one the things that God
had done among the Gentiles through
his ministry. 20 And when they heard
it, they glorified God. And they said
to him, "You see, brother, how many
thousands there are among the Jews
of those who have believed; they are
all zealous for the law, 21 and they have
been told about you that you teach all
the Jews who are among the Gentiles
to forsake Moses, telling them not to
circumcise their children or observe
the customs. 22 What then is to be
done? They will certainly hear that
you have come. 23 Do therefore what
we tell you. We have four men who are
under a vow; 24 take these men and pu-
rify yourself along with them and pay
their expenses, so that they may shave
their heads. Thus all will know that
there is nothing in what they have
been told about you but that you your-
self live in observance of the law. 25 But
as for the Gentiles who have believed,
we have sent a letter with our judg-
ment that they should abstain from
what has been sacrificed to idols and
from blood and from what is stran-
gled[a] and from unchastity." 26 Then
Paul took the men, and the next day
he purified himself with them and
went into the temple, to give notice
when the days of purification would
be fulfilled and the offering presented
for every one of them.

PAUL ARRESTED IN THE TEMPLE

27 When the seven days were al-
most completed, the Jews from Asia,
who had seen him in the temple,
stirred up all the crowd, and laid
hands on him, 28 crying out, "Men of
Israel, help! This is the man who is
teaching men everywhere against the
people and the law and this place;
moreover he also brought Greeks into
the temple, and he has defiled this
holy place." 29 For they had previously
seen Troph´imus the Ephesian with
him in the city, and they supposed that
Paul had brought him into the temple.
30 Then all the city was aroused, and
the people ran together; they seized
Paul and dragged him out of the tem-
ple, and at once the gates were shut.
31 And as they were trying to kill him,
word came to the tribune of the cohort
that all Jerusalem was in confusion.
32 He at once took soldiers and centuri-
ons, and ran down to them; and when
they saw the tribune and the soldiers,
they stopped beating Paul. 33 Then the
tribune came up and arrested him,
and ordered him to be bound with
two chains. He inquired who he was
and what he had done. 34 Some in the

[a] Other early authorities omit *and from what is strangled*

crowd shouted one thing, some anoth-
er; and as he could not learn the facts
because of the uproar, he ordered him
to be brought into the barracks. 35And
when he came to the steps, he was ac-
tually carried by the soldiers because
of the violence of the crowd; 36for the
mob of the people followed, crying,
"Away with him!"

PAUL DEFENDS HIMSELF

37 As Paul was about to be brought
into the barracks, he said to the tri-
bune, "May I say something to you?"
And he said, "Do you know Greek?
38Are you not the Egyptian, then, who
recently stirred up a revolt and led the
four thousand men of the Assassins
out into the wilderness?" 39Paul re-
plied, "I am a Jew, from Tarsus in
Cili´cia, a citizen of no mean city; I
beg you, let me speak to the people."
40And when he had given him leave,
Paul, standing on the steps, motioned
with his hand to the people; and when
there was a great hush, he spoke to
them in the Hebrew language, saying:

22 "Brethren and fathers, hear the
defense which I now make before
you."

2 And when they heard that he ad-
dressed them in the Hebrew language,
they were the more quiet. And he said:

3 "I am a Jew, born at Tarsus in
Cili´cia, but brought up in this city
at the feet of Gama´li-el, educated
according to the strict manner of the
law of our fathers, being zealous for
God as you all are this day. 4I perse-
cuted this Way to the death, binding
and delivering to prison both men
and women, 5as the high priest and
the whole council of elders bear me
witness. From them I received let-
ters to the brethren, and I journeyed
to Damascus to take those also who
were there and bring them in bonds to
Jerusalem to be punished.

PAUL TELLS OF HIS CONVERSION

6 "As I made my journey and drew
near to Damascus, about noon a great
light from heaven suddenly shone
about me. 7And I fell to the ground
and heard a voice saying to me, 'Saul,
Saul, why do you persecute me?' 8And
I answered, 'Who are you, Lord?' And
he said to me, 'I am Jesus of Nazareth
whom you are persecuting.' 9Now
those who were with me saw the
light but did not hear the voice of the
one who was speaking to me. 10And I
said, 'What shall I do, Lord?' And the
Lord said to me, 'Rise, and go into
Damascus, and there you will be told
all that is appointed for you to do.'
11And when I could not see because of
the brightness of that light, I was led
by the hand by those who were with
me, and came into Damascus.

12 "And one Anani´as, a devout
man according to the law, well spo-
ken of by all the Jews who lived
there, 13came to me, and standing by
me said to me, 'Brother Saul, receive
your sight.' And in that very hour I
received my sight and saw him. 14And
he said, 'The God of our fathers ap-
pointed you to know his will, to see
the Just One and to hear a voice from
his mouth; 15for you will be a witness
for him to all men of what you have
seen and heard. 16And now why do
you wait? Rise and be baptized, and
wash away your sins, calling on his
name.'

PAUL SENT TO THE GENTILES

17 "When I had returned to
Jerusalem and was praying in the
temple, I fell into a trance 18and saw
him saying to me, 'Make haste and get
quickly out of Jerusalem, because they
will not accept your testimony about
me.' 19And I said, 'Lord, they them-
selves know that in every synagogue
I imprisoned and beat those who be-
lieved in thee. 20And when the blood
of Stephen thy witness* was shed, I
also was standing by and approving,
and keeping the garments of those
who killed him.' 21And he said to me,
'Depart; for I will send you far away to
the Gentiles.'"

PAUL AND THE ROMAN TRIBUNE

22 Up to this word they listened to
him; then they lifted up their voices
and said, "Away with such a fellow
from the earth! For he ought not
to live." 23And as they cried out and
waved their garments and threw dust
into the air, 24the tribune commanded
him to be brought into the barracks,
and ordered him to be examined by
scourging, to find out why they shout-
ed thus against him. 25But when they
had tied him up with the thongs, Paul
said to the centurion who was stand-
ing by, "Is it lawful for you to scourge
a man who is a Roman citizen, and
uncondemned?" 26When the centurion
heard that, he went to the tribune and
said to him, "What are you about to
do? For this man is a Roman citizen."
27So the tribune came and said to him,
"Tell me, are you a Roman citizen?"
And he said, "Yes." 28The tribune an-
swered, "I bought this citizenship for
a large sum." Paul said, "But I was
born a citizen." 29So those who were
about to examine him withdrew from
him instantly; and the tribune also
was afraid, for he realized that Paul
was a Roman citizen and that he had
bound him.

PAUL BEFORE THE COUNCIL

30 But on the morrow, desiring to
know the real reason why the Jews ac-
cused him, he unbound him, and com-
manded the chief priests and all the
council to meet, and he brought Paul
down and set him before them.

23 And Paul, looking intently at the
council, said, "Brethren, I have
lived before God in all good con-
science up to this day." 2And the high
priest Anani´as commanded those
who stood by him to strike him on the
mouth. 3Then Paul said to him, "God
shall strike you, you whitewashed
wall! Are you sitting to judge me ac-
cording to the law, and yet contrary to
the law you order me to be struck?"
4Those who stood by said, "Would
you revile God's high priest?" 5And
Paul said, "I did not know, brethren,
that he was the high priest; for it is
written, 'You shall not speak evil of a
ruler of your people.'"

6 But when Paul perceived that one
part were Sad´ducees and the other
Pharisees, he cried out in the council,
"Brethren, I am a Pharisee, a son of
Pharisees; with respect to the hope
and the resurrection of the dead I am
on trial." 7And when he had said this,
a dissension arose between the Phar-
isees and the Sad´ducees; and the as-
sembly was divided. 8For the Sad´du-
cees say that there is no resurrection,
nor angel, nor spirit; but the Phari-
sees acknowledge them all. 9Then a
great clamor arose; and some of the
scribes of the Pharisees' party stood
up and contended, "We find nothing
wrong in this man. What if a spirit or
an angel spoke to him?" 10And when
the dissension became violent, the tri-
bune, afraid that Paul would be torn
in pieces by them, commanded the
soldiers to go down and take him by
force from among them and bring him
into the barracks.

11 The following night the Lord
stood by him and said, "Take courage,
for as you have testified about me at
Jerusalem, so you must bear witness
also at Rome."

THE PLOT TO KILL PAUL

12 When it was day, the Jews made
a plot and bound themselves by an
oath neither to eat nor drink till they
had killed Paul. 13There were more
than forty who made this conspiracy.
14And they went to the chief priests
and elders, and said, "We have strictly
bound ourselves by an oath to taste
no food till we have killed Paul. 15You
therefore, along with the council, give
notice now to the tribune to bring him
down to you, as though you were go-
ing to determine his case more exact-
ly. And we are ready to kill him before
he comes near."

16 Now the son of Paul's sister
heard of their ambush; so he went

and entered the barracks and told
Paul. 17And Paul called one of the
centurions and said, "Bring this
young man to the tribune; for he has
something to tell him." 18So he took
him and brought him to the tribune
and said, "Paul the prisoner called
me and asked me to bring this young
man to you, as he has something to
say to you." 19The tribune took him
by the hand, and going aside asked
him privately, "What is it that you
have to tell me?" 20And he said, "The
Jews have agreed to ask you to bring
Paul down to the council tomorrow,
as though they were going to in-
quire somewhat more closely about
him. 21But do not yield to them; for
more than forty of their men lie in
ambush for him, having bound them-
selves by an oath neither to eat nor
drink till they have killed him; and
now they are ready, waiting for the
promise from you." 22So the tribune
dismissed the young man, charging
him, "Tell no one that you have in-
formed me of this."

PAUL SENT TO FELIX THE GOVERNOR

23 Then he called two of the cen-
turions and said, "At the third hour
of the night get ready two hundred
soldiers with seventy horsemen and
two hundred spearmen to go as far as
Caesare´a. 24Also provide mounts for
Paul to ride, and bring him safely to
Felix the governor." 25And he wrote a
letter to this effect:

26 "Claudius Lys´ias to his
Excellency the governor Felix, greet-
ing. 27This man was seized by the
Jews, and was about to be killed by
them, when I came upon them with
the soldiers and rescued him, having
learned that he was a Roman citizen.
28And desiring to know the charge on
which they accused him, I brought
him down to their council. 29I found
that he was accused about ques-
tions of their law, but charged with
nothing deserving death or imprison-
ment. 30And when it was disclosed to
me that there would be a plot against
the man, I sent him to you at once,
ordering his accusers also to state
before you what they have against
him."

31 So the soldiers, according to
their instructions, took Paul and
brought him by night to Antip´atris.
32And on the morrow they returned
to the barracks, leaving the horsemen
to go on with him. 33When they came
to Caesare´a and delivered the letter
to the governor, they presented Paul
also before him. 34On reading the let-
ter, he asked to what province he be-
longed. When he learned that he was
from Cili´cia 35he said, "I will hear
you when your accusers arrive." And
he commanded him to be guarded in
Herod's praetorium.

PAUL BEFORE FELIX AT CAESAREA

24 And after five days the high
priest Anani´as came down
with some elders and a spokesman,
one Tertul´lus. They laid before the
governor their case against Paul;
2and when he was called, Tertul´lus
began to accuse him, saying: "Since
through you we enjoy much peace,
and since by your provision, most ex-
cellent Felix, reforms are introduced
on behalf of this nation, 3in every
way and everywhere we accept this
with all gratitude. 4But, to detain you
no further, I beg you in your kind-
ness to hear us briefly. 5For we have
found this man a pestilent fellow, an
agitator among all the Jews through-
out the world, and a ringleader of the
sect of the Nazarenes. 6He even tried
to profane the temple, but we seized
him.[a] 8By examining him yourself
you will be able to learn from him
about everything of which we accuse
him."

9 The Jews also joined in the
charge, affirming that all this was so.

[a]Other ancient authorities add *and we would have judged him according to our law. 7But the chief captain Lysias came and with great violence took him out of our hands, 8commanding his accusers to come before you.*

PAUL'S DEFENSE BEFORE FELIX

10 And when the governor had mo-
tioned to him to speak, Paul replied:
"Realizing that for many years you
have been judge over this nation, I
cheerfully make my defense. 11As you
may ascertain, it is not more than
twelve days since I went up to worship
at Jerusalem; 12and they did not find
me disputing with any one or stir-
ring up a crowd, either in the temple
or in the synagogues, or in the city.
13Neither can they prove to you what
they now bring up against me. 14But
this I admit to you, that according to
the Way, which they call a sect, I wor-
ship the God of our fathers, believ-
ing everything laid down by the law
or written in the prophets, 15having a
hope in God which these themselves
accept, that there will be a resurrec-
tion of both the just and the unjust.
16So I always take pains to have a clear
conscience toward God and toward
men. 17Now after some years I came to
bring to my nation alms and offerings.
18As I was doing this, they found me
purified in the temple, without any
crowd or tumult. But some Jews from
Asia 19they ought to be here before
you and to make an accusation, if they
have anything against me. 20Or else
let these men themselves say what
wrongdoing they found when I stood
before the council, 21except this one
thing which I cried out while stand-
ing among them, 'With respect to the
resurrection of the dead I am on trial
before you this day.'"

22 But Felix, having a rather accu-
rate knowledge of the Way, put them
off, saying, "When Lys´ias the tribune
comes down, I will decide your case."
23Then he gave orders to the centuri-
on that he should be kept in custody
but should have some liberty, and that
none of his friends should be prevent-
ed from attending to his needs.

PAUL HELD IN CUSTODY

24 After some days Felix came
with his wife Drusil´la, who was
a Jewess; and he sent for Paul and
heard him speak upon faith in Christ
Jesus. 25And as he argued about jus-
tice and self-control and future judg-
ment, Felix was alarmed and said,
"Go away for the present; when I
have an opportunity I will summon
you." 26At the same time he hoped
that money would be given him by
Paul. So he sent for him often and
conversed with him. 27But when two
years had elapsed, Felix was succeed-
ed by Porcius Festus; and desiring to
do the Jews a favor, Felix left Paul in
prison.

PAUL APPEALS TO THE EMPEROR

25 Now when Festus had come into
his province, after three days he
went up to Jerusalem from Caesare´a.
2And the chief priests and the prin-
cipal men of the Jews informed him
against Paul; and they urged him,
3asking as a favor to have the man
sent to Jerusalem, planning an am-
bush to kill him on the way. 4Festus
replied that Paul was being kept at
Caesare´a, and that he himself intend-
ed to go there shortly. 5"So," said he,
"let the men of authority among you
go down with me, and if there is any-
thing wrong about the man, let them
accuse him."

6 When he had stayed among them
not more than eight or ten days, he
went down to Caesare´a; and the next
day he took his seat on the tribunal
and ordered Paul to be brought. 7And
when he had come, the Jews who had
gone down from Jerusalem stood
about him, bringing against him many
serious charges which they could
not prove. 8Paul said in his defense,
"Neither against the law of the Jews,
nor against the temple, nor against
Caesar have I offended at all." 9But
Festus, wishing to do the Jews a favor,
said to Paul, "Do you wish to go up to
Jerusalem, and there be tried on these
charges before me?" 10But Paul said, "I
am standing before Caesar's tribunal,
where I ought to be tried; to the Jews I

have done no wrong, as you know very
well. 11 If then I am a wrongdoer, and
have committed anything for which I
deserve to die, I do not seek to escape
death; but if there is nothing in their
charges against me, no one can give
me up to them. I appeal to Caesar."
12 Then Festus, when he had conferred
with his council, answered, "You have
appealed to Caesar; to Caesar you
shall go."

FESTUS CONSULTS KING AGRIPPA

13 Now when some days had
passed, Agrippa the king and Ber-
ni´ce arrived at Caesare´a to welcome
Festus. 14 And as they stayed there
many days, Festus laid Paul's case be-
fore the king, saying, "There is a man
left prisoner by Felix; 15 and when I
was at Jerusalem, the chief priests
and the elders of the Jews gave in-
formation about him, asking for
sentence against him. 16 I answered
them that it was not the custom of
the Romans to give up any one before
the accused met the accusers face to
face, and had opportunity to make
his defense concerning the charge
laid against him. 17 When therefore
they came together here, I made no
delay, but on the next day took my
seat on the tribunal and ordered the
man to be brought in. 18 When the
accusers stood up, they brought no
charge in his case of such evils as
I supposed; 19 but they had certain
points of dispute with him about
their own superstition and about one
Jesus, who was dead, but whom Paul
asserted to be alive. 20 Being at a loss
how to investigate these questions, I
asked whether he wished to go to Je-
rusalem and be tried there regarding
them. 21 But when Paul had appealed
to be kept in custody for the decision
of the emperor, I commanded him
to be held until I could send him to
Caesar." 22 And Agrippa said to Fes-
tus, "I should like to hear the man
myself." "Tomorrow," said he, "you
shall hear him."

PAUL BROUGHT BEFORE AGRIPPA

23 So on the morrow Agrippa and
Berni´ce came with great pomp, and
they entered the audience hall with
the military tribunes and the prom-
inent men of the city. Then by com-
mand of Festus Paul was brought
in. 24 And Festus said, "King Agrippa
and all who are present with us, you
see this man about whom the whole
Jewish people petitioned me, both at
Jerusalem and here, shouting that he
ought not to live any longer. 25 But I
found that he had done nothing de-
serving death; and as he himself ap-
pealed to the emperor, I decided to
send him. 26 But I have nothing defi-
nite to write to my lord about him.
Therefore I have brought him before
you, and, especially before you, King
Agrippa, that, after we have examined
him, I may have something to write.
27 For it seems to me unreasonable, in
sending a prisoner, not to indicate the
charges against him."

PAUL DEFENDS HIMSELF BEFORE AGRIPPA

26 Agrippa said to Paul, "You have
permission to speak for yourself."
Then Paul stretched out his hand and
made his defense:

2 "I think myself fortunate that it
is before you, King Agrippa, I am to
make my defense today against all the
accusations of the Jews, 3 because you
are especially familiar with all cus-
toms and controversies of the Jews;
therefore I beg you to listen to me
patiently.

4 "My manner of life from my
youth, spent from the beginning
among my own nation and at Jerusa-
lem, is known by all the Jews. 5 They
have known for a long time, if they are
willing to testify, that according to the
strictest party of our religion I have
lived as a Pharisee. 6 And now I stand
here on trial for hope in the promise
made by God to our fathers, 7 to which
our twelve tribes hope to attain, as
they earnestly worship night and day.
And for this hope I am accused by

Jews, O king! 8Why is it thought in-
credible by any of you that God raises
the dead?
9 "I myself was convinced that I
ought to do many things in opposing
the name of Jesus of Nazareth. 10And
I did so in Jerusalem; I not only shut
up many of the saints in prison, by
authority from the chief priests, but
when they were put to death I cast my
vote against them. 11And I punished
them often in all the synagogues and
tried to make them blaspheme; and in
raging fury against them, I persecuted
them even to foreign cities.

PAUL TELLS OF HIS CONVERSION

12 "Thus I journeyed to Damascus
with the authority and commission of
the chief priests. 13At midday, O king,
I saw on the way a light from heaven,
brighter than the sun, shining round
me and those who journeyed with me.
14And when we had all fallen to the
ground, I heard a voice saying to me
in the Hebrew language, 'Saul, Saul,
why do you persecute me? It hurts
you to kick against the goads.' 15And
I said, 'Who are you, Lord?' And the
Lord said, 'I am Jesus whom you are
persecuting. 16But rise and stand upon
your feet; for I have appeared to you
for this purpose, to appoint you to
serve and bear witness to the things
in which you have seen me and to
those in which I will appear to you,
17delivering you from the people and
from the Gentiles—to whom I send
you 18to open their eyes, that they may
turn from darkness to light and from
the power of Satan to God, that they
may receive forgiveness of sins and a
place among those who are sanctified
by faith in me.'

PAUL TELLS OF HIS PREACHING

19 "Wherefore, O King Agrippa, I
was not disobedient to the heavenly
vision, 20but declared first to those
at Damascus, then at Jerusalem and
throughout all the country of Judea,
and also to the Gentiles, that they
should repent and turn to God and
perform deeds worthy of their re-
pentance. 21For this reason the Jews
seized me in the temple and tried to
kill me. 22To this day I have had the
help that comes from God, and so I
stand here testifying both to small
and great, saying nothing but what
the prophets and Moses said would
come to pass: 23that the Christ must
suffer, and that, by being the first to
rise from the dead, he would proclaim
light both to the people and to the
Gentiles."

PAUL APPEALS TO AGRIPPA TO BELIEVE

24 And as he thus made his de-
fense, Festus said with a loud voice,
"Paul, you are mad; your great learn-
ing is turning you mad." 25But Paul
said, "I am not mad, most excellent
Festus, but I am speaking the sober
truth. 26For the king knows about
these things, and to him I speak free-
ly; for I am persuaded that none of
these things has escaped his notice,
for this was not done in a corner.
27King Agrippa, do you believe the
prophets? I know that you believe."
28And Agrippa said to Paul, "In a
short time you think to make me a
Christian!" 29And Paul said, "Whether
short or long, I would to God that not
only you but also all who hear me this
day might become such as I am—ex-
cept for these chains."
30 Then the king rose, and the
governor and Berni´ce and those who
were sitting with them; 31and when
they had withdrawn, they said to one
another, "This man is doing nothing
to deserve death or imprisonment."
32And Agrippa said to Festus, "This
man could have been set free if he had
not appealed to Caesar."

PAUL SAILS FOR ROME

27 And when it was decided that we
should sail for Italy, they deliv-
ered Paul and some other prisoners to
a centurion of the Augustan Cohort,
named Julius. 2And embarking in a

ship of Adramyt´tium, which was
about to sail to the ports along the
coast of Asia, we put to sea, accompa-
nied by Aristar´chus, a Macedo´nian
from Thessaloni´ca. 3The next day
we put in at Sidon; and Julius treated
Paul kindly, and gave him leave to go
to his friends and be cared for. 4And
putting to sea from there we sailed
under the lee of Cyprus, because the
winds were against us. 5And when we
had sailed across the sea which is off
Cili´cia and Pamphyl´ia, we came to
Myra in Ly´cia. 6There the centurion
found a ship of Alexandria sailing for
Italy, and put us on board. 7We sailed
slowly for a number of days, and ar-
rived with difficulty off Cni´dus, and
as the wind did not allow us to go
on, we sailed under the lee of Crete
off Salmo´ne. 8Coasting along it with
difficulty, we came to a place called
Fair Havens, near which was the city
of Lase´a.

9 As much time had been lost, and
the voyage was already dangerous
because the fast had already gone by,
Paul advised them, 10saying, "Sirs, I
perceive that the voyage will be with
injury and much loss, not only of the
cargo and the ship, but also of our
lives." 11But the centurion paid more
attention to the captain and to the
owner of the ship than to what Paul
said. 12And because the harbor was
not suitable to winter in, the majority
advised to put to sea from there, on
the chance that somehow they could
reach Phoenix, a harbor of Crete,
looking northeast and southeast,[a] and
winter there.

THE STORM AT SEA

13 And when the south wind blew
gently, supposing that they had ob-
tained their purpose, they weighed
anchor and sailed along Crete, close
inshore. 14But soon a tempestuous
wind, called the northeaster, struck
down from the land; 15and when the
ship was caught and could not face
the wind, we gave way to it and were
driven. 16And running under the lee
of a small island called Cauda,[b] we
managed with difficulty to secure the
boat; 17after hoisting it up, they took
measures[c] to undergird the ship; then,
fearing that they should run on the
Syr´tis, they lowered the gear, and so
were driven. 18As we were violently
storm-tossed, they began next day to
throw the cargo overboard; 19and the
third day they cast out with their own
hands the tackle of the ship. 20And
when neither sun nor stars appeared
for many a day, and no small tempest
lay on us, all hope of our being saved
was at last abandoned.

21 As they had been long without
food, Paul then came forward among
them and said, "Men, you should have
listened to me, and should not have
set sail from Crete and incurred this
injury and loss. 22I now bid you take
heart; for there will be no loss of life
among you, but only of the ship. 23For
this very night there stood by me an
angel of the God to whom I belong and
whom I worship, 24and he said, 'Do
not be afraid, Paul; you must stand
before Caesar; and lo, God has grant-
ed you all those who sail with you.'
25So take heart, men, for I have faith
in God that it will be exactly as I have
been told. 26But we shall have to run
on some island."

27 When the fourteenth night
had come, as we were drifting across
the sea of A´dria, about midnight
the sailors suspected that they were
nearing land. 28So they sounded and
found twenty fathoms; a little farther
on they sounded again and found
fifteen fathoms. 29And fearing that
we might run on the rocks, they let
out four anchors from the stern, and
prayed for day to come. 30And as the
sailors were seeking to escape from
the ship, and had lowered the boat
into the sea, under pretense of laying

[a] Or *southwest and northwest*
[b] Other ancient authorities read *Clauda*
[c] Greek *helps*

out anchors from the bow, 31Paul said
to the centurion and the soldiers,
"Unless these men stay in the ship,
you cannot be saved." 32Then the sol-
diers cut away the ropes of the boat,
and let it go.

33 As day was about to dawn, Paul
urged them all to take some food,
saying, "Today is the fourteenth day
that you have continued in suspense
and without food, having taken noth-
ing. 34Therefore I urge you to take
some food; it will give you strength,
since not a hair is to perish from the
head of any of you." 35And when he
had said this, he took bread, and giv-
ing thanks to God in the presence
of all he broke it and began to eat.
36Then they all were encouraged and
ate some food themselves. 37(We were
in all two hundred and seventy-six[a]
persons in the ship.) 38And when they
had eaten enough, they lightened the
ship, throwing out the wheat into the
sea.

THE SHIPWRECK

39 Now when it was day, they did
not recognize the land, but they no-
ticed a bay with a beach, on which
they planned if possible to bring the
ship ashore. 40So they cast off the an-
chors and left them in the sea, at the
same time loosening the ropes that
tied the rudders; then hoisting the
foresail to the wind they made for the
beach. 41But striking a shoal[b] they ran
the vessel aground; the bow stuck and
remained immovable, and the stern
was broken up by the surf. 42The sol-
diers' plan was to kill the prisoners,
lest any should swim away and es-
cape; 43but the centurion, wishing to
save Paul, kept them from carrying
out their purpose. He ordered those
who could swim to throw themselves
overboard first and make for the land,
44and the rest on planks or on pieces
of the ship. And so it was that all es-
caped to land.

PAUL ON THE ISLAND OF MALTA

28 After we had escaped, we then
learned that the island was called
Malta. 2And the natives showed us
unusual kindness, for they kindled a
fire and welcomed us all, because it
had begun to rain and was cold. 3Paul
had gathered a bundle of sticks and
put them on the fire, when a viper
came out because of the heat and
fastened on his hand. 4When the na-
tives saw the creature hanging from
his hand, they said to one another,
"No doubt this man is a murderer.
Though he has escaped from the sea,
justice has not allowed him to live."
5He, however, shook off the creature
into the fire and suffered no harm.
6They waited, expecting him to swell
up or suddenly fall down dead; but
when they had waited a long time and
saw no misfortune come to him, they
changed their minds and said that he
was a god.

7 Now in the neighborhood of
that place were lands belonging to
the chief man of the island, named
Publius, who received us and enter-
tained us hospitably for three days. 8It
happened that the father of Publius
lay sick with fever and dysentery;
and Paul visited him and prayed, and
putting his hands on him healed him.
9And when this had taken place, the
rest of the people on the island who
had diseases also came and were
cured. 10They presented many gifts to
us;[c] and when we sailed, they put on
board whatever we needed.

PAUL ARRIVES AT ROME

11 After three months we set sail
in a ship which had wintered in the
island, a ship of Alexandria, with the
Twin Brothers as figurehead. 12Putting
in at Syracuse, we stayed there for
three days. 13And from there we made
a circuit and arrived at Rhe´gium; and
after one day a south wind sprang up,
and on the second day we came to

[a] Other ancient authorities read *seventy-six* or *about seventy-six*
[b] Greek *place of two seas*
[c] Or *honored us with many honors*

Pute´oli. 14There we found brethren,
and were invited to stay with them for
seven days. And so we came to Rome.
15And the brethren there, when they
heard of us, came as far as the Forum
of Ap´pius and Three Taverns to meet
us. On seeing them Paul thanked God
and took courage. 16And when we
came into Rome, Paul was allowed to
stay by himself, with the soldier that
guarded him.

PAUL AND JEWISH LEADERS IN ROME

17 After three days he called to-
gether the local leaders of the Jews;
and when they had gathered, he
said to them, "Brethren, though I
had done nothing against the peo-
ple or the customs of our fathers,
yet I was delivered prisoner from
Jerusalem into the hands of the
Romans. 18When they had examined
me, they wished to set me at liber-
ty, because there was no reason for
the death penalty in my case. 19But
when the Jews objected, I was com-
pelled to appeal to Caesar—though
I had no charge to bring against my
nation. 20For this reason therefore I
have asked to see you and speak with
you, since it is because of the hope
of Israel that I am bound with this
chain." 21And they said to him, "We
have received no letters from Judea
about you, and none of the brethren
coming here has reported or spoken
any evil about you. 22But we desire
to hear from you what your views
are; for with regard to this sect we
know that everywhere it is spoken
against."

PAUL PREACHES IN ROME

23 When they had appointed a
day for him, they came to him at his
lodging in great numbers. And he
expounded the matter to them from
morning till evening, testifying to the
kingdom of God and trying to con-
vince them about Jesus both from the
law of Moses and from the prophets.
24And some were convinced by what
he said, while others disbelieved. 25So,
as they disagreed among themselves,
they departed, after Paul had made
one statement: "The Holy Spirit was
right in saying to your fathers through
Isaiah the prophet:

26'Go to this people, and say,
You shall indeed hear but never
understand,
and you shall indeed see but
never perceive.
27For this people's heart has
grown dull,
and their ears are heavy of
hearing,
and their eyes they have closed;
lest they should perceive with
their eyes,
and hear with their ears,
and understand with their
heart,
and turn for me to heal them.'

28Let it be known to you then that
this salvation of God has been sent to
the Gentiles; they will listen."[d]

30 And he lived there two whole
years at his own expense,[e] and wel-
comed all who came to him, 31preach-
ing the kingdom of God and teaching
about the Lord Jesus Christ quite
openly and unhindered.

[d]Other ancient authorities add verse 29, *And when he had said these words, the Jews departed, holding much dispute among themselves*

[e]Or *in his own hired dwelling*

THE LETTER OF PAUL TO THE
ROMANS

SALUTATION

1 Paul, a servant[a] of Jesus Christ,
called to be an apostle, set apart for
the gospel of God 2which he promised
beforehand through his prophets in
the holy scriptures, 3the gospel con-
cerning his Son, who was descended
from David according to the flesh
4and designated[b] Son of God in power
according to the Spirit of holiness by
his resurrection from the dead, Jesus
Christ our Lord, 5through whom we
have received grace and apostleship
to bring about the obedience of faith
for the sake of his name among all the
nations, 6including yourselves who are
called to belong to Jesus Christ;
7 To all God's beloved in Rome,
who are called to be saints: Grace to
you and peace from God our Father
and the Lord Jesus Christ.*

PRAYER OF THANKSGIVING

8 First, I thank my God through
Jesus Christ for all of you, because
your faith is proclaimed in all the
world. 9For God is my witness, whom
I serve with my spirit in the gospel of
his Son, that without ceasing I men-
tion you always in my prayers, 10asking
that somehow by God's will I may now
at last succeed in coming to you.* 11For
I long to see you, that I may impart to
you some spiritual gift to strengthen
you, 12that is, that we may be mutu-
ally encouraged by each other's faith,
both yours and mine. 13I want you to
know, brethren, that I have often in-
tended to come to you (but thus far
have been prevented), in order that I
may reap some harvest* among you as
well as among the rest of the Gentiles.
14I am under obligation both to Greeks
and to barbarians, both to the wise
and to the foolish: 15so I am eager to
preach the gospel to you also who are
in Rome.

THE POWER OF THE GOSPEL

16 For I am not ashamed of the
gospel: it is the power of God for sal-
vation to every one who has faith, to
the Jew first and also to the Greek.
17For in it the righteousness of God is
revealed through faith for faith; as it
is written, "He who through faith is
righteous shall live."[c]

THE GUILT OF MANKIND

18 For the wrath of God is revealed
from heaven against all ungodliness
and wickedness of men who by their
wickedness suppress the truth. 19For
what can be known about God is plain
to them, because God has shown it to
them. 20Ever since the creation of the
world his invisible nature, namely,
his eternal power and deity, has been
clearly perceived in the things that
have been made. So they are without
excuse; 21for although they knew God
they did not honor him as God or give
thanks to him, but they became futile
in their thinking and their senseless
minds were darkened. 22Claiming to
be wise, they became fools, 23and ex-
changed the glory of the immortal
God for images resembling mortal
man or birds or animals or reptiles.
24 Therefore God gave them up in
the lusts of their hearts to impurity, to
the dishonoring of their bodies among
themselves, 25because they exchanged
the truth about God for a lie and wor-
shiped and served the creature rather
than the Creator, who is blessed for
ever! Amen.
26 For this reason God gave them
up to dishonorable passions. Their
women exchanged natural relations

[a] Or *slave*
[b] Or *constituted*
[c] Or *The righteous shall live by faith*

for unnatural, 27and the men likewise
gave up natural relations with women
and were consumed with passion for
one another, men committing shame-
less acts with men and receiving in
their own persons the due penalty for
their error.

28 And since they did not see fit
to acknowledge God, God gave them
up to a base mind and to improper
conduct. 29They were filled with all
manner of wickedness, evil, covet-
ousness, malice. Full of envy, mur-
der, strife, deceit, malignity, they are
gossips, 30slanderers, haters of God,
insolent, haughty, boastful, inventors
of evil, disobedient to parents, 31fool-
ish, faithless, heartless, ruthless.
32Though they know God's decree that
those who do such things deserve to
die, they not only do them but approve
those who practice them.

THE RIGHTEOUS JUDGMENT OF GOD

2 Therefore you have no excuse, O
man, whoever you are, when you
judge another; for in passing judg-
ment upon him you condemn yourself,
because you, the judge, are doing the
very same things. 2We know that the
judgment of God rightly falls upon
those who do such things. 3Do you
suppose, O man, that when you judge
those who do such things and yet do
them yourself, you will escape the
judgment of God? 4Or do you presume
upon the riches of his kindness and
forbearance and patience? Do you not
know that God's kindness is meant to
lead you to repentance? 5But by your
hard and impenitent heart you are
storing up wrath for yourself on the
day of wrath when God's righteous
judgment will be revealed. 6For he
will render to every man according to
his works: 7to those who by patience
in well-doing seek for glory and honor
and immortality, he will give eternal
life; 8but for those who are factious
and do not obcy thc truth, but obey
wickedness, there will be wrath and
fury. 9There will be tribulation and
distress for every human being who
does evil, the Jew first and also the
Greek, 10but glory and honor and
peace for every one who does good,
the Jew first and also the Greek. 11For
God shows no partiality.

12 All who have sinned without the
law will also perish without the law,
and all who have sinned under the
law will be judged by the law. 13For it
is not the hearers of the law who are
righteous before God, but the doers of
the law who will be justified. 14When
Gentiles who have not the law do by
nature what the law requires, they are
a law to themselves, even though they
do not have the law. 15They show that
what the law requires is written on
their hearts, while their conscience
also bears witness and their conflict-
ing thoughts accuse or perhaps excuse
them 16on that day when, according to
my gospel, God judges the secrets of
men by Christ Jesus.

THE JEWS AND THE LAW

17 But if you call yourself a Jew and
rely upon the law and boast of your re-
lation to God 18and know his will and
approve what is excellent, because
you are instructed in the law, 19and if
you are sure that you are a guide to
the blind, a light to those who are in
darkness, 20a corrector of the foolish, a
teacher of children, having in the law
the embodiment of knowledge and
truth 21you then who teach others,
will you not teach yourself? While
you preach against stealing, do you
steal? 22You who say that one must
not commit adultery, do you commit
adultery? You who abhor idols, do you
rob temples? 23You who boast in the
law, do you dishonor God by breaking
the law? 24For, as it is written, "The
name of God is blasphemed among
the Gentiles because of you."

25 Circumcision indeed is of value
if you obey the law; but if you break
the law, your circumcision becomes
uncircumcision. 26So, if a man who is
uncircumcised keeps the precepts of

the law, will not his uncircumcision
be regarded as circumcision? 27 Then
those who are physically uncircum-
cised but keep the law will condemn
you who have the written code and
circumcision but break the law. 28 For
he is not a real Jew who is one out-
wardly, nor is true circumcision some-
thing external and physical. 29 He is
a Jew who is one inwardly, and real
circumcision is a matter of the heart,
spiritual and not literal. His praise is
not from men but from God.

3 Then what advantage has the Jew?
Or what is the value of circumci-
sion? 2 Much in every way. To begin
with, the Jews are entrusted with the
oracles of God. 3 What if some were
unfaithful? Does their faithlessness
nullify the faithfulness of God? 4 By no
means! Let God be true though every
man be false, as it is written,

> "That thou mayest be justified
> in thy words,
> and prevail when thou art
> judged."

5 But if our wickedness serves to
show the justice of God, what shall
we say? That God is unjust to inflict
wrath on us? (I speak in a human
way.) 6 By no means! For then how
could God judge the world? 7 But if
through my falsehood God's truth-
fulness abounds to his glory, why am
I still being condemned as a sinner?
8 And why not do evil that good may
come?—as some people slanderously
charge us with saying. Their condem-
nation is just.

NONE IS RIGHTEOUS

9 What then? Are we Jews any bet-
ter off?[a] No, not at all; for I[b] have al-
ready charged that all men, both Jews
and Greeks, are under the power of
sin, 10 as it is written:

> "None is righteous, no, not
> one;
> 11 no one understands, no one
> seeks for God.
> 12 All have turned aside, together
> they have gone wrong;
> no one does good, not even
> one."
> 13 "Their throat is an open grave,
> they use their tongues to
> deceive."
> "The venom of asps is under
> their lips."
> 14 "Their mouth is full of curses
> and bitterness."
> 15 "Their feet are swift to shed
> blood,
> 16 in their paths are ruin and
> misery,
> 17 and the way of peace they do not
> know."
> 18 "There is no fear of God before
> their eyes."

19 Now we know that whatever the
law says it speaks to those who are
under the law, so that every mouth
may be stopped, and the whole world
may be held accountable to God. 20 For
no human being will be justified in
his sight by works of the law, since
through the law comes knowledge of
sin.

RIGHTEOUSNESS THROUGH FAITH

21 But now the righteousness
of God has been manifested apart
from law, although the law and the
prophets bear witness to it, 22 the
righteousness of God through faith
in Jesus Christ for all who believe.
For there is no distinction; 23 since
all have sinned and fall short of the
glory of God, 24 they are justified by
his grace as a gift, through the re-
demption which is in Christ Jesus,
25 whom God put forward as an expi-
ation by his blood, to be received by
faith. This was to show God's righ-
teousness, because in his divine for-
bearance he had passed over former
sins; 26 it was to prove at the present
time that he himself is righteous and
that he justifies him who has faith
in Jesus.

[a] Or *at any disadvantage?*
[b] Greek *we*

27 Then what becomes of our
boasting? It is excluded. On what
principle? On the principle of works?
No, but on the principle of faith.*
28For we hold that a man is justified
by faith apart from works of law. 29Or
is God the God of Jews only? Is he
not the God of Gentiles also? Yes, of
Gentiles also, 30since God is one; and
he will justify the circumcised on the
ground of their faith and the uncir-
cumcised through their faith. 31Do we
then overthrow the law by this faith?
By no means! On the contrary, we up-
hold the law.

THE EXAMPLE OF ABRAHAM

4 What then shall we say about[c]
Abraham, our forefather accord-
ing to the flesh? 2For if Abraham was
justified by works, he has something
to boast about, but not before God.
3For what does the scripture say?
"Abraham believed God, and it was
reckoned to him as righteousness."
4Now to one who works, his wages are
not reckoned as a gift but as his due.
5And to one who does not work but
trusts him who justifies the ungodly,
his faith is reckoned as righteousness.
6So also David pronounces a blessing
upon the man to whom God reckons
righteousness apart from works:

7"Blessed are those whose iniq-
uities are forgiven, and
whose sins are covered;
8blessed is the man against whom
the Lord will not reckon
his sin."

9 Is this blessing pronounced only
upon the circumcised, or also upon
the uncircumcised? We say that faith
was reckoned to Abraham as righ-
teousness. 10How then was it reckoned
to him? Was it before or after he had
been circumcised? It was not after,
but before he was circumcised. 11He
received circumcision as a sign or seal
of the righteousness which he had
by faith while he was still uncircum-
cised. The purpose was to make him
the father of all who believe without
being circumcised and who thus have
righteousness reckoned to them, 12and
likewise the father of the circumcised
who are not merely circumcised but
also follow the example of the faith
which our father Abraham had before
he was circumcised.

GOD'S PROMISE REALIZED THROUGH FAITH

13 The promise to Abraham and
his descendants, that they should in-
herit the world, did not come through
the law but through the righteousness
of faith. 14If it is the adherents of the
law who are to be the heirs, faith is
null and the promise is void. 15For the
law brings wrath, but where there is
no law there is no transgression.

16 That is why it depends on faith,
in order that the promise may rest
on grace and be guaranteed to all his
descendants—not only to the adher-
ents of the law but also to those who
share the faith of Abraham, for he is
the father of us all, 17as it is written,
"I have made you the father of many
nations"—in the presence of the God
in whom he believed, who gives life to
the dead and calls into existence the
things that do not exist. 18In hope he
believed against hope, that he should
become the father of many nations; as
he had been told, "So shall your de-
scendants be." 19He did not weaken
in faith when he considered his own
body, which was as good as dead be-
cause he was about a hundred years
old, or when he considered the bar-
renness of Sarah's womb. 20No dis-
trust made him waver concerning the
promise of God, but he grew strong
in his faith as he gave glory to God,
21fully convinced that God was able
to do what he had promised. 22That is
why his faith was "reckoned to him as
righteousness." 23But the words, "it
was reckoned to him," were written
not for his sake alone, 24but for ours
also. It will be reckoned to us who be-
lieve in him that raised from the dead

[c]Other ancient authorities read *was gained by*

Jesus our Lord, 25who was put to death
for our trespasses and raised for our
justification.

RESULTS OF JUSTIFICATION

5 Therefore, since we are justi-
fied by faith, we[a] have peace with
God through our Lord Jesus Christ.
2Through him we have obtained ac-
cess[b] to this grace in which we stand,
and we[c] rejoice in our hope of sharing
the glory of God. 3More than that, we[d]
rejoice in our sufferings, knowing that
suffering produces endurance, 4and
endurance produces character, and
character produces hope, 5and hope
does not disappoint us, because God's
love has been poured into our hearts
through the Holy Spirit who has been
given to us.

6 While we were yet helpless, at
the right time Christ died for the un-
godly. 7Why, one will hardly die for a
righteous man—though perhaps for a
good man one will dare even to die.
8But God shows his love for us in that
while we were yet sinners Christ died
for us. 9Since, therefore, we are now
justified by his blood, much more
shall we be saved by him from the
wrath of God. 10For if while we were
enemies we were reconciled to God by
the death of his Son, much more, now
that we are reconciled, shall we be
saved by his life. 11Not only so, but we
also rejoice in God through our Lord
Jesus Christ, through whom we have
now received our reconciliation.

ADAM AND CHRIST

12 Therefore as sin came into the
world through one man and death
through sin, and so death spread to
all men because all men sinned* 13sin
indeed was in the world before the
law was given, but sin is not count-
ed where there is no law. 14Yet death
reigned from Adam to Moses, even
over those whose sins were not like
the transgression of Adam, who was a
type of the one who was to come.

15 But the free gift is not like the
trespass. For if many died through
one man's trespass, much more have
the grace of God and the free gift in
the grace of that one man Jesus Christ
abounded for many.* 16And the free
gift is not like the effect of that one
man's sin. For the judgment follow-
ing one trespass brought condem-
nation, but the free gift following
many trespasses brings justification.
17If, because of one man's trespass,
death reigned through that one man,
much more will those who receive the
abundance of grace and the free gift
of righteousness reign in life through
the one man Jesus Christ.

18 Then as one man's trespass led
to condemnation for all men, so one
man's act of righteousness leads to
acquittal and life for all men. 19For as
by one man's disobedience many were
made sinners, so by one man's obe-
dience many will be made righteous.
20Law came in, to increase the tres-
pass; but where sin increased, grace
abounded all the more, 21so that, as
sin reigned in death, grace also might
reign through righteousness to eter-
nal life through Jesus Christ our Lord.

DYING AND RISING WITH CHRIST

6 What shall we say then? Are we
to continue in sin that grace may
abound? 2By no means! How can we
who died to sin still live in it? 3Do
you not know that all of us who have
been baptized into Christ Jesus were
baptized into his death? 4We were
buried* therefore with him by bap-
tism into death, so that as Christ was
raised from the dead by the glory of
the Father, we too might walk in new-
ness of life.

5 For if we have been united with
him in a death like his, we shall
certainly be united with him in a

[a] Other ancient authorities read *let us*
[b] Other ancient authorities add *by faith*
[c] Or *let us*
[d] Or *let us*

resurrection like his. 6 We know that our old self was crucified with him so that the sinful body might be destroyed, and we might no longer be enslaved to sin. 7 For he who has died is freed from sin. 8 But if we have died with Christ, we believe that we shall also live with him. 9 For we know that Christ being raised from the dead will never die again; death no longer has dominion over him. 10 The death he died he died to sin, once for all, but the life he lives he lives to God. 11 So you also must consider yourselves dead to sin and alive to God in Christ Jesus.

12 Let not sin therefore reign in your mortal bodies, to make you obey their passions. 13 Do not yield your members to sin as instruments of wickedness, but yield yourselves to God as men who have been brought from death to life, and your members to God as instruments of righteousness. 14 For sin will have no dominion over you, since you are not under law but under grace.

SLAVES OF RIGHTEOUSNESS

15 What then? Are we to sin because we are not under law but under grace? By no means!* 16 Do you not know that if you yield yourselves to any one as obedient slaves, you are slaves of the one whom you obey, either of sin, which leads to death, or of obedience, which leads to righteousness? 17 But thanks be to God, that you who were once slaves of sin have become obedient from the heart to the standard of teaching to which you were committed, 18 and, having been set free from sin, have become slaves of righteousness. 19 I am speaking in human terms, because of your natural limitations. For just as you once yielded your members to impurity and to greater and greater iniquity, so now yield your members to righteousness for sanctification.

20 When you were slaves of sin, you were free in regard to righteousness. 21 But then what return did you get from the things of which you are now ashamed? The end of those things is death. 22 But now that you have been set free from sin and have become slaves of God, the return you get is sanctification and its end, eternal life. 23 For the wages of sin is death, but the free gift of God is eternal life in Christ Jesus our Lord.

AN ANALOGY FROM MARRIAGE

7 Do you not know, brethren—for I am speaking to those who know the law—that the law is binding on a person only during his life? 2 Thus a married woman is bound by law to her husband as long as he lives; but if her husband dies she is discharged from the law concerning the husband. 3 Accordingly, she will be called an adulteress if she lives with another man while her husband is alive. But if her husband dies she is free from that law, and if she marries another man she is not an adulteress.

4 Likewise, my brethren, you have died to the law through the body of Christ, so that you may belong to another, to him who has been raised from the dead in order that we may bear fruit for God. 5 While we were living in the flesh, our sinful passions, aroused by the law, were at work in our members to bear fruit for death. 6 But now we are discharged from the law, dead to that which held us captive, so that we serve not under the old written code but in the new life of the Spirit.

THE LAW AND SIN

7 What then shall we say? That the law is sin? By no means! Yet, if it had not been for the law, I should not have known sin. I should not have known what it is to covet if the law had not said, "You shall not covet." 8 But sin, finding opportunity in the commandment, wrought in me all kinds of covetousness. Apart from the law sin lies dead. 9 I was once alive apart from

the law, but when the commandment
came, sin revived and I died; [10]the
very commandment which promised
life proved to be death to me. [11]For
sin, finding opportunity in the com-
mandment, deceived me and by it
killed me. [12]So the law is holy, and the
commandment is holy and just and
good.

THE INNER CONFLICT

13 Did that which is good, then,
bring death to me?* By no means! It
was sin, working death in me through
what is good, in order that sin might
be shown to be sin, and through the
commandment might become sinful
beyond measure. [14]We know that the
law is spiritual; but I am carnal, sold
under sin. [15]I do not understand my
own actions. For I do not do what I
want, but I do the very thing I hate.
[16]Now if I do what I do not want, I
agree that the law is good. [17]So then it
is no longer I that do it, but sin which
dwells within me. [18]For I know that
nothing good dwells within me, that
is, in my flesh. I can will what is right,
but I cannot do it. [19]For I do not do the
good I want, but the evil I do not want
is what I do. [20]Now if I do what I do
not want, it is no longer I that do it,
but sin which dwells within me.

21 So I find it to be a law that
when I want to do right, evil lies close
at hand. [22]For I delight in the law of
God, in my inmost self, [23]but I see in
my members another law at war with
the law of my mind and making me
captive to the law of sin which dwells
in my members. [24]Wretched man that
I am! Who will deliver me from this
body of death? [25]Thanks be to God
through Jesus Christ our Lord! So
then, I of myself serve the law of God
with my mind, but with my flesh I
serve the law of sin.

LIFE IN THE SPIRIT

8 There is therefore now no condem-
nation for those who are in Christ
Jesus. [2]For the law of the Spirit of life
in Christ Jesus has set me free from
the law of sin and death. [3]For God has
done what the law, weakened by the
flesh, could not do: sending his own
Son in the likeness of sinful flesh
and for sin,[a] he condemned sin in the
flesh, [4]in order that the just require-
ment of the law might be fulfilled in
us, who walk not according to the
flesh but according to the Spirit. [5]For
those who live according to the flesh
set their minds on the things of the
flesh, but those who live according
to the Spirit set their minds on the
things of the Spirit. [6]To set the mind
on the flesh is death, but to set the
mind on the Spirit is life and peace.
[7]For the mind that is set on the flesh
is hostile to God; it does not submit
to God's law, indeed it cannot; [8]and
those who are in the flesh cannot
please God.

9 But you are not in the flesh,
you are in the Spirit, if the Spirit
of God really dwells in you. Any
one who does not have the Spirit
of Christ does not belong to him.
[10]But if Christ is in you, although
your bodies are dead because of sin,
your spirits are alive because of righ-
teousness. [11]If the Spirit of him who
raised Jesus from the dead dwells in
you, he who raised Christ Jesus from
the dead will give life to your mortal
bodies also through his Spirit who
dwells in you.

12 So then, brethren, we are debt-
ors, not to the flesh, to live according
to the flesh [13]for if you live according
to the flesh you will die, but if by the
Spirit you put to death the deeds of
the body you will live. [14]For all who
are led by the Spirit of God are sons of
God. [15]For you did not receive the spir-
it of slavery to fall back into fear, but
you have received the spirit of son-
ship. When we cry, "Abba! Father!"
[16]it is the Spirit himself bearing wit-
ness with our spirit that we are chil-
dren of God, [17]and if children, then

[a]Or *and as a sin offering*

heirs, heirs of God and fellow heirs
with Christ, provided we suffer with
him in order that we may also be glo-
rified with him.

FUTURE GLORY

18 I consider that the sufferings
of this present time are not worth
comparing with the glory that is to
be revealed to us. 19 For the creation
waits with eager longing for the re-
vealing of the sons of God;* 20 for the
creation was subjected to futility, not
of its own will but by the will of him
who subjected it in hope; 21 because the
creation itself will be set free from its
bondage to decay and obtain the glo-
rious liberty of the children of God.
22 We know that the whole creation
has been groaning in travail together
until now; 23 and not only the creation,
but we ourselves, who have the first
fruits of the Spirit, groan inwardly as
we wait for adoption as sons, the re-
demption of our bodies. 24 For in this
hope we were saved. Now hope that
is seen is not hope. For who hopes
for what he sees? 25 But if we hope for
what we do not see, we wait for it with
patience.

26 Likewise the Spirit helps us in
our weakness; for we do not know
how to pray as we ought, but the
Spirit himself intercedes for us with
sighs too deep for words. 27 And he
who searches the hearts of men
knows what is the mind of the Spirit,
because[b] the Spirit intercedes for the
saints according to the will of God.

28 We know that in everything
God works for good[c] with those who
love him,[d] who are called according
to his purpose. 29 For those whom he
foreknew he also predestined to be
conformed to the image of his Son, in
order that he might be the first-born
among many brethren. 30 And those
whom he predestined he also called;
and those whom he called he also
justified; and those whom he justified
he also glorified.

GOD'S LOVE IN CHRIST JESUS

31 What then shall we say to this?
If God is for us, who is against us?
32 He who did not spare his own Son
but gave him up for us all, will he
not also give us all things with him?
33 Who shall bring any charge against
God's elect? It is God who justifies;
34 who is to condemn? Is it Christ
Jesus, who died, yes, who was raised
from the dead, who is at the right
hand of God, who indeed intercedes
for us?[e] 35 Who shall separate us from
the love of Christ? Shall tribulation,
or distress, or persecution, or famine,
or nakedness, or peril, or sword? 36 As
it is written,

"For thy sake we are being
killed all the day long;
we are regarded as sheep to be
slaughtered."

37 No, in all these things we are
more than conquerors through him
who loved us. 38 For I am sure that
neither death, nor life, nor angels,
nor principalities, nor things present,
nor things to come, nor powers, 39 nor
height, nor depth, nor anything else in
all creation, will be able to separate us
from the love of God in Christ Jesus
our Lord.

GOD'S ELECTION OF ISRAEL

9 I am speaking the truth in Christ, I
am not lying; my conscience bears
me witness in the Holy Spirit, 2 that I
have great sorrow and unceasing an-
guish in my heart. 3 For I could wish
that I myself were accursed and cut
off from Christ for the sake of my
brethren, my kinsmen by race. 4 They
are Israelites, and to them belong the
sonship, the glory, the covenants, the
giving of the law, the worship, and the
promises; 5 to them belong the patri-
archs, and of their race, according to

[b] Or *that*
[c] Other ancient authorities read *in everything he works for good*, or *everything works for good*
[d] Greek *God*
[e] Or *It is Christ Jesus... for us*

the flesh, is the Christ, who is God
over all, blessed for ever.[a] Amen.

6 But it is not as though the word
of God had failed. For not all who are
descended from Israel belong to Israel,
7and not all are children of Abraham
because they are his descendants; but
"Through Isaac shall your descen-
dants be named." 8This means that it
is not the children of the flesh who are
the children of God, but the children
of the promise are reckoned as de-
scendants. 9For this is what the prom-
ise said, "About this time I will return
and Sarah shall have a son." 10And not
only so, but also when Rebecca had
conceived children by one man, our
forefather Isaac, 11though they were
not yet born and had done nothing ei-
ther good or bad, in order that God's
purpose of election might continue,
not because of works but because of
his call, 12she was told, "The elder will
serve the younger." 13As it is written,
"Jacob I loved, but Esau I hated."

14 What shall we say then? Is
there injustice on God's part? By no
means! 15For he says to Moses, "I will
have mercy on whom I have mercy,
and I will have compassion on whom
I have compassion." 16So it depends
not upon man's will or exertion, but
upon God's mercy. 17For the scripture
says to Pharaoh, "I have raised you up
for the very purpose of showing my
power in you, so that my name may
be proclaimed in all the earth." 18So
then he has mercy upon whomever
he wills, and he hardens the heart of
whomever he wills.

GOD'S WRATH AND MERCY

19 You will say to me then, "Why
does he still find fault? For who can
resist his will?"* 20But who are you,
a man, to answer back to God? Will
what is molded say to its molder,
"Why have you made me thus?" 21Has
the potter no right over the clay, to
make out of the same lump one ves-
sel for beauty and another for menial
use? 22What if God, desiring to show
his wrath and to make known his
power, has endured with much pa-
tience the vessels of wrath made for
destruction, 23in order to make known
the riches of his glory for the vessels
of mercy, which he has prepared be-
forehand for glory, 24even us whom he
has called, not from the Jews only but
also from the Gentiles? 25As indeed he
says in Hose′a,

"Those who were not my
people
I will call 'my people,'
and her who was not beloved
I will call 'my beloved.'"
26"And in the very place where it
was said to them, 'You are
not my people,'
they will be called 'sons of the
living God.'"

27 And Isaiah cries out concern-
ing Israel: "Though the number of
the sons of Israel be as the sand of
the sea, only a remnant of them will
be saved; 28for the Lord will execute
his sentence upon the earth with
rigor and dispatch." 29And as Isaiah
predicted,

"If the Lord of hosts had not
left us children,
we would have fared like
Sodom and been made
like Gomor′rah."

ISRAEL'S UNBELIEF

30 What shall we say, then? That
Gentiles who did not pursue righ-
teousness have attained it, that is,
righteousness through faith; 31but that
Israel who pursued the righteousness
which is based on law did not succeed
in fulfilling that law. 32Why? Because
they did not pursue it through faith,
but as if it were based on works. They
have stumbled over the stumbling
stone, 33as it is written,

"Behold, I am laying in Zion
a stone that will make
men stumble,
a rock that will make them fall;

[a] Or *Christ. God who is over all be blessed for ever*

and he who believes in him will
not be put to shame."

10 Brethren, my heart's desire and
prayer to God for them is that they
may be saved.* 2 I bear them witness
that they have a zeal for God, but it is
not enlightened. 3 For, being ignorant
of the righteousness that comes from
God, and seeking to establish their
own, they did not submit to God's
righteousness. 4 For Christ is the end
of the law, that every one who has
faith may be justified.

SALVATION IS FOR ALL

5 Moses writes that the man who
practices the righteousness which is
based on the law shall live by it. 6 But
the righteousness based on faith says,
Do not say in your heart, "Who will
ascend into heaven?" (that is, to bring
Christ down) 7 or "Who will descend
into the abyss?" (that is, to bring
Christ up from the dead). 8 But what
does it say? The word is near you, on
your lips and in your heart (that is,
the word of faith which we preach);
9 because, if you confess with your
lips that Jesus is Lord and believe in
your heart that God raised him from
the dead, you will be saved. 10 For man
believes with his heart and so is jus-
tified, and he confesses with his lips
and so is saved. 11 The scripture says,
"No one who believes in him will be
put to shame." 12 For there is no dis-
tinction between Jew and Greek; the
same Lord is Lord of all and bestows
his riches upon all who call upon him.
13 For, "every one who calls upon the
name of the Lord will be saved."

14 But how are men to call upon
him in whom they have not believed?
And how are they to believe in him
of whom they have never heard? And
how are they to hear without a preach-
er? 15 And how can men preach unless
they are sent? As it is written, "How
beautiful are the feet of those who
preach good news!" 16 But they have
not all heeded the gospel; for Isaiah
says, "Lord, who has believed what he
has heard from us?" 17 So faith comes
from what is heard, and what is heard
comes by the preaching of Christ.

18 But I ask, have they not heard?
Indeed they have; for

"Their voice has gone out to all
the earth,
and their words to the ends of
the world."

19 Again I ask, did Israel not under-
stand? First Moses says,

"I will make you jealous of
those who are not a
nation;
with a foolish nation I will
make you angry."

20 Then Isaiah is so bold as to say,

"I have been found by those
who did not seek me;
I have shown myself to those
who did not ask for me."

21 But of Israel he says, "All day
long I have held out my hands to a dis-
obedient and contrary people."

ISRAEL'S REJECTION IS NOT FINAL

11 I ask, then, has God rejected
his people? By no means! I my-
self am an Israelite, a descendant of
Abraham, a member of the tribe of
Benjamin. 2 God has not rejected his
people whom he foreknew. Do you
not know what the scripture says
of Eli′jah, how he pleads with God
against Israel? 3 "Lord, they have
killed thy prophets, they have demol-
ished thy altars, and I alone am left,
and they seek my life." 4 But what is
God's reply to him? "I have kept for
myself seven thousand men who have
not bowed the knee to Ba′al." 5 So too
at the present time there is a remnant,
chosen by grace. 6 But if it is by grace,
it is no longer on the basis of works;
otherwise grace would no longer be
grace.

7 What then? Israel failed to ob-
tain what it sought. The elect ob-
tained it, but the rest were hardened,
8 as it is written,

"God gave them a spirit of
stupor,

eyes that should not see and
ears that should not
hear,
down to this very day."
9And David says,
"Let their feast become a snare
and a trap,
a pitfall and a retribution for
them;
10let their eyes be darkened so
that they cannot see,
and bend their backs for ever."

THE SALVATION OF THE GENTILES

11 So I ask, have they stumbled so
as to fall? By no means! But through
their trespass salvation has come
to the Gentiles, so as to make Israel
jealous. 12Now if their trespass means
riches for the world, and if their fail-
ure means riches for the Gentiles,
how much more will their full inclu-
sion mean!

13 Now I am speaking to you
Gentiles. Inasmuch then as I am an
apostle to the Gentiles, I magnify my
ministry 14in order to make my fellow
Jews jealous, and thus save some of
them. 15For if their rejection means
the reconciliation of the world, what
will their acceptance mean but life
from the dead? 16If the dough offered
as first fruits is holy, so is the whole
lump; and if the root is holy, so are the
branches.

17 But if some of the branches
were broken off, and you, a wild ol-
ive shoot, were grafted in their place
to share the richness[a] of the olive
tree, 18do not boast over the branch-
es. If you do boast, remember it is
not you that support the root, but
the root that supports you. 19You will
say, "Branches were broken off so
that I might be grafted in." 20That is
true. They were broken off because
of their unbelief, but you stand fast
only through faith. So do not become
proud, but stand in awe. 21For if God
did not spare the natural branches,
neither will he spare you. 22Note
then the kindness and the severity of
God: severity toward those who have
fallen, but God's kindness to you,
provided you continue in his kind-
ness; otherwise you too will be cut
off. 23And even the others, if they do
not persist in their unbelief, will be
grafted in, for God has the power to
graft them in again. 24For if you have
been cut from what is by nature a
wild olive tree, and grafted, contrary
to nature, into a cultivated olive tree,
how much more will these natural
branches be grafted back into their
own olive tree.

ALL ISRAEL WILL BE SAVED

25 Lest you be wise in your own
conceits, I want you to understand
this mystery, brethren: a hardening
has come upon part of Israel, until the
full number of the Gentiles come in,
26and so all Israel will be saved; as it
is written,
"The Deliverer will come from
Zion,
he will banish ungodliness
from Jacob";
27"and this will be my covenant
with them
when I take away their sins."
28As regards the gospel they are
enemies of God, for your sake; but as
regards election they are beloved for
the sake of their forefathers. 29For the
gifts and the call of God are irrevo-
cable. 30Just as you were once disobe-
dient to God but now have received
mercy because of their disobedience,
31so they have now been disobedient
in order that by the mercy shown to
you they also may[b] receive mercy.
32For God has consigned all men to
disobedience, that he may have mercy
upon all.

33 O the depth of the riches and
wisdom and knowledge of God! How
unsearchable are his judgments and
how inscrutable his ways!

[a]Other ancient authorities read *rich root*
[b]Other ancient authorities add *now*

34"For who has known the mind of
the Lord,
or who has been his
counselor?"
35"Or who has given a gift to him
that he might be repaid?"
36For from him and through him
and to him are all things. To him be
glory for ever. Amen.

THE NEW LIFE IN CHRIST

12 I appeal to you therefore, breth-
ren, by the mercies of God, to
present your bodies as a living sac-
rifice, holy and acceptable to God,
which is your spiritual worship. 2Do
not be conformed to this world[c] but
be transformed by the renewal of your
mind, that you may prove what is the
will of God, what is good and accept-
able and perfect.[d]
3 For by the grace given to me I bid
every one among you not to think of
himself more highly than he ought to
think, but to think with sober judg-
ment, each according to the measure
of faith which God has assigned him.
4For as in one body we have many
members, and all the members do
not have the same function, 5so we,
though many, are one body in Christ,
and individually members one of an-
other. 6Having gifts that differ accord-
ing to the grace given to us, let us use
them: if prophecy, in proportion to
our faith; 7if service, in our serving;
he who teaches, in his teaching; 8he
who exhorts, in his exhortation; he
who contributes, in liberality; he who
gives aid, with zeal; he who does acts
of mercy, with cheerfulness.

MARKS OF THE TRUE CHRISTIAN

9 Let love be genuine; hate what is
evil, hold fast to what is good; 10love
one another with brotherly affection;
outdo one another in showing honor.
11Never flag in zeal, be aglow with
the Spirit, serve the Lord. 12Rejoice in
your hope, be patient in tribulation,
be constant in prayer. 13Contribute
to the needs of the saints, practice
hospitality.
14 Bless those who persecute you;
bless and do not curse them. 15Rejoice
with those who rejoice, weep with
those who weep. 16Live in harmony
with one another; do not be haughty,
but associate with the lowly;[e] never
be conceited. 17Repay no one evil for
evil, but take thought for what is no-
ble in the sight of all. 18If possible, so
far as it depends upon you, live peace-
ably with all. 19Beloved, never avenge
yourselves, but leave it[f] to the wrath
of God; for it is written, "Vengeance
is mine, I will repay, says the Lord."
20No, "if your enemy is hungry, feed
him; if he is thirsty, give him drink;
for by so doing you will heap burning
coals upon his head." 21Do not be over-
come by evil, but overcome evil with
good.

BEING SUBJECT TO AUTHORITIES

13 Let every person be subject to the
governing authorities. For there
is no authority except from God, and
those that exist have been instituted
by God. 2Therefore he who resists
the authorities resists what God has
appointed, and those who resist will
incur judgment. 3For rulers are not
a terror to good conduct, but to bad.
Would you have no fear of him who
is in authority? Then do what is good,
and you will receive his approval, 4for
he is God's servant for your good.
But if you do wrong, be afraid, for he
does not bear the sword in vain; he
is the servant of God to execute his
wrath on the wrongdoer. 5Therefore
one must be subject, not only to avoid
God's wrath but also for the sake of
conscience. 6For the same reason you
also pay taxes, for the authorities are
ministers of God, attending to this
very thing. 7Pay all of them their dues,

[c] Greek *age*
[d] Or *what is the good and acceptable and perfect will of God*
[e] Or *give yourselves to humble tasks*
[f] Greek *give place*

taxes to whom taxes are due, revenue
to whom revenue is due, respect to
whom respect is due, honor to whom
honor is due.

LOVE FOR ONE ANOTHER

8 Owe no one anything, except to
love one another; for he who loves his
neighbor has fulfilled the law. 9The
commandments, "You shall not com-
mit adultery, You shall not kill, You
shall not steal, You shall not covet,"
and any other commandment, are
summed up in this sentence, "You
shall love your neighbor as yourself."
10Love does no wrong to a neighbor;
therefore love is the fulfilling of the
law.

AN URGENT APPEAL

11 Besides this you know what
hour it is, how it is full time now for
you to wake from sleep. For salvation
is nearer to us now than when we
first believed; 12the night is far gone,
the day is at hand. Let us then cast
off the works of darkness and put on
the armor of light; 13let us conduct
ourselves becomingly as in the day,
not in reveling and drunkenness, not
in debauchery and licentiousness, not
in quarreling and jealousy. 14But put
on the Lord Jesus Christ, and make
no provision for the flesh, to gratify
its desires.

DO NOT JUDGE ANOTHER

14 As for the man who is weak in
faith, welcome him, but not for
disputes over opinions.* 2One believes
he may eat anything, while the weak
man eats only vegetables. 3Let not
him who eats despise him who ab-
stains, and let not him who abstains
pass judgment on him who eats; for
God has welcomed him. 4Who are you
to pass judgment on the servant of
another? It is before his own master
that he stands or falls. And he will be
upheld, for the Master is able to make
him stand.

5 One man esteems one day as bet-
ter than another, while another man
esteems all days alike. Let every one
be fully convinced in his own mind.
6He who observes the day, observes
it in honor of the Lord. He also who
eats, eats in honor of the Lord, since
he gives thanks to God; while he who
abstains, abstains in honor of the Lord
and gives thanks to God. 7None of us
lives to himself, and none of us dies
to himself. 8If we live, we live to the
Lord, and if we die, we die to the Lord;
so then, whether we live or whether
we die, we are the Lord's. 9For to this
end Christ died and lived again, that
he might be Lord both of the dead and
of the living.

10 Why do you pass judgment on
your brother? Or you, why do you
despise your brother? For we shall
all stand before the judgment seat of
God; 11for it is written,

"As I live, says the Lord, every
knee shall bow to me,
and every tongue shall give
praise[a] to God."

12So each of us shall give account
of himself to God.

DO NOT MAKE ANOTHER STUMBLE

13 Then let us no more pass judg-
ment on one another, but rather de-
cide never to put a stumbling block or
hindrance in the way of a brother. 14I
know and am persuaded in the Lord
Jesus that nothing is unclean in it-
self; but it is unclean for any one who
thinks it unclean.* 15If your brother is
being injured by what you eat, you are
no longer walking in love. Do not let
what you eat cause the ruin of one for
whom Christ died. 16So do not let what
is good to you be spoken of as evil.
17For the kingdom of God does not
mean food and drink but righteous-
ness and peace and joy in the Holy
Spirit; 18he who thus serves Christ is
acceptable to God and approved by
men. 19Let us then pursue what makes
for peace and for mutual upbuilding.

[a]Or *confess*

20 Do not, for the sake of food, destroy
the work of God. Everything is indeed
clean, but it is wrong for any one to
make others fall by what he eats; 21 it
is right not to eat meat or drink wine
or do anything that makes your brother
stumble.[b] 22 The faith that you have,
keep between yourself and God; happy
is he who has no reason to judge
himself for what he approves. 23 But
he who has doubts is condemned, if
he eats, because he does not act from
faith; for whatever does not proceed
from faith is sin.[c]

PLEASE OTHERS, NOT YOURSELVES

15 We who are strong ought to bear
with the failings of the weak, and
not to please ourselves; 2 let each of us
please his neighbor for his good, to
edify him. 3 For Christ did not please
himself; but, as it is written, "The
reproaches of those who reproached
thee fell on me." 4 For whatever was
written in former days was written
for our instruction, that by steadfastness
and by the encouragement of the
scriptures we might have hope. 5 May
the God of steadfastness and encouragement
grant you to live in such
harmony with one another, in accord
with Christ Jesus, 6 that together you
may with one voice glorify the God
and Father of our Lord Jesus Christ.

THE GOSPEL FOR JEWS AND GENTILES ALIKE

7 Welcome one another, therefore,
as Christ has welcomed you, for the
glory of God. 8 For I tell you that Christ
became a servant to the circumcised
to show God's truthfulness, in order
to confirm the promises given to
the patriarchs, 9 and in order that the
Gentiles might glorify God for his
mercy. As it is written,

"Therefore I will praise thee
among the Gentiles,
and sing to thy name";

10 and again it is said,

"Rejoice, O Gentiles, with his
people";

11 and again,

"Praise the Lord, all Gentiles,
and let all the peoples praise
him";

12 and further Isaiah says,

"The root of Jesse shall come,
he who rises to rule the
Gentiles;
in him shall the Gentiles
hope."

13 May the God of hope fill you with
all joy and peace in believing, so that
by the power of the Holy Spirit you
may abound in hope.

PAUL'S REASON FOR WRITING SO BOLDLY

14 I myself am satisfied about you,
my brethren, that you yourselves
are full of goodness, filled with all
knowledge, and able to instruct one
another. 15 But on some points I have
written to you very boldly by way of
reminder, because of the grace given
me by God 16 to be a minister of Christ
Jesus to the Gentiles in the priestly
service of the gospel of God, so that
the offering of the Gentiles may be
acceptable, sanctified by the Holy
Spirit.* 17 In Christ Jesus, then, I have
reason to be proud of my work for
God. 18 For I will not venture to speak
of anything except what Christ has
wrought through me to win obedience
from the Gentiles, by word and deed,
19 by the power of signs and wonders,
by the power of the Holy Spirit, so
that from Jerusalem and as far round
as Illyr´icum I have fully preached the
gospel of Christ, 20 thus making it my
ambition to preach the gospel, not
where Christ has already been named,
lest I build on another man's foundation,
21 but as it is written,

"They shall see who have never
been told of him,
and they shall understand who
have never heard of him."

[b] Other ancient authorities add *or be upset or be weakened*
[c] Other authorities, some ancient, insert here Ch 16.25-27

PAUL'S PLAN TO VISIT ROME

22 This is the reason why I have so often been hindered from coming to you. 23But now, since I no longer have any room for work in these regions, and since I have longed for many years to come to you, 24I hope to see you in passing as I go to Spain, and to be sped on my journey there by you, once I have enjoyed your company for a little. 25At present, however, I am going to Jerusalem with aid for the saints. 26For Macedo´nia and Acha´ia have been pleased to make some contribution for the poor among the saints at Jerusalem; 27they were pleased to do it, and indeed they are in debt to them, for if the Gentiles have come to share in their spiritual blessings, they ought also to be of service to them in material blessings. 28When therefore I have completed this, and have delivered to them what has been raised,[a] I shall go on by way of you to Spain; 29and I know that when I come to you I shall come in the fulness of the blessing[b] of Christ.

30 I appeal to you, brethren, by our Lord Jesus Christ and by the love of the Spirit, to strive together with me in your prayers to God on my behalf, 31that I may be delivered from the unbelievers in Judea, and that my service for Jerusalem may be acceptable to the saints, 32so that by God's will I may come to you with joy and be refreshed in your company. 33The God of peace be with you all. Amen.

PERSONAL GREETINGS

16 I commend to you our sister Phoebe, a deaconess of the church at Cen´chre-ae, 2that you may receive her in the Lord as befits the saints, and help her in whatever she may require from you, for she has been a helper of many and of myself as well.

3 Greet Prisca and Aq´uila, my fellow workers in Christ Jesus, 4who risked their necks for my life, to whom not only I but also all the churches of the Gentiles give thanks; 5greet also the church in their house. Greet my beloved Epae´netus, who was the first convert in Asia for Christ. 6Greet Mary, who has worked hard among you. 7Greet Androni´cus and Ju´nias, my kinsmen and my fellow prisoners; they are men of note among the apostles, and they were in Christ before me. 8Greet Amplia´tus, my beloved in the Lord. 9Greet Urba´nus, our fellow worker in Christ, and my beloved Stachys. 10Greet Apel´les, who is approved in Christ. Greet those who belong to the family of Aristobu´lus. 11Greet my kinsman Hero´dion. Greet those in the Lord who belong to the family of Narcis´sus. 12Greet those workers in the Lord, Tryphae´na and Trypho´sa. Greet the beloved Persis, who has worked hard in the Lord. 13Greet Rufus, eminent in the Lord, also his mother and mine. 14Greet Asyn´critus, Phlegon, Hermes, Pat´robas, Hermas, and the brethren who are with them. 15Greet Philol´ogus, Julia, Nereus and his sister, and Olym´pas, and all the saints who are with them. 16Greet one another with a holy kiss. All the churches of Christ greet you.*

FINAL INSTRUCTIONS

17 I appeal to you, brethren, to take note of those who create dissensions and difficulties, in opposition to the doctrine which you have been taught; avoid them. 18For such persons do not serve our Lord Christ, but their own appetites,[c] and by fair and flattering words they deceive the hearts of the simple-minded. 19For while your obedience is known to all, so that I rejoice over you, I would have you wise as to what is good and guileless as to what

[a] Greek *sealed to them this fruit*
[b] Other ancient authorities insert *of the gospel*
[c] Greek *their own belly* (Phil 3. 19)

is evil; 20then the God of peace will
soon crush Satan under your feet.
The grace of our Lord Jesus Christ
be with you.[d]

21 Timothy, my fellow worker,
greets you; so do Lucius and Jason and
Sosip´ater, my kinsmen.

22 I Tertius, the writer of this let-
ter, greet you in the Lord.

23 Ga´ius, who is host to me and
to the whole church, greets you.
Eras´tus, the city treasurer, and our
brother Quartus, greet you.[e]

FINAL DOXOLOGY

25 Now to him who is able to
strengthen you according to my gos-
pel and the preaching of Jesus Christ,
according to the revelation of the
mystery which was kept secret for
long ages 26but is now disclosed and
through the prophetic writings is
made known to all nations, according
to the command of the eternal God,
to bring about the obedience of faith
27to the only wise God be glory for ev-
ermore through Jesus Christ! Amen.

[d]Other ancient authorities omit this sentence
[e]Other ancient authorities insert verse 24, *The grace of our Lord Jesus Christ be with you all. Amen*

THE FIRST LETTER OF PAUL TO THE
CORINTHIANS

SALUTATION

1 Paul, called by the will of God to be
an apostle of Christ Jesus, and our
brother Sos´thenes,

2 To the church of God which is at
Corinth, to those sanctified in Christ
Jesus, called to be saints* together
with all those who in every place call
on the name of our Lord Jesus Christ,
both their Lord and ours:

3 Grace to you and peace from God
our Father and the Lord Jesus Christ.

4 I give thanks to God[a] always for
you because of the grace of God which
was given you in Christ Jesus, 5that in
every way you were enriched in him
with all speech and all knowledge
6even as the testimony to Christ was
confirmed among you 7so that you are
not lacking in any spiritual gift, as
you wait for the revealing of our Lord
Jesus Christ; 8who will sustain you
to the end, guiltless in the day of our
Lord Jesus Christ. 9God is faithful, by
whom you were called into the fellow-
ship of his Son, Jesus Christ our Lord.

DIVISIONS IN THE CHURCH

10 I appeal to you, brethren, by the
name of our Lord Jesus Christ, that
all of you agree and that there be no
dissensions among you, but that you
be united in the same mind and the
same judgment. 11For it has been re-
ported to me by Chlo´e's people that
there is quarreling among you, my
brethren. 12What I mean is that each
one of you says, "I belong to Paul," or
"I belong to Apol´los," or "I belong
to Cephas,"* or "I belong to Christ."
13Is Christ divided? Was Paul crucified
for you? Or were you baptized in the
name of Paul? 14I am thankful[b] that I
baptized none of you except Crispus
and Ga´ius; 15lest any one should say
that you were baptized in my name.
16(I did baptize also the household
of Steph´anas. Beyond that, I do not
know whether I baptized any one
else.) 17For Christ did not send me
to baptize but to preach the gospel,
and not with eloquent wisdom, lest
the cross of Christ be emptied of its
power.

CHRIST THE POWER AND WISDOM OF GOD

18 For the word of the cross is folly
to those who are perishing, but to us
who are being saved it is the power of
God. 19For it is written,

> "I will destroy the wisdom of
> the wise,
> and the cleverness of the clever
> I will thwart."

20Where is the wise man? Where
is the scribe? Where is the debater of
this age? Has not God made foolish
the wisdom of the world? 21For since,
in the wisdom of God, the world did
not know God through wisdom, it
pleased God through the folly of what
we preach to save those who believe.
22For Jews demand signs and Greeks
seek wisdom, 23but we preach Christ
crucified, a stumbling block to Jews
and folly to Gentiles, 24but to those
who are called, both Jews and Greeks,
Christ the power of God and the wis-
dom of God. 25For the foolishness of
God is wiser than men, and the weak-
ness of God is stronger than men.

26 For consider your call, brethren;
not many of you were wise according
to worldly standards, not many were
powerful, not many were of noble
birth; 27but God chose what is foolish
in the world to shame the wise, God
chose what is weak in the world to
shame the strong, 28God chose what
is low and despised in the world,
even things that are not, to bring to

[a] Other ancient authorities read *my God*
[b] Other ancient authorities read *I thank God*

nothing things that are, 29so that no
human being might boast in the pres-
ence of God. 30He is the source of
your life in Christ Jesus, whom God
made our wisdom, our righteousness
and sanctification and redemption;
31therefore, as it is written, "Let him
who boasts, boast of the Lord."

PROCLAIMING CHRIST CRUCIFIED

2 When I came to you, brethren, I did
not come proclaiming to you the
testimony[c] of God in lofty words or
wisdom. 2For I decided to know noth-
ing among you except Jesus Christ
and him crucified.* 3And I was with
you in weakness and in much fear and
trembling; 4and my speech and my
message were not in plausible words
of wisdom, but in demonstration of
the Spirit and power, 5that your faith
might not rest in the wisdom of men
but in the power of God.

THE TRUE WISDOM OF GOD

6 Yet among the mature we do im-
part wisdom, although it is not a wis-
dom of this age or of the rulers of this
age, who are doomed to pass away.
7But we impart a secret and hidden
wisdom of God, which God decreed
before the ages for our glorification.
8None of the rulers of this age under-
stood this; for if they had, they would
not have crucified the Lord of glory.
9But, as it is written,

"What no eye has seen, nor ear
heard,
nor the heart of man conceived,
what God has prepared for
those who love him, "

10God has revealed to us through
the Spirit. For the Spirit searches
everything, even the depths of God.
11For what person knows a man's
thoughts except the spirit of the man
which is in him? So also no one com-
prehends the thoughts of God except
the Spirit of God. 12Now we have re-
ceived not the spirit of the world, but
the Spirit which is from God, that we
might understand the gifts bestowed
on us by God. 13And we impart this in
words not taught by human wisdom
but taught by the Spirit, interpreting
spiritual truths to those who possess
the Spirit.[d]

14 The unspiritual[e] man does not
receive the gifts of the Spirit of God,
for they are folly to him, and he is
not able to understand them because
they are spiritually discerned. 15The
spiritual man judges all things, but is
himself to be judged by no one. 16"For
who has known the mind of the Lord
so as to instruct him?" But we have
the mind of Christ.

ON DIVISIONS IN THE CORINTHIAN CHURCH

3 But I, brethren, could not address
you as spiritual men, but as men
of the flesh, as babes in Christ. 2I fed
you with milk, not solid food; for you
were not ready for it; and even yet
you are not ready, 3for you are still of
the flesh. For while there is jealousy
and strife among you, are you not of
the flesh, and behaving like ordinary
men? 4For when one says, "I belong
to Paul," and another, "I belong to
Apol´los," are you not merely men?

5 What then is Apol´los? What is
Paul? Servants through whom you be-
lieved, as the Lord assigned to each.
6I planted, Apol´los watered, but God
gave the growth. 7So neither he who
plants nor he who waters is anything,
but only God who gives the growth.
8He who plants and he who waters are
equal, and each shall receive his wag-
es according to his labor. 9For we are
God's fellow workers;[f] you are God's
field, God's building.

10 According to the commission of
God given to me, like a skilled mas-
ter builder I laid a foundation, and

[c] Other ancient authorities read *mystery* (or *secret*)
[d] Or *interpreting spiritual truths in spiritual language;* or *comparing spiritual things with spiritual*
[e] Or *natural*
[f] Or *fellow workers for God*

another man is building upon it. Let
each man take care how he builds
upon it. 11For no other foundation can
any one lay than that which is laid,
which is Jesus Christ. 12Now if any one
builds on the foundation with gold,
silver, precious stones, wood, hay,
stubble 13each man's work will become
manifest; for the Day* will disclose it,
because it will be revealed with fire,
and the fire will test what sort of work
each one has done. 14If the work which
any man has built on the foundation
survives, he will receive a reward. 15If
any man's work is burned up, he will
suffer loss, though he himself will be
saved, but only as through fire.

16 Do you not know that you are
God's temple* and that God's Spirit
dwells in you? 17If any one destroys
God's temple, God will destroy him.
For God's temple is holy, and that
temple you are.

18 Let no one deceive himself. If
any one among you thinks that he
is wise in this age, let him become a
fool that he may become wise. 19For
the wisdom of this world is folly with
God. For it is written, "He catches the
wise in their craftiness," 20and again,
"The Lord knows that the thoughts
of the wise are futile." 21So let no one
boast of men. For all things are yours,
22whether Paul or Apol´los or Cephas
or the world or life or death or the
present or the future, all are yours;
23and you are Christ's; and Christ is
God's.

THE MINISTRY OF THE APOSTLES

4 This is how one should regard us,
as servants of Christ and stewards
of the mysteries of God. 2Moreover it
is required of stewards that they be
found trustworthy. 3But with me it
is a very small thing that I should be
judged by you or by any human court.
I do not even judge myself. 4I am not
aware of anything against myself, but
I am not thereby acquitted. It is the
Lord who judges me. 5Therefore do
not pronounce judgment before the
time, before the Lord comes, who will
bring to light the things now hidden
in darkness and will disclose the pur-
poses of the heart. Then every man
will receive his commendation from
God.

6 I have applied all this to myself
and Apol´los for your benefit, breth-
ren, that you may learn by us not to go
beyond what is written, that none of
you may be puffed up in favor of one
against another. 7For who sees any-
thing different in you? What have you
that you did not receive? If then you
received it, why do you boast as if it
were not a gift?

8 Already you are filled! Already
you have become rich! Without us you
have become kings! And would that
you did reign, so that we might share
the rule with you! 9For I think that
God has exhibited us apostles as last
of all, like men sentenced to death; be-
cause we have become a spectacle to
the world, to angels and to men. 10We
are fools for Christ's sake, but you are
wise in Christ. We are weak, but you
are strong. You are held in honor, but
we in disrepute. 11To the present hour
we hunger and thirst, we are ill-clad
and buffeted and homeless, 12and we
labor, working with our own hands.
When reviled, we bless; when perse-
cuted, we endure; 13when slandered,
we try to conciliate; we have become,
and are now, as the refuse of the
world, the offscouring of all things.

FATHERLY ADMONITION

14 I do not write this to make you
ashamed, but to admonish you as
my beloved children. 15For though
you have countless guides in Christ,
you do not have many fathers. For I
became your father in Christ Jesus
through the gospel. 16I urge you, then,
be imitators of me. 17Therefore I sent[a]
to you Timothy, my beloved and faith-
ful child in the Lord, to remind you
of my ways in Christ, as I teach them

[a] Or *am sending*

everywhere in every church. 18Some
are arrogant, as though I were not
coming to you. 19But I will come to you
soon, if the Lord wills, and I will find
out not the talk of these arrogant peo-
ple but their power. 20For the kingdom
of God does not consist in talk but in
power. 21What do you wish? Shall I
come to you with a rod, or with love in
a spirit of gentleness?

SEXUAL IMMORALITY DEFILES THE CHURCH

5 It is actually reported that there
is immorality among you, and of
a kind that is not found even among
pagans; for a man is living with his
father's wife.* 2And you are arrogant!
Ought you not rather to mourn? Let
him who has done this be removed
from among you.

3 For though absent in body I am
present in spirit, and as if present, I
have already pronounced judgment 4in
the name of the Lord Jesus on the man
who has done such a thing. When you
are assembled, and my spirit is pres-
ent, with the power of our Lord Jesus,
5you are to deliver this man to Satan*
for the destruction of the flesh, that
his spirit may be saved in the day of
the Lord Jesus.[b]

6 Your boasting is not good. Do you
not know that a little leaven leavens
the whole lump? 7Cleanse out the old
leaven that you may be a new lump, as
you really are unleavened. For Christ,
our paschal lamb, has been sacrificed.
8Let us, therefore, celebrate the festi-
val, not with the old leaven, the leaven
of malice and evil, but with the un-
leavened bread of sincerity and truth.

SEXUAL IMMORALITY MUST BE JUDGED

9 I wrote to you in my letter not
to associate with immoral men;* 10not
at all meaning the immoral* of this
world, or the greedy and robbers, or
idolaters, since then you would need
to go out of the world. 11But rath-
er I wrote[c] to you not to associate
with any one who bears the name of
brother if he is guilty of immorality*
or greed, or is an idolater, reviler,
drunkard, or robber—not even to eat
with such a one. 12For what have I to
do with judging outsiders? Is it not
those inside the church whom you are
to judge? 13God judges those outside.
"Drive out the wicked person from
among you."

LAWSUITS AMONG BELIEVERS

6 When one of you has a grievance
against a brother, does he dare go
to law before the unrighteous* in-
stead of the saints? 2Do you not know
that the saints will judge the world?
And if the world is to be judged by
you, are you incompetent to try triv-
ial cases? 3Do you not know that we
are to judge angels? How much more,
matters pertaining to this life! 4If
then you have such cases, why do you
lay them before those who are least
esteemed by the church? 5I say this
to your shame. Can it be that there
is no man among you wise enough
to decide between members of the
brotherhood, 6but brother goes to
law against brother, and that before
unbelievers?

7 To have lawsuits at all with one
another is defeat for you. Why not
rather suffer wrong? Why not rath-
er be defrauded? 8But you yourselves
wrong and defraud, and that even
your own brethren.

9 Do you not know that the un-
righteous will not inherit the king-
dom of God? Do not be deceived;
neither the immoral,* nor idolaters,
nor adulterers, nor homosexuals,[d]*
10nor thieves, nor the greedy, nor
drunkards, nor revilers, nor robbers
will inherit the kingdom of God.
11And such were some of you. But you
were washed, you were sanctified,
you were justified in the name of the
Lord Jesus Christ and in the Spirit of
our God.

[b] Other ancient authorities omit *Jesus*
[c] Or *now I write*
[d] Two Greek words are rendered by this expression

GLORIFY GOD IN BODY AND SPIRIT

12 “All things are lawful for me,”
but not all things are helpful. “All
things are lawful for me,”* but I will
not be enslaved by anything. 13“Food
is meant for the stomach and the
stomach for food”—and God will
destroy both one and the other. The
body is not meant for immorality,*
but for the Lord, and the Lord for the
body. 14And God raised the Lord and
will also raise us up by his power. 15Do
you not know that your bodies are
members of Christ? Shall I therefore
take the members of Christ and make
them members of a prostitute? Never!
16Do you not know that he who joins
himself to a prostitute becomes one
body with her? For, as it is written,
“The two shall become one.”[a] 17But
he who is united to the Lord becomes
one spirit with him. 18Shun immorali-
ty.* Every other sin which a man com-
mits is outside the body; but the im-
moral man sins against his own body.
19Do you not know that your body is a
temple of the Holy Spirit within you,
which you have from God? You are
not your own; 20you were bought with
a price. So glorify God in your body.

DIRECTIONS CONCERNING MARRIAGE

7 Now concerning the matters about
which you wrote. It is well for a man
not to touch a woman. 2But because of
the temptation to immorality, each
man should have his own wife and
each woman her own husband.* 3The
husband should give to his wife her
conjugal rights, and likewise the wife
to her husband. 4For the wife does
not rule over her own body, but the
husband does; likewise the husband
does not rule over his own body, but
the wife does. 5Do not refuse one an-
other except perhaps by agreement
for a season, that you may devote
yourselves to prayer; but then come
together again, lest Satan tempt you
through lack of self-control. 6I say
this by way of concession, not of com-
mand. 7I wish that all were as I myself
am. But each has his own special gift
from God, one of one kind and one of
another.

8 To the unmarried and the wid-
ows I say that it is well for them to
remain single as I do. 9But if they can-
not exercise self-control, they should
marry. For it is better to marry than
to be aflame with passion.

10 To the married I give charge, not
I but the Lord, that the wife should
not separate from her husband 11(but
if she does, let her remain single or
else be reconciled to her husband)—
and that the husband should not di-
vorce his wife.

12 To the rest I say, not the Lord,
that if any brother has a wife who is
an unbeliever, and she consents to live
with him, he should not divorce her.
13If any woman has a husband who
is an unbeliever, and he consents to
live with her, she should not divorce
him. 14For the unbelieving husband
is consecrated through his wife, and
the unbelieving wife is consecrated
through her husband. Otherwise,
your children would be unclean, but
as it is they are holy. 15But if the unbe-
lieving partner desires to separate, let
it be so; in such a case the brother or
sister is not bound. For God has called
us[b] to peace. 16Wife, how do you know
whether you will save your husband?
Husband, how do you know whether
you will save your wife?

THE LIFE THAT THE LORD HAS ASSIGNED

17 Only, let every one lead the life
which the Lord has assigned to him,
and in which God has called him.
This is my rule in all the churches.
18Was any one at the time of his call
already circumcised? Let him not seek
to remove the marks of circumcision.
Was any one at the time of his call
uncircumcised? Let him not seek cir-
cumcision. 19For neither circumcision

[a] Greek *one flesh*
[b] Other ancient authorities read *you*

counts for anything nor uncircumci-
sion, but keeping the commandments
of God. 20Every one should remain
in the state in which he was called.
21Were you a slave when called? Never
mind. But if you can gain your free-
dom, avail yourself of the opportu-
nity.[c] 22For he who was called in the
Lord as a slave is a freedman of the
Lord. Likewise he who was free when
called is a slave of Christ. 23You were
bought with a price; do not become
slaves of men. 24So, brethren, in what-
ever state each was called, there let
him remain with God.

THE UNMARRIED AND THE WIDOWS

25 Now concerning the unmar-
ried,[d] I have no command of the Lord,
but I give my opinion as one who by
the Lord's mercy is trustworthy. 26I
think that in view of the impending[e]
distress it is well for a person to re-
main as he is. 27Are you bound to a
wife? Do not seek to be free. Are you
free from a wife? Do not seek mar-
riage. 28But if you marry, you do not
sin, and if a girl[f] marries she does not
sin. Yet those who marry will have
worldly troubles, and I would spare
you that. 29I mean, brethren, the ap-
pointed time has grown very short;
from now on, let those who have wives
live as though they had none, 30and
those who mourn as though they were
not mourning, and those who rejoice
as though they were not rejoicing, and
those who buy as though they had no
goods, 31and those who deal with the
world as though they had no dealings
with it. For the form of this world is
passing away.

32 I want you to be free from anx-
ieties. The unmarried man is anxious
about the affairs of the Lord, how to
please the Lord; 33but the married man
is anxious about worldly affairs, how
to please his wife, 34and his interests
are divided. And the unmarried wom-
an or girl[g] is anxious about the affairs
of the Lord, how to be holy in body
and spirit; but the married woman is
anxious about worldly affairs, how
to please her husband. 35I say this for
your own benefit, not to lay any re-
straint upon you, but to promote good
order and to secure your undivided
devotion to the Lord.

36 If any one thinks that he is not
behaving properly toward his be-
trothed,[h] if his passions are strong,
and it has to be, let him do as he
wishes: let them marry—it is no sin.
37But whoever is firmly established in
his heart, being under no necessity
but having his desire under control,
and has determined this in his heart,
to keep her as his betrothed,[i] he will
do well. 38So that he who marries his
betrothed[j] does well; and he who re-
frains from marriage will do better.

39 A wife is bound to her husband
as long as he lives. If the husband dies,
she is free to be married to whom she
wishes, only in the Lord. 40But in my
judgment she is happier if she remains
as she is. And I think that I have the
Spirit of God.

FOOD OFFERED TO IDOLS

8 Now concerning food offered to
idols:* we know that "all of us pos-
sess knowledge.""Knowledge" puffs
up, but love builds up. 2If any one
imagines that he knows something,
he does not yet know as he ought to
know. 3But if one loves God, one is
known by him.

4 Hence, as to the eating of food
offered to idols, we know that "an idol
has no real existence," and that "there
is no God but one." 5For although

[c] Or *make use of your present condition instead*
[d] Greek *virgins*
[e] Or *present*
[f] Greek *virgin*
[g] Greek *virgin*
[h] Greek *virgin*
[i] Greek *virgin*
[j] Greek *virgin*

there may be so-called gods in heav-
en or on earth—as indeed there are
many "gods" and many "lords" 6yet
for us there is one God, the Father,
from whom are all things and for
whom we exist, and one Lord, Jesus
Christ, through whom are all things
and through whom we exist.

7 However, not all possess this
knowledge. But some, through being
hitherto accustomed to idols, eat food
as really offered to an idol; and their
conscience, being weak, is defiled.
8Food will not commend us to God.
We are no worse off if we do not eat,
and no better off if we do. 9Only take
care lest this liberty of yours some-
how become a stumbling block to
the weak. 10For if any one sees you, a
man of knowledge, at table in an idol's
temple, might he not be encouraged, if
his conscience is weak, to eat food of-
fered to idols? 11And so by your knowl-
edge this weak man is destroyed,
the brother for whom Christ died.
12Thus, sinning against your brethren
and wounding their conscience when
it is weak, you sin against Christ.
13Therefore, if food is a cause of my
brother's falling, I will never eat meat,
lest I cause my brother to fall.

THE RIGHTS OF AN APOSTLE

9 Am I not free? Am I not an apostle?
Have I not seen Jesus our Lord? Are
not you my workmanship in the Lord?
2If to others I am not an apostle, at
least I am to you; for you are the seal
of my apostleship in the Lord.

3 This is my defense to those who
would examine me.* 4Do we not have
the right to our food and drink? 5Do
we not have the right to be accompa-
nied by a wife,[a]* as the other apostles
and the brethren* of the Lord and
Cephas? 6Or is it only Barnabas and
I who have no right to refrain from
working for a living? 7Who serves as
a soldier at his own expense? Who
plants a vineyard without eating any
of its fruit? Who tends a flock without
getting some of the milk?

8 Do I say this on human author-
ity? Does not the law say the same?
9For it is written in the law of Moses,
"You shall not muzzle an ox when
it is treading out the grain." Is it for
oxen that God is concerned? 10Does
he not speak entirely for our sake? It
was written for our sake, because the
plowman should plow in hope and the
thresher thresh in hope of a share in
the crop. 11If we have sown spiritual
good among you, is it too much if we
reap your material benefits? 12If oth-
ers share this rightful claim upon you,
do not we still more? Nevertheless,
we have not made use of this right,
but we endure anything rather than
put an obstacle in the way of the gos-
pel of Christ. 13Do you not know that
those who are employed in the temple
service get their food from the temple,
and those who serve at the altar share
in the sacrificial offerings? 14In the
same way, the Lord commanded that
those who proclaim the gospel should
get their living by the gospel.

15 But I have made no use of any
of these rights, nor am I writing this
to secure any such provision. For I
would rather die than have any one
deprive me of my ground for boast-
ing. 16For if I preach the gospel, that
gives me no ground for boasting. For
necessity is laid upon me. Woe to me
if I do not preach the gospel! 17For if
I do this of my own will, I have a re-
ward; but if not of my own will, I am
entrusted with a commission. 18What
then is my reward? Just this: that in
my preaching I may make the gospel
free of charge, not making full use of
my right in the gospel.

19 For though I am free from all
men, I have made myself a slave to
all, that I might win the more. 20To
the Jews I became as a Jew, in order
to win Jews; to those under the law I
became as one under the law—though
not being myself under the law—that
I might win those under the law. 21To

[a]Greek *woman, sister*

those outside the law I became as one
outside the law—not being without
law toward God but under the law of
Christ—that I might win those out-
side the law. 22To the weak I became
weak, that I might win the weak. I
have become all things to all men,
that I might by all means save some.
23I do it all for the sake of the gospel,
that I may share in its blessings.

24 Do you not know that in a race
all the runners compete, but only one
receives the prize? So run that you
may obtain it. 25Every athlete exercis-
es self-control in all things. They do it
to receive a perishable wreath, but we
an imperishable. 26Well, I do not run
aimlessly, I do not box as one beating
the air; 27but I pommel my body and
subdue it, lest after preaching to oth-
ers I myself should be disqualified.

WARNINGS FROM ISRAEL'S HISTORY

10 I want you to know, brethren, that
our fathers were all under the
cloud, and all passed through the sea,
2and all were baptized into Moses in
the cloud and in the sea, 3and all ate
the same supernatural[b] food 4and all
drank the same supernatural[c] drink.
For they drank from the supernatural[d]
Rock which followed them, and the
Rock was Christ. 5Nevertheless with
most of them God was not pleased;
for they were overthrown in the
wilderness.

6 Now these things are warnings
for us, not to desire evil as they did.
7Do not be idolaters as some of them
were; as it is written, "The people sat
down to eat and drink and rose up to
dance." 8We must not indulge in im-
morality as some of them did, and
twenty-three thousand fell in a single
day. 9We must not put the Lord[e] to the
test, as some of them did and were de-
stroyed by serpents; 10nor grumble, as
some of them did and were destroyed
by the Destroyer. 11Now these things
happened to them as a warning, but
they were written down for our in-
struction, upon whom the end of the
ages has come. 12Therefore let any one
who thinks that he stands take heed
lest he fall. 13No temptation has over-
taken you that is not common to man.
God is faithful, and he will not let you
be tempted beyond your strength, but
with the temptation will also provide
the way of escape, that you may be
able to endure it.

14 Therefore, my beloved, shun the
worship of idols. 15I speak as to sen-
sible men; judge for yourselves what
I say. 16The cup of blessing which we
bless, is it not a participation[f] in the
blood of Christ? The bread which we
break, is it not a participation[g] in the
body of Christ? 17Because there is one
bread, we who are many are one body,
for we all partake of the one bread.
18Consider the practice of Israel; are
not those who eat the sacrifices part-
ners in the altar? 19What do I imply
then? That food offered to idols is
anything, or that an idol is anything?
20No, I imply that what pagans sacri-
fice they offer to demons and not to
God. I do not want you to be partners
with demons.* 21You cannot drink the
cup of the Lord and the cup of de-
mons. You cannot partake of the table
of the Lord and the table of demons.
22Shall we provoke the Lord to jealou-
sy? Are we stronger than he?

DO ALL TO THE GLORY OF GOD

23 "All things are lawful," but not
all things are helpful. "All things
are lawful," but not all things build
up. 24Let no one seek his own good,
but the good of his neighbor. 25Eat
whatever is sold in the meat market
without raising any question on the

[b] Greek *spiritual*
[c] Greek *spiritual*
[d] Greek *spiritual*
[e] Other ancient authorities read *Christ*
[f] Or *communion*
[g] Or *communion*

ground of conscience. 26For "the earth
is the Lord's, and everything in it."
27If one of the unbelievers invites you
to dinner and you are disposed to go,
eat whatever is set before you without
raising any question on the ground of
conscience. 28(But if some one says to
you, "This has been offered in sacri-
fice," then out of consideration for
the man who informed you, and for
conscience' sake 29I mean his con-
science, not yours—do not eat it.) For
why should my liberty be determined
by another man's scruples? 30If I par-
take with thankfulness, why am I de-
nounced because of that for which I
give thanks?

31 So, whether you eat or drink, or
whatever you do, do all to the glory of
God. 32Give no offense to Jews or to
Greeks or to the church of God, 33just
as I try to please all men in everything I
do, not seeking my own advantage, but
that of many, that they may be saved.

11 Be imitators of me, as I am of
Christ.

HEAD COVERINGS

2 I commend you because you re-
member me in everything and main-
tain the traditions even as I have de-
livered them to you. 3But I want you
to understand that the head of every
man is Christ, the head of a woman is
her husband, and the head of Christ is
God. 4Any man who prays or prophe-
sies with his head covered dishonors
his head, 5but any woman who prays
or prophesies with her head unveiled
dishonors her head—it is the same
as if her head were shaven. 6For if a
woman will not veil herself, then she
should cut off her hair; but if it is dis-
graceful for a woman to be shorn or
shaven, let her wear a veil. 7For a man
ought not to cover his head, since he
is the image and glory of God; but
woman is the glory of man. 8(For
man was not made from woman, but
woman from man. 9Neither was man
created for woman, but woman for
man.) 10That is why a woman ought
to have a veil[a] on her head, because
of the angels. 11(Nevertheless, in the
Lord woman is not independent of
man nor man of woman; 12for as wom-
an was made from man, so man is
now born of woman. And all things
are from God.) 13Judge for yourselves;
is it proper for a woman to pray to God
with her head uncovered? 14Does not
nature itself teach you that for a man
to wear long hair is degrading to him,
15but if a woman has long hair, it is her
pride? For her hair is given to her for
a covering. 16If any one is disposed to
be contentious, we recognize no other
practice, nor do the churches of God.

ABUSES AT THE LORD'S SUPPER

17 But in the following instructions
I do not commend you, because when
you come together it is not for the bet-
ter but for the worse. 18For, in the first
place, when you assemble as a church,
I hear that there are divisions among
you; and I partly believe it, 19for there
must be factions among you in order
that those who are genuine among
you may be recognized. 20When you
meet together, it is not the Lord's sup-
per that you eat.* 21For in eating, each
one goes ahead with his own meal,
and one is hungry and another is
drunk. 22What! Do you not have hous-
es to eat and drink in? Or do you de-
spise the church of God and humiliate
those who have nothing? What shall
I say to you? Shall I commend you in
this? No, I will not.

THE INSTITUTION OF THE LORD'S SUPPER

23 For I received from the Lord
what I also delivered to you, that the
Lord Jesus on the night when he was
betrayed took bread, 24and when he
had given thanks, he broke it, and
said, "This is my body which is for[b]
you. Do this in remembrance of me."
25In the same way also the cup, after

[a]Greek *authority* (the veil being a symbol of this)
[b]Other ancient authorities read *broken for*

supper, saying, "This cup is the new
covenant in my blood. Do this, as of-
ten as you drink it, in remembrance
of me." 26For as often as you eat this
bread and drink the cup, you proclaim
the Lord's death until he comes.

PARTAKING OF THE SUPPER UNWORTHILY

27 Whoever, therefore, eats the
bread or drinks the cup of the Lord in
an unworthy manner will be guilty of
profaning the body and blood of the
Lord. 28Let a man examine himself,
and so eat of the bread and drink of
the cup. 29For any one who eats and
drinks without discerning the body
eats and drinks judgment upon him-
self. 30That is why many of you are
weak and ill, and some have died.[c]
31But if we judged ourselves truly, we
should not be judged. 32But when we
are judged by the Lord, we are chas-
tened[d] so that we may not be con-
demned along with the world.

33 So then, my brethren, when you
come together to eat, wait for one an-
other 34if any one is hungry, let him eat
at home—lest you come together to be
condemned. About the other things I
will give directions when I come.

SPIRITUAL GIFTS

12 Now concerning spiritual gifts,
brethren, I do not want you to be
uninformed.* 2You know that when
you were heathen, you were led astray
to dumb idols, however you may have
been moved. 3Therefore I want you to
understand that no one speaking by
the Spirit of God ever says "Jesus be
cursed!" and no one can say "Jesus is
Lord" except by the Holy Spirit.

4 Now there are varieties of gifts,
but the same Spirit; 5and there are va-
rieties of service, but the same Lord;
6and there are varieties of working,
but it is the same God who inspires
them all in every one. 7To each is giv-
en the manifestation of the Spirit for
the common good. 8To one is given
through the Spirit the utterance of
wisdom, and to another the utterance
of knowledge according to the same
Spirit, 9to another faith by the same
Spirit, to another gifts of healing by
the one Spirit, 10to another the work-
ing of miracles, to another prophecy,
to another the ability to distinguish
between spirits, to another various
kinds of tongues, to another the in-
terpretation of tongues. 11All these are
inspired by one and the same Spirit,
who apportions to each one individu-
ally as he wills.

ONE BODY WITH MANY MEMBERS

12 For just as the body is one and
has many members, and all the mem-
bers of the body, though many, are
one body, so it is with Christ. 13For by
one Spirit we were all baptized into
one body—Jews or Greeks, slaves or
free—and all were made to drink of
one Spirit.

14 For the body does not consist
of one member but of many. 15If the
foot should say, "Because I am not a
hand, I do not belong to the body,"
that would not make it any less a part
of the body. 16And if the ear should
say, "Because I am not an eye, I do not
belong to the body," that would not
make it any less a part of the body.
17If the whole body were an eye, where
would be the hearing? If the whole
body were an ear, where would be the
sense of smell? 18But as it is, God ar-
ranged the organs in the body, each
one of them, as he chose. 19If all were
a single organ, where would the body
be? 20As it is, there are many parts,
yet one body. 21The eye cannot say to
the hand, "I have no need of you," nor
again the head to the feet, "I have no
need of you." 22On the contrary, the
parts of the body which seem to be
weaker are indispensable, 23and those
parts of the body which we think less
honorable we invest with the greater
honor, and our unpresentable parts

[c] Greek *have fallen asleep* (as in 15.6, 20)
[d] Or *when we are judged we are being chastened by the Lord*

are treated with greater modesty, 24which our more presentable parts do not require. But God has so adjusted the body, giving the greater honor to the inferior part, 25that there may be no discord in the body, but that the members may have the same care for one another. 26If one member suffers, all suffer together; if one member is honored, all rejoice together.

27 Now you are the body of Christ and individually members of it. 28And God has appointed in the church first apostles, second prophets, third teachers, then workers of miracles, then healers, helpers, administrators, speakers in various kinds of tongues. 29Are all apostles? Are all prophets? Are all teachers? Do all work miracles? 30Do all possess gifts of healing? Do all speak with tongues? Do all interpret? 31But earnestly desire the higher gifts. And I will show you a still more excellent way.*

THE GIFT OF LOVE

13 If I speak in the tongues of men and of angels, but have not love, I am a noisy gong or a clanging cymbal. 2And if I have prophetic powers, and understand all mysteries and all knowledge, and if I have all faith, so as to remove mountains, but have not love, I am nothing. 3If I give away all I have, and if I deliver my body to be burned,[a] but have not love, I gain nothing.

4 Love is patient and kind; love is not jealous or boastful; 5it is not arrogant or rude. Love does not insist on its own way; it is not irritable or resentful; 6it does not rejoice at wrong, but rejoices in the right. 7Love bears all things, believes all things, hopes all things, endures all things.

8 Love never ends; as for prophecies, they will pass away; as for tongues, they will cease; as for knowledge, it will pass away. 9For our knowledge is imperfect and our prophecy is imperfect; 10but when the perfect comes, the imperfect will pass away. 11When I was a child, I spoke like a child, I thought like a child, I reasoned like a child; when I became a man, I gave up childish ways. 12For now we see in a mirror dimly, but then face to face. Now I know in part; then I shall understand fully, even as I have been fully understood. 13So faith, hope, love abide, these three; but the greatest of these is love.

GIFTS OF PROPHECY AND TONGUES

14 Make love your aim, and earnestly desire the spiritual gifts, especially that you may prophesy. 2For one who speaks in a tongue speaks not to men but to God; for no one understands him, but he utters mysteries in the Spirit. 3On the other hand, he who prophesies speaks to men for their upbuilding and encouragement and consolation. 4He who speaks in a tongue edifies himself, but he who prophesies edifies the church. 5Now I want you all to speak in tongues, but even more to prophesy. He who prophesies is greater than he who speaks in tongues, unless some one interprets, so that the church may be edified.

6 Now, brethren, if I come to you speaking in tongues, how shall I benefit you unless I bring you some revelation or knowledge or prophecy or teaching? 7If even lifeless instruments, such as the flute or the harp, do not give distinct notes, how will any one know what is played? 8And if the bugle gives an indistinct sound, who will get ready for battle? 9So with yourselves; if you in a tongue utter speech that is not intelligible, how will any one know what is said? For you will be speaking into the air. 10There are doubtless many different languages in the world, and none is without meaning; 11but if I do not know the meaning of the language, I shall be a foreigner to the speaker and the speaker a foreigner to me. 12So with yourselves; since you are eager

[a]Other ancient authorities read *body that I may glory*

for manifestations of the Spirit, strive to excel in building up the church.

13 Therefore, he who speaks in a tongue should pray for the power to interpret. 14For if I pray in a tongue, my spirit prays but my mind is unfruitful. 15What am I to do? I will pray with the spirit and I will pray with the mind also; I will sing with the spirit and I will sing with the mind also. 16Otherwise, if you bless[b] with the spirit, how can any one in the position of an outsider[c] say the "Amen" to your thanksgiving when he does not know what you are saying? 17For you may give thanks well enough, but the other man is not edified. 18I thank God that I speak in tongues more than you all; 19nevertheless, in church I would rather speak five words with my mind, in order to instruct others, than ten thousand words in a tongue.

20 Brethren, do not be children in your thinking; be babes in evil, but in thinking be mature. 21In the law it is written, "By men of strange tongues and by the lips of foreigners will I speak to this people, and even then they will not listen to me, says the Lord." 22Thus, tongues are a sign not for believers but for unbelievers, while prophecy is not for unbelievers but for believers. 23If, therefore, the whole church assembles and all speak in tongues, and outsiders or unbelievers enter, will they not say that you are mad? 24But if all prophesy, and an unbeliever or outsider enters, he is convicted by all, he is called to account by all, 25the secrets of his heart are disclosed; and so, falling on his face, he will worship God and declare that God is really among you.

ORDERLY WORSHIP

26 What then, brethren? When you come together, each one has a hymn, a lesson, a revelation, a tongue, or an interpretation. Let all things be done for edification. 27If any speak in a tongue, let there be only two or at most three, and each in turn; and let one interpret. 28But if there is no one to interpret, let each of them keep silence in church and speak to himself and to God. 29Let two or three prophets speak, and let the others weigh what is said. 30If a revelation is made to another sitting by, let the first be silent. 31For you can all prophesy one by one, so that all may learn and all be encouraged; 32and the spirits of prophets are subject to prophets. 33For God is not a God of confusion but of peace. As in all the churches of the saints, 34the women should keep silence in the churches. For they are not permitted to speak, but should be subordinate, as even the law says. 35If there is anything they desire to know, let them ask their husbands at home. For it is shameful for a woman to speak in church. 36What! Did the word of God originate with you, or are you the only ones it has reached?

37 If any one thinks that he is a prophet, or spiritual, he should acknowledge that what I am writing to you is a command of the Lord. 38If any one does not recognize this, he is not recognized. 39So, my brethren, earnestly desire to prophesy, and do not forbid speaking in tongues; 40but all things should be done decently and in order.

THE RESURRECTION OF CHRIST

15 Now I would remind you, brethren, in what terms I preached to you the gospel, which you received, in which you stand, 2by which you are saved, if you hold it fast—unless you believed in vain.

3 For I delivered to you as of first importance what I also received, that Christ died for our sins in accordance with the scriptures, 4that he was buried, that he was raised on the third day in accordance with the scriptures, 5and that he appeared to Cephas, then

[b]That is, *give thanks to God*
[c]Or *him that is without gifts*

to the twelve. 6Then he appeared to more than five hundred brethren at one time, most of whom are still alive, though some have fallen asleep. 7Then he appeared to James, then to all the apostles. 8Last of all, as to one untimely born, he appeared also to me. 9For I am the least of the apostles, unfit to be called an apostle, because I persecuted the church of God. 10But by the grace of God I am what I am, and his grace toward me was not in vain. On the contrary, I worked harder than any of them, though it was not I, but the grace of God which is with me. 11Whether then it was I or they, so we preach and so you believed.

THE RESURRECTION OF THE DEAD

12 Now if Christ is preached as raised from the dead, how can some of you say that there is no resurrection of the dead? 13But if there is no resurrection of the dead, then Christ has not been raised;* 14if Christ has not been raised, then our preaching is in vain and your faith is in vain. 15We are even found to be misrepresenting God, because we testified of God that he raised Christ, whom he did not raise if it is true that the dead are not raised. 16For if the dead are not raised, then Christ has not been raised. 17If Christ has not been raised, your faith is futile and you are still in your sins. 18Then those also who have fallen asleep in Christ have perished. 19If for this life only we have hoped in Christ, we are of all men most to be pitied.

20 But in fact Christ has been raised from the dead, the first fruits of those who have fallen asleep. 21For as by a man came death, by a man has come also the resurrection of the dead. 22For as in Adam all die, so also in Christ shall all be made alive. 23But each in his own order: Christ the first fruits, then at his coming those who belong to Christ. 24Then comes the end, when he delivers the kingdom to God the Father after destroying every rule and every authority and power. 25For he must reign until he has put all his enemies under his feet. 26The last enemy to be destroyed is death. 27"For God[a] has put all things in subjection under his feet." But when it says, "All things are put in subjection under him," it is plain that he is excepted who put all things under him. 28When all things are subjected to him, then the Son himself will also be subjected to him who put all things under him, that God may be everything to every one.

29 Otherwise, what do people mean by being baptized on behalf of the dead? If the dead are not raised at all, why are people baptized on their behalf?* 30Why am I in peril every hour? 31I protest, brethren, by my pride in you which I have in Christ Jesus our Lord, I die every day! 32What do I gain if, humanly speaking, I fought with beasts at Ephesus? If the dead are not raised, "Let us eat and drink, for tomorrow we die." 33Do not be deceived: "Bad company ruins good morals." 34Come to your right mind, and sin no more. For some have no knowledge of God. I say this to your shame.

THE RESURRECTION BODY

35 But some one will ask, "How are the dead raised? With what kind of body do they come?" 36You foolish man! What you sow does not come to life unless it dies. 37And what you sow is not the body which is to be, but a bare kernel, perhaps of wheat or of some other grain. 38But God gives it a body as he has chosen, and to each kind of seed its own body. 39For not all flesh is alike, but there is one kind for men, another for animals, another for birds, and another for fish. 40There are celestial bodies and there are terrestrial bodies; but the glory of the celestial is one, and the glory of the terrestrial is another. 41There is one glory of the sun, and another glory of the moon, and another glory

[a]Greek *he*

of the stars; for star differs from star
in glory.
42 So is it with the resurrection of
the dead. What is sown is perishable,
what is raised is imperishable. 43It is
sown in dishonor, it is raised in glory.
It is sown in weakness, it is raised in
power. 44It is sown a physical body, it
is raised a spiritual body. If there is a
physical body, there is also a spiritual
body. 45Thus it is written, "The first
man Adam became a living being"; the
last Adam became a life-giving spir-
it. 46But it is not the spiritual which
is first but the physical, and then the
spiritual. 47The first man was from
the earth, a man of dust; the second
man is from heaven. 48As was the man
of dust, so are those who are of the
dust; and as is the man of heaven, so
are those who are of heaven. 49Just
as we have borne the image of the
man of dust, we shall[b] also bear the
image of the man of heaven. 50I tell
you this, brethren: flesh and blood
cannot inherit the kingdom of God,
nor does the perishable inherit the
imperishable.
51 Lo! I tell you a mystery. We
shall not all sleep, but we shall all be
changed, 52in a moment, in the twin-
kling of an eye, at the last trumpet.
For the trumpet will sound, and the
dead will be raised imperishable, and
we shall be changed. 53For this perish-
able nature must put on the imper-
ishable, and this mortal nature must
put on immortality. 54When the per-
ishable puts on the imperishable, and
the mortal puts on immortality, then
shall come to pass the saying that is
written:

> "Death is swallowed up in
> victory."
> 55"O death, where is thy victory?
> O death, where is thy sting?"

56The sting of death is sin, and the
power of sin is the law. 57But thanks
be to God, who gives us the victory
through our Lord Jesus Christ.
58 Therefore, my beloved breth-
ren, be steadfast, immovable, always
abounding in the work of the Lord,
knowing that in the Lord your labor
is not in vain.

THE COLLECTION FOR THE SAINTS

16 Now concerning the contribution
for the saints:* as I directed the
churches of Galatia, so you also are
to do. 2On the first day of every week,
each of you is to put something aside
and store it up, as he may prosper, so
that contributions need not be made
when I come. 3And when I arrive, I
will send those whom you accredit by
letter to carry your gift to Jerusalem.
4If it seems advisable that I should go
also, they will accompany me.

PLANS FOR TRAVEL

5 I will visit you after passing
through Macedo´nia, for I intend to
pass through Macedo´nia, 6and per-
haps I will stay with you or even spend
the winter, so that you may speed me
on my journey, wherever I go. 7For I do
not want to see you now just in pass-
ing; I hope to spend some time with
you, if the Lord permits. 8But I will stay
in Ephesus until Pentecost, 9for a wide
door for effective work has opened to
me, and there are many adversaries.
10 When Timothy comes, see that
you put him at ease among you, for
he is doing the work of the Lord, as I
am. 11So let no one despise him. Speed
him on his way in peace, that he may
return to me; for I am expecting him
with the brethren.
12 As for our brother Apol´los, I
strongly urged him to visit you with
the other brethren, but it was not at
all his will[c] to come now. He will come
when he has opportunity.

FINAL MESSAGES AND GREETINGS

13 Be watchful, stand firm in your
faith, be courageous, be strong. 14Let
all that you do be done in love.

[b] Other ancient authorities read *let us*
[c] Or *God's will for him*

15 Now, brethren, you know that
the household of Steph´anas were the
first converts in Acha´ia, and they
have devoted themselves to the service
of the saints; 16I urge you to be subject
to such men and to every fellow work-
er and laborer. 17I rejoice at the com-
ing of Steph´anas and Fortuna´tus and
Acha´icus, because they have made up
for your absence; 18for they refreshed
my spirit as well as yours. Give recog-
nition to such men.
19 The churches of Asia send greet-
ings. Aq´uila and Prisca, together with
the church in their house, send you
hearty greetings in the Lord. 20All the
brethren send greetings. Greet one an-
other with a holy kiss.
21 I, Paul, write this greeting with
my own hand. 22If any one has no love
for the Lord, let him be accursed. Our
Lord, come![a] 23The grace of the Lord
Jesus be with you. 24My love be with
you all in Christ Jesus. Amen.

[a]Greek *Maranatha*

THE SECOND LETTER OF PAUL TO THE CORINTHIANS

SALUTATION

1 Paul, an apostle of Christ Jesus by
the will of God, and Timothy our
brother. To the church of God which
is at Corinth, with all the saints who
are in the whole of Acha´ia:
2 Grace to you and peace from God
our Father and the Lord Jesus Christ.

PAUL'S THANKSGIVING AFTER AFFLICTION

3 Blessed be the God and Father
of our Lord Jesus Christ, the Father
of mercies and God of all comfort,
4who comforts us in all our afflic-
tion, so that we may be able to com-
fort those who are in any affliction,
with the comfort with which we our-
selves are comforted by God. 5For as
we share abundantly in Christ's suf-
ferings, so through Christ we share
abundantly in comfort too.[a] 6If we
are afflicted, it is for your comfort
and salvation; and if we are com-
forted, it is for your comfort, which
you experience when you patiently
endure the same sufferings that we
suffer. 7Our hope for you is unshak-
en; for we know that as you share in
our sufferings, you will also share in
our comfort.
8 For we do not want you to be
ignorant, brethren, of the affliction*
we experienced in Asia; for we were
so utterly, unbearably crushed that we
despaired of life itself. 9Why, we felt
that we had received the sentence of
death; but that was to make us rely
not on ourselves but on God who rais-
es the dead; 10he delivered us from so
deadly a peril, and he will deliver us;
on him we have set our hope that he
will deliver us again. 11You also must
help us by prayer, so that many will
give thanks on our behalf for the
blessing granted us in answer to many
prayers.

THE POSTPONEMENT OF PAUL'S VISIT

12 For our boast is this, the testi-
mony of our conscience that we have
behaved in the world, and still more
toward you, with holiness and godly
sincerity, not by earthly wisdom but
by the grace of God. 13For we write
you nothing but what you can read
and understand; I hope you will un-
derstand fully, 14as you have under-
stood in part, that you can be proud
of us as we can be of you, on the day
of the Lord Jesus.
15 Because I was sure of this, I
wanted to come to you first, so that
you might have a double pleasure;[b]
16I wanted to visit you on my way to
Macedo´nia, and to come back to you
from Macedo´nia and have you send
me on my way to Judea. 17Was I vac-
illating when I wanted to do this? Do
I make my plans like a worldly man,
ready to say Yes and No at once? 18As
surely as God is faithful, our word to
you has not been Yes and No. 19For the
Son of God, Jesus Christ, whom we
preached among you, Silva´nus and
Timothy and I, was not Yes and No;
but in him it is always Yes. 20For all
the promises of God find their Yes in
him. That is why we utter the Amen
through him, to the glory of God.
21But it is God who establishes us with
you in Christ, and has commissioned
us; 22he has put his seal upon us and
given us his Spirit in our hearts as a
guarantee.
23 But I call God to witness
against me—it was to spare you that
I refrained from coming to Corinth.
24Not that we lord it over your faith;
we work with you for your joy,
for you stand firm in your faith.
2 For I made up my mind not to make
you another painful visit. 2For if I
cause you pain, who is there to make

[a] Or *For as the sufferings of Christ abound for us, so also our comfort abounds through Christ*
[b] Other ancient authorities read *favor*

me glad but the one whom I have
pained? 3And I wrote as I did, so that
when I came I might not be pained by
those who should have made me re-
joice, for I felt sure of all of you, that
my joy would be the joy of you all. 4For
I wrote you out of much affliction and
anguish of heart and with many tears,
not to cause you pain but to let you
know the abundant love that I have
for you.

FORGIVENESS FOR THE OFFENDER

5 But if any one has caused pain,
he has caused it not to me, but in
some measure—not to put it too se-
verely—to you all. 6For such a one
this punishment by the majority is
enough; 7so you should rather turn to
forgive and comfort him, or he may
be overwhelmed by excessive sorrow.
8So I beg you to reaffirm your love
for him. 9For this is why I wrote, that
I might test you and know whether
you are obedient in everything. 10Any
one whom you forgive, I also forgive.
What I have forgiven, if I have forgiv-
en anything, has been for your sake
in the presence of Christ, 11to keep
Satan from gaining the advantage
over us; for we are not ignorant of his
designs.

PAUL'S ANXIETY IN TROAS

12 When I came to Tro´as to
preach the gospel of Christ, a door
was opened for me in the Lord; 13but
my mind could not rest because I did
not find my brother Titus there. So
I took leave of them and went on to
Macedo´nia.

14 But thanks be to God, who in
Christ always leads us in triumph,
and through us spreads the fra-
grance of the knowledge of him ev-
erywhere. 15For we are the aroma of
Christ to God among those who are
being saved and among those who
are perishing, 16to one a fragrance
from death to death, to the other a
fragrance from life to life. Who is
sufficient for these things? 17For we
are not, like so many, peddlers of
God's word; but as men of sincerity,
as commissioned by God, in the sight
of God we speak in Christ.

MINISTERS OF THE NEW COVENANT

3 Are we beginning to commend our-
selves again? Or do we need, as
some do, letters of recommendation
to you, or from you? 2You yourselves
are our letter of recommendation,
written on your[a] hearts, to be known
and read by all men; 3and you show
that you are a letter from Christ de-
livered by us, written not with ink but
with the Spirit of the living God, not
on tablets of stone but on tablets of
human hearts.

4 Such is the confidence that we
have through Christ toward God. 5Not
that we are sufficient of ourselves to
claim anything as coming from us;
our sufficiency is from God, 6who has
qualified us to be ministers of a new
covenant, not in a written code but in
the Spirit; for the written code kills,
but the Spirit gives life.

7 Now if the dispensation of death,
carved in letters on stone, came with
such splendor that the Israelites could
not look at Moses' face because of its
brightness, fading as this was, 8will
not the dispensation of the Spirit be
attended with greater splendor? 9For
if there was splendor in the dispensa-
tion of condemnation, the dispensa-
tion of righteousness must far exceed
it in splendor. 10Indeed, in this case,
what once had splendor has come to
have no splendor at all, because of
the splendor that surpasses it. 11For if
what faded away came with splendor,
what is permanent must have much
more splendor.

12 Since we have such a hope, we
are very bold, 13not like Moses, who
put a veil over his face so that the
Israelites might not see the end of
the fading splendor. 14But their minds
were hardened; for to this day, when

[a]Other ancient authorities read *our*

they read the old covenant, that same
veil remains unlifted, because only
through Christ is it taken away. 15 Yes,
to this day whenever Moses is read a
veil lies over their minds; 16 but when
a man turns to the Lord the veil is re-
moved. 17 Now the Lord is the Spirit,
and where the Spirit of the Lord is,
there is freedom. 18 And we all, with
unveiled face, beholding[b] the glory of
the Lord, are being changed into his
likeness from one degree of glory to
another; for this comes from the Lord
who is the Spirit.*

TREASURE IN CLAY JARS

4 Therefore, having this ministry by
the mercy of God,[c] we do not lose
heart. 2 We have renounced disgrace-
ful, underhanded ways; we refuse to
practice cunning or to tamper with
God's word, but by the open state-
ment of the truth we would commend
ourselves to every man's conscience
in the sight of God. 3 And even if our
gospel is veiled, it is veiled only to
those who are perishing. 4 In their
case the god of this world has blinded
the minds of the unbelievers, to keep
them from seeing the light of the gos-
pel of the glory of Christ, who is the
likeness of God. 5 For what we preach
is not ourselves, but Jesus Christ as
Lord, with ourselves as your servants[d]
for Jesus' sake. 6 For it is the God who
said, "Let light shine out of dark-
ness," who has shone in our hearts to
give the light of the knowledge of the
glory of God in the face of Christ.

7 But we have this treasure* in
earthen vessels, to show that the
transcendent power belongs to God
and not to us. 8 We are afflicted in ev-
ery way, but not crushed; perplexed,
but not driven to despair; 9 persecuted,
but not forsaken; struck down, but
not destroyed; 10 always carrying in
the body the death of Jesus, so that
the life of Jesus may also be manifest-
ed in our bodies. 11 For while we live
we are always being given up to death
for Jesus' sake, so that the life of Jesus
may be manifested in our mortal
flesh. 12 So death is at work in us, but
life in you.*

13 Since we have the same spirit
of faith as he had who wrote, "I be-
lieved, and so I spoke," we too believe,
and so we speak, 14 knowing that he
who raised the Lord Jesus will raise
us also with Jesus and bring us with
you into his presence. 15 For it is all for
your sake, so that as grace extends to
more and more people it may increase
thanksgiving, to the glory of God.

LIVING BY FAITH

16 So we do not lose heart. Though
our outer nature is wasting away, our
inner nature is being renewed every
day. 17 For this slight momentary af-
fliction is preparing for us an eternal
weight of glory beyond all compar-
ison, 18 because we look not to the
things that are seen but to the things
that are unseen; for the things that
are seen are transient, but the things
that are unseen are eternal.

5 For we know that if the earthly tent
we live in is destroyed, we have a
building from God, a house not made
with hands, eternal in the heavens.
2 Here indeed we groan, and long to
put on our heavenly dwelling, 3 so
that by putting it on we may not be
found naked. 4 For while we are still
in this tent, we sigh with anxiety; not
that we would be unclothed, but that
we would be further clothed, so that
what is mortal may be swallowed up
by life. 5 He who has prepared us for
this very thing is God, who has given
us the Spirit as a guarantee.

6 So we are always of good cour-
age; we know that while we are at
home in the body we are away from
the Lord, 7 for we walk by faith, not by
sight. 8 We are of good courage, and
we would rather be away from the
body and at home with the Lord. 9 So

[b] Or *reflecting*
[c] Greek *as we have received mercy*
[d] Or *slaves*

whether we are at home or away, we
make it our aim to please him. 10For
we must all appear before the judg-
ment seat of Christ, so that each one
may receive good or evil, according to
what he has done in the body.

THE MINISTRY OF RECONCILIATION

11 Therefore, knowing the fear of
the Lord, we persuade men; but what
we are is known to God, and I hope it
is known also to your conscience. 12We
are not commending ourselves to you
again but giving you cause to be proud
of us, so that you may be able to an-
swer those who pride themselves on
a man's position and not on his heart.
13For if we are beside ourselves, it is
for God; if we are in our right mind,
it is for you. 14For the love of Christ
controls us, because we are convinced
that one has died for all; therefore all
have died. 15And he died for all, that
those who live might live no longer for
themselves but for him who for their
sake died and was raised.

16 From now on, therefore, we
regard no one from a human point
of view; even though we once re-
garded Christ from a human point of
view, we regard him thus no longer.
17Therefore, if any one is in Christ, he
is a new creation;[a] the old has passed
away, behold, the new has come. 18All
this is from God, who through Christ
reconciled us to himself and gave us
the ministry of reconciliation; 19that
is, God was in Christ reconciling[b]
the world to himself,* not counting
their trespasses against them, and
entrusting to us the message of rec-
onciliation. 20So we are ambassadors
for Christ, God making his appeal
through us. We beseech you on behalf
of Christ, be reconciled to God. 21For
our sake he made him to be sin* who
knew no sin, so that in him we might
become the righteousness of God.

6 Working together with him, then,
we entreat you not to accept the
grace of God in vain. 2For he says,

"At the acceptable time I have
listened to you,
and helped you on the day of
salvation."

3We put no obstacle in any one's
way, so that no fault may be found
with our ministry, 4but as servants of
God we commend ourselves in every
way: through great endurance, in af-
flictions, hardships, calamities, 5beat-
ings, imprisonments, tumults, labors,
watching, hunger; 6by purity, knowl-
edge, forbearance, kindness, the
Holy Spirit, genuine love, 7truthful
speech, and the power of God; with
the weapons of righteousness for the
right hand and for the left; 8in honor
and dishonor, in ill repute and good
repute. We are treated as impostors,
and yet are true; 9as unknown, and yet
well known; as dying, and behold we
live; as punished, and yet not killed;
10as sorrowful, yet always rejoicing;
as poor, yet making many rich; as
having nothing, and yet possessing
everything.

11 Our mouth is open to you,
Corinthians; our heart is wide. 12You
are not restricted by us, but you are
restricted in your own affections. 13In
return—I speak as to children—widen
your hearts also.

THE TEMPLE OF THE LIVING GOD

14 Do not be mismated with un-
believers. For what partnership
have righteousness and iniquity? Or
what fellowship has light with dark-
ness? 15What accord has Christ with
Be´lial?[c] Or what has a believer in
common with an unbeliever? 16What
agreement has the temple of God with
idols? For we are the temple of the liv-
ing God; as God said,

"I will live in them and move
among them,
and I will be their God,
and they shall be my people.
17Therefore come out from them,

[a] Or *creature*
[b] Or *in Christ God was reconciling*
[c] Greek *Beliar*

and be separate from them,
says the Lord,
and touch nothing unclean;
then I will welcome you,
18and I will be a father to you,
and you shall be my sons and
daughters,
says the Lord Almighty."

7 Since we have these promises, be-
loved, let us cleanse ourselves from
every defilement of body and spirit,
and make holiness perfect in the fear
of God.

PAUL'S JOY AT THE CHURCH'S REPENTANCE

2 Open your hearts to us; we have
wronged no one, we have corrupted
no one, we have taken advantage of
no one. 3I do not say this to condemn
you, for I said before that you are in
our hearts, to die together and to live
together. 4I have great confidence in
you; I have great pride in you; I am
filled with comfort. With all our af-
fliction, I am overjoyed.

5 For even when we came into
Macedo´nia, our bodies had no rest
but we were afflicted at every turn—
fighting without and fear within.
6But God, who comforts the down-
cast, comforted us by the coming of
Titus, 7and not only by his coming
but also by the comfort with which
he was comforted in you, as he told
us of your longing, your mourning,
your zeal for me, so that I rejoiced
still more. 8For even if I made you
sorry with my letter, I do not regret
it (though I did regret it), for I see
that that letter grieved you, though
only for a while. 9As it is, I rejoice,
not because you were grieved, but be-
cause you were grieved into repent-
ing; for you felt a godly grief, so that
you suffered no loss through us. 10For
godly grief produces a repentance
that leads to salvation and brings
no regret, but worldly grief produc-
es death. 11For see what earnestness
this godly grief has produced in you,
what eagerness to clear yourselves,
what indignation, what alarm, what
longing, what zeal, what punish-
ment! At every point you have proved
yourselves guiltless in the matter.
12So although I wrote to you, it was
not on account of the one who did the
wrong, nor on account of the one who
suffered the wrong, but in order that
your zeal for us might be revealed to
you in the sight of God. 13Therefore
we are comforted. And besides our
own comfort we rejoiced still more
at the joy of Titus, because his mind
has been set at rest by you all. 14For if
I have expressed to him some pride
in you, I was not put to shame; but
just as everything we said to you was
true, so our boasting before Titus has
proved true. 15And his heart goes out
all the more to you, as he remembers
the obedience of you all, and the fear
and trembling with which you re-
ceived him. 16I rejoice, because I have
perfect confidence in you.

ENCOURAGEMENT TO BE GENEROUS

8 We want you to know, brethren,
about the grace of God which
has been shown in the churches of
Macedo´nia, 2for in a severe test of
affliction, their abundance of joy
and their extreme poverty have over-
flowed in a wealth of liberality on
their part. 3For they gave according
to their means, as I can testify, and
beyond their means, of their own
free will, 4begging us earnestly for
the favor of taking part in the relief
of the saints 5and this, not as we ex-
pected, but first they gave themselves
to the Lord and to us by the will of
God. 6Accordingly we have urged
Titus that as he had already made a
beginning, he should also complete
among you this gracious work. 7Now
as you excel in everything—in faith,
in utterance, in knowledge, in all ear-
nestness, and in your love for us—see
that you excel in this gracious work
also.

8 I say this not as a command, but
to prove by the earnestness of others
that your love also is genuine. 9For

you know the grace of our Lord Jesus
Christ, that though he was rich, yet
for your sake he became poor, so that
by his poverty you might become rich.
10 And in this matter I give my advice:
it is best for you now to complete
what a year ago you began not only to
do but to desire, 11 so that your read-
iness in desiring it may be matched
by your completing it out of what you
have. 12 For if the readiness is there, it
is acceptable according to what a man
has, not according to what he has not.
13 I do not mean that others should be
eased and you burdened, 14 but that as
a matter of equality your abundance
at the present time should supply
their want, so that their abundance
may supply your want, that there
may be equality. 15 As it is written,
"He who gathered much had nothing
over, and he who gathered little had
no lack."

COMMENDATION OF TITUS

16 But thanks be to God who
puts the same earnest care for you
into the heart of Titus. 17 For he not
only accepted our appeal, but being
himself very earnest he is going to
you of his own accord. 18 With him
we are sending the brother who is
famous among all the churches for
his preaching of the gospel; 19 and not
only that, but he has been appoint-
ed by the churches to travel with us
in this gracious work which we are
carrying on, for the glory of the Lord
and to show our good will. 20 We in-
tend that no one should blame us
about this liberal gift which we are
administering, 21 for we aim at what
is honorable not only in the Lord's
sight but also in the sight of men.
22 And with them we are sending our
brother whom we have often tested
and found earnest in many matters,
but who is now more earnest than
ever because of his great confidence
in you. 23 As for Titus, he is my part-
ner and fellow worker in your ser-
vice; and as for our brethren, they
are messengers[a] of the churches, the
glory of Christ. 24 So give proof, be-
fore the churches, of your love and of
our boasting about you to these men.

THE COLLECTION FOR CHRISTIANS AT JERUSALEM

9 Now it is superfluous* for me to
write to you about the offering for
the saints, 2 for I know your readiness,
of which I boast about you to the peo-
ple of Macedo´nia, saying that Acha´ia
has been ready since last year; and
your zeal has stirred up most of them.
3 But I am sending the brethren so that
our boasting about you may not prove
vain in this case, so that you may be
ready, as I said you would be; 4 lest if
some Macedo´nians come with me and
find that you are not ready, we be hu-
miliated—to say nothing of you—for
being so confident. 5 So I thought it
necessary to urge the brethren to go
on to you before me, and arrange in
advance for this gift you have prom-
ised, so that it may be ready not as an
exaction but as a willing gift.

6 The point is this: he who sows
sparingly will also reap sparingly, and
he who sows bountifully will also reap
bountifully. 7 Each one must do as he
has made up his mind, not reluctant-
ly or under compulsion, for God loves
a cheerful giver. 8 And God is able to
provide you with every blessing in
abundance, so that you may always
have enough of everything and may
provide in abundance for every good
work. 9 As it is written,

> "He scatters abroad, he gives to
> the poor;
> his righteousness[b] endures for
> ever."

10 He who supplies seed to the sow-
er and bread for food will supply and
multiply your resources[c] and increase

[a] Greek *apostles*
[b] Or *benevolence*
[c] Greek *sowing*

the harvest of your righteousness.[d] 11You will be enriched in every way for great generosity, which through us will produce thanksgiving to God; 12for the rendering of this service not only supplies the wants of the saints but also overflows in many thanksgivings to God. 13Under the test of this service, you[e] will glorify God by your obedience in acknowledging the gospel of Christ, and by the generosity of your contribution for them and for all others; 14while they long for you and pray for you, because of the surpassing grace of God in you. 15Thanks be to God for his inexpressible gift!

PAUL DEFENDS HIS MINISTRY

10 I, Paul, myself entreat you, by the meekness and gentleness of Christ—I who am humble when face to face with you, but bold to you when I am away!* 2I beg of you that when I am present I may not have to show boldness with such confidence as I count on showing against some who suspect us of acting in worldly fashion. 3For though we live in the world we are not carrying on a worldly war, 4for the weapons of our warfare are not worldly but have divine power to destroy strongholds. 5We destroy arguments and every proud obstacle to the knowledge of God, and take every thought captive to obey Christ, 6being ready to punish every disobedience, when your obedience is complete.

7 Look at what is before your eyes. If any one is confident that he is Christ's, let him remind himself that as he is Christ's, so are we. 8For even if I boast a little too much of our authority, which the Lord gave for building you up and not for destroying you, I shall not be put to shame. 9I would not seem to be frightening you with letters. 10For they say, "His letters are weighty and strong, but his bodily presence is weak, and his speech of no account." 11Let such people understand that what we say by letter when absent, we do when present. 12Not that we venture to class or compare ourselves with some of those who commend themselves. But when they measure themselves by one another, and compare themselves with one another, they are without understanding.

13 But we will not boast beyond limit, but will keep to the limits God has apportioned us, to reach even to you. 14For we are not overextending ourselves, as though we did not reach you; we were the first to come all the way to you with the gospel of Christ. 15We do not boast beyond limit, in other men's labors; but our hope is that as your faith increases, our field among you may be greatly enlarged, 16so that we may preach the gospel in lands beyond you, without boasting of work already done in another's field. 17"Let him who boasts, boast of the Lord." 18For it is not the man who commends himself that is accepted, but the man whom the Lord commends.

PAUL AND THE FALSE APOSTLES

11 I wish you would bear with me in a little foolishness. Do bear with me! 2I feel a divine jealousy for you, for I betrothed you to Christ to present you as a pure bride to her one husband. 3But I am afraid that as the serpent deceived Eve by his cunning, your thoughts will be led astray from a sincere and pure devotion to Christ. 4For if some one comes and preaches another Jesus than the one we preached, or if you receive a different spirit from the one you received, or if you accept a different gospel from the one you accepted, you submit to it readily enough. 5I think that I am not in the least inferior to these superlative apostles. 6Even if I am unskilled in speaking, I am not in knowledge; in every way we have made this plain to you in all things.

[d]Or *benevolence*
[e]Or *they*

7 Did I commit a sin in abasing my-
self so that you might be exalted, be-
cause I preached God's gospel without
cost to you? 8I robbed other churches
by accepting support from them in
order to serve you. 9And when I was
with you and was in want, I did not
burden any one, for my needs were
supplied by the brethren who came
from Macedo′nia. So I refrained and
will refrain from burdening you in
any way. 10As the truth of Christ is in
me, this boast of mine shall not be si-
lenced in the regions of Acha′ia. 11And
why? Because I do not love you? God
knows I do!

12 And what I do I will continue to
do, in order to undermine the claim
of those who would like to claim that
in their boasted mission they work
on the same terms as we do. 13For
such men are false apostles, deceitful
workmen, disguising themselves as
apostles of Christ. 14And no wonder,
for even Satan disguises himself as an
angel of light. 15So it is not strange if
his servants also disguise themselves
as servants of righteousness. Their
end will correspond to their deeds.

PAUL'S SUFFERINGS AS AN APOSTLE

16 I repeat, let no one think me
foolish; but even if you do, accept
me as a fool, so that I too may boast
a little. 17(What I am saying I say not
with the Lord's authority but as a fool,
in this boastful confidence; 18since
many boast of worldly things, I too
will boast.) 19For you gladly bear with
fools, being wise yourselves! 20For you
bear it if a man makes slaves of you,
or preys upon you, or takes advantage
of you, or puts on airs, or strikes you
in the face. 21To my shame, I must
say, we were too weak for that! But
whatever any one dares to boast of—I
am speaking as a fool—I also dare to
boast of that. 22Are they Hebrews?
So am I. Are they Israelites? So am I.
Are they descendants of Abraham? So
am I. 23Are they servants of Christ? I
am a better one—I am talking like a
madman—with far greater labors, far
more imprisonments, with countless
beatings, and often near death. 24Five
times I have received at the hands
of the Jews the forty lashes less one.
25Three times I have been beaten with
rods; once I was stoned. Three times I
have been shipwrecked; a night and a
day I have been adrift at sea; 26on fre-
quent journeys, in danger from rivers,
danger from robbers, danger from my
own people, danger from Gentiles,
danger in the city, danger in the wil-
derness, danger at sea, danger from
false brethren; 27in toil and hardship,
through many a sleepless night, in
hunger and thirst, often without food,
in cold and exposure. 28And, apart
from other things, there is the daily
pressure upon me of my anxiety for all
the churches. 29Who is weak, and I am
not weak? Who is made to fall, and I
am not indignant?

30 If I must boast, I will boast of the
things that show my weakness. 31The
God and Father of the Lord Jesus, he
who is blessed for ever, knows that I
do not lie. 32At Damascus, the gover-
nor under King Ar′etas guarded the
city of Damascus in order to seize
me, 33but I was let down in a basket
through a window in the wall, and es-
caped his hands.

PAUL'S VISIONS AND REVELATIONS

12 I must boast; there is nothing to
be gained by it, but I will go on to
visions and revelations of the Lord.
2I know a man in Christ who four-
teen years ago was caught up to the
third heaven—whether in the body or
out of the body I do not know, God
knows. 3And I know that this man
was caught up into Paradise—wheth-
er in the body or out of the body I do
not know, God knows 4and he heard
things that cannot be told, which man
may not utter. 5On behalf of this man I
will boast, but on my own behalf I will
not boast, except of my weaknesses.
6Though if I wish to boast, I shall not
be a fool, for I shall be speaking the

truth. But I refrain from it, so that
no one may think more of me than
he sees in me or hears from me. 7And
to keep me from being too elated by
the abundance of revelations, a thorn*
was given me in the flesh, a messen-
ger of Satan, to harass me, to keep me
from being too elated. 8Three times I
besought the Lord about this, that it
should leave me; 9but he said to me,
"My grace is sufficient for you, for my
power is made perfect in weakness."
I will all the more gladly boast of my
weaknesses, that the power of Christ
may rest upon me. 10For the sake of
Christ, then, I am content with weak-
nesses, insults, hardships, persecu-
tions, and calamities; for when I am
weak, then I am strong.

PAUL'S CONCERN FOR THE CORINTHIAN CHURCH

11 I have been a fool! You forced
me to it, for I ought to have been
commended by you. For I am not at
all inferior to these superlative apos-
tles, even though I am nothing. 12The
signs of a true apostle were performed
among you in all patience, with signs
and wonders and mighty works. 13For
in what were you less favored than the
rest of the churches, except that I my-
self did not burden you? Forgive me
this wrong!*

14 Here for the third time I am
ready to come to you. And I will not
be a burden, for I seek not what is
yours but you; for children ought not
to lay up for their parents, but par-
ents for their children. 15I will most
gladly spend and be spent for your
souls. If I love you the more, am I to
be loved the less? 16But granting that
I myself did not burden you, I was
crafty, you say, and got the better of
you by guile. 17Did I take advantage of
you through any of those whom I sent
to you? 18I urged Titus to go, and sent
the brother with him. Did Titus take
advantage of you? Did we not act in
the same spirit? Did we not take the
same steps?

19 Have you been thinking all along
that we have been defending ourselves
before you? It is in the sight of God
that we have been speaking in Christ,
and all for your upbuilding, beloved.
20For I fear that perhaps I may come
and find you not what I wish, and that
you may find me not what you wish;
that perhaps there may be quarreling,
jealousy, anger, selfishness, slander,
gossip, conceit, and disorder. 21I fear
that when I come again my God may
humble me before you, and I may have
to mourn over many of those who
sinned before and have not repented
of the impurity, immorality, and licen-
tiousness which they have practiced.

FURTHER WARNING

13 This is the third time I am com-
ing to you. Any charge must be
sustained by the evidence of two or
three witnesses. 2I warned those who
sinned before and all the others, and I
warn them now while absent, as I did
when present on my second visit, that
if I come again I will not spare them
3since you desire proof that Christ
is speaking in me. He is not weak in
dealing with you, but is powerful in
you. 4For he was crucified in weak-
ness, but lives by the power of God.
For we are weak in him, but in dealing
with you we shall live with him by the
power of God.

5 Examine yourselves, to see
whether you are holding to your faith.
Test yourselves. Do you not realize
that Jesus Christ is in you?—unless
indeed you fail to meet the test! 6I
hope you will find out that we have
not failed. 7But we pray God that you
may not do wrong—not that we may
appear to have met the test, but that
you may do what is right, though we
may seem to have failed. 8For we can-
not do anything against the truth, but
only for the truth. 9For we are glad
when we are weak and you are strong.
What we pray for is your improve-
ment. 10I write this while I am away
from you, in order that when I come

I may not have to be severe in my use of the authority which the Lord has given me for building up and not for tearing down.

FINAL GREETINGS AND BENEDICTION

11 Finally, brethren, farewell. Mend your ways, heed my appeal, agree with one another, live in peace, and the God of love and peace will be with you. 12Greet one another with a holy kiss. 13All the saints greet you.

14 The grace of the Lord Jesus Christ and the love of God and the fellowship of[a] the Holy Spirit be with you all.

[a]Or *and participation in*

THE LETTER OF PAUL TO THE
GALATIANS

SALUTATION

1 Paul an apostle—not from men nor
through man, but through Jesus
Christ and God the Father, who raised
him from the dead 2and all the breth-
ren who are with me, To the churches
of Galatia:

3 Grace to you and peace from God
the Father and our Lord Jesus Christ,
4who gave himself for our sins to de-
liver us from the present evil age,
according to the will of our God and
Father; 5to whom be the glory for ever
and ever. Amen.

THERE IS NO OTHER GOSPEL

6 I am astonished that you are
so quickly deserting him who called
you in the grace of Christ and turn-
ing to a different gospel—* 7not that
there is another gospel, but there
are some who trouble you and want
to pervert the gospel of Christ. 8But
even if we, or an angel from heaven,
should preach to you a gospel contrary
to that which we preached to you, let
him be accursed. 9As we have said be-
fore, so now I say again, If any one is
preaching to you a gospel contrary to
that which you received, let him be
accursed.

10 Am I now seeking the favor of
men, or of God? Or am I trying to
please men? If I were still pleasing
men, I should not be a servant[a] of
Christ.*

PAUL'S VINDICATION OF HIS APOSTLESHIP

11 For I would have you know,
brethren, that the gospel which was
preached by me is not man's[b] gospel.
12For I did not receive it from man, nor
was I taught it, but it came through
a revelation of Jesus Christ. 13For
you have heard of my former life in
Judaism, how I persecuted the church
of God violently and tried to destroy
it; 14and I advanced in Judaism beyond
many of my own age among my peo-
ple, so extremely zealous was I for the
traditions of my fathers. 15But when
he who had set me apart before I was
born, and had called me through his
grace, 16was pleased to reveal his Son
to[c] me, in order that I might preach
him among the Gentiles, I did not
confer with flesh and blood, 17nor did I
go up to Jerusalem to those who were
apostles before me, but I went away
into Arabia; and again I returned to
Damascus.

18 Then after three years I went up
to Jerusalem to visit Cephas, and re-
mained with him fifteen days. 19But I
saw none of the other apostles except
James the Lord's brother. 20(In what
I am writing to you, before God, I do
not lie!) 21Then I went into the regions
of Syria and Cili´cia. 22And I was still
not known by sight to the churches of
Christ in Judea; 23they only heard it
said, "He who once persecuted us is
now preaching the faith he once tried
to destroy." 24And they glorified God
because of me.

PAUL AND THE OTHER APOSTLES

2 Then after fourteen years I went up
again to Jerusalem with Barnabas,
taking Titus along with me. 2I went up
by revelation; and I laid before them
(but privately before those who were
of repute) the gospel which I preach
among the Gentiles, lest somehow I
should be running or had run in vain.
3But even Titus, who was with me,
was not compelled to be circumcised,
though he was a Greek. 4But because
of false brethren secretly brought in,
who slipped in to spy out our freedom

[a] Or *slave*
[b] Greek *according to man*
[c] Greek *in*

which we have in Christ Jesus, that
they might bring us into bondage 5to
them we did not yield submission
even for a moment, that the truth
of the gospel might be preserved for
you. 6And from those who were re-
puted to be something (what they
were makes no difference to me; God
shows no partiality)—those, I say,
who were of repute added nothing to
me; 7but on the contrary, when they
saw that I had been entrusted with
the gospel to the uncircumcised, just
as Peter had been entrusted with the
gospel to the circumcised 8(for he who
worked through Peter for the mission
to the circumcised worked through
me also for the Gentiles), 9and when
they perceived the grace that was giv-
en to me, James and Cephas and John,
who were reputed to be pillars, gave
to me and Barnabas the right hand of
fellowship, that we should go to the
Gentiles and they to the circumcised;
10only they would have us remember
the poor, which very thing I was ea-
ger to do.

PAUL REBUKES PETER AT ANTIOCH

11 But when Cephas came to
Antioch I opposed him to his face,
because he stood condemned. 12For
before certain men came from James,
he ate with the Gentiles; but when
they came he drew back and separat-
ed himself, fearing the circumcision
party. 13And with him the rest of the
Jews acted insincerely, so that even
Barnabas was carried away by their
insincerity. 14But when I saw that they
were not straightforward about the
truth of the gospel, I said to Cephas
before them all, "If you, though a Jew,
live like a Gentile and not like a Jew,
how can you compel the Gentiles to
live like Jews?" 15We ourselves, who
are Jews by birth and not Gentile
sinners, 16yet who know that a man
is not justified[a] by works of the law*
but through faith in Jesus Christ, even
we have believed in Christ Jesus, in
order to be justified by faith in Christ,
and not by works of the law, because
by works of the law shall no one be
justified. 17But if, in our endeavor to
be justified in Christ, we ourselves
were found to be sinners, is Christ
then an agent of sin? Certainly not!
18But if I build up again those things
which I tore down, then I prove my-
self a transgressor. 19For I through the
law died to the law, that I might live
to God. 20I have been crucified with
Christ; it is no longer I who live, but
Christ who lives in me; and the life
I now live in the flesh I live by faith
in the Son of God, who loved me and
gave himself for me. 21I do not nullify
the grace of God; for if justification[b]
were through the law, then Christ
died to no purpose.

LAW OR FAITH

3 O foolish Galatians! Who has be-
witched you, before whose eyes
Jesus Christ was publicly portrayed as
crucified? 2Let me ask you only this:
Did you receive the Spirit* by works
of the law, or by hearing with faith?
3Are you so foolish? Having begun
with the Spirit, are you now ending
with the flesh? 4Did you experience so
many things in vain?—if it really is in
vain. 5Does he who supplies the Spirit
to you and works miracles among you
do so by works of the law, or by hear-
ing with faith?

6 Thus Abraham "believed God,
and it was reckoned to him as righ-
teousness." 7So you see that it is men
of faith who are the sons of Abraham.
8And the scripture, foreseeing that
God would justify the Gentiles by
faith, preached the gospel beforehand
to Abraham, saying, "In you shall
all the nations be blessed." 9So then,
those who are men of faith are blessed
with Abraham who had faith.

10 For all who rely on works of the
law are under a curse; for it is written,

[a]Or *reckoned righteous;* and so elsewhere
[b]Or *righteousness*

"Cursed be every one who does not
abide by all things written in the book
of the law, and do them." 11Now it is
evident that no man is justified before
God by the law; for "He who through
faith is righteous shall live";[c] 12but the
law does not rest on faith, for "He
who does them shall live by them."
13Christ redeemed us from the curse
of the law, having become a curse for
us—for it is written, "Cursed be ev-
ery one who hangs on a tree" 14that in
Christ Jesus the blessing of Abraham
might come upon the Gentiles, that
we might receive the promise of the
Spirit through faith.

THE PROMISE TO ABRAHAM

15 To give a human example, breth-
ren: no one annuls even a man's will,[d]
or adds to it, once it has been ratified.
16Now the promises were made to
Abraham and to his offspring. It does
not say, "And to offsprings," referring
to many; but, referring to one, "And
to your offspring," which is Christ.
17This is what I mean: the law, which
came four hundred and thirty years
afterward, does not annul a cove-
nant previously ratified by God, so
as to make the promise void. 18For if
the inheritance is by the law, it is no
longer by promise; but God gave it to
Abraham by a promise.

THE PURPOSE OF THE LAW

19 Why then the law? It was add-
ed because of transgressions, till the
offspring should come to whom the
promise had been made; and it was or-
dained by angels through an interme-
diary. 20Now an intermediary implies
more than one; but God is one.

21 Is the law then against the
promises of God? Certainly not; for
if a law had been given which could
make alive, then righteousness would
indeed be by the law. 22But the scrip-
ture consigned all things to sin, that
what was promised to faith in Jesus
Christ might be given to those who
believe.

23 Now before faith came, we were
confined under the law, kept under re-
straint until faith should be revealed.
24So that the law was our custodian
until Christ came, that we might be
justified by faith. 25But now that faith
has come, we are no longer under a
custodian; 26for in Christ Jesus you are
all sons of God, through faith. 27For
as many of you as were baptized into
Christ have put on Christ. 28There is
neither Jew nor Greek, there is nei-
ther slave nor free, there is neither
male nor female; for you are all one in
Christ Jesus. 29And if you are Christ's,
then you are Abraham's offspring,
heirs according to promise.

4 I mean that the heir, as long as he
is a child, is no better than a slave,
though he is the owner of all the es-
tate; 2but he is under guardians and
trustees until the date set by the fa-
ther. 3So with us; when we were chil-
dren, we were slaves to the elemental
spirits of the universe. 4But when the
time had fully come, God sent forth
his Son, born of woman, born under
the law, 5to redeem those who were
under the law, so that we might re-
ceive adoption as sons. 6And because
you are sons, God has sent the Spirit
of his Son into our hearts, crying,
"Abba! Father!" 7So through God you
are no longer a slave but a son, and if a
son then an heir.

PAUL REPROVES THE GALATIANS

8 Formerly, when you did not know
God, you were in bondage to beings
that by nature are no gods; 9but now
that you have come to know God, or
rather to be known by God, how can
you turn back again to the weak and
beggarly elemental spirits, whose
slaves you want to be once more?
10You observe days, and months, and
seasons, and years! 11I am afraid I have
labored over you in vain.

[c] Or *the righteous shall live by faith*
[d] Or *covenant* (as in verse 17)

12 Brethren, I beseech you, become
as I am, for I also have become as you
are. You did me no wrong; 13you know
it was because of a bodily ailment that
I preached the gospel to you at first;
14and though my condition was a trial
to you, you did not scorn or despise
me, but received me as an angel of
God, as Christ Jesus. 15What has be-
come of the satisfaction you felt? For
I bear you witness that, if possible,
you would have plucked out your eyes
and given them to me. 16Have I then
become your enemy by telling you the
truth?[a] 17They make much of you, but
for no good purpose; they want to shut
you out, that you may make much of
them. 18For a good purpose it is always
good to be made much of, and not only
when I am present with you. 19My lit-
tle children, with whom I am again in
travail until Christ be formed in you!
20I could wish to be present with you
now and to change my tone, for I am
perplexed about you.

THE ALLEGORY OF HAGAR AND SARAH

21 Tell me, you who desire to be
under law, do you not hear the law?
22For it is written that Abraham had
two sons, one by a slave and one by a
free woman. 23But the son of the slave
was born according to the flesh, the
son of the free woman through prom-
ise. 24Now this is an allegory: these
women are two covenants. One is
from Mount Sinai, bearing children
for slavery; she is Hagar. 25Now Hagar
is Mount Sinai in Arabia;[b] she corre-
sponds to the present Jerusalem, for
she is in slavery with her children.
26But the Jerusalem above is free, and
she is our mother. 27For it is written,

> "Rejoice, O barren one that
> dost not bear;
> break forth and shout, thou
> who art not in travail;
> for the desolate hath more
> children
> than she who hath a husband."

28Now we,[c] brethren, like Isaac,
are children of promise. 29But as at
that time he who was born according
to the flesh persecuted him who was
born according to the Spirit, so it is
now. 30But what does the scripture
say? "Cast out the slave and her son;
for the son of the slave shall not in-
herit with the son of the free woman."
31So, brethren, we are not children of
the slave but of the free woman.

5 For freedom Christ has set us free;
stand fast therefore, and do not sub-
mit again to a yoke of slavery.

THE NATURE OF CHRISTIAN FREEDOM

2 Now I, Paul, say to you that if you
receive circumcision, Christ will be of
no advantage to you. 3I testify again to
every man who receives circumcision
that he is bound to keep the whole
law. 4You are severed from Christ, you
who would be justified by the law;
you have fallen away from grace. 5For
through the Spirit, by faith, we wait
for the hope of righteousness. 6For in
Christ Jesus neither circumcision nor
uncircumcision is of any avail, but
faith working through love. 7You were
running well; who hindered you from
obeying the truth? 8This persuasion is
not from him who called you. 9A lit-
tle leaven leavens the whole lump. 10I
have confidence in the Lord that you
will take no other view than mine;
and he who is troubling you will bear
his judgment, whoever he is. 11But if
I, brethren, still preach circumcision,
why am I still persecuted? In that case
the stumbling block of the cross* has
been removed. 12I wish those who un-
settle you would mutilate themselves!

13 For you were called to freedom,
brethren; only do not use your free-
dom as an opportunity for the flesh,
but through love be servants of one
another. 14For the whole law is ful-
filled in one word, "You shall love
your neighbor as yourself." 15But if
you bite and devour one another take

[a] Or *by dealing truly with you*
[b] Other ancient authorities read *For Sinai is a mountain in Arabia*
[c] Other ancient authorities read *you*

heed that you are not consumed by
one another.

THE WORKS OF THE FLESH AND THE FRUIT OF THE SPIRIT

16 But I say, walk by the Spirit,
and do not gratify the desires of the
flesh. 17For the desires of the flesh
are against the Spirit, and the desires
of the Spirit are against the flesh;
for these are opposed to each other,
to prevent you from doing what you
would. 18But if you are led by the Spirit
you are not under the law. 19Now the
works of the flesh are plain: immorali-
ty, impurity, licentiousness, 20idolatry,
sorcery, enmity, strife, jealousy, anger,
selfishness, dissension, party spir-
it, 21envy,[d] drunkenness, carousing,
and the like. I warn you, as I warned
you before, that those who do such
things shall not inherit the kingdom
of God. 22But the fruit of the Spirit is
love, joy, peace, patience, kindness,
goodness, faithfulness, 23gentleness,
self-control; against such there is no
law. 24And those who belong to Christ
Jesus have crucified the flesh with its
passions and desires.

25 If we live by the Spirit, let us
also walk by the Spirit. 26Let us have
no self-conceit, no provoking of one
another, no envy of one another.

BEAR ONE ANOTHER'S BURDENS

6 Brethren, if a man is overtaken in
any trespass, you who are spiritual
should restore him in a spirit of gen-
tleness. Look to yourself, lest you too
be tempted. 2Bear one another's bur-
dens, and so fulfil the law of Christ.
3For if any one thinks he is something,
when he is nothing, he deceives him-
self. 4But let each one test his own
work, and then his reason to boast
will be in himself alone and not in his
neighbor. 5For each man will have to
bear his own load.

6 Let him who is taught the word
share all good things with him who
teaches.

7 Do not be deceived; God is not
mocked, for whatever a man sows,
that he will also reap. 8For he who
sows to his own flesh will from the
flesh reap corruption; but he who
sows to the Spirit will from the Spirit
reap eternal life. 9And let us not grow
weary in well-doing, for in due season
we shall reap, if we do not lose heart.
10So then, as we have opportunity, let
us do good to all men, and especially
to those who are of the household of
faith.

FINAL ADMONITIONS AND BENEDICTION

11 See with what large letters I am
writing to you with my own hand. 12It
is those who want to make a good
showing in the flesh that would com-
pel you to be circumcised, and only in
order that they may not be persecut-
ed for the cross of Christ. 13For even
those who receive circumcision do not
themselves keep the law, but they de-
sire to have you circumcised that they
may glory in your flesh. 14But far be it
from me to glory except in the cross of
our Lord Jesus Christ, by which[e] the
world has been crucified to me, and
I to the world. 15For neither circumci-
sion counts for anything, nor uncir-
cumcision, but a new creation. 16Peace
and mercy be upon all who walk by
this rule, upon the Israel of God.

17 Henceforth let no man trouble
me; for I bear on my body the marks
of Jesus.

18 The grace of our Lord Jesus
Christ be with your spirit, brethren.
Amen.

[d] Other ancient authorities add *murder*
[e] Or *through whom*

THE LETTER OF PAUL TO THE

EPHESIANS

SALUTATION

1 Paul, an apostle of Christ Jesus by
the will of God, To the saints who
are* also faithful[a] in Christ Jesus:
2 Grace to you and peace from
God our Father and the Lord Jesus
Christ.

SPIRITUAL BLESSINGS IN CHRIST

3 Blessed be the God and Father of
our Lord Jesus Christ, who has bless-
ed us in Christ with every spiritual
blessing in the heavenly places, 4 even
as he chose us in him before the foun-
dation of the world, that we should
be holy and blameless before him.
5 He destined us in love[b] to be his sons
through Jesus Christ, according to
the purpose of his will, 6 to the praise
of his glorious grace which he freely
bestowed on us in the Beloved. 7 In
him we have redemption through his
blood, the forgiveness of our trespass-
es, according to the riches of his grace
8 which he lavished upon us. 9 For he
has made known to us in all wisdom
and insight the mystery of his will,
according to his purpose which he
set forth in Christ 10 as a plan for the
fulness of time, to unite* all things in
him, things in heaven and things on
earth.
11 In him, according to the purpose
of him who accomplishes all things
according to the counsel of his will,
12 we who first hoped in Christ have
been destined and appointed to live
for the praise of his glory. 13 In him
you also, who have heard the word
of truth, the gospel of your salvation,
and have believed in him, were sealed
with the promised Holy Spirit, 14 who
is the guarantee of our inheritance
until we acquire possession of it, to
the praise of his glory.

PAUL'S PRAYER

15 For this reason, because I have
heard of your faith in the Lord Jesus
and your love[c] toward all the saints,
16 I do not cease to give thanks for you,
remembering you in my prayers, 17 that
the God of our Lord Jesus Christ, the
Father of glory, may give you a spir-
it of wisdom and of revelation in the
knowledge of him, 18 having the eyes
of your hearts enlightened, that you
may know what is the hope to which
he has called you, what are the rich-
es of his glorious inheritance in the
saints, 19 and what is the immeasur-
able greatness of his power in us who
believe, according to the working of
his great might 20 which he accom-
plished in Christ when he raised him
from the dead and made him sit at
his right hand in the heavenly places,
21 far above all rule and authority and
power and dominion, and above every
name that is named, not only in this
age but also in that which is to come;
22 and he has put all things under his
feet and has made him the head over
all things for the church, 23 which is his
body, the fulness of him who fills all
in all.

FROM DEATH TO LIFE

2 And you he made alive, when you
were dead through the trespasses
and sins 2 in which you once walked,
following the course of this world,
following the prince of the power of
the air, the spirit that is now at work
in the sons of disobedience. 3 Among
these we all once lived in the passions
of our flesh, following the desires of
body and mind, and so we were by
nature children of wrath, like the
rest of mankind. 4 But God, who is
rich in mercy, out of the great love

[a] Other ancient authorities read *[who are at Ephesus and faithful]*
[b] Or *[before him in love, having destined us]*
[c] Other ancient authorities omit *[your love]*

with which he loved us, 5even when we were dead through our trespasses, made us alive together with Christ (by grace you have been saved), 6and raised us up with him, and made us sit with him in the heavenly places in Christ Jesus, 7that in the coming ages he might show the immeasurable riches of his grace in kindness toward us in Christ Jesus. 8For by grace you have been saved through faith; and this is not your own doing, it is the gift of God 9not because of works, lest any man should boast. 10For we are his workmanship, created in Christ Jesus for good works, which God prepared beforehand, that we should walk in them.

ONE IN CHRIST

11 Therefore remember that at one time you Gentiles in the flesh, called the uncircumcision by what is called the circumcision, which is made in the flesh by hands 12remember that you were at that time separated from Christ, alienated from the commonwealth of Israel, and strangers to the covenants of promise, having no hope and without God in the world. 13But now in Christ Jesus you who once were far off have been brought near in the blood of Christ. 14For he is our peace, who has made us both one, and has broken down the dividing wall* of hostility, 15by abolishing in his flesh the law of commandments and ordinances, that he might create in himself one new man in place of the two, so making peace, 16and might reconcile us both to God in one body through the cross, thereby bringing the hostility to an end. 17And he came and preached peace to you who were far off and peace to those who were near; 18for through him we both have access in one Spirit to the Father. 19So then you are no longer strangers and sojourners, but you are fellow citizens with the saints and members of the household of God, 20built upon the foundation of the apostles and prophets, Christ Jesus himself being the cornerstone, 21in whom the whole structure is joined together and grows into a holy temple in the Lord; 22in whom you also are built into it for a dwelling place of God in the Spirit.

PAUL'S MINISTRY TO THE GENTILES

3 For this reason I, Paul, a prisoner for Christ Jesus on behalf of you Gentiles 2assuming that you have heard of the stewardship of God's grace that was given to me for you, 3how the mystery* was made known to me by revelation, as I have written briefly. 4When you read this you can perceive my insight into the mystery of Christ, 5which was not made known to the sons of men in other generations as it has now been revealed to his holy apostles and prophets by the Spirit; 6that is, how the Gentiles are fellow heirs, members of the same body, and partakers of the promise in Christ Jesus through the gospel.

7 Of this gospel I was made a minister according to the gift of God's grace which was given me by the working of his power. 8To me, though I am the very least of all the saints, this grace was given, to preach to the Gentiles the unsearchable riches of Christ, 9and to make all men see what is the plan of the mystery hidden for ages in[d] God who created all things; 10that through the church the manifold wisdom of God might now be made known to the principalities and powers in the heavenly places. 11This was according to the eternal purpose which he has realized in Christ Jesus our Lord, 12in whom we have boldness and confidence of access through our faith in him. 13So I ask you not to[e] lose heart over what I am suffering for you, which is your glory.

[d]Or [*by*]
[e]Or [*I ask that I may not*]

PRAYER FOR THE READERS

14 For this reason I bow my knees
before the Father, 15 from whom ev-
ery family in heaven and on earth is
named, 16 that according to the rich-
es of his glory he may grant you to
be strengthened with might through
his Spirit in the inner man, 17 and
that Christ may dwell in your hearts
through faith; that you, being rooted
and grounded in love, 18 may have pow-
er to comprehend with all the saints
what is the breadth and length and
height and depth, 19 and to know the
love of Christ which surpasses knowl-
edge, that you may be filled with all
the fulness of God.

20 Now to him who by the power at
work within us is able to do far more
abundantly than all that we ask or
think, 21 to him be glory in the church
and in Christ Jesus to all generations,
for ever and ever. Amen.

UNITY IN THE BODY OF CHRIST

4 I therefore, a prisoner for the Lord,
beg you to lead a life worthy of the
calling to which you have been called,
2 with all lowliness and meekness,
with patience, forbearing one anoth-
er in love, 3 eager to maintain the uni-
ty of the Spirit in the bond of peace.
4 There is one body and one Spirit, just
as you were called to the one hope
that belongs to your call, 5 one Lord,
one faith, one baptism, 6 one God and
Father of us all, who is above all and
through all and in all. 7 But grace was
given to each of us according to the
measure of Christ's gift. 8 Therefore it
is said,

"When he ascended on high he
led a host of captives,
and he gave gifts to men."

9 (In saying, "He ascended," what
does it mean but that he had also
descended into the lower parts of
the earth? 10 He who descended is he
who also ascended far above all the
heavens, that he might fill all things.)
11 And his gifts were that some should
be apostles, some prophets, some
evangelists, some pastors and teach-
ers, 12 for the equipment of the saints,
for the work of ministry, for building
up the body of Christ, 13 until we all at-
tain to the unity of the faith and of the
knowledge of the Son of God, to ma-
ture manhood, to the measure of the
stature of the fulness of Christ; 14 so
that we may no longer be children,
tossed to and fro and carried about
with every wind of doctrine, by the
cunning of men, by their craftiness in
deceitful wiles. 15 Rather, speaking the
truth in love, we are to grow up in ev-
ery way into him who is the head, into
Christ, 16 from whom the whole body,
joined and knit together by every joint
with which it is supplied, when each
part is working properly, makes bodi-
ly growth and upbuilds itself in love.

THE OLD LIFE AND THE NEW

17 Now this I affirm and testify
in the Lord, that you must no longer
live as the Gentiles do, in the futility
of their minds; 18 they are darkened in
their understanding, alienated from
the life of God because of the igno-
rance that is in them, due to their
hardness of heart; 19 they have become
callous and have given themselves
up to licentiousness, greedy to prac-
tice every kind of uncleanness. 20 You
did not so learn Christ! 21 assuming
that you have heard about him and
were taught in him, as the truth is in
Jesus. 22 Put off your old nature which
belongs to your former manner of life
and is corrupt through deceitful lusts,
23 and be renewed in the spirit of your
minds, 24 and put on the new nature,
created after the likeness of God in
true righteousness and holiness.

RULES FOR THE NEW LIFE

25 Therefore, putting away false-
hood, let every one speak the truth
with his neighbor, for we are mem-
bers one of another. 26 Be angry but do
not sin; do not let the sun go down
on your anger, 27 and give no oppor-
tunity to the devil. 28 Let the thief no

longer steal, but rather let him labor,
doing honest work with his hands, so
that he may be able to give to those
in need. [29]Let no evil talk come out of
your mouths, but only such as is good
for edifying, as fits the occasion, that
it may impart grace to those who
hear. [30]And do not grieve the Holy
Spirit of God, in whom you were
sealed for the day of redemption.
[31]Let all bitterness and wrath and
anger and clamor and slander be put
away from you, with all malice, [32]and
be kind to one another, tenderheart-
ed, forgiving one another, as God in
Christ forgave you.

5 Therefore be imitators of God, as
beloved children. [2]And walk in love,
as Christ loved us and gave himself up
for us, a fragrant offering and sacri-
fice to God.

RENOUNCE PAGAN WAYS

3 But immorality and all impuri-
ty or covetousness must not even be
named among you, as is fitting among
saints. [4]Let there be no filthiness,
nor silly talk, nor levity, which are
not fitting; but instead let there be
thanksgiving. [5]Be sure of this, that
no immoral or impure man, or one
who is covetous (that is, an idolater),
has any inheritance in the kingdom
of Christ and of God. [6]Let no one
deceive you with empty words, for
it is because of these things that the
wrath of God comes upon the sons of
disobedience. [7]Therefore do not asso-
ciate with them, [8]for once you were
darkness, but now you are light in the
Lord; walk as children of light [9](for
the fruit of light is found in all that
is good and right and true), [10]and try
to learn what is pleasing to the Lord.
[11]Take no part in the unfruitful works
of darkness, but instead expose them.
[12]For it is a shame even to speak of
the things that they do in secret; [13]but
when anything is exposed by the light
it becomes visible, for anything that
becomes visible is light. [14]Therefore it
is said,

"Awake, O sleeper, and arise
from the dead,
and Christ shall give you
light."*

15 Look carefully then how you
walk, not as unwise men but as wise,
[16]making the most of the time, be-
cause the days are evil. [17]Therefore
do not be foolish, but understand
what the will of the Lord is. [18]And
do not get drunk with wine, for that
is debauchery; but be filled with
the Spirit, [19]addressing one another
in psalms and hymns and spiritual
songs, singing and making melody to
the Lord with all your heart, [20]always
and for everything giving thanks in
the name of our Lord Jesus Christ to
God the Father.

THE CHRISTIAN HOUSEHOLD

21 Be subject to one another out
of reverence for Christ. [22]Wives, be
subject to your husbands, as to the
Lord. [23]For the husband is the head
of the wife as Christ is the head of
the church, his body, and is himself
its Savior. [24]As the church is subject
to Christ, so let wives also be sub-
ject in everything to their husbands.
[25]Husbands, love your wives, as Christ
loved the church and gave himself up
for her, [26]that he might sanctify her,
having cleansed her by the wash-
ing of water with the word, [27]that he
might present the church to himself in
splendor, without spot or wrinkle or
any such thing, that she might be holy
and without blemish. [28]Even so hus-
bands should love their wives as their
own bodies. He who loves his wife
loves himself. [29]For no man ever hates
his own flesh, but nourishes and cher-
ishes it, as Christ does the church,
[30]because we are members of his body.
[31]"For this reason a man shall leave
his father and mother and be joined
to his wife, and the two shall become
one flesh." [32]This is a great mystery,
and I mean in reference to Christ and
the church; [33]however, let each one
of you love his wife as himself, and

let the wife see that she respects her
husband.

CHILDREN AND PARENTS

6 Children, obey your parents in the
Lord, for this is right. 2"Honor your
father and mother" (this is the first
commandment with a promise), 3"that
it may be well with you and that you
may live long on the earth." 4Fathers,
do not provoke your children to anger,
but bring them up in the discipline
and instruction of the Lord.

SLAVES AND MASTERS

5 Slaves, be obedient to those who
are your earthly masters, with fear
and trembling, in singleness of heart,
as to Christ; 6not in the way of eye-ser-
vice, as men-pleasers, but as servants[a]
of Christ, doing the will of God from
the heart, 7rendering service with a
good will as to the Lord and not to
men, 8knowing that whatever good
any one does, he will receive the same
again from the Lord, whether he is a
slave or free. 9Masters, do the same to
them, and forbear threatening, know-
ing that he who is both their Master
and yours is in heaven, and that there
is no partiality with him.

THE WHOLE ARMOR OF GOD

10 Finally, be strong in the Lord
and in the strength of his might.
11Put on the whole armor of God, that
you may be able to stand against the
wiles of the devil. 12For we are not
contending against flesh and blood,
but against the principalities, against
the powers, against the world rulers
of this present darkness, against the
spiritual hosts of wickedness in the
heavenly places. 13Therefore take the
whole armor of God, that you may
be able to withstand in the evil day,
and having done all, to stand. 14Stand
therefore, having girded your loins
with truth, and having put on the
breastplate of righteousness, 15and
having shod your feet with the equip-
ment of the gospel of peace; 16above
all taking the shield of faith, with
which you can quench all the flaming
darts of the evil one. 17And take the
helmet of salvation, and the sword of
the Spirit, which is the word of God.
18Pray at all times in the Spirit, with
all prayer and supplication. To that
end keep alert with all perseverance,
making supplication for all the saints,
19and also for me, that utterance may
be given me in opening my mouth
boldly to proclaim the mystery of the
gospel, 20for which I am an ambassa-
dor in chains; that I may declare it
boldly, as I ought to speak.

PERSONAL MATTERS AND BENEDICTION

21 Now that you also may know
how I am and what I am doing,
Tych´icus the beloved brother and
faithful minister in the Lord will tell
you everything. 22I have sent him to
you for this very purpose, that you
may know how we are, and that he
may encourage your hearts.

23 Peace be to the brethren, and
love with faith, from God the Father
and the Lord Jesus Christ. 24Grace
be with all who love our Lord Jesus
Christ with love undying.

[a]Or *[slaves]*

THE LETTER OF PAUL TO THE

PHILIPPIANS

SALUTATION

1 Paul and Timothy, servants[a] of
Christ Jesus, To all the saints in
Christ Jesus who are at Philippi, with
the bishops[b] and deacons:
2 Grace to you and peace from God
our Father and the Lord Jesus Christ.

PAUL'S PRAYER FOR THE PHILIPPIANS

3 I thank my God in all my remem-
brance of you, 4always in every prayer
of mine for you all making my prayer
with joy, 5thankful for your partner-
ship in the gospel from the first day
until now. 6And I am sure that he who
began a good work in you will bring
it to completion at the day of Jesus
Christ. 7It is right for me to feel thus
about you all, because I hold you in
my heart, for you are all partakers
with me of grace, both in my impris-
onment and in the defense and confir-
mation of the gospel. 8For God is my
witness, how I yearn for you all with
the affection of Christ Jesus. 9And it is
my prayer that your love may abound
more and more, with knowledge and
all discernment, 10so that you may
approve what is excellent, and may
be pure and blameless for the day of
Christ, 11filled with the fruits of righ-
teousness which come through Jesus
Christ, to the glory and praise of God.

PAUL'S PRESENT CIRCUMSTANCES

12 I want you to know, brethren,
that what has happened to me has re-
ally served to advance the gospel, 13so
that it has become known throughout
the whole praetorian guard[c] and to
all the rest that my imprisonment is
for Christ; 14and most of the brethren
have been made confident in the Lord
because of my imprisonment,* and are
much more bold to speak the word of
God without fear.
15 Some indeed preach Christ from
envy and rivalry, but others from good
will. 16The latter do it out of love,
knowing that I am put here for the de-
fense of the gospel; 17the former pro-
claim Christ out of partisanship, not
sincerely but thinking to afflict me in
my imprisonment. 18What then? Only
that in every way, whether in pretense
or in truth, Christ is proclaimed; and
in that I rejoice.
19 Yes, and I shall rejoice. For I
know that through your prayers and
the help of the Spirit of Jesus Christ
this will turn out for my deliverance,
20as it is my eager expectation and
hope that I shall not be at all ashamed,
but that with full courage now as al-
ways Christ will be honored in my
body,* whether by life or by death.
21For to me to live is Christ, and to die
is gain. 22If it is to be life in the flesh,
that means fruitful labor for me. Yet
which I shall choose I cannot tell. 23I
am hard pressed between the two. My
desire is to depart and be with Christ,
for that is far better. 24But to remain
in the flesh is more necessary on your
account. 25Convinced of this, I know
that I shall remain and continue with
you all, for your progress and joy in
the faith, 26so that in me you may have
ample cause to glory in Christ Jesus,
because of my coming to you again.
27 Only let your manner of life
be worthy of the gospel of Christ,
so that whether I come and see you
or am absent, I may hear of you that
you stand firm in one spirit, with one
mind striving side by side for the faith
of the gospel, 28and not frightened in
anything by your opponents. This is a

[a] Or *slaves*
[b] Or *overseers*
[c] Greek *in the whole praetorium*

clear omen to them of their destruction, but of your salvation, and that from God. 29For it has been granted to you that for the sake of Christ you should not only believe in him but also suffer for his sake, 30engaged in the same conflict which you saw and now hear to be mine.

IMITATING CHRIST'S HUMILITY

2 So if there is any encouragement in Christ, any incentive of love, any participation in the Spirit, any affection and sympathy, 2complete my joy by being of the same mind, having the same love, being in full accord and of one mind. 3Do nothing from selfishness or conceit, but in humility count others better than yourselves. 4Let each of you look not only to his own interests, but also to the interests of others. 5Have this mind among yourselves, which was in Christ Jesus, 6who, though he was in the form of God,* did not count equality with God a thing to be grasped, 7but emptied himself,* taking the form of a servant,[a] being born in the likeness of men. 8And being found in human form he humbled himself and became obedient unto death, even death on a cross. 9Therefore God has highly exalted him and bestowed on him the name which is above every name, 10that at the name of Jesus every knee should bow, in heaven and on earth and under the earth, 11and every tongue confess that Jesus Christ is Lord, to the glory of God the Father.

SHINING AS LIGHTS IN THE WORLD

12 Therefore, my beloved, as you have always obeyed, so now, not only as in my presence but much more in my absence, work out your own salvation with fear and trembling; 13for God is at work in you, both to will and to work for his good pleasure.

14 Do all things without grumbling or questioning, 15that you may be blameless and innocent, children of God without blemish in the midst of a crooked and perverse generation, among whom you shine as lights in the world, 16holding fast the word of life, so that in the day of Christ I may be proud that I did not run in vain or labor in vain. 17Even if I am to be poured as a libation upon the sacrificial offering of your faith, I am glad and rejoice with you all. 18Likewise you also should be glad and rejoice with me.

TIMOTHY AND EPAPHRODITUS

19 I hope in the Lord Jesus to send Timothy to you soon, so that I may be cheered by news of you. 20I have no one like him, who will be genuinely anxious for your welfare. 21They all look after their own interests, not those of Jesus Christ. 22But Timothy's worth you know, how as a son with a father he has served with me in the gospel. 23I hope therefore to send him just as soon as I see how it will go with me; 24and I trust in the Lord that shortly I myself shall come also.

25 I have thought it necessary to send to you Epaphrodi´tus my brother and fellow worker and fellow soldier, and your messenger and minister to my need, 26for he has been longing for you all, and has been distressed because you heard that he was ill. 27Indeed he was ill, near to death. But God had mercy on him, and not only on him but on me also, lest I should have sorrow upon sorrow. 28I am the more eager to send him, therefore, that you may rejoice at seeing him again, and that I may be less anxious. 29So receive him in the Lord with all joy; and honor such men, 30for he nearly died for the work of Christ, risking his life to complete your service to me.

BREAKING WITH THE PAST

3 Finally, my brethren, rejoice in the Lord. To write the same things to you is not irksome to me, and is safe for you.

[a]Or *slave*

2 Look out for the dogs, look out for the evil-workers, look out for those who mutilate the flesh. [3]For we are the true circumcision, who worship God in spirit,[b] and glory in Christ Jesus, and put no confidence in the flesh. [4]Though I myself have reason for confidence in the flesh also. If any other man thinks he has reason for confidence in the flesh, I have more: [5]circumcised on the eighth day, of the people of Israel, of the tribe of Benjamin, a Hebrew born of Hebrews; as to the law a Pharisee, [6]as to zeal a persecutor of the church, as to righteousness under the law blameless. [7]But whatever gain I had, I counted as loss for the sake of Christ. [8]Indeed I count everything as loss because of the surpassing worth of knowing Christ Jesus my Lord. For his sake I have suffered the loss of all things, and count them as refuse, in order that I may gain Christ [9]and be found in him, not having a righteousness of my own, based on law, but that which is through faith in Christ, the righteousness from God that depends on faith; [10]that I may know him and the power of his resurrection, and may share his sufferings, becoming like him in his death, [11]that if possible I may attain the resurrection from the dead.

PRESSING TOWARD THE GOAL

12 Not that I have already obtained this or am already perfect; but I press on to make it my own, because Christ Jesus has made me his own.* [13]Brethren, I do not consider that I have made it my own; but one thing I do, forgetting what lies behind and straining forward to what lies ahead, [14]I press on toward the goal for the prize of the upward call of God in Christ Jesus. [15]Let those of us who are mature be thus minded; and if in anything you are otherwise minded, God will reveal that also to you. [16]Only let us hold true to what we have attained.

17 Brethren, join in imitating me, and mark those who so live as you have an example in us. [18]For many, of whom I have often told you and now tell you even with tears, live as enemies of the cross of Christ. [19]Their end is destruction, their god is the belly, and they glory in their shame, with minds set on earthly things.* [20]But our commonwealth is in heaven, and from it we await a Savior, the Lord Jesus Christ, [21]who will change our lowly body to be like his glorious body, by the power which enables him even to subject all things to himself.

4 Therefore, my brethren, whom I love and long for, my joy and crown, stand firm thus in the Lord, my beloved.

EXHORTATIONS

2 I entreat Eu-o´dia and I entreat Syn´tyche to agree in the Lord. [3]And I ask you also, true yokefellow, help these women, for they have labored side by side with me in the gospel together with Clement and the rest of my fellow workers, whose names are in the book of life.

4 Rejoice in the Lord always; again I will say, Rejoice. [5]Let all men know your forbearance. The Lord is at hand. [6]Have no anxiety about anything, but in everything by prayer and supplication with thanksgiving let your requests be made known to God. [7]And the peace of God, which passes all understanding, will keep your hearts and your minds in Christ Jesus.

8 Finally, brethren, whatever is true, whatever is honorable, whatever is just, whatever is pure, whatever is lovely, whatever is gracious, if there is any excellence, if there is anything worthy of praise, think about these things. [9]What you have learned and received and heard and seen in me, do; and the God of peace will be with you.

[b]Other ancient authorities read *worship by the Spirit of God*

ACKNOWLEDGMENT OF THE PHILIPPIANS' GIFT

10 I rejoice in the Lord greatly
that now at length you have revived
your concern for me; you were indeed
concerned for me, but you had no op-
portunity. 11Not that I complain of
want; for I have learned, in whatev-
er state I am, to be content. 12I know
how to be abased, and I know how to
abound; in any and all circumstanc-
es I have learned the secret of facing
plenty and hunger, abundance and
want. 13I can do all things in him who
strengthens me.

14 Yet it was kind of you to share
my trouble. 15And you Philippians
yourselves know that in the beginning
of the gospel, when I left Macedo´nia,
no church entered into partnership
with me in giving and receiving except
you only; 16for even in Thessaloni´ca
you sent me help[a] once and again.
17Not that I seek the gift; but I seek
the fruit which increases to your cred-
it. 18I have received full payment, and
more; I am filled, having received
from Epaphrodi´tus the gifts you sent,
a fragrant offering, a sacrifice accept-
able and pleasing to God. 19And my
God will supply every need of yours
according to his riches in glory in
Christ Jesus. 20To our God and Father
be glory for ever and ever. Amen.

FINAL GREETINGS AND BENEDICTION

21 Greet every saint in Christ Jesus.
The brethren who are with me greet
you. 22All the saints greet you, espe-
cially those of Caesar's household.

23 The grace of the Lord Jesus Christ be with your spirit.

[a] Other ancient authorities read *money for my needs*

THE LETTER OF PAUL TO THE

COLOSSIANS

SALUTATION

1 Paul, an apostle of Christ Jesus by
the will of God, and Timothy our
brother,
2 To the saints and faithful breth-
ren in Christ at Colos´sae: Grace to
you and peace from God our Father.

PAUL THANKS GOD FOR THE COLOSSIANS

3 We always thank God, the Father
of our Lord Jesus Christ, when we
pray for you, 4because we have heard
of your faith in Christ Jesus and of the
love which you have for all the saints,
5because of the hope laid up for you in
heaven. Of this you have heard before
in the word of the truth, the gospel
6which has come to you, as indeed in
the whole world it is bearing fruit and
growing—so among yourselves, from
the day you heard and understood the
grace of God in truth, 7as you learned
it from Ep´aphras our beloved fellow
servant. He is a faithful minister of
Christ on our[a] behalf 8and has made
known to us your love in the Spirit.
9 And so, from the day we heard of
it, we have not ceased to pray for you,
asking that you may be filled with the
knowledge of his will in all spiritual
wisdom and understanding, 10to lead
a life worthy of the Lord, fully pleas-
ing to him, bearing fruit in every good
work and increasing in the knowledge
of God. 11May you be strengthened
with all power, according to his glo-
rious might, for all endurance and
patience with joy, 12giving thanks to
the Father, who has qualified us[b] to
share in the inheritance of the saints
in light. 13He has delivered us from the
dominion of darkness and transferred
us to the kingdom of his beloved Son,
14in whom we have redemption, the
forgiveness of sins.

THE SUPREMACY OF CHRIST

15 He is the image of the invisible
God, the first-born* of all creation;
16for in him all things were created, in
heaven and on earth, visible and in-
visible, whether thrones or dominions
or principalities or authorities—all
things were created through him and
for him. 17He is before all things, and
in him all things hold together. 18He is
the head of the body, the church; he
is the beginning, the first-born from
the dead, that in everything he* might
be pre-eminent. 19For in him all the
fulness of God was pleased to dwell,
20and through him to reconcile to him-
self all things, whether on earth or in
heaven, making peace by the blood of
his cross.
21 And you, who once were es-
tranged and hostile in mind, doing
evil deeds, 22he has now reconciled in
his body of flesh by his death, in order
to present you holy and blameless and
irreproachable before him, 23provided
that you continue in the faith, stable
and steadfast, not shifting from the
hope of the gospel which you heard,
which has been preached to every
creature under heaven, and of which
I, Paul, became a minister.

PAUL'S INTEREST IN THE COLOSSIANS

24 Now I rejoice in my sufferings
for your sake, and in my flesh I com-
plete what is lacking* in Christ's af-
flictions for the sake of his body, that
is, the church, 25of which I became a
minister according to the divine of-
fice which was given to me for you, to
make the word of God fully known,
26the mystery hidden for ages and
generations[c] but now made manifest
to his saints. 27To them God chose to
make known how great among the

[a] Other ancient authorities read *your*
[b] Other ancient authorities read *you*
[c] Or *from angels and men*

Gentiles are the riches of the glory of
this mystery, which is Christ in you,
the hope of glory. [28]Him we proclaim,
warning every man and teaching ev-
ery man in all wisdom, that we may
present every man mature in Christ.
[29]For this I toil, striving with all the
energy which he mightily inspires
within me.

2 For I want you to know how greatly
I strive for you, and for those at La-
odice´a, and for all who have not seen
my face, [2]that their hearts may be en-
couraged as they are knit together in
love, to have all the riches of assured
understanding and the knowledge of
God's mystery, of Christ, [3]in whom are
hid all the treasures of wisdom and
knowledge. [4]I say this in order that
no one may delude you with beguil-
ing speech. [5]For though I am absent
in body, yet I am with you in spirit,
rejoicing to see your good order and
the firmness of your faith in Christ.

FULLNESS OF LIFE IN CHRIST

6 As therefore you received Christ
Jesus the Lord, so live in him, [7]rooted
and built up in him and established
in the faith, just as you were taught,
abounding in thanksgiving.

8 See to it that no one makes a
prey of you by philosophy and empty
deceit, according to human tradition,
according to the elemental spirits of
the universe, and not according to
Christ. [9]For in him the whole fulness
of deity dwells bodily, [10]and you have
come to fulness of life in him, who is
the head of all rule and authority. [11]In
him also you were circumcised with
a circumcision made without hands,
by putting off the body of flesh in
the circumcision of Christ; [12]and you
were buried with him in baptism, in
which you were also raised with him
through faith in the working of God,
who raised him from the dead. [13]And
you, who were dead in trespasses and
the uncircumcision of your flesh, God
made alive together with him, having
forgiven us all our trespasses, [14]hav-
ing canceled the bond which stood
against us with its legal demands; this
he set aside, nailing it to the cross.
[15]He disarmed the principalities and
powers and made a public example of
them, triumphing over them in him.[a]

16 Therefore let no one pass judg-
ment on you in questions of food and
drink or with regard to a festival or
a new moon or a sabbath. [17]These are
only a shadow of what is to come;
but the substance belongs to Christ.
[18]Let no one disqualify you, insisting
on self-abasement and worship of
angels, taking his stand on visions,
puffed up without reason by his sen-
suous mind, [19]and not holding fast to
the Head, from whom the whole body,
nourished and knit together through
its joints and ligaments, grows with a
growth that is from God.

WARNINGS AGAINST FALSE TEACHERS

20 If with Christ you died to the
elemental spirits of the universe, why
do you live as if you still belonged
to the world? Why do you submit to
regulations, [21]"Do not handle, Do not
taste, Do not touch" [22](referring to
things which all perish as they are
used), according to human precepts
and doctrines? [23]These have indeed an
appearance of wisdom in promoting
rigor of devotion and self-abasement
and severity to the body, but they are
of no value in checking the indulgence
of the flesh.[b]

THE NEW LIFE IN CHRIST

3 If then you have been raised with
Christ, seek the things that are
above, where Christ is, seated at the
right hand of God. [2]Set your minds on
things that are above, not on things
that are on earth. [3]For you have died,
and your life is hid with Christ in God.
[4]When Christ who is our life appears,
then you also will appear with him in

[a]Or *in it* (that is, the cross)
[b]Or *are of no value, serving only to indulge the flesh*

glory.

5 Put to death therefore what is earthly in you: immorality, impurity, passion, evil desire, and covetousness, which is idolatry. 6On account of these the wrath of God is coming.[c] 7In these you once walked, when you lived in them. 8But now put them all away: anger, wrath, malice, slander, and foul talk from your mouth. 9Do not lie to one another, seeing that you have put off the old nature with its practices 10and have put on the new nature, which is being renewed in knowledge after the image of its creator. 11Here there cannot be Greek and Jew, circumcised and uncircumcised, barbarian, Scyth´ian, slave, free man, but Christ is all, and in all.

12 Put on then, as God's chosen ones, holy and beloved, compassion, kindness, lowliness, meekness, and patience, 13forbearing one another and, if one has a complaint against another, forgiving each other; as the Lord has forgiven you, so you also must forgive. 14And above all these put on love, which binds everything together in perfect harmony. 15And let the peace of Christ rule in your hearts, to which indeed you were called in the one body. And be thankful. 16Let the word of Christ dwell in you richly, as you teach and admonish one another in all wisdom, and as you sing psalms and hymns and spiritual songs with thankfulness in your hearts to God. 17And whatever you do, in word or deed, do everything in the name of the Lord Jesus, giving thanks to God the Father through him.

RULES FOR CHRISTIAN HOUSEHOLDS

18 Wives, be subject to your husbands, as is fitting in the Lord.* 19Husbands, love your wives, and do not be harsh with them. 20Children, obey your parents in everything, for this pleases the Lord. 21Fathers, do not provoke your children, lest they become discouraged. 22Slaves, obey in everything those who are your earthly masters, not with eyeservice, as men-pleasers, but in singleness of heart, fearing the Lord. 23Whatever your task, work heartily, as serving the Lord and not men, 24knowing that from the Lord you will receive the inheritance as your reward; you are serving the Lord Christ. 25For the wrongdoer will be paid back for the wrong he has done, and there is no partiality.

4 Masters, treat your slaves justly and fairly, knowing that you also have a Master in heaven.

FURTHER INSTRUCTIONS

2 Continue steadfastly in prayer, being watchful in it with thanksgiving; 3and pray for us also, that God may open to us a door for the word, to declare the mystery of Christ, on account of which I am in prison, 4that I may make it clear, as I ought to speak.

5 Conduct yourselves wisely toward outsiders, making the most of the time. 6Let your speech always be gracious, seasoned with salt, so that you may know how you ought to answer every one.

FINAL GREETINGS AND BENEDICTION

7 Tych´icus will tell you all about my affairs; he is a beloved brother and faithful minister and fellow servant in the Lord. 8I have sent him to you for this very purpose, that you may know how we are and that he may encourage your hearts, 9and with him One´simus, the faithful and beloved brother, who is one of yourselves. They will tell you of everything that has taken place here.

10 Aristar´chus my fellow prisoner greets you, and Mark the cousin of Barnabas* (concerning whom you have received instructions—if he comes to you, receive him), 11and Jesus who is called Justus. These are the only men of the circumcision among my fellow workers for the kingdom

[c] Other ancient authorities add *upon the sons of disobedience*

of God, and they have been a comfort to me. 12Ep´aphras, who is one of
yourselves, a servant[a] of Christ Jesus,
greets you, always remembering you
earnestly in his prayers, that you may
stand mature and fully assured in
all the will of God. 13For I bear him
witness that he has worked hard for
you and for those in La-odice´a and
in Hi-erap´olis. 14Luke the beloved
physician* and Demas greet you.
15Give my greetings to the brethren
at La-odice´a, and to Nympha and the
church in her house. 16And when this
letter has been read among you, have
it read also in the church of the La-odice´ans; and see that you read also
the letter from La-odice´a. 17And say
to Archip´pus, "See that you fulfil the
ministry which you have received in
the Lord."

18 I, Paul, write this greeting with
my own hand. Remember my fetters.
Grace be with you.

[a]Or *slave*

THE FIRST LETTER OF PAUL TO THE
THESSALONIANS

SALUTATION

1 Paul, Silva´nus, and Timothy,* To
the church of the Thessalo´nians
in God the Father and the Lord Jesus
Christ: Grace to you and peace.

THE THESSALONIANS' FAITH AND EXAMPLE

2 We give thanks to God always for
you all, constantly mentioning you in
our prayers, 3remembering before our
God and Father your work of faith
and labor of love and steadfastness of
hope in our Lord Jesus Christ. 4For we
know, brethren beloved by God, that
he has chosen you; 5for our gospel
came to you not only in word, but also
in power and in the Holy Spirit and
with full conviction. You know what
kind of men we proved to be among
you for your sake. 6And you became
imitators of us and of the Lord, for
you received the word in much afflic-
tion, with joy inspired by the Holy
Spirit; 7so that you became an exam-
ple to all the believers in Macedo´nia
and in Acha´ia. 8For not only has the
word of the Lord sounded forth from
you in Macedo´nia and Acha´ia, but
your faith in God has gone forth ev-
erywhere, so that we need not say
anything. 9For they themselves report
concerning us what a welcome we had
among you, and how you turned to
God from idols, to serve a living and
true God, 10and to wait for his Son
from heaven, whom he raised from
the dead, Jesus who delivers us from
the wrath to come.

PAUL'S MINISTRY IN THESSALONICA

2 For you yourselves know, breth-
ren, that our visit to you was not
in vain; 2but though we had already
suffered and been shamefully treat-
ed at Philippi, as you know, we had
courage in our God to declare to you
the gospel of God in the face of great
opposition. 3For our appeal does not
spring from error or uncleanness, nor
is it made with guile; 4but just as we
have been approved by God to be en-
trusted with the gospel, so we speak,
not to please men, but to please God
who tests our hearts. 5For we never
used either words of flattery, as you
know, or a cloak for greed, as God is
witness; 6nor did we seek glory from
men, whether from you or from oth-
ers, though we might have made de-
mands as apostles of Christ. 7But we
were gentle[a] among you, like a nurse
taking care of her children. 8So, be-
ing affectionately desirous of you, we
were ready to share with you not only
the gospel of God but also our own
selves, because you had become very
dear to us.

9 For you remember our labor and
toil, brethren; we worked night and
day, that we might not burden any
of you, while we preached to you the
gospel of God. 10You are witnesses,
and God also, how holy and righteous
and blameless was our behavior to
you believers; 11for you know how, like
a father with his children, we exhort-
ed each one of you and encouraged
you and charged you 12to lead a life
worthy of God, who calls you into his
own kingdom and glory.

13 And we also thank God con-
stantly for this, that when you re-
ceived the word of God which you
heard from us, you accepted it not as
the word of men but as what it really
is, the word of God, which is at work
in you believers. 14For you, breth-
ren, became imitators of the church-
es of God in Christ Jesus which are
in Judea; for you suffered the same
things from your own countrymen as
they did from the Jews, 15who killed
both the Lord Jesus and the prophets,

[a]Other ancient authorities read *babes*

and drove us out, and displease God
and oppose all men [16]by hindering us
from speaking to the Gentiles that
they may be saved—so as always to
fill up the measure of their sins. But
God's wrath has come upon them at
last![a]

PAUL'S DESIRE TO VISIT THE THESSALONIANS AGAIN

17 But since we were bereft of you,
brethren, for a short time, in person
not in heart, we endeavored the more
eagerly and with great desire to see
you face to face; [18]because we wanted
to come to you—I, Paul,* again and
again—but Satan hindered us. [19]For
what is our hope or joy or crown of
boasting before our Lord Jesus at his
coming? Is it not you? [20]For you are
our glory and joy.

3 Therefore when we could bear it
no longer, we were willing to be
left behind at Athens alone, [2]and we
sent Timothy, our brother and God's
servant in the gospel of Christ, to es-
tablish you in your faith and to exhort
you, [3]that no one be moved by these
afflictions. You yourselves know that
this is to be our lot. [4]For when we
were with you, we told you before-
hand that we were to suffer affliction;
just as it has come to pass, and as you
know. [5]For this reason, when I could
bear it no longer, I sent that I might
know your faith, for fear that some-
how the tempter had tempted you and
that our labor would be in vain.

TIMOTHY'S ENCOURAGING REPORT

6 But now that Timothy has come
to us from you, and has brought us the
good news of your faith and love and
reported that you always remember
us kindly and long to see us, as we
long to see you [7]for this reason, breth-
ren, in all our distress and affliction
we have been comforted about you
through your faith; [8]for now we live, if
you stand fast in the Lord. [9]For what
thanksgiving can we render to God for
you, for all the joy which we feel for
your sake before our God, [10]praying
earnestly night and day that we may
see you face to face and supply what is
lacking in your faith?

11 Now may our God and Father
himself, and our Lord Jesus, direct our
way to you; [12]and may the Lord make
you increase and abound in love to
one another and to all men, as we do
to you, [13]so that he may establish your
hearts unblamable in holiness before
our God and Father, at the coming of
our Lord Jesus with all his saints.

A LIFE PLEASING TO GOD

4 Finally, brethren, we beseech and
exhort you in the Lord Jesus, that
as you learned from us how you ought
to live and to please God, just as you
are doing, you do so more and more.
[2]For you know what instructions we
gave you through the Lord Jesus. [3]For
this is the will of God, your sanctifica-
tion:* that you abstain from immorali-
ty;* [4]that each one of you know how to
control his own body in holiness and
honor, [5]not in the passion of lust like
heathen who do not know God; [6]that
no man transgress, and wrong his
brother in this matter,[b] because the
Lord is an avenger in all these things,
as we solemnly forewarned you. [7]For
God has not called us for uncleanness,
but in holiness. [8]Therefore whoever
disregards this, disregards not man
but God, who gives his Holy Spirit to
you.

9 But concerning love of the breth-
ren you have no need to have any
one write to you, for you yourselves
have been taught by God to love one
another; [10]and indeed you do love all
the brethren throughout Macedo´nia.
But we exhort you, brethren, to do so
more and more, [11]to aspire to live qui-
etly, to mind your own affairs, and to
work with your hands, as we charged
you;* [12]so that you may command the

[a] Or *completely,* or *for ever*
[b] Or *defraud his brother in business*

respect of outsiders, and be depen-
dent on nobody.

THE COMING OF THE LORD

13 But we would not have you igno-
rant, brethren, concerning those who
are asleep, that you may not grieve as
others do who have no hope.* [14]For
since we believe that Jesus died and
rose again, even so, through Jesus,
God will bring with him those who
have fallen asleep. [15]For this we de-
clare to you by the word of the Lord,
that we who are alive, who are left un-
til the coming of the Lord, shall not
precede those who have fallen asleep.
[16]For the Lord himself will descend
from heaven with a cry of command,
with the archangel's call, and with the
sound of the trumpet of God. And the
dead in Christ will rise first; [17]then we
who are alive, who are left, shall be
caught up together with them in the
clouds to meet the Lord in the air; and
so we shall always be with the Lord.*
[18]Therefore comfort one another with
these words.

5 But as to the times and the seasons,
brethren, you have no need to have
anything written to you. [2]For you
yourselves know well that the day of
the Lord will come like a thief in the
night. [3]When people say, "There is
peace and security," then sudden de-
struction will come upon them as tra-
vail comes upon a woman with child,
and there will be no escape. [4]But you
are not in darkness, brethren, for that
day to surprise you like a thief. [5]For
you are all sons of light and sons of
the day; we are not of the night or of
darkness. [6]So then let us not sleep, as
others do, but let us keep awake and
be sober. [7]For those who sleep sleep
at night, and those who get drunk are
drunk at night. [8]But, since we belong
to the day, let us be sober, and put on
the breastplate of faith and love, and
for a helmet the hope of salvation. [9]For
God has not destined us for wrath, but
to obtain salvation through our Lord
Jesus Christ, [10]who died for us so that
whether we wake or sleep we might
live with him. [11]Therefore encourage
one another and build one another up,
just as you are doing.

FINAL EXHORTATIONS, GREETINGS, AND BENEDICTION

12 But we beseech you, brethren,
to respect those who labor among you
and are over you in the Lord and ad-
monish you, [13]and to esteem them very
highly in love because of their work.
Be at peace among yourselves.[c] [14]And
we exhort you, brethren, admonish
the idle, encourage the fainthearted,
help the weak, be patient with them
all. [15]See that none of you repays evil
for evil, but always seek to do good to
one another and to all. [16]Rejoice al-
ways, [17]pray constantly, [18]give thanks
in all circumstances; for this is the
will of God in Christ Jesus for you.
[19]Do not quench the Spirit, [20]do not
despise prophesying, [21]but test every-
thing; hold fast what is good, [22]abstain
from every form of evil.

23 May the God of peace himself
sanctify you wholly; and may your
spirit and soul and body be kept
sound and blameless at the coming of
our Lord Jesus Christ. [24]He who calls
you is faithful, and he will do it.

25 Brethren, pray for us.

26 Greet all the brethren with a
holy kiss.

27 I adjure you by the Lord that
this letter be read to all the brethren.

28 The grace of our Lord Jesus
Christ be with you.

[c]Or *with them*

THE SECOND LETTER OF PAUL TO THE
THESSALONIANS

SALUTATION

1 Paul, Silva´nus, and Timothy, To
the church of the Thessalo´nians
in God our Father and the Lord Jesus
Christ:

2 Grace to you and peace from God
the Father and the Lord Jesus Christ.

THANKSGIVING

3 We are bound to give thanks to
God always for you, brethren, as is
fitting, because your faith is growing
abundantly, and the love of every one
of you for one another is increasing.
4 Therefore we ourselves boast of you
in the churches of God for your stead-
fastness and faith in all your persecu-
tions and in the afflictions which you
are enduring.

THE JUDGMENT AT CHRIST'S COMING

5 This is evidence of the righteous
judgment of God, that you may be
made worthy of the kingdom of God,
for which you are suffering 6 since in-
deed God deems it just to repay with
affliction those who afflict you, 7 and
to grant rest with us to you who are
afflicted, when the Lord Jesus is re-
vealed from heaven with his mighty
angels in flaming fire, 8 inflicting ven-
geance upon those who do not know
God and upon those who do not obey
the gospel of our Lord Jesus. 9 They
shall suffer the punishment of eternal
destruction and exclusion from the
presence of the Lord and from the glo-
ry of his might, 10 when he comes on
that day to be glorified in his saints,
and to be marveled at in all who have
believed, because our testimony to
you was believed. 11 To this end we al-
ways pray for you, that our God may
make you worthy of his call, and may
fulfil every good resolve and work of
faith by his power, 12 so that the name
of our Lord Jesus may be glorified in
you, and you in him, according to the
grace of our God and the Lord Jesus
Christ.

THE MAN OF LAWLESSNESS

2 Now concerning the coming of
our Lord Jesus Christ and our as-
sembling to meet him, we beg you,
brethren, 2 not to be quickly shaken
in mind or excited, either by spirit or
by word, or by letter purporting to be
from us, to the effect that the day of
the Lord has come.* 3 Let no one de-
ceive you in any way; for that day will
not come, unless the rebellion comes
first, and the man of lawlessness[a]* is
revealed, the son of perdition, 4 who
opposes and exalts himself against
every so-called god or object of wor-
ship, so that he takes his seat in the
temple of God, proclaiming himself
to be God. 5 Do you not remember
that when I was still with you I told
you this? 6 And you know what is re-
straining him now so that he may be
revealed in his time. 7 For the mystery
of lawlessness is already at work; only
he who now restrains it will do so
until he is out of the way.* 8 And then
the lawless one will be revealed, and
the Lord Jesus will slay him with the
breath of his mouth and destroy him
by his appearing and his coming. 9 The
coming of the lawless one by the ac-
tivity of Satan will be with all power
and with pretended signs and won-
ders, 10 and with all wicked deception
for those who are to perish, because
they refused to love the truth and
so be saved. 11 Therefore God sends
upon them a strong delusion, to make
them believe what is false, 12 so that
all may be condemned who did not
believe the truth but had pleasure in
unrighteousness.

[a] Other ancient authorities read *sin*

CHOSEN FOR SALVATION

13 But we are bound to give
thanks to God always for you, breth-
ren beloved by the Lord, because God
chose you from the beginning[b] to be
saved, through sanctification by the
Spirit[c] and belief in the truth. 14To
this he called you through our gos-
pel, so that you may obtain the glory
of our Lord Jesus Christ. 15So then,
brethren, stand firm and hold to the
traditions which you were taught by
us, either by word of mouth or by
letter.

16 Now may our Lord Jesus Christ
himself, and God our Father, who
loved us and gave us eternal comfort
and good hope through grace, 17com-
fort your hearts and establish them in
every good work and word.

REQUEST FOR PRAYER

3 Finally, brethren, pray for us, that
the word of the Lord may speed
on and triumph, as it did among you,
2and that we may be delivered from
wicked and evil men; for not all have
faith. 3But the Lord is faithful; he will
strengthen you and guard you from
evil.[d] 4And we have confidence in
the Lord about you, that you are do-
ing and will do the things which we
command. 5May the Lord direct your
hearts to the love of God and to the
steadfastness of Christ.

WARNING AGAINST IDLENESS

6 Now we command you, brethren,
in the name of our Lord Jesus Christ,
that you keep away from any broth-
er who is living in idleness and not
in accord with the tradition that you
received from us. 7For you yourselves
know how you ought to imitate us; we
were not idle when we were with you,
8we did not eat any one's bread with-
out paying, but with toil and labor we
worked night and day, that we might
not burden any of you. 9It was not be-
cause we have not that right, but to
give you in our conduct an example
to imitate. 10For even when we were
with you, we gave you this command:
If any one will not work, let him not
eat. 11For we hear that some of you are
living in idleness, mere busybodies,
not doing any work. 12Now such per-
sons we command and exhort in the
Lord Jesus Christ to do their work in
quietness and to earn their own liv-
ing. 13Brethren, do not be weary in
well-doing.

14 If any one refuses to obey what
we say in this letter, note that man,
and have nothing to do with him, that
he may be ashamed. 15Do not look on
him as an enemy, but warn him as a
brother.

FINAL GREETINGS AND BENEDICTION

16 Now may the Lord of peace him-
self give you peace at all times in all
ways. The Lord be with you all.

17 I, Paul, write this greeting with
my own hand. This is the mark in ev-
ery letter of mine; it is the way I write.
18The grace of our Lord Jesus Christ be
with you all.

[b] Other ancient authorities read *as the first converts*
[c] Or *of spirit*
[d] Or *the evil one*

THE FIRST LETTER OF PAUL TO
TIMOTHY

SALUTATION

1 Paul, an apostle of Christ Jesus by
command of God our Savior and of
Christ Jesus our hope,
2 To Timothy, my true child in the
faith:* Grace, mercy, and peace from
God the Father and Christ Jesus our
Lord.

WARNING AGAINST FALSE TEACHERS

3 As I urged you when I was go-
ing to Macedo´nia, remain at Ephesus
that you may charge certain persons
not to teach any different doctrine,
4 nor to occupy themselves with myths
and endless genealogies* which pro-
mote speculations rather than the di-
vine training[a] that is in faith; 5 where-
as the aim of our charge is love that
issues from a pure heart and a good
conscience and sincere faith. 6 Certain
persons by swerving from these have
wandered away into vain discussion,
7 desiring to be teachers of the law,
without understanding either what
they are saying or the things about
which they make assertions.
8 Now we know that the law is
good, if any one uses it lawfully, 9 un-
derstanding this, that the law is not
laid down for the just but for the law-
less and disobedient, for the ungodly
and sinners, for the unholy and pro-
fane, for murderers of fathers and
murderers of mothers, for manslayers,
10 immoral persons, sodomites, kid-
napers, liars, perjurers, and whatever
else is contrary to sound doctrine, 11 in
accordance with the glorious gospel
of the blessed God with which I have
been entrusted.

GRATITUDE FOR MERCY

12 I thank him who has given me
strength for this, Christ Jesus our
Lord, because he judged me faithful by
appointing me to his service, 13 though
I formerly blasphemed and persecuted
and insulted him; but I received mer-
cy because I had acted ignorantly in
unbelief, 14 and the grace of our Lord
overflowed for me with the faith and
love that are in Christ Jesus. 15 The say-
ing is sure and worthy of full accep-
tance, that Christ Jesus came into the
world to save sinners. And I am the
foremost of sinners; 16 but I received
mercy for this reason, that in me, as
the foremost, Jesus Christ might dis-
play his perfect patience for an ex-
ample to those who were to believe
in him for eternal life. 17 To the King
of ages, immortal, invisible, the only
God, be honor and glory for ever and
ever.[b] Amen.
18 This charge I commit to you,
Timothy, my son, in accordance with
the prophetic utterances which point-
ed to you, that inspired by them you
may wage the good warfare, 19 hold-
ing faith and a good conscience. By
rejecting conscience, certain per-
sons have made shipwreck of their
faith, 20 among them Hymenae´us and
Alexander, whom I have delivered
to Satan* that they may learn not to
blaspheme.

INSTRUCTIONS CONCERNING PRAYER

2 First of all, then, I urge that suppli-
cations, prayers, intercessions, and
thanksgivings be made for all men,
2 for kings and all who are in high po-
sitions, that we may lead a quiet and
peaceable life, godly and respectful
in every way. 3 This is good, and it is
acceptable in the sight of God our
Savior, 4 who desires all men to be
saved and to come to the knowledge of
the truth. 5 For there is one God, and
there is one mediator between God
and men, the man Christ Jesus, 6 who

[a] Or *stewardship,* or *order*
[b] Greek *to the ages of ages*

gave himself as a ransom for all,* the
testimony to which was borne at the
proper time. 7For this I was appointed
a preacher and apostle (I am telling
the truth, I am not lying), a teacher of
the Gentiles in faith and truth.

8 I desire then that in every place
the men should pray, lifting holy
hands without anger or quarreling;
9also that women should adorn them-
selves modestly and sensibly in seem-
ly apparel, not with braided hair or
gold or pearls or costly attire 10but
by good deeds, as befits women who
profess religion. 11Let a woman learn
in silence with all submissiveness. 12I
permit no woman to teach or to have
authority over men; she is to keep
silent. 13For Adam was formed first,
then Eve; 14and Adam was not de-
ceived, but the woman was deceived
and became a transgressor. 15Yet wom-
an will be saved through bearing chil-
dren,[c] if she continues[d] in faith and
love and holiness, with modesty.

QUALIFICATIONS OF BISHOPS

3 The saying is sure: If any one as-
pires to the office of bishop,* he
desires a noble task. 2Now a bishop
must be above reproach, the husband
of one wife, temperate, sensible, dig-
nified, hospitable, an apt teacher, 3no
drunkard, not violent but gentle, not
quarrelsome, and no lover of money.
4He must manage his own household
well, keeping his children submissive
and respectful in every way; 5for if a
man does not know how to manage
his own household, how can he care
for God's church? 6He must not be a
recent convert, or he may be puffed
up with conceit and fall into the con-
demnation of the devil;[e] 7moreover he
must be well thought of by outsiders,
or he may fall into reproach and the
snare of the devil.[f]

QUALIFICATIONS OF DEACONS

8 Deacons likewise must be serious,
not double-tongued, not addicted to
much wine, not greedy for gain; 9they
must hold the mystery of the faith with
a clear conscience. 10And let them also
be tested first; then if they prove them-
selves blameless let them serve as dea-
cons. 11The women* likewise must be
serious, no slanderers, but temperate,
faithful in all things. 12Let deacons be
the husband of one wife, and let them
manage their children and their house-
holds well; 13for those who serve well as
deacons gain a good standing for them-
selves and also great confidence in the
faith which is in Christ Jesus.

THE MYSTERY OF OUR RELIGION

14 I hope to come to you soon, but
I am writing these instructions to you
so that, 15if I am delayed, you may
know how one ought to behave in the
household of God, which is the church
of the living God, the pillar and bul-
wark of the truth. 16Great indeed, we
confess, is the mystery of our religion:

He[g] was manifested in the
flesh,
vindicated[h] in the Spirit,
seen by angels,
preached among the nations,
believed on in the world,
taken up in glory.

FALSE ASCETICISM

4 Now the Spirit expressly says that in
later times some will depart from the
faith by giving heed to deceitful spirits
and doctrines of demons, 2through the
pretensions of liars whose consciences
are seared, 3who forbid marriage*
and enjoin abstinence from foods*
which God created to be received with
thanksgiving by those who believe and
know the truth. 4For everything creat-
ed by God is good, and nothing is to be

[c] Or *by the birth of the child*
[d] Greek *they continue*
[e] Or *slanderer*
[f] Or *slanderer*
[g] Greek *Who;* other ancient authorities read *God;* others, *Which*
[h] Or *justified*

rejected if it is received with thanksgiv-
ing; 5for then it is consecrated by the
word of God and prayer.

A GOOD MINISTER OF JESUS CHRIST

6 If you put these instructions be-
fore the brethren, you will be a good
minister of Christ Jesus, nourished
on the words of the faith and of the
good doctrine which you have fol-
lowed. 7Have nothing to do with god-
less and silly myths. Train yourself in
godliness; 8for while bodily training
is of some value, godliness is of value
in every way, as it holds promise for
the present life and also for the life to
come. 9The saying is sure and worthy
of full acceptance. 10For to this end we
toil and strive,[a] because we have our
hope set on the living God, who is the
Savior of all men, especially of those
who believe.

11 Command and teach these
things. 12Let no one despise your
youth, but set the believers an exam-
ple in speech and conduct, in love, in
faith, in purity. 13Till I come, attend
to the public reading of scripture, to
preaching, to teaching. 14Do not ne-
glect the gift you have, which was giv-
en you by prophetic utterance when
the elders laid their hands upon you.
15Practice these duties, devote your-
self to them, so that all may see your
progress. 16Take heed to yourself and
to your teaching; hold to that, for by
so doing you will save both yourself
and your hearers.

DUTIES TOWARD BELIEVERS

5 Do not rebuke an older man but
exhort him as you would a father;
treat younger men like brothers, 2old-
er women like mothers, younger wom-
en like sisters, in all purity.

3 Honor widows who are real
widows.* 4If a widow has children or
grandchildren, let them first learn
their religious duty to their own
family and make some return to
their parents; for this is acceptable
in the sight of God. 5She who is a
real widow, and is left all alone, has
set her hope on God and continues
in supplications and prayers night
and day; 6whereas she who is self-in-
dulgent is dead even while she lives.
7Command this, so that they may be
without reproach. 8If any one does
not provide for his relatives, and es-
pecially for his own family, he has
disowned the faith and is worse than
an unbeliever.

9 Let a widow be enrolled if she is
not less than sixty years of age, having
been the wife of one husband; 10and
she must be well attested for her good
deeds, as one who has brought up
children, shown hospitality, washed
the feet of the saints, relieved the
afflicted, and devoted herself to do-
ing good in every way. 11But refuse to
enrol younger widows; for when they
grow wanton against Christ they de-
sire to marry, 12and so they incur con-
demnation for having violated their
first pledge.* 13Besides that, they learn
to be idlers, gadding about from house
to house, and not only idlers but gos-
sips and busybodies, saying what they
should not. 14So I would have young-
er widows marry, bear children, rule
their households, and give the enemy
no occasion to revile us. 15For some
have already strayed after Satan. 16If
any believing woman[b] has relatives
who are widows, let her assist them;
let the church not be burdened, so
that it may assist those who are real
widows.

17 Let the elders who rule well be
considered worthy of double honor, es-
pecially those who labor in preaching
and teaching; 18for the scripture says,
"You shall not muzzle an ox when it
is treading out the grain," and, "The
laborer deserves his wages." 19Never
admit any charge against an elder ex-
cept on the evidence of two or three
witnesses. 20As for those who persist

[a]Other ancient authorities read *suffer reproach*
[b]Other ancient authorities read *man or woman;* others, simply *man*

in sin, rebuke them in the presence of
all, so that the rest may stand in fear.
21 In the presence of God and of Christ
Jesus and of the elect angels I charge
you to keep these rules without favor,
doing nothing from partiality. 22 Do
not be hasty in the laying on of hands,
nor participate in another man's sins;
keep yourself pure.

23 No longer drink only water, but
use a little wine for the sake of your
stomach and your frequent ailments.

24 The sins of some men are con-
spicuous, pointing to judgment, but
the sins of others appear later. 25 So
also good deeds are conspicuous; and
even when they are not, they cannot
remain hidden.

6 Let all who are under the yoke of
slavery regard their masters as
worthy of all honor, so that the name
of God and the teaching may not be
defamed. 2 Those who have believing
masters must not be disrespectful on
the ground that they are brethren;
rather they must serve all the better
since those who benefit by their ser-
vice are believers and beloved.

FALSE TEACHING AND TRUE RICHES

Teach and urge these duties. 3 If
any one teaches otherwise and does
not agree with the sound words of
our Lord Jesus Christ and the teach-
ing which accords with godliness, 4 he
is puffed up with conceit, he knows
nothing; he has a morbid craving for
controversy and for disputes about
words, which produce envy, dissen-
sion, slander, base suspicions, 5 and
wrangling among men who are de-
praved in mind and bereft of the
truth, imagining that godliness is a
means of gain. 6 There is great gain
in godliness with contentment; 7 for
we brought nothing into the world,
and[c] we cannot take anything out
of the world; 8 but if we have food
and clothing, with these we shall be
content. 9 But those who desire to be
rich fall into temptation, into a snare,
into many senseless and hurtful de-
sires that plunge men into ruin and
destruction. 10 For the love of money
is the root of all evils; it is through
this craving that some have wandered
away from the faith and pierced their
hearts with many pangs.

THE GOOD FIGHT OF FAITH

11 But as for you, man of God,
shun all this; aim at righteousness,
godliness, faith, love, steadfastness,
gentleness. 12 Fight the good fight of
the faith; take hold of the eternal
life to which you were called when
you made the good confession in the
presence of many witnesses. 13 In the
presence of God who gives life to all
things, and of Christ Jesus who in his
testimony before Pontius Pilate made
the good confession, 14 I charge you to
keep the commandment unstained
and free from reproach until the
appearing of our Lord Jesus Christ;
15 and this will be made manifest at
the proper time by the blessed and
only Sovereign, the King of kings and
Lord of lords, 16 who alone has immor-
tality and dwells in unapproachable
light, whom no man has ever seen or
can see. To him be honor and eternal
dominion. Amen.

17 As for the rich in this world,
charge them not to be haughty, nor
to set their hopes on uncertain rich-
es but on God who richly furnishes us
with everything to enjoy. 18 They are to
do good, to be rich in good deeds, lib-
eral and generous, 19 thus laying up for
themselves a good foundation for the
future, so that they may take hold of
the life which is life indeed.

PERSONAL INSTRUCTIONS AND BENEDICTION

20 O Timothy, guard what has been
entrusted to you. Avoid the godless
chatter and contradictions of what is
falsely called knowledge, 21 for by pro-
fessing it some have missed the mark
as regards the faith. Grace be with
you.

[c] Other ancient authorities insert *it is certain that*

THE SECOND LETTER OF PAUL TO
TIMOTHY

SALUTATION

1 Paul, an apostle of Christ Jesus by
the will of God according to the
promise of the life which is in Christ
Jesus,
2 To Timothy, my beloved child:
Grace, mercy, and peace from God the
Father and Christ Jesus our Lord.

THANKSGIVING AND ENCOURAGEMENT

3 I thank God whom I serve with
a clear conscience, as did my fathers,
when I remember you constantly
in my prayers. 4As I remember your
tears, I long night and day to see you,
that I may be filled with joy. 5I am re-
minded of your sincere faith, a faith
that dwelt first in your grandmother
Lo´is and your mother Eunice and
now, I am sure, dwells in you. 6Hence I
remind you to rekindle the gift of God
that is within you through the laying
on of my hands; 7for God did not give
us a spirit of timidity but a spirit of
power and love and self-control.
8 Do not be ashamed then of testi-
fying to our Lord, nor of me his prison-
er, but take your share of suffering for
the gospel in the power of God, 9who
saved us and called us with a holy
calling, not in virtue of our works but
in virtue of his own purpose and the
grace which he gave us in Christ Jesus
ages ago, 10and now has manifested
through the appearing of our Savior
Christ Jesus, who abolished death and
brought life and immortality to light
through the gospel. 11For this gospel
I was appointed a preacher and apos-
tle and teacher, 12and therefore I suf-
fer as I do. But I am not ashamed, for
I know whom I have believed, and I
am sure that he is able to guard until
that Day what has been entrusted to
me.[a] 13Follow the pattern of the sound
words which you have heard from
me, in the faith and love which are
in Christ Jesus; 14guard the truth that
has been entrusted to you by the Holy
Spirit who dwells within us.
15 You are aware that all who are in
Asia* turned away from me, and among
them Phy´gelus and Hermog´enes.
16May the Lord grant mercy to the
household of Onesiph´orus, for he of-
ten refreshed me; he was not ashamed
of my chains, 17but when he arrived in
Rome he searched for me eagerly and
found me 18may the Lord grant him
to find mercy from the Lord on that
Day—and you well know all the ser-
vice he rendered at Ephesus.

A GOOD SOLDIER OF CHRIST JESUS

2 You then, my son, be strong in the
grace that is in Christ Jesus, 2and
what you have heard from me before
many witnesses entrust to faithful
men who will be able to teach oth-
ers also. 3Take your share of suffer-
ing as a good soldier of Christ Jesus.
4No soldier on service gets entangled
in civilian pursuits, since his aim is
to satisfy the one who enlisted him.
5An athlete is not crowned unless
he competes according to the rules.
6It is the hard-working farmer who
ought to have the first share of the
crops. 7Think over what I say, for the
Lord will grant you understanding in
everything.
8 Remember Jesus Christ, risen
from the dead, descended from David,
as preached in my gospel, 9the gospel
for which I am suffering and wearing
fetters like a criminal. But the word
of God is not fettered. 10Therefore
I endure everything for the sake of
the elect, that they also may obtain
the salvation which in Christ Jesus
goes with eternal glory. 11The saying
is sure:

[a] Or *what I have entrusted to him*

If we have died with him, we
shall also live with
him;
12if we endure, we shall also reign
with him;
if we deny him, he also will
deny us;
13if we are faithless, he remains
faithful—
for he cannot deny himself.

A WORKER APPROVED BY GOD

14 Remind them of this, and charge
them before the Lord[b] to avoid disput-
ing about words, which does no good,
but only ruins the hearers. 15Do your
best to present yourself to God as
one approved, a workman who has no
need to be ashamed, rightly handling
the word of truth. 16Avoid such god-
less chatter, for it will lead people into
more and more ungodliness, 17and
their talk will eat its way like gan-
grene. Among them are Hymenae´us
and Phile´tus, 18who have swerved
from the truth by holding that the
resurrection is past already.* They
are upsetting the faith of some. 19But
God's firm foundation stands, bear-
ing this seal: "The Lord knows those
who are his," and, "Let every one who
names the name of the Lord depart
from iniquity."

20 In a great house there are not
only vessels of gold and silver but also
of wood and earthenware, and some
for noble use, some for ignoble. 21If
any one purifies himself from what
is ignoble, then he will be a vessel for
noble use, consecrated and useful to
the master of the house, ready for any
good work. 22So shun youthful pas-
sions and aim at righteousness, faith,
love, and peace, along with those who
call upon the Lord from a pure heart.
23Have nothing to do with stupid,
senseless controversies; you know
that they breed quarrels. 24And the
Lord's servant must not be quarrel-
some but kindly to every one, an apt
teacher, forbearing, 25correcting his
opponents with gentleness. God may
perhaps grant that they will repent
and come to know the truth, 26and
they may escape from the snare of the
devil, after being captured by him to
do his will.[c]

GODLESSNESS IN THE LAST DAYS

3 But understand this, that in the
last days there will come times of
stress. 2For men will be lovers of self,
lovers of money, proud, arrogant,
abusive, disobedient to their parents,
ungrateful, unholy, 3inhuman, impla-
cable, slanderers, profligates, fierce,
haters of good, 4treacherous, reck-
less, swollen with conceit, lovers of
pleasure rather than lovers of God,
5holding the form of religion but de-
nying the power of it. Avoid such peo-
ple. 6For among them are those who
make their way into households and
capture weak women, burdened with
sins and swayed by various impulses,
7who will listen to anybody and can
never arrive at a knowledge of the
truth. 8As Jannes and Jambres op-
posed Moses, so these men also op-
pose the truth, men of corrupt mind
and counterfeit faith; 9but they will
not get very far, for their folly will be
plain to all, as was that of those two
men.

PAUL'S CHARGE TO TIMOTHY

10 Now you have observed my
teaching, my conduct, my aim in life,
my faith, my patience, my love, my
steadfastness, 11my persecutions,
my sufferings, what befell me at
Antioch, at Ico´nium, and at Lystra,
what persecutions I endured; yet
from them all the Lord rescued me.
12Indeed all who desire to live a godly
life in Christ Jesus will be persecut-
ed, 13while evil men and impostors
will go on from bad to worse, deceiv-
ers and deceived. 14But as for you,
continue in what you have learned

[b] Other ancient authorities read *God*
[c] Or *by him, to do his* (that is, God's) *will*

and have firmly believed, knowing from whom you learned it 15and how from childhood you have been acquainted with the sacred writings which are able to instruct you for salvation through faith in Christ Jesus. 16All scripture is inspired by God and[a] profitable for teaching, for reproof, for correction, and for training in righteousness,* 17that the man of God may be complete, equipped for every good work.

4 I charge you in the presence of God and of Christ Jesus who is to judge the living and the dead, and by his appearing and his kingdom: 2preach the word, be urgent in season and out of season, convince, rebuke, and exhort, be unfailing in patience and in teaching. 3For the time is coming when people will not endure sound teaching, but having itching ears they will accumulate for themselves teachers to suit their own likings, 4and will turn away from listening to the truth and wander into myths. 5As for you, always be steady, endure suffering, do the work of an evangelist, fulfil your ministry.

6 For I am already on the point of being sacrificed;* the time of my departure has come. 7I have fought the good fight, I have finished the race, I have kept the faith. 8Henceforth there is laid up for me the crown of righteousness, which the Lord, the righteous judge, will award to me on that Day, and not only to me but also to all who have loved his appearing.

[a]Or *Every scripture inspired by God is also*
[b]Other ancient authorities read *Gaul*

PERSONAL INSTRUCTIONS

9 Do your best to come to me soon. 10For Demas, in love with this present world, has deserted me and gone to Thessaloni´ca; Crescens has gone to Galatia,[b] Titus to Dalmatia. 11Luke alone is with me. Get Mark and bring him with you; for he is very useful in serving me. 12Tych´icus I have sent to Ephesus. 13When you come, bring the cloak that I left with Carpus at Tro´as, also the books, and above all the parchments. 14Alexander the coppersmith did me great harm; the Lord will requite him for his deeds. 15Beware of him yourself, for he strongly opposed our message. 16At my first defense no one took my part; all deserted me. May it not be charged against them! 17But the Lord stood by me and gave me strength to proclaim the word fully, that all the Gentiles might hear it. So I was rescued from the lion's mouth. 18The Lord will rescue me from every evil and save me for his heavenly kingdom. To him be the glory for ever and ever. Amen.

FINAL GREETINGS AND BENEDICTION

19 Greet Prisca and Aq´uila, and the household of Onesiph´orus. 20Eras´tus remained at Corinth; Troph´imus I left ill at Mile´tus. 21Do your best to come before winter. Eubu´lus sends greetings to you, as do Pudens and Linus* and Claudia and all the brethren.

22 The Lord be with your spirit. Grace be with you.

THE LETTER OF PAUL TO TITUS

SALUTATION

1 Paul, a servant[a] of God and an apos-
tle of Jesus Christ, to further the
faith of God's elect and their knowl-
edge of the truth which accords with
godliness, 2in hope of eternal life
which God, who never lies, promised
ages ago 3and at the proper time mani-
fested in his word through the preach-
ing with which I have been entrusted
by command of God our Savior;
4 To Titus, my true child in a com-
mon faith: Grace and peace from God
the Father and Christ Jesus our Savior.

TITUS IN CRETE

5 This is why I left you in Crete,
that you might amend what was de-
fective, and appoint elders* in every
town as I directed you, 6if any man is
blameless, the husband of one wife,
and his children are believers and not
open to the charge of being profli-
gate or insubordinate. 7For a bishop,
as God's steward, must be blameless;
he must not be arrogant or quick-tem-
pered or a drunkard or violent or
greedy for gain, 8but hospitable, a
lover of goodness, master of himself,
upright, holy, and self-controlled;
9he must hold firm to the sure word
as taught, so that he may be able to
give instruction in sound doctrine and
also to confute those who contradict
it. 10For there are many insubordinate
men, empty talkers and deceivers, es-
pecially the circumcision party; 11they
must be silenced, since they are up-
setting whole families by teaching for
base gain what they have no right to
teach. 12One of themselves, a prophet
of their own, said, "Cretans are always
liars, evil beasts, lazy gluttons." 13This
testimony is true. Therefore rebuke
them sharply, that they may be sound
in the faith, 14instead of giving heed to
Jewish myths or to commands of men
who reject the truth. 15To the pure all
things are pure, but to the corrupt
and unbelieving nothing is pure; their
very minds and consciences are cor-
rupted. 16They profess to know God,
but they deny him by their deeds; they
are detestable, disobedient, unfit for
any good deed.

TEACH SOUND DOCTRINE

2 But as for you, teach what befits
sound doctrine. 2Bid the older men
be temperate, serious, sensible, sound
in faith, in love, and in steadfastness.
3Bid the older women likewise to be
reverent in behavior, not to be slan-
derers or slaves to drink; they are to
teach what is good, 4and so train the
young women to love their husbands
and children, 5to be sensible, chaste,
domestic, kind, and submissive to
their husbands, that the word of God
may not be discredited. 6Likewise
urge the younger men to control
themselves. 7Show yourself in all re-
spects a model of good deeds, and in
your teaching show integrity, gravity,
8and sound speech that cannot be cen-
sured, so that an opponent may be put
to shame, having nothing evil to say
of us. 9Bid slaves to be submissive to
their masters and to give satisfaction
in every respect; they are not to be
refractory, 10nor to pilfer, but to show
entire and true fidelity, so that in ev-
erything they may adorn the doctrine
of God our Savior.
11 For the grace of God has ap-
peared for the salvation of all men,
12training us to renounce irreligion
and worldly passions, and to live so-
ber, upright, and godly lives in this
world, 13awaiting our blessed hope,
the appearing of the glory of our great
God and Savior[b]* Jesus Christ, 14who

[a] Or *slave*
[b] Or *of the great God and our Savior*

gave himself for us to redeem us from all iniquity and to purify for himself a people of his own who are zealous for good deeds.

15 Declare these things; exhort and reprove with all authority. Let no one disregard you.

MAINTAIN GOOD DEEDS

3 Remind them to be submissive to rulers and authorities, to be obedi-
ent, to be ready for any honest work,
2to speak evil of no one, to avoid
quarreling, to be gentle, and to show
perfect courtesy toward all men. 3For
we ourselves were once foolish, dis-
obedient, led astray, slaves to vari-
ous passions and pleasures, passing
our days in malice and envy, hated
by men and hating one another; 4but
when the goodness and loving kind-
ness of God our Savior appeared, 5he
saved us, not because of deeds done
by us in righteousness, but in virtue
of his own mercy, by the washing
of regeneration and renewal in the
Holy Spirit, 6which he poured out
upon us richly through Jesus Christ
our Savior, 7so that we might be jus-
tified by his grace and become heirs
in hope of eternal life.* 8The saying
is sure. I desire you to insist on these
things, so that those who have be-
lieved in God may be careful to ap-
ply themselves to good deeds;[a] these
are excellent and profitable to men.
9But avoid stupid controversies, ge-
nealogies, dissensions, and quarrels
over the law, for they are unprofit-
able and futile. 10As for a man who
is factious, after admonishing him
once or twice, have nothing more to
do with him, 11knowing that such a
person is perverted and sinful; he is
self-condemned.

FINAL MESSAGES AND BENEDICTION

12 When I send Ar´temas or Tych´-
icus to you, do your best to come to
me at Nicop´olis, for I have decided
to spend the winter there. 13Do your
best to speed Zenas the lawyer and
Apol´los on their way; see that they
lack nothing. 14And let our people
learn to apply themselves to good
deeds,[b] so as to help cases of urgent
need, and not to be unfruitful.

15 All who are with me send greetings to you. Greet those who love us in the faith. Grace be with you all.

[a] Or *enter honorable occupations*
[b] Or *enter honorable occupations*

THE LETTER OF PAUL TO

PHILEMON

SALUTATION

1 Paul, a prisoner for Christ Jesus,
and Timothy our brother, To Phile´mon
our beloved fellow worker [2]and Ap-
ph´ia our sister and Archip´pus our
fellow soldier, and the church in your
house:

3 Grace to you and peace from God
our Father and the Lord Jesus Christ.

PHILEMON'S LOVE AND FAITH

4 I thank my God always when I
remember you in my prayers, [5]because
I hear of your love and of the faith
which you have toward the Lord Jesus
and all the saints, [6]and I pray that the
sharing of your faith may promote the
knowledge of all the good that is ours
in Christ. [7]For I have derived much joy
and comfort from your love, my broth-
er, because the hearts of the saints
have been refreshed through you.

PAUL'S PLEA FOR ONESIMUS

8 Accordingly, though I am bold
enough in Christ to command you
to do what is required, [9]yet for love's
sake I prefer to appeal to you—I, Paul,
an ambassador[a] and now a prisoner
also for Christ Jesus [10]I appeal to you
for my child, One´simus, whose father
I have become in my imprisonment.
[11](Formerly he was useless to you, but
now he is indeed useful[b] to you and
to me.) [12]I am sending him back to
you, sending my very heart. [13]I would
have been glad to keep him with me,
in order that he might serve me on
your behalf during my imprisonment
for the gospel; [14]but I preferred to do
nothing without your consent in order
that your goodness might not be by
compulsion but of your own free will.

15 Perhaps this is why he was
parted from you for a while, that you
might have him back for ever, [16]no lon-
ger as a slave but more than a slave,
as a beloved brother, especially to me
but how much more to you, both in
the flesh and in the Lord. [17]So if you
consider me your partner, receive him
as you would receive me. [18]If he has
wronged you at all, or owes you any-
thing, charge that to my account. [19]I,
Paul, write this with my own hand, I
will repay it—to say nothing of your
owing me even your own self. [20]Yes,
brother, I want some benefit from
you in the Lord. Refresh my heart in
Christ.

21 Confident of your obedience, I
write to you, knowing that you will
do even more than I say. [22]At the same
time, prepare a guest room for me, for
I am hoping through your prayers to
be granted to you.

FINAL GREETINGS AND BENEDICTION

23 Ep´aphras, my fellow prisoner
in Christ Jesus, sends greetings to
you, [24]and so do Mark, Aristar´chus,
Demas, and Luke, my fellow workers.

25 The grace of the Lord Jesus
Christ be with your spirit.

[a] Or *an old man*
[b] The name Onesimus means *useful* or (compare verse 20) *beneficial*

THE LETTER TO THE

HEBREWS

GOD HAS SPOKEN BY HIS SON

1 In many and various ways God spoke
of old to our fathers by the prophets;
2 but in these last days he has spoken
to us by a Son, whom he appointed the
heir of all things, through whom also
he created the world. 3 He reflects the
glory of God and bears the very stamp
of his nature, upholding the universe
by his word of power. When he had
made purification for sins, he sat
down at the right hand of the Majesty
on high, 4 having become as much su-
perior to angels as the name he has ob-
tained is more excellent than theirs.*

THE SON IS SUPERIOR TO ANGELS

5 For to what angel did God ever
say,

"Thou art my Son,
today I have begotten thee"?
"I will be to him a father,
and he shall be to me a son"?

6 And again, when he brings the
first-born into the world, he says,

"Let all God's angels
worship him."

7 Of the angels he says,

"Who makes his angels winds,
and his servants flames of
fire."

8 But of the Son he says,

"Thy throne, O God, [a] is for
ever and ever,
the righteous scepter is the
scepter of thy[b] kingdom.
9 Thou hast loved righteousness
and hated lawlessness;
therefore God, thy God, has
anointed thee
with the oil of gladness beyond
thy comrades."

10 And,

"Thou, Lord, didst found the
earth in the beginning,
and the heavens are the work
of thy hands;
11 they will perish, but thou
remainest;
they will all grow old like a
garment,
12 like a mantle thou wilt roll them
up,
and they will be changed.[c]
But thou art the same,
and thy years will never end."

13 But to what angel has he ever
said,

"Sit at my right hand,
till I make thy enemies
a stool for thy feet"?

14 Are they not all ministering spir-
its sent forth to serve, for the sake of
those who are to obtain salvation?

WARNING TO PAY ATTENTION

2 Therefore we must pay the closer at-
tention to what we have heard, lest
we drift away from it. 2 For if the mes-
sage declared by angels* was valid and
every transgression or disobedience
received a just retribution, 3 how shall
we escape if we neglect such a great
salvation? It was declared at first by
the Lord, and it was attested to us by
those who heard him, 4 while God also
bore witness by signs and wonders
and various miracles and by gifts of
the Holy Spirit distributed according
to his own will.

EXALTATION THROUGH ABASEMENT

5 For it was not to angels that God
subjected the world to come, of which
we are speaking. 6 It has been testified
somewhere,

"What is man that thou art
mindful of him,
or the son of man, that thou
carest for him?

[a] Or *God is thy throne*
[b] Other ancient authorities read *his*
[c] Other ancient authorities add *like a garment*

7Thou didst make him for a
little while lower than the
angels,
thou hast crowned him with
glory and honor,[d]
8putting everything in subjection
under his feet."
Now in putting everything in subjec-
tion to him, he left nothing outside his
control. As it is, we do not yet see ev-
erything in subjection to him. 9But we
see Jesus, who for a little while was
made lower than the angels, crowned
with glory and honor because of the
suffering of death, so that by the grace
of God he might taste death for every
one.

10 For it was fitting that he, for
whom and by whom all things exist,
in bringing many sons to glory, should
make the pioneer of their salvation
perfect through suffering.* 11For he
who sanctifies and those who are
sanctified have all one origin. That
is why he is not ashamed to call them
brethren, 12saying,

"I will proclaim thy name to
my brethren,
in the midst of the congrega-
tion I will praise thee."

13And again,

"I will put my trust in him."
"Here am I, and the children
God has given me."

14 Since therefore the children
share in flesh and blood, he himself
likewise partook of the same nature,
that through death he might destroy
him who has the power of death, that
is, the devil, 15and deliver all those
who through fear of death were sub-
ject to lifelong bondage. 16For surely it
is not with angels that he is concerned
but with the descendants of Abraham.
17Therefore he had to be made like his
brethren in every respect, so that he
might become a merciful and faith-
ful high priest in the service of God,
to make expiation for the sins of the
people. 18For because he himself has
suffered and been tempted, he is able
to help those who are tempted.

MOSES A SERVANT, CHRIST A SON

3 Therefore, holy brethren, who share
in a heavenly call, consider Jesus,
the apostle and high priest of our con-
fession. 2He was faithful to him who
appointed him, just as Moses also was
faithful in[e] God's house. 3Yet Jesus has
been counted worthy of as much more
glory than Moses as the builder of a
house has more honor than the house.
4(For every house is built by some one,
but the builder of all things is God.)
5Now Moses was faithful in all God's
house as a servant, to testify to the
things that were to be spoken later,
6but Christ was faithful over God's[f]
house as a son. And we are his house
if we hold fast our confidence and
pride in our hope.[g]

WARNING AGAINST UNBELIEF

7 Therefore, as the Holy Spirit
says,

"Today, when you hear his
voice
8do not harden your hearts as in
the rebellion,
on the day of testing in the
wilderness,
9where your fathers put me to
the test
and saw my works for forty
years.
10Therefore I was provoked with
that generation,
and said, 'They always go
astray in their hearts;
they have not known my ways.'
11As I swore in my wrath,
'They shall never enter my
rest.'"*

12Take care, brethren, lest there be in
any of you an evil, unbelieving heart,
leading you to fall away from the liv-
ing God. 13But exhort one another

[d]Other ancient authorities insert *and didst set him over the works of thy hands*
[e]Other ancient authorities insert *all*
[f]Greek *his*
[g]Other ancient authorities insert *firm to the end*

every day, as long as it is called "to-
day," that none of you may be hard-
ened by the deceitfulness of sin. 14For
we share in Christ, if only we hold
our first confidence firm to the end,
15while it is said,

> "Today, when you hear his
> voice,
> do not harden your hearts as in
> the rebellion."

16Who were they that heard and yet
were rebellious? Was it not all those
who left Egypt under the leadership
of Moses? 17And with whom was he
provoked forty years? Was it not with
those who sinned, whose bodies fell
in the wilderness? 18And to whom did
he swear that they should never enter
his rest, but to those who were dis-
obedient? 19So we see that they were
unable to enter because of unbelief.

THE REST THAT GOD PROMISED

4 Therefore, while the promise of en-
tering his rest remains, let us fear
lest any of you be judged to have failed
to reach it. 2For good news came to us
just as to them; but the message which
they heard did not benefit them, be-
cause it did not meet with faith in the
hearers.[a] 3For we who have believed
enter that rest, as he has said,

> "As I swore in my wrath,
> 'They shall never enter my
> rest,'"

although his works were finished from
the foundation of the world. 4For he
has somewhere spoken of the seventh
day in this way, "And God rested on
the seventh day from all his works."
5And again in this place he said,

> "They shall never enter my
> rest."

6Since therefore it remains for
some to enter it, and those who for-
merly received the good news failed to
enter because of disobedience, 7again
he sets a certain day, "Today," saying
through David so long afterward, in
the words already quoted,

> "Today, when you hear his
> voice,
> do not harden your hearts."

8For if Joshua had given them rest,
God[b] would not speak later of anoth-
er day. 9So then, there remains a sab-
bath rest for the people of God; 10for
whoever enters God's rest also ceases
from his labors as God did from his.

11 Let us therefore strive to enter
that rest, that no one fall by the same
sort of disobedience. 12For the word
of God is living and active, sharper
than any two-edged sword, piercing
to the division of soul and spirit, of
joints and marrow, and discerning the
thoughts and intentions of the heart.
13And before him no creature is hid-
den, but all are open and laid bare to
the eyes of him with whom we have
to do.

JESUS THE GREAT HIGH PRIEST

14 Since then we have a great high
priest who has passed through the
heavens, Jesus, the Son of God, let
us hold fast our confession. 15For we
have not a high priest who is unable
to sympathize with our weakness-
es, but one who in every respect has
been tempted as we are, yet without
sinning. 16Let us then with confidence
draw near to the throne of grace, that
we may receive mercy and find grace
to help in time of need.

5 For every high priest chosen from
among men is appointed to act on
behalf of men in relation to God, to
offer gifts and sacrifices for sins. 2He
can deal gently with the ignorant and
wayward, since he himself is beset
with weakness. 3Because of this he is
bound to offer sacrifice for his own
sins as well as for those of the peo-
ple. 4And one does not take the honor
upon himself, but he is called by God,
just as Aaron was.

5 So also Christ did not exalt him-
self to be made a high priest, but was
appointed by him who said to him,

[a] Other manuscripts read *they were not united in faith with the hearers*
[b] Greek *he*

"Thou art my Son,
today I have begotten thee";*
6as he says also in another place,
"Thou art a priest for ever,
after the order of
Melchiz′edek."
7 In the days of his flesh, Jesus[c]
offered up prayers and supplications,
with loud cries and tears, to him who
was able to save him from death,
and he was heard for his godly fear.
8Although he was a Son, he learned
obedience through what he suffered;
9and being made perfect he became
the source of eternal salvation to all
who obey him, 10being designated by
God a high priest after the order of
Melchiz′edek.

WARNING AGAINST FALLING AWAY

11 About this we have much to say
which is hard to explain, since you
have become dull of hearing. 12For
though by this time you ought to be
teachers, you need some one to teach
you again the first principles of God's
word. You need milk, not solid food;
13for every one who lives on milk is un-
skilled in the word of righteousness,
for he is a child. 14But solid food is for
the mature, for those who have their
faculties trained by practice to distin-
guish good from evil.

THE PERIL OF FALLING AWAY

6 Therefore let us leave the elemen-
tary doctrines of Christ and go on
to maturity, not laying again a foun-
dation of repentance from dead works
and of faith toward God, 2with in-
struction[d] about ablutions, the laying
on of hands, the resurrection of the
dead, and eternal judgment. 3And this
we will do if God permits.[e] 4For it is
impossible* to restore again to repen-
tance those who have once been en-
lightened, who have tasted the heav-
enly gift, and have become partakers
of the Holy Spirit, 5and have tasted
the goodness of the word of God and
the powers of the age to come, 6if they
then commit apostasy, since they cru-
cify the Son of God on their own ac-
count and hold him up to contempt.
7For land which has drunk the rain
that often falls upon it, and brings
forth vegetation useful to those for
whose sake it is cultivated, receives
a blessing from God. 8But if it bears
thorns and thistles, it is worthless
and near to being cursed; its end is to
be burned.
9 Though we speak thus, yet in
your case, beloved, we feel sure of
better things that belong to salvation.
10For God is not so unjust as to over-
look your work and the love which
you showed for his sake in serving
the saints, as you still do. 11And we
desire each one of you to show the
same earnestness in realizing the full
assurance of hope until the end, 12so
that you may not be sluggish, but imi-
tators of those who through faith and
patience inherit the promises.

THE CERTAINTY OF GOD'S PROMISE

13 For when God made a prom-
ise to Abraham, since he had no one
greater by whom to swear, he swore by
himself, 14saying, "Surely I will bless
you and multiply you." 15And thus
Abraham,[f] having patiently endured,
obtained the promise. 16Men indeed
swear by a greater than themselves,
and in all their disputes an oath is fi-
nal for confirmation. 17So when God
desired to show more convincingly
to the heirs of the promise the un-
changeable character of his purpose,
he interposed with an oath, 18so that
through two unchangeable things, in
which it is impossible that God should
prove false, we who have fled for ref-
uge might have strong encouragement
to seize the hope set before us. 19We
have this as a sure and steadfast an-
chor of the soul, a hope that enters

[c] Greek *he*
[d] Other ancient manuscripts read *of instruction*
[e] Other ancient manuscripts read *let us do this if God permits*
[f] Greek *he*

into the inner shrine behind the cur-
tain, 20where Jesus has gone as a fore-
runner on our behalf, having become
a high priest for ever after the order of
Melchiz′edek.

THE PRIESTLY ORDER OF MELCHIZEDEK

7 For this Melchiz′edek, king of Sa-
lem, priest of the Most High God,
met Abraham returning from the
slaughter of the kings and blessed
him; 2and to him Abraham appor-
tioned a tenth part of everything. He
is first, by translation of his name,
king of righteousness, and then he
is also king of Salem, that is, king of
peace. 3He is without father* or moth-
er or genealogy, and has neither be-
ginning of days nor end of life,* but
resembling the Son of God he contin-
ues a priest for ever.

4 See how great he is! Abraham
the patriarch gave him a tithe of the
spoils. 5And those descendants of Levi
who receive the priestly office have
a commandment in the law to take
tithes from the people, that is, from
their brethren, though these also are
descended from Abraham. 6But this
man who has not their genealogy
received tithes from Abraham and
blessed him who had the promises. 7It
is beyond dispute that the inferior is
blessed by the superior. 8Here tithes
are received by mortal men; there,
by one of whom it is testified that he
lives. 9One might even say that Levi
himself, who receives tithes, paid
tithes through Abraham, 10for he was
still in the loins of his ancestor when
Melchiz′edek met him.

ANOTHER PRIEST, LIKE MELCHIZEDEK

11 Now if perfection had been at-
tainable through the Levit′ical priest-
hood (for under it the people received
the law), what further need would
there have been for another priest to
arise after the order of Melchiz′edek,
rather than one named after the order
of Aaron? 12For when there is a change
in the priesthood, there is necessarily
a change in the law as well. 13For the
one of whom these things are spoken
belonged to another tribe, from which
no one has ever served at the altar.
14For it is evident that our Lord was
descended from Judah, and in connec-
tion with that tribe Moses said noth-
ing about priests.

15 This becomes even more evi-
dent when another priest arises in
the likeness of Melchiz′edek, 16who
has become a priest, not according to
a legal requirement concerning bodily
descent but by the power of an inde-
structible life. 17For it is witnessed of
him,

"Thou art a priest for ever,
after the order of
Melchiz′edek."

18On the one hand, a former com-
mandment is set aside because of its
weakness and uselessness 19(for the
law made nothing perfect); on the
other hand, a better hope is intro-
duced, through which we draw near
to God.

20 And it was not without an oath.
21Those who formerly became priests
took their office without an oath, but
this one was addressed with an oath,

"The Lord has sworn
and will not change his mind,
'Thou art a priest for ever.'"

22This makes Jesus the surety of a bet-
ter covenant.

23 The former priests were many in
number, because they were prevented
by death from continuing in office;
24but he holds his priesthood perma-
nently, because he continues for ever.
25Consequently he is able for all time
to save those who draw near to God
through him, since he always lives to
make intercession for them.

26 For it was fitting that we should
have such a high priest, holy, blame-
less, unstained, separated from sin-
ners, exalted above the heavens. 27He
has no need, like those high priests,
to offer sacrifices daily, first for his
own sins and then for those of the
people; he did this once for all when

he offered up himself. 28Indeed, the
law appoints men in their weakness
as high priests, but the word of the
oath, which came later than the law,
appoints a Son who has been made
perfect for ever.

MEDIATOR OF A BETTER COVENANT

8 Now the point in what we are saying
is this: we have such a high priest,
one who is seated at the right hand of
the throne of the Majesty in heaven, 2a
minister in the sanctuary and the true
tent[a] which is set up not by man but
by the Lord. 3For every high priest is
appointed to offer gifts and sacrific-
es; hence it is necessary for this priest
also to have something to offer. 4Now
if he were on earth, he would not be
a priest at all, since there are priests
who offer gifts according to the law.
5They serve a copy and shadow of the
heavenly sanctuary; for when Moses
was about to erect the tent,[b] he was
instructed by God, saying, "See that
you make everything according to the
pattern which was shown you on the
mountain." 6But as it is, Christ[c] has
obtained a ministry which is as much
more excellent than the old as the
covenant he mediates is better, since
it is enacted on better promises. 7For if
that first covenant had been faultless,
there would have been no occasion for
a second.

8 For he finds fault with them
when he says:

"The days will come, says the
Lord,
when I will establish a new
covenant with the house
of Israel
and with the house of Judah;
9not like the covenant that I made
with their fathers
on the day when I took them by
the hand
to lead them out of the land of
Egypt;
for they did not continue in my
covenant,
and so I paid no heed to them,
says the Lord.
10This is the covenant that I will
make with the house of
Israel
after those days, says the Lord:
I will put my laws into their
minds,
and write them on their hearts,
and I will be their God,
and they shall be my people.
11And they shall not teach every
one his fellow
or every one his brother, say-
ing, 'Know the Lord,'
for all shall know me,
from the least of them to the
greatest.*
12For I will be merciful toward
their iniquities,
and I will remember their sins
no more."

13In speaking of a new covenant he
treats the first as obsolete. And what
is becoming obsolete and growing old
is ready to vanish away.

THE EARTHLY AND THE HEAVENLY SANCTUARIES

9 Now even the first covenant had
regulations for worship and an
earthly sanctuary. 2For a tent[d] was
prepared, the outer one, in which
were the lampstand and the table and
the bread of the Presence;[e] it is called
the Holy Place. 3Behind the second
curtain stood a tent[f] called the Holy
of Holies, 4having the golden altar of
incense and the ark of the covenant
covered on all sides with gold, which
contained a golden urn holding the
manna, and Aaron's rod that budded,
and the tables of the covenant; 5above

[a] Or *tabernacle*
[b] Or *tabernacle*
[c] Greek *he*
[d] Or *tabernacle*
[e] Greek *the presentation of the loaves*
[f] Or *tabernacle*

it were the cherubim of glory over-
shadowing the mercy seat. Of these
things we cannot now speak in detail.

6 These preparations having thus
been made, the priests go continually
into the outer tent,[a] performing their
ritual duties; 7but into the second only
the high priest goes, and he but once
a year, and not without taking blood
which he offers for himself and for
the errors of the people. 8By this the
Holy Spirit indicates that the way into
the sanctuary is not yet opened as
long as the outer tent[b] is still stand-
ing 9(which is symbolic for the present
age). According to this arrangement,
gifts and sacrifices are offered which
cannot perfect the conscience of the
worshiper, 10but deal only with food
and drink and various ablutions, regu-
lations for the body imposed until the
time of reformation.

11 But when Christ appeared as
a high priest of the good things that
have come,[c] then through the greater
and more perfect tent[d] (not made with
hands, that is, not of this creation)
12he entered once for all into the Holy
Place, taking[e] not the blood of goats
and calves but his own blood, thus se-
curing an eternal redemption. 13For if
the sprinkling of defiled persons with
the blood of goats and bulls and with
the ashes of a heifer sanctifies for the
purification of the flesh, 14how much
more shall the blood of Christ, who
through the eternal Spirit offered
himself without blemish to God, pu-
rify your[f] conscience from dead works
to serve the living God.

15 Therefore he is the mediator of
a new covenant, so that those who
are called may receive the promised
eternal inheritance, since a death has
occurred which redeems them from
the transgressions under the first cov-
enant.[g] 16For where a will[h] is involved,
the death of the one who made it must
be established. 17For a will[i] takes ef-
fect only at death, since it is not in
force as long as the one who made it is
alive. 18Hence even the first covenant
was not ratified without blood. 19For
when every commandment of the law
had been declared by Moses to all the
people, he took the blood of calves
and goats, with water and scarlet wool
and hyssop, and sprinkled both the
book itself and all the people, 20say-
ing, "This is the blood of the covenant
which God commanded you." 21And in
the same way he sprinkled with the
blood both the tent[j] and all the ves-
sels used in worship. 22Indeed, under
the law almost everything is purified
with blood, and without the shedding
of blood there is no forgiveness of sins.

CHRIST'S SACRIFICE TAKES AWAY SIN

23 Thus it was necessary for the
copies of the heavenly things to be pu-
rified with these rites, but the heav-
enly things themselves with better
sacrifices than these. 24For Christ has
entered, not into a sanctuary made
with hands, a copy of the true one,
but into heaven itself, now to appear
in the presence of God on our behalf.
25Nor was it to offer himself repeated-
ly, as the high priest enters the Holy
Place yearly with blood not his own;
26for then he would have had to suf-
fer repeatedly since the foundation of
the world. But as it is, he has appeared
once for all at the end of the age to
put away sin by the sacrifice of him-
self. 27And just as it is appointed for
men to die once, and after that comes

[a] Or *tabernacle*
[b] Or *tabernacle*
[c] Other manuscripts read *good things to come*
[d] Or *tabernacle*
[e] Greek *through*
[f] Other manuscripts read *our*
[g] The Greek word here used means both *covenant* and *will*
[h] The Greek word here used means both *covenant* and *will*
[i] The Greek word here used means both *covenant* and *will*
[j] Or *tabernacle*

judgment, 28so Christ, having been of-
fered once to bear the sins of many,
will appear a second time, not to deal
with sin but to save those who are ea-
gerly waiting for him.

CHRIST'S SACRIFICE ONCE FOR ALL

10 For since the law has but a shadow
of the good things to come instead
of the true form of these realities,
it can never, by the same sacrifices
which are continually offered year
after year, make perfect those who
draw near.* 2Otherwise, would they
not have ceased to be offered? If the
worshipers had once been cleansed,
they would no longer have any con-
sciousness of sin. 3But in these sacri-
fices there is a reminder of sin year af-
ter year. 4For it is impossible that the
blood of bulls and goats should take
away sins.

5 Consequently, when Christ[k]
came into the world, he said,

"Sacrifices and offerings thou
hast not desired,
but a body hast thou prepared
for me;
6in burnt offerings and sin offer-
ings thou hast taken no
pleasure.
7Then I said, 'Lo, I have come to
do thy will, O God,'
as it is written of me in the roll
of the book."

8When he said above, "Thou hast
neither desired nor taken pleasure in
sacrifices and offerings and burnt of-
ferings and sin offerings" (these are
offered according to the law), 9then
he added, "Lo, I have come to do thy
will." He abolishes the first in order
to establish the second. 10And by that
will we have been sanctified through
the offering of the body of Jesus
Christ once for all.

11 And every priest stands dai-
ly at his service, offering repeatedly
the same sacrifices, which can never
take away sins. 12But when Christ[l] had
offered for all time a single sacrifice
for sins, he sat down at the right hand
of God, 13then to wait until his ene-
mies should be made a stool for his
feet. 14For by a single offering he has
perfected for all time those who are
sanctified. 15And the Holy Spirit also
bears witness to us; for after saying,

16"This is the covenant that I will
make with them
after those days, says the Lord:
I will put my laws on their
hearts,
and write them on their
minds,"

17then he adds,

"I will remember their sins
and their misdeeds no
more."

18Where there is forgiveness of
these, there is no longer any offering
for sin.

A CALL TO PERSEVERE

19 Therefore, brethren, since we
have confidence to enter the sanctu-
ary by the blood of Jesus, 20by the new
and living way which he opened for us
through the curtain, that is, through
his flesh, 21and since we have a great
priest over the house of God, 22let us
draw near with a true heart in full
assurance of faith, with our hearts
sprinkled clean from an evil con-
science and our bodies washed with
pure water. 23Let us hold fast the con-
fession of our hope without wavering,
for he who promised is faithful; 24and
let us consider how to stir up one an-
other to love and good works, 25not
neglecting to meet together, as is the
habit of some, but encouraging one
another, and all the more as you see
the Day drawing near.

26 For if we sin deliberately after
receiving the knowledge of the truth,
there no longer remains a sacrifice for
sins, 27but a fearful prospect of judg-
ment, and a fury of fire which will
consume the adversaries. 28A man

[k]Greek *he*
[l]Greek *this one*

who has violated the law of Moses
dies without mercy at the testimo-
ny of two or three witnesses. 29How
much worse punishment do you think
will be deserved by the man who has
spurned the Son of God, and profaned
the blood of the covenant by which
he was sanctified, and outraged the
Spirit of grace? 30For we know him
who said, "Vengeance is mine, I will
repay." And again, "The Lord will
judge his people." 31It is a fearful
thing to fall into the hands of the liv-
ing God.

32 But recall the former days
when, after you were enlightened,
you endured a hard struggle with
sufferings, 33sometimes being pub-
licly exposed to abuse and affliction,
and sometimes being partners with
those so treated. 34For you had com-
passion on the prisoners, and you
joyfully accepted the plundering of
your property, since you knew that
you yourselves had a better posses-
sion and an abiding one. 35Therefore
do not throw away your confidence,
which has a great reward. 36For you
have need of endurance, so that you
may do the will of God and receive
what is promised.

37"For yet a little while,
and the coming one shall come
and shall not tarry;
38but my righteous one shall live
by faith,
and if he shrinks back,
my soul has no pleasure in
him."

39But we are not of those who shrink
back and are destroyed, but of those
who have faith and keep their souls.

THE MEANING OF FAITH

11 Now faith is the assurance of
things hoped for, the conviction of
things not seen. 2For by it the men of
old received divine approval. 3By faith
we understand that the world was cre-
ated by the word of God, so that what
is seen was made out of things which
do not appear.

THE EXAMPLES OF ABEL, ENOCH, AND NOAH

4 By faith Abel offered to God a
more acceptable sacrifice than Cain,
through which he received approv-
al as righteous, God bearing witness
by accepting his gifts; he died, but
through his faith he is still speaking.
5By faith Enoch was taken up so that
he should not see death; and he was
not found, because God had taken
him. Now before he was taken he was
attested as having pleased God. 6And
without faith it is impossible to please
him. For whoever would draw near to
God must believe that he exists and
that he rewards those who seek him.*
7By faith Noah, being warned by God
concerning events as yet unseen, took
heed and constructed an ark for the
saving of his household; by this he
condemned the world and became an
heir of the righteousness which comes
by faith.

THE FAITH OF ABRAHAM

8 By faith Abraham obeyed when
he was called to go out to a place
which he was to receive as an inher-
itance; and he went out, not know-
ing where he was to go. 9By faith he
sojourned in the land of promise, as
in a foreign land, living in tents with
Isaac and Jacob, heirs with him of
the same promise. 10For he looked
forward to the city which has foun-
dations, whose builder and maker is
God. 11By faith Sarah herself received
power to conceive, even when she
was past the age, since she consid-
ered him faithful who had promised.
12Therefore from one man, and him as
good as dead, were born descendants
as many as the stars of heaven and as
the innumerable grains of sand by the
seashore.

13 These all died in faith, not hav-
ing received what was promised, but
having seen it and greeted it from
afar, and having acknowledged that
they were strangers and exiles on the

earth. 14For people who speak thus make it clear that they are seeking a homeland. 15If they had been thinking of that land from which they had gone out, they would have had opportunity to return. 16But as it is, they desire a better country, that is, a heavenly one. Therefore God is not ashamed to be called their God, for he has prepared for them a city.

17 By faith Abraham, when he was tested, offered up Isaac, and he who had received the promises was ready to offer up his only son, 18of whom it was said, "Through Isaac shall your descendants be named." 19He considered that God was able to raise men even from the dead; hence he did receive him back, and this was a symbol. 20By faith Isaac invoked future blessings on Jacob and Esau. 21By faith Jacob, when dying, blessed each of the sons of Joseph, bowing in worship over the head of his staff. 22By faith Joseph, at the end of his life, made mention of the exodus of the Israelites and gave directions concerning his burial.[a]

THE FAITH OF MOSES

23 By faith Moses, when he was born, was hid for three months by his parents, because they saw that the child was beautiful; and they were not afraid of the king's edict. 24By faith Moses, when he was grown up, refused to be called the son of Pharaoh's daughter, 25choosing rather to share ill-treatment with the people of God than to enjoy the fleeting pleasures of sin. 26He considered abuse suffered for the Christ greater wealth than the treasures of Egypt, for he looked to the reward. 27By faith he left Egypt, not being afraid of the anger of the king; for he endured as seeing him who is invisible. 28By faith he kept the Passover and sprinkled the blood, so that the Destroyer of the first-born might not touch them.

THE FAITH OF OTHER ISRAELITE HEROES

29 By faith the people crossed the Red Sea as if on dry land; but the Egyptians, when they attempted to do the same, were drowned. 30By faith the walls of Jericho fell down after they had been encircled for seven days. 31By faith Rahab the harlot did not perish with those who were disobedient, because she had given friendly welcome to the spies.

32 And what more shall I say? For time would fail me to tell of Gideon, Barak, Samson, Jephthah, of David and Samuel and the prophets 33who through faith conquered kingdoms, enforced justice, received promises, stopped the mouths of lions, 34quenched raging fire, escaped the edge of the sword, won strength out of weakness, became mighty in war, put foreign armies to flight. 35Women received their dead by resurrection. Some were tortured, refusing to accept release, that they might rise again to a better life. 36Others suffered mocking and scourging, and even chains and imprisonment. 37They were stoned, they were sawn in two,[b] they were killed with the sword; they went about in skins of sheep and goats, destitute, afflicted, ill-treated 38of whom the world was not worthy—wandering over deserts and mountains, and in dens and caves of the earth.

39 And all these, though well attested by their faith, did not receive what was promised, 40since God had foreseen something better for us, that apart from us they should not be made perfect.

THE EXAMPLE OF JESUS

12 Therefore, since we are surrounded by so great a cloud of witnesses, let us also lay aside every weight, and sin which clings so closely, and let us run with perseverance the race that is set before us,* 2looking to Jesus the pioneer and perfecter of our faith,

[a]Greek *bones*

[b]Other manuscripts add *they were tempted*

who for the joy that was set before
him endured the cross, despising the
shame, and is seated at the right hand
of the throne of God.

3 Consider him who endured from
sinners such hostility against himself,
so that you may not grow weary or
fainthearted. 4In your struggle against
sin you have not yet resisted to the
point of shedding your blood. 5And
have you forgotten the exhortation
which addresses you as sons?—

> "My son, do not regard lightly
> the discipline of the
> Lord,
> nor lose courage when you are
> punished by him.
> 6For the Lord disciplines him
> whom he loves,
> and chastises every son whom
> he receives."

7It is for discipline that you have to en-
dure. God is treating you as sons; for
what son is there whom his father does
not discipline? 8If you are left without
discipline, in which all have participat-
ed, then you are illegitimate children
and not sons. 9Besides this, we have
had earthly fathers to discipline us and
we respected them. Shall we not much
more be subject to the Father of spirits
and live? 10For they disciplined us for a
short time at their pleasure, but he dis-
ciplines us for our good, that we may
share his holiness. 11For the moment
all discipline seems painful rather
than pleasant; later it yields the peace-
ful fruit of righteousness to those who
have been trained by it.

WARNINGS AGAINST REJECTING GOD'S GRACE

12 Therefore lift your drooping
hands and strengthen your weak
knees, 13and make straight paths for
your feet, so that what is lame may
not be put out of joint but rather be
healed. 14Strive for peace with all men,
and for the holiness without which no
one will see the Lord. 15See to it that
no one fail to obtain the grace of God;
that no "root of bitterness" spring up
and cause trouble, and by it the many
become defiled; 16that no one be im-
moral or irreligious like Esau, who
sold his birthright for a single meal.
17For you know that afterward, when
he desired to inherit the blessing, he
was rejected, for he found no chance
to repent, though he sought it with
tears.

18 For you have not come to what
may be touched, a blazing fire, and
darkness, and gloom, and a tempest,
19and the sound of a trumpet, and a
voice whose words made the hear-
ers entreat that no further messages
be spoken to them. 20For they could
not endure the order that was given,
"If even a beast touches the moun-
tain, it shall be stoned." 21Indeed, so
terrifying was the sight that Moses
said, "I tremble with fear." 22But you
have come to Mount Zion and to the
city of the living God, the heavenly
Jerusalem, and to innumerable an-
gels in festal gathering, 23and to the
assembly[a] of the first-born who are
enrolled in heaven, and to a judge
who is God of all, and to the spir-
its of just men made perfect, 24and
to Jesus, the mediator of a new cov-
enant, and to the sprinkled blood
that speaks more graciously than the
blood of Abel.

25 See that you do not refuse him
who is speaking. For if they did not
escape when they refused him who
warned them on earth, much less
shall we escape if we reject him who
warns from heaven. 26His voice then
shook the earth; but now he has
promised, "Yet once more I will shake
not only the earth but also the heav-
en." 27This phrase, "Yet once more,"
indicates the removal of what is shak-
en, as of what has been made, in order
that what cannot be shaken may re-
main. 28Therefore let us be grateful for
receiving a kingdom that cannot be
shaken, and thus let us offer to God

[a]Or *angels, and to the festal gathering and assembly*

acceptable worship, with reverence
and awe; 29for our God is a consuming
fire.

SERVICE WELL-PLEASING TO GOD

13 *Let brotherly love continue.
2Do not neglect to show hospi-
tality to strangers, for thereby some
have entertained angels unawares.
3Remember those who are in prison,
as though in prison with them; and
those who are ill-treated, since you
also are in the body. 4Let marriage be
held in honor among all, and let the
marriage bed be undefiled; for God
will judge the immoral and adulter-
ous. 5Keep your life free from love of
money, and be content with what you
have; for he has said, "I will never fail
you nor forsake you." 6Hence we can
confidently say,

"The Lord is my helper,
I will not be afraid;
what can man do to me?"

7 Remember your leaders, those
who spoke to you the word of God;
consider the outcome of their life,
and imitate their faith. 8Jesus Christ
is the same yesterday and today and
for ever. 9Do not be led away by di-
verse and strange teachings; for it is
well that the heart be strengthened
by grace, not by foods, which have not
benefited their adherents.* 10We have
an altar from which those who serve
the tent[b] have no right to eat. 11For the
bodies of those animals whose blood
is brought into the sanctuary by the
high priest as a sacrifice for sin are
burned outside the camp. 12So Jesus
also suffered outside the gate in or-
der to sanctify the people through his
own blood. 13Therefore let us go forth
to him outside the camp, bearing
abuse for him.* 14For here we have
no lasting city, but we seek the city
which is to come. 15Through him then
let us continually offer up a sacrifice
of praise to God, that is, the fruit of
lips that acknowledge his name. 16Do
not neglect to do good and to share
what you have, for such sacrifices are
pleasing to God.

17 Obey your leaders and submit to
them; for they are keeping watch over
your souls, as men who will have to
give account. Let them do this joyful-
ly, and not sadly, for that would be of
no advantage to you.

18 Pray for us, for we are sure that
we have a clear conscience, desiring
to act honorably in all things. 19I urge
you the more earnestly to do this in
order that I may be restored to you the
sooner.

BENEDICTION

20 Now may the God of peace who
brought again from the dead our Lord
Jesus, the great shepherd of the sheep,
by the blood of the eternal covenant,
21equip you with everything good that
you may do his will, working in you[c]
that which is pleasing in his sight,
through Jesus Christ; to whom be glo-
ry for ever and ever. Amen.

FINAL EXHORTATION AND GREETINGS

22 I appeal to you, brethren, bear
with my word of exhortation, for
I have written to you briefly. 23You
should understand that our broth-
er Timothy has been released, with
whom I shall see you if he comes
soon. 24Greet all your leaders and all
the saints. Those who come from Italy
send you greetings. 25Grace be with all
of you. Amen.

[b] Or *tabernacle*
[c] Other ancient authorities read *us*

THE LETTER OF
JAMES

SALUTATION

1 James, a servant of God and of the
Lord Jesus Christ,
To the twelve tribes* in the
Dispersion:
Greeting.

FAITH AND WISDOM

2 Count it all joy, my brethren,
when you meet various trials, 3for
you know that the testing of your
faith produces steadfastness. 4And
let steadfastness have its full effect,
that you may be perfect and complete,
lacking in nothing.

5 If any of you lacks wisdom, let
him ask God, who gives to all men
generously and without reproaching,
and it will be given him. 6But let him
ask in faith, with no doubting, for he
who doubts is like a wave of the sea
that is driven and tossed by the wind.
7,8For that person must not suppose
that a double-minded man, unstable
in all his ways, will receive anything
from the Lord.

POVERTY AND RICHES

9 Let the lowly brother boast in
his exaltation, 10and the rich in his
humiliation, because like the flower
of the grass he will pass away. 11For
the sun rises with its scorching heat
and withers the grass; its flower falls,
and its beauty perishes. So will the
rich man fade away in the midst of his
pursuits.

TRIAL AND TEMPTATION

12 Blessed is the man who en-
dures trial, for when he has stood
the test he will receive the crown
of life which God has promised to
those who love him. 13Let no one say
when he is tempted, "I am tempted
by God"; for God cannot be tempted
with evil and he himself tempts no
one; 14but each person is tempted
when he is lured and enticed by his
own desire. 15Then desire when it has
conceived gives birth to sin; and sin
when it is full-grown brings forth
death.

16 Do not be deceived, my beloved
brethren. 17Every good endowment
and every perfect gift is from above,
coming down from the Father of lights
with whom there is no variation or
shadow due to change.[a] 18Of his own
will he brought us forth by the word
of truth that we should be a kind of
first fruits of his creatures.

HEARING AND DOING THE WORD

19 Know this, my beloved brethren.
Let every man be quick to hear, slow
to speak, slow to anger, 20for the anger
of man does not work the righteous-
ness of God. 21Therefore put away all
filthiness and rank growth of wicked-
ness and receive with meekness the
implanted word, which is able to save
your souls.

22 But be doers of the word, and
not hearers only, deceiving your-
selves.* 23For if any one is a hearer of
the word and not a doer, he is like a
man who observes his natural face in
a mirror; 24for he observes himself and
goes away and at once forgets what
he was like. 25But he who looks into
the perfect law, the law of liberty, and
perseveres, being no hearer that for-
gets but a doer that acts, he shall be
blessed in his doing.

26 If any one thinks he is religious,
and does not bridle his tongue but de-
ceives his heart, this man's religion is
vain. 27Religion that is pure and un-
defiled before God and the Father is
this: to visit orphans and widows in
their affliction, and to keep oneself
unstained from the world.

[a]Other ancient authorities read *variation due to a shadow of turning*

WARNING AGAINST PARTIALITY

2 My brethren, show no partiality
as you hold the faith of our Lord
Jesus Christ, the Lord of glory. 2For
if a man with gold rings and in fine
clothing comes into your assembly,
and a poor man in shabby clothing
also comes in, 3and you pay atten-
tion to the one who wears the fine
clothing and say, "Have a seat here,
please," while you say to the poor
man, "Stand there," or, "Sit at my
feet," 4have you not made distinctions
among yourselves, and become judg-
es with evil thoughts? 5Listen, my be-
loved brethren. Has not God chosen
those who are poor in the world to be
rich in faith and heirs of the kingdom
which he has promised to those who
love him? 6But you have dishonored
the poor man. Is it not the rich who
oppress you, is it not they who drag
you into court? 7Is it not they who
blaspheme that honorable name by
which you are called?*

8 If you really fulfil the royal law,
according to the scripture, "You shall
love your neighbor as yourself," you
do well. 9But if you show partiality,
you commit sin, and are convicted by
the law as transgressors. 10For who-
ever keeps the whole law but fails in
one point has become guilty of all of
it.* 11For he who said, "Do not com-
mit adultery," said also, "Do not kill."
If you do not commit adultery but do
kill, you have become a transgres-
sor of the law. 12So speak and so act
as those who are to be judged under
the law of liberty. 13For judgment is
without mercy to one who has shown
no mercy; yet mercy triumphs over
judgment.

FAITH WITHOUT WORKS IS DEAD

14 What does it profit, my breth-
ren, if a man says he has faith but has
not works? Can his faith save him?*
15If a brother or sister is ill-clad and
in lack of daily food, 16and one of you
says to them, "Go in peace, be warmed
and filled," without giving them the
things needed for the body, what does
it profit? 17So faith by itself, if it has no
works, is dead.

18 But some one will say, "You
have faith and I have works." Show me
your faith apart from your works, and
I by my works will show you my faith.
19You believe that God is one; you
do well. Even the demons believe—
and shudder. 20Do you want to be
shown, you foolish fellow, that faith
apart from works is barren? 21Was
not Abraham our father justified by
works, when he offered his son Isaac
upon the altar? 22You see that faith
was active along with his works, and
faith was completed by works, 23and
the scripture was fulfilled which says,
"Abraham believed God, and it was
reckoned to him as righteousness";
and he was called the friend of God.
24You see that a man is justified by
works and not by faith alone. 25And in
the same way was not also Rahab the
harlot justified by works when she re-
ceived the messengers and sent them
out another way? 26For as the body
apart from the spirit is dead, so faith
apart from works is dead.

TAMING THE TONGUE

3 Let not many of you become teach-
ers, my brethren, for you know
that we who teach shall be judged
with greater strictness. 2For we all
make many mistakes, and if any one
makes no mistakes in what he says
he is a perfect man, able to bridle the
whole body also. 3If we put bits into
the mouths of horses that they may
obey us, we guide their whole bodies.
4Look at the ships also; though they
are so great and are driven by strong
winds, they are guided by a very small
rudder wherever the will of the pilot
directs. 5So the tongue is a little mem-
ber and boasts of great things. How
great a forest is set ablaze by a small
fire!

6 And the tongue is a fire. The
tongue is an unrighteous world
among our members, staining the

whole body, setting on fire the cycle
of nature,[a] and set on fire by hell.[b]
7For every kind of beast and bird, of
reptile and sea creature, can be tamed
and has been tamed by humankind,
8but no human being can tame the
tongue—a restless evil, full of dead-
ly poison. 9With it we bless the Lord
and Father, and with it we curse men,
who are made in the likeness of God.
10From the same mouth come blessing
and cursing. My brethren, this ought
not to be so. 11Does a spring pour
forth from the same opening fresh
water and brackish? 12Can a fig tree,
my brethren, yield olives, or a grape-
vine figs? No more can salt water yield
fresh.

TWO KINDS OF WISDOM

13 Who is wise and understanding
among you? By his good life let him
show his works in the meekness of
wisdom. 14But if you have bitter jeal-
ousy and selfish ambition in your
hearts, do not boast and be false to
the truth. 15This wisdom is not such as
comes down from above, but is earth-
ly, unspiritual, devilish. 16For where
jealousy and selfish ambition exist,
there will be disorder and every vile
practice. 17But the wisdom from above
is first pure, then peaceable, gentle,
open to reason, full of mercy and good
fruits, without uncertainty or insin-
cerity. 18And the harvest of righteous-
ness is sown in peace by those who
make peace.

FRIENDSHIP WITH THE WORLD

4 What causes wars, and what caus-
es fightings among you? Is it not
your passions that are at war in your
members? 2You desire and do not
have; so you kill. And you covet[c] and
cannot obtain; so you fight and wage
war. You do not have, because you do
not ask. 3You ask and do not receive,
because you ask wrongly, to spend
it on your passions. 4Unfaithful
creatures! Do you not know that
friendship with the world is enmity
with God? Therefore whoever wish-
es to be a friend of the world makes
himself an enemy of God. 5Or do you
suppose it is in vain that the scrip-
ture says, "He yearns jealously over
the spirit which he has made to dwell
in us"? 6But he gives more grace;
therefore it says, "God opposes the
proud, but gives grace to the hum-
ble." 7Submit yourselves therefore to
God. Resist the devil and he will flee
from you. 8Draw near to God and he
will draw near to you. Cleanse your
hands, you sinners, and purify your
hearts, you men of double mind. 9Be
wretched and mourn and weep. Let
your laughter be turned to mourning
and your joy to dejection. 10Humble
yourselves before the Lord and he
will exalt you.

WARNING AGAINST JUDGING ANOTHER

11 Do not speak evil against one
another, brethren. He that speaks
evil against a brother or judges his
brother, speaks evil against the law
and judges the law. But if you judge
the law, you are not a doer of the law
but a judge. 12There is one lawgiver
and judge, he who is able to save and
to destroy. But who are you that you
judge your neighbor?

BOASTING ABOUT TOMORROW

13 Come now, you who say, "Today
or tomorrow we will go into such and
such a town and spend a year there
and trade and get gain"; 14whereas
you do not know about tomorrow.
What is your life? For you are a mist
that appears for a little time and then
vanishes. 15Instead you ought to say,
"If the Lord wills, we shall live and
we shall do this or that." 16As it is,
you boast in your arrogance. All such
boasting is evil. 17Whoever knows
what is right to do and fails to do it,
for him it is sin.

[a] Or *wheel of birth*
[b] Greek *Gehenna*
[c] Or *you kill and you covet*

WARNING TO RICH OPPRESSORS

5 Come now, you rich, weep and howl
for the miseries that are coming
upon you. 2 Your riches have rotted
and your garments are moth-eaten.
3 Your gold and silver have rusted, and
their rust will be evidence against
you and will eat your flesh like fire.
You have laid up treasure[d]* for the
last days. 4 Behold, the wages of the
laborers who mowed your fields,
which you kept back by fraud, cry
out; and the cries of the harvesters
have reached the ears of the Lord of
hosts. 5 You have lived on the earth in
luxury and in pleasure; you have fat-
tened your hearts in a day of slaugh-
ter. 6 You have condemned, you have
killed the righteous man; he does not
resist you.

PATIENCE IN SUFFERING

7 Be patient, therefore, brethren,
until the coming of the Lord. Behold,
the farmer waits for the precious fruit
of the earth, being patient over it until
it receives the early and the late rain.
8 You also be patient. Establish your
hearts, for the coming of the Lord is
at hand. 9 Do not grumble, brethren,
against one another, that you may not
be judged; behold, the Judge is stand-
ing at the doors. 10 As an example of
suffering and patience, brethren, take
the prophets who spoke in the name
of the Lord. 11 Behold, we call those
happy who were steadfast. You have
heard of the steadfastness of Job,
and you have seen the purpose of the
Lord, how the Lord is compassionate
and merciful.

12 But above all, my brethren, do
not swear, either by heaven or by
earth or with any other oath, but let
your yes be yes and your no be no, that
you may not fall under condemnation.

THE PRAYER OF FAITH

13 Is any one among you suffer-
ing? Let him pray. Is any cheerful? Let
him sing praise. 14 Is any among you
sick? Let him call for the elders of the
church, and let them pray over him,
anointing him with oil in the name of
the Lord; 15 and the prayer of faith will
save the sick man, and the Lord will
raise him up; and if he has committed
sins, he will be forgiven.* 16 Therefore
confess your sins to one another, and
pray for one another, that you may
be healed. The prayer of a righteous
man has great power in its effects.
17 Eli′jah was a man of like nature with
ourselves and he prayed fervently that
it might not rain, and for three years
and six months it did not rain on the
earth. 18 Then he prayed again and
the heaven gave rain, and the earth
brought forth its fruit.

19 My brethren, if any one among
you wanders from the truth and some
one brings him back, 20 let him know
that whoever brings back a sinner
from the error of his way will save his
soul from death and will cover a mul-
titude of sins.

[d] Or *will eat your flesh, since you have stored up fire*

THE FIRST LETTER OF
PETER

SALUTATION

1 Peter, an apostle of Jesus Christ,
To the exiles of the Dispersion in
Pontus, Galatia, Cappado´cia, Asia,
and Bithyn´ia,* 2chosen and destined
by God the Father and sanctified
by the Spirit for obedience to Jesus
Christ and for sprinkling with his
blood: May grace and peace be multiplied to you.

A LIVING HOPE

3 Blessed be the God and Father
of our Lord Jesus Christ! By his great
mercy we have been born anew to a
living hope through the resurrection
of Jesus Christ from the dead, 4and
to an inheritance which is imperishable, undefiled, and unfading, kept in
heaven for you, 5who by God's power
are guarded through faith for a salvation ready to be revealed in the last
time. 6In this you rejoice,[a] though
now for a little while you may have to
suffer various trials, 7so that the genuineness of your faith, more precious
than gold which though perishable is
tested by fire, may redound to praise
and glory and honor at the revelation of Jesus Christ. 8Without having
seen[b] him you[c] love him; though you
do not now see him you[d] believe in
him and rejoice with unutterable and
exalted joy. 9As the outcome of your
faith you obtain the salvation of your
souls.

10 The prophets who prophesied
of the grace that was to be yours
searched and inquired about this salvation; 11they inquired what person
or time was indicated by the Spirit
of Christ* within them when predicting the sufferings of Christ and the
subsequent glory. 12It was revealed
to them that they were serving not
themselves but you, in the things
which have now been announced to
you by those who preached the good
news to you through the Holy Spirit
sent from heaven, things into which
angels long to look.

A CALL TO HOLY LIVING

13 Therefore gird up your minds,
be sober, set your hope fully upon
the grace that is coming to you at the
revelation of Jesus Christ. 14As obedient children, do not be conformed
to the passions of your former ignorance, 15but as he who called you is
holy, be holy yourselves in all your
conduct; 16since it is written, "You
shall be holy, for I am holy." 17And if
you invoke as Father him who judges
each one impartially according to his
deeds, conduct yourselves with fear
throughout the time of your exile.
18You know that you were ransomed
from the futile ways inherited from
your fathers, not with perishable
things such as silver or gold, 19but
with the precious blood of Christ,
like that of a lamb without blemish
or spot. 20He was destined before
the foundation of the world but was
made manifest at the end of the
times for your sake. 21Through him
you have confidence in God, who
raised him from the dead and gave
him glory, so that your faith and
hope are in God.[e]

22 Having purified your souls by
your obedience to the truth for a sincere love of the brethren, love one
another earnestly from the heart.
23You have been born anew, not of
perishable seed but of imperishable,

[a] Or *Rejoice in this*
[b] Other ancient authorities read *known*
[c] Or omit *you*
[d] Or omit *you*
[e] Or *so that your faith is hope in God*

through the living and abiding word
of God; 24for

"All flesh is like grass
and all its glory like the flower of grass.
The grass withers, and the flower falls,
25but the word of the Lord abides for ever."

That word is the good news which was
preached to you.

THE LIVING STONE AND A CHOSEN PEOPLE

2 So put away all malice and all guile
and insincerity and envy and all
slander. 2Like newborn babes, long
for the pure spiritual milk, that by
it you may grow up to salvation; 3for
you have tasted the kindness of the
Lord.

4 Come to him, to that living stone,
rejected by men but in God's sight
chosen and precious; 5and like living
stones be yourselves built into a spir-
itual house, to be a holy priesthood,
to offer spiritual sacrifices acceptable
to God through Jesus Christ. 6For it
stands in scripture:

"Behold, I am laying in Zion
a stone, a cornerstone chosen and precious,
and he who believes in him
will not be put to shame."

7To you therefore who believe, he is
precious, but for those who do not
believe,

"The very stone which the builders rejected
has become the head of the corner,"

8and

"A stone that will make men stumble,
a rock that will make them fall";

for they stumble because they dis-
obey the word, as they were destined
to do.

9 But you are a chosen race, a royal
priesthood, a holy nation, God's own
people,[f] that you may declare the
wonderful deeds of him who called
you out of darkness into his marvel-
ous light. 10Once you were no people
but now you are God's people; once
you had not received mercy but now
you have received mercy.

LIVE AS SERVANTS OF GOD

11 Beloved, I beseech you as
aliens and exiles to abstain from the
passions of the flesh that wage war
against your soul. 12Maintain good
conduct among the Gentiles, so that
in case they speak against you as
wrongdoers, they may see your good
deeds and glorify God on the day of
visitation.

13 Be subject for the Lord's sake
to every human institution,[g] whether
it be to the emperor as supreme, 14or
to governors as sent by him to pun-
ish those who do wrong and to praise
those who do right. 15For it is God's
will that by doing right you should
put to silence the ignorance of fool-
ish men. 16Live as free men, yet with-
out using your freedom as a pretext
for evil; but live as servants of God.
17Honor all men. Love the brother-
hood. Fear God. Honor the emperor.

THE EXAMPLE OF CHRIST'S SUFFERING

18 Servants, be submissive to your
masters with all respect, not only to
the kind and gentle but also to the
overbearing. 19For one is approved
if, mindful of God, he endures pain
while suffering unjustly. 20For what
credit is it, if when you do wrong
and are beaten for it you take it pa-
tiently? But if when you do right and
suffer for it you take it patiently, you
have God's approval. 21For to this
you have been called, because Christ
also suffered for you, leaving you an
example, that you should follow in
his steps. 22He committed no sin; no

[f] Greek *a people for his possession*
[g] Or *every institution ordained for men*

guile was found on his lips. 23When he was reviled, he did not revile in return; when he suffered, he did not threaten; but he trusted to him who judges justly. 24He himself bore our sins in his body on the tree,[a] that we might die to sin and live to righteousness. By his wounds you have been healed. 25For you were straying like sheep, but have now returned to the Shepherd and Guardian of your souls.

WIVES AND HUSBANDS

3 Likewise you wives,* be submissive to your husbands, so that some, though they do not obey the word, may be won without a word by the behavior of their wives, 2when they see your reverent and chaste behavior. 3Let not yours be the outward adorning with braiding of hair, decoration of gold, and wearing of robes, 4but let it be the hidden person of the heart with the imperishable jewel of a gentle and quiet spirit, which in God's sight is very precious. 5So once the holy women who hoped in God used to adorn themselves and were submissive to their husbands, 6as Sarah obeyed Abraham, calling him lord. And you are now her children if you do right and let nothing terrify you.

7 Likewise you husbands, live considerately with your wives, bestowing honor on the woman as the weaker sex, since you are joint heirs of the grace of life, in order that your prayers may not be hindered.

SUFFERING FOR DOING RIGHT

8 Finally, all of you, have unity of spirit, sympathy, love of the brethren, a tender heart and a humble mind. 9Do not return evil for evil or reviling for reviling; but on the contrary bless, for to this you have been called, that you may obtain a blessing. 10For

"He that would love life
and see good days,
let him keep his tongue from
evil
and his lips from speaking
guile;
11let him turn away from evil and
do right;
let him seek peace and pursue
it.
12For the eyes of the Lord are
upon the righteous,
and his ears are open to their
prayer.
But the face of the Lord is
against those that do
evil."

13 Now who is there to harm you if you are zealous for what is right? 14But even if you do suffer for righteousness' sake, you will be blessed. Have no fear of them, nor be troubled, 15but in your hearts reverence Christ as Lord. Always be prepared to make a defense to any one who calls you to account for the hope that is in you, yet do it with gentleness and reverence; 16and keep your conscience clear, so that, when you are abused, those who revile your good behavior in Christ may be put to shame. 17For it is better to suffer for doing right, if that should be God's will, than for doing wrong. 18For Christ also died[b] for sins once for all, the righteous for the unrighteous, that he might bring us to God, being put to death in the flesh but made alive in the spirit; 19in which he went and preached to the spirits in prison, 20who formerly did not obey, when God's patience waited in the days of Noah, during the building of the ark, in which a few, that is, eight persons, were saved through water. 21Baptism, which corresponds to this, now saves you, not as a removal of dirt from the body but as an appeal to God for a clear conscience, through the resurrection of Jesus Christ, 22who has gone into heaven and is at the right hand

[a] Or *carried up... to the tree*
[b] Other ancient authorities read *suffered*

of God, with angels, authorities, and
powers subject to him.

GOOD STEWARDS OF GOD'S GRACE

4 Since therefore Christ suffered in
the flesh,[c] arm yourselves with
the same thought, for whoever has
suffered in the flesh has ceased from
sin,* 2so as to live for the rest of the
time in the flesh no longer by hu-
man passions but by the will of God.
3Let the time that is past suffice for
doing what the Gentiles like to do,
living in licentiousness, passions,
drunkenness, revels, carousing, and
lawless idolatry. 4They are surprised
that you do not now join them in the
same wild profligacy, and they abuse
you; 5but they will give account to
him who is ready to judge the liv-
ing and the dead. 6For this is why
the gospel was preached even to the
dead, that though judged in the flesh
like men, they might live in the spirit
like God.

7 The end of all things is at hand;
therefore keep sane and sober for
your prayers. 8Above all hold un-
failing your love for one another,
since love covers a multitude of sins.
9Practice hospitality ungrudgingly to
one another. 10As each has received
a gift, employ it for one another, as
good stewards of God's varied grace:
11whoever speaks, as one who utters
oracles of God; whoever renders ser-
vice, as one who renders it by the
strength which God supplies; in order
that in everything God may be glori-
fied through Jesus Christ. To him be-
long glory and dominion for ever and
ever. Amen.

SUFFERING AS A CHRISTIAN

12 Beloved, do not be surprised at
the fiery ordeal which comes upon
you to prove you, as though some-
thing strange were happening to you.
13But rejoice in so far as you share
Christ's sufferings, that you may also
rejoice and be glad when his glory is
revealed. 14If you are reproached for
the name of Christ, you are blessed,
because the spirit of glory[d] and of God
rests upon you. 15But let none of you
suffer as a murderer, or a thief, or a
wrongdoer, or a mischief-maker; 16yet
if one suffers as a Christian, let him
not be ashamed, but under that name
let him glorify God. 17For the time has
come for judgment to begin with the
household of God; and if it begins
with us, what will be the end of those
who do not obey the gospel of God?
18And

"If the righteous man is scarce-
ly saved,
where will the impious and
sinner appear?"

19Therefore let those who suffer ac-
cording to God's will do right and en-
trust their souls to a faithful Creator.

TENDING THE FLOCK OF GOD

5 So I exhort the elders among you,
as a fellow elder and a witness of
the sufferings of Christ as well as
a partaker in the glory that is to be
revealed. 2Tend the flock of God that
is your charge,[e] not by constraint but
willingly,[f] not for shameful gain but
eagerly, 3not as domineering over
those in your charge but being ex-
amples to the flock. 4And when the
chief Shepherd is manifested you will
obtain the unfading crown of glory.
5Likewise you that are younger be sub-
ject to the elders. Clothe yourselves,
all of you, with humility toward one
another, for "God opposes the proud,
but gives grace to the humble."

6 Humble yourselves therefore un-
der the mighty hand of God, that in
due time he may exalt you. 7Cast all
your anxieties on him, for he cares
about you. 8Be sober, be watchful.
Your adversary the devil prowls
around like a roaring lion, seeking

[c] Other ancient authorities add *for us; some for you*
[d] Other ancient authorities insert *and of power*
[e] Other ancient authorities add *exercising the oversight*
[f] Other ancient authorities add *as God would have you*

some one to devour. 9Resist him, firm
in your faith, knowing that the same
experience of suffering is required
of your brotherhood throughout the
world. 10And after you have suffered a
little while, the God of all grace, who
has called you to his eternal glory in
Christ, will himself restore, establish,
and strengthen[a] you. 11To him be the
dominion for ever and ever. Amen.

FINAL GREETINGS AND BENEDICTION

12 By Silva´nus, a faithful brother
as I regard him, I have written briefly
to you, exhorting and declaring that
this is the true grace of God; stand fast
in it. 13She who is at Babylon,* who is
likewise chosen, sends you greetings;
and so does my son Mark. 14Greet one
another with the kiss of love. Peace to
all of you that are in Christ.

[a]Other ancient authorities read *restore, establish, strengthen and settle*

THE SECOND LETTER OF
PETER

SALUTATION

1 Simon Peter, a servant and apostle
of Jesus Christ, To those who have
obtained a faith of equal standing
with ours in the righteousness of our
God and Savior Jesus Christ:[a]

2 May grace and peace be multi-
plied to you in the knowledge of God
and of Jesus our Lord.

THE CHRISTIAN'S CALL AND ELECTION

3 His divine power has granted to
us all things that pertain to life and
godliness, through the knowledge of
him who called us to[b] his own glo-
ry and excellence, 4 by which he has
granted to us his precious and very
great promises, that through these
you may escape from the corruption
that is in the world because of pas-
sion, and become partakers of the
divine nature.* 5 For this very rea-
son make every effort to supplement
your faith with virtue, and virtue
with knowledge, 6 and knowledge
with self-control, and self-control
with steadfastness, and steadfast-
ness with godliness, 7 and godliness
with brotherly affection, and broth-
erly affection with love. 8 For if these
things are yours and abound, they
keep you from being ineffective or
unfruitful in the knowledge of our
Lord Jesus Christ. 9 For whoever lacks
these things is blind and shortsight-
ed and has forgotten that he was
cleansed from his old sins. 10 There-
fore, brethren, be the more zealous
to confirm your call and election, for
if you do this you will never fall; 11 so
there will be richly provided for you
an entrance into the eternal kingdom
of our Lord and Savior Jesus Christ.

12 Therefore I intend always to re-
mind you of these things, though you
know them and are established in the
truth that you have. 13 I think it right,
as long as I am in this body,[c] to arouse
you by way of reminder, 14 since I know
that the putting off of my body[d] will
be soon, as our Lord Jesus Christ
showed me. 15 And I will see to it that
after my departure you may be able at
any time to recall these things.

EYEWITNESSES OF CHRIST'S GLORY

16 For we did not follow cleverly
devised myths when we made known
to you the power and coming of our
Lord Jesus Christ, but we were eye-
witnesses of his majesty.* 17 For when
he received honor and glory from God
the Father and the voice was borne to
him by the Majestic Glory, "This is my
beloved Son,[e] with whom I am well
pleased," 18 we heard this voice borne
from heaven, for we were with him on
the holy mountain. 19 And we have the
prophetic word made more sure. You
will do well to pay attention to this as
to a lamp shining in a dark place, until
the day dawns and the morning star
rises in your hearts. 20 First of all you
must understand this, that no prophe-
cy of scripture is a matter of one's own
interpretation, 21 because no prophecy
ever came by the impulse of man, but
men moved by the Holy Spirit spoke
from God.[f]

FALSE PROPHETS AND THEIR PUNISHMENT

2 But false prophets also arose among
the people, just as there will be
false teachers among you, who will
secretly bring in destructive heresies,
even denying the Master who bought

[a] Or *of our God and the Savior Jesus Christ*
[b] Or *by*
[c] Greek *tent*
[d] Greek *tent*
[e] Or *my Son, my* (or *the*) *Beloved*
[f] Other authorities read *moved by the Holy Spirit holy men of God spoke*

them, bringing upon themselves swift
destruction. 2And many will follow
their licentiousness, and because of
them the way of truth will be reviled.
3And in their greed they will exploit
you with false words; from of old their
condemnation has not been idle, and
their destruction has not been asleep.*

4 For if God did not spare the an-
gels when they sinned, but cast them
into hell[a] and committed them to pits
of nether gloom to be kept until the
judgment; 5if he did not spare the
ancient world, but preserved Noah,
a herald of righteousness, with sev-
en other persons, when he brought a
flood upon the world of the ungodly;
6if by turning the cities of Sodom and
Gomor´rah to ashes he condemned
them to extinction and made them
an example to those who were to
be ungodly; 7and if he rescued righ-
teous Lot, greatly distressed by the
licentiousness of the wicked 8(for by
what that righteous man saw and
heard as he lived among them, he
was vexed in his righteous soul day
after day with their lawless deeds),
9then the Lord knows how to rescue
the godly from trial, and to keep the
unrighteous under punishment until
the day of judgment, 10and especially
those who indulge in the lust of de-
filing passion and despise authority.
Bold and wilful, they are not afraid
to revile the glorious ones, 11where-
as angels, though greater in might
and power, do not pronounce a revil-
ing judgment upon them before the
Lord. 12But these, like irrational an-
imals, creatures of instinct, born to
be caught and killed, reviling in mat-
ters of which they are ignorant, will
be destroyed in the same destruction
with them, 13suffering wrong for their
wrongdoing. They count it pleasure to
revel in the daytime. They are blots
and blemishes, reveling in their dis-
sipation,[b] carousing with you. 14They
have eyes full of adultery, insatiable
for sin. They entice unsteady souls.
They have hearts trained in greed.
Accursed children! 15Forsaking the
right way they have gone astray; they
have followed the way of Balaam, the
son of Be´or, who loved gain from
wrongdoing, 16but was rebuked for his
own transgression; a dumb ass spoke
with human voice and restrained the
prophet's madness.

17 These are waterless springs and
mists driven by a storm; for them the
nether gloom of darkness has been re-
served. 18For, uttering loud boasts of
folly, they entice with licentious pas-
sions of the flesh men who have bare-
ly escaped from those who live in er-
ror. 19They promise them freedom, but
they themselves are slaves of corrup-
tion; for whatever overcomes a man,
to that he is enslaved. 20For if, after
they have escaped the defilements of
the world through the knowledge of
our Lord and Savior Jesus Christ, they
are again entangled in them and over-
powered, the last state has become
worse for them than the first. 21For it
would have been better for them never
to have known the way of righteous-
ness than after knowing it to turn
back from the holy commandment
delivered to them. 22It has happened
to them according to the true proverb,
The dog turns back to his own vomit,
and the sow is washed only to wallow
in the mire.

THE PROMISE OF THE LORD'S COMING

3 This is now the second letter that
I have written to you, beloved, and
in both of them I have aroused your
sincere mind by way of reminder;
2that you should remember the pre-
dictions of the holy prophets and the
commandment of the Lord and Savior
through your apostles. 3First of all you
must understand this, that scoffers
will come in the last days with scoff-
ing, following their own passions 4and
saying, "Where is the promise of his

[a]Greek *Tartarus*
[b]Other ancient authorities read *love feasts*

coming? For ever since the fathers fell
asleep, all things have continued as
they were from the beginning of cre-
ation." 5They deliberately ignore this
fact, that by the word of God heavens
existed long ago, and an earth formed
out of water and by means of water,
6through which the world that then
existed was deluged with water and
perished. 7But by the same word the
heavens and earth that now exist have
been stored up for fire, being kept un-
til the day of judgment and destruc-
tion of ungodly men.

8 But do not ignore this one fact,
beloved, that with the Lord one day is
as a thousand years, and a thousand
years as one day. 9The Lord is not slow
about his promise as some count slow-
ness, but is forbearing toward you,[c]
not wishing that any should perish,
but that all should reach repentance.
10But the day of the Lord will come
like a thief, and then the heavens will
pass away with a loud noise, and the
elements will be dissolved with fire,
and the earth and the works that are
upon it will be burned up.

11 Since all these things are thus
to be dissolved, what sort of persons
ought you to be in lives of holiness
and godliness, 12waiting for and has-
tening[d] the coming of the day of God,
because of which the heavens will
be kindled and dissolved, and the
elements will melt with fire! 13But
according to his promise we wait for
new heavens and a new earth in which
righteousness dwells.

FINAL EXHORTATION AND DOXOLOGY

14 Therefore, beloved, since you
wait for these, be zealous to be found
by him without spot or blemish, and
at peace. 15And count the forbearance
of our Lord as salvation. So also our
beloved brother Paul wrote to you
according to the wisdom given him,
16speaking of this* as he does in all
his letters. There are some things in
them hard to understand, which the
ignorant and unstable twist to their
own destruction, as they do the other
scriptures. 17You therefore, beloved,
knowing this beforehand, beware
lest you be carried away with the er-
ror of lawless men and lose your own
stability. 18But grow in the grace and
knowledge of our Lord and Savior
Jesus Christ. To him be the glory
both now and to the day of eternity.
Amen.

[c]Other ancient authorities read *on your account*
[d]Or *earnestly desiring*

THE FIRST LETTER OF

JOHN

THE WORD OF LIFE

1 *That which was from the begin-
ning, which we have heard, which
we have seen with our eyes, which we
have looked upon and touched with
our hands, concerning the word of life
2the life was made manifest, and we
saw it, and testify to it, and proclaim
to you the eternal life which was with
the Father and was made manifest to
us 3that which we have seen and heard
we proclaim also to you, so that you
may have fellowship* with us; and
our fellowship is with the Father and
with his Son Jesus Christ. 4And we
are writing this that our[a] joy may be
complete.

GOD IS LIGHT

5 This is the message we have
heard from him and proclaim to you,
that God is light and in him is no
darkness* at all. 6If we say we have
fellowship with him while we walk
in darkness, we lie and do not live ac-
cording to the truth; 7but if we walk
in the light, as he is in the light, we
have fellowship with one another, and
the blood of Jesus his Son cleanses us
from all sin. 8If we say we have no sin,
we deceive ourselves, and the truth is
not in us. 9If we confess our sins, he
is faithful and just, and will forgive
our sins and cleanse us from all un-
righteousness. 10If we say we have not
sinned, we make him a liar, and his
word is not in us.

CHRIST OUR ADVOCATE

2 My little children, I am writing this
to you so that you may not sin; but
if any one does sin, we have an ad-
vocate with the Father, Jesus Christ
the righteous; 2and he is the expiation
for our sins, and not for ours only but
also for the sins of the whole world.
3And by this we may be sure that we
know him, if we keep his command-
ments.* 4He who says "I know him"
but disobeys his commandments is a
liar, and the truth is not in him; 5but
whoever keeps his word, in him tru-
ly love for God is perfected. By this
we may be sure that we are in him:
6he who says he abides in him ought
to walk in the same way in which he
walked.

A NEW COMMANDMENT

7 Beloved, I am writing you no
new commandment, but an old com-
mandment which you had from the
beginning; the old commandment
is the word which you have heard.
8Yet I am writing you a new com-
mandment, which is true in him
and in you, because[b] the darkness
is passing away and the true light is
already shining. 9He who says he is
in the light and hates his brother is
in the darkness still. 10He who loves
his brother abides in the light, and
in it[c] there is no cause for stumbling.
11But he who hates his brother is in
the darkness and walks in the dark-
ness, and does not know where he
is going, because the darkness has
blinded his eyes.

12 I am writing to you, little chil-
dren, because your sins are forgiven
for his sake. 13I am writing to you,
fathers, because you know him who
is from the beginning. I am writ-
ing to you, young men, because you
have overcome the evil one. I write to
you, children, because you know the
Father. 14I write to you, fathers, be-
cause you know him who is from the
beginning. I write to you, young men,
because you are strong, and the word

[a] Other ancient authorities read *your*
[b] Or *that*
[c] Or *him*

of God abides in you, and you have
overcome the evil one.
15 Do not love the world or the
things in the world. If any one loves
the world, love for the Father is not
in him. 16For all that is in the world,
the lust of the flesh and the lust of
the eyes and the pride of life, is not of
the Father but is of the world. 17And
the world passes away, and the lust
of it; but he who does the will of God
abides for ever.

WARNING AGAINST ANTICHRISTS

18 Children, it is the last hour;*
and as you have heard that antichrist
is coming, so now many antichrists
have come; therefore we know that
it is the last hour. 19They went out
from us, but they were not of us; for
if they had been of us, they would
have continued with us; but they
went out, that it might be plain that
they all are not of us. 20But you have
been anointed by the Holy One, and
you all know.[d] 21I write to you, not be-
cause you do not know the truth, but
because you know it, and know that
no lie is of the truth. 22Who is the
liar but he who denies that Jesus is
the Christ? This is the antichrist, he
who denies the Father and the Son.
23No one who denies the Son has the
Father. He who confesses the Son has
the Father also. 24Let what you heard
from the beginning abide in you. If
what you heard from the beginning
abides in you, then you will abide in
the Son and in the Father. 25And this
is what he has promised us,[e] eternal
life.
26 I write this to you about those
who would deceive you; 27but the
anointing which you received from
him abides in you, and you have no
need that any one should teach you;
as his anointing teaches you about
everything, and is true, and is no lie,
just as it has taught you, abide in him.

CHILDREN OF GOD

28 And now, little children, abide
in him, so that when he appears we
may have confidence and not shrink
from him in shame at his coming. 29If
you know that he is righteous, you
may be sure that every one who does
right is born of him.
3 See what love the Father has given
us, that we should be called chil-
dren of God; and so we are. The rea-
son why the world does not know us
is that it did not know him. 2Beloved,
we are God's children now; it does
not yet appear what we shall be, but
we know that when he appears we
shall be like him, for we shall see
him as he is. 3And every one who thus
hopes in him purifies himself as he
is pure.
4 Every one who commits sin is
guilty of lawlessness; sin is lawless-
ness. 5You know that he appeared to
take away sins, and in him there is no
sin. 6No one who abides in him sins;*
no one who sins has either seen him
or known him. 7Little children, let no
one deceive you. He who does right is
righteous, as he is righteous. 8He who
commits sin is of the devil; for the
devil has sinned from the beginning.
The reason the Son of God appeared
was to destroy the works of the devil.
9No one born of God commits sin; for
God's[f] nature abides in him, and he
cannot sin because he is[g] born of God.
10By this it may be seen who are the
children of God, and who are the chil-
dren of the devil: whoever does not do
right is not of God, nor he who does
not love his brother.

LOVE ONE ANOTHER

11 For this is the message which
you have heard from the beginning,
that we should love one another, 12and
not be like Cain who was of the evil
one and murdered his brother. And
why did he murder him? Because his

[d] Other ancient authorities read *you know everything*
[e] Other ancient authorities read *you*
[f] Greek *his*
[g] Or *for the offspring of God abide in him, and they cannot sin because they are*

own deeds were evil and his brother's
righteous. 13 Do not wonder, brethren,
that the world hates you. 14 We know
that we have passed out of death into
life, because we love the brethren. He
who does not love remains in death.
15 Any one who hates his brother is a
murderer, and you know that no mur-
derer has eternal life abiding in him.
16 By this we know love, that he laid
down his life for us; and we ought to
lay down our lives for the brethren.
17 But if any one has the world's goods
and sees his brother in need, yet clos-
es his heart against him, how does
God's love abide in him? 18 Little chil-
dren, let us not love in word or speech
but in deed and in truth.

19 By this we shall know that we
are of the truth, and reassure our
hearts before him 20 whenever our
hearts condemn us; for God is greater
than our hearts, and he knows every-
thing. 21 Beloved, if our hearts do not
condemn us, we have confidence be-
fore God; 22 and we receive from him
whatever we ask, because we keep his
commandments and do what pleases
him. 23 And this is his commandment,
that we should believe in the name of
his Son Jesus Christ and love one an-
other, just as he has commanded us.
24 All who keep his commandments
abide in him, and he in them. And by
this we know that he abides in us, by
the Spirit which he has given us.

TESTING THE SPIRITS

4 Beloved, do not believe every spirit,
but test the spirits* to see whether
they are of God; for many false proph-
ets have gone out into the world. 2 By
this you know the Spirit of God: ev-
ery spirit which confesses that Jesus
Christ has come in the flesh is of
God, 3 and every spirit which does not
confess Jesus is not of God. This is
the spirit of antichrist, of which you
heard that it was coming, and now it is
in the world already. 4 Little children,
you are of God, and have overcome
them; for he who is in you is greater
than he who is in the world. 5 They are
of the world, therefore what they say
is of the world, and the world listens
to them. 6 We are of God. Whoever
knows God listens to us, and he who
is not of God does not listen to us. By
this we know the spirit of truth and
the spirit of error.

GOD IS LOVE

7 Beloved, let us love one another;
for love is of God, and he who loves
is born of God and knows God. 8 He
who does not love does not know
God; for God is love. 9 In this the love
of God was made manifest among us,
that God sent his only Son into the
world, so that we might live through
him. 10 In this is love, not that we loved
God but that he loved us and sent his
Son to be the expiation for our sins.
11 Beloved, if God so loved us, we also
ought to love one another. 12 No man
has ever seen God; if we love one an-
other, God abides in us and his love is
perfected in us.

13 By this we know that we abide
in him and he in us, because he has
given us of his own Spirit. 14 And we
have seen and testify that the Father
has sent his Son as the Savior of the
world. 15 Whoever confesses that Jesus
is the Son of God, God abides in him,
and he in God. 16 So we know and be-
lieve the love God has for us. God is
love, and he who abides in love abides
in God, and God abides in him. 17 In
this is love perfected with us, that
we may have confidence for the day
of judgment, because as he is so are
we in this world. 18 There is no fear in
love, but perfect love casts out fear.
For fear has to do with punishment,
and he who fears is not perfected in
love. 19 We love, because he first loved
us. 20 If any one says, "I love God,"
and hates his brother, he is a liar;
for he who does not love his brother
whom he has seen, cannot[a] love God
whom he has not seen. 21 And this

[a] Other ancient authorities read *how can he*

commandment we have from him,
that he who loves God should love his
brother also.

FAITH CONQUERS THE WORLD

5 Every one who believes that Jesus
is the Christ is a child of God, and
every one who loves the parent loves
the child. 2By this we know that we
love the children of God, when we
love God and obey his command-
ments. 3For this is the love of God,
that we keep his commandments. And
his commandments are not burden-
some. 4For whatever is born of God
overcomes the world; and this is the
victory that overcomes the world, our
faith. 5Who is it that overcomes the
world but he who believes that Jesus
is the Son of God?

TESTIMONY CONCERNING THE SON OF GOD

6 This is he who came by water
and blood, Jesus Christ, not with the
water only but with the water and the
blood. 7And the Spirit is the witness,
because the Spirit is the truth. 8There
are three witnesses, the Spirit, the
water, and the blood; and these three
agree.* 9If we receive the testimony of
men, the testimony of God is great-
er; for this is the testimony of God
that he has borne witness to his Son.
10He who believes in the Son of God
has the testimony in himself. He who
does not believe God has made him a
liar, because he has not believed in the
testimony that God has borne to his
Son. 11And this is the testimony, that
God gave us eternal life, and this life
is in his Son. 12He who has the Son has
life; he who has not the Son of God
has not life.

EPILOGUE

13 I write this to you who believe in
the name of the Son of God, that you
may know that you have eternal life.
14And this is the confidence which
we have in him, that if we ask any-
thing according to his will he hears
us. 15And if we know that he hears
us in whatever we ask, we know that
we have obtained the requests made
of him. 16If any one sees his brother
committing what is not a mortal sin,
he will ask, and God[b] will give him
life for those whose sin is not mortal.
There is sin which is mortal; I do not
say that one is to pray for that. 17All
wrongdoing is sin, but there is sin
which is not mortal.

18 We know that any one born of
God does not sin, but He who was
born of God keeps him, and the evil
one does not touch him.

19 We know that we are of God,
and the whole world is in the power
of the evil one.

20 And we know that the Son of
God has come and has given us un-
derstanding, to know him who is true;
and we are in him who is true, in his
Son Jesus Christ. This is the true God
and eternal life. 21Little children, keep
yourselves from idols.

[b]Greek *he*

THE SECOND LETTER OF JOHN

SALUTATION

1 The elder* to the elect lady* and
her children, whom I love in the truth,
and not only I but also all who know
the truth, 2because of the truth which
abides in us and will be with us for
ever:

3 Grace, mercy, and peace will be
with us, from God the Father and
from Jesus Christ the Father's Son, in
truth and love.

TRUTH AND LOVE

4 I rejoiced greatly to find some
of your children following the truth,
just as we have been commanded by
the Father. 5And now I beg you, lady,
not as though I were writing you a
new commandment, but the one we
have had from the beginning, that we
love one another. 6And this is love,
that we follow his commandments;
this is the commandment, as you have
heard from the beginning, that you
follow love. 7For many deceivers have
gone out into the world, men who will
not acknowledge the coming of Jesus
Christ in the flesh; such a one is the
deceiver and the antichrist. 8Look
to yourselves, that you may not lose
what you[a] have worked for, but may
win a full reward. 9Any one who goes
ahead and does not abide in the doc-
trine of Christ does not have God; he
who abides in the doctrine has both
the Father and the Son. 10If any one
comes to you and does not bring this
doctrine, do not receive him into the
house or give him any greeting; 11for
he who greets him shares his wicked
work.

FINAL GREETINGS

12 Though I have much to write to
you, I would rather not use paper and
ink, but I hope to come to see you and
talk with you face to face, so that our
joy may be complete.

13 The children* of your elect sister
greet you.

[a]Other ancient authorities read *we*

THE THIRD LETTER OF
JOHN

SALUTATION

1 The elder to the beloved Ga´ius,
whom I love in the truth.

GAIUS COMMENDED FOR HIS HOSPITALITY

2 Beloved, I pray that all may go
well with you and that you may be in
health; I know that it is well with your
soul. 3For I greatly rejoiced when some
of the brethren arrived and testified
to the truth of your life, as indeed you
do follow the truth. 4No greater joy
can I have than this, to hear that my
children follow the truth.

5 Beloved, it is a loyal thing you
do when you render any service to
the brethren, especially to strangers,
6who have testified to your love before
the church. You will do well to send
them on their journey as befits God's
service. 7For they have set out for his
sake and have accepted nothing from
the heathen. 8So we ought to sup-
port such men, that we may be fellow
workers in the truth.

DIOTREPHES AND DEMETRIUS

9 I have written something to the
church; but Diot´rephes, who likes to
put himself first, does not acknowl-
edge my authority. 10So if I come, I
will bring up what he is doing, prating
against me with evil words. And not
content with that, he refuses himself
to welcome the brethren, and also
stops those who want to welcome
them and puts them out of the church.

11 Beloved, do not imitate evil but
imitate good. He who does good is of
God; he who does evil has not seen
God. 12Deme´trius* has testimony from
every one, and from the truth itself; I
testify to him too, and you know my
testimony is true.

FINAL GREETINGS

13 I had much to write to you, but
I would rather not write with pen and
ink; 14I hope to see you soon, and we
will talk together face to face.

15 Peace be to you. The friends
greet you. Greet the friends, every one
of them.

THE LETTER OF
JUDE

SALUTATION

1 Jude, a servant of Jesus Christ
and brother of James, To those who
are called, beloved in God the Father
and kept for Jesus Christ:

2 May mercy, peace, and love be
multiplied to you.

OCCASION OF THE LETTER

3 Beloved, being very eager to
write to you of our common salvation,
I found it necessary to write appeal-
ing to you to contend for the faith
which was once for all delivered to
the saints. 4For admission has been
secretly gained by some who long ago
were designated for this condemna-
tion, ungodly persons who pervert the
grace of our God into licentiousness
and deny our only Master and Lord,
Jesus Christ.[a]

JUDGMENT ON FALSE TEACHERS

5 Now I desire to remind you,
though you were once for all fully in-
formed, that he[b] who saved a people
out of the land of Egypt, afterward
destroyed those who did not believe.
6And the angels that did not keep
their own position but left their prop-
er dwelling have been kept by him in
eternal chains in the nether gloom un-
til the judgment of the great day;* 7just
as Sodom and Gomor′rah and the sur-
rounding cities, which likewise acted
immorally and indulged in unnatural
lust, serve as an example by undergo-
ing a punishment of eternal fire.

8 Yet in like manner these men
in their dreamings defile the flesh,
reject authority, and revile the glori-
ous ones.[c] 9But when the archangel
Michael, contending with the devil,
disputed about the body of Moses, he
did not presume to pronounce a re-
viling judgment upon him, but said,
"The Lord rebuke you."‡ 10But these
men revile whatever they do not un-
derstand, and by those things that
they know by instinct as irrational
animals do, they are destroyed. 11Woe
to them! For they walk in the way of
Cain, and abandon themselves for the
sake of gain to Balaam's error, and
perish in Korah's rebellion. 12These
are blemishes[d] on your love feasts, as
they boldly carouse together, looking
after themselves; waterless clouds,
carried along by winds; fruitless trees
in late autumn, twice dead, uprooted;
13wild waves of the sea, casting up the
foam of their own shame; wandering
stars for whom the nether gloom of
darkness has been reserved for ever.

14 It was of these also that Enoch
in the seventh generation from Adam
prophesied, saying, "Behold, the Lord
came with his holy myriads, 15to exe-
cute judgment on all, and to convict
all the ungodly of all their deeds of
ungodliness which they have com-
mitted in such an ungodly way, and
of all the harsh things which ungod-
ly sinners have spoken against him."
16These are grumblers, malcontents,
following their own passions, loud-
mouthed boasters, flattering people
to gain advantage.

WARNINGS AND EXHORTATIONS

17 But you must remember, be-
loved, the predictions of the apostles
of our Lord Jesus Christ; 18they said
to you, "In the last time there will be
scoffers, following their own ungod-
ly passions." 19It is these who set up
divisions, worldly people, devoid of
the Spirit. 20But you, beloved, build

[a] Or *the only Master and our Lord Jesus Christ*
[b] Ancient authorities read *Jesus* or *the Lord* or *God*
[c] Greek *glories*
[d] Or *reefs*

yourselves up on your most holy faith;
pray in the Holy Spirit; 21keep your-
selves in the love of God; wait for the
mercy of our Lord Jesus Christ unto
eternal life. 22And convince some, who
doubt; 23save some, by snatching them
out of the fire; on some have mercy
with fear, hating even the garment
spotted by the flesh.[e]

BENEDICTION

24 Now to him who is able to keep
you from falling and to present you
without blemish before the presence
of his glory with rejoicing, 25to the
only God, our Savior through Jesus
Christ our Lord, be glory, majesty, do-
minion, and authority, before all time
and now and for ever. Amen.

[e]The Greek text in this sentence is uncertain at several points

THE
REVELATION TO JOHN
(THE APOCALYPSE)

INTRODUCTION AND SALUTATION

1 The revelation of Jesus Christ,
which God gave him to show to his
servants what must soon take place;
and he made it known by sending his
angel to his servant John, 2who bore
witness to the word of God and to the
testimony of Jesus Christ, even to all
that he saw. 3Blessed is he who reads
aloud the words of the prophecy, and
blessed are those who hear, and who
keep what is written therein; for the
time is near.

4 John to the seven churches that
are in Asia:* Grace to you and peace
from him who is and who was and
who is to come, and from the seven
spirits who are before his throne,
5and from Jesus Christ the faithful
witness, the first-born of the dead,
and the ruler of kings on earth. To
him who loves us and has freed us
from our sins by his blood 6and made
us a kingdom, priests to his God and
Father, to him be glory and dominion
for ever and ever. Amen. 7Behold, he
is coming with the clouds, and ev-
ery eye will see him, every one who
pierced him; and all tribes of the
earth will wail on account of him.
Even so. Amen.

8 "I am the Alpha and the Omega,"
says the Lord God, who is and who
was and who is to come, the Almighty.

A VISION OF CHRIST

9 I John, your brother, who share
with you in Jesus the tribulation and
the kingdom and the patient endur-
ance, was on the island called Patmos
on account of the word of God and
the testimony of Jesus. 10I was in the
Spirit on the Lord's day, and I heard
behind me a loud voice like a trum-
pet 11saying, "Write what you see
in a book and send it to the seven
churches, to Ephesus and to Smyrna
and to Per′gamum and to Thyati′ra
and to Sardis and to Philadelphia and
to La-odice′a."

12 Then I turned to see the voice
that was speaking to me, and on turn-
ing I saw seven golden lampstands,
13and in the midst of the lampstands
one like a son of man,* clothed with
a long robe and with a golden girdle
round his breast; 14his head and his
hair were white as white wool, white
as snow; his eyes were like a flame
of fire, 15his feet were like burnished
bronze, refined as in a furnace, and
his voice was like the sound of many
waters; 16in his right hand he held
seven stars, from his mouth issued
a sharp two-edged sword, and his
face was like the sun shining in full
strength.

17 When I saw him, I fell at his feet
as though dead. But he laid his right
hand upon me, saying, "Fear not, I
am the first and the last, 18and the liv-
ing one; I died, and behold I am alive
for evermore, and I have the keys of
Death and Hades. 19Now write what
you see, what is and what is to take
place hereafter. 20As for the mystery
of the seven stars which you saw in
my right hand, and the seven gold-
en lampstands, the seven stars are
the angels of the seven churches and
the seven lampstands are the seven
churches.

THE MESSAGE TO EPHESUS

2 "To the angel of the church in
Ephesus write: 'The words of him
who holds the seven stars in his right
hand, who walks among the seven
golden lampstands.

2 "'I know your works, your toil
and your patient endurance, and how
you cannot bear evil men but have

tested those who call themselves
apostles but are not, and found them
to be false; 3I know you are endur-
ing patiently and bearing up for my
name's sake, and you have not grown
weary. 4But I have this against you,
that you have abandoned the love you
had at first. 5Remember then from
what you have fallen, repent and do
the works you did at first. If not, I will
come to you and remove your lamp-
stand from its place, unless you re-
pent. 6Yet this you have, you hate the
works of the Nicola´itans, which I also
hate. 7He who has an ear, let him hear
what the Spirit says to the churches.
To him who conquers I will grant to
eat of the tree of life, which is in the
paradise of God.'

THE MESSAGE TO SMYRNA

8 "And to the angel of the church
in Smyrna write: 'The words of the
first and the last, who died and came
to life.

9 "'I know your tribulation and
your poverty (but you are rich) and
the slander of those who say that they
are Jews and are not, but are a syn-
agogue of Satan. 10Do not fear what
you are about to suffer. Behold, the
devil is about to throw some of you
into prison, that you may be tested,
and for ten days* you will have trib-
ulation. Be faithful unto death, and I
will give you the crown of life. 11He
who has an ear, let him hear what the
Spirit says to the churches. He who
conquers shall not be hurt by the sec-
ond death.'

THE MESSAGE TO PERGAMUM

12 "And to the angel of the church
in Per´gamum write: 'The words of
him who has the sharp two-edged
sword.

13 "'I know where you dwell,
where Satan's throne is; you hold
fast my name and you did not deny
my faith even in the days of An´tipas
my witness, my faithful one, who
was killed among you, where Satan
dwells. 14But I have a few things
against you: you have some there
who hold the teaching of Balaam,
who taught Balak to put a stumbling
block before the sons of Israel, that
they might eat food sacrificed to idols
and practice immorality. 15So you also
have some who hold the teaching
of the Nicola´itans. 16Repent then.
If not, I will come to you soon and
war against them with the sword of
my mouth. 17He who has an ear, let
him hear what the Spirit says to the
churches. To him who conquers I will
give some of the hidden manna, and
I will give him a white stone, with
a new name written on the stone
which no one knows except him who
receives it.'

THE MESSAGE TO THYATIRA

18 "And to the angel of the church
in Thyati´ra write: 'The words of the
Son of God, who has eyes like a flame
of fire, and whose feet are like bur-
nished bronze.

19 "'I know your works, your love
and faith and service and patient en-
durance, and that your latter works
exceed the first. 20But I have this
against you, that you tolerate the
woman Jez´ebel, who calls herself a
prophetess and is teaching and be-
guiling my servants to practice im-
morality* and to eat food sacrificed
to idols. 21I gave her time to repent,
but she refuses to repent of her im-
morality.* 22Behold, I will throw her
on a sickbed, and those who commit
adultery with her I will throw into
great tribulation, unless they repent
of her doings; 23and I will strike her
children dead. And all the churches
shall know that I am he who search-
es mind and heart, and I will give to
each of you as your works deserve.
24But to the rest of you in Thyati´ra,
who do not hold this teaching, who
have not learned what some call the
deep things of Satan,* to you I say, I
do not lay upon you any other bur-
den; 25only hold fast what you have,

until I come. 26 He who conquers and
who keeps my works until the end,
I will give him power over the na-
tions, 27 and he shall rule them with
a rod of iron, as when earthen pots
are broken in pieces, even as I my-
self have received power from my
Father; 28 and I will give him the
morning star.* 29 He who has an ear,
let him hear what the Spirit says to
the churches.'

THE MESSAGE TO SARDIS

3 "And to the angel of the church in
Sardis write: 'The words of him
who has the seven spirits of God and
the seven stars. "'I know your works;
you have the name of being alive, and
you are dead. 2 Awake, and strength-
en what remains and is on the point
of death, for I have not found your
works perfect in the sight of my God.
3 Remember then what you received
and heard; keep that, and repent. If
you will not awake, I will come like
a thief, and you will not know at
what hour I will come upon you. 4 Yet
you have still a few names in Sardis,
people who have not soiled their gar-
ments; and they shall walk with me in
white, for they are worthy. 5 He who
conquers shall be clad thus in white
garments, and I will not blot his name
out of the book of life; I will confess
his name before my Father and before
his angels. 6 He who has an ear, let
him hear what the Spirit says to the
churches.'

THE MESSAGE TO PHILADELPHIA

7 "And to the angel of the church
in Philadelphia write: 'The words of
the holy one, the true one, who has
the key of David, who opens and no
one shall shut, who shuts and no one
opens.

8 "'I know your works. Behold,
I have set before you an open door,
which no one is able to shut; I know
that you have but little power, and
yet you have kept my word and have
not denied my name. 9 Behold, I will
make those of the synagogue of Satan
who say that they are Jews and are
not, but lie—behold, I will make
them come and bow down before
your feet, and learn that I have loved
you. 10 Because you have kept my word
of patient endurance, I will keep you
from the hour of trial which is com-
ing on the whole world, to try those
who dwell upon the earth. 11 I am com-
ing soon; hold fast what you have, so
that no one may seize your crown.
12 He who conquers, I will make him a
pillar in the temple of my God; never
shall he go out of it, and I will write
on him the name of my God, and the
name of the city of my God, the new
Jerusalem which comes down from
my God out of heaven, and my own
new name.* 13 He who has an ear, let
him hear what the Spirit says to the
churches.'

THE MESSAGE TO LAODICEA

14 "And to the angel of the church
in La-odice´a write: 'The words of the
Amen, the faithful and true witness,
the beginning of God's creation.

15 "'I know your works: you are
neither cold nor hot. Would that you
were cold or hot! 16 So, because you
are lukewarm, and neither cold nor
hot, I will spew you out of my mouth.
17 For you say, I am rich, I have pros-
pered, and I need nothing; not know-
ing that you are wretched, pitiable,
poor, blind, and naked. 18 Therefore I
counsel you to buy from me gold re-
fined by fire, that you may be rich,
and white garments to clothe you and
to keep the shame of your nakedness
from being seen, and salve to anoint
your eyes, that you may see. 19 Those
whom I love, I reprove and chasten;
so be zealous and repent. 20 Behold, I
stand at the door and knock; if any
one hears my voice and opens the
door, I will come in to him and eat
with him, and he with me. 21 He who
conquers, I will grant him to sit with
me on my throne, as I myself con-
quered and sat down with my Father

on his throne. 22He who has an ear,
let him hear what the Spirit says to
the churches.'"

THE HEAVENLY WORSHIP

4 After this I looked, and lo, in heav-
en an open door! And the first
voice, which I had heard speaking
to me like a trumpet, said, "Come
up hither, and I will show you what
must take place after this." 2At once
I was in the Spirit, and lo, a throne
stood in heaven, with one seated on
the throne! 3And he who sat there
appeared like jasper and carnelian,
and round the throne was a rain-
bow that looked like an emerald.*
4Round the throne were twenty-four
thrones, and seated on the thrones
were twenty-four elders,* clad in
white garments, with golden crowns
upon their heads. 5From the throne
issue flashes of lightning, and voic-
es and peals of thunder, and before
the throne burn seven torches of fire,
which are the seven spirits of God;
6and before the throne there is as it
were a sea of glass, like crystal. And
round the throne, on each side of the
throne, are four living creatures,*
full of eyes in front and behind: 7the
first living creature like a lion, the
second living creature like an ox, the
third living creature with the face of
a man, and the fourth living creature
like a flying eagle. 8And the four liv-
ing creatures, each of them with six
wings, are full of eyes all round and
within, and day and night they never
cease to sing,

"Holy, holy, holy,* is the Lord
God Almighty,
who was and is and is to come!"

9And whenever the living creatures
give glory and honor and thanks to
him who is seated on the throne, who
lives for ever and ever, 10the twen-
ty-four elders fall down before him
who is seated on the throne and wor-
ship him who lives for ever and ever;
they cast their crowns before the
throne, singing,

11"Worthy art thou, our Lord and
God,
to receive glory and honor and
power,
for thou didst create all things,
and by thy will they existed
and were created."

THE SCROLL AND THE LAMB

5 And I saw in the right hand of him
who was seated on the throne a
scroll* written within and on the back,
sealed with seven seals; 2and I saw a
strong angel proclaiming with a loud
voice, "Who is worthy to open the
scroll and break its seals?" 3And no
one in heaven or on earth or under the
earth was able to open the scroll or
to look into it, 4and I wept much that
no one was found worthy to open the
scroll or to look into it. 5Then one of
the elders said to me, "Weep not; lo,
the Lion of the tribe of Judah, the Root
of David, has conquered, so that he can
open the scroll and its seven seals."

6 And between the throne and
the four living creatures and among
the elders, I saw a Lamb standing, as
though it had been slain, with seven
horns and with seven eyes,* which are
the seven spirits of God sent out into
all the earth; 7and he went and took
the scroll from the right hand of him
who was seated on the throne. 8And
when he had taken the scroll, the four
living creatures and the twenty-four
elders fell down before the Lamb,
each holding a harp, and with golden
bowls full of incense, which are the
prayers of the saints; 9and they sang a
new song, saying,

"Worthy art thou to take the
scroll and to open its
seals,
for thou wast slain and by thy
blood didst ransom men
for God
from every tribe and tongue
and people and nation,
10and hast made them a kingdom
and priests to our God,
and they shall reign on earth."

11 Then I looked, and I heard around
the throne and the living creatures
and the elders the voice of many an-
gels, numbering myriads of myriads
and thousands of thousands, 12 say-
ing with a loud voice, "Worthy is the
Lamb who was slain, to receive pow-
er and wealth and wisdom and might
and honor and glory and blessing!"
13 And I heard every creature in heaven
and on earth and under the earth and
in the sea, and all therein, saying, "To
him who sits upon the throne and to
the Lamb be blessing and honor and
glory and might for ever and ever!"
14 And the four living creatures said,
"Amen!" and the elders fell down and
worshiped.

THE SEVEN SEALS

6 *Now I saw when the Lamb opened
one of the seven seals, and I heard
one of the four living creatures say, as
with a voice of thunder, "Come!" 2 And
I saw, and behold, a white horse, and
its rider had a bow; and a crown was
given to him, and he went out con-
quering and to conquer.

3 When he opened the second seal,
I heard the second living creature
say, "Come!" 4 And out came another
horse, bright red; its rider was permit-
ted to take peace from the earth, so
that men should slay one another; and
he was given a great sword.

5 When he opened the third seal,
I heard the third living creature say,
"Come!" And I saw, and behold, a
black horse, and its rider had a bal-
ance* in his hand; 6 and I heard what
seemed to be a voice in the midst of
the four living creatures saying, "A
quart of wheat for a denarius,[a] and
three quarts of barley for a denarius;[b]
but do not harm oil and wine!"

7 When he opened the fourth
seal, I heard the voice of the fourth
living creature say, "Come!" 8 And I
saw, and behold, a pale horse, and its
rider's name was Death, and Hades
followed him; and they were given
power over a fourth of the earth, to
kill with sword and with famine and
with pestilence and by wild beasts of
the earth.

9 When he opened the fifth seal,
I saw under the altar the souls of
those who had been slain for the word
of God and for the witness they had
borne; 10 they cried out with a loud
voice, "O Sovereign Lord, holy and
true, how long before thou wilt judge
and avenge our blood on those who
dwell upon the earth?" 11 Then they
were each given a white robe and told
to rest a little longer, until the num-
ber of their fellow servants and their
brethren should be complete, who
were to be killed as they themselves
had been.

12 When he opened the sixth
seal, I looked, and behold, there was
a great earthquake; and the sun be-
came black as sackcloth, the full
moon became like blood, 13 and the
stars of the sky fell to the earth as the
fig tree sheds its winter fruit when
shaken by a gale; 14 the sky vanished
like a scroll that is rolled up, and ev-
ery mountain and island was removed
from its place. 15 Then the kings of
the earth and the great men and the
generals and the rich and the strong,
and every one, slave and free, hid in
the caves and among the rocks of the
mountains, 16 calling to the mountains
and rocks, "Fall on us and hide us
from the face of him who is seated
on the throne, and from the wrath of
the Lamb; 17 for the great day of their
wrath has come, and who can stand
before it?"

THE 144,000 OF ISRAEL SEALED

7 After this I saw four angels stand-
ing at the four corners of the earth,
holding back the four winds of the
earth, that no wind might blow on
earth or sea or against any tree. 2 Then
I saw another angel ascend from the

[a] The denarius was a day's wage for a laborer
[b] The denarius was a day's wage for a laborer

rising of the sun, with the seal of
the living God, and he called with
a loud voice to the four angels who
had been given power to harm earth
and sea, 3saying, "Do not harm the
earth or the sea or the trees, till we
have sealed the servants of our God
upon their foreheads." 4And I heard
the number of the sealed, a hundred
and forty-four thousand* sealed, out
of every tribe of the sons of Israel,
5twelve thousand sealed out of the
tribe of Judah, twelve thousand of
the tribe of Reuben, twelve thousand
of the tribe of Gad, 6twelve thousand
of the tribe of Asher, twelve thou-
sand of the tribe of Naph´tali, twelve
thousand of the tribe of Manas´seh,
7twelve thousand of the tribe of
Simeon, twelve thousand of the tribe
of Levi, twelve thousand of the tribe
of Is´sachar, 8twelve thousand of the
tribe of Zeb´ulun, twelve thousand of
the tribe of Joseph, twelve thousand
sealed out of the tribe of Benjamin.

THE MULTITUDE FROM EVERY NATION

9 After this I looked, and be-
hold, a great multitude which no
man could number, from every na-
tion, from all tribes and peoples and
tongues, standing before the throne
and before the Lamb, clothed in white
robes, with palm branches in their
hands, 10and crying out with a loud
voice, "Salvation belongs to our God
who sits upon the throne, and to the
Lamb!" 11And all the angels stood
round the throne and round the elders
and the four living creatures, and they
fell on their faces before the throne
and worshiped God, 12saying, "Amen!
Blessing and glory and wisdom and
thanksgiving and honor and power
and might be to our God for ever and
ever! Amen."

13 Then one of the elders ad-
dressed me, saying, "Who are these,
clothed in white robes, and whence
have they come?" 14I said to him, "Sir,
you know." And he said to me, "These
are they who have come out of the
great tribulation;* they have washed
their robes and made them white in
the blood of the Lamb.

15Therefore are they before the
throne of God,
and serve him day and night
within his temple;
and he who sits upon the
throne will shelter them with his
presence.
16They shall hunger no more, neither thirst any more;
the sun shall not strike
them, nor any scorching heat.
17For the Lamb in the midst of
the throne will be their
shepherd,
and he will guide them to
springs of living
water;
and God will wipe away every
tear from their eyes."

THE SEVENTH SEAL AND THE GOLDEN CENSER

8 When the Lamb opened the seventh
seal, there was silence in heaven
for about half an hour. 2Then I saw
the seven angels who stand before
God, and seven trumpets were given
to them. 3And another angel came
and stood at the altar with a golden
censer; and he was given much in-
cense to mingle with the prayers of
all the saints upon the golden altar
before the throne; 4and the smoke of
the incense rose with the prayers of
the saints from the hand of the an-
gel before God. 5Then the angel took
the censer and filled it with fire from
the altar and threw it on the earth;*
and there were peals of thunder, loud
noises, flashes of lightning, and an
earthquake.

THE SEVEN TRUMPETS

6 Now the seven angels who had
the seven trumpets made ready to
blow them.

7 The first angel blew his trum-
pet, and there followed hail and fire,
mixed with blood, which fell on the
earth; and a third of the earth was
burnt up, and a third of the trees were
burnt up, and all green grass was
burnt up.
8 The second angel blew his trum-
pet, and something like a great moun-
tain, burning with fire, was thrown
into the sea; 9and a third of the sea
became blood, a third of the living
creatures in the sea died, and a third
of the ships were destroyed.
10 The third angel blew his trum-
pet, and a great star fell from heaven,
blazing like a torch, and it fell on a
third of the rivers and on the foun-
tains of water. 11The name of the star
is Wormwood. A third of the waters
became wormwood, and many men
died of the water, because it was made
bitter.
12 The fourth angel blew his trum-
pet, and a third of the sun was struck,
and a third of the moon, and a third
of the stars, so that a third of their
light was darkened; a third of the day
was kept from shining, and likewise a
third of the night.
13 Then I looked, and I heard an
eagle crying with a loud voice, as it
flew in midheaven, "Woe, woe, woe to
those who dwell on the earth, at the
blasts of the other trumpets which the
three angels are about to blow!"
9 And the fifth angel blew his trum-
pet, and I saw a star* fallen from
heaven to earth, and he was given the
key of the shaft of the bottomless pit;
2he opened the shaft of the bottomless
pit, and from the shaft rose smoke
like the smoke of a great furnace, and
the sun and the air were darkened
with the smoke from the shaft. 3Then
from the smoke came locusts on the
earth, and they were given power like
the power of scorpions of the earth;
4they were told not to harm the grass
of the earth or any green growth or
any tree, but only those of mankind
who have not the seal of God upon
their foreheads; 5they were allowed
to torture them for five months, but
not to kill them, and their torture was
like the torture of a scorpion, when it
stings a man. 6And in those days men
will seek death and will not find it;
they will long to die, and death will
fly from them.
7 In appearance the locusts were
like horses arrayed for battle; on
their heads were what looked like
crowns of gold; their faces were like
human faces, 8their hair like wom-
en's hair, and their teeth like lions'
teeth; 9they had scales like iron
breastplates, and the noise of their
wings was like the noise of many
chariots with horses rushing into
battle. 10They have tails like scorpi-
ons, and stings, and their power of
hurting men for five months lies in
their tails. 11They have as king over
them the angel of the bottomless pit;
his name in Hebrew is Abad´don,
and in Greek he is called Apol´lyon.[a]
12 The first woe has passed; be-
hold, two woes are still to come.
13 Then the sixth angel blew his
trumpet, and I heard a voice from the
four horns of the golden altar before
God, 14saying to the sixth angel who
had the trumpet, "Release the four
angels who are bound at the great
river Euphra´tes."* 15So the four an-
gels were released, who had been
held ready for the hour, the day, the
month, and the year, to kill a third of
mankind. 16The number of the troops
of cavalry was twice ten thousand
times ten thousand; I heard their
number. 17And this was how I saw
the horses in my vision: the riders
wore breastplates the color of fire
and of sapphire[b] and of sulphur, and
the heads of the horses were like li-
ons' heads, and fire and smoke and
sulphur issued from their mouths.
18By these three plagues a third of

[a] Or Destroyer
[b] Greek hyacinth

mankind was killed, by the fire and
smoke and sulphur issuing from their
mouths. 19For the power of the horses
is in their mouths and in their tails;
their tails are like serpents, with
heads, and by means of them they
wound.

20 The rest of mankind, who were
not killed by these plagues, did not
repent of the works of their hands
nor give up worshiping demons and
idols of gold and silver and bronze
and stone and wood, which cannot
either see or hear or walk; 21nor did
they repent of their murders or their
sorceries or their immorality* or their
thefts.

THE ANGEL WITH THE LITTLE SCROLL

10 Then I saw another mighty an-
gel coming down from heaven,
wrapped in a cloud, with a rainbow
over his head, and his face was like
the sun, and his legs like pillars of
fire. 2He had a little scroll open in
his hand. And he set his right foot on
the sea, and his left foot on the land,
3and called out with a loud voice, like
a lion roaring; when he called out, the
seven thunders sounded. 4And when
the seven thunders had sounded, I
was about to write, but I heard a voice
from heaven saying, "Seal up what
the seven thunders have said, and do
not write it down." 5And the angel
whom I saw standing on sea and land
lifted up his right hand to heaven 6and
swore by him who lives for ever and
ever, who created heaven and what is
in it, the earth and what is in it, and
the sea and what is in it, that there
should be no more delay, 7but that
in the days of the trumpet call to be
sounded by the seventh angel, the
mystery of God,* as he announced to
his servants the prophets, should be
fulfilled.

8 Then the voice which I had heard
from heaven spoke to me again, say-
ing, "Go, take the scroll which is
open in the hand of the angel who is
standing on the sea and on the land."
9So I went to the angel and told him to
give me the little scroll; and he said to
me, "Take it and eat; it will be bitter
to your stomach, but sweet* as hon-
ey in your mouth." 10And I took the
little scroll from the hand of the an-
gel and ate it; it was sweet as honey
in my mouth, but when I had eaten it
my stomach was made bitter. 11And I
was told, "You must again prophesy
about many peoples and nations and
tongues and kings."

THE TWO WITNESSES

11 *Then I was given a measuring
rod like a staff, and I was told:
"Rise and measure the temple of God
and the altar and those who worship
there, 2but do not measure the court
outside the temple; leave that out,
for it is given over to the nations,
and they will trample over the holy
city for forty-two months.* 3And I
will grant my two witnesses* power
to prophesy for one thousand two
hundred and sixty days, clothed in
sackcloth."

4 These are the two olive trees
and the two lampstands which stand
before the Lord of the earth. 5And
if any one would harm them, fire
pours from their mouth and con-
sumes their foes; if any one would
harm them, thus he is doomed to be
killed. 6They have power to shut the
sky, that no rain may fall during the
days of their prophesying, and they
have power over the waters to turn
them into blood, and to smite the
earth with every plague, as often as
they desire. 7And when they have
finished their testimony, the beast
that ascends from the bottomless pit
will make war upon them and con-
quer them and kill them, 8and their
dead bodies will lie in the street of
the great city* which is allegorically[c]
called Sodom and Egypt, where their
Lord was crucified. 9For three days
and a half men from the peoples and

[c] Greek spiritually

tribes and tongues and nations gaze
at their dead bodies and refuse to let
them be placed in a tomb, 10and those
who dwell on the earth will rejoice
over them and make merry and ex-
change presents, because these two
prophets had been a torment to those
who dwell on the earth. 11But after
the three and a half days a breath of
life from God entered them, and they
stood up on their feet, and great fear
fell on those who saw them. 12Then
they heard a loud voice from heaven
saying to them, "Come up hither!"
And in the sight of their foes they
went up to heaven in a cloud. 13And
at that hour there was a great earth-
quake, and a tenth of the city fell;
seven thousand people were killed
in the earthquake, and the rest were
terrified and gave glory to the God of
heaven.

14 The second woe has passed; be-
hold, the third woe is soon to come.

THE SEVENTH TRUMPET

15 Then the seventh angel blew his
trumpet, and there were loud voices
in heaven, saying, "The kingdom of
the world has become the kingdom
of our Lord and of his Christ, and he
shall reign for ever and ever." 16And
the twenty-four elders who sit on
their thrones before God fell on their
faces and worshiped God, 17saying,

"We give thanks to thee, Lord
God Almighty, who art
and who wast,
that thou hast taken thy
great power and
begun to reign.
18The nations raged, but thy wrath
came,
and the time for the dead to
be judged,
for rewarding thy servants, the
prophets and saints,
and those who fear thy
name, both small and
great,
and for destroying the destroy-
ers of the earth."

19 Then God's temple in heaven
was opened, and the ark of his cove-
nant was seen within his temple; and
there were flashes of lightning, loud
noises, peals of thunder, an earth-
quake, and heavy hail.

THE WOMAN AND THE DRAGON

12 *And a great portent appeared in
heaven, a woman clothed with the
sun, with the moon under her feet,
and on her head a crown of twelve
stars; 2she was with child and she
cried out in her pangs of birth, in
anguish for delivery. 3And another
portent appeared in heaven; behold,
a great red dragon, with seven heads
and ten horns, and seven diadems
upon his heads. 4His tail swept down
a third of the stars of heaven, and
cast them to the earth. And the drag-
on stood before the woman who was
about to bear a child, that he might
devour her child when she brought it
forth; 5she brought forth a male child,
one who is to rule all the nations
with a rod of iron, but her child was
caught up to God and to his throne,
6and the woman fled into the wilder-
ness, where she has a place prepared
by God, in which to be nourished for
one thousand two hundred and sixty
days.

MICHAEL DEFEATS THE DRAGON

7 Now war arose in heaven,
Michael and his angels fighting
against the dragon; and the dragon
and his angels fought, 8but they were
defeated and there was no longer
any place for them in heaven. 9And
the great dragon was thrown down,
that ancient serpent, who is called
the Devil and Satan, the deceiver of
the whole world—he was thrown
down to the earth, and his angels
were thrown down with him. 10And I
heard a loud voice in heaven, saying,
"Now the salvation and the power
and the kingdom of our God and the
authority of his Christ have come, for
the accuser of our brethren has been

thrown down, who accuses them day and night before our God. 11And they have conquered him by the blood of the Lamb and by the word of their testimony, for they loved not their lives even unto death. 12Rejoice then, O heaven and you that dwell therein! But woe to you, O earth and sea, for the devil has come down to you in great wrath, because he knows that his time is short!"

THE DRAGON FIGHTS AGAIN ON EARTH

13 And when the dragon saw that he had been thrown down to the earth, he pursued the woman who had borne the male child. 14But the woman was given the two wings of the great eagle that she might fly from the serpent into the wilderness, to the place where she is to be nourished for a time, and times, and half a time.* 15The serpent poured water like a river out of his mouth after the woman, to sweep her away with the flood. 16But the earth came to the help of the woman, and the earth opened its mouth and swallowed the river which the dragon had poured from his mouth. 17Then the dragon was angry with the woman,* and went off to make war on the rest of her offspring, on those who keep the commandments of God and bear testimony to Jesus. And he stood[a] on the sand of the sea.

THE FIRST BEAST

13 And I saw a beast* rising out of the sea, with ten horns and seven heads, with ten diadems upon its horns and a blasphemous name upon its heads. 2And the beast that I saw was like a leopard, its feet were like a bear's, and its mouth was like a lion's mouth. And to it the dragon gave his power and his throne and great authority. 3One of its heads seemed to have a mortal wound, but its mortal wound was healed, and the whole earth followed the beast with wonder. 4Men worshiped the dragon, for he had given his authority to the beast, and they worshiped the beast, saying, "Who is like the beast, and who can fight against it?"

5 And the beast was given a mouth uttering haughty and blasphemous words, and it was allowed to exercise authority for forty-two months; 6it opened its mouth to utter blasphemies against God, blaspheming his name and his dwelling, that is, those who dwell in heaven. 7Also it was allowed to make war on the saints and to conquer them.[b] And authority was given it over every tribe and people and tongue and nation, 8and all who dwell on earth will worship it, every one whose name has not been written before the foundation of the world in the book of life of the Lamb that was slain. 9If any one has an ear, let him hear:

10If any one is to be taken captive,
to captivity he goes;
if any one slays with the sword,
with the sword must he be
slain.

Here is a call for the endurance and faith of the saints.

THE SECOND BEAST

11 Then I saw another beast* which rose out of the earth; it had two horns like a lamb and it spoke like a dragon. 12It exercises all the authority of the first beast in its presence, and makes the earth and its inhabitants worship the first beast, whose mortal wound was healed. 13It works great signs, even making fire come down from heaven to earth in the sight of men; 14and by the signs which it is allowed to work in the presence of the beast, it deceives those who dwell on earth, bidding them make an image for the beast which was wounded by the sword and yet lived; 15and it was allowed to

[a] Other ancient authorities read *And I stood*, connecting the sentence with 13.1
[b] Other ancient authorities omit this sentence

give breath to the image of the beast
so that the image of the beast should
even speak, and to cause those who
would not worship the image of the
beast to be slain. 16Also it causes
all, both small and great, both rich
and poor, both free and slave, to
be marked on the right hand or the
forehead, 17so that no one can buy or
sell unless he has the mark, that is,
the name of the beast or the number
of its name. 18This calls for wisdom:
let him who has understanding reck-
on the number of the beast, for it is
a human number, its number is six
hundred and sixty-six.[a]*

THE LAMB AND THE 144,000

14 Then I looked, and lo, on Mount
Zion stood the Lamb, and with
him a hundred and forty-four thou-
sand who had his name and his
Father's name written on their fore-
heads. 2And I heard a voice from
heaven like the sound of many waters
and like the sound of loud thunder;
the voice I heard was like the sound
of harpers playing on their harps,
3and they sing a new song before the
throne and before the four living
creatures and before the elders. No
one could learn that song except the
hundred and forty-four thousand who
had been redeemed from the earth. 4It
is these who have not defiled them-
selves with women, for they are
chaste;[b]* it is these who follow the
Lamb wherever he goes; these have
been redeemed from mankind as first
fruits for God and the Lamb, 5and in
their mouth no lie was found, for they
are spotless.

THE MESSAGES OF THE THREE ANGELS

6 Then I saw another angel flying
in midheaven, with an eternal gospel
to proclaim to those who dwell on
earth, to every nation and tribe and
tongue and people; 7and he said with
a loud voice, "Fear God and give him
glory, for the hour of his judgment
has come; and worship him who made
heaven and earth, the sea and the
fountains of water."

8 Another angel, a second, fol-
lowed, saying, "Fallen, fallen is
Babylon* the great, she who made all
nations drink the wine of her impure
passion."

9 And another angel, a third, fol-
lowed them, saying with a loud voice,
"If any one worships the beast and
its image, and receives a mark on his
forehead or on his hand, 10he also
shall drink the wine of God's wrath,
poured unmixed into the cup of his
anger, and he shall be tormented with
fire and brimstone in the presence of
the holy angels and in the presence of
the Lamb. 11And the smoke of their
torment goes up for ever and ever; and
they have no rest, day or night, these
worshipers of the beast and its image,
and whoever receives the mark of its
name."

12 Here is a call for the endurance
of the saints, those who keep the
commandments of God and the faith
of Jesus.

13 And I heard a voice from heav-
en saying, "Write this: Blessed are
the dead who die in the Lord hence-
forth." "Blessed indeed," says the
Spirit, "that they may rest from their
labors, for their deeds follow them!"

REAPING THE EARTH'S HARVEST

14 Then I looked, and lo, a white
cloud, and seated on the cloud one
like a son of man, with a golden
crown on his head, and a sharp sick-
le in his hand. 15And another angel
came out of the temple, calling with
a loud voice to him who sat upon the
cloud, "Put in your sickle, and reap,
for the hour to reap has come, for the
harvest of the earth is fully ripe." 16So
he who sat upon the cloud swung his
sickle on the earth, and the earth was
reaped.

[a]Other ancient authorities read six hundred and sixteen
[b]Greek *virgins*

17 And another angel came out
of the temple in heaven, and he too
had a sharp sickle. 18Then another an-
gel came out from the altar, the an-
gel who has power over fire, and he
called with a loud voice to him who
had the sharp sickle, "Put in your
sickle, and gather the clusters of the
vine of the earth, for its grapes are
ripe." 19So the angel swung his sickle
on the earth and gathered the vintage
of the earth, and threw it into the
great wine press of the wrath of God;
20and the wine press was trodden out-
side the city, and blood flowed from
the wine press, as high as a horse's
bridle, for one thousand six hundred
stadia.[c]

THE ANGELS WITH THE SEVEN LAST PLAGUES

15 Then I saw another portent in
heaven, great and wonderful, sev-
en angels with seven plagues, which
are the last, for with them the wrath
of God is ended.

2 And I saw what appeared to be
a sea of glass mingled with fire, and
those who had conquered the beast
and its image and the number of its
name, standing beside the sea of glass
with harps of God in their hands.
3And they sing the song of Moses,* the
servant of God, and the song of the
Lamb, saying,

"Great and wonderful are thy
deeds,
O Lord God the Almighty!
Just and true are thy ways,
O King of the ages![d]
4Who shall not fear and glorify
thy name, O Lord?
For thou alone art holy.
All nations shall come and wor-
ship thee,
for thy judgments have been
revealed."

5 After this I looked, and the tem-
ple of the tent of witness in heaven
was opened, 6and out of the temple
came the seven angels with the seven
plagues, robed in pure bright linen,
and their breasts girded with golden
girdles. 7And one of the four living
creatures gave the seven angels seven
golden bowls full of the wrath of God
who lives for ever and ever; 8and the
temple was filled with smoke from the
glory of God and from his power, and
no one could enter the temple until
the seven plagues of the seven angels
were ended.

THE BOWLS OF GOD'S WRATH

16 Then I heard a loud voice from
the temple telling the seven an-
gels, "Go and pour out on the earth
the seven bowls of the wrath of
God."

2 So the first angel went and
poured his bowl on the earth, and foul
and evil sores came upon the men who
bore the mark of the beast and wor-
shiped its image.

3 The second angel poured his
bowl into the sea, and it became like
the blood of a dead man, and every
living thing died that was in the sea.

4 The third angel poured his bowl
into the rivers and the fountains of
water, and they became blood. 5And I
heard the angel of water say,

"Just art thou in these thy
judgments,
thou who art and wast, O Holy
One.
6For men have shed the blood of
saints and prophets,
and thou hast given them blood
to drink.
It is their due!"

7And I heard the altar cry,

"Yea, Lord God the Almighty,
true and just are thy
judgments!"

8 The fourth angel poured his
bowl on the sun, and it was allowed
to scorch men with fire; 9men were
scorched by the fierce heat, and they
cursed the name of God who had

[c] About two hundred miles
[d] Other ancient authorities read *the nations*

power over these plagues, and they
did not repent and give him glory.
10 The fifth angel poured his
bowl on the throne of the beast, and
its kingdom was in darkness; men
gnawed their tongues in anguish 11and
cursed the God of heaven for their
pain and sores, and did not repent of
their deeds.
12 The sixth angel poured his bowl
on the great river Euphra´tes, and
its water was dried up, to prepare
the way for the kings from the east.
13And I saw, issuing from the mouth
of the dragon and from the mouth of
the beast and from the mouth of the
false prophet, three foul spirits like
frogs; 14for they are demonic spirits,
performing signs, who go abroad to
the kings of the whole world, to as-
semble them for battle on the great
day* of God the Almighty. 15("Lo, I am
coming like a thief! Blessed is he who
is awake, keeping his garments that
he may not go naked and be seen ex-
posed!") 16And they assembled them
at the place which is called in Hebrew
Armaged´don.*
17 The seventh angel poured his
bowl into the air, and a great voice
came out of the temple, from the
throne, saying, "It is done!" 18And
there were flashes of lightning,
loud noises, peals of thunder, and a
great earthquake such as had never
been since men were on the earth,
so great was that earthquake. 19The
great city was split into three parts,
and the cities of the nations fell, and
God remembered great Babylon, to
make her drain the cup of the fury
of his wrath. 20And every island fled
away, and no mountains were to be
found; 21and great hailstones, heavy
as a hundredweight, dropped on men
from heaven, till men cursed God for
the plague of the hail, so fearful was
that plague.

THE GREAT WHORE AND THE BEAST

17 Then one of the seven angels
who had the seven bowls came
and said to me, "Come, I will show
you the judgment of the great har-
lot* who is seated upon many waters,
2with whom the kings of the earth
have committed fornication, and
with the wine of whose fornication*
the dwellers on earth have become
drunk." 3And he carried me away
in the Spirit into a wilderness, and
I saw a woman sitting on a scarlet
beast which was full of blasphemous
names, and it had seven heads and
ten horns. 4The woman was arrayed
in purple and scarlet, and bedecked
with gold and jewels and pearls,
holding in her hand a golden cup full
of abominations and the impurities
of her fornication; 5and on her fore-
head was written a name of mystery:
"Babylon the great, mother of harlots
and of earth's abominations." 6And
I saw the woman, drunk with the
blood of the saints and the blood of
the martyrs of Jesus. When I saw her
I marveled greatly. 7But the angel said
to me, "Why marvel? I will tell you
the mystery of the woman, and of the
beast with seven heads and ten horns
that carries her. 8The beast that you
saw was, and is not, and is to ascend
from the bottomless pit and go to
perdition; and the dwellers on earth
whose names have not been written
in the book of life from the founda-
tion of the world, will marvel to be-
hold the beast, because it was and is
not and is to come. 9This calls for a
mind with wisdom: the seven heads
are seven hills on which the woman
is seated; 10they are also seven kings,
five of whom have fallen, one is, the
other has not yet come, and when he
comes he must remain only a little
while. 11As for the beast that was and
is not, it is an eighth but it belongs
to the seven, and it goes to perdition.
12And the ten horns that you saw are
ten kings who have not yet received
royal power, but they are to receive
authority as kings for one hour, to-
gether with the beast. 13These are of
one mind and give over their power

and authority to the beast; 14they will
make war on the Lamb, and the Lamb
will conquer them, for he is Lord of
lords and King of kings, and those
with him are called and chosen and
faithful."

15 And he said to me, "The waters
that you saw, where the harlot is seat-
ed, are peoples and multitudes and
nations and tongues. 16And the ten
horns that you saw, they and the beast
will hate the harlot; they will make
her desolate and naked, and devour
her flesh and burn her up with fire,
17for God has put it into their hearts
to carry out his purpose by being of
one mind and giving over their royal
power to the beast, until the words
of God shall be fulfilled. 18And the
woman that you saw is the great city
which has dominion over the kings of
the earth."

THE FALL OF BABYLON

18 After this I saw another angel
coming down from heaven, hav-
ing great authority; and the earth was
made bright with his splendor. 2And
he called out with a mighty voice,

"Fallen, fallen is Babylon the great!
It has become a dwelling place of demons,
a haunt of every foul spirit,
a haunt of every foul and hateful bird;
3for all nations have drunk[a] the wine of her impure passion,
and the kings of the earth have committed fornication with her,
and the merchants of the earth have grown rich with the wealth of her wantonness."

4Then I heard another voice from
heaven saying,

"Come out of her, my people,
lest you take part in her sins,
lest you share in her plagues;

[a] Other ancient authorities read *fallen by*

5for her sins are heaped high as heaven,
and God has remembered her iniquities.
6Render to her as she herself has rendered,
and repay her double for her deeds;
mix a double draught for her in the cup she mixed.
7As she glorified herself and played the wanton,
so give her a like measure of torment and mourning.
Since in her heart she says, 'A queen I sit,
I am no widow, mourning I shall never see,'
8so shall her plagues come in a single day,
pestilence and mourning and famine,
and she shall be burned with fire;
for mighty is the Lord God who judges her."

9 And the kings of the earth, who
committed fornication and were wan-
ton with her, will weep and wail over
her when they see the smoke of her
burning; 10they will stand far off, in
fear of her torment, and say,

"Alas! alas! thou great city,
thou mighty city, Babylon!
In one hour has thy judgment come."

11* And the merchants of the
earth weep and mourn for her, since
no one buys their cargo any more,
12cargo of gold, silver, jewels and
pearls, fine linen, purple, silk and
scarlet, all kinds of scented wood, all
articles of ivory, all articles of cost-
ly wood, bronze, iron and marble,
13cinnamon, spice, incense, myrrh,
frankincense, wine, oil, fine flour
and wheat, cattle and sheep, horses
and chariots, and slaves, that is, hu-
man souls.

14"The fruit for which thy soul longed has gone from thee,

and all thy dainties and thy
splendor are lost to
thee, never to be found
again!"

15The merchants of these wares,
who gained wealth from her, will
stand far off, in fear of her torment,
weeping and mourning aloud,

16"Alas, alas, for the great city
that was clothed in fine linen,
in purple and scarlet,
bedecked with gold, with jewels,
and with pearls!
17In one hour all this wealth has
been laid waste."

And all shipmasters and seafaring
men, sailors and all whose trade
is on the sea, stood far off 18and cried
out as they saw the smoke of her
burning,

"What city was like the great
city?"

19And they threw dust on their
heads, as they wept and mourned,
crying out,

"Alas, alas, for the great city
where all who had ships at
sea grew rich by her
wealth!
In one hour she has been laid
waste.
20Rejoice over her, O heaven,
O saints and apostles and
prophets,
for God has given judgment for
you against her!"

21 Then a mighty angel took up a
stone like a great millstone and threw
it into the sea, saying,

"So shall Babylon the great city
be thrown down with
violence,
and shall be found no more;
22and the sound of harpers and
minstrels, of flute players
and trumpeters,
shall be heard in thee no
more;
and a craftsman of any craft
shall be found in thee no
more;
and the sound of the millstone
shall be heard in thee no
more;
23and the light of a lamp
shall shine in thee no more;
and the voice of bridegroom
and bride
shall be heard in thee no
more;
for thy merchants were the
great men of the earth,
and all nations were
deceived by thy
sorcery.
24And in her was found the blood
of prophets and of saints,
and of all who have been
slain on earth."

THE REJOICING IN HEAVEN

19After this I heard what seemed to
be the mighty voice of a great multitude
in heaven, crying,

"Hallelujah! Salvation and
glory and power belong
to our God,
2for his judgments are true and
just;
he has judged the great
harlot who corrupted
the earth with her
fornication,
and he has avenged on her the
blood of his servants."

3Once more they cried,

"Hallelujah! The smoke from
her goes up for ever and
ever."

4And the twenty-four elders and
the four living creatures fell down and
worshiped God who is seated on the
throne, saying, "Amen. Hallelujah!"
5And from the throne came a voice
crying,

"Praise our God, all you his
servants,
you who fear him, small and
great."

6Then I heard what seemed to be
the voice of a great multitude, like
the sound of many waters and like
the sound of mighty thunderpeals,
crying,

coming down out of heaven from
God, 11having the glory of God, its
radiance like a most rare jewel, like
a jasper, clear as crystal. 12It had a
great, high wall, with twelve gates,
and at the gates twelve angels, and
on the gates the names of the twelve
tribes of the sons of Israel were in-
scribed; 13on the east three gates, on
the north three gates, on the south
three gates, and on the west three
gates. 14And the wall of the city had
twelve foundations, and on them the
twelve names of the twelve apostles
of the Lamb.

15 And he who talked to me had a
measuring rod of gold to measure the
city and its gates and walls. 16The city
lies foursquare, its length the same
as its breadth; and he measured the
city with his rod, twelve thousand
stadia;[d] its length and breadth and
height are equal. 17He also measured
its wall, a hundred and forty-four cu-
bits by a man's measure, that is, an
angel's. 18The wall was built of jasper,
while the city was pure gold, clear as
glass. 19The foundations of the wall
of the city were adorned with every
jewel; the first was jasper, the second
sapphire, the third agate, the fourth
emerald, 20the fifth onyx, the sixth
carnelian, the seventh chrysolite,
the eighth beryl, the ninth topaz, the
tenth chrysoprase, the eleventh ja-
cinth, the twelfth amethyst. 21And the
twelve gates were twelve pearls, each
of the gates made of a single pearl,
and the street of the city was pure
gold, transparent as glass.

22 And I saw no temple in the
city, for its temple is the Lord God
the Almighty and the Lamb. 23And
the city has no need of sun or moon
to shine upon it, for the glory of God
is its light, and its lamp is the Lamb.
24By its light shall the nations walk;
and the kings of the earth shall bring
their glory into it, 25and its gates shall
never be shut by day—and there shall
be no night there; 26they shall bring
into it the glory and the honor of the
nations. 27But nothing unclean shall
enter it, nor any one who practices
abomination or falsehood, but only
those who are written in the Lamb's
book of life.

THE RIVER OF LIFE

22 Then he showed me the river of
the water of life, bright as crystal,
flowing from the throne of God and of
the Lamb 2through the middle of the
street of the city; also, on either side
of the river, the tree of life[e] with its
twelve kinds of fruit, yielding its fruit
each month; and the leaves of the tree
were for the healing of the nations.
3There shall no more be anything ac-
cursed, but the throne of God and of
the Lamb shall be in it, and his ser-
vants shall worship him; 4they shall
see his face, and his name shall be on
their foreheads. 5And night shall be
no more; they need no light of lamp
or sun, for the Lord God will be their
light, and they shall reign for ever and
ever.

6 And he said to me, "These words
are trustworthy and true. And the
Lord, the God of the spirits of the
prophets, has sent his angel to show
his servants what must soon take
place. 7And behold, I am coming
soon." Blessed is he who keeps the
words of the prophecy of this book.

EPILOGUE AND BENEDICTION

8 I John am he who heard and saw
these things. And when I heard and
saw them, I fell down to worship at
the feet of the angel who showed them
to me; 9but he said to me, "You must
not do that! I am a fellow servant with
you and your brethren the prophets,
and with those who keep the words of
this book. Worship God."

10 And he said to me, "Do not seal
up the words of the prophecy of this
book, for the time is near. 11Let the

[d] About fifteen hundred miles

[e] Or *the Lamb. In the midst of the street of the city, and on either side of the river, was the tree of life,* etc.

evildoer still do evil, and the filthy
still be filthy, and the righteous still
do right, and the holy still be holy."
12 "Behold, I am coming soon,
bringing my recompense, to repay ev-
ery one for what he has done. 13I am the
Alpha and the Omega, the first and the
last, the beginning and the end."
14 Blessed are those who wash
their robes,[a] that they may have
the right to the tree of life and that
they may enter the city by the gates.
15Outside are the dogs and sorcerers
and fornicators and murderers and
idolaters, and every one who loves and
practices falsehood.
16 "I Jesus have sent my angel to you
with this testimony for the churches. I
am the root and the offspring of David,
the bright morning star."
17 The Spirit and the Bride say,
"Come." And let him who hears say,
"Come." And let him who is thirsty
come, let him who desires take the
water of life without price.
18 I warn every one who hears the
words of the prophecy of this book:
if any one adds to them, God will
add to him the plagues described
in this book, 19and if any one takes
away from the words of the book of
this prophecy, God will take away
his share in the tree of life and in the
holy city, which are described in this
book.
20 He who testifies to these things
says, "Surely I am coming soon."
Amen. Come, Lord Jesus!
21 The grace of the Lord Jesus be
with all the saints.[b] Amen.

[a]Other ancient authorities read *do his commandments*
[b]Other ancient authorities omit *all*; others omit *the saints*

LIST OF MAPS OF
THE BIBLE

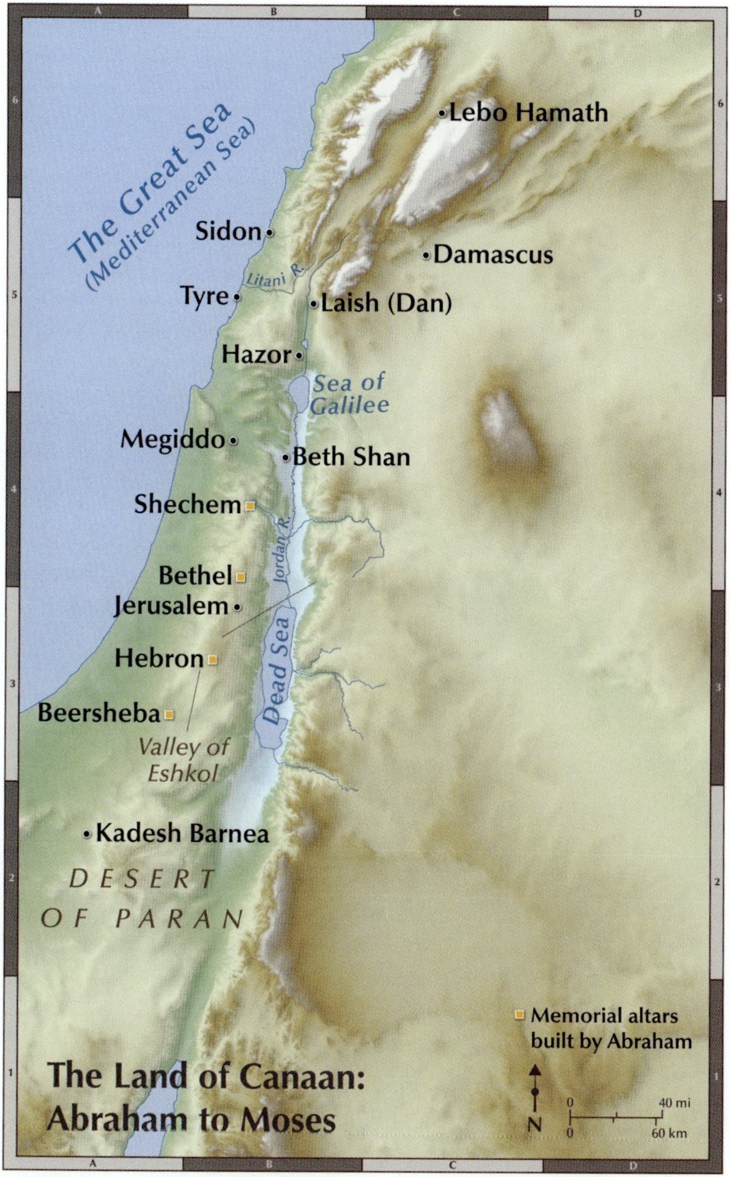
The Great Sea
(Mediterranean Sea)
Lebo Hamath
Sidon
Damascus
Litani R.
Tyre
Laish (Dan)
Hazor
Sea of
Galilee
Megiddo
Beth Shan
Shechem
Jordan R.
Bethel
Jerusalem
Dead Sea
Hebron
Beersheba
Valley of
Eshkol
Kadesh Barnea
DESERT
OF PARAN
Memorial altars
built by Abraham
N
0
40 mi
0
60 km
The Land of Canaan:
Abraham to Moses

Probable route of wandering in the Sinai
Entry into and conquest of Canaan
The Great Sea (Mediterranean Sea)
BASHAN
Heshbon
Shittam
Mt. Nebo
Jericho
Jerusalem
Dibon
Hebron
AMMON
Dead Sea
MOAB
Beersheba
LOWER EGYPT
Rameses
GOSHEN
Kadesh Barnea
Punon
EDOM
SINAI
Ezion-geber
Nile R.
(Gulf of Suez)
(Gulf of Aqaba)
MIDIAN
UPPER EGYPT
Mt. Sinai
Red Sea
N
0 60 mi
0 90 km
The Exodus

Israel in Canaan: Joshua, Samuel, and Saul

A
B
C
D
6
5
4
3
2
1
N
0
20 mi
0
30 km
Kingdom of Saul
Area conquered by David
Sidon
PHOENICIA
Tyre
Hazor
The Great Sea
(Mediterranean Sea)
Sea of Chinnereth
Megiddo
ISRAEL
PHILISTIA
Gezer
Lower Beth-horon
Rabbah
Baalath
Jerusalem
Sea of Arabah
(The Salt Sea)
Gaza
JUDAH
Kir-hareseth
The United Monarchy
Tamar

The Great Sea
(Mediterranean Sea)
Sea of Chinnereth
ISRAEL
Samaria
Tirzah
Shechem
Shiloh
Gibeon
Gibeah
Heshbon
Ashdod
Jerusalem
Hebron
The Salt Sea
(The Dead Sea)
JUDAH
40 mi
60 km
N
The Kingdoms of
Israel and Judah

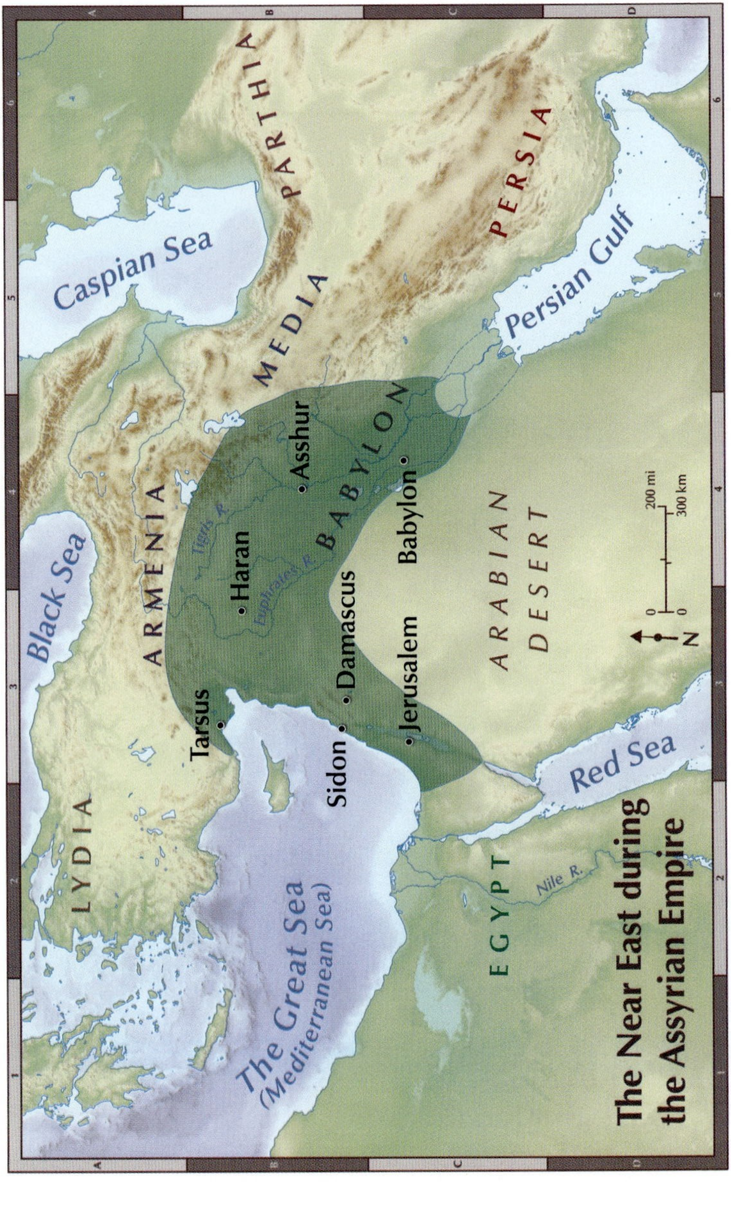

The Near East during the Assyrian Empire

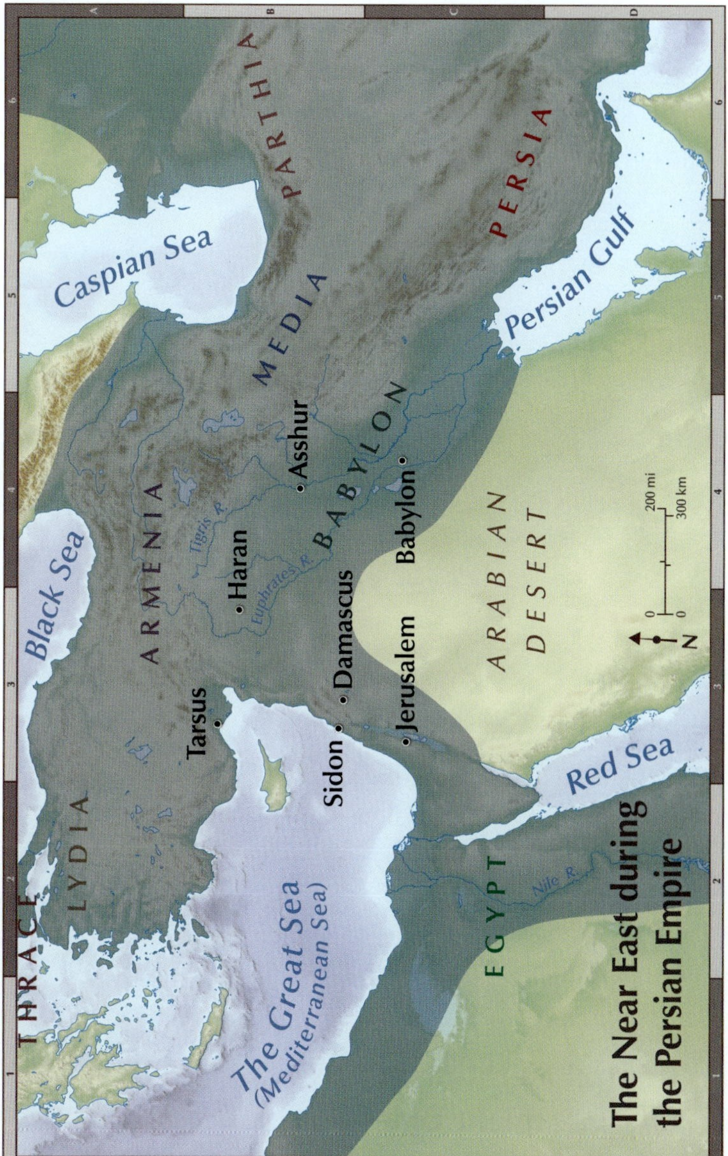
The Near East during the Persian Empire
Caspian Sea
Black Sea
Persian Gulf
Red Sea
The Great Sea
(Mediterranean Sea)
PARTHIA
PERSIA
MEDIA
ARMENIA
BABYLON
ARABIAN DESERT
LYDIA
THRACE
EGYPT
Tigris R.
Euphrates R.
Nile R.
Asshur
Haran
Babylon
Damascus
Jerusalem
Tarsus
Sidon
0 200 mi
0 300 km
N

Central Palestine in Old Testament Times

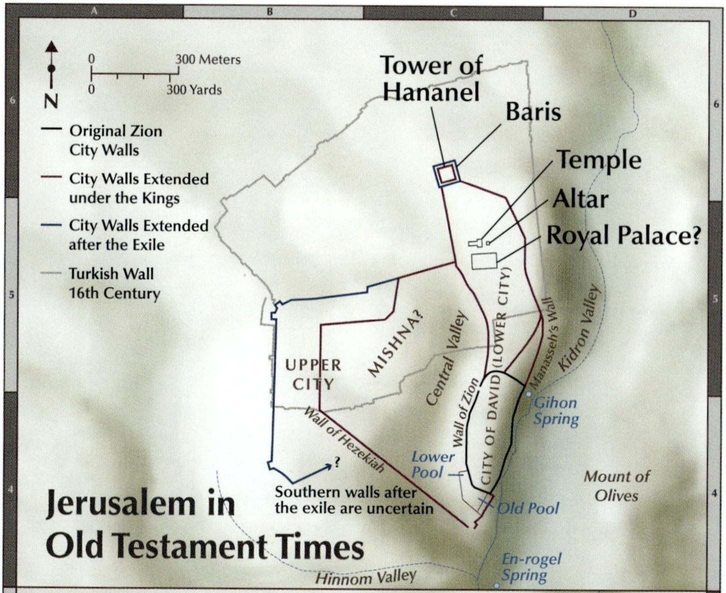

N
0 300 Meters
0 300 Yards
Original Zion City Walls
City Walls Extended under the Kings
City Walls Extended after the Exile
Turkish Wall 16th Century
Tower of Hananel
Baris
Temple
Altar
Royal Palace?
UPPER CITY
MISHNA?
Central Valley
CITY OF DAVID
(LOWER CITY)
Wall of Zion
Manasseh's Wall
Kidron Valley
Gihon Spring
Wall of Hezekiah
Lower Pool
Old Pool
Southern walls after the exile are uncertain
Mount of Olives
En-rogel Spring
Hinnom Valley
Jerusalem in Old Testament Times

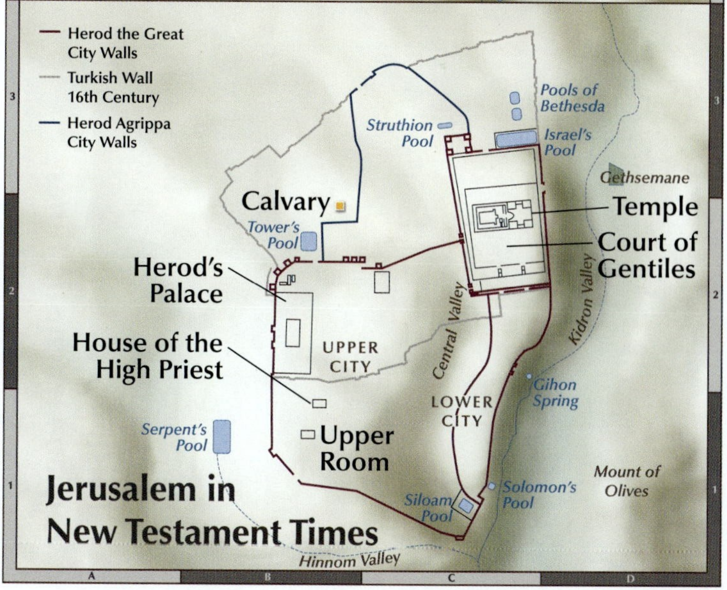

Herod the Great City Walls
Turkish Wall 16th Century
Herod Agrippa City Walls
Pools of Bethesda
Struthion Pool
Israel's Pool
Gethsemane
Calvary
Tower's Pool
Temple
Court of Gentiles
Herod's Palace
House of the High Priest
UPPER CITY
Central Valley
Kidron Valley
LOWER CITY
Gihon Spring
Serpent's Pool
Upper Room
Mount of Olives
Solomon's Pool
Siloam Pool
Hinnom Valley
Jerusalem in New Testament Times

Black Sea
Caspian Sea
PHYGRIA
CILICIA
Tarsus
Haran
Tigris R.
Euphrates R.
The Great Sea
(Mediterranean Sea)
Sidon
Damascus
Asshur
MEDIA
PARTHIA
Amu Darya
Maracanda
BACTRIA
ARACHOSIA
Babylon
BABYLONIA
Jerusalem
Memphis
EGYPT
Nile R.
Persepolis
PERSIS
Persian Gulf
GEDROSIA
Indus R.
ARABIAN
DESERT
Red Sea
Arabian Sea
Palenstine in
Persian-Hellenistic Times
N
0
200 mi
0
300 km

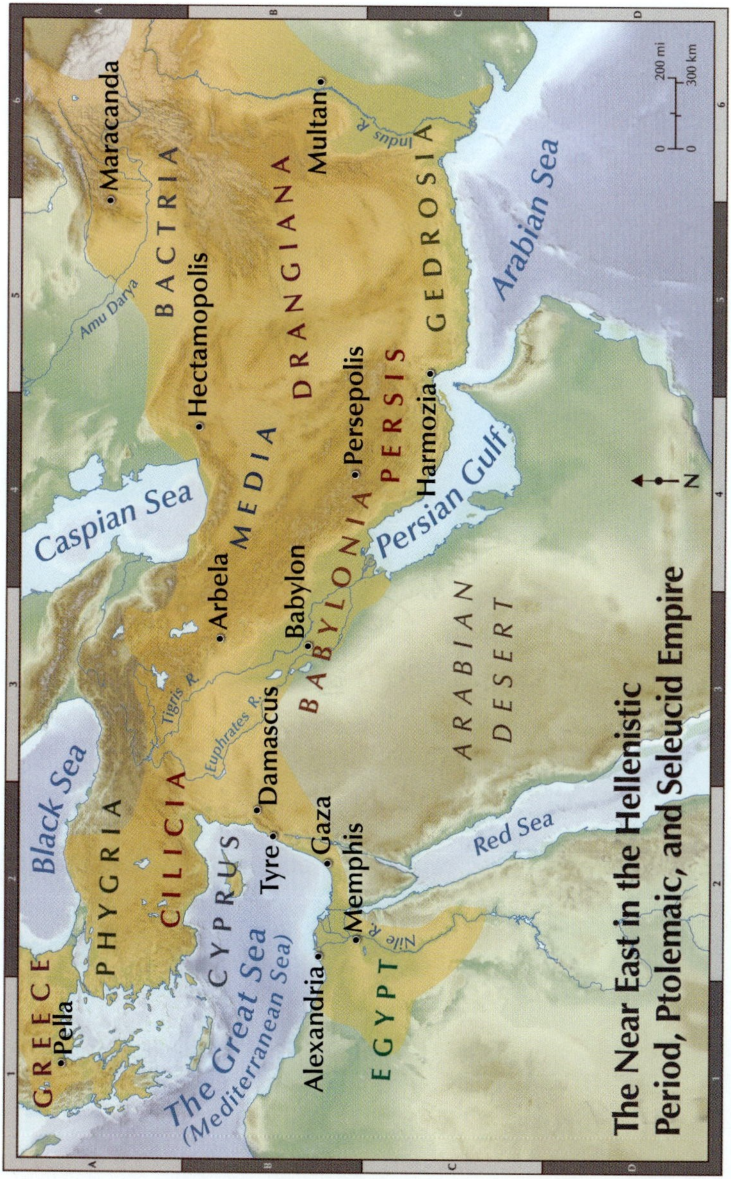

The Near East in the Hellenistic Period, Ptolemaic, and Seleucid Empire

Palestine under the Herods

North and Central Palestine at the Time of the Ministry of Jesus

St. Paul's First Journey
Euxine Sea (Black Sea)
MACEDONIA
THRACE
ASIA
GALATIA
Aegean Sea
CRETE
The Great Sea (Mediterranean Sea)
CYPRUS
SYRIA
Tigris R.
Euphrates R.
Antioch (Pisidian)
Perga
Lystra
Iconium
Derbe
Tarsus
Seleucia
Aleppo
Antioch (Syrian)
Salamis
Paphos
Damascus
Jerusalem
0 200 mi
0 300 km
N

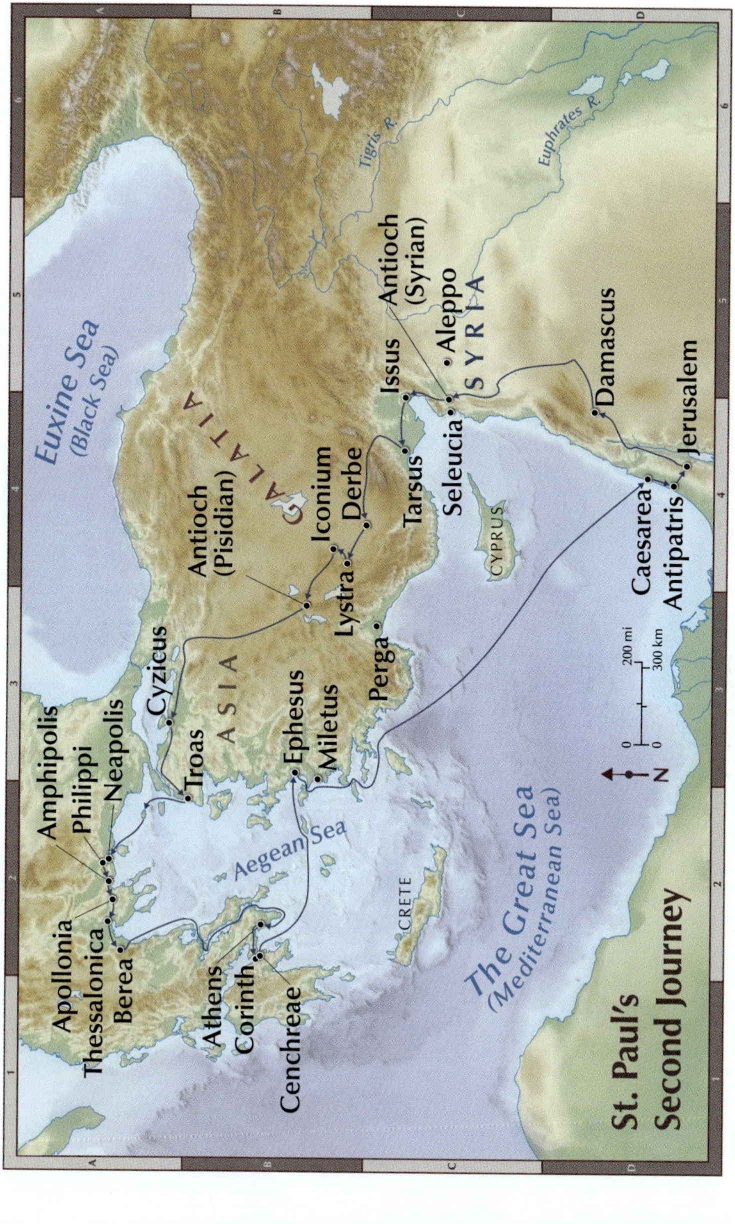
St. Paul's Second Journey
Euxine Sea
(Black Sea)
The Great Sea
(Mediterranean Sea)
Aegean Sea
GALATIA
ASIA
SYRIA
CYPRUS
CRETE
Tigris R.
Euphrates R.
Apollonia
Thessalonica
Berea
Amphipolis
Philippi
Neapolis
Athens
Corinth
Cenchreae
Troas
Cyzicus
Ephesus
Miletus
Perga
Antioch
(Pisidian)
Iconium
Lystra
Derbe
Tarsus
Issus
Seleucia
Antioch
(Syrian)
Aleppo
Damascus
Caesarea
Antipatris
Jerusalem
0 200 mi
0 300 km
N

St. Paul's Third Journey
Euxine Sea
(Black Sea)
Aegean Sea
The Great Sea
(Mediterranean Sea)
CRETE
CYPRUS
GALATIA
ASIA
SYRIA
Tigris R.
Euphrates R.
Apollonia
Thessalonica
Berea
Amphipolis
Philippi
Neapolis
Athens
Corinth
Cenchreae
Troas
Assos
Miletus
Cyzicus
Pergamum
Smyrna
Ephesus
Laodicea
Miletus
Patara
Antioch
(Pisidian)
Lystra
Iconium
Derbe
Tarsus
Issus
Seleucia
Antioch
(Syrian)
Aleppo
Tyre
Ptolemais
Caesarea
Antipatris
Jerusalem
0 200 mi
0 300 km
N